PENGUIN HANDBOOKS

The Penguin Guide to Compact Discs

EDWARD GREENFIELD has been Record Critic of the *Guardian* since 1954, and from 1964 Music Critic too. At the end of 1960 he joined the reviewing panel of *Gramophone*, specializing in operatic and orchestral issues. He is a regular broadcaster on music and records for the BBC and has a weekly record programme on the BBC World Service. In 1958 he published a monograph on the operas of Puccini. More recently he has written studies on the recorded work of Joan Sutherland and André Previn. He has been a regular juror on International Record awards and has appeared with such artists as Elisabeth Schwarzkopf and Joan Sutherland in public interviews.

ROBERT LAYTON studied at Oxford with Edmund Rubbra for composition and with Egon Wellesz for the history of music. He spent two years in Sweden at the universities of Uppsala and Stockholm. He joined the BBC Music Division in 1959 and has been responsible for such programmes as *Interpretations on Record*. He has contributed 'A Quarterly Retrospect' to *Gramophone* for a number of years and he has written books on Berwald and Sibelius and has specialized in Scandinavian music. His recent publications include a monograph on the Dvořák symphonies and concertos for the BBC Music Guides, of which he is General Editor, and the first two volumes of his translation of Erik Tawastsjerna's definitive study of Sibelius. In 1987 he was awarded the Sibelius Medal and in the following year was made a Knight of the Order of the White Rose of Finland for his services to Finnish music.

IVAN MARCH is a former professional musician and a regular contributor to *Gramophone*. He studied at Trinity College of Music, London, and at the Royal Manchester College. After service in the RAF Central Band, he played the horn professionally for the BBC and travelled with the Carl Rosa and D'Oyly Carte opera companies. Now director of the Long Playing Record Library, the largest commercial lending library· for classical music on compact discs in the British Isles, he is a well-known lecturer, journalist and personality in the world of recorded music.

The present volume is dedicated with much warmth, admiration and respect (but, alas, without permission) to

ARTHUR HADDY
(1906–89)
Chief Recording Engineer of Decca

without whom so much would not have happened.

Arthur Haddy began his recording career with the Crystalate Gramophone Company which, before the Second World War, was making records that were as excellent as they were inexpensive. In 1937 Crystalate was taken over by British Decca (London Records in the USA) and Haddy became that company's Chief Recording Engineer, a position he held with the utmost distinction for fifty years. His wartime achievement with ffrr (full frequency range recording) established for his new company a technical lead that was never relinquished. In 1950, under his guidance Decca issued the first British ffrr LPs, at least two years ahead of its major competitor, having already begun to export them to the USA. Arthur Haddy understood all about stereo from his earliest recording experiences, and even in the mono era he used microphone placings which optimized the hall ambience, one reason why Decca ffrr recordings had so much bloom, to balance their brilliance. In 1957 he expended enormous energy, extending his personal influence internationally to ensure that a world-wide standard was established for stereo LPs from their inception, and Decca ffrr became ffss (full frequency stereophonic sound). During that vintage period of the late 1950s and the 1960s, Haddy's technical team underpinned the remarkable artistic achievements of John Culshaw and his colleagues in what for those days were mighty projects, ranging from first recordings of Britten's *Peter Grimes* and the *War Requiem* to Solti's epoch-making cycle of Wagner's *Der Ring* – recordings which still have never been surpassed. Haddy went on to play a leading part in the cassette revolution, taking musicassettes seriously while others scoffed and making them technically viable by championing the adoption of the Dolby Noise Reduction System. He must have been well satisfied with Decca's continuing progress in the era of the CD for, even though the company was absorbed into the Polygram group, it maintained its technical independence and went on to produce state-of-the-art recordings with Charles Dutoit in Montreal, notably that astonishing early CD of Ravel's *Daphnis et Chloé*, which uncannily echoed the work of Ernest Ansermet in Geneva of four decades earlier: his equally famous record of another Diaghilev ballet, Stravinsky's *Petrushka*.

The Penguin Guide to Compact Discs

Edward Greenfield, Robert Layton and Ivan March

Edited by Ivan March

Penguin Books

PENGUIN BOOKS

Published by the Penguin Group
27 Wrights Lane, London W8 5TZ, England
Viking Penguin, a division of Penguin Books USA Inc.
375 Hudson Street, New York, New York 10014, USA
Penguin Books Australia Ltd, Ringwood, Victoria, Australia
Penguin Books Canada Ltd, 2801 John Street, Markham, Ontario, Canada L3R 1B4
Penguin Books (NZ) Ltd, 182—190 Wairau Road, Auckland 10, New Zealand

Penguin Books Ltd, Registered Offices: Harmondsworth, Middlesex, England

First published 1990
10 9 8 7 6 5 4 3 2 1

Printed in England by Clays Ltd, St Ives plc
Typeset in 8 on 9½ pt Times

Contents

Editor's Comment

During the preparation of this book we came to understand how Noah must have felt. Indeed, new recordings of the major musical species did not arrive singly, or even two by two; they were much more likely to appear in threes and fours and – in the case of key works like Vivaldi's *Four Seasons* – could almost be 'reckoned up by dozens'. Moreover, if our survey was to be of a manageable size, we felt we had to stay within the limitations of a single volume, with all the restrictions that implied. So, for the first time since we started publishing regular assessments of available recorded music (in 1960), we were faced with the situation that any new survey would by definition have to be selective, and that we would have to make the decision – in some cases quite arbitrarily – what to put in and what to leave out.

The present volume therefore combines a re-evaluation of older issues and reissues, among which are still to be found much of the cream of the repertoire, together with a careful appraisal of what seems to us to be most important among the newer records – many of which, especially in the area of the major popular classics, have proved disappointing when compared with past excellence.

Although the major companies continually seek to renew their recordings of the standard classics (to which each new generation of music-lovers rightly gives priority), we are reassured to observe that the edges of the repertoire are forever being pushed back. One of the great joys of conducting a continuing survey is the regular discovery of music of astonishingly high quality of which we were hitherto entirely unaware. Often the recorded performance can reflect a similar joy of new discovery, and this gives the record an even greater appeal. One such instance, which appeared just seven days before we finally went to print, is the Gimell CD collection of Portuguese Renaissance music by Frei Manuel Cardosa, whose strikingly original *Requiem* is a glorious addition to known music from the first quarter of the seventeenth century.

Our other great source of pleasure has been the growing profusion of outstanding bargain and mid-priced reissues now appearing from the major labels. The early volumes of Peter Hurford's (originally Argo) integral recording of Bach's organ music on Decca are outstanding value in the amount of music offered on each CD, while the first distinguished releases in EMI's Beecham Edition are comparably generous. Even more striking are some of the releases on the Philips and DG bargain labels with, on the former, Stephen Bishop-Kovacevich's exemplary versions of the Beethoven *Piano concertos* with Sir Colin Davis and, on the latter, Karajan's mid-1960s coupling of Brahms's *Second* and *Third Symphonies* and Abbado's pairing of Tchaikovsky's *Second* and *Fourth Symphonies*, both offering astonishing value.

It seems very likely that this unexpected generosity from the major companies (who continue to maintain high prices for their premium issues) has been stimulated by the new super-bargain CDs (Hungaroton White Label, LaserLight and Naxos) from Eastern Europe, where recording costs are made artificially low by the need for hard currency and the desire of East European musicians to gain exposure and recognition in the West. Our exploration of this area has only just begun and we hope to evaluate many more of these inexpensive CDs in our 1991 Yearbook, when we shall also fill in other gaps in the repertoire for which there was simply no room in the present volume.

Older readers will imagine my great personal reluctance to bid farewell to the musicassette so soon after abandoning the LP, for they both retain a nostalgia that is very much a part of our musical experience. Many desirable, inexpensive cassettes are still available, and their technology is now so reliable that comment on individual issues seldom seems useful. But it was the arrival of the 'super-bargain CD' at a time when price increases brought the cost of some premium-range cassettes up to that of a mid-priced CD which made us decide that, except for use in the car, tapes were no longer a realistic alternative to compact discs, with the latter's infinitely greater ease of access.

Ivan March
August 1990

Preface

The compact disc is now firmly established as the major sound-carrier for prerecorded music, with no serious rival in sight. Digital tape, once vaunted as an alternative, has had no apparent impact on the marketplace, and its most obvious use is for those who wish to make their own recordings, or for copying. CDs offer a recording medium combining fidelity and clarity against a silent or near-silent background. They are also perceived as having a robust resistance to damage, given reasonable care in handling (though, regrettably, this does not apply to the plastic 'jewel cases' in which they are individually packaged) and they offer convenient and instant internal access to their musical contents.

Documentation still leaves a good deal to be desired, seldom approaching the standard we took for granted during the vintage LP era. Sometimes, in the case of mid-priced series, major opera reissues appear without libretto translations into English and, even where there is a synopsis of the action, it is not always co-ordinated with the relevant cues on the CDs. But the situation is particularly unfortunate in the case of bargain reissues on major labels: here essential musical information often is non-existent in the very area where it is most needed. These are records which are likely to be among the first purchases made by those seeking an entry into a musical world which already puts up too many barriers! Such a policy from companies which otherwise seek to maintain the highest standards is as astonishing as it is disgraceful, more particularly since some of the super-bargain CDs from less famous sources have more than adequate information accompanying them.

Transfer technology for the remastering of older recordings to CD continues to be controversial. With analogue stereo issues of vintage orchestral recordings made within natural concert-hall acoustics, there is usually minimal ambient loss in the digitalization; the body and firmness of the sound is retained, with the achievement of enhanced definition. One thinks at once of Fritz Reiner's marvellous recordings made in Orchestra Hall, Chicago, in the very earliest days of stereo, or of the series of Karajan/Berlin Philharmonic recordings made in the Berlin Jesus-Christus- Kirche, or again of Beecham's music-making at Walthamstow, the Paris Salle Wagram, the London Kingsway Hall, or EMI's No. 1 Studio which, with the right producer, can sound surprisingly like a concert hall. Then there are the many fine Philips records made in the Amsterdam Concertgebouw, and of course the famous Decca ventures in the Vienna Sofiensaal. But, alas, it is all too easy for an excellent analogue master to become degraded by an attempted facelift, if it is clumsily handled. A sharply etched aural image is not necessarily a more agreeable one musically, and if the ambience of the master recording was very resonant, attempts to improve internal clarity can be false, resulting in a combination of an added harshnesss with a certain fuzziness. Where the analogue original was brightly lit, the remastering can bring a glare to the violins, ill balanced by a reduction of fullness in the bass. Moreover a curious effect is sometimes produced that can best be described as 'dehydration', in which the body and substance of the recording seem to evaporate. The digital remastering process seems to be applied fairly uniformly to all discs; this sometimes works to advantage and is remarkably successful in refining the detailed focus and adding a sense of presence; but too often it produces a treble emphasis, even bringing an edginess on top. This is difficult to smooth with the playback controls, particularly on high-quality systems which faithfully reproduce everything transmitted by the laser beam tracking the CD.

With much older recordings, especially those of the human voice, the added presence of CD can be striking. The introduction of CEDAR (Computer Enhanced Digital Audio Restoration) can also bring a dramatic improvement to recordings made in the pre-LP era. This is a system which, with guidance from a musical operator, uses a series of computerized processes to eliminate clicks and various background noises, including hiss and swish, inherent in the old, 78-r.p.m. shellac discs, leaving the original musical signal totally intact. However, it is the human ear which must be the final arbiter of new technology; we already have one instance where the collector can compare an EMI CEDAR-remastered version of Beecham's late-1930s recording of Mozart's *Die Zauberflöte* with a relatively uncomplicated transfer to CD taken straight from commercial 78-r.p.m. shellac pressings on the Pearl label. The latter offers less presence but sound-quality with far more bloom and natural realism.

Nimbus have approached the problem of transferring vintage vocal recordings from 78s to CD by a radical but ingenious method: playing the original discs back on an acoustic gramophone with an enormous horn in a small hall, and re-recording the results digitally. The use of thorn needles for playback acts as a 'natural' filter of background noise and, while this also limits the reproduced frequency range, the result is friendly to the ear, often subduing peakiness. Comparison with electronically managed transfers of similar material shows that the latter can bring greater immediacy and character, even if exposing the voice more and giving it less bloom. Neither system offers the ideal answer, but both give fascinating demonstrations of alternative possibilities.

The continuing strong influence of the 'authentic' lobby in current recordings of Baroque music has now extended to embrace the nineteenth century, with Beethoven's as well as Mozart's keyboard concertos available on the fortepiano, together with the more obviously Romantic solo piano music of Schubert. Even such an orchestral showpiece as Berlioz's *Symphonie fantastique* has been brought into sharper focus by the authenticists. Fortunately, the 'second generation' of performances on original instruments seems less intimidated by strict stylistic rituals. The players are able to breathe more life into phrasing and more readily bring a natural warmth into the the shaping of melodic lines. String timbres are without the degree of cutting edge which has been fashionable hitherto, even if speeds often remain on the hectic side. It is salutary to recall that Anton Stadler, the clarinettist for whom Mozart wrote his *Clarinet quintet*, possessed a timbre which a contemporary described as 'so soft and lovely that nobody who has a heart can resist it', and it is no less reasonable to conjecture that Mozart's much-quoted dislike for the flute may have derived from the somewhat anaemic timbre which some early instruments can produce.

However, there is no question that authenticity of a more invigorating and life-enhancing character – such as one can expect, for instance, from performances directed by an artist like John Eliot Gardiner – can be a very stimulating experience. Moreover Sigiswald Kuijken, who as a solo violinist has given us some outstanding authentic performances of Bach's *Violin sonatas*, provides some of the most enjoyable period performances of Haydn ever in his complete set of Haydn's *Paris symphonies* with the Orchestra of the Age of Enlightenment. The influence of the authentic movement has undoubtedly been profound, now even extending to performances in which modern instruments are in use. The most striking current example is Sir Yehudi Menuhin's new recordings of the last four Mozart symphonies, with the hand-picked orchestra of which he is principal conductor, the Sinfonia Varsovia. These have all the benefits of the authentic approach, including freshly transparent textures, without sacrificing sweetness of string timbre. It is of course the transparency of sound in earlier Baroque music which makes the claims of the authenticists especially strong, when the harpsichord continuo can make its presence felt without the artificial balancing that can only be achieved electronically when modern instruments are used.

Our loyalties to traditional performances directed by artists of the calibre of Sir Thomas Beecham, Bruno Walter and, more recently, Leonard Bernstein, Sir Colin Davis and Sir Neville Marriner remain undiminished. As to the use of the fortepiano (with its drier sonority but obvious freshness and clarity of texture) for nineteenth-century music, one's reactions must inevitably be subjective. It is easy to conjecture that Beethoven composed his *Hammerklavier sonata* or *Emperor concerto* with an idealized piano-image in mind, not unlike that of the modern concert grand; yet creative artists are usually happiest in the sound-world with which they are familiar.

Fortunately the current CD catalogue offers a profusion of alternatives for listeners of all tastes and persuasions, and in the world of recorded music we can all make our own choices.

Introduction

The object of *The Penguin Guide to Compact Discs* is to give the serious collector a comprehensive survey of the finest recordings of permanent music on CD. As most records are issued almost simultaneously on both sides of the Atlantic and use identical international catalogue numbers, this *Guide* should be found to be equally useful in Great Britain and the USA. The internationalization of repertoire and numbers is increasingly applying to CDs issued by the major international companies and by many smaller ones too, while most of the smaller European labels are imported in their original formats into both Britain and the USA.

The sheer number of records of artistic merit now available causes considerable problems in any assessment of overall and individual excellence. While in the case of a single popular repertoire work it might be ideal for the discussion to be conducted by a single reviewer, it has not always been possible for one person to have access to every version, and division of reviewing responsibility becomes inevitable. Also there are certain works and certain recorded performances for which one or another of our team has a special affinity. Such a personal identification can often carry with it a special perception too. We feel that it is a strength of our basic style to let such conveyed pleasure or admiration for the merits of an individual recording come over directly to the reader, even if this produces a certain ambivalence in the matter of choice between competing recordings. Where disagreement is more positive (and this has rarely happened), then readers will find an indication of this difference in the text.

We have considered and rejected the use of initials against individual reviews, since this is essentially a team project. The occasions for disagreement generally concern matters of aesthetics, for instance in the manner of recording balance, where a contrived effect may trouble some ears more than others, or in the matter of style, where the difference between robustness and refinement of approach appeals differently to listening sensibilities, rather than involving a question of artistic integrity. But over the years our views seem to grow closer together, rather than to diverge; perhaps we are getting mellower, but we are seldom ready to offer strong disagreement following the enthusiastic reception by one of the team of a controversial recording, if the results are creatively stimulating. Our perceptions of the advantages and disadvantages of performances of early music on original (as against modern) instruments seem fairly evenly balanced; again, any strong feelings are indicated in the text.

EVALUATION

Most recordings issued today by the major companies are of a high technical standard and offer performances of a quality at least as high as is experienced in the concert hall. In adopting a starring system for the evaluation of records, we have decided to make use of from one to three stars. Brackets round one or more of the stars indicate some reservations about its inclusion, and readers are advised to refer to the text. Brackets round all the stars usually indicate a basic qualification: for instance, a mono recording of a performance of artistic interest, where considerable allowances have to be made for the sound quality, even though the recording may have been digitally remastered.

Our evaluation system may be summarized as follows:

*** An outstanding performance and recording in every way.
** A good performance and recording of today's normal high standard.
* A fair performance, reasonably well or well recorded.

Our evaluation is normally applied to the record as a whole, unless there are two main works or groups of works, and by different composers. In this case, each is dealt with separately in its appropriate place. In the case of a collection of shorter works, we feel that there is little point in giving a separate starring to each item, even if their merits are uneven, since the record has to be purchased as a complete programme.

ROSETTES

To a very few records we have awarded a rosette: ✿.

Unlike our general evaluations, in which we have tried to be consistent, a rosette is a quite arbitrary compliment by a member of the reviewing team to a recorded performance which, he finds, shows special illumination, magic, or a spiritual quality, or even outstanding production values, that places it in a very special class. The choice is essentially a personal one (although often it represents a shared view), and in some cases it is applied to an issue where certain reservations must also be mentioned in the text of the review. The rosette symbol is placed before the usual evaluation and the record number. It is quite small – we do not mean to imply an 'Academy Award' but a personal token of appreciation for something uniquely valuable. We hope that, once the reader has discovered and perhaps acquired a 'rosetted' CD, its special qualities will soon become apparent.

DIGITAL RECORDINGS

Nearly all new compact discs are recorded digitally, but an increasingly large number of digitally remastered, reissued analogue recordings are now appearing, and we think it important to include a clear indication of the difference:

Dig. This indicates that the master recording was digitally encoded.

BARGAIN AND SUPER-BARGAIN ISSUES

Since the publication of our last volume we have seen a huge expansion of the mid- and bargain-price labels from all the major companies. These are usually standard-repertoire works in excellent analogue recordings, digitally remastered. Often these reissue CDs are generous in playing time, increasing their value to the collector. The record chain stores are now also offering even cheaper classical CDs at super-bargain price, usually featuring performances by artists whose names are not internationally familiar. Most of these recordings dervive from Eastern Europe, where recording costs are currently much lower than in the West. Many of them are digitally encoded and some offer outstanding value, both technically and musically. Thus the collector has plenty of scope in deciding how much to pay for a recorded performance, with a CD range from about £4 up to over three times that amount.

Our listing of each recording first indicates if it is not in fact in the premium-price category, as follows:

(M) Medium-priced label, with the CD costing between £6 and £9.

(B) Bargain-priced label, with the CD costing £4–£6.

(BB) Super-bargain label, with the CD costing under £4.

Some chain stores may have special offers from time to time, when prices are even lower.

It is possible that, in the current inflationary times, prices may rise during the lifetime of this volume so that the above price ranges become out of date, but the major manufacturers generally maintain the price ratios between labels when an overall increase is made.

LAYOUT OF TEXT

We have aimed to make our style as simple as possible, even though the catalogue numbers of recordings are no longer as straightforward as they once were. So, immediately after the evaluation and before the catalogue number, the record make is given, usually in abbreviated form (a key to the abbreviations is provided on pages xx–xxi). In the case of a set of two or more CDs, the number of units involved is given in brackets after the catalogue number.

AMERICAN CATALOGUE NUMBERS

The numbers which follow in square brackets are US catalogue numbers, while the abbreviation [id.] indicates that the American number is identical to the European, which is increasingly the case.

There are certain small differences to be remembered by American readers. For instance, a CBS number could have a completely different catalogue number on either side of the Atlantic, or use the same digits with different alphabetical prefixes. Both will be clearly indicated. EMI/Angel use extra digits for their British compact discs; thus the US number CDC 47001 becomes CDC7 47001-2 in Britain (the -2 is the European indication that this is a compact disc). We have taken care to check catalogue information as far as is possible, but as all the editorial work has been done in England there is always the possibility of error; American readers are therefore invited, when ordering records locally, to take the precaution of giving their dealer the fullest information about the music and recordings they want.

The indications (M), (B) and (BB) immediately before the starring of a disc refer only to the British record, as pricing systems are not always identical on both sides of the Atlantic.

Where no American catalogue number is given, this does not necessarily mean that a record is not available in the USA; the transatlantic issue may not have been made at the time of the publication of this *Guide*. Readers are advised to check the current *Schwann* catalogue and to consult their local record store.

ABBREVIATIONS

To save space we have adopted a number of standard abbreviations in listing orchestras and performing groups (a list is provided below), and the titles of works are often shortened, especially where they are listed several times. Artists' forenames are sometimes omitted if they are not absolutely necessary for identification purposes. Also we have not usually listed the contents of operatic highlights and collections; these can be found in *The Classical Catalogue*, published by *Gramophone* magazine (177–179, Kenton Road, Kenton, Harrow, Middlesex, England, HA3 0HA).

We have followed common practice in the use of the original language for titles where it seems sensible. In most cases, English is used for orchestral and instrumental music and the original language for vocal music and opera. There are exceptions, however; for instance, the Johann Strauss discography uses the German language in the interests of consistency.

ORDER OF MUSIC

The order of music under each composer's name broadly follows that adopted by *The Classical Catalogue*: orchestral music, including concertos and symphonies; chamber music; solo instrumental music (in some cases with keyboard and organ music separated); vocal and choral music; opera; vocal collections; miscellaneous collections.

The Classical Catalogue now usually includes stage works alongside opera; in the main we have not followed this practice, preferring to list, say, ballet music and incidental music (where no vocal items are involved) in the general orchestral group. Within each group our listing follows an alphabetical sequence, and couplings within a single composer's output are *usually* discussed together instead of separately with cross-references. Occasionally and inevitably because of this alphabetical approach, different recordings of a given work can become separated when a record is listed and discussed under the first work of its alphabetical sequence. The editor feels that alphabetical consistency is essential if the reader is to learn to find his or her way about.

CONCERTS AND RECITALS

Most collections of music intended to be regarded as concerts or recitals involve many composers, and it is quite impractical to deal with them within the alphabetical composer index. They are grouped separately, at the end of the book, in three sections. In each section, recordings are usually arranged in alphabetical order of the performers' names: concerts of orchestral and concertante music under the name of the orchestra, ensemble or, if more important, conductor or soloist; instrumental recitals under the name of the instrumentalist; operatic and vocal recitals under the principal singer or vocal group, as seems appropriate.

In certain cases where the compilation features many different performers, it is listed alphabetically under its collective title, or the key word in that title (thus *Favourite operatic duets* is listed under 'Operatic duets'). Sometimes, for complicated collections, and especially compilations of favourite operatic arias, only brief details of contents and performers are given; fuller information can usually be found in *The Classical Catalogue*.

CATALOGUE NUMBERS

Enormous care has gone into the checking of CD catalogue numbers and contents to ensure that all details are correct, but the editor and publishers cannot be held responsible for any mistakes that may have crept in despite all our zealous checking. When ordering CDs, readers are urged to provide their record-dealer with full details of the music and performers, as well as the catalogue number.

DELETIONS

Compact discs, especially earlier, full-priced issues not too generous in musical content, are now steadily succumbing to the deletions axe, and more are likely to disappear during the lifetime of this book. Sometimes copies may still be found in specialist shops, and there remains the compensatory fact that most really important and desirable recordings are eventually reissued, usually costing less!

COVERAGE

As the output of major and minor labels continues to expand, it will obviously be impossible for us to mention *every* CD that is available, within the covers of a single book; this is recognized as a practical limitation if we are to update our survey regularly. We have to be carefully selective in choosing the discs to be included (although on rare occasions a recording has been omitted simply because a review copy was not available); anything which eludes us can always be included next time. However, we do welcome suggestions from readers about such omissions if they seem to be of special interest, and particularly if they are inexpensive. But borderline music on specialist labels that are not readily and reliably obtainable on both sides of the Atlantic cannot be given any kind of priority.

Acknowledgements

For the first time this completely new edition of *The Penguin Guide to Compact Discs* has been written and compiled by all three authors using compatible computers. This has meant that combining the major contents of our previous (1988) *New Penguin Guide* with the *1989 Yearbook* has been inherently straightforward, and that re-editing and updating earlier reviews has been achieved with an ease that would have been unthinkable using more traditional, paper-and-paste methods. We have also been able to exchange listings and reviews of new material readily among ourselves on miniature 'not-so-floppy' discs. It was then possible for the Editor to bring everything together – old reviews, reissues, and new recordings – into two basic sections, which we called 'Old Book' and 'New Book'; these could be quickly printed out as page proofs and proofread independently. Finally, closely following the Editor's detailed instructions about order and layout, our Copy Editor, Roger Wells, combined the two sections in their final sequence on his computer and encoded the complicated 'instructions' for the printer. A few days later we received finished page-proofs to check, and not long after that actual copies of the 1990/1991 *Penguin Guide* were being printed. With such a short time-period between the final reviews being written and the actual printing process, our survey is almost unbelievably up to date.

It all sounds so simple! But when we began, only one of us had any real experience of computer techniques, and no one had met our formidable word-processing software (WordPerfect), which at first seemed to exercise far greater control over events than we did. Any reader who has personally experienced such a baptism, with their computer ready and willing to swallow up everything at the touch of a wrong key, will understand how fraught was our learning process.

The whole experiment – about which Penguin Books at first had some misgivings – would not have succeeded without the enormous patience and skill of Roger Wells, who had mastered the intricacies of WordPerfect well in advance and who was ready at almost any hour of the day or night to rescue his determined but not especially talented group of authors whenever disaster struck. Without him this book would certainly not have appeared on time, nor would it have been so comprehensive (we were under great pressure from the endless flood of new issues, and our new technology meant that we were able to cope with them all and make rational decisions about the book's final contents). So we need to say a heartfelt thankyou for R.W.'s consistently creative help, over and above the demands of duty, which proved indispensable and which was always given with good humour.

Our thanks are due to others too, not least to Kathleen March for her zealous checking of the finished proofs. It was she who first decided that, contrary to our first revised draft, Mozart was 8½ – not 82 – when he wrote his early *London symphonies* in Chelsea in 1764. We also appreciate the stamina and eagle eyes of Winifred Greenwood, who spent countless hours checking every catalogue number in both our old and new material. The Editor wishes also to thank Barbara Menard who, with considerable word-processing experience, stood by to restore his nerve when complicated text had to be moved about or copied, and especially at those moments when reviews that had already been integrated into the main draft seemed to disappear from his computer without trace.

Finally the authors gratefully acknowledge the many letters of encouragement and appreciation from readers which have supported us in our marathon task, and whose comments about errata and suggestions concerning omitted recordings have helped to make the present text more comprehensive and more precise in its detail than its predecessor.

E.G.
R.L.
I.M.

An International Mail-Order Source for Recordings

Readers are urged to support a local dealer if he is prepared and able to give a proper service, and to remember that obtaining many CDs involves perseverance. If, however, difficulty is experienced locally, we suggest the following mail-order alternative, which operates world-wide:

Squires Gate Music Centre
Squires Gate Station Approach
Blackpool
Lancashire FY8 2SP
England

This organization (which is operated under the direction of the Editor of *The Penguin Guide to Compact Discs*) patiently extends compact disc orders until they finally come to hand. A full guarantee of safe delivery is made on any order undertaken. Please write for further details, enclosing a stamped and self-addressed envelope if within the UK.

American readers seeking a domestic mail-order source may write to the following address where a comparable supply service is in operation (for both American and imported European labels). Please write for further details (enclosing a stamped, self-addressed envelope if within the USA) or send your order to:

PG Dept
Serenade Records
1713 G St, N.W.
Washington DC 20006
USA

Abbreviations

Ac.	Academy, Academic
AAM	Academy of Ancient Music
Amb. S.	Ambrosian Singers
Ang.	Angel
Ara.	Arabesque
arr.	arranged
ASMF	Academy of St Martin-in-the-Fields
ASV	Academy Sound and Vision
Bar.	Baroque
Bav.	Bavarian
BPO	Berlin Philharmonic Orchestra
Cal.	Calliope
Cap.	Caprice
CBSO	City of Birmingham Symphony Orchestra
CfP	Classics for Pleasure
Ch.	Choir; Chorale; Chorus
Chan.	Chandos
CO	Chamber Orchestra
COE	Chamber Orchestra of Europe
Col. Mus. Ant.	Musica Antiqua, Cologne
Coll.	Collegium
Coll. Aur.	Collegium Aureum
Coll. Mus.	Collegium Musicum
Concg. O	Royal Concertgebouw Orchestra of Amsterdam
cond.	conductor, conducted
Cons.	Consort
CRD	Continental Record Distributors
DG	Deutsche Grammophon
Dig.	digital recording
E.	England, English
ECO	English Chamber Orchestra
EMI	Electrical and Mechanical Industries
Ens.	Ensemble
Fest.	Festival
Fr.	French
GO	Gewandhaus Orchestra
HM	Harmonia Mundi France
HM/RCA	Deutsche Harmonia Mundi
Hung.	Hungaroton
Hyp.	Hyperion
L.	London

LAPO	Los Angeles Philharmonic Orchestra
LCO	London Chamber Orchestra
LMP	London Mozart Players
LOP	Lamoureux Orchestra of Paris
LPO	London Philharmonic Orchestra
LSO	London Symphony Orchestra
Mer.	Meridian
Met.	Metropolitan
MoC	Ministry of Culture
movt	movement
N.	North
nar.	narrated
Nat.	National
NY	New York
O	Orchestra, Orchestre
O-L	Oiseau-Lyre
Op.	Opera (in performance listings); opus (in music titles)
orch.	orchestrated
ORTF	L'Orchestre de la radio et télévision française
Ph.	Philips
Phd.	Philadelphia
Philh.	Philharmonia
PO	Philharmonic Orchestra
PRT	Precision Records & Tapes
Qt	Quartet
R.	Radio
RCA	distributed in UK by BMG
ROHCG	Royal Opera House, Covent Garden
RPO	Royal Philharmonic Orchestra
RSO	Radio Symphony Orchestra
S.	South
SCO	Scottish Chamber Orchestra
Sinf.	Sinfonietta
SNO	Scottish National Orchestra
SO	Symphony Orchestra
Soc.	Society
Sol. Ven.	I Solisti Veneti
SRO	Suisse Romande Orchestra
Sup.	Supraphon
trans.	transcription, transcribed
V.	Vienna
Van.	Vanguard
VCM	Vienna Concentus Musicus
VPO	Vienna Philharmonic Orchestra
VSO	Vienna Symphony Orchestra
W.	West

Abel, Carl Friedrich (1723–87)

6 Symphonies, Op. 7.
**(*) Chan. Dig. CHAN 8648 [id.]. Cantilena, Shepherd.

The *Six Symphonies* of Op. 7 were composed in 1764. The symphonies speak much the same language as J. C. Bach or early Mozart, but they are often quite characterful and well worth hearing. The performances are not the last word in elegance, but they are both lively and enjoyable as well as being well recorded. An eminently serviceable issue that fills a gap in the catalogue.

Adam, Adolphe (1803–56)

Giselle (ballet): complete recording.
*** Decca Dig. 417 505-2 (2) [id.]. ROHCG O, Bonynge.

Giselle (ballet): original score (abridged).
(M) **(*) Decca 417 738-2 [id.]. VPO, Karajan.

Giselle (1841) is the first of the great classical ballets. Bonynge's performance offers the complete original score, exactly as Adam scored it, with all repeats. Also included are the *Peasants' Pas de deux* in Act I with music by Frédéric Bürgmuller, and two other insertions, possibly by Minkus. The playing is polished and warmly sympathetic. Bonynge's tempi are very much of the ballet theatre, but the overall tension is maintained well and detail is affectionately vivid. Recorded in London's Henry Wood Hall, with its glowing acoustics, the sound is richly coloured and sumptuous, the bass resonance almost too expansive, and this is one of the most successful and satisfying of Bonynge's many ballet recordings made for Decca over the years.

Karajan's performance offers sixty minutes of music: he effectively combines drama with an affectionate warmth, and the phrasing of the lyrical passages produces much lovely – if sometimes suave – playing from the Vienna strings. The more robust writing has plenty of vigour and colour. The recording was made in the Sofiensaal in 1961, and its original excellence is enhanced by the digital remastering, rather like the cleaning of a painting. Karajan is particularly good in the closing pages: when Giselle leaves her lover for ever, he creates a tellingly spacious romantic apotheosis.

Adams, John (born 1947)

Shaker loops.
*** Ph. 412 214-2 [id.]. San Francisco SO, De Waart – REICH: *Variations for winds.****

Shaker loops is one of the more appealing of minimalist works. John Adams's inspiration was from the Shakers, the religious sect whose devotions regularly led to shaking and trembling. In his four linked movements Adams reproduces the shaking in prolonged ostinatos and trills, making the result sound like Sibelius stuck in the groove. Whatever the limitations, there is a genuine poetic imagination here; both performance and recording are outstanding on CD.

Addinsell, Richard (1904-77)

Warsaw concerto.
*** Ph. Dig. 411 123-2 [id.]. Dichter, Philh. O, Marriner (with *Concert of concertante music* ***).
*** Decca Dig. 414 348-2 [id.]. Ortiz, RPO, Atzmon – LITOLFF: *Scherzo*; GOTTSCHALK: *Grande fantaisie*; RACHMANINOV: *Concerto No. 2*.***

Richard Addinsell's pastiche miniature concerto, written for the film *Dangerous moonlight* in 1942, is perfectly crafted and its atmosphere combines all the elements of the Romantic concerto to great effect; moreover it has a truly memorable main theme. It is beautifully played here, with Marriner revealing the most engaging orchestral detail. The sound is first rate.

The alternative from Cristina Ortiz is a warmly romantic account, spacious in conception, with the resonant ambience of Walthamstow Assembly Hall providing beguilingly rich string timbres. If the couplings are suitable, this is a rewarding collection, more substantial than Dichter's. The recording is first class.

Aguado, Dionisio (1784-1849)

Adagio, Op. 2/1; Polonaise, Op. 2/2; Introduction and Rondo, Op. 2/3.
(*) RCA Dig. RD 84549 [RCD1 4549]. Julian Bream (guitar) – SOR: *Fantaisies* etc.(*)

Aguado was a contemporary of Sor, with whom his music is coupled – the two composers played duets together in Paris. The *Adagio* is the most striking piece, serene and introspective; it might have been even more effective had Bream been slightly less deliberate and reflective and chosen to move the music on a little more. However, the other pieces have plenty of life, and all are played with Bream's characteristic feeling for colour. The New York recording is truthful and realistic.

Aho, Kalevi (born 1949)

(i) *Violin concerto; Hiljaisuus (Silence); Symphony No. 1.*
*** BIS Dig. CD 396 [id.]. (i) Manfred Gräsbeck; Lahti SO, Vänskä.

The Finnish composer Kalevi Aho is now in his early forties. He was a pupil of Rautavaara, under whose guidance he composed his *First Symphony* in 1969. Its serious tone betokens an impressive musical personality at work: the first movement has something of the gravity of Nielsen, Bartók or Shostakovich. The second has the latter's macabre sense of humour, perhaps with a touch of Britten. The least successful of the four movements is probably the baroque-like third; the finale, however, has an impressive eloquence. Those who like Robert Simpson's music will feel at home here. *Silence* (1982) is an imaginative piece whose stillness and glowing colours recall the luminous wind chords of the *Prelude* to Sibelius's *Tempest* incidental music, as well as the tone-clusters of the avant-garde. It is related to (and was conceived as an introduction to) the post-expressionist and more 'radical' and trendy *Violin concerto* (1981). All the same, it is a work of considerable resource and imaginative intensity. Good performances and recording.

Albéniz, Isaac (1860–1909)

Suite española (arr. Frühbeck de Burgos).
(M) *** Decca 417 786-2 [id.]. New Philh. O, Frühbeck de Burgos – FALLA: *El amor brujo**** (with GRANADOS: *Goyescas: Intermezzo****).

Here is a multi-coloured orchestral arrangement, by the conductor Raphael Frühbeck de Burgos, of Albéniz's early *Suite española* (which Alicia de Larrocha gives us in its original piano format). It offers light music of the best kind, colourful, tuneful, exotically scored and providing orchestra and recording engineers alike with a chance to show their paces, the sound bright and glittering. We are given here seven pieces from the suite plus *Cordoba*, which is one of the *Cantos de españa* and has a very fetching melody to end the group graciously. The Granados *Intermezzo* from *Goyescas* makes a lusciously brilliant bonus item.

Cantos de España: Córdoba, Op. 232/4; Mallorca (Barcarola), Op. 202; Piezás caracteristicás: Zambra Granadina; Torre Bermaja, Op. 92/7, 12; Suite española: Granada; Sevilla; Cádiz; Asturias, Op. 47/1, 3–5.
*** CBS Dig. MK 36679 [id.]. John Williams (guitar).

Some of Albéniz's more colourful miniatures are here, and John Williams plays them most evocatively. His mood is slightly introvert, and the underlying technical skill is hidden in his concern for atmosphere. A most engaging recital, recorded with great faithfulness and not over-projected.

Cantos de España: Córdoba, Op. 234/4; Mallorca, Op. 202. Suite española, Op. 47: Cádiz; Granada; Sevilla.
⊛ *** RCA Dig. RCD 14378 [id.]. Julian Bream (guitar) – GRANADOS: *Collection.**** ⊛

Julian Bream is in superb form in this splendid recital, his own favourite record, vividly recorded in the pleasingly warm acoustic of Wardour Chapel, near his home in Wiltshire. The CD is electrifying, giving an uncanny impression of the great guitarist sitting and making music just beyond the loudspeakers. The playing itself has wonderfully communicative rhythmic feeling, great subtlety of colour, and its spontaneity increases the impression that one is experiencing a 'live' recital. The performance of the haunting *Córdoba*, which ends the group, is unforgettable.

Iberia; Navarra; Suite española.
⊛ *** Decca Dig. 417 887-2 [id.]. Alicia de Larrocha.

Iberia comprises four books of impressions which Albéniz composed during the last few years (1906–9) of his all-too-short life. Alicia de Larrocha brings an altogether beguiling charm and character to these rewarding miniature tone-poems and makes light of their sometimes fiendish technical difficulties. There is plenty of atmosphere, lyricism and warmth, a masterly command of keyboard and colour, crisp, light articulation and beautifully judged rubato. Miss Larrocha completes the set with the early *Suite española*, begun in the 1880s, and *Navarra*, with which Albéniz had originally intended to end *Iberia*. The recording is among the most successful of piano sounds Decca has achieved.

Albinoni, Tommaso (1671–1750)

Adagio in G min. for organ and strings (arr. Giazotto).
*** Ph. Dig. 410 606-2 [id.]. I Musici (with *Baroque Concert.****)

*** Virgin Dig. VCy 791081-2 [id.]. LCO, Warren-Green – VIVALDI: *Four seasons;*
PACHELBEL: *Canon.****
(M) *** Decca 417 712-2 [id.]. SCO, Münchinger – PACHELBEL: *Canon ****; VIVALDI: *4 Seasons.***(*)
(B) *** Pickwick Dig. PCD 802. Scottish CO, Laredo (with *String masterpieces.****)

Albinoni's *Adagio* in Giazotto's cunning arrangement combines features from both the baroque and romantic eras, which have made it a world-wide hit with the musical public. I Musici gave it its CD début; collectors who have a soft spot for the piece will find this performance thoroughly recommendable, with nicely judged expressive feeling giving the melodic line a restrained nobility. The sound is excellent too, and the rest of the programme is equally successful.

Christopher Warren-Green's version is as impressive as any in the catalogue, opening with an attractively volatile violin solo and leading to a richly upholstered climax, with the strings matching the organ in sonority. Splendid sound.

Münchinger's sumptuous yet stylish version is also available within a mid-priced concert of baroque lollipops (Decca 417 781-2) and he has re-recorded it digitally in a similar collection (411 973-2) – see Concerts, below.

No less telling is the bargain-priced, digitally recorded Pickwick account, strongly contoured and most responsively played by the Scottish Chamber Orchestra under Jaime Laredo.

12 Concerti a cinque, Op. 5.
(M) *** Ph. Dig. 422 251-2 [id.]. Pina Carmirelli, I Musici.

Albinoni has been quite unjustly overshadowed by many of his contemporaries. His invention is unfailingly fresh and vital, and this fine body of concertos has variety and resource to commend it. I Musici, with Pina Carmirelli as the solo player, are every bit as fresh as the music, and they are accorded altogether first-rate sound. The digital recording is early (1982) but sounds excellent. Modern instruments are used to most convincing effect.

Concerti a cinque, Op. 7/2, 3, 5, 6, 8, 9, 11 & 12.
(M) *** DG 427 111-2 [id.]. Holliger, Elhorst, Berne Camerata.

Oboe concertos, Op. 7/3, 6, 9 & 12; Op. 9/2, 5, 8 & 11.
*** Unicorn Dig. DKPCD 9088 [id.]. Sarah Francis, L. Harpsichord Ens.

This splendid DG reissue contains eight of the twelve concertos comprising Albinoni's Op. 7, which were published in Amsterdam in 1715. Four of them are double oboe concertos (Nos. 2, 5, 8 and 11), four are for solo oboe, and the remainder are for strings. The ideas are memorable and there is a touching charm about many of the slow movements. The playing of Heinz Holliger, Hans Elhorst and the Berne Camerata is refined, persuasive and vital, and the CD could hardly be more truthful or better detailed.

Those looking for a selection of *Oboe concertos* from both Opp. 7 and 9 could hardly better this generous digital collection (over 73 minutes) from Unicorn-Kanchana. Sarah Francis is an immensely stylish and gifted soloist: her decoration is nicely judged, her legato playing is as appealing as her light, clean articulation of allegros. She is accompanied with warmth and grace, and the recording is first class, transparent yet full and naturally balanced.

Concerti a cinque, Op. 9/1, 4, 6, 7, 10 & 12.
(M) *** Ph. 426 080-2 [id.]. Ayo, Holliger, Bourgue, Garatti, I Musici.

Concerti a cinque, Op. 9/2, 3, 5, 8, 9 & 11.
(M) *** Ph. 426 449-2 [id.]. Holliger, Bourgue, Garatti, I Musici.

This excellent pair of mid-priced CDs between them offer Albinoni's complete Op. 9, concertos in five parts featuring one or two oboe soloists, or a violin. The recordings were first issued in 1968 and are played with characteristic finesse and style. There is much delightful music here and the recording, excellent for its period, sounds fresh and vivid, if a little dry. The first disc (426 080-2) includes the concertos with violin, plus two of the double oboe concertos; the second includes all the solo oboe concertos plus the other two double concertos. Both discs are well worth exploring.

Alfvén, Hugo (1872–1960)

Symphony No. 1 in F min., Op. 7; Andante religioso; Drapa (Ballad for large orchestra); Uppsala rhapsody, Op. 24.
*** BIS Dig. CD 395 [id.]. Stockholm PO, Neeme Järvi.

Järvi's version of the *First Symphony* supersedes the earlier Westerberg version; it is superior both artistically and technically and leaves the listener more persuaded as to its merits. Though the symphony has a certain warmth and freshness, it remains amiable rather than memorable, likeable rather than lovable. The *Uppsala rhapsody* is based on student songs, but it is pretty thin stuff compared with its predecessor, the justly celebrated *Midsummer vigil*. The *Andante religioso* is rather let down by its sugary closing pages. *Drapa* opens with some fanfares, full of sequential clichés and with a certain naïve pomp and splendour that verges on bombast.

Symphony No. 2 in D, Op. 11; Swedish rhapsody No. 1 (Midsummer vigil).
*** BIS Dig. CD 385 [id.]. Stockholm PO, Neeme Järvi.

Like those of its predecessor, the ideas of the *Second Symphony* are pleasing though they do not possess a particularly individual stamp. If you expect anything as characteristically Swedish or as fresh as the *Midsummer vigil* (1903), you will surely be disappointed, but there is still much to enjoy. On the whole, Järvi is very persuasive in the symphony and gives a delightful performance of the popular *Midsummer vigil*.

Aliabiev, Alexander (1787–1851)

(i; ii) *Introduction and theme with variations in D min.; (iii; ii) Souvenir de Moscou, Op. 6; (iv) Piano trio in A min.; (v) 12 Romances.*
*** Olympia OCD 181 [id.]. (i) Venyavsky; (ii) USSR Ac. SO, Verbitsky; (iii) Grauch; (iv) Voskresensky, Ambarpumyan, Knyasev; (v) Pluzhnikov, Mishuk.

Aliabiev's (or Alyabiev's) *Trio in A minor* is a delightful piece with something of the fluency of Weber and Mendelssohn, and it is heard to good advantage here. (Mikhail Voskresensky is a refined and brilliant pianist.) The *Introduction and theme with variations in D minor* is sandwiched between two groups of songs, nearly all of which have great charm and appeal. The *Trio* and the songs are well recorded, though the piano is placed rather backwardly in relation to the violin, to which the engineers give a slight hardness. The recording of the two insubstantial pieces for violin and orchestra comes off less well, though the *Souvenir de Moscou* variations bring splendid playing from Eduard Grauch. This disc almost gives the lie to the impression that Russian music begins with Glinka.

Violin sonata in E min.
** Olympia OCD 184 [id.]. Ambarpumyan, Voskresensky – GLINKA: *Quartet.***

This *Sonata*, a fluent piece in the style of Weber and Mendelssohn, shows more charm than originality. The sleeve suggests that its second group takes Glinka as a model, and the ideas throughout are attractive and the music well crafted. Not essential but far from unpleasing music, and eminently well played by Lievon Ambarpumyan and Mikhail Voskresensky.

Alkan, Charles (1813–88)

Barcarolle; Gigue, Op. 24; Marche, Op. 37/1; Nocturne No. 2, Op. 57/1; Saltarelle, Op. 23; Scherzo diabolico, Op. 39/3; Sonatine, Op. 61.
(M) *** HM HMA 190 927 [id.]. Bernard Ringeissen.

Bernard Ringeissen is slightly less flamboyant than Ronald Smith, but he is fully equal to the cruel technical demands of this music. The *Sonatine*, an extended, big-boned piece, is particularly successful, but all this music is of interest. The recording, from the beginning of the 1970s, is first class; it has splendid presence and body in its remastered format.

3 Études de bravoure (Scherzi), Op. 16; 3 Grandes Études, Op. 76.
(M) *** EMI CDM7 69630-2 [id.]. Ronald Smith.

Ronald Smith's virtuosity in this repertoire is pretty well transcendental. Although Alkan was no Chopin (the *Études de bravoure* appeared, as Smith reminds us, in the same year as Chopin's *B flat minor Scherzo*), he is a composer of some stature and much originality. These are new recordings of excellent quality.

Grande sonate (Les quatre ages), Op. 23; Sonatine.
(M) *** EMI CDM7 69421-2. Ronald Smith.

The *Grande sonate* dates from 1847, some six years before the Liszt *Sonata*, and is a rather extraordinary piece. Its four movements describe four decades of a man's life: his twenties, thirties, forties and fifties, each getting progressively slower. The first movement is a whirlwind of a scherzo whose difficulties Ronald Smith bestrides almost nonchalantly; the second, *Quasi-Faust*, is perhaps the most Lisztian, while the last two are the most searching and individual. It goes without saying that the performance here is a remarkable piece of virtuosity. The *Sonatine*, by no means a small-scale piece, is given a comparably strong performance, and the 1971 recordings are realistic and clean.

Allegri, Gregorio (1582–1652)

Miserere.
*** Gimell CDGIM 339 [id.]. Tallis Scholars, Phillips – MUNDY: *Vox patris caelestis*; PALESTRINA: *Missa Papae Marcelli.***
(M) *** Decca 421 147-2 [id.]. King's College Ch., Willcocks – PALESTRINA: *Collection.* ***
(*) DG Dig. 415 517-2 [id.]. Westminster Abbey Ch., Preston – PALESTRINA: *Missa Papae Marcelli* etc.*

Mozart was so impressed with Allegri's *Miserere* when he heard it in the Sistine Chapel (which originally claimed exclusive rights to its performance) that he wrote the music out from memory so that it could be performed elsewhere. On the much-praised Gimell version, the soaring treble solo is taken by a girl, Alison Stamp, and her memorable contribution is enhanced by the recording itself. The Tallis Scholars are ideally balanced in Merton College Chapel, Oxford, and Peter Phillips, their conductor, emphasizes his use of a double choir by placing the solo group in the echoing distance and the main choir directly in front of the listener. The contrasts are dramatic and hugely effective.

It is good to see the famous King's performance of Allegri's *Miserere*, with its arresting treble solo so beautifully and securely sung by Roy Goodman, now appear on CD, coupled with Palestrina at mid-price. The sound remains first class; the background quiet of the medium is a great blessing in this music, with the soaring treble line elysian in its purity.

In Preston's account with the Westminster choristers, the treble solo, though sung confidently, is more positive, less easeful in style; and the result is not quite so memorable as with its two main competitors. However, the coupling includes an outstanding performance of Palestrina's *Missa Papae Marcelli*.

Alwyn, William (1905–85)

(i) *Rhapsody for piano quartet; String quartet No. 3; String trio.*
*** Chan. Dig. CHAN 8440 [id.]. (i) David Willison; Qt of London.

Alwyn's serialism is skin deep and never strays far from a fundamentally tonal language. Although the other two works are impressive, the *Third Quartet* is the most important work on this record; like its two predecessors, it is a concentrated and thoughtful piece of very considerable substance, elegiac in feeling. The playing of the Quartet of London throughout (and of David Willison in the *Rhapsody*) is both committed and persuasive. As a recording, this is in the very first flight and the recording brings the musicians vividly into one's living-room.

Fantasy-Waltzes; 12 Preludes.
**(*) Chan. Dig. CHAN 8399 [id.]. John Ogdon (piano).

The *Fantasy-Waltzes* are highly attractive and are excellently played by John Ogdon, who is also responsible for a perceptive insert-note. The *12 Preludes* are equally fluent and inventive pieces that ought to be better known and well repay investigation. The recording, made at The Maltings, Snape, is first rate and carries the imprimatur of the composer in whose presence it was made. Recommended.

Arensky, Anton (1861–1906)

(i) *Piano concerto No. 2 in F min., Op. 2;* (ii) *Egyptian nights, Op. 50a.*
** Olympia OCD 107 [id.]. (i) Cherkassov; USSR RSO, (i) Alexeev; (ii) Demchenko –
IPPOLITOV-IVANOV: *Caucasian sketches.***

Arensky's *F minor Concerto* is something of a rarity; the work is worth investigating, for the performance is a good one; Alexei Cherkassov brings sensibility and a convincing sense of rubato to the lyrical writing. The recording is somewhat two-dimensional and the piano timbre is not ideally rich but remains fully acceptable. The *Egyptian nights suite* is not the most potent of cheap music – it has something in common with Luigini's *Ballet Egyptien*, even if thematically much less indelible. The bright brash playing here projects the music quite effectively, though the recording has a degree of coarseness; the interest of the repertoire (including the coupling) earns the disc its place in the catalogue.

Violin concerto in A min., Op. 54.
*** Olympia Dig. OCD 106 [id.]. Stadler, Leningrad PO, Chernushenko –
TCHAIKOVSKY: *Suite No. 3.****

This concerto is a much later work than the *Piano concerto* and is a winning piece with a particularly endearing second-subject group theme. The work is most persuasively played by Sergei Stadler, who has a firm rich line and a full understanding of the work's nostalgic feeling; the accompaniment is quite admirable. If the soloist is balanced a shade closely, in all other respects the clear recording, which has excellent presence and detail, is worthy of the performance and should make many new friends for this engaging work.

Symphonies Nos. 1 in B min., Op. 4; 2 in A, Op. 22; Dream on the Volga overture.
(M) ** Olympia OCD 167 [Mobile Fidelity MFCD 878 (without *Overture*)]. USSR Ac. SO, Svetlanov.

Arensky was a pupil of Rimsky-Korsakov and a close friend of both Tchaikovsky and Taneyev. His *First Symphony*, composed shortly after his graduation in 1882, is a work of great fluency and charm. It is beautifully put together and has considerable melodic freshness. The *Second* is the more individual of the two and is full of highly attractive ideas: its four movements are linked together, the finale returning to the material of the opening movement; however, there is little serious attempt at organic cohesion. The *Overture* to the opera, *Dream on the Volga* (1888), based on Ostrovsky's *The Voyvode* which had twice inspired Tchaikovsky, opens bombastically but also has its attractive moments, though its inspiration is less consistent than either of the symphonies. The analogue recordings date from 1983; the performances are spirited though the brass are at times raw in climaxes.

Variations on a theme of Tchaikovsky, Op. 35a.
*** ROH ROH 304/5 [id.]. ROHCG O, Ermler – TCHAIKOVSKY: *Nutcracker ballet.***
(B) **(*) Van. VNC 7532 [VCD 72012 with TCHAIKOVSKY & BORODIN: *Nocturne*].
ECO, Somary – PROKOFIEV: *Classical symphony*; TCHAIKOVSKY: *String serenade.***

Warm and easy on the ear, particularly in this ripely recorded performance, Arensky's unpretentious string work – new to the CD catalogue – makes an attractive fill-up for Mark Ermler's Covent Garden recording of Tchaikovsky's Nutcracker.

It is good to have the fine Vanguard catalogue available again – especially at bargain price – when the remastering is so natural and clear. Somary's performance of Arensky's delightful *Variations*, which amount almost to Tchaikovskian pastiche, has an unaffected simplicity and charm. The slight dryness of the acoustic brings refreshingly cool string textures to prevent the stylish music-making from sounding inflated.

Piano trio No. 1 in D min., Op. 32.
*** Chan. Dig. CHAN 8477 [id.]. Borodin Trio – GLINKA: *Trio.****
*** Delos Dig. DE 3056 [id.]. Cardenes, Solow, Golabek – TCHAIKOVSKY: *Trio.***(*)

The shades of Mendelssohn, Borodin and Tchaikovsky can clearly be discerned in the *Piano trio*, while the invention is fertile and has an endearing period charm; at the same time the ideas have undoubted freshness. The Borodins give a lively and full-blooded account of the *Trio*. The *Scherzo* comes off well, and the whole does justice to the Borodins' genial playing.

The Cardenes group on Delos also give an admirable account of this attractive work, catching the full measure of its charm. It is not an assertive performance, yet it is full of affection. In the scherzo there is a scintillating contribution from the pianist, Mona

Golabek, and all the playing is polished and nicely blended. The recording is realistically balanced, not too forward, and a highly appropriate and generous coupling makes this well worth considering.

Arne, Thomas (1710–78)

Organ concertos Nos. 1 in C; 2 in G; 3 in A; 4 in B flat; 5 in G min.; 6 in B flat.
*** Chan. Dig. CHAN 8604/5 (2) [id.]. Roger Bevan Williams, Cantilena, Shepherd.

Though Arne's concertos are simpler in style and construction than those of Handel, their invention is consistently fresh; their *galant* tunefulness and vigour give lasting pleasure. While their basic structural layout looks forward classically, the baroque influence remains strong, and the orchestral ritornellos recall both Vivaldi and the orchestral suites of Bach. The performances here have admirable style and spirit, and the recording (made in the Henry Wood Hall, Glasgow) is wonderfully fresh and ideally balanced – the organ seems perfectly chosen for this consistently engaging music. A highly recommendable set in every respect.

Symphonies Nos. 1 in C; 2 in F; 3 in E flat; 4 in C min.
** Chan. Dig. CHAN 8403 [id.]. Cantilena, Shepherd.

Arne began writing these symphonies late in his career, when Handel reigned supreme in England. He was stimulated to produce works as electric in their way as those of Haydn's middle period, though there is an obvious influence by J. C. Bach. The symphonies receive business-like performances from the Cantilena and Adrian Shepherd, perhaps a little short on charm and subtlety, though the rather close recording may exaggerate this defect. A serviceable issue that falls short of real distinction.

Cymon and Iphigenia; Frolic and free (cantatas); Jenny; The Lover's recantation; The Morning (cantata); Sigh no more, ladies; Thou soft flowing Avon; What tho' his guilt.
*** Hyp. Dig. CDA 66237 [id.]. Emma Kirkby, Richard Morton, Parley of Instruments, Goodman.

The present collection admirably shows the ingenuous simplicity of Arne's vocal writing, very much in the mid-eighteenth-century English pastoral school with its 'Hey down derrys'. Emma Kirkby has the perfect timbre and all the vocal freshness to bring this music charmingly to life. Richard Morton sings well too; though his style has not always quite the easy manner of Kirkby, he is always responsive. Excellent, warm recording, with the voices naturally projected. A most entertaining concert.

Arnold, Malcolm (born 1921)

(i) *Clarinet concerto No. 1;* (ii) *Flute concertos Nos. 1–2;* (i) *Horn concerto No. 2; Oboe concerto; Trumpet concerto.*
(M) *** EMI CDM7 63491-2. (i) Janet Hilton, Alan Civil, Gordon Hunt, John Wallace; Bournemouth Sinf., Del Mar; (ii) John Solum, Philh. O, Dilkes.

Malcolm Arnold has more than eighteen concertos to his credit. Both his *Flute concertos* are charming and resourceful and John Solum plays them excellently. Janet Hilton in the *First Clarinet concerto* and Alan Civil in the *Second Horn concerto* are hardly less brilliant, while the *Oboe concerto*, written for Leon Goossens, is played with quite superb panache and virtuosity by Gordon Hunt. Having been a trumpeter, Arnold writes with uncommon skill for the instrument and John Wallace's articulation is dazzling. All this music is well crafted, enormously facile and easy to enjoy. The accompaniments, under Norman Del Mar and Neville Dilkes respectively, are excellent and the recordings are comparably vivid.

(i) *Clarinet concerto No. 1, Op. 20;* (ii) *Flute concerto No. 1, Op. 45;* (iii) *Horn concerto No. 2, Op. 58;* (iv) *Double violin concerto, Op. 77.*
*** Conifer Dig. CDCF 172 [id.]. (i) Collins; (ii) Jones; (iii) Watkins; (iv) Sillito and Fletcher; L. Musici, Mark Stephenson.

These four works – all involving string orchestra alone – provide outstanding examples of a genre which Arnold has cultivated with conspicuous success and which might be described as 'the quarter-hour concerto'. Within this frame, neo-classical in scale and aim, he has consistently shown his brilliance in compressing his arguments, writing with jewelled concision for particular performers. Often he adopts neo-classical stylistic patterns – as in the *Double Violin concerto* written with Yehudi Menuhin and Alberto Lysy in mind – but that rarely gets in the way of his lyrical gift, which regularly blossoms in amiable, often catchy tunes. In that *Double concerto*, with the two soloists chasing each other's tail in rapid figuration, Kenneth Sillito and Lyn Fletcher are sweetly matched in writing which presents the most severe demands on purity of intonation. The clarinet and flute works are both Arnold's first essays in these genres – though the Conifer labelling does not indicate the fact – and both Michael Collins and Karen Jones give urgent, exhilarating readings of works which aim for brilliance above all, with the solo writing in the *Flute concerto* concentrating on spiky lines, and with the low chalumeau register of the clarinet surprisingly avoided. The horn soloist, Richard Watkins, may not quite match the wonderfully wide tonal range that the late Alan Civil achieves on the earlier recording, but he is weightier in the slow movement and even brisker in the finale. Remarkable in all four works is the rich resonance of the London Musici string ensemble. Mark Stephenson, who founded this talented chamber orchestra, draws out a sound from his players that would do credit to a much larger ensemble, set against the helpful acoustic of The Maltings at Snape.

(i) *Flute concerto No. 1, Op. 45;* (ii) *Oboe concerto, Op. 39; Sinfoniettas Nos. 1–3, Opp. 48, 65 & 81.*
*** Hyp. Dig. CDA 66332 [id.]. (i) Beckett, (ii) Messiter; L. Fest. O, Ross Pople.

It makes a delightful programme having Arnold's three *Sinfoniettas* framing two wind concertos that come from the same early period, the 1950s. Though, particularly in his later works, Arnold's music has grown much darker, these all reveal him at his most accessible. Crisp allegros and freely lyrical slow movements never outstay their welcome for a moment, with five minutes seemingly set as an outside limit for each. The *Third Sinfonietta*, written slightly later than the rest in 1964 on a commission from the Philharmonia Orchestra, maintains that pattern in its four brief movements. The performances here are all excellent, with warm, well-balanced sound. Anyone hesitating between this version of the *Flute concerto No. 1* and the rival accounts on Conifer and EMI can safely make the choice on preference of coupling.

8 English dances.
(M) (***) Decca mono 425 661-2 [id.]. LPO, Boult – WALTON: *Façade* etc.*** ⊛

Arnold's first essay in writing colourful regional pieces as a latterday equivalent of Dvořák's and Brahms's orchestral dances is still a winner, and it receives a colourful performance under Boult, with the mono recording still sounding remarkably well, an unexpected but attractive coupling for a classic account of Walton's *Façade*.

(i) *Symphony No. 2, Op. 40;* (ii) *Symphony No. 5, Op. 74.*(i) *Peterloo: overture.*
(M) *** EMI CDM7 63368-2 [id.]. (i) Bournemouth SO, Groves; (ii) CBSO, composer.

The recoupling of two of Arnold's most impressive symphonies can be warmly welcomed. Both recordings date from the 1970s. The *Second Symphony* is one of Malcolm Arnold's best pieces, far more complex in structure than it may initially seem. Arnold has developed the habit of hiding his deeper emotions behind a bright, extrovert manner and his *Fifth Symphony* brings out this dichotomy very clearly. It is a consciously elegiac work, written in memory of friends who died young; it contains some of his most intense and emotional music but remains easily approachable. The composer secures an excellent response from the Birmingham orchestra, as Groves, in Bournemouth, is equally dedicated. The compact disc transfer is outstandingly successful; indeed the sound approaches the demonstration class in its vivid detail, body and spaciousness. The *Overture* makes a highly effective encore. Splendid value at mid-price.

Divertimento for flute, oboe and clarinet, Op. 37; Duo for flute and viola, Op. 10; Flute sonata, Op. 121; Oboe quartet, Op. 61; Quintet for flute, violin, viola, horn and piano, Op. 7; 3 Shanties for wind quintet, Op. 4.
*** Hyp. Dig. CDA 66173 [id.]. Nash Ens.

Duo for 2 cellos, Op. 85; Piano trio, Op. 54; Viola sonata No. 1, Op. 17; Violin sonatas Nos. 1, Op. 15; 2, Op. 43; Pieces for violin and piano, Op. 54.
*** Hyp. Dig. CDA 66171 [id.]. Nash Ens.

Clarinet sonatina, Op. 29; Fantasies for wind, Opp. 86–90; Flute sonatina, Op. 19; Oboe sonatina, Op. 28; Recorder sonatina, Op. 41; Trio for flute, bassoon and piano, Op. 6.
*** Hyp. Dig. CDA 66172 [id.]. Nash Ens.

There is much here that belies Malcolm Arnold's image as just an entertaining and genial tunesmith. All the pieces on the first disc show conspicuous resource in the handling of the instruments, whether in the *Duo for flute and viola* or in the *Oboe quartet*, composed for Leon Goossens, a fine piece let down by an empty finale. The *Flute sonata* is the most recent piece, written in 1977, and has a vaguely Satie-like *Andantino* movement, with a touch of Poulenc in the finale. The second disc includes two *Violin sonatas*, which exhibit some Gallic traits: they are cool, civilized and intelligent. The *Piano trio* of 1956 has a powerful sense of direction; it is a vital and ingenious piece, and for the most part the music on this disc is worth getting to know. As a glance at the third listing shows, this collection concentrates on the wind music. This is perhaps more for admirers of Arnold's music than for the generality of collectors. The playing is brilliant and sympathetic throughout all three discs and the recording first rate.

Arriaga, Juan (1806–26)

String quartets Nos. 1 in D min.; 2 in A; 3 in E flat.
*** CRD CRD 33123 (2) [id.]. Chilingirian Qt – WIKMANSON: *String quartet No. 2.****

String quartets Nos. 1 in D min.; 2 in A; 3 in E flat.
**(*) HM Dig. L 3236. Voces Qt.

These CRD recordings come from the mid-1970s and still sound good. The Chilingirians play with both conviction and feeling. There are times perhaps when they could have more lightness of touch (the minuet and finale of the *D minor* are a case in point). However, these are generally very satisfying performances, and their reappearance on CD must be warmly welcomed. These three *Quartets* are marvellous works of great warmth and spontaneity that can hold their own in the most exalted company. It is barely credible that a boy still in his teens could have produced them.

If you want to save money and possess all three *Quartets* on a single compact disc, the more recent set made in 1985 by the Voces String Quartet is well worth considering. The performances though cultured are at times a little too suave; the Chilingirian are the more gutsy and characterful. However, there are many felicitous and musicianly touches here, and the Voces are scrupulous in matters of dynamics. Tempi are well judged throughout, and there is much that gives pleasure.

Atterberg, Kurt (1887–1974)

Symphony No. 6 in C, Op. 31.
(**) Dell'Arte mono CDDA 9019 [id.] NBC SO, Toscanini – SIBELIUS: *Symphony No. 2.*(**)

Toscanini's performance comes from a 1943 broadcast (there is applause after the first movement). It is odd that this endearing piece with its merry finale has never been recorded since the days of Beecham (Columbia) and Atterberg himself (Polydor). The *Symphony* won the 1928 Schubert centenary competition and was for many years scorned for its light-hearted (but ingenious) allusions to other composers. This reading has the imprimatur of the composer himself and has previously only been available coupled in a Society edition with Toscanini's very brisk Sibelius No. 4. The sound is very dated, though not quite as thin as the 1939 Sibelius with which it is coupled.

Auber, Daniel (1782–1871)

Manon Lescaut (complete).
(M) **(*) EMI CMS7 63252-2 (2). Mesplé, Orliac, Runge, Bisson, Greger, Ch. & O Lyrique of R. France, Marty.

Ending, like Puccini's setting of the same story, in 'a desert in Louisiana', Auber's opera, written in the 1850s when he was already seventy-four, bears little resemblance to that example of high romanticism. But the music demonstrates that the liveliness we know from his overtures persisted to the end of his career. Scribe's libretto is a free and often clumsy adaptation of the Prévost novel, but the sequence of arias and ensembles, conventional in their way, restores some of the original poetry. Manon herself is a coloratura soprano (here the tweety but agile Mady Mesplé) and Des Grieux a lyric tenor (here the lightweight Jean-Claude Orliac). A recording as lively as this, with excellent sound in a vivid CD transfer, is very welcome.

La muette de Portici.
*** EMI CDS7 49284-2 (2). Aler, Anderson, Kraus, Lamont, Vassar, La Forge, Ch. & Monte Carlo PO, Fulton.

Auber's opera is well worth investigating. Among the lively ensembles, there is even one chorus that anticipates Gilbert and Sullivan in *Mikado*, a cross between *Three little maids from school* and Pish-Tush's song. The writing may not, as a rule, be very distinguished, but it has striking melodic ideas, and there is a magnificent aria for the hero. In that role, the Spanish tenor Alfredo Kraus sings as stylishly as ever, even if the heroic voice shows signs of age. There is another important tenor role, that of Alphonse, the thoughtless Duke's son who seduces and then leaves Masaniello's sister, the dumb girl of the title. The American tenor, John Aler, provides an ideal contrast with Kraus, singing most beautifully; and June Anderson in the principal soprano role of Elvira, Alphonse's bride-to-be, sounds sweeter than often heretofore on record. Strongly cast and vigorously conducted by Thomas Fulton, it makes an attractive two-disc set, warmly recorded.

Auric, Georges (1899–1983)

L'Eventail de Jeanne: (complete ballet, including music by Delannoy, Ferroud, Ibert, Milhaud, Poulenc, Ravel, Roland-Manuel, Roussel, Florent Schmitt).
Les Mariés de la Tour Eiffel: (complete ballet, including music by Honegger, Milhaud, Poulenc, Tailleferre).
⊛ *** Chan. Dig. CHAN 8356 [id.]. Philh. O, Simon.

A carefree spirit and captivating wit run through both these composite works. The Ravel *Fanfare* is among the shortest and most original of the contributions to *L'Eventail de Jeanne*, and there are many other charming things apart from the best-known number, Poulenc's *Pastourelle*. In fact these pieces are full of imagination and fun – even the Ibert *Valse* quotes the Ravel *Valses nobles*. Geoffrey Simon and the Philharmonia Orchestra give a very good account of themselves and the Chandos recording is little short of spectacular. Its detail is quite marvellously sharp on CD.

Bach, Carl Philipp Emanuel (1714–88)

Cello concertos: in A min., Wq.170; in B flat, Wq.171; in A, Wq.172.
*** Virgin Dig. VC7 90800-2 [id.]. Anner Bylsma, O of Age of Enlightenment, Leonhardt.

Cello concertos: in B flat, Wq.171; in A, Wq.172.
(BB) **(*) Hung. White Label HRC 117 [id.]. Csába Onczay, Liszt CO, Rolla (with CHERUBINI: *13 Contredanses***).

Cello concerto in A, Wq.172.
** DG Dig. 429 219-2. Matt Haimovitz, ECO, A. Davis – BOCCHERINI; HAYDN: *Concertos.***

These concertos also have alternative versions for both keyboard and flute, but they suit the cello admirably. The allegros are full of life, and slow movements are impressive, particularly the hauntingly volatile *Largo con sordini, mesto* of H.439. It is difficult to imagine a better partnership to provide authentic versions of these three fine works. Outer allegros are engagingly lighthearted and alert, and in slow movements Bylsma's expressive intensity communicates strongly, without ever taking the music outside its boundaries of sensibility. These artists convey their commitment to this music persuasively and Bylsma underlines his sure understanding of its style in his excellent cadenzas. One has to accept that the strings of the Orchestra of the Age of Enlightenment can (at times) be somewhat meagre in their upper-range timbre, especially in comparison with competitors using modern instruments. But many listeners are already so indoctrinated by the claims of those who choose even thinner sounds that this will surely not be a drawback, particularly as the recording is so faithful and the acoustic pleasing. Incidentally, Leonhardt makes one concession to modernity: he conducts these performances, rather than leading from the keyboard, which partly accounts for the buoyantly crisp articulation of the allegros.

Onczay, who has a warm, well-focused tone, also plays very sympathetically. The accompaniments for him are polished, elegant and alert, and the recording has a pleasing

13

ambience. As an encore, we are given some attractive country dances by Cherubini, in which the recording is more confined but still agreeable. The disc has good documentation too. Excellent value.

Matt Haimovitz is still a student in his teens, and a very gifted one. His account of the *A major Concerto* may lack something in refinement, but there is no lack of intensity – indeed the slow movement is a bit too introspective and there is some overheated vibrato which will not be to all tastes. The cello is rather up-front, but the recording has no lack of body or warmth.

Flute concerto in D min., Wq. 22.
(B) **(*) ASV CDQS 6012. Dingfelder, ECO, Mackerras – HOFFMEISTER: *Concertos Nos. 6 & 9.***(*)

Flute concertos: in D, Wq. 22; in A min., Wq. 166; in B flat, Wq. 167; in A, Wq. 168; in G, Wq. 169.
*** Capriccio Dig. 10 104 (Wq. 22, 166, 168); 10 105 (Wq. 167, 169) [id.]. Eckart Haupf, C. P. E. Bach CO, Haenchen.

Flute concertos: in A min.; in B flat, Wq. 166/7.
(M) **(*) DG 427 132-2 [id.]. Stephen Preston, E. Concert, Pinnock.

Eckart Haupf gives lively, cleanly articulated performances of these concertos, written for the court of Frederick the Great, well supported by the strong, full-bodied and vigorous accompaniments of the C. P. E. Bach Chamber Orchestra under Hartmut Haenchen. Full, atmospheric recording from East German VEB engineers.

Stephen Preston plays a period instrument which is inevitably less strong in the bottom octave than the modern flute. He gives performances of considerable accomplishment and virtuosity; he makes much of the introspection of the slow movement of the *A minor* and tosses off the finales with enormous facility. He receives excellent support from Pinnock, and the recording quality has fine presence and detail; however, some ears may find this coupling, with its slightly abrasive upper string-sound, a little lacking in charm.

Those who are interested in the Hoffmeister coupling rather than a C. P. E. Bach collection will find Ingrid Dingfelder's playing both spirited and stylish, while Mackerras's accompaniments match polish with vigour. The sound-quality too is admirably vivid and this CD reissue is competitively priced.

Harpsichord concertos, Wq. 43/1–6.
*** EMI Dig. CDS7 49207-8 (2). Van Asperen, Melante 81 Orchestra.

These six concertos come from 1771 during Bach's Hamburg period, and they are disturbingly original and volatile in temperament. Period instruments are used to produce an excellently light and transparent texture. The playing of Bob van Asperen is a delight: bright, vital and intelligent; and the recording is very fine indeed. Another indispensable issue for collectors interested in this intriguing composer.

Harpsichord concerto in G, Wq. 43/5.
(*) CRD CRD 3411 [id.]. Pinnock, E. Concert – VIVALDI: *Trial between harmony and invention* etc.(*)

An excellent performance of an attractive work, using original instruments, a filler for Vivaldi's Op. 8.

Double concerto in E flat for harpsichord and fortepiano; Double concerto in F for 2 harpsichords, Wq. 46.

*** Erato/WEA Dig. 2292 45306-2 [id.]. Koopman, Mathot, Amsterdam Baroque O.

(i) *Double concerto in E flat for harpsichord and fortepiano; Organ concerto in G, Wq. 34;* (ii) *Double harpsichord sonatina No. 2 in D, Wq. 109.*
**(*) ASV Novalis Dig. 150 025-2 [id.]. Haselböck, (i) Fuller; (ii) Rainer; V. Academy.

Double harpsichord concerto in F, Wq. 46.
*** DG Dig. 419 256-2 [id.]. Staier, Hill, Col. Mus. Ant., Goebel – w. f. bach: *Double concerto* etc.***

This spirited and delightful *E flat Concerto for harpsichord and fortepiano*, which comes from Bach's last year, is recorded in this Erato version with period instruments and the inevitably lower pitch, but this does not seem to have dampened its spirits, and the textures are lucid and transparent. The *F major Concerto for two harpsichords* comes from a different world: it was composed almost half a century earlier for Frederick II's court. The recording is as good as the playing. The only grumble: at 43 minutes this is short measure – but what it wants in quantity it certainly makes up for in quality.

The *Double concerto in F* is played with vitality, imagination and dedication by the artists on the alternative DG record; the recording is exceptionally well balanced, with the two solo instruments taking up the right amount of aural space in relation to the orchestra. And how dazzling they are in the finale!

An alternative version of the *E flat Concerto for harpsichord and fortepiano* comes from Martin Haselböck, Richard Fuller and a Viennese ensemble. The *Organ concerto* finds Carl Philipp Emanuel at his most inventive and, in its slow movement, most poetic. The *Sonatina* is another highly interesting piece. The Vienna Academy is a period-instrument group who play with much spirit though their violins are disagreeably nasal at times. The Erato issue is to be preferred.

Oboe concertos: in B flat, Wq. 164; in E flat, Wq. 165.
** Capriccio Dig. 10 069 [id.]. Glaetzner, New Bach Coll. Mus., Pommer – j. c. bach: *Concerto.***

Max Pommer and his Leipzig players are less lively and imaginative in these C. P. E. Bach *Oboe concertos* than their Berlin colleagues in the flute works. Burkhardt Glaetzner's very reedy, piping oboe tone is distinctive but makes for monotony. The two concertos are both fine works with their abrupt changes of mood. The recording, full but rather bass-heavy, emphasizes the discrepancy between Leipzig and Berlin performances in the Capriccio series.

Organ concertos: in G; in E flat, Wq. 34–5; Fantasia and fugue in C min., Wq. 119/7; Prelude in D, Wq. 70/7.
*** Capriccio Dig. 10 135 [id.]. Roland Munch, C. P. E. Bach CO, Haenchen.

With much of the writing involving simple alternation of orchestra and soloist, Hartmut Haenchen and his admirable C. P. E. Bach Chamber Orchestra reinforce the lively expressiveness of the music, alongside the soloist, Roland Munch, on a Berlin baroque organ of the 1750s. The two solo pieces are impressive too, though here the scale is much less ambitious. Full, atmospheric recording.

Berlin sinfonias: in C; in F, Wq. 174/5; in E min.; in E flat, Wq. 178/9; in F, Wq. 181.
*** Capriccio Dig. 10 103 [id.]. C. P. E. Bach C O, Haenchen.

The *Berlin sinfonias* are most welcome as they have not previously been recorded. The playing of Haenchen's excellent C. P. E. Bach group is alert and vigorous, with airy textures and attractively sprung rhythms. Modern instruments are used in the best possible way. Slow movements have expressive commitment without any suggestion of romanticism, and there is a fine sense of balance so that the boldness of Bach's inspiration is well projected. Excellent sound.

6 Hamburg sinfonias, Wq. 182/1 – 6.
*** DG 415 300-2 [id.]. E. Concert, Pinnock.
*** Capriccio Dig. 10 106 [id.]. C. P. E. Bach C O, Haenchen.
*** O-L 417 124-2 [id.]. AAM, Hogwood.

The six *Hamburg string sinfonias* are magnificent examples of Bach's later style when, after the years at the Berlin court, he had greater freedom in Hamburg. They are particularly striking in their unexpected twists of imagination, with wild, head-reeling modulations and sudden pauses which suggest the twentieth century rather than the eighteenth. The abrasiveness of such music comes out sharply in the kind of authenticity favoured by the Academy of Ancient Music. However, many listeners may find the angularity does not make for relaxed listening; they can turn to the English Concert under Pinnock which offers a performing style no less authentic than Hogwood's but with more concern for eighteenth-century poise and elegance. The 1960 analogue recording sounds splendidly fresh and clear in its remastered format. Hogwood's set dates from 1979.

Hartmut Haenchen and the strings of the C. P. E. Bach Chamber Orchestra give attractively warm, red-blooded performances. Though ensemble is not always ideally refined, allegros are strong and vigorous, and the extra sweetness of the lovely *Adagios* is most welcome. Vivid, full recording to match.

4 Hamburg Sinfonias, Wq. 183/1 – 4.
*** Erato/WEA Dig. 2292 45430-2 [id.]. Amsterdam Bar. O, Koopman.
**(*) Capriccio Dig. 10 175 [id.]. C.P.E. Bach CO, Haenchen.

4 Hamburg sinfonias, Wq. 183/1 – 4; Sinfonias: in E min., Wq. 177; in C, Wq. 182/3.
(M) *** Ph. 426 081-2 [id.]. ECO, Leppard.

Unlike the six *Hamburg sinfonias* which C. P. E. Bach wrote earlier for Baron von Swieten, these four later works involve wind as well as strings, pairs of horns, flutes and oboes, as well as a bassoon. The writing is just as refreshing in its unexpectedness and originality, product of Bach's years of relative freedom in Hamburg, after his long stint at the Prussian court in Berlin. Unlike the rival Capriccio version from the C. P. E. Bach Chamber Orchestra, this one from Koopman and his talented Amsterdam players is on period instruments, and the performances gain from that, not only in transparency of texture and natural balance but in their easy-sounding spontaneity, for Koopman tends to favour relatively relaxed speeds. Excellent Erato recording.

Like their predecessors, the four *Sinfonias*, Wq. 183, are not merely interesting historically but are often characterized by an emotional insistence that is disturbing and by a capacity to surprise that is quite remarkable. The other two works also boast some unpredictable modulations, many of them abrupt and not always totally convincing. Leppard's performances are full of drive and have an alert intensity appropriate to this astonishing composer. The recordings too are fresh and impeccably balanced; and this generous mid-priced Philips disc can be strongly recommended to those not insisting on original instruments.

Hartmut Haenchen gives lively and spirited performances of the second set of *Hamburg symphonies*, played on modern instruments at today's pitch; they are well recorded, if not quite as present or detailed as Pinnock's set of Wq. 182 with the English Concert on Archiv. All the same, eminently recommendable, even if not as a first choice.

CHAMBER AND INSTRUMENTAL MUSIC

Fantasia (Fantasy-sonata) in F sharp min. (Empfindungen), Wq. 80; Sonatas for piano and violin in B min., Wq. 76; C min., Wq. 78.
*** Denon Dig. CO 72434 [id.]. Huguette Dreyfus, Eduard Melkus.

These little-known pieces are primarily keyboard sonatas with violin obbligato, not violin sonatas in the same sense as those of Mozart or Beethoven. The subtitle of the *Fantasy-sonata, Empfindungen* (*The Sentiments*), gives some idea of its introspective character, which emerges immediately in the first of its twelve sections; it finds Bach at his most individual. Its two companions are less striking – though in their different way they are rewarding. They are excellently played, though the recording places Melkus marginally more forward than is ideal. In the earlier *Sonatas* Huguette Dreyfus uses a harpsichord (a Hemsch of 1754) and for the *Fantasy* a Neupert fortepiano. Strongly recommended.

Flute sonatas: in D, Wq. 83; in E, Wq. 84; in G, Wq. 85; in G, Wq. 86.
** Denon Dig. C37 7807 [id.]. András Adorján, Huguette Dreyfus.

These sonatas are less exploratory in idiom and less unpredictable than is often the case with this composer. They are pleasing if somewhat bland. The recordings were made in Tokyo in 1976 and are well balanced, with the players neither too forward nor recessed. András Adorján, the Hungarian-born flautist, has an agreeably sweet tone. The CD offers a total playing time of 47 minutes.

Flute sonatas: in E min., Wq. 124; in G; in A min.; in D, Wq. 127–9; in G, Wq. 133; in G, Wq. 134.
*** Capriccio Dig. 10 101 [id.]. Eckart Haupf, Siegfried Pank, Armin Thalheim.

This issue in the C. P. E. Bach series collects six of the composer's eleven flute sonatas in fresh, lively performances, well recorded. The six pieces last, in all, less than 50 minutes, ending with one written in Bach's Hamburg period, two years before he died, altogether lighter and more conventionally classical, presenting an interesting perspective on the rest.

Quartets (Trios) for fortepiano, flute and viola: in A min., D & G, Wq.93/95.
(M) *** HM/BMG GD 77052. Les Adieux.

Although these works were designated by Bach as *Quartets*, no bass part survives, and the players tell us that they decided against an improvised addition 'because a cello running along in the good old basso continuo style would be directly contrary to the outstandingly progressive composition of the pieces. Piano, flute and viola are musically handled so equally, and everything is so minutely written out, that an added cello would always remain the fifth wheel on the wagon.' Certainly the bright, transparent textures of the original instruments are as delightful as Bach's invention. The playing, too, matches the music in its finish, lightness of touch and spontaneity.

Trio sonatas: in A min., Wq. 148; in D, Wq. 151.
(*) Denon Dig. C37 7093 [id.]. Nicolet, Holliger, Jaccottet – J. S. BACH: *Trio sonatas.*(*)

Originally written for flute and violin (or two violins) and continuo, these *Trio sonatas* sound attractive enough in the combination of flute and oboe, although one would have welcomed a greater degree of dynamic variation in the playing. Both playing and recording are admirably vivid.

Sinfonia a tre voci in D; 12 Variations on La Folia, Wq. 118/9; Trio sonatas: in B flat, Wq. 158; in C min. (Sanguineus & Melancholicus), Wq. 161/1; Viola da gamba sonata in D, Wq. 137.
*** Hyp. Dig. CDA 66239 [id.]. Purcell Qt.

The *Variations on La Folia* are fresh and inventive, particularly in Robert Woolley's hands, but the remaining pieces are hardly less rewarding. The *C minor Trio sonata* of 1749 presents a most imaginative dialogue between two players, depicting two of the four temperaments. It is as individual – indeed, quirky – as much of his later music. The Purcell Quartet play with sensitivity and seem well attuned to the particularly individual sensibility of this composer, and in the *Gamba sonata* Richard Boothby is most persuasive. The Hyperion recording is well balanced, faithful and present.

Keyboard sonatas Nos. 1–6, Wq. 63/1–6.
** Capriccio Dig. 10 107 [id.]. Armin Thalheim (clavichord).

Important though they may be for an understanding of C. P. E. Bach, these *Clavichord sonatas* give much less satisfaction musically than the big sets of keyboard sonatas. It goes without saying that the disc should be played at a very low volume indeed; a clavichord is barely audible, and if this is listened to with the level set at normal there is a great deal of clatter. Armin Thalheim plays an instrument made by Johann Augustin Straube in 1787, the last year of Bach's life, in the Leipzig University collection.

VOCAL MUSIC

Anbetung dem Erbamer (Easter cantata) Wq. 243; Auf, shicke dich trecht feierlich (Christmas cantata), Wq. 249; Heilig, Wq. 217; Klopstocks Morgengesang am Schöpfungfeste, Wq. 239.
*** Capriccio Dig. 10 208 [id.]. Schlick, Lins, Pregardien, Elliott, Varcoe, Schwarz, Rheinische Kantorei, Kleine Konzert, Hermann Max.

Carl Philipp Emanuel Bach was a friend of the poet, Klopstock, who was to write his epitaph; and *Klopstocks Morgengesang am Schöpfungfeste* (*Klopstock's morning song on the celebration of Creation*) bears eloquent witness to their friendship, for it is a work of many beauties and is well performed by these artists. *Anbetung dem Erbamer* (*Worship of the merciful*) is another late work, written for the Easter celebrations of 1784, and full of modulatory surprises. *Auf, shicke dich trecht feierlich* (*Up, be reconciled*) was written for Christmas 1775, though the subject-matter is only tenuously seasonal. *Heilig* (*Holy*) (1779) was also part of a Christmas work. A record of unusual interest, very well performed and naturally recorded.

(i) *Die Auferstehung und Himmelfahrt Jesu (The Resurrection and Ascension of Jesus), Wq. 240;* (ii) *Gott hat den Herrn auferweckt (Easter cantata), Wq. 244.*
*** Capriccio Dig. 10 206/7 (2) [id.]. (i) Schlick, Lins, Pregardien; (ii) Elliott, Varcoe, Schwarz; Rheinische Kantorei, Kleine Konzert, Hermann Max.

Carl Philipp Emanuel numbered *Die Auferstehung und Himmelfahrt Jesu* among his finest works. It was composed in the late 1770s and was highly regarded by Mozart, who conducted three performances of it in 1788. This two-CD set offers good solo singing and generally very good playing; the choral singing for the most part is respectable without being distinguished. The oratorio lasts about 75 minutes and the second CD offers an earlier *Easter cantata* from 1756. Impressive music which no one with an interest in this composer should pass over.

Die letzten Leiden des Erlösers (The Last Sufferings of the Saviour), Wq. 233.
(M) *** HM/BMG GD 77042. Schlick, Reyghere, Patriasz, Prégardien, Egmond, Ghent Coll. Vocale, La Petite Bande, Kuijken.

Die letzten Leiden des Erlösers (1770) has moments of great inspiration; its invention has nobility and originality – though it must be admitted that there are some passages which are routine. However, the restless intelligence and sensibility which pervade so much of Bach's music are all in evidence. *Die letzten Leiden* has good claims to be considered one of Carl Philipp Emanuel's masterpieces, and it is given a first-class performance by the excellent team of soloists assembled here. The singing of the Collegium Vocale of Ghent is also eloquent, and the playing of La Petite Bande under Sigiswald Kuijken is predictably vivid and alive. Fine, well-balanced recording.

Cantatas: *Wer ist so wurdig als du, Wq. 222; Zur Einfuhrung des H. P. Gasie, Wq. 250; Der Herr lebet, Wq. 251.*
** Capriccio Dig. 10 209 [id.]. Schlick, Helling, Jochens, Schwarz, Rheinische Kantorei, Kleine Konzert, Hermann Max.

Although there are some felicitous moments, such as the tenor aria, *Abgehärmter Wangen Tränen*, there is a certain blandness about some of the invention in the cantata *Zur Einfuhrung des H. P. Gasie*, and the overall impression is one of intelligence rather than of depth. *Wer ist so wurdig als du (There is none worthier than Thee)* is an adaptation for chorus and orchestra of an earlier Psalm setting and comes from the previous decade. The material of the other substantial cantata, *Der Herr lebet, und gelobet sei mein Hort (The Lord liveth, and blessed be my rock)*, is fresh and pleasing. The performances and recordings are eminently serviceable without being really distinguished.

Magnificat, Wq. 215.
(M) *** Decca 421 148-2 [id.]. Palmer, Watts, Tear, Roberts, King's College Ch., ASMF, Ledger – BACH, J.S.: *Magnificat.* ***

The magnificent opening chorus of C. P. E. Bach's *Magnificat* (repeated later in the setting of the *Gloria*) presents King's College Choir at its most exhilarating. This irresistible movement, here taken challengingly fast, leads to a whole series of sharply characterized numbers, including a sparkling tenor aria on *Quia fecit*. With vividly atmospheric recording, the performance under Philip Ledger comes electrically to life, with choir, soloists and orchestra all in splendid form. Aptly coupled with Johann Sebastian's earlier setting, this CD can be strongly recommended. It sounds extremely vivid.

Bach, Johann Christian (1735–82)

Bassoon concertos: in B flat; in E flat.
(BB) ** Hung. White Label HRC 041 [id.]. Gábor Janota, Liszt CO, Rolla; or József Vajda, Budapest SO, Lehel – HUMMEL: *Bassoon concerto.***

These are smoothly straightforward works in the *galant* style. Both have agreeably Italianate slow movements, but the most striking movement is the vivacious *Presto* finale of the *B flat Concerto*. Good playing from both soloists (especially from Janota in the latter) and warm, polished accompaniments. The recording is full and pleasing, the overall effect a shade bland.

Cello concerto in C min.; Sinfonia concertante in A for violin, cello and orchestra.
** Chan. Dig. CHAN 8470 [id.]. Yuli and Eleonora Turovsky, I Musici di Montreal, Y. Turovsky – BOCCHERINI: *Cello concerto.***

The *Cello concerto* would seem to be a conjectural reconstruction. The *A major Sinfonia concertante* has all the charm and grace one associates with its composer. Yuli Turovsky's playing has warmth and good taste, though his intonation is not always completely true. He directs his Canadian ensemble with style and spirit, and the recording, too, is well defined and warm.

Clavier concertos, Op. 7/5 – 6; Op. 13/1 – 2.
(M) *** Ph. 426 085-2 [id.]. Haebler (fortepiano), V. Capella Ac., Melkus.

Bach wrote three sets of keyboard concertos, of which Opp. 7 and 13 were designated for either harpsichord or fortepiano. Op. 7 have string accompaniments and Op. 13 include effective parts for oboes and horns. Moreover, in the engaging slow movement of Op. 13/2 Bach substitutes flutes for oboes, to add special colour to his variations on the Scottish air, *O saw ye my daddy,* clearly aiming to charm his London audience; the effect is most winning. It would be difficult to find a more suitable or persuasive advocate than Ingrid Haebler; she is excellently acccompanied and most truthfully recorded. J. C. Bach is at his freshest and most appealing in some of these concerto movements, and this realistically recorded disc cannot be recommended too strongly.

Oboe concerto in F.
** Capriccio Dig. 10 069 [id.]. Glaetzner, New Bach Coll. Mus., Pommer – C. P. E. BACH: *Concertos.***

This appealing concerto is included with the recordings of Carl Philipp Emanuel *Oboe concertos* in Capriccio's integral series of that composer's music, but the performance, like those of its couplings, is acceptable rather than outstanding – see above.

6 Sinfonias, Op. 3 (ed. Erik Smith).
(M) *** Ph. 422 498-2 [id.]. ASMF, Marriner.

These Op. 3 symphonies are recorded here for the first time. Erik Smith, who has edited them, describes them as 'in essence Italian overtures, though with an unusual wealth of singing melody'. They are beguilingly played by the Academy of St Martin-in-the-Fields under Sir Neville Marriner, and beautifully recorded. The 1970 recording sounds wonderfully fresh and transparent.

Sinfonias, Op. 6/3; Op. 9/2; Op. 18/2 & 4.
(B) *** CfP CD-CFP 4550. Bournemouth Sinf., Montgomery.

Very good playing and excellent 1978 sound make this Bournemouth collection, directed by Kenneth Montgomery, an attractive proposition. Everything is fresh: the two Op. 18 pieces are the most substantial, but all four works are well worth having. With realistic remastering, clear and firm, this is a bargain.

Sinfonia concertante in A for violin, cello and orchestra; Grand Overture in E flat.
(*) CBS MK 39964 [id.]. Yo-Yo Ma, Zukerman, St Paul CO – BOCCHERINI: *Cello concerto* (arr. Grützmacher).*

Generally this is an enjoyable pairing and the playing of the soloists in the *Sinfonia concertante* establishes a fine musical interplay, although the cadenza is over-elaborated. Good sound, with excellent stereo effects.

Sinphonias concertantes in A for violin, cello and orchestra, SC 3; E flat for 2 violins, 2 violas, cello and orchestra (MSC E flat 1); E flat for 2 clarinets, bassoon and orchestra (MSC E flat 4); G for 2 violins, cello and orchestra, SC 1.
*** ASV CDDCA 651 [id.]. London Fest. O, Ross Pople.

There are some 18 *Sinphonias concertantes*, and the four recorded here are delightfully fresh and inventive. The performances are eminently vital and enthusiastic – this band is obviously composed of excellent players, and the recording is very bright and present. This is an invigorating disc which can be recommended strongly. (The numbering above is based on Ernest Warburton's system, SC indicating works published in the eighteenth century, and MSC those printed only recently.)

Oboe quartet in B flat, Op. 8/6.
*** Denon Dig. C37 7119 [id.]. Holliger, Salvatore Qt – M. HAYDN: *Divertimenti*; MOZART: *Adagio.********

The unpretentious elegance of J. C. Bach's *Oboe quartet* is beautifully caught by the incomparable Holliger and his stylish partners. An excellent coupling for even more compelling works, all vividly recorded.

Quintets: in C, Op. 11/1; in D, Op. 11/6; in D, Op. 22/1. Sextet in C.
*** DG Dig. 423 385-2 [id.]. English Concert.

This is a self-recommending collection. The music, delectably scored for unexpected combinations of instruments, is wonderfully fresh and inventive in these spirited performances, with the sounds of the original instruments adding bite and colour and readily finding the music's charm. The sound has splendid realism and presence.

Bach, Johann Christoph (1642–1703)   **Bach, Georg Christoph** (1642–97)

Bach, Johann Michael (1648–94)   **Bach, Heinrich** (1615–92)

J. C. BACH: Cantatas: *Ach, dass ich Wassers g'nug hätte; Er erhub sich Streit; Die Furcht des Herren; Herr wende dich und sei mir gnädig; Meine Freundin; Wir bist du denn.* J. M. BACH: Cantatas: *Ach bleib uns, Herr Jesu Christ; Ach, wie sehnlich wart' ich der Zeit; Auf lasst uns den Herren loben; Es ist ein grosser Gewinn; Liebster Jesu, hör mein Flehen.* G. C. BACH: Cantata: *Siehe, wie fein und lieblich.* H. BACH: *Ich danke dir, Gott.*
*** DG 419 253-2 (2) [id.]. Soloists, Rheinische Kantorei, Col. Mus. Ant., Goebel.

These two CDs include all the cantatas and vocal concertos by Bach's forefathers that he preserved, with, in addition, a vocal concerto, *Herr, wende dich*, by Johann Christoph Bach. This set breaks new ground for the gramophone and does so with great distinction, for the performances and recording are of the very highest quality. An invaluable issue and indispensable for collectors with an interest in Johann Sebastian.

Bach, Johann Sebastian (1685–1750)

The Art of fugue; Canons, BWV 1072/8 and 1086/7; Musical offering, BWV 1079.
** DG Dig. 413 642-2 (3). Col. Mus. Ant., Goebel.

How to perform *The Art of fugue* has always presented problems, since Bach's own indications are so sparse. In the Cologne performance, the movements are divided between strings and solo harpsichord. The two harpsichord players are often imaginative and expressive, to contrast with the rhythmic vigour of the playing of the strings. But there are snags to the authentic style, which is at times exaggerated. However, this is generally much to be preferred to the somewhat joyless *Musical offering* with which it comes in harness on the CD set, together with some newly found *Canons*. The recording is remarkably clean and present.

Brandenburg concertos Nos. 1–6, BWV 1046/51; Suites Nos. 1–4, BWV 1066/9.
(M) **(*) DG 423 492-2 (3) [id.]. E. Concert, Pinnock.
(B) *** Ph. 426 145-2 (3) [id.]. ECO, Raymond Leppard.
**(*) EMI Dig. CDS7 47881-8 (3). ASMF, Marriner.

The merits of Pinnock's *Brandenburg concertos* are considerable - see below - but the *Suites* are somewhat more controversial, bringing a distinct loss of breadth and grandeur. However, at mid-price many will be tempted to this package. The *Suites* come from analogue masters, but are vividly transferred. Leppard's *Brandenburgs* and *Suites* are highly recommendable at bargain price and the sound is excellent. They are discussed below in greater detail; however, unless original instruments are mandatory, this set should give every satisfaction.

Marriner's latest, EMI digital recordings of the *Brandenburgs* and *Suites* are linked together on three CDs. This is his third recording, with fine teamwork, superb ensemble and well-judged speeds, never too hectic. However, although the playing is freshly conceived, it also has a certain urbane quality (although this does not apply to George Malcolm's harpsichord contribution, notably in the special link provided in No. 3). Many will like performances with a little more eccentricity, not quite so safe, and they will turn to Marriner's earlier Philips set (see below) or, if original instruments are required, to Gardiner, or to Pinnock. Marriner's new recording of the *Suites* is a worthy successor to his earliest, Argo set, and the vividness of the playing is enhanced by the excellent sound, full in texture yet transparent, too.

Brandenburg concertos Nos. 1–6, BWV 1046/51.
*** DG Dig. 410 500/1-2 [id.]. E. Concert, Pinnock.
*** Ph. 400 076/7-2 (2) [id.]. ASMF, Marriner.
(B) *** Pickwick Dig. PCD 830 (1–3); PCD 845 (4–6) [MCA MCAD 25956/7]. ECO, Ledger.
(M) *** Ph. 420 345/6-2 [id.]. ECO Leppard.
**(*) Virgin Dig. VCD 790747-2 (2) [id.]. O. of Age of Enlightenment.
**(*) Ph. Dig. 412 790-2 (2) [id.]. I Musici.
**(*) O-L Dig. 414 187-2 (2) [id.]. AAM, Hogwood.

Brandenburg concerti Nos. 1–6; Harpsichord concerto No. 2 in D, BWV 1054.
(BB) *(*) LaserLight 15 508 (*Nos. 1–3* & BWV 1054); ** 15 509 (*Nos. 4–6*). Berlin CO, Peter Wohlert.

Pinnock's DG performances represent the peak of his achievement as an advocate of authentic performance, with sounds that are clear and refreshing but not too abrasive. Interpretatively he tends to opt for faster speeds in outer movements, relatively slow in *Andantes*, with a warm but stylish degree of expressiveness, but from first to last there is no routine. Soloists are outstanding, and so is the recording, with the CDs transferred at a very high level, giving the sound great immediacy.

For those who still cannot quite attune their ears to the style of string playing favoured by the authentic school, there are several excellent alternatives. Marriner's analogue Philips set has been remastered since it was first issued and the sound is both natural and lively. Above all, these performances communicate warmth and enjoyment; and they are strong in personality, with star soloists adding individuality to the concertos without breaking the consistency of beautifully sprung performances. George Malcolm is the ideal continuo player, as he is in the later EMI recording. However, this set has to face strong competition in the mid-priced range.

On Pickwick, Ledger has the advantage of fresh and detailed digital recording. He directs resilient, well-paced readings of all six concertos, lively yet never over-forced. The slow movements in particular are most beautifully done, persuasively and without mannerism. Flutes rather than recorders are used in No. 4.

Leppard's Philips set, also in the mid-priced range, is higher-powered than Ledger's, whose gentler manner will for many be easier to live with. But the exhilaration of the Leppard set is undeniable; there is much to enjoy here. The remastered analogue sound is full and ample.

With the direction shared among four violinists, Monica Huggett (Nos. 2, 4 and 6), Catherine Mackintosh (No. 1), Alison Bury (No. 3) and Elizabeth Wallfisch (No. 5), the Orchestra of the Age of the Enlightenment presents an amiable set of *Brandenburgs* on period instruments. These performances bring all the advantages of light, clear textures and no sense of haste, even when a movement is taken faster than has become traditional. With generally excellent recording, this makes a good alternative to the outstanding version by Trevor Pinnock on DG Archiv; but the OAE ensemble cannot quite match that of the English Concert in crispness.

I Musici – like Marriner's Academy – are joined by distinguished soloists. The readings are strong and direct. Where I Musici fall short is on rhythmic imagination in slow movements, with bass lines at times too evenly stressed, perhaps owing to the absence of a director, but the plainness and honesty of these invigorating accounts will appeal to many. The digital recording is strikingly 'present' on CD.

Though Hogwood's set of *Brandenburgs* is notably less persuasive than Pinnock's, also on period instruments, with often brisk speeds, more metrical and less well sprung, the distinctive point is that unlike most rivals he has chosen the original Cöthen score rather than the usual text as sent to the Margrave of Brandenburg. Besides many detailed differences, this version has no *Polonaise* in the *First Concerto*, and the harpsichord cadenza in No. 5 is much less elaborate, 'more convincingly proportioned' as Hogwood himself suggests.

Those chancing upon Peter Wohlert's set in the bargain basement should not be too disappointed. The sound, made by a small group using modern instruments, is pleasingly full and clear. The performances are in the older German tradition associated with Münchinger and Richter. Tempi are very relaxed, though the finale of No. 3 has an attractive lightness of articulation; only in the first movement of No. 2 is tuning less than ideally defined. The second disc, including the last three concertos, is consistently enjoyable, with excellent solo playing. The keyboard concerto with an unnamed soloist, included as a bonus on the first disc, is not an asset, rhythmically rigid and emphatic in its accents.

Marriner's earlier (1971–2) Philips set (reissued at mid-price on 426 088/9-2) in Thurston Dart's controversial edition must reluctantly be passed over, as his later versions have far greater appeal.

Concerto for flute, violin and harpsichord in A min., BWV 1044; Concerto for oboe and violin in C min., BWV 1060; Concerto for oboe d'amore in A, BWV 1055.
*** DG Dig. 413 731-2 [id.]. Beznosiuk, Standage, Reichenberg, Pinnock, E. Concert.

As in their other Bach concerto recordings for DG Archiv, Pinnock and the English Concert prove the most persuasive practitioners of authentic performance, both vigorous and warm, with consistently resilient rhythms. The recorded sound is exceptionally vivid in its sense of presence.

Harpsichord concertos Nos. 1 in D min.; 2 in E; 3 in D, 4 in A; 5 in F; 6 in F; 7 in G min., BWV 1052/8.
*** DG Dig. 415 991-2 (1–3); 415 992-2 (4–7) [id.]. Pinnock, E. Concert.

Trevor Pinnock plays with real panache, his scholarship tempered by excellent musicianship. There are occasions when one feels his tempi are a little too fast and unrelenting, but for the most part there is little cause for complaint. On the contrary, the performances give much pleasure and the period instruments are better played than on most issues of this kind. Both CDs have the advantage of great clarity of texture. Apart from the very quick tempi, which may strike an unsympathetic note, this set is thoroughly recommendable.

Clavier concertos Nos. 1–7, BWV 1052/8.
** EMI Dig. CDS7 47629-8 (2). Gavrilov (piano), ASMF, Marriner.

In terms of dexterity and clarity of articulation Andrei Gavrilov cannot be faulted and he produces some beautiful sound when his playing is lyrical and relaxed. If at times one feels he pushes on relentlessly and his incisive touch can be a bit unremitting in some movements, there are a lot of memorable things, too. Indeed, in the slow movement of the *D minor* and *F minor concertos*, there is playing of real poetry and delicacy – and, for that matter, in the finale of the *A major*. The recordings are excellently balanced, with the piano well integrated into the overall picture.

Clavier concertos Nos. 1 in D min., BWV 1052; 3 in D, BWV 1054; 5 in F min., BWV 1056; 6 in F, BWV 1057.
*** Teldec/WEA Dig. 2292 43113-2 [id.]. Katsaris (piano), Liszt CO, Rolla.

Cyprien Katsaris possesses the most remarkable technique and feeling for colour, which are to be heard to excellent advantage in this vividly recorded and well-filled disc. He has an astonishingly vital musicality and keyboard resource. The playing of the Liszt Chamber Orchestra, surely one of the very finest chamber ensembles in the world, is splendidly supportive. Exhilarating and imaginative performances all round. A most distinguished issue.

Clavier concertos Nos. 1 in D min., BWV 1052; 4 in A, BWV 1055; 5 in F min., BWV 1056.
*** Denon Dig. C37 7236 [id.]. András Schiff (piano), ECO, Malcolm.

András Schiff never tries to pretend that he is not using a modern piano, and the lightness of his touch and his control of colour are a constant delight to the ear. George Malcolm's accompaniments are alert and resilient, and the actual sound of the strings is perfectly in scale. This is an example of digital recording at its most believable, although the upper strings are soft-grained and not brightly lit.

Clavier concertos Nos. 1 in D min.; 4 in A; 5 in F min., BWV 1052 & 1055/6; (i) *Brandenburg concerto No. 5 in D, BWV 1050.*
(M) (***) EMI mono CDH7 63039-2. Edwin Fischer & CO; (i) Philh. O.

Edwin Fischer recorded the *Clavier concertos* with his own chamber orchestra in the 1930s and the *Fifth Brandenburg* in 1953 with the Philharmonia. Even the latter was also recorded for 78 r.p.m. discs, since there are long rallentandos as the side draws to a close. But these performances are riveting and have a compelling eloquence and sensitivity that banish all thoughts of sound-quality. It is good to hear Gareth Morris and Manoug Parikian again in the *Brandenburg*. Excellent transfers.

Clavier concertos Nos. 2 in E, BWV 1053; 3 in D, BWV 1054; 4 in A, BWV 1055; 6 in F, BWV 1057.
(M) **(*) Olympia OCD 127. Gavrilov, (USSR) CO, Yuri Nikolaevsky.

Exhilarating performances from Gavrilov and the unnamed Soviet chamber orchestra, with sparkling allegros, briskly paced, and thoughtfully poetic accounts of the central slow movements, where the soloist's delicate flexibility is appealingly responsive. Passage-work is sparklingly incisive and decoration crisp. The full-bodied string group brings an almost astringent freshness to tuttis, and Nikolaevsky is rhythmically assertive without being heavy-handed. Very good 1982 recording. This is not for authenticists, but is strong in baroque spirit.

Harpsichord concertos Nos. 1 in D min., BWV 1052; 5 in F min., BWV 1056; Double harpsichord concerto No. 1 in C min., BWV 1060; Triple harpsichord concerto No. 2 in C, BWV 1064; Quadruple harpsichord concerto in A min., BWV 1065.
(M) *** Ph. 422 497-2 [id.]. Leppard, Andrew Davis, Ledger, Verlet, ECO, Leppard.

Harpsichord concertos Nos. 2 in E, BWV 1053; 4 in A, BWV 1055; Double harpsichord concerto No. 2 in C, BWV 1061; Triple harpsichord concerto No. 1 in D min., BWV 1063.
(M) *** Ph. 426 084-2 [id.]. Leppard, Andrew Davis, Ledger, ECO, Leppard.

Harpsichord concerto Nos. 3 in D, BWV 1054; 6 in F, BWV 1057; 7 in G min., BWV 1058; (i) *Double harpsichord concerto No. 3 in C min., BWV 1062.*
(M) *** Ph. 426 448-2 [id.]. Leppard; (i) Ledger, ECO, Leppard.

These performances derive from a boxed set, recorded in 1973/4. Leppard and Davis play with skill and flair, as do their colleagues in the multiple concertos; the ECO shows plenty of life and, if the performances overall are less incisive than the English Concert versions with Pinnock, they have resilience and communicate such joy in the music that criticism is disarmed. The Philips sound is very realistic, the harpsichords life-size and not too forward; one does reflect that modern strings, however refined, create a body of tone which tends slightly to outweigh the more slender keyboard timbres. However, in the works for two or more harpsichords there is a pleasing absence of jangle.

Double harpsichord concertos: Nos. 1 in C min.; 2 in C; 3 in C min., BWV 1060/2.
**(*) DG Dig. 415 131-2 [id.]. Pinnock, Gilbert, E. Concert.

The character of the Pinnock performances is robust, with the balance forward and the performances very strongly projected. The combination of period instruments and playing of determined vigour certainly makes a bold impression, but the relatively unrelaxed approach to the slow movements will not appeal to all ears. The lively recording has very striking presence on CD.

Double clavier concertos Nos. 1 in C min., BWV 1060; 2 in C, BWV 1061; Triple clavier concerto in D min., BWV 1063; Quadruple clavier concerto in A min., BWV 1065.
*** DG Dig. 415 655-2 [id.]. Eschenbach, Frantz, Oppitz, Schmidt (pianos), Hamburg PO, Eschenbach.

Helmut Schmidt, the German ex-Chancellor, joins his friends, Eschenbach and Frantz, alongside Gerhard Oppitz in the *Quadruple concerto* – and very enjoyable it is. The other concertos are presented with comparable vigour, with slow movements correspondingly thoughtful and responsive. The recording is rather resonant, but the spirit of this record is very communicative. In spite of the resonance the overall sound-picture is very believable.

Triple harpsichord concertos Nos. 1 in D min.; 2 in C, BWV 1063/4; Quadruple harpsichord concerto in A min., BWV 1065.
**(*) DG Dig. 400 041-2 [id.]. Pinnock, Gilbert, Mortensen, Kraemer, E. Concert.

Fine playing here but the slightly aggressive style of the music-making – everything alert, vigorously paced and forwardly projected – emphasizes the bravura of Bach's conceptions.

Oboe concertos: in A (from BWV 1055); in D min. (from BWV 1059); in F (from BWV 1053).
*** Ph. Dig. 415 851-2 [id.]. Heinz Holliger, ASMF, Iona Brown.

Stylish, pointed performances (leaning at times towards Romantic expressiveness in slow movements) of two concertos better known in their harpsichord versions (BMW 1053 and 1055) and a third reconstruction from seemingly independent movements. Excellent recording.

Violin concertos Nos. 1 in A min.; 2 in E; Double concerto in D min., BWV 1041/3; Sonata in E min., BWV 1023 (arr. Respighi for violin and strings); Suite 3, BWV 1068: Air.
(BB) **(*) Naxos Dig. 8.550194 [id.]. Nishizaki, Jablokov, Capella Istropolitana, Oliver Dohnányi.

The first thing about the Naxos recording that strikes the ear is the attractively bright, gleaming sound of the orchestral string group, who play with fine resilience. Neither soloist is a strong personality and the espressivo in the *Adagio* of the *E major* solo *Concerto* and in the famous lyrical dialogue of the slow movement of the *Double concerto* brings rather deliberate phrasing. Yet these players are certainly musical and there is a sense of style here and plenty of vitality in allegros. The Respighi arrangement is effective enough and the concert ends with Bach's most famous string tune, played simply and eloquently.

(i) Violin concertos Nos. 1–2, BWV 1041-2; (ii) Violin concerto in G min. (from BWV 1056); (i; ii) Double violin concerto, BWV 1053.
*** EMI CDC7 47856-2 [id.]. (i) Perlman, (ii) Zukerman, ECO, Barenboim.

Violin concertos Nos. (i) 1, BWV 1041; (ii) 2, BWV 1042; (iii) Double violin concerto, BWV 1053; (iv) Double concerto for violin & oboe in D min., BWV 1060.
⊛ (M) *** Ph. 420 700-2 [id.]. Grumiaux; (iii) Krebbers, (iv) Holliger; (i–iii) Les Solistes Romandes, Arpad Gerecz; (iv) New Philh. O, Edo de Waart.
(B) ** Ph. 426 075-2 [id.]. (i; iii; iv) Michelucci; (ii; iii) Ayo; (iv) Leo Driehuys; I Musici.

Violin concertos Nos. 1–2; (i) Concerto for violin & oboe.
*(*) EMI Dig. CDC7 49862-2 [id.]. Zimmermann, (i) Black; ECO, Tate.

Arthur Grumiaux has recorded the violin concertos before in stereo (see below), but the present Swiss versions were made in 1978, when he was joined in the *Double concerto* by Hermann Krebbers. The result is an outstanding success. The way Grumiaux responds to the challenge of working with another great artist comes over equally clearly in the concerto with oboe, reconstructed from the *Double harpsichord concerto in C minor*. There the interplay of phrasing with Holliger is enchanting and, although the recording is earlier (1970), the sound is still good. Grumiaux's performances of the two solo concertos are equally satisfying, with a purity of line and an expressive response in slow movements that communicate very positively. Les Solistes Romandes under Gerecz provide crisply rhythmic allegros and are sensitively supportive in the expressive music. The digital remastering produces transparently fresh yet warm sound and gives the soloists great presence – indeed some may feel that the soloists are too forward, perhaps robbing the playing of some of its dynamic range.

The EMI CD combines the Perlman/Zukerman recordings of BWV 1041-3. Zukerman is the soloist in the *G minor Concerto*. The two famous violinists, with their friend and colleague Barenboim, are inspired to give a very fine account of the *Double violin concerto*, but neither is quite so impressive without the challenge of the other in the solo concertos. The digital remastering provides a full and agreeable balance and the sound is acceptable.

On the Philips bargain label it is Felix Ayo who plays the *E major Violin concerto*, and with rather more flair than his colleague, Roberto Michelucci, shows in the *A minor Concerto*; but the two players join together for a spirited account of the *Double concerto*, and the work featuring the oboe is also a success. The clear, unaffected approach to all four concertos gives pleasure; the only snag is the reverberant acoustic, which rarely allows the harpsichord continuo to come through with any bite. But the sound itself is pleasing and this is acceptable value.

At under 50 minutes Zimmermann's coupling is poor value by today's standards, and the substitution of the *Violin and oboe concerto* for the *Double violin concerto* hardly makes it any more attractive. Zimmermann's silkily romantic style is very pleasing in what now sounds a rather old-fashioned way, with speeds extreme in both directions and warm vibrato colouring the slow movements. Tate draws sympathetic playing from the ECO, who are well recorded.

Violin concertos Nos. 1 in A min.; 2 in E; (i) *Double concerto, BWV 1041/3.*
*** EMI Dig. CDC7 47011-2 [id.]. Mutter, ECO, Accardo.
*** DG Dig. 410 646-2 [id.]. Standage, Wilcock, E. Concert, Pinnock.
(M) *** DG 427 114-2 [id.]. Melkus, (i) Rantos; Vienna Capella Academica (with VIVALDI: *Concerto for viola d'amore and lute, RV 540****).
(M) (***) EMI mono CDH7 61018-2 (with *Partita No. 2, BWV 1004: Chaconne*) [MCA MCAD 25931]. Menuhin, Paris SO, Enescu or Monteux; (i) with Enescu (violin).
(B) **(*) Pickwick Dig. PCD 808. Laredo, Scottish CO.

CDs including only BWV 1041/3 seem ungenerous, even if they offer considerable artistic satisfaction. However, Anne-Sophie Mutter's variety of timbre as well as the imagination of her phrasing is extremely compelling; her performance of the slow movement of the *E major Concerto* is finer than any other version, except Grumiaux's, with marvellous shading within a range of hushed tones. Accardo's accompaniments are splendidly stylish and alert. In principle the slow movement of the *Double concerto* – where Accardo takes up his bow to become a solo partner, scaling down his timbre – is too slow, but the result could hardly be more beautiful, even if the soloists are rather forwardly balanced.

If you want the three favourite Bach *Violin concertos* on original instruments, then Pinnock's disc is the one to go for. Rhythms are crisp and lifted at nicely chosen speeds – not too fast for slow movements – but, as so often with authentic performances of violin concertos, the edge will not please everyone. Good clear recording.

Menuhin's 78 r.p.m. recording of the *Double concerto* with George Enescu his partner (and teacher) is legendary for its rapport and simple expressive beauty; the two solo *Concertos* are hardly less remarkable. All these records were made when Menuhin was between sixteen and nineteen years of age and show his unique instinctive musical vision, which came from within rather than from outside influences. The famous *Partita* is very impressive too, and all admirers of this great artist will not want to miss this reissue, even if the orchestral sound is dry and limited.

Melkus has the advantage of well-balanced DG recording from the early 1970s. He is not a soloist with a 'big' personality like Menuhin or Oistrakh, but he is a musician of uncommon sensibility, and the way the recording balance allows him to form part of the overall ensemble, rather than enjoying a spotlight, gives special character to the music-making. Throughout, one has the impression of a happy balance between scholarship and musical freshness. His coupling is Vivaldi's *Concerto for viola d'amore and lute*, RV 540, in which he is ably partnered by Konrad Ragossnig. This is most memorably played and beautifully recorded.

On the bargain-priced Pickwick CD, Laredo directs sympathetic traditional performances. The excellent Scottish Chamber Orchestra is well recorded with a realistic, well-judged balance except for the rather too prominent harpsichord continuo which in its relentlessness sometimes detracts from the generally well-sprung rhythms. Laredo's tone is a little thin at times, but that is a fault on the right side.

Double concerto for violin and oboe in D min., BWV 1060.
*** Ph. Dig. 411 466-2 [id.] (with *Easter oratorio: Sinfonia*). Holliger, Kremer – VIVALDI: *Oboe; Violin concertos.***(*)
(*) ASV Dig. CDCOE 803 [id.]. Blankenstein, Boyd, COE, Schneider – MOZART: *Sinfonia concertante*; VIVALDI: *Concerto, RV 556.*(*)

Double concerto for violin and oboe; Triple concerto for flute, violin and harpsichord in A min., BWV 1044.
**(*) Denon Dig. C37 7064 [id.]. Kantorow, Bourgue, Adorján, Dreyfus, Netherlands CO, Bakels.

Holliger is at his distinguished best in the *Double concerto*, and Kremer makes a good partner in a fresh performance with a serene central *Adagio*. But what makes this coupling memorable is the improvisatory quality which Holliger brings to his beautiful account of the solo in the *Sinfonia* from the *Easter oratorio* which sounds just like the slow movement of a concerto. The recording is first class, the ambience nicely judged, and the oboe is especially tangible in the CD format.

In the Denon version the *Double concerto* is dominated by Maurice Bourgue, with phrasing and tonal nuances that consistently ensnare the ear. Jean-Jacques Kantorow makes another fine contribution, not quite so individual but producing immaculate playing. The *Triple concerto* is less compellingly done, and there one is more aware of the often inappropriately beefy style of the Netherlands Chamber Orchestra, as recorded here. Huguette Dreyfus's harpsichord is rather aggressively recorded, but otherwise the sound is very good.

Recorded live, with stage and audience noises audible, the ASV version from the Chamber Orchestra of Europe is not immaculate, with the opening allegro rather sluggish of rhythm, but the solo playing from the oboist Douglas Boyd and the violinist Marieka Blankenstein is outstanding. Atmospheric recording, not ideally balanced.

The Musical offering, BWV 1079.
*** Ph. 412 800-2 [id.]. ASMF, Marriner.
(M) ** Teldec/WEA 2292 42748-2 [id.]. VCM, Harnoncourt.

Sir Neville Marriner uses his own edition and instrumentation: strings with three solo violins, solo viola and a solo cello; flute, organ and harpsichord. He places the three-part *Ricercar* (scored for organ) at the beginning and the six-part *Ricercar* at the very end, scored for strings. As the centrepiece comes the *Trio sonata* (flute, violin and continuo), and on either side the *Canons*. The performance here is of high quality, though some of the playing is a trifle bland. It is, however, excellently recorded and overall must be numbered among the most successful accounts of the work.

Harnoncourt's recording dates from the early 1970s. It is musically sound, somewhat plain-spun and a little lacking in imaginative vitality; but it is well recorded and offered at mid-price.

Orchestral suites Nos. 1–4, BWV 1066/9.
*** O-L Dig. 417 834-2 (2) [id.]. AAM, Hogwood.
(M) *** HM/BMG Dig. GD 77008 (2) [77008-2-RG]. La Petite Bande, Kuijken.
*** Hung. Dig. HCD 31018 [id.]. Liszt CO, Janos Rolla.
**(*) Capriccio 10 011/2 (available separately). Leipzig New Bach Coll., Pommer.

Orchestral suites Nos. 1–4; Double violin concerto, BWV 1043; Double concerto for violin & oboe, BWV 1060.
(M) ** Ph. 426 462-2 (2). Kremer, Szeryng, Hasson, Holliger, ASMF, Marriner.

Orchestral suites Nos. 1 in C; 3 in D; 4 in D, BWV 1066, 1068 & 1069.
(M) *** Ph. 420 888-2 [id.]. ECO, Leppard.

Orchestral suite No. 2 in B min., BWV 1067; (i) Violin concertos Nos. 1 in A min.; 2 in E, BWV 1041/2; (ii) Triple concerto for flute, violin and harpsichord in A min., BWV 1044.
(M) *** Ph. 420 889-2 [id.]. (i) Grumiaux; (ii) Garcia, Adeney, Leppard; ECO, Leppard.

Hogwood's set of the Bach orchestral *Suites*, one of his more recent recordings, illustrates how the Academy of Ancient Music has developed in refinement and purity of sound, modifying earlier abrasiveness without losing period-instrument freshness. That comes out in the famous *Air* from the *Suite No. 3* where, with multiple violins and an avoidance of the old squeezed style, the tone is sweet even with little or no vibrato – a movement which in the Pinnock version on DG Archiv, for example, sounds very sour. *Allegros* tend to be on the fast side, but are well sprung, not breathless. The refinement of the ensemble is enhanced by the slight distancing of the recording, giving sharper, leaner ensembles than in most rival versions, but with less-defined contrasts between solo and ripieno passages. Hogwood aficionados need not hesitate.

Kuijken with La Petite Bande shows that authentic performance need not be acidly over-abrasive. Set against a warm acoustic – more comfortable for the trumpet-sound, if not always helpful to clarity – these are brightly attractive performances with their just speeds and resilient rhythms. Solo work is most stylish, though ensemble is not always immaculate and intonation is somewhat variable. Nevertheless a good medium-price alternative to Hogwood if you are looking for performances on original instruments. The

CDs are certainly impressive in their spaciousness, and definition is excellent. Now reissued at mid-price, these CDs are very competitive.

To have all four Bach *Orchestral suites* on a single CD (at less than premium price) playing for 74 minutes is bounty indeed. Rolla's tempi are brisk, with rhythms consistently resilient, but not always swifter than those of others; he misses the repeats of the second parts of the overture, a practice most listeners will accept. The performances are alive, straightforward and stylish. Even if they are not 'authentic' (in the sense that modern instruments are used), the woodwind colours and incisive trumpets have a true Baroque sound. Most important, the music-making is spontaneous; other versions may have more individuality (especially in the matter of embellishment), but these are direct in the best possible way, and the recording is excellent.

For Philips's Silverline mid-price reissue of the four Bach *Orchestral suites*, Grumiaux's 1964 performances of the two solo *Violin concertos* have been added (with their purity of line and matching vitality) plus an attractive version of the *Triple concerto*, its slow movement striking for the colourful interchanges of timbre. The *Suites* come from the pre-authentic era, but they are sparklingly played with excellent soloists; overall, Leppard's conception balances gravitas and elegance with baroque ebullience. The 1968 recording has been remastered successfully for CD, with the sound remaining full as well as being better defined.

Pommer's version, issued as part of the Leipzig Bach Edition to celebrate Bach's Tercentenary, brought the first complete set of the *Suites* on CD using modern pitch. Anyone not wanting authentic performance might consider these lively and fresh versions with generally brisk but not unfeeling speeds, rhythmically buoyant. Good atmospheric recording, but with a slightly boomy bass.

Fine as it is – and despite the inclusion of two *Double concertos* – Marriner's second recording of the *Suites* for Philips is no match for his first, Argo/Decca set. The movements where he has changed his mind – for example in the famous *Air* from the *Suite No. 3*, which is here ponderously slow – are now almost always less convincing, and that reflects the very qualities of urgency and spontaneity which made the earlier Argo version so enjoyable. At present only Nos. 2 and 3 from that set are available on CD – see below.

Orchestral suites Nos. 2–3, BWV 1067/8; (i) *Flute concerto, BWV 1056;* (ii) *Concerto for violin and oboe, BWV 1060.*

(M) **(*) Decca 417 715-2 [id.]. ASMF, Marriner; (i) with Bennett; (ii) Kaine, Miller.

These spirited and polished performances come from Marriner's Argo recordings of the 1970s. The digital remastering has emphasized the bright lighting of the recording in the *Suites*, the violin timbre is thin (some might feel the effect to be more 'authentic') and the overall sound-balance rather dry in the bass. The two concertos (which date from 1975) are noticeably more expansive in quality.

CHAMBER MUSIC

(Unaccompanied) *Cello suites Nos. 1–6, BWV 1007/12.*
*** EMI Dig. CDS7 47471-8 (2). Heinrich Schiff.
(M) (***) EMI mono CHS7 61027-2 (2) [Ang. CDH 61028/9]. Pablo Casals.
*** EMI Dig. CDC7 47035-2 (1, 4 & 5); 47036-2 (2, 3 & 6). Paul Tortelier.
(M) *** Ph. 422 494-2 (*Nos. 1, 4 & 6*); 422 495-2 (*Nos. 2, 3 & 5*). Maurice Gendron.
(M) **(*) EMI CMS7 69431-2 (2). Paul Tortelier.
**(*) Decca Dig. 414 163-2 (2) [id.]. Lynn Harrell.
**(*) CBS Dig. M2K 37867 (2) [id.]. Yo-Yo Ma.

Schiff blows any cobwebs away from these dark and taxing works, not with consciously authentic performances that risk desiccation but with sharply direct ones, tough in manner and at speeds generally far faster than usual. For once one is constantly reminded that these are suites of dance movements, with Schiff's rhythmic pointing a delight. So even the *Sarabandes* emerge as stately dances, not unfeeling but freed of the heavy romanticism which is often plastered on them. Equally, the fast movements are given a lightness and resilience which make them sound fresh and new. Strong and positive, producing a consistent flow of beautiful tone at whatever dynamic level, Schiff here establishes his individual artistry very clearly. He is treated to an excellent recording, with the cello given fine bloom against a warm but intimate acoustic. The CDs have striking presence and realism.

It was Casals who restored these pieces to the repertory after long decades of neglect. Some of the playing is far from flawless; passage-work is rushed or articulation uneven, and he is often wayward. But he brought to the *Cello suites* insights that remain unrivalled. Casals brings one closer to this music than do most (one is tempted to say, any) of his rivals. Listen to the *Sarabandes* from the *D minor* or *C minor Suites* and the humanity, nobility and wisdom of this playing will be immediately evident. The sound is inevitably dated but still comes over well in this transfer.

Recorded in the reverberant acoustic of the Temple Church in London, Tortelier's 1983 performances of the *Suites* present clear contrasts with his version of twenty years earlier. His approach remains broadly romantic by today's purist standards, but this time the rhythms are steadier, the command greater, with the preludes of each suite strongly characterized to capture the attention even in simple chattering passage-work. Some will prefer a drier acoustic than this, but the digital sound is first rate, with striking presence on CD.

No one artist holds all the secrets in this repertoire, but few succeed in producing such consistent beauty of tone as Maurice Gendron, with the digital remastering firming up the focus of what was originally an excellent and truthful analogue recording. His phrasing is unfailingly musical and, although these readings have a certain sobriety (save perhaps for No. 6, which has distinct flair), their restraint and fine judgement command admiration. At mid-price (with the two discs available separately) they can certainly be given a warm welcome back to the catalogue.

With Tortelier's 1983 digital set already holding an honoured place in the catalogue, EMI have now reissued his earlier analogue recording at mid-price. Some might prefer it for its drier acoustic, and undoubtedly Tortelier's rhythmic grip is strong, his technique masterly and his intonation true. At the same time, however, there are touches of reticence: it is as if he is consciously resisting the temptation to give full rein to his musical and lyrical instinct. Nevertheless the faster movements are splendidly played, and the *Prelude* to the *E flat major Suite* finds him at his most imposing. The set is good value and the recording, though made in the first half of the 1960s, sounds most realistic.

The spareness and restraint of Harrell's performances contrast strongly with the more extrovert manner of most virtuosi, but rarely if ever is he guilty of understatement. The simple dedication of the playing, combined with cleanness of attack and purity of tone, bring natural unforced intensity. One might disagree with the occasional tempo, but the overall command is unassailable. Excellent, aptly intimate recorded quality.

Yo-Yo Ma gives deeply satisfying performances. He commands the highest artistry, and his playing invariably offers both technical mastery and elevation of spirit. Moreover, the CBS engineers have given him truthful and well-balanced sound. However, his intonation is not always absolutely impeccable: his present set cannot be counted a first recommendation.

Flute sonatas Nos. 1–6, BWV 1030/35; in G min., BWV 1020; Partita in A min. (for solo flute), *BWV 1013.*
*** CRD CRD 33145 (2) [id.]. Stephen Preston, Trevor Pinnock, Dordi Savall.
(M) **(*) Ph. 422 943-2 (2) [id.]. Maxence Larrieu, Rafael Puyana, Wieland Kuijken.
(BB) ** Hung. White Label HRC 119 [id.] (*Nos. 2, 4–6 & BWV 1020*). Lóránt Kovács, János Sebestyén, Ede Banda.

Flute sonatas Nos. 1 in B min, BWV 1030; 3 in A, BWV 1032; 5 in E min., BWV 1034; 6 in E, BWV 1035; Partita in A min., BWV 1013.
**(*) Denon Dig. C37 7331 [id.]. Nicolet, Jaccottet, Fujiwara.

(i) *Flute sonatas Nos. 1, 3, 5 & 6; Partita in A min., BWV 1013* (2 versions); (ii) *Concerto in D for strings* (arr. Brüggen from *BWV 1031*).
(M) ** HM/BMG GD 71964 (2). Brüggen, Leonhardt, Bylsma; Kuijken Ens.

Two of these *Sonatas*, BWV 1031 and 1033, are unauthenticated, but still contain attractive music. Using an authentic one-key instrument, Stephen Preston plays all six with a rare delicacy. By its nature, the baroque instrument he uses can cope with only a limited dynamic range; but Preston is finely expressive, not least in the splendid *Partita* for solo flute. Unfortunately, its inclusion in the set has contributed to an uneconomic layout on a pair of CDs. Of the works with continuo, the two minor-key sonatas, BWV 1030 and BWV 1034, are particularly fine. A reconstruction of the first movement of the *A major*, where bars are missing, is featured here. Throughout, the continuo playing, led by Trevor Pinnock, is of the highest standard; for those willing to stretch to the expense of two premium-priced records, this is a clear first choice for this repertoire.

The Philips set comes from 1967 and places the flute very much in the foreground, though it is otherwise well enough recorded. Maxence Larrieu plays a modern flute, Rafael Puyana an instrument modelled on a large German harpsichord of the eighteenth century, and Wieland Kuijken a seven-stringed viola da gamba from the Tyrol and probably dating from the second half of the eighteenth century. The performances are highly accomplished and often persuasive. Moreover the *G minor Sonata*, BWV 1020, is also included. There are doubts about its authenticity, but Carl Philipp Emanuel has claimed that his father wrote it; if so, it almost certainly pre-dates the other works included. Puyana has made a sensible, fairly straightforward reconstruction of the incomplete first movement of BWV 1032. The set, which is economically priced, makes very agreeable listening, although it would not be a first choice.

The five *Flute sonatas* which are accepted as authentic by the editors of the *Neuen Bach-Ausgabe* are included on this well-filled Denon CD. The music itself comes from Bach's days at Cöthen. The later *E major sonata* was written when Bach visited Potsdam in 1741, and it is beautifully played – as for that matter are they all. Naturally when a modern flute is blended with harpsichord, it tends to dominate. The recordings were made in Switzerland in 1984 and are otherwise well balanced.

Lóránt Kovács makes an arbitrary selection of five *Sonatas*, and makes a good case for the unauthenticated works as well as for those confirmed as belonging to Bach. This is not for authenticists, as his timbre is rich; but he plays quite winningly and the continuo is more than adequate. Apart from the rather forward balance of the flute, the sound is very good and this inexpensive CD includes proper documentation.

Brüggen's RCA set is a curiosity. He plays those four *Sonatas* which he considers authentic very beautifully, and the flute timbre is nicely in scale with the continuo. Then come two versions of the *Partita*, one for solo flute, the second with the movements divided up between flute and various stringed instruments. Lastly we are offered

Brüggen's own arrangement for strings of part of the *Sonata*, BWV 1031, which he admits is sketchy and 'still leaves much to be desired'. The 1975 sound is very good.

Lute music transcribed for guitar

Lute suites (arr. for guitar): *Nos. 1–4, BWV 995/7 and 1006a.*
*** CBS MK 42204 [id.]. John Williams (guitar).
With all four *Suites* conveniently fitted on to a single compact disc, this CBS issue offers a clear first choice in this repertoire. John Williams shows a natural feeling for Bach; the flair of his playing with its rhythmic vitality and sense of colour is always telling. His is a first-class set in every way: the linear control and ornamentation are equally impressive. The CD transfer is made at the highest level; but with the volume control turned down a bit, the close balance does not affect the fullness of timbre.

Suites Nos. 1–2, BWV 996/7; Fugue in G min., BWV 1000.
*** DG Dig. 410 643-2 [id.]. Göran Söllscher (guitar).

Suites Nos. 3, BWV 995; 4, BWV 1006a; Prelude in C min., BWV 999; Prelude, fugue and allegro in E flat, BWV 998.
*** DG Dig. 413 719-2 [id.]. Göran Söllscher (guitar).

Göran Söllscher is a highly musical player. He is well attuned to Bach, his style is fluent and there is a judicious use of light and shade. The playing is technically impeccable – as is the recorded sound, which is suitably intimate, though not to be reproduced at too high a volume level.

Lute suites (arr. for guitar): *Nos. 1 in E min., BWV 996; 2 in A min. (originally C min.), BWV 997;* (i) *Trio sonatas Nos. 1 in E flat, BWV 525; 5 in C, BWV 529* (ed. Bream).
**(*) RCA RD 89654 [RCD1 5841]. Julian Bream (guitar/lute); (i) with George Malcolm.

Bream's compilation comes from records made in the 1960s. The *Lute suites* are played with great subtlety and mastery on the guitar; the *Trio sonatas* are usually heard on the organ, but Bream's arrangement for lute and harpsichord is effective, even if one may prefer the originals. They are elegantly played and crisply recorded, though the harpsichord remains a shade less well defined in the bass register than is ideal.

Lute suites Nos. 3 in G min., BWV 995; 4 in F (trans. of Solo Violin partita in E), BWV 1006a; Prelude in C min. and fugue in G min., BWV 999/1000.
**(*) Saydisc Amon Ra CD-SAR 23 [id.]. Nigel North (baroque lute).

Nigel North plays this music on a baroque lute and he is convincingly recorded in a slightly dry acoustic which is yet not too enclosed. These works lie awkwardly for the lute, and his style is freer and less rhythmically precise than John Williams using the guitar; some may prefer the firmer outline of the latter's playing. Nigel North is at his finest in the transcription of the *E major Violin partita*, which he plays in the key of F (even though the autograph is in the key of the original), as apparently E major offers problems for the lute. Certainly it is both enjoyable and very convincing in North's arrangement where there are a few minor changes in the chordal layout.

Trio sonatas Nos. 1 in D min., 2 in C, 3 & 4 in G, BWV 1036/9.
*** HM Dig. HMC 901173 [id.]. L. Bar.

This disc contains two sonatas of established authenticity, the *G major*, BWV 1039, and (perhaps less certain) its companion in the same key, BWV 1038, which exists in a set of parts in Bach's own hand. The other two are of less certain authorship. The playing of the London Baroque has great freshness and spirit, and readers wanting this repertoire need not hesitate. The recording is eminently satisfactory, too.

Trio sonatas: in G min., BWV 1029; in D min., BWV 1036; in F, BWV 1040 (for flute, oboe and continuo).
(*) Denon Dig. C37 7093 [id.]. Nicolet, Holliger, Jaccottet – c. p. e. bach: *Trio sonatas.*(*)

The *Sonata in D minor*, BWV 1036, although attractive, is almost certainly spurious; indeed, its content seems too mellifluously *galant* to come from the pen of Johann Sebastian. BWV 1029 certainly is Bach, as its opening movement makes obvious, deriving from a sonata for viola da gamba. All three are enjoyable when given performances so spirited and polished. One would have welcomed rather more light and shade, but the resonant ambience has contributed to this. In all other respects the recording is excellent.

Viola da gamba sonatas Nos. 1–3, BWV 1027/9.
*** CBS Dig. MK 37794 [id.]. Yo-Yo Ma (cello), Kenneth Cooper.
*** DG Dig. 415 471-2 [id.]. Mischa Maisky (cello), Martha Argerich (piano).

Yo-Yo Ma plays with great eloquence and natural feeling. His tone is warm and refined and his technical command remains, as ever, irreproachable. Kenneth Cooper is a splendid partner. The CD has wonderful clarity and presence, and admirers of this cellist will undoubtedly want to acquire this issue.

Mischa Maisky is also a highly expressive cellist and, unlike Yo-Yo Ma, he opts for the piano – successfully, for Martha Argerich is a Bach player of the first order. In fact the sonority of the cello and the modern piano seems a happier marriage than the compromise Ma and Cooper adopt. The recording is extremely well balanced too, and the acoustic pleasingly warm. A most enjoyable account for collectors who do not care for period instruments.

(Unaccompanied) Violin sonatas Nos. 1–3, BWV 1001, 1003 & 1005; Violin partitas Nos. 1–3, BWV 1002, 1004 & 1006.
⊛ *** EMI Dig. CDS7 49483-2 (2) [id.]. Itzhak Perlman.
*** ASV CDDCD 454 (2) [id.]. Oscar Shumsky.
(m) *** DG 423 294-2 (2) [id.]. Milstein.
(m) *** Ph. 422 940-2 (2). Felix Ayo.
(m) *** HM/BMG GD 77043 (2) [77043-2-RG]. Sigiswald Kuijken.
*** Orfeo C 130853H (2) [id.]. Dmitry Sitkovetsky.
(m) (***) EMI mono CHS7 693035-2 (2). Yehudi Menuhin.
(m) (**(*)) RCA mono GD 87708 (2) [7708-2-RC]. Jascha Heifetz.
* Claves Dig. 2897 943 (2). Mark Lubotsky.

The range of tone in Perlman's playing adds to the power of these performances, infectiously rhythmic in dance movements but conveying the intensity of live performance in the great slow movements in hushed playing of great refinement. Some may still seek a greater sense of struggle conveyed in order to bring out the full depth of the writing, but the sense of spontaneity, of the player's own enjoyment in the music, makes this set a unique, revelatory experience. Perlman's finest achievement comes in the supreme test of the great *Chaconne* which concludes the *D minor Partita*, the Everest of violin music. Here the scale of the playing is all-embracing. The climax which Perlman builds at the end of the first big group of minor-key variations is almost orchestral in its power, and the tempo allows him to give the complete illusion, ventriloquial, of voices answering one another – as also in the fugues. Then the sudden dramatic moment of hush, as the first major-key variation begins, has rarely been caught on record with such intensity. Perlman here triumphantly demonstrates his insight in bringing out the deepest qualities of these six searching masterpieces.

Shumsky's clean attack and tight vibrato, coupled with virtuosity of the highest order, make for strong and refreshing readings, full of flair and imagination. If you want big-scale playing of Bach, this supplies the need splendidly, though the dry, close acoustic reduces the scale and undermines tenderness.

Milstein's set from the mid-1970s has been most realistically remastered and makes a first-class mid-price recommendation. Every phrase is beautifully shaped and there is a highly developed feeling for line. Intonation is not always absolutely impeccable, but there is no want of virtuosity and it is always put at the service of the music. The DG engineers served this artist well on the original LPs, and the CDs have not lost the lifelike sound-balance, while there is the usual gain in presence. These performances have an aristocratic poise and a classical finesse which are very refreshing.

Felix Ayo, closely associated with I Musici, is also renowned for his purity of intonation and fine musicianship, both of which are in evidence here. His beautiful tone brings a feeling of Italian sunshine to Bach; tempi are often more relaxed than with Milstein and his approach is mellower, although this is playing of much feeling. Ayo's readings are unmannered but have a distinct personality, and they are very easy to live with; they also have the advantage of very realistic sound, the violin image smoother and warmer than Milstein's, though not as opulent as with Perlman.

Using a Grancino violin of 1700 restored to its original condition, Sigiswald Kuijken aims in his set to present an authentic period performance. Those who tire of the sweetness and beauty of even the finest modern performances will find the sharper sounds of Kuijken very refreshing. With wonderfully true intonation and G-string tone of gutty firmness, these accounts are as little painful or scratchy as you are ever likely to get in the authentic field. The recording is full and faithful, yet conveys chamber intimacy.

Dmitry Sitkovetsky is not only a player of exceptional virtuosity but a real stylist. He conveys no sense of haste and he has a splendidly fluid sense of line and firm rhythms. The excellence and naturalness of the recording make the claims of this set very strong indeed.

The Menuhin set brings together a masterly series he recorded between May 1934 and February 1936, mostly in Paris, rounding off his golden teenage. For anyone wanting to appreciate the impact his playing had at that period – strong, pure and disciplined, as well as warmly expressive in the way always associated with his name – this provides the most compelling evidence. Though the digital transfer reveals the occasional bump in the original recording, the vivid sense of presence quickly makes one forget any limitations.

The dry and limited mono sound of Heifetz's classic set, dating from the 1950s, does not prevent one being thrilled by the astonishing bravura of his playing. Speeds are often extremely fast – phenomenally so in the fugues – yet rhythms are superbly controlled. Though the power of the performances is overwhelming, the closeness and dryness of the acoustic give a kind of drawing-room intimacy. Heifetz's creative imagination in his phrasing has one consistently registering the music afresh.

Mark Lubotsky is an impressive player, but his account of the solo *Sonatas* and *Partitas* is effortful and suffers from some rough tone and unglamorous recorded sound. Merits it undoubtedly has, but it represents no challenge to its main competitors.

(Unaccompanied) *Violin partita No. 1 in B min., BWV 1002.*
*** Ph. Dig. 420 948-2 [id.]. Viktoria Mullova – BARTÓK: *Sonata**** (also with
PAGANINI: *Introduction and variations on Nel cor più non misento****).

There is no doubt that Viktoria Mullova is an artist of remarkable intelligence as well
as enormous technical accomplishment. Her account of the *B minor Partita* is undeniably
impressive and is in every way compelling. Apart from the tonal finesse which she
commands, there is a strong sense of line and pure intonation. Good if forward recording.

Violin sonatas (for violin and harpsichord) *Nos. 1–6, BWV 1014/9.*
*** Ph. Dig. 410 401-2 (2) [id.]. Monica Huggett, Ton Koopman.
(M) *** HM/BMG GD 77170 (2). Sigiswald Kuijken, Gustav Leonhardt.

*Violin sonatas Nos. 1–6, BWV 1014/9; 1019a; Sonatas for violin and continuo, BWV
1020/4.*
⊛ (M) *** Ph. 426 452-2 (2) [id., without *BWV 1024*]. Arthur Grumiaux, Christiane
Jaccottet, Philippe Mermoud (in *BWV 1021 & 1023*).

*Violin sonatas Nos. 1–6, BWV 1014/9; in G, BWV 1019a; Sonatas for violin and
continuo, BWV 1021/4.*
(M) **(*) DG Dig. 427 152-2 (2) [id.]. Reinhard Goebel, Robert Hill, Jaap ter Linden.

Violin sonatas (for violin and harpsichord) *Nos. 1–6, BWV 1014/9; Sonatas for violin and
continuo, BWV 1021 & 1023.*
**(*) Virgin Dig. VCD 790741-2 (2) [id.]. John Holloway, Davitt Moroney, Susan
Sheppard.

The Bach *Sonatas for violin and harpsichord* and *violin and continuo* are much less well
known than the works for unaccompanied violin or cello, but they contain music of great
character and beauty. Who can forget the Siciliana which opens No. 4 or the charm of the
brief *Largo* of BWV 1019; while the polyphony of the allegros is always engagingly fresh.
Grumiaux's performances were recorded in 1978 and 1980, but are new to the UK
catalogue. They are marvellously played, with all the beauty of tone and line for which he
is renowned; they have great vitality too. His admirable partner is Christiane Jaccottet,
and in BWV 1021 and 1023 Philippe Mermoud (cello) joins the continuo. Grumiaux's
collection is all-embracing, even though the *Sonatas*, BWV 1020 and 1022, are not
considered authentic. There is endless treasure to be discovered here, particularly when
the music-making is so serenely communicative. The balance rather favours the violin,
but the recording is very realistic and Grumiaux's tone is ravishingly pure.

Monica Huggett, one of the outstanding exponents of authentic performance, plays
with refined expressiveness in a beautifully unified conception of these six endlessly
inventive works. Other versions may be more vigorous but, with excellent recording,
detailed and well balanced, period instruments are projected most persuasively. Two
alternative versions are given of the slow movement of BWV 1019.

Sigiswald Kuijken uses a baroque violin, and both he and Gustav Leonhardt give us
playing of rare eloquence. This reissue is an admirable example of the claims of
authenticity and musical feeling pulling together rather than apart. The violinist does not
shrink from the intelligent use of vibrato, and both artists demonstrate in every bar that
scholarship is at their service and is not an inhibiting taskmaster. As so often from this
source, the harpsichord is very well recorded and the texture is lighter and cleaner than
usual. This is a wholly delightful set and the transparency of the sound is especially
appealing. It is also reasonably priced.

The Goebel/Hill recordings offer vigorous performances on period instruments, somewhat abrasive in the violin tone, bringing dance-based movements in particular vividly to life. With the reservation that some ears may find Goebel's timbre too acerbic over a long listening span, these performances can be recommended. The recording is first rate in its presence and clarity, with no lack of ambience.

In addition to the six *Sonatas for violin and harpsichord*, the Virgin set presents the two surviving *Sonatas for violin and continuo* (in the latter, Davitt Moroney uses a chamber organ) known to be authentic. John Holloway has long experience in the early-music field, but violin tone is as much a matter of personal taste as is the human voice. Some will find the actual sound he makes unpleasing: it is vinegary and at times downright ugly. Yet those who take a different view will find him not wanting in artistry. Both Davitt Moroney and Susan Sheppard give excellent support, and the recording cannot be faulted in its clarity and presence; for those who must have original-instrument performances, first choice remains with Monica Huggett and Ton Koopman who, although they omit BWV 1021 and 1023, are no less authentic.

KEYBOARD MUSIC

The Art of fugue, BWV 1080 (see also orchestral versions).
*** HM HMC 901169/70 [id.]. Davitt Moroney (harpsichord).
**(*) DG Dig. 427 673-2 [id.]. Kenneth Gilbert (harpsichord).

The Art of fugue, BWV 1080; Italian concerto, BWV 971; Partita in B min., BWV 831; Prelude, fugue and allegro in E flat, BWV 998.
(M) *** HM/BMG GD 77013 (2). Gustav Leonhardt (harpsichord).

Gustav Leonhardt uses a copy by Martin Skowroneck of a Dulcken harpsichord of 1745, a responsive and beautiful instrument. Under the fingers of Leonhardt every strand in the texture emerges with clarity and every phrase is allowed to speak for itself. In the 12th and 18th fugues Leonhardt is joined by Bob van Asperen. Leonhardt does not include the unfinished fugue, but that will be the only reservation to cross the minds of most listeners. This is a very impressive and rewarding set, well recorded and produced.

Davitt Moroney's account commands not only the intellectual side of the work but also the aesthetic, and his musicianship is second to none. Moroney makes some alterations in the order of the various contrapuncti but he argues his case persuasively – and he is eminently well served by the engineers. Davitt Moroney has imagination as well as scholarship.

Kenneth Gilbert's is a version of special interest. He turns to the earlier autograph version, edited by Christoph Wolff and published by Peters Edition in 1987. It differs from the 1751 edition primarily in omitting four of the movements familiar from 1751 and fits conveniently on to a single CD. Kenneth Gilbert plays a fine 1671 harpsichord by Jan Couchet of Antwerp, enlarged by the Parisian makers, Blanchet (c. 1759) and Taskin (1778). He is splendidly recorded, though some may be troubled by the rather literal, almost Teutonic approach he adopts. A valuable supplementary issue, but not a first recommendation for obvious reasons.

Capriccio in B flat, BWV 992; Fantasia and fugue in A min., BWV 904; Prelude, fugue and allegro in E flat, BWV 998; Suite in E min., BWV 996 (originally for lute); *Toccata in E min., BWV 914.*
*** Ph. Dig. 416 141-2 [id.]. Gustav Leonhardt (harpsichord).

Gustav Leonhardt plays a William Dowd harpsichord, modelled on an instrument by Mietke of Berlin dating from 1715. The sonorities are rich and the great Dutch player exploits them with characteristic resourcefulness. His well-planned recital has vitality, freshness and imagination, and everything comes vividly to life, thanks perhaps to a splendidly articulate recording.

Chaconne in D min. (arr. Busoni from (unaccompanied) *Violin partita No. 2 in D min., BWV 1004).*
*** RCA RD 85673 [RCA 5673-2-RC]. Artur Rubinstein – LISZT: *Sonata***(*); FRANCK: *Prelude, chorale & fugue****.

Busoni's arrangement of the celebrated *Chaconne* for solo violin is a piece which has to be presented with flair as virtuoso piano music, and Rubinstein is an ideal choice of pianist. He recorded this performance in Rome in 1970, when he was already in his eighties, but the freshness and spirit are a delight. The recording is clangy but not unpleasantly so.

Chromatic fantasia and fugue in D min., BWV 903; Chorale Preludes: Ich ruf zu dir, BWV 639; Nun komm' der Heiden Heiland, BWV 659 (both arr. Busoni); *Fantasia in A min., BWV 922; Fantasia and fugue in A min., BWV 904; Italian concerto in F, BWV 971.*
*** Ph. 412 252-2 [id.]. Alfred Brendel (piano).

Brendel's fine Bach recital originally appeared in 1978. The performances are of the old school with no attempt to strive after harpsichord effects, and with every piece creating a sound-world of its own. The *Italian concerto* is particularly imposing, with a finely sustained sense of line and beautifully articulated rhythms. The recording is in every way truthful and present, bringing the grand piano very much into the living-room before one's very eyes. Masterly.

Chromatic fantasia & fugue in D min., BWV 903; 4 Duets, BWV 802/5; Italian concerto, BWV 971; Partita in B min., BWV 831.
*** EMI Dig. CDC7 49800-2 [id.]. Robert Woolley (harpsichord).

Robert Woolley's recital begins with a very persuasive account of the *B minor Partita.* This he presents with an apparently effortless sense of style and evident delight. The playing has spontaneity and sense of spirit and is greatly helped by the quality both of his instrument and of the warm, well-defined but not over-projected recording. His version of the *Chromatic fantasia and fugue* has no less authority or panache, and both the *Four Duets* and the *Italian concerto* come off well. There is a refreshing absence of didacticism here. Woolley uses a modern copy by Bruce Kennedy of an instrument from 1702 by Michael Mietke.

Chromatic fantasia & fugue in D min., BWV 903; Fantasias: in C min., BWV 906; G min., BWV 917; C min., BWV 919; Fantasia & fugue in A min., BWV 904; Preludes: in C min., BWV 921; A min., BWV 922; Preludes & fugues: in A min., BWV 894; F, BWV 901; G, BWV 902.
*** HM/BMG RD 77039 [RCA 77039-2-RC]. Andreas Staier (harpsichord).

Andreas Staier will be familiar to most collectors as a member of the Cologne Musica Antiqua, but in recent years he has pursued a solo career both on harpsichord and fortepiano. On this CD he plays a copy of an instrument from 1702–4 by the Berlin maker, Michael Mietke, and alongside the familiar *Chromatic fantasia and fugue,* he offers less-often-recorded repertoire, always with imagination and flair. What is good about his playing is its air of freedom, for although he keeps a firm grip on rhythm he is never rigid or inflexible, and his approach and registration are varied enough for his programme to be heard at one sitting. The recording has impressive clarity and presence and is made in a pleasingly warm acoustic. Strongly recommended.

Chromatic fantasia and fugue in D min., BWV 903; Fantasia in C min., BWV 906; Italian concerto in F, BWV 971; Prelude and fugue in A min., BWV 894.
**(*) Denon Dig. C37 7233 [id.]. Huguette Dreyfus (harpsichord).

Eminently straightforward accounts, perhaps a little unyielding at times but cleanly and truthfully recorded. Huguette Dreyfus plays with an admirable style and taste, without any ostentatious changes of registration. The recording is processed at a high level and for best results should be played at a low volume setting.

Chromatic fantasia and fugue, BWV 903; Italian concerto in F, BWV 971; Partita No. 1 in B flat, BWV 825; Prelude, fugue and allegro, BWV 998; Toccata, adagio and fugue, BWV 916.
*** Virgin Dig. VC 790712-2 [id.]. Maggie Cole (piano).

This is Maggie Cole's first solo recital, and very good it is too. She uses a Ruckers harpsichord of 1612 from the Royal Collection, tuned in unequal temperament. Her playing is splendidly unfussy, free from interpretative mannerisms and not bound by rigid rhythms; her virtuosity in the *Chromatic fantasia and fugue* seems effortless and unforced, and there is an agreeable naturalness about the whole recital. The recording is thoroughly faithful and the acoustic lively, if small.

4 Duets, BWV 802–5; English suite No. 6 in D min., BWV 811; Italian concerto, BWV 971; Toccata in C minor, BWV 911.
(m) *** DG Dig. 429 975-2 [id.]. Angela Hewitt (piano).

In both the *Italian concerto* and the *English suite* Angela Hewitt's playing is enormously alive and stimulating. Textures are clean, with every strand in perfect focus and every phrase clearly articulated. She plays with vital imaginative resource, totally free from idiosyncrasy and affectation. The piano is beautifully captured on this recording, which must be numbered as one of the most successful DG have given us, with fresh, life-like sound and vivid presence.

English suites, Nos. 1–6, BWV 806–11.
*** EMI Dig. CDS7 49000-8 (2) [Ang. CDCB 49000]. Gustav Leonhardt (harpsichord).
*** Decca Dig. 421 640-2 (2) [id.]. András Schiff (piano).

Gustav Leonhardt uses a 1755 instrument by Nicholas Lefebre of Rouen, recently restored by Martin Skowroneck, and very beautiful it sounds too in this clear but not too forwardly balanced recording. Leonhardt's playing here has a flair and vitality that one does not always associate with him, and there is no doubt that he makes the most of the introspective *Sarabande* of the *G minor Suite*. He is well served by the EMI engineers; his performances, too, are flexible and relaxed. The CD transfer retains the atmospheric sound-balance; the harpsichord is present without being right on top of the listener.

Schiff is straightforward, finely articulated, rhythmically supple and vital. Ornamentation is stylishly and sensibly observed. Everything is very alive, without being in the least over-projected or exaggerated in any way. The Decca recording is altogether natural and present and places the odd- and even-numbered *Suites* together. Readers looking for the complete set played on the piano are unlikely to be disappointed.

English suite No. 2 in A min., BWV 807; Partita No. 2 in C min., BWV 826; Toccata in C min., BWV 911.

(M) *** DG 423 880-2 [id.]. Martha Argerich (piano).

Martha Argerich does not disappoint: her playing is alive and keenly rhythmic but also wonderfully flexible and rich in colour. Her finger control is consistently impressive. The textures are always varied and clean, and there is an intellectual and musical vitality here that is refreshing. Moreover Miss Argerich is very well recorded.

English suites Nos. 2 in A min.; 3 in G min., BWV 807/8.
*** DG Dig. 415 480-2 [id.]. Ivo Pogorelich (piano).

The young Yugoslav pianist plays both *Suites* with a welcome absence of affectation. He observes all repeats and, although some of the *Sarabandes* are really rather slow, which may strain the allegiance of some listeners, there is generally speaking an impressive feeling of movement. It is all beautifully articulate and fresh. The recording is one of DG's best, with natural piano sound and an excellent sense of presence.

French suites Nos. 1–6, BWV 812/7.
**(*) HM HMC 90437/8 [id.]. Kenneth Gilbert (harpsichord).
(M) **(*) HM/BMG GD 71963 (2). Gustav Leonhardt (harpsichord). ⋅
**(*) EMI Dig. CDS7 49293-2 [Ang. CDCB 49293]. Andrei Gavrilov (piano).

French suites Nos. 1–6; Suites: in A min., BWV 818a; in E flat, BWV 819; Allemande, BWV 819a.
*** O-L Dig. 411811-2 (2) [id.]. Christopher Hogwood (harpsichord).

Christopher Hogwood uses two harpsichords, a Ruckers of 1646 enlarged and modified by Taskin in 1780, and a 1749 instrument, basically the work of Jean-Jacques Goujon and slightly modified by Jacques Joachim Swanen in 1784. They are magnificent creatures and Hogwood coaxes superb sounds from them: his playing is expressive, and the relentless sense of onward momentum that disfigures so many harpsichordists is pleasingly absent. These performances have both style and character and can be recommended with some enthusiasm. To the *French suites* themselves he adds the two others that Bach had obviously intended to include as Nos. 5 and 6. The useful notes describe the tuning which was adopted for each suite.

Kenneth Gilbert's recording dates from the mid-1970s. He uses a 1636 Ruckers, rebuilt by Hemsch, which is made to sound full and robust by the forward balance. One needs to set the volume control cautiously and perhaps make further adjustments at times. As in his set of the *English suites*, the playing has a natural flow; there is an obvious feeling for the strongly rhythmic French style, yet his flexibility prevents any sense of rigidity. Tempi are well judged and ornamentation is discreet. This is fine playing, but Hogwood has the advantage of digital recording and offers more music. Gilbert's set is played a semitone lower than normal present-day pitch.

Leonhardt's recordings were made in 1975. He uses a Rubio, modelled on a Taskin, and it sounds well, the recording only a shade close. The playing is generally flexible; perhaps the rhythmic French style is over-assertive at times, but the livelier dance movements, like the famous *Gavotte* in BWV 816, have plenty of character. Not a first choice, but good value at mid-price.

Gavrilov's set is full of interesting things, and there is some sophisticated, not to say masterly, pianism. The part-writing is keenly alive and the playing full of subtle touches. He draws a wide range of tone-colour from the keyboard and employs a wider dynamic range than might be expected. There is an element of the self-conscious here and a measure of exaggeration in some of the *Gigues*, but there is also much that is felicitous. The recording is excellent.

Goldberg variations, BWV 988.
*** DG 415 130-2 [id.]. Trevor Pinnock (harpsichord).
*** Decca Dig. 417 116-2 [id.]. András Schiff (piano).
*** HM Dig. HMC 901240 [id.]. Kenneth Gilbert (harpsichord).
**(*)EMI Dig. CDC7 49058-2 [id.]. Scott Ross (harpsichord).

Goldberg variations, BWV 988; Chromatic fantasia and fugue, BWV 903; Italian concerto in F, BWV 971.
(M) (**) EMI mono CDH7 61008-2 [id.]. Wanda Landowska (harpsichord).

Trevor Pinnock uses a Ruckers dating from 1646, modified over a century later by Taskin and restored most recently in 1968 by Hubert Bédard. He retains repeats in more than half the variations – which seems a good compromise, in that variety is maintained yet there is no necessity for an additional disc. The playing is eminently vital and intelligent, with alert, finely articulated rhythm. The recording is very truthful and vivid.

For those who enjoy Bach on the piano, András Schiff's set can receive the most enthusiastic advocacy. The part-writing emerges with splendid definition and subtlety: Schiff does not play as if he is performing a holy ritual but with a keen sense of enjoyment of the piano's colour and sonority. The Decca recording is excellent in every way, clean and realistic.

Kenneth Gilbert gives a refreshingly natural performance of the *Goldberg*. He uses a recent copy of a Ruckers–Taskin, and it makes a very pleasing sound. His is an aristocratic reading; he avoids excessive display and there is a quiet, cultured quality about his playing that is very persuasive. An essentially introspective account, recorded in a rather less lively acoustic than is Pinnock on Archiv, and he is a thoughtful and thought-provoking player.

Scott Ross observes every repeat of the *Goldberg* in this 1988 account, though still accommodating the whole work on one CD at just over 75 minutes. He takes the theme a good deal faster than many rivals, and his ornamentation is in exemplary taste, neither excessive nor arbitrary. There is plenty of energy and a strong sense of rhythm which at times tends towards rigidity. On the whole, however, he is a sound guide in this masterpiece and, were he not at times just a shade prosaic, this would be a wholehearted recommendation. He is certainly well recorded.

Wanda Landowska's version from the 1930s was the first ever complete recording of Bach's *Goldberg variations*; though on a clangy Pleyel – not helped by the close recording – the result is aggressive, the imagination of the soloist is endlessly illuminating on her own terms, as are her classic performances of the two other favourite Bach keyboard works.

15 2-part Inventions, BWV 772/786; 15 3-part Inventions, BWV 787/801.
*** Capriccio Dig. 10 210 [id.] (with *6 Little preludes, BWV 933/8*). Ton Koopman (harpsichord).
*** Denon Dig. C37 7566 [id.]. Huguette Dreyfus (harpsichord).
*** DG Dig. 415 112-2 [id.]. Kenneth Gilbert (harpsichord).
**(*) Decca Dig. 411 974-2 [id.]. András Schiff (piano).

Begun in 1720 for his eldest son, ten-year-old Wilhelm Friedemann, these pieces were originally placed in order of difficulty, but Bach subsequently arranged them in ascending key order. Ton Koopman scores over such rivals as Kenneth Gilbert and Huguette Dreyfus in offering the *Six Little preludes* in addition to the two sets of *Inventions*. The disc does not identify Koopman's instrument, but it is obviously a fine one and Koopman plays with somewhat greater spontaneity and sparkle than does Gilbert. As usual, the recording places us too close to the instrument and one has to listen at a rather low-level setting to achieve a truthful and realistic result.

Dreyfus is very impressive, her playing relaxed though rhythmically vital. Her instrument is a Hemsch and her recording was made at Notre Dame in 1978. Mme Dreyfus is a shade warmer and freer than Gilbert and some will prefer her record.

Kenneth Gilbert plays a magnificent 1671 harpsichord by the Antwerp maker, Jan Couchet, which was restored in 1980 by Bédard. It has a rich, almost pearl-like sound, which is enhanced by the acoustic of Chartres Museum, where it was recorded. Gilbert's playing has exemplary taste and sense of musical purpose.

Readers who prefer their Bach on the piano will welcome András Schiff's excellent recording on Decca. His playing is (for this repertoire) rather generous with rubato and other expressive touches, but elegant in the articulation of part-writing. This is at times a bit overdone; such is his musicianship and pianistic sensitivity, however, that the overall results are likely to persuade most listeners. There is a lot of life and colour in the playing and much to enjoy. The recording is excellent; the instrument sounds extraordinarily lifelike, as if in one's very room.

Partitas Nos. 1–6, BWV 825/30.
*** DG Dig. 415 493-2 (2) [id.]. Trevor Pinnock (harpsichord).
*** Erato/WEA Dig. 2292 45345-2 (2) [id.]. Scott Ross (harpsichord).
*** Decca Dig. 411 732-2 (2) [id.]. András Schiff (piano).
**(*) EMI Dig. CDS7 47996-8 (2) [Ang. CDCB 47996]. Gustav Leonhardt (harpsichord).
(***) HM Dig. HMC 901144/6 [id.]. Kenneth Gilbert (harpsichord).

Trevor Pinnock uses a copy of a Hemsch (*c.* 1760) by David Jacques Way, tuned to unequal temperament and sounding marvellously present in this recording. Tempi are generally well judged, rhythms vital yet free, and there is little to justify the criticism that he rushes some movements. He also conveys a certain sense of pleasure that is infectious and he has great spirit and panache.

Scott Ross uses an unidentified instrument and is recorded with both warmth and clarity. He plays with style and panache and, despite one or two minor points (in the *B flat Gigue* not every note speaks evenly and at times elsewhere greater rhythmic freedom would be welcome), his readings make an eminently competitive alternative recommendation.

Schiff is a most persuasive advocate of Bach on the piano, consistently exploiting the modern instrument's potential in range of colour and light and shade, not to mention its sustaining power. Though few will cavil at his treatment of fast movements, some may find him a degree wayward in slow movements, though the freshness of his rubato and the sparkle of his ornamentation are always winning. The sound is outstandingly fine.

Gustav Leonhardt's set was recorded on a Dowd (modelled on an eighteenth-century German instrument by Michael Mietke) in the excellent acoustic of the Doopsgezinde Gemeente Kerk in Haarlem. In terms of sheer sound it is among the most satisfactory available versions, and in terms of style it combines elegance, spontaneity and authority. There is nothing didactic about this playing, but it is never less than thought-provoking. In many respects it is musically the most satisfying of current sets, save for the fact that Leonhardt observes no repeats. This will undoubtedly diminish its appeal, which is a great pity since both illumination and pleasure are to be had from this set.

There is no doubting the excellence of Kenneth Gilbert's set on Harmonia Mundi which, in terms of scholarship and artistry, has much to recommend it. All the same it is handicapped by being spread over three discs. Professor Gilbert uses

J. S. BACH

a Couchet–Taskin–Blanchet (1671–1778) and is well enough recorded – but the differences between the Gilbert and the Pinnock versions do not justify the additional outlay.

Partitas Nos. 1–3, BWV 825/7.
**(*) Olympia OCD 146. Tatiana Nikolaeva (piano).

Tatiana Nikolaeva articulates cleanly but is still pleasingly flexible, and she exploits the piano's range of timbre and dynamic within the bounds of the music itself. Everything is alive, and here gentle pianissimos can be very appealing. The 1980 recording is realistic, if perhaps a trifle dry. Presumably the remaining works are to follow.

8 Preludes for W. F. Bach, BWV 924/32; 6 Little preludes, BWV 933/8; 5 Preludes, BWV 939/43; Prelude, BWV 999; Prelude, fugue and allegro in E flat, BWV 998; Preludes and fughettas: in F and G, BWV 901/2; Fantasia and fugue in A min., BWV 904.
**(*) DG Dig. 419 426-2 [id.]. Kenneth Gilbert (harpsichord).

Splendid artistry from this scholar-player; he is predictably stylish and authoritative. He uses a harpsichord by a Flemish maker, Jan Couchet, enlarged by Blanchet in 1759 and by Taskin in 1778, overhauled by Hubert Bédard. Even played at the lowest setting, the sound seems a bit unrelieved and overbright. This really has 'presence' with a vengeance. The excellence of the playing however is not in question.

The Well-tempered Clavier (48 Preludes & fugues), BWV 846/983.
*** DG Dig. 413 439-2 (4) [id.]. Kenneth Gilbert (harpsichord).
**(*) HM Dig. HMC 901285/8 [id.]. Davitt Moroney (harpsichord).
(M) (**(*)) EMI mono CHS7 63188-2 (3) [id.]. Edwin Fischer.

The Well-tempered Clavier, Book I, Preludes and fugues Nos. 1–24, BWV 846/69.
*** EMI CDS7 49727-2 (2) [Ang. CDCB 49727]. Bob van Asperen (harpsichord).
⊛ *** Decca Dig. 414 388-2 (2) [id.]. András Schiff (piano).
(M) *(**) HM/BMG GD 77011 (2) [RCA 770ll-2-RG]. Gustav Leonhardt (harpsichord).
** Teldec/WEA Dig. 2292 44918-2 (2) [id.]. Glen Wilson (harpsichord).
(M) (***) RCA mono GD 86217 (2) [6217-2-RC]. Wanda Landowska (harpsichord).

The Well-tempered Clavier, Book II, Preludes and fugues Nos. 25–48, BWV 870/93.
*** EMI CDS7 49658-2 (2) [Ang. CDCB 49658]. Bob van Asperen (harpsichord).
⊛ *** Decca Dig. 417 236-2 (2) [id.]. András Schiff (piano).
(M) *(**) HM/BMG GD 77012 (2) [RCA 77012-2-RG]. Gustav Leonhardt (harpsichord).
**(*) Teldec/WEA Dig. 2292 44934-2 (2) [id.]. Glen Wilson (harpsichord).
(M) (***) RCA mono GD 87825 (3) [7825-2-RC]. Wanda Landowska (harpsichord).

Gilbert has made some superb harpsichord records, but his set of the '48' crowns them all. By a substantial margin it now supplants all existing harpsichord versions, with readings that are resilient and individual, yet totally unmannered. Though Gilbert deliberately refuses to use the sort of wide changes of registration which are now thought unauthentic, the range of his expression and the beauty of his instrument, made originally in Antwerp in 1671 and later enlarged in France, give all the variety needed. There is a concentration and purposefulness about each performance over the widest range of moods and expression, and the quality of recording, immediate without being too aggressive, adds to that, although some might feel that the acoustic is just a shade too resonant.

Bob van Asperen was a pupil of Gustav Leonhardt, and his account of the 'Forty-Eight' enshrines many of the finest of his master's qualities and outshines most of his rivals on

CD. His playing is marked by consistent vitality, elegance and concentration: he plays every note as if he means it and is refreshingly unmetronomic without being too free. He plays a 1728 harpsichord by Christian Zell from the Hamburg Museum, which the engineers capture vividly. The acoustic is less resonant than with Gilbert, which is an advantage, and this set can certainly be considered alongside the DG set.

There are no advocates of Bach on the piano more imaginative or persuasive than András Schiff. His set of the '48', conveniently divided into two boxes of two discs, one for each book, is a delight throughout. Schiff – who at an early age found a mentor in Bach with the harpsichordist, George Malcolm – often takes a very individual view of particular preludes and fugues but, as with a pianist like Wilhelm Kempff, his unexpected readings regularly win one over long before the end. Consistently he translates this music into pianistic terms, rarely if ever imitating the harpsichord, and though his very choice of the piano will rule him out with those seeking authenticity, his voyage of discovery through this supreme keyboard collection is the more riveting, when the piano is an easier instrument to listen to over long periods. First-rate sound.

Davitt Moroney uses a modern harpsichord (built in 1980), which has a full-bodied yet cleanly focused image, but is rather too closely balanced. Yet the effect is certainly tangible and realistic, the perspective more convincing than with Leonhardt. His thoughtful, considered approach is satisfying in its way, stylistically impeccable, although the playing is less concentrated than with Gilbert, the result less exuberantly spontaneous than with Van Asperen. But it will suit those who like a thoughtful, unostentatious approach to Bach, yet one that does not lack rhythmic resilience.

Gustav Leonhardt plays a copy of a Taskin by David Rubio for Book I and an instrument by Martin Skowroneck for Book II. It must be said straight away that the attractions of this reissue are diminished by their close balance. Even when the volume is reduced, the perspective seems unnatural, as if one were leaning into each instrument itself. Tastes in the matter of registration are bound to differ, but there is little with which to quarrel and much to admire, while Leonhardt's technique is effortless. His interpretative insights too are most impressive and, were the sound more sympathetic and appealing, this would be very highly recommendable, for Leonhardt combines scholarship, technique and sensibility in no small measure.

Glen Wilson uses a copy of the Zell instrument used by Bob van Asperen and has equally fluent fingers to commend him. He is often thoughtful and never less than accomplished. However, he is inclined to rush through some of the pieces in Book I, though in Book II his approach is more considered. Though there is much to admire here and he is well recorded, his account would not be a first choice.

It is good that RCA have restored Landowska's celebrated records of the '48' to circulation, together with her original notes. They were recorded between 1949 and 1954 and are now accommodated on five well-filled CDs. They still sound marvellous and have a colour, vitality, authority and grandeur that make it difficult to stop listening to them. Styles in Bach playing may have changed over the intervening forty years – it would be strange if they had not – but this playing still carries all before it. The CD transfer has the usual advantages of the medium. Strongly recommended.

Older collectors will recall Edwin Fischer's Bach with particular affection. His was the first ever 'Forty-Eight' to be put on shellac, being recorded in 1933–6. After more than half a century the sound is inevitably dated and the piano tone papery and shallow but – make no mistake – there is nothing shallow about these interpretations. Fischer has often been spoken of as an artist of intellect, but the approach here is never remote or cool. Moreover he produces a beauty of sound and a sense of line that is an unfailing source of musical wisdom and nourishment. The performance is economically laid out on three mid-price CDs, each accommodating close on 80 minutes. These discs are indispensable to the serious Bach collector.

ORGAN MUSIC

Complete organ music

Volume 1: *Fantasias, BWV 562, 570, 572; Fantasias & fugues, BWV 537, 542, 561; Fugues, BWV 575/577, 579, 581, 946; Kleines harmonisches Labyrinth, BWV 591; Passacaglia & fugue, BWV 582; Pedal-Exercitium, BWV 598; Preludes & fugues, BWV 531/533, 535, 548/551; Toccata, adagio & fugue, BWV 564; Toccatas & fugues, BWV 538, 540, 565; Trios, BWV 583, 585.*
(M) *** Decca 421 337-2 (3) [id.]. Peter Hurford (organs of Ratzeburg Cathedral, West Germany, Church of Our Lady of Sorrows, Toronto).

Volume 2: *Chorale preludes, BWV 672/675, 677, 681, 683, 685, 687, 689); 24 Kirnberger Chorale preludes, BWV 690/713; Clavier-Übung, Part 3: German organ Mass (Prelude & fugue in E flat, BWV 552 & Chorale preludes, BWV 669/671, 676, 678, 680, 682, 684, 686, 688); 6 Trio sonatas, BWV 525/530.*
(M) *** Decca 421 341-2 (3) [id.]. Peter Hurford (organs of Chapels at New College, Oxford, & Knox Grammar School, Sydney; Church of Our Lady of Sorrows, Toronto, Ratzeburg Cathedral).

Volume 3: *Canonic variations: Vom Himmel hoch, BWV 769; Chorale partitas: Christ, der du bist; O Gott, du frommer Gott; Sei gegrüsset, Jesu gütig, BWV 766/768; Chorale preludes, BWV 726/740; Schübler chorale preludes, BWV 645/650; Chorale variations: Ach, was soll ich sünder machen; Allein Gott in der Höh' sei Ehr, BWV 770/771. Concertos Nos. 1–6, BWV 592/597.*
⊛ (M) *** Decca 421 617-2 (3) [id.]. Peter Hurford (organs as above, & Melk Abbey, Austria, and Eton College, Windsor).

Volume 4: *35 Arnstedt chorale preludes, BWV 714, 719, 742, 957 & 1090/1120 (from Yale manuscript, copied Neumeister); 18 Leipzig chorale preludes, BWV 651/58. Chorale preludes, BWV 663/668 & BWV 714/725.*
(M) *** Decca Dig./Analogue 421 621-2 (3) [id.]. Peter Hurford (Vienna Bach organ, Augustinerkirche, Vienna, & organs of All Souls' Unitarian Church, Washington, DC, St Catharine's College Chapel, Cambridge, Ratzeburg Cathedral, Knox Grammar School, Sydney, and Eton College, Windsor).

With the exception of the *Arnstedt chorale preludes*, which were added in 1986 (and are digital), Peter Hurford recorded his unique survey of Bach's organ music for Decca's Argo label over a period of eight years, 1974–1982. Originally the recordings were issued on LP and tape in a series of recitals; for their reissue, the different genres are sensibly grouped together since, with the ease of CD access, one can pick and choose readily from each box of three records. Performances are consistently fresh and engrossing in their spontaneity; there is no slackening of tension and the registration features a range of baroque colour that is almost orchestral in its diversity. Hurford plays a number of different organs, moving, say, from Sydney to Toronto, then on to Washington, DC, back to Ratzeburg Cathedral in West Germany, and thence home again to Oxford and Windsor. The digital recording of the Vienna Bach organ, used for the recently discovered *Arnstedt chorale preludes*, is particularly beautiful. Hurford here omits the three pieces which were already familiar (BWV 601, 639 and 737) but includes BWV 714 (which in the Neumeister manuscript is 27 bars longer than previously known versions), BWV 719 and 742 (hitherto not thought to be authentic Bach), and BWV 957 (until now not regarded as an organ work). This brings about a duplication of BWV 714 and 719, which were also recorded in Sydney in 1977.

Anyone wishing to explore the huge range of this repertoire could hardly do better than begin with one of these boxes, and perhaps a good jumping-off point would be Volume 3, to which we award a token Rosette: this includes many of the *Chorale preludes* and *Chorale variations*, in particular the splendid half-dozen chorales which were published at the very end of Bach's life and which commemorate the name of an otherwise unknown music-engraver called Schübler. They are all especially beautifully recorded, demonstrating the character of the six organs which feature most importantly in this undertaking. Their embroidery is always registered imaginatively, with every strand of texture clear; Hurford's approach may be gentle or reedily robust, but always the most fascinating sounds reach the ears, with stimulating alternation of beauty and piquancy of timbre. Hurford understands the structural needs of all this music, yet he ceaselessly fascinates with his feeling for colour and care for detail. Both here and in the more ambitious works, Hurford's pacing always seems apt to the point of inevitability. There is never the faintest hint of routine nor of the fugues trundling on endlessly, as in some performances in the German pedagogic Bach tradition. Sometimes there is dash, at others a clear, unforced momentum, depending on the character of the writing, while the bigger set-pieces have no want of breadth. In the so-called *German organ Mass*, Hurford's approach is direct, with powerful contrasts made between weight and serenity. The recordings were originally in the demonstration class; the CD remastering marginally sharpens the focus and at times brightens the sound-picture at higher dynamic levels. In Volume 4, for instance, at the close of the Neumeister collection (recorded with digital smoothness) the analogue *Leipzig chorale preludes* immediately follow. The ear notices that in the first of these, BWV 651, there is an abrasive pungency on the reeds of the Washington organ, brought about by the slight treble emphasis; and elsewhere there is occasionally a slight element of harshness, with the upper partials not always quite clean. But this effect should not be overemphasized; the warm basic ambience is very appealing; the sound never clouds over and has great presence and depth. The only real drawback to these otherwise admirable reissues is their sparse documentation. The organ specifications are included, but too little about the music itself. Volume 1, which includes many of the fantasias and fugues, preludes and fugues, and toccatas and fugues, is disgracefully inadequate in this respect, although Volumes 3 and 4 are much better. But with generous measure of music in each of the boxes, this remains overall the most rewarding assessment of Bach's organ music ever committed to record.

Adagio in C (from BWV 565); Chorales: Herzlich tut mich verlangen, BWV 727; Liebster Jesu, BWV 730; Wachet auf, BWV 645; Fantasia and fugue in G min., BWV 542; Fugue in E flat (St Anne), BWV 552; Passacaglia and fugue in C min., BWV 582; Toccata and fugue in D min., BWV 565.
(M) *** Decca 417 711-2 [id.]. Peter Hurford (various organs).

An admirable popular recital. Performances are consistently alive and the vivid recording projects them strongly. A self-recommending issue.

Allabreve in D, BWV 589; Chorale prelude: Ach Gott und Herr, BWV 714; Preludes and fugues, BWV 532 and BWV 553/560; Toccata and fugue in D min., BWV 565.
*** Meridian ECD 84081 [id.]. David Sanger (organ of St Catherine's College, Cambridge).

The organ at St Catherine's College, Cambridge, was completely rebuilt in 1978/9. The result is a great success, and its reedy clarity and brightness of timbre are especially suitable for Bach, as is immediately shown in the famous opening *D minor Toccata and fugue* which David Sanger presents with fluent vigour. His playing throughout is thoughtful and well structured; registration shows an excellent sense of colour without being flamboyant. The *Preludes and fugues* are laid out simply before the listener and, although Sanger's style is essentially relaxed, the forward momentum is maintained convincingly and Bach's music is allowed to speak for itself. The *Preludes and fugues in B flat*, BWV 560, and *in D*, BWV 532 (which ends the recital) are particularly convincing, and the latter makes a fine demonstration item alongside BWV 565 for its delightful registration in the fugue as well as for the light clarity of Sanger's touch.

33 Arnstadt chorale preludes (from Yale manuscript).
*** HM Dig. HMC 905158 [id.]. Joseph Payne (organ of St Paul's, Brookline, Mass.).

38 Arnstadt chorale preludes (Yale); 8 Short preludes & fugues, BWV 553/60.
*** EMI Dig. CDS7 49296-2 (2) [Ang. CDCB 49296]. Werner Jacob (Silbermann organ, Arlesheim).

These pieces recently came to light in a volume of 82 chorale preludes in the Lowell Mason collection at Yale. Of the 38 Bach chorale preludes in the MS, 33 were previously unknown, and it is these that Joseph Payne gives us on his compact disc. Payne uses the 1983 Bozeman-Gibson organ at St Paul's Church, Brookline, near Boston, which makes very suitable noises. The sound has a splendid definition, though the acoustic is not particularly warm.

In addition to the 33 newly discovered chorale preludes authenticated by Christoph Wolff, Werner Jacob gives us the other five present in the collection but known from other sources. This entails going on to a second CD and offering a fill-up, the *Eight Short preludes and fugues*, BWV 553–60, attributed to Bach. Werner Jacob uses the Silbermann organ of Arlesheim Cathedral in Switzerland and has the advantage of an altogether more pleasing acoustic. It may not match the American recording in terms of clarity, but in every other respect it has much to recommend it, including a much warmer ambience and sense of atmosphere.

Chorale partita on Sei gegrüsset, Jesu gutig, BWV 768; Fantasia in G, BWV 572; 6 Schübler chorale preludes, BWV 645/50.
*** Ph. 412 117-2 [id.]. Daniel Chorzempa (Silbermann organ, Arlesheim Cathedral).

Both the *Sei gegrüsset partita* and the *Schübler chorales* are admirably designed to demonstrate the palette of a fine organ in the hands of an imaginative player; and here Daniel Chorzempa is on top form, in matters of both registration and musical judgement. His playing is always alive rhythmically. The *Fantasia* is comparatively sober but ends with impressive, almost orchestral flair. The Silbermann organ at Arlesheim is justly famous for its colours and bright focus; it sounds splendid here.

Chorale partita on Sei gegrüsset, Jesu gutig, BWV 768; Prelude and fugue in D, BWV 532; Prelude in G, BWV 568; Sonata No. 4 in E min., BWV 528.
*** Denon Dig. C37 7376 [id.]. Jacques Van Oortmerssen (organ of Walloon Church, Amsterdam).

The organ of the Waalse Kerk is a magnificent instrument. The opening *Prelude in G* massively demonstrates the power and variety of timbre it commands and Jacques Van Oortmerssen, although not an international virtuoso, is fully its master in the buoyant performance of the *Prelude and fugue in D*. His registration in the *Andante* of the *E minor*

Sonata is a delight; in the extended variations of the *Sei gegrüsset partita* he is consistently imaginative in his choice of colouring. The playing, always alive, is traditional in the best sense, and the CD recording is superbly realistic. A most rewarding recital.

Chorale preludes Nos. 1–45 (Orgelbüchlein), BWV 599/644.
**(*) Denon Dig. CO 1711/2 [id.]. Jørgen Hansen (organ of Holmens Church, Copenhagen).

The forty-five chorale variations which make up the *Orgelbüchlein* (Little Organ Book) were devised by Bach to train organists in the working-out of chorale themes. So that the chorale is absolutely clear to the listener, the melody invariably appears in the top line. Bach's elaborations are intended to illuminate the spirit of the text with which the melody is associated; Jørgen Hansen follows Bach's intentions with appropriate registration, erring on the side of sobriety in certain instances. However, his playing is consistently clear and direct and the chosen tempi are usually apt. A little more extroversion would have been welcome at times, but the simplicity of approach brings its own rewards. The colourful Danish organ (sometimes reedy, sometimes mellifluous) is rather closely observed by the engineers; a shade more ambient effect would have been ideal; however, the sound is not dry but very faithful and present.

Chorale preludes, BWV 614, 622, 683, 727; Chorale fughetta, BWV 703; Fantasia and fugue in A min., BWV 561; Fugue in G min., BWV 578; Preludes and fugues: in G min., BWV 542; in E flat, BWV 552; Toccata and fugue in D min., BWV 565.
(BB) * LaserLight 15 507 [id.]. Gabor Lehotka or Hannes Kästner.

The sound, though not from a digital master, is very good here, but the performances are in the deliberate German tradition of Bach playing. Even Bach's genial *G minor Fugue* (beloved of Stokowski) fails to take off and the *Chorale preludes* are also slow. The documentation fails to identify the organs used.

Chorale preludes: Ich ruf' zu dir, Herr Jesu Christ, BWV 639; Nun komm der Heiden Heiland, BWV 659; Schübler chorale: Wachet auf, BWV 645; Fantasia and fugue in G min., BWV 542; Partita: O Gott, du frommer Gott, BWV 767; Prelude and fugue in E flat (St Anne), BWV 552; Toccata and fugue in D min., BWV 565.
*** Novalis Dig. 150 005-2 [id.]. Ton Koopman (Christian Müller organ, Waalse Kerk, Amsterdam).

This splendid recital is the first in a series undertaken by Ton Koopman for Novalis, perhaps to cover all Bach's organ music, and it augurs well for those to follow. He opens with three of Bach's most powerfully structured works for this instrument. The *Prelude* and *Fugue*, BWV 552, were designed separately to frame the third part of the *Clavierübung* (the so-called *German organ Mass*) and, heard together, they extend to just over 14 minutes. The *Partita* based on *O Gott, du frommer Gott* has eight diverse variations but is by no means lightweight. Then follows the *Fantasia and fugue in G minor*: the *Fantasia* bold and improvisatory, the *Fugue* swiftly moving and here buoyantly paced. The three chorales make a contrasting centrepiece with *Nun komm der Heiden Heiland* poignantly serene and the famous Schübler chorale, *Wachet auf*, infectiously jaunty. For the most popular of all Bach's organ pieces Ton Koopman then changes to a more flamboyant style, which he establishes immediately by decorating the opening flourishes so that they become almost a series of trills. The fugue proceeds with exhilarating momentum and ends in a blaze of bravura, a very free reading and a most exciting one that would deserve a standing ovation at a live recital. The organ is itself a 'co-star' of the programme, producing magnificent, unclouded sonorities in the spacious tapestry of BWV 552 and a wide palette of colour, which Koopman uses so effectively in the *Partita* and *Chorale preludes*. The recording is in the demonstration bracket, the microphones in exactly the right place for a proper illusion of reality.

Chorale preludes: Vater unser im Himmelreich, BWV 682; Jesu Christus, unser Heiland, BWV 688; Fantasia in G, BWV 572; Partita: Sei gegrüsset, Jesu gütig, BWV 768; Prelude and fugue in A min., BWV 543; Toccata and fugue in D min. (Dorian), BWV 538; Trio sonata in G, BWV 530.
*** Novalis Dig. 150 036-2 [id.]. Ton Koopman (organ of Grote Keerk, Leeuwarden).

An outstanding recital, extremely well played and splendidly recorded, using an organ admirably suited to Bach's music. The effect has resonance and power yet never really clouds detail, so that the engagingly light bravura of the playing of the brilliant *Fantasia in G* is as effective as the colourful variants of the famous *Partita, Sei gegrüsset, Jesu gütig*. Ton Koopman is strikingly fluent in the fugues; that of the *A minor* work, BWV 543, has an exhilarating momentum, while the *Trio sonata* is given apt contrasts of registration. The programme runs for over 70 minutes and is very well laid out for continuous listening.

Chorale variations on Vom himmel hoch, BWV 769; Fantasia in G, BWV 572; Pastorella in F, BWV 590; Preludes & fugues: in D, BWV 532; in E flat, BWV 552; Toccata & fugue in D min., BWV 565.
**(*) DG Dig. 427 668-2 [id.]. Simon Preston (organ of Kreuzbergkirche, Bonn).

The Klaus-Gerd organ in Bonn makes an attractive sound in Bach, though here it is rather closely observed by the digital recording, and some action noises are included. These are lively yet highly considered performances, very crisply articulated, sensibly paced and direct. Registrations show a degree of flair, notably the *Pastorale*; but Preston's individuality seems at times too contained, particularly in the *Chorale variations*, which could flow more readily. Even so, this is an impressive recital and the presence and realism of the recording are very striking.

Concertos (for solo organ) Nos. 1 in G (after ERNST: Concerto); 2 in A min. (after VIVALDI: Concerto, Op. 3/8); 3 in C (after VIVALDI: Concerto, Op. 7/11); 4 in C (after ERNST: Concerto); 5 in D min. (after VIVALDI: Concerto, Op. 3/11), BWV 592/6.
*** DG Dig. 423 087-2 [id.]. Simon Preston (organ of Lübeck Cathedral).

It was Prince Johann Ernst who introduced Bach to the Italian string concertos; these are Bach's arrangements, with the music for the most part left with little alteration or embellishment. The two Ernst works show a lively and inventive if not original musicianship. The performances are first class and the recording admirably lucid and clear, yet with an attractively resonant ambience.

Fantasia in G, BWV 572; Preludes and fugues: in C, BWV 545; in C min.; in G, BWV 549/50; in G min., BWV 535; Pastorale, BWV 590; Toccata and fugue in D min., BWV 565.
(M) *** Ph. 420 860-2 [id.]. Wolfgang Rübsam (organ of Frauenfeld, Switzerland).

A splendid collection of early works, nearly all dating from Bach's Arnstadt and Weimar periods and full of exuberance of spirit. The *Fugue in G*, BWV 550, is especially memorable, but undoubtedly the highlight of the recital is the superb performance of the *Fantasia in G*. It opens with an exhilarating *Très vitement* and after a massive *Grave* middle section comes a brilliantly lightweight bravura finale. Wolfgang Rübsam's articulation is deliciously pointed. The recording of the Metzler organ has a fairly long reverberation period, and Rübsam anticipates this in his playing most successfully. The quality of the recorded sound is splendid. Highly recommended.

Fantasia and fugue in G min., BWV 542; Prelude and fugue in F min., BWV 534; Toccata and fugue in D min., BWV 565; Toccata, adagio and fugue in C, BWV 564; Trio sonata No. 1 in E flat, BWV 525.
(M) ** DG 419 047-2 [id.]. Helmut Walcha (organ of St Laurenskerk, Alkmaar).

These recordings, made in 1963/4, sound extremely well in their CD format: the brightness is supported by an underlying depth and there is a sense of perspective too, particularly in the interplay of the famous *D minor Fugue* which shows Walcha at his most extrovert. The other performances are often very effectively registered, notably the *C major Fugue*, BWV 564, and the first movement of the *Trio sonata*, but Walcha's pulse seems determinedly steady in most of this music. Structures are well controlled and detail is lucid, but there is also a sense of ponderousness which will not appeal to everyone.

Passacaglia and fugue in C min., BWV 582; Preludes & fugues: in D, BWV 532; in A min., BWV 543; in E flat, BWV 552; Toccata and fugue in D min., BWV 565.
(B) ** Ph. 422 965-2 [id.]. Daniel Chorzempa (organs of Our Lady's Church, Breda, or (in BWV 552) Bovenkerk, Kampen, Holland).

This is a beautifully recorded disc, with notable depth and resonance. All the items but one come from a successful 1970 recital, and here Chorzempa's playing is impressive throughout and often stimulating, even if his occasional dalliance with matters of colour can sometimes interfere with the music's forward impulse. In the great *Passacaglia and fugue in C minor* this certainly adds to the interest and individuality of the performance. Unfortunately this bargain reissue omits Chorzempa's own original sleeve-notes, which indicated the reasons for his elaborations of Bach's basic text; despite his apparently free approach, the playing has a pontificating character in places. The *E flat Prelude and fugue*, BWV 552, was recorded separately, in 1982, and is something of an artistic disaster. It is incredibly slow (23 minutes 19 seconds overall), and at its opening the fugue is leaden and sounds as though it will go on for ever. However, the rest of the recital is well worth its modest cost.

Passacaglia and fugue in C min., BWV 582; Toccata and fugue in C, BWV 564; Toccata and fugue in D min. (Dorian), BWV 538; Toccata and fugue in D min., BWV 565.
*** Argo 411 824-2 [id.]. Peter Hurford (organs of Ratzeburg Cathedral, West Germany, and Church of Our Lady of Sorrows, Toronto, Canada).

Another excellent sampler of Hurford's Bach recordings, opening with his massively extrovert *Toccata and fugue in D minor*, BWV 565, but with a variety of mood in the other works, the *Dorian fugue* quite relaxed, the *C minor Passacaglia and fugue* unhurried but superbly controlled. The sound is first class.

6 Schübler chorales, BWV 645/650; Pastorale in F, BWV 590; Passacaglia in C min., BWV 582; Toccata, adagio & fugue in C, BWV 564; Toccata & fugue in D min., BWV 565.
(M) *** DG Dig. 427 801-2 [id.]. Ton Koopman (organs of Grote Kerk, Maassluis, & Waalse Kerk, Amsterdam).

Ton Koopman uses two different organs here, principally the Grote Kerk, Maassluis, but the *Schübler chorales* are recorded on the Waalse Kerk, Amsterdam, whose reeds are livelier almost to the point of stridency, emphasized by the emphatically rhythmic style of the playing. The effect is certainly full of character. The programme includes the famous

D minor Toccata and fugue, BWV 565, and this performance has an engaging eccentricity in that Koopman introduces decoration into the opening flourishes. The performance has an excitingly paced fugue and is superbly recorded. Excellent contrast is provided by the *Pastorale* (an extended piece of some twelve minutes), where the registration features the organ's flute stops piquantly. The other performances are well structured and alive, if sometimes rather considered in feeling. The sound is generally first class, extremely vivid throughout.

Toccatas and fugues: in D min. (Dorian), BWV 538; in D, BWV 540; in D min., BWV 565; Toccata, adagio and fugue in C, BWV 564.
(B) ** DG 427 191-2 [id.]. Helmut Walcha (organ of St Laurenskerk, Alkmaar).

Helmut Walcha plays the most famous *Toccata and fugue*, in D minor, with some flair, and he is at his most buoyant in the *Fugue* of BWV 564, which is also most attractively registered. Elsewhere he is perhaps a shade didactic; but everything is laid out clearly and the performances, it hardly needs saying, are structurally impeccable. The famous Alkmaar organ sounds bright and reedy, but the remastering has dried out the bass a little, and one would have liked a degree more amplitude from the pedals. However, at bargain price this is well worth considering.

Trio sonatas Nos. 1–6, BWV 525/530.
(M) * Ph. 422 946-2 (2) [id.]. Daniel Chorzempa (organ of Reformed Church, Meppel, Netherlands).

Chorzempa's set is very disappointing. The playing is relaxed to the point of lethargy, the registration mellifluous, and the music-making, although technically immaculate, fails to generate much tension and too readily disengages the attention of the listener.

VOCAL MUSIC

Cantatas Nos. 1: Wie schön leuchtet uns der Morgenstern; 2: Ach Gott, vom Himmel; 3: Ach Gott, wie manches Herzeleid; 4: Christ lag in Todesbanden.
(M) *** Teldec/WEA 2292 42497-2 (2) [id.]. Treble soloists from V. Boys' Ch., Esswood, Equiluz, Van Egmond, V. Boys' Ch., Ch. Viennensis, VCM, Harnoncourt.

Cantatas Nos. 4: Christ lag in Todesbanden; 56: Ich will den Kreuzstab gerne tragen; 82: Ich habe genug.
(M) **(*) DG 427 128-2 [id.]. Fischer-Dieskau, Munich Bach Ch. & O, Karl Richter.

In No. 4 the chorale melody is quoted in plain or varied form in each movement and dominates proceedings. This is a cantata which, given the wrong approach, can all too readily sound dull and sombre, but Richter seems wholly in sympathy with the work and secures some splendid and dignified playing from the orchestra. The solo singing is distinguished. Perhaps in the two later cantatas Fischer-Dieskau is at times a little too expressive and over-sophisticated; yet these are certainly sensitive performances, even if here Richter is sometimes a trifle heavy-handed. The recording still sounds extremely well.

(i) *Cantatas Nos. 5: Wo soll ich fliehen; 6: Bleib bei uns;* (ii) *7: Christ unser Herr zum Jordan kam; 8: Liebster Gott.*
(M) *** Teldec/WEA 2292 42498-2 (2) [id.]. Esswood, Equiluz, Van Egmond, (i) Treble soloists from V. Boys' Ch., Ch. Viennensis, V. Boys' Ch., VCM, Harnoncourt; (ii) Regensburg treble soloists, King's College Ch., Leonhardt Cons., Leonhardt.

(i) *Cantatas Nos. 9: Es ist das Heil; 10: Meine Seele erhebt den Herrn;* (ii) *11: Lobet Gott in seinen Reichen.*
(M) *** Teldec/WEA 2292 42499-2 (2) [id.]. Esswood, Equiluz, Van Egmond; (i) Regensburg treble soloists, King's College Ch., Leonhardt Cons., Leonhardt; (ii) Treble soloists from V. Boys' Ch., Ch. Viennensis, V. Boys' Ch., VCM, Harnoncourt.

The remarkable Teldec project, a complete recording of all Bach's cantatas, began in the early 1970s and has now reached completion. The first CDs appeared during the tercentenary year and the digital remastering proved consistently successful. The original LP packaging included full scores. Inevitably, the CDs omit these but retain the English translations of the texts and excellent notes by Alfred Dürr. The authentic character of the performances means that boys replace women, not only in the choruses but also as soloists, and the size of the forces is confined to what we know Bach himself would have expected. The simplicity of the approach brings its own merits, for the imperfect yet other-worldly quality of some of the treble soloists refreshingly focuses the listener's attention on the music itself. Less appealing is the quality of the violins, which eschew vibrato – and, it would sometimes seem, any kind of timbre! Generally speaking, there is a certain want of rhythmic freedom and some expressive caution. Rhythmic accents are underlined with some regularity and the grandeur of Bach's inspiration is at times lost to view. Where there are no alternatives for outstanding cantatas, such as the marvellously rich and resourceful sonorities of the sinfonia to *Ach Gott, vom Himmel* (No. 2), with its heavenly aria, *Durchs Feuer wird das Silber rein*, choice is simple, and here the performance too is a fine one. There is more grandeur to John Eliot Gardiner's account of *Christ lag in Todesbanden* (at the moment withdrawn from the catalogue), but there is so much fine music in Cantatas 2 and 3, not otherwise obtainable on record, that the first of these volumes is a must.

Volumes 4–29 and 32–40 of the series have been temporarily withdrawn by Teldec/WEA but should reappear during the lifetime of this book, albeit with new catalogue numbers, and we hope to include reviews of them in our next edition.

Cantata No. 10: Meine Seele erhebt den Herrn.
(M) *** Decca 425 650-2 [id.]. Ameling, Watts, Krenn, Rintzler, V. Ac. Ch., Stuttgart CO, Münchinger – *Easter oratorio.****

An excellent coupling for a first-rate account of the surprisingly little-recorded *Easter oratorio.* This fine cantata is very well sung and played, with all the performers at their best. The recording too is freshly vivid.

Cantatas Nos. 26: Ach wie flüchtig; 80: Ein feste Burg; 116: Du Friedefürst, Herr Jesu Christ.
(M) ** DG 427 130-2 [id.]. Mathis, Schmidt, Schreier, Fischer-Dieskau, Munich Bach Ch. & O, Karl Richter.

It is pleasant to return to the vigorous, full-bodied Richter approach to Bach after an overdose of Leonhardt and Harnoncourt. The opening fugal chorus of *Ein feste Burg* and its later, more straightforward presentation are agreeably robust, and the music-making overall has plenty of vitality. The solo contributions are good too, particularly those of Schreier and Fischer-Dieskau. The sound is full and immediate, even if the choral focus is not absolutely clean; and these performances still have a place in the catalogue.

Cantatas Nos. 35: Geist und Seele wird verwirret; 53: Schlage doch, gewunschte Stunde; 82: Ich habe genug.

**(*) HM Dig. HMC 901273 [id.]. René Jacobs, Ens. 413, Banchini.

This CD offers three solo vocal cantatas, sung by the Belgian counter-tenor, René Jacobs. No. 82, *Ich habe genug*, was originally written for bass, but subsequently Bach arranged it for soprano, and in 1735 for alto, replacing the oboe with a flute. Jacobs elects to retain the oboe and sings it with great intelligence, though his tone at the top end of his tessitura is not always pleasing. The instrumental contribution is expert (incidentally, the Ensemble 413 takes its name from one of the tuning pitches used in the baroque period) and the recording is first class.

Cantata No. 51: Jauchzet Gott in allen Landen.
*** Ph. Dig. 411 458-2 [id.]. Emma Kirkby, E. Bar. Soloists, Gardiner – *Magnificat.****

Jauchzet Gott is one of Bach's most joyful cantatas; Emma Kirkby follows the example of the opening trumpeting (Crispian Steele-Perkins – in excellent form) when she begins. It is a brilliantly responsive performance, admirably accompanied and very well recorded.

Cantatas Nos. 51: Jauchzet Gott in allen Landen; 93: Wer nur den lieben Gott lässt walten; 129: Gelobet sei der Herr, mein Gott.
(M) ** DG 427 115-2 [id.]. Mathis, Reynolds, Schreier, Fischer-Dieskau, Munich Bach Ch. & O, Karl Richter.

These performances come from the early 1970s and are distinguished by some predictably fine singing from Anna Reynolds, Peter Schreier and Fischer-Dieskau. In No. 51, *Jauchzet Gott in allen Landen*, Mathis sings with great brilliance, and here the trumpeter also deserves special mention. As always, Karl Richter is sound, if a little stolid; but the recordings as such come up well.

Cantatas Nos. 54: Widerstehe doch der Sünde; 169: Got soll allein; 170: Vergnügte Ruh'.
*** Hyp. Dig. CDA 66326 [id.]. James Bowman, King's Consort, King.

James Bowman is on impressive form and his admirers need not hesitate here. In No. 54 he comes into competition only with Paul Esswood in the complete Teldec series, and this particular volume is currently withdrawn and awaiting reissue. In any case, their different musical insights and vocal quality are not mutually exclusive. The present disc is very desirable and the King's Consort under Robert King give excellent support. Good recorded sound.

Cantatas Nos. 57: Selig ist der Mann; 58: Ach Gott, wie manches; 59: Wer mich lieber; 152: Tritt auf die Glaubensahn.
*** Hung. Dig. HCD 12897 [id.]. Zádori, Polgár, Savaria Vocal Ens., Capella Savaria, Pál Németh.

These dialogue cantatas are well served by the Capella Savaria, a Hungarian period-instrument ensemble of considerable quality, and the two soloists. Mária Zádori and László Polgár are obviously singers of no mean accomplishment (the soprano sings with great spirit) and have a good sense of style. A rewarding, well-recorded issue and good value at slightly less than full price.

Cantatas Nos. 78: Jesu, der du meine Seele; 198: Lass, Furstin nich einen Strahl (Trauerode).
**(*) HM Dig. HMC 901270 [id.]. Schmithüsen, Brett, Crook, Kooy, Paris Chapelle Royale Ch. & O, Herreweghe.

The *Trauerode* is a huge piece in ten numbers, divided into two parts which were separated by the funeral oration. This recording has been well received and, indeed, there are many felicitous touches, some good solo singing and beautifully transparent orchestral textures. At the same time, Herreweghe takes the opening chorus far too briskly: the effect is jaunty (one is almost tempted to say bouncy) and there is a resultant loss of both dignity and breadth. However, it is only fair to say that much else here is well judged. This also has the advantage of offering another masterpiece, *Jesu, der du meine Seele*, which offers some excellent solo contributions from Ingrid Schmithüsen and Charles Brett. The balance of the recording is exemplary, with cleanly focused and well-defined detail.

Cantatas Nos. 80: Ein' feste Burg ist unser Gott; 140: Wachet auf, ruft uns die Stimme.
**(*) Decca Dig. 414 045-2 [id.]. Fontana, Hamari, Winbergh, Krause, Hymnus Boys' Ch., SCO, Münchinger.
(M) ** Ph. 422 490-2 [id.]. Ameling, Finnie, Baldin, Ramey, L. Voices, ECO, Leppard.

Münchinger, who uses the trumpets and timpani added by Bach's eldest son, Wilhelm Friedemann, has the advantage of excellently transparent and well-detailed Decca digital recording and a fine team of soloists. Karl Münchinger does not bring quite the warmth or musicality that distinguishes the finest performances of Bach, but there is little of the pedantry that has at times afflicted his music-making. Extra pleasure is afforded by the attractive ambience – the concert-hall balance is expertly managed – and by the tangibility of the chorus, whose vigorous contribution is given striking body and presence.

In *Ein' feste Burg* Leppard also uses the parts for three trumpets and drums. It is a well-prepared, straightforward account with some responsive singing from the chorus. *Wachet auf* is the less successful of the two and, even apart from the rather too measured tempo of the first of the duets, Elly Ameling's intonation is not completely true. There are good things, of course, and the actual sound is very good.

Cantata No. 82: Ich habe genug.
⊛ (M) *** EMI CDH7 63198-2 [id.]. Hans Hotter, Philh. O, Bernard – BRAHMS: *Lieder.*** ⊛

One of the greatest cantata performances ever. Glorious singing from Hans Hotter and wonderfully stylish accompanying from Anthony Bernard and the Philharmonia. This 1950 mono recording was never reissued on LP, and it sounds eminently present in this fine transfer.

Cantatas Nos. 106: Gottes Zeit ist die allerbeste Zeit; 131: Aus der Tiefen.
*** O-L Dig. 417 323-2 [id.]. Monoyios, Rickards, Brownlees, Opalach, Bach Ens., Rifkin.

Rifkin's one-voice-to-a-part principle is applied here, and readers who do not respond to it will doubtless take avoiding action. In doing so, however, they will miss a performance of considerable merit: the opening of *Gottes Zeit* is one of the most beautiful moments in all Bach and is beautifully done. *Aus der Tiefen* is hardly less fine, and the singers are all first class. One feels the need for greater weight and a more full-blooded approach at times, but this is outweighed by the sensitivity and intelligence that inform these excellently balanced recordings.

Cantatas Nos. 120: Gott, mann lobet dich in der Stille; 121: Christum wir sollen loben; 122: Das neugebor'ne Kindelein; 123: Liebster Immanuel, Herzog der Frommen.
(M) *** Teldec/WEA 2292 42609-2 (2) [id.]. Treble soloists from Tölz Ch., Esswood, Equiluz, Huttenlocher or Holl, Tölz Ch., VCM, Harnoncourt.

No serious grumbles about any of the performances here, even if one or two numbers fall short of perfection. The recordings are exemplary in every way.

Cantatas Nos. (i) *124: Meinen Jesum lass ich nicht; 125: Mit Fried und Freud ich fahrt dahin; 126: Erhalt uns, Herr, bei deinen Wort;* (ii) *127: Herr Jesu Christ, wahr' Mensch.*
(M) *** Teldec/WEA 2292 42615-2 (2) [id.]. (i) Bergius, Rampf, Esswood, Equiluz, Thomaschke, Tölz Ch., VCM, Harnoncourt; (ii) Hennig, Van Egmond, Hanover Boys' Ch., Ghent Coll. Vocale, Leonhardt Cons., Leonhardt.

Cantatas Nos. (i) *128: Auf Christi Himmelfahrt allein; 129: Gelobet sei der Herr, mein Gott;* (ii) *130: Herr Gott, dich loben alle wir; 131: Aus der Tiefen rufe ich, Herr, zu dir.*
(M) **(*) Teldec/WEA 2292 42617-2 (2) [id.]. Hennig, Bergius, Jacobs, Rampf, Equiluz, Van Egmond, Heldwein, Holl; (i) Hanover Boys' Ch., Ghent Coll. Vocale, Leonhardt Consort, Leonhardt; (ii) Tölz Boys' Ch., VCM, Harnoncourt.

Cantatas Nos. (i) *128: Auf Christi Himmelfahrt allein; 129: Gelobet sei der Herr, mein Gott;* (ii) *130: Herr Gott.*
(M) **(*) Teldec WEA 2292 43055-2 [id.]. (recordings as above).

Auf Christi Himmelfahrt allein is an Ascension cantata and is quite richly scored, while its companions, *Gelobet sei der Herr* and *Herr Gott*, are even more elaborate, with three trumpets and timpani. The singers are excellent, but the strings have an edge that is razor-sharp and not pleasing. The brass playing in No. 129 is pretty rough; but the treble, Sebastian Hennig, acquits himself excellently in the glorious aria which forms the centrepiece of the cantata. No. 130 has a powerful opening chorus, whose trumpets proclaim the Kingdom of God. All three cantatas are short and can be accommodated on a single CD. The two-CD set adds No. 131, the earliest of Bach's cantatas, not only more extended but a marvellous, inspired piece, whose grave beauty is eloquently conveyed by Harnoncourt, and it alone is almost worth the price of this volume. The recordings are of the high standard set by the series.

Cantatas Nos. 140: Wachet auf; 147: Herz und Mund und Tat und Leben.
**(*) Teldec/WEA 2292 43109-2 [id.]. Bergius, Rampf, Esswood, Equiluz, Hampson, Tölz Boys' Ch., VCM, Harnoncourt.

A coupling of two familiar cantatas, both made famous by their chorales. In No. 147 some may be a little disconcerted by the minor swelling effect in the phrasing of *Jesu, joy of man's desiring*, but otherwise the authentic approach brings much to enjoy. In No. 140 there are two beautiful duets between treble and bass soloists, representing dialogues between Jesus and the human soul, which are sung memorably. The production and recording are well up to standard.

Cantatas Nos. 161: Komm, du süsse Todesstunde; 169: Gott soll allein mein Herze haben.
(BB) ** Hung. White Label HRC 124 [id.]. Hamari, Réti, Liszt Ac. of Music Ch. & O, Sándor.

Julia Hamari's contribution here is sound rather than outstandingly eloquent, but her tenor partner in No. 161, József Réti, has a pleasing voice, and the choral singing is beautiful in both *Cantatas*. A pair of flutes add colour to the orchestra in No. 161, whereas No. 169 begins with an attractive sinfonia which is a bit like a Handel organ concerto; the excellent organist, Gábor Lehotka, also makes contributions elsewhere. This is all fine music, very well recorded; and these works are otherwise available only in the Harnoncourt/Leonhardt series, offering an entirely different sound-world.

Cantatas Nos (i) *180: Schmücke dich, o liebe Seele; 181: Leichtgesinnte Flattergeister;* (ii) *182: Himmelskönig, sei wilkommen; 183: Sie werden euch in den Bann tun;* (i) *184: Erwunschtes Freudenlicht.*
(M) *** Teldec/WEA Dig. 2292 42738-2 (2) [id.]. (i) O'Farrell, Esswood, Equiluz, Van Egmond, Hanover Boys' Ch., Coll. Vocale, Leonhardt Cons., Leonhardt; (ii) Wittek, Holl, Hampson, Tölz Boys' Ch., VCM, Harnoncourt.

In No. 180 the orchestral playing under Leonhardt is a little pedestrian and the young soloist (Jan Patrick O'Farrell) at times is swamped. Paul Esswood is in splendid form. No. 181 receives a much livelier performance, with excellent singing, and has a more confident treble in Alexander Heymann. The Palm Sunday cantata, No. 182, is in every way a delight and the performance under Harnoncourt is expressive and unforced. Its companions, *Sie werden euch in den Bann tun* and *Erwunschtes Freudenlicht*, are no less interesting and the level of inspiration is high.

Cantatas Nos. (i) *185: Barmherziges Herze der ewigen Liebes; 186: Ärgre dich, o Seele, nicht;* (ii) *187: Es wartet alles auf dich;* (i) *188: Ich habe meine Zuversicht.*
(M) **(*) Teldec/WEA Dig. 2292 44179-2 (2). (i) Wittek, Equiluz, Hampson, Holl, Tölz Boys' Ch., VCM, Harnoncourt; (ii) Emmermann, Esswood, Van Egmond, Hanover Boys' Ch., Ghent Coll. Vocale, Leonhardt Cons., Leonhardt.

Barmherziges Herze der ewigen Liebes exists in a second version which Bach made for Leipzig, but Harnoncourt opts for the 1715 Weimar with only small changes. It is a lovely piece and finds both Esswood and Hampson in excellent form. Four of the arias from No. 186 come originally from Weimar (1716) but form the basis of a much bigger cantata, also from Leipzig. The chromatic soprano aria is one of its highlights, but inspiration throughout is high and the singing good, even though the young boy soprano is under some strain. Kurt Equiluz is in impressive form both here and in No. 188. No. 187, probably performed most often of the four, finds Leonhardt at the helm. On the whole the set is rewarding, though the choral contribution is not always secure.

Cantatas Nos. (i) *192: Nun danket alle Gott;* (ii) *194: Höchsterwünschtes Freudenfest;* (iii) *195: Dem Gerechten muss das Licht immer wieder aufgehen.*
**(*) Teldec/WEA Dig. 2292 44193-2 [id.]. (i) Wittek, (i; ii) Hampson, (ii) Stricker, Gienger, Equiluz, (iii) O'Farrell, Jacobs, Elwes, Van der Kamp; (i & ii) Tölz Boys' Ch., VCM, Harnoncourt; (iii) Hanover Boys' Ch., Ghent Coll. Vocale, Leonhardt Consort, Leonhardt.

With Volumes 44 and 45 Teldec achieve their remarkable enterprise of recording the complete cycle of Bach cantatas, and it is a great pity that for the moment so many of the series have been temporarily withdrawn. Also tidy minds will note that Leonhardt and Harnoncourt omit cantatas Nos. 190–91 and 193. No. 190, *Singet dem Herrn ein neues Lied*, was partly lost, though a conjectural reconstruction of it (BWV 190a) has been recorded; No. 191, *Gloria in excelsis Deo*, is a Latin cantata, and contains music which Bach 're-cycled' in the *B minor Mass*, while 193, *Ihr Tore zu Zion*, is incomplete. The biggest cantata here is *Höchsterwünschtes Freudenfest*, a twelve-movement two-part work with (as Alec Robertson put it in his book on the *Cantatas*) some charming music but not very interesting recitatives. The performance under Harnoncourt reveals some scrawny string-tone but there is some good singing. No. 195, under Leonhardt, is let down by some undistinguished choral singing in the fugal opening, but otherwise there is much to enjoy in this fine piece.

Cantatas Nos. (i) *196: Der Herr denket an uns;* (ii) *197: Gott ist unsrer Zuversicht;* (iii) *198: Lass, Fürstin, lass noch einen Strahl;* (iv) *199: Mein Herze schwimmt im Blut.*
** Teldec/WEA Dig.2292 44194-2 (2) [id.]. (i) Wittek, Equiluz, Hampson, (ii; iii) O'Farrell, Jacobs, Van der Kamp, (iii) Elwes, (iv) Bonney; (i) Tölz Boys' Ch., (ii; iii) Hanover Boys' Ch., Ghent Coll. Vocale; (i; iv) VCM, Harnoncourt; (ii; iii) Leonhardt Consort, Leonhardt.

In the last volume in the series some measure of exhaustion must be noted. The choral singing both in No. 197, a wedding cantata from the late 1730s, and in No. 198, probably the best-known of the present set, is distinctly tired, and there is also some less than distinguished instrumental playing. However, there are good things too from the soloists, in particular from René Jacobs and young Jan Patrick O'Farrell.

Cantata No. 208: Was mir behagt, ist nur die muntre Jagd (Hunt cantata).
*** Hyp. Dig. CDA 66169 [id.]. Jennifer Smith, Emma Kirkby, Simon Davis, Michael George, Parley of Instruments, Goodman.

This delightful piece comes from 1713, when Bach was in his twenties, and celebrates the birthday of the Duke of Sachsen-Weissenfels, whose passion was hunting. It is a cantata rich in melodic invention of the highest quality. On this record the cantata is framed by movements from the *Sinfonia, BWV 1046a,* the original version of the *First Brandenburg concerto.* The performance has the benefit of excellent soloists and first-class instrumental playing.

Cantatas Nos. 211: Schweigt stille, plaudert nicht (Coffee cantata); 212: Mer hahn en neue Oberkeet (Peasant cantata).
*** O-L Dig. 417 621-2 [id.]. Kirkby, Rogers, Covey-Crump, Thomas, AAM, Hogwood.

Emma Kirkby is particularly appealing in the *Coffee cantata* and her father is admirably portrayed by David Thomas. Hogwood opts for single strings, and those accustomed to hearing these pieces with more substantial forces may find they sound thin. However, there is a corresponding gain in lightness and intimacy. The recording is altogether first class and strikes an excellent balance between voices and instruments.

Christmas oratorio, BWV 248.
*** DG Dig. 423 232-2 (2) [id.]. Rolfe-Johnson, Argenta, Von Otter, Blochwitz, Bär, Monteverdi Ch., E. Bar. Soloists, Gardiner.
(***) Ph. Dig. 420 204-2 (3) [id.]. Donath, Ihle, Lipovsek, Schreier, Buchner, Holl, Leipzig R. Ch., Dresden State O, Schreier.

Christmas oratorio, BWV 248; Magnificat, BWV 243.
(M) *** Decca 425 441-2 (3) [id.]. Ameling, Watts, Pears, Krause, Ch., Stuttgart CO, Münchinger.

The freshness of the singing and playing in the DG set is a constant pleasure, with Gardiner's often brisk speeds sounding bright and eager, not breathless. Far more than usual, one registers the joyfulness of the work, from the trumpets and timpani at the start onwards. The haunting shepherds' music of the second cantata is lightly sprung and the celebrations of the third, with trumpets again prominent, are typical. Solo voices are light and clear. Anthony Rolfe-Johnson makes a pointful and expressive Evangelist, and also outstanding is Anne-Sophie von Otter with her natural gravity and exceptionally beautiful mezzo. Beauty of tone consistently marks the singing of Nancy Argenta and Hans-Peter Blochwitz; though Olaf Bär is a baritone rather than a bass, his detailed expressiveness, lieder-like, makes up for any lack of weight. The whole oratorio is neatly contained on only two discs, with three cantatas on each instead of two. The sound is full and atmospheric without clouding detail, a fine addition to an excellent series.

Münchinger directs an admirably fresh performance of the *Christmas oratorio*, sharp in tone and bright in recording (which dates from 1967). With an excellent team of soloists and with Lübeck trebles adding to the freshness, this is a good middle-of-the-road version, representative of modern scholarship as determined in the immediate pre-authentic era. Münchinger's recording of the *Magnificat* dates from 1969 and was one of his finest Bach performances. The soloists are uniformly good and so are the contributions of the Vienna Academy Choir and the Stuttgart Chamber Orchestra. Münchinger tends to stress the breadth and spaciousness of the *Magnificat* – though his reading has plenty of spirit – and the Decca engineers have captured the detail with admirable clarity and naturalness. The trumpets sound resplendent.

Peter Schreier contributes a fine, fresh version of the *Christmas oratorio*, similarly taking on the double duties of conducting and singing the central part of the Evangelist. As in the *St Matthew*, the Leipzig Radio Choir sings responsively; though modern instruments are used, Schreier consistently shows how he has been influenced by new ideas of authentic performance on period instruments. Though the scale is larger than in a period performance, the speeds are regularly very fast, sprightly rather than breathless, with string articulation crisp and light. None of the other soloists quite matches Schreier, but they make a strong, consistent team. Full, bright and atmospheric recording, but the layout on three CDs makes this issue uncompetitive alongside Gardiner.

Easter oratorio.
(M) *** Decca 425 650-2 [id.]. Ameling, Watts, Krenn, Krause, Stuttgart CO, Münchinger – *Cantata No. 10.****

Münchinger is at his finest in the *Easter oratorio*, giving a spacious and impressive reading. He is well supported by his splendid team of soloists, and the Decca recording is well up to the lively standard of his Stuttgart series. With a generous and attractive coupling, this makes a reliable recommendation for this surprisingly little-recorded work.

Magnificat in D, BWV 243.
*** Ph. Dig. 411 458-2 [id.]. Argenta, Kwella, Kirkby, Brett, Rolfe-Johnson, David Thomas, E. Bar. Soloists, Gardiner – *Cantata No. 51.****
(M) *** Decca 421 148-2 [id.]. Palmer, Watts, Tear, Roberts, King's College Ch., ASMF, Ledger – BACH, C.P.E.: *Magnificat.* ***

The better-known D major version of the *Magnificat* receives an exhilarating performance from John Eliot Gardiner. Tempi are consistently brisk, but the vigour and precision of the chorus are such that one never has the feeling that the pacing is hurried; when there is need to relax, Gardiner does so convincingly. A splendid team of soloists, and the accompaniment is no less impressive. This is first class in every way, and the recorded sound is well balanced, fresh and vivid.

Philip Ledger's account, recorded by Argo in the late 1970s, is a most attractive alternative, highly recommendable if boys' voices are preferred in the chorus. The women soloists are outstanding, as is the St Martin's Academy; and the CD transfer brings added clarity and improves the overall balance.

Magnificat in E flat (original version), BWV 243a.
*** O-L 414 678-2 [id.]. Nelson, Kirkby, Watkinson, Elliot, D. Thomas, Christ Church Ch., AAM, Preston – VIVALDI: *Gloria.****

The original version of the *Magnificat* is textually different in detail (quite apart from being a semitone higher) and has four interpolations for the celebration of Christmas. Preston and the Academy of Ancient Music present a characteristically alert and fresh performance, and the Christ Church Choir is in excellent form. One might quibble at the use of women soloists instead of boys, but these three specialist singers have just the right incisive timbre and provide the insight of experience.

Mass in B min., BWV 232.
*** DG Dig. 415 514-2 [id.]. Argenta, Dawson, Fairfield, Knibbs, Kwella, Hall, Nichols, Chance, Collin, Stafford, Evans, Milner, Murgatroyd, Lloyd-Morgan, Varcoe, Monteverdi Ch., E. Bar. Soloists, Gardiner.
*** EMI Dig. CDS7 47293-8 [Ang. CDCB 47292] (2). Kirkby, Van Evera, Iconomou, Immler, Kilian, Covey-Crump, David Thomas, Taverner Cons. and Players, Parrott.
**(*) Ph. 416 415-2 (2) [id.]. Marshall, Baker, Tear, Ramey, Ch. and ASMF, Marriner.
**(*) RCA/Eurodisc 610 089 (2). Popp, C. Watkinson, Bluchner, Lorenz, Adam, Leipzig R. Ch., New Bach Coll. Mus., Schreier.
**(*) None. Dig. CD 79036-2 (2) [id.]. Nelson, Baird, Dooley, Minter, Hoffmeister, Brownlees, Opalach, Schultze, Bach Ens., Rifkin.
(M) ** EMI CMS7 63364-2 (2). Giebel, J. Baker, Gedda, Prey, Crass, BBC Ch., New Philh. O, Klemperer.
(M) ** DG 415 622-2 (2) [id.]. Janowitz, Ludwig, Schreier, Kerns, Ridderbusch, V. Singverein, Karajan.
** Ph. Dig. 426 238-2 (2). Jennifer Smith, Michael Chance, Van der Meel, Van der Kamp, Netherlands Chamber Ch., O of 18th Century, Frans Brüggen.

John Eliot Gardiner gives a magnificent account of the *B minor Mass*, one which attempts to keep within an authentic scale but which also triumphantly encompasses the work's grandeur. Where latterly in 'authentic' performances we have come to expect the grand six-part setting of the *Sanctus* to trip along like a dance movement, Gardiner masterfully conveys the majesty (with bells and censer-swinging evoked) simultaneously with a crisply resilient rhythmic pulse. The choral tone is luminous and powerfully projected. In the earlier parts of the *Mass*, Gardiner generally has four voices per part, but key passages – such as the opening of the first *Kyrie* fugue – are treated as concertinos for soloists alone. The later, more elaborate sections, such as the *Sanctus*, have five voices per part, so that the final *Dona nobis pacem* is subtly grander than when it appears earlier as *Gratias agimus tibi*. The regular solo numbers are taken by choir members making a cohesive whole. The alto, Michael Chance, deserves special mention for his distinctively warm and even singing in both *Qui sedes* and *Agnus Dei*. The recording is warmly atmospheric but not cloudy.

Parrott, hoping to re-create even more closely the conditions Bach would have expected in Leipzig, adds to the soloists a ripieno group of five singers from the Taverner Consort for the choruses. The instrumental group is similarly augmented with the keenest discretion. Parrott's success lies in retaining the freshness and bite of the Rifkin approach – see below – while creating a more vivid atmosphere. Speeds are generally fast, with rhythms sprung to reflect the inspiration of dance; however, the inner darkness of the *Crucifixus*, for example, is conveyed intensely in its hushed tones, while the *Et resurrexit* promptly erupts with a power to compensate for any lack of traditional weight. Soloists are excellent, with reduction of vibrato still allowing sweetness as well as purity. If you want a performance on a reduced scale, Parrott scores palpably over Rifkin in the keener, more dramatic sense of contrast, clearly distinguishing choruses and solos. The recording, made in St John's, Smith Square, is both realistic and atmospheric.

Predictably, many of Marriner's tempi are daringly fast; *Et resurrexit*, for example, has the Academy chorus on its toes, but the rhythms are so resiliently sprung that the result is exhilarating, never hectic. An even more remarkable achievement is that in the great moments of contemplation such as *Et incarnatus* and *Crucifixus* Marriner finds a degree of inner intensity to match the gravity of Bach's inspiration, with tempi often slower than usual. That dedication is matched by the soloists, the superb soprano Margaret Marshall as much as the longer-established singers. This is a performance which finds the balance between small-scale authenticity and recognition of massive inspiration, neither too small nor too large, and with good atmospheric recording, not quite as defined as it might be on inner detail; this is fully recommendable.

The refreshing distinctiveness of Schreier's reading is typified by his account of the great *Sanctus*, dancing along lightly and briskly, not at all weighty in the usual manner. His speeds are consistently fast, but that does not prevent Schreier from capturing a devotional mood, as for example in the final *Dona nobis pacem* which, in powerful crescendo, begins in meditation and ends in joy. Schreier has opted for modern pitch and instruments, yet with bright, keen choral singing and very good work from the soloists (Theo Adam occasionally excepted, with his sour tone), this is an excellent version for anyone wanting a resilient, lightweight view, using authentically small forces but without the problems of authentic performance. Good, spacious recording.

Whether or not you subscribe to the controversial theories behind the performance under Joshua Rifkin, the result is undeniably refreshing and often exhilarating. Rifkin here presents Bach's masterpiece in the improbable form of one voice to a part in the choruses and one gets a totally new perspective when, at generally brisk speeds, the complex counterpoint is so crisp and clean, with original (relatively gentle) instruments in the orchestra adding to the freshness and intimacy. The soloists also sing with comparable brightness, freshness and precision, even if lack of choral weight means that dramatic contrasts are less sharp than usual. An exciting pioneering set, crisply and vividly recorded, which rightly won *Gramophone*'s choral award in 1983.

Although the CD transfer of the 1967 Kingsway Hall recording is impressively full and clear, Klemperer's performance is disappointing. Leaving aside any questions of authenticity of scale, the sobriety of his reading, with plodding tempi and a dogged observance of the *Neue Bach-Ausgabe* (Bärenreiter), utterly unornamented, was no doubt predictable. Only when the drama of the Mass takes over in the *Crucifixus* and *Et resurrexit* does the majesty of Klemperer's conception become apparent. Dame Janet Baker stands out among the soloists with superb accounts of the *Qui sedes* and *Agnus Dei*. Whatever the initial shortcomings, Klemperer's *Sanctus* (faster than usual) has wonderful momentum, the *Osanna* is genuinely joyful and the concluding sections of this sublime work come vividly to life.

Karajan conveys intensity, even religious fervour, and the very opening brings an impressive first entry of the choir on *Kyrie*. But then, after the instrumental fugue, the contrapuntal entries are sung in a self-consciously softened tone. There is a strong sense of the work's architecture, and the highly polished surfaces do not obscure the depths of the music, but (despite a fine solo team) this is hardly a first choice.

Among period-performance specialists Frans Brüggen is one of the most positive and characterful, and his live recording of the *B minor Mass* with excellent soloists fully measures up to the greatness of the work. Like most of his other recordings, it was edited together from a series of performances, and though some may find his inflecting of rhythm and phrase too individual, the result is consistently compelling. The singing of

Michael Chance is outstanding, here taking all the alto solos, not just some as in the Gardiner version. Sadly, what prevents this version from being a serious contender with the very finest is the variable balance of the recording, above all the distancing of the chorus. The overall effect of this work depends on the power and immediacy of the choral singing – the opposite of what happens here.

Motets: *Singet dem Herrn ein Neues Lied, BWV 225; Der Geist hilft unser Schwachheit, BWV 226; Jesu meine Freude, BWV 227; Der Gerechte Kommt um Fürchte dich nicht, BWV 228; Komm, Jesu Komm, BWV 229; Lobet den Herrn, BWV 230; Sei Lob und Preis mit Ehren, BWV 231.*

*** Conifer Dig. CDCF 158 [id.] (without *BWV 231*). Trinity College, Cambridge, Ch., Marlow, G. Jackson and R. Pearce.

(M) *** DG 427 227-2 [id.] (without *BWV 231*). Regensberger Domspätzen, V. Capella Academica, Schneidt.

(M) **(*) EMI CDM7 63237-2 (without *BWV 231*). King's Coll. Ch., Willcocks.

**(*) HM HMC 901231 [id.] (without *BWV 231*). Soloists, Ghent Coll. Vocale, Chapelle Royale Ch. & O, Herreweghe.

**(*) EMI Dig. CDC7 49204-2 (2) (without *BWV 231*). Trebles of Hanover Boys' Ch., Hilliard Ens., L. Bar., Hillier.

The Conifer issue of Bach's great motets by Richard Marlow and the Trinity College Choir brings delightfully crisp and resilient performances of the six regular motets, marked by refined ensemble and transparent textures. With discreet organ accompaniment, this is a fine version for those who prefer traditional performances using sopranos instead of boy trebles, consistently stylish, set against a helpful acoustic, with plenty of presence.

At mid-price on DG's Archiv Galleria label, Hans-Martin Schneidt's version with the Regensburger Domspätzen (literally 'cathedral sparrows') brings highly enjoyable performances which have a lusty freshness, enhanced by the brightness of boy trebles. The accompaniments on period instruments at lower pitch add to the bluffness and, though speeds are often on the slow side, the resilience of the playing and singing makes them consistently convincing. Excellent atmospheric recording.

Recorded in King's College Chapel in 1967 and 1970, the King's College versions represent an older order of Bach performance; however, with their fresh attack, warmly atmospheric sound and clean rhythms, and with no accompanying instruments, they are undistractingly satisfying for all but period-performance specialists. The characteristic timbre of the Cambridge trebles is caught well, with voices closely focused against the Chapel's lively acoustic and with the stereo spread underlining the antiphonal double-choir effects of *Singet dem Herrn.*

Under Philippe Herreweghe the *Motets* are presented in fresh, meticulously clean performances, with instruments doubling vocal lines. One oddity is that the extended five-part motet, *Jesu meine Freude*, is sung by soloists and not the choir. Any gain in intimacy must be measured against an obvious loss of dramatic contrast in Bach's vivid setting of the words. Excellent sound.

Paul Hillier opts for simple continuo instrumentation of cello, violone, organ and lute. That goes with small choral forces to match the intimate approach. The results are fresh, light and alert, thoughtful too, but, as with Herreweghe, the element of grandeur in the elaborate *Singet dem Herrn* is undermined. Very good atmospheric sound.

St John Passion, BWV 245.
*** DG Dig. 419 324-2 (2) [id.]. Rolfe-Johnson, Varcoe, Hauptmann, Argenta & soloists, Monteverdi Ch., E. Bar. Sol., Gardiner.
(M) ****(*)** Decca 414 068-2 (2) [id.]. Ellenbeck, Berry, Ahrans, Ameling, Hamari, Hollweg, Prey, Ackermann, Stuttgart Hymnus Boys' Ch., Stuttgart CO, Münchinger.
**(*) Chan. Dig. CHAN 0507-8 (2) [id.]. Partridge, Wilson-Johnson, Kwella, James, Kendall, The Sixteen Ch. & O, Christophers.
**(*) Ph. Dig. 422 088-2 (2) [id.]. Schreier, Holl, Scheibner, Alexander, Lipovsek, Bär, Leipzig R. Ch., Dresden State O, Schreier.
(M) ****(*)** Teldec/WEA 2292 42492-2 (2) [id.]. Equiluz, Van t'Hoff, Van Egmond, Villisech, Schneeweis, treble soloists from V. Boys' Ch., Ch. Viennensis, VCM, Harnoncourt.

Gardiner conducts an exhilarating performance, so dramatic in its approach and so wide-ranging in the emotions conveyed it might be a religious opera. Speeds are regularly on the fast side but, characteristically, Gardiner consistently keeps a spring in the rhythm and urgently intensifies such points as the violence of the *Kreuzige* (Crucify) choruses and the section involving the casting of lots. The very opening chorus is made the more agonizing when the wind writing itself seems to suggest howls of pain. Yet Gardiner's refusal to dawdle even at the moment of the Crucifixion does not prevent the whole performance from conveying necessary dedication. Chorales are treated in contrasted ways, which may not please the more severe authenticists but, as with so much of Gardiner's work, here is a performance using authentic scale and period instruments which speaks in the most vivid way to anyone prepared to listen, not just to the specialist. Soloists – regular contributors to Gardiner's team – are all first rate, with Anthony Rolfe-Johnson light and resilient as the Evangelist, and Nancy Argenta exceptionally sweet-toned. The alto solos are beautifully taken by the counter-tenor Michael Chance, bringing necessary gravity to *Es ist vollbracht*. Warm and atmospheric, yet clear and detailed recording. A selection of arias and choruses is available on DG 427 319-2.

Münchinger's set dates from 1975, and the recording is excellent. The dynamic range is strikingly wide and the sound itself fresh and full. Münchinger's reading matches his other 'pre-authentic' recordings of Bach's choral works, with a superb line-up of soloists, all of them clear-toned and precise, and with a fresh and young-sounding tenor, Dieter Ellenbeck, as the Evangelist. The musical balance of the score is pointed most satisfyingly without idiosyncrasy, using organ continuo with no harpsichord.

Recorded (like The Sixteen's previous Hyperion sets of Handel's *Messiah* and the Monteverdi *Vespers*) at a series of live performances at St John's, Smith Square, in London, Harry Christophers' version brings a period performance that has warmth as well as freshness. It is chiefly remarkable for the uniquely mellifluous singing of Ian Partridge as the Evangelist, deeply expressive as well as sweet to the ear, and he is well matched by David Wilson-Johnson as Jesus in the dramatic exchanges of extended recitative. What mars the set is the backward balance of the chorus, and at times of the other soloists as well. The great opening and closing choruses are beautifully sung but lack inner clarity and bite. Happily, the chorales and brief turba (crowd) choruses fare much better, being simpler, for Christophers' direction has plenty of vigour. With first-rate performances from all the soloists to back up Partridge's glowing contribution, there is much to enjoy.

Schreier's telling of the Crucifixion story is riveting in its variety of tone, expression and pace. With his dry, piercing sound, he is even better suited to the biting drama of the *St John* than to the visionary expansiveness of the *St Matthew*. The arias too find him in his freshest voice, not least two extra ones, formidably difficult and never recorded before, which Bach wrote for performance in 1725, the year following the first accredited performance. In also directing the performance, Schreier – still using modern instruments – applies the lessons taught by the Authentic Movement. Two reservations have to be made. Schreier has taken the idea of detached phrasing to such an extreme that in places – notably in the great choruses at the beginning and end – the flow is impaired and the music becomes choppy. Schreier's treatment of the chorales is also controversial, when he so markedly uses rubato to give the words of these hymns extra expressiveness; the singers of the superb Leipzig Radio Choir, thirty-five strong, respond with ensemble of the highest polish, but the result is fussy. The three other principal soloists are first rate too – notably Olaf Bär, who sings the first and most original of the extra (1725) arias, in which briskly angular writing for the soloist is set against a chorale. Particularly for that supplement, this is an essential set for Bach devotees and comes on two generously filled discs, very well recorded.

Harnoncourt's version, using male voices only and period instruments, dates from 1971. This is a fresh, brisk tour through Bach's most dramatic choral work, helped by the light, distinctive narration of Kurt Equiluz and the bright singing of the Viennese choristers, men and boys. Soloists from the Vienna Boys' Choir sing the soprano and alto arias, and within its chosen approach this remains a positive and characterful reading, vigorous if not as resilient as some more recent performances using period instruments. The sound in the CD transfer is excellent.

St Matthew Passion, BWV 244.
*** DG Dig. 427 648-2 (3) [id.]. Rolfe-Johnson, Schmidt, Bonney, Monoyios, Von Otter, Chance, Crook, Bär, Hauptmann, Monteverdi Ch., E. Bar. Soloists, Gardiner.
*** Ph. Dig. 412 527-2 (3) [id.]. Schreier, Adam, Popp, Lipovsek, Holl, Dresden Children's Ch., Leipzig R. Ch., Dresden State O, Schreier.
(M) *** EMI CMS7 63058-2 (3). Pears, Fischer-Dieskau, Schwarzkopf, Ludwig, Gedda, Berry, Hampstead Parish Church Ch., Philh. Ch. & O, Klemperer.
(M) **(*) Decca 414 057-2 (3) [id.]. Pears, Prey, Ameling, Höffgen, Wunderlich, Krause, Stuttgart Hymnus Boys' Ch., Stuttgart CO, Münchinger.
*** Decca Dig. 421 177-2 (3) [id.]. Te Kanawa, Von Otter, Rolfe-Johnson, Krause, Blochwitz, Bär, Chicago Ch., Children's Ch. & SO, Solti.
**(*) HM HMC 901155/7 [id.]. Crook, Cold, Schluck, Jacobs, Blochwitz, Kooy, Chapelle Royale Ch., Ghent Coll. Mus., Herreweghe.
(M) ** Teldec/WEA 2292 42509-2 (3) [id.]. Equiluz, Esswood, Sutcliffe, Bowman, Rogers, Ridderbusch, Van Egmond, Schopper, Regensburger Boys' Ch., King's College, Cambridge, Ch., VCM, Harnoncourt.

Gardiner's version of the *St Matthew Passion*, the culminating issue in his Bach choral series for DG Archiv, brings an intense, dramatic reading which now makes a clear first choice, not just for period-performance devotees but for anyone not firmly set against the new authenticity. As Gardiner sees it, Bach's plan was to divide both parts of the Passion into scenes, 12 in the first part, 15 in the second, each rounded off with a commentary, either collective in the form of a chorale, or individual in the form of an aria. As he says, 'The cumulative effect is similar to that of the 14 stations of the Cross in Catholic tradition, with the same arbitrary but carefully considered division of the Passion story.' The result is an invigorating, intense telling of the story, with Gardiner favouring high dynamic contrasts and generally fast speeds which are still geared to the weighty purpose of the whole work. He and his performers were recorded in what proved an ideal venue, The Maltings at Snape, where the warm acoustic gives body and allows clarity to period textures. Anthony Rolfe-Johnson excels himself as the Evangelist, sweeter-toned than he has sometimes been on record, underlining the dramatic tensions in his narration. Andreas Schmidt makes an aptly young-sounding, virile Jesus, while no current recording of this work has a finer line-up of other soloists, singers with young, clear voices like the tenor, Howard Crook, and the baritone, Olaf Bär. Crowning the team are two singers in the alto parts – not just the vividly characterful Anne Sofie von Otter (delectable in *Buss und Reu*) but also the counter-tenor, Michael Chance, whose performance of the longest aria of all, *Erbarme dich*, brings a high point in the performance. It is good too that the chorales bring no gimmicks; they are expressive and pointed without mannerism. The substantial but not over-ample chorus – with boy trebles and teen-age girls for the chorale descant of the great opening number – sings with all the freshness and bite that is characteristic of Gardiner's work, not least in the dramatic crowd (turba) choruses which favour relatively relaxed speeds. Excellent Erato recording.

Schreier's aim in Bach interpretation is to bring new lightness without following the full dictates of authentic performance, and in this he succeeds superbly. Such meditative arias as the contralto's *Erbarme dich* or the soprano's *Aus liebe* bring a natural gravity and depth of expression, though Marjana Lipovsek has a tendency to sit on the flat side of the note, and Lucia Popp's silvery soprano is not always caught at its sweetest. The end result is a refreshing and cohesive performance, ideal for records, when there is no tendency for the piece to drag. The recording is first rate, with the choral forces well separated.

While it certainly will not appeal to the authentic lobby, Klemperer's 1962 Philharmonia recording of the *St Matthew Passion* represents one of his greatest achievements on record, an act of devotion of such intensity that points of style and interpretation seem insignificant. Klemperer's way is to take the chorales slowly, with pauses at the end of each line; he makes no concessions to recent scholarship on the question of introducing ornamentation. There is a matchless team of soloists, with Peter Pears at his peak in the role of Evangelist and Fischer-Dieskau deeply expressive as Jesus. The Philharmonia Choir sings with the finest focus. The whole cast clearly shared Klemperer's own intense feelings, and one can only sit back and share them too, whatever one's preconceptions.

Münchinger's direction does not attain the spiritual heights of an interpretation such as Klemperer's, but his version is consistently fresh and alert, and it has the degree of authenticity of its period (1965) – although much has happened to Bach performances since then. All the soloists are excellent, and Peter Pears shows that no tenor of his generation rivalled his insight as the Evangelist. Elly Ameling is sweet-toned and sensitive. The recording is first class, clear and brilliant and very well balanced, with the chorus sounding incisive and well defined, with just the right degree of weight. Some may object to the deliberate closeness with which the voice of Hermann Prey as Jesus has been recorded.

Solti uses a reduced-size Chicago Symphony Orchestra and himself hand-picked the choir. With him the *Passion* is less devotional than celebratory. With speeds on the fast side, resilient rhythms and bright choral tone, he brings it closer than usual to the *St John Passion*, with its message of heavenly joy. Clean, fresh solo singing, too, with Hans-Peter Blochwitz the sweetest-toned Evangelist on record. Olaf Bär as Jesus is youthfully virile, Anne Sofie von Otter makes a radiant alto soloist, giving natural gravity to *Erbarme dich*. Brilliant, full, Decca recording with fine presence and clarity.

Herreweghe's version presents a good choice for anyone wanting a performance on period instruments at lower pitch. Howard Crook is an excellent, fresh-toned Evangelist, and the other tenor, Hans-Peter Blochwitz, is first rate too. The alto part is taken by the celebrated counter-tenor, René Jacobs, rather hooty in *Erbarme dich*; but Barbara

Schluck, with her bright, clear soprano voice, sings radiantly. The instrumental group plays in authentic style but not abrasively so; Herreweghe's control of rhythm, however, tends to be too heavy. Chorales are often slow and over-accented, and heavy stressing mars the big numbers too.

Harnoncourt's vocal sound remains unique in its total reliance on male voices (including boy trebles); the choral singing is incisive and lightweight. Among the soloists, Karl Ridderbusch and Paul Esswood are outstanding. Some of the other contributions are less reliable, and the use of boy trebles for the soprano arias produces a strangely detached effect, although the singing itself is usually technically good. Vivid recording.

Vocal collections

Arias: *Bist du bei mir; Cantata 202: Weichet nur, Betrubte Schatten. Cantata 209: Ricetti gramezza. St Matthew Passion: Blute nur; Ich will dir mein Herze schenken.*
(*) Delos Dig. D/CD 3026 [id.]. Arleen Augér, Mostly Mozart O, Schwarz – HANDEL: *Arias.*(*)

Arleen Augér's pure, sweet soprano, effortlessly controlled, makes for bright performances of these Bach arias and songs, ideally suited to *Bist du bei mir*, less so to such a dark aria as *Blute nur* from the *St Matthew Passion*, not helped by relatively coarse accompaniment, over-recorded. Still very recommendable for admirers of this delightful singer, well coupled with Handel arias.

Arias: *Mass in B min.: Agnus Dei; Qui sedes. St John Passion: All is fulfilled. St Matthew Passion: Grief for sin.*
(***) Decca mono 414 623-2. Kathleen Ferrier, LPO, Boult – HANDEL: *Arias.*(***) ⊛

On 7th and 8th October 1952, Kathleen Ferrier made her last and perhaps greatest record in London's Kingsway Hall, coupling four arias each by Bach and Handel. The combined skill of John Culshaw and Kenneth Wilkinson ensured a recording of the utmost fidelity by the standards of that time. Now it re-emerges with extraordinary naturalness and presence. Boult's mono accompaniments were beautifully balanced and orchestral detail is clarified further, with the harpsichord continuo coming through the more transparent texture in *Grief for sin* and Ambrose Gauntlett's viola da gamba obbligato for *All is fulfilled* more tangible. Of course the upper strings sound thinner, but that adds an 'authentic' touch. The pre-Dolby background noise is still apparent but is in no way distracting.

Arrangements: Bach–Stokowski

Chorale prelude: Wir glauben all' an einen Gott ('Giant' fugue), BWV 680. Easter cantata, BWV 4: Chorale. Geistliches Lied No. 51: Mein Jesu, BWV 487. Passacaglia and fugue in C min., BWV 582. Toccata and fugue in D min., BWV 565. Well-tempered Clavier, Book 1: Prelude No. 8 in E flat min., BWV 853.
(B) **(*) Decca 421 639-2 [id.]. Czech PO, Stokowski.

Stokowski challenges his players in expansive tempi but, although he is mannered, he is also passionate in concentration. The recording is spectacular, big, bold and sumptuous, if not always absolutely clean in focus. However, those looking for the ultimate sonic experience will find that a marvellously recorded Telarc CD by the Cincinnati Pops Orchestra under Kunzel called 'The Stokowski sound' (CD 80129) includes the famous transcription of the *Toccata and fugue in D minor*, BWV 565, resplendent in modern digital sound.

Bach, Wilhelm Friedemann (1710-84)

Double harpsichord concerto in E flat, Falck 46; Sonata in F for 2 harpsichords, Falck 10, BWV Anh. 188.
*** DG Dig. 419 256-2 [id.]. Staier, Hill, Coll. Mus. Ant., Goebel – c. p. e. bach: *Double harpsichord concerto.****

The concerto has an expressive depth that confirms the impression that Wilhelm Friedemann was potentially the most gifted of Bach's sons. The finale is certainly highly inventive and the playing, both here and in the equally impressive *Sonata*, has enormous sparkle. Readers normally allergic to period instruments should note that such is the liveliness and imagination of these performances that only the good things – clarity and lightness of texture, etc. – and none of the drawbacks, are in evidence.

Keyboard fantasias: Nos. 1–8 & 10, F.14–21 & F.23.
*** Denon Dig. CO 72588 [id.]. Huguette Dreyfus (harpsichord).

The *E minor Fantasia* (Falck 21), which opens the disc, comes from Wilhelm Friedmann's period in Dresden (1733–46) and is highly dramatic (at times almost operatic). These works are engagingly unpredictable, all bringing quite bold and daring harmonic sleights of hand, and this holds as good of the earlier ones – such as the *A minor* (F.23) – as of the later. The *E minor* (F.20) is from 1770, and two others come from the last year of his life. They are full of flair. So, too, is the excellent playing of Huguette Dreyfus, who has the advantage of an outstanding recording.

Baermann, Heinrich (1784-1847)

Adagio for clarinet and orchestra.
*** ASV Dig. CDDCA 559 [id.]. Emma Johnson, ECO, Groves – crusell: *Concerto No. 2**** ⊛; rossini: *Introduction, theme and variations****; weber: *Concertino.****
(m) **(*) Decca 417 643-2 [id.]. Boskovsky, V. Octet (members) – brahms: *Quintet***(*); mozart: *Quintet.***

Heinrich Baermann's rather beautiful *Adagio*, once attributed to Wagner, is offered by a young clarinettist who plays the work warmly and sympathetically. Boskovsky, too, is particularly languorous – and both are well accompanied and recorded. Couplings should dictate choice here.

Balakirev, Mily (1837-1910)

Islamey (orch. Lyapunov).
** Olympia OCD 129 [id.]. USSR Ac. SO, Svetlanov – lyapunov: *Hashish* etc.**(*)

An effective performance here of Lyapunov's effective (and once much-played) orchestration of *Islamey*. It makes a logical coupling for an interesting disc of Lyapunov's very Balakirevian orchestral music. Rough-and-ready but acceptable recording.

Russia (symphonic poem).
(m) ** EMI CDM7 63093-2 [id.]. Bournemouth SO, Brusilov – borodin: *Symphony No. 2*; rimsky-korsakov: *Skazka.***

This is the second overture on Russian themes that Balakirev composed. It receives a straightforward performance that will give pleasure, even if one would have welcomed a greater sense of characterization and poetry. The recording is forward, but the sound has plenty of colour and the remastering is vivid.

Symphony No. 1 in C; Tamara (symphonic poem).
(M) *** EMI CDM7 63375-2 [id.]. RPO, Beecham.

This is a splendid symphony with a highly original first movement, a sparkling scherzo, an agreeably lyrical *Andante* and a breezy finale. It is an extended piece (40 minutes) but Balakirev's material and treatment can easily sustain the length, particularly when the performance is as persuasive as Beecham's. Admittedly Karajan (whose Philharmonia mono version is included in an EMI box – see Concerts, below) was more dynamic and passionate in his old recording, but Beecham offers many felicities and he coaxes the sinuous oriental melodies of the slow movement with characteristically stylish languor. The early (1955) stereo has responded quite well to the CD face-lift: there is plenty of colour and atmosphere, although ideally one needs a great amplitude of string-tone. *Tamara* was recorded a year earlier and the mono sound-balance compares very favourably with the stereo in the *Symphony*. The performance has the characteristic Beecham panache; there is also flamboyance and subtlety, and he is especially fine in conveying the bitter-sweet atmosphere of the work's close.

Islamey (oriental fantasy).
(M) *** EMI CDM7 69125-2 [id.]. Andrei Gavrilov – TCHAIKOVSKY: *Piano concerto No. 1 etc.***(*)

Gavrilov's dazzling account of Balakirev's fantasy is outstandingly charismatic. It is well recorded too; but unfortunately it comes in harness with a performance of the Tchaikovsky *B flat minor Concerto* which is rather less convincing.

Piano sonata in B flat min.
(*) Archduke Dig. DARC2 [id.]. Donna Amato – DUTILLEUX: *Sonata.*(*)
(*) Kingdom Dig. KCLCD 2001 [id.]. Gordon Fergus-Thompson – SCRIABIN: *Sonata No. 3 etc.*(*)
(*) Nimbus Dig. NI 5187 [id.]. Ronald Smith – MUSSORGSKY: *Pictures*; SCRIABIN: *Sonata No. 9.*(*)

The Balakirev is arguably the greatest Russian piano sonata of the pre-1914 era. Donna Amato gives a musicianly account of it, well paced and authoritative – not surprisingly, since she studied with Louis Kentner, who made the very first recording of it after the war. The recording is very lifelike, and this is a most desirable issue, even if the playing time at 47 minutes is not particularly generous.

Gordon Fergus-Thompson, too, is fully equal to the considerable demands of the Balakirev *Sonata* and offers excellent playing, though the recording is reverberant and the piano not always dead in tune. Fergus-Thompson also includes Balakirev's arrangement of Glinka's *The Lark* as an encore.

Ronald Smith also seems to have a real feeling for this repertoire and gives a very persuasive account of the work. In the second-movement *Mazurka*, however, one senses a feeling of caution: it needs to be played with just that touch more panache and abandon.

Bantock, Granville (1868–1946)

The Pierrot of the Minute: overture.
*** Chan. CHAN 8373 [id.]. Bournemouth Sinf., Del Mar – BRIDGE: *Summer*, etc.;
BUTTERWORTH: *Banks of green willow.****

67

Bantock's overture is concerned with Pierrot's dream in which he falls in love with a Moon Maiden who tells him their love must die at dawn, but he will not listen. He wakes to realize that his dream of love lasted a mere minute. The writing is often delicate and at times Elgarian, and the piece is well worth investigating. The recording sounds remarkably fresh.

Barber, Samuel (1910–81)

Adagio for strings.
*** Argo 417 818-2 [id.]. ASMF, Marriner – COPLAND: *Quiet city*; COWELL: *Hymn*; CRESTON: *Rumor*; IVES: *Symphony No. 3.****
(M) *** DG Dig. 427 806 [id.]. LAPO, Bernstein – BERNSTEIN: *Overture Candide; West Side Story; On the Town****; GERSHWIN: *Rhapsody in blue.***(*)
*** DG Dig. 413 324-2 [id.]. LAPO, Bernstein – BERNSTEIN: *Candide overture*; COPLAND: *Appalachian spring*; SCHUMAN: *American festival overture.****

Marriner's 1976 performance of Barber's justly famous *Adagio* is arguably the most satisfying version we have had since the war, although Bernstein's alternative has the advantage of digital recording. The quality of sound on the remastered Argo CD retains most of the richness and body of the analogue LP, but at the climax the brighter lighting brings a slightly sparer violin texture than on the original LP.

Bernstein's version has an expansively restrained elegiac feeling, but his control of the climax – in what is substantially a live recording – is unerring. Bernstein's recording is also available within a generally attractive mid-priced compilation, coupled with Gershwin and some of his own music.

Adagio for strings; (i) *Piano concerto, Op. 38; Medea's meditation and Dance of vengeance, Op. 23a.*
*** ASV Dig. CDDCA 534 [id.]. (i) Joselson; LSO, Schenck.

In Barber's *Concerto* Tedd Joselson is marvellously and dazzlingly brilliant, as well as being highly sensitive and poetic. What also shows this score to better advantage than before is the greater richness and detail of the ASV recording and the unforced and poetic orchestral contribution from the LSO under Andrew Schenck. The LSO also give a singularly fine account of the *Medea* excerpt (not to be confused with the Suite) and a restrained and noble one of the celebrated *Adagio*.

Adagio for strings; Essays Nos. 1–3; Medea's Dance of vengeance, Op. 23a; School for scandal: Overture, Op. 5.
*** EMI Dig. CDC7 49463-2 [id.]. St Louis SO, Slatkin.

The *Adagio for strings* and the *First Essay for orchestra* were the works by which Barber was first introduced to the public and which gained him the advocacy of Toscanini and Ormandy. But this disc also includes another youthful piece of consummate skill: his graduation exercise, the *Overture* to *The School for scandal*. What an inspired piece it is and what a marvellous second subject! The more familiar *Second Essay* and the later *Third* are given expert performances by the St Louis orchestra under Leonard Slatkin and are vividly recorded.

Cello concerto, Op. 22.
*** CBS Dig. MK 44900 [id.]. Yo-Yo Ma, Baltimore SO, Zinman – BRITTEN: *Cello symphony.****

*** Chan. Dig. CHAN 8322 [id.]. Wallfisch, ECO, Simon – SHOSTAKOVICH: *Cello concerto No. 1.****

With his masterly sense of line, Yo-Yo Ma gives a richly lyrical reading of Barber's beautiful *Cello concerto*. The subtleties in the reading are enhanced by having the soloist naturally placed, not spotlit, in relation to the well-balanced orchestra. This work of 1945 makes an unusual but apt and attractive coupling for Ma's superb account of the Britten *Cello symphony*.

Wallfisch also gives an impressive and eloquent reading, and the elegiac slow movement is especially fine. Wallfisch is forwardly balanced, but otherwise the recording is truthful; the orchestra is vividly detailed. Indeed the sound is outstandingly realistic; given the excellence of the coupling, this must also receive the strongest recommendation.

Violin concerto, Op. 14.
*** EMI Dig. CDC7 47850-2. Oliviera, St Louis SO, Slatkin – HANSON: *Symphony No. 2.****
*** ASV Dig. CDRPO 8013 [id.]. Anne Meyers, RPO, Seaman – BRUCH: *Concerto No. 1.***(*)

(i) *Violin concerto; Essay for orchestra No. 2; School for Scandal: overture; Vannesa: Prelude and Intermezzo.*
*** Pro Arte Dig. CCD 241 [id.]. (i) Silverstein; Utah SO.

Anyone who enjoys Barber's *Adagio for strings* must respond to the *Violin concerto*. It is genuinely beautiful and has consistent warmth, freshness and humanity. Elmer Oliviera's version responds to the nostalgia of the *Andante* with a vein of bitter-sweet yearning that is most affecting. It is a fine performance overall with a brilliantly played finale and is warmly and realistically recorded, with Slatkin directing an entirely sympathetic accompaniment. Rich, atmospheric sound.

The merit of Anne Meyers' performance lies in its unforced naturalness. The sleeve material tells us nothing about the soloist, who is an artist of quality. Her playing has an effortless lyrical flow and she captures its world of feeling and sense of youthful rapture marvellously. This is not high-powered, jet-setting playing, though there is no want of virtuosity or, in the slow movement, tenderness. She is well supported by the RPO under Christopher Seaman, and the recording is as musically balanced and as lifelike as the playing. An altogether first-class performance; it is a pity the coupling was not more imaginatively chosen.

The alternative version from Joseph Silverstein is in some ways an even stronger performance than Oliviera's, with the Utah orchestra providing a fervently passionate accompaniment. Both soloist and orchestra are forwardly projected by the extremely vivid Pro Arte recording, at the expense of some fierceness on the fortissimo massed violins, but in consequence Silverstein's image is bigger than Oliviera's, which suits the style of the playing. Silverstein also directs the other works, which are well worth having.

Essay No. 3 for orchestra, Op. 47.
*** New World Dig. NW 309-2 [id.]. NYPO, Mehta – CORIGLIANO: *Clarinet concerto.*
***

The *Third Essay* for orchestra was Samuel Barber's very last work; it is more dramatic, less overtly romantic and lyrical than either of its predecessors. It is powerfully organized and crafted with all of Barber's command of musical resource. The playing of the New York Philharmonic under Zubin Mehta is expert and the recording is first class.

Summer music.
*** Crystal CD 750 [id.]. Westwood Wind Quintet – CARLSSON: *Nightwings*; LIGETI: *Bagatelles*; MATHIAS: *Quintet.***

Samuel Barber's *Summer music* is an evocative mood-picture of summer, a gloriously warm and lyrical piece whose neglect on record is difficult to understand. This is superbly committed and sensitive playing and vivid, warm recording.

Agnus Dei.
*** Hyp. Dig. CDA 66129 [id.]. Corydon Singers, Matthew Best – BERNSTEIN: *Chichester Psalms*; COPLAND: *In the beginning* etc.***

Barber's *Agnus Dei* is none other than our old friend the *Adagio*, arranged for voices by the composer in 1967. Matthew Best's fine performance moves spaciously and expansively to an impressive climax. The sound is very fine, with the acoustics of St Jude-on-the-Hill, Hampstead, admirably suited to the music.

Vanessa (opera): complete.
(M) *** RCA GD 87899 (2) [7899-2-RG]. Steber, Elias, Resnik, Gedda, Tossi, Met. Op. Ch. & O, Mitropoulos.

For long *Vanessa* was looked down on as plush and old-fashioned, but it is a work of much charm and warmth. It inhabits much the same civilized world as Strauss or Henry James. Although it has not held the stage, its melodic freshness and warmth will ensure a reversal of its fortunes some day. This, its only recording so far, was made at the time of its first performance in 1958, but no apologies are needed for its quality; it stands the test of time as well as does the opera itself. Eleanor Steber is in good voice in the title-role, as are Gedda as Anatol and Resnik as the old Baroness. In fact the first-production cast has no real weakness, and the orchestral playing under Mitropoulos is wholly committed; it is good to have this lovely opera back, sounding better than ever.

Bartók, Béla (1881–1945)

Concerto for orchestra.
(M) *** Decca 417 754-2 [id.]. Chicago SO, Solti – MUSSORGSKY: *Pictures.***
(*) Decca Dig. 425 694-2 [id.]. Cleveland O, Dohnányi – LUTOSLAWSKI: *Concerto for orchestra.*
(*) Telarc Dig. CD 80174 [id.]. LAPO, Previn – JANÁČEK: *Sinfonietta.*(*)

Concerto for orchestra; 2 Images, Op. 10.
** Ph. Dig. 411 132-2 [id.]. Concg. O, Dorati.

Concerto for orchestra; Music for strings, percussion and celesta.
(M) **(*) RCA GD 60175 [60175-2-RG]. Chicago SO, Fritz Reiner.
*** Decca Dig. 421 443-2 [id.]. Montreal SO, Dutoit.
** DG 415 322-2 [id.]. BPO, Karajan.

Solti gave Bartók's *Concerto for orchestra* its compact disc début. The upper range of the sound is very brightly lit indeed, which brings an aggressive feeling to the upper strings. This undoubtedly suits the reading, fierce and biting on the one hand, exuberant on the other. With superlative playing from Solti's own Chicago orchestra and such vivid sound, this will be an obvious choice for most readers, particularly as it comes at mid-price.

Decca has made a speciality of brilliant recordings of this showpiece work, and Dohnányi's brings an even fuller, richer sound than Solti's with the Chicago orchestra or Dutoit's with the Montreal Symphony. Dohnányi's reading is relatively straight – the night music of the third movement lacks mystery, and the humour of the fourth-movement trio is a little stiff – but, with ensemble even crisper than on either rival disc, the bite and power of much of the playing is sharply contrasted with the extreme refinement and delicacy of the string articulation, as in the scurrying main theme of the finale.

Reiner's version of the *Concerto for orchestra* was recorded in 1955, but the sound is unbelievably good, spacious and vivid. The performance is most satisfying, surprisingly straightforward from one brought up in Central Europe but with plenty of cutting edge. The *Music for strings, percussion and celesta*, recorded three years later, suffers from a forward balance which prevents any true pianissimo quality, even in the first movement. Moreover Reiner tends to iron out some of Bartók's complicated speed changes. However, the performance has plenty of atmosphere and grip and is by no means to be ignored.

Helped by warm and atmospheric recording, Dutoit conducts performances of both these masterpieces – an ideal and generous coupling – which convey the message that Bartók is a composer of warmth and refinement rather than of barbarism. Dutoit is particularly successful in bringing out the vein of humour, too, not only in the *Concerto* but also in the *Music for strings, percussion and celesta*. There have been more electrifying performances of both works than these, but none more beautiful; some listeners might seek a greater degree of bite, and they can turn to Solti.

Previn and the Los Angeles Philharmonic give a comfortable, relaxed reading of Bartók's *Concerto*. Previn is at his best in the fun of the couple-play in the second movement or the Shostakovich parody of the fourth movement. For him, it is above all a work of fun. The Telarc recording captures the full bloom of the orchestra as few recordings from Los Angeles have. The coupling is unique. However, those seeking a relatively mellow account of the Bartók *Concerto* will probably find Dutoit more satisfying.

Dorati's is a surprisingly lyrical account of Bartók's most popular work, consistently bringing out the folk-dance element along with the fun of the inspiration. It is well coupled with the two atmospheric *Pictures: Blossoming* and *Village dance*. The CD is clear and faithful.

On DG, in both the *Concerto* and the *Music for strings, percussion and celesta* the Berlin Philharmonic, in superb form, give performances that are rich, romantic and smooth – for some ears perhaps excessively so. With Solti, any rubato is linked with the Hungarian folksong idiom, where Karajan's moulding of phrases is essentially of the German tradition. The effect produces a certain urbanity. Nevertheless, the playing of the Berlin strings is a pleasure in itself, and the sound is impressive and sumptuous.

Concerto for orchestra; Miraculous Mandarin: suite.
* Sony Dig. SK 45748 [id.]. BPO, Zubin Mehta.

Mehta provides a most desirable coupling, but the performances do not bite sharply enough, sounding too plushy, and the recording is no help, murky and with strings oddly recessed.

(i) *Piano concertos Nos. 1–3; Rhapsody for piano and orchestra; Concerto for orchestra.*
(M) *** DG 427 410-2 (2) [id.]. (i) Géza Anda, Berlin RSO, Fricsay.

Piano concertos Nos. 1–3; Music for strings, percussion & celesta; Rhapsody for piano and orchestra; Scherzo for piano and orchestra.
*** Ph. Dig. 416 831-2 (3) [id.]. Kocsis, Budapest Fest. O, Fischer.

Piano concerto No. 3 in E; Scherzo for piano and orchestra.
*** Ph. Dig. 416 835-2 [id.]. Kocsis, Budapest Fest. O, Fischer.

(i) *Piano concertos Nos. 1–3*; (ii) *Sonata for 2 pianos and percussion.*
(M) *** Decca Dig./Analogue 425 573-2 (2) [id.]. Vladimir Ashkenazy; (i) LPO, Solti; (ii) Vovka Ashkenazy, D. Corkhill, Andrew Smith.

Piano concerto No. 3 in E.
(*) Decca 411 969-2 [id.]. Vladimir Ashkenazy, LPO, Solti – PROKOFIEV: *Concerto No. 3.**

This outstanding Philips set dominates the catalogue in this repertoire. Kocsis recorded the *First* and *Second Piano concertos* in the early 1970s for Hungaroton; but these new versions are even more vibrant, and the *Third* is superbly done, to make it perhaps the finest on record. The inclusion of the *Music for strings, percussion and celesta* may be counted a disadvantage by some, particularly as the resonant acoustic and rather forward balance prevent an absolute pianissimo and detract from the feeling of mystery; but this is still an exciting and involving performance. We have had the *Rhapsody* before, and the account here is as fine as the *Concertos*; what is especially welcome is the *Scherzo*. Its style is fascinatingly eclectic, but the writing is extremely spontaneous and the work springs to life when the performers are so obviously enjoying themselves. The full-bodied recording with a rich, tangible piano-image is very satisfying.

Ashkenazy's versions of both the *First Concerto* and the *Sonata* (with his son, Vovka) are tough, even aggressive performances, biting, never relaxing, spectacularly caught in (1984) digital sound with the widest range of dynamics. The *Second* and *Third Concertos*, recorded four years earlier, are analogue, but the recording, although reverberant, is comparably vivid and present. With the Slavonic bite of the soloist aptly matching the Hungarian fire of the conductor, the readings of both works are urgently involving and incisive, and these two concertos, from very different periods in Bartók's career, are made to seem far closer kin than usual. Tempi tend to be fast, while slow movements bring hushed inner concentration, beautifully captured in Decca's atmospheric recording. If anything, the *Third Concerto* is even more gripping than the *Second*. The separate coupling with Prokofiev remains at full price.

Anda's recordings of the Bartók *Concertos* and the *Rhapsody*, which is attractively volatile, have acquired classic status. Anda seems ideally cast as soloist and Fricsay is a natural Bartókian. The performances are refined yet urgent, incisive but red-blooded too. The recording from 1960–61 has been vividly enhanced by the CD transfers. Fricsay's *Concerto for orchestra* was recorded in 1957 and is a first-class example of DG's expertise in the pre-stereo era. The Berlin Radio orchestra plays with considerable virtuosity, especially in the finale, and the pairs of instruments in the second movement combine wit with finesse. A most enjoyable performance and no apologies for the sound.

Piano concertos Nos. 1 in A; 2 in G.
*** DG 415 371-2 [id.]. Pollini, Chicago SO, Abbado.

The DG issue forms an exuberant partnership between two of the most distinguished Italian musicians of the day. Virtuosity goes with a sense of spontaneity. Rhythms in fast movements are freely and infectiously sprung to bring out bluff Bartókian high spirits.

The Chicago orchestra, vividly recorded, is in superb form and the CD gives a new lease of life to the 1979 analogue recording.

Piano concerto No. 2.
** EMI Dig. CDC7 49861-2 [id.]. Barto, LPO, Eschenbach – RACHMANINOV: *Concerto No. 3.* *

Tzimon Barto's account of the percussive *Second Concerto* leaves no doubts as to his dazzling pianism and, though he does not resist all the temptations which assailed him in the Rachmaninov with which it is coupled, this is very much better. It still has a self-conscious, sensational feel to it with dynamic extremes, and practically everything else a bit exaggerated, and it would not be a first choice. All the same, it is a version to reckon with and the performance is very well recorded with plenty of body and detail, particularly at the bottom end of the register.

Concerto for 2 pianos, percussion and celesta.
*** Ph. Dig. 416 378-2 [id.]. Freire, Argerich, L. and J. Pustjens, Concg. O, Zinman – KODÁLY: *Dances of Galánta.* ***

(i) *Concerto for 2 pianos, percussion and celesta; Sonata for 2 pianos, percussion and celesta.*
*** EMI Dig. CDC7 47446-2. K. and M. Labèque, Gualda, Drouet; (i) CBSO, Rattle.

Comparing the *Sonata for two pianos, percussion and celesta* and the *Concerto* which Bartók drew from it, one might wonder why a full orchestra was needed to add relatively little extra. The Labèque sisters give brilliant, intense performances of both works which can be enjoyed equally; however, with the percussion relatively close in the *Sonata* the focus is sharper, with xylophone and timpani particularly impressive.

Martha Argerich with Stephen Bishop-Kovacevich recorded a fierily vibrant performance of the *Sonata*, and there is much of the same high-voltage electricity in her recording of the orchestral version with Nelson Freire. The recording with pianos placed relatively close is well detailed but lacks something in mystery.

Violin concerto No. 1, Op. posth.
*** Decca Dig. 411 804-2 [id.]. Kyung Wha Chung, Chicago SO, Solti – BERG: *Concerto.* ***

Violin concertos Nos. 1; 2 in B min.
(M) **(*) Decca Dig./Analogue 425 015-2 [id.]. Kyung Wha Chung, Chicago SO or LPO, Solti.

In Bartók's early *Concerto* – inspired, like Berg's late one, by a woman – the tender intensity of Chung's playing is established in the opening phrase, and the whole performance is comparably magnetic, brimming with poetry to make one forget the relative immaturity of the writing. Solti and the Chicago orchestra could not be more understanding, and the recording is brilliant and warm to match.

Kyung Wha Chung's digital version of No. 1 is also reissued, coupled with her earlier analogue recording of No. 2, also partnered by Solti. It is a fiery, diamond-bright performance in which the Hungarian inflexions are sharply brought out. Though the angularity will not suit everyone, it is a strongly characterful reading, very brightly recorded and with very forward placing of the solo violin.

(i) *Violin concerto No. 2 in B min.;* (Solo) *Violin sonata.*
(M) (***) EMI mono CDH7 69804-2 [id.]. Yehudi Menuhin; (i) Philh. O, Furtwängler.

73

Menuhin's coupling of Bartók's two greatest violin works brings together historic recordings from the last days of 78 r.p.m. discs, here beautifully transferred, if with obvious limitations. One hardly associates Furtwängler with Bartók, but here in collaboration with Menuhin he is an inspired, warm interpreter, strongly co-ordinating a work that needs holding together tautly. Menuhin was also at his most inspired, both in the *Concerto* and in the solo *Violin sonata*, the work which he himself commissioned. This is among the very finest performances that Menuhin has ever put on record: strong, intense and deeply poetic.

Divertimento for strings; Music for strings, percussion and celesta.
*** Hung. Dig. HCD 12531 [id.]. Liszt CO, Rolla.

Divertimento for strings; Rumanian folk dances.
(*) DG 415 668-2 [id.]. Orpheus CO – JANÁCEK: *Mládi.*(*)

On Hungaroton both performances are expert and distil a powerful atmosphere in the slow movements of each piece. They command beautifully rapt *pianissimo* tone and keen intensity. The sound is less reverberant than some rivals, but there is no lack of ambience.

The American Orpheus Chamber Orchestra also give an eminently well-prepared account of the *Divertimento*. Good though their performance is, it is not quite as idiomatic in its sense of mystery or intensity of feeling as the Hungaroton, even if it possesses both in good measure. The recording, though very clean and well balanced, is not so atmospheric. The popular *Rumanian folk dances* are also attractively done.

The Miraculous Mandarin (complete ballet), *Op. 19.*
(*) Delos Dig. DE 3083 [id.]. Seattle SO, Gerard Schwarz – KODÁLY: *Háry Janos; Galánta dances.**

(i) *The Miraculous Mandarin* (complete ballet), *Op. 19;* (ii) *2 Portraits, Op. 5.*
*** DG Dig. 410 598-2 [id.]. (i) Amb. S.; LSO, Abbado; (ii) with Minz – PROKOFIEV: *Scythian suite.****

The Miraculous Mandarin (complete ballet), *Op. 19; Music for strings, percussion and celesta.*
** Decca Dig. 411 894-2 [id.]. (i) Kenneth Jewell Chorale; Detroit SO, Dorati.

Abbado directs a fiercely powerful performance of Bartók's barbarically furious ballet – including the wordless chorus in the finale – but one which, thanks to the refinement of the recording, makes the aggressiveness of the writing more acceptable while losing nothing in power. The Prokofiev coupling is highly appropriate and equally successful; before that, however, the ear is sweetened by Minz's warmth in the *Portraits*.

On their finest record yet, Gerard Schwarz directs the Seattle orchestra in a powerfully atmospheric account of Bartók's malignant ballet score, not as idiomatically aggressive as some, but with plenty of grip and excitement at the climax. The expansive acoustics of Seattle Opera House bring an unexpected richness of colour to the scoring. The entry of the wordless chorus is particularly telling, beautifully balanced within a recording that is at once highly spectacular while giving a spacious concert-hall effect. Aptly and generously coupled with Kodály, this can be strongly recommended as a genuine alternative to Abbado's more pungent approach.

The range and brilliance of Decca's Detroit recording are spectacular. Though the playing in the complete score of the early ballet is polished enough, it finally lacks the flamboyance needed, the bold display of controlled barbarism. The *Music for strings, percussion and celesta* lacks the final degree of intensity, too.

Music for strings, percussion and celesta.
(M) **(*) EMI CDM7 69242-2 [id.]. BPO, Karajan – HINDEMITH: *Mathis der Maler.****

Karajan's EMI version comes from 1960. Though not so well recorded as the 1973 remake for DG (see above), it is a marvellously atmospheric and committed account, in some ways fresher and more spontaneous than the later version, and this is still very well worth considering.

The Wooden prince (ballet), *Op. 13* (complete); *Dance suite.*
(M) ** CBS MK 44700 [id.]. NYPO, Boulez.

In *The Wooden prince* Bartók adopted his sweetest manner to match a fairy story which, for all its unintended Freudian overtones, essentially has a warm simplicity. Boulez is the most compelling of advocates, maintaining his concentration throughout; the coupling of the *Dance suite* brings a performance just as warm, but a degree less precise. The recording, originally among CBS's best, emerges vividly in its remastered format, although the upper strings sound somewhat fierce.

CHAMBER AND INSTRUMENTAL MUSIC

Contrasts for clarinet, violin and piano.
*** Delos Dig. D/CD 3043 [id.]. Shifrin, Bae, Lash – MESSIAEN: *Quatuor.****
(***) CBS MK 42227 [id.]. Benny Goodman, Joseph Szigeti, composer – BERNSTEIN: *Prelude, fugue and riffs*; COPLAND: *Concerto*; STRAVINSKY: *Ebony concerto*; GOULD: *Derivations.*(***)

David Shifrin and his colleagues from Chamber Music Northwest admirably capture the diverse moods of Bartók's triptych, including the mordant wit and vitality of the outer sections and the dark colouring of the centrepiece. They are very well recorded in an agreeable acoustic.
Benny Goodman's recording with Szigeti and the composer, from the 78 r.p.m. era, is part of an enterprising and worthwhile anthology demonstrating the remarkable range of this famous clarinettist in twentieth-century music. This Bartók work was written for him. The 1940 recording sounds fully acceptable and the authority of the music-making is obvious.

Sonata for 2 pianos and percussion.
*** CBS Dig. MK 42625 [id.]. Perahia, Solti, Corkhill, Glennie – BRAHMS: *Variations on a theme by Haydn.****

An unexpected and highly creative partnership produces a vivid and strongly characterized performance. The combination of star conductor, taking time off from the rostrum, and his distinguished associate, each striking sparks off the other, with Solti bringing Hungarian flair to the proceedings, makes for great eloquence in this powerful work. The recording is vivid to match, giving the players great presence.

(i) *Sonata for 2 pianos and percussion;* (ii) (Solo) *Violin sonata.*
*** Accord Dig. 149047. (i) Janka and Jurg Wyttenbach, Schmid, Huber; (ii) Schneeberger.

The Accord recordings were made in Basle in the wake of the Bartók centenary celebrations. Hans-Heinz Schneeberger is obviously an accomplished artist and his account can withstand comparison with most if not all rivals. The *Sonata for 2 pianos and percussion* receives an exhilarating performance, and the CD recording is astonishingly good and also very natural. There is impressive range and the percussion players sound as if they are there in one's living-room.

String quartets Nos. 1–6.
*** DG Dig. 423 657-2 (2) [id.]. Emerson Qt.
**(*) EMI Dig. CDS7 47720-8 (3) [Ang. CDCC 47720]. Alban Berg Qt.
(**(*)) ASV Dig. CDDCS 301 (3) [id.]. Lindsay Qt.

The Emerson Quartet's set comes on only two CDs (the odd-numbered quartets on one and the even-numbered on the other) so that, in economy alone, it scores over past rivals. They project very powerfully and, in terms of virtuosity, finesse and accuracy, outstrip most of their rivals. At times their projection and expressive vehemence are a bit too much of a good thing. The *pesante* idea that opens the main section of the first movement of the *Sixth Quartet* is one such moment; the Tokyo Quartet on a now-deleted DG recording kept some sonority in reserve and had a more natural expressive eloquence. All the same, these are concentrated and brilliant performances that are very well recorded.

The Alban Berg Quartet is one of the great ensembles of the day; in terms of sheer virtuosity and attack, as well as great beauty of sound, they are unsurpassed. These are very impressive performances indeed, technically almost in a class of their own. They are very well recorded too, but the presentation, on three full-priced CDs, now seems uneconomic. At times the Alban Berg appear to treat this music as a vehicle for their own supreme virtuosity.

The Lindsay performances, searching, powerful and expressive, are now reissued together. The digital recording, though first class, occupies three discs which, like the Alban Berg set, places it at a distinct disadvantage to the DG Emerson version.

String quartets Nos. 1, Op. 7; 2, Op. 17.
**(*) Chan. Dig. CHAN 8588 [id.]. Chilingirian Qt.

String quartets Nos. 3, 4 & 5.
*** Chan. Dig. CHAN 8634 [id.]. Chilingirian Qt.

String quartet No. 6; (i) Piano quintet.
*** Chan. Dig. CHAN 8660 [id.]. (i) Steven De Groote; Chilingirian Qt.

The Chilingirian performances have a warm, gutsy quality, based on boundless rhythmic energy and orchestrally rich textures, rather than on knife-edged precision of ensemble. There is the consistent feeling of live communication and, in the slow movements of Nos. 4 and 5 especially, the concentration and intensity of the playing are magnetic. These red-blooded performances receive warm and immediate recording to match. Chandos have then coupled No. 6 with the *Piano quintet* but, for those wanting the six *Quartets*, the Emersons have an added economy of layout and remain first choice.

Violin sonatas Nos. 1 and 2.
(M) **(*) Hung. HCD 11655-2. Kremer, Smirnov.

Both *Sonatas* come from the early 1920s and are among Bartók's most original compositions. Kremer and Smirnov play with total commitment and their performances can only be described as masterly. The recording (from the early 1970s) is rather closely balanced and the acoustic somewhat drier than is ideal, otherwise this would receive a full three-star recommendation, for the performances merit it.

(Solo) *Violin sonata.*
*** Ph. Dig. 420 948-2 [id.]. Viktoria Mullova – BACH: *Partita No. 1 in B min.**** (with
PAGANINI: *Introduction and variations on Nel cor più non misento****).
*** EMI Dig. CDC7 47621-2 [id.]. Nigel Kennedy – ELLINGTON: *Mainly black.****

Viktoria Mullova's account of the Bartók *Sonata* is undoubtedly the best now before
the public. She brings keener musical insights and more finesse to this remarkable score
than Kennedy on EMI. She is much closer to Bartók's own timing, too, and has the
benefit of excellent recording.

Nigel Kennedy also gives a deeply felt reading of the Bartók solo *Violin sonata.* With
vivid recording, full of presence, Kennedy draws beautiful sounds from his instrument
and the immediacy of his response communicates strongly.

*Allegro barbaro; Andante; 3 Burlesques; 10 Easy pieces; 3 Rondos on folk tunes; Rumanian
folk dances; 2 Rumanian dances.*
*(**) ASV Dig. CDDCA 687 [id.]. Peter Frankl.

Peter Frankl plays with splendid fire and spirit, and with no lack of sensitivity. He is
totally inside this music and is wholly persuasive, but he is let down by a rather
unflattering and not fully focused recording balance. The piano itself sounds as if it is in
less than first-class condition and the acoustic is reverberant. This disc has much in its
favour artistically, but its sonic deficiences make a recommendation difficult.

Dance suite; Hungarian peasant songs; 3 Rondos on folk tunes; Rumanian dances.
*** Denon Dig. C37 7092 [id.]. András Schiff (piano).

András Schiff, whose reputation rests on his keenly imaginative readings in the classical
repertory, here demonstrates his red-blooded Hungarian fervour. His range of mood, tone
and expression brings vivid colouring and these *Rumanian dances* have rarely been
played with such infectious rhythms. The piano sound is first rate, with plenty of bite,
and losing inner clarity only with the heaviest textures of the *Dance suite.*

Piano sonata.
*** EMI Dig. CDC7 49916-2 [id.]. Peter Donohoe – BERG; LISZT: *Sonatas.****

Donohoe is very well recorded and plays with the appropriate abandon and no small
degree of imagination. He has a wider range and colour than Foldes' mono version (still
available within a rather unsubtle mid-priced recital: DG 423 958-2) and, with interesting
couplings, this is well worth considering.

OPERA

Bluebeard's Castle (sung in Hungarian).
*** CBS Dig. MK 44523 [id.]. Eva Marton, Samuel Ramey, Hungarian State O, Adam
Fischer.
**(*) Decca 414 167-2 [id.]. Ludwig, Berry, LSO, Kertesz.
(M) **(*) DG 423 236-2 [id.]. Varady, Fischer-Dieskau, Bav. State O, Sawallisch.

The glory of the CBS version is the magnificent singing of Samuel Ramey in the title-
role. With his dark bass, firm and true, beautiful up to a high F, he carries the necessary
threat but equally brings nobility to the part. With him, Bluebeard is virile and even
heroic, the master of his fate; and that goes with a tellingly rugged account of the score
from Hungarian forces under a Hungarian conductor who understand this music from the
inside. Eva Marton, also Hungarian-born, may lack the vulnerability as well as the darker

tone-colours of the ideal Judith but, with more than a touch of abrasiveness in the voice, she still gives a powerful reading. The recording brings full and brilliant sound, well balanced and clear. The single CD comes with libretto in a separate box.

Kertesz's outstanding Decca version is admirably vivid and present, with voices and orchestra beautifully balanced. The serious snag – astonishing in a reissue at full price – is that, unlike the rival versions, it provides no libretto, very important in a work that consists entirely of spoken exchanges and with the sparest of plots.

The reissue of the Sawallisch version at mid-price makes an excellent bargain, particularly when libretto and notes are included. The performance is warmly expressive rather than biting, as you might expect from Sawallisch and the Bavarian State Orchestra. Varady and Fischer-Dieskau give a Lieder-like intensity to the exchanges, full of refined detail. The voices are more forward than on some versions; but the separation from the orchestra is far cleaner than it was on LP and the sound of the Bavarian State Orchestra has satisfying weight.

Bax, Arnold (1883–1953)

(i) *Cello concerto; Cortège; Mediterranean; Northern Ballad No. 3; Overture to a picaresque comedy.*
*** Chan. Dig. CHAN 8494 [id.]. (i) Wallfisch; LPO, Bryden Thomson.

The *Cello concerto* (1934) was Bax's first major work after the *Fifth Symphony*. It is rhapsodic in feeling and Raphael Wallfisch plays it with marvellous sensitivity and finesse, given splendid support by the LPO under Bryden Thomson. The other pieces are of mixed quality: the *Third Northern Ballad* is a dark, brooding score, while the *Overture to a picaresque comedy* is first-rate Bax, high-spirited and inventive. Here Bryden Thomson sets rather too measured a pace for it to sparkle as it should. The recording maintains the high standards of the Bax Chandos series.

The Garden of Fand; The happy forest; November woods; Summer music.
*** Chan. Dig. CHAN 8307 [id.]. Ulster O, Bryden Thomson.

The Celtic twilight in Bax's music is ripely and sympathetically caught in the first three items, while *Summer music*, dedicated to Sir Thomas Beecham and here given its first ever recording, brings an intriguing kinship with the music of Delius. The Chandos recording is superb.

In the faery hills; Into the twilight; Rosc-Catha; The tale the pine-trees knew.
*** Chan. Dig. CHAN 8367 [id.]. Ulster O, Bryden Thomson.

The tale the pine-trees knew is one of the better-known as well as one of the most evocative of Bax's tone-poems, here done with total sympathy. The other three tone-poems form an Irish trilogy. The first two are filled with typically Baxian Celtic twilight, but the last (*Rosc-Catha* meaning 'battle hymn') presents the composer in vigorous, extrovert mood, making an excellent contrast. The performances and recording are well up to the high standard of this series.

On the sea-shore.
*** Chan. Dig. CHAN 8473 [id.]. Ulster O, Handley – BRIDGE: *The Sea*; BRITTEN: *Sea interludes.****

Bax's Prelude, *On the sea-shore*, sensitively orchestrated by Graham Parlett from the composer's short-score, makes a colourful and atmospheric companion to the masterly

Bridge and Britten pieces on the disc, played and recorded with similar warmth and brilliance.

Phantasy for viola and orchestra.
(*) Conifer Dig. CDCF 171 [id.]. Golani, RPO, Handley – ELGAR: *Concerto* etc.

Bax's *Phantasy* is in effect a three-movement viola concerto, drawing heavily on his Irish vein in its use of folk-material. The first movement tends to meander in Bax's semi-improvisatory style, an amiable example of Celtic twilight in music. For all Vernon Handley's devoted advocacy, the piece sounds flabby next to the Elgar with which it is coupled. Excellent recorded sound.

Spring Fire; Northern Ballad No. 2; Symphonic scherzo.
*** Chan. Dig. CHAN 8464 [id.]. RPO, Vernon Handley.

Spring Fire is an early work, but Bax's command of the orchestra is already richly in evidence. The second *Northern Ballad* is dark and bleak, strongly tied to the landscape of the rugged northern coasts. The *Symphonic scherzo* is of less moment than its companions. Highly idiomatic playing from Vernon Handley and the RPO, and a thoroughly lifelike and characteristically well-detailed recording from Chandos.

Symphonic variations for piano and orchestra; Morning Song (Maytime in Sussex).
*** Chan. Dig. CHAN 8516 [id.]. Margaret Fingerhut, LPO, Bryden Thomson.

The *Symphonic variations* is an ambitious score, almost 50 minutes in duration. Margaret Fingerhut reveals it as a work of considerable substance with some sinewy, powerful writing in the more combative variations, thoughtful and purposeful elsewhere. The balance between piano and orchestra could hardly be better judged and more natural; and the orchestral playing under Bryden Thomson is first class. The amiable but discursive *Morning song* makes an agreeable bonus. This CD is in the demonstration class.

Symphony No. 1 in E flat; Christmas Eve.
*** Chan. Dig. CHAN 8480 [id.]. LPO, Bryden Thomson.

Bax's *First Symphony* began life as a piano sonata in 1921. Bryden Thomson is completely inside the idiom and is boldly expressive, relaxing his pace when the natural flow of the music suggests it; and the results carry total conviction. *Christmas eve* is an earlier work, coming from the Edwardian era, but it is a less developed and less interesting piece. Bax's splendid scoring is heard to excellent advantage in the Chandos recording.

Symphony No. 2; Nympholept.
*** Chan. Dig. CHAN 8493 [id.]. LPO, Bryden Thomson.

The *Second Symphony* comes from 1924–6; it is a rich and engrossing work, closely related to nature. The strength of Bryden Thomson's account lies in its breadth and sweep: its evocation of and identification with the natural and spiritual world of this composer. He seems totally at one with Bax's sensibility and secures orchestral playing of total commitment. *Nympholept* means 'possessed by nymphs' and is an imaginative piece, making an admirable fill-up to the *Symphony*. As with other issues in the series, the recording is of spectacular clarity and definition.

Symphony No. 3; Paean; The Dance of Wild Irravel.
*** Chan. Dig. CHAN 8454 [id.]. LPO, Bryden Thomson.

The *Third* is arguably the best, though the *Second* also has strong claims to be so regarded. The opening is one of the composer's finest inspirations and has a searching, visionary quality about it, while the slow movement is wholly unlike anything else in English music. Bryden Thomson is closely attuned to the Bax idiom, and it would be difficult to overpraise him and his fine players. The two companion pieces, the *Paean* and *The Dance of Wild Irravel*, may perhaps strain the allegiance of some – but no matter, the symphony is a sufficient feast; it is Bax's longest at nearly 50 minutes. The Chandos recording does full justice to Bax's sumptuous and opulent orchestral textures.

Symphony No. 4; Tintagel.
*** Chan. Dig. CHAN 8312 [id.]. Ulster O, Bryden Thomson.

The *Fourth Symphony* was written in 1930–31; the seascapes that the score brings to mind are mainly those of the coast and islands of the Western Highlands where Bax spent each winter during the 1930s. The ideas may not be quite as memorable as those of the *Third* and *Fifth*, but the moods are still powerful and the colours vivid. The performance is altogether splendid. The CD is a demonstration disc even by the high standards Chandos have established in this field.

Symphony No. 5; Russian suite.
*** Chan. Dig. CHAN 8669 [id.]. LPO, Bryden Thomson.

With the *Fifth* Bryden Thomson again proves himself completely inside the music's idiom, catching the breadth and sweep of Bax's inspiration and identifying himself consistently with the composer's natural and spiritual world. The playing of the LPO is totally committed and responsive and the Chandos recording well up to the high standards of the house.

Symphony No. 6; Festival overture.
*** Chan. Dig. CHAN 8586 [id.]. LPO, Bryden Thomson.

The *Sixth Symphony* of 1934 is the last major work to find Bax in the fullness of his creative power. Bryden Thomson is scrupulously attentive to the dynamic and agogic markings of the score, and the LPO respond admirably. The makeweight is an early overture of 1912, never recorded before. First-class recording, well up to the high standard of this series.

Symphony No. 7 in A flat; (i) *4 Songs: Eternity; Glamour; Lyke-wake; Slumber song.*
*** Chan. Dig. CHAN 8628 [id.]. (i) Martyn Hill; LPO, Bryden Thomson.

The *Seventh Symphony* comes from 1938, when Bax's creative fires were beginning to burn less brightly, but the slow movement, *In Legendary mood*, is particularly fine, and there is an epic breadth about the first which is impressive. The four songs could not be more different. Martyn Hill does them sensitively, and the playing of the LPO for Bryden Thomson is exemplary in its passion and refinement in both the *Symphony* and the songs. The recording has first-rate presence and body.

Tintagel.
*** EMI CDC7 47984-2 [id.]. LSO, Barbirolli – DELIUS: *Collection*; IRELAND: *London Overture.* ***

Sir John Barbirolli's performance of *Tintagel*, dating from the late 1960s, was the first to be recorded in stereo, and it remains unsurpassed. The sea vistas (with their musical reminders of Debussy as well as Wagner) are magnificently painted by players and recording engineers alike, and Sir John ensures that the memorable principal tune is given a fine romantic sweep. The remastering is highly successful; only a little of the original opulence has been lost, and detail is firmer and clearer with the ambience perfectly judged for the music. If the couplings are suitable, this remains highly recommendable.

Winter Legends; Saga fragment.
*** Chan. Dig. CHAN 8484 [id.]. Margaret Fingerhut, LPO, Bryden Thomson.

The *Winter Legends*, for piano and orchestra, comes from much the same time as the *Third Symphony*, to which at times its world seems spiritually related. The keyboard writing is ambitious; this is in some ways a sinfonia concertante for piano and orchestra rather than a concerto proper. The soloist proves an impressive and totally convincing advocate for the score and it would be difficult to imagine the balance between soloist and orchestra being more realistically judged. The companion piece is a transcription of his one-movement *Piano quartet* of 1922. A quite outstanding disc.

CHAMBER AND INSTRUMENTAL MUSIC

Clarinet sonata.
(*) Chan. CHAN 8683 [id.]. Janet Hilton, Keith Swallow – BLISS: *Clarinet quintet*; VAUGHAN WILLIAMS: *6 Studies.* *

Bax's *Clarinet sonata* opens most beguilingly, and Janet Hilton's phrasing is quite melting. Perhaps the second-movement *Vivace* is less individual, but the playing is very persuasive and on CD the sound is realistically focused within its resonant acoustic. Moreover the Bliss coupling is indispensable.

(i) *Harp quintet;* (ii) *Piano quartet; String quartet No. 1.*
*** Chan. Dig. CHAN 8391 [id.]. (i) Skaila Kanga, (ii) John McCabe; English Qt.

The *First String quartet* has a strong folk element in the finale and the first movement comes close to the sound-world of the Dvořák quartets. Perhaps the finest of the three movements is its elegiac centrepiece. But it is all music with a strong and immediate appeal. The *Harp quintet* is more fully characteristic and has some evocative writing to commend it. The *Piano quartet*, with its winning lyricism, was reworked in the early 1930s for piano and small orchestra as was the *Saga fragment* (see above). These may not be Bax's most important scores, but they are rewarding; and the performances are thoroughly idiomatic and eminently well recorded.

Oboe quintet.
*** Chan. Dig. CHAN 8392 [id.]. Sarah Francis, English Qt – HOLST: *Air & variations*, etc.; MOERAN: *Fantasy Qt*; JACOB: *Quartet.****

Bax's *Oboe quintet*, written for Leon Goossens, is a confident, inventive piece with a hauntingly inspired *Lento* and a gay Irish jig for its finale, though even this movement has a reflective inner core. Sarah Francis proves a most responsive soloist – though she is balanced too close; in all other respects the recording is up to Chandos's usual high standards, and the playing of the English Quartet is admirable.

Piano trio in B flat.
(*) Chan. Dig. CHAN 8495 [id.]. Borodin Trio – BRIDGE: *Trio No. 2.*(*)

The *Piano trio* was Bax's last chamber work, dating from 1946 when his creative fires burned less fiercely. The playing of the Borodin Trio is very distinguished indeed and they seem completely attuned to the idiom. Even if it is not Bax at his best, this is most welcome, particularly in view of the excellence of both performance and recording.

Rhapsodic Ballad (for solo cello).
*** Chan. Dig. CHAN 8499 [id.]. Raphael Wallfisch – BRIDGE: *Cello sonata*; DELIUS: *Cello sonata*; WALTON: *Passacaglia.****

The *Rhapsodic Ballad* for cello alone comes from 1939 and is a freely expressive piece, played with authority and dedication by Raphael Wallfisch. The recording has plenty of warmth and range.

Violin sonatas Nos. 1 in E; 2 in D.
*** Chan. Dig. CHAN 8845 [id.]. Erich Gruenberg, John McCabe.

Both *Sonatas* are early and pre-date the symphonies. The *Second* is the finer of the two and is thematically linked with *November woods*. Rhapsodic and impassioned, this is music full of temperament. Erich Gruenberg is a selfless and musicianly advocate, though some may find his tone not always uniformly beautiful; John McCabe makes an expert partner.

Apple-blossom time; Burlesque; The maiden with the daffodil; Nereid; O dame get up and bake your pies (Variations on a north country Christmas carol); On a May evening; The princess's rose-garden (Nocturne); Romance; 2 Russian tone pictures: Nocturne (May night in the Ukraine; Gopak); Sleepy-head.
**(*) Chan. Dig. CHAN 8732 [id.]. Eric Parkin.

The smaller pieces have considerable charm, and often substance too, as with the *Russian Nocturne* and the comparable *Princess's rose-garden*. They are not among Bax's most important works but in Eric Parkin's hands they certainly sound pleasingly spontaneous.

Piano sonatas Nos. 1 & 2; Country Tune; Lullaby (Berceuse); Winter waters.
**(*) Chan. Dig. CHAN 8496 [id.]. Eric Parkin (piano).

Piano sonatas Nos. 3 in G sharp min.; 4 in G; A Hill tune; In a vodka shop; Water music.
**(*) Chan. Dig. CHAN 8497 [id.]. Eric Parkin.

These *Sonatas* are grievously neglected in the concert hall and even on the gramophone; they are far from negligible, even if they do not show the fires of Bax's inspiration burning at white heat. Eric Parkin proves a sympathetic guide in this repertoire. The recording is on the resonant side and on the second disc the piano is not absolutely perfectly tuned in some of the shorter pieces, but the playing is outstandingly responsive.

Beethoven, Ludwig van (1770–1827)

Piano concertos Nos. 1–5.
(M) *** CBS M3K 44575 (3) [id.]. Perahia, Concg. O, Haitink.
** O-L Dig. 421 408-2 (3) [id.]. Steven Lubin, AAM, Hogwood.

Piano concertos Nos. 1–5; Andante favori; Polonaise in C, Op. 89.
(**) Arabesque mono Z 6549 (*Nos. 1–2*); Z 6550 (*Nos. 3–4*); Z 6551 (*No. 5, Andante* and *Polonaise*) [id.]. Artur Schnabel, LSO or LPO, Sargent.

(i) *Piano concertos Nos. 1–5. 6 Bagatelles, Op. 126; Für Elise.*
(M) ** Decca 425 582-2 (3) [id.]. Ashkenazy (i) Chicago SO, Solti.

Piano concertos Nos. 1–5; (i) *Choral fantasia, Op. 80.*
(M) *** EMI CMS7 63360-2 (3). Daniel Barenboim, New Philh. O, Klemperer, (i) with John Alldis Ch.
(B) **(*) Ph. 422 937-2 (3). Alfred Brendel, LPO, Haitink, (i) with LPO Ch.
**(*) Decca Dig. 421 781-2 (3) [id.]. Ashkenazy, Cleveland O; (i) with Ch.

(i) *Piano concertos Nos. 1–5; Piano sonata No. 32 in C min., Op. 111.*
(B) *** DG 427 237-2 (3) [id.]. Kempff; (i) BPO, Leitner.

CBS have repackaged Murray Perahia's performances at mid-price, which further enhances their attractions. This music always has greater depth than any single interpretation can fathom, but among recent versions the Perahia brings us as close to the heart of this music as any. These are masterly performances, and it is good that their more competitive price will bring them within the reach of an even wider audience. The sound is full and well balanced.

Kempff's accounts offer an additional price advantage since, although the individual issues are all at mid-price, the set is offered at bargain price; the magisterial account of Op. 111 remains coupled with the *Emperor.* The performances all come from the early 1960s and still sound remarkably good for their age, and the wisdom Kempff dispensed is as fresh as ever. He opts for his own cadenzas in Nos. 2–4, which makes a refreshing change – and very authoritative they are. No collector should restrict himself to a single version of these masterpieces for no one pianist can uncover all their profundities, and the Kempff set is undoubtedly among the handful that occupy classic status in the catalogue.

The combination of Barenboim and Klemperer, recording together in 1967/8, is nothing if not stimulating, and for every wilfulness of a measured Klemperer, there is a youthful spark from the spontaneously combusting Barenboim. The recordings were made much more quickly than usual, with long takes allowing a sense of continuity rare on record. The spontaneity easily compensates for any minor shortcomings (in the *Emperor,* for example, Barenboim has some slight fluffs of finger), but the concentration is formidable and especially compelling in the slow movements, whether in the earliest concerto, No. 2 – here given an interpretation that is anything but Mozartian, splendidly strong – or in the later concertos. No. 3 brings the most obviously wilful slow tempi but, with fine rhythmic points from soloist and orchestra, the result is still vivid and compelling. No. 4 is anything but a delicate, feminine work, with basic tempi measured enough to avoid the need for much slowing, when the lyrical counter-subjects emerge. The *Choral fantasia* too is given an inspired performance, with the weaknesses of Beethoven's writing wonderfully concealed when the the music-making is so intense. The remastered sound is vivid and clear and quite full, but orchestral tuttis are less refined than in the Bishop-Kovacevich/Davis Philips recordings.

Given an artist of Brendel's distinction, it would be surprising if his analogue set with Haitink were not artistically in the first flight, even if there are moments (for instance in the *Emperor*) when one's mind returns to his earlier Vox Turnabout recordings, which sounded less studied. Generally, however, there is no lack of spontaneity and the recordings are full and well balanced in the best Philips tradition. The perspective between soloist and orchestra is very well judged and the piano tone itself is lifelike, clean and well focused throughout its register.

Steven Lubin uses four different reproduction fortepianos, each of them contemporary with a given work. Only in No. 4 does the performance seem to miniaturize Beethoven, partly a question of balance, and here the *Andante* dialogue is disappointing. The

Emperor, with the same instrument, sounds far fuller, providing overall weight and the necessary flair to the opening flourishes. Lubin uses the extra clarity of the fortepiano very tellingly and, though speeds are on the brisk side, he is never extreme, and slow movements are allowed to breathe and find poetry and repose. Hogwood accompanies with freshness and resilience, and the recording is attractively vivid.

When Ashkenazy's earlier CD set appeared – with the Vienna Philharmonic under Zubin Mehta – barely five years before the Cleveland one, the dispiritingly limp accompaniment in Nos. 3 and 4 led some commentators to suggest that he would have done better without a conductor. Quicker than anyone had expected, the pianist took up that idea, directing from the keyboard not just in the first three concertos – where that practice has become relatively common – but in Nos. 4 and 5 too. Though some of the easy sparkle has disappeared under the burden of his added duties – as for example in the galloping 6/8 finale of No. 2 – there is a sharp consistency in the Cleveland cycle which puts it ahead both of his Vienna series and of his earlier, Chicago recordings with Solti. At times the onus of conducting shows in the heavy-handedness of tuttis, where the beat is often too rigid and too evenly stressed, so that the music loses its spring and fails to match the solo playing. But that is a relatively unimportant shortcoming, and Ashkenazy scores powerfully in the simple dedication of the slow movements in Nos. 4 and 5, making his earlier versions seem self-conscious by comparison. Like Barenboim and Klemperer, Ashkenazy includes a superb account of the *Choral fantasia* as fill-up in a three-disc set. The Cleveland sound is first rate.

The partnership of Ashkenazy and Solti is fascinating. Where Solti is fiery and intense, Ashkenazy provides an introspective balance. Ashkenazy brings a hushed, poetic quality to every slow movement, while Solti's urgency maintains a vivid forward impulse in outer movements. Sometimes, as in the *C minor Concerto*, one feels that the music-making is too intense. Here a more relaxed and lyrical approach can find in the first movement a warmth that Solti misses. But for the most part the listener is given an overriding impression of freshness, and the *Emperor* performance, while on the grandest scale, has a marvellous individual moment in the first movement when Ashkenazy lingers over the presentation of the second subject. The Chicago orchestral playing is characteristically brilliant, and the one real snag is the very bright recording, which on CD is made to sound uncomfortably fierce at times, while the piano timbre is not as full in sonority as Decca usually provides.

Schnabel's performances fall into a special category. The concertos were recorded in 1932–3, save for the *B flat*, which dates from 1935; the solo pieces come from 1938 and some were unpublished. His playing has such enormous character that it transcends the limitations of sound that are inevitable at this period. The orchestral playing is occasionally lacking in the finesse that we take for granted nowadays, but Schnabel's impulsive, searching and poetic playing offers special rewards. Not everything is equally successful: there is some roughness in the first movement of No. 3, but there are also some marvellously spirited touches. The CD transfers are crystal clear and very little of the 78 r.p.m. hiss is apparent. However, for modern ears some adjustment is necessary to the dry orchestral texture, especially for the listener beginning with No. 1, where there is no bloom on the strings; the *Emperor*, however, sounds surprisingly well. Such is the electricity of the playing that one soon forgets the primitive recording and succumbs to Schnabel's spell. The three CDs are available separately.

(i) *Piano concerto No. 1; Symphony No. 7 in A, Op. 92.*
**(*) Sony Dig. SK 45830 [id.]. (i) Daniel Barenboim; BPO, Barenboim.

Barenboim's Beethoven disc is a live recording of the concert he gave in November

1989 after the Berlin Wall was breached. It was a free concert in the Philharmonie for East German visitors, and something of the emotional tension of the occasion comes over, in warmly spontaneous if not always polished performances, reasonably well recorded. A fair recommendation for a unique coupling.

Piano concertos Nos. 1–2.
(B) *** Ph. 422 968-2 [id.]. Bishop-Kovacevich, BBC SO, Sir Colin Davis.
*** CBS Dig. MK 42177 [id.]. Perahia, Concg. O, Haitink.
(M) *** DG 419 856-2 [id.]. Kempff, BPO, Leitner.
*** DG Dig. 415 682-4 [id.]. Argerich, Philh. O, Sinopoli.
*** EMI Dig. CDC7 49509-2 [id.]. Tan (fortepiano), L. Classical Players, Norrington.
(M) *** Ph. 420 882-2 [id.]. Brendel, LPO, Haitink.
(M) *** Decca Dig. 425 012-2 [id.]. Radu Lupu, Israel PO, Mehta.

There is no finer cycle of the Beethoven *Piano concertos* than Stephen Bishop-Kovacevich's with Sir Colin Davis. These first two works, ideally coupled, bring characteristically crisp and refreshing readings which convey their conviction with no intrusive idiosyncrasies. Bishop opts for the longest and weightiest of Beethoven's own cadenzas for the first movement of No. 1, and his account of the finale has rarely been matched in its sparkle and exhilaration, with wonderfully clear articulation. In No. 2, the pianist plays with a weight and intensity to heighten such visionary passages as the hushed quasi-recitative at the end of the slow movement, while keeping the whole reading in scale with early Beethoven. That these model performances and recordings come on the cheapest Philips label is something to marvel at.

Murray Perahia's coupling of Nos. 1 and 2 brings strong and thoughtful performances very characteristic of this pianist, which yet draw a sharp distinction between the two works. No. 2, the earlier, brings a near-Mozartian manner in the first movement, but then rightly a deep and measured account of the slow movement takes Beethoven into another world, hushed and intense, looking directly forward to the slow movement of the *Fourth Concerto*. The *First Concerto* finds Perahia taking a fully Beethovenian view from the start, bringing a weight to it which leads naturally to his choice of cadenza, the longest that Beethoven wrote, here given with dash and fantasy. In the finale, too, the cadenza brings special point, when Perahia records for the first time an extended version discovered only recently among the composer's sketches. Bernard Haitink proves a lively and sympathetic partner, with the Concertgebouw playing superbly. The recording sets the orchestra in a pleasingly warm acoustic, with the piano sound agreeable if a little dull. There is separate cueing for the cadenzas.

Kempff's coupling is second to none, and the digitally remastered recording sounds remarkably fresh and vivid. The sense of repose is notable in the slow movements, the very profundity of Kempff's sense of calm creating an aura of great serenity. Leitner's contribution, too, is strong and sympathetic, and the orchestral response is memorable throughout. In the finales the playing sparkles joyously. The balance between piano and orchestra is particularly natural.

The conjunction of Martha Argerich and Giuseppe Sinopoli in Beethoven produces performances which give off electric sparks, daring and volatile. Argerich's contribution in phrase after phrase brings highly individual pointing. She is jaunty in allegros rather than lightweight – one might even ask for more *pianissimo* – and slow movements are songful, not solemn. Very distinctive and stimulating performances, given full, vivid – albeit not ideally balanced – sound in a rather reverberant acoustic.

Melvyn Tan's coupling of the first two concertos (using a Derek Adlam reproduction of an 1814 fortepiano) brings performances of natural, unselfconscious expressiveness which will delight those looking for versions on period instruments. Norrington with his London Classical Players observes the fast metronome markings in the score, in this instance put there by Czerny who, as his pupil, should have known Beethoven's mind. Even when Tan's speeds for slow movements are very fast indeed, his ease of expression makes them very persuasive, avoiding breathlessness while simultaneously conveying more gravity than you might expect. It is good too to have the very fast *Allegros* so clean and clear in warm, well-balanced recording.

Surprisingly, there is a spontaneity in Brendel's 1979 studio recordings with Haitink which eluded his later partnership with Levine in the concert hall. Nowhere is this more compelling than in the *First Concerto*, though both he and Haitink convey both the strength and charm of the *Second*, not least in the capriciousness of the finale, even if the slow movement could have been treated more gently. With very good recording, admirers of Brendel need not hesitate.

Lupu's readings with Mehta favour fast, resilient speeds. Slow movements are treated with lightness too, and throughout it is the pianist who dominates. Lupu's playing has both sparkle and sensitivity and its poetry is ever apparent. These are marvellously articulated readings, and if the playing of the Israel Philharmonic is sometimes not very refined it is always sympathetic. Those looking for a mid-priced digital coupling of these works will find the balance is excellently judged and the sound both natural and clear.

Piano concerto No. 2 in B flat, Op. 19.
** Telarc Dig. CD 80064 [id.]. Serkin, Boston SO, Ozawa – *Concerto No. 4.***
** Decca Dig. 411 901-2 [id.]. Ashkenazy, VPO, Mehta – *Concerto No. 4.***

The natural gravitas of Serkin's view of Beethoven's earliest piano concerto – presaging last-period gravity at the end of the *Adagio* – is lightened by the humour of the playing, the inescapable sense of a great musician approaching the music afresh, spontaneously and without a hint of routine. Excellent support from Ozawa and full, vivid recording, but this early digital recording would be more competitive at mid-price.

Ashkenazy's Vienna account of the *Second Piano concerto* is at once restrained and sparkling, thoughtful in the amazingly prophetic quasi-recitative which closes the slow movement, yet keeping the whole work well within an apt scale for early Beethoven. Mehta is an attentive rather than an imaginative accompanist. Excellent recording, bright and atmospheric.

Piano concertos Nos. 2–3.
**(*) RCA RD 85675 [RCA 5675-2-RC]. Rubinstein, Boston SO, Leinsdorf.

Rubinstein's readings in both No. 2 and No. 3 (recorded in 1967 and 1965 respectively) reflect his mastery as a Chopin interpreter. The rubato may be subtle but often is not very Beethovenian, and some may find it mannered. But the sparkle and spontaneity of Rubinstein's playing are vividly conveyed in bright, forward recording, made cleaner on CD, even as the close balance of the soloist is made the more apparent. However, this is another CD which needs reissuing at mid-price.

Piano concertos Nos. 2; 5 (Emperor), Op. 73.
(M) **(*) Decca 417 703-2 [id.]. Ashkenazy, Chicago SO, Solti.
(BB) **(*) Naxos Dig. 8.550121 [id.]. Stefan Vladar (fortepiano), Capella Istropolitana, Barry Wordsworth.

In both concertos the partnership of Ashkenazy and Solti works well, with the vivid orchestral articulation matched by the responsive solo playing. The slow movement of No. 2 is strikingly beautiful and its hushed close creates a memorable feeling of serenity before the sparkling finale. The *Emperor* is an excitingly dramatic performance on the largest possible scale, yet one which is consistently imbued with poetry. The remastered recording is brilliantly vivid, the piano clear and believably focused, but the orchestral textures are leaner than the originals, and some will want a more ample sound in the *Emperor*.

Vladar's fine account of the *Emperor* (see below) is also available coupled with an infectiously vigorous performance of the *Second Concerto*, again very well accompanied by Wordsworth and his chamber group. The sound is full and open, though again the 'twangy' keyboard timbre suggests a fortepiano is in use even if it is not credited.

Piano concerto No. 3 in C min., Op. 37.
** Telarc Dig. CD 80063 [id.]. Serkin, Boston SO, Ozawa – *Choral fantasia.***
(M) ** EMI CDM7 69013-2 [id.]. Sviatoslav Richter, Philh. O, Muti – MOZART: *Piano Concerto No. 22.***

Piano concerto No. 3. Andante favori, WoO 57; Für Elise, WoO 50.
** Decca Dig. 411 902-2 [id.]. Ashkenazy, VPO, Mehta.

All the performances in Ashkenazy's Vienna series with Mehta are more relaxed than in his earlier Chicago set with Solti, but the first movement of the *Third Piano concerto* brings the most striking contrast of all, noticeably slower and less forceful. The result remains compelling, because it sounds so spontaneous. The slow movement is more easily lyrical than before, the finale lighter, more sparkling and with more charm than Ashkenazy usually allows himself. Good, but the coupling is both ungenerous and slight, although both pieces are played persuasively.

Serkin's Telarc version of the *Third Concerto* comes with the bonus of the *Choral fantasia* as coupling. Though the octogenarian soloist's playing lacks some of its old fire, and the *Adagio* – taken relatively fast – is a little casual, the mastery of Serkin's conception is not in doubt. Though piano tone is a little twangy, the recording is outstandingly vivid and full.

Richter's 1978 version may be controversial – like its Mozart coupling – but clearly a master is at the keyboard and Muti draws a sympathetic accompaniment from the Philharmonia players. The performance is consciously wayward, essentially lyrical, but it has undoubted authority, and the remastered recording sounds well.

Piano concertos Nos. 3–4.
(B) *** Ph. 426 062-2 [id.]. Bishop-Kovacevich, BBC SO, Sir Colin Davis.
*** CBS Dig. MK 39814 [id.]. Murray Perahia, Concg. O, Haitink.
(M) *** DG 419 467-2 [id.]. Kempff, BPO, Leitner.
*** EMI Dig. CDC7 49815-2 [id.]. Melvyn Tan (fortepiano), L. Classical Players, Norrington.
(M) **(*) Ph. 420 861-2 [id.]. Brendel, LPO, Haitink.
(M) **(*) Decca 425 000-2 [id.]. Radu Lupu, Israel PO, Mehta.
** EMI CDC7 47714-2 [id.]. Emil Gilels, Cleveland O, Szell.
(M) ** Decca 417 740-2 [id.]. Ashkenazy, Chicago SO, Solti.

The Philips versions of Nos. 3 and 4 from Bishop-Kovacevich and Sir Colin Davis would be top recommendations even if they cost far more. In both works the playing of the soloist has a depth and thoughtful intensity that have rarely been matched, and in his concentration he totally avoids the sort of wilfulness which becomes obtrusive on repeated hearing. The *Third Concerto* brings a first movement which erupts in a commanding account of the big cadenza and, after a central *Largo* taken very slowly and intensely, Bishop-Kovacevich plays the finale with sparkling clarity. His account of the *Fourth Concerto* has a similar combination of strength, dedication and poetry. The refined Philips recording has transferred admirably to CD: the balance is altogether excellent.

Perahia gives readings that are at once intensely poetic and individual, but also strong. In many ways he gives reminders of Wilhelm Kempff, a supreme Beethovenian of his time, with pointing and shading of passage-work that consistently convey the magic of the moment caught on the wing. As with Kempff, the diamond clarity and the touches of poetry may suggest for some an approach not rugged enough for Beethoven; but with Haitink and the Concertgebouw giving firmly sympathetic support, power is conveyed through sharpness of contrast, helped by fine, spacious and open recorded sound.

The Kempff/Leitner performances on DG bring an outstanding mid-priced recommendation. The digital remastering has perceptibly clarified the sound without loss of bloom. In the *C minor Concerto* Kempff's approach is relatively measured, somewhat serious in mood; but in its unforced way, happily lyrical, brightly sparkling in articulation, it is refreshingly spontaneous. Again, in the *Fourth Concerto* Kempff's delicacy of fingerwork and his shading of tone-colour are as effervescent as ever, and the fine control of the conductor ensures the unity of the reading. In both concertos the recording of the orchestra is bright and resonant, the piano tone warm as well as clear.

With the fortepiano balanced naturally against the orchestra of period instruments, not at all spotlit, Melvyn Tan gives fresh and individual performances of both concertos that will delight those who want to hear Beethoven in period style. Though Norrington – relying on the composer's metronome markings – has tended to surprise listeners by his fast speeds in the Beethoven symphonies, that is not a problem here; these accounts of the concertos, using Czerny's metronome marks, bring speeds that would be apt enough for performances with modern instruments. Tan's individual expressiveness comes over naturally and unforcedly, to make these readings characterful without unwanted wilfulness. Naturally balanced, undistracting sound-quality.

Brendel in No. 3 provides an easy, relaxed account of the first movement, spontaneous-sounding, with the timpani raps of the coda even more measured and mysterious than usual. If the other two movements are less tense, with the finale thrown off in a mercurial manner, this adds up to a strong, persuasive performance. No. 4 brings a contrastingly strong, even tough reading, not as immaculate as one might expect on detail, but producing an almost impressionistic thrust of urgency in the first movement. The slow movement is rapt in its simplicity, and the finale is treated almost flippantly, with some slips of ensemble which suggest the immediacy of live music-making, rather than the extra care of the studio. The remastered sound is impressively firm and realistic.

Lupu's versions were originally issued in 1981 and 1978 respectively. Though only the *Third* was recorded digitally, the sound is very good in both concertos. Lupu's reading of No. 3 is forthright and dramatic, yet attentive to every detail of colour and dynamic nuance. He is unfailingly perceptive and musical, though unsmiling at those moments when a gentle poetry surfaces. He is even finer in No. 4, bringing an inner serenity and repose to this magical concerto. Had he enjoyed the advantage of more sensitive orchestral support, this would be a very formidable reissue, but in No. 3 the first desks of the Israel Philharmonic are not heard to flattering effect, and in No. 4 the opening of the slow movement is distinctly coarse. At no time does one feel that Mehta's sensibility is a match for his soloist.

Gilels was one of the keyboard giants of our century and the reissue of his magisterial accounts of the *C minor* and *G major Concertos*, made with the Cleveland Orchestra and Szell in the late 1960s, is naturally welcome; they have been in and out of the LP and cassette catalogues for many years. Szell's contribution is just a little hard-driven. All the same, Gilels is Gilels, and these performances are still very well worth having. One sees no reason, however, why they should have been reissued at full price.

The Ashkenazy/Solti combination also brings playing full of character. The fierce intensity of the orchestral tuttis of the outer movements of the *C minor* may be counted controversial, emphasized by the coarsely lit recording. But the strength of the playing is in no doubt, and the slow movement is finely done, the contrasts stronger than usual. A more relaxed atmosphere pervades the *G major*; here the contrast between the personalities of soloist and conductor is most striking in the interplay of the *Andante*, where Solti's gruff boldness contrasts so tellingly with Ashkenazy's melting response. The 1973 recording produces an attractive piano image, but the orchestra is a bit fierce..

Piano concerto No. 4 in G, Op. 58.
** Telarc Dig. CD 80064 [id.]. Serkin, Boston SO, Ozawa – *Concerto No. 2.***
** Decca Dig. 411 902-2 [id.]. Ashkenazy, VPO, Mehta – *Concerto No. 2.***

Serkin in his eighties may lack some of the brio which made his earlier recordings of the *Fourth Piano concerto* so memorable, but his concentration and sense of spontaneity are as powerful as ever. Though strength is the keynote of his view in the outer movements, and the compression of the slow movement finds him at his most intense, the detailed poetry comes as the magic of the moment, a studio performance that captures the essence of what a live account should be. Excellent recording.

The relaxation and sense of spontaneity which mark Ashkenazy's Vienna cycle bring a performance of the *Fourth* which may lack something in heroic drive, but which in its relative lightness never loses concentration and brings a captivating sparkle to the finale. Though this may not be as powerful as Ashkenazy's earlier Chicago recording with Solti, it is fresher and more natural, with fewer expressive hesitations. Excellent recording to match the rest of the series.

Piano concertos Nos. 4 in G, Op. 58; 5 (Emperor), Op. 73.
(B) *** EMI CDZ7 62607-2. Gieseking, Philh. O, Galliera.
**(*) RCA RD 85676 [RCA 5676-2-RC]. Rubinstein, Boston SO, Leinsdorf.
(M) (**) Decca mono 425 962-2 [id.]. Backhaus, VPO, Clemens Kraus.

To have both of Beethoven's last two concertos on a single disc in EMI's very low-priced Laser series is bargain enough, but these readings are from one of the greatest Beethoven pianists of the first half of the century. These are the recordings that Gieseking made in stereo in September 1955 and which were never issued at the time. Galliera's conducting is not always imaginative, but the Philharmonia gives strong and refined support for Gieseking's magnetic readings. Power was never his watchword, any more than it was with Kempff; yet the concentration and poetry in his playing, the ability to turn a phrase or passage-work in a totally individual way, make this record a fascinating document. He is at his finest in No. 4, where the delicacy of his playing is a constant delight. The slow movement of the *Emperor* tends to be over-inflected, beautiful though the playing is. The stereo sound is very good for its period, generally clear and with plenty of presence.

Rubinstein gives brilliant, spontaneous-sounding performances of both works. In the gentle opening solo of No. 4 the manner is easy and confidential, with no hush or sense of great arguments impending. The exchanges of the slow movement are cleanly and sharply contrasted, with no inner intensity but with keen, bright persuasion. The finale is wonderfully volatile with rhythms neatly pointed. In the *Emperor*, though passage-work is a little sketchy and the slow movement, at a fast speed, becomes a bright untroubled interlude, Rubinstein's totally individual freshness is winning from first to last. The 1960s recordings are bright and sharply focused, with the piano given close balance; this is another candidate for mid-price reissue.

Backhaus's mono recordings date from the early 1950s. The readings have undoubted individuality and No. 4 is lyrically more flexible than his later, stereo version with Schmidt-Isserstedt. The snag here is the sound of the orchestral violins, which have a steely edge, exaggerated by the CD transfer, although the piano image is impressively bold and full. The *Emperor* is characteristically commanding, and here the advantage over the later version (not available on CD), which has striking power and authority, is less certain, although the orchestral sound is fuller.

Piano concerto No. 5 in E flat (Emperor), Op. 73.
*** Ph. Dig. 416 215-2 [id.]. Arrau, Dresden State O, Sir Colin Davis.
*** CBS Dig. MK 42330 [id.]. Perahia, Concg. O, Haitink.
(M) (***) RCA mono GD 87992 [7992-2-RG]. Horowitz, RCA Victor SO, Reiner –
TCHAIKOVSKY: *Piano concerto No. 1.*(***) ✸
**(*) Telarc Dig. CD 80065 [id.]. Serkin, Boston SO, Ozawa.

(i) *Piano concerto No. 5 in E flat (Emperor);* (ii) *Piano sonata No. 15 in D (Pastoral), Op. 28.*
(BB) **(*) Naxos Dig. 8.550290 [id.]. (i) Stefan Vladar (fortepiano), Capella Istropolitana, Barry Wordsworth; (ii) Jenö Jandó.

(i) *Piano concerto No. 5 (Emperor); Piano sonata No. 28 in A, Op. 101.*
(M) **(*) Ph. 426 106-2 [id.]. Casadesus; (i) Concg. O, Hans Rosbaud.

(i) *Piano concerto No. 5 in E flat (Emperor); Piano sonata No. 30 in E, Op. 109.*
✸ (M) *** Ph. 422 482-2 [id.]. Bishop-Kovacevich; (i) LSO, C. Davis.

Piano concerto No. 5 (Emperor); Piano sonata No. 32 in C min., Op. 111.
(M) *** DG 419 468-2 [id.]. Kempff, BPO, Leitner.

(i) *Piano concerto No. 5 (Emperor);* (ii) *Overtures: Coriolan; Leonora No. 2.*
(BB) ** LaserLight Dig. 15 523 [id.]. (i) Anton Dikov, Sofia PO, Emil Tabakov; (ii) Dresden PO, Herbert Kegel.

Piano concerto No. 5 (Emperor); (i) *Choral fantasia, Op. 80.*
✸ *** EMI Dig. CDC7 49965-2. Melvyn Tan, (i) Schütz Ch.; L. Classical Players, Roger Norrington.
(M) **(*) Ph. 420 347-2 [id.]. Brendel, LPO, Haitink, (i) with Alldis Ch.

The wonder is that Arrau, for long an inhibited artist in the studio, should in his newest *Emperor* recording, made when he was over eighty, sound so carefree. There are technical flaws, and the digital recording is rather resonant in bass, but with Sir Colin Davis and the Dresden State Orchestra as electrifying partners, the voltage is even higher than in his earlier versions of the mid-1960s. One would expect Arrau in his eighties to become more reflective, but the opposite is the case. The slow movement flows more freely, less hushed and poised than before, while the finale at a relaxed speed is joyful in its jaunty rhythms. Intensely individual, the very opposite of routine, this is from first to last a performance which reflects new searching by a deeply thinking musician. This is a thrillingly expansive *Emperor* which will give much satisfaction.

Bishop-Kovacevich offers one of the most deeply satisfying versions of this much-recorded concerto ever made. His is not a brash, extrovert way. With alert, sharp-edged accompaniment from Sir Colin Davis, he gives a clean, dynamic performance of the outer movements, then in the central slow movement finds a depth of intensity that completely explodes any idea of this as a lighter central resting-point. Even so he avoids weighing down the simple plan with unstylistic mannerisms: he relies only on natural, unforced concentration in the most delicate, hushed tones. After such raptness, the panache of the finale is all the more exhilarating. The 1969 sound begins to show its age, with the bass a little boomy and the piano rather clattery on fortissimos, though well defined. With volume set high, the recording is still very agreeable, and the magic of the performance is never impaired. On Philips's cheapest Concert Classics label this is an outstanding bargain, particularly when for coupling there is one of the most deeply perceptive performances of a late Beethoven sonata on record. The recording, made in 1978, could be brighter but presents a natural piano tone over the full dynamic range.

Perahia's account of the *Emperor*, strong and thoughtful yet with characteristic touches of poetry, rounds off an outstanding cycle of the Beethoven concertos. The approach is spacious, and with Bernard Haitink and the Concertgebouw Orchestra firm, responsive partners, each movement immediately takes wing, though a touch of bass-heaviness in the recording needs correcting, even on CD.

Kempff's version remains very desirable. Although it is not on an epic scale, it has power in plenty and excitement, too. As ever, Kempff's range of tone-colour is extraordinarily wide, from the merest half-tone as though the fingers were barely brushing the keys to the crisp impact of a dry fortissimo. Leitner's orchestral contribution is of high quality and the Berlin orchestral playing has vigour and warmth. Some reservations need to be made about the sound of the digitally remastered CD. The bass is somewhat over-resonant and the orchestral tuttis are slightly woolly; the piano timbre is natural, but the slight lack of firmness in the orchestral focus is a drawback though it does not seriously detract from the music-making. Opus 111 is undoubtedly a great performance and makes a generous coupling.

Melvyn Tan plays with real flair and musical imagination. He has a poetic fire and brilliance all his own. The disc conveys the feeling of a live performance rather than an academic exercise, and the artists follow Czerny's brisk (and authoritative) tempo markings. The inspiriting account of the *Choral fantasia* possesses a mercurial quality and a panache that show this sometimes underrated work in a most positive light. Norrington and the chorus and orchestra are no less persuasive. In the *Concerto* Tan plays a copy of an 1814 Nanette Streicher, a maker much admired by Beethoven (and with which Tan is associated on record), and in the *Choral fantasia* a copy by Neupert of an instrument from 1815 by Louis Dulcken. A splendidly natural recording completes the attractiveness of this fine disc. The physical effect of the original instruments makes an obvious contrast with Bishop-Kovacevich's splendid Philips version (to which we have also given a Rosette), yet the insights here are every bit as stimulating.

Horowitz's fine record was made in Carnegie Hall in 1952 and few apologies need be made for the sound, which is full and resonant, although the piano timbre seems to harden a little at the opening of the finale. The *Emperor* was the work given in 1933, when the pianist was soloist for the first time with Toscanini. During rehearsals Horowitz met Toscanini's daughter, Wanda, and that December they were married in Milan. However, here Reiner is at the helm and the two great artists form a splendid partnership. Horowitz's virtuosity is always put at Beethoven's service and, for all the excitement of the outer movements, it is the *Adagio* that stays in the mind, classical in line, tender in poetic feeling.

With extraordinarily vivid recording, Serkin's Telarc *Emperor* is very satisfying. The great pianist is almost as commanding as ever, with fire and brilliance in plenty in the outer movements; yet there is also a degree of relaxation, of conscious enjoyment, that increases the degree of communication. The hushed expressive pianism that provides the lyrical contrast in the first movement is matched by the poised refinement of the *Adagio*; the finale is vigorously joyful. Ozawa's accompaniment is first class.

Casadesus and Rosbaud give a most beautiful interpretation, satisfyingly detailed and refined, and with a wonderfully serene Adagio. The Op. 101 *Sonata* is also impressively done, with the recording reasonably full and clear throughout. However, Bishop-Kovacevich and Sir Colin Davis in a similar coupling are even more searching, and they cost less.

Those wanting a fortepiano version of the *Emperor* and who prefer not to make the outlay on a premium-priced disc will find Stefan Vladar's super-bargain version on Naxos both commanding and exciting. The bold opening flourish immediately indicates the very characteristic fortepiano timbre and, although no identification is given in the accompanying documentation, the picture of Beethoven's Broadwood on the cover indicates the nature of the instrument used. The performance, while powerfully direct, still has many individual touches to indicate the degree of imagination at work both from the soloist and in Wordsworth's strong, sympathetic accompaniment. The *Adagio*, which is persuasively shaped, may lack something in idiosyncrasy but there is a real sensitivity here, and the finale is appropriately vigorous and joyful. The sound is splendidly full, with the solo instrument dominating, yet with the orchestra well in the picture. For an encore Jenö Jandó offers an appealing performance of the *Pastoral sonata*, also well recorded. The first two movements are a trifle subdued, but the scherzo is nicely buoyant and the finale catches the spirit of the work's sobriquet engagingly.

Brendel's earlier (1977) account with Haitink is beautifully balanced with a wide range and warmth, and the piano timbre is outstandingly natural. It goes without saying that there is much to admire from the artistic point of view, too. The reading is spaciously conceived and the phrasing has no lack of eloquence. Yet there is also a studied quality about the music-making, particularly in the first movement, that prevents this from being at the top of the list. One has only to turn to the coupling, a splendid performance of the *Choral fantasia*, to have the difference highlighted by the electrifying solo playing at the very opening, where Brendel has a long solo cadenza. However, at mid-price this issue remains very good value, with the recording projecting well on CD.

Anton Dikov gives a strong, forthright performance of the *Emperor*. The music-making is energetically committed, even if it does lack the subtlety of Bishop-Kovacevich's version and the playing of the Sofia Orchestra, although very good, does not have the refinement of the LSO under Davis. Dikov's thundering octaves just before the recapitulation in the first movement are arresting indeed, while the score's gentler moments are also brought out well, and the slow movement has poise and a sense of line. The finale is appropriately joyful. Kegel's *Overtures* are exciting, and the Dresden orchestra displays greater polish and a full sonority – one wishes they could have accompanied the *Concerto*. But with vivid, modern digital sound, this whole record is invigoratingly enjoyable.

Violin concerto in D, Op. 61.
*** EMI Dig. CDC7 47002-2. Perlman, Philh. O, Giulini.
*** Denon Dig. C37 7508 [id.]. Kantorow, Netherlands CO, Ros-Marba.
(M) *** EMI CD-EMX 2069. Yehudi Menuhin, VPO, Silvestri.
*** DG 413 818-2 [id.]. Mutter, BPO, Karajan.
(*) RCA RD 85402 (RCD1 4502). Heifetz, Boston SO, Munch – BRAHMS: *Concerto*.*

(M) (***) EMI mono CDH7 69799-2 [id.]. Yehudi Menuhin, Philh. O, Furtwängler – MENDELSSOHN: *Concerto*.(***)

(M) **(*) RCA Dig. GD 86536 [6536-2-RG]. Ughi, LSO, Sawallisch – MENDELSSOHN: *Concerto*.**(*)

(M) **(*) EMI CDM7 69261-2 [id.]. David Oistrakh, Fr. Nat. R. O, Cluytens – BRUCH: *Concerto No. 1*.(***)

(B) Pickwick Duet 9 CD [CBS MGT 31418]. Stern, NYPO, Bernstein – BRAHMS: *Violin concerto.*

(i) *Violin concerto in D, Op. 61;* (ii) *Romances Nos. 1 in G, Op. 40; 2 in F, Op. 50.*
*** EMI Dig. CDC7 49567-2 [id.]. Perlman, BPO, Barenboim.
🏵 (B) *** DG 427 197-2 [id.]. (i) Schneiderhan, BPO, Jochum; (ii) D. Oistrakh, RPO, Goossens.
(B) *** Ph. 426 064-2 [id.]. Grumiaux; (i) New Philh. O, Galliera; (ii) Concg. O, Haitink.
(M) *** Ph. 420 348-2 [id.]. Grumiaux, Concg. O, C. Davis, or New Philh. O, De Waart.
*** RCA Dig. RD 87777 [7777-2-RC]. Joseph Swensen, RPO, Previn.
*** Ph. 416 418-2 [id.]. Szeryng, Concg. O, Haitink.
*** CRD CRD 3353 [id.]. Ronald Thomas, Bournemouth Sinf.
(B) **(*) EMI CDZ7 62510-2. Josef Suk; (i) New Philh. O, Boult; (ii) ASMF, Marriner.

Violin concerto in D, Op. 61; Romance No. 2 in F, Op. 50.
*** ASV Dig. CDDCA 614 [id.]. Shumsky, Philh. O, Andrew Davis.

Violin concerto in D, Op. 61; Overture Egmont, Op. 84.
(B) *** Ph. 422 971-2 [id.]. Hermann Krebbers, Concg. O, Haitink.

Perlman's Berlin recording was made at a live performance in the Philharmonie in Berlin in 1986. The live occasion prompts the soloist to play with extra flair and individuality, spontaneous in imagination, with depth of insight married to total technical command. The power and purposefulness of Perlman's playing are established on his very first entry after the opening tutti; from then on he plays with a persuasiveness even beyond the similarly spacious reading he recorded in the studio just a little over five years earlier, with Giulini conducting (EMI CDC7 47002-2, which is still available). Like most latterday recordings, this one has the Kreisler cadenzas, and in playing them Perlman caps all rivals in sheer excitement and bravura. Though (as always with Perlman) the solo violin is balanced well forward, the sound is not overbearing. Anyone wanting a modern digital version cannot do better than opt for this. The two *Romances*, recorded by the same performers in the studio, are just as persuasive, with Perlman particularly sweet and tender in his expansive account of No. 2.

Perlman's outstanding early EMI digital recording of Beethoven's *Violin concerto* must be counted among the great recordings of this work, but his newest recording, which has also the *Romances*, now takes its place in the catalogue.

One of the joys of Oscar Shumsky's version of Beethoven's *Violin concerto* with the Philharmonia is its sense of naturalness and style. His playing is distinguished by a total lack of affectation and by great purity of line, and there seems to be good rapport between soloist and orchestra. The performance is unhurried and refreshingly unanxious to impress: he is agreeably old-fashioned without being overtly romantic (he pulls back for the G minor episode in the first movement, as did Kreisler, whose cadenzas he plays). The only reservation of note is that Shumsky is placed slightly too much to the fore in the aural picture, though this emphasis is in no sense excessive (indeed, there are many worse offenders: EMI for Perlman, DG for Mutter, Philips for Szeryng, and so on), and orchestral detail is never obscured. He has sympathetic support from the Philharmonia and Andrew Davis.

Kantorow, who has also recorded a very successful set of the Mozart concertos for Denon, follows a performing tradition in the Beethoven *Violin concerto* whose most distinguished recent advocate was Wolfgang Schneiderhan. Kantorow's playing has a comparable incandescent classical lyricism and unforced naturalness of line and phrasing, and his reading takes its place alongside the very finest recorded versions. The slow movement is very moving in its gentle sustained intensity, while the finale is nimble in articulation, yet with lyrical feeling still very much to the fore. The use of a chamber-sized accompanying group enhances the classical scale of the performance, with Ros-Marba providing an understanding if relaxed supporting role. The recording is first class, very well balanced in a spacious acoustic framework which never clouds detail.

Schneiderhan's outstanding version of the Beethoven *Concerto*, recorded in 1962, is most welcome on CD. The serene spiritual beauty of the slow movement is truly memorable; throughout, Jochum's accompaniment has a dignified breadth which provides an ideal backcloth for the beautiful silver thread of tone from the soloist. David Oistrakh's accounts of the *Romances* are of high quality too, and the remastering is well managed. It is fascinating to compare Oistrakh's strong, aristocratic way with Beethoven with Schneiderhan's pure inspirational lyricism.

It is good, too, to have Menuhin's first stereo recording with Silvestri back in the catalogue; it is far preferable to his more recent versions with Klemperer and Masur. This is a noble performance, very comparable with his mono record with Furtwängler, but of course the sound is greatly improved. Silvestri is surprisingly classical in his outlook and the VPO provide an accompaniment of great character. Menuhin's warmth and humanity show in his instinctive shaping of phrases, and his slightly slower tempi add breadth and boldness to a design that can easily be spoiled by ill-judged emphasis. His playing in the slow movement is particularly lovely, and the intonation here is rock-steady. The remastering is vividly successful, with the orchestra full-bodied and rich in the bass.

Grumiaux recorded the Beethoven *Violin concerto* twice for Philips in stereo, the first occasion in the late 1960s with Galliera in London, and again in the mid-1970s with Sir Colin Davis in Amsterdam. The balance of advantage between the two versions – both among the finest ever committed to disc – is very difficult to resolve, although the earlier version has a price advantage. The Concertgebouw recording is fuller and richer, even if there is not absolute clarity, and there is less background noise. With sharper orchestral ensemble under Davis, the outer movements seem even more impressive than with the New Philharmonia under Galliera. Grumiaux imbues both performances with a spirit of classical serenity. But in the slow movement there is not quite the same sense of repose or of spontaneous magic in the later account. Both discs include the *Romances*, appealingly played, and in each instance the recording is of a slightly different vintage, brighter and clearer.

The slow basic tempi of Anne-Sophie Mutter's beautiful reading on DG were her own choice, she claims, and certainly not forced on her by her superstar conductor. The first two movements have rarely, if ever, been more expansively presented on record, but the purity of the solo playing and the concentration of the whole performance make the result intensely convincing. The finale is relaxed too, but is well pointed, at a fair tempo, and presents the necessary contrast. Good atmospheric recording against the warm acoustic of the Philharmonie Hall in Berlin.

Joseph Swensen is an American player, born in 1960, with a mixture of Norwegian and Japanese ancestry. His account of the *Concerto* is one of the most thoughtful to have appeared in recent years. He gives an unemphatic, reflective account of the solo part in which overstatement plays no part and, as one would expect, is immaculate in matters of intonation and technique. He uses the four cadenzas which Beethoven wrote for the transcription of the work as a piano concerto (commissioned by Clementi). The RPO under André Previn are supportive and the recording produces a very natural balance. The two *Romances* are well played too. Not the most powerful version, but a most satisfying one.

As a soloist Hermann Krebbers has not quite the commanding 'star' quality of David Oistrakh, Menuhin or even Grumiaux, but he plays with an appealing naturalness and a totally unforced spontaneity. In his hands the slow movement has a tender simplicity which is irresistible, and it is followed by a delightfully relaxed and playful reading of the finale. In the first movement Haitink and his soloist form a partnership which brings out the symphonic strength more than almost any other reading. If the balance of the soloist is a shade too close, the recording is otherwise excellent, and it has transferred with vivid fullness to CD.

Szeryng's 1974 recording with Haitink brings a superb balance between lyricism and power. The orchestral introduction is immediately riveting in its breadth and sense of scale, and throughout the first movement Szeryng's playing has great beauty. His use of the Joachim cadenza is an added attraction. The slow movement blossoms with a richly drawn line; after this, the link into the finale is managed with a fine sense of spontaneity. The dance-like mood which follows completes an interpretation that is as satisfying in its overall shape as in its control of mood and detail. The recording is full and resonant. Fine performances of the *Romances* (recorded two years earlier) are offered as a bonus.

Heifetz's unique coupling of the Beethoven and Brahms *Concertos* on a single disc is only possible because of his consistent refusal to linger. RCA's digital transfer of a recording originally made in the very earliest days of stereo has a fine sense of realism and presence, with the soloist only a little closer than is natural. The extra immediacy of CD reinforces the supreme mastery of a performance which may adopt fast speeds but never sounds rushed, finding time for individuality and imagination in every phrase. For some listeners, the comparative lack of serenity in the first movement (though not in the *Larghetto*) will be a drawback, but the drama of the reading is unforgettable. Heifetz's unique timbre is marvellously captured; the assured aristocracy of the playing confounds criticism.

Recorded only months before the conductor's death, Menuhin's version with Furtwängler is a classic which emerges with extraordinary freshness. The bond between the wrongly reviled conductor and his Jewish champion brought an extra intensity to a natural musical alliance between two inspirational artists, here both at their peak. Rarely if ever has the Beethoven *Violin concerto* been recorded with such sweetness and tenderness, yet with firm underlying strength. With its generous coupling, it is a compact disc which defies the years. One hardly registers that this is mono recording.

Ronald Thomas, directing from the violin, gives a thoughtful and direct reading which in its beauty and poise is most refreshing, particularly as the recorded sound is excellent and the playing of the Bournemouth Sinfonietta first rate. Thomas may miss the finest flights of individual poetry, but the unity of the performance is totally compelling. The *Romances*, too, are beautifully played and the remastered recording is naturally balanced.

Ughi's version has first-class digital recording, realistic and very well balanced: this mid-priced CD is coupled with a strikingly fine performance of the Mendelssohn *Concerto* (also digitally recorded). The performance of the Beethoven is first rate, fresh and unaffected, marked by consistent purity of tone in every register. If the last degree of imagination, of the kind which creates special magic in the slow movement, is missing here, nevertheless this remains well worth considering for those with limited budgets.

Suk's version with the New Philharmonia under Boult was very well recorded in its day (1971) and still sounds good, though there is a touch of thinness on the violin timbre, and the orchestra, though clearer, has lost a little of its fullness. The reading is characteristically assured, the soloist's phrasing and sense of line impeccable and the slow movement, although restrained, is serenely beautiful. With the two *Romances* comparable in mood, this is good value on EMI's Laser bargain label.

David Oistrakh's strong, aristocratic reading dates from 1958, but the EMI recording still sounds well, with a spacious acoustic and resonant orchestral tone. The balance, however, places the soloist unnaturally forward, although he is recorded truthfully. The reading is characteristically assured, the soloist's phrasing and sense of line impeccable; but for some there is a suggestion of aloofness in the slow movement.

Stern's early stereo recording – issued on Pickwick's Duet bargain label coupled with the Brahms *Concerto* – established an intense creative relationship with Bernstein. The reading has a tremendous onward flow, counterbalancing its lyrical beauty. Its energy is compulsive. The snag is that the close CBS recording prevents any pianissimo in the slow movement, while the CD transfer brings unacceptably shrill orchestral tuttis.

(i) *Violin concerto in D;* (ii) *Violin sonata No. 9 (Kreutzer).*
(M) (***) EMI mono CDH7 63194-2 [id.]. Bronislaw Huberman; (i) VPO, Szell; (ii) Ignaz Friedman.

Huberman's is a legendary reading, recorded with George Szell and the Vienna Philharmonic in June 1934. What must strike the modern listener is that – whether or not influenced by the restrictions of short-playing 78-r.p.m. sides – the basic speed for the first movement is markedly faster than on most modern versions; yet there is no feeling of haste, and Huberman's immaculate intonation makes for ravishing sounds, particularly in the topmost register. Rarely has any later recording matched the rapt, sweet intensity of the coda in this version. The lovely third theme in the slow movement brings comparable intensity, though the close balance of the violin, typical of 78 recording, is not helpful, and Huberman, like other violinists of his generation, uses more portamento than is expected nowadays. The account of the *Kreutzer sonata*, which Huberman recorded with Ignaz Friedman in 1930, has similar bite and intensity, though with heavy surface hiss the sound shows its age more, and the piano is backwardly balanced. A generous coupling that gives a superb idea of the artistry of a master violinist long neglected.

(i) *Piano concerto in D* (arr. from *Violin concerto*), *Op. 61;* (ii) *Romances Nos. 1–2, Opp. 40 & 50.*
(M) **(*) DG 429 179-2 [id.]. (i) Barenboim, ECO; (ii) Zukerman, LPO, Barenboim.

Beethoven's transcription of his *Violin concerto* into this piano version made little or no effort to rework the solo part in pianistic terms. The result is to alter the character of the music, bringing down the emotional scale and substituting charm where in the original there is great spiritual depth. The work could not receive a more dedicated or affectionate performance than it does here: Barenboim makes the most of the limited piano part, and he is delightful in the slow movement. (Incidentally, the special cadenzas featuring the timpani can also be heard in the outstanding Schneiderhan and Swensen versions of the original.) Zukerman's performances of the *Romances* are a welcome makeweight.

Triple concerto for violin, cello and piano in C, Op. 56.
(B) *** Pickwick Dig. PCD 917. Trio Zingara, ECO, Heath – BOCCHERINI: *Concerto No. 7.****
(B) **(*) EMI CDZ7 62854-2 [id.]. D. Oistrakh, Knushevitzky, Oborin, Philh. O, Sargent – BRAHMS: *Double concerto.****
*** Capriccio Dig. 10 150 [id.]. Funke, Timm, Rösel, Dresden PO, Kegel – *Choral fantasia.****

Triple concerto, Op. 56; Overtures: Coriolan; Egmont; Fidelio.
**(*) DG 415 276 [id.]. Mutter, Zeltser, Yo-Yo Ma, BPO, Karajan.

Triple concerto, Op. 56; Romances for violin and orchestra Nos. 1 in G, Op. 40; 2 in F, Op. 50.
*** EMI Dig. CDC7 47427-2 [id.]. Hoelscher, Schiff, Zacharias, Leipzig GO, Masur.

(i) *Triple concerto, Op. 56; Variations on 'Ich bin der Schneider Kakadu', Op. 121a.*
**(*) Ph. 420 231-2 [id.]. Beaux Arts Trio; (i) LPO, Haitink.

(i) *Triple concerto, Op. 56; Piano sonata No. 17 in D min. (Tempest), Op. 31/2.*
(M) **(*) EMI CDM7 69032-2 [id.]. David Oistrakh, Rostropovich, Sviatoslav Richter, (i) BPO, Karajan.

The cellist in the Trio Zingara is Felix Schmidt, who is also the soloist in the Boccherini. In the Beethoven *Triple concerto* it is that instrument which continually takes the lead, and Schmidt plays with consistently beautiful, firm and clean tone, well matched by his two partners. It is not just a question of a regular trio working naturally together, but of them jointly – together with the conductor, Edward Heath – creating the illusion of live performance, full of bounce and vigour. At mid-price, in full and vivid digital sound and well coupled with the Boccherini, it makes an excellent recommendation.

Led by the cellist, Heinrich Schiff – a balance of responsibility suggested by Beethoven's own priorities in this work – the soloists in Masur's version make a characterful but finely integrated trio. The long span of the first movement is firmly held together, the brief slow movement has inner intensity without being overweighted, while the finale is ideally clean and light. The sound is both full and detailed, far preferable to Karajan on DG. The two *Romances* are persuasively done and make a generous fill-up, with the most engaging orchestral detail in the accompaniment.

The star-studded cast on the other EMI recording make a breathtaking line-up, and to have Karajan as well seems almost too good to be true. The results are predictably arresting, with Beethoven's priorities among the soloists well preserved in the extra dominance of Rostropovich over his colleagues. This is warm, expansive music-making that confirms even more clearly than before the strength of the piece. The resonant recording suffers from loss of focus in some climaxes, but this is not too serious. Richter's powerful reading of Beethoven's *D minor Sonata* makes a good coupling.

The EMI Laser recording, with its distinguished alternative Russian solo group, dates from the early days of stereo, but the balance (with Walter Legge producing) is very successful. Sargent does not direct the proceedings with Karajan's flair but he is authoritative and musical, and his soloists make a good team, as well as displaying plenty of individual personality. The slow movement is strikingly eloquent. In EMI's Laser series and with an outstanding version of the Brahms *Double concerto* as coupling, the bargain status is obvious.

As an alternative, the choice of the world's most distinguished piano trio is a natural casting for this great but wayward concerto. Consistently the joy of this performance –

with the soloists sharply focused in front of the orchestra – is to relish the interplay between the instruments. Haitink's splendid direction helps, too. The engineers have found the problems of balance difficult to resolve, but the sound nevertheless has the beauty and refinement of the best Philips analogue offerings and the CD transfer enhances the overall clarity. The *Variations* make a refreshing encore piece.

In the East German performance the three soloists, Christian Funke, Jürnjacob Timm and Peter Rösel, play rather as a team in the outer movements, but in the slow movement their personalities blossom, particularly that of the fine cellist, while in the finale there is a striking lightness of articulation and a lively rhythmic emphasis from the conductor, Herbert Kegel. The recording is realistically balanced. While other versions may offer stronger projection up front, this performance has plenty of energy and momentum and also an outstanding coupling, a most successful version of the *Choral fantasia*.

For their CD issue, DG have added three overtures as a reasonably generous makeweight, while the detail of the analogue recording has been sharpened, but the point is emphasized that after Karajan's formidable crescendo, within his very positive opening tutti, the soloists seem rather small-scale. But there are benefits from the unity brought by the conductor when each of the young players has a positive contribution to make, no less effectively when the recording balance for once in this work does not favour the solo instruments unduly. But the urgency, spontaneity and – in the slow movement – the depth of expressiveness make for an enjoyable version, well recorded.

The Creatures of Prometheus: Overture and ballet music, Op. 43 (complete).
*** DG Dig. 419 608-2 [id.]. Orpheus CO.

As this splendid recording demonstrates, there is much to admire in this lesser-known Beethoven score, often anticipating later, greater works in sudden flashes, with moods varying widely from tragedy to country-dance felicity. The very talented conductorless orchestra plays most stylishly, helped by bright, clean recording.

March for wind sextet, WoO 29; Military marches, WoO 18–21; 24; Ecossaise, WoO 22.
** DG 419 624-2 [id.]. BPO Wind, Priem-Bergrath – *Egmont***(*); *Wellington's victory.***

This seems a strange coupling for *Egmont*; the performances are routine ones, though well played. The 1969 recording, made in the Jesus-Christus Kirche, Berlin (a curious venue), is not very sharply defined.

OVERTURES

Overtures: The Consecration of the house, Op. 124; Coriolan, Op. 62; The Creatures of Prometheus, Op. 43; Egmont, Op. 84; Fidelio, Op. 72c; King Stephen, Op. 117; Leonora Nos. 1–3, Opp. 138; 72a; 72b; The Ruins of Athens, Op. 113; Zur Namensfeier, Op. 115.
(M) *** DG 427 256-2 (2) [id.]. BPO, Karajan.

Karajan's set of overtures was recorded in the mid- and late 1960s. They are impressive performances that have stood the test of time. They show an imposing command of structure and detail as well as the customary virtuosity one expects from this conductor and the Berlin Philharmonic. The sound is fresh and bright in its remastered format; at Privilege price, this set is excellent value.

Overtures: The Consecration of the house, Op. 124; Coriolan, Op. 62; The Creatures of Prometheus, Op. 43; Egmont, Op. 84; Fidelio, Op. 72c; King Stephen, Op. 117; Leonora No. 2, Op. 72a; The Ruins of Athens, Op. 113.
(M) **(*) Nimbus NI 5205 [id.]. Hanover Band, Roy Goodman or Monica Huggett.

Recorded at various periods in conjunction with the Hanover Band's other Beethoven recordings for Nimbus, this compilation makes a generous and attractive collection, an admirable supplement to this orchestra's Beethoven symphony cycle. Anyone who wants the principal Beethoven overtures played on period instruments will be well pleased.

Overtures: Coriolan, Op. 62; The Creatures of Prometheus, Op. 43; Egmont, Op. 84; Leonora No. 1, Op. 138; Leonora No. 3, Op. 72b; The Ruins of Athens, Op. 113.
(M) *** CBS Dig. MDK 44790 [id.]. Bav. RSO, C. Davis.

This CBS CD is very well recorded – the sound is spacious and beautiful, full yet refined, and has a remarkably wide dynamic range. Sir Colin Davis secures playing of distinction from the Bavarian orchestra and while it was a pity that *Leonora No. 2* was omitted, this remains a distinguished collection. Now reissued at mid-price, it too can be recommended with enthusiasm.

Romances for violin and orchestra Nos. 1 in G, Op. 40; 2 in F, Op. 50.
*** Ph. Dig. 420 168-2 [id.]. Zukerman, St Paul CO – DVORÁK: *Romance*; SCHUBERT: *Konzertstücke* etc.***

Beethoven's two *Romances* could hardly be played more winningly than they are within this attractively chosen collection of short concert pieces for violin and orchestra. A disc which is more than the sum of its parts.

SYMPHONIES

Symphonies Nos. 1–9.
(B) *** DG 429 036-2 (5) [id.]. Janowitz, Rössl-Majdan, Kmentt, Berry & V. Singverein (in No. 9), BPO, Karajan.
(BB) **(*) LaserLight Dig. 15 900 (5). Hungarian PO, Ferencsik (with Andor, Szirmay, Korondy, Solyom-Nagy & Budapest Philharmonic Ch. in No. 9).
**(*) Nimbus Dig. NI 5144/8 (5). Soloists, Ch., Hanover Band, Monica Huggett (*Nos. 1, 2 & 5*), Roy Goodman (*Nos. 3, 4, 6, 7–9*).
(M) ** Telarc Dig. CD 80200 (5) [id.]. Soloists, Ch., Cleveland O, Dohnányi.

Symphonies Nos. 1–9; Overtures: Coriolan; Creatures of Prometheus; Egmont.
**(*) EMI Dig. CDS7 49852-2 (6). Kenny, Walker, Power, Salomaa, Schütz Ch. (in No. 9), L. Classical Players, Norrington.

Symphonies Nos. 1–9; Overtures: Coriolan; Creatures of Prometheus; Egmont; Fidelio; King Stephen; Leonora No. 3.
(M) ** DG 423 481-2 (6) [id.]. VPO, Bernstein (with soloists & V. State Op. Ch. in No. 9).

Symphonies Nos. 1–9; Overtures: Coriolan; The Creatures of Prometheus; Egmont; Fidelio; Leonora No. 3; The Ruins of Athens.
(M) *** DG 429 089-2 (6). Tomowa-Sintow, Baltsa, Schreier, Van Dam, V. Singverein, BPO, Karajan.

Symphonies Nos. 1–9; Overtures: Coriolan; Egmont.
**(*) O-L Dig. 425 696-2 (6) [id.]. Augér, Robbin, Rolfe-Johnson, Reinhard, LSO Ch. (in No. 9); AAM, Hogwood.

Symphonies Nos. 1–9; Overtures: Coriolan; Egmont; Fidelio; Leonora No. 3.
** DG Dig. 415 066-2 (6) [id.]. Soloists, V. Singverein, BPO, Karajan.
(M) ** Ph. 416 274-2 (6) [id.]. Leipzig GO, Masur (with soloists and chorus).

Symphonies Nos. 1–9; Overtures: Coriolan; Egmont; Leonora No. 3.
(M) (**) Decca 421 673-2 (6) [id.]. Chicago SO, Solti (with soloists & Ch. in No. 9).

Symphonies Nos. 1–9; Overture Leonore No. 3.
(M) (***) RCA mono GD 60324 (5) [60324-2-RG]. Farrell, Merriman, Peerce, Scott, Shaw Chorale (in No. 9), NBC SO, Toscanini.

Symphonies Nos. 1–9; 10 (realized Cooper): *1st movt; Overtures: Coriolan; The Creatures of Prometheus* (with rehearsals of *Symphonies Nos. 6 & 10*).
*** Chan. CHAN 8712/7 (6) [id.]. Barstow, Finnie, Rendall, J. Tomlinson, CBSO Ch., CBSO, Weller.

When over the winter of 1961–2 Karajan and the Berlin Philharmonic recorded all nine *Symphonies*, it marked a breakthrough in the history of recording. The project was conceived from the start as a cycle in a way never attempted on record before. It then made its first appearance in boxed format, another important innovation which pointed to the future. Of Karajan's four recorded cycles this is the most consistent and in many ways the most compelling, combining high polish with a biting sense of urgency and spontaneity. There is one major disappointment, in the over-taut reading of the *Pastoral*, which in addition omits the vital repeat in the scherzo. Otherwise these are incandescent performances, superbly played. Designedly, Karajan left the *Eroica* and the *Ninth* till last in the intensive recording sessions, and that helped to give extra power of communication to those supreme masterpieces. On CD the sound is still excellent, the best balanced in any of his Beethoven series and with a keener sense of presence, helped by the acoustic of the Jesus-Christus-Kirche in Berlin. On five CDs at bargain price, this makes outstanding value for money.

Karajan's 1977 cycle is offered on six CDs at mid-price, including the major overtures. Interpretatively his view on Beethoven had changed relatively little, but some differences are significant. The *Eroica* presents the one major disappointment of this cycle, at least in the outer movements, which are faster and slightly rushed, though the Funeral march remains measured and direct. As against this, the first movement of the *Pastoral*, angular and tense in the 1962 cycle, has more elegance and joyfulness at tempi barely any slower. Otherwise the middle symphonies remain very much the same in both cycles, although in 1977 finales tend to be a little faster than before. Just as the cycle of 1962 established standards which were hard for any rival to match, so the 1977 cycle, different in emphasis on certain symphonies, is also very satisfying. The cycle is capped by a version of the *Choral symphony* that is among the finest ever committed to disc. However, in terms of sound the later cycle does not necessarily show an improvement, and for most collectors the earlier set will prove the more rewarding purchase.

Walter Weller's Beethoven cycle for Chandos is by far his finest achievement on record. Although this is the City of Birmingham Symphony Orchestra, there is a warm, refined, Viennese quality in the playing and interpretation, to remind you that this conductor started his career as concertmaster of the Vienna Philharmonic. The Chandos sound is full and glowing to match, by far the finest to date given to any conductor in a collected Beethoven cycle. The sixth (supplementary) disc brings Dr Barry Cooper's re-creation of the first movement of No. 10, plus substantial extracts of rehearsal and two overtures. Broadly speaking, one might categorize Weller as a Beethovenian whose sympathies centre on the even-numbered symphonies, rather than on the odd-numbered works with their cataclysmic symphonic statements. Not that the great odd-numbered symphonies lose freshness or bite under Weller; but these are all friendly performances which, in their continuing alertness and the feeling of live communication, give consistent pleasure.

There is an exuberance and a sense of joyful adventure running through all of them, so that even the first movement of the *Eroica* (with exposition repeat observed) is presented in happy optimism rather than in epic grandeur. The *Seventh* and the *Pastoral*, incidentally, are the only two symphonies in which Weller omits exposition repeats. These are not the most monumental readings you will find, but they are the most companionable; and that applies too to the final culmination, the *Ninth*.

Of the Beethoven cycles on period instruments Hogwood's with the Academy of Ancient Music in many ways makes the safest recommendation. It is the most vividly recorded, with the keenest sense of presence and, above all, the sound adds appropriate weight to the *Ninth*, with the LSO Chorus fuller and more vivid than rival choirs for Norrington and Goodman. Hogwood also has the finest quartet of soloists, though in the first movement he is too rigid. Like his rivals, Hogwood has taken note of Beethoven's metronome markings, but he applies them rather less consistently. His pointing of rhythms is not always as alert or imaginative as that of his direct rivals; as a whole, the cycle may lack something in individual moments of insight but, with clean and generally well-disciplined playing, it is consistently satisfying.

Of the first three recorded Beethoven cycles to appear using period instruments, Norrington's is the most strongly characterized. It is also the most controversial, when he makes it a point of principle to observe Beethoven's often questionable metronome markings, generally very fast, and at times with breathless results. Yet with the tang of authentic brass and timpani steadfastly brought out, and with imaginative detail that regularly magnetizes the ear, they make a consistent and satisfying series. Even more than his rivals, Norrington makes you listen afresh. The recording is not always as clean or well focused as it might be, but the only major blot is the disappointing singing of the male soloists in the finale of the *Ninth*.

With Bernstein's electricity – partly achieved by recording at live performances – matched against the traditional warmth of Viennese playing, the results are consistently persuasive, culminating in a superb, triumphant account of the *Ninth* with a fast, tense first movement, a resilient scherzo, a hushed expansive reading of the *Adagio* and a dramatic account of the finale. Balances are not always perfect, with microphones placed in order to eliminate audience noise, but the results are generally undistracting. The CD transfers, as one would expect, clarify and freshen the sound, removing any gauziness; but they also make the occasional oddities of balance more obvious.

Ferencsik's excellent set of Beethoven *Symphonies* with the Hungarian Philharmonic Orchestra comes on five CDs at super-bargain price. Each has its own individual jewel-case, within a slip-case, and there is adequate documentation. These CDs are almost unbelievably inexpensive and well worth their modest price. The orchestral playing is of good quality, if without quite the finesse or rhythmic resilience of Jochum's comparable Philips set – as is noticeable immediately in the *First Symphony* – but ensemble is always impressive, and the players' undoubted commitment conveys a sense of enjoyment and usually a feeling of spontaneity. Often the playing is really exciting, as in the outer movements of the *Seventh* (a performance which grips from beginning to end) and in the rhythmically strong *Eroica* (given without the first-movement exposition repeat) and in the allegros of the earlier symphonies. Nos. 4 and 8 are particularly successful, and no one could fault the *Fifth* for lack of energy or impetus. The *Pastoral* is mellow and pleasingly paced. (Jochum is warmer, but more relaxed in his tempi.) The series is capped by a performance of the *Choral symphony* which, while not lacking strength, begins a little soberly, offers a simple, rather withdrawn slow movement, and then explodes into a finale of great fervour, with soloists and chorus – most effectively balanced – joining in an exultant celebration of human joy, thrillingly caught by the engineers. Throughout, the recording is full and lively and without edge; the acoustics are resonant, but not excessively so.

Squeezed on to only five discs and presented in chronological order, two symphonies per disc with No. 9 taking up the last, the Hanover Band's set makes a very attractive package. Though the performances are variable, the big challenges are splendidly taken: these readings convey the fire and exuberance of live performance. In characteristic Nimbus manner, the recordings are set in a reverberant acoustic, which means that the woodwind sometimes appear a little disembodied; but the sound is warm and undistracting. In Nos. 1 and 2, the string-playing is scrawnier than it later became, and the sound has less body. No. 5, also recorded early, is different: a strong and biting performance, full of energy and imagination. In the later recordings Goodman draws consistently fresh, individual readings from his team, with rhythms well sprung in exhilarating *allegros*. Even more remarkable is the way he can convey hushed intensity in slow movements, even when, following Beethoven's metronome markings, his speeds are much faster than we are used to. That is true also of the slow movement of the *Ninth*, in contrast to Norrington's exploratory version; but so too even more strikingly of the *Eroica* Funeral march. In the *Allegretto* of No. 7 too, the wistful melancholy of the main theme has rarely been so touchingly conveyed. Consistently the feeling of spontaneity is most winning.

As one of the first batch in the Toscanini Collection, RCA/BMG's big project to reissue all the recordings that the maestro himself approved, this uniquely intense cycle amply reinforces the claims of Toscanini as a supreme conductor in his time. These NBC versions are faster and more tense than the earlier Beethoven readings that he committed to records, but they are far from rigid or unloving, and they are crowned by performances of breathtaking power in the *Eroica* and the *Ninth*. Far more than memory has come to suggest, Toscanini drew out melodic lines with Italianate affection, even while he was presenting the whole at a high voltage, rarely matched. Listening to this Beethoven is never a relaxing experience, but it is a uniquely involving one. The new transfers have been lovingly remastered under the direction of John Pfeiffer, one of Toscanini's last recording producers. In the *Ninth*, treble emphasis needs taming, and the *Fourth* and *Fifth* are given in live (as opposed to studio) recordings, with more variable results. The recordings sound at their best at a high volume, but the intrusive hum which marred the first CD transfers has been virtually eliminated. Once one adjusts to the dry acoustic that Toscanini demanded – 'like seeing the score spread before you' was his comment – there is much pleasure to be had in these incandescent performances. *Leonore No. 3* was recorded much earlier, from a 1939 broadcast.

In Karajan's last, digital set, the recording seems to have been affected by the need to have a video version recorded at the same sessions. The gain is that these performances have keener spontaneity, the loss that they often lack the brilliant, knife-edged precision of ensemble one has come to regard as normal with Karajan. Though there is relatively little homing-in of microphones to spotlight individual detail, the sound too often grows thick and congested in big fortissimo tuttis. However, with the earlier recordings now issued at mid-price or less, the attractions of this digital box are much reduced, even if interpretatively with speeds generally a little less extreme, there are a number of movements which sound more persuasive than before.

Kurt Masur's Beethoven cycle with the Leipzig Gewandhaus Orchestra has a very great deal to recommend it. In sheer naturalness of utterance, unforced expressiveness and the superlatively disciplined response of the orchestral playing, the Gewandhaus set has a good deal to offer. The *Eroica* is uncommonly fine, particularly its nobly paced slow movement which is totally free from excessive emphasis in expression. In the *Fourth*

Symphony Masur is particularly successful, and the Gewandhaus Orchestra respond with marvellously alert playing. The digital remastering has produced sound which is considerably livelier than the originals; the violins above the stave are very brightly lit, though not edgy.

Superbly played and very well recorded, Dohnányi's Cleveland cycle brings straight, satisfying performances that can hardly be faulted on points of interpretation. No one will be seriously disappointed with this five-disc package, yet these are not readings which grip the attention as live performances do, but civilized run-throughs rather.

Solti's epic cycle, recorded in the mid-1970s with his own Chicago orchestra, has a firm centrality to it, following the outstandingly successful version of the *Ninth* with which he started the cycle. The performance of the *Eroica* has comparable qualities, with expansive, steady tempi and a dedicated, hushed account of the slow movement. Here and elsewhere Solti shows a willingness to relax, as well as to press dramatically forward, and there is plenty of sunshine in the even-numbered symphonies, though Nos. 1 and 8 are arguably too weighty in their tone of voice. For the very first time on record, every repeat is observed throughout, but this means that the *Ninth* has the first movement on the fifth disc, with the rest on the sixth. That break is to be deplored; but, more seriously, the digital transfers underline the aggressive brightness of the Chicago sound, emphasizing the brilliance of the performances to the detriment of their more thoughtful qualities.

Symphony No. 1 in C, Op. 21.
(*) Ph. Dig. 416 329-2 [id.]. O of the 18th Century, Brüggen – MOZART: *Symphony No. 40.*(*)

Symphonies Nos. 1; 2 in D, Op. 36.
(B) *** CBS MBK 44775 [id.]. Columbia SO, Walter.
**(*) O-L Dig. 414 338-2 [id.]. AAM, Hogwood.
** DG Dig. 415 505-2 [id.]. BPO, Karajan.
** Ph. Dig. 420 537-2 [id.]. Concg. O, Haitink.

Symphonies Nos. 1–2; Overture: Leonora No. 1.
(B) *** Ph. 422 966-2 [id.]. Concg. O, Jochum.

With his talented band of 45 players, Frans Brüggen directs an individual and compelling reading of Beethoven's *First*, which gains interpretatively from being recorded live. This has a degree of warmth and expressiveness not often associated with recordings on period instruments. One snag is that recording balances are not ideal, and the timpani booms away very loudly.

Eugen Jochum recorded three sets of Beethoven *Symphonies*, the first for DG in the early years of stereo, the second for Philips in the late 1960s, and then in the 1970s came a further series with the LSO for EMI. The Philips set has tended to be eclipsed by the others, but now, reissued at bargain price, its merits are striking. The recording sounds particularly well in remastered form, the playing of the Concertgebouw Orchestra has warmth and finesse, and the performances have an appealing energy and spontaneity. No. 1 sounds particularly fresh, the Andante poised, the finale wonderfully light and sparkling. No. 2 is even finer, with its characterful introduction, and the vitality and power of the outer allegros, balanced by a richly eloquent *Larghetto. Leonora No. 1* makes a splendid encore: the opening is particularly beautifully played.

In the *First Symphony* Walter achieves a happy medium between its eighteenth-century ancestry and its forward-looking qualities. The most controversial point about his interpretation of the *Second Symphony* is the slow movement, which is taken very slowly indeed, with plenty of rubato. But the rich warmth of the recording makes the effect very involving. For the rest, the speeds are well chosen, with a fairly gentle allegro in the finale which allows the tick-tock accompaniment to the second subject to have a delightful lift to it. On technical grounds this reissue can stand alongside most of the more recent competition. A superb disc.

Though Hogwood's performances do not have quite the exhilaration of his Haydn recordings, they are undistractingly attractive. Some may want more positive, individual readings of this music; however, with sensible speeds, often fast but not gabbled, these versions with clean, finely balanced recording bring out the freshness and transparency of authentic textures.

Karajan's new digital Beethoven series brings some surprisingly slack ensemble in the recording of the first two symphonies. The performances are relaxed in good ways too, but the heavy reverberation of the recording makes the result arguably too weighty for these works and pianissimos are rarely gentle enough. The 1977 versions – see below – are more satisfying, both as performances and as recordings.

Haitink gives strong and straightforward readings, beautifully played, but the recording is disappointingly opaque by Concertgebouw standards.

Symphonies Nos. 1 and 2 (trans. Liszt).
*** Teldec/WEA Dig. 2292 43661-2 [id.]. Cyprien Katsaris (piano).

Transcendental technique and a fine musical intelligence are the distinguishing features of these performances, which remain without peer in the Beethoven – Liszt discography. The recordings are finer than in earlier issues in the cycle.

Symphonies Nos. 1; 4 in B flat, Op. 60.
(B) **(*) DG 419 152-2 [id.]. VPO, Boehm.

Symphonies Nos. 1; 4 in B flat, Op. 60; Egmont overture.
(M) *** DG 419 048-2 [id.]. BPO, Karajan.

Karajan's 1977 series of Beethoven symphonies has been digitally remastered and reissued at mid-price. In almost all respects, without consideration of price, it is superior to the newer, digital recordings. Certainly the sound is preferable, more realistically balanced, clear yet still weighty. No. 1 is exciting, polished and elegant; in No. 4 the balance is closer, exposing every flicker of tremolando. Yet the body and ambience of the recording combine to give a realistic presence, and overall this is very impressive. Karajan conveys weight and strength and there is a wider range of dynamic than in the later, digital version. Only the extremely fast tempo for the finale marks a controversial development, but even there the brilliance and excitement are never in doubt.

Boehm's recordings come from his Vienna cycle of the early 1970s, centrally satisfying readings, brightly recorded, though with a good deal of resonance in the lower range. What these mature readings may lack is the sort of sharp idiosyncrasy which makes for dramatic memorability. So the first movement of the *C major Symphony* is spacious and mellow (the effect emphasized by the richly upholstered sound). The *Andante* is beautifully played, and the remaining movements have both character and vitality although there is comparatively little extrovert excitement. In the *Fourth*, Boehm's reading notes the kinship with the *Pastoral symphony*. The *Allegro vivace* is relatively easy-going, but with big, satisfying contrasts; the slow movement is warmly lyrical, and the last two movements bounce along joyfully. If Boehm misses some of the tension, there is no lack of strength or weight.

Symphonies Nos. 1 in C; 5 in C min., Op. 67.
**(*) Ph. Dig. 426 782-2. Leipzig GO, Masur.

It is fascinating to compare Masur's new digital versions of these two symphonies, the first in a new complete cycle, with the unobtrusively satisfying readings he recorded with the Gewandhaus Orchestra in the early 1970s. Those were interpretatively reticent, whereas here Masur is both more individual and more thrustful, consistently adopting speeds faster than before, sometimes markedly so, as in the first movement of the *Fifth* and the *Andante* of the *First.* More clearly, these go far beyond faithful studio performances, and the wider-ranging sound conveys the bloom of the Leipzig string-sound far more realistically, though the recording for No. 1 is both fuller and more forward than that for No. 5. These are the first recordings to use the Peters Critical Editions, which research in detail the variant readings from different sources. In No. 1, that makes relatively little difference, but in No. 5 Masur has opted to follow Beethoven's original plan of having a 'grand repetition' in the Scherzo, as in the *Fourth* and *Seventh Symphonies*, even though the composer later changed his mind. Masur sustains that expansion well, and also observes the exposition repeat in the finale, which he omitted before.

Symphonies Nos. 1; 6 in F (Pastoral), Op. 68.
(M) *** RCA GD 60002 [60002-2-RG]. Chicago SO, Reiner.
** EMI Dig. CDC7 49746-2 [id.]. L. Classical Players, Norrington.
(B) *(*) Decca 421 403-2 [id.]. VPO, Schmidt-Isserstedt.

In its newly remastered form, Reiner's 1961 *Pastoral* sounds wonderfully warm and full, yet again demonstrating the beauty of the acoustics of the Chicago Orchestral Hall at that time. The performance too is among the finest ever recorded, outstandingly fresh and enjoyable. Throughout Reiner adopts a straightforward, unmannered approach, his shading is subtle, and there is atmosphere without any confusion of texture. The slow movement is particularly beautiful and all the tempi sound utterly unforced and natural. It is true that Reiner's speed in the finale is somewhat faster than usual, but with this degree of lyrical fervour it does not sound over-pressed, and his choice is justified in the firmness achieved. The exposition repeat is observed in the first movement, to add to the architectural strength. The *First Symphony*, recorded in the same year, is weighty and direct, less incandescent but still a considerable account.

Norrington fails in this coupling of Nos. 1 and 6 quite to live up to expectations. In refinement and clarity of sound, the EMI recording does not match that of the rival Oiseau-Lyre version of the *Pastoral*, and Norrington is at times surprisingly fussy in his treatment. The *Scene by the brook* in the *Pastoral*, for example, fails to flow when the phrasing is so obsessively short-winded. Nor in either symphony is there quite the same lively energy which made the earlier performances in the series so refreshing.

Though inexpensive and well transferred to CD, with sound that is full and clear, this is not one of the best of the Schmidt-Isserstedt series. In No. 1 tempi are unusually slow, giving each movement a hint of ponderousness, although the measured finale is the exception, engagingly revealing detail that is too often submerged. The *Pastoral* also is disappointing: a good, clean, straightforward classical reading but with a lack of atmosphere and warmth, in the approach rather than the playing, and certainly lacking charm.

Symphonies Nos. 1; 7 in A, Op. 92.
*(**) DG 419 434-2 [id.]. VPO, Bernstein.

(M) **(*) EMI CDM7 63354-2 [id.]. Philh. O, Klemperer.

The recoupling for CD of the *Seventh*, one of the outstanding successes of Bernstein's Vienna cycle, with the *First* makes an attractive issue. In the first movement of the *Seventh* the lilting rhythms are sprung with delightful point, while the *Allegretto* is finely detailed at a flowing speed without dragging. In the last two movements the adrenalin flows in a vintage Bernstein manner. The recording is among the brightest of the series. In No. 1 the allegros are fast but not hectic, the slow introductions and slow movements carefully moulded but not mannered. In that work the live recording is not ideally clear, but very acceptable. However, ideally this should have been reissued at mid-price.

With Klemperer the slow speeds and heavyweight manner in both works – in principle not apt for No. 1, while undermining the dance-like element in No. 7 – will for many get in the way of enjoyment. That said, the compulsion of Klemperer in Beethoven remains strong, with rhythmic pointing consistently preventing stagnation. The recordings (1958 and 1961 respectively) are full and vivid, if not quite among the best of the series.

Symphony No. 2 in D, Op. 36.
(M) **(*) EMI CDM7 69811-2 [id.]. RPO, Beecham – MOZART: *Symphony No. 41.***(*)

Beecham's speed for the slow movement verges on the eccentric in its extreme expansiveness and loving manner, a romantic reading which yet has plenty of Beecham elegance. The *Allegro con brio* of the first movement is extreme in the opposite direction, exhilaratingly fast to challenge the RPO players at their peak; while the last two movements are both taken easily and wittily. It is a strong, individual performance. The digital transfer of this 1956/7 recording brings some stridency, and the analogue hiss is relatively high; but the Beecham magic is undiluted.

Symphonies Nos. 2; 4 in B flat, Op. 60.
(M) *** EMI CDM7 63355-2 [id.]. Philh. O, Klemperer.

The coupling for CD emphasizes the consistency of Klemperer's approach to Beethoven, with both the *Second* and *Fourth* symphonies sounding the more powerful through weighty treatment. Only in the finale is the result rather too gruff. The *Fourth* brings one of the most compelling performances of all, with Klemperer's measured but consistently sprung pulse allowing for persuasive lyricism alongside power. Exposition repeats are observed in the first movements of both symphonies. The sound is fresh yet full.

Symphonies Nos. 2 in D; 5 in C min., Op. 67.
**(*) Chan. Dig. CHAN 8752 [id.]. CBSO, Weller.

Consistent with his approach in the rest of the cycle, Weller makes the first movement of the *Fifth* optimistic rather than bitingly tragic. For some, the first three movements at least will be too comfortable, at broad speeds lacking something in dramatic tension. But in the finale the performance conveys the sort of eager enjoyment that marks the rest of the cycle. With an unusual coupling in Weller's beautifully sprung version of the *Second Symphony*, the disc has its place. Full, warm sound.

Symphonies Nos. 2; 7 in A, Op. 92.
(M) *** DG 419 050-2 [id.]. BPO, Karajan.

As with Karajan's coupling of Nos. 1 and 4, the digitally remastered versions of the 1977 recordings of the *D* and *A major Symphonies* are remarkably successful, the sound vivid and clear, yet with plenty of body. In No. 2 the firm lines give the necessary strength. The tempo for the slow movement is particularly well judged; the recording is now clearer in its newest format. The *Seventh* is tense and exciting, with the conductor emphasizing the work's dramatic rather than its dance-like qualities. The slow introduction, taken at a fastish tempo, is tough rather than monumental, and the main *Allegro* is fresh and bright, and not very lilting in its 6/8 rhythm.

Symphonies Nos. 2; 8 in F, Op. 93.
*** EMI Dig. CDC7 47698-2 [id.]. L. Classical Players, Norrington.

The coupling of Nos. 2 and 8 was the first of Norrington's Beethoven series and showed the London Classical Players as an authentic group with a distinctive sound, sweeter and truer in the string section than most, generally easier on non-specialist ears. Though the recording is warmly reverberant, Norrington secures admirably transparent textures, with the braying of the natural, valveless horns adding an apt tang and with the authentic small-size timpani adding military bite. In following Beethoven's own metronome markings for both symphonies the results are exhilarating, never merely breathless, bringing far more than proof of an academic theory. Formidable as the scholarship is, the important point is the freshness and imagination of the communication.

Symphony No. 3 in E flat (Eroica), Op. 55.
*** Ph. Dig. 410 044-2 [id.]. ASMF, Marriner.
(M) *** Ph. 420 853-2 [id.] (with rehearsal). Concg. O, Monteux.
*** Decca 417 235-2 [id.]. AAM, Hogwood.

Symphony No. 3 (Eroica); 12 Contredanses, WoO 14.
**(*) CBS Dig. MDK 44516 [id.]. St Luke's CO, Tilson Thomas.

Symphony No. 3 (Eroica); Grosse Fuge, Op. 133.
(M) *** EMI CDM7 63356-2 [id.]. Philh. O, Klemperer.

(i) *Symphony No. 3 (Eroica);* (ii) *Overture, Coriolan.*
(B) *** Pickwick Dig. PCD 900 [MCA MCAD 25237]. LSO, Wyn Morris.
(B) **(*) CBS MBK 42599 [id.]. Columbia SO, Walter.
(B) *** Sup. SUP 000004. Czech PO, (i) Von Matačić; (ii) Kletzki.

Symphony No. 3 (Eroica); Creatures of Prometheus: Overture.
*** EMI Dig. CDC7 49101-2. L. Classical Players, Norrington.

Symphony No. 3 (Eroica); Overtures: The Creatures of Prometheus; Egmont; Fidelio.
(B) **(*) EMI CDZ7 62623-2. BPO, Kempe.

Symphony No. 3 (Eroica); Egmont overture.
**(*) DG Dig. 415 506-2 [id.]. BPO, Karajan.
** Decca Dig. 430 087-2 [id.]. Chicago SO, Solti.

(i) *Symphony No. 3 (Eroica);* (ii) *Egmont: Overture and incidental music, Op. 84.*
(M) **(*) Decca 421 024-2 [id.]. VPO; (i) Schmidt-Isserstedt, (ii) Szell, with Pilar Lorengar.

Symphony No. 3 in E flat (Eroica); Overtures: Fidelio; Leonora No. 3.
(B) *** Ph. 426 066-2 [id.]. Concg. O, Jochum.

Symphony No. 3 (Eroica); Overture: Leonora No. 3.
(M) **(*) DG 419 049-2 [id.]. BPO, Karajan.

The digital remastering of Klemperer's spacious 1961 version reinforces its magnificence, keenly concentrated to sustain speeds slower than in his earlier mono account. The stoically intense reading of the *Funeral march* is among the most impressive on record, and only in the coda to the finale does the slow tempo bring some slackening. The reissue includes the stereo version of the *Grosse Fuge*, dating from 1957, now available for the first time, and the sound is first rate, vivid and well balanced.

Sir Neville Marriner's version is in every way outstanding, for although the Academy may use fewer strings, the impression is of weight and strength, coupled with a rare transparency of texture and extraordinary resilience of rhythm. The dance-rhythms of the fast movements are brought out captivatingly with sforzandos made clean and sharp. The *Funeral march* may emerge as less grave and dark than it can be, but Marriner's unforced directness is most compelling. The recorded sound is among the best ever in a Beethoven symphony.

Norrington's account of the *Eroica* is among the most enjoyable of his Beethoven symphony series with the London Classical Players, well coupled with the *Prometheus overture*. He is consistently even faster than his two closest period-performance rivals – Hogwood on Oiseau-Lyre and Goodman on Nimbus – yet one quickly forgets any feeling of haste when rhythms are so crisp and supple in their spring, and the great *Funeral march* has natural gravity. The recording has more presence than most of the others, with clearer perspectives.

Wyn Morris on the Pickwick label conducts a taut reading of the *Eroica*, dark and intense, with allegros consistently urgent. The *Funeral march* too is strong and positive, braving the tragedy. Morris observes the important exposition repeat in the first movement, and has the benefit of first-rate sound; and the LSO responds with both bite and refinement. At budget price and with a coupling, it makes an excellent bargain, matching and even outshining most full-price rivals.

Jochum's 1969 Philips record offers a fine, fresh and intense performance, made the more impressive by his inclusion of the first-movement exposition repeat, giving the epic argument its proper proportions. The simple, hushed dedication of the *Funeral march* is most moving, and Jochum rounds the work off with an exceptionally fast and exciting presto coda. With two overtures as substantial makeweights, equally well played, this is a bargain, for the sound is excellent, full and clear and with the usual Concertgebouw bloom.

The gain in Karajan's digital version of the *Eroica* over his previous recordings lies most of all in the *Funeral march*, very spacious and intense, with dynamic contrasts intensified. Here, and even more noticeably in the allegros, the playing is marginally less polished than before, lacking something of the knife-edged bite associated with Karajan. As with others in the series, the oddly balanced recording grows congested in big tuttis. Nevertheless, the power and concentration make it an epic reading.

Monteux's 1962 *Eroica* comes up electrically fresh, direct and intense. The disc is the more cherishable for including 15 minutes of rehearsal (in French), with the voice of the 87-year-old maestro sounding astonishingly young.

The sharpness of attack and the clarity of rhythms and textures in Hogwood's version make for an unusually refreshing account of the first movement. Speeds are fast there and elsewhere, but not breathlessly so. Though the great *Funeral march*, at a flowing andante rather than an adagio, lacks the meditative weight that we expect in traditional performances, nevertheless its darkness is strongly established, with contrasts just as clearly marked. The recording is fresh and full to match.

Walter's interpretation has all the ripeness of the best of his work with the Vienna Philharmonic Orchestra between the wars. The digitally remastered recording retains the amplitude one needs for such a reading: its expansive qualities bring rich horns as well as full-bodied strings. The disc opens with a superb account of the *Coriolan overture*, spacious, warm and dramatic, and the sound-balance is especially telling.

Michael Tilson Thomas's version of the *Eroica* was recorded in America with the St Luke's Chamber Orchestra, on this showing an excellent band. The players respond freshly and vigorously to the conductor's direction, as in the brisk and dramatic account of the first movement, which comes with exposition repeat. The great *Funeral march*, unmannered in its expressiveness, sustains that tension, leading to effervescent accounts of the scherzo and finale. The fill-up – Beethoven at his most winningly relaxed in light music – makes a sparkling appendix. The recording is warm and full, giving little impression of chamber scale.

A warm welcome to Lovro von Matačić's commanding performance of the *Eroica*, one of the classic accounts of the 1960s. This has an impressive tension and grandeur, and was one of the few *Eroicas* to recall the famous pre-war Weingartner set. The playing has tremendous grip but is never overdriven. The sound remains remarkably fresh and realistic; this is still a most competitive release.

Kempe recorded the *Eroica* with the Berlin Philharmonic in 1961, and the *Overtures* date from the late 1950s. It is enormously civilized, well rounded, flawlessly played, beautifully recorded – and a joy to listen to. Some will find it just a touch *too* civilized, and it is true that the tension does sag a little in the first movement. However, this is a very fine record, one that can stand alongside the best modern accounts. Amazingly good value at its modest price.

Not everyone will identify readily with the fiery intensity of fast tempi in the outer movements of Karajan's 1977 performance, even if this version includes a more intense account of the *Funeral march* than in earlier recordings. A point to consider is the absence of the exposition repeat in the first movement; but this is among the most polished as well as the most dramatic accounts available. An exciting performance of *Leonora No. 3* makes a very generous bonus. The sound, although it has ample fullness and weight, is better defined than the newer, digital version.

Schmidt-Isserstedt's 1966 *Eroica* may not have quite the same power as some of the other symphonies in his cycle, but this is a very satisfying reading, thoughtfully detailed, not lacking in dramatic weight. The generous coupling is Szell's splendid 1970 version of the *Egmont overture and incidental music*. For the reissue, the spoken narration included on the original LP has been excised, although the songs, movingly sung by Pilar Lorengar, remain. Both recordings have been very satisfactorily remastered, with the ambience of the Sofiensaal providing warmth and atmosphere so that the brilliance and added clarity of the CD are in proper perspective.

Solti's 1989 recording of the *Eroica* provides an extraordinary contrast over tempo with the version he recorded almost twenty years earlier with the same orchestra. All four movements are substantially swifter, notably the first two. In the three fast movements this makes for a tauter, more dramatic reading, flowing more easily, with the third movement made into an exhilarating dance. In the *Funeral march* it is different: where in his earlier, spacious reading Solti found a hushed gravity, with the fragmentation of the theme at the end deeply moving, the faster speed of the new performance sounds too easily lyrical, not quite tense enough. Well recorded, if without transparency, with the *Egmont overture* as fill-up, it fits well in Solti's latest Beethoven series, though ideally one wants to borrow the second movement from the earlier reading.

Symphony No. 4 in B flat, Op. 60.
(M) (*) DG mono 427 777-2 [id.]. BPO, Furtwängler (with HANDEL: *Concerto grosso Op. 6/10).*

Taken from tapes of Furtwängler's wartime broadcasts, his DG account of Beethoven's *Fourth* is a fascinating document but, with a very noisy audience, it hardly compares with his later studio recording, particularly when coupled with an elephantine account of the Handel *Concerto grosso*.

Symphonies Nos. 4 in B flat, Op. 60; 5 in C min., Op. 67.
*** EMI Dig. CDC7 49656-2 [id.]. L. Classical Players, Norrington.
(B) *** Pickwick Dig. PCD 869 [MCA MCAD 25172]. LSO, Wyn Morris.
*** O-L Dig. 417 615-2 [id.]. AAM, Hogwood.

Though the knocking of Fate at the start of the *Fifth* may initially seem perfunctory as Norrington briskly presents it, it is surprising how one adjusts, even by the time the exposition repeat returns, barely a minute later. This coupling of Nos. 4 and 5 – the same as Oiseau-Lyre offers in the rival Hogwood series – shows Norrington at his most refreshing and inspired, relishing his fast speeds, showing how even a fast *Adagio* in the slow movement of No. 4 can flow easefully and lyrically, always finding new detail to bring out, thanks to imaginative use of period instruments. So the woodwind copes with fine clarity in the rapid passage-work of No. 4, and the finale of No. 5 has infectious swagger even at a very fast speed. The sound is up to the high standard of the series, though in the blazing of brass it cannot match the exceptionally vivid Decca recording for Hogwood which, in its extra weight, provides far less of a contrast with traditional performance than the Norrington.

Wyn Morris's coupling of Nos. 4 and 5 makes a first-rate budget recommendation. He generally adopts speeds close to those of Karajan and, though he cannot match that master in sharpness of focus or pointed intensity, his urgency goes with fine, biting strength, helped by some first-rate playing from the LSO. These are readings which, more than most, convey the varying tensions of a live performance, and one suspects that the studio recordings were done in long takes. The sound is bright and slightly abrasive, but with enough body to sustain that. The weight of the readings is enhanced by the observance of all repeats. A bargain.

Hogwood's generous coupling of Nos. 4 and 5 brings fresh, lively readings which, with generally fast speeds, present excellent alternative versions for anyone wanting performances on period instruments. Dramatic contrasts are strongly marked, with no feeling of miniaturization, and the clarity of textures is admirable, with natural horns in particular braying out superbly. Vivid sound, set in a believable acoustic.

Symphonies Nos. 4 in B flat; 7 in A, Op. 92.
*** Chan. Dig. CHAN 8753 [id.]. CBSO, Weller.
(B) **(*) Ph. 422 967-2 [id.]. Concg. O, Jochum.
** DG Dig. 415 121-2 [id.]. BPO, Karajan.

It is surprising that Nos. 4 and 7 are not coupled together more often, when structurally they are so closely related. Each begins with a massive slow introduction, and exceptionally brings a scherzo in A-B-A-B-A form. Weller and the CBSO are at their finest in both works, warm and companionable, giving the impression of live communication. Warm, full recording.

Jochum's Philips coupling comes from 1967/8 and offers a strong, compelling reading of No. 4, with a satisfying *Seventh*. The slow movement of the *B flat Symphony* is rather serious in mood (less radiant than in his earlier performance on Heliodor) and the outer movements of the *A major* find more extrovert excitement in some other performances; but overall this is rewarding, with the Concertgebouw playing as eloquent and polished as in the rest of this excellent series. The sound too is clear, with a full Concertgebouw sonority.

Karajan's digital coupling of the *Fourth* and *Seventh* symphonies gives an impression of more spontaneous, less meticulous performances than in his previous versions of these works. There is no doubt about the command of Karajan's never-routine view of Beethoven – but too much is lost. The slow movement of the *Fourth* is beautifully moulded but is never hushed; and the *Allegretto* of No. 7, taken characteristically fast, is so smooth that the dactylic rhythm at the start is almost unidentifiable. Recording, not as detailed or analytical as usual, is undistracting.

Symphonies Nos. 4; 8 in F (trans. Liszt).
*** Teldec/WEA Dig. 2292 43259-2 [id.]. Cyprien Katsaris (piano).

Simply astonishing! The opening of the finale of the *Eighth Symphony* is an extraordinary feat of articulation. Apart from his dazzling technique, Katsaris has enormous musicianship, a great range of colour and a real sense of scale. It is as if one is encountering this music for the first time.

Symphony No. 5 in C min., Op. 67.
(***) DG Dig. 410 028-2 [id.]. LAPO, Giulini.
(***) DG 415 861-2 [id.]. LAPO, Carlos Kleiber.

Symphony No. 5; Overtures: The Creatures of Prometheus; Egmont.
**(*) Nimbus Dig. NI 5007 [id.]. Hanover Band, Monica Huggett.

Symphony No. 5 in C min., Op. 67; Overtures: Fidelio; Leonora No. 3.
**(*) RCA Dig. RD 87894 [7894-2-RC]. RPO, Previn.

Symphony No. 5; Overture: Leonora No. 3.
(***) Decca 400 060-2 [id.]. Philh. O, Ashkenazy.

Symphonies Nos. 5; 6 in F (Pastoral), Op. 68.
(M) **(*) DG 423 203-2 [id.]. BPO, Karajan.
** DG Dig. 413 932-2 [id.]. BPO, Karajan.

Symphonies Nos. 5; 7 in A, Op. 92.
**(*) Ph. Dig. 420 540-2 [id.]. Concg. O, Haitink.
(M) (**(*)) EMI mono CDH7 69803-2 [id.]. VPO, Furtwängler.
** Telarc Dig. CD 80163 [id.]. Cleveland O, Dohnányi.
(M) (*) DG mono 427 775-2 [id.]. BPO, Furtwängler.

Symphonies Nos. 5; 8 in F, Op. 93.
(B) *** Ph. 422 474-2 [id.]. Concg. O, Jochum.
(B) **(*) Decca 421 166-2 [id.]. VPO, Schmidt-Isserstedt.
(M) **(*) EMI CDM7 63357-2 [id.]. Philh. O, Klemperer.

Symphonies Nos. 5; 8; Fidelio: overture.
(M) *** DG 419 051-2 [id.]. BPO, Karajan.

Those issues which offer the *Fifth Symphony* either alone or with just an overture as fill-up on premium-priced CD now seem uneconomic. Giulini certainly has the advantage of excellent digital sound, and his performance possesses majesty in abundance and conveys the power and vision of this inexhaustible work, but DG need to withdraw this, add some more music and perhaps bring the price down, too. Carlos Kleiber's electrifying *Fifth* similarly needs coupling, perhaps to his version of the *Seventh* if the combined playing time allows this. It remains an exceptional performance: the gradation of dynamics from the hushed pianissimo at the close of the scherzo to the weight of the great opening statement of the finale has not been heard on disc with such overwhelming effect since Toscanini. Ashkenazy's is a vivid and urgent reading, notable for its rich Kingsway Hall recording. Well-adjusted speeds here (the *Andante* on the slow side, the finale on the fast side), with joyful exuberance a fair substitute for grandeur. The overture, also fast, finds Ashkenazy at his freshest, but overall this is short measure. Far more than Previn's earlier version of No. 5 for EMI, his RCA issue brings a fresh, rhythmically alert reading, full of thoughtful detail, readily sustaining speeds that are on the broad side. It is very well played and recorded, and the only serious reservation is that the coupling of two overtures is ungenerous.

Recorded while Monica Huggett was still directing, the Hanover Band's version of the *Fifth Symphony* is strong and lithe, with the doctrine of period performance imaginatively rather than ruthlessly applied. The Nimbus recording helps in that, full and natural enough to convey the dramatic impact of the outer movements, yet mellow in a church acoustic, although the balance is not entirely convincing.

Karajan's 1977 version of the *Fifth* is magnificent in every way, tough and urgently incisive, with fast tempi bringing weight as well as excitement but no unwanted blatancy, even in the finale. The recording has satisfying body and a wide dynamic range. The coupling of an electrically intense performance of the *Eighth* plus the *Fidelio overture* is certainly generous. The earlier (1962) coupling of Nos. 5 and 6 is just as generous. Here the *Fifth* is, if anything, even more intense, and more spacious in the *Andante*, with blazing horns in the finale. The *Pastoral* is a brisk lightweight performance, marred only by the absence of the repeat in the scherzo.

The alternative, digital versions of the *Fifth* and *Sixth* present characteristically strong and incisive readings, recorded in longer takes than previously. The sound is not as cleanly focused as in his earlier Berlin versions, and with Karajan's approach the power of No. 5 is more effective than the atmospheric poetry of No. 6.

Jochum provides a highly satisfying bargain-price coupling of the *Fifth* and *Eighth Symphonies*. He launches into a vigorous reading of the *Fifth*, unmarred by any romantic exaggeration, but gripping in a totally natural and unforced way. The finale is especially fine and beautifully prepared, like Carlos Kleiber's. The *Eighth*, too, is attractively unmannered, satisfyingly paced and superbly played. The sound is extremely good. An outstanding bargain.

Schmidt-Isserstedt offers strong readings of both symphonies and includes exposition repeats in both the first movements. The first movement of No. 8 is slower than usual in the interests of emphasizing that this is not simply Beethoven's 'little one' but a powerful, symphonic argument. In the *Fifth* the first movement has both bite and breathing-space, a nicely measured *Andante* and a triumphant finale. Only the scherzo invites controversy in its slow tempo. Excellent recording, vividly transferred to CD.

As with the others in his mid-priced series on EMI, Klemperer's renditions of Nos. 5 and 8 bring a clean and natural sound on top, notably in violin tone. The *Fifth* is plainly less electric than his earlier mono version but, with exposition repeats observed in both outer movements, this retains its epic quality.

Haitink's coupling of Nos. 5 and 7 brings strong, unmannered readings of both works, well played and warmly if not brilliantly recorded. He observes the exposition repeat in the *Seventh* and he does so too in the first movement of the *Fifth* but not in the finale. The sound is rich and generally spacious, though it lacks transparency in tuttis.

Furtwängler's coupling of the *Fifth* and the *Seventh Symphonies* on EMI brings together two of his finest Beethoven recordings, both made in the Musikvereinsaal in Vienna under studio conditions. Furtwängler's rhythmic control and his mastery of line exert a magnetic hold over the listener; the fateful power of No. 5 and the dance-apotheosis of No. 7 are celebrated with equal intensity. In both symphonies the recording is rather dry and limited, but in a good transfer this is undistracting enough to give much pleasure.

Dohnányi directs clean, efficent performances of both *Symphonies*, generally at brisk speeds, but lacking something in dramatic bite, partly the result of slightly recessed recording. It all sounds rather too easy. No exposition repeats are observed in the outer movements of the *Seventh* or in the finale of the *Fifth*.

Like other Fürtwangler recordings taken from wartime tapes, his DG coupling of Nos. 5 and 7 conveys electricity but is marred by poor sound and a very noisy audience. His later versions are preferable.

Symphony No. 5 in C min., Op. 67 (trans. Liszt); *Variations & fugue on a theme from Prometheus (Eroica variations), Op. 35.*
** Teldec/WEA Dig. 2292 44921-2 [id.]. Cyprien Katsaris (piano).

Katsaris plays a Steinway here, as opposed to the instrument by Mark Allen used for his recordings of Nos. 4, 6, 8 and 9 or a Bechstein for Nos. 1 – 3. The *Fifth* is perhaps a slight disappointment after his astonishing *Eroica*, *Eighth* and *Ninth*. If the sound is not claustrophobic, it is too close and airless, and the climaxes are often overemphatic, hectoring rather than imposing. The scherzo is slow – almost portentous. The *Eroica variations* are brilliantly played; but this does not displace current recommendations.

Symphony No. 6 in F (Pastoral), Op. 68.
*** Decca Dig. 410 003-2 [id.]. Philh. O, Ashkenazy.
(M) *** DG 413 721-2 (2) [id.]. VPO, Boehm – *Symphony No. 9.****

Symphony No. 6 (Pastoral); Overture: The Consecration of the house.
**(*) Ph. Dig. 416 385-2 [id]. ASMF, Marriner.
**(*) Nimbus Dig. NI 5099 [id.]. Hanover Band, Goodman.

Symphony No. 6 (Pastoral); Overtures: Coriolan; Creatures of Prometheus; Ruins of Athens.
** DG 415 833-2 [id.]. BPO, Karajan.

Symphony No. 6 (Pastoral); Overtures: Coriolan; Egmont.
*** O-L Dig. 421 416-2 [id.]. AAM, Hogwood.

Symphony No. 6 (Pastoral); Overture: Creatures of Prometheus; (i) Egmont: Overture; Die Trommel geruhet; Freudvoll und leidvoll; Klarchens Tod, Op. 84.
(M) *** EMI CDM7 63358-2 [id.]. Philh. O, Klemperer; (i) with Birgit Nilsson.

Symphony No. 6 (Pastoral); Overture Egmont, Op. 84.
(B) **(*) Pickwick Dig. PCD 912 [MCA MCAD 25858]. LSO, Wyn Morris.
**(*) RCA Dig. RD 87747 [7747-2-RC]. RPO, Previn.
** Ph. Dig. 420 541-2 [id.]. Concg. O, Haitink.

Symphony No. 6 (Pastoral); Overture: Leonora No. 2, Op. 72a.
(B) *** CBS MYK 42536 [id.]. Columbia SO, Walter.
(B) *** Ph. 426 061-2 [id.]. Concg. O, Jochum.
** Decca Dig. 421 773-2 [id.]. Chicago SO, Solti.

Ashkenazy's is essentially a genial reading, almost totally unmannered. But the performance has a beguiling warmth and it communicates readily. With generally spacious tempi, the feeling of lyrical ease and repose is most captivating, thanks to the response of the Philharmonia players and the richness of the recording, made in the Kingsway Hall. After a *Storm* that is civilized rather than frightening, the performance is crowned by a radiant account of the *Shepherds' thanksgiving*. The sound, with its fairly reverberant acoustic, is particularly impressive.

Boehm's reading of the *Pastoral* has a natural, unforced beauty and is very well played (with strings, woodwind and horns beautifully integrated). In the first movement he observes the exposition repeat (not many versions do); although the dynamic contrasts are never underplayed and the phrasing is affectionate, there is a feeling of inevitable rightness about Boehm's approach, no sense of an interpreter imposing his will. The sound is warm and glowing and has been enhanced by its CD remastering. This is coupled with a fine digital version of the *Choral Symphony* on a pair of mid-priced discs. Among earlier versions of the *Pastoral*, Fritz Reiner's should also be considered, one of the finest ever recorded and sounding gloriously rich in its remastered format coupled with No. 1 – see above.

Bruno Walter's recording dates from the beginning of the 1960s. The whole performance glows, and the gentle warmth of phrasing is comparable with Klemperer's famous version. The slow movement is taken slightly fast, but there is no sense of hurry, and the tempo of the *Peasants' merrymaking* is less controversial than Klemperer's. It is an affectionate and completely integrated performance from a master who thought and lived the work all his life. The sound is beautifully balanced, with sweet strings and clear, glowing woodwind, and the bass response is firm and full. The quality is very slightly shallower in the *Overture Leonora No. 2* which opens the disc, but this splendid performance shows Walter at his most dramatically spontaneous.

Klemperer's account of the *Pastoral* is one of the very finest of all his records. The scherzo may be eccentrically slow but, with superbly dancing rhythms, it could not be more bucolic, and it falls naturally into place within the reading as a whole. The exquisitely phrased slow movement and the final *Shepherds' hymn* bring peaks of beauty, made the more intense by the fine digital transfer, reinforcing the clarity and balance of the original sound, with violin tone amazingly fresh and clean for 1958, although thinner than we would expect today. The *Egmont* music follows the *Symphony*, an unusual but valuable coupling with Nilsson in her prime, unexpectedly but effectively cast in the two simple songs, the first made to sound almost Mahlerian. The CD also offers the *Creatures of Prometheus overture*.

Jochum's Philips recording of the *Pastoral* dates from the end of the 1960s. It sounds extremely well in remastered form, resonantly full, vivid and clear. It is an essentially leisurely reading, the countryside relaxing in the sunshine. In the first movement Jochum is essentially undramatic until the radiant final climax in the coda, which he links with the similar burst of energy in the finale. The slow movement has an Elysian stillness and repose; the *Storm* is not over-romanticized. With beautiful playing from the Concertgebouw Orchestra, the reading is sustained without a hint of lethargy.

The clarity and vivid sense of presence in Hogwood's period performance of the *Pastoral* go with fresh, resilient playing from the Academy of Ancient Music. As in this conductor's earlier Beethoven recordings, the extra detail is presented without fussiness, and the sense of live rather than canned performance reflects Hogwood's ever-increasing assurance in this repertory. The *Storm* comes over with particular excitement, thanks to the clarity of texture, with piccolo and dry-toned timpani cutting through superbly. The *Overtures* too – not a generous coupling by today's standards, but more than many old LPs provided – bring similarly invigorating performances.

Morris takes a characteristically fresh and direct view of the *Pastoral*. The speed for the first movement is brisk, and he does not allow even a momentary easing for the entry of the second subject, let alone a slowing of tempo. Next to more relaxed readings, Morris sounds tense; on his own terms, however, it works well, as does his brisk treatment of the other movements. The piece becomes less atmospheric – with the entry into the *Storm* hardly suggesting raindrops – but one appreciates the structural originality the more. With a similarly taut account of the *Egmont overture* for fill-up, and with first-rate playing from the LSO, it makes a characterful bargain-price recommendation.

Marriner's view of the *Pastoral* is genial, with a relaxed account of the first movement leading to an unusually spacious reading of the *Scene by the brook*, and with the *Shepherds' thanksgiving* mingling joy and elegance. There are more powerful and individual performances but, beautifully played and recorded, it is a happy reading, well coupled – if not generously – with the still under-appreciated *Consecration of the house overture*.

André Previn's version of the *Pastoral*, with rhythms beautifully sprung, has all the freshness of a visit to the countryside on a spring day. Speeds are brisk and alert but unexaggerated. This first instalment of a projected Beethoven cycle augurs well for a set in which – somewhat exceptionally – the conductor never seeks to get in the way of the composer. With excellent playing and recording, no one will be disappointed, though by latterday CD standards the coupling is ungenerous.

Roy Goodman directs the Hanover Band in an appealingly bright account, clear and intense yet more relaxed in its manners than those of period-performance rivals. With the *Consecration of the house overture* (taken fast) as coupling, this separate issue is not such a bargain as the complete set from which it comes.

Karajan's 1977 performance is fresh and alert, consistent with the rest of the cycle, a good dramatic version, with polished playing and recording which is wide-ranging but suffers from the odd balances which mark this cycle. The sound is fuller in the three overtures which are also included, but in the *Symphony* there is still plenty of bloom and weight, as well as more refined detail.

Though Solti's later series of Beethoven performances with the Chicago orchestra brings greater spontaneity, his reading of the *Pastoral* is still heavyweight, rather lacking the joys of spring; and the digital recording brings little or no improvement over his earlier version.

Symphonies Nos. 6 in F (Pastoral); 8 in F, Op. 93.
***Chan. Dig. CHAN 8754 [id.]. CBSO, Walter Weller.

Weller directs a glowing, amiable account of the *Pastoral*, one of the most treasurable performances in his cycle. The first three movements are very relaxed; the *Storm*, even more than usual, then provides an electrifying contrast, with the finale bringing the most joyous apotheosis, with the violins of the CBSO playing with heady sweetness. The *Eighth* is relatively weighty, with broad speeds underlining the symphonic strength in the outer movements, contrasted with easy-going accounts of the *Allegretto* and Minuet. Warmly atmospheric recording.

Symphony No. 7 in A, Op. 92.
(**(*)) DG 415 862-2 [id.]. VPO, Carlos Kleiber.

Symphony No. 7; Overtures: Coriolan; The Creatures of Prometheus.
**(*) RCA Dig. RD 87748 [7748-2-RC]. RPO, Previn.

Symphony No. 7; Overtures: Coriolan; Creatures of Prometheus; Egmont.
(B) *** DG 429 509-2 [id.]. VPO, Boehm.

Symphony No. 7; Overtures: Coriolan; Egmont.
* Decca Dig. 411 941-2 [id.]. Philh. O, Ashkenazy.
* EMI Dig. CDC7 49816-2 [id.]. L. Classical Players, Norrington.

Symphony No. 7; Overture: The Creatures of Prometheus.
(M) ***** EMI CDM7 69183-2 [id.]. Philh. O, Klemperer.

Symphony No. 7; (i) *The Ruins of Athens (Overture and incidental music), Op. 113.*
(M) ***** EMI CDM7 69871-2 [id.]. RPO, Beecham; (i) with Beecham Choral Soc.

(i) *Symphonies Nos. 7;* (ii) *8 in F, Op. 93.*
* DG Dig. 423 364-2 [id.]. VPO, Abbado.
*(*) O-L Dig. 425 695-2 [id.]. AAM, Hogwood.
(B) ***(*)** Pickwick Dig. PCD 918. LSO, Wyn Morris.
(M) ***(*)** EMI CDM7 69031-2 [id.]. (i) Chicago SO; (ii) LSO, Giulini.
(M) ***** CBS MYK 44829 [id.]. Columbia SO, Walter.
* Decca Dig. 425 525-2. Chicago SO, Solti.

Once again strong reservations have to be expressed about the CDs offering only a single symphony, without coupling, which have become uncompetitive at premium price in the current marketplace. Carlos Kleiber's DG version dates back to 1976, but the digital remastering has improved the sound and this is an incisively dramatic reading, marked with sharp dynamic contrasts and thrustful rhythms. Like his father, Kleiber maintains the pizzicato for the strings on the final brief phrase of the *Allegretto*, a curious effect.

Of those compact discs which include overtures as makeweights, Ashkenazy's Philharmonia performance takes pride of place. This is a warmly spontaneous, generally direct reading, taken steadily at unexaggerated speeds, and the result is glowingly convincing, thanks to fine playing and recording that sets new standards in this work, full and spacious yet warmly co-ordinated. The two coupled overtures are contrasted: *Coriolan* is given a weighty reading at a measured speed, while *Egmont*, equally dramatic, is on the fast side.

With sforzandos sharply accented and rhythms lightly sprung, Norrington is at his finest in the *Seventh*. Even when he adopts characteristically fast speeds in obedience to Beethoven's metronome markings – as in the second-movement *Allegretto* – he finds time for detail and fine moulding of phrase. The recording is warm, but not ideally clear on inner detail. The *Overtures* are given performances of comparable point.

Klemperer's 1955 recording of the *Seventh* is among his very finest Beethoven interpretations on disc, and it sounds all the more vivid and full of presence in the stereo version, issued for the first time. Speeds are consistently faster, the tension more electric, with phrasing more subtly moulded, than in the later Philharmonia version. Though the later recording carries extra weight with its wider range, the 1955 sound is very acceptable, with good inner detail. The 1959 *Prometheus* is not a generous makeweight, but the disc comes at mid-price in the EMI Studio series.

Boehm's 1972 version with the VPO stands high among the lower-priced versions of this symphony. The recording is excellent, full and fresh, and the whole performance has lift and spontaneity. Boehm's direct style is most satisfying: in the first movement the well-articulated playing keeps the music very much alive, even though his basic speed isn't fast. The slow movement has a grave eloquence which is most moving, and the spirited scherzo makes way for a striking finale, full of impetus, yet with plenty of weight. The overtures go well too, especially *Egmont*.

Beecham's *Seventh* is one of the briskest accounts of the symphony ever; yet, such is his rhythmic control and his ability to clarify textures – well realized in the recording, which is astonishingly vivid for the late 1950s – that the result is exhilarating. Only the slow movement reverts to old-fashioned slow manners in what is in effect an *Andante* rather than an *Allegretto*, but Beecham's rhythmic sense and care for phrasing still avoid heaviness. The fill-up of incidental music makes a valuable and enjoyable rarity, with Beecham roaring through the *Chorus of Dervishes* (finely sung by the Beecham Choral Society), whiskers obviously bristling. The 1958 sound has also been transferred well.

André Previn's view is totally natural and unselfconscious: fresh, rhythmic and unexaggerated, joyful in the dance. It makes an excellent choice with its first-rate playing and recording, if with what now seems an ungenerous coupling.

The *Seventh* has always been a favourite symphony with Abbado, and the main allegro of the first movement is beautifully judged at a fastish speed, which is yet made resilient. Similarly, the finale blazes fearlessly but never becomes a gabble and, though the live recording is not ideally clear on inner detail, the sound is full and atmospheric, as it also is in the *Eighth* which, with such weight, is instantly established as more than a little symphony. As in the *Seventh*, speeds are beautifully judged, and the tensions of a live occasion are vividly conveyed, as they were not in the first issues of the series. A splendid coupling.

Hogwood gives clean performances of both *Symphonies*, well played and recorded, but rhythmically a degree less resilient than those of his direct period-performance rivals. In the *Seventh* in particular, that brings moments of stodginess; but they are hardly serious enough to undermine a recommendation for those who want this particular coupling on period instruments.

Wyn Morris directs strong, spontaneous-sounding readings of both *Symphonies*, not always as refined in execution as the finest, but superbly recorded. In a generous coupling on the bargain Pickwick label, they make an excellent recommendation. Though there are some distracting fluctuations of speed, Morris draws consistently resilient playing from the LSO, a vital quality in these two works written in parallel, with No. 8 becoming, like No. 7, an apotheosis of the dance.

Giulini's CD comes from the early 1970s – the two symphonies were originally differently coupled. With the Chicago orchestra in commanding form and Giulini less mannered than he has sometimes been in Beethoven, his *Seventh* is a formidable version. The *Eighth Symphony* is rather less distinguished but in its lyrical, moulded way is certainly enjoyable. The remastered recordings sound well enough, with the resonant Chicago acoustic clearer than on the original LP.

Walter's *Seventh* has a comparatively slow first-movement allegro, but he had rehearsed his players well in the tricky dotted 6/8 rhythm and the result dances convincingly, even if the movement seems to lumber somewhat. The *Allegretto* also seems heavier than usual, but the important point is that genuine tension is created with the illusion of an actual performance. The scherzo is also rather wayward and the Trio takes its time, but in contrast the finale goes with a splendid lift to the playing and very brilliant horns and trumpets in the exciting coda. The coupled *Eighth* has similarly slow speeds, especially in the inner movements. The first goes well enough, but after that the pacing hampers the sustaining of any high degree of intensity. The sound is full and well balanced.

Solti in his coupling of Nos. 7 and 8 directs weighty performances which, at rather faster speeds, still have generally more resilience than those in his earlier Chicago cycle. As usual with Solti, this Beethoven is more remarkable for its power than for sparkle or charm. Only in the finale of No. 7 does the speed tend to bring cloudy textures. By contrast, in the finale of No. 8 the result is transparent and refined. This recording, unlike the last, omits the second repeat in the Scherzo of No. 7. The sound is fuller and more sympathetic than in most in this series.

Symphony No. 7 (trans. Liszt).
(*) Teldec/WEA Dig. 2292 43065-2 [id.]. Cyprien Katsaris (with SCHUMANN: *Exercises on Beethoven's Seventh Symphony*).
(*) Nimbus NI 5013 [id.]. Ronald Smith (with BACH/BUSONI: *Chaconne**).

Cyprien Katsaris does wonders in translating Liszt's transcription into orchestral terms. His is very clean, precise playing, often powerful, with textures commendably clear and with generally steady, unexceptionable tempi. The *Schumann Exercises* make an apt if hardly inspiring fill-up, based on the main theme of the symphony's *Allegretto*. But the symphony is another matter, providing an unexpectedly illuminating listening experience. The sound is excellent.

Ronald Smith, much more than Katsaris, turns the Liszt transcription into a pianistic essay, treating the music with more expressive freedom, often more seductively. He is daring in the Presto scherzo, then unexpectedly light and easy in the finale, with an attractive spring in the rhythm. The performance is not technically flawless but here, and even more in the superb Bach–Busoni transcription, he consistently plays with virtuosic flair. The reverberant recording is pleasantly atmospheric, but not every note is clear.

Symphony No. 8 in F, Op. 93.
(M) *** Trax TRXCD 127. Sydney SO, Serebrier – DVOŘÁK: *Symphony No. 8.***
(M) (***) EMI mono CDM7 63398-2 [id.]. RPO, Beecham – MENDELSSOHN: *Symphony No. 4*; SCHUBERT: *Symphony No. 8.*(***)
(*) Telarc Dig. CD 80090 [id.]. Cleveland O, Dohnányi – SCHUBERT: *Symphony No. 8.*

Symphony No. 8; Overtures: Coriolan; Fidelio; Leonora No. 3.
**(*) DG Dig. 415 507-2 [id.]. BPO, Karajan.

A first-class mid-priced version of No. 8 from Serebrier with a good modern recording, well balanced by the Australian Broadcasting Commission studio engineers. Serebrier's reading has both vigour and weight, and the powerful climax of the first movement is matched by the energy of the finale; the *Allegretto* is contrastingly nimble, with a nice *scherzando* feeling. The full reverberation does not cloud detail; those for whom the coupling is suitable will find this excellent value.

Though Beecham was never very sympathetic to the Beethoven of the great odd-numbered symphonies, he loved the *Eighth*, as this characteristic reading makes plain, rescued by EMI for the Beecham Edition from the CBS archive. Speeds tend to be on the relaxed side, but Beecham's rhythmic spring never lets them drag. Such moments as the entry of the recapitulation in the first movement at the very culmination of the development have the thrill of first discovery, and the delicate pointing of that movement's gentle pay-off is very Beechamesque. The mono recording does not help the strings to sound very sweet, but this EMI transfer is far clearer than ever the original LPs were.

Karajan's more relaxed view of the *Eighth* (compared with his 1977 Berlin version) is almost always pure gain. Nevertheless, Karajan's is a massive view of what has often been dubbed Beethoven's 'little symphony', taking it well into the powerful world of the nineteenth century, with fierceness part of the mixture in the outer movements. The three overtures are made massively Olympian too, with *Coriolan* especially impressive. The recording is marginally brighter and clearer than in most of the series, though there is still some congestion in fortissimos.

Dohnányi with his Cleveland Orchestra gives a lively, resilient performance, exceptionally well played. The recording is not as bright as one expects from this source, but is acceptable. The coupling – once adopted in a classic Beecham record – could be, for some, an extra attraction.

Symphony No. 9 in D min. (Choral), Op. 125.
(M) *** DG 415 832-2 [id.]. Tomowa-Sintow, Baltsa, Schreier, Van Dam, V. Singverein, BPO, Karajan.

(M) *** DG 423 204-2 [id.]. Janowitz, Rössl-Majdan, Kmentt, Berry, V. Singverein, BPO, Karajan.

*** DG 429 861-2 [id.]. Anderson, Walker, König, Rootering, various Chs., Bav. RSO, Dresden State O, etc., Bernstein.

(B) *** Ph. 422 464-2 [id.]. Rebmann, Reynolds, de Ridder, Feldhoff, Netherlands R. Ch., Concg. O, Jochum.

(B) *** Decca 421 636-2 [id.]. Harper, Watts, Young, McIntyre, LSO Ch., LSO, Stokowski.

*** O-L Dig. 425 517-2 [id.]. Augér, Robbin, Rolfe-Johnson, Reinhart, LSO Ch., AAM, Hogwood.

(M) *** DG 431 026-2 [id.]. Gwyneth Jones, Schwarz, Kollo, Moll, V. State Op. Ch., VPO, Bernstein.

*** Chan. Dig. CHAN 8750 [id.]. Barstow, Finnie, Rendall, Tomlinson, CBSO Ch., CBSO, Weller.

(M) *** DG 427 802-2 [id.]. Norman, Fassbaender, Domingo, Berry, Concert Singers of V. State Op., VPO, Boehm.

(M) *** DG 413 721-2 (2) [id.]. Norman, Fassbaender, Domingo, Berry, Concert Singers of V. State Op., VPO, Boehm – *Symphony No. 6.****

**(*) ASV Dig. CDDCA 628 [id.]. Harper, Hodgson, Tear, Howell, Sinfonia Ch., LSO Ch. (members), N. Sinfonia, Hickox.

**(*) EMI Dig. CDC7 49221-2 [id.]. Kenny, Walker, Power, Salomaa, L. Schutz Ch., L. Classical Players, Norrington.

**(*) Decca Dig. 417 800-2 [id.]. Norman, Runkel, Schunk, Sotin, Chicago Ch. & SO, Solti.

(B) **(*) CBS MBK 42532 [id.]. Addison, Hobson, Lewis, Bell, Cleveland Ch. & O, Szell.

(M) **(*) Ph. 420 701-2 [id.]. Tomowa-Sintow, Burmeister, Schreier, Adam, Leipzig R. Ch. & GO, Masur.

**(*) DG Dig. 410 987-2 [id.]. Perry, Baltsa, Cole, Van Dam, V. Singverein, BPO, Karajan.

(M) **(*) CBS Dig. MDK 44646 [id.]. Murphy, Watkinson, O'Neill, Howell, Tallis Chamber Ch., ECO, Tilson Thomas.

(M) (***) EMI mono CDH7 69801-2 [id.]. Schwarzkopf, Höngen, Hopf, Edelmann, Bayreuth Fest. Ch. & O, Furtwängler.

**(*) Nimbus Dig. NI 5134 [id.]. Harrhy, Bailey, Murgatroyd, George, Oslo Cathedral Ch., Hanover Band, Goodman.

(M) *(**) EMI CDM7 69030-2 [id.]. Te Kanawa, Hamari, Burrows, Holl, LSO Ch., LSO, Jochum.

(M) ** EMI CDM7 63359-2 [id.]. Lövberg, Ludwig, Kmentt, Hotter, Philh. Ch. and O, Klemperer.

** Ph. Dig. 420 542-2 [id.]. Popp, Watkinson, Schreier, Holl, Netherlands R. Ch., Concg. O, Haitink.
*(*) Ph. Dig. 426 252-2 [id.]. Karita Mattila, Anne Sofie von Otter, Francisco Araiza, Samuel Ramey, ASMF Ch. & ASMF, Marriner.
(M) *(*) Pickwick Dig. PCD 923. Hargan, Della Jones, Rendall, Howell, LSO Ch., LSO, Wyn Morris.

Of the three stereo recordings Karajan has made of the *Ninth*, his 1977 account is the most inspired in its insight, above all in the *Adagio*, where he conveys spiritual intensity at a slower tempo than in his earlier, 1962 version and more searchingly than in the later, digital recording, where the effect is more lyrical in its beauty. In the finale, the concluding eruption has an animal excitement rarely heard from this highly controlled conductor. The soloists make an excellent team, with contralto, tenor and bass all finer than their predecessors and the soprano markedly more secure than her successor in 1985. The sound has tingling projection and drama. Though Karajan's 1962 version is less hushed and serene in the slow movement, the finale blazes even more intensely, with Janowitz's contribution radiant in its purity. This reflected the Berlin sessions when it rounded off a cycle, recorded over two weeks.

Recorded live on the morning of Christmas Day 1989, Bernstein's Berlin version may have been issued to commemorate a particular occasion of celebration, but it is far more than just a memento of a historic event, the destruction of the Berlin Wall. It brings a performance that has something special to say, even after all the many recordings of this work, and not only because Bernstein substitutes the word '*Freiheit*', 'Freedom', for '*Freude*' in the choral finale, something of which Beethoven himself might well have approved. The ensemble may have the odd blemish, and noises from the audience and other sources – not least from the conductor in his more balletic movements – intrude at times; but, at speeds far more spacious than in his previous recordings, and notably in a dedicated account of the slow movement, the tensions of a live occasion are thrillingly conveyed. The orchestra, drawn mainly from Germany, both East and West, the Bavarian RSO and Dresden Staatskapelle, also included members of the Kirov Theatre Orchestra in Leningrad, the New York Philharmonic, the Orchestre de Paris and the LSO. The choirs similarly came from East and West Germany, while the soloists represented four countries: America (June Anderson), Britain (Sarah Walker), Germany (Klaus König) and Holland (Jan-Hendrik Rootering). Rootering above all makes a splendid impact in his '*Freiheit*' solo, helped by amazingly vivid sound, with the chorus full-bodied to achieve a thrilling culmination. For many, the uniqueness of this version and the emotions it conveys will make it a first choice, despite obvious flaws.

On Philips's cheapest Concert Classics label, Jochum's 1969 version makes an excellent recommendation, powerfully conducted and intense, beautifully played with exceptionally crisp wind articulation and with the glory of the Concertgebouw string-tone well caught by the recording despite obvious signs of age. There is a demonic quality in Jochum's reading, whether in the rugged power of the first movement, the fierce dance of the scherzo or the sharp disruption at the start of the finale. That quality is strongly set against a rapt and spacious account of the slow movement and a reading of the finale which underlines the joy of the writing. Soloists are a clear and fresh team with no wobblers, and the chorus is powerful and responsive, not helped by being set behind the orchestra. The sound has good presence and clarity, though lacking a little in body and failing to expand as a more modern recording would.

Stokowski's 1969 version, also reissued on bargain label, makes another impressive choice for the *Ninth*. The recording – originally Phase 4 – has been vividly remastered and retains its fullness, both vocally and orchestrally. There is the sort of tension about this recorded performance which one expects from a great conductor in the concert hall, and that compulsion carries one over all Stokowski's idiosyncrasies, including a fair amount of retouching in the orchestration. The first movement is strong and dramatic, taken at a Toscanini pace; the scherzo is light and pointed, with timpani cutting through; the slow movement has great depth and *Innigkeit*, and that perhaps more than anything confirms the greatness of the performance, for the finale, with some strangely slow tempi, is uneven, despite fine singing, yet ends resplendently.

Hogwood with his period forces is very well recorded. The ensemble is clear and well balanced both in the instrumental movements and in the choral finale, where an apt scale is achieved, neither too large nor too small. Like his direct rivals among period performers, Hogwood has taken close note of Beethoven's controversial metronome markings; so it is that the first and third movements are faster than usual, the second and fourth generally slower. But Hogwood's manner is not too rigorous and he scores significantly over his direct rivals, not just in the sound-quality but in the quality of solo and choral singing. Though rhythms are not always ideally resilient, this is the most recommendable period performance of the *Ninth* currently available.

Bernstein – recorded live, as in the rest of his Vienna cycle – directs a powerful and distinctive reading of the *Ninth*. The very start conveys immediate electricity, the scherzo is resilient, the *Adagio* deeply convincing in its distinctive contrasting of inner meditation with lighter, more carefree interludes. Though in the choral finale Gwyneth Jones has her raw moments, overall it is a superb account, sung and played with dedication. The recording is among the finest in the series, given extra space and presence in the CD transfer.

In Weller's reading, the choral finale explodes in joy, with John Tomlinson firm and commanding in his opening solo. The tenor, David Rendall, is a shade tremulous and the soprano, Josephine Barstow, cannot sing gently in her highest register; but all the soloists are responsive and intelligent. The Birmingham Chorus, trained by another talented conductor, Simon Halsey, is superb, and the balance between voices and orchestra is among the most natural yet. Weller gives positive, well-sprung readings of the first three movements. The first and third may lack something in mystery, the one full and strong rather than cataclysmic, the other sweet and easily lyrical; but, helped by rich recording quality with an impressively wide range, this is one of the most satisfying of the modern digital versions.

Just a few months before he died, Karl Boehm made his final statement on the work in this resplendent digital recording. With generally slow tempi, his reading is spacious and powerful – the first movement even has a certain stoic quality – and in its broad concept it has much in common with Klemperer's version. Yet overall there is a transcending sense of a great occasion; the concentration is unfailing, reaching its peak in the glorious finale, where ruggedness and strength well over into inspiration. With a fine, characteristic team of soloists and a freshly incisive chorus formed from singers of the Vienna State Opera, this is strongly recommendable. It is available separately at mid-price, and also coupled to another outstanding Boehm recording – of the *Pastoral Symphony*.

Hickox's performance, using an orchestra of the size Beethoven originally had, brings some of the advantages of period performance: clarity of articulation and texture; otherwise one might not realize that the string band is any smaller than one on a regular recording of the *Ninth*. In his pacing throughout the work, Hickox is unerring and conveys from first to last the tension of a genuine performance, in a way that some of his rivals among international stars do not manage. This is the most successful issue in his Beethoven series for ASV. The performance culminates in a glowing account of the choral finale with four excellent soloists. The sole reservation one has is that, in a reverberant acoustic, the slight distancing of the players and chorus gets in the way of full expansion on crescendos. In the performance there is no lack of power at all.

Much of the sharp intensity and exhilaration of Norrington's reading of the *Ninth* comes over on his record, with many of his contentions over observing Beethoven's fast metronome markings validated in the success of the performance. What has to remain controversial is the slow movement which, at tempi far swifter than we are used to, becomes a sweet interlude rather than a meditation, far shorter than the other movements. A more serious snag is the contribution of the male soloists. Petteri Salomaa's tremulous, aspirated singing on the command '*Nicht diese Töne*' is painful, while Patrick Power's plaintive tenor timbre goes with a very slow pace for the drum-and-fife march passage. Nevertheless, the impact of the whole performance is considerable, with reverberant recording still allowing the bite of timpani and valveless horns to cut through the texture. In no sense, except in the number of performers involved, is this a small-scale performance, rather an intensely refreshing view of a supreme masterpiece.

The spaciousness of Solti's reading, with unusually slow basic speeds in the first and third movements, has remained constant, with basic tempi even a fraction slower than before. The biting drama of the first movement and the resonant lyricism of the third are as intense as ever, though lines are now sculpted a shade more carefully. The choral finale is exuberant, with fine solo singing led by the dominant Jessye Norman. It is a pity that with rather backward balance the glowing contribution of the Chicago Symphony Chorus is not more sharply focused; otherwise, the sound is of excellent Chicago vintage, bright and full.

As bitingly dramatic as Toscanini in the first movement and electrically intense all through, Szell directs a magnetic, seemingly inevitable account of the *Ninth* which demonstrates the glories of the Cleveland Orchestra. With speeds never as extreme as Toscanini's, he yet captures a comparable fire. Though with close-up CBS recording, the slow movement never conveys anything like a pianissimo, the beauty of line in immaculate legato gives persuasive warmth and sweetness. The chorus sings with similarly knife-edged ensemble, set behind the orchestra but not too distantly. Soloists are well forward, so that words are exceptionally clear. The 1961 sound, bright and forward, has come up satisfyingly full-bodied, if with some analogue hiss. At mid-price a first-rate recommendation for those wanting a commanding reminder of a great conductor's work.

Masur's Leipzig *Ninth* comes from his complete set of the mid-1970s. It is a spacious, well-proportioned and noble account, more conventional in its speeds than some, and less weighty, yet in the excellent digital remastering the choral sound is full and immediate and the extra clarity extends to the other movements.

The high point of Karajan's digital version of the *Ninth* is the sublime slow movement, here exceptionally sweet and true, with the lyricism all the more persuasive in a performance recorded in a complete take. The power and dynamism of the first two movements are striking too, but the choral finale is flawed above all by the singing of the soprano, Janet Perry, far too thin of tone and unreliable. The sound of the choir has plenty of body but is rather ill-defined.

Michael Tilson Thomas's version of the *Ninth* may – like the rest of his Beethoven cycle – involve limited forces approximating to the size of those originally used, but there is nothing miniature here. This is an unusually powerful reading, sharply rhythmic and with a fine sense of drama, well paced at traditional rather than 'authentic' tempi. The very opening has nothing of mystery in it, with the tremolos firmly placed in clear and immediate sound. That forwardness gives the first movement ample power, and the clarity of detail in the second adds to the joyful resilience of the dance rhythms. Paradoxically, one misses a full body of violins most of all in the lyrical expanses of the slow movement, which is done very sweetly. The whole of the last movement – often taken faster than usual – comes at white heat, with some first-rate solo work, notably from Gwynne Howell in a magnificent account of the opening solo, though the forward balance militates against any gentle singing. The Tallis Chamber Choir rather belies its name when, with more immediacy than choruses often get in the *Ninth*, the sound is so full as well as clear.

It is thrilling to have a CD transfer of the historic recording made at the re-opening of the Festspielhaus in Bayreuth in 1951. The chorus may sound washy in the distance, almost as though placed at the bottom of the Rhine, and the lack of perspective in the mono sound is brought out the more on CD (along with audience noises), but the extra clarity and freshness impressively enhance a reading without parallel. The spacious, lovingly moulded account of the slow movement is among Furtwängler's finest achievements on record and, with an excellent quartet of soloists, the finale crowns a great performance.

Goodman's reading of the *Ninth* is just as refreshing and even more sympathetic than Roger Norrington's mould-breaking rival version on period instruments. Like the rest of the set, the performances convey a sense of spontaneity. Though – like Norrington on EMI – Goodman broadly follows Beethoven's controversial metronome markings – very fast in the slow movement, with some of the *allegros* in the finale unusually slow – he applies the doctrine less ruthlessly. Though the slow movement flows along very briskly, he introduces a degree of easing which conveys necessary gravity, a sense of repose. His springing of rhythm in the 6/4 section of the finale is then rather more winning than in Norrington's version, and the soloists have fewer flaws. With characteristically reverberant Nimbus recording, generally undistracting, it makes an attractive recommendation overall, quite apart from its authenticity of approach.

Jochum's later EMI recording could have been even more recommendable than the earlier, Philips Concertgebouw version, but unfortunately the CD transfer has lost some of the bloom of the analogue master and is edgy and not ideally focused. The interpretation is similar, with the scherzo almost violent in its urgency and speeds generally on the fast side, the massive structures of the first and third movements held together seamlessly. With youthful-sounding voices among the soloists as well as in the chorus, the effect balances vitality with weight, and it is a pity that the sound is so disappointing.

Klemperer's 1958 sound is amazingly good for its period, with the finale fresher and better balanced than in many recent recordings. However, Klemperer's weighty vision is marred by a disappointing quartet of soloists; and the slow speeds for the first two movements – the scherzo seems to go on for ever – come to sound ponderous. Yet the flowing account of the slow movement shows Klemperer at his finest. The CD offers extra refinement, with the choral sound in the finale given astonishing presence and clarity.

Haitink's version of the *Ninth* is the third he has recorded; this is the one that rounded off his disappointing set of all nine Beethoven *Symphonies*, recorded not long before he resigned from the Concertgebouw. Though the reading displays the strong, direct manner which typifies his Beethoven, the performance as a whole fails to lift, and the recording quality falls well short of what one expects of Philips's engineers working in the Concertgebouw.

The surprise when Marriner recorded the *Eroica* with the Academy, very early in his Beethoven series, was that there was no suspicion of miniaturization, but the *Ninth* is rather different. This well-behaved performance seems too small-scale, partly a question of the slightly distant recording, partly the absence of dramatic bite. The slow movement is surprisingly plain and unmoulded, and the chorus in the finale lacks body, but the quartet of soloists is an outstanding one of fresh and young voices.

Wyn Morris's Beethoven cycle for Pickwick came to a disappointing conclusion with this account of the *Ninth* which displayed too many signs of haste in the recording; where most of the earlier issues in the series found the LSO in excellent form, the ensemble here is often slack. Even at mid-price, there are many versions finer than this; though it has the benefit of modern digital recording, the sound here is little more faithful than that on some of the vintage versions.

Symphony No. 9 (trans. Liszt).
**(*) Teldec/WEA Dig. 2292 42985-2 [id.]. Cyprien Katsaris (piano).

Liszt made no attempt to create pianistically 'effective' arrangements, yet in his transcription of the *Ninth Symphony* he conveys so much of the character of an orchestra storming the heavens. Cyprien Katsaris's performance is nothing short of a *tour de force*: his virtuosity is altogether remarkable and there is a demonic Beethovenian vehemence and drive. He must have as many hands as an octopus has tentacles, for his ability to convey the teeming activity of the finale, to bring various strands to the foreground and then disappear into the mêlée, is astonishing. The piano is closely observed in a reverberant acoustic ambience and listeners may at times be disturbed by its somewhat jangly quality.

Symphony No. 10 in E flat: 1st movement (realized and completed by Dr Barry Cooper – includes lecture by Dr Cooper).
(B) *** Pickwick Dig. PCD 911 [MCA MCAD 6269]. LSO, Wyn Morris.

As re-created from Beethoven's sketches by Dr Barry Cooper, this movement from what was planned as the *Tenth Symphony* is, as Dr Cooper says, no more than an 'artist's impression'. What he has put together from those and other sketch sources makes a fascinating and satisfying symphonic concept: a noble slow movement in E flat with obvious echoes of the *Ninth Symphony*, in the centre of which is a compressed *Allegro* sonata-form movement in C minor, the whole lasting almost 20 minutes. The broad *Andante* sections with their *Ninth*-like descants to the *Pathétique*-like main theme are plausibly Beethovenian. What is far less convincing is the *Allegro*, based as it is on relatively feeble material, with conventional working-out but with one or two surprising strokes culled from the sketches which, for all their oddity, must be counted Beethovenian. The master would have moulded this into something far greater, but it is well worth hearing music that so dwells in the mind.

Wyn Morris in this first recording directs a broad, strong reading, very well played and recorded. Dr Cooper's half-hour lecture fascinatingly amplifies and illustrates his detailed notes, making clear his scholarly credentials as well as his devotion to what Beethoven planned.

Wellington's victory (Battle symphony), Op. 91.
** DG 419 624-2 [id.]. BPO, Karajan – *Egmont***(*); *Marches.***
** Telarc Dig. CD 80079 [id.]. Cincinnati SO, Kunzel – LISZT: *Hunnenschlacht.***

Karajan's version is very well played, and the digital remastering adds presence to the opening assembly to left and right; but there is no sense of occasion and the battle-sounds are not entirely convincing, with the resonant acoustics of the Berlin Jesus-Christus Kirche bringing atmosphere but not helping to focus the spectacle. However, Karajan's *Egmont* coupling is much more worth while than the alternatives offered by his competitors.

With a characteristically natural overall sound-balance, Kunzel's Telarc recording is technically the most sophisticated presentation of Beethoven's 'Battle' Symphony on record, though the real musketry and cannon featured in the recording sound curiously like a fireworks display. The performance is musically conceived and well played, but has no special individuality.

CHAMBER MUSIC

Cello sonatas Nos. 1–5, Op. 5/1–2; Op. 69; Op. 102/1–2.
* Decca Dig. 417 628-2 [id.]. Lynn Harrell, Vladimir Ashkenazy.
* Ph. 412 256-2 [id.]. Mstislav Rostropovich, Sviatoslav Richter.
**(*) CBS Dig. M2K 42446 (2) [id.]. Yo-Yo Ma, Emanuel Ax.
(M) ****(*)** EMI CMS7 69196-2 (2). Paul Tortelier, Eric Heidsick.

Cello sonatas Nos. 1–5; 7 Variations on Bei Männern (from Mozart's Die Zauberflöte), WoO 45; 12 Variations on 'See the conqu'ring hero comes' (from Handel's Judas Maccabaeus), WoO 46; 12 Variations on Ein Mädchen, Op. 66.
(M) ******* EMI CMS7 63015-2 (2). Jacqueline Du Pré, Daniel Barenboim.
(M) ******* DG 423 297-2 (2) [id.]. Pierre Fournier, Wilhelm Kempff.
**(*) Hyp. Dig. CDA 66281/2 (available separately). Anthony Pleeth, Melvyn Tan (fortepiano).

Cello sonatas Nos. 3 in A, Op. 69; 5 in D, Op. 102/2.
*** CBS Dig. MK 39024 [id.]. Yo-Yo Ma, Emanuel Ax.
(M) ******* EMI CDM7 69179-2 [id.]. Jacqueline du Pré, Bishop-Kovacevich.

Lynn Harrell and Vladimir Ashkenazy have the advantage of superb recording: they are sensibly balanced, neither instrument being too prominent or too reticent. Artistically, too, these performances are in the first league – they are unfailingly sensitive and alert, well thought-out and yet seemingly spontaneous. They will be a first recommendation for many collectors, especially those interested in first-class sound.

The set of performances by Jacqueline Du Pré with Daniel Barenboim was recorded live for the BBC during the Edinburgh Festival of 1970. The playing may not have the final polish that studio performances would no doubt have achieved, but the concentration and intensity of the playing are wonderfully caught; and though the Scottish audience was often maddeningly bronchial, the performances remain totally compelling, with Barenboim bringing discipline, his wife drawing out lyrical intensity. The recording emerges with good presence on CD, not as full as it might be.

By a strange coincidence, Fournier and Kempff also recorded their cycle of the *Sonatas* at live festival performances. However, the Paris audience is considerably less intrusive than the Edinburgh ones on EMI and, like their younger colleagues, these artists were inspired by the occasion to produce intensely expressive playing, performances which are marked by light, clear textures and rippling scale-work, even in the slow introductions which are taken relatively fast. Some of the weight is missing; but such a stylish spontaneity is irresistible, and admirers of both artists can be warmly recommended to the set. The balances are not ideal, but there is no lack of CD presence.

Made in the early 1960s, the classic Philips performances by Mstislav Rostropovich and Sviatoslav Richter, two of the instrumental giants of the day, have withstood the test of time astonishingly well and sound remarkably fresh in this compact disc transfer. Apart from the usual gains in continuity and freedom from background, there is so much greater presence and realism. But this should now be reissued at mid-price.

With the CBS set by Yo-Yo Ma and Emanuel Ax there are balance problems in the coupling of the two Op. 5 *Sonatas*, where the piano often masks the refined lines that Yo-Yo Ma draws. In Opp. 69 and 102, the internal balance is much better judged. Emanuel Ax often produces a big, wide-ranging tone which must have posed problems, when related to the more introvert style of the cellist. Yo-Yo Ma plays with extraordinary sensitivity and imagination, even if there are times when one might think his pianissimo a bit overdone. The sound-quality is well focused and truthful.

Though the cello is rather forwardly balanced in relation to the fortepiano, the Hyperion collection of Beethoven's cello and piano music – not just the five *Sonatas* but the three sets of variations too – makes an attractive issue for anyone wanting period performances. Tan recorded these performances with Pleeth in 1987, not long before he began his Beethoven series for EMI, and his imagination is comparably keen here. The two discs, both generously filled, are available separately.

Tortelier's performances with Eric Heidsick lie somewhere in between the Du Pré/Barenboim and Kempff/Fournier sets. They are highly musical, classical in feeling and not lacking imaginative detail. The studio balance is well managed and the recording is very good; but without the *Variations* they offer short measure.

The Du Pré/Bishop-Kovacevich recordings of Nos. 3 and 5 come from 1966, the year after Jacqueline had made her definitive record of the Elgar *Concerto*. The very opening of the *D major Sonata* underlines an unbuttoned quality in Beethoven's writing and when, after the hushed intensity of the slow introduction of Op. 69, the music launches into the allegro, both artists soar away fearlessly. More remarkable still is the range of expressiveness in the slow movement of Op. 102/2. Du Pré's tone ranges from full-blooded fortissimo to the mere whisper of a half-tone, and these artists allow the most free range of expressive rubato. With excellent recording, these performances are most welcome on CD, sounding crisp and present in their new format.

Clarinet trio in B flat, Op. 11.
*** Decca 414 576-2 [id.]. Peter Schmidl, New V. Octet (members) – *Septet.****

The New Vienna Octet makes a better case for the Op. 11 *Trio* than most previous rivals. The playing is wonderfully alert and has both sparkle and warmth. Taken on artistic merit alone, this is second to none, but the coupling brings an added inducement. The 1981 analogue recording is admirably balanced and has transferred smoothly and realistically to CD.

Piano quartet in E flat; Op. 16; Serenade in D for string trio, Op. 16.
** Mer. CDE 84154 [id.]. Nelly Ben-Or, Jerusalem String Trio.

The *Piano quartet* is Beethoven's own arrangement of the *Piano and wind quintet*; it sounds more homogeneous using strings but inevitably loses some of its colour. It is well played here, the *Andante* taken rather slowly, to good effect. The *Serenade* is pleasingly done too, although at times the mood seems rather too serious. Good, smooth recording.

Piano trios Nos 1–9; 10 (Variations on an original theme in E flat), Op. 44; 11 (Variations on 'Ich bin der Schneider Kakadu'), Op. 121a; Allegretto in E flat, Hess 48.
*** EMI Dig. CDS7 47455-8 [Ang. CDCD 47455] (4). Ashkenazy, Perlman, Harrell.

Piano trios Nos. 1–3; 5–7; 9–10 (Variations on an original theme in E flat); 11 (Variations on 'Ich bin der Schneider Kakadu'); Allegretto in E flat, Hess 48.
(M) **(*) EMI CMS7 63124-2 (3) [Ang. CDMC 63124]. Daniel Barenboim, Pinchas Zukerman, Jacqueline du Pré.

Piano trios Nos. 1 – 3; 5 – 7.
(M) **(*) DG 415 879-2 (3) [id.]. Kempff, Szeryng, Fournier.

Piano trios Nos. 1 in E flat; 2 in G, Op. 1/1 – 2.
*** Hyp. Dig. CDA 66197 [id.]. L. Fortepiano Trio.

Piano trio No. 5 in D (Ghost), Op. 70/1.
(M) *** Ph. 420 716-2 [id.]. Beaux Arts Trio – SCHUBERT: *Trout quintet.***

Piano trios Nos. 5 in D (Ghost), Op. 70/1; 7 in B flat (Archduke), Op. 97.
(M) **(*) DG 429 712-2 [id.]. Kempff, Szeryng, Fournier.

Piano trio No. 7 (Archduke); 9 in B flat, WoO 39.
*** EMI Dig. CDC7 47010-2 [id.]. Ashkenazy, Perlman, Harrell.

Piano trios Nos. 7 (Archduke); 11 (Variations on 'Ich bin der Schneider Kakadu').
(B) *** Pickwick Dig. PCD 874 [MCA MCAD 25193]. Kalichstein, Laredo, Robinson.

Ashkenazy, Perlman and Harrell lead the field in this repertoire. Their four CDs comprise all of Beethoven's output for the piano trio. They also include the various additional works for the medium, the *Kakadu variations*, the isolated movements with WoO suffixes (works without opus numbers) and the early *Allegretto in E flat*, which most ensembles omit from their complete surveys. The recordings have been made over a period of five years and at various locations, but the sound is consistently fresher, warmer, more richly detailed and more present than with most other rivals. The playing is unfailingly perceptive and full of those musical insights that make one want to return to the set. The *Archduke*, coupled with *No. 9 in B flat*, is available separately on CD.

The Barenboim/Zukerman/du Pré set (by omitting Nos. 4 and 8) is fitted economically on to three mid-priced CDs. Even more than usual, the individual takes involved long spans of music, often complete movements, sometimes even a complete work. The result is music-making of rare concentration, spontaneity and warmth. Any tendency to self-indulgence – and this aspect of the playing may seem intrusive to some ears – plus a certain leaning towards romantic expressiveness, is counterbalanced by the urgency and intensity. Speeds tend to be extreme in both directions, and the *Innigkeit* of some of the slow movements, especially in the *Ghost trio*, Op. 70, No. 1, has the depth of really mature artistry, extraordinary in the work of musicians so young at the time of the recordings. The excellent recording has been freshened on CD, and the players are given a natural presence; although at times the definition is not absolutely clean and there is a touch of dryness on fortissimo tuttis, overall the effect is pleasingly natural.

The Kempff–Szeryng–Fournier team recorded their survey of the Beethoven *Trios* in the early 1970s, and the DG engineers have been outstandingly successful in transferring them to the new medium. These are performances of distinction and well worth adding to any collection, given the excellence of the sound-quality. Wilhelm Kempff is an unfailingly interesting artist, and both Henryk Szeryng and that aristocrat of cellists, Pierre Fournier, are in impressive form throughout. On their separate coupling of the two most famous works, Kempff and his colleagues give a crystalline reading of the *Archduke*, and the performance of the *Ghost trio* is again relatively restrained. These are essentially lyrical readings and it is the clarity and imagination of Kempff's playing which grip the listener's attention with his many individual touches so that, by comparison, Szeryng and Fournier sound less inspired. The CD transfers are fresh and clear and the 1970 recording has plenty of fullness as well as a natural presence.

The Kalichstein–Laredo–Robinson Trio's interpretations of both the *Archduke* and the *Variations* are unaffected, supremely musicianly and thoughtful. Indeed their first movement of the *Archduke* is splendidly unhurried, and tempi throughout are excellently judged. There is formidable and distinguished opposition, but this team has nothing to fear from it. A marvellous performance and a very good, splendidly clean recording, even if it is bright and forward.

At present the London Fortepiano Trio have the field to themselves in the realm of 'authentic' performances. Monica Huggett and her partner, Linda Nicholson, play with considerable virtuosity, particularly in the finales, which are taken at high speed and to considerable effect. The use of a fortepiano serves to enhance clarity of texture in this particular repertoire, and readers should make an effort to sample what one assumes will be a complete cycle.

On Philips the Beaux Arts Trio couple the *Ghost trio* with an enjoyable version of Schubert's *Trout quintet*. The *Ghost* comes off marvellously and sounds very fresh, and the 1979 recording has responded well to digital remastering; the sound is firm, clear and truthfully balanced. The *Trout*, however, is rather less successful; the violinist Isidore Cohen's timbre is made to sound thinner and edgier than it is.

Piano and wind quintet in E flat, Op. 16.
*** CBS Dig. MK 42099 [id.]. Perahia, members of ECO – MOZART: *Quintet.****
*** Decca Dig. 414 291-2 [id.]. Lupu, De Vries, Pieterson, Zarzo, Pollard – MOZART: *Quintet.****
(M) *** Decca 421 151-2 [id.]. Ashkenazy, L. Wind Soloists – MOZART: *Quintet.****
(*) Ph. Dig. 420 182-2 [id.]. Brendel, Holliger, Brunner, Baumann, Thunemann – MOZART: *Quintet.**

The view that Beethoven's *Piano and wind quintet* is less interesting than its Mozartian predecessor (which plainly inspired it) is almost confounded by Perahia's CBS version, recorded at The Maltings. The first movement is given more weight than usual, with a satisfying culmination. In the *Andante*, Perahia's playing is wonderfully poetic and serene and the wind soloists are admirably responsive. The pacing of the finale is ideally judged; and with the recording most realistically balanced, this issue can be recommended with all enthusiasm.

Radu Lupu and his colleagues also give a glorious account of the Beethoven *Quintet* and, while it would not necessarily weaken allegiance to Perahia and members of the ECO on CBS, it can certainly be recommended alongside it. The balance achieved by the Decca engineers is very natural and true to life. Lupu's playing has sparkle and freshness, and the first movement has real elegance and, when required, wit. The wind offer beautifully blended and cultured playing; this is a glorious performance, superbly recorded.

Ashkenazy's recording from 1966 stands up well to the competition. The *Andante cantabile* of the Beethoven is given a particularly appealing tranquillity, and the *Rondo* is both gracious and sprightly. The sound is first class in every way, the balance rather forward but very vivid and real. A splendid mid-priced alternative to the versions featuring Perahia and Lupu.

Brendel and his colleagues are hardly less impressive in the Beethoven than they are in the Mozart coupling. The quality of the recording is remarkably clean and fresh and, generally speaking, the sound is well in the demonstration bracket. This will rightly delight admirers of these artists.

Septet in E flat, Op. 20.
*** Decca 414 576-2 [id.]. New V. Octet (members) – *Clarinet trio.****
(M) *** Decca 421 093-2 [id.]. V. Octet (members) – MENDELSSOHN: *Octet.***(*)

(i) *Septet in E flat, Op. 20;* (ii) *Duo for clarinet and bassoon in B flat, WoO 27/3.*
*** Novalis Dig. 150 021-2 [id.]. (i) Schweizer Soloists; (ii) Kurt Weber, Tomas Sosnowski.

Septet in E flat, Op. 20; (i) *Sextet in E flat, Op. 81b.*
(M) **(*) Ph. 426 091-2 [id.]. BPO Octet (members); (i) with Manfred Klier.

The splendid new digital CD, made by a young Swiss group, in almost all respects supersedes the distinguished older versions on Decca. At the very outset one is struck by the freshness of their playing, by the excellent internal blending, helped by a naturally balanced recording, and by the spirit and warmth of their music-making. Tempi are consistently apt and the ear revels in the interplay between these artists. The finale is particularly fluent and infectious, as indeed is the whole performance. With such realistic recording one has the sense of live music-making taking place in one's very room. The *Duo* which follows is also played with much charm and confirms the natural partnership between clarinet and bassoon that had already blossomed in the *Septet.*

These Decca recordings were made by different generations of the Vienna Octet, which consists of the first desks of the VPO. Their performances have elegance, but also convey a sparkle and a sense of enjoyment that are thoroughly exhilarating. In terms of spirit and exuberance, the newer version is altogether special. Both CD transfers are very successful.

An amiably refined performance from the excellent Berlin Philharmonic group, with plenty of life in the outer movements, but with rather a solemn view taken of the slow movement. The recording is first class; many will like its warmth and amplitude. The *Sextet*, for two horns and string quartet, is also very well played and recorded.

Serenade in D for flute, violin and viola, Op. 25.
⊛ (B) *** Pickwick/CDI Dig. PWK 1139. Israel Flute Trio (with Recital: '*Flute Serenade*'***).

The light and charming combination of flute, violin and viola inspired the youthful Beethoven to write in an unexpectedly carefree and undemanding way. The sequence of tuneful, unpretentious movements reminds one of Mozart's occasional music, and this delectable Israel performance brings out all its charm. Er'ella Talmi is a superb flautist and she receives admirable support from her colleagues. The recording is wonderfully natural in sound and balance: it is as if the players were making music in one's own room.

Serenades: in D for violin, viola & cello, Op. 8; in D for flute, violin & viola, Op. 25.
(M) ** Ph. 426 090-2 [id.]. Grumiaux Trio with Maxence Larrieu.

This is a sensible coupling, as both works were probably composed at about the same time. The *Serenade* for strings alone does not match its better-known companion in charm, and the performance here, though polished, is not especially persuasive, with slightly dry string-timbres as recorded. The Op. 25, however, freshly played, is enjoyable, although it is not as spontaneous in effect as the Israel version.

Serenades: (i) *in D, Op. 25* (for flute, violin and viola); (ii) *in D, Op. 8 ; Sonata in B flat* (both arr. for flute and piano).
**(*) RCA Dig. RD 87756 [7756-2-RC]. James Galway; (i) Joseph Swensen & Paul Neubauer; (ii) Phillip Moll.

A fine, polished account of the *D major Serenade*, with plenty of sparkle, if not quite as winning as the Israel version. The balance is good, but the resonance prevents an absolutely sharp focus. Instead of using the trio version of Op. 8, Galway opts for an arrangement for flute and piano, which provides less diversity of texture, although his vivacious bravura turns the fourth-movement *Allegretto alla Polacca* into something of a lollipop. Phillip Moll makes a strong contribution, both here and in the *Sonata* which probably is not by Beethoven at all. It is a pleasing enough piece and both artists relish the operatic line of its *Largo* slow movement.

String quartets

String quartets Nos. 1–16; Grosse Fugue, Op. 133.
*** Valois V 4401 (*Nos. 1 & 5*); V 4402 (*Nos. 2–4*); V 4403 (*Nos. 6–7*); V 4404 (*Nos. 8–9*); V 4405 (*Nos. 10 & 12*); V 4406 (*Nos. 11 & 15*); V 4407 (*Nos. 13 & Grosse Fugue*); V 4408 (*Nos. 14 & 16*) [id.]. Végh Qt.
(M)**(*) DG 423 473-2 (7) [id.]. Amadeus Qt.

The Végh performances were recorded in the mid-1970s; they have been rightly hailed for their simplicity and depth. Intonation may not always be absolutely immaculate, but flaws are few and trivial when one considers the wisdom and experience the Végh communicate. In short they are in a different league from most of their rivals: there is no cultivation of surface polish though there is both elegance and finesse. They observe all the first-movement exposition repeats, which is why they don't fit the Op. 18 set on two records. The Végh bring very special insights to this music; their playing is deep and searching, and when listening to them you are conscious only of Beethoven's voice. The CD transfers are successful in producing an altogether cleaner image and a slightly firmer focus than the original analogue LPs, although the imbalance towards the cello remains.

The Amadeus are at their best in the Op. 18 quartets, where their mastery and polish are heard to good advantage. In the middle-period and late quartets their sumptuous tone and refinement of balance are always in evidence, but they do not always penetrate very far beneath the surface, particularly in the late quartets. There is some superb quartet playing in this cycle, but there are more searching accounts to be found. The recording, from the beginning of the 1960s, is fresh and lifelike and the set is economically priced on seven CDs, but the Végh Quartet are worth the extra cost.

String quartets Nos. 1–6, Op. 18/1–6.
*** EMI Dig. CDS7 47127-8 [Ang. CDC 47126] (3). Alban Berg Qt.
(M) **(*) Ph. 426 046-2 (3) [id.]. Italian Qt.
**(*) Cal. CAL 9633/4 [id.]. Talich Qt.

String quartets Nos. 1 in F; 2 in G, Op. 18/1–2.
**(*) HM HMC 901222 [id.]. Brandis Qt.
*(*) Hyp. Dig. CDA 66401 [id.]. New Budapest Qt.

String quartets Nos. 1–3, Op. 18/1–3.
*** Nimbus Dig. NI 5173 [id.]. Medici Qt.

String quartets Nos. 5 in A; 6 in B flat, Op. 18/5–6.
(B) **(*) Ph. 426 049-2 [id.]. Italian Qt.

The Alban Berg undoubtedly offer a polish and tonal finesse that put them in a class of their own. The playing is immaculate and the sound has all the usual advantages of the new medium: excellent definition, presence and body. The CDs are also available separately (CDC7 47127/8/9-2).

The Italian performances are in superb style. The only reservations concern Nos. 2 and 4: the latter is perhaps a little wanting in forward movement, while the conventional exchanges at the opening of No. 2 seem a shade too deliberate. The recordings were made between 1972 (Nos. 1 and 3) and 1975 (Nos. 2 and 4) and while the balance is truthful, the digital remastering does draw the ear to a certain thinness in the treble, slightly more noticeable in the earliest recordings. If all the recordings are issued on Philips's bargain label, they will remain highly competitive.

The Medici offer all but a few seconds short of 80 minutes of playing time, and without sacrificing first-movement exposition repeats. They are not a jet-set ensemble; their playing is refreshingly unglamorous and yet thoroughly polished; nor do they fail to penetrate the depths – their account of the slow movement of the *F major* is far from superficial. They are given a very natural and well-balanced recording, and these performances will give considerable satisfaction.

The Talich offer all six Op. 18 *Quartets* on two CDs. Their performances have the merit of directness and simplicity of utterance; as music-making there is a refreshing naturalness about this approach. Sometimes they are inclined to be a little measured and wanting in urgency, but if there is some prose in this set there is no want of poetry either. First-movement exposition repeats are preserved except in Nos. 1 and 6. The Calliope recording is very clean and present, if a trifle dry.

The Brandis Quartet can more than hold their own with their current rivals. Tempi are well chosen, there is an enviable unanimity of ensemble and no lack of polish. The slow movement of the *F major* does not obliterate memories of the greatest performances of the past but, generally speaking, no one investing in these well-recorded performances need fear disappointment.

The New Budapest Quartet give well-prepared but slightly undervitalized performances. They tend to iron out dynamics so that the overall effect sounds a little bland. Their playing is eminently civilized and they are often perceptive (as in the slow movement of Op. 18, No. 1) but if the complete cycle which is promised proceeds as it has started, it will not displace the best of current recommendations.

String quartets Nos. 7–9 (Rasumovsky Nos. 1–3), Op. 59/1–3; 10 in E flat (Harp), Op. 74; 11 in F min., Op. 95.
(M) *** Ph. 420 797-2 (3) [id.]. Italian Qt.
**(*) EMI Dig. CDS7 47131-8 [Ang. CDC 47130] (3). Alban Berg Qt.

String quartet No. 7 in F (Rasumovsky No. 1), Op. 59/1.
*** ASV Dig. CDDCA 553 [id.]. Lindsay Qt.
**(*) EMI CDC7 47131-2 [id.]. Alban Berg Qt.

String quartets Nos. 8 in E min.; 9 in C (Rasumovsky Nos. 2–3), Op. 59/2–3.
*** ASV Dig. CDDCA 554 [id.]. Lindsay Qt.

String quartets Nos. 7, Op. 59/1; 10 (Harp), Op. 74.
*** Cal. CAL 9636 [id.]. Talich Qt.

String quartets Nos. 8, Op. 59/2; 10 (Harp), Op. 74.
(BB) *** Hung. White Label HRC 063. Bartók Qt.

String quartets Nos. 8, Op. 59/2; 11 in F min., Op. 95.
**(*) EMI CDC7 47132-2 [id.]. Alban Berg Qt.

String quartets Nos. 8, Op. 59/2; 13 in B flat, Op. 130.
*** Cal. CAL 9637 [id.]. Talich Qt.

String quartets Nos. 9, Op. 59/3; 10 (Harp), Op. 74.
**(*) EMI CDC7 47133-2 [id.]. Alban Berg Qt.

String quartets Nos. 9, Op. 59/3; 14 in C sharp min., Op. 131.
*** Cal. CAL 9638 [id.]. Talich Qt.

The remastered Italian set still sounds well: the original recordings, made between 1971 and 1974, were strikingly natural in balance and there is now only a slight thinness on top to betray their age, with no lack of body and warmth in the middle range. Their superiority in terms of sheer quartet playing is still striking: purity of intonation, perfectly blended tone and superb ensemble and attack. Their tempi are perfectly judged and every phrase is sensitively shaped. Yet there is no attempt to 'beautify' Beethoven, and these performances remain very recommendable at mid-price.

The Lindsay set contains performances of real stature; and though they are not unrivalled in some of their insights, among modern recordings they are not often surpassed. The *F major*, Op. 59/1, available separately on CD, is very impressive indeed. This is the most masterly account to have appeared for many decades. In each movement of the *E minor*, Op. 59/2, the Lindsays find the *tempo giusto* and all that they do as a result has the ring of complete conviction. The opening of Op. 59/3 has real mystery and awe, and how splendidly they convey the pent-up torrent of energy released in the fugal onrush of the *Allegro molto*. The two remaining quartets, Opp. 74 and 95, are also highly competitive. As a recording, this set is comparable with most of its competitors and superior to many; artistically, it can hold its own with the best.

The Talich have an impressive technical address, no less formidable than any of their current rivals, and they win our confidence by the essentially private character of their performances. One feels a privileged eavesdropper on an intimate discourse rather than a concert-hall listener waiting for another jet-setting, over-projecting ensemble. There is a real understanding of what this music is about. The recordings, which seemed a bit bottom-heavy when they first appeared, are more firmly defined and better focused than on LP and, while the sound is not in the demonstration class, the instruments are well placed and the timbre truthful – in fact, one quickly forgets about it and loses oneself in the music. Each of these three CDs offers exceptionally good value, containing over 70 minutes of music.

The Bartók Quartet give strong, well-paced readings of both middle-period works, with slow movements to match any rival versions at whatever price. With excellent Hungaroton recording, this is an outstanding bargain in the very inexpensive White Label series.

The Alban Berg recordings favour rather brisk tempi in first movements, which they dispatch with exemplary polish and accuracy of intonation. There is much perceptive music-making but there is also a distinct tendency to exaggerate dynamic extremes. The introduction to Op. 59/3 suffers in this respect and the results sound self-conscious. In the first movements of Op. 59/2 and Op. 95 the brilliance of the attack almost draws attention to itself and perhaps the recording quality, which is closely balanced, gives it a slightly more aggressive quality than it really has. The three CDs are also available separately.

String quartet No. 10 in E flat (Harp), Op. 74.
(B) ** Pickwick Dig. PCD 831. Brodsky Qt – SCHUBERT: *String quartet No. 13.***

The Brodsky recording comes from the mid-1980s. It marks the début of a very good British quartet named after Adolf Brodsky, dedicatee of the Tchaikovsky *Violin concerto*, and – in his time – Principal of the Royal Manchester College of Music, the predecessor of the Royal Northern College of Music, where these players were students. Their account of the *Harp quartet* is full of spirit and they are not lacking in imagination. But there are some rough edges here and there, and their vehemence in fortissimos is not helped by a rather forward recording balance.

String quartets Nos. 10 (Harp); 11 in F min., Op. 95.
** Hyp. Dig. CDH 88032 [id.]. Delmé Qt.
* Teldec/WEA Dig. 2292 44929-2 [id.]. Vermeer Qt.

The playing from the Delmé Quartet is refreshingly natural and free from exaggeration – the kind of performance you might expect to encounter under domestic conditions. Yet their account of the *Harp quartet* needs more dramatic tension: the first movement is not taut enough, and one feels the need for greater concentration and density of feeling throughout Op. 95. However, rather this musicianly and selfless playing than the thrustful, glamorized sonority of some of the starry ensembles now on disc.

The technical command, intonation and tonal blend of the Vermeer Quartet are impeccable. That said, it must be admitted that these are pretty unappealing performances without much warmth or spontaneity. It is all very efficient and rather soulless, with aggressive sforzandi and spot-on ensemble. As with other records in this cycle, the acoustic is inclined to be a trifle dry, and the quartet is rather forward.

String quartets Nos. 10 (Harp), Op. 74; 14 in C sharp min., Op. 131.
*(*) Ph. Dig. 422 341-2 [id.]. Guarneri Quartet.

The Guarneri play with all the expertise and technical address one would expect but, as was the case with earlier records in this series, their imaginative insights are rather less impressive. Playing Beethoven immaculately and with enormous technical polish is no encumbrance if it does not draw attention to itself; but in this instance their brilliance prevents one penetrating far beneath the surface. There is little depth in the opening movement of Op. 131 and no sense of its profound mystery. Marvellous playing as such, and very good recorded sound – but that by itself is not enough in this music.

String quartets Nos. 11 in F min., Op. 95; 12 in E flat, Op. 127; Grosse Fuge, Op. 133.
*** Cal. CAL 9635 (id.]. Talich Qt.

String quartets Nos. 15 in A min., Op. 132; 16 in F, Op. 135.
*** Cal. CAL 9639 [id.]. Talich Qt.

Having Opp. 132 and 135 on one disc is quite a bargain, especially so, given the quality of the performances. These penetrating accounts can hold their own with the very finest, and the quality of the recorded sound – though not spectacular in any way – is more than acceptable. Indeed in the new format it is eminently clean and well focused though not as warm or as alive as in some of the most recent rivals.

String quartets Nos. 11 (Serioso), Op. 95; 15 in A min., Op. 132.
* Ph. Dig. 422 388-2 [id.]. Guarneri Qt.

Sensibly paced and impeccably played though these are, neither performance fully succeeds in reaching the heart either of the music or of the listener.

String quartets Nos. 12 in E flat, Op. 127; 13 in B flat, Op. 130; 14 in C sharp min., Op. 131; 15 in A min., Op. 132; 16 in F, Op. 135; Grosse Fuge in B flat, Op. 133.
*** ASV DCS 403 (4) [id.]. Lindsay Qt.
(M) **(*) Ph. 426 050-2 (4) [id.]. Italian Qt.

**(*) DG Dig. 415 676-2 (3) [id.]. Melos Qt.
**(*) EMI Dig. CDS7 47135-8 (4) [Ang. CDC 47134]. Alban Berg Qt.

String quartet No. 15 in A min., Op. 132.
**(*) EMI CDC7 47138-2 [id.]. Alban Berg Qt.

The Lindsays get far closer to the essence of this great music than most of their rivals. They have the benefit of very well-balanced recording (better than the Végh and the Talich, which are both a little bottom-heavy – see above); the sound of the ASV set is more present. They seem to find tempi that somehow strike the listener as completely right and which enable them to convey so much of both the letter and the spirit of the music. They bring much rich musical characterization and musical strength. Taken overall, these are among the very finest versions to have been made in recent years.

The merits of the Italian Quartet's performances are considerable. The sonority that they produce is beautifully blended and splendidly focused and yet their prime concern is with truth, not beauty. The transfers to compact disc have been effected well, though the gain in clarity also entails a slight loss of warmth in the middle register. Now they do not sound as sumptuous as some modern quartet recordings, but their reissue on four medium-price CDs is less competitive than it might be, when DG have been able to place the newer Melos set on three. However, these are at premium price, and for many the Italians' searching and thoughtful interpretations will ultimately prove more satisfying than the more extrovert Melos approach.

The Melos Quartet seem more naturally attuned to the late quartets than to the early or middle-period works. Overall these are warmly satisfying readings, and the players are particularly impressive in their powerful reading of the *Grosse Fuge*. Though speeds are not excessively fast, all six works are fitted on to three CDs with vividly immediate sound. A small but important final point: the pauses between movements are often too short (only three seconds between the second movement of Op. 132 and the *Heiliger Dankegesang*).

Some listeners may find the sheer polish of the Alban Berg Quartet gets in the way. Others dig deeper into the soul of this music – the Lindsays do – and this tells in movements like the *Heiliger Dankegesang* of Op. 132 or the *Cavatina* of Op. 130. The CDs have great clarity of focus, particularly at the bottom end of the spectrum, and a distinct presence, yet it is difficult to suppress the feeling that others convey even more of the stature and depth of these great and profound works. The CDs are also available separately (CDC7 47135/6/7/8-2).

String quartets Nos. 12 in E flat, Op. 127; 14 in C sharp min., Op. 131.
(BB) *** Hung. White Label HRC 125. Bartók Qt.

The Bartók Quartet's very generous coupling of Opp. 127 and 131 comes in the very inexpensive White Label series, making it another outstanding bargain, particularly when the performances – well recorded by Hungaroton in good analogue sound – have such concentration. The sweetness and purity of the string-playing matches that of any rival versions; but the sureness of control over the span of the sublime slow movements still makes this an outstanding version, even taking no account of price.

String quartets Nos. 12 in E flat, Op. 127; 16 in F, Op. 135.
(M) *** Ph. 422 840-2 [id.]. Italian Quartet.
**(*) EMI CDC7 47135-2 [id.]. Alban Berg Qt.

The Italians give a most searching account of the first movement of Op. 127 and their firmness of tone and accuracy of ensemble compel admiration; indeed, their account of the whole work goes far deeper than that of many full-priced rivals. Some may quarrel with their tempi in the inner movements of Op. 135; but on the whole this is a magnificent account which readers will find musically satisfying and sounding very fresh and immediate on this remastered CD.

String quartet No. 13 in B flat, Op. 130; Grosse Fuge in B flat, Op. 133.
*** ASV CDDCA 602 [id.]. Lindsay Qt.
**(*) EMI CDC7 47136-2 [id.]. Alban Berg Qt.

The Lindsay's account of Op. 130 includes both the *Grosse Fuge* as an ending and also the finale Beethoven substituted, so that listeners can choose for themselves. The merits of their performance are well known, and in its CD format their interpretation ranks very high indeed – along with the Végh and the Talich. They also have the advantage of better recording than either.

String quartet No. 14 in C sharp min., Op. 131.
*** ASV CDDCA 603 [id.]. Lindsay Qt.
**(*) EMI CDC7 47137-2 [id.]. Alban Berg Qt.

The Lindsay's account of Op. 131 is as fine as any in the catalogue. It must be remembered that the competing Talich disc (Cal. CAL 9638) offers also Op. 59/3 and, with fine performances of both works, represents even better value; but the ASV recording is somewhat clearer in focus, with the digital remastering very successful.

(i) *String quintet in C, Op. 29; String quartet No. 7 in F (Rasumovsky), Op. 59/1.*
** Nimbus Dig. NI 5207 [id.]. Medici Qt; (i) with S. Rowland-Jones.

The neglect of the *String quintet* is unaccountable. Dating from the year before the *First Symphony*, it is full of memorable ideas. Its opening (and much of the invention in the finale) foreshadows Schubert, and readers who enjoy the Op. 18 *Quartets* will find this more than their equal; yet the Medici account on Nimbus remains its only current representation on CD. This performance does it justice: tempi are well judged and there is no glamorization or any kind of egocentric mannerism. The interpretation is sensible and straightforward, and the recording, made at The Maltings, Snape, is truthful. The *Rasumovsky*, however, is another matter. The first movement is very fast (though not faster than the Alban Berg on EMI) and not unacceptable. The third movement is the disappointment for, though the playing is beautiful, the Medici players do not penetrate its depths as do the Végh, Lindsay and Talich versions.

String trios Nos. 1 in E flat, Op. 3; 2 in G; 3 in D; 4 in C min., Op. 9/1–3; Serenade in D (for string trio), Op. 8.
**(*) DG Dig. 427 687-2 (2) [id.]. Mutter, Giuranna, Rostropovich.

String trio No. 1 in E flat, Op. 3; Serenade in D, Op. 8.
*** Unicorn Dig. DKPCD 9059 [id.]. Cummings Trio.

String trios Nos. 2 in G; 3 in D; 4 in C min., Op. 9/1–3.
*** Unicorn Dig. DKPCD 9042 [id.]. Cummings Trio.

The playing of the Cummings Trio is cultured but not overcivilized; there is an unforced naturalness about it all, nothing glamorous at all and nothing which ever takes one's attention away from Beethoven. The *G major* is of particular interest, as its scherzo includes a newly discovered second trio. The *Serenade* is, of course, entertainment music. These players let Beethoven speak for himself and in quieter moments there is a winning sense of repose: in short, this is real chamber-music-making, with excellent recording; indeed it is in the demonstration class.

The *String trios* come in a two-CD package from Anne-Sophie Mutter, Bruno Giuranna and Mstislav Rostropovich, and they are splendidly played; however, the less glamorous but highly accomplished Cummings Trio is to be preferred. The sound in the DG is rather forward and dry.

Violin sonatas Nos. 1–10.
(M) *** Decca 421 453-2 (4) [id.]. Itzhak Perlman, Vladimir Ashkenazy.
(M) *** DG 415 874-2 (3) [id.]. Yehudi Menuhin, Wilhelm Kempff.
(M) (***) Ph. mono 422 140-2 (3) [id.]. Arthur Grumiaux, Clara Haskil.
*(*) ASV Musicmasters Dig. CDAMM 151/4 [MMCD 60121; 60143; 60182/3]. Robert Mann, Stephen Hough.

Perlman and Ashkenazy's set of the *Violin sonatas*, now reissued on four mid-priced CDs, is self-recommending. It was for the 1970s what Kreisler and Rupp were for the 1930s and 1940s, Grumiaux and Haskil for the 1950s and David Oistrakh and Oborin for the 1960s; and it will be difficult to surpass. These performances offer a blend of classical purity and spontaneous vitality that it is hard to resist; moreover the realism and presence of the recording in its CD format are very striking.

Inspirational artists of genius, Menuhin and Kempff met together in London in June 1970 to record this cycle of the Beethoven *Violin sonatas* in Conway Hall. Though these are not always the most immaculate performances on disc, they consistently reflect the joy and sense of wonder of pianist and violinist alike, often relaxed in tempo but magnetic from first to last. The brightness of the CD transfer at times gives too much edge to the violin tone, but these vintage recordings still sound well, with the rippling articulation of Kempff a constant delight.

Arthur Grumiaux and Clara Haskil made their celebrated recordings in 1956–7 and they sound remarkably well for their age. The performances are wonderfully civilized and aristocratic, and no one investing in them will regret it. They accommodate all ten *Sonatas* on three CDs at mid-price, as opposed to the four of Perlman and Ashkenazy.

Robert Mann is best known – on this side of the Atlantic at least – as the leader of the Juilliard Quartet and brings a lifetime's experience to this repertoire. His artistry is considerable, and though his vibrato may not be to all tastes there are some valuable insights here. This is live music-making: the recordings were made at concerts in New York and have the merit of spontaneity. All the same (and despite the undoubted excellence of Stephen Hough) it would be difficult to recommend their set in preference to such partnerships as Oistrakh and Oborin (Philips) or Perlman and Ashkenazy (Decca). Decent, rather than distinguished, recording. The four discs are available separately, but differently coupled in Britain and the USA.

Violin sonatas Nos. 1 in D; 2 in A; 3 in E flat, Op. 12/1–3.
*** DG Dig. 415 138-2 [id.]. Gidon Kremer, Martha Argerich.
*** Decca 417 573-2 [id.]. Itzhak Perlman, Vladimir Ashkenazy.

The partnership of Kremer and Argerich, two inspirational artists, works superbly in the first three sonatas. Each sparks the other into individual, but never wilful, expression, with the to-and-fro exchanges typical of early Beethoven consistently delightful. The CD gives a keen sense of presence.

The musicianship and vitality of Perlman and Ashkenazy are matched by a poise and elegance that give consistent pleasure; tempi are excellently judged and articulation could hardly be more alive. The recording balance remains exemplary between the two instruments, but the digital remastering has added a degree of edge to the image, particularly striking at the opening of the *First Sonata*.

Violin sonatas Nos. 4 in A min., Op. 23; 5 in F (Spring), Op. 24.
**(*) DG Dig. 419 787-2 [id.]. Gidon Kremer, Martha Argerich.

The ungenerous coupling of Op. 23 and the *Spring sonata* yet brings characteristically compelling and individual readings from Kremer and Argerich, an inspired and characterful – if at times wilful – duo. In all but one movement, but that arguably the most important, they match their earlier issue of the three Op. 12 *Sonatas* in sparkle and imagination. However, in the first movement of the *Spring*, Kremer's refusal to keep a steady tempo, even within phrases, sounds fussy and uncomfortable.

Violin sonatas Nos. 4 in A min., Op. 23; 6 in A; 8 in G, Op. 30/1 & 3.
*** Decca 417 574-2 [id.]. Itzhak Perlman, Vladimir Ashkenazy.

A further outstanding recoupling from the Perlman/Ashkenazy series, well up to the standard of the rest. The digital remastering is highly successful: the sound gives both violin and piano admirable presence and reality.

Violin sonatas Nos. 5 in F (Spring), Op. 24; 7 in C min., Op. 30/2.
(M) (***) EMI CDH7 63494-2. Adolf Busch, Rudolf Serkin (with BACH: *Violin partita No. 2 (***)).

Music-making from another age, unhurried, humane and of supreme integrity. It seems as if the music plays itself, so selfless and musical are these great artists. The *Sonatas* were recorded in the early 1930s and the *Partita* in 1929, though the latter sounds more vivid, since the violin is placed more forwardly. Playing of such naturalness and artistry transcends the inevitable sonic limitations.

Violin sonatas Nos. 5 in F (Spring), Op. 24; 9 in A (Kreutzer), Op. 47.
(M) *** EMI CDM7 69021-2. Pinchas Zukerman, Daniel Barenboim.
*** Decca 410 554-2 [id.]. Itzhak Perlman, Vladimir Ashkenazy.
(M) *** DG 427 251-2 [id.]. Yehudi Menuhin, Wilhelm Kempff.
**(*) EMI Dig. CDC7 47353-2 [id.]. Yehudi Menuhin, Jeremy Menuhin.
(BB) *(*) Hung. White Label HRC 105 [id.]. Dénes Kovács, Mihály Bächer.

Zukerman and Barenboim's coupling of the two favourites among Beethoven's *Violin sonatas*, taken from their 1973 cycle, brings disarmingly spontaneous-sounding performances. The CD transfer has warm, natural sound that scarcely betrays its age.

On Decca an obvious recoupling from the Perlman/Ashkenazy series. The dynamism is there but never becomes too extrovert, and the music unfolds naturally and spontaneously. The recording quality is excellent and has transferred smoothly to CD, though the EMI transfer of the Zukerman/Barenboim recordings is even more impressive.

Menuhin has recorded three different versions of this coupling in the catalogue, two on EMI with partners from his own family, and the version on DG. There is no doubt that Menuhin and Kempff give inspirational accounts of both works, and the recording has striking presence on CD.

In 1959, while still at the peak of his form, Yehudi Menuhin recorded inspirational accounts of these two sonatas with his sister, Hephzibah. Then in 1986 Menuhin repeated the formula, in digital stereo, this time with his son, Jeremy, who plays remarkably well – if not quite matching Hephzibah in the slow movement of the *Kreutzer*. Menuhin's timbre is less rounded now and his technique less refined, but the nobility of line is still apparent, and the spontaneity and family chemistry are as potent as ever. The *Kreutzer* finale is joyfully spirited. Excellent recording in a resonant acoustic.

Those with limited budgets should find the Hungaroton White Label coupling very acceptable, though Kovács' timbre as recorded is a little on the thin side. The balance, though, is good and these are fresh, straightforward performances.

Violin sonatas Nos. 7 in C min., Op. 30/2; 10 in G, Op. 96.
*** Decca 411 948-2 [id.]. Itzhak Perlman, Vladimir Ashkenazy.

These Decca performances emanate from the 1977 set and the sound is improved, firmer and fresher than ever. No phrase is unimaginatively handled, and the playing of Perlman and Ashkenazy is masterly.

Violin sonata No. 8 in G, Op. 30/3.
(M) ** RCA GD 86264 [6264-2-RG]. Szeryng, Rubinstein – BRAHMS: *Sonatas Nos. 1 & 3.***

A particularly successful account of the *G major Sonata* from Szeryng and Rubinstein, well recorded if rather drily, makes a good coupling for the two Brahms *Sonatas.*

Violin sonatas Nos. 8 in G, Op. 30/3; 9 in A (Kreutzer), Op. 47.
**(*) Amon Ra CDSAR 16 [id.]. Ralph Holmes, Richard Burnett.

Ralph Holmes recorded these two Beethoven sonatas not long before he died. They reveal his art at its freshest and most alert in a period performance, accompanied by Richard Burnett on a sweet-toned Graf fortepiano of around 1820. Inevitably Holmes's Stradivarius overtops the fortepiano but, with recording realistically set in a helpful but intimate acoustic, the textures are admirably clear. The twanginess of the instrument is distracting only in sustained melodic passages, and Burnett's clean articulation is as much a delight as Holmes's strong and imaginative phrasing.

(Wind) *Octet in E flat, Op. 103; Quintet in E flat for oboe, 3 horns & bassoon; Rondino in E flat for wind octet, WoO 25; Sextet in E flat, Op. 71.*
*** ASV Dig. CDCOE 807 [id.]. Wind Soloists of COE.

(Wind) Octet in E flat, Op. 103; Rondino in E flat, WoO 25; Sextet in E flat, Op. 71.
**(*) Amon Ra Dig. CDSAR 26 [id.]. Classical Winds.

The wind soloists of the Chamber Orchestra of Europe give strong and stylish performances of this collection of Beethoven's wind music, marked by some outstanding solo work, notably from the first oboe, Douglas Boyd. With the little *Rondino* included alongside Opus 103, as well as the three-movement *Quintet*, it makes a generous collection, recorded in warm but clear sound with good presence.

Using period instruments, Classical Winds give bright, sometimes abrasive performances of Beethoven's two major wind works, including the *Rondino* not as a separate work but as the fourth movement of Opus 103 immediately before the finale, citing interesting evidence for that incorporation. Generally these are fresh, lively performances very well recorded, not as stylish or persuasive as those from the COE soloists using modern instruments, but recommendable to anyone who prefers period style at a lower pitch.

Piano sonatas Nos. 1–32 (complete).
(M) *** EMI CZS7 62863-2 (10). Daniel Barenboim.
(M) **(*) Decca 425 590-2 (10). Vladimir Ashkenazy.
**(*) Nimbus Dig. NI 5050 (*Nos. 1, 22 & 23 (Appassionata)*); NI 5051 (*Nos. 2, 24 & 28*);

NI 5052 (*Nos. 3, 19 & 21* (Waldstein)); NI 5053 (*Nos. 4, 10 & 26* (Les Adieux)); NI 5054 (*Nos. 5–7*); NI 5055 (*Nos. 11, 15 (Pastoral) & 20*); NI 5056 (*Nos. 17 (Tempest), 18 & 25*); NI 5057 (*Nos. 13 & 29 (Hammerklavier)*); NI 5058 (*Nos. 9, 16 & 30*); NI 5059 (*Nos. 12, 14 (Moonlight) & 31*); NI 5060 (*Nos. 8 (Pathétique), 27 & 32*) [id.]. Bernard Roberts.

Piano sonatas Nos. 1–32; Andante favori in F, G.170.
**(*) Ph. 412 575-2 (11) [id.]. Alfred Brendel.

Piano sonatas Nos. 1–15.
**(*) DG Dig. 413 759-2 (6) [id.]. Daniel Barenboim.

Piano sonatas Nos. 16–32.
**(*) DG Dig. 413 766-2 (6) [id.]. Daniel Barenboim.

Barenboim's earlier set of the Beethoven *Sonatas*, recorded for EMI when he was in his late twenties, remains one of his very finest achievements on record. Reissued on ten CDs at mid-price, it offers very good value, with truthful recording and unique interpretations. The readings are sometimes idiosyncratic, with unexpected tempi both fast and slow, but the spontaneous style is unfailingly compelling. At times Barenboim's way is mercurial, with an element of fantasy, a charm that is missing in Brendel, for instance. But overall this is a keenly thoughtful musician living through Beethoven's great piano cycle with an individuality that puts him in the line of master pianists. All three of the wonderful Op. 10 sonatas are given superb performances, and the last five show remarkable concentration, with the *Hammerklavier* providing a fitting culmination to the series.

Ashkenazy's comparable set occupied him over a decade or longer. These are eminently sound, well-recorded performances that deserve to rank among the best. Crisply articulated, intelligently shaped, not always inspired, they are never less than musically satisfying, although there is at times a hint of self-consciousness in the playing. The recording was generally of Decca's best quality in its LP format, but the CDs are not always as full and natural as the EMI transfers of the Barenboim cycle.

With eleven hours of music on eleven CDs, the Brendel cycle makes full use of the extra convenience of the new medium, though the CD transfers bring out the discrepancies between different recordings made between 1970 and 1977. As to the performances, though they lack some of the fighting spontaneity of the young Brendel many years ago on Turnabout, they have a dark, thoughtful, deeply satisfying quality that consistently gives pleasure.

Spontaneity and electricity, extremes of expression in dynamic, tempo and phrasing as well as mood, mark Barenboim's DG cycle, as they did his much earlier one for EMI. Some of his more extreme readings – such as the sleep-walking tempo for the finale of the *Waldstein* – have been modified to fall short of provocation or eccentricity. This time he has a tendency to rush his fences, particularly in the early sonatas, giving a hint of breathlessness to already fast speeds. That is exceptional, and so is the hint of technical stress. The first movement of the *Appassionata* is given with all his old flair, even more a vehicle for display thanks to dramatic extremes of light and dark. Conversely, the second and third movements are now plainer and simpler. The plainness in the first movement of the *Moonlight* is disappointing, however, less poetic, with little veiled tone; but the light, flowing finale of the *Tempest*, Op. 31, No. 2, is now more magically Mendelssohnian than ever. All three movements of the *Waldstein* this time are more lyrical, and that applies in the late sonatas too, not just in slow movements but equally strikingly in the great fugal movements, where inner parts are brought out more clearly and warmly. Only in the final Adagio variations of Op. 111 does a hint of self-consciousness develop, thanks to agogic hesitations at a tempo even slower than before.

The lyrical opening movement of Op. 101 in A is delectably done, flowing and simple. The sound is warm and spacious, much more consistent than before. The CDs – taking the sonatas in consecutive order but on one more disc than Brendel's rival set – come in two separate boxes. However, the earlier set, now available on EMI at bargain price, remains preferable on almost all counts.

Bernard Roberts's series for Nimbus has an inspired directness, with few if any distracting idiosyncrasies but with fine concentration and comparable intensity. The sound on CD is vivid, a full-bodied recording well focused in a helpful but fairly intimate setting. These readings consistently reflect Roberts's dedication as a chamber-music pianist intent on presenting the composer's argument as clearly as possible, not drawing attention to himself. The layout allows one to appreciate the pianist's consistency, when his treatment has an element of toughness even in the early sonatas, and the mature sonatas are marked by rugged power, with Roberts's virtuosity given full rein, as in the finale of the *Appassionata*. That favourite comes on the first disc of the series, coupled with the very first sonata of all and the little Op. 54. The second, third and fourth discs similarly lead in well-balanced programmes to one of the great middle or late sonatas. The fifth disc groups together the three Op. 10 sonatas, including the magnificent *D major*, Op. 10, No. 3, and the sixth has two of the most inspired of the early sonatas, Op. 22 and Op. 28 (*Pastoral*) as well as the sonatina-like Op. 49, No. 2. Volume seven has the second and third of the Opus 31 sonatas, launching into the middle period, coupled with the deceptively simple-looking Op. 79. The *Hammerklavier* comes in volume eight with the first of the *Sonatas quasi una fantasia*, Op. 27, and the last three volumes couple early sonatas with last-period masterpieces, respectively Op. 109, 110 and 111. The eleven discs are available separately, not in a box. In sound, this is the finest Beethoven sonata-cycle yet on CD.

Piano sonatas Nos. 1 in F min., Op. 2/1; 9 in E, Op. 14/1; 23 (Appassionata), Op. 57; 27 in E min., Op. 90.
* Olympia Dig. OCD 330 [id.]. Edith Fischer.

Edith Fischer is a respected artist who studied with Arrau. She is a capable player, but these recordings do not, perhaps, do her full justice: the bass is thin and the dynamic range insufficiently wide. Given her considerable reputation, her interpretations are a bit wanting in personality and colour.

Piano sonatas Nos. 2 in A, Op. 2/2; 4 in E flat, Op. 7.
*** DG Dig. 415 481-2 [id.]. Emil Gilels.

Gilels's magisterial Beethoven sonatas are one of the glories of the catalogue, and his leonine strength was tempered by a delicacy and poetry that few matched and none have surpassed. His accounts of the *A major Sonata* and the *E flat*, Op. 7, are as masterly as one expects and silence criticism. The recording is clear and well lit in the DG fashion, and does not perhaps do the fullest justice to the sound he produced in the concert hall; but, given such playing, there is no need to withhold the strongest recommendation.

Piano sonatas Nos. 5 in C min.; 6 in F; 7 in D, Op. 10/1 – 3.
*** Decca 417 662-2 [id.]. Vladimir Ashkenazy (piano).

Ashkenazy gives characteristically thoughtful and alert performances. Tempi are not always conventional – that of the finale of Op. 10/2 is questionably fast – but Ashkenazy's freshness of manner is disarming and the account of the *D major*, Op. 10/3, is masterly. With such excellent sound this is outstanding.

Piano sonatas Nos. 5 in C min.; 10 in G, Op. 14/2; 19 in G min.; 20 in G, Op. 49/1–2.
**(*) DG Dig. 419 172-2 [id.]. Emil Gilels.

Gilels manages to make one believe that his is exactly the *tempo giusto* even when one feels tempted to question the very deliberate speed he adopts in the slow movement of the *C minor*, Op. 10, No. 1. He can even almost convince one in what at first seems (and is) an eccentricity: the explosive opening to the second group of the first movement, a staccato sforzando sustained on the middle pedal. This really disturbs the balance of the phrase. However, such is his magic that, while under his spell, doubts are silenced. He is well recorded, too.

Piano sonatas Nos. 7 in D, Op. 10/3; 18 in E flat, Op. 31/3; 15 Variations and fugue on a theme from Prometheus (Eroica variations), Op. 35.
*** DG 423 135-2 [id.]. Emil Gilels.

Gilels's account of the *Eroica variations* is masterly. In the *D major Sonata* he is hardly less impressive, though there are odd mannerisms. Op. 31, No. 3 is distinguished, too, though the recording acoustic is somewhat drier than that of its companions.

Piano sonatas Nos. 7 in D; 23 in F min. (Appassionata), Op. 57.
*** CBS Dig. MK 39344 [id.]. Murray Perahia.

Intense, vibrant playing from Perahia in the *D major Sonata*, with great range of colour and depth of thought. The slow movement is a model of sensitivity and keyboard colour, and the *Appassionata* is a performance of comparable stature. These are among the few interpretations to have appeared in recent years that can be recommended alongside Gilels. The recorded sound is truthful.

Piano sonatas Nos. 8 (Pathétique); 9 in E; 10 in in G, Op. 14/1–2; 13 in E flat; 14 (Moonlight), Op. 27/1–2.
(B) ** EMI CDZ7 62857-2 [id.]. Walter Gieseking.

These recordings were made in the early days of stereo, not long before Gieseking's death. He was undoubtedly a great pianist and there is distinguished playing here, of course; but there is something a little remote and cool about his approach to these *Sonatas*, and they cannot be said to compete in interpretative insight with the very finest versions now available. Even so, at bargain price they are by no means to be dismissed.

Piano sonatas Nos. 8 (Pathétique), Op. 13; 13; 14 (Moonlight), Op. 27/1–2.
**(*) DG Dig. 400 036-2 [id.]. Emil Gilels.

Gilels's compact disc, coupling the two Op. 27 sonatas and the *Pathétique*, does not quite rank among his very best (such as the *Waldstein* and Op. 101). The opening movement of the *Moonlight* is wonderfully serene, and there are many felicities. But the first movement of the *E flat Sonata* is strangely reserved, as if Gilels feared the charge of self-indulgence or out-of-period sentiment. However, such are the strengths of this playing that few will quarrel with the magnificence of his conceptions of all three pieces. The digital recording is lifelike, although the balance is very close.

Piano sonatas Nos. 8 (Pathétique); 14 (Moonlight), Op. 27/2; 15 (Pastoral), Op. 28; 24 in F sharp, Op. 78.
(M) *** DG 415 834-2 [id.]. Wilhelm Kempff.

Kempff's masterly recordings show so well his ability to rethink Beethoven's music within the recording studio. Everything he does has his individual stamp; above all, he never fails to convey the deep intensity of a master in communion with Beethoven. The recording has undoubtedly gained in firmness.

Piano sonatas Nos. 8 (Pathétique); 14 (Moonlight), Op. 27/2; 23 (Appassionata), Op. 57.
*** Decca 410 260-2 [id.]. Vladimir Ashkenazy.
**(*) Ph. 411 470-2 [id.]. Alfred Brendel.
(B) ** Pickwick Dig. PCD 828 [MCA MCAD 25921]. John Ogdon.
*(*) DG Dig. 427 767-2 [id.]. Gerhard Oppitz.
(B) * Ph. 422 970-2 [id.]. Claudio Arrau.

Ashkenazy's *Pathétique* is perhaps slightly understated for so ebulliently youthful a work, with the finale unusually gentle; nevertheless the performance conveys the underlying power. The *Moonlight* is generally successful, and the *Appassionata* is admirable. He is well served by the engineers and the analogue recordings are very well transferred to CD. However, the *Moonlight* and the *Appassionata* are also available at mid-price – see below.

Brendel's performances, too, are undoubtedly impressive, the *Moonlight* beautifully played, the others strong and thoughtful, yet not lacking power. The sound is full-bodied and clear, although plainly from an analogue source.

John Ogdon's mid-1980s record for Pickwick is far from negligible, even if it is not always completely satisfying. He is impressive in the outer movements of the *Moonlight* (the finale has admirable spirit and fire) but less so in the *Pathétique* and the *Appassionata* finale, which are wanting in concentration and at times are touched by routine. Yet Ogdon is a pianist of undoubted insights; the first movement of Op. 57 has great power. His admirers will want this, even if it does not represent him at his most consistently inspired.

Gerhard Oppitz's Beethoven playing has won him acclaim, particularly in his home country, Germany, as the 'successor' to Kempff, who enshrined the highest and noblest in the German Beethoven tradition. These well-recorded performances are much closer to Backhaus, strong and fleet of finger, intelligent and with a good feeling for architecture, but plain and wanting in fantasy. The slow movement of the *Pathétique*, for example, is terribly prosaic.

This is one of Arrau's least successful Beethoven records. The *Grave* introduction of the *Pathétique*, the *Adagio* of the same sonata, the *Andante* of the *Appassionata* and the opening of the *Moonlight sonata* are curiously studied and unspontaneous and, though there is impressive playing elsewhere and the recording is good if rather dry, this record can give but limited enjoyment.

Piano sonatas Nos. 8 (Pathétique); 14 (Moonlight); 23 (Appassionata); 26 (Les Adieux).
(M) * RCA GD 60356 [60356-2-RG]. Van Cliburn.

A disappointing collection. Van Cliburn takes the opening of the *Moonlight* quite fast and finds absolutely no atmosphere in the music; the slow movement of the *Pathétique* is similarly direct. The *Appassionata* comes off best here.

Piano sonatas Nos. 11 in B flat, Op. 22; 18 in B flat, Op. 31/3.
**(*) Dell'Arte DBS 7004. Earl Wild.

These are distinguished performances. The interrelationships of mood and pacing of the *B flat Sonata* are particularly finely judged. Its good-tempered character is caught well, and the *Adagio*'s songful *con molto expressione* is a highlight of the reading. Op. 31/2 is equally successful, with Wild's technical command at its most impressive in the strongly articulated Scherzo and the brilliant closing *Presto con fuoco*. These performances have the excitement of live music-making, and the clear, bold, 1984 recording brings out the special colour and sonority of Wild's chosen Bösendorfer. But it is a pity that a third sonata was not included – there was plenty of room for one.

Piano sonatas Nos. 13 in E flat, Op. 27/1; 15 (Pastoral), Op. 28; 21 (Waldstein), Op. 53.
*** DG Dig. 423 577-2 [id.]. Daniel Barenboim.

This triptych shows Barenboim at his best, with the lyrical flow in both the *Waldstein* and the *Pastoral* as evident as the undoubted spontaneity of the music-making. Good recording.

Piano sonatas Nos. 14 (Moonlight); 17 in D min. (Tempest); 26 (Les Adieux).
(M) **(*) DG Dig. 427 803-2 [id.]. Daniel Barenboim.

A good example of Barenboim's spontaneous studio style in his second set of Beethoven sonatas, recorded digitally for DG in 1984. The slow movements of *Les Adieux* and the *Tempest* are memorable, and the finale of the latter work is infectiously communicative. Perhaps the opening of the *Moonlight* could be less withdrawn, but the rest of the work springs readily to life. Realistic recording, with a natural presence.

Piano sonatas Nos. 14 in C sharp min. (Moonlight), Op. 27/2; 21 in C (Waldstein), Op. 53; 23 in F min. (Appassionata), Op. 57.
*** Virgin Dig. VC 790737-2 [id.]. Mikhail Pletnev.
(M) *** Decca 417 732-2 [id.]. Vladimir Ashkenazy.
(M) **(*) RCA GD 60375 [60375-2-RG]. Vladimir Horowitz.

Pletnev is an artist of stature, strong in personality and with a commanding sense of keyboard colour. Some will find the *Moonlight* a bit mannered (the second movement is undoubtedly quirky), but he has the capacity to make you listen intently – as every great pianist does. The clarity of articulation is altogether remarkable in the finale, and in the *Waldstein*; he also finds the right depths in its slow movement and finale. The account of the *Appassionata* is masterly: it has a sense of scale and grand design, and a feeling for both line and refinement of detail. The engineering is immaculate and does justice to Pletnev's individual sound-world.

An excellent mid-priced grouping of three popular sonatas from Ashkenazy. All three recordings are given fine presence on CD. The *Waldstein* (1975) is splendidly structured and the *Appassionata* (1973) superb, although those who feel strongly about matters of tempo may well find Ashkenazy a little too free in the first movement.

Horowitz was not thought of primarily as a Beethoven pianist, but these recordings, made in 1956 (the *Moonlight* and *Waldstein*) and 1959, show how powerful he could be in the music of this composer. His delicacy, too, is equally impressive, as in the gentle *Adagio* which opens the *Moonlight sonata* or in the way the lyrical theme steals in at the beginning of the finale of the *Waldstein*, where his reading has much in common with Kempff. There is prodigious bravura, too, as in the finale of the *Appassionata*, where he matches – and perhaps even surpasses – Richter in exuberance. The sound has been improved in the remastering process; there is some hardness on top but little shallowness, and the bass sonority is telling.

Piano sonatas Nos. 15 in D (Pastoral), Op. 28; 17 in D min. (Tempest), Op. 31/2.
** DG Dig. 419 161-2 [id.]. Emil Gilels.

Gilels's *Pastoral* is a strange performance – a laboured, almost hectoring first movement, very deliberate in tempo and character, with little sense of flow and only occasional glimpses of the wisdom and humanity one associates with this great artist. The

Tempest sonata, Op. 31, No. 2, is another matter; this performance has excited universal acclaim, and rightly so. The balance of the recording is excessively close.

Piano sonatas Nos. 15 in D (Pastoral), Op. 28; 21 in C (Waldstein); 26 in E flat (Les Adieux).
(B) ** Ph. 426 068-2 [id.]. Claudio Arrau.

These are sound readings. Arrau is impressive in the *Andante* of the *Pastoral*, and he finds a similar lightness of touch in his introduction of the famous melody in the finale of the *Waldstein*. But the slow movement of the same sonata is overtly serious in mood, and elsewhere the impulsive and spontaneous character of these works is less readily brought out. The recordings were made between 1962 and 1966; the recording is truthful, if lacking something in colour in the middle range.

Piano sonatas Nos. 16 in G; 17 in D min. (Tempest); 18 in E flat, Op. 31/1 - 3.
*** Decca 417 663-2 [id.]. Vladimir Ashkenazy (piano).

The CD grouping of the Op. 31 sonatas is highly successful. The performances are among the best of Ashkenazy's Beethoven cycle: he brings concentration of mind, together with spontaneity of feeling. The command of keyboard colour is, as always, impressive and in terms of both dramatic tension and the sense of architecture these are thoroughly satisfying performances. The recordings date from 1976/7.

Piano sonatas Nos. 17 in D min., Op. 31/2; 18 in E flat, Op. 31/3; 26 in E flat (Les Adieux), Op. 81a.
*** CBS Dig. MK 42319 [id.]. Murray Perahia.

Wonderfully concentrated performances. The *D minor*, Op. 31, No. 2, is magisterial in its control and command of poetic feeling: the finest since Solomon. All these readings have the blend of authority, finesse and poetry that distinguishes this great artist at his best. The recording is acceptable.

Piano sonatas Nos. 17 in D min. (Tempest), Op. 31/2; 21 in C (Waldstein), Op. 53; 25 in G, Op. 79; 26 in E flat (Les Adieux), Op. 81a.
**(*) DG 427 642-2 [id.]. Maurizio Pollini.

Pollini's impeccable keyboard mastery is always evident, though the recital as a whole is a little problematic: the opening of the 'little' *G major*, Op. 79, is tossed off rather uncaringly, and there is little of the lightness of touch it calls for. The *Waldstein* has a fine sense of pace and *Les Adieux* is impressive, if a little lacking in poetic intensity. Op. 31, No. 2, brings a perfectly proportioned account, but one that seems to draw us into its world only sporadically. The engineers do not allow too much of the ambience of the acoustic to help him and, though the piano sound is not dry, it is somewhat close and clinical.

Piano sonatas Nos. 17 in D min.; 29 (Hammerklavier), Op. 106.
(M) *** DG 419 857-2 [id.]. Wilhelm Kempff.

Kempff's *Hammerklavier* performance represents his interpretative approach to Beethoven at its most extreme and therefore controversial. Here his preference for measured allegros and fastish andantes gives a different weighting to movements from the usual, but there is a thoughtfulness of utterance which brings profundity, while in the finale Kempff's clarity of fingerwork brings a new freshness that lacks nothing in excitement. The coupling also has its own special insights, and the sound is clean and clear.

Piano sonatas Nos. 21 in C (Waldstein), Op. 53; 23 in F min. (Appassionata), Op. 57; 26 in E flat (Les Adieux), Op. 81a.
⊛ *** DG 419 162-2 [id.]. Emil Gilels.
*** EMI Dig. CDC7 49330-2 [id.]. Melvyn Tan (fortepiano).
(M) *** DG 419 053-2 [id.]. Wilhelm Kempff.

This recoupling offers three of Gilels's finest analogue recordings dating from 1972–5. The piano is believably present, but much less closely observed than in his later digital recordings, to great advantage. The account of the *Appassionata* has previously been hailed by us as among the finest ever made, and much the same must be said of the *Waldstein*. It has a technical perfection denied even to Schnabel, and Gilels is hardly less searching and profound. Moreover, Gilels's fastidiously sensitive yet commanding *Les Adieux* is also one of the most impressive ever committed to disc. These are all performances to relish, to study and to keep for special occasions.

Melvyn Tan offers a CD for those who are unconverted to the fortepiano and find its exponents tame. Tan has a strong musical personality and attacks his instrument with tremendous spirit and flair; every phrase lives and he is not afraid to present the widest dynamic spectrum and expressive range. In all three sonatas he exhibits consummate artistry and real temperament and fire. Nor is there any want of poetic feeling. He plays on a copy by Derek Adlam of a Streicher (1814), an instrument for which Beethoven himself expressed a strong preference. The EMI recording is excellent: in short, an outstanding issue.

Kempff's individuality in Beethoven is again established here. The *Appassionata* is characteristically clear, classically straight in the same way that the *Waldstein* is cooler and fresher than usual with a wonderful classical purity in the rippling quavers. *Les Adieux*, like the *Appassionata*, may be less weightily dramatic than in other readings, but the concentration is irresistible. The digital remastering has brought clean sound to match.

Piano sonatas Nos. 21 in C (Waldstein), Op. 53; 26 in E flat (Les Adieux), Op. 81a; 27 in E min., Op 90.
*** Decca 414 630-2 [id.]. Vladimir Ashkenazy.

Taking a broadly lyrical view, Ashkenazy gives a deeply satisfying reading of the *Waldstein sonata*. *Les Adieux* brings a vehement first movement and memorable concentration, while the account of the *E minor Sonata*, Op. 90, is masterly. The analogue recordings are first class and sound full, firm and clear in their CD transfer. Readers will note that Ashkenazy's *Waldstein* is also available on mid-priced CD (coupled with the *Moonlight* and the *Appassionata*) – see above.

Piano sonata No. 23 in F min. (Appassionata), Op. 57.
(M) *** RCA GD 86518 [RCA 6518-2-RG]. Sviatoslav Richter – BRAHMS: *Piano concerto No. 2.****

Richter's thrilling 1960 *Appassionata* is a superb example of a studio recording sounding like a live performance, with the wide dynamic range bringing out both the drama and passion of this boldly contrasted sonata. Some might feel that Richter goes over the top in the coda of the finale but the fervour is unmistakable, and this is an undeniably great interpretation. The recording brings out the percussive qualities of Richter's playing. But the remastering has made the most of the possibilities of the master-tape.

Piano sonatas Nos. 24 in F sharp, Op. 78; 29 in B flat (Hammerklavier), Op. 106.
**(*) Ph. 412 723-2 [id.]. Alfred Brendel.

Piano sonata No. 29 (Hammerklavier).
*** DG Dig. 410 527-2 [id.]. Emil Gilels.

Gilels's *Hammerklavier* is a performance of supreme integrity, Olympian, titanic, subtle, imperious, one of the finest accounts ever recorded. Speeds for the outer movements are surprisingly spacious and relaxed, with clarity of texture and refinement of detail brought out. Yet the concentration brings the most powerful impact – not just in those movements but in all four. The recording is close and bright and harder than ideal.

The CD coupling of the *Hammerklavier* and Opus 78 comes not from Brendel's complete sonata cycle but from a live recording made at the Queen Elizabeth Hall in London a decade later. Though there is greater urgency and dramatic tension in the allegro movements, the great *Adagio* of the *Hammerklavier*, intense as it is, lacks the spacious sublimity of his earlier (1972) version, taken even more slowly.

Piano sonatas Nos. 28 in A, Op. 101; 29 (Hammerklavier), Op. 106.
(M) *** DG Dig. 429 485-2 [id.]. Daniel Barenboim.

In his second digital cycle for DG, Barenboim was at his finest in the late *Sonatas*, and the sustained concentration of the slow movement of the *Hammerklavier* is like a live performance, with the finale hardly less eloquent. In Op. 28, another fine performance with a melting opening, the brief Adagio before the *attaca* into the finale is another passage of Barenboim magic. Excellent recording, with real presence.

Piano sonatas Nos. 28 in A, Op. 101; 29 (Hammerklavier), Op. 106; 30 in E, Op. 109; 31 in A flat, Op. 110; 32 in C min., Op. 111.
*** Decca 417 150-2 (2) [id.]. Vladimir Ashkenazy.
**(*) DG 429 569-2 (*28 & 29*); 429 570-2 (*30–32*) [id.]. Pollini.

Distinguished performances on Decca, as one would expect, and an impressive sense of repose in the slow movement of Op. 109, while the account of No. 28 is searching and masterly. This was Ashkenazy's second recording of the *Hammerklavier*, the performance fresher, more spontaneous than the earlier version, but the total experience is less than monumental. The last two sonatas are played with a depth and spontaneity which put them among the finest available. In the slow movement of Op. 111 Ashkenazy matches the concentration of the slowest possible speed which marks out the reading of his friend Barenboim, but there is an extra detachment. If anything, the interpretation of Op. 110 is even more remarkable, consistently revealing. The analogue recordings date from between 1974 and 1982, and the remastering is very successful.

Pollini's recordings of the late *Sonatas* (which on LP originally included No. 27) won the 1977 *Gramophone* Critics' award for instrumental music and they contain playing of the highest order of mastery. Joan Chissell spoke of the 'noble purity' of these performances, and that telling phrase aptly sums them up, if also hinting perhaps at a missing dimension, which the CD transfer seems to emphasize. The sound has great presence but on the first disc there is hardness to the timbre in Opus 101 which becomes almost brittle in the fortissimos of the *Hammerklavier* with an adverse effect on the music-making. Pollini's *Hammerklavier* is undoubtedly eloquent, and so is Op. 111, which has a peerless authority and power. However, the slow movement of Op. 110 may be a trifle fast for some tastes, and in the A major work Gilels has greater poetry and humanity. The second disc brings a close balance to Opp. 109 and 110 but the recordings seem fractionally mellower, although a touch of hardness comes back in Op. 111. The two discs are now reissued separately, with no price reduction.

Piano sonatas Nos. 30 in E, Op. 109; 31 in A flat, Op. 110.
* DG Dig. 419 174-2 [id.]. Emil Gilels.

The opening movement of Op. 110 is enormously spacious and its breadth of vision (and tempo) can only be called Olympian. Both sonatas are given performances of stature that seek out their profoundest truths. Even when Gilels storms the greatest heights in the closing fugue of Op. 110, no fortissimo ever sounds percussive or strained. DG seem to have found a more truthful sound-balance here than they did for his *Moonlight* and *Pathétique.*

Piano sonatas Nos. 30 in E, Op. 109; 31 in A flat, Op. 110; 32 in C min., Op. 111.
* Calliope CAL 9648 [id.]. Inger Södergren.
** DG Dig. 427 498-2 [id.]. Rudolf Serkin.

Inger Södergren is a Swedish pianist, little known in her native country, who lives in France where she enjoys a considerable reputation; indeed her performances and recordings are regarded there with as much respect as those of Brendel. Her analogue accounts of Opp. 110 and 111 come from 1979, when they earned golden opinions. They are musically most impressive. She is obviously a pianist of keen musical insights. Her recording of Op. 109 is new: it is brighter and more forward; while Op. 110 reminds one a little of Myra Hess's old mono LP, but this reading is even stronger. These performances are fit to keep exalted company even if the recordings of Opp. 110 and 111 are not quite three-star.

Rudolf Serkin's recording comes from a recital he gave in 1987 in the Vienna Konserthaus and recorded by Austrian Radio. There is always something to learn from artists of this stature even when they are past their prime. Serkin's control is pretty remarkable, given the fact that he is in his mid-eighties (though nowhere near as remarkable as the nonogenarian Horszowski). Pianistically, it is wanting the lyrical refinement and range of keyboard colour he has brought to this repertoire in the past. He is often brusque and plain (not in itself unBeethovenian) and, as often in recitals, he stamps noisily on the pedal. However, he conveys a lifelong understanding of this repertoire, its structure and pacing, even if he no longer commands the beauty of sonority of Gilels or Solomon.

Piano sonatas Nos. 31 in A flat, Op. 110; 32 in C min., Op. 111.
**(*) DG Dig. 423 371-2 [id.]. Daniel Barenboim.

Though Barenboim's readings of the last two sonatas – taken from his DG cycle of all 32 – are not as spaciously spontaneous-sounding as they were in his earlier series for EMI, they make a splendid coupling, deeply thoughtful and strongly expressed.

Piano sonata No. 32, Op. 111.
**(*) DG Dig. 410 520-2 [id.]. Ivo Pogorelich – SCHUMANN: *Études symphoniques* etc.*(*)

Ivo Pogorelich produces consistent beauty of tone throughout the sonata, and his account of this masterpiece contains many felicities. It is imposing piano playing and impressive music-making. There are self-indulgent touches here and there, but also moments of illumination. The CD is admirably clear and realistically balanced, but the clarity of the recording and its background silence tend to emphasize the slightly dry bass quality.

Miscellaneous piano music

Allegretto in C min., WoO 53; Andante favori, WoO 57; Für Elise, WoO 59; 6 Variations in F, Op. 34.
*** EMI CDC7 49793-2 [id.]. Melvyn Tan (fortepiano) – SCHUBERT: *Moments musicaux* etc.***

Melvyn Tan plays a copy by Richard Adlam of an 1814 fortepiano by Nanette Streicher, and brings to these pieces his customary flair and panache. He is a spirited artist and an enormously persuasive exponent of the fortepiano. The *F major Variations* come off splendidly: there is plenty of colour and imagination throughout. Despite his rather brisk *Andante favori*, this is a thoroughly enjoyable recital and is recorded with great realism and presence in The Maltings at Snape.

6 Bagatelles, Op. 126; 6 Écossaises, WoO 83; Für Elise, WoO 59; 15 Variations and fugue on a theme from Prometheus (Eroica variations), Op. 35.
*** Ph. 412 227-2 [id.]. Alfred Brendel.

Brendel may lack some of the sheer bravura of his own early playing in this collection of shorter pieces, but his consistent thoughtfulness and imagination bring out the truly Beethovenian qualities of even the most trivial pieces. The *Eroica variations*, not as flamboyant as with some, plainly point to the magnificence of their culminating development in the *Eroica* finale. Excellent recording: the CD is outstandingly realistic.

Bagatelles, Op. 26; Polonaise in C, Op. 89; Variations and fugue on a theme from Prometheus (Eroica variations), Op. 35.
*** Nimbus Dig. NIM 5017 [id.]. Bernard Roberts.

Bernard Roberts gives a characteristically fresh and forthright reading of the *Eroica variations*, recorded in exceptionally vivid sound. He may not have quite the dash of Brendel, but the crispness and clarity of his playing are most refreshing. The shorter pieces bring performances even more intense, with the *Bagatelles* for all their brevity given last-period intensity.

32 Variations in C min., WoO 80.
(B) *** Decca 417 773-2. Radu Lupu – MOZART: *Piano concertos Nos. 12 and 21.***(*)

Originally coupled with a less memorable version of Beethoven's *Third Piano concerto*, Lupu's fine account of the *32 Variations in C minor* makes a worthwhile addition to Decca's Weekend reissue of Mozart *Concertos*.

33 Variations on a Waltz by Diabelli, Op. 120.
(B) *** Ph. 422 969-2 [id.]. Stephen Bishop-Kovacevich.
*** Ph. Dig. 426 232-2 [id.]. Alfred Brendel.
**(*) Ph. 416 295-2 [id.]. Claudio Arrau.

Bishop-Kovacevich gives one of the most deeply satisfying performances ever recorded. Avoiding the idiosyncrasies of most other interpreters, Bishop-Kovacevich may at times seem austere, but his concentration is magnetic from first to last, and the variety of expression within his unmannered approach has one thinking direct to Beethoven, with fearless dynamic contrasts enhanced in the CD transfer. The reading culminates in the most dedicated account of the concluding variations, hushed in meditation and with no hint of self-indulgence. On the cheapest Philips label, it is a bargain that no Beethovenian should miss, and the remastering – with separate tracks for each variation – fully matches that of the other, full-price Philips version.

Unlike his previous CD version, taken from a live performance given at the Queen Elizabeth Hall in London in 1977, Brendel's later recording was done in digital sound in the studio. The glory of the earlier performance was its daring, with the mercurial side of Brendel given full rein; to an amazing degree Brendel, here working in the studio, recaptures that earthshaking dynamism, the sense of an irresistible force building up this immense structure, section by section. It would be hard to imagine a more dramatic reading, sparked off by the cheeky wit of Brendel's treatment of the Diabelli theme itself. The keynotes are power and urgency, and it follows that Brendel is reluctant to treat the great slow variations, Nos. 14, 29, 30 and 31, as deeply meditative, even avoiding half-tones. But the whirlwind power of the whole performance is irresistible, and the piano sound is full and immediate.

Arrau in his eighties demonstrates formidable virtuosity in tackling this Everest of the keyboard, even if at times the strain shows. What matters is the concentration of his playing, his ability to hold the whole massive structure together, whatever the problems of detail, full of new insights. The sound is very immediate, perhaps too much so for such a work.

VOCAL MUSIC

An die ferne Geliebte, Op. 98. Lieder: *Adelaide; L'amant impaziente; Es war einmal ein König; In questa tomba oscura; Maigesang; Zärtliche Liebe.*
(*) DG 415 189-2 [id.]. Dietrich Fischer-Dieskau, Joerg Demus – BRAHMS: *Lieder.*(*)

Recorded in 1966, Fischer-Dieskau's DG Beethoven selection finds him at his vocal peak, and though Demus's accompaniment is not as imaginative as the singer received in other versions of these songs, Fischer-Dieskau's individuality is as positive as ever, with detail touched in as with no one else.

An die ferne Geliebte, Op. 98. Lieder: *Adelaide; Andenken; An die Hoffnung; Aus Goethes Faust (Song of the flea); Busslied; Ich liebe dich; Der Kuss; Mailied; Neue Liebe; Resignation; Der Wachtelschlag; Der Zufriedene.*
**(*) Amon Ra CDSAR 15. Ian Partridge, Richard Burnett.

Partridge, accompanied on an 1800 fortepiano, gives delightful performances of a wide-ranging and generous collection of Beethoven songs. The honeyed tones of Partridge's tenor and his finely detailed feeling for words come over well – particularly suited not only to the song-cycle but also to such soaring lyrical songs as *Adelaide* and *An die Hoffnung*. The twangy fortepiano is recorded much more dully.

Bundeslied, Op. 122; Eligischer Gesang, Op. 118; King Stephen (incidental music), *Op. 117; Meeresstille und glückliche Fahrt (Calm sea and a prosperous voyage), Op. 112; Opferlied, Op. 121b.*
*** CBS Dig. CD 76404 [MK 33509]. Amb. S., LSO, Tilson Thomas.

With the 1975 CBS sound fresher and more atmospheric than ever on CD, Tilson Thomas's collection of Beethoven choral rarities plus the *King Stephen* incidental music makes an attractive out-of-the-way disc for Beethovenians. Except for *Meeresstille (Calm sea and a prosperous voyage)* with its deeply meditative, highly original first half, these are no more than random chips from the master's workbench; but with excellent singing and playing they are all enjoyable.

Choral fantasia in C, Op. 80.
*** Capriccio Dig. 10 150 [id.]. Rösel, Leipzig R Ch., Dresden PO, Kegel – *Triple concerto.****
** Telarc Dig. CD 80063 [id.]. Serkin, Boston Ch. & SO, Ozawa – *Piano concerto No. 3.***

With four excellent vocal soloists from the chorus and a splendid contribution from the pianist, Peter Rösel, Hubert Kegel shapes a highly convincing account of Beethoven's *Choral fantasia*, clearly looking ahead to the *Choral symphony* in the closing pages, with the chorus making a thrilling climax. The recording is first rate, very well balanced and vivid.

As a fill-up for Serkin's version of the *Third Piano concerto*, the *Choral fantasia* is most welcome, even though the long opening solo lacks something in brio, the necessary evocation of Beethoven himself improvising. But Ozawa draws committed performances from chorus and orchestra, though vocal balances are odd, with the chorus close and the soloists rather distant in a reverberant acoustic.

The famous Brendel/Haitink version from the late 1970s is available on CD, coupled with the *Emperor concerto* (see above).

Christus am Ölberge, Op. 85.
(M) **(*) Sony MPK 45878 [id.]. Raskin, Lewis, Herbert Beattie, Temple University Choirs, Phd. O, Ormandy.
**(*) HM HMC 905181 [id.]. Pick-Hieronimi, Anderson, Von Halem, Ch. & O Nat. de Lyon, Baudo.

With Beethoven depicting Christ as another Florestan, it is appropriate that Monica Pick-Hieronimi, a singer of some power, should bring Leonore-like qualities to her role as Seraph. Baudo directs an energetic and lively account of it which, if lacking the utmost refinement of detail, generates urgency and breadth in the fine closing section. The chorus sings vividly and the Lyon orchestra is committed too in a recording which projects well and is convincingly balanced.

This oratorio is a stronger and more interesting work than has often been thought. Though the Ormandy version dates from the mid-1960s, the CBS sound as transferred on the Sony disc is full and forward, with satisfyingly resonant strings. At mid-price there is a strong case for preferring it, when Ormandy is at his most purposeful and warmly understanding without self-indulgence, and the soloists are outstandingly fine, with the pure-toned Judith Raskin very aptly cast as the Seraph and with Richard Lewis at his freshest and most expressive as Jesus.

Egmont: Overture and incidental music, Op. 84.
(*) DG 419 624-2 [id.]. Janowitz, Schellow, BPO, Karajan – *Wellington's victory; Marches.*

There is no lack of drama and Gundula Janowitz sings the two Lieder impressively; Erich Schellow's narration is reduced to a single melodrama before the finale. The sound is clear and vivid but ideally needs more sonority. The couplings too are uninspiring.

Folksong arrangements: *Again my love; Bonnie laddie; The deserter; Helpless woman; Judy lovely; March Megan; Oh! who, my dear Dermot; The parting kiss; The sweetest lad was Jamie.*
*** EMI Dig. CDC7 47420-2 [id.]. Robert White, Sanders, Peskanov, Rosen, Wilson – WEBER: *Folksong arrangements.****

Beethoven may not even have seen the words of these songs – the publisher George

Thomson often fitted new words to old tunes – but the charm and imagination of the music are delightful. In *Helpless woman* we even have a Beethoven setting of a Robert Burns poem. White's heady tenor and sharply expressive delivery are ideally suited to this music, and he is warmly accompanied by his instrumental ensemble. Warm recording, but with no lack of presence.

(i) *King Stephen* (incidental music), *Op. 117: Overture and excerpts. The Ruins of Athens* (incidental music), *Op. 113: Overture and excerpts.* (ii) *The Creatures of Prometheus overture.*
(BB) *** Hung. White Label HRC 118 [id.]. (i) Hungarian R. & TV Ch., Budapest PO, Oberfrank; (ii) Hungarian State O, Kórodi.

This is a particularly useful issue in Hungaroton's enterprising super-bargain White Label series, as it will surely encourage collectors with limited budgets to explore repertoire that might otherwise be overlooked. Beethoven's incidental music, though not always characteristic, is full of imagination and vitality. The choruses (and five are included here from each score) bring a whiff of Weber, yet the finales of both scores have an epic, Beethovenian grandeur. *The Ruins of Athens* has an unexpectedly bizarre Turkish element, but it also includes a duet for baritone and soprano (the excellent Margit László and Sándor Sólyom-Nagy) that recalls *Fidelio*. The fervour of the singing of the Hungarian Radio Chorus adds much to the sparkle of the performances, admirably conducted by Géza Oberfrank; as an apt encore, András Kórodi directs a lively account of *The Creatures of Prometheus overture*.

Mass in C, Op. 86.
(B) ** DG 429 510-2 [id.]. Janowitz, Hamari, Laubenthal, Schramm, Munich Bach Ch. & O, Richter – MOZART: *Mass No. 16.***(*)

(i) *Mass in C, Op. 86; Meeresstille und glückliche Fahrt (Calm sea and a prosperous voyage), Op. 112.*
**(*) Decca Dig. 417 563-2 [id.]. (i) Dunn, Zimmermann, Beccaria, Krause; Berlin RIAS Chamber Ch. & RSO, Chailly.

Beethoven's *Mass in C* has been consistently underrated. It was designed as a successor to the late great Haydn masses, like them being commissioned for the Princess Esterházy's name-day. The Chailly performance is on the right expansive scale; the singing of the Berlin RIAS Chorus has vigour and exuberance, yet conveys the full range of emotions expressed in the *Kyrie* and *Sanctus*. The solo team is also very good although the tenor, Bruno Beccaria, is too histrionically operatic in style. The recording has the widest dynamic range, and this adds drama to the fine performance of the rare cantata which is used as an encore (it is comparatively short, just over 8 minutes). The balance favours the singers, but the recording overall is admirably vivid.

Richter's account seems a little earthbound alongside Chailly's, but it is soundly conceived and not without eloquence. The soloists are good and the 1970 recording has been given a highly effective facelift: the whole impression is fresher than on the original LPs; moreover it is coupled, at bargain price, with an excellent version of Mozart's *Coronation Mass*.

Missa solemnis in D, Op. 123.
(M) *** DG 423 913-2 (2) [id.]. Janowitz, Ludwig, Wunderlich, Berry, V. Singverein, BPO, Karajan – MOZART: *Mass No. 16.***(*)
*** EMI Dig. CDC7 49950-2 [id.]. Vaness, Meier, Blochwitz, Tschammer, Tallis Chamber Ch., ECO, Tate.

*** DG 413 780-2 (2) [id.]. Moser, Schwarz, Kollo, Moll, Netherlands Ch., Concg. O, Bernstein.

(M) **(*) EMI CMS7 69246-2 (2) [Ang. CDMB 69246]. Janowitz, Baltsa, Schreier, Van Dam, V. Singverein, Philh. O, Karajan.

**(*) DG Dig. 419 166-2 (2) [id.]. Cuberli, Schmidt, Cole, Van Dam, V. Singverein, BPO, Karajan.

(*) Telarc Dig. CD 80150 (2) [id.]. McNair, Taylor, Aler, Krauss, Atlanta Ch. & SO, Robert Shaw – MOZART: *Mass No. 18.*

**(*) Nimbus Dig. NI 5109 [id.]. Hirsti, Watkinson, Murgatroyd, George, Oslo Cathedral Ch., Hanover Band, Kvam.

(M) * Decca 425 844-2 (2). Popp, Minton, Walker, Howell, Chicago Ch. & SO, Solti – VERDI: *Sacred pieces.***(*)

(i) *Missa solemnis in D;* (ii) *Choral fantasia in C, Op. 80.*
(M) *** EMI CMS7 69538-2 (2) [Ang. CDMB 69538-2]. (i) Söderström, Höffgen, Kmentt, Talvela, New Philh. Ch.; (ii) Barenboim, Alldis Ch.; New Philh. O, Klemperer.

Karajan's earlier DG version of the *Missa solemnis* comes up marvellously well in the digital transfer to CD, far clearer and more faithful in sound than either of his later versions (for EMI and DG), to make it an outstanding recommendation on two mid-price discs, with a generous fill-up in Mozart's *Coronation Mass.* Both the chorus and, even more strikingly, the superbly matched quartet of soloists, never surpassed as a team in this work, convey the intensity and cohesion of Beethoven's deeply personal response to the liturgy, not so much a statement of conventional religious faith as of belief in humanity. Gundula Janowitz is even more meltingly beautiful here than in her later EMI recording for Karajan. Christa Ludwig, as there, is a firm and characterful mezzo, while Walter Berry is a warmly expressive bass. Best of all is the ill-fated Fritz Wunderlich, whose lovely, heroic but unstrained tenor adds supremely to the radiance of the performance, one of his great recordings. The balance between soloists, chorus and orchestra is far clearer and more precise than in most recent recordings, and the clarity of detail is exemplary.

Tate's EMI version has powerful advantages over its rivals in presenting the whole work on a single disc, the only other to do so being the Hanover Band's period performance. Tate, with chorus and orchestra on a modest chamber scale, gains in incisiveness and loses hardly at all in weight, with bright, fresh singing from the Tallis Chamber Choir, challenged at times by Tate's fast speeds for some of the big fugatos. For the controversial case of *Pleni sunt coeli* he opts to use the soloists – as the score says – rather than chorus, as has become customary. The soloists make an outstanding quartet, with Hans Tschammer adding to Tate's deeply devotional treatment of the *Agnus Dei.* Both there and at a number of other points, Tate is marginally slower than Klemperer, and nowhere is there a feeling of excessive haste, just one of dramatic urgency. The well-balanced recording is at rather a low level, but sounds well at full volume. There is no finer digital version.

Bernstein's DG version with the Concertgebouw was edited together from tapes of two live performances, and the result has a spiritual intensity matched by very few rivals. Edda Moser is not an ideal soprano soloist, but the others are outstanding, and the *Benedictus* is made angelically beautiful by the radiant playing of the Concertgebouw concertmaster, Hermann Krebbers. The recording is a little light in bass, but outstandingly clear as well as atmospheric. The CD clarifies the sound still further.

Klemperer's set has been transferred to CD very successfully. Its glory is the superb choral singing of the New Philharmonia Chorus; it is not just their purity of tone and their fine discipline but the real fervour with which they sing that makes the choral passages so moving. The soloists are less happily chosen: Waldemar Kmentt seems unpleasantly hard and Elisabeth Söderström does not sound as firm as she can be. It was a happy idea to include the *Choral fantasia* as a bonus.

Karajan's EMI version is dedicated and dramatic. Though the resonance obscures some detail, the urgency of Karajan's view here is compelling. There is no feeling that he is skating over the surface of a spiritual experience, and the solo team are excellent. However, the analogue DG version is preferable and is even more successfully remastered. It also offers more music.

The later, digital set for DG was one of Karajan's recordings made in conjunction with a video film, and that brings both gains and losses. The sense of spontaneity, of a massive structure built dramatically with contrasts underlined, makes for extra magnetism, but there are flaws of ensemble and at least one serious flaw of intonation in the singing of Lella Cuberli, otherwise a full, sweet-toned soprano.

Shaw with his Atlanta forces directs a fine performance of the *Missa solemnis*, notable for its unforced good manners, with beautifully matched and moulded choral sound and intelligent pacing, but it lacks the full bite of tension, whether in spiritual meditation or in the dramatic uplift of the liturgy. This impression of reticence is reinforced by the slightly backward balance of the chorus, refined rather than immediate.

On Nimbus, the first ever recording of the *Missa solemnis* on period instruments brings a brisk, refreshing performance which has the incidental advantage of also being the first CD version on a single disc. The conductor, Terje Kvam, is chorus-master of the Oslo Cathedral Choir; not surprisingly, he is no match for such high-powered conductors as Klemperer and Bernstein in weight or gravity, but the simple intensity of the performance, with period instruments giving extra clarity and bite, brings a scale and manner to make it seem more liturgical than usual, partly because of the reverberant acoustic.

Solti's view of the work is essentially dramatic, hardly at all spiritual; moreover it is let down by less than crisp orchestral ensemble and poor co-ordination with the chorus. Thus the necessary bite is not always forthcoming. The solo team is balanced much too forwardly and is not well matched either: the women outweigh the men, and the contribution of the tenor, Mallory Walker, is indifferent. His colleagues all have splendid moments but overall, given the competition, this is a non-starter, not helped by a recording with a narrow range of dynamic.

OPERA

Fidelio (complete).

⊛ (M) *** EMI CMS7 69324-2 (2) [Ang. CDMB 69324]. Ludwig, Vickers, Frick, Berry, Crass, Philh. Ch. & O, Klemperer.

(M) *** EMI CMS7 69290-2 (2) [Ang. CDMB 69290]. Dernesch, Vickers, Ridderbusch, Van Dam, Kelemen, German Op. Ch., BPO, Karajan.

*** DG 419 436-2 (2) [id.]. Janowitz, Kollo, Sotin, Jungwirth, Fischer-Dieskau, Popp, V. State Op. Ch., VPO, Bernstein.

Klemperer's great set of *Fidelio* arrives on CD at last, sounding admirably fresh, to sweep the board in its new format. Its incandescence and spiritual strength are unique, with wonderful performances from all concerned and with a final scene in which, more than in any other recording, the parallel with the finale of the *Choral symphony* is underlined.

Comparison between Karajan's strong and heroic reading and Klemperer's version is fascinating. Both have very similar merits, underlining the symphonic character of the work with their weight of utterance. Both may miss some of the sparkle of the opening scene, but it is better that seriousness should enter too early than too late. Since seriousness is the keynote, it is rather surprising to find Karajan using bass and baritone soloists lighter than usual. Both the Rocco (Ridderbusch) and the Don Fernando (Van Dam) lack something in resonance in their lower range. Yet they sing dramatically and intelligently, and there is the advantage that the Pizarro of Zoltan Kelemen sounds the more biting and powerful as a result – a fine performance. Jon Vickers as Florestan is if anything even finer than he was for Klemperer; and though Helga Dernesch as Leonore does not have quite the clear-focused mastery of Christa Ludwig in the Klemperer set, this is still a glorious, thrilling performance, outshining lesser rivals than Ludwig. The orchestral playing is superb.

Bernstein, as one would expect, directs a reading of *Fidelio* full of dramatic flair. The recording was made in conjunction with live performances by the same cast at the Vienna State Opera. Lucia Popp as Marzelline is particularly enchanting, and though Bernstein later rises splendidly to the high drama of Act II, it remains a drama on a human scale. Gundula Janowitz sings most beautifully as Leonore. Kollo as Florestan is intelligent and musicianly but indulges in too many intrusive aitches, and the rest of the cast make strong contributions.

Fidelio: highlights.
(M) *** EMI CDM7 63077-2 (from above set; cond. Karajan).

Those who acquire Klemperer's classic set will welcome just under an hour of well-chosen highlights from the fine alternative Karajan recording, made in 1970. It opens with the *Overture* and includes key items like Pizzaro's Act I aria, the *Abscheulicher!*, the *Prisoners' chorus* and the closing scene, all vividly presented in bright, clear sound. There is a brief synopsis but no libretto.

Bellini, Vincenzo (1801–35)

Norma (complete).
**(*) Decca Dig. 414 476-2 (3) [id.]. Sutherland, Pavarotti, Caballé, Ramey, Welsh Nat. Op. Ch. & O, Bonynge.
(M) *** Decca 425 488-2 (3). Sutherland, Horne, Alexander, Cross, Minton, Ward, LSO Ch., LSO, Bonynge.
(***) EMI mono CDS7 47304-8 [CDCB 47303] (3). Callas, Filippeschi, Stignani, Rossi-Lemeni, La Scala, Milan, Ch. and O, Serafin.
(M) **(*) EMI CMS7 63000-2 (3) [Ang. CDMC 63000]. Callas, Corelli, Ludwig, Zaccharia, Ch. & O of La Scala, Milan, Serafin.

Norma: highlights.
(M) **(*) EMI CDM7 63091-2 [Ang. CDMC 63091] (from above complete set with Callas, Corelli; cond. Serafin).

Dame Joan Sutherland was fifty-eight when her second Norma recording was made. The coloratura is still remarkably flexible, but the conjunction of Sutherland with Pavarotti and Caballé does not always work easily. Though Pavarotti is in some ways the set's greatest strength, easily expressive yet powerful as Pollione, Caballé as Adalgisa seems determined to outdo Sutherland in mooning manner, cooing self-indulgently. However, in the big Act II Trio the three principals effectively and excitingly sink their stylistic differences. Bonynge, as in the earlier Sutherland recording (which would still make a first choice if it were to appear on CD), paces Bellini well, and the Welsh National Opera Orchestra and Chorus respond most sympathetically. Full, brilliant, well-balanced recording of the complete score.

In her first, mid-1960s recording of *Norma*, Sutherland was joined by an Adalgisa in Marilyn Horne whose control of florid singing is just as remarkable as Sutherland's own, and who sometimes even outshines the heroine in musical imagination. The other soloists are very good indeed, John Alexander and Richard Cross both young, clear-voiced singers. Sutherland's own contribution is dramatically very much after the school of Callas, while at the same time ensuring that something as near as possible to musical perfection is achieved, even if occasionally at the expense of masked diction. But overall this is a most compelling performance, helped by the conducting of Richard Bonynge, who keeps musical interest alive in the many conventional accompaniment figures with sprung rhythm and with the most subtle attention to the vocal line. The Walthamstow recording is vivid but also atmospheric in its new format.

Though the flatness of the 1954 mono recording is emphasized by the precision of CD, the sense of presence gives wonderful intensity to one of Callas's most powerful performances, recorded at the very peak of her powers. The chorus could hardly be dimmer, but this is a classic, irreplaceable recording, one of the jewels of the CD catalogue. Ebe Stignani as Adalgisa gives Callas a worthily characterful partner in the sisters' duets. Filippeschi is disappointing by comparison, thin-toned and at times strained, and Rossi-Lemeni is not well treated by the microphone either.

By the time Callas came to record her 1960 stereo version, the tendency to hardness and unsteadiness in the voice above the stave, always apparent, had grown more serious, but the interpretation was as sharply illuminating as ever, a unique assumption, helped – as the earlier mono performance was not – by a strong cast. Christa Ludwig as Adalgisa brings not just rich, firm tone but a real feeling for Italian style and, despite moments of coarseness, Corelli sings heroically. Serafin as ever is the most persuasive of Bellini conductors, and the recording is very good for its period – not surprisingly, as Walter Legge masterminded the original production.

Those who already have the mono set will surely want the generous (63 minutes) highlights disc which includes, of course, *Casta diva* and the three principal Norma/Adalgisa duets.

I Puritani (complete).
*** Decca 417 588-2 (3). Sutherland, Pavarotti, Ghiaurov, Luccardi, Caminada, Cappuccilli, ROHCG Ch. & O, Bonynge.
(***) EMI mono CDC7 47308-8 [Ang. CDCB 47308] (3). Callas, di Stefano, Panerei, Rossi-Lemeni, La Scala, Milan, Ch. & O, Serafin.

Whereas her earlier set was recorded when Sutherland had adopted a soft-grained style, with consonants largely eliminated and a tendency to lag behind the beat, this time her singing is fresher and brighter. The lovely aria *Qui la voce* is no longer a wordless melisma, and though the great showpiece *Son vergin vezzosa* is now taken dangerously fast, the extra bite and tautness are exhilarating. Pavarotti shows himself a remarkable Bellini stylist, rarely if ever coarsening a legato line, unlike so many of his Italian colleagues. Ghiaurov and Cappuccilli make up an impressive cast, and the only disappointing contributor is Anita Caminada in the small role of Enrichetta – Queen Henrietta Maria in disguise. Vivid, atmospheric recording, enhanced and given added presence by the digital remastering.

In 1953, when Callas made the recording, her voice was already afflicted with hardness on top and with some unsteadiness, and for sheer beauty of sound Sutherland is consistently preferable. But Callas, once heard, is unforgettable, for the compulsion of her singing is irresistible. None of the other soloists is ideally stylish, though most of the singing is acceptable. As can be heard at the very opening, the upper range of the sound is restricted, though later the recording opens up and the solo voices project vividly.

La Sonnambula (complete).
*** Decca Dig. 417 424-2 (2) [id.]. Sutherland, Pavarotti, Della Jones, Ghiaurov, L. Op. Ch., Nat. PO, Bonynge.
(***) EMI mono CDS7 47378-8 (2) [CDCB 47377]. Callas, Monti, Cossotto, Zaccaria, Ratti, La Scala, Milan, Ch. and O, Votto.

Sutherland's singing here is even more affecting and more stylish than her earlier version, generally purer and more forthright, if with diction still clouded at times. The challenge of singing opposite Pavarotti adds to the bite of the performance, crisply and resiliently controlled by Bonynge. The star tenor may be stylistically coarser than Nicola Monti on Sutherland's earlier set, but the beauty and size of the voice help to focus the whole performance more positively, not least in such ensembles as the finale of Act I. The rest of the cast is vocally strong too, and the early digital recording comes up very vividly.

Substantially cut, the Callas version was recorded in mono in 1957, yet it gives a vivid picture of the diva at the peak of her powers. By temperament she may not have related closely to Bellini's heroine, but the village girl's simple devotion through all trials is touchingly caught, most of all in the recitatives. The recording has transferred remarkably well to CD. Nicola Monti makes a strong rather than a subtle contribution but blends well with Callas in the duets; and Fiorenza Cossotto is a good Teresa. Callas admirers will find this enjoyable as an overall performance.

Benjamin, George (born 1960)

(i) *Ringed by the flat horizon.* (ii) *At first light. A Mind of winter.*
*** Nimbus Dig. NI 5075 [id.]. (i) BBC SO, Elder; (ii) Penelope Walmsley-Clark, L. Sinf., composer.

Ringed by the flat horizon is a 20-minute orchestral piece that conceals the detailed complexity of its argument in warmly expressive, evocative use of the orchestra, with the big climax masterfully built. *A Mind of winter* is a 9-minute setting of *The Snowman* by Wallace Stevens, beautifully sung by the soprano Penelope Walmsley-Clark, with Benjamin himself conducting the London Sinfonietta. It has been aptly described as a winter equivalent of Debussy's *L'après-midi d'un faune.* Sound of great warmth and refinement to match the music make this a collection well worth exploring.

Berg, Alban (1885–1935)

(i) *Chamber concerto;* (ii) *4 Pieces for clarinet and piano, Op. 5; Piano sonata, Op. 1.*
*** DG 423 237-2 [id.]. Barenboim with (i) Zukerman & Ens. Intercontemporain, Boulez; (ii) Antony Pay.

Boulez sets brisk tempi in the *Chamber concerto*, seeking to give the work classical incisiveness; but the strong and expressive personalities of the pianist and violinist tend towards a more romantic view. The result is characterful and convincing, though unaccountably Boulez omits the extended repeat in the finale. The apt coupling combines the high-romantic *Piano sonata* in one movement with the *Clarinet pieces*; here Antony Pay is an outstanding soloist.

Violin concerto.
*** DG 413 725-2 [id.]. Itzhak Perlman, Boston SO, Ozawa – STRAVINSKY: *Concerto.****
*** Decca Dig. 411 804-2 [id.]. Kyung Wha Chung, Chicago SO, Solti – BARTÓK: *Concerto.****
(M) ******* Ph. 422 136-2 [id.]. Grumiaux, Concg. O, Markevitch – STRAVINSKY: *Violin concerto.****

Violin concerto; 3 Orchestral pieces, Op. 6.
**(*) Ph. 412 523-2 [id.]. Gidon Kremer, Bav. RSO, Sir Colin Davis.

Perlman's performance is totally commanding. The effortless precision of the playing goes with great warmth of expression, so that the usual impression of 'wrong-note Romanticism' gives way to total purposefulness. The Boston orchestra accompanies superbly and, though the balance favours the soloist, the recording is excellent. It has been convincingly remastered for CD, although the detail is less sharp than in either the Decca or Philips alternative.

Chung may not be as powerful as Perlman, but her tenderness and poetry bring an added dimension to the music. The violin is placed well in front of the orchestra, but not aggressively so. The recording is brilliant in the Chicago manner, but more spacious than some from this source.

Grumiaux's splendid account is by no means an also-ran, even though it is an older recording. As a performance it could hardly be bettered, and Markevitch gives him highly sympathetic support. There is a warmth and melancholy that make this as moving and convincing as any committed to disc, and the recording emerges freshly, besides having a price advantage.

Kremer's performance of the *Concerto* is more problematic, for it too is often intensely felt and enormously accomplished. However, there is an element of narcissism here, and Kremer often stresses the music's self-pity. The Bavarian Radio Orchestra give a fine account of the Op. 6 *Pieces*, and Sir Colin makes much of their refined textures and powerful atmosphere. This is a really compelling performance. The Philips recording is of altogether remarkable clarity and definition.

Lyric suite: 3 Pieces; 3 Pieces for orchestra, Op. 6.
(M) ******* DG 427 424-2 (3) [id.]. BPO, Karajan – SCHOENBERG; WEBERN: *Orchestral pieces.****

Karajan's justly famous collection of music by the Second Viennese School has now been reissued as a set of three mid-priced CDs. No more persuasive view could be taken, though, next to Schoenberg and Webern, Berg appears here as the figure who overloaded his music, rather than as the most approachable of the three composers. Beautiful, refined recording, admirably transferred to CD.

3 Pieces for orchestra, Op. 6.
*** DG Dig. 419 781-2 [id.]. BPO, Levine – SCHOENBERG; WEBERN: *Pieces.****

Levine gives a powerful, warmly emotional reading of Berg's Opus 6. He is particularly impressive in the big build-up of the third and last piece, the *March*, though there as elsewhere odd emphasis of individual lines is intrusive in an otherwise full and vivid recording.

Piano sonata.
*** EMI Dig. CDC7 49916-2 [id.]. Peter Donohoe – BARTÓK; LISZT: *Sonatas.****

Donohoe gives a thoughtful and searching performance of Berg's one-movement *Sonata*. He is better recorded than most rivals from the recent past, and readers wanting this piece are unlikely to do much better at present.

Lulu: symphonic suite.
*** EMI Dig. CDC7 49857-2 [id.]. Arleen Augér, CBSO, Rattle – SCHOENBERG: *5 Pieces*; WEBERN: *6 Pieces.***

Rattle steers a perfect course between traditional austerity and overtly romantic warmth in this music. Augér's pure, true soprano in the vocal passages of the *Lulu suite* is presented as an adjunct to the orchestra, rather than as a salient solo. The sound is of demonstration quality, one of the very finest recordings that Rattle and the CBSO have received, adding enormously to the attractiveness of the disc, and the couplings are equally positive and red-blooded.

Lulu: symphonic suite. 3 Pieces for orchestra, Op. 6; 5 Orchestral songs, Op. 4.
(M) ******* DG 423 238-2 [id.]. M. Price; LSO, Abbado.

Abbado makes it clear above all how beautiful Berg's writing is, not just in the *Lulu* excerpts but in the early Opus 4 *Songs* and the Opus 6 *Orchestral pieces*, among which even the formidable march movement has sumptuousness as well as power. The recording from the early 1970s is still outstanding.

Lulu (with orchestration of Act III completed by Friedrich Cerha).
*** DG 415 489-2 (3) [id.]. Stratas, Minton, Schwarz, Mazura, Blankenheim, Riegel, Tear, Paris Op. O, Boulez.

The full three-Act structure of Berg's *Lulu*, first unveiled by Boulez in his Paris Opéra production and here treated to studio recording, was a revelation with few parallels. The very end of the opera, with Yvonne Minton singing the Countess Geschwitz's lament, is most moving, though Lulu remains to the last a repulsive heroine. Teresa Stratas's bright, clear soprano is well recorded, and there is hardly a weak link in the cast. Altogether this is an historic issue, presenting an intensely involving performance of a work which in some ways is more lyrically approachable than *Wozzeck*.

Wozzeck (complete).
*** Decca Dig. 417 348-2 (2) [id.]. Waechter, Silja, Winkler, Laubenthal, Jahn, Malta, Sramek, VPO, Dohnányi – SCHOENBERG: *Erwartung.***
**(*) DG 423 587-2 (2) [id.]. Grundheber, Behrens, Haugland, Langridge, Zednik, V. State Op. Ch., VPO, Abbado.
**(*) CBS M2K 79251 [M2K 30852] (2). Berry, Isabel Strauss, Weikenmeier, Uhl, Doench, Paris Op. Ch. & O, Boulez.

Dohnányi, with refined textures and superb playing from the Vienna Philharmonic, presents an account of *Wozzeck* that not only is more accurate than any other on record but also is more beautiful. It may lack some of the bite of Pierre Boulez's CBS version, but with superb digital sound the Decca set stands as first choice. Unfortunately the beauty of the performance does not extend to Eberhard Waechter's vocal quality in the name-part, but he gives a thoughtful, sensitive performance. The edge of Anja Silja's voice and her natural vibrancy of character make her a memorable Marie, first cousin to Lulu. An excellent supporting cast too, and the recording has a spectacular sense of presence and clarity; unlike its CD rivals, it comes with a substantial coupling in Schoenberg's monodrama, *Erwartung*, also with Silja.

The Abbado version, recorded live in the opera house, is very compelling in its presentation of the drama, given extra thrust through the tensions of live performance. However, there are drawbacks, too. Not only do you get the stage noises; the voices are also set behind the orchestra, with the instrumental sound putting a gauze between listener and singers. The cast is a good one, headed by a clear-toned if lightweight Wozzeck in Franz Grundheber. Hildegard Behrens sings affectingly as Marie, but the microphones exaggerate the flutter in her voice and she produces unpleasantly curdled tones, even in the scene where she sings a lullaby to her child. The Decca Dohnányi set is clearly preferable.

Walter Berry's view of the hero's character includes a strong element of brutishness, and Boulez's uncompromising, thrustful view of the whole score matches this conception; he is less concerned with pure atmosphere than with emotional drive, and undoubtedly he provides a powerful experience. One is made to suffer. The forward recording gives strong projection on CD, but the sound is brightly lit to the point of harshness.

Bergman, Erik (born 1911)

Bim bam bum; Fåglarna; Hathor Suite; Nox.
*** Chan. Dig. CHAN 8478 [id.]. Walmsley-Clark, Varcoe, Potter, New London Chamber Ch., Endymion Ens., James Wood.

The Finnish composer, Erik Bergman, is at his best and most characteristic in writing for voices. *Nox* (1970) is a setting of four poems on the theme of Night, while for *Bim bam bum* (1976) he turns to Morgenstern, whose gallows-songs inspired earlier works. *Fåglarna* (*The Birds*) is earlier (1962) but is no less resourceful in its use of choral colour; and the *Hathor Suite* is based on ancient Egyptian cult texts dedicated to the goddess Hathor. All four are well performed and recorded, and the record forms an invaluable introduction to a highly imaginative and sensitive artistic personality.

Berio, Luciano (born 1925)

A-Ronne; The Cries of London.
(M) *** Decca 425 620-2 [id.]. Swingle II, composer.

One of the highlights of the first release in Decca's new Enterprise reissue series, this definitive recording was originally used for a memorable BBC television film. *A-Ronne*, literally 'A–Z', is an extraordinary setting of a multilingual poem by Edoardo Sanguinetti. From time to time the eight voices briefly break into singing, but for the most part the characteristic musical collage consists of shouts, snarls and organized crowd-noises, with the fragmentary word-sequence run through some twenty times. *The Cries of London* is almost equally surrealistic, an updating of the cries used by Elizabethan madrigal composers but with musical references to medieval patterns. There is some jokiness, but much of the music in this cycle of seven vocal pieces is immediately beautiful. The performances by Swingle II are nothing less than brilliant and they are recorded with stunning immediacy. There are few more stimulating examples of the avant garde than this.

Coro (revised version).
*** DG 423 902-2 [id.]. Cologne R. Ch. and SO, composer.

Coro is one of the most ambitious of Berio's works, with each of forty singers paired with an instrumentalist and with folk verse on basic themes contrasted with poems of

159

Pablo Neruda. Of his generation of leading avant-gardists Berio remains the most approachable. The composer directs a committed performance here, helped by the impact of the forward sound.

Berkeley, Lennox (1903-89)

Improvisation on a theme of Falla, Op. 55/2; Mazurka, Op. 101/2; 3 Mazurkas (Hommage à Chopin), Op. 32; Paysage; 3 Pieces; Polka, Op. 5a; 6 Preludes, Op. 23; 5 Short pieces, Op. 4; Sonata, Op. 20.
**(*) Kingdom KCLCD 2012 [id.]. Christopher Headington.

With the exception of the *Sonata*, all these pieces are miniatures, some of considerable elegance. Christopher Headington is a sympathetic exponent. Sometimes (as in the third of the *Six Preludes*) his playing is wanting the last ounce of finish, but it is not lacking in charm, and he is completely attuned to the idiom. The recording is eminently serviceable and truthful, but not in the demonstration class.

Berkeley, Michael (born 1948)

Or shall we die? (oratorio).
(M) *** EMI Dig. CDM7 69810-2. Harper, Wilson-Johnson, LSO Ch., LSO, Hickox.

Michael Berkeley's oratorio on the pain and problems of a nuclear world confidently uses an openly eclectic style that communicates immediately to any listener. The pity is that the biggest blemish comes at its very peak, where the Woman's agony as the mother of a nuclear bomb victim is most tenderly brought home, only to be resolved in banality, when doggerel verses are set in pop parody, intended bathos which defeats its own object. Despite the flaws, it is a strong, confident and colourful work which it is good to have on record. The recording is first rate.

Berlioz, Hector (1803-69)

(i) *Harold in Italy, Op. 16; Overture: Le Carnaval romain, Op. 9.*
*** DG Dig. 415 109-2 [id.]. (i) Christ; BPO, Maazel.

(i) *Harold in Italy; Overture: Le Carnaval romain, Op. 9; La damnation de Faust: Rákóczy march. Roméo et Juliette: Queen Mab scherzo.*
(***) RCA mono RD 85755 [RCA 5755-2]. (i) Cooley; NBC SO, Toscanini.

(i) *Harold in Italy, Op. 16; Overtures: Le Corsaire, Op. 21; Rob Roy.*
**(*) Decca Dig. 421 193-2 [id.]. (i) Zukerman; Montreal SO, Dutoit.

(i) *Harold in Italy; (ii) Tristia: (Méditation religieuse; La mort d'Ophélie; Marche funèbre pour la dernière scène de Hamlet), Op. 18; Les Troyens à Carthage: Prelude to Act II.*
*** Ph. 416 431-2 [id.]. (i) Imai; (ii) Alldis Ch.; LSO, C. Davis.

The Philips account offers splendid value. In addition to a noble account of *Harold* in which Nobuko Imai is on top form, this CD offers the *Tristia*, which includes the haunting *Funeral march for the last scene of Hamlet* given with chorus, as well as the *Prelude* to the second Act of *Les Troyens*. The sound is completely natural and realistic, and has impressive transparency and detail. The recordings emanate from the 1970s but still lead the field. A first recommendation.

Maazel's *Harold* is undoubtedly very fine; the structure is held together well, with a vivid sense of forward movement and no lack of poetic feeling; there is some imaginative phrasing, and he invariably finds the *tempo giusto*. Wolfram Christ is an eloquent and dignified protagonist. Moreover, the overture, *Le Carnaval romain*, combines exhilaration with an infectious sparkle. The DG recording is marvellously clean and vivid.

Dutoit's version of *Harold in Italy* is very richly recorded. With as characterful a soloist as Zukerman, highly individual and warmly expressive, if not always at his purest, the centre of gravity of the work is shifted. Though the beauty of the writing is very satisfying, the work seems to lose some of its purpose when the soloist comes to be phased out. With the viola's contribution all but eliminated, the *Orgy* seems just a little tame, and speeds throughout tend to be on the broad side. *Rob Roy* and *Le Corsaire* make appropriate Byronic couplings.

Toscanini's account of the *Roman carnival overture* is of very high voltage and so, of course, is the famous recording of *Harold* with Carlton Cooley an excellent soloist. The demonic fires glow with great intensity in the *Orgy of the Brigands* – perhaps the *Pilgrims' march* is just a shade hard driven. The *Queen Mab scherzo* is absolutely magical and wonderfully delicate. The RCA engineers have accomplished much in the transfer to the new medium but the sound calls for tolerance, particularly in the *Rákóczy march*.

Overtures: *Béatrice et Bénédict; Benvenuto Cellini; Le Carnaval romain; Le Corsaire; Les Francs-juges.*
(M) **(*) EMI CD-EMX 2159. LSO, André Previn.

Previn offers the five most popular Berlioz *Overtures*, brilliantly played. *Le Corsaire* is less hectic than Previn has been known to present it in the concert hall, but it hardly loses from that. *Béatrice et Bénédict* fizzes with wit, while the swing-along melody of *Les Francs-juges* swaggers boldly. There is certainly no lack of panache here, but on CD the very spectacular recording is made to sound somewhat over-brilliant at fortissimo level, although there is plenty of warmth and atmosphere.

Overtures: *Béatrice et Bénédict; Le Carnaval romain, Op. 9; Le Corsaire, Op. 21; Rob Roy; Le Roi Lear, Op. 4.*
**(*) Chan. Dig. CHAN 8316 [id.]. SNO, Gibson.

Rob Roy is the rarity of Sir Alexander Gibson's Berlioz collection. It adds an aptly Scottish tinge to the record, even when traditional melodies – *Scots wha hae* at the opening – are given distinctly Berliozian twists, and finds Gibson and the SNO at their most dashingly committed. *King Lear*, another rarity, also comes out most dramatically, and though *Béatrice et Bénédict* is not quite so polished, the playing is generally excellent. With first-rate digital recording, this can be generally recommended.

Overtures: *Le Carnaval romain, Op. 9; Le Corsaire, Op. 21; Les Francs Juges, Op. 3; Le Roi Lear, Op. 4; Waverley, Op. 26.*
**(*) Ph. 416 430-2. LSO, C. Davis.

Sir Colin Davis's collection of overtures dates from the mid-1960s and, while the CD transfer has freshened the recording, the original balance was not ideal, although the woodwind detail remains well integrated. This is music which ideally calls for modern digital sound; in spite of this, Sir Colin's collection can hold its own, even though it should now be in the mid-price bracket. The playing undoubtedly has fire and brilliance, *Les Francs Juges* is exhilarating and the performance of *King Lear* is outstanding, challenging comparison with Beecham.

Symphonie fantastique, Op. 14.
*** Ph. 411 425-2 [id.]. Concg. O, C. Davis.
*** Denon Dig. CO 73208 [id.]. Frankfurt RSO, Inbal.
**(*) EMI Dig. CDC7 49541-2 [id.]. L. Classical Players, Norrington.
(M) **(*) EMI CDM7 69002-2 [id.]. O Nat. de France, Bernstein.
**(*) EMI Dig. CDC7 47278-2 [id.]. Phd. O, Muti.
**(*) DG 415 325-2 [id.]. BPO, Karajan.
**(*) DG Dig. 410 895-2 [id.]. Chicago SO, Abbado.
(M) **(*) DG 423 957-2 [id.]. LOP, Markevitch – ROUSSEL: *Bacchus et Ariane.***
**(*) Decca Dig. 414 203-2 [id.]. Montreal SO, Dutoit.
** Chan. Dig. CHAN 8727 [id.]. LSO, Skrowaczewski.

(i) *Symphonie fantastique, Op. 14;* (ii) *Overtures: Le Carnaval romain, Op. 9; Benvenuto Cellini, Op. 23; Les Troyens: Trojan march.*
(B) **(*) EMI CDZ7 62605-2. (i) Philh. O, Cluytens; (ii) CBSO, Frémaux.

(i) *Symphonie fantastique;* (ii) *Overtures: Le Carnaval romain, Op. 9; Le Corsaire, Op. 21.*
**(*) ASV Dig. CDDCA 590 [id.]. RPO, Bátiz.
(M) **(*) RCA GD 86720 [RCA-6720-2RG]. Boston SO, (i) Prêtre; (ii) Munch.

Sir Colin Davis's 1974 Concertgebouw recording – his first with that orchestra – remains a primary recommendation. The Philips recording was always a fine one, but the digital remastering for CD has been outstandingly successful and there is a very striking improvement in the firmness of focus, detail is clearer, while in brilliance and definition the overall balance is very satisfying. The Concertgebouw performance has superb life and colour. The slow movement, most beautifully played, is wonderfully atmospheric and the final two movements are very exciting indeed, with a fine rhythmic spring given to the *March to the scaffold* and the finale gripping to the last bar.

Eliahu Inbal with the Frankfurt Radio Symphony Orchestra brings to his recording of the *Symphonie fantastique* the same clear-headed perception that marks his fine series of Mahler recordings, also for Denon; moreover the digital sound is exceptionally full and atmospheric. Inbal's freshness and directness have a similar impact to that of Sir Colin Davis but, for all the brilliance of the Frankfurt performance, Inbal cannot quite match Davis in his electricity, not helped in the first two movements by speeds that are marginally slower. Nevertheless this stands out among recent versions and, for anyone insisting on a spectacular modern digital recording, this is a first-rate recommendation.

Though Berlioz was writing so soon after the death of Beethoven, he represented a leap forward in the art of orchestration. The gains from using period instruments are less striking here than in Beethoven, but the rasp of heavy brass and the bite of authentic timpani stand out more vividly. As in his Beethoven, Norrington does his utmost to observe the composer's metronome markings; but where his Beethoven is consistently fast, some of these speeds are more relaxed than we are used to – as in the *March to the scaffold* and the *Ronde du sabbat.* As usual, his lifting of rhythms prevents the music from dragging, at the same time giving new transparency; and his revelations here certainly give his version a key place. The sound is warm and well balanced, more firmly focused than some recordings by the London Classical Players at the EMI studio.

André Cluytens's 1959 account was superbly recorded (with Walter Legge producing). It is a sensitive and intelligent reading which can safely be ranked among the very best, and it still sounds amazingly good. The two overtures are of later provenance (mid-1970s) and are eminently well played by the Birmingham orchestra under Louis Frémaux. This disc is well worth considering, and though it does not displace Colin Davis it is to be preferred to many of the brash digital recordings that enjoy currency.

Bernstein directs a brilliant and understanding performance which captures the wild, volatile quality of Berlioz's inspiration. Sir Colin Davis may give a clearer idea of the logic of the piece, but Bernstein (omitting the exposition repeat, unlike Davis) has even more urgency, and his reading culminates in superb accounts of the *March to the scaffold* and the *Witches' sabbath*, full of rhythmic swagger and natural flair. The remastering of the late-1970s analogue recording gives some over-emphasis to the brilliance with its tendency to shrillness in the upper strings; however, the warm resonance of the recording retains the body of the orchestral sound.

Muti holds the thread of argument together firmly without ever underplaying excitement. The sound is among the best which he has had in Philadelphia – full in range, if not always ideally clear in texture – but cannot equal Dutoit on Decca in realism or fidelity of balance.

Karajan's reading is highly individual in its control of tempo in the first movement, but the Berlin Philharmonic are fully equal to his quixotic pacing, and the effect is certainly compelling. In the slow movement, the intensity of pianissimo playing is enhanced by the beautiful orchestral sound; the *Waltz* has characteristic panache and the spacious yet immensely dramatic finale sends the adrenalin racing. Unlike Sir Colin Davis, Karajan does not observe the first-movement repeat, and there is no doubt that Davis's structural control and overall pacing are more convincing. Karajan's 1965 performance, now on DG's bargain Privilege label, with two dances from the *Damnation de Faust* as a bonus (429 511-2), is altogether too erratic to be entirely convincing.

Abbado brings the right dreamy atmosphere and feverish intensity to this score, and the playing of the Chicago Symphony Orchestra has all the polish and finesse one could expect. There is much poetic feeling, the slow movement is outstandingly fine, and he observes the exposition repeat in the first movement (also in the *March to the scaffold*). The DG recording is rich in texture but the balance is less than ideal. The effect is recessed and the resonance sometimes clouds finer points of detail.

Markevitch's 1960 account is characteristically impulsive and full of nervous intensity. Even the *Waltz*, though basically warm and elegant, has its underlying neurosis; while the *Adagio*'s serene pastoral atmosphere is shattered by a climax of explosive power, with the tension relaxing spontaneously afterwards. The compulsion of the *March to the scaffold* is carried forward grippingly into the finale, with its doom-laden church bell tolling remorselessly and the *Dies irae* echoing with sinister force on the brass. The whole reading holds the listener under its spell. The digital remastering retains the ambient fullness of what was originally a highly praised analogue recording, and only the focus of the upper strings reveals the early recording date.

Bátiz has a first-class modern digital recording, brilliant yet full-bodied and very well balanced. As always in the recording studio, he brings the score vividly to life, and his consistent warmth and intensity are highly persuasive. Points of detail may be less subtle than with Davis, but one has the feeling here of live music-making, and the two overtures are equally strong and spontaneous.

The spectacular, wide-ranging recorded sound is the first point to note with the Dutoit version. But he tends to prefer slower speeds than usual, and that sometimes makes him seem less exciting than his finest rivals. Yet by keeping the pulse steady, he adds to structural strength while never limiting expressive warmth in lyrical passages or the crisp lifting of rhythm in allegros, and the power is most impressive.

Prêtre's early stereo recording suffers from thin, overlit violins, but the Boston ambience brings weight and the sound is otherwise resonantly full, with exciting projection for the brass. It is a highly volatile performance but his sense of neurosis is convincing. The heart of the interpretation lies in the beautiful slow movement, but the *March to the scaffold* has a jaunty sense of melodrama, and the finale combines an element of the grotesque with high adrenalin flow. An individual and involving account. With the two overtures, recorded earlier in 1958, the upper range becomes shrill, although the recording undoubtedly makes the strongest impact. They have great panache and excitement. At mid-price one can accept the need to cut back the treble and enjoy the music-making for its exuberance.

Skrowaczewski's performance opens rather marvellously and shows real vision; he observes the first-movement exposition repeat, and there are lots of good things here, including an exciting *Marche au supplice*. However, he does indulge in agogic exaggerations (in the opening movement there is a massive pull-back before the famous oboe entry – about 12 minutes in), and the slow movement is really much too slow and has its longueurs. He manages to take an hour over the whole work, and the opening of the finale does not quite work. The recording is splendidly natural, but this cannot be counted among the most convincing available versions.

Symphonie fantastique, Op. 14; (i) *Lélio (Le retour à la vie), Op. 14b.*
(M) *** EMI CZS7 62739-2 (2) [id.]. (i) Gedda, Burles, Van Gorp, Sendrez, Topart, Ch. of R. France; ORTF Nat. O, Martinon.

Berlioz intended *Lélio* as a sequel to the *Symphonie fantastique*, and Martinon conveniently offers the works paired at bargain price. His account of the *Symphonie* shows a unique seductiveness. In its way it is as magically compelling as Beecham's version with the same orchestra. Martinon gives the first-movement exposition repeat and provides the often omitted extra brass parts; though the result is brilliant, he never presses on too frenetically. The *March to the scaffold* is aptly menacing. But most of all this reading is outstanding for its warm shaping of phrase, even if the finale, with its tolling bells of doom, has a flamboyance and power to match any available. The 1973 sound remains remarkably vivid.

Lélio is a strange work but, as so often with an oddity, the gramophone allows one to appreciate its genuine merits more clearly. Though the spoken narration and music for soloists (including a Goethe ballad setting for tenor with piano!) doesn't help the piece hold together, the six musical numbers make a fascinating suite. The work quotes the *idée fixe* from the *Symphonie*, which helps the listener to feel at home. It is difficult to imagine this performance being bettered, and the 1974 sound is suitably atmospheric.

VOCAL MUSIC

Cantatas: (i) *Le 5 mai; L'impériale;* (ii) *La mort d'Orphée;* (iii) *Scène héroïque.*
** Denon Dig. CO 72886 [id.]. (i) Lieuwe Visser, (ii) Gérard Garino, (iii) Ruud van der Meer; Dutch R. Ch. & SO, Fournet.

Le 5 mai (subtitled *Chant sur la mort de l'Empereur Napoléon*) was written between 1831 and 1835, fourteen years after Napoleon's death (on 5 May 1821). It is an imaginative piece and is given eloquent advocacy here. *L'impériale* is the Second Empire's equivalent of this century's *Odes to Stalin* – and just about as hollow! It is a eulogy in extravagant terms, addressed to Napoleon III, and the orchestral forces are particularly grandiose: a half-dozen each of cornets and trumpets, eight trombones, five tubas, and so on. The earliest work, *Scène héroïque*, is frankly the least interesting: it is most characteristic when it is least grandiloquent – but that is not very often. However, the pastoral opening of *La mort d'Orphée* is magical; there are some characteristic touches elsewhere and the closing *Larghetto* is beautiful. The performances derive from a public concert in Utrecht and offer some good solo singing. The recording is good rather than outstanding: the large forces involved rather strain the acoustic space.

La damnation de Faust, Op. 24.
*** Ph. 416 395-2 (2) [id.]. Veasey, Gedda, Bastin, Amb. S., Wandsworth School Boys' Ch., LSO Ch., LSO, C. Davis.
*** Decca Dig. 414 680-2 (2) [id.]. Riegel, Von Stade, Van Dam, King, Chicago Ch. & SO, Solti.
**(*) Ph. Dig. 416 199-2 (2) [id.]. Myers, Lafont, Von Otter, Schirrer, Edinburgh Fest. Ch., Lyon Opera O, Gardiner.
(M) **(*) DG 423 907-2 (2) [id.]. Mathis, Burrows, McIntyre, Paul, Tanglewood Fest. Ch., Boston Boys' Ch. & Boston SO, Ozawa.

La damnation de Faust: highlights.
**(*) Decca Dig. 410 181-2 [id.] (from above recording; cond. Solti).

Both Gedda as Faust and Bastin as Mephistopheles are impressive in the 1974 Philips set. The response of the chorus and orchestra is never less than intelligent and, in the quieter passages, highly sensitive and the recording perspective is outstandingly natural and realistic. The subtlety and fantasy of Davis's reading are finely matched. The only snag is the tape-hiss, but that is easily ignored.

Solti's performance, searingly dramatic, is given stunning digital sound to make the *Ride to Hell* supremely exciting. But with Von Stade singing tenderly, this is a warmly expressive performance too; and the *Hungarian march* has rarely had such sparkle and swagger. The extra brightness matches the extrovert quality of the performance, less subtle than Davis's.

Gardiner's version was recorded live by Radio France at the Berlioz Festival in Lyon in September 1987; though this means that sound-balances are not always ideal, there is a natural sense of presence to bring out the vitality and dramatic thrust of the performance. Gardiner persuasively draws on the spark of humour in this work, lifting rhythms, finding the sparkle in Berlioz's inspiration more readily than his current rivals. His solo team is a strong one: Michael Myers as Faust gives a warm, relaxed performance, producing beautiful tenor tone, a believable, vulnerable hero; Anne Sofie von Otter makes an appealingly tender Marguerite, but Jean-Philippe Lafont is a lightweight – if lively – Mephistopheles, not firm or dark enough. The singing of the Edinburgh Festival Chorus adds to the bite of the drama, even though they are balanced a little too distantly.

Ozawa's performance provides an admirable mid-priced alternative, in a much more moulded style. The relative softness of focus is underlined by the reverberant Boston acoustics; with superb playing and generally fine singing, however, the results are seductively enjoyable. The digital remastering has improved definition without losing the effect of the hall ambience.

La damnation de Faust: Dance of the Sylphs.
(M) *** Decca 417 779-2 [id.]. LSO, Stokowski – DEBUSSY: *La Mer* etc.; RAVEL: *Daphnis et Chloé.****

This was recorded as a *bonne-bouche* at the end of the *La Mer* sessions (part of the coupling). The performance is very slow and affectionate – more Stokowski than Berlioz, perhaps, but delicious of its kind, with exquisite playing from the LSO violins. The sound is very good indeed.

L'enfance du Christ, Op. 25.
**(*) Ph. 416 949-2 (2) [id.]. Baker, Tappy, Langridge, Allen, Herincx, Rouleau, Bastin, Alldis Ch., LSO, C. Davis.

(i; ii) *L'enfance du Christ*; (ii; iii) *Méditation religieuse; La mort d'Ophélie; Sara la baigneuse*; (iii; iv) *La mort de Cléopâtre.*
(M) *** Decca 425 445-2 (2) [id.]. (i) Pears, Morison, Cameron, Rouleau, Frost, Fleet, Goldsbrough O; (ii) St Anthony Singers, (iii) ECO; (iv) Anne Pashley; Sir Colin Davis.

Davis's 1961 recording of *L'enfance du Christ* (originally made for L'Oiseau-Lyre) is by no means inferior to his later, Philips set. At times the earlier performance was fresher and more urgent, and Peter Pears was a sweeter-toned, more characterful narrator. Elsie Morison and John Cameron are perfectly cast as Mary and Joseph, and Joseph Rouleau makes an impressive contribution as the Ishmaelite Father. Not all the French pronunciation is immaculate, but Davis and his singers revel in the sheer originality of the melody. Such moments as the famous *Shepherds' chorus* and the angelic hosannas which end Part 2 are ravishingly beautiful, particularly when the recording has transferred so freshly and atmospherically to its new format. Moreover this Decca reissue offers (within a pair of mid-priced CDs) the entire contents of a third LP, issued in 1968 and also sounding freshly minted. This is an invaluable collection of off-beat vocal works, with fine choral singing and a splendid contribution from Anne Pashley. In a wonderfully intense account of the early scena, *La mort de Cléopâtre*, she even manages to rival Dame Janet Baker's version; in this most substantial of pieces Miss Pashley is if anything the more dramatic: the closing section, where Cleopatra in her death throes can merely mutter disconnected phrases, is most affectingly done. The other three pieces are for chorus: the gentle *Méditation religieuse* is a setting of Thomas Moore in translation; *La mort d'Ophélie*, for women's chorus, brings overtones of the choruses in *Roméo et Juliette*; and *Sara la baigneuse* is a strong, flowing setting of a Victor Hugo poem.
In Sir Colin Davis's second recording for Philips the beautifully balanced recording intensifies the colour and atmosphere of the writing, so that for example the *Nocturnal march* in the first part is wonderfully mysterious. There is a fine complement of soloists, and though Eric Tappy's tone as narrator is not always sweet, his sense of style is immaculate. Others are not always quite so idiomatic, but Dame Janet Baker and Thomas Allen, as ever, both sing beautifully. However, at full price and with no filler, this is now distinctly uncompetitive, compared with the reissued Decca set.

(i) *Herminie; La mort de Cléopâtre;* (ii) *La belle voyageuse;* (iii) *La captive;* (iv) *Le chasseur danois;* (v) *Le jeune pâtre breton;* (ii) *Zaïde.*
*** Ph. 416 960-2 [id.]. (i) Dame Janet Baker; (ii) Sheila Armstrong; (iii) Josephine Veasey; (iv) John Shirley-Quirk; (v) Frank Patterson; LSO, C. Davis.

These two dramatic scenes, *Herminie* and *La mort de Cléopâtre*, make an apt coupling, early works which yet give many hints of the mature Berlioz. Dame Janet Baker sings with passionate intensity while Sir Colin Davis draws committed playing from the LSO. Sheila Armstrong is very successful in her two songs provided as the fill-up; Josephine Veasey's contribution is also an individual one; but Frank Patterson, the weakest of the soloists, lacks the necessary charm. Nevertheless this compilation is a major addition to the Berlioz CD discography.

(i) *Lélio, Op. 14b* (without narration); (ii) *Les nuits d'été. Op. 7.*
**(*) Ph. 416 961-2 [id.]. (i) Carreras, Allen, Alldis Ch.; (ii) Armstrong, Veasey, Patterson, Shirley-Quirk; LSO, C. Davis.

By not using the spoken dialogue, Sir Colin Davis is able to include on his record not only the music of *Lélio* but also his interesting version of Berlioz's deeply expressive song-cycle, with different voices singing different songs. (The tessitura here ranges so wide that it is hard for any one singer to encompass them all.) Yet the success of this apparently logical venture is limited. Davis's insight is not in doubt, but the unity of the work is undermined and the contribution of the four singers involved is uneven. Sheila Armstrong is at her finest in her two songs (including the final exhilarating *L'île inconnue*), but Frank Patterson's opening *Villanelle* is less appealing. *Lélio* is altogether more convincing within its structural limitations.

(i) *La Mort de Cléopâtre;* (ii) *Les Nuits d'été, Op. 7* (see also below).
*** DG Dig. 410 966-2 [id.]. (i) Jessye Norman; (ii) Kiri Te Kanawa, O de Paris, Barenboim.

The coupling of Jessye Norman in the scena and Dame Kiri Te Kanawa in the song-cycle makes for one of the most ravishing of Berlioz records, with each singer at her very finest. Norman has natural nobility and command as the Egyptian queen in this dramatic scena, while Te Kanawa encompasses the challenge of different moods and register in *Les Nuits d'été* more completely and affectingly than any singer on record in recent years.

Les Nuits d'été (song-cycle), *Op. 7* (see also above).
*** Decca 417 813-2 [id.]. Régine Crespin, SRO, Ansermet (with *Recital of French songs****).
** Ph. 412 493-2 [id.]. Jessye Norman, LSO, Sir Colin Davis – RAVEL: *Shéhérazade.***

Crespin's richness of tone and a style which has an operatic basis do not prevent her from bringing out the subtlety of detail. *Le spectre de la rose* (a wonderful song) has a breadth of line and colouring and an immediate sense of drama that conjure up the opera house at once and, with Ansermet accompanying brilliantly, this glowing performance is a *tour de force*. The remastered sound (from the 1960s) retains the atmosphere of the original most successfully, while adding presence.

Jessye Norman is in fine voice here but does not get fully inside this most magical of orchestral song-cycles. There is no lack of voluptuousness, but the word-meanings are less subtly registered than in the finest rival versions.

(i)*Les Nuits d'été* (song-cycle), *Op. 7;* (ii) *La mort de Cléopâtre* (lyric scene); (ii; iii) *Les Troyens, Act V Scenes ii & iii.*
⊛ (M) *** EMI CDM7 69544-2. Dame Janet Baker, (i) New Philh. O, Barbirolli; (ii) LSO, Gibson; (iii) with Greevy, Erwen, Howell & Amb. Op. Ch.

The collaboration of Dame Janet Baker at the peak of her powers and Sir John Barbirolli in what is probably the most beautiful of all orchestral song-cycles produces ravishing results. The half-tones in the middle songs are exquisitely controlled, and the elation of the final song, *L'île inconnue*, with its vision of an idyllic island, has never been captured more rapturously on record. Berlioz's early scena on the death of a famous classical heroine is also beautifully performed. But even more desirable is Dame Janet's deeply moving rendering of the concluding scenes of Berlioz's epic opera. This makes an essential supplement to the complete recording for any dedicated Berliozian. Baker, helped by a warm and sympathetic accompaniment under Gibson's direction, allows herself a range of tone-colour and a depth of expressiveness not matched by Josephine Veasey, the Dido in the Philips set. Fine remastered sound.

Requiem mass (Grande messe des morts), Op. 5.
** Telarc Dig. CD 80109 (2) [id.]. Aler, Atlanta Ch. & SO, Robert Shaw – BOITO: *Mefistofele: Prologue*; VERDI: *Te Deum.***

(i) *Requiem Mass, Op. 5;* Overtures: *Benvenuto Cellini; Le carnaval romain; La Damnation de Faust: Hungarian march; Dance of the sylphs; Minuet of the Will-o'-the-wisps. Les Troyens: Royal hunt & storm; Trojan march.*
(M) ** EMI CMS7 69932-2 (2) (i) Tear, CBSO Ch.; CBSO, Frémaux.

(i) *Requiem mass; Symphonie fantastique.*
*(**) RCA RD 86210 (2) [RCA 6210-2-RC]. (i) Simoneau, New England Conservatory Ch., Brass bands; Boston SO, Munch.

(i) *Requiem mass;* (ii) *Symphonie funèbre et triomphale, Op. 15.*
**(*) Ph. 416 283-2 (2) [id.]. (i) Dowd, Wandsworth School Boys' Ch., LSO Ch.; (ii) John Alldis Ch.; LSO, Sir Colin Davis.

For Sir Colin Davis's recording of the *Requiem* Philips went to Westminster Cathedral, which should have been atmospheric enough; but then the engineers managed to negate the massiveness of the forces in anything but the loudest fortissimos, thanks to the closeness of the microphones: in many passages one can hear individual voices in the choir. However, the large-scale brass sound is formidably caught and the choral fortissimos are glorious, helped by the fresh cutting edge of the Wandsworth School Boys' Choir. It was Davis's idea, not Berlioz's, to have boys included, but it is entirely in character. The LSO provides finely incisive accompaniment, and there is no doubt that the CD remastering has added to the overall impact and tangibility. The *Symphonie funèbre et triomphale* is a fascinating product of Berlioz's eccentric genius, designed as it was to be performed not just in the open air but on the march. The *Funeral march* itself provides the most haunting music, but it needs more persuasive handling than Sir Colin's if it is not to outstay its welcome.

Munch's Boston version was recorded as early as 1959 and is an astonishing technical achievement for its time. The four brass groups make a bold effect within the resonant Boston acoustics and the big climaxes of the *Dies irae* and the *Tuba mirum*, though not perfectly focused, are still thrilling. Munch's overall direction has a fine lyrical flow; he brings powerful expressive feeling to the *Lacrymosa*, where the chorus is at its finest. The *Sanctus* – where Leopold Simoneau, with headily beautiful tone, does full justice to the tenor solo – is particularly moving. All in all, this is a most distinguished set; it is a great pity that it is offered in harness with an unsatisfactory version of the *Symphonie fantastique*. There are erratic speed-changes in the first movement, yet a low level of tension and seldom a convincing sense of spontaneity.

Robert Shaw directs a fresh and straightforward reading of Berlioz's monumental score, with attractively clean and well-disciplined choral singing. The Telarc recording has a better sense of presence on instruments than on voices, with the massive forces contained in a pleasant but not at all ample acoustic. Male voices in the choir lack bite in exposed passages. More seriously, what the performance misses is grandeur and a sense of occasion. John Aler makes an excellent tenor soloist in the *Sanctus*, but the following *Hosanna* is pedestrian.

It is a pity that for Frémaux's performance the EMI engineers fell into the same trap as the Philips technical personnel in the Davis set: the choir and orchestra are recorded relatively close, to make the result seem too small-scale for such a work. Detail is vivid, but the absence of a true pianissimo is just as serious as the failure to expand in the big climaxes, making a potentially fine performance far less effective than it might be. The chorus work, too, is surprisingly variable. The *Overtures* and orchestral excerpts are disappointing: they do not catch fire as one might expect from a Gallic conductor who is well experienced in the recording studio.

Roméo et Juliette, Op. 17.
**(*) Ph. 416 962-2 (2) [id.]. Kern, Tear, Shirley-Quirk, Alldis Ch., LSO Ch. & O, C. Davis.

(i) *Roméo et Juliette, Op. 17. Symphonie funèbre et triomphale, Op. 15.*
*** Decca 417 302-2 (2) [id.]. (i) Quivar, Cupido, Krause, Tudor Singers, Montreal Ch. & SO, Dutoit.

Roméo et Juliette, Op. 17; Les nuits d'été.
**(*) DG Dig. 427 665-2 (2) [id.]. Von Otter, Langridge, Morris, Berlin RIAS Chamber Ch., Ernest Senff Ch., BPO, Levine.

Dutoit's is a masterly, heart-warming reading of Berlioz's curious mixture of symphony, cantata and opera, superbly recorded in richly atmospheric sound, with a triumphantly successful account of the *Symphonie funèbre et triomphale* as a generous coupling. Dutoit consistently brings out the romantic lyrical warmth of the work, not least in the great orchestral love-scene. When that is coupled with brilliant choral singing, incisive and atmospheric, it is an unassailable mixture. Though the mezzo, Florence Quivar, is less steady than she should be, the other soloists are first rate, Alberto Cupido witty in his scherzetto, Tom Krause aptly firm and resonant. In the *Symphonie funèbre*, Dutoit is at his most uninhibited, brilliantly skirting the very edge of vulgarity in this outgoing ceremonial piece.

Sir Colin Davis – it hardly needs saying – has a rare sympathy with this score and secures playing of great vitality and atmosphere from the LSO. His soloists are excellent too, and so is the chorus. The 1968 recording still sounds excellent; it is natural in tone and balance, and the CDs bring added presence. But with no coupling and at full price, this is not very competitive, especially compared with Dutoit.

Levine gives a powerful performance of Berlioz's great dramatic symphony, marked by playing of exceptional polish and precision from the Berlin Philharmonic, and with Anne Sofie von Otter outstanding alongside two other very positive soloists. Von Otter adds to the attractions of the set in the generous fill-up, *Les nuits d'été*, again fresh and radiant, underlining the dramatic contrasts between the songs. Levine is nevertheless rather heavy-handed in his treatment of Berlioz. Compare him in the music for the Capulets' party with such an outstanding rival as Dutoit on Decca and, for all the precision and power, he has less feeling of jollity. There is also less sparkle in the *Queen Mab Scherzo*, for all the high brilliance of the playing, while the night music of the love scene emerges in the full brightness of day. Yet the very weight of Levine's reading, his electricity, still puts this version high on the list. The recording, made in the Jesus Christus Kirche in Berlin, is very full and weighty to match, while catching pianissimo strings most delicately, even if it falls short of the Decca in transparency.

Te Deum, Op. 22.
*** DG Dig. 410 696-2 [id.]. Araiza, LSO Ch., LPO Ch., Woburn Singers, Boys' Ch., European Community Youth O, Abbado.
**(*) Ph. 416 660-2 [id.]. Tagliavini, Wandsworth School Boys' Ch. LSO Ch. & O, N. Kynaston (organ), C. Davis.

The newest DG recording from Abbado is very impressive. The sound is wide-ranging, with striking dynamic contrasts and a much greater sense of presence than its predecessors. Artistically, too, it is of considerable merit: Abbado brings great tonal refinement and dignity to this performance, and the spacious sound helps. Francisco Araiza is altogether first class. The choirs are responsive, as are the young players Abbado has assembled.

Davis's 1969 Philips recording has been successfully remastered. He conveys massiveness without pomposity, drama without unwanted excesses of emotion, and his massed forces with the LSO respond superbly. The expansive choral climaxes and Nicolas Kynaston's fine organ contribution are impressively contained; but this reissue should have been offered at mid-price.

OPERA

Béatrice et Bénédict (complete).
*** Ph. 416 952-2 (2) [id.]. Baker, Tear, Eda-Pierre, Allen, Lloyd, Van Allan, Watts, Alldis Ch., LSO, C. Davis.

Béatrice et Bénédict here reveals itself as less an opera than a dramatic symphony, one of the important Berlioz works which refuse to fit in a conventional category. The score presents not just witty and brilliant music for the heroine and hero (Dame Janet Baker and Robert Tear at their most pointed) but sensuously beautiful passages such as the duet for Hero and Ursula at the end of Act I and the trio they later share with Beatrice, both incidental to the drama but very important for the musical structure. First-rate solo and choral singing, brilliant playing and sound refined and clear in texture, bright and fresh, even if minimal hiss betrays an analogue source.

Les Troyens, Parts 1 & 2 (complete).
⊛ *** Ph. 416 432-2 (4) [id.]. Veasey, Vickers, Lindholm, Glossop, Soyer, Partridge, Wandsworth School Boys' Ch., ROHCG Ch. & O, C. Davis.

Throughout this long and apparently disjointed score Davis compels the listener to concentrate, to appreciate its epic logic. His tempi are generally faster than in the theatre, and the result is exhilarating but with no hint of rush. Only in the great love scene of *O nuit d'ivresse* would one have welcomed the more expansive hand of a Beecham. It is interesting too to find Davis pursuing his direct, dramatic line even in Dido's death scene at the end. Veasey on any count, even next to Dame Janet Baker, makes a splendid Dido, single-minded rather than seductive, singing always with fine heroic strength. Of the rest, Berit Lindholm as Cassandra, in the first half of the opera, is the only soloist who falls short – the voice is not quite steady – otherwise one cannot imagine a more effective cast, with Vickers a ringing Aeneas. The Covent Garden Chorus and Orchestra excel themselves in virtuoso singing and playing, while CD brings out the superb quality of sound all the more vividly, and the Acts are arranged on the four discs with no break within any Act.

Les Troyens à Carthage: ballet music.
** Decca Dig. 411 898-2 [id.]. Nat. PO, Bonynge – LECOCQ: *Mam'zelle Angot*; WEBER: *Invitation to the dance.****

Berlioz's ballet music sounds insubstantial, heard away from its source. Although it has characteristic fingerprints, it does not show its composer at his finest. It is very well played here and the brightly lit recording is vivid.

Bernstein, Leonard (born 1918)

Candide: overture.
*** DG Dig. 413 324-2 [id.]. LAPO, Bernstein – BARBER: *Adagio*; COPLAND:
Appalachian spring; SCHUMAN: *American festival overture.****

Bernstein's *Candide overture* is one of the most dazzlingly brilliant of the century, and
the composer directs it in this live recording with tremendous flair, his speed a fraction
slower than in his New York studio recording for CBS.

(i) *Candide: overture;* (ii) *Divertimento; On the Town: 3 Dance episodes. On the Waterfront
(Symphonic suite);* (i) *West Side story: Symphonic dances.*
**(*) DG Dig. 423 198-2 [id.]. (i) LAPO, (ii) Israel PO, composer.

This collection is entitled 'The best of Bernstein' which may not be strictly true, but
certainly some of the best of him is here, from the vivacious overture to the marvellous
tunes encapsulated in the *Symphonic dances* from *West Side story.*

(i) *Candide: overture;* (ii) *On the Town: 3 Dance episodes;* (i) *West Side story: Symphonic
dances;* (iii) *America.*
(M) *** DG Dig. 417 806-2 [id.]. (i) LAPO; (ii) Israel PO; (iii) Troyanos with O; composer
– BARBER: *Adagio****; GERSHWIN: *Rhapsody in blue.***(*)

A mid-priced collection, duplicating others, to show the popular side of Bernstein's
genius at its most electrifying.

Fancy Free (ballet); (i) *Serenade after Plato's Symposium* (for solo violin, string orchestra,
harp and percussion).
*** DG 423 583-2 [id.]. Israel PO, composer, (i) with Kremer.

The *Serenade* must rank among Bernstein's most resourceful and inspired creations,
full of ideas, often thrilling and exciting, and equally often moving. Gidon Kremer has all
the nervous intensity and vibrant energy to do justice to this powerful and inventive
score. The ballet, *Fancy Free*, is an attractive example of Bernstein's freely eclectic style,
raiding Stravinsky, Copland or Gershwin and putting the result together effectively,
thanks to his exuberant sense of colour and rhythm. The Israel Philharmonic Orchestra
plays with tremendous spirit and also enjoys the benefit of outstanding recording quality.

Divertimento for orchestra; (i) *Halil (Nocturne);* (ii) *3 Meditations from Mass; On the Town
(3 Dance episodes).*
**(*) DG 415 966-2 [id.]. (i) Rampal; (ii) Rostropovich; Israel PO, composer.

Early Bernstein is well represented in the colourful and vigorous dances from *On the
Town* while the other three works show the later Bernstein sharply sparked off by specific
commissions. The *Divertimento*, easily and cheekily moving from one idiom to another,
is often jokey, but amiably so. The two concertante pieces, *Halil* for flute and strings and
the *Meditations* for cello and orchestra, both beautifully reflect the individual poetry of
the two artists for whom they were written and who perform masterfully here. The
aggressive digital sound of the original recording bites even more on CD, with a brilliant
top and spectacular bass leaving the middle light. With Bernstein, such sound does little
harm.

Prelude, fugue and riffs.
(***) CBS MK 42227. Goodman, Columbia Jazz Combo, composer – COPLAND:

Clarinet concerto; STRAVINSKY: *Ebony concerto;* BARTÓK: *Contrasts;* GOULD: *Derivations.*(***)
*** RCA Dig. RD 87762 [7762-2-RC]. Stolzman, LSO, Leighton Smith – COPLAND; CORIGLIANO: *Concertos.****

Bernstein's exuberant, sometimes wild, yet structured *Prelude, fugue and riffs* fits well within this CBS collection of jazz-inspired pieces in a vintage performance, directed by the composer. It sounds exceptionally vivid on CD.

Like Benny Goodman before him, Richard Stolzman couples Bernstein's *Prelude, fugue and riffs* with Copland's masterly concerto and makes the most of its unbuttoned jazziness. He is better recorded than Goodman, and his record can be recommended strongly on all counts.

Symphonies Nos. 1 (Jeremiah); (i) 2 (The age of anxiety) for piano and orchestra.
*** DG 415 964-2 [id.]. Israel PO, composer; (i) with Lukas Foss.

The *Jeremiah symphony* dates from Bernstein's early twenties and ends with a moving passage from Lamentations for the mezzo soloist. As its title suggests, the *Second Symphony* was inspired by the poem of W. H. Auden. These performances with the Israel Philharmonic are not always quite as polished or as forceful as those Bernstein recorded earlier in New York, but with excellent recording they never fail to reflect the warmth of Bernstein's writing. In No. 2 the concertante piano part is admirably played by Lukas Foss.

(i) Symphony No. 3 (Kaddish), rev. 1977; (ii) *Dybbuk* (ballet): *Suite No. 2.*
*** DG 423 582-2 [id.]. (i) Caballé, Wagner, V. Jeunesse Ch., Berlin Boys' Ch., Israel PO; (ii) NYPO; composer.

The impressive *Third Symphony,* written in memory of President Kennedy, is recorded here in its revised version (with a male speaker), which concentrates the original concept of a dialogue between man and God, a challenge from earth to heaven. With excellent sound, the performance with the Israel Philharmonic is extremely vivid. The shorter, more contemplative *Second Suite* from his powerful ballet score, *Dybbuk* (on the sinister subject of a lost spirit), makes a splendid foil for the symphony – a strong and colourful performance, cleanly recorded.

Arias and Barcarolles. On the Town: Some other time; Lonely town; Carried away; I can cook. Peter Pan: Dream with me. Songfest: Storyette, H. M.; To what you said. Wonderful Town: A little bit in love.
*** Koch International Classics Dig. 37000-2 [id.]. Judy Kaye, William Sharp; Michael Barrett, Steven Blier.

Arias and Barcarolles for two soloists and piano duet is a family charade of a work that, thanks to Bernstein's genius in simultaneously writing with complex ingenuity and immediate attractiveness, skirts all the potential embarrassments of baby talk, nursery stories and numbers telling of Jewish weddings and insubordinate children. Completed in 1988, it draws on some earlier material, as in a touching celebration of fatherhood, *Greeting,* and in the final, wordless number, *Nachspiel,* with the two soloists humming a slow nostalgic waltz. It is a charming piece, here given – with the composer himself approving the performance – in the original version with piano and excellent, characterful soloists. The bizarre title relates to a comment made by President Eisenhower, after he had heard Bernstein play a Mozart concerto: 'I like music with a theme, not all them arias and barcarolles.' It became a Bernstein family joke. That half-hour work, very well recorded, is coupled with an equivalent collection of eight of Bernstein's most haunting songs and duets, including three from *On the Town* of 1944 and two from *Songfest* of 1977.

Chichester Psalms.
*** ASV Dig. CDRPO 8004 [id.]. Aled Jones, LSO Ch. RPO, Hickox – FAURÉ: *Requiem.****
(M) *** CBS MK 44710 [id.]. John Bogart, Camerata Singers, NYPO, composer – POULENC: *Gloria****; STRAVINSKY: *Symphony of Psalms.**** ⊛

Chichester Psalms (reduced score).
*** Hyp. Dig. CDA 66219 [id.]. Martelli, Corydon Singers, Masters, Kettel, Trotter; Best – BARBER: *Agnus Dei*; COPLAND: *In the beginning* etc.***

(i) *Chichester Psalms; Missa brevis.*
** Telarc Dig. CD 80181 [id.].(i) Ragin; Atlanta Ch. & SO, Shaw – WALTON: *Belshazzar's feast.***

Bernstein's *Chichester Psalms* make an instant communication and respond to familiarity too, especially in Richard Hickox's fresh and colourful reading, with Aled Jones bringing an ethereal contribution to the setting of the 23rd Psalm. As a bonus for a fresh and sympathetic account of the Fauré *Requiem*, this can be recommended strongly. The recorded sound is firm and well focused.

Martin Best uses the composer's alternative reduced orchestration, which omits the three trumpets and three trombones specified in the original commission and settles for a single harp (instead of a pair), organ and percussion, spectacularly played here by Gary Kettel. The treble soloist, Dominic Martelli, cannot match Aled Jones, but his chaste contribution is persuasive and the choir scales down its pianissimos to accommodate him, with elegiac effect. Indeed the singing of the Corydon Singers is first rate, rising well to the catchy 7/4 rhythms in Psalm 100. Excellent sound, with the acoustic of St Jude-on-the-Hill, Hampstead, creating the right atmosphere.

Bernstein's own version of the *Chichester Psalms* is exceptionally vivid, and the recording is given striking presence by the CD remastering. Coupled with outstanding performances of Poulenc and Stravinsky, this is a most valuable reissue.

As in the Walton coupling, Shaw secures singing of phenomenal precision in the *Chichester Psalms*, but the jazz rhythms do not swing as they do under the composer's direction. As well as using a mixed chorus, Shaw opts to have a male alto soloist, the outstanding counter-tenor, Derek Lee Ragin. The little *Missa brevis* is a delight, a charming setting adapted by Bernstein – on the suggestion of Shaw – from incidental music he wrote many years earlier for the Anouilh play about St Joan, *The Lark*. Full, well-balanced recording.

Mass (for the death of President Kennedy): complete.
(M) *** CBS M2K 44593 (2) [M2K 31008]. Titus (celebrant), Scribner Ch., Berkshire Boys' Ch., Rock band and O, composer

Outrageously eclectic in its borrowings from pop and the avant-garde, Bernstein's *Mass* presents an extraordinary example of the composer's irresistible creative energy. With a scenario that boldly defies all sense of good taste, the celebrant smashing the holy vessel before the altar, its impact is even more remarkable in the CD format, which loses nothing in atmosphere but increases the sense of spectacle. The recording was made partly at the J. F. Kennedy Center, Washington, DC, supplemented by New York studio sessions in 1971. It now assumes an historical as well as a musical significance, for

Bernstein's all-embracing emotional theatricality sums up a decade in recent American history when all conventional beliefs were put in question by a new generation. Bernstein characteristically encapsulated both the doubt and the optimistic self-confidence in the future which is so much a part of the American experience.

(i) *Songfest* (cycle of American poems); (ii) *Chichester Psalms.*
*** DG 415 965-2 [id.]. (i) Dale, Elias, Williams, Rosenshein, Reardon, Gramm, Nat. SO of Washington; (ii) Soloist from V. Boys' Ch., V. Jeunesse Ch., Israel PO; composer.

Songfest, one of Bernstein's most richly varied works, is a sequence of poems which ingeniously uses all six singers solo and in various combinations. Characteristically, Bernstein often chooses controversial words to set, and by his personal fervour welds a very disparate group of pieces together into a warmly satisfying whole. The *Chichester Psalms* were recorded live in 1977. One might have slight reservations over the treble soloist from the Vienna Boys' Choir, but otherwise the performance is first class, with the music's warmth and vigour compellingly projected.

Songs: *La bonne cuisine* (French and English versions); *I hate music* (cycle); *2 Love songs; Piccola serenata; Silhouette; So pretty; Mass: A simple song; I go on. Candide: It must be so; Candide's lament. 1600 Pennsylvania Ave: Take care of this house. Peter Pan: My house; Peter Pan; Who am I; Never-Never Land.*
*** Etcetera Dig. KTC 1037 [id.]. Roberta Alexander, Tan Crone.

A delightful collection, consistently bearing witness to Bernstein's flair for a snappy idea as well as his tunefulness. There is a charming artlessness about the four songs he wrote for a 1950 production of *Peter Pan* with Jean Arthur and Boris Karloff; even earlier is the cycle of five *Kid songs*, *I hate music*; while it is good to have the haunting number from the unsuccessful bicentennial musical, *1600 Pennsylvania Avenue.* Roberta Alexander's rich, warm voice and winning personality are well supported by Tan Crone at the piano. The recording is lifelike and undistracting.

Stage works

Candide (revised 1982 version).
*** New World Dig. NWCD 340/1 [id.]. John Lankston, David Eisler, Erie Mills, Scott Reeve, Joyce Castle, NY City Op. Ch. & O, Mauceri.

For the New World recording of *Candide* John Mauceri edited together a text incorporating as much as possible of the material that had been written for the piece at its various revivals from the first production in 1956 onwards. The result on record makes a splendid, fizzing entertainment, necessarily episodic but held together by the electricity of Mauceri's direction and the singing of a cast that nicely bridges the demands of opera and musical. Some of the numbers quoted in the brilliant overture, like *The best of all possible worlds* and *Oh, happy we*, are a particular delight. The recording is aptly bright and clear, with voices placed in firm focus well in front of the orchestra.

Candide (musical): *Overture and excerpts.*
(M) *** CBS MK 38732 [id.]. Adrian, Cook, Rounseville and original New York cast, Krachmalnick.

This exhilarating CBS record encapsulates the original 1956 Broadway production and has all the freshness of discovery inherent in a first recording, plus all the zing of the American musical theatre. Its highlight, the Rossini-style *Glitter and be gay*, is given a scintillating coloratura performance here by Barbara Cook. Max Adrian is hardly less memorable, and the Gilbert and Sullivan influences will surely endear the score to British listeners. The lyrics, by Richard Wilbur, give pleasure in themselves. Brilliantly lively sound.

Candide (opera/musical): highlights.
** That's Entertainment Dig. CDTER 1156 [id.]. Grace, Beudert, Hill-Smith, Bottone, Howard, Tinkler, Scottish Op. Ch. & O, Justin Brown.

Based on the imaginative Scottish Opera production, the TER disc of highlights from *Candide* was recorded well before the stage performances. Almost inevitably that made for less electric results, though it is a strong and characterful cast. Rather disappointingly, the selection of items is relatively conventional, not drawing on the extra material revived in this production. The recording, set in a rather dry acoustic, is apt for most of the music, if a little constricting in the ensembles.

A Quiet place (complete).
*** DG Dig. 419 761-2 (2) [id.]. Wendy White, Chester Ludgin, Beverly Morgan, John Brandstetter, Peter Kazaras, Vocal Ens., Austrian RSO, composer.

In flashbacks in Act II of *A Quiet place*, Bernstein incorporates his 1951 score, *Trouble in Tahiti*, with its popular style set in relief against the more serious idiom adopted for the main body of the opera. The opening Act is sharply conceived, set in a funeral parlour. The wife from *Trouble in Tahiti* has just died in a car crash, and for the first time in years the family is reunited, along with an assortment of relatives and friends, all sharply characterized. Sadly, those characters never reappear; the central figures of the family quickly seem to have come not from a grand opera but from a soap opera. Bernstein's score is full of thoughtful and warmly expressive music, but nothing quite matches the sharp, tongue-in-cheek jazz-influenced invention of *Trouble in Tahiti*. The recording was made in Vienna, with an excellent cast of American singers, and with the Austrian Radio orchestra responding splendidly on its first visit to the Vienna State Opera. Considering the problems of live recording of opera, the sound is excellent, remarkably well balanced.

West Side story: complete recording; *On the Waterfront (Symphonic suite).*
⊛ *** DG Dig. 415 253-2 (2) [id.]. Te Kanawa, Carreras, Troyanos, Horne, Ollman, Ch. and O, composer.

Bernstein's recording of the complete score of his most popular work – the first time he had ever conducted the complete musical himself – takes a frankly operatic approach in its casting, but the result is highly successful, for the great vocal melodies are worthy of voices of the highest calibre. Dame Kiri Te Kanawa may not be a soprano who would ever be cast as Maria on stage, and José Carreras may be apparently miscast, but the beauty of such songs as *Maria* or *Tonight*, or even a sharp number like *Something's coming*, with floated pianissimos and subtly graded crescendos, has one admiring the score the more. Tatiana Troyanos, herself brought up on the West Side, spans the stylistic dichotomy to perfection in a superb portrayal of Anita, switching readily from full operatic beauty to a New York snarl and back, and Kurt Ollman as Riff equally finds a nice balance between the styles of opera and the musical. The clever production makes the best of both musical worlds, with Bernstein's son and daughter speaking the dialogue most affectingly. Bernstein conducts a superb instrumental group of musicians 'from on and off Broadway', and they are recorded with a bite and immediacy that is captivating, whether in the warm, sentimental songs or, above all, in the fizzing syncopated numbers, sounding even more original when precisely played and balanced as here. The power of the music is greatly enhanced by the spectacularly wide dynamic range of the recording, with a relatively dry acoustic keeping the sound-picture within an apt scale but without losing bloom. The two-disc set includes, besides the musical, the vivid *Symphonic suite*, which was arranged from Bernstein's film music for the Marlon Brando film, *On the Waterfront*, written about the same period.

West Side story: highlights.
(M) **(*) DG Dig. 431 027-2 [id.] (from above recording; cond. composer).

By cutting the dialogue, all the main numbers are included here, presented as vividly as on the complete set; but with only just over 53 minutes of music included this is not especially good value, even though the highlights disc is now offered at mid-price. The moving *Tonight* sequence, for example, loses much without the spoken interchanges between the lovers, and clearly there was room for this on the disc.

West Side story: Symphonic dances.
*** DG Dig. 410 025-2 [id.]. LAPO, composer – GERSHWIN: *Rhapsody in blue* etc.**
(*) DG 419 625-2 [id.]. San Francisco SO, Ozawa – GERSHWIN: *An American in Paris*; RUSSO: *Street music.*

Bernstein, recorded live, is at his most persuasive conducting a highly idiomatic account of the orchestral confection devised from his most successful musical, with the players contributing the necessary shouts in the *Mambo* representing a street fight. Vivid if close-up sound.

Ozawa's performance is highly seductive, with an approach which is both vivid and warm yet which conceals any sentimentality. The 1973 recording has responded well to its digital remastering, but this should have been reissued at mid-price.

Bertrand, Anthoine de (1540–81)

Amours de Ronsard, Book 1; *Amours de Cassandre:* excerpts.
** HM Dig. HMC 901147 [id.]. Clément Janequin Ens.

Anthoine de Bertrand's chansons as recorded here by the Clément Janequin Ensemble show him to be, if not a great master, at least a composer of feeling and considerable resource. (*Mon Dieu, mon Dieu que ma maistresse est belle*, for instance, is both touching and memorable.) They are interspersed with four short, rather anonymous pieces by the French lutenist and composer, Guillaume de Morlaye, active in the 1550s. The performances are excellent throughout, and admirably recorded.

Berwald, Franz (1797–1868)

Symphonies Nos. 1 in G min. (Sérieuse); 2 in D (Capricieuse); 3 in C (Singulière); 4 in E flat.
*** DG Dig. 415 502-2 [id.]. Gothenburg SO, Järvi.

Franz Berwald's first four symphonies receive a distinguished and auspicious CD début. The present set of recordings outclasses the previous Björlin versions on EMI and almost all previous rivals. First, the orchestral playing has abundant spirit and energy: this is music that is wholly in the life-stream of the Gothenburg orchestra; and secondly, the excellent acoustic of the Gothenburg Hall shows the scores to great advantage. Neeme Järvi sets generally brisk tempi, yet the pacing feels right. The sound is altogether superb, with every detail coming through with great clarity, and this can be strongly recommended.

Grand septet in B flat.
*** CRD CRD 3344 [id.]. Nash Ens. – HUMMEL: *Septet.****

Berwald's only *Septet* is a work of genuine quality and deserves a secure place in the repertory instead of on its periphery. It dates from 1828 and is for the same forces as the Beethoven and Kreutzer *Septets*; the invention is lively and the ideas have charm. It is eminently well played by the Nash Ensemble, and finely recorded.

Birtwistle, Harrison (born 1934)

Carmen Arcadiae mechanicae perpetuum; Secret theatre; Silbury air.
*** Etcetera Dig. KTC 1052 [id.]. L. Sinf., Elgar Howarth.

Silbury air, named after an archaeological site in south-west England, is one of Birtwistle's 'musical landscapes', bringing ever-changing views and perspectives on the musical material and an increasing drawing-out of melody. With melody discarded, *Carmen Arcadiae mechanicae perpetuum* (*The perpetual song of Mechanical Arcady*) superimposes different musical mechanisms to bring a rhythmic kaleidoscope of textures and patterns. The title of *Secret theatre* is taken from a poem by Robert Graves which refers to 'an unforeseen and fiery entertainment', and there is no doubting the distinctive originality of the writing, utterly typical of the composer. Howarth and the Sinfonietta could hardly be more convincing advocates, recorded in vivid, immediate sound.

Bizet, Georges (1838–75)

L'Arlésienne (complete incidental music; ed. Riffaud).
*** EMI Dig. CDC7 47460-2 [id.]. Orféon Donstiarra, Toulouse Capitole O, Plasson.

The two *L'Arlésienne* suites constitute just over half of the total music. Bizet himself made just one suite from the score; the second was by Ernest Guiraud and incorporates a minuet from *La jolie fille de Perth*. The score that Michel Plasson and his excellent French forces have recorded is based on the 1872 autograph, and the singing of the Orféon Donstiarra is as excellent as the orchestral playing. The less familiar music is every bit as captivating as the suites so that the performance has great charm, and the EMI recording is very good indeed. Strongly recommended.

L'Arlésienne (incidental music): *suites Nos. 1–2.*
*** EMI CDC7 47794-2 [id.]. RPO, Beecham – *Symphony.****
L'Arlésienne: suites Nos. 1–2; Carmen: suite No. 1.
(M) *** DG 423 472-2 [id.]. LSO, Abbado.
**(*) DG Dig. 415 106-2 [id.]. BPO, Karajan.

L'Arlésienne (incidental music): *suites Nos. 1 & 2; Carmen* (opera): *suites Nos. 1 & 2.*
*** Decca Dig. 417 839-2 [id.]. Montreal SO, Dutoit.
(BB) **(*) Naxos Dig. 8.550061 [id.]. Slovak PO, Anthony Bramhall.
(B) *(*) LaserLight Dig. 15 614 [id.]. Budapest SO, Janos Sandor.

L'Arlésienne: suites Nos. 1–2; Carmen: suite No. 1; suite No. 2: excerpts.
(B) **(*) Pickwick Dig. PCD 905 [MCA MCAD 6278]. LSO, Frühbeck de Burgos.

(i) *L'Arlésienne: suite No. 1; suite No. 2: Farandole. Carmen: suites 1 & 2;* (ii) *Fair maid of Perth suite.*
(B) ** Decca 421 632-2. (i) New Philh. O, Munch; (ii) SRO, Ansermet.

With playing that is both elegant and vivid, and with superb, demonstration-worthy sound, Dutoit's polished yet affectionate coupling of the *L'Arlésienne* and *Carmen* suites makes a clear first choice. The inclusion of 73 minutes of music means that a good deal of *Carmen* involves orchestral instruments standing in for voices, but the various wind and string soloists are always persuasive; the overall stylishness, particularly of the string phrasing, is a constant pleasure. All the colour of Bizet's palette is glowingly caught by the Decca engineers and the percussion component is never overdone.

Most recordings of Bizet's enchanting incidental music for *L'Arlésienne* are overshadowed by Beecham's magical set, dating from 1957 but still sounding remarkably well. Besides the beauty and unique character of the wind solos, Beecham's deliciously sprightly *Minuet* and his affectingly gentle sense of nostalgia in the *Adagietto* (both from the first suite) are as irresistibly persuasive as the swaggering brilliance of the closing *Farandole* of the second.

Karajan, too, secures marvellous playing from the Berlin Philharmonic Orchestra, but he is less naturally at home in this repertoire, and tempi are not always ideally apt. The modern digital recording has the widest possible range of dynamic, but the effect sometimes seems rather inflated in tuttis. The *Carmen* suite, taken from his complete opera recording of 1983, is vividly played throughout – Karajan is at his best here.

Those looking for a bargain can also turn to the CD of the 1981 Abbado performances. The orchestral playing is characteristically refined, the wind solos cultured and eloquent, especially in *L'Arlésienne*, where the pacing of the music is nicely judged. With vivid and truthful recording, this is very attractive.

Raphael Frühbeck de Burgos offers three more items than Abbado, and in an even cheaper price-range; he also has the advantage of full, modern digital recording, made in Watford Town Hall. The LSO playing is bright-eyed and polished but Frühbeck's tempi are not always as naturally apt as those of Abbado or Dutoit (who offers even more music), and the effect is rather less spontaneous than either. Nevertheless the Pickwick disc remains good value for those wanting an inexpensive modern recording of this colourful coupling.

Anthony Bramhall makes his Naxos début directing excellent performances with the Slovak Philharmonic Orchestra. The solo wind playing has an appealing delicacy of colour, the principal flute plays with finesse, and only the violin substituting for Michaela's aria is a little below the generally high standard. There is plenty of flair in the *Danse bohémienne* and the closing *Farandole* from *L'Arlésienne*; with vivid digital sound and a nicely atmospheric ambience, this inexpensive disc is most attractive.

Munch's disc was originally issued in 1967 as a Decca Phase 4 recording, and there is no doubt that the sound is both atmospheric and extraordinarily vivid. Generally the readings are stylish; if the last ounce of swagger is missing, the playing is still infectiously lively. Ansermet's *Fair maid of Perth* suite dates from 1960; it offers clean string-playing, and the overall effect has plenty of warmth and colour. A good bargain coupling, offering generous measure.

Sandor's selection is comprehensive, with over an hour of music; but the orchestral playing lacks the necessary zip and panache for these scores. The digital sound is good but not outstanding.

Jeux d'enfants (children's games), Op. 22.
(B) ** Pickwick Dig. PCD 932. LSO, Wordsworth – SAINT-SAENS: *Carnival***; RAVEL: *Ma Mère l'Oye.***(*)

Barry Wordsworth draws crisp and sympathetic playing from the LSO, although there could be greater individuality. The recording is vivid at higher dynamic levels but seems to recede somewhat at pianissimos, and it is difficult to find a volume setting which suits both the gentle *Berceuse* and the brightly coloured opening *Marche.*

Symphony in C.
*** DG Dig. 423 624-2 [id.]. Orpheus CO – BRITTEN: *Simple symphony*; PROKOFIEV: *Symphony No. 1.****
(M) *** Decca 417 734-2 [id.]. ASMF, Marriner – PROKOFIEV: *Symphony No. 1*; STRAVINSKY: *Pulcinella.****
*** EMI CDC7 47794-2 [id.]. French Nat. R. O, Beecham – *L'Arlésienne.****
(*) Virgin Dig. VC 790744-2 [id.]. SCO, Saraste – RAVEL: *Ma Mère l'Oye* etc.(*)

Symphony in C; Jeux d'enfants: suite.
*** Ph. 416 437-2 [id.]. Concg. O, Haitink – DEBUSSY: *Danses sacrée et profane.****

The freshness of the seventeen-year-old Bizet's *Symphony* is well caught by the Orpheus group who present it with all the flair and polished ensemble for which they are famous. They offer the first-movement exposition repeat and make an excellent case for including it, while in the *Adagio* the oboe solo is wistful and tender. After a characterful minuet, the sparkling *moto perpetuo* finale is joyfully exhilarating, helped by the bouncing rhythms and crisp articulation. First-rate sound, most realistic in effect.

Marriner's performance is played with all the polish and elegance characteristic of the vintage ASMF records of the early 1970s; the slow movement has a delectable oboe solo and the finale is irrepressibly gay and high-spirited. The recording, originally rather reverberant, is now drier, the bass less expansive, not entirely to advantage; but at mid-price and with highly desirable couplings, this remains excellent value.

Beecham's version from the beginning of the 1960s above all brings out its spring-like qualities. The playing of the French orchestra is not quite as polished as that of Marriner's group or the Concertgebouw, but Beecham's panache more than compensates and the slow movement is delightfully songful, even if there is a moment of suspect intonation at its opening and close. The remastered sound is bright on top, without glare.

The warmest, most pleasing sound comes from Haitink's sunny 1979 Concertgebouw performance. His reading obviously takes into account the Amsterdam acoustics for it is essentially spacious, although the finale does not lack vivacity. The serene slow movement is particularly eloquent, with a beautiful oboe solo. *Jeux d'enfants* is also delectably played; here, the recording is demonstration-worthy in its sparkling detail.

Saraste gives a rhythmically strong and bold, if somewhat unrelenting account of the first movement; the *Adagio* with a rich-timbred oboe solo blossoms romantically in the strings, and the scherzo has striking impetus to lead to a high-spirited finale. The effect of the recording is fuller than that provided by the Orpheus group on DG, and the Scottish performance is enjoyable in its own way.

Jeux d'enfants, Op. 22.
*** Ph. Dig. 420 159-2 [id.]. Katia and Marielle Labèque – FAURÉ: *Dolly*; RAVEL: *Ma Mère l'Oye.****

Even were other versions to appear, it would not be easy to surpass the Labèque sisters. They characterize Bizet's wonderfully inventive cycle of twelve pieces with vitality, great wit and delicacy of feeling and touch. Superb recording in the best Philips tradition.

OPERA

Carmen (complete).

*** DG Dig. 410 088-2 (3) [id.]. Baltsa, Carreras, Van Dam, Ricciarelli, Barbaux, Paris Op. Ch., Schoenberg Boys' Ch., BPO, Karajan.

(M) *** RCA GD 86199 (3) [6199-2-RG]. Leontyne Price, Corelli, Merrill, Freni, Linval, V. State Op. Ch., VPO, Karajan.

**(*) Decca 414 489-2 (2) [id.]. Troyanos, Domingo, Van Dam, Te Kanawa, John Alldis Ch., LPO, Solti.

**(*) DG 419 636-2 (3) [id.]. Berganza, Domingo, Cotrubas, Milnes, Amb. S., LSO, Abbado.

**(*) EMI CDC7 49240-2 (3) [Ang. CDCB 49240]. De los Angeles, Gedda, Blanc, Micheau, Fr. R. Ch. and O, Petits Chanteurs de Versailles, Beecham.

** EMI CDS7 47313-8 (3) [Ang. CDC 47312]. Callas, Gedda, Massard, René Duclos Ch., Children's Ch., Paris Nat. Op. O, Prêtre.

* Ph. Dig. 422 366-2 (3) [id.]. Jessye Norman, Schicoff, Estes, Freni, O. Nat. de France, Ozawa.

Karajan's newest DG set of *Carmen* makes a clear first choice among currently available versions, with the performance combining affection with high tension and high polish, using the Oeser edition with its extra passages and spoken dialogue. In Carreras he has a Don José, lyrical and generally sweet-toned, who is far from a conventional hero-figure, more the anti-hero, an ordinary man caught up in tragic love. The Micaela of Katia Ricciarelli is similarly scaled down, with the big dramatic voice kept in check. José van Dam – also the Escamillo for Solti – is incisive and virile, the public hero-figure; which leaves Agnes Baltsa as a vividly compelling Carmen, tough and vibrant yet musically precise and commanding, larger than life but still a believable figure, with tenderness under the surface. As for Karajan, he draws richly resonant playing from the Berlin Philharmonic, sparkling and swaggering in the bullfight music but delicate and poetic too. The digital recording is almost aggressively bright, but atmospheric too, if not always ideally balanced, with a tendency to bass-lightness. The spoken dialogue distractingly sounds like the soundtrack of a French film.

With Karajan's earlier RCA version, made in Vienna in 1964, much depends on the listener's reaction to the conductor's tempi and to Leontyne Price's smoky-toned Carmen. Corelli has moments of coarseness, but his is still a heroic performance. Robert Merrill sings with gloriously firm tone, while Mirella Freni is, as ever, enchanting as Micaela. With often spectacular recording, this set, now offered at mid-price, remains a keen competitor.

Solti's Decca performance is remarkable for its new illumination of characters whom everyone thinks they know inside out. Tatiana Troyanos is quite simply the subtlest Carmen on record. Escamillo too is more readily sympathetic, not just the flashy matador who steals the hero's girl, whereas Don José is revealed as weak rather than just a victim. Troyanos's singing is delicately seductive too, with no hint of vulgarity, while the others make up a most consistent singing. Solti, like Karajan, uses spoken dialogue and a modification of the Oeser edition, deciding in each individual instance whether to accept amendments to Bizet's first thoughts. Though the CD transfer brings out the generally excellent balances of the original analogue recording, it exaggerates the bass to make the orchestra sound boomy, although the voices retain their fine realism and bloom.

Through the four Acts of the Abbado set there are examples of idiosyncratic tempi, but the whole entertainment hangs together with keen compulsion, and the discipline is superb. Conductor and orchestra can take a large share of credit for the performance's success, for though the singing is never less than enjoyable, it is on the whole less characterful than on some rival sets. Teresa Berganza is a seductive Carmen – not without sensuality, and producing consistently beautiful tone, but lacking some of the flair which makes for a three-dimensional portrait. Ileana Cotrubas as Micaela is not always as sweetly steady as she can be; Sherrill Milnes makes a heroic matador. The spoken dialogue is excellently produced, and the sound is vivid and immediate.

Beecham's approach to Bizet's well-worn score is no less fresh and revealing. His speeds are not always conventional but they always *sound* right. It seems he specially chose De los Angeles to be his Carmen, although she had never sung the part on the stage before making the recording. He conceived the *femme fatale* as someone winning her admirers not so much by direct assault and high voltage as by genuine charm and real femininity. De los Angeles's characterization of Carmen is absolutely bewitching. Gedda is pleasantly light-voiced as ever, Janine Micheau is a sweet Micaela, and Ernest Blanc makes an attractive Escamillo. There seems to have been little attempt at stage production, but in the CD transfer the recording does not show its age too greatly.

Though in so many ways the vibrant, flashing-eyed personality of Maria Callas was ideally suited to the role of Carmen, her complete recording – unlike two separate aria recordings she made earlier – is disappointing. One principal trouble is that the performance, apart from her, is so slipshod. The moment the heroine enters, the tension rises, but by Callas standards this is a characterization rough-hewn and strong but lacking the full imaginative detail of her finest work.

It was a bold idea to cast Jessye Norman as Carmen, and it says much for her artistry that hers is the most compelling performance in a disappointing set. The sound she produces is glorious and the command of detail formidable, with the voice as rounded in speaking as in singing – but this is a monumental rather than a vivacious Carmen. She scales her voice down beautifully where necessary, but it is not unlike watching a great and beautiful ocean-liner threading its way through the Panama Canal. The set is well worth hearing for Jessye Norman alone; but, with slow speeds for the key solos and with a large-sounding chorus set too distantly, well behind any action, in a church-like acoustic, you might even describe this as 'Carmen the oratorio'. One's disappointment is sealed by the contributions of the other soloists, not to mention that of the conductor, Ozawa. Freni, many years ago a superb Micaela for Karajan, is here shrill and grainy, Shicoff makes a coarse Don José, belting out the *Flower song*, and Simon Estes is surprisingly rough both in his singing and in his speaking of the French dialogue (which at times is unintentionally comic). It is sad that such a set should have achieved such wide circulation thanks to hype from the publicity machine.

Carmen: highlights.
*** DG Dig. 413 322-2 [id.] (from above recording with Baltsa, Carreras; cond. Karajan).
(M) *** Decca 421 300-2 [id.] (from above recording with Troyanos, Domingo; cond. Solti).
(M) ** EMI CDM7 63075-2 (from above recording with Callas, Gedda; cond. Prêtre).
* Ph. Dig. 426 040-2 [id.] (from above recording with J. Norman; cond. Ozawa).

A good representative selection from Karajan's DG set, with recording to match, is first choice here, but the reissued compilation of 'scenes and arias' from Solti's sharply characterful set is generous, and the remastered recording sounds better than the complete set. The selection from the Callas set, which is very generous with a playing time of 71 minutes 35 seconds, is not designed so much to highlight the heroine as to provide as many 'pops' as possible from the opera. In isolation, Callas's shortcomings – dramatic as well as vocal – are just as clear as in the complete set, and Prêtre is hardly a sensitive or understanding Bizet conductor. This single disc of highlights from the Philips set was for many weeks at the top of the classical charts in Britain, but few issues have deserved such an accolade less.

Carmen (ballet): suite (arr. and scored for strings & percussion by Rodion Shchedrin).
**(*) Olympia Dig. OCD 108 [id.]. Moscow Virtuoso CO, Armenian State Ch. Ens. &
Percussion Ens., Spivakov – SHCHEDRIN: *Frescoes of Dionysius*.**

Rodion Shchedrin's free adaptation of Bizet's *Carmen* music uses Bizet's tunes,
complete with harmony, and reworks them into a new tapestry using only strings and
percussion (including vibraphone). The playing of the Moscow Virtuoso group justifies its
name; Vladimir Spivakov maintains the electricity throughout an exciting performance.
He is helped by the concert-hall acoustics of the brilliant digital recording; however, the
brightness of the upper strings does bring a degree of harshness in the vivid climax of the
Flower song.

La jolie fille de Perth (complete).
*** EMI Dig. CDS7 47559-8 (2). Anderson, Kraus, Quilico, Van Dam, Zimmermann,
Bacquier, Ch. and New PO of R. France, Prêtre.

Based on Scott's *Fair Maid of Perth*, the plot of Bizet's opera is as improbable as many
others of the Romantic period, yet it inspired Bizet to one delectable number after
another, not just the famous *Serenade* for the tenor hero, Henry Smith. Here, as in
Carmen, you have a principal gypsy role for mezzo soprano contrasted against a purer-
toned soprano heroine; but this time it is the soprano who is the deliberately provocative
one, leaving Henry Smith almost as wounded as Don José in *Carmen*. Unlike *Carmen*,
however, this piece ends happily, with the crazed heroine delivering a Lucia-like mad
song (coloratura delightfully done by June Anderson) before being shocked into sanity for
the final curtain. As the hero, Alfredo Kraus sings stylishly and Gino Quilico is superb as
the predatory Duke of Rothsay; José van Dam as the apprentice Ralph is aptly lugubrious
in his drunken song, and the veteran Gabriel Bacquier makes a delightfully bluff figure of
the heroine's father. Margarita Zimmermann (not always treated well by the microphone)
as Mab, queen of the gypsies, makes an equivocal role convincing. Georges Prêtre's
conducting is warm and understanding, even if ensemble is not always ideally crisp. Full,
warm recording to match.

(i) *Les pêcheurs de perles* (complete). (ii) *Ivan IV: highlights*.
** EMI Dig. CDS7 49837-2 (2) [Ang. CDCB 49837]. Hendricks, Aler, Quilico, Capitole,
Toulouse, Ch. & O, Plasson.
(M) ** EMI CMS7 69704-2 (2) [Ang. CDMB 69704]. (i) Micheau, Gedda, Blanc, Mars,
Paris Opéra-Comique O, Dervaux; (ii) Roux, Micheau, Legay, Sénéchal, Noguera, French
R. Ch. & O, Tzipine.

EMI's new version of *Pearlfishers*, well recorded, should have provided an ideal
recommendation for this lovely opera, but, for all its qualities, it falls well short of that.
Michel Plasson with the choir and orchestra of the Capitole, though sympathetic, fails to
draw out as warmly committed a performance as he usually does in his French opera
recordings. John Aler and Gino Quilico as the two fishermen sing cleanly and with lyrical
freshness, but often their phrasing could be more affectionate. Barbara Hendricks is aptly
alluring as Leila, beloved of both of them, but too often she attacks notes from below,
coming near to crooning her lovely Act II solo, *Comme autrefois*, as well as the following
love-duet. The original text has been used but, rightly, this new set (unlike EMI's last)
gives the listener the choice of versions of the great *Pearlfishers duet*. The original version,
given as an appendix, is maddening when it fails to bring a reprise for the big tune and
instead launches into a trivial *Polonaise-cabaletta*.

Paul Dervaux is no more than an efficient conductor, and his lack of affection infects the principals, who are all stylish artists but who here sing below their best, even the dependable Nicolai Gedda. On two mid-priced CDs the set might still be worth considering, however, when it also includes selections from the opera which Bizet wrote immediately after *Pearl-fishers*, *Ivan IV*. There is a fine scena for the heroine, beautifully sung by Janine Micheau; and the heady-toned tenor, Henri Legay, an outstanding artist, sings superbly in his vengeance aria. It is also good to hear the fine bass, Pierre Savignol. The package includes the libretto of *Pearl-fishers* but, as yet, no translation, and only garbled notes and synopsis for *Ivan IV*. The CD transfers hardly betray the age of the recordings.

Blake, Howard (born 1938)

Clarinet concerto.
*** Hyp. Dig. CDA 66215 [id.]. Thea King, ECO, composer – LUTOSLAWSKI: *Dance preludes*; SEIBER: *Concertino.****

Howard Blake provides a comparatively slight but endearing *Clarinet concerto*, which is played here with great sympathy by Thea King, who commissioned the work. With its neo-classical feeling, it is improvisatory and reflective in its basic style, but produces plenty of energy in the finale with its whiff of Walton. Both couplings are extremely attractive; admirers of the clarinet and of Miss King will find this a most rewarding collection. It is extremely vividly recorded on CD – there is almost a sense of over-presence.

Bliss, Arthur (1891–1975)

(i) *Piano concerto; March of homage.*
(M) **(*) Unicorn Dig. UKCD 2029 [id.]. (i) Philip Fowke; Royal Liverpool PO, David Atherton.

Bliss wrote his *Piano concerto* for British Week at the New York World Fair in 1939 and he attempted a bravura work on a very large scale. From the dashing double octaves at the start the pianistic style throughout has much of Rachmaninov and Liszt in it, though the idiom is very much Bliss's own, with some of his most memorable material. It is a work which needs a passionately committed soloist, and that is what it finds in Philip Fowke, urgent and expressive, well matched by David Atherton and the Liverpool orchestra. The occasional piece is also given a lively performance. The digital recording is full and vivid, with the piano naturally balanced, less forward than is common. There is a tendency for the acoustic to be a shade over-resonant in the *Concerto* (noticeable at the opening) but the internal definition is somewhat improved on CD which also brings a degree of fierceness to orchestral fortissimos.

A Colour symphony; Checkmate (ballet): *suite.*
*** Chan. Dig. CHAN 8503 [id.]. Ulster O, Handley.

(i) *A Colour symphony;* (ii) *Edinburgh overture;* (iii) *Miracle in the Gorbals* (ballet): suite.
(M) *** EMI CDM7 69388-2. (i) RPO, Groves; (ii) CBSO, Handley; (iii) Bournemouth SO, Berglund.

Bliss's *Colour symphony* comes from the early 1920s. Each of its movements evokes the heraldic symbolism of four colours – purple, red, blue and green – and the quality of his invention and imagination is fresh. Vernon Handley directs with complete authority and evident enthusiasm; the *Checkmate* ballet is less of a rarity on record and is given with equal success. Chandos has an enviable reputation for the quality of its engineering, and this issue is one of its very best.

The work is also well projected in Groves's highly sympathetic performance, and the remastered EMI recording from the late 1970s offers vintage sound from that period and is effectively remastered. The extended selection from the *Miracle in the Gorbals* ballet also shows Bliss at his most imaginative; the orchestral playing under Berglund has fine life and spontaneity, and the somewhat earlier recording is spectacularly vivid. The *Edinburgh overture* is an engagingly extrovert piece and Handley's advocacy is predictably spirited; this mid-priced EMI issue remains fully competitive.

Conversations; Madam Noy; (i; ii) *Rhapsody;* (ii) *Rout; The Women of Yueh; Oboe quintet.*
*** Hyp. CDA 66137 [id.]. Nash Ens., (i) Anthony Rolfe-Johnson; (ii) Elizabeth Gale.

The predominant influence in *Rout*, for soprano and chamber orchestra, and in the *Rhapsody*, with its two wordless vocal parts, is Ravel – one readily forgets how strong it was in that period, even in the light-hearted and diverting *Conversations* for flute and oboe (and their relatives, the bass flute and cor anglais) and string trio. *Madam Noy* sets a poem of F. W. H. Meyerstein that is close to *Old Mother Hubbard*. The longest piece on the disc is the *Oboe quintet*, also a work of considerable quality. The music assembled here represents Bliss at his very best. A lovely disc – and eminently well engineered, too – it can be warmly recommended even to those who do not normally admire this composer.

Clarinet quintet.
*** Chan. Dig. CHAN 8683 [id.]. Hilton, Lindsay Qt – BAX: *Sonata*; VAUGHAN WILLIAMS: *Studies.***

The *Clarinet quintet*, composed in the early 1930s, is arguably Bliss's masterpiece; the present performance is a worthy successor to the 1963 recording by Gervase de Peyer and members of the Melos Ensemble. These artists have the measure of its autumnal melancholy; the recording is natural and well focused, and the music-making is of the highest quality.

String quartets Nos. 1 in B flat; 2 in F min.
*** Hyp. CDA 66178 [id.]. Delmé Qt.

These performances by the Delmé Quartet are not only thoroughly committed but enormously persuasive and can be recommended even to readers not normally sympathetic to this composer. Both quartets are fine pieces: the *First* is a work of strong character, finely proportioned and not dissimilar in quality of inspiration to the *Music for strings*, written a few years earlier. Bliss regarded the *Second* as his finest chamber work, and the Delmé certainly do it justice. Strongly recommended.

VOCAL MUSIC

Lie strewn the white flocks.
*** Hyp. CDA 66175 [id.]. Shirley Minty, Judith Pierce (flute), Holst Singers & O, Hilary Davan Wetton – BRITTEN: *Gloriana: Choral dances*; HOLST: *Choral hymns from Rig Veda.***

Bliss's *Pastoral* may be severely classical in its inspiration, from Pan and the world of shepherds and shepherdesses, but its warm and natural expressiveness makes it one of Bliss's most immediately appealing works. It is given a winning performance by the Holst

Singers and Orchestra, with the choral sections (the greater part of the work) aptly modest in scale but powerful in impact. With glowing sound and very attractive works for coupling, this is an outstanding issue.

Bloch, Ernest (1880–1959)

Schelomo: Hebrew rhapsody (for cello and orchestra).
*** EMI CDC7 49307-2 [id.]. Rostropovich, O. Nat. de France, Bernstein – SCHUMANN: *Cello concerto.**(*)
*** Virgin Dig. VC 790735-2 [id.]. Isserlis, LSO, Hickox – ELGAR: *Cello concerto.***(*)
(B) **(*) DG 429 155-2 [id.]. Fournier, BPO, Wallenstein – DVOŘÁK: *Cello concerto***(*); BRUCH: *Kol Nidrei.***
*DG Dig. 427 347-2 [id.]. Maisky, Israel PO, Bernstein – DVOŘÁK: *Cello concerto.*

Schelomo calls for a large, though by no means outsize, orchestra including celeste and two harps. The collaboration of the great Russian cellist with Leonard Bernstein is a triumph. The rich expressiveness of both artists – with the French orchestra also persuaded into passionately committed playing – blends superbly, so that the rhapsodic flow conveys total concentration. The recording is full to match, but spotlights the soloist. It is a great pity that the Schumann on the reverse is not nearly so successful.

The dark intensity of Isserlis's solo playing and the sharp, dramatic focus of Hickox in the big climactic orchestral tuttis are here magnetic, preventing Bloch's youthful outpouring on Solomon and the Song of Songs from sounding self-indulgent. Warm, refined recording.

Fournier's fervent advocacy of Bloch's *Hebrew rhapsody* is given sympathetic support by Alfred Wallenstein. Fournier is closely balanced, but the 1976 recording is warmly atmospheric and, if orchestral detail is not always fully revealed, the CD sound is otherwise impressive.

Maisky's consistently heavy vibrato gives a wailing quality to his tone which may be apt for this intensely Jewish inspiration, but he fails to give the work the light and shade it really needs. The close balance of the soloist in this live recording and the dehydrated sound of the Israel Philharmonic in the tuttis also make it disappointing as the fill-up for Maisky and Bernstein's self-indulgent reading of the Dvořák *Concerto*.

Sacred service.
**(*) Chan. CHAN 8418 [id.]. Berkman, L. Chorale and Concord Singers, LSO, Simon.

Bloch's *Sacred service* does not deserve its current neglect. The singing here is perhaps wanting in ardour and intensity, and there could be greater attention to dynamic nuances. However, it would be unfair to dwell on the shortcomings of this performance in the light of so much that is good, not least of which is the orchestral playing. The recording is spacious and well focused.

Blow, John (1649–1708)

(i) *Ode on the death of Mr Henry Purcell*; (ii) *Amphion Angelicus* (song collection): *Ah heaven! What is't I hear?; Cloe found Amintas lying all in tears; Loving above himself; Shepherds deck your crooks; Why weeps Asteria?* ; *Epilogue: Sing, sing, ye muses.*
(M) **(*) HM/BMG GD 71962. (i) René Jacobs, James Bowman; (ii) Yamamoto, Van der Speek, Jacobs, Van Altena, Van Egmond, Ens., Leonhardt.

John Blow's *Ode on the death of Purcell*, a highly eloquent setting of an allegorical poem by John Dryden, makes a worthy memorial to the great English composer. It is an extended three-part structure some 25 minutes long, with René Jacobs and James Bowman ideally matched in the vocal centrepiece. The other items in the programme are taken from a collection of 50 songs, published in 1700, and admirably demonstrate the range and variety of Blow's art. Apart from the opening *Cloe found Amintas lying all in tears*, where the two soprano soloists, Nobuko Yamamoto and Nelly van der Speek, could blend more pleasingly, they are all effectively presented, especially the closing *Epilogue* for vocal quartet. Gustav Leonhardt and his chamber ensemble (two recorders are used in the main work) accompany authentically, and the 1973 recording has a good ambience and no lack of presence.

Ode on the death of Mr Henry Purcell: Mark how the lark and linnet sing. Ah, heav'n! What is't I hear.
*** Hyp. Dig. CDA 66253 [id.]. James Bowman, Michael Chance, King's Consort, King
– PURCELL: *Collection.****

James Bowman's re-recording of Blow's fine Purcellian *Ode for Hyperion* not only comes within an entirely different context – a collection of counter-tenor duets and solos, concentrating mainly on Purcell – but is also different in character. Where Leonhardt on RCA is spacious in his concept and more detailed in his concern for word-meanings, the result also more polished, Robert King's spontaneous style is infectious with the orchestral comments engagingly animated. Bowman's voice blends more readily with that of Michael Chance so that their interchanges are smoother, but that is not necessarily an advantage, for the stronger vocal contrast with René Jacobs is attractively characterful. Both performances are highly rewarding, and in the last resort couplings will dictate choice. The Hyperion disc is more expensive but includes a quarter of an hour more music.

Venus and Adonis.
*** HM Dig. HMC 90 1276 [id.]. Argenta, Dawson, Varcoe, Covey-Crump, L. Bar. & Ch., Medlam.

Charles Medlam with London Baroque gives a sprightly account of John Blow's delightful masque, one of the few that have survived today as a living entertainment. Though this is a period performance, the ensemble is substantial, and Medlam takes care that the early instruments are well blended rather than edgy and the choral sound is full, bright and clean. The *Huntsmen's chorus* in Act I has splendid bite and panache. The soloists too are all remarkable for sweetness and freshness of tone, with the bright, clear tones of Nancy Argenta as Cupid and Lynne Dawson as Venus nicely counterpointed, and with Stephen Varcoe a clear, youthful-sounding Adonis.

Boccherini, Luigi (1743–1805)

Cello concerto No. 2 in D, G.479.
(M) *** DG 429 098-2 [id.]. Rostropovich, Zurich Coll. Mus., Sacher – TARTINI; VIVALDI: *Concertos.****

Although essentially a performance in the grand manner (with Rostropovich providing his own cadenzas), the music-making has tremendous vitality, with extremely lively outer movements to balance the eloquence of the *Adagio*. The forceful nature of the performance is short on charm and so perhaps a little out of character for an essentially elegant composer like Boccherini; but Rostropovich is so compelling that reservations are swept aside. He is given an alert accompaniment by Sacher, and the recording has fine body and presence.

Cello concerto No. 7 in G, G.480.
(B) *** Ph. 422 481-2 [id.]. Gendron, LSO, Leppard – HAYDN: *Cello concerto in C.****
(B) *** Pickwick Dig. PCD 917. Felix Schmidt, ECO, Heath – BEETHOVEN: *Triple concerto.****

It was Maurice Gendron who originally unearthed this *G major Concerto* and made its first recording. It is admirably played and usefully coupled with Haydn's lesser-known *C major Concerto.*
The Boccherini *Concerto No. 7* makes an unusual but apt and attractive coupling for the Trio Zingara's excellent version of the Beethoven *Triple concerto.* This is the concerto from which Grützmacher extracted the slow movement in his phoney, cobbled-together 'Boccherini Concerto', the movement everyone remembers. The recording, as in the Beethoven, is full and vivid, an excellent recommendation on the bargain-price IMP label.

Cello concerto No. 9 in B flat, G. 482 (original version).
** Chan. Dig. CHAN 8470 [id.]. Turovsky, I Musici di Montréal – J. C. BACH: *Cello concerto etc.***

Yuli Turovsky, who directs as well as plays, has elegance and warmth, and gets an alert response from the orchestra. Tiny insecurities of intonation make one wonder whether it is always wise to combine both functions, but they are not serious enough to inhibit a recommendation. The recording is truthful and well balanced.

Cello concerto in B flat (arr. Grützmacher).
*** CBS MK 39964 [id.]. Yo-Yo Ma, St Paul CO, Zukerman – J. C. BACH: *Sinfonia concertante etc.***(*)
(*) EMI CDC7 47840-2 [id.]. Jacqueline du Pré, ECO, Barenboim – HAYDN: *Concerto in D.**
** DG Dig. 429 219-2. Haimovitz, ECO, A. Davis – C. P. E. BACH; HAYDN: *Concertos.***

Like Jacqueline du Pré before him, Yo-Yo Ma chooses the Grützmacher version of the Boccherini *Concerto,* romantically derived from three different Boccherini works, but highly effective in its own right. He plays it with taste and finesse, not wearing his heart on his sleeve as obviously as du Pré, but with his warm, if refined, timbre and style not missing the romanticism. The recording is first class.
Working for the first time in the recording studio with Daniel Barenboim, du Pré was inspired to some really heart-warming playing, broadly romantic in style – but then that is what Grützmacher plainly asks for. The 1967 recording has retained much of its fullness and atmosphere, and the solo cello has good presence, but the orchestral sound is rather less well focused than the Haydn coupling. An endearing performance none the less.
Matt Haimovitz produces a big (almost schmalzy) tone – there are more refined players in this generation – and is rather impulsive, pressing forward and then holding back, albeit slightly, but disturbing the natural flow of the piece.

Symphonies: in D; in C, Op. 12/3; in D min., Op. 12/4; in B flat, Op. 35/6; in D min., Op. 37/3; in A, Op. 37/4.
** Chan. Dig. CHAN 8414-5 (3) [id.]. Cantilena, Adrian Shepherd.

In all, Boccherini composed twenty symphonies, seven of which are included in this set. The *D minor,* Op. 12, No. 4, is the celebrated *La casa del diavolo,* whose finale is based on the chaconne of Gluck's *Don Juan* ballet. Adrian Shepherd and his Cantilena have the measure of this music's grace and gentleness, and are scrupulous in observing repeats. These are sympathetic rather than high-powered performances and will give considerable pleasure, though lacking the last ounce of finish. But there is no want of feeling for this unjustly neglected repertoire, and the symphonies are well recorded.

Symphonies: in D min. (La casa del diavolo), Op. 12/4; in A, Op. 12/6; in A, Op. 21/6.
*** Hyp. Dig. CDA 66236 [id.]. L. Fest. O, Ross Pople.

Ross Pople's record duplicates only one work included in the more ambitious Chandos collection, *La casa del diavolo*, Op. 12/4; in his account the demons are certainly let loose in the finale, with the most frantically energetic playing from the strings. Elsewhere the performances are the soul of elegance; in the sunny *A major*, Op. 12/6, where the flutes add a helping of cream to the strawberries, the finesse of the playing gives much pleasure in itself; altogether this well-played and well-recorded collection can be given the warmest welcome.

Guitar quintets Nos. 3 in B flat, G.447; 9 in C (La ritirata di Madrid), G.453.
(M) ****(*)** Ph. 426 092-2 [id.]. Pepe Romero, ASMF Chamber Ens.

Both works here are arrangements. No. 3 comes from the *Piano quintet*, Op. 57/2; the first three movements of No. 9 originate in the *Piano quintet*, Op. 56/3, and the finale, which gives it its subtitle, *La ritirata di Madrid*, is familiar from the *String quintet*, Op. 30/6. The picturesque evocation of Spanish life is created with a set of twelve short variations set in a long, slow crescendo, followed by a similarly graduated decrescendo, a kind of Spanish patrol with the 'night watch' disappearing into the distance at the close. Both works are melodically engaging in Boccherini's elegant rococo style, and they are beautifully played. The guitar is well balanced within the string group, yet is able to dominate when required. On CD, detail is cleaner, but the string timbre is slightly more astringent than it was on the original LP, not entirely to Boccherini's advantage. However, this remains an attractive coupling.

Guitar quintets Nos. 4 in D (Fandango); 5 in D; 6 in G, G. 448/50.
*** Ph. 420 385-2 [id.]. Pepe Romero, ASMF Chamber Ens.

The *D major* and *G major Quintets*, G. 449–50, are eminently agreeable but possess no darker undercurrents. The work subtitled *Fandango* produces a sudden burst of Spanish fireworks in the finale, complete with rattling castanets. All three performances are spontaneous and have plenty of warmth, and this makes excellent late-evening background listening. The digital remastering of the 1978/9 originals brings a fine sense of reality and presence, though the string focus seems just a little fuzzy.

Guitar quintets Nos. (i) 4 in D (Fandango); 7 in E min., G.451; 9 in C (La ritirata di Madrid).
(B) ******* DG 429 512-2 [id.]. Yepes, Melos Qt; (i) with Lucero Tena.

Guitar quintets Nos. 4 (Fandango); 9 (La ritirata di Madrid).
(BB) ****** Hung. White Label HRC 055 [id.]. Laszlo Szendrey-Karper, Tátrai Qt.

The DG bargain compilation (from 1971) offers a cleaner sound-picture than its Philips competitors: indeed the sound is very good, full yet lively and well projected. The playing is expert and, in the boisterous *Fandango* finale of No. 4, Lucero Tena makes a glittering contribution with his castanets.

The Hungaroton CD is in the bargain basement and is not to be dismissed; the performances have vitality and the recording is vivid, if a trifle thin in string timbre. But the DG disc is worth its small extra cost.

Cello quintet, Op. 37/7 (Pleyel).
(B) **(*) Decca 421 637-2. ASMF – MENDELSSOHN: *Octet.***(*)

This is an inspired piece: it would be worth getting for its own sake – and the coupled performance of the Mendelssohn *Octet* is a particularly fine one. Reissued on Decca's Weekend label, this is a bargain, even if the recording shows its age just a little in the upper range.

String quintets: in E, Op. 11/5, G 275; in D min., Op. 13/4, G 280; in D, Op. 39/3, G 339; in C min., Op. 51/2, G 377.
**(*) Denon Dig. CO 2199 [id.]. Berlin Philh. Ens.

Boccherini composed more than 100 string quintets, of which the first recorded here, containing the famous *Minuet*, is the best known. The whole disc offers music-making of great elegance and charm (perhaps too much at times, as the first movement of Op. 11, No. 5, is just a little undervitalized). There is depth and pathos in some of these *Quintets* (the *Andante* of the *D minor* or the *Andantino con innocenza* of the *C minor*, for example) as well as the customary finish. There is some beguiling music in the *D major* (the *Pastorale*) as well. These fine musicians play with dedication, though at times there is a degree of caution as if they are a little inhibited by courtly manners. Good if rather forward recording.

Boito, Arrigo (1842–1918)

Mefistofele (complete).
**(*) Decca Dig. 410 175-2 [id.]. Ghiaurov, Pavarotti, Freni, Caballé, L. Op. Ch., Trinity Boys' Ch., Nat. PO, Fabritiis.

Boito's *Mefistofele* is a strange episodic work to come from the hand of the master-librettist of Verdi's *Otello* and *Falstaff*, but it has many fine moments. The modern digital recording given to the Fabritiis set brings obvious benefits in the extra weight of brass and percussion – most importantly in the heavenly prologue. With the principal soloists all at their best – Pavarotti most seductive in *Dai campi, dai prati*, Freni finely imaginative on detail, Caballé consistently sweet and mellifluous as Elena, Ghiaurov strongly characterful if showing some signs of strain – this is a highly recommendable set, though Fabritiis in his last recording lacks a little in energy, and the chorus is placed rather distantly.

Mefistofele: Prologue.
** Telarc Dig. CD 80109 [id.]. John Cheek, Young Singers of Callanwolde, Atlanta Ch. and SO, Shaw – BERLIOZ: *Requiem*; VERDI: *Te Deum.***

Despite some excellent choral singing, finely disciplined, the Atlanta performance remains obstinately earth-bound, though the heavenly choirs are more convincing than their infernal counterparts, which lack demonry. Fine, clear recording, with massed forces all precisely placed.

Nerone (complete).
**(*) Hung. Dig. HCD 12487/9-2 [id.]. Nagy, Tokody, Dene, Miller, Takács, Gregor, Hungarian R. and TV Ch., Hungarian State Op. O, Queler.

Eve Queler conducts a powerful and atmospheric performance of Boito's massive, uncompleted opera. There are plenty of marvellous ideas here, starting with the strikingly original opening, sliding in like *Aida* updated. Later too the piece is full of prayers and ceremonial music, all of it richly colourful and superbly performed by the company of the Hungarian State Opera, whose soloists are far less afflicted with Slavonic wobbles than is common in Eastern Europe. Notable in the cast are Ilona Tokody as the heroine, Klara Takács, Lajos Miller as the Christian leader, and Janos Nagy as a disconcertingly engaging Nero, a tenor role. The recording is of outstanding quality, with the atmospheric perspectives demanded by the score most realistically conveyed.

Borodin, Alexander (1833–87)

Petite suite (arr. Glazunov).
*** Olympia OCD 114 A/B (2) [id.]. USSR RSO, Cherkassov – MUSSORGSKY: *Sorochinsky Fair.***

Not long before Borodin died, he compiled a suite of piano pieces for the Belgian countess who had been his patroness in France, and these became the *Petite suite* which Glazunov orchestrated after Borodin's death. It is a colourful, undemanding work, very well played and recorded.

Symphonies Nos. 1 in E flat; 2 in B min.; 3 in A min.
** ASV Dig. CDDCA 706 [id.]. O Sinfonica di Roma (RAI), Serebrier.

It is generous and useful to have all three symphonies on one disc, as this demonstrates how the *First* (although its scherzo is highly delectable in its own right) was very much a model for the *Second*, Borodin's masterpiece. Serebrier's performances, recorded live, are sensibly paced and direct, rather than vividly characterized; perhaps not surprisingly they are not very Russian in feeling. This is partly the effect of the studio-ish recorded sound, which lacks glitter and bite. Although the strings are still able to bring a warm, Italianate espressivo to slow movements, there is a lack of real passion.

Symphonies Nos. 1 and 3.
** Chant du Monde LDC 278 781. USSR Ac. SO, Svetlanov.

Symphony No. 2 in B min.
(M) ** EMI CDM7 63093-2 [id.]. Bournemouth SO, Brusilov – BALAKIREV: *Russia*; RIMSKY-KORSAKOV: *Skazka.***

Symphony No. 2 in B min.; In the Steppes of central Asia; (i) Prince Igor: Polovtsian dances.
** Chant du Monde LDC 278 272 [id.]. USSR Ac. SO; (i) and Ch.; Svetlanov.

Symphony No. 2 in B min.; Prince Igor: Overture; Polovtsian dances.
(B) ** ASV Dig. CDQS 6018 [id.]. Mexico State SO, Bátiz.

Svetlanov gives vivid and well-characterized readings of the Borodin symphonies; they may not be the most subtle performances but nevertheless have plenty of spirit. The sound is very acceptable without being in any way outstanding. On the second of the two CDs the *Polovtsian dances* make a vivid and exciting bonus. The recording dates from 1966.

Bátiz's bright, modern digital recording certainly makes a vivid impression and the performances are extremely spirited, although one is made to realize that the Mexican State orchestra, though impressively rehearsed, cannot match the finest European orchestras in virtuosity and finesse. The *Polovtsian dances* are without a chorus, and the effect is slightly shrill; but the energy of the performance is arresting. This is issued in the budget range and is very good value.

Brusilov's opening of the *Second Symphony* is emphatic to the point of portentousness, and the overall shape of the first movement is not held together very tautly. The scherzo sparkles and there are moments of excitement in the development of the first movement and the finale; but for the most part the performance is not in any way distinctive, though it offers lively (if not always absolutely refined) sound and interesting couplings.

String quartets Nos. 1 in A; 2 in D.
*** EMI CDC7 47795-2 [id.]. Borodin Qt.

String quartet No. 2 in D.
*** Olympia Dig. OCD 138 [id.]. Borodin Qt – TANEYEV: *Quintet.****
(M) **(*) Decca 425 541-2 [id.]. Borodin Qt – SHOSTAKOVICH; TCHAIKOVSKY: *Quartets.***(*)
** Telarc Dig. CD 80178 [id.]. Cleveland Qt – SMETANA: *Quartet No. 1 in E min.***

The EMI performances from the eponymous Borodin Quartet are admirable in all respects. They are completely effortless and idiomatic; indeed, so total is their sense of identification with these scores that one is scarcely conscious of the intervention of the interpreter. The quality achieved by the Melodiya engineers has fine clarity; on CD the focus of the first violin line is firmer than before. The ambient warmth remains, although the sound is perhaps just a shade harder than on the original (1980) analogue LP.

On Olympia, the alternative version from the Borodin Quartet is equally masterly. The performance is virtually indistinguishable in quality from their EMI version and they are beautifully recorded. The Olympia CD has a slight price advantage, and the Taneyev *Quintet* is certainly well worth investigating.

The Borodins' first version on Decca was recorded in 1962; this performance is hardly less fine than the later versions and it is very generously coupled. However, the forward recording, though rich-textured, is given a boldly outlined treble, approaching fierceness in the CD transfer, and some will prefer a softer-grained effect.

The Cleveland give a brilliantly prepared and vital account of the Borodin on their four Stradivariuses – but, as is the case with the Smetana, their performances are stronger on polish than they are on spontaneity. Not a first choice, though it is impossible not to admire their expertise or gainsay the excellence of the recording.

The famous *Nocturne* from the *Second Quartet* is included as a bonus on the Philips coupling of Dvořák's *American quartet* and Schubert's *Death and the Maiden* by the Italian Quartet (420 876-2), a mid-priced bargain.

Songs: *Arabian melody; Arrogance; The beauty no longer loves me; The false note; The fisher-maiden; From my tears; From the shores of thy far native land; Listen to my song little friend; The magic garden; The queen of the sea; The sea; The sleeping princess; Song of the dark forest; There is poison in my songs; Those people; Why art thou so early, dawn?*
(M) *** EMI CMS7 63386-2 (3) [Ang. CDMC 63386]. Christoff, Tcherepnin, Reiss, Lamoureux O, Tzipine – *Prince Igor.***(*)

Accompanied at the piano in all but three of the songs by the composer, Alexander Tcherepnin, Christoff gives glorious performances of these rare items. They were recorded in the 1960s, when the voice was at its richest and most expressive, providing an invaluable makeweight for Semkow's cut version of *Prince Igor*.

BORODIN

Prince Igor (opera) complete.
*** Sony Dig. S3K 44878 (3) [id.]. Martinovich, Evstatieva, Kaludov, Ghiuselev, Ghiaurov, Miltcheva, Sofia Nat. Op. Ch. & Fest. O, Tchakarov.
(M) **(*) EMI CMS7 63386-2 (3) [Ang. CDMC 63386]. Chekerliiski, Christoff, Todorov, Sofia Nat. Theatre Op. Ch. & O, Jerzy Semkow – *Songs*.***

Issued as one of the first offerings on the new Sony Classical label, Tchakarov's complete recording of *Prince Igor* fills one of the most important gaps in the catalogue. It may give an idea of the quality of the singing that the soloist over whom there are most reservations, Nicola Ghiuselev as Galitsky, powerful but rather unsteady, is one of the two most celebrated international stars in the Sofia cast. The other, Nicolai Ghiaurov, makes a splendid Konchak, if not quite as characterful as Christoff on the EMI set. Boris Martinovich makes a firm, very virile Igor, and both the principal women have vibrantly Slavonic voices which still never distract as with wobbling: Stefka Evstatieva very moving and young-sounding as Igor's wife, Yaroslavna, and Alexandrina Miltcheva as Konchak's daughter. Kaludi Kaludov sings with Slavonic tightness at times, but that too is apt. Tchakarov takes a generally brisk view of the score. The dramatic tension in this long work is held very well and its richness of invention over its very episodic span comes across vividly, notably in all its memorable melody and high colour. The performance is particularly moving in Act III, where – thanks to the 'creative editing' of Rimsky-Korsakov and Glazunov – the score is enhanced by the ideas they also used in the *Overture*, culminating in the glorious final trio between Igor, his son and Konchak's daughter. Full, brilliant recording to match the orchestration.

Recorded in Paris in 1966, the colourful EMI recording of *Prince Igor* was never given international circulation – except briefly in a highlights disc – until this mid-price CD transfer appeared in 1990. Its great flaw is that Act III is completely omitted, on the grounds that it was almost entirely the work of Rimsky-Korsakov and Glazunov. The great glory of the performance is the singing of Boris Christoff as both Galitzky and Konchak, easily outshining all rivals. Jerzy Semkow with his Sofia Opera forces is most sympathetic, but the other soloists are almost all disappointing, with the women sour-toned and the men often strained and unsteady. There is no libretto; but EMI is very generous with cueing points, and you can follow the story easily by checking them against the very detailed synopsis. The sound is limited but agreeably atmospheric.

Prince Igor: Overture and Polovtsian dances.
(B) *** Decca 417 689-2 [id.]. LSO Ch., LSO, Solti – MUSSORGSKY: *Khovanshchina prelude; Night;* GLINKA: *Russlan overture*.***
*** Telarc Dig. CD 80039. Atlanta Ch. and SO, Shaw – STRAVINSKY: *Firebird suite*.**(*)

Prince Igor: Polovtsian dances.
*** EMI CDC7 47717-2 [id.]. Beecham Choral Soc., RPO, Beecham – RIMSKY-KORSAKOV: *Scheherazade*.***
(M) *** DG 419 063-2 [id.]. BPO, Karajan – RIMSKY-KORSAKOV: *Scheherazade*.***
(M) *** EMI CDM7 69041-2 [id.]. Philh. O, Karajan – GOUNOD: *Faust ballet****; OFFENBACH: *Gaîté parisienne***(*); PONCHIELLI: *Dance of the hours*.***
(M) **(*) Decca 417 753-2 [id.]. Welsh Nat. Op. Ch., RPO, Stokowski – RIMSKY-KORSAKOV: *Scheherazade* etc.*(**)

Beecham's 1957 recording of the *Polovtsian dances*, made in EMI's Abbey Road studios, sweeps the board, even though it omits the percussion-led opening *Dance of the Polovtsi Maidens*. Beecham draws an almost Russian fervour from his choristers, who sing with enormous enthusiasm, and the orchestral playing creates a comparable excitement, building to a tremendous climax. The recorded sound is little short of astonishing in its fullness, vividness and clarity.

Karajan's Berlin Philharmonic version does include the introductory section missing on the Beecham record (so does Solti) and his account has great flair and excitement too, though not a chorus. The alternative Philharmonia account comes from 1960 but hardly shows its age – the recording sounds full as well as brilliant.

Solti's performance is also among the finest ever recorded, with good choral singing – even if the chorus takes a little longer to warm up than Sir Thomas's group. The *Overture* too has fine dash, with the LSO players consistently on their toes.

On Telarc the choral singing is less clearly focused in the lyrical sections of the score than at climaxes, but the singers undoubtedly rise to the occasion. The entry of the bass drum is riveting and the closing section very exciting. The vivid sound-balance is equally impressive in the *Overture*, and if the Atlanta orchestra does not possess the body of string timbre to make the very most of the sweeping second subject, the playing has vitality and spontaneity in its favour.

Stokowski misses out the percussion-led opening dance. His performance is a mannered one, but there is no question of the sheer excitement he creates as the work reaches its final climax. The remastered 1969 recording is impressively vivid, with a sense of spectacle, even if the effect is not absolutely refined.

Bottesini, Giovanni (1821–89)

Gran duo concertante for violin, double-bass and orchestra; Gran concerto in F sharp min. for double-bass; Andante sostenuto for strings; Duetto for clarinet and double-bass.
**(*) ASV Dig. CDDCA 563 [id.]. Garcia, Martin, Emma Johnson, ECO, Andrew Litton.

The ASV recording combines the *Gran duo concertante* with another *Duo for clarinet and double-bass* which Emma Johnson ensures has plenty of personality. The *Andante sostenuto for strings* is pleasant enough, but the *Double-bass concerto* fails to convince. To be frank, none of this amiable music is very distinctive. The recording is excellent, well balanced and truthful.

Capriccio di bravura; Elegia in Re; Fantasia on Beatrice di Tenda; Fantasia on Lucia di Lammermoor; Grand allegro di concerto; Introduzione e Bolero; Romanza drammatica; (i) Romanza: Une bouche aimée.
** ASV Dig. CDDCA 626 [id.]. Thomas Martin, Anthony Halstead; (i) with J. Fugelle.

The mechanical limitations of the double-bass mean that harmonics performed with scientific accuracy are out of tune. Thomas Martin is a superb virtuoso of the instrument, and he obviously relishes these display pieces, but some of the high tessitura is inevitably uncomfortable. In *Une bouche aimée* he is joined by the charmingly eloquent voice of Jacquelyn Fugelle and the double-bass provides the obbligato, which makes a welcome central interlude. There are excellent accompaniments from Anthony Halstead, better known as a fine horn player. The recording is most realistic.

Boughton, Rutland (1878–1960)

(i) *Oboe concerto; Symphony No. 3 in B min.*
*** Hyp. Dig. CDA 66343 [id.]. (i) Sarah Francis; RPO, Vernon Handley.

Rutland Boughton's *Third Symphony* comes from 1937 and proves something of a surprise. It is old-fashioned in idiom; some of it would not be out of place in Dvořák or Borodin, and its debt to Elgar above all is overwhelming. However, it is expertly fashioned, often imaginative and (save in the rumbustious scherzo, where the closing pages are clumsily scored) hardly puts a foot wrong. The *Oboe concerto* of 1936, which Boyd Neel took to Salzburg in the same year as he presented Britten's *Variations on a theme of Frank Bridge*, is hardly less rewarding. The recording is in the demonstration class and the performances are totally committed, even if the strings of the RPO are not quite on top form.

The Immortal hour (opera): complete.
*** Hyp. Dig. CDA 66101/2 [id.]. Kennedy, Dawson, Wilson-Johnson, Davies, Geoffrey Mitchell Ch., ECO, Melville.

There is far more to *The Immortal hour* than the still-celebrated *Faery song*, which hauntingly is heard first at the end of Act I, sung by a chorus in the distance. Analysed closely, much of it may seem like Vaughan Williams and water; but this fine performance, conducted by a lifelong Boughton devotee, brings out the hypnotic quality which had 1920s music-lovers attending performances many times over, entranced by its lyrical evocation of Celtic twilight. The simple tunefulness goes with a fine feeling for atmosphere. The excellent cast of young singers includes Anne Dawson as the heroine, Princess Etain, and Maldwyn Davies headily beautiful in the main tenor rendering of the *Faery song*. Warm, reverberant recording, undoubtedly enhanced in its CD format.

Boulez, Pierre (born 1926)

Rituel: In memoriam Bruno Maderna; Éclat-Multiples.
(M) *** Sony SK 45839 [id.]. BBC SO, Ens. InterContemporain, composer.

This mid-priced CD reissue of two of Boulez's strongest and most immediately approachable works in his own authoritative performances could not be more welcome. *Éclat-Multiples* is a piece, begun in 1964, which may well never be completed to the composer's satisfaction. It started simply as *Éclat*, a brilliant showpiece, an exuberant mosaic of sounds, but then, in 1970, it started developing from there in the pendant work, *Multiples*. On this recording the two sections are played without a break. *Rituel* is even more remarkable, the most moving music that Boulez has ever written, inspired by the premature death of his friend and colleague, Bruno Maderna. Conceived more broadly than most of Boulez's music, this half-hour span, in fifteen clearly defined sections, brings what even an uninitiated listener will recognize as a great funeral procession, darkly intense, building up with an emotional intensity hardly less involving than a Mahler funeral march. Boulez himself does not resist the idea of the work being appreciated first on a direct emotional level, so long as the listener does not just wallow, but looks below the surface. This record, very well played and recorded, provides both a challenge and a reward.

Boyce, William (1710–79)

Symphonies Nos. 1–8.
*** DG Dig. 419 631-2 [id.]. E. Concert, Pinnock.
*** CRD CRD 3356 [id.]. Bournemouth Sinf., Ronald Thomas.

Pinnock's disc of the Boyce *Symphonies* is a delight, the first recording to use period instruments. It wears its scholarship very easily and in so doing brings not only lively,

BRAHMS

resilient playing but fresh revelation in the treatment of the *vivace* movements, which are normally taken faster than is authentic, when that marking in eighteenth-century England did not have its modern connotation of speed. Nicely scaled recording, bright but atmospheric.

Thomas's tempi are often brisk, and certainly swifter-paced than Pinnock's 'new look'. But even against such strong competition as this, the buoyant playing of the Bournemouth Sinfonietta still gives much pleasure by its sheer vitality. Bright, clear sound.

Solomon (serenata).
*** Hyp. Dig. CDA 66378 [id.]. Bronwen Mills, Howard Crook, Parley of Instruments, Goodman.

William Boyce's *Solomon* could hardly provide a stronger contrast with the magnificent oratorio of the same name that Handel wrote in 1748, six years after Boyce's gentle *Serenata* had been completed. It is a totally secular piece, a dialogue between She and He, with the verses freely based on the *Song of Solomon*. The only actual reference to the King is in the opening chorus; the rest of this gentle entertainment is a sequence of recitatives and airs, plus two duets, with the chorus making only brief contributions. By the nineteenth century it had fallen out of the repertory, when the erotic overtones of the text had become less acceptable and choral societies did not want to perform a work almost entirely devoted to two soloists. But, as this stylish and alert period performance using young, fresh-voiced soloists makes clear, it has some delightful inspirations, less influenced by Italian models than by popular English song. First-rate sound.

Brahms, Johannes (1833–97)

Piano concertos Nos. 1–2; Fantasias, Op. 116.
*** DG 419 158-2 (2). Gilels, BPO, Jochum.

These performances from the early 1970s still dominate the catalogue. Gilels brings a combination of magisterial strength and a warmth, humanity and depth that are altogether inspiring. Jochum is a superb accompanist. The digital remastering has improved definition and the sound is full in an appropriately Brahmsian way. In the *Fantasias*, Op. 116, Gilels displays artistry of an order that silences criticism.

Piano concerto No. 1 in D min., Op. 15.
*** Ph. Dig. 420 071-2 [id.]. Brendel, BPO, Abbado.
*** Decca Dig. 410 009-2 [id.]. Ashkenazy, Concg. O, Haitink.
(B) *** CfP CD-CFP 4553. Martino Tirimo, LPO, Sanderling.
**(*) RCA RD 85668 [RCA 5668-2-RC]. Rubinstein, Chicago SO, Reiner.
(M) **(*) Ph. 420 702-2 [id.]. Arrau, Concg. O, Haitink.
(*) Chan. Dig. CHAN 8724 [id.]. Margalit, LSO, Thomson (with MENDELSSOHN: *Capriccio brillant*).
** RCA Dig. RD 87780 [7780-2-RC]. Barry Douglas, LSO, Skrowaczewski.

Piano concerto No. 1; Intermezzi: in E flat, Op. 117/1; in C, Op. 119/3.
**(*) Decca 417 641-2 [id.]. Clifford Curzon, LSO, Szell.

Piano concerto No. 1; 2 Rhapsodies, Op. 79.
(M) *** Decca 417 776-2 [id.]. Radu Lupu, LPO, Edo de Waart.

195

(i) *Piano concerto No. 1; Variations and fugue on a theme of Handel, Op. 24.*
(M) **(*) RCA GD 60357 [60357-2-RG]. Van Cliburn; (i) Boston SO, Leinsdorf.

(i) *Piano concerto No. 1 in D min., Op. 15;* (ii) *Variations on a theme by Schumann, Op. 23.*
*** Decca Dig. 425 110-2 [id.]. (i) Schiff, VPO, Solti; (ii) Schiff, Solti.

Brendel produces a consistently beautiful sound and balances the combative and lyrical elements of the work with well-nigh perfect judgement. With Claudio Abbado and the Berlin Philharmonic as understanding partners,the result is both strong and spontaneous. His control of Brahmsian rubato is masterly, when it is easily flexible but totally unexaggerated, and the basic tempi are well and steadily set. The balance is not too forward and the effect is warmly satisfying.

Clifford Curzon's 1962 recording sounds fuller on some reproducers than on others, but the piano tone is consistently good. Curzon penetrates both the reflective inner world of the slow movement and the abundantly vital and massive opening movement, while Szell provides plenty of nervous energy in his accompaniment. The piano balance is most satisfying. As a bonus for the reissue, Decca have added two beautifully played *Intermezzi*, recorded in the Vienna Sofiensaal.

Ashkenazy gives a commanding and magisterial account of the solo part that is full of poetic imagination. The performance is very impressive indeed and there is superlative playing from the Concertgebouw Orchestra. The recording is enormously vivid, though the balance may worry some collectors. The forward placing of the soloist gives the lower and middle registers of the piano a disproportionate amount of aural space.

Schiff's performance has an imposing sense of line and is powerful and rich in sonority. Like the Lupu on Decca, it presents a very truthful and realistic balance between piano and orchestra, with the soloist not given undue prominence. The playing of the Vienna orchestra under Solti is glorious. It is worth considering not only for its own sake but in particular for the Schumann duet *Variations* in which, once again, Solti reminds us that he is a pianist of finesse.

Radu Lupu eschews *Sturm und Drang*. His is a deeply reflective and intelligent performance, full of masterly touches and an affecting poetry that falls short of the combative power we experience with Curzon and Szell. De Waart provides sensitive support and matches Lupu's approach admirably. The reading is a valuable corrective to the accepted view of this masterpiece. The Decca recording from the mid-1970s achieves an ideal relationship between piano and orchestra; the sound is wide-ranging and full, with the CD adding presence. The *Rhapsodies* are also finely done and make a good bonus.

With consistently measured tempi, Sanderling and Tirimo amply justify their straight and measured manner in the thoughtful concentration of the whole reading. One has no feeling of the performance dragging, for the crisp, lifted rhythms prevent that in the outer movements, and the slow movement has a rapt quality, holding one's attention as a live performance would. With such excellent sound, this makes a highly satisfying CD bargain. The recording dates from 1980.

With its rugged opening, Van Cliburn's account of the *D minor Concerto* soon develops a full head of steam. Leinsdorf is hardly less sympathetic than he is for Richter in No. 2, and this is a compelling reading, full of spontaneous vigour. The slow movement has eloquence and atmosphere, and the finale plenty of fire. What makes the disc especially attractive is the splendid account of the *Handel variations*, which acts as an exhilarating (26-minute) encore. Van Cliburn plays with splendid dash and often with great bravura, displaying a wide range of timbre and dynamic. He is never heavy-handed, yet the closing fugue is a *tour de force*. The 1964 sound in the *Concerto* is good if not always ideally expansive, in spite of the Boston acoustics, but the solo work, recorded a decade later, gives little if any cause for complaint. This is one of Van Cliburn's best records.

Rubinstein's is a poetic and essentially lyrical reading, impulsive and avoiding Brahmsian stodginess – though it is by no means without power, for Reiner's control of the orchestra, volatile and imaginative, has a spacious strength. The only snag is the forward balance of the piano, which means that a real pianissimo fails to register, although the 1954 recording attractively brings out the brightness of Rubinstein's tone against the warm Chicago backcloth.

Arrau's reading has vision and power and, though there are some characteristic agogic distortions that will not convince all listeners, he is majestic and eloquent. There is never an ugly sonority even in the moments of the greatest vehemence. By the side of Curzon he seems idiosyncratic but, given the excellence of the digitally remastered recording and the warmth of Haitink's support, this is well worth considering in the medium-price range.

Israela Margalit is a most musical exponent of this most leonine of concertos, and she is certainly given a recording of some sumptuousness. Her account is far more than just an also-ran, but the overall impression makes it less commanding than the finest available versions. However, there is much to admire.

Barry Douglas possesses ample technical command and takes a cool, dispassionate view of the first movement. He is a big player but can also produce impressive pianissimo quality in the slow movement – even if, by comparison with the greatest players, he is a little short on poetic feeling. The finale needs a little more momentum, but there is still much in this performance that will give satisfaction to his admirers.

Piano concerto No. 2 in B flat, Op. 83.
(M) *** RCA GD 86518 [RCA 6518-2-RG]. Sviatoslav Richter, Chicago SO, Leinsdorf –
BEETHOVEN: *Piano sonata No. 23.****
(M) *** DG 419 471-2 [id.]. Pollini, VPO, Abbado.
(M) **(*) Ph. 420 885-2 [id.]. Arrau, Concg. O, Haitink.
(B) **(*) CfP CD-CFP 4563. Martino Tirimo, LPO, Yoel Levi.
(M) (**(*)) DG mono 427 778-2 [id.]. Edwin Fischer, BPO, Furtwängler.
(M) ** Ph. 426 633-2 [id.]. Brendel, Concg. O, Haitink.

(i) *Piano concerto No. 2; Intermezzi, Op. 117/1–2; Op. 119/1–3.*
(M) ** RCA GD 87942 [7942-2-RG]. Van Cliburn, (i) Chicago SO, Reiner.

Piano concerto No. 2; Intermezzi: in E min., Op. 116/5; in B flat min., Op. 117/2; Rhapsody in G min., Op. 79/2.
*** RCA RD 85671. Rubinstein, RCA SO, Josef Krips.

(i) *Piano concerto No. 2; Variations on a theme of Haydn.*
*(*) Telarc Dig. CD 80197 [id.]. Guitérrez, RPO, Previn.

Richter's 1960 performance has all the intensity of a live occasion and finds him in splendid form. It is wayward, mannered in places, but the basic structure is always kept in sight; there is impressive weight and authority as well as a warm Brahmsian lyrical feeling, and it is far more spontaneous and dashing than his later recording with Maazel and the Orchestre de Paris for EMI. The Chicago acoustics ensure that the orchestral texture is full-bodied and atmospheric and the piano timbre sounds fuller than before. With an exciting account of Beethoven's *Appassionata Sonata* as coupling, this remains highly recommendable.

Pollini's 1977 recording makes a good alternative choice, also at mid-price. Pollini's account is powerful, in many ways more classical in feeling than Gilels's or Richter's. He has the measure of the work's scale and breadth and is given first-rate support by the Vienna Philharmonic under Abbado. The remastered sound has a Brahmsian body and warmth and, although the upper range is not as open as a digital recording would be, it sounds more modern than the RCA CD.

Rubinstein was at his peak (in 1958) and his technical mastery brings a scintillating response to the changing moods of the first movement, while the finale is a delight with its deftness of articulation and rippling lyricism. Krips brings a Viennese touch to the orchestra and matches Rubinstein's spontaneity. This is a reading which emphasizes the bright and luminous aspects of the work and is all the more refreshing for that, even if the piano, for all its vivid realism, is almost in one's lap, and the close balance means that a true pianissimo is never registered. The three substantial encores are well chosen to make a miniature (15-minute) solo recital after the concerto; once again, the sound is realistic and the playing distinguished.

Arrau's account of the concerto is competitive at medium price. There are one or two idiosyncratic touches, but the playing has a splendid combination of aristocratic finesse and warmth of feeling, and Haitink and the Concertgebouw Orchestra give excellent support. The engineers strike the right balance between the piano and orchestra, and the orchestral texture is better focused and cleaner than in the earlier Arrau recording.

This was Tirimo's début recording, made in 1982. He gives a commanding if measured account of the first movement, not always quite tidy in its occasional impulsiveness (but then neither is Richter). The second and fourth movements too have slow basic tempi, but the clarity of articulation gives a sharpness of focus to conceal that, and both are made exuberant and joyful. The recording has fine weight and range. Well worth considering in the bargain range.

Van Cliburn could not have a more committed or sympathetic accompanist than Reiner, and the Chicago orchestra create a richly spacious background tapestry for their soloist. Cliburn plays powerfully and shows a ready response to Brahmsian lyricism. There is much that is fine here, but the first movement lacks something in overall grip and the tension is not sustained consistently. The recording, from the early 1970s, is faithful and very well transferred. As a bonus, Cliburn offers five *Intermezzi*, but these are disappointingly lacking in spontaneity.

The DG mono performance comes from a set recorded during the war on 14-inch reels of iron-oxide tape at 30 i.p.s, which was (rightly) considered remarkable in its time. There is some distortion, but the playing of Edwin Fischer has an impressive humanity and dignity, and there is a special intensity and inspiration to the music-making here that is quite memorable.

Brendel's is a finely recorded performance, but the performance falls a little below expectations.. He seems too judicious and adopts a deliberately restrained approach, so keen is he to eschew the grand manner. The results, though always commanding respect, are not wholly convincing, but the engineers produce excellent sound.

In spite of the generous playing time, the Guitérrez/Previn recording has nothing special to recommend it. It is the kind of performance which you would hear with approval in the concert hall but which does not have quite the distinction or character to prompt you to return to it.

Violin concerto in D, Op. 77.
(M) *** Ph. 420 703-2 [id.]. Grumiaux, New Philh. O, C. Davis – BRUCH: *Concerto No. 1.***(*)

*** RCA RD 85402 [RCD1 5402]. Heifetz, Chicago SO, Reiner – BEETHOVEN: *Concerto*.**(*)

**(*) DG Dig. 400 064-2 [id.]. Mutter, BPO, Karajan.

(M) (***) EMI mono CDH7 61011-2 [id.]. Ginette Neveu, Philh. O, Issay Debrowen – SIBELIUS: *Concerto*.(***)

(M) **(*) EMI CDM7 69034-2 [id.]. David Oistrakh, French Nat. R. O, Klemperer.

**(*) EMI CDC7 47166-2 [id.]. Perlman, Chicago SO, Giulini.

(B) Pickwick Duet 9 CD [CBS MGT 31418]. Stern, Phd. O, Ormandy – BEETHOVEN: *Violin concerto*.

(i) *Violin concerto; Academic festival overture, Op. 80.*
**(*) DG Dig. 423 617-2 [id.]. Mintz, BPO, Abbado.

(i) *Violin concerto;* (ii) *Hungarian dances Nos. 1, 3, 5, 6, 17–21.*
(B) *** EMI CDZ7 62608-2. (i) Menuhin, BPO, Kempe; (ii) RPO, Kubelik.

(i) *Violin concerto in D; Tragic overture, Op. 81.*
(B) *** Ph. 422 972-2 [id.]. (i) Hermann Krebbers; Concg. O, Haitink.

(i) *Violin concerto in D;* (ii) *Violin sonata No. 1 in G, Op. 78.*
(B) **(*) DG 429 513-2 [id.]. Ferras, (i) BPO, Karajan; (ii) Pierre Barbizet.

Hermann Krebbers, concertmaster of the Concertgebouw Orchestra, but also a master violinist of the first order in his own right, gives here one of the most deeply satisfying readings of the Brahms *Violin concerto* ever recorded: strong and urgent yet tenderly poetic too, and always full of spontaneous imagination. The total commitment behind the performance is not just the achievement of the soloist, but also that of his colleagues and their conductor, who perform as at a live concert. The vintage, 1973 recording has been successfully remastered: the effect, with the violin slightly forward but not too obtrusively so, is full and immediate. The *Tragic overture* makes a suitable encore after the *Concerto*.

Reissued in EMI's bargain Laser series, with Kubelik's group of *Hungarian dances* offered as an engaging additional incentive, Menuhin's recording from the end of the 1950s can be given the strongest recommendation. He was in superb form, producing tone of great beauty, while the reading is memorable for its warmth and nobility. He was splendidly accompanied by Kempe, and the Berlin Philharmonic was inspired to outstanding playing – the oboe solo in the slow movement is particularly fine. The sound remains satisfyingly well balanced and now compares very favourably indeed with any of the top recommendations for this work.

Grumiaux's performance of the Brahms *Concerto*, it goes without saying, is full of insight and lyrical eloquence, and Sir Colin Davis lends his soloist the most sympathetic support; at mid-price, coupled with the Max Bruch *G minor Concerto* (a work with which Grumiaux, with his essentially classical style, has slightly less natural affinity), this excellent CD could well be first choice for many readers, particularly in view of the excellence of the remastered Philips sound, which is firm, detailed and refined, with believable presence and a warm ambience.

Like the Beethoven on the reverse, the CD transfer of Heifetz's dazzling performance makes vivid and fresh what on LP was originally a rather harsh Chicago recording, more aggressive than the Boston sound in the Beethoven. With the CD, the excellent qualities of RCA's Chicago balance for Reiner come out in full, giving a fine three-dimensional focus. The speeds for all three movements may be fast, but Heifetz's ease and detailed imagination make them more than just dazzling, while the central *Andante*, at a flowing speed, is delectably songful.

In many ways the playing of Anne-Sophie Mutter combines the unforced lyrical feeling of Krebbers with the flair and individuality of Perlman. There is a lightness of touch, a gentleness in the slow movement that is highly appealing, while in the finale the incisiveness of the solo playing is well displayed by the clear (yet not clinical) digital recording. Needless to say, Karajan's accompaniment is strong in personality and the Berlin Philharmonic play beautifully; the performance represents a genuine musical partnership between youthful inspiration and eager experience. The recording is given vivid presence, although its clarity emphasizes the close balance of the soloist, and there is a touch of fierceness in the orchestral upper range in tuttis. The lack of any coupling must also reduce the claims of this version.

Shlomo Mintz and Claudio Abbado give a beautifully cultured reading that is both relaxed and lyrical. Mintz is less than generously coupled, but he does have the advantage of a superbly balanced recording and predictably fine orchestral playing. Only in the rather heavy-handed finale does it fall short of real excellence; it belongs among the best without actually being a first choice – not that there can be any in these days of such duplication – but no one investing in it will be greatly disappointed. The *Academic festival overture*, well played though it is, hardly affects choice.

Ginette Neveu's is a magnificent performance, urgently electric, remarkable not just for the sweetness of tone and pinpoint intonation but for the precision and clarity of even the most formidable passages of double-stopping. This is a reading as remarkable for its toughness and power as for the warmth and poetry one would expect from an outstanding woman virtuoso. Though dynamic contrasts are limited, the transfer from the original 78s brings satisfyingly full-bodied sound, surprisingly good on detail. Coupled with the Sibelius on a mid-price Références disc, it makes an outstanding bargain.

The conjunction of two such positive artists as Oistrakh and Klemperer makes for a reading characterful to the point of idiosyncrasy, monumental and strong rather than sweetly lyrical. Oistrakh sounds superbly poised and confident, and in the finale, if the tempo is a shade deliberate, the total effect is one of clear gain. The 1961 recording is quite full, but the bright CD transfer has brought an element of steeliness to the solo violin timbre.

A distinguished account of the solo part from Perlman, finely supported by Giulini and the Chicago Symphony Orchestra, a reading of darker hue than is customary, with a thoughtful, searching slow movement rather than the autumnal rhapsody which it so often becomes; granted a certain want of impetus in the first movement, this is an impressive and convincing performance. However, with no coupling this seems too highly priced.

Much depends on one's attitude to Ferras's tone-colour whether the Ferras/Karajan CD version is a good recommendation or not. DG have placed him close to the microphone so that the smallness of tone that in the concert hall is disappointing is certainly not evident here. Moreover there is a jewelled accuracy about the playing that is most appealing, and Karajan conducts vividly. The recording is of good quality and the CD transfer is of striking liveliness, bright on top though not shrill. The *Violin sonata*, which is very pleasingly done, appropriately sounds more intimate and subdued.

Stern's 1959 recording, with Ormandy, made when he was at the peak of his career, is undoubtedly a great performance, although the mid-priced CD issue has lost some of its orchestral body and the ear is drawn to the artificial, forward balance of the soloist. However, Stern's playing still emerges as ripely full-bodied, and Ormandy contributes a wonderfully positive Brahmsian warmth to a reading that carries the listener forward in its expressive spontaneity and fire. The alternative Pickwick coupling has been further remastered, so that the highlighting of the soloist is even more striking and brings impossibly shrill orchestral fortissimos, which are too fierce to give any listening satisfaction.

Double concerto for violin, cello and orchestra in A min., Op. 102.
*** CBS Dig. MK 42387 [id.]. Isaac Stern, Yo-Yo Ma, Chicago SO, Abbado – *Piano quartet No. 3.***
(B) *** EMI CDZ7 62854-2 [id.]. D. Oistrakh, Fournier, Philh. O, Galliera – BEETHOVEN: *Triple concerto.***(*)
(B) **(*) CBS MYK 44771 [id.]. Francescatti, Fournier, Columbia SO, Bruno Walter – SCHUMANN: *Piano concerto.***(*)
(M) **(*) EMI Dig. CDM7 63022-2. Menuhin, Tortelier, LPO, Berglund – DELIUS: *Double concerto***(*)

Double concerto; Tragic overture, Op. 81.
**(*) DG Dig. 410 603-2 [id.]. Mutter, Meneses, BPO, Karajan.

The CBS version with Isaac Stern, Yo-Yo Ma and the Chicago Symphony Orchestra under Claudio Abbado is one of the more successful of recent years and deserves a full recommendation. The balance is well judged, not too up-front as is the case with some rivals. There are occasional moments when Yo-Yo Ma reduces his tone to the barest whisper rather than a pianissimo, but for the most part expressive exaggeration is minimal and the playing of both soloists and orchestra alike is glorious. The *Piano quartet* coupling, however, is rather less successful.

With two young soloists, Karajan conducts an outstandingly spacious and strong performance. Anne-Sophie Mutter conveys a natural authority comparable to Karajan's own, and the precision and clarity of Meneses' cello as recorded make an excellent match. The central slow movement in its spacious way has a wonderful Brahmsian glow, and all these qualities come out the more vividly on CD, though the relatively close balance of the soloists – particularly the cellist – is evident, too. However, the coupling is not remarkably generous.

David Oistrakh's recording with Fournier dates from 1959, but it was balanced by Walter Legge and the sound remains remarkably satisfying. The performance is distinguished, strong and lyrical – the slow movement particularly fine – and, with Galliera and the Philharmonia providing excellent support, this version, coupled with Beethoven's *Triple concerto*, makes a good choice for bargain-hunters.

Bruno Walter's recording with Francescatti and Fournier dates from 1959 and the compact disc represents another example of successful digital remastering which enhances the original balance within an attractively warm ambience. Fournier is magnificent and, if one can adjust to Francescatti's rather intense vibrato, this can stand among the most satisfying of available versions. Walter draws playing of great warmth from the Columbia orchestra and oversees the reading as a whole with his customary humanity, yet tuttis are thrillingly expansive and vital.

In the version by Menuhin and Tortelier the soloists are placed well forward, but the result is more genial, as well as big and positive. The challenge between two volatile, inspirational artists brings the best out of both of them, with the slow movement sweet and relaxed and the finale slower than usual but nicely lilting and crisply pointed. Excellent, full recording, debatable only on the question of the forwardness of the soloists.

Hungarian dances Nos. 1–21 (complete).
*** Ph. Dig. 411 426-2 [id.]. Leipzig GO, Masur.
*** DG Dig. 410 615-2 [id.]. VPO, Abbado.
(BB) ** LaserLight Dig. 15501 [id.]. Hungarian PO, János Sándor.

In Nos. 5 and 6 Masur uses Parlow's scoring instead of Martin Schmelling (as preferred by Abbado) and in Nos. 7 and 8 he opts for Schollum rather than Hans Gál. Masur is just a shade more relaxed and smiling and the timbre of the strings is generally richer and warmer than that achieved by the DG engineers in Vienna. Abbado has great sparkle and lightness, but the Leipzig orchestra is hardly less dazzling than the Viennese. The Philips issue has the finer sound.

The Hungarian performances are essentially mellow, and the feeling of warmth is emphasized by the resonant acoustics of the auditorium. Even though this is a digital recording, it is comfortably subdued in the upper range. Some might feel, too, that these dances, although very well played and obviously idiomatic, could use a little more dash.

Hungarian dances Nos. 1, 5–7, 12–13, 19, 21.
(B) **(*) Decca 417 696-2. VPO, Reiner – DVORÁK: *Slavonic dances.***(*)

Reiner's collection was a favourite record of the late John Culshaw, and the recording (from the beginning of the 1960s) wears its years fairly lightly. Reiner indulges himself in rubato and effects of his own (witness No. 12); but the affection of the music-making is obvious, and the sound balances a bright upper range with ambient warmth.

Serenades Nos. 1 in D, Op. 11; 2 in A, Op. 16.
**(*) Orfeo C 008101A [id.]. VSO, Gary Bertini.
(B) **(*) Decca 421 628-2 [id.]. LSO, Kertesz.

Serenade No. 1 in D, Op. 11.
** DG Dig. 410 654-2 [id.]. BPO, Abbado.
** RCA Dig. RD 86247 [RCA 6247-2]. St Louis SO, Slatkin.

Bertini's account of the opening movement of the *D Major Serenade*, with its rollicking horns, has a boisterous geniality which is engaging, and throughout both works he draws much fine playing from the Vienna Symphony Orchestra; the woodwind provide appealing colour, beautifully blended at the opening and in the *Rondo* finale of the A major work, and charming the ear in the Minuets of both. Bertini maintains a fairly strong momentum for the *Adagio* slow movements, which is sensible enough, but he captures the relaxed atmosphere better in Op. 16 than in Op. 11. The resonant recording sounds really lovely at lower dynamic levels (with more bloom than on the remastered Decca sound for Kertesz), but in fortissimos the opulence also brings a suggestion of heaviness, at times giving a rather 'symphonic' impression. However, there is much agreeable Brahmsian warmth here; in general the greater amplitude of the sound is an advantage, and this is marginally preferable to the Kertesz coupling.

Both Kertesz performances are beautifully relaxed but at the same time alert, and the 1968 Decca recording emerges clearer in detail, with a drier effect at the bass end, yet with the hall ambience retaining most of the bloom. A bargain; but in some ways the original LPs sounded sweeter.

Neither of the alternative versions of Brahms's delightful *D major Serenade* is ideal. Abbado's performance is a fine one, vital, imaginative and sensitive, but the digital recording is rather dry and lacking in bloom, though clear enough in its CD format. Leonard Slatkin gives a very well-paced and tautly conceived performance, but with no want of personality. The recording is perfectly good without being in the demonstration bracket: although the acoustic here is far from dry, it could do with a little more warmth.

Serenade No. 2 in A, Op. 16 – see also below under *Symphony No. 3.*

Symphonies Nos. 1–4.
(M) **(*) DG 429 644-2 (3) [id.]. BPO, Karajan.

Symphonies Nos. 1–4; Academic festival overture, Op. 80; Tragic overture, Op. 81.
(M) **(*) Decca 421 074-2 (4) [id.]. Chicago SO, Solti.

Symphonies Nos. 1–4; Tragic overture; Variations on a theme of Haydn.
**(*) DG Dig. 427 602-2 (3) [id.]. BPO, Karajan.

Broadly, Karajan's 1978 cycle shows that his readings of the Brahms *Symphonies*, with lyrical and dramatic elements finely balanced, changed little over the years. It is worth noting that his approach to No. 3 is stronger and more direct, with less mannered phrasing in the third movement, but that he continues to omit the first-movement exposition repeat. The playing of the Berlin Philharmonic remains uniquely cultivated: the ensemble is finely polished, yet can produce tremendous bravura at times, as in the finales to the *First* and *Second symphonies*. The remastering has freshened the sound: textures are clear and clean, but the effect is slightly polarized, with a bright, clean treble and a strong, firmly focused bass. There is less emphasis in the middle frequencies so that the Brahmsian richness is conveyed less readily. On three mid-priced discs, this apppears to be good value, but there was plenty of room on the first and third discs to include the *Overtures* and the *Haydn variations*.

With variably focused sound, Karajan's last cycle of the Brahms *Symphonies* is not his finest; but he remained a natural Brahmsian to the last, and this compilation, with Nos. 2 and 3 on the second disc, and No. 4 coupled with the *Variations*, makes a better investment than the original issues, for those who must have digital sound.

Sir Georg Solti's Chicago cycle of the four symphonies in a mid-price box makes a satisfying, individual set. These are all spacious rather than impetuous readings, marked by beautifully refined, poised playing by the Chicago orchestra, notably the strings. Even at slow speeds, tension and electricity remain not always relaxed enough in lyricism. The recording is warmly atmospheric with a weighty – at times over-weighty – bass.

Symphony No. 1 in C min., Op. 68.
(B) **(*) CBS MYK 44827. Columbia SO, Bruno Walter.
**(*) DG Dig. 423 141-2 [id.]. BPO, Karajan.
** Decca 414 458-2 [id.]. Chicago SO, Solti.
(M) ** EMI Dig. CD-EMX 2160. LPO, Tennstedt.
(M) ** DG Dig. 427 804-2 [id.] (with SCHUMANN: *Manfred overture*). LAPO, Giulini.

Symphony No. 1; Academic festival overture, Op. 80.
(B) *** Pickwick Dig. PCD 882 [MCA MCAD 25188]. Hallé O, Skrowaczewski.

Symphony No. 1; Academic festival overture; Tragic overture.
(M) *** EMI CDM7 69651-2 [id.]. Philh. O, Klemperer.

(i) *Symphony No. 1*; (ii) *Tragic overture, Op. 81.*
(B) *** EMI CDZ7 62604-2. LPO, Jochum.
(M) *** EMI CDM7 69251-2 [id.]. (i) LPO; (ii) LSO, Boult.

Symphony No. 1; Variations on a theme of Haydn, Op. 56a.
(M) *** DG 427 253-2 [id.]. BPO, Karajan.
(BB) **(*) Naxos Dig. 8.550278 [id.]. Belgian R. PO, Brussels, Alexander Rahbari.

(M) (***) DG mono 427 402-2 [id.]. BPO, Furtwängler.
(BB) * Hung. White Label HRC 109 [id.]. (i) Budapest SO, Lehel; (ii) Hungarian State O, Németh.

Klemperer's monumental performance was recorded in the Kingsway Hall over a long time-span (between December 1955 and March 1957), yet the interpretation lost nothing in consistency. The spacious opening with its thundering, relentless timpani strokes is as compelling as ever and the close of the work has a comparable majesty. Elsewhere, other versions may find greater incandescence, but the reading remains unique for its feeling of authority and power, supported by consistently fine Philharmonia playing. The remastered recording has gained in clarity while retaining its fullness, but has lost a little in weight, although the bass is firmer and clearer than on LP. Even those who find Klemperer's approach too marmoreal must respond to its integrity. The *Tragic overture* suits Klemperer particularly well, but the *Academic festival overture* is made to sound grand rather than high-spirited.

On EMI's cheapest label, Laser, Jochum's outstanding coupling of the *First Symphony* with the two overtures is not only generous but brings excellent performances, vividly recorded, of three of the composer's most approachable works. Taken from Jochum's Brahms series for EMI, recorded in 1977, the *Symphony* is given an exceptionally strong reading, broad in the outer movements – with the exposition repeat observed in the first – and seamlessly lyrical in the *Andante*. The expectant opening of the *Academic festival overture* is most telling, when the first-rate EMI recording captures the bass drum so vividly.

Walter's first two movements have a white-hot intensity that shows this conductor at his very finest. He conveys the architecture of the first movement strongly. The second movement too is most impressive, warm and with natural, unforced phrasing. The third movement begins with a less than ravishing clarinet solo and, though the 6/8 section is lively enough, the playing is not as crisp as in the first two movements. In the finale the performance reasserts itself, although some might find the big string tune too slow. The remastered recording makes the strings sound richly beautiful here; and later the brass is comparably sonorous. The 1960 recording is full and well balanced; as sound, this is preferable to many more recent versions.

Karajan in his 1987 recording draws a typically powerful and dramatic performance from the Berlin Philharmonic. The sound is full and weighty to match on CD, but tends to be thick and generalized in tuttis. It is comfortable enough overall but could be better defined. Characteristically Karajan does not observe the first-movement exposition repeat; with any reservations about that and the relative lack of inner clarity, this still takes its place among the list of top recommendations. However, Karajan's 1964 analogue recording - his fourth - is still highly recommendable (especially at mid-price) and the sound is still remarkably good. Many will prefer it to the the digital version: the superbly committed response of the Berlin Philharmonic players, in repertoire to which they are completely attuned, is a joy in itself.

Boult's is a noble and impressive performance, among the most distinguished of the LP era. There is no attempt to score interpretative points; the reading is admirably classical and objective. Boult observes the exposition repeat in the first movement and is true to every indication of Brahms's score. It is splendidly played, too, and is very satisfying for repeated listening – a sound mid-priced recommendation. The *Tragic overture* is also well done, but is not as fine as the *Symphony*.

Opening powerfully with thundering timpani in the manner of Klemperer, though with generally more relaxed tempi, Alexander Rahbari gives an account of Brahms's *First* that is certainly recommendable. It is a strong, direct reading, spacious yet with plenty of impetus. The inner movements are well contrasted, with soaring eloquence in the *Andante*, and though there are one or two minor idiosyncrasies in the finale the reading holds together convincingly, even the broadening at the end. The sound is full and rich, yet detail is clear. The *Variations* bring a lighter, more lyrical Brahms style but are no less spontaneously successful. A very good choice for those with limited budgets, although Jochum's Laser version is even finer.

Skrowaczewski conducts the Hallé in a powerful performance of No. 1, both warmly sympathetic and refined, with sound which is fresh, bright and clear and with a good, open atmosphere. The first movement is ideally paced, purposeful without undue rush – and also without the exposition repeat. Few other accounts of the slow movement are as delicate as Skrowaczewski's, with the hushed opening given simple gravity. His view of the finale is big and bold, but with a rather old-fashioned slowing for the final appearance of the chorale theme in the coda. With an account of the *Academic festival overture* textured with similar refinement, it makes an excellent bargain-price digital choice.

Despite a limited recording – taken from a live 1952 broadcst – which becomes ill-focused in heavy tuttis, the weight and grandeur of Furtwängler's reading, as well as its spontaneous poetry, come out magnificently. After the richness of the first movement, the slow movement is spacious and loving, and though characteristically in the finale Furtwängler moulds the tempo freely, he conceals the gear-changes far more cunningly than most, ending with a thrilling coda, where booming timpani adds to the excitement. The *Variations*, given a similarly weighty and personal reading, make a useful fill-up. This was one of the finest of DG's issues for the Furtwängler centenary.

With the Chicago orchestra's playing as refined as any on record, Solti directs a performance both spacious and purposeful, with the first movement given a single pulse, preserved as far as possible. Some will want more relaxation, for the tension and electricity remain here even when tempi are expansive. The recording is both atmospheric and clear. However, there is excessive bass resonance to cut back; otherwise, the original analogue sound is freshened.

Tennstedt's EMI recording has plenty of body and presence, although at the very opening the timpani are a shade boomy, and the LPO strings are less sumptuous in tone and less sophisticated in colour than some rival accounts. The reading is plain and unadorned and has something of Klemperer's integrity and directness. It is an honest and sober account, rather than an inspired one.

Giulini's spacious, 1982 digital recording with the Los Angeles Philharmonic Orchestra has been reissued at mid-price, coupled with Schumann's *Manfred overture*. His keen control of rhythm generally means that the slowness does not deteriorate into heaviness, but the speed for the big C major theme in the finale is so slow that it sounds self-conscious and the movement loses its concentration.

Although the Hungaroton disc is also in the bargain basement, collectors would do better to look elsewhere. The sound is good, but the outer movements of the *Symphony* are lacking in thrust and momentum. The *Variations* (which shrewdly have been placed first) are more successful.

Symphony No. 2 in D, Op. 73.
(M) *** EMI CDM7 69227-2 [id.]. Philh. O, Karajan – SCHUBERT: *Symphony No. 8.****

Symphony No. 2; Academic festival overture, Op. 80.
(B) *** CBS MYK 44870 [id.]. Columbia SO, Bruno Walter.
* Ph. Dig. 422 334-2 [id.]. Phd. O, Muti.

Symphony No. 2 in D; Academic festival overture; (i) *Song of destiny.*
(M) **(*) EMI CDM7 63221-2 [id.]. (i) Beecham Ch. Soc.; RPO, Beecham.

Symphony No. 2; Tragic overture, Op. 81.
(B) **(*) Pickwick Dig. PCD 857 [MCA MCAD 25160]. Hallé O, Skrowaczewski.
** Decca 414 487-2 [id.]. Chicago SO, Solti.

Symphony No. 2; Variations on a theme of Haydn, Op. 56a.
*** DG Dig. 423 142-2 [id.]. BPO, Karajan.

Symphony No. 2; (i) *Alto rhapsody, Op. 53.*
*** DG Dig. 427 643-2 [id.]. (i) Lipovšek, Senff Ch.; BPO, Abbado.
(M) *** EMI CDM7 69650-2 [id.]. (i) Ludwig, Philh. Ch.; Philh. O, Klemperer.

This was the first recording to be issued from Abbado with the Berlin Philharmonic after his appointment was announced as chief conductor of the orchestra. Though the recording was made before the decision was taken, its glowing intensity from first to last reflects a special relationship, one of his very finest discs in years, bringing DG sound of exceptional fullness, vividness and reality. Among modern versions this now stands as an easy first choice, particularly when, with Marjana Lipovšek a radiant soloist, it also contains a gravely beautiful account of the *Alto rhapsody.* Abbado's approach to Brahms is generally direct, but his control of rhythm and phrase makes the performance instantly compelling. He observes the exposition repeat in the first movement; and there, as well as in the slow movement, the nobility of Brahms's inspiration is fully brought out, while in the finale, through his rhythmic control, Abbado makes a relatively measured speed sound much more exciting than it does with any of the speed-merchants. This is an outstanding version in every way.

Walter's performance is wonderfully sympathetic, with an inevitability, a rightness which makes it hard to concentrate on the interpretation as such, so cogent is the musical argument. As though to balance the romanticism of his approach on detail, Walter keeps his basic speeds surprisingly constant, yet little of the passion is lost in consequence. It is a masterly conception overall and one very easy to live with. The CD opens with a vigorous and yet expansive account of the *Academic festival overture,* sumptuously recorded; in the remastering of the *Symphony* there is some loss in the lower middle and bass, which is less richly resonant than in the *First Symphony.* But the bloom remains and the middle string timbre is always fresh and warm.

In his 1987 Brahms series, Karajan's reading of the *Second Symphony* suffers less than the *First* from the thick, undifferentiated recording, when textures in this later work tend to be lighter. It is a magnificent reading, even warmer and more glowing than his previous versions, with consistently fine playing from the Berlin Philharmonic, who approach with striking freshness a symphony which they must have played countless times. As in the *First Symphony,* Karajan omits the first-movement exposition repeat, but compensates with an appealing performance of the *Haydn variations.* However, his splendid mid-1960s version is now available, coupled with No. 3 and offered at bargain price – see below.

Klemperer's is also a great performance, the product of a strong and vital intelligence. He may seem a trifle severe and uncompromising; but he was at his peak in his Brahms cycle and he underlines the power of the *Symphony* without diminishing its eloquence in any way. The *Alto rhapsody,* with Klemperer at his most masterful and Ludwig on fine form, is a beautifully expressive performance that brings out the work's strength as well as its lyricism. Ludwig sings gloriously in the opening section, and later her voice blends beautifully with the male chorus. The remastered recording is outstanding here; the *Symphony* sounds full and clear, with telling viola and cello timbre; but there is a degree of shrillness on the *ff* massed violins.

Karajan's 1957 EMI account with the Philharmonia unfolds with an unforced naturalness that is warmly compelling. Yet for all the relaxed atmosphere, the grip that all his Berlin accounts have shown is strongly evident here. The recording has less range than modern accounts, but it is beautifully balanced, and the substantial Schubert coupling is no less distinguished.

Though the CD transfer of the *Symphony* brings some rough sound – less well focused than in the two fill-up items – the Beecham magic makes this volatile reading consistently compelling. The accompanying booklet reveals that it was recorded at no fewer than six separate recording sessions, spread between November 1958 and November 1959. The quirkiness of the performance rather reflects that. The horns at the opening may be disappointing, but the first movement is then urgently riveting at speeds faster than usual. Beecham is on the fast side too in the second-movement Adagio, but his fine detailing there and in the third movement are totally distinctive, and the finale, rough at times, predictably brings an exhilarating close. The fill-ups are equally desirable, particularly the rare *Song of destiny*, sung in Denis Vaughan's English translation.

A powerful, weighty performance from Solti, its lyrical feeling passionately expressed in richly upholstered textures. The reading displays a broad nobility, but the charm and delicately gracious qualities of the music are much less a part of Solti's view. Solti includes the first-movement exposition repeat and offers a splendidly committed account of the *Tragic overture* as a bonus. On CD, the bass has to be tamed if boominess is not to spoil the otherwise pleasing analogue sound.

With beautifully open and transparent sound, Skrowaczewski and the Hallé Orchestra give a measured and restrained reading, unsensational, fresh and thoughtful. The opening may seem sleepy, but Skrowaczewski's broad speeds and patient manner build up increasingly as the work progresses. With exposition repeat observed and a generous fill-up, plus excellent digital recording, luminous to match the performance, it is a good bargain-priced recommendation.

Like the version of No. 4 which began Muti's Brahms cycle for Philips, his account of No. 2 is disappointing, partly because of murky sound, with even the famed Philadelphia violins sounding scrawny. The interpretation is inconsistent too, with the first movement warmly (if sometimes self-consciously) moulded, and the rest surprisingly plain and unlifted until the dashing finale. The *Overture* sounds pedestrian.

Symphonies Nos. 2–3.
(B) *** DG 429 153-2 [id.]. BPO, Karajan.
(M) **(*) Ph. 426 632-2 [id.]. Concg. O, Haitink.

Karajan's 1964 reading of the *Second* is among the sunniest and most lyrical accounts, and its sound is fully competitive even now. The companion performance of the *Third* is marginally less compelling, but still very fine. He takes the opening expansively – which makes it surprising that he omits the exposition repeat. But clearly he sees the work as a whole: the third movement is also slow and perhaps slightly indulgent, but the closing pages of the finale have a memorable autumnal serenity. A bargain.

Haitink's account of No. 2 opens soberly. The tempo is slow, the manner bald and uncompromising. The sunshine quickly breaks through, however, so that the gentle high entry of the violins is magically sweet. This is a thoughtful reading, marked by beautifully refined string playing, but in a way it is too controlled. The *Third* is much more impressive. The playing of the Concertgebouw Orchestra here is distinguished by unanimity of attack and chording, wonderfully true intonation and homogeneity of tone; and Haitink's firmness of grip and lyrical eloquence make this a very satisfying account. The sound is fresh yet full in the Philips manner.

Symphony No. 3 in F, Op. 90.
(M) *** EMI CDH7 63085-2 [id.]. Philh. O, Cantelli – SCHUMANN: *Symphony No. 4.*(***)
(M) ** Decca 417 744-2 [id.]. VPO, Karajan – DVOŘÁK: *Symphony No. 8.**(**)

Symphony No. 3; Academic festival overture, Op. 80.
** Decca 414 488-2 [id.]. Chicago SO, Solti.

(i) *Symphony No. 3;* (ii) *Serenade No. 2 in A, Op. 16; Academic festival overture.*
(M) **(*) EMI CDM7 69203-2 [id.]. (i) LSO; (ii) LPO, Sir Adrian Boult.

Symphony No. 3; Tragic overture.
** DG Dig. 427 496-2 [id.]. BPO, Karajan.

Symphony No. 3; Variations on a theme of Haydn, Op. 56a.
(B) *** Pickwick Dig. PCD 906 [MCA MCAD 25857]. Hallé O, Skrowaczewski.

Guido Cantelli's 1955 version with the Philharmonia offers one of the most glowing performances of the work ever put on record; and the early stereo CD transfer is astonishingly full and vivid. The *Andante* is taken broadly and expressively but without sentimentality; and the incandescence of the outer movements makes one regret all the more that such a genius of a conductor died so young. Coupled with his other great symphony recording with the Philharmonia, Schumann's *Fourth*, this is an outstanding issue in EMI's Références series.

Skrowaczewski chooses consistently slow tempi for the central movements, yet with refined playing there is no hint of dragging. In the third movement he underlines the tender wistfulness, with a gorgeous horn solo in the reprise, full and spacious. The hush at the start of the finale then leads to a powerfully rhythmic performance, ending with a beautifully refined account of the gentle coda. Only in the high violin lines at the very start of the work does the sound grow edgy, and that is more marked on some machines than on others. An excellent digital bargain-price version, well coupled with a fresh reading of the *Haydn variations*.

If there are slight reservations about the sound – which isn't ideally open, although there is no lack of Brahmsian warmth – Boult's mid-priced CD offers a happily unusual coupling. The 1971 performance of the *Third Symphony* has great dignity and spaciousness. Boult captures the autumnal feeling of the slow movement with great success, after including the exposition repeat in the first. It is essentially a mellow performance, keenly lyrical in feeling, but the LSO play with great enthusiasm and fire, so the music-making exudes vitality. After an expansive account of the *Academic festival overture*, the *Serenade in A major* is again glowingly lyrical.

Solti takes a big-scale view of the *Third*. The epically grand opening, Solti seems to say, demands an equivalent status for the rest; and the result, lacking a little in Brahmsian idiosyncrasy, is most compelling. However, as in the others of the cycle, there is too much bass emphasis on the CD transfer.

Karajan's Decca recording from the early 1960s is not without substance in its remastered format, but the strings are fierce, the upper range exaggerated. He takes the opening expansively but, by omitting the exposition repeat – even though the account of the third movement is slow – leaves room for Dvořák's *Eighth Symphony*, a vintage performance but one also suffering from very bright lighting in its CD incarnation.

Karajan's last recording of Brahms's *Third* disappointingly brings a relatively perfunctory reading, seeming the more so when, at a fastish tempo, the first movement has no exposition repeat. However, this was Karajan's customary approach to this movement which, he presumably felt, lost something of its forward impetus if the repeat was observed. The sound too is disappointing, not clear enough in tuttis and a little shrill. The short measure also makes it poor value, especially when Karajan's first stereo recordings of Nos. 2 and 3 for DG are available on a bargain-price disc.

Symphonies Nos. 3–4.
(M) *** EMI CDM7 69649-2 [id.]. Philh. O, Klemperer.

With slow speeds and all repeats taken, Klemperer's timing in No. 3 is much more extended than usual. For all his expansiveness, however, Klemperer does not make the music sound opulent. There is a severity about his approach which may at first seem unappealing but which comes to underline the strength of the architecture. Similarly in No. 4, Klemperer's granite strength and his feeling for Brahmsian lyricism make his version one of the most satisfying ever recorded. The finale may lack something in sheer excitement, but the gravity of Klemperer's tone of voice, natural and unforced in this movement as in the others, makes for a compelling result. The remastering, like the others in the Klemperer/Brahms series, brings brightly lit violin timbre, with a hint of shrillness immediately noticeable at the surging opening of No. 3 but less so in No. 4. The orchestral focus is admirably clear, with woodwind fairly forward, and there is no lack of body in the middle, while the bass is firmer.

Symphony No. 4 in E min., Op. 98.
**(*) DG Dig. 400 037-2 [id.]. VPO, Carlos Kleiber.
(M) **(*) EMI CDM7 69228-2 [id.]. Philh. O, Karajan – LISZT: *Les Préludes.****
**(*) Decca 414 563-2 [id.]. Chicago SO, Solti.
** DG Dig. 427 497-2 [id.]. BPO, Karajan.

Symphony No. 4; Academic festival overture, Op. 80.
**(*) Telarc Dig. CD 80155 [id.]. RPO, Previn.

Symphony No. 4; Academic festival overture; Tragic overture.
(BB) * Hung. White Label HRC 108 [id.]. Budapest SO, Lehel.
(BB) (*) Naxos Dig. 8.550281 [id.]. Belgian R. PO, Brussels, Alexander Rahbari.

Symphony No. 4; Hungarian dances Nos. 1, 3 & 10.
(B) *** Pickwick Dig. PCD 897 [MCA MCAD 25230]. Hallé O, Skrowaczewski.

Symphony No 4; Tragic overture, Op. 81.
(B) *** CBS MYK 44776 [id.]. Columbia SO, Bruno Walter.
*** DG Dig. 410 084-2 [id.]. VPO, Bernstein.
(M) (***) EMI mono CDH7 69783-2 [id.]. BBC SO, Toscanini.

Symphony No. 4; Tragic overture; Variations on a theme of Haydn, Op. 56a.
*** DG 423 205-2 [id.]. BPO, Karajan.

Walter's opening is simple, even gentle, and the pervading lyricism is immediately apparent; yet power and authority are underlying. The conductor's refusal to linger by a wayside always painted in gently glowing colours adds strength and impetus, building a cumulative effect. The slow movement, essentially serene yet intense at its central climax, is balanced by a vivacious, exhilarating scherzo. The finale has an underlying impetus so that Walter creates a feeling of inevitability throughout. The *Tragic overture* opens the record powerfully, so that the mellow opening of the *Symphony* is the more striking. The

CD brings full, well-balanced sound in an attractively spacious ambience, with glowing detail. Few versions are sonically balanced more appealingly.

Karajan's 1964 version has been reissued, aptly and very generously coupled with both the *Tragic overture* and the *Haydn variations*. The performance is richer and more relaxed than the Philharmonia account, more spacious in all four movements, yet the *Passacaglia* has splendid grip in Karajan's hands and so too does the slow movement. The recording also is firmer and more wide-ranging.

Bernstein's Vienna version of Brahms's *Fourth*, recorded live, is exhilaratingly dramatic in fast music, while the slow movement brings richly resonant playing from the Vienna strings, not least in the great cello melody at bar 41, which with its moulded rubato comes to sound surprisingly like Elgar.

Any record from Carlos Kleiber is an event, and his is a performance of real stature. Everything is shaped with the attention to detail one would expect from this great conductor. A gripping and compelling performance. However, the limitations of the early digital recording are exposed here. The strings above the stave sound a little shrill and glassy, while there is a want of opulence in the bass.

The refinement of the very opening in Skrowaczewski's Pickwick version leads to an exceptionally satisfying reading, outstanding in the bargain-price range and finer than many full-price versions. The phrasing is affectionate without ever sounding self-conscious, and the alertness as well as the refinement of the Hallé playing confirms the excellence; if the coupling of only three *Hungarian dances* is hardly generous, they are certainly attractively presented.

Karajan's glowing EMI performance almost holds its own with his later, mid-1960s Berlin version. The keynote of the performance is its complete naturalness; the symphony unfolds at an unforced pace and possesses a glowing eloquence that is unfailingly impressive. The sound is remarkably good, given that it is over thirty years old. The Philharmonia play marvellously for Karajan and, with its Liszt bonus, this is a bargain.

The most distinctive point about Solti's reading, after a very direct, fast and steady first movement, is that the *Andante moderato* of the second movement is more an *Adagio*. Not everyone will like the result, but it is unfailingly pure and strong, not only in the slow movement but throughout. The playing of the Chicago orchestra is magnificent and the recording is full and precise. However, on CD the very resonant bass needs cutting well back.

Toscanini's version was recorded live in June 1935, and though the sound is inevitably limited and the playing is fallible, the interpretation brings out not only the tension of a Toscanini performance but also his warmth in freely expressive phrasing, very different from his much later NBC recording. The *Tragic overture* too has more colour and freedom than other versions he recorded.

There is a Boultian directness about the opening of Previn's account, fresh and alert, which immediately commands attention, helped by naturally balanced Telarc digital sound, just a little distanced. The finale is similarly strong and energetic, well drawn together; only in the bold third movement does the distancing detract from the impact of the performance, while allowing some clouding of inner detail. The coupling is well managed, if hardly generous.

Though this DG digital version brings the most satisfying performance from Karajan's last Brahms cycle, it lacks the spontaneous imagination of his earlier readings, also available on CD, notably the 1960s' DG version.

György Lehel's leisurely approach to Brahms comes off better in the *Fourth Symphony* than in the *First*, but the overall effect is still somewhat enervating, especially in the finale; moreover the orchestral playing lacks polish and wind textures could ideally be more homogeneous. The two *Overtures* frame the main work.

After the success of his recording of Brahms's *First*, Rahbari's account of the *Fourth* is a great disappointment. His weighty approach to the outer movements brings a serious lack of momentum and the reading entirely fails to take off.

CHAMBER MUSIC

Cello sonatas Nos. 1 in E min., Op. 38; 2 in F, Op. 99.
*** DG Dig. 410 510-2 [id.]. Mstislav Rostropovich, Rudolf Serkin.
*** Decca 414 558-2. Lynn Harrell, Vladimir Ashkenazy.
*** Hyp. Dig. CDA 66159 [id.]. Steven Isserlis, Peter Evans.
**(*) RCA Dig. RD 87022 [RCA 1-7022]. Yo-Yo Ma, Emanuel Ax.
(M) ** EMI CDM7 63298-2 [id.]. Jacqueline du Pré, Daniel Barenboim.

The partnership of the wild, inspirational Russian cellist and the veteran Brahmsian pianist is a challenging one. It proves an outstanding success, with inspiration mutually enhanced, whether in the lyricism of Op. 38 or the heroic energy of Op. 99. Good if close recording.

Harrell and Ashkenazy give almost ideal performances of the two Brahms *Cello sonatas*, strong and passionate as well as poetic. However, although they are naturally recorded and well balanced, the acoustic is resonant and the imagery lacks the last degree of sharpness of focus.

Using gut strings, Isserlis produces an exceptionally warm tone, here nicely balanced in the recording against the strong and sensitive playing of his regular piano partner. In every way these perceptive and well-detailed readings stand in competition with the finest. The heroic power of the opening of the *F major* is presented with all the projection – if at less sheer volume – that Brahms himself would have expected. Warm, unaggressive Hyperion sound.

The partnership of Yo-Yo Ma and Emanuel Ax favours the piano, for Ax sometimes produces too thick a sound in climaxes and Ma is, as always, sensitive and smaller in tone, though the grace and tenderness of his playing are not in question. Theirs is an essentially romantic view and certainly more measured in tempi than almost any of their rivals, but they have splendid rapport. The RCA recording is very truthful.

This coupling shows the Du Pré/Barenboim partnership at its stylistically most self-indulgent. Many listeners will find the blatant change of tempo between the first and second subjects in the earlier work hard to accept. At least the players tackle the second and more taxing of the *Sonatas* with a sense of its heroic size. This on the whole is the more successful of the two performances, but neither is lacking in Brahmsian warmth and flair. The remastered recording is well balanced.

Clarinet quintet in B min., Op. 115.
(M) *** EMI CDM7 63116-2 [id.]. Gervase de Peyer, Melos Ens. – MOZART: *Quintet.***
(B) *** Pickwick Dig. PCD 883 [MCA MCAD 25214]. Keith Puddy, Delmé Qt – DVORÁK: *Quartet No. 12.***
(M) **(*) Decca 417 643-2 [id.]. Boskovsky, V. Octet (members) – BAERMANN: *Adagio***(*); MOZART: *Quintet.***
(*) CRD Dig. CRD 3445 [id.]. Michael Collins, Nash Ens. – MOZART: *Clarinet quintet.*

(i) Clarinet quintet in B min., Op. 115; (ii) Clarinet trio in A min., Op. 114.
*** Hyp. CDA 66107 [id.]. King, (i) Gabrieli Qt; (ii) Georgian, Benson (piano).

(i) *Clarinet trio in A min., Op. 114;* (ii) *Horn trio in E flat, Op. 40.*
**(*) Decca Dig. 410 114-2 [id.]. (i) Schmidl, (ii) Hogner; András Schiff, New Vienna Octet (members).

Thea King and the Gabrieli Quartet give a radiantly beautiful performance of the *Clarinet quintet,* as fine as any put on record, expressive and spontaneous-sounding, with natural ebb and flow of tension as in a live performance. Not only does Thea King produce heavenly pianissimos, above all in the slow movement, she plays with exceptional bite and point in such a passage as the central Hungarian section in that movement. The *Trio,* a gentler work, brings a less positive performance – but still a most sensitive one. The recording of the strings is on the bright side, very vivid and real.

Gervase de Peyer's vintage performance of the *Clarinet quintet* with the Melos Ensemble, recorded in 1964, returns to the catalogue at mid-price in an apt and generous coupling with Mozart. It is a warmly lyrical reading, dominated by the clarinettist, who brings out wistfully autumnal overtones. The sound is full and immediate, set in a relatively dry acoustic.

Keith Puddy's warm tone is well suited to Brahms and, with spacious speeds in all four movements, this is a consistently sympathetic reading; the recording is equally fine, vivid and full. Excellent value.

Boskovsky's is a rich-toned, relaxed account; the first movement could be tauter and the slow movement is on the gentle side; with generous couplings and good sound, however, this is certainly attractive.

Michael Collins plays beautifully on CRD and the recording is most naturally balanced, but contrasts are not strong enough to bring out all the mood changes in which the work abounds. It is attractive playing, nevertheless, and the sound is first class.

With members of the New Vienna Octet joining András Schiff on Decca, the *Clarinet trio* is given a delightful performance, relaxed and warm. The *Horn trio* has less urgency, though dramatic contrasts of dynamic are strongly brought out. Schiff's incisive playing is brightly caught on the full and realistic digital recording.

(i) *Clarinet quintet, Op. 115;* (ii) *Piano quintet, Op. 34; String quintets Nos. 1–2, Opp. 88 & 111; String sextets Nos. 1–2, Opp. 18 & 36.*
(M) **(*) DG 419 875-2 (3) [id.]. (i) Leister; (ii) Eschenbach; augmented Amadeus Qt.

These performances were first issued in 1969. The playing is consistently polished and tempi are well chosen. Karl Leister plays with considerable sensitivity in the *Clarinet quintet,* while in the *Piano quintet* Christoph Eschenbach gives a powerful account of the piano part. Perhaps it is at times over-projected, but the performance has no want of life. Elsewhere the element of suavity which at times enters the Amadeus contribution seems minimized by the immediacy of the sound, and there is much to enjoy here.

(i) *Clarinet quintet in B min., Op. 115; String quintet No. 2 in G, Op. 111.*
**(*) Delos Dig. DE 3066 [id.]. (i) David Shifrin; Chamber Music NorthWest.

David Shifrin plays most beautifully in the *Clarinet quintet* and fully catches its serenity and autumnal nostalgia. He receives highly sympathetic support from Chamber Music NorthWest who find a parallel in the atmosphere of the *Adagio* of the *String quintet,* which is also played with a natural Brahmsian feeling. The recording projects Shifrin's rich, yet never too opulent timbre beautifully in a warm acoustic, but the microphones are a shade too near the strings and there is a hint of wiriness in the violins, especially in the *String quintet.*

Clarinet sonatas Nos. 1 in F min.; 2 in E flat, Op. 120/1–2.
*** Chan. Dig. CHAN 8562 [id.]. Gervase de Peyer, Gwenneth Prior.
*** Virgin Dig. VC 791076-2. Collins, Pletnev – WEBER: *Grand Duo concertante in E flat, Op. 48.****
**(*) Hyp. Dig. CDA 66202 [id.]. Thea King, Clifford Benson.
(M) **(*) RCA GD 60036 [60036-2-RG]. Richard Stoltzman, Richard Goode.

Superb performances from Gervase de Peyer and Gwenneth Prior, commanding, aristocratic, warm and full of subtleties of colour and detail. The recording too is outstandingly realistic.

Another fine version of the *Clarinet sonatas* comes from Michael Collins and Mikhail Pletnev, and this has an impressive range of feeling and colour to commend it. These are commanding, strongly masculine performances without being in the least overpowering: they embrace the greatest delicacy of feeling and sensitivity of phrasing. The artists are excellently recorded and this makes a strong alternative recommendation to the Chandos disc.

Thea King and Clifford Benson give finely paced, warm and musicianly accounts of both works. Even if it is possible to imagine readings of greater intensity, the performances will give pleasure on all counts, and the recording is well balanced and truthful.

Stoltzman's readings of both works have a relaxed, improvisatory style. Richard Goode makes a sensitive partner, but his piano timbre as recorded is a little dry, although the sound overall is balanced truthfully.

Horn trio in E flat, Op. 40 (see also above).
*** Decca 414 128-2 [id.]. Tuckwell, Perlman, Ashkenazy – FRANCK: *Violin sonata.****

A superb performance of Brahms's marvellous *Horn trio* from Tuckwell, Perlman and Ashkenazy. They realize to the full the music's passionate impulse, and the performance moves forward from the gentle opening, through the sparkling scherzo and the more introspective but still outgiving *Adagio* to the gay, spirited finale. The recording is worthy of the playing although, in their care not to out-balance the violin with the horn, the engineers have placed the horn rather backwardly. The CD brings an essentially analogue sound-picture, atmospheric rather than sharp in detail.

Piano quartet No. 1 in G min., Op. 25.
*** CBS Dig. MK 42361 [id.]. Murray Perahia, Amadeus Qt (members).

Piano quartets Nos. 1 in G min.; 3 in C min., Op. 60.
*** Virgin Dig. VC 790709-2 [id.]. Domus.
(M) **(*) RCA GD 85677 [5677-2-RG]. Rubinstein, Guarneri Qt.

This Perahia version of the *G minor Piano quartet* has an expressive power and eloquence that silence criticism. The sound has both warmth and presence in its CD format and this is arguably the finest account of the work since Gilels recorded it with the same string group. However, Domus offer not only the *G minor Quartet* but also the *C minor*, and they give marvellously spontaneous accounts of both works, urgent and full of warmth, yet with no lack of subtlety. The full, vivid recording can be recommended strongly.

Rubinstein can be a persuasive Brahms advocate and here he is at his most commanding, clearly inspiring the Guarneri players to match his power and emotional warmth. The performances have tremendous spontaneity and conviction; however, the remastered recording, although well blended and properly balanced and clear, lacks something in warmth in the middle frequencies, although the upper range is not shrill.

Piano quartet No. 1 in G min., Op. 25 (orch. Schoenberg).
*** EMI Dig. CDS7 47301-8 (2) [Ang. CDCB 47300]. CBSO, Rattle – MAHLER: *Symphony No. 10.****

Schoenberg's orchestral transcription of the Brahms *Piano quartet* was a labour of love. The use of a xylophone in the finale strikes some listeners as bizarre, but it is the thickness of some passages that seems surprising, given Schoenberg's mastery of the orchestra. However, the playing of the Birmingham orchestra for Rattle is so inspiriting that many doubts are silenced. The EMI recording is natural and wide-ranging.

Piano quartet No. 2 in A, Op. 26.
*** Virgin Dig. VC 790739-2 [id.]. Domus – MAHLER: *Quartet movement.****

With this CD, Domus complete their set of the Brahms *Piano quartets*, and one need hardly say more than that this record is fully worthy of its companion. This is real chamber-music-making that conveys a sense of pleasure; although the recording acoustic seems less than ideal, the ear soon adjusts and it is only in tutti passages that one becomes conscious of excessive reverberation.

Piano quartet No. 3 in C min., Op. 60.
** CBS Dig. MK 42387 [id.]. Stern, Ma, Laredo, Ax – *Double concerto.****

Excellent playing from all concerned on the CBS disc, even if Emanuel Ax delivers too thick a fortissimo tone at times – though he can produce beautiful pianissimo tone as well. There are pianists more sensitive in this respect on rival recordings.

Piano quintet in F min., Op. 34.
*** Ph. 412 608-2 [id.]. André Previn, Musikverein Qt.
**(*) DG 419 673-2 [id.]. Pollini, Italian Qt.

André Previn is much better recorded than Pollini, and the balance between pianist and quartet is very well judged. The work is beautifully shaped; the only reservation that might worry some collectors is the rather sweet vibrato of the leader, Rainer Küchl. However, the playing has fine vigour, warmth and spontaneity.

There is some electrifying and commanding playing from Pollini, and the Italian Quartet is eloquent too. The balance, however, is very much in the pianist's favour and occasionally masks the lower strings. The CD has opened up the sound somewhat, but at fortissimo levels the piano and strings could ideally be better separated.

Piano trio No. 1 in B min., Op. 8.
*** Teldec/WEA Dig. 2292 44924-2 [id.]. Trio Fontenay – IVES: *Trio.****

The Trio Fontenay are excellent in Op. 8 and hardly put a foot wrong throughout. They are also given an excellently clear but not oppressively close recording.

Piano trio No. 2 in C, Op. 87.
*** Teldec/WEA Dig. 2292 44177-2 [id.]. Trio Fontenay – DVORÁK: *Piano trio No. 1.****

A very good performance from the Trio Fontenay which has sparkle and drama without being over-projected. The recording is first class too.

Piano trios Nos. 1 in B, Op. 8; 2 in C, Op. 87.
(M) *** Decca 421 152-2 [id.]. Julius Katchen, Josef Suk, Janos Starker.

Piano trio No. 3 in C min., Op. 101; Cello sonata No. 2 in F, Op. 99; Scherzo for violin and piano in C min.
(M) *** Decca 425 423-2 [id.]. Katchen, Suk, Starker.

The Katchen/Suk/Starker recordings were made in The Maltings in July 1968, representing Katchen's last sessions before his untimely death. The performances are warm, strong and characterful. The richness of the acoustics at The Maltings adds to the Brahmsian glow; and if the sound of the remastered disc is a little limited in the upper range, it provides a real Brahmsian amplitude which is very satisfying. The *Scherzo in C minor*, added for the reissue on CD, is an attractive bonus, not otherwise available.

Piano trios Nos. 1 in B, Op. 8; 2 in C, Op. 87; 3 in C min., Op. 101; 4 in A, Op. posth.
*** Ph. Dig. 416 838-2 (2) [id.]. Beaux Arts Trio.

Piano trios Nos. 1–3.
**(*) Chan. Dig. CHAN 8334/5 (2) [id.]. Borodin Trio.

Piano trios Nos. 1 in B, Op. 8; 3 in C min., Op. 101.
**(*) CRD CRD 3432 [id.]. Israel Piano Trio.

Piano trio No. 2 in C, Op. 87.
(*) CRD CRD 3433 [id.]. Israel Piano Trio – SCHUMANN: *Piano trio No. 1.*(*)

The new digital recordings by the Beaux Arts Trio were made in La Chaux-de-Fonds, Switzerland, and they bring one close to the artists, the bottom end of the piano being larger than life, at times strikingly so. The playing, however, is always highly vital and sensitive. There is a splendid, finely projected sense of line and the delicate, sensitive playing of Menahem Pressler is always a delight.

The Borodin Trio give most musical and sensitive accounts of the three *Trios* that convey the sense of music-making in the home. Theirs are not high-powered performances and they are accorded strikingly natural recording. There is strength when it is called for, lightness of touch and a sense of repose. They are not always perfectly in tune, and this might well prove tiresome on repetition. However, the odd imperfections should not stand in the way of a recommendation.

The Israel Piano Trio give powerful accounts of all three *Trios*. In the first movements they tend towards 'public' rather than chamber performances, the pianist at times sounding as if he is tackling a concerto, but they have no lack of eloquence or feeling. Throughout, however, the intensity is such that they always hold one's attention. Their intonation is very accurate and their playing shows a Brahmsian feel and is commanding and spontaneous. The CDs offer fine presence and tangibility.

String quartets Nos. 1–3.
*** DG Dig. 423 670-2 (3) [id.]. Melos Qt – SCHUMANN: *Quartets Nos. 1–3.* **(*)

String quartets Nos. 1 in C min.; 2 in A min., Op. 51/1–2.
*** DG Dig. 427 641-2 [id.]. Melos Qt.
*** Chan. Dig. CHAN 8562 [id.]. Gabrieli Qt.

These Melos performances are generally well-shaped accounts with no want of fire and free from exaggeration, though they are at times short on charm – as, for example, in the *B flat Quartet*. The recordings are well (some may find them too well) lit and a bit forward, but on the whole this makes a marginal first choice for the Op. 51 *Quartets*.

Richly recorded in an agreeably expansive ambience, the Gabrielis also give warm, eloquent performances of both the Op. 51 *Quartets*, deeply felt and full-textured without being heavy; the *Romanze* of Op. 51, No. 1, is delightfully songful. There are both tenderness and subtlety here, and the sound is first class.

String quintets Nos. 1 in F, Op. 88; 2 in G, Op. 111.
(M) **(*) Ph. 426 094-2 [id.]. BPO Octet (members).

These splendid works are quite well served by the 1970 Philips reissue. Although the remastering has brought a thinner, more astringent treble response than the original LP, the underlying sound is full and well balanced. The performances by the Berlin Philharmonic group are searching and artistically satisfying, combining freshness with polish, warmth with well-integrated detail.

String sextets Nos. 1 in B flat, Op. 18; 2 in G, Op. 36.
*** Hyp. Dig. CDA 66276 [id.]. Raphael Ens.

The *Sextets* are among Brahms's most immediately appealing chamber works; they have a breadth of scale and texture that relates them closely to the orchestral music, yet they have the added freshness and transparency of writing in which there is one player to each part. The Raphael Ensemble are fully responsive to all their subtleties as well as to their vitality and warmth. In short, these are superb performances; the recording is very vivid and immediate, although some ears might find it a shade too present.

String sextet No. 1 in B flat, Op. 18.
(*) CRD CRD 3334 [id.]. Augmented Alberni Qt – SCHUBERT: *String quartet No. 12.**

The Alberni performance of the *First Sextet* is transferred well to CD and remains highly attractive, with a ripely blended recording to match the warmth of the playing. At times one might feel that a degree more fire would be welcome, but there is no lack of spontaneity. However, the coupling now seems rather short measure.

String sextet No. 2 in G, Op. 36.
(*) CRD CRD 3346 [id.]. Augmented Alberni Qt – BRUCKNER: *Intermezzo and trio.**

A fine account of the *Second String sextet* to match the excellence of the *First* by this same Alberni group. The playing is splendidly alive and succeeds in combining expressive feeling with vigour. The sound is full-bodied, with a fresh, bright, clean treble; however, as with the companion CD, the coupling is not very generous.

Viola sonatas Nos. 1 in F min.; 2 in E flat, Op. 120/1 & 2.
(*) Chan. Dig. CHAN 8550 [id.]. Imai, Vignoles – SCHUMANN: *Märchenbilder.*(*)

Viola sonatas Nos. 1 in F min.; 2 in E flat, Op. 120, 1/2; (i) *Trio in A min. for viola, violin and piano, Op. 114.*
(***) Olympia OCD 175 [id.]. Yuri Bashmet, Mikhail Muntyan; (i) Valentin Berlinsky.

Nobuko Imai is an almost peerless violist and it is difficult to find a flaw in her accounts of the two Op. 120 *Sonatas* with Roger Vignoles. She brings great warmth and a splendid feeling for line to these fine works, and has altogether excellent support from her partner. The reverberant acoustic does not show the piano to good advantage but, apart from that, this is an impressive issue.

Yuri Bashmet is the Rostropovich of the viola; the tone is big, the virtuosity is transcendental and there is enormous energy and expressive warmth. He encompasses great tonal variety, and the performances, given at the Moscow Conservatoire, have all the electricity of live music-making. But Bashmet is placed very far forward and the sonority of the piano, rather backwardly placed, is unappealing, lacking in bloom and freshness. These are all wonderful performances, but the less-than-ideal sound-quality prevents the full three-star recommendation they deserve.

Violin sonatas Nos. 1 in G, Op. 78; 2 in A, Op. 100; 3 in D min., Op. 108.
*** EMI Dig. CDC7 47403-2 [id.]. Itzhak Perlman, Vladimir Ashkenazy.
*** DG 415 989-2 [id.]. Pinchas Zukerman, Daniel Barenboim.
(M) **(*) Decca 421 092-2 [id.]. Josef Suk, Julius Katchen.
(M) ** Ph. 426 093-2 [id.]. Arthur Grumiaux, György Sebok.

Perlman and Ashkenazy bring out the trouble-free happiness of these lyrical inspirations, fully involved yet avoiding underlying tensions. In their sureness and flawless confidence at generally spacious speeds, they are performances which carry you along, cocooned in rich sound.

Zukerman and Barenboim are inspired to take a more expansive view of Brahms to produce songful, spontaneous-sounding performances that catch the inspiration of the moment. Compared with Perlman and Ashkenazy, the manner is warmer, less self-conscious – if at times less refined. Recorded in 1975, the sound is ripe and warm to match. But either of these two CDs will give much pleasure.

Suk's personal blend of romanticism and the classical tradition is warmly attractive but small in scale. These are intimate performances and, in their way, very enjoyable, since the remastered 1967 recording remains smoothly realistic, with only a hint of rawness on top.

Mellifluous playing from Grumiaux, expertly partnered by György Sebok, but not helped by the remastered mid-1970s recording, which is very slightly thin on top. This is acceptable, but is no match for Suk and Katchen in the same price range.

Violin sonatas Nos. 1 in G, Op. 78; 3 in D min., Op. 108.
(M) ** RCA GD 86264 [6264-2-RG]. Szeryng, Rubinstein – BEETHOVEN: *Sonata No. 8.***

Szeryng and Rubinstein were recorded together in the early 1960s. Their performances are sophisticated yet committed, strongly felt yet careful in matters of detail and balance. The remastered recording is, however, rather dry in acoustic; ideally, Brahms chamber music needs a warmer acoustic than this and a richer piano sound. But this remains very distinguished playing.

PIANO MUSIC

4 Ballades, Op. 10 (see also below).
*** DG Dig. 400 043-2 [id.]. Michelangeli – SCHUBERT: *Sonata No. 4.***

4 Ballades, Op. 10; 8 Pieces, Op. 76; Scherzo in E flat, Op. 4.
*** Ph. Dig. 411 103-2 [id.]. Stephen Bishop-Kovacevich.

4 Ballades, Op. 10; Variations and fugue on a theme of Handel, Op. 24; Variations on a theme of Schumann, Op. 9.
*** ASV Dig. CDDCA 616 [id.]. Jorge-Federico Osorio.

Michelangeli gives the *Ballades* a performance of the greatest distinction and without the slightly aloof quality that at times disturbs his readings. He is superbly recorded and this compact disc approaches demonstration standard.

Bishop-Kovacevich is a distinguished Brahmsian; his fine performances of the *Ballades* and of the Op. 76 *Klavierstücke* have both fire and tenderness, and are most truthfully recorded. The CD is wonderfully realistic and has the utmost presence.

Jorge-Federico Osorio's account of the *Variations and fugue on a theme of Handel* is tremendously impressive. There is no want of clarity, but the texture has plenty of warmth and colour and he balances the sonorities in a most musical way. He possesses an unfailing sense of the Brahms style, and this is undoubtedly his best record to date, for the Schumann set and the four *Ballades* are also played with fine sensitivity and character. ASV provide excellent, well-focused sound with plenty of depth.

7 Fantasias, Op. 116; 3 Intermezzi, Op. 117; 4 Pieces, Op. 119.
*** Ph. 411 137-2 [id.]. Stephen Bishop-Kovacevich.

3 Intermezzi, Op. 117; 6 Pieces, Op. 118; 4 Pieces, Op. 119; 2 Rhapsodies, Op. 79.
*** Decca 417 599-2 [id.]. Radu Lupu.

6 Pieces, Op. 118; 2 Rhapsodies, Op. 79; 12 Waltzes, Op. 39.
*** Ph. Dig. 420 750-2 [id.]. Stephen Bishop-Kovacevich.

The pair of well-recorded discs from Stephen Bishop-Kovacevich can receive the strongest recommendation. He finds the fullest range of emotional contrast in the Op. 116 *Fantasias*, but he is at his finest in the Op. 117 *Intermezzi* and four *Klavierstücke*, Op. 119, which contain some of Brahms's most beautiful lyrical inspirations for the keyboard. The companion disc offers playing of comparable distinction. The playing is not only thoughtful but full of the sharpest contrasts. The result is most compelling, both in the much-loved *Waltzes* and in the later, more demanding pieces.

Radu Lupu's late Brahms is quite outstanding in every way. The analogue recordings date from 1971 and 1978, and the CD transfer has brought greater emphasis on the middle and lower sonorities in the earlier recordings (Op.79/1 and Op. 117). The quality of the recorded sound is otherwise wide in range and Lupu's warmth and delicacy of colouring are most truthfully conveyed. There is great intensity and inwardness when these qualities are required and a keyboard mastery that is second to none. This is undoubtedly one of the most rewarding Brahms recitals currently before the public.

Piano sonatas Nos. 1 in C, Op. 1; 2 in F sharp min., Op. 2; 3 in F min., Op. 5; 4 Ballades, Op. 10; Scherzo in E flat, Op 4.
**(*) DG 423 401-2 (2) [id.]. Krystian Zimerman.

Krystian Zimerman's account of the lesser-known *C major Sonata* is powerful and concentrated. The work emerges with altogether fresh urgency and expressive power. His version of the *F minor*, Op. 5, is also particularly commanding and is worthy to stand alongside the great performances of the past. There is leonine power, tempered with poetic feeling. There is no want of tenderness as well as strength in the Op. 10 *Ballades*, while the recording sound is very good, although in adding presence the digital remastering has brought a degree of hardness to the upper range at higher dynamic levels.

Piano sonata No. 2 in F sharp min., Op. 2.
** Denon Dig. CO 73336 [id.]. Hélène Grimaud – SCHUMANN: *Kreisleriana.***

There is nothing wrong with Hélène Grimaud's playing in the Brahms *F sharp minor Sonata* – indeed she is a remarkably mature and authoritative young artist (not yet in her twenties). However, enthusiasm is tempered by the oppressively close and rather bottom-heavy recording.

Piano sonata No. 3 in F min., Op. 5.
**(*) Hung. Dig. HCD 12601 [id.]. Zoltán Kocsis.

Piano sonata No. 3 in F min., Op. 5; 2 Rhapsodies, Op. 79; Theme and variations in D min. (from String sextet, Op. 18).
*** Teldec/WEA Dig. 2292 44186-2 [id.]. Cyprien Katsaris.

Piano sonata No. 3; Theme and variations in D min. (from String sextet, Op. 18).
*** Decca Dig. 417 122-2. Radu Lupu.

Noble, dignified and spacious are the adjectives that spring to mind when listening to Lupu's Op. 5; he does not, perhaps, have the youthful ardour of Kocsis or the communicative qualities of Krystian Zimerman's account; Lupu's view is inward, ruminative and always beautifully rounded. The recording is most realistic, the piano set slightly back, the timbre fully coloured, and the focus natural.

Cyprien Katsaris possesses a pretty breathtaking technique and his Brahms *F minor Sonata* is second to none. While it does not displace Lupu or Zimerman, it can certainly be recommended alongside them. Katsaris takes few of the agogic liberties that have sometimes distinguished him in the romantic repertoire and, although he does not have quite the same grasp of structure as Zimerman or the same classical purity, this is strong, exciting playing, and the recording is excellent.

Kocsis gives an ardent account of the *F minor Sonata*. His performance is spacious and expansive, and there is no lack of warmth. The slow tempo (an *adagio* rather than *andante*) he adopts in the second and fourth movements is not quite as disturbing as the small agogic exaggerations in which he indulges. Yet what wonderful points he makes elsewhere. For all one's reservations, this is playing of great imagination and artistry, and the recording is eminently truthful.

Variations and fugue on a theme by Handel, Op. 24.
(M) *** Decca 417 791-2 [id.]. Jorge Bolet – REGER: *Variations.****

This was Jorge Bolet's début record for Decca, and very impressive it is. His playing in Brahms's best-loved set of piano variations is incisive and brightly revealing, intensely refreshing and concentrated. With excellently remastered analogue sound, this makes a first-class coupling with music by Reger which is much less familiar.

Variations on a theme of Haydn, Op. 56a (arr. for piano duet).
*** CBS Dig. MK 42625 [id.]. Murray Perahia, Sir Georg Solti – BARTÓK: *Sonata for 2 pianos and percussion.****

It seems likely that Brahms wrote out his *Variations* in piano score (for two pianos, four hands) before completing the orchestration. Murray Perahia and Solti bring out the fullest possible colouring in their performance, so that one hardly misses the orchestra. Highly spontaneous music-making which gives great pleasure, and very well recorded too.

VOCAL MUSIC

Lieder: *Abendregen; Alte Liebe; Feldensamkeit; Immer leiser wird mein Schlummer; Der Jäger; Liebestreu; Mädchenfluch; Mädchenlied; Das Mädchen spricht; Meine Liebe is grün; Regenlied; Salome; Der Schmied; Sommerabend; Therese; Der Tod, das ist die kühle Nachte; Von ewiger Liebe; Vor dem Fenster; Wir wandelten.*
*** Orfeo C 058831A [id.]. Margaret Price, James Lockhart.

Margaret Price gives a delightful Brahms recital; sensitively supported by James

Lockhart, she sings radiantly, with the voice ideally suited to the soaring lines of many of these songs, finely coloured over the changes of mood in a song such as *Alte Liebe*. Clean, bright recording.

Lieder: *Alte Liebe; Auf dem Kirchhofe; Feldeinsamkeit; Nachklang; O wusst' ich doch; Verzagen. Vier ernste Gesänge (4 Serious Songs), Op. 121.*
(*) DG 415 189-2 [id.]. Dietrich Fischer-Dieskau, Joerg Demus – BEETHOVEN: *Lieder.*(*)

Recorded in the late 1960s, Fischer-Dieskau's Brahms selection on CD brings consistently imaginative singing. His darkness and intensity in the *Four Serious Songs* are hardly matched in the relatively lightweight accompaniments from Demus – placed at a disadvantage by the recording balance; but, with excellent transfers, the disc can be recommended.

(i) *Alto rhapsody, Op. 53;* (ii; iii) *German requiem, Op. 45; Nänie, Op. 82;* (iv) *Rinaldo, Op. 50; Song of destiny, Op. 54; Song of the Fates, Op. 89;* (iii) *Song of triumph, Op. 55.*
*** DG Dig. 419 737-2 (3) [id.]. (i) Fassbaender; (ii) Popp; (iii) Wolfgang Brendel; (iv) Kollo; Prague Philharmonic Ch., Czech PO, Sinopoli.

Sinopoli's box of the choral music brings performances both challenging and controversial which – particularly in the rare works – are a revelation. Brigitte Fassbaender makes a strong, noble soloist in the *Alto rhapsody*, but it is the other works which command first attention in such a collection, not least the one generally dismissed as mere occasional music, the *Triumphlied* of 1870. Sinopoli, helped by incandescent singing from the Czech choir, gives it Handelian exhilaration. There is freshness and excitement too in the other rare works, with Sinopoli lightening rhythms and textures. In *Rinaldo* for example, Sinopoli moulds the sequence of numbers dramatically. René Kollo is the near-operatic soloist. The recording of the whole box, made in Prague, is warm and sympathetic with the orchestra incisively close and the chorus atmospherically behind.

(i) *Alto rhapsody, Op. 53; Funeral ode, Op. 13; Nänie, Op. 82; Song of the Fates, Op. 89.*
**(*) HM Orfeo C 025821A [id.]. (i) Alfreda Hodgson; Bav. R. Ch. and SO, Haitink.

(i) *Alto rhapsody, Op. 53;* (ii) *Vier ernste Gesange (4 Serious Songs), Op. 121;* (iii) *2 Songs with viola, Op. 91.*
(***) Decca 421 299-2. Kathleen Ferrier, (i) LPO Ch., LPO, Krauss; (ii) John Newmark; (iii) Gilbert, Spurr – MAHLER: *Rückert Lieder.*(***)

Alfreda Hodgson and Bernard Haitink make a good partnership in the *Alto rhapsody*. The other works combine refinement and moments of fervour in much the same way, and there is some splendid singing from the Bavarian choir, especially in the *Funeral ode*. The 1981 analogue recording was made in a concert-hall setting. Not everything is crystal clear, but the overall impression suits the music admirably and gives a convincing sense of realism.

This vintage Ferrier record brings together a group of the great contralto's early recordings for Decca. The earliest of all here, first issued in 1948, is of the *Alto rhapsody*, a glowing performance which culminates in a heart-warming final section. The *Four Serious Songs*, issued three years later, are even more intense, with the voice more suited to these dark, weighty songs than to most Lieder. The digital transfers capture the voice fairly enough, but present the accompaniments less agreeably.

Lieder: *Dein blaues Auge hält; Dort in den Weiden; Immer leiser wird mein Schlummer; Klage I & II; Liebestreu; Des Liebsten Schwur; Das Mädchen; Das Mädchen spricht;*

Regenlied; Romanzen und Lieder, Op. 84; Salome; Sapphische Ode, Op. 94/4; Der Schmied; (i) *2 Songs with viola, Op. 91; Therese; Vom Strande; Wie Melodien zieht es; Zigeunerlieder, Op. 103.*
*** DG Dig. 413 311-2 [id.]. Jessye Norman, Daniel Barenboim; (i) Wolfram Christ.

The task of recording a complete set of women's songs seems in this instance to have added to the warmth and sense of spontaneity of both singer and pianist in the studio, while Wolfram Christ makes a distinguished contribution to Op. 91. The heroic scale of *Der Schmied* is superb, as is the open simplicity of the *Zigeunerlieder*, while the gentler songs find Norman's gloriously ample voice exquisitely scaled down. The recording is wonderfully vivid, giving the artists a tangible presence. This is one of the finest Lieder collections in the CD catalogue.

Vier ernste Gesänge, Op. 121; Lieder: *Auf dem Kirchhofe; Botschaft; Feldeinsamkeit; Im Waldeseinsamkeit; Minnelied III; Mondenschein; O wüsst ich doch den Weg züruck; Sapphische Ode; Sommerabend; Ständchen.*
⊛ (M) (***) EMI CDH7 63198-2 [id.]. Hotter, Moore – BACH: *Cantata No. 82: Ich habe genug.**** ⊛

Glorious singing from Hans Hotter, wonderfully accompanied by Gerald Moore. Those who have treasured the old LP will know how eloquent this is; others should not pass over singing and artistry of this eloquence. An excellent transfer.

German requiem, Op. 45.
*** Teldec/WEA Dig. 2292 43200-2 [id.]. M. Price, Ramey, Amb. S., RPO, Previn.
*** EMI CDC7 47238-2 [id.]. Schwarzkopf, Fischer-Dieskau, Philh. Ch. & O, Klemperer.
(M) *** DG Dig. 429 486-2 [id.]. Lucia Popp, Wolfgang Brendel, Prague Philharmonic Ch., Czech PO, Sinopoli.
(M) **(*) EMI CDM7 69229-2 [id.]. Tomowa-Sintow, Van Dam, V. Singverein, BPO, Karajan.
(M) (***) EMI mono CDH7 61010-2 [id.]. Schwarzkopf, Hotter, V. Singverein, VPO, Karajan.
(*) DG Dig. 410 521-2 (2) [id.]. Hendricks, Van Dam, V. Singverein, VPO, Karajan – BRUCKNER: *Te Deum.
(M) **(*) Sony SK 45853 [id.]. Cotrubas, Prey, New Philh. Ch. & O, Maazel.
(M) ** DG 427 252-2 [id.]. Janowitz, Waechter, V. Singverein, BPO, Karajan.
** RCA Dig. RD 85003 [RD-1 5003]. Battle, Hagegard, Chicago Ch. & SO, Levine.

It is the seeming simplicity of Previn's dedicated approach, with radiant singing from the chorus and measured speeds held steadily, that so movingly conveys an innocence in the often square writing, both in the powerful opening choruses and in the simple, songful *Wie lieblich*. The great fugatos are then powerfully presented. Both soloists are outstanding, Margaret Price golden-toned, Samuel Ramey incisively dark. The recording is warmly set against a helpful church acoustic with the chorus slightly distanced.

Measured and monumental, Klemperer's performance defies preconceived doubts. The speeds are consistently slow – too slow in the *vivace* of the sixth movement, where Death has little sting – but, with dynamic contrasts underlined, the result is uniquely powerful. The solo singing is superb, and the Philharmonia singers were at the peak of their form. The CD transfer is excellent, with voices and instruments placed in a realistic sound-spectrum.

Sinopoli's DG version brings a performance of extremes: generally measured but consistently positive and often dramatically thrilling, helped by the wide-ranging recording, excellent soloists and an incisive contribution from the Prague Philharmonic Chorus. The hushed opening pianissimo soon expands powerfully, and the dynamic and emotional contrast is even more striking in the penultimate section (with baritone and chorus), which uses texts made famous in Handel's *Messiah*. The 1983 digital recording is full, clear and realistically balanced.

The reissue of Karajan's 1977 EMI set on a mid-priced CD offers considerable competition to the later, digital version. The chorus is both full and clearly focused, and soloists and orchestral detail are vividly projected. Indeed the most striking difference between this and the digital DG set lies in the choral sound, bigger and closer, with sharp dramatic contrasts. The soloists are both excellent: Tomowa-Sintow sings with a rich vocal colour, while José van Dam is equally expressive with firm tone. The remastering is certainly a success and this is generally preferable to the alternative mid-priced Karajan reissue from DG. Though there is a good deal to praise and enjoy on this analogue DG disc, the EMI version brings better choral sound and solo contributions at least as fine.

Recorded in October 1947 and issued on ten short-playing 78-r.p.m. discs, Karajan's mono version of the *German requiem* was – surprisingly – the first ever complete recording of this work. It was also something of a breakthrough in Karajan's early career. It is in part a tribute to his unique collaboration with Walter Legge, not only that this is a performance which has been rarely matched since on record, incandescent and intense, but that even now the sound has such vivid presence. There is inevitably some surface noise, but nothing too distracting, and the brightness and fullness of the sound is astonishing. The chorus is in superb, incisive form, and the two soloists are both at their peak, the young Schwarzkopf fresh-toned and Hotter far firmer than he later became.

The chorus of the Vienna Singverein sounds disappointingly opaque in Karajan's latest DG version, but that is the only serious shortcoming in a performance which brings out the warmth and spontaneity of Brahms's writing, not merely its devotional or monumental qualities. The soloists provide characterful contributions, even if the rapid vibrato of Barbara Hendricks detracts from a feeling of innocence in *Ihr habt nun Traurigkeit*. The relative closeness of the orchestra in the recording balance adds to the feeling of constriction in the sound.

Maazel on his mid-priced Sony disc gives a strong, unaffected performance, marked by superbly disciplined singing from the New Philharmonia Chorus, though the 1976 recording is not as clear on inner detail as it might be. Maazel sustains slow speeds most convincingly, and the two soloists, balanced rather close, are both warmly expressive, maybe too much so for some, with Cotrubas's vibrato giving a richer sound than is common in this work. Helpfully, Sony have put tracks on different sections within the seven movements.

Levine's version features the Chicago Symphony Chorus, which is probably the finest in America, while his two soloists both prove excellent, Kathleen Battle pure and sweetly vulnerable-sounding, Hagegard clear-cut and firm. Levine is not the most illuminating conductor in this work, and his pacing is not always convincing; yet the performance is alive, with power as well as impetus, and it undoubtedly gives pleasure. The recording is not ideal, with inner textures growing cloudy in tuttis.

6 Gesänge, Op. 3; Lieder und Gesänge, Op. 32; Lieder und Gesängen von Georg Friedrich Daumer, Op. 57; 4 Lieder, Op. 96; 2 Lieder, Op. 59.
*** EMI Dig. CDC7 49723-2 [id.]. Olaf Bär, Geoffrey Parsons.

Recorded in warm and well-balanced sound in the Lukaskirche in Dresden, this beautiful collection of Brahms songs was one of Olaf Bär's early successes, establishing him as a major artist, one who naturally invites comparison in both tonal beauty and musical imagination with Dietrich Fischer-Dieskau. On that level, Bär may not so regularly produce those sparks of spontaneous imagination that, with Fischer-Dieskau, suddenly illuminate a song; but on any level this is a most attractive collection, the more so for including rarities like the very early Opus 3 songs, when the composer was still very much under Schumann's influence.

Liebeslieder waltzes, Op. 52; New Liebeslieder waltzes, Op. 65; 3 Quartets, Op. 64.
*** DG Dig. 423 133-2 [id.]. Mathis, Fassbaender, Schreier, Fischer-Dieskau; Engel and Sawallisch (pianos).

For its Brahms edition, DG assembled these characterful yet well-matched voices. The result brought one of the most successful recordings yet of the two seductive but surprisingly difficult sets of *Liebeslieder waltzes*. The CD has fine realism and presence.

Motets, Opp. 10, 12, 27, 30, 37, 74, 109–10 (complete).
*** Conifer Dig. CDCF 178 [id.]. Trinity College, Cambridge, Ch., Richard Marlow.

Richard Marlow and his excellent Cambridge choir add to their distinguished list of records with this invaluable collection, bringing together all sixteen of the motets – mostly unaccompanied but some with organ – which Brahms wrote over the course of his long career. Early in life he was choirmaster at both Detmold and Hamburg, and that experience brought him the gift of writing with a warm understanding of singers and voices. What is surprising here is to discover how close Brahms regularly comes to the example of Bach, whether in the chorales or in such a delightful motet as the lively setting for women's voices of *Regina coeli*, with its brightly rhythmic contrapuntal entries. Most ambitious is the first of the two Opus 74 motets, *Warum ist das Licht gegeben*, with linked sections setting carefully chosen texts from the Book of Job, the Epistle of St James and Martin Luther, a fine work with something of the solemnity of the *German requiem*. With superb singing recorded vividly, this is an outstanding issue.

Die schöne Magelone.
** DG Dig. 427 334-2 [id.]. Andreas Schmidt, Joerg Demus.

The collaboration of the young German baritone, Andreas Schmidt, with the veteran pianist, Joerg Demus, brings a compelling reading of one of Brahms's most neglected works. *Die schöne Magelone* is not exactly helped by its text, which inconsistently illustrates a story of the days of chivalry without linking it into a dramatic whole. Though Demus is at times overtaxed by the heavy accompaniment, he proves a strong, thrustful partner for Schmidt, whose youthful ardour is most persuasive, even though he cannot efface memories of the fine performances recorded by Fischer-Dieskau. First-rate sound.

Brian, Havergal (1876–1972)

Symphony No. 3 in C sharp min.
**(*) Hyp. Dig. CDA 66334. Ball, Jacobson, BBC SO, Friend.

A welcome addition to the growing representation of Havergal Brian in the catalogue. The *Third Symphony* began life as a concerto for piano; this perhaps explains the prominent role given to two pianos in the score, splendidly played here by Andrew Ball and Julian Jacobson. The work is full of extraordinarily imaginative and original touches, but the overall lack of rhythmic variety is a handicap. The playing of the BBC Symphony Orchestra under Lionel Friend is well prepared and dedicated, but the recording does not open out sufficiently in climaxes. However, this is an important and interesting record of a challenging and thought-provoking work.

Symphonies Nos. 7 in C; 31. The Tinker's wedding: comedy overture.
*** EMI Dig. CDC7 49558-2. Royal Liverpool PO, Mackerras.

This record brings together the last of the expansive works, No. 7, completed in 1948, allying Brian's earlier style with the often elliptical manners of his later, more concentrated manner in the penultimate symphony of the whole series, written just twenty years later. The brilliant comedy overture, *The Tinker's wedding*, provides an attractive makeweight. This collection presents him and his achievement more effectively than any other disc. Beautifully played and vividly recorded, it can be recommended to anyone fascinated by an extraordinary, offbeat composer.

Symphonies Nos. 8 in B flat min.; 9 in A min.
(M) *** EMI CDM7 69890-2. Royal Liverpool PO, Groves.

Groves gives a splendid account of the *Ninth*, a work of undoubted power and atmosphere. No. 8 is a rather more complex and enigmatic piece, and the performance is marginally less assured. There is fine orchestral playing throughout and the coupling merits the strongest recommendation, for the music's harmonic language is not too 'difficult' for anyone who enjoys Mahler to come to terms with. The first-class recording sounds a little drier in its digital remastering, but is still admirably vivid.

Symphonies Nos. 10 in C min.; 21 in E flat.
(M) **(*) Unicorn UKCD 2027 [id.]. Leicestershire Schools SO, Loughran or Pinkett.

Both these *Symphonies* are works of old age; No. 10, a powerfully wrought and original one-movement piece, is the more appealing of the two; No. 21 dates from the composer's late eighties. There need be no serious reservations about the recordings, and the performances are astonishingly accomplished.

Bridge, Frank (1879–1941)

Cherry Ripe; Enter Spring (rhapsody); *Lament; The Sea* (suite); *Summer* (tone-poem).
(M) *** EMI CDM7 69870-2. Royal Liverpool PO, Groves.

Writing in the early years of the century, the composer confidently produced a magnificent seascape in the wake of Debussy, *The Sea*, but already by 1914 his responses were subtler, more original. *Summer*, written in that fateful year, was free of conventional pastoral moods, while in the last and greatest of Bridge's tone-poems, *Enter Spring*, he was responding to still wider musical horizons in experimentation which matches that of European contemporaries. Groves's warm advocacy adds to the impressiveness. First-rate recording, most successfully remastered.

Enter spring (rhapsody); (i) Oration (Concerto elegiaco).
*** Pearl SHECD 9601 [id.]. (i) Baillie; Cologne RSO, Carewe.

Oration is in effect a massive cello concerto in nine linked sections, an elegiac work which reflects the composer's continuing desolation over the deaths of so many of his friends in the First World War. Alexander Baillie is certainly an eloquent advocate, at times wearing his heart unashamedly on his sleeve, at others more thoughtfully reticent. John Carewe matches his rhapsodic approach and secures wholly idiomatic playing from the fine Cologne orchestra, both here and in a splendidly fluid account of the expansive

BRIDGE

tone-poem, *Enter spring*, which is wholly spontaneous and generates considerable power. The studio recording is vivid and wide-ranging.

2 Entr'actes: Rosemary; Canzonetta. Heart's ease. 3 Lyrics for piano: No. 1, Heart's ease (orch. Cornford). *Norse legend;* (i) *Suite for cello and orchestra (Morning song; Elegie; Scherzo),* arr. & orch. Cornford. *Threads* (incidental music); *2 Intermezzi. 3 Vignettes de danse. The turtle's retort* (one-step), orch. Wetherell.
*** Pearl SHECD 9600 [id.]. (i) Lowri Blake; Chelsea Op. Group O, Howard Williams.

Those who enjoy Elgar's lighter music will surely find much to delight them in this diverse and very tuneful collection, even if a number of the items are arrangements by other hands. The *Norse legend* is quite brief; then comes the Elgarian *Rosemary*; but the *Suite for cello and orchestra* is by no means insubstantial and it has a sympathetic, rich-toned soloist in Lowri Blake. The incidental music for *Threads* brings more nostalgia; *Heart's ease* has a delicious oriental delicacy and the *Three Vignettes* recall three lady friends, obviously of very contrasting dispositions. *The turtle's retort* ends the concert in good rhythmic spirits, and Eric Wetherell's scoring is nicely judged. Altogether this is a most entertaining concert that is more than the sum of its constituents. The Chelsea orchestra are a semi-professional group, but no apologies need be made for their response or their ensemble, and Howard Williams directs with spontaneous warmth and an apt sense of pacing. The recording is first rate, with plenty of colour and ambient warmth.

Phantasm for piano and orchestra.
*** Conifer Dig. CDFC 175 [id.]. Kathryn Stott, RPO, Handley – IRELAND: *Piano concerto*; WALTON: *Sinfonia concertante.****

Bridge's curiously titled *Phantasm* is a large-scale piano concerto, some 26 minutes long, in a single, massive movement. It makes a generous and very welcome coupling for two of the most colourful of concertante piano works written by English composers. Completed in 1931, *Phantasm* is one of Bridge's later works and seriously disconcerted his admirers with its tough, uncompromising idiom, very different from his easier, more lyrical early style. Starting with an extended slow introduction, the sections are clearly defined – though, sadly, Conifer fail to provide any CD tracks for them – with an energetic main allegro relaxing into a waltz-like second subject. That in turn subsides into a central *Andante*, before the allegro material is recapitulated, building to a formidable climax which finally dies away in a mood of disillusion. Kathryn Stott, most sympathetically accompanied by Vernon Handley and the RPO, proves a persuasive, committed interpreter, matching her achievement in the other two works on the disc. Warm, generally well-balanced recording.

The Sea (suite).
*** Chan. Dig. CHAN 8473 [id.]. Ulster O, Handley – BAX: *On the sea-shore*; BRITTEN: *Sea interludes.****

The Sea was a work which Benjamin Britten heard as a boy at the Norwich Festival in 1924. It impressed him so deeply that before long it led to his taking composition lessons with the older composer. It receives a brilliant and deeply sympathetic performance from Handley and the Ulster Orchestra, recorded with a fullness and vividness to make this a demonstration disc.

Suite for strings.
*** Chan. Dig. CHAN 8390 [id.]. ECO, Garforth – IRELAND: *Downland suite; Holy Boy; Elegiac meditations.****

*** Nimbus Dig. NI 5068 [id.]. E. String O, Boughton – BUTTERWORTH: *Banks of green willow; Idylls; Shropshire lad;* PARRY: *Lady Radnor's suite.****

Suite for strings; Summer; There is a willow grows aslant a brook.
*** Chan. CHAN 8373 [id.]. Bournemouth Sinf., Del Mar – BANTOCK: *Pierrot of the minute*; BUTTERWORTH: *Banks of green willow.****

Summer is beautifully played by the Bournemouth Sinfonietta under Norman Del Mar. The same images of nature permeate the miniature tone-poem, *There is a willow grows aslant a brook*, an inspired piece, very sensitively managed. The *Suite for strings* is equally individual. Its third movement, a *Nocturne*, is lovely. The CD transfer is excellent and one can relish its fine definition and presence.

The ECO also play well for David Garforth in the *Suite for strings*. This performance, though not scrupulous in observing the composer's metronome markings, is extremely committed; it is certainly excellently recorded, with great clarity and presence. The slow movement in particular is played with great eloquence. The disc does not score high marks on playing time – it runs for under 50 minutes – but it scores on every other point.

The Nimbus collection is more generous and is certainly well chosen. Here Bridge's *Suite* again receives a lively and responsive performance, from William Boughton and his excellent Birmingham-based orchestra, treated to ample, sumptuously atmospheric recording, more resonant than its competitors.

Cello sonata.
*** Chan. Dig. CHAN 8499 [id.]. Raphael and Peter Wallfisch – BAX: *Rhapsodic ballad*; DELIUS: *Sonata*; WALTON: *Passacaglia.****

At first sight the *Cello sonata* seems to bear all the imprints of the English pastoral school with its pastel colourings and gentle, discursive lines, but there is no lack of fibre here and a pervasive sense that the pre-war Edwardian world was gone beyond recall. It is a distinctive world that Bridge evokes and one to which Raphael Wallfisch and his father, Peter, are completely attuned. There is a sense of scale about their reading which is impressive, and they are beautifully recorded.

(i) *Phantasie (quartet) in F sharp min.; Phantasie trio in C min.; Piano trio No. 2.*
*** Hyp. Dig. CDA 66279 [id.]. Dartington Trio; (i) with P. Ireland.

Piano trio No. 2.
(*) Chan. Dig. CHAN 8495 [id.]. Borodin Trio – BAX: *Piano trio.**

Even those who do not usually respond to Bridge's early music should be persuaded by this playing of the *Phantasie trio*; it is of exceptional eloquence and sensitivity. The Dartington group are no less persuasive in the *F sharp minor Phantasy*. Their account of the visionary post-war *Piano trio No. 2* of 1929 is more completely inside this score than is the Borodins' very well-recorded version on Chandos. The Hyperion recording is altogether superb, in the demonstration bracket, perfectly natural and beautifully proportioned.

The playing of the Borodin Trio is also very distinguished, if not quite as compelling as that by the Dartington group on Hyperion; but, given such advocacy and the excellence of the Chandos recording, let us hope that this will win more new friends for this music.

Britten, Benjamin (1913–76)

An American overture, Op. 27; Occasional overture, Op. 38; Sinfonia da Requiem. Op. 20; Suite on English folk tunes: A time there was, Op. 90.
*** EMI Dig. CDC7 47343-2 [id.]. CBSO, Rattle.

While the most ambitious piece here is the *Sinfonia da Requiem*, written after the death of Britten's parents, the *Folk tunes suite* is a good deal more diverse in mood than one might expect, and the early *American overture*, with its attractive whiff of Copland, is matched by the much later *Occasional overture* in its brilliant orchestral command. The whole programme is splendidly played by the City of Birmingham orchestra under Rattle, whose passionate view of the *Sinfonia da Requiem* is unashamedly extrovert, yet finding subtle detail too. The recording is admirably vivid and clear.

Piano concerto, Op. 13.
** Hyp. Dig. CDA 66293 [id.]. Servadei, LPO, Giunta – KHACHATURIAN: *Piano concerto.***

(i) *Piano concerto, Op. 13;* (ii) *Violin concerto, Op. 15.*
(M) *** Decca 417 308-2. (i) Sviatoslav Richter; (ii) Lubotsky; ECO, composer.

Richter is incomparable in interpreting the *Piano concerto*, not only the thoughtful, introspective moments but the Liszt-like bravura passages (many of them surprising from this composer). With its highly original sonorities the *Violin concerto* makes a splendid vehicle for another Soviet artist, Mark Lubotsky. Recorded in The Maltings, the playing of the ECO under the composer's direction matches the inspiration of the soloists. The 1971 recording sounds splendid on this reissued CD.
With good, well-balanced digital recording, Annette Servadei gives a strong, dedicated, muscular performance. However, Richter remains first choice.

Violin concerto, Op. 15.
** Olympia OCD 242 [id.]. Boris Gutnikov, Leningrad PO, Dmitriev – ELGAR: *Violin concerto.***

Gutnikov's strong, red-blooded reading of Britten's *Violin concerto*, bringing out the romantic warmth of the writing, makes a generous and unexpectedly apt coupling for the Elgar *Concerto* on a reasonably priced Olympia disc. After all, Britten himself chose a young Soviet violinist, Mark Lubotsky, as soloist when he recorded this work for Decca. Now transferred to CD, that vintage recording is hardly matched here, however committed the performance, when the exaggeratedly close balance of the soloist coarsens the interpretation. Despite that basic flaw, this version is well worth investigating by anyone wanting to get away from a parochial view of English music.

(i) *Lachrymae (Reflections on a song by John Dowland), Op. 48a; Prelude and fugue for 18-part string orchestra, Op. 29; Simple symphony, Op. 4.* PURCELL, arr. Britten: *Chacony in G min.*
**(*) Virgin Dig. VCy 791080-2 [id.]. (i) Roger Chase; LCO, Christopher Warren-Green.

Though Christopher Warren-Green's Britten programme is not quite as successful as his Elgar/Vaughan Williams coupling, the playing here has comparable commitment and ardour. The sheer energy of the opening movement of the *Simple symphony* is breathtaking; this is surely too fast, even for a *Boisterous bourrée,* but with bold articulation the effect is certainly exhilarating. The *Sentimental saraband,* by contrast, is very relaxed and winningly nostalgic; the incandescent energy returns in the finale. The players of the LCO obviously enjoy themselves in Britten's arrangement of the great Purcell *Chaconne*, expanded from its sparer original version into a grand – even sumptuous – affair for a full string orchestra.

Matinées musicales, Op. 25; Soirées musicales, Op. 9.
*** Decca Dig. 410 139-2. Nat. PO, Bonynge – ROSSINI: *La Boutique fantasque.****

Matinées musicales; Soirées musicales; Variations on a theme of Frank Bridge, Op. 10.
(M) **(*) EMI CD-EMX 2111. ECO, Gibson.

(i) *Matinées musicales; Soirées musicales;* (ii; iv) *Young person's guide to the orchestra;* (iii; iv) *Peter Grimes: 4 Sea interludes & Passacaglia.*
(M) *** Decca 425 659-2 [id.]. (i) Nat. PO, Bonynge; (ii) LSO; (iii) ROHCG O; (iv) composer.

Britten wrote his *Soirées musicales* for a GPO film-score in the 1930s; the *Matinées* followed in 1941 and were intended as straight ballet music. Both are wittily if rather sparsely scored, deriving their musical content directly from Rossini. Bonynge's versions are brightly played and extremely vividly recorded in the best Decca manner. They are now also reissued at mid-price, generously coupled with Britten's brilliant account of the *Young person's guide to the orchestra* and the *Sea interludes* and *Passacaglia* from *Peter Grimes*. The latter are taken from the complete recording, and this means that odd extracts from the vocal parts are included and the general effect is not as tidy as the concert version. That proviso apart, these are wonderfully vital accounts of some superbly atmospheric music.

The ECO play very well for Alexander Gibson and, apart from giving a characterful account of the *Variations*, the charm and high spirits of Britten's two sets of *Musicales* are splendidly conveyed. The recording has a very tangible presence in its CD format, although the upper range of the violins is now very brightly lit and there is a hint of shrillness at fortissimo levels in the *Variations*. The two sets of *Musicales* sound attractively lively and sparkling.

Men of goodwill; The young person's guide to the orchestra, Op. 34; Peter Grimes: 4 Sea interludes.
** EMI Dig. CDC7 49300-2 [id.]. Minnesota O, Marriner.

The brief orchestral piece, *Men of goodwill*, is a set of variations on *God rest ye merry, gentlemen*. The Minnesota performances of the well-known music are a little stiff but enjoyable enough. First-rate digital sound, clean and clear.

Prelude and fugue for 18 solo strings, Op. 29; Reflections on a song of Dowland; Simple symphony, Op. 4; Variations on a theme of Frank Bridge, Op. 10.
**(*) Nimbus Dig. NI 5025 [id.]. Roger Best, E. String O, William Boughton.

Prelude and fugue for 18 solo strings, Op. 29; Simple symphony, Op. 4; Variations on a theme of Frank Bridge, Op. 10.
*** ASV Dig. CDDCA 591 [id.]. Northern Sinfonia, Hickox.
**(*) Chan. CHAN 8376 [id.]. Bournemouth Sinf., Ronald Thomas.

Among these three collections of Britten's string music, the ASV issue is notable for an outstandingly fine account of the *Frank Bridge variations*, which stands up well alongside the composer's own version. Throughout, the string playing is committedly responsive, combining polish with eloquence, the rich sonorities resonating powerfully in the glowing ambience of All Saints' Quayside Church, Newcastle. The reverberation also recalls Britten's own famous account of the *Simple symphony*, made in The Maltings, even if Hickox does not quite match the composer's rhythmic bounce in the *Playful pizzicato*. The *Prelude and fugue* is comparably eloquent, although here the playing is marginally less assured. The recording is first class, with the bright upper range well supported by the firm bass.

Warmly recorded in the Great Hall at Birmingham University, Boughton's collection of Britten pieces brings sympathetic and lively performances not just of the popular *Variations* and *Simple symphony* but also of the relative rarities, the ingenious *Prelude and fugue* and the *Dowland reflections*.

The Chandos coupling is also most attractive; the performances have a natural expressive warmth which is most engaging; not least, the recording has a ripeness and resonance which are most satisfying, particularly in the bass registers, especially telling in the *Variations*.

The Prince of the Pagodas (complete).
⊛ *** Virgin Dig. VCD 791103-2 (2) [id.]. L. Sinf., Knussen.

(i) *The Prince of the Pagodas* (ballet), *Op. 57* (complete); (ii) *Diversions for piano (left hand) and orchestra, Op. 21.*
*** Decca 421 855-2 (2) [id.]. (i) ROHCG O; (ii) Julius Katchen, LSO, composer.

The multicoloured instrumentation – much influenced by Britten's visit to Bali – is caught with glorious richness in Oliver Knussen's really complete version for Virgin of the full-length ballet. Knussen confesses to having loved Britten's own recording from childhood, and his own performance is no less dramatic and persuasive. But in addition he scores significantly in opening out more than 40 cuts, most of them small, which Britten only sanctioned to fit the three Acts on to four LP sides. So Knussen includes four whole numbers omitted before, as well as important transitions and 'middle-eights' which, as Knussen explains, are integral to the musical argument. The tracking on the CD is very generous and is complemented by a detailed synopsis of the plot, which cues in the track-numbers.

The composer's own recording was originally made after the first performances at Covent Garden, early in 1957, with Britten drawing playing of electric intensity and knife-edged precision from the orchestra. The stereo sound has come up with astonishing vividness on CD, with some thinness only on violin tone to betray the age. Britten's many offbeat fanfares ring out superbly, and his re-creation of oriental textures is caught magically. With Julius Katchen as soloist in the distinctive left-hand piano part, Britten conducts the LSO in an equally inspired account of the most neglected of his full-scale concertante works. The 1954 sound is amazingly vivid too, though (without acknowledgement on the CD box) this is in mono only, and the sound is inevitably flatter than in the complete ballet.

Simple symphony (for strings), *Op. 4.*
*** DG Dig. 423 624-2 [id.]. Orpheus CO – BIZET: *Symphony*; PROKOFIEV: *Symphony No. 1.****

(i) *Simple symphony, Op. 4; Variations on a theme of Frank Bridge, Op. 10;* (ii) *The Young person's guide to the orchestra (Variations and fugue on a theme of Purcell), Op. 34.*
**(*) Decca 417 509-2. (i) ECO, (ii) LSO; composer.

These Decca recordings arrive on CD with very tangible strings and great clarity and presence overall; some ears, however, might decide that the violins are *too* brightly lit.

Britten takes a very brisk view of his *Young person's guide*, so brisk that even the LSO players cannot always quite match him. But every bar has a vigour which makes the music sound more youthful than usual, and the headlong, uninhibited account of the final fugue (trombones as vulgar as you like) is an absolute joy. In the *Frank Bridge variations* Britten goes more for half-tones and he achieves an almost circumspect coolness in the waltz-parody of the *Romance*; in the Viennese waltz section later, he is again subtly atmospheric; and in the *Funeral march* he is relatively solemn. The *Simple symphony* makes a splendid foil, with its charm and high spirits; no one else has found quite the infectious bounce in the *Playful pizzicato* that the composer does, aided by the glowing resonance of The Maltings where the recording was made.

The *Simple symphony* goes nicely alongside the Bizet and Prokofiev works, especially when played as freshly and characterfully as here by the Orpheus group. They are especially gentle and touching in the *Sentimental saraband*, and the *Boisterous bourrée* is contrastingly robust. Britten himself found more fun in the *Playful pizzicato*, and perhaps the Orpheus account of the *Frolicsome finale* could be more inconsequential in spirit; but the reading is all-of-a-piece and enjoyably spontaneous. Excellent, realistic sound.

(i) *Sinfonia da requiem, Op. 20;* (ii) *Symphony for cello and orchestra, Op. 68;* (iii) *Cantata misericordium, Op. 69.*
(M) *** Decca 425 100-2 [id.]. (i) New Philh. O; (ii) Rostropovich, ECO; (iii) Pears, Fischer-Dieskau, LSO Ch., LSO; composer.

Symphony for cello and orchestra, Op. 68.
*** CBS Dig. MK 44900 [id.]. Yo-Yo Ma, Baltimore SO, Zinman – BARBER: *Cello concerto.****

(i) *Symphony for cello and orchestra, Op. 68; Death in Venice: suite, Op. 88* (arr. Bedford).
*** Chan. Dig. CHAN 8363 [id.]. (i) Wallfisch; ECO, Bedford.

Britten's own 1964 recordings of the *Sinfonia da requiem* and the *Cello symphony* appear on CD with the *Cantata misericordium* added for good measure. All the performances are definitive, and Rostropovich's account of the *Cello symphony* in particular is everything one could ask for. It is a marvellous piece, very much a new landscape in Britten's world. The CD transfers are admirably managed.

With a comparison ready to hand, it is the more remarkable how closely Wallfisch manages to match the earlier version. If Wallfisch's tone is not as resonant as Rostropovich's, the slight help from the recording balance gives it all the power needed. Sounding less improvisatory than Rostropovich, he and Bedford give a more consistent sense of purpose, and the weight and range of the brilliant and full Chandos recording quality add to the impact, with Bedford's direction even more spacious than the composer's, the effect emphasized by the Chandos ambience, spacious and warm. Steuart Bedford's encapsulation of Britten's last opera into this rich and colourful suite makes a splendid coupling, but it is a pity that the CD does not have bands between the separate sections.

Yo-Yo Ma, in partnership with David Zinman, gives a superb performance of the Britten *Cello symphony*. The wayward mystery in the first movement, rather than its more aggressive qualities, is what predominates, and in the scherzo Ma is masterly in bringing out the lightness and fantasy. The third-movement *Adagio* is softer-grained than usual, with the soloist placed naturally, leading on to an account of the finale, a shade faster than usual, compellingly purposeful, which brings out the Copland-like swagger of the main *passacaglia* theme. The orchestra plays with brilliance and commitment in a full and well-balanced recording.

Sinfonia da requiem, Op. 20; The Young person's guide to the orchestra, Op. 34; Peter Grimes: 4 Sea interludes & Passacaglia, Op. 34.
**(*) Virgin Dig. VC 790834-2 [id.]. Royal Liverpool PO, Libor Pešek.

Though Pešek fails to convey the full ominous weight of the first movement of the *Sinfonia da requiem*, he then directs a dazzling account of the central *Dies Irae* scherzo, taken breathtakingly fast, and finds an intense repose in the calm of the final *Requiem aeternam*. The *Sea interludes* – given here complete with the fine *Passacaglia* – are also well played, though they sound very literal, not ideally atmospheric. *The Young person's guide* lacks a degree of tension, with the fugue not dashing enough. The recording is comfortably reverberant and full, but takes some of the bite from the playing.

Variations on a theme of Frank Bridge, Op. 10.
(M) *** Decca 421 391-2 [id.]. ASMF, Marriner – BUTTERWORTH: *Banks of green willow* etc.; WARLOCK: *Capriol suite.****

Although not even Marriner quite matches the natural warmth of expression of the composer himself in this music, his is a superb performance, if anything even more polished, and recorded with remarkable vividness, the CD giving the impression of great presence and immediacy. With beautiful Butterworth pieces plus the Warlock *Capriol suite* for coupling, this is a very attractive reissue.

The Young person's guide to the orchestra (Variations and fugue on a theme of Purcell), Op. 34.
(B) **(*) Pickwick IMPX 9002. Sean Connery, RPO, Dorati – PROKOFIEV: *Peter and the wolf.***(*)
(M) **(*) EMI CDM7 63177-2 (without narration). Royal Liverpool PO, Groves – PROKOFIEV: *Peter;* SAINT-SAENS: *Carnival.****

The Young person's guide to the orchestra; Gloriana: Courtly dances (suite).
(*) Telarc Dig. CD 80126 [id.] (without narration). RPO, Previn – PROKOFIEV: *Peter.**

Sean Connery's voice is very familiar and his easy style is attractive. His narration should go down well with young people, even if some of the points are made rather heavily. The orchestral playing is first rate and the vivid, forwardly balanced recording – with a Decca Phase 4 source – is effective enough in this context. The performance has plenty of colour and vitality.

Unlike Previn's earlier, EMI version, in which he gave a spoken narration, the Telarc disc brings a straight performance, rather relaxed compared with the composer's own – see above – too well-behaved at times (as in the percussion section) but ending with a fizzing account of the finale. The *Gloriana dances*, done with great flair, make a welcome filler. The CD has only four tracks but plentiful index points for the different variations and movements.

The EMI triptych of Britten, Prokofiev's *Peter and the wolf* and Saint-Saëns's *Carnival of the animals* arrives on CD, rather brashly transferred; if the performance of the *Young person's guide* lacks that last degree of finesse, it is nevertheless well paced and has plenty of vitality.

CHAMBER MUSIC

Cello sonata, Op. 65.
(*) CBS Dig. MK 44980 [id.]. Yo-Yo Ma, Emanuel Ax – R. STRAUSS: *Sonata.*(*)

(i) *Cello sonata in C, Op. 65;* (Unaccompanied) *Cello suites Nos. 1, Op. 72; 2, Op. 80.*
(M) *** Decca 421 859-2 [id.]. Rostropovich; (i) with composer.

This strange five-movement *Cello sonata* was written specially for Rostropovich's appearance at the Aldeburgh Festival of 1961, and the recording was made soon after the first performance. Each of the five movements is poised and concentrated and it is an excellent work to wrestle with on a record, particularly when the performance is never likely to be outshone. Here it is coupled with the two *Suites for unaccompanied cello.* This is rough, gritty music in Britten's latterday manner, but Rostropovich gives such inspired accounts that the music reveals more and more with repetition. The CD transfers serve to add presence to recordings which are already very impressive.

Yo-Yo Ma and Emanuel Ax give an account of the *Cello sonata* which is very carefully thought out – perhaps too carefully, for one is left with the impression that these artists are striving too hard to shed new light on the piece. It is at times just too self-aware, with exaggerated pianissimi and self-conscious phrasing. The recording is very truthful, though the sound Decca provide for Rostropovich and the composer is more present. However, this is still very good and worth considering.

(i) *Suite for harp, Op. 83;* (ii) *2 Insect pieces, for oboe & piano; 6 Metamorphoses after Ovid* (for oboe solo), *Op. 49.*
*** Mer. CDE 84119 [id.]. (i) Osian Ellis; (ii) Sarah Watkins; Ledger – *Tit for Tat* etc.***.

It was for Osian Ellis that Britten wrote the *Harp suite*, which sounds surprisingly unlike any other harp music at all. Ellis remains the ideal performer. A younger artist, the oboist Sarah Watkins, gives biting and intense performances of the unaccompanied *Metamorphoses*, as well as the two early *Insect pieces*, with Philip Ledger – a long-time Aldeburgh associate – at the piano. The sound is full and immediate, set convincingly in a small but helpful hall. This is part of a cleverly planned recital which includes *Tit for Tat* and six folksong arrangements with their original harp accompaniments (see below).

(i) *Sinfonietta, Op. 1;* (ii) *String quartets Nos. 2, Op. 36; 3, Op. 94.*
(M) *** Decca 425 715-2 [id.]. (i) Vienna Octet; (ii) Amadeus Qt.

Britten's Opus 1 was written when he was in his teens. It has some characteristic fingerprints but points atypically towards Central Europe – reflection no doubt of his desire at the time to study with Berg in Vienna. Its mixture of seriousness and assurance is not unappealing and its astringency is brought out well in this appropriately Viennese chamber performance. The *Third Quartet*, a late work, was written for the Amadeus, who play it so convincingly. It is spare, seemingly wayward, but with an underlying depth of feeling which comes to the surface in its brooding *Passacaglia.* The *Second*, ending with a forceful *Chaconne*, was written in 1945 to commemorate the 250th anniversary of Purcell's death. The contrasts of style and mood are developed well here, in performances that could be regarded as definitive. On CD the recording is full, vivid and realistic.

String quartet No. 1 in D, Op. 25a.
*** CRD CRD 3351 [id.]. Alberni Qt – SHOSTAKOVICH: *Piano quintet.***(*)

String quartets Nos. 2 in C, Op. 36; 3, Op. 94.
*** CRD CRD 3395 [id.]. Alberni Qt.

The Alberni Quartet have good ensemble and intonation, and they play with considerable feeling; moreover the CDs are available separately. The recording is vivid and clear in its remastered format.

String quartet No. 3, Op. 94.
*** ASV Dig. CDDCA 608 [id.]. Lindsay Qt – TIPPETT: *Quartet No. 4.****

The Lindsay performance brings the most expansive and deeply expressive reading on record. The commitment of the performers makes the final slow movement all the more affecting, baring the inner heart of Britten's rarefied inspiration. The ASV recording is vivid, with fine presence; but extraneous sounds are intrusive at times: heavy breathing, snapping of strings on finger-board, etc.

Suites for unaccompanied cello Nos. 1, Op. 72; 2, Op. 80; 3, Op. 87.
*** BIS Dig. CD 446 [id.]. Torleif Thedéen.

Torleif Thedéen is a young Swedish cellist, still in his twenties, who came to international prominence in the mid-1980s. He has magnificent tonal warmth and eloquence, and he proves a masterly advocate of these *Suites*, which were composed for Rostropovich but which sound no less convincing in his hands. However, Rostropovich's record – see above – offers the *Sonata* as well and is at mid-price.

VOCAL MUSIC

A.M.D.G.; (i) *A Boy was born; Hymn to St Cecilia; A Shepherd's carol.*
*** Virgin Dig. VC 790728-2 [id.]. London Sinf. Voices, (i) St Paul's Cathedral Choristers, Terry Edwards.

A.M.D.G. (*Ad majorem Dei gloriam, To the greater glory of God*, the motto of the Jesuit order) is a collection of choral settings of poems by Gerard Manley Hopkins. As is plain from this beautiful and brilliant first recording of what is in effect a choral suite, they contain some masterly inspirations, ending with the loveliest song of all, a *Prayer*. The Sinfonietta Voices sing with the same sensitive virtuosity in the equally taxing set of choral variations on a Christmas theme, *A Boy was born*, firmer and more dramatic than the rival one from the Corydon Singers on Hyperion. Using solo voices, with Edwards himself singing the bass part, the record also has a fresh and incisive account of *A Hymn to St Cecilia*, made the sharper and cleaner in its gently jazzy rhythms by the slimmer texture. As a charming supplement comes another rarity, the *Shepherd's carol*, written in 1944 for a BBC radio play. Fine recording, both atmospheric and clear.

A Birthday Hansel, Op. 92: Afton Water; My Hoggie; Wee Willie; The winter. A Charm of Lullabies. Folksong arrangements: *The ash grove; Come you not from Newcastle?; How sweet the answer; The last rose of summer; The minstrel boy; O can ye sew cushions; O Waly Waly; Quand j'étais chez mon père; The trees they grow so high.*
** HM Dig. KTC 1046 [id.]. Yvonne Kenny, Carolyn Watkinson, Tan Crone.

This collection of Britten songs refreshingly brings together two of his rarer cycles, and a generous collection of folksongs. Yvonne Kenny's voice, with vibrato sometimes obtrusive, is not ideally suited to recording; but these are sensitive and intelligent performances, well recorded.

A boy was born, Op. 3; Festival Te Deum, Op. 32; Rejoice in the Lamb, Op. 30; A Wedding anthem, Op. 46.
*** Hyp. CDA 66126 [id.]. Corydon Singers, Westminster Cathedral Ch., Best; Trotter (organ).

All the works included here are sharply inspired, usually to match the requirements of particular occasions. *Rejoice in the Lamb* is the most masterly of the pieces, poignantly matching the pain as well as the innocence of the words of the mad poet, Christopher Smart. The refinement and tonal range of the choirs could hardly be more impressive, and the recording is refined and atmospheric to match.

The Burning fiery furnace (2nd Parable), Op. 77.
(M) *** Decca 414 663-2. Pears, Tear, Drake, Shirley-Quirk, Ch. & O of E. Op. Group, composer and Viola Tunnard.

Britten's conception of the church parable, so highly individual with its ritual elements (the audience turned into a medieval congregation), yet allows the widest variety of construction and expression. The story of *Burning fiery furnace* is obviously dramatic in the operatic sense, with vivid scenes like the Entrance of Nebuchadnezzar, the Raising of the Idol, and the putting of the three Israelites into the furnace. Britten is as imaginative as ever in his settings, and one must mention also the marvellous central interlude where the instrumentalists process round the church, which is stunningly well conveyed by the recording. The performers, both singers and players, are the same hand-picked cast that participated in the first performance at Orford Parish Church, where this record was made. This is another example of the way Decca served Britten in providing definitive versions of his major scores for the guidance of all future performers, as well as for our enjoyment at home. The recording now emerges on CD with even greater vividness and presence.

Canticles Nos. 1, My beloved is mine, Op. 40; 2, Abraham and Isaac, Opp. 51; 3, Still falls the rain, Op. 55; 4, Journey of the Magi, Op. 86; 5, Death of St. Narcissus, Op. 89. A birthday hansel. (iii) Arr. of P U R C E L L: *Sweeter than roses.*
(M) *** Decca 425 716-2 [id.]. Peter Pears, Hahessy, Bowman, Shirley-Quirk, Tuckwell, Ellis, composer.

This CD brings together on a single record all five of the miniature cantatas to which Britten gave the title 'Canticle', most of them performed by their original performers. To the new collection, the *Birthday hansel*, written in honour of the seventy-fifth birthday of Queen Elizabeth the Queen Mother, and a Purcell song-arrangement are added for good measure. The *Canticles* all share the spiritual intensity which stemmed from the composer's religious faith. A beautiful collection as well as a historical document, with recording that still sounds well.

A Ceremony of carols; Deus in adjutorium meum; Hymn of St Columba; Hymn to the Virgin; Jubilate Deo in E flat; Missa brevis, Op. 63.
*** Hyp. Dig. CDA 66220 [id.]. Westminster Cathedral Ch., David Hill; (i) with S. Williams; J. O'Donnell (organ).

It was for the trebles of Westminster Cathedral Choir – when directed by George Malcolm – that Britten wrote his *Missa brevis*. Under David Hill, the present choir shows brilliantly how well standards have been kept up, not least in the treble section. Particularly impressive is the boys' singing in the *Ceremony of carols*, where the ensemble is superb, the solo work amazingly mature, and the range of tonal colouring a delight. Along with the other, rarer pieces, this is an outstanding collection, beautifully and atmospherically recorded.

A Ceremony of carols; Hymn to St Cecilia, Op. 17; Hymn to St Peter; Hymn to the Virgin; Te Deum in C.
(B) **(*) ASV Dig. CDQS 6030 [id.]. Christ Church Cathedral, Oxford, Ch., Grier; Kelly.

There is an earthy quality in these performances which reflects the composer's own rejection of over-refined choirboy tone, but the *Hymn to St Cecilia* with its setting of a brilliant Auden poem (text not included) is a degree too rough, and it loses some impact when the choir is rather backwardly balanced. The coupling, however, is apt and most desirable; and for the rest the sound is excellent. For those wanting a budget digital collection including the *Ceremony of carols*, this is excellent value.

(i) *A Ceremony of carols, Op. 28; Hymn to St Cecilia, Op. 17;* (ii) *Jubilee Deo;* (i) *Missa brevis, Op. 63;* (ii; iii) *Rejoice in the Lamb, Op. 30; Te Deum in C.*
*** EMI CDC7 47709. King's College, Cambridge, Ch., (i) Willcocks with Ellis; (ii) Ledger with James Bowman, D. Corkhill, J. Lancelot.

The King's trebles under Willcocks may have less edge in the *Ceremony of carols* than some of their rivals, while the *Missa brevis* can certainly benefit from throatier sound. Yet these Willcocks performances, made towards the end of his stay at Cambridge, are dramatic as well as beautiful, and well recorded, too. To make a particularly generous concert, EMI have added Philip Ledger's new version of the cantata, *Rejoice in the Lamb*, with timpani and percussion added to the original organ part. The biting climaxes are sung with passionate incisiveness, while James Bowman is in his element in the delightful passage which tells you that 'the mouse is a creature of great personal valour'. The *Te Deum* setting and the *Jubilate* make an additional bonus and are no less well sung and recorded.

4 chansons françaises; Les illuminations; Serenade for tenor, horn and strings.
**(*) Chan. Dig. CHAN 8657 [id.]. Felicity Lott, Anthony Rolfe-Johnson, Michael Thompson, SNO, Bryden Thomson.

The *Four French songs* were written when Britten was only fourteen. These are colourful and evocative settings of Victor Hugo and Verlaine, scored with astonishing finesse, if with occasional echoes of Debussy and Ravel. The boy composer's response to the words has remarkable maturity and emotional depth, with flashes of genius worthy of Britten at his finest. Felicity Lott gives a strong and sensitive performance, as she does of the other early French cycle on the disc, *Les illuminations*, bringing out the tough and biting element rather than the sensuousness. Anthony Rolfe-Johnson, soloist in the *Serenade*, gives a finely controlled performance, but is not always helped by the slight distancing of the voice in the recording balance. Nor is Michael Thompson as evocative in the horn solo as his most distinguished predecessors have been. Bryden Thomson draws crisp, responsive playing from the SNO, and the recording is warm and spacious, with plenty of presence.

The Company of Heaven. Paul Bunyan: Overture; Inkslinger's aria; Lullaby of dream shadows.
*** Virgin Dig. VC 791107-2 [id.]. Allen, Barkworth (narrators), Pope, Dressen, LPO Ch., ECO, Brunelle.

Britten wrote this big cantata, *The Company of Heaven*, for radio in 1937 as an offering for the Feast of St Michael and All Angels, but the score was lost for many years. The music, some half-hour of it, links extensive readings from texts on the theme of angels, and there is much that echoes such works of the time as the *Frank Bridge variations* and *Les illuminations*, with Britten's use of a congregational hymn in the last item anticipating both *Noye's Fludde* and *St Nicolas*. It was here too that Britten wrote, with the voice of Peter Pears in mind, a jaunty setting of Emily Brontë. Also very striking is the movement, *War in heaven*, with the men in the chorus delivering the words in sing-speech. Philip Brunelle made this recording soon after the first concert performance at

The Maltings in 1989, using the same excellent forces, with the spoken contributions more effective on record than in concert. The brief excerpts from *Paul Bunyan* include an infectious 'Overture' (completed from sketches, by Colin Matthews) and a rather engaging *Lullaby*, here performed most persuasively. The recording throughout is excellent, spacious and with fine balance and presence.

Curlew River (1st parable for church performance).
(M) *** Decca 421 858-2 [id.]. Pears, Shirley-Quirk, Blackburn, soloists, Instrumental Ens., composer and Viola Tunnard.

Few dramatic works have been based on a more unlikely idea than *Curlew River*, and the result is a dramatic entertainment that defies all convention. The work was initially inspired by Britten's recollection of a Noh-play which he saw in Japan. There are overtones too of Eastern music (Balinese rather than Japanese) in the highly original instrumentation and often free approach to rhythm, but mainly the work's ultimate success stems from the vividness of atmosphere within a monastery setting. Harold Blackburn plays the Abbot of the monastery, who introduces the drama, while John Shirley-Quirk plays the ferryman who takes people over the Curlew River, and Peter Pears sings the part of the madwoman who, distracted, searches fruitlessly for her abducted child. The recording is outstanding even by Decca standards, as the vivid CD transfer readily demonstrates.

Folksong arrangements: *The ash grove; La belle est au jardin d'amour; The bonny Earl o' Moray; The brisk young widow; Ca' the yowes; Come you not from Newcastle?; The foggy, foggy dew; The Lincolnshire poacher; Little Sir William; The minstrel boy; O can ye sew cushions; Oliver Cromwell; O Waly, Waly; The plough boy; Quand j'étais chez mon père; Le roi s'en va-t'en chasse; The Sally Gardens; Sweet Polly Oliver; The trees they grow so high.*
(M) *** EMI CDM7 69423-2. Robert Tear, Philip Ledger.

Close as Robert Tear's interpretations are to those of Peter Pears, he does have a sparkle of his own, helped by resilient accompaniment from Philip Ledger. In any case, some of these songs are unavailable in the Pears versions, and the record is a delight on its own account. *Oliver Cromwell* is among the most delectable of pay-off songs ever written. Fine recording.

(i) *The Golden Vanity*; (ii) *Noye's Fludde.*
(M) *** Decca 425 161-2 [id.]. (i) Wandsworth School Boys' Ch., Burgess, composer (piano); (ii) Brannigan, Rex, Anthony, East Suffolk Children's Ch. & O, E. Op. Group O, Del Mar.

The Golden Vanity is a 'vaudeville' written for the Vienna Boys' Choir. The tale of the cabin boy who sinks the threatening pirate ship and is then drowned by his wicked captain is simply and vividly told, with the help of the well-known folksong, and the recording does wonders in recapturing the fun of performance, with its play ritual round the stage. The Wandsworth Boys are completely at home in the music and sing with pleasing freshness. The coupling, Britten's infectious children's oratorio, setting words from the Chester Miracle Play, was recorded during the 1961 Aldeburgh Festival, and not only the professional choristers but the children too have the time of their lives to the greater glory of God. All the effects have been captured miraculously here, most strikingly the entry into the Ark; while a bugle band blares out fanfares which finally turn into a rollicking march. Altogether this coupling makes a wonderful record, with the stereo readily catching the sense of occasion and particularly the sound of *Eternal father* rising above the storm at the climax of *Noye's Fludde.*

(i; iii) *The Holy sonnets of John Donne, Op. 35;* (ii; iii) *Songs and proverbs of William Blake, Op. 74.*
*** Decca 417 428-2 (3) [id.]. (i) Peter Pears; (ii) Dietrich Fischer-Dieskau; (iii) composer – *Billy Budd.****

This performance of the John Donne cycle sets a definitive standard, with Pears's voice still amazingly even, coping beautifully with both the dramatic outbursts and the lyrical soaring which in fine contrast put this among the richest of modern song-cycles. The Blake cycle makes an excellent coupling. It is just as tough and intense a setting of equally visionary words but it presents fewer moments of sweetness or relaxation. Ideal performances, with the composer re-creating his inspiration.

(i) *Les Illuminations* (song-cycle), *Op. 18;* (ii) *Nocturne;* (iii) *Serenade for tenor, horn and strings, Op. 31.*
*** Decca 417 153-2 [id.]. Peter Pears, (i; iii) ECO; (iii) with Barry Tuckwell; (ii) wind soloists, LSO strings; composer.
**(*) Virgin Dig. VC 790792-2 [id.]. Martyn Hill, (iii) with Frank Lloyd; City of L. Sinfonia, Hickox.

With dedicated accompaniments under the composer's direction, these Pears versions of *Les Illuminations* and the *Serenade* (with its horn obbligato superbly played by Barry Tuckwell) make a perfect coupling. For the CD release Decca have added the recording of the *Nocturne* from 1960. It is a work full – as so much of Britten's output is – of memorable moments. Each song has a different obbligato instrument (with the ensemble unified for the final Shakespeare song), and each instrument gives the song it is associated with its own individual character. Pears as always is the ideal interpreter, the composer a most efficient conductor, and the fiendishly difficult obbligato parts are played superbly. The recording is brilliant and clear, with just the right degree of atmosphere.

From his student days onwards, Martyn Hill has been an outstanding interpreter of Britten's song-cycles, and here he gives heartfelt performances of three great orchestral cycles, to provide rewarding alternatives to the classic recordings by their inspirer, Peter Pears. With Richard Hickox a warmly sympathetic interpreter, relishing delicate textures, Hill produces ravishing half-tones in such delicate songs as the opening Cotton item in the *Serenade.* He is able to give heroic weight when necessary, though the recording balance does not help him; placed among the orchestra rather than in front of it, he is not always able to bite through heavy textures, though it is very satisfying to have such a weighty orchestral climax in the deeply moving final Shakespeare setting of the *Nocturne.* Most remarkable of all in some ways is the dashingly fast account of *Queen and huntress* in the *Serenade,* with the horn soloist, Frank Lloyd, extraordinarily agile in playing the fast triplets. It is a pity that he is barely audible in his offstage solo at the end, yet the atmospheric beauty of the digital recording presents a powerful case for this Virgin issue, even next to the Pears.

(i) *Les Illuminations* (song-cycle), *Op. 18;* (ii) *Phaedra, Op. 93;* French folksong arrangements: *La belle est au jardin d'amour; Eho! Eho!; Fileuse; Quand j'étais chez mon père; Le roi s'en va-t'en chasse.*
*** EMI Dig. CDC7 49259-2 [id.]. (i) Jill Gomez; (ii) Felicity Palmer; Endymion Ens., Whitfield.

Though Felicity Lott has recorded a fine performance of *Les Illuminations* (see above),

Jill Gomez, ably backed by John Whitfield and the Endymion Ensemble, is far more seductively sensuous, matching the exotic quality of the Baudelaire poems. Felicity Palmer, contrasting strongly, gives intense performances both of the late dramatic cantata, *Phaedra* (tougher and less tender than the dedicatee, Janet Baker – see below) and of the five French folksong arrangements not previously recorded in this colourful orchestral form. Vivid, well-balanced recording.

(i) *Les Illuminations* (song-cycle), *Op. 18;* (ii) *Serenade for tenor, horn and strings, Op. 31;* (iii) *Young person's guide to the orchestra.*
**(*) DG 423 239-2 [id.]. (i; ii) Robert Tear; (i) Philh. O; (ii) Clevenger, Chicago SO; (i; ii) Giulini; (iii) French Nat. R. O, Maazel.

The fact that these two excellent performances were recorded on opposite sides of the Atlantic adds to the attractiveness, for the Philharmonia produces playing of warmth and resonance to match that of the Chicago orchestra. Tear is at his finest in both cycles, more open than in his earlier recording of the *Serenade*. Dale Clevenger is a superb horn-player, and though some may find him unidiomatic in places it is good to have a fresh view in such music. Soloists are balanced rather close in an otherwise excellent, vivid recording. The Maazel version of the *Young person's guide to the orchestra* was recorded much earlier and, though well played, was hardly an imaginative way of offering a bonus.

The Prodigal Son (3rd parable), Op. 81.
(M) *** Decca 425 713-2 [id.]. Pears, Tear, Shirley-Quirk, Drake, E. Op. Group Ch. & O, composer & Viola Tunnard.

The last of the parables is the sunniest and most heart-warming. Britten cleverly avoids the charge of oversweetness by introducing the Abbot, even before the play starts, in the role of Tempter, confessing he represents evil and aims to destroy contentment in the family he describes: 'See how I break it up' – a marvellous line for Peter Pears. An ideal performance is given here with a characteristically real and atmospheric Decca recording.

St Nicholas; Hymn to St Cecilia.
*** Hyp. Dig. CDA 66333 [id.]. Rolfe-Johnson, Corydon Singers, St George's Chapel, Windsor, Ch., Girls of Warwick University Chamber Ch., Ch. of Christ Church, Southgate, Sevenoaks School, Tonbridge School, Penshurst Ch. Soc., Occasional Ch., Edwards, Alley, Scott, ECO, Best.

For the first time in a recording, the congregational hymns are included in Matthew Best's fresh and atmospheric account of *St Nicholas*. That adds enormously to the emotional impact of the whole cantata, for they have an effect which is similar to the hymns Britten was to incorporate into his later children's piece, *Noyes Fludde*. Though the chorus is distanced slightly, the contrasts of timbre are caught well, with the waltz-setting of *The birth of Nicholas* and its bath-tub sequence delightfully sung by boy-trebles alone. The unaccompanied *Hymn to St Cecilia* makes an apt and generous coupling, also beautifully sung, with gentle pointing of the jazzy syncopations in crisp, agile ensemble and with sweet matching among the voices.

(i) *Serenade for tenor, horn and strings; Now sleeps the crimson petal.* PURCELL, orch. Britten: *Orpheus Britannicus:* suite of songs. SCHUBERT, orch. Britten: *Die Forelle.* SCHUMANN, orch. Britten: *Frühlingsnacht.* Folksong arrangements: *The bonny Earl o'Moray; Oliver Cromwell. Rossini suite* (film music).
*** EMI Dig. CDC7 49480-2 [id.]. Neil Mackie, (i) Tuckwell; Paisley Ch., SCO, Bedford.

Neil Mackie's version of the *Serenade* not only brings radiantly sweet and true singing and idiomatic playing, but also has an indispensable supplement in a haunting setting, newly discovered, of Tennyson's *Now sleeps the crimson petal*, which Britten originally intended for this work. The disc also features other rarities recorded for the first time, such as Britten's orchestration of Schubert's *Trout* and of Schumann; also the original film-track instrumentation of the music he wrote for a film, *The Tocher*, made by the GPO Film Unit, and which later provided material for his Rossini ballets, *Soirées* and *Matinées Musicales*. Excellent sound.

Songs and proverbs of William Blake, Op. 74; Tit for Tat; 3 Early songs: Beware that I'd ne'er been married; Epitaph; The clerk. Folksong arrangements: *Bonny at morn; I was lonely; Lemady; Lord! I married me a wife!; O Waly, Waly; The Sally Gardens; She's like the swallow; Sweet Polly Oliver.*
**(*) Chan. Dig. CHAN 8514 [id.]. Benjamin Luxon, David Williamson.

Benjamin Luxon's lusty baritone gives an abrasive edge whether to early songs, folksong settings or the Blake cycle originally written for Dietrich Fischer-Dieskau. Only rarely does he become too emphatic. The Blake cycle is commandingly done, despite some signs of strain, and the most valuable items of all are the five very late folksong settings, originally with harp accompaniment, ending with the most touching, the hauntingly melancholy *She's like the swallow*. Excellent, sensitive accompaniment and first-rate recording.

(i) *Tit for Tat;* (ii) Folksong arrangements: *Bird scarer's song; Bonny at morn; David of the White Rock; Lemady; Lord! I married me a wife!; She's like the swallow.*
*** Mer. CDE 84119 [id.]. Shirley-Quirk; (i) Ledger; (ii) Ellis – *Suite for harp* etc.***

This Meridian collection celebrates a nicely varied group of works which Britten wrote for friends to perform at the Aldeburgh Festival. John Shirley-Quirk was the baritone who first sang the cycle, *Tit for Tat*, with the composer at the piano, and he is still unrivalled in the sharp yet subtle way he brings out the irony in these boyhood settings of De la Mare poems. It is also good to have him singing the six late folk-settings with harp accompaniment, here played by Osian Ellis for whom (with Peter Pears) they were originally written – much more distinctive in these original versions than with piano accompaniment. The recording is naturally balanced and immediate.

War Requiem, Op. 66.
*** Decca 414 383-2 [id.]. Vishnevskaya, Pears, Fischer-Dieskau, Bach Ch., LSO Ch., Highgate School Ch., Melos Ens., LSO, composer.
*** EMI Dig. CDS7 47034-8 [id.]. Söderström, Tear, Allen, Trebles of Christ Church Cathedral Ch., Oxford, CBSO Ch., CBSO, Rattle.
** Telarc Dig. CD 80157 (2) [id.]. Lorna Haywood, Rolfe-Johnson, Luxon, Atlanta Boy Ch., Atlanta Ch. & SO, Robert Shaw.

The vivid realism of Britten's own 1963 recording of the *War Requiem*, one of the outstanding achievements of the whole analogue stereo era, comes over the more strikingly in the CD transfer, with uncannily precise placing and balancing of the many different voices and instruments; and John Culshaw's contribution as producer is all the more apparent. The recorded performance comes near to the ideal, but it is a pity that Britten insisted on Vishnevskaya for the soprano solos. Having a Russian singer was emotionally right, but musically Heather Harper would have been so much better still. The digital remastering, as with *Peter Grimes*, brings added textural refinement and makes the recording sound newly minted; it also reveals a degree of background hiss.

The most striking difference between Rattle's interpretation and that of Britten himself lies in the relationship between the settings of Owen's poems and the setting of the liturgy in Latin. With Söderström a far more warmly expressive soloist than the oracular Vishnevskaya, the human emotions behind the Latin text come out strongly with less distancing than from the composer. If Tear does not always match the subtlety of Pears on the original recording, Allen sounds more idiomatic than Fischer-Dieskau. Rattle's approach is warm, dedicated and dramatic, with fine choral singing (not least from the Christ Church Cathedral trebles). The dramatic orchestral contrasts are superbly brought out, as in the blaze of trumpets on *Hosanna*. The various layers of perspective are impressively managed by the superb digital recording. Yet in its combination of imaginative flair with technical expertise, the Culshaw recording of two decades earlier is by no means surpassed by this new EMI venture, although the EMI set has the considerable digital advantage of a silent background.

Sharpness of focus is not always a help in evoking the mystery and drama of a work such as the *War Requiem*, and though Shaw's Telarc recording has sound of spectacular clarity and detail, it fails to match either of its predecessors in the qualities of this moving work which matter most. The clarity of the recording lets the fine precision of ensemble in chorus and orchestra come over very tellingly, but it also emphasizes how literal the performance is, often lacking the dramatic tensions implicit in Britten's evocative mingling of Latin liturgy and Wilfred Owen poems. So the setting of *Bugles sang* is more remarkable for beautiful textures than for mystery, and when the excited chorus, *Confutatis maledictis*, erupts into *Be slowly lifted up*, there is no feeling of horror in the resolution, even though Benjamin Luxon sings most sympathetically, as does Anthony Rolfe-Johnson in the tenor part. Lorna Haywood with her bright, clear soprano completes a fine trio of soloists, and the Atlanta Chorus produces incandescent tone, thrilling in fortissimos, with the trebles of the Atlanta Boy Chorus beautifully set at a distance.

OPERA

Albert Herring (complete).
**(*) Decca 421 849-2 (2) [id.]. Pears, Fisher, Noble, Brannigan, Cantelo, ECO, Ward, composer.

The CD transfer of Britten's own 1964 recording of the comic opera, *Albert Herring*, is a delight. The comedy comes over with an immediacy and sense of presence which have you involved straight away in the improbable tale of the May King, chosen when no local girl is counted suitable. Peter Pears's portrait of the innocent Albert was caught only just before he grew too old for the role, but it is full of unique touches. Sylvia Fisher is a magnificent Lady Billows, and it is good to have so wide a range of British singers of the 1960s so characterfully presented – as, for example, Sheila Rex, whose tiny portrait of Albert's mother is a gem. The recording, made in Jubilee Hall, remains astonishingly vivid.

Billy Budd (complete).
*** Decca 417 428-2 (3) [id.]. Glossop, Pears, Langdon, Shirley-Quirk, Wandsworth School Boys' Ch., Amb. Op. Ch., LSO, composer – *Holy sonnets of John Donne* etc.***

The libretto of *Billy Budd*, by E. M. Forster and Eric Crozier, with its all-male cast is more skilled than those Britten usually set, and the range of characterization – so apparently limited in a tale of good and evil directly confronting one another – is masterly, with Peter Pears's role of Captain Vere presenting the moral issue at its most moving. Britten's master-stroke of representing the confrontation of Vere and the condemned Billy in a sequence of 34 bare common chords is irresistible, and the many richly imaginative strokes – atmospheric as well as dramatic – are superbly managed. An ideal cast, with Glossop a bluff, heroic Billy, and Langdon a sharply dark-toned Claggart, making these symbol-figures believable. Magnificent sound. The layout on three CDs begins with the *John Donne Holy sonnets* and *Songs and proverbs of William Blake*, with the *Prologue* and Act I of the opera beginning thereafter.

Death in Venice (complete).
*** Decca 425 669-2 (2) [id.]. Pears, Shirley-Quirk, Bowman, Bowen, Leeming, E. Op. Group Ch., ECO, Bedford.

Thomas Mann's novella, which made an expansively atmospheric film, far removed from the world of Mann, here makes a surprisingly successful opera, totally original in its alternation of monologue for the central character (on two levels, inner and external) and colourful set-pieces showing off the world of Venice and the arrival of the plague. Britten's inspiration, drawing together threads from all his earlier operas from *Peter Grimes* to the *Church parables*, is nothing less than exuberant, with the chamber orchestra producing the richest possible sounds. Pears's searching performance in the central role of Aschenbach is set against the darkly sardonic singing of John Shirley-Quirk in a sequence of roles as the Dionysiac figure who draws Aschenbach to his destruction. The recording is extremely vivid in its CD format and, though Steuart Bedford's assured conducting lacks some of the punch that Britten would have brought, the whole presentation makes this a set to establish the work outside the opera house as the very culmination of Britten's cycle of operas.

Gloriana: Choral dances.
*** Hyp. CDA 66175 [id.]. Martyn Hill, Thelma Owen, Holst Singers & O, Hilary Davan Wetton – BLISS: *Lie strewn the white flocks*; HOLST: *Choral hymns from the Rig Veda.****

It is little short of a scandal that so great an opera as *Gloriana* still remains to be recorded complete. The composer's own choral suite, made up of unaccompanied choral dances linked by passages for solo tenor and harp, makes a valuable if tantalizing sample, an excellent coupling for the equally attractive Bliss and Holst items. Excellent, atmospheric recording.

A Midsummer Night's Dream (complete).
*** Decca 425 663-2 (2) [id.]. Deller, Harwood, Harper, Veasey, Watts, Shirley-Quirk, Brannigan, Downside and Emmanuel School Ch., LSO, composer.

Britten and Pears together prepared the libretto for this opera by careful compression of the Shakespeare words. What this recording confirms – with the aid of the score – more than any live performance, is how compressed the music is, as well as the words. At first one may regret the absence of rich and memorable tunes, but there is no thinness of argument, and the atmosphere of every scene is brilliantly re-created in the most evocative orchestral sounds. The beauty of instrumental writing comes out in this recording even more than in the opera house, for John Culshaw, the recording manager, put an extra halo round the fairy music to act as a substitute for visual atmosphere. The problem of conveying the humour of the play-scene at the end with the 'rude mechanicals' cavorting about the stage proved more intractable. Humour is there all right, but the laughter of the stage audience is too ready for comfort. Britten again proves himself an ideal interpreter of his own music and draws virtuoso playing from the LSO (marvellous trumpet sounds for Puck's music). Among the singers Peter Pears has shifted from his original role as Flute (the one who has the Donizetti mad-scene parody to sing) to the straight role of Lysander. The mechanicals are admirably led by Owen Brannigan as

Bottom; and among the lovers Josephine Veasey (Hermia) is outstanding. Deller, with his magical male alto singing, is the eerily effective Oberon.

Paul Bunyan (complete).
⊛ *** Virgin Dig. VCD 790710-2 (2) [id.]. James Lawless, Dan Dressen, Elisabeth Comeaux Nelson, soloists, Ch. & O of Plymouth Music Series, Minnesota, Philip Brunelle.

Aptly, this first recording of Britten's choral operetta comes from the state, Minnesota, where the story of this legendary giant is set. The Plymouth Music Series under Philip Brunelle fields a team not of international singers but of enthusiasts. That they are American brings an immediate advantage not just in the spoken and sung accents but in the idiomatic feeling for the syncopated rhythms in this bold but initially unsuccessful attempt of the poet, W. H. Auden, and Britten to invade Broadway. When the principal character is a giant who can appear only as a disembodied voice, the piece works rather better on record or radio than on stage. Musically, Britten's conscious assumption of popular American mannerisms does not prevent his invention from showing characteristic originality. It is not just the jazzy, ballad-like songs and ensembles that stick in the memory but such charming numbers as *Tiny's song* (sung very freshly and sweetly by Elisabeth Comeaux Nelson). Also most memorable is the choral section of the *Prologue*, with its lines by Auden which moved Britten particularly: *But once in a while the odd thing happens, / Once in a while the dream comes true.* He confessed many years later that he was thinking how he met Peter Pears. Recorded in clean, vivid sound, with Philip Brunelle a vigorous conductor, this excellent first recording richly deserves the prizes it won for the Virgin Classics label.

Peter Grimes (complete).
⊛ *** Decca 414 577-2 [id.]. Pears, Claire Watson, Pease, Jean Watson, Nilsson, Brannigan, Evans, Ch. and O of ROHCG, composer.

The Decca recording of *Peter Grimes* was one of the first great achievements of the stereo era. Few opera recordings can claim to be so definitive, with Peter Pears, for whom it was written, in the name-part, Owen Brannigan (another member of the original team) and a first-rate cast with Claire Watson a highly sympathetic Ellen Orford. James Pease, as the understanding Captain Balstrode, is brilliantly incisive musically and dramatically; but beyond that it becomes increasingly unfair to single out individual performances. Britten conducts superbly and secures splendidly incisive playing, with the whole orchestra on its toes throughout. The recording, superbly atmospheric, has so many felicities that it would be hard to enumerate them, and the Decca engineers have done wonders in making up aurally for the lack of visual effects. Moreover, the digital remastering for CD miraculously has improved the sound still further. The striking overall bloom remains, yet solo voices and chorus are vividly clear and fully projected. Some background noise remains, of course, but it is not really intrusive and, that apart, one might believe this to be a modern digital set.

Peter Grimes: 4 Sea interludes and Passacaglia.
*** Chan. Dig. CHAN 8473 [id.]. Ulster O, Handley – BAX: *On the Sea-shore*; BRIDGE: *The Sea.****

Britten's suite is made up of four interludes, taken from an opera consistently rich in evocation, that with the *Passacaglia* make a finely balanced concert piece. Handley draws brilliant and responsive playing from the Ulster Orchestra in readings that fully capture the atmospheric beauty of the writing, helped by vivid recording of demonstration quality.

(i) *The Rape of Lucretia* (complete); (ii) *Phaedra, Op. 93.*
*** Decca 425 666-2 (2) [id.]. (i) Pears, Harper, Shirley-Quirk, J. Baker, Luxon, ECO, composer; (ii) J. Baker, ECO, Bedford.

In combining on CD *The Rape of Lucretia* with *Phaedra*, Decca celebrates two outstanding performances by Dame Janet Baker, recorded at the peak of her career. In particular her performance as Lucretia underlines the depth of feeling behind a work which, in its formal classical frame, may superficially seem to hide emotion. The logical problems of the story remain – why *should* Lucretia feel so guilty? – but with Baker the heart-rending tragedy of the heroine is conveyed with passionate conviction, her range of tone-colours, her natural feeling for words and musical phrase used with supreme artistry. Similarly *Phaedra* – written at the very end of Britten's life – provides vocal writing which brings out every glorious facet of her voice. Setting words from Robert Lowell's fine translation of Racine's play, the composer encapsulated the character of the tragic heroine. The use of harpsichord in the recitatives linking the sections of this scena is no mere neo-classical device but a sharply dramatic and atmospheric stroke. Among other distinguished vocal contributions to the opera, Peter Pears and Heather Harper stand out, while Benjamin Luxon makes the selfish Tarquinius into a living character. The stylization of the drama with its frame of Christian comment comes over even more effectively when imagined rather than seen. The seductive beauty of the writing – Britten then at his early peak – is splendidly caught, the melodies and tone-colours as ravishing as any that he ever conceived.

Bruch, Max (1838–1920)

Violin concerto No. 1 in G min., Op. 26.
(M) *** Decca 417 707-2 [id.]. Kyung Wha Chung, RPO, Kempe – SAINT-SAENS: *Havanaise*; TCHAIKOVSKY: *Concerto.****
*** ASV Dig.CDDCA 680. Xue Wei, Philh. O, Bakels – SAINT-SAENS: *Concerto No. 3.****
(B) *** CfP Dig CD-CFP 4566 [Ang. CDB 62920]. Tasmin Little, Royal Liverpool PO, Handley – DVORÁK: *Concerto.****
*** EMI Dig. CDC7 49663-2 [id.]. Nigel Kennedy, ECO, Tate – MENDELSSOHN: *Concerto*; SCHUBERT: *Rondo.****
(B) *** Pickwick Dig. PCD 829 [MCA MCAD 25934]. Jaime Laredo, SCO – MENDELSSOHN: *Concerto.****
*** DG 419 629-2. Shlomo Mintz, Chicago SO, Abbado (also with KREISLER: *Caprice viennoise; Liebeslied; Liebesfreud*) – MENDELSSOHN: *Concerto.***(*)
*** DG Dig. 400 031-2 [id.]. Mutter, BPO, Karajan – MENDELSSOHN: *Concerto.****
(M) *** EMI CDM7 69003-2 [id.]. Menuhin, Philh. O, Susskind – MENDELSSOHN: *Concerto.****
(M) *** Decca 417 793-2y [id.]. Ricci, LSO, Gamba – MENDELSSOHN: *Concerto***(*); SAINT-SAENS: *Havanaise* etc.***
(M) (***) EMI mono CDM7 69261-2 [id.]. David Oistrakh, LSO, Lovro von Matačić – BEETHOVEN: *Concerto.***(*)
(B) **(*) EMI CDZ7 62519-2. Menuhin, LSO, Boult – MENDELSSOHN: *Violin concerto.***(*)
(*) ASV Dig. CDRPO 8013 [id.]. Anne Meyers, RPO, Seaman – BARBER: *Violin concerto.**
(*) Decca Dig. 421 145-2 [id.]. Joshua Bell, ASMF, Marriner – MENDELSSOHN: *Concerto.*(*)

(M) **(*) Ph. 420 703-2 [id.]. Grumiaux, New Philh. O, Wallberg – BRAHMS: *Concerto*.**(*)

(B) **(*) CBS MBK 44717 [id.]. Zukerman, LAPO, Mehta – LALO: *Symphonie espagnole*.**(*)

Even against all the formidable competition, the magic of Kyung Wha Chung, a spontaneously inspired violinist if ever there was one, comes over very beguilingly in her (mid-priced) Decca interpretation, while Kempe and the Royal Philharmonic give a sympathetic, if not always perfectly polished accompaniment, well caught in a glowing recording from the early 1970s which has responded well to its remastering. There may be more glossily perfect accounts of the concerto, but Chung goes straight to the heart, finding mystery and fantasy as well as more extrovert qualities.

Xue Wei (Xue as in *Schweppes*; Wei as in *way*) is a Chinese soloist of very considerable calibre. His approach to the *Concerto* is at once passionately committed and refined in its delicacy of detail. Fortunately he is accompanied superbly by Kees Bakels, who provides exciting orchestral tuttis to lead the ear on from the ardour of the solo playing, while Wei can equally seduce the listener with a most magical pianissimo. The slow movement is ravishing in its poetic flair, and the finale is full of fire. The recording balance is a shade artificial, with a bold presence for the soloist and bright orchestral violins against an essentially resonant acoustic, but it is fully acceptable. An outstanding début.

It was the Classics for Pleasure/Eminence label that promoted Nigel Kennedy's first concerto recording, and that enterprise is here followed up in the first recording by another highly talented young violinist, Tasmin Little, a generous and unique coupling of Bruch and Dvořák. The movement in the Bruch where Little's individuality comes out most clearly is the central *Adagio*, raptly done, with a deceptive simplicity of phrasing, totally unselfconscious, that matches the purity of her sound. Her speeds in the outer movements are broader than those of such rivals as Kennedy and Lin. The finale may not have quite the thrusting excitement of Lin's in particular, but the clarity and precision of her playing are fair compensation, along with the fuller, more faithful sound. At full price this would be a first-rate recommendation: on CfP it is an outstanding bargain.

Kennedy's is a warm, positive performance, consistently sympathetic, with the English Chamber Orchestra anything but lightweight. Kennedy's masculine strength goes with a totally unsentimental view of Bruch's lyricism, as in the central slow movement. This may not have quite the individual poetry of the very finest versions; but, coupled with an outstanding account of the Mendelssohn and a bonus to that usual coupling in the rare Schubert *Rondo*, it makes an excellent recommendation. The recording is full, warm and well balanced.

Jaime Laredo with consistently fresh and sweet tone gives a delightfully direct reading, warmly expressive but never for a moment self-indulgent. His is a beautiful, reflective account of the slow movement. The orchestral ensemble is particularly impressive, when no conductor is involved. With first-rate modern digital recording, this is a bargain, a highlight of the Pickwick budget-price catalogue.

Shlomo Mintz certainly makes the listener hang on to every phrase and his playing is undoubtedly compelling. The vibrato is wide but his approach is so distinctive and interesting that few listeners will not be fired. The Chicago Symphony Orchestra plays with great brilliance and enthusiasm, and Abbado's direction is most sympathetic. The vivid recording has transferred splendidly to CD. As an encore Mintz plays the three Kreisler lollipops with great flair.

In Anne-Sophie Mutter's hands the concerto has an air of chaste sweetness, shedding much of its ripe, sensuous quality but retaining its romantic feeling. There is a delicacy and tenderness here which are very appealing and, although the tuttis have plenty of fire,

Karajan sensitively scales down his accompaniment in the lyrical passages to match his soloist. The digital recording provides a natural balance and a vivid orchestral texture.

Menuhin's performance has long held an honoured place in the catalogue. It was a work to which he made a particularly individual response, and he was in very good form when he made the disc. The performance has a fine spontaneity, the work's improvisatory quality very much part of the interpretation, and there is no doubt about the poetry Menuhin finds in the slow movement, or the sparkle in the finale. The bright forward sound of the 1960 recording has transferred vividly to CD.

Ricci's performance of the *G minor Concerto* has a fine intensity and there is a natural warmth. Ricci's timbre is personal and instantly recognizable, and his manner full of temperament; Gamba accompanies persuasively. The Decca sound remains vivid, with good definition and plenty of depth. For the CD reissue, two Saint-Saëns showpieces have been added.

David Oistrakh's 1954 mono recording of this *Concerto* is rightly admired. His restraint brings a moving eloquence to the slow movement, especially its closing pages. The polished accompaniment matches the aristocratic feeling of the soloist, yet has plenty of impetus. Overall this makes a valuable corrective to more histrionic versions of this famous work and it shows the soloist at his finest. No apologies need be made for the excellently balanced recording.

Menuhin's second stereo recording of the Bruch *Concerto* was made in the early 1970s. While he is obviously on familiar ground, there is no sign of over-familiarity and the lovely slow movement is given a performance of great warmth and humanity. Boult accompanies admirably and the recording is obviously fuller and more modern than the earlier version with Susskind, even if the solo playing is technically less immaculate. On EMI's bargain Laser label, this coupling with Mendelssohn remains very competitive.

Anne Meyers' performance with the RPO under Christopher Seaman is keenly musical, though competition is stiffer here than in the Barber coupling. Her performance is both refined and lyrical, though she is perhaps slightly lacking in dramatic scale; but it is still a satisfying account, if the fine Barber coupling is wanted.

Joshua Bell demonstrates a flawless technique and plays with plenty of warmth and poetry, if missing something of the withdrawn, 'inner' quality of the slow movement. He is not helped by a very forward balance which places him in a spotlight at the expense of the orchestra, although Marriner's fine accompaniment is not entirely masked. The effect is to boost the romantic boldness of his playing, but the uneven partnership between soloist and orchestra prevents the fullest recommendation.

Grumiaux's version with Wallberg would not be counted a first choice; but as a coupling for an outstanding performance of the Brahms *Concerto* it offers a refreshingly different view, civilized, classical in its refinement, if slightly cool. Yet Grumiaux brings all his beauty of tone and expressive technique to this music-making, and he is well accompanied and recorded.

Zukerman's account of the *G minor Concerto* is splendidly eloquent, and the slow movement is played most beautifully. The late 1970s recording is also good and the balance convincing within a fairly resonant acoustic. On the whole the transfer is successful, and those seeking a coupling with Lalo might consider this at bargain price.

Violin concerto No. 1 in G min., Op. 26; Scottish fantasy, Op. 46.
⊛ *** CBS Dig. MK 42315 [id.]. Cho-Liang Lin, Chicago SO, Slatkin.
*** RCA RD 86214 [RCA 6214-2-RC]. Heifetz, New SO of L., Sargent – VIEUXTEMPS: *Concerto No. 5.***

Cho-Liang Lin gives radiantly beautiful performances of Bruch's two most popular concertante works for violin, totally compelling in their combination of passion and purity, strength and dark, hushed intensity. Lin is particularly imaginative and moving in the longer and lesser-known of the two works, the *Scottish fantasy*, which emerges as far more than a collection of Scottish melodies. There have been few accounts on record of the slow movement of the *G minor* that begin to match the raptness of Lin, most sensitively accompanied by Slatkin and the Chicago orchestra.

Heifetz plays with supreme assurance, and the slow movement shows this fine artist in top romantic form. All lovers of great violin playing should at least hear this coupling, for Heifetz's panache and the subtlety of his bowing and colour bring a wonderful freshness to Bruch's charming Scottish whimsy. Sargent accompanies sympathetically, and it is noticeable that though the soloist is balanced much too closely, there is never any doubt that Heifetz can still produce a true *pianissimo*.

Violin concerto No. 2 in D min., Op. 44; Scottish fantasy, Op. 46.
**(*) EMI Dig. CDC7 49071-2 [id.]. Perlman, Israel PO, Mehta.

Perlman attractively couples Bruch's two 'next-best' concertante violin works in performances full of characteristic brilliance and panache, recorded in rather bright, aggressive sound at the Mann Auditorium, Tel Aviv. Perlman may be less intimately reflective in both works than he was when he recorded this coupling before with the New Philharmonia, but in the fast movements there are ample compensations in the sharp concentration from first to last.

Kol Nidrei, Op. 47.
*** DG Dig. 427 323-2 [id.]. Matt Haimovitz, Chicago SO, Levine – LALO: *Concerto*; SAINT-SAENS: *Concerto No. 1.****
(*) Decca Dig. 410 144-2. Harrell, Philh. O, Ashkenazy – DVOŘÁK: *Cello concerto.*
(B) ** DG 429 155-2 [id.]. Fournier, LAP, Martinon – DVOŘÁK: *Cello concerto*; BLOCH: *Schelomo.***(*)

Bruch was not himself Jewish, but his *Kol Nidrei* sensitively draws on Hebrew melodies associated with the Day of Atonement. Matt Haimovitz, born in Israel, has a natural feeling for the piece and his performance, balancing restraint with expressive intensity, is serenely moving, yet not without romantic feeling. He is subtly accompanied and very well recorded.

This withdrawn, prayerful Bruch piece also finds a natural response in Lynn Harrell, whose musical personality is often comparatively reticent; his account with Ashkenazy is both eloquent and atmospheric and certainly very well recorded.

Fournier's performance, while not without feeling, is slightly lacking in romantic urgency. The recording is fully acceptable.

Symphonies Nos. 1 in E flat, Op. 28; 2 in F min., Op. 36; 3 in E, Op. 51. 7 Swedish dances, Op. 63.
** Ph. Dig. 420 932-2 (2) [id.]. Leipzig GO, Masur.

When the first of Bruch's three symphonies is the one that is most striking in its invention and each has its weaknesses, one has to deduce that he was more a symphonist by default than by nature. Yet this collected edition contains much attractive music, beautifully played and recorded, guaranteed to delight anyone wanting undemanding symphonies as alternatives to those of Brahms and Schumann. Masur's performances with the Leipzig Gewandhaus Orchestra are characteristically warm and refined, with smooth recording to match, but sparkle is largely missing. The *Swedish dances*, dating from much later, make an apt and attractive fill-up; but when the disc is not generously filled, it is a pity that only seven from the full set of fifteen are included.

4 Pieces for clarinet, viola and piano, Op. 83/1, 2, 5 & 6.
*** EMI CDC7 49736-2. Meyer, Zimmermann, Holl – MOZART: *Clarinet trio;* SCHUMANN: *Märchenerzählungen.****

Four of Bruch's *Eight Pieces*, Opus 83 – Nos. 1, 2, 5 and 6 – make up a delightful collection of music for this rare combination, and these highly individual artists are very winning in bringing out the amiable Mendelssohnian qualities without any sentimentality. Excellent recording.

Bruckner, Anton (1824–96)

Symphonies Nos. 1–9 (original editions).
(M) ** Teldec/WEA Dig. 2292 46068-2 (10) [id.]. Frankfurt RSO, Inbal.

Eliahu Inbal's performances with the Frankfurt Radio Orchestra are obviously not a first choice since they commit to disc Bruckner's first thoughts rather than the finished works of art. The differences are most striking in the case of the 1874 version of No. 4, where the familiar scherzo is not to be found, and in the opening of the finale. There are, of course, major divergences in Nos. 3 and 8: Inbal gives us the 1873 edition of No. 3, the form in which it was first presented to Wagner. Inbal has a good feeling for Bruckner and there is no lack of atmosphere, but the set as a whole is variable. Nos. 5 and 6 do not come off well and, generally speaking, readers would be better advised to stick with rival versions, supplementing them for the sake of interest with Inbal's accounts of 1, 3, 4 and 8. The recordings are good though not top-drawer.

Symphonies Nos. 1–9.
(M) *** DG 429 648-2 (9) [id.]. BPO, Karajan.
(M) *** DG 429 079-2 (9) [id.]. BPO or Bav. RSO, Jochum.
(M) **(*) HM/BMG GD 60075 (10) [60075-2-RG]. Cologne RSO, Wand.

The reappearance of Karajan's magnificent cycle, long a yardstick by which others were measured – and at mid-price, too – must be warmly welcomed. The *Symphonies* have been re-coupled: Nos. 1 and 5, which were coupled together, are now given a record each, as indeed is No. 8, one of the peaks of the cycle. This is his 1976 account, which is only marginally less magisterial than his recent Vienna performance. In No. 1, Karajan (like Günther Wand) opts for the 1891 edition, while Jochum gives us the Linz version of 1865–6. We have sung the praises of these recordings loud and long, and in their new format they are outstanding value.

Jochum's cycle was recorded between 1958 (No. 5) and 1967 (No. 2), all but four (Nos. 2, 3, 5 and 6) with the Berlin Philharmonic. Like the Karajan set, it enjoys the advantage of accommodating one symphony per disc. No apology need be made for either the performances or the quality of the recorded sound, which wears its years lightly. Indeed one of the finest is the 1958 *Fifth.* Jochum brought a sense of mystery and atmosphere to Bruckner that was quite unique, and it more than compensates for the occasional freedom he permitted himself. His was the first overview of Bruckner on record – followed not long afterwards by Haitink on Philips – and he still has special claims as a guide in this terrain. He communicates a lofty inspiration to his players, and many of these readings can more than hold their own with later rivals.

Honours are almost (but not quite) evenly divided between Jochum and Günther

Wand's more recent survey (1974–81) with the Cologne Radio Symphony Orchestra. Wand is a dedicated Brucknerian who rarely falters in his majestic progress. His accounts of Nos. 5 and 6 do not match Jochum but elsewhere (in Nos. 2 and 8) he is perhaps to be preferred. The *Eighth* may be the least successful of the Jochum set, and the planners were wise to choose Wand's 1979 recording rather than his more recent and less convincing account. Except in No. 6, Wand is never less than perceptive and at times he and his fine orchestra achieve real inspiration.

Symphony No. 0 in D min.; Overture in G min.
**(*) Decca Dig. 421 593-2 [id.]. Berlin RSO, Chailly.

Riccardo Chailly's Bruckner recordings have the merit of clarity and definition but are sometimes short on atmosphere and warmth. His account of the unnumbered *D minor* (the so-called *Die Nullte*), which actually comes between the *First* and *Second Symphonies*, does not have the eloquence of the long-deleted Haitink LP (Philips) but is still eminently acceptable. The Berlin Radio Orchestra respond well to Chailly's direction and, both as a recording and as a performance, this deserves recommendation. There is at present no satisfactory alternative.

Symphony No. 1 in C min.
*** Orfeo Dig. C 145851A [id.]. Bav. State O, Sawallisch.

Symphonies Nos. 1 in C min.; 5 in B flat.
**(*) DG 415 985-2 (2) [id.]. BPO, Karajan.

Sawallisch's account of the *First* is probably the best-sounding of the CDs before the public and his interpretation is impressive in its honesty and dignity. There is warmth and some beautiful playing from the fine Bavarian orchestra, which is recorded in a spacious, yet not over-reverberant acoustic.

Karajan's versions of Nos. 1 and 5 come yoked together, which saves a disc but may not suit all collectors. No. 1 is digital (1982) but the recording is brightly lit and not always ideally expansive at the bottom end. It is still an incisive and powerful reading. Karajan, like Sawallisch, uses the revised Linz version and here as elsewhere shows a clear-headed concentration, making light of the problems of co-ordinating arguments which in lesser hands can seem rambling. In the *Fifth Symphony* the ear registers a greater resonant warmth in the (1977) analogue sound, for the recording generally is richer and more spacious than its digital companion. The reading is not just poised and polished; it is superbly structured on every level, clear on detail as well as on overall architecture. Karajan takes a patrician view of this great and individual symphonist; even if the slow movement lacks some of the simple dedication which makes Jochum's earlier version with the same orchestra so compelling, the result is undoubtedly satisfying. The playing of the Berlin Philharmonic is magnificent.

Symphony No. 2 in C min.
*** DG Dig. 415 988-2 [id.]. BPO, Karajan.

Karajan's reading is not only powerful and polished, it is distinctive on matters both of tempi and of text. He modifies the Nowak edition by opening out some of the cuts, but by no means all. He starts reticently, only later expanding in grandeur. The scherzo at a fast speed is surprisingly lightweight, the finale relatively slow and spacious. It is a noble reading, not always helped by rather bright digital recording. However, the CD brings a firmer sound-image than the LP, with more weight at the bottom than some in this series, and the strings do not lack amplitude in the *Andante*.

Symphony No. 2 in C min. (original Haas 1872 version).
** Teldec/WEA Dig. 2292 43718-2 [id.]. Frankfurt RSO, Inbal.

In his Frankfurt performance, Inbal, so the label tells us, offers the revised version of 1877, but what we get is something much closer to the 1872 Haas version. This retains the scherzo and trio with all its repeats and uses the original horn instead of the clarinet, substituted by Herbeck in 1876 at the end of the slow movement. Incidentally, the closing string chords are missing here, which brings one up with a start. The playing is for the most part good without being outstanding, and the recording, made at the Frankfurt Opera, is very good. Karajan really does play the 1877 (Nowak) edition and remains first choice.

Symphony No. 3 in D min.
*** DG Dig. 421 362-2 [id.]. BPO, Karajan.
**(*) Decca Dig. 417 093-2 [id.]. Berlin RSO, Chailly.

Karajan's account of the *Third Symphony* is very impressive indeed. He opts for the Nowak edition of 1888–9. One is awe-struck by the eloquence and beauty of the orchestral playing and the command of architecture here. Karajan achieves a sense of majesty in the opening movement and an other-worldliness and spirituality in the slow movement that cannot fail to move the listener. At the same time, fine though it is, this is not a state-of-the-art recording and it is not as transparent or detailed as, say, Chailly's Bruckner *Seventh* on Decca.

Vividly recorded and beautifully played, Chailly's version of No. 3 – using the 1889 text, as Karajan does – has admirable qualities. It is a broad, spacious view of the work but, by the standards of the finest Bruckner recordings, it is undercharacterized.

Symphony No. 4 in E flat (Romantic) (original 1874 version).
**(*) Teldec/WEA Dig. 2292 42960-2 [id.]. Frankfurt RSO, Inbal.

Like the *Third*, there are three versions of the *Romantic symphony*, and no one has recorded the original before. The differences are most obvious in the scherzo, a completely different and more fiery movement, but the opening of the finale is also totally different. Inbal's performance is more than adequate – indeed he has a genuine feeling for the Bruckner idiom and pays scrupulous attention to dynamic refinements. The recording is well detailed, though the climaxes almost (but not quite) reach congestion. An indispensable and fascinating issue.

Symphony No. 4 in E flat (Romantic).
(B) *** DG 427 200-2 [id.]. BPO, Jochum.
*** DG 415 277-2 [id.]. BPO, Karajan.
*** Decca Dig. 425 613-2 [id.]. Concg. O, Riccardo Chailly.
(B) *** CBS MYK 44871 [id.]. Columbia SO, Walter.
*** Denon Dig. C37 7126 [id.]. Dresden State O, Blomstedt.
(M) **(*) EMI CDM7 69006-2 [id.]. BPO, Karajan.
(M) **(*) Ph. 420 881-2 [id.]. Concg. O, Haitink.
(M) **(*) EMI CDM7 69127-2 [id.]. Philh. O, Klemperer.
**(*) Decca Dig. 410 550-2 [id.]. Chicago SO, Solti.
(BB) ** Naxos Dig. 8.550154 [id.]. Royal Flanders PO, Günther Neuhold.

Jochum's way with Bruckner is unique. So gentle is his hand that the opening of each movement or even the beginning of each theme emerges into the consciousness rather than starting normally. And when it is a matter of leading from one section to another over a difficult transition passage – as in the lead-in to the first-movement recapitulation – no one can match Jochum in his subtlety and persuasiveness. The purist may object that, in order to do this, Jochum reduces the speed far below what is marked, but Jochum is for the listener who wants above all to love Bruckner. The recording from the late 1960s still sounds vivid and firm.

Karajan's opening (on his DG version) also has more beauty and a greater feeling of mystery than almost anyone else on CD. As in his earlier, EMI record, Karajan brings a keen sense of forward movement to this music as well as showing a firm grip on its architecture. His slow movement is magnificent. The DG analogue recording lacks the transparency and detail of the very finest of his records, but there is no doubt that this is a performance of considerable stature.

Chailly's new account has two things in its favour: the incomparable Concertgebouw Orchestra at their most resplendent, and a Decca recording of magnificent opulence. The results are very enjoyable, and Chailly himself is a far from unimpressive Brucknerian, who can evoke a strong sense of atmosphere. Perhaps he does not quite match the greatest of his rivals in strength of personality, but this account has a great deal to commend it and, like his version of the *Seventh*, will have a high priority with those who enjoy sound which, while naturally balanced, is undoubtedly in the demonstration bracket.

Although not quite as impressive as his Bruckner *Ninth*, Bruno Walter's 1960 recording is transformed by its CD remastering, with textures clearer, strings full and brass sonorous. It is not quite as rich as the Blomstedt Dresden recording on Denon, but is still pretty impressive, and the superbly played 'hunting horn' scherzo is wonderfully vivid. Walter makes his recording orchestra sound remarkably European in style and timbre. The reading is characteristically spacious. Walter's special feeling for Bruckner means that he can relax over long musical paragraphs and retain his control of the structure, while the playing has fine atmosphere and no want of mystery.

Blomstedt, like Solti, opts for the Nowak edition, and the spacious and resonant acoustic in which his version is recorded lends it a pleasing sense of atmosphere. The performance has a certain ardour and conviction that impress. The slow movement has more feeling and poetry than one normally associates with this conductor, and the sumptuous tone produced by the Dresden orchestra is a joy in itself. This is less bright and analytical than Solti's, for instance, but it is a beautiful sound and it suits Bruckner; many will prefer it to the greater detail of the Decca.

Karajan's earlier reading for EMI had undoubted electricity and combines simplicity and strength. The playing of the Berlin Philharmonic is very fine. The snag is the considerable resonance, which has led to a degree of harshness appearing in the tuttis with the added brilliance of the digital remastering, while pianissimos are relatively diffuse. The (more expansive) DG performance is tauter and more crisply disciplined, while keeping all the qualities of strength and mystery.

Haitink's earlier, Concertgebouw version of the *Fourth* dates from the late 1960s and has been reissued several times. In its new CD format it sounds firm and clear; the performance is noble and unmannered. In the budget range, this remains competitive and is a better investment than Haitink's later, digital, Vienna recording.

Klemperer's performance with the Philharmonia is for those primarily seeking architectural strength. The reading is magisterial and the finale has impressive weight and strength. Alongside Jochum's flexible account Klemperer's view seems severe, even marmoreal. But there is no question concerning its power or the vividness of the remastered EMI recording, although there is a hint of fierceness on fortissimos.

As a Brucknerian, Solti can hardly be faulted, choosing admirable tempi, keeping concentration taut through the longest paragraphs, and presenting the architecture of the work in total clarity. Raptness is there too, and only the relative lack of Brucknerian idiosyncrasy will disappoint those who prefer a more loving, personal approach. Like Blomstedt, Solti prefers the Nowak edition with the opening motif brought back on the horns at the end of the finale. The Decca sound is almost excessively brilliant.

Günther Neuhold uses the Nowak edition, and his is a wayward, if often powerful account. His basic tempi are slow – he begins very slowly – but his pacing is very volatile. The Royal Flanders orchestra produces a rich sonority with spectacular brass sounds, and they are obviously responsive. The digital recording has plenty of atmosphere, though the resonance means that the most expansive fortissimos are almost overwhelming. This could be regarded as an interesting and very free alternative reading; but Jochum, who is also inspirational in approach, brings more grip to the score.

Symphony No. 5 in B flat.
(M) *(**) Ph. 426 107-2 [id.]. Concg. O, Jochum.

Symphony No. 5 in B flat; (i) *Te Deum.*
*** Ph. Dig. 422 342-2 (2) [id.]. (i) Mattila, Mentzer, Cole, Holl, Bav. R. Ch., VPO, Haitink.

Bernard Haitink earned his Brucknerian spurs in the Concertgebouw with his late-1960s/early-1970s cycle. One of the most impressive was the *Fifth*, but his new recording with the Vienna Philharmonic is, if anything, even finer. It is superbly recorded and the orchestral playing is predictably of the very highest quality. The only snag, perhaps, is the slow movement, which is rather on the brisk side. He knocks four minutes off Karajan's reading, yet at the same time he succeeds in conveying an unhurried effect. Anyway this is a performance of nobility and it presents undeniably the best sound so far. The *Te Deum* is an added inducement to invest in this set.

Jochum's Concertgebouw version was made at a concert in the Ottobeuren Abbey, West Germany, in 1964. The acoustic of the Philips recording is confined, with two-dimensional brass sonorities. The string timbre too is curiously dry and studio-ish for an ecclesiastical ambience. The performance undoubtedly has the electricity of live music-making, but most listeners will want a more expansive sound in this work.

Symphony No. 6 in A (original version).
*(*) Teldec/WEA Dig. 2292 44182-2 [id.]. Frankfurt RSO, Inbal.

Eliahu Inbal secures good playing from the Frankfurt Radio Orchestra and he is generally well served by the engineers. Nevertheless this performance is a little short on personality and is ultimately bland. The *Sixth* is one of the least well-served of the cycle, and this version is something of an also-ran.

Symphony No. 6 in A.
*** Orfeo Dig. C 024821 [id.]. Bav. State O, Sawallisch.
(M) *** EMI CDM7 63351-2 [id.]. New Philh. O, Klemperer.
**(*) DG 419 194-2 [id.]. BPO, Karajan.
**(*) Decca 417 389-2 [id.]. Chicago SO, Solti.
** RCA Dig. RD 69010. Schleswig-Holstein Fest. O, Eschenbach.

Sawallisch's account of the *Sixth Symphony* is beautifully shaped, spacious yet never portentous or inflated. Tempi – never too slow but never hurried – are beautifully judged, and the Bavarian State Orchestra respond splendidly to his direction. The acoustic has plenty of warmth but is not too reverberant, and the recording sounds excellent.

Klemperer's version was recorded in the Kingsway Hall in 1964. Starting with a spacious account of the first movement, grandly majestic, sharply architectural, he directs a characteristically strong and direct reading. It is disarmingly simple rather than expressive in the slow movement (faster than usual) but is always concentrated and strong, and the finale is particularly well held together. Splendid playing from the orchestra and clear, bright recording. Bruckner's massive climaxes are accommodated without strain and the brass is very telling. A little more warmth in the sound would have been ideal, but it is always clear and the brightness never harshens.

Karajan is not as commanding here as in his other Bruckner recordings. This is still a compelling performance, tonally very beautiful and with a glowing account of the slow movement that keeps it in proportion – not quite the match of the sublime slow movements of Nos. 8 and 9. The transfer of the 1980 analogue recording is well enough managed, although the bright upper range is more noticeable than the lower, which might ideally have been more expansive.

Solti offers a strong, rhetorical reading, powerfully convincing in the outer movements and helped by playing and recording of outstanding quality. Where he is less persuasive is in the slow movement, which fails to flow quite as it should; the expressiveness does not sound truly spontaneous. The analogue recording emerges vividly enough in its CD format.

Christoph Eschenbach proves a sympathetic Bruckner interpreter and gets very good results from the Schleswig-Holstein Festival Orchestra, a youth orchestra whose members are drawn from all over the world. The playing is at a high level of accomplishment and moves with the right kind of momentum. Given the fact that these young players have so little time to develop a corporate identity, theirs is an impressive response. The recording is really a shade over-reverberant, which poses problems in climaxes.

Symphony No. 7 in E.
*** Decca Dig. 414 290-2 [id.]. Berlin RSO, Chailly.
*** Ph. 420 805-2 [id.]. Concg. O, Haitink.
*** DG 419 195-2 [id.]. BPO, Karajan.
*** Denon Dig. C37 7286 [id.]. Dresden State O, Blomstedt.
(M) *** EMI CDM7 69923-2. BPO, Karajan.
*** DG Dig. 429 226-2 [id.]. VPO, Karajan.
*(*) ASV Dig. CDDCA 625 [id.]. Philh. O, Francesco D'Avalos.

While Karajan and Haitink both give of their finest in this work, Chailly's account, with its superb Decca digital recording, also ranks among the best available. He obtains some excellent playing from the Berlin Radio Symphony Orchestra and, though he may not attain the warmth and, indeed, the spirituality of Karajan and Jochum, his is a committed performance, and the apparent lack of weight soon proves deceptive. He has a considerable command of the work's architecture and controls its sonorities expertly. The recording, made in the Jesus-Christus Kirche, Berlin, is outstanding in every way. Warm, full tone throughout all the departments of the orchestra, yet a clean and refined sound, which is especially impressive on CD.

Both the Haitink and Karajan/DG CDs offer analogue recordings from the late 1970s, but the Philips remastering is conspicuously the more successful. The recording is wide in range and refined in detail, yet retains much of the ambient warmth of the Concertgebouw. Haitink's reading is more searching than his earlier version, made in the 1960s. The first movement is considerably slower and gains in mystery and atmosphere, and the *Adagio* expands in vision, too. The Concertgebouw play with their accustomed breadth of tone and marvellously blended ensemble – the closing section of the *Adagio* is wonderfully serene.

A well-shaped account of the *Seventh* comes from Herbert Blomstedt and the Staatskapelle, Dresden. It is not quite as moving as his version of the *Fourth*, but it is still very fine, and the beautiful playing of the Dresden orchestra and the expansive acoustic of the Lukaskirche are strong points in its favour. The reading is totally dedicated and Blomstedt has both strength and imagination to commend him.

Like Bruckner's *Fourth*, Karajan recorded the *Seventh* for EMI five years before his DG version, and both have now resurfaced simultaneously. The earlier reading showed a superb feeling for the work's architecture, and the playing of the Berlin Philharmonic was gorgeous. The recording has striking resonance and amplitude, sounding well if not absolutely refined in its remastered format and making a good medium-price choice for this favourite Bruckner symphony. In the newer, DG version, Karajan draws enormously compelling playing from the same orchestra and this performance shows even greater power and nobility. This is undoubtedly a great performance, and the recording was one of the best in Karajan's analogue series, with rich strings and sonorous yet biting brass. The digital remastering, however, is not quite as successful in freshening the sound as is Haitink's Philips CD.

Karajan's digital account of the *Seventh* was his last recording and he secures a marvellous response from the Vienna Philharmonic. This features high in the lists, without displacing his earlier accounts: in fact the 1977 version has slightly more grip and the 1971 EMI account has a sense of mystery that is also rather special. Those who have either need not make the change.

There is some respectable orchestral playing from the Philharmonia Orchestra under Francesco D'Avalos on ASV and the quality of the recorded sound gives no ground for complaint. But the performance is not strong on personality and it would be impossible to recommend it while such excellent accounts as those by Chailly, Karajan and Blomstedt remain in currency.

Symphony No. 8 in C min.
⊛ *** DG Dig. 427 611-2 [id.]. VPO, Karajan.
(M) *** EMI CMS7 63469-2 (2) [Ang. CDMB 63469]. BPO, Karajan – WAGNER: *Lohengrin; Parsifal: Preludes.****
*** DG 419 196-2 (2) [id.]. BPO, Karajan – WAGNER: *Siegfried idyll.****
*** Ph. Dig. 412 465-2 (2) [id.]. Concg. O, Haitink – WAGNER: *Siegfried idyll.****
**(*) DG Dig. 415 124-2 (2) [id.]. VPO, Giulini.
** Chan. Dig. CHAN 8843/4 [id.]. LPO, Järvi – REGER: *Beethoven variations.***
Olympia OCD 238 [id.]. USSR Ac. SO, Svetlanov.

Karajan recorded the *Eighth Symphony* in the late 1950s and again in 1976, on both occasions with the Berlin Philharmonic. His last version is with the Vienna Philharmonic Orchestra and is the most impressive of them all. The sheer beauty of sound and opulence of texture is awe-inspiring but never draws attention to itself: this is a performance in which beauty and truth go hand in hand. We are not far into the first movement when one simply forgets the performance and marvels at the composer's vision. The recording is superior to either of its predecessors in terms of naturalness of detail and depth of perspective, though they were both of good quality. This is quite an experience!

The transfer of Karajan's 1958 Berlin Philharmonic recording is amazingly successful. The EMI sound is wonderfully full and spacious, yet with excellent detail; the strings are gloriously rich and brass sonorities are thrilling. The performance has much in common with the later versions and has compelling power. The slow movement is very fine indeed, conveying darker and more tragic feelings than the 1976 analogue version which is more freely lyrical, though not lacking in intensity. Those with limited budgets will find this very much worthwhile: as well as the advantage of economy, it offers outstanding performances of the *Preludes* to Acts I and III of both *Lohengrin* and *Parsifal*.

Karajan's 1976 analogue set had striking richness and refinement of texture and it has transferred to CD with impressive clarity, the Berlin Philharmonic string timbre very real and tangible. The performance is majestic, massive in scale, yet immaculate in detail, the reading both noble and searching. However, at full price this takes third place to the new VPO version and to the remastered, mid-price EMI set which is much more generously coupled, although Karajan's glorious account of Wagner's *Siegfried idyll* also sounds full and fresh in remastered form.

Haitink's is a noble reading of this massive symphony, using the extended Haas edition. Never one to force the pace, Haitink's degree of restraint will please those who find Karajan too powerfully concentrated. The spaciousness of the slow movement brings a rare clarity and refinement; the tempo is relentlessly steady, even slower than Karajan's. On compact disc, the resonant Concertgebouw ambience has all the more atmospheric bloom, as well as fine detail, an aptly beautiful sound.

Giulini elects to use the Nowak edition, which may worry some collectors and incline them towards Haitink or Karajan, who opt for the Haas. If these considerations do not worry you, the Giulini will be a strong contender, for he is a conductor of vision, and the Vienna orchestra give him wonderful support. This reading has undoubted spirituality and power, and the DG recording is spacious and clean. However, the absence of any coupling limits the fullest recommendation.

Neeme Järvi on Chandos is far from negligible though he enters a crowded market. His is a reading which one would applaud in the concert hall; it has freshness, as one would expect, and is free from interpretative idiosyncrasy. The slow movement is given with much eloquence, but the reverberance of All Saints', Tooting, sometimes clouds climaxes.

Svetlanov's version, recorded in 1981, does not lack passion, but its fervour, aided and abetted by the braying Russian brass, brings coarseness rather than excitement. The reverberantly vivid sound gives an overblown effect and this is altogether unsatisfactory.

Symphony No. 9 in D min. (1896 original version).
** Teldec/WEA Dig. 2292 43175-2 [id.]. Frankfurt RSO, Inbal.

Eliahu Inbal's reading of the *Ninth* with the Frankfurt Radio orchestra is far from negligible, even though it may not be a performance of the highest stature. The playing is often very fine, and Inbal is scrupulously attentive to detail; however, there is not the sense of scale that is to be found in the finest of his rivals.

Symphony No. 9 in D min.
⊛ (M) *** CBS MYK 44825 [id.]. Columbia SO, Bruno Walter.
*** DG Dig. 427 345-2 [id.]. VPO, Giulini.
(B) **(*) DG 429 514-2 [id.]. BPO, Jochum.
**(*) DG 419 083-2 [id.]. BPO, Karajan.
**(*) Decca Dig. 425 405-2 [id.]. Cleveland O, Dohnányi.
**(*) Ph. Dig. 410 039-2 [id.]. Concg. O, Haitink.
** Decca Dig. 417 295-2 [id.]. Chicago SO, Solti.
** Orfeo Dig. C 160851A [id.]. Bav. State O, Sawallisch.

Bruno Walter's 1959 recording is a superb achievement. This was one of the most beautiful results of Walter's Indian summer in the CBS studio, and now the results are immeasurably enhanced, with a blend of rich, clear strings and splendidly sonorous brass.

Walter's mellow, persuasive reading leads one on through the leisurely paragraphs so that the logic and coherence seem obvious where other performances can sound aimless. Perhaps the scherzo is not vigorous enough to provide the fullest contrast – though the sound here has ample bite – yet it exactly fits the overall conception. The final slow movement has a nobility which makes one glad that Bruckner never completed the intended finale. After this, anything would have been an anticlimax.

Giulini's *Ninth* is a performance of great stature, the product of deep thought. As always, there is the keenest feeling for texture and beauty of contour, and he distils a powerful sense of mystery from the first and third movements. The DG recording has a welcome sense of space and transparency of texture. Although this does not displace Walter, it is a record that all Brucknerians should possess.

Jochum's reading has greater mystery than any other and the orchestral playing (at the individual level) reaches a degree of eloquence that disarms criticism. If at times Jochum tends to phrase too affectionately and in consequence the architecture does not emerge unscathed, he is still magnetic in everything he does. The 1966 recording sounds remarkably good and this issue is a genuine bargain, especially if treated as a supplement to Walter's version.

DG have understandably chosen Karajan's 1977 recording for CD remastering. In this later reading Karajan clearly wanted to convey a tougher, more majestic impression, and the interpretation concentrates on strength and impact. As before, however, the playing of the Berlin Philharmonic is both technically immaculate and dedicated. The recording balance is closer than before but the digital transfer is not without ambient atmosphere and is truthful in matters of orchestral timbre.

Decca provide the Cleveland Orchestra and Christoph von Dohnányi with a recording of enormous clarity and presence. Dohnányi's reading makes the most of the dramatic tensions inherent in the score – at the expense, perhaps, of its sense of mystery. It gives the impression of a newly cleaned and restored painting, with the colours in bold relief and the drama highlighted.

The extremely measured speed of the first movement in Haitink's pure and dedicated reading may be taken as a deciding factor; he underlines the elegiac mood. Though the great dynamic contrasts are superbly and fearlessly caught, this is not as thrustful an interpretation as Solti's or Karajan's. The spaciousness of the sound against an ambient Concertgebouw acoustic gives a degree of distancing which matches the interpretation.

Solti's is a large-scale reading of the *Ninth*, spacious in its view. The brilliance and concentration of the Chicago orchestra's playing are matched by the wide-ranging Decca sound. Others may be more deeply meditative – Walter for one – but the power of Solti and the brilliance of the playing and the recording are formidable.

After Sawallisch's fine versions of Nos. 1 and 6, this is disappointingly underpowered, with the first movement taken fairly briskly and the rest of the work well played, but without the concentration found in the finest versions. Good but not outstanding recording.

Intermezzo and trio for string quintet.
*** CRD CRD 3346 [id.]. Augmented Alberni Qt – BRAHMS: *Sextet No. 2.***(*)

Following on after the vigorous finale of the Brahms *Sextet* the autumnal feeling of the Bruckner with its lighter (but still rich) textures makes a most pleasing encore. The recording is excellent and the CD transfer is freshly vivid.

VOCAL MUSIC

(i) *Masses Nos. 1 in D min.; 2 in E min.; 3 in F min.;* Motets: *Afferentur regi; Ave Maria;*

Christus factus est pro nobis; Ecce sacerdos magnus; Locus iste; Os justi medititur; Pange lingua; Tota pulchra es, Maria; Vexilla regis; Virga Jesse. (ii) *Psalm 150; Te Deum.*
(M) **(*) DG 423 127-2 (4) [id.]. (i) Soloists, Bav. R. Ch. & SO; (ii) Soloists, Ch. of German Op., Berlin, BPO; Jochum.

Bruckner's choral music, like the symphonies, spans his musical career. Now Brucknerians have an excellent chance to get to know this unjustly neglected music, in highly sympathetic and dedicated performances from one of the composer's most understanding and eloquent advocates. With excellent soloists, including Maria Stader, Edith Mathis, Ernst Haefliger, Kim Borg and Karl Ridderbusch, the performances of the large-scale works have fine eloquence and admirable breadth and humanity, and no lack of drama, although other accounts – of the *Te Deum*, for instance – have had more blazing intensity. But that is not Jochum's way, and the concentration of these performances is never in doubt, with much magic distilled, notably in the early *D minor Mass*, a noble and moving account. The original recordings tended to be distanced; in making the sound more present and clear, the CD remastering has lost some of the atmospheric fullness, although the effect is undoubtedly fresher and brighter, if not always absolutely clean on top. The beautiful motets are particularly successful.

Motets: *Afferentur regi; Ave Maria; Christus factus est; Ecce sacerdos magnus; Inveni David; Locus iste; Os justi medititur; Pange lingua; Tota pulchra es, Maria; Vexilla regis; Virga Jesse.*
**(*) Hyp. CDA 66062 [id.]. Salmon, Corydon Singers, Best; Trotter (organ).

The Corydon Singers under Matthew Best are not quite as well blended or as homogeneous in tone as the Bavarian Radio Chorus, but Best's direction is often imaginative and he achieves a wide tonal range. The motets span the best part of Bruckner's creative life; given their devotional character, though, they are best heard two or three at a time rather than at one sitting.

Requiem in D min.; Psalms 112 and 114.
**(*) Hyp. CDA 66245 [id.]. Rodgers, Denley, Maldwyn Davies, George, Corydon Singers, ECO, Best; T. Trotter (organ).

Matthew Best here tackles the very early setting of the *Requiem* which Bruckner wrote at the age of twenty-five; often gauche in the string-writing, but with a number of pointers to the future, notably in the *Benedictus*. The quality of the writing in the Psalm settings also varies; but with fine, strong performances from singers and players alike, including an excellent team of soloists, this is well worth investigating by Brucknerians. First-rate recording.

Te Deum.
* DG Dig. 410 521-2 (2) [id.]. Perry, Müller-Molinari, Winbergh, Malta, V. Singverein, VPO, Karajan – BRAHMS: *German requiem.***(*)

With Janet Perry a shrill soprano soloist, and with the big choral tuttis constricted in sound, the Bruckner *Te Deum* makes a disappointing fill-up for Karajan's latest version of the Brahms *Requiem*, though the majesty of his vision is never in doubt.

Burgon, Geoffrey (born 1951)

Acquainted with night; Cançiones del Alma; Lunar beauty; Nunc dimittis; This ean night; Worldes blissè.

*** EMI Dig. CDC7 49762-2. Bowman, Brett, Steele-Perkins, Hulse, Henderson, City of L. Sinfonia, Hickox.

This collection of Geoffrey Burgon's music for counter-tenor makes a hauntingly unusual record. Appropriately, it has at the centre his most celebrated piece, the setting of the *Nunc dimittis*, used as theme-music in the television adaptation of John Le Carré's *Tinker, Tailor, Soldier, Spy*, originally for treble but well within counter-tenor range. Some of the other works are just as striking. The performances are strongly committed, with James Bowman taking the lion's share of solos. The recording gives an aptly ecclesiastical glow to the sound while keeping essential clarity.

At the round earth's imagined corners; But have been found again; Laudate Dominum; Magnificat; Nunc dimittis; A prayer to the Trinity; Short mass; This world; Two hymns to Mary.
**(*) Hyp. Dig. CDA 66123 [id.]. Chichester Cathedral Ch., Alan Thurlow.

Burgon's famous *Nunc dimittis* is well matched here with the *Magnificat* that he later wrote to complement it and a series of his shorter choral pieces, all of them revealing his flair for immediate, direct communication, and well performed. First-rate recording.

Busoni, Ferruccio (1866–1924)

Piano concerto, Op. 39.
(M) *** EMI CDM7 69850-2. John Ogdon, Alldis Ch., RPO, Revenaugh.
*** Telarc Dig. CD 80207 [id.]. Garrick Ohlsson, Cleveland O and Men's Ch., Dohnányi.

Busoni's marathon *Piano concerto* is unique, running to 70 minutes, roughly the same time as Beethoven's *Choral symphony*, with which it has another parallel in its choral finale. With such an ambitious design it must be expected that the music's inspiration will be uneven. Much of the most important material lies with the orchestra, the piano often tending to act more as a poetic obbligato to the work's main argument. John Ogdon's magisterial and powerful advocacy is matched by both his brilliance and his passionate commitment, making the music surge forward, and he is well supported by Daniel Revenaugh and the RPO, with an incandescent contribution from the John Alldis Choir. The EMI recording, from the late 1960s, sounds bold and immediate in its new CD format. This issue makes an outstanding bargain at mid-price.

The full-price alternative from Telarc can be warmly recommended too, even if the first-rate modern digital sound brings fewer advantages than expected, other than highlighting the solo piano. In the choral finale the John Alldis Choir on EMI has far more impact than the men of the Cleveland Orchestra Chorus, making it into a genuine culmination. With extra prominence given to the solo instrument, Garrick Ohlsson's bravura display is very exciting, and the pianist's own enjoyment in virtuosity enhances his electricity and flair.

Fantasia contrappuntistica; Fantasia after J. S. Bach; Toccata.
**(*) Altarus AIR-2-9074. John Ogdon.

It is a bizarre thought that Busoni's remarkable *Fantasia contrappuntistica* was begun, as Ronald Stevenson reminds us, on board a transatlantic liner in 1910 and completed in New Orleans. Stevenson calls it a masterpiece and, listening to John Ogdon's performance, one is tempted to agree. The *Fantasia after J. S. Bach* was written a year earlier and is among Busoni's most concentrated and powerful piano works. The balance places Ogdon rather far back and, as the acoustic is somewhat reverberant, the piano sounds a little clangy (for example, at the opening of the *Toccata*).

Sarabande and cortège (Doktor Faust), Op. 51.
ⓑ (M) *** EMI CDM7 69840-2. RPO, Revenaugh – SCHMIDT: *Variations*; LUTOSLAWSKI: *Postlude; Symphonic variations.****** ⓑ

While he was working on his last and greatest opera, *Doktor Faust*, Busoni made these two orchestral studies using ideas he intended for the opera. The *Sarabande* and *Cortège* instantly draw one into his imaginative world: this music has a powerful sense of mystery and a quiet and haunting depth. These two fragments take 20 minutes and are coupled with other repertoire of equally exceptional interest. Performances are excellent, the digitally remastered recordings first rate, and the price is extraordinarily competitive. Recommended with all possible enthusiasm.

3 Album Leaves; An die Jugend; Ballet scene No. 4, Op. 33a; Chamber fantasy on Bizet's Carmen; Chorale prelude on a fragment by Bach; Ciaccona; 2 Dance pieces, Op. 30a; Elegies; Fantasia contrappuntistica; Fantasy after J. S. Bach; Indian diary, Book 1; Machiette mediaevali, Op. 33; Notturni; Nuit de Noel; Perpetuum mobile; Pieces, Op. 33b; 24 Preludes, Op. 37; Prelude & Etude in arpeggios; Preludio-Fantasia; Prologo; Racconti fantastici, Op. 12; 7 Short Pieces; Sonatinas 1–2; Sonatina ad usum infantis; Sonatina brevis: In signo Joannis Sebastiani Magni; Sonatina in diem navita is Christi MCMXVII; Sonatina super Carmen; Suite campestre, Op. 18; Toccata; Variations & fugue on Chopin's C minor Prelude (Op. 28/20), Op. 22; 10 Variations on a Chopin Prelude, Op. 22 (2nd version).
** Ph. Dig. 420 740-2 (6) [id.]. Geoffrey Douglas Madge.

An important and long-overdue undertaking. Such is its scale that it deserves an unqualified welcome: six well-filled CDs, including so much that is technically demanding and forbidding. Geoffrey Douglas Madge, an Australian pianist who teaches in The Hague, has a formidable rather than a transcendental technique. He produces less than beautiful tone in climaxes, where he tends to overpedal. Gratitude for this mammoth undertaking should be unstinting, however, for much of this repertoire is new to record, even if in the *Elegies*, for example, he does not outclass those who have recorded Busoni before and the piano sound is not up to the high standard we expect of Philips: it lacks transparency and tends to coarsen on climaxes. Busoni needs the most persuasive advocacy and beauty of sonority. However, this set is a must for those who care about this repertoire and, these shortcomings apart, must be given a warm welcome.

Doktor Faust (opera) complete.
(M) *** DG 427 413-2 (3) [id.]. Fischer-Dieskau, Kohn, Cochran, Hillebrecht, Bav. Op. Ch. & R. O, Leitner.

Busoni's epic *Doktor Faust* was left incomplete at the composer's death. Unfortunately, this recording is full of small but tiresome cuts; however, with a magnificent performance from Fischer-Dieskau in the name-part and superb, fierily intense conducting from Leitner, it fully conveys the work's wayward mastery, the magnetic quality which establishes it as Busoni's supreme masterpiece, even though it was finished by another hand. This performance, recorded in conjunction with a broadcast mounted by the European Broadcasting Union, fully substantiates the vision and originality of the opera. Being offbeat in its layout, the piece works more predictably on record than on stage. The cast is dominated by Fischer-Dieskau, here in 1969 at his very finest; and the only weak link among the others is Hildegard Hillebrecht as the Duchess of Parma. In the CD transfer the vividness of the sound is intensified. Though this is a mid-price set, the documentation is generous, with essays and synopsis and the complete libretto in English translation as well as the original German.

Butterworth, George (1885–1916)

The Banks of green willow.
*** Chan. CHAN 8373 [id.]. Bournemouth Sinf., Del Mar – BANTOCK: *Pierrot of the minute*; BRIDGE: *Suite for strings* etc.***

The Banks of green willow; 2 English idylls; A Shropshire lad (rhapsody).
(M) *** Decca 421 391-2 [id.]. ASMF, Marriner – BRITTEN: *Variations on a theme of Frank Bridge*; WARLOCK: *Capriol suite.****
*** Nimbus Dig. NI 5068 [id.]. E. String O, Boughton – BRIDGE: *Suite*; PARRY: *Lady Radnor's suite.****

The banks of green willow; A Shropshire lad (rhapsody).
(M) **(*) EMI CDM7 69419-2 [id.]. E. Sinfonia, Dilkes – MOERAN: *Symphony* etc.**(*)

Butterworth's *Shropshire lad* represents the English folksong school at its most captivatingly atmospheric, and the other works are in a similarly appealing pastoral vein. Marriner's performances with the Academy are stylishly beautiful, without the last degree of finesse but very fine indeed, with vivid, wide-ranging recording quality. The recording dates from 1976 and the CD remastering shows just how good it was.

The four Butterworth pieces, done with tender simplicity in sumptuously atmospheric sound, provide the centrepiece for a Nimbus issue that has become one of that company's best-sellers. As in the Parry and Bridge items, Boughton secures from his Birmingham-based orchestra warm and refined playing in well-paced readings. In an ample acoustic, woodwind is placed rather behind the strings.

On Chandos, Del Mar gives a glowingly persuasive performance of *The Banks of green willow*, which comes as part of another highly interesting programme of English music, devoted also to Butterworth's somewhat older contemporaries, Bantock and Frank Bridge. The digital transfer of a 1979 analogue recording has the benefit of even greater clarity without loss of atmosphere.

The performances by Dilkes and the English Sinfonia are also sensitive if perhaps a shade too immediate for this atmospheric music; with fine, immediate recording, this makes an attractive coupling for an excellent mid-priced version of the Moeran *Symphony*.

Buxtehude, Diderik (c. 1637–1707)

Trio sonatas: in G; B flat and D min., Op. 1/2, 4 & 6, (BuxWV 253, 255 & 257); in D and G min., Op. 2/2–3, (BuxWV 260–1).
*** ASV/Gaudeamus CDGAU 110. Trio Sonnerie.

Make no mistake, this is music of real quality: its invention is fertile and distinguished by a lightness of touch and colour that is quite individual; the melodic lines are vivacious and engaging, and their virtuosity inspiriting. The Trio Sonnerie play this music with real enthusiasm and expertise, and their virtuosity is agreeably effortless and unostentatious. Most musical performances – and very well recorded, too. This is highly recommended, especially to those who regard Buxtehude as merely a name in the musical history books.

Canzona in E min., BuxWV 169; Canzonetta in G, BuxWV 171; Ciacona in E min., BuxWV 160; Chorales: Ach Herr, mich armen Sünder, BuxWV 178; In dulci jubilo, BuxWV 197; Komm, Heiliger Geist, Herre Gott, BuxWV 199; Vater unser im Himmelreich, BuxWV 219; Magnificat primi toni, BuxWV 203; Preludes: in C, BuxWV 137; in D, BuxWV 139.
**(*) Chan. Dig. CHAN 0514 [id.]. Piet Kee (organ of St Laurens Church, Alkmaar) –
SWEELINCK: Collection.***

The splendid Schnitger organ at Alkmaar has recently been restored and it is good to have it in use for fine modern recordings of the music of Buxtehude – for which it is eminently suited – in the hands of an authoritative exponent. Kee's performance of the opening *Magnificat primi toni* is little short of magnificent. In his words, the piece consists of 'a prelude, four fugues with interludes and a sparkling fugal finale', and it is fully worthy to be compared with Bach. The closing *Ciacona in E minor* is pretty impressive too, while the *Canzonetta in G* is deliciously registered, with piping flute colouring. One's reservations, however, concern the presentation of the chorales which, Kee suggests, 'require poetic expression'. Perhaps they do, but they also need to be moved on rather faster; *In dulci jubilo*, in particular, loses much of its character when the pacing is so studied, even though the detail emerges admirably. The Chandos recording is superb.

Ciaconas: in C min.; E min., BuxWV 159/60; Passacaglia in D min., BuxWV 161; Preludes and fugues: in D; D min.; E; E min.; BuxWV 139/142; in F; F sharp min., BuxWV 145/146; in G min., BuxWV 149.
(M) *** DG 427 133-2 [id.]. Helmut Walcha (organ of Church of SS Peter and Paul, Cappel, West Germany).

Buxtehude's organ music has a character of its own: his *Preludes and fugues* are more complex than Bach's straightforward two-part structures. Toccata-like passages and fugal sections alternate, and the writing here and in the *Ciaconas* is often exuberantly florid. Helmut Walcha has the full measure of this repertoire and these performances on the highly suitable Arp Schnitger organ in Cappel, Lower Saxony, are authoritative and spontaneous. The 1978 recording is excellent and the disc comprises generous measure: 73 minutes.

Byrd, William (1543–1623)

Browning a 5; Fantasia a 3; Fantasia a 3 in C (No. 1); Fantasia a 3 in C (No. 3); Fantasia a 4 in G min; Fantasias a 6 in G min. (Nos 1–2); Pavan & Galliard a 6 in C; Pavana Bray; La Volta.
*** Virgin Dig. VC 790795-2 [id.]. Fretwork, with Christopher Wilson – DOWLAND: Lachrimae.***

These consort pieces of Byrd have much greater variety of mood and feeling than the unrelieved melancholy of the Dowland *Lacrimae*, with which they are interspersed. They are given performances of both authority and freshness. Good recording, too.

Pavans and galliards (collection).
*** HM HMC 901241/2 [id.]. Davitt Moroney (harpsichord).

On the first of the two discs Davitt Moroney presents the sequence of nine pavans and galliards Byrd composed in the 1570s and '80s, which come from *My Ladye Nevell's Booke* (1591), and the second creates a second cycle of pieces on the same lines. Between them, Davitt Moroney constructs a sequence of Byrd's finest late pavans, taking care to model it on the same lines of symmetry and contrast that distinguish Byrd's own. Moroney contributes a thorough and scholarly note which sets out the thinking behind his compilation. The playing is totally committed and authoritative though a trifle didactic. His recording, made on an Italian instrument of 1677, is very naturally recorded, though collectors will have to use a very low-level setting to get realistic results. This pair of CDs comprises half of Byrd's output in this field and is a most valuable contribution to the catalogue. The documentation is excellent.

Anthems: *Praise our Lord, all ye Gentiles; Sing joyfully; Turn our captivity.* Motets: *Attolite portas; Ave verum corpus; Christus resurgens; Emendemus in melius; Gaudeamus omnes; Justorum animae; Laudibus in sanctis; Non vos relinquam; O magnum mysterium; O quam suavis; Plorans plorabit; Siderum rector; Solve iubente Deo; Veni sancte spiritus; Visita quaesumus Domine.*
*** Coll. Dig. COLCD 110 [id.]. Cambridge Singers, John Rutter.

This is the first of a projected series intended to cover all Byrd's music, so it is not surprising that the beautifully sung *Ave verum corpus* and the jubilant anthem, *Sing joyfully*, were included, alongside much that is less familiar. Officially Byrd wrote for the Anglican Church, but much of his finest music was for the Roman liturgy, at that time officially banned but still performed clandestinely. There is no better example here than *Emendemus in melius*, which was chosen by the composer jointly with Tallis to open their 1575 collection of *Cantiones sacrae*. John Rutter brings a composer's understanding to these readings, which have a simple, direct eloquence, the music's serene spirituality movingly caught; and the atmospheric recording is very faithful, even if detail could be sharper. The programme is divided into four groups, first Anthems, and then Motets: of penitence and prayer; of praise and rejoicing; and for the Church year.

Ave verum corpus; Masses for 3, 4 and 5 voices.
*** Gimell Dig. CDGIM 345 [id.]. Tallis Scholars, Phillips.

Mass for four voices; Mass for five voices.
(M) **(*) EMI Dig. CD-EMX 9505 [Ang. CDM 62015]. St John's College, Cambridge, Ch., Guest.

Peter Phillips's performances are altogether more ardent than those recorded by Argo at King's, and some might prefer the greater serenity of the latter. But Phillips is a master of this repertoire; undoubtedly these performances have more variety and great eloquence so that, when the drama is varied with a gentler mood, the contrast is the more striking. This enormously rewarding music lends itself to an imaginatively varied treatment, and certainly the sound made by the Scholars in Merton College Chapel is beautiful, both warm and fresh.

There is no lack of enthusiasm in the performances of the Choir of St John's College, Cambridge, and they can at times be more persuasive than are professional groups. The *Five-part Mass* fares best and is given with genuine fervour. The balance of the recording is rather closer than is usual in this venue, though there is a reasonable glow round the singers. George Guest features rather more pronounced cadential ritardandi than are favoured in Early Music circles, but there is a sense of real music-making here.

Cantiones sacrae, Book 1: Aspice Domine; Domine secundum multitudinem; Domine tu iurasti; In resurrectione tua; Ne irascaris Domine; O quam gloriosum; Tristitia et anxiestas; Vide Domine afflic-tionem; Virgilate.
**(*) CRD Dig. CRD 3408 [id.]. New College, Oxford, Ch., Higginbottom.

Cantiones sacrae, Book 2: Circumdederunt me; Cunctis diebus; Domine, non sum dignus; Domine, salva nos; Fac sum servo tuo; Exsurge, Domine; Haec dicit Dominus; Haec dies; Laudibus in sanctis Dominum; Miserere mei, Deus; Tribulatio proxima est.
**(*) CRD Dig. CRD 3439 [id.]. New College, Oxford, Ch., Higginbottom.

Though the New College Choir under its choirmaster Edward Higginbottom does not sing with the variety of expression or dynamic which marks its finest Oxbridge rivals, it is impossible not to respond to the freshness of its music-making. The robust, throaty style suggests a Latin feeling in its forthright vigour, and the directness of approach in these magnificent *cantiones sacrae* is most attractive, helped by recording which is vividly projected, yet at once richly atmospheric.

The Great Service (with anthems).
*** Gimell Dig. CDGIM 011 [id.]. Tallis Scholars, Phillips.
*** EMI Dig. CDC7 47771-2. King's College, Cambridge, Ch., Cleobury; Richard Farnes (organ).

Peter Phillips and the Tallis Scholars give a lucid and sensitively shaped account of Byrd's *Great Service*. Theirs is a more intimate performance than one might expect to encounter in one of the great English cathedrals; they are fewer in number and thus achieve greater clarity of texture. Of course, the top lines are sung by women – excellently, too – and the firmer focus will not be seen as a disadvantage by many collectors. The recording is quite excellent: it is made in a church acoustic (the Church of St John, Hackney) and captures detail perfectly. It includes three other anthems, two of which (*O Lord make thy servant Elizabeth* and *Sing joyfully unto God our strength*) are included on the rival EMI disc. This CD will give great musical satisfaction.

Collectors wanting *The Great Service* in a cathedral acoustic will turn to the King's version, which is beautifully recorded on EMI. They have the advantages of boy trebles, a larger complement of singers who can offer more contrast between solo and full verses, and a well-played organ accompaniment, which it probably had in the 1580s. Stephen Cleobury also sets the music in a more authentic liturgical background: he offers the *Kyrie* and puts the two canticles for *Evensong* into their context with anthems and responses.

'Songs of sundrie natures': Christ is rising again; Come to me griefe for ever (Funeral songs of Phillip Sydney Knight). *Come wofull Orpheus; Elegy on the death of Thomas Tallis: Ye sacred muses. From Virgin's wombe; A carowle for Christmas Day; Have mercy upon me, O God; Lulla, lullaby; Make ye joy to God; Praise our Lord all yee gentiles; Though Amaryllis daunce in greene; Turne our captivitie; Who made thee Hob* (Dialogue between two shepherds).
*** EMI Dig. CDC7 47961-2. Hilliard Ens., L. Bar., Hillier.

Although 'naturally disposed to Gravity and Piety', Byrd included a number of livelier pieces in his 1589 collection – but even so, the overall mood here is melancholy. The white, vibrato-less tone and a certain uniformity of timbre leave a slightly mannered impression. A special point of interest is that the Hilliard adopt contemporary pronunciation – presumably the speech favoured in the 1590s – and this may to some extent account for a slight feeling of self-consciousness. There is the usual high level of accomplishment about these performances and a beautifully natural recording.

Cage, John (born 1912)

Sonatas and Interludes for prepared piano.
*** Denon Dig. C37 7673 [id.]. Yuji Takahashi.

The sixteen sonatas included here, each in binary form not very different from Scarlatti's, are – by Cage's standards – closely structured, and in their sequence are punctuated by four interludes, very similar in style. One can readily appreciate the attraction of an Eastern performer to this music with its pentatonic passages as well as its odd textures and unexpected sounds – induced by the insertion of bolts, screws, coins, etc., on most of the piano strings. Takahashi's commitment is reinforced by close, rather dry recording, apt for this music.

Campra, André (1660–1744)

Requiem Mass.
**(*) HM HMC 901251 [id.]. Baudry, Zanetti, Benet, Elwes, Varcoe, Chapelle Royale Ch. & O, Herreweghe.

André Campra's *Requiem* is a lovely work, with luminous textures and often beguiling harmonies, and its neglect is difficult to understand. Herreweghe's performance, with refined solo and choral singing, makes a good alternative to John Eliot Gardiner's (currently withdrawn) version, for those who prefer a cooler approach to church music of 1700. The recording is refined, to match the performance.

L'Europe galante (opera-ballet).
(M) *** HM/BMG GD 77059 (2). Yakar, Kweksilber, René Jacobs, La Petite Bande, Leonhardt – LULLY: *Bourgeois gentilhomme.****

The sheer tunefulness of *L'Europe galante* has ensured its appeal over the years. This record, the first with period instruments, dates from 1973 and gives us the complete entertainment – and very delightful it is. Like Couperin's *Les Nations*, though in a very different fashion, this enchanting divertissement attempts to portray various national characteristics: French, Spanish, Italian and Turkish. The three soloists all shine and the instrumentalists, directed by Leonhardt, are both expert and spirited. The recording too is well balanced and sounds very fresh on CD. The only snag is that this now comes in harness with Lully's *Le bourgeois gentilhomme*, which is musically much thinner. Full translations are provided.

Tancrède (opera); complete.
** Erato/WEA Dig. 2292 45001-2 (2). François Le Roux, Evangelatos, Dubosc, Le Maigat, Reinhart, Alliot-Lugaz, Visse, The Sixteen, La Grande Écurie et la Chambre du Roy, Malgoire.

André Campra had an extraordinary melodic facility (on which Milhaud drew of course in his *Suite provençale*) and collectors who do not have it should seek out the BMG/Harmonia Mundi reissue of his delightful ballet, *L'Europe galante*, written at the end of the seventeenth century (see above). *Tancrède*, the first of his tragédies lyriques, comes at the beginning of the eighteenth: it is very much in the tradition of Lully but is stronger in its blend of lyricism and dance than in dramatic coherence. This recording was made at a performance in Aix-en-Provence in 1986 and, though there are stage noises and at times some less than polished playing, it is well worth investigating, even if the original production at Aix must presumably have taken much longer than the two hours presented here.

Canteloube, Marie-Joseph (1879–1957)

Chants d'Auvergne: Series 1–5.
*** EMI CDC7 47970-2 [id.]. Victoria de los Angeles, LOP, Jacquillat.

The warmth and sweetness of De los Angeles' tone when the recordings were made (1973 and 1975) match the allure of Canteloube's settings. Now the twenty-four songs have been reissued, squeezed on to one CD. In the lighter songs, the *Bourrées*, for instance, the singing combines sparkle with a natural feeling for the folk idiom; elsewhere, De los Angeles can be ravishing with her fine-spun vocal timbre. The accompaniments are highly sympathetic and the atmospheric recording is attractive too, although at times not ideally clear in focusing orchestral detail. But overall this is most enjoyable, and excellent value.

Chants d'Auvergne: Baïlèro; 2 Bourrées; 3 Bourrées; Lou Boussu; Brezairola; Lou coucut; Chut, chut; La Delaïssâdo; Lo Fiolairé; Malurous qu'o uno fenno; Oï Ayaï; Passo pel prat.
(M) *** Van. VECD 7522 [id.]. Netania Davrath, O, Pierre de la Roche.

It was Netania Davrath who, alongside Victoria de los Angeles on EMI, made the pioneering stereo recordings of this now very popular repertoire. Her performances are folksier in feeling than almost any others, with a simple, essentially lyrical, but very characterful vocal production which gives a special kind of colour to these infinitely varied songs. De los Angeles' tone is warmer and more alluring, but Davrath has her own special appeal, and the accompaniments are idiomatic. Hers is a very successful presentation, which appeals to a wide range of musical tastes, and a good selection is offered here at bargain price.

Chants d'Auvergne: L'Antouèno; Baïlèro; 3 Bourrées; Lou Boussu; Brezairola; Lou coucut; Chut, chut; La Delaïssâdo; Lo Fiolairé; Jou l'pount d'o Mirabel; Malurous qu'o uno fenno; Passo pel prat; Pastourelle; Postouro, sé tu m'aymo; Tè, l'co tè.
⊛ (M) *** EMI Dig. CD-EMX 9500 [Ang. CDM 62010]. Jill Gomez, Royal Liverpool PO, Handley.

Jill Gomez's selection of these increasingly popular songs, attractively presented on a mid-price label, makes for a memorably characterful record which, as well as bringing out the sensuous beauty of Canteloube's arrangements, keeps reminding us, in the echoes of rustic band music, of the genuine folk base. Jill Gomez's voice could not be more apt, for the natural radiance and the range of tone-colour go with a strong feeling for words and sentiment, helped by her intensive study of Provençal pronunciation. Vernon Handley's accompaniments have a directness as well as a warmth which supports the voice admirably, and the recording is outstandingly full and vivid. A splendid bargain.

Chants d'Auvergne: L'Antouèno; Baïlèro; 3 Bourrées; 2 Bourrées; Brezairola; La Delaïssâdo; Lo Fiolairé; Lou Boussu; Malurous qu'o uno fenno; La pastrouletta è lou chibalie; Passo pel prat; La pastoura als camps; Pastourelle.
*** Decca Dig. 410 004-2 [id.]. Te Kanawa, ECO, Tate.

In Dame Kiri Te Kanawa's recital the warmly atmospheric Decca recording brings an often languorous opulence to the music-making. In such an atmosphere the quick songs lose a little in bite and *Baïlèro*, the most famous, is taken extremely slowly. With the sound so sumptuous, this hardly registers and the result remains compelling, thanks in great measure to sympathetic accompaniment from the ECO under Jeffrey Tate.

Chants d'Auvergne: L'Antouèno; Baïlèro; 3 Bourrées; 2 Bourrées; Brezairola; Lou coucut; Chut, chut; La Delaïssàdo; Lo Fiolairé; Oï ayaï; Passo pel prat; Pour l'enfant; Tè, l'co, tè; Uno jionto postouro.
**(*) CBS Dig. MK 37299 [id.]. Frederica von Stade, RPO, Almeida.

Fine as Frederica von Stade's singing is, she is stylistically and temperamentally not always completely at home in Canteloube's lovely folksong settings and the result is far less persuasively sensuous. The CD is clean and immediate but not as richly beautiful as the Decca, nor indeed as vividly atmospheric as Jill Gomez's EMI CD.

Chants d'Auvergne: L'Aio dè rotso; L'Antouèno; Baïlèro; Brezairola; Malurous qu'o uno fenno; Passo pel prat; Pastourelle.
(M) *** RCA GD 87831 [7831-2-RG]. Anna Moffo, American SO, Stokowski – RACHMANINOV: *Vocalise*; VILLA-LOBOS: *Bachianas Brasileiras No. 5.****

Moffo gives radiant performances, helped by the sumptuous accompaniment which Stokowski provides. The result is sweet, seductively so. The recording, from the early 1960s, is opulent to match. With several favourites included, this makes an excellent shorter selection from Canteloube's famous settings, and the couplings are vintage Stokowski.

Chants d'Auvergne: Baïlèro; 3 Bourrées; Brezairola; Lou Boussu; Lou coucut; Chut, chut; La Délaïssàdo; Lo Fiolairé; Jou l'pount d'o Mirabel; Malurous qu'o uno fenno; Oï ayaï; Pastourelle; La pastrouletta; Postouro, sé tu m'aymo; Tè l'co tè; Uno jionto postouro.
*** Virgin Dig. VC 790714-2 [id.]. Arleen Augér, ECO, Yan Pascal Tortelier.

Arleen Augér's lovely soprano is ravishing in the haunting, lyrical songs like the ever-popular *Baïlèro*. In the playful items she conveys plenty of fun, though in the more boisterous numbers the recording catches an unexpected edge in her voice. With excellent recording, however, this stands alongside other recommended selections.

Chants d'Auvergne: Hé! beyla-z-y dau fè; Jou l'pount d'o Mirabel; Là-haut, sur le rocher; Lou boussu; Lou diziou bé; Malurous qu'o uno fenno; Obal din lo coumbèlo; La pastoura als camps; Pastorale; Pastourelle; La pastrouletta è lou chibalie; Postouro sé tu m'aymo; Quand z'eyro petitoune. Triptyque: Offrande à l'eté; Lunair; Hymne dans l'aurore.
*** CBS Dig. MK 37837 [id.]. Frederica von Stade, RPO, Almeida.

Frederica von Stade's second collection not only has more charm and personal identification than the first but also includes Canteloube's haunting *Triptyque*, written in 1914. This is its first recording in stereo. Von Stade's performance is eloquent and the recording suitably atmospheric, if not quite as sumptuous as the Decca sound for Kiri Te Kanawa.

Chants d'Auvergne, 4th and 5th series (complete).
(*) Decca 411 730-2 [id.]. Te Kanawa, ECO, Tate – VILLA-LOBOS: *Bachianas Brasileiras No. 5.**

This second collection of Canteloube folksong arrangements from Kiri Te Kanawa, again with Jeffrey Tate providing richly beautiful accompaniments, presents all remaining items in the five sets of the songs. There is less variety here, partly a question of Dame Kiri's preference for producing a continuous flow of sensuously beautiful sounds rather than giving a folk-like tang.

Cardosa, Frei Manuel (c. 1566-1650)

Requiem: Magnificat; Motets, Mulier quae erat; Non mortui; Nos autem gloriari; Sitivit anima mea.
⊛ *** Gimell CDGIM 021 [id.]. Tallis Scholars, Phillips.

This is quite a discovery. Renaissance music in Portugal is a closed book to most collectors, and unaccompanied choral polyphony continued to flourish there long after Monteverdi had changed the course of music in Italy. Cardosa was a member of the Carmelite order and published five collections of motets and Masses between 1613 and 1648. The *Requiem* comes from the 1625 Book of Masses and opens in striking and original fashion. The polyphony unfolds in long-breathed phrases of unusual length and eloquence, and both the motets, *Mulier quae erat* (A woman, a sinner in that city) and the short *Nos autem gloriari* (Yet should we glory), are rich in texture and have great expressive resplendence. Cardosa's use of the augmented chord at the opening of the *Requiem* gives his music some of its distinctive stamp. The Tallis Scholars sing with characteristic purity of tone and intonation, and they are splendidly recorded. A glorious issue.

Carissimi, Giacomo (1605-74)

Duos & cantatas: *A piè d'un verde alloro; Bel tempo per me; Così volete, così sarà; Deh, memoria è che più chiedi; Hor che si Sirio; Il mio cor è un mar; Lungi homai deh spiega; Peregrin d'ignote sponde; Rimati in pace homai; Scrivete, occhi dolente (Lettera amorosa); Tu m'hai preso à consumare; Vaghi rai, pupille ardenti.*
*** HM Dig. HMC 901262 [id.]. Concerto Vocale, René Jacobs.

Carissimi's achievement as a sacred composer has long overshadowed his secular music, whose riches are generously displayed here and whose inspiration and mastery are immediately evident. These are performances of great style and are beautifully recorded.

Jepthe; Judicium Salomonis (The Judgement of Solomon); Jonas (oratorios).
*** Mer. Dig. CDE 84132 [id.]. Coxwell, Hemington Jones, Harvey, Ainsley, Gabrieli Cons. 8 Players, Paul McCreesh.

The present disc collects three of the best known of Carissimi's chamber oratorios. No opening sinfonia survives for *Jepthe* and the editor chooses to preface the oratorio with a Frescobaldi *Toccata*, which works well. *Jepthe* is affectingly presented in this well-prepared and intelligent performance, which is let down only by some vocal insecurities at the very top. The continuo part is imaginatively realized with some pleasing sonorities (organ, double harp, chitarrone, etc.). Despite some undoubted shortcomings, these are most convincing accounts of all three works.

Carlsson, Mark (born 1952)

Nightwings.
*** Crystal Dig. CD 750 [id.]. Westwood Wind Quintet – BARBER: *Summer music*; LIGETI: *Bagatelles*; MATHIAS: *Quintet.***

In *Nightwings* the flute assumes the persona of a dreamer, the taped music may be perceived as a dream-world, and the other four instruments appear as characters in a dream. The music is almost wholly diatonic and immediately accessible, but it is not an unimaginative conception. On this evidence, however, the conception is in some respects more interesting than the piece itself. Excellent playing and recording.

Carmina Burana (c. 1300)

Carmina Burana – songs from the original manuscript.
*** O-L Dig. 417 373-2 [id.]. New L. Cons., Pickett.
**(*) HM HMC 90335 [id.]. Clemencic Cons., René Clemencic.

Carmina Burana – songs from the original manuscript, Vol. 2.
*** O-L Dig. 421 062-2 [id.]. New L. Cons., Pickett.

This was the collection on which Carl Orff drew for his popular cantata. The original manuscript comprises more than 200 pieces from many countries, dating from the late eleventh to the thirteenth century, organized according to subject-matter: love songs, moralizing and satirical songs, eating, drinking, gambling and religious texts. The performances on these well-filled Oiseau-Lyre discs have the merit of excellent singing from Catherine Bott and Michael George, and sensitive playing from the instrumentalists under Pickett. The engineering is excellent and strikes a virtually ideal balance between voice and instruments. There is a pleasing acoustic ambience. This makes a clear first choice, given the clarity and warmth of the sound.

René Clemencic's performances, recorded in 1977, have immense spirit and liveliness, and there is much character. The presentation suffers slightly in comparison with its rival from slightly over-reverberant sound, though this at times brings a gain in atmosphere. Most collectors will prefer the better-focused sound of its immediate rival.

Carter, Elliott (born 1908)

(i) *Piano concerto; Variations for orchestra.*
*** New World NWCD 347 [id.]. (i) Ursula Oppens; Cincinnati SO, Gielen.

The *Concerto* comes from the mid-1960s and is a densely argued piece, complex in its structure, contrasting an isolated soloist (Ursula Oppens its heroine) whose character is 'free, fanciful and sensitive' with an orchestra that functions as a massive and mechanical ensemble, and with a concertino of seven instruments, surrounding the piano, who act as 'a well-meaning but impotent intermediary'. It is a strange work that seems at first impenetrable but which is undeniably powerful and disturbing. The *Concerto* and the *Variations* date from two different stylistic periods; the *Variations* is an inventive and fascinating work, splendidly played by these Cincinnati forces. The recording was made at concert performances and is excellent.

Castelnuovo-Tedesco, Mario (1895–1968)

Guitar concerto in D, Op. 99.
*** Ph. Dig. 416 357-2 [id.]. Pepe Romero, ASMF, Marriner – RODRIGO: *Sones en la Giralda*; VILLA-LOBOS: *Concerto.****
(*) Decca Dig. 417 199-2 [id.]. Fernández, ECO, Martinez – RODRIGO: *Concierto; Fantasia.*(*)

Castelnuovo-Tedesco's innocently romantic *Concerto*, with its slow-movement melody that faintly recalls another even more famous tune, is splendidly played by Pepe Romero, while Sir Neville Marriner's accompaniments are affectionate, polished and full of character. With a good balance, natural sound and tempting couplings, this will be hard to beat.

Eduardo Fernández is also given warmly atmospheric recording on Decca, and his too is a highly agreeable performance, but in the finale Marriner's articulation has a markedly greater degree of rhythmic bite, helped by the slightly clearer Philips recording.

Cavalli, Francesco (1602–76)

Giasone (complete).
*** HM Dig. HMC 901282/4 [id.]. Chance, Schopper, Dubosc, Deletré, Mellon, Banditelli, Visse, De Mey, Concerto Vocale, Jacobs.

With the brilliant and sensitive counter-tenor, Michael Chance, in the title-role of an opera that roams far away from the authentic tale of Jason and the Argonauts, René Jacobs's recording of Cavalli's opera is a remarkable achievement. Based on a stage production given in Innsbruck, it brings fine, stylish singing and playing which uses period performance positively to communicate with a modern audience. Drawing from no fewer than twelve textual sources, Jacobs drew up a text which necessarily omits much material but still runs for almost four hours of music. In the instrumentation Jacobs adds recorders in particular to the strings, to give greater variety. The admixture of comedy that can be embarrassing in operas of this period is here handled splendidly. The vividly characterful Dominique Visse in particular scores a huge success in the drag-role of the nurse, Delfa, very much in the tradition of Hugues Cuenod's performances for Raymond Leppard in Cavalli at Glyndebourne. It is a pity that none of the others characterize like Visse, beautifully as they sing. Clean, well-balanced sound.

Xerse (complete).
*** HM HMC 901175/8 [id.]. René Jacobs, Nelson, Gall, Poulenard, Mellon, Feldman, Elwes, De Mey, Visse, Instrumental Ens., Jacobs.

'*Ombra mai fù,*' sings King Xerxes in the opening scene, addressing a plane tree, and most listeners will have a double-take, remembering Handel's *Largo*, which comes from a later setting of the same libretto. Cavalli's opera, even longer than Handel's *Serse* but just as brisk in its action, can be presented just as winningly, as here in the first ever recording. Jacobs' presentation is piquant to match the plot, often genuinely funny, sustaining the enormous length very well. As well as directing his talented team, Jacobs sings the title-role, only one of the four counter-tenors, nicely contrasted, who take the castrato roles. The fruity alto of Dominique Visse in a comic servant role is particularly striking, and among the women – some of them shrill at times – the outstanding singer, Agnès Mellon, takes the other servant role, singing delightfully in a tiny laughing song. The three Acts of the opera are preceded by an allegorical prologue. Excellent sound, which consistently allows the fresh, young voices of the principals to make every word plain. Notes and libretto are first rate.

Chabrier, Emmanuel (1841–94)

Bourrée fantasque; Danse slave; España; Fête polonaise; Marche joyeuse; Menuet pompeux; Prélude pastoral; Suite pastorale.
**(*) EMI Dig. CDC7 49652-2. Capitole Toulouse O, Plasson.

Chabrier is Beecham territory and calls for playing of elegance and charm. Michel Plasson and his excellent Toulouse forces bring just the right note of exuberance and *joie de vivre* to this delightful music. The recording is eminently satisfactory, though it is a shade resonant and as a result lacks the last ounce of transparency.

Air de ballet; Bourrée fantasque; Caprice; Impromptu in C; Marche des Cipayes; 10 Pièces pittoresques.
** Cal. CAL 9268 [id.]. Annie d'Arco.

Chabrier's piano music – like his songs – is underrated though it left its mark on later French composers. Annie d'Arco's survey puts us in her debt and has a certain charm, but the 1974 recording is somewhat lacklustre.

OPERA

L'Étoile (complete).
⊛ *** EMI Dig. CDS7 47889-8 (2) [Pathé id.]. Alliot-Lugaz, Gautier, Bacquier, Raphanel, Damonte, Le Roux, David, Lyon Opéra Ch. and O, Gardiner.

This fizzing operetta is a winner: the subtlety and refinement of Chabrier's score go well beyond the usual realm of operetta, and Gardiner directs a performance that from first to last makes the piece sparkle bewitchingly. Central to the story, the star of *L'Étoile* is the pedlar, Lazuli, a breeches role, and Gardiner has been lucky to include in his company at the Lyon Opéra a soprano with just the personality, presence and voice to carry it off, Colette Alliot-Lugaz. Except for Gabriel Bacquier as the Astrologer, Sirocco, the others are not well known either, but all are first rate. The helpful French dialogue adds to the sparkle (just long enough to give the right flavour), and numbers such as the drunken duet between King and Astrologer are hilarious. Outstandingly good recording, with excellent access.

Chadwick, George (1854–1931)

Symphony No. 2, Op. 21.
*** New World Dig. NWCD 339 [id.]. Albany SO, Julius Hegyi – PARKER: *Northern Ballad.****

George Chadwick's *Second Symphony* (1883–6) breathes much the same air as Brahms and Dvořák; the scoring is beautifully clean and the ideas appealing, if perhaps wanting the distinctive stamp of an original. The scherzo had to be repeated at its first performance – independently of the whole symphony – when one critic noted that it 'positively winks at you'. It is quite delightful. The symphony as a whole is cultivated, well crafted and civilized. Very natural recorded sound and an excellent performance from these New England forces. An interesting disc.

Charpentier, Marc-Antoine (1634–1704)

Concert à 4 (for viols), *H.545; Musique de théâtre pour Circé et Andromède; Sonata à 8* (for 2 flutes & strings), *H.548.*
**(*) HM Dig. HMC 901244 [id.]. London Baroque, Medlam.

Marc-Antoine Charpentier's music for Thomas Corneille's *Circé* was written in 1675, and its companion for Pierre Corneille's *Andromède* followed seven years later. The pieces are most expertly played here by the members of London Baroque (though the string sound still does not entirely escape the faint suspicion that it has been marinaded in vinegar) and well reward investigation. As usual in recordings from this source, the sound is excellent.

Le malade imaginaire.
*** Erato/WEA Dig. 2292 45002-2 [id.]. Poulenard, Feldman, Ragon *et al.*, Les musiciens du Louvre, Marc Minkowski.

Molière, having fallen out with Lully, dictator of French music in Louis XIV's time and not an agreeable man, turned instead to Charpentier for the music he needed for his last comedy, *Le malade imaginaire*. This sequence of extended prologue and three *intermèdes* tingles with energy, and is superbly realized on this first recording of the complete incidental music, much of which was lost for three centuries. The extended allegorical prologue works like a miniature comic opera, fresh and speedy, amply confirming that the long-underappreciated Charpentier was a master at least equal to Lully. Eight first-rate soloists and a lively period orchestra are spurred by the consistently animated direction of Marc Minkowski, and the vivid recording adds to the illusion of live performance.

Motets: *Alma Redemptoris; Amicus meus; Ave regina; Dialogus inter Magdalenam et Jesum; Egredimini filiae Sion; Elevations; O pretiosum; O vere, o bone, Magdalena lugens; Motet du saint sacrement; O vos omnes; Pour le passion de notre Seigneur* (2 settings); *Salve regina; Solva vivebat in antris Magdalena lugens.*
*** HM HMC 901149 [id.]. Concerto Vocale.

Half of the motets on this record are for solo voice and the others are duets. Among the best and most moving things here are the *O vos omnes* and *Amicus meus*, which are beautifully done. Another motet to note is *Magdalena lugens*, in which Mary Magdalene laments Christ's death at the foot of the Cross. Expressive singing from Judith Nelson and René Jacobs, and excellent continuo support. Worth a strong recommendation.

Caecilia, virgo et martyr; Filius prodigus (oratorios); *Magnificat.*
*** HM Dig. HMC 90066 [id.]. Grenat, Benet, Laplenie, Reinhard, Studer, Les Arts Florissants, Christie.

The two works recorded here come from different periods of his life: *Caecilia, virgo et martyr* was composed in 1675, when he wrote a number of works on the subject of St Cecilia; the second, on the theme of the Prodigal Son, is later and is richer in expressive harmonies and poignant dissonances. The music's stature and nobility are fully conveyed here. The *Magnificat* is a short piece for three voices and has an almost Purcellian flavour. One thing that will immediately strike the listener is the delicacy and finesse of the scoring. All this music is beautifully recorded; the present issues can be recommended with enthusiasm.

In navitatem Domini nostri Jésus Christi (canticum), H.414; Pastorale sur la naissance de notre Seigneur Jésus Christ, H.483.
*** HM HMC 901082. Les Arts Florissants Vocal & Instrumental Ens., Christie.

This *Canticum* has much of the character of an oratorio (indeed, the word 'canticum' was loosely used to indicate both the motet and the oratorio) and affirms the composer's debt to his master, Carissimi. The invention has great appeal and variety. The *Pastorale* is not new to the gramophone, but the present performance offers music that was not included in the previously recorded Guy Lambert edition. It is a most rewarding piece, and the grace and charm of the writing continue to win one over to this eminently resourceful composer. This collection by William Christie is self-recommending, so high are the standards of performance and recording, and so fertile is Charpentier's imagination. The CD remastering is very successful; the only snag in the presentation is the minuscule print of the accompanying texts.

In navitatem Domini nostri Jésus Christ, H.416; Pastorale sur la naissance de notre Seigneur Jésus Christ.
*** HM HMC 905130 [id.]. Les Arts Florissants Vocal & Instrumental Ens., Christie.

The cantata, *In navitatem*, is one of some 35 which Charpentier composed in this genre (the French call them *histoires sacrées*). It is one of his grandest, a finely balanced edifice in two complementary halves, separated by an instrumental section, an eloquent evocation of the night. The little *pastorale* was written in the tradition of the ballet de cour or divertissement. This is enchanting music, elegantly played and excellently recorded.

Leçons de ténèbres.
*** HM HMC 901005 [id.]. Jacobs, Nelson, Verkinderen, Kuijken, Christie, Junghänel.

These *Leçons de ténèbres* are eloquent and moving pieces, worthy of comparison with Purcell and more substantial musically than Couperin's later setting. Since the falsetto tradition was weak, it seems unlikely that any of the music was intended for male alto, a fact that the counter-tenor René Jacobs readily concedes in his notes. Yet his performance (like that of his colleagues) is so authentic in every respect that it is difficult to imagine it being surpassed. The music has depth and these artists reveal its stature to fine effect. The recording is as distinguished as the performances.

Méditations pour le Carême; Le reniement de St Pierre.
*** HM Dig. HMC 905151 [id.]. Les Arts Florissants, William Christie.

Le reniement de Saint Pierre is one of Charpentier's most inspired and expressive works and its text draws on the account in all four Gospels of St Peter's denial of Christ. The *Méditations pour le Carême* are a sequence of three-voice motets for Lent with continuo accompaniment (organ, theorbo and bass viol) that may not have quite the same imaginative or expressive resource but which are full of nobility and interest. The performances maintain the high standards of this ensemble, and the same compliment can be paid to the recording.

(i) *Messe de minuit pour Noël (Midnight Mass for Christmas Eve);* (ii) *Te Deum.*
** EMI CDC7 63135-2. (i) Cantelo, Gelmar, Partridge, Bowman, Keyte, King's College Ch., ECO, Willcocks; (ii) Lott, Harrhy, Brett, Partridge, Roberts, King's College Ch., ASMF, Ledger.

There is a kinship between Charpentier's lovely *Christmas Mass* and Czech settings of the Mass that incorporate folk material; and the combination of verse anthems and carol-like pieces is attractive, even the *Kyrie* having a jolly quality about it. The King's performance is warm and musical, but there isn't much Gallic flavour. The organist, Andrew Davis, intelligently uses realizations of the organ interludes – which the composer directs shall be based on the carol themes – by Nicolas Le Bègue. The recording comes from the late 1960s and certainly now has more bite than it did; but reservations remain about the basic style of the singing. The coupling is the best known of the *Te Deum* settings, and this time the King's performance has a vitality and boldness to match the music and catches also its *douceur* and freshness. The recording, made a decade later than the coupling, is also very successful and has been transferred well to CD.

Miserere, H.219; Motets: pour la seconde fois que le Saint Sacrament vien au même reposoir, H.372; pour le Saint Sacrement au reposoir, H.346. Motet pour une longue offrande, H.434.
*** HM Dig. HMC 901185 [id.]. Mellon, Poulenard, Ledroit, Kendall, Kooy, Chapelle Royale, Herreweghe.

Charpentier's *Motet pour une longue offrande* is one of his most splendid and eloquent works. There are some poignant dissonances in the *Deus justus et patiens* section. The *Miserere*, the last of four settings Charpentier made of Psalm 50, was written for the Jesuit Church on Rue Saint-Antoine, whose ceremonies were particularly sumptuous. All four works on the disc are powerfully expressive and beautifully performed. The recording, made in collaboration with Radio France, is most expertly balanced.

OPERA

Actéon (complete).
*** HM HMC 901095 [id.]. Visse, Mellon, Laurens, Feldman, Paut, Les Arts Florissants Vocal & Instrumental Ens., Christie.

Actéon is a short work in six scenes; the sheer fecundity and, above all, quality of invention take one by surprise – though, by this time, one should take for granted Charpentier's extraordinarily rich imagination. Actéon is particularly well portrayed by Dominique Visse; his transformation in the fourth tableau and his feelings of horror are almost as effective as anything in nineteenth-century opera! Although scholarship is an important ingredient in this undertaking, musicianship and flair are even more important, and these are in welcome evidence. The other singers are first rate, in particular the Diane of Agnès Mellon. Alert playing and an altogether natural recording which is truthfully balanced and sounds splendidly fresh, as well as excellent presentation, make this a most desirable issue.

David et Jonathas (complete).
**(*) HM Dig. HMC 90 1289/90 [id.]. Lesne, Zanetti, Gardeil, Visse, Les Arts Florissants, Christie.

The action of *David et Jonathas* follows the biblical narrative in broad outline, and much of the music is fresh and inventive, remarkably free from period cliché. Christie's version on Harmonia Mundi may not always be especially dramatic, but it has a notably sure sense of authentic Baroque style and scale, as well as fine choral singing. However, only one of Christie's soloists is really outstanding, the characterfully distinctive counter-tenor, Dominique Visse, who gives a vivid, highly theatrical performance. The others are relatively colourless; but those who relish authenticity above all else will clearly take to this version, very well recorded.

Medée (complete).
⊛ *** HM HMC 901139/41 [id.]. Feldman, Ragon, Mellon, Boulin, Bona, Cantor, Les Arts Florissants Ch. & O, Christie.

Few records of early Baroque opera communicate as vividly as this, winner in 1985 of the International record critics' award and the Early Music prize in the *Gramophone* record awards. Despite the classical convention of the libretto and a strictly authentic approach to the performance, Christie's account has a vitality and a sense of involvement which bring out the keen originality of Charpentier's writing, his implied emotional glosses on a formal subject. This was Charpentier's only tragédie-lyrique, and richly extends our knowledge of a long-neglected composer. Les Arts Florissants, in the stylishness of its playing on period instruments, matches any such group in the world, and the soloists are all first rate. Excellent recording.

Chausson, Ernest (1855-99)

Poème for violin and orchestra, Op. 25.
*** EMI CDC7 47725-2 [id.]. Perlman, O de Paris, Martinon – RAVEL: *Tzigane*; SAINT-SAENS: *Havanaise* etc.***
*** DG Dig. 423 063-2 [id.]. Perlman, NYPO, Mehta – RAVEL: *Tzigane*; SAINT-SAENS: *Havanaise* etc.: SARASATE: *Carmen fantasy*.***
*** Decca 417 118-2 [id.]. Kyung Wha Chung, RPO, Dutoit – RAVEL: *Tzigane*; SAINT-SAENS: *Havanaise* etc.***
(M) **(*) EMI Dig. CDC7 47623-2 [id.]. Nigel Kennedy, LPO, Kamu – TCHAIKOVSKY: *Violin concerto*.**(*)

Chausson's beautiful *Poème* has been generously represented on records; Perlman's 1975 recording with the Orchestre de Paris under the late Jean Martinon is a classic account by which newcomers are measured. What a glorious and inspired piece it is when played with such feeling! The digital transfer exchanges some of the opulence of the original for a gain in presence (not that Perlman isn't near enough already) but still sounds full. Perlman's glorious tone is undiminished, even if now the ear perceives a slightly sharper outline to the timbre.

Perlman's 1987 digital version is also a very fine one and will not disappoint. The sound is immediate and refined in detail, while the balance of the soloist is very slightly less forward. The New York Philharmonic players are undoubtedly responsive under Mehta; yet Martinon displays a more subtle feeling for the atmosphere of the piece. In making a choice, some readers will wish to bear in mind that the DG compact disc includes a stunning bonus performance of Sarasate's *Carmen fantasy*.

Chung's performance of Chausson's beautiful *Poème* is deeply emotional; some may prefer a more restrained approach but, with committed accompaniment from the RPO and excellent recording, this makes an admirable foil for the virtuoso pieces with which it is coupled.

Nigel Kennedy's version of the *Poème*, unusually expansive and sensuous with ripe and powerful build-up of climaxes, comes as a welcome if not very generous coupling for his warmly romantic reading of the Tchaikovsky *Concerto*, recorded in similarly rich, full sound.

Symphony in B flat min., Op. 20; Soir de Fête, Op. 32; The Tempest, Op. 18: 2 Scenes.
**(*) Chan. Dig. CHAN 8369 [id.]. Radio-Télévision Belge SO, Serebrier.

Serebrier succeeds in drawing playing of real conviction and some sensitivity from his players. He also offers the *Soir de Fête*, which makes an excellent effect in this recording. In addition, the Chandos disc includes two dances from the incidental music which he composed for *The Tempest*. They are slight but attractive. The recording is very good indeed, without being in the demonstration class.

CHAMBER MUSIC

Concert in D for piano, violin and string quartet, Op. 21; String quartet in C min., Op. 35 (comp. d'Indy).
*** EMI Dig. CDC7 47548-2 [id.]. Collard, Dumay, Muir Qt.

273

Concert for piano, violin and string quartet, Op. 21.
(*) Essex CDS 6044. Accardo, Canino, Levin, Batjer, Hoffman, Wiley – SAINT-SAENS: *Violin sonata No. 1.**

Jean-Philippe Collard and Augustin Dumay unquestionably lead the field. These artists are completely attuned to the sensibility of the period, and they bring an impressive authority to the work. Both Dumay and Collard are scrupulous in their observance of the dynamic markings, and there is an authenticity of feeling that is completely involving. The *C minor String quartet* that was left incomplete, and to which Vincent d'Indy put the finishing touches, provides a splendid makeweight, and this is not otherwise available. The playing is effortless and unforced, and the recording is extremely vivid and lifelike.

Salvatore Accardo and Bruno Canino and their four colleagues convey a sense of effortless music-making and of pleasure in making music in domestic surroundings. Accardo is particularly songful in the third movement, light and delicate elsewhere. While it does not displace the Dumay–Collard version on EMI, which is more concentrated and powerful, it is a thoroughly enjoyable account, recorded in a warm acoustic.

Piano quartet in A, Op. 30; Piano trio in G min., Op. 3.
** HM HMC 901115 [id.]. Les Musiciens.

The Op. 30 *Piano quartet* of 1896 is one of Chausson's finest works and reinforces the oft-quoted claim that he is the connecting link between Franck and Debussy. Les Musiciens comprise the Pasquier Trio and Jean-Claude Pennetier, but they are recorded in a less than ample acoustic, and their performance is lacking the subtlety and colour one knows this ensemble can command. The effect both here and in the early *G minor Trio*, Op. 3, is somewhat monochrome. A pity, since this is enormously civilized music.

Piano trio in G min., Op. 3.
*** Ph. Dig. 411 141-2 [id.]. Beaux Arts Trio – RAVEL: *Trio in A min.****

The early *G minor Trio* will come as a pleasant surprise to most collectors, for its beauties far outweigh any weaknesses. There are many glimpses of the promise to come, and the invention is strong. The playing of the Beaux Arts Trio is superbly eloquent and the recording is very impressive on CD, even if the piano looms a little too large in the picture. A distinguished issue.

(i) *Chanson perpétuelle, Op. 37;* (ii) *Poème de l'amour et de la mer, Op. 19;* (iii) *5 mélodies, Op. 2/2–5 & 7 (Le charme; Le colibri; La dernière feuille; Sérénade italienne; Les papillons).*
*** Erato/WEA 2292 45368-2 [id.]. Jessye Norman, (i) Monte Carlo Qt, Dalberto; (ii) Monte Carlo PO, Jordan; (iii) Michel Dalberto.

Although Jessye Norman's account of the glorious *Poème de l'amour et de la mer* does not wholly eclipse memories of Dame Janet Baker's version, it is still very competitive in its own right. The orchestral texture is splendidly opulent and atmospheric, and Jessye Norman makes an impressive sound throughout. Sometimes her voice seems a bit too big for these pieces – and the closer-than-ideal balance does not help here – but her artistry is never for a moment in doubt. Few will be disappointed with this disc, although its playing time is comparatively short.

Poème de l'amour et de la mer.
(M) (***) EMI CMS7 63549-2 (3) [id.]. Victoria de los Angeles, Lamoureux O, Jacquillat – MASSENET: *Manon(*(**)).*

Victoria de los Angeles, the most seductive Manon on record, is in just as glorious voice for Chausson's sensuous cantata, a generous fill-up on EMI's mid-price set of the opera.

Chávez, Carlos (1899–1978)

Symphonies Nos. 1 (Sinfonia de Antigona); 2 (Sinfonia India); 4 (Sinfonia romantica).
(M) **(*) Ph. 422 305-2 [id.]. NY Stadium O, composer.

Symphonies Nos. 1 (Sinfonia de Antigona); 4 (Sinfonia romantica).
*** ASV Dig. CDDCA 653 [id.]. RPO, Bátiz – REVUELTAS: *Caminos* etc.***

The *Sinfonia de Antigona* (1933) was reworked from incidental music Chávez composed for a production of Sophocles' *Antigone*. It is a primitive, highly exotic piece with plenty of colour and a large wind section; the extravagant scoring includes heckelphone, eight horns, two harps and plenty of percussion. The effect is appropriately primeval. The *Fourth Symphony* is perhaps less blatantly exotic but is full of character. Excellent playing from the RPO, offering demonstration sound of great impact, detail and presence.

The Philips performances carry the authority of the composer's own direction and include the best-known, *Sinfonia India*, which is based on true Indian melodies. It has a savage, primitive character that is very attractive. The recording is detailed and bright, if not absolutely sharp in focus and somewhat wanting in real depth and weight. It derives from the Everest catalogue and dates from the early days of stereo (1958).

Cherubini, Luigi (1760–1842)

String quartets Nos 1–6.
(M) *** DG 429 185-2 (3) [id.]. Melos Qt.

Cherubini's *Quartets* are new to the CD catalogue and here have the advantage of authentic performing texts. No. 1 was composed when Cherubini was already in his fifties; the last four were written in the 1830s, when he was advanced in years. *No. 2 in C* is a reworking of the *Symphony in D*, though he composed a fresh slow movement. Cherubini's melodic inspiration is often both distinguished and distinctive, although there are times when it falls short of true memorability; but a fine musical intelligence and a polished craftsmanship are always in evidence. The Melos Quartet play these works with real commitment and authority, while the remastered recorded sound is well balanced and clear.

(i) *Coronation Mass for King Charles X; Marche religieuse.* (ii) *Requiem in C min.;* (iii) *Requiem in D min. for male voices;* (iv) *Solemn mass in G for the Coronation of Louis XVIII.*
(M) *** EMI Dig./Analogue CMS7 63161-2 (4). (i) Philh. Ch. & O; (ii) Amb. S., Philh. O; (iii) Amb. S., New Philh. O; (iv) LPO Ch., LPO; Muti.

Three of these records are digital, the *D minor Requiem* (recorded in 1975) is analogue. They come in a handsome slip-case and, at mid-price, should bring this fine repertoire to a wider audience. Three of the four works are currently still available separately at full price, although they may disappear during the lifetime of this book. The *C minor Requiem*, the best known, was called by Berlioz 'the greatest of the greatest of his [Cherubini's] work', and he went on to claim that 'no other production of this great master can bear any comparison with it for abundance of ideas, fullness of form and sustained sublimity of style'. Muti directs a tough, incisive reading, underlining the drama, to remind one that this was a work also recorded by Toscanini some three decades earlier. Muti is well served both by his orchestra and by the relatively small professional choir; and the full, clear recording is most satisfying.

Coronation mass for King Charles X; Marche religieuse.
*** EMI Dig. CDC7 49302-2 [id.]. Philh. Ch. & O, Muti.

The *Coronation Mass for Charles X* dates from 1825 and there are signs in the *Gloria* that Cherubini was influenced by both *Fidelio* and the *Ninth Symphony*, and in the *Incarnatus* and *Crucifixus* by the *Missa solemnis*. But Cherubini's church music has a character of its own, beautifully crafted, with moments of real inspiration, such as the closing bars of the *Kyrie*. Muti presents the music with an intensity to hide any limitations, and both chorus and orchestra respond superbly. He secures the widest dynamic refinements and the digital sound is bold and full, with ceremonial trumpets braying magnificently. There is an instrumental appendix in the form of a *Marche religieuse*, a very fine piece.

Solemn Mass in G for the Coronation of Louis XVIII.
*** EMI Dig. CDC7 49553-2 [id.]. LPO Ch., LPO, Muti.

The *G major Mass* was finished in 1819, but meanwhile Louis XVIII had postponed his coronation a number of times, and in the end it never took place, so Cherubini's *Mass* remained unperformed and the full score was prepared for publication only recently. As is so often the case with Cherubini, the musical inspiration is not merely dignified but noble – and on occasion inspired. Muti seems persuaded of its distinction and performs the work with dedication and conviction.

Requiem in C min.
**(*) RCA Dig. RD 60059 [60059-2-RC]. Berlin Radio Ch. & SO, Flor.

Cherubini's *C minor Requiem* has an impressive nobility and dignity – and, in Claus Peter Flor's hands, humanity. All the same, his performance does not have the dramatic intensity of the Muti (EMI), let alone the legendary Toscanini version, and the singing of the Berlin Radio Choir is not as firmly focused in tone or as accurate in intonation as the Ambrosians on EMI. Their soprano line is not as strong; and Muti's account, which is not overdriven, remains a first choice.

Requiem in D min.
*** EMI CDC7 49301-2 [id.]. Amb. S., Philh. O, Muti.

The darkness of tone in the use of male voices in Cherubini's *D minor Requiem* goes with much solemn minor-key music (a little inflated by Beethovenian standards) and some striking anticipations of Verdi. In Muti's fine, committed performance the listener forgets the scarcity of really memorable melodies, and relishes the drama and the distinctive textures, particularly as the recording is outstandingly fine.

OPERA

Medea.
*** Hung. HCD 11904/5 [id.]. Sass, Luchetti, Kováts, Takács, Kalmár, Gregor, Hungarian Radio and TV Ch., Budapest SO, Gardelli.

Gardelli conducts a powerful performance of Cherubini's formidable opera, explaining very clearly why Beethoven so admired this composer. This Hungarian set, originally made in 1978 but sounding very fresh and vivid on CD, shows off the formidable strengths of the Hungarian State Opera, and in particular the artistry of Sylvia Sass, who has rarely if ever sounded as impressive on disc as here, full and firm, the tone creamier than it has latterly become, unexaggerated in expression yet intensely dramatic. One hardly misses the extra individuality of a Callas in a consistently gripping performance, helped by fine support from the other principals, not to mention Gardelli and the orchestra. Kolos Kováts as Creon and Klára Takács as Neris are particularly fine, and Veriano Luchetti is stronger and more individual than he has generally been on disc. Well-balanced sound, cleanly transferred.

Chopin, Frédéric (1810–49)

CONCERTANTE AND ORCHESTRAL MUSIC

Piano concertos Nos. 1 in E min., Op. 11; 2 in F min., Op. 21.
*** DG 415 970-2 [id.]. Zimerman, LAPO, Giulini.
*** Sony Dig. SK44922 [id.]. Perahia, Israel PO, Mehta.
(BB) *** Naxos Dig. 8.550123 [id.]. István Székely, Budapest SO, Gyula Németh.
(B) *** DG 429 515-2 [id.]. Tamás Vásáry, BPO, Semkow or Kulka.
**(*) RCA RD 85612 [RCA 5612-2-RC]. Rubinstein, London New SO, Skrowaczewski or Symphony of the Air, Wallenstein.
**(*) Olympia OCD 149 [id.]. Yevgeny Kissin, Moscow Philh. Ac. SO, Dmitri Kitaenko.
(BB) ** Hung. White Label HRC 084 [id.]. Sándor Falvai, Budapest PO, András Kórodi.

Piano concerto No. 1.
(BB) **(*) Naxos Dig. 8.550292 [id.]. Székely, Budapest SO, Németh – LISZT: *Concerto No. 1.***(*)
(*) DG 415 061-2 [id.]. Argerich, LSO, Abbado – LISZT: *Concerto No. 1.*(*)
(M) (**) EMI mono CDH7 63497-2 [id.]. Lipatti, Zurich Tonhalle O, Ackermann – GRIEG: *Piano concerto.*(***)

(i) *Piano concerto No. 1 in E min., Op. 11; Andante spianato et Grande polonaise, Op. 22; Waltz No. 1 in E flat (Grande valse brillante), Op. 18.*
(M) *** DG 419 054-2. Krystian Zimerman, (i) Concg. O, Kondrashin.

Piano concerto No. 1; Ballade No. 1, Op. 23; Nocturnes Nos. 4 & 5, Op. 15/1–2.
(M) *** EMI CDM7 69004-2 [id.]. Pollini, Philh. O, Kletzki.

Pollini's classic recording still remains the best available of the *E minor Concerto*. This is playing of such total spontaneity, poetic feeling and refined judgement that criticism is silenced. The digital remastering has been generally successful. Orchestral texture is drier and clearer, with slight loss of bass, but there is better definition; the piano timbre is unimpaired. The additional items come from Pollini's first EMI solo recital, and the playing is equally distinguished, the recording truthful.

The CD coupling of Zimerman's performances of the two Chopin *Concertos* with Giulini is also hard to beat. In the *First Concerto* Zimerman is fresh, poetic and individual in his approach; this is a sparkling, beautifully characterized performance. His reading of the *F minor Concerto* has also won much acclaim, and rightly so. Elegant, arisocratic, sparkling, it has youthful spontaneity and at the same time a magisterial authority, combining sensibility with effortless pianism. Both recordings are cleanly detailed. While the balance favours the soloist too much, this coupling leads the field, without question.

Zimerman's alternative, mid-priced version of the *E minor Concerto* comes from a live performance at the Concertgebouw in 1979. Zimerman gives a characteristically authoritative and poised performance and seems to have established a particularly good rapport with Kondrashin. He is again balanced rather forwardly, and there is a little more spontaneity (particularly in the slow movement and finale) than in the studio account. The *Andante spianato* and the *Waltz* are drier and less open in acoustic; otherwise the sound is altogether excellent and in no way inferior to the later version.

Perahia's earlier record of the Chopin *E minor Concerto* was with Mehta and the New York Philharmonic, but this is much finer. His remarkable sensitivity and virtuosity have not been heard to better effect since his Mozart cycle. His effortless brilliance and refinement of touch recall artists like Hoffman and Lipatti. Mehta provides a highly sensitive accompaniment once the soloist enters but is curiously offhand and matter-of-fact (indeed almost brutal) in the orchestral ritornelli. The sound is an improvement on anything else we have had from the Mann Auditorium, Tel Aviv – which it would need to be – though it is still dryish and far from ideal. The three stars are for Perahia's playing, not the sound!

István Székely is particularly impressive in the *E minor Concerto*, but in both works he finds atmosphere and poetry in slow movements and an engaging dance spirit for the finales, with rhythms given plenty of character. Németh accompanies sympathetically, building the uncut opening ritornelli impressively, and the Budapest strings caress Chopin's lyrical melodies affectingly. The orchestral contribution here is more refined than the accompaniment Mehta provides for Perahia. The recording is resonantly full in the Hungarian manner, not absolutely clear on detail, but the piano image is bold and realistic, and the brilliance of the pianist's articulation is crisply caught. A splendid bargain in every sense of the word.

Vásáry's approach is much more self-effacing: his gentle poetry is in clear contrast with the opulent orchestral sound (especially in No. 1, where the recording is more resonantly expansive than in No. 2). Yet soloist and orchestra match their styles perfectly in both slow movements, which are played most beautifully, and the finales have no lack of character and sparkle. In their way, these performances will give considerable pleasure and, with recording that retains its depth and bloom, this makes a fine bargain coupling.

Rubinstein's performances are no less welcome and there is much that is unforgettably magical in the solo playing. Rubinstein's shaping of the secondary theme of the first movement of the *E minor* is memorable, and in the *Larghetto* his control of colour and rubato are inimitable. Again in the *F minor Concerto*, although the Carnegie Hall sound is less than ideal, Rubinstein's contribution is an object lesson in the delicate playing of Chopin's poetic moments; his rubato is so natural that the music sounds as if it were extemporized. As with nearly all the CD issues of Rubinstein's early recordings, the piano timbre is much fuller and less twangy than it sounded on the original LPs, although the orchestral quality is more variable.

Superb playing from the twelve-year-old Yevgeny Kissin in this extraordinary début recording: these are bold, Romantic readings, full of flair and with a remarkable amount of poetry, too. Kissin's approach is unashamedly extrovert, yet his rubato is ever responsive to the the musical flow. Passage-work is glitteringly alive and the finales of both *Concertos* sparkle with bravura, while there is a winning delicacy in the music's lyrical pages. The playing has all the adrenalin and spontaneity one expects at a live concert, and the orchestra creates positive, full-bodied tuttis, yet does not want for refined feeling, and there is some lovely playing from the strings. A thrilling coupling, given an excellent, well-balanced recording, made in the concert hall of the Moscow Conservatoire. The applause at the end is well justified.

In the *E minor Concerto* Martha Argerich's affectionate phrasing provides some lovely playing, especially in the slow movement. Perhaps in the passage-work she is sometimes rather too intense, but this is far preferable to the rambling style we are sometimes offered. With excellent recording, this is one of the most satisfactory versions available of this elusive concerto. The recording was originally of high quality, and it sounds remarkably fresh in its CD format.

The Hungaroton performances are highly musical and pleasing, and the sound is smooth; but overall the impression is rather subdued and lacks a feeling of projection.

Lipatti's is a lovely performance but, despite the expert ministrations of Keith Hardwick, its sonic limitations and limited frequency range will prove something of an obstacle to all but specialist collectors.

Piano concerto No. 2 in F min., Op. 21.
(M) *** Decca 417 750-2 [id.]. Ashkenazy, LSO, Zinman – TCHAIKOVSKY: *Piano concerto No. 1.****
(B) ** ASV CDQS 6003 [id.]. Vásáry, N. Sinfonia – SCHUMANN: *Concerto.***

Ashkenazy's 1965 recording is a distinguished performance: his sophisticated use of light and shade in the opening movement, and the subtlety of phrasing and rubato, are a constant source of pleasure. The recitativo section in the *Larghetto*, which can often sound merely rhetorical, is here shaped with mastery, and there is a delectable lightness of touch in the finale. David Zinman and the LSO are obviously in full rapport with their soloist, and the vintage recording has been remastered most satisfactorily.

Vásáry's newest recording on ASV in which he not only plays but directs the Northern Sinfonia from the keyboard has the advantage of fresher and well-balanced sound, but the playing, while it has much delicacy and refinement, is not so boldly characterized nor so full of ardour and flair as was his earlier account.

Les Sylphides (ballet; orch. Douglas).
⊛ (B) *** DG 429 163-2 [id.]. BPO, Karajan – DELIBES: *Coppélia*; OFFENBACH: *Gaîté parisienne.****

Karajan conjures consistently beautiful playing with the Berlin Philharmonic Orchestra, and he evokes a delicacy of texture which consistently delights the ear. The woodwind solos are played gently and lovingly, and one can feel the conductor's touch on the phrasing. The upper register of the strings is bright, fresh and clearly focused, the recording is full and atmospheric, and this is one of Karajan's very finest recordings. At bargain price it is unbeatable, coupled on CD with not only *Coppélia* (although the suite is not complete) but also Offenbach's *Gaîté parisienne.*

Cello sonata in G min., Op. 65.
*** Claves CD 50-703 [CD 703]. Claude Starck, Ricardo Requejo – GRIEG: *Cello sonata.****
(M) **(*) EMI CMS7 63184-2 [id.]. Du Pré, Barenboim – FRANCK: *Cello sonata.***(*)
*(*) ASV Dig. CDDCA 672 [id.]. Bernard Gregor-Smith, Yolande Wrigley – RACHMANINOV: *Cello sonata.**(*)

The Claves performance is fluent and well characterized and the recording, if not in the very highest flight, is still eminently truthful. The playing has authority and dedication, and collectors need not hesitate to choose this version if the Grieg coupling is suitable.

The easy romanticism of the *Cello sonata* is beautifully caught by Jacqueline du Pré and Daniel Barenboim. Though the cellist phrases with all her usual spontaneous-sounding imagination, this is one of her more reticent records, while still bringing an autumnal quality to the writing which is very appealing. The recording is excellently balanced.

Bernard Gregor-Smith, the cellist of the Lindsay Quartet, is an artist of discerning musicianship – as indeed is his partner, Yolande Wrigley. However, these artists are not helped by a balance that distinctly favours the piano.

Piano trio in G min., Op. 8.
*** Teldec/WEA Dig. 2292 43715-2 [id.]. Trio Fontenay – SMETANA: *Piano trio.***

The Trio Fontenay give a vividly characterized and well-projected account of the Op. 8 *Trio*, written when Chopin was eighteen, and not exactly one of his greatest works. It is well worth hearing, all the same. Good clear recording.

SOLO PIANO MUSIC

Albumblatt in E; Allegro de concert, Op. 46; Barcarolle, Op. 60; Berceuse, Op. 57; Boléro, Op. 19; 2 Bourrées; Cantabile in B flat; Contredanse in G flat; 3 Écossaises, Op. 72/3; Fugue in A min.; Galop marquis; Largo in E flat; Marche funèbre, Op. 72/2; 3 Nouvelles Études; Rondos, Opp. 1, 5, 16 & 73; Sonata No. 1 in C min., Op. 4; Tarantelle, Op. 43; Variations brillantes, Op. 12; Variation No. 6 from Hexameron; Variations on a German National air; Variations (Souvenir de Paganini); (i) *Variations for piano duet.* (i) *Wiosna from Op. 74/2.*
*** Decca 421 035-2 (2) [id.]. Vladimir Ashkenazy; (i) with Vovka Ashkenazy.

Many of the shorter pieces presented here are very early, the *Écossaises*, for instance, the *Rondos*, Opp. 1 and 5, and the ingenious *Variations on a German National air (Der Schweizerbub)*. Here as elsewhere Ashkenazy's playing is often magical, fresh and direct, full of touches of insight. But there are substantial works too, including the *Barcarolle* and *Berceuse*, both superbly done, as is the *Allegro de concert*. In the *D major Variations* Ashkenazy is joined by his son. The *C major Sonata* is not deeply characteristic, but Ashkenazy makes out a more persuasive account for it than anyone who has recorded it so far. The piano transcription of Chopin's song, *Wiosna*, is particularly fetching. Throughout, Ashkenazy's playing is authoritative and poetic, and the recordings are excellent. A number of venues were used, and while the ear registers the slight differences of balance and acoustics, the quality of the digital remastering offers consistent realism and presence.

Andante spianato et Grande polonaise brillante, Op. 22; Barcarolle in F sharp min., Op. 60; Berceuse in D flat, Op. 57; Bólero in C, Op. 19; Impromptus Nos. 1–4; Fantaisie-impromptu, Op. 66; 3 Nouvelles études, Op. posth.; Tarantelle in A flat, Op. 43.
*** RCA RD 89911 [RCA 5617-2-RC]. Artur Rubinstein.

In Chopin piano music generally Rubinstein has no superior. The *Andante spianato and Grande polonaise* obviously inspires him, and his clear and relaxed accounts of the *Impromptus* make most other interpretations sound forced by comparison. The magnificent *Barcarolle* and *Berceuse* contain some of Chopin's finest inspirations – and if the *Tarantelle* may appear musically less interesting and not very characteristic, in Rubinstein's hands it is a glorious piece, full of bravura.

Allegro de concert, Op. 45; Ballades Nos. 1–4; Introduction & variations on Je vends des scapulaires, Op. 12.
*** CRD CRD 3360. Hamish Milne.

Ballades Nos. 1–4; Scherzi Nos. 1–4.
*** RCA RD 89651 [RCD1 7156]. Artur Rubinstein.
*** Decca 417 474-2 [id.]. Vladimir Ashkenazy.

Rubinstein's readings are unique and the digital remastering has been highly successful. The performances of the *Ballades* are a miracle of creative imagination, with Rubinstein at his most inspired. The *Scherzi*, which gain most of all from the improved sound (they were originally very dry), are both powerful and charismatic.

Ashkenazy's playing is full of poetry and flair, as the opening *G minor Ballade* readily demonstrates, while the *Ballade in A flat* has exceptional warmth and sonority. The *Scherzi* have characteristic panache and the whole programme is imbued with imaginative insights and a recital-like spontaneity.

Hamish Milne gives thoughtful and individual performances of the *Ballades*. They may initially sound understated, but in their freshness and concentration they prove poetic and compelling. Similarly he plays the two rarities with total conviction, suggesting that the *Allegro de concert* at least (originally a sketch for a third piano concerto) is most unjustly neglected. The recorded sound is first rate.

Barcarolle, Op. 60; Berceuse, Op. 57; Fantaisie in F min., Op. 49; Impromptu No. 1 in A flat, Op. 29; Impromptu No. 2 in F sharp, Op. 36; Impromptu No. 3 in G flat, Op. 51.
*** CBS Dig. MK 39708 [id.]. Murray Perahia.

Perahia is a Chopin interpreter of the highest order. There is an impressive range of colour and an imposing sense of order. This is highly poetic playing and an indispensable acquisition for any Chopin collection. The CBS recording does him justice.

Barcarolle in F sharp, Op. 60; Berceuse in D flat, Op. 57; Fantaisie in F. min., Op. 49; Nocturne No. 4 in F, Op. 15/1; Polonaise No. 4 in C min., Op. 40/2; Sonata No. 3 in B min., Op. 58.
(B) **(*) Pickwick Dig. PCD 834 [MCA MCAD 25202]. John Ogdon.

John Ogdon's collection presents fresh and thoughtful performances, not as electrifying as some he recorded earlier in his career but often bold and full of individual insights. His speeds for the slower pieces are at times daringly extreme, but he sustains them well, and the delicacy of much that he does is a delight, set in contrast to his natural strength in bravura. Bright, clear, realistic recording, giving the piano a powerful presence.

Barcarolle in F sharp, Op. 60; Berceuse in D flat, Op. 57; Fantaisie in F min., Op. 49; Polonaise No. 7 (Polonaise-Fantaisie), Op. 61; Souvenir de Paganini in A; Variations brillantes, Op. 12.
(M) *** EMI CD-EMX 2117. Daniel Barenboim.

Barenboim's 1974 recital now makes a distinguished entry into the mid-priced CD catalogue; highly imaginative, spontaneous playing, with the rarities made just as enticing as the more familiar works. Recommended – the sound is excellent.

Études, Op. 10/1–12; Op. 25/1–12; 3 Nouvelles études.
*** Chan. Dig. CHAN 8482 [id.]. Louis Lortie.

Études, Op. 10, Nos. 1–12; Op. 25, Nos. 1–12.
*** EMI Dig. CDC7 47452-2 [id.]. Andrei Gavrilov.
*** Decca 414 127-2 [id.]. Vladimir Ashkenazy.
*** DG 413 794-2 [id.]. Maurizio Pollini.

Andrei Gavrilov's performances bring an exuberant virtuosity that it is impossible to resist, even if some of the tempi are breathtakingly fast. Yet the sustained legato of the famous *No. 3 in E major* is lovely, and his poetic feeling, both here and in *No. 6 in E flat minor*, is indisputable. The impulsive bravura is often engulfing, so that one sometimes feels the need to take a breath on the soloist's behalf, but this is prodigious playing, given a bold forward recording to match.

Louis Lortie's set of the 24 *Études* can hold its own with the best. His playing has a strong poetic feeling and an effortless virtuosity. He is beautifully recorded at The Maltings, Snape (whose acoustic occasionally clouds the texture), but collectors wanting a first-class account of these extraordinary pieces will find that the Chandos disc is the only CD also to include the three *Nouvelles études* of 1839.

Ashkenazy's 1975 version sounds wonderfully vivid in its CD form, and the fine transfer that Decca provide may well make this a first choice for some collectors. However, honours are very evenly divided between these performances and those by Gavrilov and Lortie, and both those artists have the advantage of modern digital sound.

Pollini's record also comes from 1975 and sounds splendidly fresh in its digitally remastered form. This is playing of much stature. These are vividly characterized accounts, masterly and with the sound eminently present, although not as full in sonority as the more recent versions.

Mazurkas Nos. 1–51.
*** RCA RD 85171 (2) [RCA 5614-2-RC]. Artur Rubinstein.
*** Decca 417 584-2 (2) [id.]. Vladimir Ashkenazy.

The *Mazurkas* contain some of Chopin's most characteristic music. All are delightful, even if there is no need to linger very long over some of them. Rubinstein could never play in a dull way to save his life, and in his hands these fifty-one pieces are endlessly fascinating, though on occasion in such unpretentious music one would welcome a completely straight approach. As with the *Ballades* and *Scherzi*, the digital remastering has brought a much more pleasing piano timbre.

Ashkenazy's recordings were made at various times between 1975 and 1985. His are finely articulated, aristocratic accounts and the sound is amazingly fresh and consistent, considering the time-span involved. He includes the posthumously published *Mazurkas* and the recording quality is more modern and more natural than that afforded to Rubinstein, with a believable presence.

Nocturnes Nos. 1–19.
*** RCA RD 89563 (2) [RCA 5613-2-RC]. Artur Rubinstein.

Nocturnes Nos. 1–21.
*** Decca 414 564-2 (2) [id.]. Vladimir Ashkenazy.
*** Hyp. Dig. CDA 66341/2 [id.]. Livia Rév.
*** Ph. 416 440-2 (2) [id.]. Claudio Arrau.
(M) *** DG Dig. 423 916-2 (2) [id.]. Daniel Barenboim.

Rubinstein in Chopin is a magician in matters of colour; his unerring sense of nuance and the seeming inevitability of his rubato demonstrate a very special musical imagination in this repertoire. The recordings were the best he received in his Chopin series for RCA, and the quality is now finer still in these excellent CD transfers. There is no appreciable background noise.

Ashkenazy's set includes the two posthumously published *Nocturnes*: the performances were recorded over a decade from 1975 to 1985. The disparity in dates seems not to have affected the consistency of sound that the Decca engineers have achieved. The playing is splendidly ruminative and atmospheric. As always, Ashkenazy is completely attuned to Chopin's unique sound-world, though occasionally some may feel that his tone is too big in fortissimo passages for these intimate pieces – as if he is playing in a large concert hall rather than in a late-night salon.

Livia Rév is an artist of refined musicianship and impeccable taste, selfless and unconcerned with display or self-projection. Indeed there are times when she comes too close to understatement. But still these are lovely performances and the recording has great warmth.

Arrau's approach clearly reflects his boyhood training in Germany, creating tonal warmth coupled with inner tensions of the kind one expects in Beethoven. In this he has something in common with Barenboim. With the *Nocturnes* it can be apt to have an element of seriousness, and this is a very compelling cycle, full of poetry, the rubato showing an individual but very communicable sensibility. This is among Arrau's very finest Chopin recordings.

Barenboim's playing is of considerable eloquence, the phrasing beautifully moulded, and he is superbly recorded. While Rubinstein reigns supreme in this repertoire, Barenboim's set will still give much pleasure with its relaxed, less impetuous style, although occasionally there is just a hint of blandness.

Nocturnes Nos 1–7, 9–12, 13, 15, 19–20.
(B) ** DG 429 154-2 [id.]. Tamás Vásáry.

This is playing of character and the selection is generous. Vásáry can mould a Chopin phrase with the best, but here he often seems too positive, although there are moments of poetry too. But the clean, rather dry piano timbre does not help provide a feeling of warm relaxation.

Nocturnes Nos. 2, 4–7, 9, 11–15, 18–19.
**(*) DG Dig. 415 117-2 [id.]. Daniel Barenboim.

Barenboim's performances, taken from his complete set, are intense, thoughtful and poetic readings, the phrasing lovingly moulded, following rather in the mid-European tradition. Compared with Rubinstein, they lack a mercurial dimension, and the chosen selection tends to emphasize their repose. The sound is first class.

Polonaises Nos. 1–7.
*** RCA RD 89814 [RCA 5615-2]. Artur Rubinstein.
*** DG 413 795-2 [id.]. Maurizio Pollini.
(B) ** DG 429 516-2 [id.]. Shura Cherkassky.

Master pianist that he was, Rubinstein seems actually to be rethinking and re-creating each piece, even the hackneyed '*Military*' and *A flat* works, at the very moment of performance in this recording, made in Carnegie Hall. His easy majesty and natural sense of spontaneous phrasing gives this collection a special place in the catalogue.

Pollini offers playing of outstanding mastery as well as subtle poetry, and the DG engineers have made a decent job of the transfer. This is magisterial playing, in some ways more commanding than Rubinstein (and rather better recorded) though not more memorable.

Shura Cherkassky is sometimes an idiosyncratic artist and his playing has certain eccentricities of style and tempo. Compared with Pollini, he sometimes sounds wilful, and the famous *A major Polonaise* is rather deliberate. But for the most part his playing shows a redeeming spontaneity. The recording is good though not distinguished, bold but a little hard.

24 Preludes, Op. 28.
*** DG 413 796-2 [id.]. Maurizio Pollini.
** DG Dig. 429 227-2. Ivo Pogorelich.

24 Preludes, Op. 28; Preludes Nos. 25, Op. 43; 26, Op. posth.
** EMI Dig. CDC7 47662-2. Dmitri Alexeev.

24 Preludes, Op. 28; Preludes Nos. 25 – 26; Barcarolle, Op. 60; Polonaise No. 6 in A flat, Op. 53; Scherzo No. 2 in B flat min., Op. 31.
(M) **(*) DG 415 836-2 [id.]. Martha Argerich.

Preludes, Op. 28; Preludes Nos. 25 – 26; Berceuse, Op. 57; Fantasy in F min., Op. 4.
*** Hyp. Dig. CDA 66324 [id.]. Livia Rév.

24 Preludes, Op. 28; Preludes Nos. 25 – 26; Impromptus Nos. 1 – 4; Fantaisie-impromptu, Op. 66.
*** Decca 417 476-2 [id.]. Vladimir Ashkenazy.

Ashkenazy's 1979 set of the *Preludes* combines drama and power with finesse and much poetic delicacy when called for. The presence of the four *Impromptus* and the *Fantaisie-impromptu* makes this CD even more attractive. There is an aristocratic quality about these excellently recorded performances that is wholly Chopinesque.

Pollini's set is also highly distinguished. He has impeccable taste in handling rubato, the firmest sense of line and form, and the reading evinces an effortless and complete mastery. However, the absence of later *Preludes* or of any other additional items is not in this issue's favour.

Livia Rév's playing has an unforced naturalness that is most persuasive. She is an artist to her fingertips and, though she may not have the outsize musical personality of some great pianists, she does not have the outsize ego either. A scrupulous musician and a dedicated artist, even if at times one wishes she would let rip. She includes not only the extra *Preludes*, but two other substantial pieces as well.

The *Preludes* show Martha Argerich at her finest, spontaneous and inspirational, though her moments of impetuosity may not appeal to all tastes. But her instinct is sure, with many poetic individual touches. The other pieces are splendidly played. The digital remastering gives the piano image striking presence but at fortissimo levels the timbre becomes hard.

In some of the *Preludes* Alexeev is second to none and he is rarely unilluminating. However, although he carries all before him much of the time, elsewhere he leaves one impressed but unmoved. There is much fine artistry here, but this is not a first choice.

Pogorelich is superbly recorded but it would be difficult to call his interpretation selfless, and his playing is not free from posturing.

Sonata No. 2 in B flat min. (Funeral march), Op. 35; Andante spianato et Grande Polonaise brillante, Op. 22; Études, Op. 10/3 – 4; Nocturne No. 8 in D flat, Op. 27/2.
**(*) Mer. ECD 84070 [id.]. John Bingham.

Sonata No. 2 (Funeral march); Ballade No. 1 in G min., Op. 23; Barcarolle, Op. 60; Nocturnes: in F, F sharp, Op. 15/1 – 2; Scherzo No. 2 in B flat min., Op. 31.
(M) *** Decca 417 729-2 [id.]. Vladimir Ashkenazy.

Ashkenazy's 1972 recording of the *Second Sonata* (plus the two *Nocturnes*) was made during a live recital at Essex University; the piano has splendid resonance and realism, and now the applause has been edited out. The performance of the *Sonata* is of the highest distinction; if the final *Presto* is not absolutely immaculate, who will cavil, with music-making of this quality? The two *Nocturnes*, recorded at the same time, have a comparable spontaneity; the rest of the programme, recorded earlier, is also distinguished.

John Bingham's account of the *Sonata* is highly sensitive and most musicianly; if it lacks the sense of scale or range of rivals such as Ashkenazy or Rubinstein, it has a special dimension of its own. There is also some most beautiful playing in the *Nocturne* and the two studies. The Meridian recording is not made in an ideal acoustic; but this playing is certainly full of individuality.

Piano sonatas Nos. 2 in B flat min. (Funeral march), Op. 35; 3 in B min., Op. 58.
*** DG Dig. 415 362-2 [id.]. Maurizio Pollini.
*** CBS CD 76242 [MK 37280]. Murray Perahia.
(M) *** EMI Dig. CD-EMX 9515. Philip Fowke.

Sonatas Nos. 2 (Funeral march); 3 in B min., Op. 58; Fantaisie in F min., Op. 49.
*** RCA RD 89812 [RCA 5616-2-RC]. Artur Rubinstein.
*** Decca 417 475-2 [id.]. Vladimir Ashkenazy.

Sonatas Nos. 2 in B flat min. (Funeral march), Op. 35; 3 in B min., Op. 58; Scherzo No. 3 in C sharp min., Op. 39.
(M) **(*) DG 419 055-2 [id.]. Martha Argerich.

Sonata No. 2 in B flat min. (Funeral march), Op. 35; Andante spianato et Grande Polonaise brillante, Op. 22; Ballade No. 3 in A flat, Op. 47; 4 Mazurkas, Op. 24; Variations brillantes, Op. 12.
**(*) Olympia OCD 193 [id.]. Peter Katin.

Sonata No. 3 in B min., Op. 58; Ballade No. 4 in F min., Op. 52; Barcarolle, Op. 60; Mazurkas, Op. 59/1–3; Polonaise-Fantaisie, Op. 61.
**(*) Olympia OCD 186 [id.]. Peter Katin.

Rubinstein's readings of the *Sonatas* are unsurpassed, with a poetic impulse that springs directly from the music and a control of rubato to bring many moments of magic. The sound is improved, too, though both Pollini and Ashkenazy gain in this respect.

Pollini's performances are enormously commanding; his mastery of mood and structure gives these much-played *Sonatas* added stature. The slow movement of Op. 35 has tremendous drama and atmosphere, so that the contrast of the magical central section is all the more telling. Both works are played with great distinction, but the balance is just a shade close.

Murray Perahia's technique is remarkable, but it is so natural to the player that he never uses it for mere display; always there is an underlying sense of structural purpose. The dry, unrushed account of the finale of the *B flat Sonata* is typical of Perahia's freshness, and the only pity is that the recording of the piano is rather clattery and close.

Philip Fowke, who in the past has displayed inhibitions in the recording studio, gives highly impressive readings of both *Sonatas*, wide-ranging in their expression, dramatic and poetic, as when he is playing live. The recording is admirably realistic and full in timbre and presence, with the warm acoustics of St Barnabas Church, Finchley, creating an agreeable background ambience without clouding detail.

Ashkenazy's *B flat minor Sonata* is the version released in 1981. Both this and its companion are impressive, though not necessarily a first choice – if such there can be – in this field. There is a shade less tenderness and vision in the slow movement of the *B minor* than there is in some rival versions, though the *B flat minor* has wonderful panache. An authoritative account of the *F minor Fantasy* provides an excellent makeweight. The recordings still sound first class.

Katin produces a consistently refined sonority throughout the dynamic range and there is much sensitivity and poetic feeling in the *Andante spianato* and *Mazurkas*. His is an essentially ruminative and private approach, and in both the *Ballades* and *Sonatas* one misses a sense of scale and the narrative grip one finds in Rubinstein and Ashkenazy. But there is much that is felicitous and responsive here. Admirers of this fine artist need not hesitate.

Martha Argerich's recordings date from 1975 and 1968 respectively. Both are fiery, impetuous and brilliant performances, with no want of poetic vision to command them. They hold their own with many in the catalogue, though each has a highly strung quality that will not be to all tastes. The recording is vivid and clear, but a little dry.

Waltzes Nos. 1–19.
*** Decca 414 600-2 [id.]. Vladimir Ashkenazy.

Waltzes Nos. 1–19; Impromptus Nos. 1–3.
(b) **(*) EMI CDZ7 62602-2. Agustin Anievas.

Waltzes Nos. 1–14.
*** RCA RD 89564 [RCD1-5492]. Artur Rubinstein.

Waltzes Nos. 1–14; Barcarolle, Op. 60; Mazurka in C sharp min., Op. 50/3; Nocturne in D flat, Op. 27/2.
⊛ (m) (***) EMI CDH7 69802-2. Dinu Lipatti.

Waltzes Nos. 1–16.
(b) **(*) Decca 417 045-2 [id.]. Peter Katin.

Lipatti's classic performances were recorded by Walter Legge in the rather dry acoustic of a Swiss Radio studio at Geneva in the last year of Lipatti's short life, and with each LP reincarnation they seem to have grown in wisdom and subtlety. Their appearance on a mid-priced CD, together with the *Barcarolle* and *Nocturne*, recorded in 1947, cannot be too warmly welcomed and the transfer has been most successfully accomplished. The reputation of these meticulous performances is fully deserved.

Ashkenazy's recordings were made over the best part of a decade (1977–85) but, despite the time-span, the sound is expertly matched by the engineers. There is an impressive feeling for line throughout, an ability to make these *Waltzes* seem spontaneous and yet as carefully wrought as a tone-poem.

Rubinstein's performances have a chiselled perfection, suggesting the metaphor of finely cut and polished diamonds, emphasized by the crystal-clear quality of the RCA recording. The digital remastering has softened the edges of the sound-image, and there is an illusion of added warmth. Rubinstein's pacing is always perceptive, his rubato subtle and his phrasing elegant; and now the playing seems less aloof, more directly communicative.

Peter Katin does not play the *Waltzes* in numerical order, as is customary, but in chronological order, which seems eminently sensible. The playing is thoughtful and affectionate, certainly assured and positive, especially in the more brilliant pieces, which are presented with flair. The bright, yet quite full recording (from 1972) is very cleanly focused on CD and the piano is given striking presence. An excellent bargain recommendation.

Anievas gives us all the *Waltzes*, including the five published posthumously, and, to make this bargain-priced reissue even more generous, includes three *Impromptus*. He is more appealing in the reflective pieces than in providing glitter; yet the remastered recording brings an added brightness to the piano timbre and the playing is technically secure.

RECITAL COLLECTIONS

Andante spianato & Grande polonaise, Op. 22; Ballades Nos. 1, Op. 23; 4, Op. 52; Barcarolle, Op. 60; Études: in G flat, Op. 10/5; in C sharp min., Op. 25/7; Polonaise-fantaisie, Op. 61; Waltz in A flat, Op. 69/1.
(M) *** RCA GD 87752 [7752-2-RG]. Vladimir Horowitz.

All these performances derive from live recitals. The *Andante spianato* (offering wonderful delicacy of articulation) was recorded in 1945 but still sounds well; the remaining performances date from between 1979 and 1982. The sound is modern: the *Polonaise-fantaisie*, the *Ballades* and the *Waltz* are digital, the rest analogue. The performances are fabulous; to the end of his career Horowitz's technique was transcendental and his insights remarkable. There is much excitement – but even more that is unforgettably poetic, and not a bar is predictable. With the sound so realistic, his presence is very tangible.

Andante spianato, Op. 22; Ballade No. 4 in F min., Op. 52; Études: in C min. (Revolutionary), Op. 10/12; in A min. (Winter wind), Op. 25/11; Impromptu in A flat, Op. 29/1; Fantaisie-impromptu, Op. 66; Mazurkas: in B flat min., Op. 24/4; in C, Op. 67/3; Nocturnes: in F, Op. 15/1; in C min., Op. 48/1; Scherzo No. 3 in C sharp min., Op. 39; Waltzes: in D flat (Minute); in C sharp min., Op. 64/1–2; in A flat, Op. 69/1.
(B) **(*) Pickwick Dig. PCD 872. Cristina Ortiz.

In the hands of Cristina Ortiz the *Andante spianato* sounds particularly engaging when it is presented with attractive simplicity. In the *Mazurkas* she does not show Rubinstein's subtle feeling for rubato; but in general her playing is agreeably flexible and highly musical, even if her structural approach is a shade impulsive at times. There are many favourites here, and the two *Impromptus* are particularly successful, while the bravura in the *Études* is impressive. Excellent recording.

Ballade No. 1 in G min., Op. 23; Barcarolle, Op. 60; Fantaisie-Impromptu, Op. 66; Mazurkas: in B flat, Op. 7/1; in D, Op. 33/2; Nocturnes: in E flat, Op. 9/2; in F sharp, Op. 15/2; in D flat, Op. 27/2; in G min., Op. 37/1; Polonaises: in A (Military), Op. 40/1; in A flat, Op. 53; Waltzes: in A flat, Op. 34/1; in D flat (Minute); in C sharp min., Op. 64/1–2.
(M) *** RCA GD 87725 [7725-2-RG]. Artur Rubinstein.

An outstanding mid-priced recital – there is no more distinguished miscellaneous Chopin collection in the catalogue – with fourteen contrasted pieces, well programmed. The recording is surprisingly consistent and Rubinstein's inimitable touch gives consistent pleasure. The programme ends admirably with the lovely *Nocturne in D flat*, followed by the *G minor Ballade*, coaxing and dazzling by turns.

'Favourites': Ballade No. 1 in G min., Op. 23; Fantaisie-impromptu, Op. 66; Mazurkas: in B flat, Op. 7/1; in D, Op. 33/2; Nocturnes: in E flat, Op. 9/2; in F sharp, Op. 15/2; in B, Op. 32/1; Polonaise in A flat, Op. 53; Scherzo in B flat min., Op. 31; Waltzes: in E flat (Grand valse brillante), Op. 18; in A min., Op. 34/2; in A flat; B min., Op. 69/1–2; in G flat, Op. 70/1.
(M) *** Decca Dig. 417 798-2 [id.]. Vladimir Ashkenazy.

An exceptionally attractive recital, with many favourites, played with Ashkenazy's customary poetic flair and easy brilliance. The digital recordings were made at different times during the early 1980s but match surprisingly well: the sound has striking realism and presence.

Ballade No. 1 in G min., Op. 23; Mazurkas Nos. 19 in B min., 20 in D flat, Op. 30/2–3; 22 in G sharp min., 25 in B min., Op. 33/1 and 4; 34 in C, Op. 56/2; 43 in G min., 45 in A min., Op. 67/2 and 4; 46 in C; 47 in A min., 49 in F min., Op. 68/1–2 and 4; Prelude No. 25 in C sharp min., Op. 45; Scherzo No. 2 in B flat min., Op. 31.
**(*) DG 413 449-2 [id.]. Arturo Benedetti Michelangeli.

Although this recital somehow does not quite add up as a whole, the performances are highly distinguished. Michelangeli's individuality comes out especially in the *Ballade* and is again felt in the *Mazurkas*, which show a wide range of mood and dynamic. The *Scherzo* is extremely brilliant, yet without any suggestion of superficiality. The piano tone is real and lifelike, and has been most realistically transferred to CD.

'Favourite Chopin': Ballade No. 3 in A flat, Op. 47; Barcarolle in F sharp, Op. 60; Études, Op. 10, Nos. 3 in E (Tristesse); 5 in G flat (Black keys); 12 in C min. (Revolutionary); Op. 25, No. 11 in A min. (Winter wind); Nocturne in F min., Op. 55/1; Polonaise in A., Op. 40/1; Preludes: in D sharp (Raindrop), Op. 28/15; in C sharp min., Op. 45; Waltzes: in D flat; C sharp min., Op. 64/1 & 2.
**(*) Decca 410 180-2 [id.]. Vladimir Ashkenazy.

Ashkenazy is shown here at his most commanding, though perhaps the inclusion of more *Nocturnes* would have given a better-balanced picture of his special sensibilities in this repertoire. The digital remastering, however, produces a brightly lit treble, often bringing an edge to fortissimos, although the middle range is full, and the bass firm and resonant.

Ballade No. 3 in A flat, Op. 47; Barcarolle in F sharp, Op. 60; Fantaisie in F min., Op. 49; Fantaisie-impromptu, Op. 66; Nocturnes Nos. 2 in E flat, Op. 9/2; 5 in F sharp, Op. 15/2; Prelude in D flat, Op. 28/15; Waltzes Nos. 7 in C sharp min., Op. 64/2; 9 in A flat, Op. 69/1.
(M) *** Ph. 420 655-2 [id.]. Claudio Arrau.

A fine recital, showing both poetry and the thoughtful seriousness which distinguishes Arrau's Chopin, which is West rather than East European in spirit. The CD is admirably transferred, bringing the fullness of timbre and natural balance we expect of Philips.

Barcarolle, Op. 60; Berceuse, Op. 57; 24 Preludes, Op. 28; Sonata No. 2 (Funeral march), Op. 35.
(M) (**) RCA mono GD 60047. Artur Rubinstein.

These recordings were made in 1946 and have been transferred very well from the original 78s; although the acoustic is dry and studio-ish, the piano image is truthful and reasonably full. The performance of the *Sonata* is authoritative, its slow movement especially fine; but in the *Preludes* Rubinstein sometimes seems to rush his fences, and the fast passage-work is not always clearly articulated.

Fantasy in F min., Op. 49; Mazurkas: in C; in B flat min., Op. 24/2 & 4; in C sharp min., Op. 50/3; in C min., Op. 56/3; in C sharp min., Op. 63/3; Nocturnes: in F, Op. 15/1; in C sharp min., Op. 17/1; Scherzos Nos. 2 in B flat min., Op. 31; 3 in C sharp min., Op. 39.
(M) *(*) Polskie Nagrania PNCD 022. Witold Malcuzynski.

Malcuzynski made some famous recordings for EMI in the earliest days of stereo, notably a glittering set of *Waltzes* and some characterful *Mazurkas*. The present recital dates from the mid-1970s and is not helped by piano recording which is hard as well as bold and which even in the *Nocturnes* produces an unrelenting effect. The playing is at its most charismatic in the *Mazurkas* and the two *Scherzos*.

Sonata No. 2 in B flat min., Op. 35; Barcarolle in F sharp, Op. 60; Nocturnes Nos. 5 in F sharp, Op. 15/2; 13 in C min., Op. 48/1; 15 in E, Op. 62/2; 20 in C sharp min., Op. posth.; Scherzo No. 2 in B flat min., Op. 31.
*(**) Virgin Dig. VC 790738-2. Mikhail Pletnev.

Pletnev is a master pianist: in his hands the finale of the *Sonata* has a wizardry comparable only with Horowitz and Rachmaninov. However, whatever it *is*, this is not a self-effacing performance, and the expressive posturing will disappoint his growing circle of admirers. Of course there are marvellous things here – the *C minor Nocturne* is one – but on the whole this is masterly pianism first and Chopin second.

VOCAL MUSIC

Songs: *The bridegroom; The double end; Enchantment; Handsome lad; I want what I have not; Leaves are falling; Lithuanian song; Melody; Merrymaking; The messenger; My darling; Out of my sight; Reverie; The ring; The sad river; Spring; The warrior; What she likes; The wish.*
*** Decca Dig. 414 204-2 [id.]. Elisabeth Söderström, Vladimir Ashkenazy.

Söderström and Ashkenazy find an ideal balance in this group of songs, bringing out endless niceties of expression in pointing of word, phrase and rhythm, but keeping the essential freshness of inspiration. The recital builds towards three of the most individual: *The bridegroom* with its dramatic picture of a lover finding his bride dead, the *Lithuanian song* with its innocent folk-style exchanges, and *Leaves are falling*, more extended than the rest, a Pole's response to the Russians' callous treatment of his country in 1830. Well-balanced sound, full of presence.

Cilea, Francesco (1866–1950)

Adriana Lecouvreur (complete).
(M) **(*) CBS CD 79310 (2) [M2K 34588]. Scotto, Domingo, Obraztsova, Milnes, Amb. Op. Ch., Philh. O, Levine.
** RCA Dig. RD 71206 (2). Kabaivanska, Cupido, D'Orazi, Milcheva, Bulgarian Ch., TV & RSO, Arena.

Renata Scotto gives a vibrant, volatile, dramatically strong account of the title-role, not as electrifying as Callas would have been (to judge by her recordings of the two big arias) but vividly convincing as a great actress. The tendency for her voice to spread on top is exaggerated by the closeness of the balance of the voices on CD, but her control of legato and a beautiful line amply compensate. Domingo, Milnes and Obraztsova make a strong supporting team, not always idiomatic but always relishing the melodrama, while Levine draws committed playing from the Philharmonia.
Just as Hungaroton has produced some very enjoyable, well-recorded sets of Italian opera in Budapest, so Bulgarian Balkanton shows what Sofia can produce, with a cast assembled by Bulgarian Radio and Television. Raina Kabaivanska, Bulgarian born but long domiciled in Italy, makes a characterful, vibrant heroine. The recording exaggerates

her vibrato only a little, and her performance is strongly presented from the first aria onwards, *Io son l'umile ancella*, the grand tune of which then proceeds to pervade the whole opera. Alberto Cupido sings capably as Maurizio, even if his rather unrounded tenor shows signs of strain under pressure. In some ways the most memorable singing comes from Alexandrina Milcheva as the Princesse de Bouillon, rival to Adriana for the love of Maurizio. She is a trumpet-toned Slavonic mezzo whose fire-eating style and keen projection strike home powerfully.

Cimarosa, Domenico (1749–1801)

Concertante in G for flute, oboe and orchestra.
*** Ph. Dig. 416 359-2 [id.]. Nicolet, Holliger, ASMF, Sillito – SALIERI; STAMITZ: *Double concertos.****

Cimarosa's engaging *Concertante* is notably operatic in feeling. The music is not without substance, but the singing, lyrical secondary theme in the first movement and the interplay of flute and oboe in the *Largo* show a distinct vocal style. With such superb playing from Nicolet and Holliger, nicely turned accompaniments and first-rate recording, this CD, with its attractive coupling, is most entertaining.

Double flute concerto in G.
(B) **(*) Decca 421 630-2 Aurèle and Christiane Nicolet, Stuttgart CO, Münchinger – MOZART: *Flute concertos.****

Although not momentous music, Cimarosa's *Concerto for two flutes* has undeniable charm, and its gay final rondo is quite memorable. The only drawback is the composer's emphasis on florid writing, with the two solo instruments playing consistently in thirds and sixths. The performance here is warmly gracious, with a good accompaniment and excellent sound.

Requiem (rev. Negri).
(M) *** Ph. 422 489-2 [id.]. Ameling, Finnila, Van Vrooman, Widmer, Montreux Fest. Ch., Lausanne CO, Negri.

The choral writing in Cimarosa's *Requiem* is most assured, whether in the big contrapuntal numbers or in the more homophonic passages with solo interpolations, and it is a pity that the chorus is so reverberantly recorded. However, the CD transfer has improved the projection and Vittorio Negri secures excellent playing from the Lausanne orchestra. A recommendable reissue.

Il Maestro di Capella.
*** Hung. Dig. HCD 12573 [id.]. József Gregor, Boys of Schola Hungarica, Corelli CO, Pál – TELEMANN: *Der Schulmeister.****

Gregor's firm rich bass goes with a comparably strong personality and a striking ability to act the buffoon in this romp of an intermezzo with its comic conflict between the maestro di cappella and the orchestra. Plainly, Gregor's performance has benefited from stage experience. Though his comic style is on the broad side, his magnetism pulls the piece together very effectively, with Thomás Pál a responsive conductor. It is aptly if ungenerously coupled with the more heavily Germanic Telemann cantata. First-rate recording.

Il pittor parigino (complete).
(M) **(*) Hung. Dig. HCD 12972/3-2 (2) [id.]. Szucs, Kincses, Garino, Gregor, Klietmann, Salieri CO, Pál.

The Parisian painter of the title is the beloved of the heroine, who will lose her inheritance if she marries anyone but a baron she detests. With plenty of misunderstandings and disguises and with some nice touches of parody of operatic tradition in Cimarosa's frothy score, it makes a delightful entertainment in a performance, recorded – rather dryly in the studio – after a stage production given in both Budapest and Monte Carlo. Tamás Pál is an efficient conductor, himself playing harpsichord recitatives, and he draws a lively performance – using modern instruments – from the Salieri Chamber Orchestra. The cast is a strong one, using a number of soloists from the Budapest Opera who are becoming increasingly well-known on record, though Marta Szucs as the heroine, Eurilla, is less sweet on the ear than Veronika Kincses as her scheming cousin, Cintia. The outstanding performance comes from the veteran buffo bass, József Gregor, brilliant as the Baron.

Clemens non Papa, Jacob *(c. 1510/15 – c. 1555/6)*

Missa Pastores quidnam vidistis; Motets: *Pastores quidnam vidistis; Ego flos campi; Pater peccavi; Tribulationes civitatum.*
⊛ *** Gimell Dig. CDGIM 013 [id.]. Tallis Scholars, Peter Phillips.

This admirable disc serves as an introduction to the music of Jacob Clement or Clemens non Papa (who was jokingly known as Clemens-not-the-Pope, so as to distinguish him from either Pope Clement VII or the Flemish poet, Jacobus Papa). He was one of the later representatives of the Renaissance Flemish school, following on after Dufay, Ockeghem and Josquin. The beauty of line and richness of texture in the masterly *Missa Pastores quidnam vidistis* are unforgettable in this superb performance by the Tallis Scholars. Tempi are flexible, while the overall momentum is convincingly controlled and Peter Phillips heightens the tension by quickening the pace in the closing phrases of different parts of the Mass, as in *Cum Sancto Spiritu* in the *Gloria* and in *Hosanna in excelsis* which acts as a 'coda' for the *Benedictus*. The programme opens with the parody motet associated with the Mass, which has a glorious eloquence. Of the other motets, *Pater peccavi*, solemnly rich-textured, is especially memorable; but the whole programme is designed to reveal to twentieth-century ears another name hitherto known only to scholars. The recording is uncannily real and superbly balanced. It was made in the ideal acoustics of the Church of St Peter and St Paul, Salle, Norfolk.

Clementi, Muzio *(1752–1832)*

Piano sonatas: in F min., Op. 13/6; in B flat, Op. 24/2; in F sharp min., Op. 25/5; in G, Op. 37/1.
*** Accent ACC 67911D [id.]. Jos van Immerseel.

Very fleet and brilliant performances from Jos van Immerseel, playing on an instrument made by Michael Rosenberger in 1795, recorded at Finchcocks in 1979 – and very well, too. As Horowitz showed us in the 1950s, Clementi is a very considerable composer and possessed a fertile imagination. The slow movements of these sonatas have some considerable expressive depth, and the outer ones are full of a brilliance that is well served by this eminently skilful and excellent artist.

Keyboard sonatas: in F min., Op. 14/3; in F sharp min., Op. 26/2; in C (quasi concerto), Op. 33/3; in G min., Op. 34/2; Rondo (from Sonata, Op. 47/2).
(M) *** RCA GD 87753 [7753-2-RC]. Vladimir Horowitz (piano).

These electrifying performances from the 1950s show a Clementi of greater substance and sterner mettle than the composer we thought we knew. In Horowitz's commanding hands these *Sonatas* sound almost worthy of Beethoven and, though the piano sound is shallow by the side of most up-to-date recordings, the quality is a great improvement upon either of the vinyl transfers with which we have compared it.

Piano sonatas: in E flat, Op. 24/3; in D, Op. 26/3; in C; in G, Op. 39/1-2.
(BB) **(*) Hung. White Label HRC 092 [id.]. Donatella Failoni.

Donatella Failoni is a thoughtful and intelligent player, with a clean, direct style. She is particularly persuasive in the *D major Sonata*, which in her hands almost has the calibre of Mozart; throughout, she makes a good case for these underrated works and she is given a bold, faithful recording. This is well worth exploring at its very reasonable price.

Coates, Eric (1886–1958)

(i) *By a sleepy lagoon;* (ii) *Calling all workers* (march); (iii) *Cinderella* (phantasy); *From meadow to Mayfair: suite; London suite; London again suite;* (i) *The Merrymakers overture;* (iii) *Music everywhere* (march); (iv) *Saxo-rhapsody;* (i) *The three bears* (phantasy); (ii) *The three Elizabeths* (suite); (i) *The three men* (suite): *Man from the Sea.* (iii) *Wood nymphs* (valsette).
(B) *** CfP CD-CFP 4456 (2) [id.]. (i) LSO, Mackerras; (ii) CBSO, Kilbey; (iii) Royal Liverpool PO, Groves; (iv) with Jack Brymer.

This collection of the music of Eric Coates with its breezy tunefulness is now issued on a pair of very inexpensive CDs, cleanly transferred. It includes, besides some very lively performances from Sir Charles Mackerras, several outstanding ones from the CBSO under Reginald Kilbey who proves the ideal Coates conductor. The marches are splendidly alive and vigorous. Although the CDs bring out the brittleness in the upper range, notably in the Groves recordings, the ambient effect helps to prevent too great an imbalance towards the treble. This remains much the best Coates compilation currently available.

Songs: *Always as I close my eyes; At sunset; Bird songs at eventide; Brown eyes I love; Dinder courtship; Doubt; Dreams of London; Green hills o'Somerset; Homeward to you; I heard you singing; I'm lonely; I pitch my lonely caravan; Little lady of the moon; Reuben Ranzo; Song of summer; A song remembered; Stonecracker John; Through all the ages; Today is ours.*
*** ASV Dig. CDDCA 567. Brian Rayner-Cook, Raphael Terroni.

Eric Coates, as well as writing skilful orchestral music, also produced fine Edwardian ballads, which in many instances transcended the limitations of the genre, with melodies of genuine refinement and imagination. Most date from earlier in his career, prior to the Second World War. Brian Rayner-Cook, with his rich baritone beautifully controlled, is a superb advocate and makes a persuasive case for every one of the nineteen songs included in this recital. The recording is admirably clear.

Coleridge-Taylor, Samuel (1875–1912)

(i) *Hiawatha's wedding feast;* (ii) *Petite suite de concert.*
(M) *** EMI CDM7 69689-2. (i) Lewis, Royal Choral Soc., Philh. O, Sargent; (ii) Philh. O, Weldon.

In its day *Hiawatha's wedding feast* blew a fresh breeze through a turgid British Victorian choral tradition; since then, the work has been kept alive in fairly frequent performances by amateur choral societies. Everything about Sargent's performance is a success, including of course Richard Lewis's stylish performance of *Onaway! Awake, Beloved!* The remastered sound is first rate and for the reissue EMI have generously added a bonus in George Weldon's polished Philharmonia recording of the *Petite suite de concert,* a salon pastiche of great charm.

Copland, Aaron (born 1900)

(i) *Appalachian spring* (ballet; original version). *Billy the Kid* (ballet suite); (ii) *Lincoln portrait.*
(M) **(*) CBS MK 42431 [id.]. (i) NY Instrumental Ens. or LSO, composer; (ii) with Henry Fonda.

Appalachian spring: ballet suite; *Fanfare for the common man; Rodeo: 4 Dance episodes;* (i) *Old American songs.*
(M) *** CBS MK 42430 [id.]. LSO or (i) William Warfield & Columbia SO; composer.

Danzón Cubano; El Salón México; 3 Latin-American sketches; Our town; The Red pony (film music): suite.
(M) *** CBS MK 42429 [id.]. New Philh. O or LSO, composer.

Copland made his series of recordings for CBS over the decade between 1962 and 1973. Most were done in London at Walthamstow or at EMI's Abbey Road Studio, although the *Old American songs* and the original full chamber score of *Appalachian spring* (which, appropriately, brings a slightly drier acoustic) had a New York venue. The recording is of consistently high quality throughout: atmospheric, naturally balanced and with the ambient bloom this music ideally needs in order to create its evocative feeling of the wide open spaces of the American landscape. While Bernstein's early New York recordings of *Billy the Kid* and *Rodeo* have never been surpassed for their exuberant orchestral virtuosity and rhythmic bite, Copland himself is unrivalled in implying emotion even in the apparently light-hearted genre pieces: the *Walk to the bunkhouse* from the film score for *The Red pony* is hauntingly memorable in his hands. Over the years he built a splendid rapport with his English players, whether the LSO or Philharmonia, and it would be hard to find any rival interpreter to nudge his dance rhythms more seductively, especially in the classic *El Salón México* or the entertaining *Danzón Cubano.* While it is good to have the original extended chamber score of *Appalachian spring* played by a hand-picked chamber group of fifteen players, and Copland makes much of its clean, transparent textures, he achieves equally refined results in the full orchestral version; here the playing of the LSO has an innocence and a fresh purity which are most appealing. The only disappointment is the *Lincoln portrait,* where Henry Fonda seems ill at ease with Lincoln's ringing prose: Katharine Hepburn on Telarc is indispensable in this fine piece. All the rest gives enormous pleasure, however, and William Warfield brings gloriously robust colouring to the *Old American songs,* every one a delight. The CBS engineers who remixed these recordings for CD are to be congratulated for avoiding any artificial brilliance in the upper range. Perhaps the gunshots in *Billy the Kid* would have more transient bite in a more modern digital recording, but there is certainly no lack of impact.

Appalachian spring: ballet suite.
*** DG Dig. 413 324-2 [id.]. LAPO, Bernstein – BARBER: *Adagio*; BERNSTEIN: *Candide overture*; SCHUMAN: *American festival overture.****

Appalachian spring (ballet suite); Fanfare for the common man.
(M) *** Decca 417 716-2 [id.]. LAPO, Mehta – GERSHWIN: *American in Paris; Cuban overture; Rhapsody in blue.***

(i) *Appalachian spring (suite);* (ii) *Fanfare for the common man; Orchestral variations;* (i) *El Salón México.*
(B) ** Van. VNC 7530 [CSRV 399]. (i) V. State Op. O, Litschauer; (ii) Hartford SO, Mahler.

Appalachian spring: ballet suite; Fanfare for the common man; Rodeo: 4 Dance episodes.
**(*) Telarc CD 80078 [id.]. Atlanta SO, Lane.

Appalachian spring (ballet); *3 Latin-American sketches; Quiet city; Short symphony.*
*** DG 427 335-2 [id.]. Orpheus CO.

Appalachian spring: ballet suite; Short symphony.
*** Pro Arte Dig. CDD 140 [id.]. St Paul CO, Russell Davies – IVES: *Symphony No. 3.****

With exceptionally vivid sound, bright and immediate, giving a realistic sense of presence, the Orpheus Chamber Orchestra's collection makes for a very distinctive Copland record of four works in which the composer is at his most approachable. The version of *Appalachian spring* here is the shortened text of the suite allied to the original 13-instrument ballet scoring. With strings discreetly augmented, the 'wide-open spaces' freshness of Copland's invention is underlined, with rhythmic bite sharpened. In the *Short symphony* the intimacy underlines the jagged Stravinskian echoes. *Quiet city* on this scale may lack some of its usual misty, evocative qualities, but it is all the more intense. The three *Latin-American sketches* are bitingly colourful, characteristic little squibs of pieces. The performances, immaculately drilled, have a consistent sense of corporate purposefulness, of live communication made the more intense by the realism of the recording.

Bernstein's newest version was recorded at a live performance, and the conductor communicates his love of the score in a strong, yet richly lyrical reading, and the compulsion of the music-making is obvious. The recording is close but not lacking atmosphere, and it sounds extremely vivid.

Mehta's performance is one of the most distinguished of several fine recordings he made for Decca in the late 1970s which also included the spectacular *Fanfare for the common man.* Here the digital remastering gives riveting presence to the percussion at the opening, without quite going over the top like the Telarc version. The sound is excellent in the ballet also, which is powerfully atmospheric: the work's climax is exhilarating and the closing pages movingly serene. The couplings are generous but less distinctive.

The Telarc coupling is given recording of demonstration quality. Lane's account of *Appalachian spring* has an attractive feeling of the ballet theatre about it, with the strings lightly rhythmic. *Rodeo* too is not as bitingly dramatic and incisive as some versions, but is essentially lyrical and atmospheric. The snag, however, is the extremely forward balance of the bass drum and tam tam at the opening of the *Fanfare for the common man*. The sheer force and amplitude of that simultaneous opening crash is unnerving.

Using a smaller ensemble than is usual, Russell Davies conducts fresh and immediate performances of both the *Short symphony* and the well-known suite from *Appalachian spring*, which was originally conceived for chamber orchestra. The recording is bright and forward to match the performances. An excellent and recommendable anthology.

Viennese performances of Copland are rare indeed, but Franz Litschauer produces a strongly rhythmic account of *Appalachian spring* to show how universal this score has now become. He is less naturally idiomatic in *El Salón México* but makes a spectacular display with the *Fanfare*. What makes this bargain disc of special interest is the inclusion of the *Orchestral variations*, by no means to be regarded as a straightforward transcription of the equivalent piano work, for the colouring and texture of the music are completely altered. The recording is vividly forward throughout, which means that the range of dynamic contrast is narrowed, although not too seriously to mar enjoyment.

Billy the Kid (complete ballet); *Rodeo* (complete ballet).
*** EMI Dig. CDC7 47382-2 [id.]. St Louis SO, Slatkin.

Slatkin's record of two favourite Copland works is specially valuable for presenting the ballet scores complete. In practice this means the inclusion of a number of passages which Copland excised from *Billy the Kid* solely out of concern for length. *Rodeo* also has substantially more music, including a piano interlude in *Saturday night waltz*. Slatkin conducts strong and colourful performances, very well recorded with plenty of detail as well as bloom on the sound. The atmospheric bite in Billy's gun-battle with its fortissimo timpani is very impressive. It is a pity, though, that the CD has only one track for the whole of *Billy the Kid*; *Rodeo* has four tracks.

Ceremonial fanfare; John Henry (A railroad ballad); Jubilee variations; (i) *Lincoln portrait;* (ii) *Old American songs, set 1; An Outdoor overture; The Tender Land: The promise of living.*
*** Telarc Dig. CD 80117 [id.]. Cincinnati Pops O, Kunzel; (i) with Katharine Hepburn (nar.); (ii) Sherrill Milnes.

Katharine Hepburn's remarkable delivery of Abraham Lincoln's words quite transcends any limitations in Copland's *Lincoln portrait* and makes it an undeniably moving experience, and Kunzel, clearly inspired by the authority of her reading, punctuates the text with orchestral comments of singular power. Incidentally there is much fine orchestral writing in this piece before the narration begins, which Kunzel delivers eloquently. The shorter pieces are also given splendid life. Sherrill Milnes's highly infectious performance of the first set of *Old American songs* shows a spirited boisterousness that recalls Howard Keel in *Seven Brides for Seven Brothers*. Altogether a collection that is more than the sum of its parts, given superlative Telarc recording, highly spectacular and realistic, yet with natural balance.

Clarinet concerto.
*** RCA Dig. RD 87762 [7762-2-RC]. Stolzman, LSO, Leighton Smith – CORIGLIANO: *Concerto*; BERNSTEIN: *Prelude, fugue and riffs.****
*** CBS MK 42227 [id.]. Benny Goodman, Columbia SO, composer – BERNSTEIN: *Prelude, fugue and riffs*; GOULD: *Derivations*; STRAVINSKY: *Ebony concerto****; BARTÓK: *Contrasts.*(***)

*** Chan. Dig. CHAN 8618 [id.]. Janet Hilton, SNO, Bamert – NIELSEN: *Concerto*;
LUTOSLAWSKI: *Dance preludes.****
*** ASV Dig. CDDCA 568 [id.]. MacDonald, N. Sinfonia, Bedford – FINZI: *Concerto*;
MOURANT: *Pied Piper.****

Copland's splendid *Clarinet concerto* is at last coming into its own, on record at least.
Stolzman is effectively cool in the serene opening and catches the work's later quirky jazz
elements to perfection; in this he is well matched by Lawrence Leighton Smith and the
LSO players, who let their hair down without losing rhythmic sharpness or crispness of
ensemble. The finale's flair is exhilarating and, with first-rate RCA recording, this bids to
upstage even Benny Goodman in its combination of idiomatic understanding, natural
virtuosity and superior sound.

Benny Goodman gives a splendid account of the concerto he commissioned in 1947,
and the recording from the early 1960s sounds admirably fresh in remastered form – the
slight astringency in the violin timbre suits the music. With the composer directing the
accompaniment, this performance is eminently recommendable.

Janet Hilton's performance is softer-grained and has a lighter touch than Stolzman's,
yet she finds plenty of sparkle for the finale and her rhythmic felicity is infectious. She is
at her very finest, however, in the gloriously serene opening, where her tender poetic line
is ravishing. The performance is attractively spontaneous and the change of mood from
lyricism to jaunty extroversion is managed beautifully.

George MacDonald gives a virtuoso performance, not quite as dramatic and full of flair
as that of the dedicatee, Benny Goodman, but in many ways subtler in expression and
particularly impressive in the long lyrical paragraphs of the first of the two movements.

(i) *Clarinet concerto; Dance panels; Music for the theatre; Quiet city.*
*** EMI Dig. CDC7 49095-2 [id.]. (i) David Shifrin, NY Chamber Symphony, Schwarz.

David Shifrin's account of the *Clarinet concerto* is among the best, the opening radiant
in timbre and showing a natural fluency of phrasing, the later jazzy elements also well
caught. What makes this collection especially attractive, apart from the beautifully played
and evocative account of *Quiet city*, is the inclusion of the rare *Dance panels*. Those who
enjoy *Appalachian spring* will surely respond to this inspired and diverse score, which
typically moves with great ease from lyric tonal painting to jazzy dance rhythms. The
Music for the theatre has comparable contrasts. The performances are of a high standard
and the recording vivid and with a particularly attractive ambience.

*Dance symphony; Danzón cubano; El salón México; Fanfare for the common man; Quiet
city; Rodeo* (ballet): *4 Dance episodes.*
(M) **(*) EMI Dig. CD-EMX 2147. Mexico City PO, Bátiz.

Bátiz is a lively interpreter of Copland and he is particularly good with *El salón México*
and the *Danzón cubano*. The *Dance symphony* is derived from an unperformed ballet
composed with Diaghilev in mind. It was devised to fit a bizarre scenario involving
dancing corpses, coffins and a vampire called Grohg, but as a ballet was stillborn; the
music turned up in its present format in 1929. Bátiz has the full measure of its sparky
rhythms and vivid scoring. Ensemble is not ideally polished overall, but the playing
throughout has splendid vitality; the gentler moments of *Rodeo* are atmospherically
caught, even if the orchestra could do with more body here and in the evocative *Quiet city*.

Dance symphony; El salón México; Fanfare for the common man; Rodeo (ballet): *4 dance
episodes.*
**(*) Decca Dig. 414 273-2 [id.]. Detroit SO, Dorati.

There is a bright, extrovert brilliance about Dorati's attractive collection of Copland works, chosen for their immediate, cheerful, wide-open-spaces qualities. The only reservation is that, rather surprisingly, Dorati's treatment of jazzy syncopations is very literal, lacking the lift we think of as idiomatic. As sound, this is very impressive.

Quiet city.
*** Argo 417 818-2 [id.]. ASMF, Marriner – BARBER: *Adagio*; COWELL: *Hymn*; CRESTON: *Rumor*; IVES: *Symphony No. 3.****

Marriner's 1976 version is both poetic and evocative, and the playing of the trumpet and cor anglais soloists is of the highest order. The digital remastering has brought added clarity without loss of atmosphere.

Symphony No. 3; Music for the theatre.
** Telarc Dig. CD 80201 [id.]. Atlanta SO, Yoel Levi.

Symphony No. 3; Quiet city.
*** DG Dig. 419 170-2 [id.]. NYPO, Bernstein.

With Bernstein conducting Copland's *Third Symphony*, you appreciate more than with rival interpreters that this is one of the great symphonic statements of American music. He consciously exaggerates the rhetoric, leading up to the fantasy on the *Fanfare for the common man*, which opens the finale. In absolute terms he may be accused of going over the top but, recorded at live concerts, the electricity of the performance is irresistible. The recording is full-bodied and bright, but its brashness is apt for the performance. The hushed tranquillity of *Quiet city*, another of Copland's finest scores, is superbly caught by Bernstein in the valuable fill-up.

In brilliant Telarc sound Levi and the Atlanta Symphony Orchestra give a powerful performance of Copland's most ambitious symphony, but the weight tends to iron out imagination, making for squareness, and in thrust and urgency this cannot compare with the versions by Copland and Bernstein. This account of *Music for the theatre* equally misses some of the jazzy vigour of Copland's inspiration.

Piano quartet.
** Pro Arte CDD 120 [id.]. Frank Glazer, Cantilena Chamber Players – FOSS: *Round a common center*; WYNER: *Intermezzi.***

The *Piano quartet* of 1950 is one of Copland's most masterly and challenging works. It is an imaginative but at times austere score. It receives an impressive performance from the Cantilena Chamber Players – though by the standards of, say, the best Philips chamber-music issues, the recording might be called synthetic and unventilated. However, it is more than adequate, and the playing of these artists is both accomplished and dedicated.

VOCAL MUSIC

(i) *In the Beginning; Help us, O Lord; Have mercy on us, O my Lord; Sing ye praises to our King.*
*** Hyp. Dig. CDA 66219 [id.]. (i) Catherine Denley; Corydon Singers, Best – BARBER: *Agnus Dei*; BERNSTEIN: *Chichester Psalms.****

In the Beginning is a large-scale, fifteen-minute motet for unaccompanied chorus and soprano solo, written in 1947. The open harmonies and clean textures and lines are very characteristic of the composer at his most approachable, and the long span of the work is well structured with the help of the soprano soloist, here the fresh-toned Catherine Denley. The chorus is just as clear and alert in its singing, not just in the big motet but also in the three delightful little pieces which come as an appendix. The last is vigorous, like a carol; but all three bring out Copland's deft use of voices. Vivid recording, full of presence.

The Tender Land (opera): complete.
*** Virgin Dig. VCD 791113-2 (2) [id.]. Comeaux, Dressen, Soloists, Ch. and O of Plymouth Music Series, Philip Brunelle.

Commissioned by Rodgers and Hammerstein to write a piece to celebrate the thirtieth anniversary of the American League of Composers, Copland wrote as guileless an opera as could be, innocent-seeming in its diatonic harmony, sparing of dissonance, to match the rustic simplicity of the story of a farm family. The graduation from high school of the daughter, Laurie, is being celebrated when two drifters arrive, Martin and Top. Laurie and Martin fall instantly in love, but what follows is not just a story of love's young dream with a happy ending. Copland himself likened *The Tender Land* to the ballet, *Appalachian spring*, but the opera is gentler. The key passage is the big quintet at the end of Act I, *The promise of living*. It brings a simple tune that builds up to a memorable, moving climax, and, though not quoted, fragments of the melody then seem to underpin the rest of the score, with its set-numbers including a square-dance ensemble and a big love-duet. Nothing has quite the sharpness of *Appalachian spring*, but it is an amiable piece, beautifully performed here in a rather lighter style than Copland himself adopted on a much earlier recording of excerpts. Elizabeth Comeaux and Dan Dressen make an affecting pair of lovers, and the recording is open and atmospheric, conveying the stage picture very effectively.

Corelli, Arcangelo (1653–1713)

Concerti grossi, Op. 6/1–12.
*** DG Dig. 423 626-2 (2) [id.]. E. Concert, Pinnock.
(M) *** HM/BMG GD 77007 (2). La Petite Bande, Kuijken.
(M) **(*) Ph. 426 453-2 (2) [id.]. I Musici.
**(*) Denon Dig. CO 74168/9 [id.]. I Solisti Italiani.

What strikes one immediately here is the freshness and vitality of Corelli's invention, and the DG performances bring not only an enthusiasm for this music but a sense of its breadth and nobility. The English Concert are entirely inside its sensibility, and the playing of the concertino group (Simon Standage, Micaela Comberti and Jaap Ter Linden) is wonderfully fresh-eyed and alert, yet full of colour. The recordings are bright without being in the least overlit. Collectors wanting an authentic-instrument version need look no further.

La Petite Bande offers a useful mid-priced alternative to Pinnock's set. Again authentic instruments are used to excellent effect, and the playing is always expressive and musical. The 1977 recordings were made in a highly sympathetic acoustic, that of Cedernsaal at Schloss Kirchheim, and besides being splendidly lifelike are especially impressive in conveying the the the nobility and grandeur of Corelli.

I Musici bring a full sonority and expert musicianship to these *Concertos*. They are especially good in slow movements, where the playing has an agreeable lightness of touch and often creates delicately radiant textures. In allegros, rhythms are less bouncy than with Pinnock, and the effect is less exhilarating. Yet there is an appealing warmth here, and certainly the Philips recording provides beautifully rich string-sound.

Older collectors will recall the Virtuosi di Roma's pioneering LPs of Vivaldi and will wonder what became of them. Well, here they are under their new name and without the late Renato Fasano at the helm. They play modern instruments and do so with warmth, vitality and good taste. Readers who can't abide period instruments will find these finely recorded accounts well worth investigation. All the same, it must be conceded that they sound a little bland alongside Pinnock's set.

Trio sonatas, Op. 1/1, 3, 7, 9, 11 – 12; Op. 2/4, 6, 9, 12.
*** DG Dig. 419 614-2 [id.]. E. Concert (members), Pinnock.

Trio sonatas, Op. 1/9, 10 & 12 (Ciacona); Op. 2/4; Op. 3/5; Op. 4/1; Violin sonata, Op. 5/3; Concerto grosso in B flat, Op. 6/5.
**(*) EMI Dig. CDC7 47965-2 [id.]. L. Baroque, Medlam.

Trio sonatas: in G, Op. 1/9; in G, Op. 2/12; in B min.; in E min.; in F min.; in A, Op. 3/4, 7, 9 & 12; in D min.; in B min., Op. 4/8 & 12.
*** Ph. Dig. 416 614-2 [id.]. Huggett, Bury, Ter Linden, H. Smith, Koopman.

Trio sonatas, Op. 1/9; Op. 2/4 & 12 (Ciacona); Op. 3/12; Op. 4/3; Op. 5/3, 11 & 12 (La Follia).
*** Hyp. Dig. CDA 66226 [id.]. Purcell Qt.

Corelli is a composer more praised than played, and the quality of invention in these pieces underlines the injustice of their neglect. The players from the English Concert dispatch them with a virtuosity and panache that is inspiriting, and their evident enthusiasm for this music is infectious. This is a most impressive and rewarding issue – and excellently recorded into the bargain.

The Philips CD makes a comparably fine introduction to the Corellian *Trio sonata* repertoire, offering a cross-section of his first four collections, encompassing the period 1681 – 94. The invention is both rich and varied, and rarely falls below a high level. Collectors fearful of the vinegary tone often produced by period violins will find their ears beguiled by sounds of great beauty. This CD should make many friends for this composer; all the performers play with effortless virtuosity and an expressive freedom that is totally convincing.

The London Baroque collection mixes church and chamber sonatas, with an impeccable feeling for the style of the period and a continuo which includes archlute and organ, appropriately. Ornamentation is judicious and intonation is secure. Though not lacking vitality, the performances here are graceful and comparatively restrained, lighter in feeling and texture than Pinnock and his English Concert, and thus providing a genuine alternative approach.

The Hyperion disc is one of six designed to illustrate the widespread use in the eighteenth century of the famous *La Follia* theme. It includes a varied collection of *sonate da chiesa* and *sonate da camera*. Excellent performances from all concerned, and recording to match. The acoustic has warmth and resonance, while the detail is admirably defined. A thoroughly enjoyable issue which deserves wide currency.

Violin sonatas, Op. 5/1 – 12.
(M) **(*) DG 427 161-2 (2) [id.]. Eduard Melkus, Huguette Dreyfus, Garo Atmacayan, Karl Scheidt (No. 7 only: V. Capella Academica).

Both Melkus and his fine continuo support show scrupulous scholarship combined with real musical flair. However, Melkus plays extremely elaborate embellishments of slow movements, taken from an early edition, though in the last group he uses decorations that are by Corelli's immediate successors. These may strike some listeners as too much of a good thing, blurring the effect of Corelli's beautiful melodic lines. Melkus plays marvellously (not on a period instrument) and is truthfully recorded; to add extra variety to the set, *No. 7 in D minor* is played in its concerto grosso arrangement by Geminiani; anyone wanting the complete set will find there is much to enjoy here. However, those content with a selection will find the Accent disc will give even greater satisfaction.

Violin sonatas, Op. 5/1, 3, 6, 11 and 12 (La Follia).
*** Accent Dig. ACC 48433D [id.]. Sigiswald & Wieland Kuijken, Robert Kohnen.

When authenticity of spirit goes hand in hand with fine musical feeling and accomplishment, the results can be impressive, as they undoubtedy are here, drawing one into the sensibility of the period. This is a thoroughly recommendable issue which deserves to reach a wider audience than early-music specialists; the recording is natural and the musicianship refined and totally at the service of Corelli.

Corigliano, John (born 1928)

Clarinet concerto.
*** New World Dig. NW 309-2 [id.]. Drucker, NYPO, Mehta – BARBER: *Essay No. 3.* ***
*** RCA Dig. RD 87762 [7762-2-RC]. Stolzman, LSO, Leighton Smith – COPLAND: *Concerto*; BERNSTEIN: *Prelude, fugue and riffs.****

In its slow movement John Corigliano's *Clarinet concerto* pays elegiac tribute to the composer's father, who for more than two decades was concertmaster of the New York Philharmonic; not surprisingly, it shows considerable feeling for orchestral colour. The sonorities are always fascinating, and there are moments of some depth too. The playing both of Stanley Drucker, its dedicatee, and of the orchestra is quite superb, and the recording does them full justice.

Stolzman also gives an outstanding account of the *Concerto*, his richly expressive treatment of the slow movement balanced by superb flair and virtuosity in the finale. This is every bit as good a performance as that offered on the New World disc; and many will prefer Stolzman's couplings, which are distinguished. The RCA recording is first class.

Flute concerto (Pied Piper fantasy); Voyage.
**(*) RCA Dig. RD 86602 [6602-2-RC]. James Galway, Eastman Philh. O, David Effron.

Galway is at his inimitable best in Corigliano's *Flute concerto*; however, this is a longer and far less concentrated piece than the *Clarinet concerto*. The picaresque qualities of its invention in detailing the *Pied Piper* narrative are spread thinly in memorability of material, although the closing section when the children are led away into the distance is right up Galway's street. The serene *Voyage* is shorter and more memorable; but in spite of fine playing and excellent recording the main work outstays its welcome.

Cornysh, William (c. 1468–1523)

Adieu, adieu my heartes lust; Adieu, courage; Ah Robin; Ave Maria, mater Dei; Gaude, virgo, mater Christi; Magnificat; Salve regina; Stabat Mater; Woefully arrayed.
⊛ *** Gimell Dig. CDGIM 014 [id.]. Tallis Scholars, Phillips.

The nine pieces recorded here all derive from the Eton Choir Book and will surely come as a revelation to collectors unfamiliar with this period and a joy to those who are. Much of Cornysh's music has disappeared, including several Masses, and even the opening section of the *Stabat Mater* lacks treble, counter-tenor and tenor parts (Peter Phillips uses Frank Lloyd Harrison's ingenious reconstruction). The music is quite unlike much other polyphony of the time and is florid, wild, complex and, at times, grave. The Tallis Scholars give a magnificent, totally committed account of these glorious pieces – as usual their attack, ensemble and true intonation and blend are remarkable. For those who do not know this music, this will be one of the discoveries of the year. Excellent recording.

Couperin, Armand-Louis (1727–89)

Pièces: L'Intrépide; Rondeau; L'arlequine ou la Adam.
*** Ph. Dig. 420 939-2 [id.]. Gustav Leonhardt – François and Louis COUPERIN: *Keyboard pieces.****

Collectors can be forgiven for not knowing much of the music of Armand-Louis Couperin, who was François-le-Grand's second cousin. These pieces are slight but far from uninteresting, particularly in the expert hands of Gustav Leonhardt.

Couperin, François (1668–1733)

L'apothéose de Corelli; L'apothéose de Lully; Concert 'dans le goût théatral'.
*** Erato/WEA Dig. 2292 45011-2 [id.]. Bury, Wilcock, Campbell, E. Bar. Soloists, Gardiner.

Gardiner here presents an ideal Couperin coupling in superb performances, bringing together the two great instrumental works, both called *apothéoses*, celebrating first Corelli and then, even more grandly, Lully. Each one, in linking its sequence of movements, has a stylized classical programme. In the Corelli work Couperin imagines the composer in communication with the Muses, while the Lully work starts with the composer in the Elysian fields making music with the Lyric Shades, before being abducted to Parnassus. It is all an excuse for inspired music. The disc is completed with a fine *Concerto* 'in the theatrical style', in which the instrumentation has been realized by Peter Holman. First-rate sound.

L'Apothéose de Lulli; La Parnasse ou l'apothéose de Corelli; Pièces de clavecin: 9e Ordre: Allemande à deux. 14e Ordre: La Juilliet. 15e Ordre: Muséte de Choisi; Muséte de Taverni. 16e Ordre: La Létiville.
*** HM Dig. HMC 901269 [id.]. William Christie, Christophe Rousset (harpsichords).

Couperin's preface explains that he himself played these works on two harpsichords with members of his family and pupils; and William Christie has chosen to follow his example. Surprisingly, they sound rather more exciting in this form than in the more familiar instrumental versions, largely perhaps because of the sheer sparkle and vitality of these performers. The accompanying notes are very informative and helpful, and the two larger pieces are supplemented by four shorter movements from the *Pièces de Clavecin*. Hugely enjoyable and stimulating listening, splendidly recorded.

L'art de toucher le clavecin: Préludes 1–8; Pièces de clavecin, Book 3: 15e ordre.
*** Ph. Dig. 420 939-2 [id.]. Gustav Leonhardt – Armand-Louis and Louis COUPERIN: *Keyboard pieces.****

L'art de toucher le clavecin (1716), apart from its pedagogical dimension, includes eight preludes that were intended to be performed with great rhythmic freedom. Gustav Leonhardt plays with much poetic feeling and in a free style born of authority. Couperin has been called the Chopin of the harpsichord – listening to this playing, one can understand why. The descriptive character-studies in the *Quinzième ordre* are beautifully realized.

Concerts Royaux Nos. 1 in G; 2 in D; 3 in A; 4 in E min.
*** ASV Gaudeamus CDGAU 101 [id.]. Trio Sonnerie.

The *Concerts Royaux* can be performed in a variety of forms (violin, flute, oboe, viol and bassoon) and in pre-war days they were played in rich chamber-orchestral transcriptions. The Trio Sonnerie give them in the most economical fashion (violin, viola da gamba and harpsichord). Monica Huggett's violin playing in particular is distinguished by subtlety of phrasing and keenness of musical response, and the contribution of all three musicians is unfailingly imaginative. Excellent recording.

Concerts royaux Nos 1–4.
(M) *** DG 427 119-2 [id.]. A. and C. Nicolet, Holliger, Sax, Brandis, Ulsamer, Jaccottet.

Les Goûts-réunis ou Nouveaux concerts Nos 5–14.
(M) *** DG 427 167-2 (2) [id.]. Brandis, Banchini, Holliger, Schüpbach, A. and C. Nicolet, Ulsamer, Strehl, Sax, Jaccottet.

The *Concerts royaux* and *Nouveaux concerts* are nearly all first-rate music, and we certainly need a recording to do justice to their excellence. The present set, using modern instruments, has lively musicality to commend it and the recording is clearly focused and natural; indeed it sounds highly realistic in its CD format. If there are some reservations, it is because these distinguished artists do not seek to find the music's peculiarly French flavour. *Notes inégales* are not always observed and there are inconsistencies in matters of ornamentation. But the non-specialist listener will find that there is much to delight the ear, for the playing itself is sensitive and expert.

Les Goûts-réunis: Nouveaux concerts Nos. 8; 9 (Ritratto dell'amore).
(M) **(*) HM/BMG GD 71968 [id.]. Kuijken Ens.

The Kuijken Ensemble use original instruments, and one only has to sample the *Overture* of the *Eighth Concert* to find how attractive is their sound-world. The *Ninth Concert* has a linking programme and its eight dance movements contrast the many facets of love. The first, *Le charme*, marked *Gracieusement et gravement*, has all the delicacy of mood one would expect; and all these vignettes are engaging in their different ways. The playing here is idiomatic and pleasing; but the disc offers short measure: there is plenty of room for another *Concert*.

Harpsichord suites, Book 1, Ordres 1–5.
(M) *** HM HMA 190351/3 [id.]. Kenneth Gilbert.

Harpsichord suites, Book 2, Ordres 6–12.
(M) *** HM HMA 190354/6 [id.]. Kenneth Gilbert.

Harpsichord suites, Book 3, Ordres 13–19.
(M) *** HM HMA 190357/8 [id.]. Kenneth Gilbert.

Harpsichord suites, Book 4, Ordres 20–27.
(M) *** HM HMA 190359/60 [id.]. Kenneth Gilbert.

The Canadian scholar Kenneth Gilbert has edited the complete keyboard works of Couperin, and his recording of them is made on an exact copy of an instrument by Henry Hemsch (1750) made by Hubbard in Boston. Professor Gilbert's performances are scrupulous in matters of registration, following what is known of eighteenth-century practice in France. There is no want of expressive range throughout the series and Gilbert plays with authority and taste – and, more to the point, artistry. He is also well served by the engineers. Readers should note that the sound throughout the series is of excellent quality and altogether on a par with the performances. It is impossible to dwell on the individual felicities of each *Ordre*. As with the *48*, there is little to be gained in making recommendations to start with any particular disc; the important thing is to start somewhere. Once started, the listener will want to explore this rewarding world more fully, and there is no doubt that Kenneth Gilbert is an eminently authoritative guide.

Harpsichord suites, Book 2, Ordres 8 & 9.
*** Denon Dig. CO 1719 [id.]. Huguette Dreyfus (harpsichord).

Huguette Dreyfus chooses an eighteenth-century instrument by Jacques Goerman, restored by Mercier-Ythier and tuned in accordance with Marpurg temperament (A = 415). Its colours are rather sombre and subdued, and Huguette Dreyfus plays with her customary authority and restraint. The *Huitième Ordre* includes the famous *Passacaille* that Landowska played with such panache and flair. Excellent balance and recording.

Harpsichord suites, Book 2, Ordre 11; Book 3, Ordre 13.
*** Denon Dig. C37 7070 [id.]. Huguette Dreyfus (harpsichord).

For *Ordres 11* and *13*, Huguette Dreyfus plays a Dowd and shows herself yet again to have great understanding of this style; Mme Dreyfus certainly has the poetic sensibility and the grasp of rubato so necessary in the interpretation of Couperin's art. She is impeccably recorded.

Pièces de clavecin, Book 2, Ordre 11; Book 3, Ordres 13 & 15.
(M) ** Ph. 426 087-2 [id.]. Rafael Puyana (harpsichord) with Christopher Hogwood in Musète de Choisi & Muséte de Taverni in the 15th Ordre, Book 3.

By comparison with Kenneth Gilbert, Rafael Puyana seems larger than life, thanks mainly to the close balance. But there is no want of panache or excitement here and he has obviously thought about his presentation. Some of his chosen registration will not be to all tastes and there are also some inconsistencies of interpretation, but the collection is generous and certainly not to be ignored.

Messe a l'usage ordinaire des paroisses.
*** HM HMC 90714 [id.]. Michel Chapuis (organ of St Mazimin-en-Var).

Couperin was an organist all his working life, but the two *Organ Masses* which constitute his entire output for the instrument were composed in 1690 when he was twenty-two. Michel Chapuis uses the organ of St Mazimin-en-Var, completed in the 1770s by Jean-Esprit Isnard, a beautiful instrument that sounds excellent in this recording which, dating from 1967, sounds remarkably vivid. The performance has all the scholarship, authority and style one would expect from this fine player.

Messe Propre pour les Couvents.
*(*) Denon CO-74396 [id.]. Harry Geraerts, Pierre-Yves Asselin.

Pierre-Yves Asselin's 1978 analogue recording was made on the fine Alexandre Clicquot of 1734 in the Église St-Christopher, Houdan, and the Dutch tenor, Harry Geraerts, intersperses the plainsong. The playing is just a little stiff and readers will be better advised to wait until Decca eventually reissue their Hurford recordings.

Les Nations.
* Denon Dig. CO 74408/9 [id.]. European Bar. Soloists.

Denon's new account of *Les Nations* comes from the European Baroque Soloists using modern instruments. The group includes some distinguished players, including Hansjörg Schellenberg, Milan Turković and Peter Moll, and they are well served by the engineers. Alas, the welcome must be muted, for these turn out to be inflexible, rather heavy-handed and, above all, dull. Those who grew up with Thurston Dart's Oiseau-Lyre versions of the late 1950s, and who want something as stylish and as alive as that, will be disappointed by this set.

Motets: *Domine salvum fac regem; Jacunda vox ecclesiae; Laetentur coeli; Lauda Sion salvatorem; Magnificat; O misterium ineffabile; Regina coeli; Tantum ergo sacramentum; Venite exultemus Domine; Victoria, Christo resurgenti.*
** HM HMC 901150 [id.]. Feldman, Poulenard, Reinhart, Linden, Moroney.

The consensus of informed opinion is that the *Tenebrae* represent Couperin's sacred music at its best, but there is much here that is well worth investigating, and the motets on this record cover a wider spectrum of feeling and range of expressive devices than might at first be imagined. The performances are eminently acceptable, with some particularly good singing from Jill Feldman; the recording is made in a spacious and warm acoustic. There is no doubting that this is an issue of special interest to all lovers of French Baroque music.

Couperin, Louis (c. 1626–61)

Suite in D min.
*** Ph. Dig. 420 939-2 [id.]. Gustav Leonhardt – François and Armand-Louis COUPERIN: *Keyboard pieces.****

Louis' output remained unpublished during his lifetime, but his manuscripts were sufficiently admired for copies to be made; some 120 keyboard pieces have come down to us. His music, though of quality, is not quite as characterful as that of his illustrious nephew. Gustav Leonhardt gives a sympathetic and authoritative account of these pieces.

Cowell, Henry (1897–1965)

Hymn and fuguing tune No. 10 for oboe and strings.
*** Argo 417 818-2 [id.]. Nicklin, ASMF, Marriner – BARBER: *Adagio;* COPLAND: *Quiet City;* CRESTON: *Rumor;* IVES: *Symphony No. 3.****

This likeable *Hymn and fuguing tune*, by a composer otherwise little known, is well worth having and is expertly played and recorded here. The digital remastering has slightly clarified an already excellent recording.

Creston, Paul (born 1906)

A Rumor.
*** Argo 417 818-2 [id.]. ASMF, Marriner – BARBER: *Adagio*; COPLAND: *Quiet City*; COWELL: *Hymn*; IVES: *Symphony No. 3*.***

A Rumor is a witty and engaging piece and is played here with plenty of character by the Academy under Sir Neville Marriner. It completes a thoroughly rewarding and approachable disc of twentieth-century American music that deserves the widest currency. The sound is first class.

Crusell, Bernhard (1775–1838)

Clarinet concertos Nos. 1–3.
** BIS Dig. CD 345 [id.]. Karl Leister, Lahti SO, Osmo Vänskä.

Clarinet concertos Nos. 1 in E flat, Op. 1; 3 in E flat, Op. 11.
*** Hyp. CDA 66055 [id.]. Thea King, LSO, Francis.

Crusell, born in Finland in 1775 but working in Stockholm most of his career, was himself a clarinettist, and these delightful concertos demonstrate his complete understanding of the instrument. There are echoes of Mozart, Weber and Rossini in the music, with a hint of Beethoven, and though the writing is demanding for the soloist, Crusell generally avoided cadenzas. Thea King with her beautiful liquid tone makes an outstanding soloist, well accompanied by Francis and the LSO. The recording is first class, with an attractive ambient effect.

With speeds consistently on the fast side, Karl Leister neatly fits all three Crusell *Clarinet concertos* on to a single disc. The performances are both sensitive and brilliant, with the fast speeds rarely seeming rushed, even though the Finnish players from the Lahti orchestra are sometimes stretched. Nevertheless Leister is a little lacking in character and sense of fantasy or fun. Nor is the recorded sound ideal, with No. 2 (placed first on the disc) noticeably cleaner and more atmospheric than the other two.

Clarinet concerto No. 2 in F min., Op. 5.
⊛ *** ASV Dig. CDDCA 559 [id.]. Emma Johnson, ECO, Groves – BAERMANN: *Adagio*; ROSSINI: *Introduction, theme and variations*; WEBER: *Concertino*.***
*** Hyp. CDA 66088 [id.]. Thea King, LSO, Francis – WEBER: *Concerto No. 2*.***

Crusell's *Second Clarinet concerto* made Emma Johnson a star, and in return she put Crusell's engagingly lightweight piece firmly on the map. Her delectably spontaneous performance is now caught on the wing and this recording sounds very like a live occasion. There is an element of daring in the music-making, the sparkling virtuosity of the outer movements bringing a lilting bravura that has one relishing the sense of risks being taken and brought off with ease, and the songful *Andante* is no less appealing. Groves is a lively and sympathetic accompanist, and the balance is a natural one.

Thea King's approach makes this *Concerto* seem more serious, suggesting an almost Beethovenian character to the first movement, while the *Andante pastorale* slow movement is played with a wide range of tone-colour to contrast with the jaunty *Allegretto* finale. It is not the obvious coupling for the better-known Weber *Concerto*, but an attractive one. The digital recording is full and atmospheric, with the soloist balanced forward.

Introduction, theme and variations on a Swedish air.
*** ASV Dig. CDDCA 585 [id.]. Emma Johnson, ECO, Yan Pascal Tortelier – DEBUSSY: *Rapsodie*; TARTINI: *Concertino*; WEBER: *Concerto No. 1.****

Emma Johnson, a naturally inspirational artist, skates lightly over any banalities in Crusell's *Variations*, giving a carefree performance, often witty, youthfully daring. Well recorded in a helpful acoustic, it makes an attractive item in a mixed collection of concertante pieces which show contrasted sides of a winning young instrumentalist.

Clarinet quartets Nos. 1 in E flat, Op. 2; 2 in C min., Op. 4; 3 in D, Op. 7.
*** Hyp. CDA 66077 [id.]. Thea King, Allegri Qt (members).

These are captivatingly sunny works, given superb performances, vivacious and warmly sympathetic. Thea King's tone is positively luscious, as recorded, and the sound is generally excellent. The CD transfer is highly successful.

Clarinet quintet in C min., Op. 4.
*** Orfeo C 141861A [id.]. Karl Leister, Pražák Qt – MOZART: *Clarinet quintet.***(*)

Aptly, Karl Leister plays this extrovert Scandinavian piece with more dash and flair than its Mozart coupling. One feels that he is actually enjoying it – at this stage of his career – more than the Mozart masterpiece.

Divertimento in C, Op. 9.
*** Hyp. CDA 66143 [id.]. Francis, Allegri Qt – KREUTZER: *Grand quintet*; REICHA: *Quintet.****

Crusell has become something of a light industry at Hyperion, who seem to be recording his complete works. (All three *Clarinet concertos* and *Quartets* enrich their enterprising list.) His music certainly has charm and grace, and the *Divertimento*, Op. 9, is no exception. No one wanting this slight but charming piece and its companions need look further than this nicely played and well-recorded account.

Danzi, Franz (1763–1826)

Flute concertos Nos. 1 in G, Op. 30; 2 in D min., Op. 31; 3 in D min., Op. 42; 4 in D, Op. 43.
*** Orfeo Dig. C 00381-2H [id.]. András Adorjan, Munich CO, Stadlmair.

Danzi was an almost exact contemporary of Beethoven. He wrote four *Flute concertos*, all included here, which suggest a style midway between eighteenth-century classicism and the more romantic manner of Weber. The *D minor Concerto*, Op. 31, is an excellent example, with three strongly contrasted movements including an engaging *Polacca* finale. All three performances by András Adorjan and Stadlmair with his Munich Chamber Orchestra are impeccably stylish and have plenty of vitality, and the recording is both full and transparent and is well balanced.

Dargomizhky, Alexander (1813–69)

(i) *Baba Yaga, or From Volga to Riga* (fantasy); *Bolero; Chukchi fantasy; Kasatchok (Fantasy on the theme of the Ukrainian Kasatchok);* (ii) *St Petersburg serenades.*
** Olympia OCD 216 [id.]. (i) USSR Ac. SO, Svetlanov; (ii) Leningrad R. & TV Ch., Sandler.

Dargomizhky wrote relatively little orchestral music; the music here owes much to Glinka. Perhaps the most individual is *Baba Yaga*, though the orchestration is not polished. Together they take little more than 25 minutes, the remainder of the CD being devoted to the *St Petersburg serenades*, for unaccompanied choir, which have some charm. The playing of this fine orchestra under Svetlanov is good and the analogue recording serviceable rather than brilliant.

Debussy, Claude (1862–1918)

Berceuse héroïque; Marche écossaise; La Mer; Musiques pour le Roi Lear; Nocturnes; Prélude à l'après-midi d'un faune.
(M) **(*) EMI CDM7 69587-2. French R. & TV Ch. & O, Martinon.

Martinon's account of *La Mer* first appeared in the mid-1970s. It still has plenty of atmosphere and enjoys the idiomatic advantage of fine French orchestral playing. The *Musiques pour le Roi Lear* is a real rarity; the colourful *Fanfare* remains impressive, and *Le Sommeil de Lear* is highly evocative. The *Nocturnes* are not quite the equal of the finest versions, but are still beautifully played. At mid-price, this is again a competitive recommendation, though in the digital remastering there is a slight edge at the upper end of the range, where the trumpets are shrill.

La Boîte à joujoux (orch. Caplet): complete.
*** Chan. Dig. CHAN 8711 [id.]. Ulster O, Yan Pascal Tortelier – RAVEL: *Ma Mère l'Oye.****

Debussy's enchanting ballet score depicts adventures in a children's box of toys, and is full of delights. Although the ballet has its robust moments (often humorous), its essential feeling is impressionistic, like a series of etchings. It is beautifully played by the Ulster Orchestra under Yan Pascal Tortelier, who clearly relishes the witty quotations from Gounod's *Faust* and Debussy's own *Golliwog's Cake-walk*. The subtlety and atmosphere are captured admirably by the splendid Chandos recording, which is in the demonstration class.

La Boîte à joujoux; Children's corner (orch. Caplet); (i) *Danses sacrée et profane; Petite suite* (orch. Büsser).
(M) *** EMI CDM7 69589-2. (i) Marie-Claire Jamet, Fr. R. & TV O, Martinon.

Caplet's orchestration of *Children's corner* and *La Boîte à joujoux*, both of them containing much to enchant the ear, and Henri Büsser's orchestration of the tuneful *Petite suite* are welcome together in this mid-priced compilation. The performances are sympathetic and authoritative, and the recordings have been remastered successfully and remain very competitive.

Danse (orch. Ravel); (i) *Fantaisie for piano and orchestra;* (ii) *La plus que lente;* (iii) *Khamma;* (iv) *Première Rhapsodie for clarinet and orchestra;* (v) *Rhapsodie for saxophone.*
(M) **(*) EMI CDM7 69668-2. (i) Aldo Ciccolini; (ii) John Leach; (iii) Fabienne Boury; (iv) Guy Dangain; (v) Londe; Fr. R. & TV O, Martinon.

The rarity here is *Khamma*, which Ansermet recorded in the 1960s, a ballet whose scoring Debussy entrusted to Charles Koechlin. The two *Rhapsodies* are underrated, and although there are alternative versions of all these pieces on CD, none is more generously coupled or more economically priced. Very acceptable performances and recordings.

Danse (Tarantelle styrienne); Sarabande (orch. Ravel).
*** Virgin Dig. VC7 91098-2 [id.]. Lausanne CO, Zedda – MILHAUD: *Création du monde*; PROKOFIEV: *Sinfonietta* etc.*******

Zedda's performances with the Lausanne Chamber Orchestra are neat and polished, full of character and well recorded. But it is the couplings that make his disc specially attractive.

Danses sacrée et profane.
*** Ph. 416 437-2 [id.]. Vera Badings, Concg. O, Haitink – BIZET: *Symphony* etc.*******

A ravishingly beautiful account of Debussy's contrasting *Danses*, matching elegance and refinement with warmth. The sound is suitably warm and glowing, atmospheric rather than sharply defined.

(i) *Danses sacrée et profane; Images; Jeux; La Mer;* (ii) *Nocturnes; Prélude à l'après-midi d'un faune; Printemps;* (iii) *Rhapsody for clarinet and orchestra.*
(M) ****** CBS M2YK 45620 [id.]. New Philh. O or Cleveland O, Boulez, with (i) Alice Chailifoux, (ii) Alldis Ch., (iii) Gervase de Peyer.

Recorded between 1969 and 1971, Boulez's Debussy performances are much admired, but in these clearly remastered reissues the original CBS sound-balance tells against them. Although there is no lack of clarity, string tone is undernourished in the CBS American manner of that time and the balance is often too close and artificially contrived. The performance of *Images* is carefully shaped and *Gigues* has plenty of atmosphere, but in the *Danses sacrée et profane* the exaggerated harp image assumes an importance equal to that of the strings. In his set of *Nocturnes*, Boulez immediately sets a brisk tempo in *Nuages*, only to abandon it a few bars later; that inconsistency apart, his performance has atmosphere, though *Fêtes* lacks electricity and *Sirènes* is rather languid. Both *Printemps* and the *Clarinet rhapsody*, however, are given convincing performances. *Jeux* and *La Mer* are equally persuasive; they are also available separately with the *Prélude* – see below.

Fantasy for piano and orchestra.
(M) ******* Erato/WEA 2292 45086-2 [id.]. Anne Queffélec, Monte Carlo Op. O, Jordan – RAVEL: *Concertos.********

Debussy's *Fantasy*, an early work, does not find his musical language fully formed, but it is well worth investigating, for in Anne Queffélec's hands it makes a good impression. The warm recording too is persuasive.

Images (complete).
(M) *(*) DG Dig. 429 487-2 [id.]. O de Paris, Barenboim – RAVEL: *Daphnis* etc.**

Images; Jeux; Printemps.
(M) **(*) EMI CDM7 69588-2. French R. & TV O, Martinon.

Images; Jeux; Le Roi Lear (incidental music).
*** EMI Dig. CDC7 49947-2. CBSO, Rattle.

Images; Le Martyre de Saint Sébastien (symphonic fragments).
**(*) Ph. 420 392-2 [id.]. LSO, Monteux.

(i) *Images;* (ii) *La Mer.*
(M) ******* DG 419 473-2 [id.]. (i) Boston SO, Tilson Thomas; (ii) LAPO, Giulini.

Images; (i) *Nocturnes.*
*** Decca Dig. 425 502-2 [id.]. Montreal SO, Dutoit; (i) with chorus.

Images; Prélude à l'après-midi d'un faune.
*** EMI Dig. CDC7 47001-2. LSO, Previn.

Simon Rattle's version of the *Images* is memorably atmospheric. *Gigues* is wonderfully languorous and *Ibéria* is quite intoxicating with its heady perfumes and subtle colourings. In fact some may even find it a trace too exotic and its sensuousness a shade too voluptuous. The *Rondes de printemps* is also very fine. *Jeux*, too, comes off well. Rattle is just a touch more expansive than most rivals, and also more evocative, though he does not depart from the basic metronome markings. Haitink probably remains a first choice in this score, for he has atmosphere and a tauter grip on the music's flow, but Baudo's mid-priced EMI version should not be forgotten either. The *King Lear* excerpts sound splendid. First-rate recording, very vivid but beautifully balanced.

Dutoit and his Montreal Symphony Orchestra give performances of both these great Debussy works which, in their idiomatic expressiveness, echo their achievement earlier in Ravel, helped, as there, by some of the richest and most luminous orchestral sound ever put on disc. In comparison with such rivals as Previn and Rattle in the *Images*, and with Haitink in the *Nocturnes*, Dutoit is freer in his use of rubato, as well as in his warm, espressivo moulding of phrase. His sharp pointing of rhythm, as in the Spanish dances of *Ibéria* or the processional march in *Fêtes*, is also highly characteristic of his approach to French music. Some will prefer a cooler manner in Debussy, but for those who like these impressionistic masterpieces to be presented in full colour, with a vivid feeling for atmosphere, this is an ideal choice, and it has the merit of providing an exceptionally generous coupling.

In Previn's account of *Images* every colour and sonority, however subtle, registers; so vivid is the picture that there seems no intermediary between the musicians and the listener. There is much to admire in Previn's performance, too. Dynamic nuances are carefully observed; there is much felicitous wind-playing and no lack of intelligent and musical phrasing. There does seem to be a want of atmosphere in *Gigues*, and perhaps the last ounce of concentration and electricity that is the hallmark of a great performance is not always felt in the other movements, particularly *Rondes de printemps*. Previn has given us more atmospheric accounts of the *Prélude à l'après-midi d'un faune* than this, though none is more vividly captured by the engineers.

Monteux's classic coupling makes a splendid addition to the Debussy discography; indeed one would hardly suspect that the recording dates from 1963, for the woodwind colouring is translucent and there is a fine sheen of sensuousness to the string tone. Monteux's performance of the *Images* was notable for its freshness and impetus. There is a vivid yet refined feeling for colour which is carried through into the orchestral sections from *Le Martyre*. The delicacy of texture of Debussy's exquisite scoring is marvellously balanced by Monteux and he never lets the music become static. There is very little background noise, and our only real reservation is that this might more reasonably have been reissued in Philips's mid-priced series.

Michael Tilson Thomas's set of *Images*, from the early 1970s, is extremely well played and very atmospheric; it conveys the flavour of *Gigues* and the languor of the middle movement of *Ibéria* far more convincingly than most of its rivals. Moreover, the recording, though it must yield to the EMI sound-picture for Previn, is very good indeed. There is plenty of presence and body, and it has lost none of its warmth and atmosphere. The *Images* are particularly vivid and translucent. Giulini's DG version of *La Mer* is also very fine. There is much excitement here, as well as poetry. The sound is fully acceptable, though perhaps here the balance is not quite natural.

Martinon's is a very good *Images*, tauter and more characterful than Previn's, but the ORTF's wind section are less well blended than the LSO's, either for Previn or for Monteux. There is also a slightly raucous quality to the brass in climaxes. Martinon's *Jeux* does not displace Haitink or Baudo, though it is undoubtedly good. *Printemps*, too, is beautifully played and Martinon penetrates its charm.

Barenboim's 1982 recording of *Images* is now coupled with music of Ravel on an impressively engineered mid-priced reissue. The sound is well balanced, atmospheric and vivid; Barenboim secures a good response from the Orchestre de Paris and there are many felicitous touches. However, there is nothing very special here: the performance remains serviceable rather than distinguished and there is an ultimate lack of real profile which in the last resort is disappointing.

Images: Ibéria.
⊛ (M) *** RCA GD 60179. Chicago SO, Fritz Reiner – RAVEL: *Alborada* etc.*** ⊛

(i) *Images: Ibéria* (only); *La Mer; Prélude à l'après-midi d'un faune.*
*** Ph. 416 444-2 [id.]. Concg. O, Haitink.

Fritz Reiner and the Chicago orchestra give a reading that is immaculate in execution and magical in atmosphere. There have been superb modern accounts since this first appeared, over 30 years ago, but none that are more refined in terms of characterization. This marvellously evocative performance, and the Ravel with which it is coupled, has been underrated by the wider record-loving public over the years and has long been out of circulation. It should not be overlooked now, for the recorded sound with its natural concert-hall balance is greatly improved in terms of body and definition. It is amazingly realistic even without considering its vintage.

Haitink's response to the atmosphere of *Ibéria* is less Latin in feeling than some versions, but the subtlety of the orchestral playing is constantly telling. In *La Mer* he secures playing of great sensitivity and virtuosity. *De l'aube à midi sur la mer* has real atmosphere and the *Dialogue du vent et de la mer* is both fast and exciting. An interesting point is that the brief fanfares that Debussy removed eight bars before fig. 60 are restored, but Haitink gives them on horns. The *Prélude à l'après-midi d'un faune* is also atmospherically played. The Philips recording is truthful and natural, with beautiful perspective and realistic colour, a marvellously refined sound.

Images: Ibéria. Prélude à l'après-midi d'un faune; (i) *La damoiselle élue.*
*** DG Dig. 423 103-2 [id.]. (i) Maria Ewing, Brigitte Balleys, LSO Ch.; LSO, Abbado.

The London Symphony Orchestra has rarely sounded as sensuously beautiful on record as in Abbado's Debussy collection, bringing together two favourite works, in coupling with the exotic early cantata inspired by Rossetti's Blessèd Damozel, *La damoiselle élue.* With a warm church resonance adding to the bloom not just of the orchestral sound but of the voices, the cantata brings the most distinctive performance, poised and spacious. Maria Ewing has never sounded sweeter on record, and Brigitte Balleys, a touch raw-toned on some notes, sings with attractive freshness. The purely orchestral works bring more urgent, even impulsive performances, marked by a warmly persuasive rubato style. Though balances are not always quite natural, the ambient warmth of All Saints', Tooting, seems ideal for the music, orchestral as well as vocal, and the effect is very vivid and glowing, without loss of detail.

Jeux; La Mer; Prélude à l'après-midi d'un faune.
⊛ (M) *** EMI Dig. CD-EMX 9502 [Ang. CDM 62012]. LPO, Baudo.
(B) **(*) CBS MYK 42546 [MYK 37261]. New Philh. O, Boulez.

Serge Baudo's version of *La Mer* is first class and can be ranked alongside the finest accounts now on disc. The recording is beautifully natural and expertly balanced. The same may be said for his lovely account of *Prélude à l'après-midi d'un faune*, as atmospheric as any in the catalogue and more beautifully shaped than many. In the faster sections, *Jeux* is at times brisker than we are used to and well conveys the sense of the playfulness of the tennis match. Its competitive price makes it even more enticing.

There is no doubt about the grip Boulez exerts on *La Mer* nor the excellence and electricity of the playing. *Jeux* too is persuasively given, and the control of rhythm and colour here has considerable subtlety. The *Prélude à l'après-midi d'un faune*, however, lacks the last degree of atmosphere and poetry. The snag is the recording balance which, while acceptable in gramophone terms, is artificially contrived to spotlight detail. In *La Mer* the fortissimo strings are somewhat bleak, even if the digital remastering still allows the necessary ambient atmosphere.

Jeux; (i) *Nocturnes.*
*** Ph. 400 023-2 [id.]. Concg. O, Haitink, (i) with women's Ch. of Coll. Mus.

Haitink's reading of *Jeux* is wonderfully expansive and sensitive to atmosphere. In the *Nocturnes*, the cruel vocal line in *Sirènes* taxes the women of the Collegium Musicum Amstelodamense, but few versions are quite as beguiling and seductive as Haitink's. Add to this an equally admirable recorded quality, with transparent textures, splendidly defined detail and truthful perspective – in short, demonstration sound – and the result is very distinguished indeed.

La Mer.
(M) (**) EMI mono CDH7 69784-2 [id.]. BBC SO, Toscanini – ELGAR: *Enigma variations.*(***)

La Mer; (i) *Nocturnes.*
(M) *** EMI CDM7 69184-2 [id.]. Philh. O, Giulini, (i) with Ch.
**(*) Ph. Dig. 411 433-2 [id.]. Boston SO, Sir Colin Davis; (i) with Tanglewood Fest. Ch.

La Mer; (i) *Nocturnes. Prélude à l'après-midi d'un faune.*
(B) *** Pickwick Dig. PCD 915. LSO, (i) with Ch., Frühbeck de Burgos.

La Mer; Nocturnes; Prélude à l'après-midi d'un faune; Printemps.
**(*) EMI Dig. CDC7 49472-2 [id.]. Capitole Toulouse O, Plasson.

La Mer; Prélude à l'après-midi d'un faune.
(M) *** DG 427 250-2 [id.]. BPO, Karajan – RAVEL: *Boléro; Daphnis et Chloé.****
** DG Dig. 413 589-2 [id.]. BPO, Karajan – RAVEL: *Daphnis.***

(i) *La Mer; Prélude à l'après-midi d'un faune;* (ii) *Prélude: La cathédrale engloutie* (orch. Stokowski).
(M) *** Decca 417 779-2 [id.]. (i) LSO; (ii) New Philh. O, Stokowski – BERLIOZ: *Dance of the Sylphs;* RAVEL: *Daphnis et Chloé.****

After more than two decades, Karajan's 1964 DG account of *La Mer* is still very much in a class of its own. So strong is its evocative power that one feels one can almost see and smell the ocean, and the superb playing of the Berlin orchestra, for all its virtuosity and beauty of sound, is totally at the service of the composer. The performance of the *Prélude à l'après-midi d'un faune* is no less outstanding, the cool perfection of the opening flute solo matched by ravishing string-playing in the central section.

Stokowski's 1970 *La Mer* is thrilling, showing the maestro at his most magnetic. He chooses surprisingly slow basic tempi, but the playing has great intensity, with marvellously moulded phrasing, and the effect of the remastered CD is breathtaking in its power and impact. For the reissue a sensuous account of the *Prélude à l'après-midi d'un faune* has been added, plus Stokowski's characteristically expansive orchestration of the piano prelude, *La cathédrale engloutie*.

Giulini's early EMI version of *La Mer* is also very distinguished. The Philharmonia are in splendid form, and the coupled *Nocturnes* are also played with great delicacy of feeling and refinement of detail. Giulini's sound-world is more subtle than Stokowski's, and if *Nuages* is perhaps a little too dreamy it is nevertheless full of atmosphere. *Sirènes*, however, is somewhat lacking in a sense of movement, slow to the point of sluggishness. Nevertheless, overall this is an impressive reissue.

Although strong in Mediterranean atmosphere, Frühbeck de Burgos's account of *La Mer* has an underlying grip, so he can concentrate on evocation at the opening and create a real pianissimo, helped by the wide dynamic range of the Walthamstow recording. Later he indulges in a moment of sultry rubato in the early part of the *Dialogue du vent et de la mer*, and yet he continues to lead the ear on spontaneously. Overall there is plenty of excitement, with the LSO's virtuosity in the finale matched by the rich-toned ardour of the strings when they rise to the emotional peak of *Jeux de vagues*. There is much subtlety of detail, both here and in the *Nocturnes*, where textures again have the sensuousness of southern climes, while the processional of *Fêtes* proceeds spectacularly, glittering with colour. The *Prélude à l'après-midi d'un faune* brings lovely, delicate flute playing from Paul Edmund-Davies and a richly moulded string climax. If these are not conventional readings, they are full of impulse and superbly recorded.

Michel Plasson and the Orchestre du Capitole de Toulouse offer value for money in that the traditional coupling of *La Mer* and the *Nocturnes* is supplemented by what a decade ago would have been an additional LP side: *Printemps* and the *Prélude à l'après-midi d'un faune*. The two orchestral *Nocturnes* have plenty of atmosphere but *Sirènes* is let down by some uncertain intonation and poor tone from the female voices of the Choeurs de Toulouse Midi-Pyrénées. Plasson gives a lovely performance of *Printemps*, one of the best of recent years, very refined and beautifully recorded, and he also offers a very well-characterized and finely played account of *La Mer* that can hold its own with the best. The reverberance of the Halle-aux-Grains poses problems, but they are more completely overcome here than in many earlier recordings.

The waters that Sir Colin Davis's reading evokes are somewhat cold and grey, and there is always the sense of tremendous power used with restraint. The set of *Nocturnes* is also very fine. Sir Colin's measured approach to *Sirènes* is convincing, marvellously sustained in both feeling and atmosphere. *Nuages* is hardly less concentrated in poetic feeling, slow and ethereal. Both works are sumptuously recorded; the snag is that the acoustics of the Boston Hall tend to blur inner detail, although the definition of the CD is better than that of the original LP.

Karajan's 1964 recording of *La Mer* for DG remains pre-eminent; his re-make for EMI was not quite so successful, and nor is the newest digital version. The orchestral playing is eminently satisfactory – and if one takes an individual excerpt from it, there seems to be no cause for complaint. But the sheer magic that informed the 1964 account is missing.

Toscanini's 1935 recording of *La Mer* is extremely vivid and the sense of occasion is striking. However, it cannot quite compare with his much later NBC recording which, with far crisper ensemble, bites harder; the London recording, well handled by the engineers, is seriously marred by audience noises (there are some appalling coughs to disfigure the quiet opening section).

Prélude à l'après-midi d'un faune.
(M) ** Decca 417 704-2 [id.]. Chicago SO, Solti – RAVEL: *Boléro***; STRAVINSKY: *Rite of spring.****

On CD, Solti's version of *L'après-midi* is coupled with his powerful version of Stravinsky's *Rite of spring*, music to which he is more readily attuned.

Rhapsody for clarinet and orchestra.
*** ASV Dig. CDDCA 585 [id.]. Emma Johnson, ECO, Yan Pascal Tortelier – CRUSELL: *Introduction, theme & variations*; TARTINI: *Concertino*; WEBER: *Concerto No. 1.****

Debussy's lovely *First Rhapsody* brings out the most persuasive qualities in Emma Johnson's artistry. The range of expression with extreme contrasts of tone and dynamic makes this an exceptionally sensuous performance, yearningly poetic, and recorded in a helpful acoustic.

COLLECTION

La Boîte à joujoux: Valsette. Children's corner: The little shepherd. Danses sacrée et profane; Petite suite: Ballet. La petite nègre; Prélude: La fille aux cheveux de lin. Rêverie; Sonata for flute, viola and harp. Syrinx for solo flute.
**(*) RCA Dig. RD 87173 [RCD1-7173]. Galway, Robles, Oppenheimer; COE, Galway.

An agreeable and well-recorded late-evening Debussy collection, mostly lightweight (although both the *Danses* and the *Sonata* add attractive ballast) and distinctly appealing when the artists concerned are of the calibre of Marisa Robles, Graham Oppenheimer and the excellent Chamber Orchestra of Europe. James Galway's performance of *Syrinx* is memorable, and the *Trio* is very fine too.

CHAMBER MUSIC

Cello sonata; Petite pièce for clarinet and piano; Première Rapsodie for clarinet and piano; Sonata for flute, viola and harp; Violin sonata; Syrinx for solo flute.
*** Chan. CHAN 8385 [id.]. Athena Ens.

(i) *Cello sonata in D min.;* (ii; iii) *Sonata for flute, viola and harp;* (iv) *Violin sonata in G min.;* (ii) *Syrinx.*
(M) *** Ph. 422 839-2 [id.]. (i) Gendron, Françaix; (ii) Bourdin; (iii) Lequien, Challan; (iv) Grumiaux, Hajdu.

Though these excellent performances on Philips do not wholly dislodge others from one's affections, for example Rostropovich's account of the *Cello sonata* or the Chung version on Decca of the *Violin sonata*, they are very nearly as fine. Gendron's version of the *Cello sonata* is most eloquent and is splendidly recorded. In the quality of both the performances and the recording, this is every bit as attractive as the full-priced Chandos collection.

The well-recorded Chandos set from 1981 scores in being generously filled. The most ethereal of these pieces is the *Sonata for flute, viola and harp*, whose other-worldly quality is beautifully conveyed here; indeed, this version can hold its own with the best in the catalogue. In the case of the other sonatas, there are strong competitors but, as a collection, this is certainly recommendable.

Cello sonata in D min.
*** Decca 417 833-2 [id.]. Rostropovich, Britten – SCHUBERT: *Arpeggione sonata***(*);
SCHUMANN: *5 Stücke.****

(i) *Cello sonata;* (ii) *Violin sonata.*
**(*) Chan. Dig. CHAN 8458 [id.]. (i) Yuli Turovsky; (ii) Rostislav Dubinsky; Luba
Edlina – RAVEL: *Piano trio.****

Like Debussy's other late chamber works, the *Cello sonata* is a concentrated piece,
quirkily original. The classic version by Rostropovich and Britten, now restored to the
catalogue at premium price, has a clarity and point which suit the music perfectly. The
recording is first class, and if the couplings are suitable, this holds its place as first choice.

In the *Cello sonata*, Turovsky gives a well-delineated, powerful account, with Luba
Edlina, less reticent, perhaps – and, some might feel, less refined in feeling – than some
of the great performances of the past. In the *Violin sonata*, Rostislav Dubinsky and Luba
Edlina (his wife) are in excellent form, though this is red-blooded Slavonic Debussy rather
than the more ethereal, subtle playing of a Grumiaux.

Piano trio in G.
**(*) Denon Dig. CO 72508 [id.]. Rouvier, Kantorow, Müller – FAURÉ; RAVEL:
Trios.**(*)

Debussy's *Trio* probably comes from his student years; it is a work more of promise
than of fulfilment, of facility rather than of individuality. Jean-Jacques Kantorow,
Philippe Müller and Jacques Rouvier are an accomplished ensemble and give a
persuasive account of the piece; they are excellently recorded.

String quartet in G min.
*** DG 419 750-2 [id.]. Melos Qt – RAVEL: *Quartet.****
(M) *** EMI CD-EMX 2156 [id.]. Chilingirian Qt – RAVEL: *Quartet.****
(M) *** Ph. 420 894-2 [id.]. Italian Qt – RAVEL: *Quartet.****
(BB) **(*) Hung. White Label HRC 122 [id.]. Bartók Qt – RAVEL: *Quartet***(*);
DVORÁK: *Quartet No. 12.****
(*) Denon Dig. C37 7830 [id.]. Nuovo Qt – RAVEL: *Quartet.*(*)
(*) Virgin Dig. VC 791077-2 [id.]. Borodin Qt – RAVEL: *Quartet.*
(*) EMI Dig. CDC7 47347-2 [id.]. Alban Berg Qt – RAVEL: *Quartet.*(*)
(*) Telarc Dig. CD 80111 [id.]. Cleveland Qt – RAVEL: *Quartet.*(*)
** DG Dig. 427 320-2. Emerson Qt – RAVEL: *Quartet.***

The playing of the Melos Quartet is distinguished by perfect intonation and ensemble,
scrupulous accuracy in the observance of dynamic markings, a natural sense of flow and
great tonal beauty. It would be difficult to imagine a finer account of the Debussy than
this; and though the Italian Quartet recording on Philips has long been a yardstick against
which newcomers are measured, the Melos have the advantage of excellent recorded
sound, wider in range and sonority than the Philips; the balance is neither too forward
nor too reticent, and is truthful in matters of perspective as well as of timbre. The transfer
of the analogue recording to CD is eminently successful.

At mid-price the Chilingirian coupling is in every way competitive. They give a
thoroughly committed account with well-judged tempi and very musical phrasing. The
scherzo is vital and spirited, and there is no want of poetry in the slow movement. The
recording has plenty of body and presence and has the benefit of a warm acoustic: the
sound is fuller than on the competing version by the Italian Quartet.

It need hardly be said that the playing of the Italian Quartet is also outstanding. Perfectly judged ensemble, weight and tone make this a most satisfying alternative choice, and the recording engineers have produced a vivid and truthful sound-picture, with plenty of impact. For CD collectors, this is only marginally a second-best alternative to the Melos issue and there is a considerable price advantage.

If not quite as refined as the Chilingirians, the account by the Bartók Quartet is full of character, and the *Andante* is certainly *doucement expressif.* The recording is good, too, and well balanced; with three quartets on offer, this record is a genuine bargain.

The Nuovo Quartet are very musical and there is a natural, unforced quality about their playing that is likeable. There are some moments of affectation and they pull the development section of the first movement around. The scherzo is marvellously delicate and a delight – and their slow movement, too, is appropriately thoughtful and inward-looking. They blend very beautifully and the recording is well focused in an acoustic that has warmth and space. This can be recommended to those seeking a digital version of this coupling.

If one is talking just about perfection of ensemble, purity of intonation and tonal blend, the Borodins' account has to be a three-star recommendation. The opening of the scherzo is quite breathtaking in its body and sheer technical perfection. However, their reading is at times over-sophisticated, with some expressive slides from the leader which will not enjoy universal appeal and a slowing-up for the second group in the first movement. Recording quality is superb, and readers should undoubtedly try to hear this – but the Melos allow the music to speak for itself.

Technically the Alban Berg Quartet are in a class of their own – yet, strangely enough, one finishes listening to this with greater admiration than involvement; the performance beautifies the work and has little spontaneous feeling.

The Cleveland performance is all high voltage, with impressive attack, a rich sonority and splendid tone, a wide dynamic range and a keen sensitivity to the changing tempo indications, but there is also a certain loss of intimacy. The recording has plenty of body and presence.

The Emersons play with amazing precision and body of sound on DG, but their performances, though less affected than the Borodins', are too high-powered to do full justice to the sensibility of Debussy's score. The playing dazzles – but then, so does strip-lighting!

Violin sonata in G min.
(M) *** Ph. 420 777-2 [id.]. David Oistrakh, Frida Bauer – PROKOFIEV: *Mélodies*; RAVEL: *Sonata*; YSAYE: *Sonata.****
DG Dig. 415 683–2 [id.]. Shlomo Mintz, Yefim Bronfman – FRANCK; RAVEL: *Sonatas.*
** Virgin Dig. VC 790760-2 [id.]. Dmitry Sitkovetsky, Pavel Gililov – JANÁCEK; R. STRAUSS: *Violin sonatas.****
*(*) Decca Dig. 421 817-2 [id.]. Joshua Bell, Jean-Yves Thibaudet – FAURÉ; FRANCK: *Sonatas.**(*)

Violin sonata in G min.; Prélude: Minstrels.
(M) (***) EMI mono CDH7 63032-2. Jacques Thibaud, Alfred Cortot – FAURÉ; FRANCK: *Sonatas* etc.(***)

(i) *Violin sonata in G min.*; (ii) *Sonata for flute, viola and harp.*
⊛ (M) *** Decca 421 154-2 [id.]. (i) Kyung Wha Chung, Radu Lupu; (ii) Melos Ens. (members) – FRANCK: *Violin sonata*; RAVEL: *Introduction and allegro.**** ⊛

Kyung Wha Chung and Radu Lupu are superbly balanced and most truthfully recorded. Miss Chung plays with marvellous character and penetration, and her partnership with Radu Lupu could hardly be more fruitful. Nothing is pushed to extremes, and everything is in perfect perspective so far as both the playing and the recording are concerned. The *Sonata for flute, viola and harp* and the Ravel *Introduction and allegro* come from a famous Oiseau-Lyre record made in 1962. In both works the playing is wonderfully sensitive and the music's ethereal atmosphere well caught. The recording sounds admirably real.

David Oistrakh produces a rich yet finespun line and conveys all the poetry and atmosphere of the score. Frida Bauer's imaginative response is no less keen. This is beautifully proportioned and well transferred to CD, and the couplings are no less appealing.

Shlomo Mintz and Yefim Bronfman give a performance that is difficult to fault and gives much pleasure. They can be recommended alongside – though not in preference to – Chung and Lupu. This is undoubtedly a magnificent account and excellently recorded, too.

The Debussy *Sonata* and the transcription of *Minstrels* were recorded by Thibaud and Cortot as long ago as 1929 but are vibrant performances. Despite the dated sound, this performance brings one closer to the Debussy than almost any modern rival.

Dmitry Sitkovetsky and Pavel Gililov are much stronger in the Janáček and Strauss *Sonatas* than they are in the Debussy. They give a responsive performance, but there is a change of perspective which finds the balance favouring the piano, with the result that Sitkovetsky seems all too reticent. Nor do these artists seem to have the same natural feeling for this repertoire that they have for Janáček.

Joshua Bell is a gifted young American player whose début on the Decca label was loudly trumpeted. He and Jean-Yves Thibaudet play the *Sonata* with no want of ardour and much accomplishment, but they are not fully attuned to its spirit. Dynamic markings are carefully observed, but this performance makes more of the work's outward virtuosity than its searching, intimate quality. The rather up-front recording balance does not help either artist, and competition is very keen here.

MUSIC FOR TWO PIANOS

Danses sacrée et profane; En blanc et noir; Lindaraja; Nocturnes (trans. Ravel); *Prélude à l'après-midi d'un faune.*
*** LDR Dig. LDRCD 1009 [id.]. Stephen Coombs & Christopher Scott.

An outstanding début. Stephen Coombs and Christopher Scott have the full measure of this repertoire and play with great vividness and subtlety of colour. Ravel's skill in transcribing the *Nocturnes* is exploited to the full. *Nuages* has a gentle luminosity that is quite magical and they build an arresting climax from the processional in *Fêtes*. The bravura of the playing is always at the service of the composer, while their languorous feeling for the famous *Prélude à l'après-midi d'un faune* is such that one hardly misses the orchestra. The recording, made in the Cranleigh School Chapel, is most faithfully balanced, with realistic separation and an ideal ambient effect.

PIANO MUSIC

2 Arabesques; Ballade; Images, Book 1; L'isle joyeuse; La plus que lente; Rêverie; Suite bergamasque.
*** Conifer Dig. CDCF 148 [id.]. Kathryn Stott.

After her extremely successful Fauré disc, Kathryn Stott repeats the formula with Debussy, assembling an admirable recital which spans Debussy's composing career from the *Deux Arabesques* of 1888, through to *La plus que lente* (1910). She is unerringly sensitive to atmosphere, there is no lack of finesse and her impetuosity always sounds spontaneous. This is a very refreshing programme, given excellent realism and presence.

2 Arabesques; Ballade; Images, Book 1: Reflets dans l'eau; Mouvement. Book 2: Poissons d'or. L'isle joyeuse; Préludes, Book 2: Feux d'artifice. Suite bergamasque.
(M) *** EMI CD-EMX 2055-2. Daniel Adni.

This collection dates from 1972 and was a follow-up to a similarly successful Chopin recital, which had served as Daniel Adni's gramophone début the previous year and was equally well recorded. It is outstanding in every way: this young Israeli pianist proves himself a Debussian of no mean order. His recital is well planned and offers playing that is as poetic in feeling as it is accomplished in technique.

2 Arabesques; Berceuse héroïque; D'un cahier d'esquisses; Hommage à Haydn; Images Books 1 & 2; L'isle joyeuse; Page d'album; Rêverie.
⊛ *** Ph. Dig. 422 404-2 Zoltán Kocsis.

Zoltán Kocsis's Debussy recital is quite outstanding. The recording of the piano is among the most realistic we have heard. Artistically, this new recital is if anything even more distinguished in terms of pianistic finesse, sensitivity and tonal refinement than his earlier, 1983 Debussy collection – see below.

2 Arabesques; Children's corner; Estampes; Pour le piano.
** Virgin Dig. VC 790847-2 [id.]. Jean-Bernard Pommier.

Accomplished playing comes from Jean-Bernard Pommier, an intelligent artist with a good feeling for Debussy and excellent technical address. He is often perceptive; but there is strong competition here, and the good must yield to the better. The recording is basically truthful, but somewhat bottom-heavy.

2 Arabesques; Children's corner; Images I and II; Suite bergamasque.
(M) *** Decca 417 792-2 [id.]. Pascal Rogé.

Pascal Rogé's playing is distinguished by a keen musical intelligence and sympathy, as well as by a subtle command of keyboard colour. Apart from the *Images* with their finesse and highly accomplished pianism, the *Suite bergamasque* is particularly successful, with genuine poetry in the famous *Clair de lune*. The well-defined Decca sound is most realistic. The quality is eminently secure and the bottom end of the piano reproduces in a most lifelike fashion.

2 Arabesques; Images, Books I and II; Suite bergamasque.
**(*) EMI Dig. CDC7 49497-2. Cécile Ousset.

The music here is well played and Cécile Ousset pays due regard to pianissimo markings and distils good atmosphere in *Et la lune descend sur le temple qui fut*. She is a virile, muscular player who, at the other end of the dynamic spectrum, can at times produce some hardness of tone at fortissimo, but this is relatively slight. Not a first choice, but recommendable if you like your Debussy strong.

2 Arabesques; L'Isle joyeuse; Masques; La plus que lente; Pour le piano; Suite bergamasque; Tarantelle styrienne (Danse).
(B) *** DG 429 517-2 [id.]. Tamás Vásáry.

Vásáry is at his very best in the *Suite bergamasque,* and *Clair de lune* is beautifully played, as are the *Arabesques. La plus que lente* receives the least convincing performance. Here Vásáry's rubato sounds slightly unspontaneous. But overall this is a satisfying recital and makes an excellent bargain, particularly as the piano is so realistic.

Berceuse héroïque; Children's corner suite; Danse; D'un cahier d'esquisses; Mazurka; Morceau de concours; Nocturne; Le petit nègre; La plus que lente; Rêverie.
*** Denon Dig. C37 7372 [id.]. Jacques Rouvier.

An enjoyable and interesting Debussy recital from Jacques Rouvier, which has the advantage of very truthful recording. This serves as a very useful addition to the catalogue and can be thoroughly recommended.

Berceuse héroïque; Élégie; 6 Épigraphes antiques; Études, Books 1–2; Hommage à Haydn; Page d'album.
(**) Nimbus NI 5164 [id.]. Martin Jones.

La boîte à joujoux; Jeux; Khamma.
*(**) Nimbus Dig. NI 5163 [id.]. Martin Jones.

Artistically, Martin Jones's series on Nimbus can hold its head high among the burgeoning discography of Debussy piano music but, by comparison with rival accounts, the sound is not well focused. The previous issues, NI 5160 (which includes *Pour le piano,* the *Suite bergamasque* and shorter pieces) and NI 5161 (with *Children's corner, Estampes, L'isle joyeuse* and the *Images*), have been praised by us on artistic but not technical grounds, and NI 5164 brings much the same reservations. NI 5163 is the most recommendable issue so far. It is a bizarre experience to hear *Jeux* in black-and-white, so to speak, though it would be difficult to conceive of it in more imaginative or sympathetic hands, while monochrome certainly underlines the diffuseness of *Khamma. La boîte à joujoux* is given with great sensitivity and feeling for colour, but again there is too much studio ambience (though it is not as bad as in some of these recordings). Were the sound better focused, it would receive a stronger recommendation, for the artistic impression the playing leaves is strong.

Children's corner; Images, Sets 1 & 2.
*** DG 414 372-2 [id.]. Michelangeli.

Michelangeli is outstanding in this repertoire. It is a magical and beautifully recorded disc. Michelangeli has made few records, but this is one of his best. It is also among the most distinguished Debussy playing in the catalogue. The remastering of the 1971 recording has been wonderfully successful.

Estampes; Images I & II; Images oubliées (1894); Pour le piano.
*** Denon Dig. CD 1411 [id.]. Jacques Rouvier.

Jacques Rouvier is very well recorded; there is plenty of atmosphere and space round the sound. His account of the *Cloche à travers les feuilles* has great poise and *Et la lune descend sur le temple qui fut* has wonderful atmosphere and repose. In the *Images oubliées* he is not quite as imaginative (or as outstandingly recorded) as Zoltán Kocsis on Philips, but all the same this is an impressive issue.

Estampes; Images oubliées (1894); Pour le piano; Suite bergamasque.
*** Ph. Dig. 412 118-2 [id.]. Zoltán Kocsis.

An exceptionally atmospheric and intelligently planned recital from Zoltán Kocsis. The playing is enormously refined and imaginative, and every nuance is subtly graded; and the Philips engineers have captured the piano with exceptional realism and fidelity.

Études, Books 1–2.
*** Ph. Dig 422 412-2 [id.]. Mitsuko Uchida.
*(*) Denon Dig. CO 2200 [id.]. Jacques Rouvier.

The *Études* are not yet well represented on CD – but, even if they were, this Uchida disc would be in a class of its own: superfine delicacy of touch, without the slightest hint of preciosity, and the widest possible range of dynamics and colouring. This CD has won wide acclaim both here and abroad – and fully deserves it. Superbly vivid piano-sound, among the very best on record.

Jacques Rouvier is a fine Debussy interpreter, many of whose earlier records we have admired. This could be recommended alongside them, were it not for the rather undistinguished recording, which is wanting in ambience and bloom.

Préludes, Books 1–2 (complete).
⊛ (M) *** EMI mono CDH7 61004-2 [id.]. Walter Gieseking.
(M) (***) CBS mono MPK 45688 [id.]. Robert Casadesus.

In his day, Walter Gieseking was something of a legend as a Debussy interpreter, and this excellent CD transfer testifies to his magic. Background is almost vanquished; our copy produced some very slight noise near the opening, but for the most part this is simply not a problem. Gieseking penetrates the atmosphere of the *Préludes* more deeply than almost any other artist. This is playing of rare distinction and great evocative quality. However, the documentation is concerned solely with the artist and gives no information about the music save the titles and the cues.

Robert Casadesus's accounts of the *Préludes* are like Gieseking's: legendary. His recordings were made in 1953/4 and the piano sound is faithful, though the second book has a warmer, fuller piano image. The performances of Book 2 show the pianist at his very finest: *Brouillards* and *Feuilles mortes*, for instance, are superbly atmospheric and *Feux d'artifice* glitters with fiery brilliance. At times in Book 1 he is a trifle cool. Nevertheless this is all distinguished playing and this CD is a must for Debussyans.

Préludes, Book 1; Estampes; Images, Book 1.
*** Ph. 420 393-2 [id.]. Claudio Arrau.

Préludes, Book 1.
**(*) Denon Dig. C37 7121 [id.]. Jacques Rouvier.
*(**) DG 413 450-2 [id.]. Arturo Benedetti Michelangeli.

Préludes, Book 2; Images, Book 2.
*** Ph. 420 394-2 [id.]. Claudio Arrau.

Arrau's tempi are unhurried, but that is no bad thing. His playing combines sensitivity with warmth; there are some beautifully coloured details and a fine sense of atmosphere. He is helped by the richness of timbre provided by the Philips engineers; indeed the piano in these 1978/9 analogue recordings has a consistent body and realism typical of this company's finest work.

Jacques Rouvier's playing has atmosphere and elegance; though Michelangeli exhibits the greater keyboard control and (sometimes) evocation of character, Rouvier has greater warmth and a pleasing humanity. He is given an excellent recording, too.

It goes without saying that Michelangeli's accounts reveal the highest pianistic distinction. However, this playing seems even cooler and more aloof on CD and it must be conceded that not all collectors will find his readings sympathetic.

Préludes, Book 2.
**(*) Denon Dig. C37 7043 [id.]. Jacques Rouvier.

There is some beautiful playing from Jacques Rouvier, and there are very few points with which one would quarrel. *La terrasse des audiences de clair de lune* is more measured than many interpreters on record, but Rouvier succeeds in shaping it with considerable mastery and makes the most of its different moods. All in all, this is most responsive playing and Rouvier is very well recorded.

Préludes, Books 1 & 2, excerpts: *Bruyères; Canope; La cathédrale engloutie; Ce qu'a vu le vent d'ouest; La danse de Puck; Danseuses de Delphes; Des pas sur la neige; Feux d'artifice; La fille aux cheveux de lin; General Lavine – eccentric; Minstrels; Ondine; La puerta del vino; La sérénade interrompue; La terrasse des audiences au clair de lune; Le vent dans la plaine.*
* Decca Dig. 425 518-2 [id.]. Jorge Bolet.

Jorge Bolet is curiously unatmospheric in his finely recorded Debussy recital on Decca. His playing excites more admiration than it gives pleasure. For some reason he gives us only two-thirds of the set and moves freely from one book to the other. A disappointment.

VOCAL MUSIC

Mélodies: Ariettes oubliées; Fêtes galantes; 5 poèmes de Charles Baudelaire.
** EMI Dig. CDC7 47888-2. Barbara Hendricks, Michel Béroff.

There is much that is vocally beautiful here, although Barbara Hendricks does not always succeed in using her middle and lower register to produce the intimacy she seeks, and the microphones are not always kind to her. Words are clear and word-meanings are conveyed with considerable artistry; both artists clearly have a feeling for this repertoire, but the end result is uneven.

Mélodies: Beau soir; 3 Chansons de Bilitis; 3 Chansons de France; Les cloches; Fêtes galantes, Set 2; Mandoline.
*** Unicorn DKPCD 9035 [id.]. Sarah Walker, Roger Vignoles – ENESCU: *Chansons***; ROUSSEL: *Mélodies.***(*)

Sarah Walker's Debussy collection makes an outstandingly fine disc of French songs. With deeply sympathetic accompaniment from Roger Vignoles, Sarah Walker's positive and characterful personality comes over vividly, well tuned to the often elusive idiom. Excellent recording in a warm acoustic.

OPERA

Pelléas et Mélisande (complete).
*** EMI CDS7 49350-2 (3). Stilwell, Von Stade, Van Dam, Raimondi, Ch. of German Op., Berlin, BPO, Karajan.

Karajan sets Debussy's masterpiece as a natural successor to Wagner's *Tristan* rather than its antithesis, a rich and passionate performance with the orchestral tapestry at the centre and the singers providing a verbal obbligato. Paradoxically, the result of this approach is more, not less, dramatic, for Karajan's concentration carries one in total involvement through a story that can seem inconsequential. The playing of the Berlin Philharmonic is both polished and deeply committed, and the cast comes near the ideal, with Frederica von Stade a tenderly affecting heroine and Richard Stilwell a youthful, upstanding hero, set against the dark incisive Golaud of Van Dam. The balance ensures that voices are particularly vivid, with the orchestra, pleasantly mellow, set rather behind, and the layout could hardly be better.

Delibes, Léo (1836–91)

Coppélia (ballet): complete.
*** Decca Dig. 414 502-2 (2) [id.]. Nat. PO, Bonynge.
(M) *** Decca 425 472-2 (2) [id.]. SRO, Richard Bonynge – MASSENET: *Le Carillon.****

Bonynge's later digital recording of Delibes' sparkling and tuneful complete ballet was made with the National Philharmonic with its personnel of expert British sessions musicians, who bring a polished and spirited ensemble, with the wind solos a constant delight. The only slight drawback is the relatively modest number of violins, which the clarity of the digital recording makes apparent. In moments like the delicious *Scène et valse de la poupée*, which Bonynge points very stylishly, the effect is Mozartian in its grace. But the full body of strings above the stave lacks something in amplitude and the fortissimos bring a digital emphasis on brilliance that is not wholly natural. In all other respects the recording is praiseworthy, not only for its vividness of colour, but for the balance within a concert-hall acoustic (Walthamstow Assembly Hall).

Bonynge secures a high degree of polish from the Swiss Romande Orchestra, with sparkling string and wind textures and sonority and bite from the brass. The Decca recording sounds freshly minted and, with its generous Massenet bonus, little-known music of great charm, this set is very competitive.

Coppélia (ballet): suite: excerpts.
(B) *** DG 429 163-2 [id.]. BPO, Karajan – CHOPIN: *Les Sylphides*** ⊛; OFFENBACH: Gaîté parisienne.***

(i) Coppélia (ballet): suite; *(ii) Sylvia* (ballet): suite.
(BB) *** LaserLight Dig. 15 616. (i) Berlin RSO, Fricke; (ii) Budapest PO, Sandor – GOUNOD: *Faust ballet.****

Although the playing of the (East German) Berlin Radio orchestra is not quite as cultured as that of the Berlin Philharmonic under Karajan, it is still very fine, and Fricke displays a lighter touch in the *Csárdás*. He also includes more music, both at the opening and in the delectable *Music of the Automatons*, one of Delibes' most piquant and memorable inspirations. The digital recording is first class, with sparkle and warmth and an attractively warm ambient effect. The Budapest performance of *Sylvia* is also graceful and vividly coloured, and the recording again is first rate. A genuine super-bargain.

Karajan secures some wonderfully elegant playing from the Berlin Philharmonic Orchestra, and generally his lightness of touch is sure. The *Csárdás*, however, is played very slowly and heavily, and its curiously studied tempo may spoil the performance for some. The recording is very impressive; but it is a pity that in assembling the CD the suite had to be truncated (with only 71 minutes' playing time, at least one more number could have been included). As it is, the *Scène et Valse de la Poupée*, *Ballade de l'Épi* and the *Thème slav varié*, all present on the original analogue LP, are omitted here.

La Source (ballet): Act II; Act III, scene i.
*** Decca Dig. 421 431-2 (2). ROHCG O, Bonynge – MINKUS: *La Source* (Act I; Act III, scene ii); DRIGO: *La Flûte magique.****

It is not clear why the composition of the music for *La Source* was divided between two composers, the established Minkus and the younger Delibes who had not yet tried his hand in the field of ballet and for whom the commission was a godsend. He begins the Second Act in the elegantly lightweight style of his colleague, but soon his stronger musical personality asserts itself with a romantic horn tune and, later, an even more memorable melody in the strings. His felicitous use of the orchestral palette is readily discernible; but, even so, this is clearly a forerunner for *Coppélia* and *Sylvia* from a composer whose style is not yet fully individualized. However, the ballet was to become a success and establish Delibes' reputation in the field, for Minkus returned to Russia and left the French composer in charge. Bonynge makes the music sparkle throughout, and the warm yet vivid sound is out of Decca's top drawer.

Sylvia (ballet): complete.
(M) *** Decca 425 475-2 (2) [id.]. New Philh. O, Richard Bonynge – MASSENET: *Le Cid*.***

If the score for *Sylvia* does not quite brim over with hits in the way that *Coppélia* does, and some of the best tunes are presented more than once, it still contains much delightful music and characteristically felicitous scoring. It is played here with wonderful polish and affection, and the recording is full, brilliant and sparkling in Decca's best manner. The CDs offer a splendid Massenet bonus, another recording out of Decca's top drawer.

Lakmé (complete).
(M) *** Decca 425 485-2 (2). Sutherland, Berbié, Vanzo, Bacquier, Monte Carlo Op. Ch. and O, Bonynge.

Lakmé is a strange work, not at all the piece one would expect knowing simply the famous *Bell song*. Predictably enough, at the beginning it has its measure of orientalism, but quickly comedy is introduced in the shape of Britons abroad, and Delibes presents it with wit and charm. This performance (with Monica Sinclair a gloriously outrageous Governess) seizes its opportunities with both hands, while the more serious passages are sung with a regard for beautiful vocal line that should convert anyone. Sutherland swallows her consonants, but the beauty of her singing, with its ravishing ease and purity up to the highest register, is what matters; and she has opposite her one of the most pleasing and intelligent of French tenors, Alain Vanzo. Excellent contributions from the others too, spirited conducting and brilliant, atmospheric recording. Highly recommended in this mid-price reissue which costs little more than the original LPs.

Lakmé: highlights.
(M) ** EMI CDM7 63447-2 [id.]. Mesplé, Burles, Soyer, Millet, Paris Opéra-Comique Ch. & O, Lombard.

The *Flower duet*, made into a top classical pop by a British Airways TV commercial, is quite nicely sung here by Mady Mesplé and Danielle Millet, and those who seek it could choose this highlights disc. Otherwise the performance is marred by the thin and wobbly – if idiomatic – singing of Mesplé in the title-role. The rest of the cast give adequate support and Lombard conducts with understanding.

Delius, Frederick (1862–1934)

Air and dance; Fennimore and Gerda: Intermezzo; Hassan: Intermezzo and serenade; Koanga: La Calinda; On hearing the first cuckoo in spring; A Song before sunrise; Summer night on the river; A Village Romeo and Juliet: The Walk to the Paradise Garden.
(M) *** Decca 421 390-2 [id.]. ASMF, Marriner.

No grumbles here: these are lovely performances, warm, tender and eloquent. They are played superbly and recorded in a flattering acoustic. The recording is beautifully balanced – the distant cuckoo is highly evocative – though, with a relatively small band of strings, the sound inevitably has less body than with a full orchestral group. Excellent value at mid-price.

Air and dance for string orchestra; Fennimore and Gerda: Intermezzo. Hassan: Intermezzo & Serenade (arr. Beecham). *Irmelin: Prelude. Koanga: La Calinda. On hearing the first cuckoo in spring; Sleigh ride; A song before sunrise; Summer evening* (ed. Beecham); *Summer night on the river.*
*** EMI Dig. CDC7 47610-2. N. Sinfonia, Richard Hickox.

Richard Hickox's Delius collection neatly brings together most of the shorter pieces in finely shaped, well-played readings, recorded in aptly atmospheric sound. This is currently the best recorded of the post-Beecham collections of this repertoire.

Air and dance for string orchestra; On hearing the first cuckoo in spring; Summer evening; Summer night on the river.
*** Chan. CHAN 8330 [id.]. LPO, Handley – VAUGHAN WILLIAMS: *Serenade* etc.***

Handley's refusal to sentimentalize – which can miss some of the more sweetly evocative qualities of the music – goes with the most subtle nuances in performance, fresh as well as beautiful and atmospheric. The tonal richness of the LPO's playing is well caught in the Chandos recording.

American rhapsody (Appalachia); Norwegian suite (Folkeraadet: The Council of the people); Paa Vidderne (On the heights); Spring morning.
** Marco Polo 8.220452 [id.]. Slovak PO, Bratislava, John Hopkins.

A fascinating collection of early Delius, mostly uncharacteristic, but with pre-echoes of his later work. *Paa Vidderne*, the most substantial piece, is rather melodramatic but has a distinct melodic interest. *Spring morning* is shorter and similarly picaresque, but the *Folkeraadet suite* displays a sure orchestral touch and is most attractive in its diversity of invention. The *American rhapsody* is a concise version of *Appalachia* without the chorus, given here in its original 1896 format. John Hopkins brings a strong sympathy and understanding to this repertoire and secures a committed and flexible response from his Czech players in music which must have been wholly unknown to them.

2 Aquarelles (arr. Fenby); *Fennimore and Gerda: Intermezzo* (arr. Beecham). *Hassan: Intermezzo & Serenade* (arr. Beecham). *Irmelin: Prelude. Late swallows* (arr. Fenby); *On hearing the first cuckoo in spring; Song before sunrise; Summer night on the river.*
*** Chan. CHAN 8372 [id.]. Bournemouth Sinf., Del Mar.

Norman Del Mar's 1977 performances are warmly atmospheric and have a strong sense of line. Full recording to match and a successful digital transfer, the sound fresh yet with an excellent overall bloom.

2 Aquarelles; Fennimore and Gerda: Intermezzo. On hearing the first cuckoo in spring; Summer night on the river.
*** DG 419 748-2 [id.]. ECO, Barenboim – VAUGHAN WILLIAMS: *Lark ascending* etc.; WALTON: *Henry V.****

Barenboim's luxuriant performances have a gorgeous sensuousness and their warm, sleepy atmosphere should seduce many normally resistant to Delius's pastoralism. The couplings are no less enticing; indeed, some might feel that this music-making has a touch of decadence in its unalloyed appeal to the senses.

Brigg Fair; Dance rhapsody No. 2; Fennimore and Gerda: Intermezzo. Florida suite; Irmelin: Prelude. Marche-caprice; On hearing the first cuckoo in spring; Over the hills and far away; Sleigh ride; Song before sunrise; Summer evening; Summer night on the river; (i) *Songs of sunset.*
⊛ ***** EMI CDS7 47509-8 (2) [id.]. RPO, Beecham;** (i) with Forrester, Cameron, Beecham Choral Society.

The remastering of the complete stereo orchestral recordings of Delius's music, plus the choral *Songs of sunset*, is something of a technological miracle, and it fully deserved *Gramophone* magazine's 1987 award for remastering 'historical' material. The result is far from historical in effect, for it brings Beecham's ravishing performances into our own time with an uncanny sense of realism and presence. Beecham's fine-spun magic, his ability to lift a phrase, is apparent throughout. The shorter pieces bring superb wind solos, while the great conductor often conjures a hazy sentient warmth from the strings which no other conductor has matched since. In the *Songs of sunset* the choral focus is soft-grained, but the words are surprisingly audible, and the backward balance of the soloists is made to sound natural against the rich orchestral textures. The CD documentation includes a booklet in which Lyndon Jenkins describes the relationship between the composer and his great interpreter. The gramophone here offers music-making which is every bit as rewarding as the finest live performances.

Brigg Fair; Eventyr; In a summer garden; A song of summer.
(B) ***** CfP CD-CFP 4568. Hallé O, Vernon Handley.**

Although the tempi are sometimes controversial, Handley is an understanding and exciting Delian, and these pieces are beautifully played. The woodwind and horn solos in *Brigg Fair* are particularly delectable and the strings throughout make some lovely translucent sounds. The digital recording is of EMI's best quality, matching clarity of definition with ambient lustre and rich colouring. A bargain.

Cello concerto.
*** RCA RD 70800. Lloyd Webber, Philh. O, Handley – HOLST: *Invocation*; VAUGHAN WILLIAMS: *Fantasia.****

Lloyd Webber is inside the idiom and plays the *Concerto* with total conviction. Its lyricism is beguiling enough, but the *Concerto* proceeds in wayward fashion, and the soloist must play every note as if he believes in it ardently – and this Lloyd Webber and his partners do. The RCA balance is ideal and conveys an almost chamber-like quality at times, with great warmth and clarity.

Violin concerto; Légende for violin and orchestra; Suite for violin and orchestra.
*** Unicorn Dig. DKPCD 9040 [id.]. Ralph Holmes, RPO, Handley.

Ralph Holmes gives a strong and beautiful performance of one of Delius's supreme masterpieces, the *Violin concerto*. Holmes and Handley, an ideal partnership, bring out the Delian warmth in their shaping of phrase and pointing of rhythm, while keeping firm control of the overall structure. The *Légende* – long forgotten in this orchestral form – and the early *Suite* make ideal couplings, played with equal understanding. Holmes's beautifully focused playing is nicely balanced, against the wide span of the orchestra behind him, in first-class digital recording.

Double concerto for violin, cello and orchestra.
(M) **(*) EMI CDM7 63022-2. Menuhin, Tortelier, RPO, Meredith Davies – BRAHMS: *Double concerto.***(*)

The partnership of two master musicians, Menuhin and Tortelier, is highly productive, even if this is a somewhat lighter view of the work than is its first stereo recording with Raymond Cohen and Gerald Warburg, in which Norman Del Mar drew more richly expressive playing from the RPO than Meredith Davies does. But the four-square power of the work is never in doubt here, and the remastered sound is full and wide-ranging.

(i) *Dance rhapsody No. 1; Eventyr;* (ii) *Life's dance; North country sketches; A Song of summer.*
(M) **(*) EMI CDM7 63171-2 [id.]. (i) Royal Liverpool PO; (ii) RPO, Sir Charles Groves.

Recorded in 1971 in the Philharmonic Hall, Liverpool, and in EMI's Abbey Road No. 1 Studio in 1974, these Delius performances make an attractively generous (80 minutes) CD anthology. The collection contains a virtually unknown piece, *Lebenstanz*, or *Life's dance*, which was written in the 1890s immediately before the tone-poem *Paris*. It presents a fascinating contrast, beginning with an urgency not always associated with this composer. *Song of summer*, a typically evocative piece, comes from the other end of Delius's career; it was conceived just before he lost his sight and was subsequently dictated to his amanuensis, Eric Fenby. The *North country sketches*, depicting with Delian impressionism the seasons of the year, are equally welcome, as are the *Dance rhapsody* and *Eventyr*. Groves is a sensitive interpreter, even if he rarely matches the irresistible persuasiveness of a Beecham. The balance is vivid and warm, almost too close in sound to do justice to such delicately atmospheric music. The CD transfer is successful in retaining the fullness and bloom, although orchestral textures are not ideally transparent.

Eventyr; Fennimore and Gerda: Intermezzo. Irmelin: prelude. Over the hills and far away; Paris, the song of a great city.
(***) Beecham Trust mono BEECHAM 2. LPO, Sir Thomas Beecham.

These recordings date from between 1935 and 1939. The transfers from the original 78 r.p.m. discs were made by the highly skilled Anthony Griffiths, and the further remastering for CD seems to have been entirely beneficial.

Fennimore and Gerda: Intermezzo. Irmelin: Prelude. Koanga: La Calinda (arr. Fenby). *On hearing the first cuckoo in spring; Sleigh ride; A Song before sunrise; Summer night on the river; A Village Romeo and Juliet: The Walk to the Paradise Garden.*
(B) *** CfP CD-CFP 4304. LPO, Vernon Handley.

This is a successful anthology, with expansive and imaginative phrasing; the woodwind playing of the LPO is particularly fine. Those looking for a bargain collection of Delius should find this very good value, although Handley's approach to *The Walk to the Paradise Garden* is strongly emotional, closer to Barbirolli than to Beecham. The CD brings enhanced clarity, if with slightly less sumptuous violin timbre.

Florida suite; North Country sketches.
*** Chan. Dig. CHAN 8413 [id.]. Ulster O, Handley.

Handley's choice of tempi is always apt and it is fascinating that in the *North Country sketches* which evoke the seasons in the Yorkshire moors a Debussian influence is revealed. The delicious tune we know as *La Calinda* appears in the first movement of the *Florida suite*; elsewhere, the local influences absorbed by the young composer in America bring parallels with Dvořák. But Handley's refined approach clearly links the work with later masterpieces. The recording is superbly balanced within the very suitable acoustics of the Ulster Hall; one's only real criticism is the lack of sumptuous weight to the violins when they have an eloquent musical line in the *Florida suite*; otherwise, tuttis are superbly expansive.

Irmelin: Prelude. A Song of summer; A Village Romeo and Juliet: The Walk to the Paradise Garden.
*** EMI CDC7 47984-2 [id.]. LSO, Barbirolli – BAX: *Tintagel*; IRELAND: *London Overture.* ***

Barbirolli brings an almost Italianate romanticism to Delius's arching string-phrases, yet there is some rapturously delicate playing in the music's gentler moments. Lovely music-making throughout: all three performances are memorable. The late-1960s recording, outstanding in its day, has lost a little of the opulence in the violin timbre, but the ambient warmth ensures that the effect remains warmly beguiling.

Cello sonata.
*** Chan. Dig. CHAN 8499 [id.]. Raphael and Peter Wallfisch – BAX: *Rhapsodic ballad*; BRIDGE: *Cello sonata*; WALTON: *Passacaglia.****

The Delius *Sonata* is a less concentrated, more discursive piece than the Bridge with which it is coupled, but there is a highly personal atmosphere, and these Chandos performers give as strong and sympathetic an account of it as is to be found. They are also excellently recorded.

String quartet.
*** ASV Dig. CDDCA 526 [id.]. Brodsky Qt – ELGAR: *Quartet.****

The Brodsky Quartet give a richly expressive performance of Delius's *String quartet* with its evocative slow movement, *Late swallows*. In this music the ebb and flow of tension and a natural feeling for persuasive but unexaggerated rubato is vital; with fine ensemble but seeming spontaneity, the Brodsky players consistently produce that. First-rate recording.

VOCAL MUSIC

(i) *An Arabesque; Dance rhapsody No. 2; Fennimore and Gerda: Intermezzo.* (i; ii) *Songs of sunset.*
*** Unicorn Dig. DKPCD 9063 [id.]. (i) Thomas Allen; (ii) Sarah Walker, Amb. S., RPO, Fenby.

The present collection follows up Fenby's earlier two-disc set for Unicorn (see below), and brings equally warm, well-sung and well-played performances, atmospherically recorded. What emerges as a Delius masterpiece is *An Arabesque*, a 15-minute work for baritone, mixed chorus and orchestra, setting a Pan-worship poem (in English translation) of the Norwegian poet and biologist, Jens Peter Jacobsen. The emotional thrust of the opening sequence, superbly sung by Thomas Allen and with passionate singing from the chorus too, subsides into characteristic Delian reflectiveness, but with a distinction and sense of purpose to put it among the composer's finest works. The *Songs of sunset* also bring ravishing sounds, with Sarah Walker as deeply expressive as Allen. The *Dance rhapsody No. 2* is crisply sprung in this performance, while the sensuousness of the *Fennimore and Gerda Intermezzo* returns us to gorgeously characteristic orchestral textures. Warm, full sound, yet refined and transparent.

2 Aquarelles. (i) *Caprice & elegy. Fantastic dance; Irmelin: Prelude. Koanga: La Calinda. A Song of Summer.* (ii) *Cynara.* (ii; iii) *Idyll.* (iv) *A Late Lark.* (v) *Songs of Farewell.*
*** Unicorn Dig. DKPCD 9008/9 [id.]. Fenby, with (i) Lloyd Webber; (ii) Allen; (iii) Lott; (iv) Rolfe-Johnson; (v) Amb. S.; RPO.

Eric Fenby draws loving, dedicated performances from the RPO. *A Song of Summer* is the finest of the works which Fenby took down from the dictation of the blind, paralysed and irascible composer, but the *Songs of Farewell* (to words of Whitman) and the love scene entitled *Idyll*, rescued from an abortive opera project, are most beautiful too, with Felicity Lott and Thomas Allen especially impressive in the *Idyll*. These major works were based on earlier sketches, while other items here were arranged by Fenby with the composer's approval. The transfer to CD is expertly managed, with Delius's comparatively thick choral textures here sounding fresh and almost transparent.

Part-songs: *Durch den Wald; Frühlingsanbruch; Midsummer songs; On Craig Ddu; Sonnenscheinlied; The splendour falls; 2 unaccompanied part songs.*
(*) Conifer Dig. CDCF 162 [id.]. CBSO Ch., Simon Halsey – GRAINGER: *Part-songs.**

These Delius part-songs make an apt supplement to the CBSO Chorus's record of Grainger items, warmer and smoother because of full choral treatment but lacking some of the sharpness of performance that comes with one voice per line. Nevertheless Halsey draws crisp, refined singing from his excellent team, helped by atmospheric recording.

Hassan (incidental music).
(M) **(*) EMI CMS7 69891-2 (2). Hill, Rayner-Cook, Ch., Bournemouth Sinf., Handley – ELGAR: *Starlight Express.***(*)

Handley secures clean-cut, enjoyable performances of all the pieces Delius wrote for Flecker's play *Hassan* (including a choral version of the famous *Serenade*). Both playing and singing are first rate, and though the often picaresque writing is uneven in appeal – the *Serenade* is the best number by far – this is a most valuable issue for Delians.

4 Old English lyrics. Songs: *Brasil; Indian love song; Love's philosophy; The nightingale; The nightingale has a lyre of gold; Secret love; Sweet Venevil; Twilight fancies.*
(*) Chan. Dig. CHAN 8539 [id.]. Benjamin Luxon, David Willison – ELGAR: *Songs.*(*)

Benjamin Luxon aptly chooses a group of Delius songs to couple with his selection of those by Elgar. They are just as delightful in their unpretentiousness, as near a meeting-point between the two sharply contrasted masters as can be found in any genre, and they draw most persuasive performances from Luxon and Willison, sadly marred by the rough tone which has latterly afflicted this fine baritone. Excellent, well-balanced recording.

327

Song of the high hills. Songs: *The bird's story; Le ciel est pardessus le toit; I-Brasil; Il pleure dans mon coeur; Let springtime come; La lune blanche; To daffodils; Twilight fancies; Wine roses.*
⊛ *** Unicorn Dig. DKPCD 9029 [id.]. Lott, Sarah Walker, Rolfe-Johnson, Amb. S., RPO, Fenby.

Even among Delius issues, this stands out as one of the most ravishingly beautiful of all. Eric Fenby draws a richly atmospheric performance from Beecham's old orchestra in one of the most ambitious and beautiful, yet neglected, of Delius's choral works. Inspired by the hills of Norway, Delius evocatively conveys the still, chill atmosphere above the snow-line by episodes for wordless chorus, here finely balanced. The coupling of Delius songs in beautiful, virtually unknown orchestral arrangements is ideally chosen, with all three soloists both characterful and understanding.

Destouches, André (1672–1749)

Première Suite des éléments (ballet music).
*** O-L 421 656-2 [id.]. AAM, Hogwood – REBEL: *Les Élémens.****

A few years before Rebel composed his highly original ballet on *'les élémens'*, André Destouches, even better connected as a court composer, wrote this ballet on the same theme. The result is less original but still well worth hearing, especially in this refreshing performance on original instruments. The vividness of the recording is undoubtedly enhanced on CD but, with 45 minutes' playing time, this reissue is not especially generous.

Dett, R. Nathaniel (1882–1943)

8 Bible vignettes; In the bottoms; Magnolia suite.
**(*) New World Dig. NWCD 367 [id.]. Denver Oldham.

Robert Nathaniel Dett was born in Drummondsville, Quebec, which was populated largely by the descendants of slaves. He showed natural gifts as a pianist, developing his talents while working as a bell-hop in a hotel at Niagara Falls. He graduated from Oberlin Conservatory in 1908, the first Negro to gain a Bachelor of Music degree. His music is full of echoes of Dvořák and MacDowell, as well as the influence of the Negro spiritual. His writing is at times colourful and, though limited in its range of expressive devices, is attractive, particularly so in the suite *In the bottoms*, which evokes the moods and atmosphere of Negro life in the 'river bottoms' of the Deep South. However, this is not a disc to be taken all at once. Denver Oldham is a persuasive enough player and he is decently recorded.

Dickinson, Peter (born 1934)

4 Auden songs; 3 Comic songs; A Dylan Thomas cycle; An e. e. cummings cycle; Let the florid music praise; 3 Songs from The Unicorns.
*** Conifer Dig. CDCF 154 [id.]. Marilyn Hill Smith, Meriel Dickinson, Martyn Hill, Henry Herford, Peter Dickinson, Robin Bowman.

Peter Dickinson's settings of Auden – several of them poems already memorably set by Britten – are crisply rhythmic, not least *Over the heather* from the *Three Comic songs*, also known as *Roman wall blues* as sung by a Roman centurion. The Dylan Thomas songs are aptly rhetorical, while the uncapitalized freedom of e. e. cummings prompts a more abrasive style. The three songs to words by John Heath Stubbs strike a warmer note and together provide a fine emotional climax to the whole sequence. The four soloists make a well-contrasted group. Though not always ideally sweet of tone, they and the piano accompanists are very well recorded.

4 Blues; Blue rose; Concerto rag; Extravagances; Hymn-tune rag; Quartet rag; A red, red rose; So, we'll go no more a roving; Stevie's tunes; Wild rose rag.
**(*) Conifer Dig. CDCF 134 [id.]. Meriel Dickinson, Peter Dickinson.

Dickinson's eclectic style and ingenious mind are well illustrated in this collection of miniatures, with musical references and allusions adding to the point of the pieces. His love of American popular music provides a basic element. With the composer accompanying his sister, Meriel, in the songs, it makes an entertaining disc, with clear sound, just a little dry on piano tone.

Mass of the Apocalypse; Outcry; The Unicorns.
*** Conifer Dig. CDCF 167 [id.]. Maggs, Söderström, Dickinson, Reeves, St James's Singers, L. Concert Ch., City of L. Sinfonia, Cleobury; Solna Brass, Björklund.

Peter Dickinson is an unashamed communicator in his music, and these three works for voices and orchestra are excellent examples, nodding in the direction of minimalism without indulging in the art of near-boredom. The *Mass* brings a setting of the liturgy in English for soloists, chorus, piano and percussion, which is punctuated by readings from the Book of Revelation. The melodic writing is simple and direct to match the needs of an ordinary congregation. *Outcry* is a cantata of protest on the theme of man's cruelty to animals. It may not have the sharp originality of Britten's early cantata on the same subject to words selected by Auden, *Our hunting fathers*, but the dedication is equally clear. *The Unicorns* is a suite in six movements drawn from a projected opera, and here the singing of Elisabeth Söderström rises above all else on the record, not least in the final movement picturing a heavenly world of happiness and repose, where unicorns can live. First-rate recording.

Diepenbrock, Alphons (1862-1921)

Elektra suite; (i) Hymn for violin & orchestra; Marsyas suite; Overture: The Birds.
*** Chan. Dig. CHAN 8821 [id.]. (i) Emmy Verhey; Hague Residentie O, Hans Vonk.

For most non-native collectors, Dutch music is a closed book, save possibly for Pijper and Badings. Diepenbrock was something of a polymath and was self-taught as a composer. *The Birds Overture* (1917), written for a student production of Aristophanes, is rather delightful if very Straussian, with some vaguely Impressionist touches. The *Marsyas* music (1910) is expertly and delicately scored with touches of Strauss, Reger and Debussy. Try also the second movement of *Elektra* (track 9) which has a haunting, melancholy charm that is most appealing. Diepenbrock does not possess a strongly distinctive musical personality but his music is eminently civilized and melodically inviting. Good performances from the Residentie Orchestra under Hans Vonk and eminently truthful recording quality. Recommended.

Dittersdorf, Carl Ditters von (1739–99)

6 Symphonies after Ovid's Metamorphoses.
**(*) Chan. Dig. CHAN 8564/5 (2). Cantilena, Shepherd.

All the *Ovid symphonies* have a programmatic inspiration and relate episodes from the *Metamorphoses* of Ovid, such as *The fall of Phaeton*, which are vividly portrayed. *The rescue of Andromeda by Perseus* is a particularly effective work (it has an inspired *Adagio*) and the slow movement of the *D major, The petrification of Phineus and his friends*, is a delight. One well appreciates the contemporary verdict that Ditters 'spoke to the heart'. *The transformation of the Lycian peasants into frogs* could hardly be more graphic and is full of wit. This is inventive and charming music that will give much pleasure, and it is generally well served by Cantilena under Adrian Shepherd. The performances are not outstanding but they are very musical, and the recording, made in a lively and warm acoustic, is very clean and well detailed.

Dohnányi, Ernst von (1877–1960)

Konzertstück for cello and orchestra, Op. 12.
*** Chan. Dig. CHAN 8662 [id.]. Wallfisch, LSO, Mackerras – DVOŘÁK: *Cello concerto.***

Dohnányi's *Konzertstück*, in effect a full-scale cello concerto lasting 24 minutes, is a delightful rarity which makes an unusual and attractive coupling for Wallfisch's outstanding version of the Dvořák. It may not be a great work but it has many rich, warm ideas, not least a theme in the slow movement all too close to *Pale hands I loved beside the Shalimar*, and none the worse for that. Wallfisch's performance, as in the Dvořák, is strong, warm and committed, and the Chandos sound is first rate.

(i) *Ruralia hungarica, Op. 32b;* (i; ii) *Variations on a nursery tune, Op. 25;* (iii) *Serenade in C (for string trio), Op. 10.*
⊛ (BB) *** Hung. White Label HRC 121 [id.]. (i) Budapest SO, Lehel; (ii) with István Lantos; (iii) Kovács, Bársony, Botvay.

Ruralia hungarica, although a cultivated score, still has an element of peasant earthiness. There is also, in its five movements, wide variety of mood, and the music rises to considerable eloquence; it was admired by Bartók for its colourful scoring. György Lehel and the Budapest orchestra successfully convey its exuberance and poetry, and the pianist in the famous *Variations*, István Lantos, is characterful as well as brilliant. To make this record even more attractive, we are offered the *Serenade*, Op. 10, an expressive and inventive piece with a particularly beautiful slow movement. Again the playing here is accomplished and spontaneous. With excellent, well-balanced sound, this is one of the outstanding bargains on Hungaroton's White Label and as such we award it a token Rosette.

(i) *Suite in F sharp min., Op. 19;* (ii) *Variations on a nursery tune, Op. 25.*
(M) *** EMI CDM7 63183-2. (i) RPO, Sargent; (ii) composer, RPO, Boult.

Variations on a nursery tune (for piano and orchestra), Op. 25.
(*) Decca Dig. 417 294-2 [id.]. Schiff, Chicago SO, Solti – TCHAIKOVSKY: *Piano concerto No. 1.*

** Ph. Dig. 422 380-2 [id.]. Zoltán Kocsis, Budapest Fest. O, Iván Fischer – LISZT: *Piano concertos 1–2.***(*)

Dohnányi was nearly eighty when he recorded his famous *Nursery tune variations* in 1956, but his playing is extraordinarily vital and characterful, and still amazingly witty and sprightly. Sir Adrian gets splendid playing from the RPO. Sargent's account of the delightful *F sharp minor Suite* is slightly later (1961) and also comes up well. What a marvellously resourceful piece this is, inventive, expertly scored and full of charm! The remastering for CD has produced extraordinarily vivid sound, especially in the *Variations*. A mid-priced issue which is not to be missed.

Solti dominates the Decca performance and his vehemence in the orchestral introduction sounds as if he is trying to consign the pianist to the flames of the burning Valhalla. But this points up the contrast with the piquant piano entry, and although later Solti's lyrical climaxes have a certain pungency there are moments of wit too, and Schiff's neat, crisp articulation makes a sparkling foil for the more aggressive orchestral response.

Zoltán Kocsis plays with dazzling brilliance, though the orchestral playing could be more subtle. By the side of past recordings of this masterpiece the Kocsis/Fischer account is rather plain and, though not wanting in humour, rarely commands real wit.

Piano quintet in C min., Op. 1; (i) *Sextet in C for piano, violin, viola, cello, clarinet and horn, Op. 37.*
**(*) Decca Dig. 421 423-2 [id.]. András Schiff, Takács Qt, (i) Berkes, Vlatkovic.

(i) *Piano quintet in C min., Op. 1; String quartet No. 2 in D flat, Op. 15.*
**(*) Chan. Dig. CHAN 8718 [id.]. (i) Wolfgang Manz; Gabrieli Qt.

Dohnányi's *Piano quintet*, Op. 1, is a student work, heavily indebted to Brahms. The *Sextet* for the unusual combination of piano, clarinet, horn and string trio was written while Dohnányi was recovering from an illness, hence the autumnal feeling of much of the slow movement. The first movement has real charm. These Hungarian artists play with grace and a genuine delight in this music. The recording is made in the resonant acoustic of the Schubertsaal in the Konserthaus in Vienna, and the piano is rather backwardly placed so that textures are a little too woolly, which inhibits the three-star recommendation the performances themselves deserve.

Manz's performance of the Dohnányi *Quintet* has slightly less fantasy and lightness of touch than Schiff's; the overall effect is bigger-boned and more Brahmsian than that achieved by the Decca team. This does not have quite the charm of the Schiff/Takács record, nor the advantage of the *Sextet*. The scherzo of the *Second Quartet* is reminiscent of the opening of *Die Walküre* and there are reminders of Dvořák and Reger as well as Brahms. It is a strong piece, splendidly played by the Gabrielis and beautifully recorded.

Études de concert, Op. 28, Nos. 4–6; 3 Pieces, Op. 23; Rhapsody in F sharp min., Op. 11, No. 2; Ruralia hungarica, Op. 32a, Nos. 1, 3–5, 7.
(M) (*) Ph. 422 308-2 [id.]. Composer (with BEETHOVEN: *Andante favori*).

Dohnányi was one of the great pianists of his day; these performances, recorded in his early eighties only a month before his death, give some idea of how remarkable he must have been. However, at this stage in his career he did not possess the transcendental technique required to cope with the demands of the *Études de concert* or some of the other virtuoso pieces. It is nevertheless pretty amazing that he plays as well as he does. Unfortunately, the recording is rather shallow and wanting in range, and this is primarily of documentary interest.

Donizetti, Gaetano (1797-1848)

Il Barcaiolo; Cor anglais concertino in G; Oboe sonata in F; (Piano) *Waltz in C* (with PASCULLI: *Concerto on themes from La Favorita; Fantasia on Poliuto.* LISZT: *Réminsciences de Lucia di Lammermoor*).
*** Mer. CDE 84147 [id.]. Jeremy Polmear, Diana Ambache.

The *Sonata in F* is an agreeable piece with a fluent *Andante* and a catchy finale; and the vignette, *Il Barcaiolo*, is even more engaging. The *Cor anglais concerto* centres on a set of variations which are not unlike the fantasias on themes from his operas by Pasculli. However, these demand the utmost bravura from the soloist. Diana Ambache proves a sympathetic partner and gives a suitably flamboyant account of Liszt's famous *Lucia* paraphrase. The recording, made in Eltham College, London, is a shade too reverberant here, though the resonance is more agreeable in the duos.

String quartet No. 13 in A.
*** CRD CRD 3366 [id.]. Alberni Qt – PUCCINI: *Crisantemi*; VERDI: *Quartet.****

This is an endearing work, with a scherzo echoing that in Beethoven's *Eroica*, and with many twists of argument that are attractively unpredictable. It is well coupled here with other works for string quartet by Italian opera composers, all in strong, committed performances and well recorded. The CD transfer is fresh and vivid.

Miserere in D min.
** Hung. HCD 12147-2 [id.]. Pászthy, Bende, Slovak Ch. and PO, Maklári.

From the solemn opening you would not readily recognize this *Miserere* as the work of Donizetti. Other movements are less ambitious, with one or two jolly secular touches to give a hint of the opera composer to come. The clarinet obbligato in the second number is rather raw, but the horn in the fifth is splendid, and both the soprano, Julia Pászthy, and the baritone, Zsolt Bende, sing with fresh, clear tone, though at times challenged by the technical difficulties. The 1980 analogue recording comes up very freshly.

OPERA

Anna Bolena (complete).
*** Decca Dig. 421 096-2 (3) [id.]. Sutherland, Ramey, Hadley, Mentzer, Welsh Nat. Op. Ch. & O, Bonynge.

In this 1987 recording of *Anna Bolena*, Sutherland crowns her long recording career with a commanding performance. Dazzling as ever in coloratura, above all exuberant in the defiant final cabaletta, she poignantly conveys the tragedy of the wronged queen's fate with rare weight and gravity. Ramey as the king is outstanding in a fine, consistent cast. Excellent recording.

Il Campanello (complete).
*** CBS Dig. MK 38450 [id.]. Baltsa, Dara, Casoni, Romero, Gaifa, V. State Op. Ch., VSO, Bertini.

This sparkling one-act piece is based on something like the same story which Donizetti developed later in *Don Pasquale*. Enzo Dara as the apothecary, Don Annibale, and Angelo Romero as the wag, Enrico, are delightful in their patter duet, and Agnes Baltsa is a formidable but sparkling Serafina. Gary Bertini is a sympathetic conductor who paces things well, and the secco recitatives – taking up rather a large proportion of the disc – are well accompanied on the fortepiano. Generally well-balanced recording.

Don Pasquale (complete).
*** EMI Dig. CDS7 47068-2 (2) [Ang. CDCB 47068]. Bruscantini, Freni, Nucci, Winbergh, Amb. Op. Ch., Philh. O, Muti.

With sparkle and spring on the one hand and easily flexible lyricism on the other, Muti's is a delectably idiomatic-sounding reading, one which consistently captures the fun of the piece. It helps that three of the four principals are Italians. Freni is a natural in the role of Norina, both sweet and bright-eyed in characterization, excellent in coloratura. The buffo baritones, the veteran Bruscantini as Pasquale and the darker-toned Leo Nucci as Dr Malatesta, steer a nice course between vocal comedy and purely musical values. They sound exhilarated, not stressed, by Muti's challenging speeds for the patter numbers. On the lyrical side, Muti is helped by the beautifully poised and shaded singing of Gösta Winbergh, honey-toned and stylish as Ernesto. Responsive and polished playing from the Philharmonia and excellent studio sound.

L'Elisir d'amore (complete).
*** Decca 414 461-2 (2) [id.]. Sutherland, Pavarotti, Cossa, Malas, Amb. S., ECO, Bonynge.
(M) *** CBS CD 79210 (2) [M2K 34585]. Cotrubas, Domingo, Evans, Wixell, ROHCG Ch. & O, Pritchard.
**(*) Eurodisc 601 097 (3) [RCA ARE3-5411]. Popp, Dvorský, Weikl, Nesterenko, Munich R. Ch. & O, Wallberg.

Joan Sutherland makes Adina a more substantial figure than usual, full-throatedly serious at times, at others jolly like the rumbustious Marie. Malibran, the first interpreter of the role, was furious that the part was not bigger, and got her husband to write an extra aria. Richard Bonynge found a copy of the piano score, had it orchestrated, and included it here, a jolly and brilliant waltz song. Though that involves missing out the cabaletta *Il mio fugor dimentica*, the text of this frothy piece is otherwise unusually complete, and in the key role of Nemorino Luciano Pavarotti proves ideal, vividly portraying the wounded innocent. Spiro Malas is a superb Dulcamara, while Dominic Cossa is a younger-sounding Belcore, more of a genuine lover than usual. Bonynge points the skipping rhythms delectably, and the recording is sparkling to match, with striking presence.

Originating from a successful Covent Garden production, the CBS reissue presents a strong and enjoyable performance, well sung and well characterized. Delight centres very much on the delectable Adina of Ileana Cotrubas. Quite apart from the delicacy of her singing, she presents a sparkling, flirtatious character to underline the point of the whole story. Placido Domingo by contrast is a more conventional hero and less the world's fool that Nemorino should be. It is a large voice for the role and *Una furtiva lagrima* is not pure enough in its legato, but otherwise his singing is stylish and vigorous. Sir Geraint Evans gives a vivid characterization of Dr Dulcamara, though the microphone sometimes brings out roughness of tone and this is all the more noticeable with the added projection of CD. Ingvar Wixell is an upstanding Belcore. The stereo staging is effective and the remastered recording bright and immediate.

Wallberg conducts a lightly sprung reading, marked by a charming performance of the role of Adina from Lucia Popp, comparably bright-eyed, with delicious detail both verbal and musical. Nesterenko makes a splendidly resonant Dr Dulcamara with more comic sparkle than you would expect from a great Russian bass. Dvorský and Weikl, both sensitive artists, sound much less idiomatic, with Dvorský's tight tenor growing harsh under pressure, not at all Italianate, and Weikl failing similarly to give necessary roundness to the role of Belcore. Like other sets recorded in association with Bavarian Radio, the sound is excellent, naturally balanced with voices never spotlit.

La Fille du régiment (complete).
*** Decca 414 520-2 (2) [id.]. Sutherland, Pavarotti, Sinclair, Malas, Coates, ROHCG Ch. & O, Bonynge.

It was with this cast that *La Fille du régiment* was revived at Covent Garden, and Sutherland immediately showed how naturally she takes to the role of Marie, a *vivandière* in the army of Napoleon. This original French version favoured by Richard Bonynge is fuller than the Italian revision and, with a cast that at the time of the recording sessions was also appearing in the theatre, the performance could hardly achieve higher spirits with keener assurance. Sutherland is in turn brilliantly comic and pathetically affecting, and Pavarotti makes an engaging hero. Monica Sinclair is a formidable Countess, and even if the French accents are often suspect it is a small price to pay for such a brilliant, happy opera set, a fizzing performance of a delightful Donizetti romp that can be confidently recommended both for comedy and for fine singing. Recorded in Kingsway Hall, the CD sound has wonderful presence and clarity of focus.

Lucia di Lammermoor (complete).
*** Decca 410 193-2 (2) [id.]. Sutherland, Pavarotti, Milnes, Ghiaurov, Ryland Davies, Tourangeau, ROHCG Ch. & O, Bonynge.
(M) *** Decca 411 622-2 (2) [id.]. Sutherland, Cioni, Merrill, Siepi, St Cecilia Academy, Rome, Ch. & O, Pritchard.
**(*) EMI CDS7 47440-8 (2) [Ang. CDCB 47440]. Callas, Tagliavini, Cappuccilli, Ladysz, Philh. Ch. & O, Serafin.
(M) (***) EMI mono CMS7 69980-2 (2) [Ang. CDMB 69980]. Callas, Di Stefano, Gobbi, Arie, Ch. & O of Maggio Musicale Fiorentino, Serafin.

It was hardly surprising that Decca recorded Sutherland twice in the role with which she is inseparably associated. Though some of the girlish freshness of voice which marked the 1961 recording disappeared in the 1971 set, the detailed understanding was intensified, and the mooning manner, which in 1961 was just emerging, was counteracted. Power is there as well as delicacy, and the rest of the cast is first rate. Pavarotti, through much of the opera not as sensitive as he can be, proves magnificent in his final scene. The sound-quality is superb on CD, though choral interjections are not always forward enough. In this set, unlike the earlier one, the text is absolutely complete.

The earlier Sutherland version remains an attractive proposition in the mid-price range. Though in 1961 consonants were being smoothed over, the voice is obviously that of a younger singer and dramatically the performance was closer to Sutherland's famous stage appearances of that time, full of fresh innocence. Though the text is not quite as full as the later version, a fascinating supplement is provided in an aria (from *Rosmonda d'Inghilterra*) which for many years was used as a replacement for the big Act I aria, *Regnava nel silenzio*). The recording remains very fresh and vivid, though not everyone will like the prominent crowd noises. Sutherland's coloratura virtuosity remains breathtaking, and the cast is a strong one, with Pritchard a most understanding conductor.

The Callas stereo version was recorded in Kingsway Hall in 1959, at the very same time that Serafin was conducting this opera at Covent Garden for the newly emergent Joan Sutherland. The sound is very good for its period. Callas's flashing-eyed interpretation of the role of Lucia remains unique, though the voice has its unsteady moments to mar enjoyment. Serafin's conducting is a model of perception. The score has the cuts which used to be conventional in the theatre.

Callas's earlier mono set, which dates from 1954, is given an effective remastering, which brings out the solo voices well, although the acoustic is confined and the choral sound less well focused. Here, needless to say, is not the portrait of a sweet girl, wronged and wilting, but a formidably tragic characterization. The diva is vocally better controlled than in her later stereo set (indeed some of the coloratura is excitingly brilliant in its own right), and there are memorable if not always perfectly stylish contributions from Di Stefano and Gobbi. As in the later set, the text has the usual stage cuts, but Callas's irresistible musical imagination, her ability to turn a well-known phrase with unforgettable inflexions, supremely justifies the preservation of an historic recording.

Lucrezia Borgia (complete).
(M) *** Decca 421 497-2 (2) [id.]. Sutherland, Aragall, Horne, Wixell, London Op. Voices, Nat. PO, Bonynge.
(M) *(*) RCA GD 86642 (2) [6642-2-RG2]. Caballé, Verrett, Kraus, Flagello, RCA Italiana Op. Ch. & O, Perlea.

Sutherland is in her element here. In one or two places she falls into the old swooning style but, as in the theatre, her singing is masterly, not only in its technical assurance but in its power and conviction, making the impossible story of poisoner-heroine moving and even sympathetic. Aragall sings stylishly too, and though Wixell's timbre is hardly Italianate he is a commanding Alfonso. Marilyn Horne in the breeches role of Orsini is impressive in the brilliant *Brindisi* of the last Act, but earlier she has moments of unsteadiness. Thanks to researches by Richard Bonynge, the set also includes extra material for the tenor, including an aria newly discovered, *T'amo qual dama un angelo.* The recording is characteristically full and brilliant.

Lucrezia Borgia was the opera which brought Montserrat Caballé overnight fame when she stepped in at the last minute at a stage performance in New York; so one approaches this 1966 recording with expectation. But in no way does she enter into the character of the wicked Lucrezia caught out by fate and, though there is much beautiful singing, the uninspired direction of Perlea does not help. Even when Caballé in the final Act enters the banquet where her enemies (and, unknown, her son) are being entertained to poisoned wine, she sounds like a hostess asking whether her guests would like more tea. Alfredo Kraus is the most successful soloist here, for even Shirley Verrett seems to have been affected by the prevailing lassitude. However, the remastered recording is excellent.

Maria Stuarda (complete).
(M) *** Decca 425 410-2 (2) [id.]. Sutherland, Tourangeau, Pavarotti, Ch. & O of Teatro Comunale, Bologna, Bonynge.
** Ph. Dig. 426 233-2 (2) [id.]. Gruberová, Baltsa, Vermillion, Araiza, D'Artegna, Alaimo, Bav. R. Ch., Munich RSO, Patanè.

In Donizetti's tellingly dramatic opera on the conflict of Elizabeth I and Mary Queen of Scots the confrontation between the two Queens is so brilliantly effective that one regrets that history did not actually manage such a meeting between the royal cousins. Here the contrast between the full soprano Maria and the dark mezzo Elisabetta is underlined by some transpositions, with Tourangeau emerging as a powerful villainess in this slanted version of the story. Pavarotti turns Leicester into a passionate Italian lover, not at all an Elizabethan gentleman. As for Sutherland, she is at her most fully dramatic too, and the great moment when she flings the insult *Vil bastarda!* at her cousin brings a superb snarl. In the lovely prayer before the Queen's execution with its glorious melody, Sutherland is richly forthright but does not quite efface memories of Dame Janet Baker. Otherwise she remains the most commanding of Donizetti sopranos, and Richard Bonynge directs an urgent account of an unfailingly enjoyable opera. Unusually for Decca, the score is slightly cut. The recording is characteristically bright and full and the CD transfer first rate. This version is now offered at mid-price.

Giuseppe Patanè, in one of his last recordings, conducts a refined account of *Maria Stuarda*, very well sung and well recorded. The manner is lighter, the speeds often faster than in the immediate CD rivals, and that makes the result less sharply dramatic, a point reflected in the actual singing of Gruberová and Baltsa which, for all its beauty and fine detail, is less intense than that of Sutherland and Tourangeau (Decca) or Baker and Plowright (EMI). Whether it is Mary singing nostalgically of home in her first cantilena or leading the surgingly memorable Scottish prayer in Act III, or even in the confrontation between the two Queens, this account keeps a degree of restraint – even on the thrusting insult from Mary to Elizabeth, *Vil bastarda!*. Some may prefer this, particularly if they have not seen the opera on stage. Araiza sings well as Leicester, but again gives a less rounded performance than Pavarotti with Sutherland. Not that the rivalry is exact, when the EMI is a live performance in English, and the Decca uses a slightly different text. This is the only digital version. The Philips sound is well balanced, but there is less sense of presence than in the fine analogue Decca.

Mary Stuart (complete in English).
(M) **(*) EMI Dig. CMS7 69372-2 (2). Dame Janet Baker, Plowright, Rendall, Opie, Tomlinson, E. Nat. Op. Ch. and O, Mackerras.

Mary Stuart was the opera chosen at the ENO just before Dame Janet decided to retire from the opera stage in 1982; happily, EMI took the opportunity to make live recordings of a series of performances at the Coliseum. Though far from ideal, the result is strong and memorable, with Dame Janet herself rising nobly to the demands of the role, snorting fire superbly in her condemnation of Elizabeth as a royal bastard, and above all making the closing scenes before Mary's execution deeply moving. Her performance is splendidly matched by that of Rosalind Plowright, though the closeness of the recording of the singers makes the voice rather hard. The singing of the rest of the cast is less distinguished, with chorus ensemble often disappointingly ragged, a point shown up by the recording balance. The acoustic has the listener almost on stage, with the orchestra relatively distant. It is a valuable and historic set, but the Decca version (in Italian) with Sutherland gives a fuller idea of the work's power.

Poliuto (complete).
*** CBS Dig. M2K 44821 (2) [id.]. Carreras, Ricciarelli, Pons, Polgar, V. Singakademie Ch., VSO, Oleg Caetani.

Set in Rome in the early Christian period, *Poliuto* is based on Corneille's tragedy, *Polyeucte*, a story of martyrdom. Written in 1838, it was originally banned by the censor and was first heard in a version that Donizetti arranged for Paris under the title *Les martyrs*. It is a piece that was revived at various periods, thanks to the advocacy of such tenors as Tamagno and Lauri-Volpi; Maria Callas, attracted to the dramatic role of the heroine, Paolina, appeared opposite Franco Corelli in a revival at La Scala, Milan, in 1960. This version was recorded in the Vienna Konzerthaus in 1986. That was before Carreras's serious illness, and the voice is in splendid form. Ricciarelli as Paolina lacks something in dramatic bite, but she gives the heroine an inward warmth and tenderness. Pons and Polgar are also excellent and, though the piece is not remarkable for any depth of character-drawing, it is well worth investigating for the foretastes it brings of middle-period Verdi, and specifically for one of Donizetti's most inspired ensembles in the Act II finale. The recording is clear and vivid, hardly betraying the fact that it was made live at a concert performance.

Arias from: *Don Pasquale; Don Sebastiano; Il Duca d'Alba; L'elisir d'amore; La Favorita; La Fille du régiment; Lucia di Lammermoor; Maria Stuarda.*
*** Decca 417 638-2 [id.]. Luciano Pavarotti with various orchestras & conductors.

A cleverly chosen compilation of Pavarotti recordings of Donizetti from various sources – not just complete sets but previous recital discs. It is good to have one or two rarities along with the favourite numbers, including Tonio's celebrated 'High-C's' solo from the Act I finale of *La Fille du régiment*. Sound from different sources is well co-ordinated.

Dowland, John (1563–1626)

Consort music: *Captain Digorie Piper, his pavan and galliard; Fortune my foe; Lachrimae; Lady Hunsdon's almain; Lord Souch's galliard; Mistress Winter's jump; The shoemaker's wife (a toy); Sir George Whitehead's almain; Sir Henry Guildford's almain; Sir Henry Umpton's funeral; Sir John Smith's almain; Sir Thomas Collier's galliard; Suzanna.*
*** Hyp. Dig. CDA 66010 [id.]. Extempore String Ens.

The Extempore Ensemble's technique of improvising and elaborating in Elizabethan consort music is aptly exploited here in an attractively varied selection of pieces by Dowland. Performers in turn are each allowed what the jazz musician would recognize as a 'break', and on record, as in concert, the result sounds the more spontaneous. Excellent recording, given added presence on CD.

First Book of Songes (1597): 1, Unquiet thoughts; 2, Whoever thinks or hopes; 3, My thoughts are wing'd with hopes; 4, If my complaints; 5, Can she excuse my wrongs; 6, Now, O now I needs must part; 7, Dear, if you change; 8, Burst forth my tears; 9, Go crystal tears; 10, Think'st thou then; 11, Come away, come sweet love; 12, Rest awhile; 13, Sleep wayward thoughts; 14, All ye who love or fortune; 15, Wilt thou unkind; 16, Would my conceit; 17, Come again; 18, His golden locks; 19, Awake, sweet love; 20, Come, heavy sleep; 21, Away with these self-loving lads.
*** O-L 421 653-2 [id.]. Cons. of Musicke, Rooley.

Rooley and the Consort of Musicke he directs have recorded all the contents of the *First Book of Songes* of 1597 in the order in which they are published, varying the accompaniment between viols, lute with bass viol, voices and viols, and even voices alone. There is hardly any need to stress the beauties of the music itself, which is eminently well served by this stylish ensemble, and beautifully recorded.

Lachrimae, or Seaven Teares.
*** BIS Dig. CD 315 [id.]. Dowland Consort, Jakob Lindberg.
**(*) O-L Dig. 421 477-2 [id.]. Consort of Musicke, Rooley.

Jakob Lindberg and his consort of viols give a highly persuasive account of Dowland's masterpiece. The texture is always clean and the lute clearly present. The recording is made in the pleasing acoustic of Wik Castle, near Uppsala, and needs to be reproduced at a low-level setting. Beautiful playing, expertly recorded.

The Oiseau-Lyre alternative, good though it is, has now been displaced by Jakob

337

Lindberg's record with the Dowland Consort. This has greater atmosphere and warmth, and carries a first recommendation.

Lachrimae or Seaven Teares: excerpts.
*** Virgin Dig. VC7 90795-2 [id.]. Fretwork, with Christopher Wilson – BYRD: *Consort music*.***

This record differs from rival accounts in that it intersperses the *Lachrimae* (which are unbroken in the fine Jakob Lindberg record) with consort music of Byrd, thus bringing greater variety of mood and feeling. The performances are of undoubted merit and can be recommended as offering an interesting alternative.

Lute music: *Almaine; Dowland's first galliard; Earl of Derby, his galliard; Earl of Essex, his galliard; Farewell (fancy); Forlorne hope (fancy); Frog galliard; Lachrimae antiquae; Lachrimae verae; Lady Rich, her galliard; Lord d'Lisle, his galliard; Melancholie galliard; Mrs Vaux's gigge; My Lady Hunsdon's puffe; My Lord Willoughby's welcome home; Piper's pavan; Resolution; Semper Dowland, Semper dolens; The Shoemaker's wife (a toy); Sir Henry Gifford, his almaine.*
*** RCA RD 89977. Julian Bream (lute).

Julian Bream captures the melancholy (the piece entitled *Semper Dowland, semper dolens* is certainly autobiographical) and the eloquence of these endlessly imaginative miniatures. He produces an astonishing range of colour from the lute: each phrase shows distinction, nothing is in the least routine. The CD gives Bream the most realistic presence, though care should be exercised with the volume control – a lower-level setting is advisable for a truthful image.

Part songs: *Awake sweet love; Cease these false sports; Disdain me still; Go christall teares; His golden locks; Lamentation Henrici Noel; Now, O now I needs must part; A shepherd in a shade; Tell me true love; Thou mighty God; Welcome black night; What if I never speed.*
*** EMI Dig. CDC7 49805-2 [id.]. Hilliard Ens., Paul Hillier.

As Paul Hillier reminds us, many of Dowland's songs were also originally published in four-part chamber form so that the singers and lutenist could gather round a table and read from one copy 'provided their eyesight was fair and they could tolerate a certain degree of intimacy'. This CD gives us four songs from the 1597 Books, one each from the Second and Third, and seven from *A Pilgrim's Solace*, between which comes the less inspired *Lamentation Henrici Noel*. As always with this group, the singing is impeccable in blend and intonation, but at times the effect is slightly bland.

Drigo, Riccardo (1846–1930)

La Flûte magique (ballet; complete).
*** Decca Dig. 421 431-2 [id.]. ROHCG O, Bonynge – DELIBES; MINKUS: *La Source*.***

Drigo's *ballet* has nothing whatsoever to do with Mozart's *opera*, but its storyline does have something in common with *The Red shoes*, for, once the hero starts playing his flute, no one can stop dancing. It has a happy ending, and the score is appropriately vivacious, the invention inconsequential but so prettily scored and amiably tuneful that it makes a very agreeable entertainment when played as wittily and elegantly as here. Richard Bonynge is in his element and, with Decca's finest sound, this cannot fail to entertain.

Dukas, Paul (1865-1935)

L'apprenti sorcier (The sorcerer's apprentice).
*** DG Dig. 419 617-2 [id.]. BPO, Levine – SAINT-SAENS: *Symphony No. 3.***
*** RCA RD 86205 [RCA 6205-2-RC]. NBC O, Toscanini – (with Concert: *Light classics*
(***)).
**(*) Decca Dig. 421 527-2 [id.]. Montreal SO, Dutoit (with Concert: *'Fête à la française'*
***).
(B) **(*) RCA Dig. VD 87727 [7727-2-RV]. Dallas SO, Mata (with Concert ***).
(B) **(*) Pickwick Dig. PCD 921. Nat. Youth O of Great Britain, Christopher Seaman –
STRAVINSKY: *Firebird ballet.***(*)

Levine chooses a fast basic tempo, though not as fast as Toscanini (who managed with
only two 78 sides), but achieves a deft, light and rhythmic touch to make this a real
orchestral scherzo. Yet the climax is thrilling, helped by superb playing from the Berlin
Philharmonic; in the gentle 'epilogue' the picture of a crestfallen apprentice handing the
broom back to his master comes readily into the mind's eye. The sound is suitably
expansive and its clarity reveals the brilliance of Dukas's scoring. The CD has an
amplitude and sparkle which are especially telling.

Toscanini's overall timing is 10 minutes 9 seconds. He creates memorably translucent
textures at the opening and then sets off with great dash at the entry of the main theme.
The effect is undoubtedly exhilarating, and the Studio 8-H recording (clear and clean, if
not ideally resonant) has been most satisfactorily remastered from an excellent 1950
mono LP, so that the sound-quality is fully acceptable. The performance is unique.

Neither Dutoit nor Mata quite matches their zest (nor indeed achieves the sense of
calamity at the climax that Levine does), but both are genially enjoyable and are featured
within desirable collections, given demonstration-worthy recording – see our Concerts
section. There is also an excellent earlier Ansermet version included in Decca's
ingeniously planned 'Children's Weekend' anthology; and Previn, too, has made a lively
recording with the LSO, included in a popular compilation of 'Classical Favourites':
again, see our Concerts section, below.

Under Christopher Seaman, the National Youth Orchestra of Great Britain give a most
attractive account of Dukas's orchestral scherzo, with ensemble and commitment that
leave little to be desired. There is plenty of impulse here, and the modern digital
recording is full and brilliant.

(i) *L'apprenti sorcier (The sorcerer's apprentice);* (ii) *Ariane et Barbe-bleue: Act III Prelude;
La péri;* (iii) *Symphony in C.*
(M) **(*) EMI CDM7 63160-2. (i) (mono): Philh. O, Markevitch; (ii) (stereo): Paris Op. O,
Dervaux, (iii) ORTF, Martinon.

The Dukas is one of the finest of the post-Franck symphonies, more vital in argument
and more independent in outlook than the Chausson or either of the d'Indy symphonies.
Martinon brings real vigour and feeling to it, and the (slightly but not excessively
reverberant) 1974 recording comes up well. *La péri* was recorded in 1957 and wears its
years well, though the orchestral playing is not first class (the wind intonation is not
always true). Markevitch's 1953 Philharmonia account of *L'apprenti sorcier* (mono, of
course) is brilliantly played, but there is an ugly edit (cut-off reverberation) halfway
through. Still, this is worth having.

Duparc, Henri (1848–1933)

Mélodies (complete): *Au pays où se fait la guerre; Chanson triste; Élégie; Extase; La fuite* (duet); *Le galop; L'invitation au voyage; Lamento; Le Manoir de Rosamonde; Phidylé; Romance de Mignon; Sérénade; Sérénade florentine; Soupir; Testament; La vague et la cloche; La vie antérieure.*
*** Hyp. Dig. CDA 66323 [id.]. Sarah Walker, Thomas Allen, Roger Vignoles.

The Hyperion issue is as near an ideal Duparc record as could be. Here are not only the thirteen recognized songs but also four early works – three songs and a duet – which have been rescued from the composer's own unwarranted suppression. The singers are ideally matched and contrasted, both of them characterful and searching; and the layout of songs on the record is itself most happily devised, with the singers alternating and with the programme framed by Sarah Walker's inspired singing of two of the finest songs of all, both of them settings of Baudelaire, *L'invitation au voyage* and *La vie antérieure*, a late inspiration. Roger Vignoles is the ever-sensitive accompanist; and the recording captures voices and piano beautifully, bringing out the tang and occasional rasp of Walker's mezzo and the glorious tonal range of Allen's baritone.

Mélodies: *Au pays où se fait la guerre; Chanson triste; L'invitation au voyage; Le manoir de Rosamonde; Phidylé; La vie antérieure.*
*** EMI Dig. CDC7 49689-2 [id.]. Barbara Hendricks, Lyon Op. O, Gardiner – RAVEL: *Mélodies.****

Barbara Hendricks with John Eliot Gardiner accompanying is just as seductive in these orchestrated Duparc songs as in the Ravel, with which they are coupled. The finely balanced, warmly atmospheric recording ensures that the voice rides over the exotic instrumental textures in a way generally impossible in the concert hall, yet there is no impression of the singer being spotlit. Best of all is *Phidylé*, made yearningly erotic, with the rising temperature finding its fulfilment in the climax of the third stanza. The only complaint is that two of the eight songs which Duparc orchestrated are omitted – a pity when there is plenty of room on the CD.

Dupré, Marcel (1886–1971)

Symphony in G minor for organ and orchestra, Op. 25.
*** Telarc Dig. CD 80136 [id.]. Michael Murray, RPO, Ling – RHEINBERGER: *Organ concerto No. 1.****

If you enjoy Saint-Saëns's *Organ symphony* you'll probably enjoy this. The organ's contribution is greater, though it is not a concerto. It is a genial, extrovert piece, consistently inventive if not as memorably tuneful as its predecessor. The performance has warmth, spontaneity and plenty of flair, and the recording has all the spectacle one associates with Telarc in this kind of repertoire.

Chorale and fugue, Op. 57; 3 Esquisses, Op. 41; Preludes and fugues: in B; G min., Op. 7/1 & 3; Le tombeau de Titelouse: Te lucis ante terminum; Placare Christe servulis, Op. 38/6 & 16; Variations sur un vieux Noël, Op. 20.
*** Hyp. Dig. CDA 66205 [id.]. John Scott (St Paul's Cathedral organ).

An outstandingly successful recital, more spontaneous and convincing than many of the composer's own recordings in the past. Dupré's music is revealed as reliably inventive and with an atmosphere and palette all its own. John Scott is a splendid advocate and the St Paul's Cathedral organ is unexpectedly successful in this repertoire. The reverberation does bring some clouding of detail, but the swirling sounds are always pleasing to the ear, and details focus well at lower dynamic levels.

Duruflé, Maurice (born 1902)

Fugue sur la thème du Carillon des heures de la Cathédrale de Soissons; Prélude, adagio et choral varié sur la thème du Veni Creator; Prélude sur l'Introit de l'Épiphanie; Prélude et fugue sur le nom d'Alain, Op. 7; Scherzo, Op. 2; Suite, Op. 5.
**(*) Delos Dig. D/CD 3047 [id.]. Todd Wilson (Schudi organ of St Thomas Aquinas, Dallas, Texas.

The producer of this record, which contains all Duruflé's organ music, consulted the composer before choosing the present organ, which has recently been modified to make it even more suitable for the purpose. Even so, it possesses a mellifluous palette and, coupled with the cathedral-like reverberation of Dallas's Catholic church, the effect has less reedy bite than that of a typical French instrument. But the performances of Duruflé's often powerful and always engagingly inventive music are of the highest quality, and Todd Wilson builds thrilling climaxes as well as articulating cleanly and showing a fine ear for colour, notably in the *Scherzo*, Op. 2. Obviously, he also relishes the Alain quotations (from *Litanies*) in the ingenious piece that commemorates his name. The account of the closing *Toccata* of the *Suite*, Op. 5, has breathtaking bravura and if here, as elsewhere, detail is not sharply registered, the spontaneity and power of the playing are compulsive. The recording is immensely spectacular in its amplitude and range, although once or twice saturation point seems to be approached at the forceful closing cadences.

Requiem, Op. 9.
(*) EMI Dig. CDC7 49880-2 [id.]. Murray, Bär, King's Coll. Ch., ECO, Cleobury – FAURÉ: *Requiem.**

(i) *Requiem, Op. 9;* (ii) *4 Motets, Op. 10.*
**(*) Erato/WEA Dig. 2292 45230-2 [id.]. (i) Berganza, Van Dam, Colonne Ch. & O; (ii) Jean Sourisse, Philippe Corboz (organ); (i; ii) Audite Nova Vocal Ens., cond. Michel Corboz.

Requiem, Op. 9 (3rd version); *4 Motets, Op. 10.*
*** Hyp. Dig. CDA 66191 [id.]. Ann Murray, Thomas Allen, Corydon Singers, ECO, Best; Trotter (organ).

Using the chamber-accompanied version, with strings, harp and trumpet – a halfway house between the full orchestral score and plain organ accompaniment – Best conducts a deeply expressive and sensitive performance of Duruflé's lovely setting of the *Requiem*. With two superb soloists and an outstandingly refined chorus, it makes an excellent recommendation, well coupled with motets, done with similar freshness, clarity and feeling for tonal contrast. The recording is attractively atmospheric yet quite clearly focused.

Corboz conducts a warmly idiomatic reading. He uses the full orchestral version; the slight haziness of the sound, merging textures richly, adds to the sense of mystery. However, the Hyperion version strikes a happy medium in this respect. The Erato soloists are excellent, but even on CD the lack of internal focus remains apparent.

It makes a generous and ideal coupling having the Duruflé *Requiem* coupled with the work which it clearly seeks to emulate, the Fauré *Requiem*. Cleobury takes a rather recessive view of the Duruflé, bringing out its meditative repose rather than any dramatic tension. But with beautiful, polished – if very English – singing from the King's Choir, and excellent contributions from the two soloists, this can certainly be recommended – although, considered individually, neither performance would be a first choice.

Dusik, Jan Ladislav (1760–1812)

Sonata in F min. (L'Invocation), Op. 77; 12 Études mélodiques, Op. 16; Rondo (Les Adieux).
** Sup. SUP 001853 [id.]. Jan Panenka.

Dusik is one of the most interesting of Beethoven's contemporaries, and the *F minor Sonata*, Op. 77, is one of his most powerful contributions to the genre. Panenka plays this and the other pieces with tremendous spirit and gusto on a fortepiano by Graff. He shapes phrases with an imagination and fire that will pleasantly surprise those who imagine early-music performances to be bloodless. There are two snags: the acoustic is resonant, which makes the instrument sound unnecessarily clattery, and at 45 minutes it offers short measure. Artistically, however, it is first class.

Dutilleux, Henri (born 1916)

L'Arbre des Songes (Violin concerto).
*** CBS Dig. MK 42449 [id.]. Stern, O Nat. de France, Maazel – MAXWELL DAVIES: *Violin concerto.****

In his *Violin concerto* Dutilleux, always the perfect craftsman and consistently writing with refinement, yet shows how taut self-discipline can go with natural expressive warmth. There are passages in this tightly knit structure of seven linked sections which sound very like Walton updated; and the underlying romantic fervour finds Stern playing with warm commitment, strongly accompanied by Maazel and the Orchestre National. First-rate recording.

Symphony No. 1; Timbres, espace, mouvement.
⊛ *** HM Dig. HMC 905159 [id.]. O Nat. de Lyon, Serge Baudo.

In Dutilleux's *First Symphony* there is a mercurial intelligence and a vivid imagination at work, and the orchestral textures are luminous and iridescent. What is particularly impressive is its sense of forward movement: you feel that the music is taking you somewhere. *Timbres, espace, mouvement* is a more recent work, dating from 1978. Serge Baudo is an authoritative interpreter of this composer and the Lyon orchestra also serve him well. The engineering is superb: there is plenty of space round the various instruments, and the balance is thoroughly realistic.

Piano sonata.
(*) Archduke Dig. DARC 2 [id.]. Donna Amato (piano) – BALAKIREV: *Sonata.*(*)

The Dutilleux *Sonata* has an almost symphonic breadth and sense of scale; it is tonal – the first movement is in F sharp minor and its centrepiece, a *Lied*, is finely wrought and original, and skilfully linked to the final chorale and variations. Donna Amato, a young American pianist, gives a totally committed and persuasive account of it, and the recording is very truthful; given the interest and rarity of the coupling, this is a most desirable issue.

Dvořák, Antonin (1841–1904)

Overtures: Carnaval, Op. 92; In Nature's realm, Op. 91; Othello, Op. 93. Scherzo capriccioso, Op. 66.
* Chan. Dig. CHAN 8453 [id.]. Ulster O, Handley.

Dvořák wrote this triptych immediately before his first visit to America in 1892. Until now, Opp. 91 and 93 have tended to be eclipsed by the just public acclaim for the *Carnaval overture.* Handley's superb performances put the three works in perspective. A splendid issue, superbly recorded in the attractive ambience of Ulster Hall, Belfast.

Cello concerto in B min., Op. 104.
* DG 413 819-2 [id.]. Rostropovich, BPO, Karajan – TCHAIKOVSKY: *Rococo variations.******
* Chan. Dig. CHAN 8662 [id.]. Wallfisch, LSO, Mackerras – DOHNÁNYI: *Konzertstück.******
(M) ***** RCA GD 86531 (6531-2-RG]. Harrell, LSO, Levine – SCHUBERT: *Arpeggione sonata.******
(M) ***** EMI CDM7 69169-2. Tortelier, LSO, Previn – TCHAIKOVSKY: *Rococo variations.******
(B) ***** DG 429 155-2 [id.]. Fournier, BPO, Szell – BLOCH: *Schelomo;* BRUCH: *Kol Nidrei.***(*)**
*(*) EMI CDC7 47614-2 [id.]. Jacqueline du Pré, Chicago SO, Barenboim – HAYDN: *Concerto in C.***(*)**
(B) ***** DG 429 155-2 [id.]. Fournier, BPO, Szell – BLOCH: *Schelomo;* BRUCH: *Kol Nidrei.***(*)**
*(*) Ph. 412 880-2 [id.]. Heinrich Schiff, Concg. O, C. Davis – ELGAR: *Concerto.***(*)**
* Decca Dig. 410 144-2 [id.]. Harrell, Philh. O, Ashkenazy – BRUCH: *Kol Nidrei.***(*)**
DG Dig. 427 347-2 [id.]. Maisky, Israel PO, Bernstein – BLOCH: *Schelomo.***

(i) *Cello concerto; Carnaval overture, Op. 92; Rusalka: Polonaise.*
*(*) Ph. Dig. 422 387-2 [id.]. (i) Julian Lloyd Webber; Czech PO, Neumann.

Cello concerto; Rondo in G, Op. 94.
(B) ***(*)** Ph. 422 467-2 [id.]. Gendron, LPO, Haitink – FAURÉ: *Élégie*(*)*; SAINT-SAENS: *Concerto No. 1.***

Cello concerto; Silent woods, Op. 68.
*(*) BIS CD 245 [id.]. Helmerson, Gothenburg SO, Järvi.

If Rostropovich can sometimes sound self-indulgent in this most romantic of cello concertos, the degree of control provided by Karajan gives a firm yet supple base, and there have been few recorded accounts so deeply satisfying. The result is unashamedly romantic, with many moments of dalliance, but the concentration is never in doubt. Splendid playing by the Berliners, and a bonus in the shape of Tchaikovsky's glorious *Rococo variations.* The analogue recording dates from 1969 and the original sound was both rich and refined; the effect is certainly enhanced in the first-class CD transfer.

Rafael Wallfisch's is an outstanding version, strong and warmly sympathetic, masterfully played and with fewer expressive distortions than is common, and with its rich Chandos recording full of presence. This is a performance which, in its taut co-ordination between soloist, conductor and orchestra, far more than usual establishes the unity of the work. This is not to say that the soloist lacks individuality but that he is so confident and commanding that rhythms which are usually distorted come out with emphatic precision. The excitement as well as the warmth of the piece comes over as in a live performance, and Wallfisch's tone remains rich and firm in even the most taxing passages. Above all – helped by a natural balance for the solo cello – this is a performance which conveys the deepest expressiveness without any hint of self-indulgence. The orchestral playing, the quality of sound and the delightful, generous and unusual coupling all make it a recommendation which must be given the strongest advocacy.

In Lynn Harrell's first RCA recording, made in the mid-1970s, his collaboration with James Levine proved a powerful and sympathetic one. Richly satisfying accounts of the first and second movements culminate in a reading of the finale which proves the most distinctive of all. The main body of the movement is finely integrated, but it is the *andante* epilogue which brings the most memorable playing, very expansive but not at all sentimental, with a wonderful sense of repose. The recording is bright and full and has been most successfully remastered for CD.

The richness of Tortelier's reading of Dvořák's *Cello concerto* has long been appreciated on record; his 1978 recording with Previn has a satisfying centrality, not as passionately romantic as Rostropovich's recording on DG, but with the tenderness as well as the power of the work held in perfect equilibrium. What is rather less perfect is the balance of the recording, favouring the cellist too much, although the digital remastering has improved overall clarity without loss of bloom.

Jacqueline du Pré's reading conveys the spontaneous passion which marked her playing in public. The pity is that the recording is badly balanced, the cello too forward, while the trumpet solo at the end of the first movement is too backward. Nevertheless it is an interpretation which captures very vividly the urgent flair of the music-making.

Fournier's reading has a sweep of concentration and richness of tone and phrasing which carry along the melodic lines with the mixture of tension and nobility that the concerto demands. Fournier can relax and beguile the ear in lyrical passages and yet, with Szell's strong accompaniment, catch the listener up in the exuberance of the exciting finale. The remastered recording has lost some of its original warmth and amplitude but still sounds vivid, with the solo timbre well focused. Now reissued with unusual but worthwhile couplings of music by Bloch and Bruch, this remains competitive at bargain price.

Julian Lloyd Webber's version boasts an obvious advantage in having as collaborators the Czech Philharmonic under the Dvořák specialist, Neumann – although not everyone will like the fruity, slightly whiny horn tone in the great second-subject melody when it first appears in the introduction. Some of the advantage is dissipated by the recording, which is agreeable and atmospheric but not ideally clear on inner detail; other versions bring orchestral playing of even sharper intensity. Not that there is any lack of intensity in Lloyd Webber's playing. This is a strong and warmly sympathetic performance, marked by ripe, rich tone and opulent vibrato; but there are places where the stress on the soloist shows in unwanted agogics and uneven rhythms, even in an occasional forced easing of tempo. Only next to the very finest versions does this appear as anything like a flaw, and anyone who fancies the non-cello Dvořák coupling will not be disappointed.

Gendron's performance is unidiosyncratic, attractively fresh and lyrical, and it has the advantage of impeccable orchestral support under Haitink. There is a real spontaneity about this playing and its responsiveness is given good support by the Philips engineers. The *Rondo* makes an engaging bonus; alas, the other couplings, although generous, are less appealing.

Schiff's reading has an unexaggerated vein of poetry more akin to Yo-Yo Ma, and its range of emotion is satisfying on a smaller scale. It sounds extremely well in its CD transfer and, with a generous and successful Elgar coupling, is well worth considering.

Frans Helmerson may not have the outsize personality of Rostropovich, but he plays with eloquence and feeling, and the orchestra provide exemplary support.

Lynn Harrell's newest recording of the Dvořák *Concerto* for Decca is a little disappointing and does not match his earlier, RCA version with the LSO under James Levine, although it is superbly recorded.

Maisky and Bernstein in their live recording spread the *Concerto* to an extraordinary 43½ minutes. Even that might have been acceptable, had Maisky's playing been less perverse. His fluctuations of tempo and rhythm are so wilful that he sounds jerky, not persuasive. With the soloist too closely balanced and with dry orchestral sound in tuttis, this is not recommended.

Piano concerto in G min., Op. 33.
*** EMI CDC7 47967-2. Sviatoslav Richter, Bav. State O, Carlos Kleiber – SCHUBERT: *Wanderer Fantasia.****
(*) Decca Dig. 417 802-2 [id.]. András Schiff, VPO, Dohnányi – SCHUMANN: *Introduction and allegro appassionato.**

Much has been made of the *Piano concerto*'s pianistic deficiencies, but Richter plays the solo part in its original form and his judgement is triumphantly vindicated. This is the most persuasive and masterly account of the work ever committed to disc; its ideas emerge with an engaging freshness and warmth, while the greater simplicity of Dvořák's own keyboard writing proves in Richter's hands to be more telling and profound. Carlos Kleiber secures excellent results from the Bavarian orchestra, and the 1977 recording has clarity and good definition to recommend it, although the digital remastering for CD has produced an over-bright and relatively unrefined sound for the violins in their upper-range fortissimos. However, this responds satisfactorily to the controls.

Like Richter, Schiff opts for the original piano part rather than the more 'pianistic' version of Kurz. Schiff's excellent performance derives from a public concert in the Musikverein, and he is given splendid support from the Vienna Philharmonic under Dohnányi. In the Decca recording, the piano is very up-front and the perspective in this respect is not wholly natural. All the same, this is an excellent performance.

Violin concerto in A min., Op. 53.
(B) *** CfP Dig. TC-CFP 4566 [Ang. CDB 62920]. Tasmin Little, Royal Liverpool PO, Handley – BRUCH: *Concerto No. 1.****
(M) *** Ph. 420 895-2 [id.]. Accardo, Concg. O, C. Davis – SIBELIUS: *Violin concerto.****
(B) *** Sup. 110601-2. Josef Suk, Czech PO, Ančerl – SUK: *Fantasy.****

Violin concerto in A min., Op. 53; Romance in F min., Op. 11.
*** EMI Dig. CDC7 49858-2 [id.]. Kyung Wha Chung, Phd. O, Muti.
*** EMI CDC7 47168-2 [id.]. Perlman, LPO, Barenboim.
(***) CBS Dig. MK 44923 [id.]. Midori, NYPO, Mehta (with *Carnaval overture*).
*** DG Dig. 419 618-2 [id.]. Mintz, BPO, Levine – SIBELIUS: *Concerto.***(*)

Kyung Wha Chung in her first recording under her exclusive EMI contract gives a heartfelt reading of a work that can sound wayward. The partnership with Muti and the Philadelphia Orchestra is a happy one, with the sound warmer and more open than it has usually been in the orchestra's recording venue. Chung may not always generate the tense excitement of such rivals as Perlman and Midori, with their generally faster speeds, but in each movement she uses the extra elbow-room to bring out subtler detail, more fantasy.

So in the first movement, using a warm vibrato, she draws out the Slavonic melancholy to the full, and in the finale she is able to give light and shade to the dance rhythms, with the 'giocoso' element bubbling out in a happy and genial reading. She finds similar concentration in the *Romance*, which is also the coupling on Perlman's and Midori's versions.

Perlman and Barenboim still sound pretty marvellous and show all the warmth and virtuosity one could desire. This CD also has the eloquent and touching *F minor Romance*. Perlman is absolutely superb in both pieces: the digital remastering undoubtedly clarifies and cleans the texture, though there is a less glowing aura about the sound above the stave.

On the Classics for Pleasure label, Tasmin Little in her first concerto recording offers a bargain version that fully matches top-price rivals, and is more generously coupled too. If Chung finds more fantasy in this concerto and Midori is more fierily volatile, Little brings to it an open freshness and sweetness, very apt for this composer, that are equally winning. The firm richness of her sound, totally secure on intonation up to the topmost register, goes with an unflustered ease of manner and, unlike the American recordings for Chung and Midori, this one brings little or no spotlighting of the soloist. She establishes her place firmly with full-ranging, well-balanced sound that co-ordinates the soloist along with the orchestra. She is particularly successful in the finale where, at a speed between Midori's and Chung's, she plays the syncopations of the dance-like main theme with a happy lilt that yet has no hint of rushing.

Midori, still in her teens, gives an astonishing display not merely of virtuosity but of artistic maturity. From the similarities with Perlman's version, not least over tempo, one might have guessed that she too has been guided by the great New York teacher, Dorothy DeLay. Yet, even more than Perlman, Midori finds a vein of tenderness, using a wider range of tone-colour and dynamic; and the finale, at a speed even faster than Perlman's, becomes a bitingly brilliant Slavonic dance, with the passage-work only occasionally showing signs of haste. A most exciting performance. The *Romance* too finds Midori a deeply sympathetic Dvořákian; but collectors should not be swayed too much by the presence of the extra item, the *Carnaval overture*, for the sound is coarse, with brass over-prominent. The recording for the main items is warm and undistracting, if not ideally well defined.

In his Philips recording, Accardo is beautifully natural and unforced, with eloquent playing from both soloist and orchestra. Shlomo Mintz and Levine are similarly paired, but they are at full price and Accardo is equally poised and more relaxed. The engineering is altogether excellent, and in a competitive field this must rank high, especially at mid-price.

Suk's earlier performance is back in the catalogue at bargain price, effectively remastered, recoupled with the Suk *Fantasy*. Its lyrical eloquence is endearing, the work is played in the simplest possible way and Ančerl accompanies glowingly.

There is dazzling playing from Schlomo Mintz, whose virtuosity is effortless and his intonation astonishingly true. There is good rapport between soloist and conductor, and the performance has the sense of joy and relaxation that this radiant score needs. The digital sound is warmer and more natural in its upper range than the remastered EMI recording.

In Nature's realm, overture, Op. 91.
(*) Ph. Dig. 420 607-2 (2) [id.]. Concg. O, Dorati – SMETANA: *Má Vlast.*(*)

An ungenerous coupling for *Má Vlast* (there is no reason why the complete triptych,

Opp. 91–3, could not have been offered). Dorati's performance is excitingly direct and very well played and recorded.

Romance, Op. 11.
*** Ph. Dig. 420 168-2 [id.]. Zukerman, St Paul CO – BEETHOVEN: *Romances*; SCHUBERT: *Konzertstücke* etc.***

Zukerman gives a simple, heartwarming performance of this beguiling work within a most attractive concert of short pieces for violin and orchestra, and he is beautifully recorded.

Rondo in G min., Op. 94.
*** ASV Dig. CDRPO 8012 [id.]. Tortelier, RPO, Groves – ELGAR: *Concerto***(*); TCHAIKOVSKY: *Rococo variations.****

The Dvořák *Rondo* is one of Tortelier's party-pieces, and its point and humour are beautifully caught here.

Serenade for strings in E, Op. 22.
*** DG Dig. 400 038-2 [id.]. BPO, Karajan – TCHAIKOVSKY: *String serenade.****
(M) **(*) Ph. 420 883-2. ECO, Leppard – TCHAIKOVSKY: *String serenade.***(*)
(M) ** Decca 417 736-2 [id.]. ASMF, Marriner – TCHAIKOVSKY: *String serenade***(*) (with SIBELIUS: *Valse triste***).
(M) *(*) DG Dig. 429 488-2 [id.]. Orpheus CO – ELGAR: *Serenade *(*); TCHAIKOVSKY: *Serenade.***

Serenade for strings, Op. 22; Romance, Op. 11.
(B) *** Pickwick Dig. PCD 928. Laredo, SCO, Laredo – WAGNER: *Siegfried idyll.****

Serenade for strings, Op. 22; Serenade for wind in D min., Op. 44.
*** ASV Dig. CDCOE 801 [id.]. COE, Alexander Schneider.
*** Ph. 400 020-2 [id.]. ASMF, Marriner.
*** Decca Dig. 417 452-2 [id.]. LPO, Hogwood.

Serenade for strings, Op. 22; Slavonic dances Nos. 9–16, Op. 72/1–8.
(BB) **(*) LaserLight Dig. 15 605 [id.]. Berlin CO, Peter Wohlert.

The young players of the Chamber Orchestra of Europe give winningly warm and fresh performances of Dvořák's *Serenades*. The distinction of the wind soloists in this fine orchestra has been demonstrated many times on disc, and the *Wind serenade* brings a particularly distinguished performance. Schneider's approach in the *String serenade* is no less persuasive, with the COE string players producing beautifully refined playing, vividly caught in the ASV recording.

The earlier Marriner version is coupled with the Tchaikovsky and also includes Sibelius's *Valse triste* as a lollipop encore. With its rather mannered opening, it was not numbered among Marriner's vintage ASMF performances. It dates from 1970 and the originally excellent recording has suffered from its digital remastering – the violin timbre now sounds excessively thin on CD. The later, Philips performance is far preferable, more direct without loss of warmth, with speeds ideally chosen and refined, yet spontaneous-sounding and consistently resilient string playing. It still remains very competitive; in the *Wind serenade* the Academy are comparably stylish, with beautifully sprung rhythms, and the recording has a fine sense of immediacy.

A fresh, bright and spring-like account of both works from Hogwood and the LPO in clean, slightly recessed sound. Textually this version of the *String serenade* is unique on record when it uses the original score, newly published, in which two sections (one of 34 bars in the scherzo and the other of 79 bars in the finale), missing in the normal printed edition, are now included. Though these performances are not quite as winning or as rhythmically subtle as those of Schneider or Marriner, they are still very enjoyable, and the inclusion of the extra material brings added interest.

Karajan's digital version of the *String serenade* is given a recording of striking finesse. Karajan's approach is warmly affectionate in the opening movement and there is greater expressive weight than with Marriner, with the colouring darker. Yet the playing is both sympathetic and very polished; though the focus is slightly more diffuse and less firm in the bass than the Tchaikovsky coupling, many will feel that the softer delineation suits the music.

Laredo's performance of Dvořák's lovely *Serenade* is volatile, full of spontaneous lyrical feeling. The SCO strings play beautifully, and their bright rich tone above the stave adds to the feeling of freshness. The recording, made in City Hall, Glasgow, is admirably balanced to give a true concert-hall effect and add ambient lustre to the string timbre. As an encore Laredo takes the solo role in the *F minor Romance*, which he plays with appealing simplicity.

Although the same artists are credited for both recordings on the LaserLight disc, the effect is entirely different. The *Serenade* is played simply and gracefully by a small body of strings. Wohlert's tempi are well chosen and the acoustic is both fresh and warm. For the *Slavonic dances* a larger group is used and the recording is more resonant, with the bass fairly weighty. But the playing itself is never heavy, and there are some felicitous woodwind solos. Peter Wohlert is again very sympathetic, his pacing and feeling for rubato find the music's Czech spirit. Some may want less reverberation, but otherwise the digital sound is well defined, with plenty of bloom on the wind and strings alike.

The reissue of Leppard's fine Philips ECO recording from the late 1970s is welcome at mid-price. The remastering has taken away a little (but not much) of the bloom on the violins above the stave. Leppard is more robust than Marriner, and the tempi of his allegros have a strong momentum, but the natural flexibility of the playing prevents the brisk manner from losing its resilience. The finale is strikingly fresh and invigorating, making this a good mid-price recommendation.

The Orpheus Chamber Orchestra starts with a disconcertingly limp and wayward account of the first movement at a very slow speed, and elsewhere, though the playing is refined, there is little feeling of the bright folk element. Good, clean recording.

Serenade for wind, Op. 44.
*** CRD CRD 3410 [id.]. Nash Ens. – KROMMER: *Octet-Partita.****
** HM Orfeo Dig. C 051831A [id.]. Munich Wind Ac., Brezina – GOUNOD: *Petite symphonie.***

The Nash Ensemble can hold their own with the competition in the *D minor Serenade*, and their special claim tends to be the coupling, a Krommer rarity that is well worth hearing. The CRD version of the Dvořák is very well recorded and the playing is very fine indeed, robust yet sensitive to colour, and admirably spirited.

The sumptuously weighty ensemble of the Munich players at the opening of Dvořák's first movement sets the scene for a performance that is essentially robust, yet very well played. The recording (made in St Stephen's Church, Munich) is amply textured throughout, yet detail is not clouded and there is individuality and character in the solo playing. The CD brings fine presence, but is short on playing time – there would have been plenty of room for another piece alongside the Gounod coupling.

Slavonic dances Nos. 1–8, Op. 46; 9–16, Op. 72.
*** BIS Dig. CD 425 [id.]. Rheinland-Pfalz State PO, Leif Segerstam.
(M) *** DG 419 056-2 [id.]. Bav. RSO, Kubelik.
(M) **(*) Decca Dig. 411 749-2 [id.]. RPO, Dorati.
(M) **(*) Sup. Dig. SUP 000812 [id.]. Czech PO, Neumann.
**(*) Chan. Dig. CHAN 8406 [id.]. SNO, Järvi.

Slavonic dances Nos. 1–16, Opp. 46 & 72; Carnaval overture, Op. 92.
(B) ** Pickwick DUET 2CD (2). Cleveland O, Szell.

Anyone looking for a first-class modern digital recording of the complete *Slavonic dances* could be well satisfied with this BIS collection. The sound is full and vivid, the orchestral playing does not lack imaginative touches, and Segerstam's approach is suitably volatile and with plenty of lyrical exuberance, while the opening *Furiant* readily demonstrates the zest of the music-making. There is delicacy of rhythm and colour from both strings and woodwind. Generally speaking, this would seem to be a 'best buy' for this repertoire, though Kubelik's 1975 analogue set with the Bavarian Radio Symphony Orchestra offers strong competition at mid-price.

Kubelik's *Slavonic dances* are long admired; the recording dates from 1975 and is of excellent quality. The orchestral playing is first rate and the performances are infectiously full of flair. Kubelik is a natural Dvořákian and his feeling for the subtlety and rubato of this music is always attractive, especially so in the second set, where Dvořák's ideas are often particularly imaginative. The sound (as with other DG Bavarian recordings made at this time) is a little dry in the bass, but the middle response is full and there is no shrillness on top.

Dorati's performances have characteristic brio, the RPO response is warmly lyrical when necessary, and the woodwind playing gives much pleasure. Sparkle is the keynote and there is no lack of spontaneity. The Kingsway Hall venue with its natural resonance seems to have offered more problems than usual, and on CD the louder tuttis are not as sweet in the upper range of the strings as one would expect. However, the digital sound is generally superior to Kubelik's DG alternative.

Neumann's Supraphon set was recorded in the House of Artists, Prague. The *Dances* are very well played, with much felicitous detail from the Czech orchestra, who clearly have not grown tired of this engaging music. The recording is clear and naturally balanced, with no artificial digital brightness; it is also a little dry at the lower end. But the alert vivacity of the music-making is winning.

Järvi has the measure of this repertoire and secures brilliant and responsive playing from the SNO. The recording, made in the SNO Centre, Glasgow, has the orchestra set back in an acoustic of believable depth, but the upper strings are brightly lit and fortissimos bring some loss of body and a degree of hardness on top, so that after a while the ear tends to tire.

It is good to have Szell's performances – famous for their orchestral exuberance – back in the catalogue. But the layout on a pair of bargain-price CDs, with only the *Carnaval overture* added, gives an overall playing time of only 84 minutes, which almost nullifies the low price! However, the orchestral playing has tremendous bravura and polish, to say nothing of absolute unanimity of attack and ensemble. Szell's rubato is most skilfully managed to entice the ear, and the bright Cleveland sound suits the extrovert style.

Slavonic dances Nos. 1, 3, 8, 9–10.
(B) **(*) Decca 417 696-2. VPO, Reiner – BRAHMS: *Hungarian dances.***(*)

Reiner's way with Dvořák's dance music is indulgent but has plenty of sparkle, and the Vienna Philharmonic are clearly enjoying themselves; any reservations about the conductor's idiosyncrasies are soon forgotten in the pleasure of listening to such colourful music so vivaciously and spontaneously played. This much-reissued compilation now reappears in a good transfer on Decca's Weekend series; it shows its age very slightly in the upper range.

Symphonies Nos. 1–9; Carnaval overture; Scherzo capriccioso; The Wood Dove, Op. 110.
(M) **(*) DG 423 120-2 (6). BPO, Kubelik.

Kubelik's set has much to recommend it: first and foremost the glorious playing of the Berlin Philharmonic and the natural warmth that Kubelik brings to his music-making. He seems less convinced by the earliest symphonies than Järvi and in No. 3 he sounds almost routine by the side of the Chandos recording. In spite of some idiosyncratic but not unidiomatic touches, however, he achieves glowing performances of Nos. 6–9. At mid-price this remains a desirable set; the bonus items are all well played and recorded and are equally idiomatic.

Symphony No. 1 in C min. (The Bells of Zlonice), Op. 3; The Hero's song, Op. 111.
*** Chan. Dig. CHAN 8597 [id.]. SNO, Järvi.

The first of Dvořák's nine symphonies is on the long-winded side. Dvořák never had a chance to revise it, which he certainly would have done, had the score not been lost for over half a century. Yet whatever its structural weaknesses, it is full of colourful and memorable ideas, often characteristic of the mature composer. Järvi directs a warm, often impetuous performance, with rhythms invigoratingly sprung in the fast movements and with the slow movement more persuasive than in previous recordings. Tense and energetic as the SNO performance remains throughout the last two movements, there are some signs of the ensemble growing slacker. The real rarity here is *The Hero's song*, Dvořák's very last orchestral work. It has no specific programme, though the journey from darkness to light in the unspecified hero's life is established clearly enough. Järvi's strongly committed, red-blooded performance minimizes any weaknesses. The recording, warmly atmospheric in typical Chandos style, is among the best in this series, not always clean on detail but firmly focused.

Symphony No. 2 in B flat, Op. 4; Slavonic rhapsody No. 3 in A flat, Op. 45.
**(*) Chan. Dig. CHAN 8589 [id.]. SNO, Järvi.

Järvi directs a characteristically warm and urgent performance of this exuberant inspiration of the 24-year-old composer. A jubilant work, it is by far the longest symphony Dvořák ever wrote, and was originally longer still, before the composer revised it. Unfortunately, the Chandos sound, characteristically reverberant but washier than usual, misses the necessary sharpness. The tangy Czech flavour of the music loses some of its bite, and the results are often too smooth; one might easily miss even the entry of the second subject. The generous fill-up, the *Slavonic rhapsody No. 3*, is done with delicious point and humour, and with sound back to Chandos's normally high standard.

Symphony No. 3 in E flat, Op. 10; Carnaval overture; Scherzo capriccioso.
*** Virgin Dig. VC 790797-2 [id.]. Royal Liverpool PO, Pešek.

Symphony No. 3 in E flat, Op. 10; Carnaval overture, Op. 92; Symphonic variations, Op. 78.
*** Chan. Dig. CHAN 8575 [id.]. SNO, Järvi.

This was the first of Dvořák's symphonies to show the full exuberance of his genius. The music certainly betrays the influence of Wagner, but nowhere do the Wagnerian ideas really conceal the essential Dvořák. Pešek's strong, direct manner in Dvořák here works to bring out the rhythmic freshness of the writing in a most persuasive reading. Pešek gives a radiant account of the lovely second subject and is masterly in controlling the long development section. He has similar concentration in sustaining a very slow speed for the central *Adagio*, keeping it clean and taut, where Järvi, much faster, sounds relatively unsettled. The clarity of the recording, beautifully set against a believable acoustic, adds to the rhythmic freshness, not least in Pešek's urgent performance of the finale. He is warmly sympathetic as well in his account of the *Scherzo capriccioso*, in which he observes the central repeat.

Järvi's is a highly persuasive reading, not ideally sharp of rhythm in the first movement but totally sympathetic. His account of the *Adagio* blossoms, and the finale effectively combines energy with weight. The recording is well up to the standards of the house and the fill-ups are particularly generous, with an exhilarating performance of *Carnaval* followed by a strongly characterized set of variations, with a rich, lyrical emphasis.

Symphony No. 4 in D min., Op. 13; (i) *Biblical songs, Op. 99.*
*** Chan. Dig. CHAN 8608 [id.]. SNO, Järvi, (i) with Brian Rayner-Cook.

Järvi's affectionate reading of this early work brings out the Czech flavours in Dvořák's inspiration and makes light of the continuing Wagner influences, notably the echoes of *Tannhäuser* in the slow movement. Allowing himself ample rubato, Järvi completely avoids any *Tannhäuser*-like squareness and, in the bold march-time trio of the *Scherzo* with its jangling cymbal and triangle, edges away from vulgarity in his persuasive rhythmic pointing, as well as giving a delectable swagger to the *Allegro feroce* main section. This is a performance to win converts to a work often underrated. The generous coupling has Brian Rayner-Cook giving positive and clean-cut, if not very Slavonic-sounding, performances of the ten *Biblical songs* which Dvořák wrote in America at the same period as the *Cello concerto*. The recording is well up to the Chandos standard.

Symphonies Nos. 4 in D min., Op. 13; 8 in G, Op. 33.
(BB) **(*) Naxos Dig. 8.550269 [id.]. Slovak PO, Stephen Gunzenhauser.

Gunzenhauser's *Fourth* is very convincing. In his hands the fine lyrical theme of the first movement certainly blossoms and the relative lack of weight in the orchestral textures brings distinct benefit in the Scherzo, where the outer sections are rhythmically buoyant and the forceful centrepiece has an infectious vigour without crudeness. The slow movement, too, is lyrical without too much Wagnerian emphasis and the rhythmically repetitive finale avoids heaviness. The naturally sympathetic orchestral playing helps to make the *Eighth* a refreshing experience, even though the first two movements are rather relaxed and without the impetus of the finest versions. The digital sound is excellent, vivid and full, with a natural concert-hall ambience.

Symphony No. 5 in F, Op. 76; Othello overture, Op. 93; Scherzo capriccioso, Op. 66.
⊛ *** EMI Dig. CDC7 49995-2 [id.]. Oslo PO, Jansons.

Symphony No. 5 in F, Op. 75; The Water Goblin, Op. 107.
*** Chan. Dig. CHAN 8552 [id.]. SNO, Järvi.

Jansons directs a delectable account of this radiant symphony, drawing the most affectionate playing from his Oslo orchestra. The pastoral opening, with its theme for two clarinets over shimmering strings, has never been done more subtly or relaxedly on record, leading on to a performance both warmly lyrical and highly dramatic. More than in previous recordings, the EMI engineers here put a bloom on the Oslo sound, apparently having overcome the acoustic problems of the Oslo Konzerthus, where the recordings are made. This is just as persuasive a reading in all four movements as Järvi's on Chandos, but the playing is consistently more refined. The finale in particular is far more telling, with the minor mode of the opening vigorously pressed home to make the astonishingly belated arrival of the home key of F major all the more exhilarating. Then at last the main theme bursts out in glory, superbly realized here. Jansons, unlike his rivals, omits the exposition repeat in the first movement, which is a pity, but there is ample evidence that Dvořák inclined against having those conventional repeats. The *Scherzo capriccioso* brings another exuberant performance, with the central *Poco tranquillo* lovingly drawn out. The superb *Othello overture* makes up a very generous coupling.

Neeme Järvi and the Scottish National Orchestra present the pastoral opening of Dvořák's *F major Symphony* with an airy beauty never matched on record before. The reverberant Chandos recording adds to the open-air feeling of this shimmering nature music, also adding warmth to the robust ideas which quickly follow. Järvi is most effective in moulding the structure, subtly varying tempo between sections to smooth over the often abrupt links. His persuasiveness in the slow movement, relaxed but never sentimental, brings radiant playing from the SNO, and Czech dance-rhythms are sprung most infectiously, leading to an exhilarating close to the whole work, simulating the excitement of a live performance. The fill-up is unusual and colourful, a piece based on a gruesome little fairy-story full of sharp dramatic contrasts. It is a highly rewarding piece and a substantial bonus when the advocacy is so strong.

Symphonies Nos. 5 in F, Op. 76; 7 in D min., Op. 70.
(BB) *** Naxos Dig. 8.550270 [id.]. Slovak PO, Stephen Gunzenhauser.

Gunzenhauser's coupling, the finest so far of his super-bargain Naxos series, is recommendable even without the price advantage. Both symphonies are very well played and truthfully recorded within a convincing concert-hall acoustic. The beguiling opening of the *Fifth*, with its engaging Slovak wind solos, has plenty of atmosphere, and the reading generates a natural lyrical impulse. The *Seventh* has something in common with Païta's famous version, spontaneous throughout and with an eloquent *Poco adagio*, a lilting scherzo, and a finale that combines an expansive secondary theme with plenty of excitement and impetus.

Symphony No. 5 in F; Czech suite, Op. 39.
**(*) Virgin Dig. VC 790769-2 [id.]. Czech PO, Pešek.

Pešek's version is characteristically fresh and direct, markedly cooler than Jansons' or Järvi's, but consistent with the rest of his cycle, crisp and clean-cut. The recording, rather distant but refined, adds to the coolness but, with native Czechs performing, there is plenty of power as well as authenticity. The coupling is particularly apt with its five folk-based movements, their pastoral mood linking with what was once the nickname of the *F major Symphony*.

Symphony No. 6 in D, Op. 60; The Noon Witch, Op. 108.
*** Chan. Dig. CHAN 8530 [id.]. SNO, Järvi.

Symphony No. 6; Overture, In nature's realm, Op. 91.
** Virgin Dig. VC 790791-2 [id.]. Czech PO, Pešek.

Järvi and the Scottish National Orchestra give a wonderfully sympathetic reading of Dvořák's *Sixth*, underlining the direct links with Brahms's *Second Symphony*, notably at the start of the first and fourth movements. The big grandioso sunburst when the first theme opens out is superbly presented, with Järvi moulding the tempo naturally and without mannerism. The bloom on the Chandos sound adds to the lyrical warmth and sweetness of the slow movement, ripely and relaxedly done but without self-indulgence. The *Furiant*, rhythmically sprung like a jolly dance, leads to a finale taken challengingly fast but with lifted rhythms too, and with sharp contrasts of mood. In the fill-up, Järvi brings out the programmatic story-telling of the piece, with tremolo strings breathtakingly delicate on the entry of the witch. The recording is in the demonstration bracket.

Pešek takes a slow and relaxed view of the first movement, which should have brought out the sunshine in this happy D major movement, with its clear echoes of Brahms's *Second*, also in D. Unfortunately, with less body to the sound than the music needs – a question of recording, rather edgy and bright, not full enough – the result lacks the dramatic tension of the finest versions. This is more like a refined run-through, hardly a match for the finest in Pešek's Dvořák series for Virgin. He omits the exposition repeat in observance of a note that the composer put on the autograph after an early performance.

Symphonies Nos. 7–9 (New World).
*** Decca Dig. 421 082-2 (2) [id.]. Cleveland O, Dohnányi.

By placing the last three symphonies on a pair of CDs, Decca in effect offer these splendid Dohnányi performances at 'mid-price', so perhaps it seems churlish to complain that with Nos. 7 and 8 coupled on the first disc (72 minutes 48 seconds) there was room on the second – which offers only the *New World*, and without the first-movement exposition repeat (barely 40 minutes) – for the *Scherzo capriccioso* (originally coupled with No. 8). Nevertheless these are all among the finest available CD versions – see below – and with top-drawer Decca sound this is an excellent way of acquiring these works as economically as possible on compact disc.

Symphony No. 7 in D min., Op. 70.
*** Decca Dig. 417 564-2 [id.]. Cleveland O, Dohnányi.

Symphony No. 7; The Golden spinning wheel, Op. 109.
*** Chan. Dig. CHAN 8501 [id.]. SNO, Järvi.

Symphony No. 7; My home overture, Op. 62.
**(*) Telarc Dig. CD 80173 [id.]. LAPO, Previn.

We have long praised Carlos Païta's outstanding, inspirational version of Dvořák's *D minor Symphony*, a reading of striking lyrical ardour, matching excitement with warmth. This music-making has the kind of spontaneity one experiences only at the most memorable of live performances, helped by a natural concert-hall balance and the strikingly wide dynamic range of the CD format. However, Païta has his own label; this record has become increasingly difficult (and expensive) to obtain and is only intermittently available (Lodia LOD-CD 782).

Although Dohnányi's fine Decca Cleveland performance also stands out, the CD is distinctly short measure (36 minutes), and it is better approached in conjunction with the two other late symphonies, offered complete on a pair of CDs – see above. The performance, if not quite as gripping as Païta's, is still an extremely fine one. Tempi are all aptly judged, and while the work's Brahmsian inheritance is acknowledged in the slow movement, the lighter Dvořákian lyrical flavour is dominant, notably in the nicely sprung scherzo, liltingly articulated and rhythmically infectious. The outer movements are strong, with the exciting climaxes. The Decca recording is first rate, brilliant yet with a convincing concert-hall ambience.

Järvi's Chandos version is just a little plain-spun. He secures playing of considerable lyrical ardour from his excellent SNO players, but the articulation of the scherzo misses out that engaging 'comma' which is an essential part of the presentation of the main idea. However, it would be wrong to make too much of this; Chandos offer a very substantial bonus in including one of Dvořák's most memorable symphonic poems. Järvi's account has plenty of drama and atmosphere. The CD brings a fine bloom to a warmly resonant orchestral sound-image.

Previn directs a tautly rhythmic account of the *Seventh*. The opening could be more mysterious, but the toughness of argument is immediately clear, bringing out the symphonic cohesion. The slow movement is warmly done, with fine horn solos; but some of the lightness of the last two movements is lost. *My home*, a welcome but none-too-generous fill-up, is also given emphatic treatment. The recording is first rate, with good detail, the timpani dramatically prominent; but the high violins sound edgy under pressure, losing their bloom.

Symphonies Nos. 7 in D min., Op. 70; 8 in G, Op. 88.
*** Virgin Dig. VC 790756-2 [id.]. Royal Liverpool PO, Pešek.
(M) *** Ph. 420 890-2 [id.]. Concg. O, C. Davis.
** EMI Dig. CDC7 49948-2 [id.]. Phd. O, Sawallisch.

It makes a generous coupling in Pešek's Dvořák series to have both Nos. 7 and 8 on a single disc, the more welcome when these are among the most refreshing of his recordings yet. The opening of the *D minor*, the darkest of the cycle, may lack the ominous and mysterious atmosphere of some performances, but the fresh, direct manner relates it readily to other Dvořák. The slow movement is warm and relaxed, and the scherzo becomes a happy folk-like dance, despite the minor key, while Pešek's speed in the finale also allows him to give a lift to the stamping dance-rhythms. No. 8 receives a similarly refreshing performance, persuasive in a light, relaxed way, with the folk element again brought out, above all in the middle movements. The scherzo is liltingly light; and again the performance benefits from the full, clear sound.

The coupling of Sir Colin Davis's analogue recordings of the *D minor* and *G major Symphonies* makes an outstanding bargain. The recordings (from 1975 and 1978 respectively) have been remastered most successfully: there is very little loss to the body of the string timbre (indeed in the *Allegretto grazioso* third movement of No. 8 the violins sound engagingly fresh) and the Concertgebouw ambience casts a warm glow on woodwind and horns, while detail is cleaner, with the bass firm. Davis's performances, with their bracing rhythmic flow and natural feeling for Dvořákian lyricism, are appealingly direct, yet have plenty of life and urgency. In the famous scherzo of No. 7, with its striking cross-rhythms, he marks the sforzandos more sharply than usual, keeping rhythms very exact. The *Adagio* of No. 8 is hardly less eloquent, and there is an engagingly zestful exuberance in the outer movements.

After Sawallisch's honeyed account of the *New World*, also recorded with the Philharmonia Orchestra, it is disappointing to find that the playing this time is not so easily spontaneous-sounding, particularly in No. 7. Sawallisch gives thoughtful, sympathetic readings of both symphonies, but the glow of enjoyment is less obvious here, even in No. 8. Additionally, the sound presents the violins with an edge in loud tuttis which is very un-Philadelphian.

Symphony No. 8 in G, Op. 88.
(B) *** CBS MYK 44872 [id.]. Columbia SO, Bruno Walter – WAGNER: *Parsifal* excerpts.***
(M) *** Trax TRXCD 127. Sydney SO, Serebrier – BEETHOVEN: *Symphony No. 8.****
(M) (***) EMI mono CDM7 63399-2 [id.]. RPO, Beecham – SIBELIUS: *Symphony No. 2.(***)*
(M) *(**) Decca 417 744-2 [id.]. VPO, Karajan – BRAHMS: *Symphony No. 3.***

(i) *Symphony No. 8 in G, Op. 88;* (ii) *Carnaval overture, Op. 92.*
(B) **(*) ASV Dig. CDQS 6006 [id.]. (i) Royal Liverpool PO; (ii) LPO; Bátiz.

Symphony No. 8 in G, Op. 88. Carnaval overture; The wood dove, Op. 110.
(B) *** DG 429 518-2 [id.]. BPO or Bav. RSO, Kubelik.

Symphony No. 8 in G, Op. 88; Nocturne for strings, Op. 40.
**(*) Chan. Dig. CHAN 8323 [id.]. LPO, Handley.

Symphony No. 8 in G, Op. 88; Scherzo capriccioso, Op. 66.
*** Decca Dig. 414 422-2 [id.]. Cleveland O, Dohnányi.

Symphony No. 8 in G, Op. 88; Scherzo capriccioso; Notturno for strings.
*** Telarc Dig. CD 80206 [id.]. LAPO, Previn.

Symphony No. 8 in G, Op. 88; The Wood dove, Op. 110.
*** Chan. Dig. CHAN 8666 [id.]. SNO, Järvi.

Previn and the Los Angeles Philharmonic give a delectable performance of the *Eighth*. Warmth and freshness go with the finest recorded sound yet achieved with this orchestra in Royce Hall, full and with a vivid sense of presence that allows fine inner clarity. Characteristically, Previn's Dvořák style is sharply rhythmic, and his idiomatic use of rubato brings affectionate moulding of phrase and rhythm, generally kept within a steady pulse. The tenderness that Previn brings to the delicate second subject is a fine instance, and the delectable counter-theme in the slow movement with its descending demisemiquaver scales has rarely been so lightly done. The natural lilt of the first contrasting episode in the scherzo is also a delight, with Previn providing an exuberant pay-off in the *furiant* coda to that movement. Previn's fill-up is equally attractive, with the infectiously sprung account of the *Scherzo capriccioso* scarcely harmed by the omission of the central repeat.

Järvi's highly sympathetic account of the *Eighth* underlines the expressive lyricism of the piece, the rhapsodic freedom of invention rather than any symphonic tautness, with the SNO players reacting to his free rubato and affectionate moulding of phrase with collective spontaneity. Ensemble is excellent, and speeds are never eccentric. The finale is marginally slower than usual, but the changes of mood are made to sound easy and natural. *The Wood dove* makes a good if not generous fill-up, atmospherically telling. The warm Chandos sound has plenty of bloom, with detail kept clear, and is very well balanced.

Kubelik's *Eighth* is appealingly direct and without idiosyncrasy, except for a minor indulgence in the phrasing of the richly contoured string theme in the trio of the scherzo. The polished, responsive playing of the Berlin Philharmonic adds to the joy and refinement of the performance. The Bavarian Radio Orchestra provide the substantial encores, which are splendidly done. This is well worth considering in DG's bargain range:

the 1966 sound is bright and clear, if a little dry; the *Overture* and *Symphonic poem*, which were recorded a decade later, are only slightly more atmospheric.

Walter's famous account of Dvořák's *Eighth* was recorded in 1962, just before he died. It is a strong yet superbly lyrical reading; but the overall lyricism never takes the place of virility and Walter's mellowness is most effective in the *Adagio*. His pacing is uncontroversial until the finale, which is steadier than usual, more symphonic, although never heavy. The sound was always warm and full but now is more naturally clear, the focus of all sections of the orchestra firmer, with upper strings sweet and the violas, cellos and basses expansively resonant. With its equally inspired coupling of the *Prelude and Good Friday music* from *Parsifal*, this bargain-priced issue ranks high in the CBS legacy.

Dohnányi's performance is attractively alive and spontaneous, although it includes a few self-conscious nudgings here and there. But the playing of the Cleveland Orchestra is so responsive that the overall impression is one of freshness. The coupling with the *Scherzo capriccioso* is apt, when the performance finds an affinity with the *Symphony* in bringing out the Slavonic dance sparkle and moulding the lyrical secondary theme with comparable affectionate flair. The recording is in the demonstration class. The layout of the orchestra is convincingly natural, the internal definition achieved without any kind of digital edge.

Serebrier's first movement is exciting and well paced, and he has the measure of the *Adagio*, balancing lyricism with drama. His scherzo, too, has a lilting rhythmic impetus, and the finale develops plenty of exuberance. The recording is bright, well balanced and full, though less amply resonant than its Beethoven coupling.

Beecham always got rousing results, and this is an infectiously spirited and rumbustious performance, but full of glowing Dvořákian lyricism. The 'live' recording comes from 1959 and the Royal Festival Hall acoustics bring a somewhat dry ambience, with a bright sheen on the strings and a less than ideal balance for the brass – the trumpet fanfare in the finale is much too close and tuttis can be a bit fierce. Nevertheless the sound is fully acceptable and every bar of the music is alive.

With exceptionally full and brilliant sound, Handley's Chandos version makes a strong, fresh impact. The manner is direct, with the opening relatively straight, not eased in. Though some will miss a measure of charm, the life and spontaneity of the reading are most winning, with the CD brightly vivid and with good inner clarity. The *Nocturne* makes a most agreeable bonus and is beautifully played.

Karajan's 1965 Decca version of Dvořák's *Eighth* has far more charisma than his most recent digital version with the same orchestra. There are moments of indulgence from Karajan in the scherzo, but this too stems from affection and, overall, this is a most winning performance, blending polish and spontaneity. The vintage analogue recording was full and fresh and well detailed; the digital remastering has brightened the strings above the stave to the point of fierceness and some of the amplitude has been lost.

An excellent digital bargain CD comes from Bátiz with consistently spirited playing from the Royal Liverpool Philharmonic Orchestra. The reading is direct, responsive and structurally sound and enjoyable in its easy spontaneity. The recording is vivid, yet does not lack warmth, although there is a touch of fierceness on climaxes. The overture is slightly less successful, but this is certainly good value.

Symphonies Nos. 8; 9 (New World).
*** Lodia Dig. LO-CD 789 [id.]. RPO, Païta.

Païta's generous coupling of Dvořák's two most popular symphonies brings a thrustful new version of No. 8 and an equally positive and fiery account of the *New World*, marked by extreme speeds, slow as well as fast. The full-bodied, larger-than-life recording has a vivid sense of presence, enhancing the dramatic impact of performances which – to judge by the occasional flaw in ensemble – were done in long takes, adding to the sense of spontaneity. The RPO string playing is particularly beautiful in the *Largo* slow movement of the *New World*, taken very slowly but steadily too. Only in the main *Allegro con fuoco* of the finale does Païta's fondness for fast speeds lose some of the music's weight and breadth. But those who have enjoyed Païta's *Seventh Symphony* will find that these performances have much in common with that, even if the balance is less natural in its simulation of the concert hall.

Symphony No. 9 in E min. (From the New World), Op. 95.
*** Decca Dig. 400 047-2 [id.]. VPO, Kondrashin.
*** Decca Dig. 414 421-2 [id.]. Cleveland O, Dohnányi.
(B) *** DG 429 676-2 [id.]. BPO, Karajan – SCHUBERT: *Symphony No. 8.****
(M) **(*) EMI CDM7 69005-2 [id.]. BPO, Karajan – SMETANA: *Vltava.****
(B) **(*) Decca 417 678-2. VPO, Kertesz – SMETANA: *Vltava.***(*)
(M) **(*) DG 423 384-2 [id.]. BPO, Fricsay – LISZT: *Les Préludes***(*); SMETANA: *Vltava.****
** EMI Dig. CDC7 49860-2 [id.]. Oslo PO, Jansons (with SMETANA: *Vltava****).

Symphony No. 9 (New World); American suite, Op. 98b.
**(*) Virgin Dig. VC 790723-2 [id.]. Royal Liverpool PO, Pešek.

Symphony No. 9 (New World); Carnaval overture, Op. 92; Humoresque (arr. Foster).
(M) **(*) RCA GD 86530 (6530-2-RG]. Boston Pops O, Fiedler – ENESCU: *Rumanian rhapsody.***(*)

Symphony No. 9 (New World); Carnaval overture; Scherzo capriccioso, Op. 66.
(M) **(*) Decca 417 724-2 [id.]. LSO, Kertesz.
(B) **(*) EMI CDZ7 62514-2. Philh. O, Giulini.

Symphony No. 9 (New World); My home overture, Op. 62.
*** Chan. Dig. CHAN 8510 [id.]. SNO, Järvi.

(i) *Symphony No. 9 (New World);* (ii) *Scherzo capriccioso.*
(B) *** DG 427 202-2 [id.]. (i) BPO; (ii) Bav. RSO, Kubelik.

Symphony No. 9 (From the New World); Slavonic dances Nos. 1, 3 & 8, Op. 46.
(**) DG Dig. 427 346-2 [id.]. Israel PO, Bernstein.

(i) *Symphony No. 9 (New World);* (ii) *Symphonic variations, Op. 78.*
(B) *** CfP Dig. CD-CFP 9006. LPO, Macal.
(BB) **(*) Naxos Dig. 8.550271 [id.]. Slovak PO, Stephen Gunzenhauser.
(M) **(*) Ph. 420 349-2 [id.]. (i) Concg. O; (ii) LSO; C. Davis.

Dohnányi's *New World*, superbly played and recorded like the companion recordings of Nos. 7 and 8, should by rights be a first recommendation, but it falls down by failing to observe the first-movement exposition repeat. That said, there is much to praise in this grippingly spontaneous performance, generally direct and unmannered but glowing with warmth. In the first movement Dohnányi, without any stiffness, allows himself relatively little easing of tempo for the second and third subjects while the great cor anglais melody in the *Largo* and the big clarinet solo in the finale are both richly done, with the ripe and very well-balanced Decca recording adding to their opulence. The sound is spectacularly full and rich. However, without a coupling this is short measure and readers are referred to the Decca box, which includes his versions of the last three symphonies – see above.

Kondrashin's Vienna performance *does* include the exposition repeat, and the recording's impact remains quite remarkable although it was one of Decca's earliest CDs. Recorded in the Sofiensaal, the range of the sound is equalled by its depth; every detail of Dvořák's orchestration is revealed within a highly convincing perspective. Other performances may show a higher level of tension, but there is a natural spontaneity here, the cor anglais solo in the *Largo* is easy and songful, and the finale is especially satisfying, with the wide dynamic range adding drama and the refinement and transparency of the texture noticeably effective as the composer recalls ideas from earlier movements. This version is surely now due for reissue at mid-price.

Karajan's 1964 DG recording held a strong place in the catalogue for two decades, and it is certainly far preferable to his digital version. It has a powerful lyrical feeling and an exciting build-up of power in the outer movements. The *Largo* is played most beautifully, and Karajan's element of detachment lets the orchestra speak for itself, which it does, gloriously. The rustic qualities of the scherzo are affectionately brought out, and altogether this is very rewarding. The recording is full, bright and open. This is now reissued at bargain price, generously coupled with Schubert's *Unfinished*, as a sampler for DG's Karajan Symphony Edition.

Kubelik's marvellously fresh account of the *New World*, recorded in the early 1970s, has now been reissued on DG's bargain Privilege label in digitally remastered form, which has brought a firmer bass and slightly clearer detail. The coupling is a reading of comparable freshness of the *Scherzo capriccioso*, with much felicitous detail from the Bavarian orchestra. The performance of the *Symphony* is certainly among the finest; the *Largo* has a compelling lyrical beauty, with playing of great radiance from the Berlin Philharmonic. After a scherzo of striking character and a finale of comparable urgency, Kubelik then relaxes magically, when the composer recalls earlier themes as in a reverie.

Macal as a Czech takes a fresh and unsentimental view, with speeds far steadier than usual in the first movement. His inclusion of the repeat balances the structure convincingly. With idiomatic insights there is no feeling of rigidity, with the beauty of the slow movement purified, the scherzo crisp and energetic, set against pastoral freshness in the episodes, and the finale again strong and direct, bringing a ravishing clarinet solo. The *Symphonic variations*, which acts as coupling, is less distinctive, but well characterized. The digital recording is strikingly believable in its natural balance, with body as well as brilliance, and excellent definition. A fine bargain recommendation.

Järvi's opening introduction establishes the spaciousness of his view, with lyrical, persuasive phrasing and a very slow speed, leading into an allegro which starts relaxedly, but then develops in big dramatic contrasts. The expansiveness is underlined, when the exposition repeat is observed. The *Largo* too is exceptionally spacious, with the cor anglais player taxed to the limit but effectively supported over ravishingly beautiful string playing. The scherzo is lilting rather than fierce, and the finale is bold and swaggering. *My home* overture is also given an exuberant performance, bringing out the lilt of dance rhythms.

Among earlier analogue accounts Kertesz's LSO version stands out, with a most exciting first movement (exposition repeat included), in which the introduction of the second subject group is eased in with considerable subtlety; the *Largo* brings playing of hushed intensity to make one hear the music with new ears. Kertesz's exuberant *Carnaval overture* and his brilliant and lilting account of the *Scherzo capriccioso* are as attractive as any in the catalogue.

Karajan's 1977 *New World* for EMI is robust and spontaneous-sounding, but refined too, and the cor anglais solo of the *Largo* is fresh, at a nicely flowing tempo. The digital remastering has brightened the sound and given it excellent projection but, as usual with

EMI's remastered analogue recordings of this period, the bass is drier and the overall effect slightly less atmospheric than the original. As in the earlier, DG version, the first-movement exposition repeat is omitted.

Gunzenhauser's is a vibrantly exciting reading, helped by sound that is more present and brilliant than in the earlier issues in his Dvořák cycle. Indeed the climaxes of the first movement (exposition repeat included) have just a hint of stridency. But the impact of the performance is undeniable, particularly the finale, which moves forward with a consistently dramatic impetus. There is fine playing in the *Largo*, but this is not as melting as some versions. Where Gunzenhauser scores is in also offering a highly spontaneous account of Dvořák's engaging *Symphonic variations*, where the vivid orchestral response blows all the cobwebs off this underrated piece, full of the most attractive Dvořákian invention.

Kertesz's VPO recording dates from the beginning of the 1960s. It is a highly dramatic reading, made the more so by the unnaturally forward balance of the timpani – especially striking in the introduction; but in most other respects the vivid sound remains full-bodied and brilliant in its CD format. The performance is agreeably fresh, if not without its occasional idiosyncrasy; in general, Kertesz's later LSO version is preferable, with more appropriate couplings.

Ferenc Fricsay's style is somewhat old-fashioned, unashamedly romantic, including an affectionate and considerable *ritardando* at the entry of the first movement's secondary theme. The Berlin Philharmonic, on top form, are highly responsive and everything sounds spontaneous. The *Largo* is most beautiful and the finale is splendid, with a very exciting coda. The recording is generally brilliant in the digital remastering, although there is a degree of stridency in the fortissimo passages.

Giulini's EMI record was made when the Philharmonia was at its peak in 1962. The result has a refinement, coupled to an attractive directness, which for some will make it an ideal reading. The remastering gives the sound plenty of projection and, if the performance is not as physically exciting as with Fricsay, the playing, with its beautiful moulding of phrase, is very refreshing. With two attractive couplings (the lyrical side of the *Scherzo capriccioso* appealingly affectionate), this is a bargain on EMI's low-price Laser label.

Pešek's version, though very well played and impressively recorded, is just a little lacking in spontaneity and grip. It is enjoyable in its way – at its best in the Scherzo which has striking character, the Trio nicely relaxed – but elsewhere Pešek's mellowness produces a reading which could use a degree more adrenalin. The *American suite* also has clear influences from the *New World*; it is slight but charming music and is presented with a beguilingly affectionate touch.

Sir Colin Davis's very directness has its drawbacks. The cor anglais solo in the slow movement has an appealing simplicity, yet the effect is not very resilient, and later, when the horns echo the theme at the end of the opening section, the impression is positive rather than seductively nostalgic. The reading is completely free from egotistic eccentricity and, with beautiful orchestral playing throughout, this is satisfying in its way. The CD transfer is well managed, rich and full-bodied. The coupling, a first-class performance of the *Symphonic variations* – one of Dvořák's finest works, much underrated by the public – is very welcome and sounds fresh.

Arthur Fiedler's performance was recorded in 1959 and the sound is most naturally balanced and vivid, characteristic of RCA's early stereo techniques. The performance is satisfying in its direct simplicity, with responsive playing from every section of the orchestra, no interpretative eccentricities, and an attractively relaxed feeling, as if all the players were enjoying the music. Fiedler observes the first-movement exposition repeat, by no means an automatic procedure in the late 1950s, and his feeling for the work's structure is conveyed well. The dashing account of the *Carnaval overture* comes from 1964, and here the recording brightens and is slightly less natural in the matter of string timbre. After the very welcome Enesco *Rhapsody*, Fiedler provides an agreeable lollipop encore, Stephen Foster's outrageous arrangement of the *Humoresque*, intertwined with his own *Swanee River*.

Jansons offers a coupling much favoured over the years by Karajan, but Jansons' performance of the *New World* hardly matches that of the Smetana fill-up, which is characteristically full of vigour, warmth and fantasy. Jansons' direct view of the *Symphony* is rather undermined by recorded sound that is far from the best achieved in the admittedly difficult Oslo Concert House; the timpani in particular are disappointingly shallow-sounding and withdrawn. There are many points to praise in the reading, for example the breadth of the main theme in the finale, which becomes a quasi-patriotic march song, but in so competitive a field one needs more.

Bernstein's live recording with the Israel Philharmonic brings an extraordinary reading, the first ever on disc to break the 50-minute barrier for what usually comes nearer to being a 40-minute work. When Bernstein conveys such personal electricity, it makes for a fascinating experience heard once, but can hardly be recommended for a record likely to be played frequently. By contrast with the rest, after an astonishingly slow account of the *Largo* – 18½ minutes as against the more normal 12 – the scherzo is hectically fast, but is delightfully sprung in the contrasting episodes. As always, Bernstein compels attention, but the recording – better than most from this source – is inclined to be boomy in the bass, with some fuzzing in tuttis.

Symphony No. 9 in E min. (From the New World) (trans. Yamashita).
*** RCA Dig. RD 87929 [7929-2-RC]. Kazuhita Yamashita (guitar) (with STRAVINSKY: *Firebird suite****).

Kazuhita Yamashita is a young Japanese guitarist, still in his twenties. The present transcriptions (or 're-writings', as he calls them) of the *New World symphony* and the *Firebird* are extremely imaginative and resourceful, and he exhibits astonishing virtuosity and artistry in their execution. This is an amazing disc, compelling and gripping, and vividly recorded.

CHAMBER AND INSTRUMENTAL MUSIC

Flute sonatina in G min. (trans. Galway).
*** RCA Dig. RD 87802 [7802-2-RC]. James Galway, Phillip Moll – FELD; MARTINŮ: *Sonatas.****

What the flute version of Dvořák's *Sonatina* underlines more than the violin original is how close this tuneful, unpretentious piece, written for the composer's young children, is to the *New World symphony* of the same year, 1893. The skipping *Molto vivace* of the third movement emerges as almost an Irish jig, and similarly the finale might be inspired by the whistling of an errand-boy. Well recorded, with characterful performances and an unusual and attractive coupling of two modern Czech flute works, it makes an excellent recommendation for anyone wanting a Galway record out of the ordinary.

Piano quartets Nos. 1 in D, Op. 23; 2 in E flat, Op. 87.
⊛ *** Hyp. Dig. CDA 66287 [id.]. Domus.

The Dvořák *Piano quartets* are glorious pieces, and the playing of Domus is little short of inspired. This is real chamber-music-playing: intimate, unforced and distinguished by both vitality and sensitivity. As one would expect, the *E flat* is the more mature and concentrated piece, and the playing in the slow movement is quite magical. Domus are recorded in an ideal acoustic and in perfect perspective; they sound wonderfully alive and warm. An altogether outstanding chamber-music record.

Piano quartet No. 2 in E flat, Op. 87.
(*) RCA RD 86256 [RCA 6256-2-RC]. Rubinstein, Guarneri Qt – FAURÉ: *Piano quartet No. 1.*(*)

Rubinstein's recording, made in December 1970, is here enhanced and is now fuller than originally – though not especially transparent – and the close balance prevents a real pianissimo. Nevertheless this is infectious music-making and there is much to enjoy.

Piano quintet in A, Op. 81.
(M) *** Decca 421 153-2 [id.]. Clifford Curzon, VPO Qt – FRANCK: *Quintet.***

Piano quintet in A, Op. 81; Piano trio No. 4 in E min. (Dumky), Op. 90.
**(*) Virgin Dig. VC 790736-2 [id.]. Nash Ens.

(i) *Piano quintet in A, Op. 81; String quartet No. 12 in F (American), Op. 96.*
*** RCA RD 86263 [6263-2-RC]. (i) Rubinstein; Guarneri Qt.

This wonderfully warm and lyrical (1962) performance of Dvořák's *Piano quintet* by Clifford Curzon is a classic record, one by which all later versions have come to be judged, and the CD transfer has not lost the richness and ambient glow of the original analogue master, yet has improved definition and presence. The piano timbre remains full and real.

It is surprising that the obvious coupling of the *Piano quintet* and the *String quartet No. 12* has not been made more often. Both the RCA performances are memorably warm and spontaneous; tempi tend to be brisk, but the lyrical element always underlies the music and the playing has both great vitality and warmth. Needless to say, Rubinstein's contribution to the *Quintet* is highly distinguished. The recordings, made in April 1971 and 1972 respectively, are well balanced, detailed and fairly full, helped by the attractive studio ambience.

The Nash offer a useful alternative coupling of the *Piano quintet* and the *Dumky trio*. Good, musicianly performances that are eminently well recorded and give satisfaction, without being as memorable as such classic accounts as that with Clifford Curzon.

Piano trio No. 1 in B flat, Op. 21.
*** Teldec/WEA Dig. 2292 44177-2 [id.]. Trio Fontenay – BRAHMS: *Piano trio No. 2.***

First-class playing and recording from the Trio Fontenay, and a useful coupling as well, of rewarding music.

Piano trios Nos. 1 in B flat, Op. 21; 3 in F min., Op. 65.
*(*) Decca Dig. 421 118-2 [id.]. Chung Trio.

The *F minor Trio* is placed first, not the *B flat* (as stated in the booklet, on the back of the Decca CD and on its label). Myung Whun Chung is very much the dominant partner, as he was in their recent EMI account of the Tchaikovsky *Piano trio*; and here the two sisters take even more of a back seat, and the cellist is far too reticent. His inflammable and flamboyant playing is often captivating but is more appropriate to the concerto repertoire than to an intimate chamber group. It goes without saying that there is much that inspires pleasure, but this is not ideal chamber-music-making and the rather big, reverberant acoustic does not help matters.

Piano trio No. 3 in F min., Op. 65.
*** Chan. Dig. CHAN 8320 [id.]. Borodin Trio.

Piano trios No. 3 in F min., Op. 65; 4 in E min. (Dumky), Op. 90.
*** CBS Dig. MK 44527 [id.]. Emanuel Ax, Young-Uck Kim, Yo-Yo Ma.
(M) **(*) Ph. 426 095-2. Beaux Arts Trio.

Piano trio No. 4 in E min. (Dumky), Op. 90.
*** Chan. Dig. CHAN 8445 [id.]. Borodin Trio – SMETANA: *Piano trio.****
(*) Ph. Dig. 416 297-2 [id.]. Beaux Arts Trio – MENDELSSOHN: *Piano trio No. 1.*(*)

The *F minor Trio* is given a powerful yet sensitive performance by the Ax/Kim/Ma trio. There is the occasional moment when one feels that expressive feeling is just a little too explicit, yet on the whole this is a fine performance and, like the *Dumky*, has warmth and freshness. Occasionally Ax, for all his sensitivity, produces too thick a sound in fortissimo passages, but for the most part his playing is full of musical insight. The recording is faithful and natural.

The Beaux Arts' 1969 performances of Op. 65 and the *Dumky* still sound fresh and sparkling, though the recording on CD is a little dry in violin timbre ; the *F minor*, arguably the finer and certainly the more concentrated of the two, is played with great eloquence and vitality.

The playing of the Borodin Trio has great warmth and fire; such imperfections as there are arise from the natural spontaneity of a live performance, for one feels this is what it must have been, with few if any retakes. The pianist, Luba Edlina, is balanced rather forward but otherwise the wide-ranging Chandos recording has transferred with impressive presence to CD; however, this now seems short measure.

Those unfamiliar with Dvořák's marvellous *E minor Piano trio* might think the sobriquet 'Dumky' indicates some kind of national dance. It is in fact the plural of the Russian word, *dumka* (a term also found in both Poland and Czechoslovakia), which can be broadly translated as a lament. Musically, it implies alternating slow and fast movements, with brightness lightening the melancholy. Dvořák's six-movement *Trio* follows this pattern, with contrasting sequences inherent in the structure of each. It is the spontaneous flexibility of approach to the constant mood-changes that makes the splendid Borodin performance so involving, as well as the glorious playing from each of the three soloists. The recording is naturally balanced and the illusion of a live occasion is striking.

The latest digital Beaux Arts performance is rather more assertive than their earlier approach and, although not lacking dramatic contrast and refinement of detail (Menahem Pressler's playing always gives pleasure), has a degree less spontaneity than before. The new recording has striking realism and presence; and for those who like high drama, this version should be very satisfactory.

String quartets Nos. 1–14; Cypresses, B.152; Fragment in F, B.120; 2 Waltzes, Op. 54, B.105.
(M) *** DG 429 193-2 (9) [id.]. Prague Qt.

Dvořák's *Quartets* span the whole of his creative life: the *A major*, Op. 2, pre-dates the *First Symphony* and the *G major*, Op. 106, comes two years after the *New World*. This set was made in 1973–7 and first appeared on 12 LPs. In the new format, *No. 3 in D* (which, remarkably, takes 69 minutes 42 seconds) can be accommodated complete on one CD. The glories of the mature *Quartets* (Opp. 34, 51, 61, 80, 96 and 105–6) are well known, though it is only the so-called *American* which has achieved real popularity. The beauty of the present set is that it offers seven more *Quartets* (not otherwise available) plus two *Quartet movements*, in *A minor* (1873) and *F major* (1881), plus two *Waltzes* and *Cypresses* for good measure, all in eminently respectable performances and decent recordings.

String quartet No. 12 in F (American), Op. 96.
(B) *** Pickwick Dig. PCD 883 [MCA MCAD 25214]. Delmé Qt – BRAHMS: *Clarinet quintet.****
(BB) *** Hung. White Label HRC 122 [id.]. Bartók Qt – DEBUSSY; RAVEL: *Quartets.***(*)
*** Ph. Dig. 420 803-2 [id.]. Guarneri Qt – SMETANA: *String quartet No. 1.****
*** Ph. 420 396-2 [id.]. Orlando Qt – MENDELSSOHN: *String quartet No. 1.****
(M) *** Ph. 420 876-2 [id.]. Italian Qt – SCHUBERT: *String quartet No.14**** (also with BORODIN: *Nocturne****).
* Teldec/WEA Dig. 2292 44187-2 [id.]. Vermeer Qt – MENDELSSOHN: *Quartet No. 2.**

String quartet No. 12 (American); Cypresses.
*** DG Dig. 419 601-2 [id.]. Hagen Qt – KODÁLY: *Quartet No. 2.****

The Delmé Quartet on a superbly recorded Pickwick disc at bargain price give a winningly spontaneous-sounding performance, marked by unusually sweet matching of timbre between the players, which brings out the total joyfulness of Dvořák's American inspiration. The exuberant finale in particular has its rhythms sprung with delectable lightness, leading to an exhilarating close. The unusual coupling, a similarly warm reading of the Brahms *Clarinet quintet*, is both attractive and generous.

A splendidly alive and spontaneous account from the Bartók Quartet too, polished yet with plenty of warmth and lyrical feeling, and with a dance-like sparkle in the Scherzo and finale. Good sound, generous couplings and the bargain status of this issue ensure its value.

The Guarneri performance is warmly romantic; the articulation of the lovely secondary theme of the first movement is particularly affectionate, and both here and in the *Largo sostenuto* one notices the rich cello line of David Soyer, within a responsive texture of finely blended lyricism. Of course there is plenty of life too, and the dance-like finale has an agreeable rhythmic lightness. The recording is full in timbre and most natural in balance and presence.

The Hagen Quartet make an uncommonly beautiful sound and their account of this masterly score is very persuasive indeed. Their playing is superbly polished, musical and satisfying, and few will fail to respond. In the finale, for example, they are marvellously spirited, and they play the enchanting *Cypresses*, which Dvořák transcribed from the eponymous song-cycle, with great tenderness. The recording is altogether superb, very present and full-bodied.

The digital remastering of the 1980 Orlando recording brings very striking presence and immediacy; it emphasizes that their approach, while still romantic, has more drama than the Guarneri account. But again the slow movement is beautifully played and the finale has the most sparkling articulation and dash. With such realistic sound, this still ranks among the best versions of the *Quartet*, with the finely balanced and well-blended tone, excellent musical judgement and great sensitivity, and perhaps it will appear soon at mid-price.

Another outstanding account from the Italian Quartet, notable for its spontaneous, unforced naturalness. It was splendidly recorded by the Philips engineers in 1968 and still sounds realistic, warm and full in texture as well as clearly defined. This version is made more enticing in this reissue by the inclusion of the famous *Nocturne* from Borodin's

Second Quartet, which comes as an encore at the very end of the CD, the Schubert coupling being placed first.

The Vermeer Quartet, though a magnificent ensemble, give relatively little pleasure in Op. 96. They are forwardly balanced in a rather dry acoustic with little ambience. Their playing has no want of attack or musical intelligence – but there is little sense of spontaneity or of music-making in the home, and less grace.

String quartets Nos. 12 in F (American); 14 in E flat, Op. 105.
(BB) ** Naxos 8.550251 [id.]. Moyzes Qt.

The members of the Moyzes Quartet are drawn from the ranks of the Slovak Philharmonic Orchestra and they are obviously at home in this repertoire. The slow movement of the *American quartet* is played with much warmth, and their account of Op. 105 has comparable intensity. The bright recording projects them forwardly and, although the acoustic is quite sympathetic, the effect could ideally be more intimate. However, this coupling remains very good value.

(i) *String quartet No. 12 (American);* (ii) *String quintet in E flat, Op. 97.*
(M) *** Decca 425 537-2 [id.]. (i) Janáček Qt; (ii) Vienna Octet (members).

The Janáček performance of the *American quartet* is strikingly fresh, the superb playing and ensemble ensuring that the fast tempi chosen for the outer movements are exciting without being rushed, while the *Lento* is warmly eloquent. This is virtuosity of a high order put completely at the service of the composer, and the fine 1964 recording has depth as well as realistic definition. The coupled *E flat Quintet*, another of the greatest works of Dvořák's American period, is given a comparably eloquent and characterful performance by members of the Vienna Octet. Again the recording is full, with an attractive ambience, and the focus is firmer than the orginal LP.

String quintet in E flat, Op. 97; String sextet in A, Op. 48.
*** Hyp. Dig. CDA 66308 [id.]. Raphael Ens.

The *E flat major Quintet*, Op. 97, is one of the masterpieces of Dvořák's American years, and it is most persuasively given by the Raphael Ensemble. It is also very well recorded, though we are placed fairly forward in the aural picture.

Slavonic dances Nos. 1–16, Opp. 46 & 72.
**(*) Ara. Dig. Z 6559 [id.]. Artur Balsam, Gena Raps (piano, four hands).
**(*) Hyp. Dig. CDA 66204 [id.]. Peter Noke, Helen Krizos (piano, four hands).

Generally fine performances from Artur Balsam and Gena Raps, who respond to the music in a spirit of relaxed enjoyment, yet do not miss its brio. The recording too is well balanced in a pleasing acoustic.

Peter Noke and Helen Krizos often play with more dash, but some of the more reflective moments are less sensitively observed here although their impetuous verve is undoubtedly exhilarating at times. The Hyperion recording is more resonant and, coupled to a fairly close microphone placing, the effect is less convincing, although there is no lack of focus and brightness to the sound on CD.

VOCAL AND CHORAL MUSIC

Requiem, Op. 89.
(M) *** Decca 421 810-2 (2) [id.]. Lorengar, Komlóssy, Isofalvy, Krause, Amb. S., LSO, Kertesz – KODÁLY: *Hymn of Zrinyi; Psalmus Hungaricus.****

The *Requiem* reflects the impact on Dvořák of the English musical world of the day and has a good deal of relatively conventional writing in it. Kertesz conducts with a total commitment to the score and secures from both singers and orchestra an alert and sensitive response. Pilar Lorengar's vibrato is at times a trifle disturbing, but it is the only solo performance that is likely to occasion any reserve. The recording matches the performance: it has a lifelike balance and the CD remastering adds freshness and bite.

(i) *Stabat Mater, Op. 58*; (ii) *Legends, Op. 59.*
(M) *** DG 423 919-2 (2) [id.]. (i) Mathis, Reynolds, Ochman, Shirley-Quirk, Bav. R. Ch. & O; (ii) ECO, Kubelik.

Dvořák's devout Catholicism led him to treat this tragic religious theme with an open innocence that avoids sentimentality, and though a setting of a relatively short poem which stretches to 80 minutes entails much repetition of words, this idiomatic DG performance, with fine solo and choral singing and responsive playing, holds the attention from first to last. Kubelik is consistently persuasive and this is a work which benefits from his imaginative approach. The recording, made in the Munich Herkules-Saal, is of very good quality; the remastering adds presence (especially for the soloists) without too much loss of the attractive hall ambience. There are ten *Legends*, lyrical and romantic equivalents of the *Slavonic dances* but less robust in rhythmic style and more delicately coloured. They are presented here most persuasively and the 1976 recording, made in the London Henry Wood Hall, is pleasingly vivid and atmospheric.

OPERA

Rusalka (complete).
*** Sup. Dig. C37 7201/3 [id.]. Beňačková-Čápová, Novak, Soukupová, Ochman, Drobkova, Prague Ch. & Czech PO, Neumann.

Dvořák's fairy-tale opera is given a magical performance by Neumann and his Czech forces, helped by full, brilliant and atmospheric recording which, while giving prominence to the voices, brings out the beauty and refinement of Dvořák's orchestration. Written right at the end of the composer's career in his ripest maturity but with Wagnerian influences at work, the piece has a unique flavour; where on stage it can seem too long for its material, on record it works beautifully. The title-role is superbly taken by Gabriela Beňačková-Čápová. The voice is creamy in tone, characterfully Slavonic without disagreeable hooting or wobbling, and the famous *Invocation to the Moon* is enchanting. Vera Soukupová as the Witch is just as characterfully Slavonic in a lower register, though not so even; while Wieslaw Ochman sings with fine, clean, heroic tone as the Prince, with timbre made distinctive by tight vibrato. Richard Novak brings out some of the Alberich-like overtones as the Watersprite, though the voice is not always steady. The banding is both generous and helpful.

Rusalka: highlights.
(B) *** Sup. Dig. 110617-2 (from above recording with Soukupová; cond. Neumann).

There is a first-class selection available on a bargain-priced disc, offering an hour of music, although only a synopsis is provided.

Dyson, George (1883–1964)

At the Tabard Inn: overture; (ii) In honour of the City; (i; ii) Sweet Thames run softly.
*** Unicorn Dig. DKPCD 9048 [id.]. RPO with (i) Stephen Roberts; (ii) Royal College of Music Chamber Ch., Willcocks.

There could hardly be a better introduction to Sir George Dyson's music than this collection, with two vigorously sung choral works preceded by the overture based upon themes from his best-known work, *The Canterbury Pilgrims. In honour of the City*, Dyson's setting of William Dunbar, uses a modern translation of Dunbar's Chaucerian English and to fine, direct effect. The third work here shows Dyson at his most spontaneous. *Sweet Thames run softly* has words by Spenser taken from his *Prothalamion*, celebrating a famous marriage of 1596 when the two young daughters of the Earl of Worcester sailed up the Thames as far as the Temple. The score is full of imaginative touches, with a pair of virginal flutes to represent the brides-to-be. With Stephen Roberts an excellent baritone soloist in the more ambitious cantata, these performances, full of life and warmth, could hardly be bettered; and the recording is first class.

(Organ) Fantasia and Ground bass. 3 Choral hymns; Hierusalem; Psalm 150; 3 Songs of praise.
*** Hyp. CDA 66150 [id.]. Vakery Hill, St Michael's Singers, Thomas Trotter, RPO, Jonathan Rennert.

In his old age Dyson returned to Winchester, the city where he had spent his happiest years teaching, and there he wrote the two major items here, not only the ecstatic hymn, *Hierusalem*, for soprano, chorus, string quartet and orchestra, but the strongly argued *Fantasia and Ground bass* for organ, beautifully played here by Jonathan Rennert, choirmaster of the St Michael's Singers. Where the organ piece unashamedly builds on an academic model, *Hierusalem* reveals the inner man more surprisingly, a richly sensuous setting of a medieval poem inspired by the thought of the Holy City, building to a jubilant climax. Just under 20 minutes long, it is a splendid work, and is backed here by the six hymns and the Psalm setting, all of them heartwarming products of the Anglican tradition. Performances are outstanding, with Rennert drawing radiant singing and playing from his team, richly and atmospherically recorded.

Benedicte; Benedictus; Evening services in D; Hail, universal Lord; Live forever, glorious Lord; Te Deum; Valour. (i) *(Organ) Prelude; Postlude; Psalm-tune prelude (I was glad); Voluntary of praise.* (with HOWELLS: *Dyson's delight*).
*** Unicorn Dig. DKPCD 9065 [id.]. St Catherine's College, Cambridge, Ch., Owen Rees; (i) Owen Rees (organ).

Sir George Dyson's writing may not always be strikingly individual, but every so often its invention soars. There are some well-made organ pieces too (plus an admiring contribution from Herbert Howells based on two themes from Dyson's *Canterbury Pilgrims*), but it is the vocal music that is the more memorable. It is all sung with striking freshness by choristers who, young as some of them may be, seem to have its inflexions in their very being. Excellent recording too, in a properly spacious acoustic, though the words come over well.

The Blacksmiths. The Canterbury Pilgrims: suite. Quo vadis: Nocturne. 3 Rustic songs. Song on May morning; Spring garland; A Summer day; To music.

*** Unicorn Dig. DKPCD 9061 [id.]. Neil Mackie, Royal College of Music Chamber Ch., RPO, Willcocks.

Sir George Dyson spent most of his life teaching in public schools, notably Winchester, finally becoming Principal of the Royal College of Music in London. Yet he came from a humble Yorkshire background, and *The Blacksmiths* – done here with a reduced orchestra (two pianos, timpani, percussion and strings), as suggested by the composer – has an earthiness that sets it apart from the regular English choral tradition. *The Canterbury Pilgrims*, the work for which Dyson is best known, is here represented by a suite assembled by Christopher Palmer, who also acted as record producer, making one want to hear the full work. The other items, most of them more conventional, make up an appealing disc, played and recorded well.

Elgar, Edward (1857–1934)

Adieu (arr. Geehl). *Beau Brummel: Minuet. Sospiri, Op. 70. The Spanish Lady: Burlesco. The Starlight Express: Waltz. Sursum corda, Op. 11.*
(*) Chan. CHAN 8432 [id.]. Bournemouth Sinf., Hurst – VAUGHAN WILLIAMS: *Collection.*(*)

A collection of delightful Elgar rarities. *Sursum corda* has real *nobilmente* depth; the *Burlesco*, a fragment from the unfinished Elgar opera, is delightfully done; and each one of these items has its charms. Well coupled with rare Vaughan Williams, warmly performed and atmospherically recorded, although the violins sound a little thin above the stave.

3 Bavarian dances, Op. 27. Caractacus, Op. 35: Woodland interludes. Chanson de matin, Op. 15/2; Chanson de nuit, Op. 15/1. Contrasts, Op. 10/3. Dream children, Op. 43. Falstaff, Op. 68: 2 Interludes. Salut d'amour. Sérénade lyrique. (i) *Soliloquy for oboe* (orch. Jacob).
*** Chan. CHAN 8371. Bournemouth Sinf., Del Mar, (i) with Goossens.

Elgar wrote his *Soliloquy* right at the end of his life for Leon Goossens, a wayward, improvisatory piece which yet has a character of its own. Here the dedicatee plays it with his long-recognizable tone-colour and feeling for phrase in an orchestration by Gordon Jacob. Most of the other pieces are well known, but they come up with new warmth and commitment in splendid performances under Del Mar. The analogue recording is of high quality, full and vivid.

3 Bavarian dances, Op. 27. Caractacus, Op. 35: Triumphal march. The Light of Life, Op. 29: Meditation. Polonia, Op. 76. Wand of Youth suites Nos. 1 & 2, Op. 1a–b.
(M) *** EMI CDM7 69207-2 [id.]. LPO, Boult.

Sir Adrian's outstanding performances of the *Wand of Youth suites* catch both the innocence and the intimacy of this music, which is very much part of Elgar's personal world. The orchestral playing is first rate and carries through the conductor's obvious affection to the listener. The 1968 recording has adapted splendidly to CD remastering; even if the roisterous scoring for the *Wild Bear* portrait becomes a little noisy because of the resonance, the string-tone retains the warmth and bloom of the analogue original.

3 Bavarian dances, Op. 27; Pomp and circumstance marches Nos. 1–5, Op. 39; Wand of youth suite No. 2, Op. 1b.
**(*) Nimbus Dig. NI 5136 [id.]. E. String O (augmented), William Boughton.

William Boughton, with his English String Orchestra augmented, proves a winningly relaxed Elgarian both in the marches and in the genre pieces, *Wand of youth* and the *Bavarian dances*. There is an easy swagger about the marches. The warmly reverberant acoustic of the Great Hall in Birmingham University gives the performances a spacious scale that is entirely apt. What is much more questionable is the scale conveyed by the recording (in the same acoustic) for the other, much lighter and more intimate pieces. Moreover it is a pity that only the second of the *Wand of youth suites* is included.

Caractacus, Op. 35: Woodland interlude. Crown of India (suite), Op. 66; Grania and Dermid, Op. 42: Funeral march. Light of Life, Op. 29: Meditation. Nursery suite; Severn suite, Op. 87.
(M) **(*) EMI CDM7 63280-2 [id.]. Royal Liverpool PO, Groves.

It is good to have these performances by Sir Charles Groves – recorded while he was principal conductor of the Royal Liverpool Philharmonic Orchestra – restored to the catalogue. This is all music that he understands warmly, and the results give much pleasure. One does not have to be an imperialist to enjoy any of the occasional pieces, and it is interesting to find the patriotic music coming up fresher than the little interlude from *The Light of Life*, beautiful as that is. Both the *Nursery suite* (written for the Princesses Elizabeth and Margaret Rose) and the orchestral version of the *Severn suite* (written for a brass band contest) come from Elgar's very last period, when his inspiration came in flashes rather than as a sustained searchlight. The completely neglected *Funeral march* was written in 1901 for a play by W. B. Yeats and George Moore; it is a splendid piece. The CD transfer retains the bloom of the original recordings and adds to the vividness.

Chanson de matin, Op. 15/2; Chanson de nuit, Op. 15/1; Elegy, Op. 58; Introduction and allegro, Op. 47; Serenade in E min., Op. 20; The Spanish Lady (suite).
**(*) Nimbus NI 5008 [id.]. E. String O, William Boughton.

Boughton conducts warm, sympathetic performances of an attractive selection of shorter Elgar works – including the suite drawn from his unfinished opera, *The Spanish Lady*. The reverberant recording is less crisply detailed than is ideal – like the actual playing – but, with the clarification of CD, presents a pleasingly natural ensemble.

Chanson de matin; Chanson de nuit (arr. Fraser); *Elegy for strings, Op. 58; Introduction and allegro for strings, Op. 47; Mazurka, Op. 10/1; Salut d'amour* (arr. Fraser); *Serenade for strings in E min., Op. 20.*
**(*) Ara. Dig. Z 6563 [id.]. ECO, Sir Yehudi Menuhin.

Sir Yehudi Menuhin on the Arabesque disc couples Elgar's three substantial string pieces with string arrangements of favourite trifles as well as the *Mazurka*. Well played, it makes an attractive collection, with the solo quartet in the *Introduction and allegro* particularly sensitive and with warm, atmospheric recording. However, neither this piece nor the *Serenade* is quite as strongly characterized as the Warren-Green versions.

Cockaigne overture, Op. 40; Crown of India suite, Op. 66; Pomp and circumstance marches Nos. 1–5, Op. 39.
*** Chan. CHAN 8429 [id.]. SNO, Gibson.

Overtures: Cockaigne; Froissart; In the South. Overture in D min. (arr. from Handel: *Chandos anthem No. 2*).
*** Chan. Dig. CHAN 8309 [id.]. SNO, Gibson.

(i) *Cockaigne overture, Op. 40;* (ii) *Froissart overture, Op. 19; Pomp and circumstance marches, Op. 39, Nos* (i) *1 in D;* (ii) *2 in A min.; 3 in C min.;* (i) *4 in G;* (ii) *5 in C.*
(M) *** EMI CDM7 69563-2 [id.]. (i) Philh. O; (ii) New Philh. O; Barbirolli.

(i) *Cockaigne overture, Op. 40; Pomp and circumstance marches Nos. 1–5, Op. 39;* (ii) *Variations on an original theme (Enigma), Op. 36.*
(M) **(*) Decca 417 719-2. (i) LPO; (ii) Chicago SO; Solti.

It is good to have Barbirolli's ripe yet wonderfully vital portrait of Edwardian London at last on CD where the recording retains its atmosphere as well as its vividness. *Froissart* is very compelling too, and Barbirolli makes a fine suite of the five *Pomp and circumstance marches*, with plenty of contrast in Nos. 2 and 3 to offset the Edwardian flag-waving of Nos. 1 and 4.

Sir Alexander Gibson's *Cockaigne* is attractively spirited, and although the Scottish orchestra misses something of the music's opulence, this is undoubtedly very enjoyable. The *Pomp and circumstance marches* are taken at a spanking pace, but with no lack of swagger, and there is a strong feeling of pageantry too. The music has great forward thrust, and the recording acoustic is suitably reverberant. In the *Crown of India suite* Gibson is consistently imaginative in attention to detail, and the playing of the Scottish orchestra here is warmly sensitive. In all this music the CD transfer of the 1978 analogue recording is first rate in every way.

Gibson's later Chandos collection is given a brilliantly truthful digital recording. The Scottish orchestra makes a vividly cohesive sound, although again the strings are just a little lacking in richness of timbre. The picture of London is full of bustle and pageantry, with bold brass and flashing percussion, and the closing pages have striking impact. *In the South* has strong impetus, and Gibson's directness serves *Froissart* and the Handel arrangement equally well.

Solti's *Cockaigne* is sharply dramatic and exciting; his view of the *Marches* is both vigorous and refined, with sharp pointing in the outer sections, spaciousness in the great melodies. In the *Marches* the CD remastering brings vivid sound with full-bodied strings; *Cockaigne* is somewhat brighter, especially in the brass, and there is a touch of glare. Although the opening of *Enigma* is affectionately Elgarian, with Solti the work becomes essentially a dazzling showpiece. *Nimrod* opens elegiacally but, with a basic tempo faster than usual, Solti allows himself to get faster and faster still, although there is a broadening at the end. This won't be to all tastes, but the brilliant recording suits the drama of the playing.

Cello concerto in E min., Op. 85.
⊛ *** EMI CDC7 47329-2 [id.]. Du Pré, LSO, Sir John Barbirolli – *Sea Pictures.**** ⊛
*** CBS Dig. MK 39541 [id.]. Yo-Yo Ma, LSO, Previn – WALTON: *Cello concerto.****
(B) *** Pickwick Dig. PCD 930. (i) Felix Schmidt; LSO, Frühbeck de Burgos – VAUGHAN WILLIAMS: *Tallis fantasia; Greensleeves.***(*)
(M) *** Decca 421 385-2 [id.]. Lynn Harrell, Cleveland O, Maazel – WALTON: *Violin concerto.****
(*) Ph. Dig. 412 880-2 [id.]. Heinrich Schiff, Dresden State O, Marriner – DVOŘÁK: *Cello concerto.(*)
(*) Virgin Dig. VC 790735-2 [id.]. Isserlis, LSO, Hickox – BLOCH: *Schelomo.**
(*) ASV Dig. CDRPO 8012 [id.]. Tortelier, RPO, Groves – DVOŘÁK: *Rondo;* TCHAIKOVSKY: *Rococo variations.**

(i) *Cello concerto; Elegy for strings, Op. 58; In the South, Op. 50.*
(B) **(*) CfP CD-CFP 9003. (i) Robert Cohen; LPO, Del Mar.

(i) *Cello concerto; Variations on an original theme (Enigma), Op. 36.*
*** Ph. Dig. 416 354-2 [id.]. (i) Julian Lloyd Webber; RPO, Menuhin.

(i) *Cello concerto;* (ii) *Cockaigne overture, Op. 40; Variations on an original theme (Enigma), Op. 36.*
*** CBS MK 76529. (i) Du Pré, Phd. O; (ii) LPO; Barenboim.

(i) *Cello concerto in E min.; Overtures: Froissart, Op. 19; In the South (Alassio), Op. 50. Introduction and allegro for strings, Op. 47.*
(M) **(*) EMI CDM7 69200-2 [id.]. (i) Tortelier; LPO, Boult.

Jacqueline du Pré was essentially a spontaneous artist, no two performances by her were exactly alike; wisely, Barbirolli at the recording sessions of Elgar's *Cello concerto* encouraged her above all to express emotion through the notes. Her style is freely rhapsodic, but the result produced a very special kind of meditative feeling. The tempi, long-breathed in the first and third movements, are allowed still more elbow-room when du Pré's expressiveness requires it; in the very beautiful slow movement, brief and concentrated, her inner intensity conveys a depth of espressivo rarely achieved by any cellist on record. Brilliant virtuoso playing too in scherzo and finale. CD brings a subtle extra definition to heighten the excellent qualities of the 1965 recording, with the solo instrument firmly placed. This performance is now also available at mid-price, the only reservation being that it comes in a box of two discs, also offering her recordings of Haydn and Beethoven (EMI CMS7 69707-2 – see our Concerts section).

The Philips coupling of the *Cello concerto* and the *Enigma variations*, the two most popular of Elgar's big orchestral works, featuring two artists inseparably associated with Elgar's music, made the disc an immediate bestseller, and rightly so. These are both warmly expressive and unusually faithful readings, the more satisfying for fidelity to the score and the absence of exaggeration. The speeds – as in the flowing *Moderato* in the first movement of the *Concerto* – are never extreme, always well judged, and Julian Lloyd Webber in his playing has never sounded warmer or more relaxed on record, well focused in the stereo spectrum.

Jacqueline du Pré's second recording of the Elgar *Cello concerto* was taken from live performances in Philadelphia in November 1970, and this is a superb picture of an artist in full flight. Here on CBS you have the romantic view of Elgar at its most compelling. The mastery of du Pré lies not just in her total commitment from phrase to phrase but in the feeling for the whole, setting her sights on the moment in the Epilogue where the slow-movement theme returns, the work's innermost sanctuary of repose. Barenboim's most distinctive point in *Enigma* is his concern for the miniature element, giving the delicate variations sparkle and emotional point, while the big variations have full weight, and the finale brings extra fierceness at a fast tempo. *Cockaigne* is comparably lively and colourful. The sound of the CBS transfer lacks something in body and amplitude.

In its rapt concentration Yo-Yo Ma's recording with Previn is second to none. The first movement is lighter, a shade more urgent than the Du Pré/Barbirolli version, and in the scherzo he finds more fun, just as he finds extra sparkle in the main theme of the finale. The key movement with Ma, as it is with du Pré, is the *Adagio*, echoed later in the raptness of the slow epilogue, and there his range of dynamic is just as daringly wide, with a thread of pianissimo at the innermost moment, poised in its intensity. Warm, fully detailed recording, finely balanced, with understanding conducting from Previn.

On bargain-price Pickwick, Felix Schmidt, a young cellist with the widest expressive range, gives a bold, emotionally intense reading which finds a most satisfying middle ground between the romantic freedom typified by the unique Jacqueline du Pré and the steadier, more restrained way of a Paul Tortelier. Schmidt's hushed, deeply meditative account of the slow movement is among the most moving of all. With his rich, full tone opulently recorded, his account can be recommended beside the very finest versions, depending on preference as to coupling, in this instance an unconventional linking with two of Vaughan Williams's most popular works.

Lynn Harrell's outstanding account with the Cleveland Orchestra on Decca offers a strong challenge. With eloquent support from Maazel and this fine orchestra (the woodwind play with appealing delicacy), this reading, deeply felt, balances a gentle nostalgia with extrovert brilliance. The slow movement is tenderly spacious, the scherzo bursts with exuberance and, after a passionate opening, the finale is memorable for the poignantly expressive reprise of the melody from the *Adagio*, one of Elgar's greatest inspirations. The recording of the orchestra is brightly lit; the solo cello is rich-timbred, a little larger than life, but convincingly focused.

On his earlier EMI recording, Tortelier gives a noble and restrained performance; Boult accompanies with splendid tact, and in addition gives fine accounts of the *Introduction and allegro*, the early *Froissart overture* – which combines orchestral links with Brahms with emergent fingerprints of the later Elgar – and *In the South*.

The Classics for Pleasure CD is a good bargain. Robert Cohen's performance is firm and intense, with steady tempi, the colouring more positive, less autumnal than usual, relating the work more closely to the *Second Symphony*. Yet there is no lack of inner feeling. Del Mar's accompaniment is wholly sympathetic, underlining the soloist's approach. He also directs an exciting account of *In the South*, recorded in a single take and highly spontaneous in effect. The *Elegy* makes an eloquent bonus. The recording is wide-ranging and well balanced, but shows Cohen's tone as bright and well focused rather than as especially resonant in the bass.

Schiff gives a warm, thoughtful account, at his most successful in the lovely slow movement and the epilogue, both played with soft, sweet tone. The sound is excellent, to match the orchestra's richness.

The most distinctive point about Steven Isserlis's version on Virgin is his treatment of the slow movement, not so much elegiac as songful. Using a mere thread of tone, with vibrato unstressed, the simplicity of line and the unforced beauty are brought out. The very placing of the solo instrument goes with that, rather more distant than is usual, with the refinement of Elgar's orchestration beautifully caught by both conductor and engineers.

Tortelier's latest version of the Elgar, issued on the RPO's own label to celebrate the cellist's seventy-fifth birthday in March 1989, may not be as firm and powerful as his earlier account with Boult. In the finale the septuagenarian shows signs of strain; but the performance has a spontaneity and a new tenderness which make it very compelling.

Cello concerto (arr. for viola by Lionel Tertis); *3 Characteristic pieces, Op. 10.*
** Conifer Dig. CDCF 171 [id.]. Rivka Golani, RPO, Handley – BAX: *Phantasy.***(*)

Lionel Tertis's arrangement for viola of the Elgar *Cello concerto* is a curiosity. When set against the original, the losses far outweigh any gain; but the recording provides a fascinating sidelight on a masterpiece. The middle two movements work well: the scherzo is clean and volatile, with the soloist's articulation sharply focused, and Golani's tone is at its warmest in the slow movement. The outer movements bring problems. For all Golani's power, there is an inevitable lack of weight in the great rhetorical double-stopping. More seriously, the tone of the viola in its upper register is often disagreeably sour, with the soloist indulging far too much in under-the-note coloration. The record also includes as a makeweight the three charming Opus 10 *Pieces*, originally designed as an answer to Edward German's *Henry VIII dances*, and here given with a full – not a chamber – orchestra. The recording is outstandingly full and vivid.

(i) *Cello concerto in E min., Op. 85*; (ii) *Violin concerto in B min., Op. 61.*
(M) (***) EMI mono CDH7 69786-2. (i) Beatrice Harrison, New SO, (ii) Menuhin, LSO, composer.

Even though the original master of the 1932 Menuhin/Elgar recording of the *Violin concerto* was wilfully destroyed many years ago, the tape transfer (originally made by A. C. Griffith) was of the highest quality and it emerges on CD with a superb sense of atmosphere and presence. As for the performance, its classic status is amply confirmed: in many ways no one has ever matched – let alone surpassed – the seventeen-year-old Menuhin in this work, even if the first part of the finale lacks something in fire. The response of conductor, soloist and orchestra has extraordinary magic, with great warmth but no self-indulgence. The performance of the *Cello concerto* has nothing like the same inspiration, when Beatrice Harrison's playing is at times fallible, and there are moments which seem almost perfunctory; but there is still much Elgarian feeling. A bad swish on the side of the 78 record devoted to the scherzo has been cleaned away marvellously, thanks to the use of CEDAR (Computer Enhanced Digital Audio Restoration). Even with reservations about the *Cello concerto*, this record is indispensable for Menuhin's totally compulsive account of the *Violin concerto*, a very moving experience.

Violin concerto in B min., Op. 61.
⊛ *** EMI Dig. CDC7 47210-2 [id.]. Nigel Kennedy, LPO, Handley.
(M) (***) RCA mono GD 87966 [7966-2-RG]. Heifetz, LSO, Sargent – WALTON: *Concerto.*(***)
** Olympia OCD 242 [id.]. Igor Oistrakh, Moscow SO, Zhuk – BRITTEN: *Violin concerto.***

Violin concerto in B min.; Salut d'amour; La Capricieuse.
(M) *** Decca 421 388-2 [id.]. Kyung-Wha Chung, LPO, Solti.

Kennedy's is a commanding reading, arguably even finer than the long line of versions with star international soloists from outside Britain. With Vernon Handley as guide, it is at once the most centrally Elgarian of all those on record in its warm expressiveness; equally, in its steady pacing it brings out more than is usual the clear parallels with the Beethoven and Brahms concertos. Yet the example of Yehudi Menuhin is also clear, not least in the sweetness and repose of the slow movement and in the deep meditation of the accompanied cadenza which comes as epilogue. The recording, with the soloist balanced more naturally than is usual, not spotlit, is outstandingly faithful and atmospheric.

The extra clarity and sense of presence in the CD transfer intensify the impact of Kyung-Wha Chung's heartfelt performance, with Solti responding with warmth to the wide-ranging expressiveness of the soloist. Chung's dreamily expansive playing in that middle movement is ravishing in its beauty, not least in the ethereal writing above the stave, and so too are the lyrical pages of the outer movements. The bravura passages draw from her a vein of mercurial fantasy, excitingly volatile, and no other recording brings a wider range of dynamic or tone in the soloist's playing. The two little violin pieces, accompanied by Philip Moll, act as encores. The 1977 analogue recording for the *Concerto* has been beautifully transferred.

Heifetz's view of Elgar, with speeds unusually fast, may not be idiomatic, but this recording brings a masterly example of his artistry, demonstrating very clearly that, for all the ease and technical perfection, he is in no way a cold interpreter of romantic music. The mono recording is limited, not helped by a low hum in the transfer, and the solo instrument is balanced very close; but such an historic document should not be missed, generously coupled at mid-price with Heifetz's authoritative reading of the Walton, with the composer conducting.

Igor Oistrakh's commanding virtuosity has rarely been demonstrated so formidably on record as in this urgent, vigorous reading of the Elgar *Violin concerto*. It is quite a revelation to have Russian performers tackling Elgar with a red-blooded commitment that has you relating him closely to Tchaikovsky and Rachmaninov. Sadly, for all the beauty and purity – as well as the brilliance – of Oistrakh's playing, the performance misses many of the subtleties of the work, largely a question of the excessively close balance of the soloist. Yet with the Britten *Violin concerto* in an equally red-blooded reading as an exceptionally generous coupling, this is well worth investigating on a lower-than-premium-price label.

Coronation march, Op. 65; Froissart: concert overture, Op. 19; In the South (Alassio): concert overture, Op. 50; The Light of life: Meditation, Op. 29.
*** ASV Dig. CDDCA 619 [id.]. RPO, Yondani Butt.

Yondani Butt draws warm and opulent performances from the RPO. Both the overtures have splendid panache, well shaped and with the joins smoothed over; and he brings out the purely musical, non-jingoistic quality of the *Coronation march*. *The Light of life meditation*, taken very slowly, is prevented from becoming soupy by Butt's direct, simple expressiveness. Warm, atmospheric recording, yet with plenty of brilliance – an excellent Elgar sound, in fact.

Elegy for strings, Op. 58; Introduction and allegro for strings, Op. 47; Serenade for strings in E min., Op. 20; Sospiri, Op. 70; The Spanish Lady; suite (ed. Young).
(M) **(*) Decca 421 384-2 [id.]. ASMF, Marriner – WARLOCK: *Serenade.****

Elegy for strings, Op. 58; Serenade for strings, Op. 20; Sospiri, Op. 70.
*** EMI Dig. CDC7 47671-2. City of L. Sinfonia, Hickox – PARRY: *English suite* etc.***

Marriner's somewhat stiff manner of the *Introduction and allegro* will not appeal to everyone, but the subtlety and strength of Marriner's unique band of string players are never in doubt. The collection has the added interest of including the brief snippets arranged by Percy Young from Elgar's unfinished opera *The Spanish Lady*. Marriner's version of the *Serenade*, warm and resilient, shows him at his finest. The (1968) sound on CD is fresh and full – but with just a touch of astringency in the violins, which adds to the bite of the *Introduction and allegro*. The Warlock *Serenade* has also been included for this reissue.

Hickox draws beautifully refined string-playing from his City of London Sinfonia, notably in the three elegiac movements, the slow movement of the *Serenade* as well as the two separate pieces. An excellent coupling for the rare Parry items, excellently recorded.

(i) *Falstaff, Op. 68;* (ii) *Variations on an original theme (Enigma), Op. 36.*
(M) *** EMI CDM7 69185-2 [id.]. (i) Hallé O, (ii) Philh. O, Barbirolli.
*** Chan. CHAN 8431 [id.]. SNO, Gibson.
**(*) EMI Dig. CDC7 47416-2. LPO, Mackerras.

Falstaff (symphonic study), *Op. 68; The Sanguine Fan* (ballet), *Op. 81;* BACH, arr. ELGAR: *Fantasia and fugue in C min. (BWV 537), Op. 86.*
(M) *** EMI CDM7 63133-2 [id.]. LPO, Boult.

Ripe and expansive, Barbirolli's view of *Falstaff* is colourful and convincing; it has fine atmospheric feeling too, and the interludes are more magical here than in the Boult version. *Enigma*, too, was a work that Barbirolli, himself a cellist, made especially his own, with wonderfully expansive string-playing and much imaginative detail; the recording was made when he was at the very peak of his interpretative powers. The massed strings have lost some of their amplitude, but detail is clearer and the overall balance is convincing, with the Kingsway Hall ambience ensuring a pleasing bloom.

Boult treats *Falstaff* essentially as a symphonic structure. It follows therefore that some of the mystery, and the delicate sense of atmosphere that impregnates the interludes for example, is undercharacterized. But the crispness of the playing and Boult's unfailing alertness amply compensate for that. The little-known ballet score written during the First World War makes for an unexpected and enjoyable coupling, and Elgar's Bach arrangement is richly expansive. The remastering, as with Boult's other Elgar recordings, clarifies textures without too much loss of ambience and weight.

Sir Alexander Gibson's *Falstaff* is particularly spontaneous; Gibson generates a strong forward momentum from the very opening bars, yet detail is consistently imaginative and the closing section is most touchingly played. Like the symphonic study, *Enigma* moves forward from variation to variation in a refreshingly direct manner, each portrait full of character, and without self-consciousness in its presentation; *Nimrod* has genuine eloquence, and the finale goes splendidly. The 1978 recording, made in Glasgow City Hall, has a natural perspective, and has been most successfully remastered for CD.

Mackerras's reading of *Falstaff* is superb, among the most electrically compelling put on disc; but *Enigma* is marred by mannered and self-conscious phrasing in the opening statement of the theme and first variation, as well as in *Nimrod*. The recording, very resonant, could be more clearly detailed.

Falstaff, Op. 68; Introduction and allegro for strings, Op. 47; arr. of BACH: *Fantasia and fugue in C min., Op. 86.*
(B) *** Pickwick Dig. PCD 934 [MCA MCAD 25892]. National Youth O of Great Britain), Christopher Seaman.

These works have rarely been given such heartfelt performances as those by Christopher Seaman and the National Youth Orchestra. The weight of string sound, combined with the fervour behind the playing, makes this an exceptionally satisfying reading of the *Introduction and allegro*, while *Falstaff* demonstrates even more strikingly how, working together intensively, these youngsters have learnt to keep a precise ensemble through the most complex variations of expressive rubato. There the weight of string tone contrasts with the lightness of touch and wit that the players bring to the many scherzando passages, keeping keen concentration from first to last, not easy in this work. Some of the solo string passages betray that these are not adult professionals, but they are momentary and very rare, and most Elgarians will enjoy these performances – including the Bach arrangement, also done passionately – far more than cooler ones, however polished. Warm, full, digital recording adds to an outstanding bargain, though irritatingly there is no tracking of sections in *Falstaff*, over half an hour long.

Grania and Diarmid (incidental music), Op. 42; The Sanguine Fan (ballet; complete), *Op. 81; Variations on an original theme (Enigma), Op. 36;* (i) *There are seven that pull the thread.*
*** Chan. Dig. CHAN 8610 [id.]. LPO, Bryden Thomson, (i) with Jenny Miller.

Bryden Thomson conducts a broad, characterful reading of *Enigma*, warmly expressive but never mannered, leading the ear on persuasively in a purposefully structured whole. He finds all the charm of *The Sanguine Fan* ballet, characterizing it well without inflating it; while the unexpected mixture of Elgar and Celtic twilight in the *Grania and Diarmid* incidental music brings a similarly agreeable response, notably in the fine, measured *Funeral march.* The little Yeats song, *There are seven,* is warmly sung by Jenny Miller, though the microphone exaggerates her generous vibrato. First-class Chandos sound.

In the South (Alassio): concert overture, Op. 50; Serenade for strings in E min., Op. 20; Variations on an original theme (Enigma), Op. 36.
*** Virgin Dig. VC 790727-2 [id.]. RPO, Andrew Litton.

Andrew Litton brings a natural flair to this repertoire. His recording of *Enigma* may not be traditional in every detail – *Nimrod* is intense and strong rather than elegiac – but each variation is vividly characterized without eccentricity. *In the South* and the *Serenade* also confirm Litton's innate feeling for Elgarian rubato, phrasing and rhythm, the qualities which are implied rather than specified in the score. The programme is warmly and atmospherically recorded in EMI's St John's Wood studio.

Introduction and allegro for strings, Op. 47; Serenade for strings in E min., Op. 20.
⊛ *** Virgin Dig. VCy 790819-2 [id.]. LCO, Christopher Warren-Green – VAUGHAN WILLIAMS: *Tallis fantasia* etc.*** ⊛

(i) *Introduction and allegro for strings, Op. 47; Serenade for strings, Op. 20;* (ii) *Elegy, Op. 58; Sospiri, Op. 70.*
*** EMI CDC7 47537-2. (i) Sinfonia of L. with Allegri Qt; (ii) New Philh. O, Barbirolli – VAUGHAN WILLIAMS: *Tallis fantasia* etc.***

Introduction and allegro for strings, Op. 47; Serenade for strings, Op. 20; Variations on an original theme (Enigma), Op. 36.
(M) **(*) EMI Dig. CD-EMX 9503. LPO, Vernon Handley.

Repeating a coupling made famous by Sir John Barbirolli, Christopher Warren-Green, directing and leading his reborn London Chamber Orchestra, could hardly have made a more impressive début. The account of the *Introduction and allegro* has tremendous ardour: the great striding theme on the middle strings is unforgettable, while the fugue has enormous bite and bravura. The whole work moves forward in a single sweep and the sense of a live performance, tingling with electricity and immediacy, is thrillingly tangible. It is very difficult to believe that the group contains only seventeen players (6-5-2-3-1), with the resonant but never clouding acoustics of All Saints' Church, Petersham, helping to create an engulfingly rich body of tone. Appropriately, the *Serenade* is a more relaxed reading yet has plenty of affectionate warmth, with the beauty of the *Larghetto* expressively rich but not overstated.

Barbirolli brings an Italianate ardour and warmth to this music without in any way robbing it of its Englishness; and the response of the string players, full-throated or subtle as the music demands, was matched by superb analogue recording, notable for its combination of clarity and ambient richness. For CD, the *Elegy,* like the *Serenade* showing Barbirolli in more gentle, beguiling mood, and the passionate *Sospiri* have been

375

added for good measure. The CD transfer, however, while retaining the fullness and amplitude, seems more restricted on top and has lost some of the original bite.

Vernon Handley's generously full Eminence collection is given brilliantly wide-ranging digital sound. In the string works, the CD makes the emphasis of the upper range at the expense of the middle the more striking; one needs more amplitude here. Handley's strong personal identification with the music brings a consciously moulded style that tends at times to rob the *Enigma variations* of its forward impulse. The performances of the string works are more direct.

Nursery suite; Wand of Youth suites Nos. 1 and 2, Op. 1a and 1b.
*** Chan. Dig. CHAN 8318 [id.]. Ulster O, Bryden Thomson.

Although Boult's performances of the more robust items from the *Wand of Youth* brought marginally more exuberance, the playing in Ulster is attractively spirited; in the gentle pieces (the *Sun dance*, *Fairy pipers* and *Slumber dance*) which show the composer at his most magically evocative, the music-making engagingly combines refinement and warmth. The *Nursery suite* is strikingly well characterized, and with first-class digital sound this is highly recommendable.

Overtures: Cockaigne, Op. 40; Froissart, Op. 19; Variations on an original theme (Enigma), Op. 36.
* RCA Dig. RD 60073 [60073-2-RC]. LPO, Slatkin.

Slatkin, a persuasive Elgarian in the *Symphonies* and in *The Kingdom*, is most disappointing in his reading of *Enigma*. The theme and *Nimrod* are both done sluggishly, and the whole performance fails to catch fire. Though *Froissart* is on the stiff side, the overtures are more successful, but they hardly compensate for the shortcomings in the main work.

(i) *Pomp and circumstance marches Nos. 1–5, Op. 39;* (ii) *Variations on an original theme (Enigma), Op. 36.*
(M) *** DG 429 713-2 [id.]. RPO, Norman Del Mar.
*** Ph. Dig. 416 813-2 [id.]. RPO, André Previn.
(B) **(*) Decca 417 878-2 [id.]. LSO, (i) Bliss; (ii) Monteux.

In the *Enigma variations* Del Mar comes closer than any other conductor to the responsive rubato style of Elgar himself, using fluctuations to point the emotional message of the work with wonderful power and spontaneity. Recorded in Guildford Cathedral, with plentiful reverberation, this version has the advantage of a splendid contribution from the organ at the end. The RPO plays superbly, both here and in the *Pomp and circumstance marches*, given Proms-style flair and urgency – although some might feel that the fast speeds miss some of the nobilmente. The reverberant sound here adds something of an aggressive edge to the music-making; however, at mid-price this is a very competitive reissue.

In his RPO version, Previn's reading is rather in the Boult mould, noble and unexaggerated in *Nimrod*, very delicate in the *Romanza* and *Dorabella*, and particularly impressive in the surging accelerando of the final variation. The five *Pomp and circumstance marches* make an attractive coupling, not quite as flamboyant as some versions but beautifully sprung. The recording is warm and slightly recessed.

Monteux's *Enigma* is famous for its individual account of *Nimrod*, where his electric pianissimo at the opening (the playing scarcely above a whisper) benefits from the background quiet of CD, enhancing the superb climax, built up in elegiac fashion. Bliss's

Pomp and circumstance marches have a rumbustious vigour; here the recording sounds more dated; but in Decca's bargain range this makes an impressive coupling.

Serenade for strings in E min., Op. 20.
(B) *** Pickwick Dig. PCD 861 [MCA MCAD 25162]. Serenata of London – GRIEG: *Holberg suite*; MOZART: *Eine kleine Nachtmusik* etc.***
** ASV Dig. CDDCA 518 [id.]. ASMF, Marriner – TIPPETT: *Fantasia concertante***; VAUGHAN WILLIAMS: *Lark ascending* etc.**(*)
(M) *(*) DG Dig. 429 488-2 [id.]. Orpheus CO – DVOŘÁK: *Serenade**(*); TCHAIKOVSKY: *Serenade.***

A particularly appealing account of Elgar's *Serenade*, with unforced tempi in the outer movements admirably catching its mood and atmosphere so that the elegiac *Larghetto*, beautifully and sensitively phrased, finds a natural place in the overall scheme. The Serenata of London is led rather than conducted by Barry Wilde; but this is a performance of undoubted personality, and it is recorded with remarkable realism and naturalness. With excellent couplings, this is an outstanding bargain.

Sir Neville Marriner's recording of the *Serenade*, for ASV, offers well-defined and cleanly focused sound; perhaps it is just a little too 'present' and forward, though not unreasonably so. The performance adds nothing to his earlier recording on Argo, made in the late 1960s, which generated greater atmosphere – see above – and the newer version can certainly be recommended if the couplings are suitable.

The recording by the Orpheus Chamber Orchestra is disappointing. The sharply focused, vividly realistic recording of a string group that is plainly too few in number to be fully effective in this music also emphasizes the lack of ripeness in the reading.

Symphonies Nos. 1–2; Chanson de matin; Chanson de nuit; Cockaigne overture; Pomp and circumstance marches Nos. 1–5; Serenade for strings; Variations on an original theme (Enigma).
(M) *** EMI CMS7 63099-2 (3) [Ang. CDMC 63099]. LPO or LSO, Boult.

Boult's final recordings of the Elgar *Symphonies* are likely to reappear on individual records at mid-price during the lifetime of this book. Both are richly satisfying, with the architecture clearly established. In each the slow movement, concentrated in lyrical intensity, becomes the emotional peak of the reading. This box gathers together almost all the vintage performances which Sir Adrian recorded right at the end of his career. All except the two salon pieces, *Chanson de matin* and *Chanson de nuit*, were recorded in the 1970s. His characteristic glow of intensity is enhanced by the exceptionally full-bodied and well-balanced EMI recordings. The three CDs have not been re-pressed but come boxed in their original packages, not quite consistent with one another. The cost is about the same as that of the original premium-priced CD issues of the two symphonies.

Symphony No. 1 in A flat, Op. 55.
(B) *** CfP CD-CFP 9018. LPO, Vernon Handley.
*** Ph. Dig. 416 612-2 [id.]. RPO, André Previn.

Symphony No. 1 in A flat, Op. 55; Cockaigne overture.
(M) *** Decca 421 387-2 [id.]. LPO, Solti.

Vernon Handley directs a beautifully paced reading which can be counted in every way outstanding, even making no allowance for price. The LPO has performed this symphony many times before but never with more poise and refinement than here. It is in the slow movement above all that Handley scores, spacious and movingly expressive. With very good sound, well transferred to CD, this is a clear first choice.

Solti's version of the *First Symphony* is in Decca's mid-price British Collection series, aptly coupled with his sharply dramatic account of *Cockaigne*. The CD transfers bring out the fullness as well as the brilliance of the excellent 1970s sound, and though Solti's thrusting manner will give the traditional Elgarian the occasional jolt, his clearing away of the cobwebs stems from his study of the composer's own recording before he ever attempted to conduct the work at all.

Previn's view of the first movement is spacious; his espressivo style tends towards accelerando rather than tenuto, towards fractional anticipation rather than hesitation, which makes for alert allegros and a slow movement that is warm but not self-indulgent. The syncopations of the scherzo/march theme have an almost jazzy swagger, and the reading is crowned by a flowing account of the finale which has the necessary heart-tug. The Philips sound is more refined than the typical Elgar sound from EMI, but there is no lack of richness or bite.

Symphony No. 2 in E flat, Op. 63.
(B) *** CfP CD-CFP 9023. LPO, Vernon Handley.
**(*) DG Dig. 423 085-2 [id.]. Philh. O, Sinopoli.

Symphony No. 2 in E flat; Overture: In the South.
(M) *** Decca 421 386-2 [id.]. LPO, Solti.

Symphony No. 2; Serenade for strings.
*** RCA Dig. RD 60072 [60072-2-RC]. LPO, Slatkin.

Handley's is the most satisfying modern version of a work which has latterly been much recorded. What Handley conveys superbly is the sense of Elgarian ebb and flow, building climaxes like a master and drawing excellent, spontaneous-sounding playing from an orchestra which, more than any other, has specialized in performing this symphony. The sound is warmly atmospheric and vividly conveys the added organ part in the bass, just at the climax of the finale, which Elgar himself suggested 'if available': a tummy-wobbling effect. This would be a first choice at full price, but as a bargain CD there are few records to match it.

Slatkin's account of the *Second Symphony* is splendid, timed beautifully to deliver authentic frissons, and it has extra power in the finale from the addition of pedal notes on the organ, just before the epilogue – as Elgar once suggested to Sir Adrian Boult. Previously, only Vernon Handley had included them on his equally outstanding version for CfP. Though the new Slatkin is much more expensive than that, it also includes a strong account of the *Serenade for strings*. Those looking for a first-class modern digital recording of the symphony should be well satisfied.

Solti's brilliant version of the *Second Symphony* is now very generously coupled with *In the South*. Rather more than in the *First Symphony*, his study of Elgar's own recording of the work brings results – surprisingly clipped and urgent – that traditional Elgarians may resist. But the result is incandescent, benefiting from virtuoso playing by the LPO and by brilliant sound, made all the more vivid on CD. The sound for *In the South* is a degree brighter than for the *Symphony*, but with plenty of body it suits the brilliance and flamboyance of the reading, with Solti responding warmly to this most Straussian of Elgar's works.

Sinopoli's version lasts an amazing 65 minutes – or some 20 minutes longer than Elgar's own, which admittedly was cramped by 78-r.p.m. side-lengths. The result has consistent spontaneity and conveys emotional thrust; it is true that in the first movement

Sinopoli misses the leaping exhilaration which the compound time should ideally have, but that and the slow movement have a glow which endows the score with Brucknerian majesty. The recording is exceptionally beautiful, both full and refined, with the Philharmonia strings playing radiantly.

Variations on an original theme (Enigma), Op. 36.
(M) (***) EMI mono CDH7 69784-2 [id.]. BBC SO, Toscanini – DEBUSSY: *La Mer.*(**)

Toscanini's freely expressive reading makes a fascinating contrast with his much later NBC orchestra recording, done live but in much more clinical conditions. Where the American orchestra plays the notes brilliantly but, as it seems, too literally, what is basically the same interpretation comes over with a far greater sense of fantasy, of idiomatic warmth and flair in the electric atmosphere of Queen's Hall, ending with a dazzling account of the finale, which promptly inspires an eruption of joy and excitement from the audience. Though elsewhere audience noises intrude, the sound – superbly mastered by Keith Hardwick, but given extra space on CD – is astonishingly vivid, especially for a transfer from 78 r.p.m., roughening at times as at the very end of the finale.

CHAMBER AND INSTRUMENTAL MUSIC

Piano quintet in A min., Op. 84; String quartet in E min., Op. 83.
*** EMI Dig. CDC7 47661-2 [id.]. Bernard Roberts, Chilingirian Qt.
**(*) Mer. ECD 84082. John Bingham, Medici Qt.

(i; ii) *Piano quintet in A min., Op. 84*; (iii) *Violin sonata in E min., Op. 82*; (i) (Piano) *Concert allegro, Op. 46; Serenade; Sonatina.*
(M) *** EMI CDM7 69889-2. (i) John Ogdon; (ii) Allegri Qt; (iii) Hugh Bean, David Parkhouse.

Bernard Roberts and the Chilingirian Quartet are well attuned to the Elgarian sensibility: they have dignity and restraint, and capture the all-pervading melancholy of the *Quintet*'s slow movement. In the *String quartet*, the Chilingirians are excellent, too, though they do not quite match the ardour of the Medicis; indeed some people have found them too low-voltage. However, they are excellently recorded in a warm acoustic and there is plenty of space round the aural image. An impressive and rewarding issue.

John Bingham and the Medici Quartet play with a passionate dedication and bring an almost symphonic perspective to the *Piano quintet*, and there is no denying their ardour and commitment, particularly in the slow movement. They also give a fine and thoroughly considered account of the *Quartet*, more extrovert in its expressive feeling than with the Chilingirians; and overall their reading is full of perceptive and thought-provoking touches. There will be many who will respond to the higher voltage. Unfortunately they are far too close in the *Quartet* (though less so in the *Quintet*) and it still remains difficult for a real *pp* to register, while tone tends to harden somewhat on climaxes.

John Ogdon and the Allegri Quartet give a strong performance of the *Piano quintet* which misses some of the deeper, warmer emotions in the music but which still gives considerable satisfaction. The *Concert allegro* is a valuable oddity, resurrected by Ogdon (the music was long thought to be lost) and splendidly played; and the shorter pieces also bring some charming ideas, even if they reveal Elgar's obvious limitations when writing for the keyboard. There is an autumnal quality about the *Violin sonata* and it responds to ripe treatment such as Hugh Bean and David Parkhouse bring to it. The remastered sound is most realistic, fresh, full and clear, and this generous collection is excellent value.

String quartet in E min., Op. 83.
*** Chan. Dig. CHAN 8474 [id.]. Gabrieli Qt – WALTON: *Quartet.* ***
*** ASV Dig. CDDCA 526 [id.]. Brodsky Qt – DELIUS: *Quartet.****

Apart from its intrinsic excellence, the Gabrieli playing has a far-from-autumnal vitality and much eloquence; and the recording, made in the excellent acoustic of The Maltings, Snape, is up to the high standards one expects from this source.

The young players of the Brodsky Quartet take a weightier view than usual of the central, interlude-like slow movement but amply justify it. The power of the outer movements, too, gives the lie to the idea of this as a lesser piece than Elgar's other chamber works. First-rate recording.

Violin sonata in E min., Op. 82.
(*) ASV Dig. CDDCA 548 [id.]. Lorraine McAslan, John Blakely – WALTON: *Sonata.*(*)

Violin sonata in E min., Op. 82; Canto popolare; Chanson de matin, Op. 15/2; Chanson de nuit, Op. 15/1; Mot d'amour, Op. 13/1; Salut d'amour, Op. 12; Sospiri, Op. 70; 6 Easy pieces in the first position.
*** Chan. Dig. CHAN 8380 [id.]. Nigel Kennedy, Peter Pettinger.

At the start of the *Sonata*, Kennedy establishes a concerto-like scale, which he then reinforces in a fiery, volatile reading of the first movement, rich and biting in its bravura. The elusive slow movement, *Romance*, is sharply rhythmic in its weird Spanishry, while in the finale Kennedy colours the tone seductively. As a coupling, Kennedy has a delightful collection of shorter pieces, not just *Salut d'amour* and *Chanson de matin* but other rare chips off the master's bench. Kennedy is matched beautifully throughout the recital by his understanding piano partner, Peter Pettinger, and the recording is excellent.

Though Lorraine McAslan cannot match the virtuoso command and warmth of tone of Nigel Kennedy's Chandos recording of the *Sonata*, hers is an impressive and warm-hearted version, full of natural imagination, helped by the incisive playing of John Blakely. Good, forward recording, which gives the violin tone less bloom than it might.

PIANO MUSIC

Adieu; Carissima; Chantant; Concert allegro; Dream children, Op. 43; Griffinesque; In Smyrna; May song; Minuet; Pastorale; Presto; Rosemary; Serenade; Skizze; Sonatina.
**(*) Chan. Dig. CHAN 8438 [id.]. Peter Pettinger.

This record includes all of Elgar's piano music. He did not have anywhere near the same feeling for the keyboard as many of his contemporaries – and the earlier writing is both derivative and poorly laid out for the instrument. It has not established itself in the piano repertoire but, as Peter Pettinger shows, there are interesting things in this byway of English music (such as the *Skizze* and *In Smyrna*). We get both the 1889 version of the *Sonatina* and its much later revision. Committed playing from this accomplished artist, and a pleasing recording too, with fine presence on CD.

VOCAL AND CHORAL MUSIC

Songs: *After; Arabian serenade; Is she not passing fair; Like to the damask rose; Oh, soft was the song; Pleading; Poet's life; Queen Mary's song; Rondel; Shepherd's song; Song of autumn; Song of flight; Through the long days; Twilight; Was it some golden star?*
(*) Chan. Dig. CHAN 8539 [id.]. Benjamin Luxon, David Willison – DELIUS: *Songs.*(*)

Benjamin Luxon seemingly cannot avoid the roughness of production which has marred some of his later recordings, but gives charming freshness to this delightful selection. Such a simple invention as the *Shepherd's song* is hauntingly beautiful. Brilliant and sensitive accompaniment, and a very fine recording balance.

Angelus, Op. 56/1; Ave Maria; Ave maris stella; Ave verum corpus, Op. 2; Ecce sacerdos magnus; Fear not, O land; Give unto the Lord, Op. 74; Great is the Lord, Op. 67; I sing the birth; Lo! Christ the Lord is born; O hearken thou, Op. 64; O salutaris hostia Nos. 1–3.
*** Hyp. Dig. CDA 66313 [id.]. Worcester Cathedral Ch., Donald Hunt; Adrian Partington.

Though one misses the impact of a big choir in the *Coronation anthem, O hearken thou,* and in the grand setting of Psalm 48, *Great is the Lord,* the refinement of Dr Hunt's singers, their freshness and bloom as recorded against a helpful acoustic, are ample compensation, particularly when the feeling for Elgarian phrasing and rubato is unerring. Most of these fourteen items are more intimate, and the Worcester performances are near ideal, with clean ensemble, fine blending and taut rhythmic control. Vividly atmospheric recording, which still allows full detail to emerge.

The Banner of St George, Op. 33; (i) *Great is the Lord (Psalm 48), Op. 67; Te Deum and Benedictus, Op. 34.*
*** EMI Dig. CDC7 47658-2 [id.]. (i) Stephen Roberts; LSO Ch., N. Sinfonia, Hickox.

In telling the story of St George slaying the dragon and saving the Lady Sylene, Elgar is at his most colourful, with the battle sequence leading to beautifully tender farewell music (bringing one of Elgar's most yearningly memorable melodies) and a final rousing chorus. The three motets, written at the same period, bring 'Pomp and circumstance' into church and, like the cantata, stir the blood in Hickox's strong, unapologetic performances, richly recorded.

(i) *Coronation ode, Op. 44; The Spirit of England, Op. 80.*
*** Chan. CHAN 8430 [id.]. Cahill, SNO Ch. and O, Gibson; (i) with Anne Collins, Rolfe-Johnson, Howell.

Gibson's performances combine fire and panache, and the recorded sound has an ideal Elgarian expansiveness, the choral tone rich and well focused, the orchestral brass given plenty of weight, and the overall perspective highly convincing. He is helped by excellent soloists, with Anne Collins movingly eloquent in her dignified restraint when she introduces the famous words of *Land of hope and glory* in the finale; and the choral entry which follows is truly glorious in its power and amplitude. *The Spirit of England,* a wartime cantata to words of Laurence Binyon, is in some ways even finer, with the final setting of *For the fallen* rising well above the level of his occasional music.

The Dream of Gerontius, Op. 38.
*** EMI CDS7 47208-8 (2). Helen Watts, Gedda, Lloyd, John Alldis Ch., LPO, Boult – *The Music Makers.***(*)
*** Chan. Dig. CHAN 8641/2 (2) [id.]. Palmer, Davies, Howell, LSO Ch. & O, Hickox – PARRY: *Anthems.****
(M) **(*) Decca 421 381-2 (2) [id.]. Pears, Minton, Shirley-Quirk, King's College Ch., LSO Ch., LSO, Britten – HOLST: *Hymn of Jesus.****
**(*) EMI Dig. CDS7 49549-2 (2) [Ang. CDCB 49549]. J. Baker, Mitchinson, Shirley-Quirk, CBSO Ch. & O, Rattle.
**(*) CRD CRD 3326/7 [id.]. Tear, Hodgson, Luxon, SNO Ch. & O, Gibson.

(M) (**(*)) EMI mono CHS7 63376-2 [Ang. CDHB 63376]. Lewis, Thomas, Cameron, Huddersfield Ch. Soc., Royal Liverpool PO, Sargent – WALTON: *Belshazzar's Feast*.(**(*))

(i) *The Dream of Gerontius; Sea Pictures.*
(M) **(*) EMI CMS7 63185-2 (2). Dame Janet Baker, Hallé O, Barbirolli; (i) with Richard Lewis, Kim Borg, Hallé & Sheffield Philharmonic Ch., Amb. S.

Boult's total dedication is matched by his sense of drama. The spiritual feeling is intense, but the human qualities of the narrative are also fully realized. Boult's controversial choice of Nicolai Gedda in the role of Gerontius brings a new dimension to this characterization, and he brings the sort of echoes of Italian opera that Elgar himself – perhaps surprisingly – asked for. He is perfectly matched by Helen Watts as the Angel. The dialogues between the two have a natural spontaneity as Gerontius's questions and doubts find a response which is at once gently understanding and nobly authoritative. It is a fascinating vocal partnership, and it is matched by the commanding manner which Robert Lloyd finds for both his roles. The orchestral playing is always responsive and often, like the choral singing, very beautiful, while the dramatic passages bring splendid incisiveness and bold assurance from the singers. The fine 1976 analogue recording is extremely well balanced and has responded admirably to its CD remastering. There is slight loss of ambience, but the extra clarity adds impact to the big choral climaxes, and the magical opening and closing pages of Part II are not robbed of their atmosphere and sense of mystery. However, in order to make room for *The Music Makers*, a welcome enough bonus, at the end of the first disc Part I of *Gerontius* is broken immediately before the Priest's dramatic *Proficiscere, anima Christiana*, a most unfortunate choice, robbing the listener of the surprise entry of the brass.

Barbirolli's red-blooded reading of *Gerontius* is the most heart-warmingly dramatic ever recorded; here it is offered, in a first-rate CD transfer, in coupling with one of the greatest Elgar recordings ever made: Dame Janet Baker's rapt and heartfelt account of *Sea Pictures*, originally the coupling for Jacqueline du Pré's first version of the *Cello concerto*. No one on record can match Dame Janet in this version of *Gerontius* for the fervent intensity and glorious tonal range of her singing as the Angel, one of her supreme recorded performances; and the clarity of CD intensifies the experience. In pure dedication the emotional thrust of Barbirolli's reading conveys the deepest spiritual intensity, making most other versions seem cool by comparison. Barbirolli also scores even over the finest modern rivals in the forward immediacy of the chorus. The recording may have its hints of distortion, but the sound is overwhelming, not least in the great outburst of *Praise to the Holiest*, and in the surge of emotion behind the radiant choruses ending each half. Richard Lewis gives one of his finest recorded performances, searching and intense, and, though Kim Borg is unidiomatic in the bass roles, his bass tones are rich in timbre, even if his projection lacks the dramatic edge of Robert Lloyd on the Boult set – however, that has the comparably unidiomatic Nicolai Gedda in the role of Gerontius. The Barbirolli reissue has rather a high tape-hiss, but in such a performance one quickly forgets it after the Prelude; and the layout is preferable to the Boult set, opening with the *Sea Pictures*, then offering Part One of the main work on the first CD, and Part Two complete on the second.

Hickox's version outshines all rivals in the range and quality of its sound. Quite apart from the fullness and fidelity of the recording, Hickox's performance is deeply understanding, not always ideally powerful in the big climaxes but most sympathetically paced, with natural understanding of Elgarian rubato. The soloists make a characterful team. Arthur Davies is a strong and fresh-toned Gerontius; Gwynne Howell in the bass roles is powerful if not always ideally steady; and Felicity Palmer, though untraditionally bright of tone with her characterful vibrato, is strong and illuminating. Though on balance Boult's soloists are even finer, Hickox's reading in its expressive warmth conveys much love for this score, and the last pages with their finely sustained closing *Amen* are genuinely moving.

The Britten version brings searching and inspired conducting from a fellow-composer not generally associated with Elgar. Britten's approach is red-blooded, passionate and urgent, and with speeds never languishing – as in this oratorio they can. The LSO Chorus – supplemented by the King's Choir – is balanced backwardly in the warmly atmospheric recording made at The Maltings, but the extra projection and precision of CD brings out how bitingly dramatic the singing is, even if the actual choral sound is not sharply focused. The soloists are a fine, responsive team, with Pears an involving if sometimes over-stressed Gerontius, and Yvonne Minton and John Shirley-Quirk both excellent. On CD the layout, with the Holst work placed first, allows the break between discs to come in the ideal place, between the oratorio's two parts.

Rattle's flamboyant operatic style is certainly not lacking in dynamism and there is much that is moving, but his control of the ebb and flow of tempo and tension is not always convincing. In *Praise to the holiest in the height*, the chorus, while producing gloriously rich and luminous sounds, is pressed into an impetuous accelerando at the close, so that the climax is approached at breakneck speed, in complete contrast to the broad and heavily accented opening section. Similarly the brief but profound orchestral interlude, where the soul of Gerontius goes forward to meet his Maker, is robbed of dignity by a sudden quickening of pace, so that the apocalyptic fortissimo chord conveys the bizarre impression that the Lord has smitten him down for his eagerness. John Mitchinson sings powerfully and dramatically in Part I and Rattle's accompaniment throbs with fervour; but the voice soon develops an uncomfortably wide vibrato under pressure, which is less congenial in Part II. Dame Janet Baker's assumption of the Angel's role is justly famous, but the close microphones are not kind to her high fortissimos; she comes into her own, however, at the work's valedictory close, helped by the rapturously lovely sounds made by chorus and orchestra alike. The recording has the widest possible dynamic range and, with the solo voices recessed and pianissimos having a tendency to recede, it is difficult to achieve a setting which is comfortable in the work's lyrical sections and yet not overwhelming at climaxes.

Gibson's performance is impressively spontaneous and very dramatic. When in his opening section Gerontius (Robert Tear) describes 'this strange innermost abandonment, this emptying out of each constituent', the orchestral response sends a shiver down the spine. The same sense of drama attends the demons (who are forthright rather than sinister), although here the brightness of the CD transfer verges on fierceness. The male soloists match Gibson's urgency, although there is no lack of repose in the dialogue between the Angel (sensitively portrayed by Alfreda Hodgson) and Gerontius at the opening of Part II. With Gibson, the closing pages are sensitively done but lack the magical feeling of blissful infinity that Boult evokes. The CRD recording is generally excellent but, like Rattle's EMI set, it has almost too wide a dynamic range; also the internal cueing is much too limited.

Sargent directs a thoughtful and moving account of *Gerontius*, with the 1950s sound coming up remarkably well, but it is sad that his earlier (1945) recording, the first complete one ever issued, was not chosen instead, more intense, more dedicated, more spontaneous-sounding. But with three excellent soloists and the Huddersfield Choral Society at its traditional peak, this is an excellent example of Sargent's work in his most successful area, conducting an amateur chorus. The coupling is both generous and apt and, with Walton coming before Part 1 of the Elgar, it means that the break between discs is ideally placed between the two Parts.

King Arthur: suite; (i) *The Starlight Express, Op. 78: suite.*
**(*) Chan. CHAN 8428 [id.]. Bournemouth Sinf., Hurst, (i) with Glover, Lawrenson.

The *King Arthur suite*, though not great music at all, is full of surging, enjoyable ideas and makes an interesting novelty on record. *The Starlight Express suite* is from very much the same world as the *Wand of Youth suites*, with a song or two included. Though the singers here are not ideal interpreters, the enthusiasm of Hurst and the Sinfonietta is conveyed well, particularly in the *King Arthur suite.* The recording is atmospheric if rather over-reverberant.

(i) *The Kingdom* (with BACH, arr. ELGAR: *Fantasia and fugue in C min.(BWV 537), Op. 86;* HANDEL, arr. ELGAR: *Overture in D min.* from *Chandos anthem No. 2*).
*** RCA Dig. RD 87862 (2) [7862-2-RC]. (i) Kenny, Hodgson, Gillett, Luxon, LPO Ch.; LPO, Slatkin.

The Kingdom; Sursum corda; Sospiri.
*** Chan. Dig. CHAN 8788/9 [id.]. Marshall, Palmer, Davies, Wilson-Johnson, LSO Ch., LSO, Hickox.

Hickox is a passionate Elgarian, confident in his dramatic timing and in his use of an expressive rubato which never has any feeling of self-consciousness or over-indulgence. This fine Chandos version provides a strong contrast with the classic Boult recording (currently awaiting reissue), the first ever made and which, above all, brings out the oratorio's nobility. On his RCA version Slatkin, like Hickox, proves a warmly understanding Elgarian, but Hickox's manner is more ripely idiomatic. With a more consistent team of soloists and richer recording, the Chandos is to be preferred – though there is still a strong case for choosing the Boult, which has the finest soloists of all and, in an excellent CD transfer, brings an exceptionally generous coupling. Hickox's soloists make a characterful quartet. Margaret Marshall is the sweet, tender soprano, rising superbly to a passionate climax in her big solo, *The sun goeth down*, and Felicity Palmer is a strong and positive – if not ideally warm-toned – Mary Magdalene. David Wilson-Johnson points the words of St Peter most dramatically, and Arthur Davies is the radiant tenor. The fill-ups are not generous: the intense little string adagio, *Sospiri*, and the early *Sursum corda*; but both similarly reveal Hickox as a deeply understanding Elgarian.

Slatkin's contribution to the RCA set is outstandingly fine, passionate and red-blooded. Slatkin is more daring and less restrained than is Boult in his (currently withdrawn) version; Slatkin sometimes jumps the gun in unleashing his forces, but he makes nonsense of any suggestion that this is an undramatic, merely meditative piece. Urgent as his view of Elgar is, Slatkin has a natural feeling for Elgarian rubato and is never rigid or breathless. When it comes to the gentler moments, he conveys a hushed dedication surpassing even Boult's. The choral singing is incandescent; but sadly the set falls short in the choice of soloists. All four in varying degrees (Alfreda Hodgson less than the others) sing with uneven production and with noticeable flutter or vibrato amounting to wobble. The sound is full, rich and atmospheric, as it also is in the two ripely characteristic transcriptions of Bach and Handel that come as fill-ups.

The Music Makers, Op. 69.
(*) EMI CDS7 47208-8 (2). Dame Janet Baker, LPO Ch., LPO, Boult – *Dream of Gerontius.**

The Music Makers, Op. 69; Sea pictures, Op. 37.
**(*) EMI Dig. CDC7 47674-2 [id.]. Felicity Palmer, LSO Ch. & O, Hickox.

It is some measure of the musical material in *The Music Makers* that the passages which stand out are those where Elgar used themes from his earlier works. If only the whole piece lived up to the uninhibited choral setting of the *Nimrod* variation from *Enigma*, it would be another Elgar masterpiece. Dame Janet Baker sings with dedicated mastery, though unfortunately her example is not always matched in Boult's recording by the comparatively dull-sounding choir.

Hickox's generous coupling of *Sea pictures* and the big cantata, *The Music Makers*, brings strong, powerful performances, very individual in the song-cycle thanks to the urgent, tough singing of Felicity Palmer, very different from that of Dame Janet Baker or Bernadette Greevy (see below), but just as characterful. Though Hickox in *The Music Makers* cannot quite match the finesse of Sir Adrian Boult's recording, it is a convincing, red-blooded reading, atmospherically recorded with voices well caught, but with reverberation masking some of the orchestral detail.

4 Partsongs, Op. 53; 5 Partsongs from the Greek anthology, Op. 45. Choral songs: *Christmas greeting; Death on the hills; Evening scene; The fountain; Fly, singing bird; Goodmorrow; Go, song of mine; The herald; How calmly the evening; Love's tempest; My love dwelt; Prince of sleep; Rapid stream; Reveille; Serenade; The shower; Snow; Spanish serenade; They are at rest; The wanderer; Weary wind of the West; When swallows fly; Woodland stream; Zut! zut! zut!*
*** Hyp. Dig. CDA 66271/2 [id.]. Worcester Cathedral Ch.; Donald Hunt Singers, Hunt; K. Swallow, J. Ballard; R. Thurlby.

Though many of the partsongs, particularly the early ones, show Elgar at his most conventional, they bring many delights and at least one extraordinarily original item in the last of the *Four Partsongs* Opus 53 of 1908, *Owls*. Set to words of Elgar himself, it is dedicated (in Latin) to his daughter Carice's pet rabbit, and presents a weirdly chromatic and pauseful piece, quite unlike the rest. The finest item is the last, in which both choirs join, the eight-part setting of *Cavalcanti* in translation by Rossetti, *Go, song of mine*. It is also fascinating to find Elgar in 1922, with all his major works completed, writing three charming songs for boys' voices to words by Charles Mackay, as refreshing as anything in the whole collection. He was plainly enjoying himself over such trifles. Atmospherically recorded – the secular singers rather more cleanly than the cathedral choir – it is a delightful collection for anyone fascinated by Elgar outside the big works.

Scenes from the Saga of King Olaf, Op. 30.
⊕ *** EMI Dig. CDS7 47659-8 (2). Cahill, Langridge, Rayner-Cook, LPO Ch., LPO, Handley.

The emotional thrust in Handley's reading confirms *King Olaf* as the very finest of the big works Elgar wrote before the *Enigma variations* in 1899. The wonder is that Elgar's inspiration rises high above the doggerel of the text (Longfellow, adapted by Harry Acworth), and though the episodic dramatic plan tails off towards the end, it is the opposite with Elgar's music, which grows even richer. Though strained at times by the high writing, Philip Langridge makes a fine, intelligent Olaf; Teresa Cahill sings with ravishing silver purity and Brian Rayner-Cook brings out words with fine clarity; but it is the incandescent singing of the London Philharmonic Chorus that sets the seal on this superb set, ripely recorded, one of the finest in EMI's long Elgar history. The CDs are in the demonstration class.

Sea pictures (song cycle), *Op. 37.*
⊛ *** EMI CDC7 47329-2 [id.]. Dame Janet Baker, LSO, Barbirolli – *Cello concerto.****
⊛

(i) *Sea pictures, Op. 37; Pomp and circumstance marches Nos. 1–5, Op. 39.*
(B) *** CfP CD-CFP 9004. (i) Bernadette Greevy; LPO, Handley.

Sea pictures hardly matches the mature inspiration of the *Cello concerto* with which it is coupled on EMI, but it is heartwarming here none the less. Like du Pré, Baker is an artist who has the power to convey on record the vividness of a live performance. With the help of Barbirolli she makes the cycle far more convincing than it usually seems, with often trite words clothed in music that seems to transform them. On CD, the voice is caught with extra bloom, and the beauty of Elgar's orchestration is enhanced by the subtle added definition.

Bernadette Greevy – in glorious voice – gives the performance of her recording career in an inspired partnership with Vernon Handley, whose accompaniments are no less memorable, and with the LPO players finding a wonderful rapport with the voice. The singer's imaginative illumination of the words is a constant source of delight. In the last song Handley uses a telling *ad lib.* organ part to underline the climaxes of each final stanza. The recording balance is excellent, although the CD suggests that the microphone was rather close to the voice, rich and clear against an orchestral background shimmering with atmospheric detail. The coupled *Marches* are exhilarating, and if Nos. 2 and (especially) 3 strike some ears as too vigorously paced, comparison with the composer's own tempi reveals an authentic precedent.

Scenes from the Bavarian Highlands, Op. 27 (original version).
*** Conifer Dig. CDCF 142 [id.]. CBSO Ch, Halsey; Richard Markham – HOLST: *Dirges & Hymeneal etc.****

Scenes from the Bavarian Highlands, Op. 27 (orchestral version).
*** EMI CDC7 49738-2. Bournemouth Ch. & SO, Del Mar – VAUGHAN WILLIAMS: *In Windsor Forest; Towards the Unknown Region.****

Three movements from this choral version of *Scenes from the Bavarian Highlands* were later to become the *Bavarian dances* for orchestra; but with piano accompaniment this original version is if anything even more charming, particularly when sung as freshly as by the Birmingham choir, vividly recorded.

The EMI recording uses the orchestral version of the score; although the choral recording is agreeably full, balances are not always ideal, with the choral descant in the *Lullaby* outweighing the attractive orchestral detail. However, the performances are infectiously spirited, conveying warmth as well as vigour.

The spirit of England, Op. 80; Give unto the Lord (Psalm 29); Land of hope and glory; O hearten Thou (Offertory); *The snow.*
*** EMI Dig. CDC7 49481-2 [id.]. Felicity Lott, LSO Ch., N. Sinfonia, Hickox.

Hickox, in his series of lesser Elgar choral works for EMI, conducts a rousing performance of *The spirit of England*, magnificently defying the dangers of wartime bombast. He adds three short choral pieces, including a setting of Psalm 29, and ends with *Land of hope and glory* in all its splendour. The London Symphony Chorus is in radiant form. Felicity Lott in *The spirit of England* is not quite as sweet as Teresa Cahill on the Chandos version under Sir Alexander Gibson – see above. It is extremely well recorded; but the EMI CD has the advantage of the finest EMI digital sound, with a wide amplitude.

The Starlight Express (incidental music), *Op. 78.*
(M) **(*) EMI CMS7 69891-2 (2). Masterson, Hammond-Stroud, LPO, Handley – DELIUS: *Hassan.***(*)

Handley's fine recording of Elgar's incidental music for *The Starlight Express* was just too long to fit on to a single CD, and one cannot help reflecting, as it is somewhat repetitive, that a few judicious cuts might have been justified. Here, of necessity, Act III scene ii (which is quite short) had to be placed on a second disc. Much of the writing reveals the composer at his most charming; in this dedicated reconstruction, the ear is continually beguiled. Both soloists are good and Derek Hammond-Stroud – who has the most sympathetic vocal writing – makes a splendid Organ Grinder, while the LPO plays with warmth and sympathy. It is all rather insubstantial, but the warmly atmospheric recording helps to create an evocative feeling throughout.

Eller, Heino (1887–1970)

Dawn (tone poem); (i) *Elegia for harp & strings; 5 pieces for strings.*
*** Chan. Dig. CHAN 8525 [id.]. (i) Pierce; SNO, Järvi – RAID: *Symphony No. 1.***

Heino Eller was an Estonian composer and his earliest work here is a tone-poem, *Dawn*, written at the end of the First World War, which is frankly romantic – with touches of Grieg and early Sibelius as well as the Russian nationalists. The *Five Pieces for strings* of 1953 are transcriptions of earlier piano miniatures and have a wistful, Grieg-like charm. The *Elegia for harp and strings* of 1931 strikes a deeper vein of feeling and has nobility and eloquence, tempered by quiet restraint; there is a beautiful dialogue involving solo viola and harp which is quite haunting. Excellent performances and recording, too. Strongly recommended.

Ellington, Edward Kennedy 'Duke' (1899–1974)

Mainly black (suite, arr. Kennedy).
*** EMI Dig. CDC7 47621-2 [id.]. Nigel Kennedy, Alec Dankworth – BARTÓK: *Violin sonata.***

As a fascinating and surprisingly apt coupling for the Bartók *Solo Violin sonata*, Nigel Kennedy gives an equally brilliant account of his own free arrangement of Duke Ellington's suite for big band, *Black, Brown and Beige.* With only a double-bass as partner, the haunting beauty of the melody in *Come Sunday* is all the more intense. In other movements the bass sharpens the impact of Kennedy's always vital playing. The sound is outstandingly vivid and full of presence.

Enescu, Georges (1881–1955)

Romanian rhapsody No. 1.
(*) RCA Dig. VD 87727 [7727-2-RV]. Dallas SO, Mata (with *Concert*(*)).
(M) **(*) RCA GD 86530 (6530-2-RG]. Boston Pops, Fiedler – DVORÁK: *Symphony No. 9.***(*)

Enescu's chimerical *First Roumanian rhapsody* combines a string of glowing folk-derived melodies with glittering scoring, to make it the finest genre piece of its kind in laminating East European gypsy influences under a bourgeois orchestral veneer. The Dallas performance, with the help of superbly lustrous digital sound, brings out all the colour and much of the sparkle, although Mata does not quite find the flair and exhilaration in the closing pages which distinguished the best analogue versions. But the RCA compact disc is truly demonstration-worthy in its natural vividness.

Fiedler's version has more dash than Mata's; this was music the conductor of the Boston Pops did uncommonly well, and the orchestral playing is first rate. The recording, however, is not so rich as Mata's.

Symphony No. 3 in C, Op. 21; Chamber symphony for 12 solo instruments, Op. 33.
(**) Marco Polo 8.223143 [id.]. Cluj-Napoco Ch. & PO, Ion Baciu.

Enescu is a grossly underrated composer, and there is much else besides the *Roumanian rhapsody No. 1* and the *Third Violin sonata* that deserves to be heard. The *Third Symphony* (1916–21) is richly imaginative, with overtones of Strauss, Ravel and the music of its time, and it is scored with considerable flair. It deserves a better recording than this, which is very synthetic in balance and coarse-toned with no air round the aural image. It is difficult to believe that this sound dates from 1988! The *Chamber symphony for 12 instruments* is a late work of some subtlety; it is inventive and individual, dating from 1954, and though the sound is two-dimensional, it is an improvement on the *Symphony.*

7 Chansons de Clément Marot.
*** Unicorn Dig. DKPCD 9035 [id.]. Sarah Walker, Roger Vignoles – DEBUSSY: *Songs***; ROUSSEL: *Songs.***(*)

The set of Enescu songs, written in 1908, makes a rare, attractive and apt addition to Sarah Walker's recital of French song. As a Romanian working largely in Paris, Enescu was thinking very much in a French idiom, charming and witty as well as sweetly romantic. Ideal accompaniments and excellent recording.

Erkel, Ferenc (1810–93)

Hunyadi László (opera): complete.
*** Hung. HCD 12581/3 [id.]. Gulyás, Sass, Molnár, Dénes, Sólyom-Nagy, Gáti, Hungarian People's Army male Ch., Hungarian State Op. Ch. & O, Kovács.

Like the much later Erkel opera, *Bank ban, Hunyadi László* has never been out of the repertory in Hungary, and this recording makes one understand why. The end of Act I even brings a rousing chorus which, like *Va pensiero* in Verdi's *Nabucco,* has all the qualities of a pop tune. Erkel's use of national music may not be as strikingly colourful as Smetana's in Czechoslovakia or Glinka's in Russia – both comparable figures – but the flavour is both distinctive and attractive, strongly illustrating a red-blooded story. Janos Kovács conducts with a vigour suggesting long experience of this work in the opera house. Denes Gulyás is a heroic, heady-toned hero, while Andras Molnár is equally effective as the villainous king, surprisingly another tenor role. Sylvia Sass is excellent as the hero's mother, in this version allowed to sing the beautiful prayer just before Laszlo's execution, excised from the earlier recording. First-rate sound. An excellent, unusual set, full of strong ideas, making easy listening.

Falla, Manuel de (1876–1946)

El amor brujo (original version, complete with dialogue); (i) (Piano) *Serenata; Serenata andaluza; 7 Canciones populares Españolas.*
*** Nuovo Era Dig. 6809 [id.]. Martha Senn, Carme Ens., Luis Izquierdo; (i) Maria Rosa Bodini.

(i) *El amor brujo* (original version); (ii) *El corregidor y la molinara.*
*** Virgin Dig. VC7 90790-2 [id.]. (i) Claire Powell; (ii) Jill Gomez; Aquarius, Cleobury.

By including the dialogue, spoken over music, the Nuovo Era issue provides the complete original conception of *El amor brujo*, rather like a one-act zarzuela, with chamber scoring and a narrative line somewhat different from the ballet we know in its full orchestral dress. This works admirably; a complete translation enables the listener to enjoy the dramatic and musical experience fully. Martha Senn is perfectly cast in the role of the gypsy heroine. She sings flamboyantly and often ravishingly, both here and in the delectable *Canciones populares* and the other two songs offered as coupling, and she is accompanied very sympathetically. Luis Izquierdo directs the main work atmospherically and finds plenty of gusto for the piece we know as the *Ritual fire dance*. He lets the tension slip a little only in the closing sequence, when the coming of dawn should bring a greater sense of exultation. Apart from a rather shrill opening fanfare, the recording is suitably atmospheric and vivid.

The Virgin alternative, by omitting the dialogue, finds room for the original version of the *Three-cornered hat*, also conceived for chamber orchestra, which first appeared as a mime play with music. Much is missing from the ballet we know today, including the glorious opening fanfare, while the finales for both Acts end relatively limply without the extra music which Falla added later. Nevertheless each score is aurally fascinating in its original format. Claire Powell makes an admirable gypsy in *El amor brujo*, while Jill Gomez is equally vibrant in her contributions to the companion work. Nicholas Cleobury concentrates on atmosphere rather than drama and, helped by the transluscent textures of the outstanding Virgin Classics recording, certainly seduces the ear, though his *Ritual fire dance* (here the 'Dance at the end of the day') has less pungency than Izquiero's.

El amor brujo; The Three-cornered hat (ballet): complete.
⊛ *** Decca Dig. 410 008-2 [id.]. Boky, Tourangeau, Montreal SO, Dutoit.
(M) *** Decca 417 786-2 [id.]. Nati Mistral, New Philh. O, Frühbeck de Burgos –
ALBÉNIZ: *Suite española.****

(i; ii) *El amor brujo* (complete); (iii) *Nights in the gardens of Spain;* (ii) *The Three-cornered hat* (ballet): *suite.*
** EMI CDM7 69037-2 [id.]. (i) De los Angeles; (ii) Philh. O, Giulini; (iii) Soriano, Paris Conservatoire O, Frühbeck de Burgos.

(i) *El amor brujo* (complete); (ii) *Nights in the gardens of Spain; La vida breve: Interlude and dance.*
*** Chan. Dig. CHAN 8457 [id.]. (i) Sarah Walker; (ii) Fingerhut, LSO, Simon.

Dutoit provides the ideal and very generous coupling of Falla's two popular and colourful ballets, each complete with vocal parts. Few more atmospheric records have ever been made. Performances are not just colourful and brilliantly played, they have an idiomatic feeling in their degree of flexibility over phrasing and rhythm. The ideal instance comes in the tango-like seven-in-a-bar rhythms of the *Pantomime* section of *El amor brujo* which is lusciously seductive. The sound is among the most vivid ever; this remains in the demonstration class for its vividness and tangibility.

Raphael Frühbeck de Burgos provides us with a completely recommendable mid-priced version of *El amore brujo*, attractively coupled with Albéniz. The score's evocative atmosphere is hauntingly captured and, to make the most striking contrast, the famous *Ritual fire dance* blazes brilliantly. Nati Mistral has the vibrant open-throated projection of the real flamenco artist, and the whole performance is idiomatically authentic and compelling. Brilliant Decca sound to match.

The brightly lit Chandos recording emphasizes the vigour of Geoffrey Simon's very vital account of *El amor brujo*, and Sarah Walker's powerful vocal contribution is another asset, her vibrantly earthy singing highly involving. In the more atmospheric sections of the score, however, Dutoit finds a degree of extra subtlety, which gives the Montreal performance its distinction. The Simon/Fingerhut version of *Nights in the gardens of Spain* also makes a strongly contrasted alternative to Alicia de Larrocha's much-praised reading (see below). Here the Chandos sound has a sharper focus than the Decca and the effect is more dramatic, with the soloist responding chimerically to the changes of mood, playing with brilliance and power, yet not missing the music's delicacy. The *Interlude* and *Dance* from *La vida breve* make a very attractive encore.

Giulini's performances come from the mid-1960s and include Soriano's excellent account of *Nights in the gardens of Spain*. The Philharmonia playing is polished and responsive, and Giulini produces civilized and colourful performances. But the recording, though brightly coloured, has lost some of its bloom in the digital remastering, and in any case *El amor brujo* is not as red-blooded here as it is in the hands of either Dutoit or Geoffrey Simon.

Nights in the gardens of Spain.
*** Decca Dig. 410 289-2 [id.]. De Larrocha, LPO, Frühbeck de Burgos – TURINA: *Rapsodia Sinfónica**** (with ALBÉNIZ: *Rapsodia española****).

(i) *Nights in the gardens of Spain; El amor brujo: Ritual fire dance.*
(*) RCA RD 85666. Rubinstein; (i) Phd. O, Ormandy – FRANCK: *Symphonic variations*; SAINT-SAENS: *Concerto No. 2.*(*)

(i) *Nights in the gardens of Spain;* (ii) *The Three-cornered hat* (ballet): complete; *La vida breve: Interlude and dance.*
(M) *** Decca 417 771-2 [id.]. (i) De Larrocha, SRO, Comissiona; (ii) SRO, Ansermet.

Alicia de Larrocha's newest digital version of *Nights in the gardens of Spain* – made in Walthamstow Town Hall – has the advantage of superb digital sound, rich and lustrous, with refined detail. Miss de Larrocha's playing has undoubted poetry and this beguiling and atmospheric performance makes for a very desirable issue indeed. There is a thoughtful, improvisatory quality about the reading and the closing pages, consciously moulded, are particularly beautiful.

Her alternative, earlier (1971) recording makes an excellent mid-priced recommendation, coupled with Ansermet's lively and vividly recorded complete *Three-cornered hat*; she receives admirable support from Comissiona. The Decca analogue recording was outstanding in its day and is very well balanced: it sounds first class in its remastered format, as does the Ansermet coupling, which entirely belies its age (1962). The *La vida breve* excerpts make an agreeable bonus.

Rubinstein's version dates from 1970. His is an aristocratic reading, treating the work as a brilliantly coloured and mercurial concert piece, rather than a misty evocation, with flamenco rhythms glittering in the finale. The two encores which follow are even more arresting.

PIANO MUSIC

4 piezas españolas; Fantasia Baetica; El amor brujo: suite; The Three-cornered hat: 3 dances.
*** Decca 417 816-2 [id.]. Alicia de Larrocha.

This welcome and attractive issue fills an admirable place in the catalogue. It assembles the main piano music of Falla on one CD in exemplary performances and good recordings from 1974 which have transferred with pleasing naturalness to the new medium.

OPERA

La vida breve (complete).
(M) *** EMI CDM7 69590-2 [id.]. De los Angeles, Higueras, Rivadeneyra, Cossutta, Moreno, Orfeon Donostiarra Ch., Nat. O of Spain, Frühbeck de Burgos.

La vida breve is a kind of Spanish *Cavalleria Rusticana* without the melodrama. Unquestionably the opera's story is weak, the heroine expiring with a broken heart when her lover deserts her for another; but if the music for the final scene is weakened by a fundamental lack of drama in the plot, Frühbeck de Burgos makes the most of the poignancy of the closing moments. Victoria de los Angeles deepened her interpretation over the years, and her imaginative colouring of the words gives a unique authority and evocation to her performance. *Vivan les que ri'an* is most expressively done, with Frühbeck following the soloist with great skill. The flamenco singer in Act II (Gabriel Moreno) also matches the realism of the idiom with an authentic 'folk' style. The other members of the cast are good without being memorable; but when this is primarily a solo vehicle for De los Angeles, and the orchestral interludes are managed so colloquially, this is readily recommendable. The recording remains atmospheric, as well as having increased vividness and presence. It now fits conveniently on a single CD.

Fauré, Gabriel (1845–1924)

(i) *Ballade for piano and orchestra, Op. 19;* (ii) *Berceuse for violin and orchestra, Op. 16; Caligula, Op. 52; Les Djinns* (orchestral version), *Op. 12;* (iii) *Elégie for cello and orchestra, Op. 24;* (i) *Fantaisie for piano and orchestra, Op. 111; Pénélope: Prélude.*
*** EMI CDC7 47939-2 [id.]. (i) Collard; (ii) Yan Pascal Tortelier; (iii) Paul Tortelier; Toulouse Capitole O, Plasson.

Masques et bergamasques (complete), *Op. 112; Pelléas et Mélisande* (incidental music), *Op. 80; Shylock, Op. 57.*
*** EMI CDC7 47938-2 [id.]. Von Stade, Gedda, Bourbon Vocal Ens., Toulouse Capitole O, Plasson.

This set of Fauré's orchestral music contains much that is highly rewarding, including the delightful *Masques et bergamasques* and the *Pelléas et Mélisande* and *Shylock* music, as well as such rarities as *Les Djinns* and *Caligula*. Michel Plasson gets an alert and spirited response from the Toulon orchestra and is blessed with very decent orchestral sound. The two works for piano and orchestra are particularly valuable; Jean-Philippe Collard gives a really distinguished account of both the early *Ballade* and the seldom-heard *Fantaisie*, Op. 111, though the piano sound is a trifle hard (not the playing, of course).

Ballade for piano and orchestra, Op. 19.
*** Chan. Dig. CHAN 8773 [id.]. Louis Lortie, LSO, Frühbeck de Burgos – RAVEL: *Piano concertos.***(*)

Louis Lortie's account of the Fauré *Ballade* comes as a fill-up to the Ravel *Concertos* and has the measure of its tenderness and refinement. This young Canadian pianist is a thoughtful artist and his playing has both sensitivity and strength. This is as penetrating and well recorded an account of Fauré's lovely piece as any now available; however, the coupling is not one of the preferred versions of the Ravel *Concertos*.

(i) *Ballade for piano and orchestra, Op. 19;* (ii) *Requiem, Op. 48; Cantique de Jean Racine, Op. 11.*
(M) **(*) EMI CDM7 69841-2. (i) John Ogdon; (ii) Burrowes, Rayner-Cook, CBSO Ch.; CBSO, Frémaux.

The elusive and delicate essence of Fauré's *Ballade* is not easy to capture, but Ogdon's warmly affectionate approach is enjoyable and is notably sensitive in the central and closing sections of the work. Frémaux has a moulded style in the *Requiem* which does not spill over into too much expressiveness, and there is a natural warmth about this performance that is persuasive. Norma Burrowes sings beautifully; her innocent style is most engaging. The originally reverberant recording has been refocused somewhat and does not lose too much of its warmth.

(i) *Berceuse, Op. 16; Violin concerto;* (ii) *Élégie. Masques et bergamasques: Overture, Op. 112; Pelléas et Mélisande: suite, Op. 80; Shylock: Nocturne, Op. 57.*
** ASV Dig. CDDCA 686. (i) Bonucci; (ii) Ponomarev; Mexico City PO, Bátiz.

Fauré's projected *Violin concerto* was composed in the late 1870s; the allegro, which is all that survives, was first performed in 1880. Although it is no masterpiece, it is good to have it on record and students of the composer will certainly want to hear it. Rodolfo Bonucci plays it with affection, as he does the charming *Berceuse* – though his tone above the stave can be a little wiry. Viocheslav Ponomarev produces a big, rich sonority in the celebrated *Élégie*, and Enrique Bátiz plays the orchestral pieces with evident feeling, even if he rather overstates matters at times in the *Nocturne* from *Shylock* and the ravishing *Prélude* of *Pelléas*. Good rather than distinguished recorded sound.

Élégie in C min. (for cello and orchestra), *Op. 24.*
*** Decca Dig. 414 387-2 [id.]. Harrell, Berlin RSO, Chailly – LALO: *Concerto;* SAINT-SAENS: *Cello concerto No. 2.****
(B) *(*) Ph. 422 467-2 [id.]. Gendron, Monte Carlo Op. O, Benzi – DVOŘÁK: *Concerto* etc.**(*); SAINT-SAENS: *Concerto No.1.***

A most distinguished performance of Fauré's *Élégie*, played with eloquence and restraint by Lynn Harrell and admirably accompanied by Chailly.

Gendron's performance is an excellent one, but it is disfigured by an undistinguished accompaniment, notably by some poor woodwind intonation.

(i) *Fantaisie for flute and orchestra, Op. 79* (orch. Aubert); *Masques et bergamasques, Op. 112; Pavane, Op. 50; Pelléas et Mélisande: suite, Op. 80.*
** Argo Dig. 410 552-2 [id.]. (i) Bennett; ASMF, Marriner.

This ASMF Fauré recital certainly offers excellent sound; detail is well defined and there is excellent body. Were the performances in quite the same league, this would be an indispensable issue for all lovers of the French composer. Not that the playing is second-rate or routine, and William Bennett is most sensitive in the *Fantaisie*, but there could be greater freshness and charm.

CHAMBER MUSIC

(i) *Andante in B flat, Op. 75; Berceuse, Op. 16;* (ii) *Cello sonatas Nos. 1 in D min., Op. 109; 2 in G min., Op. 117; Élégie, Op. 24;* (iii) *Fantaisie, Op. 79;* (iii) *Morceau de concours;* (i) *Morceau de lecture;* (ii) *Papillon, Op. 77;* (i) *Romance, Op. 69;* (ii) *Sicilienne, Op. 78;* (i) *Violin sonatas Nos. 1 in A, Op. 13; 2 in E min., Op. 108;* (i; ii) *Trio in D min., Op. 120.*
(M) *** EMI CMS7 62545-2 (2). Jean-Philippe Collard, (i) Augustin Dumay; (ii) Frédéric Lodéon; (iii) Michel Debost.

Cello sonatas Nos. 1 in D min., Op. 109; 2 in G min., Op. 117; Élégie, Op. 24; Sicilienne, Op. 78.
**(*) CRD CRD 3316 [id.]. Thomas Igloi, Clifford Benson.

Noble performances from the late Thomas Igloi and Clifford Benson that do full justice to these elusive and rewarding Fauré sonatas. Igloi plays with fervour and eloquence within the restrained expressive limits of the music and the recording is clear, if not one of CRD's finest in terms of ambient effect.

Cello sonata No. 2 in G min., Op. 117; Après un rêve, Op. 7, No. 1; Berceuse, Op. 16; Élégie, Op. 24; Papillon, Op. 77; Romance, Op. 69; Sicilienne, Op. 78.
*** Hyp. Dig. CDA 66235 [id.]. Steven Isserlis, Pascal Devoyon.

Strange that Hyperion did not record both sonatas: the *D minor* could easily have been accommodated; at under 44 minutes, this is as short on quantity as it is strong on quality! But the *G minor* is one of the most rewarding of Fauré's late works and is played with total dedication and eloquence by Steven Isserlis and Pascal Devoyon.

Piano quartets Nos. 1 in C min., Op. 15; 2 in G min., Op. 45; (i) *Piano quintets Nos. 1 in C min., Op. 89; 2 in D min., Op. 115;* (i) *String quartet in E min., Op. 121.*
(M) *** EMI CMS7 62548-2 (2). Jean-Philippe Collard, Augustin Dumay, Bruno Pasquier, Frédéric Lodéon, (i) Parrenin Qt.

An essential acquisition. Dumay and Collard bring different and equally valuable insights, and their performance of the *Piano quartets* is masterly. In addition, there are authoritative and idiomatic readings of the two *Piano quintets*, the *Piano trio*, the two *Cello sonatas*, on the first set, above (what a fine player Lodéon is!) and the enigmatic and other-worldly *Quartet*, Fauré's last utterance, plus all the smaller pieces. This is enormously civilized music whose rewards grow with each hearing.

Piano quartet No. 1 in C min., Op. 15.
(*) RCA RD 86256 [RCA 6256-2-RC]. Rubinstein, Guarneri Qt – DVORÁK: *Piano quartet No. 2.*(*)

Piano quartets Nos. 1 in C min., Op. 15; 2 in G min., Op. 45.
⊛ *** Hyp. CDA 66166 [id.]. Domus.
*** CRD Dig. CRD 3403 [id.]. Ian Brown, Nash Ens.
(M) (*) EMI mono CDH7 69794-3 [id.]. Marguerite Long, Pasquier Trio.

Lovely playing from all concerned in this immensely civilized music. Domus have the requisite lightness of touch and subtlety, and just the right sense of scale and grasp of tempi. Their nimble and sensitive pianist, Susan Tomes, can hold her own in the most exalted company. The recording is excellent, too, though the balance is a little close, but the sound is not airless.

The Nash Ensemble's readings are perhaps less inward and searching than the Hyperion team's, but they do not fall short of excellence, and the clarity and presence of the recording very much tell in its favour. A three-star issue then, but the wonderfully responsive Domus performance has something special which gives it preference.

The RCA coupling was recorded in December 1970 and, like other Rubinstein reissues from this period, is affected by a rather close balance which prevents a real pianissimo. The performance is warm and spontaneous and readily conveys the players' highly musical response to this attractive music.

Marguerite Long, who was closely associated with Ravel, made the celebrated first recording of the *Piano concerto*, but by the time these recordings were made she was past her prime and the delicacy and finesse associated with her playing were less in evidence. A disappointment.

(i) *Piano quartet No. 1 in C min., Op. 15; Piano trio in D min., Op. 120.*
*** Ph. Dig. 422 350-2. Beaux Arts Trio, (i) with Kim Kashkashian.

Collectors of the Fauré chamber music will have to have this, even if it involves duplication. In some ways (notably in subtlety and charm) it surpasses even the Domus account on Hyperion. Theirs has the grace and lightness of youth; the Beaux Arts have the gentle wisdom of maturity. It is almost invidious to say that Menahem Pressler surpasses himself throughout, since he inspires his partners to equal heights. The *Piano trio* has never sounded so persuasive, even in the hands of Dumay, Collard and Lodéon. The recording is absolutely first rate.

Piano quintets Nos. 1 in D min., Op. 89; 2 in C min., Op. 115.
*** Claves Dig. CD 50-8603 [id.]. Quintetto Fauré di Roma.

These two quintets are much less popular than the two piano quartets and inhabit a more private world. These artists have the measure of Fauré's subtle phrasing and his wonderfully plastic melodic lines, and their performances are hard to fault. The pianist is Maureen Jones, and the quartet are members of I Musici. The recording, made in a Swiss church, is warm and splendidly realistic. This music, once you get inside it, has a hypnotic effect and puts you completely under its spell.

Piano trio in D min., Op. 120.
(*) Denon Dig. CO 72508 [id.]. Rouvier, Kantorow, Müller – DEBUSSY; RAVEL: *Trios.*(*)

A vital performance of one of Fauré's loveliest and most inward-looking late works which succeeds also in conveying its *tendresse*, particularly in the slow movement. It is vividly recorded, if rather closely balanced.

Piano trio in D min., Op. 120; (i) *La bonne chanson, Op. 61.*
*** CRD CRD 3389 [id.]. Nash Ens., (i) with Sarah Walker.

The characterful warmth and vibrancy of Sarah Walker's voice, not to mention her positive artistry, come out strongly in this beautiful reading of Fauré's early settings of Verlaine, music both tender and ardent. The passion of the inspiration is underlined by the use of a long-neglected version of the cycle in which the composer expanded the accompaniment by adding string quartet and double-bass to the original piano. Members of the Nash Ensemble give dedicated performances both of that and of the late, rarefied

Piano trio, capturing both the elegance and the restrained concentration. The atmospheric recording is well up to CRD's high standard in chamber music. In the vocal work the CD quality is a little subdued in the upper range, but that is no real disadvantage: the effect is suitably evocative.

String quartet in E min., Op. 121.
*(*) Nimbus Dig. NI 5114 [id.]. Medici Qt – FRANCK: *Piano quintet.***(*)

The Medici seem only intermittently at ease in the other-worldly atmosphere of Fauré's only string quartet. Their tempi are just a bit too slow and rhythmic, and accompaniments are at times a little plodding. The players obviously like this music, but they have yet to come fully to terms with it. They are very well recorded. Readers wanting this elusive work should turn to the Parrenin on EMI – see above.

Violin sonatas Nos. 1 in A, Op. 13; 2 in E min., Op. 108.
⊛ (M) *** Ph. 426 384-2 [id.]. Arthur Grumiaux, Paul Crossley – FRANCK: *Sonata.***(*)
*** Hyp. Dig. CDA 66277 [id.]. Krysia Osostowicz, Susan Tomes.

Violin sonatas Nos. 1 in A, Op. 13; 2 in E min., Op. 108; Andante, Op. 75; Berceuse, Op. 16.
**(*) ASV Dig. CDDCA 705. Mayumi Fujikawa, Jorge Federico Osorio.

The two Fauré *Sonatas* are immensely refined and rewarding pieces, with strange stylistic affinities and disparities: the second movement of the *E minor* actually uses a theme intended for a symphony that Fauré had discarded more than thirty years earlier. Although they have been coupled before, they have never been so beautifully played or recorded as on the Philips issue. Indeed, this is a model of its kind: there is perfect rapport between Grumiaux and Crossley, and both seem totally dedicated to and captivated by Fauré's muse. Moreover the two artists sound as if they are in the living-room; the acoustic is warm, lively and well balanced. Reissued on Philips's 'Musica da camera' at mid-price and vividly transferred to CD, this coupling is more desirable than ever.

Outstanding performances of both the Fauré *Sonatas*, beautifully played by Krysia Osostowicz and Susan Tomes. There is an appealingly natural, unforced quality to their playing and they are completely persuasive, particularly in the elusive *Second Sonata*. The acoustic is a shade resonant but, such is the eloquence of these artists, the ear quickly adjusts.

Mayumi Fujikawa and Jorge Federico Osorio produce playing of the highest accomplishment and finesse. There is genuine passion here and real commitment, but they do not penetrate Fauré's world as completely as do rivals Grumiaux and Crossley on Philips or Krysia Osostowicz and Susan Tomes on Hyperion, nor are they quite as well recorded.

Violin sonata No. 1 in A, Op. 13.
** Chan. Dig. CHAN 8417 [id.]. Lydia Mordkovitch, Gerhard Oppitz – R. STRAUSS: *Violin sonata.***(*)
*(*) Decca Dig. 421 817-2 [id.]. Joshua Bell, Jean-Yves Thibaudet – DEBUSSY; FRANCK: *Sonatas.*(*)

Violin sonata No. 1; Dolly (suite): *Berceuse.*
(M) (***) EMI mono CDH7 63032-2. Jacques Thibaud, Alfred Cortot – DEBUSSY; FRANCK: *Sonatas* etc.(***)

It is a salutary thought that the glorious performance by Thibaud and Cortot was put on shellac only three years after Fauré's death and is probably the first ever recording of the work. Despite the 1927 sound, which is naturally limited in range and colour, there is tremendous ardour and lyricism here. The recording of the *Dolly Berceuse*, made with Tasso Janopoulo, is much later and comes from 1944.

Lydia Mordkovitch gives a sensitive account of the popular *A major Sonata* but her other-worldly, disembodied pianissimo tone does not draw playing of comparable dynamic range and sensitivity from the pianist, though the acoustic (St Luke's Church, Chelsea) may have posed problems for him. All the same, the playing of both artists will still give pleasure.

While Joshua Bell and Jean-Yves Thibaudet have the measure of Fauré's ardour, his reticence and subtlety register less successfully. The recording is far from airless but there could be more space round the aural image.

SOLO PIANO MUSIC

Ballade in F sharp, Op. 19; Mazurka in B flat, Op. 32; 3 Songs without words, Op. 17; Valses caprices Nos. 1–4.
*** CRD Dig. CRD 3426 [id.]. Paul Crossley.

Crossley's playing seems to have gone from strength to strength in his series, and he is especially good in the quirky *Valses caprices*, fully equal to their many subtleties and chimerical changes of mood. He is extremely well recorded too.

Barcarolles Nos. 1–13 (complete).
*** EMI CDC7 47358-2 [id.]. Jean-Philippe Collard.
*** CRD CRD 3422 [id.]. Paul Crossley.

Jean-Philippe Collard displays unerring judgement in this music and an instinctive feeling for its shifting moods and colours. The recordings were made in 1970 in the Salle Wagram, but the acoustic sounds confined. Collard's *ff* sounds more overpowering in this enclosed environment than it does in real life, but the playing is totally idiomatic.

Paul Crossley is also a fine interpreter of the gentle yet powerful French master. He has a highly sensitive response to the subtleties of this repertoire and is fully equal to its shifting moods. The CRD version was made in the somewhat reverberant acoustic of Rosslyn Hill Chapel, and is more vivid than the 1971 EMI recording of Jean-Philippe Collard. Honours are pretty evenly divided between the two players; both will give pleasure and, if Collard's account is not displaced, the CRD is still a strong challenger.

Barcarolles Nos. 1, 2, 4, Opp. 26, 41, 44; Impromptus Nos. 2 & 3, Opp. 31, 34; Nocturnes Nos. 4 & 5, Opp. 36–7; 3 Romances sans paroles, Op. 17; Valse caprice, Op. 30.
*** Decca Dig. 425 606. Pascal Rogé.

Pascal Rogé is ideally suited by temperament and sensibility to this repertoire. It makes an ideal introduction to Fauré's piano music, and anyone wanting to explore this rewarding world could not do better than set out from here. Rogé brings warmth and charm as well as all his pianistic finesse to this anthology, and his artistry is well served by the Decca engineers.

Barcarolles Nos. 1, 4–6; Impromptus 1–3; Nocturnes 1, 4, 6; 3 Romances sans paroles, Op. 17.
*** Conifer Dig. CDCF 138 [id.]. Kathryn Stott.

A lovely recital. Kathryn Stott produces not only a wide dynamic range but a rich and subtle variety of colours in this well-chosen Fauré anthology. This is a most intelligently planned and boldly executed recital. She has a strong artistic personality and has thought deeply and to good purpose about this wonderful music. The recording is excellent, and this fine recital would make a highly rewarding introduction for any newcomer to Fauré's piano music.

Dolly, Op. 56.
*** Ph. Dig. 420 159-2 [id.]. Katia and Marielle Labèque – BIZET: *Jeux d'enfants*; RAVEL: *Ma Mère l'Oye.****

Fauré's touching suite was written for Hélène Bardac, who was known as *Dolly* and whose mother was Debussy's second wife. The *Kitty waltz* was a gift for her fourth birthday. The Labèque sisters give a beautiful account of it, their playing distinguished by great sensitivity and delicacy. The recording is altogether first class, totally natural and very realistic in its CD format.

Impromptus Nos. 1–5; 9 Préludes, Op. 103; Theme and variations in C sharp min., Op. 73.
*** CRD CRD 3423 [id.]. Paul Crossley.

The *Theme and variations in C sharp minor* is one of Fauré's most immediately attractive works; Paul Crossley plays it with splendid sensitivity and panache, so this might be a good place to start for a collector wanting to explore Fauré's special pianistic world. Crossley never forces the music, yet his purity of style is never chaste, and his concentration and sense of scale demonstrate his full understanding of this repertoire. The recorded sound, too, is extremely well judged, with a most realistic piano image, nicely placed in relation to the listener.

Nocturnes (complete); Pièces brèves, Op. 84.
**(*) CRD CRD 3406-7 [id.]. Paul Crossley.

Here the recording is rather closely balanced, albeit in an ample acoustic, but the result tends to emphasize a percussive element that one does not normally encounter in this artist's playing. The beautifully inward *F sharp minor Nocturne*, Op. 104, No. 1, almost loses the intimate, private quality of which Crossley speaks in his excellent notes, and it is not the only one to do so. There is much understanding and finesse, however, and the *Pièces brèves* are a valuable fill-up.

VOCAL MUSIC

La bonne chanson, Op. 61; Poème d'un jour, Op. 21; Les berceaux; La chanson d'Ève: Eau vivante; O mort, poussière d'étoiles. Le horizon chimérique; Le jardin clos: Exaucement; Je me poserai sur ton coeur. 5 Mélodies de Venise; Mirages.
*** Ph. 420 775-2 [id.]. Gérard Souzay, Dalton Baldwin.

This is a self-recommending recital. Gérard Souzay had a unique sensibility in this repertoire, and his control of colour and feeling for the words is magical. The songs are drawn from two records, made in 1961 and 1965, and the sound is fresh, with good presence. Baldwin accompanies impeccably and is well in the picture.

La chanson d'Ève, Op. 95; Mélodies: Après un rêve; Aubade; Barcarolle; Les berceaux; Chanson du pêcheur; En prière; En sourdine; Green; Hymne; Des jardins de la nuit; Mandoline; Le papillon et la fleur; Les présents; Rêve d'amour; Les roses d'Ispahan; Le secret; Spleen; Toujours!.
🏵 *** Hyp. Dig. CDA 66320 [id.]. Dame Janet Baker, Geoffrey Parsons.

Starting with the boy Fauré's Opus 1, No. 1, a charming, Gounod-like waltz-song, *Le papillon et la fleur*, Dame Janet Baker gives magical performances of a generous collection of 28 songs, representing the composer throughout his long composing career. The rare song-cycle, *La chanson d'Ève*, represents Fauré's rarefied later style, written long after everything else here; but the youthful composer was a much more striking melodist, and here he is represented by many of his most winning songs. Early copies had a couple of incorrect texts in the booklet, but that does not alter the glowing, magical singing of Dame Janet, still golden-toned at the very period when she announced her retirement from public performance. Geoffrey Parsons is at his most compellingly sympathetic, matching every mood. Many will be surprised at Fauré's variety of expression over this extended span of songs.

Requiem, Op. 48.
(M) (**(*)) EMI mono CDH7 61025-2. Gisele Peyron, Doda Conrad, Ch. & O, Nadia Boulanger – MONTEVERDI: *Madrigals.*(***)

It was Nadia Boulanger who conducted the first British performance of the Fauré *Requiem* as recently as 1936. Her magnetism immediately established a new pattern of taste, but it was not until 1948 that she made this recording, and by then her principal baritone, Doda Conrad, was losing his voice, and the ensemble was none too precise. Yet Boulanger's magnetism remains, to convince the listener – at least momentarily – that, for example, so slow a speed for *Piê Jesu* is right, particularly with the silvery Gisele Peyron as soloist. As a generous coupling for the still-magical Boulanger performances of Monteverdi madrigals, so historic an account is most welcome.

Requiem, Op.48.
*** EMI Dig. CDC7 49880-2 [id.]. Murray, Bär, King's College Ch., ECO, Cleobury – DURUFLÉ: *Requiem.***(*)

Requiem, Op. 48 (1893 version). *Ave Maria, Op. 67/2; Ave verum corpus, Op. 65/1; Cantique de Jean Racine, Op. 11; Maria, Mater gratiae, Op. 47/2; Messe basse; Tantum ergo, Op. 65/2.*
*** Collegium COLCD 109 [id.]. Ashton, Varcoe, Cambridge Singers, L. Sinfonia (members), Rutter.

Requiem, Op. 48 (1893 version); *Ave verum corpus, Op. 65/1; Cantique de Jean Racine, Op. 11; Messe basse; Tantum ergo, Op. 65/2.*
*** Hyp. Dig. CDA 66292 [id.]. Mary Seers, Isabelle Poulenard, Michael George, Corydon Singers, ECO, Matthew Best.

Requiem, Op. 48 (1894 version); *Messe des pêcheurs de Villerville.*
*** HM Dig. HMC 90 1292 [id.]. Mellon, Kooy, Audoli, Petits Chanteurs de Saint-Louis, Paris Chapelle Royale Ch., Musique Oblique Ens., Herreweghe.

Requiem, Op. 48.
*** ASV Dig. CDRPO 8004 [id.]. Aled Jones, Stephen Roberts, LSO Ch., RPO, Hickox – BERNSTEIN: *Chichester Psalms.****

Requiem, Op. 48; Maria Mater gratiae, Op. 47/2; Tantum ergo, Op. 65/2.
(B) **(*) Pickwick Dig. PCD 896 [MCA MCAD 25231]. Aidan Oliver, Harry Escott, David Wilson-Johnson, Westminster Cathedral Ch., City of L. Sinfonia, David Hill.

Requiem; Pavane, Op. 50.
(M) *** EMI CDM7 69038-2 [id.]. Sheila Armstrong, Fischer-Dieskau, Edinburgh Fest. Ch., O de Paris, Barenboim.

(i; ii) *Requiem, Op. 48;* (i) *Pavane, Op. 50; Pelléas et Mélisande: suite, Op. 80.*
*** Decca Dig. 421 440-2 [id.]. (i) Kiri Te Kanawa, Sherrill Milnes; (ii) Montreal Philharmonic Ch.; Montreal SO, Dutoit.

(i) *Requiem. Pelléas et Mélisande; Masques et bergamasques.*
(B) *(*) Decca 421 026-2. (i) Danco, Souzay, Peilz Ch. Union; SRO, Ansermet.

John Rutter's inspired reconstruction of Fauré's original 1893 score, using only lower strings and no woodwind, opened our ears to the extra freshness of the composer's first thoughts. Rutter's fine, bright recording now makes a welcome reappearance on the Collegium label with more music added, equally beautifully sung, including the *Messe basse* and four motets, of which the *Ave Maria* setting and *Ave verum corpus* are particularly memorable. The recording is first rate but places the choir and instruments relatively close, with less space round the sound than on the two even more recent rival versions using original instrumentation.

Matthew Best's performance with the Corydon Singers also uses the Rutter edition but presents a choral and orchestral sound that is more refined, set against a helpful church acoustic. *In paradisum* is ethereally beautiful. Best's soloists are even finer than Rutter's, and he too provides a generous fill-up in the *Messe basse* and other motets, though two fewer than Rutter.

In many ways Philippe Herreweghe scoops both of them in his quest for authenticity, for he has had access to a score which makes use of the recently discovered instrumental parts of the original 1894 performance of the seven-movement version; unlike Rutter and Best, however, he tends to adopt speeds that are a degree slower than those marked. His soloists are more sophisticated than their British rivals, tonally very beautiful but not quite so fresh in expression. What makes the Harmonia Mundi version also particularly attractive is the fill-up, the joint Mass-setting which the young Messager and the young Fauré wrote together over one happy summer holiday in Normandy in 1881. The recording has chorus and orchestra relatively close, but there is a pleasant ambience round the sound.

Following on from John Rutter's and Matthew Best's recordings, the EMI version from King's also uses Rutter's reconstruction of the original 1893 score with limited chamber orchestra. It can also claim ancestry from Sir David Willocks's EMI version of the 1960s using the King's Choir of an earlier generation; now, as then, the refinement and responsiveness of the young King's choristers is unsurpassed among collegiate or cathedral choirs. Like Willcocks, Cleobury uses a boy treble for the *Pié Jesu*, with Richard Eteson clear and bright. Generously coupled with the Duruflé *Requiem*, which was directly inspired by Fauré's example, this makes a worthwhile coupling, although neither performance considered individually would be a first choice.

Not surprisingly, the acoustics of St Eustache, Montreal, are highly suitable for recording the regular full orchestral score of Fauré's *Requiem*, and the Decca sound is superb. Dutoit's is an essentially weighty reading, matched by the style of his fine soloists, yet the performance has both freshness and warmth and does not lack transparency. The generous coupling of the choral version of the *Pavane* plus a beautifully played and similarly full-textured suite from *Pelléas et Mélisande* adds to the attractiveness of the Decca issue.

Richard Hickox opts for the regular full-scale text of the *Requiem*, yet at speeds rather faster than usual – no faster than those marked – he presents a fresh, easily flowing view, rather akin to John Rutter's using the original chamber scoring on his Conifer issue. Aled

399

Jones sings very sweetly in *Piè Jesu*. With its generous and equally successful coupling, this makes a strong alternative recommendation to the Dutoit version.

The Edinburgh Festival Chorus is freshly responsive in Barenboim's 1975 recording so that, although the sound is beefier than with Rutter, the effect is never heavy and the performance is given a strong dimension of drama. Yet there is splendidly pure singing from Sheila Armstrong, and although Fischer-Dieskau is not quite as mellifluous as in his earlier account with Cluytens he brings a greater sense of drama. Including a sensitive account of the *Pavane*, this is well worth considering in the budget range.

Using the usual full orchestral score, David Hill yet gives a performance which keeps a modest scale, set within a warm church acoustic – St Jude's, Hampstead, not Westminster Cathedral itself. Its special quality among current versions is that it uses boy trebles and male altos from the cathedral choir instead of women's voices. There is a very boyish, earnest quality to Aidan Oliver's singing of the *Piè Jesu* which is most winning, even if there are still more angelic accounts. The snag is that the choir is set at rather too great a distance in relation to the orchestra.

Ansermet's clear Decca recording serves only to emphasize the rather thin-toned contribution from the chorus. The solo singing is good but not memorable. This disc is most notable for the orchestral items, sympathetic and stylish performances, highly regarded in their day and still sounding well.

Feld, Jindrich (born 1925)

Flute sonata.
*** RCA Dig. RD 87802 [7802-2-RC]. James Galway, Phillip Moll – DVOŘÁK: *Sonatina*; MARTINŮ: *Sonata.****

Jindrich Feld writes in a relatively conservative idiom, only occasionally betraying a specifically Czech flavour. What matters is his understanding of the flute, when it prompts Galway to play with characteristic flair. The piece makes an unusual and attractive coupling to the Dvořák and Martinů works, all of them vividly recorded in a relatively dry acoustic.

Ferguson, Howard (born 1908)

(i) *Concerto for piano and string orchestra, Op. 12;* (ii) *Amore langueo, Op. 18.*
*** EMI Dig. CDC7 49627-2. (i) Howard Shelley; (ii) Martyn Hill, LSO Ch., City of L. Sinfonia, Hickox – FINZI: *Eclogue.****

Ferguson's *Concerto* has something in common with the lyrical feeling of John Ireland's comparable work. Howard Shelley's performance is admirable and Hickox secures a highly sympathetic response from the City of London Sinfonia string section. Although *Amor langueo* is subtitled *Christ's complaint to Man* and concerns Christ's spiritual love for mankind, its imagery also explicitly draws distinctly erotic associations with romantic sexual passion. To the medieval mind, spiritual and secular love were not always seen as separate experiences. The setting, for tenor solo and semi chorus, with a strong contribution from Martyn Hill, brings a powerful response in the present performance. An unusual and rewarding piece, recorded with great vividness.

Ferlendis, Giuseppe (1755–1802)

Oboe concerto No. 1 in F.
(*) Ph. Dig. 420 179-2 [id.]. Holliger, ASMF, Sillito – MOZART: *Concerto* etc.(*)

Ferlendis's *Oboe concerto* was, for a time, also attributed to Mozart although it is difficult to see why. It makes a less than completely enticing coupling for Holliger's latest recording of Mozart's illustrious work, although it is impeccably played and well recorded.

Ferranti, Marco Aurelio Zani de (1801–78)

Exercice, Op. 50/14; Fantaisie variée sur le romance d'Otello (Assisa à piè), Op. 7; 4 Mélodies nocturnes originales, Op. 41a/1–4; Nocturne sur la dernière pensée de Weber, Op. 40; Ronde des fees, Op. 2.
⊛ *** Chan. Dig. CHAN 8512 [id.]. Simon Wynberg (guitar) – FERRER: *Collection.****

Ferranti, now virtually forgotten, was a famous figure in his day. Let Berlioz sum up the contemporary view of his prowess: 'With a Paganinian technique Zani combines a communicative sensibility and an ability to sing that few, as far as I know, have ever possessed before. He soothes you, magnetizes you; it should be added that he writes excellent music for the guitar and that, to a large degree, the charm of his compositions contributes to the spell over the listener.' Here Simon Wynberg's playing fully enters the innocently compelling sound-world of the Bolognese composer; it is wholly spontaneous and has the most subtle control of light and shade. Ferranti's invention is most appealing, and this makes ideal music for late-evening reverie; moreover the guitar is most realistically recorded.

Ferrer, José (1835–1916)

Belle (Gavotte); La danse de naïades; L'étudiant de Salamanque (Tango); Vals.
*** Chan. Dig. CHAN 8512 [id.]. Simon Wynberg (guitar) – FERRANTI: *Collection.**** ⊛

José Ferrer is a less substantial figure than Ferranti, but these four vignettes (each lasting two to three minutes) are almost as winning as that composer's music. They form a centrepiece in Simon Wynberg's excellent and enterprising recital which is most enjoyable. The recording has striking realism and presence.

Fibich, Zdeněk (1850–1900)

Symphony No. 1 in F, Op. 17; The Tempest (symphonic poem), Op. 46.
** Sup. SUP 001091 [id.]. Brno State PO, Vronsky.

Fibich is a fine craftsman, writing in a genial idiom, and his music gives undoubted pleasure. His first published symphony comes from his early thirties and is an attractive piece with appealing melodic ideas; the exhilarating scherzo is its best movement. *The Tempest* is a later and less interesting work, full of stock-in-trade dramatic gestures. Good performances, but a rather indifferent recording: tuttis need more room to expand. All the same, for all those who like Smetana and Dvořák, this is worth investigating.

(i) *Symphonies Nos. 2 in E flat, Op. 38;* (ii) *3 in E min., Op. 53.*
**(*) Sup. SUP 001256 [id.]. Brno State PO, (i) Waldhans; (ii) Bělohlávek.

Fibich's *Second Symphony* is the most often played. At times the music proceeds in a somewhat predictable way, yet the *Adagio* is undoubtedly eloquent, and the scherzo is stirring and colourful. The Brno orchestra under Jiŕá Waldhans give a straightforward performance and the 1976 recording is clear, with plenty of body and a convincing ambient effect. In the *Third Symphony* the invention is fresher than that of its predecessor, and the scherzo with its catchy syncopations has great charm. The performance, directed by Jiří Bělohlávek, is sympathetic and alive; the 1981 recording has a concert-hall balance and vividness, while being kinder to the excellent strings of the Brno orchestra than the balance for the *First Symphony*.

Finzi, Gerald (1901–56)

Cello concerto in A min., Op. 40.
*** Chan. Dig. CHAN 8471 [id.]. Wallfisch, Royal Liverpool PO, Handley – K. LEIGHTON: *Veris gratia.****

Finzi's *Cello concerto*, perhaps the most searching of all his works, should certainly be in the repertory. Wallfisch's performance is stronger and more direct than that of Yo-Yo Ma, who recorded it on LP for Lyrita at the end of the 1970s. Wallfisch finds all the dark eloquence of the central movement, and the performance overall has splendid impetus, with Handley providing the most sympathetic backing and the Royal Liverpool Philharmonic Orchestra on their finest form. The Chandos recording has an attractively natural balance.

Clarinet concerto, Op. 31.
*** Hyp. CDA 66001 [id.]. Thea King, Philh. O, Francis – STANFORD: *Concerto.****
*** ASV Dig. CDDCA 568 [id.]. MacDonald, N. Sinfonia, Bedford – COPLAND: *Concerto*; MOURANT: *Pied Piper.****

Finzi's *Clarinet concerto* is among his very finest music. The expressive intensity of the slow movement communicates immediately, and the joyous pastoral lyricism of the finale has sharp memorability. On the Hyperion label, Thea King gives a definitive performance, strong and clean-cut. Her characterful timbre, using little or no vibrato, is highly telling against a resonant orchestral backcloth. The accompaniment of the Philharmonia under Alun Francis is highly sympathetic. With Stanford's even rarer concerto, this makes a most attractive issue, and the sound is excellent.

The coupling of Finzi and Copland makes an unexpected but attractive mix, with the Canadian clarinettist, George MacDonald, giving a brilliant and thoughtful performance, particularly impressive in the spacious, melismatic writing of the slow movement. The finale with its carefree 'travelling' theme could be handled more lightly. Refined recording, with the instruments set slightly at a distance.

(i) *Clarinet concerto;* (ii) *Dies natalis; Farewell to arms.*
**(*) Virgin Dig. VC 790718-2 [id.]. (i) Michael Collins, (ii) Martyn Hill; City of L. Sinfonia, Hickox.

Dies natalis is quintessential Finzi: a setting of words by Traherne, it reflects the composer's preoccupations with the evanescent nature of life and the corruption of innocence by experience. Martyn Hill is set rather far back: his voice is balanced very much as one would expect it to be in real life, and some listeners will want him to be brought further forward. He also suffers from a pronounced vibrato which takes a lot of getting used to, both in *Dies natalis* and in the *Farewell to arms*. The *Clarinet concerto* is brilliantly played by Michael Collins. Throughout all three works Richard Hickox and the City of London Sinfonia give thoroughly sympathetic support, and the Virgin recording is eminently natural and pleasing.

(i) *Clarinet concerto; Love's labour's lost: suite; Prelude for string orchestra; Romance for strings.*
(M) *** Nimbus Dig. NI 5101 [id.]. (i) Alan Hacker; E. String O, Boughton.

Alan Hacker's reading of the *Concerto* is improvisatory in style and freely flexible in tempi, with the slow movement at once introspective and rhapsodic. The interpretation finds a release from its essentially elegiac feeling in the songful exhilaration of the finale, with William Boughton's sensitive accompaniment following the changes of mood of his soloist most persuasively. The concert suite of incidental music for Shakespeare's *Love's labour's lost* begins with attractive fanfares and a melody in the Bliss/Elgar/Walton tradition, and the rest of the suite is amiably atmospheric and pleasing in invention and in the colour of its scoring. The two string pieces are by no means slight and are played most expressively; the *Romance* is particularly eloquent in William Boughton's hands. The recording, made in the Great Hall of Birmingham University, has the characteristic richness and ambient warmth we associate with Nimbus's fine series of recordings with this group.

Eclogue for piano and string orchestra.
*** EMI Dig. CDC7 49627-2. Howard Shelley, City of L. Sinfonia, Hickox – FERGUSON: *Piano concerto* etc.***

This is the central movement of an uncompleted piano concerto which the composer decided could stand on its own. The mood is tranquil yet haunting, and the performance brings out all its serene lyricism. The recording is admirably realistic.

Dies natalis.
(M) *** EMI CDM7 63372-2. Wilfred Brown, ECO, composer – HOWELLS: *Hymnus paradisi.***

Finzi's sensitive setting of words by the seventeenth-century poet, Thomas Traherne, is sung well here by Wilfred Brown. In a way, one may regard this as a preparation for Britten's later achievement in his orchestral song-cycles, and this record must be recommended to all interested in modern English song setting. The remastered recording sounds wonderfully fresh and is naturally balanced within a glowing acoustic. What a beautiful work this is!

Fiorillo, Federigo (1755– after 1823)

Violin concerto No. 1 in F.
*** Hyp. Dig. CDA 66210 [id.]. Oprean, European Community CO, Faerber – VIOTTI: *Violin concerto No. 13.***

Fiorillo's *Concerto* is charmingly romantic; the *Larghetto* is not ambitious, but the finale is agreeably gay. Adelina Oprean's playing can only be described as quicksilver: her lightness of bow and firm, clean focus of timbre are most appealing. She is given a warm, polished accompaniment by this first-class chamber orchestra, conducted with vitality and understanding by Joerg Faerber. The recording, made in the attractive ambience of the London Henry Wood Hall, is eminently truthful and well balanced.

Flotow, Friedrich (1812–83)

Martha (complete).
*** Eurodisc 352 878 (2) [7789-2-RG]. Popp, Soffel, Jerusalem, Nimsgern, Ridderbusch, Bav. R. Ch. and O, Wallberg.
(M) **(*) EMI CMS7 69339-2 (2) [Ang. CDMB 69339]. Rothenberger, Fassbaender, Weller, Gedda, Prey, Bav. State Op. Ch. & O, Heger.

Martha: highlights.
(M) *** EMI CDM7 69211-2 (from above recording; cond. Heger).

Martha is a charming opera that should be much better known in Britain than it is. The Eurodisc cast is as near perfect as could be imagined. Lucia Popp is a splendid Lady Harriet, the voice rich and full (her *Letzte Rose* is radiant) yet riding the ensembles with jewelled accuracy. Doris Soffel is no less characterful as Nancy, and Siegfried Jerusalem is in his element as the hero, Lionel, singing ardently throughout. Siegmund Nimsgern is an excellent Lord Tristan, and Karl Ridderbusch matches his genial gusto, singing Plunkett's *Porter-Lied* with weight as well as brio. Wallberg's direction is marvellously spirited, and the opera gathers pace as it proceeds. The Bavarian Radio Chorus sings with joyous precision and the orchestral playing sparkles. With first-class recording, full and vivid, this is highly recommended, for the transfer to CD has been managed admirably.

Curiously, the veteran conductor, Robert Heger, for all the delicacy of his pointing, sometimes chooses slow tempi. Gedda sings agreeably, but his characterization of Lionel is a little stiff; otherwise there is stylishness and jollity all round, with Rothenberger in clear, fresh voice as the heroine and Fassbaender at her finest as Nancy. Prey, agreeably expressive in a light-toned way, makes a youthful-sounding Plunkett. Minimal cuts and bright, atmospheric recording, and a distinct price advantage; but the Eurodisc set remains first choice. However, there is also an excellent set of highlights from the Heger recording, and this can be strongly recommended to those wanting just a selection from this tuneful opera.

Foss, Lukas (born 1922)

Round a common center.
** Pro Arte Dig. CDD 120 [id.]. Orson Welles, Elaine Bonazzi, Yehudi Menuhin, Cantilena Chamber Players – COPLAND: *Piano quartet*; WYNER: *Intermezzi.***

Foss's *Round a common center*, here heard in its optional layout for speaker plus violin quintet, is a setting of *The Runner*, a poem by Auden, and the work is tonal and highly resourceful. He suggests it is a piece 'strictly for virtuosi' and it receives a thoroughly committed reading on this recording, well, if rather forwardly, balanced and sympathetic. Not great music perhaps, but a compelling, thoughtful piece with strong atmosphere.

Foulds, John (1880–1939)

String quartets Nos. 9 (Quartetto intimo), Op. 89; 10 (Quartetto geniale), Op. 97. Aquarelles, Op. 32.
⊛ *** Pearl SHECD 9564 [id.]. Endellion Qt.

The *Quartetto intimo*, written in 1931, is a powerful five-movement work in a distinctive idiom more advanced than that of Foulds' British contemporaries, with echoes of Scriabin and Bartók. Also on the disc is the one surviving movement of his tenth and last quartet, a dedicated hymn-like piece, as well as three slighter pieces which are earlier. Passionate performances and excellent recording, which is enhanced by the CD transfer. A uniquely valuable issue.

Franck, César (1822–90)

Le chasseur maudit (The accursed huntsman): symphonic poem.
(*) RCA RD 85750 [RCA 5750-2-RC]. Boston SO, Munch – POULENC: *Organ concerto*(*); SAINT-SAENS: *Symphony No. 3.****

Munch's recording dates from 1962 and sounds quite spectacular, with plenty of fullness, if with a touch of inflation, provided by the warm acoustics of Symphony Hall, Boston. Franck's horn calls come over arrestingly.

Symphonic variations for piano and orchestra.
(*) RCA RD 85666. Rubinstein, NY Symphony of the Air, Wallenstein – FALLA: *Nights* etc.; SAINT-SAENS: *Concerto No. 2.*(*)

(i) *Symphonic variations for piano and orchestra; Prélude, aria and final; Prélude, chorale et fugue.*
*** Decca Dig. 421 714-2 [id.]. Jorge Bolet, (i) Concg. O, Chailly.

Jorge Bolet's accounts of both the solo pieces are very persuasive, although the balance is very present. The *Variations symphoniques* have appeared before, in harness with Chailly's record of the *Symphony*, but this is a more attractive and useful coupling. Bolet never makes an ugly sound and plays the works with evident dedication.

There is refinement and charm from Rubinstein, yet his bravura tautens the structure while his warmth and freedom prevent it from seeming hard or in any way aggressive. The sound is dry but its intimacy is attractive.

Symphony in D min.
⊛ (M) **(*) RCA GD 86805 [6805-2-RG]. Chicago SO, Monteux – D'INDY: *Symphonie sur un chant montagnard français***(*) (with BERLIOZ: *Overture: Béatrice et Bénédict***). **(*) DG Dig. 400 070-2 [id.]. O Nat. de France, Bernstein (with SAINT-SAENS: *Rouet d'Omphale***).

Symphony in D min.; Le chasseur maudit.
**(*) EMI Dig. CDC7 47849-2 [id.]. Phd. O, Muti.

Symphony in D min; (i) *Symphonic variations for piano and orchestra.*
**(*) RCA RD 60146 [60146-2-RC]. (i) Rudolf Firkušný; RPO, Claus Peter Flor.
(M) **(*) EMI CDM7 69008-2. (i) Weissenberg; BPO, Karajan.

Symphony in D min.; (i) *Symphonic variations;* (ii) *Prelude, choral et fugue.*
(M) *** Erato/WEA 2292 45088-2 [id.]. Fr. ORTF O, Martinon; (i) with Entremont; (ii) Pascal Devoyon.

Monteux exerts a unique grip on this highly charged Romantic symphony, and his control of the continuous ebb and flow of tempo and tension is masterly, so that any weaknesses of structure in the outer movements are disguised. The splendid playing of the Chicago orchestra is ever responsive to the changes of mood: the fervour of the thrusting chromatic secondary tune of the first movement is matched by the dynamism of the transformation of the main theme of the *Andante* when it reappears in the finale, before the superbly prepared apotheosis of the coda. The sound on this new CD is greatly improved; the ingredient of harshness, caused by Franck's scoring of trumpets in his tuttis, now seems hardly a problem, merely adding a degree of pungency and providing a true French accent. The Chicago ambience ensures that the overall effect is properly spacious.

Martinon's account of the *Symphony* has splendid thrust and impulse and is much better recorded than Monteux's, with full, rich strings. After the beautifully played slow movement, the finale surges forward to get the adrenalin going. To make this record even more attractive, the disc includes a fine account of the *Symphonic variations* from Entremont, combining drama with poetry, and a convincing performance of the *Prelude, choral et fugue* from Pascal Devoyon, also very well recorded.

It is good to have a first-class modern digital recording of this coupling, and Flor's RCA recording is superb, with the resonant acoustics of London's Henry Wood Hall exactly right for Franck's *Symphony*, with its dependence on the richness and body of the strings and the sonority of the brass. The *Symphonic variations*, a splendid account with Firkušný both poetic and brilliant, was made at EMI's Abbey Road studio and is equally successful. Flor exerts a firm grip on the intractable first movement of the *Symphony*; his conception is essentially spacious and in some ways convincing, but one longs for more thrust: the chromatic secondary theme sings out agreeably but not with the impulsive fervour that Monteux generates. The *Allegretto* is nicely done, and the finale opens powerfully, but when Franck returns to reconsider his earlier ideas Flor again lets the impetus flag.

Karajan's performance is given strong projection by the CD remastering of the 1970 recording, now sounding more brightly lit but with textures still full and bold. Karajan's tempi are all on the slow side, but his control of rhythm prevents any feeling of sluggishness or heaviness. There is always energy underlying the performance and, by facing the obvious problems squarely, Karajan avoids the perils. Weissenberg's account of the *Symphonic variations* has less distinction, but the poetry of the lyrical sections is not missed. The balance favours the orchestra slightly more than usual, but the pianist is realistically defined.

Bernstein conducts a warmly expressive performance which, thanks in part to a live recording, carries conviction in its flexible spontaneity. It has its moments of vulgarity, but that is part of the work; the reservations are of less importance next to the glowing positive qualities of the performance. The recording is vivid and opulent, but with the brass apt to sound strident.

Muti's is a strongly committed but unsentimental reading. The fill-up is welcome, a vividly dramatic symphonic poem, strongly presented; but with Karajan's version at mid-price, this is not especially competitive, except for those seeking a digital master. The 1983 recording, robust and vivid, is among EMI's better Philadelphia records made in the 1980s.

Piano quintet in F min.
(M) **(*) Decca 421 153-2 [id.]. Clifford Curzon, VPO Qt – DVOŘÁK: *Quintet.****
**(*) Nimbus Dig. NI 5114 [id.]. John Bingham, Medici Qt – FAURÉ: *String quartet.*(*)

Not as seductive a performance on Decca as the glorious Dvořák coupling, partly because the sound, though basically full, has a touch of astringency on top. But there is a case for not having too luscious textures and not letting the emotion spill over in this work, and Curzon and the VPO players are sensitive and firm at the same time. Curzon's playing is particularly fine. The CD transfer has undoubtedly enhanced the detail of the (1960) sound.

Ardent playing from the Medici and an especially imaginative contribution from their pianist, John Bingham. Artistically this is very impressive, for the players seem more fully inside César Franck's world than they are in the Fauré coupling. Unfortunately the recording venue is reverberant; but there is much here that will give pleasure.

String quartet in D.
(M) **(*) Decca 425 424-2 [id.]. Fitzwilliam Qt – RAVEL: *Quartet.***

Franck's *Quartet*, highly ambitious in its scale, contains some of the composer's most profound, most compelling thought; and this magnificent performance by the Fitzwilliam Quartet, triumphing superbly over the technical challenge with totally dedicated, passionately convincing playing, completely silences any reservations. Very well recorded, with the thick textures nicely balanced, this was one of the finest chamber records of the 1980s. However, the CD transfer, in attempting to clarify the sound, has brought a degree of fierceness to the fortissimo violin timbre.

Violin sonata in A.
🏵 (M) *** Decca 421 154-2 [id.]. Kyung Wha Chung, Radu Lupu – DEBUSSY: *Sonatas*; RAVEL: *Introduction and allegro* etc.*** 🏵
*** DG Dig. 415 683-2 [id.]. Shlomo Mintz, Yefim Bronfman – RAVEL; DEBUSSY: *Sonatas.***
*** Decca 414 128-2 [id.]. Itzhak Perlman, Vladimir Ashkenazy – BRAHMS: *Horn trio.***
(M) **(*) Ph. 426 384-2 [id.]. Arthur Grumiaux, György Sebok – FAURÉ: *Sonatas.*** 🏵
(*) EMI Dig. CDC7 49890-2 [id.]. Dumay, Collard – MAGNARD: *Sonata.*
(M) (***) EMI mono CDH7 63032-2. Jacques Thibaud, Alfred Cortot – DEBUSSY; FAURÉ: *Sonatas* etc.(***)
*(*) Decca Dig. 421 817-2 [id.]. Joshua Bell, Jean-Yves Thibaudet – DEBUSSY; FAURÉ: *Sonatas.*(*)

Kyung Wha Chung and Radu Lupu give a glorious account, full of natural and not over-projected eloquence, and most beautifully recorded. The slow movement has marvellous repose and the other movements have a natural exuberance and sense of line that carry the listener with them. The 1977 recording is enhanced on CD and, with outstanding couplings, this record is in every sense a genuine bargain.

On DG, Shlomo Mintz and Yefim Bronfman give a superbly confident account of the *Sonata*. It is impeccably played and splendidly recorded, too. This can rank alongside the best, and it has the advantage of a digital master.

With Perlman and Ashkenazy the first movement catches the listener by the ears with its forward impulse and flexible lyrical flow. The CD transfer is admirably done, and the 1980 analogue sound is enhanced, although there is not the sharpness of detail one would expect in a digital recording.

Grumiaux's account, if less fresh than Kyung Wha Chung's, has nobility and warmth to commend it. He is slightly let down by his partner, who is not as imaginative as Lupu in the more poetic moments, including the hushed opening bars. The balance favours the violin, but remains lifelike.

Right from the start it is clear that Augustin Dumay and Jean-Philippe Collard are going to give us something out of the ordinary. Their playing has strong personality and great authority; they treat the first movement with great freedom and Dumay produces tone of great sweetness. They are full of fire in the scherzo and give a commandingly thoughtful account of the slow movement. Theirs is a strongly felt and marvellously played reading that would be a three-star recommendation, were it not for the recording which, though good, places the two players rather too forward.

The celebrated Thibaud/Cortot recording comes from 1929 and has an ardour and lyricism that are altogether special. The sound may be primitive – but the playing is anything but and leaps off the silver disc as vividly as it did from the shellac 78s.

Joshua Bell and Jean-Yves Thibaudet bring no want of passion and an impressive technical address to the *Sonata*. Theirs is an outgoing performance that would fire enthusiasm in the heat of the concert hall. But while it would be quite unjust to call them shallow, it must be said that their insights are not as penetrating as those of some of their distinguished rivals. The acoustic in which they are recorded is less than ideal, for there is too little ambience to help them.

Cello sonata in A (arr. of *Violin sonata*).
(M) **(*) EMI CDM7 63184-2 [id.]. Du Pré, Barenboim – CHOPIN: *Sonata*.**(*)

Du Pré and Barenboim give a fine, mature, deeply expressive reading of a richly satisfying work. They are well balanced, but the effect of the work when transferred to the cello is inevitably mellower, less vibrant.

Prelude, choral et fugue.
*** RCA RD 85673 [5673-2RC]. Artur Rubinstein – BACH: *Chaconne***; LISZT: *Sonata*.**(*)

In music like this, strangely poised between classic form and Romantic expression, between the piano and the organ loft, no one is more persuasive than Rubinstein. This performance, recorded (like the Bach) in Rome in 1970, has fire and spontaneity. The piano tone is firm and clear.

ORGAN MUSIC

(i) *Andantino in A flat; Final in B flat, Op. 21; Grand pièce symphonique, Op. 17; Pièce héroïque*; (ii) *Prélude, fugue et variation in B min., Op. 18.*
(BB) **(*) Hung. White Label HRC 120 [id.]. (i) Gábor Lehotka (organ of Kodaly Music Centre, Kecskemét); (ii) Ferenc Gergely (organ of Péc Cathedral).

As recorded here, Czech organs seem to suit Franck's music rather well. The sound is fresh and bright, and detail emerges vividly. Both organists are sympathetic: the *Final* has plenty of impulse and the extended *Grand pièce symphonique* is very well structured, the listener's interest readily held throughout. Gergely's account of the last item is attractively registered and well contrasted. This makes an excellent survey in the lowest price range.

Cantabile; Chorale No. 1; Fantaisie in C; Pièce héroïque; Prélude, fugue and variation.
**(*) Unicorn Dig. DKPCD 9013 [id.]. Jennifer Bate.

Chorale No. 2 in B min.; Fantaisie in C, Op. 16; Grande pièce symphonique, Op. 17.
**(*) Unicorn Dig. DKPCD 9014 [id.]. Jennifer Bate.

Chorale No. 3 in A min.; Final in B flat, Op. 21; Pastorale, Op. 19; Prière in C sharp min., Op. 20.
** Unicorn Dig. DKPCD 9030 [id.]. Jennifer Bate.

Jennifer Bate plays the Danion-Gonzalez organ at Beauvais Cathedral and is given the benefit of an excellent digital recording. The spacious acoustic contributes an excellent ambience to the aural image, and Miss Bate's brilliance is always put at the service of the composer. The *Pièce héroïque* seems rather well suited to the massive sounds which the Beauvais organ can command and all the music in the third volume shows the instrument to good advantage. However, Bate rushes the opening of the *A minor Chorale*, some of whose detail does not register in this acoustic at the speed.

Fantaisie in A; Pastorale.
*** Telarc Dig. CD 80096 [id.]. Michael Murray (organ of Symphony Hall, San Francisco) – JONGEN: *Symphonie concertante.****

Michael Murray plays these pieces very well, although the San Francisco organ is not tailor-made for them. The Telarc recording is well up to standard.

Frumerie, Gunnar de (1908–87)

Singoalla.
**(*) Cap. Dig. CAP 22023 (2) [id.]. Wahlgren, von Otter, Olsson, Haugen, Saeden, Andersson, Tysklind, Blom, Bergström, Hägersten Motet Ch., Stockholm PO, Ahronovich.

Gunnar de Frumerie's *Singoalla* is set in Sweden during the fourteenth century, just before the onset of the Black Death, and is a story of love and betrayal. De Frumerie's style is resolutely diatonic with a strong modal flavour. If it lacks dramatic sophistication, variety of invention or any real sense of scale, there is a certain freshness and atmosphere. Björn Haugen gives a thoroughly committed account of the leading role, and Anne Sofie von Otter is a good Singoalla. The rest of the cast is also excellent, though the boy soprano is often strained by the awkward writing in Act III. The recording itself is good and so, too, is the orchestral playing under Ahronovich.

Gabrieli, Giovanni (1557–1612)

Canzon per sonar a 4; Canzoni Nos. 4 a 6; 12 a 8; In ecclesiis; Jubilate Deo; O Jesu mi dulcissime; O magnum mysterium; Quem vidistis pastores?; Timor et tremor.
*** Argo Dig. 417 468-2 [id.]. King's College, Cambridge, Ch., P. Jones Brass Ens., Cleobury.

The widely resonant acoustics of King's College Chapel make an admirable alternative to St Mark's for this repertoire. *In ecclesiis*, with its three choirs, plus organ and instrumental accompaniment, is thrilling (although here the trebles – not quite the strongest contingent this choir has ever fielded – can only just compete). Other highlights include the Christmas motet, *Quem vidistis pastores?*, the light and joyful *Jubilate Deo* and the highly atmospheric *O magnum mysterium*. The programme is given variety by the inclusion of canzoni, sonorously played by the Philip Jones brass group. Altogether a fine achievement; this CD is very much in the demonstration bracket.

Gade, Niels (1817–90)

Symphonies Nos. 1 in C min. (On Sjønland's fair plains), Op. 5; 8 in B min., Op. 47.
*** BIS Dig. CD 339 [id.]. Stockholm Sinf., Järvi.

Mendelssohn conducted the première of Gade's *First Symphony* (1841–2) and, although his influence is all-pervasive, it is a charming piece. Thirty years separate it from his *Eighth* and last symphony, still much indebted to Mendelssohn. Despite this debt, there is still a sense of real mastery and a command of pace. The Stockholm Sinfonietta and Neeme Järvi give very fresh and lively performances, and the recording is natural and truthful.

Symphonies Nos. 2 in E, Op. 10; 7 in F, Op. 45.
**(*) BIS Dig. CD 355 [id.]. Stockholm Sinf., Järvi.

Schumann thought No. 2 'reminiscent of Denmark's beautiful beechwoods'. The debt to Mendelssohn is still enormous here, but it is very likeable, more spontaneous than the *Seventh*, written twenty years later in 1864–5, though this work has a delightful scherzo. Splendid playing from the Stockholm Sinfonietta under Järvi, and good recording too.

Symphonies Nos. 3 in A min., Op. 15; 4 in B flat, Op. 20.
*** BIS Dig. CD 338 [id.]. Stockholm Sinf., Järvi.

The key of Gade's *Third* naturally prompts one's thoughts to turn to Mendelssohn's *Scottish symphony*, composed only five years before it. Yet there is great freshness and a seemingly effortless flow of ideas and pace, and a fine sense of musical proportion. No. 4 was more generally admired in Gade's lifetime, but its companion here is the more winning. It is beautifully played and recorded.

Symphonies Nos. (i) 5 in D min., Op. 35; 6 in G min., Op. 32.
*** BIS Dig. CD 356 [id.]. Stockholm Sinf., Järvi; (i) with Roland Pöntinen.

The *Fifth Symphony* is a delightfully sunny piece which lifts one's spirits; its melodies are instantly memorable, and there is a lively concertante part for the piano, splendidly played by the young Roland Pöntinen. The *Sixth Symphony* is rather more thickly scored and more academic. The recording is perhaps less transparent and open than others in the series but, given the charm of the *Fifth Symphony* and the persuasiveness of the performance, this coupling must be warmly recommended.

Gallo, Domenico (c. 1730– ?)

Trio sonatas: No. 2: Moderato; No. 3: Presto I; Presto II; No. 7: Allegro.
*** Decca Dig. 425 614-2 [id.]. St Paul CO, Hogwood – PERGOLESI: *Sinfonia*; STRAVINSKY: *Pulcinella* etc.***

These tiny movements come as a valuable and delightful appendix to Hogwood's fine recording of Stravinsky's *Pulcinella*, showing how he transformed such sources as these.

Geminiani, Francesco (1687–1762)

6 Concerti grossi, Op. 3.
*** O-L 417 522-2 [id.]. AAM, Schröder; Hogwood.

Hogwood's approach reveals the vigour and freshness of Geminiani's melodious and resourceful invention. The concerti are given performances of genuine quality by the Academy of Ancient Music under their Dutch leader, and readers normally resistant to the cult of authentic instruments can be reassured that there is no lack of body and breadth here. They are also extremely well recorded (analogue, 1976), although the CD transfer notices some studio noise and there is a curious moment of background hum which comes up suddenly and disappears on track 8 (Op. 3/2).

Concerti grossi: in D min. (La Folia, from CORELLI: *Sonata in D min., Op. 5/12); in G min., Op. 7/2; Trio sonatas Nos. 3 in F (from Op. 1/9); 5 in A min. (from Op. 1/11); 6 in D min. (from Op. 1/12); Violin sonatas: in E min., Op. 1/3; in A, Op. 4/12.*
*** Hyp. Dig. CDA 66264 [id.]. Purcell Band & Qt.

This record comes from Hyperion's '*La Folia*' series, though the only piece here using that celebrated theme is the arrangement Geminiani made of Corelli's *D minor Sonata.* Apart from the *G minor Concerto,* Op. 7, No. 2, the remainder of the disc is given over to chamber works. The Purcell Quartet play with dedication and spirit and convey their own enthusiasm for this admirably inventive music to the listener.

German, Edward (1862–1936)

Welsh rhapsody.
(M) *** EMI CDM7 69206-2. SNO, Gibson – HARTY: *With the Wild Geese*; MACCUNN: *Land of Mountain and Flood*; SMYTH: *The Wreckers overture.****

Edward German is content not to interfere with the traditional melodies he uses, relying on his orchestral skill to retain the listener's interest, in which he is very successful. The closing pages, based on *Men of Harlech,* are prepared in a Tchaikovskian manner to provide a rousing conclusion. The CD transfer is very well managed, though the ear perceives a slight limitation in the upper range.

Merrie England (opera): complete (without dialogue).
(B) ** CfP CD-CFPD 4710 (2) [id.]. Bronhill, Sinclair, Kern, McAlpine, Glossop, Glynne, Williams Singers, O, Michael Collins.

Taken as a whole, the score of *Merrie England* does not wear too well. But if the moments of coarseness in the libretto can be forgiven, there is much pleasing lyricism in German's music and one or two really outstanding tunes which will ensure that the work survives. Among the soloists Howell Glynne is splendid as King Neptune, and Monica Sinclair sings with her usual richness and makes *O peaceful England* more moving than usual. Patricia Kern's mezzo is firm and forward, while McAlpine as Sir Walter Raleigh sings with fine, ringing voice. The Rita Williams Singers are thoroughly professional even if just occasionally their style is suspect. The 1960 recording has atmosphere but a tendency to edginess.

Gershwin, George (1898–1937)

An American in Paris.
** DG 419 625-2 [id.]. San Francisco SO, Ozawa – BERNSTEIN: *West Side Story: Symphonic dances***(*); RUSSO: *Street music.***

An American in Paris; (i) *Piano concerto in F;* (ii) *Rhapsody in blue.*
(B) *** Pickwick Dig. PCD 909. (i; ii) Gwenneth Pryor; LSO, Richard Williams.
**(*) EMI CDC7 47161-2 [id.]. André Previn with LSO.
(B) **(*) Van. VECD 7518 [id.]. (i) Jerome Lowenthal; Utah SO, Abravanel.
(M) **(*) Ph. 420 492-2 [id.]. (i; ii) Werner Haas; Monte Carlo Op. O, De Waart.
(B) **(*) CfP CD-CFP 9012. (i; ii) Blumenthal; ECO, Steuart Bedford.
(M) **(*) DG Dig. 427 806-2 [id.]. Bernstein with LAPO – BARBER: *Adagio*; BERNSTEIN: *Candide overture* etc. ***

An American in Paris; (i) *Piano concerto in F; Rhapsody in blue; Variations on 'I got rhythm'.*
(M) **(*) RCA GD 86519 [RCA 6519-2-RG]. (i) Earl Wild; Boston Pops O, Fiedler.

An American in Paris; Cuban overture; (i) *Rhapsody in blue.*
(M) ** Decca 417 716-2 [id.]. (i) Ivan Davis; Cleveland O, Maazel – COPLAND: *Appalachian spring* etc.***

An American in Paris; Cuban overture; (i) *Rhapsody in blue; Porgy and Bess: Symphonic picture* (arr. R. R. Bennett).
**(*) Decca Dig. 425 111-2 [id.]. (i) Louis Lortie; Montreal SO, Charles Dutoit.

(i) *An American in Paris;* (ii) *Rhapsody in blue.*
⊛ *** CBS MK 42264 [id.]. (i) NYPO, Bernstein; (ii) Bernstein with Columbia SO (with GROFÉ: *Grand Canyon suite***).
** Telarc Dig. CD 80058 [id.]. Eugene List, Cincinnati SO, Kunzel.

Bernstein's 1959 CBS coupling was recorded when (at the beginning of his forties) he was at the peak of his creativity, with *West Side Story* only two years behind him. This record set the standard by which all subsequent pairings of these two works came to be judged. It still sounds astonishingly well as a recording; the *Rhapsody* in particular has better piano-tone than CBS often provided in the 1970s. Bernstein's approach is inspirational, exceptionally flexible but completely spontaneous. Although the jazzy element is not masked, it is essentially a concert performance, fully justifying the expanded orchestration, masterly in every way, with much broader tempi than in the composer's piano-roll version, but quixotic in mood, rhythmically subtle and creating a life-enhancing surge of human warmth at the entry of the big central tune. The performance of *An American in Paris* is vividly characterized, brash and episodic; an unashamedly American view, with the great blues tune marvellously timed and phrased as only a great American orchestra can do it. Though the Grofé bonus is by no means indispensable, the Gershwin performances certainly are.

From the opening glissando swirl on the clarinet, the performance of the *Rhapsody in blue* by Gwenneth Pryor and the LSO under Richard Williams tingles with adrenalin, and the other performances are comparable. The *Rhapsody* has splendid rhythmic energy, yet the performers can relax to allow the big expressive blossoming at the centre really to expand. Similarly in the *Concerto,* the combination of vitality and flair and an almost voluptuous response to the lyrical melodies is very involving. *An American in Paris,* briskly paced, moves forward in an exhilarating sweep, with the big blues tune vibrant and the closing section managed to perfection. The performances are helped by superb recording, made in the EMI No. 1 Studio; but it is the life and spontaneity of the music-making that enthral the listener throughout all three works.

The digital remastering of Previn's EMI set, made at the beginning of the 1970s, has brought a striking enhancement of the recording itself. There is now much more sparkle, and the extra vividness comes without loss of body; indeed, in the *Concerto* the strings sound particularly full and fresh and the piano timbre clean and natural. The performance of the *Concerto* was always a fine one by any standards, but now in the *Rhapsody* one senses many affinities with the famous Bernstein account. *An American in Paris* is exuberantly volatile, and the entry of the great blues tune on the trumpet has a memorable rhythmic lift. This is generally preferable to Previn's later, Philips CD, made in Pittsburgh, but now should be reissued at mid-price.

Jerome Lowenthal forms a stimulating partnership with Abravanel and these are vividly spontaneous performances. Perhaps the end of *An American in Paris* is made too grandly spacious, but the earlier sequences have plenty of colour and zest. The full, resonant Utah sound is particularly attractive in the *Concerto*.

Among the other British and European compilations, the Philips collection from Monte Carlo stands out. Again, digital remastering has brought noticeable improvement in the sound, which always had appealing body and warmth; now the treble is brighter but not edgier and, although the upper range is still not as wide as on more recent versions, there is no real feeling of restriction. The *Concerto* is particularly successful; its lyrical moments have a quality of nostalgia which is very attractive. Werner Haas is a volatile and sympathetic soloist, and his rhythmic verve is refreshing. Edo de Waart's *An American in Paris* is not only buoyant but glamorous, too – the big blues melody is highly seductive and, as with all the best accounts of this piece, the episodic nature of the writing is hidden. There is a cultured, European flavour to this music-making that does not detract from its vitality, and the jazz inflexions are not missed, with plenty of verve in the *Rhapsody*.

Daniel Blumenthal gives performances of the two concertante pieces which convincingly combine Ravelian delicacy of articulation with genuine feeling for the jazz-based idiom. The syncopations are often naughtily pointed, to delightful effect, and Bedford and the ECO, unlikely accompanists as they may be, give warm and understanding support. *An American in Paris* is warmly done too but with less panache, the episodic nature of the piece undisguised. For those seeking a cultured flavour in this music, however, this can be strongly recommended as an alternative to Haas.

The mid-priced RCA CD is particularly generous (70 minutes) in including, besides the usual triptych, the *'I got rhythm' variations*, given plenty of rhythmic panache. Indeed these are essentially jazzy performances: Earl Wild's playing is full of energy and brio, and he inspires Arthur Fiedler to a similarly infectious response. The outer movements of the *Concerto* are comparably volatile and the blues feeling of the slow movement is strong. At the end of *An American in Paris* Fiedler adds to the exuberance by bringing in a bevy of motor horns. The brightly remastered recording suits the music-making, though the resonant Boston acoustics at times prevent absolute sharpness of focus: ideally, the spectacular percussion at the beginning of the *Concerto* should sound cleaner.

Ozawa's *American in Paris* (1977) sounds well in digitally remastered form. It is easy to respond to such opulence, with the performers revealing the music's vivid tunefulness and rich scoring, but this is clearly overpriced and should have been reissued on DG's mid-priced label – the Russo coupling is far more indispensable.

Eugene List has also recorded the *Rhapsody in blue* for Turnabout. On that occasion he used the original scoring; on Telarc he is accompanied by a full symphony orchestra and is recorded very sumptuously indeed. The rich sound is ideal for those who like to wallow in the melodic richness of *An American in Paris*. The blues tune certainly sounds expansive and there is no real lack of vitality, although in both works the hi-fi-conscious engineers have provided rather too much bass drum (a characteristic of Telarc CDs).

The Montreal players bring a mischievous Gallic flair and an attractively light touch to *An American in Paris* which, if not entirely idiomatic, is certainly infectious. The *Cuban overture* has a comparable racy vitality and the *Rhapsody in blue* is strong in rhythmic feeling. But several more convincing versions of the latter piece exist, and the famous *Symphonic picture* from *Porgy and Bess* sounds more opulently magical in Dorati's hands. The Decca engineers have sought here to achieve an essentially bright and vivid effect by placing their microphones fairly close, and some of the lustre of the St Eustache ambience has been lost: the result is comparatively brash.

Maazel's triptych dates from 1974. The performances of all three works are strikingly energetic (Ivan Davis both brilliant and sophisticated in the *Rhapsody*) and the boisterous account of the *Cuban overture* is immensely spirited, almost disguising its emptiness. But the big tune at the centre of the *Rhapsody* and the blues melody in *An American in Paris* (given an upbeat reading) are lacking in sensuous warmth, which means that a dimension is missing in both works.

(i) *An American in Paris;* (ii) *Broadway overtures: Girl crazy; Funny face; Let 'em eat cake; Of thee I sing; Oh Kay!; Strike up the band.* (iii) *Rhapsody in blue* (original version).
** CBS MK 42240 [id.]. (i) NYPO; (ii) Buffalo PO; (iii) George Gershwin (piano-roll), Columbia Jazz Band; Tilson Thomas.

The remastered Tilson Thomas CD anthology centres on the famous 1976 recording of the *Rhapsody in blue*, which added to the piano-rolls of the composer's own performance of the piano part an exhilarating accompaniment (1920s style) by the Columbia Jazz Band, using the original Whiteman score. The result proved refreshingly controversial – there is one tutti which sounds like an old film speeded up. Tilson Thomas's direction of *An American in Paris* has comparable flair, and the Broadway overtures are given expert and idiomatic performances, with the Buffalo Philharmonic clearly on their toes and enjoying themselves, but the remastering has lost some of the body of the original analogue sound and is a little flat and two-dimensional.

Piano concerto in F.
(*) Virgin Dig. VC 790780-2 [id.]. Andrew Litton, Bournemouth SO – RAVEL: *Piano concerto in G.**

Directing the orchestra, of which he is principal conductor, from the keyboard Andrew Litton gives an exceptionally refined account of the *Concerto in F*. If he brings out links with French music, as typified by the Ravel *Concerto* which comes as coupling, he will not always please those who seek an idiomatic, conventional reading. The Bournemouth players, for all their incisiveness and precision, sound rather literal in the big, expansive moments. But as a coupling for an outstanding, totally idiomatic version of the Ravel, it is well worth considering since, with textures made luminous, it is most beautifully recorded.

Rhapsody in blue.
(M) **(*) DG Dig. 427 806-2 [id.]. Bernstein with LAPO – BARBER: *Adagio;* BERNSTEIN: *Candide overture* etc. ***

Rhapsody in blue; Prelude for piano No. 2.
** DG Dig. 410 025-2 [id.]. Bernstein with LAPO – BERNSTEIN: *West Side Story: Symphonic dances.****

Rhapsody in blue; Second Rhapsody; Preludes for piano; Short story (1925); *Violin piece; For Lily Pons* (1933); *Sleepless night* (1936); *Promenade (Walking the dog).*
** CBS Dig. MK 39699 [id.]. Michael Tilson Thomas (piano), LAPO.

Rhapsody in blue (original version); *Who cares?* (ballet from Gershwin Songbook, arr. Hershy Kay); arr. of songs for piano: *Clap your hands; Do, do, do it again; Nobody but you; Swanee.*
** ASV Dig. CDRPO 8008. Andrew Litton with RPO.

In his most recent recording for DG, Bernstein rather goes over the top with his jazzing of the solos in Gershwin. The encore too brings seductively swung rhythms, one of the three solo piano *Preludes*. Such rhythmic freedom was clearly the result of a live rather than a studio performance. The big melody in *Rhapsody in blue* is rather too heavily pointed for comfort. The immediacy of the occasion is most compellingly projected, but this does not match Bernstein's inspired 1959 analogue coupling for CBS. This version has been reissued at mid-price, coupled with Barber's *Adagio* and two extracts from Bernstein's own *West Side story*, but without the *Prelude*.

Michael Tilson Thomas's newest Gershwin record supplements rather than displaces his earlier account of *Rhapsody in blue* accompanying the composer's 1924 piano-roll, and there is not quite the same hell-for-leather excitement and zest for life that the earlier performance generated. Moreover the *Second Rhapsody* is far from being one of Gershwin's best pieces. What is a real discovery, however, is *Sleepless night*, an altogether enchanting miniature, poignant and touching. This and some of the other piano works that Tilson Thomas plays with such style are new to the catalogue. The *Violin piece* is previously unpublished.

Andrew Litton follows in Michael Tilson Thomas's footsteps by adopting the original Whiteman score of the *Rhapsody in blue*. The performance is lively enough and thoughtful too, so it has some elements of the Bernstein approach. In its way, this is very enjoyable and far better recorded than the CBS version; but the rhythmic inflexions are clearly from this side of the Atlantic, and this applies even more strikingly to the (attractively) amiable performance of Hershy Kay's ballet-score adapted from Gershwin's own 'Song Book for Balanchine'. Litton then usefully plays as solo piano items the four remaining songs which Kay discarded, and very well too.

Arrangements of songs: *Embraceable you; Fascinatin' rhythm; A foggy day; Funny face; He loves and she loves; I got rhythm; Lady be good; Liza; Love is here to stay; The man I love; Nice work if you can get it; Soon; Summertime; S'wonderful; They all laughed; They can't take that away from me.*
(M) *** EMI CDM7 69218-2 [id.]. Yehudi Menuhin, Stéphane Grappelli.

This is an attractive re-assembly of the Gershwin numbers taken from the famous Menuhin/Grappelli series of studio collaborations in which two distinguished musicians from different musical backgrounds struck sparks off each other to most entertaining effect. The songs are all famous and the treatments highly felicitous. The sound has excellent presence.

Catfish Row (suite from *Porgy and Bess*).
*** Telarc Dig. CD 80086 [id.]. Tritt, Cincinnati Pops O, Kunzel – GROFÉ: *Grand Canyon suite.****

Catfish Row was arranged by the composer after the initial failure of his opera and already existed when in 1941 Fritz Reiner commissioned Robert Russell Bennett's more sumptuous *Symphonic picture*, which uses much of the same material. It includes a brief piano solo, played with fine style by William Tritt in the highly sympathetic Telarc performance which is very well recorded.

Concerto in F; 'I got rhythm' variations; Rhapsody in blue; Rialto ripples rag.
** Telarc Dig. CD 80166 [id.]. William Tritt, Cincinnati Pops O, Kunzel.

The original jazz-band version of the *Rhapsody* is here without the breathless momentum of the famous piano-roll version with the composer on CBS, but it is notable in including some 44 bars of music later cut out by the composer (not always to disadvantage). The *Concerto* has a nostalgically memorable slow movement, but the outer movements are somewhat lacking in sheer verve. However, both the *Rialto ripples rag* and the engaging *'I got rhythm' variations* are played with attractive and stylish flair.

Broadway music: *Damsel in Distress: Stiff upper lip (Funhouse dance sequence). Overtures: Girl crazy; Of thee I sing; Oh Kay!; Primrose; Tip-toes.*
** EMI Dig. CDC7 47977-2 [id.]. New Princess Theatre O, John McGlinn.

John McGlinn has recorded his selections, using the original scores. The extended dance-sequence, *Stiff upper lip*, comes from a 1937 movie and has some good tunes. So has *Oh Kay!* (half a dozen) while *Girl crazy* offers the irresistible *I got rhythm*. Elsewhere, the famous melodies are more thinly spread, but the marvellous playing of the New York pick-up orchestra (gorgeous saxes and brass) has splendid pep. On CD the presence of the close-miked instruments brings edginess with a touch of shrillness on the strings, though the background ambience is voluptuous enough. There is only 42 minutes' music overall.

VOCAL MUSIC

'Kiri sings Gershwin': Boy wanted; But not for me; By Strauss; Embraceable you; I got rhythm; Love is here to stay; Love walked in; Meadow serenade; The man I love; Nice work if you can get it; Somebody loves me; Someone to watch over me; Soon; Things are looking up. Porgy and Bess: Summertime.
**(*) EMI Dig. CDC7 47454-2 [id.]. Kiri Te Kanawa, New Theatre O, McGlinn (with Chorus).

In Dame Kiri's gorgeously sung *Summertime* from *Porgy and Bess*, the distanced heavenly chorus creates the purest kitsch. But most of the numbers are done in an upbeat style, which has the advantage of carrying the vocal introductions before the verse and preventing their sounding superfluous out of stage context. Dame Kiri is at her most relaxed and ideally there should be more variety of pacing: *The man I love* is thrown away at the chosen tempo. But for the most part the ear is seduced by the lovely sounds and the direct rhythmic style of the presentation; however, the pop microphone techniques bring excessive sibilants in the CD format.

Songs: *But not for me; Embraceable you; I got rhythm; The man I love; Nice work if you can get it; Our love is here to stay; They can't take that away from me. Blue Monday: Has anyone seen Joe? Porgy and Bess: Summertime; I loves you, Porgy.*
**(*) Ph. 416 460-2 [id.]. Barbara Hendricks, Katia and Marielle Labèque.

Barbara Hendricks is at her finest in the operatic numbers (*I loves you, Porgy* is particularly eloquent), and the warm beauty of the voice gives much pleasure throughout the programme. The performances of the songs are lushly cultured, often indulgently slow (even the faster numbers lack something in vitality). The piano arrangements are elaborate; the playing is elegantly zestful, not out of style but giving the presentation a European veneer that in its way is very beguiling. The sound is first class.

Let 'em Eat Cake; Of Thee I Sing (musicals).
*** CBS Dig. M2K 42522 (2) [id.]. Jack Gilford, Larry Kert, Maureen McGovern, Paige O'Hara, David Garrison, NY Choral Artists, St Luke's O, Tilson Thomas.

Of Thee I Sing and *Let 'em Eat Cake* are the two operettas that George Gershwin wrote in the early 1930s on a political theme, the one a sequel to the other. Though the aim is satirical in both works, the musical tone of voice has the easy tunefulness of typical Gershwin shows, with only the occasional hint of Kurt Weill to suggest a more international source of inspiration. What the British listener will immediately register is the powerful underlying influence of Gilbert and Sullivan, not just in the plot – with

Gilbertian situations exploited – but also in the music, with patter-songs and choral descants used in a very Sullivan-like manner.

In every way these two very well-filled discs are a delight, offering warm and energetic performances by excellent artists under Michael Tilson Thomas, not just a star conductor but a leading Gershwin scholar. Both Larry Kert and Maureen McGovern as his wife make a strong partnership, with Jack Gilford characterful as the Vice-Presidential candidate, Alexander Throttlebottom, and Paige O'Hara excellent as the interloping Diana in *Of Thee I Sing*. With the recording on the dry side and well forward – very apt for a musical – the words are crystal clear, not least from the splendidly disciplined chorus that, for much of the time, is protagonist. The well-produced booklets (one for each operetta) give full words – though, as with many CD sets, you need a magnifying glass to read them.

OPERA

Porgy and Bess (complete).
⊛ *** EMI Dig. CDS7 49568-2 (3) [Ang. CDCC 49568]. Willard White, Cynthia Haymon, Harolyn Blackwell, Cynthia Clarey, Damon Evans, Glyndebourne Ch., LPO, Rattle.
**(*) Decca 414 559-2 (3) [id.]. White, Mitchell, Boatwright, Quivar, Hendricks, Clemmons, Thompson, Cleveland Ch., Children's Ch., Cleveland O, Maazel.
**(*) RCA RD 82109 (3) [RCD3 2109]. Ray Albert, Dale, Andrew Smith, Shakesnider, Marschall, Children's Ch., Houston Grand Op. Ch. and O, DeMain.

EMI's gloriously rich and colourful recording of Gershwin's masterpiece directly reflects the spectacular success enjoyed by the Glyndebourne production. Simon Rattle here conducts the same cast and orchestra as in the opera house, and the EMI engineers have done wonders in re-creating what was so powerful at Glyndebourne, establishing more clearly than ever the status of *Porgy* as grand opera, not a mere jumped-up musical or operetta. The impact of the performance is consistently heightened by the subtleties of timing that come from long experience of live performances. By comparison, Lorin Maazel's Decca version sounds a degree too literal, and John DeMain's RCA set, also associated with a live stage production and dating from the mid-1970s, is less subtle. More than their rivals, Rattle and the LPO capture Gershwin's rhythmic exuberance with the degree of freedom essential if jazz-based inspirations are to sound idiomatic. The chorus is the finest and most responsive of any on the three sets, and the bass line-up is the strongest. Willard White, not as youthful-sounding as for Maazel, but warmer and weightier, is superbly matched by the magnificent Jake of Bruce Hubbard, singing as characterfully as in the role of Joe in the EMI *Show Boat* set, and by the dark and resonant Crown of Gregg Baker. As Sportin' Life, Damon Evans gets nearer than any of his rivals to the original scat-song inspiration without ever short-changing on musical values, heightening them with extra expressive intensity and characterization. The women principals too are first rate, if no more striking than their opposite numbers on Decca and RCA: Cynthia Haymon as Bess movingly convincing in conveying equivocal emotions, Harolyn Blackwell as Clara sensuously relishing Rattle's slow speed for *Summertime*, and Cynthia Clarey an intense and characterful Serena. EMI's digital sound is exceptionally full and spacious. Voices are naturally balanced, not spotlit, so that words are not always as crystal clear as on Decca and RCA; but the atmosphere and sense of presence are the more winning.

Maazel also includes the complete text. The vigour and colour are irresistible, and the recording is one of the most vivid that even Decca has produced. Willard White is a magnificent Porgy, dark of tone; while Leona Mitchell's vibrant Bess has a moving streak of vulnerability, and François Clemmons as Sportin' Life achieves the near-impossible by actually singing the role and making one forget Cab Calloway. But above all it is Maazel's triumph, a tremendous first complete recording with dazzling playing from the Cleveland Orchestra.

Where Maazel easily and naturally demonstrates the operatic qualities of Gershwin's masterpiece, DeMain presents a performance clearly in the tradition of the Broadway musical. There is much to be said for both views; the casts are equally impressive vocally, with the RCA singers a degree more characterful. Donnie Ray Albert, as Porgy, uses his bass-like resonance impressively, though not everyone will like the suspicion of hamming, which works less well in a recording than on stage.

Porgy and Bess: highlights.
(M) ** RCA GD 85234 [5234-2-RG]. Leontyne Price, William Warfield, John Bubbles, McHenry Boatwright, RCA Victor Ch. & O, Skitch Henderson.
** RCA RD 84680 (from above recording; cond. DeMain).
** Ph. Dig. 412 720-2 [id.]. Estes, Alexander, Curry, Berlin R. Ch. and SO, Slatkin.

The RCA studio compilation was recorded in 1963, a decade before the complete Decca and RCA versions appeared. Both Price and Warfield sing magnificently, and the supporting group is given lively direction by Skitch Henderson, while the DeMain disc is taken from the robust and colourful, highly idiomatic complete recording made by RCA in the late 1970s.

Slatkin's collection is totally geared to the glorious voices of Simon Estes and Roberta Alexander. Naturally, each soloist sings numbers from several characters, not just hero and heroine. The rich darkness of Estes' voice is clearly operatic in style, but tough and incisive too, not just as Porgy but equally impressively as Sportin' Life in *It ain't necessarily so*. Only the Berlin Chorus lacks sharpness, but the sound on CD is particularly rich.

COLLECTIONS

But not for me (medley); *Nice work if you can get it* (medley). Songs: *Do it again; Fascinatin' rhythm; A foggy day; I've got a crush on you; The man I love; My man's gone now; Sweet and low-down. Porgy and Bess: Overture and medley.*
** CBS MK 73650. Sarah Vaughan and Trio; LAPO, Tilson Thomas.

This is live recording at its most impressive. The sound is vivid and one can readily forgive the beat in the voice and the occasional strident moment. The accompaniments are worthy of the occasion, with the orchestra under Tilson Thomas exciting in its own right. With any reservations about the soloist, not always at her best vocally, this remains a compelling musical experience.

Gesualdo, Carlo (*c.* 1561–1613)

Ave, dulcissima Maria; Ave, regina coelorum; Maria mater gratiae; Precibus et meritus beatae Mariae (motets). *Tenebrae responsories for Holy Saturday.*
*** Gimell Dig. CDGIM 015 [id.]. Tallis Scholars, Peter Phillips.

The astonishing dissonances and chromaticisms may not be as extreme here as in some of Gesualdo's secular music but, as elaborate as madrigals, they still have a sharp, refreshing impact on the modern ear which recognizes music leaping the centuries. The rule-breaking is akin to the uninhibited self-expression of today's composers, freed from academic rules; and similarly it communicates intensely when genuine emotion lies behind the inspiration. The Tallis Scholars give superb performances, finely finished and beautifully blended, with women's voices made to sound boyish, singing with freshness and bite to bring home the total originality of the writing with its awkward leaps and intervals. Beautifully recorded, this is another of the Tallis Scholars' ear-catching discs, powerful as well as polished.

Getty, Gordon (20th century)

The White election (song-cycle).
*** Delos Dig. D/CD 3057 [id.]. Kaaren Erickson, Armen Guzelimian.

The simple, even primitive, yet deeply allusive poetry of Emily Dickinson is sensitively matched in the music of Gordon Getty. Here he tackles a sequence of 32 songs, building them into an extended cycle in four linked parts, lasting in all an hour and a quarter. His style, direct and spare, easy and fluent, has links with the Britten of *Winter words* on the one hand and with the minimalists on the other, but with no hint of mindless repetition. Everything is aimed, in as simple a way as possible, at bringing out the meaning of the poems, which have been selected (as Getty puts it) 'to tell Emily's story in her own words'. He adds that 'The most salient features of Emily's life were taken to be the white election, with its theme of union in death, and her unsuspected poetic genius.' The poet's obsession with the colour white and its many-sided symbolism here prompts the composer to heighten the emotional overtones of a life at once unfulfilled in marriage but secretly fulfilled in her verse. If at times the tinkly tunes seem to be an inadequate response to profound emotions, the total honesty of the writing disarms criticism, particularly in a performance as dedicated and sensitive as this, with Kaaren Erickson a highly expressive artist with a naturally beautiful voice. The pianist too is very responsive.

Gibbons, Orlando (1583–1625)

Anthems & Verse anthems: *Almighty and Everlasting God; Hosanna to the Son of David; Lift up your heads; O Thou the central orb; See, see the word is incarnate; This is the record of John.* Canticles: *Short service: Magnificat and Nunc dimittis. 2nd Service; Magnificat and Nunc dimittis.* Hymns & Songs of the church: *Come kiss with me those lips of thine; Now shall the praises of the Lord be sung; A song of joy unto the Lord. Organ fantasia: Fantasia for double organ; Voluntary.*
*** ASV Dig. CDDCA 514 [id.]. King's College Ch., Ledger; London Early Music Group; John Butt.

An invaluable first CD anthology of Gibbons that contains many of his greatest pieces; this accommodates seventeen items in all, including superlative accounts of such masterpieces of the English repertoire as *This is the record of John* and *Almighty and Everlasting God*. Not only are the performances touched with distinction, the recording too is in the highest flight. Strongly recommended.

Ginastera, Alberto (1865–1936)

(i) *Harp concerto, Op. 25;* (ii) *Piano concerto No. 1; Estancia* (ballet suite), *Op. 89.*
*** ASV Dig. CDDCA 654 [id.]. (i) Nancy Allen; (ii) Oscar Tarrago; Mexico City PO, Bátiz.

The *Harp concerto* is a highly inventive and rewarding work whose brilliant colours are brought fully to life here by Nancy Allen and the Mexican orchestra. *Estancia* is a comparably vivid piece of Coplandesque macho, its character also very successfully realized. The *First Piano concerto* is mildly serial but far from unattractive – and very brilliantly (and sensitively) played by Oscar Tarrago. An excellent introduction to this composer, and excellently recorded – perhaps a bit over-bright and up-front, but well balanced all the same – and with plenty of range. Strongly recommended.

Giordano, Umberto (1867–1948)

Andrea Chénier (complete).
(M) *** RCA GD 82046 (2) [RCD-2-2046]. Domingo, Scotto, Milnes, Alldis Ch., Nat. PO, Levine.
(M) (***) EMI mono CHS7 69996-2 (2) [Ang. CDHB 69996]. Gigli, Caniglia, Bechi, Huder, Simionato, La Scala, Milan, Ch. & O, Fabritiis.
**(*) Decca Dig. 410 117-2 (2) [id.]. Pavarotti, Caballé, Nucci, Kuhlmann, Welsh Nat. Op. Ch., Nat. PO, Chailly.
(M) **(*) Decca 425 407-2 (2) [id.]. Tebaldi, Del Monaco, Bastianini, Ch. & O of St Cecilia Ac., Rome, Gavazzeni.

Giordano always runs the risk – not least in this opera with its obvious parallels with *Tosca* – of being considered only in the shadow of Puccini, but this red-blooded score can, as here, be searingly effective with its defiant poet hero – a splendid role for Domingo at his most heroic – and the former servant, later revolutionary leader, Gérard, a character who genuinely develops from Act to Act, a point well appreciated by Milnes. Scotto gives one of her most eloquent and beautiful performances, and Levine has rarely displayed his powers as an urgent and dramatic opera conductor more potently on record, with the bright recording intensifying the dramatic thrust of playing and singing.

The title-role in this opera was always among Gigli's top favourites; if he could, he would always choose it for his début in a house new to him. Here, in a recording made in 1941 in wartime Italy, he gives a glowing and characterful performance, full of totally distinctive touches. There is the occasional hint of the lachrymose Gigli, but it is of little importance next to the golden assurance of the singing, with the voice showing remarkably few signs of wear. And where most of Gigli's complete opera sets are simply star vehicles, this one brings some fine performances from the others too, including the young Giulietta Simionato, Giuseppe Taddei and Italo Tajo, all early in their careers, in small character-roles. Gino Bechi gives a thrillingly resonant performance as Gerard, and Maria Caniglia – who regularly recorded with Gigli – was never finer on record than here. The transfers from 78s are first rate.

Pavarotti may motor through the role of the poet-hero, singing with his usual fine diction but in a conventional barnstorming way; nevertheless, the red-blooded melodrama of the piece comes over powerfully, thanks to Chailly's sympathetic conducting, incisive but never exaggerated. Caballé, like Pavarotti, is not strong on characterization but produces beautiful sounds, while Leo Nucci makes a superbly dark-toned Gérard. A number of veterans have also been brought in to do party turns; Hugues Cuénod as Fléville delightfully apt, Piero de Palma as the informer, Christa Ludwig superb as Madelon, and Astrid Varnay well over the top caricaturing the Contessa di Coigny. Though this cannot replace the Levine set with Domingo, Scotto and Milnes, it is a colourful substitute with its demonstration sound.

Apart perhaps from *La Forza del destino*, the 1960 Decca set represents the most desirable of the Tebaldi/Del Monaco collaborations in Italian opera. The blood and thunder of the story suits both singers admirably and Gavazzeni is also at his best.

Sample the final duet if you have any doubts concerning the power of this performance. Finer still than the soprano and tenor is Bastianini as Gérard. His finely focused voice is caught beautifully and he conveys vividly the conflicts in the man's character. Bold, vivid sound projects the drama splendidly.

Giuliani, Mauro (1781–1828)

Sonata for violin and guitar.
*** CBS MK 34508 [id.]. Itzhak Perlman, John Williams – PAGANINI: *Cantabile* etc.***

Giuliani's *Sonata* is amiable enough but hardly substantial fare; but it is played with such artistry here that it appears better music than it is. The recording is in need of more ambience, but sound is invariably a matter of taste, and there is no reason to withhold a strong recommendation. The CD transfer is admirably managed.

Glass, Philip (born 1937)

Dance Pieces: Glasspieces; In the Upper Room: Dances Nos. 1, 2, 5, 8 & 9.
*** CBS Dig. MK 39539 [id.]. Ens., dir. Michael Riesman.

These two ballet scores bring typical and easily attractive examples of Glass's minimalist technique. *Glasspieces* was choreographed by Jerome Robbins for the New York City Ballet. The scoring features woodwind, piano and strings, often heard in separate groups, plus voices, synthesizer and rhythm. Heard away from the stage, the music seems to have a subliminally hypnotic effect, even though rhythmic patterns often repeat themselves almost endlessly.

OPERA

Akhnaten (complete).
*** CBS M2K 42457 (2) [id.]. Esswood, Vargas, Liebermann, Hannula, Holzapfel, Hauptmann, Stuttgart State Op. Ch., Russell Davies.

Akhnaten, Glass's powerful third opera, is set in the time of Ancient Egypt. Among the soloists, Paul Esswood in the title-role is reserved, strong and statuesque; perhaps a more red-blooded approach would have been out of character – this is an opera of historical ghosts, and its life-flow lies in the hypnotic background provided by the orchestra; indeed the work's haunting closing scene with its wordless melismas is like nothing else in music. It offers a theatrical experience appealing to a far wider public than usual in the opera house, as the English National Opera production readily demonstrated; and here the Stuttgart chorus and orchestra give the piece impressively committed advocacy.

Einstein on the beach (complete).
(***) CBS Dig. M4K 38875 (4) [id.]. Childs, Johnson, Mann, Sutton, Ch., Zukovsky (violin), Philip Glass Ens., Riesman.

As the surreal title implies, *Einstein on the beach* is more dream than drama. In this, his first opera, Glass translated his use of slowly shifting ostinatos on to a near-epic scale. The opera takes significant incidents in Einstein's life as the basis for the seven scenes in three Acts, framed by five 'Knee Plays'. Einstein's life is then linked with related visual images in a dream-like way, reflecting the second half of the title, *On the Beach*, a reference to Nevil Shute's novel with its theme of nuclear apocalypse. Other works of

Glass are more communicative than this on record. Dedicated performances and first-rate recording. The booklet gives copious illustrations of the stage production.

Satyagraha (complete).
*** CBS Dig. M3K 39672 (3) [id.]. Perry, NY City Op. Ch. and O, Keene.

The subject here is the early life of Mahatma Gandhi, pinpointing various incidents; and the text is a selection of verses from the Bhagavadgita, sung in the original Sanskrit and used as another strand in the complex repetitive web of sound. The result is undeniably powerful. With overtones of Indian Raga at the very start, Glass builds long crescendos with a relentlessness that may anaesthetize the mind but which have a purposeful aesthetic aim. Where much minimalist music in its shimmering repetitiveness becomes static, a good deal of this conveys energy as well as power. The writing for chorus is often physically thrilling, and individual characters emerge in only a shadowy way. The recording, using the device of overdubbing, is spectacular.

Glazunov, Alexander (1865–1936)

Chant du ménestrel (for cello and orchestra) *Op. 71.*
*** Chan. Dig. CHAN 8579 [id.]. Wallfisch, LPO, Bryden Thomson – KABALEVSKY; KHACHATURIAN: *Cello concertos.****

Glazunov's *Chant du ménestrel* (*Song of the troubadour*) shows the nostalgic appeal of 'things long ago and far away'. It is a short but appealing piece and a welcome makeweight on this excellently played and recorded CD.

Violin concerto in A min., Op. 82.
*** RCA RD 87019 [RCD1-7019]. Heifetz, RCA SO, Hendl – PROKOFIEV: *Concerto No. 2*; SIBELIUS: *Violin concerto.****
*** EMI Dig. CDC7 49814-2 [id.]. Perlman, Israel PO, Mehta – SHOSTAKOVICH: *Violin concerto No. 1.****
(*) Erato/WEA Dig. 2292 45343-2 [id.]. Mutter, Nat. SO, Washington, Rostropovich – PROKOFIEV: *Violin concerto No. 1*; SHCHEDRIN: *Stihira.*

(i) *Violin concerto; The Seasons* (ballet), *Op. 67.*
*** Chan. Dig. CHAN 8596 [id.]. (i) Oscar Shumsky; SNO, Järvi.

Heifetz is incomparable here; his account is the strongest and most passionate (as well as the most perfectly played) in the catalogue. In his hands the *Concerto*'s sweetness is tempered with strength. It is altogether a captivating performance that completely absolves the work from any charge of synthetic sweetness. The RCA orchestra under Hendl gives splendid support, and although the 1963 recording is not beyond reproach, the disc is a must.

The command and panache of Perlman are irresistible in this showpiece concerto, and the whole performance, recorded live, erupts into a glorious account of the galloping final section, in playing to match that even of the supreme master in this work, Heifetz. The acoustic of the Mann Auditorium in Tel Aviv is not an easy one for the engineers, and tuttis are rather rough, but this is more atmospheric than most from that source. It makes an unexpected but rewarding coupling for the more substantial Shostakovich *First Concerto*.

Neeme Järvi obtains good results from the Scottish National Orchestra in *The Seasons*, though tempi tend to be brisk. The Chandos acoustic is reverberant and the balance recessed. In the *Violin concerto*, Oscar Shumsky is perhaps wanting the purity and effortless virtuosity of Heifetz, but the disc as a whole still carries a three-star recommendation.

Anne-Sophie Mutter is in excellent form. No doubt encouraged by Rostropovich, she does not shrink from expressive exaggeration but this is generally tastefully done. Her playing, it must be said, is pretty dazzling and the playing of the Washington orchestra is certainly first class. All the same, Shumsky's less self-conscious version is to be preferred. The recording sounds as if it was made in a packed auditorium, though detail registers satisfactorily.

From the middle ages, Op. 79; Scènes de ballet, Op. 52.
*** Chandos Dig. CHAN 8804 [id.]. SNO, Järvi (with LIADOV: *Musical snuffbox****).

Järvi makes out an excellent case for these charming – though at times rather thickly scored – Glazunov suites. He has the advantage of an excellently balanced and wide-ranging recording and gets good playing from the SNO. Although this music is obviously inferior to Tchaikovksy, Järvi has the knack of making you think it is better than it is. The disc also includes a fine account of Liadov's delightful *A Musical snuffbox*.

Raymonda (ballet), *Op. 57:* extended excerpts from Acts I & II.
*** Chan. Dig. CHAN 8447 [id.]. SNO, Järvi.

Järvi chooses some 56 minutes of music from the first two Acts, omitting entirely the Slavic/Hungarian *Wedding Divertissement* of the closing Act, and this contributes to the slight feeling of lassitude. But with rich Chandos recording this is a record for any balletomane to wallow in, even if a Russian performance would undoubtedly have more extrovert fire. There are 24 dividing bands, and it is a pity that they are not directly related to the fairly detailed synopsis.

(i) *Les ruses d'amour* (ballet), *Op. 61;* (ii) *The Sea* (fantasy), *Op. 28;* (iii) *March on a Russian theme.*
**(*) Olympia OCD 141 [id.]. (i) USSR RSO, Ziuraitis; (ii) Provatorov; (iii) USSR Ministry of Defence O, Maltsiev.

Les ruses d'amour is new to the UK domestic catalogue. The analogue recording is one of Olympia's better CD transfers, with plenty of body, along with its Russian brightness and colour. There are some 55 minutes of ballet music here, not unlike *Raymonda* though not perhaps quite as fine as *The Seasons*. *The Sea*, though not really memorable, has undoubtedly effective pictorial content and is not too long for its material; the *March* is ingenuous. All are very well played, especially the main work which reveals Algis Ziuraitis as a deft exponent of his compatriot's music.

The Sea (fantasy), Op. 28; Spring, Op. 34.
*** Chan. Dig. CHAN 8611 [id.]. SNO, Järvi – KALINNIKOV: *Symphony No. 1.****

The tone-poem, *Spring*, was written two years after *The Sea* and is infinitely more imaginative; in fact, it is as fresh and delightful as its companion is cliché-ridden. At one point Glazunov even looks forward to *The Seasons*. Persuasive and well-recorded performances from the Scottish National Orchestra under Neeme Järvi. The spacious and vivid recording sounds well.

The Seasons (ballet) *Op. 67.*
(BB) **(*) Naxos Dig. 8.550079 [id.]. Czech RSO (Bratislava), Ondrej Lenard – TCHAIKOVSKY: *Sleeping Beauty suite.***

Ondrej Lenard gives a pleasing account of Glazunov's delightful score, finding plenty of delicacy for the vignettes of *Winter: Frost, Ice* and *Snow*, and an appropriate warmth for the *Waltz of the cornflowers and poppies* of *Summer*. The entry of Glazunov's most famous tune at the opening of the *Autumn Bacchanale* is very virile indeed, helped by a slight rise in the recording level. The sound is first class, transparently atmospheric yet with plenty of fullness and weight at climaxes. The ear has an impression of a fairly modest string section, but the sounds they make are pleasing and graceful.

Stenka Razin (symphonic poem), *Op. 13*.
*** Chan. Dig. CHAN 8479 [id.]. SNO, Järvi – RIMSKY-KORSAKOV: *Scheherazade*.***

Stenka Razin has its moments of vulgarity – how otherwise with the *Song of the Volga Boatmen* a recurrent theme? – but it makes a generous and colourful makeweight for Järvi's fine version of *Scheherazade*. The recording is splendid.

Symphonies Nos. 1 in E, Op. 5; 5 in B flat, Op. 55.
**(*) Orfeo Dig. C 093101A [id.]. Bav. RSO, Järvi.

Symphonies Nos. 1 in E, Op. 5; 7 in F, Op. 77.
*** Olympia Dig. OCD 100 [id.]. USSR MoC SO, Rozhdestvensky.

Glazunov composed his prodigious *First Symphony* in the early 1880s (it is not only remarkably accomplished but delightfully fresh) and the last in 1906 when he had just turned forty. Rozhdestvensky's persuasive advocacy enhances the appeal of all this music. Under his direction the *First Symphony* sounds even more mature, and its slow movement is eloquently shaped, as is that of the 'Pastoral' *Seventh*. Throughout, the woodwind playing has an agreeable lyrical lightness. The scherzos, always Glazunov's best movements, are a delight, helped by the sparkling ensemble of this fine new Soviet orchestra. The digital recording is very bright but full and vividly detailed, not quite as sophisticated as a Western recording yet not coarsening the sound-picture.

The playing of the Bavarian Radio Symphony Orchestra under Neeme Järvi is highly sympathetic and polished. The music is made to sound cogent and civilized, if perhaps a little bland at times. The Orfeo recording is more naturally balanced and ample in texture but, like the performances, lacks something in glitter, although the scherzos remain highly effective. Overall the Russian performances project more vitality, although in their way Järvi's versions are certainly enjoyable.

Symphony No. 2 in F sharp min., Op. 16; Concert waltz No. 1, Op. 47.
**(*) Orfeo Dig. C 148101A [id.]. Bamberg SO, Järvi.

(i) *Symphony No. 2 in F sharp min., Op. 16; Romantic intermezzo, Op. 69; Stenka Razin, Op. 13*.
**(*) Olympia Dig. OCD 119 [id.]. (i) USSR MoC SO, Rozhdestvensky; USSR RSO, Dimitriedi.

The melodic material of the *Second Symphony* has an unmistakably Slavic feeling and, in Rozhdestvensky's hands, is played with enormous eloquence, with glowingly colourful woodwind solos from this splendid orchestra. The snag is the recording which, although it has a most attractive basic ambience, produces problems at fortissimo levels, where the brass bray fiercely and the violins above the stave lose a good deal of body and tend to shrillness. Both the *Romantic intermezzo*, which also generates considerable fervour, and *Stenka Razin*, which is very exciting indeed, especially in its vulgarly thrilling closing section, are analogue recordings and have considerably more body at climaxes.

Järvi's Orfeo sound is altogether more comfortable, and the music-making is more comfortable too. However, within its boundaries, which are more inhibited than

Rozhdestvensky's, this is a very good performance: the playing is eloquent; the scherzo is beautifully cultivated and undoubtedly fresh, although the finale sounds relatively lame without the added histrionics. The recording is full-bodied and naturally balanced, but could do with just a bit more brilliance. The *Concert waltz* makes an attractive encore.

Symphony No. 3 in D, Op. 33.
*** ASV CDDCA 581 [id.]. LSO, Yondani Butt.

Symphony No. 3; Concert waltz No. 2 in F, Op. 51.
*** Orfeo Dig. C 157101A [id.]. Bamberg SO, Järvi.

Symphony No. 3 in D, Op. 33; Poème lyrique, Op. 12; Solemn procession.
**(*) Olympia Dig. OCD 120 [id.]. USSR MoC SO, Rozhdestvensky.

In Järvi's hands the engaging opening of Glazunov's *Third Symphony*, with its lyrical string melody soaring over throbbing wind chords, is richer and more cultivated than Rozhdestvensky's version, where the entry of the Russian brass coarsens the effect. In the lovely *Andante*, there is some fine woodwind playing and the Bamberg violins are warmly expansive when they are given the melody; the scherzo too is delectably played. The finale has plenty of energy and almost doesn't seem too long, when the momentum is so well sustained. The *Concert waltz* too has a charming elegance.

Butt starts with the disadvantage of having no coupling. But the ASV recording is brighter and more open than the Orfeo, and this gives an added freshness to the textures of the slow movement. The response of the LSO catches both its colour and its gentle melancholy; the scherzo too has an extra sparkle here. Butt's reading lies somewhere between those of Järvi and Rozhdestvensky.

In Rozhdestvensky's performance the very opening has a Mendelssohnian lightness of touch, but when the brazen Russian trombones enter, they take the music into a distinctly Slavic world and the Russian-ness of the lyricism soon asserts itself. Otherwise, the playing of the USSR Ministry of Culture Symphony Orchestra is well up to the excellent standard of this series (particularly in the scherzo of the *Symphony*), with notably fine woodwind solos. Rozhdestvensky is especially good in the *Solemn procession*, which is more optimistic than the title suggests, though again the rather papery sound of the violins above the stave and the edgy brass of the recording are a drawback.

Symphonies Nos. 4 in E flat, Op. 48; 5 in B flat, Op. 55.
*** Olympia Dig. OCD 101 [id.]. USSR MoC SO, Rozhdestvensky.

Symphonies Nos. 4 in E flat, Op. 48; 7 in F, Op. 77.
**(*) Orfeo C 148201A [id.]. Bamberg SO, Järvi.

Glazunov's *Fourth* is a charming and well-composed symphony, full of good things and distinctly Russian in outlook, and held together structurally by a theme which Glazunov uses in all three movements. The *Fifth* is much better known and has a particularly fine slow movement. The string playing confirms the Ministry of Culture Symphony as currently the finest Soviet orchestra. The recording is extremely vivid, among the best in this fine series of recordings which undoubtedly give the strongest advocacy to Glazunov's music.

The *Seventh* with its engaging woodwind writing, notably for the oboe in the first movement, has much to attract the listener. The *Andante* is undoubtedly eloquent in Järvi's performance and the scherzo, marked *giocoso*, is well up to form. The finale has plenty of bustle, even if here it sounds rather long. The sound, as in the rest of Järvi's series, is full and naturally balanced, lacking something in spectacle.

Symphony No. 6 in C min., Op. 58; Poème lyrique, Op. 12.
*** Orfeo Dig. C 157201 [id.]. Bamberg SO, Neeme Järvi.

Symphony No. 6 in C min., Op. 58; Scènes de ballet, Op. 52.
**(*) Olympia Dig. OCD 104 [id.]. USSR MoC SO or RSO, Rozhdestvensky.

Symphony No. 6 in C min., Op. 58; Serenades Nos. 1, Op. 7; 2, Op. 11; Triumphal march, Op. 40.
*** ASV Dig. CDDCA 699 [id.]. LSO or RPO, Yondani Butt.

Taken overall, Yondani Butt's is the preferred choice for Glazunov's *Sixth*, although of course couplings do come into the matter. But Butt's performance is marginally fresher than Järvi's, helped by the more open sound of the ASV recording, and the fine wind and brass contributions from the LSO; the brass chorale at the end of the *Variations* is effectively sonorous. There is some lovely string playing too, and Butt finds an attractive elegance in the *Intermezzo*. The finale generates unflagging energy and even a certain dignity. The two waltz-like *Serenades* have a lilting graciousness and the *March*, an American commission, builds a suitably grandiloquent climax on the song, *John Brown's body*.

Järvi makes more than usual of the first movement of the *Sixth*, building an impressive climax. The *Theme and variations* benefits greatly from the polished playing of the Bambergers, who find plenty of colour both here and in the *Intermezzo*, a slight but agreeable replacement for Glazunov's usual scherzo. The finale produces energy and vigour without too much bombast, for the Bamberg brass is sonorous without being blatant, as happens in Rozhdestvensky's alternative Russian performance. The *Poème lyrique* is full of romantic atmosphere and is beautifully played; the full yet vivid recording, which is admirably detailed but which still possesses rich string textures, seems just right for the music.

Rozhdestvensky directs the work with the kind of thrust and conviction to make the very most of it, and is suitably affectionate in the variations. Here, however, the brass chorale is a bit fierce as recorded, and the upper string sound could ideally be more glamorous. The *Scènes de ballet* is analogue: the recording is still very bright but has slightly more depth. It is characteristic of the composer's favourite genre, assured and often tuneful.

(i) *Symphony No. 8 in E flat, Op. 83; Ballade, Op. 78; Slavonic festival, Op. 26.*
*** Olympia Dig. OCD 130 [id.]. (i) USSR MoC SO, Rozhdestvensky; USSR RSO, Dimitriedi.

Symphony No. 8 in E flat, Op. 83; Overture solennelle, Op. 73; Wedding procession, Op. 21.
**(*) Orfeo C 093201A [id.]. Bav. RSO, Järvi.

Rozhdestvensky provides the most powerful advocacy, particularly in the fine first movement and the expansively eloquent *Mesto*. The scherzo is less charming, more purposive than is usual in a Glazunov symphony; it is splendidly played, and in the finale the brass chorale is without the blatancy one tends to expect from a Russian performance. Indeed this is one of Glazunov's most convincing finales, with an attractive lyrical strain. The two bonuses are well worth having. The *Ballade* contrasts expressively intense writing for the strings with a brass interlude, where again the Russian playing is colourful rather than edgy. The *Slavonic festival* is a most engaging piece, a kaleidoscope of vigorous dance-themes and sparkling orchestration. The recording throughout is more agreeable than many in Rozhdestvensky's cycle, not lacking vividness but fuller and better balanced.

As in the rest of his series, Järvi and the Bavarian players give the piece a cultivated, polished performance, not lacking commitment and vigour, and certainly with plenty of colour in the scherzo, but bringing to the music a Schumannesque quality at times. Nevertheless the performance is thoroughly musical and undoubtedly enjoyable, with spaciousness to some extent compensating for passion, when the sound is full and pleasing.

Symphony No. 9 in D min. (Unfinished).
** Olympia OCD 147 [id.]. USSR RSO, Yudin – KABALEVSKY: *Romeo and Juliet*; LVOV: *Violin concerto.***

A single movement is all that survives of the *Ninth*, and that had to be completed by the present conductor. It opens nobly and is beautifully constructed; the texture is more polyphonic in character than is generally the case with Glazunov. Had it continued as it began, this might have added a new dimension to our view of this composer. It is a beautiful piece, though the recording, whose date is not specified, sounds as if it comes from the 1960s.

String quartet No. 1 in D, Op. 1.
*** Olympia OCD 157 [id.]. Shostakovich Qt – TCHAIKOVSKY: *Trio.***(*)

Glazunov's *First Quartet* is extraordinarily assured and inventive. It dates from the year after the *First Symphony*, when its composer was eighteen. With a genuinely eloquent *Andante* – beautifully played here – and an accomplished scherzo, the piece ends appealingly with a moderately paced and tuneful finale. The performance is superb: the immaculate ensemble of the Shostakovich Quartet is matched by their warmth and body of tone. One could not imagine a better account. The recording, made in 1974, is well balanced and immediate.

String quartets Nos. 2 in F, Op. 10; 4 in A min., Op. 64.
*** Olympia OCD 173 [id.]. Shostakovich Qt.

The *Second Quartet* is clearly indebted to Borodin; its scherzo has lots of charm and its slow movement is really quite beautiful. The *Fourth* is far less obviously nationalistic and, though it cannot wholly escape the blandness of contour that often distinguishes this composer, there are undoubted rewards. The Shostakovich Quartet have obvious feeling for this music and play with real conviction; their 1974 recording is very good indeed.

Piano sonatas Nos. 1 in B flat min., Op. 74; 2 in E min., Op. 75; Grand concert waltz in E flat, Op. 41.
**(*) Pearl SHECD 9538 [id.]. Leslie Howard.

The Glazunov *Sonatas* are well worth investigating, particularly in performances as committed and as well recorded as these. Howard does not always make the most of the poetry here and is not always consistent in observing dynamic nuances, but there is more to praise than to criticize. Admirers of Glazunov's art should investigate this issue which sounds extremely impressive in its CD format. The analogue recording is most realistically transferred.

Glière, Reinhold (1875–1956)

Symphony No. 3 in B min. (Ilya Murometz), Op. 42.
(M) **(*) Unicorn Dig. UKCD 2014/5 [id.]. RPO, Farberman.

Glière's massive programme symphony manages to stretch thin material extraordinarily far. Farberman's conducting cannot be described as volatile, and he is never led into introducing urgent stringendos to add to the passion of a climax, but his very patience, helped by vivid recording, makes for very compelling results. The sound has natural balance and combines brilliance with warmth.

Glinka, Mikhail (1805–57)

Russlan and Ludmilla: Overture.
(B) *** Decca 417 689-2 [id.]. LSO, Solti – MUSSORGSKY: *Khovanshchina prelude; Night;* BORODIN: *Prince Igor:* excerpts.***
(M) *** RCA GD 60176 [60176-2-RG]. Chicago SO, Fritz Reiner – PROKOFIEV: *Alexander Nevsky* etc.***

Solti's electrifying account of the *Russlan and Ludmilla overture* is perhaps the most exciting ever recorded, with the lyrical element providing a balancing warmth, though the sound is very brightly lit.

Reiner's performance is not quite as racy as Solti's, but it is still highly infectious, and the 1959 Chicago sound brings plenty of colour and warmth.

(i; ii) Divertissement on themes from Bellini's La Sonnambula; (i) String quartet in F; (iii) Valse-fantaisie.
** Olympia OCD 184 [id.]. (i) Leningrad PO Qt, (ii) with Shakin, Yakovlev; (iii) V. Kamishov.

This, together with the Olympia Aliabiev CD, gives a very good picture of what musical life was like in the salons of St Petersburg in the 1830s. The *Quartet*, which starts the disc, comes from 1830; it has an element of pastiche but it also has a certain charm in these artists' expert hands. Valery Kamishov plays the *Valse-fantaisie* very persuasively. The *Divertissement brillante* for piano, string quartet and double-bass is unpretentious but agreeable. The recording is fully acceptable.

Grand sextet in E flat.
*** Hyp. CDA 66163 [id.]. Capricorn – RIMSKY-KORSAKOV: *Quintet.****

Glinka's *Sextet* is rather engaging, particularly when played with such aplomb as it is here. The contribution of the pianist, Julian Jacobson, is brilliantly nimble and felicitous. The recording has an attractive ambience and, if the balance places the piano rather backwardly for a resonant acoustic, the CD provides good detail and overall presence.

Trio pathétique in D min.
*** Chan. Dig. CHAN 8477 [id.]. Borodin Trio – ARENSKY: *Piano trio.****

Glinka's *Trio* is prefaced by a superscription; 'Je n'ai connu l'amour que par les peines qu'il cause' (I have known love only through the misery it causes). It is no masterpiece – but the Borodins play it for all they are worth and almost persuade one that it is. As we have come to expect from this source, the recording is vivid and has excellent presence.

Barcarolle in G; Contredanse in G; New Contredanses; Cotillon; Farewell waltz; Galop in E flat; Mazurka in F; Las Molares; Monastyrka; Polski in E flat; Reminiscences of a mazurka in B flat; Rondo on themes from Montecchi e Capuletti; Tarantella in A min.; Variations on Scottish themes; Variations on a theme from Aliabiev's The Nightingale; Variations on themes from Bellini's Montecchi e Capuletti; Variations on two themes from Kia-King; Waltz in G.
*(*) Olympia OCD 124 [id.]. Valery Kamishov.

Not even his greatest admirers would make huge claims for Glinka's piano music, and it is difficult to summon up much enthusiasm here, although some of the later works represent a considerable advance on the earlier, salon pieces. Valery Kamishov plays with undoubted skill, though the recording is undistinguished.

Gluck, Christophe (1714–87)

Alceste (complete).
** Orfeo Dig. C 02782 (3) [id.]. Jessye Norman, Gedda, Krause, Nimsgern, Weikl, Bav. R. Ch. and SO, Baudo.

The French version of *Alceste* in this very well-cast set has Jessye Norman commanding in the title-role, producing gloriously varied tone in every register. What is rather lacking – even from her performance – is a fire-eating quality such as made Janet Baker's performance so memorable and which comes out to hair-raising effect in Callas's recording of *Divinités du Styx*. Here it is beautiful but relatively tame. That is mainly the fault of the conductor, who makes Gluck's score sound comfortable rather than tense. The other principals sing stylishly; however, as a set, this does not quite rebut the idea that in Gluck 'beautiful' means 'boring'. Good, well-focused sound from Bavarian Radio engineers.

(i) *La Corona* (complete). (ii) *La Danza* (dramatic pastoral).
**(*) Orfeo Dig. C 135872H (2) [id.]. (i) Slowakiewicz, Gorzynska, Nowicks, Bav. R. Ch; (ii) Ignatowicz, Myriak, Warsaw CO; Bugaj.

Hunting-calls set the scene evocatively in the three-movement sinfonia of *La Corona*, which is followed by six arias (including a particularly brilliant one for Atalanta), a delightful duet and a final quartet. This performance, originally recorded for Bavarian Radio, is fresh and direct, with first-rate singing from the three sopranos. The much shorter fill-up, described as a dramatic pastoral, is less interesting and is less reliably done. It is none the less welcome as an extension of the Gluck repertory.

Echo et Narcisse (opera).
(**) HM HMC 905201/2 [id.]. Boulin, Streit, Massell, Galliard, Hoffstedt, Hogman, Hamburg Op. Ch., Cologne Concerto, Jacobs.

In this delightful performance directed by René Jacobs, who is better known as a counter-tenor but who is also a great inspirer of others, one can understand why *Echo et Narcisse* was a failure initially. With its gently swinging triple-time rhythms, much of this is very different from the solid Gluck we encounter in the big operas. Jacobs' direction in this live Schwetzingen Festival performance carries you winningly from one number to the next, right up to the jolly final chorus, a *Hymn to Love*. Though one or two of the singers are disappointing, notably the tremulous Sophie Boulin as Echo, the singing is generally good, with excellent choral support from the Hamburg Opera Chorus. The big snag – which may well make enjoyment impossible for many – is that the live recording captures all too faithfully the incessant background noises of the stage production. At times the bangs, shufflings and clonks, directionally reproduced, are so loud, improbable and unfortunately timed that one might be listening to a Goon Show. Those who can ignore that background will find great pleasure here, as they would have done in the intimate Schwetzingen theatre.

Iphigénie en Aulide (complete).
***Erato/WEA Dig. 2292 45003-2 (2). Van Dam, Anne Sophie von Otter, Dawson, Aler, Monteverdi Ch., Lyon Op. O, Gardiner.

Following up the success of his recording of the more celebrated *Iphigénie en Tauride*, John Eliot Gardiner here tackles the earlier of the two *Iphigénie* operas, much more neglected. *Iphigénie en Aulide* was written in 1774 – Gluck's first piece in French – and anticipated the *Tauride* opera in its speed and directness of treatment, so different from the leisurely and expansive traditions of *opera seria*. Based on Euripides by way of Racine, this does not have quite the emotional variety of the later opera, but it is just as moving. Gardiner here eliminates the distortions of the piece which the long-established Wagner edition created and reconstructs the score as presented in the first revival of 1775. Though the original final chorus was then omitted, Gardiner rightly includes it here, amazingly original, with the bass drum prefacing a number which is less a celebration than a dramatic call to war, very different from the conventional happy ending. The darkness of the piece is established at the very start, with men's voices eliminated, and a moving portrait built up of Agamemnon, here superbly sung by José van Dam, with his extended solo at the end of Act II tellingly contrasted with the brevity and economy of the rest. In the title-role Lynne Dawson builds up a touching portrait of the heroine from the contrasted sequence of brief arias, a character developing in adversity, always vulnerable. Her sweet, pure singing is well contrasted with the positive strength of Anne Sofie von Otter as Clytemnestra, and John Aler brings clear, heroic attack to the tenor role of Achille. The performance is crowned by the superb ensemble-singing of the Monteverdi Choir in the many choruses. Based on a production at the Aix-en-Provence Festival, the recording conveys the tensions of a live performance without the distractions of intrusive stage noise. Gardiner persuades the Lyon Opera Orchestra, using modern instruments, to adopt some of the manners of period players, minimizing any disappointment that – like Gardiner's recording of *Iphigénie en Tauride* – this is not a true period performance.

Iphigénie en Tauride (complete).
⊛ *** Ph. Dig. 416 148-2 (2) [id.]. Montague, Aler, Thomas Allen, Argenta, Massis, Monteverdi Ch., Lyon Op. O, Eliot Gardiner.

Gardiner's electrifying reading of *Iphigénie en Tauride* is a revelation. Anyone who has found Gluck operas boring should hear this dramatically paced performance of an opera that is compact and concentrated in its telling of a classical story. Gardiner is an urgent advocate, bringing out the full range of expression from first to last; though his Lyon orchestra does not use period instruments, its clarity and resilience and, where necessary, grace and delicacy are admirable. The cast is first rate. Diana Montague in the name-part sings with admirable bite and freshness, making the lovely solo *O malheureuse Iphigénie* pure and tender. Thomas Allen is an outstanding Oreste, characterizing strongly – as in his fury aria – but singing with classical precision. John Aler is a similarly strong and stylish singer, taking the tenor role of Pylade, with some fine singers from Gardiner's regular team impressive in other roles. The recording is bright and full, with the balance favouring voices but not inappropriately so.

Orfeo ed Euridice (complete).
*** EMI Dig. CDS7 49834-2 (2). Hendricks, Von Otter, Fournier, Monteverdi Ch., Lyon Opera O, Gardiner.
(M) **(*) RCA GD 87896 (2) [7896-2-RG]. Verrett, Moffo, Raskin, Rome Polyphonic Ch., Virtuosi di Roma, Fasano.
**(*) Decca 417 410-2 (2) [id.]. Horne, Lorengar, Donath, ROHCG Ch. & O, Solti.
**(*) Ariola 302588. Lucia Popp, Lipovšek, Kaufman, Munich R. O, Hager.
**(*) Capriccio Dig. 60 008-2 (2) [id.]. Kowalski, Schellenberger-Ernst, Fliegner, Berlin R. Ch., C. P. E. Bach CO, Hartmut Haenchen.

Gardiner here cuts through the problem of which text to use in this opera – the original Vienna version with alto in the title-role or the Paris version with tenor – by opting broadly for the Berlioz edition, which aimed at combining the best of both. At Glyndebourne under Raymond Leppard, much the same solution was adopted, and one hopes that Erato will issue on CD its fine recording with Dame Janet Baker from that source. For Gardiner, Anne Sofie von Otter is a superb Orfeo, tougher than Dame Janet, less vulnerable but less feminine too, and dramatically most convincing. The masculine forthrightness of her singing matches the extra urgency of Gardiner's direction; and both Barbara Hendricks as Eurydice and Brigitte Fournier as Amour are also excellent. The chorus is Gardiner's own Monteverdi Choir, superbly clean and stylish. Unlike the Leppard/Glyndebourne production, Gardiner's omits the celebratory ballet at the end of the opera. The recording is full and well balanced.

Clearly, if you have a mezzo as firm and sensitive as Shirley Verrett, then everything is in favour of your using the original Italian version rather than the later, Paris version with tenor. Quite apart from making a sensible decision over the text, Fasano uses the right-sized orchestra (of modern instruments) and adopts an appropriately classical style. Anna Moffo and Judith Raskin match Verrett in clean, strong singing, and the Rome Polyphonic Chorus is far more incisive than most Italian choirs. The recording is vivid and atmospheric, but on CD the close balance of the voices emphasizes the music's dramatic qualities rather than its tenderness. However, this makes a good mid-priced recommendation.

The surprise of the Decca set is the conducting of Georg Solti, which combines his characteristic brilliance and dramatic bite with a feeling for eighteenth-century idiom which is most impressive. Solti and Horne opt to conclude Act I, not as the Gluck score prescribes, but with a brilliant display aria, *Addio, o miei sospiri*, taken from the contemporary opera, *Tancredi*, by Ferdinando Bertoni. That may sound like cavalier treatment for Gluck, but stylistically Solti justifies not only that course but his whole interpretation, which combines drama with delicacy. Marilyn Horne makes a formidably strong Orfeo, not as deeply imaginative as Dame Janet Baker, but wonderfully strong and secure, with fine control of tone. Pilar Lorengar sings sweetly, but is not always steady, while Helen Donath is charming in the role of Amor. Recording quality is outstandingly fine.

Hager's Munich version brings a good, enjoyable middle-of-the-road performance. Marjana Lipovšek has a beautiful, rich mezzo inclined to fruitiness, which yet in this breeches role is well able to characterize Orfeo strongly and positively. So *Che farò* is warm and direct in its expressiveness, with Lipovšek avoiding distracting mannerism both here and in recitative. Lucia Popp makes a delightful Euridice and Julie Kaufman, though less distinctive, is fresh and bright as Amor. The chorus is on the heavyweight side for Gluck, but that adds to the power of the performance which uses the 1762 Vienna version of the score, though with instrumental numbers added from the Paris version.

The big attraction of the Capriccio version is the inspired singing of the German counter-tenor, Jochen Kowalski, in the title-role. The main shortcoming can be assessed at the very start, when the washy acoustic obscures rapid figuration in the overture, and the whole scale of the performance seems too big. Haenchen, with a good chamber orchestra using modern instruments, opts for the Vienna version of the opera, using Italian, more compact than the later Paris score; but he provides as an appendix the Paris ballet with its *Dance of the blessed spirits*, an essential item. The extra sharpness of the Vienna score is unfortunately countered not only by the recording and the conductor's occasionally heavy direction, but also by the murkiness of the large-sounding chorus. None of these shortcomings need weigh very heavily against the glories of the solo singing, notably that of Kowalski who, with his firm, characterful voice, generally warm-toned in a masculine way, creates an exceptionally convincing portrait of the bereaved Orpheus. More than usual he brings out the full poignant agony of the hero's situation. *Che farò* is taken effectively fast, but tenderly and with big rallentandos, and his intensity is matched by the fresh vehemence of his Eurydice, Dagmar Schellenberger-Ernst. Having a boy-treble as Amour is more controversial, though, as between Orpheus and Eurydice the sharp contrasts of timbre add to dramatic realism, and why not have a real boy in the role of Cupid, particularly when his voice is as pure and true as Christian Fliegner's? He comes from the Tölzer Boy Singers, and sings with commendably clean attack, fine rhythmic sense and no hooting.

Opera arias from *Alceste; Armide; Iphigénie en Aulide; Iphigénie en Tauride; Orfeo ed Euridice; Paride ed Elena; La rencontre imprévue.*
(M) *** Ph. 422 950-2 [id.]. Dame Janet Baker, ECO, Raymond Leppard.

Helped by alert and sensitive accompaniments, Dame Janet Baker's singing of Gluck completely undermines any idea of something square or dull. The most famous arias bring unconventional readings – *Divinités du Styx* from *Alceste* deliberately less commanding, more thoughtful than usual – but the rarities are what inspire her most keenly: the four arias from *Paride ed Elena*, for example, are vividly contrasted in their sharply compact form. Outstanding recording, vividly remasterd.

Godowsky, Leopold (1870–1938)

18 Studies on Chopin Études.
** Ara. Dig. Z 6537 [id.]. Ian Hobson.

Godowsky's studies are bizarre inventions and at times highly disconcerting. Ian Hobson takes their difficulties in his stride, but these pieces call for transcendental keyboard powers and must be tossed off with enormous aplomb and dazzling virtuosity. Hobson has formidable technique but he communicates comparatively little sense of abandon or joy; he is distinctly short on charm.

Goldmark, Karl (1830–1915)

Violin concerto No. 1 in A min., Op. 28.
*** EMI CDC7 47846-2 [id.]. Perlman, Pittsburgh SO, Previn – KORNGOLD: *Violin concerto.****

The first of Goldmark's two violin concertos is a pleasing and warm-hearted concerto in the Romantic tradition that deserves to be better known. Perlman is placed very much in the foreground – so much so that orchestral detail does not always register as it should. However, this is very charming and likeable music, and Perlman plays it most winningly. The CD transfer is clear and refined, losing perhaps a little of the warmth of the analogue master.

Overtures: Der gefesselte Prometheus, Op. 38; Im Frühling, Op. 36; In Italien, Op. 49; Sakuntala, Op. 13.
** Hung. Dig. HCD 12552 [id.]. Budapest PO, Korodi.

The overtures recorded here are expertly crafted and, in the case of *Im Frühling*, have good inventive ideas and no mean charm. Two of them, *Sakuntala* and *Der gefesselte Prometheus*, are longer than one would expect and, indeed, rather outstay their welcome. The playing of the Budapest orchestra under Andreas Korodi is very good; so, too, is the recording, which has considerable depth.

Die Königin von Saba (opera).
** Hung. HCD 12179/82 [id.]. Nagy, Gregor, Kincses, Jerusalem, Miller, Takács, Hungarian State Op. Ch. and O, Fischer.

With the Queen of Sheba representing evil and the lovely Sulamit representing good, the theme of this opera has a link with Wagner's *Tannhäuser*, yet in style Goldmark rather recalls Mendelssohn and Gounod, with a touch of Meyerbeer. In the tenor role of Asad, Siegfried Jerusalem gives a magnificent performance, not least in his aria *Magische Töne*. Klára Takács is dramatic and characterful as the Queen of Sheba, but on top the voice is often raw. Sándor Nagy is an impressive Solomon, and Adam Fischer, one of the talented family of conductors, draws lively performances from everyone. The recording is very acceptable, but even on CD there are many details which do not emerge as vividly as they might. The documentation, too, is poorly produced.

Gottschalk, Louis (1829–69)

Grande fantaisie triomphale sur l'Hymne Nationale Brésilien, Op. 69 (arr. Hazel).
*** Decca Dig. 414 348-2 [id.]. Ortiz, RPO, Atzmon – ADDINSELL: *Warsaw concerto*; LITOLFF: *Scherzo*; RACHMANINOV: *Concerto No. 2*.***

Gottschalk's *Grand fantasia* has naïvety and a touch of vulgarity, too, but the performers here give it an account which nicely combines flair and a certain elegance, and the result is a distinct success.

Gould, Morton (born 1913)

Derivations for clarinet and band.
*** CBS MK 42227 [id.]. Benny Goodman, Columbia Jazz Combo, composer – BARTÓK: *Contrasts*; BERNSTEIN: *Prelude, fugue and riffs*; COPLAND: *Concerto*; STRAVINSKY: *Ebony concerto*.(***)

Gould's *Derivations* is in Gershwinesque mould. The first-movement *Warm-up* is well managed, but the central *Contrapuntal blues* and (especially) the *Rag* are the most memorable of these four miniatures. Benny Goodman is in his element and the accompaniment under the composer is suitably improvisatory in feeling.

Gounod, Charles (1818–93)

Petite symphonie for wind in B flat.
** HM Orfeo Dig. C 051831A [id.]. Munich Wind Ac., Brezina – DVOŘÁK: *Wind serenade.***

The playing of the Munich Academy is first class: they have an impressive overall blend and the solo contributions have plenty of individuality. The finale is especially engaging and the scherzo is deft. In the first two movements the musicians' geographical location is felt in the style, which is less vital and fresh than the famous Netherlands version under Edo de Waart which we hope may reappear on a mid-priced CD during the lifetime of this book.

Messe solennelle de Saint Cécile.
*** EMI Dig. CDC7 47094-2 [id.]. Hendricks, Dale, Lafont, Ch. and Nouvel O Philharmonique of R. France, Prêtre.
(M) *** DG 427 409-2 [id.]. Seefried, Stolze, Uhde, Czech Ch. & PO, Markevitch.

Gounod's *Messe solennelle*, with its blatant march setting of the *Credo* and sugar-sweet choral writing, may not be for sensitive souls, but Prêtre here directs an almost ideal performance, vividly recorded, to delight anyone not averse to Victorian manners. Prêtre's subtle rhythmic control and sensitive shaping of phrase minimize the vulgarity and bring out the genuine dramatic contrasts of the piece, with glowing singing from the choir as well as the three soloists.

In DG's mid-price Dokumente series, Markevitch's vintage version, recorded in the mid-1960s, still sounds remarkably well. In his straight-faced way Markevitch makes the incongruity of Gounod's jolly and vulgar tunes all the more delectable, and soloists, chorus and orchestra are all first rate. A good alternative to Prêtre's modern EMI version, costing a good deal less.

Faust (complete).
(M) **(*) EMI CMS7 69983-2 (3) [Ang. CDMC 69983]. De los Angeles, Gedda, Blanc, Christoff, Paris Nat. Op. Ch. and O, Cluytens.
**(*) Ph. Dig. 420 164-2 (3) [id.]. Te Kanawa, Araiza, Nesterenko, Bav. R. Ch. and SO, C. Davis.

In the reissued Cluytens set the seductiveness of de los Angeles's singing is a dream and it is a pity that the recording hardens the natural timbre slightly. Christoff is magnificently Mephistophelian; the dark, rich bass voice with all its many subtle facets of tone-colour is a superb vehicle for the part, at once musical and dramatic. Gedda, though showing some signs of strain, sings intelligently, and among the other soloists Ernest Blanc has a pleasing, firm voice, which he uses to make Valentin into a sympathetic character. Cluytens's approach is competent but somewhat workaday. He rarely offers that extra spring which adds so much to Gounod's score in sheer charm, and he shows a tendency to over-drive in the more dramatic passages. The recording is well balanced on the whole, although at times some of the soloists are oddly placed on the stereo stage. The layout of the five Acts over three CDs is just as it should be, and the libretto includes a full translation.

Sir Colin Davis, with his German orchestra and with no French singer among his principals, may not always be idiomatic but, with fine singing from most of them, it is a refreshing version. Dame Kiri, more than you might expect, makes a light and innocent-sounding Marguerite, with the *Jewel Song* made to sparkle in youthful eagerness leaping off from a perfect trill. Evgeni Nesterenko as Mephistopheles is a fine saturnine tempter; Andreas Schmidt as Valentin sings cleanly and tastefully in a rather German way; while Pamela Coburn as Siebel is sweet and boyish. The big snag is the Faust of Francisco Araiza, a disappointing hero with the voice, as recorded, gritty in tone and frequently strained. The sound is first rate.

Faust: ballet music (suite).
(M) *** EMI CDM7 69041-2 [id.]. Philh. O, Karajan – BORODIN: *Polovtsian dances****; OFFENBACH: *Gaîté parisienne***(*); PONCHIELLI: *Dance of the Hours.****
(*) Decca Dig. 411 708-2 [id.]. Montreal SO, Dutoit – OFFENBACH: *Gaîté parisienne.*(*)

Karajan's 1960 recording offers elegant, sparkling playing from the Philharmonia at their peak. The sound is pleasingly full as well as bright.

Gounod's attractive suite is warmly and elegantly played by the Montreal orchestra under Dutoit, although the conductor's touch is not as light as one would have expected. The CD sounds first rate, however.

Grainger, Percy (1882–1961)

Blithe bells (Free ramble on a theme by Bach: Sheep may safely graze): Country gardens; Green bushes (Passacaglia); Handel in the Strand; Mock morris; Molly on the shore; My Robin is to the greenwood gone; Shepherd's hey; Spoon River; Walking tune; Youthful rapture; Youthful suite; Rustic dance; Eastern intermezzo.
*** Chan. CHAN 8377 [id.]. Bournemouth Sinf., Montgomery.

Montgomery's anthology of Grainger's music stands out for the sparkling and sympathetic playing of the Bournemouth Sinfonietta and an engaging choice of programme. Among the expressive pieces, the arrangement of *My Robin is to the greenwood gone* is highly attractive, but the cello solo in *Youthful rapture* is perhaps less effective. Favourites such as *Country gardens*, *Shepherd's hey*, *Molly on the shore* and *Handel in the Strand* all sound as fresh as paint, and among the novelties the *Rustic dance* and *Eastern intermezzo* have undoubted period charm.

Part songs: Australian up-country song; Brigg Fair; Danny Deever; Irish tune from County Derry; The lost lady found; Morning song in the jungle; The peora hunt; Shallow Brown; Six dukes went afishin'; Skye boat song; There was a pig.
*** Conifer Dig. CDCF 162 [id.]. CBSO Ch., Simon Halsey – DELIUS: *Part songs.***(*)

Robust and engaging, these songs emerge just as characterfully when treated chorally, as here, instead of with the sharper focus of single voices. Some of the more evocative gain from this larger-scale treatment, particularly when the CBSO Chorus sings so responsively and with such fine ensemble under Simon Halsey. Atmospheric recording.

Duke of Marlborough fanfare; Green bushes (Passacaglia); Irish tune from County Derry; Lisbon; Molly on the shore; My Robin is to Greenwood gone; Shepherd's hey; Piano duet: Let's dance gay in green meadow; Vocal & choral: Bold William Taylor; Brigg Fair; I'm seventeen come Sunday; Lord Maxwell's goodnight; The lost lady found; The pretty maid milkin' her cow; Scotch strathspey and reel; Shallow Brown; Shenandoah; The sprig of thyme; There was a pig went out to dig; Willow willow.
(M) *** Decca 425 159-2 [id.]. Pears, Shirley-Quirk, Amb. S. or Linden Singers, Wandsworth Boys' Ch., ECO, Britten or Steuart Bedford; Britten and V. Tunnard (pianos).

This is an altogether delightful anthology, beautifully played and sung by these distinguished artists. Grainger's talent was a smaller one than his more fervent advocates would have us believe, but his imagination in the art of arranging folksong was prodigious. The *Willow song* is a touching and indeed haunting piece and shows the quality of Grainger's harmonic resource. The opening fanfare too is strikingly original, and so is *Shallow Brown*. Vocal and instrumental items are felicitously interwoven, and the recording is extremely vivid, though the digital remastering has put a hint of edge on the voices.

Granados, Enrique (1867–1916)

Cuentos de la juventud, Op. 1: Dedicatoria. Spanish dances, Op. 37/4 & 5; Tonadillas al estilo antiguo: La Maja de Goya. Valses poéticos.
⊛ *** RCA RCD 14378 [RCD1 4378]. Julian Bream – ALBENIZ: *Collection.**** ⊛

Like the Albéniz items with which these Granados pieces are coupled, these performances show Julian Bream at his most inspirational. The illusion of the guitar being in the room is especially electrifying in the middle section of the famous *Spanish dance No. 5*, when Bream achieves the most subtle pianissimo. Heard against the background silence, the effect is quite magical. But all the playing here is wonderfully spontaneous. This is one of the most impressive guitar recitals ever recorded.

Allegro de concierto; Capricho espagnol, Op. 39; Carezza vals, Op. 38; 2 Impromptus; Oriental; Rapsodia aragonesa; Valses poéticos.
*** CRD CRD 3323 [id.]. Thomas Rajna.

Thomas Rajna's recital overlaps with Alicia de Larrocha's distinguished collection (see below) only in the *Allegro de concierto*. Not all of Granados's works are as inventive as the *Goyescas*, but some of his finest music for piano is included here. Thomas Rajna plays it with great sympathy and flair, and the piano has good presence within a warm acoustic.

Allegro de concierto; 6 escenas románticas; 6 piezas sobre cantos populares españoles.
*** Decca Dig. 410 288-2 [id.]. Alicia de Larrocha.

The spirited *Allegro de concierto*, the colourful and folk-orientated *Seis piezas*, and the more subtle, expressively ambitious *Escenas románticas* show the surprisingly wide range of Granados's piano music and Alicia de Larrocha's natural accord with his sound-world. Her authority in this programme is matched by her ability to communicate. The recording is first class.

12 Danzas españolas, Op. 37.
*** Decca 414 557-2 [id.]. Alicia de Larrocha.
*** CRD CRD 3321 [id.]. Thomas Rajna.

Alicia de Larrocha has an aristocratic poise to which it is difficult not to respond, and plays with great flair and temperament. There have been other fine accounts, but this is undoubtedly the most desirable and best-recorded version in circulation. The transfer of the analogue master to CD has been very successful and the sound has enhanced presence.
Rajna's performances are first class: his feeling for the idiom is assured and the playing is delectably spontaneous. The CRD recording has transferred realistically to CD, and those collecting his complete series will not be disappointed here.

Goyescas (complete).
*** Decca 411 958-2 [id.]. Alicia de Larrocha.
**(*) CRD CRD 3301 [id.]. Thomas Rajna.

The Decca recording is most distinguished. Alicia de Larrocha brings special insights and sympathy to the *Goyescas*; her playing has the crisp articulation and rhythmic vitality that these pieces call for, and the overall impression could hardly be more idiomatic in flavour nor more realistic as a recording.

Thomas Rajna's *Goyescas* is persuasive and clearly recorded; but with Alicia de Larrocha's outstanding Decca CD available, this must inevitably take second place.

Grieg, Edvard (1843–1907)

Piano concerto in A min., Op. 16.
*** Ph. 412 923-2. Bishop-Kovacevich, BBC SO, Sir Colin Davis – SCHUMANN: *Piano concerto.****
*** CBS Dig. MK 44899 [id.]. Perahia, Bav. RSO, C. Davis – SCHUMANN: *Concerto.****
(M) *** EMI CD-EMX 2002. Solomon, Philh. O, Menges – SCHUMANN: *Piano concerto.****
(*) EMI Dig. CDC7 47611-2 [id.]. Ousset, LSO, Marriner – MENDELSSOHN: *Piano concerto No. 1.*(*)
(M) **(*) Decca 417 728-2 [id.]. Radu Lupu, LSO, Previn – SCHUMANN: *Concerto.***(*)
(B) **(*) Decca 417 676-2 [id.]. Curzon, LSO, Fjelstad – TCHAIKOVSKY: *Piano concerto No. 1.***(*)
(M) (***) EMI mono CDH7 63497-2 [id.]. Lipatti, Philh. O, Galliera – CHOPIN: *Piano concerto No. 1.*(**)

The freshness and imagination displayed in the coupling of the Grieg and Schumann *Concertos* by Stephen Bishop-Kovacevich and Sir Colin Davis offers a recording collaboration which continues to dominate the catalogue. Whether in the clarity of virtuoso fingerwork or the shading of half-tone, Bishop-Kovacevich is among the most illuminating of the many great pianists who have recorded the Grieg *Concerto*. He plays with bravura and refinement, the spontaneity of the music-making bringing a sparkle throughout, to balance the underlying poetry. The 1972 recording has been freshened most successfully.

Perahia revels in the bravura as well as bringing out the lyrical beauty in radiantly poetic playing. He is commanding and authoritative when required, with the blend of spontaneity, poetic feeling and virtuoso display this music calls for. The performance gains from having been recorded at a live concert, though there are no intrusive audience noises to betray that, and the sound is as full and well balanced as in most ordinary studio recordings. He is given sympathetic support by Sir Colin Davis and the fine Bavarian Radio Symphony Orchestra. Bishop-Kovacevich's simpler, even more dedicated manner in the same coupling on Philips is even more moving in the first two movements, but there is no finer version of the Grieg recorded in the digital age than this.

Solomon's poetic lyricism has a special appeal in this work, and the sound has been improved, especially the piano tone and the overall balance. Menges' orchestral contribution is sympathetic, if not inspired, but Solomon dominates the performance, and the Philharmonia strings play very sensitively in the slow movement.

Ousset's is a strong, dramatic reading, not lacking in warmth and poetry but, paradoxically, bringing out what we would generally think of as the masculine qualities of

437

power and drive. A good choice for anyone wanting this unusual coupling of the Mendelssohn *Concerto*, except that the measure is rather short for CD, although the sound is full, firm and clear.

Radu Lupu's recording dates from 1974 and is now even more brightly lit than it was originally, not entirely to advantage. But the performance is a fine one; there is both warmth and poetry in the slow movement; the hushed opening is particularly telling. There is a hint of calculation at the coda of the first movement; but the performance does not lack spontaneity, and the orchestral contribution under Previn is a strong one.

The sensitivity of Clifford Curzon in the recording studio is never in doubt, and his has been a favourite performance since it was first issued at the beginning of the 1960s. Curzon's approach is not as individual as Bishop-Kovacevich's – there is a suggestion of self-effacement – but the performance has strength and power, as well as freshness. The sound is fully acceptable.

The famous 1947 Lipatti performance remains eternally fresh, and its return to the catalogue is a cause for rejoicing. Although the recording has greater clarity and definition, particularly at the top, put this CD alongside one of the LP transfers of the 1970s and the ear now notices a slightly drier quality and a marginal loss of bloom.

(i; ii) *Piano concerto; Peer Gynt* (incidental music): *suites Nos.* (ii) *1, Op. 46;* (iii) *2, Op. 55.*
(BB) * LaserLight Dig. 15 617 [id.]. (i) Jenö Jandó; (ii) Budapest PO, János Sándor; (iii) VSO, Ahronovitch.

Jandó's account of the *Concerto* is bold and brilliant, missing much of its delicacy of romantic feeling, and Sándor's performance of the first *Peer Gynt suite* is rather square and unimaginative; *Anitra's dance* comes off best. Ahronovitch is much more convincing in the *Second Suite*, although he is melodramatic too, but *Solveig's song* is beautifully played. Full, brilliant, digital sound.

2 Elegiac melodies, Op. 34; Holberg suite, Op. 40; Lullaby, Op. 68/5; 2 Melodies, Op. 53; 2 Melodies, Op. 56.
** BIS CD 147 [id.]. Norwegian CO, Tønnensen.

Holberg suite, Op. 40.
*** DG Dig. 400 034-2 [id.]. BPO, Karajan – MOZART: *Eine kleine Nachtmusik*; PROKOFIEV: *Symphony No. 1.****
(B) *** Pickwick Dig. PCD 861 [MCA MCAD 25162]. Serenata of London – ELGAR: *Serenade*; MOZART: *Eine kleine Nachtmusik.****

Holberg suite, Op. 40; 2 Lyric pieces: Evening in the mountains; At the cradle, Op. 68/5.
(*) Ph. Dig. 412 727-2 [id.]. ASMF, Marriner – SIBELIUS: *Karelia; Swan.*

Karajan's performance of the *Holberg suite* is the finest currently available. The playing has a wonderful lightness and delicacy, with cultured phrasing not robbing the music of its immediacy. There are many subtleties of colour and texture revealed here by the clear yet full digital sound with its firm bass-line.

The performance by the Serenata of London is also first class in every way, spontaneous, naturally paced and played with considerable eloquence. The ensemble is led rather than conducted by Barry Wilde, and he asserts his personality much in the way Marriner did in the early days of the ASMF. The digital recording is most realistic and very naturally balanced. A bargain.

Otherwise the most attractive collection here is the BIS CD, which includes all of Grieg's music for strings. The playing, if not really distinctive, is enjoyably fresh. These young players, fourteen in number, produce clean attack, vital rhythms and sensitive phrasing, and though a larger ensemble would have provided greater weight, the texture is eminently transparent.

Sir Neville Marriner's performance of the *Holberg suite* is even more beautifully recorded than Karajan's, with more air round the string textures and a natural balance. However, his performance is less distinguished. Brisk tempi in the odd-numbered movements (with even a sense of hurry in the *Gavotte*) are not balanced by a comparable serenity in the *Sarabande* and *Air*. The *Lyric pieces* are much more evocative.

Lyric suite, Op. 54; Norwegian dances, Op. 35; Symphonic dances, Op. 64.
*** DG Dig. 419 431-2 [id.]. Gothenburg SO, Järvi.

Excellent playing from the Gothenburg orchestra under Neeme Järvi. He secures light and transparent textures and finely balanced sonorities throughout. His *Lyric suite* includes *Klokkeklang* (Bell-ringing); taken rather slowly, it sounds far more atmospheric than in the piano version, where it is placed last. Very fine, wide-ranging recording, which makes excellent use of the celebrated acoustic of this orchestra's hall.

Symphony in C; In Autumn: Overture, Op. 11; Old Norwegian melody with variations, Op. 51; Funeral march in memory of Rikard Nordraak.
*** DG Dig. 427 321-2 [id.]. Gothenburg SO, Järvi.

This is the best recording of the Grieg *Symphony* to appear so far, both as a performance and as a recording. Indeed Järvi produces excellent, fresh accounts of all four works on the disc. Enterprisingly, he includes the orchestral transcription of the Op. 51 *Variations* for two pianos and the arrangement for wind of the *Funeral march for Nordraak*. Most natural and unaffected performances, beautifully balanced.

INSTRUMENTAL MUSIC

Cello sonata in A min.
*** Claves CD 50-703 [CD 703]. Claude Starck, Ricardo Requejo – CHOPIN: *Cello sonata.****

The Grieg *Sonata* is gratefully written for both instruments. Its slow movement is related to the *Homage march* from *Sigurd Jorsalfar*, and the work undoubtedly enriches the cellist's relatively small repertoire. Both Starck and his Spanish partner play with a superb and compelling artistry.

PIANO MUSIC

Ballade, Op. 24; 4 Lyric Pieces: March of the dwarfs; Notturno, Op. 54/3–4; Wedding day at Troldhaugen, Op. 65/6; Peace of the woods, Op. 71/4. Sonata in E min., Op. 7; arr. of songs: Cradle song; I love thee; The princess; You cannot grasp the wave's eternal course. Peer Gynt: Solveig's song.
**(*) Olympia OCD 197 [id.]. Peter Katin.

The *Sonata* is not one of Grieg's finest works, but it has a touching *Andante* and is agreeably inventive, if perhaps conventionally so. Katin gives it a clean, direct performance, and he is impressive in the rather dolorous set of variations which forms the *Ballade*. The song arrangements, too, come off well, and the four *Lyric pieces* are presented very appealingly, if without quite the distinction of the much-praised Gilels recital devoted entirely to these works.

Holberg suite, Op. 40; Lyric pieces from Opp. 12, 38, 43, 47, 54, 57, 68, 71; Norwegian dance No. 2, Op. 35; Peer Gynt: Morning.

**(*) Teldec/WEA Dig. 2292 42964-2 [id.]. Cyprien Katsaris.

Katsaris is accorded quite outstanding recording quality; the piano sound is particularly realistic and 'present', with plenty of range and colour. He plays with character and combines both temperament and sensitivity, and is generally scrupulous in observing dynamic nuances; there are occasions here when this young artist is a shade impetuous, but for the most part these are strong and idiomatic performances – perhaps too 'strong' in the *Holberg suite*, where he is masterful and exuberant and where more finesse could be in order.

Lyric pieces: Op. 12/1; Op. 38/1; Op. 43/1–2; Op. 47/2–4; Op. 54/4–5; Op. 57/6; Op. 62/4 and 6; Op. 68/2, 3 and 5; Op. 71/1, 3 and 6–7.
⊛ *** DG 419 749-2 [id.]. Emil Gilels.

A generous selection of Grieg's *Lyric pieces*, from the well-known *Papillon*, Op. 43/1, to the less often heard and highly poetic set, Op. 71, written at the turn of the century. With Gilels we are in the presence of a great keyboard master whose characterization and control of colour and articulation are wholly remarkable. An altogether outstanding record in every way. The CD has brought a rather soft-focused piano sound, but the result is ideal for this repertoire.

VOCAL MUSIC

Peer Gynt (incidental music), *Op. 23* (complete).
(M) *** Unicorn UKCD 2003/4 [id.]. Carlson, Hanssen, Björköy, Hansli, Oslo PO Ch., LSO, Dreier.

Peer Gynt (incidental music), *Op. 23* (complete); *Sigurd Jorsalfar* (incidental music), *Op. 56* (complete).
*** DG Dig. 423 079-2 (2) [id.]. Bonney, Eklöf, Sandve, Malmberg, Holmgren; Foss, Maurstad, Stokke (speakers); Gösta Ohlin's Vocal Ens., Pro Musica Chamber Ch., Gothenburg SO, Järvi.

Neeme Järvi's recording differs from its predecessor by Per Dreier in offering the Grieg Gesamtausgabe *Peer Gynt*, which bases itself primarily on the twenty-six pieces he included in the 1875 production rather than the final published score, prepared after Grieg's death by Halvorsen. This well-documented set comes closer to the original by including spoken dialogue, as one would have expected in the theatre. The CDs also offer the complete *Sigurd Jorsalfar* score, which includes some splendid music. The performances by actors, singers (solo and choral) and orchestra alike are exceptionally vivid, with the warm Gothenburg ambience used to creative effect; the vibrant histrionics of the spoken words undoubtedly add to the drama.

Those who prefer not to have the Norwegian spoken dialogue can rest content with the excellent Unicorn analogue set from the end of the 1970s, which sounds admirably fresh in its CD format, the sound not tampered with in the transfer. Per Dreier achieves very spirited results from his soloists, the Oslo Philharmonic Chorus and our own LSO, with some especially beautiful playing from the woodwind; the recording is generally first class, with a natural perspective between soloists, chorus and orchestra. The Unicorn set (without *Sigurd Jorsalfar*) may be thought less generous, but it includes thirty-two numbers in all, including Robert Henrique's scoring of the *Three Norwegian dances*, following the revised version of the score Grieg prepared for the 1886 production in Copenhagen. Whichever version one chooses, this music, whether familiar or unfamiliar, continues to astonish by its freshness and inexhaustibility.

Peer Gynt: extended excerpts.
*** DG Dig. 427 325-2 [id.]. Bonney, Eklöf, Malmberg, Maurstad, Foss, Gothenburg Ch. & SO, Järvi.
*** Decca Dig. 425 448-2 [id.]. Urban Malmberg, Mari-Ann Haeggander, San Francisco Ch. & SO, Blomstedt.
*** CBS Dig. MK 44528 [id.]. Hendricks, Oslo PO, Salonen.
**(*) EMI Dig. CDC7 47003-2 [id.]. Popp, ASMF, Marriner.

(i) *Peer Gynt*: extended excerpts; *Overture In Autumn, Op. 11; Symphonic dance No. 2.*
(M) *** EMI CDM7 69039-2 [id.]. (i) Ilse Hollweg, Beecham Ch. Soc.; RPO, Beecham.

All the single-disc compilations from *Peer Gynt* rest under the shadow of Beecham's, which is not ideal as a recording (the choral contribution lacks polish and is rather too forwardly balanced) but which offers moments of magical delicacy in the orchestral playing. Beecham showed a very special feeling for this score, and to hear *Morning*, the gently textured *Anitra's dance*, or the eloquent portrayal of the *Death of Aase* under his baton is a uniquely rewarding experience. Ilse Hollweg makes an excellent soloist. The recording dates from 1957 and, like most other Beecham reissues, has been enhanced by the remastering process. The most delectable of the *Symphonic dances*, very beautifully played, makes an ideal encore after *Solveig's lullaby*, affectingly sung by Hollweg. The final item, the *Overture In Autumn*, not one of Grieg's finest works, is most enjoyable when Sir Thomas is so affectionately persuasive.

Neeme Järvi's disc offers more than two-thirds of the 1875 score, and the performance has special claims on the collector who wants one CD rather than two (half the second CD of the set is taken up by *Sigurd Jorsalfar*).

Decca's set of excerpts makes a useful alternative to the Järvi disc. All but about 15 minutes of the complete score is here and the spoken text is included too, all admirably performed. Perhaps the Gothenburg acoustic is to be preferred to the Davies Hall, San Francisco, and there is a marginally greater sense of theatre in the Swedish account. However, there is really not much to choose between them, and the Decca recording approaches the demonstration class.

Salonen's selection is generous too, offering some seventeen numbers: all those included in the suites plus one or two more than have previously been included in single-disc highlights. Anyone investing in this version with Barbara Hendricks and the Oslo Philharmonic is unlikely to be disappointed.

Sir Neville Marriner's account of *Peer Gynt* is not a performance that attains real distinction or character and, in spite of the excellence of the engineering, it does not displace Beecham. The compact disc is freshly detailed and glowing, but the music-making does not really lift off here.

Peer Gynt: extended excerpts; *Sigurd Jorsalfar: suite;* (i) *Songs: Efterårsstormen; Jeg giver mit digt til våren; Og jeg vil ha mig en hjaertenskjaer; Til én Nos. 1–2.*
(B) *(**) Decca 425 512-2 [id.]. LSO, Øivin Fjeldstad, (i) with Kirsten Flagstad.

Fjeldstad's wonderfully fresh *Peer Gynt* selection was one of the most beautiful records in Decca's early stereo catalogue. The digital remastering, while adding vividness, has not been beneficial to the string tone – originally radiant, now thin and edgy. Moreover, while Kirsten Flagstad's performances of the songs are very welcome, no translations or synopses are provided, and their reissue is almost pointless without them.

Peer Gynt: suites Nos. 1, Op. 46; 2, Op. 55.
*** DG Dig. 410 026-2 [id.]. BPO, Karajan – SIBELIUS: *Pelléas et Mélisande.****

Peer Gynt: suite No. 1; suite No. 2: Ingrid's lament; Solveig's song.
(M) **(*) Decca 417 722-2 [id.]. VPO, Karajan – TCHAIKOVSKY: *Romeo and Juliet***(*)
(with R. STRAUSS: *Till Eulenspiegel***(*)).

Peer Gynt: suites Nos. 1 & 2; Holberg suite; Sigurd Jorsalfar: suite.
(M) *** DG 419 474-2 [id.]. BPO, Karajan.

Grieg's perennially fresh score is marvellously played in Karajan's latest recording, though there are small differences between this and his earlier DG version with the same orchestra: Anitra danced with greater allure though no less elegance in 1972 and there was greater simplicity and repose in *Aase's Death*. The digital recording is one of the best to have emerged from the Berlin Philharmonie. Karajan's earlier, analogue set remains available on a mid-priced CD, where the highly expressive performances were played with superlative skill and polish. The coupling is again different so that any reader preferring the *Holberg suite* will not be disappointed. This is the 1982 digital version, which still sounds first class – see above. There is a touch of fierceness on the *Sigurd Jorsalfar* climaxes, but otherwise the earlier performances are given good sound.

To offer a further choice, Decca have also reissued Karajan's Vienna recording of the *First Suite* plus two favourite items from the *Second*, which come from ten years earlier. The digital remastering is successful, the new sound-image, if not lustrously rich, is quite full and firm and with good ambient effect.

(i) *Peer Gynt: suites Nos. 1–2; Lyric suite, Op. 54; Sigurd Jorsalfar: suite.*
(M) *** DG Dig. 427 807-2 [id.]. Soloists, Ch., Gothenburg SO, Järvi.

Järvi's excerpts from *Peer Gynt* and *Sigurd Jorsalfar* are extracted from his complete sets, so the editing inevitably produces a less tidy effect than normal recordings of the *Suites*. However, the performances are first class and so is the recording, and this comment applies also to the *Lyric suite*, taken from an earlier, digital orchestral collection – see above.

4 Psalms, Op. 74.
**(*) Nimbus Dig. NI 5171 [id.]. Håkan Hagegård, Oslo Cathedral Ch., Terje Kvam –
MENDELSSOHN: *3 Psalms.***(*)

The *Four Psalms* are based on old Norwegian church melodies. They are rarely heard except on the radio and are dignified, beautiful pieces, very well sung here by the choir and the Swedish baritone, Håkan Hagegård. The recording is eminently faithful, though the pauses between the Psalms are not long enough and, at under 45 minutes, this CD offers short measure.

(i) *Sigurd Jorsalfar, Op. 22:* incidental music; *Funeral march in memory of Rikard Nordraak* (orch. Halvorsen); (i) *The Mountain spell, Op. 32.*
(M) *** Unicorn UKCD 2019 [id.]. (i) Kåre Björköy; Oslo Philharmonic Ch., LSO, Per Dreier.

Even though it does not claim to be a first recording, *Den Bergtekne* (*The Mountain spell*) for baritone, strings and two horns is something of a rarity. *The Mountain spell* (or 'thrall', as it is sometimes translated) is somewhat later than *Sigurd Jorsalfar* and was one of Grieg's favourite pieces. It is a song of great beauty and alone is worth the price of the CD. The Oslo Philharmonic Choir give a spirited account of themselves, as do the LSO, who play sensitively for Per Dreier. Kåre Björköy is an excellent soloist with well-focused tone. The recording is very good indeed and the perspective is agreeably natural.

GROFÉ

Griffes, Charles (1884-1920)

(i) *The Pleasure Dome of Kubla Khan, Op. 8;* (ii) *3 Tone pictures, Op. 5;* (ii; iii) *3 Poems of Fiona Macleod;* (iv) *4 German songs; 4 Impressions; Song of the Dagger.*
** New World NW 273/4 [id.]. (i) Boston SO; (ii) New World CO; Ozawa; (iii) with P. Bryn-Julson; (iv) Stapp, Milnes, Richardson, Spong.

Charles Griffes studied in Berlin with Humperdinck, who persuaded him to concentrate on composition rather than pursue a career as a concert pianist. His early works are Brahmsian but he soon succumbed to the influence of the Russians and Debussy. He wrote most of his music in the free time left over from his teaching at Hackley School in Tarrytown, New York. He was a gifted artist in watercolour and made some fine etchings in copper. The four *German songs* come from the early years of the century when he was much influenced by Brahms; they are well sung here by Sherrill Milnes, but the four *Impressions* (1912–16) are less well served. Ozawa's performance of *The Pleasure Dome* lacks something of the warmth of the old RCA version with Charles Gerhardt but it conveys much of the work's strong atmosphere. By far the most persuasive performance comes from Phyllis Bryn-Julson in the Op. 11 settings of Fiona Macleod. The recordings date from the 1970s and are eminently acceptable.

Fantasy pieces; Legend; The Pleasure Dome of Kubla Khan; 3 Preludes; Rhapsody in B min.; Sonata; 3 Tone pictures.
** Kingdom Dig. KCLCD 2011 [id.]. James Tocco.

The *Sonata* is the most radical and expressionistic work here and *The Pleasure Dome of Kubla Khan* the best known. Like *The White Peacock*, it began life as a piano piece, though it is a little too congested to make its best effect. Griffes was obviously an accomplished pianist (he had originally planned a solo career) and his music makes considerable demands on the performer. The most interesting pieces are the three late *Preludes* (1919), which have a keen sense of mystery and concentration. So, too, have the three *Tone pictures*. James Tocco plays with insight and sensitivity; he meets the virtuoso demands of the *Sonata* and is keenly responsive to the dynamic nuances of these scores. He is not well served by the acoustic, which has far too little space round the aural image and as a result proves tiring on the ear. All the same, such is the interest of the music and the quality of the playing that this shortcoming should not be exaggerated.

Grofé, Ferde (1892-1972)

Grand Canyon suite.
*** Decca Dig. 410 110-2 [id.]. Detroit SO, Dorati (with GERSHWIN: *Porgy and Bess****).
*** Telarc Dig. CD 80086 [id.] (with additional *Cloudburst*, including real thunder). Cincinnati Pops O, Kunzel – GERSHWIN: *Catfish Row.****

Antal Dorati has the advantage of superlative Decca recording, very much in the demonstration class, with stereophonically vivid detail. Yet the performance combines subtlety with spectacle, and on compact disc the naturalness of the orchestral sound-picture adds to the sense of spaciousness and tangibility.

The Cincinnati performance is also played with great commitment and fine pictorial splendour, although Dorati scores at *Sunrise*, where his powerful timpani strokes add to the power of the climax, while at the opening of *Sunset* the Detroit strings have greater body and richness. Yet the Cincinnati *On the trail* has fine rhythmic point and piquant

443

colouring. What gives the Telarc CD its special edge is the inclusion of a second performance of *Cloudburst* as an appendix. Over a period of five years the Telarc engineers had been recording genuine thunderstorms in both Utah and Arizona, and an edited version of their most spectacular successes is laminated into the orchestral recording. The result is overwhelmingly thrilling, except that in the final thunderclap God quite upstages the orchestra, who are left trying frenziedly to match its amplitude in their closing peroration.

Hahn, Reynaldo (1875–1947)

Le bal de Béatrice d'Este (ballet suite).
*** Hyp. Dig. CDA 66347 [id.]. New London O, Ronald Corp – POULENC: *Aubade; Sinfonietta.****

Le bal de Béatrice d'Este is a rather charming pastiche, dating from the early years of the century and scored for the unusual combination of wind instruments, two harps, piano and timpani. It is dedicated to Saint-Saëns and evokes an evening in the palazzo of an Italian noblewoman. Ronald Corp and the New London Orchestra play it with real panache and sensitivity.

Songs: *À Chloris; L'Air; L'Automne; 7 Chansons Grises; La chère blessuré; D'une prison; L'enamourée; Les étoiles; Fêtes galantes; Les fontaines; L'Incrédule; Infidélité; Offrande; Quand je fus pris au pavillon; Si mes vers avaient des ailes; Tyndaris.*
**(*) Hyp. CDA 66045 [id.]. Hill, Johnson.

It is partly because swift or brisk songs are so few here that the classical pastiches of *Chloris* and *Quand je fus pris au pavillon* come as quite a refreshment. If Hahn never quite matched the supreme inspiration of his most famous song, *Si mes vers avaient des ailes*, the delights here are many, the charm great. Martyn Hill, ideally accompanied by Graham Johnson, modifies his very English-sounding tenor to give delicate and stylish performances, well recorded. There is a touch of pallor about this singing, but in general it suits the music.

Halévy, Jacques Fromental (1799–1862)

La juive (opera): complete.
*** Ph. Dig. 420 190-2 (3). Varady, Anderson, Carreras, Gonzalez, Furlanetto, Amb. Op. Ch., Philh. O, Almeida.

La juive (The Jewess), was the piece which, along with the vast works of Meyerbeer, set the pattern for the epic French opera, so popular last century. Eleazar was the last role that the great tenor, Enrico Caruso, tackled, and it was in this opera that he gave his very last performance. Yet in its entirety it was probably never performed on a single night, and the Philips recording is not absolutely complete, even if much more is included here than you will find in the published edition. The cuts are mainly of crowd scenes, drinking choruses and the like, many of which simply hold up the action. As it is, over three hours of music on three CDs makes an attractive package. There are three great character-roles: not just the tenor role of Eleazar, the Jew, and that of the heroine, Rachel, his adoptive daughter, but also the dark bass role of Cardinal Brigni, who in this story of the Spanish Inquisition pronounces anathema on these Jewish infidels. The final scene vies with that of *Il Trovatore* in its melodrama. At the very moment when Rachel is being thrown into a cauldron of boiling oil, Eleazar reveals to the vengeful Cardinal that she is really the long-lost daughter he had always been looking for. The greater part of the recording was completed in 1986, but that was just at the time when José Carreras was diagnosed as having leukaemia. The recording was made without him, and it was only in 1989 that he contributed his performance through 'overdubbing'. It is a tribute to the Philips engineers that the results rarely if ever betray that deception, sounding naturally balanced even when Carreras is contributing to the many complex ensembles. He sings astonishingly well, but the role of the old Jewish father really needs a weightier, darker voice, such as Caruso had in his last years. Julia Varady as Rachel makes that role both the emotional and the musical centre of the opera, responding both tenderly and positively. In the other soprano role, that of the Princess Eudoxia, June Anderson is not so full or sweet in tone, but she is particularly impressive in the dramatic coloratura passages, such as her Act III Boléro. Ferruccio Furlanetto makes a splendidly resonant Cardinal in his two big solos, and the Ambrosian Opera Chorus brings comparable bite to the powerful ensembles. Antonio de Almeida as conductor proves a dedicated advocate. Halévy is more lyrical in his writing than his contemporary, Meyerbeer, writing melodies that almost – but not quite – stick in the mind. As a massive music-drama, this is at least as impressive and moving as anything Meyerbeer wrote. As a recording, it is a formidable achievement.

Handel, George Frideric (1685–1759)

Amaryllis: suite (arr. Beecham); *Music for the Royal Fireworks; Water music: suite* (both arr. Baines).
**(*) ASV Dig. CDRPO 8002 [id.]. RPO, Menuhin.

Like the well-known *Fireworks* and *Water music*, the latter in an arrangement by Anthony Baines that claims to use a contemporary source for re-ordering the movements, Beecham's own arrangement of *Amaryllis* is warmly and vigorously done by his old orchestra, helped by full, well-balanced recording. With any reservations duly noted concerning style, this is persuasive music-making, with the Beecham arrangement particularly light and delectable.

Amaryllis (suite): *Gavotte; Scherzo. The Gods go a-begging* (ballet): suite. *The Great elopement: Serenade.* (i) *Love in Bath* (complete).
(M) *** EMI CDM7 63374-2 [id.]. RPO, Sir Thomas Beecham, (i) with Ilse Hollweg.

This delightful CD collects together many of Beecham's most famous Handel arrangements and – unless you are an out-and-out purist – the result is irresistible. One must remember that in Beecham's time little of this music was often (if at all) heard in its original format. The new name, *Love in Bath*, in fact conceals the identity of Beecham's intended ballet, *The Great elopement*. It never received a stage performance, although Beecham recorded a suite under this title, from which the *Serenade*, an aria from *Il pastor fido* (*Un sospiretto d'un labro pallido*), is presented in its purely orchestral form as an appendix. In the (virtually complete) version of *Love in Bath* it is charmingly sung by Ilse Hollweg. The score also includes a *Rondeau* purloined from yet another Handel suite, while the introduction of the famous *Largo* in the finale, floating serenely over a rhythmically busy accompaniment, is an inspired highlight. The earlier ballet, *The Gods go a-begging*, was produced for the stage with choreography by Balanchine, and nine of its eleven numbers are included here; its delectable woodwind scoring is a special feature. Needless to say, the Royal Philharmonic play like angels – if occasionally not perfectly disciplined angels! – and the originally mellow sound has been freshly remastered with great skill: there is greater transparency and little loss of bloom.

Concerto grosso in C (Alexander's Feast); Oboe concertos Nos. 1–3; Sonata a 5 in B flat.
*** DG Dig. 415 291-2 [id.]. E. Concert, Pinnock.

Concerto grosso in C (Alexander's Feast); Oboe concertos Nos. 1–2; Organ concerto in D min.; Sonata a 5 in B flat.
(M) **(*) Teldec/WEA 2292 43032-2 [id.]. Schaeftlein, Tachezi, VCM, Harnoncourt.

Rhythms are sprightly, and Pinnock's performance of the *Alexander's Feast concerto* has both vitality and imagination and is as good as any now available. The *B flat Sonata* (HWV 288) is to all intents and purposes a concerto, and it is given with great sensitivity and taste by Simon Standage and his colleagues. David Reichenberg is the excellent soloist in the *Oboe concertos*. Excellently balanced and truthful recording, but the record could have been filled more generously.

There is nothing wrong with Harnoncourt's collection, dating from 1974, especially now it is available at mid-price. Jurg Schaeftlein is a fine oboist, but he omits the third concerto (HWV 287) in favour of Herbert Tachezi's spirited performance of a fairly attractive hybrid organ concerto, based on a sonata from the first set of Telemann's *Tafelmusik*. Alice Harnoncourt is the third soloist in the *Sonata a 5*. Good performances, all well recorded and cleanly transferred to CD; but Pinnock's concert is generally preferable, not least because of the fine modern digital recording.

Concerti grossi, Op. 3/1–6.
*** DG 413 727-2 [id.]. E. Concert, Pinnock.
*** Ph. Dig. 411 482-2 [id.]. ASMF, Marriner.
(M) *** Ph. 422 487-2 [id.]. ECO, Leppard.
**(*) Hung. Dig. HCD 12463-2. Liszt CO, Janos Rolla.
(B) **(*) ASV CDQS 6024 [id.]. Northern Sinfonia, Malcolm.

The six Op. 3 *Concertos* with their sequences of brief jewels of movements find Pinnock and the English Concert at their freshest and liveliest, with plenty of sparkle and little of the abrasiveness associated with 'authentic' performance. For a version on period instruments, this could hardly be better, with its realistic, well-balanced sound. The playing has breadth as well as charm.

In Sir Neville Marriner's latest version with the Academy, tempi tend to be a little brisk, but the results are inspiring and enjoyable. The continuo is divided between organ and harpsichord, though the latter is reticently balanced. Not unexpectedly, textures are fuller here than on Pinnock's competing Archiv recording, and the CD quality is admirably fresh.

Among budget versions of Handel's Op. 3, Leppard's set stands out. The playing is lively and fresh, and the remastered recording sounds very good. Leppard includes oboes and bassoons and secures excellent playing all round. At times, one wonders whether he isn't just a shade too elegant, but in general this CD offers one of the best versions of Op. 3 on modern instruments.

A fourth version from Hungaroton also uses modern instruments to good effect, in some ways striking a happy medium between Pinnock's 'authentic' leanness of texture and Marriner's briskness. The Hungaroton digital recording combines fullness with clarity, although the harpsichord continuo could make a stronger effect, not entirely a matter of balance; the organist in the sixth concerto is a more striking player.

George Malcolm's performances are infectiously spirited and stylish, though rhythms are sometimes jogging rather than sprightly. The recording is strikingly vivid in its CD transfer, but the forward balance reduces the dynamic range, though the contrasts of light and shade within the strings are effective.

12 Concerti grossi, Op. 6/1–12.
⊛ *** Ph. Dig. 410 048-2 (3) [id.]. ASMF, Iona Brown.
(M) **(*) Ph. 426 465-2 (3). ECO, Leppard.
**(*) DG Dig. 410 897-2 (1–4); 410 898-2 (5–8); 410 899-2 (9–12) [id.]. E. Concert, Pinnock.
**(*) RCA Dig. RD 87895 [7895-2-RC] (*Nos. 1–4*); RD 87907 [7907-2-RC] (*Nos. 5–8*); RD 87921 [7921-2-RC] (*Nos. 9–12*). Guildhall String Ens., Robert Salter.
** Ph. Dig. 422 370-2 (3) [id.]. I Musici, Maria Teresa Garatti (harpsichord; organ).

Handel's set of twelve *Concerti grossi*, Op. 6 – the high-water mark of Baroque orchestral music – has a distinguished recording history. The young Iona Brown participated at Marriner's late-1960s recording sessions, but the new readings have many new insights to offer and Miss Brown sets her own personality firmly on the proceedings. In the expressive music (and there are some memorable Handelian tunes here) she is freer, warmer and more spacious than Marriner. Where allegros are differently paced, they are often slightly slower, yet the superbly crisp articulation and the rhythmic resilience of the playing always bring added sparkle. On recording grounds, the Philips set gains considerably: the sound is fuller and fresher and more transparent. The contrast between the solo group and the ripieno is even more tangible. This can be recommended strongly.

Leppard's 1967 set sounds splendid in its newly remastered format, not in the least dated. The main group is comparatively full-bodied, which means that his soloists stand out in greater relief. There is grace and elegance here, but rather less gravitas than with Brown and the ASMF. These performances, too, have plenty of spirit and lively rhythmic feeling, while the richer orchestral texture brings added breadth in slow movements. With the sound newly minted, this is excellent value at mid-price, though Leslie Pearson's harpsichord continuo is dwarfed by the tuttis.

In his pursuit of authentic performance on original instruments, Pinnock finds a fair compromise between severe principle and sweetened practice. For all its 'authenticity', this is never unresponsive music-making, with fine solo playing set against an attractively atmospheric acoustic. Ornamentation is often elaborate – but never at the expense of line. These are performances to admire and to sample, but not everyone will warm to them. If listened through, the sharp-edged sound eventually tends to tire the ear, and there is comparatively little sense of grandeur and few hints of tonally expansive beauty. The recording is first class and each of the three CDs is available separately.

The Guildhall String Ensemble offer fresh, modestly scaled performances, with plenty of life about them. Although modern instruments are used, textures are lighter, more transparent, than those of the ASMF. The effect is very real and tangible, with the soloists nicely separated from the ripieno, although their forward balance means that there is not the degree of dynamic contrast that Handel obviously intended. However, tempi are generally apt, and this music-making has a buoyantly rhythmic sparkle and a nicely balanced espressivo feeling in Handel's songful slow movements.

I Musici bring plenty of Italian sunshine to their playing, and the performances are not without vitality. But their recording, with its glowingly expansive textures, often gives the impression of Corelli rather than of Handel, and, although the Philips sound is first class, this set would not be a first choice.

Concerti grossi, Op. 6/4, 6, 9 & 11.
(BB) ** Hung. White Label HRC 133 [id.]. Liszt CO, Rolla.

These performances use a double continuo but, while the organ increases the sonority of the ripieno, the harpsichord contribution is barely audible. Nevertheless the playing, both of soloists and of the main group, is attractively warm, alive and sympathetic and has plenty of personality. Those looking for a super-bargain sampler of Op. 6 will not be disappointed by the recording quality, which is resonantly full and firmly focused.

Harp concerto in B flat, Op. 4/5.
(B) *** DG 427 206-2 [id.]. Zabaleta, Paul Kuentz CO – MOZART: *Flute and harp concerto*; WAGENSEIL: *Harp concerto.****

The DG recording sounds clear and immediate and the crystalline stream of sound is attractive. Zabaleta's approach is agreeably cool, with imaginative use of light and shade. The Privilege reissue also includes a set of variations by Spohr.

Oboe concertos Nos 1–3, HWV 301, 302a & 287; Concerto grosso, Op. 3/3; Hornpipe in D, HWV 356; Overture in D, HWV 337/8; Sonata a 5 in B flat, HWV 288.
(M) **(*) Ph. 426 082-2 [id.]. Heinz Holliger, ECO, Raymond Leppard.

Holliger, being a creative artist as well as a masterly interpreter, does not hesitate to embellish repeats; his ornamentation may overstep the boundaries some listeners are prepared to accept. His playing and that of the other artists in this collection is exquisite, and the recording is naturally balanced and fresh.

Organ concertos, Op. 4/1–6; in A, HWV 296.
*** DG Dig. 413 465-2 (2) [id.]. Simon Preston, E. Concert, Pinnock.

Organ concertos, Op. 7/1–6; in F (Cuckoo and the nightingale); in D min., HWV 304.
*** DG Dig. 413 468-2 (2) [id.]. Simon Preston, E. Concert, Pinnock.

Organ concertos, Op. 7/1–6; in D min., HWV 304; in F, HWV 305 & Appendix.
*** Decca Dig. 417 560-2 (2) [id.]. Peter Hurford, Concg. CO, Rifkin.

Simon Preston's set of the Handel *Organ concertos* comes in two separate packages. In the first, containing the six Op. 4 works, plus the *A major* (the old No. 14), though the balance of the solo instrument is not ideal, the playing of both Preston and the English Concert is admirably fresh and lively. Ursula Holliger is outstanding on a baroque harp in Op. 4, No. 6, and she creates some delicious sounds; however, it seems perverse not to include the organ version of this work, with the harp arrangement already available on other records. The second of the two boxes, containing the six Op. 7 works, plus the 'Cuckoo and the nightingale' and the old *No. 15 in D minor*, was recorded on the organ at St John's, Armitage, in Staffordshire, and is even more attractive, not only for the extra delight of the works but for the warmth and assurance of the playing, which comes near the ideal for an 'authentic' performance. These are all recordings which positively invite re-hearing, with full, clear sound, all the fresher on CD.

Peter Hurford's Decca Op. 7 set has comparable sparkle, but the effect (especially of the first four concertos) seems rather lightweight compared with Simon Preston's Archiv alternatives. This remains the preferred version, in spite of Peter Hurford's considerable bonuses, which include a useful appendix.

Organ concertos, Op. 4/1 & 2; Op. 7/1 & 2.
(M) ** Teldec/WEA 2292 43434-2 [id.]. Karl Richter with CO.

Organ concertos, Op. 4/3 & 4; Op. 7/3 & 4.
(M) *** Teldec/WEA 2292 43540-2 [id.]. Karl Richter with CO.

Organ concertos, Op. 4/5 & 6; Op. 7/5 & 6.
(M) *** Teldec/WEA 2292 42412-2 [id.]. Karl Richter with CO.

Organ concertos, Op. 4/1 & 4; Op. 7/1; in F (Cuckoo and the nightingale).
**(*) DG Dig. 419 634-2 [id.]. Simon Preston, E. Concert, Pinnock.

These Teldec recordings come from a complete set which Karl Richter recorded in 1959. The sound is surprisingly undated and the performances have the merit of exactly the right kind of organ (St Mark's, Munich) and a small, flexible orchestral group which Richter directs from the keyboard. The element of extemporization is a limited feature, at first, especially in Op. 4; but later, in Op. 7, organ *ad libs* are effectively included. Throughout, the playing is attractively buoyant; the full sound of the strings, contrasted with imaginative registration, makes this series increasingly attractive. The latter two discs can be recommended strongly, and overall the set is excellent value.

On DG Archiv, a useful sampler of the Preston/Pinnock recordings, although the choice of works is arbitrary.

Overtures: Admeto; Alcina; Ariodante; Esther; Lotario; Orlando; Ottone; Partenope; (i) Il pastor fido; Poro.
(M) *** Ph. 422 486-2 [id.]. ECO or (i) New Philh. O, Leppard.

Characteristically elegant performances from Leppard, richly recorded. The orchestral playing is gracious and polished, and the recording is bright and well balanced. The reissue includes two extra overtures, *Il pastor fido* and *Ariodante* (taken from the complete set), not included on the original LP. There is some fine music here: Handel's overtures are consistently tuneful and inventive and, at budget price, this disc is well worth exploring.

Overtures: Agrippina; Alceste; Il pastor fido; Samson; Saul (Acts I & II); Teseo.
*** DG Dig. 419 219-2 [id.]. E. Concert, Pinnock.

Trevor Pinnock directs vigorous, exhilarating performances of these Handel overtures, most of them hardly known at all but full of highly original ideas, even in the most formally structured pieces. All are freshly and cleanly recorded.

Music for the Royal Fireworks (original version); (i) *Coronation anthems* (see also below).
*** Hyp. Dig. CDA 66350 [id.]. (i) New College, Oxford, Ch.; augmented King's Consort, Robert King.

King directs his Consort and the choir of New College, Oxford, in amiable and relaxed accounts of Handel's four *Coronation anthems*, not as incisively dramatic as some but still conveying the joy of the inspiration. Either Marriner or Simon Preston remain a first choice here; but King evens the balance by providing as an extra item the first ever period performance of Handel's *Royal fireworks music* to use the full complement of instruments Handel demanded. It was quite an achievement assembling no fewer than 24 baroque oboists ('foreman Paul Goodwin') and 12 baroque bassoonists, nine trumpeters, nine exponents of the hand horn and four timpanists. It all makes for a glorious noise, and for once the fill-up provides what is probably the main attraction. King's Handel style has plenty of rhythmic bounce, and the recording in its warmly atmospheric way gives ample scale.

Music for the Royal Fireworks (original wind scoring).
*** Telarc Dig. CD 80038 [id.]. Cleveland Symphonic Winds, Fennell – HOLST: *Military band suites.*** ⊛

Music for the Royal Fireworks; Concerti a due cori Nos. 2 and 3.
*** DG Dig. 415 129-2 [id.]. E. Concert, Pinnock.
**(*) Ph. Dig. 411 122-2 [id.]. E. Bar. Soloists, Gardiner.

Music for the Royal Fireworks; Water music (complete).
*** Argo 414 596-2 [id.]. ASMF, Marriner.
(M) **(*) Decca Dig. 417-743-2 [id.]. Stuttgart CO, Münchinger.

Music for the Royal Fireworks; Water music: Suite in F.
**(*) O-L Dig. 400 059-2 [id.]. AAM, Hogwood.

Music for the Royal Fireworks; Water music: extended suite.
(M) *** Ph. 420 354-2 [id.]. ECO, Leppard.

Music for the Royal Fireworks: suite; Water music; suite (arr. Harty and Szell); *The Faithful shepherd: Minuet* (ed. Beecham); *Xerxes: Largo* (arr. Reinhardt).
(B) *** Decca 417 694-2. LSO, Szell.

In 1978, in Severance Hall, Cleveland, Ohio, Frederick Fennell gathered together the wind and brass from the Cleveland Symphony Orchestra and recorded a performance to demonstrate spectacularly what fine playing and digital sound could do for Handel's open-air score. The overall sound-balance tends to favour the brass (and the drums), but few will grumble when the result is as overwhelming as it is on the CD, with the sharpness of focus matched by the presence and amplitude of the sound-image.

Pinnock works on a smaller scale and does not attempt to compete with the outdoor performances, except in spirit. The playing has tremendous zest, and for those wanting a period-instrument version this is not only the safest but the best recommendation. The DG recording is among the finest Archiv has given us.

Marriner directs a sparkling account of the complete *Water music*, using modern instruments. All the well-loved movements we once knew only in the Harty suite come out refreshed, and the rest is similarly stylish. Scholars may argue that textures are too thick; but for many listeners the sounds which reach the ears have a welcome freedom from acerbity. It is a substantial advantage that the CD (for the transfer is very successful) also includes the complete *Fireworks music* – unlike most of its rivals. Here Marriner deliberately avoids a weighty manner, even at the magisterial opening of the overture. But with full, resonant recording, this coupling makes sound sense and the remastered Argo recording still sounds both full and fresh.

Münchinger's similar coupling has first-class 1982 digital recording: the effect is vivid and well focused. His style is a compromise between authenticity and the German tradition. Some other versions of this music are more buoyant, but Münchinger is consistently sympathetic and never dull. With the additional advantage of economy, this is well worth considering.

Leppard's mid-priced Philips reissue offers an excellent alternative. The remastering is very successful and the resonance of the sound in the *Fireworks music* matches the broad and spectacular reading, while the substantial extract from Leppard's complete *Water music* recording has comparable flair, combining rhythmic resilience with an apt feeling for ceremony.

In the *Fireworks music* Hogwood's Academy certainly make a vivid impact. The added clarity of the CD does emphasize some faults in balance; nevertheless, this version can be counted among the best available and has lively rhythms and keen articulation. Hogwood gives a strong impression of the score, even if no attempt is made to reproduce the forces heard in 1749. In the *Water music*, the timbres of the original instruments are consistently attractive, with vibrato-less string-tone never squeezed too painfully.

Many readers will, like us, have a nostalgic feeling for the Handel–Harty suites from which earlier generations got to know these two marvellous scores. George Szell and the LSO offer a highly recommendable coupling of them on a Decca lower-mid-priced issue, with Handel's *Largo* and the *Minuet* from Beecham's *Faithful Shepherd suite* thrown in for good measure. The orchestral playing throughout is quite outstanding, and the strings are wonderfully expressive in the slower pieces. The horns excel, and the crisp new Decca re-transfer makes for a good bargain.

John Eliot Gardiner secures an excellent response from his players. Tempi are a bit on the fast side: there are the usual string bulges favoured by period-instrument groups, and wind intonation is good, though not always impeccable. Fine though this is, it does not displace Pinnock and the English Concert on Archiv.

Music for the Royal Fireworks; Water music: suite in F (both arr. Howarth); *The Harmonious blacksmith* (arr. Dodgson). *Berenice: Minuet. Occasional oratorio: March. Solomon: Arrival of the Queen of Sheba. Xerxes: Largo* (arr. Archibald or Hazell).
*** Decca Dig. 411 930-2 [id.]. Philip Jones Brass Ens., Howarth.

This is a fun concert played with true Baroque spirit, combining polish with bravura, and spectacularly recorded. The *Arrival of the Queen of Sheba* is disconcertingly vivid in her very different costume, while *The Harmonious blacksmith* stands at his anvil in similarly bold relief. In the *Berenice Minuet* and the famous *Largo*, the sentiment of the bandstand is handsomely avoided, though the playing is warmly expressive, but it is the fast pieces with their intricately exhilarating detail that catch the ear.

Water music: Suites Nos. 1–3 (complete).
*** DG Dig. 410 525-2 [id.]. E. Concert, Pinnock.
*** ASV Dig. CDDCA 520 [id.]. ECO, Malcolm.
**(*) Chan. Dig. CHAN 8382 [id.]. Scottish CO, Gibson.
(M) **(*) Delos Dig. D/CD 3010 [id.]. LAPO, Schwarz.
**(*) Ph. 416 447-2 [id.]. ASMF, Marriner.

Water music: Suites Nos. 1–3 (complete); *Solomon: Arrival of the Queen of Sheba. Ode for St Cecilia's Day: Minuet.*
(BB) ** LaserLight Dig.15 607 [id.]. Budapest Strings, Bela Banfalvi.

Pinnock's version on DG Archiv is very enticing. Speeds are consistently well chosen and are generally uncontroversial. One test is the famous *Air*, which here remains an engagingly gentle piece. The recording is beautifully balanced and clear, but with bloom on the sound to balance the CD presence.

Those whose taste does not extend to 'authentic' string textures should be well satisfied with George Malcolm's splendid digital recording for ASV. The playing is first class, articulation is deft and detail admirable. Decoration is nicely judged and the alertness of the music-making, combined with full, vivid sound, makes a strong impact. There is a sense of delight in the music which makes this version especially appealing.

Sir Alexander Gibson's pacing of the allegros is brisk and he points the rhythms with infectious zest. There is fine lyrical playing too, notably from the principal oboe, while the horns are robust. The combination of energy and warmth comes as a welcome relief after prolonged exposure to period instruments. The ample acoustic of the Glasgow City Hall is attractive and this is a very likeable performance which could well be a first choice for many readers.

The Los Angeles performance under Gerard Schwarz is hardly less enjoyable, its character more athletic, with playing that is both polished and sprightly. It has an attractive freshness of spirit, yet is without the abrasiveness of early-instrumental timbres. The sound is first class and the clear detail does not prevent an overall ambient warmth.

The Philips account of the *Water music* brings Sir Neville Marriner's second complete recording – and characteristically he has taken the trouble to correct several tiny textual points read wrongly before. The playing too is even finer. However, given the competition, this now seems over-priced.

The Budapest Strings carry a wind contingent too, and – if the overture could be rhythmically more telling – on the whole the playing is quite fresh, though this is a case where the absence of a conductor has brought a somewhat anonymous impression. However, the recording is vivid and, with the attractive encores at the end also nicely done, this is fair value.

CHAMBER MUSIC

Flute sonatas, Op. 1/1a; in D; in A min., E min., and B min. (Halle Nos. 1–3).
*** Ph. Dig. 412 606-2 [id.]. Bennett, Kraemer, Vigay.

William Bennett's compact disc comprises the three *Halle sonatas* and two others: one from the Op. 1 set and the other a more recent discovery from a Brussels manuscript. Bennett uses a modern flute very persuasively, and Nicholas Kraemer and Denis Vigay provide admirable support. The recording is most realistic and and present.

Oboe sonatas (for oboe and continuo), *Op. 1/5 and 8; in B flat, HWV 357; Sinfonia in B flat for 2 violins and continuo, HWV 338; Trio sonatas: in E min. for 2 flutes, HWV 395; in F for 2 recorders, HWV 405.*
*** Ph. Dig. 412 598-2 [id.]. ASMF Chamber Ens.

Marvellously accomplished accounts of the three oboe sonatas. Indeed there are no reservations whatsoever about any of the performances or the recording quality, which is among Philips's best.

Recorder sonatas, Op. 1/2, 4, 7, 9 and 11; in B flat.
*** Ph. Dig. 412 602-2 [id.]. Petri, Malcolm, Vigay, Sheen.
*** CRD Dig. CRD 3412 [id.]. L'École d'Orphée.

Michala Petri plays with her accustomed virtuosity and flair, and it would be difficult to imagine her performances being improved upon. She has the advantage of excellent rapport with her continuo players, and the Philips engineers have produced a natural and spacious sound.

The CRD performances have already won much acclaim. There is some elegant and finished playing from the two recorder players, and this makes a rewarding alternative to Petri for those preferring 'authentic' timbres.

Trio sonatas, Op. 2/1–6; Sonatas for 2 violins: in F, HWV 392; in G min., HWV 393.
*** Ph. Dig. 412 595-2 [id.]. ASMF Chamber Ens.

Trio sonatas, Op. 5/1–7; Sonatas for 2 violins: in E, HWV 394; in C, HWV 403.
*** Ph. Dig. 412 599-2 (2) [id.]. ASMF Chamber Ens.

The performances from Michala Petri, William Bennett, Kenneth Sillito, Malcolm Latchem and others are wonderfully accomplished and have a refreshing vigour and warmth. In these sonatas, Handel's invention seems inexhaustible and it is difficult to imagine readers not responding to them. The sound is excellent in every way.

Trio sonatas (for flute and violin), *Op. 2/1;* (for violins), *Op. 2/3; Op. 5/2 & 4; Violin sonata in A, Op. 1/3; Sonata for 2 violins in G min., HWV 393.*
*** DG Dig. 415 497-2 [id.]. E. Concert, Pinnock.

Rhythms are vital, and the playing of the two violinists (Simon Standage and Micaela Comberti) has panache and style – as, for that matter, have the other contributors. The flautist, Lisa Beznosiuk, is particularly expert and imaginative in the *B minor Sonata*, Op. 2, No. 1; the whole enterprise gives pleasure and stimulus and can be recommended even to those normally unresponsive to period instruments or their copies, while the recording has excellent ambience and warmth.

Violin sonatas, Op. 1/3, 6, 10, 12, 13–15; in D min., HWV 359a; in D min., HWV 367a; Fantasia in A, HWV 406.
*** Ph. Dig. 412 603-2 (2) [id.]. Iona Brown, Nicholas Kraemer, Denis Vigay.

Iona Brown plays with vigour and spirit, and there is a welcome robustness about this music-making; many will find it a relief to turn to the modern violin after the Gillette-like strains of the Baroque variety.

KEYBOARD MUSIC

Chaconne in G, HWV 435; Suites Nos. 3 in D min.; 4 in E min.; 13 in B flat; 14 in G.
** DG Dig. 410 656-2 [id.]. Trevor Pinnock (harpsichord).

Suites Nos. 2 in F; 3 in D min.; 5 in E; 6 in F sharp min.; 7 in G min.
**(*) HM HMC 90447 [id.]. Kenneth Gilbert (harpsichord).

Gilbert uses a copy of a Taskin harpsichord by Bédard. He observes most first-half repeats but not the second, and he is as imaginative in the handling of decoration and ornamentation as one would expect. Perhaps some grandeur, some larger-than-life vitality, is missing; but so much else is here that there is no cause for qualifying the recommendation. The recording is much better balanced and more natural than recent rivals.

Although Trevor Pinnock's playing has undoubted flair and imagination, the CD is transferred at a thunderous level and is altogether overpowering. The result conveys expertise in plenty but rather less in the way of enjoyment.

VOCAL AND CHORAL MUSIC

Acis and Galatea (masque).
*** DG 423 406-2 (2) [id.]. Burrowes, Rolfe-Johnson, Martyn Hill, Willard White, E. Bar. Soloists, Gardiner.

(i) *Acis and Galatea;* (ii) *Cantata: Look down, harmonious saint.*
*** Hyp. Dig. CDA 66361/2. (i; ii) Ainsley; (i) McFadden, Covey-Crump, George, Harre-Jones; King's Cons., Robert King.

Certain of John Eliot Gardiner's tempi are idiosyncratic (some too fast, some too slow), but the scale of the performance, using original instruments, is beautifully judged, with the vocal soloists banding together for the choruses. The acoustic is rather dry, the balance fairly close, but the soloists are consistently sweet of tone, although the singing is less individually characterful than in some previous versions. Willard White is a fine Polyphemus, but his *O ruddier than the cherry* has not quite the degree of genial gusto that Owen Brannigan brought to it. The authentic sounds of the English Baroque Soloists are finely controlled and the vibrato-less string timbre is clear and clean without being abrasive. A thoroughly rewarding pair of CDs.

Robert King directs a bluff, beautifully sprung reading of *Acis and Galatea* that brings out its domestic jollity. Using the original version for five solo singers and no chorus, this may be less delicate in its treatment than John Eliot Gardiner's reading of the original version on DG Archiv but, at speeds generally a little faster and with warmer, fuller sound, it is if anything even more winning. The soloists are first rate, with John Mark Ainsley among the most stylish of the younger generation of Handel tenors, and the bass, Michael George, characterizing strongly as Polyphemus, yet never at the expense of musical values. Claron McFadden's vibrant soprano is girlishly distinctive. This Hyperion issue scores somewhat on price too and provides a valuable makeweight in the florid solo cantata, thought to be originally conceived as part of *Alexander's Feast*, nimbly sung by Ainsley.

(i) *Aci, Galatea e Polifemo.* (ii) *Recorder sonatas in F; C & G* (trans. to *F*).
*** HM Dig. HMC 901253/4 [id.]. (i) Kirkby, C. Watkinson, Thomas, L. Bar., Medlam; (ii) Michel Piquet, John Toll.

Aci, Galatea e Polifemo proves to be quite a different work from the always popular English masque, *Acis and Galatea*, with only one item even partially borrowed. In effect it is a one-act opera, full of delightful brief numbers, far more flexible in scale and layout than later full-scale Italian operas. Charles Medlam directs London Baroque in a beautifully sprung performance with three excellent soloists, the brightly characterful Emma Kirkby as Aci, Carolyn Watkinson in the lower-pitched role of Galatea (often – a little confusingly – sounding like a male alto), and David Thomas coping manfully with the impossibly wide range of Polifemo's part. The three recorder sonatas are comparably delightful, a welcome makeweight. Excellent sound, full of presence.

Ah, che pur troppo è vero; Mi palpita il cor. Duets: *A miravi io son intento; Beato in ver chi può; Conservate, raddioppiate; Fronda leggiera e mobile; Langue, geme e sospira; No, di voi non vuo fidarni; Se tu non lasci amore; Sono liete, fortunate; Tanti strali al sen; Troppo cruda* (cantatas).
*** Hung. Dig. HCD 12564-5 [id.]. Zádori, Esswood; Falvay, Németh, Ella (cello, flute and harpsichord).

The two vocal soloists, the clear-voiced soprano Maria Zádori and the counter-tenor Paul Esswood, sing delightfully throughout this generous collection of very rare Handel duet cantatas, most of them charmers when the singing is so sweet and accomplished and the coloratura so brilliantly turned. Excellent recording, the voices most naturally focused and the accompaniment sounding very refined, with the harpsichord particularly realistic.

(i) *Alceste* (incidental music); (ii) *Comus* (incidental music).
*** O-L 421 479-2 [id.]. (i) Nelson, Kirkby, Elliott; (i; ii) Cable, Thomas; (ii) Kwella; AAM, Hogwood.

Commissioned to write incidental music for a play by Smollett, the composer was stopped in his tracks by the abandonment of the whole project. Nevertheless there is much to enjoy in what he wrote for *Alceste*, not just solo items but also some simple tuneful choruses, all introduced by an impressive, dramatic overture in D minor. The incidental music for *Comus* makes equally refreshing listening, intended as it was to be an epilogue for a performance of the Milton masque. Performances of all this music have the freshness and vigour one associates with the Academy under Hogwood at their finest. The sound, too, is first rate.

Alexander's Feast; Concerto grosso in C (Alexander's Feast).
**(*) Ph. Dig. 422 053-2 (2) [id.]. Carolyn Watkinson, Robson, Donna Brown, Stafford, Varcoe, Monteverdi Ch., E. Bar. Soloists, Eliot Gardiner.

Gardiner's version of *Alexander's Feast* was recorded live at performances given at the Göttingen Festival. The sound is not distractingly dry, but it is still harder than usual on singers and players alike, taking away some of the bloom. What matters is the characteristic vigour and concentration of Gardiner's performance, which winningly explains how this now neglected piece could, in Handel's lifetime, have been his most frequently performed work after *Messiah* and *Acis and Galatea*. Among the most striking numbers are the two big arias for the bass, both with brilliant brass obbligato: the drinking song *Bacchus ever fair and young* (with two horns) and the Victorian favourite, *Revenge, Timotheus cries* (with trumpet). Stephen Varcoe may lack the dark resonance of a traditional bass, but he projects his voice well. Nigel Robson's tenor suffers more than do the others from the dryness of the acoustic. The soprano, Donna Brown, sings with boyish freshness, and the alto numbers are divided very effectively between Carolyn Watkinson and the soft-grained counter-tenor, Ashley Stafford. The two discs also include the *Concerto grosso in C* that was given with the oratorio at its first performance and which still bears its name.

L'Allegro, il penseroso, il moderato.
*** Erato/WEA 2292 45377-2 (2). Kwella, McLaughlin, Jennifer Smith, Ginn, Davies, Hill, Varcoe, Monteverdi Ch., E. Bar. Soloists, Gardiner.

Taking Milton as his starting point, Handel illustrated in music the contrasts of mood and character between the cheerful and the thoughtful. Then, prompted by his librettist, Charles Jennens, he added compromise in *Il moderato*, the moderate man. The final chorus may fall a little short of the rest (Jennens's words cannot have provided much inspiration), but otherwise the sequence of brief numbers is a delight, particularly in a performance as exhilarating as this, with excellent soloists, choir and orchestra. The recording is first rate.

Italian cantatas: *Alpestre monte; Mi palpita il cor; Tra le fiamme; Tu fedel? Tu costante?*
*** O-L Dig. 414 473-2 [id.]. Emma Kirkby, AAM, Hogwood.

The four cantatas here, all for solo voice with modest instrumental forces, are nicely contrasted, with the personality of the original singer by implication identified with *Tu fedel*, a spirited sequence of little arias rejecting a lover. Even 'a heart full of cares' in *Mi palpita il cor* inspires Handel to a pastorally charming aria, with a delectable oboe obbligato rather than anything weighty, and even those limited cares quickly disperse. Light-hearted and sparkling performances to match.

Aminta e Fillide (cantata).
*** Hyp. CDA 66118 [id.]. Fisher, Kwella, L. Handel O, Darlow.

In writing for two voices and strings, Handel presents a simple encounter in the pastoral tradition over a span of ten brief arias which, together with recitatives and final duet, last almost an hour. The music is as charming and undemanding for the listener as it is taxing for the soloists. This lively performance, beautifully recorded with two nicely contrasted singers, delightfully blows the cobwebs off a Handel work till now totally neglected.

Anthem for the Foundling Hospital; Ode for the birthday of Queen Anne.
*** O-L 421 654-2 [id.]. Nelson, Kirkby, Minty, Bowman, Hill, Thomas, Ch. of Christ Church Cathedral, Oxford, AAM, Preston – HAYDN: *Missa brevis in F.****

The *Ode* is an early work, written soon after Handel arrived in England. It has its Italianate attractions, but it is the much later *Foundling Hospital anthem* which is the more memorable, not just because it concludes with an alternative version of the *Hallelujah chorus* (sounding delightfully fresh on this scale with the Christ Church Choir) but because the other borrowed numbers are also superb. An extra tang is given by the accompaniment on original instruments. The CD adds Haydn's early *Missa brevis* as an attractive bonus.

Apollo e Dafne (cantata).
**(*) HM HMC 905157 [id.]. Judith Nelson, David Thomas; Hayes, San Francisco Bar. O, McGegan.

Apollo e Dafne is one of Handel's most delightful cantatas, with at least two strikingly memorable numbers, a lovely siciliano for Dafne with oboe obbligato and an aria for Apollo, *Come rosa in su la spina*, with unison violins and a solo cello. Both soloists are first rate, and Nicholas McGegan is a lively Handelian, though the playing of the orchestra could be more polished and the sound more firmly focused.

Athalia (oratorio).
*** O-L Dig. 417 126-2 (2) [id.]. Sutherland, Kirkby, Bowman, Aled Jones, Rolfe-Johnson, David Thomas, New College, Oxford, Ch., AAM, Hogwood.

As Queen Athalia, an apostate Baal-worshipper who comes to no good, Dame Joan Sutherland sings boldly with a richness and vibrancy to contrast superbly with the pure silver of Emma Kirkby, not to mention the celestial treble of Aled Jones, in the role of the boy-king, Joas. That casting is perfectly designed to set the Queen aptly apart from the good Israelite characters led by the Priest, Joad (James Bowman in a castrato role), and Josabeth (Kirkby). Kirkby's jewelled ornamentation is brilliant too, and Aled Jones's singing – despite a few moments of caution – is ethereally beautiful, if only a little more remarkable than that of the three trebles from the Christ Church Choir who do the little trios for Three Virgins at the end of Act II. Christopher Hogwood with the Academy brings out the speed and variety of the score that has been described as Handel's first great English oratorio. The recording is bright and clean, giving sharp focus to voices and instruments alike.

Duets: *Beato in ver; Langue, geme; Tanti strali.* Cantatas: *Parti, l'idolo mio; Sento là che ristretto.*
*** HM HMC 901004 [id.]. Judith Nelson, René Jacobs, William Christie, K. Jünghanel.

These Handel duets (two of them very early from his Italian period) and the two cantatas – more substantial works – contain some delightful music, Handel at his most charming. With outstanding solo singing from both Judith Nelson and René Jacobs, they are given very stylish performances, cleanly recorded.

Brockes Passion.
**(*) Hung. Dig. HCD 12734/6-2 [id.]. Klietmann, Gáti, Zádori, Minter & soloists, Halle Stadtsingechor, Capella Savaria, McGegan.

The relatively crude Passion text by Barthold Brockes prompted a piece of some thirty or so arias, two duets and a trio, most of them brief but full of superb ideas, many of which Handel raided for his later oratorios. Thus, the deeply moving duet between Christ and the Virgin Mary just before the *Crucifixion* later became the duet for Esther and King Ahasuerus in *Esther*. Generally, this degree of depth – worthy to be compared with Bach's Passion music – is missing, but there is still much to enjoy. Nicholas McGegan with the excellent Capella Savaria using period instruments directs a lively, refreshing account of the piece that easily outshines previous versions. The team of soloists has no weak link, and the only comparative reservation concerns the singing of the chorus, fresh but less polished than the rest. The Hungaroton recording is bright and well focused, with a fine sense of presence.

Carmelite Vespers.
*** EMI Dig. CDS7 49749-2 (2) [Ang. CDCB 49749]. Feldman, Kirkby, Van Evera, Cable, Nichols, Cornwell, David Thomas, Taverner Ch. & Players, Parrott.

What Andrew Parrott has recorded here is a reconstruction by Graham Dixon of what might have been heard in July 1707 at the church of the Carmelite Order in Rome for the Festival of Our Lady of Mount Carmel. Dixon has put the motets and Psalm settings in an order appropriate for the service of Second Vespers, noting that it is not the only possible reconstruction. So *Dixit Dominus* is introduced by plainchant and a chanted antiphon, with similar liturgical links between the other Handel settings – in turn *Laudate pueri, Te decus Virgineum, Nisi Dominus, Haec est Regina Virginum, Saeviat Tellus* and *Salve Regina*. Of these, the only unfamiliar Handel piece is *Te decus Virgineum* – which makes this not quite the new experience promised but an enjoyable way of hearing a magnificent collection of Handel's choral music. In a liturgical setting in 1707, women's voices would not have been used, but the sopranos and altos of the Taverner Choir produce an aptly fresh sound, as does the fine group of soloists, headed by an outstanding trio of sopranos: Emma Kirkby, Jill Feldman and Emily van Evera. The recording, made in St Augustine's, Kilburn, has a pleasant and apt ambience, which however does not obscure detail.

(i) *Cecilia vogi un sguardo* (cantata); *Silete venti* (motet).
*** DG Dig. 419 736-2 [id.]. Jennifer Smith, Elwes, E. Concert, Pinnock.

These two fine cantatas come from a later period than most of Handel's Italian-language works in this genre. Both reveal him at his most effervescent, a quality superbly caught in these performances with excellent singing and playing, most strikingly from Jennifer Smith whose coloratura has never been more brilliantly displayed on record. Excellent recording.

Chandos anthems Nos. 1: O be joyful in the Lord; 2: In the Lord put I my trust; 3: Have mercy on me, HWV 246/8.
*** Chan. Dig. CHAN 8600 [id.]. Lynne Dawson, Ian Partridge, The Sixteen Ch. & O, Christophers.

Handel based the first *Chandos anthem, O be joyful*, setting the *Jubilate*, Psalm 100, on his *Utrecht Te Deum*; grandly, he uses three soloists as well as chorus. The second, though rather longer, uses tenor alone with chorus, while the third has soprano and tenor, both in solo and duet. The impact of the performances is affected strongly by the recorded sound, set in a warm acoustic characteristic of Chandos but with rather a close balance; that makes the choir sound bigger and with a greater body of weight than on The Sixteen's recording of *Messiah*. Ian Partridge is the radiant-voiced linchpin of these performances and is superbly matched by Lynne Dawson with her gloriously pure, silvery soprano. Michael George's much briefer contribution is also most stylish. The closeness of sound makes the instrumental sonatas which start each *Anthem* more abrasive than they might be, but not uncomfortably so.

Chandos anthems Nos. 4: O sing unto the Lord a new song; 5: I will magnify thee; 6: As pants the hart for cooling streams.
*** Chan. Dig. CHAN 0504 [id.]. Lynne Dawson, Ian Partridge, The Sixteen Ch. & O, Christophers.

The second volume of the Chandos series is hardly less appealing than the first. There are some splendidly vigorous choruses, while in No. 6 there is a lovely adagio chorus, *As pants the hart for cooling streams*, and an equally memorable soprano aria, beautifully sung by Lynne Dawson. Indeed the performances are well up to standard, as is the recording.

Chandos anthems Nos. 10: The Lord is my light; 11: Let God arise.
*** Chan. Dig. CHAN 0509. Lynne Dawson, Ian Partridge, The Sixteen Ch. & O, Christophers.

Although he is framed by some splendidly ambitious choruses, the tenor soloist dominates No. 10, and Ian Partridge sings with his customary style and sweetness of timbre. Lynn Dawson makes her entry on the penultimate number. The two soloists share the honours in No. 11: they have one aria each, and here the chorus is again in exhilarating form, especially in the closing *Alleluja*. The recording is spacious while continuing to preserve the music's intimate feeling.

Coronation anthems (1, Zadok the Priest; 2, The King shall rejoice; 3, My heart is inditing; 4, Let Thy hand be strengthened).
*** DG Dig. 410 030-2 [id.]. Westminster Abbey Ch., E. Concert, Preston; Pinnock (organ).

(i) *Coronation anthems;* (ii) *Chandos anthem No. 9: O praise the Lord.*
(M) *** Decca 421 150-2 [id.]. (i) King's College Ch., Willcocks; (ii) with E. Vaughan, A. Young, Forbes Robinson; ASMF, Willcocks.

(i) *Coronation anthems;* (ii) *Dixit Dominus.*
(M) ** EMI CDM7 69753-2. (i) King's College Ch., ECO, Ledger; (ii) Zylis-Gara, J. Baker, Lane, Tear, Shirley-Quirk, King's College Ch., Willcocks.

Coronation anthems (complete); *Judas Maccabaeus; See the conqu'ring hero comes; March; Sing unto God.*
*** Ph. Dig. 412 733-2 [id.]. ASMF Ch., ASMF, Marriner.

The extra weight of the Academy of St Martin-in-the-Fields Chorus compared with the Pinnock version seems appropriate for the splendour of music intended for the pomp of royal ceremonial occasions, and the commanding choral entry in *Zadok the Priest* is gloriously rich in amplitude, without in any way lacking incisiveness. The instrumental accompaniments are fresh and glowing. Sir Neville Marriner's direction is full of imaginative detail, and the Philips recording, with its wide dynamic range, is admirably balanced and excitingly realistic in its CD format. The excerpts from *Solomon* are delightful.

Those who prefer sparer, more 'authentic' textures can choose Pinnock where, although the overall effect is less grand, the element of contrast is even more telling. After the lightness and clarity of the introduction to *Zadok the Priest*, to have the choir enter with such bite and impact underlines the freshness and immediacy. The recording gives ample sense of power, and the use of original instruments gives plenty of character to the accompaniments. An exhilarating version.

The reissued 1961 Argo recording makes an admirable mid-priced alternative, particularly as the extra clarity and presence given to the choir improve the balance in relation to the orchestra. The *Chandos anthem* makes a fine bonus.

Ledger directs a reading of the *Coronation anthems* which favours measured speeds. Though the choir is small, the recording balance in excellent digital sound has the voices standing out clearly to reinforce the weight of the reading. The use of a modern string sound also increases this effect. The inclusion of *Dixit Dominus* is generous, but this performance is rather less successful. The intonation of the soloists is not above reproach and the trio, *Dominus a dextris*, is not very comfortable. Vigour and enthusiasm are here, but not always the last degree of finesse.

Dettingen Te Deum; Dettingen anthem.
*** DG Dig. 410 647-2 [id.]. Westminster Abbey Ch., E. Concert, Preston.

The *Dettingen Te Deum* is a splendidly typical work and continually reminds the listener of *Messiah*, written the previous year. Preston's new Archiv performance from the English Concert makes an ideal recommendation, with its splendid singing, crisp but strong (Stephen Varcoe does the two brief airs beautifully), excellent recording and a generous, apt coupling. This setting of *The King shall rejoice* should not be confused with the *Coronation anthem* of that name. It is less inspired, but has a magnificent double fugue for finale. The recording is first class, although the Westminster Abbey reverberation prevents a sharp choral focus.

Dixit Dominus; Nisi Dominus; Salve Regina.
*** DG Dig. 423 594-2 [id.]. Westminster Abbey Ch. & O, Simon Preston.

Dixit Dominus; Zadok the Priest.
*** Erato/WEA 2292 45136-2. Palmer, Marshall, Brett, Messana, Morton, Thomson, Wilson-Johnson, Monteverdi Ch. and O, Gardiner.

On DG Archiv *Dixit Dominus* is very aptly coupled with fine performances of another – less ambitious – Psalm setting, *Nisi Dominus*, and a votive antiphon, *Salve Regina*, which Handel composed between the two. Preston here draws ideally luminous and resilient singing from the Westminster Abbey Choir, with a fine team of soloists in which Arleen Augér and Diana Montague are outstanding. Their duet together in *Dixit Dominus, De torrente in via bibet*, is ravishingly beautiful, with clashing suspensions made up to add emotional depth. The playing of the orchestra of period instrumentalists, led by Roy Goodman, in every way matches the fine qualities of the singing.

John Eliot Gardiner catches the music's brilliance and directs an exhilarating performance, marked by strongly accented, sharply incisive singing from the choir and outstanding solo contributions. In high contrast to the dramatic choruses, the duet for two sopranos, *De torrente*, here beautifully sung by Felicity Palmer and Margaret Marshall, is languorously expressive, but stylishly so. However, the Erato coupling is less generous than the two works offered on DG.

Esther (complete).
**(*) O-L Dig. 414 423-2 (2) [id.]. Kwella, Rolfe-Johnson, Partridge, Thomas, Kirkby, Elliott, Westminster Cathedral Boys' Ch., Ch. and AAM, Hogwood.

Hogwood has opted for the original 1718 score with its six compact scenes as being more sharply dramatic than the 1732 expansion, and his rather abrasive brand of authenticity goes well with the bright, full recorded sound which unfortunately exaggerates the choir's sibilants. The Academy's own small chorus is joined by the clear, bright trebles of Westminster Cathedral Choir, and they all sing very well (except that the elaborate passage-work is far too heavily aspirated, at times almost as though the singers are laughing). The vigour of the performance is unaffected and the team of soloists is strong and consistent, with Patrizia Kwella sounding distinctive and purposeful in the name-part.

Israel in Egypt (oratorio).
(M) **(*) DG 429 530-2 (2) [id.]. Harper, Clark, Esswood, Young, Rippon, Keyte, Leeds Fest. Ch., ECO, Mackerras.

(i) *Israel in Egypt;* (ii) *Chandos anthem No. 10: The Lord is my light.*
(M) *** Decca 421 602-2 [id.]. (i) Gale, Watson, Bowman, Partridge, McDonell, Watt, Christ Church Ch., Oxford, ECO, Preston; (ii) Cantelo, Partridge, ASMF, Willcocks.

(i) *Israel in Egypt; The Ways of Zion* (funeral anthem).
**(*) Erato/WEA 2292 45399-2 (2) [id.]. (i) Knibbs, Clarkson, Elliot, Varcoe, Monteverdi Ch. & O, Gardiner.

Simon Preston, using a small choir with boy trebles and an authentically sized orchestra, directs a performance of this great dramatic oratorio which is beautifully in scale. He starts with the *Cuckoo and the nightingale organ concerto* – a procedure sanctioned by Handel himself at the first performance – and, though inevitably the big plague choruses lack the weight which a larger choir would give them, the vigour and resilience are ample compensation. Though Elizabeth Gale is not always absolutely firm in the soprano role, overall the band of soloists is impressive, and the ECO is in splendid form. The recording is realistically balanced within an attractively warm acoustic, and the remastering has splendidly enhanced the vividness. The *Chandos anthem* makes an enjoyable bonus, memorable for some remarkable fugal writing, and throughout these two discs the sound is outstandingly fresh and full.

Though the solo singing shared between principals in the chorus is variable on Erato, the choruses are what matter in this work, making up a high proportion of its length, and the teamwork involved brings tingling excitement. It is good to have the moving funeral anthem as an extra item. Both Simon Preston's version on Decca and the DG/Mackerras account have superior solo contributions; but Gardiner's chorus remains the finest of the three.

Mackerras's performance represents a dichotomy of styles, using the English Chamber Orchestra, sounding crisp, stylish and lightweight in the opening overture (borrowed from *Solomon*) and the full texture of the fairly large amateur choir, impressively weighty rather than incisive, but given strong projection on CD. Thus the work makes its effect by breadth and grandiloquence rather than athletic vigour. The recording balance also reflects the problems of the basic set-up, with the chorus sometimes virtually drowning the orchestra in the epic pieces, and then suddenly coming to the fore for the lighter moments of the score. The solo singing is distinguished, but its style is refined rather than earthy – thus again contrasting with the choral manner (although this contrast is not unfamiliar in the English tradition of live performance) and it is the choruses which are the glory of this oratorio.

Jephtha.
*** Ph. Dig. 422 351-2 (3) [id.]. Robson, Dawson, Anne Sofie von Otter, Chance, Varcoe, Holton, Monteverdi Ch., E. Bar. Soloists, Gardiner.

(i) *Jephtha;* (ii) *Chandos anthem No. 2: In the Lord I put my trust.*
(M) *** Deccca 425 701-2 (3) [id.]. (i) Rolfe-Johnson, Marshall, Hodgson, Esswood, Keyte, Kirkby, Southend Boys' Ch., ASMF Ch., ASMF, Marriner; (ii) Langridge, King's College Ch., ASMF, Willcocks.

Whatever Handel's personal trials in writing what, in all but name, is a biblical opera, the result is a masterpiece, containing some magnificent music, not least in the choruses. There are only three *da capo* arias out of ten, and the beautiful accompanied recitatives – not least Jephtha's celebrated *Deeper and deeper still* in Act II – give a cohesion to the whole. John Eliot Gardiner's recording was made live at the Göttingen Festival in 1988 and, though the sound does not have quite the bloom of his finest studio recordings of Handel, the exhilaration and intensity of the performance come over vividly, with superb singing from both chorus and an almost ideal line-up of soloists. Nigel Robson's tenor may be on the light side for the title-role, but in such a lovely aria as *Waft her, angels* the clarity of sound and the sensitivity of expression are very satisfying. Lynne Dawson, with her bell-like soprano, sings radiantly as Iphis; and the counter-tenor, Michael Chance, as her beloved, Hamor, is also outstanding. Anne Sofie von Otter is powerful as Storge, and Stephen Varcoe with his clear baritone, again on the light side, is a stylish Zebul. As for the Monteverdi Choir, their clarity, incisiveness and beauty are a constant delight.

Marriner's performance, helped by the bright tones of trebles in the choruses, is refreshing from first to last, well sprung but direct in style. The soloists are excellent, with Emma Kirkby nicely distanced in the role of the Angel, her clean vibrato-less voice made the more ethereal. It is a very long oratorio, but in this performance it hardly seems so, with such beautiful numbers as Jephtha's *Waft her, angels* given a finely poised performance by Rolfe-Johnson. The recording is first rate, and the CD transfer has lively presence and detail. The *Chandos anthem* makes a pleasing encore. The choral singing is well up to the King's standard and Philip Langridge is notable for his eloquence and simplicity of approach. The CD transfer produces strikingly real and vivid sound.

Lucrezia (cantata). Arias: *Ariodante: Oh, felice mio core . . . Con l'ali do constanza; E vivo ancore? . . . Scherza infida in grembo al drudo; Dopo notte. Atalanta: Care selve. Hercules: Where shall I fly? Joshua: O had I Jubal's lyre. Rodelinda: Pompe vane di morte! . . . Dove sei, amato bene? Serse: Frondi tenere e belle . . . Ombra mai fù (Largo).*
(M) *** Ph. 426 450-2 [id.]. Dame Janet Baker, ECO, Leppard.

Even among Dame Janet's most impressive records this Handel recital marks a special contribution, ranging as it does from the pure gravity of *Ombra mai fù* to the passionate virtuosity in *Dopo notte* from *Ariodante*. Two extra items have been added to the original, 1972 selection. Leppard gives sparkling support and the whole is recorded with natural and refined balance. An outstanding disc, with admirable documentation.

Messiah (complete).
*** DG Dig. 423 630-2 (2). Augér, Anne Sofie von Otter, Chance, Crook, J. Tomlinson, E. Concert Ch., E. Concert, Pinnock.
*** Hyp. Dig. CDA 66251/2 [id.]. Lynne Dawson, Denley, Maldwyn Davies, Michael George, The Sixteen Ch. & O, Christophers.
(***) Ph. Dig. 411 041-2 (3) [id.]. Marshall, Robbin, Rolfe-Johnson, Brett, Hale, Shirley-Quirk, Monteverdi Ch., E. Bar. Soloists, Gardiner.

*** Decca Dig. 414 396-2 (2) [id.]. Te Kanawa, Gjevang, Keith Lewis, Howell, Chicago Ch. & SO, Solti.

(M) *** Ph. 420 865-2 (2) [id.]. Harper, Watts, Wakefield, Shirley-Quirk, LSO Ch., LSO, C. Davis.

**(*) EMI CDS7 49027-2 (2) [Ang. CDCB 49027]. Battle, Quivar, Aler, Ramey, Toronto Mendelssohn Ch. & SO, Andrew Davis.

**(*) O-L 411 858-2 (3) [id.]. Nelson, Kirkby, Watkinson, Elliott, Thomas, Christ Church Cathedral Ch., Oxford, AAM, Hogwood.

**(*) ASV Dig. CDRPD 001R (2). Lott, Palmer, Langridge, Lloyd, Huddersfield Choral Soc., RPO, Mackerras.

(M) ** Decca 421 234-2 (2) [id.]. Ameling, Reynolds, Langridge, Howell, Ch. & ASMF, Marriner.

** EMI Dig. CDS7 49801-2 (2) [Ang. CDCB 49801]. Kirkby, Van Evera, Cable, Bowman, Cornwell, Thomas, Taverner Ch. & Players, Parrott.

Pinnock presents a performance using authentically scaled forces which, without inflation, rise to grandeur and magnificence, qualities Handel himself would have relished. With a choir of thirty-two voices, cleanly and powerfully recorded in a warm acoustic, the result is thrilling, not least when timpani decorate the cadences. The fast contrapuntal choruses, such as *For unto us a Child is born*, are done lightly and resiliently in the modern manner, but there is no hint of breathlessness, and Pinnock (more than his main rivals) balances his period instruments to give a satisfying body to the sound. There is weight too in the singing of the bass soloist, John Tomlinson, firm, dark and powerful, yet marvellously agile in divisions. Arleen Augér's range of tone and dynamic is daringly wide and, with radiant purity in *I know that my Redeemer liveth*, she and Pinnock, at a slow tempo, find a vein of tenderness too often lacking in period performance. The contralto aria, *He was despised*, is even more extreme in slowness, yet Anne Sofie von Otter sustains it superbly with her firm, steady voice. Some alto arias are taken by the outstanding counter-tenor, Michael Chance, who in some ways is even more remarkable. The tenor, Howard Crook, is less distinctive but still sings freshly and attractively. With full, atmospheric and well-balanced recording, this is a set not to be missed, even by those who already have a favourite version of *Messiah*.

Harry Christophers' brilliant and stylish choir, The Sixteen, have also made a highly appealing performance, one of the most attractive ever on disc. The scale is compact – with three extra sopranos added to the regular sixteen singers – but the bloom on the sound of chorus and instruments alike gives them brightness and clean projection with no sense of miniaturization. Christophers consistently adopts speeds more relaxed than those we have grown used to in modern performances and the effect is fresh, clear and resilient. Alto lines in the chorus are taken by male singers; a counter-tenor, David James, is also used for the *Refiner's fire*, but *He was despised* is rightly given to the contralto, Catherine Denley, warm and grave at a very measured tempo. The team of five soloists is at least as fine as that on any rival set, with the soprano, Lynne Dawson, singing with silvery purity to delight traditionalists and authenticists alike. The band of thirteen strings sounds as clean and fresh as the choir. Even the *Hallelujah chorus* – always a big test in a small-scale performance – works well, with Christophers in his chosen scale, through dramatic timpani and trumpets conveying necessary weight. The sound has all the bloom one associates with St John's recordings, but – thanks to the dampening effect of an audience – no clouding from reverberation.

Gardiner chooses bright-toned sopranos instead of boys for the chorus, on the grounds that a mature adult approach is essential, and conversely he uses, very affectingly, a solo treble to sing *There were shepherds abiding*. Speeds are fast and light, and the rhythmic buoyancy in the choruses is very striking. There is drama and boldness, too. *Why do the nations* and *The trumpet shall sound* (both sung with great authority) have seldom come over more strongly. The soloists are all first class, with the soprano Margaret Marshall finest of all, especially in *I know that my Redeemer liveth* (tastefully decorated). There are times when one craves for more expansive qualities; the baroque string sound can still give cause for doubts. Yet there are some wonderful highlights, not least Margaret Marshall's angelic version of *Rejoice greatly*, skipping along in compound time. Unfortunately, the set is extravagantly presented on three discs but with each of the three parts complete and separate. The CDs bring most items individually cued and the sound is outstandingly beautiful.

Surprisingly, Sir Georg Solti had never conducted *Messiah* before this recording, but he inspires the most vitally exciting reading on record. The Chicago Symphony Orchestra and Chorus respond to some challengingly fast but never breathless speeds, showing what lessons can be learnt from authentic performance in clarity and crispness. Yet the joyful power of *Hallelujah* and the *Amen chorus* is overwhelming. Dame Kiri Te Kanawa matches anyone on record in beauty of tone and detailed expressiveness, while the other soloists are first rate too, even if Anne Gjevang has rather too fruity a timbre. Brilliant, full sound and great tangibility, breadth and clarity on the CDs.

The earlier Philips recording has not lost its impact and sounds brightly lit and fresh in its digitally remastered format. Textures are beautifully clear and, thanks to Davis, the rhythmic bounce of such choruses as *For unto us* is really infectious. Even *Hallelujah* loses little and gains much from being performed by a chorus of this size. Excellent singing from all four soloists, particularly Helen Watts who, following early precedent, is given *For He is like a refiner's fire* to sing, instead of the bass, and produces a glorious chest register. The performance is absolutely complete and is excellent value at mid-price.

Andrew Davis's 1987 recording seeks to step back a little in time to a recently traditional style of performance; nevertheless his presentation follows current practice in using judicious decoration in *da capo* arias, and his tempi for choruses are lively, even though he uses a modern orchestra and a large amateur choral group. They are well trained and generally cope well with the demands placed on them. The special strength of the set lies in the soloists, a team without weakness. Kathleen Battle's sweet purity of timbre in *How beautiful are the feet* suggests a boy treble, yet *I know that my Redeemer liveth* has mature expressive feeling. Florence Quivar's *He was despised* is comparably eloquent and both male singers display a fine sense of drama. Overall the sound is first class, full, clear and believably balanced, and those who relish a more traditional approach to Handel's masterpiece will find a great deal to enjoy here.

By aiming at re-creating an authentic version, reproducing a performance of 1754, Christopher Hogwood has achieved a reading which is consistently vigorous and refreshing. The trebles of Christ Church are superb, and though the soloists cannot match the tonal beauty of the finest of their rivals on other sets, the consistency of the whole conception makes for most satisfying results. As to the text, it generally follows what we are used to, but there are such oddities as *But who may abide* transposed for a soprano and a shortened version of the *Pastoral symphony*. The recording is superb, clear and free to match the performance.

The big disappointment of Sir Charles Mackerras's digital set with the Huddersfield Choral Society is that this great choir sounds relatively feeble, conveying less weight and bite than many of the small choirs on period recordings. It is largely a question of recording balance, which gives the choral ensemble too little body. The quartet of soloists is a strong and distinctive one – Felicity Lott, Felicity Palmer, Philip Langridge and Robert Lloyd – but hardly traditional-sounding. It is interesting to have Mozart's arrangement used, with its trombones and clarinets, but the traditional cuts are made here; this means that Part One comes complete on the first disc and the other two Parts complete on the second. Inconsistently but aptly for a British recording, the original English text is used, not the German actually set by Mozart.

Marriner's conception was to present *Messiah* as nearly as possible in the text followed at the first London performance of 1743. The losses are as great as the gains, but the result has unusual unity, thanks also to Marriner's direction. His tempi in fast choruses can scarcely be counted as authentic in any way: with a small professional chorus he has gone as far as possible towards lightening them and has thus made possible speeds that almost pass belief. Although Anna Reynolds' contralto is not ideally suited to recording, this is otherwise an excellent band of soloists – and in any case Miss Reynolds sings *He was despised* on a thread of sound. Vivid recording.

Parrott for EMI has assembled a fine team of performers, as well as his own Taverner Choir and Players. Emma Kirkby is even more responsive here than she was in her earlier recording, for Oiseau-Lyre; but, for all its great merits, the performance lacks the zest and the sense of live communication that mark out a version like Pinnock's, another period performance which also dares to adopt slow, expressive speeds for such arias as *He was despised* and *I know that my Redeemer liveth*.

Messiah: highlights.
*** Ph. Dig. 412 267-2 [id.] (from above set, cond. Gardiner).
*** Decca Dig. 417 449-2 [id.] (from above set, cond. Solti).
*** O-L Dig. 440 086-2 [id.] (from above set, cond. Hogwood).
(M) *** EMI CDM7 69040-2 [id.]. Harwood, Janet Baker, Esswood, Tear, Herinx, Amb. S., ECO, Mackerras.
(B) **(*) CfP CD-CFP 9007. Morison, Marjorie Thomas, R. Lewis, Milligan, Huddersfield Ch. Soc., Royal Liverpool PO, Sargent.
(B) **(*) Pickwick Dig. PCD 803 [MCA MCAD 25852]. Lott, Finnie, Winslade, Herford, Scottish Philharmonic Singers, Scottish SO, Malcolm.
(M) **(*) Decca 417 735-2 [id.]. Ameling, Reynolds, Langridge, Howell, Ch. & ASMF, Marriner.
(B) **(*) ASV Dig. CDQS 6001. Kwella, Cable, Kendal, Drew, Jackson, Winchester Cathedral Ch., L. Handel O, Neary.
(M) **(*) Decca 417 879-2. Sutherland, Bumbry, McKellar, Ward, LSO Ch. & O, Boult.

Here Gardiner's collection reigns supreme with the single caveat that *The trumpet shall sound* is missing. The *Amen* chorus is included, however, and rounds off a satisfying musical experience. Solti's selection is undoubtedly generous, including all the key numbers and much else besides. The sound is thrillingly vivid and full. There is in addition a selection including all the important choruses (Decca 421 059-2), but this has a much more limited appeal.

The digitally remastered CD of highlights from the Hogwood recording was issued before the complete set, and acts as an excellent sampler for it. Sir Charles Mackerras's 1967 EMI recording was a landmark in its day, and this makes a clear mid-priced recommendation.

The great and pleasant surprise among the bargain selections is the Classics for Pleasure CD of highlights from Sir Malcolm Sargent's 1959 recording. This offers an amazing improvement in sound and restores his reputation in this repertoire – his pacing is sure and spontaneous throughout, whether or not one agrees with it. There is some splendid solo singing, notably from Elsie Morison and Richard Lewis, and Marjorie Thomas's *He was despised* is very moving in its simplicity and vocal warmth. The choruses emerge vigorously out of the fog of the old analogue master, with the words audible and the heaviness dissipated; no one will be disappointed with *Hallelujah*, while the closing *Amen* has a powerful sense of apotheosis.

Beautifully sung by excellent soloists (especially Felicity Lott) and choir, the Pickwick issue makes another good bargain-priced CD, very naturally and beautifully recorded in warmly atmospheric sound, though the performance at times could be livelier.

A highlights disc is probably the best way to sample the Marriner performance, and the same comment might apply to Boult's 1961 version, where Sutherland alone pays any attention to the question of whether or not to use ornamentation in the repeats of the *da capo* arias.

Brightly if reverberantly recorded in Winchester Cathedral, Martin Neary's collection of excerpts gives a pleasant reminder of the work of one of our finest cathedral choirs. In its authentic manner Neary's style is rather too clipped to convey deep involvement, but the freshness is attractive, with some very good solo singing.

Ode for the birthday of Queen Anne (Eternal source of light divine); Sing unto God (Wedding anthem); Te deum in D (for Queen Caroline).
*** Hyp. Dig. CDA 66315 [id.]. Fisher, Bowman, Ainsley, George, New College, Oxford, Ch., King's Consort, Robert King.

Handel wrote this *Birthday Ode for Queen Anne* near the beginning of his years in England (before his master, the Elector of Hanover, became George I), combining Purcellian influences with Italianate writing to make a rich mixture. King's performance may not quite match Hogwood's on the rival Oiseau-Lyre disc in vigour (see above), but it is richly enjoyable, with warm, well-tuned playing from the King's Consort and with James Bowman in radiant form in the opening movement. There is excellent singing from the other soloists too. The other two items are far rarer. Though less consistently inspired, they have some charming moments, to make an attractive coupling. Warmly atmospheric recording, not ideally clear on detail.

Ode for St Cecilia's Day.
*** DG Dig. 419 220-2 [id.]. Lott, Rolfe-Johnson, Ch. & E. Concert, Pinnock.
*** ASV Dig. CDDCA 512 [id.]. Gomez, Tear, King's College Ch., ECO, Ledger.

Trevor Pinnock's account of Handel's magnificent setting of Dryden's *Ode* comes near the ideal for a performance using period instruments. Not only is it crisp and lively, it has deep tenderness too, as in the lovely soprano aria, *The complaining flute*, with Lisa Beznosiuk playing the flute obbligato most delicately in support of Felicity Lott's clear singing. Anthony Rolfe-Johnson gives a robust yet stylish account of *The trumpet's loud clangour*, and the choir is excellent, very crisp of ensemble. Full, clear recording with voices vivid and immediate.

Those seeking a version with modern instruments will find Ledger's ASV version a splendid alternative. With superb soloists – Jill Gomez radiantly beautiful and Robert Tear dramatically riveting in his call to arms – this delightful music emerges with an admirable combination of freshness and weight. Ledger uses an all-male chorus; the style of the performance is totally convincing without being self-consciously authentic. The recording is first rate, rich, vivid and clear.

La Resurrezione.
*** O-L Dig. 421 132-2 (2) [id.]. Kirkby, Kwella, C. Watkinson, Partridge, Thomas, AAM, Hogwood.

Though *La Resurrezione* does not have the great choral music which is so much the

465

central element of later Handel oratorios, it is a fine and many-faceted piece. Hogwood directs a clean-cut, vigorous performance with an excellent cast of singers highly skilled in the authentic performance of Baroque music. Emma Kirkby is at her most brilliant in the coloratura for the Angel, Patrizia Kwella sings movingly as Mary Magdalene and Carolyn Watkinson as Cleophas adopts an almost counter-tenor-like tone. Ian Partridge's tenor has a heady lightness as St John, and though David Thomas's Lucifer could have more weight, he too sings stylishly. Excellent recording, well balanced and natural in all respects, with an attractive ambient bloom.

Solomon (complete).
⊛ *** Ph. Dig. 412 612-2 (2) [id]. C. Watkinson, Argenta, Hendricks, Rolfe-Johnson, Monteverdi Ch., E. Bar. Soloists, Gardiner.

This is among the very finest of all Handel oratorio recordings. With panache, Gardiner shows how authentic-sized forces can convey Handelian grandeur even with clean-focused textures and fast speeds. The choruses and even more magnificent double-choruses stand as cornerstones of a structure which may have less of a story-line than some other Handel oratorios – the Judgement apart – but which Gardiner shows has consistent human warmth. Thus in Act I, the relationship of Solomon and his Queen is delightfully presented, ending with the ravishing Nightingale chorus, *May no rash intruder*; while the Act III scenes between Solomon and the Queen of Sheba, necessarily more formal, are given extra warmth by having in that role a singer who is sensuous in tone, Barbara Hendricks. Carolyn Watkinson's pure mezzo, at times like a male alto, is very apt for Solomon himself (only after Handel's death did baritones capture it), while Nancy Argenta is clear and sweet as his Queen. In the Judgement scene, Joan Rodgers is outstandingly warm and characterful as the First Harlot, but the overriding glory of the set is the radiant singing of Gardiner's Monteverdi Choir. Its clean, crisp articulation matches the brilliant playing of the English Baroque Soloists, regularly challenged by Gardiner's fast speeds, as in the *Arrival of the Queen of Sheba*; and the sound is superb, coping thrillingly with the problems of the double choruses.

The Triumph of time and truth.
*** Hyp. CDA 66071/2 [id.]. Fisher, Kirkby, Brett, Partridge, Varcoe, L. Handel Ch. and O, Darlow.

Darlow's performance of Handel's very last oratorio, with the London Handel Choir and Orchestra using original instruments, has an attractive bluffness. This is broader and rougher than the authentic recordings by John Eliot Gardiner, but it is hardly less enjoyable. The soloists all seem to have been chosen for the clarity of their pitching – Emma Kirkby, Gillian Fisher, Charles Brett and Stephen Varcoe, with the honey-toned Ian Partridge singing even more beautifully than the others, but with a timbre too pure quite to characterize 'Pleasure'. Good atmospheric recording; though the chorus is a little distant, the increase in overall immediacy which has come with the CD transfer makes this less striking.

Utrecht Te Deum and Jubilate.
*** O-L 414 413-2 [id.]. Nelson, Kirkby, Brett, Elliot, Covey-Crump, Thomas, Ch. of Christ Church Cathedral, Oxford, AAM, Preston.

Handel wrote the Utrecht pieces just before coming to London, intending them as a sample of his work. Using authentic instruments and an all-male choir with trebles, Preston directs a performance which is not merely scholarly but characteristically alert and vigorous, particularly impressive in the superb *Gloria* with its massive eight-part chords. With a team of soloists regularly associated with the Academy of Ancient Music, this can be confidently recommended.

OPERA

Alcina (complete).
*** EMI Dig. CDS7 49771-2 (3) [Ang. CDCB 49771]. Augér, Della Jones, Kuhlmann, Harrhy, Kwella, Maldwyn Davies, Tomlinson, Opera Stage Ch., City of L. Bar. Sinfonia, Hickox.

It would be hard to devise a septet of Handelian singers more stylish than the soloists here. Though the American, Arleen Augér, may not have the weight of Joan Sutherland (who in a much-edited text sang the title-role both at Covent Garden and on record), she is just as brilliant and pure-toned, singing warmly in the great expansive arias. Even next to her, Della Jones stands out in the breeches role of Ruggiero, with an extraordinary range of memorable arias, bold as well as tender. Eiddwen Harrhy as Morgana is just as brilliant in the aria, *Tornami a vagheggiar*, usually 'borrowed' by Alcina, while Kathleen Kuhlmann, Patrizia Kwella, Maldwyn Davies and John Tomlinson all sing with a clarity and beauty to make the music sparkle. As for the text, it is even more complete than any known performance ever, when it includes as appendices two charming items that Handel cut even at the première. Hickox underlines the contrasts of mood and speed, conveying the full range of emotion. There are few Handel opera recordings to match this, with warm, spacious sound, recorded at EMI's Abbey Road studio.

Atalanta (complete).
*** Hung. Dig. HCD 12612/4 [id.]. Farkas, Bartfai-Barta, Lax, Bandi, Gregor, Polgar, Savaria Vocal Ens. & Capella, McGegan.

The fresh precision of the string playing of the Capella Savaria demonstrates – even without the help of vibrato – what Hungarian string quartets have been proving for generations: a superfine ability to match and blend. This is an opera crammed with dozens of sparkling, light-hearted numbers with no flagging of the inspiration, the opposite of weighty Handel. Led by the bright-toned Katarin Farkas in the name-part, the singers cope stylishly, and the absence of Slavonic wobbles confirms the subtle difference of Magyar voices; Joszef Gregor with his firm, dark bass is just as much in style, for example, as he regularly is in Verdi. First-rate recording.

Flavio (complete).
*** HM Dig. HMC 901312/13 (2) [id.]. Gall, Ragin, Lootens, Fink, *et al.*, Ens. 415, Jacobs.

Based on a staging of this unjustly neglected Handel opera at the 1989 Innsbruck Festival, René Jacobs' recording vividly captures the consistent vigour of Handel's inspiration. Unlike most Handel operas, this one has principal soloists in all four registers and keeps well within modern ideas of length, with some two and a half hours of music squeezed on to the two CDs. That and the quality of invention make it surprising that *Flavio* has never enjoyed popular success, even in Handel's time. The plot is no stiffer or more improbable than most of the period, and Handel's score was brilliantly written for some of the most celebrated singers of the time, including the castrato, Senesino. His four arias are among the highspots of the opera, all sung superbly here by the warm-toned and characterful counter-tenor, Derek Lee Ragin. The first three are brilliant coloratura arias; but the last, in the rare key of B flat minor, touches a darker, more tragic note. The other tragic aria is for the heroine, Emilia, again in a distant key, F sharp minor; but almost every other aria is open and vigorous, with the whole sequence rounded off in a rousing ensemble. René Jacobs' team of eight soloists is a strong one, with only the strenuous tenor of Gianpaolo Fagotto occasionally falling short of the general stylishness. Full, clear sound.

Giulio Cesare (Julius Caesar); abridged.
(M) ** RCA GD 86182 (2) [6182-2-RG]. Treigle, Sills, Forrester, Wolff, Malas, NY City Op. Ch. & O, Julius Rudel.

This RCA recording of *Julius Caesar* (first issued on LP in 1968) is fairly complete and based on a New York stage production. The conductor's approach is intelligent and tries to pay homage to scholarship, but one is not sure that the solution to the *da capo* arias – having a bare initial statement and reserving all the decoration to the reprise – is entirely successful. Nor does the singing of the name-part by a baritone (while effective on the stage) mean that the music lies exactly right for the voice. But with all reservations, the overall effect is accomplished, and the lively, atmospheric recording gives considerable enjoyment.

Hercules (complete).
*** DG Dig. 423 137-2 (3) [id.]. Tomlinson, Sarah Walker, Rolfe-Johnson, Jennifer Smith, Denley, Savidge, Monteverdi Ch., E. Bar. Soloists, Gardiner.

Gardiner's generally brisk performance of *Hercules* using authentic forces may at times lack Handelian grandeur in the big choruses, but it conveys superbly the vigour of the writing, its natural drama. Writing in English, Handel concentrated on direct and involving human emotions more than he generally did when setting classical subjects in Italian. Numbers are compact and memorable, and the fire of this performance is typified by the singing of Sarah Walker as Dejanira in her finest recording yet. John Tomlinson makes an excellent, dark-toned Hercules with florid passages well defined except for very occasional sliding. Youthful voices consistently help in the clarity of the attack – Jennifer Smith as Iole, Catherine Denley as Lichas, Anthony Rolfe-Johnson as Hyllus and Peter Savidge as the Priest of Jupiter. Refined playing and outstanding recording quality.

Julius Caesar (complete; in English).
(M) *** EMI Dig. CMS7 69760-2 (3) [id.]. Dame Janet Baker, Masterson, Sarah Walker, Della Jones, Bowman, J. Tomlinson, E. Nat. Op. Ch. & O, Mackerras.

Dame Janet, in glorious voice and drawing on the widest range of expressive tone-colours, shatters the old idea that this alto-castrato role should be transposed down an octave and given to a baritone. Valerie Masterson makes a charming and seductive Cleopatra, fresh and girlish, though the voice is caught a little too brightly for caressing such radiant melodies as those for *V'adoro pupille* (*Lamenting, complaining*) and *Piangero* (*Flow my tears*). Sarah Walker sings with powerful intensity as Pompey's widow; James Bowman is a characterful counter-tenor Ptolemy and John Tomlinson a firm, resonant Achillas, the other nasty character. The ravishing accompaniments to the two big Cleopatra arias amply justify the use by the excellent ENO Orchestra of modern, not period, instruments. The full, vivid studio sound makes this one of the very finest of the invaluable series of ENO opera recordings in English.

Il pastor fido (opera) complete.
**(*) Hung. Dig. HCD 12912 (2) [id.]. Esswood, Farkas, Lukin, Kállay, Flohr, Gregor, Savaria Vocal Ens., Capella Savaria, McGegan.

Drawn largely from material originally written for other operas, and revised three times with still more mixing of sources, *Il pastor fido* is an unpretentious pastoral piece, which charms gently rather than compelling attention. Though there is some fussiness in the orchestral playing (on period instruments) in this welcome recording, Nicholas McGegan demonstrates what talent there is in Budapest, among singers as among instrumentalists. Singers better known in much later operatic music translate well to Handel, for example the celebrated bass, József Gregor, but the most stylish singing comes from the British counter-tenor, Paul Esswood, in the castrato role of Mirtillo. Good sound and excellent documentation.

COLLECTIONS

Arias from: *Acis and Galatea; Alexander's Feast; Orlando; Samson; Theodora.*
(M) **(*) EMI CD-EMX 2158. Owen Brannigan, Handel Op. Soc. Ch., L. Philomusica –
MOZART: *Arias.***(*)

It is good to have a reminder of a much-loved British artist, with recordings made when he was still at his prime in the late 1970s. His endearingly genial style was such that he could almost make a virtue out of intrusive aitches in Handel's florid divisions by the twinkle in his delivery. His diction was splendid and he is especially characterful here as Polyphemus in *Acis and Galatea*, a part he was surely born to play. The transfer to CD is vivid but, unfortunately, adds a degree of edge to the voice.

Arias: *Alexander's Feast: The Prince, unable to conceal his pain; Softly sweet in Lydian measures. Atalanta: Care selve. Giulio Cesare: Piangero. Messiah: Rejoice greatly; He shall feed his flock. Rinaldo: Lascia ch'io pianga. Samson: Let the bright Seraphim.*
(*) Delos Dig. D/CD 3026 [id.]. Arleen Augér, Mostly Mozart O, Schwarz – BACH: *Arias.*(*)

Arleen Augér's bright, clean, flexible soprano is even more naturally suited to these Handel arias than to the Bach items with which they are coupled. The delicacy with which she tackles the most elaborate divisions and points the words is a delight, and the main snag is that the orchestral accompaniment, recorded rather too close, is coarse, though the sound is bright and clear.

Hanson, Howard (1896–1981)

Symphonies Nos. 1 in E min. (Nordic); 2 (Romantic); Elegy in memory of Serge Koussevitzky.
*** Delos Dig. D/CD 3073 [id.]. Seattle SO, Gerard Schwarz.

Hanson's *First Symphony* is a sombre, powerful work. Hanson was of Swedish descent and his music has a strong individuality of idiom and colour. The *Second* is warmly appealing and melodically memorable with an indelible theme which permeates the structure. These Seattle performances have plenty of breadth and ardour, and Schwarz's feeling for the ebb and flow of the musical paragraphs is very satisfying. The recording, made in Seattle Opera House, is gloriously expansive and the balance is convincingly natural. This is demonstration sound in the best sense. As a bonus, the record includes the *Elegy* written to commemorate the conductor who commissioned the *Second Symphony* and who gave its first performance in 1930.

Symphony No. 2 (Romantic), Op. 30.
*** EMI Dig. CDC7 47850-2 [id.]. St Louis SO, Slatkin – BARBER: *Violin concerto.****

The *Romantic* subtitle is wholly appropriate, for the *Second Symphony* is very much in a post-Rachmaninov vein. Apart from the memorable opening motif which finds its way into all three movements, the melody of the *Andante* is justly renowned in America, where it has been used as theme music for TV. Such incidental use in no way detracts from the appeal of the symphony itself which, if harmonically not breaking any new ground, is structurally sound, imaginatively laid out and by no means lightweight. Slatkin's performance is a very satisfying one, responding to the expressive nostalgia of the slow movement and bringing an exhilarating attack to the finale – there are only three movements. The full, atmospheric recording, beautifully balanced and rich in its washes of string tone, is a pleasure in itself.

Harris, Roy (1898–1979)

(i) *Violin concerto; Symphonies Nos. 1; 5.*
** Albany AR012 [id.]. (i) Gregory Fulkerston; Louisville O, Leighton Smith; Mester or Whitney.

The *Third Symphony* has overshadowed all of Roy Harris's other compositions so that the appearance of the present issue offers a chance of filling out our picture of him. Many people think of him as a one-work composer; although there is some truth in this, in that the *Third* encapsulates Harris's characteristics, there is much else that is fine, including the 1933 symphony, recorded here. No. 1 is strong stuff, hardly less impressive than No. 3, but neither No. 5 nor the *Violin concerto* adds greatly to our picture of him. Gregory Fulkerston gives a persuasive account of the solo part, but the strings of the enterprising Louisville Orchestra are wanting in body and lustre. The recordings are serviceable rather than distinguished.

Symphony No. 3 in one movement.
*** DG Dig. 419 780-2 [id.]. NYPO, Bernstein – SCHUMAN: *Symphony No. 3.****

Roy Harris's *Third* is the archetypal American Symphony. There is a real sense of the wide open spaces, of the abundant energy and independent nature of the American pioneers, and an instinctive feeling for form. The music moves forward relentlessly from the very opening bars until the massive eloquence of its coda. Like Samuel Barber's *First*, it is a one-movement work, but it is held together more convincingly, is far less episodic, grander and more deeply original. Bernstein gives a keenly felt but essentially softer-grained account of the work than the famous first Koussevitzky recording. There is no lack of punch or weight, but the ends of some paragraphs are carefully rounded. However, this is a great symphony – splendidly played and well recorded.

Harty, Hamilton (1879–1941)

(i) *Piano concerto in B min.;* (ii) *In Ireland (Fantasy for flute, harp and orchestra); With the wild geese.*
*** Chan. Dig. CHAN 8321 [id.]. (i) Binns, (ii) Fleming, Kelly; Ulster O, Thomson.

Harty's *Piano concerto*, written in 1922, has strong Rachmaninovian influences, but the melodic freshness remains individual and in this highly sympathetic performance the work's magnetism increases with familiarity, in spite of moments of rhetoric. The *In Ireland fantasy* is full of delightful Irish melodic whimsy, especially appealing when the playing is so winning. Melodrama enters the scene in the symphonic poem, *With the wild geese*, but its Irishry asserts itself immediately in the opening theme. Again a splendid performance and a high standard of digital sound.

Violin concerto in D; Variations on a Dublin air.
*** Chan. CHAN 8386 [id.]. Ralph Holmes, Ulster O, Thomson.

Though the *Violin concerto* has no strongly individual idiom, the invention is fresh and often touched with genuine poetry. Ralph Holmes gives a thoroughly committed account of the solo part and is well supported by an augmented Ulster Orchestra under Bryden Thomson. The *Variations* are less impressive though thoroughly enjoyable. These are accomplished and well-recorded performances.

An Irish symphony; A Comedy overture.
*** Chan. Dig. CHAN 8314 [id.]. Ulster O, Thomson.

The *Irish symphony* dates from 1904 and arose from a competition for a suite or symphony based on traditional Irish airs, inspired by the first Dublin performance of Dvořák's *New World symphony.* Harty's symphony won great acclaim for its excellent scoring and good craftsmanship. The scherzo is particularly engaging. It is extremely well played by the Ulster Orchestra under Bryden Thomson, and the overture is also successful and enjoyable. The recording is absolutely first class in every respect.

With the wild geese (symphonic poem).
(M) *** EMI CDM7 69206-2. SNO, Gibson – GERMAN: *Welsh rhapsody*; MACCUNN: *Land of Mountain and Flood*; SMYTH: *The Wreckers overture.****

With the wild geese is a melodramatic piece about the Irish soldiers fighting on the French side in the Battle of Fontenoy. The ingredients – a gay Irish theme and a call to arms among them – are effectively deployed; although the music does not reveal a strong individual personality, it is carried by a romantic sweep which is well exploited here. The 1968 recording still sounds most vivid.

VOCAL MUSIC

The Children of Lir; Ode to a nightingale.
*** Chan. Dig. CHAN 8387 [id.]. Harper, Ulster O, Thomson.

Harty's setting of Keats' *Ode to a nightingale* is richly convincing, a piece written for his future wife, the soprano, Agnes Nicholls. The other work, directly Irish in its inspiration, evocative in an almost Sibelian way, uses the soprano in wordless melisma, here beautifully sung by Heather Harper. The performances are excellent, warmly committed and superbly recorded.

Haydn, Josef (1732–1809)

Cello concerto in C, Hob VIIb/1.
(B) *** Ph. 422 481-2 [id.]. Gendron, LSO, Leppard – BOCCHERINI: *Cello concerto.****
(*) EMI CDC7 47614-2. Jacqueline du Pré, ECO, Barenboim – DVORÁK: *Concerto.*(*)
** DG Dig. 429 219-2. Matt Haimovitz, ECO, A. Davis – C. P. E. BACH; BOCCHERINI: *Concertos.***

Cello concertos in C and D, Hob VIIb/1–2.
*** Ph. Dig. 420 923-2 [id.]. Heinrich Schiff, ASMF, Marriner.
*** O-L Dig. 414 615-2 [id.]. Christophe Coin, AAM, Hogwood.
(M) **(*) EMI CDM7 69299-2 [id.]. Tortelier, Württemberg CO, Faerber.
**(*) CBS MK 36674 [id.]. Yo-Yo Ma, ECO, Garcia.

(M) ** EMI CDM7 69009-2 [id.]. Lynn Harrell, ASMF, Marriner.
** EMI CDC7 49305-2 [id.]. Rostropovich, ASMF.

Cello concerto in D, Hob VIIb/2.
*** EMI CDC7 47840-2 [id.]. Jacqueline du Pré, LSO, Barbirolli – BOCCHERINI: *Concerto.***(*)

Cello concertos in C and D, Hob VIIb/1–2; in G (arr. of *Violin concerto, Hob VIIa/4*).
**(*) DG Dig. 419 786-2 [id.]. Mischa Maisky, COE.

Even in a competitive field, Heinrich Schiff is a strong contender. His playing has not only an effortless fluency but also a zest for life. As always, he produces a beautiful sound, as indeed do the Academy under Marriner. These are impressively fresh-sounding performances with lyrical and affectionate (but not too affectionate) playing from all concerned. Schiff plays his own cadenzas – and very good they are. The recording has the realistic timbre, balance and bloom one associates with Philips.

Christophe Coin, too, is a superb soloist and, provided the listener has no reservations about the use of original instruments, Hogwood's accompaniments are equally impressive. The style is not aggressively abrasive but gives extra clarity and point to the music, not least in the breathtakingly brilliant account of the finale of the *C major Concerto*. Certainly no fresher or more vital performance of these two works has been put on disc, although Coin's own cadenzas – undoubtedly stylish – are on the long side. Excellent sound.

Tortelier gives warmly expressive performances of the two *Concertos*, more relaxed than some of his rivals, but not lacking spontaneity. He is sympathetically if not always immaculately accompanied by the Württemberg Chamber Orchestra. Clear yet warm digital sound to match, very pleasingly balanced. At mid-price this remains fully competitive.

Ma's refinement has its own rewards, though some may prefer a bolder approach to music firmly belonging to the classical eighteenth century. Apart from one or two odd points of balance, the recording is clean and full.

Harrell, rather after the manner of Rostropovich, seeks to turn these elegant concertos into big virtuoso pieces, helped by Marriner's beautifully played accompaniments, although touches of over-romantic expressiveness tend to intrude. Cadenzas are distractingly and unstylishly long. The remastered recording is vivid but not absolutely clean in focus.

Mischa Maisky gives beautifully cultured readings of both concertos, which he also directs himself. He has much warmth and refinement, though his tempi are generally a bit too fast. He adds a bonus in the shape of an arrangement of the *G major Violin concerto*. The recordings, made in the Vienna Konzerthaus, have admirable body and presence, and detail is well placed. Marvellous playing, but not a first choice.

With Barbirolli to partner her, Jacqueline du Pré's performance of the best-known *D major Concerto* is warmly expressive. Though purists may object, the conviction and flair of the playing are extraordinarily compelling, and the romantic feeling is matched by an attractively full, well-balanced recording which belies its age (1969).

Rostropovich's virtuosity in the reissued EMI coupling is astonishing. With modern recording, this has some claims on the collector; however, quite apart from the extra haste (which brings its moments of breathless phrasing) Rostropovich's style has acquired a degree of self-indulgence in the warmth of expressiveness, and this is reflected in the accompaniment, which he also directed.

Gendron's account of the *C major Concerto* is highly musical and is sensitively accompanied by Leppard. This coupling with Boccherini shows him at his finest, and the recording is of good Philips quality.

Du Pré gives a performance of characteristic warmth and intensity. Her style, as in the D major work, is sometimes romantic in a way that, strictly speaking, is inappropriate in this music – yet the very power of her personality is strongly conveyed. This is the sort of music-making that defies cold analysis. Good recording.

Matt Haimovitz's account of the *C major Concerto* is well worth hearing, although there is an unrelieved emotional intensity about his playing that is a bit overheated, and there are one or two moments of inelegance. That said, his fresh enthusiasm and good technique tell, even if his account does not disturb current recommendation.

Cello concerto in C; Violin concerto No. 1 in C, Hob VIIa/1; Double concerto for violin and harpsichord in F, Hob XVIII/6.
**(*) Mer. CDE 84177 [id.]. William Conway, Malcolm Layfield, David Francis, Goldberg Ens., Layfield.

The gleamingly fresh opening tutti of the *Violin concerto*, full of vitality, is immediately welcoming. Malcolm Layfield makes an appealing soloist, and the *Double concerto* is also enjoyably done and excellently balanced. The *Cello concerto* has vigorous allegros, but the melodic line in the slow movement is rather less convincing. The overall sound is impressive, except for a small amount of background hiss, which suggests a non-digital master.

(i) *Cello concerto in D;* (ii) *Trumpet concerto in E flat;* (iii) *Violin concerto in C.*
**(*) CBS Dig. MK 39310 [id.]. (i) Yo-Yo Ma, ECO, Garcia; (ii) Marsalis, Nat. PO, Leppard; (iii) Lin, Minnesota O, Marriner.

All these performances are still available with their original couplings and are discussed above and below. The CBS recording has excellent clarity and its presence is striking.

Harpsichord concerto in D, Hob XVIII/2; Double concerto for violin and harpsichord, Hob XVIII/6. Symphony No. 31 in D (Horn signal).
(BB) ** Hung. White Label HRC 088 [id.]. Zsuzsa Pertis, János Rolla, Liszt CO, Rolla.

Engagingly vivacious accounts of Haydn's best-known keyboard concerto and the equally personable *Double concerto*, with a convincing balance for the harpsichord, especially considering the full-timbred orchestral sound. In the *Symphony*, which has some splendid horn playing, the recording becomes slightly more opaque with greater bass emphasis, but this inexpensive disc is worth having for the *Concertos* alone.

Horn concerto No. 1 in D, Hob VIId/3.
(M) *** Decca 417 767-2 [id.]. Barry Tuckwell, ASMF, Marriner – MOZART: *Concertos Nos 1–4.****

Horn concertos Nos. 1–2 in D, Hob VIId/3–4; (i) *Double horn concerto in E flat* (attrib. M. Haydn & Rosetti).
(*) Ph. Dig. 422 346-2 [id.]. Baumann; (i) Timothy Brown; ASMF, Iona Brown (with POKORNY: *Horn concerto in D*).

(i) *Horn concertos Nos. 1–2;* (ii) *Trumpet concerto in E flat;* (i) *Divertimento a 3 in E flat.*
**(*) Nimbus NI 5010 [id.]. (i) Thompson; (ii) Wallace; Philh. O, Warren-Green.

In his interesting notes for the Nimbus CD, Michael Thompson suggests that Haydn wrote his *First* and *Second Concertos* for his first and second horn players, Thaddäus Steinmüller and Carl Franz. Yet both works explore the widest range, and it was the

Divertimento, an attractive bonus, that exploited Steinmüller's ability to slip easily into the stratosphere of the horn register. Thompson manages it too, with aplomb, and he gives bold, confident accounts of the two concertos, with a sprinkling of decoration. John Wallace's trumpet timbre is strikingly brilliant, as recorded, and his playing in the *Trumpet concerto* is full of personality. He too likes to decorate and there are some attractive surprises in the finale. The recording was made in the resonant ambience of All Saints', Tooting, but the CD provides good definition under the circumstances, even if the harpsichord tends to get lost.

Haydn's *First Horn concerto* is a fine work, technically more demanding than any of the Mozart concertos – especially as played by Barry Tuckwell on Decca, with a profusion of ornaments and trills, witty or decorative. The finale is in the 'hunting' style of the period, but the highlight of the work is the *Adagio*, a beautifully shaped cantilena for the soloist. Tuckwell's playing throughout is of the highest order, and Marriner's vintage accompaniments are equally polished and full of elegance and vitality. The remastering is admirably fresh, though there is a hint of shrillness on the violins above the stave.

Baumann plays both solo concertos splendidly, with a strong sense of line in the cantilena of No. 1; but it is the *Double concerto*, probably not by Haydn at all, that most impresses here, with the two horns carolling joyously together in the outer movements. Predictably, Iona Brown produces elegant, polished accompaniments, a major pleasure of the disc. The Pokorny *Concerto* makes a good bonus with its engaging finale, showing Baumann at his very best. The recording is full and natural, if rather resonant.

(i) *Horn concerto No. 1 in D, Hob VII/d3;* (ii) *Organ concerto No. 1 in C, Hob XVIII/1;* (iii) *Trumpet concerto in E flat, Hob VIIe/1*.
**(*) O-L Dig. 417 610-2 [id.]. (i) Timothy Brown; (ii) Christopher Hogwood; (iii) Friedmann Immer, AAM, Hogwood.

An admirable collection aimed directly at authenticists. Timothy Brown uses a valveless instrument, and he 'stops' the missing notes convincingly. It is an attractive account in its eighteenth-century scale. Hogwood plays the *Organ concerto* with elegance and spirit on a chamber organ, which produces piquant and colourful registration. But the real novelty here is a performance of the *Trumpet concerto* on the instrument for which it was written, a keyed *Klappentrompete*. Immer's intonation and execution are very impressive, and the sounds have a character all their own, even if he is unable to produce the soaring melisma and glittering bravura possible on the modern instrument.

Oboe concerto in C, Hob VIIg/C1.
*** Capriccio Dig. 10 308 [id.]. Lajos Lencsés, Stuttgart RSO, Marriner – HUMMEL: *Intro., theme & variations*; MARTINŮ: *Concerto*.***

Haydn's *Oboe concerto* is of doubtful authenticity and in Lajos Lencsés' hands it is given an almost Italianate sunny grace. The *Andante* is played with appealing delicacy and the Minuet finale has an elegantly light touch. Marriner brings a touch of classical gravitas to the tuttis of the first movement and is altogether a most sympathetic accompanist. The balance is natural and the sound excellent. So are the couplings.

Organ concertos, Hob XVIII/1, 2, 5, 7, 8 and 10.
*** Ph. 416 452-2 (2) [id.]. Koopman, Amsterdam Bar. O.

Ton Koopman has chosen the organ of St Bartholomew at Beek-Ubbergen near Nijmegen which is reproduced to vivid effect in this excellently engineered pair of discs. The sonorities blend perfectly with those of the Amsterdam Baroque Orchestra and the performances have great personality and spirit. This is not great music but, played like this, it affords much stimulus and pleasure. Slow movements have the right expressive feeling, and 'authentic' bulges in the melodic line are minimal and unobtrusive.

(i) *Piano concerto in D, Hob XVII/11;* (ii) *Violin concerto in C, Hob VIIa/1. Sinfonia concertante in B flat.*
**(*) RCA Dig. RD 87948 [7948-2-RC]. (i) Kissin; (ii) Spivakov; Moscow Virtuosi, Spivakov.

The fleet-fingered young Soviet star gives a trim, nimble account of the *D major concerto*. Spivakov's reading of the *C major Violin concerto* is pure-toned, though the first-movement allegro is on the slow side and by no means as vibrant or as light in touch as Cho-Liang Lin on CBS. However, taken on its own merits, it is musically satisfying. The most substantial work here is the *Sinfonia concertante*, which also comes off best. The recording is clean and decent, though there is little front-to-back depth and the solo instruments are forwardly placed.

Trumpet concerto in E flat.
❀ *** Ph. Dig. 420 203-2 [id.]. Håkan Hardenberger, ASMF, Marriner – HERTEL***; HUMMEL*** ❀; STAMITZ: *Concertos.***
*** Delos Dig. D/CD 3001 [id.]. Schwarz, New York 'Y' CO – HUMMEL: *Concerto.***
*** CBS CD 37846 [id.]. Marsalis, Nat. PO, Leppard – HUMMEL: *Concerto*** (with L. MOZART: *Concerto***).

The only possible reservation about Hardenberger's vividly recorded version of Haydn's finest concerto is that the acoustic in which the orchestra is set is a shade over-reverberant. The trumpet, however, placed well forward, is right in the room with the listener and its physical presence is highly involving. Hardenberger's playing of the noble line of the *Andante* is no less telling than his fireworks in the finale and, with Marriner providing warm, elegant and polished accompaniments throughout, this is probably the finest single collection of trumpet concertos in the present catalogue.

George Schwarz's account on Delos is hardly less memorable, but the Delos CD now seems distinctly short measure, although the Hummel coupling is equally desirable. Indeed, Schwarz's stylish command, richly gleaming timbre and easy bravura are impossible to resist, and in the lovely *Andante* he adds a little decoration to the melody, played with a warm, serene elegance. The finale combines wit and sparkle. The recording is attractively reverberant without inflating the lively accompaniment which Schwarz himself directs.

Marsalis is splendid too, his bravura no less spectacular, with the finale a *tour de force*, yet never aggressive in its brilliance. He is cooler than Schwarz in the slow movement, but his way with Haydn is eminently stylish, as is Leppard's lively and polished accompaniment. The CBS recording is faithful and the CD gives a very vivid projection, although the orchestral sound is slightly artificial in its immediacy.

Violin concerto in C, Hob VIIa/1.
** CBS Dig. CD 37796 [id.]. Lin, Minnesota O, Marriner – VIEUXTEMPS: *Concerto No. 5.***(*)

Cho-Liang Lin's performance has both strength and drive and is not wanting in character, but it is lacking in charm, notably in the slow movement. Moreover, the CBS coupling seems ill-considered, although the recording is impressive.

Sinfonia concertante in B flat, Hob I/105.
(*) ASV Dig. CDDCA 580. L. Fest. O, Ross Pople – MOZART: *Sinfonia concertante, K.297b.*(*)

Sinfonia concertante in B flat; Symphony No. 94 in G (Surprise).
**(*) DG Dig. 419 233-2 [id.]. VPO, Bernstein.

Sinfonia concertante in B flat; Symphonies Nos. 94 in G (Surprise); 100 in G (Military).
**(*) Nimbus Dig. NI 5159 [id.]. Austro-Hungarian Haydn O, Adám Fischer.

Sinfonia concertante in B flat; Symphony No. 96 in D (Miracle).
*** DG Dig. 423 105-2 [id.]. COE, Abbado.

Abbado conducts the Chamber Orchestra of Europe in winning performances of both works, lively and sparkling. With outstanding solo contributions – the violinist and cellist just as stylish as their wind colleagues who have already appeared as soloists on several records – this issue of the *Sinfonia concertante* even outshines other excellent versions from Vienna and London with more mature soloists. The symphony too brings some brilliant playing, capturing the fun of Haydn's inspiration without any hint of undue haste or breathlessness. Abbado has rarely made a record as happy as this.

Bernstein adopts challengingly fast speeds in the finales of both works, with his flair superbly illustrated in the alternations of orchestral flourish and violin solo which open that of the *Sinfonia concertante.* The slow movements are taken relaxedly, with the *Andante* of the *Sinfonia concertante* beautifully done over accompaniment figures that are elegantly lifted. Bernstein is never more winning than in Haydn; and this disc brings splendid examples, edited as usual from live recordings.

These are relaxed readings on Nimbus, marked by broad speeds and resilient rhythms. The *Sinfonia concertante* shares two of the four soloists with Bernstein's Vienna version for DG and brings performances of the outer movements just as lively, with soloists less spotlit, better integrated with the ensemble.

Directing the players from the solo cello, Ross Pople draws a strong and alert rather than an elegant performance from his London Festival Orchestra, well recorded in bright, firmly focused sound. Though the solo playing is not always ideally refined, there is a winning sense of musicians acting out a drama, at speeds that are comfortable, never exaggerated.

SYMPHONIES

Symphonies Nos. 1–5.
Chan. Dig. CHAN 8737 [id.]. Cantilena, Shepherd.

These performance do not have to compete in a crowded market but anyway they are not well enough rehearsed to do so.

Symphonies Nos. 6 in D (Le Matin); 7 in C (Le Midi); 8 in G (Le Soir).
*** DG Dig. 423 098-2 [id.]. E. Concert, Pinnock.
(M) *** Decca 421 627-2 [id.]. Philh. Hungarica, Dorati.
*** Ph. Dig. 411 441-2 [id.]. ASMF, Marriner.

These were almost certainly the first works that Haydn composed on taking up his appointment as Kapellmeister to the Esterhazys and it seems very likely that their highly imaginative content and frequent use of instrumental solos were designed as much to stimulate the interest of his players as to make a grand effect on his employer. Pinnock's players clearly relish their opportunities here and take them with strong personality. The performances are polished and refined, yet highly spirited, with infectious allegros and expressive feeling. The size of the string group (4.4.2.2.1) is made to seem expansive by the warm acoustics of the Henry Wood Hall and there is certainly weight here, yet essentially this is a bracing musical experience with the genius of these early works fully displayed.

Dorati's recordings, made in 1973, come from his integral set of Haydn symphonies and their combination of exhilaration and stylishness is irresistible in these relatively well-known named symphonies, with their marvellous solos for members of the Esterhazy orchestra. The remastered recording sounds fresh and clear, but just a little of the body has been lost from the strings.

Admirers of Marriner and his Academy should not be disappointed with their (1982) alternative. The ASMF is nothing if not a band of soloists and there is plenty of character throughout this set, the best of its kind for some years, fresh and polished and very well balanced and recorded, though the harpsichord is only just distinguishable.

Symphonies Nos. 21 in A; 96 in D (Miracle); (i) *Cello concerto No. 1 in C.*
**(*) Delos Dig. D/CD 3062 [id.]. (i) Janos Starker, SCO, Schwarz.

Symphonies Nos. 22 in E flat (Philosopher); 104 in D (London); (i) *Piano concerto in D.*
**(*) Delos Dig. D/CD 3061 [id.]. (i) Carol Rosenberger, SCO, Schwarz.

Symphonies Nos. 51 in B flat; 100 in G (Military); (i) *Piano concerto in G.*
**(*) Delos Dig. D/CD 3064 [id.]. (i) Carol Rosenberger, SCO, Schwarz.

Each of Gerard Schwarz's records with the Scottish Chamber Orchestra presents a complete concert, with a concerto framed by a pair of symphonies, one early and one late. The performances are full of character – indeed the *Adagio* opening of the *Philosopher* seems almost too solemn. However, the comparable first movement in No. 21 is well judged, and both the *Miracle* and (especially) the *London symphony* are full of vitality. The playing is polished and phrasing is sympathetic, while the horns cover themselves in glory in No. 51. The resonant acoustics of Queen's Hall, Edinburgh, emphasize the fact that this is a modern approach, while Carol Rosenberger's playing of the two keyboard concertos makes no concessions whatsover and the piano image is big and bold.

Symphonies Nos. 22 in E flat (Philosopher); 24 in D; 45 in F sharp min. (Farewell).
**(*) Nimbus Dig. NI 5179 [id.]. Austro-Hungarian Haydn O, Adám Fischer.

With horns more forwardly balanced than in some of the Nimbus recordings of the later symphonies, Fischer draws some exhilarating playing from his regular team, working in the Haydnsaal of the Esterhazy Palace. In such a setting the flute solo in the slow movement of No. 24 has a Gluckian 'Elysian field' quality, and the warm acoustic takes away some of the abrasiveness of the cor anglais in the opening *Adagio* of No. 22, *The Philosopher*. That leads to brisk and light accounts of the two *Presto* movements, with phenomenal articulation from the horn. In the *Farewell symphony*, the fast movements bristle with energy, and the *Sturm und Drang* power of the first movement is enhanced by the observance of the second-half repeat, leading to a very measured account of the slow movement and an ungimmicky reading of the final *Adagio*. This is unconventional but stimulating music-making.

Symphonies Nos. 22 in E flat (Philosopher); 63 in C (La Roxelane); 80 in D min.
*** DG Dig. 427 337-2 [id.]. Orpheus CO.

The three symphonies offered here span twenty of Haydn's most creative years, from the highly original *Philosopher* (1764) to the mature D minor work with its serenely beautiful *Adagio* and characteristic interplay of drama and benign yet twinkling humour in the outer movements. *La Roxelane* is so nicknamed because its not-so-slow second movement brings characteristically felicitous variations on an *entr'acte* which Haydn had previously written as part of the incidental music for a play: La Roxelane was its heroine. The rest of the work is typically inventive, and the Orpheus players give all three symphonies with that sense of style, polish and intelligent commitment we have come to expect from them. Pacing, suppleness of phrase and precision of ensemble again demonstrate that for them a conductor isn't necessary, and the DG sound is well up to the previous high standard of their Haydn series.

Symphonies Nos. 26 in D min. (Lamentatione); 44 in E min. (Trauer); 45 in F sharp min. (Farewell).
(BB) **(*) Hung. White Label HRC 102 [id.]. Hungarian CO, Vilmos Tátrai.

Symphonies Nos. 27 in G; 88 in G; 100 in G (Military).
(BB) **(*) Hung. White Label HRC 090 [id.]. Hungarian CO, Tátrai or Adám Fischer.

Symphonies Nos. 43 in E flat (Mercury); 82 in C (The Bear); 94 in G (Surprise).
(BB) **(*) Hung. White Label HRC 123 [id.]. Hungarian CO, Tátrai or János Ferencsik.

Symphonies Nos. 49 in F min. (La Passione); 59 in A (Fire); 73 in D (La Chasse).
(BB) **(*) Hung. White Label HRC 103 [id.]. Hungarian CO, Vilmos Tátrai.

This excellent series by the Hungarian Chamber Orchestra offers alert, well-characterized performances, played with zest and style. There is no lack of polish here and the expressive playing in slow movements is appealingly phrased and spontaneous. In short, this excellent chamber orchestra convey their enjoyment of the music. The recording is resonant and full but remains clear. Tempi are apt (in No. 88, for instance, they are somewhat measured, but this is still a fine performance) and for those with limited budgets this is an excellent way to explore this repertoire.

Symphonies Nos. 26 in D min. (Lamentatione); 49 in F min. (La Passione); 58 in F.
*** DG Dig. 427 662-2 [id.]. E. Concert, Pinnock.

This disc – sadly containing only three symphonies instead of the four in volume one of Pinnock's *Sturm und Drang* series – still has two of the very finest, both with evocative nicknames, *Lamentatione*, misleadingly numbered No. 26, and *La Passione*, No. 49. The chant quoted in the vigorous first movement of No. 26 is brought out perfectly here, made clear but not spotlit, and, though the slow movement finds Pinnock – with period authority – adopting what we would think of as *Andante* rather than *Adagio*, the result flows relaxedly. The great first-movement *Adagio* of No. 49 is then aptly measured, a genuine lament, sharply contrasted with the two fast movements following. Though the storm and stress in No. 58 is less marked, the clear, vivid, closely balanced recording sharpens the dissonances of the first movement and underlines the harmonic and rhythmic surprises of the finale. Like the first in the series, an outstanding issue.

Symphonies Nos. 26 in D min. (Lamentatione); 52 in C min.; 53 in D (L'Imperiale).
*** Virgin Dig. VC 790743-2 [id.]. La Petite Bande, Sigiswald Kuijken.

Two of the toughest of Haydn's *Sturm und Drang* symphonies plus one of the celebratory works which he wrote on emerging from that self-questioning period make an excellent coupling in lively and stylish period performances. As recorded in a Haarlem church in the Netherlands, the light-textured string sound is more abrasive than usual and the oboe timbre is both plangent and sonorous; but the ear quickly adjusts. These are fresh, vital, cleanly articulated performances which wear their authenticity lightly and even indulge in speeds for slow movements that are more expansive and affectionate than many purists would allow. The '*Lamentatione*' refers to the Gregorian chant Haydn used in both the first two movements. No. 53 is thought to derive its title from a performance given before the Empress Maria Theresia.

Symphonies Nos. 28 in A; 44 in E min. (Trauer); 49 in F min. (La Passione).
**(*) Olympia OCD 169 [id.]. Moscow CO.

Very good playing indeed from the conductorless Moscow Chamber Orchestra, catching the warm intensity of the *Adagios* in the two named symphonies, balanced against keenly alert playing in allegros. No. 28, gay and extrovert, makes a happy centrepiece. The recording is bright and vivid, only occasionally a little hard on top.

Symphonies Nos. 35 in B flat; 38 in C (Echo); 39 in G min.; 49 in F min. (La Passione); 58 in F; 59 in A (Fire).
**(*) CBS Dig. M2K 37861 (2) [id.]. L'Estro Armonico, Solomons.

Like Derek Solomons' other Haydn recordings in this stimulating series, this set from 1766–8 is recorded in chronological order. The style (using original instruments and a small band) is fresh and lively, though ensemble is not always immaculate and not everyone will like the 'squeeze' style of slow movements with vibrato virtually eliminated. On their intimate scale these make an attractive alternative to versions using modern instruments, though the playing is less appealing than Pinnock's Archiv recordings. The sound on CD is admirably fresh and clear.

Symphonies Nos. 35 in B flat; 38 in C (Echo); 39 in G min.; 59 in A (Fire).
*** DG Dig. 427 661-2 [id.]. E. Concert, Pinnock.

This is the first of a projected series of six discs, under the title, *Sturm und Drang symphonies*, scheduled to contain all the symphonies that Haydn wrote between 1776 and 1783, during his early years as Kapellmeister at Esterháza. The idea is to present them all in the order in which they were written, not the order of the regular Hoboken catalogue numbering. Though the first two symphonies have little 'storm and stress', the sharp incisiveness of the playing, coupled with the exhilarating rhythmic lift which Pinnock gives in his direction from the keyboard, makes the results very refreshing. The ceremonial panache of the first movement of *No. 38 in C* is typical. Each work makes you want to go on to the next and, when it comes to the full *Sturm und Drang* drama of *No. 39 in G minor*, the surprising pauses in the first movement have you sitting up sharply. That is partly a question of the very limited string forces used, but also of the apt acoustic. It is a new experience to have Haydn symphonies of this period recorded in relatively dry and close sound, with inner detail crystal clear (harpsichord never obscured) and made the more dramatic by the intimate sense of presence, yet with a fine bloom on the instruments. Those attuned to Pinnock's authentic style need not hesitate.

Symphonies Nos. 41 in C; 48 in C (Maria Theresia); 65 in A.
*** DG Dig. 423 399-2 [id.]. E. Concert, Pinnock.

This group of three symphonies sits rather oddly in Pinnock's *Sturm und Drang* series; they are all outstanding examples, not of storm or stress, but of Haydn's ceremonial application of symphonic form. No. 48, *Maria Theresia*, is perhaps the most magnificent of all, by tradition associated with Empress Maria Theresia's visit to Esterháza in 1773, but in fact written at least three years earlier. The opening with its imperious horn calls sets the pattern of grandeur, and the rest develops on an aptly ambitious scale. Though

Pinnock's forces are modest (with 6.5.2.2.1 strings, as in the rest of the series) the panache of the performance conveys the necessary grandeur and, unlike many other period performers, Pinnock opts for a spacious *Adagio* in the second movement. The other two symphonies are done just as winningly, with the hunting-horn calls in the finale of No. 65 especially exhilarating. However, those used to the performance tradition as represented by Beecham, Sir Colin Davis and others may quarrel with the very brisk one-in-a-bar minuet and – dare one say it – even find finales a bit rushed. Converts to the authentic school will surely find such misgivings of little import. Excellent, well-balanced sound, as in the rest of the series.

Symphonies Nos. 43 in E flat (Mercury); 51 in B flat; 52 in C min.
*** DG Dig. 423 400-2 [id.]. E. Concert, Pinnock.

The symphony which more than any in Haydn's whole output sums up the spirit of *Sturm und Drang* is *No. 52 in C minor*, with its dramatic opening, its chromatic writing and sharp contrasts, made the more intense in a minor key. Though the second-movement *Andante* is relatively easy-going, the Minuet and finale, both also in C minor, bring anticipations of the romantic movement. *No. 51 in B flat* also has an element of wildness, very close to *Sturm und Drang*, notably in the extraordinary writing for horns in the slow movement, the one rising in a few bars to its highest compass, the second growling away at its lowest. The nickname, *Mercury*, was not given to No. 43 by Haydn but was appended much later in the nineteenth century, reflecting the light-hearted quality in the triple-time first movement, leading to a slow movement using muted strings. As in the rest of his series, Pinnock draws model performances from the English Concert, although for some ears there is a lack of charm. Once again the one-in-a-bar minuets preclude any feeling of dignity (the gracious dance element lost altogether). Those listeners thoroughly acclimatized to period performances will find that they don't come any better than this; others may reflect that these works have been performed before on disc with greater humanity.

Symphony No. 44 in E min. (Trauer).
(B) *** Pickwick Dig. PCD 820 [MCA MCAD 25846 with *Symphony No. 49*]. O of St John's, Smith Square, Lubbock – MOZART: *Symphony No. 40.***(*)

Symphonies Nos. 44 in E min. (Trauer); 77 in B flat.
*** DG Dig. 415 365-2 [id.]. Orpheus CO.

Symphonies Nos. 45 in F sharp min.; 81 in G.
*** DG Dig. 423 376-2 [id.]. Orpheus CO.

Symphonies Nos. 48 in C (Maria Theresia); 49 in F min. (La Passione).
*** DG Dig. 419 607-2 [id.]. Orpheus CO.

Symphony No. 49 in F minor (La Passione).
(B) **(*) Pickwick Dig. PCD 819 [MCA MCAD 25846 with *Symphony No. 44*]. O of St John's, Smith Square, Lubbock – SCHUBERT: *Symphony No. 5.***

The Orchestra of St John's are on their toes throughout their splendidly committed account of the *Trauersymphonie*. Outer movements are alert and vivacious – the finale has striking buoyancy and spring – and there is some lovely espressivo playing in the beautiful *Adagio* slow movement which brings out the forward-looking qualities of the writing. The recording too is in the demonstration class.

The Orpheus Chamber Orchestra certainly seem to be of one mind in No. 44, which they give with great freshness and spirit. All the players are expert, and so keenly do they listen to each other that they blend, almost as if they had a fine conductor in front of them. They capture the urgency of feeling of the *Trauersymphonie*, and No. 77 is given with a lightness of touch and infectious high spirits. Its humour and vivacity are beautifully realized, and the DG engineers provide excellent recording, too. Strongly recommended; as sound, this CD is especially believable.

The Orpheus group are at their very finest in their coupling of the *Farewell symphony* and *No. 81 in G*, a splendid work which comes first on the CD. The opening is rhythmically strong, but the players most appealingly catch the charming touch of melancholy which underlies the first movement's second group, while the bassoon solo that lies at the centre of the Minuet is equally characterful. In the *Farewell symphony*, the tenderly refined *espressivo* of the strings in the *Adagio* is most beautiful, while the departing players in the finale present their solos with personable finesse.

The *Maria Theresia symphony* is a splendidly festive piece and is comparably served here by this excellent conductorless ensemble. They take its first movement very briskly – perhaps a shade too much so. The two horns playing at pitch, rather than an octave lower, give a particularly bright colouring; the Orpheus also omit the trumpets and drums which are of dubious authenticity. *La Passione* makes an excellent foil and these players capture the dark *Sturm und Drang* introspection of the piece.

John Lubbock's version of Haydn's *La Passione* is not quite as convincing as his fine account of No. 44. With the opening *Adagio* overtly expressive and the allegros boldly assertive in their fast, crisp articulation, this is certainly responsive playing, but there is at times a sense of over-characterization of an already powerfully contrasted work. The recording is first class.

Symphonies Nos. 59 in A (Fire); 100 in G (Military); 101 in D (Clock).
(M) *** Ph. 420 866-2 [id.]. ASMF, Marriner.

Marriner's recordings derive from the mid-1970s and the performances are very satisfactory, as is the remastering. The *Clock* is vital and intelligent, the playing of the Academy very spruce and elegant. There is perhaps not quite the depth of character that informs Sir Colin Davis's performances of this repertoire, but they do display finesse, and the readings are never superficial in expressive terms.

Symphonies Nos. 78 in C min.; 102 in B flat.
**(*) DG Dig. 429 218-2 [id.]. Orpheus CO.

For Haydn symphonies on modern instruments, there are no more refined or polished performances than those on this disc, one of the Orpheus Chamber Orchestra's series. The underappreciated *No. 78 in C minor*, with its darkly chromatic first movement, comes in coupling with the magnificent No. 102, its slow movement containing one of the most beautiful of all Haydn melodies. These are model performances, yet they provide very short measure for a full CD, and the high polish makes them a little unsmiling.

Symphonies Nos. 80 in D min.; 87 in A; 89 in F.
*** ASV Dig. CDDCA 635 [id.]. L. Mozart Players, Jane Glover.

Jane Glover conducts the reinvigorated London Mozart Players in strong and energetic performances of these three relatively rare symphonies. No. 87 is the least known of the *Paris symphonies*; but all three of these works show Haydn at his most inventive. *No. 80 in D minor* begins as though it were a throwback to the *Sturm und Drang* period, but then at the end of the exposition Haydn gives a winning smile, as though to say, 'I fooled you!' No. 89 ends with a dance movement which contains delectable *strascinando* (dragging) passages, where the music hesitates before launching into reprises, done with great zest by the LMP. No. 87 has its delights too, notably in the lyrical *Adagio* with lovely flute and oboe solos. Though textures are not as transparent as we are beginning to demand in an age of period performance – largely a question of the ambient recorded sound – these modern-instrument performances are as winning as they are lively.

(Paris) Symphonies Nos. 82 in C (The Bear); 83 in G min. (The Hen); 84 in E flat.
⊛ *** Virgin Dig. VC7 90793-2. O of Age of Enlightenment, Kuijken.

(Paris) Symphonies Nos. 85 in B flat (La Reine); 86 in D; 87 in A.
⊛ *** Virgin Dig. VC7 90844-2. O of Age of Enlightenment, Kuijken.

These two discs, well filled, with three symphonies apiece, together present an outstanding set of Haydn's six *Paris symphonies*, between them offering among the most enjoyable period-performance recordings of Haydn ever. Kuijken and the players of the OAE wear their authenticity lightly and even allow themselves spacious speeds in slow movements, where expansion seems needed, as in the *Andante* of No. 83. There is a warm bloom on the sound, with woodwind well defined but not over-prominent. Textures are airily transparent, even when in the finale of No. 86 Kuijken opts for a very fast *allegro* indeed. Kuijken's one-in-a-bar treatment of the Minuets is a delight, giving them a Laendler-like swing. With dynamic contrasts underlined, the grandeur of Haydn's inspiration is fully brought out, along with the vigour; yet Kuijken gives all the necessary sharpness to the reminiscence of *Sturm und Drang* in the near-quotation from the *Farewell* in the first movement of No. 85, *La Reine*. The magnificence of that movement is underlined by the observance of the second-half repeat. Above all, Kuijken and his players convey the full joy of Haydn's inspiration in every movement.

Symphonies Nos. 82 in C (The Bear); 83 in G min. (The Hen).
*** Ph. Dig. 420 688-2 [id.]. Concg. O, C. Davis.

These splendid performances very much perpetuate the spirit of Sir Thomas Beecham's Haydn in their combination of humanity and elegance and a lively communication of the music's joy. Rhythms are crisp and allegros are energetic without a suspicion of hurry, while slow movements are full of grace. Tempi always seem just right, especially in the minuets which some conductors find elusive. Sir Colin Davis has made no finer record than this, and the Philips engineers capture the seductive Concertgebouw string-textures more transparently than ever, without loss of warmth and weight.

Symphonies Nos. 86 in D; 87 in A.
**(*) Ph. 412 888-2 [id.]. ASMF, Marriner.

It is possible to imagine performances of greater character and personality than these (slow movements do bring a hint of blandness), but they have a certain charm and are, generally speaking, lively and musical. Moreover they sound admirably vivid in their CD format.

Symphony No. 88 in G.
(M) (***) DG mono 427 404-2 [id.]. BPO, Furtwängler – SCHUMANN: *Symphony No. 4; Manfred.*(***)

Symphonies Nos. 88 in G; 89; 92 (Oxford).
(B) *** DG 429 523-2 [id.]. VPO, Boehm.

Symphonies Nos. 88 in G; 92 in G (Oxford).
**(*) DG Dig. 413 777-2 [id.]. VPO, Bernstein.

Furtwängler's coupling of Haydn's *Symphony No. 88* with Schumann's *Fourth* is deservedly one of his most famous records and can be universally recommended, even to those collectors who usually find his interpretations too idiosyncratic. The Berlin Philharmonic play marvellously well for him and the 1951 recording, made in the attractive ambience of the Jesus Christ Church, West Berlin, needs no apology.

Enjoyably cultured performances from Boehm and the Vienna Philharmonic, who play with great polish and tonal refinement. The finale of No. 88 and the Andante of No. 89 are most beautifully done and the slow movement of the former is gravely expansive. The remastering is very successful indeed in freshening the sound without losing its body and depth; some will want a less weighty effect, possible with a smaller group, but Boehm's touch can charm in allegros, as in the sprightly finale of the *Oxford symphony*.

A warmly glowing account of both symphonies from Bernstein with the full strings of the Vienna orchestra and a richly upholstered recording. Bernstein observes the repeat of the development and restatement in the first movement of No. 88 and gives a romantic and really rather beautiful account of the *Largo*. Both performances emanate from concerts at the Musikvereinsaal.

Symphonies Nos. 88 in G; 104 in D (London).
*** CRD CRD 3370 [id.]. Bournemouth Sinf., Ronald Thomas.

Although the orchestra is smaller than the Concertgebouw or LPO, the playing has great freshness and vitality; indeed it is the urgency of musical feeling that Ronald Thomas conveys which makes up for the last ounce of finesse. They are uncommonly dramatic in the slow movement of No. 88 and bring great zest and eloquence to the rest of the symphony too. In No. 104 they are not always as perceptive as Sir Colin Davis, but this brightly recorded coupling can be recommended alongside his version.

Symphonies Nos. 90 in C; 93 in D.
**(*) Ph. Dig. 422 022-2 [id.]. O of 18th Century, Frans Brüggen.

As in his recordings of Mozart symphonies, Brüggen's approach to Haydn brings contradictions of style. The openings of both works are large-scale and portentous, generating an almost Beethovenian atmosphere, to contrast with the restrained, 'authentic' string style in the *Largo cantabile* of No. 93. The performances have plenty of life and vigour and both finales are snappily rhythmic. The resonant acoustic increases the feeling of size, but the focus of the dynamically expansive tuttis is not absolutely clean.

Symphonies Nos. 91 in E flat; 92 in G (Oxford).
*** Ph. Dig. 410 390-2 [id.]. Concg. O, C. Davis.

The *Oxford* and its immediate predecessor in the canon, No. 91 in E flat, are here given performances that are refreshingly crisp and full of musical life. The sheer joy, vitality and, above all, sanity that these performances radiate is inspiriting and heart-warming. Excellent recorded sound.

Symphonies Nos. 92 in G (Oxford); 101 in D (Clock).
(BB) **(*) Hung. White Label HRC 089 [id.]. Hungarian State O, Ervin Lukács.

A useful supplement to the Hungarian Chamber Orchestra series, using a bigger band for late Haydn. The performances have plenty of life and are unidiosyncratic without losing character. The sound is full but not clouded.

Symphonies Nos. 92 in G (Oxford); 104 in D (London).
(B) *** Pickwick Dig. PCD 916. E. Sinfonia, Groves.

Sir Charles Groves makes an admirable case for a modern orchestra, especially when it is recorded so faithfully (in EMI's Abbey Road studio, but sounding like a concert hall), with agreeable ambient warmth, a bloom on strings and woodwind alike, yet with good definition. The performances are robust yet elegant as well; both slow movements are beautifully shaped, with Haydn's characteristic contrasts unfolding spontaneously. In the last movement of the *Oxford*, the dancing violins are a special delight in what is one of the composer's most infectious finales. The closing movement of the *London symphony* is altogether stronger and has a satisfying feeling of apotheosis.

Symphonies Nos. 93–104 (London symphonies).
(M) **(*) DG Dig. 429 658-2 (4). BPO, Karajan.

Symphonies Nos. 93 in D; 94 in G (Surprise); 100 in G (Military).
(M) **(*) DG Dig. 427 809-2 [id.]. BPO, Karajan.

Karajan offers big-band Haydn – but what a band! At times the Berlin Philharmonic do not seem fully involved in this music, and many of the minuets are wanting in the sparkle and humour that distinguished Beecham's performances on a similar scale. But there is often tenderness in slow movements – witness the close of *No. 98 in B flat* – and there is no want of dignity and breadth. The sound of the Berlin Philharmonic is itself a joy. This set, we gather, enjoyed the imprimatur of no less an authority than H. C. Robbins Landon; but it inspires admiration rather than affection. As a fine sampler, the triptych of Nos. 93, 94 and 100 can be recommended. First-movement exposition repeats are observed and the playing undoubtedly has distinction. The sound is first class.

Symphonies Nos. 93–104 (London symphonies).
**(*) Nimbus NI 5200/04 (5) [id.]. Austro-Hungarian Haydn O, Adám Fischer.

With three symphonies apiece on the first two discs of the five-disc Nimbus set, Fischer's cycle of all twelve *London symphonies* makes a neat and attractive package, with consistently fresh, resilient and refined performances. When much trouble has been taken to record this specially assembled orchestra in the authenic venue of the Haydnsaal in the Esterhazy Palace, it is surprising that in style these are rather old-fashioned readings, relatively uninfluenced by the example of period performance. Though these works were first given in the intimate surroundings of the Hanover Square Rooms in London, they were very quickly heard in this much grander setting, and the performances reflect the fact, with broad speeds made weightier by the reverberant Nimbus recording, so that in sound the tuttis relate rather to a Karajan or Bernstein performance than to one by a regular chamber orchestra. Only in lightly scored passages does one register the true scale of the orchestra, and such a movement as the lovely *Adagio* of No. 102 with its soaring melody is given added beauty by the ambience and slow speed. The set can be warmly recommended to most who resist period performance when, even at broad speeds, rhythms are light and resilient. Never sounding breathless, Fischer's Haydn consistently brings out the happiness of the inspiration. The first-movement allegro of No. 93 gets the cycle off to a delectable start, with the three-in-a-bar rhythms given a delicious lift. Not everyone will like the reverberance of the Nimbus recording, but these are very much performances to relax with.

Symphonies Nos. 93 in D; 94 in G (Surprise); 96 in D (Miracle).
*** Ph. Dig. 412 871-2 [id.]. Concg. O, C. Davis.

Finely paced and splendidly recorded in clean but warm digital sound, Sir Colin Davis's performances top the present lists for those listeners not requiring period instruments. To the original LP coupling of Nos. 93 and 94 the *Miracle* has been added, a refreshing and substantial bonus. Do not look to this CD for sharply defined inner detail, rather a very well-balanced overall perspective that gives a convincing illusion of the concert hall.

Symphonies Nos. 93 in D; 99 in E flat.
⊛ *** Decca Dig. 417 620-2 [id.]. LPO, Solti.

In this pairing of Nos. 93 and 99, two favourites of Sir Thomas Beecham, the atmosphere is sunny and civilized; there is no lack of brilliance – indeed the LPO are consistently on their toes – but the music-making is infectious rather than hard-driven. The string phrasing is as graceful as the woodwind articulation is light and felicitous, and pacing is wholly sympathetic. The lovely slow movement of No. 93 has both delicacy and gravitas and that of No. 99 is serenely spacious. The minuets are shown to have quite different characters, but both finales sparkle in the happiest manner. The sound on CD is very much in the demonstration class in its transparency, warmth and naturalness.

Symphonies Nos. 94 in G (Surprise); 96 in D (Miracle).
*** O-L Dig. 414 330-2 [id.]. AAM, Hogwood.

The playing here is superb: polished, feeling, and full of imaginative detail. The oboe solo in the Trio of the third movement of the *Miracle symphony* is a delight, and the sparkle in the finale with its crisp articulation and spirited pacing is matched by the elegance given to the engaging second subject of the first movement. The account of No. 94 is particularly dramatic and in the *Andante* there is not just the one 'surprise' (and that pretty impressive, with the contrast afforded by gentle strings at the opening) but two more *forte* chords to follow at the beginning of each subsequent phrase – a most telling device. The presence of Hogwood's fortepiano can also be subtly felt here, and later the wind solos are full of character. The minuet is fast, but this follows naturally after the drama of the slow movement, while the finale makes a light-hearted culmination. With superb recording, full yet transparent, this is an issue to make converts to the creed of authenticity.

Symphonies Nos. 94 in G (Surprise); 96 in D (Miracle); 100 in G (Military).
(M) *** Decca 417 718-2 [id.]. Philh. Hungarica, Dorati.

These three symphonies, collected from Dorati's historic complete Haydn cycle, make a delightful group. Allegros are well sprung, with phrasing elegant and the wind playing a special delight. The only controversial speed comes in the *Andante* of the *Surprise*, much faster than usual, but the freshness of the joke is the more sharply presented. Dorati's flair comes out in the bold reading of the military section of the slow movement of No. 100, and though the digital transfer exaggerates the brightness of upper frequencies, the warm acoustic of the hall in Marl, West Germany, where the recordings were done makes the result very acceptable.

Symphonies Nos. 94 in G (Surprise); 96 in D (Miracle); 102 in B flat.
(B) (**) CfP mono CD-CFP 4559. RPO, Beecham.

These performances of Nos. 94 and 96 derive from mono masters and the timbre of the violins is distinctly thin; No. 102 comes from 1960 and seems somewhat fuller. The performances are characteristically spirited and elegant, but the sound counts against the fullest enjoyment.

Symphonies Nos. 94 (Surprise); 100 (Military); 101 (Clock).
(B) *(*) Ph. 422 973-2 [id.]. VSO, Sawallisch.

Although well played and recorded (between 1961 and 1963), these are not very subtle performances. Tempi are on the fast side (the finales are infectious) but Sawallisch's direct, robust style brings an element of routine, and central movements are unmemorable.

Symphonies Nos. 94 in G (Surprise); 101 in D (Clock).
(M) *** DG 423 883-2 [id.]. LPO, Jochum.

Jochum's are marvellously fresh, crisp accounts of both symphonies, elegantly played and always judiciously paced. The sound remains first class, with added clarity but without loss of bloom, the bass cleaner and only slightly drier.

Symphonies Nos. 95 in C min; 104 in D (London).
*** Decca Dig. 417 330-2 [id.]. LPO, Solti.

Solti's LPO coupling of the little-known but splendid *No. 95 in C minor* and the *London symphony* is altogether superb and the LPO playing – smiling and elegant, yet full of bubbling vitality – is a constant joy. No. 95 has a striking sense of cohesion and purpose, and there is no finer version of No. 104. Solti uses a full body of strings and all the resources of modern wind instruments with the greatest possible finesse, yet the spontaneity of the music and the music-making is paramount. Top-drawer Decca sound (the record was made in the attractive acoustics of London's Henry Wood Hall) makes this an exceptionally natural-sounding CD.

Symphonies Nos. 96 in D (Miracle); 102 in B flat; Overture: La fedelta premiata.
**(*) Nimbus Dig. NI 5135 [id.]. Austro-Hungarian Haydn O, Adám Fischer.

Though the coupling of the sparkling overture to *La fedelta premiata* is rather less than generous, this separate issue can be warmly recommended alongside the complete cycle of the *London symphonies*, from which the two symphony recordings are taken. The *Adagio* of No. 102 is particularly sympathetic.

Symphonies Nos. 99 in E flat; 101 in D (Clock).
*** EMI Dig. CDC7 49634-2 [id.]. ECO, Jeffrey Tate.

Tate's coupling of No. 99 and the *Clock* completes his set of the last six Haydn symphonies. With comparable success, he generally adopts speeds broader than have become customary in the age of period performance, but with light, transparent textures. The 6/8 finale of the *Clock* is particularly delightful at Tate's relaxed speed, with rhythms skipping instead of rushing headlong. A fine recommendation for traditionalists.

Symphonies Nos. 100 in G (Military); 104 in D (London).
*** Ph. 411 449-2 [id.]. Concg. O, C. Davis.
*** O-L Dig. 411 833-2 [id.]. AAM, Hogwood.

Sir Colin Davis's coupling has genuine stature and can be recommended without reservation of any kind. The playing of the Concertgebouw Orchestra is as sensitive as it is brilliant, and Davis is unfailingly penetrating. The performances also benefit from excellent recorded sound, with fine clarity and definition.

Those looking for performances on period instruments will find Hogwood's accounts are uncommonly good ones and offer much better playing than was the case in some of his Mozart cycle. The wind execution is highly accomplished and the strings well blended and in tune. The change in the balance in the orchestral texture is often quite striking, particularly where the bassoon cuts through the lower strings. The 'Turkish' percussion instruments in the *Military symphony* are most effectively placed, and the performances are not only vital but also splendidly paced. The recording has clarity and presence. An altogether impressive issue.

Symphonies Nos. 101 in D (Clock); 103 in E flat (Drum Roll).
(B) *** CfP CD-CFP 4530. RPO, Beecham.

Beecham's 1960 coupling is self-recommending at bargain price (it would still be if it cost far more). He does not use authentic texts – he was a law unto himself in such matters – but the spirit of Haydn is ever present – just listen to the delicious way he handles the tick-tock of the *Clock symphony*, especially at its reprise. These works have rarely sounded as captivating and glowing as they do in his hands. The CD remastering provides fresh, clean sound, slightly fuller in the *Drum Roll* than in its companion. There is some background noise, but it is not intrusive.

Symphony No. 104 in D (London).
(M) (**) DG mono 427 776-2 [id.]. BPO, Furtwängler – MOZART: *Symphony No. 39.*(**)

As one of Furtwängler's recently rediscovered wartime recordings, this account of No. 104 brings limited sound that tends to crumble in tuttis, but the performance consistently reveals what a fine classicist he could be, with an exuberant *allegro* in the first movement, a spaciously lyrical slow movement (but with appoggiatura interpreted oddly), a solidly weighty minuet and an exhilarating, sunny finale. This and the Mozart coupling are among the finest of the wartime Furtwängler series.

CHAMBER MUSIC

Baryton trios Nos. 63 in D; 64 in D; 82 in C; 87 in A min.; 88 in A; 107 in D, 110 in C.
(M) *** EMI CDM7 69836-2 [id.]. Esterhazy Baryton Trio.

These EMI recordings were made in 1980 and they sound admirably fresh. The playing is expert and lively. Although Haydn did not pour his finest inspiration into this medium, there are some good moments in all these *Trios*, and this disc has a price advantage over its competitors.

Baryton trios Nos. 71 in A; 96 in B min.; 113 in D; 126 in C.
*** Gaudeamus CDGAU 109 [id.]. John Hsu, Miller, Arico.

Baryton trios Nos. 87 in A min.; 97 in D (Fatto per la felicissima nascita de S:ai:S Principe Estorhazi); 101 in C; 111 in G.
*** Gaudeamus CDGAU 104 [id.]. John Hsu, Miller, Arico.

Prince Esterházy was particularly fond of the baryton, whose delicate sonorities much appealed to him, and was a keen amateur player himself. During his years at Eisenstadt, Haydn composed 126 trios for his delectation. As John Hsu puts it on the sleeve, 'the baryton is a kind of viola da gamba with a broadened neck, behind which is a harp . . . the metal harp-strings are exposed within the open-box-like back of the neck so that they may be plucked by the thumb of the left hand'. These are most beguiling performances which have subtlety and finesse. Natural and well-balanced recorded sound. The second collection is no less desirable than the first.

Duo sonatas for violin and viola Nos. 1–6.
(BB) *** Hung. White Label HRC 071 [id.]. Dénes Kovács, Géza Németh.

Haydn composed these six duos some time in the late 1760s. They are all structured similarly: a central adagio is framed by a moderately fast opening movement and a closing Minuet; but Haydn's diversity of invention seems inexhaustible. The performances here are expert and spontaneous – the players are obviously enjoying the music, and so do we. The recording too is well balanced and has fine presence and realism. Ideal repertoire for a super-bargain label!

Piano trios, Hob XV, Nos. 24–27.
(M) *** Ph. 422 831-2 [id.]. Beaux Arts Trio.

These are all splendid works. No. 25 with its *Gypsy rondos* is the most famous, but each has a character of its own, showing the mature Haydn working at full stretch (they are contemporary with the *London symphonies*). The playing here is peerless and the recording truthful and refined.

String quartets: in E flat, Op. 1/0; Nos. 43 in D min., Op. 42; 83 in B flat, Op. 103.
**(*) Mer. ECD 88117 [id.]. English Qt.

This disc explores off-the-beaten-track and rarely played Haydn. The Op. 1, 'No. 0', is no masterpiece but has distinct charm, particularly when it is as well played as it is here. These fine players rise to all the challenges posed by this music, and the recorded sound is eminently truthful. There would have been room for another *Quartet* on this disc, which offers rather short measure at 43 minutes.

String quartets Nos. 1 in B flat, Op. 1/1; 67 in D, Op. 64/5 (Lark); 74 in G min., Op. 74/3 (Rider).
*** DG Dig. 423 622-2 [id.]. Hagen Qt.

The Hagen are supple, cultured and at times perhaps a little overcivilized, but in these three Haydn quartets they play flawlessly and are wonderfully alert and intelligent. This is real chamber-music-making; and the recording, made in the Cologne Radio Sendesaal, is perfectly balanced: in fact it could not be improved upon.

String quartets Nos. 17 in F (Serenade), Op. 3/5; 38 in E flat (Joke), Op. 33/2; 76 in D min. (Fifths), Op. 76/2.
(M) *** Decca 425 422-2 [id.]. Janáček Qt.

These performances are strong and dedicated, and careful to sense that the style of Haydn is not that of either Beethoven or Mozart. The music itself is highly civilized; whether Haydn or Hoffstetter wrote that delicious tune which forms the slow movement of the *Serenade quartet* seems irrelevant; it is an attractive little work and makes a good foil for the really splendid music of its companions. The recording (mid-1960s' vintage) always had good presence; the CD brings even more striking tangibility and plenty of body, within a well-judged ambience.

String quartets Nos. 17 in F (Serenade), Op. 3/5; 63 in D (Lark), Op. 64/5; 76 in D min. (Fifths), Op. 76/2.
(M) *** Ph. 426 097-2 [id.]. Italian Qt.

First-class playing here, although the first movement of the *Lark* is a bit measured in feeling and could do with more sparkle. The *Serenade quartet* is made to sound inspired, its famous slow movement played with exquisite gentleness. The *D minor Quartet* is admirably poised and classical in feeling. This rivals the grouping by the Janáček Quartet on Decca, but the remastered Philips recording, although refined, is drier: the Decca has more bloom and warmth.

String quartets Nos. 32 in C, Op. 20/2; 44 in B flat, Op. 50/1; 76 in D min. (Fifths), Op. 76/2.
*** ASV Dig. CDDCA 622 [id.]. Lindsay Qt.

Obviously, since these are public performances, one has to accept music-making reflecting the heat of the occasion, the odd sense of roughness (the finale of Op. 76, No. 2), for these artists take risks – and this is perhaps a shade faster than it would be in a studio. There is splendid character in these performances and plenty of musical imagination. These readings have a spontaneity which is refreshing in these days of retakes! The recordings are eminently truthful and audience noise is minimal.

String quartets Nos. 37–42, Op. 33/1–6.
*** Hung. HCD 11887/8-2 [id.]. Tátrai Qt.

The Tátrai recording comes from 1979 and maintains the generally high standard of the cycle; in other words, the playing is unfailingly musical and intelligent, and the recording eminently acceptable. There is no current alternative, though it can be only a matter of time before the Lindsays record them.

String quartets Nos. 50–56 (The Seven Last Words of our Saviour on the cross), Op. 51.
*** Olympia Dig. OCD 171 [id.]. Shostakovich Qt.
**(*) Ph. Dig. 412 878-2 [id.]. Kremer, Rabus, Causse, Iwasaki.

String quartets Nos. 50–56 (The Seven Last Words of our Saviour on the Cross), Op. 51; 83 in B flat, Op. 103.
(BB) ***** Naxos Dig. 8.550346 [id.]. Kodály Qt.**

The Kodály Quartet give an outstanding performance, strongly characterized and beautifully played, with subtle contrasts of expressive tension between the seven inner slow movements. They also offer an appropriate bonus in Haydn's last, unfinished, two-movement *Quartet*. He was working on this in 1803, at about the same time as he directed his last public concert, which was *The Seven Last Words*. The recording is first rate, vividly present yet naturally balanced, like the other isssues in this attractive Naxos series.

The Shostakovich Quartet gives an eloquent and thoughtful account of Haydn's score. There is no overstatement and no point-making, yet the playing is tremendously felt – and they are a quartet who produce a beautifully integrated and cultured sound, not a body of distinguished soloists as is the case with Kremer on Philips. This present performance sounds totally natural and unforced.

This Philips account does not displace the Shostakovich, either as a performance or as a recording; but it is a useful addition to the catalogue. Moreover, the CD brings sound of remarkable realism, recorded within a most attractive ambience.

String quartets Nos. 57 in G; 58 in C; 59 in E, Op. 54/1–3.
*** ASV Dig. CDDCA 582 [id.]. Lindsay Qt.
*** Virgin Dig. VC 790719-2 [id.]. Endellion Qt.

This is a relatively neglected set, though the second, the *C major* (placed last on this ASV recording), is a profound and searching masterpiece, while the *G major* gives a taste of the high-flying violin writing that distinguishes the set. The playing of the Lindsay Quartet is splendidly poised and vital, and the recording is very fine indeed.

The Endellion Quartet on Virgin are recorded at The Maltings, Snape, which provides the ideal acoustic environment. The playing is bright-eyed, fresh and vital. The overall sound is beautifully integrated and there are many moments of musical insight. Yet the Lindsays' insights go deeper into this movement, even if at times they have marginally less surface polish. All the same, if theirs remains a first preference, the Endellions are so good and so well recorded that they deserve a strong recommendation.

String quartets Nos. 69 in B flat; 70 in D; 71 in E flat, Op. 71/1–3; 72 in C; 73 in F; 74 in G min. (Reiter), Op. 74/1–3 (Apponyi quartets).
(BB) *** Naxos Dig. 8.550394 (*Nos. 69–71*); 8.550396 (*Nos. 72–74*) [id.]. Kódaly Qt.
*** Hung. HCD 12246/7-2 [id.]. Tátrai Qt.

The *Apponyi quartets* (so named because their 'onlie begetter' was Count Antal Apponyi) are among the composer's finest. The Naxos recordings by the Kodály Quartet are outstanding in every way and would be highly recommendable even without their considerable price advantage. The performances are superbly shaped, naturally paced and alive; the playing is cultivated, yet it has depth of feeling too, and the group readily communicate their pleasure in this wonderful music. The second disc, offering the three Op. 74 *Quartets*, is particularly fine, although the performance of Op. 71/3, a superb work, is hardly less memorable. The digital recording has vivid presence and just the right amount of ambience: the effect is entirely natural.

Hungaroton have chosen to issue these performances by the Tátrai Quartet, rather than commission new ones from their expert younger ensembles such as the Eder or the Takács – a wise decision, since these are civilized, selfless readings that never deflect the listener's attention away from Haydn's inexhaustible invention. The sound is natural.

String quartets Nos. 69 in B flat; 70 in D, Op. 71/1–2.
*** Hyp. CDA 66095 [id.]. Salomon Qt.

String quartets Nos. 71 in E flat, Op. 71/3; 72 in C, Op. 74/1.
*** Hyp. CDA 66098 [id.]. Salomon Qt.

String quartets Nos. 73 in F; 74 in G min., Op. 74/2–3.
*** Hyp. CDA 66124 [id.]. Salomon Qt.

The Opp. 71 and 74 *Quartets* belong to the same period as the first set of *Salomon symphonies* (1791–2) and are grander and more 'public' than any of their predecessors. The appropriately named Salomon Quartet use period instruments. They are vibrato-less but vibrant; the sonorities, far from being nasal and unpleasing, are clean and transparent. There is imagination and vitality here, and the Hyperion recording is splendidly truthful. Its clarity is further enhanced in the CD transfers.

String quartets Nos. 69 in B flat; 70 in D; 71 in E flat, Op. 71/1–3; 72 in C; 73 in F; 74 in G min. (Reiter), Op. 74/1–3; Op. 77/1–2; in D min., Op. 103.
(M) *** DG 429 189-2 (3) [id.]. Amadeus Qt.

This excellent set shows the Amadeus on their finest form; there is a sense of spontaneity as well as genuine breadth to these readings. Haydn's late quartets have much the same expansiveness and depth as the symphonies, and here the Amadeus succeed in conveying both their intimacy and their scale. The recordings have a warm acoustic and plenty of presence.

String quartets Nos. 72 in C; 73 in F; 74 in G min., Op. 74/1–3.
*** Virgin Dig. VC 791097-2 [id.]. Endellion Qt.

The Endellion Quartet are also proving sound guides to this rewarding repertoire; this record can be recommended alongside their comparably well-played and -recorded set of Op. 54.

String quartets Nos. 75 in G; 76 in D min. (Fifths); 77 in C (Emperor); 78 in B flat (Sunrise); 79 in D; 80 in E flat, Op. 76/1–6.
*** Hung. mono HCD 12812/3-2 [id.]. Tátrai Qt.
(M) **(*) DG 415 867-2 (2) [id.]. Amadeus Qt.

The Tátrai's classic set of the *Erdödy Quartets* is ageless and always much admired. These performances are unforced and natural, as intimate as if they were playing for pleasure, and as authoritative as one could hope for. The splendours of this set are as inexhaustible as those of the Beaux Arts set of the *Trios*. What will surprise many collectors is the quality of the mono sound, which is in many ways more congenial than some more recent records. A very strong recommendation on all counts – artistic and technical.

The Amadeus performances are certainly polished but, by the side of the Tátrai, relatively mannered. Norbert Brainin's vibrato is a little tiresome on occasion; but, generally speaking, there is much to reward the listener here; the recordings are vivid and they have enhanced realism and presence in their new CD format. They are also offered at mid-price. But the Tátrai mono set is the one to buy.

String quartets Nos. 76 in D min. (Fifths); 77 in C (Emperor); 78 in B flat (Sunrise), Op. 76/2–4.
*** Teldec/WEA Dig. 2292 43062-2 [id.]. Eder Qt.

The Eder is a Hungarian quartet whose players command a refined and beautiful tone, with generally excellent ensemble and polish. These are elegant performances that are unlikely to disappoint even the most demanding listener, save perhaps in the finale of the *Emperor*, which they take a little too quickly. But this is unfailingly thoughtful quartet-playing whose internal balance and tonal blend are practically flawless. The recording is altogether excellent.

String quartet No. 77 in C (Emperor), Op. 77/3.
* DG Dig. 427 657-2 [id.]. Emerson Qt – MOZART: *String quartets Nos. 17 & 19.**

The Emerson group produce quartet-playing of remarkable virtuosity and stunning ensemble. One can only wonder in amazement at their brilliance, definition and clarity. However, it is all very thrustful and over-projected, and quite uncongenial as Haydn playing. The Mozart with which it is coupled is even worse. In terms of skill, this deserves more than three stars – but as a musical experience one is at a loss to rate it!

String quartets Nos. 78 in B flat (Sunrise); 80 in E flat, Op. 76/4 & 6.
*** Ph. Dig. 410 053-2 [id.]. Orlando Qt.

One of the best Haydn quartet records currently available. The playing has eloquence, vitality and warmth; there is a keen sense of rhythm, and phrases breathe with refreshing naturalness. Moreover Philips have given this fine ensemble first-rate recorded sound.

KEYBOARD MUSIC

Piano sonatas Nos. 31 in A flat, Hob XVI/46; 33 in C min., Hob XVI/20; 60 in C, Hob XVI/50; Andante with variations in F min., Hob XVII/6.
** LDR Dig. LDRCD 1010 [id.]. Yeo Ean Mei.

Yeo Ean Mei is an intelligent player who gives sympathetic accounts of all these pieces. Her *F minor Variations* are a good deal less controversial than Pletnev's, though she is not an artist of his calibre. For all the merits of these performances, there are more characterful accounts of these *Sonatas* in the catalogue.

Piano sonatas: No. 33 in C min., Hob XVI/20; 38 in F, Hob XVI/23; 58 in C, Hob XVI/48; 60 in C, Hob XVI/50.
*** CBS Dig. MK 44918 [id.]. Emanuel Ax.

Emanuel Ax offers four *Sonatas*, two of which duplicate Mikhail Pletnev's remarkable disc. Ax is a fine stylist and his playing is full of colour, without being quite so personal. He brings sparkle, refined musicianship and fluent fingers to these pieces and he is well enough recorded. There is a faint halo of resonance round the aural image, but the reverberation is not excessive. An enjoyable recital.

Piano sonatas Nos. 33 in C min., Hob XVI/20; 47 in B min., Hob XVI/32; 53 in E min., Hob XVI/34; 50 in D, Hob XVI/37; 54 in G, Hob XVI/40; 56 in D, Hob XVI/42; 58 in C; 59 in E flat; 60 in C; 61 in D; 62 in E flat, Hob XVI/48–52; Adagio in F, Hob XVII/9; Andante with variations in F min., Hob XVII/6; Fantasia in C, Hob XVII/4.
*** Ph. 416 643-2 (4). Alfred Brendel.

This collection offers some of the best Haydn playing on record – and some of the best Brendel, too. There are eleven sonatas in all, together with the *F minor Variations* and the *C major Fantasia* (or *Capriccio*). They have been recorded over a number of years and are splendidly characterized and superbly recorded. The first is analogue, the remainder digital.

Piano sonatas Nos. 33 in C min., Hob XVI/20; 58 in C, Hob XVI/48; 60 in C, Hob XVI/50.
*** Denon Dig. C37 7801 [id.]. András Schiff.

Those who do not respond to Brendel's strong keyboard personality and find his Haydn a shade self-conscious should consider this disc. Schiff plays with an extraordinary refinement and delicacy; he is resourceful and highly imaginative in his use of tone-colour; his phrasing and articulation are a constant source of pleasure. Superb in every way and beautifully recorded, too.

Piano sonatas: 33 in C min., Hob XVI/20; 60 in C, Hob XVI/50; 62 in E flat, Hob XVI/52; Andante & Variations in F min., Hob XVII/6.
*** Virgin Dig. VC 790839-2 [id.]. Mikhail Pletnev.

Pletnev's reading of the *Sonatas* is full of personality and character. The *C major* is given with great elegance and wit, and the great *E flat Sonata* is magisterial. This playing has a masterly authority, and Pletnev is very well recorded. No Haydn collection should be without these thoughtful and individual performances. Three stars for everything in this recital except the *F minor Variations*, which is shorn of repeats and gravitas.

Piano sonatas Nos. 38 in F, Hob XVI/23; 51 in E flat, Hob XVI/38; 52 in G, HobXVI/39.
*** Mer. CDE 84155 [id.]. Julia Cload.

Julia Cload's cool, direct style is heard at its best in her second group of sonatas. The clean articulation in the first movement of the *F major* is matched by her thoughtfulness in the *Adagio*, and the other performances have the same mixture of boldness and introversion. The piano image is bright and clear, with just a touch of hardness on *fortes*;

one wonders, incidentally, why Meridian have not recorded her digitally; there is a degree of background noise here.

Piano sonatas Nos. 47 in B min., Hob XVI/32; 53 in E min., Hob XVI/34; 56 in D, Hob XVI/42; Adagio in F, Hob XVII/9; Fantasia in C, Hob XVII/4.
*** Ph. Dig. 412 228-2 [id.]. Alfred Brendel.

These performances are held together marvellously, self-aware at times, as many great performances are, but inspiriting and always governed by the highest intelligence. The *B minor Sonata* has a *Sturm und Drang* urgency, and Brendel's account has vitality and character. Moreover the recording is splendidly realistic.

Piano sonatas Nos. 50 in D, Hob XVI/37; 54 in G, Hob XVI/40; 55 in B flat, Hob XVI/41; Adagio in F, Hob XVII/9.
*** Mer. ECD 84083 [id.]. Julia Cload.

Julia Cload's playing is fresh, characterful and intelligent, and will give considerable pleasure. She has the advantage of very truthful recorded sound.

Piano sonatas Nos. 50 in D, Hob XVI/37; 54 in G, Hob XVI/40; 62 in E flat, Hob XVI/52; Andante with variations in F min., Hob XVII/6.
*** Ph. Dig. 416 365-2 [id.]. Alfred Brendel.

Brendel at his finest, and Philips, too: he is splendidly recorded. The playing has a jewelled precision – not perhaps to all tastes (some will find it too self-aware). However, its intelligence and artistry will win over most collectors.

VOCAL MUSIC

The Creation (Die Schöpfung).
*** DG Dig. 419 765-2 (2) [id.]. Blegen, Popp, Moser, Ollmann, Moll, Bav. R. Ch. & SO, Bernstein.
*** Ph. 416 449-2 [id.]. Mathis, Fischer-Dieskau, Baldin, Ch. & ASMF, Marriner.
**(*) DG Dig. 410 718-2 (2) [id.]. Mathis, Araiza, Van Dam, V. Singverein, VPO, Karajan.

(i) *The Creation;* (ii) *Mass No. 7 in B flat (Little organ mass): Missa brevis Sancti Johannis de Deo.*
(M) *** Decca 425 968 (2). (i; ii) Ameling; (i) Krenn, Krause, Spoorenberg, Fairhurst; (ii) P. Planyavsky (organ); (i; ii) V. State Op. Ch., VPO, Münchinger.

Bernstein's version, recorded at a live performance in Munich, uses a relatively large chorus, encouraging him to adopt rather slow speeds at times. What matters is the joy conveyed in the story-telling, with the finely disciplined chorus and orchestra producing incandescent tone, blazing away in the big set-numbers, and the performance is compulsive from the very opening bars. Five soloists are used instead of three, with the parts of Adam and Eve sung by nicely contrasted singers. So the charming, golden-toned Lucia Popp is a warmly human Eve, to contrast with the more silvery and ethereal Gabriel of Judith Blegen; and Kurt Ollmann as Adam is lighter and less magisterial than his angelic counterpart, Kurt Moll as Raphael who, with his dark bass tone, produces the most memorable singing of all. Bernstein's tenor, Thomas Moser, combines a lyrical enough quality with heroic weight, confirming this as an unusually persuasive version, well recorded in atmospheric sound.

With generally fast tempi Marriner draws consistently lithe and resilient playing and singing from his St Martin's team. There is no lack of weight in the result, although you might count Dietrich Fischer-Dieskau in the baritone role as too weighty, recorded rather close, but his inflexion of every word is intensely revealing. The soprano Edith Mathis is very sweet of tone if not always quite as steady as some of her rivals on record. The one notable snag is that Aldo Baldin's tenor is not well focused by the microphones. Otherwise the 1980 analogue recording still sounds first rate.

Münchinger provides an excellent mid-price *Creation*. It is a fine performance that stands up well, even in comparison with Karajan's digital set, and the Decca recording is much better balanced. Münchinger has rarely conducted with such electric tension on record and although his direct style is squarer by comparison with Marriner, his soloists make a satisfying team. The set also includes Haydn's *Little organ mass*, so called because the solo organ is used to add colour to the soprano's *Benedictus*, a most delightful setting. Ameling here matches her appealing contribution to the main work and the choral singing is pleasingly crisp. The sound is first class, the remastering highly successful.

Karajan's digital recording is taken from a live performance given at the Salzburg Festival in 1982. Not surprisingly, it cannot match the perfection of his earlier one either in musical ensemble or in recording balance, but there are many compensations, for there is greater warmth in the later version and the choruses brim with joy at speeds generally a degree more relaxed. Edith Mathis gives a sweeter-toned performance than she did for Marriner on Philips, though the close balancing of voices is hardly flattering to any of the soloists. The sense of presence is what matters, and this is a fine memento of a powerful, glowing occasion.

The Creation: Arias and choruses.
(M) **(*) DG Dig. 429 489-2 [id.] (from above recording with Mathis, Murray, VPO; cond. Karajan).

This is a generous disc of excerpts, offering 72 minutes' playing time, but, without the continuity of the complete work, the ear is drawn even more to notice the contrived balance.

The Creation (complete; in English).
(M) **(*) EMI CMS7 69894-2 (2) [id.]. Harper, Tear, Shirley-Quirk, King's College Ch., ASMF, Willcocks.

Quite apart from the fact that it is based on Milton, the idea of *The Creation* was first presented to Haydn in the form of an English libretto provided by the impresario Salomon. David Willcocks captures the work's genial, spirited vigour and it is good to have 'the flexible tiger' and 'the nimble stag' so vividly portrayed. Though Heather Harper is not always quite as steady or sweet-toned as usual, this is a first-rate team of soloists, and the choral singing and the playing of the Academy could hardly be more stylish.

Mass No. 2 in F (Missa brevis).
*** O-L 421 654-2 [id.]. Kirkby, Nelson, Ch. of Christ Church Cathedral, Oxford, AAM, Preston – HANDEL: *Anthem for Foundling Hospital* etc.***

Haydn wrote the early *Missa brevis* when he was seventeen. The setting is engagingly unpretentious; some of its sections last for under two minutes and none takes more than three and a half. The two soprano soloists here match their voices admirably and the effect is delightful.

Mass No. 3 in C (Missa Cellensis): Missa Sanctae Caeciliae.
*** O-L Dig. 417 125-2 [id.]. Nelson, Cable, Hill, Thomas, Ch. of Christ Church
Cathedral, AAM, Preston.

The *Missa Cellensis* (also known as the *Missa Sanctae Caeciliae*) is Haydn's longest
setting of the liturgy; the *Gloria* alone (in seven cantata-like movements) lasts nearly half
an hour. Preston directs an excellent performance with fine contributions from choir and
soloists, set against a warmly reverberant acoustic.

Masses Nos (i) *5 in E flat (Missa in honorem Beatissimae Virginis Mariae), Hob XXII/4;*
(ii) *6 in G (Missa Sancti Nicolai), Hob XXII/6; Missa rorate coeli desuper, Hob XXII/3.*
*** O-L 421 478-2 [id.]. Christ Church Cathedral Ch., Oxford, AAM, Preston, with (i)
Nelson, Watkinson, Hill, Thomas; (ii) Nelson, Minty, Covey-Crump, Thomas.

In the early *E flat Mass* Haydn followed the rococo conventions of his time, dutifully
giving weight to the *Gloria* and *Credo* in culminating fugues but generally adopting a style
featuring Italianate melody which to modern ears inevitably sounds operatic. One
intriguing point is Haydn's use of a pair of cors anglais, which add a touch of darkness to
the scoring. The *Missa Sancti Nicolai* dates from 1772 but has a comparable freshness of
inspiration. The performance is first rate in every way, even finer than that of the earlier
Mass, beautifully sung, with spontaneity in every bar and a highly characterized
accompaniment. The little *Missa rorate coeli desuper* was written by Haydn when he was
still a choirboy in Vienna, and it may well be his earliest surviving work. Not everything
is perfunctory, for the *Agnus Dei* has a touching gravity. The whole work lasts for just
under eight minutes. Excellent recording ensures that this CD receives a warm welcome.

Masses Nos. 7 in B flat: Missa brevis Sancti Joannis de Deo (Little organ mass); 13 in B
flat (Schöpfungsmesse).
** EMI Dig. CDC7 54002-2 [id.]. Hendricks, Murray, Blochwitz, Hölle, Leipzig R. Ch.,
Dresden State O, Marriner.

Marriner couples the last but one of the masterpieces which Haydn wrote during his
retirement for the nameday of Princess Esterhazy with a fascinating work written a
quarter-century earlier. In the manner of a *Missa brevis*, it compresses the liturgy by
getting different voices to sing different lines simultaneously, so that the *Gloria* takes only
48 seconds. Both in that and in the much later work, Marriner favours brisk speeds,
defying the weight of his forces, which is increased by the bass-heavy Dresden recording.
Though the Leipzig Radio Choir is sometimes stressed, as are the soloists, these are
enjoyably vigorous readings. It is worth noting that Decca may well reissue this same
coupling – as it did for a time on LP and cassette – in the classic versions made by St
John's College Choir and Marriner's Academy of St Martin's. Those are more in scale –
with fresh trebles in the choir – and more infectiously resilient.

Mass No. 11 in D min. (Nelson): Missa in angustiis.
(M) ******* Decca 421 146-2. Stahlman, Watts, Wilfred Brown, Krause, King's College,
Cambridge, Ch., LSO, Willcocks – VIVALDI: *Gloria.********

Mass No. 11 in D min. (Nelson); Te Deum in C, Hob XXIIIc/2.
*** DG Dig. 423 097-2 [id.]. Lott, C. Watkinson, Maldwyn Davies, Wilson-Johnson, Ch.
& E. Concert, Pinnock.

The *Nelson Mass* (*Missa in angustiis*: Mass in times of fear) brings a superb choral
offering from Trevor Pinnock and the English Concert. Using a larger band of strings

than in his highly successful recordings of Baroque instrumental music, Pinnock brings home the high drama of Haydn's autumnal inspiration. The extraordinary instrumentation at the very start, with organ replacing wind, and horns and trumpets made all the more prominent, has never sounded more menacing. With incandescent singing from the chorus and fine matching from excellent soloists (Felicity Lott in exceptionally sweet voice), the exuberance of the *Gloria* is then brought home all the more by contrast. Misplaced accents, almost jazzy, add to the joyful exhilaration. Similarly exuberant syncopations mark the magnificent setting of the *Te Deum*, which comes as a very valuable makeweight. The inspiration of such music leaps forward from the eighteenth century all the more excitingly in an authentic performance such as this. Excellent, full-blooded sound, with good definition.

The CD of the famous Willcocks account, recorded by Argo in 1962, does not quite manage to control the focus of the resonant King's acoustic, but the effect is admirably full-bodied and vivid; those not wanting to stretch to Pinnock's full-priced digital CD will find this a satisfactory alternative with its very generous Vivaldi coupling.

Mass No. 14 in B flat (Harmoniemesse).
**(*) Hung. Dig. HCD 12360 [id.]. Tokody, Takács, Gulyas, Gregor, Slovak Philh. O and Ch., Ferencsik.

With four of Hungary's outstanding singers as soloists, Ferencsik conducts a recording of Haydn's last, masterly setting of the Mass with speeds generally on the slow side, and the weight of sound from the relatively large choir brings some lack of clarity, if no lack of vigour. Ferencsik gains in such a passage as the *Gratias* in the *Gloria*. The pure originality of the writing, with Haydn determined not simply to repeat himself in words he had set so often, is consistently brought out – as in the minor-key switch on *Et resurrexit* and the light, molto allegro *Benedictus*, not to mention the explosive triumph of the final *Dona nobis pacem*. Excellent digital recording.

Il ritorno di Tobia (oratorio).
** Hung. HCD 11660/2-2 (3) [id.]. Bende, Takács, Fülöp, Kincses, Kalmár, Budapest Madrigal Ch., Hungarian State O, Szekeres.

Il ritorno di Tobia, telling the biblical story of Tobit, was Haydn's first oratorio, an extended parable of light after darkness. This is a worthy attempt to revive it, but, even with first-rate playing and generally good singing, Ferenc Szekeres fails to conceal the longueurs, not helped by unimaginative continuo playing. The finest singing comes from the two sopranos, Magda Kalmár and Veronika Kincses – the latter brilliant in her extended aria with its multiple obbligato. The tenor, Attila Fülöp, is disappointing in the title-role, but the choral singing is fresh and bright, to match the recording.

The Seasons (Die Jahreszeiten; oratorio): complete (in German).
(M) *** DG 423 922-2 (2) [id.]. Janowitz, Schreier, Talvela, VSO, Boehm.
*** Ph. Dig. 411 428-2 (2) [id.]. Mathis, Jerusalem, Fischer-Dieskau, Ch. & ASMF, Marriner.
(M) **(*) Decca 425 708-2 (2). Cotrubas, Krenn, Sotin, Brighton Fest. Ch., RPO, Dorati.
(M) **(*) EMI CMS7 69224-2 (2) [Ang. CDMB 69224]. Janowitz, Hollweg, Berry, Ch. of German Op., BPO, Karajan.

The Seasons: highlights.
(M) **(*) EMI CDM7 69010-2 [id.] (from above recording; cond. Karajan).

This work, essentially genial, is an expression of a simple faith and of a human being to whom life on the whole has been kind, and who was duly grateful to record the many earthly pleasures he had enjoyed. Boehm's performance enters totally into the spirit of the music. The soloists are excellent and characterize the music fully; the chorus sing enthusiastically and are well recorded. But it is Boehm's set. He secures fine orchestral playing throughout, an excellent overall musical balance and real spontaneity in music that needs this above all else. The CD transfer of the 1967 recording is admirably managed; the sound overall is a little drier, but the chorus have plenty of body and there is an excellent sense of presence.

Sir Neville Marriner offers (at full price) a superbly joyful performance of Haydn's last oratorio. Edith Mathis and Dietrich Fischer-Dieskau are as stylish and characterful as one would expect, pointing the words as narrative. Siegfried Jerusalem is both heroic of timbre and yet delicate enough for Haydn's most elegant and genial passages. The chorus and orchestra, of authentic size, add to the freshness. The recording, made in St John's, Smith Square, is warmly reverberant, with vivid detail.

Dorati brings to the work an innocent dedication, at times pointing to the folk-like inspiration, which is most compelling. This is not as polished an account as Boehm's in the same price range but, with excellent solo singing and bright chorus work, is enjoyable in its own right. The choruses of peasants in Part 3, for instance, are boisterously robust. Textually there is an important difference in that Dorati has returned to the original version and restored the cuts in the introductions to *Autumn* and *Winter*, the latter with some wonderfully adventurous harmonies. The performance as a whole is highly animated. With Dorati, this is above all a happy work, a point made all the more telling by the immediacy of the new transfer.

Karajan's 1973 recording of *The Seasons* offers a fine, polished performance which is often very dramatic too. The characterization is strong, and in Karajan's hands the exciting Hunting chorus of Autumn (*Hört! Hört! Hört das laute Getön*) with its lusty horns anticipates *Der Freischütz*. The remastered sound is drier than the original but is vividly wide in dynamic range. Choruses are still a little opaque, but the soloists are all caught well and are on good form; and the overall balance is satisfactory. However, both Boehm and Marriner display a lighter, more human touch here; those drawn to Karajan might try the fairly generous (53 minutes) highlights CD.

Stabat Mater.
**(*) Erato/WEA Dig. 2292 45181-2 [id.]. Armstrong, Murray, Hill, Huttenlocher, Lausanne Vocal Ens. & CO, Corboz.

Haydn's *Stabat Mater*, one of his first major masterpieces, showing him at full stretch, was written in his early years at Esterháza. Scored for strings with oboes, the work is far bigger in aim than that scale might suggest, and some of the choruses include harmonic progressions which in their emotional overtones suggest music of a much later period. The Erato version offers brisk speeds; but it has an excellent quartet of soloists, fine choral singing of the kind we have come to expect from the Lausanne choir, and first-rate digital recording.

Te Deum in C, Hob XXIIIc/2.
(M) **(*) RCA GD 86535 [6535-2-RG]. V. Boys' Ch., Ch. Viennensis, VCO, Gillesberger
– MOZART: *Requiem mass; Ave verum.***(*)

A fine, vigorous account of the *Te Deum* by these Viennese forces, very vividly recorded, coupled to a not inconsiderable account of Mozart's *Requiem*. At mid-price it is excellent value.

COLLECTIONS

English songs: *Content; Despair; Fidelity; The lady's looking glass; Mermaid's song; O tuneful voice; Pastoral song; Piercing eyes; Pleasing pain; Recollection; Sailor's song; She never told her love; Spirit's song; Sympathy; The wanderer.* Folksong settings: *Cupido; Eine sehr gewöhnliche Geschichte; Der erste Kuss; Pensi a me si fido amante; Das strickende Mädchen; Un tello umil.*
*** Ph. 420 217-2 [id.]. Elly Ameling, Joerg Demus.

This very attractive recital displays the artless charm of Elly Ameling to perfection. The songs are simple but often touching. The celebrated ones like *The Sailor's song* (with its improbable refrain of 'hurly-burly') and *The Mermaid's song* are well matched by many others, equally rewarding, some with clear anticipations of nineteenth-century Lieder. Joerg Demus is a brightly sympathetic accompanist. The recording is sparkling and fresh and the playing time is generous.

OPERA

Armida: excerpts; *La vera constanza*: excerpts.
(M) *** Ph. 426 641-2 [id.]. Jessye Norman, Claes Ahnsjö, Lucerne CO, Dorati.

With both these operas currently out of the catalogue, this set of arias and duets is the more attractive, to whet the musical appetite for the complete works. Jessye Norman's voice is superbly captured in fine recording, with Claes Ahnsjö also impressive in two duets. Lively and sympathetic conducting from Dorati.

L'Infedeltà delusa.
**(*) HM/BMG RD 77099 (2) [77099-2-RC]. Argenta, Lootens, Prégardien, M. Schäfer, Varcoe, La Petite Bande, Sigiswald Kuijken.

More than Haydn's other operas, *L'infedeltà delusa* makes one wonder whether Mozart and Da Ponte had access to it before they created their three supreme operatic masterpieces. When the Act III finale is launched by the jealous Vespina slapping her beloved's face, it might almost be Susanna in *Figaro*. As there, the effect is totally refreshing, with sudden realism in the midst of formality. Some of the scenes are very complex for their period too. Musically, the surprises come less in the melodic writing which, in one jolly number after another, is relatively conventional, than in ear-catching twists and striking instrumental effects. Haydn was proud of the Esterhazy horns, for example, and they have some marvellous whooping to do. The plot of the opera is unusual for the time in giving the role of the heavy father to the tenor (well taken by Christoph Prégardien), reflecting the fact that it was expressly designed for Karl Friberth, literary adviser to Prince Esterhazy as well as a singer. This performance on period instruments nicely captures the flavour of a semi-domestic performance in the prince's country palace. Both the sopranos, Nancy Argenta and Lena Lootens, are agile and precise, if a little edgy. Both tenors, Markus Schäfer as well as Prégardien, are stressed by the range demanded; but, like the bass, Stephen Varcoe, they have clean voices, apt for Haydn on a small scale. The scale of the whole work, much shorter than was common in the late eighteenth century, makes it the more apt for revival today. *L'infedeltà delusa* may be no *Così fan tutte*, but this is a most enjoyable set, even if a reissue of Dorati's pioneering version for Philips using modern instruments, more strongly cast, will be a powerful contender when issued on CD.

Haydn, Michael (1737-1806)

Flute concerto in D.
(BB) ** Hung. White Label HRC 107 [id.]. Lóránt Kovács, Györ PO, Sándor – MOZART: *Flute concertos Nos. 1-2.***(*)

An agreeable if not distinctive work, well played and recorded.

Serenade in D; Symphony in D, P.11.
(BB) ** Hung. White Label HRC 100 [id.]. Budapest PO, János Sándor.

Michael Haydn's music represents a happy medium between the baroque and early classical styles. The *Serenade,* for small orchestra, is fairly ambitious, with six movements and an extended *Andante with variations* at its centre. It is undemanding but agreeably inventive, with anticipations of Mozart, notably in the lively first movement. Like the better-known *Symphony in D,* it receives an alert and stylish performance, and the sound is full and bright.

Divertimenti: in C, P. 98; in C, P. 115.
*** Denon Dig. C37 7119 [id.]. Holliger, Salvatore Qt – J. C. BACH: *Oboe quartet;* MOZART: *Adagio.****

Josef Haydn's brother is seriously neglected on record. Both these *Divertimenti* contain captivating and original inspirations. The longer of the two, P. 98, has a fizzing first movement and a joyful *Presto* finale, while P. 115 brings unexpected timbres. Well coupled and vividly recorded.

Hebden, John (18th century)

6 Concertos for strings (ed. Wood).
**(*) Chan. Dig. CHAN 8339 [id.]. Cantilena, Shepherd.

Little is known about John Hebden except that he was a Yorkshire composer who also played the cello and bassoon. These concertos are his only known works, apart from some flute sonatas. Although they are slightly uneven, at best the invention is impressive. The concertos usually feature two solo violins and are well constructed to offer plenty of contrast. The performances here are accomplished, without the last degree of polish but full of vitality. The recording is clear and well balanced, and given good presence.

Herbert, Victor (1859-1924)

Cello concertos Nos. 1 in D, Op. 8; 2 in E min., Op. 30; 5 Pieces for cello and strings (arr. Dennison).
*** Decca Dig. 417 672-2 [id.]. Lynn Harrell, ASMF, Marriner.

Herbert was himself a cello virtuoso and his *Second Cello concerto* was the piece which prompted Dvořák in his American period to take on the idea of writing his own great concerto. The note to this Decca record specifies the detailed points of resemblance observed by Lynn Harrell, and certainly his commanding performance presents the most convincing case for it. He couples it with the *First Concerto,* which is hardly less attractive. Harrell plays both works with endearing warmth and is given an accompaniment of comparable sympathy and flair. Most of the *Five pieces* were derived from piano music, but they do include one item conceived for cello and piano; each

499

movement here demonstrates Herbert's ability immediately to attract the attention with a striking gesture or idea, the gift which stood him in such good stead later when writing for the world of operetta. A most attractive disc: all the music repays repeated listening, and the performances and recording could hardly be more winning.

Hérold, Ferdinand (1791–1833)

La Fille mal gardée: extended excerpts.
🏵 *** EMI Dig. CDC7 49403-2. Royal Liverpool PO, Wordsworth.

Barry Wordsworth's scintillating account of a generous extended selection from the ballet on CD includes all the important sequences. With playing from the Royal Liverpool Philharmonic Orchestra that combines refinement and delicacy with wit and humour, this is very highly recommendable, with the EMI recording in the demonstration bracket.

Hertel, Johann (1727–89)

Trumpet concerto in D.
*** Ph. Dig. 420 203-2 [id.]. Hardenberger, ASMF, Marriner – HAYDN *** 🏵; HUMMEL *** 🏵; STAMITZ: *Concertos.***

Johann Hertel's *Trumpet concerto* is typical of many works of the same kind written in the Baroque era, with a highly placed solo line, a touch of melancholy in the *Largo* and plenty of opportunities for crisp tonguing in the finale. Håkan Hardenberger clearly relishes every bar and plays with great flair. He is stylishly accompanied and vividly recorded, though the acoustic is a shade resonant.

Hildegard of Bingen (1098–1179)

Hymns and sequences: *Ave generosa; Columba aspexit; O Ecclesia; O Euchari; O Jerusalem; O ignis spiritus; O presul vere civitatis; O viridissima virga.*
*** Hyp. CDA 66039 [id.]. Gothic Voices, Muskett, White, Page.

Abbess Hildegard of Bingen was one of the great mystics of her age. From 1141 onwards she was Abbess of the Benedictine order at Disibodenberg near Bingen, twenty-five miles south-west of Mainz. She was a naturalist, playwright and poetess as well as composer. Her series of visions, *Scivias*, occupied her for the best part of a decade (1141–51); this record draws on her collection of music and poetry, the *Symphonia armonie celestium revelationum* – 'the symphony of the harmony of celestial revelations'. These hymns and sequences, most expertly performed and recorded, have excited much acclaim – and rightly so. A lovely CD.

Hindemith, Paul (1895–1963)

Concert music for strings and brass, Op. 50; (i) *Horn concerto; Noblissima visione (suite); Symphony in B flat for concert band.*
(M) *** EMI CDH7 63373-2 [id.]. (i) Dennis Brain; Philh. O, composer.

Recorded in 1956, Hindemith's own performances with the Philharmonia Orchestra of four of his most characteristic works come out with astonishing vividness in this digital transfer of well over three decades later; indeed the sheer bloom of the sound and the naturalness of the balance suggest that it could have been made in the 1970s. The *Horn concerto* – distinctly laid out in two fast movements followed by a longer, more formal slow movement as summary – is dazzlingly played by its original performer, Dennis Brain. That has been available in stereo before this latest issue, but it is a revelation to have the other three works, notably the fine ballet score, *Nobilissima visione.* Though there is much in his output that is manufactured and arid, *Nobilissima visione,* the work he composed in the 1930s on the theme of St Francis, shows Hindemith at his most inspired. The slow movement has a grave beauty that is quite haunting, and its eloquence here should touch even those who regard him as normally outside their reach. There is also dignity and nobility in its splendid opening, and the composer proves a most persuasive interpreter of his own music, drawing refined and committed performances and finding wit in the *Symphony for concert band.* These 73 minutes of music make an ideal introduction to Hindemith's orchestral writing, and collectors can rest assured that the transfers are well managed throughout.

(i) *Concert music for brass and strings; Mathis der Maler* (symphony); (ii) *Viola concerto (Der Schwanendreher).*
(M) **(*) DG 423 241-2 [id.]. (i) Boston SO, Steinberg; (ii) Benyamini, O de Paris, Barenboim.

William Steinberg's accounts of *Mathis* and the *Concert music* were recorded in the early 1970s and are first class, even if the balance is a little recessed. The CD now carries a bonus in the shape of Daniel Benyamini's 1979 version of *Der Schwanendreher.* Hindemith was a fine violist and *Der Schwanendreher* is his third concerto for the instrument; it was completed only three months after he had finished work on *Mathis.* It is based on folksongs and the unusual title (*The Swan-Turner*) is of the tune he uses in the finale. Benyamini and the Orchestre de Paris under Barenboim give a very full-bodied account of it; Benyamini is rather forwardly balanced, but his rich (almost over-ripe) tone is glorious.

Cello concerto; (i) *Clarinet concerto.*
*** Etcetera KTC 1006 [id.]. Tibor de Machula; (i) George Pieterson; Concg. O, Kondrashin.

The 1940 *Cello concerto* is exhilarating and inventive, and Tibor de Machula proves an excellent protagonist. As always with Hindemith, the musical argument is rich in incident. The *Clarinet concerto* was written in 1947 for Benny Goodman, who gave its première with Ormandy and the Philadelphia Orchestra. It is not, however, jazz-inspired and is lyrical and eventful. The recordings (made in the Concertgebouw, Amsterdam) are public performances and emanate from the Hilversum Radio archives. Rewarding scores in eminently serviceable recordings.

Horn concerto.
(***) EMI CDC7 47834-2 [id.]. Brain, Philh. O, composer – R. STRAUSS: *Horn concertos.*(***)

This CD has been produced by Angel, the American offshoot of EMI International, and the transfer is acceptable. Unfortunately, the remastering of the Richard Strauss couplings has been inexpertly managed, with uningratiatingly thin orchestral textures. The CD documentation, too, is unsatisfactory.

(i) *The Four temperaments; Nobilissima visione.*
**(*) Delos Dig. D/CD 1006 [id.]. (i) Carole Rosenberger; RPO, James de Preist.

The Four temperaments, a set of variations on a three-part theme for piano and strings of 1940, is one of Hindemith's finest and most immediate works. Carole Rosenberger gives a formidable reading of this inventive and resourceful score. James de Preist also secures responsive playing from the RPO strings and gives a sober, well-shaped account of the *Nobilissima visione* suite, doing justice to its grave nobility. The recording is natural and well balanced but could be more transparent, particularly at the top end of the spectrum.

Mathis der Maler (Symphony).
(M) *** EMI CDM7 69242-2 [id.]. BPO, Karajan – BARTÓK: *Music for strings, percussion and celesta.***(*)
(*) Chan. CHAN 8533 [id.]. LSO, Horenstein – R. STRAUSS: *Death and transfiguration.*

Mathis der Maler (Symphony); *Symphonic metamorphoses on themes of Carl Maria von Weber; Trauermusik.*
*** Decca Dig. 421 523-2 [id.]. San Francisco SO, Blomstedt.

Mathis der Maler (Symphony); *Symphonic metamorphoses on themes of Carl Maria von Weber;* (i) *Theme and variations (The Four Temperaments).*
(M) (**(*)) DG mono 427 407-2 [id.]. (i) Hans Otte (piano); BPO, composer.

Blomstedt has a strong feeling for *Mathis der Maler* and presents a finely groomed and powerfully shaped performance, with lucid and transparent textures. The famous *Trauermusik*, written on the death of King George V, has an affecting quiet eloquence and dedication, and is infinitely more responsive to dynamic shading than any previous account: the solo viola, Geraldine Walther, is exceptionally sensitive. Blomstedt's reading of the *Symphonic metamorphoses on themes of Carl Maria von Weber* is appropriately light in touch; and the recording is exemplary in the naturalness of its balance.

Karajan's 1960 version of the *Mathis symphony* is beautifully spacious and among the very finest accounts of the work ever made. Karajan succeeds in producing a more refined and transparent texture, and both dynamic nuances and details of phrasing are attentively followed, without creating a sense of beautification. The recording is atmospheric too and has more body than the original LP, even if it is not as fine as Blomstedt's new Decca CD.

Horenstein's *Mathis der Maler* was the last record he made, and it has the merit of breadth and weight. The recording, originally issued by Unicorn, has been remastered satisfactorily; but this issue is overpriced: there are a number of stunning accounts of Richard Strauss's *Death and transfiguration* which eclipse Horenstein's. Nevertheless his admirers will probably want this reissue.

Hindemith made his recordings in 1955, just before the advent of stereo. In fact there is some constriction, particularly on climaxes, but the mono balance is remarkably good and the ears adjust quickly. The composer's tempi are more leisurely than most modern conductors'. The piano timbre in *The Four Temperaments* is a bit dry (the soloist is impressive) and, generally speaking, the quality in this fine piece is less confined than we remembered from the 1950s. Dated sound it may be, but it is good to have Hindemith himself back on CD. Let us hope DG will follow this with *Die Harmonie der Welt* and the marvellous *Symphonic dances.*

When lilacs last in the dooryard bloom'd.
*** Telarc Dig. CD 80132 [id.]. DeGaetani, Stone, Atlanta Ch. & SO, Robert Shaw.

Robert Shaw's record carries special authority, since it was he who commissioned

Hindemith to compose this 'Requiem for those we loved' at the end of the 1939–45 war. It is one of the composer's most deeply felt works and one of his best. Hindemith took Whitman's poem in memory of Lincoln and fashioned from it a requiem that is both non-liturgical and highly varied – not just recitatives and arias, but marches, passacaglias and fugue. Robert Shaw gives a performance of great intensity and variety of colour and nuance. Both his soloists are excellent, and there is both weight and subtlety in the orchestral contribution. Splendid recording.

Hoffmeister, Franz (1754–1812)

Flute concertos: in D; in G.
(B) **(*) ASV CDQS 6012 [id.]. Dingfelder, ECO, Mackerras; Leonard – C. P. E. BACH: *Concerto.***(*)

Franz Hoffmeister's two *Flute concertos* are elegantly inventive, if not distinctive. They are well recorded and make pleasant late-evening listening. The performances are sprightly and polished, and the accompaniments have plenty of spirit. The sound is brightly lit, but not excessively so.

Holst, Gustav (1874–1934)

(i) *Beni Mora (oriental suite), Op. 29/1;* (ii) *Brook Green suite;* (iii) *Egdon Heath, Op. 47; The Perfect Fool: ballet suite, Op. 39;* (iv) *St Paul's suite, Op. 29/2;* (v) *Festival Te Deum;* (vi) *Psalm 86.*
*** EMI CDC7 49784-2. (i) BBC SO, Sargent; (ii) ECO, Bedford; (iii) LSO, Previn; (iv) RPO, Sargent; (v) LSO Ch., St Paul's Cathedral choristers, LPO, Groves; (vi) Partridge, Purcell Singers, ECO, Imogen Holst.

An admirable and generous anthology, recorded during the 1960s and 1970s. All the performances are good ones and many are distinctive. *Beni Mora*, an attractively exotic piece that vividly shows Holst's flair for orchestration, is well played here under Sir Malcolm Sargent, while the account of the *St Paul's suite* is equally accomplished, full of verve and character. The *Brook Green suite* from Steuart Bedford is also lively and spontaneous. Previn gives a darkly intense performance of *Egdon Heath*, illuminatingly different from Boult's earlier version which was much more coolly detached. The rip-roaring ballet music from *The Perfect Fool* presents a colourful contrast. The *Short Festival Te Deum* comes from 1919; it takes only a little over four minutes and is an 'occasional' piece, less original than the *Hymn of Jesus*, written in the same year. The setting of Psalm 86, with its expressive tenor part sung beautifully by Ian Partridge, is also included in this bountiful compilation and is very well recorded; the success of this performance owes much to the inspired direction of the composer's daughter. The CD transfers are all well managed, and this compilation is indispensable for any true Holstian.

Invocation for cello and orchestra, Op. 19/2.
*** RCA RD 70800. Lloyd Webber, Philh. O, Handley – DELIUS: *Concerto;* VAUGHAN WILLIAMS: *Folksongs fantasia.****

Holst's *Invocation for cello and orchestra* is a highly attractive and lyrical piece, well worth reviving and a valuable addition to the growing Holst discography. Both the performance and recording are of admirable quality. The CD brings increased vividness, yet is strikingly refined. Recommended.

Military band suites Nos. 1–2.
⊛ *** Telarc Dig. CD 80038 [id.]. Cleveland Symphonic Winds, Fennell – HANDEL: *Royal Fireworks music.****

Military band suites Nos. 1–2. Hammersmith: Prelude & scherzo, Op. 52.
(B) *** ASV CDQS 6021 [id.]. L. Wind O, Denis Wick – VAUGHAN WILLIAMS: *English folksong suite* etc.***

Holst's two *Military band suites* contain some magnificent music. Frederick Fennell's new versions have more gravitas though no less *joie de vivre* than his old Mercury set. They are magnificent, and the recording is truly superb – digital technique used in a quite overwhelmingly exciting way. Perhaps there is too much bass drum, but no one is going to grumble when the result is so telling. The *Chaconne* of the *First Suite* makes a quite marvellous effect here. The playing of the Cleveland wind group is of the highest quality, smoothly blended and full in slow movements, vigorous and alert and with strongly rhythmic articulation in fast ones.

The London performances have great spontaneity, even if they are essentially lightweight, especially when compared with the Fennell versions. *Hammersmith*, however, is well worth having on CD, although the approach is freshly direct rather than seeking to evoke atmosphere. The sound is first class and the Vaughan Williams couplings are no less successful; this reissue is very competitively priced.

The Planets (suite), *Op. 32.*
*** Decca Dig. 417 553-2 [id.]. Montreal Ch. & SO, Dutoit.
*** Collins Dig. 1036-2 [id.]. LPO & Ch., Hilary Davan Wetton.
*** EMI CDC7 47160-2 [id.]. Amb. S., LSO, Previn.
(M) *** EMI CDM7 69045-2 [id.]. LPO, Boult (with G. Mitchell Ch.).
(M) *** Decca 417 709-2 [id.]. V. State Op. Ch., VPO, Karajan.
(B) *** Decca 417 677-4. LAPO & Master Chorale, Mehta.
**(*) DG Dig. 400 028-2 [id.]. Berlin Ch. & BPO, Karajan.
(M) **(*) DG 419 475-2 [id.]. Boston Ch. & SO, Steinberg – LIGETI: *Lux aeterna.****
(B) **(*) Pickwick Dig. PCD 890 [MCA MCAD 25208]. LSO & Ch., Hickox.
**(*) Ph. Dig. 422 403-2 [id.]. Berlin R. Ch., BPO, Sir Colin Davis.
**(*) Telarc Dig. CD 80133 [id.]. RPO with Ch., Previn.
(M) **(*) EMI Dig. CD-EMX 9513 [Ang. CDM 62030]. Amb. S., Philh. O, Rattle.
**(*) Chan. Dig. CHAN 8302 [id.]. SNO & Ch., Gibson.
(M) (***) EMI mono CDH7 63097-2. BBC SO & Ch., Boult (with ELGAR: *Introduction and allegro* (***)).
(B) * CfP CD-CFP 4243. Hallé Ch. & O, James Loughran.

(i) *The Planets;* (ii) *Egdon Heath, Op. 47; The Perfect Fool* (suite); *Op. 39.*
(M) **(*) Decca 425 152-2 [id.]. LPO, (i) Solti; (ii) Boult (with LPO Choir).

The Planets; The Perfect Fool: suite.
(M) ** Virgin Dig. VC 790825-2 [id.]. Royal Liverpool PO & Ch., Mackerras.

Charles Dutoit's natural feeling for mood, rhythm and colour, so effectively used in his records of Ravel, here results in an outstandingly successful version, both rich and brilliant, and recorded with an opulence to outshine all rivals. It is remarkable that, whether in the relentless build-up of *Mars*, the lyricism of *Venus*, the rich exuberance of *Jupiter* or in much else, Dutoit and his Canadian players sound so idiomatic. The final account of *Saturn* is chillingly atmospheric. This marvellously recorded disc is a clear first choice on CD.

Hilary Davan Wetton's set of *Planets* is among the most successful of recent records. It has a superb digital recording, made in All Saints', Tooting, which creates a gripping sense of spectacle in *Mars*, given with a biting attack and forceful rhythms. Pacing is measured, but the wild bursts from the tam-tam add to the ferocity which is hammered home in the powerful final chords. After a delicately translucent *Venus*, combining serenity with restrained ardour, the delicacy of *Mercury* lacks the sharpest definition. But the resonance adds to the impact of *Jupiter* with its ebullient horns, although here the big tune could be more expansive. With potent, measured melancholy, *Saturn* moves to a forceful climax, dominated by the timpani; then *Uranus*, with its ringing brass chords and rollicking horns, makes a dramatic contrast, while *Neptune*'s ethereal chorus returns us to a silent infinity.

Previn's remastered EMI analogue version of 1974 remains highly desirable. Though it does not have quite the range of a digital recording, the focus is firm and the realistic perspective gives an admirable illusion of depth. Previn's interpretation is an outstandingly attractive one, with many of Holst's subtleties of orchestral detail telling with greater point than on many other versions. The performance is basically traditional, yet has an appealing freshness. However, this is now surely due for reissue at mid-price.

It was Sir Adrian Boult who, over sixty years ago, first 'made *The Planets* shine', as the composer put it, and if the opening of *Mars* – noticeably slower than in Boult's previous recordings – suggests a slackening, the opposite proves true: that movement gains greater weight at a slower tempo. *Mercury* has lift and clarity, not just rushing brilliance, and it is striking that in Holst's syncopations – as in the introduction to *Jupiter* – Boult allows himself a jaunty, even jazzy freedom which adds an infectious sparkle. The great melody of *Jupiter* is more flowing than previously but is more involving too, and *Uranus* as well as *Jupiter* has its measure of jollity, with the lolloping 6/8 rhythms delectably pointed. The recording has gained presence and definition with its digital remastering and yet not lost its body and atmosphere. At mid-price, this could well be a first choice for many.

Still very competitive indeed is Karajan's earlier Decca version which still sounds remarkably vivid with its brilliantly remastered recording, now more precise in detail but retaining its atmospheric analogue sound-picture. There are many individual touches, from the whining Wagnerian tubas of *Mars*, *Venus* representing ardour rather than mysticism, the gossamer textures of *Mercury*, and the strongly characterized *Saturn* and *Venus*, with splendid playing from the Vienna brass, now given more bite. The upper range of the strings, however, has a touch of fierceness at higher dynamic levels.

Karajan's later digital CD (for DG) is undoubtedly spectacularly wide-ranging, while the marvellously sustained pianissimo playing of the Berlin Philharmonic Orchestra – as in *Venus* and the closing pages of *Saturn* – is the more telling against a background of silence. But the 'digital edge' on the treble detracts from the overall beauty of the orchestra in fortissimos. *Jupiter* ideally needs a riper body of tone, although the syncopated opening now erupts with joy and the big melody has a natural flow and nobility. *Venus* has sensuous string phrasing, *Mercury* and *Uranus* have beautiful springing in the triplet rhythms, and the climax of that last movement brings an amazing glissando on the organ.

When it was first issued in 1971, the Los Angeles Decca recording set a new standard for sonic splendour in a work which has since the days of 78s put the recording engineers on their mettle. The power and impact of *Mars* are still impressive; and the brass and timpani in *Uranus* have fine body and bite. In short this was vintage Decca analogue sound, and the splendid CD remastering has given it a new lease of life. Mehta's performance is fresh, strongly characterized and very well played. There is plenty of atmosphere and genuine spontaneity throughout. A bargain.

Also recorded in 1971, Steinberg's Boston set of *Planets* was another outstanding version from a vintage analogue period. It remains one of the most exciting and involving versions and sounds brighter and sharper in outline, though with some loss of opulence. Steinberg draws sumptuous playing from the Boston Symphony, and anyone who wants to wallow in the colour and power of this extrovert work will certainly be delighted. *Mars* in particular is intensely exciting. At his fast tempo, Steinberg may get to his fortissimos a little early, but rarely has the piece sounded so menacing on record. The testing point for most will no doubt be *Jupiter*, and here Steinberg the excellent Elgarian comes to the fore, giving a wonderful nobilmente swagger.

The Decca recording for Solti's Chicago version is extremely brilliant, with *Mars* given a vivid cutting edge at the fastest possible tempo. Solti's directness in *Jupiter* (with the trumpets coming through splendidly) is certainly riveting, the big tune red-blooded and with plenty of character. In *Saturn* the spareness of texture is finely sustained and the tempo is slow, the detail precise; while in *Neptune* the coolness is even more striking when the pianissimos are achieved with such a high degree of tension. The analogue recording has remarkable clarity and detail, and Solti's clear-headed intensity undoubtedly brings refreshing new insights to this multi-faceted score, even if some will prefer a less tense, more atmospheric viewpoint. The CD gives the orchestra great presence, and the addition of Boult's classic versions of *Egdon Heath* and *The Perfect Fool* ballet music makes this reissue very competitive.

Richard Hickox's *Mars* is given an unremittingly fast pace and is angrily aggressive, the climax topped by ferocious percussion. The emphasized dissonance makes *Venus*, with its translucent serenity, the more striking, the playing cool and withdrawn. *Mercury* is attractively fleet, with a proper element of fantasy, and *Saturn* has an elegiac gravity of mood. The disappointments are *Jupiter* and *Uranus*: the former lacking in real jubilation, with the central melody rather square – though there is no lack of energy – and *Uranus* has a forcefulness of accentuation which precludes any geniality. The recording, with its wide dynamic range, is certainly spectacular; it has excellent transparency and detail but rather misses out on expansive warmth.

Sir Colin Davis's *Mars* is menacingly fast, with weighty Berlin brass and barbaric accents adding to the forcefulness. The resonant recording brings sumptuous textures to *Venus*, while even *Saturn* has a degree of opulence. *Mercury*, however, is infectiously spirited and *Jupiter*, with a grand central tune, is bucolic in its amplitude. *Uranus* brings galumphing brass and the closing *Neptune* is both ethereal and sensuous, an unusual combination, brought about partly by the warm reverberation. There are more subtle versions than this, but it is easy to enjoy.

André Previn's Telarc version broadly preserves the magnificent concept of *The Planets* contained in his superb EMI account with the LSO; however, with sound that is wide-ranging and atmospheric but slightly diffused, and with a rather more relaxed approach to some of the movements, it lacks the final bite which made the earlier record so compelling.

For Simon Rattle, EMI's digital recording provides wonderfully atmospheric sound, and the quality in *Venus* and *Mercury* is also beautiful, clear and translucent. Otherwise it is not as distinctive a version as one might have expected from this leading young conductor; it is sensibly paced but neither so polished nor so bitingly committed as Karajan, Previn or Boult.

Gibson's reading is characteristically direct and certainly well played. Other versions have greater individuality and are more involving, but there is no doubt that the Chandos recording has fine bite and presence, although there are moments when one would have expected a greater degree of transparency. With sound this vivid, the impact of such a colourful score is enhanced, but at full price this now seems uncompetitive alongside Dutoit, where the recording is equally clear but better detailed and more opulent.

Mackerras's usual zestful approach communicates readily and the Liverpool orchestra bring a lively response, but the over-reverberant recording tends to cloud the otherwise pungently vigorous *Mars*, and both *Venus* and *Saturn* seem a little straightforward and marginally undercharacterized, while again in the powerful climax of *Uranus* there is some blurring from the resonance. *The Perfect Fool*, with its vivid colouring and irregular rhythms, has much in common with *The Planets* and makes a fine coupling, especially when played with such flair.

Sir Adrian Boult's 1945 recording of *The Planets* is also most welcome on CD, if only to show nostalgic collectors how vividly the EMI engineers captured the music at the time, when Decca's first FFRR 78 r.p.m. discs were also extending the boundaries of recorded sound, prior to the arrival of LPs. The *Introduction and allegro* also sounds amazing for its period; of course Boult has since recorded both works in greatly improved sound.

Loughran finds plenty of atmosphere in Holst's score, but the music-making is relatively pedestrian, even though the playing itself is often very fine. Moreover the remastered recording has lost some of its bloom and the overall focus is not always quite clean.

Air and variations; 3 Pieces for oboe & string quartet, Op. 2.
*** Chan. Dig. CHAN 8392 [id.]. Francis, English Qt – BAX: *Quintet*; MOERAN: *Fantasy quartet*; JACOB: *Quartet.****

The three pieces here are engagingly folksy, consisting of a sprightly little *March*, a gentle *Minuet* with a good tune, and a *Scherzo*. Performances are first class, and so is the recording.

VOCAL MUSIC

Choral hymns from the Rig Veda (Groups 1–4), *H. 97–100; 2 Eastern pictures for women's voices and harp, H. 112; Hymn to Dionysus, Op. 31/2.*
**(*) Unicorn Dig. DKPCD 9046 [id.]. Royal College of Music Chamber Ch., RPO, Willcocks; Ellis.

The *Choral hymns from the Rig Veda* show Holst writing with deep understanding for voices, devising textures, refined, very distinctively his, to match atmospherically exotic texts. Though performances are not always ideally polished, the warmth and thrust of the music are beautifully caught. The *Hymn to Dionysus*, setting words from the *Bacchae* of Euripides in Gilbert Murray's translation, a rarity anticipating Holst's *Choral symphony*, makes a welcome and substantial fill-up, along with the two little *Eastern pictures*. Beautifully clean and atmospheric recording.

Choral hymns from the Rig Veda (Group 3), *H. 99, Op. 26/3.*
*** Hyp. CDA 66175 [id.]. Holst Singers & O; Davan Wetton; T. Owen – BLISS: *Lie strewn the white flocks*; BRITTEN: *Gloriana: Choral dances.****

The third group of *Choral hymns from the Rig Veda*, like the whole series, reveals Holst in his Sanskritic period at his most distinctively inspired. In this responsive performance, it makes an excellent coupling for the attractive Bliss and Britten items, atmospherically recorded.

Dirge and Hymeneal, H. 124; 2 Motets, H. 159/60; 5 Part-songs, H. 61.
*** Conifer Dig. CDCF 142 [id.]. CBSO Ch., Halsey, R. Markham (piano) – ELGAR: *Scenes from the Bavarian Highlands.****

It is fascinating to find among these Holst part-songs the original musical idea that he used later in the *Saturn* movement of *The Planets* suite, with the piano accompaniment pivoting back and forth. That is from the *Dirge and Hymeneal*. The other items – all unaccompanied – bring writing just as hauntingly beautiful and original, not least the most demanding and ambitious of them, the motet *The evening watch*, in eight parts, slow and hushed throughout. Beautiful, refined performances, atmospherically recorded.

The Evening watch, H.159; 6 Choruses, H.186; Nunc dimittis, H.127; 7 Partsongs, H.162; 2 Psalms, H.117.
*** Hyp. Dig. CDA 66329 [id.]. Holst Singers & O, Hilary Davan Wetton.

Having given us a splendid set of *Planets*, Hilary Davan Wetton now turns to the often more austere but no less inspired choral music. The second of the two Psalm settings, using a very famous tune, has a frisson-creating climax, as affecting as any in the more famous orchestral work. *The Evening watch* creates a rapt, sustained pianissimo until the very closing bars, when the sudden expansion is quite thrilling. The *Six Choruses* for male voices show the composer at his most imaginative, with a characteristically original use of vocal colour, while the comparable *Partsongs* for women, set to words by Robert Bridges, often produce a ravishingly dreamy, mystical beauty. The final song, *Assemble all ye maidens*, is a narrative ballad about a lost love, and its closing section is infinitely touching. The performances are gloriously and sensitively sung and unerringly paced, while St Paul's Girls' School, Hammersmith, is not only an appropriate recording venue but produces a lovely bloom on voices and accompanying strings alike.

Hymn of Jesus, Op. 37.
(M) *** Decca 421 381-2 (2) [id.]. BBC Ch., BBC SO, Boult – ELGAR: *Dream of Gerontius.***(*)

Boult's superb performance of *The Hymn of Jesus*, a visionary masterpiece that brings some of Holst's most searching inspirations, comes as a generous and apt – if unusual – coupling for Elgar's great oratorio. The spatial beauty of Holst's choral writing is vividly caught with fine presence in the early-1960s recording.

(i) *Savitri* (complete); (ii) *Dream city* (song cycle, orch. Matthews).
**(*) Hyp. Dig. CDA 66099 [id.]. (i) Langridge, Varcoe, Palmer, Hickox Singers; (ii) Kwella; City of L. Sinfonia, Hickox.

The simple story is taken from a Sanskrit source – Savitri, a woodcutter's wife, cleverly outwits Death, who has come to take her husband – and Holst with beautiful feeling for atmosphere sets it in the most restrained way. Felicity Palmer is more earthy, more vulnerable as Savitri than Janet Baker was in the earlier Argo recording, her grainy mezzo well caught. Philip Langridge and Stephen Varcoe both sing sensitively with fresh, clear tone, though their timbres are rather similar. Hickox is a thoughtful conductor both in the opera and in the orchestral song-cycle arranged by Colin Matthews (with Imogen Holst's approval) from Holst's settings of Humbert Wolfe poems. Patrizia Kwella's soprano at times catches the microphone rather shrilly.

Honegger, Arthur (1892–1955)

(i) *Concerto da camera for flute, cor anglais and strings; Prelude, arioso et fughetta on the name of Bach; Symphony No. 2.*
** Chan. Dig. CHAN 8632 [id.]. (i) Hutchins, Plante; I Musici de Montreal, Yuli Turovsky.

The pastoral *Concerto da camera for flute, cor anglais and strings* comes from the same period as the *Fourth Symphony* (*Deliciae Basiliensis*), a good vintage, and has something of its harmonic resource and charm. The soloists play with effortless virtuosity, though they are placed a little forward in the aural picture. Their version is better played and scores over their only rival, on Nonesuch, which offers very short measure. The recording is made in a somewhat reverberant acoustic but is well balanced and warm. In the *Prelude, arioso et fughetta*, the short *Prelude* is in the style of the '*Forty-Eight*', while the four notes, B.A.C.H., dominate the *Arioso*. This is vividly presented; but the *Second Symphony* needs a larger force of strings if it is to make its full effect, and Turovsky makes rather heavy weather of the middle movement.

Symphony No. 1; Pastorale d'été; 3 Symphonic movements: Pacific 231; Rugby; No. 3.
*** Erato/WEA Dig. 2292 45242-2 [id.]. Bav. RSO, Dutoit.

Honegger's *First Symphony* is a highly stimulating and rewarding piece. Charles Dutoit gets an excellent response from the Bavarian Radio Symphony Orchestra, who produce a splendidly cultured sound and particularly beautiful phrasing in the slow movement. Dutoit also gives an atmospheric and sympathetic account of the *Pastorale d'été* and in addition offers the *Three Symphonic movements*, of which *Pacific 231* with its robust and vigorous portrait of a railway engine is by far the best known.

Symphony No. 2; Napoleon (film incidental music); *Phedre* (suite; both ed. Rozhdestvensky).
** Olympia Dig. OCD 212 [id.]. USSR MoC Chamber Ch. & SO, Rozhdestvensky.

Rozhdestvensky's account of Honegger's wartime *Symphony No. 2* is no match for Karajan's classic account. The strings of the Soviet orchestra are not in the same league as those of the Berlin Philharmonic and, partly because of the acoustic, the trumpet in the finale has a slightly raw quality. Nevertheless the record is well worth considering for the suite of incidental music to d'Annunzio's *Phedre*. It is stronger in atmosphere than in argument but is none the less hauntingly powerful and casts a strong spell. The three short movements of the score for Gance's epic *Napoleon* are by no means so atmospheric or powerful.

Symphonies Nos. 2 & 3 (Symphonie liturgique).
⊛ (M) *** DG 423 242-2 [id.]. BPO, Karajan.

This reissue includes arguably the finest versions of any Honegger works ever put on record. The Berlin strings in No. 2 have extraordinary sensitivity and expressive power, and Karajan conveys the sombre wartime atmosphere to perfection. At the same time, there is astonishing refinement of texture in the *Liturgique*, whose slow movement has never sounded more magical. The recording was always one of DG's best, and this transfer brings to life more detail and greater body and range. A great record, completely in a class of its own.

Christmas cantata (Cantate de Noël).
*** EMI Dig. CDC7 49559-2. Sweeney, Waynflete Singers, Winchester Cathedral Ch., ECO, Neary – POULENC: *Mass; Motets.****

At last a recording of Honegger's charming *Cantate de Noël* to do it full justice. Ansermet's mid-1960s account has served us well for the last two decades, but this new EMI version is incomparably superior in every way. It was Honegger's last completed work and deserves to be more popular at the festive season outside France. The CD is impressively wide-ranging and well defined.

Le Roi David.
(M) **(*) Decca 425 621-2 [id.]. Audel (nar.), Danco, De Montmollin, Martin, Hamel, Ch. & SRO, Ansermet.

(i) *Le Roi David* (oratorio). *Mouvement symphonique No. 3; Le Tempête: Prélude.*
**(*) Sup. Dig. SUP 001412/13 [id.]. (i) Eda Pierre, Senn, Raffalli, Mesgluch, Gaillard, Prague Philharmonic Ch., Kuhn's Children's Ch., Czech PO, Serge Baudo.

Le Roi David is a powerful, dramatic canvas for narrators and soloists which in the course of its three short Acts recounts the slaying of Goliath, the jealousy of Saul and David's coronation and reign. The music is highly imaginative if perhaps a bit short-breathed; but its savagery, colour and poetry are splendidly conveyed under Baudo and the balance is excellent, though the acoustic of the House of Artists is over-reverberant and slightly glassy on top. Supraphon also includes the *Mouvement symphonique No. 3*, a companion piece to *Pacific 231*, and *Rugby*, commissioned by Furtwängler, and a rarity – the *Prelude* to *The Tempest*, an exciting and brilliantly evocative piece. Strongly recommended.

Ansermet's Decca recording dates from the mid-1950s and the sound lacks the body of the Supraphon set. However, it is economically fitted on to a single CD and, as the recording generally wears its years lightly, can be considered a serious alternative. Judged by the highest standards, the orchestral playing is a little wanting in finish, but the cast is distinguished and Ansermet fully reveals the vivid detail of Honegger's rich tapestry.

Hovhaness, Alan (born 1911)

(i) *Armenian rhapsody No. 1;* (ii) *Prayer of St Gregory;* (iii) *Symphony No. 11 (All men are brothers);* (i; iv) *Tzaikerk (Evening song) for flute, violin, strings & timpani.*
** Crystal CD 801 [id.]. (i) Crystal CO, Ernest Gold, with (ii) Stevens; (iv) Shapiro, Shanley; (iii) RPO, composer.

The *Symphony* is of little real substance. It is rather like film music, atmospheric and well scored, but wanting in distinctive personality or any sense of real movement. Nor is there too much to the companion pieces. Repetitive, modal doodling, spectacularly uninventive!

(i) *Artik concerto for horn and strings, Op. 78;* (ii) *Symphony No. 9 (St Vartan), Op. 180.*
*** Crystal CD 802 [id.]. (i) Meir Romin, Israel PO strings, David Amos; (ii) Nat. PO of London, composer.

The *Saint Vartan symphony* shows little or no evidence of mastery, and precious little invention. Both works are static and wanting in rhythmic variety; the mysticism of the symphony borders on the unctuous and its pursuit of simplicity is unremitting. The three stars are to indicate good performances and excellent recording.

Symphony No. 24 (Majnun symphony), Op. 273.
* Crystal CD 803 [id.]. Hill, Wilbraham, Sax, John Alldis Ch., Nat. PO of London, composer.

The *Majnun symphony* was composed in 1973 in response to a commission from the International Center for Arid and Semi-arid Land Studies for Focus on the Arts Series at Texas Technical University. Unlikely though it may seem, we are not making this up – and arid is certainly the word for this musically uneventful and naïve composition. It draws for its inspiration on *Salaman and Absal* by the Persian poet, Jami, and tells of the love of Majnun for Layla. The recording is eminently satisfactory.

Howells, Herbert (1892–1983)

Collegium regale: canticles; Behold, O God our defender; Like as the hart; St Paul's service: Canticles. Take him to earth for cherishing. (Organ): *Psalm prelude: De profundis; Master Tallis's testament.*
* Hyp. Dig. CDA 66260 [id.]. St Paul's Cathedral Ch., Scott; Christopher Dearnley.

This well-planned programme of Howells' music is framed by the two fine sets of canticles; in between come the organ solos and motets, *Take him to earth for cherishing* being dedicated to John F. Kennedy. All the music is of high quality and the recording gives it resonance, in both senses of the word, with the St Paul's acoustic well captured by the engineers. A fine representation of a composer who wrote in the mainstream of English church and cathedral music but who had a distinct voice of his own.

Hymnus paradisi.
(M) ***** EMI CDM7 63372-2. Harper, Tear, Bach Ch., King's College Ch., New Philh. O, Willcocks – FINZI: *Dies natalis.******

Hymnus paradisi is a dignified and beautifully wrought work but also and more importantly is both moving and powerful. Howells is not among the most original of English composers but, on the strength of this work, he is surely among the most civilized and disciplined. The performance is eloquently and warmly persuasive within the glowing Kingsway Hall acoustics, and the 1970 recording has been enhanced further in its CD transfer.

Requiem.
(M) ***** Hyp. CDA 66076 [id.]. Corydon Singers, Best – VAUGHAN WILLIAMS: *Mass; Te Deum.******

Howells' *Requiem* was composed in the immediate aftermath of his son's death, and some of its material was reworked in the *Hymnus Paradisi*. This is a most moving piece and one of the crowns of English church music. The Corydon Singers sing with conviction and eloquence, and the recording, made in a spacious acoustic, serves them and the composer well.

Hummel, Johann (1778–1837)

Bassoon concerto in F.
(BB) ****** Hung. White Label HRC 041 [id.]. Gábor Janota, Liszt CO, Frigyes Sándor – J. C. BACH: *Concertos.*******

Hummel's *Concerto* has much more florid and, generally, more interesting passage-work for the bassoon than its two J. C. Bach couplings, and its central *Romanza* has a distinctly *galant* charm. The work is very well played and nicely recorded within a characteristically reverberant Hungaroton acoustic. Not an indispensable disc, but a pleasant one.

Piano concertos: in A min., Op. 85; B min., Op. 89.
*** Chan. Dig. CHAN 8505 [id.]. Stephen Hough, ECO, Bryden Thomson.

The *A minor* is Hummel's most often-heard piano concerto, never better played, however, than by Stephen Hough on this Chandos disc. The coda is quite stunning; it is not only his dazzling virtuosity that carries all before it but also the delicacy and refinement of colour he produces. The *B minor*, Op. 89, is more of a rarity, and is given with the same blend of virtuosity and poetic feeling which Hough brings to its companion. He is given expert support by Bryden Thomson and the ECO – and the recording is first class.

Trumpet concerto in E.
⊛ *** Ph. Dig. 420 203-2 [id.]. Hardenberger, ASMF, Marriner – HAYDN *** ⊛; HERTEL***; STAMITZ: *Concertos.****

Trumpet concerto in E flat.
*** Delos Dig. D/CD 3001 [id.]. Schwarz, New York 'Y' CO – HAYDN: *Concerto.****
*** CBS CD 37846 [id.]. Marsalis, Nat. PO, Leppard – HAYDN: *Concerto**** (with L. MOZART: *Concerto****).

Hummel's *Trumpet concerto* is usually heard in the familiar brass key of E flat, but the brilliant Swedish trumpeter, Håkan Hardenberger, uses the key of E, which makes it sound brighter and bolder than usual. Neither he nor Marriner miss the genial lilt inherent in the dotted theme of the first movement, yet this seductive element is set off by the brassy masculinity of the actual timbre. The slow-movement cantilena soars beautifully over its jogging pizzicato accompaniment, and the finale captivates the ear with its high spirits and easy bravura; Hardenberger's crisp tonguing and tight trills are of the kind to make you smile with pleasure. This is the finest version of the piece in the catalogue, for Marriner's accompaniment is polished and sympathetic. The recording projects the vibrant trumpet image forward with great presence, and the only slight complaint is that the orchestral recording is a shade too reverberant.

Both Schwarz and Marsalis give fine accounts of Hummel's *Concerto*, but neither player quite catches its full *galant* charm. In matters of bravura, however, neither can be faulted; both artists relish the sparkling finale. If Marsalis is more reserved in the slow movement, he has the advantage of very fine accompaniment from Leppard, and the CBS record includes a substantial extra work.

Introduction, theme and variations in F min./maj., Op. 102.
*** Capriccio Dig. 10 308 [id.]. Lajos Lencsés, Stuttgart RSO, Marriner – HAYDN; MARTINŮ: *Concertos.****

Lajos Lencsés – the principal oboe of the Stuttgart orchestra – plays with both poise and an obvious relish for Hummel's engaging invention. His account is relaxed but matches Holliger's in elegance and charm. He is very well recorded and has worthwhile couplings.

Grand military septet in C, Op. 114.
*** CRD CRD 3390 [id.]. Nash Ens. – C. KREUTZER: *Septet.****

Hummel's *Military septet* is not really as grand as its name implies. It features a trumpet, certainly, but that makes a major contribution only in the third movement, although in the first its fanfare-like interjections do bring in a somewhat refined reminder of the work's title. There is sparkle and warmth here, and the playing itself has beguiling elegance. The recording is superb and the balance of the trumpet part (very nicely played by James Watson) is most felicitous. Highly recommended, especially in view of the apt coupling.

Septet in D min., Op. 74.
*** CRD CRD 3344 [id.]. Nash Ens. – BERWALD: *Septet.****

Hummel's *Septet* is an enchanting and inventive work with a virtuoso piano part, expertly dispatched here by Clifford Benson. The *Septet* is full of vitality, and its scherzo in particular has enormous charm and individuality. A fine performance and excellent recording make this a highly desirable issue, particularly in view of the enterprising coupling.

Violin sonatas: in E flat, Op. 5/3; in D, Op. 50; Nocturne, Op. 99.
*** Amon Ra CD-SAR 12 [id.]. Ralph Holmes, Richard Burnett.

Ralph Holmes's violin timbre is bright and the Graf fortepiano under the fingers of Richard Burnett has plenty of colour and does not sound clattery. The *D major Sonata*, which comes first, is a very striking work with hints of early Beethoven; but the *D flat Sonata*, written a decade and a half earlier in 1798, has a memorably eloquent slow movement which shows Ralph Holmes at his finest. Richard Burnett has a chance to catch the ear in the finale of the *D major Sonata* when he uses the quaintly rasping cembalo device (without letting it outstay its welcome). The *Nocturne* is an extended piece (nearly 16 minutes) in variation form, and it is a pity that the CD, while banding the movements of the two sonatas, does not provide more internal cues. A thoroughly worthwhile issue, 'authentic' in the most convincing way, which shows this engaging composer at his most assured and inventive.

Piano sonatas: Nos. 1 in C, Op. 2/3; 6 in D, Op. 106.
** Ara. Dig. Z 6564 [id.]. Ian Hobson.

Piano sonatas: Nos. 2 in E flat, Op. 13; 5 in F sharp min., Op. 81.
** Ara. Dig. Z 6565 [id.]. Ian Hobson.

Piano sonatas: Nos. 3 in F min., Op. 20; 4 in C, Op. 38.
** Ara Dig. Z 6566 [id.]. Ian Hobson.

As one might expect from hearing the record of the two *Concertos*, these are enormously fluent works, close to Clementi at the early end of his career and to Weber in the brilliant finale of No. 4. They are not innovative in style but they have undoubted charm. Though the music offers great expressive depths to explore, it is always accomplished and well crafted, the product of fine intelligence. Ian Hobson plays with enormous facility and clarity of articulation. The recordings are alive and present, though the instrument goes out of tune in the slow movement of No. 4. Of the six, this and the *F sharp minor Sonata* (No. 5) make a good starting point.

Humperdinck, Engelbert (1854–1921)

Hänsel und Gretel (complete).
(M) *** EMI CMS7 69293-2 (2) [Ang. CDMB 69293]. Schwarzkopf, Grümmer, Metternich, Ilsovay, Schürhoff, Felbermayer, Children's Ch., Philh. O, Karajan.
*** CBS M2K 79217 (2) [M2K 35898]. Cotrubas, Von Stade, Ludwig, Nimsgern, Te Kanawa, Söderström, Cologne Op. Children's Ch., Cologne Gürzenich O, Pritchard.
** Decca 421 111-2 (2) [id.]. Fassbaender, Popp, Berry, Hamari, Schlemm, Burrowes, Gruberová, V. Boys' Ch., VPO, Solti.

Karajan's classic 1950s set of Humperdinck's children's opera, with Schwarzkopf and Grümmer peerless in the name-parts, is enchanting; this was an instance where everything in the recording went right. The original mono LP set was already extremely atmospheric. In most respects the sound has as much clarity and warmth as rival recordings made in the 1970s. There is much to delight here; the smaller parts are beautifully done and Else Schürhoff's Witch is memorable. The snag is that the digital remastering has brought a curious orchestral bass emphasis, noticeable in the Overture and elsewhere, but notably in the *Witch's ride*.

Beautifully cast, the Pritchard version from CBS was the first in genuine stereo to challenge the vintage Karajan set. Cotrubas – sometimes a little grainy as recorded – and Von Stade both give charming characterizations, and the supporting cast is exceptionally strong, with Söderström an unexpected but refreshing and illuminating choice as the Witch. Pritchard draws idiomatic playing from the Gürzenich Orchestra; the recording is pleasingly atmospheric and very realistically balanced.

Solti directs a strong, spectacular version with the Vienna Philharmonic, emphasizing the Wagnerian associations of the score. It is well sung – both principals are engaging – but just a little short on charm. The solo singing is not as steady in tone as on the EMI set, and the lack of geniality in the atmosphere is a drawback in a work of this nature. Needless to say, Solti does the *Witch's ride* excitingly, and the VPO are encouraged to play with consistent fervour throughout. Brilliant sound.

Königskinder (complete).
(M) *** EMI CMS7 69936-2 (3). Donath, Prey, Dallapozza, Schwarz, Unger, Ridderbusch, Bav. R. Ch., Tolz Boys' Ch., Munich R. O, Wallberg.

The success of *Hänsel und Gretel* has completely overshadowed this second fairy-tale opera of Humperdinck, which contains much fine music. Humperdinck had expanded his incidental music for a play to make this opera, which was given its première in New York in 1910. In an entertainment for children, the sadness and cruelty of a typical German fairy-tale, not to mention the heavy vein of moralizing, are a serious disadvantage, but in a recording as fine as this it is a piece well worth investigation. Both the conducting and the singing of the principals are most persuasive.

Ibert, Jacques (1890–1962)

Les amours de Jupiter; Escales; (i) *4 Chansons de Don Quichotte.*
(M) (**) EMI mono CDM7 63416-2 [id.]. Paris Nat. Theatre Op. O, composer; (i) with Chaliapine.

An interesting historical rarity. *Escales* ideally calls for the most opulent sound, which it doesn't exactly find here; but it is most beautifully played by the Orchestra of the Paris

Opéra under the composer. The mono recording dates from 1954, as does the ballet, *Les amours de Jupiter*. Neither was issued in the UK at the time, though the producer was John Culshaw; the 1933 Chaliapine records of the *Don Quichotte* songs are more familiar. The ballet is relaxing music with a whiff of the French cinema, pleasing but ultimately unmemorable. The *Chansons de Don Quichotte* were commissioned for a film to be directed by Pabst, and Ibert's songs were chosen in preference to Ravel, who was also approached. Good though they are, they are not better than his.

Divertissement.
(b) *(**) Decca 421 173-2 [id.]. Paris Conservatoire O, Martinon – OFFENBACH: *Gaîté parisienne* etc.(**)

Martinon's 1960 account of Ibert's *Divertissement* has never been surpassed for its wit and infectious bravado, with the *Valse* just skirting the edge of vulgarity and the finale carrying all before it in sheer high spirits. Alas, the digital remastering of an outstanding recording is almost impossibly shrill.

Escales.
** Ph. Dig. 426 255-2 [id.]. LAPO, Previn (with Concert of French Music**).

Ibert's exoticism is the kind of territory in which one would expect Previn to thrive – but expectations are not completely fulfilled either in terms of the performance, which is deficient in atmosphere, or in the recording which, though very good, is not as transparent as, say, his outstanding Prokofiev recordings.

d'India, Sigismondo (c. 1582–c. 1630)

Amico hai vint'io; Diana (Questo dardo, quest' arco); Misera me (Lamento d'Olympia); Piangono al pianger mio; Sfere fermate; Torna il sereno zefiro.
*** Hyp. CDA 66106 [id.]. Emma Kirkby, Anthony Rooley (chitarone) – MONTEVERDI: *Lamento d'Olympia* etc.***

All these pieces are rarities. They are also of very great interest. Sigismondo d'India's setting of the *Lamento d'Olympia* makes a striking contrast to Monteverdi's and is hardly less fine. This is an affecting and beautiful piece and so are its companions, particularly when they are sung as superbly and accompanied as sensitively as they are here. A very worthwhile CD début.

d'Indy, Vincent (1851–1931)

Symphonie sur un chant montagnard français (Symphonie cévenole).
*** Conifer Dig. CDFC 146 [id.]. Michel Block, Berne SO, Peter Maag – MARTINŮ: *Rhapsody-Concerto.***
(bb) *** Hung. White Label HRC 106 [id.]. Gabriella Torma, Budapest PO, Tamás Pál – LALO: *Symphonie espagnole.***(*)
(m) **(*) RCA GD 86805 [6805-2-RG]. Nicole Henriot-Schweitzer, Boston SO, Munch – FRANCK: *Symphony.***(*) ⊛

Michel Block, a sensitive and intelligent player, gives a sympathetic account of this strange but, in his hands, appealing work. The recording is well balanced and the perspective natural: it could perhaps open out more at climaxes and the very top of the piano is less transparent than is ideal. However, few would regret investing in this thoroughly recommendable issue.

A sensitive and atmospheric account also from Gabriella Torma and the Budapest Philharmonic under Pál. The Hungaraton recording is warmly atmospheric and the piano is balanced well with the orchestra. There is no lack of vividness here, and these artists show great sympathy for this attractive music. The Lalo coupling is recommendable, too. A bargain.

Nicole Henriot-Schweitzer and Munch present a fresh and crisp performance which is certainly true to the atmosphere of the composer's inspiration, which he found in the mountains of the Cevennes. Munch's natural affinity and the bright-eyed response of the Boston players make for the happiest results, and Henriot-Schweitzer plays the piano part most sympathetically. The early (1958) stereo recording comes up well; there is not always absolute internal clarity, but the Boston acoustics are effective in this music, and the piano focus is bright and sharp.

Ippolitov-Ivanov, Mikhail (1859–1935)

Caucasian sketches (suite), *Op. 10.*
** Olympia OCD 107 [id.]. USSR RSO, Fedoseyev – ARENSKY: *Piano concerto etc.***

The *Caucasian sketches* are justly famed for a single number, the *Procession of the Sardar*, much loved on bandstands and, in the past, on seaside piers. The other three items rely mainly on atmosphere for their appeal; nevertheless their picaresque writing is effectively presented here, and the recording is fully acceptable.

Ireland, John (1879–1962)

Piano concerto in E flat.
*** Conifer Dig. CDCF 175 [id.]. Kathryn Stott, RPO, Handley – BRIDGE: *Phantasm*; WALTON: *Sinfonia concertante.***
*** Unicorn Dig. DKPCD 9056 [id.]. Tozer, Melbourne SO, Measham – RUBBRA: *Violin concerto.***

Piano concerto in E flat; Legend for piano and orchestra; Mai-Dun (symphonic rhapsody).
*** Chan. Dig. CHAN 8461 [id.]. Parkin, LPO, Thomson.

John Ireland's only *Piano concerto* has a distinctive melodic inspiration throughout all three movements and its poetic lyricism is in the best traditions of the finest English music. Kathryn Stott gives the most sympathetic reading on record since the original interpreter on disc, Eileen Joyce. Spaciously expressive in the lyrical passages – not least the lovely slow movement – and crisply alert in the jazzy finale, Stott plays with a sense of spontaneity, using freely idiomatic rubato. Generously and aptly coupled with the much more neglected Walton and Bridge works, and very well recorded, this version, the third on CD, makes an easy first choice for the work.

Eric Parkin gives a splendidly refreshing and sparkling performance and benefits from excellent support from Bryden Thomson and the LPO. They are no less impressive in *Mai-Dun* and the beautiful *Legend for piano and orchestra*.

Geoffrey Tozer also gives a characterful account of Ireland's lyrical and often whimsical *Concerto*. It wears well and its charms have not faded in the half-century or more since it was composed. Tozer conveys the poetic feel of the slow movement and, though he takes a rather measured tempo in the finale, the music loses none of its freshness. The recording is a little studio-bound, and a slightly more open acoustic would have been preferable – but too much should not be made of this. Doubtless the coupling will decide matters for most collectors.

A Downland suite; Elegiac meditation; The Holy Boy.
*** Chan. Dig. CHAN 8390 [id.]. ECO, David Garforth – BRIDGE: *Suite for strings.****

David Garforth and the ECO play with total conviction and seem wholly attuned to Ireland's sensibility. *A Downland suite* was originally written for brass band, and in 1941 Ireland began to make a version for strings. As was the case with the *Comedy overture* for brass band which he rewrote in 1936, he completely reconceived it. However, his reworking was interrupted and the present version was finished and put into shape by Geoffrey Bush, who also transcribed the *Elegiac meditation*. The recording is first class, clear and naturally balanced.

A London Overture.
*** EMI CDC7 47984-2 [id.]. LSO, Barbirolli – BAX: *Tintagel*; DELIUS: *Collection.* ***

One of Ireland's most immediately attractive works; and Barbirolli's performance of it is a great success, as is the remastering of an outstanding recording: the effect is tangible and real in its crisply vivid focus. The main theme (rhythmically conjuring up the bus conductor's call of 'Piccadilly') is made obstinately memorable, and the ripe romanticism of the middle section is warmly expansive in Barbirolli's hands. The freshness of the sound makes the performance sound newly minted.

Ives, Charles (1874–1954)

Central Park in the dark; New England Holidays symphony; The unanswered question (original and revised versions).
*** CBS Dig. MK 42381 [id.]. Chicago Symphony Ch. & O, Tilson Thomas.

The *New England Holidays symphony* comprises four fine Ives pieces normally heard separately. The performance from Michael Tilson Thomas and his Chicago forces is in every way superb, while the wide-ranging CBS recording provides admirable atmosphere for the magical opening of *Washington's birthday* and is fully equal to the complex textures and spectacle of *Decoration Day* and the great climax of the finale. This is now among the most impressive Ives records in the catalogue, for the other pieces – shorter but no less characteristically original works – are made to sound as breathtakingly original as the day they were written.

Symphony No. 2; Central Park in the dark; The gong on the hook and ladder; Hallowe'en; Hymn for strings; Tone roads No. 1; The Unanswered question.
*** DG Dig. 429 220-2 [id.]. NYPO, Bernstein.

Bernstein's disc brings one of the richest offerings of Ives yet put on record, offering the *Symphony No. 2*, with its array of references and parodies, extravagant even by this wild composer's standards, plus six shorter orchestral pieces. They include two of his very finest, *Central Park in the dark* and *The Unanswered question*, both characteristically quirky but deeply poetic too. In a note on the record, Bernstein explains in plain words the depth of his feelings towards this 'greatly gifted primitive'; and the superb performances, recorded live, consistently reflect that in their electricity and concentration. The *Symphony No. 2* was a work which Bernstein recorded with this orchestra for CBS many years ago, but this DG version with its radiant string-sound is much warmer still. The extra tensions and expressiveness of live performance here heighten the impact of each of the works. The difficult acoustic of Avery Fisher Hall in New York has rarely sounded more sympathetic on record.

Symphony No. 3 (The Camp meeting).
*** Argo 417 818-2 [id.]. ASMF, Marriner – BARBER: *Adagio*; COPLAND: *Quiet City*; COWELL: *Hymn*; CRESTON: *Rumor*.***
*** Pro Arte Dig. CDD 140 [id.]. St Paul CO, Russell Davies – COPLAND: *Appalachian spring* etc.***

Symphony No. 3 (The Camp meeting); (i) Orchestral set No. 2.
*** CBS Dig. MK 37823 [id.]. Concg. O, Tilson Thomas; (i) with Concg. Ch.

Tilson Thomas's version of Ives's most approachable symphony is the first to use the new critical edition, prepared with reference to newly available Ives manuscripts. Thanks to that and to Tilson Thomas's clear, incisive manner, it avoids any hint of blandness; the *Second Orchestral set*, with its three substantial atmosphere pieces, brings performances of a sharpness to back up the characteristically wordy titles – *An elegy to our forefathers, The rockstrewn hills join in the people's outdoor meeting* and *From Hanover Square North at the end of a tragic day the voice of the people again arose.* First-rate recording to match the fine performances.

Russell Davies does not use the new edition of Ives's score; nevertheless, he gives a fine account of this gentlest of Ives's symphonies, with its overtones of hymn singing and revivalist meetings. It makes a good coupling for the fine Copland works. Though the forward, relatively intimate acoustic may not evoke a church atmosphere at all, the beauty of the piece still comes over strongly.

Marriner's account is first rate in every way. It does not have the advantage of a digital master, but the 1976 analogue recording has slightly sharper detail in this remastered format. The performance has plenty of conviction; moreover it comes as part of an anthology that is of unusual interest and merit.

Symphony No. 4.
**(*) Chan. Dig. CHAN 8397 [id.]. John Alldis Ch., LPO, Serebrier.

Ives's most intense inspirations came when he limited himself to a single piece; though he was a big enough man to encompass symphony-length, it was difficult for him to fit the pieces together. Even so, no Ives enthusiast should miss this preposterous work, scored for an immense orchestra. José Serebrier acted as subsidiary conductor for Stokowski when he conducted the world première. In this English performance he somehow manages to find his way through multi-layered textures which have deliberately conflicting rhythms. The players respond loyally, and the movement representing *Chaos* is particularly colourful and dramatic in its sharp contrasts of dynamic, brutal but somehow poetic. *Order* is represented by a fugue, and the finale brings an apotheosis: a vivid, gripping work, but perhaps not as great as some American commentators originally thought. For the record collector at least, it provides a store-house of fantastic orchestral sound in a recording as vivid as this.

Piano trio (1904).
*** Teldec/WEA Dig. 2292 44924-2 [id.]. Trio Fontenay – BRAHMS: *Piano trio No. 1.****
** Delos D/CD 1009 [id.]. Pacific Piano Trio – KORNGOLD: *Piano trio.***

The Ives *Trio* is an amazing piece for 1904 and it is excellently played by the Trio Fontenay. Whether collectors wanting Brahms's Op. 8 will want it too is another matter –

and vice versa, of course. Anyway, they play it with great spirit and are given eminently clear but not overbright recording.

A good performance on Delos, though recorded rather close in a less than spacious acoustic. It is perfectly acceptable, though, and the coupling is apt.

Songs: *Autumn; Berceuse; The cage; Charlie Rutlage; Down East; Dreams; Evening; The greatest man; The Housatonic at Stockbridge; Immortality; Like a sick eagle; Maple leaves; Memories: 1, 2, 3; On the counter; Romanzo di Central Park; The see'r; Serenity; The side-show; Slow march; Slugging a vampire; Songs my mother taught me; Spring song; The things our fathers loved; Tom sails away; Two little flowers.*
*** Etcetera Dig. KTC 1020 [id.]. Roberta Alexander, Tan Crone.

Roberta Alexander presents her excellent and illuminating choice of Ives songs – many of them otherwise unavailable on record – in chronological order, starting with one written when Ives was only fourteen, *Slow march*, already predicting developments ahead. Sweet, nostalgic songs predominate, but the singer punctuates them with leaner, sharper inspirations. Her manner is not always quite tough enough in those, but this is characterful singing from an exceptionally rich and attractive voice. Tan Crone is the understanding accompanist, and the recording is first rate.

Jacob, Gordon (1895–1987)

Divertimento for harmonica and string quartet.
*** Chan. Dig. CHAN 8802 [id.]. Tommy Reilly, Hindar Qt – MOODY: *Quintet; Suite.****

Gordon Jacob's set of eight sharply characterized miniatures shows the composer at his most engagingly imaginative. The variety of invention, whether in the *Romance* and *Siciliano*, the *Elegy* or the final *Jig*, constantly beguiles the ear, and the performances are deliciously piquant in colour and feeling. The recording could hardly be more successful, for the harmonica's special timbre can blend and yet stand out from the string textures.

Oboe quartet.
*** Chan. Dig. CHAN 8392 [id.]. Francis, English Qt – BAX: *Quintet*; HOLST: *Air and variations* etc.; MOERAN: *Fantasy quartet.****

Gordon Jacob's four-movement *Oboe quartet* is the slightest of the four works included in this admirable anthology, but is none the less very welcome. It is well crafted and entertaining, particularly the vivacious final Rondo. The performance could hardly be bettered, and the recording is excellent too.

Janáček, Leoš (1854–1928)

Mládi.
(*) DG Dig. 415 668-2 [id.]. Orpheus CO – BARTÓK: *Divertimento* etc.(*)

Mládi (Youth) is a work of Janáček's old age. On the DG version, the playing is excellent and the recording very realistic. Tempi may at times seem brisker by comparison with some past performances on record, but the music is never made to seem hurried. This makes a fine choice for those wanting the pairing with Bartók.

Sinfonietta.
*** EMI Dig. CDC7 47504-2 [id.]. Philh. O, Rattle – *Glagolitic Mass.****
(M) *** Decca 425 624-2 [id.]. LSO, Abbado – *Glagolitic Mass.****

(*) Telarc Dig. CD 80174 [id.]. LAPO, Previn – BARTÓK: *Concerto for orchestra.*(*)

Sinfonietta; Taras Bulba (rhapsody).
*** Decca Dig. 410 138-2. VPO, Mackerras.

Mackerras's coupling comes as a superb supplement to his Janáček opera recordings with the Vienna Philharmonic. The massed brass of the *Sinfonietta* has tremendous bite and brilliance as well as characteristic Viennese ripeness, thanks to a spectacular digital recording. *Taras Bulba* too is given more weight and body than is usual, the often savage dance rhythms presented with great energy.

Rattle gets an altogether first-class response from the orchestra and truthful recorded sound from the EMI engineers. The rival Decca recording is a hi-fi spectacular with rather forward placing and a hint of aggression; many collectors may find the EMI sound more pleasing. The Decca has greater clarity and presence in its favour, as well as Mackerras's authority in this repertoire. However, Rattle's coupling with the *Glagolitic Mass* is very attractive indeed and will be first choice for many collectors.

Abbado gives a splendid account of the *Sinfonietta* and evokes a highly sympathetic response from the LSO. His acute sensitivity to dynamic nuances and his care for detail are felt in every bar, without any sense of excessive fastidiousness, and this is thoroughly alive and fresh playing. The recording balance, too, allows the subtlest of colours to register while still having plenty of impact. In its remastered CD format it sounds quite splendid.

The amiability of Janáček's colourful and brassy work is what dominates Previn's performance rather than any more dramatic qualities. It matches his relaxed view of the Bartók *Concerto for orchestra*, which comes as a unique coupling. The Los Angeles Philharmonic has never been recorded with a warmer and more realistic bloom than here by Jack Renner of Telarc in Royce Hall, UCLA. However, those looking for more bite and brilliance in this work will probably be happier with either the splendidly vital Mackerras recording, coupled with *Taras Bulba*, or the Rattle version.

String quartets Nos. 1 (Kreutzer sonata); 2 (Intimate letters).
**(*) Nimbus Dig. NI 5113 [id.]. Medici Qt.
** DG Dig. 427 669-2 [id.]. Hagen Qt (with WOLF: *Italian Serenade***).

(i) *String quartets Nos. 1–2;* (ii) *On an overgrown path: suite No. 1.*
*** Calliope Dig. CAL 9699 [id.]. (i) Talich Qt; (ii) Radoslav Kvapil.

Pride of place must go to the Talich Quartet on Calliope, not because their recording is the best – it is by no means as vivid as the DG or, for that matter, the Medici – but because of their extraordinary qualities of insight. They play the *Intimate letters* as if its utterances came from a world so private that it must be approached with great care. Their understanding of and love for this music comes across in every bar, and their insights are deeper than almost any of their predecessors on disc. This is a clear first choice and its value is much enhanced by a fill-up in the form of the *First suite, On an overgrown path*. Radoslav Kvapil is thoroughly inside this repertoire.

The Medici offer eminently enjoyable and thoroughly sound readings, not quite as penetrating or as fully characterized as those by the Talich Quartet, but nevertheless musically satisfying. Given the truthful recording and good balance, this is well worth considering.

The Hagen performances are every bit as carefully thought out and as superbly played as their earlier records of Slavonic repertoire (Dvořák and Kodály) but suffer from an expressive vehemence that will strike some listeners as out of key. Theirs is an impassioned, larger-than-life, rather sensationalized account that is stunningly played and very well recorded. The Wolf *Serenade* makes an agreeable encore.

Violin sonata.
*** Virgin Dig. VC 790760-2 [id.]. Dmitry Sitkovestsky, Pavel Gililov – DEBUSSY: *Sonata***; R. STRAUSS: *Sonata.****

Janáček composed two violin sonatas in his youth, neither of which survives. The present work was finalized in 1921. It is a rarity both in the concert hall and on record, and Dmitry Sitkovestsky and Pavel Gililov seem completely attuned to its thoughtful, impulsive, improvisatory idiom. There is excellent rapport between the two players, and the engineers produce a natural, well-balanced sound.

VOCAL MUSIC

Amarus (cantata).
*** Sup. Dig. SUP 007735 [id.]. Němečková, Vodička, Zítek, Czech Philharmonic Ch. and O, Mackerras – MARTINŮ: *Field mass.****

Amarus is relatively early, coming from 1897, well before *Jenůfa*. It is a powerfully written piece whose individuality was acknowledged by Dvořák, to whom Janáček sent the score. It is full of atmosphere and has a real sense of movement. The choral writing is powerful and the orchestration skilful and imaginative. The performance is a fine one; the recording is excellent on CD, which enjoys the usual advantages of the medium, greater range and body; the only minor grumble is that the soloists are a little too closely balanced. But this is strongly recommended and supersedes the earlier version by Vaclav Neumann on all counts.

Glagolitic Mass.
*** EMI Dig. CDC7 47504-2 [id.]. Palmer, Gunson, Mitchinson, King, CBSO & Ch., Rattle – *Sinfonietta.****
(M) *** Decca 425 624-2 [id.]. Kubiak, Collins, Tear, Schone, Brighton Fest. Ch., RPO, Kempe – *Sinfonietta.****

(i) *Glagolitic Mass; Taras Bulba.*
(M) ** DG 429 182-2 [id.]. (i) Lear, Rössl-Majdan, Haefliger, Crass, Bav. R. Ch.; Bav. RSO, Kubelik.

Written when Janáček was over seventy, this is one of his most important and most exciting works, full of those strikingly fresh uses of sound that make his music so distinctive. The opening instrumental movement has much in common with the opening fanfare of the *Sinfonietta*, and all the other movements reveal an original approach to the church service. The text is taken from native Croatian variations of the Latin text, but its vitality bespeaks a folk inspiration. Rattle's performance, aptly paired with the *Sinfonietta*, is strong and vividly dramatic, with the Birmingham performers lending themselves to Slavonic passion. The recording is first class. An outstanding coupling.

The Decca recording is also an extremely good one. Kempe's reading is somewhat broader than Rattle's but has plenty of vitality, and the Brighton chorus sings vigorously. The playing of the Royal Philharmonic too is wonderfully committed and vivid, and there is first-rate solo singing, with Teresa Kubiak particularly impressive. The sound on CD is splendidly lively and colourful, of vintage Decca quality.

The reissued DG coupling under Kubelik has considerable merits: there is some very fine playing in *Taras Bulba*. In a less competitive marketplace it would have been very welcome, but at medium price Kempe is preferable – the effect marginally less refined, perhaps, but with greater overall impact, even though the DG remastering gives a very lively effect.

Mass in E flat; (i) *Otčenáš (The Lord's Prayer).*
*** EMI Dig. CDC7 49092-2 [id.]. King's College, Cambridge, Ch., Cleobury; Stephen Layton; (i) with Arthur Davies, Osian Ellis – KODÁLY: *Missa brevis.****

The *Mass* was never completely finished. It is possible that Janáček used some of it twenty years later in the *Glagolitic Mass*. Janáček's pupil, Vilém Petrželka, discovered the *Kyrie* and *Agnus Dei* and a part of the *Credo*, which he completed. It is a beautiful piece. *Otčenáš (The Lord's Prayer)* was written originally for tenor, chorus and harmonium (or piano); the accompaniment was later replaced by organ and harp. The singing is generally good, though the sound is (not unnaturally) English rather than Slavonic. There is no alternative version of either work, and they are both valuable additions to the Janáček discography.

OPERA

The Cunning little vixen (complete); *Cunning little vixen* (suite, arr. Talich).
*** Decca Dig. 417 129-2 (2) [id.]. Popp, Randová, Jedlická, V. State Op. Ch., Bratislava Children's Ch., VPO, Mackerras.

Mackerras's thrusting, red-blooded reading is spectacularly supported by a digital recording of outstanding, demonstration quality. That Janáček deliberately added the death of the vixen to the original story points very much in the direction of such a strong, purposeful approach. The inspired choice of Lucia Popp as the vixen provides charm in exactly the right measure, a Czech-born singer who delights in the fascinating complexity of the vixen's character: sparkling and coquettish, spiteful as well as passionate. The supporting cast is first rate, too. Talich's splendidly arranged orchestral suite is offered as a bonus in a fine new recording.

Jenůfa (complete).
⊛ *** Decca Dig. 414 483-2 (2) [id.]. Söderström, Ochman, Dvorský, Randová, Popp, V. State Op. Ch., VPO, Mackerras.

This is the warmest and most lyrical of Janáček's operas, and it inspires a performance from Mackerras and his team which is deeply sympathetic, strongly dramatic and superbly recorded. After Mackerras's previous Janáček sets, it was natural to choose Elisabeth Söderström for the name-part. Mature as she is, she creates a touching portrait of the girl caught in a family tragedy. The two rival tenors, Peter Dvorský and Wieslav Ochman as the half-brothers Steva and Laca, are both superb; but dominating the whole drama is the Kostelnitchka of Eva Randová. For the first time on record one can register the beauty as well as the power of the writing for this equivocal central figure. Some may resist the idea that she should be made so sympathetic but, particularly on record, the drama is made stronger and more involving.

Osud (complete).
*** EMI Dig. CDC7 49993-2 [id.]. Langridge, Field, Harries, Bronder, Kale, Welsh National Op. Ch. & O, Mackerras.

This single-disc recording of Janáček's – most unjustly neglected – opera, richly lyrical, more sustained and less fragmented than his later operas, is not just a valuable rarity but makes an ideal introduction to the composer. It is a piece that was for generations rejected for being unstageable, thanks to the oddities of the libretto; that was until the

English National Opera presented it at the Coliseum in London in an unforgettable production by David Pountney. Though this recording, one of the series sponsored by the Peter Moores Foundation, was made with Welsh National Opera forces, its success echoes the ENO production too, with Philip Langridge, as at the Coliseum, superb in the central role of the composer, Zivny, well supported by Helen Field as Mila, the married woman he loves, and by Kathryn Harries as her mother – a far finer cast than was presented on a short-lived Supraphon set. That was done in the original Czech, whereas this performance, following ENO, uses Rodney Blumer's excellent English translation, adding to the immediate impact. Sir Charles Mackerras matches his earlier achievement in the prize-winning series of Janáček opera recordings for Decca, capturing the full gutsiness, passion and impetus of the composer's inspiration, from the exhilarating opening waltz ensemble onwards, a passage that vividly sets the scene in a German spa at the turn of the century. The warmly atmospheric EMI recording, made in Bragnwyn Hall, Swansea, brings out the unusual opulence of the Janáček sound in this work written immediately after *Jenufa*, yet it allows words to come over with fine clarity. With a playing-time of nearly 80 minutes, the single disc comes complete with English libretto and excellent notes.

Jolivet, André (1905–74)

(i) *Concertino for trumpet, piano and strings; Trumpet concerto.*
*** CBS Dig. MK 42096 [id.]. Wynton Marsalis, (i) Craig Shepherd, Philh. O, Salonen – TOMASI: *Concerto.****

As crossover music goes, this is rather successful, with the brilliant musicianship, dizzy bravura and natural idiomatic feeling of Wynton Marsalis tailor-made for this repertoire. There is not a great deal for Craig Shepherd to do in the duet concertino, but he does it well enough. This is certainly a flamboyant piece – but the solo concerto is the finer work, with the Latin-American dance-rhythms fully laminated to the music itself. The recording is not especially clear, but this does not seem to matter too much, though some ears will detect background hum at times. The CD offers poor value at only 35 minutes.

Jongen, Joseph (1873–1953)

Symphonie concertante, Op. 18.
*** Telarc Dig. CD 80096 [id.]. Murray, San Francisco SO, De Waart – FRANCK: *Fantaisie* etc.***

Anyone who likes the Saint-Saëns *Third Symphony* should enjoy this. Even if the music is on a lower level of inspiration, the passionate *Lento misterioso* and hugely spectacular closing *Toccata* make a favourable impression at first hearing and wear surprisingly well afterwards. The performance here is undoubtedly persuasive in its verve and commitment, and Michael Murray has all the necessary technique to carry off Jongen's hyperbole with the required panache. He receives excellent support from Edo de Waart and the San Francisco Symphony Orchestra. The huge Ruffatti organ seems custom-built for the occasion and Telarc's engineers capture all the spectacular effects with their usual aplomb. A demonstration disc indeed.

Joplin, Scott (1868–1917)

Elite syncopations (ballet).
**(*) CRD CRD 3329 [id.]. Gammon (piano), members of the Royal Ballet O.

These are authentic arrangements, many of them by Günther Schuller, and they are played with a fine sense of style. Most of the favourite rags are included (though not *The Entertainer*), plus some novelties, and the orchestrations are nicely varied, with the solo piano often left to play alone. The recording is really first class, and Joplin fans will find this very enjoyable, although some might feel that the playing is *too* sophisticated.

Rags (arr. Perlman): *Bethena; The Easy Winners; Elite syncopations; The Entertainer; Magnetic rag; Pineapple rag; Ragtime dance; Solace; The strenuous life; Sugar cane rag.*
*** EMI CDC7 47170-2 [id.]. Perlman, Previn.

Perlman and Previn letting their hair down present a winning combination in a whole sequence of Joplin's most naggingly haunting rags. This is very much Previn's country, and his rhythmic zest infects his brilliant partner. The naturally balanced 1975 sound is enhanced by the freshness of the CD transfer, and though the focus is not quite as sharp as one would expect in a more modern digital recording, the violin image is pleasingly without edge.

Rags: *A Breeze from Alabama; The Cascades; The Chrysanthemum; Easy winners; Elite syncopations; The Entertainer; Maple leaf rag; Original rags; Palm leaf rag; Peacherine rag; Something doing; The Strenuous life; Sunflower slow drag; Swipesy; The Sycamore.*
(M) *** RCA GD 87993 [7993-2-RG]. Dick Hyman.

Dick Hyman's playing is first rate. His rhythmic spring (the crisp snap of the main phrase of *Original rags* is a splendid example), clean touch and sensibility in matters of light and shade – without ever trying to present this as concert music – mean that pieces which can easily appear stereotyped remain fresh and spontaneous-sounding throughout. The recording has fine presence; the piano image (not too rich, but not shallow either) seems just right. There is nearly an hour of playing time and this is essentially a recital to be dipped into rather than listened to at a single sitting.

Josephs, Wilfred (born 1927)

Concerto for brass.
(M) *** Trax Dig. TRXCD 114 [id.]. L. Collegiate Brass, Stobart – LLOYD: *Symphony No. 10.****

Josephs' *Concerto* is an engaging set of variations (twenty-five in all) which, after an opening cornet flourish, sets off genially with its catchy theme. It is a slight work, but the invention is ingenious and entertaining, and the climax is a bizarre Sousa-esque march. With superbly clear, resonant brass recording and fine playing, this makes a very useful coupling for George Lloyd's more ambitious *Tenth Symphony*.

Josquin des Prés (c. 1450–1521)

Motets: *Absolom, fili mi; Ave Maria, gratia plena; De profundis clamavi; In te Domine speravi per trovar pietà; Veni, Sanctus Spiritus;* Chansons: *La déploration de la mort de Johannes Ockeghem; El grillo; En l'ombre d'ung buissonet au matinet; Je me complains;*

Je ne me puis tenir d'aimer; Mille regretz; Petite camusette; Scaramella va alla guerra; Scaramella va la galla.
*** EMI Dig. CDC7 49209-2 [id.]. Hilliard Ens.

Josquin spent much of his life in Italy, first as a singer in the choir of Milan Cathedral and subsequently in the service of the Sforza family. His fusion of learned polyphony and tuneful rhythmic gaiety laid the foundations of the Italian madrigal. The chansons recorded here have both variety of colour and lightness of touch, while the motets are sung with dignity and feeling by the Hilliard Ensemble. Indeed, these performances will kindle the enthusiasm of the uninitiated as few others can. The recording is expertly balanced and eminently truthful.

Motets: *Ave Maria, gratia plena; Ave, nobilissima creatura; Miserere mei, Deus; O bone et dulcissime Jesu; Salve regina; Stabat mater dolorosa; Usquequo, Domine, obliviceris me.*
*** HM Dig. HMC 901243 [id.]. Chapelle Royale Ch., Herreweghe.

A valuable Josquin anthology which gives us the *Miserere*, so much admired by the doyen of Josquin scholars, Edward Lowinsky. The Chapelle Royale comprises some nineteen singers, but they still produce a clean, well-focused sound and benefit from excellent recorded sound. Their account of the expressive *Stabat mater* sounds thicker-textured than the New College forces under Edward Higginbottom, but there is a refreshing sense of commitment and strong feeling. They are well served by the recording engineers.

Antiphons, Motets and Sequences: *Inviolata; Praeter rerum serium; Salve regina; Stabat mater dolorosa; Veni, sancte spiritus; Virgo prudentissima; Virgo salutiferi.*
*** Mer. ECD 84093 [id.]. New College, Oxford, Ch., Higginbottom.

The Meridian anthology collects some of Josquin's most masterly and eloquent motets in performances of predictable excellence by Edward Higginbottom and the Choir of New College, Oxford. Higginbottom does not shrink from expressive feeling and at the same time secures both purity of tone and clarity of texture. An admirable introduction to Josquin, and an essential acquisition for those who care about this master.

Missa: Faisant regretz; Missa di dadi.
*** O-L Dig. 411 937-2 [id.]. Medieval Ens. of London, Peter and Timothy Davies.

The two Josquin Masses recorded here are both new to the catalogue; both are parody Masses based on English music of the period. The *Missa: Faisant regretz* acquires its name from the fact that its four-note cantus firmus occurs on the words, 'Faisant regretz', in the chanson *Tout a par moy*. They are both ingenious works and, more to the point, very beautiful, particularly when sung with such dedication and feeling as here. Nine singers are used for this recording, the number that would have been available in an average-size choir of one of the smaller religious establishments before the 1480s, the last decade when these Masses could have been composed. The Medieval Ensemble of London sing superbly; they not only blend perfectly but are blessed with perfect intonation. This deserves the strongest recommendation to all with an interest in this period.

Missa – L'homme armé super voces musicales.
*** DG 415 293-2 [id.]. Pro Cantione Antiqua, Bruno Turner – OCKEGHEM: *Missa pro defunctis.****

This Mass on the *L'homme armé* theme is both one of the most celebrated of all Mass settings based on this secular melody and at the same time one of Josquin's most masterly and admired works. It was written in the late 1480s or early '90s and is called *super voces musicales* to distinguish it from his *Missa L'homme armé in sexti toni* (in the sixth mode). Jeremy Noble's edition is used in the present (1977) performance, which must be numbered among the very finest accounts not only of a Josquin but of any Renaissance Mass to have appeared on record. On CD, the transparency of each strand in the vocal texture is wonderfully clear and the singers are astonishingly present. An outstanding issue.

Missa Pange lingua.
**(*) HM Dig. HMC 901239 [id.]. Clément Janequin Ens.

Missa Pange lingua; Missa La sol fa re mi.
*** Gimell Dig. CDGIM 009 [id.]. Tallis Scholars, Peter Phillips.

The Gimell recording of the *Missa Pange lingua* has collected superlatives on all counts and was voted record of the year in the *Gramophone* magazine's 1987 awards. The tone the Tallis Scholars produce is perfectly blended, each line being firmly defined and yet beautifully integrated into the whole sound-picture. Their recording, made in the Chapel of Merton College, Oxford, is first class, the best of the *Missa Pange lingua* and the first of the ingenious *Missa La sol fa re mi*. Not to be missed.

The Clément Janequin Ensemble also can hardly be flawed. They use eight singers but also make considerable use of solo voices. The Mass is interspersed with chant appropriate to the Feast of Corpus Christi, sung by the Organum Ensemble under Marcel Peres; CD players can be programmed to omit some or all of these bands – but, even so, it puts rival versions at something of an advantage when they can accommodate another Mass.

Kabalevsky, Dmitri (1904-87)

Cello concerto No. 1 in G min.
*** CBS Dig. MK 37840 [id.]. Yo-Yo Ma, Phd. O, Ormandy – SHOSTAKOVICH: *Cello concerto No. 1.****

Both of Kabalevsky's *Cello concertos* have been recorded before, though neither with such persuasive force as Yo-Yo Ma brings to the *First*. This is an amiable piece and is well crafted and pleasing. The excellence of the performance is matched by a fine recording which adds considerably to the refinement and presence of the sound, and its vividness is such as to seem to add stature to the music itself.

Cello concerto No. 2, Op. 77.
*** Chan. Dig. CHAN 8579 [id.]. Wallfisch, LPO, Thomson – GLAZUNOV: *Chant du ménestrel*; KHACHATURIAN: *Concerto.****
*** Virgin Dig. VC 790811-2 [id.]. Isserlis, LPO, Litton – PROKOFIEV: *Concertino; Cello sonata.****

The *Second* is the darker of the two *Cello concertos* and touches on a deeper vein of feeling than one encounters in, say, his more familiar *Second Symphony*. It is played eloquently – and with the greatest virtuosity – by Rafael Wallfisch, who is well supported by Bryden Thomson and the LPO. Excellent recording too.

Steven Isserlis on Virgin gives as compelling and ardent an account of the *Concerto* as does Wallfisch on Chandos and, since the LPO play as well for Andrew Litton as they did for Bryden Thomson, there is little to choose between them. As far as recorded sound is concerned, both are impressive: perhaps Virgin use a slightly less resonant acoustic. The coupling will probably settle matters for most collectors; Isserlis offers two rarities, both new to CD.

Violin concerto in C, Op. 48.
(**) Chant du Monde mono LDC 278883 [id.]. David Oistrakh, USSR Nat. O, composer – KHACHATURIAN: *Violin concerto.**** ⊛

If the style of Kabalevsky's gay, extrovert *Concerto* is essentially old-fashioned, the work is spontaneous and tuneful. David Oistrakh's 1955 mono recording is in most ways definitive, with the composer helping to make the delightfully atmospheric slow movement quite memorable. Oistrakh's clean articulation and sparkle in the finale are also outstanding – and it is a pity that so much allowance has to be made for the sound, which is papery, with a shrill solo image and whistly orchestral strings. At a modest volume level, with a top cut, it is listenable, however, and the playing itself is highly rewarding.

Romeo and Juliet (Musical sketches), Op. 55.
(M) ** Olympia OCD 147 [id.]. Moscow SO, Kitaenko – GLAZUNOV: *Symphony No. 9*; LVOV: *Violin concerto.***

Kabalevsky's music to *Romeo and Juliet* comes from 1956, twenty years after Prokofiev's ballet, whose influence it at times reflects. There are some beautiful episodes, as in the opening of the *Lyric dance* (the *Meeting of Romeo and Juliet*) but, although it has a good sense of theatre, the melodic substance is not really strong enough for it to sustain strong claims on the repertory. The orchestral playing under Dmitri Kitaenko is responsive but the recording is not in the first flight.

Kalinnikov, Vasily (1866–1901)

Intermezzos Nos. 1 in F sharp min.; 2 in G.
*** Chan. Dig. CHAN 8614 [id.]. SNO, Järvi - RACHMANINOV: *Symphony No. 3.****

These two colourful *Intermezzos* with a flavour of Borodin are charming examples of Kalinnikov's work, an attractive if hardly generous fill-up for Järvi's red-blooded account of Rachmaninov's *Third Symphony*.

Symphony No. 1 in G min.
*** Chan. Dig. CHAN 8611 [id.]. SNO, Järvi – GLAZUNOV: *The Sea; Spring.****

Some of the fame of Kalinnikov's *First Symphony* must be attributed to the second theme of the first movement which is irresistible and, once heard, is difficult to get out of your head. The symphony contains something akin to the flow and natural lyricism of Borodin, and the second movement has something of the atmosphere and character of early Rachmaninov or his almost exact contemporary, Glazunov. Neeme Järvi and the Scottish National Orchestra seem fired with enthusiasm for this appealing work, and the engineers serve them admirably. Strongly recommended.

Symphonies Nos. 1 in G min.; 2 in A.
** Chant du Monde LDC 278 926 [id.]. USSR State Ac. SO, Svetlanov.

The attraction of the Chant du Monde disc is that of economy in that it couples both these appealing works together, and were it at mid-price it would be highly competitive. But these recordings are not new: the *First Symphony* comes from 1975 and the *Second* from 1969; and they do not compete with Neeme Järvi's discs on Chandos. The Melodiya recording does not do full justice to the bloom of this great orchestra's strings, though it is generally acceptable.

Symphony No. 2 in A; The Cedar and the palm; Overture: Tsar Boris.
*** Chan. Dig. CHAN 8805 [id.]. SNO, Järvi.

The *Second Symphony*, though not quite as appealing as No. 1, is played by the Scottish orchestra under Neeme Järvi with enthusiasm and commitment, and the Chandos recording is in the demonstration class. The Tsar to whom the *Overture* alludes is the one celebrated by both Pushkin and Mussorgsky. *The Cedar and the palm* was Kalinnikov's last piece and was inspired by Heine's, which must have enjoyed a vogue at the turn of the century, as Sibelius also planned a work inspired by it. Both these novelties are worth having on disc.

Kálmán, Emmerich (1882–1953)

Countess Maritza: highlights (in English).
*** That's Entertainment CDTER 1051. Hill-Smith, Remedios, Barber, Livingstone, Tudor Davies, Moyle, New Sadler's Wells Op. Ch. and O, Wordsworth.

The label, 'That's Entertainment', has brought out an enterprising series of recordings of stage musicals. Here it adds a recording based on the New Sadler's Wells production (in English) of Kálmán's operetta. Voices are fresh, playing and conducting are lively and the recording is excellent. Much recommended for those who prefer their operetta in English, for the CD has fine presence.

Kancheli, Giya (born 1935)

Symphonies Nos. (i) *3* (1973); *6* (1981).
*** Olympia OCD401. (i) Gonashvili; Georgian State SO, Dzabsug Kakhidze.

The Georgian State Symphony Orchestra is absolutely first rate and their conductor, Dzabsug Kakhidze, obtains impressive results in the two symphonies recorded here. Their composer studied in his native Tiflis, where he now teaches. The *Third Symphony* is essentially static; there is little in the way of symphonic development, but the treatment of the orchestra is imaginative. There is a small role for a wordless tenor solo. The *Sixth* caused something of a stir when it was given at the 1987 Warsaw Autumn, and it has developed a small but devoted following. Like No. 3, it is strongly atmospheric but again mostly static (and rather empty). The performances have enormous conviction and the analogue recordings, made in 1979 and 1981 respectively, are very good indeed, wide in range and truthful in perspective.

Kern, Jerome (1885–1945)

Showboat (complete recording of original score).
⊛ *** EMI Dig. CD-RIVER 1 (3) [Ang. A23 49108]. Von Stade, Hadley, Hubbard, O'Hara, Garrison, Burns, Stratas, Amb. Ch., L. Sinf., John McGlinn.

In faithfully following the original score, this superb set at last does justice to a musical of the 1920s which is both a landmark in the history of Broadway and musically a work of strength and imagination hardly less significant than Gershwin's *Porgy and Bess* of a decade later. Even with spoken scenes cut and dialogue drastically pruned, the recording lasts for almost four hours – and that includes a fascinating appendix of variants and extra items alone lasting over an hour. The original, extended versions of important scenes are included, as well as various numbers written for later productions. In the modern 'crossover' manner, this recording is operatically cast, but with far more concern for idiomatic performance than usual. As the heroine, Magnolia – who dauntingly has to age 37 years between beginning and end – Frederica von Stade gives a meltingly beautiful performance, totally in style, bringing out the beauty and imagination of Kern's melodies, regularly heightened by wide intervals to make those of most of his Broadway rivals seem flat. The first half-hour alone brings a clutch of hit numbers – *Make believe, Ol' man river* and *Can't help loving that man* among them – which one would be lucky to find in a whole season of Broadway musicals today. The London Sinfonietta play with tremendous zest and feeling for the idiom, while tuba bass and banjo regularly add spice to the ensemble; the Ambrosian Chorus sings with joyful brightness and some impeccable American accents. Opposite von Stade, Jerry Hadley makes a winning Ravenal, and Teresa Stratas is charming as Julie, giving a heartfelt performance of the haunting number, *Bill* (words by P. G. Wodehouse). Above all, the magnificent black bass, Bruce Hubbard, sings *Ol' man river* and its many reprises with a firm resonance to have you recalling the wonderful example of Paul Robeson, but for once without hankering after the past. The cast of actors is also distinguished, with Lillian Gish, a star since her first appearance on the silent screen, as an old lady on the levee, right at the end. Beautifully recorded to bring out the piece's dramatic as well as its musical qualities, this is a heart-warming issue.

Ketèlbey, Albert (1875–1959)

Bells across the meadow; Chal Romano (Gypsy lad); The Clock and the Dresden figures; In a Chinese temple garden; In a monastery garden; In a Persian market; In the moonlight; In the mystic land of Egypt; Sanctuary of the heart.
*** EMI CDC7 47806-2 [id.]. Midgley, Temperley, Amb. S., Pearson (piano), Philh. O, Lanchbery.

A splendid collection in every way. John Lanchbery uses every possible resource to ensure that when the composer demands spectacle he gets it. *In the mystic land of Egypt*, for instance, uses soloist and chorus in canon in the principal tune (and very fetchingly too). In the *Monastery garden* the distant monks are realistically distant, in *Sanctuary of the heart* there is no mistaking that the heart is worn firmly on the sleeve. The orchestral playing throughout is not only polished but warmhearted – the middle section of *Bells across the meadow*, which has a delightful melodic contour, is played most tenderly and loses any hint of vulgarity. Yet when vulgarity is called for it is not shirked – only it's a stylish kind of vulgarity! The recording is excellent, full and brilliant, and it has transferred to CD with striking presence and warmth.

Khachaturian, Aram (1903–78)

Cello concerto.
*** Chan. Dig. CHAN 8579 [id.]. Wallfisch, LPO, Thomson – GLAZUNOV: *Chant du ménestrel*; KABALEVSKY: *Cello concerto No.2.***

The *Cello concerto* is a post-war work, dating from 1946, and although it is true that there are some imaginative moments and expert handling of the orchestra, it is not one of

Khachaturian's strongest pieces. Rafael Wallfisch plays with total commitment and has the benefit of excellent and sympathetic support from the LPO under Bryden Thomson. The recording is of the usual high standard we have come to expect from Chandos.

Piano concerto in D flat.
** Hyp. Dig. CDA 66293 [id.]. Servadei, LPO, Giunta – BRITTEN: *Piano concerto.***

(i) *Piano concerto in D flat; Gayaneh* (ballet) *suite; Masquerade: suite.*
**(*) Chan. Dig. CHAN 8542 [id.]. (i) Orbelian, SNO, Järvi.

The Chandos recording is splendid technically, well up to the standards of the house. Constantin Orbelian, an Armenian by birth, plays brilliantly and Järvi achieves much attractive lyrical detail. He scores in the slow movement by making the most of the curious whistly overtones of the flexitone, used with great aplomb here. The bass clarinet, too, drools sinuously at the end. Overall it is a spacious account, and though the finale has plenty of gusto, the music-making seems just a shade too easy-going in the first movement. The couplings, sumptuously played, are both generous and appealing, especially *Masquerade* – an attractively romantic account of this rather engaging music. Four famous numbers are included from *Gayaneh*, among the finest music Khachaturian ever wrote, and they are played with considerable panache.

In the Khachaturian concerto Annette Servadei makes up in clarity and point for a relative lack of weight in the outer movements, which she takes at speeds marginally slower than usual. The slow movement brings hushed and intense playing, sympathetically supported by the LPO under Joseph Giunta in a new digital recording that is well balanced and unaggressive. However, ideally this work needs a stronger grip than these artists exert – the first movement in particular could do with greater thrust.

Violin concerto in D min.
⊛ *** Chant du Monde LDC 278883 [Mobile Fidelity MFCD 899 with SIBELIUS: *Concerto*]. David Oistrakh, USSR RSO, composer – KABALEVSKY: *Violin concerto.*(**)
(*) EMI Dig. CDC7 47087-2 [id.]. Perlman, Israel PO, Mehta – TCHAIKOVSKY: *Méditation.**

David Oistrakh, for whom the *Concerto* was written, gave the work its première, and is its dedicatee. He is peerless in its performance, not only in projecting its very Russian bravura, but also in his melting phrasing and timbre in the sinuous secondary theme of the first movement, which returns in the finale, and in the equally haunting melody of the *Andante*. Indeed this quite marvellous performance is unlikely ever to be surpassed. The composer, clearly inspired by the expressive response of his soloist, creates a rapt degree of tension in the slow movement and affectionately caresses the Armenian colour and detail in the very atmospheric orchestral accompaniment. The finale has an irresistible exhilaration, and the return of the big tune on the G string is heart-warming. The (1970) Russian recording is warm and very well balanced, especially in its relationship of soloist with orchestra. The acoustic is resonant in the right way – there is bloom but no muddiness or fierceness. This must be listed among the all too few great stereo recordings in which the composer has been able to participate. The *Concerto* is coupled differently in the USA.

Perlman's performance sparkles too – indeed it is superb in every way, lyrically persuasive in the *Andante* and displaying great fervour and rhythmic energy in the finale. He is well accompanied by Mehta (who nevertheless does not match the composer's feeling for detail); were the Oistrakh version not available, this would be a ready choice. However, on CD one's ear is drawn to the very forward balance of the soloist, and the generally bright lighting becomes rather fierce at the opening tutti of the finale – the comparatively dry Israeli acoustic does not provide an ideal bloom on the music-making.

Flute concerto (arr. Rampal/Galway); *Gayaneh: Sabre dance. Masquerade: Waltz. Spartacus: Adagio of Spartacus and Phrygia.*
*** RCA Dig. RD 87010. Galway, RPO, Myung-Whun Chung.

Khachaturian's *Flute concerto* is a transcription of the *Violin concerto* made by Jean-Pierre Rampal, with the composer's blessing. Galway has prepared his own edition of the solo part 'which goes even further in its attempts to adapt the solo line to the characteristics of the flute'. He has the advantage of a modern digital recording, but the resonant acoustic of Watford Town Hall tends to coarsen the orchestral tuttis very slightly, especially the big fortissimo flare-up towards the end of the slow movement, which is fierce. Needless to say, the solo playing is peerless; if in the finale even Galway cannot match the effect Oistrakh makes with his violin, the ready bravura is sparklingly infectious. As encores, he offers three of Khachaturian's most famous melodies. They are marvellously played, with the *Sabre dance* elegant rather than boisterously noisy.

Gayaneh (ballet): original score: highlights.
(***) RCA RD 70952. Nat. PO, Tjeknavorian.

Gayaneh: suite.
(B) *** RCA VD 87734 [7734-2-RV]. Boston Pops O, Fiedler – OFFENBACH: *Gaîté parisienne.****

Gayaneh (ballet): highlights; *Spartacus* (ballet): highlights.
(M) **(*) EMI CD-EMX 2119. LSO, composer.

Gayaneh: suite; Masquerade suite; Spartacus: suite.
(B) **(*) Decca 417 062-2 [id.]. LSO, Stanley Black.

Gayaneh (ballet): *suite; Spartacus* (ballet): *suite.*
**(*) EMI Dig. CDC7 47348-2 [id.]. RPO, Temirkanov.
(M) **(*) Decca 417 737-2 [id.]. VPO, composer – PROKOFIEV: *Romeo and Juliet.****

Loris Tjeknavorian made a pretty definitive recording of Khachaturian's *Gayaneh* in 1977 using the original score. The RCA highlights disc, which plays for 71 minutes, includes the kernel of the ballet and offers at least a dozen numbers with strong melodic and rhythmic appeal and apt scoring. The performance is first class, with polished and alive orchestral playing directed by the sympathetic Tjeknavorian, himself an Armenian by birth. Unfortunately, the CD transfer produces artificially brightened sound which is very wearing to listen to – for there is much that is noisy. While the gentler numbers still sound beautiful, the bass is light, which emphasizes the brightly lit treble.

Temirkanov opens *Gayaneh* with the boisterous but engaging *Gopak*, rather than the *Sabre dance* (which follows on soon enough); in the nine items from this ballet and the slightly shorter selection from *Spartacus* musical characterization is strong, rhythms are well sprung and the lyrical music is treated with contrasting tenderness. The RPO respond with playing that is both alert and polished. In the famous *Adagio* from *Spartacus* Temirkanov refuses to go over the top – the composer's own recording is more passionate – but the element of slight reserve is not unattractive. The digital sound is brilliant but not edgy.

Fiedler's offering is a miniature suite; it includes the *Lesginka, Dance of the Rose Maidens* and *Dance of the Kurds*, plus an exhilarating *Sabre dance*, all played with zest and flair – but, alas, it omits the *Lullaby*. Fiedler and his Bostonians are at their best, and the RCA sound is pretty good too. An excellent coupling for an outstanding bargain version of Offenbach's *Gaîté parisienne* ballet.

The composer's own first selection on Decca was recorded in 1962 and offers five items from *Gayaneh* and four from *Spartacus*, coupled to an intelligent selection from Maazel's complete Cleveland set of Prokofiev's *Romeo and Juliet*, dating from a decade later. Khachaturian achieves a brilliant response from the VPO and everything is most vivid, notably the famous *Adagio* from *Spartacus* which is both expansive and passionate. It is a pity that the Decca remastering process has brought everything into such strong focus; the presence of the sound certainly makes an impact, but the massed violins now have an added edge and boldness of attack, at the expense of their richness of timbre.

Khachaturian's 1977 pairing for EMI of suites from his two famous ballets offers one more item from *Gayaneh* than on his 1962 Decca coupling. The EMI sound was originally both reverberant and more voluptuous; the digital remastering creates a drier effect, without achieving absolute clarity of focus. The recording is less brightly lit than the Decca – but that is much more generous in including also a suite from Prokofiev's *Romeo and Juliet*. In terms of sound, the EMI issue is perhaps marginally fuller.

Stanley Black understands the spirit of this music and the LSO make a colourful and vibrant response. The recording is forwardly balanced but extremely vivid, and this is an inexpensive way of acquiring some of the composer's most memorable ideas.

Symphony No. 2; Gayaneh: suite.
(M) (***) Decca 425 619-2 [id.]. VPO, composer.

The *Symphony* was a propaganda piece, written during the war when the composer was evacuated from Moscow. Khachaturian lays the Armenian colour on very thickly but, unlike the splendid *Violin concerto* of two years earlier, this does not develop into a coherent argument. If the musical value is roughly in inverse proportion to the amount of noise made (and it is a long and very loud score indeed), one can still find the composer's earnest attempts to create a symphonic structure curiously endearing, and the lyrical moments are often quite attractive. The performance gives the music passionate advocacy and the recording is superbly spectacular (although the CD remastering doesn't help its garish qualities). When one turns to the *Gayaneh* coupling, splendidly done, one realizes where Khachaturian's talent really lies.

Knipper, Lev (1898–1974)

(i) *Concert poem for cello and orchestra; Sinfonietta for strings.*
** Olympia OCD 163 [id.]. (i) Shakhovskaya; Moscow Conservatoire CO, Teryan – MIASKOVSKY: *Symphony No. 7.***

Lev Knipper was a respected figure in Soviet music and a pupil of Glière in Moscow. This *Sinfonietta* comes from 1953 and is well-fashioned but rather anonymous music, albeit with some moments of beauty. The *Concert poem* opens strikingly and is played magnificently, but is not strongly individual either. The recording is rather forwardly balanced.

Knussen, Oliver (born 1952)

Where the Wild Things are (complete).
*** Unicorn Dig. DKPCD 9044 [id.]. Rosemary Hardy, Mary King, Herrington, Richardson, Rhys-Williams, Gallacher, L. Sinf., composer.

Oliver Knussen has devised a one-act opera that beautifully matches the grotesque fantasy of Maurice Sendak's children's book of the same name, with its gigantic monsters or Wild Things which prove to have hearts of gold and make the naughty boy, Max, their king. The record presents the piece with all the bite and energy of a live performance. It helped that the sessions took place immediately after a series of stage performances. The final rumpus music, which Knussen managed to complete only after the rest, here feels like the culmination intended. Rosemary Hardy makes a superb Max, not just accurate but giving a convincing portrait of the naughty child with little or no archness. Mary King sings warmly in the small part of the Mother. The brilliant recording vividly conveys a sense of presence and space.

Kodály, Zoltán (1882–1967)

(i) *Concerto for orchestra; Summer evening;* (ii) *Háry János: suite.*
(M) **(*) DG 427 408-2 [id.]. (i) Budapest PO, composer; (ii) Berlin RSO, Fricsay.

Kodály's *Concerto for orchestra* does not set out to rival the Bartók *Concerto*, but in its own way it is attractive and easy to listen to. *Summer evening*, a pleasantly rhapsodic pastoral piece, dates from ten years earlier. Kodály's own recordings come from 1960 and originally sounded recessed, with little immediacy of impact. The improvement on CD is dramatic and the performances of both works sound much more vital, even if Kodály does not display the fervour and intensity which Fricsay brings to the *Háry János suite* (recorded a year later), with *The Battle and defeat of Napoleon* made very dramatic indeed. The Berlin Radio orchestra play splendidly and the sound is sparkling and clear.

Dances of Galánta.
*** Ph. 416 378-2 [id.]. Concg. O, Zinman – BARTÓK: *Concerto for 2 Pianos, percussion & celesta.****

Dances of Galánta; Dances of Marosszék; Variations on a Hungarian folksong (Peacock).
**(*) Hung. Dig. HCD 12252 [id.]. Budapest SO, Lehel.

Lehel conducts warmly idiomatic readings of three of Kodály's most colourful and approachable orchestral works, lacking only the last degree of virtuoso brilliance. The bright, immediate recorded sound makes up for that lack, with the instruments well defined within a helpful but hardly reverberant acoustic.

David Zinman offers an attractively vivid performance of the *Dances of Galánta*. Although this is not a very generous coupling for the Bartók *Concerto*, the recording is very much in the demonstration class. Philips experimentally used simple microphone techniques, and the result brings an uncanny sense of presence and realism, indeed of sitting in the concert hall.

Háry János suite.
(BB) *** Naxos Dig. 8.550142 [id.]. Hungarian State O, Mátyás Antal (with Concert: 'Hungarian festival'***).

The Hungarian performance of the *Háry János suite* is wonderfully vivid, with the cimbalom – perfectly balanced within the orchestra – particularly telling. The grotesque elements of *The Battle and defeat of Napoleon* are pungently and wittily characterized and the *Entrance of the Emperor and his Court* also has an ironical sense of spectacle. The brilliant digital sound adds to the vitality and projection of the music-making, yet the lyrical music is played most tenderly. Incidentally, CBS have reissued George Szell's comparably brilliant account from the 1960s (CD 45509 [MYK 38527]), coupled with Prokofiev's *Lieutenant Kijé*, demonstrating the superb flair and virtuosity of the Cleveland Orchestra at that time. The Hungarians cannot quite match the Americans in polish, but they have this music in their bones. The CBS remastering has brought a tingling brightness to the sound which makes it tiring to the ear; the Naxos recording is more naturally atmospheric.

Háry Janos: suite; Dances of Galánta.
*** Delos Dig. DE 3083 [id.]. Seattle SO, Garard Schwarz – BARTÓK: *Miraculous Mandarin.***(*)

The Seattle Symphony Orchestra play Kodály's music with great vividness and warmth. The *Háry Janos suite* is more spaciously Romantic in feeling than some versions – helped by the rich acoustics of Seattle Opera House – and there is less surface glitter. But *The Battle and defeat of Napoleon* and the *Entrance of the Emperor and his Court* have all the necessary mock-drama and spectacle, and it is good to hear the cimbalom again balanced so effectively within the orchestra. The *Galánta dances* have splendid dash. The recording is outstandingly real, yet very naturally balanced.

(Unaccompanied) *Cello sonata, Op. 8;* (i) *Duo for violin and cello.*
*** Delos D/CD 1015 [id.]. Janos Starker, (i) Josef Gingold.
**(*) Chan. Dig. CHAN 8427 [id.]. Yuri Turovsky, (i) with Eleonora Turovsky.

Starker's version, his fourth, was made in 1970 in Japan. When, not long before the composer's death, Kodály heard him playing it, he apparently said: 'If you correct the ritard in the third movement, it will be the Bible performance.' To judge from this record, his prediction was not far from the truth. The recording is made in a smaller studio than is perhaps ideal, though it has a certain nostalgic attraction since it calls to mind the somewhat boxy sound of his first LP. But generally the sound is good; the *Duo*, impressively played by Starker and Josef Gingold, is made in a slightly more open acoustic. There is a small makeweight in the form of Starker's own arrangement of the Bottermund *Paganini variations*. Authoritative and eloquent playing throughout.

Yuri Turovsky plays with considerable intensity and understands the work's rhapsodical nature. He is given striking body and presence by the recording. The *Duo* is another fine work and, with Eleonora Turovsky taking the lead, this performance is even more compellingly spontaneous. The recording is very well balanced.

String quartets Nos. 1 and 2.
**(*) Hung. Dig. HCD 12362 [id.]. Kodály Qt.

String quartet No. 2, Op. 10.
*** DG Dig. 419 601-2 [id.]. Hagen Qt – DVOŘÁK: *String quartet No. 12* etc.***

The two performances from this eponymous quartet make an excellent coupling, warmly committed and spontaneous. Though the playing is not as refined as from the most polished Hungarian quartet groups, the natural understanding brings out the sharply contrasted character of the two works very convincingly. Much the more ambitious and more passionate is the *First*, Kodály's Op. 2, written in 1909; in its luxuriant span it inhabits very much the same world as Bartók's *First Quartet* of the same period, yearningly lyrical but bitingly dramatic too, with its characteristic folk element. The *Second Quartet* of 1918 is altogether simpler and less intense, a delightful, compact piece, which reveals Kodály's own character more clearly, very different from that of his close colleague. Excellent, immediate recording.

The Hagen give a marvellously committed and beautifully controlled performance of the *Second* – indeed as quartet playing it would be difficult to surpass. They might strike some collectors as almost too polished – Hungarian peasants in their best Sunday suits, rather than in everyday attire – but, in range of dynamic response and sheer beauty of sound, this is thrilling playing and welcome advocacy of a neglected but masterly piece. The recording is well balanced and admirably present.

Budavári Te Deum; Missa brevis.
*** Hung. HCD 11397-2 [id.]. Andor, Ekert, Makkay, Mohácsi, Szirmay, Réti, Gregor, Hungarian R. & TV Ch., Budapest SO, Ferencsik.

The *Budavári Te Deum* is predictably nationalist in feeling. The *Missa brevis* is also one of Kodály's strongest works, almost comparable in stature to the *Psalmus Hungaricus*. The performances first appeared on record in the early 1970s but sound remarkably fresh in their CD incarnation. The singing is accurate and sensitive, and the playing of the Budapest orchestra under Ferencsik absolutely first class.

Budavári Te Deum; Missa brevis; Psalmus Hungaricus, Op. 13.
(M) (**) Ph. mono 426 102-2 (2) [id.]. Rossler, Szecsodi, Tiszay, Udvardy, Farago, Gyurkovios, Ganos, Cser, Littasy, Budapest Ch., Hungarian Nat. PO, composer.

The *Psalmus Hungaricus* and the *Budavári Te Deum* share the first CD and the *Missa brevis* has the second to itself. These mono recordings were made in 1956–8 and first appeared on Hungaroton LPs in the early 1980s. They do not wear their years quite as gracefully as does the slightly later DG disc of the *Concerto for orchestra* and *Summer evening*. However, the ear rapidly adjusts and the performances are of considerable spirit and obvious authority: there is some particularly fine singing in the *Te Deum*.

Háry János (musical numbers only).
**(*) Hung. HCD 12837/8-2 [id.]. Sólyom-Nagy, Takács, Sudlik, Póka, Mésozöly, Gregor, Palcsó, Hungarian R. & TV Children's Ch., Hungarian State Op. Ch. and O, Ferencsik.

For the CD transfer the dialogue has been cut out, which means there is no dramatic continuity but, when Kodály's score is so colourful, the piece becomes a rich chocolate-box of delights. Ferencsik's performance with Hungarian singers and players is committedly idiomatic, with strong singing, not always ideally well characterized but very stylish, from some of the most distinguished principals of the Budapest Opera.

(i) *Hymn of Zrinyi*; (ii) *Psalmus Hungaricus*.
(M) *** Decca 421 810-2 (2) [id.]. (i) Luxon, Brighton Fest. Ch., Heltay; (ii) Kozma, Brighton Fest. Ch., Wandsworth School Boys' Ch., LSO, Kertesz – DVORÁK: *Requiem*.***

Psalmus Hungaricus is Kodály's most vital choral work, and this Decca version comes as close to an ideal performance as one is likely to get. Here, with a chorus trained by a Hungarian musician, the results are electrifying, and the recording is outstandingly brilliant too. The light tenor tone of Lajos Kozma is not ideal for the solo part, but again the authentic Hungarian touch helps. The *Hymn of Zrinyi*, for unaccompanied chorus and baritone solo, celebrates a Magyar hero, and Heltay is persuasive. With first-class remastered sound, this generous coupling with Dvořák is strongly recommended.

Missa brevis.
*** EMI Dig. CDC7 49092-2 [id.]. King's College, Cambridge, Ch., Cleobury; Stephen Layton – JANÁCEK: *Mass in E flat; Otčenáš.****

The *Missa brevis* is one of Kodály's strongest and most deeply felt works, every bit as powerful as the *Psalmus Hungaricus*. Ferencsik's recording was of the orchestral version, whereas Stephen Cleobury gives it in its earlier form as did Laszlo Heltay in the early 1970s. Some of the treble lines could be more secure, but for the most part this is a good performance, even if it lacks the bite and intensity that Hungarian singers would bring to it.

Kokkonen, Joonas (born 1921)

(i) *Cello concerto; Symphonic sketches; Symphony No. 4.*
*** BIS Dig. CD 468 [id.]. (i) Torleif Thedéen, Lahti SO, Osmo Vänskä.

Kokkonen is the leading composer of the older generation in Finland; this is the first CD in a project to record all his orchestral works. The *Fourth Symphony* is the strongest work here: its ideas are symphonic, its structure organic and its atmosphere powerful. The *Cello concerto* is a lyrical piece, very accessible – indeed some may find it insufficiently astringent (there is a slightly sanctimonious streak to the composer). The Swedish cellist, Torleif Thedéen, still in his twenties, gives a performance of great restraint, mastery and sensitivity. Good orchestral playing and recording.

Korngold, Erich (1897–1957)

Violin concerto in D, Op. 35.
*** EMI CDC7 47846-2 [id.]. Perlman, Pittsburgh SO, Previn – GOLDMARK: *Concerto.****

The *Violin concerto* draws its material largely from film scores. It was written for Huberman, but was a favourite of Heifetz's. It has to be played as if it is a masterpiece and with consummate virtuosity if it is to carry conviction. Perlman, dashing and romantic, with more of a sense of fun than the older maestro, gives such a superlative account, and though he is placed too close to the microphone, the recording overall is vivid, with Previn and the Pittsburgh orchestra warmly committed in their accompaniment. Although it is pure kitsch, there is something endearing about this piece and it deserves a place in the catalogue, if only to remind us of the calibre of this famous Hollywood musician. It is also marvellous violin music. The remastered sound has gained in presence, but lost a little amplitude and warmth.

Film scores: excerpts from: *Anthony Adverse; Between Two Worlds;* (i) *The Constant Nymph; Deception; Devotion; Escape Me Never; King's Row; Of Human Bondage; The Sea Hawk* (suite); *The Sea Wolf* (suite).
(M) *** RCA GD 87890 [7890-2-RG]. Nat. PO, Gerhardt; (i) with Procter, Amb. S.

A generous anthology of Korngold's film scores, showing the richness of his lyrical invention and vivid sense of orchestral colour. The spacious recording, with its panoply of brass and strings, sounds even more spectacular on CD. Hollywoodian hyperbole is heard at its most overwhelming in the *Between Two Worlds* sequence, while *The Constant Nymph* (about a composer) brings a characteristically flamboyant setting for contralto soloist (here Norma Procter) and chorus. *The Sea Wolf* contrasts a snarlingly pungent portrait of the main character (played by Edward G. Robinson) with a tenderly nostalgic romantic interlude. The *Elegy* for *Devotion* is equally touching, while the music for *The Sea Hawk* (an Errol Flynn vehicle) is vigorously exhilarating.

Piano trio, Op. 1.
** Delos D/CD 1009 [id.]. Pacific Art Trio – IVES: *Piano trio.***

Not for nothing did Sibelius call Korngold a 'young eagle' when he heard his *Sinfonietta* in 1914. This *Piano trio* was composed in 1909–10 and finished just before the composer's thirteenth birthday. It is a work of astonishing musical maturity (Bruno Walter played the piano part at its first performance). You could easily pass it off as by Strauss or Reger. A good performance, though rather closely balanced.

String quartets Nos. 1; 3.
(M) **(*) RCA GD 87889 [7889-2-RG]. Chilingirian Qt.

The *First* is the finer of the two quartets. It comes from 1923 and was written for Arnold Rosé, the brother-in-law of Mahler, whose string group gave its first performance. It comes from a period of some creative vitality and its inspiration is fresher than its later companion. The *Third Quartet*, dedicated to Bruno Walter, comes from 1945 and is a much feebler work, incorporating ideas used in some of Korngold's Hollywood scores. The Chilingirian give a good account of themselves and the 1977 recording still sounds very good.

Die tote Stadt (complete).
(M) *** RCA GD 87767 (2) [7767-2-RG]. Neblett, Kollo, Luxon, Prey, Bav. R. Ch., Tölz Ch., Munich R. O, Leinsdorf.

At the age of twenty-three Korngold had his opera, *Die tote Stadt*, presented in simultaneous world premières in Hamburg and Cologne! It may not be a great work, but in a performance like this, splendidly recorded, it is one to revel in on the gramophone. The score includes many echoes of Puccini and Richard Strauss, but its youthful exuberance carries the day. Here René Kollo is powerful, if occasionally coarse of tone, Carol Neblett sings sweetly in the equivocal roles of the wife's apparition and the newcomer, and Hermann Prey, Benjamin Luxon and Rose Wagemann make up an impressive cast. Leinsdorf is at his finest.

Violanta (complete).
**(*) CBS CD 79229 [MK 35909]. Marton, Berry, Jerusalem, Stoklassa, Laubenthal, Hess, Bav. R. Ch., Munich R. O, Janowski.

Korngold was perhaps the most remarkable composer-prodigy of this century; he wrote this opera at the age of seventeen. It was given its first triumphant performance under Bruno Walter, and even Ernest Newman seriously compared Korngold to Mozart. Though luscious of texture and immensely assured, the writing lets one down by an absence of really memorable melody but, with a fine, red-blooded performance with Siegfried Jerusalem a youthfully fresh hero, it makes a fascinating addition to the recorded repertory. Eva Marton, not always beautiful of tone, combines power and accuracy in the key role of the heroine, suddenly floating high pianissimos with unexpected purity. The recording is quite full if not especially refined.

Kraus, Joseph Martin (1756–92)

Funeral music on the death of Gustav III.
*** Cap. MSCD 416E [id.]. Martinpelto, Högman, Ahnsjö, Lander, Uppsala University Chamber Ch., Drottningholm Bar. Ens., Parkman.

Gluck is the predominant influence in the *Funeral music* and informs almost every page of the opening *Mortuary music*. The cantata itself is an extended piece of some 45 minutes' duration, but the *Mortuary music* (or *Symphonie funèbre*, as it is called in the autograph) is altogether new to disc and is every bit as impressive as the cantata. The music is powerful, deeply felt and restrained; it has something of the lyrical intensity of Mozart, who is the obvious model in the aria, *High on his throne the tyrant boasts*. Kraus may be an uneven composer, but the quality of invention in the *Funeral music* is extraordinarily high: it is a work of real passion and dignity, and both the performance and the recording are admirable.

Kreutzer, Conradin (1780–1849)

Septet in E flat, Op. 62.
*** CRD CRD 3390 [id.]. Nash Ens. – HUMMEL: *Military septet.****

Kreutzer's *Septet* is a delightful work, and it is given a thoroughly engaging performance here by the Nash Ensemble, whose playing is as lyrically elegant as it is full of refined detail. The Hummel coupling too is most apt, as both works date from the same period (around 1830). The recording is first class in every way and beautifully balanced.

Kreutzer, Rodolphe (1766–1831)

Grand quintet in C.
*** Hyp. CDA 66143 [id.]. Sarah Francis (oboe), Allegri Qt – CRUSELL: *Divertimento*; REICHA: *Quintet.****

This is the Kreutzer of the Beethoven sonata – not to be confused with Conradin. The *Grand quintet* is a rather bland but very pleasing piece when it is played as beautifully as it is here. The CD has fine presence.

Krommer, Franz (Kramar, František) (1759–1831)

Clarinet concertos: in E flat, Op. 36; in E min., Op. 86; (i) Double clarinet concerto in E flat, Op. 35.
**(*) Claves Dig. CD 50-8602 [id.]. Friedli; (i) Pay, ECO, Pay.

Both the solo concertos here are fine works, tuneful and full of character. Op. 36 is an outgoing piece, with a fine expressive *Adagio* and a lilting, genial finale, in which Thomas Friedli is in his element. Op. 86 is rather more serious, with even a sombre touch to the *Adagio*, but the clouds clear away in the Rondo. Friedli's tone is full and luscious in both works. Antony Pay directs spirited accompaniments and then joins him on the first desk in the *Double concerto*, which has a grand opening and even a hint of melodrama as the slow movement unfolds. The only fault with the solo playing is a relative lack of dynamic light and shade, but the shared enjoyment of the duo is readily conveyed, especially in the bouncing last movement, which is infectious. The recording might ideally be more transparent, but it is full and pleasing and well balanced.

Flute concerto in G, Op. 30; Flute and oboe concertino, Op. 65; Oboe concerto in F, Op. 52.
**(*) Claves Dig. CD 50-8203 [id.]. Graf, Holliger, ECO.

Krommer's harmonic sense was highly developed, as in the slow movement of the Op. 52 *Oboe concerto*; it is these unpredictable felicities that lend his work its charm. Peter-

Lukas Graf is the flautist and directs the performance of the *Oboe concerto*, while in the *Concerto for flute* Heinz Holliger returns the compliment for him. The playing is expert, though the recording places the soloists are a little too forward and there is a need for greater transparency.

Octet-Partita in E flat, Op. 79.
*** CRD CRD 3410 [id.]. Nash Ens. – DVOŘÁK: *Wind serenade.****

The Nash Ensemble give an excellent and lively account of this attractive Krommer piece. It is not great music but it is highly agreeable, and the Nash readily demonstrate its charm in a direct way for which the bright recording is admirably suited.

Kuhlau, Friedrich (1786–1832)

Flute quintets: in D; E and A, Op. 51/1–3.
*** CBS Dig. MK 44517 [id.]. Rampal, Juilliard Qt.

Those who have enjoyed Mozart's *Flute quartets* will surely derive pleasure from these slighter, though rather longer works (using the full string quartet), well crafted, pleasingly inventive and certainly not without vitality. Rampal is supported well by the Juilliard players and the recording has both presence and depth.

Lulu (opera) complete.
*** Kontrapunkt/HM 32009/11 [id.]. Saarman, Frellesvig, Kiberg, Cold, Danish R. Ch. & SO, Schonwandt.

This *Lulu* comes from 1824 and enjoyed some success in its day; it would probably have enjoyed more, but contemporary audiences complained that both the text and the music were too long. They certainly had a point: the spoken passages are omitted here – but, even so, the music takes three hours. The opening of Act II has overtones of the Wolf's Glen scene in *Der Freischütz* and the dance of the black elves in the moonlight is pure Mendelssohn – and has much charm. The invention is generally fresh and engaging, though no one would claim that it has great depth. The largely Danish cast cope very capably with the not inconsiderable demands of Kuhlau's vocal writing, and the title-role, sung by the Finnish tenor, Risto Saarman, is admirable. The weakest member of the cast is Anne Frellesvig's rather white-voiced Princess Sidi. The Danish Radio recording is eminently truthful and vivid, and Michael Schonwandt draws excellent results from the Danish Radio Chorus and Orchestra.

Kuhnau, Johann (1660–1722)

Biblische Historien Sonatas Nos. 1, 2, 3 & 6.
(BB) ** Hung. White Label HRC 130 [id.]. Anikó Horváth (harpsichord).

This early example of keyboard programme music was written by Bach's predecessor at St Thomas's Church, Leipzig. Bible stories are used and the chosen examples here include descriptions of *The fight between David and Goliath, Saul cured by David through music, Jacob's wedding* (lasting nearly twenty minutes!) and *death and burial*. It is very doubtful whether anyone could begin to guess the narrative detail from the music itself, even knowing the subject-matter, although the music is strongly presented. The recording of the harpsichord is bold, a shade over-resonant. A curiosity.

Lalo, Eduard (1823-92)

Cello concerto in D min.
*** CBS Dig. MK 35848 [id.]. Yo-Yo Ma, O Nat. de France, Maazel – SAINT-SAENS: *Concerto No. 1.****
*** Decca Dig. 414 387-2 [id.]. Harrell, Berlin RSO, Chailly – FAURÉ: *Élégie*; SAINT-SAENS: *Cello concerto No. 2.****
*** DG Dig. 427 323-2 [id.]. Matt Haimovitz, Chicago SO, Levine – SAINT-SAENS: *Concerto No. 1*; BRUCH: *Kol Nidrei.****

Yo-Yo Ma's account of the Lalo *Concerto* must rank as the finest now available. It has great sensitivity, beauty of tone and expressive feeling to commend it, and indeed it makes the work seem better than in fact it is. Moreover, Maazel and the Orchestre National de France give understanding support, matching the sensitivity of the soloist. The quality of the recorded sound is excellent, beautifully balanced and spacious, yet with detail admirably refined in its CD format.

Lynn Harrell's Decca account was recorded within the attractive acoustic of the Jesus Christ Church, Berlin (the venue of many of Furtwängler's successful mono LPs of the 1950s). The orchestra is given vivid colour and presence. Chailly's accompaniment is attractively bold, more assertive than Maazel's for Yo-Yo Ma. Lynn Harrell's performance is an extremely fine one, perhaps less subtle but no less ardent than Ma's, and certainly no less convincing. Harrell's couplings are more generous than Ma's, including not only the attractive and virtually unknown *Second Concerto* of Saint-Saëns, but also a splendid account of Fauré's *Élégie*.

An outstandingly impressive début from the young cellist, Matt Haimovitz, just nineteen at the time of making his first recording. Levine's opening flourishes are boldly dramatic, immediately eliciting a warm response, and in the second movement the contrasts are again emphasized; the performance throughout combines vitality with expressive feeling in the most spontaneous manner. The recording is very well balanced indeed and highly realistic. The competition from Yo-Yo Ma and Lynn Harrell is strong, but Haimovitz emerges with flying colours, and many will be attracted by his bonus of Bruch's *Kol Nidrei.*

(i) *Cello concerto in D min.;* (ii) *Symphonie espagnole, Op. 21.*
(M) *(*) Erato/WEA 2292 45087-2 [id.]. (i) Lodéon, Philh. O, Dutoit; (ii) Pierre Amoyal, Monte Carlo Op. O, Paray.

Lodéon's performance of the *Cello concerto* is recommendable in every way, with the Philharmonia under Dutoit providing excellent backing. For the coupling, Amoyal gives a warm and polished account of the *Symphonie espagnole*, rhythmically infectious and with many a seductive turn of phrase. Unfortunately here the Erato recording has a middle and bass emphasis which causes a muddy orchestral resonance, although the violin timbre remains sweet.

Violin concerto in F, Op. 20; Symphonie espagnole, Op. 21.
*** EMI CDC7 49833-2 [id.]. Augustin Dumay, Toulouse Capitole O, Plasson.

This is an ideal coupling, not only because it introduces us to the hitherto virtually unknown *Violin concerto* but also because Dumay's sparkling account of the *Symphonie espagnole* is as fine as any available, and the recording, made in the Halle aux Grains, Toulouse, is full and natural, much better balanced than Perlman's DG version. The *Symphonie espagnole* lifts off rhythmically from the very opening bars, and the sultry feeling of the secondary theme is caught delectably. Inner movements are full of flair, the *Andante* passionately lyrical, while the finale scintillates, with the orchestral colour just as ear-catching as the easy bravura of the soloist. The *Violin concerto* (also written for Sarasate, who premièred both works) has a tenderly songful *Andante* and another genially high-spirited finale, and here the solo playing is ravishing and exciting by turns, while Plasson's accompaniments are admirably supportive throughout. Dumay's account of the *Symphonie espagnole* is second to none; he is a glorious player, an aristocrat among violinists.

Symphonie espagnole (for violin and orchestra), *Op. 21.*

(M) *** DG Dig. 429 977-2]id.]. Perlman, O de Paris, Barenboim – SAINT-SAENS: *Concerto No. 3.****

*** Decca Dig. 411 952-2 [id.]. Kyung Wha Chung, Montreal SO, Dutoit – SAINT-SAENS: *Concerto No. 1.****

(B) **(*) Ph. 422 976-2 [id.]. Szeryng, Monte Carlo Op. O, Van Remoortel – PAGANINI: *Violin concerto No. 3.****

(BB) **(*) Hung. White Label HRC 106 [id.]. Miklós Szenthelyi, Hungarian State O, Lukács – D'INDY: *Symphonie.****

(B) **(*) CBS CD 44717 [MBK 44717]. Zukerman, LAPO, Mehta – BRUCH: *Concerto No. 1.***(*)

** Decca Dig. 425 501-2 [id.]. Joshua Bell, Montreal SO, Dutoit – SAINT-SAENS: *Concerto No. 3.****

Lalo's brilliant five-movement distillation of Spanish sunshine is well served here. The strongly articulated orchestral introduction from Barenboim combines rhythmic buoyancy with expressive flair and the lyrical material is handled with great sympathy. The richness and colour of Perlman's tone are never more telling than in the slow movement, which opens tenderly but develops a compelling expressive ripeness. The brilliance of the scherzo is matched by the dancing sparkle of the finale. The recording is extremely lively but fairly dry, and the forward balance of the soloist does not obscure orchestral detail.

Kyung Wha Chung has the advantage of a first-class Decca digital recording, fuller than the DG alternative, and with a highly effective, natural balance. Hers is an athletic, incisive account, at its most individual in the captivatingly light-weight finale, with an element almost of fantasy. Miss Chung does not have quite the panache of Perlman, but Charles Dutoit's accompaniment is first class and the orchestral characterization is strong throughout.

Szeryng's performance was recorded in 1970. He is in splendid form and brings out the work's Spanish sparkle, especially in the brilliant finale. The accompaniment is less distinctive, and the spotlighting of the soloist means that some of the orchestral detail, which is less strong in personality, is almost lost. Yet Szeryng's flair carries the day, and his Paganini coupling is outstanding too.

On Hungaroton, Miklós Szenthelyi brings an added Hungarian sparkle to this music without losing its seductive Spanish character. He is a first-class, full-timbred player and this is an attractively spontaneous performance, well accompanied and with an effervescent finale. Although the resonant recording makes tuttis somewhat bass-heavy, detail is well observed and the slow movement is richly sonorous.

Zukerman's account of Lalo's five-movement *Symphonie espagnole* is first class in every way. The solo playing has real panache, Mehta accompanies vividly, and the recording is transferred well to CD, even if the balance is not ideal in its relationship of the soloist to the orchestra.

Dutoit opens rather heavily and Bell's reading of the secondary theme is rather bland, missing its Mediterranean languor. Overall, the performance lacks spontaneity and fire until it springs to life in the finale. Splendidly glowing Montreal sound and a good balance hardly compensate, although the coupling is much more successful.

Symphony in G min.; Rapsodie norvégienne; Le Roi d'Ys overture; Scherzo in D min.
** ASV Dig. CDDCA 709 [id.]. RPO, Yondani Butt.

Lalo's *Symphony* was a favourite work of Sir Thomas Beecham, and no doubt his version will soon return to the catalogue. It is, however, a far from outstanding piece: the opening movement can easily sound turgid and, although Butt makes the most of it and does his best with the livelier finale, the heavy scoring (an amalgam of the influences of Schumann and Wagner) is not helped by the resonance of the ecclesiastical acoustic chosen for this ASV recording. The *Adagio* has a degree of eloquence, although the entry of the heavy brass at the end is somewhat overwhelming; the Scherzo is by far the best movement. It is not as fine, however as the independent orchestral scherzo also included here; *Le Roi d'Ys* is an endearingly rumbustious piece and the RPO present it with exuberant relish. The *Rapsodie norvégienne* is an arrangement of a concertante work for solo violin in two movements: the first tuneful and rather engaging, the second more energetic but also repetitive.

Le roi d'Ys (complete).
*** Erato/WEA Dig. 2292 45015-2 (2) [id.]. Courtis, Ziegler, Hendricks, Villa, Fr. R. Ch. & PO, Jordan.
(M) ** EMI CMS7 69858-2 (2) [id.]. Gorr, Micheau, Legay, Borthayre, Fr. R. O, Cluytens (with Gorr singing French arias**).

The Erato version gains enormously in presenting this opulent score in sumptuous modern sound, with Jordan underlining the colourful dramatic contrasts between the exotic scene-setting and the sharply rhythmic choruses. The women soloists are particularly fine, preferable to those on previous sets. The American mezzo-soprano, Delores Ziegler, is very convincingly cast in what – thanks to the celebrated example of Rosa Ponselle, among others – used to be counted a soprano role. Her dramatic, unfruity voice is perfectly contrasted against the ravishing Rozenn of Barbara Hendricks. Eduardo Villa as the hero, Mylio, may not be as stylish as his recorded predecessors, not delicate enough in the famous *Aubade*, but his heady tenor has no trouble with the high tessitura. Jean-Philippe Courtis as the King, in this improbable Breton legend of medieval chivalry, and Marcel Vanaud as the villain, Karnac, have dark, weighty voices, marred at times by flutter.

Recorded in 1959, the Cluytens version brings a well-paced, idiomatic performance with three characterful principal soloists. The timbres of both Janine Micheau and Rita Gorr could hardly be more authentically French, and Henri Legay, a superb recording tenor, sings radiantly, not least in the *Aubade*. On two mid-price CDs, with a generous selection of arias sung by Rita Gorr, it makes a fair recommendation, despite sound that begins to show its age.

Langlais, Jean (born 1907)

(i) *Messe solennelle;* (i; ii; iii) *Missa Salve regina;* (Organ): (i) *Paraphrases grégoriennes, Op. 5: Te Deum. Poèmes évangéliques, Op. 2: La Nativité. Triptyque grégorien: Rosa mystica.*

*** Hyp. Dig. CDA 66270 [id.]. Westminster Cathedral Ch., David Hill, (i) with J. O'Donnell; (ii) A. Lumsden; (iii) ECO Brass Ens.

Jean Langlais' organ music owes much to Dupré's example, and the two Masses are archaic in feeling, strongly influenced by plainchant and organum, yet with a plangent individuality that clearly places the music in the twentieth century. The *Missa Salve regina* is scored for male-voice chorus, unison boy trebles, two organs and an octet of brass instruments divided into two groups. The style is wholly accessible and the music enjoys fervent advocacy from these artists, who are accorded sound-quality of the high standard one expects from this label. Those unfamiliar with the music of Jean Langlais should lose no time and try this outstanding collection.

Larsson, Lars-Erik (1908–86)

Symphonies Nos. 1 in D, Op. 2; 2, Op. 17.
**(*) BIS Dig. CD 426 [id.]. Helsingborg SO, Hans-Peter Frank.

Even in his native Sweden, Larsson is not thought of as a symphonist, although he has many important works to his credit, notably the lyrical *Violin concerto* (1952) and *Music for orchestra* (1949). The *First Symphony* is a student work, written when he was nineteen and before his studies with Berg. It is derivative but a work of obvious promise, fluent and well put together. There are obvious echoes of the Russian post-nationalists as well as Nielsen and Sibelius. Much the same could be said of the more mature *Second Symphony* (1936–7), which is genial and unpretentious. After its première the composer withdrew it, allowing only the final *Ostinato* to be published. Good performances and recording, but the music itself is not Larsson at his strongest.

Symphony No. 3 in C min., Op. 34; (i) Förklädd Gud (A God in disguise), Op. 24.
** BIS CD 96 [id.]. (i) Nordin, Hagegård, Jonsson, Helsingborg Concert Ch.; Helsingborg SO, Frykberg.

A God in disguise was a production for Swedish Radio, similar in ambition to the Louis MacNeice–Benjamin Britten collaboration in *The dark tower*, and was a choral setting of poems by Hjalmar Gullberg. The choral suite for two soloists and narrator that Larsson fashioned from it has great freshness and charm. This 1978 performance has some fine singing from Håkan Hagegård, and the Helsingborg chorus and orchestra give a serviceable account of the score. Like its predecessor, the *Third Symphony* (1944–5) it was withdrawn after its first performance though, as with the *Second*, Larsson allowed the finale to be published as *Concert overture No. 3*. It is as diatonic as *A God in disguise* and, though not completely successful, is strong enough to deserve rescue.

Lassus, Orlandus (c. 1530–94)

De profundis clamavi; Exaltabo te, Domine; Missa octavi toni; Missa qual donna.
*** Nimbus Dig. NI 5150 [id.]. Christ Church Cathedral Ch., Oxford, Stephen Darlington.

The *Missa qual donna* begins this excellent CD: it is a late work, expressive and mellifluous, and very well sung by the choir of Christ Church Cathedral, Oxford. As a pendant, the disc also includes Cipriano de Rore's Petrarch setting, *Qual donna a gloriosa fama*, composed forty years earlier, which the Mass takes as its inspiration. The contrast between this and the *Missa octavi toni*, also known as the *Missa Venatorum* (or *Missa Jäger – Hunting Mass*), could hardly be more striking. The motet, *De profundis clamavi*,

543

one of the great penitential Psalms, is almost the most eloquent and expressive of the pieces here. At times one could wish for more ardent tone from the trebles; but unquestionably these are fine performances that enrich the Lassus discography, and the recording is very good indeed.

Missa Osculetur me; Motets: *Alma Redemptoris Mater; Ave regina caelorum; Hodie completi sunt; Osculetur me; Regina caeli; Salve Regina; Timor et tremor.*
*** Gimell Dig. CDGIM 018 [id.]. Tallis Scholars, Peter Phillips.

Lassus learned the technique of double-choir antiphonal music in Italy, for, although eight-part polyphony was widely practised and held in the highest esteem in the Low Countries, the massive sonorities of the Venetian School were alien. The Mass is preceded by the motet, *Osculetur me* (*Let him kiss me with the kisses of his lips*), which provides much of its motivic substance and is glorious in its sonorities and expressive eloquence. The singing of the Tallis Scholars under Peter Phillips is as impressive as it was on their earlier records, and the recording is beautifully present.

Missa Pro defunctis a 4.
** Hyp. Dig. CDA 66066 [id.]. Pro Cantione Antiqua, Mark Brown.

The Pro Cantione Antiqua sing this four-part *Requiem* one voice to a part, and the gain in clarity of texture is offset by a loss of grandeur and majesty. The singers are impressive for all that, and the *Requiem* is interspersed with plainchant from the Office for the Dead. The recording, made in the warm acoustic of St John's Church, Hackney, places the singers rather close to the listener, which again helps clarity but reduces the sense of mystery. The four singers blend well and intonation is generally true.

Sacred music: *Adoramus te, Christe; Ad te levavi oculos meos; Christus resurgens ex mortuis; Domine, dominus noster; In hora ultima; In pace, in idipsum; Pelli meae consumptis carnibus;* Plainchant, Magnificat and Motet: *Praeter rerum seriem; Resonant in laudibus; Te Deum; Tibi laus, tibi gloria.*
*** EMI CDC7 49157-2. King's Singers (with JOSQUIN DES PRÉS: Motet: *Praeter rerum seriem****).

Chansons, madrigals, motets and Lieder: *Ardo si, ma non t'amo; Au feu; Bon jour et puis quelles nouvelles?; Bon jour mon coeur; Cantai hor piango; Chi chilichi?; Come la notte ogni fiamella; Dessus le marché d'Arras; Ein guten Raht; Hört zu ein news gedicht; Il était une religieuse; Im Mayen; Matona mia cara; Musica, Dei donum optimi; La nuit froide et sombre; Omnia tempus habent; O vin en vigne; Paisible domaine; Quand mon mari vient; Toutes les nuits; Vignon, vignon.*
**(*) EMI CDC7 49158-2. King's Singers.

In their two programmes of the music of Lassus, the King's Singers are, perhaps surprisingly, more successful in the collection of sacred music. Here the rich, homogeneous style has a balancing directness and vitality which could make this often very beautiful music communicate to listeners who would normally not seek out this repertoire. The secular collection covers a wider range of styles, including French, German and Italian settings, and the manner of presentation has at times a touch of blandness in its warm, expressive feeling. After a while the ear craves a change from the almost instrumental vocal timbre, richly blended and impeccable in its intonation and polish. Yet there is much to enjoy here, not least the humorous German song of the nose, *Hört zu ein news gedicht* which the group make sound as if it were specially written for them. The recording is forward against a warm acoustic, with words clear, and there is good documentation.

Lecocq, Alexandre (1832–1918)

Mam'zelle Angot (ballet, arr. Gordon Jacob).
*** Decca Dig. 411 898-2 [id.]. Nat. PO, Bonynge – BERLIOZ: *Les Troyens: ballet***; WEBER: *Invitation to the dance.****

La Fille de Madame Angot was a highly successful operetta of the 1870s. The narrative line follows the story of the operetta, and much of the music is also drawn from that source; however, Gordon Jacob includes excerpts from other music by Lecocq. It is a gay, vivacious score with plenty of engaging tunes, prettily orchestrated in the modern French style. Offenbach's influence is strongly felt in the final carnival scene. Bonynge offers the first recording of the complete score, and its 39 minutes are consistently entertaining when the orchestral playing has such polish and wit. The Kingsway Hall recording is closely observed: the CD brings sharp detail and tangibility, especially at lower dynamic levels. Some ears may find the violin timbre a shade over-bright.

Lehár, Franz (1870–1948)

Waltzes: *Eva; Gold and silver; Gypsy love. The Count of Luxembourg: Luxembourg. Giuditta: Where the lark sings. The Merry Widow: Ballsirenen.*
**(*) EMI Dig. CDC7 47020-2 [id.]. Johann Strauss O of Vienna, Boskovsky.

Gold and silver was Lehár's waltz masterpiece; the others are his arrangements, using melodies from the operettas. They are ravishingly tuneful; given such warmly affectionate performances and a recording which is sumptuous and has sparkling detail, this is easy to enjoy. Lehár's scoring is often imaginative, but in the last resort one misses the voices. The CD is first class in every way.

The Count of Luxembourg (highlights, in English).
*** That's Entertainment CDTER 1050. Hill-Smith, Jenkins, Tierney, Nicoll, Richard, New Sadler's Wells Op. Ch. and O, Wordsworth.

Like its companion disc of selections from Kálmán's *Countess Maritza*, this record from That's Entertainment presents lively and fresh performances from the cast of the New Sadler's Wells Opera production. Particularly in the general absence of records of operetta in English, this is very welcome. Bright digital sound, which is given plenty of presence on CD.

The Land of Smiles (Das Land des Lächelns; complete in German).
*** EMI Dig. CDS7 47604-8 (2). Jerusalem, Donath, Lindner, Finke, Hirte, Bav. R. Ch., Munich R. O, Boskovsky.
(M) (***) EMI mono CHS7 69523-2 (2) [id.]. Schwarzkopf, Gedda, Kunz, Loose, Kraus, Philh. Ch. & O, Ackermann.

The Land of Smiles, with its mixture of Eastern and Western values, is a strange piece, its principal tenor a Chinese prince. Siegfried Jerusalem, who plays Sou-Chong here (a role made famous by Richard Tauber), gives a strong and sympathetic reading, lacking only a vein of implied tragedy, the wistfulness behind the smile. Helen Donath sings sweetly as his beloved Lisa, and the whole ensemble is admirably controlled in a colourful performance by Willi Boskovsky, warmly recorded.

Though Gedda does not have quite the passionate flair of Tauber in his famous *Dein ist mein ganzes Herz*, his thoughtful artistry matches a performance which effortlessly brings out the serious parallels without weighing the work down. Schwarzkopf and Kunz sing delectably and the transfer to CD of a well-balanced mono recording is very lively and full of presence.

The Merry Widow (Die lustige Witwe: complete, in German).
⊛ *** EMI CDS7 47178-8 (2) [Ang. CDCB 47177]. Schwarzkopf, Gedda, Waechter, Steffek, Knapp, Equiluz, Philh. Ch. and O, Matačić.
(M) (***) EMI mono CDH7 69520-2 [id.]. Schwarzkopf, Gedda, Kunz, Loose, Kraus, Philh. Ch. & O, Ackermann.

Matačić provides a magical set, guaranteed to send shivers of delight through any listener with its vivid sense of atmosphere and superb musicianship. It is one of Walter Legge's masterpieces as a recording manager. He had directed the earlier *Merry Widow* set, also with his wife Elisabeth Schwarzkopf as Hanna, and realized how difficult it would be to outshine it. But outshine it he did, creating a sense of theatre that is almost without rival in gramophone literature. The CD opens up the sound yet retains the full bloom, and the theatrical presence and atmosphere are something to marvel at. The layout is less than ideal, however, and only two bands are provided on each CD, though there is generous indexing.

It was the earlier set of the early 1950s which established a new pattern in recording operetta. Some were even scandalized when Schwarzkopf insisted on treating the *Viljalied* very seriously indeed at an unusually slow tempo; but the big step forward was that an operetta was treated with all the care for detail normally lavished on grand opera. Ten years later in stereo Schwarzkopf was to record the role again, if anything with even greater point and perception, but here she has extra youthful vivacity, and the *Viljalied* – ecstatically drawn out – is unique. Some may be troubled that Kunz as Danilo sounds older than the Baron, but it is still a superbly characterful cast, and the transfer to a single CD is bright and clear.

The Merry Widow (English version by Christopher Hassall): abridged.
(B) ** CfP CD-CFP 4485. Bronhill, Lowe, Glynne, McAlpine, Round, Dowling, Sadler's Wells Op. Ch. and O, William Reid.

The performance on Classics for Pleasure does not always have an *echt*-Viennese flavour; nevertheless it says much for the achievement of the Sadler's Wells production in the 1950s that their version is so successful. For many, the deciding factor will be the English words, sung in an admirable translation; but one is not sure that this is so important on a recording. The Sadler's Wells cast is strongly characterized; only in Howell Glynne's approach is there a suspicion of Gilbert and Sullivan. The chorus is outstandingly good (especially the men) in the big scenes. The 1959 recording sounds fresh, if slightly dated, but the voices and diction are clear and, though there is a touch of shrillness on top, there is an agreeable ambient feeling.

Der Zarewitsch (complete).
*** Eurodisc 610 137 (2). Kollo, Popp, Rebroff, Orth, Hobarth, Bav. R. Ch., Munich R. O, Wallberg.

René Kollo may not have the finesse of a Tauber, but he sings with a freshness and absence of mannerism that bring out the melodic beauty. Lucia Popp as the heroine, Sonya, sings ravishingly, and there is no weak link in the cast elsewhere. With two extra numbers given to the Grand Duke (Ivan Rebroff), both taken from Lehár's *Wo die Lerche singt*, the exhilaration of the entertainment comes over all the more refreshingly in the excellent CD transfer. No text is given, only notes in German.

Leighton, Kenneth (1929–88)

(i) *Cello concerto;* (ii) *Symphony No. 3 (Laudes Musicae).*
*** Chan. Dig. CHAN 8741 [id.]. (i) Wallfisch; (ii) Mackie; SNO, Bryden Thomson.

Belated attention is now being paid to this fine composer, barely known at all outside the UK and rarely featured in public concerts. This splendid CD couples the early *Cello concerto*, written in the mid-1950s, at the time of the composer's studies with Petrassi, and the *Third Symphony*, a BBC commission, written in 1984, four years before his untimely death. The symphony is in part a song-cycle, and its glowing, radiant colours and refined textures are immediately winning. Raphael Wallfisch plays the *Concerto* as if his life depended on it, and the *Symphony* draws every bit as much dedication from its performers. The recording is very immediate, and presents every strand in the orchestral texture with stunning clarity and definition.

Veris gratia (for cello, oboe and strings), Op. 9.
*** Chan. Dig. CHAN 8471 [id.]. Wallfisch, Caird, Royal Liverpool PO, Handley –
FINZI: *Cello concerto.****

Finzi is the dedicatee of Kenneth Leighton's *Veris gratia*, and so it makes an appropriate coupling for his *Cello concerto*, more particularly as its English pastoral style nods in his direction. It is in essence a miniature sinfonia concertante, featuring oboe as well as cello, written in 1950. The performance is highly sympathetic, George Caird the excellent oboist, and the naturally balanced recording is first class.

Conflicts, Op. 51; Fantasia contrappuntistica, Op. 24; Household pets, Op. 86; Sonatina No. 1; 5 Studies, Op. 22.
**(*) Abacus Dig. ABA 402-2 [id.]. Eric Parkin.

What a civilized composer Kenneth Leighton was. He was one of the most musical of pianists and wrote beautifully for the instrument. The *Household pets* is a sensitive piece, refined in craftsmanship, and the *Fantasia contrappuntistica* is comparably powerful. Eric Parkin plays it with total sympathy, and the recording, though not in the demonstration bracket, is eminently serviceable.

Lemba, Artur (1885–1960)

Symphony in C sharp min.
*** Chan. Dig. CHAN 8656 [id.]. SNO, Järvi (with Concert: *'Music from Estonia'*: Vol. 2***).

Lemba's *Symphony in C sharp minor* was composed in 1908, the first symphony ever to be written by an Estonian. It sounds as if he studied in St Petersburg: at times one is reminded fleetingly of Glazunov, at others of Dvořák (the scherzo) – and even of Bruckner (at the opening of the finale) and of Elgar. This is by far the most important item in an enterprising collection of Estonian music.

Leoncavallo, Ruggiero (1858–1919)

I Pagliacci (complete).
*** DG 419 257-2 (3) [id.]. Carlyle, Bergonzi, Benelli, Taddei, Panerai, La Scala, Milan, Ch. & O, Karajan – MASCAGNI: *Cavalleria Rusticana*.***
(***) EMI mono CDS7 47981-8 (3) [Ang. CDCC 47981]. Callas, Di Stefano, Gobbi, La Scala, Milan, Ch. & O, Serafin – MASCAGNI: *Cavalleria Rusticana*.(***)

Karajan does nothing less than refine Leoncavallo's melodrama, with long-breathed, expansive tempi and the minimum exaggeration. One would expect such a process to take the guts out of the drama, but with Karajan the result is superb. One is made to hear the beauty of the music first and foremost, and that somehow makes one understand the drama more. Karajan's choice of soloists was clearly aimed to help that – but the passions are still there; and rarely if ever on record has the La Scala Orchestra played with such beautiful feeling for tone-colour. Bergonzi is among the most sensitive of Italian tenors of heroic quality, and it is good to have Joan Carlyle as Nedda, touching if often rather cool. Taddei is magnificently strong, and Benelli and Panerai could hardly be bettered in the roles of Beppe and Silvio. As a filler, DG provides a splendid set of performances of operatic intermezzi from *Manon Lescaut, Suor Angelica*, Schmidt's *Notre Dame*, Giordano's *Fedora*, Cilea's *Adriana Lecouvreur*, Wolf-Ferrari's *Jewels of the Madonna*, Mascagni's *L'amico Fritz*, plus the *Meditation* from *Thaïs* (with Michel Schwalbé), and the *Prelude* to Act III of *La Traviata*.

It is thrilling to hear *Pagliacci* starting with the Prologue sung so vividly by Tito Gobbi. The bite of the voice and its distinctive timbres are unique. Di Stefano, too, is at his finest, but the performance inevitably centres on Callas. There are many points at which she finds extra intensity, extra meaning, so that the performance is worth hearing for her alone. Serafin's direction is strong and direct. The mono recording is dry, with voices placed well forward but with choral detail blurred, a balance underlined in the clarity and definition of CD.

Liadov, Anatol (1855–1914)

About olden times, Op. 21b; Baba-Yaga, Op. 56; The enchanted lake, Op. 62; 3 Fanfares; Kikimora, Op. 63; The musical snuff-box, Op. 32; Polonaises, Opp. 49 & 55; 8 Russian folksongs, Op. 58.
**(*) ASV Dig. CDDCA 657 [id.]. Mexico City SO, Bátiz.

Three stars for the ASV recording by Brian Culverhouse – but the performances under Enrique Bátiz fall just short of that rating: the magical world of the finest of these scores could perhaps be conveyed with a more subtle atmosphere. Bátiz sometimes allows the colours to become almost gaudy, though he draws enthusiastic playing from his Mexican orchestra. However, there is much to enjoy here and the music itself (particularly *Kikimora* and the *Eight Russian folksongs*) is full of enchantment. Recommended.

(i) *Baba Yaga, Op. 56; The enchanted lake, Op. 62; Kikimora, Op. 63;* (ii) *8 Russian folksongs.*
(BB) **(*) Naxos Dig. 8.550328 [id.]. Slovak PO, (i) Gunzenhauser (ii) Kenneth Jean – Concert: *'Russian Fireworks'*.

It is good to have inexpensive recordings of these key Liadov works, particularly the *Russian folksongs*, eight orchestral vignettes of great charm, displaying a winning sense of orchestral colour. The performances are persuasive, and the digital recording is vivid and well balanced. They are part of an attractive concert of Russian music, much of it with a more extrovert appeal.

Ligeti, György (born 1923)

Bagatelles.
*** Crystal CD 750 [id.]. Westwood Wind Quintet – CARLSSON: *Nightwings*; MATHIAS: *Quintet*; BARBER: *Summer music.****

Ligeti's folk-inspired *Bagatelles* were originally written for piano and in 1953 were arranged by the composer for wind quintet. They are highly inventive and very attractive; and they are played with dazzling flair and unanimity of ensemble by this American group.

(i) *Chamber concerto for 13 instrumentalists;* (ii) *Double concerto for flute, oboe and orchestra; Melodien for orchestra;* (iii) *10 Pieces for wind quintet.*
(M) *** Decca 425 623-2 [id.]. (i) L. Sinf., Atherton; (ii) with Nicolet, Holliger; (iii) Vienna Wind Soloists.

Over the last decade or so, Ligeti has developed a technique of micro-polyphony that produces strongly atmospheric and distinctive textures. The *Double concerto* makes great play with micro-intervals, not exactly quarter-tones but deviations. The resulting sonorities will not always please but should consistently interest or even exasperate the unprejudiced listener. The distinguished soloists and the London Sinfonietta give accomplished accounts of these complex scores and the Vienna performances of the wind pieces are hardly less stimulating.

Lux aeterna.
(M) *** DG 419 475-2 [id.]. N. German R. Ch., Helmut Franz – HOLST: *The Planets.***(*)

What seems an unexpected coupling for a performance of Holst's *Planets* is linked by the film *2001* in which this choral piece took an honoured place, fascinating the unlikeliest listeners with its evocative clouds of vocal sound. Performance and recording are first class.

Liszt, Franz (1811–86)

Ce qu'on entend sur la montagne (Bergsymphonie), G. 95.
(*) ASV Dig. CDDCA 586 [id.]. LSO, Yondani Butt – TCHAIKOVSKY: *The Tempest.*(*)

Ce qu'on entend sur la montagne is the first of Liszt's symphonic poems and the longest (28 minutes). It suffers not only from formal weakness but also from a lack of really interesting material. Yondani Butt gives the work with much conviction, and the LSO respond with some powerful and expressive playing. The recording is appropriately spectacular, with a wide dynamic range on CD. The coupling, an early symphonic poem of Tchaikovsky, more inspired music, is very appropriate.

Piano concerto No. 1 in E flat, G. 124.
*** EMI Dig. CDC7 47221-2 [id.]. Ousset, CBSO, Rattle – SAINT-SAENS: *Concerto No. 2.****
(*) DG 415 061-2 [id.]. Argerich, LSO, Abbado – CHOPIN: *Concerto No. 1.*(*)

(BB) **(*) Naxos Dig. 8.550292 [id.]. Joseph Banowetz, Czech RSO Bratislava, Oliver Dohnányi – CHOPIN: *Concerto No. 1*.**(*)

For those seeking the *First Concerto* alone, Cécile Ousset's is a magical performance, sparklingly individual, full of spontaneity, with Ousset making light of the technical difficulties. Rattle equally draws exciting and warmly expressive playing from the CBSO and the recording is first rate, save for the forward balance of the soloist, who seems to be in a slightly different acoustic. But those looking for a red-blooded modern recording should be well satisfied with this.

By the side of Ousset, Martha Argerich seems much less flamboyant. Hers is a clear, direct, even fastidious approach. She plays the *Larghetto* meltingly, and there is an excellent partnership with Abbado, who also seeks refinement without reducing the underlying tension. The CD remastering of the 1969 recording is extremely successful, the sound hardly dated at all.

A splendid, dashing account of the *First Concerto* from Banowetz, well coupled with Chopin, has the full measure of the work's flamboyance and its poetry. The only snag is that the delicacy of texture in the engaging scherzo means that the triangle solo is only just audible. Otherwise the wide-ranging sound is excellent.

Piano concertos Nos. 1 in E flat, G. 124; 2 in A, G. 125.
*** Ph. 412 006-2 [id.]. Sviatoslav Richter, LSO, Kondrashin.
(*) Ph. Dig. 422 380-2 [id.]. Zoltán Kocsis, Budapest Fest. O, Iván Fischer – DOHNÁNYI: *Nursery variations*.

Piano concertos Nos. 1–2; Années de pèlerinage, Supplement: Venezia e Napoli, G. 162.
(M) *** DG 415 839-2 [id.]. Lazar Berman, VSO, Giulini.

Piano concertos Nos. 1–2; 3 Études de concert, G. 144.
**(*) Ph. 416 461-2 [id.]. Arrau, LSO, Sir Colin Davis.

(i) *Piano concertos Nos. 1–2; Hungarian rhapsody No. 6, G.244; Concert paraphrase on Mendelssohn's Wedding march, G.410.*
(B) **(*) Decca 421 629-2. Ivan Davis, (i) RPO, Downes.

Piano concertos Nos. 1–2; Totentanz, G. 126.
⊛ *** DG Dig. 423 571-2 [id.]. Zimerman, Boston SO, Ozawa.
(M) *** Ph. 426 637-2 [id.]. Alfred Brendel, LPO, Haitink.

Krystian Zimerman's DG recording belongs in illustrious company and can be recommended alongside the Berman, Richter and Arrau versions. His record of the two *Concertos* and the *Totentanz* is altogether thrilling, and he has the advantage of excellent support from the Boston orchestra under Ozawa. It has poise and classicism and, as one listens, one feels this music could not be played in any other way – surely the mark of a great performance! The DG recording places the soloist a fraction too far forward, but the overall sound-quality is excellent. This record is outstanding in every way, and it now makes a first choice for this repertoire.

Brendel's Philips recordings from the early 1970s hold their place at or near the top of the list. There is a valuable extra work offered here and the recording is of Philips's best. The performances are as poetic as they are brilliant, and those who doubt the musical substance of No. 2 will find their reservations melt away.

Richter's 1962 recordings are particularly distinguished, not only by the power and feeling of Richter's own playing and the obvious rapport between conductor and soloist, but also because of a similar and striking communication between Richter and the orchestra. The orchestral playing throughout is of the very highest order and achieves a remarkably poetic response when orchestral soloists are called on to share a melody with the piano. The recording, which is perhaps slightly below the finest modern standard, has been vividly remastered. However, this should be withdrawn and reissued at mid-price.

Lazar Berman has the advantage of Giulini's sensitive and masterly accompaniment with the Vienna Symphony. Berman's playing is consistently poetic and he illuminates detail in a way that has the power to touch the listener. Some of his rapt, quiet tone would probably not register without the tactful assistance of the DG engineers, who enable all the detail to 'tell', but the balance is most musical and well judged. A very thoughtful account of No. 1 and a poetic reading of the *A major* make this a most desirable record. To make the Galleria issue even more desirable, DG have added the three pieces which comprise the *Années de pèlerinage Supplement*, and there is more magnificent piano-playing here.

Claudio Arrau made a stunning record of the *E flat Concerto* with Ormandy and the Philadelphia Orchestra in the 1950s, and this new account, made in his mid-seventies, is scarcely less fine. Even though some of the youthful abandon is tamed, Arrau's virtuosity is transcendent. There is a greater breadth in No. 1 here than in the earlier version, and there are many thoughtful touches throughout. This artist's Indian summer shows no loss of fire, and he brings plenty of panache to the *A major Concerto*. Curiously, the remastering for CD has resulted in a very reticent triangle in the scherzo of the *First Concerto*; in fact one has to listen very carefully to hear it at all. The CD adds Arrau's 1976 recordings of the three *Concert studies*, G. 144; but this, too, calls for a mid-price reissue.

Ivan Davis shows a genuine feeling for both concertos, revealing their poetry as well as their flamboyance. He is admirably accompanied by the RPO under Edward Downes. The recording, originally made in Decca's hi-fi-conscious Phase 4 system, has a vivid spotlighting of orchestral soloists, effective enough when the piano too is forwardly balanced and boldly recorded. This record is not expensive; with its encores, it is certainly enjoyably spirited and spontaneous.

Kocsis plays with dazzling virtuosity and panache in both *Concertos*. These are high-voltage performances, though not without moments of self-consciousness. The soloist is rather forwardly balanced and the general impression is less refined or aristocratic than with Zimerman (DG). The Philips/Hungaroton recording is good but rather bass-heavy and opaque in the heavier piano writing. Well worth hearing, but not a first choice.

Dante symphony, G. 109.
*** Hung. HCD 11918-2 [id.]. Kincses, Hungarian R. & TV Ch., Budapest SO, Lehel.

Lehel's account is second to none and better than most previous versions. Veronika Kincses is a fine singer, and Lehel gives a strongly characterized performance with well-focused singing and fiery, intense orchestral playing. The Hungaroton recording has plenty of detail and presence, and the acoustic is agreeably warm. Like Lopez-Cobos before him, Lehel offers the *Magnificat* ending, which comes off splendidly in his hands.

(i) *Fantasia on Hungarian folk tunes, G. 123. Hungarian rhapsodies, G. 359/2, 4 & 5; Mazeppa, G. 100; Mephisto waltz No. 1; Les Préludes, G. 97; Tasso, lamento e trionfo, G. 96.*
*** DG 415 967-2 (2). (i) Shura Cherkassky; BPO, Karajan.

(i) *Fantasia on Hungarian folk tunes; Hungarian rhapsodies Nos. 2 & 5.*
(B) *** DG 429 156-2 [id.]. (i) Cherkassky; BPO, Karajan (with BRAHMS: *Hungarian dances Nos. 17–20****).

For the two-disc CD collection, DG have added to the orchestral works, recorded by Karajan over the years, Shura Cherkassky's glittering 1961 recording of the *Hungarian fantasia*. It is an affectionate performance with some engaging touches from the orchestra, though the pianist is dominant and his playing is superbly assured. Here as elsewhere, the remastering for CD has improved the range and body of the sound impressively, with firm detail throughout the orchestra. The cellos and basses sound marvellous in the *Fifth Rhapsody* and *Tasso*, and even the brashness of *Les Préludes* is a little tempered. *Mazeppa* is a great performance, superbly thrilling and atmospheric. A superb achievement, showing Karajan and his Berlin orchestra at their finest. However, this set now seems overpriced. The bargain Privilege issue offers a popular grouping, centred on the *Hungarian fantasia*, although the *Hungarian rhapsody* described as No. 2 is not the famous orchestral No. 2, but an orchestration of No. 12 for piano. The four Brahms *Hungarian dances* make a scintillating, lightweight encore.

Fantasia on Hungarian folk tunes, G. 123; Malédiction, G. 121; Totentanz, G. 126 (all for piano and orchestra).
*** Decca Dig. 414 079-2 [id.]. Bolet, LSO, Ivan Fischer.

Bolet is the masterful soloist in a splendid triptych of concertante works, the second of which – using strings alone – is unjustly neglected. Bolet's performance, sensitive as well as brilliant, should do much to rectify that, and the accounts of the two well-known works, persuasive enough to paper over any structural cracks, bring out all of Bolet's characteristic bravura. Excellent accompaniments from the LSO under an understanding Hungarian conductor, and recording of demonstration quality.

A Faust symphony, G. 108.
(M) *** EMI CDM7 63371-2 [id.]. Alexander Young, Beecham Ch. Soc., RPO, Beecham.
*** EMI Dig. CDC7 49062-2 [id.]. Winberg, Westminster Ch. College Male Ch., Phd. O, Muti.
**(*) Decca Dig. 417 399-2 [id.]. Jerusalem, Chicago Ch. & SO, Solti.
**(*) Hung. HCD 12022-2 [id.]. Korondy, Hungarian Army Ch. & State O, Ferencsik.

Sir Thomas Beecham's classic 1959 recording, well transferred to CD, shows this instinctive Lisztian at his most illuminatingly persuasive. His control of speed is masterly, spacious and eloquent in the first two movements without dragging, brilliant and urgent in the finale without any hint of breathlessness. Though in the transfer string-tone is limited in body, balances are very convincing, and the sound is unlikely to disappoint anyone wanting to enjoy a uniquely warm and understanding reading of an equivocal piece, hard to interpret.

Those looking for a modern digital recording will probably turn to Muti. As an ardent Tchaikovskian, he shows a natural sympathy for a piece which can readily seem overlong, and he finds obvious affinities in the music with the style of the Russian master. Some might feel that he is too overtly melodramatic in the finale, yet his pacing of the first movement is admirable, finding tenderness as well as red-blooded excitement. In the *Gretchen* movement he conjures the most delicately atmospheric playing from the orchestra and throughout he is helped by the ambience of the Old Met. in Philadelphia which seems especially suitable for this score. The digital recording is brilliant yet full-bodied, and without glare.

It was after hearing Beecham's classic recording that Sir Georg Solti was persuaded to tackle Liszt's great *Faust* triptych, a work which – surprisingly, for a musician born in Hungary – he had not studied till then. It is a spacious, brilliant reading, marked by superb playing from the Chicago orchestra. The bright Decca recording underlines the fierce element in Solti's reading, removing some of its warmth. The Mephistophelean finale brings the most impressive playing of the set, with Solti's fierceness chiming naturally with the movement's demoniac quality. The recording is typical of Decca's work in Chicago, very brilliant but lacking the depth of focus which would set the brightness in context.

With relatively brisk speeds Ferencsik directs a very idiomatic reading of Liszt's three portraits, lacking a little in weight and dramatic tension, but ending with a biting and brilliant account of the scherzando music representing Mephistopheles. The Hungarian players are on their mettle there, and are very well recorded.

Hunnenschlacht (symphonic poem), *G. 105.*
** Telarc Dig. CD 80079 [id.]. Cincinnati SO, Kunzel – BEETHOVEN: *Wellington's victory.***

A direct, unsubtle performance of a rarely recorded piece, not one of Liszt's finest works in the genre. The Telarc sound, however, is highly spectacular, with the organ interpolation adding to the expansiveness of texture. Those wanting the *'Battle' symphony* of Beethoven won't be disappointed with this, although the CD is rather short measure.

Orpheus; (i) *Psalm 13.*
(M) *** EMI CDM7 63299-2 [id.]. (i) Beecham Ch. Soc.; RPO, Beecham – R. STRAUSS: *Ein Heldenleben.****

Beecham's account of *Orpheus* originally appeared as the fill-up to his magisterial account of the *Faust symphony.* Inspired by an Etruscan vase in the Louvre depicting Orpheus singing to his lyre, it was partly designed to preface performances of Gluck's opera at Weimar. Beecham's recording remains the most poetic and unaffected yet to be committed to disc. Most listeners would place it as being recorded in the 1970s rather than in 1958! It sounds uncommonly fresh and spacious, and the performance is magical. The performance of *Psalm 13* is hardly less impressive. It is sung in English with the legendary Walter Midgely but is drier and more monochrome. All the same, an indispensable issue.

Les Préludes, G. 97.
(M) *** EMI CDM7 69228-2 [id.]. Philh. O, Karajan – BRAHMS: *Symphony No. 4.***(*)
(M) **(*) DG 423 384-2 [id.]. BPO, Fricsay – DVOŘÁK: *Symphony No. 9***(*); SMETANA: *Vltava.****

Karajan's 1958 *Les Préludes* found much favour in its day, as well it should. It still sounds thrilling now, and demonstrates the fine musical judgement of the original balance engineers. Musically, this is the equal of any modern version.

Fricsay has exactly the right temperament for *Les Préludes.* His performance is highly romantic – the detail of the pastoral interlude is delightful – yet the performance has enormous conviction and ardour and generates great excitement without vulgarity. The recording, made in the Jesus Christus Church, Berlin, was originally outstanding, but the 'drying-out' effect of the digital remastering has coarsened the sound somewhat.

PIANO MUSIC

Albumblatt in waltz form, G. 166; Bagatelle without tonality, G. 216a; Caprice-valses Nos. 1 & 2, G. 214; Ländler in A flat, G. 211; Mephisto waltzes Nos. 1–3, G. 514–15 and 216; Valse impromptu, G. 213; 4 Valses oubliées, G. 215.
*** Hyp. Dig. CDA 66201 [id.]. Leslie Howard.

On this excellent Hyperion disc Leslie Howard collects all of Liszt's original piano pieces that might be described as waltzes. Fascinatingly, he includes a fourth *Valse oubliée* that he himself has notionally completed from material long buried. Howard, on the cool side as a recording artist, gives clean, fresh, dramatic performances, very well recorded.

Années de pèlerinage, 1st Year, G.160: Au bord d'une source; 2nd Year, G.161: Sonnetto 104 del Petrarca; 3rd Year, G.162: Les jeux d'eau à la Villa d'Este; Supplement, G.162: Tarantella. Concert paraphrases of Schubert Lieder: *Auf dem Wasser zu singen; Die Forelle.* Concert studies: *Gnomenreigen; Un sospiro. Liebestraum No. 3.* (i) SCHUBERT/LISZT: *Wanderer fantasia* (arr. for piano and orchestra).
(B) *** Decca Dig. 425 689-2 [id.]. Jorge Bolet; (i) with LPO, Solti.

Intended by Decca as a bargain sampler for Bolet's distinguished Liszt series, this makes a unique recital in its own right. Quite apart from including a splendid version of Liszt's transcription for piano and orchestra of Schubert's *Wanderer fantasia*, the recital demonstrates the composer's wide pianistic range, from the evocation of the *Années de pèlerinage* and the romanticism of *Un sospiro* and *Liebestraum* to the glittering brilliance of *Gnomenreigen*, in which Bolet's playing is breathtakingly assured. The recording is very real and present.

Années de pèlerinage, 1st Year (Switzerland), G. 160.
*** Decca Dig. 410 160-2 [id.]. Jorge Bolet.
*** DG Dig. 415 670-2 [id.]. Daniel Barenboim.

This recording of the Swiss pieces from the *Années de pèlerinage* represents Bolet at his very peak, with playing of magical delicacy as well as formidable power. So *Au bord d'une source* brings playing limpid in its evocative beauty. The piano sound is outstandingly fine, set against a helpful atmosphere.

Barenboim's set is also distinguished, rather warmer in pianistic colour and romantic feeling. Barenboim's approach is freer, more improvisatory at times (though Bolet's poetic mastery in the closing two pieces is undeniable). The DG recording projects an image of striking fullness, yet still not lacking brilliance.

Années de pèlerinage, 2nd Year (Italy), G. 161 (complete).
*** Decca Dig. 410 161-2 [id.]. Jorge Bolet.

The pianistic colourings in this fine instalment in Bolet's Liszt series are magically caught here, whether in the brilliant sunlight of *Sposalizio* or the visionary gloom of *Il penseroso*. The *Dante sonata* brings a darkly intense performance, fresh and original and deeply satisfying.

Années de pèlerinage, 2nd Year, G. 161: Après une lecture du Dante (Dante sonata); Concert paraphrase on Wagner's Isoldens Liebestod, G. 447.
(*) RCA Dig. RD 85931. Barry Douglas – MUSSORGSKY: *Pictures.*(*)

There is plenty of colour and fire in Barry Douglas's performances which are an encore for an impressive account of Mussorgsky's *Pictures at an exhibition*. The *Wagner paraphrase* is particularly strong and involving. Good full piano tone.

Années de pèlerinage, Book 2. Supplement: Venezia e Napoli (Gondoliera; Canzone; Tarantella), G. 162; 3rd Year: Les jeux d'eau à la Villa d'Este, G. 163/4; Ballade No. 2 in B min., G. 171; Harmonies poétiques et religieuses: Bénédiction de Dieu dans la solitude, G. 173/3.

*** Decca Dig. 411 803-2 [id.]. Jorge Bolet.

'A dazzling pendant to Liszt's Italian *Années de pèlerinage*', as the sleeve-note describes Bolet's performances; and the recital includes two of Liszt's weightiest conceptions, the *Bénédiction* and the *Ballade*, both spaciously conceived and far too little known. The concentration of the longer works, as well as the magically sparkling textures of the sunny Italian pieces, is masterfully conveyed. Vivid and full piano recording.

Années de pèlerinage, 3rd Year (Italy), G. 163 (complete).
*** Ph. Dig. 420 174-2 [id.]. Zoltán Kocsis.

Zoltán Kocsis gives the most compelling account of these sombre and imaginative pieces; apart from beautiful pianism, he also manages to convey their character without exaggeration. He has impeccable technical control and can convey the dark power of the music without recourse to percussive tone. He is splendidly recorded by the Philips engineers. Lisztians need not hesitate.

Années de pèlerinage, 3rd Year: Tarantella. Harmonies poétiques et religieuses: Pensées des morts; Bénédiction de Dieu dans la solitude, G. 153; Legend: St Francis of Assisi preaching to the birds, G. 175. Mephisto waltz No. 1, G. 514; Rhapsodie espagnole, G. 254.
*** Virgin Dig. VC 790700-2 [id.]. Stephen Hough.

Stephen Hough's imaginatively planned Liszt recital on the Virgin Classics label is outstanding in every way. The choice of items is both illuminating and attractive. *St Francis preaching to the birds* is magically poetic in its re-creation of birdsong, while in the *Tarantella* Hough gives an inspired performance, combining power and searing virtuosity with delicate poetry and keen wit. Full, vivid recording. This amply confirms what Hough's prize-winning record of Hummel concertos for Chandos suggested, that he is a natural, magnetic communicator in the recording studio.

Ballades Nos. 1–2, G.170/1; Berceuse, G.174; Impromptu (Nocturne), G.191; Klavierstück in A flat, G.189; 2 Légendes, G.175; 2 Polonaises, G.223.
*** Hyp. Dig. CDA 66301 [id.]. Leslie Howard.

An attractive and enjoyable recital, aided by a magnificently balanced recording. The disc includes one short piece, the *Klavierstück*, G.189, new to the catalogue. The two *Legends* are beautifully played, though it must be said that Howard is not as imaginative here as some of the great pianists who have recorded these two highly evocative pieces.

Concert paraphrases of Schubert Lieder: *Auf den Wasser zu singen; Aufenthalt; Erlkönig; Die Forelle; Horch, horch die Lerch; Lebe wohl!; Der Lindenbaum; Lob der Tränen; Der Müller und der Bach; Die Post; Das Wandern; Wohin.*
*** Decca Dig. 414 575-2 [id.]. Jorge Bolet.

Superb virtuosity from Bolet in these display arrangements of Schubert. He is not just a wizard but a feeling musician, though here he sometimes misses a feeling of fun. First-rate recording, with the CD adding the usual extra sense of presence, and gaining from the silent background.

Concert paraphrase of Verdi's: *Rigoletto, G. 434; Études d'exécution transcendante d'après Paganini: La Campanella, G. 140/6. Harmonies poétiques et religieuses: Funérailles, G. 173/7. Hungarian rhapsody No. 12, G. 244; Liebestraum No. 3, G. 541/3. Mephisto waltz No. 1, G. 514.*
*** Decca Dig. 410 257-2 [id.]. Jorge Bolet.

Bolet's playing is magnetic, not just because of virtuosity thrown off with ease (as here in the *Rigoletto* paraphrase) but because of an element of joy conveyed, even in the demonic vigour of the *Mephisto waltz No. 1*. The relentless thrust of *Funérailles* is beautifully contrasted against the honeyed warmth of the famous *Liebestraum No. 3* and the sparkle of *La Campanella*. First-rate recording.

3 Concert studies, G. 144; 2 Concert studies, G. 145; 6 Consolations, G. 172; Réminiscences de Don Juan (Mozart), G. 418.
*** Decca 417 523-2 [id.]. Jorge Bolet.

In the *Concert studies* the combination of virtuoso precision and seeming spontaneity is most compelling, and the record is particularly valuable for including a splendid account of the *Don Juan* paraphrase, a piece which is neglected on record. The *Consolations* show Bolet at his most romantically imaginative: he plays them beautifully.

Études d'exécution transcendante (1838 version).
(B) ******* Pickwick Dig. MCD 10. Janice Weber.

An interesting and impressive issue – and amazing value too. Janice Weber is an American pianist of formidable technique – and she needs it if she is to take on the 1838 version of the *Transcendental studies*. Liszt composed his *Étude en douze exercices* when he was fifteen, and in 1838 he reworked and expanded them into the present set. The form in which we know them now is the revision Liszt made in 1851. Ms Weber has not only excellent fingers but also refined musicianship and a good sense of keyboard colour. Lisztians will welcome the appearance of this excellently played and splendidly recorded account. But just as a great ballerina must make the most daunting difficulties seem easy, a virtuoso pianist must toss off the most hair-raising passage-work without apparent effort. This she does not quite manage, which is probably why Liszt made his revision.

Études d'exécution transcendante, G. 139 (complete).
*** EMI Dig. CDC7 49821-2 [id.]. Vladimir Ovchinikov.
(M) ****(*)** EMI CDM7 69111-2 [id.]. György Cziffra.
**(*) Ph. 416 458-2 [id.]. Claudio Arrau.
**(*) Decca Dig. 414 601-2 [id.]. Jorge Bolet.

Vladimir Ovchinikov is an artist first and a pyrotechnician second. There is no lack of display, stamina or virtuosity at any stage, nor does this Leeds Prizewinner lack poetic insights. He has good fingers and never produces an ugly fortissimo. The EMI recording is first class, with plenty of space round the aural image. Those wanting this work need not hesitate.

György Cziffra's set of the *Études d'exécution transcendante* was recorded in 1959 when he was at the height of his powers; the playing is highly volatile and charismatic and shows enormous technical command. The recording is not distinguished, the upper range somewhat restricted, and there is at times a bass orientation; but the panache of the playing triumphs over the early stereo technology.

Arrau made this recording in 1977 and it was a formidable achievement for an artist in his seventies. Arrau always plays with great panache and musical insight which more than compensate for the occasional smudginess of the recorded sound. On record, Cziffra brings greater obvious virtuosity to these pieces, but he is of course a much younger man. Arrau's playing is most masterly and poetic, and the recording, if too reverberant, is truthful.

If you are looking principally for pianistic fireworks, Bolet is a little disappointing, lacking a little in demonry; but as a searching interpreter of the composer and his musical argument he has few rivals. The Decca recording presents big-scale piano sound to match the performances.

Hungarian rhapsodies Nos. 1– 19.
(M) *** DG 423 925-2 (2) [id.]. Roberto Szidon.

Hungarian rhapsodies Nos. 2; 6; 9 (Carnival in Pest); 12– 14; 15 (Rákóczy march).
*** EMI CDC7 47370-2 [id.]. György Cziffra.

At mid-price, Roberto Szidon's set of the *Hungarian rhapsodies* is highly recommendable. Szidon has been missing from the concert platform in recent years – at least so far as England is concerned – and has made few records. There is plenty of fire and flair here, and much that will dazzle the listener! The recording, too, sounds very good indeed.

Cziffra's performances are dazzling. They are full of those excitingly chimerical spurts of rubato that immediately evoke the unreasonably fierce passions of gypsy music. The high degree of neurosis in the playing, with hardly two consecutive phrases at an even tempo, makes even Szidon (who has the full measure of the music) seem staid. Cziffra, with glittering rhythmic and digital dexterity, sets every bar of the music on fire. Some might find him too impulsive for comfort, but the *Rákóczy march* is a *tour de force* and his command of the keyboard is masterly. The recording, made in the Salle Wagram, Paris, in 1974/5, is a little dry, but otherwise truthful.

Liebesträume Nos. 1– 3, G. 541.
*** DG 415 118-2 [id.]. Daniel Barenboim – MENDELSSOHN: *Songs without words****; SCHUBERT: *6 Moments musicaux.***

Barenboim plays these famous Liszt pieces with unaffected simplicity and, taken as a whole, this is a rewarding CD.

Piano sonata in B min., G. 178.
(*) RCA RD 85673 [RCA 5673-2RC]. Artur Rubinstein – BACH: *Chaconne*; FRANCK: *Prelude, chorale & fugue*.*

Piano sonata; Années de pèlerinage, 2nd Year, G. 161: Il Penseroso; 3rd Year, G. 162: Les jeux d'eau à la Villa d'Este. Hungarian rhapsody No. 15 (Rákóczy march), G. 244; Mephisto waltz No. 1, G. 514.
⊛ *** Olympia Dig. OCD 172 [id.]. Mikhail Pletnev.

Piano sonata; Années de pèlerinage, 2nd Year, G. 161: Après une lecture du Dante (Dante sonata). Mephisto waltz No. 1, G. 514.
*** Denon Dig. C37 7547 [id.]. Dezsö Ránki.

Piano sonata; Bagatelle sans tonalité.
*** EMI Dig. CDC7 49916-2 [id.]. Peter Donohoe – BARTÓK; BERG: *Sonatas.***

Piano sonata; 3 Concert studies, G. 144.
*** Chan. Dig. CHAN 8548 [id.]. Louis Lortie.

Piano sonata; Grand galop chromatique, G. 219; Liebesträume Nos. 1–3; Valse impromptu, G. 213.
*** Decca Dig. 410 115-2. Jorge Bolet.

Piano sonata; 2 Légendes, G. 175; La lugubre gondola, Nos. 1 and 2, G. 200.
*** Ph. Dig. 410 040-2 [id.]. Alfred Brendel.

Mikhail Pletnev has a commanding musical authority, a highly distinctive timbre and an amazing dynamic range and variety of colour. His technique is transcendental and can be compared only with the young Horowitz, and there is a refinement and poetry that are hardly less remarkable. He dispatches the *Sonata* with an awesome brilliance and sense of drama, and his *Mephisto Waltz* is altogether thrilling. While the recording does not do full justice to his highly personal sound-world, it is eminently satisfactory. A most exciting disc.

Brendel's latest account of the *Sonata* has received wide acclaim. It is certainly a more subtle and concentrated account than his earlier version, made in the mid-1960s – brilliant though that was – and must be numbered among the very best now available. There is a wider range of colour and tonal nuance, yet the undoubted firmness of grip does not seem achieved at the expense of any spontaneity. It is most realistically recorded.

Louis Lortie gives almost as commanding a performance of the Liszt *Sonata* as any in the catalogue; its virtuosity can be taken for granted and, though he does not have the extraordinary intensity and feeling for drama of Pletnev, he has a keen awareness of its structure and a Chopinesque finesse that win one over. The Chandos recording is made at The Maltings, Snape, and, though a shade too reverberant, is altogether natural.

Donohoe's playing has a certain abandon and panache that hold the listener throughout. Pianistically this is impressive and Donohoe can hold his head high among the long list. Strangely enough, the *Bagatelle without tonality* is thrown off in a somewhat cavalier fashion.

The power, imagination and concentration of Bolet are excellently brought out in his fine account of the *Sonata*. With the famous *Liebestraum* (as well as its two companions) also most beautifully done, not to mention the amazing *Grand galop*, this is one of the most widely appealing of Bolet's outstanding Liszt series. Excellent recording.

Dezsö Ránki's account of the *Sonata* is very impressive indeed and can hold its own with almost any of its rivals. The *Mephisto waltz* and the *Dante sonata* are hardly less powerful in the hands of the young Hungarian master, the latter with real fire and a masterly control of dramatic pace. The Denon recording is absolutely first class and has admirable clarity, body and presence. This is one of the best Liszt recital programmes currently available.

Rubinstein's performance of the *Sonata* was recorded in 1965, and there is some hardness of timbre in fortissimos. But at *piano* and *mezzo forte* levels (and there is a wider range of dynamic here than on some Rubinstein records) the tone is subtly coloured and Rubinstein's mercurial approach to the music is wonderfully spontaneous, bringing an astonishing fire and brilliance for a pianist of his age, and considerable poetry to the more thoughtful moments.

ORGAN MUSIC

Am Grabe Richard Wagners; Andante maestoso; Angelus; Avé maris stella; Gebet (Ave Maria); Missa pro organo; Ora pro nobis; Praeludium; Rosario; Salve Regina; Tu es Petrus; Weimars Volkslied.
(BB) ** Hung. White Label HRC 095 [id.]. Sándor Marggittay, Endre Kovács, Gábor Lehotka (various organs).

Most of these are late works and many of the pieces were conceived in other, alternative versions. Of these the *Angelus* comes from the third year of the *Années de pèlerinage*, but sounds rather effective on the organ. The Wagner inspiration exists in three alternative versions but again suits the instrument well. Of the pieces conceived especially for the organ the *Salve Regina*, based on a Gregorian chant, has a striking, cool beauty. The most ambitious work is the *Missa pro organo*, an integral part of an organ-accompanied low Mass. All the music is presented well and the unnamed Hungarian organs sound bright and sonorous. Not an indispensable Liszt record but an interesting one.

Fantasia and fugue on 'Ad nos, ad salutarem undam'; Prelude and fugue on the name BACH, G. 260; Variations on Bach's 'Weinen, Klagen, Sorgen, Zagen', G. 673.
*** Pierre Verany Dig. PV 783041 [id.]. Chantal de Zeeuw (organ of Aix-en-Provence Cathedral).

Chantal de Zeeuw plays Liszt's ripely romantic evocations of classical forms with striking flair, and the resonant acoustic of Aix Cathedral helps to make a spectacular effect. The microphones are close enough to capture the organ's action noise, but the overall sound-picture remains convincing.

VOCAL MUSIC

Lieder: *Blume und Duft; Der drei Zigeuner; Der du von dem Himmel bist* (2 settings); *Ein Fichtenbaum steht einsam; Es muss ein Wunderbares sein; Es rauschen die Winde; Der Hirt; Ihr Auge; Ihr Glocken von Marling; Freudvoll und leidvoll; Die Loreley; O komm im Traum; Des Tages laute Stimmen schweigen; Über allen Gipfeln ist Ruh; Vergiftet sind meine Lieder.*
*** Capriccio Dig. 10 294 [id.]. Mitsuko Shirai, Hartmut Höll.

Mitsuko Shirai has already established a unique place among Lieder-singers of her generation, and now the voice has darkened to add weight and intensity to her always searchingly perceptive singing. Her accompanist husband, Hartmut Höll, equally has few rivals to match him today, and their partnership in this outstanding Liszt record, as in their previous Capriccio issues, brings one revelation after another. There are few collections of Liszt songs as searchingly persuasive as this, and none more beautiful. Provocatively the record starts with Shirai at her most vehement in *Vergiftet sind meine Lieder* (My songs are poised), written when Liszt's long relationship with the Countess d'Agoult was breaking up. Regrettably, no English translations are provided with the text, only a commentary.

Lieder: *Comment, disaient-ils; Die drei Zigeuner; Ein Fichtenbaum steht einsam; Enfant, si j'étais roi; Es muss ein Wunderbares sein; Oh, quand je dors; S'il est un charmant gazon; Über allen Gipfeln ist Ruh; Vergiftet sind meine Lieder.*
*** DG Dig. 419 238-2 [id.]. Brigitte Fassbaender, Irwin Gage – R. STRAUSS: *Lieder.****

This is singing which, in its control of detail, both in word and in note, as well as in its beauty and range of expression, is totally commanding. There are few women Lieder singers in any generation who can match this in power and intensity, with each song searchingly characterized. Fassbaender proves just as much at home in the four Victor Hugo settings in French as in the German songs. Sensitive accompaniment, well-placed recording.

Hungarian Coronation mass, G. 11.
*** Hung. HCD 12148-2 [id.]. Kincses, Takács, Gulyás, Polgár, Hungarian R. & TV Ch., Budapest SO, Lehel.

Written for the coronation of Franz Josef I as King of Hungary, this setting of the Mass shows Liszt at his most direct, freely indulging his sympathy with a wide range of sources: operatic, Hungarian (in the *Sanctus*), plainchant and, with the *Graduale*, added later, bringing in Lisztian chromaticism. Sung here with dedication by excellent Hungarian forces under György Lehel, its plain homophonic textures – with the soloists generally used together as a quartet – make a strong impact, and the reverberant recording allows plenty of detail to be heard against an apt church acoustic.

The Legend of St Elisabeth, G. 2.
*** Hung. Dig. HCD 12694/6-2 [id.]. Marton, Kováts, Farkas, Solyom-Nagy, Gregor, Gáti, Budapest Ch., Hungarian Army Male Ch., Children's Ch., Hungarian State O, Joó.

Though uneven in inspiration, Liszt's oratorio on *The Legend of St Elisabeth* contains some of his finest religious music in its span of six tableaux. Arpad Joó drives the work hard, but never to undermine the expressiveness of chorus and soloists, with Eva Marton as Elisabeth more firmly controlled than she has sometimes been in opera, and with no weak link in the rest of the team of principals.

Missa solemnis, G. 9.
**(*) Hung. HCD 11861-2 [id.]. Kincses, Takács, Korondy, Gregor, Hungarian R. & TV Ch., Budapest SO, Ferencsik.

This ambitious setting of the Mass is one of Liszt's finest choral inspirations, full of powerful, dramatic ideas, with thematic links between movements that make it stylistically more consistent than most. Ferencsik's recording, made in the mid-1970s, brings a spacious, powerful performance, well played and sung, with four of Hungary's most distinguished singers as soloists. The analogue recording is not ideal but this remains far more than a stop-gap and is a noble account of a masterly choral work.

OPERA

Don Sanche (complete).
**(*) Hung. Dig. HCD 12744/5-2 [id.]. Garino, Hamari, Gáti, Farkas, Hungarian R. & TV Ch., Hungarian State Op. O, Tamás Pál.

Don Sanche or the Castle of Love was the teenage composer's first essay at a stage work. The piece tells of a magic castle of love ruled over by a sinister magician, and how the knight, Don Sanche, finally wins the love of the disdainful Elzire. The only really Lisztian quality is the way he lights on instruments relatively exotic at the time, loading piccolos and trombones on to writing which suggests Weber or Rossini with dashes of Haydn, Schubert or even an occasional watered-down echo of Beethoven's *Fidelio*. The pity is that, after a promising start, the 90-minute one-acter tails off. Támas Pál conducts a lively performance, with some stylish singing from the lyric tenor, Gerard Garino, in the name-part. Other principals are variable, including Julia Hamari as the hard-hearted heroine; but as long as you keep firmly in mind that this is the work of a thirteen-year-old, it will give much pleasure. The sound is bright and close.

Litolff, Henri (1818–91)

Concerto symphonique No. 4, Op. 102: Scherzo.
*** Ph. Dig. 411 123-2 [id.]. Misha Dichter, Philh. O, Marriner (with Concert of concertante music***).

*** Decca Dig. 414 348-2 [id.]. Cristina Ortiz, RPO, Atzmon – ADDINSELL: *Warsaw concerto*; GOTTSCHALK: *Grand fantaisie*; RACHMANINOV: *Concerto No. 2.****

Misha Dichter gives a scintillating account of Litolff's delicious *Scherzo*, played at a sparklingly brisk tempo. Marriner accompanies sympathetically and the recording is excellent.

Cristina Ortiz's version has less extrovert brilliance but an agreeable elegance. The intimacy of this version is emphasized by the balance, which places the piano within the orchestral group, making the gentle central section especially effective. The Decca couplings are more substantial and the CD is impressively natural.

Loewe, Frederick (born 1904)

My Fair Lady (musical).
**(*) Decca Dig. 421 200-2 [id.]. Kiri Te Kanawa, Jeremy Irons, John Gielgud, Warren Mitchell, Jerry Hadley, London Voices, LSO, Mauceri.

Kiri Te Kanawa has difficulty with Eliza's cockney persona. Although she sings *I could have danced all night* ravishingly, memories of Julie Andrews are not banished; and Jeremy Irons, who gives a forceful portrayal of Higgins, does not match Rex Harrison's elegant timing, especially in his first early mono recording. Clearly this is a studio production. Having said that, it is a joy to hear the music presented with such vigour and sophistication. Warren Mitchell's Doolittle is endearingly crusty and Jerry Hadley sings *On the street where you live* very engagingly. With spirited direction from John Mauceri, this is a first-class entertainment, the recording giving depth as well as presence.

Lloyd, George (born 1913)

(i) *Piano concerto No. 4; The lily-leaf and the grasshopper; The transformation of that Naked Ape.*
*** Albany AR 004 [id.]. Kathryn Stott; (i) LSO, composer.

The *Fourth Piano concerto* is a romantic, light-hearted piece with a memorable 'long singing tune' (the composer's words), somewhat Rachmaninovian in its spacious lyricism contrasting with a 'jerky' rhythmic idea. The *Larghetto*, serene in a typical, undemanding, Lloydian way, derives from the material of the first movement, and then there is a good-humoured finale. The performance by Kathryn Stott and the LSO under the composer is ardently spontaneous from the first bar to the last. The first of the two solo pieces ingenuously but endearingly evokes a memory of an evening on the Avon when the composer saw a large lily-leaf come floating past him; on it sat a grasshopper. The second is a six-movement suite inspired by Desmond Morris's book *The Naked Ape*. The style is eclectic but still somehow Lloydian. The recording is first rate.

Symphonies Nos. 2 and 9.
*** Conifer Dig. CDCF 139 [id.]. BBC PO, composer.

Lloyd's *Second Symphony* is a light-weight, extrovert piece, conventional in form and construction, though in the finale the composer flirts briefly with polytonality, an experiment he did not repeat. The *Ninth* (1969) is similarly easygoing; the *Largo* is rather fine, but its expressive weight is in scale, and the finale, 'a merry-go-round that keeps going round and round', has an appropriately energetic brilliance. Throughout both works the invention is attractive, and in these definitive performances, extremely well recorded, the composer's advocacy is very persuasive.

Symphony No. 4.
*** Albany AR 002 [id.]. Albany SO, composer.

George Lloyd's *Fourth Symphony* was composed during his convalescence after being badly shell-shocked while serving in the Arctic convoys of 1941/2. The first movement is directly related to this period of his life, and the listener may be surprised at the relative absence of sharp dissonance – indeed the violence seems muted by subjective feeling; in the serene second movement the composer is able to recall a pre-war journey up the Norwegian coast as far as the North Cape. After a brilliant scherzo, the infectious finale is amiable, offering a series of quick, 'march-like tunes', which the composer explains by suggesting that 'when the funeral is over the band plays quick cheerful tunes to go home'. Under Lloyd's direction, the Albany Symphony Orchestra play with great commitment and a natural, spontaneous feeling. The recording is superb.

(i) *Symphonies Nos. 6;* (ii) *10 (November journeys);* (i) *Overture: John Socman.*
**(*) Albany Dig. CDTROY 015 [id.]. (i) BBC PO; (ii) BBC PO Brass, composer.

Symphony No. 10 (*November journeys*) has already been recorded by the London Collegiate Brass under James Stobart, a strikingly fine account which the composer's version does not quite match – perhaps surprisingly, since the work was written for the BBC players. The *Sixth Symphony* is amiable and lightweight; it is more like a suite than a symphony. Lloyd's performance of No. 6 is attractively spontaneous and well played, and the equally agreeable *John Socman overture* (a prelude for his opera of the same name, commissioned for the Festival of Britain in 1951) also comes off well, although it is rather inconsequential. This is not the record with which to start a Lloyd collection.

Symphony No. 7.
*** Conifer Dig. CDFC 143 [id.]. BBC PO, composer.

The *Seventh Symphony* is on a larger scale than most of Lloyd's earlier works. It is a programme symphony, using the ancient Greek legend of Proserpine. The slow movement is particularly fine, an extended soliloquy of considerable expressive power. The last and longest movement is concerned with 'the desperate side of our lives – "Dead dreams that the snows have shaken, Wild leaves that the winds have taken",' yet, as is characteristic with Lloyd, the darkness is muted; nevertheless the resolution at the end is curiously satisfying. Again he proves an admirable exponent of his own music. The recording is splendid.

Symphony No. 10 (November journeys).
(M) ******* Trax Dig. TRXCD 114 [id.]. L. Collegiate Brass, Stobart – JOSEPHS: *Concerto for brass.********

The bitter-sweet lyricism of the first movement of *November journeys* is most attractive (the use of the piccolo-trumpet a piquant added colouring), but the linear writing is more complex than usual in a work for brass. In the finale a glowing *cantando* melody warms the spirit, to contrast with the basic *Energico*. The performance by the London Collegiate Brass is expert – the *Calma* slow movement is quite haunting, no doubt reflecting the composer's series of visits to English cathedrals, the reason for the subtitle. The recording is in the demonstration class.

Symphony No. 11.
*** Conifer Dig. CDCF 144 [id.]. Albany SO, composer.

The urgently dynamic first movement of the *Eleventh* is described by the composer as being 'all fire and violence', but any anger in the music quickly evaporates, and it conveys rather a mood of exuberance, with very full orchestral forces unleashed. The second movement, *Lento*, is a songful interlude; the third, a dance, leads to the fourth, a funeral march that for all its drumbeat rhythms is not really mournful. The finale starts with cheerful carolling trumpets and sets the seal on Lloyd's basic message of optimism. With the orchestra for which the work was commissioned, Lloyd conducts a powerful performance, very well played. The recording was made in the Music Hall of Troy Savings Bank near Albany; it is spectacularly sumptuous and wide-ranging.

PIANO MUSIC

An African shrine; The aggressive fishes; Intercom baby; The road through Samarkand; St Anthony and the bogside beggar.
**(*) Albany Dig. AR 003 [id.]. Martin Roscoe.

The most ambitious piece here is *An African shrine*, in which the composer's scenario is linked (not very dissonantly) to African violence and revolution. The music is like a symphonic poem for piano and is effectively diverse in mood, but rather extended (at 23 minutes) for its material. *The road through Samarkand* (1972) has travellers from the younger generation leaving for the East; while *The aggressive fishes* are tropical and violently moody, changing from serenity to anger at the flick of a fin. The two most striking pieces are the picaresque tale of the *Bogside beggar* and the charming lullaby written for a baby whose mother is in another room listening with the aid of modern technology. Martin Roscoe's performances are thoroughly committed and spontaneous, and the recording is first class.

Lloyd Webber, Andrew (born 1948)

Variations.
(*) Ph. Dig. 420 342-2 [id.]. Julian Lloyd Webber, LPO, Maazel – W. LLOYD WEBBER: *Aurora.*
**(*) MCA DCML 1816. Julian Lloyd Webber, Airey, Argent, Hiseman, Mole, More, Thompson, composer.

Andrew Lloyd Webber's piece began life as a comparatively short, 20-minute work, composed with his brother's brilliant cello-playing very much in mind. It was then expanded to the format here recorded by MCA, about half an hour, and has since been blown up to even greater proportions for its orchestral version, scored by David Cullen. The vulgarity of the ambience of its 'pop' sections will exasperate many listeners, yet its sheer vitality cannot be ignored and the lyrical variations, featuring the flute and solo cello, are genuinely memorable. Although the earlier account sits more comfortably between the world of 'pop' and concert hall, the MCA recording does not match the Philips digital sound and most readers will probably identify more readily with the orchestral expansion, ably directed by Maazel who has been so successful with his recording of the *Requiem*.

Requiem.
*** EMI Dig. CDC7 47146-2 [id.]. Brightman, Domingo, Miles-Kingston, Drew, Winchester Cathedral Ch., ECO, Maazel; J. Lancelot (organ).

This *Requiem* may be derivative at many points, with echoes of Carl Orff – not to mention the *Requiems* of both Verdi and Fauré – but, with Maazel conducting a performance of characteristic intensity, it certainly has a life of its own. The *Pié Jesu* is a model of bridge-building, a melody beautiful and individual by any standard, which yet has all the catchiness of one of Lloyd Webber's tunes in a musical. Plainly the high, bright voice of Sarah Brightman was the direct inspiration, and the beauty of her singing certainly earns her this place alongside Placido Domingo, contributing in a rather less prominent role. Radiant sounds from the Winchester Cathedral Choir, not least the principal treble, Paul Miles-Kingston. Above all, this is music to which one returns with increasing appreciation and pleasure. The CD gives presence and clarity to the excellent sound.

Tell me on a Sunday (song cycle).
*** Polydor 833 447-2. Marti Webb, LPO, Rabinowitz.

This fine song-cycle by Andrew Lloyd Webber with splendid lyrics by Don Black chronicles the disastrous series of love affairs of an English girl living in America. The theme of the songs is nostalgic and a little sentimental, for the heroine gradually comes to terms with her failures and it is she who makes the final break. The music itself is memorable and contains more catchy tunes than most of Lloyd Webber's musicals. The performance by Marti Webb (for whom the cycle was written) is distinctive and she is very well accompanied by Harry Rabinowitz and members of the LPO. The recording is very good, and the only small snag is that the opening number, *Take that look off your face*, was stridently heated up to secure its entry into the charts as a hit single.

The Phantom of the Opera (complete).
*** Polydor 831 273-2 [id.] (2). Michael Crawford, Sarah Brightman, Steve Barton, Ch. & O of original London cast, Michael Read.

The Phantom of the Opera: highlights.
*** Polydor 831 563-2 (from above recording).

The worldwide success of *The Phantom of the Opera* means that the recording of the score needs no advocacy from us. It can be said, however, that there is far more to it than the ubiquitous *Music of the night*; and the chromatic *Phantom theme* is the real stuff of melodrama. As the anti-hero of the piece was a neglected composer, Lloyd Webber needed to write some pastiche opera for him, and this he does very skilfully. The vividly recorded highlights will be the best way to approach this score, but the complete set is also surprisingly compulsive. Extraordinarily, there are no internal cues on the CDs.

Lloyd Webber, William (1914–82)

Aurora (tone poem).
*** Ph. Dig. 420 342-2 [id.]. LPO, Maazel – A. LLOYD WEBBER: *Variations.***(*)

The world fame of Andrew Lloyd Webber has led to an interest in his father, who is shown here as a talented composer in his own right, if one without the individuality of his son. *Aurora*, a gentle evocation of the Roman goddess of Dawn, Youth and Beauty, is very well played and recorded. It is coupled with Andrew's more positively inspired, but often more vulgar *Variations*.

(i) *Missa Sanctae Mariae Magdalenae;* (ii) Arias: *The Divine compassion: Thou art the King. The Saviour: The King of Love. 5 Songs.* (iii; iv) *In the half light (soliloquy); Air varié* (after Franck); (iv) *6 Piano pieces.*
*** ASV Dig. CDDCA 584 [id.]. (i) Richard Hickox Singers, Hickox; I. Watson (organ); (ii) J. Graham Hall; P. Ledger; (iii) Julian Lloyd Webber; (iv) John Lill.

William Lloyd Webber was a distinguished academic, a virtuoso organist and a composer who in a few beautifully crafted works laid bare his heart in pure romanticism. In his varied collection, the *Missa Sanctae Mariae Magdalenae* is both the last and the most ambitious of his works, strong and characterful, building up to moments of drama, as when the organ enters for the first time, not in the opening *Kyrie* but suddenly and unexpectedly in the *Gloria* which follows, to thrilling effect. John Lill is a persuasive advocate of the *Six Piano pieces,* varied in mood and sometimes quirky, and accompanies Julian Lloyd Webber in the two cello pieces, written – as though with foresight of his son's career – just as his second son was born. Graham Hall, accompanied by Philip Ledger, completes the recital with beautiful performances of a group of songs and arias, no more remarkable than many works by talented academics, but well worth hearing. Recording, made in a north London church, is warm and undistracting.

Locatelli, Pietro (1695–1764)

Violin concertos Op. 3, Nos. 1 in D; 8 in E min.; 9 in G.
(M) *** Ph. 422 491-2 [id.]. Michelucci, I Musici.

The three concertos recorded here come from the set of concertos and caprices called *The art of the violin*. The caprices are an integral part of the concertos, taking the place of the normal cadenza. These are attractive pieces and here are beautifully played. Although not of very recent provenance, the recording sounds fresh and well detailed in its newest incarnation. What a splendid soloist Michelucci is!

Flute sonatas, Op. 2/2, 6, 7 & 10.
*** Ph. Dig. 416 613-2 [id.]. Hazelzet, Koopman, Van der Meer.

These *Sonatas* come from Locatelli's set of twelve, Op. 2, and were published in 1732. The set was sufficiently admired in its day to sell out and be reprinted, and a generous melodic fertility can be heard in the four recorded here. The performances could hardly be more sympathetic and stylish, while the recording itself, dating from 1980, is very truthful and immediate.

Lully, Jean-Baptiste (1632–87)

Le bourgeois gentilhomme (comédie-ballet; complete).
(M) *** HM/BMG GD 77059 (2). Nimsgern, Jungmann, Schortemeier, René Jacobs, Tölz Ch., La Petite Bande, Leonhardt – CAMPRA: *L'Europe galante.****

Entertainment rather than musical value: in itself, Lully's score offers no great musical rewards. The melodic invention is unmemorable and harmonies are neither original nor interesting; but if the music taken on its own is thin stuff, the effect of the entertainment as a whole is quite a different matter. This performance puts Lully's music into the correct stage perspective and, with such sprightly and spirited performers as well as good

1973 recording, this can hardly fail to give pleasure. The orchestral contribution under the direction of Gustav Leonhardt is distinguished by a splendid sense of the French style.

Atys (opera): complete.
*** HM Dig. HMC 901257/9. Guy de Mey, Mellon, Laurens, Gardeil, Semellaz, Rime, Les Arts Florissants Ch. & O, Christie.

Christie and his excellent team give life and dramatic speed consistently to the performance of *Atys*, so much so that, though this five-act piece lasts nearly three hours, one keeps thinking of Purcell's almost contemporary masterpiece on quite a different – miniature – scale, *Dido and Aeneas*. Invention is only intermittently on a Purcellian level, but there are many memorable numbers, not least those in the sleep interlude of Act III. Outstanding in the cast are the high tenor, Guy de Mey, in the name-part and Agnès Mellon as the nymph, Sangaride, with whom he falls in love.

Lumbye, Hans Christian (1810–74)

Amager polka; Amelie waltz; Champagne galop; Columbine polka mazurka; Copenhagen Steam Railway galop; Dream pictures fantasia; The Guard of Amager (ballet): Final galop. Helga polka mazurka; Hesperus waltz; Lily polka (dedicated to the ladies); Queen Louise's waltz; Napoli (ballet): Final galop. Salute to August Bournonville; Salute to our friends; Sandman galop fantastique.
⊛ *** Unicorn Dig. DKPCD 9089 [id.]. Odense SO, Peter Guth.

It is incredible that the waltzes and polkas of Hans Christian Lumbye – 'the Strauss of the North' as this CD collection rightly proclaims him – are not more widely known and loved. A representative EMI LP appeared in the mid-1960s but did not stay around very long. Now this superb Unicorn collection makes handsome amends, offering 75 minutes of the composer's best music, with wonderfully spontaneous performances demonstrating above all its elegance and gentle grace. It opens with a vigorous *Salute to August Bournonville* (he was Director of the Danish Royal Theatre ballet) and closes with a *Champagne galop* to rival Johann junior's polka; and here the hitherto silent audience joins in with enthusiastic, if undisciplined hand-claps, to recall the *Radetzky march* of Johann senior. In between comes much to enchant, not least the delightful *Amelie waltz* and the haunting *Dream pictures fantasia* with its diaphanous opening textures and lilting main theme. Another charmer is the *Sandman galop fantastique*, a vivacious pot-pourri which never wears out its welcome by becoming too vociferous, while *Queen Louise's waltz* has an appropriate melodic poise. But Lumbye's masterpiece is the unforgettable *Copenhagen Steam Railway galop*. This whimsical yet vivid portrait of a local Puffing Billy begins with the gathering of passengers at the station – obviously dressed for the occasion in a more elegant age than ours. The little engine then wheezingly starts up and proceeds on its journey, finally drawing to a dignified halt against interpolated cries from the station staff. Because of the style and refinement of its imagery, it is much the most endearing of musical railway evocations, and the high-spirited lyricism of the little train racing through the countryside, its whistle peeping, is enchanting. It is interesting, too, that the expansive melodic line of the introduction is sometimes hinted at in the opening paragraphs of Lumbye's other music. This is a superbly entertaining disc, showing the Odense Symphony Orchestra and its conductor, Peter Guth, as naturally suited to this repertoire as are the VPO under Boskovsky in the music of the Strauss family. The recording has a warm and sympathetic ambience and gives a lovely bloom to the whole programme.

Lutoslawski, Witold (born 1916)

(i) *Chain I – III;* (ii) *Symphony No. 3.*
** Polski Nagrania PNCD 044 [id.]. (i) Junge Deutsch PO, Holliger; Jakowicz, Warsaw Nat. PO, Kord; Polish Nat. R. O, (ii) Antoni Wit.

The *Third Symphony* (1983) is well played by the Polish Radio Orchestra of Katowice under Antoni Wit, and the analogue recording is very good. This would make a perfectly acceptable alternative to the composer (Philips) or Salonen (CBS) if it were priced more competitively, but the latter are to be preferred. *Chain I* was recorded (rather forwardly and less subtly) at the 1984 Warsaw Autumn by Holliger and his youthful and expert German players, *Chain II* two years later with the Warsaw forces under Kazimierz Kord, and *Chain III* with the Katowice orchestra in 1988 under the composer. More than acceptable sound throughout.

Chain II; Partita.
*** DG Dig. 423 696-2 [id.]. Mutter, BBC SO, composer – STRAVINSKY: *Violin concerto.****

Chain II, a *Dialogue for violin and orchestra*, follows up the technique which Lutoslawski developed in a work written for the London Sinfonietta, *Chain I*, contrasting fully written sections with *ad libitum* movements, where chance plays its part within fixed parameters. The *Partita* is a development of a piece for violin and piano which Lutoslawski originally wrote for Pinchas Zukerman, with the first, third and fifth movements written for violin and orchestra, the second and fourth '*ad libitum*' for violin and piano alone. With Mutter and the composer the most persuasive advocates, both pieces establish themselves as among the finest examples of Lutoslawski's latterday work, provocative and ear-catching in their fantasy. First-rate sound.

Concerto for orchestra.
*** Decca Dig. 425 694-2. Cleveland O, Dohnányi – BARTÓK: *Concerto for orchestra.***(*)

Lutoslawski's brilliant showpiece is here played with a thrust and precision to bring out the full colour and energy of the work. If it lacks the thematic memorability of the Bartók, it is just as exuberantly colourful. Dohnányi's dedicated performance makes it a perfect counterpart, an apt coupling, recorded with a fullness and brilliance outstanding even by Decca standards.

Concerto for orchestra; Funeral music; Symphony No. 1; (i) *Lacrimosa.*
*(**) Polski Nagrania PNCD 040 [id.]. Warsaw Nat. PO; Polish Nat. RSO, Rowicki; Krenz; (i) Stefania Woytowicz, Silesian Philharmonic Ch., composer.

The *Lacrimosa* is a short and moving graduation piece from 1937, somewhat in the style of Szymanowski, who died that same year. Woytowicz, alas, has now developed a wobble; but the piece, recorded in 1988, is not otherwise available. Krenz's 1964 record of the *First Symphony* is thoroughly acceptable, if not outstanding. However, Rowicki's *Concerto for orchestra*, made in 1962, if hardly better recorded, is a marvellous performance; and the 1959 account of the *Funeral music* is played with terrific intensity, though again the rough-and-ready recording calls for tolerance. These works form a good introduction to the composer and, if modern sound is not a first priority, they make a useful point of entry into his world.

(i) *Cello concerto;* (ii) *Concerto for oboe, harp and chamber orchestra;* (iii) *Dance preludes.*
*** Ph. Dig. 416 817-2 [id.]. (i) Schiff; (ii) H. and U. Holliger; (iii) Brunner; Bav. RSO, composer.

Heinrich Schiff is very impressive in the *Cello concerto* and has the advantage of the composer's direction and a recording of exceptional clarity and refinement. The *Concerto for oboe, harp and chamber orchestra* is a later piece, written for the Holligers, its expert advocates here; it mingles charm, irony and intelligence in equal measure. The *Dance preludes* are much more folk-like in idiom and speech, and are attractively presented here by Eduard Brunner. Lutoslawski himself gets splendid playing from the Bavarian Radio Symphony Orchestra and readers should find this a rewarding issue. The recording is excellent.

(i) *Cello concerto. Livre; Postlude 1;* (ii) *Parole tissées* (for tenor, strings, harp, piano & percussion).
** Polski Nagrania PNCD 042 [id.]. (i) Jablonski; (ii) Louis Devos; Polish Nat. R. SO or Warsaw Nat. PO, Krenz or composer.

The Krenz performance of *Postlude No. 1* is an earlier recording (1964) than EMI's (1977), now coupled with Busoni and Franz Schmidt; but the best-known of the performances here, Roman Jablonski's 1976 account of the *Cello concerto*, still stands up well against the competition, though it is not a first choice. Very good broadcast balances rather than a subtle concert-hall sound. An acceptable way of further exploring Lutoslawski's output, if the most up-to-date sound is not your highest priority.

Dance preludes (for clarinet and orchestra).
*** Hyp. Dig. CDA 66215 [id.]. Thea King, ECO, Litton – BLAKE: *Clarinet concerto;* SEIBER: *Concertino.****
*** Chan. Dig. CHAN 8618 [id.]. Janet Hilton, SNO, Bamert – COPLAND; NIELSEN: *Concertos.****

Lutoslawski's five folk-based vignettes are a delight in the hands of Thea King and Andrew Litton, who give sharply characterized performances, thrown into bold relief by the bright, clear recording. Janet Hilton also emphasizes their contrasts with her expressive lyricism and crisp articulation in the lively numbers. Excellent recording.

Mi-Parti; (i) *Novelette;* (ii) *7 Preludes and fugue for 13 solo strings.*
** Polski Nagrania PNCD 043 [id.]. Polish Nat. RSO; (i) Junge Deutsche Philharmonie, (ii) Warsaw Nat. CO, composer; (i) Heinz Holliger.

The *Seven Preludes and fugue* are vividly recorded and marvellously played by Warsaw forces under the composer, and the mysterious sound world of *Mi-Parti* with its dream-like opening makes a strong impression. These two pieces were recorded in the 1970s; the *Novelette,* written in 1979 for Rostropovich's Washington orchestra, was recorded at the 1984 Warsaw Autumn. Undistinguished sound, but authoritative performances.

Symphony No. 2; Venetian games; (i) *3 Poèmes d'Henri Michaux.*
** Polski Nagrania PNCD 041 [id.]. Warsaw Nat. PO, composer or Rowicki;(i) Polish Cracow R. Ch., Polish Nat. RSO, Krenz.

All these performances appeared on LP: the *Jeux vénitiens* was made in 1962, the *Trois poèmes d'Henri Michaux* under Krenz comes from 1964, and the *Second Symphony* from 1968 under Lutoslawski himself. Eminently acceptable analogue sound, and a worthwhile addition to this composer's discography.

Symphony No. 3; (i) *Les espaces du sommeil.*
*** CBS Dig. M2K 42271 (2) [id.]. (i) Shirley-Quirk; LAPO, Salonen – MESSIAEN: *Turangalîla symphony.***(*)
*** Ph. Dig. 416 387-2 [id.]. (i) Fischer-Dieskau; BPO, composer.

Even next to Lutoslawski's own interpretation, Salonen's brings an extra revelation. This is a deeply committed, even passionate account of a work which may be rigorous in its argument but which is essentially dramatic in one massive, continuous span. In *Les espaces du sommeil*, setting a surreal poem by Robert Desnos, Salonen also presents a different slant from the composer himself, making it – with the help of John Shirley-Quirk as an understanding soloist – much more evocative and sensuous in full and well-balanced sound.

The *Third Symphony* is given an authoritative reading by the composer. The performance of *Les espaces du sommeil* might also be counted definitive, with Lutoslawski joined by the dedicatee, the baritone Dietrich Fischer-Dieskau. Treated to refined, finely analytical recording, these are sharply focused performances, but in warmth and thrust of communication they finally yield to those of Esa-Pekka Salonen on his CBS version.

Postlude No. 1; Symphonic variations.
⊛ (M) *** EMI CDM7 69840-2. Polish RSO, composer – SCHMIDT: *Variations on a Hussar's song*; BUSONI: *Sarabande and cortège (Doktor Faust).**** ⊛

Lutoslawski's *Symphonic variations* is an early work. The mantle of Szymanowski, who had died only two years earlier, can still be discerned: indeed the work has the poignant and ecstatic atmosphere that one finds in that master. Lutoslawski's short *Postlude No. 1* was written twenty years later and sounds very different but no less atmospheric on this excellently transferred CD.

Epitaph for oboe & piano; Grave for cello & piano; Partita for violin & piano; String quartet; Variations on a theme of Paganini for 2 pianos; 2 Studies for piano; 5 Songs after the poems of Illalowicz.
* Polski Nagrania PNCD 045 [id.]. Holliger; Jablonski; Esztényi; Kulka, Knapik; LaSalle Qt; J. & M. Lukaszczyk; Drewnowskki; Lukomska, Polish Nat. SO, Markowski.

Variable quality here. The two piano *Studies* and the *Paganini variations* are recorded in a very small studio and make an unpleasing aural impression. The rather beautiful *Illalowicz songs* were recorded in 1967, but the sound is wanting in bloom; nor is the 1965 LaSalle recording of the *Quartet* ideal, though the quieter dynamic markings make a stronger impression than in the DG record of three years later. The other recordings come from the 1980s – the acoustic is dry and does justice neither to Holliger's playing in the *Epitaph* nor to that of Roman Jablonski in the *Grave for cello and piano*.

String quartet.
*** Olympia OCD 328 [id.]. Varsovia Qt – SZYMANOWSKI: *Quartets*; PENDERECKI: *Quartet No. 2.****

Lutoslawski tells us that in his *String quartet* he uses 'chance elements to enrich the rhythmic and expressive character of the music without in any way limiting the authority of the composer over the final shape of the piece'. Whatever its merits, it has a highly developed and refined feeling for sonority and balance and, generally speaking, succeeds in holding the listener.

Variations on a theme of Paganini.
*** Ph. Dig. 411 034-2 [id.]. Argerich, Freire – RACHMANINOV: *Suite No. 2*; RAVEL: *La valse.****

Lutoslawski's *Variations* for piano duo date from 1941; they are exhilarating and are played with great virtuosity by Martha Argerich and Nelson Freire. The recording is very realistic and natural, if reverberant.

Lvov, Alexey (1798–1872)

Violin concerto in A min.
** Olympia OCD 147 [id.]. Stadler, Leningrad PO, Chernushenko – GLAZUNOV: *Symphony No. 9*; KABALEVSKY: *Romeo and Juliet.***

Alexey Lvov's *Concerto in A minor* dates from 1840 and is characteristic of much of the virtuoso writing of the period: bland, fluent and not particularly individual. It is far from unpleasing, particularly as it is so well played by Sergei Stadler and the Leningrad orchestra. The recording is much fresher and more wide-ranging than the Glazunov or Kabalevsky couplings.

Lyapunov, Sergei (1859–1924)

Hashish, Op. 53; Polonaise, Op. 16; Solemn overture on Russian themes, Op. 7; Zelazowa Wola, Op. 37.
(*) Olympia OCD 129 [id.]. USSR Ac. SO, Svetlanov – BALAKIREV: *Islamey.*

The *Solemn overture on Russian themes* is much influenced by Balakirev's examples in this genre, and the spirited *Polonaise* is very much in the processional style of Glinka and Tchaikovsky. The tone-poem, *Zelazowa Wola* (Chopin's birthplace), is a tribute to Chopin and is inspired by the centenary celebrations in 1909 in which both Balakirev and Lyapunov played a part (there is an oblique allusion to the *A minor Mazurka*, Op. 17, No. 4). The intriguingly entitled *Hashish* takes its cue from Balakirev's *Tamara* (beloved of Sir Thomas Beecham) but is colourful stuff. If you respond to Balakirev, you should investigate this attractive music, even if you may feel that Lyapunov's indebtedness to his friend and mentor was too great. Svetlanov is in his element in this kind of repertoire and the playing is very good. The recording, though not top-drawer, is perfectly acceptable, though it comes close to overloading in climaxes.

MacCunn, Hamish (1868–1916)

Overture: Land of the Mountain and the Flood.
(M) *** EMI CDM7 69206-2 [id.]. SNO, Gibson – HARTY: *With the wild geese*; GERMAN: *Welsh rhapsody*; SMYTH: *The Wreckers: overture.****

MacCunn's descriptive overture is no masterpiece, but it has a memorable tune, is attractively atmospheric and is constructed effectively. Sir Alexander Gibson's performance is quite outstanding in its combination of warmth, colour and drama, and the recording is excellent.

MacDowell, Edward (1861-1908)

Piano concertos Nos. 1 in A min., Op. 15; 2 in D min., Op. 23.
⊛ *** Archduke Dig. DARC 1 [id.]. Donna Amato, LPO, Paul Freeman.

Of MacDowell's two *Piano concertos* the *First* is marginally the lesser of the two. Liszt's influence is strong (MacDowell studied with him) and there is plenty of dash, but the melodic content, though very pleasing, is slightly less memorable than in the *Second*, which has been recorded before. It is a delightful piece, fresh and tuneful, redolent of Mendelssohn and Saint-Saëns. Donna Amato's scintillating performance is entirely winning, and she is equally persuasive in the *A minor*, which Liszt himself played. This music needs polish and elegance as well as fire, and Paul Freeman's accompaniments supply all three. The recording, made in All Saints', Tooting, has the right resonance for the Lisztian spectacle and agreeable ambient warmth for the music's lyrical side. A highly rewarding coupling in all respects.

Piano sonatas Nos. 1 (Tragica), Op. 45; 2 (Eroica), Op. 50; 3 (Norse), Op. 57.
** Kingdom Dig. KCLCD 2029 [id.]. James Tocco.

The strongest of these sonatas is the *Eroica*, a four-movement piece of considerable quality whose invention is better sustained than in its relatively conventional companions. James Tocco makes a good case for it, though his readings are a little wanting in scale. Climaxes are not as full-bodied or impassioned as they might be. The disc is primarily of specialist interest, and the recording is serviceable rather than outstanding.

Machaut, Guillaume (1300-77)

Messe de Nostre Dame.
**(*) EMI Dig. CDC7 47949-2 [id.]. Taverner Ch. and Cons., Parrott.

Andrew Parrott's version of this great work sets it in the context of a plainsong liturgy, thus greatly enhancing its effect. This EMI issue is splendidly recorded and there are many beauties, some of them obscured by Parrott's decision to transpose the work down a fourth, thus darkening its texture, which reduces internal clarity. However, the sound of the CD brings a most realistic impression.

McLaughlin, John (20th century)

(i) Guitar concerto (Mediterranean). (ii) Duos for guitar & piano: Brise de coeur; Montana; 2 Sisters; Until such time; Zakir.
*** CBS Dig. MK 45578 [id.]. The composer, (i) LSO, Tilson Thomas; (ii) Katia Labèque.

McLaughlin's *Guitar concerto* is an amiable piece, very much modelled on Rodrigo but without the melodic distinctiveness. The outer movements generate lots of bustle and the central movement has a very Southern Mediterranean theme. The performance is alive and persuasive and the recording, if too resonant for an ideal focus, is reasonably well balanced. What McLaughlin does best is to write high-class semi-improvised music of the kind you might enjoy at a top-quality night spot. The romantic numbers have an agreeable languor, and the composer and the brilliant Katia Labèque play them very beguilingly, with a microphone hanging right over them.

Maconchy, Elizabeth (born 1907)

String quartets Nos. 1–4.
*** Unicorn Dig. DKPCD 9080 [id.]. Hanson Qt.

String quartets Nos. 5–8.
*** Unicorn Dig. DKPCD 9081 [id.]. Bingham Qt.

Elizabeth Maconchy has excited the admiration of musicians far and wide from Tovey and Sir Henry Wood to Holst and Vaughan Williams. Hopefully this Unicorn series, planned to include all her *Quartets*, will introduce her to a wider audience. The four recorded by the Hanson Quartet encompass the period 1932–43; while the second disc spans the years 1948–67, and the Bingham Quartet seem equally at home in this rewarding repertoire. All these works testify to the quality of Maconchy's mind and her inventive powers. She speaks of the quartet as 'an impassioned argument', and there is no lack of either in these finely wrought and compelling pieces. Even if there is not the distinctive personality of a Bartók or a Britten, her music is always rewarding. Though the playing may occasionally be wanting in tonal finesse, both groups play with total commitment and are well recorded.

Maderna, Bruno (1920–73)

Aura; Biogramma; Quadrivium.
*** DG 423 246-2 [id.]. N. German RSO, Sinopoli.

This record usefully brings together three of Bruno Maderna's key works, among the last he wrote before his untimely death when still in his early fifties. Earliest is *Quadrivium*, for four orchestral groups, each with percussion, a work designed 'to entertain and to interest, not to shock the bourgeoisie'. In 1972 came *Aura* and *Biogramma*; the former won the composer (posthumously) the city of Bonn's Beethoven prize. Excellent recording for dedicated performances.

Madetoja, Leevi (1887–1947)

Symphonies Nos. (i) 2; (ii) 3.
** Finlandia FACD 011 [id.]. (i) Tampere PO, Ratio; (ii) Helsinki PO, Panula.

Leevi Madetoja was one of Sibelius's two pupils. He also studied briefly with Vincent d'Indy, and his outlook and sympathies were strongly Gallic, though Sibelius too is not far away. The *Second Symphony* (1918) is a long work (42 minutes 30 seconds) but sustains interest throughout. Like its more compact successor of 1926, its Nordic provenance is never in doubt; however, here is no granite-like edifice but a more relaxed and smiling countenance: he loved France, where the *Third* was written. This is expertly crafted and well-scored music, which will give pleasure to those who like nationalist composers of the second rank. Decent performances from 1981 and 1973 respectively, and acceptable recordings.

Magnard, Albéric (1865–1914)

Violin sonata in G, Op. 13.
*** EMI Dig. CDC7 49890-2 [id.]. Dumay, Collard – FRANCK: *Sonata.***(*)

Magnard's *Violin sonata* is a welcome discovery. It is a substantial work, playing for three-quarters of an hour, and is a noble and eloquent piece. It comes from 1902 and, like the coupled Franck *Sonata*, to which it is indebted, was premièred by Ysaÿe. It is powerfully argued throughout and, though it is a long work, there are so many fine things in its course that one longs to return to it. Augustin Dumay and Jean-Philippe Collard give a dedicated and sensitive performance; though the recording balance places them rather too forward than may be ideal, the sound is still very good indeed.

Guercoeur (opera) complete.
*** EMI CDS7 49193-8 (3) [Ang. CDCC 49193]. Behrens, Van Dam, Denize, Lakes, Orfeòn Donostiarra, Toulouse Capitole O, Plasson.

With its distant echoes of Wagner's *Tristan*, its warm lyricism and superbly crafted writing, *Guercoeur* makes a fine offering on record, almost as rich and distinctive as Magnard's symphonies. It echoes specific passages in Wagner less than Chausson's *Le roi Arthus*, the other fine French opera of the period; but Magnard's lyricism is almost too rich, so regularly heightened that the key moments stand out too little. José van Dam makes a magnificent hero, the ideal singer for the role with his firm, finely shaded baritone. Hildegard Behrens makes a similarly powerful Vérité. Though some of the soprano singing among the attendant spirits in Heaven is edgily French, the casting is generally strong, with Gary Lakes a ringing Heurtal and Nadine Denize a sweet-toned Giselle. A rich rarity, warmly recorded.

Mahler, Gustav (1860–1911)

Symphony No. 1 in D (Titan).
(M) *** DG Dig. 431 036-2 [id.]. Concg. O, Bernstein.
(M) *** Decca 417 701-2 [id.]. LSO, Solti.
*** RCA RD 80894 [RCD1 0894]. LSO, Levine.
*** Decca Dig. 411 731-2 [id.]. Chicago SO, Solti.
*** CBS Dig. MK 42141 [id.]. VPO, Maazel.
(M) *** Unicorn UKCD 2012 [id.]. LSO, Horenstein.
**(*) Ph. Dig. 420 936-2 [id.]. BPO, Haitink.
(BB) **(*) LaserLight Dig. 15 529 [id.]. Prague Festival O, Pavel Urbanek.
**(*) Denon Dig. C37 7537 [id.]. Frankfurt RSO, Inbal.
(B) ** Ph. 426 067-2 [id.]. Concg. O, Haitink.
(B) *(*) Pickwick IMPX 9005. Israel PO, Mehta.

Symphony No. 1 (with *Blumine*).
(BB) **(*) Hung. White Label HRC 077 [id.]. Hungarian State O, Iván Fischer.

Symphony No. 1 in D min.; (i) *Lieder eines fahrenden Gesellen.*
(B) **(*) DG 429 157-2 [id.]. Bav. RSO, Kubelik; (i) with Fischer-Dieskau.
** Virgin Dig. 790703-2 [id.]. (i) Murray; RPO, Litton.

Bernstein and the Concertgebouw Orchestra, recorded live, give a wonderfully alert and imaginative performance of Mahler's *First*, with the opening movement conveying the youthful joys of spring in its *Wayfaring lad* associations, and the second at a relaxed Laendler tempo made more rustic than usual. In the slow movement the funeral march overtones are underlined, leading easily into what Bernstein calls the raucous 'Jewish wedding' episode. The finale has superb panache. This is among Bernstein's finest Mahler issues, very well recorded, even making no allowance for the extra problems encountered at live concerts.

The London Symphony Orchestra play Mahler's *First* like no other orchestra. They catch the magical opening with a singular evocative quality, at least partly related to the peculiarly characteristic blend of wind timbres, and throughout there is wonderfully warm string-tone. Solti's tendency to drive hard is felt only in the second movement, which is pressed a little too much, although he relaxes beautifully in the central section. Especially memorable are the poignancy of the introduction of the *Frère Jacques* theme in the slow movement and the exultant brilliance of the closing pages. The remastering for CD has improved definition without losing the recording's bloom. A fine mid-price recommendation.

Like Solti, James Levine has the LSO for this symphony, and he draws from it most exciting playing. It is a reading of high contrasts, with extremes of tempo and dynamic brought out with total conviction. In that emphasis on drama, Levine is at times less beguiling than Solti, but the result is just as convincing. The brilliant 1975 recording is noticeably more modern; even so, partly because of the balance, the LSO violins are warmer and fuller in the earlier, Decca version.

Because of the excellence of the 1964 LSO version, which has been a prime choice for many years, it was hard for Solti and the Decca engineers to match his earlier achievement, even with exceptionally high-powered playing from the Chicago orchestra and brilliant, crystal-clear digital recording. Particularly on CD, that very clarity takes away some of the atmospheric magic – the feeling of mists dispersing in the slow introduction, for example – but charm and playfulness in this *Wunderhorn* work emerge delightfully; one of the happiest of Solti's records, tinglingly fresh, with perfectly chosen speeds.

With superb playing and refined recording, Maazel's account of the *First* has the Viennese glow which marks out his CBS series and notably the *Fourth*. Though there are other versions which point detail more sharply, this performance has a ripeness and an easy lyricism that put it among the most sympathetic readings in a very long list. The sound too is full and atmospheric, as well as brilliant.

Unicorn had the laudable aim of securing a relatively modern recording of Horenstein in Mahler's *First*, and the result has a freshness and concentration which put it in a special category among the many rival accounts. With measured tempi and a manner which conceals much art, Horenstein links the work more clearly with later Mahler symphonies. Fine recording from the end of the 1960s, though the timpani is balanced rather too close.

Kubelik gives an intensely poetic reading. He is here at his finest in Mahler, and though, as in later symphonies, he is sometimes tempted to choose a tempo on the fast side, the result could hardly be more glowing. The rubato in the slow funeral march is most subtly handled. In its bargain CD reissue the quality is a little dry in the bass and the violins have lost some of their warmth, but there is no lack of body. In the *Lieder eines fahrenden Gesellen* the sound is fuller, with more atmospheric bloom. No one quite rivals Fischer-Dieskau in these songs for his range and beauty of tone, conveying the heartache of the young traveller, and, with Kubelik equally persuasive, this is a very considerable bonus.

The Berlin Philharmonic plays superbly for Bernard Haitink in this, his third recording of Mahler's *First*. There is greater gravity in his view now, to bring out the full weight of this ambitious early work, and a greater freedom of expression, though this conductor is hardly one to wear his heart on his sleeve or even to inject charm into such a passage as the Laendler trio of the second movement. The purity and refinement of the Berlin string-tone is superbly caught. The recorded sound is notably finer than many previous recordings made in the Philharmonie, even if it is not entirely free of cloudiness.

From the well-sustained opening pianissimo, the tension of the playing of the Prague Festival Orchestra under Pavel Urbanek holds the listener and, even though Urbanek's reading is unconventional in its control of Mahlerian structure, this is a highly spontaneous performance, not immaculate but full of character. The scherzo has exuberance, and the darkness of colour at the opening of the slow movement contrasts with the energetic excitement of the finale. The wide-ranging digital recording is extremely vivid, the upper strings bright but lacking just a little in body, but the ambient effect is well caught. At super-bargain price, this is distinctly competitive.

The alternative super-bargain version on Hungaroton White Label includes the original second movement, *Blumine*, placing it where the composer intended. Fischer's reading of the *Symphony* is spaciously conceived, with relaxed tempi throughout, but the Hungarian State Orchestra sustain his conception with very fine playing, especially from the strings in the last movement. With excellent analogue sound, full and well detailed, this is an inexpensive way to sample Mahler's initial layout.

Edited together from a couple of live performances, Inbal's Frankfurt version may not be as polished or high-powered as the finest from top international orchestras, but it has an easy-going charm which, coupled to recording that puts fine bloom on the sound, will please many. The happy expansiveness and gentle manners of the first three movements then lead to a powerful and urgent reading of the finale which is more tautly held together than usual.

Andrew Litton's record has the advantage of being the first version to include the most apt (and generous) of couplings, the *Lieder eines fahrenden Gesellen*, the song-cycle that provided material for the symphony. Litton's way with Mahler is fresh and generally direct, with well-chosen speeds, but the playing of the RPO strings is not always quite polished or taut enough. Ann Murray's mezzo, characterful and boyish in tone, nevertheless catches the microphone rawly at times.

Haitink's 1962 version did not stay in the catalogue very long, and he re-recorded the work a decade later. That later version is generally preferable; the earlier performance had a lower level of tension. However, everything is beautifully laid out in front of the listener and, in its thoughtful way, with refined Concertgebouw playing, this could be quite appealing for those who enjoy Haitink's laid-back Mahler style.

Mehta's 1976 Decca recording has resurfaced on Pickwick's bargain label, and the sound is vividly full and brilliant; but the hard-driving, frenetic quality of the outer movements is unattractive and the warmth of the slow movement offers insufficient compensation. This is an approach to Mahler which is essentially outside the European tradition.

Symphonies Nos. (i) *1;* (ii) *2 (Resurrection).*
(B) *** CBS M2YK 45674. (i) Columbia SO; (ii) Cundari, Forrester, Westminster College Ch., NYPO; Bruno Walter.

Bruno Walter's recordings of Mahler's *Symphonies Nos. 1* and *2* are now economically coupled together on a pair of bargain-price discs with the sound further improved over the previous CD issues. The recording of No. 1 sounds splendid in this new format. The compellingly atmospheric opening is magnetic, heard against the almost silent background, and Walter is at his most charismatic here. While the recording's dynamic range is obviously more limited than more recent versions, the balance and ambient warmth are entirely satisfying, emphasizing the Viennese character of the reading, with the final apotheosis drawn out spaciously and given added breadth and impact. The orchestral playing throughout is first class; other conductors have whipped up more animal excitement in the finale, but that is not Walter's way.

Even more than the *First Symphony*, the 1958 CBS set of the *Resurrection symphony* is among the gramophone's indispensable classics. In the first movement there is a restraint and in the second a gracefulness which provides a strong contrast with a conductor like Solti. The recording, one of the last Walter made in New York before his series with the Columbia Symphony Orchestra, was remarkably good for its period and the dynamic range is surprisingly wide. In remastering for CD, the CBS engineers have sought to remove as much as possible of the pre-Dolby background noise, and the treble response is noticeably limited, with the attractively warm ambience tending to smooth internal definition. But the glowing sound brings an evocative haze to the score's more atmospheric moments, and in the finale the balance with the voices gives the music-making an ethereal resonance, with the closing section thrillingly expansive.

Symphony No. 2 in C min. (Resurrection).
⊛ *** EMI CDS7 47962-8 (2) [Ang. CDCB 47962]. Augér, J. Baker, CBSO Ch., CBSO, Rattle.
(M) *** EMI CDM7 69662-2 [id.]. Schwarzkopf, Rössl-Majdan, Philh. Ch. & O, Klemperer.
(M) *** DG 427 262-2 (2) [id.]. Neblett, Horne, Chicago SO Ch. and O, Abbado.
*** Chan. Dig. CHAN 8838/9 [id.]. Felicity Lott, Julia Hamari, Latvian State Ac. Ch., Oslo Ch. & PO, Jansons.
*** Decca Dig. 410 202-2 (2) [id.]. Buchanan, Zakai, Chicago SO Ch. & SO, Solti.
(B) **(*) Pickwick Dig. DPCD 910 (2) [MCA MCAD 11011]. Valente, Forrester, LSO Ch., LSO, Kaplan.
**(*) DG Dig. 423 395-2 (2) [id.]. Hendricks, Ludwig, Westminster Ch., NYPO, Bernstein.

(i) *Symphony No. 2 (Resurrection);* (ii) *Lieder eines fahrenden Gesellen;* (iii) *Lieder und Gesänge (aus der Jugendzeit):* excerpts.
*** DG Dig. 415 959-2(2) [id.]. (i) Fassbaender, Plowright, Philh. Ch.; (ii) Fassbaender; (iii) Weikl; Philh. O, Sinopoli.

Simon Rattle's reading of Mahler's *Second* is among the very finest records he has yet made, superlative in the breadth and vividness of its sound and with a spacious reading which in its natural intensity unerringly sustains generally slow, steady speeds to underline the epic grandeur of Mahler's vision. This comes closer than almost any rival version to creating the illusion of a live performance, its tensions and its drama, while building on the palpable advantage of well-balanced studio sound. Rattle here establishes himself as not merely a good but a great Mahlerian with a strongly individual view, controlling tensions masterfully over the broadest span. The playing of the CBSO is inspired, matching that of the most distinguished international rivals. The choral singing, beautifully balanced, is incandescent, while the heart-felt singing of the soloists, Arleen Augér and Dame Janet Baker, is equally distinguished and characterful. Recorded in Watford Town Hall instead of the orchestra's usual Birmingham venue, the sound is full and clear even in the heavyweight textures of the finale.

The transfer of Klemperer's performance – one of his most compelling on record – on to a single CD (playing for over 79 minutes) is a considerable achievement, and the remastered sound is impressively full and clear, with the fullest sense of spectacle in the closing pages. The first movement, taken at a fairly fast tempo, is intense and earth-shaking, and that is surely as it should be in a work which culminates in a representation of Judgement Day itself. Though in the last movement some of Klemperer's speeds are designedly slow, he conveys supremely well the mood of transcendent heavenly happiness in the culminating passage, with chorus and soloists themselves singing like angels. The *Last Trump* brings a shudder of excitement, and the less grand central movements have their simple charm equally well conveyed.

Sinopoli's version of the *Resurrection* brings the additional advantage that the two CDs also include two Mahler song-cycles: the *Lieder eines fahrenden Gesellen*, beautifully sung by Brigitte Fassbaender, and the *Songs of Youth 'aus der Jugendzeit'*, skilfully orchestrated by Harold Byrns, well sung by Bernd Weikl, bringing extra anticipations of the mature *Des Knaben Wunderhorn* songs. In the symphony Sinopoli has meticulous concern for detail, yet he still conveys consistently the irresistible purposefulness of Mahler's writing, fierce at high dramatic moments and intense too, rarely relaxed, in moments of meditation, with *Urlicht* beautifully sung with warmth and purity by Fassbaender. The recorded sound, though not quite as full and vivid as that for Rattle, is among the most brilliant of any in this work. Rosalind Plowright is a pure and fresh soprano soloist, contrasting well with the equally firm, earthier-toned mezzo of Fassbaender.

The total conviction of Abbado's performance establishes itself in the very first bars, weighty yet marvellously precise on detail, with dotted rhythms sharply brought out. It proves a performance of extremes, with variations of tempo more confidently marked than is common but with concentration so intense there is no hint of self-indulgence. The delicacy of the Chicago orchestra in the second and third movements is as remarkable as its precision, while the great contrasts of the later movements prove a challenge not only to the performers but to the DG engineers, who produce sound of the finest analogue quality. Generally the singing is as splendid as the playing, but if there is even a minor disappointment, it lies in the closing pages which are just a little contained: Abbado keeps his sharpness of focus to the very end. However, at mid-price this is highly recommendable.

The crisp attack at the start of the opening funeral march sets the pattern for an exceptionally refined and alert reading of the *Resurrection symphony* from Jansons and his Oslo orchestra. Transparent textures are beautifully caught by the glowing recording – one of the last big projects of the outstanding recording producer and engineer, Jimmy Burnett. Through the first four movements, this may seem a lightweight reading, but the extra resilience and point of rhythm bring out the dance element in Mahler's *Knaben Wunderhorn* inspirations rather than ruggedness or rusticity. That Jansons intends this is confirmed when, at the finale, the whole performance erupts in an overwhelming outburst for the vision of Resurrection. That transformation is intensified by the breathtakingly rapt and intense account of the song, *Urlicht*, which precedes it. At a very measured speed, with Julia Hamari the warmly dedicated soloist, Jansons secures the gentlest of pianissimos. The chorale for pianissimo trumpets at the start is far more hushed than usual, magically distanced. In the finale, power goes with precision and meticulous observance of markings, when even Mahler's surprising diminuendo on the final choral cadence is observed. With the Oslo Choir joined by singers from Jansons' native Latvia, the choral singing is heartfelt, to crown a version which finds a special place even among the many distinguished readings on a long list.

In digital sound of extraordinary power Solti has re-recorded with the Chicago orchestra this symphony which with the LSO was one of the finest achievements of his earlier Mahler series. Differences of interpretation are on points of detail merely, with a lighter, more elegant rendering of the minuet-rhythms of the second movement. Though the digital recording is not always as well balanced as the earlier analogue (Isobel

Buchanan and Mira Zakai are too close, for example), the weight of fortissimo in the final hymn, not to mention the Judgement Day brass, is breathtaking. Interpretatively too, the outer movements are as fiercely intense as before.

It would be easy but misguided to scoff at the achievement of the rich eccentric, Gilbert Kaplan, in his best-selling version of the *Resurrection symphony*. It is the only music he ever conducts, or ever plans to; and whatever his musical training, by whatever means, the LSO plays with a biting precision and power to shame many an effort on record under a world-renowned conductor. Added to that, the sound is exceptionally brilliant and full, bringing home the impact of the big dramatic moments, which are what stand out in the performance. Though there are no *longueurs*, it becomes more a collection of salient sequences than a strongly co-ordinated whole, and in places the 'in-between bits' tend to plod a little or become less tense. The second-movement Laendler too is rhythmically heavy-handed, but even there the ensemble is splendid, with fine detail brought out. It is good to have the veteran Canadian mezzo, Maureen Forrester, as soloist, when her voice remains so rich and full. The soprano, Benita Valente, is less aptly fruity of tone; but she and Forrester as well as the fine chorus sing with a will, crowning a performance that is never less than enjoyable, thanks above all to the playing and to superb sound. The two discs come at bargain price, costing together the same as a single full-price disc. The documentation included is exceptionally generous, with a long essay and analysis by Kaplan in one booklet and a fascinating collection of Mahler's letters about the symphony in a second.

The big advantage of Bernstein's DG version over his previous CBS recording with the LSO lies in the quality of sound. Recorded live in Avery Fisher Hall, New York, the engineers have overcome the acoustic problems to a remarkable degree, presenting a weighty and wide-ranging sound, set against a warm reverberation (superimposed?) not associated with that venue. The expansion for the choral finale is well handled, and it is there in the urgency of the final chorus that Bernstein's interpretation gains over his previous one, recorded in the studio, a shade more intense. Otherwise, like earlier recordings in Bernstein's DG series, the live performance shows the conductor more self-indulgent than before, as well as more expansive, often overlaying Mahler's simplest and most tender melodies with forced expressiveness – even if, as ever, the voltage is high.

Symphony No. 3 in D min.
*** DG Dig. 410 715-2 (2) [id.]. J. Norman, V. State Op. Ch., V. Boys' Ch., VPO, Abbado.
(M) *** Unicorn UKCD 2006/7 [id.]. Procter, Wandsworth School Boys' Ch., Amb. S., LSO, Horenstein.
*** RCA RD 81757 [RCD2 1757]. Horne, Ellyn Children's Ch., Chicago Ch. & SO, Levine.
**(*) Decca Dig. 414 268-2 (2) [id.]. Dernesch, Glen Ellyn Children's Ch., Chicago Ch. & SO, Solti.
**(*) Denon Dig. C37 7828/9 [id.]. Soffel, Limburger, Domsingknaben, Frankfurter Kantorei, Frankfurt RSO, Inbal.

(i) *Symphony No. 3;* (ii) *Das klagende Lied.*
**(*) Ph. 420 113-2 (2) [id.]. (i) Forrester, Netherlands R. Ch., St Willibrod Boys' Ch.; (ii) Harper, Procter, Hollweg, Netherlands R. Ch.; Concg. O, Haitink.

Symphony No. 3; 5 Rückert Lieder.
*** CBS M2K 44553 (2) [id.]. Janet Baker, LSO Ch., LSO, Tilson Thomas.

Michael Tilson Thomas, in one of his first recordings with the LSO since being appointed its principal conductor, directs a powerful account of this challenging symphony. Predictably, he inspires the orchestra to play with bite and panache in the bold, dramatic passages and to bring out the sparkle and freshness of the *Knaben Wunderhorn* ideas; but what crowns the performance is the raptness of his reading of the noble, hymn-like finale, hushed and intense, beautifully sustained. There is a formidable bonus in Dame Janet Baker's searching performances of the five *Rückert Lieder*. She is just as moving here as she was in the classic recording of them she made twenty years earlier with Sir John Barbirolli. Excellent CBS sound, both warm and brilliant.

With sound of spectacular range, Abbado's performance is sharply defined and deeply dedicated. The range of expression, the often wild mixture of elements in this work, is conveyed with extraordinary intensity, not least in the fine contributions of Jessye Norman and the two choirs. The recording has great presence and detail on CD.

More than the earlier issue of Mahler's *First Symphony*, this account of the Mahler *Third* shows Horenstein at his most intensely committed. The manner is still very consistent in its simple dedication to the authority of the score and its rejection of romantic indulgence; but with an extra intensity the result has the sort of frisson-making quality one knew from live Horenstein performances. Above all the restraint of the finale is intensely compelling. Though the strings are rather backwardly balanced and the timpani are too prominent, the recording quality is both full and brilliant. Fine vocal contributions from Norma Procter, the Ambrosian Singers and the Wandsworth School Boys' Choir.

James Levine directs a superbly rhythmic account of the *Third Symphony*, with splendidly judged tempi which allow extra swagger (most important in the first movement), more lilt and a fine sense of atmosphere. The choral contributions, too, are outstanding. In the radiant finale Levine's tempo is daringly slow, but he sustains it superbly, though in that movement the recording has some congestion at climaxes; otherwise the 1977 sound is nicely rounded, with the posthorn beautifully balanced in the third movement. On CD, refinement is enhanced by the virtually silent background: this is plainly not a digital recording, but it represents the highest analogue standards.

In Solti's Chicago version the last movement is hushed and intense, deeply concentrated, building up superbly even though the hastening is a shade excessive towards the end. The other movements have brilliance, freshness and clarity, with Helga Dernesch a fine if rather detached soloist. Solti remains a bold Mahler interpreter, missing some of the *Wunderhorn* fun. The virtuoso playing of the Chicago orchestra is brilliantly caught by the wide-ranging recording, though the posthorn of the third movement is placed unatmospherically close.

In a work that can seem over-inflated Haitink's straightforwardness as a Mahlerian makes for a deeply satisfying performance. Though in the first movement his rather fast speed allows for less lift in the rhythm than, say, Bernstein's, he captures to perfection the fresh, wide-eyed simplicity of the second movement and the carol-like quality of the fifth movement, *Bell song*. Best of all is the wonderfully simple and intense reading of the long concluding slow movement, which here is given an inner intensity that puts it very close to the comparable movement of Mahler's *Ninth*. Haitink's soloists are excellent, the playing of the Concertgebouw is refined and dedicated. For CD the *Symphony* has been coupled with *Das klagende Lied*, a much earlier recording but one of high quality, although the performance is not ideal, lacking urgency and a sense of imaginative imagery.

Eliahu Inbal in his Frankfurt version for Denon takes a spacious view, well sustained by very fine playing from the orchestra. This marked the point in the joint project between Denon and Hesse Radio where the intensive planning of a whole Mahler cycle within a two-year span began to deliver extra intensity in the finished results as recorded. The slow speeds are sustained easily and naturally, with the *Wunderhorn* element brought out more prominently than usual. The sound, as in the rest of the series, is excellent in its natural balances; but there are readings which convey the grandeur of Mahler's vision more powerfully.

Symphony No. 4 in G.
*** CBS Dig. MK 39072 [id.]. Kathleen Battle, VPO, Maazel.
⊛ (B) *** CBS MYK 44713 [id.]. Judith Raskin, Cleveland O, Szell.
*** Denon Dig. C37 7952 [id.]. Helen Donath, Frankfurt RSO, Inbal.
*** DG 415 323-2 [id.]. Edith Mathis, BPO, Karajan.
*** Decca Dig. 410 188-2 [id.]. Kiri Te Kanawa, Chicago SO, Solti.
*** Ph. Dig. 412 119-2 [id.]. Roberta Alexander, Concg. O, Haitink.
*** RCA RD 80895 [RCD1 0895]. Judith Blegen, Chicago SO, Levine.
**(*) DG Dig. 423 607-2 [MYK 37225]. Helmut Witek (treble), Concg. O, Bernstein.
(M) **(*) EMI CDM7 69667-2 [id.]. Schwarzkopf, Philh. O, Klemperer.
(M) *(*) Chief CD 2 [id.]. LPO, Jascha Horenstein.

Maazel's VPO recording is the most completely successful issue in his cycle. The superbly refined and warmly atmospheric recording enhances a performance that – unlike other Mahler from this conductor – reflects the Viennese qualities of the work while still conveying structural strength, above all in the beautiful, wide-ranging slow movement, played with great inner intensity. Kathleen Battle with her radiant soprano brings aptly child-like overtones to the *Wunderhorn* solo in the finale, until the final stanza is given with rapt intimacy to match Maazel's whole reading.

George Szell's 1966 record of Mahler's *Fourth* represented his partnership with the Cleveland Orchestra at its highest peak. The digital remastering for CD brings out the very best of the original recording, making it sound translucently clear, yet without losing the ambient warmth. The performance remains uniquely satisfying: the interpretation has an element of coolness, but the music blossoms, partly because of the marvellous attention to detail (and the immaculate ensemble), but more positively because of the committed and radiantly luminous orchestral response to the music itself. In the finale Szell found the ideal soprano to match his conception: Judith Raskin sings without artifice, and her voice has an open colouring like a child's, yet the feminine quality subtly remains. An outstanding choice in the bargain-price range and comparable with the finest premium-priced versions.

With a rather smaller orchestra than in the other symphonies, the engineers who balanced Inbal's fine Frankfurt series were able to rely entirely on the source drawn from single-point placing of microphones. The result is outstandingly fresh and natural, matching a delightful performance of the *Symphony*, the tone of which is set by the easy, happy and relaxed manner of the opening. There is a pastoral element in Inbal's approach all through, reflecting the *Wunderhorn* basis, and even the spacious slow movement is easily songful rather than ethereal. Helen Donath brings boyish, Hansel-like timbre to her solo in the finale.

With playing of incomparable refinement – no feeling of rusticity here – Karajan directs a performance of compelling poise and purity, not least in the slow movement, with its pulse very steady indeed, most remarkably at the very end. Karajan's view of the finale is gentle, wistful, almost ruminative, with the final stanzas very slow and legato, beautifully so when Edith Mathis's poised singing of the solo is finely matched. Not that this quest for refinement means that joy has in any way been lost in the performance; with glowing sound, it is a worthy companion to Karajan's other Mahler recordings, effectively transferred to CD.

Solti's digital version gives the lie to the idea of his always being fierce and unrelaxed.

This sunniest of the Mahler symphonies receives a delightfully fresh and bright reading, beautifully paced and superbly played. The recording is bright, full and immediate in the Decca Chicago manner, without inflating the interpretation. Dame Kiri Te Kanawa sings beautifully in the child-heaven finale.

With outstandingly refined playing from the Concertgebouw, superlatively recorded, Haitink's reading has a fresh innocence that is most winning. Thus the lovely *Adagio*, rather than conveying the deepest meditation, presents an ecstatic, songful musing in the long paragraphs of the main theme, and Roberta Alexander makes a perceptive choice of soloist for such a reading, both fresh and creamy of tone.

James Levine draws a superlative performance from the Chicago orchestra, one which bears comparison with the finest versions, bringing out not merely the charm but the deeper emotions too. The subtlety of his control of tempo, so vital in Mahler, is superbly demonstrated and, though he may not quite match the nobility of Szell's famous analogue CBS version in the great slow movement, he has the advantage of more modern (1975) recording. Blegen makes a fresh, attractive soloist.

Bernstein conducts the Concertgebouw in a beautifully refined, generally expansive version which brings one highly controversial point. The subtlety of expression makes Bernstein's CBS version of thirty years earlier seem heavy-handed by comparison; but not everyone will respond to his use of a boy treble, instead of a soprano, for the solo in the child-heaven finale. Helmut Witek of the Tölzer Boys' Choir sings with delightful freshness, but the close balance of the voice tends to bring out the element of rawness. Refined Concertgebouw sound, the more commendable when it is realized that this was edited together from live performances.

Klemperer is slow in the first movement and, strangely, fractionally too fast in the slow movement. Yet the Philharmonia make some ravishing sounds, and one can easily fall under Klemperer's spell. The two highlights of the reading are the marvellously beautiful Laendler, which forms the central section of the second movement, and the simplicity of Elisabeth Schwarzkopf's singing in the finale. This is a record to enjoy, but perhaps not the one to buy as a single representation of Mahler's *Fourth* in a collection.

Admirers of Horenstein will welcome his 1971 record back to the catalogue in a good CD transfer. But his characteristic simplicity of approach here seems too deliberate, and even the great slow movement appears didactic and relatively uncommitted. Margaret Price's singing in the finale is beautiful but cool, in line with the rest of the interpretation; the sound is clear but relatively unatmospheric.

Symphony No. 5 in C sharp min.
⊛ (M) *** EMI CDM7 69186-2. New Philh. O, Barbirolli.
*** EMI Dig. CDC7 49888-2 [id.]. LPO, Tennstedt.
(M) *** DG Dig. 431 037-2 [id.]. VPO, Bernstein.
(*) DG 415 096-2 (2) [id.]. BPO, Karajan – *Kindertotenlieder*.*
*** DG Dig. 415 476-2 [id.]. Philh. O, Sinopoli.
*** Decca Dig. 425 438-2 [id.]. Cleveland O, Dohnányi.
*** Denon Dig. CO 1088 [id.]. Frankfurt RSO, Inbal.
**(*) Ph. 416 469-2 [id.]. Concg. O, Haitink.
**(*) RCA RD 89570 [RCD1 5453]. Phd. O, Levine.
**(*) Decca 413 321-2 [id.]. Chicago SO, Solti.
(M) **(*) DG Dig. 427 254-2 [id.]. Chicago SO, Abbado.
(B) ** DG 429 519-2 [id.]. Bav. RSO, Kubelik.

Barbirolli's famous 1969 version has been digitally remastered on to one mid-priced CD. On any count it is one of the greatest, most warmly affecting performances ever committed to record, expansive yet concentrated in feeling. A classic version and a fine bargain.

Tennstedt's later, digital recording of the *Fifth* was made live at the Festival Hall at a concert which marked a happy reunion between orchestra and its music director after the conductor's long and serious illness. The emotional tension of the occasion is vividly captured. As a Mahler interpretation, it is at once more daring and more idiosyncratic than Tennstedt's earlier, studio recording, but the tension is far keener. One readily accepts the expressive distortions of the moment, the little hesitations that Tennstedt introduces, when the result communicates so immediately and vividly; and the problems of recording live in this difficult acoustic have been masterfully overcome under the direction of the orchestra's managing director and former EMI recording manager, John Willan. The experience hits one at full force, whether in the exuberant, pointed account of the third-movement scherzo, the deeply hushed, expansive one of the *Adagietto* or the headlong reading of the finale, which, even at thrilling high speed, has irresistible swagger.

Bernstein's is also an expansive version, characteristic of his latterday Mahler style. The lovely *Adagietto* was the music he conducted at the funeral of President John F. Kennedy, and the tempo this time is just as slow as before and just as elegiac, though the phrasing is less heavily underlined. The whole performance (recorded, in the Bernstein manner, at live concerts) has his personal stamp on it, at times idiosyncratic but luminous and magnetically compelling, one of the best in his new DG Mahler series and one of his finest recent records. The sound is more open and refined than in many of DG's Vienna recordings.

While Karajan's recording may be a top choice for Mahler's *Fifth*, its expensive layout, involving a pair of CDs, must be counted a considerable drawback, even if Christa Ludwig's warm singing in the *Kindertotenlieder* is a worthwhile fill-up. Karajan's is among the most beautiful and the most intense versions available, starting with an account of the first movement which brings more biting funeral-march rhythms than any rival. Resplendent recording, rich and refined.

Sinopoli's version draws the sharpest distinction between the dark tragedy of the first two movements and the relaxed *Wunderhorn* feeling of the rest. Thus, the opening *Funeral march* is tough and biting, expressive but moulded less than one associates with this conductor; here, as later, Sinopoli seems intent on not overloading the big melodies with excessive emotion. This comes out the more clearly in the central movements, where relaxation is the keynote, often with a pastoral atmosphere. The third-movement Laendler has the happiest of lilts but leads finally to a frenetic coda, before the celebrated *Adagietto* brings a tenderly wistful reading, songful and basically happy, not tragic. The *Wunderhorn* mood returns in full joy in the finale, starting with a magical evocation of the Austrian countryside. Warmly atmospheric recording, not lacking brilliance, but not always ideally clear on detail.

Dohnányi conducts the Cleveland Orchestra in an exceptionally high-powered reading, superbly played and recorded, which can still relax totally in expressive warmth. The toughness of the first two movements – with superb discipline bringing immaculate articulation in the second – gives way to an equally polished but nicely lilting Laendler in the third, finely shaded. Though the hushed *Adagietto* keeps a degree of reserve, the songful freshness and purity are very sympathetic, before the thrustful and dramatic finale, dramatically done. The brilliance of the Cleveland playing is matched by the vivid recorded sound.

As in his accounts of the earlier Mahler symphonies, Inbal brings out the *Wunderhorn* element in the *Fifth* very convincingly, and that applies to all five movements. He may not be as exciting as some rivals, but, with superb playing and beautifully balanced sound, full and atmospheric, it is an exceptionally sympathetic reading. The second and third movements, unusually relaxed, lead to an account of the *Adagietto* that is warmly songful yet hushed and sweet, while the finale conveys the happiness of pastoral ideas leading logically to a joyful, triumphant close.

Haitink's fresh and direct reading, with finely judged tempi and unexaggerated observance of Mahler's markings, is supported by refined playing from the Concertgebouw. The famous *Adagietto* is relatively cool, but its beauty is as intense as ever. Good, well-balanced Philips recording which, as usual, has responded well to digital remastering.

Apart from a self-consciously slow account of the celebrated *Adagietto*, Levine directs a deeply perceptive and compelling performance, one that brings out the glories of the Philadelphia Orchestra. The other movements are beautifully paced, and the remastering for CD is vivid without losing its body and becoming fierce.

The opening *Funeral march* sets the tone of Solti's 1971 reading. At a tempo faster than usual, it is wistful rather than deeply tragic, even though the dynamic contrasts are superbly pointed and the string tone could hardly be more resonant. In the pivotal *Adagietto*, Solti secures intensely beautiful playing, but the result lacks the 'inner' quality one finds so abundantly in Karajan's interpretation.

Unlike Abbado's superb account of No. 2, his version of No. 5 lacks something in spontaneity. The *Adagietto*, for example, is hardly at all slower than with Karajan but the phrasing by comparison sounds self-conscious. Nevertheless it is a polished reading, with first-rate digital sound, which can be recommended at mid-price to those collecting Abbado's Mahler series.

Although the opening brass fanfare is given dramatic projection on CD, in the first-movement funeral march Kubelik is gentle rather than tragic, and his relative lightness of manner, coupled with refined textures, underplays the epic qualities of this work. Nor does he succeed in disguising the patchwork structure of the last movement. The CD transfer gives the performance striking immediacy. The sound is slightly lacking in depth with a rather dry bass, but there is no lack of ambient glow in the *Adagietto*.

Symphony No. 6 in A min.
*** DG 415 099-2 (2) [id.]. BPO, Karajan – *5 Rückert Lieder.***(*)
(M) *** Unicorn UKCD 2024/5 [id.]. Stockholm PO, Jascha Horenstein.
(*) Decca 414 674-2 (2) [id.]. Chicago SO, Solti – *Lieder eines fahrenden Gesellen.**

Symphony No. 6; Symphony No. 10: Adagio.
*** DG Dig. 423 082-2 (2) [id.]. Philh. O, Sinopoli.

Symphony No. 6 in A min.; (i) *Kindertotenlieder.*
**(*) DG Dig. 427 697-2 (2) [id.]. (i) Thomas Hampson; VPO, Bernstein.

Symphony No. 6; (i) *Lieder eines fahrenden Gesellen.*
** Ph. 420 138-2 (2) [id.]. Concg. O, Haitink; (i) with Hermann Prey.

With superlative playing from the Berlin Philharmonic, Karajan's reading of the *Sixth* is a revelation, above all in the slow movement which here becomes far more than a lyrical interlude. It emerges as one of the greatest of Mahler's slow movements and the whole balance of the symphony is altered. Though the outer movements firmly stamp this as the darkest of the Mahler symphonies, in Karajan's reading their sharp focus – with contrasts of light and shade heightened – makes them both compelling and refreshing. The superb DG recording, with its wide dynamics, adds enormously to the impact. On CD, Christa Ludwig's set of the *Five Rückert Songs* has been added as a bonus.

Sinopoli's version of the *Sixth* presents a strongly individual view, outstandingly convincing in the first two movements which, tough and urgent, are given rhythmic elbow room, but sounding less purposeful in the last two movements, both taken notably slower than usual. In the first movement the swaggering gait of the march rhythm has a power comparable with that of Karajan, but without his clipped militaristic fierceness. In the second-movement scherzo Sinopoli finds a haunted quality. With brass whooping and sprung rhythms, it conveys an even more sinister fantasy than with Karajan. The slow movement, taken very slowly indeed, with agogic hesitations peppered over the phrasing, lacks a warm flow, refined as it is. But, like the finale, it finds the right tensions after opening self-consciously, and overall the breadth of vision makes this one of the most compellingly individual versions of all. The *Adagio* from the *Tenth Symphony* makes a generous fill-up; but Sinopoli's very slow reading, with detail heavily underlined, takes away the dark purposefulness of the argument. The recording of both works is among DG's fullest and most brilliant.

Horenstein's Unicorn-Kanchana set originates from live performances, recorded in Stockholm in April 1966; yet the sound is amazingly faithful and well balanced, with a firm bass, full strings, and a spacious concert-hall perspective. In the first movement Horenstein finds extra weight by taking a more measured tempo than most conductors. It is a sober reading that holds together with wonderful concentration. Not that this view of Mahler lacks flexibility, for the slow movement brings the most persuasive rubato. The finale brings another broad, noble reading, and the side-break which disfigured the LPs has disappeared. Yet some will feel that 33 minutes is short measure for the second CD, especially when Horenstein's recorded reminiscences with Alan Blyth, featured in the LP set, are not included here.

Solti draws stunning playing from the Chicago orchestra and his rather extrovert approach to Mahler is here at its most impressive. His fast tempi may mean that he misses some of the deeper emotions but – with an outstandingly successful performance of the *Wayfaring Lad* cycle as fill-up (Yvonne Minton a splendid soloist) – this is a very convincing and attractive set with brilliantly immediate but atmospheric recording.

Bernstein's DG version easily outshines his earlier account for CBS on the vividness of the sound alone. His speed for the military march of the first movement still struts rather uncomfortably fast, but it brings more variety and refinement of expression than before. It is much the same with the other three movements. The special attraction of this version is the fill-up, when on the second disc Bernstein offers a searching performance of the *Kindertotenlieder* with, for once, a male soloist, the deeply responsive, rich-voiced Thomas Hampson.

Haitink, like Bernstein and Solti, takes a fast tempo for the first movement, but the performance is marked by refinement rather than fire, helped by well-balanced Philips recording. The whole performance reflects Haitink's thoughtful, unsensational approach to the composer, a characteristically satisfying reading. There is noticeably more warmth in the 1970 set of *Lieder eines fahrenden Gesellen*, which Hermann Prey sings most beautifully.

Symphony No. 7 in E min.
*** DG Dig. 413 773-2 (2) [id.]. Chicago SO, Abbado.
*** Denon Dig. CO 1553/4 [id.]. Frankfurt RSO, Inbal.
*** Decca 414 675-2 (2) [id.]. Chicago SO, Solti – *Des Knaben Wunderhorn*: excerpts.***
*** DG Dig. 419 211-2 (2) [id.]. NYPO, Bernstein.
**(*) Ph. Dig. 410 398-2 (2) [id.]. Concg. O, Haitink.

Abbado's command of Mahlerian characterization has never been more tellingly displayed than in this most problematic of the symphonies; even in the loosely bound finale, Abbado unerringly draws the threads together. The contrasts in all its movements are superbly brought out, with the central interludes made ideally atmospheric, as in the eeriness of the scherzo and the haunting tenderness of the second *Nachtmusik*. The precision and polish of the Chicago orchestra go with total commitment, and the recording is one of the finest DG has made with this orchestra.

Inbal's account of the *Seventh* is one of the high points of his Mahler series, masterfully paced, relaxed and lyrical where appropriate, but incorporating all the biting tensions that are missing in his version of the *Sixth*, the other dark, middle symphony. Inbal's easy, natural manner is particularly effective in the three middle movements, and the radiant beauty of the second *Nachtmusik*, taken at a flowing speed, has never sounded more Elysian. The easy purposefulness of the finale in its many sections brings a masterly example of his unforced, incisive control, ending exuberantly at full power. The recording is outstandingly fine in its vivid, natural balances.

The sound of Solti's Decca issue is glorious, even riper and more brilliant than that of his two earlier Chicago recordings of Mahler and, on CD, much clearer. In interpretation, this is even more successful than his fine account of the *Sixth Symphony*, extrovert in display but full of dark implications. The tempi tend to be challengingly fast – at the very opening, for example, and in the scherzo (where Solti is mercurial) and in the finale (where his energy carries shock-waves in its trail). The second *Nachtmusik* is enchantingly seductive and, throughout, the orchestra plays superlatively well. For the CD issue, Yvonne Minton's fine performance of four Lieder from *Des Knaben Wunderhorn* has been added.

Leonard Bernstein's *Seventh* for DG was recorded from live performances. It is a riveting performance from first to last, ending with a searingly exciting account of the finale which triumphantly flouts the idea of this as a weak conclusion. It is a performance to send you off cheering, while the purposeful control of earlier movements also minimizes the obvious objections in principle to wilful exaggerations in phrasing and changes of tempo. This is Mahlerian expression at its most red-blooded, and with fine playing from the New York Philharmonic – marginally finer even than in his CBS version – it is a splendid example of Bernstein's flair in Mahler. The recording, fuller than in his much earlier CBS account, is yet a little harsh at times, next to the finest modern digital sound.

Beauty is the keynote of Haitink's newer, digitally recorded version of Mahler's *Seventh*. The superb playing of the Concertgebouw Orchestra is richly and amply caught; however, with spacious speeds to match, tensions have tended to ease since Haitink's earlier account; the vision of darkness is softened a degree. The wide dynamic range is very telling, with detail clarified.

Symphony No. 8 (Symphony of 1000).
⊛ *** EMI Dig. CDS7 47625-8 (2) [Ang. CDCB 47625]. Connell, Wiens, Lott, Schmidt, Denize, Versalle, Hynninen, Sotin, Tiffin School Boys' Ch., LPO Ch., LPO, Tennstedt.
*** Decca 414 493-2 (2) [id.]. Harper, Popp, Augér, Minton, Watts, Kollo, Shirley-Quirk, Talvela, V. Boys' Ch., V. State Op. Ch. & Singverein, Chicago SO, Solti.
*** Denon Dig. CO 1564/5 [id.]. Robinson, Cahill, Heichele, Budai, Henschel, Riegel, Prey, Stamm, Bav. N., S. & W. German R. Choirs, RIAS Chamber Ch., Limburg Cathedral Ch., Hesse R. Children's Ch., Frankfurt RSO, Inbal.

Tennstedt's magnificent account of the *Eighth*, long delayed through problems of casting, marks a superb culmination, the finest of his whole cycle. Though it does not always have the searing intensity that marks Solti's overwhelming Decca version,

Tennstedt's broader, grander view makes at least as powerful an impact, and with the extra range and richness of the modern EMI recording, coping superbly with even the heaviest textures, for most listeners it will be even more satisfying. Not the least impressive point about the recording is the firm, opulent sound of the Westminster Cathedral organ, dubbed on afterwards but sounding all the better focused for that. Next to this EMI recording, the 1972 Decca sound, for all its vividness, with solo voices made more immediate, sounds a little rough, underlining the fierceness. That said, the contrasting approaches of Tennstedt and Solti make them equally cherishable in their illumination of Mahler. It is the urgency and dynamism of Solti which make his reading irresistible, ending in an earth-shattering account of the closing hymn. Tennstedt, both there and elsewhere, finds more light and shade. His soloists, though a strong, characterful team, are not as consistent as Solti's. Even Felicity Lott as Mater Gloriosa is less pure-toned than she has sometimes been, but her solo is the more moving for being ethereally balanced. The great glory of the set is the singing of the London Philharmonic Choir, assisted by Tiffin School Boys' Choir. The chorus may be rather smaller than in live performance, but diction and clarity are aided, with no loss of power. This was a worthy winner in the orchestral category of the 1987 *Gramophone* awards.

The exhilaration of Inbal's culminating performance, recorded (like earlier ones) at sessions linked to live performances, comes over vividly. Even with a very large chorus, the sound is superbly detailed as well as full and atmospheric. *Veni creator spiritus* is wonderfully fresh and eager, but the clarity of detail does at times reveal fractional imprecision of ensemble. The refinement of sound gives extra intensity to the meditations of the great second movement, and Inbal's fast speed for the closing hymn makes it all the more purposeful, exuberant in joy. The team of soloists is a strong one but, like Tennstedt's octet, cannot match Solti's in consistency. The sound, naturally balanced and with as little tampering as possible, is extremely fine, not as spectacular as Tennstedt's but deeply satisfying in its warmth and beauty.

Symphony No. 9 in D min.
*** DG Dig. 410 726-2 (2) [id.]. BPO, Karajan.
(M) *** EMI CDM7 63115-2. BPO, Barbirolli.
(M) *** EMI CMS7 63277-2 (2) [Ang. CDMB 63277]. New Philh. O, Klemperer – WAGNER: *Siegfried idyll.***(*)
**(*) Decca Dig. 410 012-2 (2) [id.]. Chicago SO, Solti.
(**(*)) EMI mono CDH7 63029-2. VPO, Bruno Walter.

Symphony No. 9; Symphony No. 10: Adagio.
*** Denon Dig. CO 1566/7 [id.]. Frankfurt RSO, Inbal.
**(*) CBS Dig. M2K 39721 (2) [id.]. VPO, Maazel.

Symphony No. 9; (i) Kindertotenlieder.
*** Ph. 416 466-2 (2) [id.]. Concg. O, Haitink; (i) with Hermann Prey.

Karajan recorded Mahler's *Ninth* twice within a space of two years, and both performances transcended his earlier Mahler. The combination of richness and concentration in the outer movements makes for a reading of the deepest intensity, and in the middle movements point and humour are found, as well as refinement and polish. For his later version he added a new dimension of glowing optimism in the finale, rejecting any Mahlerian death-wish. It is this newer performance which appears on CD, recorded at live performances in Berlin and making it a supreme achievement. Despite the problems of live recording, the sound is bright and full, if somewhat close.

Haitink is at his very finest in Mahler's *Ninth*, and the last movement, with its slow expanses of melody, reveals a unique concentration. Unlike almost all other conductors he maintains his intensely slow tempo from beginning to end. This is a great performance, beautifully recorded and, with the earlier movements performed superbly – the first movement a little restrained, the second pointed at exactly the right speed, and the third gloriously extrovert and brilliant – this will be a first recommendation for many Mahlerians. The CD transfer freshens the 1969 recording, which still sounds highly impressive in its body and natural focus. Hermann Prey's early-1970s version of the *Kindertotenlieder* is added, a fresh, intelligent account, yet lacking something in imagination and intensity of expression.

Inbal's reading may not have the epic power or the sweeping breadth of Karajan, but his simple dedication brings a performance just as concentrated in its way, simulating the varying tensions of a live performance. The second-movement Laendler brings peasant overtones in the rasping woodwind; the third movement is finely pointed, emphasizing its joyfulness; and the simple gravity of the finale, easily lyrical in the big melodies, leads to a wonderfully hushed culmination, not tragic as with Karajan, but in its rapt ecstasy looking forward to the close, on murmurs of *'Ewig'*, of *Das Lied von der Erde*. As a logical fill-up, the *Adagio* from the *Tenth Symphony* brings a similarly natural and warm reading. The sound in both works is excellent in its natural balance, a fine example of the Denon engineers' work.

Barbirolli greatly impressed the Berliners with his Mahler performances live, and this recording reflects the players' warmth of response. He opted to record the slow and intense finale before the rest, and the beauty of the playing makes it a fitting culmination. The other movements are strong and alert too, and the sound remains full and atmospheric, though now more clearly defined. An unquestionable bargain.

Klemperer's performance was recorded in 1967 after a serious illness, and his refusal to languish pays tribute to his physical and spiritual defiance. Characteristically, he insisted on a relatively close balance, with woodwind well forward, and the physical power is underlined when the sound is full-bodied and firmly focused. The sublimity of the finale comes out the more intensely, with overt expressiveness held in check and deep emotion implied rather than made explicit. In the second movement the rustic humour is beautifully pointed, and even the comparative heaviness of the third movement has its justification in bringing out Mahler's parody of academic forms. This is one of the very finest of Klemperer's later recordings and it is coupled with the much earlier Philharmonia chamber version of Wagner's *Siegfried idyll*.

Clear and certain from the first hushed murmur of the opening movement, Solti in his newest Chicago version – in forward and full digital sound – presents the power of the piece with total conviction. What he lacks in the outer movements is a sense of mystery; he is also short of charm in the central movements, which should present a necessary contrast.

Maazel may not have quite the gravity and masterful control of tension that mark the very finest versions – Karajan's, for example – but with glorious playing from the Vienna strings and with unexaggerated speeds it is hard to fault Maazel on any point. He steers a masterly course between the perils of being either too plain or too mannered. Though some may miss an element of temperament, this is one of the more satisfying in his Mahler series, and is extremely well recorded. On CD, however, the spectacular sound-quality with the widest range of dynamic does bring a feeling in the climaxes that the microphones were very near the orchestra.

Recorded live at a concert in the Musikvereinsaal on 16 January 1938, only a few weeks before Hitler invaded Austria, Bruno Walter's version with the Vienna Philharmonic was the first recording of this symphony ever issued. The opening is not promising, with coughing very obtrusive; but then, with the atmosphere of this hall caught more vividly than in most modern recordings, the magnetism of Walter becomes irresistible in music which he was the first ever to perform. Interestingly, his speeds in the great spans of the outer movements are faster than we have latterly grown used to, markedly so in the great *Adagio* finale. Ensemble is often scrappy in the first movement, but intensity is unaffected; and, even at its flowing speed, the finale brings warmth and repose with no feeling of haste.

Symphony No. 10 in F sharp (unfinished): completed Deryk Cooke.
(M) **(*) Sony MPK 45882 [id.]. Phd O, Ormandy.

At mid-price on a single CD there is much to be said for the Ormandy version, when the performance has such emotional thrust and the playing such power and resonance, particularly in the strings. The mid-1960s recording still sounds well but, with a playing time of only 70 minutes, it means that the finale in particular does not have the spacious gravity and dark intensity of other versions, even though the opening hammerblows on the bass drum are thrillingly caught. A snag too is that this uses Cooke's original performing score (as distinct from the later, revised version) with rather balder, less Mahlerian scoring in the last two movements.

Symphony No. 10 in F sharp (Unfinished) (revised performing edition by Deryck Cooke).
*** EMI Dig. CDS7 47301-8 (2) [Ang. CDCB 47300]. Bournemouth SO, Rattle –
BRAHMS/SCHOENBERG: *Piano quartet.***
**(*) RCA Dig. RD 84553 (2) [RCD2 4553]. Phd. O, Levine.
(*) Decca Dig. 421 182-2 (2) [id.]. Berlin RSO, Chailly – SCHOENBERG: *Verklaerte Nacht.*

With digital recording of outstanding quality, Simon Rattle's vivid and compelling reading of the Cooke performing edition has one convinced more than ever that a remarkable revelation of Mahler's intentions was achieved in this painstaking reconstruction. To Cooke's final thoughts Rattle has added one or two detailed amendments; the finale in particular, starting with its cataclysmic hammer-blows and growing tuba line, is a deeply moving experience, ending not in neurotic resignation but in open optimism. In the middle movements, too, Rattle, youthfully dynamic, has fresh revelations to make. The Bournemouth orchestra plays with dedication, marred only by the occasional lack of fullness in the strings.

Levine's performance reveals him as a thoughtful and searching Mahlerian; the spacious account of the first movement is splendid, with refined Philadelphia string-tone; however, the recording, digital or not, does not always do justice to the high violins, which lack something in bloom, not least in the epilogue to the finale. The sound lacks a little in bass, too.

Chailly's Decca version is superbly recorded, and his grasp of the musical structure is keen. The Berlin Radio orchestra is highly responsive, yet the internal tension of the music-making is without the high voltage of Rattle's version and, indeed, Levine's.

Symphony No. 10: Adagio. Blumine; Totenfeier.
**(*) Virgin Dig. VC 790771-2 [id.]. Bamberg SO, Rickenbacher.

Rickenbacher, inventive in his choice of repertory with the Bamberg orchestra, here brings together the three separate movements attached to Mahler's cycle of completed symphonies. The *Adagio* which he planned as the first movement of his *Tenth Symphony* – here given in the suspect Krenek/Berg edition – and the *Blumine* movement excised from the *First Symphony* are both already well known on record. *Totenfeier* (Funeral rites), is the symphonic poem which eventually became the first movement of the *Symphony No. 2*. The unprepared listener will initially notice little difference, and it is a pity that the conductor's notes completely fail to illuminate its points of distinction from the version in the symphony. There are many detailed differences, but the main point is that the instrumentation is more modest and the dynamic contrasts less extreme as marked. Rickenbacher's performance reflects that, without diminishing the impact of the piece. The other two movements are played and recorded with similar refinement.

Piano quartet movement.
*** Virgin Dig. VC 790739-2 [id.]. Domus – BRAHMS: *Piano quartet No. 2.****

Mahler's *Piano quartet movement* comes from his student days. It is in no sense characteristic of the Mahler we know from the symphonies; but even at this early stage there is a sense of scale and shape. Ideas unfold at the right pace and in a way that shows the composer to have mastered the received tradition. Domus play with sensitivity and dedication and, though the acoustic is undeniably reverberant, the sound is far from unpleasing.

LIEDER AND SONG-CYCLES

Kindertotenlieder.
*** DG 415 096-2 (2) [id.]. Christa Ludwig, BPO, Karajan – *Symphony No. 5.***(*)

Kindertotenlieder; Lieder eines fahrenden Gesellen.
** Decca 414 624-2 [id.]. Kirsten Flagstad, VPO, Boult – WAGNER: *Wesendonk Lieder.****

(i) *Kindertotenlieder;* (ii) *Lieder eines fahrenden Gesellen;* (iii) *Des Knaben Wunderhorn: Das irdische Leben; Wo die schönen Trompeten blasen. Rückert Lieder: Ich bin der Welt abhanden gekommen; Um Mitternacht; Ich atmet' einen linden Duft.*
(M) **(*) EMI CDM7 69499-2 [id.]. Christa Ludwig, Philh. O, (i) Vandernoot; (ii) Boult; (iii) Klemperer.

(i) *Kindertotenlieder; Lieder eines fahrenden Gesellen;* (ii) *5 Rückert Lieder.*
*** EMI CDC7 47793-2 [id.]. Dame Janet Baker, (i) Hallé O; (ii) New Philh. O, Barbirolli.

5 Rückert Lieder.
(*) DG 415 099-2 (2) [id.]. Christa Ludwig, BPO, Karajan – *Symphony No. 6.**

Dame Janet Baker's collaboration with Barbirolli represents the affectionate approach to Mahler at its warmest. The Hallé strings are not quite as fine as the New Philharmonia in the *Rückert Lieder*, but this generous recoupling brings results that are still intensely beautiful, full of breathtaking moments. The spontaneous feeling of soloist and conductor for this music comes over as in a live performance, and though a baritone like Fischer-Dieskau can give a stronger idea of these appealing cycles, this brings out the tenderness to a unique degree. The remastering has freshened the sound, but the ambient warmth of the original recording has not been lost. An indispensable CD.

Christa Ludwig's singing on DG is very characterful too, if not as magical as Baker's. The *Rückert Lieder* are fine positive performances. It is the distinction and refinement of the orchestral playing and conducting that make this reissue valuable, although the microphone conveys some unevenness in the voice. The transfer is clear and clean.

There is also a valuable and attractive compilation of Ludwig's EMI recordings of Mahler, made when her voice was in its early prime and at its richest. The three *Rückert Lieder* and two excerpts from *Des Knaben Wunderhorn* are substituted on the CD issue for the songs with piano on the LP. Other versions may find a deeper response to the words, but the freshness of the singing here gives much pleasure.

Flagstad sings masterfully in these two most appealing of Mahler's orchestral cycles, but she was unable to relax into the deeper, more intimate expressiveness that the works really require. The voice is magnificent, the approach always firmly musical (helped by Sir Adrian's splendid accompaniment), but this recording is recommendable for the singer rather than for the way the music is presented.

(i) *Kindertotenlieder;* (ii) *Lieder eines fahrenden Gesellen;* (i) *4 Rückert Lieder (Um Mitternacht; Ich atmet' einen linden Duft; Blicke mir nicht in die Lieder; Ich bin der Welt).*
*** DG 415 191-2 [id.]. Dietrich Fischer-Dieskau, (i) BPO, Boehm; (ii) Bav. RSO, Kubelik.

Only four of the *Rückert Lieder* are included (*Liebst du um Schönheit* being essentially a woman's song), but otherwise this conveniently gathers Mahler's shorter and most popular orchestral cycles in performances that bring out the fullest range of expression in Fischer-Dieskau at a period when his voice was at its peak. The CD transfer gives freshness and immediacy to both the 1964 recording with Boehm and the 1970 recording with Kubelik.

Das klagende Lied (complete).
*** EMI Dig. CDC 747089-2 [id.]. Döse, Hodgson, Tear, Rea, CBSO and Ch., Rattle.

Das klagende Lied (published version).
*** Nimbus NI 5085 [id.]. Anna Reynolds, Zylis-Gara, Kaposy, Amb. S., New Philh. O, Wyn Morris.

The electricity of Simon Rattle as a recording conductor has rarely been more strikingly illustrated than in this fine recording of *Das klagende Lied*, complete with the dramatically necessary first part which Mahler came to discard. Pierre Boulez was the first to record the work complete, a clean-cut and dramatic version that has been intermittently available from CBS. Like Boulez, Rattle brings out the astonishing originality but adds urgency, colour and warmth, not to mention deeper and more meditative qualities. So the final section, *Wedding Piece*, after starting with superb swagger in the celebration music, is gripping in the minstrel's sinister narration and ends in the darkest concentration on a mezzo-soprano solo, beautifully sung by Alfreda Hodgson. The ensemble of the CBSO has a little roughness, but the bite and commitment could not be more convincing.

The reissue of Wyn Morris's 1967 Delysé recording, carefully remastered on Nimbus, is most welcome. These are committed, idiomatic performances with fine solo singing; and the recording is as atmospheric as ever, with the off-stage band at the wedding celebrations caught more vividly than on Rattle's version. This is excellent value on a label at less than premium price.

Des Knaben Wunderhorn.
*** DG Dig. 427 302-2 [id.]. Lucia Popp, Andreas Schmidt, Concg. O, Bernstein.
*** EMI CDC7 47277-2. Schwarzkopf, Fischer-Dieskau, LSO, Szell.
**(*) Nimbus NI 5084 [id.]. Dame Janet Baker, Sir Geraint Evans, LPO, Morris.

Since he last recorded Mahler's *Des Knaben Wunderhorn* songs, Bernstein's approach has grown more spacious and more measured; in that, he often tests his singers sorely, but Lucia Popp – very much the dominant partner of the two soloists – characterizes most appealingly, and though Andreas Schmidt is less positive, his singing is both fresh and unmannered. The sound is spacious and atmospheric, remarkably refined and well balanced for a live recording, with the soloists naturally placed, not spotlit. As in his previous version for CBS, Bernstein includes *Urlicht*, better known as the fourth movement of the *Symphony No. 2*, in its separate song-form.

In his last years Szell on his visits to Europe made a number of records which reflect a warmth and tenderness in his nature not often revealed in his work in Cleveland. This is one of that superlative group of records, with the most refined control of pianissimo in the orchestra matching the tonal subtleties of the two incomparable soloists. Wit and dramatic point as well as delicacy mark these widely contrasted songs, and the device of using two voices in some of them is apt and effective. The EMI recording has been freshened for CD very satisfactorily.

Dame Janet and Sir Geraint recorded Mahler's cycle in 1966 for Delysé, long before they had both received the Queen's accolade. Dame Janet in particular turns her phrases with characteristic imagination, and her flexibility is not always matched by the orchestra. Baker could hardly be more ideally cast, but Sir Geraint is more variable. He points the humour of the song about the cuckoo and the donkey with typical charm, but sometimes the voice does not sound perfectly focused. That may partly be attributed to the recording which, although vivid and warmly atmospheric, is not always sharply defined, as at the very opening with its resonance in the bass.

Des Knaben Wunderhorn: excerpts *(Das irdische Leben; Verlor'ne Müh; Wo die schönen Trompeten blasen; Rheinlegendchen).*
(*) Decca 414 675-2 (2) [id.]. Minton, Chicago SO, Solti – *Symphony No. 7.**

Yvonne Minton, a singer whom Solti encouraged enormously in her career at Covent Garden, makes a splendid soloist in these colourful songs from *Des Knaben Wunderhorn*, an attractive bonus for the CD issue of the *Seventh*.

Des Knaben Wunderhorn (excerpts): *Verlor'ne Müh; Rheinlegendchen; Wo die schönen Trompeten blasen; Lob des hohen Verstandes; Aus! Aus!.* Lieder: *Erinnerung; Frühlingsmorgen; Ich ging mit Lust durch einen grünen Wald; Phantasie aus Don Juan; Serenade aus Don Juan.*
*** DG Dig. 423 666-2 [id.]. Anne Sofie von Otter, Rolf Gothoni – WOLF: *Lieder.****

The Mahler half of Anne Sofie von Otter's brilliant recital is just as assured and strongly characterized as the formidable group of Wolf songs. Von Otter's mezzo has an aptly boyish quality in the five *Knaben Wunderhorn* settings – including one of the rarer ones, *Aus! Aus!*, and Rolf Gothoni's sparkling and pointed playing, as in the Wolf couplings, makes this a genuinely imaginative partnership, bringing out the gravity as well as the humour of the writing. Excellent, well-balanced recording.

Lieder eines fahrenden Gesellen (see also above, under *Symphony No. 6*).
*** Decca 414 674-2 (2) [id.]. Minton, Chicago SO, Solti – *Symphony No. 6.***(*)

Lieder eines fahrenden Gesellen; Lieder und Gesänge (aus der Jugendzeit); Im Lenz; Winterlied.
⊛ *** Hyp. CDA 66100 [id.]. Dame Janet Baker, Geoffrey Parsons.

Dame Janet presents a superb collection of Mahler's early songs with piano, including two written in 1880 and never recorded before, *Im Lenz* and *Winterlied*; also the piano version of the *Wayfaring Lad* songs in a text prepared by Colin Matthews from Mahler's final thoughts, as contained in the orchestral version. The performances are radiant and deeply understanding from both singer and pianist, well caught in atmospheric recording. A heart-warming record.

Yvonne Minton's performance of the *Wayfaring Lad* cycle is outstandingly successful, and very well recorded too.

Das Lied von der Erde.
(M) *** DG 419 058-2 [id.]. Ludwig, Kollo, BPO, Karajan.
*** DG Dig. 413 459-2 [id.]. Fassbaender, Araiza, BPO, Giulini.
*** EMI CDC7 47231-2 [id.]. Ludwig, Wunderlich, New Philh. O and Philh. O, Klemperer.
*** Decca 414 066-2 [id.]. Minton, Kollo, Chicago SO, Solti.
(M) **(*) Decca 417 783-2 [id.]. James King, Fischer-Dieskau, VPO, Bernstein.
(**) Decca mono 414 194-2. Ferrier, Patzak, VPO, Walter.

Karajan presents *Das Lied* as the most seductive sequence of atmospheric songs, combining characteristic refinement and polish with a deep sense of melancholy. This way of presenting Mahler's orchestration in the subtlest tones rather than in full colours is arguably more apt. In any case what matters is that here Karajan conveys the ebb and flow of tension as in a live performance. He is helped enormously by the soloists, both of whom have recorded this work several times, but never more richly than here. The sound on CD is more sharply defined, and some of the ambient effect has gone, but the quality is admirably vivid and does not lack a basic warmth.

Giulini conducts a characteristically restrained reading. With Araiza a heady-toned tenor rather than a powerful one, the line *Dunkel ist das Leben* in the first song becomes unusually tender and gentle, with rapture and wistfulness keynote emotions. In the second song, Fassbaender gives lightness and poignancy rather than dark tragedy to the line *Mein Herz ist müde*; and even the final *Abschied* is rapt rather than tragic, following the text of the poem. Not that Giulini fails to convey the breadth and intensity of Mahler's magnificent concept; and the playing of the Berlin Philharmonic could hardly be more beautiful.

Klemperer's way with Mahler is at its most individual in *Das Lied von der Erde* – and that will enthral some, as it must infuriate others. With slower speeds, the three tenor songs seem initially to lose some of their sparkle and humour; however, thanks to superb expressive singing by the late Fritz Wunderlich, and thanks also to pointing of rhythm by Klemperer himself, subtle but always clear, the comparative slowness will hardly worry anyone intent on hearing the music afresh, as Klemperer intends. As for the mezzo songs, Christa Ludwig sings them with a remarkable depth of expressiveness; in particular, the final *Abschied* has the intensity of a great occasion. Excellent digitally remastered recording (1967 vintage).

As an interpretation, Solti's version may lose something in mystery because of his very precision, but the concentration, in a consciously less romantic style than normal, is highly compelling, above all in the final *Abschied*: slower than usual and in the final section bringing an unusually close observance of Mahler's *pianissimo* markings. Minton exactly matches Solti's style, consistently at her most perceptive and sensitive, while Kollo presents Heldentenor strength, combined with sensitivity.

Bernstein's tempi, although showing an individual hallmark, generally suit the music naturally. So the tenor songs sparkle as they should, and though the final *Abschied*, taken at a very slow tempo indeed, puts extra strain on everyone, Bernstein's intensity carries the performance through. Doubts do arise over the soloists. James King is a strong-voiced tenor, but at times his word-pointing and phrasing sound comparatively stiff. Fischer-Dieskau is as sensitive as ever, but it is doubtful whether even he can match the finest contralto in the role, for one needs a lightening of tone in the even-numbered songs rather than – as here – a darkening. We still eagerly await the reissue on CD of Dame Janet Baker's version, also partnering James King, with the Concertgebouw Orchestra under Haitink, which remains unsurpassed.

It is a joy to have the voice of Kathleen Ferrier so vividly caught on CD – not to mention that of the characterful Patzak – in Bruno Walter's classic Vienna recording for Decca. It is also an enormous advantage having silent background with minimum tape-hiss, to be able to appreciate the radiance of the performance, not least in the ecstatic closing pages and the final murmurs of '*Ewig*'. The sad thing is that the violin tone in high loud passages has acquired a very unattractive edge, not at all like the Vienna violins, and this makes for uncomfortable listening.

Rückert Lieder: Ich atmet' einen Linden Duft; Ich bin der Welt; Um Mitternacht.
(***) Decca 421 299-2. Kathleen Ferrier, VPO, Bruno Walter – BRAHMS: *Alto rhapsody* etc.(***)

Ferrier's recording of three of Mahler's *Rückert Lieder* was a pendant to her historic recording, also with Bruno Walter and the Vienna Philharmonic, of Mahler's *Song of the earth*. Both heartfelt and monumental, they bring weighty readings, exploratory in the world of Mahler on record, not as delicately expressive as many since, but magnetically intense. While the extra clarity of CD is not kind to the orchestral strings, the voice emerges realistically with good presence.

Manzoni, Giacomo (born 1932)

Masse: Omaggio a Edgard Varèse.
*** DG Dig. 423 307-2 [id.]. Pollini, BPO, Sinopoli – SCHOENBERG: *Chamber symphony No. 1.****

Masse has nothing to do with church liturgy, but refers to measures or quantities, and in its tribute to Varèse follows up a science-based mode of thought which proves surprisingly dramatic and colourful. Only the piano solo has much in the way of melodic interest, and Pollini exploits it all he can, not least in the elaborate cadenza-like passages. Sinopoli too reveals the feeling for texture and dynamic which so often makes his conducting so memorable.

Marais, Marin (1656–1728)

La Gamme en forme de petit opéra; Sonata à la marésienne.
*** HM HMC 901105 [id.]. L. Baroque.

La Gamme is a string of short character-pieces for violin, viole de gambe and harpsichord that takes its inspiration from the ascending and descending figures of the scale. Although it is *en forme de petit opéra*, its layout is totally instrumental and the varied pieces and dramatic shifts of character doubtless inspire the title. It plays without a break of any kind and its continuity is enlivened by much variety of invention and resource. The *Sonata à la marésienne* is less unusual, but it also has variety and character. The London Baroque is an excellent group, and they are well recorded too.

Marcello, Alessandro (1669–1747)

6 Oboe concertos (La Cetra).
(M) *** DG 427 137-2 [id.]. Heinz Holliger, Louise Pellerin, Camerata Bern, Füri.

The six concertos of *La Cetra* are concertante exercises rather than concertos in the accepted sense of the word, and they reveal a pleasing mixture of originality and convention. As a composer Alessandro was perhaps not quite as accomplished as his brother, Benedetto, and occasionally there is a reliance on relatively routine gestures; but much of the time one is surprised by a genuinely alive and refreshing individuality. These performances are vital and keen, occasionally almost aggressively bright, but full of style and character, and the recording is faithful and well projected.

Martin, Frank (1890–1974)

(i) *Ballade for piano and orchestra;* (ii) *Ballade for trombone and orchestra;* (iii) *Concerto for harpsichord and small orchestra.*
**(*) Jecklin-Disco JD 529-2. (i) Sebastian Benda; (ii) Armin Rosin; (iii) Christiane Jaccottet; Lausanne CO, composer.

These performances first appeared on LP in the early 1970s. The *Harpsichord concerto* is a highly imaginative and inventive piece, arguably the most successful example of the genre since the Falla *Concerto*. The orchestral texture has a pale, transparent delicacy that is quite haunting, and the atmosphere is powerful – as, indeed, it is in the fine *Ballade*. A disc to which this writer (R.L.) often returns, and which deserves a strong recommendation in spite of minor sonic limitations. Christiane Jaccottet is a committed advocate and her performance has the authority of the composer's direction.

(i) *Violin concerto;* (ii) *Piano concerto No. 2.*
*(**) Jecklin Disco JD 632-2 [id.]. (i) Schneiderhan; (ii) Badura-Skoda; Luxembourg RSO, composer.

The *Violin concerto* (1951) is a score of great subtlety and beauty. It is scarcely credible that Schneiderhan is the only player to have tackled it on record. Hopefully the centenary year will bring us a new and better recording, for this balances the soloist rather too closely. Don't be put off by the less-than-lustrous sound, for this is a masterpiece and has the benefit of having Martin himself at the helm. The *Second Piano concerto* (1968–9) was written for Badura-Skoda. It is not as lyrical as the *Violin concerto* but is still worth investigation for its thoughtful slow movement.

Der Cornet.
*** Orfeo Dig. S 164881A [id.]. Marjana Lipovšek, Austrian RSO, Zagrosek.

Rilke's celebrated collection of poems, *Die Weise von Liebe und Tod des Cornets Christoph Rilke*, tells of a youthful ensign who in 1660 fell under 'the sabres of the Turks into an ocean of flowers'. Writing in the middle of the Second World War, Frank Martin set all but three of the 26 poems, scoring them for a contralto soloist with a small chamber orchestra. The shadowy, half-real atmosphere often reminds one of *Pelléas*; and Martin's responsiveness to the rhythm and music of the words is thoroughly Debussian (German was not his native tongue). All his fingerprints are there, and the restrained, pale colourings provide an effective backcloth to the vivid outbursts that mark some of the settings. The performance by the contralto, Marjana Lipovšek, is a *tour de force*. Hers is a moving account of the songs, in which every word is expertly and vividly placed; and the orchestral playing under Lothar Zagrosek is highly sympathetic. The recording is very faithful, and the performance puts one completely under the spell of this strongly atmospheric work.

Requiem.
*** Jecklin Disco JD 631-2 [id.]. Speiser, Bollen, Tappy, Lagger, Lausanne Women's Ch., Union Ch., SRO, composer.
Written some three years before the composer's death, this music can only be described as seraphic. It is arguably the most beautiful *Requiem* to have been written since Fauré's and, were the public to have ready access to it, would be as popular. The recording, made at a public performance that the (then 83-year-old) composer conducted in Lausanne Cathedral, is very special. The analogue recording is not in the demonstration class, but this music and performance must have three stars.

Le vin herbé (oratorio).
*(**) Jecklin Disco JD 581/2-2 [id.]. Retchitzka, Tuscher, Comte, Morath, De Montmollin, Diakoff, De Nyzankowskyi, Tappy, Jonelli, Rehfuss, Vessières, Olsen, composer, Winterthur O (members), Desarzens.

Martin's oratorio on the Tristan legend is laid out for a madrigal choir of twelve singers, who also assume solo roles, and a handful of instrumentalists, including the piano, played here by the septuagenarian composer himself. It is powerfully atmospheric and sounds like a distant relative of *Pelléas et Mélisande*, having all the pale, dimly lit but at times luminous colouring of Debussy's world. It is powerful and hypnotic, and there is some fine singing here from Nata Tuscher (Isolde), Eric Tappy (Tristan) and Heinz Rehfuss (King Mark). The instrumental playing, though not impeccable, is dedicated (and the same must be said for the choral singing). The 1960s sound ideally needs a bit more space round it but is much improved in the CD format. *Le vin herbé* is a masterly and compelling work and is strongly recommended.

Martinů, Bohuslav (1890–1959)

La Bagarre; Half-time; Intermezzo; The Rick; Thunderbolt.
*** Sup. SUP 001669 [id.]. Brno State O, Vronsky.

La Bagarre and *Half-time* are early evocations, the latter a Honeggerian depiction of a roisterous half-time at a football match that musically doesn't amount to a great deal. The three later works are much more interesting – *Intermezzo* is linked to the *Fourth Symphony* – and the collection as a whole will be of great interest to Martinů addicts, if perhaps not essential for other collectors. All the performances are alive and full of character, and the recording is vividly immediate.

Oboe concerto.
*** Capriccio Dig. 10 308 [id.]. Lajos Lencsés, Stuttgart RSO, Marriner – HAYDN: *Concerto*; HUMMEL: *Intro., theme & variations.****

Not surprisingly, Martinů's *Concerto* is full of individual touches and has plenty of rhythmic interest, particularly in the pulsing energy of the wittily high-spirited finale. Lajos Lencsés plays with a rather more plangent timbre than in the Haydn and Hummel couplings, and the unusual *Poco andante* – with its two piano-accompanied improvisatory interludes – is memorable in its bitter-sweet lyricism. Marriner accompanies sympathetically and the recording is first rate.

Rhapsody-Concerto for viola and orchestra.
*** Conifer Dig. CDFC 146 [id.]. Golani, Berne SO, Maag – D'INDY: *Symphonie sur un chant montagnard français.****

This is not quite a viola concerto: though the elements of dialogue and display we associate with the genre are present, it is primarily gentle and reflective. The *Rhapsody* is free in its formal layout, and the quieter episodes of the *Adagio* have an impressive inner repose. The violist Rivka Golani plays with a gloriously warm tone and much musical insight, and the whole performance is agreeably natural: there is nothing high-powered or overdriven. As admirers of Peter Maag will expect, this is a selfless performance of the old school that allows this music to speak for itself and penetrates deeper below the surface. The sound is that of a very fine broadcast rather than a seat in a concert hall, but detail is kept in an excellent and believable perspective. Very strongly recommended.

Symphonies Nos. 1–4.
*** BIS Dig. CD 362-3 [id.]. Bamberg SO, Järvi.

Martinů always draws a highly individual sound from his orchestra and secures great clarity, even when the score abounds in octave doublings. He often thickens his textures in this way, yet, when played with the delicacy these artists produce, they sound beautifully transparent. On hearing the *First*, Virgil Thomson wrote, 'the shining sounds of it sing as well as shine', and there is no doubt this music is luminous and life-loving. The *Fourth* is the most popular and is coupled with the more highly charged and intensely felt *Third*. It is probably best to start with them; but few, having done so, will be able to resist their companions. The thrilling recording is in the demonstration class yet sounds completely natural, and the performances under Neeme Järvi are totally persuasive and have a spontaneous feel for the music's pulse.

Symphonies Nos. 5; 6 (Fantaisies symphoniques).
*** BIS Dig. CD 402 [id.]. Bamberg SO, Järvi.
**(*) RCA Dig. RD 87805 [7805-2-RC]. Berlin RSO, Flor.

The *Fifth*, like its predecessor, has some recourse to sectional repetition and is not as powerfully structured or as profoundly original as the *Sixth*. All the same, it is a glorious piece and Järvi brings to it that mixture of disciplined enthusiasm and zest for life that distinguishes all his work. This is vividly imagined music that enriches and enhances the spirit; it follows the Handelian precept and makes one better! Wonderfully transparent, yet full-bodied sound, in the best BIS manner.

Artistically, honours are fairly evenly divided between Claus-Peter Flor's Berlin recording and Järvi's on BIS, but the more open acoustic and better recording tip the scales in Järvi's favour.

Cello sonatas Nos. 1–3.
*** Hyp. Dig. CDA 66296 [id.]. Steven Isserlis, Peter Evans.
*** Sup. SUP 001718 [id.]. Josef Churcho, Josef Hála.

Steven Isserlis and Peter Evans have done well to collect all three Martinů *Cello sonatas* on one disc. The slow movement of the *First* is dark and inward-looking; it is a powerful, well-wrought and often moving piece, whose combative outer movements are highly effective. The more familiar *Second sonata* comes from the composer's American years – and one recognizes the kind of thinking and sense of musical pace that were developing in the symphonies. The *Third* is thoroughly characteristic Martinů. Good playing and very acceptable recording.

The Czech performances too are outstandingly committed and spontaneous. The recording is truthful and well balanced, a shade studio-ish and close, but realistic.

Flute sonata.
*** RCA Dig. RD 87802 [7802-2-RC]. James Galway, Phillip Moll – DVORÁK: *Sonatina*; FELD: *Sonata.****

With the outer movements generally jolly and extrovert, bringing distinctive Martinů touches, the main weight of the *Flute sonata* comes in the central *Adagio* with its powerful middle section and meditative close. Galway is characteristically individual but without mannerism in his performance, and is most sympathetically accompanied by Moll. Relatively dry recording, with a fine sense of presence.

4 Madrigals for oboe, clarinet and bassoon; 3 Madrigals for violin and viola; Madrigal sonata for piano, flute and violin; 5 Madrigal stanzas for violin and piano.
*** Hyp. Dig. CDA 66133 [id.]. Dartington Ens.

These delightful pieces exhibit all the intelligence and fertility of invention we associate with Martinů's music. The *Five Madrigal stanzas* of 1943 were written for Albert Einstein, no less, whose duo partner was Robert Casadesus! The playing of the Dartington Ensemble is accomplished and expert, and the recording, though resonant, is faithful. Just try the opening piece of the *Five Madrigal stanzas* to discover how melodically inviting this music is.

Nonet.
*** DG Dig. 427 640-2 [id.]. Vienna/Berlin Ens. – SPOHR: *Nonet.****

The Wien/Berlin Ensemble numbers some distinguished players including Karl Leister, Hansjörg Schellenberger and Milan Turkovič, and they give an alert and sparkling account of the *Nonet*. Martinů enthusiasts will want or already have the Dartington version listed below and they can rest assured that, though the DG has fractionally more authority as a performance, the Hyperion recording is just that bit more open.

Nonet; Trio in F for flute, cello and piano; La Revue de cuisine.
*** Hyp. CDA 66084 [id.]. Dartington Ens.

A delightful record. None of these pieces, save the *Nonet*, is otherwise available on CD and all of them receive first-class performances and superb recording. The sound has space, warmth, perspective and definition. *La Revue de cuisine* is very much of its decade and the *Charleston* is most engaging. The *Trio* is as fresh and inventive as Martinů's very best work and is played deliciously. Its *Andante* deserves to be singled out for special mention: it is a most beautiful movement. The *Nonet*, for string trio plus double-bass, flute, clarinet, oboe, horn and bassoon, is equally life-enhancing. An indispensable issue for lovers of Martinů's music.

Études and Polkas; Fantasy and Toccata; Moderato (Julietta Act II), arr. Firkušný; Les Ritournelles; Piano sonata No. 1.
**(*) RCA Dig. RD 87987 [id.]. Rudolf Firkušný.

Firkušný was long associated with Martinů and gave the first performances of most of these pieces. The *Fantasy and Toccata* was written for him in the dark days of 1940 while both musicians were waiting to escape from Vichy France to America. Although he loved the instrument, his piano music is not the finest Martinů, but Firkušný displays it in the best possible light. No doubt had he recorded it when he was younger (he is in his late seventies), the rhythmic contours would be more sharply etched and would have more bite, but it could not be more delicate in its keyboard colouring, more authoritative or refined. Firkušný is a pianist of the old school who never plays to the gallery and is supremely musical. The recording is not made in a large enough acoustic but is otherwise truthful.

Field mass.
*** Sup. Dig. SUP 007735 [id.]. Ztek, Czech Philharmonic Ch. and O, Mackerras – JANÁČEK: *Amarus.****

Martinů's *Field mass* is full of delightful and original sonorities, and this persuasive account under Mackerras shows it in the best possible light. It is scored for the unusual combination of baritone, male chorus, wind instruments, percussion, harmonium and a piano, as well as a triangle and a number of bells. The resultant sounds are as fresh and individual as one could imagine, and so is Martinů's invention. It is very impressively performed by the Czech forces under Sir Charles Mackerras, and the recording is quite outstanding.

Martucci, Giuseppe (1856–1909)

Symphony No. 1 in D min., Op. 75; Notturno, Op. 70/1; Novelletta, Op. 82; Tarantella, Op. 44.
** ASV Dig. CDDCA 675 [id.]. Philh. O, D'Avalos.

Martucci was a key figure in the renaissance of Italian instrumental music, as conductor as well as composer. Toscanini included Martucci's own music in his repertoire, and ASV are now embarked on a project to record all his orchestral works. Like so much of his music, the *First Symphony* is greatly indebted to Brahms, but elsewhere there is a vein of lyricism that is more distinctive. Both the *Novelletta* and the *Notturno* were originally for piano; the latter has the nobility and eloquence of Elgar or Fauré and deserves to be much better known. The present *Symphony* is not the equal of the beautiful *Canzone dei Ricordi* on Hyperion, but it is well worth having on disc. The performances by the Philharmonia under Francesco d'Avalos are serviceable rather than distinguished, but the recording is very truthful and well balanced.

Le canzone dei ricordi; Notturno, Op. 70/1.
*** Hyp. Dig. CDA 66290 [id.]. Carol Madalin, ECO, Bonavera – RESPIGHI: *Il tramonto.****

Le canzone dei ricordi is a most beautiful song-cycle and comes from 1886, the year of Mahler's *Lieder eines fahrenden Gesellen*. But Martucci's musical language is closer to that of Fauré or the elegiac Elgar, and its gentle atmosphere and warm lyricism are most seductive. At times Carol Madalin has a rather rapid vibrato, but she sings the work most sympathetically and with great eloquence. The *Notturno* is an inspired piece in similar vein and is beautifully played; there are echoes of Mahler and the Italian *verismo* school, but the music is free from sentimentality and has great dignity. Recommended with all possible enthusiasm.

Mascagni, Pietro (1863–1945)

L'Amico Fritz (complete).
*** EMI CDS7 47905-8 (2) [Ang. CDCB 47905]. Pavarotti, Freni, Sardinero, ROHCG Ch. and O, Gavazzeni.

The haunting *Cherry duet* from this opera whets the appetite for more, and it is good to hear so rare and charming a piece, one that is not likely to enter the repertory of our British opera houses. This performance could be more refined, though Freni and Pavarotti are most attractive artists and this was recorded in 1969 when they were both at their freshest. The Covent Garden Orchestra responds loyally; the recording is clear and atmospheric, and it has transferred very successfully to CD. While the dramatic conception is at the opposite end of the scale from *Cavalleria Rusticana*, one is easily beguiled by the music's charm.

Cavalleria Rusticana (complete).
*** RCA RD 83091. Scotto, Domingo, Elvira, Isola Jones, Amb. Op. Ch., Nat. PO, Levine.
*** DG 419 257-2 (3) [id.]. Cossotto, Bergonzi, Guelfi, Ch. & O of La Scala, Milan, Karajan – LEONCAVALLO: *I Pagliacci**** (also with collection of *Operatic intermezzi***).
(***) EMI mono CDS7 47981-8 (3) [Ang. CDCC 47981]. Callas, Di Stefano, Panerai, Ch. & O of La Scala, Milan, Serafin – LEONCAVALLO: *I Pagliacci*.(***)
(M) (***) RCA mono GD 86510 [RCA 6510-2-RG]. Milanov, Bjoerling, Merrill, Robert Shaw Chorale, RCA O, Cellini.

There is far more to recommend about the RCA issue than the fact that it is available on a single CD (libretto included). On balance, in performance it stands as the best current recommendation, with Domingo giving a heroic account of the role of Turiddu, full of defiance. Scotto, strongly characterful too, though not always perfectly steady on top, gives one of her finest performances of recent years, and James Levine directs with a splendid sense of pacing, by no means faster than his rivals (except the leisurely Karajan), and drawing red-blooded playing from the National Philharmonic. The recording is very good, strikingly present in its CD format.

Karajan pays Mascagni the tribute of taking his markings literally, so that well-worn melodies come out with new purity and freshness, and the singers have been chosen to match that. Cossotto quite as much as Bergonzi keeps a pure, firm line that is all too rare in this much-abused music. Not that there is any lack of dramatic bite. The CD transfer cannot rectify the balance, but voices are generally more sharply defined, while the spacious opulence is retained. Karajan's fine performances of various opera-interludes make a welcome filler on the three-CD set.

Dating from the mid-1950s, Callas's performance as Santuzza reveals the diva in her finest voice, with edginess and unevenness of production at a minimum and with vocal colouring at its most characterful. The singing of the other principals is hardly less dramatic and Panerai is in firm, well-projected voice. This powerful team is superbly controlled by Serafin, a master at pacing this music, giving it full power while minimizing vulgarity. However, with Callas providing the central focus, the performance seems to centre round the aria, *Voi lo sapete*, wonderfully dark and intense, and one soon adjusts to the rather mushy quality of the opera's opening choruses, brought about by the restricted range; the solo voices, however, are projected vividly.

Though Zinka Milanov starts disappointingly in the *Easter hymn*, the conjunction of three of the outstanding Met. principals of the early 1950s period brings a warmly satisfying performance. Admirers of Milanov will not want to miss her beautiful singing of *Voi lo sapete*, and in the duet Merrill's dark, firm timbre is thrilling. Bjoerling brings a good measure of musical and tonal subtlety to the role of Turiddu, normally belted out, while Cellini's conducting minimizes the vulgarity of the piece.

Iris (complete).
*** CBS Dig. M2K 45526 (2) [id.]. Domingo, Tokody, Pons, Giaiotti, Bav. R. Ch., Munich R. O, Patanè.

Iris is the opera – first given in 1898 – which, with its story of Old Japan and a heroine-victim, prompted the ever-competitive Puccini to turn his attention to the East and write *Madama Butterfly*. It has often been said that, but for *Butterfly*, *Iris* would have stayed in the repertory – but even as committed a performance as this hardly sustains such an idea. Amid the early plaudits for an opera which aims far higher than *Cavalleria Rusticana*, Puccini put his finger on the central weakness: a lack of interesting action. This heroine-as-victim is totally passive, much put upon by everyone. The rich hero, Osaka, makes advances to her in Act II, behaves insensitively and promptly finds himself bored by the reactions of a frightened child. How different that delayed duet is from the love-duet in *Butterfly*. Iris's one positive act is to throw herself to her death down a shaft when even her blind father turns against her – through an implausible misunderstanding, needless to say. Illica as librettist falls sadly short of his achievement for Puccini. Musically, *Iris* brings a mixture of typical Mascagnian sweetness and a vein of nobility often echoing Wagner. So the long symbolic prelude representing night and dawn has obvious echoes of Wagner's dawn music in the prologue to *Götterdämmerung*, and it returns at the end of the opera to represent the dead heroine's transfiguration. The comparison with the dawn interlude in *Butterfly* is also pointful, when Puccini, realistic and unsymbolic, is so much more involving. With a strong line-up of soloists including Domingo, and with Giuseppe Patanè a persuasive conductor, this recording makes as good a case for a flawed piece as one is ever likely to get. Domingo's warm, intelligent singing helps to conceal the cardboard thinness of a hero who expresses himself in generalized ardour. The most celebrated passage from the opera, the Neapolitan-like *Apri la tua finestra*, proves to be just a stylized item in a play within the play, not the hero's personal serenade at all. The Hungarian soprano, Ilona Tokody, brings out the tenderness of the heroine but, with dramatic tone, also expansively makes her into a plausible Butterfly figure, singing beautifully except when under pressure. Juan Pons, sounding almost like a baritone Domingo, is firm and well projected as Kyoto, owner of a geisha-house, and Bonaldo Giaiotti brings an authentically dark Italian bass to the role of Iris's father. Full, atmospheric recording.

Massenet, Jules (1842–1912)

Le Carillon (ballet): complete.
(M) *** Decca 425 472-2 (2) [id.]. Nat. PO, Richard Bonynge – DELIBES: *Coppélia.****

Le Carillon was written in the same year as *Werther*. The villains of the story who try to destroy the bells of the title are punished by being miraculously transformed into bronze *jaquemarts*, fated to continue striking them for ever! The music of this one-act ballet makes a delightful offering – not always as lightweight as one would expect. With his keen rhythmic sense and feeling for colour, Bonynge is outstanding in this repertory, and the 1984 Decca recording is strikingly brilliant and colourful. A fine bonus (37 minutes) for a highly desirable version of Delibes' *Coppélia*.

Cigale (ballet): complete.
(M) *** Decca 425 413-2 (3) [id.]. Enid Hartle, Nat. PO, Bonynge – TCHAIKOVSKY: *Swan Lake.***(*)

A late work, written with Massenet's characteristic finesse. *Cigale* was totally neglected after its première in 1904, until Richard Bonynge revived it in this admirable recording. The ballet recounts the La Fontaine fable about the grasshopper and the ant. The melodic invention does not match Massenet's finest, but the score is charming and colourful and is brightly and atmospherically played and sung and brilliantly recorded; and it makes a considerable coupling for Bonynge's complete set of Tchaikovsky's *Swan Lake*.

Manon (ballet) complete (arr. Lucas).
*** Decca Dig. 414 585-2 (2) [id.]. ROHCG O, Bonynge.

This confection of Massenet lollipops – with the famous *Élégie* returning as an *idée fixe* – is the work of Leighton Lucas; with characteristically lively and colourful playing from the Covent Garden Orchestra under Richard Bonynge, it makes a delightful issue, the more attractive when, as with other Bonynge recordings of ballet, the Decca engineers deliver sound of spectacular quality.

OPERA

Cendrillon (complete).
**(*) CBS CD 79323 (2). Von Stade, Gedda, Berbié, Welting, Bastin, Amb. Op. Ch., Philh. O, Rudel.

Julius Rudel directs a sparkling, winning performance of Massenet's Cinderella opera, very much a fairy story in which the magic element is vital. The Fairy Godmother is a sparkling coloratura (here the bright-toned Ruth Welting) and Cendrillon a soprano in a lower register. Von Stade gives a characteristically strong and imaginative performance, untroubled by what for her is high tessitura. The pity is that the role of the prince, originally also written for soprano, is here taken by a tenor, Gedda, whose voice is no longer fresh-toned. Jules Bastin sings most stylishly as Pandolfe, and the others make a well-chosen team. The recording is vivid, but spacious too. Worth exploring, even at full price.

Le Cid (complete).
** CBS CD 79300 (2). Bumbry, Domingo, Bergquist, Plishka, Gardner, Camp Chorale, NY Op. O, Queler.

The CBS recording is taken from a live performance in New York and suffers from boxy recording quality. Only with the entrance of Domingo in the second scene does the occasion really get going, and the French accents are often comically bad. Even so, the attractions of Massenet's often beautiful score survive all the shortcomings and this makes a valuable addition to the CD catalogue. Domingo, not always as stylish as he might be, is in heroic voice and Grace Bumbry as the proud heroine responds splendidly. The popular ballet music is given a sparkling performance. But this should have been reissued at mid-price.

Le Cid: ballet suite.
(M) *** Decca 425 475-2 (2) [id.]. Nat. PO, Richard Bonynge – DELIBES: *Sylvia*.***

Le Cid: ballet suite; *Scènes pittoresques; La Vierge: The last sleep of the Virgin.*
(M) *** CDM7 63024-2 [id.]. CBSO, Frémaux – OFFENBACH: *Overtures*.**(*)

Frémaux's record was originally one of EMI's most impressive quadrophonic issues, and the stereo master retains the sumptuous bass resonance given to the recording by the acoustics of the Great Hall of Birmingham University. In the spectacular recording of the

Le Cid ballet music, the sonic splendour is remarkable, with the CD remastering adding to the brilliance. The *Aubade*, deliciously scored for woodwind, makes a demonstration item. The performances, both of the ballet music and of the charming *Scènes pittoresques*, have great flair, and the muted strings in *Le dernier sommeil de la Vierge* are quite beautiful. This was a favourite of Sir Thomas Beecham's and Frémaux plays it lovingly.

Over the years, Decca have made a house speciality of recording the ballet music from *Le Cid* and coupling it with Constant Lambert's arrangement of Meyerbeer (*Les Patineurs*). Bonynge's version is the finest yet, with the most seductive orchestral playing, superbly recorded. Now it comes as an engaging encore for an equally recommendable complete set of Delibes' *Sylvia*, with the remastering for CD adding to the glitter and colour of Massenet's often witty scoring.

Esclarmonde (complete).
(M) *** Decca 425 651-2 (3) [id.]. Sutherland, Aragall, Tourangeau, Davies, Grant, Alldis Ch., Nat. PO, Bonynge.

The central role of *Esclarmonde*, with its Wagnerian echoes and hints of both Verdi and Berlioz, calls for an almost impossible combination of qualities. In our generation Joan Sutherland is the obvious diva to encompass the demands of great range, great power and brilliant coloratura, and her performance is in its way as powerful as it is in Puccini's last opera. Aragall proves an excellent tenor, sweet of tone and intelligent, and the other parts, all of them relatively small, are well taken too. Richard Bonynge draws passionate singing and playing from chorus and orchestra, and the recording has both atmosphere and spectacle to match the story, based on a medieval romance involving song-contests and necromancy.

Manon (complete).
(M) (*(**)) EMI mono CMS7 63549-2 (3). De los Angeles, Legay, Dens, Boirthayre, Berton, Opéra-comique, Monteux – CHAUSSON: *Poème de l'amour et de la mer.*(***)
*** EMI Dig. CDS7 49610-2 (3) [Ang. CDCB 49610]. Cotrubas, Kraus, Quilico, Van Dam, Ch. & O of Capitole, Toulouse, Plasson.

The combination of Victoria de los Angeles singing the role of the heroine with Pierre Monteux conducting is unbeatable in Massenet's most warmly approachable opera. There has never been a more winning Manon than De los Angeles, deliciously seductive from the start, making her first girlish solo, *Je suis encore tout étourdie*, sparkle irresistibly. The meeting with Des Grieux is then enchanting, with the hero's youthful wonderment breathtakingly caught by Henri Legay in his light, heady tenor. Though there are cuts – for example the end of Act I – this is a unique performance that defies the limitations of ancient mono recording. Unfortunately, the CD transfer emphasizes the top registers unduly while giving little body to lower registers. Voices can be made to sound vivid, but the orchestra remains thin and edgy. The original four LPs have been transferred to three CDs, with the bonus of De los Angeles' recording of the delightful Chausson cantata.

Plasson's set, recorded in Toulouse, presents a stylish performance, well characterized and well sung. Ileana Cotrubas is a charming Manon, more tender and vulnerable than De los Angeles on the earlier set, but not so golden-toned and with a more limited development of character from the girlish chatterbox to the dying victim. Alfredo Kraus betrays some signs of age, but this is a finely detailed and subtle reading with none of the blemishes which marred his *Werther* performance for EMI. Louis Quilico has a delightfully light touch as Lescaut, and José Van Dam is a superb Comte Des Grieux. The warm reverberation of the Toulouse studio is well controlled to give bloom to the voices, and though Plasson is rougher with the score than Monteux, his feeling for French idiom is good.

Werther (complete).
*** Ph. 416 654-2 (2) [id.]. Carreras, Von Stade, Allen, Buchanan, Lloyd, Children's Ch., ROHCG O, C. Davis.
(M) ** EMI CMS7 69573-2 (2) [id.]. Kraus, Troyanos, Manuguerra, Barbaux, Ch. & LPO, Plasson.

Sir Colin Davis has rarely directed a more sensitive or more warmly expressive performance on record than his account of *Werther*, based on a stage production at Covent Garden. Frederica von Stade makes an enchanting Charlotte, outshining all current rivals on record, both strong and tender, conveying the understanding but vulnerable character of Goethe's heroine. Carreras may not be quite so clearly superior to all rivals, but he uses a naturally beautiful voice freshly and sensitively. Others in the cast, such as Thomas Allen as Charlotte's husband Albert and Isobel Buchanan as Sophie, her sister, are excellent, too. The CD transfer on to a pair of discs has been highly successful, with a single serious reservation: the break between the two CDs is badly placed in the middle of a key scene between Werther and Charlotte, just before *Ah! qu'il est loin ce jour!* Otherwise this is one of the very finest French opera sets yet issued in the new medium.

It is sad that Alfredo Kraus, as a rule one of the most stylish of tenors, came to record *Werther* so late in his career. Listen to this account of *Pourquoi me réveiller*, and the effortful underlining, with its chopping of the melodic line, is almost unrecognizable as his work. Troyanos makes a volatile Charlotte, but the voice as recorded is grainy. Manuguerra produces rich tone as the Bailiff, but the engineers have not been kind to the LPO strings, which sound rather thin, particularly when compared with those on the Philips set.

Mathias, William (born 1934)

Lux aeterna, Op. 88.
*** Chan. Dig. CHAN 8695 [id.]. Felicity Lott, Cable, Penelope Walker, Bach Ch., St George's Chapel Ch., Windsor, LSO, Willcocks; J. Scott (organ).

Just as Britten in the *War Requiem* contrasted different planes of expression with Latin liturgy set against Wilfred Owen poems, so Mathias contrasts the full choir singing Latin against the boys' choir singing carol-like Marian anthems, and in turn against the three soloists, who sing three arias and a trio to the mystical poems of St John of the Cross. In the last section all three planes come together when the chorus chants the prayer *Lux aeterna*, and the boys sing the hymn, *Ave maris stella*, leaving the soloists alone at the end in a moving conclusion. Overall, the confidence of the writing makes the work far more than derivative, an attractively approachable and colourful piece, full of memorable ideas, especially in this excellent performance, beautifully sung and played and atmospherically balanced.

Wind quintet.
*** Crystal CD 750 [id.]. Westwood Wind Quintet – CARLSSON: *Nightwings*; LIGETI: *Bagatelles*; BARBER: *Summer music.******

Of the five movements of this spirited *Quintet* the scherzo is particularly felicitous and there is a rather beautiful *Elegy*. The playing of the Westwood Wind Quintet is highly expert and committed, though the recording is a little less transparent than in the Barber or Ligeti pieces with which it is coupled. However, it is still very good indeed.

Maxwell Davies, Peter (born 1934)

Violin concerto.
*** CBS Dig. MK 42449 [id.]. Stern, RPO, Previn: DUTILLEUX: *L'Arbre des songes.********

Maxwell Davies wrote his *Violin concerto* specifically with Isaac Stern in mind, and there are parallels here with the Walton *Violin concerto* of over forty years earlier. The composer was inspired to draw on a more warmly lyrical side such as he has rarely displayed. Yet for all its beauties, this is a work which has a tendency to middle-aged spread, not nearly as taut in expression as the Walton or, for that matter, the fine Dutilleux concerto with which it is coupled. Stern seems less involved here than in that other work, though this coupling makes a strong, meaty issue for anyone wanting to investigate the recent development of these characterful composers.

Sinfonia; Sinfonia concertante.
(M) ******* Unicorn Dig. UKCD 2026 [id.]. SCO, composer.

In his *Sinfonia* of 1962 Peter Maxwell Davies took as his inspirational starting point Monteverdi's *Vespers* of 1610. Except perhaps in the simple, grave beauty of the second of the four movements, where the analogy is directly with *Pulchra es* from the *Vespers*, it is not a kinship which will readily strike the listener, but the dedication in this music, beautifully played by the Scottish Chamber Orchestra under the composer, is plain from first to last. The *Sinfonia concertante* of twenty years later, as the title implies, is a much more extrovert piece for strings plus solo wind quintet and timpani. The balance of movements broadly follows a conventional plan, but in idiom this is hardly at all neo-classical, and more than usual the composer evokes romantic images, as in the lovely close of the first movement. Virtuoso playing from the Scottish principals, not least the horn. Well-balanced recording. The CD is offered at mid-price.

Sinfonia accademica; (i) *Into the labyrinth.*
(M) ******* Unicorn UKCD 2022 [id.]. (i) Neil Mackie; SCO, composer.

Into the Labyrinth, in five movements, might be regarded more as a song-symphony than as a cantata. The words by the Orcadian poet (and the composer's regular collaborator), George Mackay Brown, are a prose-poem inspired by the physical impact of Orkney, with the second movement a hymn of praise to fire, wind, earth and water, and the fourth – after a brief orchestral interlude in the third – bringing the centrepiece of the work, comprising almost half the total length, an intense meditation. The fine Scottish tenor, Neil Mackie, gives a superb performance, confirming this as one of Maxwell Davies's most beautiful and moving inspirations. The *Sinfonia accademica* provides a strong and attractive contrast, with its lively, extrovert outer movements and a central slow movement which again evokes the atmosphere of Orkney. Strong, intense performances under the composer, helped by first-rate recording.

(i) *Eight songs for a Mad King;* (ii) *Miss Donnithorne's maggot.*
*** Unicorn Dig. DKPCD 9052 [id.]. (i) Julius Eastman; (ii) Mary Thomas; Fires of London, composer.

Eight songs for a Mad King, first heard in 1969, was a landmark in the composer's career. It was followed five years later by another chillingly explicit depiction of madness,

Miss Donnithorne's maggot, to make this generous coupling particularly pointful. The *Songs for a Mad King* provide the more sharply powerful experience. In this unforgettable piece there are many levels of imagination at work: it is harrowing in its expressionistic venom, playing on hidden nerves; but the power of inspiration, superbly conveyed in this performance with Julius Eastman as soloist and conducted by the composer, comes over vividly. The performance of *Miss Donnithorne*, recorded in 1984, again with the composer conducting the Fires of London, is equally vivid, with Mary Thomas bringing out in her abrasive thrust and intensity the kinship with *Pierrot Lunaire*. Though sharp in expression, this is more diffuse than the *Mad King*, a celebration of the eccentric who provided Dickens with his model for Miss Havisham in *Great Expectations*. The digital recording is both vivid and immediate.

An Orkney wedding with sunrise; Dances from The two fiddlers; Farewell to Stromness; Kinloche, his Fantassie; Jimmack the Postie; Lullabye for Lucy; Renaissance Scottish dances; Seven songs home; Yesnaby ground.
*** Unicorn Dig. DKPCD 9070 [id.]. St Mary's Music School Ch., SCO, composer.

Since he settled on the Island of Hoy in the Orkneys, Sir Peter Maxwell Davies has become an ardent advocate both of Orcadian and – more generally – of Scottish culture. Mainly with the orchestra that is now closely associated with him, but also with an excellent children's choir and in two unpretentious revue pieces as solo pianist, he provides a delightful collection of Scottish inspirations. All of them find him at his most approachable, unafraid of simple diatonic writing with bright tunes. *An Orkney wedding with sunrise* for example is great fun, ending with an obbligato contribution from a genuine Highland piper, George McIlwham. Among the completely original pieces, *Kinloche, his Fantassie* and the seven *Renaissance Scottish dances* exploit Davies's love of giving a modern twist to seventeenth- and eighteenth-century music. The selection is both generous and very well recorded.

Medtner, Nikolai (1880–1951)

Dithyramb, Op. 10/2; Elegy, Op. 59/2; Skazki (Fairy tales): No. 1 (1915); in E min., Op. 14/2; in G, Op. 9/3; in D min. (Ophelia's song); in C sharp min., Op. 35/4. Forgotten melodies, 2nd Cycle, No. 1: Meditation. Primavera, Op. 39/3; 3 Hymns in praise of toil, Op. 49; Piano sonata in E min. (The Night Wind), Op. 25/2; Sonata Triad, Op. 11/1–3.
*** CRD CRD 3338/9 [id.]. Hamish Milne.

Medtner's art is subtle and elusive. He shows an aristocratic disdain for the obvious, a feeling for balance and proportion, and a quiet harmonic refinement that offer consistent rewards. In Hamish Milne's first two-disc set the most substantial piece is the *E minor Sonata (The Night Wind)*, which should dispel any doubts as to Medtner's capacity to sustain an argument on the grandest scale. Milne also includes the less ambitious single-movement sonatas, Op. 11, which are finely concentrated, elegantly fashioned works. There is hardly a weak piece here, and Milne is a poetic advocate whose technical prowess is matched by first-rate artistry. The recording too is very truthful and vivid.

Improvisation No. 2 (in variation form), Op. 47; Piano sonata in F min., Op. 5.
*** CRD Dig. CRD 3461 [id.]. Hamish Milne.

The *F minor Sonata* comes from 1905 yet finds the composer as fully formed in personality as he is masterly in his handling of sonata form. The *Second Improvisation in variation form* is a subtle and original work, and Hamish Milne plays it with the authority that distinguishes all he does.

3 Novelles, Op. 17; Romantic sketches for the young, Op. 54; Piano sonatas in G min., Op. 22; A min., Op. 30; 2 Skazki, Op. 8.
*** CRD Dig. CRD 3460 [id.]. Hamish Milne.

Like Fauré, Medtner is a composer of some subtlety, whose art offers more solid musical satisfaction than instant appeal. But listeners who are prepared to take trouble will find themselves just as rewarded by Hamish Milne's collection here as by the earlier ones. The *G minor Sonata* (1911), which Moiseiwitsch and Gilels recorded, makes a good starting point to discovering him, and there is no better guide than this splendid pianist. Sample *Daphnis and Chloe* (the first of the *Novelles*, Op. 17) or the Op. 30 *Sonata* and you will soon find out how varied and satisfying his world can be. Excellent recording.

Méhul, Étienne-Nicolas (1763–1817)

Symphonies Nos 1–4; Overtures: La chasse de jeune Henri; Le trésor supposé.
*** Nimbus Dig. NI 5184/5 [id.]. Gulbenkian Foundation O, Swierczewski.

Méhul was a contemporary of Cherubini and flourished during the years of Napoleon. He was enormously prolific and wrote no fewer than 25 operas in the period 1790–1810. The four symphonies recorded here come from 1808–10 (Nos. 3 & 4 have been discovered only in recent years by David Charlton, who has edited them) and are well worth investigating. The invention is felicitous and engaging, and in *No. 4 in E major* Méhul brings back a motif of the *Adagio* in the finale, a unifying gesture well ahead of its time. The performances are eminently satisfactory even if the strings sound a shade undernourished.

Mendelssohn, Fanny (1805–47)

Piano trio in D, Op. 11.
*** Hyp. Dig. CDA 66331 [id.]. Dartington Piano Trio – Clara SCHUMANN: *Trio in G min.****

The *Piano trio* is a late work which was not published until 1850, three years after her death. Like Clara Schumann's *G minor Trio* with which it is coupled, it has impeccable craftsmanship and great facility. Its ideas are pleasing, though not strongly individual. The Dartington Piano Trio play most persuasively and give much pleasure. Excellent recording.

Mendelssohn, Felix (1809–47)

Piano concerto No. 1 in G min., Op. 25.
(*) EMI Dig. CDC7 47611-2 [id.]. Ousset, LSO, Marriner – GRIEG: *Concerto.*(*)

Piano concertos Nos. 1 in G min.; 2 in D min., Op. 40.
*** Decca Dig. 414 672-2 [id.]. András Schiff, Bav. RSO, Dutoit.

Piano concertos Nos. 1–2; Capriccio brillant, Op. 22.
**(*) RCA Dig. RD 87988 [79882-RC]. Sergei Edelmann, Bamberg SO, Claus Peter Flor.

(i) *Piano concertos Nos. 1–2;* (ii) *Capriccio brillant, Op. 22; Rondo brillant, Op. 29.*
(B) **(*) Decca 425 504-2 [id.]. Peter Katin; (i) LSO, Collins; (ii) LPO, Martinon.

(i) *Piano concertos Nos. 1–2; Prelude and fugue, Op. 35/1; Rondo capriccioso, Op. 14; Variations sérieuses, Op. 54.*
*** CBS MK 42401 [id.]. Murray Perahia; (i) ASMF, Marriner.

Perahia's playing catches the Mendelssohnian spirit with admirable perception. There is sensibility and sparkle, the slow movements are shaped most beautifully and the partnership with Marriner is very successful, for the Academy give a most sensitive backing. The recording could be more transparent but it does not lack body, and the piano timbre is fully acceptable. Moreover this CBS issue offers three substantial bonuses from Perahia's admirable digital solo recital.

András Schiff plays marvellously, with poetry, great delicacy and fluency, while his virtuosity is effortless. He is given excellent accompaniments by Dutoit and the Bavarian players, and the Decca recording is first class. By the side of the CBS coupling, this is short measure, but the sound is far more realistic.

Katin's early (1955) coupling of the two *Piano concertos* has come up amazingly freshly on CD; the ambient warmth of the recording disguises its age and the piano recording is excellent. Katin has the full measure of these remarkably similar works. His crisp passage-work prevents the outer movements from becoming either brittle or lifeless, and he offers a pleasingly light touch in the finales. In both slow movements his style is sensitive without sentimentality, a feature mirrored in the excellent accompaniments. The two occasional pieces were recorded much later (1971) and are equally accomplished and enjoyable.

Sergei Edelmann is still in his twenties and is an artist of considerable poetic insight. The slow movement of the *G minor* is played with great delicacy of feeling and refinement of colour. He needs more dash in the first movements, which do not match such rivals as Perahia, Schiff or Katin in sheer exuberance and sparkle. By their side, the recording is also inclined to be bottom-heavy and wanting in brilliance, though the Bamberg orchestra under Claus Peter Flor give excellent support.

In the *G minor Concerto* Ousset gives a performance of power rather than of poetry, not always bringing out Mendelssohn's sparkle and charm but in her robust way establishing this as a bigger work than its length suggests. Strong accompaniment, very well recorded. An excellent choice for those who fancy the rare coupling.

(i) *Piano concerto No. 1 in G min., Op. 25;* (ii) *Violin concerto in E min., Op. 64; Symphony No. 4 in A (Italian).*
**(*) Nimbus Dig. NI 5158 [id.]. (i) Kite; (ii) Hudson; Hanover Band, Goodman.

The *G minor concerto* works surprisingly well on a fortepiano and, with the fortepiano not spotlit, presents much more of a contest between solo instrument and orchestra, when the original scale is reproduced. The *Violin concerto* is rather less successful when the relative closeness of the solo violin – played by the leader of the Hanover Band, Benjamin Hudson – exaggerates the cutting edge of the instrument, with little or no vibrato used, and each portamento, however authentic, is obtrusive. Yet, with well-chosen speeds – a really flowing *Andante* in the second movement – there is still much to enjoy. If anything, Goodman's performance of the *Italian symphony*, with string ensemble surprisingly large, is even more sympathetic than Sir Charles Mackerras's earlier period recording for Virgin Classics, when here both speeds and manner are more relaxed, notably in the first two movements.

Violin concerto in E min., Op. 64.

*** Decca Dig. 410 011-2 [id.]. Kyung Wha Chung, Montreal SO, Dutoit – TCHAIKOVSKY: *Concerto.****

*** DG Dig. 400 031-2 [id.]. Mutter, BPO, Karajan – BRUCH: *Concerto No. 1.****

*** CBS Dig. MK 39007 [id.]. Cho-Liang Lin, Philh. O, Tilson Thomas – SAINT-SAENS: *Concerto No. 3.****

*** EMI Dig. CDC7 49663-2 [id.]. Nigel Kennedy, ECO, Tate – BRUCH: *Concerto No. 1*; SCHUBERT: *Rondo.****

(B) *** Ph. 422 473-2 [id.]. Grumiaux, New Philh. O, Krenz – TCHAIKOVSKY: *Concerto.****

(B) *** Pickwick Dig. PCD 829 [MCA MCAD 25934]. Jaime Laredo, SCO – BRUCH: *Concerto No. 1.****

(M) *** EMI CDM7 69003-2 [id.]. Menuhin, Philh. O, Kurtz – BRUCH: *Concerto No. 1.****

(M) *** DG 419 067-2 [id.]. Milstein, VPO, Abbado – TCHAIKOVSKY: *Concerto.****

(M) **(*) Decca 417 793-2 [id.]. Ricci, LSO, Gamba – BRUCH: *Concerto No. 1*; SAINT-SAENS: *Havanaise* etc.***

(*) RCA RD 85933 [RCA 5933-2-RC]. Heifetz, Boston SO, Munch – TCHAIKOVSKY: *Concerto; Sérénade mélancolique* etc.(*)

(M) **(*) CBS CD 42537 [MYK 36724]. Stern, Phd. O, Ormandy – TCHAIKOVSKY: *Concerto.***(*)

(M) (***) EMI mono CDH7 69799-2 [id.]. Yehudi Menuhin, BPO, Furtwängler – BEETHOVEN: *Concerto.*(***)

(B) **(*) EMI CDZ7 62519-2. Menuhin, LSO, Frühbeck de Burgos – BRUCH: *Concerto No. 1.***(*)

(*) Decca Dig. 421 145-2 [id.]. Joshua Bell, ASMF, Marriner – BRUCH: *Concerto No. 1.*(*)

(*) Denon Dig. C37 7123 [id.]. Kantorow, Netherlands CO, Ros-Marba – BRUCH: *Concerto No. 1.*(*)

(M) **(*) Decca 417 687-2 [id.]. Ricci, Netherlands RPO, Fournet – TCHAIKOVSKY: *Concerto.***(*)

(M) **(*) RCA Dig. GD 86536 (RCA 6536-2-RG]. Ughi, LSO, Prêtre – BEETHOVEN: *Concerto.***(*)

(*) DG 419 629-2 [id.]. Shlomo Mintz, Chicago SO, Abbado (also with KREISLER: *Caprice viennoise; Liebeslied; Liebesfreud*) – BRUCH: *Concerto No. 1.**

Chung favours speeds faster than usual in all three movements, and the result is sparkling and happy, with the lovely slow movement fresh and songful, not at all sentimental. With warmly sympathetic accompaniment from Dutoit and the Montreal orchestra, amply recorded, the result is one of Chung's happiest records.

Here even more than in her Bruch coupling, the freshness of Anne-Sophie Mutter's approach communicates vividly to the listener, creating the feeling of hearing the work anew. Her gentleness and radiant simplicity in the *Andante* are very appealing, and the light, sparkling finale is a delight. Mutter is given a small-scale image, projected forward from the orchestral backcloth; the sound is both full and refined.

Cho-Liang Lin's is a vibrant and keenly intelligent performance, breathtaking in its virtuosity, and always musical. Lin also has the benefit of really excellent support from the Philharmonia Orchestra and Michael Tilson Thomas, and excellent CBS engineering.

Kennedy establishes a positive, masculine view of the work from the very start, but fantasy here goes with firm control. The slow movement brings a simple, songful view of the haunting melody, and the finale sparkles winningly, with no feeling of rush. With a bonus in the rare Schubert *Rondo* and clear, warm recording, it makes an excellent recommendation.

Grumiaux's 1973 account of the Mendelssohn is characteristically polished and refined. He plays very beautifully throughout; the pure poetry of his playing is heard at its most magical in the key moment of the downward arpeggio which introduces the second subject of the first movement.

Laredo's version on a bargain-price CD brings an attractively direct reading, fresh and alert but avoiding mannerism, marked by consistently sweet and true tone from the soloist. The orchestral ensemble is amazingly good when you remember that the soloist himself is directing. The recording is vivid and clean.

The restrained nobility of Menuhin's phrasing of the famous principal melody of the slow movement has long been a hallmark of his reading with Efrem Kurtz, who provides polished and sympathetic support. The sound of the CD transfer is bright, with the soloist dominating but the orchestral texture well detailed.

Milstein's version comes from the early 1970s. His is a highly distinguished performance, very well accompanied. His account of the slow movement is more patrician than Menuhin's, and his slight reserve is projected by DG sound which is bright, clean and clear in its CD remastering.

Ricci's earlier performance is clean and sympathetic and technically brilliant. Gamba conducts with vigour and sympathy. Ricci's later recording, with Fournet, in some ways is to be preferred, although it is not so naturally balanced. Both versions are striking for their spontaneity and vivid sound.

As one might expect, Heifetz gives a fabulous performance. His speeds are consistently fast, yet in the slow movement his flexible phrasing sounds so inevitable and easy that it is hard not to be convinced. The finale is a *tour de force*, light and sparkling, with every note in place. The recording has been digitally remastered with success and the sound is smoother than before.

Stern's performance has great bravura, culminating in a marvellously surging account of the finale. The slow movement too is played with great eloquence and feeling, but when pianissimos are non-existent – partly, but not entirely, the fault of the close recording balance – the poetic element is diminished.

Menuhin's unique gift for lyrical sweetness has never been presented on record more seductively than in his classic version of the Mendelssohn concerto with Furtwängler. The digital transfer is not ideally clear, yet one hardly registers that this is a mono recording from the early 1950s.

Menuhin's second stereo recording with Rafael Frühbeck de Burgos has its moments of roughness, but it has magic too: at the appearance of the first movement's second subject and in the slow movement. The recording sounds fuller than the earlier account with Kurtz, and this makes a good bargain on EMI's inexpensive Laser label.

Joshua Bell is given a very forward balance by the Decca engineers; but he can still achieve a genuine *pianissimo* when he wants to, as at the lead in to the first-movement cadenza, which is a moment of magic. Overall, this is a boldly romantic reading, full of warmth and not without poetry; but the spotlight on the soloist all but masks Marriner's fine accompaniment, a distinct drawback.

Jean-Jacques Kantorow gives a fresh, bright account with well-chosen speeds, excellently recorded. The restrained poetry will appeal to those who are not looking for a powerfully individual reading – Kantorow plays with flawlessly pure tone. Understanding, if not inspired, accompaniment.

Ughi's is a fresh, totally unsentimental reading; both the slow movement and the finale are very successful. Ughi lacks only the final individuality of artists like Mutter or Chung; but he is highly musical and has the advantage of an excellent digital recording, clean and well balanced and set against a believable atmosphere.

Mintz's version is powerfully conceived, less reticent than Mutter, less spontaneous than Chung. It is not quite the equal of the Bruch coupling, although Abbado gives fine support, as he does for Milstein. DG have added some *morceaux de concert* of Kreisler, which are most winningly played. The sound is good, but this should now be at mid-price.

Overtures: Athalia, Op. 74; Calm sea and prosperous voyage, Op. 27; The Hebrides (Fingal's Cave), Op. 26; The Marriage of Camacho, Op. 10; A Midsummer Night's Dream, Op. 21; Ruy Blas, Op. 95.
⊛ *** RCA Dig. RD 87905 [7905-2-RC]. Bamberg SO, Flor.

This is the most desirable collection of Mendelssohn overtures the catalogue has ever offered; the evocatively atmospheric opening of *Calm sea and prosperous voyage*, followed by an allegro of great vitality, is a demonstrable example of the spontaneous imagination of these performances, and there is no finer version of *Fingal's Cave*, with its lyrical secondary theme phrased with memorable warmth. *The Marriage of Camacho*, with its brass opening, reminds us somewhat of *Ruy Blas*, and also a little of Weber: it is a most attractive piece with some engaging writing for woodwind. *Athalia* is very enjoyable too, especially when played with such freshness and polish. The recording, made in the Dominikanerbau, Bamberg, has splendid warmth and bloom and a most attractive hall ambience.

Overtures: Calm sea and a prosperous voyage, Op. 27; Fair Melusina, Op. 32; The Hebrides (Fingal's Cave), Op. 21; A Midsummer Night's Dream, Op. 21; Ruy Blas, Op. 95; Trumpet overture, Op. 101; Overture for wind instruments, Op. 24.
*** DG Dig. 423 104-2 [id.]. LSO, Abbado.

Three of these performances were originally released with the symphonies in 1985; the rest are new, recorded in various venues – yet, even on CD, the ear is not troubled by the changing acoustics. Neither the *Overture for wind* (1824) nor the (1826) *Trumpet overture* (more notable for furiously busy strings) are forgotten masterpieces. All the other pieces sound strikingly vivid and spontaneous in Abbado's hands, and the recording, wide in range and always with plenty of ambience, suits the music admirably.

Symphonies for string orchestra Nos. 1 in C; 2 in D; 3 in E min.; 4 in C min.; 5 in B flat; 6 in E flat.
*** Nimbus Dig. NI 5141 [id.]. E. String O, William Boughton.

Symphonies for string orchestra Nos. 7 in D min.; 8 in D; 10 in B min.
*** Nimbus Dig. NI 5142 [id.]. E. String O, William Boughton.

Symphonies for string orchestra Nos. 9 in C; 11 in F; 12 in G min.
*** Nimbus Dig. NI 5143 [id.]. E. String O, William Boughton.

Mendelssohn's twelve *String symphonies*, written for family performance by one of the most brilliant boy-geniuses in the history of music, contain delectable inspirations by the dozen. William Boughton conducts the English String Orchestra in winningly energetic readings of these delightful works, not as polished in ensemble as some rivals, but with warmly atmospheric recording helping to make them very persuasive. The first disc contains the six earliest, all written in 1821; on the second disc, with Nos. 7, 8 and 10, the young composer raises his sights. In No. 7 there are clear signs of a Beethovenian influence in the dramatic sharpness of the argument. The third disc contains Nos. 9, 11 and 12, all products of 1823, when the boy was extending his range still further, the mature Mendelssohn style emerging more and more clearly despite the continuing echoes of Mozart and Haydn.

Symphonies for string orchestra Nos. 4 in C min.; 9 in C; 12 in G.
**(*) Mer. CDE 84131 [id.]. Guildhall String Ens.

The Guildhall group are very accomplished; they play with a lightness and grace that are very appealing. These are warmly spontaneous performances; if their ensemble in the Scherzo of No. 9 could be more sharply precise, the slow movement has an attractive elegiac feeling. The recording, made in the Church of St Edward the Confessor, Mottingham, Kent, is warm and natural, and detail is not clouded.

Symphonies for string orchestra, Nos. 9 in C min.; 10 in B min.; 12 in G min.
*** Hyp. CDA 66196 [id.]. L. Fest. O, Ross Pople.

Ross Pople achieves performances that are as polished and spirited as they are lyrically responsive. No. 9 has a particularly gracious slow movement following the drama of its opening, but No. 12 with its clear debt to Bach is also most impressive. Excellent sound.

Symphonies Nos. 1–5.
(M) *** DG 429 664-2 (3). Mathis, Rebman, Hollweg, German Op. Ch., BPO, Karajan.

Symphonies Nos. 1–5; Overtures: Calm sea and prosperous voyage; The Hebrides (Fingal's Cave).
(M) *** Decca 421 769-2 (3) [id.]. Soloists, V. State Op. Ch., VPO, Dohnányi.

Symphonies Nos. 1–5; Overtures: Fair Melusina, Op. 32; The Hebrides (Fingal's Cave), Op. 26; A Midsummer Night's Dream, Op. 21; Octet, Op. 20: Scherzo.
*** DG Dig. 415 353-2 (4) [id.]. LSO, Abbado (with Connell, Mattila, Blochwitz and LSO Ch. in *Symphony No. 2*).

Abbado's is a set to brush cobwebs off an attractive symphonic corner; in the lesser-known symphonies it is his gift to have you forgetting any weaknesses of structure or thematic invention in the brightness and directness of his manner. Instead of overloading this music with sweetness and sentiment, as the Victorians came to do, he presents it more as it must have appeared at the very beginning, when on good evidence the composer himself was known to favour brisk, light allegros and crisp rhythms. So the youthful *First* has plenty of C minor bite. The toughness of the piece makes one marvel that Mendelssohn ever substituted the scherzo from the *Octet* for the third movement (as he did in London), but helpfully Abbado includes that extra scherzo, so that on CD, with a programming device, you can readily make the substitution yourself. Good, bright recording, though not ideally transparent.

Karajan's distinguished set of the Mendelssohn *Symphonies* was recorded in 1971/2 and, like other DG recordings made at that period in the Berlin Jesus-Christus-Kirche, it has been successfully remastered for CD. The early C minor work sounds particularly fresh, and the *Hymn of Praise* brings the fullest sound of all; the very fine choral singing is vividly caught. The soloists make a good team, rather than showing any memorable individuality; but overall Karajan's performance is most satisfying. The *Scottish symphony* is a particularly remarkable account and the *Italian* shows the Berlin Philharmonic in sparkling form: the only drawback is Karajan's characteristic omission of both first-movement exposition repeats. The recording is brightly lit but not shrill. There are some reservations to be made about the *Reformation symphony*, but the sound has been effectively clarified without too much loss of weight. This makes a good mid-priced alternative to Abbado and occupies only three discs.

Dohnányi's economically priced Decca set (which includes also two key overtures) brings performances which are fresh and direct, often relying on faster and more flowing speeds than Abbado's, more clearly rebutting any idea that this music might be sentimental. The most striking contrast comes in the *Hymn of Praise*, where Dohnányi's speeds are often so much faster than Abbado's that the whole character of the music is changed, as in the second-movement scherzo, sharp in one, gently persuasive in the other. Many will prefer Dohnányi in that, particularly when the choral sound is brighter and more immediate too. The Decca engineers produced recording which was among the finest of its period and which still sounds well. The snag of the set is that Dohnányi, unlike Abbado, omits exposition repeats, which in the *Italian symphony* means the loss of the substantial lead-back passage in the first movement.

Symphonies Nos. 1 in C min., Op. 11; 5 in D (Reformation), Op. 107.
**(*) Teldec/WEA Dig. 2292 44933-2 [id.]. Leipzig GO, Kurt Masur.

Masur's mastery in Mendelssohn is due in good measure to his ability to adopt a relatively fast speed and make it sound easy and relaxed, not hurried and breathless. Mendelssohn himself, when conductor of this great Leipzig orchestra, is reported to have taken such a course in his own performances, and in all the movements of both symphonies Masur is consistently swifter than his principal rivals on record. It affects not only fast movements but slow, so that the *Andante* of No. 1 flows with winning ease and no suspicion of sentimentality, more affectionate than at a slower speed. As recorded, the Leipzig sound is on the heavy side for No. 1, with some clouding of tuttis, but when separate discs of No. 1 are rare, this is a welcome issue, part of Masur's latest Mendelssohn cycle. It is a pity that, unlike Abbado for example, he does not add the arrangement of the scherzo from the *Octet* that Mendelssohn used as an alternative third movement in No. 1.

Symphony No. 2 in B flat (Hymn of Praise), Op. 52.
*** DG Dig. 423 143-2 [id.]. Connell, Mattila, Blochwitz, LSO Ch., LSO, Abbado.

Abbado's view of the *Second*, brushing aside all sentimentality, is both fresh and sympathetic, and though the recording is not ideally clear on inner detail the brightness reinforces the conductor's view. The chorus, well focused, is particularly impressive, and the operatic flavour of some of the solo work comes over well, notably *Watchman, what of the night?* The sweet-toned tenor, Hans-Peter Blochwitz, is outstanding among the soloists, and Elizabeth Connell brings weight as well as purity to the main soprano part.

Symphony No. 3 (Scottish); (i) Die erste Walpurgisnacht.
**(*) Telarc Dig. CD 80184 [id.]. (i) Cairns, Garrison, Krause, Cleveland Ch.; Cleveland O, Dohnányi.

Symphony No. 3 in A min. (Scottish); Overture: The Hebrides (Fingal's Cave).
(M) *** DG 419 477-2 [id.]. BPO, Karajan.

Symphonies Nos. 3 in A min. (Scottish), Op. 56; 4 in A (Italian), Op. 90.
(M) *** DG Dig. 427 810-2 [id.]. LSO, Abbado.
(M) *** EMI CDM7 69660-2 [id.]. New Philh. O, Muti.
**(*) Teldec/WEA Dig. 2292 43463-2 [id.]. Leipzig GO, Masur.
(M) *** Decca 425 011-2 [id.]. LSO, Abbado.
(B) *** ASV CDQS 6004 [id.]. O of St John's, Lubbock.

(B) **(*) CfP CD-CFP 4565. SNO Gibson; LPO, Lockhart.
** DG Dig.427 670-2 [id.]. BPO, Levine.
** Argo 411 931-2 [id.]. ASMF, Marriner.

Symphonies Nos. 3 (Scottish); 4 (Italian); Overture: The Hebrides (Fingal's Cave).
(M) **(*) Decca 417 731-2 [id.]. VPO, Dohnányi.

Symphonies Nos. 3 (Scottish); 4 (Italian); Octet in E flat, Op. 20: Scherzo.
** ASV Dig. CDDCA 700. SCO, Serebrier.

Symphonies Nos. 3 in A min. (Scottish); 5 in D (Reformation).
(M) *** Ph. 420 884-2 [id.]. LPO, Haitink.

Karajan's account of the *Scottish* is very fine indeed. The orchestral playing is superb – the pianissimo articulation of the strings is a pleasure in itself and the conductor's warmth and direct eloquence, with no fussiness, are irresistible. The scherzo is marvellously done and becomes a highlight, while there is no doubt that Karajan's final coda has splendid buoyancy and power. However, the coupling is ungenerous.

In his more recent recording for Telarc, Dohnányi conducts the Cleveland Orchestra in a fresh, taut performance of the *Scottish*, at generally brisker speeds in all four movements than in his earlier, Vienna version for Decca. The disc is chiefly important for the coupling, the rare dramatic cantata, *Die erste Walpurgisnacht*. With plenty of vigorous if not highly original choral writing, it makes a very enjoyable piece in a performance as red-blooded as this. Not only the orchestra but the Cleveland Orchestra Chorus are superb: bright, fresh and crisply disciplined. The snag is the solo singing, which is undistinguished.

Haitink's Philips recording of the *Scottish symphony* has been attractively remastered, the upper strings glowingly fresh and woodwind rich and luminous. The combination of excitement and lyrical power makes this a memorable account, in spite of the omission of the first movement's exposition repeat. The final peroration sounds magnificent. Now linked to an almost equally fine version of the *Reformation symphony*, with the rich Concertgebouw acoustics especially effective in bringing out the rich brass writing, this makes a good mid-priced recommendation.

Abbado's fine digital recordings of the *Scottish* and *Italian symphonies*, taken from his complete set, now reappear, coupled together, to make a splendid mid-price bargain. The recording is admirably fresh and bright – atmospheric, too – and the ambience, if not absolutely sharply defined, is very attractive. Both first-movement exposition repeats are included. Allegros are exhilarating, but clean articulation means that the pace never seems forced and Abbado judges the espressivo with his usual combination of warmth and refinement.

Like Abbado, Muti observes the exposition repeats and the remastered sound is fresh and clear, yet warm too. Muti's is a smiling performance of the *Scottish* but one which, with its wide dynamic range, also gives Mendelssohn his due weight, with whooping horns giving an exhilarating lift to the final coda. The account of the *Italian symphony* is comparably glowing and fresh. He takes a strikingly uninhibited, even wild approach to the tarantella (*Saltarello*) finale which adds to the feeling of zest and excitement. The CD transfer is outstandingly successful, and this is every bit as attractive as Abbado's disc, and perhaps even more exhilarating.

Masur also observes exposition repeats in both symphonies, and his choice of speeds brings out the freshness of inspiration judiciously, avoiding any suspicion of sentimentality in slow movements, which are taken at flowing tempi. Conversely, the allegros are never hectic to the point of breathlessness. The one snag is that the reverberant Leipzig recording tends to obscure detail in tuttis; the scherzo of the *Scottish*, for example, becomes a blur, losing some of its point and charm. Otherwise, the sound of the orchestra has all the characteristic Leipzig bloom and beauty.

Abbado's outstanding 1968 Decca coupling with the LSO has now reappeared on Decca's Ovation label. His *Scottish* is beautifully played and the LSO responds to his direction with the greatest delicacy of feeling, while the *Italian symphony* has a comparable lightness of touch, matched with lyrical warmth. The vintage 1968 Kingsway Hall recording is freshly detailed yet full, with glowing wind colour, and is in some ways preferable to the DG sound; however, the absence of the first-movement exposition repeat in the *Scottish symphony* (though not in the *Italian*) is a drawback.

Lubbock's coupling of the *Scottish* and *Italian symphonies* makes another outstanding bargain issue, offering performances of delightful lightness and point, warmly and cleanly recorded. The string section may be of chamber size but, amplified by a warm acoustic, the result sparkles, with rhythms exhilaratingly lifted. The slow movements are both on the slow side but flow easily with no suspicion of sentimentality, while the *Saltarello* finale of No. 4, with the flute part delectably pointed, comes close to Mendelssohnian fairy music.

Dohnányi's mid-priced Decca reissue (part digital, part analogue) also includes a rather slow and romantic account of *The Hebrides*. It is a refreshing account of the *Italian*, never pushed too hard, though the *Saltarello* is taken exhilaratingly fast; it is a pity that the first-movement exposition repeat is omitted. The *Scottish* too is fresh and alert, and the weighty recording helps to underline the stormy quality that Dohnányi aptly finds in the first movement, although in other movements this is a rather less characterful account.

In the bargain range, the CfP coupling might also be considered. It is appropriate to have the *Scottish* actually recorded in Scotland, and Gibson and his orchestra are on top form and they play the piece with warmth and eloquence, although the first-movement exposition repeat is omitted. The string phrasing is strikingly fresh and, among the wind soloists, the clarinets distinguish themselves. The reading is agreeably relaxed, yet has plenty of vitality when called for, and the recording is full within a natural perspective. James Lockhart's account of the *Italian* is also well played; however, the music is less strongly characterized here and the two central movements are a little bland. Nevertheless this is enjoyable enough and the first-movement exposition repeat is observed.

Levine's version brings characteristically polished playing from the Berlin Philharmonic, with fine detail of expression and texture brought out in rather close-up recording which lacks something in bloom on the violins. Levine's speeds are unexceptionable, generally close to those of his DG rival, Abbado. Fine as Levine's performances are, Abbado's have more Mendelssohnian magic, with warmer, fuller digital sound, though there is still a strong case for preferring Muti's very individual New Philharmonia performances to either.

In Marriner's Argo performance, the *Adagio* of the *Scottish* is so spacious that the middle section grows heavy. The *Italian* is given without the exposition repeat. The performances are stylish and well sprung but have no special individuality. The use of a smaller-scale ensemble brings a crisper, more transparent effect than usual.

Serebrier conducts the SCO in fresh, uncomplicated readings of both symphonies, generally adopting brisk speeds but ending the *Scottish* with a disappointingly heavy account of the 6/8 epilogue. He fails to observe the exposition repeat in the *Scottish*, but adds an agreeable extra in the *Scherzo* from the *Octet* in its orchestral arrangement. In close-up sound, some minor imperfections of ensemble are exposed.

Symphony No. 4 in A (Italian), Op. 90.
*** DG Dig. 410 862-2 [id.]. Philh. O, Sinopoli – SCHUBERT: *Symphony No. 8.**** ✿

(M) *** DG 415 848-2 [id.]. BPO, Karajan – SCHUBERT: *Symphony No. 8.****

(B) *** DG 429 158-2 [id.]. BPO, Karajan – SCHUMANN: *Symphony No. 1.****

(M) (***) EMI mono CDM7 63398-2 [id.]. RPO, Beecham – BEETHOVEN: *Symphony No. 8*; SCHUBERT: *Symphony No. 8.*

Symphony No. 4 (Italian); Overtures: Fair Melusina, Op. 32; The Hebrides (Fingal's Cave), Op. 26; Son and stranger (Die Heimkehr aus der Fremde), Op. 89.

(B) *** Pickwick Dig. PCD 824 [MCA MCAD 25849]. Berne SO, Peter Maag.

Symphony No. 4 in A (Italian); A Midsummer Night's Dream: Overture, Op. 21, & orchestral incidental music, Op. 61.

*** Virgin Dig. VC 790725-2 [id.]. O of Age of Enlightenment, Mackerras.

Symphony No. 4 (Italian); A Midsummer Night's Dream: Overture, Op. 21; Incidental music, Op. 61: Scherzo; Nocturne; Wedding march.

(M) ** Ph. 420 653-2 [id.]. Boston SO, C. Davis.

Symphonies Nos. 4 (Italian); 5 (Reformation), Op. 107.

(B) ** Ph. 422 470-2 [id.]. New Philh. O, Sawallisch.

Peter Maag, making a welcome return to the recording studio with his Berne orchestra, here offers a winningly relaxed performance of the *Italian symphony* (including exposition repeat), plus an attractive group of overtures, which once more confirms him as a supreme Mendelssohnian. With fine ensemble from the Berne Symphony Orchestra – only marginally let down at times by the strings – the forward thrust is more compelling than with the taut, unyielding approach too often favoured today. *The Hebrides* receives a spacious reading and the two rarer overtures are a delight too, particularly *Son and stranger*, which in Maag's hands conveys radiant happiness. At bargain price, with full and brilliant recording, it is first rate.

Sinopoli's great gift is to illuminate almost every phrase afresh. His speeds tend to be extreme – fast in the first movement but with diamond-bright detail, and on the slow side in the remaining three. Only in the heavily inflected account of the third movement is the result at all mannered but, with superb playing from the Philharmonia and excellent Kingsway Hall recording, this rapt performance is most compelling. For refinement of detail, especially at lower dynamic levels, the CD is among the most impressive digital recordings to have come from DG.

Mackerras directs fresh, resilient, 'authentic'-style performances of both the *Symphony* and the *Midsummer Night's Dream* music. The middle two movements of the *Symphony* are marginally faster than usual but gain in elegance and transparency, beautifully played here, as is the *Midsummer Night's Dream* music. It is particularly good to have an ophicleide instead of a tuba for Bottom's music in the *Overture*, and the boxwood flute in the *Scherzo* is a delight.

Karajan's performance of the *Italian* is superbly polished and well paced. The reading is straighter than usual, notably in the third movement, though the effect of Karajan's slower pace is warm, never bland. The recording is very brightly lit in its remastered transfer and has lost some of its depth. The coupling with Schubert at mid-price.

In all four movements of the *Italian* Beecham adopts speeds slower than usual, but only in the third-movement Minuet does that make for even a hint of sluggishness. In the rest – notably the outer movements, which at Beecham's speeds can be given the rhythmic lift and pointing they cry out for – he could not be more persuasive. Though the RPO strings were not at their sweetest in 1952, this makes a most cherishable issue in the Beecham Edition, generously coupled with the Beethoven and Schubert.

Sir Colin Davis provides an exhilarating but never breathless account of the *Italian symphony* (complete with exposition repeat), coupled with the four most important items from the *Midsummer Night's Dream* music. There have been more delicate readings of the *Midsummer Night's Dream* pieces, but the ripeness of the Boston playing is most persuasive. The freshened 1976 recording offers a full yet lively orchestral balance.

Sawallisch's comparatively reticent Mendelssohnian style suits these two fine works. A fast tempo in the first movement of the *Italian* does not sound breathless, and Sawallisch's observance of the exposition repeat is to be welcomed. The *Reformation symphony* is also a work that gains from not being over-inflated. Good, clear recording.

(i) *Symphony No. 4 (Italian);* (ii) *A Midsummer Night's Dream: Overture, Op. 21; Incidental music, Op. 61: Fairy march; Wedding march; Intermezzo; Nocturne; Dance of the Clowns; Scherzo.*
(BB) *** LaserLight Dig. 15 526 [id.]. (i) Philh. O, János Sándor; (ii) Budapest PO, Kovacs.

A first-class coupling in the super-bargain range. Sándor gives a fresh and exhilarating account of the *Italian symphony*, with particularly elegant Philharmonia playing in his warm and nicely paced account of the *Andante*. Outer movements sparkle without being rushed, articulation is light and clean, and the digital sound is excellent. The performance of a generous selection from the *Midsummer Night's Dream* incidental music also shows the Budapest orchestra on top form: this is most beguiling and is recorded in a pleasingly warm acoustic which does not cloud detail.

Symphony No. 5 in D (Reformation), Op. 107.
(M) **(*) DG 419 870-2 [id.]. BPO, Karajan – SCHUMANN: *Symphony No. 3.****

Karajan's performance of the *Reformation symphony*, though outstandingly well played, is just a shade wanting in spontaneity and sparkle. The remastered recording has also lost some of the analogue bloom, and in the finale the famous chorale, *Ein' feste Burg*, has the brass less rounded than on the original LP. Karajan is at his most persuasive in the *Andante*, however, and this is still a thoroughly worthwhile coupling.

CHAMBER AND INSTRUMENTAL MUSIC

Octet in E flat, Op. 20.
(M) **(*) Decca 421 093-2 [id.]. Vienna Octet (members) – BEETHOVEN: *Septet.****
(B) **(*) Decca 421 637-2. ASMF – BOCCHERINI: *Cello quintet.***(*)

Octet in E flat, Op. 20; Symphonies for string orchestra Nos. 6 in E flat; 10 in B min.
*** Denon Dig. CO 73185 [id.]. I Solisti Italiani.

Octet in E flat, Op. 20; String quintet No. 1 in A, Op. 18.
*** EMI Dig. CDC7 49958-2. Hausmusik.

Octet in E flat, Op. 20; String quintet No. 2 in B flat, Op. 87.
*** Ph. 420 400-2 [id.]. ASMF Chamber Ens.

This Philips successor comes from just over a decade after the Academy's earlier record of Mendelssohn's *Octet* and the playing has greater sparkle and polish. The recorded sound is also superior and sounds extremely well in its CD format. The *Second Quintet* is an underrated piece and it too receives an elegant and poetic performance that will give much satisfaction.

Using period instruments, the British-based group, Hausmusik, gives a most refreshing performance of the *Octet* and couples it with another miraculous masterpiece of Mendelssohn's boyhood. The period performance gives extra weight to the lower lines compared with the violins, with the extra clarity intensifying the joyfulness of the inspiration. Most revealing of all is the way that the last two movements of the *Octet*, the feather-light Scherzo and the dashing finale, with their similar figuration, are presented in contrast, the one slower and more delicately pointed than usual, the other more exhilarating at high speed.

I Solisti Italiani are none other than the old Virtuosi di Roma, and they play with all the finesse and grace you would expect from them. The *Octet* is delightful and could be a first choice, were the acoustic not quite so resonant. The two early *Symphonies* are given with not only elegance but also a conviction that is very persuasive indeed.

The 1973 Vienna version of the *Octet* is highly competitive at mid-price, coupled with an equally attractive account of Beethoven's *Septet*. The playing is polished and spontaneous and the recording has re-emerged freshly in its CD format, although the upper register of the strings is not quite as cleanly focused as the Beethoven coupling.

The 1968 (originally Argo) performance by the ASMF is fresh and buoyant, and the recording wears its years fairly lightly. It offered fine judgement in matters of clarity and sonority, and the digital remastering has not lost the original ambient bloom, although the violin timbre now has noticeable thinness. A good bargain version.

Piano trio No. 1 in D min., Op. 49.
(*) Ph. Dig. 416 297-2 [id.]. Beaux Arts Trio – DVORÁK: *Piano trio No. 4.*(*)

Piano trios Nos. 1 in D min., Op. 49; 2 in C min., Op. 66.
**(*) Chan. Dig. CHAN 8404 [id.]. Borodin Trio.
**(*) Teldec/WEA Dig. 2292 44947-2. Trio Fontenay.

The latest Beaux Arts performance essays a rather larger scale than its predecessor but is slightly less spontaneous, particularly in the simple slow movement which has an attractive Mendelssohnian innocence, not entirely captured here. The first movement is emphatic in its drama and the effect can be rather over-forceful. The recording is appropriately full-bodied and present.

The Borodin Trio are recorded in a very resonant acoustic and are rather forwardly balanced. They give superbly committed but somewhat overpointed readings. All the same, there is much musical pleasure to be found here.

The Trio Fontenay are rather brightly recorded and they play with passionate commitment and great virility. Their performances are bigger-boned and more robust than some rivals, and they indulge in some slight (and mostly – though not always – undisturbing) expressive vehemence. Greater delicacy from the pianist in the scherzo movement of the *D minor trio* would have been welcome. Undoubtedly powerful and keenly alive though both performances are, they do not communicate much charm.

String quartets: Nos. 1 in E flat, Op. 12; 2 in A min., Op. 13; 3–5, Op. 44/1–3; 6 in F min., Op. 80; 4 Movements, Op. 81.
(M) ** DG 415 883-2 (3) [id.]. Melos Qt.

The present set has both the merit of completeness and the advantage of good engineering. However, the performances succumb to the temptation to play far too quickly. There is more to these quartets than this brilliant ensemble finds; but, in the absence of any alternatives, this set is acceptable enough. It has been freshly remastered.

String quartet No. 1 in E flat, Op. 12.
*** Ph. 420 396-2 [id.]. Orlando Qt – DVOŘÁK: *String quartet No. 12.****

The Orlando performance of Mendelssohn's *E flat Quartet* is one of the very best ever put on record. It is played with lightness of touch, delicacy of feeling and excellent ensemble. The original analogue recording was totally natural and lifelike; the CD transfer has added a touch of glare on the first violin, and the effect is almost too present. However, it responds to the controls and we see no reason to withhold a strong recommendation.

String quartet No. 2 in A min., Op. 13.
* Teldec/WEA 2292 44187-2 [id.]. Vermeer Qt – DVOŘÁK: *Quartet No. 12.**

The Vermeer give a strong, slightly chromium-plated account of the *A minor Quartet*, an impression partly due to the cramped acoustic environment they inhabit and the forward microphone placing. Mendelssohn appears as more Beethovenian in their hands, which may be no bad thing, but there is little sense of joy in their playing.

String quartets Nos. 3 in D, 5 in E flat, Op. 44/1 & 3.
** Pearl SHECD 9603 [id.]. Roth Qt.

In the Pearl recording, the Roth are rather on top of one, though not excessively so. In the first movement of the *D major* they are very alert and vital (occasionally a trifle aggressive), but there is plenty of sensitivity in the charming slow movement. The playing, though a bit rough and ready, still gives pleasure.

Violin sonatas: in F min., Op. 4; in F (1838).
*** DG Dig. 419 244-2 [id.]. Shlomo Mintz, Paul Ostrovsky.

Mendelssohn was only fourteen when he composed the *F minor Sonata*, but even so it is not wanting in individuality and is much more than a youthful exercise. The 1838 *Sonata* comes from Mendelssohn's productive Leipzig period. The performances are beyond reproach; the playing of both artists is a model of sensitivity and intelligence, and the recording is absolutely first class. Strongly recommended.

PIANO MUSIC

Andante and rondo capriccioso in E min., Op. 14; Prelude and fugue in E minor/major, Op. 35/1; Sonata in E, Op. 6; Variations sérieuses in D min., Op. 53.
*** CBS Dig. MK 37838 [id.]. Murray Perahia.

Perahia is perfectly attuned to Mendelssohn's sensibility and it would be difficult to imagine these performances being surpassed. In Perahia's hands, the *Variations sérieuses* have tenderness yet tremendous strength, and neither the popular *Rondo capriccioso* nor the *Prelude and fugue* have sounded more fresh or committed on record. The quality of the CBS recording is very good indeed.

Étude in F min.; Preludes & 3 Études, Op. 104; 6 Preludes & fugues, Op. 35; Prelude & fugue in E min.
**(*) Nimbus NI 5071 [id.]. Martin Jones.

Fantasy in F sharp min., Op. 28; 3 Fantaisies et caprices, Op. 16; Fantasy on 'The last rose of summer', Op. 15; Variations: in E flat, Op. 82; in B flat, Op. 83; Variations sérieuses in D min., Op. 53.
**(*) Nimbus NI 5072 [id.]. Martin Jones.

Sonatas: in E, Op. 6; in G min., Op. 105; in B flat, Op. 106; Kinderstücke, Op. 72.
**(*) Nimbus NI 5070]id.]. Martin Jones.

In his collection of Mendelssohn piano music, Martin Jones provides a fascinating slant on the composer, particularly his youthful inspirations. In many ways the disc of sonatas – all three written when he was in his teens – is the most interesting of all, reflecting Mendelssohn's devotion to Beethoven and his sonatas. The *Preludes and fugues* inevitably reflect his even deeper devotion to Bach, then still under-appreciated. Their style is positive and consistent, with sweet Mendelssohnian lyricism as well as dashing bravura marking the *Preludes*, and even the *Fugues* bringing far more than Bachian echoes. The sets of variations on the third disc were mostly written later in his career, examples of his high skill and love of the keyboard, rather than works of genius. Martin Jones is an excellent advocate, playing dedicatedly and persuasively but without mannerism. The recordings, made in the 1970s, come up very well in the CD transfers, with the atmosphere of a small hall realistically conveyed.

Fantasia in F sharp min. (Sonata écossaise), Op. 28; 3 Fantaisies et caprices, Op. 16; Rondo capriccioso in E, Op. 14; Sonata in E, Op. 6.
**(*) Chan. CHAN 8326 [id.]. Lydia Artymiw.

Lydia Artymiw is highly persuasive in the *Sonata*, as she is in the other, by no means inconsequential works. This is an altogether excellent disc, very well recorded – although it must be said that, fine though Miss Artymiw's playing is, she does not match Perahia in quality of imagination or subtlety of dynamic gradation.

Scherzo from A Midsummer Night's Dream, Op. 61 (trans. Rachmaninov).
*** Hyp. CDA 66009 [id.]. Howard Shelley – RACHMANINOV: *Variations* etc.***

Howard Shelley, with fabulously clear articulation and delectably sprung rhythms, gives a performance of which Rachmaninov himself would not have been ashamed. This is a delightful makeweight for an outstanding disc of Rachmaninov variations.

Songs without words, Books 1–8 (complete).
**(*) Hyp. Dig. CDA 66221/2 [id.]. Livia Rev.

Songs without words, Books 1–8 (complete); *Albumblatt, Op. 117; Gondellied; ·Kinderstücke, Op. 72; 2 Klavierstücke.*
(M) *** DG 423 931-2 (2) [id.]. Daniel Barenboim (piano).

Songs without words, Op. 19/1; Op. 30/6; Op. 38/6; Op. 62/1 and 6; Spring song, Op. 62/6; Spinning song, Op. 67/4; Op. 67/5; Op. 102/6.
*** DG 415 118-2 [id.]. Daniel Barenboim – LISZT: *Liebesträume***; SCHUBERT: Moments musicaux.**

This 1974 set of Mendelssohn's complete *Songs without words*, which Barenboim plays with such affectionate finesse, has dominated the catalogue for a decade and a half. For the mid-priced CD reissue, the six *Kinderstücke* (sometimes known as *Christmas pieces*) have been added, plus other music, so that the second of the two CDs plays for 73 minutes. The sound is first class. A selection of favourites is also available, coupled with Liszt and Schubert, but this is still at full price.

Livia Rev is a thoughtful, sensitive and aristocratic artist. Her survey of the *Songs without words* has charm and warmth, and she includes a hitherto unpublished piece. The set is handsomely presented and the recording is warm and pleasing; it is, however, somewhat bottom-heavy. Yet the slightly diffuse effect suits the style of the playing, and this can be recommended.

Songs without words: Op. 19/1, 2, 4, 5 & 6 (Venetian gondola song); Op. 30/3, 4, 5 & 6 (Venetian gondola song); Op. 38/1, 2 & 6; Op. 53/1, 2 & 3; Op. 62/1 & 6 (Spring song); Op. 67/4 (Spinning song) & 6; Op. 85/6; Op. 102/3 & 5.
**(*) Decca Dig. 421 119-2 [id.]. András Schiff.

András Schiff plays the *Songs without words* simply, coolly and directly, his style straighter than Livia Rev's. The famous *Spring song* shows him at his finest. This is his penultimate item and he ends the recital neatly with the engaging Op. 102, No. 3. The recording is most natural and realistic.

ORGAN MUSIC

Organ sonatas Nos. 2 in C min.; 3 in A; 6 in D min., Op. 65/1–6. Preludes & fugues: in C min.; in G; in D min., Op. 37/1–3.
⊛ *** Argo Dig. 414 420-2 [id.]. Peter Hurford (organ of Ratzeburg Cathedral).

Hurford's performances of Mendelssohn bring the same freshness of approach which made his Bach series so memorable. Throughout the recital the throaty reeds of the characterful Ratzeburg organ prevent any possible hint of blandness, yet in the *Andantes* – essentially songs without words for organ – the registration has engaging charm. The recording is superb, as the majestic opening of the *Third Sonata* immediately demonstrates, with the CD giving marvellous presence.

VOCAL MUSIC

Elijah (oratorio), *Op. 70.*
*** Chan. Dig. CHAN 8774/5 [id.]. White, Plowright, Finnie, A. Davies, LSO Ch., LSO, Hickox.

Richard Hickox with his London Symphony Chorus and the LSO secures a performance that both pays tribute to the English choral tradition in this work and presents it dramatically as a kind of religious opera. Though in Victorian times this was an oratorio which was notoriously treated as sentimental, Hickox shows what fresh inspiration it contains, what a wealth of memorable ideas, treated imaginatively, as for example in the way that numbers merge one into the next, with dramatic emphasis given· to each incident in the story of the prophet. The choice of soloists reflects that approach. Willard White may not be ideally steady in his delivery, sometimes attacking notes from below, but he sings consistently with fervour, from his dramatic introduction to the overture onwards. Rosalind Plowright and Arthur Davies combine purity of tone with operatic expressiveness, and Linda Finnie, while not matching the example of Dame Janet Baker in the classic EMI recording, sings with comparable dedication and directness in the solo, *O rest in the Lord*. The chorus fearlessly underlines the high contrasts of dynamic demanded in the score. The Chandos recording, full and immediate yet atmospheric too, enhances the drama. The old EMI set should by rights be reissued on CD; even when it is, the modern digital sound as well as the performance here will make this a keen contender.

A Midsummer Night's Dream: Overture, Op. 21; Incidental music, Op. 61.
*** RCA Dig. RD 87764 [7764-2-RC]. Popp, Lipovšek, Bamberg Ch. & SO, Flor.
*** EMI CDC7 47163-2 [id.]. Watson, Wallis, Finchley Children's Music Group, LSO, Previn.

(M) *** EMI Dig. CD-EMX 2132 [Ang. CDM 62039]. Wiens, Walker, LPO Ch. & O, Litton.

**(*) Ph. 411 106-2 [id.]. Augér, Murray, Amb. S., Philh. O, Marriner.

(M) *** DG 415 840-2 [id.]. Mathis, Boese, Bav. R. Ch. & SO, Kubelik – WEBER: *Overtures: Oberon; Der Freischütz.* ***

(BB) **(*) Hung. White Label Dig. HRC 049 [id.]. Kalmar, Bokor, Jeunesses Musicales Girls' Ch., Hungarian State O, Adam Fischer.

A Midsummer Night's Dream: Overture; Scherzo; Intermezzo; Nocturne; Wedding march. Overtures: Fair Melusina, Op. 32; The Hebrides (Fingal's Cave), Op. 26; Ruy Blas, Op. 95.
**(*) Decca Dig. 417 541-2 [id.]. Montreal SO, Dutoit.

Claus Peter Flor's account omits the little melodramas, which is a pity; but for those who require the major items only, this beautiful RCA CD could well be a first choice. Recorded in the warmly resonant acoustics of the Dominikanerbau, Bamberg, the orchestra is given glowingly radiant textures; but Flor's stylish yet relaxed control brings the kind of intimacy one expects from a chamber group. The very opening of the *Overture*, with its soft flute timbre and diaphanous violins, is agreeably evocative and, later, the *Wedding march*, played with much vigour and *élan*, expands splendidly. The lightly rhythmic *Scherzo*, taken not too fast, is another highlight; and Lucia Popp's vocal contribution is delightful, especially when she blends her voice so naturally with that of Marjana Lipovšek in *Ye spotted snakes*.

On EMI, Previn offers a wonderfully refreshing account of the complete score; the veiled pianissimo of the violins at the beginning of the *Overture* and the delicious woodwind detail in the *Scherzo* certainly bring Mendelssohn's fairies into the orchestra. Even the little melodramas which come between the main items sound spontaneous here, and the contribution of the soloists and chorus is first class. The *Nocturne* (taken slowly) is serenely romantic and the *Wedding march* resplendent. The recording is naturally balanced and has much refinement of detail. The CD brings the usual enhancement, with the fairy music in the *Overture* given a most delicate presence.

Andrew Litton also includes the melodramas and, like Previn, he uses them most effectively as links, making them seem an essential part of the structure. He too has very good soloists; in the *Overture* and *Scherzo* he displays an engagingly light touch, securing very fine wind and string playing from the LPO. The wide dynamic range of the recording brings an element of drama to offset the fairy music. Both the *Nocturne*, with a fine horn solo, and the temperamental *Intermezzo* are good examples of the spontaneity of feeling that permeates this performance throughout and makes this disc a bargain.

Marriner omits the inconsequential melodramas which separate the main items. The *Overture*, taken briskly, brings the most delicate articulation from the strings; the *Scherzo* too is engagingly infectious, and there is a complementary sense of joy and sparkle from soloists and chorus alike. The *Nocturne* is rather broadly romantic, yet the *Wedding march* sounds resplendent when the quality is so vivid. There is a brief cut at the end of the *Intermezzo* but, this apart, the Philips recording, warm as well as refined in detail, has much to recommend it.

The Hungaroton CD offers much lovely playing, and fine singing from the soloists too, although many will count it a disadvantage that the vocal numbers are sung in German. While the soft focus is attractively atmospheric, the resonant acoustic has to some extent subdued the sound, although the digital recording is full and natural. There is fine, delicate articulation from the woodwind and strings in the *Scherzo*; but the hint of vibrato on the horn solo of the *Nocturne* will not please all ears, although the playing is very responsive. Fischer includes the more important melodramas but omits Nos. 2, 4, 6 and 10. On Hungaroton's super-bargain White Label, this is very competitive.

Among reissues, that by the Bavarian Radio Orchestra takes pride of place. The playing and 1965 recording are strikingly fresh. Although Kubelik omits the melodramas, this makes room for an appropriate coupling of the two finest Weber overtures (both also associated with magic) and *Oberon* drawing an obvious parallel with Mendelssohn. They are marvellously played.

The acoustics of Saint-Eustache in Montreal are ideal for the music, giving a wonderful bloom to the dancing strings of the *Overture* and a very convincing concert-hall illusion for the whole programme. The performances are admirably spirited; *Ruy Blas* comes off especially well; the other highlight of the disc is the delightful *Fair Melusina*, a most affectionate portrait that recalls Beecham. But the *Midsummer Night's Dream* selection is altogether more routine: the very brisk *Scherzo* conveys little charm, although the *Wedding march* is grand without being pompous.

A Midsummer Night's Dream: Overture, Op. 21; Scherzo; Nocturne; Wedding march, Op. 61.
(B) *** Ph. 426 071-2 [id.]. Concg. O, Szell – SCHUBERT: *Rosamunde*.***

Superlative playing from the Concertgebouw Orchestra under Szell. He seldom recorded in Europe, but when he did the results were always impressive. Here the lightness and clean articulation of the violins in the *Overture* are a delight; the wonderfully nimble wind-playing in the *Scherzo* is no less engaging, and there is a fine horn solo in the *Nocturne*. The recording, unbelievably, dates from 1957 and sounds admirably clear, without loss of bloom. Szell's coupled Schubert performances are equally rewarding. A similar selection at mid-price, recorded digitally by Levine in Chicago (DG 427 817-2) and including vivacious dances from Smetana's *Bartered Bride*, might be considered, but Szell's bargain disc is the more memorable.

3 Psalms, Op. 78.
(*) Nimbus Dig. NI 5171 [id.]. Oslo Cathedral Ch., Terje Kvam – GRIEG: *4 Psalms, Op. 74*.(*)

All three *Psalms* have considerable beauty and dignity, especially the first, a setting of Psalm 11 with its ingenious four-part canon. Good performances by the Oslo Cathedral Choir, and eminently serviceable recording. However, at under 45 minutes, the CD offers short measure.

St Paul, Op. 36.
**(*) Ph. 420 212-2 (2). Janowitz, Lang, Blochwitz, Stier, Polster, Adam, Leipzig R. Ch. & GO, Masur.

Masur, always a persuasive interpreter of Mendelssohn, here directs a performance which, without inflating the piece or making it sanctimonious, conveys its natural gravity. Theo Adam is not always steady, but otherwise the team of soloists is exceptionally strong, and the chorus adds to the incandescence, although placed rather backwardly. The Leipzig recording is warm and atmospheric.

Menotti, Gian-Carlo (born 1911)

Amahl and the Night Visitors (opera): complete.
*** That's Entertainment CDTER 1124. Lorna Haywood, John Dobson, Curtis Watson, Christopher Painter, James Rainbird, ROHCG Ch. & O, David Syrus.

Recorded under the supervision of the composer himself, this Royal Opera House production of what was originally a television opera brings a fresh and highly dramatic performance, very well sung and marked by atmospheric digital sound of striking realism. Central to the success of the performance is the astonishingly assured and sensitively musical singing of the boy treble, James Rainbird, as Amahl, purposefully effective even in the potentially embarrassing moments. Lorna Haywood sings warmly and strongly as the Mother, with a strong trio of Kings. The realism of the recording makes the chamber size of the string section sound thin at the start, but the playing is both warm and polished.

Mercadante, Saverio (1795–1870)

Clarinet concerto in B flat.
*** Claves CD 50-813 [id.]. Friedli, SW German CO, Angerer – MOLTER; PLEYEL: *Concertos.****

Mercadante's *Concerto* consists of an *Allegro maestoso* and a *galant Andante with variations.* The music is agreeably fluent and very well played by the soloist. An interesting collection of works, showing the development of the clarinet as a solo instrument.

Flute concertos: in D; E; E min.
*** RCA Dig. RD 87703 [7703-2-RC]. James Galway, I Solisti Veneti, Scimone.

These three *Flute concertos* show Mercadante to be an excellent craftsman, with a nice turn for lyrical melody in the slow movements with their simple song-like cantilenas. Both the *Andante alla siciliana* of the *D major Concerto* and the *Largo* of the *E minor* are appealing, especially with Galway as soloist, while the *Rondo Russo* or *Polacca* finales are inventively spirited. Scimone makes the most of the often exuberantly florid tuttis of the opening movements and elsewhere accompanies Galway's silvery melodic line, sparkling and delicate by turns, with style and polish. The sound is excellent.

Merikanto, Aarre (1893–1958)

(i) *Fantasy for orchestra; Largo misterioso;* (ii) *Notturno;* (i) *Pan; Symphonic study.*
*** Finlandia Dig. FACD 349 [id.]. Finnish RSO, (i) Segerstam; (ii) Saraste.

The *Fantasy for orchestra* is a work of an extraordinarily rich imagination and leaves no doubt as to his distinctive orchestral sound-world. Both the *Fantasy* and the tone-poem, *Pan*, are sensitively conducted by Leif Segerstam, who successfully conveys their haunting, other-worldly atmosphere. Merikanto fell an easy victim to discouragement and was a harsh self-critic: he destroyed sections of the *Symphonic study* of 1928, but these have been expertly reconstructed by Paavo Heininen. The *Notturno* and *Largo misterioso* are also beautiful pieces that immediately cast a strong spell.

Juha (opera) complete.
**(*) Finlandia FACD 105 (2) [id.]. Lehtinen, Kostia, Krumm, Kuusoja, Finnish Nat. Op. Ch. and O, Ulf Söderblom.

The musical language of *Juha* reflects the composer's international sympathies and yet the music is far more than merely eclectic. It is atmospheric and highly expert in scoring and, in its way, bears a quite distinctive stamp. This performance derives from the early 1970s and, though it may not be ideal, every detail registers and the words are clearly projected. The singing on the whole is more than respectable, and Matti Lehtinen in the title-role is outstanding. The opera is not long – under two hours – and is very well worth investigating.

Messiaen, Olivier (born 1908)

Des canyons aux étoiles; Couleurs de la cité céleste; Oiseaux exotiques.
*** CBS Dig. MK 44762 [id.]. Paul Crossley, L. Sinf., Salonen.

The power of the writing in Messiaen's vast symphonic cycle, *Des canyons aux étoiles*, comes out vividly in Esa-Pekka Salonen's CBS version, with Paul Crossley as soloist both incisive and deeply sympathetic. Highly evocative in its American inspirations, this is the work which most satisfyingly brings together the contrasting strains in Messiaen's musical ethos, not just Christian meditation and response to the grandeur of the universe, but also the influence of birdsong, meticulously notated. Salonen's performance is not obviously devotional in the first five movements; but then, after Michael Thompson's virtuoso horn solo, in the sixth movement Salonen and his players increasingly find a sharper focus, with the playing of the London Sinfonietta ever more confident and idiomatic. The coupling is generous, with *Oiseaux exotiques* again finding Crossley in inspired form as soloist, and with *Couleurs de la cité céleste* made tough rather than evocative. The recording is sharply focused, but has good presence and atmosphere.

Turangalîla symphony.
(*) CBS Dig. M2K 42271 (2) [id.]. Crossley, Murail, Philh. O, Salonen – LUTOSLAWSKI: *Symphony No. 3* etc.*

(i) *Turangalîla symphony;* (ii) *Quartet for the end of time.*
*** EMI Dig. CDS7 47463-8 [id.] (2). (i) Donohoe, Murail, CBSO, Rattle; (ii) Gawriloff, Deinzer, Palm, Kontarsky.

Simon Rattle conducts a winning performance of *Turangalîla*, not only brilliant and dramatic but warmly atmospheric and persuasive. It is not just that his rendering of the love music is ripely sensuous: in his rhythmic control of the fast dramatic movements he is equally understanding, nudging the syncopations of the fifth movement, *Joie du sang des étoiles*, to bring out the exuberant jazz overtones. The recording is warm and richly co-ordinated while losing nothing in detail. Peter Donohoe and Tristan Murail play with comparable warmth and flair, rhythmically persuasive, and the orchestra responds superbly to the challenge of a virtuoso score. Led by the pianist, Aloys Kontarsky, the German performance of the *Quartet for the end of time* is a strong one. Recorded in 1976, it provides a contrasted approach to Messiaen from Rattle's, when atmospheric warmth is only an incidental.

Esa-Pekka Salonen's account of the *Turangalîla symphony* minimizes its atmospheric beauty, its sensuousness, and underlines the points which look forward to later composers. This is emphasized by the close balance of the piano and ondes martenot, so the passage-work for piano, beautifully played by Paul Crossley, sounds angular in a very modern way rather than evoking birdsong. Significantly, the syncopated rhythms of the energetic fifth movement are pressed home very literally, at a speed faster than usual, with little or no echo of jazz. The Philharmonia plays brilliantly and the recording underlines the sharp focus of the reading, while giving ample atmosphere.

Quatuor pour la fin du temps.
*** Delos Dig. D/CD 3043 [id.]. Chamber Music Northwest – BARTÓK: *Contrasts.****

(m) *** Ph. 422 834-2 [id.]. Beths, Pieterson, Bylsma, De Leeuw.

(m) **(*) RCA GD 87835 [7835-2-RG]. Tashi (Kavafian, Sherry, Stoltzman, Peter Serkin).

**(*) DG 423 247-2 [id.]. Yordanoff, Tetard, Desurment, Barenboim.

Messiaen's visionary and often inspired piece was composed during his days in a Silesian prison camp. Among his fellow-prisoners were a violinist, clarinettist and cellist who, with the composer at the piano, made its creation possible. It is good to have a fine modern digital recording of Messiaen's strangely haunting *Quatuor*. We already know the calibre of David Shifrin's playing from his recording of Copland's *Clarinet concerto*. Here, like his colleagues, he fully captures the work's sensuous mysticism, while the solos of Warren Lash (cello) and Williams Doppmann have a wistful, improvistory quality: both *Louange à l'eternité de Jésus* and the closing *Louange à l'immortalité de Jésus* are played very beautifully. The recording is naturally balanced and very realistic, while the ambience is suitably evocative.

The Dutch team on Philips are given the benefit of very good recording which has transferred well to CD; moreover their account has the merit of outstanding team-work and Reinbert de Leeuw has a keen sense of atmosphere, though he does not dominate the proceedings. There is also some superbly eloquent playing from George Pieterson and Anner Bylsma.

With Peter Serkin at the piano it is not surprising that the RCA performance is a distinguished one. The clarinet solo, *Abyss of the birds*, is played with memorable eloquence by Richard Stoltzman, and the cellist, Fred Sherry, plays very beautifully in his *Praise to the eternity of Jesus*, while Ida Kavafian's long violin melisma has a striking, improvisatory quality. Considerable tension is movingly created in the work's closing section; and if there are minor reservations about the forward balance, the players certainly project as real and tangible.

Barenboim and his colleagues recorded the *Quatuor pour la fin du temps* in the presence of the composer. Barenboim is a strong personality who carries much of this performance in his hands and inspires his colleagues with his own commitment to the music. The recording was originally a good one; while increasing its presence, the digital remastering has added a degree of edginess to the sound on CD, making it less attractive than the original analogue LP from which the recording derives.

PIANO MUSIC

Cantéyodjaya; Fantaisie burlesque; 4 études de rythme; Rondeau.
*** Unicorn Dig. DKPCD 9051 [id.]. Peter Hill.

Peter Hill, playing a Bösendorfer, is a sympathetic guide in this repertoire; he has a good feeling for atmosphere and makes out an excellent case for all these pieces, save perhaps for the somewhat repetitive *Fantaisie burlesque* of 1932, which outstays its welcome. The playing is consistently sensitive and has great finesse, and the *Cantéyodjaya* (1948) is particularly refined. The recording is unobtrusively natural.

Catalogue d'oiseaux, Books 1–3.
*** Unicorn Dig. DKPCD 9062 [id.]. Peter Hill.

Catalogue d'oiseaux, Books 4–6: L'alouette calandrelle; La bouscarle; La merle de roche; La rousserolle effarvatte.
*** Unicorn Dig. DKPCD 9075 [id.]. Peter Hill.

These scores derive their inspiration from Messiaen's beloved birdsong. Little of the piano writing is conventional, but there is no question as to the composer's imaginative flair, and the music is vivid and colourful to match the plumage of the creatures which Messiaen depicts so strikingly. Peter Hill prepared this music in Paris with the composer himself and thus has his imprimatur. He has great sensitivity to colour and atmosphere and evokes the wildlife pictured in this extraordinary music to splendid effect. He is recorded with the utmost clarity and definition.

ORGAN MUSIC

L'Apparition de l'église éternelle; L'Ascension; Le Banquet céleste; Diptyque.
**(*) BIS Dig. CD-409 [id.]. Hans-Ola Ericsson.

La Nativité du Seigneur.
**(*) BIS Dig. CD-410 [id.]. Hans-Ola Ericsson.

Hans-Ola Ericsson is a Swedish organist now in his early thirties, active in northern Sweden. These two discs, recorded on the Grönlund organ of Luleå Cathedral, mark the beginning of a complete cycle. His playing is introspective and inward-looking and, though these recordings do not by any means displace the authoritative (and spectacularly recorded) Jennifer Bate on Unicorn, they form a useful alternative.

Livre du Saint Sacrement.
*** Unicorn Dig. DKPCD 9067/8 [id.]. Jennifer Bate (organ of Saint-Trinité, Paris).

What a sound! This is a quite spectacular recording and carries the composer's imprimatur. The *Livre du Saint Sacrement* was composed in 1984 and consists of eighteen movements of great intensity. Jennifer Bate makes an impressive and compelling case for these hypnotic pieces, and the recording is in the demonstration bracket.

La Nativité du Seigneur (9 meditations).
(M) *** Decca 425 616-2 (2) [id.]. Simon Preston (organ of Westminster Abbey) – *La Transfiguration.****
**(*) Hyp. CDA 66230 [id.]. David Titterington (organ of Gloucester Cathedral).

La Nativité du Seigneur (9 meditations); *Le banquet céleste.*
⊛ *** Unicorn Dig. DKPCD 9005 [id.]. Jennifer Bate (organ of Beauvais Cathedral).

'*C'est vraiment parfait!*' said Messiaen after hearing Jennifer Bate's Unicorn recording of *La Nativité du Seigneur*, one of his most extended, most moving and most variedly beautiful works. For the CD issue, *Le banquet céleste* has generously been added, an intense comment on the religious experience which has inspired all of the composer's organ music. The recording of the Beauvais Cathedral organ is of demonstration quality.

Simon Preston is a convinced advocate of this score and conveys its hypnotic power most successfully. The recording reproduces with great fidelity, and in Preston's hand the Westminster Abbey organ produces the right kind of veiled colours to evoke the work's mysticism. This performance is by no means second best and makes a very generous bonus for *La Transfiguration*.

David Titterington's Hyperion record is made on the organ of Gloucester Cathedral. His playing is resourceful and intelligent, but not perhaps as totally convincing as that of Jennifer Bate, recorded at Beauvais.

La Transfiguration de Notre Seigneur Jésus-Christ.
(M) *** Decca 425 616-2 (2) [id.]. Sylvester, Aquino, Westminster Symphonic Ch., Loriod, Instrumental Soloists, Washington Nat. SO, Dorati – *La Nativité du Seigneur.****

This massive work of fourteen movements, divided into two parallel septenaries, seems to sum up the whole achievement of Messiaen. Though the unconverted may feel it has its longueurs, no one can doubt the dedication of the composer and his ability, beyond that of almost any other contemporary, to convey his personal religious exaltation through his music. Dorati magnificently holds the unwieldy structures together, and though such an evocative work might suggest a more reverberant acoustic, the brilliance and immediacy of the recording are most impressive. The opening percussion effects are very tangible, while the internal balance between singers and instrumentalists is managed ideally – the blend between chorus and orchestra rich yet transparent in detail – indeed everything is clearly interrelated within a sympathetic ambience.

Meyerbeer, Giacomo (1791–1864)

Les Patineurs (ballet; arr. Constant Lambert): *suite.*
(M) *** Decca 425 468-2 (3) [id.]. Nat. PO, Richard Bonynge – TCHAIKOVSKY: *Sleeping Beauty.***(*)

Les Patineurs was arranged by Constant Lambert using excerpts from two of Meyerbeer's operas, *Le Prophète* and *L'Étoile du Nord.* Bonynge's approach is warm and comparatively easy-going but, with such polished orchestral playing, this version is extremely beguiling. The sound too is first rate.

Les Huguenots (complete).
** Erato Dig. 2292 45027-2 (4) [id.]. Raphanel, Pollet, Borst, Leech, Cachemaille, Martinovic, Ghiuselev, Montpellier Op. Ch. & PO, Diederich.

Montpellier in the south of France is an adventurous place, promoting a lively annual festival and here sponsoring this first CD version of the most successful of Meyerbeer's blockbuster operas. The performance was recorded live in concert in the autumn of 1988 and, though inevitably it is flawed, with the soloists very variable, there is much to enjoy, with the engineers capturing the atmosphere of the occasion very vividly. The five substantial Acts are neatly contained on the four discs, with the first three Acts each complete on a disc, and with Acts IV and V together on the final CD. Outstanding among the singers is the soprano, Françoise Pollet, who sings the role of Valentine, one of the two heroines. Hers is a warm, full voice, which she uses most imaginatively, with fine clean attack in her big Act IV aria, and in the long duet with the hero, Raoul, which follows. In that role Richard Leech has a light, pleasing tenor, but his style is too lachrymose. Ghyslaine Raphanel as the other heroine, Queen Marguerite de Valois, attacks the dauntingly difficult Act II aria with total assurance in coloratura, but the voice is shrill and tweety in a very French way; and though Danielle Borst in the breeches role of the page, Urbain, is sweeter on the ear and agile, she cannot match her predecessor on record, Huguette Tourangeau in the Decca set with Joan Sutherland, and she is robbed of one of her most delicious numbers, the aria *No, no, no, no,* sung provocatively in the garden scene of Act II after the Bathers' chorus. Singing the role of the Huguenot soldier, Marcel (in both the new set and the old Decca) is Nicola Ghiuselev; but in almost twenty years the voice has grown much less steady, even though the comedy of his Act I solo, *Piff-Paff,* is again beautifully caught. The Erato version makes a fair stop-gap, but Decca is bound to reissue its Bonynge set with Sutherland before long on CD and, quite apart from Sutherland's supreme contribution as the Queen, that in every way outshines this one, even in its superb studio sound.

627

Le Prophète (complete).
**(*) CBS M3K 79400 (3) [id.]. Horne, Scotto, McCracken, Hines, Dupony, Bastin, Boys' Ch. of Haberdasher's Aske's School, Amb. Op. Ch., RPO, Henry Lewis.

This recording anticipated the 1977 production at the New York Met. with the same conductor and principal soloists. But the fact that it was recorded before the stage performances meant that the usual spadework for recording a rare opera had to be gone through, and the sessions had more than their share of crises. That is reflected in the finished recording, which lacks the last degree of assurance. None of the soloists is quite at peak form, though they all sing more than competently. Nevertheless, with vigorous direction by Henry Lewis – rather brutal in the Coronation scene – there is much to enjoy. The recording is vividly transferred to CD but would have benefited from a more atmospheric acoustic.

Miaskovsky, Nikolay (1881–1950)

(i) *Violin concerto, Op. 44;* (ii) *Symphony No. 22 in B min., Op. 54.*
**(*) Olympia OCD 134 [id.]. Grigori Feigin, USSR RSO, Dmitriev; (ii) USSR SO, Svetlanov.

The *Violin concerto* has a distinctive personality and a rich vein of lyricism. The ideas flow generously and the architecture is well held together; its slow movement in particular seems to look back nostalgically to a secure, genuinely happy world on whose passing the composer sadly muses. Grigori Feigin is the excellent soloist and plays with the right amount of warmth and virtuosity. The *Symphony* is a more powerful and ambitious piece and far more substantial than its immediate neighbours. Neither recording is new; both were made in 1974.

(i) *Lyric concertino in G, Op. 32, No. 3;* (ii) *Symphony No. 3 in A min., Op. 15.*
**(*) Olympia OCD 177 [id.]. USSR SO; (i) Verbitzky, (ii) Svetlanov.

The *Third Symphony* is an epic, ambitious work, conceived in the grand manner and cast in two long movements; its world is close to that of Glière's *Ilya Mourmetz symphony*. It is a dark, powerful piece, and Svetlanov is a persuasive advocate. The *Lyric concertino* is less satisfactorily recorded. The playing is a little less polished, too – which is a pity, as there are imaginative and original touches in the slow movement which show that Miaskovsky knew his French music.

(i) *Sinfonietta No. 2 in A min. for strings, Op. 68;* (ii) *Symphony No. 27 in C min., Op. 85.*
** Olympia OCD 168 [id.]. USSR Ac. SO; (i) Verbitzky, (ii) Svetlanov.

The *Symphony*, Miaskovsky's penultimate work, is tuneful; its harmonic vocabulary scarcely embraces a chord that would be out of place in Borodin or Brahms – and the slow movement is particularly Brahmsian. It is an endearingly old-fashioned work, and is very much better played and recorded than the *Sinfonietta*, written in a similar idiom. The recording, which dates from 1980, was made in a warm acoustic; the sound image is in excellent perspective, even if the balance will be too recessed for some tastes.

Symphonies Nos. (i) *5 in D, Op. 18;* (ii) *11 in B flat, Op. 34.*
**(*) Olympia OCD 133 [id.]. (i) USSR SO, Ivanov; (ii) Moscow SO, Dudarova.

Miaskovsky himself called the *Fifth* his 'quiet' symphony; it is also pastoral in feeling and more introspective than Glazunov. The *Eleventh* is also conservative in idiom, yet the language is unpredictable; its distinctive melodic style is particularly evident in the finale. The recording of the *Eleventh Symphony* comes from 1978, and the *Fifth* is probably earlier: if neither is outstanding, they are eminently serviceable and comprise a more than welcome addition to this composer's representation on record.

Symphony No. 7 in B min., Op. 24.
** Olympia OCD 163 [id.]. USSR RSO, Ginsburg – KNIPPER: *Concert poem* etc.**

The *Seventh Symphony* (1922) is one of Miaskovky's finest symphonies, a much shorter work than its vast predecessor; though the influence of Glière and Scriabin are discernible, they are here assimilated. The pastoral writing in the *Andante* movement has great beauty, and the performance under Leo Ginsburg is very persuasive. We suspect an earlier recording date than the 1977 given on the sleeve. However, the sound is very agreeable and better balanced than the Knipper with which it is coupled.

Cello sonata No. 2 in A min., Op. 81.
** Chan. Dig. CHAN 8523 [id.]. Yuli Turovsky, Luba Edlina – RACHMANINOV: *Cello sonata.***

Miaskovsky's *Second sonata* has a warm, lyrical beauty which should earn it a permanent place in the repertory. Yuli Turovsky and Luba Edlina certainly take their time over the first movement, which in their hands is far more *moderato* than *allegro* and should flow more; but they do give a splendid account of the finale. This is such an eloquent piece that we ought to have as many recordings of it as of the Rachmaninov. The sound here is truthfully balanced.

String quartets Nos. 3 in D min., Op. 33/3; 10 in F, Op. 67/1; 13 in A min., Op. 86.
**(*) Olympia OCD 148 [id.]. Leningrad Taneiev Qt.

The *Thirteenth Quartet* is Miaskovsky's last work, one of fastidious craftsmanship and refined musicianship. It is a beautifully wrought score, in which ideas of great lyrical fervour flow abundantly. The Leningrad Taneiev Quartet, a first-class ensemble, play with dedication in all three works and the recordings, though not of the very highest quality, are very acceptable indeed.

Piano sonatas Nos. 1 in D min., Op. 6; 2 in F sharp min., Op. 13; 3 in C min., Op. 19; 6 in A flat, Op. 64/2.
**(*) Olympia Dig. OCD 214 [id.]. Murray McLachlan.

The sonatas on this disc are all fairly early; the *First* is the longest. In its way it is an oddity; its opening, like that of the Balakirev *B flat minor Sonata* written two years earlier, is fugal – the theme is of considerable angularity – but much of the second movement is more akin to the early Scriabin sonatas. So, too, is the *Second*, though Taneyev, Glazunov and Medtner also spring to mind. The pianist, Murray McLachlan, is still in his early twenties and possesses a very considerable talent. An enterprising issue in every way, and well recorded on the whole, even though the acoustic ambience is not absolutely ideal.

Piano sonatas Nos. 4 in C min., Op. 27; 5 in B, Op. 64/1; Sonatine in E min., Op. 57; Prelude, Op. 58.
*** Olympia Dig. OCD 217 [id.]. Murray McLachlan.

The middle movement of the *Sonatine*, marked *Narrante e lugubre*, is dark and pessimistic, and quite haunting. McLachlan speaks of the 'enormous tactile pleasure' it gives to the performer, but it also grips the listener. As on the companion disc, this gifted young artist communicates his own enthusiasm for this music, and his playing is both authoritative and persuasive. Perhaps this is the record to try first, since both *Sonatas*, not just the more 'radical' *Fourth*, are of interest and substance. Good recording.

Milhaud, Darius (1892–1974)

Le boeuf sur le toit.
(*) Sup. Dig. SUP 001519 [id.]. Czech PO, Válek – POULENC: *Les Biches*; SATIE: *Parade.*(*)

Le boeuf sur le toit; La Création du monde; Saudades do Brazil Nos. 7, 8, 9 & 11.
**(*) EMI CDC7 47845-2 [id.]. O Nat. de France, Bernstein.

Vladimír Válek's account of *Le boeuf sur le toit* is on the whole preferable to Bernstein's version, even if the American conductor has a more natural affinity with its rhythmic character. The Czech Philharmonic give a very spirited account of it, and the digital Supraphon recording is firmer and cleaner. Moreover the couplings, two equally attractive Diaghilev ballet scores, are also vivacious and well played.

As one would expect, Bernstein finds this repertoire thoroughly congenial, though his performance of *La Création du monde* disappoints slightly. Nor does *Le boeuf sur le toit* have quite the sparkle and infectious gaiety that the music ideally demands. The recordings, made in 1978, have not entirely benefited from their digital remastering. The sharpening of the focus, within a fairly reverberant acoustic, has lost a little of the body in the sound.

La Création du monde (ballet).
*** Virgin Dig. VC 791098-2 [id.]. Lausanne CO, Zedda – DEBUSSY: *Danse; Sarabande*; PROKOFIEV: *Sinfonietta.***

Milhaud's ballet, with its mixture of yearning melancholy and jazzy high spirits, comes off splendidly in Alberto Zedda's highly spontaneous account, its witty syncopations and brassy exuberance bringing an unbridled effervescence to offset the restrained blues feeling of the main lyrical theme. The performance doesn't miss the Gershwin affinities, and the very vivid recording makes a bold dynamic contrast between the work's tender and abrasive moments.

La Création du monde; Suite for clarinet, violin and piano; Scaramouche; Caramel mou; 3 Rag-caprices.
** Ara. Dig. Z 6569 [id.]. Ian Hobson, Sinfonia da camera.

This is the chamber version of Milhaud's jazz-inspired ballet, not the orchestral arrangement he made later. Ian Hobson and this Illinois group give a spirited account of the piece; if at times they are a trifle too well-bred and polite, they are very civilized too. In the other pieces they capture the warmth and spontaneity of this relaxed music, if not all of its charm. The acoustic is a shade dry, but not excessively so.

Sonatina for clarinet and piano; Sonatina for flute and piano; Sonata for flute, oboe, clarinet and piano; Sonatina for oboe and piano.
*** Orfeo Dig. CO 60831A [id.]. Brunner, Nicolet, Holliger, Maisenberg.

The *Sonata* is an ingenious and delightful piece, most expertly played here. The later *Sonatinas* have no less charm and polish, and are beautifully played and very naturally recorded. A strong recommendation for a very attractive concert.

String quartets Nos. 1, Op. 5; 7 in B flat, Op. 87; 10, Op. 218; 16, Op. 303.
*** Cybella Dig. CY 804 [id.]. Aquitaine National Qt.

The *First Quartet* is a beautifully relaxed, sunny work, rather Debussian in feel. The *Seventh* speaks Milhaud's familiar, distinctive language; its four short movements are delightful, full of melody and colour. The *Tenth* is attractive too, while the *Sixteenth* was a wedding anniversary present for the composer's wife: its first movement has great tenderness and warmth. The recordings are very good, though No. 1 appears to be recorded in a slightly drier acoustic than its companions. Individual movements in the quartets are not indexed. The Aquitaine Quartet has excellent ensemble, intonation is good and their playing is polished. The recording has a wide dynamic range and a spacious tonal spectrum.

String quartets Nos. 5, Op. 64; 8, Op. 121; 11, Op. 232; 13, Op. 268.
*** Cybella Dig. CY 805 [id.]. Aquitaine National Qt.

The *Fifth Quartet* is not one of Milhaud's most inspired; the *Eighth*, on the other hand, has much to commend it, including a poignant slow movement. No. 11 has a splendid pastoral third movement and a lively jazzy finale; No. 13 has overtones of Mexico in its finale and a beguiling and charming *Barcarolle*. Both performance and recording are very good.

Minkus, Léon (1826–1917)

La Source (ballet): Act I; Act III, scene ii.
*** Decca Dig. 421 431-2 (2) [id.]. ROHCG O, Bonynge – DELIBES: *La Source* (Act II; Act III, scene i); DRIGO: *Flûte magique.****

Composed in partnership with Delibes, it is the contribution of Minkus that sets the style and atmosphere of *La Source*, very much inherited from Adam, though with less melodrama. The music is attractive, its melodic contours less positive than those characteristic of Delibes; but the writing has distinct charm and its picaresque evocation suits the slight narrative line. The score is beautifully played and Bonynge's affection is obvious; there is both grace and sparkle here. First-class Decca sound, too.

Moeran, Ernest J. (1894–1950)

(i) *Cello concerto; Sinfonietta.*
*** Chan. Dig. CHAN 8456 [id.]. (i) Raphael Wallfisch; Bournemouth Sinf., Del Mar.

Raphael Wallfisch brings an eloquence of tone and a masterly technical address to the *Cello concerto* and he receives responsive orchestral support from Norman Del Mar and the Bournemouth players. The well-crafted *Sinfonietta* is among Moeran's most successful pieces: its invention is delightfully fresh, and there is that earthy, unpretentious musicality that makes Moeran so appealing a composer. The recording is a little on the reverberant side but well balanced and present.

(i) *Violin concerto; 2 Pieces for small orchestra: Lonely waters; Whythorne's shadow.*
*** Chan. Dig. CHAN 8807 [id.]. (i) Lydia Mordkovitch; Ulster O, Vernon Handley.

The *Violin concerto* is a rarity in the concert hall and this is only its second recording. Though less striking than the *Symphony in G minor* (and not as consistent in inspiration), it is strongly lyrical in feeling. The first movement is ruminative and rhapsodic, its inspiration drawn from Moeran's love of the west coast of Ireland; the middle movement makes use of folk music; while the finale, a ruminative elegy of great beauty, is the most haunting of the three. Lydia Mordkovitch plays with great natural feeling for this music and, quite apart from his sensitive support in the *Concerto*, Vernon Handley gives an outstanding (and affecting) account of *Lonely waters*. Superb recording.

Symphony in G min.; Lonely waters; Whythorne's shadow.
(M) **(*) EMI CDM7 69419-2 [id.]. E. Sinfonia, Dilkes – BUTTERWORTH: *Banks of green willow* etc.**(*)

Symphony in G min.; Overture for a masque.
*** Chan. Dig. CHAN 8577 [id.]. Ulster O, Vernon Handley.

Moeran's superb *Symphony in G minor* is in the best English tradition of symphonic writing and worthy to rank with the symphonies of Vaughan Williams and Walton. But for all the echoes of these composers (and Holst and Butterworth, too) it has a strong individual voice. Vernon Handley gives a bitingly powerful performance, helped by superb playing from the Ulster Orchestra, totally committed from first to last. With the brass cutting through rich textures with thrilling edge, the whole symphony carries more menace with it than in previous recordings, relating to both the dark nature-music of Sibelius and the pre-war period in which it was written. The *Overture for a masque*, a brash, brassy piece in its fanfare opening and Waltonian cross-rhythms, makes an attractive and generous fill-up. The recording is superb, spacious and full, with a dramatic range of dynamic and the Ulster strings sounding exceptionally sweet.

Dilkes's fine, lusty performance is perhaps not as powerful as Handley's superb version on Chandos, nor has it quite the subtlety of rubato that Handley draws from the Ulster Orchestra. With a smaller string band, recorded relatively close, the sound is vivid and immediate; the reading remains a satisfying one and it certainly does not lack urgency. The two lovely orchestral miniatures are most beautifully played and recorded and make a very worthwhile bonus alongside the two better-known Butterworth pieces which have been added to make this mid-priced disc even more attractive, although here especially the recording ideally could be more distanced.

Fantasy quartet for oboe and strings.
*** Chan. Dig. CHAN 8392 [id.]. Francis, English Qt – BAX: *Quintet*; HOLST: *Air and variations* etc.; JACOB: *Quartet.****

Moeran's folk-influenced *Fantasy quartet*, an attractively rhapsodic single-movement work, is played admirably here, and the recording is excellent, well balanced too.

(i) *String quartet in A min.;* (ii) *Violin sonata in E min.*
*** Chan. Dig. CHAN 8465 [id.]. (i) Melbourne Qt; (ii) Donald Scotts, John Talbot.

There is a strong folksong element in the *Quartet*, and some French influence too; these pieces are stronger than they have been given credit for. Good performances and recording.

Molter, Johann (1696–1765)

Clarinet concerto in D.
*** Claves CD 50-813 [id.]. Friedli, SW German CO, Angerer – MERCADANTE; PLEYEL: *Concertos.****

Molter's *Concerto* is for D clarinet and its high tessitura means that, when heard on a modern version of the instrument for which it was written, the timbre sounds uncannily like a soft-grained trumpet – and very effective, too, especially when the playing is both expert and sympathetic. Here the accompaniment is good rather than outstanding: orchestral detail is not ideally clear, and the harpsichord contribution is only just audible. Nevertheless, this remains a most enjoyable collection, for the coupled works are equally interesting.

Monn, Georg Matthias (1717–50)

Cello concerto in D (arr. Schoenberg).
*** CBS Dig. MK 39863 [id.]. Yo-Yo Ma, Boston SO, Ozawa – R. STRAUSS: *Don Quixote.***(*)

Schoenberg's free transcription for cello and orchestra of this Monn concerto can be compared with Strauss's *Couperin suite*, though Schoenberg's scoring varies from a Regerian delicacy to altogether thicker sonorities. It is beautifully played and recorded.

Monteverdi, Claudio (1567–1643)

Ab aeterno ordinata sum; Confitebor tibi, Domine (3 settings); *Deus tuorum militum sors et corona; Iste confessor Domini sacratus; Laudate Dominum, O omnes gentes; La Maddalena: Prologue: Su le penne de venti. Nisi Dominus aedificaverit domum.*
⊛ *** Hyp. Dig. CDA 66021 [id.]. Kirkby, Partridge, Thomas, Parley of Instruments.

There are few records of Monteverdi's solo vocal music as persuasive as this. The three totally contrasted settings of *Confitebor tibi* (Psalm 110) reveal an extraordinary range of expression, each one drawing out different aspects of word-meaning. Even the brief trio, *Deus tuorum militum*, has a haunting memorability – it could become to Monteverdi what *Jesu, joy of man's desiring* is to Bach – and the performances are outstanding, with the edge on Emma Kirkby's voice attractively presented in an aptly reverberant acoustic. The accompaniment makes a persuasive case for authentic performance on original instruments. The CD sounds superb.

Il ballo dell'ingrate: Lamento della Ninfa. Madrigals: *Ardo; Chiome d'oro; Ecco mormorar l'onde; Hor ch'el ciel e la terra; Lasciatemi morire; Ohimè dov' è il mio ben; Zefira torna (ciaccona).*
(M) (***) EMI mono CDH7 61025-2. Countess Jeanne de Polignac, I. and N. Kedroff, L. Rauh, G. Peyron, P. Derenne, H. Cuenod, D. Conrad, Instrumental Ens., Boulanger – FAURÉ: *Requiem.***(*))

Nadia Boulanger's historic recordings of Monteverdi madrigals, made in 1937 with a characterful vocal ensemble including the sponsoring heiress, the Comtesse de Polignac, and Hugues Cuenod, provide a landmark in that they opened up a new area of enjoyment for a wider audience than ever before. Though the use of a piano now seems very odd indeed, the magic is as intense as ever. Each item was beautifully chosen to demonstrate the composer's mastery, and it would be hard to imagine a more haunting performance of the *Lamento della Ninfa* than the Comtesse de Polignac's or a more infectiously jaunty one of the tenor duet, *Chiome d'oro*, than that with Cuenod and Paul Derenne. The original sound, at once dry and atmospheric, has been transferred faithfully.

Madrigals: *Addio Florida bella; Ahi com'a un vago sol; E così a poco a poco torno farfalla; Era l'anima mia; Luci serene e chiare; Mentre vaga Angioletta ogn'anima; Ninfa che*

scalza il piede; O mio bene, a mia vita; O Mirtillo, Mirtill'anima mia; Se pur destina; Taci, Armelin deh taci; T'amo mia vita; Troppo ben può questo tiranno amore.
*** HM HMC 901084 [id.]. Concerto Vocale.

A highly attractive collection of generally neglected items, briskly and stylishly performed. The most celebrated of the singers is the male alto, René Jacobs, a fine director as well as soloist. With continuo accompaniment, the contrasting of vocal timbres is achieved superbly. Excellent recording.

Madrigals, Book 4 (complete).
*** O-L Dig. 414 148-2 [id.]. Cons. of Musicke, Anthony Rooley.

Under Anthony Rooley the fine, well-integrated singers of the Consort of Musicke give masterly performances of this dazzling collection of madrigals which readily encompass not only the vocal pitfalls but the deeper problems of conveying the intensity of emotions implied by both music and words. The flexibility and control of dramatic contrast, conveying consistent commitment, make this one of this group's finest records, helped by atmospheric but aptly intimate recording.

Madrigals from Books 7 and 8: *Amor che deggio far; Altri canti di Marte; Chiome d'oro; Gira il nemico insidioso; Hor ch'el ciel e la terra; Non havea Febo ancora – Lamento della ninfa; Perchè t'en fuggi o Fillide; Tirsi e Clori* (ballo concertato for 5 voices and instruments).
*** HM HMC 901068 [id.]. Les Arts Florissants, Christie.

The singing of this famous group is full of colour and feeling and, even if intonation is not absolutely flawless throughout, it is mostly excellent. Much to be preferred to the bloodless white tone favoured by some early-music groups. Good recording.

Madrigali erotici: Chiome d'oro; Come dolci hoggi l'auretta; Con che saovita; Mentre vaga Angioletta; Ogni amante e guerrier; Ohimè, dov'è il mio ben?; Parlo misero, o taccio; S'el vostro cor, Madonna; Tempro la cetra; Vorrei baciarti o Filli.
*** O-L Dig. 421 480-2 [id.]. Emma Kirkby, Nelson, Holden, Elliot, King, Thomas, Cons. of Musicke, Rooley.

Most of the madrigals on this CD come from the Seventh Book of 1619, very much a watershed in Monteverdi's output. In many instances they are for virtuoso singers and make a break with the past in that they call for instrumental accompaniment. The recording is excellently balanced. Strongly recommended.

Mass of thanksgiving (Venice 1631).
*** EMI Dig. CDS7 49876-2 (2) [Ang. CDCB 49876]. Taverner Consort, Ch. & Players, Parrott.

Following up the success of his reconstruction of Handel's *Carmelite vespers*, Parrott here presents a similar reconstruction of the *Mass of thanksgiving* as performed in Venice on 21 November 1631. Historical records show that the Mass was then celebrated in the grandest possible way in St Mark's in thanks to the Virgin Mary for the deliverance of the city from the plague, which had raged throughout the earlier part of the year. What Parrott and his team have sought to assemble is a likely sequence of music for the liturgy, surrounding it with introits, toccatas, sonatas and recessionals, as well as linking chant. At the heart of the celebration lies Monteverdi's magnificent seven-part *Gloria* from his great collection, *Selva morale e spirituale*. The *Kyrie*, sections of the *Credo* (including an amazing chromatic *Crucifixus*), the *Offertory*, *Sanctus*, *Agnus Dei* and a final *Salve regina* also come from that great collection. The only parts of the actual Mass written by another composer are the sections of the *Credo* that Monteverdi did not set. They are by Giovanni Rovetta; other contemporaries of Monteverdi contributing incidental items include Girolami Fantini, Giuseppe Scarani and Francesco Usper, to make a very grand whole. The recording is warmly atmospheric, with the brassy music at the opening and close approaching and receding and with appropriate sound-effects punctuating the ceremony. The performance is superb; the only reservation to make is that with only a little less linking material it would have been possible to fit the whole on to a single CD.

Selva morale e spirituale: Beatus vir a 6; Confitebor tibi; Deus tuorum militum a 3; Dixit Dominus a 8; Domine a 3; Jubilet tota civitas; Laudate dominum a 5; Laudate pueri a 5; Magnificat a 8; Salve Regina a 3.
** EMI CDC 747016-2 [id.]. Kirkby, Rogers, Covey-Crump, Thomas, Taverner Cons. Ch. and Players, Parrott.

The performances here really need more breadth and grandeur, and there is at times a somewhat bloodless quality about the singing of some of the pieces; but there is enough to admire, such as the attractive account of *Salve Regina* and the opening *Dixit Dominus*. A little more spaciousness in the acoustic would have given the music-making more amplitude.

Lamento d'Olympia; Maladetto sia l'aspetto; Ohimè ch'io cado; Quel sdengosetto; Voglio di vita uscia.
*** Hyp. CDA 66106 [id.]. Emma Kirkby, Anthony Rooley (chitarone) – D'INDIA: *Lamento d'Olympia* etc.***

A well-planned recital from Hyperion contrasts the two settings of *Lamento d'Olympia* by Monteverdi and his younger contemporary, Sigismondo d'India. The performances by Emma Kirkby, sensitively supported by Anthony Rooley, could hardly be surpassed; her admirers can be assured that this ranks among her best records.

Missa de cappella a 4; Missa de cappella a 6 (In illo tempore); Motets: Cantate domino a 6; Domine ne in furore a 6.
*** Hyp. Dig. CDA 66214 [id]. The Sixteen, Christophers; M. Phillips.

Harry Christophers draws superb singing from his brilliant choir, highly polished in ensemble but dramatic and deeply expressive too, suitably adapted for the different character of each Mass-setting, when the four-part Mass involves stricter, more consistent contrapuntal writing and the six-part, in what was then an advanced way, uses homophonic writing to underline key passages. Vivid, atmospheric recording.

Vespro della Beata Vergine (Vespers).
*** Hyp. Dig. CDA 66311/2 [id.]. The Sixteen, Harry Christophers.
*** EMI Dig. CDS7 47078-8 [Ang. CDCB 47077] (2). Kirkby, Nigel Rogers, David Thomas, Taverner Ch., Cons. & Players, Canto Gregoriano, Parrott.
*** Decca 414 572-2 (2) [id.]. Gomez, Palmer, Bowman, Tear, Langridge, Shirley-Quirk, Rippon, Monteverdi Ch. & O, Salisbury Cathedral Boys' Ch., Jones Brass Ens., Murrow Recorder Cons., Gardiner.
**(*) Teldec/WEA Dig. 2292 42671-2 (2) [id.]. Margaret Marshall, Palmer, Langridge, Equiluz, Korn, Tolz Boys' Ch., V. Hofburg Church Ch. Scholars, Schoenberg Ch., VCM, Harnoncourt.

The Sixteen's version of Monteverdi's 1610 *Vespers* on Hyperion, beautifully scaled, presents a liturgical performance of what the scholar, Graham Dixon, suggests as

Monteverdi's original conception. Dixon noted that this was one of the texts used in the Gonzaga family's traditional celebrations for their patron saint, St Barbara. He infers from this that Monteverdi's first idea was to be a work in her honour. In practice the occasional changes of text are minimal; the booklet accompanying the set even includes an order of tracks if anyone wishes to hear the *Vespers* in traditional form. As it is, with a liturgical approach, the performance includes not only relevant Gregorian chant but antiphon substitutes, including a magnificent motet of Palestrina, obviously relevant, *Gaude Barbara*. The scale of the performance is very satisfying, with The Sixteen augmented to 22 singers (7.4.6.5) and with members of the group taking the eight solo roles. Christophers provides a mean between John Eliot Gardiner's unashamedly grand view with modern instruments and pitch and Andrew Parrott's vital, scholarly re-creation of an intimate, princely devotion.

Though Andrew Parrott uses minimal forces, with generally one instrument and one voice per part, so putting the work on a chamber scale in a small church setting, its grandeur comes out superbly through its very intensity. Far more than usual with antiphons in Gregorian chant it becomes a liturgical celebration. Brilliant singing here by the virtuoso soloists, above all by Nigel Rogers, whose distinctive timbre may not suit every ear but who has an airy precision and flexibility to give expressive meaning to even the most taxing passages. Fine contributions too from Parrott's chosen groups of players and singers, and warm, atmospheric recording, with an ecclesiastical ambience which yet allows ample detail.

Gardiner's recording was made in 1974, before he had been won over entirely to the claims of the authentic school. Modern instruments are used and women's voices, but Gardiner's rhythms are so resilient that the result is more exhilarating as well as grander. Singing and playing are exemplary, and the recording is one of Decca's most vividly atmospheric, with relatively large forces presented and placed against a helpful, reverberant acoustic.

Harnoncourt's version, recorded live, gives a keen sense of occasion, with the grandeur of the piece linked to a consciously authentic approach. There is a ruggedness in the interpretation, entirely apt, which is lightened by the characterful refinement of the solo singing from an exceptionally strong team of soloists, not to mention the fine singing from all three choirs. Ample, atmospheric recording.

Vespri di S. Giovanni Battista.
*** Ph. Dig. 422 074-2 [id.]. Netherlands Chamber Ch., Ch. Viennensis, Amsterdam Monteverdi Ens., Gustav Leonhardt.

This is a conjectural reconstruction of an actual performance directed by the composer; although the emphasis has to be on the conjectural, both the music itself and the performances are delightful. Apart from Monteverdi's settings of *Dixit Dominus*, *Confitebor tibi*, *Laudate pueri* and *Magnificat*, there are toccatas by Giovanni Gabrieli, a motet by Alessandro Grandi (*c.* 1575–1630), and two sonatas by Dario Castello (whose dates are uncertain). The recording, made in Utrecht in an ideal acoustic, is a model of its kind.

OPERA AND OPERA-BALLET

Il ballo delle ingrate; Il combattimento di Tancredi e Clorinda (opera-ballets).
(M) *** Ph. 426 451-2 [id.]. Harpur, Watson, Howells, Alva, Wakefield, Dean, Amb. S, ECO, Leppard.

Monteverdi's mastery in these earliest examples of opera is brought out readily in these finely sung performances under Leppard. The famous dramatic narrative of *Tancredi and Clorinda*, brother and sister, tragically and unknowingly matched in mortal combat, is perfectly coupled with *Il ballo delle ingrate*, which tells of the 'ungrateful' ladies who were condemned to the domain of Pluto, not for profligacy but for refusing to yield to their lovers' caresses. (Clearly the 'moral' of the story was aimed directly at the bride of the Duke of Mantua, at whose nuptial celebrations the work received its première.) The poignant climax to this remarkably expressive piece comes with the beautiful aria sung by a 'lost spirit', who stays behind to plead the cause of her companions. The recorded sound is very beautiful, the balance excellent and the vocal projection very present and natural against an attractively warm ambience.

Il ballo delle ingrate; Sestina: Lagrime d'amante al sepolcro dell'amata.
**(*) HM Dig. HMC 901108 [id.]. Les Arts Florissants, Christie.

William Christie directs refreshingly dramatic accounts of both *Il ballo delle ingrate* and the *Sestina*. His singers have been chosen for character and bite rather than for beauty of tone, and the final lament of *Il ballo* is spoilt by exaggerated plaintiveness, but (particularly in the *Sestina*) the boldness of Christie's interpretation makes for very compelling performances, beautifully recorded. The note on the CD version irritatingly omits details of the soloists.

Il combattimento di Tancredi e Clorinda. L'Arianna: Lasciatemi Morire (Ariadne's lament) (with FARINA: *Sonata (La Desperata).* ROSSI: *Sonata sopra l'aria di Ruggiero.* FONTANA: *Sonata a tre violini.* MARINI: *Passacaglia a 4. Sonata sopra la Monica; Eco a tre violini.* BUONAMENTE: *Sonata a tre violini*).
**(*) DG 415 296-2 [id.]. C. Watkinson, Rogers, Kwella, David Thomas, Col. Mus. Ant., Goebel.

Carolyn Watkinson's singing of the *Lament* is finely controlled and certainly dramatic. So too is the performance of the touching and powerfully imaginative narrative about the battle of Tancredi and Clorinda, which understandably moved the audience to tears at its première. The other pieces are of more mixed appeal. Highlights are Fontana's engaging *Sonata for three violins* and Marini's ingenious *Eco a tre violini*, which is performed here to great effect, with the imitations echoing into the distance. Elsewhere, the slightly spiky sounds produced by the string players, with the close microphones bringing a touch of edginess, may not appeal to all tastes.

L'Incoronazione di Poppea.
*** Virgin Dig. VCT 790775-2 (3) [id.]. Arleen Augér, Della Jones, Linda Hirst, James Bowman, City of L. Bar. Sinfonia, Hickox.

The tender expressiveness of Arleen Augér in the title-role of Monteverdi's elusive masterpiece goes with a performance from Richard Hickox and the City of London Sinfonia which consistently reflects the fact that it was recorded in conjunction with a stage production. Hickox, following the latest scholarship, daringly uses a very spare accompaniment of continuo instruments, contrasting not just with the opulent score presented at Glyndebourne by Raymond Leppard, but with the previous period performance on record, that of Nikolaus Harnoncourt and the Concentus Musicus of Vienna, who has a far wider, more abrasive range of instrumental sound. Hickox overcomes the problems of that self-imposed limitation by choosing the widest possible range of speeds. So the exuberant Nero–Lucan duet after the death of Seneca is very fast and brilliant, while the heavenly final duet of the lovers – apparently not by Monteverdi at all – is extremely slow, rapt and gentle. The purity of Augér's soprano may make

Poppea less of a scheming seducer than she should be, but it is Monteverdi's music for the heroine which makes her so sympathetic in this oddly slanted, equivocal picture of Roman history, and one that has never sounded subtler or more lovely on record than here. Taking the castrato role of Nero, Della Jones sings very convincingly with full, rather boyish tone, while Gregory Reinhart is magnificent in the bass role of Seneca. James Bowman is a fine Ottone, with smaller parts taken by such excellent young singers as Catherine Denley, John Graham-Hall, Mark Tucker and Janice Watson. Linda Hirst sounds too raw of tone for Ottavia, making her a scold rather than a sympathetic suffering widow. Squeezed on to three well-filled CDs, the opera comes with libretto, translation and excellent notes by Clifford Bartlett.

Orfeo (opera): complete.
*** DG Dig. 419 250-2 (2) [id.]. Rolfe-Johnson, Baird, Lynne Dawson, Von Otter, Argenta, Robson, Monteverdi Ch., E. Bar. Soloists, Gardiner.
*** EMI Dig. CDS7 47142-8 (2) [Ang. CDCB 47141]. Nigel Rogers, Kwella, Kirkby, Jennifer Smith, Varcoe, David Thomas, Chiaroscuro, L. Bar. Ens., L. Cornett & Sackbutt Ens., Rogers & Medlam.

John Eliot Gardiner very effectively balances the often-conflicting demands of authentic performance – when this pioneering opera was originally presented intimately – and the obvious grandeur of the concept. So the 21-strong Monteverdi Choir conveys, on the one hand, high tragedy to the full, yet sings the lighter commentary from nymphs and shepherds with astonishing crispness, often at top speed. However, Gardiner is strong on pacing. He gives full and moving expansion to such key passages as the messenger's report of Euridice's death, sung with agonizing intensity by Anne Sophie von Otter. Lynne Dawson is also outstanding as the allegorical figure of Music in the Prologue, while Anthony Rolfe-Johnson shows his formidable versatility in the title-role. This is a set to take you through the story with new involvement. Though editing is not always immaculate, the recording on CD is vivid and full of presence.

In the EMI Reflexe version Nigel Rogers has the double function of singing the main part and acting as co-director. Since he first recorded the role, Rogers has modified his extraordinarily elaborate ornamentation in the hero's brilliant pleading aria before Charon, and makes the result all the freer and more wide-ranging in expression, with his distinctive fluttering timbre adding character. The sound of thunder that fatefully makes Orpheus turn around as he leads Euridice back to earth is all the more dramatic for being drily percussive; and Euridice's plaint, beautifully sung by Patrizia Kwella, is the more affecting for being accompanied very simply on the lute. The other soloists make a good team. The brightness of the cornetti is a special delight, when otherwise the instrumentation used – largely left optional in the score – is modest. Excellent, immediate recording.

Moody, James (born 1907)

(i) *Quintet for harmonica and string quartet;* (ii) *Suite dans le style français.*
*** Chan. Dig. CHAN 8802 [id.]. Tommy Reilly; (i) Hindar Qt; (ii) Skaila Kanga – JACOB: *Divertimento.****

James Moody has been Tommy Reilly's pianist for over thirty years and he learned to play the harmonica so that he could compose for his partner. His *Suite in the French style* may be pastiche but its impressionism is highly beguiling, especially when Reilly and Skaila Kanga create such exquisite textures. The *Quintet* is more ambitious, less charming perhaps, but likely to prove even more rewarding on investigation, especially the very diverse theme and variations of the finale, the longest movement. The performance and recording are hardly likely to be bettered.

Moscheles, Ignaz (1794–1870)

(i) *Double concerto for flute and oboe;* (ii) *Piano concerto No. 3 in G min. Bonbonnière musicale.*
*** Sup. SUP 001326 [id.]. (i) Valék, Mihule; (ii) Klánský; Dvořák CO, Pařík.

Ivan Klánský gives strong, attractive performances (helped by Pařík's polished accompaniment) in both the *Piano concerto* and the *Bonbonnière musicale,* an eight-movement suite, not at all trivial and often highly inventive. The *Concerto for flute and oboe* is lighter in style, and its unexpected opening demonstrates that Moscheles could be unconventional – it is a most winning work, particularly the gay finale with its complex intertwining of the two solo instruments. Excellent recording throughout, with a realistic balance in the concerto; the piano is a bit close in the suite, but the image is eminently realistic.

Mourant, Walter (born 1910)

The Pied Piper.
*** ASV Dig. CDDCA 568 [id.]. MacDonald, N. Sinfonia, Bedford – COPLAND: *Concerto*; FINZI: *Concerto.****

Walter Mourant's *Pied Piper* is a catchy, unpretentious little piece for clarinet, strings and celeste, which in a gently syncopated style effectively contrasts 3/4 and 6/8 rhythms. It makes an attractive filler after the Copland *Concerto.*

Mozart, Leopold (1719–87)

Cassation in G: Toy symphony (attrib. Haydn). (i) *Trumpet concerto in D.*
*** Erato/WEA Dig. 2292 45199-2. (i) Touvron; Paillard CO, Paillard – W. A. MOZART: *Musical Joke.****

One could hardly imagine this *Cassation* being done with more commitment from the effects department, while the music itself is elegantly played. The Minuet is particularly engaging, with its aviary of bird-sounds plus a vigorous contribution from the toy trumpet; and the finale, with its obbligato mêlée, is dispatched with an infectious sense of fun. After this, the more restrained approach to the excellent two-movement *Trumpet concerto* seems exactly right. The recording has plenty of presence and realism, with the balance very well judged, both for the solo trumpet and for the toy instruments in the *Cassation* – which are properly set back.

Cassation in G (Toy symphony).
(*) Ph. Dig. 416 386-2 [id.]. ASMF, Marriner – W. A. MOZART: *Serenade No. 13 (Eine kleine Nachtmusik)*, etc; PACHELBEL: *Canon and Gigue.*(*)

With the toy instruments played for all they are worth and more, the additions to the *Toy symphony* make the strongest contrast with Sir Neville's characteristically elegant and refined performance. This is generally effective, though the raucousness of the grotesquely mismatched cuckoo-whistle is hard to take. A good item in an attractive mixed bag, treated to warm, well-balanced recording.

Mozart, Wolfgang Amadeus (1756-91)

Cassations Nos. 1 in G, K.63; 2 in B flat, K.99; Adagio and fugue in C min., K.546.
*** Capriccio Dig. 10 192 [id.]. Salzburg Camerata, Végh.

These excellent performances of the early *Cassations*, so full of attractive invention, can be strongly recommended. The playing combines vitality with finesse and the allegros have an attractively light resilience and, to make a proper contrast, the Camerata under Végh find plenty of drama in the *Adagio and fugue*. Very good recording in a warm acoustic.

Cassation No. 2 in B flat, K.99; Divertimento No. 2 in D, K.131.
*** Ph. Dig. 420 924-2 [id.]. ASFM, Marriner.

The Academy strings bring the soul of finesse to these performances and, with the horns adding an agreeably robust element, there is sparkle as well as grace.

(i) *Bassoon concerto in B flat, K.191;* (ii) *Clarinet concerto in A, K.622.*
**(*) Claves Dig. CD 50-8205 [id.]. (i) Thunemann; (ii) Friedli; Zurich CO, Stoutz.

The performances on the Claves CD are first class, fresh and direct, sensitive without affectionate lingering, but with slow movements nicely expressive, and with plenty of vitality elsewhere. Klaus Thunemann's woody bassoon timbre has lots of character (although not all will take to his vibrato). The digital recording is bright, fresh and clean.

(i) *Bassoon concerto in B flat, K.191;* (ii) *Clarinet concerto in A, K.622;* (i; iii) *Sonata for bassoon & cello, K.292.*
**(*) Ph. Dig. 422 390-2 [id.]. (i) Thunemann, (ii) Leister, (iii) Stephen Orton, ASMF, Marriner.

Karl Leister plays the *Clarinet concerto* with his customary refinement and sensitivity, though perhaps some may find the overall impression a little bland, for which Neville Marriner must share some responsibility. Klaus Thunemann dispatches the *Bassoon concerto* with his usual virtuosity, though here Marriner's direction is a little impersonal. The *Sonata*, K.292, of 1775 is a slight makeweight and is elegantly played; and the 1989 recording has plenty of warmth and body.

Bassoon concerto; Clarinet concerto; Flute concerto No. 1, K.313; Flute and harp concerto; Oboe concerto, K.314b; Sinfonia concertante in E flat, K.297b.
(M) ** EMI CMS7 63472-2 (3) [Ang. CDMC 63472]. Soloists, BPO, Karajan.

Solo wind players who spend most of their musical lives working in orchestras develop an aptitude for blending their musical personalities to work within a team. This often means that, if they take on a solo role in a concerto, the listener is aware of a lack of individual strength of character in the player's image. So it is in this otherwise beautifully played series of performances, and Karajan's bland manner with the accompaniments does not help to give them individuality. Günther Piesk gives a highly musical account of the *Bassoon concerto* but there is a certain want of sparkle and spontaneity here, while in the *Clarinet concerto* Karl Leister is curiously self-effacing. Lothar Koch is much more successful in his fine version of the *Oboe concerto* but is backwardly balanced in relation to the fulsome orchestral tuttis. Andreas Blau's account of the *Flute concerto* too is impeccably played – though the first-movement cadenza is rather extended – and the superb artistry of James Galway and Fritz Helmis bring many details to admire in the *Flute and harp concerto*. But the blandness that afflicts Karajan's suave accompaniments is most striking in the *Sinfonia concertante* – perfectly blended as it is – though the finale has undoubted charm. The recording is rich and smooth, but detail and transparency are improved in the excellent CD transfers.

(i) *Bassoon concerto;* (ii) *Clarinet concerto;* (iii) *Oboe concerto, K.314.*
(M) *** DG 429 816-2 [id.]. (i) Zeman; (ii) Prinz; (iii) Turetschek, VPO, Boehm.

Dietmar Zeman gives a highly accomplished account of the *Bassoon concerto*, a distinguished performance by any standards. Prinz's account of the *Clarinet concerto* is also beautifully turned; both deserve a position of honour in the field. Turetschek is eminently civilized in the *Oboe concerto*, though his bright timbre is an individual one. The 1974/5 recordings are truthful and well balanced, with the upper range freshened on CD without being edgy.

Clarinet concerto in A, K.622; Bassoon concerto in B flat (arr. for clarinet).
(M) ** RCA GD 60379 [60379-2-RG]. Richard Stolzman, ECO, Schneider.

Richard Stolzman's performance of the *Clarinet concerto* is distinctive, particularly in matters of light and shade, and he plays the slow movement beautifully. The recording too has been vastly improved in its present transfer, the solo instrument both clear and full-timbred, and very present against a warmly expansive orchestral backcloth. The *Bassoon concerto*, however, loses much of its character in this transcription, and the clarinet image here is rather more reedy.

Clarinet concerto; Flute concerto No. 1, K.313; Andante for flute & orchestra, K.315; Flute & harp concerto; Oboe concerto; Horn concertos Nos. 1–4; Rondo for horn & orchestra, K.371.
(B) *** Ph. 426 148-2 (3) [id.]. Brymer, Claude Monteux, Ellis, Black, Civil, ASMF, Marriner.

A useful bargain collection on Philips. The performances of these concertos are among the finest available and, although the forward balance tends to make the soloists sound larger than life, the sound is otherwise realistic and eminently truthful in timbre. Jack Brymer's recording of the *Clarinet concerto* is the third he has made; in some ways it is his best, for he plays with deepened insight and feeling. The *Flute* and *Oboe concertos* are hardly less recommendable and the *Flute and harp concerto* is delightful, even if the instruments are made to seem jumbo-sized! Alan Civil's third recording of the *Horn concertos* is included, and this is discussed below.

(i) *Clarinet concerto;* (ii) *Flute and harp concerto in C, K.299.*
*** ASV Dig. CDDCA 532 [id.]. (i) Emma Johnson; (ii) Bennett, Ellis; ECO, Leppard.
(B) *** Pickwick Dig. PCD 852 [MCA MCAD 25965]. (i) Campbell; (ii) Davies, Masters; City of L. Sinfonia, Hickox.
(B) *** Decca 421 023-2 [id.]. (i) Alfred Prinz; (ii) Werner Tripp, Hubert Jellinek; VPO, Münchinger.

Emma Johnson's account of the *Clarinet concerto* has a sense of spontaneity, of natural magnetism which traps the ear from first to last. There may be some rawness of tone in places, but that only adds to the range of expression, which breathes the air of a live performance. Leppard and the ECO are in bouncing form, as they are too for the *Flute and harp concerto*, though here the two excellent soloists are somewhat on their best behaviour, until the last part of the finale sends Mozart bubbling up to heaven. First-rate recording.

David Campbell's agile and pointed performance of the clarinet work brings fastish speeds and a fresh, unmannered style in all three movements. Though some will prefer a weightier or more individual approach, and the reverberant recording tends not to differentiate the soloist sharply enough, his tonal shading is very beautiful. The earlier flute and harp work is just as freshly and sympathetically done, with a direct, unmannered style sounding entirely spontaneous.

The Decca bargain coupling dates from 1963 and the recording is smooth, rich and well judged in reverberation. The balance between soloists and orchestra is finely calculated and the performances are admirable, sounding as fresh as the day they were made. Refinement and beauty of tone and phrase are a hallmark throughout, and Münchinger provides most sensitive accompaniments.

(i) *Clarinet concerto in A, K.622;* (ii) *Oboe concerto in C, K.314.*
** O-L Dig. 414 339-2 [id.]. (i) Pay; (ii) Piguet, AAM, Hogwood.

Pay, using a basset clarinet, is a more restrained, less warm-toned player than his main rivals, with a relatively cool account of the beautiful slow movement; but that is apt for the 'authentic' stylistic aims of the performance. The French oboist, Michel Piguet, is an equally stylish soloist in the *Oboe concerto*, providing not a generous coupling but an attractive one. Clean, well-balanced recording.

(i) *Clarinet concerto;* (ii) *Clarinet quintet in A, K.581.*
*** Hyp. Dig. CDA 66199 [id.]. Thea King, (i) ECO, Tate; (ii) Gabrieli Qt.
(M) **(*) Ph. 420 710-2 [id.]. Brymer, (i) LSO, C. Davis; (ii) Allegri Qt.

Thea King's coupling brings together winning performances of Mozart's two great clarinet masterpieces. She steers an ideal course between classical stylishness and expressive warmth, with the slow movement becoming the emotional heart of the piece. The Gabrieli Quartet is equally responsive in its finely tuned playing. For the *Clarinet concerto* Thea King uses an authentically reconstructed basset clarinet such as Mozart wanted. Its extra range allows certain passages to be played as originally intended with octave jumps avoided. With Jeffrey Tate an inspired Mozartian, the performance – like that of the *Quintet* – is both stylish and expressive, with the finale given a captivating bucolic lilt. Excellent recording.

Jack Brymer's second recording of the *Clarinet concerto* has a warm, autumnal feeling, and its soft lyricism is appealing in the slow movement, but there is not quite the magic of the earlier version with Beecham, until a fast speed for the finale brings extra exhilaration. The *Quintet* is comparably warm and smiling; the sound is bright and fresh.

(i) *Clarinet concerto, K.622;* (ii) *Clarinet quintet, K.581;* (iii) *Clarinet trio (Kegelstatt), K.498.*
**(*) Mer. CDE 84169 [id.]. Joy Farrell, (i) Divertimenti, Nicholas Daniel; (ii) Divertimenti members; (iii) Garfield Jackson, Graham Johnson.

The idea of putting the three major Mozart chamber works featuring the clarinet on one CD is excellent, and it is a pity there are reservations to be made. Joy Farrell is a splendid soloist, phrasing with individuality and creating a full, glowing timbre. In the *Concerto* she uses a basset clarinet, and clearly relishes – often in an agreeably whimsical way – the throaty sounds it makes at the very bottom of its register, which Mozart so wittily contrasts with the rich upper range. The *Adagio* is gloriously sustained, and the finale is appropriately spirited with matching accompaniments. The *Quintet* is a fine performance too, the solo instrument warmly integrated with the strings; again the spacious account of the *Larghetto* is memorable. But the reverberant acoustics of St Edward the Confessor's Church, Mottingham, create a very ample texture and there is a loss of subtlety, even though the effect is easy on the ear. This lack of sharpness of focus is even more noticeable in the *Kegelstatt trio*, given an amiable, if not distinctive performance. While Miss Farrell dominates throughout, the pianist, Graham Johnson, does not show a very strong personality: his diffidence is noticeable at his very opening phrase.

(i) *Clarinet concerto; Symphonies Nos. 25 in G min., K.183; 29 in A, K.201.*
* DG Dig. 429 221-2 [id.]. (i) Schmidl; VPO, Bernstein.

Bernstein's coupling of the two finest of the early symphonies with the last masterpiece among the concertos makes a generous if illogical coupling; unfortunately, however, the performances are too flawed to allow much of a recommendation. In No. 29 the first three movements are rhythmically too heavy at slow speeds. The finale marks a complete transformation; conversely, it is the finale of No. 25 which tends to be slack. With the same orchestra on the same label, James Levine is far fresher and crisper, as many others are too. Peter Schmidl is a disappointing clarinet soloist in the *Concerto*, so reedy of tone that his playing often sounds pinched, with rhythms apt to sag in all three movements.

Flute concerto No. 1 in G, K.313; Andante in C, K.315; (i) *Flute and harp concerto in C, K.299.*
*** Ph. Dig. 422 339-2 [id.]. Irena Grafenauer; (i) Maria Graf; ASMF, Marriner.
(M) *** Ph. 420 880-2 [id.]. Claude Monteux; (i) Ellis; ASMF, Marriner.

Flute concertos Nos. (i) *1 in G, K.313;* (ii) *2 in D, K.314.*
(B) *** Pickwick Dig. PCD 871. Judith Hall, Philh. O, Peter Thomas.
(B) *** Decca 421 630-2. William Bennett, ECO, Malcolm – CIMAROSA: *Double flute concerto.***(*)
(B) *** Pickwick PCD 807. Galway, New Irish Chamber Ens., Prieur.
(B) ** DG 427 211-2 [id.]. (i) Linde, Munich CO, Stadlmair; (ii) Nicolet, Lucerne Fest. O, Baumgartner – SALIERI: *Concerto for flute and oboe.****

Flute concertos Nos. 1 in G, K.313; 2 in D, K.314; Andante in C, K.315.
(B) **(*) Ph. 426 074-2 [id.]. Aurèle Nicolet, Concg. O, Zinman.
(BB) **(*) Hung. White Label HRC 107 [id.] (without *Andante*). Lóránt Kovács, Hungarian State O, Ervin Lukács – M. HAYDN: *Concerto.***

Flute concertos Nos. 1 in G, K.313; 2 in D, K.314; Andante in C, K.315; Rondo in C, K.373 (originally for violin and orchestra).
**(*) Chan. CHAN 8613 [id.]. Susan Milan, ECO, Leppard.

Judith Hall produces a radiantly full timbre. Moreover she is a first-class Mozartian, as she demonstrates in her cadenzas as well as in the line of the slow movements, phrased with a simple eloquence that is disarming. There is plenty of vitality in the allegros, and Peter Thomas provides polished, infectious accompaniments to match the solo playing. The balance is most realistic and the sound overall is in the demonstration bracket.

William Bennett also gives a beautiful account of the *Flute concertos*, among the finest to have appeared in recent years. Every phrase is shaped with both taste and affection, and the playing of the ECO under George Malcolm is fresh and vital. The recording is clean, well detailed and with enough resonance to lend bloom to the sound.

Needless to say, Galway plays this music superbly and his Pickwick alternative is also a bargain. The accompaniments, ably directed by André Prieur, are reasonably polished and stylish, and the recording (although it gives a rather small sound to the violins) is excellent, clear and with good balance and perspective. It might be argued that Galway's vibrato is not entirely suited to these eighteenth-century works and that his cadenzas, too, are slightly anachronistic. But the star quality of his playing disarms criticism.

Anyone looking for a new digital recording of Mozart's *Flute and harp concerto* could be very happy with the stylishly conceived version by Irena Grafenauer and Maria Graf. Marriner's tempi are apt and the solo playing is highly sensitive, with Grafenauer's nicely focused timbre the right scale for the music. She plays with equal sensibility in the solo concerto and the *Andante*, K.315, its alternative slow movement. The recording is first class and is beautifully balanced.

Exquisite playing on the earlier Philips record (with Claude Monteux) from all concerned. The only reservation is that the solo instruments sound larger than life as balanced. In every other respect this splendidly remastered disc is highly recommendable.

Susan Milan displays a nice balance between expressive feeling and felicity of bravura in outer movements. She is effectively and sympathetically accompanied by Leppard and the ECO. The recording is resonant, and this means that textures are fairly opulent; this is especially noticeable in slow movements, where Susan Milan's phrasing is strongly contoured and her timbre quite rich.

The Nicolet/Zinman couplings are now available at bargain price, although these are fairly new recordings (1978). The performances are very positive, with the flute balanced well forward and dominating the proceedings, though David Zinman's accompaniments are alert and strong. Both finales are particularly attractive, briskly paced, and the solo playing throughout is expert and elegantly phrased. However, Galway displays a lighter touch generally and is to be preferred.

The performances by Lóránt Kovács have winning simplicity of line, and these are thoroughly musical accounts. The accompaniments are stylish too; the minuet finale of No. 1 has striking character. The recording is full, the flute forwardly balanced.

Two different soloists on the DG Privilege reissue, with Linde rather less flexible in allegros than Nicolet, but both playing impeccably and offering poised slow movements. The sound is lively and fresh, and the coupling is attractive.

Flute concertos Nos. 1–2; (i) *Flute and harp concerto, K.299.*
(M) *** DG 429 815-2 [id.]. Zöller, (i) Zabaleta; VPO, Boehm.

Karlheinz Zöller is a superb flautist. K.313 is a little cool but is played most elegantly, with pure tone and unmannered phrasing; the charming minuet finale is poised and graceful. The performance of K.314 is more relaxed and smiling. Zöller favours the use of comparatively extended cadenzas, and one wonders whether they will not seem too much of a good thing on repetition. However, the 1974 recording gives him a radiant timbre and he is very persuasive. The admirably played *Flute and harp concerto* is discussed below in its alternative bargain coupling.

Flute and harp concerto in C, K.299.
(B) *** DG 427 206-2 [id.]. Zöller, Zabaleta, BPO, Märzendorfer – HANDEL; WAGENSEIL: *Harp concertos.****

The outer movements of this DG performance have an attractive rhythmic buoyancy. The flautist is a most sensitive player and his phrasing is a constant pleasure, while Zabaleta's poise and sense of line knit the overall texture of the solo-duet together most convincingly. Märzendorfer conducts with warmth yet with a firm overall control. In short, with fresh, clear recorded sound, this is highly successful.

(i) *Flute and harp concerto in C, K.299;* (ii) *Oboe concerto in C, K.314.*
(M) ** EMI Dig. CD-EMX 9510 [Ang. CDM 62027]. (i) Snowden, Thomas; (ii) Hunt, LPO, Litton.

The performance of the *Flute and harp concerto* is the more winning here. Where Gordon Hunt in the *Oboe concerto* seems a less natural concerto soloist, the flautist Jonathan Snowden, in collaboration with Caryl Thomas on the harp, is both sparkling and sensitive, a natural soloist, regularly imaginative in his individual phrasing.

(i) *Flute and harp concerto in C, K.299;* (ii) *Sinfonia concertante for flute, oboe, horn, bassoon and orchestra in E flat, K.297b.*
**(*) CBS Dig. MK 44524 [id.]. Rampal, (i) Nordmann; (ii) Pierlot, Koster, Allard; Liszt CO, Rolla.

Rampal has a strong personality, but he forms a good partnership with Marielle Nordmann in the *Flute and harp concerto.* He is joined by a distinguished roster of other wind-players for the *Sinfonia concertante;* there is much to enjoy here, with considerable charm in the variations which make up the finale. The recording is well balanced in both works, but the resonance does prevent detail from being absolutely sharp.

Horn concertos Nos. 1 in D, K.412; 2–4 in E flat, K.417, 447 & 495.
(M) (*(**)) EMI mono CDH7 61013-2 [id.]. Dennis Brain, Philh. O, Karajan.
*** Decca Dig. 410 284-2 [id.]. Barry Tuckwell, ECO.
(M) *** Decca 417 767-2 [id.]. Barry Tuckwell, LSO, Maag – HAYDN: *Concerto No. 1.***
(M) *** Teldec/WEA 2292 42757-2 [id.]. Hermann Baumann (hand-horn), VCM, Harnoncourt.
(M) *** DG 429 817-2 [id.]. Gerd Seifert, BPO, Karajan.
(M) **(*) DG Dig. 427 814-2 [id.]. David Jolley (*1 & 4*); William Purvis (*2–3*); Orpheus CO.

Horn concertos Nos. 1–4; Concert rondo in E flat, K.371 (ed. Civil or E. Smith).
(M) *** EMI CD-EMX 2004 [Ang. CDM 69281]. Alan Civil, RPO, Kempe.
*** EMI Dig. CDC7 47453-2 [id.]. Radovan Vlatković, ECO, Tate.
(M) *** Ph. 420 709-2 [id.]. Alan Civil, ASMF, Marriner.

Horn concertos Nos. 1–4; Concert rondo, K.371 (ed. Tuckwell); *Fragment, K.494a.*
(M) *** EMI CDM7 69569-2. Barry Tuckwell, ASMF, Marriner.

Dennis Brain's famous 1954 record with Karajan is a somewhat diminished shadow in its CD format, for the remastering has been mismanaged; in seeking to achieve greater presence and clarity, the engineers have produced emaciated, shrill violin tone. Fortunately the horn timbre is unimpaired, but the orchestra has lost its bloom and some of its weight. The glorious tone and phrasing – every note is alive – is life-enhancing in its warmth; the *espressivo* of the slow movements is matched by the joy of the Rondos, spirited, buoyant, infectious and smiling. Karajan's accompaniments, too, are a model of Mozartian good manners and the Philharmonia at their peak play wittily and elegantly.
Barry Tuckwell has re-recorded the four concertos digitally – without extra items – and in the brightly focused new digital set he plays as well as ever and also directs the accompanying ECO, ensuring that the string phrasing echoes the horn in every detail. The orchestra provides crisp, polished and elegant accompaniments, to make a perfectly scaled backcloth for solo playing which again combines natural high spirits with a warmly expressive understanding of the Mozartian musical line.
Tuckwell's first (1960) stereo recording of the *Horn concertos* (perhaps even more

spontaneous) re-emerges freshly on Decca's mid-price label, now shorn of the *Fragment*, K.494a, but offering instead Haydn's best concerto, to make this earlier record more competitive. Peter Maag's accompaniments are admirably crisp and nicely scaled, giving his soloist buoyant support, and the vintage recording still sounds astonishingly well.

However, EMI have effectively remastered Tuckwell's second set with Marriner, and the 1972 recording sounds fuller, with slightly more body to the violins. Marriner's direction of the accompaniments is agreeably warm and elegant. This mid-priced CD has the advantage of including not only the *Concert rondo* but also the *Fragment in E* which ends where Mozart left it at bar 91. Altogether the vigour and grace of this music-making commend this record highly, alongside the Decca.

Alan Civil, like Tuckwell, recorded the concertos three times, but the earliest set, with Kempe, is the freshest and most rewarding. He plays with a simple eloquence, a full tone and a flawless technique. His sensitivity is present in every bar and Kempe accompanies benignly and with great affection. The warm 1967 recording has been cleanly remastered, although the RPO violins sound somewhat thinner above the stave than on the Tuckwell/Marriner recordings.

Radovan Vlatković's tone is very full, with the lower harmonics telling more resonantly than is characteristic of a British soloist; there is also the slightest hint of vibrato at times, but it is applied with great discretion and used mostly in the cadenzas. His performances are full of imaginative touches, and he has the perfect partner in Jeffrey Tate, who produces sparkling accompaniments. All in all, another outstanding set, winningly different from the playing of the British generation. Vlatković includes the *Concert rondo*, K.371, a substantial bonus.

Hermann Baumann successfully uses the original hand-horn, without valves, for which the concertos were written, and the result is a *tour de force* of technical skill, not achieved at the expense of musical literacy or expressive content. Inevitably this implies at least some alterations in timbre, as certain notes have to be 'stopped', with the hand in the bell of the instrument, if they are to be in tune. Baumann is not in the least intimidated by this problem; he lets the listener hear the stopped effect only when he decides that the tonal change can be put to good artistic effect. In his cadenzas he also uses horn chords (where several notes are produced simultaneously by resonating the instrument's harmonics), but as a complement to the music rather than as a gimmick. While the horn is given added presence and tangibility in the digital remastering, the brightness of the strings has brought some roughness of focus, since the original recording was mellow and reverberant.

Alan Civil's most recent set was made in 1973. The recording is obviously more modern and the performances are highly enjoyable, with Sir Neville Marriner's polished and lively accompaniments giving pleasure in themselves. The balance has the effect of making the horn sound slightly larger than life.

Gerd Seifert has been principal horn of the Berlin Philharmonic since 1964, and his velvety, warm tone is familiar on many records. His articulation is light and neat here and his nimbleness brings an effective lightness to the gay Rondos. Karajan almost matches his earlier accompaniments for Dennis Brain, and the orchestral playing is strong in character, although he never overwhelms his soloist. The 1969 recording now brings just a hint of over-brightness on the *forte* violins, but this adds to the sense of vitality without spoiling the elegance.

The appropriately named David Jolley is very personable in the *First* and *Fourth Concertos*. Rondos are played with a winning flair and crisp articulation, while he can fine his tone down to a pianissimo with striking sensibility, and the slow movement of K.495 (No. 4) is particularly imaginative. A comparable use of light and shade elsewhere makes both performances distinctive, in the accompaniments as well as the solo playing.

In the remaining two concertos, William Purvis plays fluently and agreeably, if not with quite the flair of his colleague; he is a shade deliberate in the slow movement of the *Third Concerto*, K.447. The recording is first class, naturally balanced and believable in scale, and anyone wanting a mid-priced digital set of these concertos might consider this reissue.

Oboe concerto in C, K.314.
*** ASV Dig. CDCOE 808 [id.]. Douglas Boyd, COE, Berglund – R. STRAUSS: *Oboe concerto.****

Oboe concerto in C, K.314; Arias: Ah se in ciel, benigne stelle, K.538; Sperai vicino il lido, K.368.
(*) Ph. Dig. 420 179-2 [id.]. Heinz Holliger, ASMF, Sillito – FERLENDIS: *Concerto.*(*)

Douglas Boyd is never afraid to point the phrasing individually, spontaneously and without mannerism. Others may be purer in their classicism, but this is a very apt reading next to Strauss. Recorded in Henry Wood Hall, the sound is full and vivid.

This is Holliger's third recording of Mozart's *Concerto*: his timbre is creamier than ever in the lovely melisma of the *Adagio*, while the finale Minuet-Rondo has the most engaging rhythmic felicity. Holliger makes less of a case for the transposition of the arias; without the words, they are much less interesting. The accompaniments are polished and stylish, but the acoustic is perhaps a shade too resonant.

Piano concertos (for piano and strings) after J. C. Bach, K.107, Nos. 1 in D; 2 in G; 3 in E flat.
*** CBS Dig. MK 39222 [id.]. Perahia, ECO – SCHROTER: *Piano concerto.****

Piano concertos: K.107/1-3; Nos. 1-6, 8, 9, 11-27; Concert rondos Nos. 1-2, K.382 and 386.
⊛ *** CBS M13K 42055 (13) [id.]. Perahia, ECO (with SCHROTER: *Concerto*).

(i) *Piano concertos Nos. 1-6; 8-9; 11-27;* (ii) *Double piano concerto in E flat. K.365;* (iii) *Triple piano concerto in F, K.242.*
(M) *** Decca Dig./Analogue 425 557-2 (12). (i) Ashkenazy, Philh. O; (ii) Ashkenazy, Barenboim, ECO, (iii) with Fou Ts'ong.

Piano concertos Nos. 1-6; 8-9; 11-27; Rondo in D, K.382.
(M) *** EMI CZS7 62825-2 (10). Daniel Barenboim, ECO.
(M) ** DG 429 001-2 (10) (without *Rondo*). Géza Anda, Salzburg Mozarteum.

Piano concertos Nos. 5, 6, 8, 9, 11-27; (i) *Double piano concertos, K.242 and K.365; Concert rondos 1-2.*
**(*) Ph. 412 856-2 (10) [id.]. Brendel, (i) Imogen Cooper; ASMF, Marriner.

Murray Perahia's cycle is a remarkable achievement and it is difficult to imagine its being surpassed. In terms of poetic insight and musical spontaneity, the performances are in a class of their own. There is a wonderful singing line and at the same time a sensuousness that is always tempered by spirituality. The CBS recordings have improved since the cycle started and the more recent are excellent – although generally the sound Decca have afforded Ashkenazy has greater bloom and a firmer focus.

The sense of spontaneity in Barenboim's performances of the Mozart concertos, his message that this is music hot off the inspiration line, is hard to resist, even though it occasionally leads to over-exuberance and idiosyncrasies. On balance, fast movements are faster than usual and slow movements slower, but that view has powerful backing and any inconsistencies or romantic touches seem merely incidental to the forward drive. These are as nearly live performances as one could hope for on record, and the playing of the English Chamber Orchestra is splendidly geared to the approach of an artist with whom the players have worked regularly. They are recorded with fullness, and the sound is generally freshened very successfully in the remastering, with the piano tone remaining natural. Certainly this is the most invigorating cycle available at less than full price.

Ashkenazy's set with the Philharmonia has appeared over more than a decade: the early *Concertos* are the most recent (1987), while the *G major*, K.453, and the *C major*, K.467, come from 1977. The account of the *E flat Concerto*, K.365, with Barenboim and the ECO and the *Triple concerto* with Fou Ts'ong to complete the trio, is earlier still (1972). These performances have won golden opinions over the years, and the clarity of both the performances and the recordings is refreshing: indeed the fine Decca sound is one of their strongest features. With the twelve CDs at mid-price, they make an attractive proposition. However, looking back over the cycle, their insights do not seem to strike as deeply as the Perahia (still at full price) or the earlier ECO set with Barenboim (EMI).

Brendel's 'complete' box does not include the four early concertos, K.37 and K.39–41, or the three based on J. C. Bach, K.107. Throughout, his thoughts are never less than penetrating. Where analogue recordings have been transferred to CD, the digital remastering has produced clean and successful results. The transfers are consistently of the very highest quality, as is the playing of the Academy of St Martin-in-the-Fields under Sir Neville Marriner.

Were the competition not so fierce, Anda's performances could carry a stronger recommendation. They are beautifully poised and have excellent feeling for style; some are quite memorable for their unidiosyncratic freshness. The recordings do not quite match those of Barenboim, and Anda is a less individual artist, but the sound is clean and well balanced and gives consistent enjoyment. But this set would have been better reissued on DG's bargain label.

Piano concertos Nos. 1 in F, K.37; 2 in B flat, K.39; 3 in D, K.40; 4 in G, K.41.
*** CBS Dig. MK 39225 [id.]. Murray Perahia, ECO.
*** EMI CDC7 47987-2 [id.]. Daniel Barenboim, ECO.

The first four concertos which occupy Perahia's present issue date from the spring or summer of 1767, when Mozart was eleven. Of course, they are not the equal of any of his more mature concertos; however, played with such grace and affection as here, they make delightful listening.

Barenboim, too, gives sensitive accounts of all four works. The 1975 recording has been remastered most successfully: the piano tone remains very natural and now the orchestral texture sounds fresher and more transparent.

Piano concertos (i) *Nos. 1 in F, K.37; 2 in B flat, K.39; 3 in D, K.40; 4 in G, K.41; 5 in D, K.175; 6 in B flat, K.238;* (ii) *Concerto in F for 3 pianos, K.242.*
*** Decca 421 577-2 (2) [id.]. (i) Ashkenazy, Philh. O; (ii) Ashkenazy, Barenboim, Fou Ts'ong, ECO, Barenboim.

The celebrated recording of the *F major Concerto*, K.242, with Barenboim and Fou Ts'ong derives from the mid-1970s, but the others are new – and very good. In many ways these are delightful recordings, well ventilated and full-bodied and, for those who have been collecting Ashkenazy, they can be confidently recommended.

Piano concertos Nos. 5 in D, K.175; 6 in B flat, K.238.
**(*) Ph. Dig. 416 366-2 [id.]. Alfred Brendel, ASMF, Marriner.

Short measure at 43 minutes, but some lively playing from Brendel in these early works. He is brightly recorded. There is prose as well as poetry here, but admirers need not hesitate.

Piano concertos Nos. 5 in D, K.175; 8 in C, K.246. Concert rondos Nos. 1 in D, K.382; 2 in A, K.386.
*** DG Dig. 415 990-2 [id.]. Malcolm Bilson (fortepiano), E. Bar. Soloists, Gardiner.

Bilson's coupling of the two early, lightweight *Concertos* with the two *Concert rondos* demonstrates the advantages of period performance at their most telling. What comes out in these early concertos, perhaps even more pointedly than in later and more individual works, is the expressive tonal range possible on the fortepiano in even the simplest passage-work. Warm, well-balanced recording.

Piano concertos Nos. 5 in D, K.175; 25 in C, K.503.
*** CBS Dig. MK 37267 [id.]. Murray Perahia, ECO.

Murray Perahia has the measure of the strength and scale of the *C major*, K.503, as well as displaying tenderness and poetry; while the early *D major*, K.175, has an innocence and freshness that are completely persuasive. The recording is good, but the upper strings are a little fierce and not too cleanly focused.

Piano concertos Nos. 6 in B flat, K.238; 13 in C, K.415.
*** CBS MK 39223 [id.]. Murray Perahia, ECO.

Perahia brings a marvellous freshness and delicacy to the *B flat Concerto*, K.238, but it is in the *C major*, with its sense of character and subtle artistry, that he is at his most sparkling and genial. Even if the acoustic ambience is less than ideally spacious, the CBS sound is still good.

Piano concertos Nos. 8 in C (Lützow), K.246; 9 in E flat (Jeunehomme), K.271.
**(*) Decca Dig. 414 543-2 [id.]. Vladimir Ashkenazy, Philh. O.

Thoroughly musical performances from Ashkenazy and the Philharmonia, though some may find the slow movements a little too relaxed. However, the playing is still sunny and the fresh Decca recording is beautifully balanced.

Piano concertos Nos. 8 in C (Lützow), K.246; 9 in E flat (Jeunehomme), K.271; Concert rondo in A, K.386.
(B) * Pickwick Dig. PCD 931. Diana Ambache, Ambache CO.

Though Diana Ambache is a sympathetic Mozartian, these performances are without a strong profile, particularly in the orchestra. The opening of K.271 (which comes first) could be more alert, and the following *Andantino* ideally needs a more positive onward flow. The first movement of K.246 has more rhythmic character, but neither of the finales sparkle as they might.

Piano concertos Nos. 8 in C, K.246; 11 in F, K.413; 14 in E flat, K.449.
**(*) EMI Dig. CDC7 49791-2 [id.]. Collard, Quatuor Muir.

Even with a pianist of Jean-Philippe Collard's distinction there seems rather little point in recording these concertos *à quattro*, particularly on a modern grand. However, Collard plays with characteristic distinction and charm, and his admirers will doubtless not want to disregard anything by him: he makes all too few records.

Piano concertos Nos. 8 in C, K.246; 26 in D (Coronation), K.537.
*** Ph. Dig. 411 468-2. Alfred Brendel, ASMF, Marriner.

Brendel's articulation and intelligence excite admiration: everything is well thought out and impressively realized. Only in the slow movement of the *Coronation concerto* does one feel a trace of didacticism. The digital recording is most naturally balanced.

Piano concertos Nos. 9 in E flat, K.271; 11 in F, K.413.
*** DG Dig. 410 905-2 [id.]. Malcolm Bilson (fortepiano), E. Bar. Soloists, Gardiner.

Malcolm Bilson here shows himself to be a lively and imaginative artist, well matched by the ever-effervescent and alert Gardiner. The recording on CD catches superbly the lightness and clarity of the textures; the darkness of the C minor slow movement of K.271 is eerily caught. Bilson chooses fast allegros, but never at the expense of Mozart.

(i) *Piano concertos Nos. 9 in E flat, K.271; 14 in E flat, K.449. Fantasia in C min., K.396.*
(B) *** Van. VCD 72022 [id.]. Alfred Brendel; (i) I Solisti di Zagreb, Janigro.

Brendel's 1968 performance of No. 9 is quite outstanding, elegant and beautifully precise. The classical-sized orchestra is just right and the neat, stylish string-playing matches the soloist. Both pianist and conductor are sensitive to the gentle melancholy of the slow movement, and in the contrasting middle section of the finale Brendel's tonal nuance is beautifully shaded. The performance of K.449 is also first rate, with a memorably vivacious finale. Altogether this is an outstanding bargain reissue with natural sound which hardly shows its age in the clean remastering. The rather serious account of the *Fantasy*, which comes first on the record, has a much drier acoustic and the forward balance brings a less natural effect.

Piano concertos Nos. 9 in E flat, K.271; 21 in C, K.467.
*** CBS MK 34562 [id.]. Murray Perahia, ECO.

Perahia's reading of K.271 is wonderfully refreshing and delicate, with diamond-bright articulation, urgently youthful in its resilience. The famous *C major Concerto* is given a more variable, though still highly imaginative performance. Faithful, well-balanced recording.

Piano concertos Nos. 11 in F, K.413; 12 in A, K.414; 14 in E flat, K.449.
*** CBS MK 42243 [id.]. Murray Perahia, ECO.

These performances remain in a class of their own. When it first appeared, we thought the *F major*, K.413, the most impressive of Perahia's Mozart concerto records so far, its slow movement wonderfully inward; and the *E flat Concerto*, K.449, is comparably distinguished.

Piano concertos Nos. 11 in F, K.413; 14 in E flat, K.449.
**(*) Decca Dig. 417 627-2 [id.]. Vladimir Ashkenazy, Philh. O.

Ashkenazy's playing is very fine indeed and he displays many subtleties in both *Concertos.* In the *F major*, Ashkenazy's slow movement, though beautiful, is not as freshly poetic as the CBS reading, nor does the finale of the *E flat* have quite the keen abandon of the Perahia. But the Decca recording is first class.

Piano concertos Nos. 11 in F, K.413; 16 in D, K.451.
*** Ph. Dig. 415 488-2 [id.]. Alfred Brendel, ASMF, Marriner.

Brendel's performances are distinguished by wonderful clarity of articulation: the ideas are always finely shaped without ever being overcharacterized. Both recordings are refreshing in sound and to the spirit.

Piano concertos Nos. 12 in A, K.414; 13 in C, K.415.
*** Decca Dig. 410 214-2 [id.]. Vladimir Ashkenazy, Philh. O.

Vladimir Ashkenazy's account of K.414 and 415 must be numbered among the most successful of his cycle. His account of the *A major* admirably combines expressive feeling with sparkle and conveys real enjoyment. The *C major* has equally strong claims and readers collecting the Ashkenazy survey will not be disappointed. The piano is forwardly balanced, but the naturalness of timbre and the transparency and bloom on the overall sound-picture are such as to confound criticism.

Piano concertos Nos. 12 in A, K.414; 14 in E flat, K.449.
*** DG Dig. 413 463-2 [id.]. Malcolm Bilson (fortepiano), E Bar. Soloists, Gardiner.
**(*) Chan. Dig. CHAN 8455 [id.]. Louis Lortie, I Musici di Montreal, Turovsky.

Malcolm Bilson's coupling of the '*Little A major*', K.414, and the tough *Concerto in E flat*, K.449, is one of the finest of the Archiv series. Gardiner and the English Baroque Soloists again prove to be ideal accompanists, matching Bilson's expressiveness on the one hand while on the other relishing the very fast speeds he prefers in finales. The extra clarity of authentic instruments makes the music seem all the stronger in its lean resilience. Fresh, clear recording.

Louis Lortie gives sensitive accounts of both *Concertos*, full of natural poetry and imagination, and the accompaniments are stylish and resilient; the only questionable point is the reverberant Chandos recording, less apt in Mozart than in Romantic music.

Piano concertos Nos. 12 in A, K.414; 21 in C, K.467.
(B) **(*) Decca 417 773-2. Lupu, ECO, Segal – BEETHOVEN: *32 Variations in C min.****

There is much that is beautiful here, including hushed playing from Radu Lupu in the slow movements of both concertos. The music-making has life and sensibility, and both performances are very enjoyable. The recording is brightly lit, but this is excellent value.

Piano concertos Nos. 12 in A, K.414; 23 in A, K.488.
(M) **(*) Hung. Dig. HCD 12472 [id.]. Zoltán Kocsis, Liszt CO, Rolla.

In the 'little' *A major Concerto*, K.414, Kocsis is marvellously sensitive and alert, and he is given excellent support by Janos Rolla. As piano playing, this can hold its own with the best; the performance of K.488 is hardly less impressive. Kocsis is unfailingly vital and imaginative, although to some ears his sparkling finale will seem rushed off its feet. The recording is a little wanting in opulence and bloom, yet there is much to delight the collector here.

Piano concertos Nos. 13 in C, K.415; 14 in E flat, K.449.
**(*) Ph. Dig. 422 359-2 [id.]. Mitsuko Uchida, ECO, Tate.

Jeffrey Tate draws splendid playing from the ECO and Uchida is unfailingly elegant. Her account of the slow movement of K.449 is a little over-civilized and the finale needs more abandon and character. There is some lovely playing in K.415, but her cultured reading of the slow movement offers more than a glimpse of Dresden china. The recording is marvellous, but this is not a first choice.

Piano concertos Nos. 13 in C, K.415; 15 in B flat, K.450.
*** DG Dig. 413 464-2 [id.]. Malcolm Bilson (fortepiano), E. Bar. Soloists, Gardiner.

Festive with trumpets, K.415 makes a striking impact here, despite the modest-sized forces (5, 4, 2, 2, 1 strings). Though Bilson opts for brisk allegros, which emerge with exceptional clarity, he and Gardiner relax well in the central andante and the two adagio episodes of the finale. K.450 brings woodwind to the fore, and the English Baroque players match their string colleagues in stylishness. The recording is nicely balanced without spotlighting, so vivid you can hear the clicking keys of the wind instruments.

Piano concertos Nos. 14 in E flat, K.449; 15 in E flat, K.450; 16 in D, K.451.
(M) *** EMI CDM7 69124-2 [id.]. Barenboim, ECO.

Barenboim's playing is spontaneous and smiling, while the orchestra respond with genuine vitality and sparkle. K.451 is particularly enjoyable, with a brisk, jaunty account of the first movement, a flowing expressive slow movement and an exuberant finale. Good recording throughout, and a sensible price.

(i) *Piano concerto No. 15 in B flat, K.450; Symphony No. 36 (Linz), K.425.*
(M) **(*) Decca 417 790-2 [id.]. (i) Bernstein (piano); VPO, Bernstein.

An enjoyably light-hearted Mozartian coupling. In the performance of the *Linz symphony*, one relishes the carefree quality in the playing. The *Concerto*, even more than the *Symphony*, conveys the feeling of a conductor enjoying himself on holiday. Bernstein's piano playing may not be poised in every detail, but every note communicates vividly – so much so that in the slow movement he even manages to make his dual tempo convincing – faster for the tuttis than for the more romantic solos. The finale is taken surprisingly slowly, but Bernstein brings it off. The sound projects vividly in its new format.

Piano concertos Nos. 15 in B flat, K.450; 16 in D, K.451.
*** CBS Dig. MK 37824 [id.]. Murray Perahia, ECO.
*** Decca 411 612-2 [id.]. Vladimir Ashkenazy, Philh. O.

Perahia's are superbly imaginative readings, full of seemingly spontaneous touches and turns of phrase very personal to him, which yet never sound mannered. His version of the *B flat Concerto* has sparkle, grace and intelligence; both these performances are very special indeed. The recording is absolutely first rate, intimate yet realistic and not dry, with the players continuously grouped round the pianist.

Ashkenazy takes a more direct view, yet there is a fine sensibility here and many imaginative touches: both slow movements are played very beautifully yet without a trace of narcissism, and the finales sparkle. There is some splendid wind playing from the Philharmonia and the result is consistently clean and refreshing. The Decca sound is excellent.

Piano concertos Nos. 15 in B flat, K.450; 21 in C, K.467.
*** Ph. Dig. 400 018-2 [id.]. Alfred Brendel, ASMF, Marriner.

Brendel's outer movements of K.467 are brisk, but tempo is not in itself a problem. Each detail of a phrase is meticulously articulated, every staccato and slur carefully observed. The finale sounds over-rehearsed, for some of the joy and high spirits are sacrificed in the sense of momentum. However, there is much to delight in both these performances. The playing is very distinguished, and so, too, is the recording.

Piano concertos Nos. 16 in D, K.451; 17 in G, K.453.
*** DG Dig. 415 525-2 [id.]. Malcolm Bilson (fortepiano), E. Bar. Soloists, Gardiner.

In K.451 the gains are greater than usual, with textures so beautifully clarified and the relationship between keyboard and orchestra revealed on record more tellingly than it would be in concert, thanks to shrewd balancing. K.453, as ever, is a delight, with Bilson allowing himself a natural degree of expressiveness within the limits of classical taste. As in the rest of the series, he uses apt ornamentation in the slow movements, in the *Andante* of K.451 adding discreetly to the decorations which Mozart himself wrote out for his sister. Warm, well-balanced recording.

Piano concertos Nos. 17 in G, K.453; 18 in B flat, K.456.
*** CBS MK 36686 [id.]. Murray Perahia, ECO.

The *G major Concerto* is one of the most magical of the Perahia cycle and is on no account to be missed. The *B flat*, too, has the sparkle, grace and finesse that one expects from him. Even if you have other versions, you should still add this to your collection, for its insights are quite special.

Piano concertos Nos. 17 in G, K.453; 21 in C, K.467.
*** Decca 411 947-2 [id.]. Vladimir Ashkenazy, Philh. O.
(B) **(*) DG 429 522-2 [id.]. Géza Anda, Camerata Academica of Salzburg Mozarteum.

Ashkenazy's performances combine a refreshing spontaneity with an overall sense of proportion and balance. There is a fine sense of movement, and yet nothing is hurried; detail is finely characterized, but nothing is fussy. Moreover the recording is clear and lucid, with the balance between soloist and orchestra finely judged.

In the *G major*, K.453, Anda, who is soloist and conductor, errs a little on the side of heaviness in style. But these Salzburg performances have both strength and poetry. Anda continues with a successful performance of K.467, notable for a beautifully poised orchestral introduction to the slow movement. One notices a certain rhythmic rigidity, and a lighter touch in the finale would have been acceptable; but on the whole this is a satisfying reading and the recording is excellent. There is plenty of life in the strings and a balancing orchestral richness; indeed this 1961 coupling wears its years lightly.

Piano concertos Nos. 17 in G, K.453; 26 in D (Coronation), K.537.
**(*) EMI CDC7 47968-2 [id.]. Daniel Barenboim, ECO.

The *G major Concerto* is phrased most musically and is full of life, but it may be spoilt for some by the unusually brisk tempo Barenboim adopts for the first movement. However, Barenboim's account of the *Coronation concerto* must be counted one of the most successful on disc. Altogether this is a fine record, worth acquiring for the sake of the *D major* alone, and the digital remastering is highly felicitous, adding presence and freshening the orchestral textures.

Piano concertos Nos. 18 in B flat, K.456; 19 in F, K.459.
(M) *** EMI CDM7 69123-2 [id.]. Barenboim, ECO.
**(*) DG Dig. 415 111-2 [id.]. Malcolm Bilson (fortepiano), E. Bar. Soloists, Gardiner.

Barenboim's account of K.456 is among the most sparkling of his cycle, full of imaginative touches which have one chuckling with delight. K.459, with its *Figaro* overtones, prompts another remarkable performance, brisk in its march rhythms in the first movement, tender in the Susanna-like sweetness of the *Andante* and strong and resilient in the finale, with its great fugal tutti. Excellent sound.

Malcolm Bilson too gives a vivacious account of the *B flat Concerto*, briskly paced but never sounding rushed, and the colour of the fortepiano made enticing in the *Andante*, by subtlety of inflexion and imaginative dynamic shading. The performance of *No. 19 in F* is rather more controversial. Gardiner's fast, crisp tempo in the first movement is initially disconcerting and, with the *Allegretto* marking for the second movement observed to the letter, there is less contrast than usual. But again the sparkle of the finale rounds off a reading that is consistent in its freshness and momentum. The clear, naturally balanced recording adds much to the pleasure of this series.

Piano concertos Nos. 18 in B flat, K.456; 20 in D min., K.466.
** Decca Dig. 414 337-2 [id.]. Vladimir Ashkenazy, Philh. O.

Ashkenazy is just a shade wanting in spontaneity in K.456 and does not convey the sparkle and delight that so often distinguish his music-making. The *D minor* is not perfunctory, but it is not as distinguished as his earlier version with Schmidt-Isserstedt (see below).

Piano concertos Nos. 19 in F, K.459; 23 in A, K.488.
⊛ *** CBS Dig. MK 39064 [id.]. Murray Perahia, ECO.
(M) *** DG 429 812-2 [id.]. Pollini, VPO, Boehm.

Murray Perahia gives highly characterful accounts of both *Concertos* and a gently witty yet vital reading of the *F Major*, K.459. As always with this artist, there is a splendidly classical feeling allied to a keenly poetic sensibility. His account of K.488 has enormous delicacy and inner vitality, yet a serenity that puts it in a class of its own. Even in a series of such distinction, this performance stands out. On CD, the sound is particularly fresh and natural.

Pollini is sparkling in the *F major*, and in the *A major* has a superbly poised, vibrant sense of line. Every phrase here seems to speak, and he is given excellent support from Boehm and the Vienna orchestra. Good, well-detailed and finely balanced analogue recording, which has transferred very freshly to CD, makes this one of the finest Mozart concerto records DG have given us. Excellent value, and it is now offered at mid-price.

Piano concertos Nos. 19 in F, K.459; 24 in C min., K.491.
*** Decca 414 433-2 [id.]. Vladimir Ashkenazy, Philh. O.

Ashkenazy has the measure of the breadth and emotional power of the *C minor Concerto*; his playing, while showing all the elegance and poise one could desire, never detracts from the coherence of the whole. He is every bit as sensitive as his most formidable rivals in the middle movement and highly characterful in the finale. The *F major Concerto* is subtle and sparkling. Clean, well-focused recording and an orchestral response that does almost as much credit to the pianist as his solo contribution.

Piano concertos Nos. 19 in F, K.459; 27 in B flat, K.595.
*** Decca Dig. 421 259-2 [id.]. András Schiff, Salzburg Mozarteum Camerata Academica, Végh.

Though Schiff's piano occupies a relatively small space in the aural image, it is not an unrealistic one. Details certainly register and the orchestral playing is a delight. This is agreeably relaxed, leisurely music-making though not in the least lacking in intensity or weight (Sandor Végh is very much the hero of the occasion). Occasionally András Schiff dots his 'i's and crosses his 't's a little too precisely, but his playing for the most part is so musicianly and perceptive that this does not seem important. These two readings can be warmly recommended – with the proviso that the resonant acoustic may trouble some listeners.

Piano concertos Nos. 20 in D min., K.466; 21 in C, K.467.
⊛ *** DG Dig. 419 609-2 [id.]. Malcolm Bilson (fortepiano), E. Bar. Soloists, Gardiner.
(M) *** RCA GD 87967 [7967-2-RG]. Rubinstein, RCA Victor SO, Wallenstein (with
HAYDN: *Andante & variations in F min.****).
(M) **(*) DG 429 811-2 [id.]. Friedrich Gulda, VPO, Abbado.
**(*) Ph. Dig. 416 381-2 [id.]. Mitsuko Uchida, ECO, Tate.

Here, even more than in the earlier masterpieces, the benefits of period performance
are striking in the way that, along with the extra transparency, the scale of the argument
and its dramatic bite, far from being minimized, are actually reinforced. These are vital,
electric performances by Bilson and the English Baroque Soloists, expressive within their
own lights, neither rigid nor too taut in the way of some period Mozart, nor
inappropriately romantic. This is a disc to recommend even to those who would not
normally consider period performances of Mozart concertos, fully and vividly recorded
with excellent balance between soloist and orchestra – better than you would readily get
in the concert hall.

Rubinstein has seldom been caught so sympathetically by the microphones, and the
remastered 1961 recording has the orchestral sound admirably freshened. In each
concerto the slow movement is the ˙ernel of the interpretation. Rubinstein's playing is
melting, and in the famous *Andante* of K.467 the silky smoothness of the string theme
catches the intensity of the pianist's inspiration. The opening of the first movement of
K.466, taken fairly briskly, is full of implied drama. Altogether Wallenstein is an excellent
accompanist, for finales have plenty of sparkle. The Haydn *Andante and variations*, a
substantial bonus recorded a year earlier, again demonstrates Rubinstein's aristocratic
feeling for a classical melodic line: it is played most beautifully.

With Gulda the piano tone is crisp and clear, with just a hint of the character of a
fortepiano about it, and admirably suited to these readings, which have an element of
classical restraint yet at the same time are committed and do not lack warmth. Abbado's
accompaniment shows him to be a first-class Mozartian, and the orchestral wind-playing
is delightful. The recording (from 1975) now has added clarity and the bass is firmer;
there is little loss of ambient bloom, but the upper string timbre has been slightly thinned
out. This is good value at mid-price, but Rubinstein is even more distinctive.

Uchida's are beautiful performances, guaranteed never to offend and most likely to
delight; but on the highest level their degree of reticence – despite the superb orchestral
work of the ECO under Tate – makes them less memorable than the very finest versions.
Excellent sound.

Piano concertos Nos. 20 in D min., K.466; 23 in A, K.488.
(B) **(*) Ph. 422 466-2. Bishop-Kovacevich, LSO, C. Davis.

If the coupling of the *D minor* and the *A major* from Bishop-Kovacevich and Davis
lacks some of the magic of their earlier pairing of the two *C major Concertos*, it is largely
that the playing of the LSO is less polished. Nevertheless the minor-key seriousness of the
outer movements of K.466 and the F sharp minor *Adagio* of K.488 come out superbly. It
is a token of the pianist's command that, without any expressive exaggeration, the K.488
slow movement conveys such depth and intensity. The recording is full and clear in its
new format.

Piano concertos Nos. (i) 20 in D min., K.466; (ii) 24 in C min., K.491.
(M) **(*) Decca 417 726-2 [id.]. Vladimir Ashkenazy, (i) LSO, Schmidt-Isserstedt; (ii)
Philh. O.

**(*) EMI CDC7 49007-2 [id.]. Daniel Barenboim, ECO.

The mid-priced Decca reissue recouples recordings from 1968 and 1979. They sound quite different: the *D minor* very immediate and fresh; the *C minor*, more distantly balanced, with sound natural but more diffuse. The former is conducted by Hans Schmidt-Isserstedt; it is a performance of some personality, although perhaps a little too regulated in emotional temperature (the *Romance* is rather precise), yet it has no want of vividness and life. Ashkenazy directs the orchestra himself in the *C minor*; his is a balanced view of the first movement: he avoids investing it with excessive intensity, yet never loses impact. He is equally impressive in the slow movement and finale.

Barenboim's performance of *No. 20 in D minor* has all the sparkle and sensitivity one could ask for. The orchestral accompaniment is admirably alive and one's only serious reservation concerns the somewhat fast tempo he adopts in the finale. K.491 brings a more controversial performance; the very first entry of the piano shows how much Barenboim wants to make it a romantic work, and some may find the first two movements too heavily dramatized for their taste, while the finale is compensatingly fast and hectic. The sound is vividly bright, the upper range not as natural as in others of this CD series.

Piano concertos Nos. 20 in D min., K.466; 24 in C min., K.491; Concert rondo No. 1 in D, K.382.
(M) *** Ph. 420 867-2 [id.]. Alfred Brendel, ASMF, Marriner.

The two minor-key *Concertos* are superbly played and the analogue recording is of Philips's best. Perhaps the last ounce of tragic intensity is missing but, at mid-price and with the *D major Rondo* now included, there is nothing to inhibit a three-star recommendation.

Piano concerto Nos. 20 in D min., K.466; 25 in C, K.503.
*(*) DG Dig. 429 353-2 [id.]. Arturo Benedetti Michelangeli, N. German RSO, Cord Garben.

Michelangeli is recorded at (obviously packed) public concerts in Bremen with the Nord-Deutscher Rundfunk Sinfonieorchester, so the sound is on the dry side. There are moments of aristocratic pianism here, but for the most part Michelangeli sounds curiously remote and uninvolved. The slow movement of the *D minor* is on automatic pilot throughout, and the finale is little better. The Beethoven cadenza in the first movement is unusually mannered. Michelangeli's reputation is such that he is greeted with a critical reverence which the actual music-making does not always justify. There are much finer versions of K.503 on the market than this rather routine account. The excellent NDR Orchestra plays well for Cord Garben.

Piano concertos Nos. 20 in D min., K.466; 27 in B flat, K.595.
*** CBS MK 42241 [id.]. Murray Perahia, ECO.
*** Decca 417 288-2 [id.]. Clifford Curzon, ECO, Benjamin Britten.

Perahia produces wonderfully soft colourings and a luminous texture in the *B flat Concerto*, yet at the same time he avoids underlining too strongly the valedictory sense that inevitably haunts this magical score. In the *D minor Concerto* none of the darker, disturbing undercurrents go uncharted, but at the same time we remain within the sensibility of the period. Not, perhaps, the only way of looking at this work, but a wonderfully compelling one. An indispensable issue, well recorded.

Anyone hearing Curzon's magical record, full of the glow and natural expressiveness which always went with Britten's conducting of Mozart, will recognize both performances as uniquely individual and illuminating, with Curzon at his very finest. The coupling was kept from issue until after Sir Clifford's death; it sounds vivid and well balanced in its CD format.

Piano concerto No. 21 in C, K.467.
(M) (*(**)) EMI mono CDH7 69792-2. Lipatti, Lucerne Fest. O, Karajan – SCHUMANN: *Concerto.*(***)

Lipatti's performance derives from a broadcast from the 1950 Lucerne Festival and there is some discoloration and, at climaxes, distortion. However, nothing can detract from the distinction of Lipatti's playing or its immaculate control. This obviously occupies a rather special place in the catalogue and will be wanted by all admirers of this great artist.

Piano concertos Nos. 21 in C, K.467; 24 in C min., K.491.
(B) *** CBS MYK 42594 [id.]. Robert Casadesus, Cleveland O, Szell.
(B) *** Pickwick Dig. PCD 832 [MCA MCAD 25228]. Howard Shelley, City of L. Sinfonia.

Casadesus is on top form: he plays most delectably in the first movement of K.467 and its ravishing central *Andante* has seldom sounded so magical. He takes the finale at a tremendous speed but brings it off; and both here and in the coupled K.491 (where, unusually, he chooses a cadenza by Saint-Saëns) this is exquisite Mozart playing, beautifully paced and articulated. Szell's precision gives a special character to the accompaniments. He is not as flexible as Davis is for Bishop-Kovacevich, but the orchestral playing is superbly crisp. The 1965 recording sounds remarkably fresh and full, and this disc should belong in any Mozartian's library.

Howard Shelley gives delightfully fresh and characterful readings of both the popular *C major* and the great *C minor* concertos, bringing out their strength and purposefulness as well as their poetry, never overblown or sentimental. His Pickwick disc makes an outstanding bargain, with accompaniment very well played and recorded.

Piano concertos Nos. 21 in C, K.467; 25 in C, K.503.
⊛ (B) *** Ph. 426 077-2 [id.]. Bishop-Kovacevich, LSO, C. Davis.

This is among the most searching and satisfying records of Mozart piano concertos available. The partnership of Bishop-Kovacevich and Davis almost invariably produces inspired music-making, and here their equal dedication to Mozart, their balancing of strength and charm, drama and tenderness, make for performances which retain their sense of spontaneity but which plainly result from deep thought. Never has the famous slow movement of K.467 sounded more ethereally beautiful on record than here, with superb LSO string tone, and the weight of both these great C major works is formidably conveyed. The 1972 recording is well balanced and refined; though the CD transfer has brightened the violins, there is plenty of supporting body and depth to the sound-picture, and the piano image is particularly appealing and cleanly focused.

Piano concertos Nos. 21 in C, K.467; 27 in B flat, K.595.
(M) * DG Dig. 427 812-2 [id.]. Rudolf Serkin, LSO, Abbado.

Serkin made some distinguished Mozart concerto records way back in the days of shellac; at the beginning of the 1980s he embarked on a new cycle as the eightieth year of his own life was fast approaching. Though his thoughtfulness as an artist is often clear, his passage-work in these performances is scrappy; indeed the playing is distressingly prosaic, with uneven scales. Refined accompaniments from Abbado – the opening of K.595 is measured and spacious – with an excellent response from the LSO, but even there the styles clash, for Serkin is wanting in the grace he once commanded. There are moments of inelegance (the theme of the slow movement is a case in point) and little real sparkle in quicker movements, where the orchestral playing tends to follow Serkin's lead. The compact disc is of first-class quality, even if it reveals some of the soloist's vocal additions.

Piano concerto No. 22 in E flat, K.482.
(M) ** EMI CDM7 69013-2 [id.]. Sviatislav Richter, Philh. O, Muti – BEETHOVEN: *Concerto No. 3.***

Richter's 1983 recording is clearly looking forward towards Beethoven, particularly in the slow movement. He plays with all the poise and authority one would expect, and there are numerous felicities. He uses cadenzas by Benjamin Britten. Muti draws lively and sympathetic support from the Philharmonia – though, following Richter's example, the finale is weighty, if not without rhythmic bounce. Good remastered sound.

Piano concertos Nos. 22 in E flat, K.482; 23 in A, K.488.
*** Ph. Dig. 420 187-2 [id.]. Mitsuko Uchida, ECO, Tate.
(M) **(*) EMI CDM7 69122-2 [id.]. Barenboim, ECO.

In balance, fidelity and sense of presence, few recordings of Mozart piano concertos can match Uchida's fine coupling of the late *E flat*, K.482, with its immediate successor, the beautiful *A major*. It makes a fascinating match, presenting illuminating contrasts rather than similarities, and Uchida's thoughtful manner, at times a little understated, is ideally set against outstanding playing from the ECO with its excellent wind soloists.

Barenboim gives a persuasive, at times even wilful account of K.482, relishing its expansiveness with dozens of spontaneous-sounding inflexions. The account of K.488 is enchanting. There are moments when his delicacy of fingerwork comes close to preciosity, but it never quite goes over the edge. Indeed his playing has all the sparkle and sensitivity one could ask for, and the orchestral accompaniment is admirably alive. One's only reservation concerns the somewhat fast tempo he adopts in the finale. Good remastered sound, firm, full and clear.

Piano concertos Nos. 22 in E flat, K.482; 24 in C min., K.491.
*** CBS MK 42242 [id.]. Murray Perahia, ECO.

Not only is Perahia's contribution inspired in the great *E flat Concerto*, but the wind players of the ECO are at their most eloquent in the slow movement. Moreover the *C minor Concerto* emerges here as a truly Mozartian tragedy, rather than as foreshadowing Beethoven, which some artists give us. Both recordings are improved in focus and definition in the CD transfer.

(i) *Piano concerto No. 22 in E flat, K.482;* (ii) *Double Piano concerto in E flat, K.365.*
** Decca 421 036-2 [id.]. (i) Ashkenazy, Philh. O; (ii) Ashkenazy, Barenboim, ECO, Barenboim.

Ashkenazy has the measure of the strength of the *E flat Concerto* and his playing is thoughtful and lyrical. He evidently does not use the *Neue Mozartausgabe* edition, as he leaves out two bars in the first movement, but that is hardly likely to weigh heavily in the balance for most collectors. This is recommendable – and nicely recorded too. Ashkenazy is joined by Barenboim in the *Double concerto*, and it finds both artists self-conscious, particularly in the slow movement, which is taken very slowly. So this coupling – new to CD – has unequal attractions, although it cannot be faulted on sound-quality.

Piano concertos Nos. 23 in A, K.488; 24 in C min., K.491.
⊛ (M) *** DG 423 885-2 [id.]. Kempff, Bamberg SO, Leitner.

(i) *Piano concertos Nos. 23 in A, K.488;* (ii) *24 in C min., K.491; Rondo in A, K.511.*
(M) *** RCA GD 87968 [7968-2-RG]. Rubinstein, RCA Victor SO, (i) Alfred Wallenstein; (ii) Josef Krips.

Kempff's outstanding performances of these *Concertos* are uniquely poetic and inspired, and Leitner's accompaniments are comparably distinguished. The 1960 recording still sounds well, and this is strongly recommended at mid-price.

Rubinstein brings characteristic finesse and beauty of phrasing to his coupling of two of Mozart's finest concertos. K.488 is especially beautiful, with Wallenstein providing a most sympathetic accompaniment. In K.491 the crystal-clear articulation is allied to the aristocratic feeling characteristic of vintage Rubinstein: the slow movement is memorable in its poise. Krips' accompaniment, like the solo part, is smoothly cultured and acts as a foil to the tragic tone of this great and wonderfully balanced work. The recordings, from 1958 and 1961 respectively, sound fresh and full, although in K.488 the violin timbre is rather bright. The *Rondo*, recorded in 1959, is equally distinguished – much more than just an encore.

Piano concertos Nos. 23 in A, K.488; 27 in B flat, K.595.
*** Decca Dig. 400 087-2 [id.]. Vladimir Ashkenazy, Philh. O.
(M) *** Ph. 420 487-2 [id.]. Alfred Brendel, ASMF, Marriner.

Ashkenazy's *A Major* is beautifully judged, alive and fresh, yet warm – one of the most satisfying accounts yet recorded. No quarrels either with the *B flat*, which is as finely characterized as one would expect. The recording focuses closely on the piano, but nevertheless no orchestral detail is masked and the overall impression is very lifelike.

On Philips, two of the best of Brendel's Mozart concertos. Both performances come from the early 1970s and sound wonderfully fresh in these digitally refurbished transfers. But allegiance to Gilels in K.595 remains strong.

Piano concerto No. 23 in A, K.488; Piano sonata No. 13 in B flat, K.333 (K.315c).
**(*) DG Dig. 423 287-2 [id.]. Vladimir Horowitz, La Scala, Milan, O, Giulini.

With Horowitz there are occasional reminders of the passage of time, but they are astonishingly few, and the artistry remains undiminished. The Busoni cadenza is an unusual (and far from unwelcome) feature of the *Concerto*. As usual, the piano is tuned within an inch of its life, and the slightly shallow sound of the instrument is not solely due to the engineers. This is very much Horowitz's record – and at times in the finale there is not too much of the orchestra, nor is there much sign of rapport between Horowitz and Giulini! Still, this is remarkable piano playing, quite unlike any other, and in the *Sonata* not free from affectation. In the *Concerto*, the recording is synthetic and dryish; the *Sonata* is slightly less constricted but far from first rate.

Piano concertos Nos. 25 in C, K.503; 26 in D (Coronation), K.537.
*** DG Dig. 423 119-2 [id.]. Malcolm Bilson (fortepiano), E. Bar. Soloists, Gardiner.
*** Decca Dig. 411 810-2 [id.]. Vladimir Ashkenazy, Philh. O.

With Bilson at his strongest and Gardiner and the English Baroque Soloists taking a dramatic view – biting down sharply on the repeated chords of the first movement – the magnificent scale of the *C major* work is formidably established. The *Coronation concerto* is also presented strongly as well as elegantly, with the authentic timpani cutting dramatically through the textures in the first movement. Full and spacious recording in a helpful acoustic.

Ashkenazy's opening of the *C major Concerto* is on the grandest scale, emphasized by the weighty bass response of the recording; but the interpretation is set in relief by the more delicate feeling of the *Andante*. In the *Coronation concerto* Ashkenazy's approach to the first movement is comparably magisterial, while he produces some exquisitely shaded playing in the *Larghetto*, with the final *Allegretto* hardly less refined. In both works the Decca recording is of the highest quality.

Piano concertos Nos. (i) *26 in D (Coronation), K.537;* (ii) *27 in B flat, K.595.*
(M) *** DG 429 810-2 [id.]. (i) Vásáry, BPO; (ii) Gilels, VPO, Boehm.
**(*) Ph. Dig. 420 951-2 [id.]. Mitsuko Uchida, ECO, Tate.
(B) ** Ph. 422 975-2 [id.]. Ingrid Haebler, LSO, Rowicki or Galliera.

Tamás Vásáry is a fine Mozartian with exemplary taste and judgement, and his account of the *Coronation concerto* has grandeur as well as vitality. The quality of the 1974 sound is very good in this transfer. Gilels's account of K.595 is in a class of its own, and those who do not require his coupling with the *Double piano concerto*, K.365 – see below – will find this a worthwhile alternative, although Vásáry's K.543 does not sparkle quite as brightly as the performances of his finest rivals.

Mitsuko Uchida and Jeffrey Tate are blessed with outstanding recorded sound; the orchestral playing is first class and Uchida produces an unfailingly pianistic refinement and elegance. But this very refinement is a bit too much of a good thing and at times one would welcome a greater robustness, a more lively inner current.

Miss Haebler's account of the first movement of the *Coronation concerto* is straightforward and dignified, but in the main theme of the slow movement she exaggerates staccato markings and even plays the top A of the theme staccato, which seems to trivialize it. In No. 27 Galliera is not the tautest of conductors, yet the LSO communicate a sense of enjoyment throughout, and within the premises of the soloist (a relaxed, poetic approach which eschews masculine drives) there is much to admire. The recording is full and spacious and has transferred very successfully to CD, with the piano colouring naturally caught.

Piano concerto No. 26 in D (Coronation), K.537; Concert rondos, Nos. 1 in D, K.382; 2 in A, K.386.
*** CBS Dig. MK 39224 [id.]. Murray Perahia, ECO.

Perahia succeeds in making K.537 mean more than do most of his rivals, and the dignity and breadth of his reading are matched in the slow movement by enormous delicacy and sensibility. This is a magical performance in which the level of inspiration runs high. The *Concerto* is coupled with superb accounts of the two *Concert rondos*, K.382 and K.386, which for the first time on record incorporate the closing bars newly discovered by Professor Alan Tyson. The recording is naturally balanced within a fairly resonant ambience.

Piano concerto No. 27 in B flat, K.595; (i) *Double piano concerto in E flat, K.365.*
⊛ (M) *** DG 419 059-2 [id.]. Emil Gilels, VPO, Boehm, (i) with Elena Gilels.

Gilels's is supremely lyrical playing that evinces all the classical virtues. No detail is allowed to detract from the picture as a whole; the pace is totally unhurried and superbly controlled. All the points are made by means of articulation and tone, and each phrase is marvellously alive. This is playing of the highest order of artistic integrity and poetic insight, while Boehm and the Vienna Philharmonic provide excellent support. The performance of the marvellous *Double concerto* is no less enjoyable. Its mood is comparatively serious, but this is not to suggest that the music's sunny qualities are not brought out; the interplay of phrasing between the two soloists is beautifully conveyed by the recording without exaggerated separation. The quality on CD is first class, refining detail yet not losing ambient warmth.

Double piano concerto in E flat, K.365; Triple piano concerto in F (Lodron), K.242 (arr. for 2 pianos).
*** Ph. 416 364-2 [id.]. Alfred Brendel, Imogen Cooper, ASMF, Marriner.

The playing here is cultured and elegant, strikingly poised – particularly in K.242 – combining vigour with tonal refinement. Marriner's accompaniments are comparably polished and the Philips engineers afford the music-making a most natural sound-balance. The analogue recording of K.365 dates from 1977; K.242 is digital and was made in 1984.

Violin concertos Nos. 1–5.
(B) *** Ph. 422 938-2 (2) [id.]. Arthur Grumiaux, LSO, C. Davis.

Violin concertos Nos. 1 in B flat, K.207; 2 in D, K.211; 4 in D, K.218.
**(*) ASV Dig. CDRPO 8018 [id.]. Young Uck Kim, LPO, Eschenbach.

Violin concertos Nos. 3 in G, K.216; 5 in A, K.219.
**(*) ASV Dig. CDRPO 8014 [id.]. Young Uck Kim, LPO, Eschenbach.

Violin concertos Nos. 1–5; Adagio in E, K.261; Rondos for violin and orchestra Nos. 1 in B flat, K.269; 2 in C, K.573.
(M) **(*) Ph. 422 256-2 (2) [id.]. Henryk Szeryng, New Philh. O, Gibson.
**(*) DG Dig. 419 184-2 (3) [id.]. Itzhak Perlman, VPO, Levine.

Grumiaux's accounts of the Mozart *Violin concertos* come from the early 1960s and are among the most beautifully played in the catalogue at any price. The orchestral accompaniments have sparkle and vitality and Grumiaux's contribution has splendid poise and purity of tone. There are many delights here and the music-making has warmth as well as refinement; the recording sounds remarkably good, with clean, fresh string-tone and well-defined bass.

Szeryng's set, which appeared originally in 1971, offers excellent value on two CDs. Szeryng plays with great purity of style and musicianly insight (though at times some might find his approach a trifle cool alongside Perlman). But Sir Alexander Gibson's orchestral support is always alive, well shaped and responsive; and the Philips recording, musically balanced and truthful in timbre, is transferred immaculately to CD. Szeryng offers worthwhile bonuses and the Philips sound has an attractive Mozartian scale.

Perlman gives characteristically assured virtuoso readings of these concertos of Mozart's youth, which, with Levine as a fresh and undistracting Mozartian, bring exceptionally satisfying co-ordination of forces. The virtuoso approach sometimes involves a tendency to hurry, and the power is emphasized by the weight and immediacy of the recording. Warmth is here rather than charm; but Perlman's individual magic makes for magnetic results all through, not least in the intimate intensity of slow movements.

The Korean-born American violinist Young Uck Kim is an artist of real quality and his playing has great purity of tone and stylistic finesse to commend it; it is a pity that in the *G major* and *A major Concertos*, the first to appear, the orchestral playing under Christoph Eschenbach is at times touched by routine. In its companion with Nos. 1, 2 and

4, the sound is slightly brighter and the playing fresher. Like Grumiaux and Colin Davis, all five *Concertos* are accommodated on two discs, but the latter – albeit at bargain price – are not available separately.

Violin concertos Nos. 1 in B flat, K.207; 2 in D, K.211; Rondo No. 1 in B flat, K.269.
*** Denon Dig. C37 7506 [id.]. Jean-Jacques Kantorow, Netherlands CO, Hager.

Violin concertos Nos. 1 in B flat, K.207; 2 in D, K.211; 3 in G, K.216.
(M) **(*) CBS Dig. MDK 44653 [id.]. Zukerman, St Paul CO.

Violin concertos Nos. 1 in B flat, K.207; 2 in D, K.211; 3 in G, K.216; Rondo in C, K.373.
(M) **(*) EMI CDM7 69176-2 [id.]. David Oistrakh, BPO.

Violin concerto No. 2; (i) Sinfonia concertante for violin and viola in E flat, K.364.
**(*) Argo Dig. 411 613-2 [id.]. Iona Brown; (i) Suk; ASMF, Marriner.

Violin concertos Nos. 1 in B flat, K.207; 4 in D, K.218; Rondo in B flat, K.269.
*** CBS MK 44503 [id.]. Cho-Liang Lin, ECO, Leppard.

Violin concertos Nos. 1 in B flat, K.207; 5 in A (Turkish), K.219; Adagio in E, K.261.
(M) **(*) DG Dig. 427 813-2 [id.]. Itzhak Perlman, VPO, Levine.

Kantorow's coupling makes an excellent start to his Mozart series. He is given alert, stylish accompaniments by Leopold Hager and the Netherlands Chamber Orchestra, and the recording is eminently realistic. Kantorow's full personality emerges gradually in K.207, although he plays strongly with a fine classical spirit. The account of K.211 is splendid in all respects. The *B flat Rondo* makes an excellent bonus. Kantorow plays his own cadenzas – and very good they are. Highly recommended.

As in his coupling of K.216 and K.219, Lin creates a ready partnership with Leppard and the ECO, and his combination of effervescence and delicacy is matched by the orchestra, with appealing tenderness in both slow movements and plenty of dash in the last movement of K.207. The *Rondo*, K.269, is of course an alternative finale for this work, so the CD listener can easily programme a substitution. Excellent recording, naturally balanced, adds to the attractions of this highly recommendable CBS disc.

David Oistrakh is predictably strong and positive as a Mozartian, and he is well accompanied by the Berlin Philharmonic Orchestra. The slow movement of the *G major*, K.216, is memorably expressive, and the *Rondo*, K.373, is also very pleasing. The original resonance means that orchestral tuttis are not always absolutely clean, but in general the quality on CD is very good.

Perlman's version of K.207 is first class in every way and, like the particularly graceful account of the *Adagio*, K.261, receives accompaniments which are beautifully played and perfectly integrated in a recording which is ideally balanced and very truthful. K.219 is also drawn from the 1986 complete set but is treated rather more like a virtuoso showpiece than is common. For some the tone will be too sweet for Mozart, though Levine and the VPO are again in good form. This is certainly enjoyable, though the soloist is balanced rather forwardly.

Zukerman's set has the advantage of excellent digital recording and a good balance, the violin forward but not distractingly so. The playing of outer movements is agreeably simple and fresh, and in the slow movements of both the *D major* and *G major Concertos* Zukerman's sweetness of tone will appeal to many, although his tendency to languish a little in his expressiveness, particularly in the *G major*, may be counted a less attractive feature. The St Paul Chamber Orchestra is clearly in rapport with its soloist/director and accompanies with stylish warmth.

Iona Brown's account of the *D major Concerto* is also a fine one, even more positively classical in spirit, with striking vitality in the outer movements. The Brown/Suk partnership works well in the *Sinfonia concertante*, but there is an element of restraint in the slow movement. Nevertheless these are both fine performances and there are no grounds for complaint about the sound, which is fresh and clear.

Violin concertos Nos. 2 in D, K.211; 4 in D, K.218.
*** EMI Dig. CDC7 47011-2 [id.]. Anne-Sophie Mutter, Philh. O, Muti.
*** DG Dig. 415 975-2 [id.]. Itzhak Perlman, VPO, Levine.
(B) **(*) Ph. 422 468-2. Krebbers, Netherlands CO, Zinman.

Anne-Sophie Mutter is given very sensitive support from the Philharmonia under Muti. Her playing combines purity and classical feeling, delicacy and incisiveness, and is admirably expressive. Its freshness too is most appealing, and she is a strong contender in a very competitive field. The EMI recording is very good; the images are sharply defined, but the balance is convincing.

Perlman's virtuosity is effortless and charismatic, and the orchestral playing is glorious. Moreover the DG recording is well balanced, with Perlman forward but not excessively so; the acoustic has warmth and the perspective on the whole is well judged.

With his immaculate intonation and subtle rhythmic sense, Krebbers gives splendid performances, very brightly recorded and with crisply alert accompaniments from the excellent Netherlands Chamber Orchestra. The earlier *D major Concerto* brings the most beautiful high-floated solo entries in the central slow movement, and relaxed tempi, beautifully sprung, in the outer movements. The only snag is that the remastering emphasizes the forward balance of the soloist.

Violin concertos Nos. 3 in G, K.216; 4 in D, K.218; 5 in A (Turkish), K.219.
(BB) **(*) LaserLight Dig. 15 525 [id.]. Christian Altenburger, German Bach Soloists, Winschermann.
(B) ** DG 429 159 [id.]. Wolfgang Schneiderhan, BPO.

Violin concertos Nos. 3 in G, K.216; 5 in A (Turkish), K.219.
(M) *** DG 429 814-2 [id.]. Anne-Sophie Mutter, BPO, Karajan.
**(*) Denon Dig. C37 7504 [id.]. Jean-Jacques Kantorow, Netherlands CO, Hager.

Violin concertos Nos. 3, K.216; 5 (Turkish); Adagio in E, K.261.
*** CBS Dig. MK 42364 [id.]. Cho-Liang Lin, ECO, Leppard.

Lin's persuasive style brings out the tenderness of both slow movements. There is an element of youthful lightness running through the performances of both *Concertos*, though there is no lack of bite and point either. Lin is full of fancy and imagination, apt for the music of a teenager, and only the first movement of K.216 brings a performance that is less fresh and sparkling on some details. Leppard and the ECO are the most responsive of partners, and the recording is first rate.

Extraordinarily mature and accomplished playing from Anne-Sophie Mutter, who was a mere fourteen years old when her recording was made. The instinctive mastery means that there is no hint of immaturity: the playing has polish, but fine artistry too and remarkable freshness. Karajan is at his most sympathetic and scales down the accompaniment to act as a perfect setting for his young soloist. The recording has been brilliantly transferred to CD; some might feel that the orchestral strings are a shade too brightly lit.

Jean-Jacques Kantorow is a highly intelligent player and has obviously studied these scores with meticulous care. In his hands they come up very freshly indeed. Kantorow uses the Ysaÿe cadenzas, which are shorter. In a way his are the best thought-out of the present set though, in terms of personality and tonal beauty, others are to be preferred.

Christian Altenburger is an appealing soloist, playing with full timbre and classical feeling, even if he is without a strong individual personality. Winschermann and the German Bach Soloists give polished and sympathetic support. Allegros are alive and the Turkish Minuet/Rondo finale of K.219 admirably contrasts elegance with sparkle. Slow movements, too, are appealingly poised, and the scale of these performances is well judged, with modern instruments used to convincing effect. Excellent digital sound, bright and open. A genuine bargain.

Schneiderhan's performances come from a complete set, made with the Berlin Philharmonic Orchestra at the end of the 1960s. He plays with effortless mastery and a strong sense of classical proportion. The Berlin orchestra accompany well for him, though there is a slightly unsmiling quality at times. The 1968 recording sounds firmer in focus in its new CD presentation, the sound very good for its period.

Violin concerto No. 4; Adagio, K.261; Rondo No. 2, K.373; (i) *Concerto for violin and fortepiano, K. Anh. 56/315f* (fragment); (ii) *Sinfonia concertante in A, K. Anh. 104/320e* (fragment).
**(*) Denon Dig. C37 7505 [id.]. Jean-Jacques Kantorow, (i) Glen Wilson, (ii) Vladimir Mendelssohn, Mari Fujiwara; Netherlands CO, Hager.

Violin concertos (i) *Nos. 4, K.218;* (ii) *5 (Turkish), K.219.*
*** Nimbus Dig. NI 5009. Oscar Shumsky, SCO, Yan Pascal Tortelier.
(M) **(*) EMI CDM7 69064-2 [id.]. David Oistrakh, BPO.

Violin concertos Nos. 4 in D, K.218; 5 in A (Turkish), K.219; Adagio in E, K.261; Rondo in C, K.373.
(M) ** CBS Dig. MDK 44654 [id.]. Pinchas Zukerman, St Paul CO.

Shumsky's performances with the Scottish Chamber Orchestra have the advantage of being totally unaffected, natural and full of character. Yan Pascal Tortelier secures a very alive and thoroughly musical response from the orchestra, and the players themselves convey enthusiasm and pleasure. The recording is nicely balanced.

David Oistrakh's performances come from his complete set of 1972. The remastering has lightened the sound, and the orchestral violins, notably in K.218, now sound just a little papery above the stave; otherwise the full ambience offsets the drier bass response, and the touch of rhythmic heaviness in the accompaniments from the Berlin Philharmonic is less striking. The slow movement of K.219 is particularly fine, and so too is the finale. At mid-price, this is more than acceptable.

Kantorow's account of the *D major Concerto* brings fresh, intelligent solo playing, essentially classical in spirit, and with an agreeable but not exaggerated warmth in the slow movement. The two shorter pieces are also splendidly done, the *Adagio*, K.261, particularly fine. There is undoubted interest in the inclusion of the two fragments, from an unfinished *Double concerto* and the *Sinfonia concertante*, featuring three soloists. However, they are disconcertingly short and break off abruptly. The recording is first class and very well balanced.

Zukerman's account of K.218 is unmannered and stylish, admirably direct in approach, though the *Andante* is taken rather slowly. The pacing of the last movement is somewhat idiosyncratic. His admirers will not be disappointed with K.219, although his sweet tone and effortless facility do not always engage one's sympathies. He languishes lovingly in the slow movement (though rather less so than in the *G major*, K.219) and is not always subtle in his expression of feeling. The shorter pieces are played with some flair, the *Adagio* most appealingly. The St Paul Chamber Orchestra obviously contains some fine players and the accompaniments, which Zukerman also directs, are polished, the recording vivid and rather brightly lit.

Violin concerto No. 5 in A (Turkish), K.219.
(M) *** RCA GD 87869 [7869-2-RG]. Heifetz with CO – *String quintet, K.516* etc.***

Marvellously exhilarating Mozart from Heifetz, though his actual entry in the first movement is quite ethereal. He directs the accompanying group himself, the only time he did so on record. The early (1954) stereo is fully acceptable and the performance memorable, with the crystalline clarity of articulation matched by warmth of timbre and aristocratic phrasing. The 'Turkish' interludes of the finale are brought off with great élan and the slow movement has a superb line and much grace and subtlety of detail.

Concertone in C for 2 violins and orchestra, K.190; Sinfonia concertante in E flat for violin, viola and orchestra, K.364.
⊛ *** DG 415 486-2 [id.]. Perlman, Zukerman, Israel PO, Mehta.
*** Chan. Dig. CHAN 8315 [id.]. Brainin, Schidlof, SNO, Gibson.
**(*) Denon Dig. C37 7507 [id.]. Kantorow, Olga Martinova, Vladimir Mendelssohn, Hans Meijer, Netherlands CO, Hager.

The responsive playing of Norbert Brainin and Peter Schidlof does bring a degree of romanticism to the slow movement of the *Sinfonia concertante*, and their phrasing employs tenutos, at times rather indulgently. Yet there is no lack of vitality in outer movements, and Sir Alexander Gibson's accompaniments are stylish and strong. The *Concertone*, where Schidlof changes from viola to violin, is also very successful, with Neil Black making an elegant contribution in the concertante oboe role. The sound is first class.

The alternative DG version of the *Sinfonia concertante* was recorded in Tel Aviv at the Huberman Festival in December 1982. It is balanced less successfully, with the soloists a fraction too near the microphones and with orchestral detail not so clearly focused as on Chandos. The performance is in a class of its own and is an example of 'live' recording at its most magnetic, with the inspiration of the occasion caught on the wing. Zubin Mehta is drawn into the music-making and accompanies most sensitively. The *Concertone* is also splendidly done (with a fine oboe contribution from Chaim Jouval); the ear notices the improvement in the sound-balance of the studio recording of this work. But the *Sinfonia concertante*, with the audience incredibly quiet, conveys an electricity rarely caught on record.

Kantorow forms an excellent partnership with Vladimir Mendelssohn in the *Sinfonia concertante*; in the *Concertone*, Olga Martinova, the violinist, and the fine oboist, Hans Meijer, distinguish themselves. In keeping with the style of Kantorow's concerto series, the playing is refined and classical in spirit. With recording which is naturally balanced and realistic this Denon CD offers performances which give much pleasure in their freshness and natural responsiveness.

Divertimenti for strings Nos. 1 in D; 2 in B flat; 3 in F, K.136–8; Serenade No. 6 in D (Serenata notturna), K.239.
*** Ph. Dig. 412 120-2 [id.]. I Musici.

Divertimenti for strings Nos. 1–3, K.136–8; Serenades Nos. 6 (Serenata notturna); 13 in G (Eine kleine Nachtmusik), K.525.
(M) **(*) Decca 417 741-2 [id.]. ASMF, Marriner.
(M) **(*) Ph. 420 712-2 [id.]. I Musici.
(M) ** DG 429 805-2 [id.]. BPO, Karajan.

The newest digital recording of the Salzburg *Divertimenti* by I Musici is particularly successful, extremely vivid and clean, bringing the players before one's very eyes. Their earlier, analogue recording from 1974, however, still sounds well in its mid-priced reissue which offers more music. The playing is spirited and beautifully stylish. With the *Night music* added to the *Serenata notturna* as couplings, this is good value.

The playing of the Academy is marvellous, with Marriner's choice of tempi equally apt. The same warm stylishness distinguishes the *Serenata notturna*, while *Eine kleine Nachtmusik* is played delightfully. However, the remastered recordings from the late 1960s and early 1970s are very brightly lit, with the violins noticeably thin above the stave in *Eine kleine Nachtmusik*; the touch of shrillness is less striking in the three *Divertimenti*.

Karajan's (late 1960s) performances of the *String divertimenti* and the *Serenata notturna* are beautifully played and as such they prompt the liveliest admiration. At the same time there is a predictably suave elegance that seems to militate against spontaneity. Cultured and effortless readings, well balanced and recorded, though the violins sound a little thin above the stave. There is too much legato and not always a balancing sparkle. The performance of *Eine kleine Nachtmusik*, however, sounds more spontaneous.

Divertimenti for strings Nos. 1–2, K.136/7; Serenades Nos. 6 (Serenata notturna), K.239; 13 (Eine kleine Nachtmusik), K.525.
*** Capriccio 10185 [id.]. Salzburg Mozarteum Camerata Academica, Végh.

These are delightfully bold, fresh and characterful performances, very well recorded. Only in the slow movement of *Eine kleine Nachtmusik*, taken rather slowly, is the playing a shade less refined. Curiously, Végh changes the regular order of movements in K.137, making it a conventional fast-slow-fast piece, though neither the label nor the note recognizes the change.

Divertimento for strings No. 1, K.136; A Musical Joke, K.522; Serenade No. 13 (Eine kleine Nachtmusik), K.525.
*** Ph. Dig. 412 269-2 [id.]. ASMF Chamber Ens.

Three popular Mozart pieces given with elegance and polish by the Academy Chamber players and recorded with complete fidelity and splendid definition by the Philips engineers.

Divertimento for strings No. 2 in B flat, K. 137; Divertimenti Nos. 1 in E flat, K.113; 11 in D, K.251.
**(*) Ph. 420 181-2 [id.]. ASMF Chamber Ens.

The *E flat Divertimento*, K.113, for 2 clarinets, 2 horns and strings is an assured and inventive piece for a fifteen-year-old; K.251 dates from five years later. It still uses horns and strings, but adds an elaborate oboe part, elegantly played here by Celia Nicklin. The *String divertimento*, played with considerable vitality – very much a *Salzburg symphony* – forms the centrepiece of an attractive concert. The playing throughout is polished and full of life, if perhaps a shade anonymous in its overall effect. The sound is extremely vivid.

Divertimento for strings No. 2, K.137; Serenade No. 3 in D, K.185; March in D, K.189.
**(*) Hung. Dig. HCD 12861 [id.]. Liszt CO, János Rolla.

János Rolla directs strongly articulated performances and also takes the solo violin role in the *Serenade*. The playing is stylish and polished, but displays rather less in the way of charm, and the *Andante grazioso* in K.185 could be more expansive. The recording is excellent.

Divertimento for strings No. 3 in F, K.138; Divertimento No. 17 in D, K.334.
** Capriccio 10153 [id.]. Salzburg Mozarteum Camerata Academica, Végh.

Végh directs his Salzburg players in bright, robust performances of these *Divertimenti*, recorded closely and vividly to show up roughnesses in the matching and blending. In the splendid *Divertimento*, K.334, Végh disappointingly omits the exposition repeat in the first movement and both repeats in the lovely fourth-movement *Adagio*, but he does include the delightful K.138, the third of the so-called *Salzburg symphonies*.

Divertimento No. 2 in D, K.131; Divertimento for wind No. 12 in E flat, K.252; Serenade No. 13 in G (Eine kleine Nachtmusik), K.525.
**(*) DG Dig. 419 192-2 [id.]. Orpheus CO.

The Orpheus group play the *D major Divertimento* with affection and spirit, and there is elegant phrasing from the strings and a strikingly buoyant contribution from the horns. The *Wind divertimento* is also most agreeable, but the famous *Night music* is rather lacking in charm with a very brisk opening movement, alert enough and very polished but somewhat unbending. The recording is excellent.

Divertimento No. 7 in D, K.205.
(M) **(*) Decca 421 155-2 [id.]. Vienna Octet (members) – SCHUBERT: *Octet.***

Mozart's *Divertimento in D* is given a peerless performance by the Vienna Octet, and its quality of invention shows the composer at his most gracious and smiling. The recording, however, dates from 1964 and betrays a certain thinness in the string timbre, although there is plenty of ambient warmth.

Divertimenti Nos. 7 in D, K.205; 17 in D, K.334; March in D, K.290.
(BB) *** Hung. White Label HRC 080 [id.]. Liszt CO, Rolla or Sándor.

An outstanding super-bargain coupling of two of Mozart's finest *Divertimenti*, in stylish chamber orchestra versions, elegantly played and truthfully recorded in a most pleasing acoustic. K.205 is scored for string trio, plus horns and bassoon, but Mozart's part-writing skilfully ensures that the basic texture is rich; and in the *Adagio* the interplay between violins and violas is especially felicitous. The work is introduced by the march used for its première at Dr Mesmer's garden party in August 1773. K.334 is perhaps the most familiar of all Mozart's large-scale works in this form, and its famous Minuet has more natural rhythmic pulse here than in the Decca version by members of the Vienna Octet.

Divertimenti Nos. 10 in F, K.247; 11 in D, K.331.
**(*) Capriccio 10 203 [id.]. Salzburg Mozarteum Camerata Academica, Végh.

The playing, as in Végh's previous issues, has striking freshness and vitality; these are chamber orchestral performances on modern instruments, but the scale is admirable and the resonance adds a feeling of breadth. Detail is well observed – there is some fine oboe playing in K.251 – and tempi are usually apt. Although slow movements tend to be on the slow side, while not lacking grace, allegros sparkle and have dash without ever seeming hurried, even if ensemble isn't always absolutely immaculate.

Divertimenti Nos 10 in F, K.247; 17 in D, K.334.
(M) **(*) Decca 425 540-2 [id.]. Vienna Octet.

This is a generous recoupling for CD of two major *Divertimenti*, recorded at the beginning of the 1960s. The performance of No. 10 is lively but not especially imaginative and the playing is rather unsmiling until towards the end, when it enlivens itself for a very spirited finale. The more familiar D major piece is given with fine verve, and here the style of the leader (Anton Fietz) in his many solo passages is exactly right for this kind of music-making. This is in fact just how to play Mozart, with no stiffness anywhere, although the rhythmic emphasis of the famous Boccherinian Minuet may strike some ears as overdone. The Viennese acoustic is warm and the sound is extremely vivid, although some of the original smoothness in the treble has been lost in the CD mastering.

Divertimento No. 11 in D for oboe, 2 horns and string quartet, K.251.
** Ph. Dig. 412 618-2 [id.]. Holliger, Baumann, Gasciarrino, Orlando Qt, Guldemond – *Oboe quartet* etc.***

A disappointing performance of an attractive work. The playing itself is polished, alive and well integrated, as one might expect from this cast list, but the approach is rhythmically heavy at times – though the gentler movements come off well – not helped by the close balance.

Divertimenti Nos. 11 in D, K.251; 14 in B flat, K.270; Serenade No. 6 in D (Serenata notturna), K.239.
*** DG Dig. 415 669-2 [id.]. Orpheus CO.

These are wholly admirable performances. Alert, crisply rhythmic allegros show consistent resilience, strong yet without a touch of heaviness, while slow movements are warmly phrased, with much finesse and imaginative use of light and shade. The *Serenata notturna*, which can easily sound bland, has a fine sparkle here, while the *B flat Wind Divertimento* makes an effective contrast. Here the oboe playing is particularly felicitous. Impeccable in ensemble, this playing has no sense of anonymity of character or style. The recording is truthful but rather closely balanced, with a touch of edginess to the violins above the stave.

Divertimento No. 15 in B flat, K.287; Divertimento for strings No. 3, K.138.
*** Ph. Dig. 412 740-2 [id.]. ASMF Chamber Ens.

Divertimento No. 15 in B flat, K.287; Serenade No. 13 (Eine kleine Nachtmusik), K.525.
**(*) DG Dig. 423 610-2 [id.]. BPO, Karajan.

The K.287 *Divertimento*, composed in Salzburg for the Countess Lodron, is a major six-movement piece, with an attractive theme with variations coming second and a central *Adagio*, led by the first violin, of considerable expressive intensity. The finale is witty and humorously based on a folksong ('The farmer's wife has lost the cat'). The ASMF performance here, with a double bass and two horns added to a string quartet, is admirable and beautifully recorded. The *String divertimento* makes an agreeable filler.

Karajan uses a full body of strings; the Berlin Philharmonic play with marvellous unanimity and their phrasing is the soul of elegance. This is an unfashionable approach to Mozart, but it is easy to enjoy. The *Divertimento* is a 1987 recording, the *Night music* (1982) has appeared before and been praised by us for its cultured playing and well-sprung rhythms. The Philharmonie sound is especially full and real in K.287, rather more brightly lit in the *Serenade*, but still very believable in its presence.

Divertimento No. 17 in D, K.334; March in D, K.445.
*** Ph. Dig. 411 102-2 [id.]. ASMF Chamber Ens.

Divertimento No. 17, K.334; Divertimento for strings No. 1, K.136.
*** Denon Dig C37 7080 [id.]. Augmented Berlin Philh. Qt.

Divertimento No. 17; Serenata notturna, K. 239.
** DG Dig. 423 375-2 [id.]. BPO, Karajan.

The engaging *D major Divertimento* with its famous Minuet has frequently been recorded in orchestral dress but nowadays is more often given in its chamber version, as it is here by the Academy. This is an expert performance with plenty of charm and a recording to match. In its CD format it is wonderfully lifelike and present.

On Denon, a hardly less successful account from the augmented Berlin Philharmonia Quartet. The music-making is polished, spirited and full of warmth. The *String divertimento* is equally attractive and makes a more substantial encore than the *March*. The recording is fresh and believable.

Karajan offers both works in orchestral full evening dress; the result, within a resonant acoustic, is opulent and gracious – with some marvellously polished playing from the Berlin violins – but, notably in the famous Minuet, is unashamedly indulgent. In the *Serenata notturna*, the timpani are backward and none too cleanly focused, and this performance lacks real zest.

German dances, K.509/1–6; K.571/1–6; K.600/1–6; K.602/1–4; K.605/1–3; 3 Marches in D, K.189 and K.335/1–2.
**(*) Ph. 416 484-2 [id.]. ASMF, Marriner.

Mozart's dances are hardly among his greatest music but they contain much attractive invention and some individual touches like the use of the hurdy-gurdy in K.602, while in K.600/5 there is a 'canary' trio. The *Sleigh ride* of K.605 is justly famous. The performances here are spirited and nicely turned, but at times perhaps a shade heavy in rhythmic feeling, although the reverberant acoustic contributes to this effect.

6 German dances, K.571; Les petites riens: ballet music, K.299b; Serenade No. 13 (Eine kleine Nachtmusik), K.525.
*** Erato/WEA Dig. 2292 45198-2 [id.]. SCO, Leppard.

An excellent collection in every way. The performance of *Les petites riens* is delightful, spirited and polished, and the *German dances* are no less lively and elegant; the famous *Nachtmusik* is nicely proportioned and very well played. The sound is especially believable on CD, giving a tangible impression of the players sitting together, out beyond the speakers.

Masonic funeral music, K.477; Overtures: Così fan tutte; The Impresario; Le nozze di Figaro; Die Zauberflöte; Serenade No. 13 (Eine kleine Nachtmusik), K.525.
(B) ****(*)** CBS MYK 42593 [id.]. Columbia SO, Bruno Walter.

Walter conducts all this music with evident affection; even if some may feel that he is almost too loving at times, particularly in *Eine kleine Nachtmusik*, there is still something very special about this music-making. His tempi in the overtures are unerringly apt. The account of the *Masonic funeral music* is particularly fine. The recording is characteristic of this highly successful CBS series, warm and full, with an ample bass, but a remarkably fresh upper range, with sweet violins.

A Musical Joke, K.522.
*** Erato/WEA Dig. 2292 45199-2 [id.]. Paillard CO, Paillard – L. MOZART: *Cassation* etc.*******

A Musical Joke, K.522; Serenade No. 13 in G (Eine kleine Nachtmusik), K.525.
*** DG 400 065-2 [id.]. Augmented Amadeus Qt.

Happily paired with a high-spirited version of Leopold Mozart's *Toy symphony*, Paillard's account of Mozart's fun piece makes the most of its outrageous jokes, with the horns in the opening movement boldly going wrong and the final discordant clash sounding positively cataclysmic; yet it takes into account the musical values, too. The recording is excellent, the orchestral group being placed within a warm ambience which yet does not cloud inner detail.

Eine kleine Nachtmusik has rarely sounded as refreshing and exhilarating as in this Amadeus chamber performance; the finale in particular is delectably resilient. The musical clowning in the *Musical Joke*, which can so often seem heavy and unfunny, is here given charm. The horn players, Gerd Seifert and Manfred Klier, are from the Berlin Philharmonic. The recording is first rate.

Notturno for four orchestras, K.286; Serenade No. 6 (Serenata notturna), K.239; Serenade No. 13 (Eine kleine Nachtmusik), K.525.
*** O-L Dig. 411 720-2 [id.]. AAM, Hogwood.

Eine kleine Nachtmusik is usually given in the four-movement form that survives. Christopher Hogwood uses an additional minuet that Mozart composed in collaboration with his English pupil, Thomas Attwood. All the repeats in every movement save one are observed – which is perhaps too much of a good thing. The performance is given one instrument to a part and is sprightly and alive. The *Serenata notturna* and the *Notturno for four orchestras* are for larger forces and are given with considerable panache. Technically, this is first class, with clean and well-defined recorded sound and great presence.

Overtures: *La clemenza di Tito; Così fan tutte; Don Giovanni; Die Entführung aus dem Serail; Idomeneo; Lucio Silla; Le nozze di Figaro; Der Schauspieldirektor; Die Zauberflöte.*
*** EMI Dig. CDC7 47014-2 [id.]. ASMF, Marriner.

Marriner's collection is strongly characterized, emphasizing the spirit of the opera house, offering plenty of drama in *Don Giovanni* and *Idomeneo* and a sense of spectacle with the percussion effects in *Die Entführung. Così fan tutte* and *Figaro* bring a lighter touch; throughout, the ASMF playing is characteristically spirited and stylish, with the string detail nicely clean and polished. The digital recording is bright and bold.

Serenade No. 3 in D, K.189.
**(*) O-L Dig. 411 936-2 [id.]. Schröder, AAM, Hogwood.

In this work Mozart established the feature of including a miniature violin concerto as part of the structure, though here its movements are interspersed with others. This presents the only drawback to the present recording, for Schröder's account of the solo role in the *Andante* is rather too straight and direct, although he offers more charm later on when he contributes to the Trio of the Minuet. The performance overall is brimming with vitality, the finales especially neat and infectious. The recording is first rate.

Serenade Nos. 4 in D (Colloredo); 6 in D (Serenata notturna); March in D, K.237.
*** Ph. Dig. 420 201-2 [id.]. ASMF, Marriner.

This performance under Marriner is highly estimable, very much in the best traditions of the Academy, with Iona Brown making a distinguished and appealing contribution as soloist. The *Serenata notturna*, too, is first class, crisply rhythmic in the first movement with the drums cleanly focused. The recording, like the playing, is strikingly warm and fresh, and this record makes a very good case for performing this consistently engaging music on modern instruments, with elegance of style a keynote of the music-making.

Serenades Nos. 6 in D (Serenata notturna), K.239; 7 in D (Haffner), K.250.
*** Telarc Dig. CD 80161 [id.]. Prague CO, Mackerras.

In Mackerras's coupling the playing is lively and brilliant, helped by warm recorded sound, vivid in its sense of presence, except that the reverberant acoustic clouds the tuttis a little. The violin soloist, Oldrich Viček, is very much one of the team under the conductor rather than a virtuoso establishing his individual line. By omitting repeats in the *Haffner*, Mackerras leaves room for the other delightful *Serenade*, just as haunting, with the terracing between the solo string quartet (in close focus) and the full string band aptly underlined.

Serenades Nos. 6 in D (Serenata notturna), K.239; 9 in D (Posthorn), K.320.
*** Novalis Dig. 150 013-2 [id.]. Bav. RSO, C. Davis.

Davis secures consistently spirited and responsive playing from the Bavarian Radio Orchestra, not only from the strings but also from the woodwind in their concertante section. The posthorn soloist is also a very stylish player; his contribution is unusually refined, yet still tonally robust. With apt tempi and a fine sense of spontaneity throughout, this is very refreshing. The *Serenata notturna* is also well done, if without quite the sparkle of K.320 – here the backwardly balanced drums sound a shade too resonant.

Serenades Nos. 6 in D (Serenata notturna), K.239; 13 in G (Eine kleine Nachtmusik), K.525.
(B) *** Pickwick Dig. PCD 861 [MCA MCAD 25162]. Serenata of London – ELGAR: *Serenade*; GRIEG: *Holberg suite.****

The performance of the *Night music* by the Serenata of London is as fine as any available. There is not a suspicion of routine here; indeed the players, for all the excellence of their ensemble, give the impression of coming to the piece for the first time. The *Serenata notturna* is perhaps not quite so inspired a work, but these excellent players make a good case for it and are agreeably sprightly whenever given the opportunity. The recording has striking naturalness and realism; this is an outstanding CD bargain.

Serenades Nos. 6 in D (Serenata notturna), K.239; 13 (Eine kleine Nachtmusik), K.525;
(i) *Sinfonia concertante in E flat, K.364.*
(B) **(*) DG 427 208-2 [id.]. BPO, Boehm; (i) with Brandis, Cappone.

Boehm's performance of *Eine kleine Nachtmusik* is very enjoyable; it is gracious and stylishly phrased, with a gentle finale. If the *Sinfonia concertante* really requires more individual solo playing (especially in the slow movement) than Messrs Brandis and Cappone provide, the strong directing personality of the conductor keeps the music alive throughout and the sound has been clarified, yet remains well balanced.

Serenade No. 7 in D (Haffner), K.250; March in D, K.249.
*** Ph. Dig. 416 154-2 [id.]. I. Brown, ASMF, Marriner.

A spacious, yet warm and polished account of the *Haffner serenade* from Marriner and his Academy players, with Iona Brown making a superb contribution in the concertante violin role. There is sparkle here as well as expressive grace. The recording is resonant,

MOZART

which increases the impression of a full orchestral performance rather than one on a chamber scale. As usual, the Philips engineers provide a natural sound-balance.

(i) *Serenade No. 7 in D (Haffner);* (ii) *Wind divertimento in B flat, K.186.*
(M) ** DG 429 806-2 [id.]. (i) BPO, Boehm; (ii) VPO Wind Ens.

The Berlin Philharmonic play with such polish and vivacity, and articulation is so beautifully crisp, that one is inclined to accept Boehm's uncharacteristic lack of mellowness and his willingness to drive the allegros rather hard. Thomas Brandis is the excellent violin soloist, but at times there is more exhilaration here than charm. The freshened recording sounds just a little fierce at times in its remastered format and is not absolutely refined in focus. The performance of the *Wind divertimento* is sympathetic, polished and well integrated, but the bright recording tends to make the wind balance slightly top-heavy.

Serenade No. 7 in D (Haffner), K.250; Symphony No. 32 in G.
**(*) Novalis Dig. 150 027-2 [id.]. Bav. RSO, C. Davis.

Sir Colin Davis's Bavarian version of the *Haffner serenade* is graced by an excellent soloist in Andreas Rohn whose playing, firm and warm of tone, is individual without being idiosyncratic. Speeds are unexceptionable, except that the third minuet is on the sluggish side. The short Italian overture, *Symphony No. 32*, makes a lively fill-up. The sound is refined and slightly distanced in the manner one expects from the Herkulessaal in Munich.

Serenade No. 9 in D (Posthorn); 2 Marches, K.335.
*** Ph. Dig. 412 725-2 [id.]. ASMF, Marriner.

(i) *Serenade No. 9 in D (Posthorn);* (ii) *Wind divertimenti: in E flat, K.166; in B flat, K.227.*
(M) **(*) DG 429 807-2 [id.]. (i) BPO, Boehm; (ii) VPO Wind Ens.

Serenades Nos. 9 in D (Posthorn); 13 (Eine kleine Nachtmusik), K.525.
(B) *** Decca 417 874-2 [id.]. V. Mozart Ens., Boskovsky.
**(*) Telarc CD 10108 [id.]. Prague CO, Mackerras.
**(*) DG Dig. 410 085-2 [id.]. VPO, Levine.

Marriner's performance is spacious, cultured and marvellously played. The Academy wind players make a compelling case for modern instruments, as do the strings in the lovely *Andantino*, where the mood darkens. The outer movements are both spirited and strong, the minuets lively and resilient. Michael Laird's contribution on the posthorn is characterful yet elegant. The two *Marches* are used as 'entrance' and 'exit' music. The recording, in a fairly resonant acoustic, adds to the feeling of breadth without blurring detail.

Bargain hunters should be well pleased with Decca's Weekend reissue of Boskovsky's performance with its natural musicality and sense of sparkle. The newest transfer is a little dry in the matter of string timbre, but there is plenty of bloom on the wind, detail is clean and the posthorn is tangible in its presence. The coupled *Night music* is one of the freshest and most attractive performances of this much-played work in any format, and the small string group is most realistically balanced and vividly projected.

The Prague strings have great warmth and Mackerras gets vital results from his Czech forces. Rhythms are lightly sprung and the phrasing is natural in every way. The Telarc acoustic is warm and spacious with a wide dynamic range (some might feel it is too wide for this music), and most ears will find the effect agreeable.

In the *Posthorn serenade* Levine's tempi are well judged, and the Vienna Philharmonic play with distinction. The recording is clean and well balanced, but with less warmth than the Telarc. Indeed there is a sharpness of outlines on the DG compact disc which suggests that the microphones were a shade too close to the musicians.

Boehm's 1971 Berlin Philharmonic recording of the *Posthorn serenade* sounds particularly fresh in its digitally remastered format. The playing is characteristically polished, warm and civilized. Incidentally, as well as naming the excellent posthorn soloist, the documentation reveals the principal flautist as James Galway and the fine oboist as Lothar Koch. Two attractive *Wind divertimenti* are now offered as couplings. Like their companion included with Boehm's *Haffner serenade*, they are sensitively played and well blended, but the digital mastering sounds a bit top-heavy.

Serenade No. 10 in B flat for 13 wind instruments, K.361.
*** ASV Dig. CDCOE 804 [id.]. COE Wind Soloists, Schneider.
*** Ph. Dig. 412 726-2 [id.]. ASMF, Marriner.
**(*) Accent ACC 68642D [id.]. Octophorus, Kuijken.
(M) **(*) EMI Dig. CD-EMX 9520. LPO Wind Ens.
(BB) **(*) Hung. White Label HRC 076 [id.]. Hungarian State Op. Wind Ens., Ervin Lukacs.
**(*) DG Dig. 423 061-2 [id.]. Orpheus CO.
(BB) ** Naxos Dig. 8.55060 [id.]. Amadeus Wind Ens.

Serenades Nos. 10 in B flat; 11 in E flat, K.375.
(M) *** Ph. 420 711-2 [id.]. Netherlands Wind Ens., Edo de Waart.
(M) *** Decca 425 421-2 [id.]. L. Wind Soloists, Jack Brymer.
(M) **(*) EMI CDM7 63349-2 [id.]. (i) London Wind Quintet & Ens.; (ii) New Philh. Wind Ens., Klemperer.

Serenade No. 10 in B flat; Wind divertimento No. 8 in F, K.213.
**(*) Chan. Dig. CHAN 8553 [id.]. SNO Wind Ens., Paavo Järvi.

The brilliant young soloists of the Chamber Orchestra of Europe, inspired by the conducting of Alexander Schneider, give an unusually positive, characterful reading. Right at the start, the flourishes from the first clarinet are far more effective when played as here, not literally, but with Schneider leading them on to the first forte chord from the full ensemble. From then on the individual artistry of the players is most winning. The only controversial point is that where the first *Adagio* – nowadays the most popular movement of all, thanks to the sound-track of the film, *Amadeus* – flows very persuasively rather faster than usual, the second *Adagio*, phrased subtly, sounds rather heavier than usual at a slower, more relaxed speed. The sound is exceptionally vivid and faithful.

The Marriner version fits very stylishly in the Academy's series of Mozart wind works, characteristically refined in its ensemble, with matching of timbres and contrasts beautifully judged, both lively and graceful with rhythms well sprung and speeds well chosen, yet with nothing mannered about the result. Full, warm recording that yet allows good detail.

The Netherlanders offer not only the *B flat Serenade* but also the *E flat*, K.375, a very substantial bonus. Their performances are fresh and alive, admirably sensitive both in feeling for line and in phrasing, but never lingering too lovingly over detail. Both works are enhanced by the presence and sonority of the recording.

Brymer's group gives a strong, stylish performance of the large-scale *B flat major Serenade* with plenty of imagination in matters of phrasing. The Decca balance is rather close, which gives excellent inner clarity but sometimes means that the overall blend is not perfectly balanced. But this has always been one of the best versions and now, with an equally fine account of K.375 added for the reissue, it is again very competitive; the digital remastering has great presence.

Admirers of Klemperer will find this reissued EMI CD worthwhile in combining two characteristic performances from 1961 and 1973 respectively. Though tempi tend to be on the slow side, the rhythmic control and fine ensemble make for performances which, despite their seriousness, remain bright and refreshing, not heavy. They are far from being conventional readings but, as the expression of a unique Mozart interpreter, they are undoubtedly illuminating. The sound is clean and clear.

On period instruments Barthold Kuijken directs his talented team in an authentic performance where the matching is never uncomfortably raw, though the distinctive character of eighteenth-century instruments brings a sparer, lighter texture, as it should. Speeds tend to be on the cautious side but the liveliness of the playing makes up for that. The recording adds to the clarity.

Outstanding playing from the wind ensemble of the London Philharmonic, richly blended in full digital recording. The articulation and rhythmic feeling of the outer movements and the Theme and variations are particularly spontaneous; however, in the slower sections, notably the third-movement *Adagio*, one feels the need of a conductor's directing hand: there is some loss of character both here and, occasionally, elsewhere.

The SNO Wind Ensemble's version under Paavo Järvi (son of a famous father) is enjoyably spontaneous-sounding, though ensemble is not quite as polished as in the finest versions. Speeds are well chosen, and the recording is warm, though the detail is sometimes masked by the lively acoustic. The little *Divertimento* makes an attractive bonus.

Of the super-bargain versions of Mozart's large-scale wind serenade the Hungaroton is the one to go for. The blending of the wind players from the Hungarian State Opera is impressive and their performance has an attractively robust character with buoyant allegros, and plenty of flexibility in slow movements. The sound is excellent, naturally vivid within an attractive ambience.

The Orpheus Chamber Orchestra give a refined, finely detailed reading, which yet rather lacks the individual character of the finest versions, though ensemble is splendid, and the slow movements are very smoothly done, with finely controlled dynamics. Good, full-toned recording.

The source of the group on the Naxos CD, the so-called Amadeus Wind Ensemble, is not made clear. They have a less characterful blend than the Hungaroton group and, although their performance is enjoyable, it has marginally less rhythmic character.

Serenades for wind Nos. 11 in E flat, K.375; 12 in C min., K.388.
*** ASV Dig. CDCOE 802 [id.]. COE, Schneider.
** Hung. Dig. HCD 12549 [id.]. Budapest Wind Ens., Berkes.
**(*) Ph. Dig. 420 183-2 [id.]. Holliger, Pellerin, Brunner, Schmid, Thunemann, Wilkie, Baumann, Vlatkovič.

With Schneider as a wise and experienced guide, the COE Wind give performances which combine brilliance and warmth with a feeling of spontaneity. Schneider very persuasively encourages the individuality of particular soloists, so that the result is both natural and compelling. K.375 in particular is a delight, as genial as it is characterful, conveying the joy of the inspiration. K.388 might have been more menacing at the C minor opening, but the result is most persuasive, with excellent digital sound set against a warm but not confusing acoustic.

The dry acoustic of the Hungaroton recording emphasizes the extraordinary precision of ensemble that marks the work of the Budapest group. Yet for all that precision, the result lacks the sort of fizz, the sense of spontaneous communication, which has been so striking a quality in the group's live performances. Nevertheless, it presents a fine, clean view of Mozart, beautifully paced, with no suspicion of mannerism, and with dazzling technical accomplishment.

Heinz Holliger leads his group of wind players in exceptionally crisp and light-textured readings, marked, as might be expected, by some winningly imaginative oboe solos. The unusually reedy, thin-sounding clarinet-tone will not please everyone, sounding almost like a period instrument; for all their stylishness, these performances do at times seem a shade cautious and lacking in character.

Serenade No. 13 in G (Eine kleine Nachtmusik), K.525.
*** Ph. Dig. 410 606-2 [id.]. I Musici (with concert of Baroque music***).
*** DG Dig. 400 034-2 [id.]. BPO, Karajan – GRIEG: *Holberg suite*; PROKOFIEV: *Symphony No. 1.****
(*) Virgin Dig. VC 790786-2 [id.]. Ac. of L., Richard Stamp – PROKOFIEV: *Peter** ⊛; SAINT-SAENS: *Carnival.****

Serenade No. 13 (Eine kleine Nachtmusik); Adagio and fugue in C min., K.546.
(*) Ph. Dig. 416 386-2 [id.]. ASMF, Marriner – L. MOZART: *Toy symphony*; PACHELBEL: *Canon and gigue.*(*)

I Musici play the music with rare freshness, giving the listener the impression of hearing the work for the first time. The playing is consistently alert and sparkling, with the *Romanze* particularly engaging. The recording is beautifully balanced.

Apart from a self-conscious and somewhat ponderous minuet, Karajan's is a very fine performance, the playing beautifully cultured, with finely shaped phrasing and well-sprung rhythms. The digital sound, well detailed and not without bloom, is a little sharp-edged.

In his miscellaneous group of popular classical and Baroque pieces, Marriner gives a polished and elegant account of *Eine kleine Nachtmusik*, clearly designed to caress the ears of traditional listeners wearied by period performance. The second-movement *Romanze* is even more honeyed than usual on muted strings. Beautifully balanced recording. The *Adagio and fugue* makes a curious encore, played quite strongly but in no way distinctive.

Anyone buying Richard Stamp's record for the Prokofiev and Saint-Saëns couplings will find this account of Mozart's *Night music* an enjoyable makeweight, if not really distinctive. It is quite direct and well paced, and the playing does not lack vitality.

Sinfonia concertante in E flat for oboe, clarinet, horn, bassoon and orchestra, K.297b.
(*) ASV Dig. CDCOE 803 [id.]. COE, Schneider – BACH: *Double violin concerto*; VIVALDI: *Concerto, RV 556.*(*)
(*) ASV Dig. CDDCA 580 [id.]. L. Fest. O, Ross Pople – HAYDN: *Sinfonia concertante.*(*)

The team of young wind soloists of the Chamber Orchestra of Europe is exceptional, and though their live recording of the *Sinfonia concertante* brings a performance less immaculate than we expect from them, it is a lively, stylish account with atmospheric if imperfectly balanced sound, not helped by audience noises.

Well coupled with the Haydn *Sinfonia concertante*, Ross Pople's version also brings a lively, alert performance, with speeds relaxed enough to allow a winning lift to rhythms, making it a genial, affectionate reading which yet never falls into sentimentality. Only in the finale is the result a little heavy, but the way the soloists appear in turn as protagonists in the variation finale is delightfully done. The sound is bright, firm and well balanced.

(i) *Sinfonia concertante in E flat, K.297b;* (ii) *Horn quintet in E flat, K.407;* (iii) *Piano and wind quintet in E flat, K.452.*
**(*) Decca Dig. 421 393-2 [id.]. (i) ECO, Tuckwell; (ii) Tuckwell, Gabrieli Qt; (iii) John Ogdon, Wickens, Hill, Tuckwell, Gatt.

Tuckwell directs as well as providing the concertante horn part in the *Sinfonia concertante*, and it is an entirely beguiling performance, beautifully shaped and aptly paced. Tuckwell also leads the *Horn quintet* – very like a concerto with string quartet instead of orchestra – with characteristic sensibility and aplomb, and is at his most infectious in the finale. The contribution of the Gabrielis is rather severe; one would have liked the string playing to smile a bit more, but they are not helped by a rather close, grainy string timbre; more ambience would have helped here. The *Piano and wind quintet* is enjoyable but not distinctive. The recording throughout has striking presence and clarity, and is especially well balanced in the *Sinfonia concertante*.

(i) *Sinfonia concertante in E flat for violin, viola and orchestra, K.364;* (ii) *Sinfonia concertante in E flat for oboe, clarinet, horn, bassoon and orchestra, K.297b.*
*** Virgin Dig. VCy 790818-2 [id.]. (i) Warren-Green, Chase; (ii) Hunt, Collins, Thompson, Alexander; LCO, Warren-Green.
(M) ** DG 429 813-2 [id.]. (i) Brandis, Cappone, BPO; (ii) Lehmayer, Schmidl, Högner, Faltl, VPO; Boehm.

In the ideal coupling of Mozart's paired *Sinfonias concertantes*, Christopher Warren-Green is joined by Roger Chase to provide a characteristically vital account of Mozart's inspired work for violin and viola. The *Andante* is slow and warmly expressive, yet without a trace of sentimentality. This is not quite as inspired as the Perlman/Zukerman account (see above), but it is still very satisfying with its full-timbred sound from soloists and orchestra alike. The coupling, K.297b, is even more delectable and it would be hard to imagine a more persuasive team of wind players than those here. The full-bodied recording has plenty of space and atmosphere and the soloists in both works remain real and tangible.

These are uneven performances on DG, recorded a decade apart. Boehm's direction of K.364 is stylish and sure, but this work really requires more positive and individual solo playing than Messrs Brandis and Cappone provide, although the performance is not without spontaneity. Moreover the 1966 recording of the orchestra is not ideally focused in its CD transfer. The 1976 Vienna account of the companion work for wind is a different matter: it sounds remarkably idiomatic and well blended. The soloists exert plenty of personality and the recording too is better. This is altogether refreshing.

Sonatas for organ (Epistle) Nos. 1–17 (complete).
*** Decca Dig. 421 297-2 [id.]. Peter Hurford, Amsterdam Mozart Players.

The *Epistle sonatas* derive their name from the fact that they were intended to be heard between the Epistle and Gospel in the Mass. Admittedly they are not great music or even first-class Mozart; however, played with relish, as they are here, and recorded with delightful freshness, they make a strong impression.

SYMPHONIES

Symphonies Nos. 1 in E flat, K.16; in A min. (Odense), K.16a; 4 in D, K.19; in F, K.19a.
(M) **(*) Unicorn Dig. UKCD 2018 [id.]. Odense SO, Vetö.

It was in Odense that the lost symphony, K.16a, was discovered by the archivist, Gunnar Thygesen. Alas for everyone's hopes, it seems very unlikely, from stylistic evidence and even the key, A minor, that it is genuine Mozart. It remains a charming work in the *Sturm und Drang* manner, and is well coupled here with an apt group of other early Mozart symphonies, done with warmer tone than those in the Hogwood complete set. First-rate recording.

Symphonies Nos. 1 in E flat, K.16; 4 in D, K.19; in F, K.19a; 5 in B flat, K.22; in D, K.32; 11 in D, K.73q; 13 in F, K.112; 44 in D, K.73e; 45 in D, K.73n; 46 in C, K.111; in D, K.111a; 47 in D, K.73m.
*** O-L 417 140-2 (2) [id.]. AAM, Schröder; Hogwood.

The earliest pieces here are the three London symphonies, written in Chelsea in 1764, when Mozart was only 8½, obviously influenced by J. C. Bach, then an arbiter of musical fashion in London. A little later come two symphonies written for The Hague, but most of the works were written for Italy. With vigour and resilience in outer movements and no lack of charm in slow movements, this is among the most successful of an important and historic series, superbly recorded. Throughout, the performances are directed by Jaap Schröder, with Christopher Hogwood contributing the continuo from the harpsichord. The CD transfers are highly successful.

Symphonies Nos. 1, 4–6, 7a, 8–20, 42–7, 55; in C, K.208/102; in D, K.45, 111/120, 141a & 196/121; in G.
*** Ph. 416 471-2 (6) [id.]. ASMF, Marriner.

The Academy play with great style, warmth and polish; the Philips engineers, having responded with alive and vivid recording, offer admirable (analogue) transfers into the CD format. As with the set of later symphonies (see below), the layout is over six compact discs (offered for the price of five). These are altogether delightful records and can be strongly recommended to non-authenticists.

Symphonies Nos. 6 in F, K.43; 7 in D, K.45; 8 in D, K.48; 40 in G min., K.550 (2nd version); in F, K.42a; in B flat, K.45b; in D, K.46a (K.51); in G (New Lambacher); in B flat, K.74g (K.216); in G, K.425a (K.444); in A min. (Odense).
*** O-L 421 135-2 (3) [id.]. AAM, Schröder; Hogwood.

This volume of the Academy's monumental series is crowned by the clarinet version of No. 40 (the original version with oboe is elsewhere) and also by the *Symphony 'No. 37'*, in fact the work of Michael Haydn but with a slow introduction by Mozart. The other works are early pieces, some of them doubtfully by Mozart, but the depth and perception of the scholarship behind the series are superbly demonstrated not only in the performances but (as in all the volumes) by the detailed and illuminating annotations of the American Mozart scholar, Neal Zaslaw. Performances are fresh, clear and alert, as in the rest of the series. Brilliant recording.

Symphonies Nos. 9 in C, K.73; 14 in A, K.114; 15 in G, K.124; 16 in C, K.128; 17 in G, K.129; in C, K.35; in D, K.38; in D, K.62a/K.100; (42) in F, K.75; in G, K.75b/K.110.
**(*) O-L 417 518-2 (2). AAM, Schröder; Hogwood.

It is vitality and sharpness of articulation which dominate the readings here. In the later symphonies, textures are sometimes thinned even further by the use of solo strings in sections of the music, which produces the feeling of a chamber ensemble, and seems a questionable practice. However, Schröder and his group are nothing if not consistent, and those collecting this series can be assured that this volume is as vigorous and dedicated as the others. The recording too is lively, although the acoustic at times seems somewhat over-resonant, especially in the earlier works.

Symphonies Nos. 18 in F, K.130; in D, K.141a; 19 in E flat, K.132; 20 in D, K.133; 21 in A, K.134; in D, K.135; 26 in E flat, K.161a; 27 in G, K.161b; 22 in C, K.162; 23 in D, K.162b; 24 in B flat, K.173dA.
*** O-L 417 592-2 (3) [id.]. AAM, Schröder; Hogwood.

This was the first box of the Academy of Ancient Music's issue of the complete recording of Mozart symphonies using authentic texts and original instruments; and very invigorating it proved. The variety of scale as well as of expression makes it a very refreshing collection, particularly as the style of performance, with its non-vibrato tang, sharply picks out detail of texture rather than moulding the sound together. The recording is excellent, and the CD transfers are bright and clean.

Symphonies No. 19 in E flat, K.132; 20 in D, K.133; 21 in A, K.134; 22 in C, K.162; 23 in D, K.162b.
*** Telarc Dig. CD 80217 [id.]. Prague CO, Mackerras.

Mackerras, having had great success with his Telarc recordings of the later symphonies, is equally lively in these early works from Mozart's Salzburg period. The surprising thing is how fast his speeds tend to be, not just swifter than a rival such as James Levine – who, with the Vienna Philharmonic, is recorded far more closely in drier sound – but also the Academy of Ancient Music. In one instance the contrast is astonishing, when at a very brisk *Andantino grazioso* Mackerras turns the slow middle movement of No. 23 into a lilting Laendler, quite different from other performances. The recording is reverberant, as in the later symphonies, giving relatively weighty textures; with such light scoring, however, there is ample clarity, with braying horns riding beautifully over the rest. Few will complain – when the five symphonies add up to a disc of over 73 minutes – that Mackerras is less meticulous about observing every single repeat than he was with the later masterpieces.

Symphonies Nos. 21–41 (complete).
*** Ph. 415 954-2 (6) [id.]. ASMF, Marriner.

Marriner, following up the success of his splendid volume of the early symphonies on modern instruments, here presents the later works in comparably stylish, well-recorded performances. The transfers are of high quality; only in No. 40 and the *Haffner* (which date from 1970, nearly a decade before the rest) does a somewhat over-resonant bass betray the age of the originals. Perhaps when he reaches the *Jupiter*, Marriner fails to capture the full weight of Mozart's argument (exposition repeat not observed in the finale); but the wonder is that so many symphonies have been performed with no hint of routine.

Symphonies Nos. 24 in B flat, K.182; 25 in G min., K.183; 26 in E flat, K.184; 27 in G, K.199; 32 in G, K.318.
*** EMI Dig. CDC7 49176-2. ASMF, Marriner.

Marriner's record stands out from others of the same repertoire for a winning combination of stylishness and polish, extrovert high spirits and strong characterization. Allegros throughout are vital and strong, never heavy, always rhythmically buoyant. In fact this whole record is immensely enjoyable, not least because the players and Marriner together convey their own joy in the music. Splendid sound.

Symphonies Nos. 24 in B flat, K.173; 26 in E flat, K.161a; 27 in G, K.161b; 30 in D, K.202.
*** Telarc Dig. CD 80186 [id.]. Prague CO, Mackerras.

With discreet use of harpsichord continuo, Mackerras's readings are consistently stylish in their refreshing Mozart manners. Where in later symphonies Mackerras chooses more relaxed speeds, here he tends to be more urgent, as in the finale of No. 26 or the *Andantino grazioso* slow movement of No. 27, where he avoids the questionable use of muted strings. The reverberation of the recording gives the impression of a fairly substantial orchestra, without loss of detail, and anyone fancying this particular group of early Mozart symphonies need not hesitate.

Symphonies Nos. 25 in G min., K.183; 28 in C, K.200; 29 in A, K.201; 30 in D, K.202; in D, K.203, 204 and 196/121.
*** O-L 417 841-2 (3) [id.]. AAM, Schröder; Hogwood.

It is a revelation to find that a symphony such as the *G minor* (No. 25) is not a 'little *G minor*' at all for, with repeats all observed, it acquires extra weight; and in as lively and fresh a performance as this the extra length from repetition proves invigorating, never tedious. The *A major* – another 'big' symphony – also has a new incisiveness and clarity, without losing anything in rhythmic bounce; so too with the less well-known works. As in the other volumes, the recording is superb, and the CDs have added presence and transparency of texture.

Symphonies Nos. 25 in G min., K.183; 28 in C, K.200; 29 in A, K.201.
*** Telarc Dig. CD 80165 [id.]. Prague CO, Mackerras.

If you want performances on modern (as opposed to period) instruments, these are at least as fine as any, fresh and light, with transparent textures set against a warm acoustic and with rhythms consistently resilient. The impression is of an aptly scaled orchestra believably set in a conventional concert hall. Mackerras's speeds are always carefully judged to allow elegant pointing but without mannerism, and the only snag is that second-half repeats are omitted in slow movements, and in the finale too of No. 29.

Symphonies Nos. 25 in G min., K.183; 29 in A, K.201; 31 (Paris); 33 in B flat, K.319; 34 in C, K.338; 35 (Haffner); 36 (Linz); 38 (Prague); 39 in E flat, K.543; 40 in G min., K.550; 41 (Jupiter).
(M) ****** EMI CMS7 63344-2 (3) [Ang. CDMD 63272]. Philh. O or New Philh. O, Klemperer.

Klemperer's Mozart performances with the Philharmonia were made over a decade between 1957 (*No. 25 in G minor* – sounding a little rough in the remastered transfer) and 1966. His achievement was uneven. The spirit of Beethoven often makes its presence felt, beneficially in the large-scale symphonies, notably in Nos. 38 and 39, but sometimes merely bringing heaviness, as in the *Haffner* and the *Linz*, where the weightiness and portentous feeling step outside the boundaries of Mozartian sensibility. Yet with wonderfully refined playing from the Philharmonia, usually in peak form, there are rare insights. The finale of No. 34 with its scampering triplets is the movement to try first: the rhythmic urgency makes it a delicious experience, while the beautiful *Andante* of the *G minor* (No. 25) has genuine incandescence. In the *Paris symphony* there is a gain in strength, while the slow movement has a memorable classical poise. The 1963 performance of *No. 40 in G minor* was chosen rather than the earlier (late-1950s) version, because of better recording, but the reading is altogether heavier. The finest performances are undoubtedly the *Prague* and *No. 39 in E flat*, which combine virility and power in the outer movements with grace and elegance in slow movements: the orchestra respond throughout with a spontaneous sense of joy. Surprisingly, however, the *Jupiter* lacks a sense of occasion: while alert and structurally impressive, it never really catches fire. The remastered recording is fresh, bright and usually clean, with no lack of weight.

Symphonies Nos. 27 in G, K.199; 28 in C, K.200; 34 in C, K.338.
(B) **(*) Pickwick Dig. PCD 933. E. Sinfonia, Sir Charles Groves.

Crisp, clean, alert performances of these early symphonies from Sir Charles Groves and no lack of finesse in the playing of the English Sinfonia. Perhaps at times accents seem a shade strong, but rhythms are not unresilient and the *Andante* of No. 34 is shaped elegantly and affectionately, while remaining thoroughly stylish. Compared with Marriner and Mackerras there is perhaps a lack of idiosyncrasy in the readings but, at bargain price and with fine modern digital sound, well balanced with the resonance nicely judged, this is excellent value.

Symphonies Nos. 29 in A, K.201; 32 in G, K.318; 33 in B flat, K.319; 35 (Haffner), 36 (Linz); 38 (Prague); 39 in E flat, K.543; 40 in G min., K.550; 41 (Jupiter).
(M) *** DG 429 668-2 (3) [id.]. BPO, Karajan.

With Nos. 29, 32 and 33 added to the original LP box, these are beautifully played and vitally alert readings, and the recordings made between 1966 and 1979 are well balanced and given full, lively transfers to CD. There are details about which some may have reservations, and the opening of the *G minor*, which is a shade faster than in Karajan's earlier Vienna performance for Decca, many not be quite dark enough for some tastes. But the *Jupiter*, although short on repeats, has weight and power as well as surface elegance.

Symphonies Nos. 29 in A, K.201; 32 in G, K.318; 33 in B flat, K.319.
(M) **(*) Pickwick Dig. PCD 922. E. Sinfonia, Sir Charles Groves.

Again Sir Charles Groves shows himself at home in this repertoire, with well-paced readings, cleanly and brightly articulated, especially the rhythmically buoyant minuets and the spirited finales which produce an attractively neat response from the strings and a light touch overall. The slow movements of all three works are gently graceful and beautifully played; the *Andante* of the *A major Symphony* has rather more warmth in Boehm's hands, but many will like Sir Charles's delicacy, helped by an appealing, transparent recording. Indeed the sound is very good indeed, with EMI's No. 1 Studio once more producing a concert-hall impression, with just the right amount of resonance.

Symphonies Nos. 29 in A, K.201; 33 in B flat, K.319.
*** Ph. Dig. 412 736-2 [id.]. E. Bar. Soloists, Gardiner.

Although the opening is deceptively gentle, the first movement of John Eliot Gardiner's *A major Symphony* soon develops an athletic strength. Delicacy returns in the *Andante*, nicely proportioned and beautifully played. The account of *No. 33 in B flat* is outstandingly successful, the outer movements a delight, full of rhythmic character. The *Andante* brings some slight squeezing of phrases, but overall this is authenticity with a winning countenance and without the abrasiveness of the Academy of Ancient Music in this repertoire. The recording is fresh and immediate and very well balanced.

Symphonies Nos. 29 in A, K.201; 35 in D (Haffner), K.385; Masonic funeral music, K.477.
(M) **(*) DG 429 803-2 [id.]. VPO, Karl Boehm.

These performances, which first appeared not long before Boehm's death, are distinguished by finely groomed playing from the Vienna Philharmonic. The first movement of the *A major* is on the slow side, but Boehm's warmth sustains it and there is some lovely expressive playing in the second. Although these performances are weightier than his earlier, complete set with the Berlin Philharmonic, they have a relaxed quality and a glowing resonance which make them endearing, the mature products of octogenarian wisdom. They may sometimes lack drive but they remain compelling. The *Masonic funeral music*, darkly characterful, makes a worthwhile bonus. The 1981 recordings have responded to CD remastering; some of the heaviness has been mitigated, while the orchestral quality is full and naturally balanced within its attractive ambience.

Symphonies Nos. 29 in A, K.201; 35 in D (Haffner), K.385; 40 in G min., K.550.
(M) **(*) Ph. 420 486-2 [id.]. ASMF, Marriner.

Marriner uses original scorings of both the later works – minus flutes and clarinets in the *Haffner*, minus clarinets in No. 40. The readings are finely detailed but dynamic too, nicely scaled against warm recording, with a degree of excess bass resonance. No. 29 was recorded in 1979, but the sound matches up quite well.

Symphonies Nos. 29 in A, K.201; 39 in E flat, K.543.
**(*) DG Dig. 423 374-2 [id.]. BPO, Karajan.

Although this is very much big-band Mozart with full, weighty sound, it is easy to respond to the warmth of Karajan's approach to the *A major Symphony*. There is some radiant string playing from the Berlin orchestra – the sounds produced utterly different from the textures of Hogwood's Academy – and if the *E flat Symphony* has a degree of heaviness (like the Minuet of K.201), the strength of the reading is in no doubt and the woodwind detail of the finale is perceptively illuminated.

Symphonies Nos. 30 in D, K.202; 33 in B flat, K.319; 34 in C, K.338.
(B) **(*) Ph. 422 978-2 [id.]. Concg. O, Josef Krips.

Krips' performances on this bargain CD and its companions listed below were recorded in 1972/3. The ample Concertgebouw sound, with its resonant bass, emphasizes the breadth of scale of the music-making, yet the digital remastering gives an attractive freshness to the violins, although the Minuets sound rather well upholstered. Krips' tempi are aptly judged and the orchestral playing is a pleasure in itself, especially nimble in finales, which are never raced. Slow movements are graciously phrased, and altogether the music-making here shows Krips as a highly sympathetic if not a specially individual Mozartian.

Symphonies Nos. 30 in D, K.202; 35 in D (Haffner), K.385; Serenade No. 13 in G (Eine kleine Nachtmusik), K.525.
(M) ** DG Dig. 427 811-2 [id.]. VPO, James Levine.

These performances are characteristic of Levine's Mozart series with the VPO. Strong and stylish, with brisk, well-polished allegros, they lack a little in distinctiveness, although in the *Night music* Levine's direct, elegant manner is in some ways more telling. The digital sound is clean and lively, less well balanced than later issues in the series (No. 30 was one of the first to be recorded).

Symphonies Nos. 31 in D (Paris), K.297; 33 in B flat, K.319; Andante, K.297.
**(*) Teldec/WEA Dig. 2292 42924-2 [id.]. Concg. O, Harnoncourt.

Harnoncourt, when he stops conducting an orchestra of original instruments, may still favour speeds rather slower than usual, but the manner is relatively romantic in its expressiveness. This is the most successful of his Mozart records with the Concertgebouw, with beautiful, cleanly articulated playing. The alternative slow movements are given for the *Paris*, the second one much lighter in weight. In No. 33, Harnoncourt overdoes his slowness in the *Andante*, but adds to the breadth of the finale by giving the repeats of both halves. Very good recording.

Symphonies Nos. 31 in D (Paris), K.207; 33 in B flat, K.319; 34 in C, K.338.
**(*) Telarc Dig. CD 80190 [id.]. Prague CO, Mackerras.

Mackerras and the Prague Chamber Orchestra give characteristically stylish and refined performances, clean of attack and generally marked by brisk speeds. As in their accounts of the later symphonies, all repeats are observed – even those in the *da capos* of minuets – and the only snag is that the reverberant Prague acoustic, more than in others of the Telarc series, clouds tuttis: the Presto finale of the *Paris* brings phenomenal articulation of quavers at the start, which then in tuttis disappear in a mush. One welcome extra on a well-filled disc is the 3/4 alternative *Andante* slow movement for this symphony, Mozart's second thoughts when his 6/8 *Andante* failed to find favour with the Paris public. Surprisingly, after that, the opportunity has not also been taken to include the *Minuet*, K.409, originally intended for No. 34.

Symphonies Nos. 31 in D (Paris), K.297 (1st version); *34 in C, K.338.*
*** Ph. 420 937-2 [id.]. E. Bar. Soloists, Gardiner.

John Eliot Gardiner repeats here the success of his coupling of Nos. 29 and 33. He offers as a bonus the alternative slow movement of the *Paris symphony*, placing it immediately after the usual movement, so that both are played unless one or the other is programmed out, a singular advantage of the CD format. In No. 34, Gardiner includes the K.409 *Minuet*, which works quite well. Throughout, the playing has characteristic incisive strength, with the allegros strong in rhythmic character and slow movements appealingly lyrical in feeling; there is no suggestion here of vinegary 'authenticity', and the sound is first class.

Symphonies Nos. 31 in D (Paris), K.297; 35 in D (Haffner), K.385.
**(*) Ph. Dig. 416 490-2 [id.]. O of 18th Century, Brüggen.

With period instruments used, textures are comparably clean, but Brüggen's emphasis is on sweetness and delicacy, with refined and distinctive blending. He moulds the music more subtly than would have been possible under the conditions of Mozart's day, making it rather mannered; but the delicacy of these performances will certainly attract many. On CD the sound is both warm and refined.

Symphonies Nos. 31 in D (Paris), K.297; 35 in D (Haffner), K.385; 36 in C (Linz), K.425.
(B) **(*) Ph. 426 063-2 [id.]. Concg. O, Josef Krips.

These are generally excellent performances, polished, alert and attractively recorded, if the warm Concertgebouw acoustics are not felt to be too weighty. Krips' pacing is relatively steady, but his readings again show a genuine Mozartian sensibility, and have vitality too.

Symphonies Nos. 31 in D (Paris) (2 versions); *35 in D (Haffner), K.385* (2nd version); *38 in D (Prague), K.504; 39 in E flat, K.543; 40 in G min., K.550* (1st version); *41 in C (Jupiter).*
**(*) O-L Dig. 421 085-2 (3) [id.]. AAM, Schröder; Hogwood.

The last and greatest of Mozart symphonies fare well in the Academy's collected edition, for performances on original instruments bring sharpness and intensity to compensate for any lack of weight or resonance expected by modern ears. Though the lack of expressive freedom typical of slow movements may be disappointing for some, only No. 40 really disappoints in its rather prosaic manner. The *Paris symphony* is given two complete performances with alternative slow movements, both using more strings than the rest, as witnessed by the first Paris performances. Excellent recording, as in the whole series.

(i) *Symphonies Nos. 31 in D (Paris), K.297; 36 in C (Linz), K.425;* (ii) *Overture: Le nozze di Figaro.*
(B) *** ASV CDQS 6033. (i) LSO; (ii) RPO, Bátiz.

After a sprightly account of the *Figaro overture* from the RPO, the LSO under Bátiz provide two spirited and polished accounts of favourite named symphonies. Tempi in outer movements are brisk, but the *Presto* finale of the *Linz* (for instance) produces some sparkling playing from the strings; and in both slow movements the phrasing is warm and gracious. With excellent digital recording, this makes an enjoyable bargain-priced pairing.

Symphonies Nos. 31 in D (Paris), K.297; 36 in C (Linz), K.425; 38 in D (Prague), K.504.
*** ASV Dig. CDDCA 647 [id.]. L. Mozart Players, Jane Glover.

Jane Glover and the London Mozart Players offer a particularly attractive and generous coupling in the three Mozart symphonies associated with cities. The only penalty is that the first-half repeats in the slow movements of the *Linz* and *Prague* are omitted, perhaps not a great loss. Happily, exposition repeats are observed in the outer movements. The performances are all fresh and vital in traditional chamber style, with little influence from period performance. Tuttis are not always ideally clear on inner detail; but the result is nicely in scale, not too weighty, with the delicacy beautifully light and airy. Speeds are never eccentric, and the feeling of live communication comes over at such a moment as in the final coda of the *Linz*, where Glover gives an extra thrust to the closing bars to seal the whole work in exhilaration.

Symphonies Nos. 31 (Paris); 40 in G min.; 41 in C (Jupiter).
(B) *** DG 427 210-2 [id.]. BPO, Boehm.

Boehm's way with Mozart is broader and heavier in texture than we are used to nowadays, and exposition repeats are the exception rather than the rule; but these are warm and magnetic performances with refined and strongly rhythmic playing, sounding remarkably vivid in their digital transfer.

Symphonies Nos. 32 in G, K.318; 33 in B flat, K.319; 34 in C, K.338; 35 in D (Haffner), K.385; 36 in C (Linz), K.425; in C, K.213c/208; in D, K.248b/250 and 320.
**(*) O-L 421 104-2 (3) [id.]. AAM, Schröder; Hogwood.

Using authentic performance style with all repeats observed as before, Hogwood's readings are always fresh and illuminating, the speeds often brisk but never rushed, though some will prefer a more relaxed, less metrical style in slow movements. The recordings – with Hogwood's harpsichord presented clearly against the full ensemble (strings 9.8.4.3.2) – are superbly faithful to the aim of re-creating the sounds Mozart originally heard.

Symphonies Nos. 32 in G, K.318; 33 in B flat, K.319; 36 in C (Linz), K.425.
(M) *** DG 429 804-2 [id.]. BPO, Karajan.

This is Karajan's big-band Mozart at its finest. Although there may be slight reservations about the Minuet and Trio of the *Linz*, which is rather slow (and one might quibble at the broadening of tempo at bar 71 of the first movement), overall there is plenty of life here and slow movements show the BPO at their most graciously expressive. The remastered sound is clear and lively, full but not over-weighted.

Symphonies Nos. 32 in G, K.318; 35 in D (Haffner), K.385; 36 in C (Linz), K.425.
*** Virgin Dig. VC 790702-2 [id.]. SCO, Saraste.
** Ph. Dig. 422 419-2 [id.]. E. Bar. Soloists, Gardiner.

More than most other versions on modern instruments, Saraste's accounts reflect the new lessons of period performance. These are more detached, less sostenuto performances than those of, for example, Jeffrey Tate and the ECO in these works and, with all repeats observed, make an excellent alternative. The recording, helpfully reverberant, yet gives lightness and transparency to textures, conveying an apt chamber scale.

The English Baroque Soloists play for Gardiner with a refinement and polish to stand out even among the finest period groups – but, surprisingly for this conductor, the performances lack sparkle and often seem over-refined. They are very well recorded.

Symphonies Nos. 32 in G, K.318; 35 in D (Haffner), K.385; 39 in E flat, K.543.
*** EMI Dig. CDC7 47327-2 [id.]. ECO, Tate.

It is the gift of Jeffrey Tate to direct meticulously detailed readings of Mozart, full of stylish touches which never sound fussy or mannered, thanks to the natural electricity which he consistently reveals, whether in fast movements or slow. As in his other late-symphony recordings, Tate is generous with repeats, and there is considerable gain from having both halves of the finale of No. 39 repeated. In the brief *Italian overture* (No. 32) and in the *Haffner* Tate achieves comparable exhilaration at relatively spacious speeds, finding elegance on the one hand while bringing out dramatic contrasts on the other. Excellent sound, weighty but apt in scale.

Symphonies Nos. 33 in B flat, K.319; 34 in C, K.338; Minuet, K.409.
*** EMI Dig. CDC7 49317-2 [id.]. ECO, Jeffrey Tate.

Tate's coupling of Nos. 33 and 34 matches the achievement of his other Mozart issues with the ECO. In No. 33 Tate brings out the fun of the fast movements to the full and makes the *Andante moderato* seem a genuine slow movement, refined, fresh and unmannered. In the first movement of No. 34 Tate gives a big-scale reading, built on dramatic contrasts, following it with a sweet and natural account of the slow movement. The extra *Minuet* (placed on the disc as a supplement) is plain and rather brisk, while in the finale Tate gives an exhilarating lift to the 6/8 jig rhythms. Warm, natural recording, as in the rest of the series.

Symphonies Nos. 34 in C, K.388; 35 in D (Haffner), K.385; 39 in E flat, K.543.
*** ASV Dig. CDDCA 615 [id.]. L. Mozart Players, Jane Glover.

Tackling three major works, Jane Glover provides freshly imaginative performances that can compete with any in the catalogue, given the most vividly realistic recorded sound; Nos. 34 and 39 are especially striking. This collection can be recommended with enthusiasm.

Symphonies Nos. 34 in C, K.338; 41 in C (Jupiter), K.551; Minuet, K.409.
**(*) Hung. HCD 12982 [id.]. Budapest Fest. O, Ivan Fischer.

Like some of the finest recent versions, Ivan Fischer gives a performance of the *Jupiter* on modern instruments that shows direct signs of having been influenced by period style. The natural vigour and superb discipline of the orchestra bring home the electric qualities of the playing. Some may seek a gentler manner in the slow movement, but the Minuet, fast and light, has winning panache; crisp articulation, with superb attack from the brass, makes for an exhilarating account of the finale. *Symphony No. 34* is given a similarly fresh and clean performance, with the military flavour of the first movement brought out. Speeds tend to be on the slow side in the first two movements, as well as in the optional *Minuet*, K.409, which is given a Laendler-like swagger. By contrast the finale is taken very fast, on the verge of sounding breathless.

Symphonies Nos. 35 (Haffner); 36 (Linz); 38 (Prague); 39 in E flat; 40 in G min.; 41 (Jupiter).
(B) *** CBS M2YK 45676 (2). Columbia SO, Bruno Walter.
*** DG Dig. 419 427-2 (3) [id.]. VPO, Bernstein.

Walter's set of Mozart's last and greatest symphonies comes from the beginning of the 1960s, his final recording period. The sound remains wonderfully fresh and full; some may feel that the bass resonance is occasionally too ample, but the upper range is sweet and clear and there is no imbalance. The performances are crisp and classical, while still possessing humanity and warmth. Slow movements are outstanding for their breadth and the natural flow of the phrasing. Melodic lines are moulded nobly and pacing always seems inevitable. Walter achieves just the right balance of tempi in the two sections of the first movement of the *Prague*, for instance, and draws from the *Andante* all the sweetness and lyrical power he is capable of. Finales are sparkling and brilliant, but never forced. The *G minor Symphony* is given a treasurable performance; in the *Jupiter*, if neither the first-movement exposition nor the finale carries repeats, Walter structures his interpretation accordingly, and the reading wears an Olympian quality.

Bernstein's recordings were taken from live performances (between 1984 and 1986) and have all the added adrenalin that is expected – but not always achieved – in such circumstances. Besides the electricity, Bernstein's Mozart also has breadth and style; only occasionally (as in No. 39) does a suspicion of self-consciousness mar the interpretation. Pacing is consistently well judged, except perhaps in finales, where the VPO are kept very much on their toes with speeds that are perilously brisk. The sound is full and well balanced.

(i) *Symphonies Nos. 35 in D (Haffner), K. 385; 36 in C (Linz);* (ii) *Rondo for violin and orchestra in B flat, K. 269.*
(M) *** CBS Dig. MDK 44647 [id.]. (i) Bav. RSO, Kubelik; (ii) Zukerman, St Paul CO.

First-class performances from Kubelik and the Bavarian Radio orchestra, well paced and alive in every bar. The *Haffner* is particularly strong, and Kubelik's spacious presentation of the *Linz* is also satisfying. Both slow movements are beautifully played. At the end, Zukerman provides a sparkling encore. The CBS recording is admirable, full, yet clear and well balanced.

Symphonies Nos. 35 (Haffner); 36 (Linz); 38 (Prague).
(B) *** DG 429 521-2 [id.]. BPO, Boehm.

A splendid bargain triptych showing Boehm on his best form. His Berlin account of the *Linz* is one of his finest Mozart performances, balancing vitality with warmth. It was recorded in 1966 and the sound is first class; its companions were made six years earlier, yet the difference in quality is only marginal and the remastering brings plenty of warmth as well as adding freshness to the violins. The *Haffner* and the *Prague* are also alert and sensitive, and the playing is again of the highest order.

Symphonies Nos. 35 in D (Haffner); 38 in D (Prague).
**(*) Ph. Dig. 416 155-2 [id.]. Dresden State O, Sir Colin Davis.

Though Davis favours big-scale Mozart, he opts for fastish allegros, and the refinement of the playing helps to make up for the bass-heavy thickness of the Dresden sound, as recorded by VEB engineers. The dramatic opening of the *Haffner* is made very weighty indeed. In slow movements Davis is less detached than he sometimes used to be in Mozart, more obviously affectionate yet without sentimentality. This makes an unusual but not over-generous coupling.

Symphonies Nos. 35 in D (Haffner), K.385; 38 in D (Prague), K.504; 39 in E flat, K.543.
(M) **(*) EMI CD-EMX 2097. ECO, Barenboim.

Barenboim is strongly vigorous in the first movement of the *Haffner*, and the slow movement is elegantly done; in the *Prague*, he obviously intends the full weight of the imposing introduction to be felt – and, to tell the truth, he miscalculates a trifle so that the listener is impatient for the allegro to begin. When it does, it is gracious yet alive and the impetus of the music is on the right scale. No. 39 is especially impressive: imaginative phrasing from the strings is matched by wind playing in which the colour is brought out well. Throughout the disc, the scale of the performances is right, with the good recording balance always helpful. However, the violin timbre now sounds thinner than originally, although this is offset to some extent by the overall ambient warmth.

Symphonies Nos. 35 in F (Haffner), K.385; 41 in C (Jupiter), K. 551.
*** DG Dig. 415 305-2 [id.]. VPO, Bernstein.
(B) **(*) Pickwick Dig. PCD 914. O of St John's, Smith Square, Oliver Gilmour.

The *Jupiter* brings one of the finest of all of Bernstein's Mozart recordings, edited together from live performances. It is exhilarating in its tensions and observes the repeats in both halves of the finale, making it almost as long as the massive first movement. Bernstein's electricity sustains that length, and one welcomes it for establishing the supreme power of the argument, the true crown to the whole of Mozart's symphonic output. Pacing cannot be faulted in any of the four movements; and the *Haffner* brings a similarly satisfying reading until the finale, when Bernstein in the heat of the moment breaks loose with a speed so fast that even the Vienna violins find it hard to articulate exactly. It remains exciting and, with recording on CD only slightly cloudy in heavy tuttis, far better than most taken from live performance. It makes an excellent recommendation.

Oliver Gilmour's coupling of the *Haffner* and the *Jupiter* has the benefit of excellent sound, setting genuine chamber-orchestra performances in a believable acoustic. The playing is consistently neat, crisp and transparent; if the finale of the *Jupiter* brings some falling away in weightiness, there is compensation in added zest and spontaneity. Next to the finest versions these are rather plain readings, lacking something in individuality, though the fast movements of the *Haffner* are winningly bold and energetic.

Symphonies Nos. 36 in C (Linz), K.425; 38 in D (Prague), K.504.
*** EMI Dig. CDC7 47442-2 [id.]. ECO, Tate.
**(*) DG Dig. 415 962-2 [id.]. VPO, Bernstein.

Tate's are very live-sounding performances translated to the studio, and his ear for detail as well as his imagination in rethinking the music gives them wit as well as weight within a scale (woodwind balanced close) which never sounds too big or inflated. One detail to note is the way that – exceptionally – Tate brings out the extraordinary originality of instrumentation in the recapitulation of the central slow movement of the *Prague*, with the widest possible span between exposed flutes, oboes and bassoons (bar 105). That movement, with the repeat observed, is given extra weight, matching the enormous span of the first movement.

Bernstein's comparable coupling, taken from live performances, brings effervescent accounts of both Nos. 36 and 38. Though speeds are dangerously fast in the finales, they are strong, stylish and characterful performances, beautifully played. In sound they cannot quite match the finest rivals, but Bernstein is a consistently winning Mozartian.

Symphonies Nos. 36 in C (Linz); 40 in G min., K.550.
*** EMI Dig. CDC7 49073-2 [id.]. ASMF, Marriner.
**(*) Ph. Dig. 422 398-2. Dresden State O, C. Davis.

Marriner's coupling of the *Linz* and No. 40 in his EMI series brings a keener sense of spontaneity, of conductor and players enjoying themselves, than his earlier issues. Brisk speeds and resilient rhythms go with subtle phrasing and refined ensemble, to make the disc a strong recommendation in this coupling.

Sir Colin Davis and the Dresdeners give elegant and refined performances on a big, traditional scale, relaxed in manner, with the scale and smoothness underlined by the warmly reverberant Dresden acoustic. Since he made his early recordings of Mozart symphonies for Philips, he has grown warmer as well as weightier in his approach, and the recording is comfortable to match.

Symphonies Nos. 38 in D (Prague), K.504; 39 in E flat, K.543.
*** Virgin Dig. VC 791078-2 [id.]. Sinfonia Varsovia, Sir Yehudi Menuhin.
(m) *** CBS Dig. MDK 44648 [id.]. Bav. RSO, Rafael Kubelik.
(m) *** DG 429 802-2 [id.]. BPO, Karajan.
*** ASV Dig. CDCOE 806 [id.]. COE, Schneider.
**(*) EMI Dig. CDC7 47334-2 [id.]. ASMF, Marriner.
**(*) DG Dig. 423 086-2 [id.]. VPO, Levine.
**(*) DG 413 735-2 [id.]. VPO, Boehm.
**(*) O-L Dig. 410 233-2 [id.]. AAM, Schröder; Hogwood.

Menuhin's Mozart with this hand-picked orchestra – of which he is the Principal Conductor – has a clear place for those who, resisting period instruments, yet want many of the benefits of an authentic approach without sacrificing sweetness of string sound. It may be surprising to some that Menuhin is such a complete classicist here, with speeds on the fast side, notably in the *Andante* of the *Prague*, where he is a shade faster even than Hogwood in his period-performance version. Yet even here Menuhin does not sound at all rushed, giving the movement a free, song-like lyricism. He treats the third-movement trio of No. 39 as a brisk Laendler, almost hurdy-gurdy-like, refusing – after consultation with the autograph – to allow a rallentando at the end. Otherwise the only other oddity is his omission of the exposition repeat in the first movement when as a rule he is generous with repeats. The fresh, immediate sound highlights the refined purity of the string-playing.

Kubelik has the advantage of first-class modern digital recording, and this coupling is well up to the standard of the other two discs in his series of late Mozart symphonies. The playing has verve and is highly responsive. No. 39 is especially invigorating in its racy finale but has plenty of strength too.

Karajan's record, too, is strongly recommended. Generally speaking, the playing is so superlative and the sense of pace so well judged that one surrenders to the sheer quality of this music-making: the impression is one of resilience as well as of strength. The remastered recording is of high quality, appropriately weightier in the bass than in the disc offering the earlier symphonies.

Schneider's might be counted old-fashioned readings of both symphonies, with measured speeds both in allegros and in slow movements, marked by fine pointing and moulding. The string band sounds larger than in some recent versions, and that is partly a question of the recording, set in a warm, helpful acoustic which brings out the sweetness of the COE violins and the bloom on the wind instruments. Schneider shows his allegiance to older fashion by not observing exposition repeats in the first movements or first halves of slow movements; but the consistent rhythmic resilience of Schneider's direction and the superb playing of the COE lightens everything.

Marriner's Academy pairing of Nos. 38 and 39 was the first of a new Mozart series, bringing characteristically polished and stylish readings of both works in full and well-defined sound. Outer movements are brisk, the style rather plain but well sprung and with no hint of overpointing or mannerism. These are strong, satisfying readings that will offend no one, even though – or perhaps because – they could be more positively characterful.

Levine's coupling of the *Prague* and No. 39 brings characteristically brisk and athletic performances, marked by superb playing from all sections of the Vienna Philharmonic. His pacing is controversially brisk in the delectable Minuet of No. 39, but the speeds have allowed every single repeat to be observed in both works – including the second halves of the finales. The sound is good.

Boehm's tempi are spacious, but the results are less markedly magisterial than in some of his Mozart records. The glow of the performances is helped by the warm DG sound, which has transferred strikingly well to CD. Detail is less sharp than on digital alternatives, but the balance is truthful and the effect pleasingly natural.

Those who prefer the acerbities of original instruments will find in the AAM coupling two splendid examples of this approach to the Mozart symphonies. The weight and scale of the *Prague* are the more keenly apparent in such a performance as this, with all repeats observed, even if the determination not to overload slow movements with anachronistic expressiveness will disappoint some.

Symphony No. 39 in E flat, K.543.
(M) (**) DG mono 427 776-2 [id.]. BPO, Furtwängler – HAYDN: *Symphony No. 104.* (**).

Though recorded in 1944 in the Berlin State Opera, after the Philharmonie had been bombed, conductor and orchestra were undeterred by any such problems, giving a strong, vigorous performance typical of Furtwängler, a far more stylish classicist than his reputation has generally allowed. The manner is often weighty – notably in the biting, un-Laendler-like account of the Minuet – but the elegance of Mozart is never far away. The sound tends to crumble in loud tuttis, but the performance remains compelling.

Symphonies Nos. 39 in E flat, K.543; 40 in G min., K.550.
**(*) DG Dig. 413 776-2 [id.]. VPO, Bernstein.

Bernstein's coupling is inconsistent, with an electrifying account of No. 40, keen, individual and stylish, and a slacker, less convincing one of No. 39, recorded three years earlier. It would be wrong, however, to exaggerate the shortcomings of No. 39, when No. 40 is one of the finest versions available, keenly dramatic, with the finale delightfully airy and fresh. Considering the problems of making live recordings, the sound is first rate, lacking only the last degree of transparency in tuttis.

Symphonies Nos. 39 in E flat, K.543; 41 in C (Jupiter), K.551.
*** Ph. Dig. 410 046-2 [id.]. Dresden State O, C. Davis.
(B) ** Ph. 422 974-2 [id.]. Concg. O, Josef Krips.

Imaginative playing from the Staatskapelle, Dresden, under Sir Colin Davis, finely paced and beautifully balanced. Davis has recorded the *Jupiter* more than once, and this newcomer is all that one would expect: alert, sensitive, perceptive and played with vitality and finesse. Philips also provide very good recording. A self-recommending coupling.

This is the least appealing of Krips' three reissued couplings. No. 39 goes well enough, but in the *Jupiter* Krips holds the tension much more slackly and there is something unmemorable and wanting in character that does not do full honour to the fine Mozartian Krips was.

Symphony No. 40 in G min., K.550.
(*) Ph. Dig. 416 329-2 [id.]. O of 18th Century, Brüggen – BEETHOVEN: *Symphony No. 1.*(*)
(B) **(*) Pickwick Dig. PCD 820 [MCA MCAD 25845 with SCHUBERT: *Symphony No. 5*]. O of St John's, Smith Square, Lubbock – HAYDN: *Symphony No. 44.****

Using only marginally fewer players than in the Beethoven coupling, Brüggen's live recording using period instruments is more warmly communicative than most authentic performances, without losing the benefits of clarity and freshness. Speeds are on the fast side without being stiff or eccentric. Good atmospheric recording, but with some exaggeration of bass.

Lubbock's is a pleasingly relaxed account of Mozart's *G minor Symphony*, well played – the Minuet particularly deft – and nicely proportioned. The last ounce of character is missing from the slow movement, but the orchestra is responsive throughout, and the recording is in the demonstration class.

Symphonies Nos. 40 in G min., K.550; 41 in C (Jupiter), K.551.
*** Virgin Dig. VC 791082-2 [id.]. Sinfonia Varsovia, Sir Yehudi Menuhin.
*** EMI Dig. CDC7 47147-2 [id.]. ECO, Tate.
*** Telarc Dig. CD 80139 [id.]. Prague CO, Mackerras.
(M) *** CBS Dig. MDK 44649 [id.]. Bav. RSO, Kubelik.
*** DG 413 547-2 [id.]. VPO, Boehm.
(B) *** CfP CD-CFP 4253. LPO, Mackerras.
(M) **(*) CBS MYK 42538 [id.]. Cleveland O, George Szell.
**(*) O-L Dig. 417 557-2 [id.]. AAM, Schröder; Hogwood.
(M) **(*) EMI CD-EMX 2074. ECO, Barenboim.

Symphonies Nos. (i) 40 in G min.; (ii) 41 (Jupiter); Die Zauberflöte: Overture.
(BB) **(*) LaserLight 15 511 [id.]. (i) Hungarian CO, Tátrai; (ii) LPO, Sándor.

Recorded in exceptionally vivid, immediate sound, Menuhin's versions of both symphonies with the Sinfonia Varsovia find a distinctive place in an overcrowded field, with playing of precision, clarity and bite which is consistently refreshing, giving a feeling of live music-making. The string tuning and refinement of expressive nuance match that of a fine string quartet, and Menuhin reveals himself again as very much a classicist, preferring speeds on the fast side, rarely indulging in romantic tricks. He is generous with repeats – observing exposition repeats in both first movement and finale of the *Jupiter*, for example. With such vivid sound, this is the best current recommendation for this favourite coupling.

For the general listener Tate's account of the *Jupiter* makes an excellent first choice, with an apt scale which yet allows the grandeur of the work to come out. On the one hand it has the clarity of a chamber orchestra performance, but on the other, with trumpets and drums, its weight of expression never underplays the scale of the argument which originally prompted the unauthorized nickname. In both symphonies exposition repeats are observed in outer movements, particularly important in the *Jupiter* finale. Those who like a very plain approach may find the elegant pointing in slow movements excessive, but Tate's keen imagination on detail, as well as over a broad span, consistently conveys the electricity of a live performance. The recording is well detailed, yet has pleasant reverberation, giving the necessary breadth.

With generally fast speeds, so brisk that he is able to observe every single repeat, Mackerras takes a fresh, direct view which, with superb playing from the Prague Chamber Orchestra, is also characterful. The speeds that might initially seem excessively fast are those for the Minuets, which – with fair scholarly authority – become crisp country dances, almost scherzos. The definition of woodwind lines is immaculate, with string textures equally clear despite the warm acoustic, though the bassoon has a distinctly East European tone. On the question of repeats, the doubling in length of the slow movement of No. 40 makes it almost twice as long as the first movement, a dangerous proportion – though it is pure gain having both halves repeated in the magnificent finale of the *Jupiter*.

Like his excellent coupling of the *Haffner* and *Linz symphonies*, these performances by Kubelik are strong and beautifully played, with well-integrated tempi and highly responsive phrasing – both slow movements are very appealingly shaped. Kubelik favours first-movement exposition repeats, but here he misses the chance of extending the finale of the *Jupiter*, although the performance certainly does not lack weight. The CBS recording is first class, and Kubelik's disc is fully competitive.

Boehm takes a relatively measured view of the outer movements of No. 40, but the resilience of the playing rivets the attention and avoids any sort of squareness. Excellent recommendations for both symphonies, though in No. 41 the original single-sided LP format prevented the observance of exposition repeats. This is the only drawback to the CD transfer, which offers full, refined sound within a very attractive ambience.

On Classics for Pleasure, Mackerras directs excellent, clean-cut performances which can stand comparison with any at whatever price. He observes exposition repeats in the outer movements of the *G minor* but not the *Jupiter*, which is a pity for so majestic a work. Some may prefer a more affectionate style in slow movements but, with clean (though not especially rich) modern recording, this is well worth considering in the bargain range.

Szell's versions are also outstanding. He is not generous with repeats but the playing of the Cleveland Orchestra has superb polish, without sounding in the least glossy. Slow movements bring great delicacy of feeling and the *Jupiter* with its rhythmic incisiveness has genuine power. The recording is very early stereo (1956) but the remastering produces a good balance and a smooth upper range, without excessive brightness on the violins.

In the super-bargain range, the LaserLight issue is highly competitive and it offers an excellent version of *The Magic flute overture* as an encore. Sándor's account of the *Jupiter* brings fine playing from the LPO and has plenty of vitality, while the overall length of the performance, with necessary repeats, is 35 minutes, fully conveying the breadth of Mozart's architectural span. Again, in the *G minor Symphony* Tátrai includes the repeats in the outer movements; the playing is polished and there is a nice sense of scale. Both works have agreeable expressive warmth in slow movements, helped by the full, resonant recording, which is obviously modern. There is not quite the individuality of Szell here, but both performances communicate strongly.

The separate issue of Nos. 40 and 41 from Hogwood's collected edition makes a first-rate recommendation for those wanting period performances, brisk and light, but still conveying the drama of No. 40 and the majesty of the *Jupiter*.

These performances by Barenboim were recorded in the late 1960s. The CD offers fresher and more transparent sound and adds to the life of Barenboim's expressive yet lively account of the *G minor*, although the *Jupiter* has somewhat less weight in the bass than before. Yet Barenboim remains very impressive in this work, observing both repeats in the finale in a reading that is full of vitality. The violin timbre is less rich than on the original LP.

Symphony No. 41 in C (Jupiter), K.551.
(M) **(*) EMI CDM7 69811-2 [id.]. RPO, Beecham – BEETHOVEN: *Symphony No. 2.***(*)

Beecham's first movement – with no exposition repeat – here takes less time than the slow movement, which is given a full romantic treatment at a slow and loving *Andante cantabile*. Even more individual is the Minuet which, at a speed slower even than a Laendler, is relaxed rather than sluggish, beautifully pointed. The outer movements bristle with strength as well as elegance. On this CD reissue the digital transfer brings some stridency with a rather heavy tape-hiss; but the Beecham magic still triumphs.

CHAMBER MUSIC

Adagio in C for cor anglais, 2 violins & cello, K.580a.
*** Denon Dig. C37 7119 [id.]. Holliger, Salvatore Qt – M. HAYDN: *Divertimenti*; J. C. BACH: *Oboe quartet.****

Though the shortest of the four works on Holliger's charming disc, this Mozart fragment is in a world apart, deeply expressive. Excellent performances and recording.

Adagio in C for cor anglais, 2 violins & cello, K.580a; Oboe quartet in F, K.370; Oboe quintet in C min., K.406.
**(*) Claves Dig. CD 50-8406 [id.]. Ingo Goritzki, Berne Qt (members).

This CD conveniently collects together Mozart's two major chamber works featuring the oboe, plus the haunting *Adagio* for cor anglais which Ingo Goritzki plays very sensitively, if not quite as memorably as Holliger. The *Oboe quartet*, too, is fresh and pleasing, if less winning than some of the finest versions – see below. However, the interesting novelty is the *Quintet*, which derives from Mozart's own arrangement of the *Wind serenade*, K.388. Ingo Goritzki makes a fairly convincing case for the choice of a broken consort and the performance is a good one, with the Berne players giving accomplished, if not highly imaginative, support. The recording is vivid and well balanced.

Clarinet quintet in A, K.581.
(M) *** EMI CDM7 63116-2 [id.]. Gervase de Peyer, Melos Ens. – BRAHMS: *Quintet.****
*** Denon Dig. C37 7038 [id.]. Sabine Meyer, BPO Qt – WEBER: *Introduction, theme & variations.****
(*) DG Dig. 419 600-2 [id.]. Eduard Brunner, Hagen Qt – WEBER: *Clarinet quintet.**
(*) Orfeo C 141861A [id.]. Karl Leister, Pražák Qt – CRUSELL: *Clarinet quintet.**
** CRD Dig. CRD 3445 [id.]. Michael Collins, Nash Ens. – BRAHMS: *Clarinet quintet.***(*)
(M) ** Decca 417 643-2 [id.]. Boskovsky, Vienna Octet (members) – BAERMANN: *Adagio*; BRAHMS: *Clarinet quintet.***(*)

Clarinet quintet in A, K.581; Clarinet quintet fragment in B flat, K.516c; (i) *Quintet fragment in F for clarinet in C, basset-horn and string trio, K.580b* (both completed by Duncan Druce).

*** Amon Ra/Saydisc CD-SAR 17 [id.]. Alan Hacker, Salomon Qt, (i) with Lesley Schatzberger.

(i) *Clarinet quintet;* (ii) *Oboe quartet in F, K.370.*

(B) *** Pickwick Dig. PCD 810. (i) Puddy; (ii) Boyd, Gabrieli Qt.

Leading the CD versions of the *Clarinet quintet* (alongside Thea King's outstanding coupling with the *Clarinet concerto* on Hyperion – see above) is a superb recording by Alan Hacker with the Salomon Quartet, using original instruments. Anton Stadler, the clarinettist for whom the work was written, possessed a timbre which was described as 'so soft and lovely that nobody who has a heart can resist it'. Alan Hacker's gentle sound on his period instrument has a similar quality, displayed at its most ravishing in the *Larghetto*. He is matched by the strings, and especially by the leader, Simon Standage, who blends his tone luminously with the clarinet. Tempi are wonderfully apt throughout the performance, the rhythms of the finale are infectiously pointed and, following a passage of rhapsodic freedom from the soloist, there is a spirited closing dash. Hacker decorates the reprise of the *Larghetto* affectionately and adds embellishments elsewhere. His chortling roulades in the last movement are no less engaging, the music's sense of joy fully projected. The recording balance is near perfect, the clarinet able to dominate or integrate with the strings at will; and the tangibility of the sound is remarkably realistic. Hacker includes a fragment from an earlier projected *Quintet* and a similar sketch for a work featuring C clarinet and basset-horn with string trio. Both are skilfully completed by Duncan Druce.

Having de Peyer's vintage account of the Mozart *Clarinet quintet* in coupling with his equally inspired reading of the Brahms *Quintet* makes an outstanding bargain on a mid-price disc. This clean, fresh, well-pointed performance with the Melos Ensemble is consistently satisfying, recorded in immediate sound in a relatively dry acoustic.

Sabine Meyer is a most gifted player whose artistry is of a high order. She produces a full, rich and well-focused tone that is a delight to the ear, and she phrases with great musicianship and sensitivity. The performance is one of the best in the catalogue and is well recorded. The only drawback to Meyer's version is the coupling which, though agreeable, is neither very substantial nor generous.

The bargain-priced Pickwick CD brings a reading of the *Clarinet quintet* which is clean and well paced and, if lacking the last degree of delicacy in the slow movement, is never less than stylish. The young oboist, Douglas Boyd, then gives an outstanding performance in the shorter, less demanding work, with the lilting finale delectably full of fun. The digital recording is vividly immediate and full of presence, with even the keys of the wind instruments often audible.

Eduard Brunner produces a mellifluous tone-quality and blends ideally with the fine Hagens. Everything is musically turned out and tempi are unfailingly sensible, relaxed and unforced. Unlike Alan Hacker and Thea King, Brunner uses a modern instrument and, despite excellent DG recording, those earlier versions take precedence.

With his warm, smooth tone, Karl Leister gives a strong, finely controlled performance which, in the occasional touch of self-consciousness in the phrasing, lacks a little in spontaneity and freshness.

Like their Brahms coupling, the Nash Ensemble give a warm, leisurely account of

Mozart's most famous chamber work, beguiling in its way but a little lacking in vitality; other versions have that bit more character.

Boskovsky's account from the mid-1960s is gracious and intimate, a little lacking in individuality, but enjoyable in its unforced way. The sound is excellent, well defined and sweet, to match the mellow approach.

(i) *Clarinet quintet, K.581;* (ii) *Flute quartet No. 1 in D, K.285;* (iii) *Oboe quartet, K.370.*
(M) *** DG 429 819-2 [id.]. (i) Gervase de Peyer; (ii) Andreas Blau; (iii) Lothar Koch; Amadeus Qt.

The Amadeus grouping, of course, is splendid. Gervase de Peyer gives a warm, smiling account of the *Clarinet quintet,* with a sunny opening movement, a gently expressive *Larghetto* and a delightfully genial finale. The performance is matched by the refinement of Koch in the *Oboe quartet.* With creamy tone and wonderfully stylish phrasing he is superb. The inclusion of just one of the four *Flute quartets* seems less than ideal, as most Mozartians will want all four. However, it must be admitted that Andreas Blau's playing is delightful, sprightly and full of grace. The Amadeus accompany with sensibility, and the recordings, which date from 1976 and 1978, are flawless, sounding fresh and immediate in their CD format.

(i) *Clarinet quintet in A, K.581;* (ii) *Horn quintet in E flat, K.407;* (iii) *Oboe quartet in F, K.370.*
(M) *** Ph. 422 833-2 [id.]. (i) Antony Pay; (ii) Timothy Brown; (iii) Neil Black; ASMF Chamber Ens.
**(*) O-L Dig. 421 429-2 [id.]. (i) Antony Pay; (ii) Michael Thompson; (iii) Stephen Hammer; AAM Chamber Ens.
**(*) Novalis Dig. 150 006-2 [id.]. (i) Reiner Wehle; (ii) Marie-Luise Neunecker; (iii) Fumiaki Miyamoto; Mannheim Qt.

It is a delightful idea to have the *Clarinet quintet, Oboe quartet* and *Horn quintet* on a single CD; and the Academy of Ancient Music Chamber Ensemble provide lively and stylish accounts on period instruments. The three wind soloists are outstanding, bringing out the extra characterful timbres of authentic instruments and never seeming troubled by any technical problems. What is more questionable is the contribution of the string-players. Needless to say, they are all most accomplished practitioners in period performance; but the slow movements, with vibrato avoided, bring a degree of acidity which – to say the very least – is an acquired taste. Many will love the results, but be warned.

However, for those to whom 'authenticity' is not paramount there is a first-class Philips analogue coupling of the same three works. Here, Antony Pay's earlier account of the *Clarinet quintet,* played on a modern instrument, with the Academy of St Martin-in-the-Fields players must be numbered among the strongest now on the market for those not insisting on an authentic basset clarinet. Neil Black's playing in the *Oboe quartet* is distinguished, and again the whole performance radiates pleasure, while the *Horn quintet* comes in a well-projected and lively account with Timothy Brown. The recording, originally issued in 1981, is of Philips's best.

Although Reiner Wehle has a full and attractive timbre, the performance of the *Clarinet quintet* on Novalis is amiable rather than distinctive; other versions have more imaginative intensity; the *Oboe quartet,* however, is played with personality, grace and charm. Best of all is the *Horn quintet,* full of character, the *Andante* producing some lovely solo playing from Marie-Luise Neunecker, while there is plenty of genial sparkle in the finale.

Clarinet trio in E flat (Kegelstatt), K.498.
*** EMI Dig. CDC7 49736-2. Meyer, Zimmermann, Holl – BRUCH: *Pieces;* SCHUMANN: *Märchenerzählungen.****

Sabine Meyer has already shown on record what an individual artist she is, a natural soloist; but Hartmut Holl, an inspired Lieder accompanist, here reveals himself as much more. In the *Kegelstatt trio* he emerges as a Mozartian of the first order, magicking the figuration of this relaxed work with a wit and point that reminds one of Murray Perahia, totally spontaneous and not at all mannered. A performance like this re-creates a private and intimate atmosphere, with the three instruments beautifully balanced.

Divertimento in E flat for string trio, K.563.
*** CBS Dig. MK 39561 [id.]. Kremer, Kashkashian, Ma.

Divertimento in E flat for string trio, K.563; Duos for violin and viola, Nos 1–2, K.423/4.
(BB) **(*) Hung. White Label HRC 072 [id.]. Dénes Kovács, Géza Németh, Ede Banda.

Divertimento in E flat for string trio, K.563; 3 Preludes and Fugues, K.404a.
**(*) Ph. 416 485-2 [id.]. Grumiaux, Janzer, Szabo.

Grumiaux is here joined by two players with a similarly refined and classical style. They may be an ad hoc group, but their unanimity is most striking, and Grumiaux's individual artistry gives the interpretation extra point. The hushed opening of the first-movement development – a visionary passage – is played with a magically intense half-tone, and the lilt of the finale is infectious from the very first bar. The 1967 recording is exceptionally vivid, but the digital remastering has brightened the treble excessively, without a compensating emphasis in the lower range, and the texture is very much dominated by the solo violin. The three *Fugues* derive from Bach's *Well-tempered Clavier*, but they are prefaced by *Preludes* written by Mozart himself. The performances are direct, clear and purposeful, and here the balance is good.

Gidon Kremer, Kim Kashkashian and Yo-Yo Ma turn in an elegant and sweet-toned account on CBS and are excellently recorded. Indeed, the sound is fresh and beautifully realistic. There are many perceptive insights, particularly in the *Adagio* movement which is beautifully done; even if there are one or two narcissistic touches from Kremer, his playing is still most persuasive.

If not quite a match in subtlety for the Grumiaux version, the account of this masterly *Divertimento* by the three Hungarian players is freshly enjoyable, the playing vital, spontaneous and agreeably without mannered idiosyncrasy. Dénes Kovács, the leader, dominates the music-making, both in the *Trio* and in the highly rewarding pair of *Duos* which make the substantial coupling. His athletic style and strong personality add to the life of the performances; if his viola colleague in K.423/4 is less forceful, this remains a proper partnership. The Hungaroton recording is forward but better balanced than the Philips disc; it has a pleasing ambience, and this inexpensive CD is well worth its very modest cost.

Flute quartets Nos. 1 in D, K.285; 2 in G, K.285a; 3 in C, K.285b; 4 in A, K.298.
(M) *** Ph. 422 835-2 [id.]. Bennett, Grumiaux Trio.
*** CBS Dig. MK 42320 [id.]. Rampal, Stern, Accardo, Rostropovich.
*** Accent ACC 48225D. Bernhard and Sigiswald Kuijken, Van Dael, Wieland Kuijken.
** Collins Dig. 1020-2 [id.]. Judith Hall, Barritt, Clarkson, Horder.

There seems to be general agreement about the merits of the William Bennett–Grumiaux Trio accounts of the *Flute quartets*. They are, to put it in a nutshell, exquisitely played and very well recorded, in every way finer than most other versions which have appeared and disappeared over the years. The freshness of both the playing and the remastered 1971 recording gives very great pleasure.

It would be hard to dream up a more starry quartet of players than that assembled on the CBS disc. But the recording was made in a relatively dry studio, and the acoustic emphasizes the dominance of Rampal's flute in the ensemble, with the three superstar string-players given little chance to shine distinctively except in the finale of K.285. A delectable record none the less.

Readers normally unresponsive to period instruments should hear these performances by Bernhard Kuijken, for they have both charm and vitality; they radiate pleasure and bring one close to this music. This record is rather special and cannot be recommended too strongly. The playing is exquisite and the engineering superb.

Though the music-making on the Collins CD is enjoyable enough, the playing is not as memorable as Judith Hall's outstanding accounts of the two *Flute concertos* on Pickwick. The choice of an ecclesiastical acoustic (All Saints', Tooting) with the players relatively closely balanced has meant a reduction in the dynamic range, and the detail of the performances here is less imaginative than in the finest versions.

Oboe quartet in F, K.370; Adagio in C for cor anglais, 2 violins & cello, K.580a.
*** Ph. Dig. 412 618-2 [id.]. Holliger, Orlando Qt – *Divertimento No. 11.***

Holliger's performance has characteristic finesse and easy virtuosity; the Orlando support is first class and so is the Philips recording. The performance of the *Adagio* – a deeper, more expressive piece – is also eloquent, though not finer than Holliger's earlier version for Denon, differently coupled – see above. The *Divertimento* coupling here is less appealing.

Piano quartets Nos. 1 in G min., K.478; 2 in E flat, K.493.
*** Ph. Dig. 410 391-2 [id.]. Beaux Arts Trio with Giuranna.
*** DG Dig. 423 404-2 [id.]. Bilson (fortepiano), Wilcock, Schlapp, Mason.
**(*) Amon Ra/Saydisc Dig. CD-SAR 31 [id.]. Richard Burnett, Salomon Qt (members).

The Beaux Arts group provide splendidly alive and vitally sensitive accounts that exhilarate the listener, just as does the Curzon–Amadeus set, and they have the advantage of first-class digital recording. The Beaux Arts play them not only *con amore* but with the freshness of a new discovery. Incidentally, both repeats are observed in the first movements, which is unusual on record. The usual high standards of Philips chamber-music recording obtain here; the sound (particularly that of the piano) is exceptionally lifelike.

Even those who find Malcolm Bilson a little wanting in temperament and too judicious will gain pleasure from these well-recorded accounts of the two *Piano quartets*. The balance between the three stringed instruments and the keyboard is immediately altered when heard on period instruments. The playing is excellent and has both sparkle and grace. The recording is outstandingly natural and lifelike.

Richard Burnett and three players from the Salomon Quartet give very persuasive accounts of both works, though there is just a touch of reticence, as if they are inhibited by what they imagine to be the expressive constraints of the period.

(i) *Piano quartets Nos 1–2;* (i) *Horn quintet in E flat, K.407.*
⊛ (M) *** Decca mono 425 960-2 [id.]. (i) Clifford Curzon, Amadeus Qt; (ii) Dennis Brain, Griller Qt.

All versions of the Mozart *Piano quartets* rest in the shadow of the recordings by

Clifford Curzon and members of the Amadeus Quartet (Norbert Brainin, Peter Schidlof and Martin Lovett). No apologies need be made for the 1952 mono recorded sound. An early example of the work of John Culshaw, it may be somewhat two-dimensional but is better balanced than many stereo recordings of chamber music. The warm integration of the strings, with the piano dominating but never dwarfing the ensemble, is ideal. The performances have a unique sparkle, slow movements are elysian, especially the beautiful account of the *Larghetto* of K.493, and the finale of the same work is the epitome of grace. One's only criticism is that the *Andante* of K.478 opens at a much lower dynamic level than the first movement, and some adjustment of the controls needs to be made. The *Horn quintet* coupling was recorded in 1944 and the transfer to CD is even more miraculous. The slight surface rustle of the 78-r.p.m. source is in no way distracting and the sound is unbelievably smooth and beautiful. Dennis Brain's horn contribution is superbly graduated to balance with the textures created by his colleagues, but again the ear registers the remarkable overall blend, with the string players (Sydney Griller, Philip Burton, Max Gilbert and Christopher Hampton) matching timbres in the true spirit of chamber music. There is not a suspicion of wiriness from the leader. The performance itself combines warmth and elegance with a spirited spontaneity, and the subtleties of the horn contribution are a continuous delight. A wonderful disc that should be in every Mozartian's library.

(i) *Piano quartets Nos 1 – 2. String quartet No. 17 in B flat (Hunt), K.458.*
(M) **(*) Decca 425 538-2 [id.]. (i) André Previn; V. Musikverein Qt.

Previn's sparkling playing gives these parallel masterpieces – especially the *G minor* – a refreshing spontaneity. Though the tuning of the Musikverein Quartet is not as sweet as that of the Beaux Arts on Philips, the vitality of the Decca coupling – recorded in the warm acoustics of the Kingsway Hall in 1981 – commands attention. For those looking for a modern mid-priced CD, this could well be the answer, particularly as the bonus is a fine version of the *Hunt quartet*. There is a relaxed, unforced quality about the playing here, though there is no want of brilliance either. This recording dates from 1979 and the CD transfer is more brightly lit, so that the upper string timbre is less smooth.

Piano quartet No. 2 in E flat, K.493.
(B) ** Van. VCD 72004 [id.]. Peter Serkin, Schneider Qt – SCHUBERT: *Trout quintet.***

Although it opens much too heavily (partly the fault of the forward balance of the 1968 recording) the Serkin performance soon settles down. This is music-making which in its way is easy to enjoy, more robust than the the Beaux Arts style, but which nevertheless brings a sensitive response to the *Larghetto* and an agreeably light-hearted finale. The sound is full and truthful.

Piano trios Nos. 1 – 6; Piano trio in D min., K.442.
*** Ph. Dig. 422 079-2 (3). Beaux Arts Trio.

Piano trios Nos. 1 – 6.
*** Chan. Dig. CHAN 8536/7 (2). Borodin Trio.

Apart from including an extra work, the Beaux Arts are more generous with repeats, which accounts for the extra disc. Their performances are eminently fresh and are no less delightful and winning. There is a somewhat lighter touch here compared with the Chandos alternative, thanks in no small degree to the subtle musicianship of Menahem Pressler. The Philips recording is strikingly realistic and present.

The Borodin Trio are slightly weightier in their approach and their tempi are generally more measured than the Beaux Arts', very strikingly so in the *Allegretto* of the *G major*. All the same, there is, as usual with this group, much sensitive playing and every evidence of distinguished musicianship. The balance in the Philips set tends to favour the piano a little; the Chandos, recorded at The Maltings, Snape, perhaps produces the more integrated sound.

Piano and wind quintet in E flat, K.452.
*** CBS Dig. MK 42099 [id.]. Perahia, members of ECO – BEETHOVEN: *Quintet.****
*** Decca Dig. 414 291-2 [id.]. Lupu, De Vries, Pieterson, Zarzo, Pollard – BEETHOVEN: *Quintet.****
(M) *** Decca 421 151-2 [id.]. Ashkenazy, L. Wind Soloists – BEETHOVEN: *Quintet.****
*** Ph. Dig. 420 182-2 [id.]. Brendel, Holliger, Brunner, Baumann, Thunemann – BEETHOVEN: *Quintet.***(*)

An outstanding account of Mozart's delectable *Piano and wind quintet* on CBS, with Perahia's playing wonderfully refreshing in the *Andante* and a superb response from the four wind soloists, notably Neil Black's oboe contribution. Clearly all the players are enjoying this rewarding music, and they are well balanced, with the piano against the warm but never blurring acoustics of The Maltings at Snape.

Lupu and his Concertgebouw colleagues also have the advantage of excellent recording: the engineers are particularly successful in capturing the piano. There is a refreshing sparkle from Lupu in the first movement and a sense of joy and spontaneity. The wind playing is beautifully blended and cultivated and the performance as a whole gives much pleasure and delight.

Ashkenazy's performance in Mozart's engaging *Quintet* is outstandingly successful, polished and urbane, yet marvellously spirited. His wind soloists are a distinguished team and their playing comes fully up to expectations. The balance and sound-quality are of the highest order and the CD sounds very natural, although the balance is forward. A first-class mid-priced alternative to the versions led by Perahia and Lupu.

Brendel and his distinguished companions on Philips convey an impressive concentration and strong personality; in the outer movements there is clarity and finesse, and in the slow movement no want of feeling. Playing of strong personality and a certain didacticism, though one is at times aware of Brendel's slightly exaggerated staccato: his pianism is very different from that of Lupu or Perahia. The recording combines a sense of immediacy with a very natural balance among the five instruments.

String quartets Nos. 1–23 (complete).
(M) *** Ph. 416 419-2 (8) [id.]. Italian Qt.

String quartets Nos. 1–23; Divertimenti, K.136/8.
(M) ** DG 423 300-2 (6) [id.]. Amadeus Qt.

The Quartetto Italiano fit all twenty-three quartets of the Mozart cycle (as well as the original *Adagio* of the *G major*, K.157) on to eight CDs and the set is offered at mid-price. There may have been more inspired accounts of some of these from individual quartets, but one is unlikely to be able to assemble a more consistently satisfying overview of these great works, or one so beautifully played and recorded.

DG amazingly accommodate the complete *Quartets* on six mid-priced CDs, so this certainly represents value for money. The performances span more than a decade, and it goes without saying that there are good things among them. However, they do not compete in naturalness of expression or tonal beauty with the Quartetto Italiano on Philips. Although the latter involves a slightly greater outlay, it is well worth the extra cost.

String quartets Nos. 14 – 19 (Haydn quartets).
⊛ *** CRD CRD 3362 (*Nos. 14 – 15*); 3363 (*Nos. 16 – 17*); 3364 (*Nos. 18 – 19*) [id.].
Chilingirian Qt.

String quartets Nos. 14 in G, K.387; 16 in E flat, K.428.
*** Hyp. Dig. CDA 66188 [id.]. Salomon Qt.

String quartets Nos. 15 in D min., K.421; 19 in C (Dissonance), K.465.
*** Hyp. Dig. CDA 66170 [id.]. Salomon Qt.

String quartets Nos. 17 in B flat (Hunt), K.458; 18 in A, K.464.
*** Hyp. Dig. CDA 66234 [id.]. Salomon Qt.

The set of six quartets dedicated to Haydn contains a high proportion of Mozart's finest works in the genre. The Chilingirian Quartet plays with unforced freshness and vitality, avoiding expressive mannerism but always conveying the impression of spontaneity, helped by the warm and vivid recording. International rivals in these works may at times have provided more poise and polish but none outshines the Chilingirians in direct conviction, and their matching of tone and intonation is second to none. Unlike most quartets, they never sound superficial in the elegant but profound slow movements. The three CDs are packaged separately and offer demonstration quality. The sound is appealingly smooth and real: there is no lack of immediacy, but the ambient effect ensures a natural balance, with no edginess on top.

The Salomon Quartet has already given us some superb Haydn, and no one sampling their Mozart will be disappointed. It goes without saying that their playing is highly accomplished and has a real sense of style; they do not eschew vibrato, though their use of it is not liberal, and there is admirable clarity of texture and vitality of articulation. There is no want of subtlety and imagination in the slow movements. The recordings are admirably truthful and lifelike, and those who seek 'authenticity' in Mozart's chamber music will not be disappointed here.

String quartets Nos. 14 in G, K.387; 15 in D min., K.421.
*(*) Ph. Dig. 426 240-2 [id.]. Guarneri Qt.

Accomplished, highly professional but rather general-purpose accounts with little feeling for Mozart. The Guarneri players produce much the same well-upholstered textures as they might do for Brahms. They find little depth in either of the slow movements and, though the sound they produce is undeniably beautiful and they are sumptuously recorded, this gives only modified pleasure.

String quartets Nos. 15 in D min., K.421; 17 in B flat (Hunt), K.458.
*** Denon C37 7003 [id.]. Smetana Qt.

Both these 1982 performances were recorded in the House of Artists, Prague. The Smetana find just the right tempo for the first movement of the *D minor*, unhurried but forward-moving. *The Hunt*, which is placed first on the disc, is given a spirited performance and is rather more polished than most of its CD rivals; it is a pleasure to report with enthusiasm on these well-paced accounts.

String quartets Nos. 16 in E flat, K.428; 17 in B flat (Hunt), K.458.
(M) **(*) Ph. 422 832-2 [id.]. Italian Qt.

String quartets Nos. 18 in A, K.464; 19 in C (Dissonance), K.465.
(M) **(*) Ph. 426 099-2 [id.]. Italian Qt.

The Italian players give a fine, unaffected account of the *Hunt quartet*, although some may feel that it is a shade undercharacterized in places. The other quartets are beautifully done, however; the *Dissonance* is especially successful, and the playing throughout is unfailingly perceptive and most musical. The remastered recording sounds fresh and transparent, if slightly dry in the treble. The ambient effect remains pleasing, but the upper range is less smooth than the CRD recording for the Chilingirians.

String quartet No. 17 in B flat (Hunt), K.458.
(M) ** DG Dig. 429 491-2 [id.]. Amadeus Qt – SCHUBERT: *Quartet No. 14.***(*)

The Amadeus Quartet previously recorded Mozart's *Hunt quartet* in the mid-1960s and it was one of their popular successes. The digital repetition does not quite match the success of the older, analogue version: there is a distinct absence of charm. Moreover, although the CD sound has striking presence, it is a little edgy in the treble. However, at mid-price and coupled with a quite recommendable version of Schubert's *Death and the Maiden quartet*, this seems fair value.

String quartets Nos. 17 in B flat (Hunt), K.458; 19 in C (Dissonance), K.465.
(M) ** DG 429 818-2 [id.]. Melos Qt.
* DG Dig. 427 657-2 [id.]. Emerson Qt – HAYDN: *String quartet No. 77 (Emperor).**

The Melos performances are soundly conceived and finely executed. The playing is unmannered and thoughtful, and the remastered 1977/8 recording is well balanced and lifelike. The *Dissonance* is certainly enjoyable and the *Hunt* has no lack of vitality. Yet the phrasing seems rather predictable, as if familiarity with these masterpieces has taken its toll of freshness of response.

The Emersons are stunningly articulate performers; they are meticulous too: every 't' is crossed and every 'i' dotted. In terms of sonority and ensemble the listener is bowled over by their virtuosity. But this is eminently self-aware, over-projected playing that might possibly be appropriate in William Schuman or Elliott Carter but is totally out of place in Mozart. They are not helped by a rather unspacious (though not unacceptable) recorded sound.

String quartets Nos. 18 in A, K.464; 19 in C (Dissonance), K.465.
(M) *** EMI CDM7 69102-2 [id.]. Smetana Qt.

The vintage analogue coupling from the Smetana Quartet is excellent in every way. The playing has impetus and feeling, finesse and vitality, and the sound is well balanced, full and clear. Excellent value at mid-price.

String quartets Nos. 20 in D (Hoffmeister), K.499; 21 in D, K.575; 22 in B flat, K.589; 23 in F, K.590 (Prussian Nos. 1–3).
*** CRD CRD 3427/8 [id.]. Chilingirian Qt.

The Chilingirian Quartet give very natural, unforced, well-played and sweet-toned accounts of the last four *Quartets* and they are extremely well recorded. Though perhaps not as highly polished as were the Melos on DG (though there is not a great deal in it), there is far more musical interest and liveliness here. They are very well recorded too, with cleanly focused lines and a warm, pleasing ambience; indeed in this respect these two discs are second to none.

String quartets Nos. 22 in B flat, K.589; 23 in F (Prussian), K.590.
*** DG Dig. 423 108-2 [id.]. Hagen Qt.

The Hagen Quartet play with great fluency, and it is difficult to resist such perfection of ensemble and refinement of blend. Slow movements in particular do not dig deep, but they have an elegance and homogeneity of tone that are remarkable and, at the present time, possibly unsurpassed. The DG recording does justice to their tonal finesse and subtlety. There is more to Mozart than they find, but what they achieve still excites the keenest admiration.

String quintets Nos. 1–6.
(M) *** Ph. 416 486-2 (3). Grumiaux Trio with Gerecz, Lesueur.
(BB) *(*) Hung. White Label HRC 085 (*Nos. 1 & 3*); HRC 086 (*Nos. 2 & 4*); HRC 096 (*Nos. 5–6*). Tátrai Qt with Anna Mauthner.

No reservations about the Grumiaux ensemble's survey of the *String quintets*: immensely civilized and admirably conceived readings. Throughout the set the vitality and sensitivity of this team are striking, and in general this eclipses all other recent accounts. The remastering of the 1973 recordings for CD is very successful.

Great disappointment has to be expressed concerning the reissues on Hungarian White Label of the Tátrai performances. Their total cost is little more than the outlay for one premium-priced CD and the performances are very good. The *Adagio* of K.515 is beautifully done and the reading of the great *G minor Quintet* is highly satisfactory. The first movement of the *C minor* (K.406) is rhythmically strong and the Andante refreshingly poised. The last two *Quintets* are splendidly alive, with slow movements thoughtful and finales sparkling. The snag is the sound-balance, with the violins in general impossibly shrill at higher dynamic levels. This seems likely to have come about with the digital remastering, since the recording is basically truthful, with firm cello tone.

String quintets Nos. 2 in C min., K.406; 6 in E flat, K.614.
**(*) Denon C37 7179 [id.]. Smetana Qt with Suk.

The Smetana Quartet and Josef Suk give extremely fine accounts of both works, though they do not quite equal the lightness of touch of the Grumiaux series. They are accorded very realistic sound.

String quintets Nos. 3 in C, K.515; 4 in G min., K.516.
** DG Dig. 419 773-2 [id.]. Melos Qt with Franz Beyer.

The Melos Quartet and their second violist, Franz Beyer, give a finely prepared and thoughtfully conceived account of both works. Tempi are well judged and phrasing thoroughly articulate, and the overall structure is well held together. But if they are sound, they are at the same time just a shade touched by routine; their dynamic range does not vary widely enough.

(i) *String quintet No. 4 in G min., K.516*; (i) *Violin sonata No. 26 in B flat, K.378.*
(M) *** RCA GD 87869 [7869-2-RG]. Heifetz, with (i) Baker, Primrose, Majewski, Piatigorsky; (ii) Brooks Smith – *Violin concerto No. 5.****

This recording of the *G minor Quintet* was made at the time of the Pilgrimage Theatre Concerts, given at Hollywood in the autumn of 1961. The illustrious ensemble adopts a very fast pace for the first movement and some might feel that its urgency is over-pressed; yet so fine is the playing that, after a minute or two, one adjusts as at a live performance. There are wonderful moments in the rest of the work, not least the viola playing of William Primrose. The great slow movement is rapt in its intensity and the opening of the finale is similarly compelling, until the allegro brings the sun out from behind the

Mozartian clouds. The acoustic is a little dry, but the sound itself is full and warmly blended, with good detail. The *Violin sonata* was recorded two years later and shows splendid rapport between the great violinist and his partner, Brooks Smith.

Violin sonatas Nos. 17–28; 32–34; Sonatina in F, K.547; 12 Variations on La bergère Célimène, K.359; 6 Variations on Au bord d'une fontaine, K.360.
*** Ph. 416 902-2 (5) [id.]. Henryk Szeryng, Ingrid Haebler.

Violin sonatas Nos. 17–28; 32–34; 6 Variations, K.360.
**(*) Ph. 412 141-2 (4) [id.]. Arthur Grumiaux, Walter Klien.

Ingrid Haebler brings an admirable vitality and robustness to her part. Her playing has sparkle and great spontaneity. Szeryng's contribution is altogether masterly, and all these performances find both partners in complete rapport. The analogue recordings from the mid-1970s provide striking realism and truthfulness, and they have been immaculately transferred to CD. The *Variations* included in the set are managed with charm; an extra set is included, plus the *Sonatina in F*, not offered by Klien and Grumiaux, which accounts for the need for five CDs.

The Grumiaux/Klien set runs to only four CDs. There is a great deal of sparkle and some refined musicianship in these performances, and pleasure remained undisturbed by the balance which, in the 1981 recordings, favours the violin. The later records from 1982 and 1983 are much better in this respect. It goes without saying that there is some distinguished playing in this set, even if the players are not quite so completely attuned as were Grumiaux and Haskil.

Violin sonatas Nos. 17 in C, K.296; 22 in A, K.305; 23 in D, K.306.
*** DG Dig. 415 102-2 [id.]. Itzhak Perlman, Daniel Barenboim.

These three *Sonatas* are the first of what Alfred Einstein described as Mozart's concertante sonatas; even here, however, the piano is dominant, a point reflected in the fact that, for all Perlman's individuality, it is Barenboim who leads. This is playing of a genial spontaneity that conveys the joy of the moment with countless felicitous details. Three sonatas on a full disc is far from generous measure for a compact disc, but the recording is undistractingly good, with the violin balanced less forwardly than is usual with Perlman, to everyone's advantage.

Violin sonatas Nos. 18–21, K.301–4.
*** DG Dig. 410 896-2 [id.]. Itzhak Perlman, Daniel Barenboim.

More very distinguished playing here from Perlman and Barenboim, with fine teamwork and alert and vital phrasing. The recording, too, is extremely lifelike, although it will be too forward for some tastes.

Violin sonatas Nos. 18 in G, K.301; 19 in G, K.302; 21 in E min., K.304; 24 in F., K.376; 26 in B flat, K.378.
(***) Ph. mono 412 253-2 [id.]. Arthur Grumiaux, Clara Haskil.

Violin sonatas Nos. 32 in B flat, K.454; 34 in A, K.526.
(***) Ph. mono 416 478-2 [id.]. Arthur Grumiaux, Clara Haskil.

This was a celebrated partnership and these classic accounts, which have excited much admiration over the years (and which will doubtless continue so to do), have been transferred excellently. Mozartians should not hesitate. The original mono recordings come from the late 1950s, yet the sound is remarkably vivid and true, and background noise has been virtually vanquished. The performances represent the musical yardstick by which all later versions were judged. However, these records need repricing.

Violin sonatas Nos. 24 in F, K.376; 25 in F, K.377; 12 Variations on La bergère Célimène, K.359; 6 Variations on Hélas, j'ai perdu mon amant, K.360.
*** DG Dig. 419 215-2 [id.]. Itzhak Perlman, Daniel Barenboim.

Though some speeds are on the fast side, these performances are characterized most winningly. The contrast between the first movements of the *Sonatas* – the one charming, the other brilliantly energetic – is strongly established in performances which make no apology, firmly presenting both as major Mozart. The two sets of variations, with their sharp changes of mood, also emerge as stronger than is generally supposed. First-rate recording.

Violin sonatas Nos. 26 in B flat, K.378; 28 in E flat, K.380; 32 in B flat, K.454; Violin sonatina in F, K.457.
*** Olympia OCD 125 [id.]. Igor Oistrakh, Natalia Zertsalova.

Igor Oistrakh has not as assertive a personality as his father, and he makes a very real partnership here with Zertsalova, who is an excellent Mozartian. These are all splendid works and they are played with fine classical feeling and impetus; the Rondo finale of K.380 is a demonstrable example of the sparkle of this music-making. The recording, too, is truthful and well balanced, and the disc costs rather less than full price.

Violin sonatas Nos. 33 in E flat, K.481; 34 in A, K.526; Violin sonatina in F, K.547.
(M) *** Decca 425 420-2 [id.]. Szymon Goldberg, Radu Lupu.

Both Goldberg and Lupu bring humanity and imagination to their performances and their response has freshness and vitality. Goldberg's playing has great depth, though at times his age perhaps begins to show (a slight lack of bloom on his tone); but this does not inhibit the strength of the recommendation, for Lupu is marvellously sensitive. The CD transfer is first class, and this is one of the most rewarding single discs of these *Sonatas*.

PIANO DUET

Sonatas for piano duet: in C, K.19d; in B flat, K.358; in D, K.381. Adagio & allegro in F min., K.584; Fantasy in F min., K.608 (both for mechanical organ); 5 Variations on an Andante in G, K.501.
(M) *** DG 429 809-2 [id.]. Christoph Eschenbach and Justus Frantz.

We thought well of these performances when they first appeared, and they stand up to the test of time. (They were made between 1972 and 1975.) The major *Sonatas* are magnificent works. Eschenbach and Frantz play with exemplary ensemble and fine sensitivity. The pieces for mechanical clock show (alongside the *Sonatas*) these artists' care for detail, and here as elsewhere they readily convey their own pleasure in the music. The recordings are clean and well balanced, if occasionally a shade dry. They are certainly given good presence on CD.

SOLO PIANO MUSIC

Piano sonatas Nos. 1–18; Adagio in B min., K.540; Gigue in G, K.574; Fantasias: in D min., K.397; C min., K.475; Rondos: in D, K.485; A min., K.511.
✿ *** Ph. Dig. 422 115-2 (6) [id.]. Mitsuko Uchida.

Piano sonatas Nos. 1–18 (complete); Fantasia in C min., K.475.
*** EMI CDS7 47336-8 (6) [Ang. CDCF 47335]. Daniel Barenboim.

On Philips a self-recommending collection, beautifully recorded – indeed the sound has consistent naturalness and distinction – in the Henry Wood Hall, London. All these performances have been praised by us for their consistent sensibility, and few boxed sets will give more pleasure.

Barenboim, while keeping his playing well within scale in its crisp articulation, refuses to adopt the Dresden china approach to Mozart's *Sonatas*. Even the little *C major*, K.545, designed for a young player, has its element of toughness, minimizing its 'eighteenth-century drawing-room' associations. Though – with the exception of the two minor-key *Sonatas* – these are relatively unambitious works, Barenboim's voyage of discovery brings out their consistent freshness, with the orchestral implications of some of the allegros strongly established. The recording, with a pleasant ambience round the piano sound, confirms the apt scale.

Piano sonatas Nos. 1 in C, K.279; 14 in C min., K.457; 17 in D, K.576.
*** Ph. Dig. 412 617-2 [id.]. Mitsuko Uchida.

Piano sonatas Nos. 2 in F, K.280; 3 in B flat, K.281; 4 in E flat, K.282; 5 in G, K.283.
*** Ph. Dig. 420 186-2 [id.]. Mitsuko Uchida.

Piano sonatas Nos. 6 in D, K.284; 16 in B flat, K.570; Rondo in D, K.485.
*** Ph. Dig. 420 185-2 [id.]. Mitsuko Uchida.

Piano sonatas Nos. 7 in C, K.309; 8 in A min., K.310; 9 in D, K.311.
*** Ph. Dig. 412 741-2 [id.]. Mitsuko Uchida.

Piano sonatas Nos. 10 in C, K.330; 13 in B flat, K.333; Adagio in B min., K.450; Eine kleine Gigue in G, K.574.
*** Ph. Dig. 412 616-2 [id.]. Mitsuko Uchida.

Piano sonatas Nos. 11 in A, K.331; 12 in F, K.332; Fantasia in D min., K.397.
*** Ph. Dig. 412 123-2 [id.]. Mitsuko Uchida.

Piano sonatas: in F, K.533/494; No. 15 in C, K.545; Rondo in A min., K.511.
*** Ph. Dig. 412 122-2 [id.]. Mitsuko Uchida.

Mitsuko Uchida's set of the Mozart *Sonatas* brings playing of consistently fine sense and sound musicianship. There is every indication that this will come to be regarded as a classic series to set alongside those of Gieseking and, more recently, András Schiff. Every phrase is beautifully placed, every detail registers, and the early *Sonatas* are as revealing as the late ones. Throughout, allegros are unerringly paced and impeccably stylish; each movement and each work is seen as a whole, yet detail is consistently illuminated. The slow movements generally bring the kind of sensibility we associate with Perahia in the concertos. The shorter pieces, too, are beautifully played: the marvellous *B minor Adagio*, K.450, is given an appropriately searching reading. As for the *Rondo in A minor*, K.511, Mitsuko Uchida delivers a reading that is so haunting and subtle that one can hardly rest until one replays it; while her realization of the closing bars of the *D minor Fantasia* combines exquisite musical taste and refinement of judgement. The piano recording is completely realistic, slightly distanced in a believable ambience.

Piano sonatas Nos. 1 in C, K.279; 4 in E flat, K.282; 12 in F, K.332; 16 in B flat, K.570.
*** Decca 421 110-2 [id.]. András Schiff.

Piano sonatas Nos. 2 in F, K.280; 5 in G, K.283; 6 in D, K.284; 10 in C, K.330.
*** Decca 421 109-2 [id.]. András Schiff.

Piano sonatas Nos. 3 in B flat, K.281; 7 in C, K.309; 9 in D, K.311; 18 in F: (Allegro, Andante & Rondo), K.533/494.
*** Decca 417 572-2 [id.]. András Schiff.

Piano sonatas Nos. 8 in A min., K.310; 11 in A, K.331; 17 in D, K.576.
*** Decca 417 571-2 [id.]. András Schiff.

Piano sonatas Nos. 13 in B flat, K.333; 14 in C min., K.457; 15 in C, K.545; Fantasia in C min., K.475.
*** Decca 417 149-2 [id.]. András Schiff.

Schiff, without exceeding the essential Mozartian sensibility, takes a somewhat more romantic and forward-looking view of the music. His fingerwork is precise, yet mellow, and his sense of colour consistently excites admiration. He is slightly prone to self-indulgence in the handling of some phrases, but such is the inherent freshness and spontaneity of his playing that one accepts the idiosyncrasies as a natural product of live performance. The piano is set just a little further back than in the Philips/Uchida recordings, and the acoustic is marginally more open, which suits his slightly more expansive manner. The realism of the piano image is very striking, and there is only a faint remnant of analogue background noise remaining. This is a fine achievement and these records are very satisfying. Moreover Decca have managed to get four *Sonatas* on to three of the CDs, and thus the whole set is presented more economically than with major rivals.

Piano sonatas Nos. 1 in C, K.279; 2 in F, K.280; 3 in B flat, K.281; 4 in E flat, K.282; 5 in G, K.283.
(M) **(*) Denon Dig. DC-8071 [id.]. Maria João Pires.

Piano sonatas Nos. 6 in D, K.284; 7 in C, K.309; 8 in A min., K.310; Rondo in D, K.485.
(M) **(*) Denon Dig. DC-8072 [id.]. Maria João Pires.

Piano sonatas Nos. 9 in D, K.311; 10 in C, K.330; 11 in A, K.331; Rondo in A min., K.511.
(M) **(*) Denon Dig. DC-8073 [id.]. Maria João Pires.

Piano sonatas Nos. 12 in F, K.332; 13 in B flat, K.333; 14 in C min., K.457.
(M) **(*) Denon Dig. DC-8074 [id.]. Maria João Pires.

Piano sonatas Nos. 15 in F, K.533/494; 16 in C, K.545; 17 in B flat, K.570; 18 in D, K.576; Fantasia in D min., K.397.
(M) **(*) Denon Dig. DC-8075 [id.]. Maria João Pires.

Maria João Pires is a good Mozartian: a refreshingly unmannered stylist with clean articulation and admirable technical address. These performances on Denon were recorded in the mid-1970s in Tokyo and show consistent intelligence and refinement. Her complete cycle, available on five separate CDs at mid-price, makes a possible alternative to the Uchida, though the recording is not as rich-toned or full-bodied as the Philips.

Piano sonatas Nos. 4 in E flat, K.282; 5 in G, K.283; 15 in C, K.545.
**(*) Ph. Dig. 416 830-2 [id.]. Claudio Arrau.

There are occasional touches here that are a little idiosyncratic, and Arrau surely invests the slow movement of the *C major Sonata* with too much reverence and feeling. On the whole, however, this is a lovely record, with particularly realistic piano sound.

Piano sonatas Nos. 8 in A min., K.310; 13 in B flat, K.333; 15 in C, K.545.
*** DG Dig. 427 768-2 [id.]. Maria João Pires.

Maria João Pires is a stylist and a fine Mozartian, as those who have heard any of her earlier cycle on Denon will already know. Pires is always refined but never wanting in classical feeling and she has a vital imagination. The recording is well-lit without being too bright and has splendid presence and definition. If DG plan to give us a complete cycle with her, this is good news.

Piano sonatas Nos. 11 in A, K.331; 14 in C min., K.457; 15 in C, K.545; Fantasy in C min., K.475; Variations on 'Ah, vous dirai-je Maman', K.265.
(M) ****** DG 429 808-2 [id.]. Christoph Eschenbach.

Eschenbach's recital calls for little detailed comment. He gives cool, elegant performances, without affectation or mannerism. The playing is not without strength of personality; if it is rather short on charm, it is very tasteful: the first movement of the *C major Sonata* is strikingly crisp and clean. The piano recording is realistic and has good presence, but in its remastered format is a trifle over-bold in focus.

Double piano sonata in D, K.448.
*** CBS MK 39511 [id.]. Murray Perahia, Radu Lupu – SCHUBERT: *Fantasia in D min.********

With Perahia taking the primo part, his brightness and individual way of illuminating even the simplest passage-work dominate the performance, producing magical results and challenging the more inward Lupu into comparably inspired playing. Pleasantly ambient recording made at The Maltings, Snape, and beautifully caught on CD.

VOCAL MUSIC

Concert arias: *A questo seno . . . Or che il cielo, K.374; Basta, vincesti . . . An non lasciarmi, K.486a; Voi avete un cor fedele, K.217. Exsultate, jubilate* (motet), *K.165. Litaniae de venerabili altaris sacramento, K.243: Dulcissimum convivium. Vesperae de Dominica, K.321: Laudate dominum.*
(B) ******* Ph. 426 072-2 [id.]. Elly Ameling, ECO, Leppard.

Elly Ameling's natural reserve can sometimes bring a coolness to her presentation, but here the singing, besides being technically very secure, has a simple radiance in the phrasing which is very beautiful. She is equally happy in the concert arias, sung with delightful flexibility of phrase, and in the ecclesiastical music, where the style has a serene simplicity, while *Exsultate jubilate* has an infectious sense of joy. With well-balanced, sympathetic accompaniments and full, vivid 1969 recording, this is well worth exploring on Philips's bargain Concert Classics label.

Lieder: *Abendempfindung; Ah, spiegarti, o Dio; Als Luise; Die Alte; An Chloë; Dans un bois solitaire; Im Frühlingsanfange; Das Lied der Trennung; Un moto di gioia; Oiseaux, si tous les ans; Ridente la calma; Sei du mein Trost; Das Traumbild; Das Veilchen; Die Verschweignung; Der Zauberer; Die Zufriedenheit.*
**(*) Etcetera KTC 1039 [id.]. Roberta Alexander, Glen Wilson.

Well accompanied on the fortepiano, Roberta Alexander gives a fresh and stylish account of these seventeen Mozart songs. Enterprisingly, they include a couple of rarities, *Im Frühlingsanfange* and *Die Alte*, though the latter is too crudely characterized. The singer's full, rounded tone is caught well in the recording, which gives a vivid sense of presence on an intimate scale.

Lieder: *Abendempfindung; Als Luise die Briefe; An Chloë; Im Frühlingsanfange; Das Kinderspiel; Die kleine Spinnerin; Oiseaux, si tous les ans; Ridente la calma; Sehnsucht nach dem Frühlinge; Der Zauberer; Die Zufriedenheit.*
*** EMI mono CDC7 47326-2 [id.]. Elisabeth Schwarzkopf, Walter Gieseking –
SCHUBERT: *Lieder.**** ⊛

Generous as this CD is, with sound clarified and the voice vividly caught, it is sad that three of the original collection were left out, including Mozart's most famous song of all, *Das Veilchen*. But we should be thankful for what we do have, as here, when great artists at their most perceptive work together.

Concert arias: *Ah! lo previdi ... Ah t'invola, K.272; Bella mia fiamma . . . Resta oh cara, K.528; Chi sa, K.582; Nehmt meinen Dank, ihr holden Gönner, K.383; Non più, tutto ascolta . . . Non temer, amato bene, K.490; Oh temerario Arbace! . . . Per quel paterno amplesso, K.79/K.73d; Vado, ma dove?, K.583.*
(M) *** Decca 417 756-2 [id.]. Kiri Te Kanawa, V. CO, György Fischer.

Concert arias: *Ch'io mi scordi di te . . . Non temer, K.505; Misera, dove son! . . . Ah! non son io che parto, K.369. Don Giovanni:* (i) *Don Ottavio, son morta! . . . Or sai chi l'onore; Calmatevi, idol mio . . . Non mi dir. Die Entführung aus dem Serail: Welcher Wechsel herrscht in meiner Seele . . . Traurigkeit ward mir zum Lose; Martern aller Arten. Mitridate, Re di Ponto: Lungi da te.*
**(*) Ph. Dig. 420 950-2 [id.]. Kiri Te Kanawa, ECO, Tate; or Mitsuko Uchida; (i) with Peter Bronder.

Kiri Te Kanawa's Decca set of Mozart's concert arias for soprano, recorded in 1982, makes a beautiful and often brilliant recital. Items range from one of the very earliest arias, *Oh temerario Arbace*, already memorably lyrical, to the late *Vado, ma dove*, here sung for its beauty rather than for its drama. Atmospheric, wide-ranging recording, which has transferred well to CD.

Her Philips digital collection was recorded six years later and produces perhaps even finer singing in the two concert arias, especially *Ch'io mi scordi di te?*, where Mitsuko Uchida provides an elegant accompaniment. However, the opera performances are more uneven; the aria from *Die Entführung* is most successful; and here, as in the excerpt from *Mitridate*, one revels in the vocal beauty. Excellent recording.

Concert arias: *Alma grande e nobil core, K.578; Ch'io mi scordi di te, K.506; Vado, ma dove?, K.583.* Arias: *Don Giovanni: Ah fuggi il traditor; In quali eccessi . . . Mi tradi quell'alma ingrata; Batti, batti, o bel Masetto; Vedrai, carino; Crudele . . . Non mi dir. Idomeneo: Zeffiretti lusinghieri. Le Nozze di Figaro: Porgi amor; E Susanna non vien! . . . Dove sono; Non so più; Voi che sapete; Giunse alfin il momento . . . Deh vieni non tardar.*
*** EMI CDC7 47950-2 [id.]. Elisabeth Schwarzkopf, LSO, Szell; Philh. O, Giulini; A. Brendel.

This generous collection of Mozart arias brings together Schwarzkopf performances recorded over the full span of her career. The recordings are presented most effectively, in reverse chronological order, taking you from the Marschallin figure of the late years presenting display arias with immaculate style and deep thoughtfulness (and with Alfred Brendel commanding in the piano obbligato of *Ch'io mi scordi di te?*), back to the radiant portraits of the Countess and Elvira, patrician in confidence with the voice still at its freshest; finally the delightful early characterizations of Cherubino as well as Susanna, of Ilia in *Idomeneo*, of Zerlina and – most strikingly, if unexpectedly – of Donna Anna in *Don Giovanni*. That last group is a *tour de force* for a singer still in her mid-twenties, but one which highlights the better-known recordings of the later years, filling in the portrait of a Mozartian with few equals. The CD transfers consistently bring out the beauty and tonal range of the voice with new clarity.

Ave verum corpus, K.618; Exsultate, jubilate, K.165; Kyrie in D minor, K.341; Vesperae solennes de confessore in C, K.339.
**(*) Ph. 412 873-2 [id.]. Te Kanawa, Bainbridge, Ryland Davies, Howell, LSO Ch., LSO, C. Davis.

This disc could hardly present a more delightful collection of Mozart choral music, ranging from the early soprano cantata *Exsultate, jubilate*, with its famous setting of *Alleluia*, to the equally popular *Ave verum*. Kiri Te Kanawa is the brilliant soloist in the cantata, and her radiant account of the lovely *Laudate Dominum* is one of the highspots of the *Solemn vespers*. That work, with its dramatic choruses, is among the most inspired of Mozart's Salzburg period, and here it is given a fine responsive performance. The 1971 recording has been remastered effectively, although the choral sound is not ideally focused.

(i; ii) *Ave verum corpus, K.618;* (iii; iv) *Exsultate, jubilate, K.165; Masses Nos.* (i; ii; iii; v) *10 in C (Missa brevis): Spatzenmesse, K.220;* (ii; iii; vi) *16 in C (Coronation), K.317.*
(M) *** DG 419 060-2 [id.]. (i) Regensburg Cathedral Ch.; (ii) Bav. RSO, Kubelik; (iii) Edith Mathis; (iv) Dresden State O, Klee; (v) Troyanos, Laubenthal, Engen; (vi) Procter, Grobe, Shirley-Quirk, Bav. R. Ch.

Kubelik draws a fine, vivid performance of the *Coronation mass* from his Bavarian forces and is no less impressive in the earlier *Missa brevis*, with excellent soloists in both works. Then Edith Mathis gives a first-class account of the *Exsultate, jubilate* as an encore. The concert ends with Bernard Klee directing a serenely gentle account of the *Ave verum corpus* (recorded in 1979). The digital remastering is entirely beneficial.

Concert arias: Bella mia fiamma, addio, K.528; Chi sa, K.582; Mitridate, re di Ponto: Lungi da te; Nehmt meinen Dank, K.383; Vado ma dove, K.583; Voi avete un cor fedele, K.217. Exsultate jubilate, K.165. Zaïde: Ruhe Sanft.
**(*) ASV Dig. CDDCA 683 [id.]. Felicity Lott, L. Mozart Players, Glover.

With Jane Glover a most sympathetic accompanist, drawing poised playing from the LMP, Felicity Lott's record of arias brings many delights, notably in the early cantata with which the recital opens, *Exsultate jubilate*, with its concluding *Alleluias*, and the two early opera arias from *Zaïde* and *Mitridate*, the latter rounding off the recital exquisitely on a floated high D. The much later concert arias bring some clean, stylish singing, but there is not so much individuality in phrasing and rhythmic pointing, with less concern for word-meaning. Full, warm recording which sets off the voice well.

Exsultate jubilate, K.165; (i) *Davidde penitente, K.469.*
*** Ph. Dig. 420 952-2 [id.]. Margaret Marshall, (i) with I. Vermillion, Blochwitz; Stuttgart RSO, Marriner.

Davidde penitente brings a fascinating example of Mozart recycling earlier material. In 1785, some eighteen months after he had abandoned the *C minor Mass* in its tragically incomplete state, he used eight movements from it for this oratorio, *Davidde penitente*, setting an Italian text taken from the penitential Psalms which, it has been suggested, may well be by Da Ponte. It was largely a question of fitting new words to the music, altering the original remarkably little, except in the great fugue set in the Mass to the words *Cum sancto spirito*. There Mozart interrupts the great strettos with a much more relaxed solo section, before resuming the weighty choral argument at the end. When Mozart omitted the sublime inspiration of *Et incarnatus* from his scheme, and the two numbers not derived from the Mass (tenor and soprano arias) are less distinctive than the rest, it hardly replaces the earlier masterpiece; but in a fizzing performance like this under Marriner, it makes a refreshing rarity, very well sung by chorus and soloists alike. Margaret Marshall is undeterred by the conductor's fast speeds in the early *Cantata*, which comes as a welcome coupling and prompts one her most brilliant performances on record.

Exsultate, jubilate, K.165 (Salzburg version); Motets: *Ergo interest, K.143; Regina coeli* (2 settings), *K.108, K.127.*
*** O-L Dig. 411 832-2 [id.]. Emma Kirkby, Westminster Cathedral Boys' Ch., AAM Ch. and O, Hogwood.

The boyish, bell-like tones of Emma Kirkby are perfectly suited to the most famous of Mozart's early cantatas, *Exsultate, jubilate*, culminating in a dazzling account of *Alleluia*. With accompaniment on period instruments, that is aptly coupled with far rarer but equally fascinating examples of Mozart's early genius, superbly recorded. A most refreshing collection, beautifully recorded.

(i) *Exsultate, jubilate, K.165;* (ii) *Litaniae lauretanae, K.195; Mass No. 16 in C (Coronation), K.137.*
(M) *** Decca 417 472-2 [id.]. (i) Erna Spoorenberg, Ledger; (ii) Cotrubas, Watts, Tear, Shirley-Quirk, Schola Cantorum of Oxford, ASMF, Marriner.

Marriner's fine 1971 coupling of two of Mozart's most appealing early choral works has been linked with Erna Spoorenberg's radiant and sparkling account of the *Exsultate, jubilate*. In the two more extended works, the solo singing is again outstandingly good, notably the contribution of Ileana Cotrubas; and the Oxford Schola Cantorum are impressively vibrant. The Academy provides the most sensitive, stylish accompaniments and, with the sound full of presence, this reissue must receive the warmest welcome.

Masses Nos. 2 in D min. (Missa brevis), K.65; 5 in G (Pastoralmesse), K.140; 7 in G (In honorem Santissimae Trinitas), K.167.
*** Ph. Dig. 422 264-2 [id.]. Donath, Markert, Blochwitz, Schmidt, Leipzig R. Ch. & SO, Kegel.

Kegel directs his splendid choir and a full modern orchestra – by latterday standards too large for this music – in fresh, vigorous performances of these three early Masses, well recorded. Nos. 2 and 5, both called *Missa brevis*, are brief to the point of perfunctoriness, but they still contain Mozartian jewels, such as the chromatic duet of K.65. Far finer is the extended setting of K.167 which, with its trumpets and drums, looks forward to later ceremonial works and is crowned by a splendid, finely structured *Credo*.

Mass No. 4 in C min. (Weisenhausmesse), K.139.
(M) *** DG 427 255-2 [id.]. Janowitz, Von Stade, Moll, Ochman, V. State Op. Ch., VPO, Abbado.

By any standards this is a remarkably sustained example of the thirteen-year-old composer's powers, with bustling allegros in the *Kyrie, Gloria* and *Credo*, as well as at the end of the *Agnus Dei*, while the *Gloria* and *Credo* end with full-scale fugues. This far from negligible piece sounds at its very best in Abbado's persuasive hands. His is a most characterful account, and the remastered DG recording sounds admirably lively, with the soloists in good perspective.

Masses Nos. 10 in C (Spatzenmesse), K.220; 16 in C (Coronation), K.317. Inter natos mulierum in G, K.72.
** Ph. Dig. 411 139-2 [id.]. Jelosits, Eder, V. Boys' Ch., VSO, Harrer.

The *Spatzenmesse* (Sparrow Mass) owes its nickname to the chirping of violins in the *Pleni sunt coeli*, a setting even more compressed than most. The *Coronation Mass* is the most famous of the period, well sung and played, with the two named soloists joined by two lusty boy singers, making a well-matched quartet. A fair recommendation for those who fancy the coupling, but there are more distinctive versions of K.317. Atmospheric recording, generally well balanced.

Masses Nos. 12 in C (Spaur), K.258; 14 in C (Missa longa), K.262.
**(*) Ph. Dig. 412 232-2 [id.]. Shirai, Schiml, Ude, Polster, Leipzig R. Ch., Dresden PO, Kegel.

Kegel with his brilliant Leipzig Radio Chorus conducts attractive performances of two of Mozart's rarer settings of the Mass, with Mitsuko Shirai outstanding among the soloists. The *Spaurmesse*, much the shorter of the two, is the more consistent, the *Missa longa* the one with sharper contrasts. The recording is good but places the singers too far in front of the orchestra.

Mass No. 16 in C (Coronation), K.317.
(M) **(*) DG 423 913-2 (2) [id.]. Tomowa-Sintow, Baltsa, Krenn, Van Dam, V. Singverein, BPO, Karajan – BEETHOVEN: *Missa solemnis.****
(B) **(*) DG 429 510-2 [id.]. Stader, Dominguez, Haefliger, Roux, Brasseur Ch., LOP, Markevitch – BEETHOVEN: *Mass in C.***

Masses Nos. 16 in C (Coronation), K.317; 17 (Missa solemnis), K.337.
**(*) Argo Dig. 411 904-2. Margaret Marshall, Murray, Covey-Crump, Wilson-Johnson, King's College Ch., ECO, Cleobury.

(i) *Mass No. 16 in C (Coronation), K.317;* (ii; iii) *Missa brevis in C (Spatzenmesse), K.220;* (iii) *Ave verum corpus;* (iv) *Exsultate jubilate, K.165; Vesperae solennes de Confessore, K.339: Laudate dominum.*
(M) **(*) DG 429 820-2 [id.]. (i) Tomowa-Sintow, Baltsa, Krenn, Van Dam, V. Singverein, BPO, Karajan; (ii) Mathis, Troyanos, Laubenthal, Engen; (iii) Regensberger Cathedral Ch., Bav. RSO, Kubelik; (iv) Mathis, Dresden Ch. & State O, Klee.

Mass No. 16 in C (Coronation), K.317; Vesperae solennes de confessore in C, K.339.
(M) **(*) EMI CDM7 69023-2 [id.]. Moser, Hamari, Gedda, Fischer-Dieskau, Bav. R. Ch. and SO, Jochum.

Karajan's 1976 recording of the *Coronation Mass* is a dramatic reading, lacking something in rhythmic resilience perhaps; but with excellent solo singing as well as an incisive contribution from the chorus there is no lack of strength, and the score's lyrical elements are sensitively managed. Kubelik draws a fine, lively account of the earlier *Missa brevis*, and again the solo singing is of high quality. Bernard Klee contributes a serene performance of the lovely *Ave verum corpus*, and Edith Mathis offers a first-class account of the *Exsultate jubilate* and a slightly less appealing *Laudate dominum* (recorded in 1979, six years after the motet). The remastering is vivid: although the choral focus in the two main works is not absolutely sharp, the sound is otherwise impressive, the ambience agreeably expansive.

The digital remastering has greatly improved the sound of Jochum's fine 1977 performance of the *Coronation Mass*, with its splendid choral response and eloquently spacious conception. Having the *Vespers* for coupling is particularly attractive; if Edda Moser is hardly the ideal choice for the heavenly *Laudate Dominum*, she sings simply and effectively.

Markevitch's performance, though not always completely refined, is incisively brilliant and its sheer vigour is infectious. That is not to say that its lyrical moments are not equally successful. He has an impressive team of soloists and they are well matched in ensemble as well as providing very good individual contributions. The *Agnus Dei* is especially fine. The brightly remastered recording has plenty of life and detail.

Though rhythmically Cleobury's performance is not as lively as the finest versions of K.317, the coupling can be recommended warmly, with its excellent soloists and fresh choral singing all beautifully recorded.

Mass No. 18 in C min. (Great), K.427.
*** Ph. Dig. 420 210-2 [id.]. McNair, Montague, Rolfe-Johnson, Hauptmann, Monteverdi Ch., E. Bar. Soloists, Gardiner.
*** Decca Dig. 425 528-2. Augér, Dawson, Ainsley, D. Thomas, Winchester Cathedral Ch. & Winchester College Quiristers, AAM, Hogwood.
*** DG Dig. 400 067-2 [id.]. Hendricks, Perry, Schreier, Luxon, V. Singverein, BPO, Karajan.
**(*) EMI CDC7 47385-2 [id.]. Cotrubas, Te Kanawa, Krenn, Sotin, Alldis Ch., New Philh. O, Leppard.
**(*) Teldec/WEA Dig. 2292 43070-2 [id.]. Láki, Dénes, Equiluz, Holl, V. State Op. Ch. Soc., VCM, Harnoncourt.
** Telarc Dig. CD 80150 (2) [id.]. Wiens, Ziegler, Aler, Stone, Atlanta Ch. & SO, Robert Shaw – BEETHOVEN: *Missa solemnis.***(*)

(i) *Mass No 18 in C min. (Great), K.427. Masonic funeral music, K.477.*
(B) **(*) DG 429 161-2 [id.]. (i) Stader, Töpper, Haefliger, Sardi, St Hedwig's Cathedral Ch.; Berlin RSO, Fricsay.

John Eliot Gardiner, using period instruments, gives an outstandingly fresh performance of high dramatic contrasts, marked by excellent solo singing – both the sopranos pure and bright-toned and Anthony Rolfe-Johnson in outstandingly sweet voice. Gardiner has made some minor corrections in the *Credo* and rewritten the string parts of *Et incarnatus* in a style closer to Mozart's – to beautiful effect, if at a relaxed speed. With the recording giving an ample scale without inflation, this can be warmly recommended to more than those simply wanting a period performance.

Hogwood's version can be recommended warmly alongside the fine Gardiner account, even though his control of rhythm is less resilient and often squarer. The soloists if anything are even finer, and many Mozartians will prefer having boy trebles in the chorus and German pronunciation of Latin. Hogwood also opts for an edition by Richard Maunder which, among other things, adds appropriate instruments to the incomplete orchestrations of the *Credo* and *Et incarnatus est*. This is particularly impressive in the *Credo*, where trumpets and timpani bring an aptly festive flavour, adding to the panache of the opening. The sound has a vivid sense of presence, with treble tone cutting through very freshly.

Karajan gives Handelian splendour to this greatest of Mozart's choral works, and though the scale is large, the beauty and intensity are hard to resist. Solo singing is first rate, particularly that of Barbara Hendricks, the dreamy beauty of her voice ravishingly caught. Woodwind is rather backward, yet the sound is both rich and vivid – though, as the opening shows, the internal balance is not always completely consistent.

Raymond Leppard uses the authentic Robbins Landon edition and favours a modest-sized professional choir. His manner is relatively affectionate, which many will prefer, even in this dark work. The sopranos are the light-givers here, and the partnership of Ileana Cotrubas and Kiri Te Kanawa is radiantly beautiful. Fine, full, clear recording, more naturally balanced than Karajan's digital version, but the digital remastering has brought just a hint of shrillness to the choral fortissimos of this 1974 recording.

Fricsay's powerful 1960 recording of the *C minor Mass* brings often bitingly dramatic choral singing. The performance is not without its eccentricities – the accelerando at the close of the *Osanna*, for instance – but the conductor's volatile approach adds to the feeling of freshness. Maria Stader distinguishes herself in the *Laudamus te* and concludes the *Credo* most beautifully. Hertha Töpper, however, is less satisfactory and in the *Domine Deus* she tends to mar the duet she shares with Stader by conveying a lack of comfort in certain high passages where a similar phrase passes from one singer to the other. But even with such blemishes this music-making communicates very directly, and the focus on CD is remarkably clear, with plenty of depth to back up the bright upper range. The performance of the *Masonic funeral music* is also distinctive, bringing out the special colour which gives this remarkable miniature its character.

Harnoncourt's version, using period instruments, is strongly characterized, with authentic performance used to enhance dramatic contrasts. The emphatic rhythmic style in both slow and fast passages will not please everyone but, with a well-chosen quartet of soloists and responsive choral singing, this fills an obvious gap. Reverberant recording is not always helpful to detail.

Shaw's version of the *C minor Mass* is presented on too big a scale for the bite of invention to make its full impact. This is an old-fashioned Mozart performance, less intense and less sharply focused than those we expect today, but with fine singing and playing to make it a comfortable experience.

Requiem Mass (No. 19) in D min., K.626.
*** DG Dig. 419 610-2 [id.]. Tomowa-Sintow, Müller Molinari, Cole, Burchuladze, V. Singverein, VPO, Karajan.
*** Ph. Dig. 411 420-2 [id.]. Margaret Price, Schmidt, Araiza, Adam, Leipzig R. Ch., Dresden State O, Schreier.
(M) *** DG 429 821-2 [id.]. Tomowa-Sintow, Baltsa, Krenn, Van Dam, V. Singverein, BPO, Karajan.
(B) **(*) EMI CZS7 62892-2 (2). Armstrong, J. Baker, Gedda, Fischer-Dieskau, Alldis Ch., ECO, Barenboim – VERDI: *Requiem.***
(M) **(*) Ph. 420 353-2 [id.]. Donath, Minton, Ryland Davies, Nienstedt, Alldis Ch., BBC SO, C. Davis.
(B) **(*) EMI CDZ7 62518-2. Donath, Ludwig, Tear, Lloyd, Philh. Ch. & O, Giulini.
(B) **(*) CfP CD-CFP 4399. Mathis, Bumbry, Shirley, Rintzler, New Philh. Ch., New Philh. O, Frühbeck de Burgos.
** Sony Dig. SK 45577 [id.]. Dawson, Jard van Nes, Keith Lewis, Estes, Philh. Ch. & O, Giulini.
(M) ** DG Dig. 431 041-2 [id.]. McLaughlin, Ewing, Hadley, Hauptmann, Ch. & Bayreuth RSO, Bernstein.

(B) ** DG 429 160-2 [id.]. Lipp, Rössl-Majdan, Dermota, Berry, V. Singverein, BPO, Karajan.

(B) *(*) Decca 417 681-2 [id.]. Ameling, Horne, Benelli, Franc, V. State Op. Ch., VPO, Kertesz.

Requiem Mass, K.626; Ave verum corpus, K.618.
(M) **(*) RCA GD 86535 [RCA 6535-2-RG]. Equiluz, Eder, Vienna Boys' Ch., V. State Op. Ch. & O, Gillesberger; or VSO, Froschauer – HAYDN: *Te Deum.***(*)

Requiem Mass, K.626; Kyrie in D min., K.341.
*** Ph. Dig. 420 197-2 [id.]. Bonney, Von Otter, Blochwitz, White, Monteverdi Ch., E. Bar. Soloists, Gardiner.

John Eliot Gardiner with characteristic panache gives a bitingly intense reading, opting for the traditional course of using the Süssmayr completion but favouring period instruments at lower pitch. The result is one of the most powerful performances ever, for while the lighter sound of the period orchestra makes for greater transparency, the weight and bite are formidable. In particular the heavy brass and the distinctively dark tones of basset horns give the piece an even more lugubrious character than usual, totally apt. The soloists are an outstanding quartet, well matched but characterfully contrasted too, and the choral singing is as bright and luminous as one expects of Gardiner's Monteverdi Choir. The superb *Kyrie in D minor* makes a very welcome and generous fill-up, to seal a firm recommendation.

Karajan's newest digital version is a large-scale reading, but one that is white-hot with intensity and energy. The power and bite of the rhythm are consistently exciting. The solo quartet is first rate, though Helga Müller Molinari is on the fruity side for Mozart. Vinson Cole, stretched at times, yet sings very beautifully, and so does Paata Burchuladze with his tangily distinctive Slavonic bass tone. The close balance adds to the excitement, though the sound, both choral and orchestral, lacks transparency.

Peter Schreier's is a forthright reading of Mozart's valedictory choral work, bringing strong dramatic contrasts and marked by superb choral singing and a consistently elegant and finely balanced accompaniment. The singing of Margaret Price in the soprano part is finer than any other yet heard on record, and the others make a first-rate team, if individually more variable. Only in the *Kyrie* and the final *Cum sanctis tuis* does the German habit of using the intrusive aitch annoy. Altogether this is most satisfying.

Unlike his earlier analogue recording (see below), Karajan's 1976 version is outstandingly fine, deeply committed. The toughness of his approach is established from the start with incisive playing and clean-focused singing from the chorus, not too large and set a little backwardly. The fine quartet of soloists is also blended beautifully. The remastered recording sounds first class.

The surprise version is Gillesberger's. Using treble and alto soloists from the Vienna Boys' Choir, who sing with confidence and no little eloquence, this performance also has the advantage of a dedicated contribution from Kurt Equiluz. Gillesberger's pacing is well judged and the effect is as fresh as it is strong and direct. The 1982 recording is excellent, vivid yet full, and the result is powerful but not too heavy. Mozart's *Ave verum* is also very well sung.

Barenboim's earlier EMI account is greatly to be preferred to his later, French recording for the same label. However, at bargain price on Laser it now comes in harness with Barbirolli's less than outstanding set of Verdi's *Requiem*. In the Mozart, Barenboim's exuberance may raise a few eyebrows. The *Dies irae*, for instance, has such zest that one senses the chorus galloping towards the Day of Judgement with enthusiasm.

Yet the underlying drama and musicality of the performance as a whole disarm criticism. The lyricism is beautifully calculated and, with a good solo team, excellent choral singing and fine orchestral playing (the opening of the *Lacrimosa* very well managed), this is a splendidly alive performance, and the remastered sound is very good.

Davis with a smaller choir gives a more intimate performance than is common, and with his natural sense of style he finds much beauty of detail. In principle the performance should have given the sort of 'new look' to the Mozart *Requiem* that was such a striking success in Handel's *Messiah*, but Davis does not provide the same sort of 'bite' that in performances on this scale should compensate for sheer massiveness of tone. The BBC Symphony Orchestra is in good form and the soloists – although varying in quality – keep up a laudably high standard. Anyone wanting a version on this scale need not hesitate, but this is plainly not the definitive version. The recording is good but not ideally sharp in focus, although it is fully acceptable on CD.

Giulini, in his bargain version also on EMI Laser, directs a large-scale performance which brings out rather more Mozartian lyricism than Mozartian drama. The choir is in excellent incisive form and the soloists are a first-rate quartet. The 1979 recording now sounds fresher and clearer, without too much loss of weight.

The glory of Frühbeck's Classics for Pleasure reissue is the singing of the New Philharmonia Chorus. Frühbeck does not have a very subtle Mozart style, but as an interpretation it stands well in the middle of the road, not too romantic, not too frigidly classic; quite apart from the choral singing – recorded with good balance – the soloists are all first rate. The remastering has brought added clarity, and this is quite competitive in the bargain-price range.

Giulini's 1989 version was his first recording for the new Sony Classical label, and it finds him even more lyrical and expansive with the same choir and orchestra than he was ten years earlier. There is more body in the digital sound but some lack of bite and inner clarity in the recording of the chorus, which gives some advantage (quite apart from price) to the earlier version. Among the soloists the young soprano, Lynne Dawson, is outstanding in the tender beauty of her singing.

Bernstein, in preparation for this recording of a work he had long neglected, made a special study not only of textual problems but also of most of the existing recordings, not least those which use period instruments. He also opted to make the recording in a church of modest size. Yet Bernstein's romantic personality engulfs such gestures towards authenticity and the result is a rich, warm-hearted reading, marked by a broad, expressive style in the slower sections. With weighty choral singing to match and with good, if flawed, solo singing, it is a strongly characterized reading, which yet hardly makes a first choice.

Karajan's earlier (1962) recording, now reissued on DG's bargain label, took a suave view of the work. The chief objection to this version is that detail tends to be sacrificed in favour of an almost bland richness of choral texture, massive in its weight. With measured tempi, in its way the effect cannot fail to be impressive, particularly as the remastered CD has firmed up the choral focus. The solo quartet are wonderfully blended, a rare occurrence in this work, and the spirited playing of the Berlin Philharmonic is another plus point. While both Karajan's later versions, digital and analogue, are greatly preferable, this is by no means without appeal.

Kertesz offers yet another large-scale view of Mozart's last work, but unfortunately he cannot rely on a really first-rate chorus. Much of the choral singing here is rather wild and smudgy, enthusiastic but not stylish enough for Mozart; and the impression is made worse by the forward balance of the singers against the orchestra.

Requiem mass (No. 19) in D min. (edited Maunder).
**(*) O-L Dig. 411 712-2 [id.]. Emma Kirkby, Watkinson, Rolfe-Johnson, David Thomas, Westminster Cathedral Boys' Ch., AAM Ch. and O, Hogwood.

Hogwood's version is strictly incomparable with any other, using as it does the edition of Richard Maunder, which aims to eliminate Süssmayr's contribution to the version of Mozart's unfinished masterpiece that has held sway for two centuries. So the *Lacrimosa* is completely different, after the opening eight bars, and concludes with an elaborate *Amen*, for which Mozart's own sketches were recently discovered. This textual clean-out goes with authentic performance of Hogwood's customary abrasiveness, very fresh and lively to underline the impact of novelty. With fine solo singing from four specialists in Baroque performance and bright choral sound, brilliantly recorded, it can be recommended to those who welcome a new look in Mozart.

OPERA

Bastien und Bastienne (complete). Lieder: *Komm liebe Zither, komm; Die Zufriedenheit.*
*** Ph. Dig. 420 163-2 [id.]. Soloists from V. Boys' Ch., VSO, Harrer.

Mozart's second opera, written at the age of twelve, is a German Singspiel so simple in style that often, as here, it is performed by boy trebles instead of the soprano, tenor and bass originally intended. Members of the Vienna Boys' Choir give a refreshingly direct performance under Uwe Christian Harrer, missing little of the piece's charm, though a recording with adult singers would still be welcome. The two songs with mandolin accompaniment, also sung by one of the trebles, make an attractive fill-up. First-rate sound.

La clemenza di Tito (complete).
*** Ph. 420 097-2 (2) [id.]. Dame Janet Baker, Minton, Burrows, Von Stade, Popp, Lloyd, ROHCG Ch. and O, C. Davis.
(M) *** DG 429 878-2 (2) [id.]. Berganza, Varady, Mathis, Schreier, Schiml, Adam, Leipzig R. Ch., Dresden State O, Boehm.

Sir Colin Davis's superb set is among the finest of his many Mozart recordings. Not only is the singing of Dame Janet Baker in the key role of Vitellia formidably brilliant, with every roulade and exposed leap flawlessly attacked; she actually makes one believe in the emotional development of an impossible character, one who progresses from villainy to virtue with the scantiest preparation. The two other mezzo-sopranos, Minton as Sesto and Von Stade in the small role of Annio, are superb too, while Stuart Burrows has rarely if ever sung so stylishly on a recording as here; he makes the forgiving emperor a rounded and sympathetic character, not just a bore. The recitatives add to the compulsion of the drama, while Davis's swaggering manner in the pageant music heightens the genuine feeling conveyed in much of the rest, transforming what used to be dismissed as a dry *opera seria*. Excellent recording, which gains in brightness and immediacy in its CD format.

In his mid-eighties Karl Boehm at last managed to record *La Clemenza di Tito*, and he gave the work warmth and charm, presenting the piece more genially than we have grown used to. The atmospheric recording helps in that, and the cast is first rate, with no weak link, matching at every point that of Sir Colin Davis on his Philips set. Yet, ultimately, even Julia Varady for Boehm can hardly rival Dame Janet Baker for Davis, crisper and lighter in her coloratura. Davis's incisiveness, too, has points of advantage; but, to summarize, any Mozartian can safely leave the preference to his feelings about the two conductors, the one more genial and glowing, the other more urgently dramatic.

Così fan tutte (complete).
⊛ (M) *** EMI CMS7 69330-2 (3) [Ang. CDMC 69330]. Schwarzkopf, Ludwig, Steffek, Kraus, Taddei, Berry, Philh. Ch. & O, Boehm.
⊛ (M) (***) EMI mono CHS7 69635-2 (3) [Ang. CDHC 69635]. Schwarzkopf, Otto, Merriman, Simoneau, Panerai, Bruscantini, Philh. Ch. & O, Karajan.
*** EMI Dig. CDS7 47727-8 (3) [id.]. Vaness, Ziegler, Watson, Aler, Duesing, Desderi, Glyndebourne Ch., LPO, Haitink.
*** Ph. 416 633-2 (3) [id.]. Caballé, Dame Janet Baker, Cotrubas, Gedda, Ganzarolli, Van Allan, ROHCG Ch. & O, C. Davis.
(M) **(*) EMI Dig. CMS7 69580-2 (3). Margaret Marshall, Battle, Baltsa, Araiza, Morris, Van Dam, V. State Op. Ch., VPO, Muti.
**(*) DG Dig. 423 897-2 (3) [id.]. Te Kanawa, Murray, McLaughlin, Blochwitz, Hampson, Furlanetto, Concert Group of Vienna State Op., VPO, Levine.
(M) **(*) DG 429 824-2 (2) [id.]. Janowitz, Fassbaender, Schreier, Prey, Panerai, V. State Op. Ch., VPO, Boehm.
(M) **(*) RCA GD 86677 [6677-2-RG] (3). L. Price, Troyanos, Raskin, Shirley, Milnes, Flagello, Amb. Op. Ch., New Philh. O, Leinsdorf.
**(*) O-L Dig. 414 316-2 (3) [id.]. Yakar, Resick, Nafé, Winberg, Krause, Feller, Drottningholm Court Theatre Ch. & O, Östman.

First choice remains with Boehm's classic set, reissued on three mid-priced CDs, with its glorious solo singing, headed by the incomparable Fiordiligi of Schwarzkopf and the equally moving Dorabella of Christa Ludwig, a superb memento of Walter Legge's recording genius. It still stands comparison with any other recordings, made before or since.

Commanding as Schwarzkopf is as Fiordiligi in the 1962 Boehm set, also with the Philharmonia, the extra ease and freshness of her singing in the earlier (1954) version makes it even more compelling. Nan Merriman is a distinctive and characterful Dorabella, and the role of Ferrando has never been sung more mellifluously on record than by Leopold Simoneau, ravishing in *Un aura amorosa*. The young Rolando Panerai is an ideal Guglielmo, and Lisa Otto a pert Despina; while Sesto Bruscantini in his prime brings to the role of Don Alfonso the wisdom and artistry which made him so compelling at Glyndebourne. Karajan has never sparkled more naturally in Mozart than here, for the high polish has nothing self-conscious about it. Though the mono recording is not as clear as some others of this period, the subtleties of the music-making are very well caught. In such a performance, one hardly worries that some recitative and one or two numbers are cut. An essential purchase for Mozartians as a supplement to the Boehm set.

With speeds often more measured than usual, Haitink's EMI version yet consistently conveys the sparkle of live performances at Glyndebourne. The excellent teamwork, consistently conveying humour, makes up for a cast-list rather less starry than that on some rival versions. This is above all a sunny performance, sailing happily over any serious shoals beneath Da Ponte's comedy. Claudio Desderi as Alfonso helps to establish that Glyndebourne atmosphere, with recitatives superbly timed and coloured. If Carol Vaness and Delores Ziegler are rather too alike in timbre to be distinguished easily, the relationship becomes all the more sisterly when, quite apart from the similarity, they respond so beautifully to each other. John Aler makes a headily unstrained Ferrando, beautifully free in the upper register; and Lilian Watson and Dale Duesing make up a strong team. The digital recording gives fine bloom and an impressive dynamic range to voices and orchestra alike.

The energy and sparkle of Sir Colin Davis are here set against inspired and characterful singing from the three women soloists, with Montserrat Caballé and Janet Baker proving a winning partnership, each challenging and abetting the other all the time. Cotrubas equally is a vivid Despina, never merely arch. Though Gedda has moments of rough tone and Ganzarolli falls short in one of his prominent arias, they are both spirited, while Richard van Allan sings with flair and imagination. Sparkling recitative and recording which has you riveted by the play of the action.

Muti's recording of *Così fan tutte* is vivid, vigorous and often very beautiful. Ensemble is not always flawless, but this is far more polished than Boehm's eightieth-birthday performance, also recorded live (for DG) at the Kleines Festspielhaus. Muti's vigour is infectiously captured, as is his ability to relax into necessary tenderness. Though purists will prefer the extra precision of a studio performance – Boehm's Philharmonia set or Karajan's stand out – this newer EMI version gives an irresistible flavour of the theatre and the sparkle of Mozartian comedy, even if the sound is rough and lacks body, compared with the best versions.

Levine's view of *Così fan tutte* is brisk and bright rather than charming or frothy. His conducting, rhythmically rather square, hardly rivals the very finest sets. Instead of sparkling, the score fizzes vigorously. There are vocal delights in the singing of Dame Kiri Te Kanawa in one of her finest Mozart performances on record; and there the conductor's taut discipline has inspired the singer to give one of the most dazzling accounts of *Come scoglio*, even if *Per pietà* lacks a full heartache. The recording was made over a concentrated period of ten days, adding to the cohesion of the whole, and with recitatives made more genial with a fortepiano instead of a harpsichord. Outstanding besides Dame Kiri is Thomas Hampson as Guglielmo, rich, firm and characterful. It is good to have his longer, more searching Act I aria included, with the usual one, *Non ti ritrasi*, given as an appendix on the same disc, so that it can be programmed instead. Hans-Peter Blochwitz is pallid by comparison but sings with heady beauty; Ferruccio Furlanetto is an urbane, rather fruity Alfonso, and Marie McLaughlin is a superb Despina, no mere soubrette but a strong character matching Alfonso. The main disappointment concerns Ann Murray's Dorabella, well characterized but with the voice straining uncomfortably above mezzo forte.

Boehm's third recording makes a delightful memento and, offered on a pair of mid-priced CDs, it is worth considering, despite its obvious flaws. It was recorded live during the Salzburg Festival performance on the conductor's eightieth birthday, and though the zest and sparkle of the occasion come over delightfully, with as splendid a cast as you could gather, the ensemble is not ideally crisp for repeated listening. The balance favours the voices, with stage noises made the more prominent on CD.

On the RCA set Leinsdorf is not an elegant Mozartian, but he was at his most relaxed in his 1967 recording of *Così fan tutte*, using a sextet of some of the finest American singers of the time. With Leontyne Price scaling her voice down well as Fiordiligi, with fine playing from the Philharmonia and with recording full of presence, it is a viable mid-price version, even though it can hardly match – except in its more complete text – its direct EMI rivals from Karajan and Boehm.

Except that soloists of international standing have been introduced – an aptly fresh-voiced team, stylishly Mozartian – this Oiseau-Lyre recording aims to reproduce one of the most successful of Arnold Östman's authentic productions in the beautiful little court opera-house at Drottningholm, near Stockholm. The point to marvel at initially is the hectic speed of almost every number, yet Östman refreshingly establishes a valid new view. Few Mozartians would want to hear *Così fan tutte* like this all the time but, with no weak link in the cast and with the drama vividly presented, it can be recommended both to those who enjoy authentic performance and to all who are prepared to listen afresh.

Così fan tutte: highlights.
(M) ** DG 429 824-2 [id.]. Janowitz, Fassbaender, Grist, Prey, Schreier, Panerai, V. State Op. Ch., VPO, Boehm.

Although an hour's playing time is indicated on the back liner-leaflet, this selection from Boehm's live 1974 Salzburg Festival recording (his third) runs to over 72 minutes, and the sparkle of the occasion is well conveyed. This is a good way of approaching a set where ensemble is at times less than perfect but which offers a splendid cast and some fine individual contributions. Unusually for DG, however, the documentation is wholly inadequate.

Don Giovanni (complete).
*** EMI CDS7 47260-8 (3) [Ang. CDCC 47260]. Waechter, Schwarzkopf, Sutherland, Alva, Frick, Sciutti, Taddei, Philh. Ch. & O, Giulini.
*** EMI Dig. CDS7 47037-8 (3) [Ang. CDCC 47036]. Thomas Allen, Vaness, Ewing, Gale, Van Allan, Keith Lewis, Glyndebourne Ch., LPO, Haitink.
*** DG Dig. 419 179-2 (3) [id.]. Ramey, Tomowa-Sintow, Baltsa, Battle, Winbergh, Furlanetto, Malta, Burchuladze, German Op. Ch., Berlin, BPO, Karajan.
*** Ph. 416 406-2 (3) [id.]. Wixell, Arroyo, Te Kanawa, Freni, Burrows, Ganzarolli, ROHCG Ch. & O, C. Davis.
(M) *** Decca 411 626-2 (3). Siepi, Danco, Della Casa, Corena, Dermota, V. State Op. Ch., VPO, Krips.
(M) (***) EMI mono CHS7 61030-2 (3). Brownlee, Souez, Von Pataky, Helletsgruber, Baccaloni, Henderson, Mildmay, Glyndebourne Fest. Ch. & O, Fritz Busch.
**(*) CBS M3K 35192 (3) [id.]. Raimondi, Moser, Te Kanawa, Berganza, Riegel, Van Dam, Paris Op. Ch. & O, Maazel.
(M) ** DG 429 870-2 (3) [id.]. Fischer-Dieskau, Arroyo, Nilsson, Grist, Schreier, Flagello, Prague Nat. Theatre Ch. & O, Boehm.

The classic Giulini EMI set, lovingly remastered to bring out even more vividly the excellence of Walter Legge's original sound-balance, sets the standard by which all other recordings have come to be judged. Not only is the singing cast more consistent than any other; the direction of Giulini and the playing of the vintage Philharmonia Orchestra give this performance an athletic vigour which carries all before it. Elisabeth Schwarzkopf, as Elvira, emerges as a dominant figure to give a distinctive but totally apt slant to this endlessly invigorating drama. The young Sutherland may be relatively reticent as Anna but, with such technical ease and consistent beauty of tone, she makes a superb foil. Taddei is a delightful Leporello, and each member of the cast – including the young Cappuccilli as Masetto – combines fine singing with keen dramatic sense. Recitatives are scintillating, and only the occasional exaggerated snarl from the Don of Eberhard Waechter mars the superb vocal standards. Even that goes well with his fresh and youthful portrait of the central character.
In Haitink's Glyndebourne set Maria Ewing's Elvira, vibrant and characterful if not ideally pure-toned, contrasts characterfully with the powerful Donna Anna of Carol Vaness and the innocent-sounding Zerlina of Elizabeth Gale. Keith Lewis is a sweet-toned Ottavio, but it is Thomas Allen as Giovanni who – apart from Haitink – dominates the recording, a swaggering Don full of charm and with a touch of nobility when, defiant to the end, he is dragged to Hell – a spine-chilling moment as recorded

here. Haitink's flawless control of pacing is not always conventional but is reliably thoughtful and convincing. Excellent playing from the LPO and warm, full recording, far more agreeable than the actual sound in the dry auditorium at Glyndebourne.

Even if ensemble is less than perfect at times in the Karajan set and the final scene of Giovanni's descent to Hell goes off the boil a little, the end result has fitting intensity and power. The very opening may be extraordinarily slow and massive, but the rest of the performance is just as remarkable for fast, exhilarating speeds as for slow. Though Karajan was plainly thinking of a big auditorium in his pacing of recitatives, having Jeffrey Tate as continuo player helps to keep them moving and to bring out word-meaning. The starry line-up of soloists is a distinctive one. Samuel Ramey is a noble rather than a menacing Giovanni, consistently clear and firm. Ferruccio Furlanetto's beautiful timbre as Leporello may not be contrasted quite enough, but both his style of singing – with sing-speech allowed into recitative – and his extrovert acting provide the necessary variation. The dark, firm bass of Paata Burchuladze as the Commendatore is thrillingly incisive, and Alexander Malta makes a bluff, mature Masetto, sharply contrasted with the fresh, sweet and innocently provocative Zerlina of Kathleen Battle. Anna Tomowa-Sintow has rarely if ever sung so animatedly on record as here in the role of Donna Anna, while the tone remains beautiful. She is well matched by the virile Ottavio of Gösta Winbergh. Most individual of all is the Donna Elvira of Agnes Baltsa. The venom and bite of her mezzo timbre go with a touch of vulnerability, so that even when – as in *Mi tradi* – ensemble falls apart, the result is memorable. Recording and editing are erratic, but the result is full and vivid.

Sir Colin Davis has the advantage of a singing cast that has fewer shortcomings than almost any other on disc and much positive strength. For once one can listen untroubled by vocal blemishes. Martina Arroyo controls her massive dramatic voice more completely than one would think possible, and she is strongly and imaginatively contrasted with the sweetly expressive Elvira of Kiri Te Kanawa and the sparkling Zerlina of Freni. As in the Davis *Figaro*, Ingvar Wixell and Wladimiro Ganzarolli make a formidable master/servant team with excellent vocal acting, while Stuart Burrows sings gloriously as Don Ottavio, and Richard Van Allan is a characterful Masetto. Davis draws a fresh and immediate performance from his team, riveting from beginning to end, and the recording, now better defined and more vivid than before, is still refined in the recognizable Philips manner.

Krips's recording of this most challenging opera has kept its place as a mid-priced version which is consistently satisfying, with a cast of all-round quality headed by the dark-toned Don of Cesare Siepi. The women are not ideal, but they form an excellent team, never overfaced by the music, generally characterful, and with timbres well contrasted. To balance Siepi's darkness, the Leporello of Corena is even more saturnine, and their dramatic teamwork is brought to a superb climax in the final scene – quite the finest and most spine-tingling performance of that scene ever recorded. The 1955 recording – genuine stereo – still sounds remarkably well.

There are those who still count the early Glyndebourne set the finest of all, with Fritz Busch an inspired Mozartian, pointing the music with a freshness and absence of nineteenth-century heaviness rare at the time. A piano is used for the *secco* recitatives and the chords are played very baldly and without elaboration; but the interplay of characters in those exchanges has never been caught more infectiously on disc. John Brownlee as Giovanni may have a rather British-stiff-upper-lip Italian accent (noticeable for the most part in the recitatives) but his is a noble performance, beautifully sung, and he is brilliantly set against the lively, idiomatically Italian Leporello of Salvatore Baccaloni. The three ladies are both contrasted and well matched, with Audrey Mildmay as Zerlina a delightful foil for the excellent, if otherwise little-known Ina Souez and Luise Helletsgruber. Koloman von Pataky uses his light, heady tenor well as Ottavio, and the British stalwarts, David Franklin and Roy Henderson, are both first rate as the Commendatore and Masetto respectively. Altogether this version is a delight, and Keith Hardwick's digital transfers are astonishingly vivid, with very little background noise.

Lorin Maazel directs a strong and urgent performance, designed to serve as soundtrack for the Losey film. An obvious strength is the line-up of three unusually firm-toned basses: José van Dam a saturnine Leporello, not comic but with much finely detailed expression; Malcolm King a darkly intense Masetto, and Ruggero Raimondi a heroic Giovanni, not always attacking notes cleanly but on balance one of the very finest on record in this role. Among the women Kiri Te Kanawa is outstanding, a radiant Elvira; Teresa Berganza as a mezzo Zerlina generally copes well with the high tessitura; and though Edda Moser starts with some fearsome squawks at her first entry, the dramatic scale is certainly impressive and she rises to the challenge of the big arias. Unfortunately the recording, made in a Paris church, has the voices close against background reverberation.

The Boehm set chosen for reissue is the earlier of his two versions for DG, recorded in Prague, with Dietrich Fischer-Dieskau singing powerfully if sometimes roughly in the title-role. Birgit Nilsson does wonders in scaling down her Wagnerian soprano for the needs of Mozart, making a characterful if hardly a flawless Donna Anna. Similarly, the Verdian, Martina Arroyo, is characterful as Elvira, even if she has ungainly moments. The partnership between Fischer-Dieskau and Ezio Flagello as Leporello is most appealing, and Reri Grist makes a charming Zerlina. A flawed set, enjoyable but scarcely matching the others in the Boehm cycle.

Don Giovanni: highlights.
(M) *** EMI CDM7 63078-2 (from above recording, cond. Giulini).
*** DG Dig. 419 635-2 [id.] (from above recording, cond. Karajan).
(M) **(*) EMI CDM7 69055-2 [id.]. Ghiaurov, Watson, Freni, Ludwig, Gedda, Berry, New Philh. Ch. & O, Klemperer.
(M) **(*) DG 429 823-2 [id.]. Milnes, Tomowa-Sintow, Zylis-Gara, Mathis, Schreier, Berry, V. State Op. Ch., VPO, Boehm.

Not surprisingly, the EMI selection concentrates on Sutherland as Donna Anna and Schwarzkopf as Donna Elvira, so that the Don and Leporello get rather short measure; but Sciutti's charming Zerlina is also given fair due.

A particularly generous selection from Karajan's digital set, most of the favourite items included and all the principals given a chance to shine, in solos, duets and ensembles. The selection opens with the *Overture* and closes with the powerful final scene.

Ghiaurov as the Don and Berry as Leporello make a marvellous pair on Klemperer's set and, among the women, Ludwig is a strong and convincing Elvira, Freni a sweet-toned but rather unsmiling Zerlina. Most of the slow tempi which Klemperer adopts, far from flagging, add a welcome spaciousness to the music.

Like its companion collection of highlights from *Così fan tutte*, Boehm's selection is very generous (76 minutes) and is taken from live performances at Salzburg (recorded in 1977). It makes a welcome representation of a set centring round Sherrill Milnes's unusually heroic assumption of the role of the Don, and he sings with a richness and commitment to match his swaggering stage presence. The rest of the cast give stylish performances without being deeply memorable but, unlike *Così* where ensembles were less than ideally crisp, this live *Giovanni* presents strong and consistently enjoyable teamwork. The balance again favours the voices but is especially vivid in the culminating scene. However, the documentation, as with *Così*, offers only period pictures and a list of contents.

Die Entführung aus dem Serail (complete).
(M) *** DG 429 868-2 (2) [id.]. Augér, Grist, Schreier, Neukirch, Moll, Leipzig R. Ch., Dresden State O, Boehm.
*** Teldec/WEA Dig. 2292 42643-2 (3) [id.]. Kenny, Watson, Schreier, Gamlich, Salminen, Zurich Op. Ch. & Mozart O, Harnoncourt.
**(*) Decca Dig. 417 402-2 (2) [id.]. Gruberová, Battle, Winbergh, Zednik, Talvela, V. State Op. Ch., VPO, Solti.
** Ph. 416 479-2 (2) [id.]. Eda-Pierre, Burrowes, Burrows, Tear, Lloyd, Jürgens, Alldis Ch., ASMF, C. Davis.

Boehm's is a delectable performance, superbly cast and warmly recorded. Arleen Augér proves the most accomplished singer on record in the role of Constanze, girlish and fresh, yet rich, tender and dramatic by turns, with brilliant, almost flawless coloratura. The others are also outstandingly good, notably Kurt Moll whose powerful, finely focused bass makes him a superb Osmin, one who relishes the comedy too. Boehm with East German forces finds a natural, unforced Mozartian expression which carries the listener along in glowing ease. The warm recording is beautifully transferred, to make this easily the most sympathetic version of the opera on CD, with the added attraction of being at mid-price.

Harnoncourt's version establishes its uniqueness at the very start of the overture, tougher and more abrasive than any previous recording, with more primitive percussion effects than we are used to in his Turkish music. It is not a comfortable sound, compounded by Harnoncourt's often fast allegros, racing singers and players off their feet. Another source of extra abrasiveness is the use of a raw-sounding flageolet instead of a piccolo. Once you get used to it, however, the result is refreshing and lively. Slow passages are often warmly expressive, but the stylishness of the soloists prevents them from seeming excessively romantic. The men are excellent: Peter Schreier singing charmingly, Wilfried Gamlich both bright and sweet of tone, Matti Salminen outstandingly characterful as an Osmin who, as well as singing with firm dark tone, points the words with fine menace. Yvonne Kenny as Constanze and Lilian Watson as Blonde sound on the shrill side – partly a question of microphones – but they sing with such style and point that one quickly accepts it. *Martern aller Arten* prompts the most brilliant coloratura from Kenny, with the coda including some extra bars, now authorized by scholarship, but doubtfully effective, one of the many textual niceties of the set. Good, clean, dryish recording.

Though Solti's speeds are disconcertingly fast at times – as in Pedrillo and Osmin's drinking duet, *Vivat Bacchus* – and the manner is consequently often too tense to be comic, the performance is magnetic overall, with the big ensembles and choruses electric in their clean, sharp focus. Gruberová makes a brilliant Constanze, but the edge on the voice is not always comfortable. Gösta Winbergh makes an ardent, young-sounding Belmonte, Kathleen Battle a seductive, minxish Blonde and Heinz Zednik a delightfully light and characterful Pedrillo, with Martti Talvela magnificently lugubrious as Osmin. With brilliant recording this makes a fresh and compelling reading, but not one likely to make you smile often.

Sir Colin Davis, using a smaller orchestra than he usually has in his Mozart opera recordings, with the St Martin's Academy produces a fresh and direct account, well but not outstandingly sung. Crisp as the ensembles are, Davis's reading rather lacks the lightness and sparkle, the feeling of comedy before our eyes, which makes Boehm's DG set so memorable.

Idomeneo (complete).
(M) *** DG 429 864-2 (3) [id.]. Ochman, Mathis, Schreier, Varady, Winkler, Leipzig R. Ch., Dresden State O, Boehm.
*** Decca Dig. 411 805-2 (3) [id.]. Pavarotti, Baltsa, Popp, Gruberová, Nucci, V. State Op. Ch., VPO, Pritchard.

Textually Boehm's version of *Idomeneo* gives grounds for regrets. The score is snipped about and, like previous recordings, it opts for a tenor in the role of Idamante. That once said, however, it is an enormously successful and richly enjoyable set. Boehm's conducting is a delight, often spacious but never heavy in the wrong way, with lightened textures and sprung rhythms which have one relishing Mozartian felicities as never before. As Idomeneo, Wieslaw Ochman, with tenor tone often too tight, is a comparatively dull dog, but the other principals are generally excellent. Peter Schreier as Idamante also might have sounded more consistently sweet, but the imagination is irresistible. Edith Mathis is at her most beguiling as Ilia, but it is Julia Varady as Elettra who gives the most compelling performance of all, sharply incisive in her dramatic outbursts, but at the same time precise and pure-toned, a Mozartian stylist through and through. Hermann Winkler as Arbace is squarely Germanic, and it is a pity that the secco recitatives are done heavily; whatever incidental reservations have to be made, however, this is a superbly compelling set which leaves one in no doubt as to the work's status as a masterpiece. The first-class recording has transferred vividly to CD.

More than any previous recorded performance, the Decca version conducted by Sir John Pritchard centres round the tenor taking the name-part. It is not just that Pavarotti has the natural magnetism of the superstar, but that he is the only tenor at all among the principal soloists. Not only is the role of Idamante given to a mezzo instead of a tenor – preferable, with what was originally a castrato role – but that of the High Priest, Arbace, with his two arias is taken by a baritone, Leo Nucci. The wonder is that though Pavarotti reveals imagination in every phrase, using a wide range of tone colours, the result remains well within the parameters of Mozartian style. By any reckoning this is not only the most heroic and the most beautiful but also the best controlled performance of this demanding role that we have on record. Casting Baltsa as Idamante makes for characterful results, tougher and less fruity than her direct rivals. Lucia Popp as Ilia tends to underline expression too much, but it is a charming, girlish portrait. Gruberová makes a thrilling Elettra, totally in command of the divisions, as few sopranos are; owing to bright Decca sound, the projection of her voice is a little edgy at times. As to Pritchard, he has relaxed a little since his Glyndebourne days – this is a bigger view than before – and (with text unusually complete) more than current rivals brings light and shade to the piece.

Le nozze di Figaro (complete).
*** Decca Dig. 410 150-2 (3). Te Kanawa, Popp, Von Stade, Ramey, Allen, Moll, LPO & Ch., Solti.
(M) *** Ph. 426 195-2 (3) [id.]. Freni, Norman, Minton, Ganzarolli, Wixell, Grant, Tear, BBC Ch. & SO, Sir Colin Davis.
(M) **(*) Decca 417 315-2 (3) [id.]. Gueden, Danco, Della Casa, Dickie, Poell, Corena, Siepi, V. State Op. Ch., VPO, Erich Kleiber.
(M) *** DG 429 869-2 (3) [id.]. Janowitz, Mathis, Troyanos, Fischer-Dieskau, Prey, Lagger, German Op. Ch. & O, Boehm.
**(*) EMI Dig. CDS7 49753-2 (3) [Ang. CDCC 49753]. Lott, Desderi, Rolandi, Stilwell, Esham, Korn, Glyndebourne Ch., LPO, Haitink.

** Decca Dig. 421 333-2 (3) [id.]. Hagegård, Augér, Salomaa, Bonney, Nafé, Jones, Feller, Gimenez, Drottningholm Theatre Ch. & O, Ostman.

Le nozze di Figaro: highlights.
*** Decca Dig. 417 395-2 [id.] (from above recording, cond. Solti).

It is important not to judge Solti's effervescent new version of *Figaro* by a first reaction to the overture, which is one of the fastest on record. Elsewhere Solti opts for a fair proportion of extreme speeds, slow as well as fast, but they rarely if ever intrude on the quintessential happiness of the entertainment. Samuel Ramey, a firm-toned baritone, makes a virile Figaro, superby matched to the most enchanting of Susannas today, Lucia Popp, who gives a sparkling and radiant performance. Thomas Allen's Count is magnificent too, tough in tone and characterization but always beautiful on the ear. Kurt Moll as Dr Bartolo sings an unforgettable *La vendetta* with triplets very fast and agile 'on the breath', while Robert Tear far outshines his own achievement as the Basilio of Sir Colin Davis's amiable recording. Frederica von Stade, as in the Karajan set, is a most attractive Cherubino, even if *Voi che sapete* is too slow; but crowning all is the Countess of Kiri Te Kanawa, challenged by Solti's spacious tempi in the two big arias, but producing ravishing tone, flawless phrasing and elegant ornamentation throughout. With superb, vivid recording this now makes a clear first choice for a much-recorded opera.

The pacing of Sir Colin Davis has a sparkle in recitative that directly reflects experience in the opera house, and his tempi generally are beautifully chosen to make their dramatic points. Vocally the cast is exceptionally consistent. Mirella Freni (Susanna) is perhaps the least satisfying, yet there is no lack of character and charm. It is good to have so ravishingly beautiful a voice as Jessye Norman's for the Countess. The Figaro of Wladimiro Ganzarolli and the Count of Ingvar Wixell project with exceptional clarity and vigour, and there is fine singing too from Yvonne Minton as Cherubino, Clifford Grant as Bartolo and Robert Tear as Basilio. The 1971 recording has more reverberation than usual, but the effect is commendably atmospheric and on CD the voices have plenty of presence. The CD transfer is altogether smoother than Decca have managed for the Kleiber set, with the break in the middle of Act II coming earlier and much better placed. This is undoubtedly one of the most enjoyable versions of this opera from the analogue era.

Kleiber's famous set was one of Decca's Mozart bicentenary recordings of the mid-1950s. It remains an outstanding bargain at mid-price, an attractively strong performance with much fine singing. Few if any sets have since matched its constant stylishness. Gueden's Susanna might be criticized but her golden tones are certainly characterful and her voice blends with Della Casa's enchantingly. Danco and Della Casa are both at their finest. A dark-toned Figaro in Siepi brings added contrast and, if the pace of the recitatives is rather slow, this is not inconsistent within the context of Kleiber's overall approach. It is a pity that the Decca remastering, in brightening the sound, has brought a hint of edginess to the voices, though the basic atmosphere remains. Also, the layout brings a less than felicitous break in Act II, which Kleiber shapes with authoritative inevitability. In this respect the cassettes were superior – and they had smoother sound, too.

Boehm's version of *Figaro* is also among the most consistently assured performances available. The women all sing most beautifully, with Janowitz's Countess, Mathis's Susanna and Troyanos's Cherubino all ravishing the ear in contrasted ways. Prey is an intelligent if not very jolly-sounding Figaro, and Fischer-Dieskau gives his dark, sharply defined reading of the Count's role. All told, a great success, with fine playing and recording, enhanced on CD, and now offered at mid-price.

As in his other Glyndebourne recordings, Haitink's approach is relaxed and mellow. Where in *Così* the results were sunny, here in *Figaro* there is at times a lack of sparkle. There is much lovely singing and fine ensemble from a strong team, yet one which does not quite match the casting of the Solti set.

Östman's version (based on the production at the Drottningholm Court Theatre) is the first to use period instruments; like his *Così*, it brings generally hectic speeds, but here such treatment undermines both the fun and the dramatic point. Östman refuses to pause or even to broaden for a second in passages which cry out for it; and with such a metrical beat even the most sparkling moments lose their brightness, and charm is far away. Nevertheless the cast is impressive. The Susanna of Barbara Bonney is delightful, and though Petteri Salomaa is rather dry-toned, he makes an engaging young Figaro. Håkan Hagegård is a splendid Count, and Arleen Augér a pure-toned Countess. Among the others, too, there are no weak links at all, and the set is valuable for generously including variant numbers that Mozart incorporated in productions at different times. Full and well-balanced recording.

Le nozze di Figaro: highlights.
(M) *** DG 429 822-3 [id.] (from above set, cond. Karl Boehm).
(M) **(*) Decca 421 317-2 [id.]. Tomowa-Sintow, Cotrubas, Von Stade, Van Dam, Bastin, Krause, VPO, Karajan.

Boehm's selection includes many of the key numbers, but with a little over an hour of music it is less generous than its companion highlights discs. Like them, it is inadequately documented but the singing is first class and the sound vivid.

Though overall Karajan's Decca Vienna recording of *Figaro* with its wilful speeds is too slick for so fizzing a comedy, such polish and refinement deserve to be sampled – notably Frederica von Stade's Cherubino.

Der Schauspieldirektor (*The Impresario*): complete.
(M) *** DG 429 877-2 (3) [id.]. Grist, Augér, Schreier, Moll, Dresden State O, Boehm – *Die Zauberflöte.***(*)

This performance of *Der Schauspieldirektor* is without dialogue, so that it is short enough to make a fill-up for Boehm's *Zauberflöte*. Reri Grist's bravura as Madame Herz is impressive, and Arleen Augér is pleasingly fresh and stylish here. The tenor and bass make only minor contributions, but Boehm's guiding hand keeps the music alive from the first bar to the last.

Die Zauberflöte (complete).
⊛ (M) *** EMI mono CHS7 69631-2 (2) [Ang. CDHB 69631]. Seefried, Lipp, Loose, Dermota, Kunz, Weber, V. State Op. Ch., VPO, Karajan.
*** EMI Dig. CDS7 47951-8 (3) [Ang. CDCC 47951]. Popp, Gruberová, Lindner, Jerusalem, Brendel, Bracht, Zednik, Bav. R. Ch. & SO, Haitink.
(M) *** EMI CMS7 69971-2 (2) [Ang. CDMB 69971]. Janowitz, Putz, Popp, Gedda, Berry, Frick; Schwarzkopf, Ludwig, Hoffgen (3 Ladies), Philh. Ch. & O, Klemperer.
*** DG Dig. 410 967-2 (3) [id.]. Mathis, Ott, Perry, Araiza, Hornik, Van Dam, German Op. Ch., Berlin, BPO, Karajan.
(M) **(*) DG 429 877-2 (3) [id.]. Lear, Peters, Otto, Wunderlich, Fischer-Dieskau, Hotter, Crass, Berlin RIAS Chamber Ch., BPO, Boehm – *Der Schauspieldirektor.****
(***) Pearl mono GEMM CDS 9371 (2) [id.]. Lemnitz, Roswaenge, Berger, Hüsch, Strienz, Ch. & BPO, Beecham.

(M) (**) EMI mono CHS7 61034-2 (2) [id.]. Lemnitz, Roswaenge, Berger, Hüsch, Strienz, Ch. & BPO, Beecham.

** Decca 414 568-2 (3) [id.]. Lorengar, Deutekom, Burrows, Fischer-Dieskau, Prey, Talvela, V. State Op. Ch., VPO, Solti.

** Teldec/WEA Dig. 2292 42716-2 (2) [id.]. Gruberová, Bonney, Salminen, Blochwitz, Scharinger, Hampson, Zurich Op. Ch. & O, Harnoncourt.

As with the companion mono version of *Così fan tutte*, there has never been a more seductive recording of *Zauberflöte* than Karajan's mono version of 1950. The Vienna State Opera cast here has not since been matched on record: Irmgard Seefried and Anton Dermota both sing with radiant beauty and great character, Wilma Lipp is a dazzling Queen of the Night, Erich Kunz as Papageno sings with an infectious smile in the voice, and Ludwig Weber is a commanding Sarastro. There is no spoken dialogue; but on two mid-priced CDs instead of three LPs, it is a Mozart treat not to be missed, with mono sound still amazingly vivid and full of presence.

Haitink in his first ever opera recording directs a rich and spacious account of *Zauberflöte*, superbly recorded in spectacularly wide-ranging digital sound. The dialogue – not too much of it, nicely produced and with sound effects adding to the vividness – frames a presentation that has been carefully thought through. Popp makes the most tenderly affecting of Paminas and Gruberová has never sounded more spontaneous in her brilliance than here as Queen of the Night: she is both agile and powerful. Jerusalem makes an outstanding Tamino, both heroic and sweetly Mozartian; and though neither Wolfgang Brendel as Papageno nor Bracht as Sarastro is as characterful as their finest rivals, their personalities project strongly and the youthful freshness of their singing is most attractive. The Bavarian chorus too is splendid. Some readers will certainly prefer Karajan's more urgent, more volatile Berlin version, but the gravitas of Haitink's approach does not miss the work's elements of drama and charm, though nothing is trivialized.

Klemperer's conducting of *The Magic Flute* is one of his finest achievements on record; indeed he is inspired, making the dramatic music sound more like Beethoven in its breadth and strength. But he does not miss the humour and point of the Papageno passages, and he gets the best of both worlds to a surprising degree. The cast is outstanding – look at the distinction of the Three Ladies alone – but curiously it is that generally most reliable of all the singers, Gottlob Frick as Sarastro, who comes nearest to letting the side down. Lucia Popp is in excellent form, and Gundula Janowitz sings Pamina's part with a creamy beauty that is just breathtaking. Nicolai Gedda too is a firm-voiced Papageno. The transfer to a pair of CDs, made possible by the absence of dialogue, is managed expertly – the whole effect is wonderfully fresh, the balance strikingly good.

In his later, digital set, *Zauberflöte* again inspired Karajan to give one of his freshest, most rhythmic Mozart performances, spontaneous-sounding to the point where vigour is preferred to immaculate precision in ensembles. The digital recording is not always perfectly balanced, but the sound is outstandingly fresh and clear. There are numbers where the tempi are dangerously slow, but Karajan's concentration helps him to avoid mannerism completely. If in principle one would want a darker-toned Sarastro than José van Dam, the clarity of focus and the fine control, not to mention the slow tempi, give the necessary weight to his arias. Francisco Araiza and Gottfried Hornik make impressive contributions, both concealing any inexperience. Karin Ott has a relatively weighty voice for the Queen of the Night, but in his tempi Karajan is most considerate to her; and the Pamina of Edith Mathis has many beautiful moments, her word-pointing always intelligent.

One of the glories of Boehm's DG set is the singing of Fritz Wunderlich as Tamino, a wonderful memorial to a singer much missed. Fischer-Dieskau, with characteristic word-pointing, makes a sparkling Papageno on record (he is too big of frame, he says, to do the role on stage) and Franz Crass is a satisfyingly straightforward Sarastro. The team of women is well below this standard – Lear taxed cruelly in *Ach, ich fühl's*, Peters shrill in the upper register (although the effect is exciting), and the Three Ladies do not blend well – but Boehm's direction is superb, light and lyrical, but weighty where necessary to make a glowing, compelling experience. Fine recording, enhanced in the CD set, which has also found room for Boehm's admirable account of *Der Schauspieldirektor*, a very considerable bonus to this mid-priced reissue.

Recorded in Berlin between November 1937 and March 1939, Beecham's recording of *Zauberflöte* was also the first opera set produced by Walter Legge. It brings a classic performance, and though Helge Roswaenge was too ungainly a tenor to be an ideal Tamino, the casting has otherwise been matched in only a few instances on record. Beecham too was at his peak, pacing each number superbly. Like other early recordings of this opera, this one omits the spoken dialogue; but the vocal delights are many, not least from Tiana Lemnitz as a radiant Pamina, Erna Berger as a dazzling Queen of the Night, and Gerhard Hüsch as a delicately comic Papageno, bringing the detailed art of the Lieder-singer to the role.

The disappointment of the EMI set is the dryness of the transfer to CD, with a limited top, little sense of presence and no bloom on the voices. As this was one of the first major issues transferred by the new CEDAR process, it provided a warning that technology should always be questioned. The shortcomings of the EMI issue were the more apparent when simultaneously Pearl issued one of its uncomplicated transfers from 78 r.p.m.s, keeping much of the surface hiss, but giving the voices an immediacy and an open warmth that transforms the experience, enhancing the joys of the performance. The orchestra too has more body than on the EMI transfer. Though the price is rather higher and Pearl, unlike EMI, provides no libretto, it is a far preferable issue. A useful essay is included, filling in the background of the recording.

Solti's reading is tough, strong and brilliant, and it is arguable that in this opera those above all are the required qualities, but the almost total absence of charm is disconcerting. The drama may be consistently vital, but ultimately the full variety of Mozart's inspiration is not achieved. Among the men, Stuart Burrows is especially impressive, with stylish and rich-toned singing; Martti Talvela and Fischer-Dieskau as Sarastro and the Speaker respectively provide a stronger contrast than usual; and Hermann Prey rounds out the character of Papageno with intelligent pointing of words. The cast of women is less consistent. Pilar Lorengar's Pamina is sweetly attractive as long as your ear is not worried by her obtrusive vibrato, while Cristina Deutekom's Queen of the Night is marred by a curious warbling quality in the coloratura. The Three Ladies make a strong team (Yvonne Minton in the middle), and it was a good idea to give the parts of the Three Boys to genuine trebles. The recording is brilliant but the libretto is poorly produced.

Harnoncourt's very opening, with sforzandos exaggerated and violin-tone thinned down in the overture, demonstrates the period-performance tendencies, but thereafter the speeds are not only on the slow side as a rule, they have a rhythmic squareness which removes much of the charm of the music. Hans-Peter Blochwitz makes a fresh and youthful Tamino, Barbara Bonney an enchanting Pamina when the voice is caught with such consistent sweetness and recorded with great immediacy. With the Papageno of Anton Scharinger and the Sarastro of Matti Salminen, the closeness is less flattering, the one sounding heavy in comedy, the other not given the space for bloom to develop on the voice. With Edita Gruberová the outstanding Queen of the Night of her generation, the forwardness adds to the dramatic bite of her singing, but equally the unevenness of production under pressure is exposed, with rawness developing. Too often Harnoncourt's fussiness as well as his slow speeds undermine the comedy. Despite the pace, the whole opera is squeezed on to only two discs. Most of the story is told – in German – by a female narrator, Gertraud Jesserer, with dialogue reduced to the odd phrase, hardly a satisfactory solution.

Die Zauberflöte: highlights.
*** EMI Dig. CDC7 47008-2 [id.] (from above recording, cond. Haitink).
*** DG Dig. 415 287-2 [id.] (from above recording, cond. Karajan).
(M) *** EMI CDM7 63451-2 (from above recording, cond. Klemperer).
(M) **(*) DG 429 825-2 [id.] (from above recording, cond. Karl Boehm).
(M) ** Decca 421 302-2 [id.] (from above set, cond. Solti).

Haitink's disc makes a good sampler with the Papageno/Papagena music well represented to make a contrast with the lyrical arias and the drama of the Queen of the Night. Both the Karajan and Solti selections similarly display the characteristics of the complete sets from which they are taken. The Karajan disc concentrates on the major arias, and very impressive it is.

Those looking for a first-rate set of highlights from *Die Zauberflöte* will find the mid-priced Klemperer disc hard to beat. It includes some seven minutes more music than Boehm's disc, mostly taken up with the final scene, and makes a good sampler of a performance which, while ambitious in scale, manages to find sparkle and humour too. A synopsis details each individual excerpt, and in this case the inclusion of the *Overture* is especially welcome. The remastered sound has plenty of presence, but atmosphere and warmth too.

The hour of (very inadequately documented) excerpts from Boehm's recording is not obviously directed towards bringing out its special qualities. One would have liked more of Wunderlich's Tamino, one of the great glories of the set. However, the key arias are all included and the sound is fresh and full.

'Famous arias': from *La clemenza di Tito; Così fan tutte; Don Giovanni; Le nozze di Figaro; Il re pastore; Zaïde; Die Zauberflöte.*
(M) **(*) Decca 421 311-2 [id.]. Berganza, Lorengar, Ghiaurov, Tom Krause, S. Burrows, Bacquier, Fassbaender, Tomowa-Sintow, Popp, Krenn, Deutekom.

It is the men who provide the most memorable singing here: Stuart Burrows melting in *Il mio tesoro* from *Don Giovanni*, Gabriel Bacquier hardly less engaging in the *Serenade (Deh! vieni alla finestra)* from the same opera, and Ghiaurov bringing a sparkle to the *Catalogue song.* Among the ladies, Brigitte Fassbaender does not let us forget that Cherubino is a breeches role when she sings *Voi che sapete* stylishly but very directly; and Anna Tomowa-Sintow's account of the Countess's *Dove sono,* also from *Figaro,* is a trifle cool too. Yet Pilar Lorengar is very moving in *Per pietà* from *Così fan tutte,* an outstanding performance; and Lucia Popp's contributions from *Il re pastore* and *Zaïde* leaven an otherwise popular collection; the recording adds a suspicion of hardness to her voice but is mostly vividly atmospheric.

Arias: La clemenza di Tito: S'altro che lagrime. Così fan tutte: Ei parte . . . Sen . . . Per pietà. La finta giardiniera: Crudeli fermate . . . Ah dal pianto. Idomeneo: Se il padre perdei. Lucio Silla: Pupille amate. Il re pastore: L'amerò, sarò costante. Zaïde: Ruhe sanft, mein holdes Leben. Die Zauberflöte: Ach ich fühl's es ist verschwunden.
*** Ph. Dig. 411 148-2 [id.]. Kiri Te Kanawa, LSO, C. Davis.

Kiri Te Kanawa's is one of the loveliest collections of Mozart arias on record, with the voice at its most ravishing and pure. One might object that Dame Kiri concentrates on soulful arias, ignoring more vigorous ones; but with stylish accompaniment and clear, atmospheric recording, beauty dominates all.

Arias (sung in English) from: *Don Giovanni; The Magic flute; The Marriage of Figaro; The Seraglio; Zaïde.*
(M) **(*) EMI CD-EMX 2158. Owen Brannigan, RPO, Susskind – HANDEL: *Arias.***(*)

In Mozart – so rarely sung in English – Owen Brannigan is completely at home. He is a singer whose whole being comes alive in everything he sings, and this is a recital to cherish. With admirably clear diction, the *Catalogue song* from *Don Giovanni* is splendidly good-natured. But he is an even more memorable Osmin, and his *When a maiden takes your fancy* is sheer delight. The transfers are lively and present; and the edge on the voice, noticed in the Handel coupling, is slightly less troublesome here.

Muldowney, Dominic (born 1952)

(i) *Piano concerto;* (ii) *Saxophone concerto.*
*** EMI Dig. CDC7 49715-2. (i) Peter Donohoe, BBC SO, Mark Elder; (ii) John Harle, L. Sinf., Masson.

Muldowney's *Piano concerto* is a formidable work in a continuous half-hour span of many different sections. It uses Bachian forms and piano figuration, to move kaleidoscopically in a kind of musical collage of references to different genres, including jazz and the popular waltz. With Peter Donohoe giving one of his finest performances on record, and with colourful playing from the BBC Symphony Orchestra under Mark Elder, the piece emerges powerfully, with occasional gruff echoes of Hindemith. The *Saxophone concerto*, written for John Harle, who plays it on the record, is a more compact, strongly characterized work in three movements, each throwing up a grateful number of warm, easy tunes without any sense of compromise or incongruity. Warm, well-balanced recording.

Mundy, William (c. 1529–c. 1591)

Vox Patris caelestis.
*** Gimell CDGIM 339 [id.]. Tallis Scholars, Phillips – ALLEGRI: *Miserere*; PALESTRINA: *Missa Papae Marcelli.****

Mundy's *Vox Patris caelestis* was written during the short reign of Queen Mary (1553–8). The work is structured in nine sections in groups of three, the last of each group being climactic and featuring the whole choir, with solo embroidery. Yet the music flows continuously, like a great river, and the complex vocal writing creates the most spectacular effects, with the trebles soaring up and shining out over the underlying cantilena. The Tallis Scholars give an account which balances linear clarity with considerable power. The recording is first class and the digital remastering for CD improves the focus further.

Mussorgsky, Modest (1839–81)

Night on the bare mountain (original version).
(M) *** Ph. 420 898-2 [id.]. LPO, Lloyd-Jones – RIMSKY-KORSAKOV: *Scheherazade.****

Although it uses some of Mussorgsky's basic material, the piece we know as *Night on the bare mountain* is much more the work of Rimsky-Korsakov, who added much music of his own. The original has undoubted power and fascination, but its construction is considerably less polished. David Lloyd-Jones's performance makes a good case for it, bringing out all the crude force of its Satanic vision. The new digital transfer is also first class , and this makes an exciting bonus for an outstanding version of Rimsky-Korsakov's *Scheherazade.*

Night on the bare mountain; Khovanshchina: Prelude (both arr. Rimsky-Korsakov).
(B) *** Decca 417 689-2 [id.]. LSO, Solti – BORODIN: *Prince Igor: Overture and Polovtsian dances;* GLINKA: *Russlan overture.****

Solti's *Night on the bare mountain* can stand up to all competition in its vintage 1967 recording with its fine amplitude and great brilliance. This remains one of Solti's finest analogue collections, offering also the highly atmospheric *Khovanshchina Prelude*, which is beautifully played.

Night on the bare mountain; Khovanshchina: Prelude (both arr. Rimsky-Korsakov); *Pictures at an exhibition* (orch. Ravel).
(*) Decca Dig. 417 299-2 [id.]. Montreal SO, Dutoit – RIMSKY-KORSAKOV: *Russian Easter festival overture.*(*)
** EMI Dig. CDC7 49797-2 [id.]. Oslo PO, Mariss Jansons.

Dutoit's *Khovanshchina prelude*, with its haunting evocation of dawn over the Moscow River, has sounded more magical in other hands. *A Night on the bare mountain* is strong and biting, but again the adrenalin does not flow as grippingly as in, say, Solti's version. Dutoit's *Pictures* have each movement strongly characterized and there is a sense of fun in the scherzando movements. But overall this is less involving than with Karajan, and the brilliant recording is not as sumptuous as some other versions, although it has the bloom characteristic of the Montreal sound.

The highlight of Jansons' record is the haunting *Khovanshchina Prelude*, which is played most beautifully, yet produces a passionate climax. *Night on the bare mountain* is diabolically pungent; but here, as in the *Pictures*, the fiercely brilliant EMI recording with its dry bass and lack of sumptuousness brings dramatic bite and sharply etched detail, but less in the way of expansiveness. The dark brass sonorities are well captured in *Catacombes* and the final climax is powerfully wrought and certainly spectacular as sound; but sonically this is less appealing than the finest versions.

Night on the bare mountain (original version); *Khovanshchina: Prelude* (orch. Rimsky-Korsakov); *Pictures at an exhibition* (orch. Ravel).
*** Collins EC 1004-2 [id.]. LSO, Kaspryzk.

Night on the bare mountain (arr. Rimsky-Korsakov); *Pictures at an exhibition* (orch. Ravel).
*** Telarc Dig. CD 80042 [id.]. Cleveland O, Maazel.

The quality of the Telarc recording is apparent at the very opening of *Night on the bare mountain* in the richly sonorous presentation of the deep brass and the sparkling yet unexaggerated percussion. With the Cleveland Orchestra on top form, the *Pictures* are strongly characterized; this may not be the subtlest reading available, but each of Mussorgsky's cameos comes vividly to life. The chattering children in the Tuileries are matched in presence by the delightfully pointed portrayal of the cheeping chicks, and if the ox-wagon (*Bydlo*) develops a climax potent enough to suggest a juggernaut, the similarly sumptuous brass in the *Catacombs* sequence cannot be counted as in any way overdramatized. After a vibrantly rhythmic *Baba-Yaga*, strong in fantastic menace, the closing *Great Gate of Kiev* is overwhelmingly spacious in conception and quite riveting as sheer sound, with the richness and amplitude of the brass which make the work's final climax unforgettable. Unfortunately the *Pictures* are not cued separately.

The LSO performance of the *Pictures* directed by Jacek Kaspryzk is superbly recorded in London's Henry Wood Hall, rivalling the famous Telarc version in its weight and brilliance and its ripe treatment of the orchestral brass: the sound is rather less sumptuous in the spectacular closing *Great Gate of Kiev* but is more sharply focused. The performance, led onwards convincingly by the various Promenades, is strongly characterized, with the nostalgia inherent in *The old castle* carried on to the portrait of the ox-wagon, which yet does not lose its juggernaut power. There is much orchestral virtuosity, exhilarating in *The Tuileries* and in the bustle of the *Limoges market place*, and the brass has subtlety as well as bite in *The hut on fowl's legs*, yet produces a powerful sonority for the *Catacombs* sequence. The spacious closing apotheosis has plenty of weight and power. Rimsky-Korsakov's glowing scoring of the beautiful *Khovanshchina Prelude* is also made radiant by fine orchestral playing, though perhaps ideally Kaspryzk could have moved the music on a little more firmly. He finds plenty of gusto, however, in the bizarre wildness of Mussorgsky's original draft for *Night on the bare mountain* (without the serene closing section).

(i) *Night on the bare mountain* (arr. Rimsky-Korsakov); *Pictures at an exhibition* (arr. Funtek). (ii) *Songs and dances of death* (arr. Aho).
*** BIS Dig. CD 325 [id.]. (i) Finnish RSO, (i) Leif Segerstam; (ii) Järvi, with Talvela.

This fascinating CD offers an orchestration by Leo Funtek, made in the same year as Ravel's (1922); it is especially fascinating for the way the different uses of colour change the character of some of Victor Hartman's paintings: the use of a cor anglais in *The old castle*, for instance, or the soft-grained wind scoring which makes the portrait of *Samuel Goldenberg and Schmuyle* more sympathetic, if also blander. The performances by the Finnish Radio Orchestra under Leif Segerstam both of this and of the familiar Rimsky *Night on the bare mountain* are spontaneously presented and very well recorded. The extra item is no less valuable: an intense, darkly Russian account of the *Songs and dances of death* from Martti Talvela with the orchestral accompaniment plangently scored by Kalevi Aho.

Pictures at an exhibition (orch. Ravel).
(B) *** DG 429 162-2 [id.]. BPO, Karajan – STRAVINSKY: *Rite of spring.****
(B) *** RCA Dig. VD 87729 [7729-2-RV]. Dallas SO, Mata – RAVEL: *La valse* etc.***
(*) DG Dig. 413 588-2 [id.]. BPO, Karajan – RAVEL: *Boléro; Rapsodie espagnole.**
*** DG Dig. 423 901-2 [id.]. LSO, Abbado – STRAVINSKY: *Petrushka.****
*** EMI Dig. CDC7 47099-2 [id.]. Phd. O, Muti – STRAVINSKY: *Firebird suite.****
(M) *** Decca Dig. 417 754-2 [id.]. Chicago SO, Solti – BARTÓK: *Concerto for orchestra.****
(M) *** DG 415 844-2 [id.]. Chicago SO, Giulini – RAVEL: *Ma mère l'Oye; Rapsodie espagnole.****

(*) Chan. Dig. CHAN 8849 [id.]. Chicago SO, Järvi – SCRIABIN: *Poème de l'extase*.(*)

(*) Ph. Dig. 426 437-2 [id.]. LPO, Gergiev – TCHAIKOVSKY: *Francesca da Rimini*.(*)

Karajan's 1966 record stands out. It is undoubtedly a great performance, tingling with electricity from the opening Promenade to the spaciously conceived finale, *The Great Gate of Kiev*, which has real splendour. Other high points are the ominously powerful climax of *Bydlo* as the Polish ox-wagon lumbers into view very weightily, and the venomously pungent bite of the brass – expansively recorded – in the sinister *Catacombs* sequence, which is given a bizarre majesty. Detail is consistently pointed with the greatest imagination, not only in the lighter moments, but for instance in *The hut on fowl's legs*, where the tuba articulation is sharp and rhythmically buoyant. Throughout, the glorious orchestral playing, and especially the brass sonorities, ensnare the ear; even when Karajan is relatively restrained, as in the nostalgic melancholy of *The old castle*, the underlying tension remains. The remastered analogue recording still sounds pretty marvellous; it is little short of demonstration standard and is very well balanced, apart from an odd spot of bass resonance.

The sumptuousness of the Dallas sound, its amplitude and richness of colouring are ideal for Mussorgsky's *Pictures*. Mata's performance has one or two idiosyncrasies – he treats *Tuileries* rather freely, with a little *tenuto* on the opening phrase – but the obvious affection justifies his indulgence. The orchestral playing is consistently responsive and the brass come into their own (after opening the work resonantly) in the *Catacombs* and the brilliant *Hut on fowl's legs*. The closing *Great Gate of Kiev* is splendidly paced, and Mata's eloquent preparation of the closing pages, measured yet purposeful, is underpinned by the gloriously full digital recording, as fine as any in the catalogue.

Karajan's 1987 record is also very impressive, very similar in many ways to the earlier account, again with superb Berlin Philharmonic playing and the weight of the climaxes contrasting with the wit of the *Tuileries* and the exhilaration of *The Market at Limoges*. Where the newest version is a shade disappointing, compared with the old, is in the finale. Here Karajan is as spacious as before but, from the beginning, is a little slack when he fails to detach the massive chords, and the culminating apotheosis falls a little short in physical excitement. The digital sound is very wide-ranging, even if the sense of presence is less keen than in his 1960s recording.

Abbado takes a straighter, more direct view of Mussorgsky's fanciful series of pictures than usual, less consciously expressive, relying above all on instrumental virtuosity and the dazzling tonal contrasts of Ravel's orchestration. He is helped by the translucent and naturally balanced digital recording; indeed, the sound is first class, making great impact at climaxes yet also extremely refined, as in the delicate portrayal of the unhatched chicks. Abbado's speeds tend to be extreme, with both this and *Tuileries* taken very fast and light, while *Bydlo* and *The Great Gate of Kiev* are slow and weighty. This performance is now recoupled with an equally distinguished and spectacularly recorded account of *Petrushka*.

Muti's reading, given the excellence of its recorded sound, more than holds its own, although the balance is forward and perhaps not all listeners will respond to the brass timbres at the opening. The lower strings in *Samuel Goldenberg and Schmuyle* have extraordinary body and presence, and *Baba-Yaga* has an unsurpassed virtuosity and attack, as well as being of a high standard as a recording. The coupling is no less thrilling. This can be recommended even to those readers who have not always responded to later records from this conductor.

Solti's performance is fiercely brilliant rather than atmospheric or evocative. He treats Ravel's orchestration as a virtuoso challenge, and with larger-than-life digital recording it undoubtedly has demonstration qualities, and the transparency of texture, given the forward balance, provides quite startling clarity. Now very generously recoupled at mid-price with Solti's outstanding version of Bartók's *Concerto for orchestra*, it makes a formidable bargain.

Giulini's 1976 Chicago recording had always been among the front runners. He is generally more relaxed and often more wayward than Karajan, but this is still a splendid performance and the finale generates more tension than Karajan's most recent, digital version, though it is not as overpowering as the earlier, analogue recording. What makes the Giulini very attractive is the generous Ravel couplings which show him at his finest.

For Järvi's Chicago version the Chandos engineers return to Orchestral Hall, where the famous Reiner recording was made, more than three decades earlier. The Chicago trumpets open the piece with bold articulation and there is a firm response from the lower strings, which later bring a comparably rich sonority to the Jewish dialogue (although here the trumpet player is rather literal). The earlier pictures are effective without being really distinctive, although in *Tuileries* there is an attractive degree of metrical freedom. Järvi is at his most evocative in *The Hut on fowl's legs*, pungently rhythmic and with a sinister grotesquerie in the contrasting middle section. The brass certainly sounds magnificent in the spectacular closing pages of *The Great Gate of Kiev*, with the tam-tam bringing an added frisson of excitement; only the bass drum doesn't resonate as the ear might expect. Just before the closing peroration Järvi has quickened the pace, but then he pulls back for a grand final statement, given a glorious amplitude by the hall acoustics.

The LPO trumpets are essentially relaxed at the opening of Gergiev's reading, the sound sonorous rather than strongly articulated; but later the brass bring a snarling pungency to the sinister portrait of *Gnomus*. The characterization brings comparable contrasts throughout, with *The Old castle* gently evocative and a comparably resigned melancholy in the tuba solo of *Bydlo*. There is plenty of bustle in the *Limoges market place*, and great charm in the evocation of the *Tuileries*, while *The Hut on fowl's legs* is dramatically forceful. The close of the piece is strong and boldly grandiloquent, with the recording expanding impressively; but in a crowded field this version doesn't stand out.

(i) *Pictures at an exhibition* (orch. Ravel); (ii) *Pictures at an exhibition* (original piano version).
(M) *** Ph. 420 708-2 [id.]. Rotterdam PO, Edo de Waart; (ii) Misha Dichter.

Those seeking the natural pairing of the original piano version of Mussorgsky's *Pictures* with Ravel's orchestration will hardly better this mid-priced Philips CD. The Rotterdam orchestra play splendidly throughout, and Edo de Waart's performance has a natural, spontaneous momentum, with each picture aptly characterized and the final climax admirably paced and excitingly powerful. The 1975 recording is rather resonant, but detail comes through well enough. The weight in the bass emphasizes the strong contribution from the drums in *Baba-Yaga* and the closing section. The surprise here, however, is Misha Dichter's outstanding performance of the original piano score, among the finest on record. Each separate picture is telling and he perceptively varies the mood of each Promenade to provide an appropriate link. After a riveting account of *Baba-Yaga*, demonstrating great keyboard flair, the closing *Great Gate of Kiev* is overwhelmingly powerful. Dichter often seems a reticent pianist in the recording studio, but not here – Mussorgsky's spectacular finale has seldom sounded more gripping; and the piano's sonority is splendidly caught by the Philips recording.

Pictures at an exhibition: (i) orch. Ashkenazy; (ii) original piano version.
**(*) Decca Dig. 414 386-2 [id.]. (i) Philh. O, Ashkenazy; (ii) Ashkenazy (piano).

A side-by-side comparison between Mussorgsky's original piano score and the orchestral version is always instructive; but here the orchestration is Ashkenazy's own, which he made after finding dissatisfaction with Ravel's transcription. His arrangement concentrates on a broader orchestral tapestry – helped by the richness of the Kingsway Hall acoustic – and he does not attempt to match Ravel in subtlety of detail or precision of effect. The character of the pictures is not always very individual, although Ashkenazy finds plenty of Russian feeling in the music itself. The recording is brightly opulent rather than glittering. Ashkenazy's digital solo account of the *Pictures* does not differ in its essentials from his earlier, analogue recording. It is distinguished by spontaneity and poetic feeling but lacks something of the extrovert flair with which pianists like Richter or Berman can make one forget all about the orchestra. The piano focus is clear with fine presence, if not quite natural in balance.

Pictures at an exhibition (original piano version).
(M) (***) Ph. mono 420 774-2 [id.]. Sviatoslav Richter (with *Recital*(***))
(*) EMI Dig. CDC7 49262-2 [id.]. Cécile Ousset – RAVEL: *Gaspard.**
(*) Nimbus Dig. NI 5187 [id.]. Ronald Smith – BALAKIREV: *Sonata*; SCRIABIN: *Sonata No. 9.*(*)
(*) RCA Dig. RD 85931. Barry Douglas – LISZT: *Dante sonata* etc.(*)

The Philips reissue offers Sviatoslav Richter's 1958 Sofia recital. The mono recording has been remastered using this company's NoNoise digital background reduction system, but alas this cannot suppress the audience's bronchial afflictions, and a troublesome tape roar also remains. Nevertheless, the magnetism of Richter's playing comes over and his enormously wide dynamic range brings a riveting final climax, even if, with the piano backwardly positioned, some of the pianissimo playing is not too cleanly focused. Besides the Mussorgsky, the recital offers a generous programme, including Schubert *Impromptus* and a *Moment musical*, the Chopin *Étude in E*, Op. 10, No. 3, two Liszt *Valses oubliées* and excerpts from the *Transcendental studies*, all readily demonstrating the Richter magic in spite of indifferent sound.

The French pianist Cécile Ousset gives a commanding account of the *Pictures*, and she is extremely well recorded. Her playing is ever responsive to the changing moods and colour of the music and is convincingly spontaneous. Hers is a big-boned and powerful reading and she is very impressive in the closing section. However, Misha Dichter's analogue version, coupled with the orchestral *Pictures* – see above – is even finer, even if the Philips recording has not quite the presence of the EMI CD.

Ronald Smith's account of the *Pictures* is impressive and often imaginative, though the acoustic of Wyastone Leys is not wholly sympathetic. Not a transcendental performance, perhaps, nor one likely to displace Richter or Horowitz, but a very fine one all the same.

Barry Douglas plays with fine impetus and much vividness of characterization, though he can also be thoughtful, as in *The old castle*. RCA's piano timbre is fully filled out, as well as being 'present', and allows Douglas plenty of weight in the finale. This is powerfully conceived but not electrifying in the manner of a Richter.

The Complete songs.
⊛ (M) (***) EMI mono CHS7 63025-2 (3). Boris Christoff, Alexandre Labinsky, Gerald Moore, French R. & TV O, Georges Tzipine.

Boris Christoff originally recorded these songs in 1958; they then appeared in a four-LP mono set with a handsome book, generously illustrated with plates and music examples, giving the texts in Russian, French, Italian and English, and copious notes on each of the

63 songs. Naturally the documentation cannot be so extensive in the CD format – but, on the other hand, one has the infinitely greater ease of access that the new technology offers. The Mussorgsky songs constitute a complete world in themselves, and they cast a strong spell: their range is enormous and their insight into the human condition deep. Christoff was at the height of his vocal powers when he made the set with Alexandre Labinsky, his accompanist in most of the songs, and its return to circulation cannot be too warmly welcomed. This was the first complete survey, and it still remains the only one.

OPERA

Boris Godunov (original version; complete).
**(*) Ph. 412 281-2 (3) [id.]. Vedernikov, Arkhipova, Koroleva, Shkolnikova, Sokolov, USSR TV and R. Ch. and SO, Fedoseyev.
** Erato/WEA Dig. 2292 45418-2 (3) [id.]. Raimondi, Vishnevskaya, Gedda, Plishka, Washington Ch. Arts Soc. & Ontario Soc., Nat. SO, Rostropovich.

Fedoseyev conducts a powerful performance of Mussorgsky's masterpiece in its original scoring, using the composer's own 1872 revision, as near an 'authentic' solution as one can get with a problematic score that never reached definitive form. The earthy strength of the music comes over superbly. Ideally for records, one needs a firmer singer than the mature Vedernikov as Boris, but this is a searingly intense performance which rises commandingly to the big dramatic moments, conveying the Tsar's neurotic tensions chillingly. Arkhipova is also too mature for the role of Marina, but equally her musical imagination is most convincing. The rest of the cast is a mixed bag, with some magnificent Russian basses but a few disappointing contributions, as from the whining tenor, Vladislav Piavko, as the Pretender. Though the recording was made over a period of years, the sound is full and satisfying, if not always ideally balanced.

Recorded live in Washington, Rostropovich's version of Mussorgsky's original score, unadulterated by Rimsky-Korsakov, is no more successful at providing the ideal version than its two predecessors. It sounds very much what it was: a well-drilled concert performance with some fine choral singing, making this great pageant-opera into an oratorio, and the choice of Ruggero Raimondi to sing the name-part is consistent with this. It is good to have so warmly Italianate a voice bringing out the lyricism of lines more often barked or grunted. Boris's death scene is refined and beautiful, wonderfully controlled in hushed intensity, but the Tsar's inner agony is missing. Even the grand Coronation scene lacks weight, though that may have something to do with the composer's own orchestration being much more subdued than Rimsky's. Taking the role of Marina, as she did in the Karajan set of twenty years earlier, is Rostropovich's wife, Galina Vishnevskaya, giving a masterly demonstration of how to eke out a voice no longer young; it remains a most vivid portrait. Of the others, Paul Plishka is a disappointingly unsteady Pimen, but Romuald Tesarowicz is a first-rate Varlaam and Vyacheslav Polozov as Dimitri is far less strained than his counterpart on the Philips Russian set. Kenneth Riegel is an excellent Shuisky and the veteran, Nicolai Gedda, makes a touching Simpleton. The sound is full and faithful, far more consistent than the Philips analogue set, but capturing the atmosphere of a concert hall, not an opera.

Boris Godunov (arr. Rimsky-Korsakov).
*** Decca 411 862-2 (3) [id.]. Ghiaurov, Vishnevskaya, Spiess, Maslennikov, Talvela, V. Boys' Ch., Sofia R. Ch., V. State Op. Ch., VPO, Karajan.
** EMI CDS7 47993-8 (3) [Ang. CDCC 47993]. Christoff, Lear, Lanigen, Ouzousov, Alexieva, Sofia Nat. Op. Ch., Paris Conservatoire O, Cluytens.

If Ghiaurov in the title-role lacks some of the dramatic intensity of Christoff on the EMI set, Karajan's superbly controlled Decca version, technically outstanding, comes far nearer than previous recordings to conveying the rugged greatness of Mussorgsky's masterpiece. Only the Coronation scene lacks something of the weight and momentum one ideally wants. Vishnevskaya is far less appealing than the lovely non-Slavonic Marina of Evelyn Lear on EMI, but overall this Decca set has much more to offer than its EMI alternative.

The EMI set is chiefly valuable for the resonant contribution of Boris Christoff, for a generation unmatched in the role of Boris. Here he takes the part not only of the Tsar but of Pimen and Varlaam too, relishing the contrast of those other, highly characterful bass roles. It is good that this glorious voice is so vividly caught on CD, but sadly the overall performance under Cluytens does not quite add up to the sum of its parts, as the earlier mono recording with Christoff did.

Sorochinsky Fair (opera) complete.
*** Olympia OCD 114 A/B (2) [id.]. Matorin, Mishchevsky, Voinarovsky, Klenov, Temichev, Chernikh, Zhakharenko, Stanislavsky Theatre Ch. & O, Esipov – BORODIN: *Petite suite.****

This first complete recording of Mussorgsky's unfinished opera uses the edition, prepared by Vissarion Shebalin, in the colourful and vigorous performance by the company of the Stanislavsky Theatre in Moscow. Though the most striking passage, *St John's Night* at the beginning of Act III, is the original choral version of what Rimsky-Korsakov turned into *Night on the bare mountain*, this is not at all a grim piece but a folk-comedy that is full of fun, as charming and attractive as any, its score spiced with characteristically individual Mussorgskian progressions. In this version, the piece ends joyfully with an exhilarating choral version of the famous *Gopak*, here brilliantly sung. The full-ranging Melodiya recording has fine immediacy and presence, though the impression is very much one of a studio rather than of the theatre, with voices sharply focused. That does not diminish the impressiveness of a company who have performed the piece on stage, with the bass, Vladimir Matorin, outstanding as the village elder, Tcherevik. An English translation of the libretto is included in the booklet.

Nicolai, Carl Otto (1810–49)

The merry wives of Windsor (Die lustigen Weiber von Windsor): complete.
(M) **(*) EMI CMS7 69348-2 (2) [Ang. CDMB 69348]. Frick, Gutstein, Engel, Wunderlich, Lenz, Hoppe, Putz, Litz, Mathis, Ch. & O of Bav. State Op., Heger.

The great glory of this fine EMI set is the darkly menacing Falstaff of Gottlob Frick in magnificent voice, even if he sounds baleful rather than comic. It is good too to have the young Fritz Wunderlich as Fenton opposite the Anna Reich of Edith Mathis. Though the others hardly match this standard – Ruth-Margret Putz is rather shrill as Frau Fluth – they all give enjoyable performances, helped by the production, which conveys the feeling of artists who have experienced performing the piece on stage. The effectiveness of the comic timing is owed in great measure to the conducting of the veteran, Robert Heger. From the CD transfer one could hardly tell the age of the recording, with the voices particularly well caught.

Nielsen, Carl (1865–1931)

Clarinet concerto, Op. 57.
*** Chan. Dig. CHAN 8618 [id.]. Janet Hilton, SNO, Bamert – COPLAND: *Concerto*; LUTOSLAWSKI: *Dance preludes.****

Janet Hilton gives a highly sympathetic account of the Nielsen *Concerto*, but it is characteristically soft-centred and mellower in its response to the work's more disturbing emotional undercurrents than Ole Schill's splendid account on BIS – see below. However, that is coupled with the *Sinfonia espansiva*; those who prefer a record offering other clarinet works will not be disappointed by Janet Hilton's alternative programme. The Chandos recording is first class.

(i) *Clarinet concerto, Op. 57;* (ii) *Symphony No. 3 (Sinfonia espansiva). Maskarade overture.*
*** BIS Dig. CD 321 [id.]. (i) Ole Schill; (ii) Pia Raanoja, Knut Skram; Gothenburg SO, Myung-Whun Chung.

The *Third Symphony* (*Sinfonia espansiva*) is an exhilarating and life-enhancing work; it radiates a confidence and well-being soon to be shattered by the First World War. The young Korean conductor secures playing of great fire and enthusiasm from the Gothenburgers, and has vision and breadth – and at the same time no want of momentum. Two soloists singing a wordless vocalise are called for in the pastoral slow movement, and their contribution is admirable. Myung-Whun Chung also gives a high-spirited and sparkling account of the *Overture* to Nielsen's comic opera, *Maskarade*. As for the *Concerto*, Ole Schill brings brilliance and insight to what is one of the most disturbing and masterly of all modern concertos. The BIS recording is marvellous, even by the high standards of this small company.

(i) *Flute concerto; Symphony No. 1; Rhapsody overture (An imaginary journey to the Faroe Islands).*
*** BIS Dig. CD 454 [id.]. (i) Patrick Gallois; Gothenburg SO, Myung-Whun Chung.

Myung-Whun Chung and the Gothenburg orchestra have an instinctive feeling for Nielsen. They play with commendable enthusiasm and warmth, and Chung shapes the *Symphony* with great sensitivity to detail and a convincing sense of the whole. The *Rhapsody overture: An imaginary journey to the Faroe Islands* is not the composer at his strongest (Nielsen called it 'nothing more than a piece of jobbery on my part'), but it has a highly imaginative opening. The *Flute concerto* is given a marvellous performance by Patrick Gallois, quite the most strongly characterized since the pioneering account by its dedicatee, Holger Gilbert-Jespersen (Decca). Gallois makes a glorious sound and eschews excessive vibrato.

Violin concerto, Op. 33.
⊛ *** CBS Dig. MK 44548 [id.]. Cho-Liang Lin, Swedish RSO, Salonen – SIBELIUS: *Violin concerto.**** ⊛

Cho-Liang Lin brings as much authority to Nielsen's *Concerto* as he does to the Sibelius and he handles the numerous technical hurdles with breathtaking assurance. The simple eloquence with which he tackles the closing pages of the introduction is most affecting. His perfect intonation and tonal purity excite admiration, but so should his command of the architecture of this piece; there is a strong sense of line from beginning to end.

Salonen is supportive here and gets good playing from the Swedish Radio Symphony Orchestra.

(i) *Violin concerto, Op. 33; Symphony No. 5, Op. 50.*
*** BIS Dig. CD 370 [id.]. (i) Dong-Suk Kang, Gothenburg SO, Myung-Whun Chung.

Dong-Suk Kang is more than equal to the technical demands of this concerto and is fully attuned to the Nordic sensibility. He brings tenderness and refinement of feeling to the searching slow movement and great panache and virtuosity to the rest. Who would have forecast at the time of the Nielsen renaissance in the 1950s that, thirty years on, two Korean artists would have produced such completely idiomatic results? The *Fifth Symphony* is hardly less successful and is certainly the best-recorded version now available. Myung-Whun Chung has a natural feeling for Nielsen's language and the first movement has real breadth.

Symphonies Nos. 1–6.
**(*) Unicorn UK CD 2000/2 [id.]. Gomez, Rayner-Cook (in No. 3), LSO, Schmidt.

These are performances that are ablaze with life, warmth and a sense of discovery. The recordings were always a bit rough, but the digital remastering represents an undoubted (though not spectacular) improvement, for the texture still remains coarse in tuttis. However, the brass is less garish and better integrated into the overall aural picture. In No. 2 and the last three symphonies Ole Schmidt is a sure and penetrating guide. Whatever quibbles one might have (Schmidt may be a little too fervent in the slow movement of the *First Symphony* for some tastes), his readings have an authentic ring to them, for he has real feeling for this glorious music. They obviously represent good value.

Symphonies Nos. 1 in G min., Op. 7; 4 (Inextinguishable), Op. 29.
**(*) RCA Dig. RD 87701 [7701-2-RC]. Royal Danish O, Berglund.

Nielsen's *First Symphony* is so fresh and characterful, so full of lyricism, that one can see why he always retained a strong affection for it. Berglund's is a thoroughly straightforward account and he holds the architecture of the symphony together in a convincing way. Phrases are affectionately turned but never pulled out of shape. Berglund's account of the *Fourth Symphony*, a work born from a totally different environment, is more problematic. Generally speaking he is close to the tempo markings but, in his desire to convey the sense of drama and urgency, he tends to be impatient to move things on. The second movement is beautifully done, and there is much to admire in the third, but the finale really does move, and at such speed that one feels rushed off one's feet, particularly in the closing paragraphs. The orchestral playing is spirited enough, but even the Royal Danish Orchestra sound a little out of breath at the end! Very well-balanced sound.

Symphonies Nos. 1 in G min., Op. 7; 6 (Sinfonia Semplice).
*** Decca Dig. 425 607-2 [id.]. San Francisco SO, Blomstedt.

Blomstedt's record of the *First Symphony* is the best to have appeared for many years. It has vitality and freshness, and there is a good feel for Nielsen's natural lyricism. He inspires the San Francisco orchestra to excellent effect and the lean, well-focused string sound and songful wind playing are lovely. In the *Sixth Symphony* he has no want of intensity, though a broader tempo would have helped generate greater atmosphere in the first movement. Ole Schmidt (Unicorn) is more penetrating here. However, the performance is undeniably impressive and enjoys the advantage of far better recording.

Indeed the quality is altogether first class, with good perspective and detail: the acoustic has more clarity than warmth, but the sound has plenty of space and front-to-back depth.

Symphony No. 2 (The Four Temperaments); Aladdin suite, Op. 34.
*** BIS CD 247 [id.]. Gothenburg SO, Myung-Whun Chung.

Symphony No. 2 (The Four Temperaments), Op. 16; (i) Aladdin suite, Op. 34; Pan and Syrinx, Op. 49.
**(*) CBS Dig. MK 44934 [id.]. Swedish RSO, (i) and Ch., Esa-Pekka Salonen.

Myung-Whun Chung has a real feeling for this repertoire and his account of the *Second Symphony* is very fine. The Gothenburg Symphony Orchestra proves an enthusiastic and responsive body of players; Chung, who studied with Sixten Ehrling at the Juilliard, does not put a foot wrong. The recording is impressive, too, and can be recommended with enthusiasm.

On CBS, by far the best Nielsen record in this series so far. Esa-Pekka Salonen is brisk and bristling in the choleric first movement (perhaps just a shade too brisk) but he captures the mood excellently. In the third movement there is genuine breadth and nobility. He inspires the Swedish Radio Orchestra to very responsive and spirited results both here and in the *Aladdin* music. Unfortunately the recording does not offer such transparent detail and presence as the BIS version from the Gothenburg orchestra under Myung-Whun Chung, who also includes *Aladdin*. Salonen's account of *Pan and Syrinx* is evocative and may sway some collectors in his favour, though it is not superior either as a recording or as a performance to the Rattle version (EMI). All the same, this is a fine issue and can be recommended.

Symphony No. 4 (Inextinguishable), Op. 29.
*** DG Dig. 413 313-2 [id.]. BPO, Karajan.

By far the best performance of Nielsen's *Fourth* ever recorded comes from Karajan. The orchestral playing is altogether incomparable and there is both vision and majesty in the reading. The strings play with passionate intensity at the opening of the third movement, and there is a thrilling sense of commitment throughout. The wind playing sounds a little over-civilized – but what exquisitely blended, subtle playing this is. It is excellently recorded, too. However, this seems ungenerous measure alongside Blomstedt's Decca coupling.

Symphonies Nos. 4 (Inextinguishable); 5, Op. 50.
*** Decca Dig. 421 524-2 [id.]. San Francisco SO, Blomstedt.

The opening of Blomstedt's *Fourth* has splendid fire: this must sound as if galaxies are forming. Blomstedt conveys Nielsen's image about the soaring string-lines in the slow movement ('like the eagle riding on the wind') most strikingly – more so than Karajan. The finale is exhilarating, yet held on a firm rein. The *Fifth Symphony*, too, is impressive: it starts perfectly and is almost as icy in atmosphere as those pioneering recordings of the 1950s. The desolate clarinet peroration also comes off most successfully. The recording balance could not be improved upon: the woodwind are decently recessed, there is an almost ideal relationship between the various orchestral sections and a thoroughly realistic overall perspective.

Symphony No. 5; En Sagadrøm, Op. 39.
(M) **(*) Unicorn UKCD 2023 [id.]. New Philh. O, Horenstein.

Horenstein gives a dignified but slightly detached account of the *Symphony*. His feeling for the overall structure of the work is strong, but poetic detail is not savoured to the same extent as in Tuxen's old set. The string-playing of the New Philharmonia is extremely fine, though they do not have quite the lyrical fervour of the new Blomstedt San Francisco version. Horenstein's record has the advantage of an interesting fill-up, the tone-poem *En Sagadrøm*, which is poetically done and beautifully recorded. In the *Symphony* the balance gives far too great a prominence to the percussion and not quite enough weight to the strings. In that respect the new Decca digital recording is infinitely better judged and, of course, although at full price, this offers also the *Fourth Symphony*.

CHAMBER MUSIC

Canto serioso; Fantasias for oboe and piano, Op. 2; The Mother (incidental music), *Op. 41; Serenata in vano; Wind quintet, Op. 43.*
**(*) Chan. CHAN 8680 [id.]. Athena Ens.

This reissue gathers together Nielsen's output for wind instruments in chamber form, with everything played expertly and sympathetically. The recording is balanced very close; nevertheless much of this repertoire is not otherwise available, and this is a valuable disc.

Complete piano music: *Chaconne; Dream of merry Christmas; Festival prelude; Humoresque bagatelles; Piano music for young and old; Piece in C; 3 Pieces; 5 Pieces; Suite; Symphonic suite; Theme and variations.*
** Hyp. Dig. CDA 66231/2 [id.]. Mina Miller.

Nielsen's keyboard music is the most important to come from Scandinavia since Grieg – and works like the *Suite*, Op. 45, and the *Three Pieces*, Op. 59, go a good deal deeper than the Norwegian master. Mina Miller knows what this music is about and, for the most part, conveys her intentions capably. Put alongside a great pianist, her playing is lacking real keyboard authority but, even if she is not impeccable pianistically, she makes up for it in terms of musical understanding.

VOCAL MUSIC

(i) *Springtime in Fünen. Aladdin suite, Op. 34.*
*** Unicorn Dig. DKPCD 9054 [id.]. (i) Ingo Nielsen, Von Binzer, Klint, Lille Muko University Ch., St Klemens Children's Ch.; Odense SO, Veto.

Springtime in Fünen is one of those enchanting pieces to which everyone responds when they hear it, yet which is hardly ever performed outside Denmark. The engaging *Aladdin* orchestral suite is well played by the Odense orchestra. This disc is a little short on playing time – but no matter, it is well worth its cost and will give many hours of delight.

Maskarade (opera; complete).
**(*) Unicorn DKPCD 9073/4 [id.]. Hansen, Plesner, Landy, Johansen, Serensen, Bastian, Brodersen, Haugland, Danish R. Ch. & SO, Frandsen.

Maskarade is new to the gramophone: only the overture and a handful of interludes have been recorded before. The plot is straightforward and simple, and to recount it would do scant justice to the charm and interest of the opera. *Maskarade* is a buoyant, high-spirited score full of strophic songs and choruses, making considerable use of dance and dance-rhythms, and having the unmistakable lightness of the *buffo* opera. It is excellently proportioned: no Act outstays its welcome, one is always left wanting more, and the scoring is light and transparent. The performance here is delightful, distinguished by generally good singing and alert orchestral support. The disappointment is the CD transfer which, in trying to clarify textures, has in fact made the focus less clean.

Novák, Vítézslav (1870–1949)

Slovak suite, Op. 32; South Bohemian suite, Op. 64.
**(*) Ṣup. Dig. SUP 001743 [id.]. Czech PO, Vajnar.

What a heavenly score the *Slovak suite* is! *Two in love*, its fourth movement – if more widely propagated – could well become as popular as any piece of music you care to think of. The *South Bohemian suite* is not quite so consistently inventive, but František Vajnar secures highly sympathetic performances of both works from the great Czech orchestra and is quite touching in the *Epilogue* to Op. 64, *Good health, my native land*. The *Slovak suite* is well balanced and has plenty of ambience; in the *South Bohemian suite* the violins have a 'digital' brightness above the stave and are lacking in body. But this is still a disc to try, if for Op. 32 alone.

Ockeghem, Johannes (c. 1410–97)

Requiem (Missa pro defunctis).
*** DG 415 293-2 [id.]. Pro Cantione Antiqua, Hamburger Bläserkreis für alte Musik, Turner – JOSQUIN DES PRÉS: *Missa – L'homme armé.****

The DG Archiv version of the *Missa pro defunctis* was originally recorded in Hamburg in 1973. The Pro Cantione Antiqua was unmatched at this period (with such artists as James Bowman and Paul Esswood as their counter-tenors, this is hardly surprising), and Bruno Turner's direction has both scholarly rectitude and musical eloquence to commend it. For most of the *Requiem*, the lines are at times doubled by the excellent Hamburger Bläserkreis für alte Musik. It is an eminently welcome addition to the compact disc catalogue.

Offenbach, Jacques (1819–80)

Cello concerto.
*** RCA RD 71003. Ofra Harnoy, Cincinnati SO, Kunzel – SAINT-SAENS: *Concerto No. 1*; TCHAIKOVSKY: *Rococo variations.****

Offenbach's *Cello concerto* is a delight, with all the effervescence and tunefulness of his operettas. It is played with verve and brio and a full range of colour by Ofra Harnoy and did much to establish her reputation, while the accompaniment from Kunzel and his Cincinnati players is just as lively and sympathetic. Excellent recording throughout.

Gaîté parisienne (ballet, arr. Rosenthal): complete.
(B) *** RCA VD 87734 [7734-2-RV]. Boston Pops O, Fiedler – KHACHATURIAN: *Gayaneh suite.****
*** Ph. Dig. 411 039-2 [id.]. Pittsburgh SO, Previn.
(*) Decca Dig. 411 708-2. Montreal SO, Dutoit – GOUNOD: *Faust: ballet music.*(*)
(M) ** EMI CDM7 63136-2 [id.]. Monte Carlo Op. O, Rosenthal – WALDTEUFEL: *Waltzes.****

(i) *Gaîté parisienne (ballet, arr. Rosenthal): complete;* (ii) *Overture: Orpheus in the Underworld.*

(B) (**) Decca 421 173-2 [id.]. (i) New Philh. O, Munch; (ii) LPO, Stanley Black – IBERT: *Divertissement*(*(**)).

A sparkling, racy – and indeed irresistible – account from Fiedler of the Rosenthal ballet, concocted from some of Offenbach's most memorable ideas. The orchestra are kept exhilaratingly on their toes throughout and are obviously enjoying themselves, not least in the elegantly tuneful waltzes and in the closing *Barcarolle*, which Fiedler prepares beautifully. The percussion, including bass drum in the *Can can*, adds an appropriate condiment, and the warm resonance of the Boston hall adds bloom yet doesn't blunt or coarsen the brilliance.

Previn realizes that tempi can remain relaxed, and the music's natural high spirits will still bubble to the surface. The orchestral playing is both spirited and elegant, with Previn obviously relishing the score's delightful detail. This is mirrored by the Philips digital sound-balance, which has substance as well as atmosphere and brilliance. Perhaps the tuba thumping away in the bass is a shade too present, but it increases one's desire to smile through this engagingly happy music. However, without a coupling this disc is ungenerous.

Dutoit has the advantage of sound that is brighter and has rather more projection than Previn's Philips disc, though the acoustic is resonant and detail is no clearer. But the recording is undoubtedly out of Decca's top drawer. He opens the music racily and there are many admirable touches, yet as the ballet proceeds there is a hint of blandness in the lyrical moments, and the *Barcarolle* is somewhat disappointing. The Decca record has the advantage of including also the *Faust* ballet music, warmly and elegantly played.

Maurice Rosenthal's absolutely complete version from the mid-1970s has now been restored to the catologue, together with the documentation giving the sources for all the music in the score, the snag being that the identification is not always accurate. The performance, though often idiomatically persuasive, has not the verve and glamour of those by Fiedler and Karajan. The sound, however, has been greatly improved, with the original excess resonance considerably tempered.

Munch's version has no lack of energy and is brilliantly played, but the closely balanced recording now sounds rather aggressive in its remastered form. There is nothing wrong with the *Overture*.

Gaîté parisienne (ballet, arr. Rosenthal): extended excerpts.
(B) *** DG 429 163-2 [id.]. BPO, Karajan – CHOPIN: *Les Sylphides**** ⍟; DELIBES: *Coppélia*: Suite excerpts.***
(M) **(*) EMI CDM7 69041-2 [id.]. Philh. O, Karajan – BORODIN: *Polovtsian dances*; GOUNOD: *Faust ballet*; PONCHIELLI: *Dance of the hours*.***

Karajan's selection is generous. On the DG disc, only Nos. 3–5, 7 and 19–21 are omitted. The remastering of the 1972 recording is highly successful. Textures have been lightened to advantage and the effect is to increase the raciness of the music-making, while its polish and sparkle are even more striking. On the whole this is preferable to the 1958 Philharmonia version. The London orchestra also plays with great brilliance, the players obviously revelling in the bravura, but the remastered sound is a little dry. However, the couplings are highly attractive.

Overtures: *Barbe-Bleue; La Belle Hélène; Les deux Aveugles; La Fille du tambour major; La Grande-Duchesse de Gérolstein; Orphée aux enfers (Orpheus in the Underworld); La Périchole; La Vie parisienne.*
*** Ph. Dig. 411 476-2 [id.]. Philh. O, Marriner.

Overtures: *La Belle Hélène; Bluebeard; La Grande-Duchesse de Gérolstein; Orpheus in the Underworld; Vert-vert. Barcarolle* from *Contes d'Hoffmann*.
**(*) DG Dig. 400 044-2 [id.]. BPO, Karajan.

Overtures: *La belle Hélène; La Grande-Duchesse de Gérolstein; Orpheus in the Underworld*.
(M) **(*) EMI CDM7 63024-2 [id.]. CBSO, Frémaux – MASSENET: *Le Cid ballet* etc.***

Other hands besides Offenbach's helped to shape his overtures. Most are on a pot-pourri basis, but the tunes and scoring are so engagingly witty as to confound criticism. *La Belle Hélène* is well constructed by Haensch, and the delightful waltz tune is given a reprise before the end. Karajan's performances racily evoke the theatre pit, and the brilliance is extrovert almost to the point of fierceness. The Berlin playing is very polished and, with so much to entice the ear, this cannot fail to be entertaining; however, the compact disc emphasizes the dryness of the orchestral sound; the effect is rather clinical, with the strings lacking bloom.

Where Karajan in his Offenbach collection tends to use inflated versions of these operetta overtures by hands other than the composer's, Marriner prefers something nearer the original scale, even though *Orpheus, Belle Hélène* and *La Périchole* are not originals. This music suits the sprightly, rhythmic style of Marriner splendidly, and the Philharmonia responds with polished playing, very well recorded. The CD sparkles attractively.

Frémaux's Offenbach overtures were recorded in 1972 in the Festival Hall, Corby. The acoustic gives a robustly large-scale effect, and some might feel that the spectacular resonance adds an element of coarseness. But the performances are infectiously spirited and stylish, with the lyrical element warmly presented, not least in the lovely waltz-tune in *La Belle Hélène*. Rumbustiousness is certainly not out of place in Offenbach, and that comes well to the fore in *Orpheus in the Underworld*. It is a pity that *La vie parisienne*, originally included, has been omitted (it is, however, included in a separate collection – see Concerts, below) but the playing time here is still generous at nearly 73 minutes overall.

Overtures: *Maître Péronilla; M. et Mme Denis; Orpheus in the Underworld* (1874 version) (with *Pastoral ballet*); *Die Rheinnixen; Le roi carotte; Le voyage dans la lune* (with *Snowflakes ballet*).
*** Ph. Dig. 422 057-2 [id.]. Philh. O, Almeida.

Offenbach's *Barcarolle* makes its début in *Die Rheinnixen*, written seventeen years before *Tales of Hoffmann*, and another item from that opera is anticipated in *Le voyage dans la lune*. The *Snowflakes ballet* from the latter source is a charmer, and the ballet from *Orpheus in the Underworld* is hardly less delectable. The other surprise is the *Orpheus overture*, not the one we know – which, it must be admitted, is a better-crafted piece – but a more extended work in pot-pourri style, with some good tunes. All the other overtures included here combine characteristic frothiness with melodic elegance. Antonio de Almeida directs them all with a plentiful supply of high spirits and much gracefulness in the lyrical numbers, and the Philharmonia's response is both polished and infectious. Excellent recording too.

Le Papillon (ballet): complete.
(M) *** Decca 425 450-2 [id.]. LSO, Richard Bonynge – TCHAIKOVSKY: Nutcracker.**(*)

Le Papillon is Offenbach's only full-length ballet and it dates from 1860. If the tunes do not come quite as thick and fast as in Rosenthal's confected *Gaîté parisienne*, the quality of invention is high and the music sparkles from beginning to end. In such a sympathic performance, vividly recorded (in 1974) it cannot fail to give pleasure. Highly recommended to all lovers of ballet and Offenbach.

OPERA

La Belle Hélène (complete).
*** EMI CDS7 47157-8 (2) [Ang. CDCB 47156]. Norman, Alliot-Lugaz, Aler, Burles, Bacquier, Lafont, Capitole Toulouse Ch. and O, Plasson.

The casting of Jessye Norman in the name-part of *La Belle Hélène* may seem too heavyweight, but the way that the great soprano can lighten her magisterial voice with all the flexibility and sparkle the music calls for is a constant delight, and her magnetism is irresistible. John Aler, another American opera-singer who readily translates to the style of French operetta, makes a heady-toned Paris, coping superbly with the high tessitura in the famous Judgement couplets and elsewhere. The rest of the cast is strong too, not forgetting Colette Alliot-Lugaz as Oreste. Michel Plasson here produces fizzing results, with excellent ensemble from the choir and orchestra of the Capitole. Excellent recording, less reverberant than in some other discs from this source, although it is very important not to set the volume level too high or the spoken dialogue will seem unrealistically close.

Les brigands (complete).
**(*) EMI Dig. CDS7 49830-2 (2). Raphanel, Alliot-Lugaz, Raffalli, Trempont, Le Roux, Lyon Opera Ch. & O, Gardiner.

This is one of Gardiner's delectably frothy French offerings, in which the Lyon Opera Company re-enacts in the studio a stage presentation. *Les brigands* has a Gilbertian plot about brigands and their unlikely association with the court of Mantua, with the carabinieri behaving very like the police in *The Pirates of Penzance*. It may not be quite such a charmer as its predecessors in Gardiner's Lyon sequence, Chabrier's *L'étoile* (EMI) and Messager's *Fortunio* (Erato), and the tone of the principal soprano, Ghislaine Raphanel, is rather edgily French, but the rest of the team is splendid. Outstanding as ever is the characterful mezzo, Colette Alliot-Lugaz, in another of her breeches roles. Warm, well-balanced recording.

Les Contes d'Hoffmann (The Tales of Hoffmann): complete.
⊛ *** Decca 417 363-2 (2) [id.]. Sutherland, Domingo, Tourangeau, Bacquier, R. Suisse Romande and Lausanne Pro Arte Ch., SRO, Bonynge.
*** EMI CDS7 49641-2 (3) [Ang. CDCC 49641]. Shicoff, Murray, Serra, Plowright, Norman, Van Dam, Tear, Ch. & O of Nat. Op., Brussels, Cambreling.
** DG Dig. 427 682-2 (2). Domingo, Gruberová, Eder, Schmidt, Bacquier, Morris, Diaz, Ludwig, Rydl, Fr. R. Ch., Fr. Nat. O, Ozawa.

On Decca the sparkling CD transfer makes Offenbach's inspired score sound even more refreshing, with the immediacy of the action even more striking, and the acoustics of Victoria Hall, Geneva, adding fullness and warmth to the vividness. Joan Sutherland gives a virtuoso performance in four heroine roles, not only as Olympia, Giulietta and Antonia but also as Stella in the Epilogue, which in this version is given greater weight by the inclusion of the ensemble previously inserted into the Venice scene as a septet, a magnificent climax. Bonynge opts for spoken dialogue, and puts the Antonia scene last, as being the more substantial. His direction is unfailingly sympathetic, while Sutherland is impressive in each role, notably as the doll Olympia and in the pathos of the Antonia scene. As Giulietta she hardly sounds like a *femme fatale*, but still produces beautiful singing. Domingo gives one of his finest performances on record, and so does Gabriel Bacquier. It is a memorable set, in every way, much more than the sum of its parts.

Sylvain Cambreling with his Belgian forces has opted for the complete text of Fritz Oeser's edition, putting together all the material which Offenbach failed to sort out before his untimely death. A good deal of that comes in the Venice scene which, as it usually stands, seems too short to sustain the sequence's dramatic weight. Here the expansions are the more attractive and the more weighty when the commanding Giulietta is Jessye Norman. Rosalind Plowright brings extra – and satisfying – power to the Antonia episode without losing charm, and Luciana Serra, as at Covent Garden, is a bright, clear Olympia. Neil Shicoff as Hoffmann makes a confident Domingo-substitute, and Ann Murray is as ever everyone's favourite Nicklausse, though the voice regularly loses focus above the stave. José van Dam sings with splendid firmness in the four villainous roles, if too nobly; while Robert Tear is excellent in the four character-tenor roles. There is no less than 214 minutes of music on the three discs. The recording is pleasantly atmospheric, if not as cleanly focused as the Decca.

In his autobiography Placido Domingo devotes special attention in whole chapters to two operatic roles only, not just Otello – which one would expect – but Hoffmann in Offenbach's opera. He finds something of Beethoven and of the mocked hunchback, Rigoletto, in the character; and DG's set conducted by Ozawa justifies itself first and last by the intelligence and strength of Domingo's performance. Yet there is no denying that the voice is no longer as fresh as it was when he recorded the same role for Decca opposite Dame Joan Sutherland, a version which, unlike this, was consistently well cast. Edita Gruberová is one of the few sopranos today who could attempt to match Sutherland's feat of singing all the strongly contrasted heroine roles. Yet even in the coloratura role of the doll, Olympia, which should suit her perfectly, she gives a limited portrait; though she sings strongly and intelligently in the other two roles, the timbre of the voice is no help. The others in the cast are disappointing, even Gabriel Bacquier, who sang all four villain roles for Decca, but here is limited to Coppélius. Though he is still characterful, he is far less firm of voice. Ozawa, generally sympathetic, makes an intelligent choice of the options now presented by the very full Oeser edition, but Bonynge's choice in the Decca set works even better, based on the text originally suggested by Tom Hammond and used by English National Opera, among others. Full, warm recording, on the reverberant side for this work.

Les Contes d'Hoffmann: highlights.
(M) *** Decca 421 866-2 [id.] (from above complete set, cond. Bonynge).
(M) ** EMI CDM7 63448-2 [id.]. Schwarzkopf, De los Angeles, D'Angelo, Gedda, Ghuiselev, London, Blanc, Duclos Ch., Paris Conservatoire O, Cluytens.

The Decca highlights disc is one of the finest compilations of its kind from any opera. With over an hour of music, it offers a superbly managed distillation of nearly all the finest items and is edited most skilfully.

With such a starry cast-list it is disappointing that the EMI set was not more successful. In particular André Cluytens proved quite the wrong conductor for this sparkling music. Fortunately, most of the best moments are included in the highlights disc, including the Schwarzkopf/Gedda duet from the Venetian scene, not to mention the famous *Barcarolle* and the brilliant *Septet*. De los Angeles (sadly out of voice) and George London (unpleasantly gruff-toned) provide the vocal disappointments.

Orphée aux enfers (Orpheus in the Underworld; 1874 version).
*** EMI CDS7 49647-2 (2). Sénéchal, Mesplé, Rhodes Burles, Berbié, Petits Chanteurs à la Croix Potencée, Toulouse Capitole Ch. and O, Plasson.

Plasson recorded his fizzing performance – the first complete set in French for thirty years – in time for the Offenbach centenary. He used the far fuller four-act text of 1874 instead of the two-act version of 1858, so adding such delectable rarities as the sparkling *Rondo* of Mercury and the *Policemen's chorus.* Mady Mesplé as usual has her shrill moments, but the rest of the cast is excellent, and Plasson's pacing of the score is exemplary. The recording is brightly atmospheric and the leavening of music with spoken dialogue just enough.

Orpheus in the Underworld: highlights of English National Opera production (in English).
**(*) That's Entertainment Dig. CDTER 1134. Kale, Watson, Angas, Squires, Bottone, Pope, Belcourt, Styx, Burgess, E. Nat. Op. Ch. & O, Mark Elder.

The sparkling English National Opera production starts not with the conventional overture but with a prelude, over which the invented character, Public Opinion, delivers a moral in unmistakable imitation of the Prime Minister. From then on the whole entertainment depends a lot for its fun on the racy new adaptation and translation by Snoo Wilson and the ENO producer, David Pountney. Offenbach devotees should be warned: there is little of Parisian elegance in this version and plenty of good knockabout British fun, brilliantly conveyed by the whole company. For this kind of performance one really needs a video, when even Bonaventura Bottone's hilariously camp portrait of a prancing Mercury is not nearly so much fun when simply heard and not seen. Bright, vivid recording to match the performance.

La Périchole (complete).
**(*) EMI Dig. CDS7 47362-8 (2) [Ang. CDCB 47361]. Berganza, Carreras, Bacquier, Sénéchal, Trempont, Delange, Toulouse Capitole Ch. and O, Plasson.

A good modern recording of this delightful piece was badly needed, and in many ways this fills the bill, for though the sound (as usual in Toulouse) is over-reverberant, the CD remastering has sharpened the impact and ensemble work is excellent, with diction surprisingly clear against full orchestral sound. The incidental roles are superbly taken, but it is odd that Spaniards were chosen for the two principal roles. José Carreras uses his always lovely tenor to fine effect but is often unidiomatic, while Teresa Berganza – who should have made the central character into a vibrant figure, as Régine Crespin used to – is surprisingly heavy and unsparkling.

Orff, Carl (1895–1982)

Carmina Burana.
*** Ph. Dig. 422 363-2 [id.]. Gruberová, Aler, Hampson, Shinyukai Ch., Knaben des Staats & Berlin Cathedral Ch., BPO, Ozawa.
*** EMI CDC7 47411-2 [id.]. Armstrong, English, Allen, St Clement Danes Grammar School Boys' Ch., LSO Ch., LSO, Previn.
(M) *** DG 423 886-2 [id.]. Janowitz, Stolze, Fischer-Dieskau, Schöneberger Boys' Ch., Berlin German Op. Ch. & O, Jochum.
(M) *** Decca 417 714-2 [id.]. Burrows, Devos, Shirley-Quirk, Brighton Fest. Ch., Southend Boys' Ch., RPO, Dorati.

(B) *** Pickwick Dig. PCD 855 [MCA MCAD 25964]. Walmsley-Clark, Graham-Hall, Maxwell, Southend Boys' Ch., LSO Ch., LSO, Hickox.

(M) *** RCA GD 86533 [RCA 6533-2-RG]. Mandac, Kolk, Milnes, New England Conservatory Ch. & Children's Ch., Boston SO, Ozawa.

**(*) RCA Dig. RCD 14550 [RCD1 4550]. Hendricks, Aler, Hagegård, St Paul's Cathedral Boys' Ch., LSO Ch. & O, Mata.

(BB) ** Naxos Dig. 8.550196 [id.]. Jenisová, Dolezal, Kusnjer, Slovak Philharmonic Ch., Czech RSO (Bratislava), Gunzenhauser.

** EMI CDC7 47100-2 [id.]. Augér, Summers, Van Kesteren, Southend Boys' Ch., Philh. Ch. & O, Muti.

Ozawa's new digital recording of Orff's justly popular cantata carries all the freshness and spontaneity of his earlier successful Boston version – still a good mid-priced competitor on RCA – yet is even finer in its overall control, matching exuberance with added breadth. The *Cours d'amours* sequence is the highlight of his reading, with the soprano, Edita Gruberová, highly seductive; and Thomas Hampson's contribution is impressive too, if not quite as imaginative as Thomas Allen's for Previn. The wide dynamic range of the recording makes a spectacular effect throughout, not least in Hampson's *Abbot's song*, where there is a cataclysmic comment from the percussion, but also in the subtly engaging interplay between chorus and semi-chorus in the rural dance-music. Ozawa's trebles are more chaste than Previn's but bring much charm to their *Amor volat undique* (*Love flies everywhere*). Ozawa's infectious rubato in *Oh, oh, oh, I am bursting out all over*, interchanged between male and female chorus towards the end of the work, is wonderfully bright and zestful, with the contrast of the big *Ave formosissima* climax which follows made to sound spaciously grand. Taken overall, this Philips version readily goes to the top of the list alongside Previn, who has a more robust fervour (his trebles deliciously earthy) which fits the hedonistic medieval poems so perfectly. It will probably be first choice for those seeking a digital version.

Previn's 1975 analogue version, vividly recorded, is even more sharply detailed than Ozawa's. It is strong on humour and rhythmic point. The chorus sings vigorously, the men often using an aptly rough tone; and the resilience of Previn's rhythms, finely sprung, brings out a strain not just of geniality but of real wit. This is a performance which swaggers along and makes you smile. The recording captures the antiphonal effects impressively, better even in the orchestra than in the chorus. Among the soloists, Thomas Allen's contribution is one of the glories of the music-making, and in their lesser roles the soprano and tenor are equally stylish. The digital remastering is wholly successful: the choral bite is enhanced, yet the recording retains its full amplitude. The background hiss has been minimized and is only really apparent in the quieter vocal solos in the latter part of the work. A triumphant success.

The CD reissue of Jochum's 1968 recording of *Carmina Burana* is also outstandingly successful. Originally the choral pianissimos lacked immediacy, but now this effect is all but banished and the underlying tension of the quiet singing is very apparent. The recording has a wide dynamic range and when the music blazes it has real splendour and excitement. Fischer-Dieskau's singing is refined but not too much so, and his first solo, *Omnia Sol temperat*, and later *Dies, nox et omnia* are both very beautiful, with the kind of tonal shading that a great Lieder singer can bring; he is suitably gruff in the Abbot's song – so much so that for the moment the voice is unrecognizable. Gerhard Stolze too is very stylish in his falsetto *Song of the roasted swan*. The soprano, Gundula Janowitz, finds a quiet dignity for her contribution and this is finely done. The closing scene is moulded by Jochum with wonderful control, most compelling in its restrained power.

Dorati's 1976 version was originally recorded in Decca's hi-fi-conscious Phase 4 system, and the balance is rather close; but the Kingsway Hall ambience helps to spread the sound and the dynamic range is surprisingly wide. It is a characteristically vibrant account; Dorati's speeds are generally brisk and the effect is exhilaratingly good-humoured, with the conductor showing a fine rhythmic sense. The characterization of the soloists is less sensuous than in some versions, but John Shirley-Quirk's account of the *Abbot's song* is very dramatic, with the chorus joining in enthusiastically. Because of Dorati's thrust, this is more consistently gripping than Hickox's otherwise first-rate Pickwick account and, if there are moments when the overall ensemble is less than perfectly polished, the feeling of a live performance is engendered throughout, even though this is a studio recording. No translation is provided and the synopsis is cursory, which earns Decca a black mark.

Richard Hickox, on his brilliantly recorded Pickwick CD, like Previn uses the combined LSO forces, but adds the Southend Boys' Choir who make sure we know they understand all about sexual abandon – their '*Oh, oh, oh, I am bursting out all over*' is a joy. Penelope Walmsley-Clark, too, makes a rapturous contribution: her account of the girl in the red dress is equally delectable. The other soloists are good but less individual. The performance takes a little while to warm up (Hickox's tempi tend to be more relaxed than Dorati's), but the chorus rises marvellously to climaxes and is resplendent in the *Ave formosissima*, while the sharp articulation of consonants when the singers hiss out the words of *O Fortuna* in the closing section is also a highlight. The vivid orchestral detail revealed by the bright digital sound adds an extra dimension. The documentation provides a vernacular narrative for each band but no translation.

On RCA Ozawa's strong, incisive performance brings out the bold simplicity of the score with tingling immediacy, rather than dwelling on its subtlety of colour. The soloists, too, are all characterful, especially Sherrill Milnes. The tenor, Stanley Kolk, sounds a little constrained with his *Roast Swan*, but otherwise the solo singing is always responsive. Overall this is a highly effective account and the blaze of inspiration of Orff's masterpiece comes over to the listener in the most direct way, when the sound is so well projected, yet without any unnatural edge. The snag is the absence of a translation or of any kind of documentation beyond a listing of the twenty-five cued sections.

Mata's alternative full-priced RCA version is most convincing as an overall performance and it also offers first-class sound. It is a volatile reading, not as metrical in its rhythms as Previn's version, and the tension is not as consistently high. The choristers of St Paul's Cathedral sing with perfect purity but are perhaps not boyish enough, though the soloists are first rate. *Pianissimo* choral detail is not sharply defined, but in all other respects the sound is superb, the background silence adding a great deal.

The Slovak Chorus sing Orff's hedonistic cantata with lusty, Slavonic enthusiasm, and it is a pity that some of the score's quieter passages are somewhat lacking in bite because of the resonance. But the Tavern scene comes across especially vividly and the culminating *Ave formosissima* and *O Fortuna* are splendidly expansive. The soprano, Eva Jenisová, is the most impressive of the three soloists, who generally do not match their Western rivals. This is an enjoyable performance, with exciting moments, but Jochum's DG version is worth the extra outlay.

The digital remastering of Muti's 1980 analogue recording is disappointing. The fullest weight of bass is much less evident on the CD, although the orchestra is affected less than the chorus and soloists, who seem to have lost a degree of immediacy. Muti's is a reading which underlines the dramatic contrasts, both of dynamic and of tempo, so the nagging ostinatos as a rule are pressed on at breakneck speed; the result, if at times a little breathless, is always exhilarating. The soloists are first rate; the Philharmonia Chorus is not quite at its most polished, but the Southend Boys are outstandingly fine and, overall, this account is as full of excitement as any available.

Pachelbel, Johann (1653-1706)

Canon in D.
*** Virgin Dig. VCy 791081-2 [id.]. LCO, Warren-Green – ALBINONI: *Adagio;* VIVALDI: *Four seasons.****
(M) *** Decca 417 712-2 [id.]. Stuttgart CO, Münchinger – ALBINONI: *Adagio****; VIVALDI: *Four Seasons.***(*)

Canon and Gigue.
(*) Ph. Dig. 416 386-2 [id.]. ASMF, Marriner – MOZART: *Serenade: Eine kleine Nachtmusik*; L. MOZART: *Toy symphony.*(*)

A lovely performance of the *Canon* from Christopher Warren-Green and his excellent London Chamber Orchestra, with a delicately graceful opening and a gorgeous climax and with radiant violins. With splendid sound this is as fine as any version in the catalogue, unless you seek an authentic performance on a much smaller scale, when you should turn to Andrew Parrott and his Taverner Players (EMI CDC7 69853-2 – see our Concerts section, below). Among budget-price recordings, Münchinger's is as good as any; Marriner turns the two pieces into a ternary structure by oddly repeating the *Canon* again after the *Gigue*, a tiny concession to the short measure on his CD. Warm, well-balanced recording.

Paganini, Niccolò (1782-1840)

Violin concertos Nos. 1 in D, Op. 6; 2 in B min. (La Campanella), Op. 7.
*** DG 415 278-2 [id.]. Accardo, LPO, Dutoit.

Violin concertos Nos. 3 in E; 4 in D min.
*** DG 423 270-2 [id.]. Accardo, LPO, Dutoit.

Violin concerto No. 5 in A min.; Maestosa sonata sentimentale; La primavera in A.
*** DG 423 578-2 [id.]. Accardo, LPO, Dutoit.

Violin concerto No. 6 in E min., Op. posth.; Sonata with variations on a theme by Joseph Weigl; Le streghe (Variations on a theme of Süssmayr), Op. 8; Variations of Non più mesta from Rossini's La Cenerentola.
*** DG 423 717-2 [id.]. Accardo, LPO, Dutoit.

Paganini's concertos can too often seem sensationally boring, or the scratchy upper tessitura can assault rather than titillate the ear. But Accardo, like Perlman, has a formidable technique, marvellously true intonation and impeccably good taste and style; it is a blend of all these that makes these performances so satisfying and enjoyable. He is accompanied beautifully by the LPO under Dutoit and the sound is very good, although the transfers seem to have generated some excess of bass resonance. Paganini's *E minor Concerto* is a relatively recent discovery and almost certainly predates the *First Concerto*. Of the additional couplings *La primavera* is a late work; ideas from Haydn turn up in the *Maestosa sonata sentimentale*. The *Variations* provide plenty of violinistic fireworks. The *Witches' dance* (*Le streghe*) is not as diabolical as the composer may have intended, but its difficulties are spectacular, including one ludicrous passage involving left-hand pizzicati. The solo playing here is stunning.

Violin concerto No. 1 in D, Op. 60.
⊛ *** EMI CDC7 47101-2 [id.]. Itzhak Perlman, RPO, Foster – SARASATE: *Carmen fantasy*.*** ⊛
*** Ph. Dig. 422 332-2 [id.]. Mullova, ASMF, Marriner – VIEUXTEMPS: *Concerto No. 5*.***
(*) Ph. Dig. 420 943-2 [id.]. Midori, LSO, Slatkin – TCHAIKOVSKY: *Sérénade mélancolique* etc.*
(*) Ara. Dig. Z 6597 [id.]. Mark Kaplan, LSO, Miller – WIENIAWSKI: *Violin concerto No. 2*.(*)

Itzhak Perlman demonstrates a fabulously clean and assured technique. His execution of the fiendish upper harmonics in which Paganini delighted is almost uniquely smooth and, with the help of the EMI engineers who have placed the microphones exactly right, he produces a gleamingly rich tone, free from all scratchiness. The orchestra is splendidly recorded and balanced too, and Lawrence Foster matches the soloist's warmth with an alive and buoyant orchestral accompaniment. Provided one does not feel strongly about Perlman's traditional cuts, there has been no better record of the *D major Concerto*.

Viktoria Mullova's account of the *D major Concerto* is second to none: her virtuosity dazzles and holds one enthralled, and she has the advantage of a bright, modern recording. She copes with all the technical hurdles effortlessly and with great brilliance, and the Academy of St Martin-in-the-Fields under Sir Neville Marriner give sterling support. Splendidly present and vivid recording (though the acoustic is bass-resonant and the timpani is somewhat prominent).

Midori is fully equal to the histrionics of Paganini's *D major Concerto*; moreover she produces a warm, singing tone for the lyrical melodies. There is effortless bravura in the finale and, with Slatkin providing admirable support, there is little to cavil at here, save perhaps that her use of the uncut version of Emile Sauret's cadenza for the first movement is perhaps too much of a good thing. Perlman's decision to shorten the cadenza is entirely justified.

Mark Kaplan is a prodigious virtuoso too, and Mitch Miller an agreeably mercurial accompanist. No one could fail to enjoy the volatile first movement in their company, and the finale positively scintillates, after a simple and eloquent slow movement. The slight snag is that the very close microphones give the soloist a glitteringly bright upper range, very realistic but in no way flattering.

Violin concertos Nos. 1 in D, Op. 6; 2 in B min. (La Campanella), Op. 7.
(B) *** DG 429 524-2 [id.]. Shmuel Ashkenasi, VSO, Esser.

At bargain price Ashkenasi's coupling of the two favourite Paganini *Concertos* is formidable value. He surmounts all the many technical difficulties in an easy, confident style and, especially in the infectious *La Campanella* finale of No. 2, shows how completely he is in control. The microphone is close and he clearly has a smaller sound than Perlman, Mullova or Accardo, but his timbre is sweet and the high tessitura and harmonics are always cleanly focused. The orchestra is set back in a warm but not too resonant acoustic and the accompaniments are nicely made. The digital remastering is smooth and does not make the upper range edgy. There is less conscious flamboyance than with his main rivals, but this playing is easy to enjoy.

Violin concerto No. 3 in F.
(B) *** Ph. 422 976-2 [id.]. Szeryng, LSO, Gibson – LALO: *Symphonie espagnole*.**(*)

Paganini kept for himself the prerogative of performing his own violin concertos and took strict security precautions to ensure that the orchestral parts could not fall into other hands. The Paganini family finally released the *Third Concerto* into the public domain at the beginning of the 1970s and, with a good deal of publicity, Henryk Szeryng gave its first posthumous performance and made the present record. The performance is dazzling technically, with assured bravura in the spectacular pyrotechnics which the composer kept in reserve for the extended finale. The first movement is even longer – the opening ritornello lasts for four minutes – but, apart from an engaging *Allegro marziale* theme, is not of great musical interest. The best movement is undoubtedly the central *Cantabile spianato*, a brief aria-like piece, its theme engagingly introduced over pizzicatos in the orchestra. Not a lost masterpiece, then, but uncommonly well played here, and given a vivid CD transfer.

Violin and guitar: *Cantabile; Centone di sonate No. 1 in A; Sonata in E min., Op. 3/6; Sonata concertata in A.*
*** CBS MK 34508 [id.]. Itzhak Perlman, John Williams – GIULIANI: *Sonata.****

Superb playing from both Perlman and John Williams ensures the listener's attention throughout this slight but very agreeable music. With a good balance, the music-making here gives much pleasure, and this is a generally distinguished disc.

24 Caprices, Op. 1.
*** EMI CDC7 47171-2 [id.]. Itzhak Perlman.
(M) *** DG 429 714-2 [id.]. Salvatore Accardo.
**(*) DG Dig. 415 043-2 [id.]. Shlomo Mintz.

These two dozen *Caprices* probably still represent the peak of violinistic difficulty, even though more than a century has gone by since their composition. Perlman's playing is flawless, wonderfully assured and polished, yet not lacking imaginative feeling. Moreover, such is the magnetism of his playing that the ear is led on spontaneously from one variation to the next. The 1972 recording is extremely natural and the transfer to CD brings a very convincing illusion of realism, without the microphones seeming too near the violin.

Accardo succeeds in making Paganini's most routine phrases sound like the noblest of utterances and he invests these *Caprices* with an eloquence far beyond the sheer display they offer. There are no technical obstacles and, both in breadth of tone and in grandeur of conception, he is peerless. Accardo observes all the repeats, whereas Perlman observes some, but not others. Accardo can be recommended alongside his famous colleague and, with an equally good CD transfer, also has a price advantage.

With Shlomo Mintz there are many breathtaking things to admire – indeed there are times when one could wish that he was not in quite so much of a hurry; but there is plenty of colour and life in the set as a whole. He is recorded with admirable clarity and definition in good digital sound, though the overall effect is not as warm as Perlman's EMI record, which is, if anything, more dazzling.

Paine, John Knowles (1839–1906)

Symphony No. 1 in C min., Op. 23; Overture, As you like it.
*** New World Dig. NW 374-2 [id.]. NYPO, Mehta.

Paine's symphonies were milestones in the history of American music, and it is good that at last Mehta's fine recordings of both of them will allow them to be appreciated more widely. No. 1, first heard in 1876, ambitiously follows up the success of the earlier, ambitious *Mass in D*. Here too Paine consciously inspires echoes of Beethoven, with little feeling of dilution – though, after his dramatic C minor opening, he tends to relax into sweeter, more Mendelssohnian manners for his second subject and the three other movements. What is striking is the bold assurance, and the overture – a concert work inspired by Shakespeare, not designed for the theatre – is also full of charming ideas. Mehta is a persuasive advocate, helped by committed playing and full, well-balanced recording.

Symphony No. 2 in A, Op. 34.
*** New World Dig. NW 350-2 [id.]. NYPO, Mehta.

Written four years after the *First Symphony*, this magnificent work is both more ambitious and more memorable than its predecessor. Though for generations Paine was dismissed by Americans as merely an academic who echoed Mendelssohn and Schumann, this work far more remarkably anticipates Mahler. The movingly expressive third-movement *Adagio* starts with the clearest foretaste of the *Adagietto* of Mahler's *Fifth Symphony* and, later, ideas richly follow that up in writing of great warmth. The idiom is notably more chromatic than that of the *First*, and the other movements – introduced by an extended slow introduction – bring an element of fantasy, as in the fragmented rhythms and textures of the scherzo. It is a work that should certainly be revived in the concert hall, and not just in America. Mehta draws a strongly committed performance from the New York Philharmonic, and the sound is first rate.

Paisiello, Giovanni (1740–1816)

Il barbiere di Siviglia (opera): complete.
*** Hung. Dig. HCD 12525/6-2 [id.]. Laki, Gulyás, Gregor, Gati, Sólyom-Nagy, Hungarian State O, Adám Fischer.

Paisiello's *Barbiere di Siviglia* may for many generations have been remembered only as the forerunner of Rossini's, but latterly stage revivals have helped to explain why, before Rossini, the opera was such a success. The musical inspiration may too often be short-winded, but the invention is full of vitality, and that is reflected captivatingly in this Hungarian performance under Adám Fischer. Jószef Gregor is a vividly characterful Bartolo, a role more important here than in Rossini, while István Gati is a strong, robust Figaro. Krisztina Laki is a brilliant Rosina and Dénes Gulyás a clean, stylish Almaviva, relishing his Don Alonso imitation. Full, vivid recording.

Palestrina, Giovanni Pierluigi di (1525–94)

Hodie Beata Virgo; Litaniae de Beata Virgine Maria in 8 parts; Magnificat in 8 parts (Primi Toni); Senex puerum portabat; Stabat Mater.
(M) *** Decca 421 147-2 [id.]. King's College Ch., Willcocks – ALLEGRI: *Miserere.****

This is an exceptionally fine collection dating from the mid-1960s. The flowing melodic lines and serene beauty which are the unique features of Palestrina's music are apparent throughout this programme, and there is no question about the dedication and accomplishment of the performance. Argo's recording is no less successful, sounding radiantly fresh and clear.

Missa Assumpta est Maria; Missa Sicut lilium.
*** Gimmell Dig. CDGIM 020 [id.]. Tallis Scholars, Peter Phillips.

After the *Missa Papae Marcelli*, the *Missa Assumpta est Maria* is probably the best-known of Palestrina's works, though it is of late provenance and was not published in his lifetime. Its companion on this CD is based on the motet, *Sicut lilium inter spinas* ('Like a lily among thorns') which comes from his First Book of Motets (1569). As is their practice, the Tallis Scholars record the Masses together with the motets on which they are based, and sing with their customary beauty of sound and well-blended tone. They are superbly recorded in the Church of St Peter and St Paul in Salle, Norfolk.

Missa Benedicta es (with Plainchant).
*** Gimell CDGIM 001 [id.]. Tallis Scholars, Peter Phillips (with JOSQUIN: Motet: *Benedicta es*).

This recording, made in the resonant acoustic of the Chapel of Merton College, Oxford, comes from 1981 and has been digitally remastered with considerable success. Palestrina's mass is coupled with the Josquin motet, *Benedicta es*, on which it is based, together with the plainchant sequence on which both drew. It would seem that this mass was the immediate predecessor of the *Missa Papae Marcelli* and was composed while the music of *Benedictus es* was still at the forefront of the composer's mind. The Tallis Scholars and Peter Phillips sing with impressive conviction and produce an expressive, excellently blended sound.

Missa brevis; Missa Nasce la gioia mia (with PRIMAVERA: Madrigal: *Nasce la gioia mia*).
*** Gimell Dig. CDGIM 008 [id.]. Tallis Scholars, Phillips.

Like the *Missa Nigra sum*, the *Missa Nasce la gioia mia* was included in the 1590 Book of Masses and is a parody Mass, modelled on the madrigal, *Nasce la gioia mia* by Giovan Leonardo Primavera, who was born in Naples in 1540. The Tallis Scholars and Peter Phillips give expressive, finely shaped accounts of both the *Missa brevis* and the Mass, which they preface by the madrigal itself. A most rewarding disc: no grumbles about the recording.

Missa Nigra sum (with motets on *Nigra sum* by LHERITIER; VICTORIA; DE SILVA).
*** Gimell Dig. CDGIM 003 [id.]. Tallis Scholars, Phillips.

Palestrina's *Missa Nigra sum* is another parody Mass, based on a motet by Jean Lheritier and follows its model quite closely. Its text comes from the Song of Solomon ('I am black but comely, O ye daughters of Jerusalem: therefore has the king loved me, and brought me into his chambers'). On this record, the plainchant and the Lheritier motet precede Palestrina's Mass, plus motets by Victoria and Andreas de Silva, a relatively little-known Flemish singer and composer who served in the Papal chapel and later in Mantua. The music is inspiring and the performances exemplary. This is a most beautiful record and the acoustic of Merton College, Oxford, is ideal.

Missa Papae Marcelli.
*** Gimell CDGIM 339 [id.]. Tallis Scholars, Phillips – ALLEGRI: *Miserere*; MUNDY: *Vox Patris caelestis.****

Missa Papae Marcelli; Stabat Mater.
(B) *** Pickwick PCD 863 [MCA MCAD 25191]. Pro Cantione Antiqua, Mark Brown.

Missa Papae Marcelli; Tu es Petrus (motet).
*** DG 415 517-2 [id.]. Westminster Abbey Ch., Preston (with ANERIO: *Venite ad me omnes*; NANINO: *Haec dies*; GIOVANNELLI: *Jubilate Deo****) – ALLEGRI: *Miserere.***(*)

The account by the Westminster Abbey Choristers transcends any Anglican stylistic limitations. It is a performance of great fervour, married to fine discipline, rich in timbre, eloquent both at climaxes and at moments of serenity. The singing is equally fine in the hardly less distinctive motet, *Tu es Petrus*. Felice Anerio, Giovanni Bernardino Nanino and Ruggiero Giovannelli represent the following generation of composers in straddling the end of the sixteenth and beginning of the seventeenth century. Their contributions to this collection are well worth having, particularly Giovannelli's *Jubilate Deo* which makes a splendid closing item. The digital recording is first class. All Saints', Tooting, was used, rather than the Abbey, and the acoustics are both intimate and expansive, while detail is beautifully caught.

Pro Cantione Antiqua on the budget-priced Pickwick label bring not only an outstandingly fresh and alert account of Palestrina's most celebrated Mass but one which involves keen scholarship. With an all-male choir and no boy-trebles, and with one voice per part, this chamber choir yet sings with power and resonance against a warm and helpful church acoustic. The authentic atmosphere is enhanced by the inclusion of relevant plainchants between the sections of the Mass. The magnificent eight-part *Stabat Mater* also receives a powerful performance, warm and resonant.

The Gimell alternative is an analogue recording from 1980, but the digital remastering produces extremely fine sound, firm, richly blended and not lacking internal detail. The acoustics of Merton College, Oxford, are admirably suited to this music; the singing has eloquence, purity of tone, and a simplicity of line which is consistently well controlled.

Motet and Mass – Tu es Petrus.
(*) Argo Dig. 410 149-2 [id.]. King's College Ch., Cleobury – VICTORIA: *O quam gloriosum.*(*)

Fine performances, positively shaped, with plenty of tonal weight and a natural flowing eloquence, with the blend secure; the King's style adapts well to this repertoire without achieving an entirely Latin feeling.

Panufnik, Andrzej (born 1914)

(i) *Autumn music; Heroic overture;* (i, ii) *Nocturne;* (iii) *Sinfonia rustica;* (i) *Tragic overture.*
(M) *** Unicorn UKCD 2016 [id.]. (i) LSO, Horenstein; (ii) with Anthony Peebles; (iii) Monte Carlo Op. O, composer.

The two overtures are early pieces and of relatively little musical interest, but the *Autumn music* and *Nocturne* are worth hearing. They may strike some listeners as musically uneventful, but the opening of the *Nocturne* is really very beautiful indeed and there is a refined feeling for texture and a sensitive imagination at work here. The *Sinfonia rustica* is the most individual of the works recorded here and has plenty of character, though its invention is less symphonic, more in the style of a sinfonietta. The performance under the composer is thoroughly committed. The LSO under Horenstein play with conviction and they are very well recorded.

(i) *Concerto festivo;* (ii) *Concerto for timpani, percussion and strings; Katyń epitaph; Landscape;* (iii) *Sinfonia sacra (Symphony No. 3).*
(M) *** Unicorn UKCD 2020. (i) LSO, (ii) with Goedicke & Frye; (ii) Monte Carlo Op. O, composer.

Andrzej Panufnik's music is invariably approachable, finely crafted and fastidiously scored. His feeling for atmosphere and colour obviously comes from a refined sensibility.

This splendidly recorded collection might be a good place for collectors to begin exploring his output. The *Concertos* are both readily communicative and the *Katyh epitaph* is powerfully eloquent. Oddly enough, at one point it is reminiscent of the atmosphere of the last pages of Britten's *A Time there was*, though the Panufnik was written some years earlier. The best of this music is deeply felt. The *Sinfonia sacra* serves to demonstrate the spectacular quality of the vividly remastered recording, with its compelling introductory 'colloquy' for four trumpets, followed by a withdrawn section for strings alone. In the finale of the second part of the work, *Hymn* (which is not separately cued as suggested by the contents details) the trumpets close the piece resplendently.

Symphony No. 8 (Sinfonia votiva).
*** Hyp. Dig. CDA 66050 [id.]. Boston SO, Ozawa – SESSIONS: *Concerto for orchestra.****

The *Sinfonia votiva* has a strongly formalistic structure, but its message is primarily emotional. It marks the response of the composer not only to the miraculous icon of the Black Madonna in his native Poland but also to the tragedy of contemporary events in that country. It begins with an extended slow movement, which is then daringly balanced against a briskly contrasted finale. Though Panufnik's melodic writing may as a rule reflect the formalism of his thought rather than tapping a vein of natural lyricism, the result is most impressive, particularly in a performance of such sharp clarity and definition as Ozawa's, very well recorded.

Parker, Horatio (1863–1910)

A Northern ballad.
*** New World Dig. NWCD 339 [id.]. Albany SO, Julius Hegyi – CHADWICK: *Symphony No. 2.****

Horatio Parker's *Northern ballad* of 1899 was an enormous success in its day and calls both Dvořák and Grieg to mind. It has remained unpublished and unperformed in recent times. Excellent playing and recording. An interesting disc.

Parry, Hubert (1848–1918)

An English suite; Lady Radnor's suite.
*** EMI Dig. CDC7 47671-2. City of L. Sinfonia, Hickox – ELGAR: *Elegy* etc.***

Parry's combination of straightforward, warm expression with hints of melancholy below the surface is very Elgarian. The Bach tributes in *Lady Radnor's suite* are surface-deep; the slow minuet for muted strings is particularly beautiful. Refined playing and first-rate recording.

Lady Radnor's suite.
*** Nimbus Dig. NI 5068 [id.]. E. String O, Boughton – BRIDGE: *Suite*; BUTTERWORTH: *Banks of Green Willow; Idylls; Shropshire lad.****

Parry's charming set of pastiche dances, now given an extra period charm through their Victorian flavour, makes an attractive item in an excellent and generous English collection, one of Nimbus's bestsellers. Warm, atmospheric recording, with refined playing set against an ample acoustic.

Nonet in B flat.
*** Hyp. Dig. CDA 66291 [id.]. Capricorn – STANFORD: *Serenade (Nonet).****

Parry's *Nonet* is an early piece, composed in 1877 while he was still in his twenties. It is for flute, oboe, cor anglais and two each of clarinets, bassoons and horns; Parry wrote it as an exercise, having acquired the score of Brahms's *Serenade in A*, and then put it on one side. Although the finale is perhaps a little lightweight, it is a delight from beginning to end. If one did not know what it was, one would think of early Strauss, for it is music of enormous accomplishment and culture as well as freshness. An excellent performance and recording.

Blest pair of sirens; I was glad (anthems).
*** Chan. Dig. CHAN 8641/2 (2) [id.]. LSO Ch. & O, Hickox – ELGAR: *Dream of Gerontius.****

Parry's two finest and most popular anthems make an attractive coupling for Hickox's fine, sympathetic reading of Elgar's *Dream of Gerontius*. The chorus for Parry is rather thinner than in the main work but is very well recorded.

Evening Service in D (Great): Magnificat; Nunc dimittis. Hear my words, ye people; I was glad when they said unto me; Jerusalem; Songs of farewell.
*** Hyp. CDA 66273 [id.]. St George's Chapel, Windsor, Ch., Christopher Robinson; Roger Judd (organ).

Everyone knows *Jerusalem*, which highlights this collection resplendently; but it is good to see Parry's other choral music being recorded. In the *Songs of farewell* trebles are used and the effect is less robust than in Marlow's version, but undoubtedly very affecting. Perhaps the stirring coronation anthem, *I was glad*, needs the greater weight of an adult choir, but it is still telling here. The excerpts from the *Great Service in D* are well worth having on record, as is the anthem, *Hear my words, ye people*. Excellent recording, the chapel ambience colouring the music without blunting the words.

Songs of farewell.
*** Conifer Dig. CDCF 155 [id.]. Trinity College, Cambridge, Ch., Richard Marlow – STANFORD: *Magnificat* etc.***

Parry's *Songs of farewell* represent his art at its deepest, beautiful inspirations that until now have been neglected on disc, even the relatively well-known setting of Henry Vaughan, *My soul, there is a country*. Finest and most searching of the set is the Donne setting, *At the round earth's imagined corners*, with its rich harmonies poignantly intense and beautiful, deeply emotional behind its poised perfection. Richard Marlow with his splendid Trinity Choir, using fresh women's voices for the upper lines instead of trebles, directs thoughtful, committed performances which capture both the beauty and the emotion. This Parry collection is very well recorded and well coupled with the Stanford items, more contained though just as beautifully written for voices.

Patterson, Paul (born 1947)

(i) *Mass of the sea, Op. 47; Sinfonia for strings, Op. 46.*
*** ASV Dig. CDRPO 8006 [id.]. (i) Brighton Fest. Ch., RPO, Geoffrey Simon.

Patterson's scheme was to frame the four main sections of the Mass – omitting the *Credo* – with apt quotations from the Bible on the subject of the sea, starting with

Genesis in the *Kyrie* movement and 'darkness on the face of the deep', and ending with Revelation and 'there was no more sea' in the *Agnus Dei* movement. Patterson's is a broadly eclectic style, which yet is so bold and inventive that echoes of other composers, notably Britten, hardly matter. With warmly committed playing and singing under Geoffrey Simon, the *Mass* makes a powerful impact. The *Sinfonia for strings*, rather more abrasive in idiom with its echoes of Bartók, also makes a welcome addition to the catalogue, deftly written with neat pay-offs in each movement. The recording is very well balanced and has atmosphere and realistically defined detail.

Penderecki, Kryszstof (born 1933)

The Awakening of Jacob; (i) *Cello concerto No. 2;* (ii) *Viola concerto; Paradise Lost: Adagietto.*
*** Polski Nagrania PNCD 020 [id.]. (i) Monighetti; (ii) Kamasa; Polish Nat. RSO, Antoni Wit.

Penderecki 'returned to melody' in the late 1970s and early '80s after his long advocacy of avant-garde techniques. The *Cello concerto No. 2* was written in 1982 for Rostropovich, and this 1984 recording is impressively played by Ivan Monighetti. The *Viola concerto* is rather like skimmed Bartók; it brings masterly playing from Stefan Kamasa and the Polish Radio Orchestra. One cannot escape the same suspicion one felt of his avant-garde period: that behind the mask of colour and orchestral trickery there is little real substance. However, others may feel differently, and these mid-1980s performances have plenty of ardour and commitment and are well recorded.

(i) *Violin concerto;* (ii) *Symphony No. 2 (Christmas symphony).*
** Polski Nagrania PNCD 019 [id.]. (i) Kulka; Polish Nat. RSO, (i) composer; (ii) Kasprzyk.

The *Violin concerto* is the long, one-movement work Penderecki composed for Isaac Stern in 1976–7. It is in the neo-romantic, post-Bartókian style he adopted at this time and it could perhaps seem more imposing on first acquaintance than it subsequently proves to be. The *Second Symphony* was commissioned by Mehta and the New York Philharmonic and is curiously anonymous, full of lugubrious, Shostakovich-like broodings and an all-purpose solemnity. It is put together well but is essentially empty. The performances here are undoubtedly committed and the recordings (1979 and 1981 respectively) are satisfactory. (An appropriate evaluation might be: three stars for the artists, two for the recording, none for the composer, and rosettes all round for those listeners who persevere to the very end of the record.)

String quartet No. 2.
*** Olympia OCD 328 [id.]. Varsovia Qt – SZYMANOWSKI: *Quartets*; LUTOSLAWSKI: *Quartet.****

Penderecki's *First quartet* of 1960 lasts seven minutes; the *Second* (1968) is not much longer and is hardly more substantial. It is full of the gimmicks and clichés of the period. Whatever its merit, it is extremely well played.

Pergolesi, Giovanni (1710–36)

Sinfonia for cello and continuo.
*** Decca Dig. 425 614-2 [id.]. Peter Howard, St Paul CO, Hogwood – GALLO: *Trio sonata movements*; STRAVINSKY: *Pulcinella* etc.***

Though Stravinsky originally thought that all his sources for his ballet, *Pulcinella*, were drawn from Pergolesi, much of the material he used was written by others. Stylishly played here, this charming *Sinfonia for cello* is genuine, providing in its finale the material for the memorable *Vivo* movement, which Stravinsky outrageously scored for trombone and double-bass.

Stabat Mater.
*** DG 415 103-2 [id.]. Margaret Marshall, Valentini Terrani, LSO, Abbado.

(i; ii) *Stabat Mater;* (ii) *In coelestibus regnis;* (i) *Salve Regina in A.*
*** Hyp. Dig. CDA 66294 [id.]. (i) Gillian Fisher; (ii) Michael Chance; King's Consort, Robert King.

Abbado's account brings greater intensity and ardour to this piece than any rival, and he secures marvellously alive playing from the LSO – this without diminishing religious sentiment. Margaret Marshall is an impressive singer; her contribution combines fervour with an attractive variety of colour, while Lucia Valentini Terrani is an excellent foil. The DG recording has warmth and good presence and the perspective is thoroughly acceptable. This is now a clear first choice.

The Hyperion recording makes a very good case for authenticity in this work. The combination of soprano and male alto blends well together yet offers considerable variety of colour. There is purity of timbre here, but also plenty of expressive intensity. The accompanying string group is led by Roy Goodman, thus ensuring a high standard, and the continuo is equally well managed. Each of the soloists is given a separate encore. Gillian Fisher's *Salve Regina* is quite a considerable piece in four sections, whereas Michael Chance's motet is brief but makes an engaging postlude. Excellent sound.

La serva padrona (opera) complete recording (includes alternative ending and insertion arias).
*** Hung. HCD 12846-2 [id.]. Katalin Farkas, Jószef Gregor, Capella Savaria, Németh.

La serva padrona is ideally suited to disc, and on this Hungaroton issue receives a delightful, sparkling performance with the excellent period-performance group, Capella Savaria. Jószef Gregor sings with splendid buffo stylishness, while Katalin Farkas, as Serpina the maid, brings out the fun of the writing, with the shrewishness of the character kept in check. Bright, clean recording.

Pfitzner, Hans (1869–1949)

Palestrina (opera) complete.
(M) *** DG 427 417-2 (3) [id.]. Gedda, Fischer-Dieskau, Weikl, Ridderbusch, Donath, Fassbaender, Prey, Tölz Boys' Ch., Bav. R. Ch. & SO, Kubelik.

This rich and glowing performance goes a long way to explaining why in Germany the mastery of this unique opera is trumpeted so loudly. Though Pfitzner's melodic invention hardly matches that of his contemporary, Richard Strauss, his control of structure and drawing of character through music make an unforgettable impact. It is the central Act, a massive and colourful tableau representing the Council of Trent, which lets one witness the crucial discussion on the role of music in the church. The outer Acts – more personal and more immediately compelling – show the dilemma of Palestrina himself and the inspiration which led him to write the *Missa Papae Marcelli*, so resolving the crisis, both personal and public. At every point Pfitzner's response to this situation is illuminating, and this glorious performance with a near-ideal cast, consistent all through, could hardly be bettered in conveying the intensity of an admittedly offbeat inspiration. This CD reissue captures the glow of the Munich recording superbly and, though this is a mid-price set, DG has not skimped on the accompanying booklet, in the way some other companies have tended to do with sets of rare operas.

Piston, Walter (1894–1976)

The Incredible flutist (complete ballet).
*** TROY 016-2. Louisville O, Jorge Mester (with KAY: *Cakewalk****).

Walter Piston's ballet *The Incredible flutist* comes from 1938 and is one of the most refreshing and imaginative of all American scores. Hitherto it has been known as a suite, in which the composer selected his more important material, ideas that are instantly memorable. The full score – here offered for the first time in an excellent mid-1970s recording – does bring a degree of dilution but a gain in cohesion. Incidentally, the Flutist does not make his appearance until well into the ballet, which is about the visit of a circus to a sleepy Spanish village. Jorge Mester directs an authoritative account; the Louisville Orchestra are highly sympathetic and play vividly throughout. The CD remastering adds presence, while retaining the original ambience.

Symphonies Nos. 5; (i) 7 and 8.
** Albany AR 011 [id.]. Louisville O, Whitney, (i) Mester.

Walter Piston's symphonies belong among the best that America has ever produced. Some authorities suggest that his music is finely crafted but more worthy than inspired. The opening of the *Fifth Symphony* belies that, and the music has a sureness of purpose and feeling for organic growth that are the hallmark of the true symphonist. The *Seventh* and *Eighth Symphonies*, though not quite the equal of the finest Piston, are powerful and rewarding works which will speak to those who are more concerned with substance than with surface appeal. The Louisville is not in the front rank of American orchestras, but the performances are thoroughly committed and good, without being outstanding. The recordings sound better than they did on LP and serve as a vehicle to acquaint us with a serious and thoughtful composer.

Pleyel, Ignaz (1757–1831)

Clarinet concerto in C.
*** Claves CD 50-813 [id.]. Friedli, SW German CO, Angerer – MERCADANTE; MOLTER: *Concertos.****

Pleyel's *Concerto*, written for C clarinet, is obviously post-Mozart, and his debt to that master is obvious. The work is engagingly inventive throughout, with the finale especially attractive. Friedli plays it skilfully and sympathetically and gets good if not outstanding support from Angerer. The CD gives good presence to the soloist; orchestral detail is a little clouded by the resonance, but the overall sound is very pleasing.

Ponchielli, Amilcare (1834–86)

La Gioconda (complete).
*** Decca Dig. 414 349-2 (3) [id.]. Caballé, Baltsa, Pavarotti, Milnes, Hodgson, L. Op. Ch., Nat. PO, Bartoletti.
*** EMI CDS7 49518-2 (3) [Ang. CDCC 49518]. Callas, Cossotto, Ferraro, Vinco, Cappuccilli, Companeez, La Scala, Milan, Ch. & O, Votto.

The colourfully atmospheric melodrama of this opera gives the Decca engineers the chance to produce a digital blockbuster, one of the most vivid opera recordings yet made. The casting could hardly be bettered, with Caballé just a little overstressed in the title-role but producing glorious sounds. Pavarotti has impressive control and heroic tone. Commanding performances too from Milnes as Barnaba, Ghiaurov as Alvise and Baltsa as Laura, firm and intense all three. Bartoletti proves a vigorous and understanding conductor, presenting the blood and thunder with total commitment but finding the right charm in the most famous passage, the *Dance of the hours*.

Maria Callas gave one of her most vibrant, most compelling, most totally inspired performances on record in the title-role of *La Gioconda*, with flaws very much subdued. The challenge she presented to those around her is reflected in the soloists – Cossotto and Cappuccilli both at the very beginning of distinguished careers – as well as the distinctive tenor Ferraro and the conductor Votto, who has never done anything finer on record. The recording still sounds well, though it dates from 1959.

La Gioconda: Dance of the hours.
(M) *** EMI CDM7 69041-2 [id.]. Philh. O, Karajan – BORODIN: *Polovtsian dances****; OFFENBACH: *Gaîté parisienne***(*); GOUNOD: *Faust ballet.****

Ponchielli's miniature romantic ballet is much more familiar than the opera from which it derives. The imaginative charm of the music is most engaging when presented with such elegance and spirit and the Philharmonia players obviously relish this attractive succession of tunes, glowingly scored. The 1960 recording, with its pleasingly full ambience, hardly sounds dated at all. Besides the listed couplings, this generous anthology also includes four minutes of Verdi's ballet from Act II of *Aida*, equally vividly played and recorded. Karajan's later DG recording of the *Dance of the hours* is also available in a mid-priced Galleria collection of opera intermezzi and ballet music (DG 415 856-2); there is a superbly recorded digital version in a similar collection on Philips, beguilingly played by the Dresden State Orchestra under Varviso (412 236-2).

Poulenc, Francis (1899–1963)

Aubade (Concerto choréographique); Piano concerto in C sharp min.; (i) Double piano concerto in D min.
*** Erato/WEA Dig. 2292 45232-2 [id.]. Duchable; (i) Collard; Rotterdam PO, Conlon.

The *Aubade* is an exhilarating work of great charm. It dates from the late 1920s and is a send-up of Mozart, Stravinsky, etc. The *Piano concerto* has a most beguiling opening theme and evokes the faded charms of Paris in the '30s. The skittish *Double concerto* is infectiously jolly. One could never mistake the tone of voice intended. The performances of the two solo works by François-René Duchable and the Rotterdam orchestra have a certain panache and flair that are most winning. The *Double concerto* too captures all the wit and charm of the Poulenc score, with the 'mock Mozart' slow movement particularly elegant. The balance is almost perfectly judged. Perhaps in the solo works Duchable is a shade too prominent, but not sufficiently so to disturb a strong recommendation, for the sound is otherwise full and pleasing.

Aubade; Sinfonietta.
*** Hyp. Dig. CDA 66347 [id.]. New London O, Ronald Corp – HAHN: *Le bal de Béatrice d'Este* (ballet suite).***

The *Sinfonietta* has enormous charm – at least it has in this winning performance! It is a fluent and effortless piece, full of resource and imagination, and Ronald Corp and the New London Orchestra, making their début on record, do it proud. This performance has a real sense of style and a Gallic elegance that promise well for this ensemble's future. Julian Evans is an alert soloist in the *Aubade*: his is a performance of real character and, though less well balanced than the *Sinfonietta*, he can hold his own artistically with the best. The Hahn rarity with which it is coupled enhances the interest and value of this release.

Les Biches (ballet): suite.
(*) Sup. Dig. SUP 001519 [id.]. Czech PO, Válek – MILHAUD: *Le boeuf sur le toit*; SATIE: *Parade*.(*)

The suite from *Les Biches* includes all the key numbers; in this spirited and well-played account by the Czech Philharmonic under Vladimír Válek it sounds attractively fresh. Válek's pacing is generally brisk, but he does not miss the music's elegance. The recording is vivid but with a good ambient effect. The couplings are well chosen and are done brightly.

Les Biches (ballet): suite; (i) *Piano concerto;* (ii) *Gloria.*
(M) *** EMI CDM7 69644-2 [id.]. (i) Ortiz; (ii) N. Burrowes, CBSO Ch.; CBSO, Frémaux.

Cristina Ortiz gives an alert and stylish account of Poulenc's disarming *Piano concerto* and is given splendid support from Louis Frémaux and the Birmingham orchestra. The latter's performance of *Les Biches*, too, is good-humoured, even if the opening trumpet tune is almost too fast in its racy vigour. The Birmingham account of the *Gloria* competes with Prêtre's fine version, but that is at full price; Frémaux also secures excellent results and he has a sympathetic soloist in Norma Burrowes. The recording, originally designed for quadraphony, is brightly remastered but retains much of its sense of spectacle.

(i) *Concert champêtre for harpsichord and orchestra;* (ii) *Concerto in G min. for organ, strings and timpani;* (iii) *Piano concerto in C sharp min.*
**(*) Virgin Dig. VC 790779-2. (i) Maggie Cole; (ii) Gillian Weir; (iii) Jean-Bernard Pommier; City of L. Sinfonia, Richard Hickox.

The *Piano concerto* receives rather laid-back treatment at the hands of Jean-Bernard Pommier, who misses the *gamin*-like charm of the opening. The instrument is also a bit laid-back and has a slightly resonant halo. The *Concert champêtre* is charming, though the perspective is not good. The harpsichord occupies an appropriately small space, but the wind and, more particularly, the percussion are far too prominent. Maggie Cole and the City of London Sinfonia produce a splendidly idiomatic performance, and so does Gillian Weir in the *Organ concerto*. Duchable is to be preferred in the *Piano concerto*, but otherwise there are good things here.

(i) *Concert champêtre; Organ concerto in G min.;* (ii) *Gloria.*
(M) *** Decca 425 627-2 [id.]. (i) Malcolm (hapsichord/organ), ASMF, Iona Brown; (ii) Greenbert, SRO Ch., SRO, Lopez-Cobos.

George Malcolm's excellent version of the *Organ concerto* is also available coupled with Saint-Saëns – see below – but pairing it with the *Concert champêtre* is even more attractive. In the latter work the engineers did not succumb to the temptation to make the harpsichord sound larger than life, and on CD the beautifully focused keyboard image contrasts wittily with the designedly ample orchestral tuttis. Some might feel that in the finale Malcolm rushes things a bit but the music effervesces, and in every other respect this is an exemplary account. Lopez-Cobos gives a fine account of the *Gloria*, expansive yet underlining the Stravinskian elements in the score. The pioneering version by Prêtre has a certain authenticity of feeling that Lopez-Cobos does not wholly capture, but his performance is enjoyable and is undoubtedly much better recorded. Indeed the sound throughout this CD is in the demonstration bracket.

Organ concerto in G min. (for organ, strings and timpani).
(M) *** Decca 417 725-2 [id.]. George Malcolm, ASMF, Iona Brown – SAINT-SAENS: *Symphony No. 3.***(*)
(*) RCA RD 85750 [RCA 5750-2-RC]. Zamkochian, Boston SO, Munch – FRANCK: *Le chasseur maudit*(*); SAINT-SAENS: *Symphony No. 3.****

Poulenc's endearing and inventive *Organ concerto* is in one continuous movement, divided into seven contrasting sections, the last of which has a devotional quality very apt for its time. The remastered 1979 Argo recording, reissued on Decca Ovation, is a triumphant success, and George Malcolm gives an exemplary account, his pacing consistently apt and with the changing moods nicely caught. The playing of the Academy is splendidly crisp and vital.

Munch's Boston recording dates from 1960; although the Boston acoustics bring slight clouding, the sound is full and hardly dated, with the strings notably warm. Munch has the full measure of the music: his account is essentially genial and relaxed, but not lacking inner vitality; he and his soloist, Berj Zamkochian, find a touching nostalgia in the closing section. Unfortunately the CD provides no internal cueing or indexing.

(i) *Organ concerto in G min.;* (ii) *Gloria in G;* (iii) *4 Motets pour un temps de pénitence.*
**(*) EMI CDC7 47723-2 [id.]. (i) Maurice Duruflé; (ii) Rosanna Carteri, R.T.F. Ch.; both with French Nat. R. & TV O; (iii) René Duclos Ch.; Prêtre.

The *Organ concerto* receives a spirited performance from Duruflé although the digital remastering of the early 1960s recording has brought a slight loss of body and refinement. The *Gloria* has an arresting theatrical quality as well as many touching moments. The soprano solo, *Domine Deus*, is especially beautiful, and the Italianate production of Rosanna Carteri's tone suits its slightly Verdian character, though her style is slightly reserved. In every other respect the performance is exemplary and – since it was recorded in the presence of the composer – presumably authoritative. Again, the new transfer has lost something of the original expansiveness, but the choral sound is undoubtedly clearer. The unaccompanied motets are among Poulenc's finest vocal music; the second, *Vinea mea electa*, has a cool memorability which is particularly well caught here, with the brightness of the choral timbre enhanced by the clean definition.

Piano concerto in C sharp min.
** EMI Dig. CDC7 47224-2 [id.]. Cécile Ousset, Bournemouth SO, Barshai –
PROKOFIEV: *Concerto No. 3.***

Ousset gives a good performance of the *Concerto*, but she is just a little lacking in
charm; nor does Barshai display an ideal lightness of touch for this delicious score. The
recording, however, is extremely good, with the CD in the demonstration bracket.

*Élégie for horn and piano; Sextet for piano, flute, oboe, clarinet, bassoon and horn;
Clarinet sonata; Sonata for 2 clarinets; Sonata for clarinet and bassoon; Flute sonata;
Sonata for horn, trumpet and trombone; Trio for piano, oboe and bassoon.*
(M) ** EMI CZS7 62736-2 (2). Civil, Wilbraham, Iveson, Menuhin, Fevrier, Fournier,
Debost, Bourgue.

*Élégie for horn and piano; Sextet for piano, flute, oboe, clarinet, bassoon and horn;
Clarinet sonata; Flute sonata; Trio for piano, oboe and bassoon.*
**(*) Decca Dig. 421 581-2 [id., without *Élégie*]. Portal, Gallois, Bourgue, Rogé, Wallez,
Cazalet.
** DG Dig. 427 639-2 id.. Vienna/Berlin Ens., Levine.

Were the recording as good as the performances, Decca's collection would warrant a
Rosette. The playing of Maurice Bourgue in the *Oboe sonata* is both masterly and
touching, and all these artists are on top form. These performances have a wonderful
freshness and convey a real sense of delight. The *Sextet* has an irresistible charm and,
whether in the melting lyrical episode in the first movement or the sparkling articulation
of the finale, these artists have an unfailing elegance. Pascal Rogé's pianism throughout is
a constant source of pleasure, and the only drawback is the reverberance of the Salle
Pleyel. Both the internal balance of the players and that of the recording engineers is
excellent, even though they do not overcome the resonant venue. All the same, an
enchanting disc.

James Levine and his colleagues of the Vienna–Berlin Ensemble give us the same
programme as is provided on the Decca CD, plus the *Élégie for horn and piano*, which
Poulenc wrote at the time of the death of Dennis Brain. This is movingly played by
Günther Högner, and the *Sextet* comes off well, though it does not have quite the same
gamin-like quality of the Decca set. The DG recording has greater clarity than its Decca
rival, but neither the *Oboe sonata* nor its companion for the clarinet quite matches the
Bourgue/Portal/Rogé partnerships. Excellent though they are, the DG team do not have
quite the same lightness and delicacy of touch as their French colleagues.

The EMI recordings of the *Trio* and *Sextet* were recorded in the mid-1960s, and the
remainder of the set in the early 1970s. Not all the performances are of equal distinction
and Jacques Fevrier's playing does not always have the finish such repertoire ideally
demands. It is good to have Fournier's elegant account of the *Cello sonata* restored to
circulation, though in the *Violin sonata* Menuhin gives less pleasure. Both the *Trio* and
the *Sextet* are rather dryly recorded; however, although the playing could be more elegant,
there is a high-spirited knockabout quality that is eminently likeable. Maurice Bourgue's
performance of the *Oboe sonata* with Fevrier is superseded by his later account with
Rogé. This is a serviceable and modestly priced introduction to some delightful music;
but the Decca disc will give greater satisfaction ultimately.

PIANO MUSIC

Badinage; Les Biches: Adagietto; Intermezzo No. 3 in A flat; 3 Mouvements perpétuels;

Napoli; 3 Pièces; Les soirées de Nazelles; Suite in C; Valse-improvisation sur le nom de Bach.
*** Chan. Dig. CHAN 8637 [id.]. Eric Parkin.

Eric Parkin's Poulenc recital competes very successfully and, though Rogé has perhaps just that extra ounce of charm and elegance, Parkin can be said to hold his own – which is some compliment. Decca score in the quality and sound of the piano. The Chandos recording is rather more resonant, though not unacceptably so. However, for anyone wanting a single disc of Poulenc's piano music, the Pascal Rogé recital must have preference.

Badinage; Bourrée au pavillon d'Auvergne; Feuillets d'album; Française; Humoresque; 6 Impromptus, Nos. 1–5; 15 Improvisations; 3 Intermezzi; Mélancolie; 3 Mouvements perpétuels; Napoli; 8 Nocturnes; 3 Novelettes; Pastourelle; 3 Pièces; Pièce brève sur le nom d'Albert Roussel; Presto in B flat; Promenades; Les soirées de Nazelles; Suite in C; Suite française; Thème varié; Valse in C; Valse-improvisation sur le nom de Bach; Villageoise.
**(*) CBS Dig. M3K 44921 (3). Paul Crossley.

Paul Crossley is a perceptive guide in this repertoire and those wanting so comprehensive a Poulenc collection can safely be directed here. Crossley is fleet-fingered and unfailingly intelligent, though he does not really have the grace and charm of Pascal Rogé. Good recording quality.

Bourrée au pavillon d'Auvergne; 15 Improvisations; 3 Intermezzi; Mélancolie; Mouvements perpétuels; Napoli; 8 Nocturnes; 3 Pièces; Pièce brève sur le nom d'Albert Roussel; Presto; Les soirées de Nazelles; Suite française; Suite in C. Thème varié; Valse-improvisation sur le nom de Bach. Villageoises.
(M) ** EMI CMS7 62551-2 (2). Gabriel Tacchino.

Gabriel Tacchino's mid-priced two-CD compilation derives from various recordings he had made between 1966 and 1983. The quality of the recordings, all made at the Salle Wagram, varies considerably; the *Nocturnes*, for example, are closely balanced and shallow, with some discomfort in climaxes. The playing is characterful but does not have anywhere near the charm or the *gamin* quality of Rogé, nor is it so well recorded. All the same, one cannot complain about the playing time.

Capriccio; Élégie; L'embarquement pour Cythère; Sonata for piano, four hands; Sonata for two pianos.
*** Chan. Dig. CHAN 8519 [id.]. Seta Tanyel, Jeremy Brown.

Delightful and brilliant playing that is not to be missed. These two artists have a very close rapport and dispatch this repertoire with both character and sensitivity. They are ebullient and high-spirited when required and also uncover a deeper vein of feeling in the *Élégie* and the *Sonata for two pianos*. The Chandos recording is excellent, very vivid and present.

Improvisations Nos. 1–3; 6–8; 12–13; 15; Mouvements perpétuels; 3 Novelettes; Pastourelle; 3 Pièces; Les soirées de Nazelles; Valse.
⊛ *** Decca Dig. 417 438-2 [id.]. Pascal Rogé.

This music is absolutely enchanting, full of delight and wisdom; it has many unexpected touches and is teeming with character. Rogé is a far more persuasive exponent of it than any previous pianist on record; his playing is imaginative and inspiriting, and the recording is superb.

VOCAL MUSIC

(i) *Le Bal masqué; Le Bestiaire. Sextet for piano & wind; Trio for piano, oboe & bassoon.*
*** CRD Dig. CRD 3437 [id.]. (i) Thomas Allen; Nash Ens., Lionel Friend.

Thomas Allen is in excellent voice and gives a splendid account of both *Le Bal masqué* and *Le Bestiaire*. The Nash play both the *Trio* and the *Sextet* with superb zest and character. The wit of this playing and the enormous resource, good humour and charm of Poulenc's music are well served by a recording of exemplary quality and definition. Not to be missed.

Gloria.
(M) *** CBS MK 44710 [id.]. Blegen, Westminster Ch., NYPO, Bernstein – STRAVINSKY: *Symphony of Psalms**** ⊛; BERNSTEIN: *Chichester Psalms.****

The *Gloria* is one of Poulenc's last compositions and among his most successful. Bernstein perhaps underlines the Stravinskian springs of its inspiration and produces a vividly etched and clean-textured account which makes excellent sense in every way and is free from excessive sentiment. Judith Blegen is an appealing soloist, and the recording, though not the last word in refinement, is really very clear, well detailed and spacious in its CD format.

(i; ii) *Gloria; Ave verum corpus; Exultate Deo;* (ii) *Litanies à la Vierge Noire; 4 Motets pour le temps de Noël; 4 Motets pour un temps de pénitence; Salve regina.*
*** Coll. COLCD 108. (i) Donna Deam, Cambridge Singers, (ii) City of L. Sinfonia, John Rutter.

A generous selection of Poulenc's choral music, much of it of great beauty and simplicity, in very fresh-sounding performances and well-focused sound. In the *Gloria*, Donna Deam is not as strong a soloist as was, say, Rosanna Cartori (with Prêtre). However, the general standard of singing is high and the results can be recommended with confidence.

Mass in G; 4 Motets pour le temps de Noël.
*** EMI Dig. CDC7 49559-2 [id.]. Mark Harris, Winchester Cathedral Ch., ECO, Neary – HONEGGER: *Christmas cantata.****

The shadow of Stravinsky hovers over the *G major Mass* and it is rather more self-conscious than his later choral pieces, certainly more so than the delightful *Quatre Motets pour le temps de Noël.* Martin Neary gets excellent results from the Winchester Cathedral Choir and his fine treble, Mark Harris. The EMI recording is also first rate, with well-defined detail and firm definition.

Mélodies: Banalités: Hôtel; Voyage à Paris. Bleuet. C; Calligrammes: Voyage. 4 Chansons pour enfants: Nous voulons une petite soeur. Les chemins de l'amour. Colloque; Hyde Park; Métamorphoses; Miroirs brûlants: Tu vois le feu du soir. Montparnasse; 2 Poèmes de Louis Aragon; 3 Poèmes de Louise Lalanne; Priez pour paix; Tel jour, telle nuit; Toréador.
*** Hyp. Dig. CDA 66147 [id.]. Songmakers' Almanac: Lott, Rolfe-Johnson, Murray, Johnson.

Graham Johnson calls his collection *Voyage à Paris*, after the title of the first song, a frothy and exuberant miniature which gets the record off to a flamboyant start. Felicity Lott sings that and the great majority of the remaining 29 songs, joyful and tender, comic and tragic by turns. The other soloists have one song apiece, done with comparable magnetism, and Richard Jackson joins Felicity Lott (one stanza each) in Poulenc's solitary 'song for two voices', *Colloque*, written in 1940 to words by Paul Valéry. Following that is another wartime song, *C*, most moving of all. First-rate recording, though Lott's soprano is not always as sweetly caught as it can be.

Stabat Mater; Litanies à la vierge noire; Salve Regina.
*** HM Dig. HMC 905149 [id.]. Lagrange, Lyon Nat. Ch. and O, Baudo.

Serge Baudo is perhaps a more sympathetic interpreter of this lovely score than was Prêtre in his earlier record, and he gets more out of it. He certainly makes the most of expressive and dynamic nuances; he shapes the work with fine feeling and gets good singing from the Lyon Chorus. Michèle Lagrange has a good voice and is an eminently expressive soloist. The coupling differs from its rival and offers the short *Salve Regina* and the *Litanies à la vierge noire*, an earlier and somewhat more severe work. A welcome and worthwhile issue.

OPERA

La voix humaine (complete).
** Chan. Dig. CHAN 8331 [id.]. Carole Farley, Adelaide SO, Serebrier.

This virtuoso monodrama, just one woman and a telephone, is ideally suited to a record if, as here, the full text is provided. Carole Farley's French is clear but not quite idiomatic-sounding, and that rather applies to the playing of the Adelaide orchestra, crisply disciplined and sharply concentrated as it is. The result has little of French finesse, but the presentation is certainly vivid.

Power, Leonel (d. 1445)

Missa, Alma redemptoris mater. Motets: *Agnus Dei; Ave Regina; Beata viscera; Credo; Gloria; Ibo michi ad montem; Quam pulchra es; Salve Regina; Sanctus.*
(M) *** EMI CDM7 63064-3 (id.). Hilliard Ens., Hillier.

Power was a contemporary of Dunstable and was born probably in the mid-1370s. One of the leading composers represented in the Old Hall MS (some twenty pieces are attributed to him), Power spent the last years of his life at Canterbury, but the music on this disc is earlier, coming from the period before 1413. The *Missa, Alma redemptoris mater* is probably the earliest, in which all the Mass sections are linked by a common cantus firmus and there is also a complex mathematical design. The music is of an austere beauty that is quite striking, as indeed is the remarkable singing of the Hilliard Ensemble. The digitally remastered recording comes from the early 1980s and is vivid and present. Strongly recommended.

Praetorius, Michael (1571–1621)

Dances from Terpsichore (extended suite).
*** Decca Dig. 414 633-2 [id.]. New L. Cons., Philip Pickett.

Dances from Terpsichore (Suite de ballets; Suite de voltes). (i) Motets: *Eulogodia Sionia: Resonet in laudibus; Musae Sionae: Allein Gott in der Höh sei Ehr; Aus tiefer Not schrei ich zu dir; Christus der uns selig macht; Gott der Vater wohn uns bei; Polyhymnia Caduceatrix: Erhalt uns, Herr, bei deinem Wort.*

(M) *** EMI CDM7 69024-2 [Ang. CDM 69024]. Early Music Cons. of L., Munrow, (i) with boys of the Cathedral and Abbey Church of St Alban.

Terpsichore is a huge collection of some 300 dance tunes used by the French-court dance bands of Henri IV. They were enthusiastically assembled by the German composer, Michael Praetorius, who also harmonized them and arranged them in four to six parts; however, any selection is conjectural in the matter of orchestration. One of the great pioneers of the 'authentic' re-creation of early music, David Munrow's main purpose was to bring the music fully to life and, at the same time, imaginatively to stimulate the ear of the listener. This record, made in 1973, is one of his most successful achievements. The sound is excellent in all respects. Munrow's instrumentation is imaginatively done: the third item, a *Bourrée* played by four racketts (a cross between a shawm and comb-and-paper in sound) is fascinating. The collection is a delightful one, the motets reminding one very much of Giovanni Gabrieli.

Philip Pickett's instrumentation (based on the illustrations which act as an appendix to the maestro's second volume of *Syntagma Musicum* of 1619) is sometimes less exuberant than that of David Munrow before him; but many will like the refinement of his approach, with small instrumental groups, lute pieces and even what seems like an early xylophone! There are also some attractively robust brass scorings (sackbuts and trumpets). The use of original instruments is entirely beneficial in this repertoire; the recording is splendid.

Christmas music: *Polyhymnia caduceatrix et panegyrica Nos. 9–10, 12 & 17. Puericinium Nos. 2, 4 & 5. Musae Sionae VI, No. 53: Es ist ein Ros' entsprungen. Terpsichore: Dances Nos. 1; 283–5; 310.*
*** Hyp. Dig. CDA 66200 [id.]. Westminster Cathedral Ch., Parley of Instruments, David Hill.

Praetorius was much influenced by the polychoral style of the Gabrielis; these pieces from the *Polyhymnia caduceatrix et panegyrica* and the *Puericinium*, which come from the last years of his life, reflect this interest. The music is simple in style and readily accessible, and its performance on this atmospheric Hyperion record is both spirited and sensitive.

Christmas music: *Polyhymnia caduceatrix et panegyrica Nos. 10, Wie schön leuchtet der Morgenstern; 12, Puer natus in Bethlehem; 21, Wachet auf, ruft uns die Stimme; 34, In dulci jubilo.*
*** EMI Dig. CDC7 47633-2 [id.]. Taverner Cons., Ch. & Players, Parrott – SCHÜTZ: *Christmas oratorio.****

This is the finest collection of Praetorius's vocal music in the current catalogue. The closing setting of *In dulci jubilo*, richly scored for five choirs and with the brass providing thrilling contrast and support for the voices, has great splendour. Before that comes the lovely, if less ambitious *Wie schön leuchtet der Morgenstern*, where the opening shows how effectively Tessa Bonner and Emily Van Evera take the place of boy trebles. Both *Wachet auf* and *Puer natus in Bethlehem* are on a comparatively large scale, their combination of block sonorities and florid decorative effects the very essence of Renaissance style. The recording is splendidly balanced, with voices and brass blending and intertwining within an ample acoustic which brings weight and resonance without clouding.

Prokofiev, Serge (1891–1953)

Boris Godunov, Op. 70 bis: Fountain scene; Polonaise. Dreams, Op. 6. Eugene Onegin, Op. 71: Minuet, Polka, Mazurka. 2 Pushkin waltzes, Op. 120. Romeo and Juliet (ballet): suite No. 2, Op. 64.
*** Chan. Dig. CHAN 8472 [id.]. SNO, Järvi.

Järvi's second suite from *Romeo and Juliet* has sensitivity, abundant atmosphere, a sense of the theatre, and is refreshingly unmannered. Of the rarities, *Dreams* is atmospheric, if derivative, with a fair amount of Debussy and early Scriabin – to whom it is dedicated. Much of the music Prokofiev wrote for a production of *Eugene Onegin* was eventually re-used in other works, but what is offered here, plus the *Two Pushkin waltzes*, are rather engaging lighter pieces. All this music is well worth having and the performances are predictably expert. The range of the recording is wide, the balance finely judged and detail is in exactly the right perspective.

Chout (The Buffoon): ballet, Op. 21.
*** Olympia Dig. OCD 126 [id.]. USSR MoC SO, Rozhdestvensky.

Chout comes from Prokofiev's time in Paris and was the first of his ballets that Diaghilev actually staged, a wonderfully imaginative score, full of colour and resource. Diaghilev never revived the ballet after 1922 and Prokofiev made a concert suite of twelve numbers. Rozhdestvensky gives a very lively account of the complete score and gets good playing from his youthful Moscow orchestra. The recording is as vivid as the music; indeed some may find it a little overbright at the top. A most rewarding issue and strongly recommended.

Chout (ballet): suite, Op. 21a; Love for 3 Oranges: suite, Op. 33a; Le pas d'acier: suite, Op. 41a.
*** Chandos Dig. CHAN 8729 [id.]. SNO, Järvi.

Chout is one of Prokofiev's most piquant and delicious scores, and the suite is full of the most beguiling invention and wonderful harmonic resource. Järvi has a natural affinity for this repertoire and gets splendid results from the SNO; and the recording is pretty spectacular. Although Järvi gives us only a half of *Le pas d'acier*, it is the better half and his is a more refined performance (and infinitely more present recording) than the complete ballet on Olympia.

Cinderella (ballet; complete), Op. 87.
*** Decca Dig. 410 162-2 (2) [id.]. Cleveland O, Ashkenazy.

Compact disc collectors wanting the complete ballet can safely invest in Ashkenazy without fear of disappointment. Some dances come off better in Previn's EMI version (not yet available on CD), and there is an element of swings and roundabouts in comparing them. Detail is more closely scrutinized by the Decca engineers; Ashkenazy gets excellent results from the Cleveland Orchestra. There are many imaginative touches in this score – as magical indeed as the story itself – and the level of invention is astonishingly high. On CD, the recording's wonderful definition is enhanced, yet not at the expense of atmosphere, and the bright, vivid image is given striking projection.

Cinderella (ballet): highlights.
**(*) RCA Dig. RD 85321 [RCD1 5321]. St Louis SO, Slatkin.

Slatkin's disc is listed as a 'suite', but the twenty numbers (from the fifty of the complete score) follow the ballet's action comprehensively. Within the flattering St Louis acoustic, the orchestra is balanced naturally and the sound is vividly spectacular. The upper range is brightly lit but the CD has amplitude and bloom so that there is no edginess. The orchestral playing is sympathetic, polished and committed; the wide dynamic range of the recording produces a riveting climax towards the end of the ballet when, at midnight, the stereoscopically ticking clock dominates the orchestra dramatically. Slatkin then creates an attractively serene contrast with the closing *Amoroso*. Earlier in the work, Slatkin's characterization is just a little tame, and the detail and rhythmic feeling of the music-making has, at times, an element of blandness.

Cinderella (ballet): *suites Nos. 1 & 2, Op. 107–8:* excerpts. (i) *Peter and the wolf, Op. 67.*
*** Chan. Dig. CHAN 8511 [id.]. (i) Lina Prokofiev; SNO, Järvi.

Järvi's Prokofiev series here offers a characterful version of *Peter and the wolf*. In time-length it is very slow, but the magnetism of Madame Prokofiev (the composer's first wife), with many memorable lines delivered in her tangily Franco-Russian accent, makes up for that leisurely manner, with beautiful, persuasive playing from the Scottish National Orchestra. The very first mention of the wolf brings an unforgettable snarl, which most children will relish. Järvi's compilation of eight movements from the two *Cinderella suites* has even more persuasive playing, with the sensuousness of much of the writing brought out. Warmly atmospheric recording, with the narration realistically balanced.

(i) *Concertino for cello and orchestra, Op. 132* (ed. Rostropovich; orch. Kabalevsky); (Solo) *Cello sonata, Op. 133* (ed. Blok).
*** Virgin Dig. VC 790811-2 [id.]. Isserlis, (i) LPO, Litton – KABALEVSKY: *Cello concerto No. 2.****

Only the first movement of the solo *Cello sonata* survived Prokofiev's death, and that in fragmentary form. Characteristic though much of it is (and the same must be said of the *Concertino*, two movements of which were fully sketched in short score), it is not vintage Prokofiev. Isserlis plays both pieces with great fervour and intelligence: he modifies Kabalevsky's scoring but also includes a rather imaginative cadenza by Olli Mustonen. These are the only recordings of either piece at present on CD and are of obvious interest to admirers of the composer.

Piano concertos Nos 1–5.
(M) **(*) Decca 425 570-2 (2) [id.]. Ashkenazy, LSO, Previn.

(i; ii) *Piano concertos Nos. 1–5;* (ii) *Overture on Hebrew themes;* (i) *Visions fugitives, Op. 22.*
(M) *** EMI CMS7 62542-2 (2). (i) Michel Béroff; (ii) Leipzig GO, Masur.

Honours are more evenly divided between Ashkenazy and Béroff than one might expect. Not that Ashkenazy's staggering virtuosity is challenged by the young Frenchman, though he too plays masterfully; rather that both sets of performances prove remarkably distinguished on closer aquaintance. However, for some the remastered Decca recording, which now has a top-heavy balance (the orginal analogue LPs were bottom-heavy!), will be a drawback. There is a fair amount of edginess and the upper strings tend to sound shrill at higher dynamic levels. The balance in the EMI version is better, although the overall sound-picture is not wholly natural. Béroff is a pianist of genuine insight where Prokofiev is concerned, and Masur gives him excellent support. He is free from some of the agogic mannerisms that distinguish Ashkenazy (in the first movement of No. 2 and the slow movement of No. 3) and he has great poetry. Ashkenazy has marvellous panache, of course; Previn is a sensitive accompanist and, for all its too-brilliant lighting, the Decca recording is extremely vivid, although the piano is made stereoscopically prominent. What may clinch the matter for many collectors is the generous bonuses offered by the EMI set.

Piano concerto No. 1 in D flat; Piano sonata No. 5 in C, Op. 38.
*** ASV Dig. CDDCA 555 [id.]. Osorio, RPO, Bátiz – RAVEL: *Left-hand concerto etc.****

Jorge Federico Osorio copes splendidly with the *Concerto* and is a thoroughly perceptive interpreter. He is accompanied well by Bátiz, and readers wanting this coupling need not fear that it is second best; they are excellently recorded. ASV offer an interesting fill-up in the form of the Prokofiev *Fifth Sonata*, which Osorio does in its post-war, revised form. It is an interesting piece from the 1920s and a welcome addition to the catalogue.

Piano concerto No. 1 in D flat, Op. 10.
**(*) Olympia OCD 190 [id.]. Moura Lympany, Philh. O, Susskind – RACHMANINOV: *Piano concertos 1 and 2.*(***)

Piano concerto No. 3 in C, Op. 26.
**(*) Olympia OCD 191 [id.]. Moura Lympany, Philh. O, Susskind – RACHMANINOV: *Piano concerto No. 3.*(***)

Moura Lympany's recordings of these two Prokofiev *Concertos* originally appeared in the late 1950s, and they wear their years lightly and still give a great deal of musical satisfaction. Her many admirers will find little to disappoint them in these authoritative and dashing performances in which her fine pianism is given excellent support by the Philharmonia under Walter Susskind.

Piano concerto No. 3 in C, Op. 26.
*** DG 415 062-2 [id.]. Argerich, BPO, Abbado – TCHAIKOVSKY: *Piano concerto No. 1.****
*** Decca 411 969-2 [id.]. Ashkenazy, LSO, Previn – BARTÓK: *Concerto No. 3.***(*)
** EMI Dig. CDC7 47224-2 [id.]. Ousset, Bournemouth SO, Barshai – POULENC: *Piano concerto.***

There is nothing ladylike about the playing of Martha Argerich but it displays countless indications of feminine perception and subtlety. The *C major Concerto* was once regarded as tough music but here receives a sensuous performance, and Abbado's direction underlines that from the very first, with a warmly romantic account of the ethereal opening phrases on the high violins. This is a much more individual performance of the Prokofiev than almost any other available and brings its own special insights. The recording remains excellent.

Ashkenazy's account of the *Third Concerto* is keen-edged and crisply articulated, and he is very sympathetically supported by Previn and the LSO. One's only reservation concerns the slow movement: Ashkenazy's entry immediately after the theme is uncharacteristically mannered. Yet his virtuosity remains thrilling and this is still a fine performance. The sound in the CD transfer is clear and more transparent than Argerich's, if with a touch of thinness on violin tone.

Cécile Ousset has the advantage of fine modern digital recording, exceptionally vivid and clear, but the performance, expert though it is, wants the dash and sparkle that artists such as Argerich and Ashkenazy bring to it. Tempi are just that bit slower than

Prokofiev's own in his pioneering recording, and Barshai's direction sounds slightly sluggish.

Piano concerto No. 5 in G, Op. 55.
*** DG 415 119-2 [id.]. Sviatoslav Richter, Warsaw PO, Witold Rowicki – RACHMANINOV: *Piano concerto No. 2.****

Richter's account of the *Fifth Piano concerto* is a classic. It was recorded in 1959, yet the sound of this excellent CD transfer belies the age of the original in its clarity, detail and vividness of colour. In any event it cannot be recommended too strongly to all admirers of Richter, Prokofiev and great piano playing.

Violin concertos Nos. 1 in D, Op. 19; 2 in G min., Op. 63.
(M) *** Decca 425 003-2 [id.]. Kyung Wha Chung, LSO, Previn – STRAVINSKY: *Concerto.****
*** DG Dig. 410 524-2 [id.]. Mintz, Chicago SO, Abbado.
*** Virgin Dig. VC 790734-2 [id.]. Sitkovetsky, LSO, C. Davis.
*** EMI Dig. CDC7 47025-2 [id.]. Perlman, BBC SO, Rozhdestvensky.
*** Chandos Dig. CHAN 8709 [id.]. Mordkovitch, SNO, Järvi.

Kyung Wha Chung gives performances to emphasize the lyrical quality of these *Concertos*, with playing that is both warm and strong, tender and full of fantasy. The melody which opens the slow movement of No. 2 finds her playing with an inner, hushed quality and the ravishing modulation from E flat to B, a page or so later, brings an ecstatic frisson. Previn's acompaniments are deeply understanding. The Decca sound has lost only a little of its fullness in the digital remastering, and the soloist is now made very present.

Mintz's performances are as fine as any; he phrases with imagination and individuality and, if he does not display quite the overwhelming sense of authority of Perlman, there is an attractive combination of freshness and lyrical finesse. He has the advantage of Abbado's sensitive and finely judged accompaniments. In short, this partnership casts the strongest spell on the listener and, with recording on CD which is both refined and full, and a realistic – if still somewhat forward – balance for the soloist, this must receive the strongest advocacy.

Dmitri Sitkovetsky conveys the demonic side of the *First Concerto* more effectively than almost any other player without losing sight of its lyricism or sense of line. His version of the scherzo touches an ironic, almost malignant nerve which he has the measure of the ice-maiden fairy-tale element at the opening. The *Second* is hardly less powerful and has a sympathetic collaborator in Sir Colin Davis. The soloist is rather more forward than is ideal, but orchestral detail is never masked and the internal orchestral balance is very natural.

Perlman's performances bring virtuosity of such strength and command that one is reminded of the supremacy of Heifetz. Though the EMI sound has warmth and plenty of bloom, the balance of the soloist is unnaturally close, which has the effect of obscuring important melodic ideas in the orchestra behind mere passage-work from the soloist. Nevertheless one is left in no doubt that both works are among the finest violin concertos written this century. Apart from the balance, the recording is very fine.

Lydia Mordkovitch enters a hotly contested field and gives readings of strong personality and character. She is well supported by the SNO and Järvi and more than holds her own with rival versions. There are some splendidly malignant sounds in the scherzo of No. 1 and much intensity and panache throughout both pieces. She does not displace Mintz (DG) or Sitkovetzky (Virgin), both of them very special, but both performances make a very satisfying alternative and have first-class sound.

Violin concerto No. 2 in G min., Op. 63.
(M) *** RCA RD 87019 [RCD1 7019]. Heifetz, Boston SO, Munch – GLAZUNOV; SIBELIUS: *Concerto.****
*** Ph. Dig. 422 364-2 [id.]. Viktoria Mullova, RPO, Previn – SHOSTAKOVICH: *Violin concerto No. 1.**(*)

In the *arioso*-like slow movement, Heifetz chooses a faster speed than is usual, but there is nothing unresponsive about his playing, for his expressive rubato has an unfailing inevitability. In the spiky finale he is superb, and indeed his playing is glorious throughout. The recording is serviceable merely, though it has been made firmer in the current remastering. But no one is going to be prevented from enjoying this ethereal performance because the technical quality is dated.

Mullova's reading is pretty dazzling though it does not displace Sitkovetsky, Mintz or Perlman. She is, however, better balanced than Perlman and is given altogether first-rate sound and predictably idiomatic support from Previn. Unfortunately the Shostakovich coupling is much less successful.

Divertimento, Op. 43; The Prodigal son, Op. 46; Symphonic song, Op. 57; Andante (Piano Sonata No. 4).
*** Chandos Dig. CHAN 8728 [id.]. SNO, Järvi.

The *Divertimento* is a lovely piece: its first movement has an irresistible and haunting second theme. It comes from 1929, the same period as *The Prodigal son*, though two of its movements derive from the ballet, *Trapeze*. Its long neglect is puzzling since it is highly attractive and ought to be popular. So, for that matter, should *The Prodigal son*, some of whose material Prokofiev re-used the following year in the *Fourth Symphony*. Another rarity is the *Symphonic song*, a strange, darkly scored piece which Miaskovsky told the composer is 'not entirely right for us . . . it lacks a familiar simplicity and breadth of contour'. It does have some interesting and characteristic colours and is more effective than the sonata transcription. The recording is in the first flight – as, indeed, are the performances. An indispensable item in any Prokofiev collection.

The Gambler: 4 Portraits, Op. 49; Semyon Kotko: Symphonic suite, Op. 81 bis.
*** Chan. Dig. CHAN 8803 [id.]. SNO, Järvi.

The interest aroused by the Brussels production of *The Gambler* in 1929 prompted Prokofiev to fashion the *Four Portraits*, which enshrine the best of the opera and are exhilarating and inventive. *Semyon Kotko* was composed after his return to the Soviet Union and, though not top-drawer Prokofiev, is still thoroughly enjoyable. The best of the eight movements are the fourth (*The Southern night*), the sixth (*The Village is burning*) and the seventh (*Funeral*), which find his inspiration flowing at a more characteristic level. The *Suite* has not been recorded since the 1950s, and Järvi gives a thoroughly sympathetic reading in vivid and present sound.

Lieutenant Kijé (suite), Op. 60; Love of three oranges (suite).
*** RCA Dig. RD 85168 [RCD1 5168]. Dallas SO, Mata – STRAVINSKY: *Suites.****

Lieutenant Kijé: suite; Love of three oranges: suite; Symphony No. 1 in D (Classical), Op. 25.
(M) **(*) Ph. 426 640-2 [id.]. LSO, Marriner.

At the evocative opening of Mata's account of *Kijé*, the distanced cornet solo immediately creates a mood of nostalgia. The orchestral playing, both here and in the suite from *Love of three oranges*, is vividly coloured and full of character, and the ambience of the Dallas auditorium adds bloom and atmosphere. The CD is bright and sharp in definition and the music-making is of the highest order; Mata shows an instinctive rapport with both these scores.

On Philips, with good playing and recording, there is nothing to disappoint. Individually these pieces are available in other versions that are as good as (or better than) this compilation, but these are lively performances, and the remastered sound is fresh and open.

On the Dnieper (ballet), *Op. 51; Le pas d'acier* (ballet), *Op. 41.*
*** Olympia Dig. OCD 103 [id.]. USSR MoC SO, Rozhdestvensky.

Earlier records of *Le pas d'acier* by Albert Coates and Rozhdestvensky have been of the suite; this gives us the newly published complete score. It is full of vitality and (apart from one or two numbers) highly attractive, very much in the *ballet mécanique* style; *On the Dnieper* is a lyrical work not dissimilar to *The Prodigal Son*. Colourful performances and recordings. Lovers of Prokofiev's ballets should not miss this welcome addition to the discography.

Peter and the wolf, Op. 67 (see also above, under *Cinderella*).
⊛ *** Virgin Dig. VC 790786-2 [id.]. Gielgud, Ac. of L., Richard Stamp – SAINT-SAENS: *Carnival****; MOZART: *Eine kleine Nachtmusik.***(*)
⊛ (B) *** Decca 421 626-2 [id.]. Richardson, LSO, Sargent – *Children's weekend* (collection).***
*** Telarc Dig. CD 80126 [id.]. André Previn, RPO, Previn – BRITTEN: *Young person's guide* etc.**(*)
*** Ph. Dig. 412 559-2 [412 556-2, with Dudley Moore]. Terry Wogan, Boston Pops O, John Williams – TCHAIKOVSKY: *Nutcracker suite.****
*** DG 415 351-2 [id.]. Hermione Gingold, VPO, Boehm – SAINT-SAENS: *Carnival.****
(B) *** ASV CDQS 6017 [id.]. Angela Rippon, RPO, Hughes – SAINT-SAENS: *Carnival.****
(M) *** EMI CDM7 63177-2. Michael Flanders, Philh. O, Kurtz – SAINT-SAENS: *Carnival****; BRITTEN: *Young person's guide.***(*)
(B) **(*) Pickwick IMPX 9002. Sean Connery, RPO, Dorati – BRITTEN: *Young person's guide.***(*)

Sir John Gielgud's highly individual presentation of Prokofiev's masterly narrative with orchestra brings a worthy successor to our previous favourite version, by Sir Ralph Richardson for Decca; moreover Richard Stamp and the Academy of London have the advantage of a superb, modern, digital recording, warmly atmospheric but with a strikingly wide dynamic range. This is never more effective than when, after a deceptively relaxed opening, the first moment of danger arrives, at the approach of the sinuous feline predator, with Sir John conveying most imaginatively the slinky cunning of the cat and the chirpy high spirits of its elusive prey. At the climax, when the wolf finally catches the duck, there is high drama so the contrast of the plaintive oboe echoing the duck's theme is the more engagingly pathetic. At the end, Sir John, who has presided over these events with a wonderfully benign involvement, becomes Grandfather himself with his restrained moral questioning of Peter's youthful bravado. Throughout, his obvious relish for the colour as well as the narrative flow of the text has been splendidly matched by the detail and impetus of Richard Stamp's accompaniment, with the orchestral soloists making the very most of all their opportunities.

Like his colleague, Sir Ralph Richardson brings a great actor's feeling for words to the narrative; he dwells lovingly on their sound as well as their meaning, and this genial preoccupation with the manner in which the story is told matches Sargent's feeling exactly. There are some delicious moments when that sonorous voice has exactly the right coloration, none more taking than Grandfather's very reasonable moral: '. . . and if Peter had not caught the wolf . . . what then?' But of course he did, and in this account it was surely inevitable. Sir Malcolm Sargent's direction of the accompaniment shows his professionalism at its very best, with finely prepared orchestral playing and many imaginative little touches of detail brought out, yet with the forward momentum of the action well sustained. Excellent, vivid sound and a cleverly chosen supporting programme of music for, or about, children.

André Previn's Telarc version, lightly pointed, lively, colourful and perfectly timed, has the enormous advantage of the conductor's own delightfully informal narration. The arrival of the wolf is marvellously sinister, yet in telling of the swallowing of the duck Previn keeps just a touch of avuncular kindness behind the horror, most delicately done. Vivid recording, with the voice balanced well against the orchestra without too much discrepancy.

Terry Wogan's amiably fresh narration is a great success. Any listener expecting a degree of archness or too much Irish whimsy will soon be disarmed by the spontaneity of the story-telling and the way the added asides point the gentle irony of the tale and the involvement of its characters. Perhaps the camped-up voice of Grandfather sounds a shade self-conscious, but the humour of the grumpy old man is nicely caught. John Williams provides imaginative orchestral backing, full of atmosphere and with marvellous detail. The recording is superb, with the nicely resonant Boston acoustic bringing an attractive overall bloom. The CD emphasizes the difference in acoustic between the separate recordings of voice and orchestra. In the American edition, Dudley Moore replaces Terry Wogan as narrator.

On DG, Hermione Gingold's narration is certainly memorable and the orchestral playing under Boehm is of a superlative standard. Some might find Miss Gingold a trifle too camp in her presentation of an amended text. However, it is difficult to resist the strength of her personality and her obvious identification with the events of the tale. The 1976 orchestral recording remains remarkably transparent and truthful. The voice itself is a little larger than life.

Angela Rippon narrates with charm yet is never in the least coy; indeed she is thoroughly involved in the tale and thus involves the listener too. The accompaniment is equally spirited, with excellent orchestral playing, and the recording is splendidly clear, yet not lacking atmosphere. This makes an excellent bargain-price recommendation.

Michael Flanders adds a touch or two of his own to the introduction and narration and, as might be expected, he brings the action splendidly alive. The pace of the accompaniment under Kurtz is attractively vibrant, and the Philharmonia are first rate. The recording is crisply vivid.

Sean Connery uses a modern script by Gabrielle Hilton which brings a certain colloquial friendliness to the narrative and invites a relaxed style, to which the actor readily responds. If you can accept such extensions as 'dumb duck' and a pussy cat who is 'smooth, but greedy and vain', you will not be disappointed with Connery's participation in the climax of the tale, where Dorati supports him admirably. Both pieces on this record start with the orchestra tuning up, to create an anticipatory atmosphere, and the introductory matter is entirely fresh and informal. The recording – from a vivid Decca source – has plenty of colour and projection.

Romeo and Juliet (ballet), *Op. 64* (complete).
*** EMI CDS7 49012-8 (2) [id.]. LSO, Previn.
*** Decca 417 510-2 (2) [id.]. Cleveland O, Maazel.
*** DG 423 268-20 (2) [id.]. Boston SO, Ozawa.
(B) **(*) CfP CD-CFPD 4452 (2). Bolshoi Theatre O, Zuraitis.

Previn's pointing of rhythm is consciously seductive, whether in fast, jaunty numbers or the soaring lyricism of the love-music. The recording quality is warm and immediate to match. Maazel by contrast will please those who believe that this score should above all be bitingly incisive. The rhythms are more consciously metrical, the tempi generally faster, and the precision of ensemble of the Cleveland Orchestra is little short of miraculous. The recording is one of Decca's most spectacular, searingly detailed but atmospheric too. Both sets have been strikingly successful in their CD transfers and are generously cued.

Immediately at the opening, one notices Ozawa's special balletic feeling in the elegance of the string phrasing and the light, rhythmic felicity. Yet he can rise to the work's drama and in the love-music his ardour is compulsive. At times, one feels, the characterization has less affectionate individuality than Previn's, whose tempi are always so apt, and the element of pungency which Maazel brings to the score is almost entirely missing in Boston. But this music-making is very easy to enjoy and the actual playing is very fine indeed, while Ozawa has the advantage of outstanding modern digital recording, full of atmosphere.

Zuraitis's bargain version includes an important supplement in addition to the usual complete ballet score. Having studied the original manuscript material, he adds three movements finally omitted in the ballet, the *Nurse and Mercutio* (using familiar material), a sharply grotesque *Moorish dance* and a so-called *Letter scene* which provides a sketch for what eight years later became the scherzo of the *Fifth Symphony*. Zuraitis has scored this last with reference to the symphony. The performance generally may lack something in orchestral refinement, compared with those of Previn and Maazel, but not Russian feeling. With strikingly bright digital sound of colour and power, not always perfectly balanced, it is excellent value. The 1982 Melodiya recording has a touch of blatancy at climaxes, mainly caused by the Russian brass style, but is otherwise vivid and full. Moreover the documentation is remarkable for a bargain issue in providing plenty of information about the music, plus a synopsis directly related to the 55 separate cues.

Romeo and Juliet (ballet): *suite*.
(M) *** Decca 417 737-2 [id.]. Cleveland O, Maazel – KHACHATURIAN: *Gayaneh; Spartacus*.**(*)

An intelligently chosen selection of six pieces (including *Juliet as a young girl*, the *Balcony scene* and *The last farewell*) makes a generous coupling for Decca's Khachaturian ballet scores.

Romeo and Juliet (ballet), *Op. 64:* highlights.
*** CBS Dig. MK 42662 [id.]. BPO, Salonen.

With magnificent playing from the Berlin Philharmonic Orchestra, Esa-Pekka Salonen's set seems marginally a first choice for those wanting merely a single disc of excerpts from Prokofiev's masterly score. The Berlin Philharmonic playing has an enormous intensity and a refined felicity in the score's more delicate moments. The portrayal of *Juliet as a young girl* is deliciously light in its detail, while the *Folk dance* and *Dance with the mandolins* are full of subtleties of colour and articulation. One is touched and deeply moved by this music-making, while the selection admirably parallels the work's narrative. The recording, made in the Philharmonie, has more resonance and amplitude than the DG engineers usually achieve in this hall for Karajan; indeed it matches sumptuousness with a potent clarity of projection, and the dynamic range is dramatically wide.

Romeo and Juliet (ballet): *suites Nos. 1 & 2, Op. 64.*
** EMI Dig. CDC7 49289-2 [id.]. Oslo PO, Jansons.

Jansons secures playing of alert sensibility, discipline and refinement from the Oslo Philharmonic and has the advantage of naturally balanced and vividly present recording. His is not as excessively well-drilled a performance as Muti's Philadelphia account of some years ago but, like that version, it is wanting in a sense of the theatre. Not a first choice.

Romeo and Juliet: suites Nos. 1 and 2: excerpts.
*** Telarc Dig. CD 80089 [id.]. Cleveland O, Yoel Levi.
**(*) Collins Dig. 1116-2 [id.]. Philh. O, Barry Wordsworth.

Levi offers one of the finest single discs of excerpts from Prokofiev's masterpiece and he draws wonderfully eloquent playing from his orchestra. He seems to have a special affinity with Prokofiev's score, for pacing is unerringly apt and characterization is strong. There are some wonderfully serene moments, as in the ethereal introduction of the flute melody in the first piece (*Montagues and Capulets*), and the delicacy of the string playing in *Romeo at Juliet's tomb* – which explores the widest expressive range – is touching. The quicker movements have an engaging feeling of the dance and the light, graceful articulation in *The child Juliet* is a delight; but the highlights of the performance are the *Romeo and Juliet love scene* and *Romeo at Juliet's before parting*, bringing playing of great intensity, with a ravishing response from the Cleveland strings leading on from passionate yearning to a sense of real ecstasy. The rich Telarc recording is in the demonstration class, and it is very difficult to choose between this fine disc and Salonen's CBS CD.

The appeal of Barry Wordsworth's selection, which follows the ballet's narrative line closely, lies in his natural feeling for the dance. His portrait of *Juliet as a young girl* is wonderfully graceful, and the Philharmonia playing throughout creates an appealing delicacy of texture, with rhythms always lifted; the more robust movements have vigour without heaviness. However, the passion of the ballet's highly charged romanticism and the despair of its tragic dénouement are conveyed with far less pungency and power here than with Levi on Telarc or Salonen on CBS. The Collins recording is of the highest quality, and those who want a record primarily to evoke the stage imagery and atmosphere should find this an excellent choice.

Romeo and Juliet (ballet): *Suite No. 2.*
*** Ph. Dig. 420 483-2 [id.]. Leningrad PO, Mravinsky – TCHAIKOVSKY: *Nutcracker*; excerpts.***

Right from the very beginning it is obvious that this is music-making of real stature. Phrases breathe and textures glow; detail stands in the proper relation to the whole. There is drama and poetry, and wonderfully rapt *pianissimi*. However, the fourth movement (*Dance*) of the printed score is omitted from this recording. Minor reservations concerning the balance of the recorded sound should not deter anyone from considering this disc.

Scythian suite, Op. 20.
*** DG 410 598-2 [id.]. Chicago SO, Abbado – BARTÓK: *Miraculous Mandarin* etc.***

Abbado's account of the *Scythian suite* has drive and fire; if it displays less savagery than some previous versions, the Chicago orchestra have no want of power, and Abbado achieves most refined colouring in the atmospheric *Night* movement. The enhancement of the CD remastering is striking: the focus is firmer, yet there is no loss of warmth and body.

Sinfonia concertante for cello and orchestra, Op. 125.
*** Erato/WEA Dig. 2292 45332-2 [id.]. Rostropovich, LSO, Ozawa – SHOSTAKOVICH: *Cello concerto No. 1.****

(i) *Sinfonia concertante in E min., Op. 125; Romeo and Juliet: suite No. 3, Op. 101.*
**(*) Chan. Dig. CHAN 8508 [id.]. (i) Raphael Wallfisch; SNO, Järvi.

It was Rostropovich's playing of the E minor original that inspired Prokofiev to rework his *Cello concerto* and replace it with the *Sinfonia concertante*, and the cellist collaborated in the writing for the solo instrument. Rostropovich has recorded it before, but his latest account of the work with Ozawa on Erato is a worthy successor. He is in glorious form throughout, and the new version also scores over its predecessor in the greater sensitivity to dynamic nuance that Ozawa shows. There is a small mannerism, a little way into the first movement, where he pulls back to make an expressive effect (no doubt at the soloist's instigation) which some will find disruptive, but this is a relatively trivial point. The orchestral balance is excellent, with a truthful perspective and transparent textures. If the coupling is suitable, this can be safely recommended.

Wallfisch has the measure of the leisurely first movement and gives a thoroughly committed account of the Scherzo and the Theme and Variations that follow, and Neeme Järvi lends him every support. It is inevitable that the cello should be given a little help by the microphone (as is the case in the previous versions) but it does seem a shade too forward. The fill-up, the third suite from *Romeo and Juliet*, is an excellent makeweight.

Sinfonietta in A, Op. 48; Symphony No. 1 in D (Classical), Op. 25.
*** Virgin Dig. VC 791098-2. Lausanne CO, Zedda – DEBUSSY: *Danse* etc.; MILHAUD: *Création du monde.****

Prokofiev could not understand why the early *Sinfonietta* failed to make an impression on the wider musical public, and neither can we. Alongside the *Classical symphony* the *giocoso* outer movements have a more fragile geniality but they are highly delectable, as are the somewhat angular *Andante*, the brief *Intermezzo* and the witty Scherzo. The use of the orchestral palette is as subtle as it is engaging and, with Alberto Zedda's affectionately light touch and fine Lausanne playing, the piece emerges here with all colours flying. The account of the *Classical symphony* is also highly persuasive, the violins exquisitely gentle at their poised entry in the *Larghetto* and the outer movements spirited, with the finale mercurial in its zestful progress. The fairly resonant sound, with the orchestra slightly recessed, adds to the feeling of warmth without blunting the orchestral articulation.

Symphony No. 1 in D (Classical), Op. 25.
*** DG Dig. 423 624-2 [id.]. Orpheus CO – BIZET: *Symphony*; BRITTEN: *Simple symphony.****

*** Decca 417 734-2 [id.]. ASMF, Marriner – BIZET: *Symphony*; STRAVINSKY: *Pulcinella*.***

*** DG Dig. 400 034-2 [id.]. BPO, Karajan – GRIEG: *Holberg suite*; MOZART: *Serenade: Eine kleine Nachtmusik*.***

*** Delos Dig. D/CD 3021 [id.]. LACO, Schwarz – SHOSTAKOVICH: *Piano concerto No. 1***(*); STRAVINSKY: *Soldier's tale suite*.***

(B) ** Van. VNC 7532 [VCD 72012 with ARENSKY & BORODIN: *Nocturne*]. ECO, Somary – ARENSKY: *Variations***(*); TCHAIKOVSKY: *Serenade*.**

Prokofiev wrote his *Classical* pastiche at the relatively advanced age of twenty-six. But the music has a certain youthful precociousness, and the Orpheus performance has comparable freshness and wit – the droll bassoon solo in the first movement against sparkling string figurations is delightful. In the cantilena of the *Larghetto*, some ears might crave a greater body of violin tone; but the playing has a fine poise, and the minuet and finale have equal flair. Excellent, truthful recording to make this a highly desirable triptych.

Marriner's famous recording has been remastered effectively and sounds very fresh; although there has been some loss of bass response, the ambient warmth ensures that the sound retains its body and bloom. Marriner's tempi are comparatively relaxed, but the ASMF are in sparkling form and play beautifully in the slow movement. Detail is stylishly pointed and the finale is vivacious, yet elegant too.

Karajan's performance is predictably brilliant, the playing beautifully polished, with grace and eloquence distinguishing the slow movement. The outer movements are wanting in charm alongside Marriner. The recording is clearly detailed, though the balance is not quite natural; the upper strings are very brightly lit, with a touch of digital edge, but the ambience is attractive. This is also available at mid-price, coupled with Karajan's superb version of the *Fifth Symphony*.

Schwarz's version, if not quite as brilliant as Karajan's, is a nicely paced performance, the slow movement particularly pleasing in its relaxed lyricism and the finale sparkling with high spirits. It is very well played; the orchestra is naturally balanced within a fairly resonant acoustic which provides plenty of air round the instruments.

Somary gives a straightforward account, very well played if with no special individuality, at its best in the high-spirited finale. If the couplings are suitable, this is good value, if not memorable. The sound is good.

Symphonies Nos. 1 in D (Classical); 4 in C, Op. 112 (revised 1947 version).
*** Chan. Dig. CHAN 8400 [id.]. SNO, Järvi.

Prokofiev drastically revised the score of the *Fourth Symphony*. The extent of this overhaul, made immediately after the completion of the *Sixth Symphony*, can be gauged by the fact that the 1930 version takes 23 minutes 8 seconds and the revision 37 minutes 12 seconds. The first two movements are much expanded and the orchestration is richer: among other things, a piano is added. Not all of Prokofiev's afterthoughts are improvements, but Järvi succeeds in making out a more eloquent case for the revision than many of his predecessors. He also gives an exhilarating account of the *Classical symphony*, one of the best on record. The slow movement has real *douceur* and the finale is wonderfully high-spirited. On CD, the recording has fine range and immediacy, but in the *Fourth Symphony* the upper range is a little fierce in some of the more forceful climaxes.

Symphonies Nos. 1 in D (Classical), Op. 25; 5 in B flat, Op. 100.
*** Decca Dig. 421 813-2 [id.]. Montreal SO, Dutoit.

(M) *** DG 423 216-2 [id.]. BPO, Karajan.
*** Ph. Dig. 420 172-2 [id.]. LAPO, Previn.
**(*) Collins Dig. 1064 [id.]. Philh. O, Barshai.

Though at a relatively expansive speed, the lyricism of the first movement of the *Fifth* is given full expressive rein by Dutoit who, with his rhythmic sharpness, balances that against the right degree of spikiness, very necessary in Prokofiev. That sharpness goes with wit in the slow movement, while the third movement, like the first, for all the lushness of the violin sound is more than just a romantic episode, its ominous side brought out potently. The finale, superbly articulated, is fresh and animated, making much of the rough, pawky humour. In the *Classical symphony* too, Dutoit points the humour infectiously, helped by beautifully sprung rhythms and crisp ensemble. The sound is warm and atmospheric, as well as brilliant.

Karajan's 1979 recording of the *Fifth* is in a class of its own. The playing has wonderful tonal sophistication and Karajan judges tempi to perfection so that proportions seem quite perfect. The Berlin Philharmonic are at the height of their form; in their hands the Scherzo is a *tour de force*. The recording has an excellent perspective and allows all the subtleties of orchestral detail to register; however, the digital remastering has brightened the upper range, while the bass response is drier. Nevertheless this remains among the most distinguished *Fifths* ever recorded, and is coupled with Karajan's 1982 digital recording of the *Classical symphony*, which is discussed above.

In the first movement of the *Fifth* Previn's pacing seems exactly right: everything flows so naturally and speaks effectively. The Scherzo is not as high voltage as some rivals, but Previn still brings it off well; and in the slow movement he gets playing of genuine eloquence from the Los Angeles orchestra. He also gives an excellent account of the perennially fresh *Classical symphony*. The recording is beautifully natural with impressive detail, range and body.

Rudolf Barshai gives a dignified and civilized performance of the *Fifth* with well-chosen, judicious tempi. He gets good, well-disciplined playing from the Philharmonia Orchestra, and if one heard this account on the radio or in the concert hall, it would be with pleasure. However, greater bite and zest are needed, the lines need to sing with greater intensity. The Collins recording more than holds its own with the best; there is abundant detail and outstanding presence at the bottom end of the register.

Symphonies Nos. 1 (Classical); 7, Op. 131; Love of 3 oranges (opera): *suite.*
(B) *** CfP CD-CFP 4523. Philh. O, Malko.

Malko's performances were recorded in 1955, and the accounts of the two symphonies were the first stereo EMI ever made. All the performances are quite excellent, and the *Seventh Symphony*, of which Malko conducted the UK première, is freshly conceived and finely shaped. What is so striking is the range and refinement of the recording: the excellence of the balance and the body of the sound are remarkable. No less satisfying is the suite from *Love of three oranges*, an additional bonus making this outstanding value.

Symphony No. 2 in D min., Op. 40; Romeo and Juliet (ballet): *suite No. 1, Op. 64.*
**(*) Chan. Dig. CHAN 8368 [id.]. SNO, Järvi.

The *Second Symphony* reflects the iconoclastic temper of the early 1920s; the violence and dissonance of its first movement betray Prokofiev's avowed intention of writing a work 'made of iron and steel'. In its formal layout (but in no other respect), the symphony resembles Beethoven's Op. 111, with two movements, the second of which is a set of variations. It is this movement that more than compensates for the excesses of its companion. It is rich in fantasy and some of the variations are wonderfully atmospheric. Neeme Järvi produces altogether excellent results from the Scottish National Orchestra; indeed, he has a real flair for this composer. The Chandos recording is impressively detailed and vivid. The *Romeo and Juliet suite* comes off well; the SNO play with real character, though the quality of the strings at the opening of the *Madrigal* is not luxurious.

Symphonies Nos. 3 in C min., Op. 44; 4 in C, Op. 47 (original, 1930 version)
*** Chan. Dig. CHAN 8401 [id.]. SNO, Järvi.

Neeme Järvi's account of the *Third* is extremely successful. He is particularly successful in the *Andante*, which derives from the last Act of the opera, *The Fiery Angel*, and succeeds in conveying its sense of magic and mystery. In the Scherzo, said to have been inspired by the finale of Chopin's *B flat minor Sonata*, he secures a very good response from the SNO strings. In many ways the original of the *Fourth Symphony* seems more like a ballet suite than a symphony: its insufficient tonal contrast tells – yet the Scherzo, drawn from the music for the Temptress in *The Prodigal Son* ballet, is particularly felicitous.

Symphonies Nos. 3, Op. 44; 4, Op. 112 (revised, 1947 version).
* Olympia Dig. OCD 260. Moscow SO, Kitaenko.

Subtlety is not Dmitri Kitaenko's strong suit, nor is the Russian recording particularly refined: it is very much a radio rather than a concert-hall balance and there is little real depth. It is good to have these two symphonies together, but Järvi on Chandos is a much better buy, although he couples No. 3 with the original 1930 version of No. 4.

Symphony No. 5 in B flat, Op. 100.
*** Chan. Dig. CHAN 8576 [id.]. Leningrad PO, Jansons.

Symphony No. 5 in B flat, Op. 100; Dreams, Op. 6.
*** Decca Dig. 417 314-2 [id.]. Concg. O, Ashkenazy.

Symphony No. 5 in B flat, Op. 100; Waltz suite, Op. 110.
*** Chan. Dig. CHAN 8450 [id.]. SNO, Järvi.

Mariss Jansons's reading with the Leningrad Philharmonic was recorded at a live concert in Dublin. Needless to say, the playing is pretty high voltage, with firm, rich string-tone, particularly from the lower strings, and distinctive wind timbre. The wind is not quite as refined as with Western orchestras, but it is good to hear Prokofiev's writing in vivid primary colours. Jansons goes for brisk tempi – and in the slow movement he really is too fast. The Scherzo is dazzling and so, too, is the finale, which is again fast and overdriven. An exhilarating and exciting performance, eminently well recorded too. For special occasions rather than everyday use perhaps, but strongly recommended.

Järvi's credentials in this repertoire are well established and his direction unhurried, fluent and authoritative. His feeling for the music is unfailingly natural. The three *Waltzes* which derive from various sources are all elegantly played. The Chandos recording is set just a shade further back than some of its companions in the series, yet at the same time every detail is clear.

Ashkenazy's Decca record has two factors in its favour: the quite superb playing of the Concertgebouw Orchestra and a splendidly vivid recording with every strand in the texture audible, yet in the right perspective. It has marvellous presence and range. The fill-up is *Dreams*, composed in 1910 while Prokofiev was still a student.

Symphony No. 5 in B flat, Op. 100; Lieutenant Kijé (suite), Op. 60.
** EMI Dig. CDC7 49469-2. RPO, Vernon Handley.

The amiability of Handley's *Kijé* performance, colourful in its illustration of the different situations, spreads over into the *Symphony*. This is a more easy-going reading than most, beautifully played but putting an emphasis on expressiveness rather than on dramatic bite. The scherzo and finale are both jolly rather than sharp; and, for all its seductive beauty, the slow movement is rather too soft-grained for Prokofiev, helped by the warmly atmospheric recording.

Symphony No. 6 in E flat min., Op. 111. Waltz suite, Op. 110, Nos. 1, 5 and 6.
*** Chan. Dig. CHAN 8359 [id.]. SNO, Järvi.

Though it lags far behind the *Fifth* in popularity, the *Sixth Symphony* goes much deeper than any of its companions; indeed it is perhaps the greatest of the Prokofiev cycle. Neeme Järvi has an instinctive grasp and deep understanding of this symphony; he shapes its detail as skilfully as he does its architecture as a whole. At times, however, one longs for greater sonority from the strings, who sound distinctly lean at the top and wanting in body and weight in the middle and lower registers, even in quieter passages – although there is no question that the orchestra play with much commitment. These artists have the measure of the music's tragic poignancy more than almost any of their predecessors on record. The fill-up, as its title implies, is a set of waltzes, drawn and adapted from various stage works: Nos. 1 and 6 come from *Cinderella* and No. 5 from *War and Peace*.

Symphony No. 7 in C sharp min., Op. 131; Sinfonietta in A, Op. 5/48.
*** Chan. Dig. CHAN 8442 [id.]. SNO, Järvi.

Neeme Järvi's account of the *Seventh Symphony* is hardly less successful than the other issues in this cycle. He gets very good playing from the SNO and has the full measure of this repertoire. Enterprisingly, Chandos offer the early *Sinfonietta* as a highly attractive coupling (what a sunny and charming piece it is!). The digital recording has great range and is excellently balanced.

CHAMBER AND INSTRUMENTAL MUSIC

Cello sonata in C, Op. 119.
*** Chan. Dig. CHAN 8340 [id.]. Yuli Turovsky. Luba Edlina – SHOSTAKOVICH: *Sonata.***
* RCA Dig. RD 87845 [7845-2-RC]. Ofra Harnoy, Michael Dussek – SCHUBERT: *Arpeggione sonata.**

Yuli Turovsky and Luba Edlina are eloquent advocates of this *Sonata*. A finely wrought and rewarding score, it deserves greater popularity, and this excellent performance and recording should make it new friends. The balance is particularly lifelike on CD.

Ofra Harnoy and Michael Dussek are handicapped by an unglamorous recording acoustic and a balance which favours but does not flatter the cellist. The sound is also very bottom-heavy. The playing is curiously listless, wanting in the character and high spirits in which this *Sonata* abounds.

5 Mélodies (for violin & piano), *Op. 35.*
(M) *** Ph. 420 777-2 [id.]. David Oistrakh, Frida Bauer – DEBUSSY; RAVEL; YSAYE: *Sonatas.***

These five pieces are rarities – surprisingly so, considering their appeal. They are inventive and charming, at times passionate, at others delectably intimate. Wonderful playing from Oistrakh and Frida Bauer, and the excellent recording is given new presence on CD without degradation of the timbre.

String quartets Nos. 1 in B min., Op. 50; 2 in F, Op. 92.
*** Olympia Dig. OCD 340 [id.]. American Qt.

Although the wartime *Second Quartet* is sometimes played, the *First* is something of a rarity. It comes from 1930 and Prokofiev subsequently arranged its slow movement, an *Andante*, for string orchestra. The American Quartet play it far more persuasively than any earlier version and reveal it to be a work of some appeal as well as substance. The *Second* incorporates folk ideas from Kabarda in the Caucasus, which Taneyev had also studied earlier in the century, but to highly characteristic ends. Although the performance does not have quite the bite and zest of the unforgettable pioneering disc by the Hollywood Quartet, it does not fall far short of it. Apart from one trifling blemish (the image recedes momentarily at one point), the recording is absolutely first class and can confidently be recommended. A rewarding issue.

Violin sonatas Nos. 1 in F min., Op. 80; 2 in D, Op. 94a.
*** DG Dig. 423 575-2 [id.]. Shlomo Mintz, Yefim Bronfman.
**(*) Chan. Dig. CHAN 8398 [id.]. Mordkovitch, Oppitz.

Violin sonatas Nos. 1 in F min., Op. 80; 2 in D, Op. 94a; 5 Melodies, Op. 35.
*(*) ASV Dig. CDDCA 667 [id.]. Mayumi Fujikawa, Craig Sheppard.

Shlomo Mintz made a great impression with his coupling of the two *Concertos*, and his recording of the *Sonatas* is hardly less successful. Mintz has a wonderful purity of line and immaculate intonation, and his partner, Yefim Bronfman, is both vital and sensitive. These are commanding performances, imaginative in phrasing and refined in approach. The DG recording is excellent. This is a clear first choice.

Lydia Mordkovitch and Gerhard Oppitz give thoughtful readings with vital contributions from both partners. They have the measure of the darker, more searching side of the *F minor*, and are hardly less excellent in the companion. They also have the benefit of well-balanced Chandos recording. Both artists bring insights of their own to this music that make these performances well worth having, but the Mintz performances on DG are finer still.

With Mayumi Fujikawa and Craig Sheppard there are many felicitous things, as one would expect. Fujikawa is an eloquent player, as indeed is her partner, but the first movement of the *F minor* is a shade ponderous and feels slow; nor do these artists fully convey the charm of the *D major Sonata*. Perhaps the recording is partly to blame, since it does not flatter Fujikawa's tone. She is an artist of quality whose representation on record is all too meagre, and it is a pity that these performances do not quite come off.

Violin sonata No. 2 in D.
** Ph. Dig. 426 254-2. Viktoria Mullova, Bruno Canino – RAVEL: *Sonata in G*; STRAVINSKY: *Divertimento.****

The *Second Sonata* is given a brilliant performance by Mullova and Canino, even if the lyrical charm and tenderness of the first movement elude them and the scherzo is rather rushed. This is musically not as impressive as the Stravinsky or the Ravel with which it is coupled. The recording is quite superb.

Piano sonatas Nos. 1 in F min., Op. 1; 4 in C min., Op. 29; 5 in C, Op. 38/135; 9 in C, Op. 103; 10 in E min., Op. 137.
**(*) Olympia Dig. OCD 255 [id.]. Murray McLachlan.

Murray McLachlan proves a sound and generally sympathetic guide to this repertoire. In addition to playing these sonatas (including a fragment – albeit only the few bars that survive – of a *Tenth*), he provides a well-informed and perceptive note. He is totally inside the idiom and makes out a very good case for the revision of the *Fifth Sonata*, though he is less convincing in the *Ninth* and does not obliterate memories of Richter. Its first movement, for example, sounds a little bland and needs greater variety of keyboard colour and a wider dynamic range than is shown here. Taken all round, however, this is accomplished playing and a remarkable feat for a pianist still in his early twenties. The recording – a bit on the close side – falls just short of three stars.

Piano sonatas Nos. 2 in D min., Op. 14; 7 in B flat, Op. 83; 8 in B flat, Op. 84.
** Olympia Dig. OCD 256 [id.]. Murray McLachlan.

By the time he came to write his *Second Sonata*, Prokofiev's keyboard style was fully formed. Murray McLachlan has excellent technique but his account of, say, the scherzo of No. 2 or the finale of No. 7 misses the last ounce of demonic fire and that transcendental virtuosity which pianists like Horowitz and Pollini brought to this music. The recording is marginally too close, though the acoustic is reasonably resonant.

Piano sonatas Nos. 3 in A min., Op. 28; 5 in C, Op. 38 (original version); 6 in A, Op. 82; Sonatine in E min., Op. 54/1; 4 Pieces, Op. 4.
** Olympia OCD 257 [id.]. Murray McLachlan.

The *Third Sonata* has plenty of fire and dash, though the rather close recording makes for a somewhat unrelieved effect. On the whole these are reliable performances from a pianist totally in sympathy with this repertoire, even though the works may have gained by being recorded over a longer time-span. There are traces of routine here and there: in the development section of the first movement of No. 5 and elsewhere. But this is unfailingly intelligent playing and a generously filled disc. It is good to have the *E minor Sonatine* (most sensitively played too) and the Op. 4 *Pieces*.

Piano sonata No. 6 in A, Op. 82.
⊛ *** DG Dig. 413 363-2 [id.]. Pogorelich – RAVEL: *Gaspard de la nuit.****

Pogorelich's performance of the *Sixth Sonata* is quite simply dazzling; indeed, it is by far the best version of it ever put on record. It is certainly Pogorelich's most brilliant record so far and can be recommended with the utmost enthusiasm in its CD format.

Piano sonata No. 7 in B flat, Op. 83.
*** DG 419 202-2 [id.]. Maurizio Pollini – *Recital.****

This is a great performance, well in the Horowitz or Richter category. It is part of a generous CD of twentieth-century music, although many readers who respond to Prokofiev and Pollini's outstanding account of Stravinsky's *Three movements from Petrushka* may find the accompanying works of Boulez and Webern less to their taste, fine as the performances are.

Piano sonatas Nos. 7 in B flat, Op. 83; 8 in B flat, Op. 84.
*** CBS Dig. MK 44680 [id.]. Yefim Bronfman.

Yefim Bronfman has a formidable technique, and neither work holds any terrors for him; his clarity of articulation and tonal finesse are unfailingly impressive. The opening of No. 8 has a good sense of forward movement, and this is much to be preferred to the slow, meandering gait favoured by some pianists. Highly accomplished playing throughout, though it is distinctly short measure these days. All the same, it is very recommendable.

Alexander Nevsky (cantata), *Op. 78.*
(M) *** EMI CDM7 63114-2. Anna Reynolds, LSO Ch., LSO, Previn – RACHMANINOV: *The Bells.****

(i) *Alexander Nevsky, Op. 78; Lieutenant Kijé* (suite), *Op. 60.*
*** DG 419 603-2 [id.]. (i) Elena Obraztsova, LSO Ch.; LSO, Abbado.
(M) *** RCA GD 60176 [60176-2-RG]. (i) Rosalind Elias, Chicago SO Ch.; Chicago SO, Reiner – GLINKA: *Russlan Overture.****

(i) *Alexander Nevsky, Op. 78; Scythian suite, Op. 20.*
*** Chan. Dig. CHAN 8584 [id.]. (i) Linda Finnie, SNO Ch.; SNO, Järvi.

The bitter chill of the Russian winter can be felt in the orchestra at the very opening of Järvi's reading and the melancholy of the choral entry has real Slavic feeling; later in their call to 'Arise, ye Russian people' there is an authentic good-humoured peasant robustness. His climactic point is the enormously spectacular *Battle on the ice*, with the recording giving great pungency to the bizarre orchestral effects and the choral shouts riveting in their force and fervour. Linda Finnie sings the final lament eloquently and Järvi's apotheosis is very affecting, but at the close Obraztsova and Abbado create an even graver valedictory feeling which is unforgettable. As coupling, Järvi chooses the ballet *Ala and Lolly*, which subsequently became the *Scythian suite*. Its motoric rhythms are characteristic of the composer at his most aggressive, but the lyrical music is even more rewarding.

Abbado's performance culminates in a deeply moving account of the tragic lament after the battle (here very beautifully sung by Obraztsova), made the more telling when the battle itself is so fine an example of orchestral virtuosity. The chorus is as incisive as the orchestra. The digital remastering of the 1980 recording has been all gain and the sound is very impressive indeed, with great weight and impact and excellent balance. *Lieutenant Kijé* also sounds splendid, and Abbado gets both warm and wonderfully clean playing from the Chicago orchestra.

All the weight, bite and colour of the score are captured by Previn, and though the timbre of the singers' voices may not suggest Russians, they cope very confidently with the Russian text; Previn's direct and dynamic manner ensures that the great *Battle on the ice* scene is powerfully effective. Anna Reynolds sings the lovely *Lament* for the dead most affectingly. The sound is sharply defined, with plenty of bite; just a little of the old analogue ambient fullness has gone. The coupling with Rachmaninov's *Bells* is an obvious (and generous) one, as Previn's performance of this other great Russian choral work is similarly successful.

Reiner's version, recorded in 1959, was another of the astonishingly vivid early achievements of the RCA stereo catalogue. The performance is gripping from the first bar to the last. The sinister evocation of the Teutonic invaders is matched by the power of the *Battle on the ice*. With choral singing of great fervour and a movingly eloquent contribution from Rosalind Elias in the great *Lament*, one hardly notices that the English-language performance inevitably sounds less idiomatic with an American accent. The *Lieutenant Kijé suite*, recorded two years earlier, is another colourful example of the Chicago orchestra at their peak, the sound again full and atmospheric.

Ivan the Terrible, Op. 116 (film music, arr. in oratorio form by Stasevich).
(M) *** EMI CDM7 69584-2 [id.]. Arkhipova, Mokrenko, Morgunov (narrator), Ambrosian Ch., Philh. O, Muti.

This oratorio was put together long after Prokofiev's death by the scholar Abram Stasevich, and the result is diffuse; the device of adding a spoken narration (in Russian) could well prove irritating on repetition. Nevertheless, with fine playing and choral singing, there are many imaginative ideas here to relish, not least those using broad, folk-like melodies. The Kingsway Hall recording is admirably spacious, and though the histrionic style of the narrator, Boris Morgunov, is unappealing, the two other soloists are excellent in their limited roles. The remastering has been highly successful and the effect is often thrillingly vivid, with the chorus especially telling.

5 Poems of Anna Akhmatova, Op. 27; 2 Poems, Op. 9; 5 Poems of Konstantin Balmont, Op. 36; 3 Romances, Op. 73.
**(*) Chan. Dig. CHAN 8509 [id.]. Carole Farley, Arkady Aronov.

Rare and valuable repertoire. The two songs of Op. 9 are vaguely impressionistic in feeling, though the first is the more imaginative. Otherwise the piano writing in these songs is thoroughly personal, nowhere more so than in the Op. 36 Balmont settings. The songs are powerful and full of resourceful and imaginative touches. The Akhmatova settings are quite beautiful. The *Three Romances*, Op. 73, to words of Pushkin, are full of the wry harmonic sleights of hand that are so characteristic of his musical speech. The American soprano, Carole Farley, responds to the different moods and character of the poems and encompasses a rather wide range of colour and tone, although at times her voice is rather edgy and uneven in timbre. The accompanying of Arkady Aronov is highly sensitive and perceptive; his playing is a joy throughout. The recording is completely truthful.

OPERA

L'amour des trois oranges (The Love of 3 oranges): complete.
**(*) Virgin Dig. VCD 791084-2 (2) [id.]. Bacquier, Bastin, Dubosc, Gautier, Viala, Lyon Opera Ch. & O, Kent Nagano.

Previous recordings of Prokofiev's sparkling charade, *The Love of three oranges*, have always been in Russian. Very reasonably, however, Virgin opted for the alternative of French, as being the original language: that was the language used when the opera was given its first, lavish production in Chicago in December 1921. French inevitably brings a degree of softening in vocal texture, but most listeners will understand far more of the words; and the brilliant young conductor, Kent Nagano, and his Lyon Opera House team make up for any loss in knife-edged precision of ensemble. The only star names in the cast are the basses in the two main character-roles, Gabriel Bacquier as the King and Jules Bastin as the monstrous Cook, guardian of the three oranges. They are well matched by the others, including Jean-Luc Viala as an aptly petulant Prince and Catherine Dubosc as a sweetly girlish Princess Ninette. A snag with the recorded sound is that the commenting chorus – very much a part of the action in commedia dell'arte style – is focused too vaguely, a pity when the timing is so crisp. Happily the focus for the solo voices is clearer. On the whole, Virgin's enterprise in going to Lyon and its outstanding new music director – successor to John Eliot Gardiner – has paid off impressively. However, it is irritating that there are so few cueing points on the CDs (just one for each scene), even if this is very much an ensemble opera, with few set solos.

The Gambler (opera): complete.
* Olympia OCD 162 A/B (2) [id.]. Ognivtsiev, Maslennikov, Kasrashvili, Korolev, Borisova, Avdeyeva, Ch. & O of USSR Bolshoi Theatre, Lazarev.

The Gambler, based on Dostoevsky, has never really established itself in the repertory, though it has been staged in the UK. There are many characteristic ideas here, several of which are included in the *Four Portraits* which Prokofiev subsequently made for orchestra. The opera is well worth investigating and the playing is thoroughly idiomatic, though the singers are characteristically Slavonic. At times the recording inclines towards the strident, and the balance is pretty disastrous, placing the singers very forward so that, if orchestral detail is to come into its own, one has to listen at an uncomfortable level. Few of the singers vary their dynamic level, which is usually high. To be approached with caution and only *faute de mieux*.

Puccini, Giacomo (1858–1924)

Capriccio sinfonico; Crisantemi; Minuets Nos. 1–3; Preludio sinfonico; Edgar: Preludes, Acts I and III. Manon Lescaut: Intermezzo, Act III. Le Villi: Prelude; La Tregenda (Act II).
*** Decca Dig. 410 007-2 [id.]. Berlin RSO, Chailly.

The *Capriccio sinfonico* of 1876 brings the first characteristically Puccinian idea in what later became the opening Bohemian motif of *La Bohème*. There are other identifiable fingerprints here, even if the big melodies suggest Mascagni rather than full-blown Puccini. *Crisantemi* has the original string quartet scoring expanded for full string orchestra. Chailly draws opulent and atmospheric playing from the Berlin Radio Symphony Orchestra, helped by richly vivid recording.

Crisantemi for string quartet.
*** CRD CRD 3366 [id.]. Alberni Qt – DONIZETTI: *Quartet No. 13*; VERDI: *Quartet.****

Puccini's brief essay in writing for string quartet dates from the late 1880s; three years later he used the main themes in his first fully successful opera, *Manon Lescaut*. The piece is given a warm, finely controlled performance by the Alberni Quartet and makes a valuable makeweight for the two full-scale quartets by fellow opera-composers. The sound is excellent.

(i) *Crisantemi; Minuets 1–3; Quartet in A min.: Allegro moderato; Scherzo in A min.*; (ii) *Foglio d'album; Piccolo tango*; (iii; ii) *Avanti Urania; E l'uccellino; Inno a Diana; Menti all'avviso; Morire?; Salve regina; Sole e amore; Storiella d'amore; Terra e mare.*
*** Etcetera KTC 1050. (i) Raphael Qt; (ii) Tan Crone; (iii) Roberta Alexander.

It is fascinating to find among early, rather untypical songs like *Storiella d'amore* and *Menti all'avviso* a charming little song, *Sole e amore*, written jokingly for a journal, 'Paganini', in 1888, which provided, bar for bar, the main idea of the Act III quartet in *La Bohème* of eight years later. Puccini's melodic flair comes out in such a song as *E l'uccellino*, written in Neapolitan style; and there is a rousing homophonic hymn for his fellow-huntsmen in *Inno a Diana*, while *Avanti Urania!* improbably was written to celebrate the launching of a titled friend's steam-yacht. The two piano pieces are simple album-leaves; among the six quartet pieces, *Crisantemi* is already well known; the rest are student pieces, including a delightful fragment of a Scherzo. Performances are good, though Roberta Alexander's soprano is not ideally Italianate. The recorded sound is vivid and immediate against a lively hall ambience.

Messa di Gloria.
*** Erato/WEA Dig. 2292 45197-2 [id.]. Carreras, Prey, Amb. S., Philh. O, Scimone.

Puccini's *Messa di Gloria* was completed when he was only twenty. The bold secularity of some of the ideas, for example the brassy march for the *Gloria* itself, is very much in the Italian tradition, perilously skirting the edge of vulgarity. Scimone and a fine team are brisker and lighter than their predecessors on record, yet effectively bring out the red-bloodedness of the writing. José Carreras turns the big solo in the *Gratias* into the first genuine Puccini aria. His sweetness and imagination are not quite matched by the baritone, Hermann Prey, who is given less to do than usual, when the choral baritones take on the yearning melody of *Crucifixus*. Excellent, atmospheric sound.

OPERA

La Bohème (complete).
(***) EMI mono CDS7 47235-8 (2) [Ang. CDCB 47235]. De los Angeles, Bjoerling, Merrill, Reardon, Tozzi, Amara, RCA Victor Ch. & O, Beecham.
*** Decca 421 049-2 (2) [id.]. Freni, Pavarotti, Harwood, Panerai, Ghiaurov, German Op. Ch., Berlin, BPO, Karajan.
**(*) RCA RD 80371 [RCD2 0371]. Caballé, Domingo, Milnes, Sardinero, Raimondi, Blegen, Alldis Ch., Wandsworth School Boys' Ch., LPO, Solti.
**(*) Decca 411 868-2 (2) [id.]. Tebaldi, Bergonzi, Bastianini, Siepi, Corena, D'Angelo, St Cecilia Ac. Ch. & O, Rome, Serafin.
(***) EMI mono CDS7 47475-8 (2) [Ang. CDCB 47475]. Callas, Di Stefano, Moffo, Panerai, Zaccaria, La Scala, Milan, Ch. & O, Votto.

Beecham's is a uniquely magical performance with two favourite singers, Victoria de los Angeles and Jussi Bjoerling, challenged to their utmost in loving, expansive singing. The voices are treated far better by the CD remastering than the orchestra, which is rather thinner-sounding than it was on LP, though as ever the benefits of silent background are very welcome in so warmly atmospheric a reading. With such a performance one hardly notices the recording, but those who want fine modern stereo can turn readily to Karajan.

Karajan too takes a characteristically spacious view of *Bohème*, but there is an electric intensity which holds the whole score together as in a live performance. Karajan unerringly points the climaxes with full force, highlighting them against prevailing pianissimos. Pavarotti is an inspired Rodolfo, with comic flair and expressive passion, while Freni is just as seductive a Mimi as she was in the Schippers set ten years earlier. Elizabeth Harwood is a charming Musetta, even if her voice is not as sharply contrasted with Freni's as it might be. Fine singing throughout the set. The reverberant Berlin acoustic is glowing and brilliant in superb Decca recording, with the clean placing of voices enhancing the performance's dramatic warmth.

The glory of Solti's set of *Bohème* is the singing of Montserrat Caballé as Mimi, an intensely characterful and imaginative reading which makes you listen with new intensity to every phrase, the voice at its most radiant. Domingo is unfortunately not at his most inspired. *Che gelida manina* is relatively coarse, though here as elsewhere he produces glorious heroic tone, and never falls into vulgarity. The rest of the team is strong, but Solti's tense interpretation of a work he had never conducted in the opera house does not quite let the full flexibility of the music have its place or the full warmth of romanticism. However, the RCA recording acquires extra brightness and clarity in the digital transfer to CD, to give extra point and sparkle to the performance.

On the earlier Decca set, Tebaldi is most affecting as Mimi: she offers some superbly controlled singing, but the individuality of the heroine is not as indelibly conveyed as with De los Angeles, Freni or Caballé. Carlo Bergonzi is a fine Rodolfo; Bastianini and Siepi are both superb as Marcello and Colline, and even the small parts of Benoit and Alcindoro (as usual taken by a single artist) have the benefit of Corena's magnificent voice. The veteran Serafin was more vital here than on some of his records. The recording, now over thirty years old, has its vividness and sense of stage perspective enhanced on CD, with minimal residue tape-hiss, though the age of the master shows in the string timbre above the stave.

Callas, flashing-eyed and formidable, may seem even less suited to the role of Mimi than to that of Butterfly, but characteristically her insights make for a vibrantly involving performance. Though Giuseppe di Stefano is not the subtlest of Rodolfos, he is in excellent voice here, and Moffo and Panerai make a strong partnership as the second pair of lovers. Votto occasionally coarsens Puccini's score but he directs with energy. The comparatively restricted dynamic range means that the singers appear to be 'front stage', but there is no lack of light and shade in Act II.

La Bohème: highlights.
*** Decca 421 245-2 [id.] (from above recording with Freni and Pavarotti, cond. Karajan).
(M) **(*) Decca 421 301-2 [id.] (from above recording with Tebaldi and Bergonzi, cond. Serafin).

It is a pity to cut anything from so taut an opera as *La Bohème*; but those who feel they can make do with a single CD instead of two will find this selection from the Karajan set ideal. Most collectors will surely want a reminder of the vintage set with Tebaldi and Bergonzi at the height of their powers. The selection is well made, and the disc is competitively priced.

La Fanciulla del West (The Girl of the Golden West; complete).
⊛ (M) *** Decca 421 595-2 (2) [id.]. Tebaldi, Del Monaco, MacNeil, Tozzi, St Cecilia Ac., Rome, Ch. & O, Capuana.
(M) **(*) DG 419 640-2 (2) [id.]. Neblett, Domingo, Milnes, Howell, ROHCG Ch. and O, Mehta.

Like Karajan's classic 1961 *Tosca* (see below), the Decca set of *La Fanciulla del West* has been remastered for CD with spectacular success. The achievement is the more remarkable when one considers that the original recording was made in 1958; but this is vintage Decca sound, both atmospheric and vivid. Tebaldi gives one of her most warm-hearted and understanding performances on record, and Mario del Monaco displays the wonderfully heroic quality of his voice to great – if sometimes tiring – effect. Cornell MacNeil as the villain, Sheriff Rance, sings with great precision and attack, but unfortunately has not a villainous-sounding voice to convey the character fully. Jake Wallace's entry and the song *Che faranno i viecchi miei* is one of the high spots of the recording, with Tozzi singing beautifully. Capuana's expansive reading is matched by the imagination of the production, with the closing scene wonderfully effective.

Mehta's manner – as he makes clear at the very start – is on the brisk side, not just in the cakewalk rhythms but even in refusing to let the first great melody, the nostalgic *Che faranno i viecchi miei*, linger into sentimentality. Sherrill Milnes as Jack Rance makes that villain into far more than a small-town Scarpia, giving nobility and understanding to the first-Act *arioso*. Domingo, as in the theatre, sings heroically, disappointing only in his reluctance to produce soft tone in the great aria *Ch'ella mi creda*. The rest of the team is excellent, not least Gwynne Howell as the minstrel who sings *Che faranno i viecchi miei*;

but the crowning glory of a masterly set is the singing of Carol Neblett as the Girl of the Golden West herself, gloriously rich and true and with formidable attack on the exposed high notes. Full, atmospheric recording to match, essential in an opera full of evocative offstage effects, but the slight drying-out process of the digital sound adds some stridency in tuttis, readily acceptable with so strong a performance.

Gianni Schicchi (complete).
*** Ariola-Eurodisc Dig. 258404 [7751-2-RC]. Panerai, Donath, Seiffert, Munich R. O, Patanè.
**(*) Hung. Dig. HCD 12541 [id.]. Melis, Kalmar, Gulya, Hungarian State Op. O, Ferencsik.

Patanè conducts a colourful and vigorous performance, very well drilled in ensembles, even when speeds are dangerously fast. Central to the performance's success is the vintage Schicchi of Rolando Panerai, still rich and firm. Peter Seiffert as Rinuccio brings a dashing contribution, consistently clean and firm of tone, making light of the high tessitura and rising splendidly to the challenge of the big central aria. Helen Donath would have sounded even sweeter a few years earlier, but she gives a tender, appealing portrait of Lauretta, pretty and demure in *O mio babbino caro*. Incredibly, the CD has only two tracks, the second starting immediately after, not before, *O mio babbino caro*!

Ferencsik conducts all-Hungarian forces in an energetic and well-drilled account of Puccini's comic masterpiece, which makes up for some unidiomatic rigidity with red-blooded commitment. The singing is variable, with the incidental characters including some East European wobblers. György Melis is not always perfectly steady, but his is a fine, characterful reading, strongly projected; though Magda Kalmar sounds too mature for the girlish Lauretta, the tone is attractively warm and finely controlled, as is Denes Gulya's tenor in the role of Rinuccio. It is a pity that the CD has no banding whatever.

Madama Butterfly (complete).
**(*) Decca 417 577-2 (3) [id.]. Freni, Ludwig, Pavarotti, Kerns, V. State Op. Ch., VPO, Karajan.
*** DG Dig. 423 567-2 (3) [id.]. Freni, Carreras, Berganza, Pons, Amb. Op. Ch., Philh. O, Sinopoli.
**(*) Decca 411 634-2 (2) [id.]. Tebaldi, Bergonzi, Cossotto, Sordello, St Cecilia Ac. Ch. & O, Serafin.
(M) *** RCA GD 84145 (2) [4145-2-RG]. Moffo, Elias, Valletti, Cesari, Catalani, Rome Op. Ch. & O, Leinsdorf.
(M) *** EMI CMS7 69654-2 (2). Scotto, Bergonzi, Di Stasio, Panerai, De Palma, Rome Op. Ch. & O, Barbirolli.
**(*) CBS M2K 35181 (2) [id.]. Scotto, Domingo, Knight, Wixell, Amb. Op. Ch., Philh. O, Maazel.
(***) EMI mono CDS7 49575-2 (2). De los Angeles, Di Stefano, Gobbi, Canali, Ercolani, Rome Op., Gavazzeni.
(***) EMI mono CDS7 47959-8 (2) [id.]. Callas, Gedda, Borriello, Danieli, La Scala, Milan, Ch. & O, Karajan.
(M) (***) EMI mono CHS7 69990-2 (2) [Ang. CDHB 69990]. Toti dal Monte, Gigli, Palombini, Basiola, Rome Opera Ch. & O, Serafin.

Karajan's set is extravagantly laid out on three discs instead of two for most of the rival sets – slow speeds partly responsible – and the advantage that each Act is complete on a single disc will not be considered adequate compensation by most collectors. However, Karajan inspires singers and orchestra to a radiant performance which brings out all the beauty and intensity of Puccini's score, sweet but not sentimental, powerfully dramatic but not vulgar. Freni is an enchanting Butterfly, consistently growing in stature from the young girl to the victim of tragedy, sweeter of voice than any rival on record. Pavarotti is an intensely imaginative Pinkerton, actually inspiring understanding for this thoughtless character, while Christa Ludwig is a splendid Suzuki. The recording is one of Decca's most resplendent, with the Vienna strings producing glowing tone.

With speeds that in principle are eccentrically slow, Sinopoli's reading is the most idiosyncratic on record, but also one of the most powerful and perhaps the most beautiful of all, certainly in the ravishing orchestral sound. However expansive his speeds, Sinopoli is never sentimental or self-indulgent. Puccini's honeyed moments are given, not sloppily, but with rapt intensity – as at the poignant close of the *Flower duet*, when '*sola e rinnegata*' is recalled from Act I. They are then set the more movingly against the biting moments, from the opening fugato of Act I, sharply incisive, through to the final aria, tough and intense, where the trumpet monotone as Butterfly dies (marked to be played as a solo but rarely done that way) nags the nerves as never before. As she was for Karajan in his classic Decca set, Freni is a model Butterfly; though the voice is no longer so girlish, she projects the tragedy even more weightily than before. José Carreras is similarly presented as a large-scale Pinkerton in this, one of his last opera-recordings before his serious illness. Juan Pons is a virile Sharpless and Teresa Berganza an equally positive, unfruity Suzuki. This is a set which in its spacious but intensely concentrated way brings a unique and unforgettable experience.

Serafin's sensitive and beautifully paced reading is on two discs merely. Tebaldi is at her most radiant. Though she was never the most deft of Butterflies dramatically, her singing is consistently rich and beautiful, sometimes breathtakingly so. The excellence of Decca engineering in 1958 is amply proved in the CD transfer, with one serious exception: the absence of bass at the very opening brings a disagreeably shrill and thin sound, improved once the orchestration grows fuller, with voices very precisely and realistically placed.

Anna Moffo's Butterfly proves delightful, fresh and young-sounding. *Un bel dì* has some sliding at the beginning, but the end is glorious, and the *Flower duet* with Rosalind Elias is enchanting. Valletti's Pinkerton has a clear-voiced, almost Gigli-like charm – preferable to most rivals – and with Corena as the Bonze the only blot on the set vocally is the unimaginative Sharpless of Renato Cesari. Leinsdorf is efficient and undistracting and, with vivid recording (balanced in favour of the voices), this makes a first-class mid-priced recommendation, costing less than half the price of the Decca Karajan set with Freni, Ludwig and Pavarotti.

Under Sir John Barbirolli, players and singers perform consistently with a dedication and intensity rare in opera recordings made in Italy, and the whole score glows more freshly than ever. There is hardly a weak link in the cast. Bergonzi's Pinkerton and Panerai's Sharpless are both sensitively and beautifully sung; Anna di Stasio's Suzuki is more than adequate, and Renata Scotto's Butterfly has a subtlety and perceptiveness in its characterization that more than make up for any shortcoming in the basic beauty of tone-colour. It is on any count a highly individual voice, used there with great intelligence to point up the drama to its tragic climax. On CD the violins have lost a little of their original opulence, but in all other respects the recording combines vividness with atmosphere.

Scotto's later version for CBS brought nothing but benefit. The voice had acquired extra richness and was recorded with a warmer tonal bloom, and in perception too Scotto's singing is far deeper, most strikingly in Butterfly's *Un bel dì*, where the narrative leads to special intensity on the words *Chiamerà Butterfly dalla lontana*. Maazel is expressive without losing his architectural sense but he has not quite the imaginative individuality of a Karajan or a Barbirolli. Other contributors are incidental, even Placido Domingo, who sings heroically as Pinkerton but arguably makes him too genuine a character for such a cad. Wixell's voice is not ideally rounded as Sharpless, but he sings sensitively, and Gillian Knight makes an expressive Suzuki. The snag is that the digital transfer, in underlining the clarity and incisiveness of Maazel's reading, makes it sound even less persuasively natural, all too tautly controlled.

Victoria de los Angeles' first recording of *Madama Butterfly*, a role which for a decade and more she made her own, was done in mono in 1954. It makes a welcome return on CD when it has many advantages over the later, stereo version (still awaited). De los Angeles' tone is even more meltingly beautiful, Di Stefano is a more ardent Pinkerton, and Tito Gobbi, unexpectedly cast as a rugged Sharpless, uses that small role to point some of the set's most memorable moments, notably the Act I toasting duet with Pinkerton and the Act II confrontation with Butterfly. The mono sound is full of presence, with voices and orchestra both vividly caught. The only drawback is that the set is offered at full price.

Callas's view, aided by superbly imaginative and spacious conducting from Karajan, gives extra dimension to the Puccinian little woman, and with some keenly intelligent singing too from Gedda as Pinkerton this is a set which has a special compulsion. The performance projects the more vividly on CD, even though the lack of stereo in so atmospheric an opera is a serious disadvantage. Yet the powerful combination of Callas and Karajan – each challenging the other both in expressive imagination and in discipline – makes a powerful effect on the listener; unlike Karajan's later and more sumptuous Decca version with Freni, this one is fitted on to two CDs only.

There has never been as endearing a portrait of Pinkerton on record as Gigli's. The perennial smile in his voice makes one immediately forget how totally caddish the American lieutenant's behaviour is. One simply revels in the beauty of the sound and the imagination of the phrasing, only occasionally self-indulgent. The Butterfly of Toti dal Monte is something of an acquired taste. The 'little-girl' sound is often exaggerated, but it is a classic performance nevertheless. Serafin as ever is a master of timing; but this mono recording of 1939, sounding very well for its age, is a set to get above all for the great tenor and his unique performance.

Madama Butterfly: highlights.
*** Decca 421 247-2 [id.]. Freni, Pavarotti, Ludwig, Kerns, V. State Op. Ch., VPO, Karajan.
**(*) Decca 417 733-2 [id.] (from above recording with Tebaldi and Bergonzi, cond. Serafin).

Karajan's disc offers an obvious first choice for a highlights CD from *Butterfly*, since it includes the *Humming chorus*, omitted from the mid-priced Tebaldi/Bergonzi selection and is excellently recorded. However, the other Decca selection gives a superb reminder of the magnetism of the Tebaldi/Bergonzi partnership. The sound is rich in ambience and the dated upper string timbre is seldom distracting, for the voices are vividly caught.

Manon Lescaut (complete).
*** DG Dig. 413 893-2 (2) [id.]. Freni, Domingo, Bruson, ROHCG Ch., Philh. O, Sinopoli.
*** Decca Dig. 421 426-2 (2) [id.]. Kiri Te Kanawa, Carreras, Paolo Coni, Ch. & O of Teatro Comunale di Bologna, Chailly.

(M) (***) EMI mono CDS7 47393-8 (2) [Ang. CDCB 47392]. Callas, Di Stefano, Fioravanti, La Scala, Milan, Ch. and O, Serafin.

With his concern for detail, his love of high dramatic contrasts, and the clear pointing of changes of mood, along with sharp control of tension, Sinopoli presents the plan of each Act with new precision, reflecting the composer's own careful crafting. This is also the most sensuous-sounding reading on record, thanks also to the fine playing of the Philharmonia and a superb contribution from the chorus. Placido Domingo's portrait of Des Grieux is here far subtler and more detailed, with finer contrasts of tone and dynamic, than in his earlier, EMI recording opposite Caballé. Freni proves an outstanding choice: her girlish tones in Act I rebut any idea that she might be too mature. *In quelle trine morbide*, in Act II, retains freshness of tone with fine concern for word detail, while the long duet and aria of the last Act present a most moving culmination, not feeling like an epilogue. Of the others, a first-rate team, Renato Bruson nicely brings out the ironic side of Lescaut's character, and having Brigitte Fassbaender just to sing the *Madrigal* adds to the feeling of luxury, as does John Tomlinson's darkly intense moment of drama as the ship's captain. The voices are more recessed than is common, but they are recorded with fine bloom, and the brilliance of the orchestral sound comes out impressively.

Dame Kiri, creamier of tone than Mirella Frèni on DG, also gives an affecting characterization, at times rather heavily underlined but passionately convincing in the development from innocent girl to fallen woman. Freni's is the subtler performance and, in the final aria, *Sola, perduta, abbandonata*, Sinopoli's ominously steady tread helps to give her the greater intensity, and the playing from Chailly's Bologna orchestra cannot quite match that of the Philharmonia. Yet Chailly is a degree more idiomatic in his pacing. Both tenors are good but Carreras, recorded just before his illness, sounds a little strained at times. The Decca sound, with voices further forward, is the more vivid.

It is typical of Callas that she turns the final scene into the most compelling part of the opera. Serafin, who could be a lethargic recording conductor, is here electrifying, and Di Stefano too is inspired to one of his finest complete opera recordings. The cast-list even includes the young Fiorenza Cossotto, impressive as the singer in the Act II *Madrigal*. The recording – still in mono, not a stereo transcription – minimizes the original boxiness and gives good detail, but for once the CD medium loses out when a break is involved in Act II between the two discs, whereas LP had that Act complete on one side.

La Rondine (complete).
*** CBS Dig. M2K 37852 [id.]. Te Kanawa, Domingo, Nicolesco, Rendall, Nucci, Watson, Knight, Amb. Op. Ch., LSO, Maazel.
(M) ** RCA GD 60489 (2) [4801-2-RG]. Moffo, Sciutti, Barioni, De Palma, Sereni, RCA Italiana Op. Ch. & O, Molinari-Pradelli.

La Rondine has never caught on, and a recording like this will almost certainly surprise anyone at the mastery of the piece, with a captivating string of catchy numbers. The story, told in Viennese-operetta style, is based on a watered-down *Traviata* situation, culminating not in tragedy but in a sad-sweet in-between ending such as the Viennese loved. It is not just a question of Puccini taking Viennese waltzes as model, but all kinds of other suitable dances such as tangos, foxtrots and two-steps; but he commandeered them completely, to make the result utterly Puccinian. Maazel's is a strong, positive reading, crowned by a superb and radiant Magda in Dame Kiri Te Kanawa, mature yet glamorous. Domingo, by age too mature for the role of young hero, yet scales his voice down most effectively in the first two Acts, expanding in heroic warmth only in the final scene of dénouement. Sadly, the second pair are far less convincing, when the voices of both Mariana Nicolesco and David Rendall take ill to the microphone. Others in the team are excellent, and though Maazel launches the very opening too aggressively, the rest is most sympathetically done, with fine playing from the LSO. One's only real criticism is the lack of access within the opera itself. Acts I and II are on the first disc, Act III on the second; but there are no cues to find individual arias.

The alternative set from RCA has a price advantage. Anna Moffo leads a good cast and the performance, though not ideal, is still highly enjoyable, with understanding direction from Molinari-Pradelli. The recording too has come up well, but the CBS set remains first choice.

Suor Angelica (complete).
**(*) Hung. Dig. HCD 12490 [id.]. Tokody, Póka, Barlay, Takács, Hungarian State Op. Ch. and O, Gardelli.

Gardelli conducts a beautifully paced reading, marked by effective characterization from the Hungarian cast (suggesting stage experience) and vivid, lifelike digital sound. Ilona Tokody makes an attractively girlish-sounding Angelica, but above the stave her voice is shrill. The Zia Principessa of Eszter Póka is breathy and wobbly and not even formidable, the one unconvincing characterization.

Il Tabarro (complete).
**(*) Ariola Eurodisc Dig. 258403 [7775-2-RC]. Nimsgern, Tokody, Lamberti, Munich R. O, Patanè.

Patanè in his larger-than-life direction may at times run the risk of exaggerating the melodrama, but the result is richly enjoyable. Ilona Tokody, already well known from Hungaroton opera sets, makes a powerful, strongly projected Giorgetta, somewhat showing up the relative weakness of the tenor, Giorgio Lamberti, as her lover, Luigi. His over-emphatic underlining mars his legato, but the main love duet comes over with gutsy strength. Siegmund Nimsgern makes a powerful Michele, a shade too explosive in the climactic final aria, but generally firm and clean in his projection, making the character more sinister. The full and brilliant recording has voices set convincingly on a believable stage and well balanced against the orchestra, though it is a pity that the 51 minutes' span brings only two tracks.

Tosca (complete).
(M) *** Decca 421 670-2 (2) [id.]. Leontyne Price, Di Stefano, Taddei, V. State Op. Ch., VPO, Karajan.
*** EMI CDS7 47175-8 (2) [id.]. Callas, Di Stefano, Gobbi, Calabrese, La Scala, Milan, Ch. and O, De Sabata.
*** DG 413 815-2 (2) [id.]. Ricciarelli, Carreras, Raimondi, Corena, German Op. Ch., BPO, Karajan.
*** Ph. 412 885-2 (2) [id.]. Caballé, Carreras, Wixell, ROHCG Ch. and O, C. Davis.
**(*) Decca Dig. 414 597-2 (2) [id.]. Te Kanawa, Aragall, Nucci, Welsh Nat. Opera Ch., Nat. PO, Solti.
**(*) EMI Dig. CDS7 49364-2 (2) [Ang. CDCB 49364]. Scotto, Domingo, Bruson, Amb. Op. Ch., St Clement Danes School Boys' Ch., Philh. O, Levine.
(M) ** EMI CMS7 69974-2 (2) [Ang. CDMB 69974]. Callas, Bergonzi, Gobbi, Paris Op. Ch. & Conservatoire O, Prêtre.

On Decca, Karajan deserves equal credit with the principal singers for the vital, imaginative performance recorded in Vienna. Some idea of its quality may be gained from the passage at the end of Act I, just before Scarpia's *Te Deum*. Karajan takes a speed far slower than usual, but there is an intensity which takes one vividly to the Church of San Andrea while at the same time building the necessary tension for the depiction of Scarpia's villainy. Taddei himself has a marvellously wide range of tone-colour, and though he cannot quite match the Gobbi snarl, he has almost every other weapon in his armoury. Leontyne Price is at the peak of her form and Di Stefano sings most sensitively. The sound of the Vienna orchestra is enthralling – both more refined and richer than usual in a Puccini opera, and it sounds quite marvellous in its digitally remastered format, combining presence with atmosphere and making a superb bargain at mid-price.

There has never been a finer recorded performance of *Tosca* than Callas's first, with Victor de Sabata conducting and Tito Gobbi as Scarpia. One mentions the prima donna first because, in this of all roles, she was able to identify totally with the heroine and turn her into a great tragic figure, not merely the cipher of Sardou's original melodrama. Gobbi too makes the unbelievably villainous police chief into a genuinely three-dimensional character, and Di Stefano as the hero, Cavaradossi, was at his finest. The conducting of De Sabata is spaciously lyrical as well as sharply dramatic, and the mono recording is superbly balanced in Walter Legge's fine production. Though there is inevitably less spaciousness than in a stereo recording, the voices are caught gloriously. Only in the big *Te Deum* scene at the end of Act I does the extra clarity of CD reveal a hint of congestion, and this is minimal. One's only real complaint is the absence of comprehensive cueing throughout the set.

For Karajan, the police chief, Scarpia, seems to be the central character, and his unexpected choice of singer, a full bass, Raimondi, helps to show why, for this is no small-time villain but a man who in full confidence has a vein of nobility in him. Katia Ricciarelli is not the most individual of Toscas, but the beauty of singing is consistent, with *Vissi d'arte* outstanding at a very slow tempo indeed. Carreras is also subjected to slow Karajan tempi in his big arias and, though the recording brings out an unevenness in the voice, it is still a powerful, stylish performance. The recording is rich and full, with the stage picture clearly established and the glorious orchestral textures beautifully caught; the CD transfer improves definition and increases the feeling of spaciousness, putting more air round the voices and adding bloom to the orchestral sound.

Sir Colin Davis rarely if ever chooses idiosyncratic tempi, and his manner is relatively straight; but it remains a strong and understanding reading, as well as a refreshing one. In this the quality of the singing from a cast of unusual consistency plays an important part. With the purity of *Vissi d'arte* coming as a key element in her interpretation, Caballé presents Tosca as a formidable siren-figure. Carreras reinforces his reputation as a tenor of unusual artistry as well as of superb vocal powers. Though Wixell is not ideally well focused as Scarpia, he presents a completely credible lover-figure, not just the lusting ogre of convention. The 1976 analogue recording is full as well as refined, bringing out the beauties of Puccini's scoring. It is given a strikingly successful CD transfer, with three-dimensional placing of voices.

Rarely has Solti phrased Italian melody so consistently *con amore*, his fiercer side subdued but with plenty of power when required. Even so, the timing is not always quite spontaneous-sounding, with transitions occasionally rushed. Scarpia's entry is presented with power but with too little of the necessary menace. Nucci in that role sings strongly but not very characterfully. Aragall as Cavaradossi produces a glorious stream of heroic tone, and the incidental characters are also strongly cast. But the principal *raison d'être* of the set must be the casting of Dame Kiri as the jealous opera-singer. Her admirers will relish the glorious sounds, but the jealous side of Tosca's character is rather muted. Her recognition of the fan shown to her by Scarpia, *E L'Attavanti!*, has no snarl of anger in it, even though she later conveys real pain in her half-tones, as Scarpia's poison begins to work.

With extreme speeds, both fast and slow, and fine playing from the Philharmonia Orchestra, Levine directs a red-blooded performance which underlines the melodrama. Domingo here reinforces his claim to be the finest Cavaradossi today, while the clean-cut, incisive singing of Renato Bruson presents a powerful if rather young-sounding Scarpia. Renata Scotto's voice is in many ways ideally suited to the role of Tosca, certainly in its timbre and colouring; as caught on record, however, the upper register is often squally, though not as distressingly so as in some other recent records. The digital recording is full and forward.

The Callas stereo *Tosca* is exciting and disappointing in roughly predictable proportions. There are few points of improvement over the old mono set, with Callas in the title-role and De Sabata conducting far more imaginatively than takes place here. When it comes to vocal reliability, the comparison of the new with the old is just as damaging, as an impartial observer might have predicted. Gobbi is magnificent still, but no more effective than he was in the mono recording, and Bergonzi's Cavaradossi, intelligent and attractive, is not helped by a recording balance not in his favour.

Tosca: highlights.
*** DG 423 113-2 [id.] (from above set with Ricciarelli and Carreras, cond. Karajan).
**(*) Decca Dig. 421 611-2 [id.] (from above set with Kiri Te Kanawa, Aragall, Nucci, cond. Solti).

The selection from Karajan's powerful, closely recorded Berlin version is welcome. The breadth of Karajan's direction is well represented in the longer excerpts; there is also Tosca's *Vissi d'arte*, but Scarpia's music is under-represented, which is a pity when Raimondi made such a distinctive Scarpia with his dark bass timbre. Dame Kiri Te Kanawa sings gloriously on Solti's set, as does Aragall; but those interested in the opera itself would do better to spend just a little more to obtain the splendid mid-priced Decca Karajan set.

Il Trittico: (i) *Il Tabarro;* (ii) *Suor Angelica;* (iii) *Gianni Schicchi.*
(M) **(*) RCA/Eurodisc Dig. GD 69043 (3) [7775-2-RC: *Il Tabarro*; 7806-2-RC: *Suor Angelica*; 7751-2-RC: *Gianni Schicchi*]. (i) Nimsgern, Lamberti, Auer, Tokody; (i; iii) Pane; (ii) Popp, Lipovšek, Schimi, Jennings; (iii) Panerai, Donath, Baniewicz, Seifert; Bav. R. Ch., Munich R. O, Patanè.
**(*) CBS CD 79312 (3) [M3K 35912]. (i; ii) Scotto, (i; iii) Domingo, (i) Wixell, Sénéchal, (ii) Horne, (ii; iii) Cotrubas, (iii) Gobbi, Amb. Op. Ch., (ii) Desborough School Ch., (i; ii) Nat. PO, (iii) LSO, Maazel.

Patanè's Munich recordings of the three *Trittico* one-acters first appeared separately, but here come, attractively packaged, on three mid-price CDs. Patanè directs consistently well-paced, idiomatic performances of all three operas, well played and atmospherically recorded. Neither Lucia Popp as Angelica nor Maria Lipovšek as the vindictive Zia principessa is ideally cast in the central opera of the triptych – the one overstressed, the other sounding too young – but these are both fine artists who sing with consistent imagination. Nimsgern as Michele in *Tabarro* gives a memorable, well-projected performance, and so does the characterful Rolando Panerai as Schicchi in the comic final opera, both central to the success of the performances. Though the cueing on CD is not generous, it is far more helpful than on the rival Maazel set. In the USA the three operas are available separately but at premium price.

Il Tabarro may most seriously lack atmosphere in Maazel's version, but his directness is certainly refreshing, and in the other two operas it results in powerful readings; the opening of *Gianni Schicchi*, for example, has a sharp, almost Stravinskian bite. In the first two operas, Scotto's performances have a commanding dominance, presenting her at her finest. In *Gianni Schicchi* the veteran Tito Gobbi gives an amazing performance, in almost every way as fine as his EMI recording of twenty years earlier – and in some ways this is even more compelling. The generally close recording has a full range and the immediacy is increased by the vivid CD transfers. The only snag is the lack of cueing; CBS provide only one track for the whole of *Il Tabarro* and only two each for *Gianni Schicchi* and *Suor Angelica*, the second in each case being used to indicate the main soprano aria.

Turandot (complete).
*** Decca 414 274-2 (2) [id.]. Sutherland, Pavarotti, Caballé, Pears, Ghiaurov, Alldis Ch., Wandsworth School Boys' Ch., LPO, Mehta.
*** DG Dig. 410 096-2 (2) [id.]. Ricciarelli, Domingo, Hendricks, Raimondi, V. State Op. Ch., V. Boys' Ch., VPO, Karajan.
(M) *** EMI CMS7 69327-2 (2) [Ang. CDMB 69327]. Nilsson, Corelli, Scotto, Mercuriali, Giaiotti, Rome Op. Ch. & O, Molinari-Pradelli.
(***) EMI mono CDS7 47971-8 (2) [id.]. Callas, Fernandi, Schwarzkopf, Zaccaria, La Scala, Milan, Ch. & O, Serafin.
** CBS M2K 39160 (2) [id.]. Marton, Carreras, Ricciarelli, Kerns, V. State Op. Ch. & O, Maazel.

The role of Turandot, the icy princess, is not one that you would expect to be in Joan Sutherland's repertory, but here on record she gives an intensely revealing and appealing interpretation, making the character far more human and sympathetic than ever before. Sutherland's singing is strong and beautiful, while Pavarotti gives a performance equally imaginative, beautiful in sound, strong on detail. To set Caballé against Sutherland was a daring idea, and it works superbly well; Pears as the Emperor is another imaginative choice. Mehta directs a gloriously rich and dramatic performance, superlatively recorded, still the best-sounding *Turandot* on CD, while the reading also remains supreme.

In Karajan's set, both the Liù of Barbara Hendricks and the Turandot of Katia Ricciarelli are more sensuously feminine than is usual. With her seductively golden tone, Hendricks is almost a sex-kitten, and one wonders how Calaf could ever have overlooked her. This is very different from the usual picture of a chaste slave-girl. Ricciarelli is a far more vulnerable figure than one expects of the icy princess, and the very fact that the part strains her beyond reasonable vocal limits adds to the dramatic point, even if it subtracts from the musical joys. By contrast, Placido Domingo is vocally superb, a commanding prince; and the rest of the cast presents star names even in small roles. The CD sound is full and brilliant, if at times rather close in the manner of DG engineers working in the Berlin Philharmonie. Ensemble is not always quite as flawless as one expects of Karajan with Berlin forces, though significantly the challenge of the manifestly less inspired completion by Alfano has him working at white heat.

The EMI set brings Nilsson's second assumption on record of the role of Puccini's formidable princess. As an interpretation it is very similar to the earlier RCA performance, but its impact is far more immediate, thanks to the conducting of Molinari-Pradelli. Corelli may not be the most sensitive prince in the world – Bjoerling is far better on detail – but the voice is in glorious condition. Scotto's Liù is very beautiful and characterful too. With vividly remastered sound, this makes an excellent mid-priced recommendation, though the documentation, as yet, does not include an English translation.

One quickly reads something of Callas's own underlying vulnerability into her portrait of Turandot. With her the character seems so much more believably complex than with others, and this 1957 recording is one of her most thrillingly magnetic performances on disc. It is made the more telling, when Schwarzkopf provides a comparably characterful and distinctive portrait as Liù, far more than a Puccinian 'little woman', sweet and wilting. Even more than usual one regrets that the confrontation between princess and slave is so brief. Next to such sopranos Eugenio Fernandi sounds relatively uncharacterful as Calaf, but his timbre is pleasing enough. By contrast, Serafin's masterly conducting exactly matches the characterfulness of Callas and Schwarzkopf, with colour, atmosphere and dramatic point all commandingly presented. With such a vivid performance, the 1957 mono sound – satisfyingly full-bodied, not boxy – hardly seems to matter, although the choral passages tend to overload at climaxes.

The strengths and shortcomings of Eva Marton as the icy princess come out at the very start of In questa reggia. The big, dramatic voice is well controlled, but there is too little variation of tone, dynamic or expression; she rarely shades her voice down. Recording balances are often odd, with Carreras – in fine voice – suffering in both directions, sometimes disconcertingly distant, at others far too close. Karajan's Turandot here becomes Liù, and the result is predictably heavyweight, though the beat in Ricciarelli's voice is only rarely apparent. In the closing Act, during the Alfano completion, Marton's confidence and command grow impressively, with her heroic tone ever more thrilling; this is recommendable to those who relish a live performance, although applause and stage noises are often distracting. Annoyingly, the CDs contain no bands within the Acts.

Turandot: excerpts.
(M) (***) EMI mono CDH7 61074-2 [id.]. Dame Eva Turner, Martinelli, Albanese, Favero, Tomei, Dua, ROHCG Ch., LPO, Barbirolli.

The Références issue of Dame Eva Turner in extracts from Turandot has live recordings made at Covent Garden during the Coronation season of 1937, with Sir John Barbirolli conducting and with Giovanni Martinelli as a unique Calaf. The excerpts were recorded at two separate performances and fascinatingly duplicate most of the items, with the second performance in each pair marginally more spacious and helpful in sound, and generally warmer and more relaxed as a performance. Martinelli's heroic timbre may be an acquired taste, but he is stirringly convincing, and Dame Eva Turner gloriously confirms all the legends, even more commanding than in her earlier studio accounts of the big aria, In questa reggia. Keith Hardwick's excellent transfers, for all the obvious limitations of recording on stage at Covent Garden, give a superb sense of presence.

Turandot: highlights.
*** Decca 421 320-2 [id.]. Sutherland, Pavarotti, Caballé, Ghiaurov, LPO, Mehta.

A generous and shrewdly chosen collection of excerpts from the glorious Decca set of Turandot. Nessun dorma, with Pavarotti at his finest, is here given a closing cadence for neatness. The vintage Decca sound is outstandingly full and vivid.

Le Villi: complete.
*** CBS MK 76890 [MK 36669]. Scotto, Domingo, Nucci, Gobbi, Amb. Op. Ch., Nat. PO, Maazel.

Maazel directs a performance so commanding, with singing of outstanding quality, that one can at last assess Puccini's first opera on quite a new level. Puccini's melodies may be less distinctive here than they later became, but one can readily appreciate the impact they had on early audiences. Scotto's voice tends to spread a little at the top of the stave but, like Domingo, she gives a powerful performance, and Leo Nucci avoids false histrionics. A delightful bonus is Tito Gobbi's contribution reciting the verses which link the scenes; he is as characterful a reciter as he is a singer. The recording is one of CBS's best.

COLLECTIONS

Arias from: *La Bohème; Fanciulla del West; Gianni Schicchi; Madama Butterfly; Manon Lescaut; Suor Angelica; Tosca; Turandot.*
(B) ** CfP CD-CFP 4569. Gedda; Scotto; Campora; Stella; Freni; ROHCG Ch. & O, Gardelli; Caballé and Marti; Charles Craig, Cavalli, Corelli, Amy Shuard.

Nicolai Gedda opens this Classics for Pleasure recital with a characteristically sensitive *Che gelida manina*, although he is not quite heroic enough in *Nessun dorma*. Charles Craig, one of the few British tenors to make a name in Italian opera, sings strongly in excerpts from *Manon Lescaut* and *Tosca*, but the remastering of these 1959 recordings does not flatter the voice. On the other hand, Amy Shuard's 1962 *In questa reggia* is thrillingly projected, and Mirella Freni is on fine form both in Liù's farewell from the same opera and in the most famous *Butterfly* aria. The rest is less distinctive, though the women are more refined than the men. As so often, a collection of histrionics like this needs singing of the highest quality to make an enjoyable continuous entertainment.

Arias: *La Bohème: Quando m'en vo' soletta. Gianni Schicchi: O mio babbino caro. Madama Butterfly: Un bel dì. Manon Lescaut: In quelle trine morbide. La Rondine: Chi il bel sogno di Doretta. Tosca: Vissi d'arte. Le Villi: Se come voi piccina.*
*** CBS Dig. CD 37298 [id.]. Kiri Te Kanawa, LPO, Pritchard – VERDI: Arias.***

The creamy beauty of Kiri Te Kanawa's voice is ideally suited to these seven lyrical arias – including such rarities as the little waltz-like song from *Le Villi*. Expressive sweetness is more remarkable than characterization, but in such music, well recorded and sounding especially believable on CD, who would ask for more?

'Puccini heroines'; *La Bohème: Sì, mi chiamano Mimì; Donde lieta uscì; Musetta's waltz song. Edgar: Addio, mio dolce amor. La Fanciulla del West: Laggiù nel Soledad. Gianni Schicchi: O mio babbino caro. Madama Butterfly: Bimba, bimba non piangere* (Love duet, with Placido Domingo); *Un bel dì. Manon Lescaut: In quelle trine morbide; Sola, perduta, abbandonata. La Rondine: Ore dolci a divine. Tosca: Vissi d'arte. Turandot: In questa reggia. Le Villi: Se come voi piccina.*
*** RCA RD 85999 [RCA 5999-2-RC]. Leontyne Price, New Philh. O or LSO, Downes; Santi.

This collection is a formidable demonstration of the art of Leontyne Price at the very peak of her career, still marvellously subtle in control (the end of Tosca's *Vissi d'arte* for example), powerfully dramatic, yet able to point the *Rondine* aria with delicacy and charm. The Love duet from *Butterfly* in which she is joined by Domingo is particularly thrilling, and there is much else here to give pleasure. The remastering is extremely vivid and the voice is given fine bloom and presence. A Puccinian feast!

Arias: *La Bohème; Sì, mi chiamano Mimì; Donde lieta uscì. Gianni Schicchi: O mio babbino caro. Madama Butterfly: Un bel dì; Tu, tu piccolo Iddio. Manon Lescaut: In quelle trine morbide; Sola, perduta, abbandonata. La Rondine: Chi il bel sogno di Doretta. Tosca: Vissi d'arte. Turandot: Signore, ascolta!; Tu che di gel sei cinta. Le Villi: Se come voi piccina.*
*** EMI CDC7 47841-2 [id.]. Montserrat Caballé, LSO, Mackerras.

Montserrat Caballé uses her rich, beautiful voice to glide over these great Puccinian melodies. The effect is ravishing, with lovely recorded sound to match the approach. This is one of the loveliest of all operatic recital discs and the comparative lack of sparkle is compensated for by the sheer beauty of the voice. The CD transfer is extremely successful, vivid yet retaining the full vocal bloom.

'Heroines': (i) *La Bohème: Musetta's waltz song;* (ii) *Sì, mi chiamano Mimì.* (iii) *Edgar: D'ogni dolor.* (i) *Gianni Schicchi: O mio babbino caro. Madama Butterfly: Un bel dì. Manon Lescaut: In quelle trine morbide;* (iii) *Sola, perduta, abbandonata.* (i) *La Rondine: Chi il bel sogno di Doretta.* (iii) *Suor Angelica: Senza mamma, o bimbo.* (i) *Tosca: Vissi d'arte.* (iv) *Turandot: Tu che di gel sei cinta (Death of Liù);* (v) *In questa reggia.* (i) *Le Villi: Se come voi piccina.*
**(*) CBS MK 39097 [id.]. (i) Kiri Te Kanawa; (ii) Ileana Cotrubas; (iii) Renata Scotto; (iv) Katia Ricciarelli; (v) Eva Marton; (iv; v) José Carreras.

Vocally these are not always immaculate performances, but the quintet of sopranos represented is exceptionally characterful, contrasting strongly with one another, where Puccini recitals from a single soprano can lack variety. However, the layout does not make as much as possible of the interplay of different voices, as Kiri Te Kanawa's seven contributions are all placed together at the start of the collection. Ileana Cotrubas's assumption of Mimi has greater feeling of the opera house; other highlights include Katia Ricciarelli's *Death of Liù* and Renata Scotto's beautiful *Senza mamma* from *Suor Angelica*. The thrilling climax of *In questa reggia* (Eva Marton and José Carreras) is spoiled by a fade-out at the end, particularly unfortunate as it is the closing item. The CD gives the voices plenty of presence, but the variations in ambience and balance are made the more striking.

Arias and duets from: *La Bohème; Gianni Schicchi; Madama Butterfly; Manon Lescaut; Tosca; Turandot.*
(B) *** EMI CDZ7 62520-2. Caballé, Domingo, Di Stefano, Gedda, Freni, Dimitrova, Bruson, De los Angeles, Bjoerling, Scotto, Corelli.

Placido Domingo opens with *Donna non vidi mai* from *Manon Lescaut* and is equally stirring in *Recondita armonia* from *Tosca*; Caballé is often ravishing in arias from *Manon Lescaut, Bohème*, a splendid *Vissi d'arte* from *Tosca*, *Un bel dì* from *Butterfly* and *Tu che di gel sei cinta*. Gedda and Freni combine passionately for *O soave fanciulla*, and Victoria de los Angeles and Jussi Bjoerling offer the Love scene from *Butterfly*. Room is also found for a fine 1957 mono version by Giuseppe di Stefano of *Che gelida manina*. The voices are given strong presence; the orchestral sound is vivid but not sumptuous. Excellent value at bargain price.

'Great arias' from: *La Bohème; La Fanciulla del West; Gianni Schicchi; Madama Butterfly; Manon Lescaut; La Rondine; Suor Angelica; Tosca; Turandot.*
(M) *** Decca 421 315-2 [id.]. Freni, Pavarotti, Harwood, Tebaldi, Milnes, Caballé, Corelli, Nilsson, Sutherland, Chiara.

Opening with Freni's *One fine day* and following with Pavarotti's *Che gelida manina* and Freni returning for *Sì, mi chiamano Mimì*, this recital begins splendidly and offers many highlights, including Caballé's *Signora ascolta* and Sutherland's *In questa reggia* (both from *Turandot*). Maria Chiara is melting in arias from *Manon Lescaut* and *Suor Angelica*; and Tebaldi reminds us how ravishingly she could turn a phrase in *O mio babbino caro* from *Gianni Schicchi.* Vivid sound throughout and few real disappointments.

Arias: *Manon Lescaut: Cortese damigella . . . Donna non vidi mai; Presto! In filia! . . . Guardate, pazzo son. Turandot: Non piangere Liù . . . Ah! Per l'ultima volta; Nessun dorma.*
*** DG Dig. 413 785-2 [id.]. Placido Domingo – VERDI: *Arias.****

These Puccini items, taken, like the Verdi, from earlier recordings made by Domingo for DG, make a fine heroic supplement, when he was challenged to some of his finest, most imaginative singing by Sinopoli and Karajan. The sound is consistently vivid.

Purcell, Henry (1659-95)

Abdelazer: suite. Bonduca: suite. The Gordian knot unty'd: suite. Timon of Athens: Overture; Curtain tune. The Virtuous wife: suite. Chacony in G min.
** Hyp. Dig. CDA 66212 [id.]. Parley of Instruments, Peter Holman.

Not a record to be played at one sitting. No relief is offered from instrumental timbres and few of the dance movements last much more than a minute. However, the performances are stylish and sensitive, all one-to-a-part as might well have been the case in some theatres of Purcell's day. The disc includes the newly discovered trumpet part for *Bonduca*, which has not been recorded before. Excellent recording, as is invariably the case with Hyperion.

Fantasias for viols Nos. 1-15.
(M) ** EMI CDM7 63066-2. London Baroque, Charles Medlam.

London Baroque are a highly accomplished group whose intonation and blend are impeccable. At the same time, it is possible to feel that, in music which is so highly charged with feeling and so richly imbued with melancholy, the constraints exercised by these artists result in playing that at times comes close to understatement. They are resonantly recorded, but the CD is not clouded.

The Gordian Knot unty'd: suite. The Old Bachelor: suite. Sonata in D for trumpet and strings.
(M) **(*) CBS MDK 44644 [id.]. ECO, Leppard – VIVALDI: *4 Seasons.***(*)

Those who like a rich orchestral tapestry in baroque music will be well satisfied with Leppard's collection of Purcell's theatre music, with its keenly resilient rhythms and nicely judged, expressive playing. The writing itself is consistently inventive. The forward balance and resonant acoustic produce attractively warm sound-quality – but it may be too well upholstered for those accustomed to the Academy of Ancient Music.

Overtures: *Abdelazer; Bonduca; Dido and Aeneas; Distressed Innocence; The Fairy Queen; The Indian Queen; King Arthur; The Married Beau; The Old Bachelor; The Rival Sisters; Timon of Athens.*
** Chan. CHAN 8424 [id.]. Bournemouth Sinf., Thomas.

Ronald Thomas directs lively performances, well recorded. His editing makes for varied repeats in some of the overtures, and the range of expression comes out well, not just a matter of extrovert energy but of heartfelt chromatic writing in adagios (as in *Bonduca*). The 1980 analogue recording – as usual with Chandos – has been pleasingly remastered.

Sonnatas of 3 parts Nos. 1–7, Z.790–6; Pavans: in A min.; B flat; G min., Z.749, Z.750, Z.752.
*** Chan. Dig. CHAN 8591 [id.]. Purcell Qt.

Sonnatas of 3 parts Nos. 8–14, Z.797/803; Chacony in G min. for 2 violins, viola and bass, Z.751; Pavan in A for 2 violins and bass, Z.748.
*** Chan. Dig. CHAN 8663 [id.]. Purcell Qt.

In these *Sonnatas*, which Purcell published when he was twenty-three, he turned from the fantasias for viol consort to the new, concerted style which had been developed in Italy. Interspersed among the *Sonnatas* are three earlier and highly chromatic *Pavans*, composed before Purcell embraced the sonata discipline. If anything, the second volume is more attractive than the first, for it includes the indelible *Chacony in G minor* (based on a song-tune, *Scocca Pur*, by Giovanni Battista Draghi, after whom Purcell named his first-born son). The Purcell Quartet give a first-class account of themselves: their playing is authoritative and idiomatic; and the Chandos recording is of exceptional clarity and definition. The artists are firmly focused in a warm but not excessively reverberant acoustic, and the sound has splendid body. Strongly recommended.

VOCAL MUSIC

Arise my muse (1690); *Now does the glorious day appear* (1689) *(Odes for Queen Mary's birthday); Ode for St Cecilia's Day: Welcome to all pleasures* (1683).
*** Hyp. Dig. CDA 66314 [id.]. Fisher, Bonner, Bowman, Chance, Daniels, Ainsley, George, Potts, King's Consort, Robert King.

Robert King directs the King's Consort and eight excellent soloists in this triptych of three of Purcell's finest ceremonial odes, including the shorter of the two *St Cecilia odes*. Ensemble could in places be sharper; but it is a delight to hear such superb artists as the counter-tenors James Bowman and Michael Chance in duet. The recording is vividly atmospheric.

Benedicte: O all ye works of the Lord. Coronation music for King James II: I was glad. Funeral music for Queen Mary: Man that is born of woman; In the midst of life; Thou knowest, Lord, the secrets of our hearts. Anthems: Blow up the trumpet in Sion; Hear my prayer, O Lord; I will sing unto the Lord; Jubilate; Lord, how long wilt Thou be angry; O God, Thou art my God; O God, Thou hast cast us out; O Lord God of Hosts; Remember not, Lord, our offences; Save me, O God.
*** Conifer Dig. CDCF 152 [id.]. Trinity College Ch., Cambridge, Marlow; Matthews; G. Jackson (organ).

Richard Marlow gets good results from his singers; such expressive anthems as *Remember not, Lord, our offences* and *Hear my prayer, O Lord* are eloquently done and beautifully recorded. Dr Peter le Huray reminds us that all the music on this disc, apart from one anthem, was composed before Purcell was twenty-five. What an extraordinary achievement! Excellent performances from all concerned – not least the Conifer recording team.

Come, ye sons of art away; Funeral music for Queen Mary (1695).
*** Erato/WEA 2292 45123-2 [id.]. Lott, Brett, Williams, Allen, Monteverdi Ch. and O, Equale Brass Ens., Gardiner.

Come, ye sons of art away. Ode on St Cecilia's day: Welcome to all pleasures. Funeral music for Queen Mary; Funeral sentences.

**(*) EMI CDC7 49635-2 [id.]. Taverner Consort, Ch. & Players, Parrott.

Come, ye sons of art away; Ode on St Cecilia's Day: Welcome to all the pleasures; Of old when heroes thought it base (Yorkshire Feast song).
*** DG Dig. 427 663-2 [id.]. J. Smith, Priday, Amps, Chance, Wilson, Ainsley, George, Richardson, E Concert Ch., E. Concert, Pinnock.

Come, ye Sons of Art, the most celebrated of Purcell's birthday odes for Queen Mary, is splendidly coupled here with the unforgettable funeral music he wrote on the death of the same monarch. With the Monteverdi Choir at its most incisive and understanding, the performances are exemplary and the recording, though balanced in favour of the instruments, is clear and refined. Among the soloists Thomas Allen is outstanding, while the two counter-tenors give a charming performance of the duet, *Sound the trumpet*. The *Funeral music* includes the well-known *Solemn march* for trumpets and drums, a *Canzona* and simple anthem given at the funeral, and two of Purcell's most magnificent anthems setting the *Funeral sentences*.

Pinnock directs exuberant performances of three of Purcell's most magnificent occasional works, and the dramatic impact is enormously enhanced by the full and immediate recording, which yet has plenty of air round it. The weight and brightness of the choral sound go with infectiously lifted rhythms, making the music dance, as in the first chorus of *Welcome to all the pleasures*, the best known of his Queen Mary *Odes*, the one for 1694. There the line, 'to celebrate this triumphant day', could not come over more infectiously. The soloists are all outstanding, with the counter-tenor duetting of Michael Chance and Timothy Wilson in *Sound the trumpet* delectably pointed. The coupling is particularly valuable, the neglected *Yorkshire Feast song*, composed in 1690 for an 'otherwise obscure annual gathering of York nobility'. It is full of wonderful inspirations, like the tenor and counter-tenor duet, *And now when the renown'd Nassau* – a reference to the new king, William III.

Though Parrott cannot quite match his rival, Trevor Pinnock, in the *St Cecilia* and *Queen Mary* odes, with speeds generally slower and rhythms rather less alert, his are still very fine performances, sounding more intimate as recorded. Parrott takes the view that Purcell would have used a high tenor and not a second counter-tenor in *Sound the trumpet*, and it works well, with John Mark Ainsley joining the counter-tenor, Timothy Wilson. The coupling is not generous but is apt and well contrasted. In his pursuit of authenticity Parrott has eliminated the timpani part from the well-known solemn march for slide trumpets (performed here on sackbuts) in the *Queen Mary Funeral music* – a pity when it becomes far less effective. The central anthem is beautifully done, and it is good also to have the three *Funeral sentence anthems*, written a few years earlier.

Duets and solos for counter-tenor: *Bonduca: Sing, sing ye Druids. Come, ye sons of art: Sound the trumpet. Elegy on the death of Queen Mary: O dive custos Auriacae domus. The Maid's last prayer: No resistance is but vain. Ode on St Cecilia's Day: In vain the am'rous flute. O solitude, my sweetest choice. The Queen's epicedium: Incassum, Lesbia rogas. Timon of Athens: Hark how the songsters.*
*** Hyp. Dig. CDA 66253 [id.]. James Bowman, Michael Chance, King's Consort, King – BLOW: *Ode* etc.***

It was a happy idea to link an outstanding performance of John Blow's *Ode on the Death of Purcell* to this sparkling collection of solos and duets which show both the composer and these fine artists in inspirational form. The performances are joyous, witty and ravishing in their Purcellian melancholy, with often subtle response to word meanings, and King's accompaniments are both supportive and have plenty of character in their own right. Excellent recording.

Funeral music for Queen Mary: March and canzona; Funeral sentences: Man that is born of woman; In the midst of life: Thou knowest, Lord. Jehova, quam multi sunt hostes.
(*) EMI Dig. CDC7 47772-2 [id.]. Winchester Cathedral Ch., Bar. Brass of L., Martin Neary (with concert: 'A Solemn musick'*).

Martin Neary's new version of the simple but magnificent *March* for drums and brass comes with a *Canzona* and four motets which, for all their brevity, find Purcell at his deepest. The choral ensemble is not ideally crisp, but the coupling of more valedictory music is very appropriate, most of it unjustly neglected. The record is pleasantly warm and atmospheric.

O sing unto the Lord; Praise the Lord, O Jerusalem; They that go down to the sea in ships (Anthems); *Ode: My heart is inditing; Te Deum and Jubilate Deo in D.*
(M) *** DG 427 124-2. Ch. of Christ Church Cathedral, Oxford, E. Concert, Preston.

This mid-priced collection includes, alongside favourite anthems, the big setting of the morning service canticles and the coronation ode, *My heart is inditing*. The performances are full of character, vigorous yet with the widest range of colour and feeling. The recording, made in London's Henry Wood Hall, is both spacious and well detailed.

Ode on St Cecilia's Day (Hail! bright Cecilia).
*** Erato/WEA Dig. 2292 45187-2 [id.]. Jennifer Smith, Stafford, Gordon, Elliott, Varcoe, David Thomas, Monteverdi Ch., E. Bar. Soloists, Gardiner.
(M) *** DG 427 159-2 [id.]. Woolf, Esswood, Tatnell, Young, Rippon, Shirley-Quirk, Tiffin Ch., Amb. S., ECO, Mackerras.
*** EMI Dig. CDC7 47490-2 [id.]. Kirkby, Chance, Kevin Smith, Covey-Crump, Elliott, Grant, George, Thomas, Taverner Ch. & Players, Parrott.

Gardiner's characteristic vigour and alertness in Purcell come out superbly in this delightful record of the 1692 *St Cecilia Ode* – not as well known as some of the other odes he wrote, but a masterpiece. Soloists and chorus are outstanding even by Gardiner's high standards, and the recording excellent.

A splendid all-male performance of Purcell's joyous *Ode* on DG, with an exceptionally incisive and vigorous choral contribution matched by fine solo singing. Simon Woolf is ideally cast here and the recording is excellent, although the balance between soloists and tutti does not make much distinction in volume between the smaller and the larger groups.

Though Parrott's EMI version lacks the exuberance of Gardiner's outstanding Erato issue, in a more reticent way it brings a performance full of incidental delights, particularly vocal ones from a brilliant array of no fewer than twelve solo singers, notably five excellent tenors. With pitch lower than usual, some numbers that normally require counter-tenors can be sung by tenors. Interestingly, Parrott includes the *Voluntary in D minor* for organ before the wonderful aria celebrating that instrument and St Cecilia's sponsorship of it, *O wondrous machine*. It holds up the flow, but at least on CD it can readily be omitted.

(i) *Ode on St Cecilia's Day (Hail! bright Cecilia)*; (ii) *Rejoice in the Lord alway* (Bell anthem).
(B) **(*) Van. VCD 72013 [id.]. (i) Cantelo, Deller, Salmon, Brown, Bevan, Frost, Amb. S., Kalmar CO, Tippett; (ii) Deller, Mary Thomas, Sheppard, Tear, Worthley, Bevan, Oriana Concert O, Deller.

The Vanguard recording, originally made in the mid-1950s, may not be of the smoothest, but it emerges vividly on CD and its shortcomings are not likely to distract anyone from the glories of the music and its inspirational performance under Sir Michael Tippett (editor as well as conductor). The magnificent principal male alto part is sung superbly by Alfred Deller. The composer originally designed it for himself and did in fact sing it (as was said at the time) 'with incredible graces'. The rest of the performance matches Deller's contribution, with Tippett obviously relishing his task and drawing wonderfully expressive playing from the Kalmar Chamber Orchestra (later to form the nucleus of the English Chamber Orchestra) and an equally responsive contribution from the Ambrosian Singers, in excellent form. George Eskdale, a famous name from the pre-LP era, is the trumpet soloist. For the CD, one of Purcell's greatest verse-anthems has been added, eloquently sung by a well-blended sextet of soloists. Unfortunately, internal access is poor with only three cues provided.

Odes for Queen Mary's birthday: Come, ye sons of art; Love's goddess sure.
(M) *** EMI CD-EMX 2134. Burrowes, Bowman, Lloyd, Brett, York, Skinner, Hill, Shaw, L. Early Music Consort, David Munrow.

While *Come, ye sons of art* is the richest of the sequence of ceremonial odes Purcell wrote for the birthday of Queen Mary, *Love's goddess sure*, though not quite so grand, brings more Purcellian delights. These early (mid-1970s) examples of the authentic approach deliberately opt for an intimate scale, using antique instruments and a matching style of string playing. The intimacy clearly detracts from the sense of grandeur and panoply apt for this music, but the late David Munrow inspires fine playing and singing from his excellent forces.

Songs: *Ah! cruel nymph; As Amoret and Thirsis lay; The fatal hour; I lov'd fair Celia; Pious Celinda.* Elegies: *Upon the death of Mr Thomas Farmer; Upon the death of Queen Mary.* Arias: *Hail bright Cecilia: 'Tis Nature's voice. History of Dioclesian: Since from my dear Astrea's sight. History of King Richard II: Retir'd from any mortal's sight. Oedipus: Music for a while. Pausanias: Sweeter than roses.*
**(*) Accent ACC 57802D [id.]. René Jacobs, W. Kuijken, K. Jünghanel.

René Jacobs' distinctive counter-tenor is well suited to Purcell; with unusually wide range, he sings this selection, weighted in favour of solemn songs, very beautifully – if with too little feeling for variety of mood. The most ambitious song is the elegy on the death of Queen Mary to Latin words, a superb piece too little known. First-rate recording.

Songs and airs: *Bess of Bedlam; Evening hymn; If music be the food of love; Lovely, lovely Albina; Not all my torments; Olinda in the shades unseen; The Plaint; O, Urge me no more; When first Amintas sued for a kiss.* Arias: *Birthday ode for Queen Mary: Crown the altar. The Fairy Queen: Hark! hark!; O, O let me weep; Ye gentle spirits of the air. The Indian Queen: I attempt from love's sickness to fly. Pausanias: Sweeter than roses. The Tempest: Dear pritty youths. Timon of Athens: The cares of lovers.*
*** O-L Dig. 417 123-2 [id.]. Emma Kirkby, Rooley, Hogwood.

The purity of Emma Kirkby's soprano – as delightful to some ears as it is disconcerting to others – suits this wide-ranging collection of Purcell songs splendidly, though you might argue for a bigger, warmer voice in the *Bess of Bedlam* song. The *Evening hymn* is radiantly done, and so are many of the less well-known airs which regularly bring new revelation. Excellent recording, if with the voice forward, and very present.

Songs: *Come, let us drink; A health to the nut brown lass; If ever I more riches; I gave her cakes and I gave her ale; Laudate Ceciliam; The miller's daughter; Of all the instruments; Once, twice, thrice I Julia tried; Prithee ben't so sad and serious; Since time so kind to us does prove; Sir Walter enjoying his damsel; 'Tis women makes us love; Under this stone; Young John the gard'ner.*
*** HM HMC 90242 [id.]. Deller Cons., Deller.

One section of this charming and stylish collection has a selection of Purcell's catches, some of them as lewd as rugby-club songs of today, others as refined as *Under this stone* – all of which the Deller Consort take in their stride. The final two pieces are extended items; *If ever I more riches*, a setting of Cowley, has some striking passages. The remastering for CD has greatly improved the sound, with voices fresh and first-rate recording of the instruments.

Songs: *The fatal hour comes on apace; Lord, what is man?; Love's power in my heart; More love or more disdain I crave; Now that the sun hath veiled his light; The Queen's Epicedium; Sleep, Adam, sleep; Thou wakeful shepherd; Who can behold Florella's charms.* Arias: *History of Dioclesian: Since from my dear Astrea's sight. Indian Queen: I attempt from love's sickness to fly. King Arthur: Fairest isle. Oedipus: Music for a while. Pausanias: Sweeter than roses. The Rival Sisters: Take not a woman's anger ill. Rule a wife and have a wife: There's not a swain.*
*** Etcetera Dig. KTC 1013 [id.]. Andrew Dalton; Uittenbosch; Borstlap.

Andrew Dalton has an exceptionally beautiful counter-tenor voice, creamy even in its upper register to make the extended '*Hallelujahs*' of *Lord, what is man?* and *Now that the sun* even more heavenly than usual. One half has sacred songs, some of them less well known, the other secular, including various favourites. Many of them require transposition, but only in some of the soprano songs such as *Fairest isle* does that distract. A delightful disc, well recorded.

Songs and dialogues: *Go tell Amynta; Hence fond deceiver; In all our Cinthia's shining sphere; In some kind dream; Lost is my quiet; Stript of their green; What a sad fate is mine; What can we poor females do; Why my poor Daphne, why complaining.* Theatre music: *Amphitryon: Fair Iris and her swain. Dioclesian: Tell me why. King Arthur: You say 'tis love; For love every creature is formed by his nature. The Old Bachelor: As Amoret and Thyrsis lay.*
*** Hyp. CDA 66056 [id.]. Kirkby, Thomas, Rooley.

This nicely planned Hyperion collection has one solo apiece for each of the singers, but otherwise consists of duets, five of them from dramatic works. The first half is the lighter in tone; the second half brings contrasting gravity, but this is just the sort of inspired material of Purcell that, unfairly, has tended to be forgotten. These near-ideal performances, beautifully sung and sensitively accompanied on the lute, make a delightful record, helped by excellent sound.

STAGE WORKS AND THEATRE MUSIC

Dido and Aeneas (complete).
*** Ph. Dig. 416 299-2 [id.]. Jessye Norman, McLaughlin, Kern, Allen, Power, ECO and Ch., Leppard.
*** Chan. Dig. CHAN 8306 [id.]. Emma Kirkby, Nelson, Thomas, Taverner Ch. & Players, Parrott.

**(*) DG Dig. 427 624-2 [id.]. Von Otter, Varcoe, Dawson, Rogers, Ch. & E. Concert, Pinnock.
(M) (***) EMI mono CDH7 61006-2 [id.]. Flagstad, Schwarzkopf, Hemsley, Mermaid Theatre Singers & O, Geraint Jones.

Authenticists should keep away, but Jessye Norman amply proves that this amazingly compressed setting of the epic *Aeneid* story has a dramatic depth and intensity to compare with Berlioz's setting. The opening phrase of *Ah Belinda* brings the most controversial moment, when Norman slows luxuriantly. But from then on the security and dark intensity of her singing make for a memorable performance, heightened in the recitatives by the equally commanding singing of Thomas Allen as Aeneas. The range of expression is very wide – with Jessye Norman producing an agonized whisper in the recitative just before Dido's *Lament* – but the unauthentic element must not be exaggerated. Marie McLaughlin is a pure-toned Belinda, Patrick Power a heady-toned Sailor, singing his song in a West Country accent, while Patricia Kern repeats her performance as the Sorceress, using conventionally sinister expression. The warm-toned counter-tenor, Derek Ragin, makes the Spirit Messenger into an eerie, other-worldly figure. Leppard's direction is relatively plain and direct, with some slow speeds for choruses. Excellent recording.

Andrew Parrott's concept of a performance on original instruments has one immediately thinking back to the atmosphere of Josias Priest's school for young ladies where Purcell's masterpiece was first given. The voices enhance that impression, not least Emma Kirkby's fresh, bright soprano, here recorded without too much edge but still very young-sounding. It is more questionable to have a soprano singing the tenor role of the Sailor in Act III; but anyone who fancies the idea of an authentic performance need not hesitate. The compact disc is exceptionally refined, the sound well focused, with analogue atmosphere yet with detail enhanced.

As in his other Purcell recordings, Pinnock pursues authenticity with more concern for the non-specialist listener than most. Significantly, an essay accompanying the libretto for this disc puts the case that the first performance of *Dido* was probably given as a Court entertainment rather than in Dr Josias Priest's girls' school in Chelsea, as has long been thought. Pinnock seeks to reproduce just such a performance at Court, rather than a school-sized entertainment; and though the reading is not as inspired as many that Pinnock has given of Purcell, the scale is attractive. Pinnock's choice of singers for the two principal women's roles is outstandingly successful, when both Anne Sofie von Otter and Lynne Dawson have voices that are at once warm and aptly pure for authentic performance. Von Otter as Dido, both fresh and mature-sounding, sings her two big arias with a combination of weight, gravity and expressive warmth which is yet completely in scale. The final lament, while faster than in traditional performances, still conveys the full tragic intensity of this epic in microcosm. Much more questionable is the casting on the male side, and that includes a tenor taking the role of the Sorceress. Nigel Rogers, not in his sweetest voice, takes that role as well as that of the Sailor. Confusingly, almost immediately after the Sailor's jolly song at the start of Act III, Rogers reappears as the Sorceress in quite a different mood, making much too quick a change. Stephen Varcoe is a rather unheroic-sounding Aeneas, but the chorus of the English Concert produces fresh, alert singing. Instead of a repetition of the final chorus, Pinnock opts for an instrumental reprise to provide an epilogue.

Though Flagstad's magnificent voice may in principle be too weighty for this music – one might point to the latter-day equivalent of Jessye Norman – she scales it down superbly in her noble reading, which brings beautiful shading and masterly control of breath and tone. Schwarzkopf is brightly characterful as Belinda, and though Thomas

Hemsley is not ideally sweet-toned as Aeneas, he sings very intelligently; even in this age of period performance, this traditional account under Geraint Jones sounds fresh and lively still, not at all heavy. The mono sound, obviously limited, yet captures the voices vividly, and this above all is Flagstad's set.

The Fairy Queen (complete).
*** DG Dig. 419 221-2 (2) [id.]. Harrhy, Jennifer Smith, Nelson, Priday, Penrose, Stafford, Evans, Hill, Varcoe, Thomas, Monteverdi Ch., E. Bar. Soloists, Gardiner.
*** HM Dig. HMC 901308/9 [id.]. Argenta, Dawson, Daniels, Loonen, Correas, Les Arts Florissants, William Christie.

Gardiner's performance is a delight from beginning to end, for though authenticity and completeness reign, scholarship is worn lightly and the result is consistently exhilarating, with no longueurs whatever. The fresh-toned soloists are first rate, while Gardiner's regular choir and orchestra excel themselves with Purcell's sense of fantasy brought out in each succeeding number. Beautifully clear and well-balanced recording, sounding all the fresher on CD, with the silent background especially telling in the light-textured music. The layout places the first three Acts complete on disc one and the remaining two Acts on the second CD.

William Christie made this recording of *The Fairy queen* immediately after a highly successful production on stage at the Aix-en-Provence Festival, also involving a presentation of the Shakespeare *Midsummer Night's Dream* text, judiciously pruned and given by the Peter Hall Theatre Company. It is a pity that not even a smattering of Shakespeare is included here – but, that said, the robust vigour of Christie's treatment is most compelling. He uses a far bigger team of both singers and instrumentalists than John Eliot Gardiner on the rival, DG Archiv set, allowing a wider range of colours. The drunken poet episode, for example, uses a glissando bassoon so that, in its earthiness, that sequence makes Gardiner's version sound too refined by comparison. The bite of the performance is increased by the relative dryness of the recorded sound. Some of the voices need more air round them to sound their best, and Gardiner's extra elegance goes with warmer, more congenially atmospheric recording. Among Christie's soloists two sopranos, well known in Britain, are outstanding: Nancy Argenta and Lynne Dawson; and the whole team is a strong one. The number of singers in solo roles allows them to be used together as chorus too – an authentic seventeenth-century practice. This makes a vigorous and refreshing alternative to the fine Gardiner set; but the Harmonia Mundi booklet is most inadequate: ingeniously, it has you chasing around in three places instead of one to identify both which number is where and who is singing. Any table of contents should be detailed enough to answer all questions.

The Indian Queen (incidental music; complete).
*** HM HMC 90243 [id.]. Knibbs, Sheppard, Mark and Alfred Deller, Elliot, Bevan, Deller Singers, King's Musick, Deller.

Deller's group is at its liveliest and most characterful in *The Indian Queen. Ye twice ten hundred deities* is sung splendidly by Maurice Bevan; and the duet for male alto and tenor, *How happy are we* (with Deller himself joined by Paul Elliot), as well as the best-known item, the soprano's *I attempt from love's sickness to fly* (Honor Sheppard), are equally enjoyable.

King Arthur (complete).
*** Erato/WEA 2292 45211-2 (2) [id.]. Jennifer Smith, Gillian Fischer, Priday, Ross, Stafford, Elliott, Varcoe, E. Bar. Soloists, Gardiner.

King Arthur may be cumbersome on stage, but here its episodic nature matters hardly at all; one can simply relish the wealth of sharply inspired and colourful numbers. Gardiner's solutions to the textual problems carry complete conviction, as for example his placing of the superb *Chaconne in F* at the end instead of the start. Solo singing for the most part is excellent, with Stephen Varcoe outstanding among the men. As the Cold Genius he helps Gardiner to make the Frost scene far more effective than usual. He is also one of the trio who give a delightfully roistering account of *Harvest home. Fairest isle* is treated very gently after that, with Gill Ross, boyish of tone, reserved just for that number. Throughout, the chorus is characteristically fresh and vigorous, and the instrumentalists beautifully marry authentic technique to pure, unabrasive sounds. The recording vividly captures a performance in an aptly intimate but not dry acoustic.

Rachmaninov, Sergei (1873–1943)

Piano concertos Nos. 1–4.
(M) *(**) Decca 425 576-2 (2) [id.]. Ashkenazy, LSO, Previn.

Piano concertos Nos. 1–4; Rhapsody on a theme of Paganini.
*** Chan. CHAN 8521/2 [id.]. Earl Wild, RPO, Horenstein.
(**(*)) RCA mono RD 86659 [RCA 6659-2-RC] (Nos. 1, 4 & Rhapsody); RD 85997 [RCA 5997-2- RC] (Nos. 2–3). The composer, Phd. O, Ormandy or Stokowski.

The composer's own performances of his four concertos are very welcome on CD, although considerable allowance has to be made for the brittle sound in Nos. 1 and 4 and particularly for No. 3, where the piano timbre is very hard indeed. These three are conducted by Ormandy and were recorded between 1939 and 1941; the *Second Concerto* and *Paganini rhapsody* are much earlier, 1929 and 1934 respectively, yet the sound is far superior – perhaps not surprisingly with Stokowski at the helm. In the *Second Concerto* the Philadelphia strings sound full at the very opening and produce radiant timbre in the *Adagio*. The *Rhapsody* is a marvellous performance; again Stokowski sees that the orchestral detail comes through splendidly, as well as ensuring that the famous eighteenth variation has great romantic panache. If the two Rachmaninov/Stokowski performances could be paired, they would make a very desirable record.

The Earl Wild set with Horenstein brought a remarkable degree of romantic ardour from the orchestra, with both artists finding the natural feeling for the ebb and flow of phrases, so readily demonstrated in the composer's own performances and which has now become a hallmark of Rachmaninovian interpretation. Earl Wild's technique is prodigious and sometimes (as in the first movement of the *Fourth Concerto* or at the end of the first movement of the *Third*) he almost lets it run away with him, though in the *Rhapsody* his sharply rhythmic articulation tingles with electricity. This is not to suggest that the bravura is exhibitionistic for its own sake, and Wild's impetuosity is very involving. There is a strong personality at work, and what is surprising is how closely the interpretations here seem to be modelled on the composer's own versions – not slavishly, but in broad conception. This applies strikingly to the *First Concerto* and the *Rhapsody*, although Horenstein does not quite match Stokowski's flair. No. 3, a most successful and spontaneous performance, finds Wild and Horenstein more poised at the very opening than the composer and Ormandy, and the slow movement has great romantic expressive feeling. All in all, this is a first-class and very rewarding set and the Kingsway Hall sumptuousness of the sound belies the age of the recording; the CDs are very believable indeed and the richness is exactly right for the music.

Decca's digital remastering of Ashkenazy's 1972 set with Previn sounds disappointingly brash. The original analogue sound cast a warm glow over the proceedings and any lack of clarity was more than compensated for by the rich atmospheric ambience. Now the sound-picture, including the piano image, is starkly clear and brilliant, and the strings have lost much of their bloom. The *Third Concerto* was originally bathed in a pleasing haze; now it is much clearer, but the fortissimo massed violins are strident. The performances are one of Ashkenazy's major achievements. The *Second Concerto*'s slow movement is particularly beautiful; and the individuality and imagination of the solo playing throughout, combined with the poetic feeling of Previn's accompaniments, provide special rewards. But the recording demands the aural equivalent of dark glasses.

Piano concertos Nos. 1 in F sharp min., Op. 1; 2 in C min., Op. 18.
(***) Olympia mono OCD 190 [id.]. Moura Lympany, Philh. O, Nicolai Malko – PROKOFIEV: *Piano concerto No. 1.***(*)

Piano concerto No. 3 in D min., Op. 30.
(***) Olympia mono OCD 191 [id.]. Moura Lympany, New SO, Anthony Collins – PROKOFIEV: *Piano concerto No. 3.***(*)

Moura Lympany's recording of the *Third* is the earliest recording and comes from a 1952 Decca LP; it sounds simply amazing for its age. Her EMI account of the *First* yields nothing in terms of virtuosity or panache to many bigger names on the international circuit, and the mono sound is very good for its age, though it is not quite as impressive as in the Decca *Third*. In No. 3, as was the custom in the 1950s, she plays Rachmaninov's later cadenza, the one he himself recorded. These are very fine performances which will give pleasure, and Olympia must be congratulated on restoring them to circulation in such excellent transfers.

(i) *Piano concerto No. 1 in F sharp min., Op. 1;* (ii) *Rhapsody on a theme of Paganini, Op. 43.*
*** Virgin Dig. VC 790724-2 [id.]. Pletnev, Philh. O, Pešek.
*** Decca Dig. 417 613-3 [id.]. Ashkenazy, (i) Concg. O; (ii) Philh. O, Haitink.

Mikhail Pletnev's accounts of the *F sharp minor Concerto* and the *Rhapsody on a theme of Paganini* with the Philharmonia Orchestra under Libor Pešek are very fine indeed. He is one of the few pianists whose technique can be (and has been) compared with the young Horowitz. The *Paganini rhapsody* is distinguished not only by quite stunning virtuosity and unobtrusive refinement but also by great feeling. This is playing that is strong in personality and musicianship – an altogether outstanding début that should acquire classic status. The CD sounds especially vivid.

This coupling also finds Ashkenazy in excellent form. The *Paganini variations* are, if anything, even better than his earlier LP with Previn. Haitink gets splendid sound from the Philharmonia in the *Variations* and Decca provides excellent recording. The *First Concerto* is no less impressive, and the Concertgebouw Orchestra under Haitink offer luxurious support.

Piano concertos Nos. 1 in F sharp min., Op. 1; 3 in D min., Op. 30.
(M) **(*) EMI CDM7 69115-2 [id.]. Jean-Philippe Collard, Capitole Toulouse O, Plasson.
(M) ** DG 429 715-2 [id.]. Tamás Vásáry, LSO, Ahronovich.

Jean-Philippe Collard's performance of No. 1 is impossible to fault; his playing is most exciting and his dazzling virtuosity very impressive indeed. Here is a performance that has one on the edge of one's seat. Its coupling is also very good, if not quite in the same class; at mid-price, this must be a strong recommendation. The recording is not of the very finest but is fully acceptable.

Ahronovich's direction is nothing if not impetuous, and this DG performance of the *First Concerto* is full of vigour, with its bursts of vivid romanticism. Vásáry's more introvert manner seems to fit well within this dashing framework and there is no doubt about the freshness of the music-making. In the *Third Concerto*, Vásáry uses the longer version of the first-movement cadenza but not always with complete spontaneity. The slow movement is indulgent, too, and lacks momentum. Vásáry's playing itself is clean, often gentle in style, but the conductor's extremes of tempi are less appropriate here than in the *First Concerto*. Taken as a whole, the performance is not without its poetry and excitement (especially in the finale) but, in the last analysis, its impetuosity of mood remains unsatisfying.

Piano concerto Nos. 1 in F sharp min., Op. 1; 4 in G min., Op. 40.
(M) **(*) Decca 425 004-2 [id.]. Ashkenazy, LSO, Previn.

The transfers of Nos. 1 and 4 are the most satisfactory of the set; the brilliance is less plangent than in Nos. 2 and 3, and the performances are certainly exciting.

Piano concerto No. 2 in C min., Op. 18.
*** RCA RD 85912 [RCA 5912-2-RC]. Van Cliburn, Chicago SO, Reiner – TCHAIKOVSKY: *Concerto No. 1.****
*** DG 415 119-2 [id.]. Sviatoslav Richter, Warsaw PO, Wislocki – PROKOFIEV: *Concerto No. 5.****
*** Decca Dig. 414 348-2 [id.]. Ortiz, RPO, Atzmon – ADDINSELL: *Warsaw concerto*; LITOLFF: *Scherzo*; GOTTSCHALK: *Grande fantaisie.****

(i) *Piano concerto No. 2 in C min., Op. 18; Études tableaux, Op. 39/1–2, 4–6 & 9.*
*** RCA Dig. RD 87982 [7982-2-RC]. Evgeny Kissin, (i) LSO, Valentin Gergiev.

With Reiner making a splendid partner, Van Cliburn's 1958 account of the Rachmaninov *C minor* is second to none. The pacing of the first movement is comparatively measured, but the climax is unerringly placed, remaining relaxed yet enormously telling. The finale too does not seek to demonstrate runaway bravura but has sparkle and excitement, with the lyrical element heart-warming to match the very beautiful account of the central *Adagio*, full of poetry and romantic feeling. The recording is wonderfully rich, with the Chicago acoustic adding a glorious ambient glow, while the piano, though forwardly placed, has an unexpected body and fullness of timbre. In the finale the cymbals demonstrate an excellent upper range, and the enhancement of the digital remastering almost makes this seem as if it was made yesterday. Coupled with an equally splendid version of the Tchaikovsky *B flat minor*, albeit not so richly recorded, this coupling is a world-beater.

Richter has strong, even controversial ideas about speeds in this concerto. The long opening melody of the first movement is taken abnormally slowly, and it is only the sense of mastery that Richter conveys in every note which prevents one from complaining. The slow movement too is spacious – with complete justification this time – and the opening of the finale lets the floodgates open the other way, for Richter chooses a hair-raisingly fast allegro, which has the Polish players scampering after him as fast as they are able. Richter does not, however, let himself be rushed in the great secondary melody, so this is a reading of vivid contrasts. The coupling is Richter's classic account of Prokofiev's *Fifth*

Concerto, so this CD combines two of Richter's very finest performances for the gramophone. The sound is very good.

Evgeny Kissin's Rachmaninov shows (as for that matter does his recording of the Chopin concertos) that he is a serious artist who phrases intelligently and resists the temptation to play to the gallery in any way. He produces a beautiful sound throughout and it is a compliment to him that any comparisons that spring to mind are with great pianists. The LSO under Valentin Gergiev give him every support. The six *Études tableaux* are imaginatively played and impressively characterized. The recording is well balanced and truthful. A remarkable CD début.

Cristina Ortiz's account has the advantage of rich Decca digital sound. The performance is warmly romantic, the first-movement climax satisfyingly expansive and the *Adagio* glowingly poetic, while the finale brings sparklingly nimble articulation from Ortiz and a fine expressive breadth from the strings in the famous lyrical melody.

Piano concerto Nos. 2 in C min.; 4 in G min., Op. 40.
**(*) Decca Dig. 414 475-2 [id.]. Ashkenazy, Concg. O, Haitink.

Unfortunately, in the *C minor Concerto* Ashkenazy's new account cannot quite match his poetic earlier reading with Previn. The opening theme is a touch ponderous this time, and elsewhere too the yearning passion of the work is rather muted, even in the lovely reprise of the main theme in the slow movement. Those reservations are relative; Ashkenazy gives a superb account of the *Fourth Concerto*, strong and dramatic and warmly passionate, with Haitink and the Concertgebouw establishing the work as more positively characterful than is often appreciated. Splendid Decca sound, with the Concertgebouw acoustics making a warmly resonant framework.

Piano concerto No. 2 in C min.; Rhapsody on a theme of Paganini, Op. 43.
(M) *** Decca 417 702-2 [id.]. Ashkenazy, LSO, Previn.
(BB) *** Naxos Dig. 8.550117. Jando, Budapest SO, Lehel.
(B) *** CfP Dig. CD-CFP 9017. Tirimo, Philh. O, Levi.
*** EMI Dig. CDC7 47223-2 [id.]. Ousset, CBSO, Rattle.
(B) **(*) Decca 417 880-2 [id.]. Katchen, LSO, Solti; or LPO, Boult.

Decca's recoupling of Ashkenazy's earlier recordings with Previn is a very desirable CD indeed. At mid-price it makes a clear first choice. In the *Concerto*, Ashkenazy's opening tempo, like Richter's, is slow, but the tension is finely graduated towards the great climax; and the gentle, introspective mood of the *Adagio* is very beautiful indeed. The finale is broad and spacious rather than electrically exciting, but the scintillating, unforced bravura provides all the sparkle necessary. The *Rhapsody* too is outstandingly successful, the opening variations exhilaratingly paced and the whole performance moving forward in a single sweep, with the eighteenth variation making a great romantic blossoming at the centre. The Kingsway Hall sound is rich and full-bodied in the best analogue sense; the digital remastering has here retained all the bloom, especially in the slow movement of the *Concerto*, among the most beautiful on record. Detail is somewhat sharper in the *Rhapsody*; in the *Concerto*, however, atmosphere rather than clarity is the predominating factor, unlike the remastered complete set above, where the focus is much sharper and the quality less sweet.

Outstanding in the Naxos super-bargain series, Jenö Jando's performances of both works are strongly recommendable. Although the *Concerto* opens modestly, the tempo relatively measured, it moves to a splendid climax, the piano astride the orchestra in a most exciting way. Jando has the full measure of the ebb and flow of the Rachmaninovian phraseology, and the slow movement is romantically expansive, the reprise particularly beautiful, while the finale has plenty of dash and ripe, lyrical feeling. The *Rhapsody* is played brilliantly, as fine as any performance in the catalogue. The digital recording is satisfyingly balanced, with a bold piano image and a full, resonant orchestral tapestry, although it is a pity that the variations in the *Rhapsody* are not separately cued.

Concentrated and thoughtful, deeply expressive yet never self-indulgent, Tirimo is outstanding in both the *Concerto* and the *Rhapsody*, making this one of the most desirable versions of this favourite coupling, irrespective of price. Speeds for the outer movements of the *Concerto* are on the fast side, yet Tirimo's feeling for natural rubato makes them sound natural, never breathless, while the sweetness and repose of the middle movement are exemplary. The digital recording is full, clear and well balanced. An outstanding bargain.

Cécile Ousset gives powerful, red-blooded performances of both works in the grand manner, warmly supported by Simon Rattle and the CBSO. Her rubato may often be extreme, but it never sounds studied, always convincingly spontaneous, though the big melody of the eighteenth variation is on the heavyweight side. The EMI recording copes well with that extreme range.

Katchen's coupling comes from 1958/60 and, while the Decca recording remains clear and vivid, the sound is slightly dated in the upper range of the *Concerto*, though the violins sound admirably full in the *Rhapsody*. The piano timbre is excellent. Katchen's accounts of both works offer drama and excitement in plenty – the outer movements of the *Concerto* reach the highest pitch of excitement, with bravura very much to the fore. Solti makes an excellent partner here; and Boult sees that the *Rhapsody* is superbly shaped and has diversity and wit, as well as romantic flair.

Piano concerto No. 3 in D min., Op. 30.
*(**) RCA RD 82633 [RCD1 2633]. Horowitz, NYPO, Ormandy.
**(*) Decca Dig. 417 239-2 [id.]. Ashkenazy, Concg. O, Haitink.
**(*) Decca Dig. 414 671-2 [id.]. Bolet, LSO, Fischer.
* EMI Dig. CDC7 49861-2 [id.]. Barto, LPO, Eschenbach – BARTÓK: *Concerto No. 2.***

(i) *Piano concerto No. 3;* (ii) *Rhapsody on a theme of Paganini, Op. 43.*
(M) **(*) RCA GD 86524 (RCA 6524-2-RG]. (i) Ashkenazy, Phd. O, Ormandy; (ii) Pennario, Boston Pops O, Fiedler.

(i) *Piano concerto No. 3 in D min.; Preludes: in C sharp min., Op. 3/2; in B flat; in G min., Op. 23/2 & 5; in B min.; in D flat, Op. 32/10 & 13.*
(M) **(*) Decca 417 764-2 [id.]. Ashkenazy; (i) LSO, Previn.

(i) *Piano concerto No. 3. Sonata No. 2 in B flat min., Op. 36; Moment musical in E flat min., Op. 16/2; Polka; Prelude in C, Op. 32/5.*
(M) (***) RCA GD 87754 [7754-2-RC-]. Vladimir Horowitz; (i) with RCA SO, Reiner.

Horowitz's legendary association with Rachmaninov's *D minor Concerto* daunted even the composer. Horowitz made it virtually his own property over half a century. In January 1978 he was persuaded to re-record the work in stereo, this time at a live concert, with Ormandy drawing a committed and romantically expansive accompaniment from the New York Philharmonic Orchestra. Perhaps just a little of the old magic is missing in the solo playing but it remains prodigious, and Horowitz's insights are countless. Not all the playing is immaculate and there is some rhythmic eccentricity in the finale; but the communicative force of the reading is unquestionable. The snag is the recording, which was originally very dry and clinical, the piano timbre lacking bloom. For CD, the remastering has altered the sound-picture radically, considerably softening the focus, to bring a more romantic aura to the music-making. The result is that at lower dynamic levels the image appears to recede. The effect is disconcerting – but one can adjust to it, and certainly the effect is more agreeable than the 'bare bones' of the original LP sound-quality.

Horowitz's RCA account with Reiner dates from 1951. As a performance it is full of poetry, yet electrifying in its excitement. In spite of its dated sound and a less than ideal balance, its magic comes over and it is to be preferred to his later performance with Ormandy. The *Sonata* comes from live concerts in 1980 and is also pretty electrifying. He plays the conflation he made (and which Rachmaninov approved) of the 1913 original and the 1931 revision plus a few further retouchings he subsequently made. An indispensible part of any Rachmaninov collection, which in its digitally remastered form sounds better than it has before.

Ashkenazy has recorded this concerto four times; as a work, it seems to prove elusive for him. In his latest Decca recording he is beautifully recorded and there is unfailing sensitivity and musicianship, but one needs a greater sense of impact and focus – his very first recording with Fistoulari had more ardour and spontaneity. So too had his 1976 RCA version, recorded in Philadelphia with Eugene Ormandy. If one can adjust to its unflattering piano sound, then the mid-1970s performance has much to offer: it has great charisma, and Ormandy, too, is at his finest. The coupling is a prodigiously brilliant account of the *Rhapsody* from Leonard Pennario and Fiedler which is certainly compulsive; the snag here is that the forward balance, coupled to the bright digital remastering, makes orchestral fortissimos sound shrill.

Ashkenazy's account with Previn has more in common with his most recent, digital version conducted by Haitink. It has moments of undoubted insight and touches of sheer magic, but in the last analysis it remains not quite satisfying as a whole. The remastering for CD is very successful, with the sound-picture clearer and firmer yet still warmly atmospheric. The well-chosen selection of *Preludes* is taken from his complete set.

Barto's pianism is in itself remarkable and, when it is not drawing attention to itself, prompts admiration and pleasure, particularly at the beginning of the *Concerto*. But he pulls this music about intolerably. His view of the first movement is mannered in the extreme, and he lingers so often over some details that the listener's tolerance is sorely tried. There is a very droopy opening to the slow movement from Eschenbach too, though he does get a good Rachmaninov sonority from the orchestra.

Piano concerto No. 4 in G min., Op. 40.
 ⊛ *** EMI CDC7 49326-2 [id.]. Michelangeli, Philh. O, Gracis – RAVEL: *Piano concerto in G.**** ⊛

As a performance this is one of the most brilliant piano records ever made. It puts the composer's own recorded performance quite in the shade and makes one wonder why the work has failed to achieve anything like the popularity of the earlier concertos. Michelangeli's performance of the climax of the first movement has an agility coupled with sheer power which has one on the edge of one's seat. The recording does not quite match the superlative quality of the playing, but in the digital remastering has been made to sound more open, the piano tone clear and not hard. There is still an attractive ambience, although the massed violins above the stave could ideally have more body.

The Isle of the dead, Op. 29; Symphonic dances, Op. 45.
*** Decca Dig. 410 124-2 [id.]. Concg. O, Ashkenazy.

The Isle of the dead, Op. 29; Symphonic dances, Op. 45; Aleko: Intermezzo & Women's dance. Vocalise, Op. 34/14.

(M) *** EMI CDM7 69025-2 [id.]. LSO, Previn.

Ashkenazy's is a superb coupling, rich and powerful in playing and interpretation. One here recognizes *The Isle of the dead* as among the very finest of Rachmaninov's orchestral works, relentless in its ominous build-up, while at generally fast speeds the *Symphonic dances* have extra darkness and intensity too, suggesting no relaxation whatever at the end of Rachmaninov's career. The splendid recording highlights both the passion and the fine precision of the playing.

Previn's original full-priced issue (from 1976) offered the same coupling as Ashkenazy, but now it has been digitally remastered with great success and the vividly wide-ranging sound is highly spectacular, among EMI's most successful analogue reissues. The added clarity and sparkle have a balancing weight in the bass and the effect is very exciting. The addition of the *Aleko* excerpts, plus a fine lyrical account of the *Vocalise*, makes a generous mid-priced CD, which competes in every respect with Ashkenazy's digital alternative.

Rhapsody on a theme of Paganini, Op. 43.
(M) *** RCA GD 87945 [7945-2-RG]. Van Cliburn, Phd. O, Ormandy – CHOPIN: *Piano concerto No. 1.**
(*) Ph. Dig. 410 052-2 [id.]. Davidovich, Concg. O, Järvi – SAINT-SAENS: *Concerto No. 2.(*)*

Van Cliburn, in repertoire for which he seems ideally suited, gives an excitingly committed account of Rachmaninov's *Rhapsody*, with much attractive detail: the scherzando playing in Variation 15 is a delight. The romantic blossoming at Variation 18 brings a wonderful expansion from Ormandy and the Philadelphia strings, a moment beautifully prepared in the previous section. With excellent 1970 recording, this stands alongside Van Cliburn's outstanding earlier coupling of Rachmaninov's *Second Concerto* and Tchaikovsky's *First* with Reiner. All the variations are cued separately.

Bella Davidovich is given the benefit of natural and vivid recorded sound and she plays with fleet-fingered fluency and no want of either brilliance or poetry; Neeme Järvi gives excellent support. This is a likeable performance, but the characterization is romantically relaxed and other versions show deeper insights.

(i) *Rhapsody on a theme of Paganini, Op. 43. Études-tableaux, Opp. 33 & 39; Piano sonata No. 2, Op. 36; Moment musical, Op. 16/3; Preludes: Op. 3/2; Op. 23/1, 2 & 4; Op. 32/12; Variations on a theme of Corelli, Op. 42.*
(M) *** EMI CZS7 62745-2 (2). Collard; (i) Capitole Toulouse O, Plasson.

These are impressive and competitive performances, recorded in the 1970s when this artist was beginning to make a name for himself. In the *Rhapsody on a theme of Paganini* he can hold his own with the finest, though he is not as well recorded as Ashkenazy or Pletnev. His account of the *Variations on a theme of Corelli* is exemplary and the *Second Sonata* no less powerful. Collard plays the 1913 version but, like Horowitz, incorporates elements of the revision. Nowadays we tend to think of Collard primarily as an interpreter of French music, and this compilation serves as a salutary reminder of his credentials as a virtuoso of the old school; moreover the set is very competitively priced.

(i) *Symphonic dances, Op. 45;* (ii) *The Bells, Op. 35.*
**(*) Olympia Dig. OCD 116 [id.]. (i) USSR RSO, Fedoseyev; (ii) Mikhailova, Larin, Bolshoi Theatre Ch., Moscow PO, Kitaenko.

The Russian performance of the *Symphonic dances* has less lyrical warmth than the

Western versions, with the drier recording emphasizing the difference. It has bountiful energy and humour assumes a hint of irony. The rhythms are sharply pointed and the reading makes a most individual effect. The digital recording is vivid and well balanced. The use of a Russian choir and soloists from the Bolshoi also adds another dimension to *The Bells*. Both soloists are eloquent, and only a touch of wobble affects the soprano contribution; the chorus sings incisively and in the final *Lento lugubre* there is a striking combination of fervour and melancholy. Again the digital recording is very lively and clear, yet the ambience provides plenty of atmosphere.

Symphonies Nos. 1–3.
**(*) Chant du Monde Dig. LDC 278 836/7 (2) [id.]. Moscow PO, Dmitri Kitaenko.

Symphonies Nos. 1–3; The Isle of the dead.
**(*) DG Dig. 419 314-2 (3) [id.]. BPO, Maazel.

Symphonies Nos. 1–3; Youth Symphony (1891).
(M) *** Decca Dig. 421 065-2 (3) [id.]. Concg. O, Ashkenazy.

Ashkenazy's set – offered at mid-price – can be given an unqualified recommendation. The performances, passionate and volatile, are intensely Russian; the only possible reservation concerns the slow movement of the *Second*, where the clarinet solo is less ripe than in some versions. Elsewhere there is drama, energy and drive, balanced by much delicacy of feeling, while the Concertgebouw strings produce great ardour for Rachmaninov's long-breathed melodies. The vivid Decca sound within the glowing Concertgebouw ambience is ideal for the music.

Russian musicians always have something extra to contribute to music from their own culture: there is a special kind of ardour and Slavonic intensity and a pungency of colouring, all of which are found in Moscow. The brass playing is less blatant (though still penetrating) than once seemed inevitable in USSR recordings. The key to all three symphonies lies with the soaring string melodies, and the Moscow orchestra here create a passionate body of string-tone whenever needed, yet are equally sensitive to Rachmaninov's gentler passages of haunted nostalgia. Dmitri Kitaenko has the full measure of each work; his control is firm, and the music's passionate elements are set in a proper perspective. In all three symphonies one has the feeling that he and the players have this music in their bones. However, the Russian recording – though extremely vivid, well balanced and transparent – is very brightly lit at the top, and at fortissimo levels the violins become shrill above the stave, a distinct drawback in music of this kind.

Maazel's set is also very impressive and offers superb playing from the Berlin Philharmonic. However, the DG engineers secured a less sumptuous sound in the Berlin Philharmonie than their Decca colleagues, and this emphasizes Maazel's fiercer way with Rachmaninov's passionate impulse. The climaxes of the *Second Symphony* in particular would have been enhanced by a warmer middle and lower range. Maazel's readings are not to be dismissed: the *First Symphony* is particularly fine; the *Third* too is distinctive, unusually fierce and intense. The result is sharper and tougher than one expects, less obviously romantic. Exhilaration is the keynote throughout and there is an abundance of adrenalin, yet the lack of expansive romantic warmth is undoubtedly a drawback. Moreover, unlike the Decca set, this is at full price.

Symphony No. 1 in D min., Op. 13.
*** Decca Dig. 411 657-2 [id.]. Concg. O, Ashkenazy.

Symphony No. 1 in D min., Op. 13; The Isle of the dead, Op. 29.
*** Virgin Dig. VC 790830-2. [id.]. RPO, Andrew Litton.

Ashkenazy's is an outstanding version, volatile and extreme in its tempi, with the Concertgebouw players responding in total conviction. The digital recording is most beautiful, for the sound is full, atmospheric and brilliant. It is superb on CD. Though the weight of the opening of the finale is magnificent, the relentless hammering rhythms are presented vividly in scale, where they can easily seem oppressive. The Scherzo at a very fast speed has Mendelssohnian lightness, the flowing *Larghetto* is presented as a lyrical interlude.

With a darkly intense account of *The Isle of the dead* as a generous fill-up, Litton's version of the *Symphony* brings exceptionally beautiful sound which captures the RPO strings in luminous form. This is a powerful performance, as the very opening indicates, but it is just as remarkable for its refinement and gentler qualities, with Litton persuasive in his free use of rubato. The magisterial fanfares at the start of the finale may be less biting or thrustful than with some others, but the resilience and clarity make the results equally compelling.

Symphony No. 2 in E min., Op. 27.
(B) *** Pickwick Dig. PCD 904. LSO, Rozhdestvensky.
**(*) Decca Dig. 400 081-2 [id.]. Concg. O, Ashkenazy.
**(*) Telarc Dig. CD 80113 [id.]. RPO, Previn.
**(*) Chan. Dig. CHAN 8423 [id.]. SNO, Gibson.
**(*) Chan. Dig. CHAN 8520 [id.]. Philh. O, Jansons.
(B) **(*) RCA VD 60132 [60132-RV]. Phd. O, Ormandy.

Symphony No. 2; The Isle of the Dead, Op. 29.
(M) **(*) DG Dig. 429 490-2 [id.]. BPO, Maazel.

Symphony No. 2; Vocalise, Op. 34/14.
*** Virgin Dig. VC 790831-2 [id.]. RPO, Andrew Litton.

Rozhdestvensky gives a very Tchaikovskian reading of Rachmaninov's *E minor Symphony*. There is plenty of vitality, but it is the conductor's affectionate warmth in the secondary material of the first two movements, with the big string melodies blossoming voluptuously, that is especially memorable. The slow movement, after a beguiling opening clarinet solo, has a climax of spacious intensity, and its power is almost overwhelming; the finale is flamboyantly broadened at the end, and the feeling of apotheosis is very much in the Tchaikovsky mould. With the LSO responding superbly, this is a most satisfying account, and the richness, brilliance and weight of the recording, made in All Saints', Tooting, adds to the compulsion of the music-making.

Refinement is the mark of Litton's well-paced reading, with the RPO caught in glowing form by the engineers as in the rest of the cycle. There is power in plenty, and Litton readily sustains his observance of the exposition repeat in the first movement, making it a very long movement indeed at over 23 minutes. But the moments of special magic are those where, as in his lightly pointed account of the Scherzo or, most of all, the lovely clarinet melody of the slow movement, subtlety of expression gives Rachmaninov's romanticism an extra poignancy. Even the red-blooded close of the finale with Litton is more subtly varied than usual, both emotionally and in execution. When the symphony alone lasts so much longer than usual, the *Vocalise*, done equally beautifully, makes a generous fill-up.

Ashkenazy's reading has a romantic urgency and drive that are missing from Previn's Telarc version, with the climaxes of the outer movements far more gripping. In the Scherzo too, the Amsterdam strings are tauter in ensemble; there is a vibrant impulse about the performance as a whole which is very Russian in its intensity. The Decca recording is full-bodied but with a degree of edge on the strings, and this extra bite suits Ashkenazy's approach.

The greater feeling of spaciousness of Previn's 1985 Telarc recording is apparent at the very opening. The whole reading is more moderately paced than those of its competitors, with long-breathed phrases moulded flexibly, with far less urgency and none of Ashkenazy's impetuosity. This expansiveness is enhanced by the finely sustained playing of the RPO strings and the sumptuous Telarc recording with its luxuriant resonance. With such superbly rich sound there are some ravishing moments, but in the last resort the lack of electricity brings a degree of disappointment.

With Gibson and the Scottish National Orchestra the brass sounds are thrilling, but the slightly recessed balance of the strings is a drawback and there is not the body of tone demonstrated by both the Telarc and Decca versions mentioned above. But this is a freshly spontaneous performance and overall the sound is admirably natural, even if it includes some strangely unrhythmic thuds at climaxes (apparently the conductor in his excitement stamping on the podium).

Jansons takes a relatively brisk pace in the first movement, but the expressive feeling, both here and in the slow movement, is less sumptuously intense than with either Rozhdestvensky or Previn. He catches the music's nostalgia very movingly, and the scherzo, with lots of bite, makes a sparkling centrepiece. The finale, however, is without the ardour and thrust that make the closing pages unforgettable. The recording is extremely good, brilliant and full.

From the brooding opening, Maazel moves the allegro away very swiftly (ignoring the composer's marking of *moderato*) and the powerful forward impulse creates considerable electricity. The scherzo is crisp and brilliant, while the *Adagio*, with long-breathed phrasing, reaches a powerful climax, only to be capped in the exhilaratingly brilliant finale with an apotheosis of even greater fervour. The brightly lit digital recording enhances the excitement; but in this work one ideally needs a warmer, more sumptuous sound. *The Isle of the Dead* makes a generous fill-up. Again choosing a fast speed, Maazel's view is less sombre than usual, but the climaxes are most powerful and the result is intensely compelling.

In 1973 Ormandy made his fourth recorded performance of the *E minor Symphony*. No doubt prodded by rivals on record, he opened out all the old disfiguring cuts and, with refined string playing and expansive recording, produced a characteristically exciting, full-blown performance. The Philadelphia strings certainly make it involving and their body of tone is well conveyed on CD. Next to the finest versions, however, it lacks subtlety in expressiveness, for Ormandy in this music tends to pull out all the emotional stops too soon.

Symphony No. 3 in A min., Op. 44.
(M) *** EMI CDM7 69564-2. LSO, Previn – SHOSTAKOVICH: *Symphony No. 6.****
*** Chandos Dig. CHAN 8614 [id.]. LSO, Järvi – KALLINIKOV: *Intermezzos.****
* RCA Dig. RD 87902 [id.]. Stockholm PO, Berglund.

Symphony No. 3 in A min., Op. 44; Symphonic dances, Op. 45.
*** Virgin Dig. VC 790832-2 [id.]. RPO, Andrew Litton.
(M) *(*) EMI Dig. CD-EMX 2153. Royal Liverpool PO, Mackerras.

Symphony No. 3; Youth Symphony (1891).
*** Decca Dig. 410 231-2 [id.]. Concg. O, Ashkenazy.

Previn's EMI CD brings an outstanding performance; the digital remastering brings plenty of body alongside the sharpened detail, even if some of the amplitude has been exchanged for clarity. There is much that is elusive in this highly original structure, and Previn conveys the purposefulness of the writing at every point, revelling in the richness, but clarifying textures. The LSO has rarely displayed its virtuosity more brilliantly in the recording studio, and, with its generous Shostakovich coupling, this is a bargain.

Ashkenazy's is a performance of extremes, volatile and passionate in a very Russian way. In the first movement the varying speeds are contrasted far more than usual, the allegros faster, the slow, lyrical passages (notably the great melody of the second subject) slower with copious rubato. The finale is fast and hectic to the point of wildness, but the Concertgebouw players respond superbly and the digital recording is full, rich and brilliant. The fragment of a projected symphony – with its first subject plainly indebted to Tchaikovsky's *Fourth* – was written when Rachmaninov was only nineteen. It is an enjoyable and unusual makeweight.

The gentleness of Litton's treatment of the great second-subject melody in the *Third Symphony* may initially sound cool, but the transparent beauty of Rachmaninov's scoring is brought out superbly by conductor, players and engineers. The slow movement has rarely been done so tenderly, and though the opening of the finale may sound a little cautious, not urgent enough, it is crisply pointed and leads on to a superbly brisk, tense conclusion. The *Symphonic dances* have similarly been given weighty performances, but the refinement and beauty of this last of Rachmaninov's orchestral works here go with sharp, clean attack, making an ideal and generous coupling for the *Symphony*.

Järvi conducts the LSO in a high-powered, red-blooded and not especially subtle performance which, in very full, bright sound, makes its points forcefully and convincingly. In his weighty, purposeful way he misses some of the subtleties of this symphony, but with superb playing from the LSO – linking back to André Previn's unsurpassed reading with them – the intensity is magnetic, with even a very slow *Adagio* for the outer sections of the middle movement made to sound convincing, and with the finale thrusting on at an equivalently extreme tempo.

With recording that sets the orchestra at a distance and undermines clarity of detail, the Mackerras disc of this ideal coupling, welcome at mid-price, can be given only a modified recommendation. The performances too often sound studied and unspontaneous in their detailed expression, lacking necessary bite and focus.

Berglund's Stockholm version is disappointing, too cautious and sounding strangely uncommitted, even in the great second-subject theme, and not helped by an overbright recording.

CHAMBER AND INSTRUMENTAL MUSIC

Cello sonata in G min., Op. 19.
** Chan. Dig. CHAN 8523 [id.]. Yuli Turovsky, Luba Edlina – MIASKOVSKY: *Sonata No. 2.***
** Unicorn Dig. DKPCD 9083 [id.]. Alexander Baillie, Piers Lane – SCHNITTKE: *Cello sonata.***(*)
*(*) ASV CDDCA 672 [id.]. Bernard Gregor-Smith, Yolande Wrigley – CHOPIN: *Cello sonata.**(*)

Cello sonata in G min., Op. 19; Vocalise, Op. 34/14 (with DVORÁK: *Polonaise*; SIBELIUS: *Malinconia*).
**(*) Ph. Dig. 412 732-2 [id.]. Heinrich Schiff, Elisabeth Leonskaja.

Schiff's performance of the *Sonata* with Elisabeth Leonskaja is not extrovert; instead, it has a thoughtful, inward quality that draws the listener to it. Its nostalgia and melancholy are undoubtedly potent. Needless to say, the Philips recording is first class. The Sibelius *Malinconia* is an uncharacteristic piece; it is not very effective, and the Dvořák *Polonaise in A* is altogether more vivid.

Yuli Turovsky produces a sound which is less than ideally rich and Luba Edlina is also more than slightly mannered; the performance nearly comes to a standstill at times in the development. There is nothing wrong with the recording, and those who like their Rachmaninov to be wayward and to wear its heart on its sleeve may well warm to it.

Alexander Baillie plays with characteristic restraint and warmth of tone; however, though his partner has an imposing technique, there have been more sensitive and imaginative accounts of the demanding piano part in recent years. The Schnittke fares better. Good and well-balanced sound.

Bernard Gregor-Smith, perhaps better known as cellist of the Lindsay Quartet, like his partner, Yolande Wrigley, is an artist of fine musicianship. His account of the *Sonata* is refined but wanting the eloquence and sweep of his finest rivals. The piano part is even more dominant than in the Chopin, and he is not helped by a balance that favours it excessively.

Trios élégiaques Nos. 1 in G min., Op. 8; 2 in D min., Op. 9.
*** Chan. Dig. CHAN 8431 [id.]. Borodin Trio.
*** Ph. Dig. 420 175-2 [id.]. Beaux Arts Trio.

The *G minor Trio* is a pensive one-movement piece lasting no more than a quarter of an hour, while Op. 9 is on a much larger scale. They are both imbued with lyrical fervour and draw from the rich vein of melancholy so characteristic of Rachmaninov. The performances by the Borodin Trio are eloquent and masterly, and the recording is admirably balanced and has plenty of warmth.

The Beaux Arts are less overtly intense and eloquent; they leave the music to speak for itself without ever being matter of fact. Their reading is lighter in colouring without being any the less deeply felt. It is difficult to make a clear choice: the Beaux Arts are splendidly aristocratic and have great refinement; the Borodins are red-blooded and ardent; either will give satisfaction.

Barcarolle in G min., Op. 10/3; Études-tableaux, Op. 39/4 & 6; Humoresque in G, Op. 10/5; Lilacs, Op. 21/5; 5 Morceaux de fantaisie, Op. 3: (Élégie in E flat min.; Prelude in C sharp min.; Mélodie in E; Polichinelle in F sharp min.; Sérénade in B flat min.); Polka de V. R.; Prelude in G min., Op. 23/5. Transcriptions: MUSSORGSKY: *Hopak.* SCHUBERT: *Wohin?.* RIMSKY-KORSAKOV: *Flight of the bumble-bee.* KREISLER: *Liebeslied; Liebesfreud. The Star spangled banner.*
(M) *** Decca 425 964-2 [id.]. Sergei Rachmaninov (Ampico Roll recordings, 1919–29).

Daisies, Op. 38/5; Études-tableaux, Op. 33/2 & 7; Op. 39/6; Humoresque, Op. 10/5; Lilacs, Op. 21/5; Mélodie, Op. 3/5; Moment musical, Op. 16/2; Oriental sketch; Polka de V. R.; Preludes: in C sharp min., Op. 3/2; in G flat, Op. 23/10; in E, F min. & F, Op. 32/3, 6 & 7; Serenade, Op. 3/5. Transcriptions: BACH: *Violin Partita No. 2: Prelude; Gavotte; Rondo; Gigue.* MENDELSSOHN: *Midsummer Night's Dream: Scherzo.* KREISLER: *Liebesfreud.* SCHUBERT: *Wohin?.* MUSSORGSKY: *Hopak.* TCHAIKOVSKY: *Lullaby, Op. 16/11.* RIMSKY-KORSAKOV: *The Flight of the bumble-bee.*
(M) (***) RCA mono GD 87766 [7766-2-RG]. Sergei Rachmaninov.

These two records make a fascinating comparison. The RCA collection includes virtually all Rachmaninov's electric 78-r.p.m. recordings, made between 1925 and 1942, with most dating from 1940. The second offers the composer's Ampico piano-roll recordings, made during a shorter time-span, between 1919 and 1929, when Rachmaninov was at his technical peak. The Ampico recordings were reproduced on a specially adapted Estonia concert grand in the Kingsway Hall and recorded in stereo in 1978/9. On CD the sound is outstandingly real and the impression on the listener is quite uncanny when the recital opens with the *Élégie in E flat minor*, which was put on roll in October 1928 yet has all the spontaneity and presence of live music-making. A number of items are common to both discs, so it is possible to make direct comparisons. The Ampico system at that time could accurately reflect what was played, including note duration and pedalling, but the *strength* at which the notes were struck had to be edited on to the roll afterwards by a skilled musician/technician, who annotated his score while the artist performed. Wrong notes could also be edited out, and the recording had finally to be approved by the performer after hearing a playback. It can only be said that listening to these Ampico recordings never brings a feeling of any mechanical tone graduation, and in pieces like the *Humoresque in G major* or the *Polka de V. R.* not only does Rachmaninov's scintillating bravura sound absolutely natural, but also his chimerical use of rubato is more convincing on the earlier recordings. On the RCA CD, the opening *Preludes* bring a curiously hollow piano timbre, and the effect throughout is shallow, partly the effect of the dry studio acoustic. Rachmaninov's performances were usually remarkably consistent – witness his sombre account of the famous *Prelude in C sharp minor*, while *The Flight of the bumble-bee*, a *tour de force* of exuberant articulation, brings only one second's difference in playing time between the two versions. However, in the closing *Liebesfreud* on the Decca disc, with its coruscating decorative cascades, his virtuosity is dazzling and the performance takes about a minute less than on the RCA version. It sounds good on both discs, but on the Decca version one has the impression of Rachmaninov sitting at the end of one's room. A remarkable achievement.

Études-tableaux, Opp. 33 & 39.
*** Hyp. CDA 66091 [id.]. Howard Shelley.

The conviction and thoughtfulness of Shelley's playing, coupled with excellent modern sound, make this convenient coupling a formidable rival to Ashkenazy's classic versions, of which only Op. 39 is so far available on CD.

Études-tableaux, Op. 39, Nos. 1–9; Variations on a theme of Corelli, Op. 42.
*** Decca Dig. 417 671-2 [id.]. Vladimir Ashkenazy.

Superb performances from Ashkenazy make this the most desirable of Rachmaninov issues. The *Corelli variations* is a rarity and a very fine work. The recording is first class.

Moments musicaux, Op. 16; Morceaux de salon, Op. 10.
*** Hyp. Dig. CDA 66184 [id.]. Howard Shelley.

Howard Shelley has a highly developed feeling for Rachmaninov and distinguishes himself here both by masterly pianism and by a refined awareness of Rachmaninov's sound-world. The recording is eminently realistic and natural.

24 Preludes (complete).
** Olympia OCD 110 A/B (2) [id.]. Peter Katin.

24 Preludes; Preludes in D min. and F; Morceaux de fantaisie, Op. 3.
*** Hyp. CDA 66081/2 [id.]. Howard Shelley.

24 Preludes (complete); *Piano sonata No. 2 in B flat min., Op. 36.*
*** Decca 414 417-2 (2). Vladimir Ashkenazy.

Considering his popularity and their quality, it is odd that Rachmaninov's *Preludes* have not been recorded complete more often. Ashkenazy's were the first to appear on CD, with the excellent recording further enhanced. There is superb flair and panache about this playing. As a bonus, the compact discs offer the *Second Piano sonata*, with Ashkenazy generally following the 1913 original score but with some variants. He plays with great virtuosity and feeling, and the result is a *tour de force*.

Shelley is a compellingly individual interpreter of Rachmaninov. Each one of the *Preludes* strikes an original chord in him. These are very different readings from those of Ashkenazy but their intensity, well caught in full if reverberant recording, makes these readings an essential recommendation alongside those of the Russian pianist.

Katin too is splendidly recorded, and the bold, clear piano image itself lends a certain romantic splendour to these performances. Katin has the measure of the lyrical music and it is only in the pieces that make their full effect with sheer bravura that he is less than completely convincing.

Preludes: Op. 3/2; Op. 23/1 – 2, 4 – 6; Mélodie, Op. 3/3; Polichinelle, Op. 3/4; Variations on a theme of Corelli, Op. 42.
*** Conifer Dig. CDCF 159 [id.]. Kathryn Stott.

Kathryn Stott has a good feeling for Rachmaninov and gives well-considered accounts of all the pieces on this generously filled CD. It would be difficult to fault her sensitive performance of the *Corelli variations*; there is a strong rhythmic grip and her phrasing is keenly articulate. In the recording one is fairly close to the piano, but not unreasonably so.

13 Preludes, Op. 32.
*** DG Dig. 427 766-2 [id.]. Lilya Zilberstein – SHOSTAKOVICH: *Sonata No. 1.****

Lilya Zilberstein came to international attention in 1987 when she won the Busoni Competition at Bolzano. She faces rather more formidable competition in the Rachmaninov *Preludes* than in the Shostakovich *Sonata*, but she takes the various hurdles in her stride. She has technique, style and finesse, and the recording is in the very first flight. This is not only a promising début but a valuable addition to the catalogue.

Piano sonatas Nos. 1 in D min., Op. 28; 2 in B flat min., Op. 36 (revised 1931).
*** Hyp. CDA 66047 [id.]. Howard Shelley.

Howard Shelley offers here the 1931 version of the *B flat Sonata*. He has plenty of sweep and grandeur and withstands comparison with the distinguished competition. He has something of the grand manner and an appealing freshness, ardour and, when required, tenderness. He is accorded an excellent balance by the engineers, which places the piano firmly in focus.

Piano sonata No. 2 in B flat min., Op. 36 (original version); Fragments in A flat; Fughetta in F; Gavotte in D; Mélodie in E; Morceau de fantaisie in G min.; Nocturnes Nos. 1 – 3; Oriental sketch in B flat; Piece in D min.; 4 Pieces; Prelude in E flat min.; Romance in F sharp min.; Song without words in D min.
*** Hyp. CDA 66198 [id.]. Howard Shelley.

Howard Shelley now gives us the original version of Op. 36 and his performances here show unfailing sensitivity, intelligence and good taste. Most of the shorter pieces are early, and not all are Rachmaninov at his very greatest – but they are persuasively played, as is the *Sonata*; they have the merit of excellent recorded sound. A valuable issue.

Suite No. 2, Op. 17.
*** Ph. Dig. 411 034-2 [id.]. Argerich, Freire – LUTOSLAWSKI: *Paganini variations*; RAVEL: *La valse.********

Argerich and Freire give a dazzling virtuoso account of the *Suite*, rushing the waltzes off their feet (the movement is marked *presto* but they play it *prestissimo*). They are fresh, idiomatic and thoughtful and their performance is thoroughly exhilarating. They are well recorded and can be recommended. The only drawback to the recording is the reverberation which seems a trifle excessive.

Song transcriptions: *Dreams; Floods of spring; In the silent night; The little island; Midsummer eve; The Muse; O, cease thy singing; On the death of a linnet; Sorrow in springtime; To the children; Vocalise; Where beauty dwells.*
**(*) Dell'Arte CD DBS 7001 [id.]. Earl Wild (piano).

Earl Wild is a pianist all too often taken for granted as a virtuoso pure and simple, rather than the great artist that he is. On this CD he plays twelve masterly transcriptions he has made of Rachmaninov songs, ranging from *In the silent night* from the Op. 4 set of 1890 to *Dreams* of Op. 38 (1916). Of course his virtuosity is dazzling – but so too is his refinement of colour and his musicianship. The recording is not of comparable distinction but is acceptable enough.

Variations on a theme of Chopin, Op. 22; Variations on a theme of Corelli, Op. 42; Mélodie in E, Op. 3/3.
*** Hyp. CDA 66009 [id.]. Howard Shelley – MENDELSSOHN: *Scherzo.********

Rachmaninov's two big sets of variations for solo piano make an excellent coupling, and Howard Shelley gives dazzling, consistently compelling performances, full of virtuoso flair. The *Corelli variations* are the better-known set; but it is the more expansive *Chopin variations* which represent the composer at his most masterly. The grouping of variations brings a kind of sonata balance, with the climax of the final section built superbly by Shelley, helped by first-rate piano sound.

RECITAL COLLECTION

Preludes Nos. 1 in C sharp min., Op. 3/2; 6 in G min.; 11 in G flat, Op. 23/5 & 10; 18 in F, Op. 32/7; 23 in G sharp min., Op. 32/11. Mélodie, Op. 3/3; Variations on a theme of Chopin, Op. 2; Arr. of KREISLER: *Liebeslied; Liebesfreud.*
*** Decca Dig. 421 061-2 [id.]. Jorge Bolet.

Bolet's Rachmaninov recital is one of the finest records he has given us for some time. It has the beautiful pianism of his Chopin, with a much stronger sense of profile. These are all aristocratic performances and eminently well recorded.

VOCAL MUSIC

The Bells, Op. 35.
(M) ******* EMI CDM7 63114-2. Sheila Armstrong, Robert Tear, John Shirley-Quirk, LSO Ch., LSO, Previn – PROKOFIEV: *Alexander Nevsky.********

The Bells, Op. 35; 3 Russian songs, Op. 41.
*** Decca Dig. 414 455-2 [id.]. Troitskaya, Karczykowski, Krause, Concg. Ch. & O, Ashkenazy.

The Bells, Op. 35; Vocalise, Op. 34/14.
**(*) Chan. Dig. CHAN 8476 [id.]. Murphy, Lewis, Wilson-Johnson, SNO Ch. & O, Järvi
– TCHAIKOVSKY: *Romeo and Juliet duet* etc.***

Ashkenazy's volatile Russian style is eminently suitable for Rachmaninov's masterly cantata. His tenor soloist has just the right touch of temperament, and in the slow movement Natalia Troitskaya's contribution combines Slavonic feeling with freshness. The chorus respond readily to the black mood of the Scherzo and bring a melancholy intensity to the finale. The Decca recording is superb, wide in range, spacious and clear.

The climaxes expand just as impressively in the Usher Hall, Edinburgh, as in the Decca set, and have great impact too, but detail is less clear and there is less bite. The three soloists all sing eloquently but without the Slavonic character of Ashkenazy's group. In short, the Decca recording has an extra degree of intensity, especially in the vehemence of the Scherzo. Järvi's Tchaikovsky couplings are unique, but Ashkenazy's choice of the *Russian folksongs* seems more apt.

In *The Bells*, as in Previn's equally fresh and direct account of the other Russian choral work included on this CD, Prokofiev's *Alexander Nevsky*, the LSO Chorus sings convincingly in the original language. The timbre may not be entirely Russian-sounding (cleaner and fresher in fact), but in what amounts to a choral symphony Previn's concentration on purely musical values as much as on evocation of atmosphere produces powerful results, even when the recording as transferred to CD has lost just a little of its ambient warmth in favour of added presence and choral brilliance.

Vespers, Op. 37.
(***) Chant du Monde 278 845 [id.]. Korkan, Ognevoi, RSFSR Ac. Russian Ch., Sveshnikov.

Rachmaninov's *Vespers* must be counted among his most profound and fascinating works. The performances can only be called superlative, and it will be a long time before they are superseded. The basses in particular have incredible richness (at one point they sing a low B flat) and the recording is in an appropriately resonant acoustic and has plenty of atmosphere. The digital remastering produces very little background noise; but some of the liveliness of the original LP has been lost, and pianissimos tend to recede, though climaxes are expansive.

Vocalise, Op. 34/14 (arr. Dubensky).
(M) *** RCA GD 87831 [7831-2-RG]. Anna Moffo, American SO, Stokowski –
CANTELOUBE: *Songs of the Auvergne;* VILLA-LOBOS: *Bachianas Brasileiras No. 5.***

Rachmaninov's *Vocalise* was a favourite showpiece of Stokowski, usually in a purely orchestral arrangement; but here with Moffo at her warmest it is good to have the vocal version so persuasively matching the accompaniment.

Aleko (opera): complete.
(B) ** AVM AVMCD 1011 [id.]. Ghiuselev, Kourchoumov, Petkov, Karnobatlova, Plovdiv PO, Raichev.

Rachmaninov's early one-Act opera is based on a Pushkin tale of love and jealousy set in a gypsy camp. If it never quite lives up to its promise of Russian *verismo*, there is some colourful, atmospheric writing and some yearning melodies. Nikola Ghiuselev sings nobly in his cavatina, and Pavel Kourchoumov brings a fresh, light tenor to the role of the Young Gypsy. Dimiter Petkov, past his best but resonant, is aptly cast as the Old Gypsy. Slavonic shrillness prevents Blagovesta Karnobatlova's singing as the heroine, Zemfira, from being as attractive as it promises. The recording, though not ideally atmospheric, is agreeable enough.

Raff, Joachim (1822–82)

Symphony No. 5 (Lenore).
(M) *** Unicorn UKCD 2031 [id.]. LPO, Bernard Herrmann.

Raff left eleven symphonies; No. 5, with its colourful programmatic writing, is generally counted the finest of his cycle. In some ways it is a very naïve work, based as it is on a high romantic ballad by the poet Bürger. A dead soldier-lover calls upon the girl he has left behind, and on a devil's ride he disconcertingly turns into a skeleton. The first two movements merely provide preparation for that dramatic development, while the third depicts the lovers' parting, with the main march heard first in crescendo then diminuendo to represent the arrival and departure of a troop of the lover's regiment – a piece much beloved by the Victorians. A thoroughly enjoyable Mendelssohnian symphony, colourfully performed with clean and vivid recording, given extra projection on CD, especially the percussion.

Raid, Kaljo (born 1922)

Symphony No. 1 in C min.
*** Chan. Dig. CHAN 8525 [id.]. SNO, Järvi – ELLER: *Dawn; Elegia* etc.***

Raid's *First Symphony* of 1944 was written when he had just passed twenty-one and was still studying with Eller; it shows a genuine feel for form and a fine sense of proportion, even though the personality is not fully formed. Well worth hearing. Neeme Järvi gets very committed playing from the Scottish National Orchestra and the recording is warm and well detailed.

Rameau, Jean Philippe (1683–1764)

Les Boréades: orchestral suite; Dardanus: orchestral suite.
*** Ph. Dig. 420 240-2 [id.]. O of 18th Century, Brüggen.

The orchestral suite from *Les Boréades* occupies the larger part of the disc. The invention is full of resource and imagination, and the playing here of both this and *Dardanus* is spirited and sensitive and will provide delight even to those normally unresponsive to authentic instruments.

Dardanus: suite.
** Erato/WEA 2292 45184-2 [id.]. E. Bar. Soloists, Gardiner.

John Eliot Gardiner offers a substantial selection from the orchestral music of both versions of Rameau's opera. There is plenty of variety here, from lightly scored dance music to the powerful closing *Chaconne*. Some of the music is slight and, out of context, does not make its full effect. The CD offers fine if not remarkable sound, with good presence but without the depth of perspective of the best recordings from this source.

Hippolyte et Aricie: orchestral suite.
(M) *** HM/BMG GD 77009 [id.]. La Petite Bande, Kuijken.

During Rameau's lifetime there were three productions of *Hippolyte et Aricie*, for which various instrumental additions were made. This record collects virtually all the orchestral music from the three in performances so lively and winning that the disc is irresistible. Sigiswald Kuijken gets delightful results from his ensemble; the melodic invention is fresh and its orchestral presentation ingenious. In every way an outstanding release – and not least in the quality of the sound.

Les Indes galantes: excerpts (harpsichord transcriptions).
*** HM HMC 901028. Kenneth Gilbert.

These transcriptions are Rameau's own, made some time after the success scored by his first opera-ballet, *Les Indes galantes*, in 1735. He grouped a number of items into four suites or '*concerts*', and these included not only dance numbers and orchestral pieces but arias as well. Kenneth Gilbert, playing a fine instrument in contemporary tuning, reveals these miniatures as the subtle and refined studies they are. He could not be better served by the recording engineers, and the CD brings added presence and background quiet.

Music for harpsichord: *Book 1* (1706); *Pièces de clavecin* (1724); *Nouvelles suites de pièces de clavecin* (c. 1728); *5 Pièces* (1741); *La Dauphine* (1747).
(M) *** DG 427 176-2 (2) [id.]. Kenneth Gilbert (harpsichord).

Rameau's keyboard music is among the finest of the whole Baroque era, and Kenneth Gilbert is not just a scholar but an artist of genuine insight and stature. He uses three harpsichords here, all from the Paris Conservatoire and all from the period: a Goujon (1749), a Hemsch (1761), and a third by Dumont (1679) restored by Pascal Taskin in 1789. They are superb instruments and are excellently recorded too (in 1977); although the CD brings added presence, the instruments remain in a good perspective. There is no need to dwell on details here, for this is an indispensable set.

Pièces de clavecin: Suite (No. 1) in A min.; L'Agaçante; La Dauphine; L'Indiscrète; La Livri; La Pantomine: La Timide.
*** CRD CRD 3320 [id.]. Trevor Pinnock.

Trevor Pinnock chose a more mellow instrument here, making his stylish, crisply rhythmic performances even more attractive. The selection includes *La Dauphine*, the last keyboard piece that Rameau wrote, brilliantly performed. Excellent recording.

Harpsichord suites: in A min. (1728); *in E min.* (1724).
*** CRD CRD 3310 [id.]. Trevor Pinnock.

Harpsichord suites: in D min./maj. (1724); *in G maj./min.* (1728).
*** CRD CRD 3330 [id.]. Trevor Pinnock.

Excellent performances. Trevor Pinnock is restrained in the matter of ornamentation, but his direct manner is both eloquent and stylish. The harpsichord is of the French type and is well recorded.

Grand motets: *In convertendo; Quam dilecta laboravi.*
*** HM HM 90 1078 [id.]. Gari, Monnaliu, Ledroit, De Mey, Varcoe, Chapelle Royale Ch., Ghent Coll. Vocale, Herreweghe.

These two motets are among Rameau's finest works. The recordings were made in the Carmelite Church in Ghent which has a warm, reverberant acoustic, and the Ghent Collegium Vocale is stiffened by forces from La Chapelle Royale in Paris. They produce excellent results and the soloists are also very fine indeed. The instrumental ensemble includes several members of La Petite Bande and so its excellence can almost be taken for granted.

OPERA-BALLET AND OPERA

Anacréon (complete).
*** HM HMC 90190 [id.]. Schirrer, Mellon, Feldman, Visse, Laplénie, Les Arts Florissants, Christie.

The music here has charm, even if it is not Rameau at his most inventive; the performance is as authoritative and stylish as one would expect from William Christie's group. It is not essential Rameau, but readers with an interest in the period will want it – and it has moments of great appeal. The recording is admirable.

Platée (complete).
** Erato/WEA Dig. 2292 45028-2 (2) [id.]. Ragon, Jennifer Smith, Guy de Mey, Le Texier, Gens, Ens. Vocale Françoise Herr, Musiciens du Louvre, Minkowski.

Platée, written in 1745, is described as a '*ballet bouffon*', in fact a comic opera comprising a Prologue and three short Acts, based on a classical theme. The central character, the nymph Platée (Plataea), is a drag part taken by a tenor, a favourite comic device of the time, as Raymond Leppard's realization of Cavalli's *La Calisto* brought out. With such a send-up of classical tradition, the performers here understandably adopt comic expressions and voices, which in a recording, as opposed to a stage performance, become rather wearing on the listener. It is like being nudged in the ribs, prompted to laugh, when the joke is not subtle. Also surprisingly, with such stylish singers as the tenor Guy de Mey, almost all the soloists aspirate heavily in florid passages. Within that convention this is a lively, brisk performance, very well conducted by Marc Minkowski, but marred by the dryness of the recording. As a joint project with French Radio, it was made in what sounds like a small Paris studio: though the sense of presence is very vivid, the sound of period instruments reminds one of the abrasiveness of much earlier recordings. Minkowski writes of the distinctive instrumentation that Rameau devised, all top and bottom, and the aggressive acoustic emphasizes that. But as a work, *Platée* certainly provides a fascinating side-glance at Rameau's mastery.

Pygmalion (complete).
(M) **(*) HM/BMG GD 77143. Elwes, Van der Sluis, Vanhecke, Yakar, Paris Chapelle Royal Ch., La Petite Bande, Leonhardt.

Leonhardt's 1980 account with John Elwes as Pygmalion and Mieke van der Sluis as Céphise is welcome back to the catalogue. Leonhardt's direction is rather leisurely, but his soloists make a good team. The use of period instruments brings attractive transparency of texture and, thanks to the excellence of the original recording, this is enhanced on CD. The documentation (including full translation) is first class.

Zoroastre (complete).
(M) **(*) HM/BMG GD 77144 (3). Elwes, De Reyghere, Van der Sluis, Nellon, Reinhart, Bona, Ghent Coll. Vocale, La Petite Bande, Kuijken.

Zoroastre was the last but one of Rameau's tragédies lyriques. It appeared 15 years before his final masterpiece, *Les Boréades*; but the original 1749 score was drastically revised to produce the text of 1756, recorded here. *Zoroastre* may not have quite the inspiration of *Les Boréades* in modifying once rigid conventions; but frequently, as in the monologue of the villain, Abramane, in Act III, Rameau was clearly taking a leaf out of

Gluck's book in the dark originality of the instrumentation, here made transparent in finely detailed recording. Though Kuijken's characteristically gentle style with his excellent authentic group, La Petite Bande, fails to give the piece the bite and urgency that John Eliot Gardiner brings to *Les Boréades* in his Erato recording, it is a fine presentation of a long-neglected masterpiece, with crisp and stylish singing from the soloists, notably John Elwes in the name-part and Gregory Reinhart as Abramane. The Ghent Collegium Vocale, placed rather close, sing with vigour in the choruses, but the individual voices fail to blend. The five Acts (with Rameau here abandoning the old convention of an allegorical Prologue) are now offered on three mid-priced CDs against the original set on four LPs. The excellent documentation (144 pages, including translations) puts the mid-priced issues of many of the large international companies to shame.

Ravel, Maurice (1875–1937)

Alborada del gracioso; Une barque sur l'océan; Boléro; (i) Piano concerto in G; Piano concerto for the left hand; Daphnis et Chloé (complete ballet); L'Éventail de Jeanne: Fanfare. Menuet antique; Ma Mère l'Oye (complete); Pavane pour une infante défunte; Rapsodie espagnole; Le tombeau de Couperin; La valse; Valses nobles et sentimentales.
⊛ (M) *** Decca 421 458-2 (4) [id.]. Montreal SO with Ch. and (i) Pascal Rogé; Dutoit.

Anyone coming new to this repertoire will find this four-disc mid-price box unbeatable value: the orchestral playing is wonderfully sympathetic and the recording ideally combines atmospheric evocation with vividness of detail. In the *Concertos*, Pascal Rogé finds gracefulness and vitality for the *G major* work and, if there is less dynamism in the *Left-hand concerto*, there is no lack of finesse. The balance is very realistic and the recording throughout is in the demonstration class.

Alborada del gracioso; Une barque sur l'océan; Ma Mère l'Oye (ballet); Pavane pour une infante défunte; Le tombeau de Couperin.
(M) *** EMI CDM7 69567-2 [id.]. O de Paris, Martinon.

Like his version of *Daphnis et Chloé*, Martinon's *Ma Mère l'Oye* is exquisite, among the finest ever put on record (and one does not forget Dutoit or Previn). The other works are also played beautifully, with the Orchestre de Paris on its finest form. The analogue recording was of EMI's vintage quality, and it has been effectively remastered.

Alborada del gracioso; Une barque sur l'océan; Menuet antique; Pavane pour une infante défunte; La valse.
**(*) DG 415 845-2 [id.]. Boston SO, Ozawa.

Ozawa is at his finest in catching the atmosphere of *Une barque sur l'océan*, and throughout this collection he secures admirable orchestral playing. If the last degree of character is missing, the 1975 recording is first class, beautifully balanced, with the hall ambience colouring the textures most naturally.

Alborada del gracioso; Une barque sur l'océan; Overture, Shéhérazade (1899); (i) Shéhérazade – song-cycle; (ii) Tzigane; La valse.
*** DG Dig. 427 314-2 [id.]. (ii) Margaret Price; (i) Salvatore Accardo; LSO, Abbado.

Highly sensitive performances of these beautiful scores. Abbado is on excellent form and brings out all the subtle colourings of Ravel's orchestration, in which he is greatly helped by the excellent DG recording. Accardo is superb in *Tzigane*, and Abbado gets delicious sounds in the two transcriptions from *Miroirs* and *La valse*. Margaret Price is a little disappointing: her voice does not float effortlessly over the texture as does Crespin on Decca and she does not seem to be quite inside the sensibility of this music. Abbado includes Ravel's early overture to *Shéhérazade*, which is completely unrelated to the cycle, and is still something of a rarity. Reservations about Price's *Shéhérazade* apart (which not everyone will share), this can be strongly recommended.

Alborada del gracioso; Boléro; Rapsodie espagnole.
(B) **(*) RCA Dig. VD 87728 [7728-2-RV]. Dallas SO, Mata.

This bargain-price reissue offers demonstration sound, sumptuously coloured – the *Alborada* flashes brilliantly – and the most spectacular dynamic range; the performances too are both vivid and subtle, and the expansive climax of *Boléro* is very compelling. However, the disc offers an overall timing of only 37 minutes 19 seconds!

Alborada del gracioso; Boléro; Rapsodie espagnole; La valse.
*** Decca 410 010-2 [id.]. Montreal SO, Dutoit.

The playing of the Montreal orchestra under Charles Dutoit is absolutely first class and thoroughly atmospheric, and the recorded sound has a clarity, range and depth of perspective that are equally satisfying. This recording defines the state of the art and, apart from the sumptuous music-making, has impressive refinement and a most musically judged and natural balance.

Alborada del gracioso; Pavane pour une infante défunte; Rapsodie espagnole; Le tombeau de Couperin; Valses nobles et sentimentales.
**(*) EMI CDC7 47468-2 [id.]. RPO, Previn.

Opening with a provocatively languorous account of the *Valses nobles et sentimentales*, lazy of tempo and affectionately indulgent, Previn's whole collection is imbued with sentient warmth. It even pervades *Le tombeau de Couperin*, although with some delectable oboe playing; this retains its lightness of character. The *Rapsodie espagnole* is unashamedly sultry, and the effect throughout is helped by the glowing EMI recording.

Alborada del gracioso; Pavane pour une infante défunte; Rapsodie espagnole; Valses nobles et sentimentales.
⊛ *** RCA GD 60179 [60179-2-RG]. Chicago SO, Reiner – DEBUSSY: *Ibéria.**** ⊛

These performances are in an altogether special class. In the *Rapsodie espagnole*, the *Prélude à la nuit* is heavy with fragrance and atmosphere; never have the colours in *Feria* glowed more luminously, while the *Malagueña* glitters with iridescence. In the thirty years since it first appeared, this is the recording we have turned to whenever we wanted to hear this work for pleasure. No one captures its sensuous atmosphere as completely as did Reiner. Its appearance on CD together with its companions is a cause for celebration, and the recorded sound with its natural concert-hall balance is greatly improved in terms of clarity and definition.

(i) *Alborada del gracioso;* (ii) *Rapsodie espagnole.*
*** EMI CDC7 47423-2 [id.]. (i) French Nat. O; (ii) LSO, Stokowski – DEBUSSY: *Ibéria; Nocturnes.****

In Stokowski's hands the *Alborada* glitters, with rhythms exhilaratingly precise; while in the *Rapsodie espagnole* the old magician beguiles the ear with his liltingly sensuous accounts of the *Malagueña* and *Habañera* and then produces a brilliant burst of colour and incandescent energy in the *Feria*. The early stereo doesn't sound dated, except that the dynamic range of the *Alborada* is not as wide as we would expect today.

Boléro.
(M) **(*) EMI CDM7 69007-2 [id.]. BPO, Karajan – DEBUSSY: *La mer* etc.**(*)
(*) Virgin Dig. VC 790729-2 [id.]. LPO, Litton – RIMSKY-KORSAKOV: *Scheherazade.*(*)
** Decca 417 704-2 [id.]. Chicago SO, Solti – DEBUSSY: *Prélude à l'après-midi d'un faune***; STRAVINSKY: *Rite of spring.****

Karajan's digitally remastered 1978 version of *Boléro* has fine presence and a splendid forward impetus. Litton's LPO version is rather reverberantly recorded, which takes some of the bite from the basic rhythmic pulse; but the climax is well prepared and not lacking in power. Metrically vigorous, Solti builds up the nagging climax with superb relentlessness. Though it lacks seductive touches, the performance is poised, the recording brightly analytical.

Boléro; Daphnis et Chloé: suite No. 2.
(M) *** DG 427 250-2 [id.]. BPO, Karajan – DEBUSSY: *La mer; Prélude.****

Karajan's 1964 *Boléro* is a very characteristic performance, marvellously controlled, hypnotic and gripping, with the Berlin Philharmonic at the top of its form. The 1965 *Daphnis et Chloé* suite is outstanding, even among all the competition, one of the very best things Karajan has ever done for the gramophone. He has the advantage of the Berlin Philharmonic at their finest and it would be difficult to imagine better or more atmospheric playing. The CD has opened up the sound spectacularly although now there is a touch of glare.

Boléro; Daphnis et Chloé: suite No. 2; Pavane pour une infante défunte.
*** EMI CDC7 47162-2 [id.]. LSO, Previn.

Previn's coupling of favourite Ravel pieces provides wonderfully rich, full and atmospheric sound for performances full of sparkle and flair. *Daphnis et Chloé* is sensuously beautiful and *Boléro*, at a slow and very steady tempo rather like Karajan's, sounds splendidly relentless. On CD, the sound is spectacular, but the playing time at 41 minutes 15 seconds is distinctly ungenerous.

Boléro; Daphnis et Chloé: suite No. 2; Pavane pour une infante défunte; La valse.
**(*) DG Dig. 400 061-2 [id.]. O de Paris, Barenboim.

At a slow speed *Boléro* brings fine balancing and smooth solos. The *Pavane* and *La valse* are also both on the slow side, but the seductive phrasing makes them sound lusciously idiomatic. The *Daphnis* suite brings the most persuasive performance of all. The recorded sound is sumptuous to match, but it could have more air round it.

Boléro; (i) *Daphnis et Chloé: suite No. 2; Pavane pour une infante défunte; La valse.*
*** Decca Dig. 414 406-2 [id.]. Montreal SO, Dutoit, (i) with chorus.

A further permutation of Dutoit's beautifully made Montreal recordings, warmly and translucently recorded at St Eustache. The *Daphnis et Chloé* suite is drawn from the highly praised complete set. If this programme is suitable, the performances and recordings cannot be bettered.

Boléro; L'éventail de Jeanne: Fanfare; Ma Mère l'Oye (complete ballet); *Pièce en forme de habañera* (arr. Arthur Horérée); *Rapsodie espagnole.*

*** CBS Dig. MK 44800 [id.]. LSO, Tilson Thomas.

Tilson Thomas is wholly attuned to the sensibility of this magical music and Ravel's sumptuous orchestral colours are vividly reproduced. There is a beautifully sultry account of the *Prélude à la nuit* and plenty of atmosphere in the *Rapsodie espagnole*. Ravel's *Vocalise-étude en forme de habañera* has the remarkable John Harle as the saxophone soloist. These are seductive, delicious performances, beautifully recorded.

Boléro; Ma Mère l'Oye (complete); *Pavane pour une infante défunte; Rapsodie espagnole.*
**(*) DG Dig. 415 972-2 [id.]. LSO, Abbado.

Abbado secures characteristically polished and refined playing from the LSO. There are some lovely gentle sounds in *Ma Mère l'Oye*, but the conductor's fastidiousness is perhaps a shade cool. However, the sultry atmosphere of the *Rapsodie espagnole* is very evocative. The *Pavane* has a grave, withdrawn melancholy. Only in *Boléro* is there any real idiosyncrasy: near the climax Abbado makes a perceptible gear-change, pressing the tempo forward arbitrarily; his involvement is also conveyed by his vocal contributions in the closing pages. The recording, with its wide dynamic range, has fine focus and detail, yet plenty of ambience and warmth.

Boléro; Ma Mère l'Oye (ballet; complete); *La valse.*
(M) **(*) Ph. 420 869-2 [id.]. LSO, Monteux.

Monteux's complete version of *Ma Mère l'Oye* is a poetic, unforced reading, given a naturally balanced sound. The 1964 recording has responded well to its digital remastering; this can be recommended, even though Monteux's reading of *Boléro* has a slight quickening of tempo in the closing pages.

Boléro; Menuet antique; Rapsodie espagnole; Shéhérazade: Overture de féerie. La valse.
(M) **(*) EMI CDM7 69565-2 [id.]. O de Paris, Martinon.

Martinon's performances are distinguished and very well played, even if *La valse* – not helped here by rather harsh fortissimo sound – is not among the finest versions available. The transfers are clearer than the originals and do not lack ambient warmth, but the upper range has a degree of shrillness under pressure.

Boléro; Rapsodie espagnole.
*** DG Dig. 413 588-2 [id.]. BPO, Karajan – MUSSORGSKY: *Pictures.***(*)

Karajan's later versions of *Boléro* and *Rapsodie espagnole* find the Berlin Philharmonic in characteristically brilliant form, recorded in very wide-ranging digital sound; the thrust of *Boléro* and the sensuousness of the *Rapsodie* are conveyed with unerring power and magnetism.

Piano concerto in G.
⊛ *** EMI CDC7 49326-2 [id.]. Michelangeli, Philh. O, Gracis – RACHMANINOV: *Concerto No. 4.*** ⊛
*** Virgin Dig. VC790780-2 [id.]. Andrew Litton, Bournemouth SO – GERSHWIN: *Concerto in F.***(*)

(i) *Piano concerto in G. Gaspard de la nuit; Sonatine.*
(M) *** DG 419 062-2 [id.]. Argerich, (i) BPO, Abbado.

Michelangeli plays with superlative brilliance which yet has great sympathy for the tender moments. He achieves exactly the right compromise between inflating the work and preventing it from seeming 'little'. The opening whipcrack could have been more biting, but the orchestra generally plays with great vigour. The exquisite playing in the slow movement makes up for any deficiencies of dimensional balance. The recording has been remastered very successfully and is of the highest quality: clear, with bold piano timbre and excellent orchestral detail.

The understanding between Andrew Litton and the orchestra of which he is principal conductor is formidably established in his seductive version of the *Concerto in G*. The players (with seeming spontaneity) respond to and mirror the subtleties of his rubato at the keyboard, making this an exceptionally characterful reading, with the wit and joyful energy of the first movement brought out alongside the yearning lyricism. The poetry of the slow movement too is most compelling, leading to an account of the finale that is full of fun. Many years ago, Bernstein performed the feat of directing this work from the keyboard, and Litton fully matches his achievement, while benefiting greatly from the beauty and refinement of the more modern sound.

Argerich's half-tones and clear fingerwork give the *G major Concerto* unusual delicacy, but its urgent virility – with jazz an important element – comes over the more forcefully by contrast. The compromise between coolness and expressiveness in the slow minuet of the middle movement is tantalizingly sensual. Her *Gaspard de la nuit* abounds in character and colour, and the *Sonatine* is a similarly telling performance. The *Concerto* balance is very successful and there is crisp detail, while the solo piano has fine presence and no want of colour.

Piano concerto in G; Piano concerto for the left hand.
(M) *** Erato/WEA 2292 45086-2 [id.]. Anne Queffélec, Strasbourg PO, Lombard – DEBUSSY: *Fantasy.***
(*) Chan. Dig. CHAN 8773 [id.]. Louis Lortie, LSO, Frühbeck de Burgos – FAURÉ: *Ballade.*

(i) *Piano concerto in G; Piano concerto for the left hand. Une barque sur l'océan; L'éventail de Jeanne: Fanfare; Menuet antique.*
**(*) Decca Dig. 410 230-2. (i) Rogé; Montreal SO, Dutoit.

(i) *Piano concerto in G;* (ii) *Piano concerto for the left hand; L'éventail de Jeanne: Fanfare. Menuet antique; Le tombeau de Couperin.*
**(*) DG Dig. 423 665-2 [id.]. (i) Argerich; (ii) Béroff; LSO, Abbado.

Piano concerto in G; Piano concerto for the left hand in D; Pavane pour une infante défunte; Jeux d'eau; (i) *La valse* (version for 2 pianos).
*** EMI CDC7 47386-2 [id.]. Collard; (i) Béroff; O Nat. de France, Maazel.

(i; ii) *Piano concerto in G; Piano concerto for the left hand;* (ii) *La valse;* (Piano) (i) *Valses nobles et sentimentales.*
(M) *** EMI CD-EMX 2146. (i) Philip Fowke; (ii) LPO, Baudo.

The performances of the *Concertos* by Philip Fowke with Baudo and the LPO are particularly attractive in the way they bring out the jazzy side of Ravel's inspiration, treating the misplaced accents and syncopations less strictly than some, but with winning results. In the slow movement of the *G major Concerto* the Spanish overtones also come out strongly, and Fowke's solo playing in the *Valses nobles et sentimentales* is clean, bright and rhythmic in a muscular way, without ever becoming brutal or unfeeling; nor does he lack poetry. Baudo and the orchestra also give a strongly characterized reading of *La valse*, brisker than some, with waltz rhythms powerfully inflected. Excellent recording, vivid and full.

Jean-Philippe Collard gives a meticulous, sparkling and refined account of the *G major*

Concerto and a marvellously brilliant and poetic account of the *Left-hand concerto*. He brings great *tendresse* to the more reflective moments and there is real delicacy of feeling throughout. Maazel gives thoroughly sympathetic support, and the Orchestre National play superbly. The CD refines the recorded sound and adds three piano items (two solos and one duet): the *Pavane, Jeux d'eau* and *La valse*, all beautifully played.

Anne Queffélec should not be passed by. Her accounts of both *Concertos* are thoughtful and imaginative. She is a thorough musician with no mean sense of poetry. The excellent Strasbourg orchestra under Alain Lombard give her admirable support, and the well-balanced recording sounds fresher in its CD format. The rare Debussy coupling is well worth having, too.

Pascal Rogé brings both delicacy and sparkle to the *G major Concerto*, which he gives with his characteristic musical grace and fluency. He produces unfailing beauty of tone at every dynamic level and brings great poetry and tenderness to the slow movement; but in the *Left-hand concerto* he is a good deal less dynamic. There is a certain want of momentum here, even though there is much to admire in the way of pianistic finesse – and charm. The Decca recording offers excellent performances of three short orchestral pieces as a makeweight, which may tip the scales in its favour for some collectors.

Louis Lortie's account of the two *Concertos* on Chandos has the advantage of altogether outstanding recording, in a field that is itself particularly strong in this respect. In the *G major* he is often highly personal without becoming unduly idiosyncratic. He has remarkable pianism and a fastidious sense of colour at his command and wonderfully clean articulation. In the *Left-hand concerto* he is perhaps less convincing; he really takes his time over the cadenzas and his agogic hesitations are sometimes over-indulgent. Immaculate playing as such, and superb recording, but ultimately not as satisfying as his major rivals, though better recorded than most of them.

In her newest digital recording, Argerich takes a very different, more ruminative view of the first movement, which she pulls out of shape: there is a gradual loss of impetus after this. These and other mannerisms do not improve upon repetition, though the playing as such is wonderfully refined. Abbado produces delicious sounds from the orchestra, both here and in the orchestral pieces which he does beautifully. In the *Concerto for the left hand*, Michel Béroff is undoubtedly impressive: there is some very sensitive and thoughtful playing in the early part of the work; he is helped by the excellence of the DG sound-balance.

(i) *Piano concerto for the left hand; Gaspard de la nuit; Pavane pour une infante défunte.*
(M) *** EMI CDM7 69026-2 [id.]. Gavrilov; (i) LSO, Rattle.

(i) *Piano concerto for the left hand. Miroirs: Alborada del gracioso.*
*** ASV Dig. CDDCA 555 [id.]. Osorio, RPO, Bátiz – PROKOFIEV: *Piano concerto No. 1* etc.***

Gavrilov's recording of the *Left-hand concerto* is altogether dazzling. He plays with effortless virtuosity, brilliance and, when required, great sensitivity. The *Pavane* is also very distinguished; apart from the strangely impulsive closing bars, this too is beautiful playing. *Gaspard de la nuit* is not quite so distinctive: both *Ondine* and *Le gibet* have an element of reserve. But *Scarbo* has superb dash, and the whole performance has impeccable style. The digital remastering is spectacular in its vividness.

Jorge-Federico Osorio's account of the *Left-hand concerto* can hold its own with the best. He also gives a crisp and colourful performance of the *Alborada*.

Daphnis et Chloé (ballet; complete).
⊛ *** Decca Dig. 400 055-2. Montreal SO and Ch., Dutoit.

* Ph. Dig. 426 260-2 [id.]. Boston SO, Tanglewood Ch., Haitink.

Daphnis et Chloé (complete); *Pavane pour une infante défunte; Rapsodie espagnole.*
(M) *** Decca 425 956-2 [id.]. ROHCG Ch., LSO, Pierre Monteux.

Daphnis et Chloé (ballet; complete); *Valses nobles et sentimentales.*
(M) *** EMI CDM7 69566-2 [id.]. Paris Op. Ch., O de Paris, Martinon.
**(*) DG Dig. 427 679-2. LSO, Abbado.

Dutoit's performance is sumptuously evocative with his splendid orchestra creating the most ravishing textures. He adopts an idiomatic and flexible style, observing the minute indications of tempo change but making every slight variation sound totally spontaneous. The final *Danse générale* finds him adopting a dangerously fast tempo, but the Montreal players – combining French responsiveness with transatlantic polish – rise superbly to the challenge, with the choral punctuations at the end adding to the sense of frenzy. The digital recording is wonderfully luminous, with the chorus ideally balanced at an evocative half-distance. It is a pity that Decca do not provide cues to guide access to the main sections of the score.

Monteux conducted the first performance of *Daphnis et Chloé* in 1912; Decca's 1959 recording, a demonstration disc in its day, captured his poetic and subtly shaded reading in the most vivid colours within an agreeably warm ambience. The performance was one of the finest things Monteux did for the gramophone. The CD transfer has opened up the sound, with generally impressive results. Perhaps just a little of the atmospheric allure has been lost (though *Daybreak* still sounds ravishing), but the sound generally is more transparent, without loss of body. Decca have added his 1962 recording of the *Pavane*, wonderfully poised and played most beautifully, and the *Rapsodie espagnole*, in which Monteux inspirationally achieves a balance and a contrast between the mood of quiet introspection for the opening and flashing brilliance for the *Feria*.

Martinon's *Daphnis et Chloé* has an intoxicating atmosphere: its sense of ecstasy and Dionysian abandon are altogether captivating. The delicacy of colouring in the *Nocturne*, the naturalness with which every phrase unfolds, and the virtuosity of the Orchestre de Paris are a constant source of delight. The *Valses nobles and sentimentales* are not quite so outstanding – there are preferable versions – but are still enjoyable. The sound, originally luminously opulent, is now clearer with only slight loss of richness.

The brilliant playing of the LSO under Abbado is a tribute to his training of the orchestra over his years as music director, and of the players' devotion. The clarity is phenomenal, helped by an exceptionally analytical DG recording which has the widest possible dynamic range – so much so that the pianissimo at the very opening is barely audible for almost thirty seconds. For all its refinement and virtuosity, this is a performance to admire rather than love, lacking the atmospheric warmth that marks, say, the Dutoit version. There is a lack of mystery in the scene-setting, and in *Daybreak* the flute and piccolo comments fail to suggest bird-song. Yet with an abundance of cueing facilities – 24 tracks plus 58 more index-points – coupled with a very detailed scenario, enjoyment is greatly enhanced. The *Valses nobles et sentimentales* is again clear rather than sensuous.

Haitink's version brings a powerful performance, marked by extremes of tempo and dynamic. Its directness is matched by the superb playing of the Boston orchestra, but sadly this is one of the relative failures by the Philips engineers working in Boston. The sound, at rather a low level, lacks body and is curiously misty, giving the Boston strings an acid edge which scarcely reflects their beauty. With no coupling and at full price, this is hardly competitive with the finest rivals.

Daphnis et Chloë: suite No. 2.
(M) *** Decca 417 779-2 [id.]. LSO Ch., LSO, Stokowski – DEBUSSY: *La Mer* etc.; BERLIOZ: *Dance of the Sylphs.****

Stokowski's 1970 recording was made using Decca's Phase 4 multi-channel technique, and this produces exactly the right disembodied, ethereal effect for the off-stage chorus. It is true that some of the woodwind bird-noises are also over-highlighted, but with the chorus the pervading presence is richly satisfying and the performance overall is glowing, with sumptuous and brilliant playing from the LSO. The digital remastering too is highly effective. Stokowski adds a fortissimo chord at the very end – but after such an involving performance few will begrudge him that.

Daphnis et Chloë: suite No. 2; La valse.
(M) ** DG Dig. 429 487-2 [id.]. O de Paris, Barenboim – DEBUSSY: *Iberia.**(*)

Barenboim's *La valse* is on the slow side, but the seductive phrasing makes it sound lusciously idiomatic. The suite from *Daphnis et Chloë* is even more persuasive. The recorded sound is sumptuous to match, but it could have more air round it; moreover the Debussy coupling is much less appealing.

Ma Mère l'Oye (complete ballet).
*** Chan. Dig. CHAN 8711 [id.]. Ulster O, Yan Pascal Tortelier – DEBUSSY: *Boîte à joujoux.****
*** Ph. Dig. 400 016-2 [id.]. Pittsburgh SO, Previn – SAINT-SAENS: *Carnival of the Animals.****
(B) **(*) Pickwick Dig. PCD 932. LSO, Barry Wordsworth – BIZET: *Jeux d'enfants*; SAINT-SAENS: *Carnival.***

Ma Mère l'Oye (complete ballet); *Pavane pour une infante défunte.*
(*) Virgin Dig. VC 790744-2 [id.]. SCO, Saraste – BIZET: *Symphony.*(*)

Ma Mère l'Oye (complete); *Rapsodie espagnole.*
(M) *** DG 415 844-2 [id.]. LAPO, Giulini – MUSSORGSKY: *Pictures.****

Ma Mère l'Oye (complete); *Le tombeau de Couperin; Valses nobles et sentimentales.*
⊛ *** Decca Dig. 410 254-2 [id.]. Montreal SO, Dutoit.

A few bars of this Decca record leave no doubt as to its excellence. This offers demonstration quality, transparent and refined, with the textures beautifully balanced and expertly placed. The performances too are wonderfully refined and sympathetic. *Ma Mère l'Oye* is ravishingly beautiful, its special combination of sensuousness and innocence perfectly caught.

More than usual, Tortelier's performance has a balletic feel to it, bringing out the affinities with *Daphnis et Chloë.* The exotic orchestration associated with *Laideronnette, Empress of the Pagodas* glitters vividly, yet the lovely closing *Jardin féerique*, opening serenely, moves to a joyous climax.

In Previn's version of the complete *Mother Goose* ballet, played and recorded with consummate refinement, the quality of innocence shines out. The temptation for any conductor is to make the music exotically sensuous in too sophisticated a way, but Previn retains a freshness apt for nursery music. The recording is superb, with the Philips engineers presenting a texture of luminous clarity.

The Giulini Los Angeles performance conveys much of the sultry atmosphere of the *Rapsodie espagnole.* Indeed some details, such as the sensuous string responses to the cor anglais tune in the *Feria*, have not been so tenderly caressed since the intoxicating Reiner version. The *Ma Mère l'Oye* suite is beautifully done too; though it is cooler, it is still beautiful.

Saraste has the measure of Ravel's *Mother Goose* score; he catches its fantasy and tenderness as well as its glitter, and the Scottish players produce lovely sounds in the gentler music, yet can flair up vividly when the composer calls for virtuosity. The *Pavane* is serenely spacious, with a very fine horn solo. However, for all its virtues, the playing does not quite match that given by the LSO to Michael Tilson Thomas, nor indeed Dutoit's superb Montreal version.

Barry Wordsworth finds the balletic grace in Ravel's beautiful score and creates some lovely diaphanous textures. There is plenty of vitality too, and the LSO response is consistently sympathetic. This hasn't the distinction of Dutoit but it is very well recorded, and the wide dynamic range suits this music rather better than the couplings.

Tzigane (for violin and orchestra).
*** EMI CDC7 47725-2 [id.]. Itzhak Perlman, O de Paris, Martinon – CHAUSSON: *Poème*; SAINT-SAENS: *Havanaise* etc.***
*** DG Dig. 423 063-2 [id.]. Itzhak Perlman, NYPO, Mehta – CHAUSSON: *Poème*; SAINT-SAENS: *Havanaise* etc.; SARASATE: *Carmen fantasy*.***
*** Decca 417 118-2 [id.]. Kyung Wha Chung, RPO, Dutoit – CHAUSSON: *Poème*; SAINT-SAENS: *Havanaise* etc.***
(M) **(*) Ph. 420 887-2. Szeryng, Monte Carlo Op. O, Remoortel – SAINT-SAENS: *Violin concerto No. 3* etc.**

Perlman's classic 1975 account of Ravel's *Tzigane* for EMI is marvellously played; the added projection of the CD puts the soloist believably at the end of the living-room. The later, digital version is very fine too and the recording is obviously more modern. The DG collection also includes a highly desirable extra Sarasate item. But the earlier performance has just that bit more charisma.

With its seemingly improvisatory solo introduction, *Tzigane* is a work which demands an inspirational artist, and Kyung Wha Chung is ideally cast, catching the atmosphere of this elusive piece with natural affinity.

Szeryng was at the height of his powers when he recorded this splendidly strong and committed account of Ravel's *Tzigane*, flexible and responsive as well as brilliant in execution. The recording spotlights him so that the rather less distinguished orchestral contribution, well enough held together by Eduard van Remoortel, emerges less strongly.

La valse; Valses nobles et sentimentales.
(B) *** RCA Dig. VD 87729 [7729-2-RV]. Dallas SO, Mata – MUSSORGSKY: *Pictures*.***

These are distinguished performances, very well played and superbly recorded – the very opening of the *Valses nobles* immediately impresses by its dynamic range, and the climax of *La valse* is engulfing.

CHAMBER MUSIC

Introduction and allegro for harp, flute, clarinet and string quartet.
⊛ (M) *** Decca 421 154-2 [id.]. Osian Ellis, Melos Ens. – DEBUSSY; FRANCK: *Sonatas*.*** ⊛

The beauty and subtlety of Ravel's sublime septet are marvellously realized by this 1962 Melos account. The interpretation has great delicacy of feeling, and the recording hardly shows its age at all.

Piano trio in A min.
*** Ph. Dig. 411 141-2 [id.]. Beaux Arts Trio – CHAUSSON: *Piano trio.****
*** Chan. Dig. CHAN 8458 [id.]. Borodin Trio – DEBUSSY: *Violin and Cello sonatas.****
(*) Denon Dig. CO 72508 [id.]. Rouvier, Kantorow, Müller – DEBUSSY; FAURÉ: *Trios.*(*)
(M) **(*) Collins Dig. 1040-2 [id.]. Trio Zingara – SHOSTAKOVICH: *Piano trio No. 2.***(*)

The most recent Beaux Arts account of the Ravel *Trio* is little short of inspired and is even finer than their earlier record of the late 1960s. The recording, too, is of high quality, even if the piano is rather forward.

The Borodin Trio pair the Ravel with the two Debussy *Sonatas*, which makes a logical and attractive coupling. They are excellently recorded and their playing has great warmth and is full of colour. Some may find them too hot-blooded by the side of the Beaux Arts, whose version is wonderfully poised and cultivated.

Jean-Jacques Kantorow, Philippe Müller and Jacques Rouvier are a highly accomplished team and are excellently recorded; their account gives much pleasure – even though the usually impressive Jacques Rouvier is not as responsive as Menahem Pressler in this work.

A fine account of the *Piano trio* comes from a young group making their début recording. The Trio Zingara was formed in 1978 and has won much acclaim and a number of prizes. Their pianist, Annette Cole, produces some beautiful *pianissimo* tone in the first movement, and the playing of all three is sensitive. If they do not match the Beaux Arts in subtlety and refinement, theirs is a thoroughly enjoyable and impressive performance, and it is recorded with great presence and clarity.

String quartet in F.
*** DG 419 750-2 [id.]. Melos Qt – DEBUSSY: *Quartet.****
(M) *** EMI CD-EMX 2156 [id.]. Chilingirian Qt – DEBUSSY: *Quartet.****
(M) *** Ph. 420 894-2 [id.]. Italian Qt – DEBUSSY: *Quartet.****
(*) Denon Dig. C37 7830 [id.]. Nuovo Qt – DEBUSSY: *Quartet.*(*)
(BB) **(*) Hung. White Label HRC 122 [id.]. Bartók Qt – DEBUSSY: *Quartet***(*);
DVOŘÁK: *Quartet No. 12.****
(*) EMI Dig. CDC7 47347-2 [id.]. Alban Berg Qt – DEBUSSY: *Quartet.*(*)
(*) Telarc Dig. CD 80111 [id.]. Cleveland Qt – DEBUSSY: *Quartet.*(*)
** Virgin Dig. VC 791077-2 [id.]. Borodin Qt – DEBUSSY: *Quartet.***(*)
(M) ** Decca 425 424-2 [id.]. Carmirelli Qt – FRANCK: *Quartet.***(*)
** DG Dig. 427 320-2. Emerson Qt – DEBUSSY: *Quartet.***

The Melos account brings artistry of the very highest order to this magical score. Their slow movement offers the most refined and integrated quartet sound; in terms of internal balance and blend it would be difficult to surpass it, and the reading has great poetry. In both the Scherzo and finale the Melos players evince the highest virtuosity, yet this is highly imaginative playing, touched with a complete identification with Ravel's sensibility. The players have the advantage of superbly truthful recording, enhanced in the digital remastering.

The Chilingirian recording has plenty of body and presence and also has the benefit of a warm acoustic. The players give a thoroughly committed account, with well-judged tempi and very musical phrasing. The scherzo is vital and spirited, and there is no want of poetry in the slow movement. At mid-price this is fully competitive and the sound is preferable to that of the Italian Quartet on Philips.

For many years the Italian Quartet held pride of place in this coupling. Their playing is perfect in ensemble, attack and beauty of tone, and their performance remains highly recommendable, one of the most satisfying chamber-music records in the catalogue. At mid-price this will prove an admirable alternative, by no means second best.

Denon's version by the Nuovo Quartet is a sympathetic and likeable account, by no means as immaculate as the finest now before the public, but for the most part these players make a beautiful sound and show considerable feeling and sensitivity. There is an agreeably unforced quality in the way they let the music unfold. Very enjoyable – despite less than absolutely spot-on intonation – and very well recorded.

The Bartók Quartet on Hungaroton's cheapest label also give a sympathetic and well-characterized reading, only marginally less perceptive than the Chilingirian and Italian versions; and they too are well recorded. Moreover they offer an additional work. Those collectors looking for a bargain will not be disappointed here.

Superb, indeed incomparable playing from the Alban Berg Quartet, and splendidly rich and sonorous recording from the EMI engineers. Yet while this is marvellously polished and has such excellence in terms of ensemble and tonal blend, there is a want of spontaneity that ultimately weighs against it.

The Cleveland on Telarc is a well-played version, not always fully observing dynamic markings at the *pianissimo* end of the spectrum. Nor do the players fully convey the atmosphere and intimacy of the slow movement. All the same, there is more that is right than is wrong in this highly accomplished and well-recorded account.

The Borodin Quartet make the most sumptuous sound; tonally this group must be in a class of its own. They not only play but seem to think as one person, and their unanimity of ensemble and perfection in matching each other in matters of phrasing is wonderful. But despite the ravishing sounds they produce, their Ravel is not unalloyed pleasure. They pull things out of shape, and they adopt a totally different tempo for the second group of the first movement, which proves most disturbing. They are beautifully recorded but their approach is too mannered to give complete artistic satisfaction. The middle section of the scherzo is disfigured by artificiality and a narcissism one had never associated with this ensemble.

It is tempting to pass over the Carmirelli, which is offered as a bonus to the Franck *Quartet*. But this would be unjust, for their playing, if not as distinguished as that of their finest competitors, is still very good, and the recording is perfectly acceptable, even though it dates from the mid-1950s. In its CD transfer it is smoother than the Franck coupling.

The Emerson have stunning ensemble, precision of attack and body of sound on DG – and are determined not to let us forget it. But their performance, though less affected than the Borodin, is just too chromium-plated and jet-powered, hardly in tune with Ravel's sensibility.

Violin sonata in G.
*** Ph. Dig. 426 254-2. Viktoria Mullova, Bruno Canino – PROKOFIEV: *Sonata***; STRAVINSKY: *Divertimento.****
(M) *** Ph. 420 777-2 [id.]. David Oistrakh, Frida Bauer – DEBUSSY; YSAYE: *Sonatas*; PROKOFIEV: *Melodies.****
*** DG Dig. 415 683-2 [id.]. Shlomo Mintz, Yefim Bronman – DEBUSSY; FRANCK: *Sonatas.****

Mullova and Canino give a beguiling performance of the Ravel *Violin sonata*, one of the finest to have appeared for many years. It is played with diamond-like precision and great character. The Philips recording is marvellous.

Oistrakh's account of the Ravel *Sonata* is most beautiful and the interest of the couplings adds to its claims on the collector. The recording is remastered using Philips's newest NoNoise system: the sound is slightly brighter than the original but well balanced.

Shlomo Mintz and Yefim Bronman's account of the Ravel comes in harness with Franck and Debussy. Impeccable, highly polished playing, even if it is not so completely inside Ravel's world in the slow movement. The glorious sounds both artists produce are a source of unfailing delight. They are beautifully recorded too.

PIANO DUET

Ma Mère L'Oye.
*** Ph. Dig. 420 159-2 [id.]. Katia and Marielle Labèque – FAURÉ: *Dolly*; BIZET: *Jeux d'enfants.****

The Labèque sisters give an altogether delightful performance of Ravel's magical score, which he later orchestrated and expanded. The recording could not be more realistic and present.

La valse.
*** Ph. Dig. 411 034-2 [id.]. Argerich, Freire – LUTOSLAWSKI: *Paganini variations*; RACHMANINOV: *Suite No. 2.****

The transcription is Ravel's own. Brilliant, atmospheric playing and good recording.

SOLO PIANO MUSIC

À la manière de Borodine; À la manière de Chabrier; Gaspard de la nuit; Jeux d'eau; Menuet antique; Menuet sur le nom de Haydn; Miroirs; Pavane pour une infante défunte; Prélude; Sérénade grotesque; Sonatine; Le tombeau de Couperin; Valses nobles et sentimentales.
*** CRD Dig. CRD 3383/4 [id.]. Paul Crossley.

Paul Crossley's accounts of all these works are beautifully fashioned and can hold their own with the available competition. He is aristocratic, with an admirable feeling for tone-colour and line, and rarely mannered (the end of *Jeux d'eau* is an exception). His version of *Le tombeau de Couperin* has a classical refinement and delicacy that are refreshing. The CRD recording is very good indeed, and this fine set deserves the warmest welcome.

À la manière de Borodine; À la manière de Chabrier; Gaspard de la nuit; Menuet antique; Menuet sur le nom de Haydn; Miroirs; Prélude; Sonatine.
*** Chan. Dig. CHAN 8647 [id.]. Louis Lortie.

The Canadian pianist, Louis Lortie, gives an impressive account of himself in *Gaspard de la nuit* and more than justifies the high hopes raised by his appearance at Leeds some years ago. His account of *Le gibet* is chilling and atmospheric, and in the *Miroirs* he produces some ravishing pianism. His rhythmic articulation in the *Alborada* is marvellously clean, and throughout the whole set his playing is elegant, virile and sensitive. The recording is made in The Maltings, Snape, and the closely observed sound perhaps robs *Ondine* and *Scarbo* of some of their sense of enchantment and eeriness respectively, but a lower-than-usual playback level helps restore a little of their mystery. This is a distinguished and stimulating recital.

À la manière de Borodine; À la manière de Chabrier; Menuet antique; Prélude; Le tombeau de Couperin; Valses nobles et sentimentales.
**(*) Nimbus NI 5011 [id.]. Vlado Perlemuter.

Gaspard de la nuit; Jeux d'eau; Miroirs; Pavane.
**(*) Nimbus NI 5005 [id.]. Vlado Perlemuter.

Though Perlemuter's technical command is not as complete as it had been, he gives delightful, deeply sympathetic readings; the sense of spontaneity is a joy. There may be Ravel recordings which bring more dazzling virtuoso displays, but none more persuasive. Nimbus's preference for an ample room acoustic makes the result naturally atmospheric on CD, with light reverberation presenting a halo of sound.

Gaspard de la nuit.
*** DG Dig. 413 363-2 [id.]. Pogorelich – PROKOFIEV: *Sonata No. 6.**** ⊛
*** EMI Dig. CDC7 49262-2 [id.]. Cécile Ousset – MUSSORGSKY: *Pictures.***(*)

Pogorelich's *Gaspard* is out of the ordinary. In *Le gibet*, there is self-conscious striving after effect. We are made conscious of the pianist's refinement of tone and colour first, and Ravel's poetic vision afterwards. But for all that, this is piano playing of astonishing quality. The control of colour and nuance in *Scarbo* is dazzling and its eruptive cascades of energy and dramatic fire have one sitting on the edge of one's seat. The coupling, Prokofiev's *Sixth Sonata*, is quite simply stunning.

Cécile Ousset's version of *Gaspard* is also very fine. Her *Scarbo* is particularly dazzling, with all the electricity of a live concert performance, even if by comparison with Pogorelich she sounds uncontrolled. She is well recorded.

Gaspard de la nuit; Jeux d'eaux; Miroirs; Valses nobles et sentimentales.
(M) *(*) Decca 425 002-2 [id.]. Pascal Rogé.

These were among Pascal Rogé's first recordings of French repertoire for Decca, made in 1974/5, and they proved to be disappointing. He does not match either Ashkenazy or Argerich in *Gaspard de la nuit* in terms of authority and panache. In the *Miroirs* he is a shade pallid and undercharacterized, though he produces some finely coloured tone; his *Jeux d'eaux*, though nicely played, is curiously faceless. He is well recorded, but he was to be much more successful in his later recordings of Debussy, Poulenc and Satie.

Gaspard de la nuit; Menuet sur le nom d'Haydn; Prélude; Sonatine; Valses nobles et sentimentales.
(M) **(*) Hung. Dig. HCD 12317-2 [id.]. Dezsö Ránki.

Ránki is thoroughly attuned to the Gallic sensibility, and in the last of the *Valses nobles* his playing has wonderful atmosphere and poignancy. Unfortunately, his rather reverberant recording does not altogether flatter him.

Gaspard de la nuit; Valses nobles et sentimentales; Pavane pour une infante défunte.
*** Decca Dig. 410 255-2 [id.]. Vladimir Ashkenazy.

Ashkenazy's new account is hardly less impressive than the old LP version and is in no way narcissistic. His *Valses nobles* are splendidly refined and aristocratic. The recording has marvellous range and is extremely vivid and open, but the newer issue offers somewhat short measure for CD.

Miroirs; Le tombeau de Couperin.
**(*) BIS Dig. CD 246. Yukie Nagai.

Yukie Nagai's account of *Noctuelles* is marvellously refined, and her range of colour at the *piano* and *pianissimo* end of the range is particularly lovely. Her account of *Oiseaux tristes* is very slow and altogether magical in atmosphere, and she is hardly less impressive elsewhere. This is distinguished playing. The recording is good – though it sounds as if it was made in a small studio.

VOCAL MUSIC

(i) *Chansons madécasses;* (ii) *Don Quichotte à Dulcinée; 5 mélodies populaires grecques;* (iii) *3 poèmes de Stéphane Mallarmé;* (iv) *Shéhérazade.*
*** CBS Dig. MK 39023 [id.]. (i) Norman, Ens. InterContemporain; (ii) José van Dam; (iii) Jill Gomez; (iv) Heather Harper; BBC SO, Boulez.

With four characterful and strongly contrasted soloists, Boulez's collection of Ravel's songs with orchestra (including arrangements) makes a delightful disc. The *Don Quichotte* and the *Greek popular songs* (both with José van Dam as soloist) are rarely heard in this orchestral form. Van Dam may not be ideally relaxed, but the dark, firm voice is very impressive. Excellent sound, with translations provided.

2 Mélodies hébraïques; 5 Mélodies populaires grecques; Shéhérazade; Vocalise en forme de habañera.
*** EMI Dig. CDC7 49689-2 [id.]. Barbara Hendricks, Lyon Op. O, Gardiner – DUPARC: *Mélodies.****

There is no version of Ravel's *Shéhérazade* more seductive than that of Barbara Hendricks with John Eliot Gardiner and the Lyon Opera Orchestra: it is both rapt and sensuous, with Hendricks's finely detailed shading of Tristan Klingsor's exotic words building an irresistible, personalized characterization, alluring but with a hint of vulnerability. The other Ravel songs in their orchestral form are just as vividly characterized, with Gardiner equally masterly in conveying physical sensuousness without a hint of excess or sentimentality. The well-balanced sound is both warmly atmospheric and finely detailed.

Shéhérazade (song-cycle).
*** Decca 417 813-2 [id.]. Régine Crespin, SRO, Ansermet (with *Recital of French songs****).
** Ph. 412 493-2 [id.]. Jessye Norman, LSO, C. Davis – BERLIOZ: *Nuits d'été.***

Crespin is right inside these songs and Ravel's magically sensuous music emerges with striking spontaneity. She is superbly supported by Ansermet who, aided by the Decca engineers, weaves a fine tonal web round the voice. As in the Berlioz *Nuits d'été* (the original coupling, which is included here within a fuller recital, offering also Poulenc and Debussy) her style has distinct echoes of the opera house; but the richness of the singer's tone does not detract from the delicate languor of *The enchanted flute*, in which the slave-girl listens to the distant sound of her lover's flute playing while her master sleeps.

Jessye Norman seems more at home in Ravel's song-cycle than in the coupled account of the Berlioz, although she and Sir Colin Davis are languorous to the point of lethargy in *L'Indifférent*. With the voice very forward, the balance is less than ideal, though otherwise the sound is rich and atmospheric.

OPERA

L'Enfant et les sortilèges (complete).
*** DG 423 718-2 [id.]. Ogéas, Collard, Berbié, Gilma, RTF Ch. & Boys' Ch., RTF Nat. O, Maazel.

L'Heure espagnole (complete).
*** DG 423 719-2 [id.]. Berbié, Sénéchal, Giraudeau, Bacquier, Van Dam, Paris Op. O, Maazel.

Maazel's recordings of the two Ravel one-Act operas were made in the early 1960s and, though the solo voices in the former are balanced too close, the sound is vivid and the performances are splendidly stylish. Neo-classical crispness of articulation goes with refined textures that convey the tender poetry of the one piece, the ripe humour of the other. The CD remastering has been very successful and both performances are given striking presence, without loss of essential atmosphere. Full librettos are included.

Rebel, Jean-Féry (1661–1747)

Les Élémens (ballet).
*** O-L 421 656-2 [id.]. AAM, Hogwood – DESTOUCHES: *Suite.****

Rebel's ballet on the elements emerging out of Chaos can startle even twentieth-century listeners with the massive discord illustrating 'chaos' at the start. The sequence of dances, beautifully performed on original instruments by Hogwood's Academy, is consistently sharp and refreshing, helping to revive an undeservedly neglected name.

Reger, Max (1873–1916)

Ballet suite; Variations on a theme of Hiller, Op. 100.
*** Orfeo C 090841 [id.]. Bav. RSO, C. Davis.

The *Hiller variations* (1907) is one of Reger's greatest works, full of wit, resource and, above all, delicacy. It culminates, as do so many Reger pieces, in a double fugue. The *Ballet suite* is a delightful piece, scored with great clarity and played, as is the *Hiller variations*, with charm and commitment. Sir Colin Davis emerges as a thoroughly *echt*-Reger conductor and the Bavarian orchestra is in excellent form. The recording is first rate, though we have one minor quibble: the individual variations are not indexed.

(i) *Symphonic prologue to a tragedy, Op. 108;* (i) *2 Romances for violin and orchestra, Op. 50.*
** Schwann CD311 076. (i) Berlin RSO, Albrecht; (ii) with Maile; cond. Lajovic.

The tragedy in question is Sophocles' *Oedipus Rex*, and Reger's *Symphonic prologue* is one of his very finest and most powerful works. Inspiration runs consistently high and Reger's score, which comes from the period of Strauss's *Elektra* and Mahler's *Das Lied von der Erde*, deserves far more exposure. The violin *Romances* are beautiful pieces and are very well played by Hans Maile and the Berlin Radio Orchestra. Strongly recommended for the sake of the marvellous music; however, it must be said that the 1982 recording is serviceable rather than distinguished (textures at climaxes are inclined to be opaque).

4 Tone poems after Böcklin, Op. 128; Variations on a theme by Hiller, Op. 100.
*** Chan. Dig. CHAN 8794 [id.]. Concg. O, Järvi.

The Swiss symbolist Arnold Böcklin (1827–1901) is best remembered by music-lovers for his painting, *Der Toteninsel* (*The Isle of the dead*), which inspired Rachmaninov's tone-poem as well as the third of Reger's four *Tone poems* of 1913. Those who still think of Reger's music as densely contrapuntal and turgidly scored will be amazed by the delicacy and refinement of his orchestration. Textures in *Der geigende Eremit* (*Hermit playing the violin*) are wonderfully transparent, and *Im spiel der Wellen* has something of the sparkle of the *Jeu de vagues* movement of *La Mer* photographed in sepia; while the *Isle of the dead* is a lovely and often very touching piece. The *Hiller variations* are gloriously inventive, full of that blend of confidence, delicacy of feeling and imagination that characterizes Reger at his best. It is beautifully recorded and Neeme Järvi's performance has the combination of sensitivity and virtuosity that this composer needs.

A Romantic suite, Op. 125; 4 Tone poems after Böcklin, Op. 128.
** Schwann Musica Mundi Dig. 311 011. Berlin RSO, Albrecht.

Good performances of the Böcklin come from the Berlin Radio orchestra, coupled less generously with the charming *Romantic suite*. The Böcklin pieces are well enough recorded, but Järvi on Chandos is a clear first choice, particularly given the excellence of the coupling.

Variations and fugue on a theme of Beethoven, Op. 86.
** Chan. Dig. CHAN 8843/4 [id.]. LPO, Järvi – BRUCKNER: *Symphony No. 8.***

Reger scored his *Beethoven variations* for two pianos in the last year of his life, after ill-health had forced him to give up his orchestral appointment at Meiningen. He reduced the number of the variations from twelve to eight and changed their sequence. It is not as strong a work as the *Mozart* and *Hiller variations*. The performance is very good, but the reverberance of All Saints', Tooting, muddles the texture.

Chorale fantasia on Straf' mich nicht in deinem Zorn, Op. 40/2; Chorale preludes, Op. 67/4, 13, 28, 40, 48; Introduction, passacaglia and fugue in E min., Op. 127.
*** Hyp. Dig. CDA 66223 [id.]. Graham Barber (organ of Limburg Cathedral).

The *Introduction, passacaglia and fugue*, which takes all of 28 minutes, is bold in conception and vision and is played superbly on this excellently engineered Hyperion disc by Graham Barber at the Klais organ of Limburg Cathedral, an instrument ideally suited to this repertoire. The five *Chorale preludes* give him an admirable opportunity to show the variety and richness of tone-colours of the instrument. The Hyperion recording captures the quality of the king of beasts marvellously on CD.

Lyrisches Andante.
*** Claves Dig. D 8502 [id.]. Deutsche Kammerakademie Neuss, Goritzki – SCHOECK: *Cello concerto.***

Reger's *Lyrisches Andante* is a short, songful and gentle piece for strings; it should make many friends for this much misunderstood composer, particularly in this dedicated performance.

Variations and fugue on a theme by Telemann, Op. 134.
(M) *** Decca 417 791-2 [id.]. Jorge Bolet – BRAHMS: *Handel variations.***

Reger's *Telemann variations*, his last major work for solo piano, makes a challenging and compelling coupling for Bolet's superb account of Brahms's *Handel* set. The virtuosity is phenomenal, not least in the fugue at the end, which was once considered unplayable. Bolet breasts all difficulties with commanding strength. A thrilling experience with first-rate remastered recording.

Reich, Steve (born 1936)

Drumming; Music for mallet instruments, voices and organ; 6 Pianos.
(M) **(*) DG 427 428-2 (2) [id.]. Instrumental & Vocal Ens., composer.

At almost 90 minutes, *Drumming* is Steve Reich's longest work, with different groups of percussion instruments exploited in each of the four long parts or movements. *Six Pianos* uses that combination in the same way; and the most attractive piece on this pair of discs is the shortest, *Music for mallet instruments, voices and organ*, where at least textures are more varied and often charm the ear. Excellent performances and recording.

Variations for winds, strings & keyboard.
*** Ph. 412 214-2 [id.]. San Francisco SO, De Waart – ADAMS: *Shaker loops.****

Reich's *Variations*, written for the San Francisco orchestra in 1980, marked a new departure in the writing of this leading minimalist, using a large orchestral rather than a small chamber scale. The repetitions and ostinatos, which gradually get out of phase, are most skilfully used to produce a hypnotic kind of poetry, soothing rather than compelling.

Reicha, Antonín (1770–1836)

Piano concerto in E flat.
** Sup. CO 1969 [id.]. Kvapil, Brno State PO, Vronsky – JOSEF REICHA: *Viola concerto.***

Reicha played the flute in the Elector of Cologne's orchestra in which Beethoven served as violist and then went to Vienna, where this *Concerto* was composed. It is of course far removed from Beethoven but is not a negligible piece. The most original of the three movements is the second with its declamatory solo part, two fortissimo chords, to which the orchestra responds with some thoughtful musings. There is a spirited finale which looks forward a few years to Hummel and Weber. A serviceable rather than distinguished performance, and the same goes for the recording.

Oboe quintet in F, Op. 107.
*** Hyp. CDA 66143 [id.]. Sarah Francis, Allegri Qt – CRUSELL: *Divertimento*; R. KREUTZER: *Grand quintet.****

Antonín Reicha's *F major Quintet* is spectacularly unmemorable but always amiable. The present performance is of high quality and very well recorded.

Wind quintets: in E flat, Op. 88/2; in F, Op. 91/3.
*** Hyp. Dig. CDA 66268 [id.]. Academia Wind Quintet of Prague.

Czech wind playing in Czech wind music has a deservedly high entertainment rating and the present performances are no exception. The music itself has great charm and geniality; it is ingenuous yet cultivated, with some delightful, smiling writing for the bassoon. The players are clearly enjoying themselves, yet they play and blend expertly. The sound too is admirable.

REICHA

Reicha, Josef (1752–95)

Viola concerto, Op. 2, No. 1
** Sup. CO 1969 [id.]. Spelina, Brno State PO, Vronsky – A. REICHA: *Piano concerto in E flat.***

Josef Reicha, an eminent cellist in his day, wrote widely for his instrument: the present work also existed in a cello version. Don't be put off by the rather conventional first movement: the other two are far more interesting, the best being the *Romanza*, which opens as if in mid-course and is quite haunting. Karel Spelina is a persuasive and accomplished soloist, though the orchestra are a lesser pleasure.

Reindl, Constantin (1738–99)

Sinfonia concertante in D for violin, two flutes, two oboes, bassoon, two horns and strings.
*** Novalis Dig. 150 031-2 [id.]. ECO, Griffiths – STALDER: *Symphony No. 5; Flute concerto.***

The *Sinfonia concertante* was written in about 1789 at the time of the outbreak of the French Revolution and, though there is nothing revolutionary about it, it is not just bland rococo music; it is fresh and inventive, and the finale has a most attractive (and obstinately memorable) main theme. A delightful performance by the ECO under Howard Griffiths and an excellent, natural and well-balanced recording.

Respighi, Ottorino (1879–1936)

Ancient airs and dances: suites Nos. 1–3.
*** Mercury 416 496-2 [id.]. Philh. Hungarica, Dorati.
(M) **(*) DG 419 868-2 [id.]. Boston SO, Ozawa.

Dorati's famous and very distinguished Mercury recording of the 1960s displays a remarkable feeling for the colour and ambience of the Renaissance dances on which Respighi's three suites (the last for strings alone) are based. The refinement and warmth of the playing (and the sound) are very striking, particularly in the *Third suite*, and the touch of astringency which the digital remastering has added increases the piquancy. Dorati finds in this music a nobility and graciousness that make it obstinately memorable.

Ozawa is at his best in the *Second suite*, where the luminous Boston wind playing combines with strong contrasts of dynamic and tempo to dramatic effect. Rhythmically very positive throughout, as so often his music-making brings a feeling of ballet to the score. He is less memorable in the *Third suite*; but with brightly vivid sound this makes an enjoyable mid-price alternative.

Ancient airs and dances: suites 1–3; The Birds (suite).
⊛ *** Omega Dig. 191007 [id.]. Australian CO, Christopher Lyndon Gee.

The performance of *The Birds* is a complete delight, opening and closing vigorously, yet providing the most refined portraits of the dove, nightingale and cuckoo, with particularly lovely oboe playing in *The dove*. The opening of the first suite of *Ancient airs and dances* has a comparable grace and delicacy of feeling; throughout, Lyndon Gee's response to Respighi's imaginative orchestration is wonderfully fresh, with the oboe (again) and bassoon distinguishing themselves among the many fine wind solos. The strings produce lovely translucent textures at the beginning of the *Third suite*; yet when a

842

robust approach is called for, the players provide it admirably. The bitter-sweet combination of nobility and melancholy that often haunts this music, especially in the *Second suite*, is not missed, and the espressivo playing has an affecting eloquence. The recording, made at the ABC Studio at Chatsworth, Sydney, is in the demonstration class.

Ancient airs and dances: suite No. 3; The Birds (suite).
*** Ph. Dig. 420 485-2 [id.]. ASMF, Marriner – ROSSINI: *La Boutique fantasque.***(*)

Ancient airs and dances: suite No. 3; The Fountains of Rome; The Pines of Rome.
*** DG 413 822-2 [id.]. BPO, Karajan.

Karajan's highly polished, totally committed performances of the two most popular Roman pieces are well supplemented by the *Third suite* of *Ancient airs and dances*, brilliantly played and just as beautifully transferred, more impressive in sound than many more recent Karajan recordings. In the symphonic poems Karajan is in his element, and the playing of the Berlin Philharmonic is wonderfully refined. The evocation of atmosphere in the two middle sections of *The Pines of Rome* is unforgettable. In *The Fountains* the tension is rather less tautly held, but the pictorial imagery is hardly less telling when the orchestral response is so magical.

Marriner too gives a very beautiful account of the *Third suite* of *Ancient airs and dances*, with gracious phrasing and luminous string textures. He catches both the music's noble melancholy and its moments of passionate feeling. The performance of *The Birds* is hardly less persuasive, the portrait of *The Dove* particularly tender, and there is much delicacy of texture elsewhere. The ASMF strings are wonderfully responsive and play as one. The sound is excellent too, but the coupling is a curious choice, acting merely as a pleasant filler.

Belkis, Queen of Sheba: suite. Metamorphoseon modi XII.
*** Chan. Dig. CHAN 8405 [id.]. Philh. O, Simon.

The ballet-suite *Belkis, Queen of Sheba*, taken from a full-length ballet written in the early 1930s, is just what you would expect: a score that set the pattern for later Hollywood biblical film music; but *Metamorphoseon* is a taut and sympathetic set of variations. It has been ingeniously based on a medieval theme, and though a group of cadenza variations relaxes the tension of argument in the middle, the brilliance and variety of the writing have much in common with Elgar's *Enigma*. Superb playing from the Philharmonia, treated to one of the finest recordings that even Chandos has produced, outstanding in every way. This is very attractive music and the sound is certainly in the demonstration bracket.

The Birds (suite); 3 Botticelli pictures.
**(*) EMI CDC7 47844-2 [id.]. ASMF, Marriner.

Sir Neville Marriner's earlier performance of *The Birds* is delightful and well recorded. The score for the *Botticelli pictures* is less well known – and understandably so, for its inspiration is less assured; with presentation of this standard, however, the music is certainly enjoyable. But at 38 minutes this is poor value at premium price.

The Birds (suite); The Fountains of Rome; The Pines of Rome.
(B) *** Decca 425 507-2 [id.]. LSO, Istvan Kertesz.

This was one of Kertesz's most impressive records and (made in 1969) it has the advantage of vintage Decca recording. It still sounds pretty spectacular and makes a fine bargain on Decca's Weekend label. *The Birds* is very engaging in its spirited elegance;

seldom before has the entry of the nightingale's song been so beautifully prepared in the central section of *The Pines of Rome*, where Kertesz creates a magical, atmospheric frisson. The iridescent brilliance of the turning-on of the Triton Fountain in the companion-piece is matched by the grandeur of the Trevi processional, when Neptune's chariot is imagined to be seen crossing the heavens. In sharpening detail the remastering loses only a little of the original ambient warmth and depth.

Brazilian impressions; Church windows (Vetrate di chiesa).
*** Chan. Dig. CHAN 8317 [id.]. Philh. O, Simon.

Respighi's set of musical illustrations of church windows is not among his finest works but is well worth having when the recording is impressively spacious and colourful. Geoffrey Simon is sympathetic and he secures very fine playing from the Philharmonia. The superb digital recording and the useful coupling (which avoids duplication with Respighi's more famous works) will be an added incentive to collectors. On CD, the wide dynamic range and a striking depth of perspective create the most spectacular effects.

Feste romane; The Fountains of Rome; The Pines of Rome (symphonic poems).
*** EMI Dig. CDC7 47316-2 [id.]. Phd. O, Muti.
*** Decca Dig. 410 145-2. Montreal SO, Dutoit.
(M) *** DG 415 846-2 [id.]. Boston SO, Ozawa.

Muti gives warmly red-blooded performances of Respighi's Roman trilogy, captivatingly Italianate in their inflexions. With brilliant playing from the Philadelphia Orchestra and warmly atmospheric recording, far better than EMI engineers have generally been producing in Philadelphia, these are exceptional for their strength of characterization. The CD version clarifies the reverberant recording very effectively, with individual soloists cleanly placed.

Dutoit, as in other brilliant and colourful pieces, draws committed playing from his fine Montreal orchestra. Where many interpreters concentrate entirely on brilliance, Dutoit finds a vein of expressiveness too, which – for example in the opening sequence of *The Pines of Rome* – conveys the fun of children playing at the Villa Borghese. There have been more high-powered, even more polished performances on record, but none more persuasive. The recorded sound is superlative on CD, where the organ pedal sound is stunning.

Ozawa's 1979 record has been digitally remastered for its Galleria reissue and remains very competitive at mid-price; however, while sharpening the focus and refining detail, the brighter treble has brought a hint of harshness to the loudest fortissimos.

Violin sonata in B min.
*** DG Dig. 427 617-2 [id.]. Kyung Wha Chung, Krystian Zimerman – R. STRAUSS: *Sonata.****

At present Kyung Wha Chung and Krystian Zimerman have the field to themselves in Respighi's fine *Sonata*. Kyung Wha Chung is at her best and has the inestimable advantage of having a great artist as her partner; Krystian Zimerman brings an enormous range of colour and dynamics to the piano part – the clarity of his articulation in the *Passacaglia* is exceptional. This is undoubtedly the finest performance to appear on record since the Heifetz version.

Il tramonto.
*** Hyp. Dig. CDA 66290 [id.]. Carol Madalin, ECO, Bonavera – MARTUCCI: *Le canzone dei ricordi; Notturno.****

Respighi's *Il tramonto* (*The sunset*) is a setting of Shelley (in Italian translation) for string quartet or full strings (as heard here). It is a glorious work which at times calls to mind the world of late Strauss. A most lovely record. Recommended with all possible enthusiasm.

OPERA

La Fiamma (complete).
*** Hung. Dig. HCD 12591/3 [id.]. Tokody, Kelen, Takács, Sólyom-Nagy, Hungarian R. and TV Ch., Hungarian State O, Gardelli.

Richly atmospheric, with choruses and ensembles both mysterious and savage, *La Fiamma* makes a fine impact in this excellent first recording, idiomatically conducted by Lamberto Gardelli. The Hungarian cast is impressive, with Ilona Tokody producing Callas-like inflexions in the central role of Silvana, the young wife of the exarch, Basilio. She falls in love with her son-in-law, shocks her husband into falling down dead, and then cannot find tongue to deny a charge of witchcraft. Sándor Sólyom-Nagy is impressive as Basilio, Peter Kelen is aptly light-toned as the son-in-law, but it is the formidable Klára Takács as the interfering Eudossia who personifies the grit in the oyster, providing high melodrama. The playing is warmly committed and, apart from some distancing of the chorus, the sound is first rate, atmospheric but also precisely focused.

Revueltas, Silvestre (1899–1940)

Caminos; Musica para charlar; Ventanas.
*** ASV Dig. CDDCA 653 [id.]. Mexico City PO, Bátiz – CHAVEZ: *Sinfonia de Antigona; Symphony No. 4.****

The music on this record is highly colourful, with moments of considerable vulgarity rubbing shoulders with very evocative and imaginative episodes, such as the depiction of *Twilight* in the second *Musica para charlar*. Revueltas is not a major musical personality but a lively and colourful one. Excellent playing from the Mexican orchestra under Bátiz and sound of demonstration quality, with great impact, detail and presence.

Rezniček, Emil (1860–1945)

Symphony No. 4 in E min.
** Schwann VMS 2091 [id.]. Philh. Hungarica, Gordon Wright.

Baron Emil Nikolaus von Rezniček is known to the wider musical public by one work only, his sparkling *Overture Donna Diana*. The *Symphony in F minor* dates from 1919. Its first movement is heavily indebted to Wagner and Bruckner, though there are occasional reminders of other composers too, such as Dvořák, Beethoven and Schubert. There are some individual touches, of course, and moments of dignity, even of nobility, but there is much that is portentous. Strangely enough, there is little real sense of mastery, and none of the melodic inventiveness or expert craftsmanship that distinguish *Donna Diana*. The playing of the Philharmonia Hungarica under Gordon Wright is serviceable rather than distinguished, and much the same goes for the recording.

Rheinberger, Joseph (1839–1901)

Organ concerto No. 1 in F, Op. 137.
*** Telarc Dig. CD 80136 [id.]. Michael Murray, RPO, Ling – DUPRÉ: *Symphony*.***

Rheinberger's *Concerto* is well made, its invention is attractive and it has suitable moments of spectacle that render it admirable for a coupling with the Dupré *Symphony*, with its use of the massive Albert Hall organ. The performance here is first rate, as is the large-scale Telarc digital recording. A fine demonstration disc.

Rimsky-Korsakov, Nikolay (1844–1908)

Christmas eve (suite); Le Coq d'or: suite; *Legend of the invisible city of Kitezh:* suite; *May night:* overture; *Mlada:* suite; *The Snow Maiden:* suite; *The Tale of the Tsar Saltan:* suite.
*** Chan. Dig. CHAN 8327-9 (3) [id.]. SNO, Järvi.

There is an essential pantheism in Rimsky's art. The *Prelude* to *The invisible city of Kitezh* is described as a hymn to nature, while the delights of the *Christmas eve suite* (an independent work) include a magical evocation of the glittering stars against a snow-covered landscape and, later, a flight of comets. The plots of his operas, drawn on Gogol and Ostrovsky, are peopled by picaresque human characters, however. In *Le Coq d'or* the bumbling King Dodon has his counterpart in the alluring Queen Shemakha, for whom Rimsky wrote one of his most sensuously languorous melodies. Apart from the feast of good tunes, the composer's skilful and subtle deployment of the orchestral palette continually titillates the ear. Neeme Järvi draws the most seductive response from the SNO; he consistently creates orchestral textures which are diaphanously sinuous. Yet the robust moments, when the brass blazes or the horns ring out sumptuously, are caught just as strikingly. The CDs have much presence, while the focus is bright and sharp. The Chandos set achieves new standards in this repertoire and the listener is assured that here is music which survives repetition uncommonly well.

Russian Easter festival overture, Op. 36.
(*) Decca Dig. 417 299-2 [id.]. Montreal SO, Dutoit – MUSSORGSKY: *Pictures* etc.(*)

Dutoit's version of the *Russian Easter festival overture* is strong, with a fine climax. The colourful Decca recording brings iridescent orchestral detail, but the music's romanticism does not blossom quite as richly as it might.

Scheherazade (symphonic suite), *Op. 35.*
⑱ *** EMI CDC7 47717-2 [id.]. RPO, Beecham – BORODIN: *Polovtsian dances*.***
*** Ph. 400 021-2 [id.]. Concg. O, Kondrashin.
(M) *** Ph. 420 898-2 [id.]. LPO, Haitink – MUSSORGSKY: *Night on the bare mountain*.***
*** Chan. Dig. CHAN 8479 [id.]. SNO, Järvi – GLAZUNOV: *Stenka Razin*.***
(M) *** DG 419 063-2 [id.]. BPO, Karajan – BORODIN: *Polovtsian dances*.***
(M) *** RCA [RDCD1 7018 (with DEBUSSY: *La Mer*)]. Chicago SO, Reiner.
(B) **(*) Pickwick Dig. PCD 880 [MCA MCAD 25187]. LSO, John Mauceri.
**(*) EMI Dig. CDC7 47023-2 [id.]. Phd. O, Muti.
(*) Virgin Dig. VC 790729-2 [id.]. LPO, Litton – RAVEL: *Boléro*.(*)
(B) *(**) RCA VD 87743 [7743-2-RV]. RPO, Stokowski.
** Collins Dig. EC 1005-2 [id.]. LPO, Louis Frémaux.

(i) *Scheherazade;* (ii) *Capriccio espagnol.*
**(*) Decca Dig. 410 253-2 [id.]. Montreal SO, Dutoit.
(M) *(**) Decca 417 753-2 [id.]. (i) LSO; (ii) New Philh. O, Stokowski – BORODIN: *Polovtsian dances.***(*)
(BB) ** LaserLight Dig. 15 608 [id.]. Hungarian State O, János Sándor.

Scheherazade; Le coq d'or: Introduction & Cortège. Sadko, Op. 5.
(BB) ** Naxos Dig. 8.550098 [id.]. Czech RSO (Bratislava), Ondrej Lenard.

(i) *Scheherazade;* (ii) *May night overture; Sadko, Op. 5.*
(B) *** Decca 421 400-2 [id.]. (i) LSO, Monteux; (ii) SRO, Ansermet.

Scheherazade; The Tale of Tsar Saltan: suite, Op. 56; The flight of the bumble bee.
**(*) Decca Dig. 417 301-2 [id.]. Philh. O, Ashkenazy.

Beecham's *Scheherazade* was recorded in London's Kingsway Hall in March 1957. It is a performance of extraordinary drama and charisma. Alongside the violin contribution of Stephen Staryk, all the solo playing has great distinction; in the second movement Beecham gives the woodwind complete metrical freedom (notably the bassoon), yet the electricity of the music-making never for a moment flickers; later the brass fanfares have great flair and bite. The sumptuousness and glamour of the slow movement are very apparent, yet a sultry, cultured refinement pervades the languor of the string phrasing. The finale has an explosive excitement, rising to an electrifying climax, which the dynamic range of the digital remastering frees from any restriction. The coupled *Polovtsian dances* have comparable dash and excitement.

Kondrashin's version with the Concertgebouw Orchestra has the advantage of splendid modern analogue recorded sound, combining richness and sparkle within exactly the right degree of resonance. Hermann Krebbers' gently seductive portrayal of Scheherazade's narrative creates a strong influence on the overall interpretation. The first movement, after Krebbers' tranquil introduction, develops a striking architectural sweep; the second is vivid with colour, the third beguilingly gracious, while in the finale, without taking unusually fast tempi, Kondrashin creates an irresistible forward impulse leading to a huge climax at the moment of the shipwreck.

Haitink's LPO record dates from 1974. The recording shows its age just a little in the string timbre, but in all other respects it is exceptionally truthful in both sound and perspective. It is a relief to hear a solo violin sounding its natural size in relation to the orchestra as a whole. Yet Rodney Friend, who plays the solos subtly, dominates the performance with his richly sinuous picture of Scheherazade herself as narrator of each episode. The playing of the LPO is both sensitive and alert, Haitink's interpretation wholly unaffected and totally fresh in impact.

Järvi's version with the SNO may not be the most high-powered or weighty; nor is it as idiosyncratic as, for instance, the Beecham or Karajan versions; but, with the episodic argument strongly held together as in the telling of a story, it is most persuasive. The playing is no less fine than in versions from the most distinguished international orchestras, and the recorded sound is spectacular in the Chandos manner, spacious and refined. Indeed for those looking for a splendid modern digital version, this could well be first choice.

Karajan's 1967 recording is greatly enhanced in its CD format. The extra vividness brings more life and sparkle to the central movements, which are superbly played, and the brass fanfares in the second have a tingling immediacy. The added presence also increases the feeling of ardour from the glorious Berlin strings in the *Andante*. The outer movements have great vitality and thrust, and the bright percussion transients add to the feeling of zest. Yet Michel Schwalbé's sinuously luxuriant violin solos are still allowed to participate in the narrative. The fill-up is a sizzling account of the Borodin *Polovtsian dances*, with no chorus, but managing perfectly well without.

The recordings from Monteux and Ansermet on the Decca Weekend CD come from the earliest days of stereo. Monteux's version of *Scheherazade* is, if anything, even more vivid than Haitink's and the recording remains brilliant and sparkling, the performance sensuous and exciting, full of charisma. Ansermet finds all the colour in the *May night overture* and *Sadko*, an exotic Rimskian fairy-tale with a colourful storm for a climax; while the Decca engineers, working in Geneva, provided both atmosphere and the fullest orchestral palette. In the finale of *Scheherazade* Monteux holds back the climax – another storm – until the last minute and then unleashes his forces with devastating effect. The orchestral playing is not as polished as the LPO under Haitink, but it has tremendous zest and spontaneity, and this makes a fine bargain recommendation, even though the upper range lacks something in opulence.

Reiner's classic 1960 recording is available in the USA on CD, coupled with Debussy's *La Mer*. The first movement has a strong forward impulse and the two central movements have beguiling colour, with Reiner's individual touches having something in common with Beecham's version, and sounding comparably spontaneous. The third movement is wonderfully languorous and the finale, brilliant and exciting, has a climax of resounding power and amplitude. The Chicago Hall ambience is very effective, making up in spaciousness for any lack of internal clarity. We look forward to this reappearing in the UK at mid-price.

In terms of playing time, Ashkenazy's Decca record is the most generous of all, offering besides the *Flight of the bumble bee* (which makes an amiable final encore) the dazzlingly scored *Tsar Saltan suite*, where Ashkenazy is in his element, and the Philharmonia players obviously relish the good tunes, sonorous brass writing and glittering effects. In the main work, with the orchestral balance set back naturally, the violin solos, sweetly played by Christopher Warren-Green, are almost ethereal in their distancing. The recording has the widest dynamic range and Ashkenazy uses its full possibilities for drama, alternating the languorous string sequences of the first movement with powerful projection for the brass entries. The inner movements are fresh and full of colourful detail, but the relatively brisk pacing of the *Andante* loses some of the music's voluptuousness. The finale is racily exciting, but Ashkenazy pulls back to broaden the climax at the dramatic gong-clash, and this sounds not entirely spontaneous.

On the bargain-price IMP label, John Mauceri conducts a powerful, dramatic reading marked by incisive, crisply disciplined playing from the LSO, just as impressive in the warmly expressive rubato of the great lyrical passages. To match this, the recording is brilliant rather than sensuously beautiful, clear, well balanced and with fine presence. Michael Davis is a persuasive violin soloist, and in Mauceri's hands the melodic line of the third movement is appealingly supple, while there is no lack of excitement in the finale.

Muti's reading is colourful and dramatic in a larger-than-life way that sweeps one along. The great string theme of the slow movement has all the voluptuousness one expects of Philadelphia strings in one of the best of EMI's latterday Philadelphia recordings, more spacious than usual, though not ideally balanced. There is a glare in the upper range to which not all ears will respond, even if the racy finale, with its exciting climax, carries all before it. The CD emphasizes the brightness of the treble, especially in climaxes.

Among recent digital recordings Andrew Litton's LPO version has a good deal to recommend it. The first movement brings strong dramatic contrasts and the violin soloist, David Nolan, plays seductively. The *Andantino* has a Beechamesque languor and the freedom given to the woodwind soloists also recalls the Beecham version. But the finale is less than overwhelming and, although the recording is opulent as well as brilliant, other performances bring a greater sense of spontaneity, although this is certainly enjoyable in its spaciousness.

Dutoit offers an exceptionally generous coupling; the recording is characteristic of the Montreal acoustic, full and warm with luminous detail. However, this is a relaxed, lyrical reading at speeds slower than usual; essentially an amiable view, lacking in virtuoso excitement. The *Capriccio espagnol* compensates to some extent for this shortcoming, again given a genial performance – though one not lacking in brilliance.

Stokowski's Decca performance is eccentric and wilful – with changes to the score – yet the LSO play brilliantly and there is no lack of excitement. But the 1964 sound is coarse-grained as remastered and lacks the necessary sumptuousness. The *Capriccio espagnol* coupling features the New Philharmonia and the recording, made a decade later, is much more acceptable. The performance brings surprisingly relaxed tempi, with jaunty gypsy rhythms deliciously underlined. In many ways this is memorable, but the score is slightly cut and rearranged by the conductor.

For the 1975 RCA recording, Stokowski turned to the RPO and, originally on LP, achieved some sensuously beautiful orchestral sound. With Erich Gruenberg providing a sweet-toned commentary, this is certainly compelling, with Stokowski at his most characteristic in the slow movement. But here his nudgings of rubato are not entirely spontaneous and, although there is no lack of drama, the reading overall does not show him at his very best. Moreover the RCA remastering brings an excess of brilliance, producing thin violin timbres and moments of shrillness.

There is not a great deal to choose between the two super-bargain versions. They both offer vivid digital sound and are well played. The Hungarian recording has slightly more glamour because of a marginally warmer recording acoustic. Neither has quite the finesse or the body of string tone of the finest Western versions but both offer excellent wind solos and plenty of excitement in the finale. Couplings could dictate choice. On the whole, those on Naxos are preferable; although it is a pity that the whole *Coq d'or suite* was not chosen, the performance of *Sadko* has plenty of atmosphere and a really spectacular climax. The *Capriccio espagnol* is also quite attractive but could be more exciting in the closing *Fandango asturiano*.

Frémaux is usually a reliable recording conductor, but his *Scheherazade* is a disappointment. The performance has warmth but is lacking in drama and charisma. The central movements have plenty of colour and the finale produces a burst of energy and spectacle, but overall the effect is amiable rather than memorable, although the sound is opulent, with weighty brass.

Skazka (fairy tale for orchestra), *Op. 29*.
(M) ** EMI CDM7 63093-2 [id.]. Bournemouth SO, Brusilow – BALAKIREV: *Russia*; BORODIN: *Symphony No. 2*.**

Skazka is a work of great charm and originality that deserves more than an occasional airing. Brusilow brings relatively little atmosphere or poetry to this score, though the recording is admirably vivid.

Symphonies Nos. 1 in E min., Op. 1; 2 (Antar), Op. 9; 3 in C, Op. 32; Capriccio espagnol, Op. 35; Russian Easter festival overture, Op. 36.
*** DG Dig. 423 604-2 (2). Gothenburg SO, Järvi.

Symphonies Nos. 1 in E min., Op. 1; 3 in C, Op. 32.
**(*) Olympia OCD 158 [id.]. USSR Ac. SO, Svetlanov.

Whatever Rimsky-Korsakov's symphonies may lack in symphonic coherence they make up for in colour and charm. Some of the material is a little thin but there is some highly attractive invention as well. *Antar*, which is far more of a symphonic suite than a symphony, is not quite as strong as some of its protagonists would have us believe, but it should surely have a stronger presence in the concert and recorded repertoire than it has. The performances under Neeme Järvi have considerable merit and, although the Gothenburg orchestra is not the equal of the USSR Academic Symphony, it is so excellently recorded that it will be the first choice for most collectors; moreover the addition of the *Capriccio espagnol* and the *Russian Easter festival overture* makes the Chandos set a very attractive proposition.

The *Third Symphony* is distinctly appealing in Svetlanov's hands. Its very opening has some delightful woodwind scoring and this makes a fine effect in Svetlanov's Olympia version, which offers a sensible coupling of Nos. 1 and 3, with the *Andante* of No. 3 particularly eloquent. The string playing has plenty of character and lyric fervour but the brass tend to bray a bit, and one could wish at times for a little more amplitude in the massed strings, although the quality is clean and clear without being too edgy.

Symphony No. 2 (Antar), Op. 9.
*** Telarc CD 80131 [id.]. Pittsburgh SO, Maazel – TCHAIKOVSKY: *Symphony No. 2.****

Maazel's taut yet sympathetic reading holds together a work which, structurally at least, might more aptly be counted as a suite (as *Scheherazade* is) but which, with strong and colourful yet refined treatment like this, is fittingly regarded as belonging to Rimsky's symphonic canon. Excellent playing – notably in the finale, where the Pittsburgh woodwind excel themselves in delicacy – and brilliant, finely balanced recording.

Tsar Saltan, Op. 57: March.
*** Telarc Dig. CD 80107 [id.]. RPO, Previn – TCHAIKOVSKY: *Symphony No. 5.****

The crisp, stylized *March* from *Tsar Saltan*, a fairy-tale piece, makes a delightful *bonne-bouche*, a welcome fill-up for Previn's fine account of the Tchaikovsky *Fifth Symphony*, equally well played and recorded.

Piano and wind quintet in B flat.
*** Hyp. CDA 66163 [id.]. Capricorn – GLINKA: *Grand Sextet.****

Rimsky-Korsakov's youthful *Quintet for piano, flute, clarinet, horn and bassoon* is a thoroughly diverting piece. It is like a garrulous but endearing friend whose loquacity is readily borne for the sake of his charm and good nature. The main theme of the finale is pretty brainless but singularly engaging, and the work as a whole leaves a festive impression. Capricorn's account has great vivacity and is very well recorded. The excellence of the pianist, Julian Jacobson (formerly Dawson Lyall), should be noted: he contributes a rare sparkle to the proceedings.

Rodrigo, Joaquín (born 1902)

(i) *Concierto Andaluz;* (ii) *Concierto madrigal.*
*** Ph. 400 024-2 [id.]. (i) Los Romeros; (ii) P. and A. Romero, ASMF, Marriner.

Los Romeros and the Academy make the very most of the *Concierto Andaluz*, with infectious spirit in the outer sections and plenty of romantic atmosphere in the slow movement. The *Concierto madrigal* was also written for the Romero family; the performance here is definitive and beautifully recorded. Sir Neville Marriner's contribution to both *Concertos* has real distinction. The analogue recordings, originally first class, have responded most convincingly to digital remastering.

Concierto de Aranjuez (for guitar and orchestra).
(M) *** Decca Dig. 417 748-2 [id.]. Carlos Bonell, Montreal SO, Dutoit (with FALLA: *Three-cornered hat****).
*** CBS Dig. CD 37848 [id.]. John Williams, Philh. O, Frémaux.
(M) *** RCA GD 86525 [6525-2-RG]. Bream, Monteverdi O, Gardiner – VILLA-LOBOS: *Concerto etc.****
*** Ph. 411 440-2 [id.]. Pepe Romero, ASMF, Marriner.
(*) Decca Dig. 417 199-2 [id.]. Eduardo Fernandez, ECO, Martinez – CASTELNUOVO-TEDESCO: *Concerto.*(*)
(BB) ** LaserLight Dig. 15 602 [id.]. Zoltán Tokos, Budapest Strings, Bela Banfalvi (with SOR: *Sonata*; GRANADOS: *Spanish dance No. 2*; ALBÉNIZ: *Castilla*; FALLA: *Homage à Debussy; Spanish dance*. Monika & Jürgen Rost).
**(*) DG 413 349-2 [id.]. Narciso Yepes, Philh. O, Navarro.

(i) *Concierto de Aranjuez; Fantasia para un gentilhombre;* (ii) *Concierto serenata for harp and orchestra.*
(M) ** Ph. 420 714-2 [id.]. (i) Lagoya, (ii) Michel; Monte Carlo Op. O, Almeida.

(i) *Concierto de Aranjuez; Fantasia para un gentilhombre. En los trigales; Pastoral; Sonata a la española.*
**(*) EMI Dig. CDC7 49050-2 [id.]. Ernesto Bitetti; (i) Philh. O, Ros-Marba.

(i) *Concierto de Aranjuez; Fantasia para un gentilhombre. Elógio de guitarra.*
*** EMI CDC7 47693-2 [id.]. Angel Romero, (i) LSO, Previn.

Having established a great success in the early days of CD with the Bonell/Dutoit coupling, Decca have made this issue even more attractive by adding a bonus of three dances from Falla's *Three-cornered hat* (taken from Dutoit's complete set) and by placing the recording on their mid-priced Ovation label, where it makes a splendid bargain. But the reasons for the original success remain unaltered: an exceptionally clear and well-balanced digital recording plus Bonell's imaginative account of the solo part, and the strong characterization of the orchestral accompaniments by Charles Dutoit and his excellent Montreal orchestra. A feeling of freshness pervades every bar of the orchestral texture. In the *Fantasia*, the balance between warmly gracious lyricism and sprightly rhythmic resilience is no less engaging; here again, the orchestral solo playing makes a strong impression.

John Williams's newest version of the *Concierto* (his third) also has the advantage of first-class digital recording. The acoustic, however, is a little dry compared with the Decca issue, while the woodwind is a shade too forward. Nevertheless, this is technically superior to Williams's previous, analogue partnership with Barenboim and the performance is even finer. The slow movement is wonderfully atmospheric and the finale is light and sparkling with an element of fantasy and much delicacy of articulation in the accompaniment. The performance of the *Fantasia* is no less memorable and this is altogether a most winning coupling, not as extrovert as the Bonell/Dutoit partnership, but no less distinguished.

Bream recorded the *Concierto de Aranjuez* twice in the analogue era before he made his digital version (again with Gardiner – see below). This is the first of his analogue recordings and it has a little more dash than the later one with Sir Colin Davis, yet the differences are too subtle for easy analysis. Sufficient to say that this is excellent value at mid-price and that the couplings are also valuable.

Pepe Romero's performance of the *Concierto de Aranjuez* has plenty of Spanish colour, the musing poetry of the slow movement beautifully caught. The account of the *Fantasia* is warm and gracious, with the Academy contributing quite as much as the soloist to the appeal of the performance. Although inner detail is less sharply focused than on either the Bonell or the Williams digital version, it hardly matters, for the warm beauty of the analogue atmosphere emphasizes the Mediterranean feeling; indeed, many will like the softer-grained Philips quality.

The Previn/Romero issue is undoubtedly very successful too. The recording sounds clearer in its remastered format; originally it was rather more atmospheric. Angel Romero does not emerge as such a strong personality as John Williams, but the skill and sensibility of his playing are in no doubt, and Previn is obviously so delighted with the orchestral scores that he communicates his enthusiasm with loving care for detail. The famous slow movement is very beautifully played indeed; the opening is especially memorable. The approach to the *Fantasia* is vividly direct, missing some of the essentially Spanish graciousness that marks the Marriner version, but its infectious quality is more than enough compensation. However, this record would have been more competitive at mid-price. There is a short patch of less than perfectly focused *tutti* at the end of the slow movement.

Eduardo Fernandez gives an amiable account of Rodrigo's famous *Concierto*, attractively ruminative in the *Adagio* and with a cheerful finale. The *Fantasia* is also played with much warmth and affectionate detail and is even more characterful. The Decca recording is warmly atmospheric, with less bite than the Bonell/Dutoit versions, which are also more distinctive interpretations. However, the couplings are generous, with the Castelnuovo-Tedesco *Concerto* offered, besides the two Rodrigo works.

The newest digital recording from EMI is attractive in combining Rodrigo's two favourite concertante guitar works with some worthwhile solo items which are very well played by Ernesto Bitetti; indeed the *Sonata a la española*, which ends this programme, was dedicated to him. He gives a rather introspective performance of it, but he is lively enough in the *Concierto*; the *Fantasia* is especially successful, with Ros-Marba and the Philharmonia providing a brilliantly coloured orchestral backing, full of bracing rhythmic vitality.

A super-bargain digital recording of Rodrigo's famous *Concierto* obviously has its attractions and Zoltán Tokos is a sympathetic soloist. He is accompanied by a chamber-sized group with good ensemble and a bright violin line: the balance is excellent. The first two movements bring an attractive intimacy, and the famous *Adagio* has an atmospheric, ruminative, improvisatory feel. The finale, however, could do with a lighter rhythmic touch and its *moto perpetuo* is interrupted when Banfalvi lets both the tension and the momentum slip at the point where the soloist is given a pizzicato accompaniment. The coupling is a recital of guitar music by an excellent duo who bring the colourful genre pieces by Granados, Albéniz and Manuel de Falla vividly to life. But the opening Op. 22 *Sonata* of Sor is curiously wan, and not only because the recording level drops after the finale of the *Concierto*.

Yepes' 1980 version of the *Concierto de Aranjuez* is an improvement on his recording of a decade earlier with the Spanish Radio and TV Orchestra, mainly because of the superior accompaniment. Even here, however, there is a lack of vitality in the outer movements, although the poetic element of the *Adagio* is well managed. The performance of the *Fantasia*, too, has character and refinement, and in both works the analogue recording balance is clear and immediate.

Lagoya is a good player, but he does not always project strongly, except perhaps in the slow movement of the *Concierto*, which he plays with considerable feeling. The outer movements are agreeable, if not as sprightly as some versions. However, we are now also offered an attractive account of the delectable *Concierto serenata* for harp, with Catherine Michel a splendid soloist and very good 1973 sound, well balanced, full and immediate.

(i) *Concierto de Aranjuez; 3 Piezas españolas (Fandango; Passacaglia; Zapateado); Invocation and dance (Homage to Manuel de Falla).*
*** RCA Dig. RD 84900 [RCD1 4900]. Julian Bream, (i) COE, Gardiner.

Bream's recording of the *Concierto* has a personality all its own. With outer movements offering strong dynamic contrasts and some pungent accents (from orchestra as well as soloist) the music's flamenco associations are underlined and the famous *Adagio* is played in a very free, improvisatory way, with some highly atmospheric wind solos in the orchestra. The balance is more natural than usual, with the guitar set slightly back and heard in a convincing perspective with the orchestra. The only slight snag is that the resonance adds a touch of harshness to the emphatic orchestral tuttis. What makes this issue especially valuable, however, is the inclusion of the *Tres Piezas españolas*, of which the second, *Passacaglia*, is one of Rodrigo's finest shorter works. No less involving is his *Invocation* for Manuel de Falla, with both performances showing Bream at his most inspirationally spontaneous.

Concierto para una fiesta (for guitar and orchestra).
*** Ph. 411 133-2 [id.]. Pepe Romero, ASMF, Marriner – ROMERO: *Concierto de Málaga.***

If in his *Concierto para una fiesta* Rodrigo does not quite repeat the success of the *Concierto de Aranjuez*, the first movement with its contrasting Valencian themes is highly engaging, and the *Andante calmo* has a hauntingly ruminative introspection, with its sombre main theme involving the dark-timbred cor anglais. The dance rhythms of the finale introduce an Andalusian *Sevillanas* as the principal idea, and the effect is unashamedly brash, in contrast to what has gone before. Pepe Romero's recording has all the freshness of new discovery, and Marriner and his Academy provide an accompaniment that is characteristically polished as well as thoroughly committed. The recording is most natural and beautifully balanced.

Sones en la Giralda.
*** Ph. Dig. 416 357-2 [id.]. Pepe Romero, ASMF, Marriner – CASTELNUOVO-TEDESCO; VILLA-LOBOS: *Concertos.****

La Giralda is the ancient tower of Seville Cathedral. Its character and its associations obviously stimulated Rodrigo's imagination so that the first of these two pieces is eerily atmospheric; then the clouds clear away and the finale sparkles with the flamenco dance rhythms of the *Sevillanas*. The work was conceived for harp and chamber orchestra; but Pepe Romero and Marriner show an immediate response to its evocation and spirit, and the result is memorable, helped by first-class recording.

Roman, Johan Helmich (1694–1758)

(i) *Violin concertos: in D min.; E flat; F min.; Sinfonias: in A; D and F.*
*** BIS Dig. CD 284 [id.]. (i) Nils-Erik Sparf; Orpheus Chamber Ens.

None of the *Sinfonias* here have appeared on disc before – and indeed only one (the *A major*) exists in print. Of the five *Violin concertos* attributed to Roman, the three recorded here are classified by Bengtsson as 'probably authentic'. They are certainly attractive pieces, particularly in such persuasive hands as those of Nils-Erik Sparf and the Orpheus Chamber Ensemble (who are not to be confused with the distinguished American group, but are drawn from the Stockholm Philharmonic). Very stylish and accomplished performances that are scholarly in approach.

The Golovin music.
*** Cap. Dig. CAP 1325. Drottningholm Bar. Ens.

Count Golovin was the Russian Ambassador to the Swedish Court at the time of the coronation of the 12-year-old tsar, Peter II, in 1728; for the festivities at his residence Roman provided what has been described as 'a generous bouquet of orchestral pieces', 45 movements in all, of which the Drottningholm Baroque Ensemble have recorded two dozen. The music has a good deal of charm; here it is recorded not only on period instruments but in the original acoustic in which the music was first heard. An attractive disc.

(i) *Assaggi for violin in A, in C min. and in G min., BeRI 301, 310 & 320;* (i; ii) *Violin and harpsichord sonata No. 12 in D, BeRI 212;* (ii) *Harpsichord sonata No. 9 in D min., BeRI 233.*
*** Cap. CAP 21344 [id.]. (i) Jaap Schröder; (ii) Johann Sönnleitner.

Assaggio (the singular form of *Assaggi*) means 'essay' in the sense of test-piece or attempt. The *Assaggi* recorded here chart an unusual path between the purely virtuosic and the introspective. They often take one by surprise, particularly when played with such imagination as they are by Jaap Schröder. The harpsichord sonata is also more inward-looking than many others of Roman's pieces, and the only work that one could possibly describe as fairly predictable is the opening *Sonata for violin and continuo*. Excellent performances and recording, as well as exemplary presentation.

Romero, Celedonio (born 1918)

Concierto de Málaga (for guitar; orch. Torroba).
** Ph. 411 133-2 [id.]. Pepe Romero, ASMF, Marriner – RODRIGO: *Concierto para una fiesta.****

Romero's *Concierto* originated as an *Andalusian suite* for solo guitar and was orchestrated by Moreno Torroba. Its material is slight and its structure more so; it will appeal most to those who like the passionate guitar-strumming effects of flamenco music, from which it is essentially derived. But this work is not on the level of its Rodrigo coupling.

Rossini, Gioacchino (1792–1868)

La Boutique fantasque (ballet, arr. Respighi); complete.
*** Decca Dig. 410 139-2 [id.]. Nat. PO, Bonynge – BRITTEN: *Matinées; Soirées.****

La Boutique fantasque: suite.
(*) Ph. Dig. 420 485-2 [id.]. ASMF, Marriner – RESPIGHI: *Ancient airs; The Birds.**

Bonynge goes for sparkle and momentum above all in Respighi's brilliant and sumptuous rescoring of Rossini, a magical ballet if ever there was one. The Decca recording has great brilliance and the orchestral colours glitter and glow within the attractive resonance of Kingsway Hall, although there is a degree of digital edge on the treble.

Marriner's suite is insubstantial, offering only about 20 minutes' music, chosen rather arbitrarily. It is elegantly played and warmly recorded.

Introduction, theme and variations in C min. for clarinet and orchestra.
*** ASV Dig. CDDCA 559 [id.]. Emma Johnson, ECO, Groves – CRUSELL: *Concerto No. 2**** ⊛; BAERMANN: *Adagio****; WEBER: *Concertino.****

As in all her recordings, Emma Johnson's lilting timbre and sensitive control of dynamic bring imaginative light and shade to the melodic line. Brilliance for its own sake is not the keynote, but her relaxed pacing is made to sound exactly right. Vivid recording.

Overtures: *Il Barbiere di Siviglia; La cambiale di matrimonio; La Cenerentola; La gazza ladra; La scala di seta; Semiramide; William Tell.*
**(*) EMI Dig. CDC7 49155-2 [id.]. ASMF, Marriner.

The highlight here is the sparkling account of *La Cenerentola*, and *William Tell* opens well and ends with great gusto. *La scala di seta* sounds more crisply spontaneous in the splendid Orpheus Chamber Orchestra's compilation on DG. Yet, in its good-humoured way, the Marriner disc is very enjoyable, the playing is clean and well mannered and the EMI recording full-bodied and clear. It was curious, though, to end with *La cambiale di matrimonio* (which by no means dispels memories of Beecham) rather than the more suitable *William Tell*.

Overtures: *Il Barbiere di Siviglia; La cambiale di matrimonio; L'inganno felice; L'Italiana in Algeri; La scala di seta; Il Signor Bruschino; Tancredi; Il Turco in Italia.*
*** DG Dig. 415 363-2 [id.]. Orpheus CO.

The Orpheus Chamber Orchestra displays astonishing unanimity of style and ensemble in this splendid collection of Rossini overtures, played without a conductor. Not only is the crispness of string phrasing a joy, but the many stylish wind solos have an attractive degree of freedom, and one never senses any rigidity in allegros which are always joyfully sprung. *La scala di seta* is an especial delight, and the opening string cantilena of *Il Barbiere* is agreeably gracious. These are performances that in their refinement and apt chamber scale give increasing pleasure with familiarity. The DG recording is marvellously real with the perspective perfectly judged.

Overtures: *Il Barbiere di Siviglia; La cambiale di matrimonio; Otello; Semiramide; Le siège de Corinthe; Tancredi; Torvaldo e Dorliska.*
**(*) Decca Dig. 414 407-2 [id.]. Nat. PO, Chailly.

This is Chailly's second collection of Rossini overtures; it shows a distinct improvement in offering cleaner ensemble and more polished detail, while retaining the high spirits and geniality of the first CD – see below. The novelties, *Otello* – played with great dash – and *Torvaldo e Dorliska*, with its witty interchanges between wind and strings, are among the highlights. *Semiramide* is also elegantly played and *The Barber* is nicely stylish. As before, detail is wonderfully clear in the music's gentler sections, but the vivid tuttis bring a touch of aggressiveness on the fortissimo strings.

Overtures: *Il Barbiere di Siviglia; La Cenerentola; La gazza ladra; L'Italiana in Algeri; Otello; La scala di seta; Semiramide; William Tell.*

*** Ph. 412 893-2 [id.]. ASMF, Marriner.

Original orchestrations are used here and the performances are characteristically neat and polished. In the remastering for CD, while the sound remains beautifully natural and refined, there has been a fractional loss of transient sparkle in achieving a virtually silent background. However, the balance remains excellent; if the last degree of presence is missing, compared with DG's Orpheus recordings, this is still very enjoyable.

Overtures: *Il Barbiere di Siviglia; La Cenerentola; La gazza ladra; L'Italiana in Algeri; Le siège de Corinthe; Il Signor Bruschino.*
(M) *** DG 419 869-2 [id.]. LSO, Abbado.

Brilliant, sparkling playing, with splendid discipline, vibrant rhythms and finely articulated phrasing – altogether invigorating and bracing. There is perhaps an absence of outright geniality here, but these are superb performances and this remains one of the very finest collections of Rossini overtures ever, for the wit is spiced with a touch of acerbity, and the flavour is of a vintage dry champagne which retains its bloom, yet has a subtlety all its own.

Overtures: *Il Barbiere di Siviglia; La Cenerentola; La gazza ladra; La scala di seta; Il Signor Bruschino; William Tell.*
⊛ (M) *** RCA GD 60387 [60387-2-RG]. Chicago SO, Fritz Reiner.

As with the others in RCA's remastered Reiner/Chicago series, the sound-quality has been improved phenomenally; no one could possibly guess that these recordings were made over thirty years ago (in 1958) for, as sound, they are preferable to most digital collections. The blaze of brass tone, supported by a rich orchestral backcloth and resonant bass drum, at the gallop in the *William Tell overture*, is all-engulfing, a thrilling moment indeed. The Chicago Symphony was always famous for its brass department, and this is an excellent reminder of how resplendent the playing could be; at the same time the scurrying violins display the utmost virtuosity. Reiner is equally impressive at the grandiloquent opening of *La gazza ladra*, where the hall acoustics again add a magnificent amplitude to the full orchestral tutti. But it is the sparkle and vivacity of these performances that one remembers above all – and, in *La Cenerentola*, the wit, as well as fizzing orchestral bravura. One would have liked the opening flourish of *La scala di seta* to be neater – it is presented too lavishly here – but this is the solitary reservation over a magnificent achievement.

Overtures: *Il Barbiere di Siviglia; La gazza ladra; L'Italiana in Algeri; La scala di seta; Semiramide; Le Siège de Corinthe; Tancredi.*
(BB) *(*) LaserLight Dig. 15 506 [id.]. Plovdiv PO, Rouslan Raychev.

These performances are quite well played by a good provincial orchestra but are not presented with much flair. The recording is bright and clear but not sumptuous. With collections by Reiner, Abbado and Karajan available inexpensively, it is false economy to invest in a record of this kind. This is music that above all needs wit and high polish.

Overtures: *Il Barbiere di Siviglia; La gazza ladra; L'Italiana in Algeri; Semiramide; Il Signor Bruschino; William Tell.*
(BB) ** Hung. White Label HRC 062 [id.]. Budapest SO, Adám Fischer.

These are lively performances – *William Tell* has splendid gusto – and the recording is both brilliant and open, while not lacking fullness. The orchestral playing is always good and generally characterful. Excellent value in the cheapest price range.

Overtures: *Il Barbiere di Siviglia; La gazza ladra; La scala di seta; Semiramide; William Tell.*
(B) **(*) Decca 417 692-2 [id.]. LSO, Pierino Gamba.

Gamba's performances are taut and involving, the orchestral playing alive and polished. A strong disciplining force is felt in every piece, and care in phrasing is noticeable at every turn. The only quality missing is a touch of geniality – but, even so, *La scala di seta* is not overdriven. The very good recording re-emerges vividly and with plenty of ambient atmosphere, but the brightly lit violins, although not edgy, have a slightly artificial timbre.

Overtures: *Il Barbiere di Siviglia; La gazza ladra; Semiramide; William Tell.*
(*) DG 415 377-2 [id.]. BPO, Karajan – SUPPÉ: *Overtures.*(*)

Overtures: *Il Barbiere di Siviglia; La gazza ladra; L'Italiana in Algeri; La scala di seta.*
(B) *** DG 429 164-2 [id.]. BPO, Karajan – VERDI: *Overtures and Preludes.****

These performances are all taken from Karajan's 1971 collection and offer orchestral playing of supreme polish and bravura. The recording is extremely realistic at *piano* and *mezzo forte* levels, with inner detail refined, and the digital remastering is fresh and vivid, if perhaps a little overbright in the treble.

Overtures: *Il Barbiere di Siviglia; La scala di seta; Semiramide; Le siège de Corinthe; Il viaggio a Reims; William Tell.*
**(*) EMI CDC7 47118-2 [id.]. Philh. O, Muti.

Muti, following the Rossini style of his great compatriot, Toscanini, generally adopts fast tempi for these sparkling overtures. The performances are brilliant and thrustful, helped by large-scale recording, but at times they are just a little short on wit and delicacy, the recording bringing some thickening of textures in tuttis.

La cambiale di matrimonio; La Cenerentola; Matilde di Shabran; Il viaggio à Reims; William Tell. La boutique fantasque (ballet, arr. Respighi): *suite.*
(BB) *(*) LaserLight Dig. 15 520 [id.]. Plovdiv PO, Rouslan Raychev.

The second LaserLight collection has some rare repertoire and quite a good horn solo in *La cambiale di matrimonio*, beloved of Sir Thomas Beecham. It also includes a really fine account of *Il viaggio à Reims*, relaxed, stylish and with an element of wit. But *William Tell* is no match for Reiner's spectacular account. The short suite from *La boutique fantasque* appears to use a reduced orchestration; it lacks the sumptuousness of Respighi's fuller version, but in any case the performance has not a great deal of balletic feeling.

Overtures: *La Cenerentola; L'Italiana in Algeri; Le Siège de Corinthe; Semiramide; Il Turco in Italia; Il viaggio a Reims.*
(B) ** Van. VECD 7525 [id.]. V. State Op. O, Mario Rossi.

Essentially robust but well-played performances, with plenty of spirit but less wit. The studio-ish acoustic emphasizes the weight of the orchestral tuttis, with the bass drum making its presence felt. Ideally the sound could be more open, but at bargain price it is fair value.

Overtures: *Elisabetta, Regina d'Inghilterra; La scala di seta; Semiramide; Tancredi; Il Turco in Italia; William Tell.*
(B) **(*) RCA VD 87814 [7814-2-RV]. LSO, Abbado.

Zestful performances from Abbado, with exhilaratingly fast tempi, the LSO players kept consistently on their toes and obviously revelling in their own virtuosity. The exuberance comes to the fore especially in *Tancredi* – there is even a brief clarinet glissando – in a revised version by Philip Gosset. But some might feel that *La scala di seta* would be more effective if a fraction more relaxed. *William Tell* opens with elegant cellos, then offers an unashamedly vulgar storm sequence and a final *Galop* taken at breakneck pace. *Elisabetta, Regina* is our old friend *The Barber of Seville* but with a subtle change (a triplet consistently repeated in the first theme of the allegro): again stylish but fast. The remastered recording is more brightly lit than the original and may need a little taming on some machines.

Overtures: *La gazza ladra; L'Italiana in Algeri; La scala di seta; Il Signor Bruschino; Il Turco in Italia; Il viaggio a Reims; William Tell.*
**(*) Decca Dig. 400 049-2. Nat. PO, Chailly.

This was the first compact disc of Rossini overtures and, while there is a degree of digital edge on tuttis, the bustle from the cellos is particularly engaging, while the overall bloom afforded by the Kingsway Hall acoustic completes the concert-hall effect. The solo playing is fully worthy of such clear presentation, although the bow tapping at the opening of *Il Signor Bruschino* is rather lazy. Just occasionally elsewhere the ensemble slips when the conductor, Riccardo Chailly, lets the exhilaration of the moment triumph over absolute discipline and poise. But under Chailly the spirit of the music-making conveys spontaneous enjoyment too, especially in *The thieving magpie* and the nicely paced account of *William Tell.*

String sonatas Nos. 1 in G; 2 in A; 3 in C; 6 in D.
(B) ** DG 429 525-2 [id.]. BPO, Karajan.

String sonatas Nos. 1 in G; 3 in C; 4 in B flat; 5 in E flat.
*** DG Dig. 413 310-2 [id.]. Bern Camerata, Füri.

String sonatas Nos. 1 in G; 3 in C; 4 in B flat; 5 in E flat; 6 in D.
(M) **(*) Ph. 422 259-2. I Musici.

These sonatas are the astonishing work of the twelve-year-old Rossini and are prodigious indeed. Although they were intended to be played one instrument to a part, with the composer himself as second violin, they are nearly always given by a small string ensemble. The Bern performances have an elegance, virtuosity and sparkle that it is going to be very difficult to beat. The playing is pretty dazzling and they are accorded recording quality of the highest order. The sound is particularly fresh and vividly focused; overall, the balance is very satisfying. This is a record that will give enormous pleasure.

I Musici offer five out of the six *String sonatas*, one more than is usual on CD. The performances are enjoyable, although they do not quite achieve the wit and sparkle of the Bern set. Nevertheless the Philips recording is fresh and clear and the playing both refined and alert.

Alongside the Berne Camerata, Karajan's Berlin Philharmonic performances sound a little suave, and the 1969 recording shows its age in the slight thinning-down of the violin timbre by the digital remastering. But there is plenty of bloom and the music cannot help but be effective when the playing is so polished and elegant; this disc also has a price advantage.

Petite messe solennelle.
*** Eurodisc 610 263 (2). Lovaas, Fassbaender, Schreier, Fischer-Dieskau, Münchner Vokalisten, Hirsch, Sawallisch (pianos), Baffalt (harmonium), Sawallisch.
*** EMI Dig. CDS7 47482-8 (2). Popp, Fassbaender, Gedda, Kavrakos, King's College, Cambridge, Ch., Katia and Marielle Labèque (pianos), Briggs (harmonium), Cleobury.

Rossini's *Petite messe solennelle* must be the most genial contribution to the church liturgy in the history of music. The description '*Petite*' does not refer to size, for the piece is comparable in length to Verdi's *Requiem*; rather it is the composer's modest evaluation of the work's 'significance'. But what a spontaneous and infectious piece of writing it is, bubbling over with characteristic melodic, harmonic and rhythmic invention. The composer never over-reaches himself. 'I was born for *opera buffa*, as well Thou knowest,' Rossini writes touchingly on the score. 'Little skill, a little heart, and that is all. So be Thou blessed and admit me to paradise.' The Sawallisch performance would surely merit the granting of the composer's wish. The soloists are first rate, the contralto outstanding in the lovely *O salutaris* and *Agnus Dei*. Good choral singing and fine, imaginative playing from the two pianists. The (originally Ariola) recording, now available on Eurodisc, dates from the early 1970s and is of high quality.

The EMI version provides a different and contrasted view from Sawallisch's. The use of the refined trebles of King's College Choir brings a timbre very different from what Rossini would have expected from boys' voices – but, arguably, close to what he would have wanted. That sound is hard to resist when the singing itself is so movingly eloquent. The work's underlying geniality is not obscured, but here there is an added dimension of devotional intensity from the chorus which, combined with outstanding singing from a fine quartet of soloists and beautifully matched playing from the Labèque sisters, makes for very satisfying results. The recording, too, attractively combines warmth with clarity.

Stabat Mater.
⊛ *** Chan. Dig. CHAN 8780 [id.]. Field, Della Jones, A. Davies, Earle, LSO Ch., City of L. Sinfonia, Hickox.
**(*) DG Dig. 410 034-2 [id.]. Ricciarelli, Valentini Terrani, Gonzalez, Raimondi, Philh. Ch. and O, Giulini.
(M) **(*) Decca 417 766-2 [id.]. Lorengar, Minton, Pavarotti, Sotin, LSO Ch., LSO, Kertesz.

In his setting of *Stabat Mater* Rossini may upset the squeamish by having rip-roaring tunes, like the tenor's rumbustious march-setting of *Cujus animam* or the jaunty quartet setting of *Sancta Mater* with its persistent oom-pah rhythms, but it is a mistake to try and over-refine the piece. Richard Hickox rightly presents it warmly with gusty strength, but then he makes sure that singing and playing have a point and polish to eliminate vulgarity. This is a most winning account which has one marvelling that a work written piecemeal should have such consistently memorable invention, much of it anticipating – or reflecting – early Verdi. All four soloists here are first rate, not Italianate of tone but full and warm. As ever in Hickox's choral recordings, the London Symphony Chorus – which he has long trained – sings with fine attack as well as producing the most refined pianissimos in the unaccompanied quartet, here as usual given to the full chorus rather than to the soloists. Full-bodied and atmospheric sound.

Some will feel that Rossini's broad, clean-cut tunes and strong rhythms should be presented more directly than in Giulini's version, but there is much here to enjoy in the singing of the chorus as well as of the soloists, though Ricciarelli is at times ungainly on top. The refined and atmospheric recording has transferred well to compact disc, giving the listener a convincing concert-hall effect, even though the balance of the soloists is well forward.

Kertesz's approach brings out an unexpected degree of beauty, notably in the fine choral singing, and even *Cujus anima* is given extra delicacy, with Pavarotti singing most beautifully and linking back to the main theme with a subtle half-tone. Some may feel that Kertesz underplays the work in removing the open-hearted vulgarity, but he certainly makes one enjoy the music afresh. Soprano, mezzo and bass may not have all the idiomatic Italian qualities, but their singing matches Kertesz's interpretation.

OPERA

Il Barbiere di Siviglia (complete).
*** Ph. Dig. 411 058-2 (3) [id.]. Baltsa, Allen, Araiza, Trimarchi, Lloyd, Amb. Op. Ch., ASMF, Marriner.
*** Decca Dig. 425 520-2 (3) [id.]. Cecilia Bartoli, Nucci, Matteuzzi, Fissore, Burchuladze, Ch. & O of Teatro Comunale di Bologna, Patanè.
*** EMI CDS7 47634-8 (2) [Ang. CDCB 47634]. Callas, Gobbi, Alva, Ollendorff, Philh. Ch. & O, Galliera.
(M) *** RCA GD 86505 (3) [RCA 6505-2-RG]. Roberta Peters, Valletti, Merrill, Corena, Tozzi, Met. Op. Ch. & O, Leinsdorf.
**(*) DG 415 695-2 (2) [id.]. Berganza, Prey, Alva, Montarsolo, Amb. Ch., LSO, Abbado.

Il Barbiere di Siviglia: highlights.
*** Ph. Dig. 412 266-2 [id.] (from above set, cond. Marriner).
(M) *** EMI CDM7 63076-2 (from complete set with Callas, Alva, Gobbi; cond. Galliera).

Il Barbiere was Sir Neville's first opera recording and he finds a rare sense of fun in Rossini's witty score. His characteristic polish and refinement – beautifully caught in the clear, finely balanced recording – never get in the way of urgent spontaneity, the sparkle of the moment. Thomas Allen as Figaro – far more than a *buffo* figure – and Agnes Baltsa as Rosina – tough and biting, too – manage to characterize strongly, even when coping with florid divisions, and though Araiza allows himself too many intrusive aitches, he easily outshines latterday rivals, sounding heroic, not at all the small-scale tenorino, but never coarse either. Fine singing too from Robert Lloyd as Basilio. The highlights are well chosen and admirably reflect the qualities of the complete set.

Giuseppe Patanè made his recording of *Il Barbiere* only months before his untimely death, but it is a performance that brims with life, very much a team effort with a cast – Burchuladze very much excepted – entirely of native Italian-speakers. Patanè is a relaxed Rossinian, generally favouring unrushed speeds, timing the delectably pointed recitatives with a keen concern for stage action. With helpful sound-effects and full and vivid sound, it makes a happy new digital recommendation for a much-recorded opera. What sets it apart is the exciting choice of singer as the heroine, Rosina. Cecilia Bartoli made this recording when she was still in her early twenties, a mezzo with a rich, vibrant voice who not only copes brilliantly with the technical demands but who also gives a sparkling, provocative characterization. In her big Act I aria, *Una voce poco fa*, she even outshines the memorable Agnes Baltsa on the excellent Marriner set. Like the conductor, Bartoli is wonderful at bringing out the fun. So is Leo Nucci, and he gives a beautifully rounded portrait of the wily barber, even though the voice is less firm and less expansive than it was, showing signs of wear. Thomas Allen for Marriner sings much better and gives a more youthful characterization. Burchuladze, unidiomatic next to the others, still gives a monumentally lugubrious portrait of Basilio, and the Bartolo of Enrico Fissore is outstanding, with the patter song wonderfully articulated at Patanè's sensible speed. The lyrical, rounded quality of William Matteuzzi's tenor makes him an attractive, if hardly memorable Almaviva. In keeping with the idiomatic style of the performance, the text is the traditional Italian one rather than the scholarly reconstruction of Alberto Zedda; but this makes a superb entertainment.

Gobbi and Callas were here at their most inspired and, with the recording quality nicely refurbished, the EMI is an outstanding set, not absolutely complete in its text, but so crisp and sparkling it can be confidently recommended. Callas remains supreme as a minx-like Rosina, summing up the character superbly in *Una voce poco fa*. In the final ensemble, despite the usual reading of the score, Rosina's verse is rightly given premier place at the very end. Though this was not among the cleanest of Philharmonia opera recordings, the early stereo sound comes up very acceptably on a pair of CDs, clarified to a degree, presenting a uniquely characterful performance with new freshness and immediacy. The highlights disc offers most of the key solo numbers from Act I, while in Act II it concentrates on Rossini's witty ensembles, including the extended Second Act *Quintet*. The *Overture* is included and, while it is stylishly played, it would have been better to have offered more of the vocal music.

Roberta Peters is a sparkling Rosina, a singer too little known in Europe, who here lives up to her high reputation at the Met., dazzling in coloratura elaborations in alt. Robert Merrill may not be a specially comic Figaro, but the vocal characterization is strong, with the glorious voice consistently firm and well focused. Valletti, Corena and Tozzi make up a formidable team, and Leinsdorf conducts with a lightness and relaxation rare for him on record. Good, clear sound of the period, set against a reverberant, helpful acoustic.

Abbado directs a clean and satisfying performance that lacks the last degree of sparkle. Berganza's interpretation of the role of Rosina remains very consistent with her earlier performance on Decca, but the Figaro here, Hermann Prey, is more reliable, and the playing and recording have an extra degree of polish. The text is not absolutely complete, but this means that the DG engineers have been able to fit the opera on to a pair of CDs.

La Cenerentola (complete).
*** Ph. Dig. 420 468-2 (2) [id.]. Baltsa, Araiza, Alaimo, Raimondi, Amb. Op. Ch., ASMF, Marriner.
** DG 423 861-2 (2) [id.]. Berganza, Alva, Montarsolo, Capecchi, Scottish Op. Ch., LSO, Abbado.

Marriner's set of *Cenerentola*, following the pattern of his first opera recording of *Il Barbiere di Siviglia*, conveys Rossinian fun to the full. As in *Il Barbiere*, the role of heroine is taken by the formidable Agnes Baltsa – not so aptly cast this time in a vulnerable Cinderella role – and that of the hero by Francisco Araiza, sweet and fresh of tone, though still allowing too many aspirants in passage-work. Ruggero Raimondi's commanding and resonant singing as Don Magnifico is very satisfying, and there is no weak link in the rest of the cast. The sound is first class in all respects, nicely resonant with plenty of atmosphere.

The DG set, although enjoyable, lacks the extrovert bravura and sparkle of an ideal performance. The atmosphere in places is almost of a concert version, with excellent balance between the participants, helped by the fine recording. Berganza, agile in the coloratura, seems too mature, even matronly, for the fairy-tale role of Cinderella. Alva sings well enough but is somewhat self-conscious in the florid writing. Abbado, though hardly witty in his direction, inspires delicate playing throughout. The CD transfer of the 1972 analogue recording brings an admirable feeling of freshness.

Le Comte Ory (complete).

⊛ *** Ph. Dig. 422 406-2 (2) [id.]. Sumi Jo, Aler, Montague, Cachemaille, Quilico, Pierotti, Lyon Op. Ch. & O, Gardiner.

Though older collectors will retain nostalgic memories of Vittorio Gui's Glyndebourne-based version of Rossini's irresistible French comic opera, Gardiner's new set admirably fills a serious gap in the catalogue. This is the piece which tells of the wicked Count Ory's attempt to seduce the virtuous Countess Adèle while her husband is away at the Crusades. In it Rossini deftly uses much of the brilliant material he had written for the occasional celebration opera, *Il viaggio a Reims*. In this re-using Rossini even introduces extra point – not surprising when the hilarious complications of the plot involve such farcical situations as the Count, disguised as a nun, believing he is addressing Countess Adèle, when it is in fact his page (played by a woman), who is himself (herself) in love with the Countess. Rossini handles such complications with unrivalled finesse. With musical argument more sustained than in other comic pieces of the period, *Le Comte Ory* stands out even among Rossini operas, as frothy as any, helped by the witty, unconventional plot. Rossini's mastery is matched by the performance here, beautifully and sparklingly sung and with ensembles finely balanced, as in the delectable Act II trio. Gardiner tends to be rather more tense than Gui was, with speeds on the fast side, and he allows too short a dramatic pause for the interruption to the Nuns' drinking choruses. But the precision and point are a delight, with not a single weak link in the casting, which is more consistent than Glyndebourne's. Though John Aler hardly sounds predatory enough as the Count, the lightness of his tenor is ideal, and Sumi Jo as Adèle and Diana Montague as the page, Isolier, are both stylish and characterful. So is the clear-toned Gino Quilico as the tutor, Raimbaud. With the cuts of the old Glyndebourne set opened out and with good and warm, if not ideally crystal-clear, recording, this set takes its place as a jewel of a Rossini issue.

La Donna del Lago (complete).
*** CBS Dig. M2K 39311 (2) [id.]. Ricciarelli, Valentini Terrani, Gonzalez, Raffanti, Ramey, Prague Philharmonic Ch., COE, Pollini.

Maurizio Pollini, forsaking the keyboard for the baton, draws a fizzing performance from the Chamber Orchestra of Europe, suggesting fascinating foretastes not just of Donizetti but of Verdi: of the *Anvil chorus* from *Il Trovatore* in the Act I *March* and of the trombone unisons of *La forza del destino* later in the finale. Katia Ricciarelli in the title-role of Elena, Lady of the Lake, has rarely sung so stylishly on record, the voice creamy, with no suspicion of the unevenness which develops under pressure, and very agile in coloratura. Lucia Valentini Terrani with her warm, dark mezzo is no less impressive in the travesti role of Elena's beloved, Malcolm; while Samuel Ramey as Elena's father, Douglas, with his darkly incisive singing makes you wish the role was far longer. Of the two principal tenors, Dalmacio Gonzalez, attractively light-toned, is the more stylish; but Dano Raffanti as Rodrigo Dhu copes with equal assurance with the often impossibly high tessitura. The recording is clear and generally well balanced and given added immediacy in the new format.

Guglielmo Tell (William Tell: complete, in Italian).
*** Decca 417 154-2 (4) [id.]. Pavarotti, Freni, Milnes, Ghiaurov, Amb. Op. Ch., Nat. PO, Chailly.
** Ph. Dig. 422 391-2 (4) [id.]. Zancanaro, Merritt, Studer, Surjan, De Grandis, Felle, D'Intino, Terranova, Noli, Roni, Cuberli, Gavazzi, La Scala, Milan, Ch. & O, Muti.

Guillaume Tell (William Tell) (sung in French).
(M) *** EMI CMS7 69951-2 (4). Bacquier, Caballé, Gedda, Mesplé, Hendrikx, Amb. Op. Ch., RPO, Gardelli.

Rossini wrote his massive opera about William Tell in French, but Chailly and his team here put forward a strong case for preferring Italian, with its open vowels, in music which glows with Italianate lyricism. Chailly's is a forceful reading, particularly strong in the many ensembles, and superbly recorded. Milnes makes a heroic Tell, always firm, and though Pavarotti has his moments of coarseness he sings the role of Arnoldo with glowing tone. Ghiaurov too is in splendid voice, while subsidiary characters are almost all well taken, with such a fine singer as John Tomlinson, for example, finely resonant as Melchthal. The women singers too are impressive, with Mirella Freni as the heroine Matilde providing dramatic strength as well as sweetness. The recording, made in 1978 and 1979, comes out spectacularly on CD. The *Pas de six* is here banded into its proper place in Act I.

The interest of the alternative 1973 EMI set is that it is sung in the original French. Gardelli proves an imaginative Rossini interpreter, allying his formidable team to vigorous and sensitive performances. Bacquier makes an impressive Tell, developing the character as the story progresses; Gedda is a model of taste, and Montserrat Caballé copes ravishingly with the coloratura problems of Mathilde's role. While Chailly's Decca set puts forward a strong case for using Italian with its open vowels, this remains a fully worthwhile alternative, with excellent CD sound. The one considerable snag is that no English translation is provided.

Recorded live, this provides a welcome memento of Muti's enterprise as music director at La Scala in presenting the grandest of Rossini's operas absolutely complete on stage for the first time in many generations. In the theatre longueurs were not avoided, even with Muti's electric direction, when the stage production was uninspired and visually bizarre. Sadly, the performance captured here on record is vocally too flawed to inspire a full recommendation. Muti is forceful, but his rhythmic thrust tends to work against lyrical warmth. The much-praised Chris Merritt is sadly strained in the tenor role of Arnoldo, no match for Pavarotti on Decca's studio recording, who is musically more imaginative too. Giorgio Zancanaro is a strong, generally reliable Tell, but is outshone by Sherrill Milnes on the earlier set. Even Cheryl Studer, warm and sympathetic as Mathilde, is below her best. The recording conveys a vivid, atmospheric impression of a performance at La Scala but, quite apart from erratic balances, inevitably suffers from the acoustic of the theatre, difficult for recording.

L'Italiana in Algeri (complete).
⊛ *** DG 427 331-2 (2) [id.]. Baltsa, Raimondi, Dara, Lopardo, V. State Op. Konzertvereinigung, VPO, Abbado.
*** CBS Dig. M2K 39048 (2) [id.]. Valentini Terrani, Ganzarolli, Araiza, Cologne R. Ch., Capella Coloniensis, Ferro.
(M) *** Decca 417 828-2 (2) [id.]. Berganza, Alva, Corena, Panerai, Maggio Musicale Fiorentino Ch. & O, Varviso.

Abbado's brilliant version was recorded in conjunction with a new staging by the Vienna State Opera, with timing and pointing all geared for wit on stage to make this the most captivating of all recordings of the opera. Agnes Baltsa is a real fire-eater in the title-role, and Ruggero Raimondi with his massively sepulchral bass gives weight to his part without undermining the comedy. The American tenor, Frank Lopardo, proves the most stylish Rossinian, singing with heady clarity in superbly articulated divisions, while both buffo baritones are excellent too. This has all the sparkle of Abbado's scintillating live recording of *Il viaggio a Reims*, plus first-rate studio sound. Like the CBS set, it uses the authentic score, published by the Fondazione Rossini in Pesaro.

The fine CBS version not only uses the critical edition of the score, it goes further towards authenticity in using period instruments including a fortepiano instead of harpsichord for the recitatives (well played by Georg Fischer). Though Ferro can at times be sluggish in slow music (even in the opening of the overture), he is generally a sparkling Rossinian, pacing well to allow a rhythmic lift to be married to crisp ensemble. The set also gains from forward and bright digital recording. Lucia Valentini Terrani here gives her finest performance on record to date, with her seductively rich, firm voice superbly agile in coloratura. Francisco Araiza as Lindoro peppers the rapid passage-work with intrusive aitches – but not too distractingly – and the strength of the voice makes the performance heroic with no suspicion of the twittering of a tenorino. Ganzarolli treats the role of the Bey, Mustafa, as a conventional buffo role, with a voice not ideally steady but full of character; the rest of the cast is strong, too.

The Decca set is offered at mid-price. Under Varviso the opera has Rossinian sparkle in abundance and the music blossoms readily. Teresa Berganza makes an enchanting Italian girl, and the three principal men are all characterful. The recording is vintage Decca, vividly remastered, and adds greatly to the sparkle of the whole proceedings. With excellent documentation this is a fine bargain, even if many may still opt for the later and more complete versions.

Maometto II (complete).
*** Ph. Dig. 412 148-2 (3) [id.]. Anderson, Zimmermann, Palacio, Ramey, Dale, Amb. Op. Ch., Philh. O, Scimone.

Claudio Scimone's account of *Maometto II* has Samuel Ramey magnificently focusing the whole story in his portrait of the Muslim invader in love with the heroine. The nobility of his singing makes Maometto's final self-sacrifice all the more convincing, even if the opera is made the less tense dramatically from having no villain. The other singing is less sharply characterized but is generally stylish, with Margarita Zimmermann in the travesti role of Calbo, June Anderson singing sweetly as Anna, not least in the lovely prayer which comes as an interlude in a massive Trio or Terzettone in Act I. Laurence Dale is excellent in two smaller roles, while Ernesto Palacio mars some fresh-toned singing with his intrusive aitches. Excellent recording.

Semiramide (complete).
(M) *** Decca 425 481-2 (3) [id.]. Sutherland, Horne, Rouleau, Malas, Serge, Amb. Op. Ch., LSO, Bonynge.

The story of *Semiramide* is certainly improbable, involving the love which almost all the male characters bear for the Princess Azema, a lady who rather curiously appears very infrequently in the opera. Instead, Rossini concentrates on the love of Queen Semiramide for the Prince Arsace (a mezzo-soprano), and musically the result is a series of fine duets, superbly performed here by Sutherland and Horne (in the mid-1960s when they were both at the top of their form). What a complete recording brings out, however, is the consistency of Rossini's drama, the music involving the listener even when the story falls short. In Sutherland's interpretation, Semiramide is not so much a Lady Macbeth as a passionate, sympathetic woman and, with dramatic music predominating over languorous cantilena, one has her best, bright manner. Horne is well contrasted, direct and masculine in style, and Spiro Malas makes a firm, clear contribution in a minor role. Rouleau and Serge are variable but more than adequate, and Bonynge keeps the whole opera together with his alert, rhythmic control of tension and pacing. The vintage Decca recording has transferred brilliantly to CD.

Tancredi (complete).
** CBS M3K 39073 (3) [id.]. Horne, Cuberli, Palacio, Zaccaria, Di Nissa, Schuman, Ch. and O of Teatro la Fenice, Weikert.

The chief glory of this live recording from Venice is the enchanting singing of Lella Cuberli as the heroine, Amenaide. The purity and beauty of her tone, coupled with immaculate coloratura and tender expressiveness, make it truly memorable. Marilyn Horne, though not quite as fresh-sounding as earlier in her career, gives a formidable performance in the breeches role of Tancredi, relishing the resonance of her chest register, but finding delicacy too in her big aria, *Di tanti palpiti*. Ernesto Palacio is an accomplished Rossini tenor, commendably agile in the role of Argirio, but the tone tends to grow tight; and Ernesto Zaccaria as Orbazzano sings with fuzzy, sepulchral tone. The conducting is efficient rather than inspired, failing to make the music sparkle or to bring the drama to life. The recording gives a realistic idea of a dryish theatre acoustic.

Il Turco in Italia (abridged).
(***) EMI mono CDS7 49344-2 (2). Callas, Gedda, Rossi-Lemeni, Calabrese, Stabile, Ch. & O of La Scala, Milan, Gavazzeni.

Callas was at her peak when she recorded this rare Rossini opera in the mid-1950s. As ever, there are lumpy moments vocally, but she gives a sharply characterful performance as the capricious Fiorilla, married to an elderly, jealous husband and bored with it. Nicola Rossi-Lemeni as the Turk of the title is characterful too, but not the firmest of singers, and it is left to Nicolai Gedda as the young lover and Franco Calabrese as the jealous husband to match Callas in stylishness. It is good too to have the veteran Mariano Stabile singing the role of the Poet in search of a plot. On CD the original mono recording has been freshened and given a degree of bloom, despite the closeness of the voices. It is a vintage Callas issue, her first uniquely cherishable essay in operatic comedy.

Il viaggio a Reims (complete).
⊛ *** DG Dig. 415 498-2 (2) [id.]. Ricciarelli, Valentini Terrani, Cuberli, Gasdia, Araiza, Gimenez, Nucci, Raimondi, Ramey, Dara, Prague Philharmonic Ch., COE, Abbado.

This DG set is one of the most sparkling and totally successful live opera recordings available, with Claudio Abbado in particular freer and more spontaneous-sounding than he generally is on disc, relishing the sparkle of the comedy. The piece has virtually no story, with the journey to Rheims never actually taking place, only the prospect of it. The wait at the Golden Lily hotel at Plombières provides the opportunity for the ten star characters each to perform in turn: and one hardly wonders that after the first performances Rossini refused ever to allow a revival, on the grounds that no comparable cast could ever be assembled. Instead, he used some of the material in his delectable comic opera, *Le comte Ory*, and it is fascinating here to spot the numbers from it in their original form. Much else is delightful, and the line-up of soloists here could hardly be more impressive, with no weak link. Apart from the established stars the set introduced two formidable newcomers in principal roles, Cecilia Gasdia as a self-important poetess (a nice parody of romantic manners) and, even finer, Lella Cuberli as a young fashion-crazed widow. The rich firmness and distinctive beauty of Cuberli's voice, coupled with amazing flexibility, proclaims a natural prima donna. Abbado's brilliance and sympathy draw the musical threads compellingly together with the help of superb, totally committed playing from the young members of the Chamber Orchestra of Europe.

Zelmira (complete).
*** Erato/WEA Dig. 2292 45419-2 (2) [id.]. Gasdia, Fink, Matteuzzi, Merritt, Amb. S., Sol. Ven., Scimone.

Zelmira, the last-but-one opera that Rossini wrote in Italy before going off to live in Paris, has always had a bad press, but this recording, well sung (with one notable exception) and very well recorded, lets us appreciate that Rossinian inspiration had certainly not dried up, even if the plot's absurdities make it hard to imagine a modern staging. Scimone conducted the recording immediately after a concert performance in Venice, and that obviously helped to give vitality to the substantial sequences of accompanied recitative. He takes a generally brisk view of both the arias and the ensembles but never seems to race his singers. Though the story of murders and usurpations in the royal family of Lesbos is too ill-motivated to be involving, it gives some splendid excuses for fine Rossini arias. There is precious little distinction in musical tone of voice between the goodies and baddies in the story, with the usurping Antenore given some of the most heroic music, for example the first aria. That is a tenor role, more robust than that of Ilo, husband of the wronged heroine, Zelmira. In this performance the choice of singers underlines the contrast between the two principal tenor-roles. Chris Merritt combines necessary agility with an almost baritonal quality as the scheming Antenore, straining only occasionally, and William Matteuzzi sings with heady beauty and fine flexibility in florid writing as Ilo. Star of the performance is Cecilia Gasdia in the name-part, projecting words and emotions very intensely in warmly expressive singing. She is well matched by the mezzo, Barbara Fink, as her friend, Emma, and only the wobbly bass of José Garcia as the deposed Polidoro mars the cast. On two generously filled CDs, with libretto in four languages and first-rate notes, this makes an attractive set for Rossinians, not least because of the fine ensembles such as the two quintets, one at the end of Act I, the other at the climax of Act II.

COLLECTION

L'assedio de Corinto: Avanziam' . . . Non temer d'un basso affetto! . . . I destini tradir ogni speme . . . Signormche tutto puio . . . Sei tu, che stendi; L'ora fatal s'appressa . . . Giusto ciel. La Donna del lago: Mura Felici; Tanti affetti. Otello: Assisa a pie d'un salice. Tancredi: Di tanti palpiti.
⊛ (M) *** Decca 421 306-2 [id.]. Marilyn Horne, Amb. Op. Ch., RPO, Henry Lewis.

Marilyn Horne's generously filled recital disc in Decca's mid-price Opera Gala series brings one of the most cherishable among all Rossini aria records ever issued. The voice is in glorious condition, rich and firm throughout its spectacular range, and is consistently used with artistry and imagination, as well as brilliant virtuosity in coloratura. By any reckoning this is thrilling singing, the more valuable for covering mostly rarities – which, with Horne, makes you wonder at their neglect. The sound is full and brilliant, showing its age hardly at all.

Arias: *La Cenerentola: Non piu mesta. La Donna del Lago: Mura felici . . . Elena! O tu, che chiamo. L'Italiana in Algeri: Cruda sorte! Amor tiranno! Pronti abbiamo . . . Pensa all patria. Otello: Deh! calma, o ciel. La Pietra del Paragone: Se l'Italie contrade . . . Se per voi lo care io torno. Tancredi: Di tanti palpiti. Stabat Mater: Fac ut portem.*
*** Decca Dig. 425 430-2 [id.]. Cecilia Bartoli, A. Schoenberg Ch., V. Volksoper O, Patanè.

Cecilia Bartoli is one of the most exciting coloratura mezzo-sopranos to have arrived in many years, a successor to Berganza, Horne and Baltsa. She is the more remarkable for having achieved so much so young. The voice is full, warm and even in its richness, which yet allows extreme flexibility. This recital of Rossini showpieces brings a formidable demonstration not only of Bartoli's remarkable voice but of her personality and artistry. As yet, she is not so much a sparkler as a commander, bringing natural warmth and imagination to each item without ever quite making you smile with delight. That may well follow, but in the meantime there are not many Rossini recitals of any vintage to match this. Vocally, the one controversial point to note is the way that Bartoli articulates her coloratura with a half-aspirate, closer to the Supervia 'rattle' than anything else, but rather obtrusive. Accompaniments under the direction of Patanè in one of his last recordings are exemplary, and Decca provided the luxury of a chorus in some of the items, with hints of staging. Full, vivid recording. Recommended.

Rott, Hans (1858–84)

Symphony in E.
*** Hyp. Dig. CDA 66366 [id.]. Cincinnati Philh. O, Gerhard Samuel.

Hans Rott, a pupil of Bruckner, spent the last four years of his short life a victim of hallucinatory insanity and succumbed to tuberculosis in his mid-twenties. During a train journey, when a fellow-traveller lit a cigar he brandished a revolver, declaring that Brahms had filled the train with dynamite. Although his *Symphony* owes much to Wagner as well as to Brahms, to whom allusion is made in the finale, it struck strong resonances in his fellow student, Gustav Mahler. It is astonishing to encounter in their pristine form ideas that took root in Mahler's *First* and *Fifth Symphonies*. Mahler wrote that 'his innermost nature is so much akin to mine that he and I are like two fruits from the same tree, produced by the same soil, nourished by the same air'. None of Rott's music has been published and we owe the present work to Dr Paul Banks, who edited it from the incomplete autograph and a set of parts that were prepared for a planned performance by Hans Richter. Structurally the work is original, each movement getting progressively longer, the finale occupying nearly 25 minutes. But the music is full of good ideas and, anticipations of Mahler apart, has a profile of its own. The Cincinnati Philharmonia is a student orchestra who produce extraordinarily good results under Gerhard Samuel. The recording sounds a trifle opaque on certain equipment but is nevertheless good. Readers should investigate this issue without delay.

Roussel, Albert (1869–1937)

Bacchus et Ariane (complete ballet), *Op. 43; Le festin de l'araignée: symphonic fragments.*
*** EMI Dig. CDC7 47376-2 [id.]. O Nat. de France, Prêtre.

Bacchus et Ariane teems with life and is full of rhythmic vitality and richness of detail. It has perhaps less of the poetic feeling of *Le festin* but is nevertheless an exhilarating score. The recording, made in the generous acoustic of the Salle Wagram, is a shade too reverberant at times but no essential detail is masked. Georges Prêtre obtains an excellent response from the Orchestre National de France in both scores. The CD freshens detail a little, although the resonance means that the improvement is relatively limited.

Bacchus et Ariane (ballet): suite No. 2.
(M) ** DG 423 957-2 [id.]. LOP, Markevitch – BERLIOZ: *Symphonie fantastique.***(*)

Markevitch's account of the *Bacchus et Ariane suite* is not quite as distinguished as its

Berlioz coupling, but its pungent rhythmic drive and abrasive lyricism have undoubted emotional force and the orchestra's response is committed.

(i) *Le festin de l'araignée;* (ii) *Songs;* (iii) *Piano works.*
(M) * Ph. (mono) 422 138-2 (2). (i) O, Roussel; (ii) Croiza, Roussel; (iii) Bouget.

It is good to have Roussel's own view of *Le festin de l'araignée* – with the 1928 sound quite serviceable – and even better to have Croiza's records of some of the songs with the composer at the piano, made between 1927 and 1929. The claims of Jean Bouget's 1969 accounts of the piano music seem less pressing, and they are not particularly well recorded either. There was enough interesting material here to fill one disc, and it is a pity that Philips have padded it out into two.

(i) *2 Idylls, Op. 44; Jazz dans la nuit; 4 Mélodies de Henri de Régnier;* (ii) *2 Mélodies, Op. 19; 2 Mélodies, Op. 20;* (i; iii) *2 Mélodies, Op. 50;* (iv) *2 Mélodies, Op. 55; La Menace;* (ii) *O bon vin, où as-tu crû?; Odes anacréontiques, Opp. 31–2;* (i; iv) *2 Poèmes chinois, Op. 12;* (i) *2 Poèmes chinois, Op. 35; 2 Poèmes chinois, Op. 47;* (i; iii; iv) *4 Poèmes de Régnier, Op. 8;* (iv) *2 Poèmes de Ronsard, Op. 26; Les rêves;* (i) *Vocalise No. 1;* (iv) *Vocalise No. 2.*
*** EMI Dig. CDS7 49271-2 (2) [Ang. CDCB 49272]. (i) Mesplé; (ii) Van Dam; (iii) Ollmann; (iv) Allioz-Lugaz; Dalton Baldwin.

This is the kind of issue you should snap up immediately; the likelihood of its remaining in circulation for long is very limited. Although such songs as *Le bachelier de Salamanque* and the *Sarabande* feature in recitals, most of these imaginative and very beautiful songs are rarities. Roussel is one of the most intelligent and resourceful of all French composers, and these generously filled CDs include many treasures. There are many good performances here – not to be missed by lovers of French song.

Songs: *Jazz dans la nuit; Mélodie, Op. 19/1: Light; 2 Mélodies, Op. 20; 2 Poèmes chinois, Op. 35.*
(*) Unicorn DKPCD 9035 [id.]. Sarah Walker, Roger Vignoles – DEBUSSY; ENESCU: *Songs.**

Sarah Walker may not plumb the full emotions of some of the deceptively deep songs in her Roussel group – *Light* for example – but the point and charm of *Jazz dans la nuit* are superbly caught, and the group makes an attractive and generous coupling for the Debussy and Enescu songs, all superbly recorded, with Vignoles a most sensitive accompanist.

Rubbra, Edmund (1901–86)

Violin concerto, Op. 103.
*** Unicorn Dig. DKPCD 9056 [id.]. Carl Pini, Melbourne SO, Measham – IRELAND: *Piano concerto.****

If the centrepiece of the *Concerto* is its reflective slow movement, the two outer movements are hardly less impressive. As always with this composer, the music unfolds with a seeming inevitability and naturalness and a strong sense of purpose. Carl Pini is the capable soloist; the Melbourne orchestra under David Measham play with a conviction that more than compensates for the somewhat unventilated recording, which makes textures sound thicker than they in fact are.

Sinfonietta (for strings), Op. 163; 4 Medieval Latin lyrics, Op. 32; 5 Spenser sonnets, Op. 42; Amoretti: 5 Spenser sonnets, 2nd series, Op. 43.

*** Virgin Dig. VC 790752-2 [id.]. Martyn Hill, Wilson-Johnson, Endellion Qt, City of L. Sinfonia, Schönzeler.

The *Sinfonietta for strings* is Rubbra's last work and alone is worth the price of the record. It is short but concentrated and is eloquently played by the City of London Sinfonia under Hans-Hubert Schönzeler. The songs are all much earlier and are rewarding pieces. Altogether a valuable contribution to the all-too-small Rubbra discography. Excellent recording.

Symphony No. 10 (Sinfonia da camera), Op. 145; Improvisations on virginal pieces by Giles Farnaby, Op. 50; A tribute to Vaughan Williams on his 70th birthday (Introduction and danza alla fuga), Op. 56.
*** Chan. CHAN 8378 [id.]. Bournemouth Sinf., Schönzeler.

Rubbra's *Tenth Symphony* is for chamber orchestra; it is a short one-movement work, whose opening has a Sibelian seriousness and a strong atmosphere that grip one immediately. Schönzeler is scrupulously attentive to dynamic nuance and internal balance, while keeping a firm grip on the architecture as a whole. The 1977 recording has been impressively remastered. It has a warm acoustic and reproduces natural, well-placed orchestral tone. The upper range is crisply defined. The *Farnaby variations* is a pre-war work whose charm Schönzeler uncovers effectively, revealing its textures to best advantage. *Loath to depart*, the best-known movement, has gentleness and vision in this performance. Strongly recommended.

Rubinstein, Anton (1829–94)

Piano sonatas Nos. 1 in F min., Op. 12; 3 in F, Op. 41.
*** Hyp. Dig. CDA 66017 [id.]. Leslie Howard.
Piano sonatas Nos. 2 in C min., Op. 20; 4 in A min., Op. 100.
*** Hyp. Dig. CDA 66105 [id.]. Leslie Howard.

Leslie Howard copes with the formidable technical demands of these *Sonatas* manfully. He proves highly persuasive in all four works, though the actual invention is scarcely distinguished enough to sustain interest over such ambitious time-spans. Rubinstein wrote these pieces for himself to play, and doubtless his artistic powers and strong personality helped to persuade contemporary audiences. The 1981 recordings sound excellent.

Russo, William (born 1928)

Street music, Op. 65.
** DG 419 625-2 [id.]. Siegel, San Francisco SO, composer – GERSHWIN: *American in Paris***; BERNSTEIN: *West Side story: dances.***(*)

William Russo has been an assiduous advocate of mixing jazz and blues traditions with the symphony orchestra, and *Street music* has its attractive side. Despite Cork Siegel on harmonica, however, it is no more successful at achieving genuine integration than other pieces of its kind, and its half-hour span is far too long for the material it contains.

Rutter, John (born 1943)

(i) *Gloria;* (ii) Anthems: *All things bright and beautiful; For the beauty of the earth; A Gaelic blessing; God be in my head; The Lord bless you and keep you; The Lord is my Shepherd; O clap your hands; Open thou my eyes; Praise ye the Lord; A prayer of St Patrick.*
*** Collegium Dig. COLCD 100 [id.]. Cambridge Singers, (i) Philip Jones Brass Ens.; (ii) City of L. Sinfonia, composer.

John Rutter is one of those British composers who has quietly gone on composing traditional English church music without recourse to atonalism or barbed wire. He has a genuine gift of melody and his use of tonal harmony is individual and never bland. The resplendent *Gloria* is a three-part piece, and Rutter uses his brass to splendid and often spectacular effect. The anthems are diverse in style and feeling and, like the *Gloria*, have strong melodic appeal – the setting of *All things bright and beautiful* is delightfully spontaneous. It is difficult to imagine the music receiving more persuasive advocacy than under the composer, and the recording is first class in every respect: the CD adds an extra dimension to the brass and organ in the *Gloria*.

(i) *Requiem; I will lift up mine eyes.*
*** Collegium Dig. COLCD 103 [id.]. (i) Ashton, Dean; Cambridge Singers, City of L. Sinfonia, composer.

John Rutter's melodic gift, so well illustrated in his carols, is here used in the simplest and most direct way to create a small-scale *Requiem* that is as beautiful and satisfying in its English way as the works of Fauré and Duruflé. The *Sanctus* has a pealing-bell effect (so like the carols) and the *Agnus Dei* is both intense and dramatic. The penultimate movement, a ripe setting of *The Lord is my Shepherd*, with a lovely oboe obbligato, sounds almost like an anglicized Song of the Auvergne, while the delightful *Pié Jesu* – which Caroline Ashton sings with the purity of a boy treble – melodically is nearly as catchy as the similar movement in the Lloyd Webber *Requiem*; it makes one reflect that these two works would make a marvellous concert double bill. The performance is wonderfully warm and spontaneous, most beautifully recorded on CD, and *I will lift up mine eyes* makes a highly effective encore piece.

Saint-Saëns, Camille (1835-1921)

Allegro appassionato for cello and orchestra, Op. 43; Caprice in D for violin and orchestra (arr. Ysaÿe); *Carnival of the animals: Le cygne. Cello concerto No. 1 in A min., Op. 33; Wedding-cake (caprice-valse) for piano and orchestra, Op. 76; Le Déluge: Prelude, Op. 45.*
(M) **(*) EMI CDM7 69386-2 [id.]. Yan Pascal and Paul Tortelier, Maria de la Pau, CBSO, Frémaux.

Paul Tortelier gives an assured account of the *A minor Cello concerto*, but fails to make much of the busy but uninspired *Allegro appassionato*. Yan Pascal Tortelier plays with charm in the *Caprice* and with pleasing simplicity in the *Prelude* to the oratorio *Le Déluge*, which has a concertante part for the solo violin. The *Wedding-cake caprice* is also nicely done, even though Maria de la Pau does not reveal a strong personality. This is quite an attractive anthology, well recorded.

Carnival of the animals.
*** Virgin Dig. VC 790786-2 [id.]. Anton Nel, Keith Snell, Ac. of L., Richard Stamp –
PROKOFIEV: *Peter**** ⊛; MOZART: *Eine kleine Nachtmusik.***(*)

*** Ph. Dig. 400 016-2 [id.]. Villa, Jennings, Pittsburgh SO, Previn – RAVEL: *Ma Mère l'Oye.****

(M) *** EMI CDM7 63177-2. H. Menuhin, Simon, Philh. O, Kurtz – BRITTEN: *Young person's guide***(*); PROKOFIEV: *Peter.***

(B) *** ASV CDQS 6017 [id.]. Goldstone, Brown, RPO, Hughes – PROKOFIEV: *Peter.***

Carnival of the animals (chamber version).

(B) ** Pickwick Dig. PCD 932 [id.]. Julian Jacobson, Nigel Hutchinson, LSO (members), Barry Wordsworth – BIZET: *Jeux d'enfants**; RAVEL: *Ma Mère l'Oye.***(*)

Carnival of the animals (with verses by Ogden Nash).

*** DG 415 351-2 [id.]. Hermione Gingold, Alfons & Aloys Kontarsky, VPO, Boehm – PROKOFIEV: *Peter.***

Richard Stamp directs an outstanding version of Saint-Saëns's witty zoology, full of affectionate humour. There is much to beguile: the *Tortoises* bringing a lethargic dignity to Saint-Saëns's geriatric treatment of Offenbach's *Can-can* and Stephen Williams's solo double-bass portrayal of *The Elephant* contrasting with the clattering, brilliant skeletal *Fossils*. After Robert Bailey's gentle, slightly recessed image of *The Swan*, the finale bursts on the listener with infectious vigour, the two pianists producing flourishes of great bravura and some telling marcato emphases for the buoyant rhythmic outlines of the *Grand parade*. Throughout, one responds to the polished overall presentation and sense of fun; although some may feel that the recording is rather resonant, it adds a genial warmth to the vitality of the proceedings.

Previn's version makes a ready alternative. The music is played with infectious rhythmic spring and great refinement. It is a mark of the finesse of this performance – which has plenty of bite and vigour, as well as polish – that the great cello solo of *Le Cygne* is so naturally presented. The shading of half-tones in Anne Martindale Williams's exquisitely beautiful playing is made all the more tenderly affecting. Fine contributions too from the two pianists, although their image is rather bass-orientated, within a warmly atmospheric recording.

Kurtz's splendid version from the end of the 1950s sounds remarkably fresh in its CD format, with some superb Philharmonia solo playing and an excellent contribution from the two pianists, although, curiously, the definition is poor for the double-basses in their portrayal of *Tortoises*. Elsewhere orchestral detail is admirably firm and vivid, and *The Swan* is memorably serene. There is plenty of sparkle and wit, the couplings are generous and the price is reasonable.

The two pianists on ASV play with point and style, and the accompaniment has both spirit and spontaneity. *The Swan* is perhaps a trifle self-effacing, but otherwise this is very enjoyable, the humour appreciated without being underlined. The recording is excellent, and this makes a good bargain-price CD recommendation.

Not everyone will care for the inclusion of Ogden Nash's verses, but those who do will find Miss Gingold's narration is splendidly performed – every inflexion of that superb voice is to be relished. Marvellous playing from the Kontarskys and the Vienna Philharmonic, and splendid 1976 analogue recording.

Barry Wordsworth opts for the original chamber version for flute, clarinet, string quintet and percussion. The two pianists make a lively contribution and the wide dynamic range of the recording means that the opening and closing sections of the work have their high spirits projected strongly. When the percussive condiment is added, the group makes a considerable impact, but in the more gentle zoological portraits the effect is a bit wan, and the imagery tends to recede. It is difficult here to achieve a volume setting which does not offer problems of changing levels within the domestic circumstances which Saint-Saëns envisaged.

Carnival of the animals; Piano trio in F, Op. 18; Septet in E flat, for trumpet, strings & piano, Op. 65.
* Virgin Dig. VC 790751-2 [id.]. Nash Ens.

A generously filled disc. Saint-Saëns wrote the first of his two *Piano trios* in his late twenties and, in the Nash's expert hands, its charms are heard here to best advantage. This is a highly persuasive account of the work, while the Nash Ensemble capture the humour of the *Septet* and the *Grand fantaisie zoölogique* excellently. The acoustic has warmth and the balance between the instruments, particularly in the *Carnival of the animals*, is admirably judged.

Cello concerto No. 1 in A min., Op. 33.
* CBS Dig. MK 35848 [id.]. Yo-Yo Ma, O Nat. de France, Maazel – LALO: *Concerto.******
* Decca Dig. 410 019-2 [id.]. Harrell, Cleveland O, Marriner – SCHUMANN: *Concerto.******
* DG Dig. 427 323-2 [id.]. Matt Haimovitz, Chicago SO, Levine – LALO: *Concerto*; BRUCH: *Kol Nidrei.******
* RCA Dig. RD 71003. Harnoy, Cincinnati SO, Kunzel – OFFENBACH: *Concerto*; TCHAIKOVSKY: *Rococo variations.******
(B) ***** Ph. 422 467-2 [id.]. Gendron, Monte Carlo Op. O, Benzi – DVOŘÁK: *Concerto* etc.***(*)**; FAURÉ: *Élégie.**(*)

Yo-Yo Ma's performance of the Saint-Saëns *Concerto* is distinguished by fine sensitivity and beautiful tone, yet there is not a trace of posturing or affectation. The Orchestre National de France respond with playing of the highest quality throughout. Superb recorded sound.

Harrell's reading of the Saint-Saëns, altogether more extrovert than Ma's, makes light of any idea that this composer always works on a small scale. The opening is positively epic, and the rest of the performance is just as compelling, with the minuet-like *Allegretto* crisply neo-classical. Recording is outstanding, beautifully balanced.

Haimovitz and Levine open the *Concerto* with a vigorous surge of passionate feeling, and the second subject is tenderly contrasted, with lovely warm timbre from Haimovitz. This strongly characterized account, full of spontaneity, competes well with the considerable competition from Ma and Harrell. Moreover it is extremely realistically recorded, with the balance between cello and orchestra nigh on perfect.

Ofra Harnoy's is also a first-rate account, the opening full of fervour and impulse, played with full tone, while later the timbre is beautifully fined down for the *Adagietto* minuet. The orchestral response is equally refined here; and this well-recorded account is in every way recommendable for its unexpected and attractive Offenbach coupling.

A good performance from Gendron with an adequate accompaniment. But the recording is not especially distinguished: the soloist is balanced too far forward.

Cello concerto No. 2 in D min., Op. 119.
* Decca Dig. 414 387-2 [id.]. Harrell, Berlin RSO, Chailly – LALO: *Concerto*; FAURÉ: *Élégie.******

The *Cello Concerto No. 2* has an attractive spontaneity and its ideas are memorable, notably the strongly rhythmic opening theme of the first movement – which returns to cap the finale – and the very engaging melody of the *Andante* (which is linked to the opening movement). At its close, Harrell refines his timbre to an exquisite half-tone and the effect is ravishing, with a gentle muted horn decoration. Chailly's accompaniment is sympathetic, polished and full of character; the attractive ambience of the Jesus Christ Church, Berlin, makes a convincing backcloth for the music-making.

Piano concertos Nos. 1-5.
*** Decca 417 351-2 (2) [id.]. Rogé, Philh. O, LPO or RPO, Dutoit.
(B) (*) CBS M2YK 45624 (2). Philippe Entremont, O du Capitole, Toulouse, Plasson.

Played as they are here, these *Concertos* can exert a strong appeal: Pascal Rogé brings delicacy, virtuosity and sparkle to the piano part and he receives expert support from the various London orchestras under Dutoit. Altogether delicious playing and excellent piano sound from Decca, who secure a most realistic balance.

Entremont is a vigorously persuasive interpreter of French music, but the (originally late-1970s) CBS recording did less than justice to his gentler qualities, with the forward balance reducing the dynamic range. The CD remastering has made matters worse, with orchestral tuttis sounding crude and fierce and no bloom given to the piano, which becomes clattery and aggressive under pressure.

Piano concerto No. 1 in D, Op. 17; Africa (fantaisie), Op. 89; Allegro appassionato, Op. 70; Rhapsodie d'Auvergne, Op. 73; Wedding-cake caprice-valse, Op. 76.
**(*) EMI Dig. CDC7 49757-2. Collard, RPO, Previn.

As always with Collard, there is splendid character and dazzling technique. He makes much of this slight Mendelssohnian concerto, though Rogé on Decca matches him in terms of charm and delicacy of feeling. Apart from the celebrated (and delightfully scatty) *Wedding-cake caprice-valse*, there are some pleasing rarities: the inventive *Rhapsodie d'Auvergne* and a sparkling account of the exuberant, pseudo-exotic *Africa fantaisie*. The recording has excellent body and presence, but we are fairly close to the piano and there is some discomfort on tutti and in fortissimo piano passages.

Piano concerto No. 2 in G min., Op. 22.
*** EMI Dig. CDC7 47221-2 [id.]. Cécile Ousset, CBSO, Rattle – LISZT: *Concerto No. 1.****
(*) Ph. Dig. 410 052-2 [id.]. Bella Davidovich, Concg. O, Järvi – RACHMANINOV: *Rhapsody on a theme of Paganini.*(*)
(*) RCA RD 85666. Rubinstein, Phd. O, Ormandy – FRANCK: *Symphonic variations*; FALLA: *Nights* etc.(*)

The most popular of Saint-Saëns's concertos has rarely received so winning a performance on record as Ousset's. The opening cadenza, so far from reflecting Bach-like qualities, is warm and urgent, genuinely romantic music, and the Scherzo, spikier than usual, brings dazzlingly clear articulation. This performance consistently conveys the flair and contrasted tensions of a live recording, though it was made in the studio. The recording favours the soloist but is rich and lively.

Bella Davidovich also gives a most sympathetic account of the *G minor Concerto*; she has the advantage of excellent orchestral support from the Concertgebouw Orchestra. The recording is very natural and Davidovich draws most sympathetic tone-quality from the instrument. This is warmly attractive music-making, but it is just a little lacking in flair.

Rubinstein's version was made in 1970, and he is partnered by that most understanding of accompanists, Eugene Ormandy. Rubinstein's secret is that, though he appears sometimes to be attacking the music, his phrasing is full of little fluctuations so that his playing never sounds stilted. The recording of the piano is rather dry, even hard at times, but the glitter seems just right for the centrepiece.

Piano concertos Nos. 2 in G min., Op. 22; 4 in C min., Op. 44.
*** EMI CDC7 47816-2 [id.]. Jean-Philippe Collard, RPO, Previn.

Jean-Philippe Collard brings panache and virtuosity to these two concertos, as well as impressive poetic feeling. Apart from the sheer beauty of sound, he commands a wide dynamic range and a subtle tonal palette, and the Royal Philharmonic under Previn give him splendid support. Although allegiance to Pascal Rogé on Decca remains unshaken, Collard with his greater dynamic range and authority makes even more of this music.

Piano concertos Nos. 3 in E flat, Op. 29; 5 in F (Egyptian), Op. 103.
*** EMI Dig. CDC7 49051-2 [id.]. Jean-Philippe Collard, RPO, Previn.

The *Third Concerto* of 1869 is not the equal of its predecessor; but there is much ingenuity in the piano writing, and it could hardly be heard to more persuasive effect than it is in Jean-Philippe Collard's hands. The *Fifth* is much better known; it was composed on a visit to Egypt just over a quarter of a century later. There is no doubting Saint-Saëns's skill in exploiting the genius of the piano to suggest Eastern sonorities. At one point Collard makes his instrument sound exactly like an Arab *qunan*, or zither. He plays throughout with superb control and finish, and Previn and the RPO are sensitive and sympathetic accompanists. The sound is very good too, slightly more transparent than the Decca for Rogé.

Violin concerto No. 1 in A, Op. 30.
*** Decca Dig. 411 952-2 [id.]. Kyung Wha Chung, Montreal SO, Dutoit – LALO: *Symphonie espagnole.****

Saint-Saëns's *First Violin concerto* is a miniature. Kyung Wha Chung makes the most of the lyrical interludes and is fully equal to the energetic bravura of the outer sections. With a clear yet full-bodied digital recording and an excellent accompaniment from Charles Dutoit, this is persuasive.

Violin concerto No. 3 in B min., Op. 61.
*** CBS Dig. MK 39007 [id.]. Cho-Liang Lin, Philh. O, Tilson Thomas – MENDELSSOHN: *Concerto.****
*** ASV Dig. CDDCA 680 [id.]. Xue Wei, Philh. O, Bakels – BRUCH: *Concerto No. 1.****
(M) *** DG Dig. 429 977-2 [id.]. Perlman, O de Paris, Barenboim – LALO: *Symphonie espagnole.****
*** Decca Dig. 425 501-2 [id.]. Joshua Bell, Montreal SO, Dutoit – LALO: *Symphonie espagnole.***

Violin concerto No. 3 in B min., Op. 61; Havanaise, Op. 83; Introduction and rondo capriccioso, Op. 28.
(M) ** Ph. 420 887-2. Szeryng, Monte Carlo Op. O, Remoortel – RAVEL: *Tzigane.***(*)

Cho-Liang Lin's account of the *B minor Concerto* with the Philharmonia Orchestra and Michael Tilson Thomas is exhilarating and thrilling. He is given excellent recording from the CBS engineers and, in terms of both virtuosity and musicianship, his version is certainly second to none and is arguably the finest yet to have appeared. The CD format is admirably 'present'.

Xue Wei's account is full of flair from the very first entry onwards. The orchestral accompaniment is strongly characterized as well: the brass chorale has a splendidly bold resonance, while the soloist creates an ideal mixture of ruminative lyricism and dash, especially in the slow movement with its delicate pianissimo near the close. The finale has plenty of vitality and the sound is vivid, even if the balance, within a church acoustic, seems artificially contrived.

On DG, Perlman achieves a fine partnership with his friend Barenboim, who provides a highly sympathetic accompaniment in a performance that is both tender and strong, while Perlman's verve and dash in the finale are dazzling. The forward balance is understandable in this work, but orchestral detail could at times be sharper.

Joshua Bell's performance is also very attractive, with the Montreal sound casting a glow over the proceedings, so that even the brass chorale sounds genial. The pianissimo opening is full of atmosphere and the *Andantino* has a pleasing lyrical simplicity, with the work's romanticism blossoming throughout. With a realistic balance for the soloist, the recording is one of Decca's most convincing.

Clean and immaculate performances from Szeryng, whose approach is aristocratic rather than indulgent. The orchestral contribution, adequate rather than distinguished, is not helped by the balance of the recording, which spotlights the violin and does not add a great deal of lustre to the accompaniment.

Havanaise, Op. 83; Introduction and rondo capriccioso, Op. 28.
*** EMI CDC7 47725-2 [id.]. Itzhak Perlman, O de Paris, Martinon – CHAUSSON: *Poème*; RAVEL: *Tzigane.****
*** DG Dig. 423 063-2 [id.]. Perlman, NYPO, Mehta – CHAUSSON: *Poème*; RAVEL: *Tzigane*; SARASATE: *Carmen fantasy.****
*** Decca 417 118-2 [id.]. Kyung Wha Chung, RPO, Dutoit – CHAUSSON: *Poème*; RAVEL: *Tzigane.****
(M) *** Decca 417 707-2 [id.] (*Havanaise* only). Chung, RPO, Dutoit – BRUCH: *Concerto No. 1*; TCHAIKOVSKY: *Concerto.****
(M) *** Decca 417 793-2 [id.]. Ricci, LSO, Gamba – BRUCH: *Concerto No. 1****; MENDELSSOHN: *Concerto.***(*)

On EMI, Perlman plays these Saint-Saëns warhorses with splendid panache and virtuosity; his tone and control of colour in the *Havanaise* are ravishing. The digital remastering brings Perlman's gorgeous fiddling right into the room, at the expense of a touch of aggressiveness when the orchestra lets rip; but the concert-hall ambience prevents this from being a problem.

Perlman's later, DG recordings are hardly less appealing. They have the advantage of an excellent digital sound-balance and the orchestral texture is fuller. Perhaps the early performances are a shade riper, but the closing pages of the *Havanaise* are particularly felicitous on DG. This disc also includes the Sarasate *Carmen fantasy* as a winning extra item.

On Decca, Kyung Wha Chung shows rhythmic flair and a touch of the musical naughtiness that gives these pieces their full charm. Dutoit accompanies most sympathetically, and the recording is excellent.

Ricci is in splendid form and shows plenty of personality in these sparkling showpieces; with vivid Decca recording, this makes an attractive bonus for his reissued coupling of Bruch and Mendelssohn.

Symphony No. 2 in A min., Op. 55; Phaëton, Op. 39; Suite algérienne, Op. 60.
*** ASV Dig. ZCDCA 599 [id.]. LSO, Butt.

The *Second Symphony* is full of excellent ideas, with a fugue delivered with characteristic aplomb in the first movement; the Scherzo is sparklingly concise and the similarly high-spirited *Tarantella* finale has something in common with Mendelssohn's *Italian symphony*. It is very well played here with the freshness of an orchestra discovering something unfamiliar and enjoying themselves; Yondani Butt's tempi are apt and he shapes the whole piece convincingly. He is equally persuasive in the picaresque *Suite algérienne*, the source of the justly famous *Marche militaire française*, and indeed in *Phaéton*. Warmly atmospheric recording

Symphonies Nos. 2 in A min., Op. 55; (i) *3 in C min., Op. 78.*
*** Chan. Dig. CHAN 8822 [id.]. Ulster O, Yan Pascal Tortelier; (i) with Gillian Weir.

Yan Pascal Tortelier's performances are very enjoyable and very well recorded. But in the *Second Symphony* Yondani Butt's account has greater freshness, and the slightly less reverberant ASV recording contributes to this. If your interest is primarily in this work, Butt's version is first choice, but if you need both *Symphonies* on one CD, then the Chandos issue has much in its favour. Certainly the hall resonance suits the *Organ symphony* and Tortelier's account of it is affectionate, well paced and alive, with plenty of vitality in the opening movement. The resonance helps the *Poco Adagio*, which begins a little soberly, to expand to a fully romantic climax; yet it does not cloud the detail of the scherzo, and Gillian Weir's organ entry in the finale is a truly impressive moment. The theme is strong in outline, yet the organ sound itself is suitably massive. The work moves to an impressive dénouement and at the end the Ulster Hall embraces the brass sonorously, and the closing moments knit together powerfully.

Symphony No. 3 in C min., Op. 78.
*** DG Dig. 419 617-2 [id.]. Simon Preston, BPO, Levine – DUKAS: *L'apprenti sorcier.****
*** RCA RD 85750 [RCA 5750-2-RC]. Zamkochian, Boston SO, Munch – POULENC: *Organ concerto;* FRANCK: *Le chasseur maudit.***(*)
*** ASV Dig. CDDCA 665 [id.]. Rawsthorne, LPO, Bátiz.
*** Decca Dig. 410 201-2 [id.]. Hurford, Montreal SO, Dutoit.
(B) *** Pickwick Dig. PCD 847 [MCA MCAD 25933]. Chorzempa, Berne SO, Maag.
*** Eurodisc 610 509. Krapp, Bamberg SO, Eschenbach (with FRANCK: *Choral No. 3***).
(M) **(*) Decca 417 725-2 [id.]. Priest, LAPO, Mehta – POULENC: *Organ concerto.****
(M) **(*) EMI CD-EMX 9511. Tracey, Royal Liverpool PO, Litton – BERLIOZ: *Le Carnaval romain.****

(i) *Symphony No. 3;* (ii) *Danse macabre; Le Déluge: Prélude, Op. 45; Samson et Dalila: Bacchanale.*
(M) *** DG 415 847-2 [id.]. (i) Litaize, Chicago SO, Barenboim; (ii) O de Paris, Barenboim.

With the Berlin Philharmonic in cracking form, Levine's is a grippingly dramatic reading, full of imaginative detail. The great thrust of the performance does not stem from fast pacing: rather it is the result of incisive articulation. After the exhilarating fervour of the first movement, the *Poco Adagio* has a mood of sombre nobility, the organ subtly underpinning the string sonority, yet leading to a climax of great intensity. The Scherzo bursts upon the listener, full of exuberance from the Berliners, bows tight on strings, and in the engaging middle section the clarity of the digital recording allows the pianistic detail to register crisply. The thunderous organ entry in the finale makes a magnificent effect, and the tension is held at white heat throughout the movement. At the close Levine draws the threads together with a satisfying final quickening.

Those looking for a bargain could hardly better Barenboim's inspirational 1976 version which dominated the catalogue for so long. Among the reissue's three attractive bonuses is an exciting account of the *Bacchanale* from *Samson et Dalila*. The performance of the *Symphony* glows with warmth from beginning to end. In the opening 6/8 section the galloping rhythms are pointed irresistibly, while the linked slow section has a poised stillness in its soaring lyricism which completely avoids any suspicion of sweetness or sentimentality. A brilliant account of the Scherzo leads into a magnificently energetic conclusion, with the Chicago orchestra excelling itself with radiant playing in every section. The digital remastering, as so often, is not wholly advantageous: while detail is sharper, the massed violins sound thinner and the bass is drier. In the finale, some of the bloom has gone, and the organ entry has a touch of hardness.

Munch's 1959 Boston recording sounds astonishingly well, still spectacular today and hardly dated – except that, in compressing the pre-Dolby background hiss, RCA have taken the edge off the treble response; in the resonance of Boston Symphony Hall, detail is foggy, especially in the Scherzo. Having said that, the effect is gorgeously rich and sumptuous, so that the *Poco Adagio* has an enveloping warmth, and in the finale there is a thrillingly sonorous contribution from the organist, Berj Zamkochian, whose powerful first entry is as arresting as any. The performance overall is very exciting, moving forward in a single sweep of great intensity; yet the feeling is always genial, never aggressively forced.

Bátiz's ASV version was the first digital success for this work, although originally the CD transfer had an unattractive digital edge. Now it has been remastered and sounds spectacularly ample, with the organ almost overwhelmingly resonant in the coda. Under an inspirational Bátiz, the orchestral playing is exhilarating in its energy and commitment, while the *Poco Adagio* balances a noble elegiac feeling with romantic warmth. After the vivacious Scherzo, the entry of the organ in the finale is a breathtaking moment, and the sense of spectacle persists, bringing an unforgettable weight and grandeur to the closing pages.

Dutoit brings his usual gifts of freshness and a natural sympathy to Saint-Saëns's attractive score. The recording is very bright, with luminous detail, the strings given a thrilling brilliance above the stave. One notices a touch of digital edge, but there is a balancing weight. The reading effectively combines lyricism with passion. In the finale, Hurford's entry in the famous chorale melody is more pointed, less massive than usual, although Dutoit generates a genial feeling of gusto to compensate. With its wide range and bright lighting, this is a performance to leave one tingling, after Dutoit's final burst of adrenalin.

Maag's extremely well-recorded Berne performance has a Mendelssohnian freshness and the sprightly playing in the Scherzo draws an obvious affinity with that composer. The first movement has plenty of rhythmic lift and the *Poco Adagio* is eloquently elegiac, yet no one could be disappointed with the organ entry in the finale, which is certainly arresting, while the rippling delicacy of the piano figurations which follow is most engaging. The closing pages have a convincing feeling of apotheosis and, although this is not the weightiest reading available, it is an uncommonly enjoyable one in which the sound is bright, full and suitably resonant.

Eschenbach's Eurodisc reading has much in common with Munch's version, with its strong and consistent forward thrust. The slow section is expansively romantic, and the bite and vigour of the Scherzo offer a fine contrast before the organ entry makes the most grandiloquent effect. The excitement is well sustained to the end and the recording is resonantly spectacular.

Mehta draws a well-disciplined and exuberant response from all departments. The slow movement cantilena sings out vividly on the strings, helped by the brightened recording.

877

The digital remastering produces a less sumptuous effect than on the original 1979 LP, and in the finale the focus of the more spectacular sounds is not absolutely clean; even so, this is very enjoyable.

In Litton's Liverpool recording the long reverberation period of Liverpool Cathedral offers problems that are not entirely solved. The finale becomes a huge swimming bath of sound, especially in the closing bars where the echoing resonance brings a physical frisson. Litton cleverly times the music to take the acoustic overhang into account, with relatively steady tempi throughout, and his lyrical feel for the work is attractive. But the balance and detail are achieved by close microphones; even though everything registers on CD, one could not count this version a complete success.

Violin sonata No. 1 in D min., Op. 75.
*** Essex CDS 6044 [id.]. Accardo, Canio – CHAUSSON: *Concert.****

The performance by Accardo and Canio is marvellously played, selfless and dedicated. The recording too is very good, and this can be recommended strongly, if the coupling is suitable.

Samson et Dalila (opera): complete.
** EMI CDS7 47895-8 (2) [Ang. CDCB 47895]. Gorr, Vickers, Blanc, Diakov, Choeurs René Duclos, O of Paris Nat. Op., Prêtre.

Jon Vickers and Rita Gorr are in commanding form, both recorded at their vocal peak. Ernest Blanc characterizes well as the High Priest, but other soloists are undistinguished. The main snag is the conducting of Prêtre, which presents the big moments of high drama effectively enough, but is coarse-grained at too many points. This is very acceptable as a stop-gap until a modern version appears on CD. The present transfer shows signs of age, with the occasional touch of distortion on the voices.

Salieri, Antonio (1750-1825)

Concerto for oboe, flute and orchestra in C.
*** Ph. Dig. 416 359-2 [id.]. Holliger, Nicolet, ASMF, Sillito – CIMAROSA: *Concertante*; STAMITZ: *Double concerto.****
(B) *** DG 427 211-2 [id.]. Holliger, Nicolet, Bamberg SO, Maag – MOZART: *Flute concertos.***

Salieri's *Concerto for flute and oboe* has great charm, with its chattering interplay in the outer movements and the elegant *Largo* bringing suitable contrast. It is played superbly by Nicolet and Holliger, and accompanied stylishly by Sillito. The recording is in the demonstration class on CD.

Heinz Holliger and Aurèle Nicolet also form an expert and sensitive partnership in their earlier version of Salieri's *Double concerto.* The recording too is fresh.

Falstaff (opera): complete.
*** Hung. Dig. HCD 21789/91 [id.]. Gregor, Zempléni, Gulyás, Gáti, Pánczél, Csura, Vámossy, Salieri Chamber Ch. & O, Tamás Pál.

Like Verdi, Salieri and his librettist ignore the Falstaff of the histories. They tell the story (minus the Anne and Fenton sub-plot and without Mistress Quickly) within the framework of the conventional two-act opera of the period. Though the opera is long, the speed is fast and furious, with the set numbers bringing many delights, as in the charming little duet, *La stessa, stessissima,* for the two wives reading their identical letters, or

Falstaff's first aria, swaggering and jolly, introduced by a fanfare motif, and a delightful laughter trio in Act II. None of the ideas, however charming or sparkling, is developed in the way one would expect in Mozart, but it is all great fun, particularly in a performance as lively and well sung as this. Jószef Gregor is splendid in the name-part, with Dénes Gulyás equally stylish in the tenor role of Ford. Maria Zempléni as Mistress Ford and Eva Pánczél in the mezzo role of Mistress Slender (not Page) are both bright and lively. The eponymous chorus and orchestra also perform with vigour under Tamás Pál; the recording is brilliant, with a fine sense of presence.

Sallinen, Aulis (born 1935)

(i) *Cello concerto, Op. 44; Shadows (Prelude for Orchestra), Op. 52; Symphony No. 4, Op. 49.*
*** Finlandia Dig. FACD 346 [id.]. (i) Arto Noras; Helsinki PO, Kamu.

The *Cello concerto* of 1977 is the most commanding piece here. It is oddly laid out, its long, expansive first movement taking almost twenty minutes and its companion only five. Yet Sallinen's ideas and his sound-world resonate in the mind. Arto Noras has its measure and plays with masterly eloquence. The *Fourth Symphony* is a three-movement work but was composed, as it were, backwards, the first movement on which Sallinen began work eventually becoming the finale. The middle movement is marked *Dona nobis pacem*; throughout the finale, bells colour the texture, as is often the case in his orchestral writing. *Shadows* is an effective short piece which reflects or 'shadows' the content of the opera, *The King goes north to France*. The performances under Okko Kamu are very impressive and the recording quite exemplary.

(i) *Symphonies Nos. 1; 3;* (ii) *Chorali;* (iii) *Cadenze for solo violin;* (iv) *Elegy for Sebastian Knight;* (v) *String quartet No. 3.*
*** BIS CD 41 [id.]. (i) Finnish RSO, Kamu; (ii) Helsinki PO, Berglund; (iii) Paavo Pohjola; (iv) Frans Helmerson; (v) Voces Intimae Qt.

The *First Symphony*, in one movement, is diatonic and full of atmosphere, as indeed is the *Third*, a powerful, imaginative piece written on an island in the Baltic which appears to be haunted by the sounds and smells of nature. The performances under Okko Kamu are excellent and this music with its subtle colourings benefits greatly from the absence of background noise. *Chorali* is a shorter piece, persuasively done by Paavo Berglund; and there are three chamber works, albeit of lesser substance. The recordings are from the 1970s and are all very well balanced. Highly recommended.

(i) *Symphony No. 5 (Washington mosaics), Op. 57;* (ii; iii) *Chamber music III: The Nocturnal dances of Don Juanquixote (for cello & orchestra), Op. 58;* (iii) *(Solo) Cello sonata, Op. 26.*
**(*) Finlandia Dig. FACD 370 [id.]. (i) Helsinki PO, or (ii) Finlandia Sinfonietta, Kamu; (iii) Arto Noras.

The success of Sallinen's short but powerful *Shadows*, which is related in atmosphere to the opera, *The King goes forth to France*, prompted Rostropovich to commission a new symphony. The result was *Washington mosaics*, a five-movement work in which the outer movements form the framework for three less substantial but highly imaginative intermezzi. There are Stravinskian overtones in the first movement, though momentum is intermittent. The three intermezzi cast a strong spell, and those who respond to the *First* and *Third Symphonies* will find comparable feeling for nature and a keen sense of its power. There are the same passing reminders of Britten and Shostakovich and the orchestral sonorities are unfailingly resourceful: the first intermezzo even has expressionistic overtones mildly reminiscent of Berg or of Sallinen's countryman, Aarre Merikanto. The performance is dedicated and the recording is in the first flight. An impressive achievement. Not so *The Nocturnal dances of Don Juanquixote*, which is pretty thin stuff. It incorporates nostalgic recollections of Sallinen's days working in a restaurant band, and the juxtaposition of such disparate elements does not really work. It is impeccably played by Arto Noras, but not even his art can persuade one of its merits. The main idea is irredeemably cheap; and the solo *Cello sonata* of 1971 is hardly a substantial makeweight, even though Noras is a masterly advocate. However, the *Symphony* is an important and rewarding work and carries a strong recommendation.

Sammartini, Giovanni Battista (1700-75)

Symphonies in D; G; String quintet in E.
*** HM HMC 901245 [id.]. Ens. 145, Banchini – Giuseppe SAMMARTINI: *Concerti grossi* etc.***

Giovanni Battista was the younger of the two Sammartini brothers; he spent his whole life in Milan. On this record, the Ensemble 145, led by Chiara Banchini, offer two of his symphonies (he composed over eighty); although neither attains greatness, they have genuine appeal. Good recording.

Sammartini, Giuseppe (c. 1693-1750)

Concerti grossi Nos. 6 & 8; (i) Recorder concerto in F.
*** HM HMC 901245 [id.]. (i) Conrad Steinmann; Ens. 145, Banchini – Giovanni SAMMARTINI: *Symphonies* etc.***

Giuseppe settled in England in the 1720s and, though influenced by the rather conservative English taste, he was a refined and inventive composer. The Ensemble 145 is a period-instrument group; they produce a firmly focused sound, even though the textures are light and the articulation lively. Excellent playing from Conrad Steinmann in the *Recorder concerto*.

Sarasate, Pablo (1844-1908)

Carmen fantasy, Op. 25.
⊛ *** EMI CDC7 47101-2 [id.]. Itzhak Perlman, RPO, Foster – PAGANINI: *Concerto No. 1.*** ⊛
*** DG Dig. 423 063-2 [id.]. Itzhak Perlman, NYPO, Mehta – CHAUSSON: *Poème*; RAVEL: *Tzigane*; SAINT-SAENS: *Havanaise* etc.***

Sarasate's *Fantasy* is a selection of the most popular tunes from *Carmen*, with little attempt made to stitch the seams between them. Played like this on EMI, with superb panache, luscious tone and glorious recording, the piece almost upstages the concerto with which it is coupled. The recording balance is admirable, with the quality greatly to be preferred to many of Perlman's more recent digital records.

As can be seen, Perlman has re-recorded the work in a fine new digital version and it is generously coupled with other famous showpieces. The new performance is beyond criticism – but the earlier one is just that bit riper and more beguiling.

Sarum Chant

Missa in gallicantu; Hymns: A solis ortus cardine; Christe Redemptor omnium; Salvator mundi, Domine; Veni Redemptor omnium.
*** Gimell Dig. CDGIM 017 [id.]. Tallis Scholars, Peter Phillips.

Filling in our knowledge of early church music, the Tallis Scholars under Peter Phillips here present a whole disc of chant according to the Salisbury rite – in other words *Sarum chant* – which, rather than the regular Gregorian style, was what churchgoers of the Tudor period and earlier in England heard at their devotions. The greater part of the record is given over to the setting of the First Mass of Christmas, intriguingly entitled *Missa in gallicantu* or *Mass at cock-crow*. Though this is simply monophonic, the men's voices alone are used, it is surprising what antiphonal variety there is. The record is completed with four hymns from the Divine Offices of Christmas Day. Ivan Moody's note helpfully presents the background of church practice from the thirteenth century through to the abandonment of the Latin rite in England. The record is warmly atmospheric in the characteristic Gimell manner.

Satie, Erik (1866-1925)

Les Aventures de Mercure (ballet); *La belle excentrique: Grand ritournelle. 5 Grimaces pour Un songe d'une nuit d'été; Parade* (ballet); *Relâche* (ballet).
(B) **(*) Van. VECD 7527 [id.]. Utah SO, Maurice Abravanel.

A generous bargain collection of Satie's orchestral music, well played and given full, vivid recording from the beginning of the 1970s. The Utah Symphony Orchestra made a number of adventurous excursions into European repertoire at that time and, if Abravanel fails to throw off some of the more pointed music with a fully idiomatic lightness of touch, these are still enjoyable performances; the ballet scores have plenty of colour and rhythmic life.

Gymnopédies Nos. 1 and 3 (orch. Debussy); *Relâche; Parade; Gnossiennes No. 3* (orch. Poulenc); *La belle excentrique; 5 grimaces pour le songe d'une nuit d'été* (orch. Milhaud).
**(*) EMI Dig. CDC7 49471-2 [id.]. Toulouse Capitole O, Plasson.

Plasson gets sensitive and lively performances from the Toulouse orchestra, though in *Parade* they do not have quite the same circus spirit and abandon as did the LSO for Dorati in the 1960s. However, few collectors will quarrel with these performances and the music has much *gamin*-like charm. Moreover this is better than many recent recordings from the Salle aux Grains in Toulouse; detail is more transparent and the textures somewhat better observed.

Parade (ballet after Jean Cocteau).
(*) Sup. Dig. SUP 001519 [id.]. Czech PO, Válek – MILHAUD: *Le boeuf sur le toit*; POULENC: *Les Biches.*(*)

Parade was written for the Diaghilev company and reflects Satie's enthusiasm for the circus and its music. Satie's surrealist score is well presented here and the special effects come off well enough. The special attraction of this Supraphon issue is its appropriate couplings, another Diaghilev ballet plus Milhaud's engaging *Le boeuf sur le toit*.

PIANO MUSIC

Avant-dernières pensées. Chapitres tournés en tous sens. Croquis et agaceries d'un gros bonhomme en bois; Descriptions automatiques; Deux rêveries nocturnes; Heures séculaires et instantanées; Nocturnes Nos. 1-3, 5; Nouvelles pièces froides; Pièces froides; Prélude de la porte héroïque du ciel. Les trois valses distinguées d'un précieux dégoûté. Véritables préludes flasques.
*** Decca Dig. 421 713-2 [id.]. Pascal Rogé.

Pascal Rogé's first Satie recital (see below) was a great success; those who have it will need no prompting to invest in its successor. His choice of repertoire on this well-filled disc ranges from the Rose-Croix pieces through to the *Nocturnes* of 1919 (No. 4 was on the earlier disc). As with the earlier recital, his playing has an eloquence and charm that are altogether rather special, and the recorded sound is very good indeed though not quite as full and realistic as that which Virgin provide for Anne Queffélec.

Avant-dernières pensées. Chapitres tournés en tous sens; Embryons desséchés; 6 Gnossiennes; 3 Gymnopédies; Heures séculaires et instantanées; Je te veux; Le Picadilly; Sonatine bureaucratique; Sports et divertissements; Pièces froides; Véritables préludes flasques; Vieux séquins et vieilles cuirasses.
*** Virgin Dig. VC 790754-2 [id.]. Anne Queffélec.

Anne Queffélec is exceptionally well served by the engineers, who produce as good a piano sound as any to have appeared on CD: it is firm, clean and fresh with a splendid tonal bloom. Their dedication is not misplaced, for her playing has great tonal subtlety and character. With the exception of the celebrated *Gnossiennes* and *Gymnopédies*, most of the music dates from the period of the First World War and is dispatched with great character and style. Nor does she possess less charm than Pascal Rogé. A most delightful issue.

Avant-dernières pensées; Croquis et agaceries d'un gros bonhomme en bois; Descriptions automatiques; 3 Gnossiennes; 3 Gymnopédies; Nocturne No. 1; Valses chantées: Je te veux; Poudre d'or. 3 Valses distinguées du précieux dégoûté.
(b) **(*) CBS MYK 45505 [id.]. Philippe Entremont.

Entremont's tempi tend to be on the slow side, and the gentler pieces have a grave melancholy and a dark colour which is very affecting. He finds plenty of wit in the picaresque items and, although the *Valses chantées* could perhaps have a lighter rhythmic touch, this is still distinctive playing. The CBS recording is modern and attractively full in timbre.

Avant-dernières pensées; Embryons desséchés; Fantaisie-Valse; 3 Gnossiennes; 3 Gymnopédies; Jack-in-the-Box; Je te veux; Le Picadilly; Poudre d'or; Prélude en tapisserie; Sports et divertissements; Les trois valses distinguées du précieux dégoûté; Valse-ballet.
(m) ** CD-EMX 9507. Angela Brownridge.

The fun of Satie is well represented in Angela Brownridge's collection. It is sensitively arranged as a programme to have *Gymnopédies* and *Gnossiennes* alternating with the lighter pieces echoing popular music. The playing is bright and stylish, sensitively reflecting the sharply changing moods and lacking only the last touches of poetry.

Avant-dernières pensées; Embryons desséchés; 6 Gnossiennes; 3 Gymnopédies; Pièces froides; Sarabande No. 3; Sonatine bureaucratique; 3 Valses distinguées du précieux dégoûté; 3 véritables préludes flasques (pour un chien).

*** BIS Dig. CD 317 [id.]. Roland Pöntinen.

Roland Pöntinen is a young Swedish pianist, still in his early twenties when this recording was made. He seems perfectly in tune with the Satiean world, and his playing is distinguished by great sensibility and tonal finesse. He is very well recorded too.

Chapitres tournés en tous sens; Croquis et agaceries d'un gros bonhomme en bois; Gnossiennes Nos. 2 and 4; 3 Gymnopédies; Heures séculaires et instantanées; Nocturnes Nos. 2 and 4; Nouvelles pièces froides; Passacaille; Le Piège de Méduse; Prélude No. 2 (Le Fils des étoiles); Sonatine bureaucratique.
(B) ** CfP CD-CFP 4329. Lawson.

Satie's deceptively simple piano writing has to be played with great sensitivity and subtlety, if justice is to be done to its special qualities of melancholy and irony. Peter Lawson's recital opens with the famous *Gymnopédies*, played coolly but not ineffectively. The highlight is a perceptive and articulate characterization of *Le Piège de Méduse*, seven epigrammatic *morceaux de concert*. Elsewhere his way is quietly tasteful, and though he catches something of Satie's gentle and wayward poetry he is less successful in revealing the underlying sense of fantasy. Good recording.

Danses gothiques; 6 Gnossiennes; Petite ouverture à danser; Prélude de la porte héroïque du ciel.
**(*) Ph. Dig. 412 243-2 [id.]. Reinbert de Leeuw.

Pièces froides; 4 Préludes; Prière; Sonneries de la rose et croix.
(M) **(*) Ph. 420 473-2 [id.]. Reinbert de Leeuw.

Reinbert de Leeuw is a sensitive player and thoroughly attuned to Satie's sensibility. He takes the composer at his word by playing many of the pieces *très lente*; indeed, he overdoes this at times, though this impression may be caused by listening to too much slow music all at once. There is no doubt that the playing creates and maintains a mood of poetic melancholy; this is helped by the beautiful recorded quality, so very effective on compact disc. As can be seen, the second of the two discs is offered at mid-price.

Embryons desséchés; 6 Gnossiennes; 3 Gymnopédies; Heures séculaires et instantanées; Nocturnes Nos. 1-5; Sonatine bureaucratique; Sports et divertissements.
*** Hyp. Dig. CDA 66344 [id.]. Yitkin Seow.

The Singapore-born pianist Yitkin Seow is a good stylist; his approach is fresh and his playing crisp and marked by consistent beauty of sound. Seow captures the melancholy of the *Gymnopédies* very well and the playing, though not superior to Rogé or Queffélec in character or charm, has a quiet reticence that is well suited to this repertoire. The recording is eminently truthful.

Embryons desséchés; 6 Gnossiennes; 3 Gymnopédies; Je te veux; Nocturne No. 4; Le Picadilly; 4 Préludes flasques; Prélude en tapisserie; Sonatine bureaucratique; Vieux séquins et vieilles cuirasses.
*** Decca Dig. 410 220-2. Pascal Rogé.

Rogé has real feeling for this repertoire and conveys its bitter-sweet quality and its grave melancholy as well as he does its lighter qualities. He produces, as usual, consistent beauty of tone, and this is well projected by the recording. Very well recorded, this remains the primary recommendation on CD for this repertoire, together with its companion above – although Anne Queffélec's recital (even more vividly recorded) should also be considered.

Saxton, Robert (born 1953)

Chamber symphony (Circles of light); Concerto for orchestra; The Ring of eternity; The Sentinel of the rainbow.
*** EMI Dig. CDC7 49915-2. BBC SO or L. Sinf., Knussen.

Robert Saxton is one of the most immediately communicative of the younger generation of British composers, using the orchestra with a panache that plainly reflects his own pleasure in rich and colourful sound. These four works, all written between 1983 and 1986, bring fine examples, notably the *Concerto for orchestra*, first given at the Proms in 1984. Its four linked sections broadly follow a symphonic shape, as do those of the *Chamber symphony* of 1986, which uses smaller forces, with solo strings. That later work has the title *Circles of light* and was inspired by a quotation from Dante, when in the *Divine Comedy* he looks into the eyes of his beloved, Beatrice, and links what he sees to the movement of the heavens. The other two works, both lasting around 15 minutes, also have evocative titles and are linked in the composer's mind to the *Concerto for orchestra* to form a sort of trilogy. Oliver Knussen draws intense, committed playing both from the BBC Symphony Orchestra in the *Concerto for orchestra* and *The Ring of eternity*, and from the London Sinfonietta in the chamber-scale works. Full, warm recording.

Scarlatti, Alessandro (1660-1725)

Sinfonie di concerti grossi Nos. 1-6.
*** Ph. Dig. 400 017-2 [id.]. Bennett, Lenore, Smith, Soustrot, Elhorst, I Musici.

These performances are taken from the complete set of twelve. All are elegantly and stylishly played. All are scored for flute and strings; in No. 2 there is a trumpet as well, in No. 5 an oboe and in Nos. 1 and 5 a second flute. No complaints about the performances, which are lively and attractive and eminently well recorded. The harpsichord is a little reticent, even on CD; but few will fail to derive pleasure from the music-making here.

Dixit Dominus.
*** DG Dig. 423 386-2 [id.]. Argenta, Attrot, Denley, Ashley Stafford, Varcoe, Ch. & E. Concert, Pinnock – VIVALDI: *Gloria.****

Of the four settings of *Dixit Dominus* (Psalm 107) that Alessandro Scarlatti composed, the one chosen by Trevor Pinnock has until now been the least well known. Pinnock, as so often, inspires his performers to sing and play as though at a live event. This Scarlatti Psalm-setting, very well recorded, makes an attractive coupling for the better known of Vivaldi's settings of the *Gloria*.

La Giuditta (oratorio).
*** Hung. Dig. HCD 12910 [id.]. Zadori, Gemes, Gregor, Minter, De Mey, Capella Savaria, McGegan.

La Giuditta, telling the biblical story of Judith, is a fascinating example of pre-Handelian oratorio as it was developing in Italy at the end of the seventeenth century. Nicholas McGegan, who has made several successful period-performance recordings for Hungaroton, here directs a fresh and stylish account, with three Hungarian principals joined by the soft-grained but agile American counter-tenor, Drew Minter, as Holofernes, and the excellent French tenor, Guy de Mey, as the Captain. The two main principals, Maria Zadori as Judith and Katalin Gemes as Prince Ozias, both have attractively bright, clear voices. Very well recorded in clean, immediate sound and with libretto and notes included in the package, it makes a most attractive disc, generously filled.

Scarlatti, Domenico (1685-1757)

Keyboard sonatas: Kk.7, 33, 49, 54, 87, 96, 105-7, 159, 175, 206-7, 240-41, 347-8, 380-81, 441-4, 518-19, 524-5.
*** HM HMC90 1164/5 [id.]. Rafael Puyana (harpsichord).

Rafael Puyana gives eminently red-blooded performances of these *Sonatas*, which are refreshing and invigorating, very much in the robust fashion of Landowska, though not always with quite the fiery imagination she brought to bear on them. Where appropriate, he presents them in pairs, as recommended by Kirkpatrick. He uses a three-manual harpsichord from 1740 by Hass of Hamburg, restored by Andrea Goble, which makes a splendidly rich sound, present and lively. Authoritative playing, though he tends, with some exceptions, to concentrate on the more outgoing and brilliant rather than the inward-looking *Sonatas*.

Keyboard sonatas: Kk. 9, 206, 259-60, 308-9, 394-5, 402-3, 429-30, 446, 460-1.
(M) *** Ph. 422 496-2 [id.]. Blandine Verlet (harpsichord).

The *Sonatas* chosen here include some of the most sharply original, dark and even tragic, as well as brilliant, and include five pairs in the same key, authentically juxtaposed, slow against fast, and to bring playing of exceptional subtlety and point, with delightful harpsichord registration. This is among the most enjoyable records of Scarlatti sonatas in the catalogue, with admirable remastering for CD to bring a most realistic and suitably intimate result. But try the opening work (Kk. 430) and you will want to explore the whole recital.

Keyboard sonatas: Kk. 39, 54, 96, 146, 162, 198, 209, 332, 335, 380, 424, 455, 466, 474, 531, 525.
(M) (***) CBS MK 42410 [id.]. Vladimir Horowitz (piano).

Recorded at various times between 1962 and 1968, the playing is of extraordinary elegance and refinement, and Horowitz's virtuosity is altogether remarkable. Unfortunately the improvement in sound-quality is minimal: the timbre is still dry and papery – so the three stars are exclusively for the playing.

Keyboard sonatas, Kk. 46, 87, 99, 124, 201, 204a, 490-92, 513, 520-21.
*** CRD CRD 3368 [id.]. Trevor Pinnock (harpsichord).

No need to say much about this: the playing is first rate and the recording outstanding in its presence and clarity. There are few better anthologies of Scarlatti in the catalogue.

Keyboard sonatas: Kk. 115-16, 144, 175, 402-3, 449-50, 474-5, 513, 516-17, 544-5.
**(*) Decca Dig. 421 422-2 [id.]. András Schiff (piano).

Exquisite and sensitive playing, full of colour and delicacy. As always, András Schiff is highly responsive to the mood and character of each piece. At times one wonders whether he is not a little too refined: in some, one would have welcomed more abandon and fire. However, for the most part this is a delightful recital, and the Decca recording is exemplary in its truthfulness.

Keyboard sonatas, Kk. 460-61, 478-9, 502, 516-17, 518-19, 529, 544-5, 546-7.
** DG Dig. 419 632-2 [id.]. Trevor Pinnock (harpsichord).

The playing here is enormously fluent and brilliant, but it excites admiration rather than pleasure. Some of the *Sonatas* seem a bit over-driven, but the slightly relentless feel to the playing may be due to the recording, which reproduces at a thunderous level. To get a realistic playback level, the volume control has to be turned right down.

Stabat Mater.
*** Erato/WEA Dig. 2292 45219-2 [id.]. Monteverdi Ch., E. Bar. Soloists, Gardiner – Concert: *'Sacred choral music'.****

The *Stabat Mater* shows Scarlatti to be a considerable master of polyphony; though it falls off in interest towards the end, it still possesses eloquence and nobility – and it is far less bland than Pergolesi's setting. Gardiner's fine performance couples three motets of interest, by Cavalli, Gesualdo and Clément, which are also splendidly done. The recording is very good indeed, notably fresh in its CD format.

Schmidt, Franz (1874-1939)

Symphonies Nos. 1 in E; 2 in E flat; 3 in A; 4 in C min.
** Opus 9350 1851/4 [id.]. Bratislava RSO, Rajter.

These symphonies can be bought separately. The *First* is an early piece, dating from 1896-9 when the composer was in his twenties; it is derivative (Strauss, Bruckner, Wagner, etc.) but well held together. The *Second* comes from 1913 and includes a highly inventive variation movement: Schmidt was a master of this form. The *Third*, written in 1928, is lighter and at times Brahmsian in feeling; the *Fourth* (1932-3) is Schmidt's masterpiece, a work of great nobility and dignity with a strong elegiac feeling, not dissimilar, perhaps, to Suk's *Asrael*. Rajter was a pupil of Schmidt and he conducts all four with great devotion and sympathy. The Bratislava Radio Orchestra respond well – though they are not the Czech Philharmonic! Neither performance nor recording is three-star, but the music is most emphatically worth investigating.

Symphony No. 2 in E flat.
*** Chan. Dig. CHAN 8779 [id.]. Chicago SO, Järvi.

The *Second Symphony* owes much to Strauss and Reger. It calls for huge orchestral forces (five clarinets, eight horns, and so on) and if it is not as individual as his later works, like the noble *Fourth Symphony*, it shows the fertility of his invention and his command of the orchestra. (The writing for the wind is particularly felicitous.) The variations comprising the second movement are a little prolix, but by and large this is a rewarding piece with many hints of what is to come. The Chicago orchestra play magnificently for Järvi and are very well recorded. It enjoys a distinct lead over the rival version made in the town of his birth, Bratislava, under Lajos Rajter.

Variations on a Hussar's song.
⊛ (M) *** EMI CDM7 69840-2. New Philh. O, Bauer – BUSONI: *Sarabande and cortège*; LUTOSLAWSKI: *Postlude; Symphonic variations.**** ⊛

The *Hussar variations* is obviously the product of a fertile and exuberant imagination with something of Strauss's confidence and Reger's delicacy. Hans Bauer and the New Philharmonia Orchestra give a thoroughly persuasive account of the piece, and the recording is superb. The couplings make this a collection of quite exceptional interest and value which cannot be too strongly recommended.

Quintet in A for clarinet, piano and strings.
**(*) Preiser Dig. 93357 [id.]. Vienna Kammermusiker.

The *A major Quintet* was written with Paul Wittgenstein in mind; Wittgenstein had lost his right arm in the First World War and commissioned a number of works for the left hand. Its layout is strange: it begins like some mysterious other-worldly scherzo which immediately introduces a pastoral idea of beguiling charm. The second movement is a piano piece in ternary form; there is a longish scherzo, full of fantasy and wit, and there is an affecting trio, tinged with the melancholy of late Brahms. The fourth sets out as if it, too, is going to be a long, meditative piano piece, but its nobility and depth almost put one in mind of the Elgar *Quintet*. The performance is good and the clarinet playing is very imaginative. Though the overall balance is a shade synthetic, do not be deterred from acquiring this glorious work.

Das Buch mit sieben Siegeln (The Book with seven seals): oratorio.
**(*) Orpheus Dig. C 143862H (2). Schreier, Holl, Greenberg, Watkinson, Moser, Rydl, V. State Op. Ch., Austrian RSO, Zagrosek.

Das Buch mit sieben Siegeln has much music of substance and many moments of real inspiration. Peter Schreier's St John is one of the glories of this set, and there are fine contributions from some of the other soloists. This performance was recorded in the somewhat unappealing acoustic of the ORF studios and is wanting in the transparency that the score deserves. Detail is less vivid than it might be and the dynamic range is somewhat compressed; however, the sound is more than acceptable.

Schnittke, Alfred (born 1934)

Violin sonata No. 1; Sonata in the olden style.
*** Chan. Dig. CHAN 8343 [id.]. Dubinsky, Edlina – SHOSTAKOVICH: *Violin sonata.****

Schnittke's *First sonata* dates from 1963 when he was still in his late twenties; it is a well-argued piece that seems to unify his awareness of the post-serial musical world with the tradition of Shostakovich. On this version it is linked with a pastiche of less interest, dating from 1977. Excellent playing from both artists, and very good recording too.

Cello sonata.
*** BIS Dig. CD 336 [id.]. Torleif Thedéen, Roland Pöntinen – STRAVINSKY: *Suite italienne*; SHOSTAKOVICH: *Sonata.****
(*) Unicorn Dig. DKPCD 9083 [id.]. Alexander Baillie, Piers Lane – RACHMANINOV: *Cello sonata.*

The *Cello sonata* is a powerfully expressive piece, its avant-garde surface enshrining a neo-romantic soul. Torleif Thedéen is a refined and intelligent player who gives a thoroughly committed account of this piece with his countryman, Roland Pöntinen.

Alexander Baillie gives a thoughtful account of this *Sonata*, less intense perhaps but by no means less searching than is usually the case, and with interesting insights. Piers Lane has an imposing technique and is often sensitive, though his playing at forte or above can be ugly in a way he does not perhaps intend.

Schoeck, Othmar (1886-1957)

Cello concerto, Op. 61.
*** Claves Dig. D 8502 [id.]. Goritzki, Deutsche Kammerakademie Neuss – REGER: *Lyrisches Andante.****

The chamber-like scoring of the *Cello concerto* gives it a rather special, private quality and, although it has its longueurs, its atmosphere is at times strong and haunting. No doubt there is an over-reliance on sequence; however, there are times when a quiet voice speaks – and one with powerful resonances. The performance is sensitive and totally dedicated, and the recording is very natural.

Das Stille Leuchten, Op. 60.
**(*) Claves Dig. CD 50-8910 [id.]. Dietrich Fischer-Dieskau, Hartmut Höll.

Das Stille Leuchten (The Silent Light or Illumination) is an altogether magnificent work and, although this record is less than ideal, collectors should seek it out. Many of the 24 songs which make up the cycle are touching and some are really inspired. Like late Strauss, they often convey a feeling of regret at life's evanescence and are full of a resigned but poignant melancholy; yet at times they also bring a great variety and range of mood. Dietrich Fischer-Dieskau sings with all his old artistry and imagination, although the voice has now lost some of its bloom and colour. Hartmut Höll is an inspired pianist.

Schoenberg, Arnold (1874-1951)

Chamber symphony No. 1, Op. 9.
*** DG Dig. 423 307-2 [id.]. BPO, Sinopoli – MANZONI: *Mass.****

A fine performance of Schoenberg's Op. 9 from Sinopoli. He links it positively back to the high romanticism of Richard Strauss, with the Berlin Philharmonic producing glorious sounds. Full recording to match.

Chamber symphonies Nos. 1, Op. 9; 2, Op. 38; Verklärte Nacht.
*** DG Dig. 429 233-2 [id.]. Orpheus CO.

Excellent value from the Orpheus Chamber Orchestra who couple their fine account of *Verklärte Nacht* with the two *Chamber symphonies* of 1906 and 1939 respectively. Their *Verklärte Nacht* is swift-moving and a bit overheated; it does not have the subtle range of colouring and dynamics that marks the classic Karajan version. Both the *Chamber symphonies* come off well and the disc is worth acquiring solely for their sake. The *Second* is an underrated piece and the Orpheus play as if they believed in every note. A rather brightly lit but very good recording.

Chamber symphony No. 2, Op. 38; Verklaerte Nacht, Op. 4.
*** EMI Dig. CDC7 49057-2. ECO, Jeffrey Tate.

Jeffrey Tate is at his most persuasive with the ECO in both these Schoenberg works. He is masterly at pacing the span of *Verklaerte Nacht*, building warmly to the great passionate moments. The *Chamber symphony No. 2* is presented with comparably heartfelt warmth, and the rich ECO ensemble, well presented in radiant EMI sound, gives it necessary weight combined with ample clarity of detail.

Piano concerto, Op. 42.
(*) DG Dig. 427 771-2 [id.]. Maurizio Pollini, BPO, Abbado – SCHUMANN: *Piano concerto.*

Pollini is much more persuasive in the Schoenberg *Concerto* than in the Schumann, where he is a little remote. His account has all the pianistic mastery one would expect and much refinement of keyboard colour, but he is not helped by a rather claustrophobic recording that is wanting in real transparency. Abbado gives dedicated support and the Berlin orchestra play splendidly.

Pelleas und Melisande (symphonic poem), *Op. 5.*
*** DG 423 132-2 [id.]. BPO, Karajan – BERG: *Lyric suite: 3 Pieces.***
(*) Chan. Dig. CHAN 8619 [id.]. SNO, Bamert – WEBERN: *Passacaglia.*(*)

The Straussian opulence of Schoenberg's early symphonic poem has never been as ravishingly presented as by Karajan and the Berlin Philharmonic in this superbly recorded version. The gorgeous tapestry of sound is both rich and full of refinement and detail, while the thrust of argument is powerfully conveyed.

Matthias Bamert gives a finely shaped account that operates at a slightly lower emotional temperature than its distinguished rival, and is none the worse for that. The playing is admirable (though the strings are not, of course, in the same class as those of the Berlin Philharmonic for Karajan) and the sound is well blended, if a bit recessed.

Pelleas und Melisande, Op. 5; Variations for orchestra, Op. 31; Verklaerte Nacht (orchestral version), *Op. 4.*
(M) *** DG 427 424-2 (3) [id.]. BPO, Karajan – BERG: *Lyric suite; 3 Pieces;* WEBERN: *Collection.***

These are superb performances which present the emotional element at full power but give unequalled precision and refinement. *Pelleas und Melisande*, written at the same time as the Debussy opera but in ignorance of the rival project, is in its way a Strauss-like masterpiece, while the Op. 31 *Variations*, the most challenging of Schoenberg's orchestral works, here receives a reading which vividly conveys the ebb and flow of tension within the phrase and over the whole plan. Superb recording, excellently remastered.

5 Pieces for orchestra, Op. 16.
*** EMI Dig. CDC7 49857-2 [id.]. CBSO, Rattle – BERG: *Lulu: suite*; WEBERN: *6 Pieces.***
*** DG Dig. 419 781-2 [id.]. BPO, Levine – BERG: *3 Pieces*; WEBERN: *5 Pieces.***

Rattle and the CBSO give an outstanding reading of this Schoenberg masterpiece, bringing out its red-blooded strength, neither too austere nor too plushy. With sound of demonstration quality and an ideal coupling, it makes an outstanding recommendation, even over Levine's similar collection of equivalent masterpieces by other leaders of the Second Viennese School.

The colour and power of Schoenberg's Opus 16 *Pieces* come over superbly in Levine's purposeful, concentrated reading. This is an interpretation designed to relate Schoenberg to his predecessors rather than to the future. Warm, full-toned recording, with some spotlighting.

Variations for orchestra, Op. 31; Verklaerte Nacht, Op. 4.
⊛ *** DG 415 326-2 [id.]. BPO, Karajan.

Verklaerte Nacht, Op. 4.
(*) Decca Dig. 410 111-2 [id.]. ECO, Ashkenazy – WAGNER: *Siegfried idyll.**
** Decca Dig. 421 182-2 (2) [id.]. Berlin RSO, Chailly – MAHLER: *Symphony No. 10.***(*)

Karajan's version of *Verklaerte Nacht* is altogether magical and very much in a class of its own. There is a tremendous intensity and variety of tone and colour: the palette that the strings of the Berlin Philharmonic have at their command is altogether extraordinarily wide-ranging. Moreover on CD the sound is firmer and more cleanly defined.

Ashkenazy conducts an outstandingly warm and lyrical reading, one which brings out the melodic richness of this highly atmospheric work, with passionate playing from the ECO. Full and brilliant recording but with a degree of edge, not always quite comfortable on high violins.

Chailly's version is very well played and recorded, but is in no way distinctive.

(i) *Verklaerte Nacht, Op. 4* (string sextet version); *String trio, Op. 45.*
(M) ** DG 423 250-2 [id.]. LaSalle Qt; (i) with D. McInnes, J. Pegis.

For those who feel that Schoenberg's *Verklaerte Nacht* is best served by the version for solo strings, the LaSalle Quartet give a superbly efficient, virtuosic account with no lack of expressive feeling. At times they are inclined to rush things, but they are well – if rather too brightly – recorded; and the *String trio*, played with effortless mastery, makes a welcome coupling.

Die eiserne Brigade (march for string quartet and piano); (i) *Pierrot lunaire, Op. 21;* (ii) *Serenade, Op. 24* (for clarinet, bass clarinet, mandolin, guitar, violin, viola, cello and bass voice).
(M) *** Decca 425 626-2 [id.]. (i) Mary Thomas; (ii) Shirley-Quirk; L. Sinf., Atherton.

These performances derive from David Atherton's distinguished 1973 survey of Schoenberg's chamber music, including vocal works. *Pierrot Lunaire* is among the most incisive and dramatic yet recorded and, although not even these performers can make the humour of the *Serenade* anything but Teutonic, the performance remains compelling.

Ode to Napoleon.
** DG Dig. 415 982-2 [id.]. Kenneth Griffiths, LaSalle Qt – WEBERN: *Quintet* etc.***

Written in 1942, the *Ode to Napoleon* sets the words of Byron in Schoenbergian *Sprechstimme* as a heartfelt protest against Nazi tyranny. With hatred at its core, it represents the composer at his most deeply committed, and that bedrock of passion is strongly brought out in the playing of the pianist, Stefan Litwin, and the LaSalle Quartet; sadly, the declamation is harshly recorded in what sounds like another acoustic.

Piano music: *3 Pieces, Op. 11; 6 Small Pieces, Op. 19; 5 Pieces, Op. 23; 3 Pieces, Op. 33a & b; Suite, Op. 25.*
*** DG 423 249-2 [id.]. Maurizio Pollini.

This CD encompasses Schoenberg's complete piano music. Pollini plays with enormous authority and refinement of dynamic nuance and colour, making one perceive this music in a totally different light from other performers. He is accorded excellent sound (very slightly on the dry side), extremely clear and well defined.

Erwartung, Op. 17.
*** Decca Dig. 417 348-2 (2) [id.]. Anja Silja, VPO, Dohnányi – BERG: *Wozzeck.****

Schoenberg's searingly intense monodrama makes an apt and generous coupling for Dohnányi's excellent version of Berg's *Wozzeck*. As in the Berg, Silja is at her most passionately committed. The sound under pressure may be raw, but the self-tortured questionings of the central character come over grippingly, and the digital sound is exceptionally vivid.

Gurrelieder.
*** Ph. 412 511-2 (2) [id.]. McCracken, Norman, Troyanos, Arnold, Scown, Tanglewood Fest. Ch., Boston SO, Ozawa.

Ozawa directs a gloriously opulent reading of Schoenberg's *Gurrelieder*. The playing of the Boston Symphony has both warmth and polish and is set against a resonant acoustic; among the soloists, Jessye Norman gives a performance of radiant beauty, at times reminding one of Flagstad in the burnished glory of her tone-colours. As the wood-dove, Tatiana Troyanos sings most sensitively, though the vibrato is at times obtrusive; and James McCracken does better than most tenors at coping with a heroic vocal line without barking. The luxuriant textures are given a degree more transparency, with detail slightly clearer on CD.

Music for chorus: 2 Canons; 3 Canons, Op. 28; Dreimal Tausend Jähre, Op. 50a; Friede auf Erden, Op. 13; 3 Folksongs, Op. 49; 3 German folksongs; Kol Nidre, Op. 39; 4 Pieces, Op. 27; 6 Pieces, Op. 35; Psalm 130, Op. 50b; Modern Psalm No. 1, Op. 50 C; A Survivor from Warsaw, Op. 46.
(M)*** Sony S2K 44571 (2) [id.]. John Shirley-Quirk, Günther Reich, BBC Singers, BBC SO, Pierre Boulez.

This superb collection of choral music, recorded by CBS between 1976 and 1986, is issued here in a handsome two-disc package by Sony. Though *A Survivor from Warsaw*, vividly dramatic and atmospheric, was issued earlier in one of CBS's Schoenberg boxes, it is shocking that the rest has had to wait so long to reappear. With passionately committed performances from the BBC Singers, the result explodes any idea that Schoenberg was a cold composer. In his choral pieces, particularly when inspired by a Jewish theme, as in the magnificent *Kol Nidre* of 1938 for narrator, mixed chorus and orchestra, his full romanticism broke out. His adoption of an idiom far removed from abrasive atonality in most of these pieces makes this one of the most approachable of Schoenberg sets, with the use of a narrator in three of the works adding spice to the mixture. The early motet, *Friede auf Erden*, very taxing for the chorus, is here made to sound mellifluous, and only the little middle-period *Pieces*, Opp. 27 and 28, show anything like the full rigour of Schoenbergian argument. The later works, written in America, use twelve-note technique with astonishingly warm, rich results. First-rate recording over the series, all done in the BBC's Maida Vale Studio. There is an extended essay in German in the booklet, but regrettably only summaries of it in English, French and Italian, though translations are given of the full texts.

OPERA

Moses und Aron.
*** Decca Dig. 414 264-2 (2) [id.]. Mazura, Langridge, Bonney, Haugland, Chicago Ch. and SO, Solti.

Solti gives Schoenberg's masterly score a dynamism and warmth which set it firmly – if perhaps surprisingly – in the grand romantic tradition. Solti instructed his performers to 'play and sing as if you were performing Brahms', and here Solti's broad romantic treatment presents a reading which in its great variety of mood and pace underlines the drama, yet finds an element of fantasy and, in places – as in the *Golden Calf* episode – a sparkle such as you would never expect from Schoenberg. It is still not an easy work. The Moses of Franz Mazura may not be as specific in his sing-speech as was Gunter Reich in the two previous versions – far less sing than speech – but the characterization of an Old Testament patriarch is the more convincing. As Aaron, Philip Langridge is lighter and more lyrical, as well as more accurate, than his predecessor with Boulez, Richard Cassilly. Aage Haugland with his firm, dark bass makes his mark in the small role of the Priest; Barbara Bonney too is excellent as the Young Girl. Above all, the brilliant singing of the Chicago Symphony Chorus matches the playing of the orchestra in virtuosity. More than ever the question-mark concluding Act II makes a pointful close, with no feeling of a work unfinished. The brilliant recording has an even sharper focus on CD.

Schreker, Franz (1878–1934)

(i) *Chamber symphony for 23 solo instruments;* (ii) *Nachtstück;* (i) *Prelude to a drama;* (ii) *Valse lente.*
**(*) Koch Int. Dig. CD 311 078. Berlin RSO, (i) Gielen, (ii) Rickenbacher.

Schreker's *Chamber symphony* is quite magical, scored with great delicacy and feeling for colour. Perhaps it is slightly over-perfumed, but it is marvellously evocative and imaginative music. There are reminders of Debussy, Strauss, Szymanowski and Puccini, but there is still an individual personality here. The other works are not quite so seductive but they, too, have a heady art-nouveau atmosphere. A most rewarding disc, with good performances and very acceptable, though not out of the ordinary, recording. But don't miss this issue.

Der Schatzgräber (opera): complete.
**(*) Capriccio Dig. 60010-2 (2) [id.]. Protschka, Schnaut, Stamm, Haage, Hamburg State O, Gerd Albrecht.

Completed at the very end of the First World War, *Der Schatzgräber* (The treasure-digger) had phenomenal success in the six years following, being given in Germany and Austria many hundreds of times. The attractions of Schreker's sweet-sour treatment of a curious morality fairy-story then waned. Schreker was forced by the Nazis to resign from his Berlin posts in 1933, and he died the following year. In idiom the comedy scenes owe much to the Wagner of *Meistersinger,* only with fewer tunes. The love music is more freely lyrical, with Schreker giving his central character, Elis – a roving minstrel with magical powers – a series of charming ballads. In Act III, before the great night of love between Elis and the heroine, Els – an innkeeper's daughter with a knack for dispatching unwanted suitors – Schreker has the temerity to have her quote her mother's simple cradle-song, a moment almost too sweet for comfort, and maybe an indication that Freudian motivation had hardly entered the composer-librettist's mind, either there or elsewhere. This first recording was made live at the Hamburg State Opera in 1989, though there are very few signs of the audience's presence, with no applause, even at the end. Josef Protschka sings powerfully as Elis, hardly ever over-strenuous, but Gabriele Schnaut finds it hard to scale down her very bright and powerful soprano and seems happiest when she is scything your ears with loud and often unsteady top notes; yet she is certainly dramatic in this equivocal role. Outstanding among the others is Peter Haage as the court jester, who in the end is the only one to take pity on the disgraced Els, even though Elis is finally persuaded to sing a ballad as she dies. *Der Schatzgräber* may be hokum, but it is enjoyable hokum, and, with Albrecht drawing committed performances from the whole company, this well-made recording is most welcome.

Schröter, Johann (1752-88)

Piano concerto in C, Op. 3/3.
*** CBS Dig. MK 39222 [id.]. Murray Perahia, ECO – MOZART: *Piano concertos Nos. 1-3, K.107.****

Johann Samuel Schröter eventually succeeded J. C. Bach as music master to the queen in 1782, six years before his death. He was a highly accomplished pianist, and this sparkling little *Concerto* explains why he was so successful. Murray Perahia gives it all his care and attention without overloading it with sophistication. His account is delightful in every way, and beautifully recorded.

Schubert, Franz (1797–1828)

Konzertstücke in D, D.935; Polonaise in B flat, D.580; Rondo in A, D.438.
*** Ph. Dig. 420 168-2 [id.]. Zukerman, St Paul CO – BEETHOVEN: *Romances*; DVOŘÁK: *Romance.****

This was the nearest Schubert came to writing a violin concerto. The engaging *Polonaise* is used separately as a foil between Beethoven and Dvořák, while the *Konzertstücke* and *Rondo* are happily linked to round off a particularly satisfying collection of short concertante works for violin and orchestra.

Rondo in A, D.438.
*** EMI Dig. CDC7 49663-2 [id.]. Nigel Kennedy, ECO, Tate – BRUCH; MENDELSSOHN: *Concertos.****

The ideas in Schubert's *Rondo* may not be very memorable, but they flow very sweetly, making this an attractive bonus to the usual Bruch–Mendelssohn coupling, with Kennedy just as understanding as in the two concertos.

Rosamunde: Overture (Die Zauberharfe), D.644; Ballet music No. 2; Entr'actes Nos. 1 & 3, D.797.
(B) *** Ph. 426 071-2 [id.]. Concg. O, George Szell – MENDELSSOHN: *Midsummer Night's Dream.****

Those looking for a bargain coupling of Schubert and Mendelssohn could hardly do better than Szell's 1957 reissue, which sounds amazingly fresh. The orchestral playing is first class, the *Overture* has an engaging rhythmic spring, and the *Ballet* and *Entr'acte* match polish with charm. Recommended. A similar digital selection from the Chicago Symphony Orchestra under Levine at mid-price (DG Dig. 427 817-2) misses out the first *entr'acte* but offers instead Smetana's dances from *The Bartered Bride*. Despite the latter's more modern recording, the Szell collection is the more memorable.

Symphonies Nos. 1–7; 8 (Unfinished); 9 (Great).
**(*) DG 419 318-2 (4) [id.]. BPO, Boehm.

Boehm's recordings were made over a decade between 1963 and 1973. The Berlin Philharmonic plays with striking warmth and finesse throughout. Boehm does not always smile as often as Schubert's music demands, but he is always sympathetic. Certainly the Berlin wind are a joy to listen to in most of these symphonies, and in Nos. 6, 8 and 9

Boehm is the best of Schubertians. It is only in the early symphonies that he does not quite capture the youthful sparkle of these delightful scores, although in its way No. 1 is brightly and elegantly done. The remastered sound is remarkably fine, fresher and clearer and without loss of bloom. But this set is over-priced.

Symphonies Nos. 1–3; 4 (Tragic); 5–7; 8 (Unfinished); 9 in C (Great); 10 in D, D.936a; Symphonic fragments in D, D.615 and D.708a (completed and orch. Newbould).
*** Ph. Dig. 412 176-2 (6) [id.]. ASMF, Marriner.

Marriner's excellent set gathers together not only the eight symphonies of the regular canon but two more symphonies now 'realized', thanks to the work of Professor Brian Newbould of Hull University. For full measure, half a dozen fragments of other symphonic movements are also included, orchestrated by Professor Newbould. Those fragments include the four-movement outline of yet another symphony – Scherzo complete, other movements tantalizingly cut off in mid-flight. Newbould's No. 7 is based on a sketch which quickly lapsed into a single orchestral line, now devotedly filled out. That work proves less rewarding than 'No. 10', written in the last months of Schubert's life, well after the *Great C major*, which now appears to have been written a year or so earlier. The set brings sparkling examples of the Academy's work at its finest, while the bigger challenges of the *Unfinished* (here completed with Schubert's Scherzo filled out and the *Rosamunde B minor Entr'acte* used as finale) and the *Great C major* are splendidly taken. These are fresh, direct readings, making up in rhythmic vitality for any lack of weight. The recordings, all digital, present consistent refinement and undistractingly good balance.

Symphonies Nos. 1–6; 8–9; Grand Duo in C, D.812 (orch. Joachim); *Rosamunde overture (Die Zauberharfe), D.644.*
*** DG Dig. 423 651-2 (5) [id.]. COE, Abbado.

Abbado's is an outstanding set. Rarely has he made recordings of the central Viennese classics which find him so naturally sunny and warm in his expression. The playing of the Chamber Orchestra of Europe is both beautiful and deeply committed, consistently refined and elegant but with ample power when necessary. Speeds are often on the fast side but never feel breathless, and the recording is refined, with fine bloom on the string-sound. Textually too, the Abbado set takes precedence over its rivals. Abbado asked one of the orchestra, Stefano Mollo, to carry out research on the original source-material in Vienna for the symphonies not yet included in the *Neue Schubert-Ausgabe*. As a result of his work, there are certain fascinating differences from what we are used to. The slip-case holds the five CD jewel-cases with a separate booklet in each. They are now also available separately – see below.

Symphonies Nos 1–6; 8–9; Rosamunde: Overture and incidental music.
(M) **(*) RCA GD 60096 (5). Cologne RSO, Wand.

The freshness and bluff honesty of Gunter Wand in Schubert shines through all his performances. Now collected on five mid-price CDs, his cycle offers first-rate sound, engineered by West German Radio. Nos. 3, 5 and 6 as well as the *Rosamunde* music are the only digital recordings. Note that the Boehm and Karajan sets take only four mid-price CDs, but have no makeweight, and are less generous over repeats.

Symphonies Nos. 1 in D, D.82; 2 in B flat, D.125.
*** DG Dig. 423 652-2 [id.]. COE, Abbado.

The coupling of the two earliest *Symphonies* brings bright and sparkling performances, reflecting the youthful joy of both composer and players. Even when he adopts a brisk speed, as in the bouncing, one-in-a-bar account of the third-movement *Allegretto* of No. 1, Abbado brings out the sunny relaxation of the writing, most exhilaratingly of all in the light-hearted finales. The recording of both captures the refined playing of the COE very vividly.

Symphonies Nos. 3 in D, D.200; 4 in C min. (Tragic), D.417.
*** DG Dig. 423 653-2 [id.]. COE, Abbado.

Crisp, fast and light, No. 3 is given a delectable performance by Abbado, with the *Presto* finale taken at a hectic speed which all the same sounds bright and easy, not at all breathless. In No. 4, the *Tragic*, Abbado makes the slow C minor introduction bitingly mysterious before a clean, elegant *Allegro*, and with this conductor the other movements are also elegant and polished as well as strong. Textually, No. 4 is particularly interesting, when the scholarly revisions by Stefano Mollo, inspired by the conductor, not only bring the excision of misread diminuendo markings (giving new sharpness to the third movement in particular) but eliminate the extra bars in the slow movement which had been inserted originally by Brahms. The slow movement is outstandingly beautiful, with the oboe solo – presumably COE's Douglas Boyd – most tenderly expressive.

Symphonies Nos. 3 in D, D.200; 5 in B flat, D.485; Overture in C in the Italian style.
**(*) Nimbus Dig. NI 5172 [id.]. Hanover Band, Roy Goodman.

As in the Hanover Band's cycle of the Beethoven symphonies, Roy Goodman presents period performances of these two favourites among Schubert's earlier symphonies which are fresh, light and resilient. The *Overture in C* makes an attractive bonus on top of the regular coupling. The Nimbus recording is characteristically reverberant and the balance between strings and wind is less well judged than on many earlier recordings. But even with that balance, the sparkle of the performances in both *Symphonies* and *Overture* is most winning.

Symphonies Nos. 3 in D, D.200; 5 in B flat, D.485; 6 in C, D.589.
⊛ (M) *** EMI CDM7 69750-2 [id.]. RPO, Beecham.

Beecham's are magical performances in which every phrase breathes. There is no substitute for imaginative phrasing and each line is shaped with affection and spirit. The *Allegretto* of the *Third Symphony* is an absolute delight. The delicacy of the opening of the *Fifth* is matched by the simple lyrical beauty of the *Andante*, while few conductors have been as persuasive as Beecham in the *Sixth* 'little' *C major Symphony*. The rhythmic point and high spirits of the first movement and scherzo are irresistible, and the finale, taken rather more gently than usual, is wonderfully graceful and delectably sprung. The sound is now just a shade drier in Nos. 3 and 6 than in their last LP incarnation but is generally faithful and spacious. This is an indispensable record for all collections and a supreme bargain in the Schubert discography.

Symphonies Nos. 3 in D, D.200; 8 in B min. (Unfinished), D.759.
(B) *** Pickwick Dig. PCD 848 [MCA MCAD 25954]. City of L. Sinfonia, Hickox.
**(*) Hung. HCD 12616-2 [id.]. Budapest Fest. O, Ivan Fischer.
** DG Dig. 415 601-2 [id.]. VPO, Carlos Kleiber.

Hickox's coupling makes a first-rate bargain recommendation on the Pickwick label. These are fresh and direct readings, never putting a foot wrong, very well recorded, with a chamber orchestra sounding full and substantial. Others may find more individuality and charm, but the crisp resilience of the playing is consistently winning.

Ivan Fischer draws bright, clean performances from the players, often at rather brisk speeds – to the point of breathlessness in the finale of No. 3 – with detached articulation that at times recalls period performance. Even though there are more searching accounts of the *Unfinished*, it is pleasing to have an intimate view so finely detailed and deeply thoughtful. First-rate recording, rather drier than some from this source.

Carlos Kleiber is a refreshingly unpredictable conductor; sometimes, however, his imagination goes too far towards quirkiness, and that is certainly so in the slow movement of No. 3, which is rattled through jauntily at breakneck speed. The effect is bizarre even for an *Allegretto*, if quite charming. The Minuet too becomes a full-blooded Scherzo, and there is little rest in the outer movements. The *Unfinished* brings a more compelling performance, but there is unease in the first movement, where first and second subjects are not fully co-ordinated, the contrasts sounding a little forced. The recording brings out the brass sharply, and is of wide range.

Symphonies Nos. 4 in C min. (Tragic), D.417; 5 in B flat, D.485.
*** Ph. Dig. 410 045-2 [id.]. ASMF, Marriner.

Here the balance is not quite ideal in the relationship between wind and strings and the recording is not as clearly defined internally as one might expect. Nevertheless this remains a highly desirable issue, for the performances are among the finest in Marriner's series.

Symphony No. 5 in B flat, D.485.
(B) ** Pickwick Dig. PCD 819 [MCA MCAD 25845 with MOZART: *Symphony No. 40*]. O of St John's, Smith Square, Lubbock – HAYDN: *Symphony No. 49.***(*)

With tempi fractionally on the brisk side, Lubbock's pacing is nevertheless convincing; there is no want of character here, and the recording is first class; but ultimately this is not a performance to resonate in the memory, though the slow movement has grace. Very good sound, and the price is very competitive.

Symphonies Nos. 5 in B flat, D.485; 6 in C, D.589.
*** DG Dig. 423 654-2 [id.]. COE, Abbado.

Abbado has rarely sounded more relaxed and winning. He brings out the happy songfulness of the slow movements in these works, as well as the rhythmic resilience of the *Allegros*. As in No. 4, so also in No. 6 Abbado eliminates the extra bars added by Brahms in his original Schubert Edition. Excellent recording, with fine bloom and good, natural contrasts.

Symphonies Nos. 5 in B flat, D.485; 8 in B min. (Unfinished), D.759.
*** Decca Dig. 414 371-2 [id]. VPO, Solti.
(M) **(*) EMI CDM7 69016 [id.]. BPO, Karajan.
**(*) DG Dig. 427 645-2 [id.]. Concg. O, Bernstein.
(B) ** Decca 417 680-2 [id.]. VPO, Istvan Kertesz.
(B) ** Ph. 422 977-2 [id.]. Dresden State O, Sawallisch.

As with Solti's fresh, resilient and persuasive reading of the *Great C major* with the Vienna Philharmonic, his coupling of Nos. 5 and 8 brings one of his most felicitous recordings. There have been more charming versions of No. 5 but few that so beautifully combine freshness with refined polish. The *Unfinished* has Solti adopting measured speeds but with his refined manner keeping total concentration. Excellent recording.

Karajan's EMI coupling is taken from the complete cycle of Schubert symphonies which he recorded in the late 1970s. The performance of the *Unfinished* may lack the mystery and dark intensity of his DG recording of the work (see below), but both No. 5 and No. 8 here find Karajan at his freshest and least complicated.

Though there is some inconsistency between Bernstein's brisk and fresh treatment of fast movements and his spacious, moulded style in the two slow movements, these are distinguished performances, beautifully played and recorded, conveying well the tensions of live music-making. The first movement of the *Unfinished*, in sharp contrast with the *Andante*, is particularly brisk, making it much more clearly a sonata-form allegro than usual, with barely any easing for the lovely second-subject melody.

In the *B flat Symphony* Kertesz does not always find the smile in Schubert's writing, but the playing of the VPO is stylishly beyond reproach. The *Unfinished* was one of the finest of his cycle, spacious and unaffected. The recording, of good quality throughout, has a wider dynamic range here, so that the woodwind solos in the second movement tend to sound a little distant, yet the pianissimo at the opening immediately creates a degree of tension that is to be sustained throughout the performance.

Sawallisch offers a fresh, nicely judged performance of No. 5, which in some ways has more character than the Kertesz version. His slow tempi in the *Unfinished* are supported by eloquent orchestral playing and natural phrasing. Of its kind this is rewarding, and the remastering of the 1967 recording is very successful: the acoustic is a little dry, but the sound lacks neither colour nor warmth in the bass. Either of these two bargain couplings will give satisfaction; Sawallisch is the more consistent, Kertesz rather more individual in the *Unfinished*.

Symphony No. 8 in B min. (Unfinished), D.759.
⊛ (M) *** DG Dig. 427 818-2 [id.]. Philh. O, Sinopoli – SCHUMANN: *Symphony No. 3.****
⊛ *** DG Dig. 410 862-2 [id.]. Philh. O, Sinopoli – MENDELSSOHN: *Symphony No. 4.****
(B) *** DG 429 676-2 [id.]. BPO, Karajan – DVORÁK: *Symphony No. 9 (New World).****
(M) *** DG 415 848-2 [id.]. BPO, Karajan – MENDELSSOHN: *Symphony No. 4.****
(M) *** EMI CDM7 69227-2 [id.]. Philh. O, Karajan – BRAHMS: *Symphony No. 2.****
(M) (***) EMI mono CDM7 63398-2 [id.]. RPO, Beecham – BEETHOVEN: *Symphony No. 8;* MENDELSSOHN: *Symphony No. 4.*(***)
** Telarc Dig. CD 80090 [id.]. Cleveland O, Dohnányi – BEETHOVEN: *Symphony No. 8.***(*)

Symphony No. 8 (Unfinished); Rosamunde: Overture (Die Zauberharfe), D.644; Incidental music, D.797; Intermezzi in D, B flat & B min.; Ballets in G & B min.
(BB) ** Hung. White Label Dig. 15 527 [id.]. Budapest PO, János Kovacs.

Sinopoli secures the most ravishingly refined and beautiful playing; the orchestral blend, particularly of the woodwind and horns, is magical. It is a deeply concentrated reading of the *Unfinished*, bringing out much unexpected detail, with every phrase freshly turned in seamless spontaneity. The contrast, as Sinopoli sees it, is between the dark – yet never histrionic – tragedy of the first movement, relieved only partially by the lovely second subject, and the sunlight of the closing movement, giving an unforgettable, gentle radiance. The exposition repeat is observed, adding weight and substance. This takes its place among the recorded classics. The warmly atmospheric recording, made in Kingsway Hall, is very impressive. As well as the original coupling with Mendelssohn, this is also available at mid-price, coupled with a superb account of Schumann's *Rhenish symphony*.

Karajan's 1965 DG recording of the *Unfinished* sounds fresher still in remastered form, yet has not lost its fullness and warmth of bass response. Its merits of simplicity and directness are enhanced by the extraordinary polish of the orchestral playing, lighting up much that is often obscured. The first movement is extremely compelling in its atmosphere; the slow movement too brings tinglingly precise attack and a wonderful sense of drama. A superb bargain in its coupling with Dvořák's *New World symphony*.

Karajan's earlier *Unfinished* with the Philharmonia dates from the late 1950s. It is without any question a most beautiful account and the quality of the playing is remarkably fine.

Beecham's 1951 mono recording, borrowed from the CBS archives for one of the first issues in the Beecham Edition, brings a magical example of his work. Though the first movement is taken relatively fast, a genuine allegro, Beecham's moulding of phrase and line could hardly be more persuasive. The build-up during the development section is thrilling, with the rasp of trombones vividly caught; and the slow movement is sweet and spacious, even though the RPO strings are not at their purest. Coupled with the Beethoven and the Mendelssohn, it makes a generous issue at mid-price.

Kovacs's account on Hungaroton is not especially dramatic, with the tempi of the two movements very similar. But the orchestral playing is warm and quite spontaneous, and the *Rosamunde overture* has a strikingly graceful touch. This selection of incidental music is more generous than is usual with this coupling and it is well characterized. The digital sound is full and natural.

If Dohnányi's reading lacks a little in poetry and magic, it presents a fresh and direct view, beautifully played, but is treated to a rather less bright recording than one expects from Telarc.

Symphony No. 8 in B min. (Unfinished); Grand Duo in C, D.812 (orch. Joachim).
*** DG Dig. 423 655-2 [id.]. COE, Abbado.

Abbado's outstandingly refined and sensitive version comes with an unusual and valuable coupling, the orchestral arrangement of the piano-duet *Grand Duo* made by Joachim, once erroneously thought to be the missing *Symphony No. 7*. The second subject in the *Unfinished* brings some slightly obtrusive agogic hesitations at the beginning of each phrase; but with such responsive playing they quickly sound fresh and natural. Abbado's choice of speeds and crisp control of dramatic contrasts are exemplary, bringing out the sunshine of Schubert as well as the darkness.

Symphony No. 9 in C (Great), D.944.
*** Virgin Dig. VC 790708-2 [id.]. O of Age of Enlightenment, Mackerras.
*** Decca 400 082-2 [id.]. VPO, Solti.
**(*) EMI Dig. CDC7 49949-2. L. Classical Players, Norrington.
(M) *** DG 419 484-2 [id.]. Dresden State O, Boehm.
(M) *** EMI CDM7 69199-2 [id.]. LPO, Boult.
(M) **(*) Decca 425 957-2 [id.]. LSO, Josef Krips – SCHUMANN: *Symphony No. 4.***
**(*) DG 427 646-2 [id.]. Concg. O, Bernstein.
**(*) Lodia Dig. LO-CD 788 [id.]. RPO, Carlos Païta.
(B) **(*) CBS MYK 44828 [id.]. Columbia SO, Bruno Walter.
**(*) EMI Dig. CDC7 47478-2 [id.]. Dresden State O, Tate.
**(*) Nimbus Dig. NI 5222 [id.]. Hanover Band, Roy Goodman.
(M) (**) DG mono 427 781-2 [id.]. BPO, Furtwängler (with WEBER: *Der Freischütz overture*(**)).

Symphony No. 9 in C (Great); Rosamunde: Overture (Die Zauberharfe), D.644.
*** DG Dig. 423 656-2 [id.]. COE, Abbado.
(M) (***) DG mono 427 405-2 [id.]. BPO, Furtwängler.

Though the COE is by definition an orchestra of chamber scale, the weight of Abbado's version, taken from his complete cycle, is ample, while allowing extra detail to be heard, thanks also to the orchestra's outstandingly crisp ensemble. Speeds are very well chosen, and the expressive detail is consistently made to sound natural. This version is important too for including textual amendments, following the scholarly researches of one of the players, Stefano Mollo. There is a striking difference in the middle of the oboe melody of the first subject in the slow movement, and the scherzo has four extra bars that were originally cut by Brahms in his early edition. The sound is beautifully refined, to match the point and polish of the playing. The *Rosamunde* (*Zauberharfe*) *overture* makes a valuable and generous fill-up.

In the first recording to use period instruments, Sir Charles Mackerras and the Orchestra of the Age of Enlightenment on the Virgin Classics label give a winning performance, one that will delight both those who prefer conventional performance and devotees of the new authenticity. The characterful rasp and bite of period brass instruments and the crisp attack of timpani are much more striking than any thinness of string tone. It is a performance of outstanding freshness and resilience. Except in the first-movement allegro, speeds are on the fast side, with characteristically light, clean articulation, and with rhythms delectably sprung, making for extra clarity. With every single repeat observed, the heavenly length is joyfully as well as powerfully sustained, and the warm, atmospheric recording gives a fine sense of presence.

Sir George Solti is not the first conductor one thinks of as a Schubertian, but the *Great C major symphony* prompted him to one of the happiest and most glowing of all his many records, an outstanding version, beautifully paced and sprung in all four movements and superbly played and recorded. It has drama as well as lyrical feeling, but above all it has a natural sense of spontaneity and freshness, beautifully caught by the richly balanced recording, confirming the Vienna Sofiensaal as an ideal recording location.

Furtwängler, too, gives the *Great C major* a glowing performance, if a highly individual one. The first movement brings an outstanding example of his wizardry, when he takes the recapitulation at quite a different speed from the exposition and still makes it sound convincing. In the *Andante*, his very slow tempo is yet made resilient by fine rhythmic pointing. Furtwängler springs the main allegro with an attractive jauntiness. No apologies need be made for the sound in the *Symphony*, made in the Jesus Christ Church in West Berlin. *Rosamunde* is not so well recorded as the *Symphony*, the effect boxier, though clear enough.

Roger Norrington's version is by far the most provocative of the period-performance versions of the *Great C major*, presenting the same sort of challenge in very fast speeds that one finds in his Beethoven, but this time without the backing-up of metronome markings, when Schubert was never able to prepare or hear a performance. Here again, the surprise is quickly modified, and one simply enjoys with new ears. The first movement brings splendid snap and swagger, exhilaratingly presented with Mendelssohnian lightness. But it will take most listeners some time to adjust to the total absence of the usual slowings in the final coda, which here sounds perfunctory. Yet in his crisp, brisk reading of the slow movement Norrington does allow himself a relaxation in the cello melody after the big climax, rightly so. Only in the finale is the speed relatively conventional, with triplets clarified. The Mackerras version with the Orchestra of the Age of Enlightenment on Virgin remains a safer choice of period performance, but those who have enjoyed Norrington in Beethoven may well prefer this, with its challenge made sharper by the recording. All repeats are observed, even those in the da capo return of the Scherzo.

Boehm's Dresden performance is more volatile than the glowing one included in his cycle of the Schubert symphonies, with a notable relaxation for the second subject in the first movement and extreme slowing before the end. The slow movement is fastish, with dotted rhythms crisply pointed and a marked slowing for the cello theme after the great dissonant climax. The Scherzo is sunny and lilting, the finale fierce and fast. It may not be quite as immaculate as the studio-recorded version, but it is equally a superb document of Boehm's mastery as a Schubertian, and the recording, though a little edgy on brass, has fine range.

A splendidly wise and magisterial account from the doyen of British conductors. Sir Adrian's tendency to understate is evident in the slow movement, just as his feeling for the overall design is undiminished. The LPO respond with playing of high quality, and the EMI engineers have produced good results too. An eminently sound recommendation alongside Boehm's at mid-price.

Josef Krips never made a finer record than his 1956 account of Schubert's *Great C major*. The performance has a direct, unforced spontaneity which shows Krips' natural feeling for Schubertian lyricism at its most engaging. The playing is polished yet flexible, strong without ever sounding aggressive. In the final two movements Krips finds an airy exhilaration which makes one wonder how other conductors can ever keep the music earthbound as they do. The pointing of the Trio in the scherzo is delectable, and the feathery lightness of the triplets in the finale makes one positively welcome every one of its many repetitions. As a whole, this reading represents the Viennese tradition at its finest. The recording, outstanding in its day, retains the glowing bloom over the orchestra; but the remastering has, alas, brought a degree of stridency to fortissimos.

Bernstein's speeds are on the fast side, and it is typical of the superb playing that he draws from the Concertgebouw that the *sempre piano* of the recapitulation has exceptional delicacy. The slow movement is fast and cleanly articulated, the scherzo tough rather than charming, and the finale brings exceptionally crisp articulation of triplets. Exposition repeats are omitted in the outer movements, as well as the second repeat in the scherzo. Full, warm recording, with a keener sense of presence than in Bernstein's Vienna recordings, also done live.

Brightly and forwardly recorded, like his comparable coupling of Dvorak's *Eighth* and *Ninth Symphonies*, Païta's reading is vibrant, with a strong forward momentum. This applies to the first movement in particular, where the coda is the culminating point of a particularly thrustful reading and must be one of the swiftest on record. The slow movement has more repose, but the feeling of vitality persists through the scherzo into the finale, which is pressed home exhilaratingly. Anyone who normally finds longueurs in this work should enjoy this, for it is nothing if not exhilarating.

Bruno Walter's 1959 CBS recording has been impressively enhanced on CD; the warm ambience of the sound – yet with no lack of rasp on the trombones – seems ideal for his very relaxed reading. The performance has less grip than Furtwängler's, while Solti shows greater spontaneity; but in the gentler passages there are many indications of Walter's mastery, not least in the lovely playing at the introduction of the second subject of the *Andante*. There is much to admire, even if this never quite achieves the distinction of the conductor's earlier recordings of this symphony.

Jeffrey Tate with the Dresden State Orchestra takes a rugged and spacious view. His choice of speeds, on the slow side, encourages a steadier pulse, with traditional, unmarked variations of tempo generally avoided. With all repeats observed, the ruggedness may be too much for some, when the finale for example is grimmer and less smiling than usual. Also the horn solo at the very start has rather wide vibrato. Otherwise the Dresden playing is characteristically refined and strong, given a pleasant bloom by the warm, helpful recording.

Goodman's Hanover Band version follows the pattern set by the two earlier discs issued in their Schubert series. Speeds are faster than is traditional with modern-instrument performances but, with warmly reverberant sound giving weight to the ensemble, the result is unlikely to shock traditionalists, and everyone will relish the clarity of violin articulation and the fat sound of the natural horns. Remember that the price of this Nimbus issue is marginally less than that of the direct rivals, though the sound is not so clear in tuttis.

It is fascinating to compare Furtwängler's wartime live account of the *Great C major* with his classic studio recording of several years later. With faster speeds and a more unsettled manner, it is not so warmly appealing but still provides an intriguing view of the master at work. The Weber *Overture* is a good alternative coupling; but in terms of sound the later version is much preferable and a much stronger recommendation for the non-specialist collector.

CHAMBER AND INSTRUMENTAL MUSIC

Arpeggione sonata, D.821 (arr. for cello).
*** Ph. Dig. 412 230-2 [id.]. Maisky, Argerich – SCHUMANN: *Fantasiestücke* etc.***
(M) *** RCA GD 86531 [RCA 6531-2-RG]. Lynn Harrell, James Levine – DVOŘÁK: *Cello concerto.***
(*) Decca 417 833-2 [id.]. Rostropovich, Britten – DEBUSSY: *Sonata*; SCHUMANN: *5 Stücke.*
* RCA Dig. RD 87845 [7845-2-RC]. Ofra Harnoy, Michael Dussek – PROKOFIEV: *Cello sonata.**

The *Arpeggione* enjoyed too brief a life for it to have an extensive literature, and Schubert's *Sonata* is about the only work written for it that survives in the repertoire. Mischa Maisky and Martha Argerich make much more of it than any of their rivals. Their approach may be relaxed, but they bring much pleasure through their variety of colour and sensitivity. The Philips recording is in the very best traditions of the house.

Lynn Harrell's account of the *Arpeggione* with James Levine makes an excellent medium-price choice. He is refreshingly unmannered and yet full of personality. Vital, sensitive playing excellently recorded, though the digitally remastered sound is rather light in bass.

Rostropovich gives a curiously self-indulgent interpretation of Schubert's slight but amiable *Arpeggione sonata*. However, the record is particularly valuable for the sake of the couplings.

Ofra Harnoy and Michael Dussek are handicapped by a somewhat unglamorous recording acoustic, though it seems less unflattering a balance than in the Prokofiev with which it comes. The cellist produces a refined and generally well-focused tone and the pianist is a sensitive and supportive artist. Yet the playing is curiously listless, as if they are recording in a heatwave! It offers little serious competition to the abundance of rivals that the catalogue boasts.

Arpeggione sonata, D.821 (arr. in G min. for clarinet & piano).
*** Chan. Dig. CHAN 8566 [id.]. Gervase de Peyer, Gwenneth Pryor – SCHUMANN: *Fantasiestücke; 3 Romances*; WEBER: *Silvana variations.***

So persuasive is the performance of Gervase de Peyer and Gwenneth Pryor that the listener is all but persuaded that the work was actually written for this combination. With rich timbre and affectionate phrasing, de Peyer brings out all its Schubertian charm. He is beautifully recorded.

Arpeggione sonata in A min. (arr. for flute); *Introduction and variations on Trock'ne Blumen* from *Die schöne Müllerin; Schwanengesang: Ständchen, D.957/4.*
**(*) RCA Dig. RD 70421. James Galway, Phillip Moll.

The *Arpeggione sonata* also transcribes surprisingly well for the flute and is played with skill and some charm by this partnership. The *Introduction and variations on Trock'ne Blumen* are as neatly played. Not distinctive, but a pleasing and well-recorded recital.

Octet in F, D.803.
*** Chan. Dig. CHAN 8585 [id.]. ASMF Chamber Ens.
*** O-L Dig. 425 519-2 [id.]. AAM Chamber Ens.
*** ASV Dig. CDDCA 694 [id.]. Gaudier Ensemble.
*** Teldec/WEA Dig. 2292 44195-2 [id.]. Berlin Soloists.
*** Ph. 416 497-2 [id.]. ASMF Chamber Ens.
(M) ** Decca 421 155-2 [id.]. Vienna Octet – MOZART: *Divertimento No. 7.***(*)
** DG Dig. 423 367-2 [id.]. Kremer, Van Keulen, Zimmermann, Geringas, Posch, Brunner, Vlatkovič, Thunemann.

Octet in F, D.803; (i) *Adagio and Rondo concertante in F, D.487.*
(M) *** EMI CDM7 69420-2. Melos Ens., (i) with Lamar Crowson.

The new Chandos version brings a performance just as delightful as the earlier one by the ASMF, less classical in style, a degree freer in expression, with Viennese overtones brought out in Schubert's sunny invention. In the *Adagio*, Andrew Marriner's clarinet solo is most delicately floated, and the dance rhythms of other movements are delightfully pointed, leading to a strong and urgent account of the finale. It has the benefit of excellent modern digital sound, cleaner on detail than before. The older version by this group remains very attractive, if now overpriced; everything is vital, yet polished and sensitive. The analogue recording is smoothly realistic.

Recorded in 1967, the Melos Ensemble's version of the *Octet* remains among the very finest ever made, full of individuality – as in Gervase de Peyer's inspired clarinet playing – but satisfyingly natural and spontaneous in expression. Now coupled with a much rarer work, the *Adagio and Rondo concertante* (Lamar Crowson the excellent pianist), it makes an outstanding choice, when the recording – closer and less reverberant than in most modern versions – reproduces very realistically.

The Academy's Chamber Ensemble using period instruments brings out the open joyfulness of Schubert's inspiration, with excellent matching and vivid recording. The reading is not at all stiff or pedantic, but personal and relaxed, with the clarinettist, Antony Pay, the obvious leader, playing his solos with yearning beauty, notably in the second-movement *Andante*, which has heavenly gentleness and repose. Lightness is the keynote, with speeds never eccentrically fast.

The Gaudier Ensemble come from the front desks of the Chamber Orchestra of Europe and the ECO, and they take their name from the brilliant French sculptor, Henri Gaudier-Brzeska, killed at the age of 25 in the First World War. They give an entirely winning account of the *Octet*, essentially spontaneous yet very relaxed and catching all the ingenuous Schubertian charm. Richard Hosford, the clarinettist, plays very gently indeed in his lovely solo which opens the *Adagio*, yet he contributes some marvellously exuberant roulades to the finale, which opens with an operatic sense of drama and then chortles along infectiously, capping the easy style of the whole performance. Excellent sound, vivid yet well balanced within a pleasing acoustic which gives a feeling of intimacy. An ideal record for a warm summer evening.

The Berlin Soloists give a strong and stylish performance which, on a bigger scale than most, designedly brings out the symphonic power of a piece lasting over an hour. Every single repeat is observed, and with such distinguished playing that length is readily sustained. This is very well characterized, not just in the big, symphonic movements but in the charming *Andante variations* too. Though the sound is not always ideally sweet on string-tone, the recording is full and clear.

The Decca record dates from as early as 1956, and while the stereo with its clean separation was always impressive, there is a thinness to the violin timbre that betrays the age of the recording. The performance has the glow of the Vienna Octet at its peak under the leadership of Willi Boskovsky, and the horn has a Viennese fruitiness to make the sound that much more authentic. The digital remastering adds clarity of focus but tends to draw the ear to the thinness of the violin timbre.

The DG version was recorded during a series of live performances and the playing communicates strongly. The only snag is in the finale, where the pacing tends to let the music seem too leisurely and there is not enough rhythmic lift in the playing to compensate.

Piano quintet in A (Trout), D.667.
*** Decca Dig. 411 975-2 [id.]. András Schiff, Hagen Qt.
*** Ph. 400 078-2 [id.]. Brendel, Cleveland Qt.
(B) ** Van. VCD 72004 [id.]. Peter Serkin, Schneider Ens. – MOZART: *Piano quartet, K.493.***
(M) ** Ph. 420 716-2 [id.]. Beaux Arts Trio (augmented) – BEETHOVEN: *Piano trio No. 5 (Ghost).***

Piano quintet in A (Trout), D.667; Adagio & Rondo concertante in F, D.487.
** Virgin Dig. VC 790801-2 [id.]. Domus (with Chi-chi Nwanoku).

(i) *Piano quintet in A (Trout)*; (ii) *Rondo in A, D.438*; (iii) *Impromptu in B flat, D.935/3.*
(BB) * LaserLight Dig. 15 522 [id.]. (i) Emmy Verhey, Colorado Qt; (ii) Dechhenne; (iii) Jenö Jandó.

(i) *Piano quintet (Trout); String quartet No. 12 (Quartettsatz).*
**(*) DG 413 453-2 [id.]. (i) Gilels; Amadeus Qt (augmented).

(i) *Piano quintet in A (Trout); (ii) String quartet No. 14 (Death and the Maiden).*
(M) **(*) Decca 417 459-2 [id.]. (i) Curzon, Vienna Octet (members); (ii) VPO Qt.

(i) *Piano quintet in A (Trout); (ii) String trios, D.471 & D.581.*
(M) *** Ph. 422 838-2 [id.]. (i) Haebler, Grumiaux, Janzer, Czako, Cazauran; (ii) Grumiaux String Trio.

(i) *Piano quintet in A (Trout); (ii) Die Forelle; (iii) Der Hirt auf dem Felsen.*
**(*) ASV Dig. CDDCA 684 [id.]. (i) Yitkin Seow, Prometheus Ens.; (ii; iii) Ann Mackay; (iii) Christopher Craker.

(i) *Piano quintet in A (Trout); (ii) Der Hirt auf dem Felsen.*
(B) **(*) Pickwick PCD 868. (i) Nash Ens.; (ii) Lott, Collins, Brown.

András Schiff and the Hagen Quartet give a delectably fresh and youthful reading of the *Trout quintet*, full of the joys of spring, but one which is also remarkable for hushed concentration, as in the exceptionally dark and intense account of the opening of the first movement. Schiff, unlike many virtuosi, remains one of a team, emphatically not a soloist in front of accompanists; the recording balance confirms that, with the piano rather behind the strings but firmly placed. The Scherzo brings a light, quick and bouncing performance, and there is extra lightness too in the other middle movements. Unlike current rivals, this version observes the exposition repeat in the finale, and with such a joyful, brightly pointed performance one welcomes that.

The Brendel/Cleveland performance may lack something in traditional Viennese charm, but it has a compensating vigour and impetus, and the work's many changes of mood are encompassed with freshness and subtlety, with Brendel at his most persuasive. The recording is well balanced and truthful. The sound is smooth and refined, but lacks something in upper range and sharpness of detail.

Clifford Curzon's 1958 recording of the *Trout* is a classic performance, with a distinguished account of the piano part and splendidly stylish support from the Vienna players. Schubert's warm lyricism is caught with remarkable freshness. Some might find the brilliant Scherzo a little too fierce to match the rest of the performance, but such vigorous playing introduces an element of contrast at the centre of the interpretation and makes possible a disarmingly relaxed account of the last movement. The Vienna Philharmonic performance treats *Death and the Maiden* with comparable affection; the playing is peerless, Boskovsky, the leader, showing all his skill and musicianship in the variations. Both recordings have a pleasingly warm ambience and, in the *Trout*, the piano timbre is appealingly full in colour, but here the upper range is noticeably thin; in the string quartet the upper range is fuller.

The Prometheus Ensemble turn in a very enjoyable and fresh account of the *Trout* on ASV which, though not a first choice, will give much pleasure to those who chance upon it. There are two bonuses in the shape of the equivalent song, charmingly done by Ann Mackay, and *The Shepherd on the rock*. The playing in the *Quintet* is alert and well shaped, and well recorded, too. There is a rather long hiatus just before the A flat section in the second movement (at about 3 minutes 30 seconds in), which is puzzling. Yitkin Seow plays with grace and finesse.

There is some admirably unassertive and deeply musical playing from Miss Haebler and from the incomparable Grumiaux; it is the freshness and pleasure in music-making that render this account memorable. These artists do not try to make 'interpretative points' but are content to let the music speak for itself. The balance is not altogether perfect, but the quality of the recorded sound is good. As an extra enticement, Philips have added a pair of *String trios*, given characteristically refined performances by Grumiaux and his companions, delightful music superbly played.

In the DG *Trout* there is a masterly contribution from Gilels, and the Amadeus play with considerable freshness. The approach is very positive, not as sunny and springlike as in some versions, but rewarding in its seriousness of purpose, and the balance is convincing.

The earlier account by the Nash Ensemble on CRD is restored to circulation now (with the *Notturno* on CRD 3352) but this is still at full price. The newer Pickwick issue also brings a fill-up in the shape of *The Shepherd on the rock*. They are rather forwardly recorded here and their account is just a little wanting in the spontaneity that distinguishes the finest of the current versions. Ian Brown is, as always, a sensitive artist.

The Domus recording on Virgin with Chi-chi Nwanoku as double-bass offers some splendid and intelligent playing, in particular from the pianist, Susan Tomes. They would enjoy a higher star-rating were the recording better balanced and the piano better focused. They offer the appealing *Adagio and Rondo concertante in F major* as a fill-up, to which they add a double-bass part, but the recording again poses problems.

Peter Serkin and Schneider's group give a bold, vigorous account of the *Trout* with a well-shaped set of variations. The wistful side of Schubert is missing here, but this music-making is easy to enjoy for its spontaneity. The recording is full and forward, the double-bass nicely resonant; but the violin timbre discloses the mid-1960s recording date.

The Beaux Arts *Trout* is a delightfully fresh performance. Every phrase is splendidly alive, there is no want of vitality or sensitivity, and the recording is basically well balanced. The snag is again the digital remastering, which gives undue prominence to Isidore Cohen's violin, lighting it up brightly and thinning down the timbre.

The LaserLight super-bargain version is a brisk, no-nonsense account, completely lacking in charm. The bright, forward recording doesn't help, with its absence of warm resonance for the double-bass, which makes a meagre impression. The *Rondo* is altogether more successful, both as a performance and as a recording, and Jandó's account of the famous *Impromptu* has an appealing simplicity.

Piano trio No. 1 in B flat, D.898.
** Chan. Dig. CHAN 8308 [id.]. Borodin Trio.
(M) ** RCA GD 86262 [6262-2-RG]. Szeryng, Fournier, Rubinstein – SCHUMANN: *Piano trio No. 1.***
(M) ** CBS MPK 45697 [id.]. Eugene Istomin, Isaac Stern, Leonard Rose.

Piano trio No. 1 in B flat; Notturno in E flat, D.897.
(M) **(*) Ph. 422 836-2 [id.]. Beaux Arts Trio.

Piano trio No. 1 in B flat, D.898; Notturno in E flat, D.897; Sonata movement in B flat, D.28.
*** EMI Dig. CDC7 49165-2. Jean-Philippe Collard, Augustin Dumay, Frédéric Lodéon.

Jean-Philippe Collard, Augustin Dumay and Frédéric Lodéon give a very good account of the sublime *B flat Trio*; not only is each a splendid performer in his own right, a fully integrated ensemble is created that sounds as if the players enjoy chamber music at home every evening, and the recording, made in a decent concert-hall acoustic, is eminently realistic.

The Beaux Arts performance has impeccable ensemble, with the pianist, Menahem Pressler, always sharply imaginative and the string playing sensitive in both line and phrase. The performance is perhaps on the lightweight side, although the slow movement has a disarming simplicity. The *Notturno*, eloquently played, makes an attractive bonus. The recording, from the late 1960s, sounds fresh, although its age shows a little in the timbre of the violin.

The Borodin Trio gives a warm and characterful interpretation, with natural expressiveness only occasionally overloaded with rubato. The impression is very much of a live performance, though in fact this is a studio recording marked by full and open sound, although the microphone balance is a little close.

Szeryng, Fournier and Rubinstein were recorded in 1974 in a rather dryish studio so that this impeccably played version sounds just a little wanting in freshness and bloom. Apart from the rather measured finale, tempi are ideally judged and there is a good sense of momentum. A fine performance.

The artists on CBS convey their enjoyment with a fairly relaxed approach to Schubert, especially the slow movement. It is a good but not distinctive account, well recorded (in 1965), if closely balanced. However, the overall playing time of 38 minutes is short measure these days.

Piano trio No. 2 in E flat, D.929.
**(*) Chan. Dig. CHAN 8324 [id.]. Borodin Trio.

Piano trio No. 2 in E flat; (i) *Fantasia in C, D.934.*
(M) (***) EMI mono CDH7 61014-2 [id.]. (i) Rudolf Serkin, (ii) with A. and H. Busch.

Piano trio No. 2 in E flat, D.929; Sonata in B flat (for piano trio), *D.28.*
(M) **(*) Ph. 426 096-2 [id.]. Beaux Arts Trio.

The Beaux Arts Trio's ensemble is superbly polished here, and the pianist's contribution is consistently imaginative, with the cellist, Bernard Greenhouse, bringing simple dedication to such key passages as the great slow-movement melody of the *E flat Trio.* The extra item gives this disc an added appeal. Written during Schubert's student days, the attractive early *Sonata in B flat* has the same kind of fluency as Beethoven's *First Piano trio,* though the lyrical flow has the unmistakable ring of Schubert. The 1967 recording has fine freshness and immediacy, but the CD remastering brings a degree of dryness to the upper range.

On the EMI Références CD by Rudolf Serkin, Adolf and Hermann Busch, the dated sound – the *Trio* from 1936 and the *Fantasy* made as long ago as 1931 – cannot dim these marvellous performances; one can only rejoice that they are again available for the musical nourishment of us all.

The Borodin Trio gives a strong and understanding performance of the *B flat Trio,* generally preferring spacious tempi. The outer movements are made the more resilient, and only in the Scherzo does the reading lack impetus. The speed for the slow movement is aptly chosen to allow a broad, steady pulse. The pianist is not always at her most subtle, but there is a sense of enjoyment here to which one responds. The compact disc is lifelike and present.

String quartets Nos. 1–15.
(M) ** DG 419 879-2 (6) [id.]. Melos Qt of Stuttgart.

The early quartets have an altogether disarming grace and innocence, and some of their ideas are most touching. The Melos are an impressive body whose accounts of this repertoire are unmannered and on the whole sympathetic. They are let down by recording quality that is less than distinguished, but the remastering has brought added presence.

String quartets Nos. 8 in B flat, D.112; 13 in A min., D.804.
*** ASV Dig. CDDCA 593 [id.]. Lindsay Qt.

In the glorious *A minor* the Lindsays lead the field. It would be difficult to fault their judgement in both these works so far as tempi and expression are concerned. Every phrase seems to arise naturally from what has gone before, and dynamics are always the result of musical thinking. The recording team has done them much credit.

String quartets Nos. 10 in E flat, D.87; 12 in C min. (Quartettsatz), D.703; 13 in A min., D.804.
** DG Dig. 419 171-2 [id.]. Hagen Qt.

The Hagen Quartet possess a quite wonderful unanimity of ensemble and great tonal finesse. They never make an ugly sound; nor, in the faster movements, do they ever cultivate virtuosity for its own sake. All the same there is more to Schubert than they find. Indeed, they come close to skating over the surface of the slow movement of the *A minor,* whose pathos they communicate only partially. One hopes they will not become the victims of their own tonal sophistication.

String quartet No. 12 in C min. (Quartettsatz), D.703.
*** CRD CRD 3334 [id.]. Alberni Qt – BRAHMS: *String sextet No. 1.****

A fresh and agreeably warm account of this fine single-movement work, and the recording is first class.

String quartets Nos. 12 in C min. (Quartettsatz), D.703; 14 in D min. (Death and the Maiden), D.810.
*** ASV Dig. CDDCA 560 [id.]. Lindsay Qt.
(M) **(*) CBS MYK 42602 [id.]. Juilliard Qt.

String quartets Nos. 13 in A min., D.804; 14 in D min. (Death and the Maiden), D.810.
**(*) EMI Dig. CDC7 47333-2 [id.]. Alban Berg Qt.

String quartet No. 14 in D min. (Death and the Maiden), D.810.
(M) *** Ph. 420 876-2 [id.]. Italian Qt – DVOŘÁK: *Quartet No. 12*** (with BORODIN: *Nocturne**).
(M) **(*) DG Dig. 429 491-2 [id.]. Amadeus Qt – MOZART: *String quartet No. 17 (Hunt).***

The Lindsays' intense, volatile account of the first movement of the *Death and the Maiden quartet*, urgently paced, played with considerable metrical freedom and the widest range of dynamic, is balanced by an equally imaginative and individual set of variations. The finale has a winning bustle and energy; and the *Quartettsatz*, which acts as the usual filler, is unusually poetic and spontaneous in feeling. The recording is excellent.

The Italian Quartet offer a fine mid-price coupling with Dvořák, and the Borodin *Nocturne* is thrown in for good measure. They bring great concentration and poetic feeling to this wonderful score, and they are free of the excessive point-making to be found in some rival versions. The sound of the reissue is vivid and clear.

The EMI issue offers two major quartets, marvellously played and cleanly recorded on one disc, and the only loss is the exposition repeat in the first movement of *Death and the Maiden*. The *A minor Quartet* is beautifully played, though the slow movement (with the theme of the *Rosamunde entr'acte*) is very fast indeed. The playing is breathtaking in terms of tonal blend, ensemble and intonation, but one is not always totally involved, except perhaps in the minuet and trio of the *A minor*. The clear, clean recording is very brightly lit in its CD format, with a slightly aggressive feeling on fortissimos.

The 1983 Amadeus version of *Death and the Maiden* offers much to admire. The performance has a powerful momentum and though there is some rough playing from Brainin, there is relatively little sentimentality. The actual sound is not as pure as in their very first mono recording, when their blend was superb and the leader's vibrato unobtrusive. Now the balance seems a trifle close.

Some might feel the Juilliard account to be a shade over-intense in the first movement, but the *Andante*, beginning and ending with a compelling pianissimo, is very fine; and the performance overall has the feeling of live music-making. Here the *Quartettsatz*, usually heard as a single movement, also includes the Andante, which ends at the moment Schubert left it as an incomplete fragment. The modern (1981) recording is closely balanced but realistic.

String quartet No. 13 in A min., D.804.
(B) ** Pickwick PCD 831. Brodsky Qt – BEETHOVEN: *String quartet No. 10.***

A promising CD début by this young British group who play with commendable vitality and spirit. There is some roughness of tone, exacerbated no doubt by the balance, but this is offset by a strong sense of line and much warmth of feeling. All the same, the greater refinement of the Hagen and Lindsays tell.

String quartets Nos. 13 in A min., D.804; 14 in D min. (Death and the Maiden), D.810.
(M) *** Ph. 426 383-2 [id.]. Italian Qt.

String quartets Nos. 13 in A min.; 14 in D min. (Death and the Maiden); 15 in G, D.887.
*** Nimbus NI 5048/9 [id.]. Chilingirian Qt.

The Italians omit the exposition repeat in the first movement of the *A minor Quartet*; the slow movement is spacious – some may feel it is a bit too slow – and has an impressive command of feeling. Their account of *Death and the Maiden* is also very fine. Here the slow movement is particularly impressive, showing a notable grip in the closing pages. Technically the playing throughout is quite remarkable. The recordings are well balanced and truthful, sounding a little dryer now in their CD remastering.

In their two-disc set of the last three *Quartets*, the Chilingirians give strongly committed, characterful and spontaneous-sounding readings, warmly recorded and full of presence. On the upper-mid-priced Nimbus label, they make a most attractive recommendation.

String quartets Nos. 14 in D min. (Death and the Maiden); 15 in G.
(M) (***) EMI (mono) CDH7 69795-2. Busch Qt.

The Busch Quartet's account is more than fifty years old, but it brings us closer to the heart of this music than any other. The slow movement of the *Death and the Maiden quartet* is a revelation, and the same must be said of the *G major*, which has enormous depth and humanity and a marvellous eloquence. For its age, the sound is still amazing, and the musical wisdom is timeless.

(i) *String quartet No. 14 (Death and the Maiden)* (arr. Mahler; ed. David Matthews and Donald Mitchell). (ii) *Der Tod und das Mädchen.*
*** EMI Dig. CDC7 47354-2 [id.]. (i) ECO, Tate; (ii) Ann Murray, Tate.

Never played complete in his lifetime, Mahler's string orchestra arrangement of *Death and the Maiden* makes a fascinating rarity. In the event, the power and bite of dramatic moments are often intensified and, with his instrumental cunning, Mahler often intensifies Schubert's poetry, giving a haunted quality to the slow movement. Obviously there are losses as well as gains in an orchestral performance where stresses are fewer. Jeffrey Tate directs the ECO in a satisfyingly dramatic reading. The original song makes an attractive prelude, intelligently sung by Ann Murray, but the disc provides short measure.

String quintet in C, D.956.
*** ASV Dig. CDDCA 537 [id.]. Lindsay Qt with Douglas Cummings.
**(*) CBS MK 39134 [id.]. Cleveland Qt with Yo-Yo Ma.
**(*) EMI Dig. CDC7 47018-2 [id.]. Alban Berg Qt with Heinrich Schiff.
** DG Dig. 419 611-2 [id.]. Amadeus Qt with Robert Cohen.
(BB) (*) Hung. White Label HRC 056 [id.]. Tátrai Qt with László Szilvásy.

String quintet in C, D.956; String quartet No. 12 in C min. (Quartettsatz), D.703.
** CRD CRD 3310 [id.]. Alberni Qt with Thomas Igloi.
(M) ** Decca 421 094-2. Weller Qt (augmented in *Quintet*).

The Lindsay version gives the impression that one is eavesdropping on music-making in the intimacy of a private concert. They observe the first-movement exposition repeat and the effortlessness of their approach does not preclude intellectual strength. The Lindsays do the amazing first movement justice, as indeed they do the ethereal *Adagio*.

Here they effectively convey the sense of it appearing motionless, suspended, as it were, between reality and dream, yet at the same time never allowing it to become static. Their reading must rank at the top of the list; it is very well recorded.

The Cleveland Quartet and Yo-Yo Ma have won golden opinions for their account of the *Quintet* on CBS. They are scrupulous in observing dynamic markings (the second subject is both restrained and *pianissimo*) and they also score by making all repeats. Their performance has feeling and eloquence, as well as a commanding intellectual grip. Moreover they are admirably recorded and thus present a strong challenge.

Few ensembles offer timbre as full-bodied or as richly burnished as that produced by the Alban Berg and Heinrich Schiff and, given the sheer polish and gorgeous sound that distinguish their playing, theirs must rank high among current recommendations. The performance is strongly projected and they have the advantage of excellent recording. However, unlike the Lindsays, they do not observe the first-movement exposition repeat.

The Amadeus version with Robert Cohen was the last recording made by that unique quartet before the death of their viola-player, Peter Schidlof. It brings a typically warm and responsive reading, strongly characterized, emphatic even, not quite as refined in ensemble as in earlier Amadeus versions, but benefiting from full, forward digital sound, and with the exposition repeat observed.

The Alberni and Thomas Igloi give an admirably unaffected and thoughtful account of the *Quintet*. The first movement is refreshingly straightforward and, like the Lindsays, they observe the exposition repeat; the slow movement has a natural simplicity of expression that is affecting. The recording has warmth and splendid definition, even if, by comparison with the Lindsays, it has less depth and bloom. Not necessarily a first choice, but a safe one.

Fine playing from the Weller Quartet, though a trifle sweet and suave. This is currently the only recommendable mid-priced version of the Schubert *Quintet*, and the *Quartettsatz* makes an attractive fill-up. The sound too is good and does not seem too dated.

The Tátrai performance is acceptable but not distinctive, with no real magic in the great *Adagio*. The players are not helped by the digital remastering, which – like the Mozart *Quintets* on the same label – makes the violins sound impossibly shrill.

Violin sonata, D.574; Violin sonatina, D.385; Fantaisie in C, D.934.
(M) **(*) Decca 425 539-2 [id.]. Szymon Goldberg, Radu Lupu.

Violin sonatinas: in D, D.384; in A min., D.385; in G min., D.408; Duo in A, D.574.
(M) **(*) Ph. 426 385-2 [id.]. Arthur Grumiaux, Robert Veyron-Lacroix.

There is an unaffected, Schubertian feeling in the Goldberg/Lupu performances that is most appealing. Indeed Goldberg is vulnerable in that he almost undercharacterizes the line, and at times one could do with a greater variety of dynamic nuance and tonal colour. Yet the presence of Radu Lupu ensures that these performances give much pleasure: his playing has a vitality and inner life that are consistently rewarding. The remastered recording also sounds full and natural, and is very realistically balanced.

Instead of reissuing Grumiaux's set with Paul Crossley, the earlier, 1972 performances with Robert Veyron-Lacroix have been chosen, and the latter does not emerge as quite so strong a personality as his partner. However, his response is admirably musical and the Philips sound is fresh and clear, even though the acoustic is resonant.

PIANO MUSIC

Allegretto in C min., D.915; Marche militaire No. 1 in D, D.733; Moments musicaux Nos. 1–6, D.780; Piano sonata No. 17 in D, D.850.
(***) Arabesque mono Z 6573 [id.]. Artur Schnabel.

(i) Allegro in A min. (Lebensstürme), D.947; Andantino varié in B min., D.823. March in E, D.606; Marches militaires Nos. 2 in G; 3 in E flat, D.733; Piano sonata No. 21 in B flat, D.960.
(***) Arabesque mono Z 6575 [id.]. Artur Schnabel; (i) with Karl-Ulrich Schnabel.

Schnabel's pioneering and magisterial accounts of the *D major* and *B flat Sonatas*, made in the late 1930s, are full of characteristic insights, though it must be admitted that later recordings of the *B flat* from Kempff and Curzon surpassed him technically. But as always with Schnabel there is imagination of a remarkable order. These recordings are now fifty years old, but some of the playing Schnabel offers – in the slow movements of both *Sonatas* – will never be less than special.

Fantasia in C (Wanderer), D.760.
*** EMI CDC7 47967-2. Sviatoslav Richter – DVOŘÁK: *Piano concerto.****
*** CBS Dig. MK 42124 [id.]. Murray Perahia – SCHUMANN: *Fantasia in C.****
(M) *** Ph. 420 644-2 [id.]. Alfred Brendel – *Sonata No. 21.****
*** DG 419 672-2 [id.]. Maurizio Pollini – *Sonata No. 16.****
** Decca Dig. 417 327-2 [id.]. Vladimir Ashkenazy – *Sonata No. 21.***

Richter's 1963 performance is masterly in every way. The piano timbre is real and the remastering gives the great pianist a compelling presence; the coupling is hardly less outstanding.

Murray Perahia's account of the *Wanderer* stands alongside the finest. In his hands it sounds as fresh as the day it was conceived, and its melodic lines speak with an ardour and subtlety that breathe new life into the score. The recording is more than acceptable, even if it does not wholly convey Perahia's wide range of sonority and dynamics.

Brendel's playing too is of a high order, and he is truthfully recorded and coupled with what is perhaps Schubert's greatest *Sonata*, so this is excellent value at mid-price.

Pollini's account is outstanding and, though he is not ideally recorded and the piano timbre is shallow, the playing still shows remarkable insights. Moreover the coupling is equally fine.

Ashkenazy's is a fine performance too, but let down by the clangorous quality of the recorded sound, acceptable here, but not suitable for the great *B flat Sonata*.

Fantasia in C (Wanderer), D.760; Impromptus, D.899/3 & 4; Piano sonata No. 21 in B flat, D. 960.
✪ *** RCA RD 86257 [RCA 6257-2-RC]. Artur Rubinstein.

Rubinstein plays the *Wanderer fantasia* with sure magnificence. The extended structure needs a master to hold it together and, particularly in the variations section, Rubinstein is electrifying. The two *Impromptus* are played with the most subtle shading of colour and delectable control of rubato, and the superb account of the *Sonata* shows Rubinstein as a magically persuasive Schubertian. The first movement is very relaxed yet the effect is wonderfully luminous, and a similar inspired and ruminative spontaneity infuses the essentially gentle *Andante*. Then the articulation in the final two movements is a joy, light and crisp in the Scherzo, bolder but never heavy in the finale. The 1965 sound is remarkably real, with fine presence and almost no shallowness.

Fantasia in D min., D.940.
*** CBS Dig. MK 39511 [id.]. Murray Perahia, Radu Lupu – MOZART: *Double piano sonata.****

Recorded live at The Maltings, the performance of Lupu and Perahia is full of haunting poetry, with each of these highly individual artists challenging the other in imagination. Where in the Mozart coupling Perahia plays primo, here it is the more recessive Lupu adding to the mellowness of this most inspired of all piano duet works. Warmly atmospheric recording.

Impromptus Nos. 1–4, D. 899; 5–8, D.935.
*** CBS Dig. CD 37291 [id.]. Murray Perahia.
*** Ph. 411 040-2 [id.]. Alfred Brendel.
*** Decca Dig. 411 711-2 [id.]. Radu Lupu.
*** Ph. Dig. 422 237-2 [id.]. Alfred Brendel.
**(*) EMI Dig. CDC7 49102-2. Melvyn Tan (fortepiano).
(M) **(*) DG 415 849-2 [id.]. Daniel Barenboim.

Perahia's account of the *Impromptus* is very special indeed and falls barely short of greatness. Directness of utterance and purity of spirit are of the essence here. As one critic has put it, Perahia's vision brings the impression of a tree opening out, whereas Brendel's suggests the moment of full bloom. The CBS recording is very good, truthful in timbre, with an increase in firmness on CD and added presence.

Brendel's analogue set of *Impromptus* is also magical. It is difficult to imagine finer Schubert playing than this; to find more eloquence, more profound musical insights, one has to go back to Edwin Fischer – and even here comparison is not always to Brendel's disadvantage. The piano image is warm and full but slightly diffuse.

Alfred Brendel's digital set of the *Impromptus* can be confidently recommended to his admirers. It offers many insights and has the benefit of immaculate recorded sound. In some respects his earlier, analogue recordings of these pieces for Vox (on LP) and Philips (411 040-2) were more affecting; not that this is lacking in warmth, but there is an element of didacticism. Recommended – but not in preference to Perahia or Lupu.

Lupu's account of the *Impromptus* is of the same calibre as the Perahia and Brendel versions, and he is most beautifully recorded on CD. Indeed, in terms of natural sound this is the most believable image of the three. Lupu brings his own special insights to these pieces. Perahia displays a fresher innocence; Brendel is more direct and wonderfully warm; but Lupu is compelling in his own way, and these performances yield much that is memorable.

Schubert on the fortepiano is, of course, quite unlike the Schubert we know from the modern pianoforte. Tan's playing is refreshingly unmannered and for the most part very persuasive: he is at pains to avoid any sentimentality, yet he succeeds in conveying the music's tenderness. He has the measure of the scale of the *F minor*, D.935/1, and brings both dramatic fire and poetic feeling to it. He is arguably a shade too brisk in the *F minor*, D.935/4, and the *B flat major*, D.935/3; but throughout the set there are valuable insights. He is excellently recorded too.

Daniel Barenboim plays the *Impromptus* with characteristic sensitivity and refinement. His tempi are rather slow and there are occasional moments of self-consciousness. Barenboim's touch is quite ethereal at times and, whatever one's response may be, the playing is enormously positive and full of character. The recording is realistic, with presence and clarity to recommend it, though the CD transfer has brought a degree of hardness. A fair mid-price choice.

Impromptus Nos. 1–4, D.889; Piano sonata No. 21 in B flat, D960.
*** Calliope Dig. CAL 9689 [id.]. Inger Södergren.

Inger Södergren's account of the first four *Impromptus* belongs in exalted company, and the *B flat Sonata* is hardly less fine. She is little known even in her native Sweden but enjoys a considerable following in France, where she is spoken of alongside the great pianists of the day – and, on the strength of this record, rightly so. Her playing is marked throughout by sensitivity and a selfless and unostentatious dedication to Schubert. The *Sonata* was recorded in 1983 and reproduces at a lower level than the *Impromptus*. The recording is acceptable rather than outstanding.

Moments musicaux Nos. 1–6, D.780.
** DG 415 118-2 [id.]. Daniel Barenboim – LISZT: *Liebesträume*; MENDELSSOHN: *Songs without words.****

Barenboim's mood is often thoughtful and intimate; at other times we are made a shade too aware of the interpreter's art, and there is an element of calculation that robs the impact of freshness. The recording is excellent, with fine presence in its CD format.

Moments musicaux Nos. 1–6, D.780; Klavierstücke, D.946.
*** EMI Dig. CDC7 49793-2 [id.]. Melvyn Tan (fortepiano) – BEETHOVEN: *Allegretto in C min.* etc.***

Melvyn Tan continues to enhance his reputation as one of the most persuasive advocates of the fortepiano now before the public. He has remarkable feeling for its colour and never approaches the music with any excess of judicious reverence that distinguishes some players using period instruments. His Schubert is consistently spirited and fresh, though he favours rather brisker tempi than is desirable. However, this is stimulating and lively playing, which has the benefit of fine and present recording.

Moments musicaux, D.780; 2 Scherzi, D.593; Piano sonata No. 14 in A min., D.784.
*** DG Dig. 427 769-2 [id.]. Maria João Pires.

Maria João Pires gives masterly accounts of the *Moments musicaux* and the *A minor Sonata* that are as good as any in the catalogue. Her playing is distinguished throughout by thoughtful and refined musicianship, and she is fully aware of the depth of feeling that inhabits the *Moments musicaux*, without ever indulging in the slightest expressive exaggeration. The digital recording is exceptionally present and clear.

Piano sonata No. 4 in A min., D.537.
** DG Dig. 400 043-2 [id.]. Michelangeli – BRAHMS: *Ballades.****

Michelangeli's Schubert is less convincing than the Brahms coupling. He rushes the opening theme and rarely allows the simple ideas of the first movement to speak for themselves. Elsewhere his playing, though aristocratic and marvellously poised, is not free from artifice, and the natural eloquence of Schubert eludes him. Splendid recording.

Piano sonatas Nos. 14–21; German dances; Impromptus; Moments musicaux; Wanderer fantasia.
*** Ph. Dig. 426 128-2 (7) [id.]. Alfred Brendel.

Piano sonatas Nos. 14 in A min., D.784; 17 in D, D.850.
*** Ph. Dig. 422 063-2 [id.] Alfred Brendel.

Piano sonatas Nos 15 in C (Relique), D.840; 18 in G, D.894.
*** Ph. Dig. 422 340-2 [id.]. Alfred Brendel.

Piano sonata No. 16 in A min., D.845; 3 Impromptus, D.946.
*** Ph. Dig. 422 075-2 [id.]. Alfred Brendel.

Piano sonata No. 21 in B flat, D.960; Wanderer fantasia, D.760.
*** Ph. Dig. 422 062-2 [id.]. Alfred Brendel.

Brendel's new digital set is perhaps more intense than his last cycle of recordings for Philips, though there was a touching freshness in the earlier set, and he has the benefit of clean, well-focused sound. Generally speaking, these are warm performances, strongly delineated and powerfully characterized, which occupy a commanding place in the catalogue. Their separate availability is also noted, and all of them can be confidently recommended to Brendel's admirers.

Piano sonatas Nos. 14 in A min., D.784; 18 in G, D.894; 12 Waltzes, D.145.
(M) *** Decca 425 017-2 [id.]. Vladimir Ashkenazy.

This is a recoupling for CD. Ashkenazy's account of the *A minor Sonata* surpasses the pianist's own high standards. There is an astonishing directness about this performance, a virility tempered by tenderness that is very compelling indeed. On the other hand, the *G major Sonata* (which comes first on the disc) is altogether more controversial. The first movement should certainly be leisurely if it is to convey the self-communing as well as the sense of peace that lies at its heart. But Ashkenazy is very slow indeed: he robs it of its normal sense of momentum. If further hearings prove more convincing, this is largely because Ashkenazy's reading is so totally felt and, equally, perceptive. He succeeds in making the piano sound exceptionally expressive. This is a most searching and poetic account, and both sonatas are given highly realistic recording, the *G major* slightly fuller in the bass. The *Waltzes* make an attractive and generous encore.

Piano sonata No. 15 in C (Relique), D. 840.
*** Ph. 416 292-2 [id.]. Sviatoslav Richter.

Richter's approach to Schubert's unfinished *Sonata* is both dedicated and strong. He treats the opening movement very spaciously indeed and the following *Andante* is comparably thoughtful; the work ends abruptly where the composer stopped, leaving the rest to the listener's imagination. The recording was made at a live performance and captures the spontaneity of the occasion and the full range of the pianist's dynamic.

Piano sonata No. 16 in A min., D.845.
*** DG 419 672-2 [id.]. Maurizio Pollini – *Fantasia in C (Wanderer).****

Pollini's account of the *A minor Sonata* is searching and profound. He is almost without rival in terms of sheer keyboard control, and his musical insight is of the same order. The piano sound as such could do with slightly more body, but the recording is musically balanced.

Piano sonatas Nos. 16 in A min., D.845; 18 in G, D.894.
⊛ *** Decca 417 640-2 [id.]. Radu Lupu.

Radu Lupu's version of the *A minor Sonata* of 1825 is searching and poetic throughout. He brings tenderness and classical discipline to bear on this structure and his playing is musically satisfying in a very Schubertian way. The coupling is hardly less fine, a superb reading, relatively straight in its approach but full of glowing perception on points of detail; moreover, the exposition repeat is observed in the first movement. The analogue recordings date from 1975 and 1979 respectively and are of Decca's finest, with timbre of warm colour yet with a striking sense of presence overall.

Piano sonatas Nos. 19 in C min., D.958; 20 in A, D.959.
*** DG Dig. 427 327-2 [id.]. Maurizio Pollini.

Piano sonata No. 21 in B flat, D.960; Allegretto in C min., D.915; Klavierstücke, D.946.
*** DG Dig. 427 326-2 [id.]. Maurizio Pollini.

In Pollini's hands these emerge as strongly structured and powerful sonatas, yet he is far from unresponsive to the voices from the other world in which these pieces resonate. Perhaps with his perfect pianism he does not always convey a sense of human vulnerability in the way that some of the greatest Schubert interpreters have. The *Sonatas* were recorded at different venues; in the *A major*, for example, the sound is not always completely natural. However, this is playing of some distinction.

Piano sonata No. 19 in C min., D.958; Moments musicaux Nos. 1–6, D.780.
*** Ph. Dig. 422 076-2 [id.]. Alfred Brendel.
(M) *** Decca Dig. 417 785-2 [id.]. Radu Lupu.

Brendel's new digital recording of the *C minor Sonata* is held on a firmer rein than before and has an almost symphonic power; even in the slow movement he does not lose the central current of nervous energy, yet nothing is overdriven. There is a tremendous sense of line throughout the *Sonata* and, although his staccato articulation may occasionally strike some listeners as exaggerated, his taut and dramatic view of the *Sonata* is masterly. The *Moments musicaux* are hardly less impressive, given with unaffected directness, and the recording is absolutely first class.

Lupu's performance has a simple eloquence that is most moving. His *Moments musicaux* are very fine indeed, though it is not possible to say that they are better than Brendel's or Curzon's, which are marvellous too. The Decca recording is very natural and, at mid-price, this is extremely competitive.

Piano sonata No. 20 in A, D.959.
*** CBS Dig. MK 44569 [id.]. Murray Perahia – SCHUMANN: *Piano sonata No. 2.****

Piano sonata No. 20 in A, D.959; Allegretto in C min., D.915; 16 German dances, D.783; Hungarian melody in B min., D.817.
**(*) Ph. Dig. 422 229-2 [id.]. Alfred Brendel.

Perahia's combination of intellectual vigour and poetic insight shows that awareness of proportion and feeling for expressive detail which distinguish the greatest interpreters. As always with this artist, every phrase speaks and each paragraph breathes naturally.

Brendel holds the *A major Sonata* on an altogether tauter rein than he did earlier. He does not convey the vulnerable quality of the slow movement as effectively as does Perahia. All the same, there is a keen sense of its tragedy. The crisp articulation in the scherzo may seem too much of a good thing, and his *vocalise* needs to be suppressed: once you notice it, it is disturbing. He is recorded with great clarity and presence.

Piano sonatas Nos. 20 in A, D.959; 21 in B flat, D.960.
*** EMI Dig. CDC7 49631-2 [id.]. Melvyn Tan (fortepiano).

Melvyn Tan uses a fortepiano much admired by Beethoven. He is a compelling artist of keen musical intelligence who makes you listen, even when you might not agree with every expressive or agogic hesitation. Generally speaking, tempi are well judged, though the *Andantino* of the *A major* and the slow movement of the *B flat* are far too fast. However, by the end of each movement he almost convinces you that he is right and, in the case of the *B flat*, he does. His account of this *Sonata* is very impressive: there is depth of feeling as well as many felicities of sonority. Whether or not you are completely persuaded, these performances will make you think afresh about this music. The recording is first class.

Piano sonata No. 21 in B flat, D.960 (see also under *Fantasia (Wanderer)*).
(M) *** Ph. 420 644-2 [id.]. Alfred Brendel – *Wanderer fantasia.****
*** Hyp. Dig. CDA 66004 [id.]. Stephen Bishop-Kovacevich.
** Decca Dig. 417 327-2 [id.]. Vladimir Ashkenazy – *Wanderer fantasia.***

Piano sonata No. 21 in B flat; Impromptu in A flat, D.935/2; 6 Moments musicaux, D.780.
⊛ *** Decca 417 642-2 [id.]. Clifford Curzon.

Piano sonata No. 21 in B flat; Impromptus, D.899/2– 3.
**(*) Denon Dig. C37 7488 [id.]. Dezsö Ránki.

Curzon's tempi are aptly judged, and everything is in fastidious taste. Detail is finely drawn but never emphasized at the expense of the architecture as a whole. It is beautifully recorded, and the piano sounds very truthful in timbre. For the reissue, the coupling has been extended to include the *Moments musicaux*. The digital remastering brings just a hint of hardness at fortissimo levels to a basically warm, full tone; some slight background remains.

Brendel's performance too is as impressive and full of insight as one would expect. He is not unduly wayward, for his recording has room for the *Wanderer fantasy* as well, and he is supported by excellent Philips sound.

Stephen Bishop-Kovacevich also gives one of the most eloquent accounts on record of this sublime *Sonata* and one which is entirely free of expressive point-making. The first-movement exposition repeat is observed. The recording reproduces the piano timbre with the same complete naturalness that Bishop-Kovacevich brings to the *Sonata* itself. However, without any couplings this seems short measure.

Ashkenazy plays with poetry and searching intensity in the ideal coupling of the great *B flat Sonata* and the *Wanderer fantasy*. What seriously mars this issue is the clangy quality of the recording, much less sympathetic than the analogue sound for Brendel in his similar coupling for Philips.

Dezsö Ránki's performance must be counted controversial in that he begins with a very expansive pacing of the opening theme, far slower than his basic speed later, and he consistently returns to this slow tempo when the famous melody recurs. The effect is to make the first movement unusually volatile, but it is also spontaneous, and he has clearly thought deeply about this approach. The slow movement is intensely poetic and, with a nimbly articulated Scherzo and a finale which balances sparkle with strength, this is a very considerable reading, matched by the two *Impromptus* which are beautifully played and nicely characterized.

VOCAL MUSIC

Lieder Vol. 1: *Der Alpenjäger; Amalia; An den Frühling; An den Mond; Erster Verlust; Die Ewartung; Der Fischer; Der Flüchtling; Das Geheimnis; Der Jüngling am Bache; Lied; Meeres Stille; Nähe des Geliebten; Der Pilgrim; Schäfers Klagelied; Sehnsucht; Thekla; Wanderers Nachtlied; Wonne der Wehmut.*
*** Hyp. Dig. CDJ 33001 [id.]. Dame Janet Baker, Graham Johnson.

Hyperion's complete Schubert song edition, master-minded by the accompanist, Graham Johnson, is planned to mix well-known songs with rarities, and that is what Dame Janet's first collection of 19 items does, demonstrating what jewels lie among unknown and insignificant songs. The whole collection is devoted to Schiller and Goethe settings, above all those he wrote in 1815, an exceptionally rich year for the 18-year-old; one marvels that, after writing his dedicated, concentrated setting of *Wanderers Nachtlied*, he could on that same day in July write two other equally memorable songs, *Der Fischer*, robustly folk-like and tuneful, and *Erster Verlust* (*First loss*), astonishingly deep for a teenager. Dame Janet is in glorious voice, her golden tone ravishing in a song such as *An den Mond* and her hushed tone caressing the ear in *Meeres Stille* and *Wanderers Nachtlied*. Presented like this, the project becomes not a marathon but a voyage of discovery.

Lieder Vol. 2: *Am Bach im Frühling; Am Flusse; Auf der Donau; Fahrt zum Hades; Fischerlied* (two settings); *Fischerweise; Der Schiffer; Selige Welt; Der Strom; Der Taucher; Widerschein; Wie Ulfru fischt.*
*** Hyp. Dig. CDJ 33002 [id.]. Stephen Varcoe, Graham Johnson.

In the accompaniments to Schubert songs, the inspiration of water is a recurrent theme and, for this second Hyperion instalment, Graham Johnson with the baritone, Stephen Varcoe, devises a delightful collection of men's songs, culminating in the rousing strophic song, *Der Schiffer*, one of the most catchily memorable that Schubert ever wrote, here exhilaratingly done. Otherwise the moods of water and wave, sea and river, are richly exploited, from the darkly brooding *Journey to Hades* (*Fahrt zum Hades*) and the urgently threatening journey to the abyss in *Der Strom*, on to the calm of *Am Bach im Frühling*. The last 28 minutes of the collection are devoted to the extended narrative, *Der Taucher* (*The Diver*), setting a long poem of Schiller which is based on an early version of the Beowulf saga. Varcoe and Johnson completely explode the long-accepted idea that this is overextended and cumbersome, giving it a thrilling dramatic intensity.

Lieder Vol. 3: *Abschied; An die Freunde; Augenlied; Iphigenia; Der Jüngling und der Tod; Lieb Minna; Liedesend; Nacht und Träume; Namenstagslied; Pax vobiscum; Rückweg; Trost im Liede; Viola; Der Zwerg.*
*** Hyp. Dig. CDJ 33003 [id.]. Ann Murray, Graham Johnson.

This is one of Ann Murray's finest records with the intimate beauty of the voice consistently well caught and with none of the stress that the microphone exaggerates on record. Graham Johnson has plainly helped in that, not only with his consistently supportive accompaniments but in a selection of songs specially suited to this sensitive, intelligent singer. Like the songs that Johnson chose for Ann Murray's husband, Philip Langridge, these too represent Schubert in his circle of friends, with their poems his inspiration, including a long flower ballad, *Viola*, by his close friend, Franz von Schober, which Murray and Johnson sustain beautifully.

Lieder Vol. 4: *Alte Liebe rostet nie; Am See; Am Strome; An Herrn Josef von Spaun (Epistel); Auf der Riesenkoppe; Das war ich; Das gestörte Glück; Liebeslauschen; Liebesrausch; Liebeständelei; Der Liedler; Nachtstück; Sängers Morgenlied* (2 versions); *Sehnsucht der Liebe.*
*** Hyp. Dig. CDJ 33004 [id.]. Philip Langridge, Graham Johnson.

Philip Langridge's contribution to Hyperion's great enterprise of recording all Schubert songs brings a collection chosen by Graham Johnson to illustrate his setting of words by poets in his immediate circle, ending with *Epistel*, a tongue-in-cheek parody song addressed to a friend who had left Vienna to become a tax collector, extravagantly lamenting his absence. It is Johnson's presentation of such rarities, complete with witty and highly illuminating as well as scholarly notes, that makes the series such a delight. With his inspired accompaniments, Johnson also draws the very finest from his singers. Langridge has rarely sounded so fresh and sparkling on record.

Lieder Vol. 5: *Die Allmacht; An die Natur; Die Erde; Erinnerung; Ferne von der grossen Stadt; Ganymed; Klage der Ceres; Das Lied im Grünen; Morgenlied; Die Mutter Erde; Die Sternenwelten; Täglich zu singen; Dem Unendlichen; Wehmut.*
*** Hyp. Dig. CDJ 33005 [id.]. Elizabeth Connell, Graham Johnson.

Elizabeth Connell's big soprano might have sounded ungainly in Schubert Lieder but, thanks in part to Johnson's choice of songs and to his sensitive support at the piano, Connell has rarely sounded so sweet and composed on record, yet with plenty of temperament. The collection of 14 songs, like others in this outstanding Hyperion series, centres round a theme, this one, Schubert and the countryside, suggested by the most popular song of the group, *Das Lied im Grünen*. As ever with this series, the joy of the record is enhanced by Johnson's brilliant, illuminating notes.

Lieder Vol. 6: *Abendlied für die Entfernte; Abends unter der Linde* (two versions); *Abendstern; Alinde; An die Laute; Des Fischers Liebesglück; Jagdlied; Der Knabe in der Wiege (Wiegenlied); Lass Wolken an Hügeln ruh'n; Die Nacht; Die Sterne; Der Vater mit dem Kind; Vor meiner Wiege; Wilkommen und Abschied; Zur guten Nacht.*
*** Hyp. Dig. CDJ 33006 [id.]. Anthony Rolfe-Johnson, Graham Johnson (with chorus).

The theme of Anthony Rolfe-Johnson's contribution to the Hyperion Schubert edition is 'Schubert and the Nocturne', making a much more varied collection than you might expect, extending even to the delectable lute-song, *An die Laute*. Two items include a small male chorus, a group of individually named singers. *Jagdlied* is entirely choral, and the final *Zur guten Nacht*, a late song of 1827, has the 'Spokesman' answered by the chorus, ending on a gentle *Gute Nacht*. As ever, Johnson's imagination in devising the programme presents the singer at his most warmly sympathetic. Rolfe-Johnson's voice has never sounded more beautiful on record, and the partnership of singer and accompanist makes light even of a long strophic song like *Des Fischers Liebesglück*, beautiful and intense.

Lieder Vol. 7: *An die Nachtigall; An den Frühling; An den Mond; Idens Nachtgesang; Idens Schwanenlied; Der Jüngling am Bache; Kennst du das Land?; Liane; Die Liebe; Luisens Antwort; Des Mädchens Klage; Meeres Stille; Mein Gruss an den Mai; Minona oder die Kunde der Dogge; Naturgenuss; Das Rosenband; Das Sehnen; Sehnsucht* (2 versions); *Die Spinnerin; Die Sterbende; Stimme der Liebe; Von Ida; Wer kauft Liebesgötter?.*
*** Hyp. Dig. CDJ 33007 [id.]. Elly Ameling, Graham Johnson.

Graham Johnson for this seventh volume of his great Schubert series has chosen an extraordinarily rewarding sequence of 24 songs, all written in the composer's *annus mirabilis*, 1815. Many of the more celebrated songs from that year have already been included in other volumes, but the relative rarities here yield extraordinary riches. With Ameling both charming and intense, Johnson's robust defence in his ever-illuminating notes of the first and longest of the songs, *Minona*, is amply confirmed, a richly varied ballad. Here too is a preliminary setting of *Meeres Stille*, less well-known than the regular version, written a day later, but just as clearly a masterpiece, sung by Ameling in a lovely intimate half-tone at a sustained pianissimo. It is fascinating too to compare the two contrasted settings of Mignon's song, *Sehnsucht*, the first of five he ultimately attempted. Singer and accompanist-annotator consistently have you involved with Schubert the man, as well as his songs.

Lieder: *Abendbilder; An die Musik; An den Mond; Bertas Lied in der Nacht; Die Blumensprache; Erster Verlust; Frühlingssehnsucht; Der Knabe; Nachthymne; Schwestergruss; Sei mir gegrüsst; Die Sterne; Wiegenlied.*
*** Ph. Dig. 410 037-2 [id.]. Elly Ameling, Dalton Baldwin.

Elly Ameling's is a fresh and enchanting collection of Schubert songs, starting with *An die Musik* and including other favourites like the *Cradle song* as well as lesser-known songs that admirably suit the lightness and sparkle of her voice. The recording gives a realistic sense of presence to the singer and the piano is unusually truthful; some ears, however, may notice that the microphone is just a little close.

Lieder: *Alinde; An die Laüte; Ariette der Claudine; Geheimes; Gott im Frühlinge;* (i) *Der Hirt auf dem Felsen; Die Junge Nonne; Lachen und Weinen; Liebhaber in allen Gestalten; Lied der Delphine; Die Männer sind méchant; Nacht und Träume; Nähe des Geliebten; Rastlose Liebe; Seligheit; Ständchen; Suleika I.*
**(*) DG Dig. 419 237-2 [id.]. Kathleen Battle, James Levine; (i) with K. Leister.

Kathleen Battle sings these songs with unfailing charm and a simplicity of approach which is disarming. At times one might seek a deeper reaction, but the beauty of the voice plus the direct response to the words is refreshing in its own way. Karl Leister provides a smooth obbligato for *Der Hirt auf dem Felsen*. Good recording in a warm acoustic.

Lieder: *Die Allmacht; An die Natur; Auf dem See; Auflösung; Erlkönig; Ganymed; Gretchen am Spinnrade; Der Musensohn; Rastlose Liebe; Suleika I; Der Tod und das Mädchen; Der Zwerg.*
*** Ph. Dig. 412 623-2 [id.]. Jessye Norman, Philip Moll.

Jessye Norman's characterization of the four contrasting voices in *Erlkönig* is powerfully effective, and the reticence which once marked her Lieder singing has completely disappeared. The poignancy of *Gretchen am Spinnrade* is exquisitely touched in, building to a powerful climax; throughout, the breath control is a thing of wonder, not least in a surpassing account of *Ganymed*. Fine, sympathetic accompaniment from Philip Moll, and first-rate recording.

Lieder: *An die Entfernte; Auf dem Wasser zu singen; Du bist die Ruh'; Der Erlkönig; Die Forelle; Heidenröslein; Das Heimweh; Der Jüngling an der Quelle; Der Jüngling und der Tod; Das Lied im Grünen; Litanei auf das Fest Aller Seelen; Nachtgesang; Der Schiffer; Sei mir gegrüsst!; Ständchen; Der Strom; Der Tod und das Mädchen; Der Wanderer; Der Winterabend; Das Zügenglöcklein; Der zürnende Barde.*
(M) *** EMI CDM7 69503-2 [id.]. Dietrich Fischer-Dieskau, Gerald Moore.

EMI's mid-price collection of vintage Fischer-Dieskau recordings makes an ideal sampler of favourite Schubert songs. Early in his career the voice was at its freshest and most beautiful, and though the comparably early stereo recording is less atmospheric than on more recent issues, there is a face-to-face immediacy which with such an artist could not be more revealing. A bargain.

Lieder: *An die Laüte; An Sylvia; Der Blumenbrief; Du liebst mich nicht; Der Einsame; Im Abendrot; Die Liebe hat gelogen; Der Liebliche Stern; Das Mädchen; Die Männer sind*

méchant; Minnelied; Nacht und Träume; Rosamunde; Romance: Schlummerlied; Seligkeit; Die Sterne.
*** Ph. 416 897-2 [id.]. Elly Ameling, Dalton Baldwin.

Elly Ameling's earlier Schubert recital of 1973, sounding undated, brings a delightful selection of songs, showing off the diamond purity of the voice at its freshest and most girlish in an attractively arranged programme. The first half takes songs on the subject of night, the second on love in all its varied moods from joy to desolation. Baldwin's playing is most sensitive in support, and the analogue recording has been transferred very well to CD, though the measure remains short.

An die Musik; An Sylvia; Auf der Bruck; Dithyrambe; Der Doppelgänger; Der Erlkönig; Erster Verlust; Die Forelle; Frühlingsglaube; Ganymed; Heidenröslein; Im Abendrot; Die Liebe hat gelogen; Der Musensohn; Nacht und Träume; Normans Gesang; Rastlose Liebe; Der Schiffer; Der Tod und das Mädchen; Der Wanderer; Wandrers Nachtlied; Der Zwerg.
(M) *** Ph. 422 418-2 [id.]. Gérard Souzay, Dalton Baldwin.

Souzay's early stereo recital includes many favourites, notably a superbly dramatic *Erlkönig*, plus the lovely *Wandrers Nachtlied*, in which he spins his tone exquisitely, and a splendid account of *Der Tod und das Mädchen*. Souzay, by skilful covering and the widening of his vibrato at points of pressure, provides consistent freshness of tone, and the consummate artistry in matter of inflexion and phrasing is always apparent. Dalton Baldwin's accompaniments are often superb, and both artists are given fine presence on this impeccably remastered CD.

Lieder: An die Musik; An Sylvia; Auf dem Wasser zu singen; Ave Maria; Du bist die Ruh'; Die Forelle; Ganymed; Gretchen am Spinnrade; Heidenröslein; Im Frühling; Die junge Nonne; Litanei; Mignon und der Harfner; Der Musensohn; Nacht und Träume; Sei mir gegrüsst; Seligkeit.
(B) *** Pickwick Dig. PCD 898 [MCA MCAD 25235]. Felicity Lott, Graham Johnson.

At bargain price, Felicity Lott's collection brings an ideal choice of songs for the general collector. With Graham Johnson the most imaginative accompanist, even the best-known songs emerge fresh and new. Though Lott's voice loses some of its sweetness under pressure, the slight distancing of the recording gives a pleasant atmosphere, and gentle songs like *Litanei* are raptly beautiful.

Lieder: An die Musik; An Sylvia; Auf dem Wasser zu singen; Du bist die Ruh'; Die Forelle; Frühlingsglaube; Gretchen am Spinnrade; Heidenröslein; Die junge Nonne; Litanei; Der Musensohn; Nacht und Träume; Rastlose Liebe; Der Tod und das Mädchen.
*** EMI CDC7 47861-2 [id.]. Dame Janet Baker, Geoffrey Parsons.

Take a poll of favourite Schubert songs, and a high proportion of these would be on the list. At the very start Dame Janet's strongly characterized reading of *Die Forelle* makes it a fun song, and similarly Parsons' naughty springing of the accompaniment of *An Sylvia* (echoed later by the singer) gives a twinkle to a song that can easily be treated too seriously. One also remembers the ravishing *subito piano* for the second stanza of *An die Musik* and the heart-felt expression of *Gretchen am Spinnrade*. The 1981 recording does not quite catch the voice at its most rounded and the digital remastering fails to achieve absolute sharpness of focus.

Lieder: An die Musik; An Sylvia; Auf dem Wasser zu singen; Ganymed; Gretchen am Spinnrade; Im Frühling; Die junge Nonne; Das Lied im Grünen; Der Musensohn; Nachtviolen; Nähe des Geliebten; Wehmut.

⊛ *** EMI mono CDC7 47326-2 [id.]. Elisabeth Schwarzkopf, Edwin Fischer – MOZART: *Lieder*.***

The radiance of the voice, the control of line and tone (vibrato an important element, varied exquisitely) set this apart even among the finest Schubert recitals. The simplest of songs inspire intensely subtle expression from singer and pianist alike, and though Fischer's playing is not always perfectly tidy, he left few records as endearing as this. The mono sound has been freshened, with the voice beautifully caught.

Lieder: *An die Nachtigall; An mein Klavier; Auf dem Wasser zu singen; Geheimnis;* (i) *Der Hirt auf dem Felsen; Ins stille Land; Liebhaben in allen Gestalten; Das Lied im Grünen; Die Mutter Erde; Romanze; Der Winterabend.*
*** HM Orfeo C 001811 A [id.]. Margaret Price, Sawallisch; (i) with H. Schöneberger.

Consistent beauty of tone, coupled with immaculately controlled line and admirably clear diction, makes Margaret Price's Schubert collection a fresh and rewarding experience. Sawallisch as ever shows himself one of the outstanding accompanists of the time, readily translating from his usual role of conductor. The rather reverberant recording gives extra bloom to the voice.

Lieder: *An Sylvia; Der blinde Knabe; Du bist die Ruh'; Der Einsame; Die Forelle; Ganymed; Gretchen am Spinnrade; Im Frühling; Der König in Thule; Lied der Mignon; Der Musensohn; Nacht und Träume; Rastlose Liebe; Suleika I & II; Der Wanderer an den Mond; Wandrers Nachtlied.*
**(*) EMI Dig. CDC7 47549-2 [id.]. Barbara Hendricks, Radu Lupu.

The duo of Barbara Hendricks and Radu Lupu makes a fascinating and characterful partnership in a delightful selection of Schubert songs, though some of these are far from conventional performances which will not please all lovers of Lieder, always beautiful if at times not well detailed. The bloom on the voice is caught well, with the singer's personality vividly conveyed – though, with such a distinguished accompanist, it is surprising that the piano is backwardly balanced.

Lieder: *Auflösung; Der Einsame; Gesänge des Harfners; Gruppe aus dem Tartarus; Herbst; Hippolits Lied; Im Abendrot; Nachtstück; Nacht und Träume; Über Wildemann; Der Wanderer; Der Wanderer an den Mond.*
*** Ph. Dig. 411 421-2 [id.]. Dietrich Fischer-Dieskau, Alfred Brendel.

The combination of Fischer-Dieskau and Brendel is particularly compelling in the dark or meditative songs which make up the majority of items here. A delicate song like *Der Einsame* loses something in lightness, but the intensity remains. A lifetime of experience in this repertoire brings a magical degree of communication from the great baritone, with the atmospheric recording naturally balanced.

Lieder: *Die schöne Mullerin: Wohin?; Des Baches Wiegenlied. Schwanengesang: Liebesbotschaft. Winterreise: Die Post; Frühlingstraum. An die Geliebte; An die Musik; An die Nachtigall; An mein Klavier; Auf dem Wasser zu singen; Ave Maria; Das sie hier gewesen; Du bist die Ruh'; Der Einsame; Des Fischers Liebesglück; Fischerweise; Die Forelle* (2 versions); *Frühlingsglaube; Geheimes; Gretchen am Spinnrade; Heidenröslein; Das Heimweh;* (i) *Der Hirt auf dem Felsen; Im Abendrot; Die junge Nonne; Der Jüngling an der Quelle; Der Jüngling und der Tod; Lachen und Weinen; Liebhabner in allen Gestalten; Das Lied im Grünen; Litanei; Das Mädchen; Der Musensohn; Nacht und Träume; Nachtviolen; Nahe des Geliebten; Nur wer die Sehnsucht kennt; Der Schmetterling; Seligkeit; So lasst mich scheinen; Ständchen; Schweizerlied; Die Vögel;*

Wiegenlied. Claudine von Villa Bella, D.239: Hin und wieder fliegen Pfeile (2 versions); *Liebe schwärmt. Rosamunde, D.797: Der Volllmond strahlt.*
(M) (***) EMI mono CHS7 63040-2 (2) [id.]. Elisabeth Schumann (various pianists); (i) Reginald Kell.

The irresistible charm and pure, silvery tones of Elisabeth Schumann make this collection of Schubert songs a delight from first to last. On the two CDs are collected 49 songs, with *Der Hirt auf dem Felsen* (*The Shepherd on the Rock*) given separate billing on the cover. The recordings were made between 1927 and 1949, but mostly come from Schumann's vintage period in the 1930s. Transfers capture the voice well but, with a brighter top than on LP, the piano sound has less body. What matters is the vivid personality of the singer, never more sparkling than in such favourite songs as *Wohin?* (one of the earliest, made in 1927), *Heidenröslein* (from 1932) or *Die Forelle*, with a fascinating contrast between the brisk 1936 account and the more cautious but more delicate version of ten years later.

Deutsche Messe with Epilogue (The Lord's prayer), D.872; Mass in G, D.167; Psalms Nos. 23, D.706; 92, D.953; Salve Regina in F, D.379.
*** EMI CDC7 47407-2 [id.]. Popp, Fassbaender, Dallapozza, Fischer-Dieskau, Bav. R. Ch. and SO, Sawallisch.

Though this does not contain the most imaginative and original music from the first volume of Sawallisch's collection of Schubert's choral music, it is a pleasing selection, easy and undemanding and superbly sung and recorded. Some of the items, such as the setting of Psalm 23, have piano accompaniment by Sawallisch.

Masses Nos. 4 in C, D.452; 5 in A flat, D.678.
(M) *** EMI CDM7 69222-2 [id.]. Popp, Donath, Fassbaender, Araiza, Dallapozza, Fischer-Dieskau, Bav. R. Ch. & SO, Sawallisch.

This medium-priced reissue from Sawallisch's excellent choral series combines two settings of the Mass, including the finest (in A flat). The singing is outstanding from chorus and soloists alike, and the remastered recording has retained most of its fullness and gained in clarity and presence.

Mass No. 6 in E flat, D.950.
**(*) DG Dig. 423 088-2 [id.]. Mattila, Lipovšek, Hadley, Pita, Holl, V. State Op. Ch. Concert Group, VPO, Abbado.

Mass No. 6 in E flat, D.950; Offertorium, D.963; Tantum ergo, D.962.
(M) *** EMI CDM7 69223-2 [id.]. Donath, Popp, Fassbaender, Schreier, Araiza, Dallapozza, Fischer-Dieskau, Bav. R. Ch. & SO, Sawallisch.

This EMI record is centred on the *E flat Mass*, Schubert's masterpiece in this form; while the *Tantum ergo* (in C) also undoubtedly has its charm. Though the chorus is not flawless in the *Mass*, Sawallisch's performances here are warmly understanding and the recording is both vivid and atmospheric.
    Abbado takes a spacious rather than a dramatic view of Schubert's most popular setting of the Mass, making Schubert look forward to Bruckner. With first-rate singing from soloists and chorus, it is certainly stimulating, with well-balanced digital sound. However, if the latest digital sound is not essential, Sawallisch's version on mid-priced EMI is even finer and more sympathetic, with a more impressive line-up of soloists and warm, full recording.

Rosamunde: Overture (Die Zauberharfe, D.644) and incidental music, D.797.
*** Ph. Dig. 412 432-2 [id.]. Ameling, Leipzig R. Ch., Leipzig GO, Masur.

The resonance of the Leipzig Gewandhaus seems over-reverberant for scoring designed for the theatre pit: the choral items are not very sharply focused and the bass is diffuse. Yet the ambient effect gives strings and woodwind a nice bloom and detail is not obscured. The superb Leipzig orchestra provides its usual cultured response to the music's drama as well as its lyricism, and the innocent eloquence of Elly Ameling's contribution is matched by the direct vigour of the chorus of spirits, with affinities found with Mozart's *Die Zauberflöte* as well as with Weber.

Die schöne Müllerin (song cycle), *D.795.*
*** DG 415 186-2 [id.]. Dietrich Fischer-Dieskau, Gerald Moore.
*** EMI CDC7 47173-2 [id.]. Dietrich Fischer-Dieskau, Gerald Moore.
*** Capriccio Dig. 10 082 [id.]. Josef Protschka, Helmut Deutsch.
*** Ph. 420 850-2 [id.]. Gérard Souzay, Dalton Baldwin.
*** EMI Dig. CDC7 47947-2 [id.]. Olaf Bär, Geoffrey Parsons.
** Capriccio Dig. 10 220 [id.]. Siegfried Lorenz, Norman Shetler.
** Chan. Dig. CHAN 8725 [id.]. Benjamin Luxon, David Willison.
(M) (*) Pickwick Dig. PCD 925. Adrian Thompson, Roger Vignoles.

With an excellent digital transfer to CD barely giving an indication of its analogue source back in 1972, Fischer-Dieskau's classic version on DG remains among the very finest ever recorded. Though he had made several earlier recordings, this is no mere repeat of previous triumphs, combining as it does his developed sense of drama and story-telling, his mature feeling for detail and yet spontaneity too, helped by the searching accompaniment of Gerald Moore. It is a performance with premonitions of *Winterreise.*

Though the voice is close in Fischer-Dieskau's earlier (1962) EMI set, it required no extra bloom at this stage of his career for its beauty to come across. The piano sound, similarly close, is bass-heavy and rather boomy by today's standards, but never enough to undermine the sensitivity of Gerald Moore's accompaniments, perfectly attuned to the singer.

Josef Protschka gives an intensely virile, almost operatic reading, which is made the more youthful-sounding in the original keys for high voice. As recorded, the voice, often beautiful with heroic timbres, sometimes acquires a hint of stridency, but the positive power and individuality of the performance make it consistently compelling, with all the anguish behind these songs caught intensely. The timbre of the Bösendorfer piano adds to the performance's distinctiveness, well if rather reverberantly recorded.

Souzay made this recording in his prime in 1965; his lyrical style is beautifully suited to this most sunny of song-cycles. Souzay's concentration on purely musical values makes for one of the most consistently attractive versions available, with the words never neglected and Dalton Baldwin giving one of his most imaginative performances on record. The sound belies the recording's age.

Olaf Bär, with Geoffrey Parsons an attentive partner, gives an attractively fresh, boyish-sounding reading of *Schöne Müllerin.* This may not have the dramatic variety of Fischer-Dieskau's strongly characterized readings but, with the songs following each other with hardly a break, it is one full of presence.

When Siegfried Lorenz uses his light, heady tenor with such imagination and 'face', it is sad that Norman Shetler's accompaniment is often so heavy and unhelpful. Nevertheless this is well worth investigating for so youthful-sounding and perceptive a reading from the singer, very well recorded. Like other Capriccio issues of Lieder, this one has no translations.

Luxon's is a heavyweight version, strongly if not always subtly characterized, with sensitive accompaniment from David Willison. Yet on record the pitching of the voice is no longer ideally clean and focused, and this hardly compares with the finest baritone versions.

It is sad that Adrian Thompson's tenor is caught so badly. As balanced, with breathing made very audible, the microphone brings out a serious unsteadiness in all sustained notes, with results so gritty that at times the vocal line almost becomes sing-speech.

Schwanengesang (Lieder collection), *D.957.*
*** Ph. Dig. 411 051-2 [id.]. Dietrich Fischer-Dieskau, Alfred Brendel.
*** EMI CDC7 49018-2 [id.]. Dietrich Fischer-Dieskau, Gerald Moore.
** Chan. Dig. CHAN 8721 [id.]. Benjamin Luxon, David Willison.

Schwanengesang (Lieder collection), *D.957;* Lieder: *An die Musik; An Sylvia; Die Forelle; Heidenröslein; Im Abendrot; Der Musensohn; Der Tod und das Mädchen.*
*** DG 415 188-2 [id.]. Dietrich Fischer-Dieskau, Gerald Moore.

Fischer-Dieskau's DG version with Moore, though recorded ten years before his CD with Brendel, brings excellent sound in the digital transfer, plus the positive advantages, first that the voice is fresher, and then that the disc also contains seven additional songs, all of them favourites. These performances represent a high-water mark in his recording of Schubert.

Fischer-Dieskau's newest version (on Philips) offers deeply reflective performances, from both the singer and his equally imaginative piano partner. His voice is not as fresh as on the earlier, DG set but this is a beautiful, compelling record.

The EMI CD was recorded in the early 1960s and represents the second wave of Fischer-Dieskau's Schubert interpretations. Though the later, DG version has greater thought and refinement, the direct power of expression here is superb too.

Luxon's reading is positive and characterful, with the mood of each song purposefully established in live communication. The boldness is most attractive, even if the voice is not of the sweetest. The Maltings' acoustic adds an agreeable bloom to voice and piano, closely balanced.

Schwanengesang. Am Fenster; Bei dir allein; Herbst; Der Wanderer an den Mond.
***Decca Dig. 425 612-2. Peter Schreier, András Schiff.

Schwanengesang. Im Freien; Der Wanderer an den Mond; Das Zügenglücklein.
*** EMI Dig. CDC 749997-2. Olaf Bär, Geoffrey Parsons.

Schreier's voice may no longer be beautiful under pressure, but the bloom on this Decca recording is far kinder to him than most recent recordings, and the range of tone and the intensity of inflexion over word-meaning make this one of the most compelling recordings ever of *Schwanengesang.* Enhancing that are the discreet but highly individual and responsive accompaniments of András Schiff. Like Bär on his fine EMI version, Schreier makes up a generous CD-length by including not just the 14 late songs published together as *Schwanengesang,* but four more, also from the last three years of Schubert's life. The 14 original songs were never intended as a cycle, anyway. The recording is vividly real, bringing out Schreier's confidential directness in communicating, his mastery in conveying facial expression as he sings. For sample, try his chillingly intense account of *Der Doppelgänger.*

Olaf Bär also amplifies the collection of late songs posthumously published as

Schwanengesang with well-chosen extra items from the same period, notably (like Schreier) *Der Wanderer an den Mond*. Where Schreier is confidential in that song at a brisk speed, Bär brings out the agony and weariness of the traveller addressing the moon. A similar contrast marks many of the other songs too – even the celebrated serenade, *Ständchen*: where Schreier is light and charming, Bär is strong and passionate. Schreier and Schiff are regularly more individual, but Bär and Parsons are the weightier and more beautiful, very well recorded too.

Winterreise (song cycle), *D.911*.
*** DG 415 187-2 [id.]. Dietrich Fischer-Dieskau, Gerald Moore.
*** Ph. Dig. 411 463-2 [id.]. Dietrich Fischer-Dieskau, Alfred Brendel.
*** EMI Dig. CDC7 49334-2 [id.]. Olaf Bär, Geoffrey Parsons.
*** EMI Dig. CDC7 49846-2 [id.]. Brigitte Fassbaender, Aribert Reimann.
**(*) DG Dig. 423 366-2 [id.]. Christa Ludwig, James Levine.
(***) EMI mono CDH7 61002-2 [id.]. Hans Hotter, Gerald Moore.

Winterreise (song cycle), *D.911; Piano sonata No. 15 in C, D.840.*
*** Ph. Dig. 416 289-2 (2) [id.]. Peter Schreier, Sviatoslav Richter.

In the early 1970s Fischer-Dieskau's voice was still at its freshest, yet the singer had deepened and intensified his understanding of this greatest of song-cycles to a degree where his finely detailed and thoughtful interpretation sounded totally spontaneous, and this DG version, now freshened, is arguably the finest of his readings on record. Moore exactly matches the hushed concentration of the singer, consistently imaginative.

The collaboration of Dietrich Fischer-Dieskau with one of today's great Schubert pianists, Alfred Brendel, brings endless illumination in the interplay and challenge between singer and pianist, magnetic from first to last. With incidental flaws, this may not be the definitive Fischer-Dieskau reading, but in many ways it is the deepest and most moving he has ever given. The recording is excellent.

Bär's is a version of this greatest of song-cycles with all the merits. The singer offers not only a beautiful voice, used with consummate artistry, but an ability to bring out with equal conviction the contrast within the cycle between the poet's ardour and the pain of rejection on the one hand, and the darker, more philosophical element. So Bär, with Geoffrey Parsons a masterly accompanist, is both intensely dramatic and deeply reflective, while finding a beauty of line and tone to outshine almost anyone. The darkness of the close is given the intensity of live communication, and the sound is outstanding, with voice and piano given intimacy in a helpful atmosphere.

Brigitte Fassbaender gives a fresh, boyishly eager reading of *Winterreise*, marked by a vivid and wide range of expression. Unlike Christa Ludwig, her predecessor on record, she demonstrates triumphantly why a woman's voice can bring special illumination to this cycle, sympathetically underlining the drama behind the tragic poet's journey rather than the more meditative qualities. Reimann, at times a wilful accompanist, is nevertheless spontaneous-sounding like the singer. Excellent sound.

Recorded live in 1985, Schreier's is an inspired version, both outstandingly beautiful and profoundly searching in its expression, helped by magnetic, highly individual accompaniment from Richter, a master of Schubert. Speeds are not always conventional – indeed are sometimes extreme – but that only adds to the vivid communication which throughout conveys the inspiration of the moment. Rarely has the agonized intensity of the last two songs been so movingly caught on record; it is a small price to pay that the winter audience makes so many bronchial contributions. A more serious snag is that the cycle spreads over on to a second CD, thanks to the slow speeds.

With James Levine a concentrated and often dramatic accompanist, consistently adding to the sense of spontaneous and immediate communication, Christa Ludwig gives a warmly satisfying performance, making use of the mature richness of the voice rather than bringing any striking new insights. Though the different sections of *Frühlingstraum*, for example, are beautifully contrasted, it is the extra darkness of the piano in low keys that adds most to the tragedy. Full, natural recording.

Hans Hotter's 1954 mono recording of *Winterreise* brings an exceptionally dark, even sepulchral performance, lightened by the imagination of Gerald Moore's accompaniment. Hotter scales down his great Wagnerian baritone so that only occasionally is the tone gritty. His concern for detail brings many moments of illumination, but the lack of animation makes this an unrelievedly depressing view.

Schuman, William (born 1910)

American festival overture.
*** DG Dig. 413 324-2 [id.]. LAPO, Bernstein – BARBER: *Adagio*; BERNSTEIN: *Candide: Overture*; COPLAND: *Appalachian spring.****

Schuman's overture is rather like a Walton comedy overture with an American accent, and it is played here with tremendous panache. Close, bright and full recording.

Symphony No. 3.
*** DG Dig. 419 780-2 [id.]. NYPO, Bernstein – HARRIS: *Symphony No. 3.****

The *Third* of William Schuman's ten symphonies has an authentic American feel to it: it certainly creates a sound-world all its own, but the world it evokes is urban. The chorale movement is particularly evocative, full of nocturnal introspection and wholly original. Schuman is also one of the few modern composers to use fugue both individually and effectively. An impressive performance. The New York Philharmonic play with excellent discipline and are well recorded. Strongly recommended.

Schumann, Clara (1819–96)

Piano trio in G min., Op. 17.
*** Hyp. Dig. CDA 66331 [id.]. Dartington Piano Trio – Fanny MENDELSSOHN: *Trio.****

In her authoritative study of the composer, Joan Chissell speaks of the *Piano trio* of 1845 as 'an outstanding testimonial to Clara's creative potential, well-proportioned and free from all procrustean strain in its use of extended forms'. It moves within the Mendelssohn–Schumann tradition with apparently effortless ease and, when played as persuasively as it is here, makes a pleasing impression. If it does not command the depth of Robert, it has a great deal of charm to commend it. Excellent recording.

Schumann, Robert (1810–56)

Cello concerto in A min., Op. 129.
*** Decca Dig. 410 019-2 [id.]. Lynn Harrell, Cleveland O, Marriner – SAINT-SAENS: *Concerto No. 1.****
*(*) EMI CDC7 49307-2 [id.]. Rostropovich, O Nat. de France, Bernstein – BLOCH: *Shelomo.****

Harrell's is a big-scale reading, strong and sympathetic, made the more powerful by the superb accompaniment from the Cleveland Orchestra. Its controversial point is that he expands the usual cadenza with a substantial sequence of his own. The digital recording is outstandingly fine.

Except in the finale, where energy triumphs, the collaboration of Rostropovich and Bernstein in Schumann sounds disappointingly self-conscious, quite unlike the Bloch performance that accompanies it. Bold recording, favouring the soloist.

(i) *Cello concerto in A min., Op. 129;* (ii) *Adagio and allegro in A flat, Op. 70; 5 Stücke im Volkston, Op. 102; Fantasiestücke, Op. 73.*
*** CBS Dig. MK 42663 [id.]. Yo-Yo Ma, (i) Bav. RSO, C. Davis; (ii) Emanuel Ax.

Yo-Yo Ma offers the whole of Schumann's music for the cello and piano. As always, Ma's playing is distinguished by great refinement of expression and his account of the *Concerto* is keenly affectionate, although at times he carries tonal sophistication to excess and drops suddenly into *sotto voce* tone and near-inaudibility. Both he and Sir Colin Davis are thoroughly attuned to the sensibility of this composer. The balance, both between soloist and orchestra and within the various departments of the orchestra, blends perfectly. The three pieces for cello and piano are well projected and full of feeling, with sensitive and well-characterized playing from Emanuel Ax.

(i) *Cello concerto in A min., Op. 129;* (ii) *Piano concerto in A min., Op. 129.*
(M) *(*) DG Dig. 427 819-2 [id.]. (i) Maisky; (ii) Frantz; VPO, Bernstein.

Both these recordings are taken from live performances. In the *Cello concerto* Bernstein seems reluctant to let the music speak for itself, and this affects the eloquent, generous-toned soloist, who similarly has moments of self-indulgence. There are reservations too about the *Piano concerto*. Justus Frantz's account seems a little wanting in spontaneity and does not have quite the delicacy of feeling or subtlety of nuance that the music requires.

Piano concerto in A min., Op. 54.
*** Ph. 412 923-2 [id.]. Bishop-Kovacevich, BBC SO, C. Davis – GRIEG: *Concerto.****
*** CBS Dig. MK 44899 [id.]. Perahia, Bav. RSO, C. Davis – GRIEG: *Concerto.****
*** Ph. 412 251-2 [id.]. Brendel, LSO, Abbado – WEBER: *Konzertstück.****
*** Decca 417 555-2 [id.]. Ashkenazy, LSO, Segal – TCHAIKOVSKY: *Concerto No. 1.****
(M) *** EMI CD-EMX 2002. Solomon, Philh. O, Menges – GRIEG: *Concerto.****
(M) (***) EMI mono CDH7 69792-2. Lipatti, Philh. O, Karajan – MOZART: *Piano concerto No. 21.*(*(**))
(B) **(*) CBS MYK 44771 [id.]. Istomin, Columbia SO, Bruno Walter – BRAHMS: *Double concerto.***(*)
(M) **(*) Decca 417 728-2 [id.]. Radu Lupu, LSO, Previn – GRIEG: *Concerto.***(*)
(B) ** ASV CDQS 6003 [id.]. Vásáry, N. Sinf. – CHOPIN: *Concerto No. 2.***
** DG Dig. 427 771-2 [id.]. Maurizio Pollini, BPO, Abbado – SCHOENBERG: *Piano concerto.***(*)

Our primary recommendation for this favourite Romantic concerto remains with the successful symbiosis of Stephen Bishop-Kovacevich and Sir Colin Davis, who give an interpretation which is both fresh and poetic, unexaggerated but powerful in its directness and clarity. More than most, Bishop-Kovacevich shows the link between the central introspective slow movement and the comparable movement of Beethoven's *Fourth Concerto*; and the spring-like element of the outer movements is finely presented by orchestra and soloist alike. The sound has been admirably freshened for its reissue and the 1972 recording date is quite eclipsed. Even though this remains at full price, it is worth it.

Perahia's version benefits – like the classic Philips account from Stephen Bishop-Kovacevich – from having the guiding hand of Sir Colin Davis directing the orchestra. The recording is taken live from performances Perahia gave in Munich, and no allowance whatever has to be made for the sound, with audience noises not at all apparent. The confident bravura in the performances presents Perahia in a rather different light from usual. He is never merely showy, but here he enjoys displaying his ardour and virtuosity as well as his ability to invest a phrase magically with poetry. In the last resort, Bishop-Kovacevich's simpler and more intimate manner is even more affecting in the first two movements but, with its full and spacious sound, the Perahia is the finest recent version of this favourite coupling.

Brendel's is a thoroughly considered, yet fresh-sounding performance, with meticulous regard to detail. There is some measure of coolness, perhaps, in the slow movement, but on the whole this is a most distinguished reading. The orchestral playing under Abbado is good, and the recorded sound is up to the usual high standards of the house.

Ashkenazy's performance, balancing the demands of drama against poetry, comes down rather more in favour of the former than one might expect, but it is a refined reading as well as a powerful one, with the finale rather more spacious than usual. The recording from the late 1970s has been remastered most successfully. Those wanting a coupling with Tchaikovsky will find this a worthwhile record.

Solomon's 1959 recording, most effectively remastered, is still among the most poetic accounts of this elusive concerto. He plays very beautifully, with the most delicate fingerwork. As in the Grieg coupling, Menges does not emerge as a strong musical personality, but his comparative reticence does not seriously mar the performance, although in the slow movement the orchestral response is slightly muted. Overall the freshness of the music-making gives much pleasure.

Dinu Lipatti's celebrated recording has acquired classic status and will more than repay study. The transfer is excellent. A splendidly aristocratic account in very acceptable sound.

Istomin's performance attractively combines strength and poetry, with bold contrasts in the first movement, a nicely lyrical *Intermezzo* and a fluent, well-paced finale. Bruno Walter's directing personality is strong and the recording sounds remarkably fine in its digital remastering, the warm ambience preventing any feeling of aggressiveness being generated by the dramatic tuttis.

Lupu's clean boldness of approach to the first movement is appealingly fresh, but the fusing together of the work's disparate masculine and feminine Romantic elements has not been solved entirely. The digital CD transfer is especially telling in the quieter moments, but tuttis are less transparent than with a digital recording.

Tamás Vásáry directing from the keyboard gives a characteristically refined yet strong account of the concerto, free from eccentricity and thoroughly straightforward. Poetic, likeable and decently recorded, this is recommendable for those wanting a bargain coupling. The recording is excellent.

Pollini's account is not without tenderness and poetry (witness the slow movement), but he is at times rather business-like and wanting in freshness. He is handicapped by rather unventilated recorded sound and an inconsistent balance. (The piano sounds much further back in the slow movement by comparison with the first.)

Violin concerto in D min., Op. posth.
(*) EMI Dig. CDC7 47110-2 [id]. Kremer, Philh. O., Muti – SIBELIUS: *Concerto.*

The Schumann *Violin concerto*, with its vein of introspection, seems to suit Gidon Kremer, who gives a generally sympathetic account of it and has very good support from the Philharmonia Orchestra under Riccardo Muti. It is not Schumann at his most consistently inspired, but there are good things in it, including a memorable second subject and a characteristic slow movement. The recording is full-bodied and vivid, balanced in favour of the soloist.

Introduction and allegro appassionato in G, Op. 92.
*** Decca Dig. 417 802-2 [id.]. András Schiff, VPO, Dohnányi – DVOŘÁK: *Piano concerto.***(*)

The *Introduction and allegro appassionato in G major* brings the full flowering of Schumann's romanticism. Schiff and Dohnányi play it with dedication and commitment, and the recording, while favouring the soloist, is more realistic in balance than for the Dvořák coupling.

Symphonies Nos. 1–4.
(M) *** DG 429 672-2 [id.]. BPO, Karajan.

Symphonies Nos. 1 in B flat (Spring), Op. 38; 4 in D min., Op. 120; Overture, scherzo and finale, Op. 52.
(M) *** EMI CDM7 69471-2 [id.]. Dresden State O, Sawallisch.

Symphonies Nos. 2 in C, Op. 61; 3 in E flat (Rhenish), Op. 97.
(M) *** EMI CDM7 69472-2 [id.]. Dresden State O, Sawallisch.

Karajan's versions of the Schumann *Symphonies* stand above all other modern recordings. No. 1 is a beautifully shaped performance, with orchestral playing of the highest distinction; Karajan has a natural feeling for the ebb and flow of the music and his control of tempo is subtly varied to follow the musical line. His No. 2 is among the most powerful ever recorded, combining poetic intensity and intellectual strength in equal proportions; and No. 3 is also among the most impressive versions ever commited to disc: its famous fourth-movement evocation of Cologne Cathedral is superbly spacious and eloquent, with quite magnificent brass playing. No. 4 can be classed alongside Furtwängler's famous record, with Karajan similarly inspirational, yet a shade more self-disciplined than his illustrious predecessor. However, the reissued complete set brings digital remastering which – as with the Brahms symphonies – has leaner textures than before, while in tuttis the violins above the stave may approach shrillness. Everything is clean and clear but, although the basic ambience remains, the brass have lost sonority and, above *mezzo forte*, textures are noticeably less warmly expansive than they were on LP. Nos. 1, 3 and 4 are also available separately – see below.

The Dresden CDs of the Schumann *Symphonies* under Sawallisch are as deeply musical as they are carefully considered; the orchestral playing combines superb discipline with refreshing naturalness and spontaneity. Sawallisch catches all Schumann's varying moods, and his direction has splendid vigour. These recordings have dominated the catalogue, alongside Karajan's, for some years and they are most welcome on CD. Unfortunately the sound was always less than ideal: the reverberant acoustic brought a degree of edge to the upper strings. Nevertheless the sound-picture has the essential fullness which the Karajan transfers lack, and the remastering has cleaned up the upper range to a considerable extent.

Symphony No. 1 in B flat (Spring), Op. 38.
(B) *** DG 429 158-2 [id.]. BPO, Karajan – MENDELSSOHN: *Symphony No. 4.****

Symphony No. 1 (Spring); Manfred overture, Op. 115; Overture, scherzo and finale, Op. 52.
**(*) Capriccio CD 10 063. Stuttgart RSO, Marriner.

Symphonies Nos. 1 (Spring); 2 in C, Op. 61; Overture: Julius Caesar.
(M) ** Decca 417 787-2 [id.]. VPO, Solti.

Symphonies Nos. 1 (Spring); 4 in D min., Op. 120.
**(*) DG Dig. 415 274-2 [id.]. VPO, Bernstein.

Bernstein's VPO versions of Nos. 1 and 4 have the extra voltage which comes with live music-making at its most compulsive; it is a pity that Bernstein, who displays a natural response to Schumann, seeks to impose personal idiosyncrasies on the performances that are not as convincing as Furtwängler's. The first movement of the *Spring symphony* is pushed very hard, while the outer movements of No. 4 are not allowed to move forward at a steady pulse. The big transitional climax before the finale of the *Fourth* is massively conceived, yet does not have the spine-tingling sense of anticipation that Furtwängler generates at this point. Even so, with splendid orchestral playing and much engaging detail, there is a great deal to admire here. The recording has an attractive ambience and is full and well balanced, with the woodwind attractively coloured.

Alongside Bernstein's performance, the bright directness of Marriner's reading of the *First Symphony* is the more striking, and there is certainly a spring-like freshness in the outer movements, with the finale sparkling in an almost Schubertian way. There is perhaps a lack of romantic weight, but throughout Sir Neville avoids interfering with the onward flow, in order to register expressive emphases. The *Overture, scherzo and finale* is strongly characterized, again very well played, with the closing apotheosis lyrically powerful without melodrama. The *Manfred overture* too is eloquently done. The digital recording is first class within a kindly studio ambience that allows detail to register admirably, yet is not too dry.

The highlight of Solti's reading, in his compelling performance of Schumann's *Second Symphony*, is the slow movement, with unwanted tensions removed and with a feeling of spontaneous lyricism paramount; and it is a pity that the companion performance of the *Spring symphony* does not quite match this degree of ardent inspiration. It is played well enough but is just a shade disappointing. The *Julius Caesar overture* is no masterpiece, but it makes an enjoyable bonus. On the CD it comes first, to emphasize the slightly dry, bright and forward recording.

Symphony No. 2 in C, Op. 61; Manfred overture.
**(*) DG Dig. 410 863-2 [id]. VPO, Sinopoli.

Sinopoli's is a performance of extremes, consciously designed to reflect the composer's own mental torment. Even the lovely slow movement broods darkly rather than finding repose. The Vienna Philharmonic play with the necessary bite, with the recording providing some mellowness, but the overall balance is not always completely convincing.

Symphony Nos. 2; 3 in E flat (Rhenish), Op. 97.
(B) *** DG 429 520-2 [id.]. BPO, Kubelik.
*** DG Dig. 423 625-2 [id.]. BPO, Levine.

An excellent bargain coupling from Kubelik. No. 2 is beautifully played and eloquently shaped, and in the *Rhenish* Kubelik's straightforward, unmannered approach, coupled to a natural warmth, provides a musical and thoroughly enjoyable account. The remastering of the 1964/5 recordings is most successful: they have more body and warmth than the Karajan complete set.

Levine conducts warm and positive readings of both *Symphonies*, drawing superb playing from the Berlin Philharmonic. The crispness of the violin articulation in his fast, athletic account of the second-movement scherzo of No. 2 is a marvel, and he gives the *Rhenish* all the rhythmic bounce it needs. Though the Berlin recording is warm and full to match – allowing thrilling crescendos in the Cologne Cathedral movement of the *Rhenish* – the inner textures are not ideally clear. The compensation is that the modern digital recording gives a satisfyingly full body to the sound.

Symphony No. 3 in E flat (Rhenish), Op. 87.
(M) *** DG 419 870-2 [id.]. BPO, Karajan – MENDELSSOHN: *Symphony No. 5.***(*)
(M) *** DG Dig. 427 818-2 [id.]. LAPO, Giulini – SCHUBERT: *Symphony No. 8 (Unfinished).**** ⊛

Symphony No. 3 (Rhenish); Manfred overture.
**(*) Ph. Dig. 411 104-2 [id.]. Concg. O, Haitink.

Giulini's *Rhenish* is completely free of interpretative exaggeration and its sheer musical vitality and nobility of spirit are beautifully conveyed. The Los Angeles players produce a very well-blended, warm and cultured sound that is a joy to listen to in itself. The recording is extremely fine, too. Now recoupled with Sinopoli's inspired version of Schubert's *Unfinished*, this makes a superb recommendation.

Haitink's is a characteristically strong and direct reading, beautifully played with outstandingly resonant and rich brass – most important in this of all the Schumann symphonies. Speeds are finely chosen, with the slower movements nicely flowing. Good Concertgebouw sound, lacking a little in brilliance but allowing textures to be registered in fair detail.

Symphonies Nos. 3 in E flat (Rhenish); 4 in D min., Op. 120.
(M) **(*) Decca 417 799-2 [id.]. VPO, Solti.

Solti's sense of rhythm in Schumann is strikingly alert so that the first movement of the *Rhenish* hoists one aloft on its soaring melodies, and the drama of the *Fourth Symphony* is given full force without ever falling into excessive tautness; there is still room to breathe. Though Karajan's account of No. 3 is even finer, Solti's coupling is still worth investigating. The 1967 recording (made in the Sofiensaal) sounds drier-textured than in its LP format, but retains most of its fullness in the bass; one certainly cannot complain that Schumann's scoring sounds too thick!

Symphony No. 4 in D min., Op. 120.
(M) (***) EMI mono CDH7 63085-2. Philh. O, Cantelli – BRAHMS: *Symphony No. 3.****
(M) **(*) Decca 425 957-2 [id.]. LSO, Josef Krips – SCHUBERT: *Symphony No. 9.****

Symphony No. 4; Manfred overture.
(M) (***) DG mono 427 404-2 [id.]. BPO, Furtwängler – HAYDN: *Symphony No. 88.*(***)

There is little doubt that Schumann's *Fourth Symphony* is one of Furtwängler's really great records. The appearance of the first movement's secondary theme is an unforgettable moment, while the *Romanze* is freshly spontaneous in its simplicity; but it is perhaps in the finale where the lack of a firm forward tempo is most striking – and equally (from the magnificently prepared 'Wagnerian' transition passage onwards) where the conductor is most successful in giving a sense of creation in the actual performance. There is superb playing from the Berlin Philharmonic, especially in the brass and strings. The 1953 mono recording has been remastered very successfully; but *Manfred* – recorded in 1949 at a public performance – has rather less congenial sound, and the strings sound thinner.

Cantelli's version of Schumann's *Fourth* brings a comparably inspired performance, with incandescent playing from the Philharmonia. Having Cantelli's two finest symphony recordings with the Philharmonia on a single CD makes the perfect memorial for a conductor who promised supreme greatness before his tragic death.

The *Fourth Symphony* with its taut cyclic form demands dramatic treatment, and Krips' lyrical manner suits the inner movements better than the outer ones. However, the work is well played and the brightly remastered 1956 Kingsway Hall recording makes more impact than the original LP.

CHAMBER MUSIC

Abendlied, Op. 85/2; Adagio and allegro in A flat, Op. 70; Fantasiestücke, Op. 73; 3 Romances, Op. 94; 3 Pieces in Folk style, Op. 102/2–4.
(M) *** Ph. 426 386-2 [id.]. Heinz Holliger, Alfred Brendel.

On this delightful record Heinz Holliger gathers together pieces written in 1849, the most fruitful of composing years for Schumann. The three *Romances* are specifically for oboe, but Holliger – pointing out that Schumann never heard any of the pieces except on the violin – suggests that the others too are suitable for oboe, since the composer himself gave different options. One misses something by not having a horn in the *Adagio and allegro*, a cello in the folk-style pieces, or a clarinet in the *Fantasiestücke* (the oboe d'amore is used here); but Holliger has never sounded more magical on record and, with superbly real recording and deeply imaginative accompaniment, the result is an unexpected revelation.

Fantasiestücke, Op. 73; 3 Romances, Op. 94.
*** Chan. Dig. CHAN 8566 [id.]. Gervase de Peyer, Gwenneth Pryor – SCHUBERT: *Arpeggione sonata*; WEBER: *Silvana variations.****

The artistry of Gervase de Peyer is heard to splendid effect in these late works of Schumann. With warmth of tone and much subtlety of colour, he gives first-class performances and is well supported by Gwenneth Pryor. The recording is most realistic.

Fantasiestücke, Op. 73; 5 Stücke in Volkston, Op. 102.
*** Ph. Dig. 412 230-2 [id.]. Maisky, Argerich – SCHUBERT: *Arpeggione sonata.****

Mischa Maisky and Martha Argerich give relaxed, leisurely accounts of these pieces that some collectors may find almost self-indulgent. Others will luxuriate in the refinement and sensitivity of this playing.

Märchenbilder, Op. 113.
(*) Chan. Dig. CHAN 8550 [id.]. Imai, Vignoles – BRAHMS: *Viola sonatas.*(*)

The *Märchenbilder* are pleasing miniatures, persuasively played here by Nobuko Imai and Roger Vignoles. The recording acoustic is not ideal, but this does not seriously detract from the value of this coupling, especially as there is no alternative account of these pieces.

Märchenerzählungen, Op. 132.
*** EMI CDC7 49736-2. Meyer, Zimmermann, Holl – BRUCH: *Pieces;* MOZART: *Clarinet trio.****

Though they are late works, Schumann's *Märchenerzählungen* – narrative tales, as he calls them – are full of musical fantasy and adventure, superbly realized in these performances by artists of keen individuality and imagination. They make ideal companions for the two other works for this rare combination of clarinet, viola and piano. The recording beautifully captures the feeling of private music-making.

Piano quartet in E flat, Op. 47; (i) Piano quintet in E flat, Op. 44.
*** Ph. 420 791-2 [id.]. Beaux Arts Trio, Rhodes, (i) with Bettelheim.
**(*) CRD CRD 3324 [id.]. Rajna, members of the Alberni Qt.

The Beaux Arts Trio (with associates) give splendid performances of both these fine chamber works. The vitality of inspiration is consistently brought out, whether in the *Quintet* or the relatively neglected *Quartet*, and with that goes the Beaux Arts' characteristic concern for fine ensemble and refined textures. The recording is beautifully clear and clean, if less atmospheric than before.

Though not quite so flawlessly polished in their playing, Rajna and the Alberni give performances that in their way are as urgent and enjoyable as those on the Philips disc. The recording is brighter and crisper, which gives an extra (and not unlikeable) edge to the performances.

Piano trio No. 1 in D min., Op. 63.
(*) CRD CRD 3433 [id.]. Israel Piano Trio – BRAHMS: *Piano trio No. 2.*(*)
(M) ** RCA GD 86262 [6262-2-RG]. Szeryng, Fournier, Rubinstein – SCHUBERT: *Piano trio No. 1.***

The Israel Piano Trio give a powerfully projected account of the *D minor Trio*; the pianist is at times rather carried away, as if he were playing a Brahms concerto. The Scherzo is too emphatically – indeed, almost brutally – articulated. There are, however, some sensitive and intelligent touches, and the recording is first class.

Szeryng, Fournier and Rubinstein are very persuasive. Their performance is taut and vital, yet gives full rein to Schumann's lyricism. The recording dates from 1972 but sounds earlier, with the piano tone a bit dry; and there is a certain want of bloom.

String quartets Nos. 1–3.
**(*) DG Dig. 423 670-2 (3). Melos Qt – BRAHMS: *String quartets 1–3.*

The Melos performances are far from negligible and are generally well shaped. However, for all their ardour they do not seem completely at one with Schumann's world: there is a certain want of tenderness and introspection. Perhaps the brightly lit and forward recording militates against them, and at present they come linked with only Brahms.

String quartets Nos. 1 in A min.; 2 in F, Op. 41/1–2.
*** CRD CRD 3333 [id.]. Alberni Qt.

The *String quartets* are not Schumann at his greatest, but they still offer many rewards. These well-recorded and sympathetic performances by the Alberni Quartet have plenty of finesse and charm and are guided throughout by sound musical instinct. Recommended.

String quartet No. 3 in A, Op. 41/3.
** BIS CD 10 [id.]. Voces Intimae Qt – SIBELIUS: *Quartet.***

An eminently serviceable account of the appealing *A major* Schumann *Quartet*, though the recording (which dates from the mid-1970s) has a touch of glare.

SCHUMANN

Funf Stücke (5 Pieces) im Volkston (for cello and piano).
(M) *** Decca 417 833-2 [id.]. Rostropovich, Britten – SCHUBERT: *Sonata***(*); DEBUSSY: *Sonata.****

Though simpler than the Debussy *Sonata* with which it is coupled, this is just as elusive a work; but in the hands of masters these *Five Pieces in folk style* have a rare charm, particularly the last, with its irregular rhythm. Excellent recording.

Violin sonatas Nos. 1 in A min., Op. 105; 2 in D min., Op. 121.
*** DG Dig. 419 235-2 [id.]. Gidon Kremer, Martha Argerich.

The *Violin sonatas* both date from 1851 and are 'an oasis of freshness' in his last creative period. Kremer and Argerich are splendidly reflective and mercurial by turn and have the benefit of an excellent recording.

PIANO MUSIC

Arabeske in C, Op. 18; Études symphoniques, Op. 13.
*** DG Dig. 410 916-2 [id.]. Maurizio Pollini.

Pollini's account has a symphonic gravitas and concentration: it also has the benefit of excellent recorded sound. Pollini includes the five additional variations that Schumann omitted from both the editions published during his lifetime, placing them as a group between the fifth and sixth variations.

Arabeske, Op. 18; Études symphoniques, Op. 13; Papillons, Op. 2.
*** Decca Dig. 414 474-2 [id.]. Vladimir Ashkenazy.

Impressive playing, and well recorded too – yet Ashkenazy's *Études symphoniques* have a breadth and splendour that are not entirely in tune with Schumann's sensibility. The *Arabeske* and *Papillons*, however, must be numbered among Ashkenazy's most impressive contributions to this repertoire.

Carnaval, Op. 9; Fantasia in C, Op. 17.
**(*) Decca Dig. 417 401-2 [id.]. Jorge Bolet.

Bolet's *Carnaval* and the *C major Fantasy* are both expansive readings, mellowed in maturity, though speeds on the slow side bring a degree of heaviness. At times there is a lack of sparkle in the lighter pieces of *Carnaval*, but these are thoughtfully poetic as well as strong performances; the piano is a little clangy in fortissimos.

Carnaval, Op. 9; Fantasiestücke, Op. 12; Romance, Op. 28/2; Waldszenen, Op. 82: The Prophet bird.
**(*) RCA RD 85667 [RCA 5667-2-RC]. Artur Rubinstein.

Rubinstein brings the fullest spectrum of colours to bear on these most romantic and lyrical of Schumann's compositions, moving with artless ease from one mood to the next, always supremely sure of himself and always superbly in tune with the musical thought. Though the piano timbre is not as rich as the best recordings from Decca or EMI, there is a directness about the sound that helps capture the attention.

5 Études, Op. posth.; Études symphoniques, Op. 13; Papillons, Op. 2.
**(*) CBS CD 76635 [MK 34539]. Murray Perahia.

Murray Perahia has a special feeling for the *Symphonic studies* and he makes every expressive point in the most natural and unfussy way. He plays the additional five studies, which Schumann omitted from the published score, as an addendum. The

Papillons are unlikely to be surpassed. The engineers give Perahia too close a balance to be ideal; the sound is of acceptable quality, but fortissimos are rather clattery.

Études symphoniques; Toccata, Op. 7.
*(*) DG Dig. 410 520-2 [id.]. Ivo Pogorelich – BEETHOVEN: *Piano sonata No. 32.***(*)

Pogorelich opens his performance of the *Études symphoniques* with a grotesquely self-conscious and studied presentation of the theme. This is pianism of the first order, but the listener's attention tends to be drawn from the music to the wilful pianism.

Fantasia in C, Op. 17.
*** CBS Dig. MK 42124 [id.]. Murray Perahia – SCHUBERT: *Wanderer fantasia.****

Murray Perahia's account of the *C major Fantasy*, perhaps the most powerful and deeply felt of all Schumann's piano works, has few peers. It is a performance of vision and breadth, immaculate in its attention to detail and refinement of nuance. The recording is good, even if it does not wholly convey the fullest range of sonority and dynamics.

Fantasia in C, Op. 17; Fantasiestücke, Op. 12.
*** Ph. Dig. 411 049-2 [id.]. Alfred Brendel.

As the very opening of the *Fantasiestücke* demonstrates, this is magically spontaneous playing, full of imaginative touches of colour, strong as well as poetic. The actual sound is rather forward, but it serves Brendel well and truthfully conveys the depth of timbre.

Fantasia in C, Op. 17; Kreisleriana, Op. 16.
*** RCA RD 86258 [RCA 6258-2-RC]. Artur Rubinstein.

Rubinstein's account of the *Fantasia in C* is wonderfully subtle in its control of tempo and colour, and the poetry of the outer sections is quite magical. In spite of the close balance, Rubinstein achieves exquisite gradations of tone; the recording, made in 1965, is among the best he received during this period. *Kreisleriana* is hardly less compelling, with the great pianist at his most aristocratic, although the impetuous opening is rather shallowly recorded.

Fantasia in C, Op. 17; Piano sonata No. 1 in F sharp min., Op. 11.
*** DG 423 134-2 [id.]. Maurizio Pollini.

This is among the most distinguished Schumann records in the catalogue. Pollini's playing throughout has a command and authority on the one hand and deep poetic feeling on the other that hold the listener spellbound. The recording is good but not outstanding – it is rather hard in its digitally remastered form.

Kinderszenen, Op. 15; Sonata No. 1 in F sharp min., Op. 11; Waldszenen, Op. 82.
*** Decca Dig. 421 290-2 [id.]. Vladimir Ashkenazy.

Ashkenazy's account of the *F sharp minor Sonata* is held on a less taut rein than Pollini's. If, in purely pianistic terms, Ashkenazy may not be so totally commanding or authoritative, nevertheless he still has his finger(s) on the pulse of Schumann's inspiration. The playing is very natural and all the more impressive for that. He proves a sound guide in the *Waldszenen*, and his *Kinderszenen* is one of the most appealing in the catalogue, again with a naturalness and directness that are attractive. The Decca recording is excellent, though the balance is closer in the *Sonata*.

Kreisleriana, Op. 16.
** Denon Dig. CO 73336 [id.]. Hélène Grimaud – BRAHMS: *Piano sonata No. 2 in F sharp min.***

Kreisleriana, Op. 16; Novelettes, Op. 21, Nos. 1 & 8.
(M) *** EMI CDM7 69537-2. Youri Egorov.

Youri Egorov's untimely death in his early thirties deprived the world of an outstanding artist. His *Kreisleriana* is very fine indeed, full of poetic feeling – indeed, one of the freshest and most ardent in the catalogue. At mid-price this is excellent value, and the digitally remastered recording comes up very well indeed.

No quarrels with Hélène Grimaud's playing, which is remarkably mature and authoritative for an artist not yet in her twenties. However, she is ill-served by a very close and bottom-heavy recording, and this greatly inhibits enjoyment.

Piano sonata No. 2 in G min., Op. 22.
*** CBS Dig. MK 44569 [id.]. Murray Perahia – SCHUBERT: *Piano sonata No. 20.***

Perahia's account of the Schumann *G minor Sonata* is fresh, ardent and vital; every phrase is beautifully moulded yet somehow seems spontaneous in feeling – and spontaneity was the essence of Schumann's youthful genius. As always, Perahia's is the art that conceals art, and it is only at the very end that one realizes what total concentration he brings to this (and what concentration it demands). The recording places the listener fairly near the piano but is eminently truthful.

VOCAL MUSIC

Dichterliebe, Op. 48; Liederkreis, Op. 24; Lieder: Dein Angesicht; Die beiden Grenadiere; Du bist wie eine Blume.
(**) Virgin Dig. VC 790787-2 [id.]. Thomas Allen, Roger Vignoles.

Allen's keenly sensitive singing of both cycles is seriously marred by the washiness of the recording, which sets singer and piano in an unsuitably reverberant acoustic, with focus blurred. Fine as the performances are, complemented by four additional songs, the disc can hardly be recommended in preference to more aptly recorded versions.

Dichterliebe (song-cycle), *Op. 48; Liederkreis* (song-cycle), *Op. 39; Myrthen Lieder, Op. 25.*
*** DG 415 190-2 [id.]. Dietrich Fischer-Dieskau, Christoph Eschenbach.

An outstandingly fine *Dichterliebe* plus the magnificent Op. 39 *Liederkreis*, made the more attractive on CD by the generous addition of seven of the *Myrthen* songs. Though a thoughtfully individual artist in his own right, Eschenbach here provides consistently sympathetic support for the singer. He is imaginative on detail without ever intruding distractingly. Very good sound for the period.

Dichterliebe, Op. 48; Liederkreis, Op. 39.
*** Ph. Dig. 416 352-2 [id.]. Dietrich Fischer-Dieskau, Alfred Brendel.
*** EMI CDC7 47397-2 [id.]. Olaf Bär, Geoffrey Parsons.

More than in his previous versions of Schumann's *Dichterliebe*, Fischer-Dieskau's latest one, done in inspired collaboration with Alfred Brendel, brings an angry, inconsolable reading, reflecting the absence of fulfilment in the poet's love – though Fischer-Dieskau's voice has more grit in it than before. The Op. 39 *Liederkreis* also brings inspired, spontaneous-sounding performances, with the voice here notably fresher.

Olaf Bär's performances are finely detailed and full of insight, but relatively reticent in expressive style. These are not such strongly characterized readings as those of Fischer-Dieskau; but in their fresher, more youthful manner they are outstandingly successful. Excellent recording on CD.

Frauenliebe und Leben, Op. 42; Liederkreis, Op. 24; 3 Heine Lieder (Abends am Strand; Lehn' deine Wang' an meine Wang'; Mein Wagen rollet langsam). Tragödie, Op. 64/3.
**(*) DG Dig. 415 519-2 [id.]. Brigitte Fassbaender, Irwin Gage.

Positively characterized, with a wide range of expression and fine detail but little sense of vulnerability, Fassbaender's reading conceals the underlying sentimentality of the poems of *Frauenliebe*. Passionate involvement also marks her singing of the Heine *Liederkreis*, of which there are surprisingly few recordings. Irwin Gage is the understanding accompanist. The recording is well balanced, with fine presence.

Lieder from Album für die Jugend, Op. 79; Gedichte der Königen Maria Stuart, Op. 135; Myrthen Lieder, Op. 25: excerpts. Abends am Strand; Die Kartenlegerin; Ständchen; Stille Tränen; Veratine Liebe.
*** CRD CRD 3401 [id.]. Sarah Walker, Roger Vignoles.

Sarah Walker's 1982 Schumann collection is most cherishable, notably the five Mary Stuart songs which, in their brooding darkness, are among Schumann's most memorable. The voice is a little weighty for some of the lighter songs from the *Myrthe* collection but, with superb accompaniment and splendid recording, this is an outstanding issue.

Mass in C min., Op. 47.
*** EMI Dig. CDC7 49763-2. Shirai, Seiffert, Rootering, Düsseldorf State Musikverein Ch., BPO, Sawallisch.

Schumann's *Mass* brings some of his finest flights of invention – not at all the tailing-off which has been ascribed to him in the period leading up to his mental illness. Of the soloists, only the soprano has much to sing (the delectable Mitsuko Shirai, sensuously beautiful in the *Offertorium* solo) and the weight of the work rests on the chorus, a fine body here warmly rather than clinically recorded. Few conductors today can match Sawallisch in this composer's music.

Das Paradies und das Peri, Op. 50 (oratorio: complete).
**(*) Erato/WEA Dig. 2292 45456-2 (2). Edith Wiens, Sylvia Herman, Ann Gjevang, Robert Gambill, Christophe Prégardien, SRO Ch. & O, Armin Jordan.

Schumann described this oratorio as 'my greatest and, I hope, my best work'. Though in the modern repertory it has almost sunk without trace, it is an important pioneering venture: as the first fully romantic oratorio using a secular text, it marked a breakthrough. Based on a quest poem by Thomas Moore, it centres on the heroine's search for gifts as a passport to heaven. From this fine recording one can understand both why the composer was so excited and why the piece has failed to gain a foothold. This was the work which rounded off Schumann's extraordinary period of creative activity prompted by his marriage to Clara, starting with the miraculous 'Year of Song', 1840. The richness and the fluency of the writing carry you on with no let-up, strongly argued, but the melodic invention is less striking than in Schumann's songs, with themes plain rather than memorable. Armin Jordan draws first-rate singing and playing from his Suisse Romande forces, helped by warmly atmospheric recording. The soloists are reliable, but not very distinctive – Edith Wiens, Ann Gjevang, Robert Gambill and Christophe Prégardien.

Requiem in D flat, Op. 148; Requiem für Mignon, Op. 98b.
*** EMI Dig. CDC7 49164-2. Donath, Lindner, Andonian, Soffel, Georg, Gedda, Fischer-Dieskau, Düsseldorf Musical Soc. Ch., Düsseldorf SO, Klee.

Like Mozart, Schumann was unable to shake off the conviction that the *Requiem* was for himself. The opening *Requiem aeternam* is affecting and dignified, and the final *Benedictus* has a haunting eloquence. Bernhard Klee extracts a very sympathetic response from his distinguished team of soloists and the fine Düsseldorf chorus and orchestra. They also give an attentive and committed account of the 1849 *Requiem for Mignon*, Op. 98b. The EMI recording is natural and well balanced.

Scenes from Goethe's Faust.
✪ (M) *** Decca 425 705-2 (2) [id.]. Harwood, Pears, Shirley-Quirk, Fischer-Dieskau, Vyvyan, Palmer, Aldeburgh Fest. Singers, ECO, Britten.

Britten made this superb recording of a major Schumann work, long neglected, in 1973, soon after a live performance at the Aldeburgh Festival. Though the reasons for neglect remain apparent – this episodic sequence of scenes is neither opera or cantata – the power and imagination of much of the music, not least the delightful garden scene and the energetic setting of the final part, are immensely satisfying. Britten inspired his orchestra and his fine cast of singers to vivid performances, which are outstandingly recorded against the warm Maltings acoustic. The CD mastering has effectively retained the ambience yet added to the projection of both solo voices and chorus. This is magnificent music, and readers are urged to explore it – the rewards are considerable.

Schütz, Heinrich (1585–1672)

Christmas oratorio (Weinachtshistorie).
*** EMI Dig. CDC7 47633-2 [id.]. Kirkby, Rogers, Thomas, Taverner Cons., Taverner Ch., Taverner Players, Parrott – PRAETORIUS: *Christmas motets.****

There is no sense of austerity here, merely a sense of purity, with the atmosphere of the music beautifully captured by these forces under Andrew Parrott. One is soon gripped by the narrative and by the beauty and simplicity of the line. Apart from a rather nasal edge on the violin tone, it is difficult to fault either this moving performance or the well-balanced and refined recording.

Italian Madrigals (complete).
*** HM HMC 901162 [id.]. Concerto Vocale, René Jacobs.

Schütz's first and only Book of Italian Madrigals reflects his encounter with the music of Giovanni Gabrieli and Monteverdi. The Concerto Vocale, led by the counter-tenor, René Jacobs, employ a theorbo which provides aural variety, and at times they offer great expressive and tonal range. They omit the very last of the madrigals, the eight-part *Vasto mar.*

Musicalische Exequien. Motets: *Auf dem Gebirge; Freue dich des Weibes Jugend; Ist nicht Ephraim mein teurer Sohn; Saul, Saul, was verfolgst du mich.*
*** DG Dig. 423 405-2 [id.]. Monteverdi Ch., E. Bar. Soloists, His Majesties Sagbutts & Cornetts, Gardiner.

Schütz's *Musical Exequien* contains music that is amazing for its period (the first half of the sixteenth century). The Monteverdi Choir responds with fiery intensity, making light of the complex eight-part writing in the second of the three *Exequies*. Four more superb motets by Schütz make an ideal coupling, with first-rate recorded sound.

St Matthew Passion.
*** EMI Dig. CDC7 49200-2 [id.]. Hilliard Ens., Hillier.

Schütz's setting of the Passion Story is exclusively vocal; its austerity extends to the absence not only of instrumental support but of any additional hymns or arias. In this version from the Hilliard Ensemble and Paul Hillier, who takes the bass part of Jesus, the solo parts on the whole are admirable and the restraint of Paul Elliot's Evangelist is impressive. The soloists double in the choral sections, which is less than ideal. In all other respects this excellently balanced and finely produced EMI version is admirable.

Scriabin, Alexander (1872 – 1915)

(i) *Piano concerto in F sharp min., Op. 20;* (ii) *Poème de l'extase, Op. 54;* (i) *Prometheus – The poem of fire, Op. 60.*
*** Decca 417 252-2 [id.]. (i) Ashkenazy, LPO; (ii) Cleveland O; Maazel.

Ashkenazy plays the *Piano concerto* with great feeling and authority, and the Decca recording has both clarity and luminosity. Moreover Maazel accompanies most sympathetically throughout. *Prometheus* too, powerfully atmospheric and curiously hypnotic, is given a thoroughly poetic and committed reading and Ashkenazy copes with the virtuoso obbligato part with predictable distinction. Given such outstanding recording and performance, this makes a splendid starting point for any Scriabin collection. Decca have added Maazel's 1979 Cleveland recording of *Le Poème de l'extase*. This is a shade too efficient to be really convincing. The playing is often brilliant and the recording is very clear but the trumpets are rather forced and strident. However, it can be regarded as a bonus for the other two works.

Le Poème de l'extase.
(*) Chan. Dig. CHAN 8849 [id.]. Chicago SO, Järvi – MUSSORGSKY: *Pictures.*(*)

Järvi's version, played superbly and recorded vividly and resonantly in Chicago's Orchestral Hall, emphasizes Scriabin's primary colours, with the trumpet solo penetrating boldly through the voluptuous texture and skirting vulgarity by a small margin. There have been more subtle performances, but this one certainly makes a strong impact.

Symphonies Nos. (i) *1 in E, Op. 26. 2 in C min., Op. 29; 3 in C min. (Le Divin Poème), Op. 43; Le Poème de l'extase, Op. 54;* (ii) *Promethée (Le Poème du feu), Op. 60.*
(M) *** Ph. 420 785-2 (3) [id.]. (i) Soffel, Tenzi; (ii) Saschowa; (i; ii) Frankfurter Kantorei, Frankfurt RSO, Eliahu Inbal.

Eliahu Inbal's set of the Scriabin *Symphonies* comes from the late 1970s. The playing of the Frankfurt Radio Orchestra is refined and well prepared, though it does not match some rivals in terms of voluptuousness, and the analogue recordings are generally well balanced and wear their years well. If they fall short of the ultimate in that overheated, heady intoxication Scriabin made so much his own, they still remain competitive in this mid-priced format.

Symphony No. 1 in E, Op. 26.
*** EMI Dig. CDC7 47349-2 [id.]. Toczyska, Myers, Westminster Ch., Phd. O, Muti.
*** Olympia Dig. OCD 159 [id.]. Gorokhovskaya, Pluzhnikov, Glinka State Ac. Ch. of Leningrad, USSR RSO, Fedoseyev.

Scriabin's *First Symphony*, a highly rhapsodic score, commands luxurious orchestral playing in Muti's new EMI recording. He brings great refinement of dynamic nuance and plasticity of phrasing to this score, showing its many beauties to the best possible advantage. It would be difficult to over-praise the sensitivity and polish of the Philadelphia wind or the sumptuous tone of the strings. The vocal contributions from Stefania Toczyska and Michael Myers in the last movement, a setting of Scriabin's own words, are also excellent. This is undoubtedly one of Muti's best records in recent years and should acquire classic status.

The new digital recording from the Soviet Union makes an admirable alternative. It is relaxed and unforced; the orchestral playing is excellent, though the brass are not as refined as those of the Philadelphia; and the two soloists, Yevgenia Gorokhovskaya and Konstantin Pluzhnikov, are every bit as fine as their EMI rivals, Stefania Toczyska and Michael Myers. This can also be recommended with confidence, and it has a slight price advantage.

Symphony No. 2 in C min., Op. 29; Rêverie, Op. 24.
*** Chan. Dig. CHAN 8462 [id.]. SNO, Järvi.

Plenty of atmosphere here in Järvi's performance and a splendid orchestral response from his Scottish players. Although it is less amorphous than its predecessor, the *Symphony* needs the most fervent advocacy if the listener is to be persuaded. This splendid account from Järvi, with its richly detailed Chandos recording, can be recommended strongly.

Symphony No. 3 in C min. (Le divin poème), Op. 43.
*** Etcetera KTC 1027 [id.]. Concg. O, Kondrashin.
(*) EMI Dig. CDC7 49115-2 [id.]. Phd. O, Muti – TCHAIKOVSKY: *Romeo and Juliet.(*)

Symphony No. 3 (Le divin poème); Le Poème de l'extase, Op. 54.
**(*) DG Dig. 427 324-2 [id.]. NYPO, Sinopoli.

Scriabin's mammoth *Third Symphony* calls for vast forces, but there is no doubt that it is original, both in layout and in substance. Kondrashin and the Concertgebouw Orchestra recorded the *Third Symphony* at a public concert in 1976, and the performance has a special authority and intensity, and is well recorded.

Muti has already shown an instinctive feeling for Scriabin in his earlier recording of the *First Symphony*, and he is pretty persuasive here. The recorded sound does not handle the more massive climaxes completely comfortably and, despite the richness of sonority this wonderful orchestra produces, one feels a certain congestion.

Sinopoli's coupling offers another bloom from the hothouse in the form of the *Poème de l'extase*. He has a good feeling for the atmosphere of the *Third Symphony* and gets responsive playing from the New York Philharmonic. However, the recording does not open out too well in climaxes. The *Poème de l'extase* is sensitively shaped and is splendidly performed. Sinopoli's version is certainly not to be dismissed, and those tempted by the coupling may feel these reservations of less importance.

Études, Op. 8/7 & 12; Op. 42/5. Preludes, Op. 11/1, 3, 9, 10, 13, 14, 16; Op. 13/6; Op. 15/2; Op. 16/1 & 4; Op. 27/1; Op. 48/3; Op. 51/2; Op. 59/2; Op. 67/1. Sonatas Nos. 3, Op. 23; 5, Op. 53.
(M) (***) RCA mono/stereo GD 86215 [6215-2-RC]. Vladimir Horowitz.

The RCA engineers have done wonders to these recordings from the 1950s though there is naturally a limit to what they can accomplish, and some of the original shallowness and clatter remains. The *Preludes* and the legendary account of the *Third Sonata* come from 1956 and give the impression of greater range and firmer focus than in their last vinyl incarnation. The *Fifth* is much later, coming from the mid-1970s, and has more bloom. The performances are obviously three star and form an essential part of any good Horowitz collection.

Preludes, Op. 11, Nos. 2, 4–6, 8–14, 16, 18, 20, 22, 24; Op. 13, Nos. 1–3; Op. 15, Nos. 1 and 5; Op. 16, Nos. 2 and 4. Prelude for the left hand in C sharp min., Op. 9/1; Étude in C sharp min., Op. 42/5. Piano sonata No. 4 in F sharp, Op. 30.
*** EMI Dig. CDC7 47346-2 [id.]. Andrei Gavrilov.

Gavrilov does not give us any set of the *Preludes* or *Studies* complete but picks and chooses – which is no doubt ideal in a piano recital designed to show his sympathies, but is less desirable from the point of view of a record collector. The playing is often exquisite and the *Fourth Sonata* is about the finest account on record. At times his approach is impetuous and dynamics can be exaggerated, but playing of this order is still pretty remarkable. The balance is not too close, yet the CD brings a tangible presence and the piano timbre is naturally caught.

Piano sonatas Nos. 1–10.
(M) *** Decca 425 579-2 (2) [id.]. Vladimir Ashkenazy.

The Scriabin *Piano sonatas* encompass two decades, the first dating from 1892 when he was twenty, while the last five were composed in quick succession from 1911 to 1913. It is good to have all ten in Vladimir Ashkenazy's commanding and authoritative performances, recorded between 1972 and 1984, all on two medium-priced discs. Ashkenazy is clearly attuned to this repertoire, though he is at his finest in the earlier sonatas. The last three are given with brilliance and vision, and there is no lack of awareness of the demonic side of Scriabin's musical personality. In Nos. 9 and 10 Horowitz had more abandon and intensity without losing any of his imperious control. However, these are fine performances and are well recorded.

Piano sonata No. 3 in F sharp min., Op. 23; 2 Poems, Op. 32; Vers la flamme, Op. 72.
(*) Kingdom Dig. KCLCD 2001. Gordon Fergus-Thompson – BALAKIREV: *Piano sonata.*(*)

Gordon Fergus-Thompson gives a splendid account of Scriabin's overheated *F sharp minor Sonata* and sensitive, atmospheric performances of the other pieces here. A reverberant but good recording, but the piano does not always sound perfectly fresh.

Piano sonata No. 9 in F (Black Mass), Op. 68.
(*) Nimbus Dig. NI 5187 [id.]. Ronald Smith – BALAKIREV: *Sonata*; MUSSORGSKY: *Pictures.*(*)

This is a powerful account of the *Ninth Sonata* (*The Black Mass*), intense and full of colour, not as concentrated in feeling or pianistically as transcendental as the Horowitz, but a far from negligible performance.

Seiber, Matyas (1905–60)

Clarinet concertino.
*** Hyp. Dig. CDA 66215 [id.]. Thea King, ECO, Litton – BLAKE: *Concerto*; LUTOSLAWSKI: *Dance preludes.****

Matyas Seiber's highly engaging *Concertino* was sketched during a train journey (in 1926, before the days of seamless rails) and certainly the opening *Toccata* has the jumpy, rhythmic feeling of railway line joints and points. Yet the haunting slow movement has a touch of the ethereal, while the Scherzo has a witty jazz element. Thea King has the measure of the piece; she is accompanied well by Litton, and very well recorded. Recommended.

Sessions, Roger (born 1896)

Concerto for orchestra.
*** Hyp. Dig. CDA 66050 [id.]. Boston SO, Ozawa – PANUFNIK: *Symphony No. 8.****

Sessions's *Concerto for orchestra* finds him at his thorniest and most uncompromising, with lyricism limited to fleeting fragments of melody; but the tapestry of sound presents its own logic with its contrasts of mood – the playful opening leading one on finally to a valedictory close – sharply defined. Ozawa makes a powerful advocate, helped by superb playing from the Boston orchestra.

Symphony No. 4; Symphony No. 5; Rhapsody for orchestra.
*** New World Dig. NWCD 345 [id.]. Columbus SO, Badea.

Roger Sessions shares with Walter Piston, his tonal contemporary (who also composed eight symphonies), a highly developed sense of structure and an integrity that remained unshaken by changes of fashion. His musical language is dense and his logic is easier to sense than to follow. The performances by the Columbus Symphony Orchestra under Christian Badea appear well prepared, and there is no doubt as to their commitment and expertise. The sound ideally needs a larger acoustic, but every strand in the texture is well placed and there is no feeling of discomfort.

Shchedrin, Rodion (born 1933)

The Frescoes of Dionysius.
** Olympia Dig. OCD 108 [id.]. Bolshoi Theatre Soloists' Ens., Lazarev – BIZET/SHCHEDRIN: *Carmen ballet.***(*)

A quite effective miniature, fairly static in feeling, owing something to minimalism in structure, inspired by the frescos of Ferapontov Monastery, near Kirilov. It is well played and recorded.

Sheppard, John (c. 1515–c. 1559)

Christe Redemptor omnium; In manus tuas; Media vita; Reges Tharsis; Sacris solemniis; Verbum caro.
*** Gimell Dig. CDGIM 016 [id.]. Tallis Scholars, Peter Phillips.

Little is known about John Sheppard save for the bare fact that he was at Magdalen College, Oxford (1543–8), and at the Chapel Royal from 1552 onwards. All the music here is based on chant, and much of it is for the six-part choir of treble, mean (or middle part), two counter-tenors, tenor and bass, which produces a particularly striking sonority. The *Media vita* ('In the midst of life we are in death') is a piece of astonishing beauty, and it is sung with remarkable purity of tone by the Tallis Scholars under Peter Phillips. There

941

are false relations as expressive as any in his Tudor contemporaries. Glorious and little-known music: the recording could hardly be improved on.

Gaude virgo Christiphera; In manus tuas; Libera nos, salva 1–2; Reges Tharsis.
*** Proudsound Dig. PROUCD 126 [id.]. Clerkes of Oxenford, David Wulstan – TYE: *Mass Euge bone.****

The Clerkes of Oxenford under David Wulstan produce a very different sonority from the Tallis group, wonderfully blended and balanced, with a tonal sophistication that is remarkable. They overlap only minimally with the Gimell disc, so both can be recommended to the enthusiast. They are placed rather more distantly than the Tallis Scholars but are splendidly recorded in a spacious but not over-reverberant acoustic.

Motets: Filiae Hierusalem venite; Haec dies; In manus tuas Domine I; In pacem in idipsum; Justi in perpetuum vivent; Lauden dicite Deo; Libera nos, salva nos I; Paschal Kyrie; Regis Tharsis et insulae; Spiritus sanctus procedens I; Verbo caro factum est.
⊛ *** Hyp. Dig. CDA 66259 [id.]. The Sixteen, Christophers.

It was merely an accident of twentieth-century scholarship – and sudden lack of funds – that prevented the Tudor Music Edition from reaching the volume on Sheppard and with it a wider dissemination of his music. Here in eleven superb responsories The Sixteen consistently convey the rapturous beauty of Sheppard's writing, above all in ethereal passages in the highest register, very characteristic of him. Even there The Sixteen's sopranos seem quite unstressed by the tessitura. There are not many more beautiful records of Tudor polyphony than this.

Shostakovich, Dmitri (1906–75)

(i; ii; iii) *The Adventures of Korzinkina* (film music): *suite, Op. 59;* (iv; ii) *Alone* (film music): *suite, Op. 26;* (v) *La Comédie Humaine* (incidental music to Balzac), *Op. 37;* (i; ii) *Scherzos: in F sharp min., Op. 1; in E flat, Op. 7; Theme & variations in B flat, Op. 3;* (vi) *Spanish songs, Op. 100.*
**(*) Olympia OCD 194 [id.]. (i) USSR MoC SO, (ii) Rozhdestvensky; (iii) with Ch.; (iv) Soloists, Ens. of USSR Ac. SO; (v) Leningrad CO, Gurdzhi; (vi) Artur Eisen, A. Bogdanova.

None of the music on this record is familiar or without interest to admirers of this composer; indeed most of it appears for the first time. The first two pieces are wholly uncharacteristic. The Op. 7 *Scherzo* is more characteristic – there is a prominent part for the piano and there is already evidence of Shostakovich's special kind of wit. The *Spanish songs* come from 1956 and are more substantial; they are splendidly sung by Artur Eisen. The film scores are from the '30s and uncover no masterpieces. Though the recordings were made during the 1980s and are not top-drawer, this disc is still well worth investigating.

Chamber symphony in C min. Op. 110a (arr. Barshai from *String quartet No. 8); Symphony for strings, Op. 118a* (arr. Barshai from *String quartet No. 10).*
*** DG Dig. 429 229-2. COE, Rudolf Barshai.
(M) *** TRAX TRXCD 110 [id.]. Phoenix CO, Julian Bigg.

The *Chamber symphony* is an arrangement for full strings of the *Eighth Quartet*, and the *Symphony for strings* is a similar transcription of the *Tenth*. Both were made by Rudolf Barshai who, in a note on his long friendship with the composer, tells how these arrangements came to be made; and he directs them both with the authority of the composer and bears his imprimatur. The young players of the Chamber Orchestra of Europe excel themselves in the tonal beauty, refinement and responsiveness of their playing, here recorded for the first time in their new home, the smaller Philharmonie Hall in Berlin. But inevitably, with such a rich string-sound, some of the darkness of the music disappears: the chill of much of the writing in No. 8, inspired by memories of the war and the bombing of Dresden. In compensation, the weight of sound gives extra impact to such movements as the *Allegro molto* in Opus 110a. These are strong performances of real eloquence and power, which are excellently recorded. It is undoubtedly the best and most authoritative version of both scores now on the market and can be confidently recommended to those who prefer the dark, brooding transcriptions to the inward-looking originals.

The Phoenix performances have great intensity and feeling and are all held together by Julian Bigg; he secures a wide dynamic range, good phrasing and a robust attack when required. The recording is made in a resonant acoustic and is well balanced.

Cello concerto No. 1 in E flat, Op. 107.
*** Erato/WEA Dig. 2292 45332-2 [id.]. Rostropovich, LSO, Ozawa – PROKOFIEV: *Sinfonia concertante.****
*** CBS Dig. MK 37840 [id.]. Yo-Yo Ma, Phd. O, Ormandy – KABALEVSKY: *Cello concerto No. 1.****
(M) *** EMI CDM7 63020-2. Tortelier, Bournemouth SO, Berglund – WALTON: *Concerto.****
*** Chan. Dig. CHAN 8322 [id.]. Raphael Wallfisch, ECO, Geoffrey Simon – BARBER: *Cello concerto.****

Cello concertos Nos. 1 in E flat, Op. 107; 2, Op. 126.
*** Ph. Dig. 412 526-2 [id.]. Heinrich Schiff, Bav. RSO, Maxim Shostakovich.

(i) *Cello concerto No. 1, Op. 107;* (ii) *Symphony No. 5.*
(M) *** CBS Dig. MYK 44903 [id.]. (i) Ma, Phd. O, Ormandy; (ii) NYPO, Bernstein.

In his newest, Erato version, Rostropovich still brings his special authority to this score and plays with demonic intensity and concentration. Ozawa gives him generally sensitive support, though he generates a less intense and brooding atmosphere in the slow movement than did Ormandy. On the other hand, the orchestral texture is placed in a more natural perspective than first time around; the recording is not only excellently balanced but very truthful. An impressive disc.

Yo-Yo Ma on CBS brings an ardent musical imagination to the *First Cello concerto*. He plays with an intensity that compels the listener and the Philadelphia Orchestra give eloquent support. The CBS recording has ample presence and warmth, with the balance slightly favouring the soloist, but very well judged overall. This has now been reissued at mid-price, generously coupled with Bernstein's exciting 1979 account of the *Fifth Symphony*, recorded in Tokyo when Bernstein and the New York Philharmonic were on tour there. Unashamedly Bernstein treats the work as a Romantic symphony. The very opening makes an impact rarely possible in the concert hall; then, exceptionally, in the cool and beautiful second-subject melody Bernstein takes a slightly detached view – though as soon as that same melody comes up for development, after the exposition, the result is altogether more warmly expressive. The *Allegretto* becomes a burlesque, but its Mahlerian roots are strongly conveyed. The slow movement is raptly beautiful, and the finale is brilliant and extrovert, with the first part dazzlingly fast and the conclusion one of unalloyed triumph, with no hint of irony. On CD, the bass is made to sound full and rich, and the slight distancing of the sound (compared with many CBS recordings) places the orchestra within a believable ambience.

Tortelier's reading of the first of Shostakovich's two *Cello concertos* does not always quite match the example of the dedicatee and first performer, Rostropovich, in sheer precision of bravura passages, but Tortelier does match the Russian master in urgency and attack. Berglund and the Bournemouth orchestra provide colourful and committed accompaniment, and the recording has retained its fullness and is even more vivid on CD.

Wallfisch handles the first movement splendidly, though there is not quite the same sense of momentum as in Yo-Yo Ma's account. However, he gives a sensitive account of the slow movement and has thoughtful and responsive support from the ECO. The Chandos recording is outstandingly fine.

Heinrich Schiff on Philips is the only cellist so far to couple the two *Concertos*. Schiff's superbly recorded account does not displace Yo-Yo Ma in the *First*, but it can hold its own, and interest inevitably centres on its companion. The *Second Concerto* offers fewer overt opportunities for display. It is a haunting piece, essentially lyrical; it is gently discursive, sadly whimsical at times and tinged with a smiling melancholy that hides deeper troubles. The recording is enormously impressive.

(i) *Cello concerto No. 1 in E flat, Op. 107*; *Piano concertos Nos.* (ii) *1 in C min., Op. 35*; (iii) *2 in F, Op. 101*.
(M) *** CBS CD 44850. (i) Rostropovich, Phd. O, Ormandy; (ii) Previn; (iii) Bernstein; NYPO, Bernstein.

Rostropovich made this recording of the *Cello concerto No. 1* within a few months of the first performance in Russia. Shostakovich himself attended the recording session in Philadelphia and gave his approval to what is a uniquely authoritative reading. Ormandy and the Philadelphia Orchestra accompany superbly, with a precision and warmth rare with new scores. The recording is clear and spacious but the balance places the soloist too prominently, and certain other features of the score are highlighted, notably the glockenspiel at the end of the first movement. CBS have now shrewdly made an attractive triptych for CD by including Bernstein's radiant account of the *Second Piano concerto*, along with Previn's equally striking account of No. 1. Though these New York performances bring somewhat dated recording, both pianists have a way of turning a phrase to catch the imagination, and a fine balance is struck between Shostakovich's warmth and his rhythmic alertness.

Piano concertos Nos. 1–2; The Unforgettable year 1919, Op. 89; The Assault on beautiful Gorky (for piano and orchestra).
(B) *** CfP Dig. CD-CFP 4547. Alexeev, Philip Jones, ECO, Maksymiuk.

Alexeev is a clear first choice in both *Concertos*, and his record would sweep the board even at full price. The digital recording is excellent in every way and scores over its rivals in clarity and presence. Artistically he has more personality than his rivals and has the advantage of sensitive and idiomatic support from the ECO and Jerzy Maksymiuk. There is a fill-up in the form of a miniature one-movement *Concerto* from a film-score called *The Unforgettable year 1919*. Given the quality of both the performance and the sound, this record should make new friends for the two *Concertos*, particularly at such an attractive price.

Piano concerto No. 1 in C min., for piano, trumpet and strings, Op. 35.
*** Olympia Dig. OCD 179 [id.]. Kissin, Moscow Virtuosi, Spivakov – *Symphony No. 15.****

(*) Delos Dig. D/CD 3021 [id]. Rosenberger, Burns, LACO, Schwarz – PROKOFIEV: *Symphony No. 1*; STRAVINSKY: *Soldier's tale.***

Yevgeny Kissin gives a first-class account of the *First Piano concerto* with the Moscow Virtuosi under Vladimir Spivakov and featuring Vladimir Kafelnikov in the important trumpet solos. With precocious mastery Kissin brings out both the youthful brightness of the outer movements and the yearning expressiveness of the slow movement.

There have been more witty accounts of the *First Concerto* than Rosenberger's, but the extra degree of gravitas in the first movement adds an unexpected depth to the music, and the *Lento* is beautifully played, with a fine expressive response from the strings of the Los Angeles Chamber Orchestra. The finale, taken fast, makes a brilliant contrast.

(i) *Piano concerto No. 2 in F, Op. 102*; (ii) *Violin concerto No. 1 in A min., Op. 99.*
**(*) Decca Dig. 425 793-2 [id.]. (i) Cristina Ortiz, (ii) Boris Belkin; RPO, Ashkenazy.

Though there are finer versions of both *Concertos*, anyone who wants this unusual coupling may safely invest in this unexpected instalment in the Ashkenazy Shostakovich series. Cristina Ortiz gives a sparkling account of the jaunty first movement, and she also brings out the fun of the finale with finely pointed playing, while the central *Andante*, taken rather more slowly than usual, is both warm and refined. Boris Belkin, in the first and more popular of the *Violin concertos*, plays immaculately with consistently sweet, pure tone; but he misses some of the work's darker, deeper undertones, whether in the meditative *Nocturne* of the first movement or in the solo leading into the cadenza in the third movement. With superb articulation he gives a brilliant account of the finale, but it is neither as sparkling nor as exciting as in the finest versions. The sound is full and well balanced, not as distanced as in other issues from Ashkenazy's series.

Piano concerto No. 2 in F, Op. 102; Symphony for strings in A flat, Op. 118a.
** Chan. Dig. CHAN 8443 [id.]. Dmitri Shostakovich, I Musici de Montreal, Montreal SO (members), Maxim Shostakovich.

Maxim Shostakovich, who gave the *Second Piano concerto* its première in 1957, on Chandos directs a performance in which his son is soloist, which ensures authenticity; and yet one must register a degree of disappointment. The outer movements are firm and crisply rhythmic, and the *Andante* avoids any suggestion of sentimentality but is a shade too straight, while the closing toccata is also somewhat anonymous in its very energetic progress. The *Symphony for strings* certainly does not lack incisiveness in the account by I Musici de Montreal, although this does not seem an apt coupling for the *Concerto*.

Violin concertos Nos. 1 in A min., Op. 99; 2 in C sharp min., Op. 129.
*** Chan. Dig. CHAN 8820. Lydia Mordkovitch, SNO, Järvi.

Mordkovitch's concentrated reading of No. 2, so much sparer than No. 1 and less immediately effective, explodes any idea that it marks a disappointing sequel. From her hushed, withdrawn account of the lyrical first theme through all three movements she is matched by Järvi and the orchestra in their total commitment. She even outshines the work's dedicatee and first interpreter, David Oistrakh, in the dark reflectiveness of her playing, even if she cannot quite match him in bravura passages. In the better-known concerto (No. 1) she is hardly less impressive, providing not a second-best, but a very valid alternative to the finest versions available. Here again, the meditative intensity of her playing is magnetic, with a fullness and warmth of tone that have not always marked her playing on record before.

Violin concerto No. 1 in A min., Op. 99.
*** EMI Dig. CDC7 49814-2 [id.]. Perlman, Israel PO, Mehta – GLAZUNOV: *Violin concerto.****
*(*) Ph. Dig. 422 364-2 [id.]. Viktoria Mullova, RPO, Previn – PROKOFIEV: *Violin concerto No. 2.****

Perlman's version of the Shostakovich *First Violin concerto* was recorded live in the Mann Auditorium in Tel Aviv, and though that involves some roughness in the sound, particularly in tuttis, the flair and electricity of this modern wizard of the violin are most compellingly caught. Excitement is the keynote: Perlman and Mehta put the work in the light of day and, in the two fast movements and the cadenza, that brings tremendous dividends. There is no violinist in the world who in sheer bravura can quite match Perlman, particularly live, and the ovation which greets his dazzling performance of the finale is richly deserved. Yet some of the mystery and the fantasy which Russian interpreters have found – from David Oistrakh onwards – is missing, and the close balance of the solo instrument, characteristic of Perlman's concerto recordings, undermines hushed intensity. However, this is not as aggressive a recording as some from this source, and anyone who fancies this unusual coupling will not be disappointed.

Viktoria Mullova does not penetrate far below the surface in the poignant opening *Nocturne*. It is all very expert, but ultimately it is routine and wanting in atmosphere.

Five days, five nights (suite), Op. 111a; Hamlet (suite), Op. 116a (film music); King Lear (suite), Op. 137.
*** RCA RD 87763 [7763-2-RC]. Belgian R. O, Serebrier.

Hamlet obviously generates powerful resonances in Shostakovich's psyche and prompts responsive and committed playing from the Belgian Radio Orchestra, while much of the score for *Five days, five nights* inhabits the bleak world of the *Eleventh Symphony*. In every way a more powerful issue than its companion (see below), this should not be passed over by collectors with an interest in either Shostakovich or the cinema.

The Gadfly (film music): Suite, Op. 97a.
(B) **(*) CfP CD-CFP 4463. USSR Cinema SO, Emin Khachaturian.

The Gadfly (film music): Suite, Op. 97a; Pirogov (film music): suite, Op. 76.
** RCA RD 86603 [6603-2-RC]. Belgian R. O, Serebrier.

The score for *The Gadfly* was turned into a twelve-movement suite, published in 1960 and recorded two years later. At times the music is quite pleasing but at others is wholly uncharacteristic. It has been brought before the public by the use of a movement called *Romance* – ripely scored with concertante solo violin – as signature theme for a TV series, *Reilly, Ace of Spies*. On CfP, a musically committed and well-recorded issue, although the brightening of the sound in the digital remastering has lost some of the smoothness of the original LP.

Pirogov also includes some colourful music but is hardly a masterpiece. The playing of the Belgian Radio Orchestra under Serebrier is eminently serviceable without being really distinguished, and the same goes for the recording. Those seeking out *The Gadfly* would do better with the Russian recording on Classics for Pleasure, which is better played and more vivid as sound.

Symphonies Nos. 1 in F min., Op. 10; 6 in B min., Op. 54.
**(*) Chan. Dig. CHAN 8411 [id.]. SNO, Järvi.
**(*) Decca Dig. 425 609-2 [id.]. RPO, Ashkenazy.

Symphonies Nos. 1 in F min., Op. 10; 9 in E flat, Op. 70.
*** Decca Dig. 414 677-2 [id.]. LPO, Haitink.

Haitink's reading of the brilliant *First Symphony* may lack something in youthful high spirits, but it is a strong, well-played performance none the less, and it is coupled with a superb account of No. 9. Without inflation Haitink gives it a serious purpose, both in the poignancy of the waltz-like second movement and in the equivocal emotions of the outer movements. The recording is outstandingly clean and brilliant.

Järvi's account of the *First Symphony* is strikingly more volatile than Haitink's in the outer movements – there is no lack of quirkiness in the finale, while the *Largo* is intense and passionate. The *Sixth* has comparable intensity, with an element of starkness in the austerity of the first movement. The Scherzo is skittish at first but, like the finale, has no lack of pungent force. In both symphonies this is emphasized by the reverberant acoustics of Glasgow City Hall, bringing an element of brutality to climaxes (which are spectacularly expansive).

Ashkenazy's coupling of Nos. 1 and 6 is a mixed bag, with the distancing of sound which has marked earlier issues in the series seriously undermining the impact of the *Sixth*. The ominous, slow first movement lacks necessary bite, and it leads to an account of the central scherzo which, at a hectic speed, becomes conventionally spiky instead of wryly comic. The finale is also taken fast, again losing some of its humour. No. 1 is far more successful, with the lightness of much of the scoring beautifully caught in a performance which captures both the spiky humour and the emotional intensity, notably in the melancholy of the slow movement. For this coupling, Järvi's Chandos disc is preferable.

Symphonies Nos. 2 (October Revolution), Op. 14; 3 (The First of May), Op. 20. The Age of gold (suite), Op. 22.
*** Decca Dig. 421 131-2 [id.]. LPO Ch. & O, Haitink.

Shostakovich was still in his early twenties when he composed these symphonies, neither of which shows him at his most inspired. Admirable performances and excellently balanced sound with great presence and body. The joky *Age of gold* suite makes an unexpected if attractive makeweight for the CD, recorded with comparable brilliance.

Symphonies Nos. 2 (October Revolution), Op. 14; 12 in D min. (1917), Op. 112.
**(*) Olympia OCD 200 [id.]. USSR MoC SO, Rozhdestvensky.

Rozhdestvensky's coupling of Nos. 2 and 12 could not be more apt, both of them inspired by the 1917 Russian Revolution but written over thirty years apart. There have been more atmospheric readings of the out-and-out programme symphony, No. 12, than Rozhdestvensky's, but the rugged strength of the writing – not merely illustrative – comes over powerfully. The bright, sometimes coarse recording is typical of the Olympia series.

Symphony No. 4 in C min., Op. 43.
*** Chan. Dig. CHAN 8640 [id.]. SNO, Järvi.
**(*) Decca 421 348-2 [id.]. LPO, Haitink.
**(*) Decca Dig. 425 693-2 [id.]. RPO, Ashkenazy.

(i) *Symphony No. 4 in C min., Op. 43;* (ii) *Jazz suite No. 1, Op. 38.*
**(*) Olympia Dig. OCD 156 [id.]. (i) USSR MoC SO, Rozhdestvensky; (ii) Soloists Ens.

Järvi gives a characteristically weighty account of this difficult work, which captures the full power and bitterness of the writing, as well as its vein of irony. He draws from the SNO playing which is both rugged and expressive, consistently conveying the emotional thrust of the piece and making the enigmatic ending, with its ticking rhythm, warmer than usual, as though bitterness is finally evaporating. He is helped by exceptionally rich, full recording.

With Rozhdestvensky the humour as well as the concentrated power of the work comes over tellingly, even if in the first movement he does nothing to mitigate rhythmic squareness, and the playing is not ideally refined. The second movement also has its slack moments, but the result is highly idiomatic, as it is in the slow, Mahlerian funeral march of the finale. The little *Jazz suite* makes a delightful extra with its *Waltz*, *Polka* and *Foxtrot*.

Haitink brings out an unexpected refinement in the *Symphony*, a rare transparency of texture. He is helped by recording of Decca's finest quality, vividly remastered. Detail is superbly caught; yet the earthiness and power, the demonic quality which can make this work so compelling, are underplayed.

Ashkenazy gives a performance of high contrasts, very well recorded but not as bitingly intense as some. He is not helped by choosing an exceptionally fast speed for the first movement, which consequently loses some of its thrust and weight, as well as some ironic overtones. The finale too is not as ominous as it might be; but, for anyone collecting the Ashkenazy series, the version is still worth considering.

Symphony No. 5 in D min., Op. 47 (see also under *Cello concerto No. 1*).
(M) *** RCA GD 86801 [6801-2-RG]. LSO, Previn (with RACHMANINOV: *The Rock***).
*** EMI Dig. CDC7 49181-2 [id.]. Oslo PO, Jansons.
**(*) Decca Dig. 410 017-2 [id.]. Concg. O, Haitink.
**(*) Telarc Dig. CD 80067 [id.]. Cleveland O, Maazel.
*(*) Denon Dig. CO 74175 [id.]. Frankfurt RSO, Eliahu Inbal.

Symphony No. 5 in D min.; The Bolt: Ballet suite No. 5.
*** Chan. Dig. CHAN 8650. SNO, Järvi.

Symphony No. 5 in D min., Op. 47; 5 Fragments, Op. 42.
*** Decca Dig. 421 120-2 [id.]. RPO, Ashkenazy.

Ashkenazy's reading of Shostakovich's most popular symphony brings one of his finest records yet as a conductor. This is an exceptionally searching and intense reading, bitingly dramatic, yet finding an element of wry humour in the second and fourth movements to outshine any rival. Ashkenazy conveys in the slow movement's spareness a rare sense of desolation, more hushed and refined than immediate rivals, with the woodwind solos adding to the chill. Unlike most versions, the Decca issue has a fill-up, the very rare *Five Fragments*, sharp little inventions, like the main work given demonstration sound quality.

Previn's version, dating from early in his recording career (1965), remains very high on the list. This is one of the most concentrated and intense readings ever, superbly played by the LSO at its peak. What has always marked out Previn's reading is the spaciousness of the first and third movements, held together masterfully. In the third movement he sustains a slower speed than anyone else, even Haitink, making it deeply meditative in its dark intensity; and the purity and beauty of the Previn have never been surpassed, notably in the long-legged second subject, while his build-up in the central development section brings playing of white heat. The bite and urgency of the second and fourth movements are also irresistible. Only in the hint of analogue tape-hiss does the sound fall short of the finest modern digital recordings – and it is more vividly immediate than most.

Jansons' EMI version with the Oslo orchestra on top form brings a tautly incisive, electrically intense reading, marked by speeds notably faster than usual that yet have the ring of authenticity. The development section in the first movement for example builds up bitingly into a thrilling climax, with the accelerando powerfully controlled. Not a first choice, but an exciting one.

One big merit of the Järvi version is the interest of the coupling, a half-hour suite from his early ballet, full of wry, quirky ideas typical of the young Shostakovich. That suits Järvi perfectly, and in the *Symphony* too he gives a warmly committed performance, even if – as in the great span of the second subject on exposed violins – the playing of the SNO is not as refined as in the finest versions. Otherwise the emotional intensity and spiky humour are very well caught indeed, and the recording is full and warm in the Chandos manner.

Haitink is eminently straightforward, there are no disruptive changes in tempo, and the playing of the Concertgebouw Orchestra and the contribution of the Decca engineers are beyond praise. There could perhaps be greater intensity of feeling in the slow movement, but, whatever small reservations one might have, it is most impressive both artistically and sonically.

Brilliant in performance, spectacular in recorded sound, Maazel's Cleveland recording for Telarc is also warm, with the Cleveland violins sweet and pure in the long-legged melody of the second subject in the first movement. Though Maazel is faster than is common in the exposition section, he allows himself less stringendo than usual in the build-up of the development. The other three movements are also on the fast side.

Without a coupling and with recording that is not always cleanly focused, the Inbal issue is hardly competitive, and the reading brings some self-conscious underlining. This would be far more acceptable in a less competitive field.

Symphonies Nos. 5 in D min., Op. 47; 9 in E flat, Op. 70.
*** Olympia Dig. OCD 113 [id.]. USSR MoC SO, Rozhdestvensky.

The *Ninth* in particular suits Rozhdestvensky's personality ideally, with the element of wit and humour brilliantly presented, and with the darker, more emotional elements emerging strongly and committedly. The Ministry of Culture Orchestra demonstrates in that work that it is second to none in Moscow, though the playing is less polished in No. 5, where violin-tone in the exposed passages is sometimes lacking fullness. Warm, vivid recording, with the players set fairly close against a reverberant acoustic.

Symphony No. 6 in B min., Op. 54.
(M) *** EMI CDM7 69564-2. LSO, Previn – RACHMANINOV: *Symphony No. 3.****

Here Previn shows his deep understanding of Shostakovich in a powerfully drawn, unrelenting account of the opening movement, his slow tempo adding to the overall impact. After that the offhand wit of the central Scherzo comes over the more delicately at a slower tempo than usual, leaving the hectic finale to hammer home the deceptively joyful conclusion to the argument. Excellent recording, impressively remastered.

Symphonies Nos. 6 in B min., Op. 54; 11 in G min. (1905), Op. 103; Overture on Russian and Kirghiz folk themes, Op. 115.
**(*) Decca Dig. 411 939-2 (2) [id.]. Concg. O, Haitink.

Haitink's performances of the *Symphonies* are characteristically refined and powerful. With superb playing from the Concertgebouw, particularly the strings, the textures have an extra transparency, helped also by the brilliant and atmospheric Decca recording. Haitink's structural control, coupled with his calm, taut manner, also brings out the weight and power of the big slow movements which open both works; the *Largo* of No. 6 is particularly impressive. Nevertheless Haitink seems almost detached, marginally lacking the concentrated tension of a genuine performance.

Symphonies Nos. 6 in B min., Op. 54; 12 in D min. (The Year 1917), Op. 112.
*** Olympia Dig. OCD 111 [id.]. USSR MoC SO, Rozhdestvensky.

No. 6 is a work that Rozhdestvensky responds to with exceptional warmth, giving weight and intensity to the magnificent opening slow movement and bringing out the spark of dark humour in the Scherzo and finale while giving them necessary bite and power. He is also most persuasive in the programmatic No. 12 with its picture of the events of the 1917 Revolution, bringing out the atmosphere and drama. Unfortunately, the disc has the full span of the work, over 40 minutes of continuous music, with no separating bands for the various sections. First-rate playing from the Ministry of Culture Orchestra and full-bodied, warm recording.

Symphony No. 7 in C (Leningrad), Op. 60.
*** Chan. Dig. CHAN 8623 [id.]. SNO, Järvi.
**(*) EMI CDC7 49494-2 [id.]. Leningrad PO, Jansons.
**(*) Olympia Dig. OCD 118 [id.]. USSR MoC SO, Rozhdestvensky.

Järvi's is a strong, intense reading, beautifully played and recorded, which brings out the full drama of this symphony in a performance that consistently gives the illusion of spontaneity in a live performance, as in the hushed tension of the slow, expansive passages. There have been more polished versions than this, but, with its spectacular Chandos sound, it makes an excellent choice as a single-disc version.

Jansons' version of the *Leningrad symphony* with the Leningrad Philharmonic is a finely wrought, superbly played reading, but only intermittently does it capture the full bite of the live performances that Jansons and the orchestra have given together. Nor can the recording compare with the very finest in vividness or amplitude. It was made, while the orchestra was on tour, in the Oslo concert hall.

Rozhdestvensky's view of the *Leningrad symphony*'s controversial first movement is unusually broad. It is undeniably powerful but runs the risk of overplaying the element of banality in the notorious *ostinato*. Many will prefer a brisker and more polished reading, but the ruggedness here is certainly authentic; the other movements too bring warmly expressive, spontaneous-sounding performances, which lack only the last degree of subtlety. The sound is full and satisfying but grows coarse at the biggest climaxes.

Symphonies Nos. 7 (Leningrad); 12 (The Year 1917), Op. 112.
**(*) Decca Dig. 412 392-2 (2). LPO or Concg. O, Haitink.

With Haitink, the long first-movement *ostinato* – now revealed as having quite different implications from the descriptive programme suggested by the Soviet propaganda-machine in the war years – is almost an interlude in a work which otherwise in its deep seriousness challenges comparison with the other wartime symphony, the epic *Eighth*. The CD includes also the *Twelfth Symphony*, but the use of two full-price compact discs makes this an expensive investment.

Symphony No. 8 in C min., Op. 65.
*** Ph. Dig. 422 442-2 [id.]. Leningrad PO, Mravinsky.
*** Decca Dig. 411 616-2 [id.]. Concg. O, Haitink.

**(*) Chan. Dig. CHAN 8757. SNO, Järvi.
** Decca Dig. 421 773-2 [id.]. Chicago SO, Solti.
* RCA Dig. RD 60145 [60145-2-RC]. St Louis SO, Slatkin.

Symphony No. 8 in C min., Op. 65; (i) *3 Satires from Op. 109.*
*** Olympia Dig. OCD 143 [id.]. USSR MoC SO, Rozhdestvensky; (i) with Bogacheva.

Mravinsky's CD is a memorial issue, a live recording in full, clear, digital sound made in 1982. It gives a superb idea of the magnetism of his reading, the way that in the massive slow first movement with its shattering climaxes he built tensions inexorably, demonstrating the firm structural strength while plumbing the deep personal emotions in this stressed wartime inspiration. Equally, a live recording maintains necessary tensions more clearly in the balancing span of the last three linked movements. Most significantly, Mravinsky's flowing speed for the elusive *Allegretto* finale makes the close of the work less equivocal than usual. It is a great performance and, though ensemble is inevitably not always quite as polished as in the finest studio recordings, discrepancies are minimal. The Leningrad audience of March 1982, evidently transfixed, even forgot to cough.

Rozhdestvensky conducts a thrustful and incisive reading of the *Eighth* with electrically intense playing that both holds the enormous structure together and brings out the element of fantasy which literal performances underplay. The spontaneity which Rozhdestvensky conveys regularly in his recordings is here combined with sharpness of focus. The digital recording is full-bodied and wide-ranging, growing a little coarse only in the biggest climaxes. The *Three Satires* are orchestral arrangements of songs from a cycle of poems by Sasha Cherny. Irina Bogacheva, a strong, very Slavonic mezzo, gives characterful performances, though her voice is balanced far too close.

Haitink characteristically presents a strongly architectural reading of this war-inspired symphony, at times direct to the point of severity. After the massive and sustained slow movement which opens the work, Haitink allows no lightness or relief in the Scherzo movements, and in his seriousness in the strangely lightweight finale (neither fast nor slow) he provides an unusually satisfying account of an equivocal, seemingly uncommitted movement.

Järvi is at his finest in the great expanses of the magnificent first movement, strong and intense from first to last, with full orchestral weight given to the rugged climaxes. The emotional thrust of this music, directly inspired by the Second World War, is conveyed powerfully, but it leads to accounts of the other movements which in their forthcoming expressiveness miss some of the chill of the work, though the wry humour of the scherzo comes out most pointedly. The resolution in the final movement is too complete, too comfortable – not tear-laden or enigmatic as it can be. But with full, warm Chandos sound this is still very impressive.

Solti recorded his account of No. 8 in preparation for his European tour with the Chicago orchestra in 1989. It is a pity that he did not wait until after the tour, when the reading would have matured. He had not previously conducted Shostakovich and, though the playing is very impressive, the fire and concentration which generally mark Solti's work are not consistently present. It is a performance to admire rather than to be moved by. The recording is characteristic of Decca's work in Chicago.

After his earlier success in Shostakovich, Slatkin is disappointing in No. 8, giving a reading which lacks both necessary weight and intensity – fatal in the long first movement – even though he draws refined playing from the St Louis orchestra. The recording, rather thin, does not help to create involvement.

Symphony No. 9 in E flat, Op. 70; Festive overture, Op. 96; Katerina Ismailova (Lady Macbeth of Mtsensk): 5 Entr'actes. Tahiti trot (arr. of Youmans's *Tea for two), Op. 16.*
*** Chan. Dig. CHAN 8567 [id.]. SNO, Järvi.

Järvi's version of the *Ninth* brings a warmly expressive, strongly characterized reading in superb, wide-ranging sound. The point and wit of the first movement go with bluff good humour, leading on to an account of the second-movement *Moderato* that is yearningly lyrical yet not at all sentimental. The weight and gravity of the fourth-movement *Largo* are then similarly contrasted with the fun and jokiness of the final *Allegretto.* The mixed bag of fill-up items is both illuminating and characterful, ending with the jolly little chamber arrangement that Shostakovich did in the 1920s of Vincent Youmans's *Tea for two,* the *Tahiti trot.*

Symphony No. 10 in E min., Op. 93.
*** DG Dig. 413 361-2 [id.]. BPO, Karajan.
**(*) Decca 421 353-2 [id.]. LPO, Haitink.
(M) *** DG 429 716-2 [id.]. BPO, Karajan.
(M) ** EMI CDM7 63096-2. Bournemouth SO, Berglund.

Symphony No. 10 in E min., Op. 93; Ballet suite No. 4.
*** Chan. Dig. CHAN 8630 [id.]. SNO, Järvi.

(i) *Symphony No. 10 in E min., Op. 93;* (ii) *Hamlet* (incidental music), *Op. 32: Fragments.*
**(*) Olympia OCD 131 [id.]. (i) USSR MoC SO, Rozhdestvensky; (ii) Leningrad CO, Serov.

Already in his 1967 recording Karajan had shown that he had the measure of this symphony; this newer version is, if anything, even finer. In the first movement he distils an atmosphere as concentrated as before, bleak and unremitting, while in the *Allegro* the Berlin Philharmonic leave no doubts as to their peerless virtuosity. Everything is marvellously shaped and proportioned. The *allegro* section of the finale is taken up to a speed much faster than most other rivals. The digital sound is altogether excellent, and this must now rank as a first recommendation.
Järvi, too, conducts an outstandingly strong and purposeful reading in superb sound, full and atmospheric. In the great span of the long *Moderato* first movement he chooses an ideal speed, which allows for moments of hushed repose but still builds up relentlessly. The curious little *Ballet suite No. 4,* with its sombre *Prelude* leading to a bouncy *Waltz* and a jolly *Scherzo tarantella,* makes a delightful bonus.
Haitink really has the measure of the first movement, whose climaxes he paces with an admirable sense of architecture, and he secures sensitive and enthusiastic playing from the LPO both here and in the scherzo. In the third movement he adopts a slower tempo than usual, which would be acceptable if there were greater tension or concentration of mood; but here and in the slow introduction to the finale the sense of concentration falters. The Decca recording is outstandingly realistic.
Karajan's earlier reading is superbly moulded, with genuine tragic feeling and authenticity. The Berlin Philharmonic plays magnificently and the 1967 recording combines ambient atmosphere with a fierce brilliance to project the score's climaxes pungently.
Following the pattern of his Shostakovich series, Rozhdestvensky conducts a strong and spontaneous-sounding reading of the *Tenth,* not as portentous or intense as some but with a vein of spikiness that is totally idiomatic. Though the digital sound is full and

bright, the bass tends to be boomy and rather vague, with internal textures coarsened at climaxes.

Berglund has a strong grip on the architecture of the work and is refreshingly straight. He draws playing of high quality from the Bournemouth orchestra and has a genuine sense of the music's scale; but ultimately he is let down by a want of inner tension. Nevertheless this performance is not without strength or atmosphere, although there is an element of literalness and sobriety.

Symphony No. 11 in G min. (1905), Op. 103.
**(*) Olympia Dig. OCD 152 [id.]. USSR MoC SO, Rozhdestvensky.

Rozhdestvensky directs a characteristically red-blooded reading, not as bitingly intense as some. He takes an exceptionally spacious view of the opening *Adagio* movement, and only in the finale does he adopt a speed that is faster than usual, losing something in weight. Like others in this series, the sound is full-bodied but coarsens a little in climaxes.

Symphony No. 13 in B flat min. (Babi-Yar), Op. 113.
*** Decca Dig. 417 261-2 [id.]. Rintzler, Concg. Male Ch. and O, Haitink.
**(*) Chan. Dig. CHAN 8540 [id.]. Storojev, CBSO, Kamu.

The often brutal directness of Haitink's way with Shostakovich works well in the *Thirteenth Symphony*, particularly in the long *Adagio* first movement, whose title, *Babi-Yar*, gives its name to the whole work. That first of five Yevtushenko settings boldly attacking anti-semitism in Russia sets the pattern for Haitink's severe view of the whole. Rintzler with his magnificent, resonant bass is musically superb but, matching Haitink, remains objective rather than dashingly characterful. The resolution of the final movement, with its pretty flutings surrounding a wry poem about Galileo and greatness, then works beautifully. Outstandingly brilliant and full sound, remarkable even for this series.

With a Russian bass soloist adding an extra touch of dark authenticity, Okku Kamu conducts a strong and sympathetic account of No. 13, well played and very well recorded. His degree of relaxation in the more pointed passages – such as the second movement, *Humour* – adds to the idiomatic feeling, though in weight and dark intensity he cannot always match Haitink, with a bass chorus rather light-toned.

(i) *Symphony No. 14 in G min., Op. 135;* (ii) *King Lear (musical fragments), Op. 58a.*
*** Olympia Dig. OCD 182 [id.]. (i) Kasrashubili, Safiulin, USSR MoC SO, Rozhdestvensky; (ii) Romanova, Leningrad CO, Serov.

(i) *Symphony No. 14, Op. 135;* (ii) *6 Poems of Marina Tsvetaeva, Op. 143a.*
*** Decca Dig. 417 514-2 [id.]. (i) Julia Varady, Fischer-Dieskau; (ii) Ortrun Wenkel; Concg. O, Haitink.

The *Fourteenth* is Shostakovich's most sombre and dark score, a setting of poems by Lorca, Apollinaire, Rilke, Brentano and Küchelbecker, all on the theme of death; Haitink's version gives each poem in its original language. It is a most powerful performance, and the outstanding recording is well up to the standard of this fine Decca series. The song-cycle, splendidly sung by Ortrun Wenkel, makes a fine bonus.

The Ministry of Culture Orchestra's performance is magnetic in drawing the sequence together; sadly, however, the booklet does not include texts, only a summary of each poem. The full, bright, digital sound is more atmospheric than some in the Olympia series. Though the voices are balanced close, their characterful Slavonic timbre will delight rather than offend Western ears. The colourful but lightweight *King Lear* pieces, recorded in warm, full, analogue sound, make a useful coupling.

Symphony No. 15 in A, Op. 141.
*** Olympia Dig. OCD 179 [id.]. USSR MoC SO, Rozhdestvensky – *Piano concerto No. 1.****
(*) Olympia OCD 224 [id.]. Leningrad PO, Mravinsky – STRAVINSKY: *Agon.*

(i) *Symphony No. 15 in A, Op. 141;* (ii) *From Jewish folk poetry* (song-cycle), *Op. 79.*
⊛ *** Decca 417 581-2 [id.]. (i) LPO; (ii) Söderström, Wenkel, Karcykowski, Concg. O, Haitink.

Early readings of the composer's last symphony seemed to underline the quirky unpredictability of the work, with the collage of strange quotations – above all the *William Tell* gallop, which keeps recurring in the first movement – seemingly joky rather than profound. Haitink by contrast makes the first movement sound genuinely symphonic, bitingly urgent. He underlines the purity of the bare lines of the second movement; after the Wagner quotations which open the finale, his slow tempo for the main lyrical theme gives it heartaching tenderness, not the usual easy triviality. The playing of the LPO is excellent, with refined tone and superb attack, and the recording is both analytical and atmospheric. The CD includes a splendidly sung version of *From Jewish folk poetry*, settings which cover a wide range of emotions including tenderness, humour and even happiness as in the final song. Ryszard Karcykowski brings vibrant Slavonic feeling to the work, which with its wide variety of mood and colour has a scale to match the shorter symphonies.

Rozhdestvensky as an interpreter of Shostakovich is particularly good at tapping the vein of wry humour in all the symphonies, a quality which comes to the fore in the equivocal *Fifteenth*. With its full, bright recording, this is one of the most recommendable of Rozhdestvensky's series with the Ministry of Culture Orchestra, particularly when it has for coupling one of the very first recordings made by the teenage prodigy, Yevgeny Kissin, soloist in a fine performance of the *Piano concerto No. 1*.

Mravinsky's authenticity of feeling and dramatic power compensate for imperfections of execution – and generally rough recording. The darkness and intensity of the slow movement come over superbly in his hands. The less than first-class quality of the recording inhibits making this a first recommendation, but Mravinsky brings special insights to the work.

CHAMBER AND INSTRUMENTAL MUSIC

Cello sonata in D min., Op. 40.
*** Chan. Dig. CHAN 8340 [id.]. Turovsky, Edlina – PROKOFIEV: *Sonata.****
*** BIS Dig. CD 336 [id.]. Thedéen, Pöntinen – SCHNITTKE: *Sonata*; STRAVINSKY: *Suite italienne.****

Yuli Turovsky and Luba Edlina play the *Cello sonata* with great panache and eloquence, if in the finale they almost succumb at times to exaggeration in their handling of its humour – no understatement here.

The Swedish cellist, Torleif Thedéen, has a real feeling for its structure and the vein of bitter melancholy under its ironic surface. Roland Pöntinen gives him excellent support and the BIS recording does justice to this partnership.

Cello sonata in D min., Op. 40; (i) *Piano trio No. 2 in E min., Op. 67.*
**(*) CBS Dig. MK 44664 [id.]. Yo-Yo Ma, Emanuel Ax; (i) with Isaac Stern.

The *Trio* receives a deeply felt performance, one which can hold its own with any issue, past or present. The *Sonata* is another matter; the playing is as beautiful as one would expect, but here Ma's self-communing propensity for reducing his tone is becoming a tiresome affectation. Ax plays splendidly and the CBS recording is very truthful.

Piano quintet in G min., Op. 57.
(*) CRD CRD 3351 [id.]. Clifford Benson, Alberni Qt – BRITTEN: *Quartet No. 1.**

Piano quintet, Op. 57; Piano trio No. 2 in E min., Op. 67.
**(*) Chan. Dig. CHAN 8342 [id.]. Borodin Trio, Zweig, Horner.
**(*) ASV ZCALH 929 [id.]. Music Group of London.

(i) *Piano quintet, Op. 57; String quartets Nos. 7 in F sharp min., Op. 108; 8 in C min., Op. 110.*
**(*) EMI Dig. CDC7 47507-2 [id.]. (i) Sviatoslav Richter; Borodin Qt.

Piano quintet, Op. 57; 2 Pieces for String quartet; (i) 7 Romances on poems of Aleksander Blok.
*** Decca Dig. 411 940-2 [id.]. Ashkenazy; (i) Söderström; Fitzwilliam Qt.

Ashkenazy's account of the *Piano quintet* with the late lamented Fitzwilliam Quartet cannot be seriously faulted and withstands comparison with the illustrious Richter and Borodin Quartet version, not least on account of the quality of the recording. The attractiveness of the issue is further enhanced not only by the *Two Pieces* but also by the *Seven Romances on Poems of Aleksander Blok* with Elisabeth Söderström, who sings these remarkable pieces with much feeling. The Decca recording is superb.

The Chandos version of the *Quintet* is bolder in character and more concentrated in feeling than its rival. The Music Group of London show rather less panache but are still impressive, and in their hands the *Trio* is played affectingly. This is a particularly painful and anguished work, dedicated to the memory of a close friend, Ivan Sollertinsky, who died in the year of its composition.

A powerful performance by Richter and the Borodins of the *Piano quintet*, recorded at a public concert at the Moscow Conservatoire, and it also goes without saying that the two *Quartets* are played superbly, although the quality of the recorded sound is on the dry side.

A vigorous and finely conceived account from Clifford Benson and the Alberni Quartet, vividly recorded; if the Britten coupling is wanted, this will be found fully satisfactory.

Piano trio No. 1, Op. 8.
*** EMI Dig. CDC7 49865-2 [id.]. Chung Trio – TCHAIKOVSKY: *Piano trio.****

The Op. 8 *Piano trio* is an early work, written when Shostakovich was only seventeen, convalescing from tuberculosis and recovering from the death of his father. It is a short piece, some 12 minutes long, but deeply felt and well worth getting to know. Readers will recognize some ideas that resurface later in the *First Symphony*. The Chungs play with great dedication and are most truthfully recorded.

Piano trio No. 2 in E min., Op. 67.
(M) **(*) Collins Dig. 1040-2 [id.]. Trio Zingara – RAVEL: *Piano trio in A min.***(*)

The *E minor Piano trio* is extremely well played by the Trio Zingara on what is their début recording. Theirs is an assured and accomplished account, extremely well recorded and sensitively phrased. One quarrel: they take the slow movement slower than marked and, as a result, do not fully sustain its atmosphere and concentration. The CBS version with Isaac Stern, Emanuel Ax and Yo-Yo Ma conveys more of the anguish and pain of this powerful score. However, those who want this particular coupling will derive much musical satisfaction from it.

String quartets Nos. 1 in C, Op. 49; 9 in E flat, Op. 117; 12 in D flat, Op. 133.
*** EMI CDC7 49266-2 [id.]. Borodin Qt.

String quartets Nos. 2 in A, Op. 68; 3 in F, Op. 73.
*** EMI CDC7 49267-2 [id.]. Borodin Qt.

String quartets Nos. 4 in D, Op. 83; 6 in G, Op. 101; 11 in F min., Op. 122.
*** EMI CDC7 49268-2 [id.]. Borodin Qt.

String quartets Nos. 5 in B flat, Op. 92; 15 in E flat min., Op. 144.
*** EMI CDC7 49270-2 [id.]. Borodin Qt.

String quartets Nos. 10 in A flat, Op. 118; 13 in B flat min., Op. 138; 14 in F sharp, Op. 142.
*** EMI CDC7 49269-2 [id.]. Borodin Qt.

The Shostakovich *Quartets* thread through his creative life like some inner odyssey and inhabit terrain of increasing spiritual desolation. This is the Borodin Quartet's second complete cycle. Two of the performances derive from concerts. The present set is made in a generally drier acoustic than its predecessors and the recordings from 1984, particularly Nos. 3 and 5, suffer in this respect. However, the ear quickly adjusts and the performances can only be described as masterly. Indeed the sheer quality of the playing on this set is unlikely to be surpassed.

String quartets Nos. 1 in C, Op. 49; 3 in F, Op. 73; 4 in D, Op. 83.
*** Teldec/WEA Dig. 2292 46009-2 [id.]. Brodsky Qt.

The Brodskys are a young quartet of real accomplishment who give well-prepared and intelligent performances of these quartets, the first of what is to be a complete cycle. They are very attentive to detail and need not fear competition, if the playing is all going to be as fine as this. The recordings are rather close, but this need not inhibit a strong recommendation for those wanting digital versions of these works.

String quartets Nos. 3 in F, Op. 73; 8 in C min., Op. 110; 13 in B flat min., Op. 138.
*** Decca 421 475-2 [id.]. Fitzwilliam Qt.

The Fitzwilliam recordings were made in the mid-to-late 1970s and are impressively realistic. The listener is forwardly placed and the sound is full-bodied and rich, the aural image very firm; in this respect they enjoy an advantage over their distinguished rivals on EMI, the Borodins. These are good performances that offer a keen challenge, but of course as a quartet the Borodins are in a class of their own.

String quartets Nos. 4 in D, Op. 83; 8 in C min., Op. 110; 11 in F min., Op. 112.
*** ASV Dig. CDDCA 631 [id.]. Coull Qt.

The *Fourth quartet* is a work of exceptional beauty and lucidity, one of the most haunting of the cycle; the *Eleventh Quartet* is a puzzling, almost cryptic work in seven short movements. The Coull is not a high-powered group; they sound as if they are playing in domestic rather than public surroundings. They are one of the most gifted of the younger British quartets and give eminently creditable accounts of all three pieces. A very good (if slightly overlit) recording on CD.

String quartet No. 8, Op. 110.
(M) **(*) Decca 425 541-2 [id.]. Borodin Qt – BORODIN; TCHAIKOVSKY: *Quartets.***(*)

As the central motif of this fine *Quartet* Shostakovich used a group of four notes derived, cipher-like, from his own name. It proves at least as fruitful as the famous one in the name 'Bach', and the argument throughout this impressive work is most intense. The Borodins' performance is outstanding and the recording real and vivid, although the balance means that in the CD transfer the effect is very forward, almost too boldly immediate.

Violin sonata, Op. 134.
*** Chan. Dig. CHAN 8343 [id.]. Dubinsky, Edlina – SCHNITTKE: *Sonata No. 1* etc.***

The *Violin sonata* is a bitter and at times arid score, thought-provoking and, unusually in this composer, not totally convincing. Rostislav Dubinsky's account is undoubtedly eloquent, and Luba Edlina makes a fine partner. The recording is excellent too, although it is balanced a shade closely.

Piano sonata No. 1.
*** DG Dig. 427 766-2 [id.]. Lilya Zilberstein – RACHMANINOV: *Preludes.***

The early *Sonata* was written in the immediate wake of the *First Symphony.* As is the case with the *Trios,* Shostakovich did not return to the medium until the Second World War. It is a radical piece, with something of the manic, possessed quality of Scriabin and the harmonic adventurousness of Berg. Lilya Zilberstein rises triumphantly to its formidable demands, and she makes a strong case for it; she is recorded with striking immediacy and impact. As piano sound, this is state of the art.

Lady Macbeth of Mtsensk (complete).
⊛ *** EMI CDS7 49955-2 (2) [Ang. CDCB 49955]. Vishnevskaya, Gedda, Petkov, Krenn, Tear, Amb. Op. Ch., LPO, Rostropovich.

Rostropovich, in his finest recording ever, proves with thrilling conviction that this first version of Shostakovich's greatest work for the stage is among the most original operas of the century. In text *Lady Macbeth* may not be radically different from the revised version, *Katerina Ismailova,* but it has an extra sharpness of focus that transforms what is much more than just a sordid love-story involving three murders by the heroine. Here the brutality of the love affair between the rich merchant's wife and Sergei, the roving-eyed workman, has maximum punch; and Rostropovich, helped by superlative recording, all the more vivid on CD, gives a performance of breathtaking power. Vishnevskaya is inspired to give an outstanding performance and provides moments of great beauty alongside aptly coarser singing; and Gedda matches her well, totally idiomatic. As the sadistic father-in-law, Petkov is magnificent, particularly in his ghostly return, and there are fine contributions from Robert Tear, Werner Krenn, Birgit Finnilä and Alexander Malta.

Sibelius, Jean (1865–1957)

Academic march; Finlandia (arr. composer); *Har du mod? Op. 31/2; March of the Finnish Jaeger Battalion, Op. 91/1;* (i) *The origin of fire, Op. 32; Sandels, Op. 28; Song of the Athenians, Op. 31/3.*

957

** BIS CD 314 [id.]. (i) Sauli Tilikainen, Laulun Ystävät Male Ch., Gothenburg SO, Järvi.

The origin of fire is by far the most important work on this record. Sauli Tilikainen is very impressive indeed, and the playing of the Gothenburg Symphony Orchestra under Neeme Järvi has plenty of feeling and atmosphere. None of the other pieces are essential Sibelius. The singing of the Laulun Ystävät is good rather than outstanding, and the Gothenburg orchestra play with enthusiasm. Fine recording in the best BIS traditions.

Andante festivo; Pelléas et Mélisande (suite), Op. 46; Rakastava, Op. 14; Romance in C, Op. 42. Suite mignonne, Op. 98a. Suite champêtre, Op. 98b. Valse triste (Kuolema), Op. 44.
** Nimbus Dig. NI 5169 [id.]. E. String O, Boughton.

The English String Orchestra is a musicianly body who produce some sensitive playing for William Boughton, but their somewhat limited sonority proves something of a handicap. Although one might take issue with Boughton's occasional choice of tempo (the *Andante festivo* is too fast and loses dignity as a result), there are many good things. He captures the charm of the *Suite mignonne* and *Valse triste* is imaginative and fresh; so, too, is *Rakastava*. Though not a first choice, these are idiomatic, unpretentious and sympathetic performances, and they are very decently recorded.

Autrefois (Scène pastorale), Op. 96b; The Bard, Op. 64; Presto in D for strings; Spring song, Op. 16; Suite caractéristique, Op. 100; Suite champêtre, Op. 98b; Suite mignonne, Op. 98a; Valse chevaleresque, Op. 96c; Valse lyrique, Op. 96a.
*** BIS Dig. CD 384 [id.]. Gothenburg SO, Järvi.

A mixed bag. *The Bard* is Sibelius at his greatest and most powerful, and it finds Järvi at his best. He penetrates its intimate musings and sounds its depths to great effect. The remaining pieces are all light: some of the movements of the *Suite mignonne* and *Suite champêtre* could come straight out of a Tchaikovsky ballet, and Järvi does them with great charm. The last thing that the *Suite*, Op. 100, can be called is *caractéristique*, while the three pieces, Op. 96, find Sibelius in Viennese waltz mood. The rarity is *Autrefois*, which has a beguiling charm and is by far the most haunting of these pastiches. Sibelius introduces two sopranos and their *vocalise* is altogether captivating. The *Presto in D major for strings* is a transcription – and a highly effective one – of the third movement of the *B flat Quartet*, Op. 4. Excellent recording, as one has come to expect from BIS.

The Bard, Op. 64; The Dryad, Op. 45/1; En Saga, Op. 9; Finlandia, Op. 26; (i) Luonnotar, Op. 70; Night ride and sunrise, Op. 55; The Oceanides, Op. 73; Pohjola's daughter, Op. 49; Tapiola, Op. 112; Varsäng (Spring song), Op. 16.
**(*) Chan. CHAN 8395/6 [id.]. SNO, Gibson, (i) with Phyllis Bryn-Julson.

Gibson's affinity with the Sibelius idiom is at its most convincing here, particularly in the more elusive pieces, like *The Bard* and *The Dryad*, although *En Saga*, which opens the collection, is also evocative and shows an impressive overall grasp. Sometimes one would have welcomed a greater degree of dramatic intensity, and both *Pohjola's daughter* and *Tapiola* fall a little short in this respect, while *Night ride and sunrise* does not fully blossom until the closing section. Nevertheless there is much here that is impressive, and the fine playing and natural perspectives of the recording contribute a great deal to the music-making. In *Luonnotar* the soprano voice is made to seem like another orchestral instrument; while there have been more histrionic versions, the singing is tonally beautiful, sensitive and well controlled.

Belshazzar's Feast (suite), Op. 54; Dance intermezzo, Op. 45/2; The Dryad, Op. 45/1; Pan and Echo, Op. 53; Swanwhite, Op. 54.

*** BIS Dig. CD 359 [id.]. Gothenburg SO, Neeme Järvi.

Belshazzar's Feast, a beautifully atmospheric piece of orientalism, and the incidental music for Strindberg's *Swanwhite* may not be Sibelius at his most powerful but both include many characteristic touches and some haunting moments. Neeme Järvi's collection with the Gothenburg orchestra is first class in every way.

Cassazione, Op. 6; Preludio; The Tempest: Prelude & suites 1–2, Op. 109; Tiera.
*** BIS Dig. CD 448 [id.]. Gothenburg SO, Järvi.

Sibelius's incidental music to *The Tempest*, written for a particularly lavish Copenhagen production in 1926, was his penultimate work and one of his most imaginative scores. Järvi's recording is the first to have appeared for a decade – and very good it is, too. It is the finest and most atmospheric since Beecham and, though it does not surpass the latter in pieces like *The Oak-tree* or the *Chorus of the winds*, it is still impressive and offers first-class modern recording. Järvi also includes the *Prelude*, omitted on Beecham's disc. The *Cassazione* comes from 1904 and is thus later than its early opus number. Sibelius never published it and intended to revise it (in character it resembles the *King Christian II* music), but it is well worth having on disc. Neither *Tiera* nor the *Preludio*, both from the 1890s, is of great interest or particularly characteristic.

Violin concerto in D min., Op. 47.
⊛ *** CBS Dig. MK 44548 [id.]. Cho-Liang Lin, Philh. O, Salonen – NIELSEN: *Violin concerto.**** ⊛
*** RCA RD 87019 [RCD1 7019]. Heifetz, Chicago SO, Hendl – GLAZUNOV: *Concerto*; PROKOFIEV: *Concerto No. 2.****
*** Ph. Dig. 416 821-2 [id.]. Mullova, Boston SO, Ozawa – TCHAIKOVSKY: *Concerto.***(*)
(M) *** Ph. 420 895-2 [id.]. Accardo, LSO, C. Davis – DVOŘÁK: *Violin concerto.****
*** EMI CDC7 47167-2 [id.]. Perlman, Pittsburgh SO, Previn – SINDING: *Suite.****
(M) (***) EMI mono CDH7 61011-2 [id.]. Ginette Neveu, Philh. O, Susskind – BRAHMS: *Concerto.*(***)
(*) DG Dig. 419 618-2 [id.]. Mintz, BPO, Levine – DVOŘÁK: *Concerto.**

(i) *Violin concerto; Symphony No. 5 in E flat, Op. 82.*
*** EMI Dig. CDC7 49717-2 [id.]. (i) Nigel Kennedy; CBSO, Rattle.

Cho-Liang Lin's playing is distinguished not only by flawless intonation and an apparently effortless virtuosity but also by great artistry. He produces a glorious sonority at the opening, which must have been exactly what Sibelius wanted, wonderfully clean and silvery, and the slow movement has tenderness, warmth and yet restraint with not a hint of the over-heated emotions which one encounters all too often. Erik Tawaststjerna makes much of the aristocratic quality which Sibelius looked for in interpreters of the *Concerto*, and there is no lack of aristocratic finesse here. At the same time, however, there is more to the *Concerto* than that, and Lin encompasses the extrovert brilliance of the finale and the bravura of the cadenza with real mastery. The Philharmonia Orchestra rise to the occasion under Esa-Pekka Salonen, and the recording is first class.

Heifetz's performance of the Sibelius *Concerto* with the Chicago Symphony Orchestra under Walter Hendl set the standard by which all other versions have come to be judged. It is also one of his finest recordings; in remastered form the sound is vivid, with the Chicago ambience making an apt setting for the finely focused violin line. The purity and luminous beauty of the violin tone at the opening put the seal on this as an interpretation of unusual depth, consummate technique and supreme artistry. There is some dryness added to the sound, which is very bright, but good results can be obtained by use of the controls.

Viktoria Mullova's account has a certain warmth, though it is mercifully free of the *zigeuner* element one so often encounters in performance. Mullova captures its magical element right from the very opening; the slow movement has a cool dignity that is impressive. The recording is excellent.

Of the mid-price versions, Salvatore Accardo and Sir Colin Davis would be a first choice. There is no playing to the gallery, and no schmaltz – and in the slow movement there is a sense of repose and nobility. The finale is exhilarating, and there is an aristocratic feel to the whole which is just right.

Itzhak Perlman plays the work as a full-blooded virtuoso showpiece and the Pittsburgh orchestra under André Previn support him to the last man and woman. In the first movement his tempo is broader than that of Heifetz, and he is at his stunning best in the first cadenza and makes light of all the fiendish difficulties in which the solo part abounds. He takes a conventional view of the slow movement, underlining its passion, and he gives us an exhilarating finale. The sound is marvellously alive and thrilling, though the forward balance is very apparent.

Ginette Neveu's reading of the Sibelius is a classic recording, a precious reminder of a great artist who died tragically young. The magnetism of Neveu in this, her first concerto recording, is inescapable from her opening phrase onwards, warmly expressive and dedicated, yet with no hint of mannerism. The finale is taken at a speed which is comfortable rather than exciting, but the extra spring of the thrumming dance-rhythms, superbly lifted, is ample compensation, providing a splendid culmination.

Nigel Kennedy's account of the *Violin concerto* is quite superbly balanced; the violin is in exactly the right perspective. Throughout, his intonation is true and he takes the considerable technical hurdles of this concerto in his stride. There is a touch of the *zigeuner* throb in the slow movement, but on the whole he plays with real spirit and panache. This can be confidently recommended if the coupling with the *Fifth Symphony* is suitable. In the symphony there is a powerful atmosphere and sense of space at the very opening, and the bassoon lament in the development is marvellously hushed and mysterious. In the famous transition – notoriously difficult to bring off – Rattle on this occasion is faster and not as finely controlled as in the Philharmonia reading. The slow movement is less spacious than the earlier one but still splendidly intense, and the ending could not be handled more sensitively or idiomatically. We are plunged too quickly into the finale, which is tremendously exhilarating; the playing of the Birmingham orchestra is excellent throughout as, indeed, is the EMI recording.

Shlomo Mintz commands unstinted admiration in this concerto; his playing is dazzlingly brilliant and full of personality. Intonation is spot-on and there seem to be no technical hurdles he cannot surmount. But there is also something too high-powered and unrelieved about his intensity, and the playing often dazzles rather more than it illuminates.

En Saga, Op. 9; Finlandia, Op. 26; Karelia suite, Op. 11; Tapiola, Op. 112.
(M) *** Decca Dig. 417 762-2 [id.]. Philh. O, Ashkenazy.

These are all digital recordings of the first order – Decca sound at its very finest. The performances are among the finest available, especially *En Saga* which is thrillingly atmospheric, while the *Karelia suite* is freshly appealing in its directness. The climax of *Tapiola* is almost frenzied in its impetus – some may feel that Ashkenazy goes over the top here; but this is the only real criticism of a distinguished collection and a very real bargain.

En Saga, Op. 9; Finlandia, Op. 26; Legend: The Swan of Tuonela, Op. 22/2; Tapiola, Op. 112.
(M) **(*) EMI CDM7 69017-2 [id.]. BPO, Karajan.

These recordings date from 1977. *En Saga* finds Karajan a brisk story-teller, more concerned with narrative than with atmosphere at the beginning; but the climax is very exciting. Here as in *Finlandia*, which is superbly played, the digital remastering gives a very brightly lit sound-picture, bringing a degree of harshness in the brass, only just stopping short of crudeness. *Tapiola* is broader and more expansive than the first DG version; at the storm section, the more spacious tempo is vindicated and again the climax is electrifying, although, with a loss of body and weight in the bass, the upper range tends to fierceness. *The Swan of Tuonela* is most persuasively done.

En Saga, Op. 9; Finlandia, Op. 26; Legend: The Swan of Tuonela, Op. 22/2; Night ride and sunrise, Op. 55; Pohjola's daughter, Op. 49.
(B) *** Decca 417 697-2 [id.]. SRO, Horst Stein.

These are distinguished and finely calculated performances offering some fine playing from the Suisse Romande Orchestra. The performance here of *Finlandia* is quite exciting and is sonorously recorded, but the achievement of the rest of the programme makes one wish that something less ubiquitous had been included. Stein shows a gift for the special atmosphere of Sibelius. The highlight of the disc is an outstandingly exciting account of *En Saga*, including the flamboyant use of the bass drum. *Night ride and sunrise* and *Pohjola's daughter* too are highly successful, although the broadening of the climax of the latter work does let the tension slip momentarily. *The Swan of Tuonela* has been added to the CD.

En saga, Op. 9; Scènes historiques, Opp. 25, 66.
*** BIS Dig. CD 295 [id.]. Gothenburg SO, Järvi.

Järvi has the advantage of modern digital sound and the Gothenburg orchestra is fully inside the idiom of this music and plays very well indeed. Järvi's *En saga* is exciting and well paced.

Finlandia; Karelia suite, Op. 11. Kuolema: Valse triste. Legends: Lemminkäinen's return, Op. 22/4; Pohjola's daughter, Op. 49.
(M) **(*) EMI CDM7 69205-2 [id.]. Hallé O, Barbirolli.

Although the orchestral playing is not as polished as that of a virtuoso orchestra, it is enthusiastic and has the advantage of excellent recording from the mid-1960s. *Pohjola's daughter* is extremely impressive, spacious but no less exciting for all the slower tempi. *Lemminkäinen's return* is also a thrilling performance. Overall, a desirable introduction to Sibelius's smaller orchestral pieces, with admirable stereo definition.

Finlandia, Op. 26; Karelia Suite, Op. 11; Scènes historiques: Festivo, Op. 25/3; The Chase; Love song; At the drawbridge, Op. 66/1-3; The Tempest (incidental music): suites Nos. 1-2, Op. 109.
❀ (M) (***) EMI mono CDM7 63397-2 [id.]. RPO, Beecham.

Beecham's mono performance of the incidental music for *The Tempest* is magical – no one has captured its spirit with such insight. A pity that he omits the *Prelude*, which he had done so evocatively on 78s, though the last number of the second suite covers much of the same ground. The four *Scènes historiques* are beautifully done, with the most vivid orchestral colouring: *The Chase* is particularly delectable. No apologies whatsoever need be made about the sound here, though in the *Intermezzo* from *Karelia* (which has a 78-r.p.m. source) the quality is curiously crumbly at the opening and close: surely a better original could have been found. The *Alla marcia* is better, although no one would buy this record for *Finlandia*.

Finlandia. Kuolema: Valse triste; Legends: The Swan of Tuonela; Lemminkäinen's return. Tapiola.
**(*) EMI Dig. CDC7 47484-2 [id.]. Philh. O, Berglund.

Berglund's Philharmonia performances of this collection of favourite Sibelius pieces have a satisfying ruggedness. They are not as vibrant as some; but they are given more impact (as in *Tapiola*) and more refinement (as in *Valse triste* or the cor anglais solo of *The Swan of Tuonela*) by the full-ranging digital recording than in his earlier, analogue versions.

Finlandia, Op. 26; Kuolema: Valse triste, Op. 44; Legends: The Swan of Tuonela, Op. 22/2; Tapiola, Op. 112.
*** DG Dig. 413 755-2 [id.]. BPO, Karajan.

This is Karajan's fourth and undoubtedly greatest account of *Tapiola*, for he has the full measure of its vision and power. Never has it sounded more mysterious or its dreams more savage; nor has the build-up to the storm ever struck such a chilling note of terror: an awesomely impressive musical landscape, while the wood-sprites weaving their magic secrets come vividly to life. *The Swan*, Karajan's third account on record, is powerful and atmospheric; and the remaining two pieces, *Valse triste* and *Finlandia*, reinforce the feeling that this Berlin/Karajan partnership has never been equalled.

Karelia suite, Op. 11; Legend: The Swan of Tuonela, Op. 22/2.
** Ph. 412 727-2 [id.]. ASMF, Marriner – GRIEG: *Holberg suite; Lyric pieces.***(*)

Marriner's performance of *Karelia* is curiously subdued and the closing *Alla marcia* could be more exuberant. Even the central *Ballade* seems to lack momentum, though the cor anglais solo is beautifully played by Barry Griffiths, who is no less eloquent in *The Swan of Tuonela*. The recording is most naturally balanced.

4 Legends, Op. 22 (Lemminkäinen and the maidens of Saari; The Swan of Tuonela; Lemminkäinen in Tuonela; Lemminkäinen's return).
*** BIS Dig. CD 294 [id.]. Gothenburg SO, Järvi.
*** Chan. CHAN 8394 [id.]. SNO, Gibson.

Järvi has the advantage of fine, modern digital sound and a wonderfully truthful balance. How good it is to hear solo violins sounding so naturally life-size. The bass drum sounds impressively realistic, too. Järvi gives a passionate and atmospheric reading of the first *Legend* and his account of *The Swan of Tuonela* is altogether magical, one of the best in the catalogue. He takes a broader view of *Lemminkäinen in Tuonela* than many of his rivals and builds up an appropriately black and powerful atmosphere, showing the Gothenburg brass to excellent advantage. The slight disappointment is *Lemminkäinen's homeward journey* which, though exciting, hasn't the possessed, manic quality of Beecham's very first record, which sounded as if a thousand demons were in pursuit.

The Scottish orchestra play freshly and with much commitment. *The Swan of Tuonela* has a darkly brooding primeval quality, and there is an electric degree of tension in the third piece, *Lemminkäinen in Tuonela*. The two outer *Legends* have ardent, rhythmic feeling, and altogether this is highly successful. The recorded sound is excellent.

The Oceanides, Op. 73; Pelléas et Mélisande: suite, Op. 46; Symphony No. 7 in C, Op. 105; Tapiola, Op. 112.
(M) *** EMI CDM7 63400-2 [id.]. RPO, Beecham.

The Oceanides, recorded at the composer's behest, is one of Beecham's greatest performances on record and is a must. It is Sibelius's most poetic evocation of the sea, and this marvellous playing captures every nuance of the score. The *Pelléas et Mélisande suite* was a yardstick by which all others have been measured ever since. Only the Karajan matches it, and even the Berlin Philharmonic textures do not sound more luminous and magical than here, for the CD transfer is wonderfully refined. However, Beecham omits the *By the sea* movement. *Tapiola* is also very impressive: it has all the requisite brooding power and must be numbered among the very finest accounts committed to disc. Only the *Seventh Symphony* disappoints – and that only relatively speaking.

Pelléas et Mélisande: suite.
*** DG Dig. 410 026-2 [id.]. BPO, Karajan – GRIEG: *Peer Gynt suites 1 & 2.****

At last a version of Sibelius's subtle and atmospheric score that can compare with the classic Beecham version; indeed in certain movements, *By the spring in the park* and the *Pastorale*, it not only matches Sir Thomas but almost surpasses him. There is also plenty of mystery in the third movement, *At the seashore*, omitted from the Beecham set. The recording is very striking indeed, with great clarity and presence.

Rakastava (suite), Op. 14; Scènes historiques, Opp. 25, 66; Valse lyrique, Op. 96/1.
*** Chan. CHAN 8393 [id.]. SNO, Gibson.

Written for a patriotic pageant, the *Scènes historiques* are vintage Sibelius. In the *Love song* Gibson strikes the right blend of depth and reticence, while elsewhere he conveys a fine sense of controlled power. Convincing and eloquent performances that have a natural feeling for the music. Gibson's *Rakastava* is beautifully unforced and natural, save for the last movement, which is a shade too slow. The *Valse lyrique* is not good Sibelius, but everything else certainly is. Gibson plays this repertoire with real commitment and the recorded sound is excellent, with the orchestral layout, slightly distanced, most believable.

Symphonies Nos. 1–7.
(M) *** Decca Dig. 421 069-2 (4) [id.]. Philh. O, Ashkenazy.

Ashkenazy's Sibelius series makes a rich and strong, consistently enjoyable cycle. Ashkenazy by temperament brings out the expressive warmth, colour and drama of the composer rather than his Scandinavian chill, reflecting perhaps his Slavonic background. The recordings are full and rich as well as brilliant, most of them of demonstration quality, even though they date from the early digital period. On four CDs at mid-price, the set makes a most attractive recommendation.

Symphony No. 1 in E min., Op. 39; Finlandia, Op. 26.
** BIS CD 221 [id.]. Gothenburg SO, Järvi.

Symphony No. 1 in E min., Op. 39; Finlandia, Op. 26; Karelia: Overture, Op. 10; Suite, Op. 11.
** RCA Dig. RD 87765 [7765-2-RC]. Finnish RSO, Saraste.

Symphony No. 1; Karelia suite, Op. 11.
*** Decca Dig. 414 534-2 [id.]. Philh. O, Ashkenazy.

(M) *** EMI Dig. CDM7 69028-2 [id.]. BPO, Karajan.

Symphony No. 1; The Oceanides, Op. 73.
**(*) EMI Dig. CDC7 47515-2 [id.]. CBSO, Rattle.

Symphonies Nos. 1; 3 in C, Op. 52.
(B) **(*) DG 429 526-2 [id.]. Helsinki R. O, Kamu.

Symphonies Nos. 1; 4 in A min., Op. 63.
(M) *** Decca 417 789-2 [id.]. VPO, Maazel.

Symphonies Nos. 1; 5 in E flat, Op. 82.
(M) **(*) EMI CDM7 63094-2. BBC SO, Sargent.

Symphonies Nos. 1; 6 in D min., Op. 104.
*** EMI Dig. CDC7 49052-2 [id.]. Helsinki PO, Berglund.

Ashkenazy's recording has superb detail and clarity of texture, and there is all the presence and body one could ask for. The bass-drum rolls are particularly realistic. Moreover, it is as successful artistically as it is in terms of recorded sound. It is well held together and finely shaped. Ashkenazy is exactly on target in the Scherzo. The resultant sense of momentum is exhilarating. Throughout, the sheer physical excitement that this score engenders is tempered by admirable control. Only at the end of the slow movement does one feel that Ashkenazy could perhaps have afforded greater emotional restraint. The playing of the Philharmonia Orchestra is of the very first order. The *Karelia* suite is very good too, the middle movement, *Ballade*, fresh and imaginative.

Maazel's VPO performance of the *First Symphony* dominated the LP catalogue during the 1970s: it has freshness of vision to commend it, along with careful attention to both the letter and the spirit of the score. The Vienna Philharmonic responds with enthusiasm and brilliance and the Decca engineers produce splendid detail (except for the important timpani part in the first movement echoing the main theme, which might have been more sharply defined). The climaxes of the outer movements are very exciting. The *Fourth* is equally impressive. The orchestral tone is less richly upholstered than in some more modern versions; but the players make the closest contact with the music, and Maazel's reading brings great concentration and power: the first movement is as cold and unremitting as one could wish. Apart from the slow movement, which could be a little more poetic, there are no real reservations to be made, and the remastered sound is brightly lit. A fine bargain.

Karajan, a great Tchaikovsky interpreter, identifies with the work's inheritance. But there is a sense of grandeur and vision here, and the opulence and virtuosity of the Berliners helps to project the heroic dimensions of Karajan's performance. The early digital recording (1981) is not top-drawer: the bass is overweighted; but the full upper strings sing out gloriously with the richest amplitude in the finale, which has an electrifying climax; the brass is comparably rich and resonant. However, in the outer movements of the *Karelia suite*, which Karajan paces quite deliberately, the extra weight at the bottom end of the spectrum is less of an advantage.

Both the playing and the interpretation of Berglund's *First* are impressive in their breadth and concentration, and his *Sixth* is particularly fine, though the Scherzo may strike some listeners as too measured. But readers wanting this coupling need not hesitate. The Helsinki orchestra produces excellent sonority and the EMI engineering is first class. If neither of these performances is necessarily a first choice, at the same time one cannot go far wrong with either.

Kamu's Helsinki version of the *First Symphony* does not lack excitement, but it is not distinctive. The *Third*, however, is among the finest ever put on disc and this bargain reissue is well worth exploring on its account alone. Tempi are invariably well judged and the atmosphere is thoroughly authentic, particularly in the slow movement, whose character seems to have eluded so many distinguished conductors. The recording is excellent, but the digital remastering, in seeking to clarify further a full-bodied sound, rich in ambience, gives an occasional hint of minor congestion. The effect is marginal and does not inhibit enjoyment of a magnificent performance overall.

Sargent was an eminently reliable Sibelius interpreter with a good feeling for this music's structural processes. In the *Fifth Symphony*, for example, he handles the difficult transition from the first movement to the scherzo section with great skill. Generally speaking, he judges tempi unerringly and gives a finely proportioned account of both symphonies. The recordings were made in 1956 and 1958 respectively, but they come up remarkably well in the present transfer. The BBC Symphony Orchestra did not have the richest string sonority at this time – indeed they sound rather opaque – but there is much more here to admire than to quarrel with. At the price it is very good value.

If the whole symphony was as fine as the first movement in Rattle's hands, this would be a clear first recommendation. He has a powerful grasp of both its structure and character, and elicits an enthusiastic response from his players. The slow movement is for the most part superb, with excellent playing from the wind and brass of the Birmingham orchestra; but he makes too much of the commas at the end of the movement, which are so exaggerated as to be disruptive. The Scherzo has splendid character but is a good deal slower than the marking. The Oceanides were the nymphs who inhabited the waters of Homeric mythology, and the opening of the piece has an atmosphere that is altogether ethereal. Simon Rattle has its measure and conveys all its mystery and poetry. This is a subtle and masterly performance.

The Gothenburg strings are clean, well focused in tone, lean and lithe; the wind are well blended and the clarinet solo at the beginning is sensitively played; and there is an excellent sense of atmosphere. The first movement is finely shaped and the slow movement is restrained and all the more effective on this count; the *Symphony* on the whole, one or two touches apart, is commendably straightforward and very well recorded.

Saraste's reading of No. 1 is pleasingly straightforward, well conceived and well held together. The tempo of the slow movement is very well judged: it is understated – and all the more affecting for that – and the scherzo is nearer the right tempo than Simon Rattle's. The *Karelia overture* comes off well, though there is nothing special about the *Suite*. Good performances with many positive merits, but of lower voltage and less distinction than the best.

Symphony No. 2 in D, Op. 43.
**(*) Decca Dig. 410 206-2 [id.]. Philh. O, Ashkenazy.
**(*) Chan. Dig. CHAN 8303 [id.]. SNO, Gibson.
(m) (***) EMI mono CDM7 63399-2 [id.]. BBC SO, Beecham – DVOŘÁK: *Symphony No. 8.*(***)
(m) (**) Dell'Arte mono CDDA 9019 [id.]. NBC SO, Toscanini – ATTERBERG: *Symphony No. 6.*(**)

Symphony No. 2; Finlandia; Kuolema: Valse triste; Legend: The Swan of Tuonela.
**(*) Ph. 420 490-2 [id.]. Boston SO, C. Davis.

Symphony No. 2: Finlandia, Op. 26; The Oceanides, Op. 73.
*** EMI Dig. CDC7 49511-2 [id.]. Helsinki PO, Berglund.

Symphony No. 2; Kuolema, Op. 44: Scene with cranes.
**(*) EMI Dig. CDC7 47222-2 [id.]. CBSO, Rattle.

Symphony No. 2; Kuolema, Op. 44: Scene with cranes; Valse triste; Nightride and sunrise, Op. 55.
*** RCA Dig. RD 87919 [7919-2-RC]. Finnish RSO, Saraste.

Symphony No. 2; Kuolema: Valse triste; Legend: The Swan of Tuonela; Pohjola's daughter.
(M) **(*) RCA GD 86528 (RCA 6528-2-RG]. Phd. O, Ormandy.

Symphony No. 2; Legend: The swan of Tuonela.
(M) ** EMI CD-EMX 2157. Hallé O, Sir John Barbirolli.

Symphony No. 2 in D; Romance for strings in C, Op. 42.
*** BIS Dig. CD 252 [id.]. Gothenburg SO, Järvi.

Järvi is very brisk in the opening *Allegretto*: this Gothenburg version has more sinew and fire than its rivals, and the orchestral playing is more responsive and disciplined than that of the SNO on Chandos. Throughout, Järvi has an unerring sense of purpose and direction and the momentum never slackens. Of course, there is not the same opulence as the Philharmonia under Ashkenazy on Decca, but the BIS performance is concentrated in feeling and thoroughly convincing. The *Romance for strings* is attractively done.

Berglund is scrupulously faithful to the letter of the score, as well as to its spirit. The build-up to the climax just before the restatement is magnificently handled. The slow movement also comes off well and its contrasting moods are effectively characterized. The scherzo and finale are of lower voltage than the finest versions. The Helsinki Philharmonic respond with no mean virtuosity and panache, but the last degree of intensity eludes them. Berglund's account of *The Oceanides* is splendidly atmospheric and can be put alongside Rattle's, which is praise indeed! The recording is well detailed and truthful, and the perspective natural.

Ashkenazy's is a passionate, volatile reading, in many ways a very Russian view of Sibelius, with Ashkenazy finding a clear affinity with the Tchaikovsky symphonies. At the very opening, the quick, flexible treatment of the repeated crotchet motif is urgent, not weighty or ominous as it can be. Ashkenazy's control of tension and atmosphere makes for the illusion of live performance in the building of each climax, and the rich digital sound adds powerfully to that impression. Yet some listeners may find it more difficult to respond positively to this reading; like R. L., they may feel the performance is wanting in firmness of grip, especially in the slow movement, with the dramatic pauses lacking spontaneity and unanimity of response.

Although Saraste's account of the *Second Symphony* is not a first choice, it is still highly recommendable. He has a good feeling for the shape of a phrase and for colour, and has the measure of this symphony's breadth. He can also handle a Sibelian climax, and there is no lack of power here. Although Rattle casts a stronger spell in the *Scene with cranes*, Saraste gets very good results both here and in *Nightride and sunrise*. The recording is well detailed and the whole disc remains strongly competitive.

Sir Alexander Gibson's version of the *Second* is honest and straightforward, free of bombast in the finale. Tempos are well judged and there is at no time any attempt to interpose the personality of the interpreter. The first movement is neither too taut nor too relaxed: it is well shaped and feels right. The strings do not possess the weight or richness of sonority of the Philharmonia, and the performance as a whole does not displace the first recommendations on CD.

The CBSO play with fervour and enthusiasm for Simon Rattle except, perhaps, in the first movement where the voltage is lower – particularly in the development, which is not easy to bring off. The slow movement is full-bodied and gutsy, convincing even when Rattle arrests the flow of the argument by underlining certain points. The Scherzo is bracing enough, though in the trio the oboe tune is caressed a little too much; however, the transition to the finale is magnificent and Rattle finds the *tempo giusto* in this movement. The Birmingham strings produce a splendidly fervent unison here – and elsewhere in the *Symphony*. The recording is very alive, though the perspective needs greater depth. As a fill-up, Simon Rattle and the CBSO give an imaginative and poetic account of the *Scene with cranes* from the incidental music to *Kuolema*.

Sir Colin Davis gives a dignified and well-proportioned account that is free from any excesses or mannerisms; it has sensitivity and freshness in its favour. The sound is not as open at the top as is desirable, and there is a certain tubbiness in the middle-to-bottom range; there is both body and impact and the violins do not lack brightness. This is satisfying in its way. Of the couplings, *Finlandia* is expansive and *The Swan of Tuonela* has a powerful atmosphere.

The overall impression of Ormandy's mid-1970s account is of a superbly disciplined response from the Philadelphians, well recorded, but wanting that extra degree of freshness and character to justify the exposure that repeated hearing will give it. Yet there is no doubt that the rich sweep of the Philadelphia strings in the big tune of the finale is very compulsive in its intensity. *Pohjola's daughter*, too, generates an exciting climax, while *The Swan of Tuonela* is darkly atmospheric. The digital remastering is vivid but not always absolutely refined, and the brass at the close of the *Symphony* has an element of coarseness.

Beecham's performance comes from a BBC tape of serviceable quality made at London's Royal Festival Hall in 1954. It is a pretty incandescent performance and the BBC orchestra, spurred on by various vocal exhortations from the conductor, play with great enthusiasm. Beecham admirers will not want to be without it.

Barbirolli's reading with the Hallé Orchestra stresses the Slav ancestry and Italianate warmth of the work. Its fill-up is an additional attraction for the singing *Swan of Tuonela*; Barbirolli's vocalizations are clearly audible. The 1967 recording, basically excellent, has a bright treble, and the CD transfer has thinned down the sound of the massed violins, though not as badly as in his version of No. l.

Besides this Dell'Arte transfer, there are two other Toscanini records, a December 1940 version which appeared on RCA with an electrifying account of *Pohjola's daughter*, and an earlier, 1938 recording with the BBC Symphony Orchestra, which will appear on CD during the lifetime of this book. In the present reading, which dates from 1938, the first movement is a little broader and more relaxed than the 1940 version: neither the quality of the recording nor the high-voltage performance really surpasses the celebrated Koussevitzky commercial records.

Symphonies Nos. 2 in D, Op. 43; 5 in E flat, Op. 82; (i) *7 in C, Op. 105; Pohjola's Daughter; Swanwhite: The Maiden with roses; Tapiola.*
(M) (***) Pearl mono GEMM CDS 9408 [id.]. Boston SO, or (i) BBC SO, Serge Koussevitzky.

Sibelians should not miss these altogether outstanding historic performances. Although Koussevitsky is not as celebrated among younger collectors as Furtwängler or Toscanini, these are stunning performances, incandescent and electrifying. The Boston strings glow as they have seldom done since. The *Seventh*, recorded when it was 'new music', barely a decade old, has tremendous urgency and grandeur. When listening to it, you feel there can be no other way of playing it, and Koussevitzky's 1939 *Tapiola* is chilling in its intensity. The sound is amazingly good for the period.

Symphony No. 3 in C, Op. 52; King Kristian II suite, Op. 27.
*** BIS Dig. CD 228 [id.]. Gothenburg SO, Järvi.

Symphonies Nos. 3 in C, Op. 52; 5 in E flat, Op. 82.
*** EMI Dig. CDC7 49175-2. Helsinki PO, Berglund.

Symphonies Nos. 3 in C, Op. 52; 6 in D min., Op. 104.
*** Decca Dig. 414 267-2 [id.]. Philh. O, Ashkenazy.

Symphonies Nos. 3 in C, Op. 52; 7 in C, Op. 105.
*** EMI Dig. CDC7 47450-2 [id.]. CBSO, Rattle.

Simon Rattle's account of the *Third* is vastly superior to his *First* and *Second*. He finds the *tempo giusto* throughout and is convincing not only in his pacing but also in his capacity to relate the parts to the whole. The slow movement is particularly fine; few have penetrated its landscape more completely, and the movement throughout is magical. The way in which he gradually builds up the finale is masterly and sure of instinct. The recording, made in the Warwick Arts Centre, sounds very well balanced, natural in perspective and finely detailed. The *Seventh* is hardly less powerful and impressive: its opening is slow to unfold and has real vision. This is one of the finest *Sevenths* of recent years.

In the first movement of the *Third*, Ashkenazy is a shade faster than the metronome marking, and so there is no want of forward momentum and thrust, either here or in the finale. The tempi and spirit of the *Andantino* are well judged; he is not helped, however, by the balance, closer than ideal, which casts too bright a light on a landscape that should be shrouded in mystery. It is clear that Ashkenazy has great feeling for the *Sixth* and its architecture and he lets every detail tell in the *Poco vivace* third movement. Indeed, this is possibly the most successful and technically impressive in the current Decca cycle, with the *Seventh* as a close runner-up.

From Berglund sober, straightforward, powerful readings which maintain the high standards of performance and recording that have distinguished his cycle. There is a good feeling for the architecture of this music and no want of atmosphere. Berglund adopts sensible tempi throughout and shapes all three movements well. He draws good playing from the Helsinki Philharmonic and evokes a feeling of inner tranquillity in the withdrawn middle section of the slow movement of No. 3, a passage where Sibelius seems to be listening to quiet voices from another planet. A successful performance and recording. In Berglund's *Fifth Symphony*, the development section of the first movement has a mystery that eluded him first time around, and there is splendid power in the closing pages of the finale. This is a very satisfying coupling and it sounds admirable on CD.

With the *Third Symphony* there is a sense of the epic in Järvi's hands and it can hold its own with any in the catalogue. In Gothenburg, the slow movement is first class and the leisurely tempo adopted here by the Estonian conductor is just right. Järvi's coupling is the incidental music to *King Christian II*; his account is splendidly committed throughout and free from the literalness that seems at times to distinguish this conductor. This is very beautifully played and recorded.

Symphony No. 4 in A min., Op. 63; Canzonetta, Op. 62/1; The Oceanides, Op. 73.
**(*) BIS Dig. CD 263 [id.]. Gothenburg SO, Järvi.

Symphony No. 4 in A min., Op. 63; Finlandia, Op. 26; (i) *Luonnotar, Op. 70.*
*** Decca Dig. 400 056-2 [id.]. Philh. O, Ashkenazy, (i) with Söderström.

Ashkenazy achieves great concentration of feeling in the *Fourth*. The brightness of the Philharmonia violins and the cleanness of attack add to the impact of this baldest of the Sibelius symphonies, and Ashkenazy's terracing of dynamic contrasts is caught superbly in the outstanding digital recording. Like his other Sibelius readings, this one has something of a dark Russian passion in it, but freshness always dominates over mere sensuousness; as ever, Ashkenazy conveys the spontaneity of live performance. There is splendid drama and intensity throughout, and this is a very impressive performance. The couplings add to the special attractions of this issue; *Finlandia* is made fresh again in a performance of passion and precision, and Elisabeth Söderström is on top form in *Luonnotar*, a symphonic poem with a voice (although some ears may find her wide vibrato and hard-edged tone not entirely sympathetic).

Neeme Järvi takes a very broad view of the first movement – and conveys much of its brooding quality. The Scherzo has a splendid strength, even if Järvi allows the pace to slacken far too much towards the end. Both Järvi and Karajan portray the bleak yet other-worldly landscape of the slow movement to excellent effect, but the tension between phrases in the Karajan makes his the more powerful experience. In the finale Järvi opts for the tubular bells rather than the glockenspiel, which Sibelius wanted. As a fill-up, he gives us the *Canzonetta for strings*, Op. 62a, which derives from the music to *Kuolema*. It has great allure and charm and is beautifully played by the Gothenburg strings. *The Oceanides* is a very fine performance, too, though less subtle than Rattle's, particularly in its observance of dynamic nuances.

Symphonies Nos. 4 in A min., Op. 63; 5 in E flat, Op. 82.
(M) *** EMI CDM7 69244-2 [id.]. BPO, Karajan.

Symphonies Nos. 4 in A min., Op. 63; 6 in D min., Op. 104.
⊛ *** DG 415 108-2 [id.]. BPO, Karajan.
*** EMI Dig. CDC7 47711-2 [id.]. CBSO, Rattle.

Karajan's 25-year-old recording of the *Fourth Symphony* is only marginally less powerful than Ashkenazy's on Decca, and his performance is of real stature. Although one is bowled over by the Ashkenazy at first, it is the Karajan that has the greater concentration and tension. DG also offer his glorious account of the *Sixth Symphony*, which remains almost unsurpassed among recent accounts. Although this DG transfer does not quite have the range and body of the BIS and Decca versions, it sounds more vivid than on its earlier appearances and, like that of No. 4, the performance is a great one.

Simon Rattle's account of the *Fourth* with the Birmingham orchestra is also one of the best to have appeared in recent years. He invokes a powerful atmosphere in its opening pages: one is completely transported to its dark landscape with its seemingly limitless horizons. The string-tone is splendidly lean without being undernourished and achieves a sinisterly whispering pianissimo in the development. The slow movement is magical. The finale is hardly less masterly: Rattle builds up most convincingly to the final climax and the enigmatic, almost resigned coda. His account of the *Sixth* is almost equally fine. In the slow movement Rattle does not have the tremendous grip that the Karajan version commands, or quite the concentration he achieves elsewhere – but make no mistake, this is still a *Sixth* to reckon with, and its closing bars are memorably eloquent.

In some ways Karajan's re-recording of the *Fourth Symphony* for EMI must be counted controversial. He gives spacious – and highly atmospheric – accounts of the first and third movements, a good deal slower than his earlier, DG version. He conveys eloquently the other-worldly quality of the landscape in the third movement. The first undoubtedly has great mystery and power. Again, in the EMI *Fifth* the opening movement is broader than the earlier, DG account, and he achieves a remarkable sense of its strength and majesty. The transition from the work's first section to the 'scherzo' is slightly more abrupt than in the 1965 recording; tempi in the work's first half are generally rather more extreme. Both the slow movement and finale are glorious and have real vision, and the recording is excellent. However, the digital remastering has brought drier, less opulent textures than in the original full-priced issues; there is now a degree of thinness on the string timbre above the stave, and the CD brings a hint of stridency on the fortissimo brass.

Symphony No. 5 in E flat, Op. 82; En Saga.
*** Decca Dig. 410 016-2 [id.]. Philh. O, Ashkenazy.

Symphony No. 5 in E flat, Op. 82; En saga, Op. 9; Tapiola, Op. 112.
*** RCA Dig. RD 87822 [7822-2-RC]. Finnish RSO, Saraste.

Symphony No. 5; Night ride and sunrise, Op. 55.
*** EMI Dig. CDC7 47006-2 [id.]. Philh. O, Rattle.

Symphonies Nos. 5; 7 in C, Op. 105.
**(*) DG 415 107-2 [id.]. BPO, Karajan.
(*) DG Dig. 427 647-2 [id.]. VPO, Bernstein.

Simon Rattle's record of the *Fifth Symphony* has collected numerous prizes in Europe – and deserves them all. Right from the very outset, one feels that he has found the *tempo giusto*. Rattle is scrupulous in observing every dynamic nuance to the letter and, one might add, spirit. What is particularly impressive is the control of the transition between the first section and the scherzo element of the first movement. This relationship is ideally balanced and enables Rattle to convey detail in just the right perspective. There is a splendid sense of atmosphere in the development and a power unmatched in recent versions, save for the Karajan. The playing is superb, with the recording to match. *Night ride* is very good but not quite so outstanding; however, this is undoubtedly an exceptional *Fifth*. The recording has range, depth and presence; it is strikingly natural and vivid, one of the best compact discs to come from EMI.

Ashkenazy's reading is a thoroughly idiomatic one and disappoints only in terms of the balance of tempi between the two sections of the first movement. This is a fine rather than a great performance. Ashkenazy's *En Saga* is the best version of that work now in the catalogue; when one considers also the outstanding excellence of the recording, this issue will obviously have its appeal. The entry of the horns in the finale – perhaps the most impressive part of the performance – is especially telling; overall, the fullness of the sound is matched by its immediacy and warmth of atmosphere, with no trace of digital edginess, although the brass has bite as well as richness of sonority.

Such is the excellence of the classic Karajan DG *Fifth* that few listeners would guess its age. It is a great performance, and this 1964 version is indisputably the finest of the four he has made. Impressive though it is, his *Seventh* is not quite in the same class, and must yield both technically and even artistically to the Ashkenazy, which is very powerful and coupled with an impressive *Tapiola*.

Jukka-Pekka Saraste offers an excellently shaped and well-thought-out reading of the *Fifth Symphony*. He handles in masterly fashion the climax at the transition to the scherzo and manages the transition extremely well, as does Rattle in his Philharmonia recording. Saraste conveys much of its breadth; his pace is measured, but the reading has weight and power. Saraste's *En saga* is no less telling in drawing the listener into its atmosphere; his *Tapiola*, on the other hand, is not so successful: this music must really chill the blood in performance – and this does not.

Bernstein's 1989 Sibelius cycle is proving no match for his mid-1960s CBS set. The *Fifth* is relatively free from the idiosyncratic distortions that marked his *Second*, but it is terribly slow. More surprisingly, it lacks both power and atmosphere – and so, too, does the *Seventh*, which is curiously deficient in electricity. The recordings, made during public performances, need greater transparency and deeper perspective. Sadly, this is a write-off!

Symphony No. 6 in D min., Op. 104; Pelléas et Mélisande: suite, Op. 46.
**(*) BIS Dig. CD 237 [id.]. Gothenburg SO, Järvi.

The response of the Gothenburg orchestra to Järvi's direction is whole-hearted; one warms to the eloquence of the opening string polyphony and the impassioned finale. Järvi takes the main section very fast. There are one or two overemphatic gestures in the closing paragraphs of the slow movement, but on the whole this is well thought out and often impressive. It can hold its own with most competition and can be recommended. Järvi produces a very atmospheric account of *Pelléas et Mélisande*, in particular the brief but concentrated *By the sea*. Yet it would be idle to pretend that it can be preferred to Karajan's performance.

Symphony No. 7 in C, Op. 105; Canzonetta, Op. 62a; Kuolema: Valse triste; Scene with cranes, Op. 44. Night ride and sunrise, Op. 55; Valse romantique, Op. 62b.
*** BIS Dig. CD 311 [id.]. Gothenburg SO, Järvi.

Symphony No. 7; Tapiola.
*** Decca Dig. 411 935-2 [id.]. Philh. O, Ashkenazy.

Ashkenazy does not build up the *Symphony* quite as powerfully as some others, but he has the measure of its nobility. His *Tapiola* is atmospheric and keenly dramatic; the only quarrel one might have is with his frenetic storm, whose very speed diminishes its overall impact and detracts from the breadth and grandeur that otherwise distinguish this reading. Apart from these minor qualifications, there is much to admire – indeed, much that is thrilling – in these interpretations; in any event, it is difficult to imagine the recorded sound being surpassed.

Neeme Järvi and the Gothenburg orchestra bring great energy and concentration to the *Seventh Symphony*. Järvi is a sympathetic and authoritative guide in this terrain. The only disappointment is the final climax, which is perhaps less intense than the best versions. However, it is a fine performance, and the music to *Kuolema* is splendidly atmospheric; *Night ride* is strongly characterized. The recording exhibits the usual characteristics of the Gothenburg Concert Hall and has plenty of body and presence.

(i) *Piano quintet in G min.; Piano trio in C (Lovisa); String quartet in E flat.*
*** Finlandia FACD 375 [id.]. Sibelius Ac. Qt, (i) with Tawaststjerna.

(i) *Piano quintet in G min.; String quartet in D min. (Voces intimae), Op. 56.*
**(*) Chan. Dig. CHAN 8742 [id.]. (i) Anthony Goldstone; Gabrieli Qt.

The last few years have seen an impressive opening up of the Sibelius repertoire. Now comes the *Piano quintet* he composed for Busoni in 1890; it was inspired by Sinding's *E minor Quintet*, which he had heard Busoni play with the Brodsky Quartet in Leipzig. It is a long and far from characteristic piece in five movements, of which only two were played in his lifetime. Anthony Goldstone and the Gabrielis reverse the order of the second and third movements so as to maximize contrast. It is far from being the 'absolute rubbish' Sibelius declared it to be, but it is no masterpiece either. The first movement is probably the finest and Anthony Goldstone, an impressive player by any standards, makes the most of Sibelius's piano writing to produce a very committed performance. The *Voces intimae Quartet* is given a reflective, intelligent reading, perhaps at times wanting in momentum but finely shaped. Good recording.

The early *Quartet* is Haydnesque and insignificant, and the *Lovisa trio*, so called because it was written in that small town in the summer of 1888, offers only sporadic glimpses of things to come. The *Piano quintet* is given a fine performance on Finlandia, and there is little to choose between it and the more expansive Goldstone/Gabrieli account on Chandos.

String quartets: in A min. (1889); in B flat, Op. 4.
**(*) Finlandia FACD 345 [id.]. Sibelius Ac. Qt.

Here, for the first time on record, are two early quartets, the *A minor*, written in 1889, his last year as a student, in Helsinki, and the *B flat*, composed the following year. Only the first violin part of the *A minor Quartet* was thought to survive, but a complete set of parts was recently discovered. There are many prophetic touches and it is interesting to see that the highly developed feeling for form we recognize from the mature Sibelius is already evident in these quartets. The playing of the Sibelius Academy Quartet is sympathetic and intelligent, very good rather than impeccable. The rather close balance of the recording does not do full justice to their dynamic range or tone colour, but it is perfectly acceptable and there is no doubt as to the commitment or expertise of the performances.

String quartets: in A min.; D min. (Voces intimae), Op. 56.
** BIS Dig. CD 463 [id.]. Sophisticated Ladies.

Good but not outstanding performances. The *A minor Quartet*, discovered a few years ago, is well worth hearing, but the Ladies do not displace the Sibelius Academy Quartet on Finlandia, who more sensibly couple it with Op. 4 of the following year. The BIS performance of *Voces intimae* is well prepared but the finale is a bit heavy-going. Good recording.

String quartet in D min. (Voces Intimae), Op. 56.
** BIS CD 10 [id.]. Voces Intimae Qt – SCHUMANN: *Quartet No. 3.***

There is some good playing here, though the first movement is a little too relaxed and wanting in concentration; and the recording is a bit forward and suffers from glare. A serviceable performance, but a stop-gap recommendation.

VOCAL MUSIC

Arioso, Op. 3; Narcissus; Pelleas and Melisande: The three blind sisters. 7 Songs, Op. 17; 6 Songs, Op. 36; 5 Songs, Op. 37; 6 Songs, Op. 88. Souda, souda, sinisorsa.
*** BIS Dig. CD 457 [id.]. Anne Sofie von Otter, Bengt Forsberg.

Anne Sofie von Otter proves herself a remarkably fine Sibelius interpreter. She gives a powerful account of the *Arioso*, Op. 3 (which is much later than the opus number implies), and is highly imaginative in the familiar Op. 37 songs. In short, she can hold her own with any of her predecessors on disc; the voice is fresh and radiant and the artistic insight is of the highest order. This is the first disc of a complete set and promises to be a delight. Fine playing from Bengt Forsberg and very acceptable recorded sound.

Kullervo Symphony, Op. 7.
** BIS Dig. CD 313 [id.]. Mattila, Hynninen, Laulun Ystävät Male Ch., Gothenburg SO, Järvi.

The *Kullervo symphony* is an ambitious five-movement work for two soloists, male-voice choir and orchestra, which Sibelius wrote at the outset of his career in 1892. It brought him national fame and a commission from Kajanus that resulted in *En Saga*. After its first performance Sibelius withdrew the score and it was never performed in its entirety until 1958, a year after his death. It is revealed as an impressive work, full of original touches, particularly in its thoroughly characteristic opening. BIS accommodate the whole work on a single CD, no mean feat considering the wide dynamic range involved. Järvi is so fast that he almost robs the symphony of its epic character and its breadth. The central movement is the high point of this performance, thanks to the superb singing of Karita Mattila and Jorma Hynninen. If only the pace were less headlong, this would have been a strong recommendation. The Gothenburg recording does justice to the large forces involved: the brass is marvellously rich and present as usual and the balance between the singers and orchestra excellently judged.

Songs with orchestra: *Arioso; Autumn evening (Höstkväll); Come away, Death! (Kom nu hit Död); The diamond on the March snow (Diamanten på marssnön); The fool's song of the spider (Sången om korsspindeln); Luonnotar, Op. 70; On a balcony by the sea (På verandan vid havet); The Rapids-rider's brides (Koskenlaskian morsiammet); Serenade; Since then I have questioned no further (Se'n har jag ej frågat mera); Spring flies hastily (Våren flyktar hastigt); Sunrise (Soluppgång).*
*** BIS CD 270 [id.]. Jorma Hynninen, Mari Anne Häggander, Gothenburg SO, Panula.

This record collects all the songs that Sibelius originally composed for voice and orchestra, together with those for voice and piano that he himself subsequently orchestrated. Jorma Hynninen is a fine interpreter of this repertoire: his singing can only be called glorious. Mari-Anne Häggander manages the demanding tessitura of *Arioso* and *Luonnotar* with much artistry, and her *Luonnotar* is certainly to be preferred to Söderström's. Jorma Panula proves a sensitive accompanist and secures fine playing from the Gothenburg orchestra. In any event, this is indispensable.

The Maiden in the tower (opera). *Karelia suite, Op. 11.*
*** BIS Dig. CD 250 [id.]. Häggander, Hynninen, Hagegård, Kruse, Gothenburg Ch. and SO, Järvi.

The Maiden in the tower falls into eight short scenes and lasts no longer than 35 minutes. Its short *Prelude* is not unappealing but does not promise great things – any more than the ensuing scene delivers them. But the orchestral interlude between the first two scenes brings us the real Sibelius, and the second scene is undoubtedly impressive; there are echoes of Wagner, such as we find in some of the great orchestral songs of the following decade. All the same, Sibelius's refusal to permit its revival was perfectly understandable, for it lacks something we find in all his most characteristic music: quite simply, a sense of mastery. Yet there are telling performances here from Mari-Anne Häggander and Jorma Hynninen and the Gothenburg orchestra. Neeme Järvi's account of the *Karelia suite* is certainly original, with its opening rather impressive in its strange way. It is difficult to imagine a more spacious account of the *Intermezzo*, which is too broad to make an effective contrast with the ensuing *Ballade*.

Simpson, Robert (born 1921)

(i) *Symphony No. 3;* (ii) *Clarinet quintet.*
(M) *** Unicorn UKCD 2028 [id.]. (i) LSO, Jascha Horenstein; (ii) Bernard Walton (clarinet), Aeolian Qt.

The *Third Symphony* (1962) is in two long movements: the first hammering home in a developed sonata structure the contrast of adjacent tonal centres, B flat against C; the second combining the functions of slow movement, scherzo and finale in a gradually accelerating tempo. There is something Sibelian about the way that, in the first movement, Simpson gradually brings together fragments of musical ideas; but generally this is a work which (within its frankly tonal idiom) asks to be considered in Simpson's own individual terms. The *Clarinet quintet* is a thoughtful, searching piece, dating from 1968 and among Simpson's profoundest utterances. It is played with total commitment here. Both works are given extremely vivid sound.

Symphonies Nos. 6; 7.
*** Hyp. Dig. CDA 66280 [id.]. Royal Liverpool PO, Handley.

Not surprisingly – since Robert Simpson has distinguished medical forebears and was originally intended for medicine – the *Sixth* is inspired by the idea of growth: the development of a musical structure from initial melodic cells in much the same way as life emerges from a single fertilized cell in nature. The *Seventh*, scored for the same chamber orchestral forces as his remarkable *Second Symphony*, is hardly less powerful in its imaginative vision and sense of purpose. Both scores are bracingly Nordic in their inner landscape and exhilarating in aural experience. The playing of the Liverpool orchestra under Vernon Handley could hardly be bettered, and the recording is altogether first class.

Symphony No. 9.
⊛ *** Hyp. Dig. CDA 66299 [id.]. Bournemouth SO, Vernon Handley (with talk by the composer).

What can one say about the *Ninth* of Robert Simpson – except that its gestures are confident, its control of pace and its material are masterly; it is a one-movement work, but at no time in its 45 minutes does it falter – nor does the attention of the listener. The CD also includes a spoken introduction to the piece that many listeners will probably find helpful. The music is a most powerful experience: concentrated, awesome, and as mysterious as some astronomical phenomenon. It is played superbly by the Bournemouth Symphony Orchestra under Vernon Handley, and is no less superbly recorded.

String quartet Nos. 3 and 6; String trio (Prelude, Adagio & fugue).
*** Hyp. Dig. CDA 66376 [id.]. Delmé Qt.

The *Third Quartet* is a two-movement piece from 1953–4, so it comes between the *First* and *Second Symphonies*. Its finale is a veritable power-house with its unrelenting sense of onward movement which, like the *Grosse Fuge*, almost strains the medium (small wonder that the composer subsequently arranged it for full strings). Its first movement is a deeply felt piece that has a powerful and haunting eloquence. The *Sixth* (1975) is the third of a set which Simpson tells us constitute a close study of Beethoven's three *Razumovsky quartets*, and is further evidence of his remarkable musical mind. The *String trio* (1987) is a marvellously stimulating and thoughtful piece. Dedicated performances and excellent recording.

String quartets Nos. 7 and 8.
(M) *** Hyp. Dig. CDA 66117 [id.]. Delmé Qt.

The *Seventh Quartet* has a real sense of vision and something of the stillness of the remote worlds it evokes. It is dedicated to Susi Jeans, the organist and widow of the astronomer, and reflects the composer's own passion for astronomy; he speaks of the universe, 'quiet and mysterious yet pulsating with energy'. The *Eighth* turns from the vastness of space to the microcosmic world of insect-life. Indeed this provides a superficial link with Bartók, but, as with so much of Simpson's music, there is a concern for musical continuity rather than beauty of incident. Excellent playing from the Delmé Quartet, and very good recorded sound too.

String quartet No. 9 (32 Variations & fugue on a theme of Haydn).
(M) *** Hyp. Dig. CDA 66127 [id.]. Delmé Qt.

What an original and, in its way, masterly conception the *Ninth Quartet* is! It is quite unlike anything in the literature of chamber music: a set of thirty-two variations and a fugue on the minuet of Haydn's *Symphony No. 47*. Like the minuet itself, all the variations are in the form of a palindrome; some of the earlier ones derive from an early piano work, thus finding an even more natural habitat in the quartet medium. Many will find it a tough nut to crack, and it certainly calls for – and repays – concentrated study. It is a mighty and serious work, argued with all the resource and ingenuity one expects from this composer. A formidable achievement in any age, and a rarity in ours. The Delmé Quartet cope with its difficulties splendidly, and the performance carries the imprimatur of the composer. The recording sounds very good in its CD format.

String quartets Nos. 10 (For Peace); 11.
*** Hyp. Dig. CDA 66225 [id.]. Coull Qt.

Robert Simpson's *Tenth* and *Eleventh quartets* form a pair. The subtitle *For Peace* of No. 10 refers to 'its generally pacific character' and aspires to define 'the condition of peace which excludes aggression but not strong feeling'. Listening to this *Quartet* is like hearing a quiet, cool voice of sanity that refreshes the troubled spirit after a long period in an alien, hostile world. The one-movement *Eleventh* draws on some of the inspiration of its predecessor. It is a work of enormous power and momentum. Excellent performances and recording.

Sinding, Christian (1856–1941)

Suite, Op. 10.
*** EMI CDC7 47167-2 [id.]. Perlman, Pittsburgh SO, Previn – SIBELIUS: *Concerto.***

Heifetz recorded this dazzling piece in the 1950s, and it need only be said that Perlman's version is not inferior. Its blend of archaism and fantasy sounds distinctively Scandinavian of the 1890s, yet altogether fresh – and quite delightful. Such is the velocity of Perlman's first movement that one wonders whether the disc is playing at the right speed. Stunning virtuosity and excellent recording.

Sinopoli, Giuseppe (born 1946)

Lou Salome (opera): suites Nos. 1 and 2.
*** DG Dig. 415 984-2 [id.]. Popp, Carreras, Stuttgart RSO, composer.

Giuseppe Sinopoli as composer writes in an approachable Bergian style, colourful and energetic by turns. In this opera, first produced in Munich in 1981, the use of the orchestra is unfailingly imaginative. The two suites are quite distinct. The first one, after an atmospheric prelude, presents a big duet between Lou and her lover, Paul Ree; the second consists of a sequence of colourful genre pieces illustrating Lou's relationships with her partners. Under the composer's direction the performance is passionately committed, and the recording full and brilliant.

Smetana, Bedřich (1824–84)

Má Vlast (complete).
*** Virgin Dig. VC 791100-2 [id.]. Royal Liverpool PO, Pešek.
(M) **(*) DG 429 183-2 [id.]. Boston SO, Rafael Kubelik.
(*) Ph. Dig. 420 607-2 (2) [id.]. Concg. O, Dorati – DVOŘÁK: *In Nature's realm*.(*)
(B) **(*) EMI CDZ7 62606-2. RPO, Sargent.
(M) ** Eurodisc/BMG GD 69074 [id.]. Bamberg SO, Gustav Kuhn.
** RCA RD 83242. SRO, Sawallisch.

Má Vlast (complete). *The Bartered Bride: Overture and dances.*
*** DG Dig. 419 768-2 (2) [id.]. VPO, Levine.

Libor Pešek's set fits conveniently on to a single disc and, although the recording is not quite as opulent as Levine's VPO version, it still offers very good sound, convincingly balanced in the Liverpool Philharmonic Hall. Pešek's reading does not miss the music's epic patriotic feeling, yet never becomes bombastic. There is plenty of evocation, from the richly romantic opening of *Vyšehrad*, to the more mysterious scene-setting in *Tábor* while the climax of *Šárka*, with its potent anticipatory horn-call, is a gripping piece of melodrama. The two key sections of the work, *Vltava* and *From Bohemia's woods and fields*, are especially enjoyable for their vivid characterization, while at the very end of *Blaník* Pešek draws together the two key themes – the *Vyšehrad* motif and the Hussite chorale – very satisfyingly.

Levine's performance of Smetana's often elusive cycle of symphonic poems is quite splendid, full of momentum and thrust, aptly paced, with much imaginative detail. The opening *Vyšehrad* immediately shows the impulse of the music-making, yet it is warmly romantic too; while the two most famous pieces, *Vltava* and *From Bohemia's woods and fields*, are full of flair and most beautifully played. In *Tábor* and *Blaník* the VPO play with great vigour and commitment, and these patriotic pieces have both fervour and plenty of colour. *The Bartered Bride Overture* and *Dances* which are used as makeweight are highly infectious: Levine offers the usual numbers plus the *Skočná*. The sound is full-bodied and vivid, with a wide amplitude and range, to give the music plenty of atmosphere. But with Pešek's account on a single disc this must be regarded only as an alternative.

Among the other single-disc versions, Kubelik's 1971 recording with the Boston Symphony Orchestra has much in its favour, not least a very reasonable price. Like Pešek, Kubelik is careful to temper the bombast which too readily comes to the surface in the later sections of the work, and his skill with the inner balance of the orchestra brings much felicitous detail. The two unquestioned masterpieces of the cycle, *Vltava* and *From Bohemia's woods and fields*, are very successful. The DG recording, however, has been brightly remastered – cymbal clashes sound very metallic – and one could have wished for more ample orchestral textures, although the sound is fully acceptable.

Dorati's is also an extremely fine account of Smetana's cycle, avoiding most of the pitfalls with readings which combine vivid drama and orchestral playing of the finest quality. The music-making has a high adrenalin level throughout, yet points of detail are not missed. The bold accents of the opening *Vyšehrad* may seem too highly stressed to ears used to a more mellow approach to this highly romantic opening piece, and *Vltava* similarly moves forward strongly. In *From Bohemia's woods and fields* the fugato for the strings is paced briskly but, because of the high level of tension, this also falls into place. In the closing *Blaník*, Dorati finds dignity rather than bombast and the pastoral episode is delightfully relaxed, with a fine rhythmic bounce to the march theme which then leads to the final peroration. The Philips sound is splendid, with a wide amplitude and a thrilling concert-hall presence. It is a pity, however, that the coupling is so ungenerous.

Sargent's version of *Má Vlast* was recorded in 1965 and emerges with striking presence on this remastered CD. The performance has all the zest and spontaneity for which he was famous in the concert hall. Though the readings are not quite as individual and imaginative as those of Pešek and Levine, they are characteristically well shaped and alive. The opening *Vyšehrad* sets the mood, with the harp balanced closely and the orchestral layout fresh and clear, the romanticism not over-indulged. *Vltava* and *From Bohemia's woods and fields* are very successful and here, as in *Tábor* and *Blaník*, Sargent's directness of manner is appealing, tempering the bombast in the last two pieces. The recording helps too, by its clarity and the bright – yet not overwhelming – brass sonorities. The strings have excellent body yet add to the feeling of freshness; in every way the remastering has given the original sound – always warm and pleasing – more life and projection, while retaining the ambient atmosphere. Good value at bargain price.

The opening, larger-than-life harp solo of Kuhn's version immediately demonstrates the orchestral balance, with bold, forward projection against a very resonant acoustic. The effect certainly gives a richly romantic aura to an essentially spacious performance (which at 79 minutes only just fits on to a single CD). But detail is muddied and the bolder tuttis – the St John's rapids in *Vltava* and the patriotic spectacle of the work's closing sections – are spectacularly ample rather than refined. Nor is the reading subtle in its rhythmic feeling; it misses the vivid Czech folk-dance influence that refreshes Pešek's version. There is no lack of impact here and the playing has plenty of impetus and weight, but there is no feeling of an imaginative freshness of approach.

Sawallisch's RCA set is very dramatic indeed, and he does not shirk the brass histrionics in *Tábor* and *Blaník*. The whole performance is very involving and vividly played, but the digital remastering is not especially refined; at full price this is no longer very competitive.

Má Vlast: Vltava.
(M) *** DG 423 384-2 [id.]. BPO, Fricsay – LISZT: *Les Préludes*; DVOŘÁK: *Symphony No. 9.***(*)
(M) *** EMI CDM7 69005-2 [id.]. BPO, Karajan – DVOŘÁK: *Symphony No. 9.****
(B) **(*) Decca 417 678-2 [id.]. Israel PO, Kertesz – DVOŘÁK: *Symphony No. 9.***(*)

In Fricsay's inspired account of *Vltava* the river is in full flood and the village wedding sequence suggests that much wine has been flowing before the dance; yet later the moonlight flickers on the water with wonderful serenity, a lovely interlude. The remastered recording is very bright and vivid, giving extra fury to the St John's Rapids.

As a fill-up for an excellent version of Dvořák's *New World symphony* Karajan's EMI account of Smetana's most popular piece is comparably vivid, sounding more robust in its digital remastering, but still expressively refined in detail and spontaneous-sounding.

Kertesz's *Vltava* is very brilliant, with fast tempi, yet not losing its picturesque qualities. The recording is perhaps over-bright, but it has plenty of ambience.

Má Vlast: Vltava; From Bohemia's woods and fields; Vyšehrad. The Bartered Bride: Overture and dances.
*** DG Dig. 427 340-2 [id.]. VPO, Levine.

Taken from Levine's highly recommended complete set, the three most popular symphonic poems from *Má Vlast* plus the *Overture* and *Dances* from *The Bartered Bride* add up to a very attractive single CD.

Piano trio in G min., Op. 15.
*** Chan. Dig. CHAN 8445 [id.]. Borodin Trio – DVORÁK: *Dumky trio.****
** Teldec/WEA Dig. 2292 43715-2 [id.]. Trio Fontenay – CHOPIN: *Piano trio.****

Writing the *Trio* was a cathartic act, following the death of the composer's four-year-old daughter, so it is not surprising that it is a powerfully emotional work. Although it has an underlying melancholy, it is by no means immersed in gloom: there is serenity too, and the powerful finale ends with a sense of lyrical release. The writing gives fine expressive opportunities for both the violin and cello, which are taken up eloquently by Rostislav Dubinsky and Yuli Turovsky, and the pianist, Luba Edlina, is also wonderfully sympathetic. In short, a superb account, given a most realistic recording balance. Highly recommended.

The Trio Fontenay take a more extrovert view of the *G minor Trio* than do earlier rivals and tend rather to dramatize its emotions. It is good to hear it played as if they believe every note, but they protest too much and do not allow this dignified, elegiac quality to speak as naturally as it might. Good recording.

String quartets Nos. 1 in E min. (From my life); 2 in D min.
*(*) Nimbus NI 5131 [id.]. Medici Qt.

Good rather than outstanding performances of both Smetana *Quartets* from the Medici. Accomplished though they are, the music is not strongly characterized.

String quartet No. 1 in E min. (From my life).
*** Ph. Dig. 420 803-2 [id.]. Guarneri Qt – DVORÁK: *String quartet No. 12.****
** Telarc Dig. CD 80178 [id.]. Cleveland Qt – BORODIN: *Quartet No. 2.*

Smetana's *E minor Quartet* is autobiographical, its heart in the glorious slow movement in which the composer recalls the happiness of his first love. The Guarneri performance of this movement is wonderfully warm, romantic without a trace of sentimentality, with rich playing from the cellist, David Soyer. The happiness of the second-movement *Polka* ('Reminiscences of youth') is nicely caught and the finale is contrasted dramatically, with the catastrophic onset of deafness heralded by a high-pitched whistle on the first violin; the performance ends in a mood of touching elegiac reverie. The Philips recording is full-textured and most naturally balanced, with unexaggerated presence.

The Cleveland play magnificently on their four Stradivariuses, but their performances are a bit short on spontaneity. There is more polish than freshness here, though there is no doubt about the accomplishment of the playing as such or the excellence of the recording.

String quartet No. 1 (From my life) – orchestral version by George Szell. *The Bartered Bride: Overture and dances.*
*** Chan. Dig. CHAN 8412 [id.]. LSO, Geoffrey Simon.

The Czech feeling of Szell's scoring is especially noticeable in the *Polka*, but overall there is no doubt that the fuller textures add a dimension to the music, though inevitably there are losses as well as gains. The powerful advocacy of Simon and the excellent LSO playing, both here and in the sparkling excerpts from *The Bartered Bride*, provide a most rewarding coupling. The recording is well up to the usual high Chandos standards.

OPERA

The Bartered Bride (complete): sung in German.
*** EMI CDS7 49279-8 (2) [id.]. Lorengar, Wunderlich, Frick, Berlin RIAS Chamber Ch., Bamberg SO, Kempe.

The Bartered Bride sung in German seems an unlikely candidate for a top recommendation, yet in the event this vivacious set is a remarkable success. This is an opera where the choruses form a basic platform on which the soloists can build their performances, and here they are sung with splendid lilt and gusto, Kempe's warm, guiding hand maintaining the lyrical flow perfectly. The discipline of the chorus and the lack of rigidity in the melodic line almost completely compensate for the absence of the idiomatic colouring that the Czech language can bring, and certainly the soloists here offer far more sophisticated singing than is usual from a Czech cast. Pilar Lorengar is most appealing as Mařenka and Fritz Wunderlich is on top form as Jeník. Gottlob Frick gives a strong, earthy characterization of Kecal, the marriage-broker. The whole production goes with a swing, and the high spirits do not drown the lyricism – Wunderlich and Lorengar see to that. The recording is bright and vivid, yet has plenty of depth. This is not an opera that calls for much 'production', but the entry of the comedians is particularly well managed. The Czech Supraphon version under Košler is currently unavailable.

Libuše (complete).
**(*) Sup. Dig. SUP 007438/40 [id.]. Beňačková-Čápová, Zítek, Švorc, Vodička, Prague Nat. Theatre Ch. and O, Košler.

This opera has a limited appeal for the non-Czech listener, with a plot essentially concerned with the Czech royal dynasty. The cast here is a very strong one, with Gabriela Beňačková-Čápová as Libuše memorable in her prophetic aria in Act III, while Václav Zítek as Přemysl, her consort, provides an attractive lyrical interlude in Act II which, with its chorus of harvesters, has affinities with *The Bartered Bride*. In Act I there is some Slavonic wobbling, notably from Eva Děpoltová as Krasava, but generally the singing is as dramatic as the plot-line will allow. Košler directs committedly; with the stage perspectives well caught, the recording is very satisfactory. The libretto booklet is clear, even if the typeface is minuscule; but this issue is for the specialist rather than the ordinary opera-lover.

Smyth, Ethel (1858–1944)

The Wreckers: overture.
(M) *** EMI CDM7 69206-2 [id.]. SNO, Gibson – HARTY: *With the Wild Geese*; MACCUNN: *Land of Mountain and Flood*; GERMAN: *Welsh rhapsody.****

Ethel Smyth's *Overture* for her opera, *The Wreckers* (first performed in England in 1909), is a strong, meaty piece, which shows the calibre of this remarkable woman's personality for, while the material itself is not memorable, it is put together most compellingly and orchestrated with real flair. The recording is full and the CD has refined detail marginally.

Soler, Vicente Martín y (1754–1806)

Canzonette: *Amor e gelosia; La costanza; L'innozenza; La mercede; La natura; La preghiera; La semplice; La volubile; Una cosa rara* (opera): *Consola le pene mia vita; Dolce mi parve un di.*
*** Ph. Dig. 411 030-2 [id.]. Teresa Berganza, José Morenzo – sor: *Seguidillas.***

Vicente Martin y Soler was regarded as a rival of Mozart, who even quoted a bar or two of his in *Don Giovanni*. These songs and one aria are charming enough in their modest way, making a fair coupling for the more characterful Sor *Canzonette*. Fine performances, well recorded.

Sor, Fernando (1778–1839)

Fantaisies, Opp. 7 and 30; Variations on a theme by Mozart, Op. 9.
(*) RCA Dig. RD 84549 [RCD1 4549]. Julian Bream (guitar) – AGUADO: *Adagio* etc.(*)

Both Sor *Fantaisies* are ambitious and each has a central set of variations. Bream's approach is spacious and his deliberation – for all the variety and skill of the colouring – means that the listener is conscious of the music's length, although it is all agreeable enough. The more concise Mozartian *Variations* remain Sor's most famous piece, and the variety and flair of the playing demonstrate why. The studio recording, made in New York, is eminently truthful.

Fantaisies, Opp. 30 and 40 (Variations on a favourite Scottish air); Fantaisie élégiaque, Op. 59. Fantaisie, Op. 7: Largo & Non tanto (only); Minuet and Andante from Op. 11; Sonata No. 2, Op. 25: Minuet; Allegro (only). Variations on a theme by Mozart, Op. 9.
*** DG Dig. 419 247-2 [id.]. Göran Söllscher (guitar).

The most substantial (and moving) piece on this CD is the *Fantaisie élégiaque*, not a set of variations but an outpouring of grief on the death of Charlotte Beslay, a pianist much admired by Rossini. Playing of great polish and elegance from the Swedish guitarist, Göran Söllscher, and excellent and truthful recording.

12 Seguidillas for voice and guitar; Andante (from Divertimento, Op. 2/3).
*** Ph. Dig. 411 030-2 [id.]. Teresa Berganza, José Morenzo – SOLER: *Canzonette.****

This recital provides a striking example of Sor's characterful vocal style in twelve *Canzonette* which with their Spanish flavour admirably match the sharpness of the words. Berganza, well accompanied and well recorded, relishes their individuality.

Sousa, John Philip (1854–1932)

Marches: *The Belle of Chicago; The Black Troop; The Crusader; El Capitan; The Fairest of the fair; The Gladiator; High school cadets; The Invincible Eagle; King Cotton; The Liberty Bell; Manhattan Beach; Semper fidelis; The Stars and Stripes forever; The Washington Post.*
*** EMI Dig. CDC7 47286-2 [id.]. H.M. Royal Marines Band, Hoskins.

Marches: *Daughters of Texas; The Diplomat; From Maine to Oregon; The gallant Seventh; Golden Jubilee; Hail to the spirit of Liberty; Hands across the sea; Kansas Wildcats; The*

Legionnaires; Powhatan's daughter; Pride of the Wolverines; Royal Welsh Fusiliers; Sound off; The Thunderer.
*** EMI Dig. CDC7 47669-2 [id.]. H.M. Royal Marines Band, Hoskins.

Marches: *Solid men to the front; Beau Ideal; Charlatan; Flor de Sevilla; Glory of the Yankee Navy; Gridiron Club; Jack Tar; The Lambs; Marquette University; National game; New York Hippodrome; Nobles of the Mystic Shrine; Northern Pines; On the campus; Rifle Regiment.*
*** EMI Dig. CDC7 47940-2 [id.]. H.M. Royal Marines Band, Hoskins.

These are the most convincing performances of Sousa marches yet to appear from a British band. Lt.-Col. Hoskins catches their breezy exuberance and his pacing is consistently well judged, while the music-making still retains a sense that the performances emanate from this side of the Atlantic. The digital recording is very much in the demonstration class.

Marches: *Bullets and bayonets; El Capitan; Glory of the Yankee Navy; Gridiron Club; Hands across the sea; High school cadets; Invincible Eagle; Kansas Wildcats; King Cotton; Liberty Bell; Manhattan Beach; National game; The Picadore; Pride of the Wolverines; Riders for the flag; The Rifle Regiment; Sabre and spurs; Sound off; The Stars and Stripes forever; The Thunderer; Washington Post; US Field Artillery.*
*** Mercury/Ph. 416 147-2 [id.]. Eastman Wind Ens., Fennell.

Whereas the EMI recordings are modern, Fennell's collection derives from analogue recordings made in the early 1960s, a vintage Mercury era, and while detail is slightly clearer in the British performances, the Mercury sound remains demonstration-worthy. The performances have characteristic American pep, yet the natural exuberance never brings a lack of essential poise. In fact Fennell is a master of this repertoire and the Eastman Ensemble play with great flair.

Spohr, Ludwig (1784–1859)

Clarinet concertos Nos. 1 in C min., Op. 26; 4 in E min.
**(*) Orfeo C 088101A [id.]. Leister, Stuttgart RSO, Frühbeck de Burgos.

Clarinet concertos Nos. 2 in E flat, Op. 57; 3 in F min.
**(*) Orfeo C 088201A [id.]. Leister, Stuttgart RSO, Frühbeck de Burgos.

The four *Clarinet concertos* of Spohr – the *Fourth* much grander than the other three – make up an attractive pair of discs, particularly when they are as beautifully played as by the long-time principal of the Berlin Philharmonic, Karl Leister. His smooth tone, the ease and agility with which he tackles virtuoso passage-work and his ability to bring out the smiling quality of much of the inspiration make for delightful performances. The radio recording has relatively little stereo spread, but is undistractingly natural.

Symphonies Nos. 6 in G (Historical), Op. 116; 9 in B min. (The Seasons), Op. 143.
** Orfeo C 094841A [id.]. Bav. RSO, Rickenbacher.

Spohr's *Sixth Symphony*, written in 1839, reminds us of the Mikado's Gilbertian quip about 'Spohr interwoven with Bach and Beethoven'. The first movement sets a Baroque atmosphere, with fugal Bach contrasting genially with a Handelian pastoral style. Karl Rickenbacher has the full measure of it and the Bavarian orchestra play it most engagingly. The element of pastiche continues throughout, but the other movements are less successful. Schumann's influence is strong in the *Ninth Symphony*'s *Spring* movement (which comes second). The finale, with its echoes of the hunt, suffers from Rickenbacher's easy-going manner. A more aleit, vivacious approach might have brought these two symphonies more fully to life, although the playing of the Bavarian Radio Orchestra is always responsive and cultured, and the attractive ambience of the recording gives pleasure in itself.

Nonet in F, Op. 31.
*** DG Dig. 427 640-2 [id.]. Vienna/Berlin Ens. – MARTINŮ: *Nonet.****

Nonet in F, Op. 31; Octet in E, Op. 32.
*** CRD CRD 3394 [id.]. Nash Ens.

Spohr's *Octet* is a work of great charm; the variations on Handel's *Harmonious blacksmith* which form one of the central movements offer that kind of naïveté which (when played stylishly) makes for delicious listening. The *Nonet* is also very attractive. Spohr's invention is again at its freshest and his propensity for chromaticism is held reasonably in check. Both works are very elegantly played here and the recording throughout is natural and lifelike. This is civilized music, well worth having.

A delightful and well-recorded account of Spohr's *Nonet* from the Vienna/Berlin Ensemble, very attractively coupled.

Piano trios Nos. 1 in E min., Op. 119; 2 in F, Op. 123.
** Kingdom Dig. KLCD 2004. Beethoven Broadwood Trio.

These performances are alive and committed but lack the last degree of polish; consequently they are without that touch of urbanity which gives Spohr's music its charm. The players are not helped by being fairly closely miked in a resonant acoustic (the Church of St John-at-Hackney, London) and the effect is not flattering to the violinist, Frances Mason, although Joy Hall's firm cello line (often very important to the textural balance) is caught well. Michael Freyhan plays a Broadwood Grand of 1823 similar to the instrument Beethoven knew, and it gives the overall sound an authentic feel. With a warmer acoustic glow, these performances would have been even more rewarding; even as it is, however, this coupling is well worth exploring by admirers of the composer. Both works have an impressive scale (the disc plays for 66 minutes overall) and their standard of invention is high.

Piano and wind quintet in C min., Op. 52; Septet in A min. for flute, clarinet, horn, bassoon, violin, cello and piano, Op. 147.
*** CRD CRD 3399 [id.]. Ian Brown, Nash Ens.

These two pieces are among Spohr's most delightful, both the sparkling *Quintet* and the more substantial but still charmingly lighthearted *Septet*. Ian Brown at the piano leads the ensemble with flair and vigour, and the recording quality is outstandingly vivid.

VOCAL MUSIC

Lieder: *An Mignon; 6 German Lieder, Op. 103; 6 Lieder, Op. 154; Lied beim Runetanz; Schlaflied; Scottische Lied; Vanitas!; Zigeuner Lied.*
*** Orfeo Dig. C 103841A [id.]. Julia Varady, Dietrich Fischer-Dieskau, Sitkovetsky, Schoneberger, Hartmut Holl.

The amiable inspiration of Spohr in his songs is delightfully presented in this collection from Dietrich Fischer-Dieskau and Julia Varady. It is characteristic of the composer that, even in his setting of *Erlkönig*, he jogs along rather than gallops, and fails to use the violin dramatically, just giving it an ordinary obbligato. The most attractive songs are the set sung by Varady with clarinet obbligato, but those sung by Fischer-Dieskau are also all highly enjoyable, as long as you do not compare them with the finest of the genre. Excellent recording.

Die letzten Dinge (The Last Judgement): oratorio.
*** Ph. Dig. 416 627-2 [id.]. Shirai, Lipovšek, Protschka, Hölle, Stuttgart Ch. & RSO, Kuhn.

Spohr's picture of the Apocalypse was designed to please rather than to startle, and the gentle first half of his oratorio comes as an amiable preparation for the Judgement Day music in the second, launched in a vigorous Handelian chorus, followed by contemplation and rejoicing. The elaborate fugal writing is very skilled (Handel the main influence). Spohr's horror music too readily relies on conventional chromatic progressions, and the gently flowing tempi provide too little contrast; well performed, as here, this historical curiosity does prove well worth reviving. Among the soloists Mitsuko Shirai is outstanding, with Matthias Hölle, an imposing bass, also impressive. Good, atmospheric recording.

Spontini, Gasparo (1774–1851)

Olympie (opera): complete.
**(*) Orfeo Dig. C 137862H (3) [id.]. Varady, Toczyska, Tagliavini, Fischer-Dieskau, Fortune, Berlin RIAS Chamber Ch., German Op. Male Ch., Berlin RSO, Albrecht.

In Spontini's *Olympie*, based on an historical play by Voltaire about the daughter of Alexander the Great, the principal characters are Olympie, Alexander's daughter, and Statire, his widow, with rival suitors for Olympie's hand setting off the dramatic conflict: the tenor, Cassandre, as the goody and the baritone, Antigone, as the baddy. The writing is lively and committed and, despite flawed singing, so is this performance. Julia Varady is outstanding in the name-part, giving an almost ideal account of the role of heroine, but Stefania Toczyska is disappointingly unsteady as Statire and Franco Tagliavini is totally out of style as Cassandre. Even Dietrich Fischer-Dieskau is less consistent than usual, but his melodramatic presentation is nevertheless most effective. The text is slightly cut.

Stainer, John (1840–1901)

The Crucifixion.
*** EMI Dig. CDC7 47502-2 [id.]. Tear, Luxon, Westminster Singers, John Scott, Hickox.
(b) *** CD-CFP 4519. David Hughes, John Lawrenson, Guildford Cathedral Ch., Barry Rose; Gavin Williams.

The newest EMI digital recording of *The Crucifixion* differs from its predecessors in using mixed voices in the choir rather than the men and trebles of the Anglican tradition. Stainer arranged further contrast by including five hymns in which the congregation are invited to join, and this device is used here. Hickox is free in their treatment, which will be a plus point for some listeners. The devotional atmosphere of the contribution of the Westminster Singers is impressive and they rise well to the famous *Fling wide the gates, the Saviour waits.* The organist, John Scott, makes a fine contribution here – as indeed he does elsewhere. Robert Tear and Benjamin Luxon are a well-matched pair of soloists, especially in their duet *So Thou liftest Thy divine petition.* The EMI recording sounds extremely vivid.

The earlier Classics for Pleasure version (from the late 1960s) is also of high quality and, although one of the congregational hymns is omitted, in every other respect this can be recommended. John Lawrenson makes a movingly eloquent solo contribution and the choral singing is excellent. When the remastered recording sounds as good as this, there seems little reason to pay more.

Stalder, Joseph Franz Xaver (1725-65)

(i) *Flute concerto in B flat; Symphony No. 5 in G.*
*** Novalis Dig. 150 031-2 [id.]. (i) William Bennett; ECO, Griffiths – REINDL: *Sinfonia concertante in D.****

Though not quite as interesting a composer as his younger compatriot, Reindl, both the short *G major Symphony* and the *Flute concerto* have freshness and charm and well repay investigation, particularly in such excellent performances and recording.

Stamitz, Johann (1717-57)

Trumpet concerto in D (arr. Boustead).
*** Ph. Dig. 420 203-2 [id.]. Hardenberger, ASMF, Marriner – HAYDN; HUMMEL: *Concertos**** ⊛; HERTEL: *Concerto.****

This recently discovered concerto was written either by Stamitz or by a composer called J. G. Holzbogen. The writing lies consistently up in the instrument's stratosphere and includes some awkward leaps. It is quite inventive, however, notably the finale which is exhilarating on the lips of Håkan Hardenberger. There is no lack of panache here and Marriner accompanies expertly. Good if reverberant recording, with the trumpet given great presence.

Stamitz, Karl (1745-1801)

Double concerto in G for flute, oboe and orchestra.
*** Ph. Dig. 416 359-2 [id.]. Nicolet, Holliger, ASMF, Sillito – CIMAROSA: *Concertante*; SALIERI: *Double concerto.****

This elegant and well-crafted *Double concerto* retains one's interest throughout and has a rather good finale to round off the piece in fine style. As in the other works on this attractive CD, the playing is most persuasive and the recording is very real and immediate.

Stanford, Charles (1852-1924)

Clarinet concerto in A min., Op. 80.
*** Hyp. CDA 66001 [id.]. King, Philh. O, Francis – FINZI: *Concerto.****

In three linked sections the *Clarinet concerto* shows Stanford characteristically fastidious in developing his ideas; the clarinet repertory is not so rich that such a well-written piece should be neglected, particularly as the final section throws inhibition aside and presents more sharply memorable themes in a warm, late-romantic manner. Thea King's crisp-toned playing is most stylish and the accompaniment thoroughly sympathetic. The recording is reverberant but full and vivid, with just a hint of edge on the upper strings.

Symphony No. 3 in F min. (Irish), Op. 28; Irish rhapsody No. 5, Op. 147.
*** Chan. Dig. CHAN 8545 [id.]. Ulster O, Handley.

This *Third* and most celebrated of the seven symphonies of Stanford is a rich and attractive work, none the worse for its obvious debts to Brahms. The ideas are best when directly echoing Irish folk music, as in the middle two movements, a skippity jig of a Scherzo and a glowing slow movement framed by harp cadenzas, while the finale gives an attractive forward glance to Stanford's pupils, Holst and Vaughan Williams. The *Irish rhapsody No. 5* dates from 1917, reflecting perhaps in its martial vigour that wartime date. Even more characteristic are the warmly lyrical passages, performed passionately by Handley and his Ulster Orchestra, matching the thrust and commitment they bring also to the *Symphony.*

Symphony No. 5 in D (L'Allegro ed il Penseroso), Op. 56; Irish rhapsody No. 4 in A min. (The Fisherman of Loch Neagh and what he saw), Op. 141.
*** Chan. Dig. CHAN 8581 [id.]. Ulster O, Handley.

Stanford's *Fifth Symphony* is colourfully orchestrated and full of easy tunes, illustrating passages from Milton's *L'Allegro* and *Il Penseroso*. The essentially jolly first movement leads to a charming, gentle pastoral movement in an easy Laendler rhythm. The last two movements more readily live up to Stanford's reputation as a Brahmsian, representing the *Penseroso* half of the work, and the slow epilogue brings reminders of Brahms's *Third.* The ease and confidence of the writing makes it a winning work in a performance as committed and full of flair as this. The *Irish rhapsody* is more distinctive of the composer, bringing together sharply contrasted, colourful and atmospheric Irish ideas under the title *The Fisherman of Loch Neagh and what he saw.* Excellent recording of the finest Chandos quality.

Symphony No. 6 in E flat (In memoriam G. F. Watts), Op. 94; Irish rhapsody No. 1 in D min., Op. 78.
*** Chan. Dig. CHAN 8627 [id.]. Ulster O, Vernon Handley.

Stanford's *Sixth Symphony* is not the strongest of the set, but it has a rather lovely slow movement, with a pervading air of gentle melancholy. The first movement has some good ideas but the finale is too long, in the way finales of Glazunov symphonies tend to overuse their material. Nevertheless Vernon Handley makes quite a persuasive case for the work and an even better one for the enjoyable *Irish rhapsody No. 1* which features and makes rather effective use of one of the loveliest of all Irish tunes, the *Londonderry air.* Excellent sound.

Serenade (Nonet) in F, Op. 95.
*** Hyp. CDA 66291 [id.]. Capricorn – PARRY: *Nonet.****

The *Serenade* is for flute, clarinet, bassoon, horn, string quartet and double-bass, and comes from the same period (1905) as the *Sixth Symphony.* Like the Parry *Nonet,* with which it is coupled, it is an inventive and delightful piece, its discourse civilized and the scherzo full of charm. Capricorn play this piece with evident pleasure and convey this to the listener. The recording is very natural and truthfully balanced.

Magnificat in B flat, Op. 164; 3 Motets, Op. 38; Motet: Eternal Father, Op. 135.
*** Conifer Dig. CDCF 155 [id.]. Trinity College, Cambridge, Ch., Marlow – PARRY: *Songs of farewell.****

These fine Stanford motets and canticles, Anglican Church music at its most assured, make a welcome and attractive coupling for the moving and beautiful Parry choral songs. The *Three Motets*, early works, are settings of Latin hymns; *Eternal Father* is an elaborate setting of Robert Bridges; while the big-scale unaccompanied *Magnificat* for double choir makes a magnificent culmination. Immaculate performances and beautifully balanced, atmospheric recording.

Magnificat and Nunc dimittis in A, Op. 12; Anthems: *For lo I raise up, Op. 145; Ye choirs of new Jerusalem, Op. 123; The Lord is my Shepherd; 3 Motets, Op. 38; Motets, Op. 135/1 & 3; Motet: O living will.*
**(*) Hyp. CDA 66030 [id.]. Worcester Cathedral Ch., Hunt; Trepte (organ).

This characteristic collection of Stanford's church music brings uneven inspiration – with even some overtones of operetta – but there are more than enough pieces which represent the Anglican tradition at its most compelling, even in easy-going performances like these. The essentially mellow recording has a fair degree of bite and presence in its CD format.

Stanley, John (1712–86)

6 Organ concertos, Op. 10.
*** CRD CRD 3409 [id.]. Gifford, N. Sinfonia.

These bouncing, vigorous performances, well recorded as they are on the splendid organ of Hexham Abbey, present these *Concertos* most persuasively. No. 4, with its darkly energetic C minor, is particularly fine. The recording is natural in timbre and very well balanced. The CD gives the attractive organ sounds added tangibility; the only disappointment is the lack of bands for individual movements.

Stenhammar, Wilhelm (1871–1927)

(i) *Piano concerto No. 1 in B flat, Op. 1; Late summer nights, Op. 33.*
**(*) Sterling CDS1004-2. (i) Irene Mannheimer; Gothenburg SO, Dutoit.

Stenhammar toured with his concerto at the turn of the century but became bored with the piece; at one time the orchestral parts were lost and the full score was reconstructed by Kurt Atterburg. It is full of beautiful ideas and the invention is fresh (there is a good deal of Brahms, Schumann and, in the scherzo, Saint-Saëns) and, even if it is too long (nearly 50 minutes), admirers of the composer will find much to reward them. It is well played in this 1977 recording, as are the charming, Brahmsian *Late summer nights*.

Serenade, Op. 31 (with the *Reverenza* movement).
*** BIS Dig. CD 310 [id.]. Gothenburg SO, Järvi.

The *Serenade for orchestra* is Stenhammar's masterpiece, his most magical work, and this version restores the second movement, *Reverenza*, which the composer had removed, to its original place. It is thoroughly characteristic, yet it has some of the melancholy charm of Elgar, as well as an occasional reminder of Reger in its modulatory patterns and its delicacy of texture. Its presence enriches rather than diminishes the effect of the work as a whole. Glorious music, sensitively played and finely recorded.

Symphony No. 1 in F.
*** BIS Dig. CD 219 [id.]. Gothenburg SO, Järvi.

The *First Symphony* displays sympathies with such composers as Brahms, Bruckner,

Berwald and, in the slow movement, even an affinity with Elgar. The composer intended to revise it but never got around to doing so. Nevertheless there is plenty of originality in it. The recording has complete naturalness and truthfulness of timbre and perspective, and on CD there is additional presence and range, particularly at the bottom end of the register.

Symphony No. 2 in G min., Op. 34.
*** Cap. CAP 21151 [id.]. Stockholm PO, Westerberg.

Symphony No. 2; Overture, Excelsior!, Op. 13.
*** BIS CD 251 [id.]. Gothenburg SO, Järvi.

This is a marvellous symphony. It is direct in utterance; its ideas have splendid character and spirit, and there is a sense of forward movement; the melodic invention is fresh and abundant, and the generosity of spirit it radiates is heart-warming. The Stockholm Philharmonic under Stig Westerberg play with conviction and eloquence; the strings have warmth and body, and they sing out as if they love playing this music. The wind are very fine too. The recording is vivid and full-bodied even by the digital standards of today: as sound, this record is absolutely first class.

Neeme Järvi takes an altogether brisker view of the first movement than Westerberg, but the playing is spirited and the recording very good indeed, though not quite as distinguished as on the Caprice rival. The special attraction of this issue, however, is the *Overture, Excelsior!* It is an opulent but inventive score in the spirit of Strauss and Elgar and is played with enormous zest. *Excelsior!* improves enormously on acquaintance and deserves to become a repertoire work.

String quartets Nos. 1 in C, Op. 2; 2 in C min., Op. 14; 3 in F, Op. 18; 4 in A min., Op. 25; 5 in C (Serenade), Op. 29; 6 in D min., Op. 35.
*** Cap. CAP 21337/9 [id.]. Fresk Qt; Copenhagen Qt; Gotland Qt.

Stenhammar was an active chamber musician as well as conductor and solo pianist. The *First Quartet* shows him steeped in the chamber music of Beethoven and Brahms, though there is a brief reminder of the shadow of Grieg; the *Second* is far more individual and one can detect the ardent voice of the real Stenhammar. By the *Third* and *Fourth*, arguably the greatest of the six, the influence of Brahms and Dvořák is fully assimilated and the *Fourth* reflects that gentle melancholy which lies at the heart of Stenhammar's sensibility. The *Fifth* is the shortest; the *Sixth* comes from the war years when the composer was feeling worn out and depressed, though there is little evidence of this in the music. The Copenhagen Quartet play this marvellously. Performances are generally excellent, as indeed is the recording. These quartets are the product of a cultivated mind and a refined sensibility, but their reticence is well worth overcoming.

(i) *The Song (Sången), Op. 44;* (ii) *Two sentimental romances, Op. 28;* (iii) *Ithaca, Op. 21.*
*** Cap. CAP 21358 [id.]. (i) Sörenson, von Otter, Dahlberg, Wahlgren, State Ac. Ch., Adolf Fredrik Music School Children's Ch., (ii) Arve Tellefsen, (iii) Håkan Hagegård, Swedish RSO; (i) Blomstedt; (ii) Westerberg; (iii) Ingelbretsen.

The first half of *The Song* has been described as 'a great fantasy' and is Stenhammar at his best and most individual: the choral writing is imaginatively laid out and the contrapuntal ingenuity is always at the service of poetic ends. The second half is less individual, masterly in its way, a lively choral allegro in the style of Handel. The solo and choral singing is superb and the whole performance has the total commitment one might expect from these forces. The superbly engineered recording does them full justice. The

Two sentimental romances have great charm and are very well played, and Hagegård is in fine voice in another rarity, *Ithaca*.

30 Songs.
*** Caprice MSCD 623. Von Otter, Hagegård, Forsberg, Schuback.

A delightful record. These songs cover the whole of Stenhammar's career: the earliest, *In the forest*, was composed when he was sixteen, while the last, *Minnesang*, was written three years before his death. This is the most comprehensive anthology yet to appear. The songs are unpretentious and charming, fresh and idyllic, nearly all are strophic. Hagegård sings the majority of them with his usual intelligence and artistry, though there is an occasional hardening of timbre. Anne Sofie von Otter is in wonderful voice and sings with great sensitivity and charm. Bengt Forsberg and Thomas Schuback accompany with great taste, and the recording is of the highest quality.

Sterndale Bennett, William (1816–75)

(i) *Piano concerto No. 4 in F min.; Symphony in G. min.;* (i) *Fantasia in A, Op. 16.*
(M) ******* Unicorn Dig. UKCD 2032 [id.]. (i) Binns; Milton Keynes CO, Hilary Wetton.

Mendelssohn conducted the first performance (in 1839) of William Sterndale Bennett's *Fourth Piano concerto* in Leipzig. The work reflects Chopin rather more than Mendelssohn himself and is agreeable and well structured. Its lollipop slow movement is a winner, an engaging *Barcarolle*, and Sterndale Bennett's device of putting a cluster of piano filigree over a gentle pizzicato accompaniment was justly admired by the critics of the day. The *Symphony* is amiable, not unlike the Mendelssohn string symphonies, and the slow movement brings another ingenious device of repeated overlapping woodwind notes. Overall it is very slight, but enjoyable enough. Both performances are uncommonly good ones. There is nothing whatsoever second rate about the Milton Keynes Chamber Orchestra; the string ensemble is spirited and clean and the wind playing is first class. Malcolm Binns is a persuasive advocate of the *Concerto*, and he has the full measure of the appealing slow movement, while Hilary Wetton paces both works admirably and clearly has much sympathy for them. The solo *Fantasia* (with echoes of Mendelssohn and Schumann – to whom it is dedicated) has been added for the CD issue, which offers excellent sound and a good balance.

Stevens, Bernard (1916–83)

(i) *Cello concerto; Symphony of liberation.*
*** Mer. CDE 84124. (i) Baillie, BBC PO, Downes.

Bernard Stevens came to wider notice at the end of the war when his *Symphony of liberation* won a *Daily Express* competition. What a fine work it proves to be, though the somewhat later *Cello concerto* is even stronger. Dedicated performances from Alexander Baillie and the BBC Philharmonic. Good recording.

(i) *Violin concerto; Symphony No. 2.*
*** Mer. CDE 84174 [id.]. (i) Ernst Kovacic; BBC PO, Downes.

The *Violin concerto* was a wartime commission by Max Rostal and was hailed in the 1940s as the equal of the Britten or Walton *Concertos* – which it is not. However, it is a good piece and well worth investigating. Stevens has not the strong personality of, say, Rawsthorne or quite the depth of Rubbra, but he is far from anonymous. Indeed he is a composer of real substance, and the *Second Symphony* (1964) is impressive in its sustained power and resource. Ernst Kovacic is persuasive in the *Concerto* and Downes and the BBC Philharmonic play well. Good (but not spectacular) recording.

Stockhausen, Karlheinz (born 1928)

Stimmung (1968).
*** Hyp. CDA 66115 [id.]. Singcircle, Gregory Rose.

Gregory Rose with his talented vocal group directs an intensely beautiful account of Stockhausen's 70-minute minimalist meditation on six notes. Though the unsympathetic listener might still find the result boring, this explains admirably how Stockhausen's musical personality can magnetize, with his variety of effect and response, even with the simplest of formulae. Excellent recording.

Donnerstag aus Licht (complete).
**(*) DG 423 379-2 (4). Soloists, Cologne RSO Ch., Hilversum R. Ch. & O, W. German R. Ens., Ens. InterContemporain, composer; Eötvös.

This Thursday episode from Stockhausen's seven-day operatic cycle, sharply eventful, has obvious concentration in its direct musical expression. The central character is the Archangel Michael, with Act I devoted to his childhood, 'moon-eve' and examination, Act II to his journey round the Earth (with trumpet and orchestra), and Act III to the return home, representing finally Judgement Day and the end of time. The recording is hardly a substitute for the full visual experience, but the originality of Stockhausen's aural imagination, not least in his use of voices, is brilliant. The complete text is omitted, and the synopsis is not always detailed enough for the action to be followed fully, a pity in a work which is baffling enough already.

Donnerstag aus Licht (excerpts); *Unsichtbare Chöre (Invisible choirs)*.
**(*) DG Dig. 419 432-2 [id.]. Suzanne Stephens (clarinet), W. German R. Ch., Cologne, composer.

This record contains just the background choruses for Acts I and III. They make a satisfying group, with Stockhausen at his most monumental in choruses which tell – with Hebrew texts – of Judgement Day and the joy of those who go to Paradise. This is very much music aimed to communicate directly, and the disc can be recommended to anyone wanting to investigate this key composer of today – with the singular drawback that there is only a single track with no banding of sections.

Strauss, Johann Snr (1804–49)   Strauss, Josef (1827–70)

Strauss, Johann Jnr (1825–99)   Strauss, Eduard (1835–1916)

(All music listed is by Johann Strauss Jnr unless otherwise stated)

Banditen-Galopp; Kaiser Franz Joseph I: Rettungs-Jubel-Marsch; Russischer Marsch. Polkas: *Champagner; Eljen a Magyar!; Neue Pizzicato; Unter Donner und Blitz.* Waltzes:

Künstlerleben; Liebeslieder; Morgenblätter; Wiener Blut; Wiener Bonbons. Josef STRAUSS: *Auf Ferienreisen polka; Dorfschwalben aus Österreich (Village swallows) waltz.*
(M) *** Decca 425 428-2 [id.]. VPO, Boskovsky.

Egyptischer Marsch. Polkas: *Annen; Auf der Jagd; Pizzicato* (with Josef); *Tritsch-Tratsch.*
Waltzes: *An der schönen, blauen Donau; Carnevals-Botschafter; Frühlingsstimmen.* Josef
STRAUSS: Polkas: *Feuerfest; Jokey; Polka-mazurka: Die Schwätzerin.* Waltzes:
Dynamiden; Sphärenklänge. Eduard STRAUSS: *Fesche Geister waltz.* Johann STRAUSS
Snr: *Wettrennen-Galopp.*
(M) *** Decca 425 425-2 [id.]. VPO, Boskovsky.

Persischer Marsch. Polkas: *Bitte schön; Leichtes Blut; 'S gibt nur a Kaiserstadt; Tik-Tak;
Vergnügungszug.* Waltzes: *Acccelerationen; Kaiser; Rosen aus dem Süden;
Schneeglöckchen.* Johann STRAUSS Snr: *Loreley-Rhein-Klänge waltz.* Josef STRAUSS: *Die
Emancipirte polka-mazurka; Delirien waltz.* Eduard STRAUSS: *Mit Extrapost polka.*
(M) *** Decca 425 429-2 [id.]. VPO, Boskovsky.

Napoleon-Marsch. Polkas: *Explosionen; Im Krapfenwaldl; Lob der Frauen (Polka-
mazurka); So ängstlich sind wir nicht!* Waltzes: *Seid umschlungen Millionen!; 1001 Nacht;
Transactionen; Wein, Weib und Gesang; Wo die Citronen blüh'n.* Josef STRAUSS: Polkas:
Heiterer Mut; Moulinet; Polka-mazurka: Die Libelle. Johann STRAUSS Snr: *Sperl-Galopp.*
(M) *** Decca 425 427-2 [id.]. VPO, Boskovsky.

Perpetuum mobile; Spanischer Marsch. Polkas: *Demolirer; Stürmisch in Lieb' und Tanz.*
Waltzes: *Du und Du; Freuet euch des Lebens; Geschichten aus dem Wienerwald; Lagunen.*
Josef STRAUSS: *Brennende Liebe polka mazurka; Eingesendet polka; Aquarellem waltz.*
Eduard STRAUSS: *Bahn frei! polka; Frauenherz polka mazurka.* Johann STRAUSS Snr:
Radetzky march. Piefke und Pufke polka.
(M) *** Decca 425 426-2 [id.]. VPO, Boskovsky.

Decca have reassembled and carefully remastered the famous vintage Boskovsky/VPO
recordings on to five CDs, each containing between 73 and 75 minutes of music. The
cream of the Strauss family repertoire is here, and that includes some memorable items
from Josef: the (so-called) *Village swallows waltz* and *Delirien*, some engaging polkas such
as *Eingesendet, Brennende Liebe* and the spectacular *Feuerfest.* Eduard too offers some
memorable pieces, of which the most famous is the infectious *Bahn frei!* with its opening
whistle. Each CD is introduced by a famous waltz from Johann and is attractively
programmed to alternate other waltzes with polkas, while the charming polka-mazurkas
and marches offer further variety. The recordings date from between 1958 and 1976 but
generally wear their years lightly, since the warm acoustics of the Vienna Sophienbad-Saal
(where many of the recordings were made) are agreeably flattering, although the upper
string sound is less sumptuous than one would expect today. But the performances
remain unsurpassed; one has only to sample the zither solo at the opening of *Tales from
the Vienna Woods* to relish the special Viennese flavour.

Overtures: *Blinde Kuh; Eine Nacht in Venedig.* Polkas: *Auf der Jagd; Champagner; Eljen a
Magyar; Im Krapfenwaldl; Neue Pizzicato.* Waltzes: *An der schönen blauen Donau;
G'schichten aus dem Wienerwald; Immer heiterer; Kaiser; Künsterleben; Neu-Wien; Rosen
aus dem Süden; Wein, Weib, und Gesang; Wiener Blut; Wo die Zitronen blühn.* Josef
STRAUSS: Polkas: *Allerlei; Künstlergruss; Plappermäulchen.* Waltz: *Perlen der Liebe.*
Eduard STRAUSS: Polkas: *Bahn frei; Ohne Aufenthalt; Ohne Bremse.* Johann STRAUSS
Snr: *Radetzky march; Seufzer galop.*
(M) **(*) EMI CZS7 62751/2-2 [id.]. Johann Strauss O of Vienna, Boskovsky.

Boskovsky's EMI recordings were made in 1972/3. They do not always have quite the freshness of the Decca series, though the waltzes have a genuine lilt, and clearly the Johann Strauss Orchestra of Vienna know what they are about in this music. The polkas go especially well, particularly the two groups by Josef and Eduard, which are placed all together at the end of the second disc, with only a single waltz to offer contrast – not exactly brilliant planning! The first disc opens with the characterful items by Johann senior, and then comes the main programme of his son's masterpieces, of which the *Blue Danube*, *Künsterleben* and *Roses from the South* are outstanding. *Tales from the Vienna woods* is less magically atmospheric here than in the earlier, Decca performance. However, all the novelties, which Boskovsky does with great affection, are memorable. The sound is bright and full, but the ambient effect is not quite as skilfully managed as on the Decca series. Nevertheless this is excellent value.

Overture: *Carneval in Rom'*; Polkas: *Kreuzfide*; *Maskenzug*; Waltzes: *Carnevalsbilder*; *Carnevals-Botschafter*; *Du und Du*; *Kuss*; *Wein, Weib und Gesang*. Eduard STRAUSS: Polkas: *Ausser Rand und Band*; *Faschingsbrief*; *Mit Vergnügen*; *Wo man lacht und lebt*. Josef STRAUSS: *Masken-Polka*.
**(*) EMI Dig. CDC7 47719-2 [id.]. Johann Strauss O. of V., Boskovsky.

Boskovsky here explores some unfamiliar repertoire, with a few favourite numbers thrown in. Eduard Strauss is well represented with polkas, although it is in fact Josef's *Masken-Polka* that is the more memorable. The performances and recordings are well up to the standard of Boskovsky's EMI series, although they do not recapture the magic of his VPO Decca recordings, made during the analogue era.

Waltzes: *An der schönen blauen Donau*; *Frühlingsstimmen*; *Geschichten aus dem Wiener Wald*; *Kaiser*; *Künstlerleben*; *Rosen aus dem Süden*; *Wiener Blut*.
**(*) EMI Dig. CDC7 47052-2 [id.]. Johann Strauss O of V., Boskovsky.

This is Boskovsky's most impressive Strauss collection since his Decca era. From the very opening of the *Blue Danube* the playing balances an evocative Viennese warmth with vigour and sparkle, rhythmic nuances are flexibly stylish and the spontaneity is enjoyably obvious. The digital sound is full and vivid, though the string timbre has less than ideal bloom, and the resonant acoustic is emphasized. But the spirit of the dance is strikingly present throughout these enjoyable performances.

'Best of the New Year Concerts' (1980–83): Overtures: *Die Fledermaus*; *Waldmeister*; *Perpetuum mobile*. Polkas: *Eljen a Magyar*; *Pizzicato* (with Josef); *Tritsch-Tratsch*; *Unter Donner und Blitz*; *Vergnügungszug*. Waltzes: *Accelerationen*; *An der schönen, blauen Donau*; *G'schichten aus dem Wienerwald*; *Kaiser*; *Morgenblätter*; *Rosen aus dem Süden*. Josef STRAUSS: Polkas: *Frauenherz*; *Die Libelle*; *Ohne Sorgen*; *Die tanzende Muse*. Waltzes: *Aquarellen*; *Delirien*; *Sphärenklänge*; *Transactionen*. Johann STRAUSS Snr: *Radetzky march*.
(M) ** DG Dig. 429 562-2 (2) [id.]. VPO, Lorin Maazel.

Waltzes: *An der schönen, blauen Donau*; *G'schichten aus dem Wienerwald*; *Kaiser*; *Rosen aus dem Süden*; *Wiener Blut*; *Wiener Bonbons*. Josef STRAUSS: *Delirien*.
(M) ** DG Dig. 427 820-2 [id.] (from above). VPO, Lorin Maazel.

Maazel did not take on Boskovsky's mantle very readily; for all the brilliance of the playing, the impression is one of energy rather than of charm. Maazel can certainly shape the beginnings and ends of the waltzes elegantly, and the performances of the *Blue Danube* and *Tales from the Vienna Woods* are not without lilt; but elsewhere the feeling of the music-making can seem too high-powered. The *Radetzky march*, for instance, for all the enthusiasm of the audience response, is tightly disciplined. The digital recording gives good presence – especially in the *Pizzicato polka* – but less atmosphere, and when the applause comes one almost registers surprise. As well as the mixed two-disc compilation, there is a collection of favourite waltzes, all at mid-price. But Boskovsky and Karajan convey greater enjoyment in this repertoire.

'1987 New Year Concert in Vienna': Overture: *Die Fledermaus*. Polkas: *Annen; Pizzicato* (with Josef); *Unter Donner und Blitz; Vergnügungszug*. Waltzes: *An der schönen blauen Donau;* (i) *Frühlingsstimmen*. J. STRAUSS Snr: *Beliebte Annen* (polka); *Radetzky march*. Josef STRAUSS: *Ohne Sorgen polka;* Waltzes: *Delirien; Sphärenklänge*.
⊛ *** DG Dig. 419 616-2 [id.]. VPO, Karajan; (i) with Kathleen Battle.

In preparation for this outstanding concert, which was both recorded and televised, Karajan re-studied the scores of his favourite Strauss pieces; the result, he said afterwards, was to bring an overall renewal to his musical life beyond the scope of this particular repertoire. The concert itself produced music-making of the utmost magic. With a minimum of gesture he coaxed the Viennese players into performances of the utmost warmth and freshness; familiar pieces sounded almost as if they were being played for the first time. Kathleen Battle's contribution to *Voices of spring* brought wonderfully easy, smiling coloratura and much charm. *The Blue Danube* was, of course, an encore, and what an encore! Never before has it been played so seductively on record, with the VPO, in Karajan's words, 'demonstrating that their feeling for waltz rhythms is absolutely unique'. In the closing *Radetzky march*, wonderfully crisp yet relaxed, Karajan kept the audience contribution completely in control merely by the slightest glance over his shoulder. The recording is superbly balanced and the acoustics of the Musikverein bring natural warmth to every department of the orchestra, but particularly to the strings. This indispensable collection makes an easy first choice among any Strauss compilations ever issued; it was an occasion when everything was right – and the only grumble is the almost unbelievable lack of accompanying documentation.

'1989 New Year Concert in Vienna': Overture: *Die Fledermaus*. Csárdás: *Ritter Pasman*. Polkas: *Bauern; Eljen a Magyar!; Im Krapfenwald'l; Pizzicato* (with Josef). Waltzes: *Accelerationen; An der schönen blauen Donau; Bei uns zu Haus; Frühlingsstimmen; Künstlerleben*. Josef STRAUSS: Polkas: *Jockey; Die Libelle; Moulinet; Plappermäulchen*. Johann STRAUSS Snr: *Radetzky march*.
(M) **(*) CBS M2K 45564 (2) [id.]. VPO, Carlos Kleiber.

In style this is very similar to Kleiber's controversial complete recording of *Fledermaus*, for though he allows all the rhythmic flexibility a traditionalist could want – and sometimes more – his pursuit of knife-edged precision prevents the results from sounding quite relaxed enough, with the Viennese lilt in the waltzes analysed to the last micro-second instead of just being played as a dance. In the delicious polka, *Im Krapfenwald'l*, the cheeky cuckoo-calls which comically punctuate the main theme are made to sound beautiful rather than rustic, and fun is muted elsewhere too. But in one or two numbers Kleiber really lets rip, as in the Hungarian polka, *Eljen a Magyar!* (*Hail to Hungary!*) and the *Ritter Pasman Csardas*. Warm, full recording, with the presence of the audience nicely implied without getting in the way. With 87 minutes of music on two discs, this is not generous measure, even at mid-price.

'1990 New Year Concert': *Einzugsmarsch* (from *Der Zigeunerbaron*). Polkas: *Explosionen; Im Sturmschritt; Tritsch-tratsch*. Waltzes: *An der schönen blauen Donau; Donauweibchen;*

Geschichten aus dem Wienerwald; Wiener Blut. Josef STRAUSS: Polkas: *Eingesendet; Die Emancipirte; Sport; Sympathie.* Johann STRAUSS Snr: *Indianer galop. Radetzky march.*
*** Sony Dig. SK 45808 [id.]. VPO, Zubin Mehta.

A worthy successor to Karajan's wonderful 1987 concert, not *quite* its equal but offering many delights of its own. After the invigorating *Entrance march* from *Zigeunerbaron*, Mehta braves the conservatism of the Viennese audience by presenting a programme of mainly novelties. The first really well-known piece (*Wiener Blut*, splendidly played) finally arrives as item number 7! Before then the applause is grudging, but the listener at home must delight in hearing so much fresh music of high quality superbly played, with all the stimulation of a live occasion. This is Mehta's finest record for years; he conjures a magical response from the VPO and is just as persuasive in the famous waltzes. In the *Blue Danube* he hardly needs forgiveness for indulging himself (as Karajan sometimes did, only slightly more so) with a gentle, rather mannered reprise of one of the subsidiary melodies, and he conjures a moment of sheer kitsch from the Vienna strings. But elsewhere his easy warmth and relaxed rhythmic style are beyond criticism. The recording is superb: the engineers capture the orchestra with complete naturalness within the glowing acoustic bloom of the Grosser Musikvereinsaal.

Kaiser Franz Josef Marsch. Polkas: *Annen; Auf der Jagd; Fata Morgana; Tritsch-Tratsch.* Waltzes: *An der schönen blauen Donau; Kaiser; Morgenblätter; Wiener Bonbons.* J. STRAUSS, Snr: *Cachucha Galop.* Josef STRAUSS: Polkas: *Moulinet; Ohne Sorgen. Aquarellen waltz.*
** Chan. Dig. CHAN 8434 [id.]. Johann Strauss O, leader Rothstein (violin).

The playing here is attractively spirited and infectious and the bright recording has plenty of bloom in its CD format. There is no lack of lilt in the waltzes, and the polkas go with an infectious swing; indeed the spontaneity of the music-making is striking throughout. Good though Rothstein is, he does not equal Boskovsky or Karajan in this repertoire.

Napoleon march. Perpetuum mobile. Die Fledermaus: Quadrille. Waltzes: *Geschichten aus dem Wiener Wald; Wiener Blut.* J. STRAUSS Snr: *Radetzky march.* Josef STRAUSS: Waltzes: *Delirien; Sphärenklänge.*
**(*) DG Dig. 410 027-2 [id.]. BPO, Karajan.

Persischer Marsch. Die Fledermaus: Overture. Polkas: *Eljen a Magyar; Leichtes Blut; Unter Donner und Blitz.* Waltzes: *Accelerationen; An der schönen blauen Donau; Künstlerleben.*
**(*) DG Dig. 400 026-2 [id.]. BPO, Karajan.

Der Zigeunerbaron overture. Polkas: *Annen; Auf der Jagd; Tritsch-Tratsch.* Waltzes: *Kaiser; Rosen aus dem Süden; Wein, Weib und Gesang.*
** DG Dig. 410 022-2 [id.]. BPO, Karajan.

These three CDs were recorded by Karajan at the beginning of the digital era; the clean, bright recording, though not lacking ambient effect, has the almost clinical clarity characteristic of the DG engineers working in the Philharmonie at that time; ideally the balance could do with a little more warmth in the lower-middle range. The first collection shows Karajan at his finest, with evocative openings to each of the four waltzes and outstanding performances of *Sphärenklänge, Delirien* and (especially) *Wiener Blut.* *Perpetuum mobile* and the engaging *Fledermaus quadrille* make a piquant contrast. On the second disc the virility and flair of the waltzes (especially *Künstlerleben*) are matched by the exuberance of the polkas, and the *Fledermaus overture* sparkles so vividly it sounds like a new discovery. The third group, however, is rather less attractive. After a refined introduction, the *Emperor* does not achieve the zest of some of the other waltzes; and although the playing is not without elegance, the noble contour of the principal melody is less potent here than in some versions. The polkas go well, and the overture is a highlight. None of these records has the full Straussian magic that Karajan later found in his 1987 New Year concert.

Overture: *Die Fledermaus.* Polkas: *Annen; Auf der Jagd; Explosionen.* Waltzes: *Frühlingsstimmen; Rosen aus dem Süden; Wein, Weib und Gesang; Windsor echoes.* Josef STRAUSS: *Feuerfest polka* (with ZIEHRER: *Kissing polka*).
(B) *** Pickwick PCD 902 [MCA MCAD 25236]. LSO, Georgiadis.

Entitled '*An Evening in Vienna*', the performances have nevertheless a British flavour – which is not to say that there is any lack of lilt or beguiling warmth in the waltzes; they are beautifully done, while the polkas all go with an infectious swing. There are no superimposed sound-effects in the *Explosions polka*; one waits until the very end, when there is a spectacular 'collapse' of the whole percussion department. The sound is very good indeed, well balanced with a pleasing ambient bloom. This is very enjoyable and is John Georgiadis's best record to date.

Overture: *Die Fledermaus.* Polkas: *Im Krapfenwald'l; Leichtes Blut.* Waltzes: *Geschichten aus dem Wiener Wald; Kaiser; 1001 Nacht.* Josef STRAUSS: Waltzes: *Dynamiden; Sphärenklänge.* Johann STRAUSS Snr: *Radetzky march.*
(B) *(*) EMI CDZ7 62855-2 [id.]. VPO, Rudolf Kempe.

A disappointing selection from the beginning of the 1960s. Kempe holds the reins loosely and, though he coaxes some fine playing from the VPO, the performances are seriously lacking in tension, with the Viennese lilt too often degenerating into slackness. The introductions are more successful than the waltzes themselves. The sound is warm and smooth.

Perpetuum mobile; Polkas: *Annen; Auf der Jagd; Pizzicato* (with Josef); *Tritsch-Tratsch; Unter Donner und Blitz.* Waltzes: *An der schönen blauen Donau; Geschichten aus dem Wiener Wald; Kaiser; Wiener Blut.* Josef STRAUSS: *Delirien waltz.*
(M) ** DG 423 221-2 [id.]. BPO, Karajan.

Here is a selection taken from the two analogue LPs made in 1967 and 1971 respectively. The performances have great flair and the playing of the Berlin Philharmonic has much ardour as well as subtlety, with the four great waltzes all finely done and the polkas wonderfully vivacious. Josef Strauss's *Delirien*, another Karajan favourite, goes especially well. But the remastering has brought such brightness of lighting to the violins that the glare tends to over-project the music-making, although the overall vividness and presence cannot be denied.

Perpetuum mobile; Polkas: *Champagne; Pizzicato* (with Josef); *Tritsch-Tratsch; Unter Donner und Blitz;* Waltzes: *An der schönen blauen Donau; Kaiser; Wiener Blut; Wo die Zitronen bluh'n.* J. STRAUSS Snr: *Radetzky march.*
(B) ** Pickwick Dig. PCD 856 [MCA MCAD 25967]. LSO, Georgiadis.

This is very spirited music-making, given brilliant, modern digital recording (the violins lacking something in sumptuousness above the stave). There is no lack of either polish or affection, but the extra magic of the best Viennese performances is missing.

Polkas: *Annen; Auf der Jagd. Geschichten aus dem Wiener Wald waltz.* Overtures: *Die Fledermaus; Der Zigeunerbaron.* Josef STRAUSS: *Delirien waltz.*
(M) **(*) Decca 417 774-2 [id.]. VPO, Karajan.

Karajan's touch with the *Gypsy Baron overture* is irresistible, and *Tales from the Vienna Woods* is really beautiful, one of the very finest recorded performances of this piece, with a perfectly judged zither solo. The polkas have the panache for which this conductor at his best is famous. The CD remastering makes the most of the recorded sound; though it does not disguise its early date, the vividness remains striking.

Polkas: *Czech; Pizzicato* (with Josef). Waltzes: *Kaiser; Rosen aus dem Süden; Sängerlust; Wiener Blut; Wiener Bonbons.* J. STRAUSS, Snr: *Radetzky march.* Josef STRAUSS: Polkas: *Feuerfest; Ohne Sorgen.*
(B) **(*) ASV CDQS 6020 [id.]. LSO, leader Georgiadis (violin).

The LSO is on top form and the rhythmic feel of the playing combines lilt with polished liveliness. There is delicacy (the *Czech polka* is enchanting) and boisterousness, as in the irresistible anvil effects in the *Feuerfest polka.* The closing *Radetzky march* is as rousing as anyone could wish, while the waltzes combine vitality and charm. With good recording in a suitably resonant acoustic, which tends to emphasize the bass, this is recommendable, especially at budget price.

Pappacoda polka; Der lustige Kreig (quadrille); *Klug Gretelein* (waltz). Josef STRAUSS: *Defilir marsch;* Polkas: *Farewell; For ever.* Eduard STRAUSS: *Weyprecht-Payer marsch;* Polkas: *Mädchenlaune; Saat und Ernte;* Waltzes: *Die Abonnenten; Blüthenkranz Johann Strauss'scher.* J. STRAUSS III (son of Eduard): *Schlau-Schlau polka.*
*** Chan. Dig. CHAN 8527. Johann Strauss O of V., Rothstein, with M. Hill-Smith.

Volume 1 of *'Vienna première'* is a concert involving other composers besides the Strauss family; it was sponsored, like the present collection (Volume 2), by the Johann Strauss Society of Great Britain. This programme is admirably chosen to include unfamiliar music which deserves recording; indeed, both the *Klug Gretelein waltz,* which opens with some delectable scoring for woodwind and harp and has an idiomatic vocal contribution from Marilyn Hill-Smith, and *Die Abonnenten* (by Eduard) are very attractive waltzes. *Blüthenkranz Johann Strauss'scher,* as its title suggests, makes a pot-pourri of some of Johann's most famous melodies. The polkas are a consistent delight, played wonderfully infectiously; indeed, above all this is a cheerful concert, designed to raise the spirits; the CD sound sparkles.

Polka: *Unter Donner und Blitz.* Waltzes: *An der schönen, blauen Donau; Kaiser; Künsterleben; Morgenblätter; Rosen aus dem Süden; Schatz; Wiener Blut.* Josef STRAUSS: Waltzes: *Dorfschwalben aus Österreich; Mein Lebenslauf ist Lieb' und Lust.*
(M) *** RCA GD 60177 [60177-2-RG]. Chicago SO, Reiner.

Reiner's collection was recorded in 1957 and 1960, and the sound is voluptuous with the warmth of the Chicago Hall ambience. The performances are memorable for their lilting zest and the sumptuous richness of the Chicago strings, although the *Thunder and lightning polka* has an unforgettably explosive exuberance. Reiner – Budapest born – fully understands how this music should be played and conveys his affection in every bar. A fine appendix for the Boskovsky series – it will give equal pleasure.

Die Fledermaus (opera): complete (gala performance).
**(*) Decca 421 046-2 (2) [id.]. Gueden, Köth, Kmentt, Waechter, Berry, Zampieri (with

guest artists: Nilsson, Tebaldi, Corena, Sutherland, Simionato, Welisch, Berganza, Leontyne Price), V. State Op. Ch., VPO, Karajan.

Die Fledermaus (complete).
(M) (***) EMI mono CHS7 69531-2 (2) [id.]. Schwarzkopf, Streich, Gedda, Krebs, Kunz, Christ, Philh. Ch. & O, Karajan.
(M) *** EMI CMS7 69354-2 (2) [Ang. CDMB 69354]. Rothenberger, Holm, Gedda, Fischer-Dieskau, Fassbaender, Berry, V. State Op. Ch., VSO, Boskovsky.
(B) **(*) CfP CD-CFPD 4702 (2) [Ang. CDMB 62566]. Lipp, Scheyrer, Ludwig, Dermota, Terkal, Waechter, Berry, Philh. Ch. & O, Ackermann.
** EMI Dig. CDC7 47480-8 (2) [Ang. CDCB 47480]. Popp, Lind, Domingo, Seiffert, Baltsa, Brendel, Bav. R. Ch., Munich Op. O, Domingo.
*(*) DG 415 646-2 (2) [id.]. Varady, Popp, Kollo, Weikl, Prey, Rebroff, Bav. State Op. Ch. & O, Carlos Kleiber.

The mono recording of Karajan's 1955 version has great freshness and clarity, along with the polish which for many will make it a first favourite. Tempi at times are unconventional, both slow and fast, but the precision and point of the playing are magical and the singing is endlessly delightful. Schwarzkopf makes an enchanting Rosalinde, not just in the imagination and sparkle of her singing but also in the snatches of spoken dialogue (never too long) which leaven the entertainment. As Adèle, Rita Streich produces her most dazzling coloratura; Gedda and Krebs are beautifully contrasted in their tenor tone, and Erich Kunz gives a vintage performance as Falke. The original recording, crisply focused, has been given a brighter edge but otherwise left unmolested.

The Boskovsky version, recorded with the Vienna *Symphoniker* instead of the Philharmonic, now heads the CD list of stereo *Fledermice*. Rothenberger is a sweet, domestic-sounding Rosalinde, relaxed and sparkling, while among an excellent supporting cast the Orlofsky of Brigitte Fassbaender must be singled out as quite the finest on record, tough and firm. The entertainment has been excellently produced for records, with German dialogue inserted, though the ripe recording sometimes makes the voices jump between singing and speaking. The remastering is admirably vivid.

The Karajan 'Gala performance' of 1960 featured various artists from the Decca roster appearing to do their turn at the 'cabaret' included in the Orlofsky ball sequence. This was a famous tradition of performances of *Die Fledermaus* at the New York Met., in the early years of this century. The party pieces now have a vintage appeal and even Tebaldi's *Viljalied* (rather heavy in style) sets off nostalgia for an earlier era. There is a breathtaking display of coloratura from Joan Sutherland in *Il Bacio*, a Basque folksong sung with delicious simplicity by Teresa Berganza, and Leontyne Price is wonderfully at home in Gershwin's *Summertime*. But the most famous item is Simionato and Bastianini's *Anything you can do, I can do better*, sung with more punch than sophistication, but endearingly memorable, over thirty years after it was recorded.

The performance of the opera itself has all the sparkle one could ask for. If anything, Karajan is even more brilliant than he was on the older mono issue, and the Decca recording is scintillating in its clarity. Where it does fall short, alas, is in the singing. Hilde Gueden is deliciously vivacious as Rosalinde, a beautifully projected interpretation, but vocally she is not perfect, and even her confidence has a drawback in showing how tentative Erika Köth is as Adèle, with her wavering vibrato. Waldemar Kmentt has a tight, German-sounding tenor, and Giuseppe Zampieri as Alfred (a bright idea to have a genuine Italian for the part) is no more than adequate. The rest of the cast are very good, but even these few vocal shortcomings are enough to take some of the gilt off the gingerbread. The sound is sparklingly clear, although the ambience now seems rather less natural and the applause in the party scene somewhat too vociferous.

On a pair of CfP CDs, with a synopsis rather than a libretto, comes another vintage *Fledermaus* from the same year as Karajan's Decca set. It makes a superb bargain, for the singing is consistently vivacious. Gerda Scheyrer's Rosalinde brings the only relative disappointment, for the voice is not ideally steady; but Wilma Lipp is a delicious Adèle and Christa Ludwig's Orlofsky is a real surprise, second only to Brigitte Fassbaender's assumption of a breeches role that is too often disappointing. Karl Terkal's Eisenstein and Anton Dermota's Alfred give much pleasure, and Erich Kunz's inebriated Frosch in the finale comes off even without a translation. Ackermann's direction has not the sparkle and subtlety of Karajan, but the final result is polished and with a real Viennese flavour. The sound has come up remarkably vividly – there is a nice combination of atmosphere and clarity.

Domingo's is a strong and amiable, rather than an idiomatically Viennese, performance. If his conducting lacks the distinction and individuality of some rivals, it is on the whole more satisfying for not drawing attention to itself in irritating mannerisms. Lucia Popp makes a delectable and provocative Rosalinde, and Seiffert a strong tenor Eisenstein, with Baltsa a superb, characterful Orlofsky. Eva Lind as Adèle sings girlishly, but the voice is not always steady or well focused. The rest of the cast has no weak link. With ensembles vigorous and urgent, this is a consistently warm and sympathetic account. More dialogue than usual is included – but, distractingly, it is recorded in a different, much less reverberant acoustic.

The glory of the DG set is the singing of the two principal women – Julia Varady and Lucia Popp magnificently characterful and stylish as mistress and servant – but much of the rest is controversial to say the least. Though Carlos Kleiber allows plenty of rhythmic flexibility, he is never easy-going, for in every rubato a first concern is for precision of ensemble; and that does not always allow the fun and sparkle of the score to emerge. But in its way the result is certainly refreshing, even compelling, and the recording quality, both clear and atmospheric, is admirable. Hermann Prey makes a forthright Eisenstein, but René Kollo sounds lumberingly heavy as Alfred, and as for the falsetto Orlofsky of Ivan Rebroff, it has to be heard to be believed, unhealthily grotesque. For some ears this is so intrusive (as is the hearty German dialogue at times) as to make this set quite unacceptable for repeated listening.

A Night in Venice (Eine Nacht in Venedig): complete.
(M) (***) EMI mono CDH7 69530-2 [id.]. Schwarzkopf, Gedda, Kunz, Klein, Loose, Dönch, Philh. Ch. & O, Ackermann.

A Night in Venice, in Erich Korngold's revision, is a superb example of Walter Legge's Philharmonia productions, honeyed and atmospheric. As a sampler, try the jaunty little waltz duet in Act I between Schwarzkopf as the heroine, Annina, and the baritone Erich Kunz as Caramello, normally a tenor role. Nicolai Gedda as the Duke then appropriates the most famous waltz song of all, the *Gondola song*; but with such a frothy production purism would be out of place. The digital remastering preserves the balance of the mono original admirably.

Wiener Blut (complete).
(M) (***) EMI mono CDH7 69529-2 [id.]. Schwarzkopf, Gedda, Köth, Kunz, Loose, Dönch, Philh. Ch. & O, Ackermann.
(M) **(*) EMI CMS7 69943-2 (2) [Ang. CDMB 69943]. Rothenberger, Gedda, Holm, Hirte, Putz, Cologne Op. Ch., Philh. Hungarica, Boskovsky.

To have Schwarzkopf at her most ravishing, singing a waltz song based on the tune of *Morning Papers*, is enough enticement for this Philharmonia version of the mid-1950s, showing Walter Legge's flair as a producer at its most compelling. Schwarzkopf was matched by the regular team of Gedda and Kunz and with Emmy Loose and Erika Köth in the secondary soprano roles. The original mono recording was beautifully balanced, and the facelift given here is most tactfully achieved.

The EMI set conducted by Willi Boskovsky makes a delightful entertainment, the performance authentic and with a strong singing cast. The recording is atmospherically reverberant, but there is no lack of sparkle. However, for some there will be too much German dialogue, which also involves two CDs.

Der Zigeunerbaron (The Gipsy Baron): complete.
(M) (***) EMI mono CDH7 69526-2 (2) [id.]. Schwarzkopf, Gedda, Prey, Kunz, Köth, Sinclair, Philh. Ch. & O, Ackermann.

This superb Philharmonia version of *The Gipsy Baron* from the mid-1950s has never been matched in its rich stylishness and polish. Schwarzkopf as the gipsy princess sings radiantly, not least in the heavenly Bullfinch duet (to the melody made famous by MGM as *One day when we were young*). Gedda, still youthful, produces heady tone, and Erich Kunz as the rough pig-breeder gives a vintage *echt*-Viennese performance of the irresistible *Ja, das schreiben und das lesen*. The CD transcription from excellent mono originals gives fresh and truthful sound, particularly in the voices.

Strauss, Richard (1864–1949)

An Alpine symphony, Op. 64.
*** DG Dig. 400 039-2 [id.]. BPO, Karajan.
*** Ph. Dig. 416 156-2 [id.]. Concg. O, Haitink.
*** RCA Dig. RD 69012 [id.]. Bamberg SO, Horst Stein.
(M) *** Decca 417 717-2 [id.]. LAPO, Mehta.

An Alpine symphony, Op. 64; Don Juan, Op. 20.
*** Decca Dig. 421 815-2. San Francisco SO, Blomstedt.

An Alpine symphony; Till Eulenspiegel.
**(*) Decca Dig. 425 112-2 [id.]. Cleveland O, Ashkenazy.

An Alpine symphony, Op. 64; (i) *Songs with orchestra: Das Bächlein; Freundlich Vision; Meinem Kinde; Morgen!*
**(*) Chan. Dig. CHAN 8557 [id.]. SNO, Järvi; (i) with Felicity Lott.

As is shown by his *Heldenleben* (as well as by some of his other Dresden records on Denon, like the Bruckner *Fourth* and *Seventh Symphonies*), Blomstedt has developed into a conductor of real stature who knows how to pace a work and relate climaxes to one another. His *Alpine symphony* is superbly shaped and has that rare quality of relating part to whole in a way that totally convinces. He gets scrupulously attentive playing from the San Francisco orchestra and a rich, well-detailed Decca recording.

Karajan's account is recorded digitally, but orchestral detail is less than ideally clear and there is a slight edge to the upper strings. But it would be wrong to give the impression that the DG sound is less than first class and, as a performance, the Karajan is in the highest flight. It is wonderfully spacious, beautifully shaped and played with the utmost virtuosity. This is certainly one of the finest versions now available.

Haitink's account on Philips is a splendid affair, a far more natural-sounding recording than the Karajan on DG, and strongly characterized throughout. The offstage horns sound suitably exciting, the perspective is excellent, and there is plenty of atmosphere, particularly in the episode of the calm before the storm. Above all, the architecture of the work as a whole is impressively laid out and the orchestral playing is magnificent. This does not quite displace Karajan, but it can hold its own with the best.

The Bamberg orchestra also produce a fine performance, and RCA provide an exceptionally good recording with plenty of detail and a spacious, warm, well-focused aural image. The Bamberg now sounds a much bigger and finer body than it did in the 1960s and '70s – though, as this CD is a co-production with Bavarian Radio, it might well be reinforced. All the same, this is not to be preferred to Blomstedt (who offers a fine *Don Juan* as well).

The Cleveland Orchestra commands as rich a sonority and as much virtuosity as any of its illustrious rivals. Ashkenazy gives a generally well-controlled and intelligently shaped reading of the score that has much to recommend it. However, it is not quite as strong in personality as the very finest versions.

Those wanting a medium-priced version could hardly do better than turn to Mehta, whose performance is among the best Strauss he has given us, and the vintage 1976 recording is successful in combining range and atmosphere with remarkable detail. It is more brightly lit in its digital transfer, but the Decca engineers let every strand of the texture tell without losing sight of the overall perspective. The effect remains spectacular.

Järvi's reading brings a roundly enjoyable performance, ripely recorded in a helpfully reverberant acoustic. Though the performance of the main work is not as electrically taut or crisp of ensemble as, say, Karajan's, tending to give too much too soon, it takes a warm, genial view of the composer's mountain-climb and its incidents. Felicity Lott is at her finest in the four songs, gentle inspirations in which the sweet purity of her voice is never disturbed.

Also sprach Zarathustra, Op. 30; Death and Transfiguration, Op. 24.
*** Telarc Dig. CD 80167 [id.]. VPO, Previn.

Also sprach Zarathustra; Death and Transfiguration; Don Juan, Op. 20.
(M) **(*) Decca 417 720-2 [id.]. VPO, Karajan.

Also sprach Zarathustra; Don Juan.
*** DG Dig. 410 959-2 [id.]. BPO, Karajan.
*** Denon Dig. CO 2259 [id.]. Dresden State O, Blomstedt.
(M) **(*) Ph. 420 521-2 [id.]. Concg. O, Haitink.

Also sprach Zarathustra; Don Juan; (i) Lieder: *Cäcile; Mütterandelei.*
** Chan. Dig. CHAN 8538 [id.]. SNO, Järvi; (i) with Felicity Lott.

Also sprach Zarathustra; Macbeth, Op. 23.
(M) ** DG Dig. 427 821-2 [id.]. VPO, Maazel.
** Decca Dig. 410 146-2 [id.]. Detroit SO, Dorati.

Also sprach Zarathustra; Till Eulenspiegel, Op. 28; Salome: Salome's dance.
(M) *** DG 415 853-2 [id.]. BPO, Karajan.

Karajan's later (1984) version (coupled with an exciting account of *Don Juan*) has the advantage of digital technology and can offer great dynamic range and presence, particularly at the extreme bass and treble. As a performance, this newest version will be very hard to beat and could well be first choice. The playing of the Berlin Philharmonic is as glorious as ever; its virtuosity can be taken for granted, along with its sumptuous tonal refinement, and in Strauss, of course, Karajan has no peer. As a recording it is very good indeed, though it does not offer the spectacular definition and transparency of detail of the Dorati CD version on Decca.

Karajan's 1974 DG version of *Also sprach Zarathustra* is also available at mid-price, coupled with his vividly characterized performance of *Till Eulenspiegel* plus his powerfully voluptuous account of *Salome's dance*. This account of *Also sprach* has long held sway and generally makes a strong recommendation. The Berlin Philharmonic plays with great fervour (the timpani strokes at the very opening are quite riveting) and creates characteristic body of tone in the strings, although the digital remastering has thrown a much brighter light on the violins, only just short of glare.

In addition, Karajan's earlier Vienna performances of *Also sprach*, *Don Juan* and *Death and transfiguration*, dating from 1959/60, are available on Decca, impressively remastered. The sound of the Vienna orchestra is more leonine than that of the Berlin Philharmonic but does not lack either body or attack. Indeed the performances of both *Don Juan* and *Death and transfiguration* are among the very finest – the *Don* has great zest and passion. *Also sprach Zarathustra* had an enormously wide dynamic range; only now, some three decades after it was made, does the technology of CD permit its degree of contrast to register without difficulty. Even so, the slightly backward balance means that the *Joys and passions* section does not sound as sumptuous as on either of the DG recordings.

Previn draws magnificent playing from the Vienna Philharmonic in powerful, red-blooded readings of both symphonic poems, and the recording is among Telarc's finest. Previn's sharp, rhythmic control at speeds that never languish brings out the structural strength of both works, yet Straussian warmth is never underplayed. Strongly recommended for anyone wanting this particular coupling, and enjoying voluptuous sound-quality.

As a recording the Denon CD could hardly be more impressive. The sound is rich, the acoustic is resonant but never clouds detail, and the range and presence are really quite stunning. The performance has all the sense of architecture and authority we have come to expect from Blomstedt, whose Strauss is always distinctive. The Denon disc also contains a very good *Don Juan*.

Haitink's 1974 *Also sprach Zarathustra* was often spoken of in the same breath as Karajan's, issued in the same year, and if the strings of the Berlin Philharmonic have greater rapture and lyrical intensity, there is no lack of ardour from the Concertgebouw players and the reading has breadth and nobility. Haitink's *Don Juan* too has a fine impetus. The snag is that the digital remastering, in attempting to clarify luxuriant textures, has lost some of the recording's inner focus, and some of the sumptuousness too.

The main attraction of Maazel's *Zarathustra* resides in the coupling, *Macbeth*, which is something of a rarity. It is powerful and does not deserve the neglect it suffers in the concert hall. It is played brilliantly here, as is the more famous work. This was one of the earliest of DG's digital recordings (1983), however, and the sound, though well balanced, is very brightly lit. It does not lack spectacle but misses the richness of texture of the finest analogue recordings, nor is it as finely detailed as the best of its current digital rivals.

Dorati's *Zarathustra* is given top-drawer Decca sound. It is well played but not so firmly held together as with Karajan and Kempe. *Macbeth* is a good rather than a distinctive account.

Järvi's account of *Also sprach Zarathustra* is the least successful of his Strauss recordings for Chandos. The reverberant acoustic characteristic of the Caird Hall at Dundee here muddles the sound without giving it compensating richness. *Don Juan* is much better, both in sound and in performance, and in the valuable song fill-ups, Felicity Lott is at her freshest in *Müttertandelei*, although the pressures of *Cäcile* bring occasional roughness.

Aus Italien, Op. 16; (i) Songs: *Befreit; Meine Auge; Das Rosenband; Winterweihe.*
*** Chan. Dig. CHAN 8744 [id.]. SNO, Järvi; (i) with Felicity Lott.

Aus Italien is early Strauss and does not do him the fullest justice; but it does have marvellous moments, including the beautiful slow movement. The finale quotes a famous Neapolitan tarantella by Denza but does not make a great deal of it. Järvi takes a spacious view of the work and his recorded sound is full-bodied, with a natural perspective, and there is plenty of warmth. The Scottish orchestra seems at home in the score, giving the finale a certain Celtic lilt. The four songs, sung simply and eloquently but not always very colourfully by Felicity Lott, make an agreeable postlude.

Le bourgeois gentilhomme: suite, Op. 60; Dance suite after keyboard pieces by Couperin.
**(*) ASV Dig. CDCOE 809 [id.]. COE, Erich Leinsdorf.

Leinsdorf is perhaps not quite as subtle or as light of touch as Tate in *Le bourgeois gentilhomme*, but he gives a very good account of the score and, for that matter, a fairly good one of the *Dance suite*, although occasionally he is a bit heavy-handed. But this is delightful music, well worth having. The recording is acceptable enough, though not as rich as the EMI, but clean and well detailed. A generally recommendable disc.

Le bougeois gentilhomme: suite, Op. 60; Metamorphosen for 23 solo strings.
*** EMI Dig. CDC7 47992-2 [id.]. ECO, Jeffrey Tate.

Tate's ECO disc provides an unusual but attractive coupling of the much-neglected incidental music to *Le bourgeois gentilhomme* and the more frequently recorded late masterpiece, *Metamorphosen*. He is a warmly expansive Straussian, building *Metamorphosen* powerfully but not letting the sparkling suite grow too heavy – quite a danger, when it is on the long side. Good EMI sound with plenty of bloom.

Le bourgeois gentilhomme (suite), Op. 60: excerpts; (i) *Don Quixote, Op. 35.*
(M) (***) EMI mono CDH7 63106-2. (i) Tortelier; RPO, Beecham.

Tortelier and Beecham recorded their *Don Quixote* in 1947 during Strauss's visit to London. The playing is pretty electrifying, with the newly formed RPO on their best form. Tortelier had performed the work under Strauss himself and here plays for all the world as if his life depended on it. There is great delicacy in *Le bourgeois gentilhomme* and some delicious playing from the RPO's then leader, Oscar Lampe.

Burleske, Op. 11; Parergon, Op. 73; Stimmungsbilder, Op. 9.
**(*) Ara. Dig. Z 6567 [id.]. Ian Hobson, Philh. O, Del Mar.

(i) *Burleske in D min.; Sinfonia domestica, Op. 53.*
*** CBS MK 42322 [id.]. (i) Barenboim; BPO, Mehta.

Mehta's version of the *Sinfonia domestica* is generally speaking the best Strauss record he has given us for some years. His account is humane and relaxed and has great warmth; he certainly gets pretty sumptuous playing from the Berlin Philharmonic and has the advantage of very good sound. As its fill-up, it has the *Burleske* for piano and orchestra, given with great brilliance and panache by Daniel Barenboim in a beautifully balanced recording. A highly recommendable disc.

Ian Hobson's account of the *D minor Burleske* is less dazzling than Barenboim's and he takes fewer risks. Nevertheless, on its own terms it is eminently satisfactory, and he is well supported by Norman Del Mar and the Philharmonia, and is well recorded. The *Parergon* for left hand is again very well played. The *Stimmungsbilder* are early, rather Schumannesque pieces, written in 1884: Hobson gives a rather touching account of *Träumerei*, and though one can imagine a performance of the *Intermezzo* with greater charm, there is still much to admire here. Decent recording.

Horn concertos Nos 1 in E flat, Op. 11; 2 in E flat.
(***) EMI CDC7 47834-2 [id.]. Dennis Brain, Philh. O, Sawallisch – HINDEMITH: *Horn concerto.*(***)
**(*) Ph. Dig. 412 237-2 [id.]. Baumann, Leipzig GO, Masur.

Dennis Brain made these *Concertos* his own, and his superlative performances of them are most welcome on CD. But the digital remastering has brought an orchestral sound without much bloom, and though the horn timbre seems unimpaired by the relative dryness of the sound, Richard Strauss ideally needs richer orchestral textures.

Baumann's broad stream of tone and consummate technique bring much pleasure throughout both works, and the florid finale of the *Second Concerto* is articulated with enviable ease. But this easy-going quality also brings some relaxation of normal tensions. The bold contrasting episode at the centre of the slow movement of Op. 11 ideally needs a kind of *Don Juan*-like fervour to make its best effect, as Dennis Brain demonstrated. The soloist here is most truthfully caught, but the orchestra, slightly recessed in the reverberant Leipzig acoustic, loses some of its edge in the brilliant tuttis, while inner detail is not sharp.

(i) *Horn concertos Nos 1 in E flat, Op. 11; 2 in E flat;* (ii) *Oboe concerto in D;* (iii) *Duet concertino for clarinet, bassoon, strings and harp.*
(M) *** EMI CDM7 69661-2. (i) Peter Damm; (ii) Manfred Clement; (iii) Manfred Weise, Wolfgang Liebscher; Dresden State O, Kempe.

Peter Damm's performances of the *Horn concertos* are second to none and although his use of a (judicious) degree of vibrato may be a drawback for some ears, his tone is gloriously rich. The big striding theme at the centre of the *Andante* of No. 1 is superbly expansive, and the articulation in the finales of both *Concertos* is joyously deft and nimble. Similarly, while Manfred Clement's *Oboe concerto* is a sensitive reading, his creamily full timbre may not appeal to those brought up on Goossens. There can be no reservations whatsoever about the *Duet concertino*, where the sounds from bassoon and clarinet are beguilingly succulent, while the intertwining of both wind soloists with the dancing orchestral violins of the finale has an irresistible, genial finesse. Throughout, the superb playing of the Dresden orchestra adds an extra dimension to the music-making. Kempe's benign control of the music's ebb and flow shows him always a warmly understanding Straussian. The remastered recording, made in the Dresden Lukaskirche, retains an agreeable ambient glow which greatly pleases the ear.

Oboe concerto in D.
*** ASV Dig. CDCOE 808 [id.]. Douglas Boyd, COE, Berglund – MOZART: *Oboe concerto.****

Douglas Boyd winningly brings out the happy glow of Strauss's inspiration of old age, and the ebb and flow of his expression with its delicate touching-in of the characteristic flourishes in the solo line sounds totally spontaneous. His warm oboe tone, less reedy than some, equally brings out the *Rosenkavalier* element in this lovely concerto. With warm, well-balanced recording, the gentle contrast of romantic and classical in this work is conveyed delectably.

(i) *Oboe concerto; Metamorphosen for 23 solo strings.*
** Capriccio Dig. 10 231 [id.]. (i) Lajos Lencses; Stuttgart RSO, Marriner.

Lajos Lencses is a characterful soloist in the *Oboe concerto;* whatever their respective merits, however, neither performance here offers much of a challenge to existing recommendations, and the recording is good rather than oustanding.

(i) *Oboe concerto; Metamorphosen for 23 solo strings;* (ii) *4 Last songs (Vier letzte Lieder).*
(M) **(*) DG 423 888-2 [id.]. (i) Koch; (ii) Janowitz; BPO, Karajan.

Karajan's 1971 account of the *Metamorphosen* is self-recommending, and it sounds excellent in its remastered format, full yet better defined. In the *Four last songs* Gundula Janowitz produces a beautiful flow of creamy soprano tone, at the same time leaving the music's deeper and more subtle emotions underexposed. Lothar Koch's oboe timbre is creamy, too: he is forwardly balanced, but Karajan's accompaniment is relatively athletic, emphasizing the neo-classical style rather than the pastoral implications.

Death and Transfiguration, Op. 24.
** Chan. CHAN 8533 [id.]. LSO, Horenstein – HINDEMITH: *Mathis der Maler.***(*)

Horenstein's account of *Death and Transfiguration* is spacious and the recorded sound, already vivid, is even more so in its digitally remastered format. However, competition is stiff and Horenstein would not displace Karajan.

Death and Transfiguration; Don Juan; Till Eulenspiegel.
*** Ph. Dig. 411 442-2 [id.]. Concg. O, Haitink.
(M) *** DG Dig. 429 492-2 [id.]. LSO, Abbado.
(B) **(*) CBS Dig. MYK 42592 [id.]. Cleveland O, Maazel.
(M) **(*) EMI Dig. CD-EMX 9501. LPO, Rickenbacher.

Death and Transfiguration; Don Juan; Till Eulenspiegel; Salome: Salome's dance.
(M) *** DG 423 222-2 [id.]. BPO, Karajan.

Among recent versions of this most popular coupling, Haitink's takes the palm. The Philips digital recording is not analytical, but the ambient bloom of the Concertgebouw is admirably suited to Strauss's rich orchestral tapestries and detail is naturally defined. Haitink's performances are undoubtedly distinguished, superbly played, persuasively and subtly characterized. He finds added nobility in *Death and Transfiguration*, while there is no lack of swagger in the characterizations of both the *Don* and *Till*. The easy brilliance of the orchestral playing is complemented by the natural spontaneity of Haitink's readings, seamless in the transition between narrative events, without loss of the music's picaresque or robust qualities.

The performances under Claudio Abbado have plenty of dash and their brilliance is tempered with sensitivity. Some may feel that *Don Juan* veers too much towards the exuberant showpiece and vehicle for display, but both this and *Till Eulenspiegel* must be numbered among the best available. *Death and Transfiguration* has a marvellously spacious opening. The strings produce some splendidly silky tone and there is much sensitive wind playing too. Compared with the Philips Concertgebouw sound for Haitink, the DG upper range is less smoothly natural, but Abbado's CD now has a price advantage.

With superbly committed support from his players, Maazel takes an extrovert view of *Death and Transfiguration;* the mortal struggle is frenzied enough, but there is comparatively little feeling of menace and, when the transformation comes, the opulent climax is endearingly sumptuous. The portrayal of *Till* is warmly affectionate, but the reading is exhilaratingly paced and has excellent detail. *Don Juan* is made totally sympathetic, with Maazel relishing every moment. In the famous love scene, the oboe solo is glowingly sensuous; the final climax is ecstatic, the tempo broadened when the strings rapturously take up the great horn tune. The CBS digital recording is sumptuous, richly glowing, but does not lack clarity, and the brass has telling bite and sonority. As sound, this is far richer and more voluptuous than Abbado.

All three Karajan performances from the mid-1970s are winningly characterized and exhilarating in impulse, the orchestral playing in the highest class; and to make this reissue even more enticing, Karajan's voluptuous account of *Salome's dance* has been added. The only snag is the very bright lighting on the violins brought by the digital remastering (it nearly amounts to glare in *Don Juan*). But the ambient effect remains to give the overall sound plenty of atmosphere.

On the mid-price Eminence label Karl Rickenbacher conducts sympathetic, unmannered readings of Strauss's three most popular symphonic poems in performances that are both well played and brilliantly recorded. They may not be quite as subtly expressive as the finest rivals, but on CD they have outstandingly good digital sound in their favour.

Death and Transfiguration; Don Juan; Metamorphosen for 23 solo strings; Salome: Dance of the 7 veils.
(M) *** EMI CDM7 63350-2 [id.]. Philh. O, Klemperer.

This generous mid-priced CD admirably assembles Klemperer's Richard Strauss recordings in convenient form at a reasonable price. In his hands it is the *Metamorphosen* and *Death and Transfiguration* that excite the greatest admiration. With Klemperer the work for strings has a ripeness that exactly fits Strauss's last essay for orchestra, while *Death and Transfiguration* is invested with a nobility too rarely heard in this work. Not everyone will respond to Klemperer's spacious treatment of the other works. His account of *Salome's dance* is splendidly sensuous and *Don Juan* is clearly seen as 'the idealist in search of perfect womanhood'. But with marvellous Philharmonia playing and a recording (made in the Kingsway Hall in 1960/61) which still sounds full-bodied and in the case of *Metamorphosen* has added refinement of detail, this collection is certainly not lacking in strength of characterization.

Death and Transfiguration; Don Juan; Salome: Dance of the 7 veils.
(B) *** RCA Dig. VD 60135 [60135-2 RV]. Dallas SO, Mata.

The sound of this bargain CD approaches the demonstration class and it is undoubtedly excellent value. These three works are all brilliantly played and, if Mata's reading of *Death and Transfiguration* does not quite match Karajan's or Klemperer's, this inexpensive CD still gives considerable satisfaction.

Death and Transfiguration; Metamorphosen for 23 solo strings.
⊛ *** DG Dig. 410 892-2 [id.]. BPO, Karajan.

Karajan's new digital account of *Metamorphosen* has even greater emotional urgency than the 1971 record he made with the Berlin Philharmonic and there is a marginally quicker pulse. The sound is fractionally more forward and cleaner but still sounds sumptuous, and the account of *Death and Transfiguration* is quite electrifying. The recording balance has no lack of vividness, and the playing of the Berliners is superbly committed. It would be difficult to improve on this coupling by the greatest Strauss conductor of his day.

Don Quixote, Op. 35.
*** EMI CDC7 49308-2 [id.]. Rostropovich, BPO, Karajan.
(*) CBS Dig. MK 39863 [id.]. Yo-Yo Ma, Boston SO, Ozawa – MONN: *Cello concerto.**

(i) *Don Quixote, Op. 35; Death and Transfiguration, Op. 24.*
(M) *** DG 429 184-2 [id.]. (i) Fournier; BPO, Karajan.

(i) *Don Quixote; Till Eulenspiegel.*
(M) **(*) DG Dig. 419 599-2 [id.]. (i) Meneses; BPO, Karajan.

(i) *Don Quixote; Salome: Salome's dance.*
**(*) Decca Dig. 417 184-2 [id.]. (i) Lynn Harrell; Cleveland O, Ashkenazy.

Karajan's 1966 recording of *Don Quixote* sounds newly minted in its remastered CD format. Detail is clarified, while there is plenty of body to the sound, and the analogue ambience remains highy effective. Fournier's partnership with Karajan is outstanding. His portrayal of the Don has no less nobility than previous rivals and compares well with more recent versions. He brings great subtlety and (when required) repose to the part. The finale and Don Quixote's death are very moving in Fournier's hands, while Karajan's handling of orchestral detail is quite splendid. Although Fournier is forwardly balanced, in every other respect the recording is of DG's very finest quality and (given its price) this can be strongly recommended, more particularly since the disc includes Karajan's superlative 1973 analogue version of *Death and Transfiguration*, which still remains a showpiece among his earlier Strauss recordings with the Berlin Philharmonic. Textures sound leaner than originally, but the quality is both vivid and refined in detail.

The 1975 Karajan/Rostropovich account of *Don Quixote* is predictably fine and its only failing is a tendency for Rostropovich to dominate the aural picture. He dominates artistically too: his Don is superbly characterized, and the expressiveness and richness of tone he commands are a joy in themselves. The recording retains its body, well-defined detail and fine perspective in its digitally remastered format, and the only slight drawback is a tendency for the bass to be somewhat over-resonant.

Yo-Yo Ma's portrait of the Don is masterly and, as always, he plays with impeccable taste and refined tone, though at times pianissimos are exaggerated and affectation comes dangerously close. Ozawa is a shade cautious in matters of characterization and, although he pays scrupulous attention to detail, the very last ounce of Straussian braggadocio is wanting. The CBS recording balance between cello and orchestra is true to life; the orchestral texture is transparent and detail is excellent, though there is a trace of hardness evident when reproduced at a high level setting.

The sound Decca give Lynn Harrell and the Cleveland Orchestra under Ashkenazy is wonderfully transparent and finely balanced. There is, perhaps, a trace of glare but, generally speaking, it is a splendidly wide-ranging and well-defined recording. Harrell gives a rich-toned and well-characterized interpretation of the Don, and is almost as eloquent as Yo-Yo Ma. There is some responsive playing from the Cleveland Orchestra under Ashkenazy, who is unaffected and direct. Nevertheless, this is not a great performance (although the *Dance of the seven veils* has an appealing allure).

Nor, for that matter, is the new Karajan with Antonio Meneses and Wolfram Christ. Both protagonists are excellent, but neither the performance nor the recording is a patch on his earlier version: the perspective is far from natural and the sound in climaxes is hard. Karajan himself is more measured and, some might feel, guides the score with a heavier hand. *Till Eulenspiegel* is far less self-conscious and is beautifully played, though it is not noticeably superior to his earlier version.

(i) *Duet concertino for clarinet & bassoon; Metamorphosen; Capriccio: Prelude.*
** CBS Dig. MK 44702 [id.]. (i) Meyer, Sönstevold, New Stockholm CO, Salonen.

Esa-Pekka Salonen's account of the *Metamorphosen* is played superbly by the New Stockholm Chamber Orchestra, who produce a rich and full-bodied sonority and are accorded fine CBS recording. Although he has an excellent feeling for the Strauss sound and despite his warmth, the young Finnish conductor does not always allow the music to flow forward at a natural pace. The two soloists in the *Duet concertino* are highly accomplished and this comes off well, as does the transcription Salonen has made of the *Prelude to Capriccio.*

Fanfare for Music Week in Vienna (1924); *Fanfare for the Vienna Philharmonic; Feier Einzug der Ritter des Johanniterordens; Festmusik der Stadt Wien; Olympic hymn* (1936); *Parade marches Nos 1 and 2* (arr. Locke).
**(*) Chan. CHAN 8419 [id.]. Locke Brass Cons., Stobart.

The two *Parade marches*, which date from 1905, offer agreeable invention but were scored by others. On the other hand the *Festmusik* is a considerable piece in the grand manner, using antiphonal effects to acknowledge its baroque heritage, although this is not emphasized by the recording layout. Otherwise the sound is first class, rich and sonorous and spacious in feeling.

Ein Heldenleben, Op. 40.
*** Denon Dig. C37 7561 [id.]. Dresden State O, Blomstedt.
(M) *** EMI CDM7 63299-2 [id.]. RPO, Beecham – LISZT: *Orpheus* etc.***
(M) *** EMI CDM7 69027-2 [id.]. BPO, Karajan.
**(*) DG Dig 415 508-2 [id.]. BPO, Karajan.
**(*) Decca Dig. 414 292-2 [id.]. Cleveland O, Ashkenazy.
**(*) Ph. Dig. 400 073-2 [id.]. Boston SO, Ozawa.

Ein Heldenleben; Don Juan, Op. 20.
(M) *** DG 429 717-2 [id.]. BPO, Karajan.

Ein Heldenleben; Macbeth.
(M) *** EMI CDM7 69171-2 [id.]. Dresden State O, Kempe.

Ein Heldenleben; Till Eulenspiegel.
*** CBS Dig. MK 44817 [id.]. LSO, Tilson Thomas.

Ein Heldenleben; (i) *4 Last songs.*
**(*) Chan. Dig. CHAN 8518 [id.]. SNO, Järvi; (i) with Felicity Lott.
** Telarc Dig. CD 80180 [id.]. (i) Arleen Augér; VPO, Previn.

Among the many fine CDs of *Ein Heldenleben*, the Blomstedt disc with the Dresden Staatskapelle for Denon comes close to the sound we used to associate with DG in the analogue era: warm, with articulate detail, but great tonal homogeneity. Blomstedt shapes his performance with both authority and poetry. One can tell from the outset that this is the real thing, for there is a genuine heroic stride and a sense of dramatic excitement here, while the Dresden orchestra, which has a long Strauss tradition, creates glorious

Straussian textures and the whole edifice is held together in a way that commands admiration. In these respects, Blomstedt's account is the most completely satisfying CD.

Karajan's 1959 *Heldenleben* still sounds amazingly fresh. It is a superb performance, and at mid-price it can certainly be recommended, in harness with *Don Juan*. Playing of great power and distinction emanate from the Berlin Philharmonic and, in the closing section, an altogether becoming sensuousness and warmth. The remastering has plenty of ambient atmosphere, combined with excellent detail; *Don Juan*, made over a decade later, brings only a marginal difference in body and none in breadth.

Beecham's valedictory *Heldenleben* sounds fabulous. He liked to work on a large scale and his 1961 performance is immensely vigorous but tender and sensuous when the music calls for it. There is also a marvellously unforced sense of naturalness in the phrasing, together with refined playing from strings and wind and an excellent solo contribution from the leader, Steven Staryk. The recording is quite full and has a transparency of texture inherent in the original balance. Beecham's magic exercises its own special pull and this reissue is a classic of the gramophone, splendidly remastered and not to be missed, particularly at its competitive price.

At mid-price, Rudolf Kempe's classic account of *Ein Heldenleben* is nothing if not a bargain. It is a noble performance in the grand manner, and the recording strikes the proper balance between richness of tone and analysis of detail. Its claims on the collector are strengthened by the fill-up, a strongly characterized account of *Macbeth*, a reading that has never been bettered on record.

Karajan's 1975 EMI *Heldenleben* received an outstanding analogue recording from the EMI engineers. A little of its sumptuousness has been lost in the digital remastering in the interests of clarified detail, but the sound remains full. The performance shows a remarkable consistency of approach on Karajan's part and an equal virtuosity of technique on the part of the Berlin Philharmonic. The performance is outstanding; as a mid-priced reissue, this remains competitive.

Karajan's digital *Heldenleben* has tremendous sweep and all the authority and mastery we have come to expect – and, indeed, take for granted. Nor is the orchestral playing anything other than glorious – indeed, in terms of sheer virtuosity the Berlin players have never surpassed this. There is also a dramatic fire and virtuosity that are quite electrifying. However, the recording falls short of the highest of present-day standards, though it has no want of firmness and body: the upper strings are a little lacking in bloom and are a shade congested.

Michael Tilson Thomas's account is also a performance of genuine authority and no less well laid out than other outstanding versions. His interpretation has an epic breadth and humanity that are impressive. If it does not displace its rivals, it can be recommended with complete confidence alongside them, and moreover it has the additional attraction of *Till Eulenspiegel*.

Järvi's reading is strongly characterized, warmly sympathetic from first to last without inflation, marked by powerfully thrustful playing from the SNO, lacking only the last degree of refinement in tone and ensemble. The Chandos recording is beautifully and naturally balanced against a reverberant acoustic. The fill-up will tip the balance for some. Though there is a degree of reserve in the singer's performance and the microphone catches an uncharacteristic roughness in Felicity Lott's voice when it is under pressure, this is a beautiful, moving account.

Ashkenazy gives a refreshing reading, with fast speeds the rule and a volatile element regularly dispelling any hint of pomposity. It has much to commend it, though something of the grandeur, the broad canvas and the sense of drama that the greatest Strauss conductors have found in it is missing. However, there is much more to admire than to deprecate and, of available recordings, it is the most impressive, with the greatest range and transparency of detail and the firmest definition.

Ozawa's view of *Heldenleben* is free-flowing, lyrical and remarkably unpompous. He consistently brings out the joy of the virtuoso writing, and though the playing of the Boston orchestra is not quite immaculate, the richness and transparency are just as seductive, superbly caught by the Philips engineers. But this is not a first choice.

André Previn is a sound guide in this terrain, but his well-recorded performance lacks the distinction and momentum, the panache and concentration of the finest rivals. Arleen Augér has great charm but is not helped by generally sluggish tempi from Previn.

Josephslegende (ballet), *Op. 63.*
** Denon Dig. CO 2050 [id.]. Tokyo Met. SO, Wakasugi.

Josephslegende (ballet): *suite, Op. 63; Sinfonia domestica, Op. 53.*
**(*) Delos Dig. DE 3082 [id.]. Seattle SO, Gerard Schwarz.

Strauss composed the *Josephslegende* for Diaghilev on the grandest scale for a large orchestra. Although the neglect of the score in the theatre is understandable on practical grounds, it contains enough good music to be of interest to Straussians. Indeed there are many felicities, the *Dance of the Turkish Boxers* a good example, while there are delicious touches in the fourth scene, *Joseph's dance.* Gerard Schwarz gives us the suite from the ballet (about half an hour's music) in addition to a very idiomatic account of the *Sinfonia domestica.* There is very good playing from the Seattle orchestra: cultured, thoroughly idiomatic and with splendid sweep; the recording, too, is splendidly detailed, if perhaps just a bit too brightly lit to be ideal.

Hiroshi Wakasugi obviously learned his Strauss with the Dresden orchestra, and the Tokyo Metropolitan Symphony Orchestra respond well. Unfortunately, although the recording is perfectly adequate, it seems a trifle congested. However, the interest of the music is very considerable.

Metamorphosen for 23 solo strings; Sonatine No. 1 in F for wind (From an invalid's workshop).
*** Ph. Dig. 420 160-2 [id.]. VPO, Previn.

André Previn's record with the Vienna Philharmonic is extremely successful. He seems to be completely attuned to the serene, darkly impassioned melancholy of this eloquent piece and he gets a glorious response from his players. The *Wind sonatine* is a relaxed and superbly wrought piece; in the persuasive hands of the Vienna wind, it is totally beguiling. The recording is first class.

Schlagobers (ballet), *Op. 70:* complete.
** Denon Dig. CO 73414 [id.]. Tokyo Met. SO, Wakasugi.

Schlagobers is a two-act ballet, lasting 75 minutes, whose action is set in a Viennese *Konditorei* (pâtisserie), full of children fresh from their confirmation ceremony. The work comes from the early 1920s (Strauss conducted its first performance for his sixtieth-birthday celebrations), but it is held in low esteem by most Strauss scholars. There are some delights, such as the *March and military exercises of marzipan, Plum soldiers and honey cakes* and the *Dance of the tea cakes* in Act I; but elsewhere his inspiration lapses into routine, as in the *Whipped cream waltz.* Hiroshi Wakasugi gets good results from the Tokyo Metropolitan Orchestra and the recording is more than acceptable, though insufficiently transparent in climaxes.

Sinphonia domestica, Op. 53.
(M) *** EMI CDM7 69571-2 [id.]. BPO, Karajan.

Sinfonia domestica, Op. 53; (i) *Death and Transfiguration, Op. 24.*
(M) *** RCA stereo/mono GD 60388 [60388-2-RG]. Chicago SO; (i) (mono) RCA Victor
O; Fritz Reiner.

Sinphonia domestica, Op. 53; Till Eulenspiegel. (i) Songs: *Die heiligen drei Könige aus
Morgenland; Zueignung.*
**(*) Chan. Dig. CHAN 8572 [id.]. SNO, Järvi; (i) with Felicity Lott.

Strauss's much-maligned *Sinphonia domestica* is quite admirably served by this mid-
priced CD of Karajan's 1973 recording. The playing is stunningly good and the Berlin
strings produce tone of great magnificence. The remastered recording demonstrates the
wide range of the original; detail is better focused and the ambient atmosphere remains.

Reiner's account of the *Sinfonia domestica* comes from 1956, the earliest days of stereo,
and is a wonderful performance, a reading of stature, worthy to rank alongside the
Karajan alternative. The Chicago orchestra play with warmth and virtuosity; the
recording is inevitably lacking a little in upper range, but it still sounds remarkably good
for its age. *Death and Transfiguration* is a 1950 mono recording, and it was perverse of
RCA not to include his marvellous 1957 Vienna Philharmonic version (in surprisingly
good stereo even now).

Järvi's is a strongly characterized, good-natured account, not as refined in ensemble as
some past rivals but gutsy and committed to remove any coy self-consciousness from this
extraordinarily inflated but delightful musical portrait of Strauss's family life. The
performance of *Till* brings out the joy of the work, too; and Felicity Lott's performance of
two of Strauss's most delightful songs makes a generous coupling. Warm, rich recording
to compensate for any occasional thinness in the SNO's violin tone.

Symphony for wind in E flat (The happy workshop).
** Orfeo C 004821A [id.]. Munich Wind Ac., Sawallisch.

Strauss's *Wind symphony*, as suggested by the subtitle, it is essentially a genial piece,
though the finale opens sombrely before the mood lightens. This comes off quite well, as
does the nicely played *Andantino*, but the focus of the first movement is less sure and the
music-making often lacks a necessary smiling quality. The recording, though full and
homogeneous in texture, does not display the inner clarity one would expect from a
digital source and the CD is poor value, playing for only 38½ minutes.

Cello sonata in F, Op. 6.
(*) CBS Dig. MK 44980 [id.]. Yo-Yo Ma, Emanuel Ax – BRITTEN: *Sonata.*(*)

Yo-Yo Ma and Emanuel Ax give a generally fine account of the *Cello sonata*, although
there are moments when Ax's fortissimos overpower the cellist and Ma is not wholly free
from self-consciousness. The recording is reasonably truthful, though the constraints of
the CBS acoustic produce a very slightly synthetic character.

String quartet in A, Op. 2.
(*) Hyp. Dig. CDA 66317 [id.]. Delmé Qt – VERDI: *Quartet.*(*)

The Strauss *Quartet* is early and derivative, as one might expect from a sixteen-year-
old, but it is amazingly assured and fluent. The Delmé version is well played; however,
although the basic acoustic is pleasing, the sound-balance remains a little on the dry side.

Violin sonata in E flat, Op. 18.
* DG Dig. 427 617-2 [id.]. Kyung Wha Chung, Krystian Zimerman – RESPIGHI: *Sonata.******
* Virgin Dig. VC 790760-2 [id.]. Dmitry Sitkovetsky, Pavel Gililov – DEBUSSY: *Sonata*******; JANÁČEK: *Sonata.******
*(*) Chan. Dig. CHAN 8417 [id.]. Lydia Mordkovitch, Gerhard Oppitz – FAURÉ: Sonata No. 1.******

In this formidable sonata, Kyung Wha Chung and Krystian Zimerman bring an impressive eloquence and commanding artistry. Collectors wanting their coupling need look no further. Among modern versions Kyung Wha Chung is *primus inter pares*, and her version of the Strauss scores over rivals also in the power and sensitivity of Krystian Zimerman's contribution and the excellence of the DG recording. This *Sonata* needs the best possible advocacy if it is to persuade the uncommitted; in the hands of these artists it is heard at its best.

Dmitry Sitkovetsky is also a passionate and characterful player, who gives a powerful account of the Strauss. Musically, his coupling is more rewarding in that the Debussy and Janáček *Sonatas* are of greater substance than the Respighi which Chung and Zimerman offer. However, theirs is a very special performance and, though Pavel Gililov is a perceptive artist, his playing is not quite the equal of Zimerman's.

Lydia Mordkovitch and Gerhard Oppitz give a compelling reading of the early Strauss *Sonata*. The piano is still a little overpowering, though not closely balanced, but Oppitz certainly gives a fine account of his demanding role.

VOCAL MUSIC

Lieder: *Allerseelen; Ach Lieb ich muss nun Scheiden; Befreit; Du meines Herzens Krönelein; Einerlei; Heimliche Aufforderung; Ich trage meine Minne; Kling!; Lob des Leidens; Malven; Mit deinen blauen Augen; Die Nacht; Schlechtes Wetter; Seitdem dein Aug; Ständchen; Stiller Gang; Traume durch die Dämmerung; Wie sollten wir geheim; Wir beide wollen springen; Zeltlose.*
* Ph. Dig. 416 298-2 [id.]. Jessye Norman, Geoffrey Parsons.

Jessye Norman's recital of Strauss brings heartfelt, deeply committed performances, at times larger than life, which satisfyingly exploit the unique glory of the voice. Quite apart from such deservedly popular songs as *Heimliche Aufforderung*, it is good to have such a rarity as Strauss's very last song, *Malven*, sung so compellingly. Some of the songs bring extreme speeds in both directions, with expression underlined in slow songs and *Ständchen* given exhilarating virtuoso treatment at high speed. But the magnetism of the singer generally silences any reservations, and Geoffrey Parsons is the most understanding of accompanists, brilliant too. Good, natural recording.

Lieder: *Allerseelen; All' mein Gedänken; Befreit; Cäcilie; Du meines Herzens Krönelein; Freundliche Vision; Heimliche Aufforderung; Ich schwebe; Kling!; Morgen; Die Nacht; Ruhe, meine Seele; Seitdem dein Aug' in meines schaute; Ständchen; Wiegenlied; Winterweihe; Zueignung.*
* EMI Dig. CDC7 47948-2 [id.]. Margaret Price, Wolfgang Sawallisch.

Margaret Price's Strauss recital brings a rich variety of mood, colour and expression, helped by exceptionally sensitive and imaginative accompaniments from Sawallisch. The evenness of her production, opening out gloriously in *Zueignung*, is typical, and so it is too in *Freundliche Vision*, well contrasted with the lightness of such a song as *All' mein*

Gedänken. If maternal tenderness is missing in *Wiegenlied,* the beauty and precision with which Price follows every marking in the music is a delight, all done with seeming spontaneity. The recording captures the voice with fine bloom.

Lieder: *Allerseelen; All' mein Gedänken; Cäcile; Du meines Herzens Krönelein; Frühlingsfeier; Heimkehr; Heimliche Aufforderung; In goldener Fülle; Mit deinen blauen Augen; Morgen; Die Nacht; Nachtgang; Ruhe meine Seele; Schlagende Herzen; Schlechtes Wetter; Ständchen; Traume durch die Dämmerung; Wiegenlied; Die Zeitlose; Zueignung.*
** Capriccio Dig. 10 258 [id.]. Dame Gwyneth Jones, Geoffrey Parsons.

Dame Gwyneth does wonders in scaling down her big, abrasive, essentially operatic voice, colouring well. With Geoffrey Parsons a thoughtful guide, she also chooses her songs carefully, but inevitably the results are at times ungainly. This is a record – in first-rate sound – for her devotees rather than for all Straussians.

Allerseelen; Am Ufer; Aus den Liedern der Trauer; Heimkehr; Liebeshymnus; Lob des Leidens; Madrigal; Morgen; Die Nacht; Winternacht; Zueignung.
*** DG Dig. 419 238-2 [id.]. Brigitte Fassbaender, Irwin Gage – LISZT: *Lieder.****

Coupled with an equally perceptive group of Liszt songs, Fassbaender's Strauss selection brings singing of exceptional command and intensity; always she communicates face to face, and the musical imagination – as in the very slow account of the popular *Morgen* – adds to the sharply specific quality she gives to each song. The voice is beautiful as recorded, but that beauty is only an incidental. Warmly understanding accompaniment; well-balanced recording.

Four Last songs; Lieder: *Das Bächlein; Freundliche Vision; Die heiligen drei Könige; Meinem Kinde; Morgen; Muttertändelei; Das Rosenband; Ruhe, meine Seele; Waldseligkeit; Wiegenlied; Winterweihe; Zueignung.*
⊛ *** EMI CDC7 47276-2 [id.]. Elisabeth Schwarzkopf, Berlin RSO, or LSO, Szell.

Four Last songs; Lieder: *Befreit; Morgen; Muttertändelei; Ruhe, meine Seele; Wiegenlied; Zueignung.*
**(*) CBS MK 76794 [id.]. Kiri Te Kanawa, LSO, Andrew Davis.

Four Last songs; Lieder: *Cäcilie; Meinem Kinde; Morgen; Ruhe, meine Seele; Wiegenlied; Zueignung.*
⊛ *** Ph. Dig. 411 052-2 [id.]. Jessye Norman, Leipzig GO, Masur.

Strauss's publisher Ernest Roth says in the score of the *Four Last songs* that this was a farewell of 'serene confidence', which is exactly the mood Jessye Norman conveys. The start of the second stanza of the third song, *Beim Schlafengehen,* brings one of the most thrilling vocal crescendos on record, expanding from a half-tone to a gloriously rich and rounded forte. In concern for word-detail Norman is outshone only by Schwarzkopf, but both in the *Four Last songs* and in the orchestral songs the stylistic as well as the vocal command is irresistible, with *Cäcilie* given operatic strength. The radiance of the recording matches the interpretations.

For the CD version of Schwarzkopf's raptly beautiful recording of the *Four Last songs,* EMI have added not just the old coupling of Strauss orchestral songs but also the extra seven which she recorded three years later in 1969, also with George Szell conducting, but with the LSO instead of the Berlin Radio Orchestra. There are few records in the catalogue which so magnetically capture the magic of a great performance, with the intensity of Schwarzkopf's singing in all its variety of tone and meaning perfectly matched by inspired playing.

Dame Kiri Te Kanawa gives an open-hearted, warmly expressive reading of the *Four Last songs*. If she misses the sort of detail that Schwarzkopf uniquely brought, her commitment is never in doubt. Her tone is consistently beautiful, but might have seemed even more so if the voice had not been placed rather too close in relation to the orchestra. The orchestral arrangements of other songs make an excellent coupling and Andrew Davis directs most sympathetically.

Four Last Songs (Vier letzte Lieder); Arabella: excerpts; *Ariadne auf Naxos: Ariadne's lament; Capriccio:* Closing scene.
(M) (**) Decca mono 425 959-2 [id.]. Lisa della Casa, Vienna PO, Boehm, Moralt, Hollreiser.

Lisa della Casa with her creamily beautiful soprano was a radiant Straussian, as these precious excerpts demonstrate. Her account of the *Four Last Songs* (given in the original order, not that usually adopted) has a commanding nobility. *Ariadne's lament* also receives a heartfelt performance, soaring to a thrilling climax, and the *Arabella* duets with Gueden, Schoeffler and Poell are hauntingly tender. When these recordings appeared in the early and mid-1950s they were always contrasted with those of Elisabeth Schwarzkopf, and so they must be now, when EMI's Schwarzkopf issue in the Références series not only has the *Four Last Songs* but the same three duets from *Arabella* and the Closing scene from *Capriccio*. Consistently Schwarzkopf is the more animated, della Casa the more restrained. Sadly, in the transfer the Decca historic issue falls far short of the EMI, with the voice not as forward and vivid, and with the orchestra shrill and papery, lacking the body of the original LPs.

(i) *Four Last songs.* (ii) *Arabella* (opera): excerpts. (i) *Capriccio* (opera): *closing scene.*
(M) (***) EMI mono CDH7 61001-2 [id.]. Elisabeth Schwarzkopf, (i) Philh. O, Ackermann; (ii) Metternich, Gedda, Philh. O, Von Matačić.

Schwarzkopf's 1953 version of the *Four Last songs* comes on the mid-price Références label with both its original coupling, the closing scene from *Capriccio*, also recorded in 1953, and the four major excerpts from *Arabella* which she recorded two years later. The *Four Last songs* are here less reflective, less sensuous, than in Schwarzkopf's later version with Szell, but the more flowing speeds and the extra tautness and freshness of voice bring equally illuminating performances. Fascinatingly, this separate account of the *Capriccio* scene is even more ravishing than the one in the complete set, and the sound is even fuller, astonishing for its period.

Four Last songs. Die heiligen drei Könige. Capriccio (opera): *Moonlight music and monologue* (closing scene).
**(*) DG Dig. 419 188-2 [id.]. Anna Tomowa-Sintow, BPO, Karajan.

Karajan directs a ravishing performance, with one of his favourite sopranos responding warmly and sympathetically, if without the final touch of individual imagination that such inspired music cries out for. Tomowa-Sintow's lovely, creamy-toned singing tends to take second place in the attention. The orchestral version of Strauss's nativity-story song makes an attractive if hardly generous extra item. Warm recording, lacking a little in sense of realism and presence.

OPERA

Arabella (complete).
*** Orfeo Dig. C 169882H (2). Varady, Fischer-Dieskau, Donath, Dallapozza, Schmidt, Berry, Bav. State Op. Ch. & O, Sawallisch.

*** Decca Dig. 417 623-2 (3) [id.]. Te Kanawa, Fontana, Grundheber, Seiffert, Dernesch, Guttstein, ROHCG Ch. & O, Tate.

This Orfeo set of *Arabella* has an immediate advantage over the Decca version with Kiri Te Kanawa in being a digital recording on two CDs against the three for the Decca. Moreover the recording is splendid in every way, not just in sound but in the warmth and understanding of Sawallisch, the characterful tenderness of Julia Varady as the heroine, and Fischer-Dieskau's fine-detailed characterization of the gruff Mandryka, *der Richtige* (Mr Right) according to the heroine's romantic view. Helen Donath too is charming as the younger sister, Zdenka, though the voice might be more sharply contrasted. If there are unappealing elements in an opera which would reach a happy ending far too quickly but for uncongenial twists of plot, this recording clothes them with an entirely Straussian glow of richness and charm. Highly recommended.

Dame Kiri Te Kanawa, in the name-part, gives one of her very finest opera performances on record. She even outshines the most famous of recorded Arabellas, Lisa della Casa, not only in the firm beauty of her voice, but in the word-pointing and detailed characterization. It is a radiant portrait, languorously beautiful, and it is a pity that so unsuited a soprano as Gabriele Fontana should have been chosen as Zdenka next to her, sounding all the more shrill by contrast. Franz Grundheber makes a firm, virile Mandryka, Peter Seiffert a first-rate Matteo, while Helga Dernesch is outstandingly characterful as Arabella's mother. Though Tate's conducting is richly sympathetic, bringing out the sumptuousness of the score – helped by brilliant Decca recording – his speeds at times are dangerously slow, which might possibly worry established Straussians, if hardly anyone else.

Ariadne auf Naxos (complete).
⊛ (M) (***) EMI mono CMS7 69296-2 (2) [id.]. Schwarzkopf, Schock, Rita Streich, Dönch, Seefried, Cuenod, Philh. O, Karajan.
*** Ph. Dig. 422 084-2 (2) [id.]. Jessye Norman, Varady, Gruberová, Asmus, Bär, Leipzig GO, Masur.
**(*) DG Dig. 419 225-2 (2) [id.]. Tomowa-Sintow, Battle, Baltsa, Lakes, Prey, VPO, Levine.

Elisabeth Schwarzkopf makes a radiant, deeply moving Ariadne, giving as bonus a delicious little portrait of the Prima Donna in the Prologue. Rita Streich was at her most dazzling in the coloratura of Zerbinetta's aria and, in partnership with the harlequinade characters, sparkles engagingly. But it is Irmgard Seefried who gives perhaps the supreme performance of all as the Composer, exceptionally beautiful of tone, conveying a depth and intensity rarely if ever matched. Rudolf Schock is a fine Bacchus, strained less than most, and the team of theatrical characters includes such stars as Hugues Cuenod as the Dancing Master. The fine pacing and delectably pointed ensemble add to the impact of a uniquely perceptive Karajan interpretation. Though in mono and with the orchestral sound a little dry, the voices come out superbly. Though the absence of translation in the libretto is a great pity, the many index-points on CD, cued to the synopsis, can be used almost as easily as a translation alongside the original German words.

Jessye Norman's is a commanding, noble, deeply felt performance, ranging extraordinarily wide; if she does not quite find the same raptness, the inner agony that still makes Elisabeth Schwarzkopf's performance unique, she yet provides the perfect focus for a cast as near ideal as anyone could assemble today. Julia Varady as the Composer brings out the vulnerability of the character, as well as the ardour, in radiant singing. The Zerbinetta of Edita Gruberová adds an extra dimension to previous recordings in the way she translates the panache of her stage performance into purely aural terms for recording. It is a thrilling performance and, even if the voice is not always ideally sweet, the range of emotions Gruberová conveys, as in her duet with the Composer, is enchanting. Paul Frey is the sweetest-sounding Bacchus on record yet, while Olaf Bär as Harlekin and Dietrich Fischer-Dieskau in the vignette role of the Music-Master are typical of the fine team of artists here in the smaller character parts. Masur proves a masterly Straussian and he is helped by the typically warm Leipzig recording, with sound rich and mellow to cocoon the listener, yet finely balanced to allow you to hear the interweaving of the piano as never before, in twentieth-century imitation of a continuo.

James Levine conducts a spacious, sumptuously textured reading of *Ariadne* which almost makes you forget that it uses a chamber orchestra. As Ariadne herself, Tomowa-Sintow with her rich, dramatic soprano adds to the sense of grandeur and movingly brings out the vulnerability of the character. But ultimately she fails to create as fully rounded and detailed a character as her finest rivals, and the voice, as recorded, loses its bloom and creaminess under pressure, marring the big climaxes. Both Agnes Baltsa as the Composer and Kathleen Battle as Zerbinetta are excellent: the one tougher than most rivals with her mezzo-soprano ring, little troubled by the high tessitura, the other delectably vivacious, dazzling in coloratura, but equally finding the unexpected tenderness in the character, the underlying sadness clearly implied in the Prologue duet with the Composer. The *commedia dell'arte* characters and the attendant theatrical team are given to stalwarts of the Vienna State Opera, among them Kurt Rydl, Hermann Prey and Heinz Zednik, while the Heldentenor role of Bacchus, always hard to cast, is strongly taken by Gary Lakes, clear-toned and firm, at times pinched but never strained.

Capriccio (complete).
(***) EMI mono CDS7 49014-8 (2) [id.]. Schwarzkopf, Waechter, Gedda, Fischer-Dieskau, Hotter, Ludwig, Moffo, Philh. O, Sawallisch.
*** DG 419 023-2 (2) [id.]. Janowitz, Fischer-Dieskau, Schreier, Prey, Ridderbusch, Troyanos, Bav. R. O, Boehm.

In the role of the Countess in Strauss's last opera, Elisabeth Schwarzkopf has had no equals. This recording, made in 1957 and 1958, brings a peerless performance from her, full of magical detail both in the pointing of words and in the presentation of the character in all its variety. Not only are the other singers ideal choices in each instance, they form a wonderfully co-ordinated team, beautifully held together by Sawallisch's sensitive conducting. Even such a vignette role as that of the Italian soprano is taken by Anna Moffo. As a performance this is never likely to be superseded, and it comes as one of the most cherishable of operatic reissues on CD. The mono sound presents the voices with fine bloom and presence, but the digital transfer makes the orchestra a little dry and relatively backward by comparison.

Janowitz is not as characterful and pointful a Countess as one really needs (and no match for Schwarzkopf), but this DG alternative is a most beautiful performance of a radiant score, well cast, beautifully sung, finely recorded and lovingly conducted. There is full documentation, including translation.

Daphne (complete).
*** EMI Dig. CDS7 49309-2 (2) [Ang. CDCB 49309]. Popp, Goldberg, Wenkel, Schreier, Bav. R. Ch. and SO, Haitink.
*** DG 423 579-2 (2) [id.]. Gueden, King, Wunderlich, Schoffler, Little, V. State Op. Ch., VPO, Boehm.

On record, this amiable telling of the story of the nymph Daphne wooed by Apollo and finally turned into a tree makes delightful entertainment. Haitink with his fine Bavarian forces takes a rather more restrained and spacious view of the piece than did Karl Boehm, the dedicatee. However, there are many gains in a studio performance with beauty of balance so important in this score. The cast is a fine one, with Lucia Popp an enchanting, girlish Daphne, Peter Schreier bringing Lieder-like feeling for detail to the role of Leukippos, and Reiner Goldberg producing heroic sounds as Apollo, with little feeling of strain and with no coarseness. Kurt Moll is a fine Peneios. The recording is exceptionally rich, yet refined too. Sadly, as in other EMI reissues of rare Strauss operas on CD, there is no translation accompanying the libretto.

The DG set is a live recording, made during the 1964 Vienna Festival, and it provides an enticing alternative. It could hardly be better cast, with the tenors James King as Apollo and Fritz Wunderlich as Leukippos both magnificent. Hilde Gueden makes a delectable Daphne and gives one of her finest performances on record, while Karl Boehm, the opera's dedicatee, brings out the work's mellowness without any loss of vitality. The DG documentation is superior to the EMI set, with full translation included.

Elektra (complete).
*** Decca 417 345-2 (2) [id.]. Nilsson, Collier, Resnik, Stolze, Krause, V. State Op. Ch., VPO, Solti.

Nilsson is almost incomparable in the name-part, with the hard side of Elektra's character brutally dominant. Only when – as in the Recognition scene with Orestes – she tries to soften the naturally bright tone does she let out a suspect flat note or two. As a rule she is searingly accurate in approaching even the most formidable exposed top notes. One might draw a parallel with Solti's direction – sharply focused and brilliant in the savage music which predominates, but lacking the languorous warmth one really needs in the Recognition scene, if only for contrast. The brilliance of the 1967 Decca recording is brought out the more in the digital transfer on CD, aptly so in this work. The fullness and clarity are amazing for the period.

Die Frau ohne Schatten (complete).
*** DG 415 472-2 (3) [id.]. Nilsson, Rysanek, Hesse, King, Berry, V. State Op. Ch. & O, Boehm.
**(*) EMI Dig. CDS7 49074-2 (3) [Ang. CDCC 49074]. Studer, Kollo, Vinzing, Muff, Schwarz, Schmidt, Kaufmann, Lipovšek, Rootering, Frey, Tölz Boys' Ch., Bav. R. Ch. & SO, Sawallisch.

Boehm's live recording of Strauss's most ambitious, most Wagnerian opera provides a magnificent reminder of the conductor at his very finest. It is a performance to love rather than just to admire, with the opera-house acoustic handled persuasively by the engineers of Austrian Radio to give the solo voices plenty of bloom without losing precision. Inevitably there are stage noises and the balance of the singers varies, but this is outstanding among live recordings. The stage cuts are an irritation, but at least they allow each of the hour-long Acts to be accommodated on a single CD. The cast is an excellent one, with Birgit Nilsson making the Dyer's Wife a truly Wagnerian character. Leonie Rysanek sings strongly in the role of the other heroine, the Empress, musically almost as demanding. Barak the Dyer is sung by Walter Berry, searchingly expressive; and James King in the Heldentenor role of the Emperor is just as remarkable for his finely shaded pianissimo singing as for heroic moments, where he is occasionally strained. On CD the perspectives are impressively caught at all levels of dynamic.

Beautifully recorded in Munich in collaboration with Bavarian Radio, EMI's version of *Die Frau ohne Schatten* with Sawallisch conducting is the first ever to include a really complete text with all the stage cuts restored. Sawallisch is a most persuasive Straussian, relaxed rather than bitingly dramatic; and the Bavarian Radio Orchestra plays ravishingly for him, helped by refined digital recording. Cheryl Studer sings radiantly as the Empress and René Kollo is a powerful Emperor, falling into coarseness only occasionally. Hanna Schwarz is superb as the Nurse, firmly establishing the magnetism of the performance in her first-scene duet with the Messenger, the excellent young baritone, Andreas Schmidt. Sadly, the whole project is undermined by the casting of the two other major roles. The central figure of the Dyer's Wife brings deeply disappointing singing from Ute Vinzing, while Alfred Muff's gritty, unattractive tone as her husband, Barak, is another blot, and his characterization is one-dimensional.

Guntram (complete).
*** CBS Dig. M2K 39737 (2) [id.]. Goldberg, Tokody, Sólyom-Nagy, Gati, Bándi, Hungarian Army Ch. & State O, Queler.

Strauss's very first opera suffers from an undramatic libretto written by the composer. Even when he consciously adopts a Wagnerian stance, the music quickly turns sweet, often anticipating the more lyrical side of *Salome*. Heading the cast as the eponymous knight is Rainer Goldberg, reliable and open-toned, only occasionally strained. Otherwise the cast is Hungarian, with Ilona Tokody strong and firm, if rarely beautiful, in the taxing role of the heroine, Freihild. Warmly sympathetic conducting from Eve Queler. The recording acoustic too is attractively rich.

Intermezzo (complete).
*** EMI CDS7 49337-2 (2) [Ang. CDCB 49337]. Popp, Brammer, Fischer-Dieskau, Bav. RSO, Sawallisch.

The central role of *Intermezzo* was originally designed for the dominant and enchanting Lotte Lehmann; but it is doubtful whether even she can have outshone the radiant Lucia Popp, who brings out the charm of a character who, for all his incidental trials, must have consistently captivated Strauss and provoked this strange piece of self-revelation. The piece inevitably is very wordy, but with this scintillating and emotionally powerful performance under Sawallisch, with fine recording and an excellent supporting cast, this set is as near ideal as could be, a superb achievement. The CD transfer is well managed but – unforgivably in this of all Strauss operas – no translation is given with the libretto, a very serious omission.

Der Rosenkavalier (complete).
⊛ *** EMI CDS7 49354-8 (3) [id.]. Schwarzkopf, Ludwig, Stich-Randall, Edelmann, Waechter, Philh. Ch. & O, Karajan.
**(*) DG Dig. 413 163-2 (3) [id.]. Tomowa-Sintow, Baltsa, Moll, Perry, Hornik, VPO Ch. & O, Karajan.
** Decca 417 493-2 (3) [id.]. Crespin, Minton, Jungwirth, Donath, Wiener, V. State Op. Ch., VPO, Solti.
** CBS M3K 42564 (3) [id.]. Ludwig, Gwyneth Jones, Berry, Popp, Gutstein, V. State Op. Ch., VPO, Bernstein.
(M) (**(*)) Decca mono 425 950-2 (3) [id.]. Reining, Weber, Jurinac, Gueden, V. State Op. Ch., VPO, Erich Kleiber.

The glory of Karajan's 1956 version, one of the greatest of all opera recordings, shines out the more delectably on CD. Though the transfer in its very clarity exposes some flaws in the original sound, the sense of presence and the overall bloom are if anything more compelling than ever. As to the performance, it is in a class of its own, with the patrician refinement of Karajan's spacious reading combining with an emotional intensity that he has rarely equalled, even in Strauss, of whose music he remains a supreme interpreter. Matching that achievement is the incomparable portrait of the Marschallin from Schwarzkopf, bringing out detail as no one else can, yet equally presenting the breadth and richness of the character, a woman still young and attractive. Christa Ludwig with her firm, clear mezzo tone makes an ideal, ardent Octavian and Teresa Stich-Randall a radiant Sophie, with Otto Edelmann a winningly characterful Ochs, who yet sings every note clearly.

Karajan's digital set brings few positive advantages, not even in recorded sound: for all the extra range of the modern recording, the focus is surprisingly vague, with the orchestra balanced too far behind the soloists. One advantage there certainly is: the Vienna Philharmonic, having been brought up with a natural feeling for waltz rhythm, is a degree more idiomatic in providing a genuine Viennese lilt, if it is also at times less precise. For the principal role Karajan chose Anna Tomowa-Sintow; the refinement and detail in her performance present an intimate view of the Marschallin, often very beautiful indeed, but both the darker and more sensuous sides of the character are muted. The Baron Ochs of Kurt Moll, firm, dark and incisive, is outstanding, and Agnes Baltsa as Octavian makes the lad tough and determined, if not always sympathetic. Janet Perry's Sophie, charming and pretty on stage, is too white and twittery of tone to give much pleasure.

The CD transfer of Solti's version is one of the more disappointing reissues from Decca. The brilliance of the original recording is exaggerated, with some of the compensating body in the sound removed, making the result too aggressive for this gloriously ripe score. Crespin is here at her finest on record, with tone well focused; the slightly maternal maturity of her approach will for many appear ideal. Manfred Jungwirth makes a firm and virile, if not always imaginative Ochs, Yvonne Minton a finely projected Octavian and Helen Donath a sweet-toned Sophie. Solti's direction is fittingly honeyed, with tempi even slower than Karajan's in the climactic moments. The one serious disappointment is that the great concluding *Trio* does not quite lift one to the tear-laden height one ideally wants.

Bernstein's CBS Vienna set captures much of the opera's ripeness with the fine, mature Marschallin of Christa Ludwig, which plainly owes much to the example of Schwarzkopf. Lucia Popp makes a charming Sophie and Walter Berry a strong, expressive Ochs, less limited in the lower register than one might expect. But Gwyneth Jones's Octavian, despite the occasional half-tone of exquisite beauty, has too many raw passages to be very appealing, a bad blot on the set. Bernstein follows traditional cuts. Surprisingly, when Decca engineers were responsible for the recording itself, the quality is more variable than one would expect, with vulgarly close horn balance.

Decca's set with Erich Kleiber was the first ever complete recording of *Rosenkavalier*, and it has long enjoyed cult status. It has many glories, quite apart from the inspired conducting of Kleiber senior. Sena Jurinac is a charming Octavian, strong and sympathetic, and Hilde Gueden a sweetly characterful Sophie, not just a wilting innocent. Ludwig Weber characterizes deliciously in a very Viennese way as Ochs; but the disappointment is the Marschallin of Maria Reining, very plain and lacking intensity, even in the great scene with Octavian at the end of Act I. She is not helped by Kleiber's refusal to linger; with the singers recorded close, the effect of age on what was once a fine voice is very clear, even in the opening solo of the culminating trio. And though the Vienna Philharmonic responds in the most idiomatic way to the waltz rhythms, ensemble is not good, with even the prelude to Act I a muddle. One recalls the notorious castigation of the VPO in rehearsal, when George Szell returned to conduct this opera after the war: 'Gentlemen, you do not seem to know this score!' On that prelude more than anywhere, the CD transfer brings out a shrillness and lack of body in the orchestral sound, though voices are well caught. On three mid-price CDs, one per Act, this remains a classic set.

Der Rosenkavalier: highlights.
(M) *** EMI CDM7 63452-2 [id.] (from above set with Schwarzkopf, cond. Karajan).
**(*) DG Dig. 415 284-2 [id.] (from above set with Tomowa-Sintow, cond. Karajan).

On EMI we are offered the Marschallin's monologue to the end of Act I (25 minutes); the Presentation of the silver rose and finale from Act II; and the Duet and closing scene, with the Trio from Act III, flawlessly and gloriously sung and transferred most beautifully to CD.

This DG highlights disc, taken from Karajan's re-recording of the complete opera, provides a generous sample of excerpts, incorporating most of the favourite passages, and includes the tenor aria, lightly sung by Vinson Cole. The richness and beauty of the score are hardly in doubt, but the flaws noted above are just as apparent.

Salome (complete).
*** Decca 414 414-2 (2) [id.]. Nilsson, Hoffman, Stolze, Kmentt, Waechter, VPO, Solti.
*** EMI CDS7 49358-8 (2) [id.]. Behrens, Bohme, Baltsa, Van Dam, VPO, Karajan.
(M) *** RCA GD 86644 (2) [6644-2-RG]. Caballé, Richard Lewis, Resnik, Milnes, LSO, Leinsdorf.

Birgit Nilsson is splendid throughout; she is hard-edged as usual but, on that account, more convincingly wicked: the determination and depravity are latent in the girl's character from the start. Of this score Solti is a master. He has rarely sounded so abandoned in a recorded performance. The emotion swells up naturally even while the calculation of impact is most precise. Waechter makes a clear, young-sounding Jokanaan. Gerhardt Stolze portrays the unbalance of Herod with frightening conviction, and Grace Hoffman does all she can in the comparatively ungrateful part of Herodias. The vivid CD projection makes the final scene, where Salome kisses the head of John the Baptist in delighted horror (*I have kissed thy mouth, Jokanaan!*), all the more spine-tingling, with a close-up effect of the voice whispering almost in one's ear.

Hildegard Behrens is also a triumphantly successful Salome, a singer who in the early scenes has one actively sympathizing with the girlish princess, and who keeps that sympathy and understanding to a point where most sopranos have been transformed into raging harpies. The sensuous beauty of tone is conveyed ravishingly, but the recording is not always fair to her fine projection of sound, occasionally masking the voice. All the same, the feeling of a live performance has been captured well, and the rest of the cast is of the finest Salzburg standard. In particular José van Dam makes a gloriously noble Jokanaan, and in the early scenes his offstage voice from the cistern at once commands attention. Karajan – as so often in Strauss – is at his most commanding and sympathetic, with the orchestra, more forward than some will like, playing rapturously. This is a performance which, so far from making one recoil from perverted horrors, has one revelling in sensuousness. If the full and warm recording cannot match the vintage Decca in brilliance or atmospheric precision, it suits Karajan's ripe reading very well.

Montserrat Caballé's formidable account of the role of Salome was recorded in 1968, utterly different from that of Birgit Nilsson, much closer to the personification of Behrens on the Karajan set. For some listeners Caballé might seem too gentle, but in fact the range of her emotions is even wider than that of Nilsson. There are even one or two moments of fantasy, where for an instant one has the girlish skittishness of Salome revealed like an evil inverted picture of Sophie. As for the vocalization, it is superb, with glorious golden tone up to the highest register and never the slightest hesitation in attack. Lewis, Resnik and Milnes make a supporting team that matches the achievement of the Decca rivals, while Leinsdorf is inspired to some of his warmest and most sympathetic conducting on record. The sound has not the pin-point atmosphere of the Decca, but is nearer to the EMI set in its fullness and vivid projection. The price advantage, too, makes this well worth considering.

Die schweigsame Frau (complete).
** EMI CDS7 49340-2 (3) [Ang. CDCC 49340]. Adam, Burmeister, Scovotti, Schmidt, Haseleu, Dresden State Op. Ch., Dresden State O, Janowski.

Janowski conducts an efficient rather than a magical performance of Strauss's exuberant comic opera, and Theo Adam's strongly characterized rendering of the central role of Dr Morosus is marred by his unsteadiness. Jeanette Scovotti is agile but shrill as the Silent Woman, Aminta. A valuable set, but of mixed success. Disappointingly, EMI includes no English translation with the libretto, an omission difficult to forgive in a full-priced set.

Stravinsky, Igor (1882–1971)

Agon (ballet): complete.
(M) ** Olympia OCD 224 [id.]. Leningrad PO, Mravinsky – SHOSTAKOVICH: *Symphony No. 15* (with WAGNER: *Lohengrin: Prelude to Act III***(*)).

Mravinsky's music-making was always distinguished by enormous intensity, even if one does sense here that the players are not completely inside this particular score; some of the jewelled, hard-edged sound-world Stravinsky evokes is missing. The sound is perfectly acceptable without being in the first flight.

Apollo (Apollon Musagète): ballet (complete).
*** DG 415 979-2 [id.]. BPO, Karajan – *Rite of spring.****
(*) Nimbus Dig. NI 5097 [id.]. E. String O, Boughton – TIPPETT: *Concerto for double string orchestra.*

Though Stravinsky tended to disparage Karajan's approach to his music as not being rugged enough, here is a work where Karajan's moulding of phrase and care for richness of string texture make for wonderful results. This neo-classical score is strong enough to stand such individual treatment, and the writing is consistently enhanced by the magnificent playing of the Berlin Philharmonic Orchestra. The recording dates from 1973 and sounds excellent in its CD format.

Boughton's version, unusually coupled with the Tippett *String concerto*, brings warm, responsive playing, lacking a little in refinement, with individual instruments often audible. The very reverberant recording, made in the Great Hall of Birmingham University, adds a pleasant halo to the sound but obscures some detail.

Apollo; Orpheus (ballets).
*** ASV CDDCA 618 [id.]. O of St John's, Lubbock.

The ASV issue offers an ideal and generous coupling, with refined performances and excellent recording. The delicacy of the rhythmic pointing in *Apollo* gives special pleasure, and there is a first-rate solo violin contribution from Richard Deakin. This is one of Stravinsky's most appealing later scores, as readily accessible as the more famous ballets of his early years.

Le baiser de la fée (ballet; complete). TCHAIKOVSKY, arr. STRAVINSKY: *Sleeping Beauty: Bluebird pas de deux.*
*** Chan. CHAN 8360 [id.]. SNO, Järvi.

Le baiser de la fée is a remarkable symbiosis of Tchaikovskian tuneful charm (as instanced by the unforgettable rhythmic theme for the horns, taken from a piano piece) and Stravinskian twentieth-century neo-classicism. The scoring here is a constant delight, much of it on a chamber-music scale; and its delicacy, wit and occasional pungency are fully appreciated by Järvi, who secures a wholly admirable response from his Scottish orchestra. The ambience seems exactly right, bringing out wind and brass colours vividly. The condensation of the scoring of the *Sleeping Beauty Pas de deux*, made for a wartime performance when only limited forces were available, also shows Stravinsky's orchestral individuality – he even introduces a piano.

Le Chant du rossignol (symphonic poem).
*** Decca Dig. 417 619-2 [id.]. Montreal SO, Dutoit – *Petrushka* etc.***
(*) Delos Dig. D/CD 3051 [id.]. Seattle SO, Schwarz – *Firebird.*(*)

The symphonic poem that Stravinsky made from the material of his opera, *Le Rossignol*, with its extraordinarily rich fantasy and vividness of colouring, deserves a more established place in the concert repertoire. Dutoit's account is full of colour and atmosphere and has the advantage of marvellous Montreal sound. The couplings too are particularly apt, and this is a very desirable disc in all respects.

The Delos Schwarz recording has the most brilliantly etched detail, yet remains reasonably atmospheric. The extremely vivid and well-focused internal detail makes for the kind of record that will thrill audiophiles with equipment capable of making the most of its projection and clarity.

Concerto in D for strings; Danses concertantes; Dumbarton Oaks concerto in E flat; (i) *Cantata on old English texts.*
(M) *** Decca 425 622-2 [id.]. ECO, Sir Colin Davis; (i) with Kern, Young, St Anthony Singers.

The *Danses concertantes* is one of Stravinsky's most light-hearted pieces and the highly original scoring is a constant delight. Together with the other two instrumental works included in this outstanding collection, it has a neo-classicism to which anyone who has enjoyed Bach's *Brandenburgs* must surely respond. Indeed Stravinsky himself admitted that the *Brandenburgs* were his starting point for the *Dumbarton Oaks concerto*. Sir Colin Davis brings enormous vitality as well as the right degree of dry humour to these works, and the 1962 recording sounds as fresh as the day it was made in this very successful CD transfer. Detail is crisp and the ambience is exactly right for the music. The *Cantata* (recorded a year later) has a much cooler atmosphere, its chilling setting of the *Lye-Wake Dirge* more relentless than Britten's; but the sharp originality of the concept makes its inspiration readily felt in a performance that so strikingly captures its harsh mood and strange beauty. Both soloists are excellent and the chorus is vividly caught.

Concerto in D for strings; Symphony in C; (i) *Symphony of Psalms* (1948 version).
(M) ** DG 423 252-2. BPO, Karajan, (i) with German Op. Ch.

These are extreme examples of Karajan's refined Stravinsky style. Though undeniably he brings elegance to the *Concerto* and to the *Symphony in C*, both these examples of

Stravinsky's late neo-classicism lose their characteristic acerbity, with lines smoothed over and rhythms weakened. The *Symphony of Psalms* is equally unidiomatic, but the greatness of this masterpiece can stand deviation, and the final *Alleluias* are most beautifully done. The originally smooth, refined recording has gained in vividness on CD and so projection is improved.

Concerto in E flat (Dumbarton Oaks); Ebony concerto; Octet; Symphonies of wind instruments (1920 and 1947 versions).
*** EMI Dig. CDC7 49786-2. Endymion Ens., John Whitfield.

The two versions of Stravinsky's masterly *Symphonies of wind* make a fascinating contrast – not strikingly different but significantly so: the second one brighter and drier. John Whitfield and the Endymion Ensemble give performances which bring out beautifully the varied moods of the writing, giving wit to the *Octet*, *Dumbarton Oaks* and the *Ebony concerto*, in which Mark van der Wiel is a dazzling soloist, very much in style. Excellent recording.

Concerto in E flat (Dumbarton Oaks); Pulcinella (suite); 8 Instrumental miniatures.
*** DG Dig. 419 628-2 [id.]. Orpheus CO.

Remarkably fine playing from this conductorless group. Their ensemble in the *Pulcinella suite* is better than that of most conducted orchestras, and the overall impression they convey is one of freshness and spontaneity. Much the same must be said of *Dumbarton Oaks*, which has great zest and brilliance. The DG recording is clean and lifelike and the perspective very natural.

Ebony concerto.
*** CBS MK 42227 [id.]. Benny Goodman, Columbia Jazz Ens., composer – COPLAND: *Concerto*; BARTÓK: *Contrasts*; BERNSTEIN: *Prelude, fugue and riffs*; GOULD: *Derivations.*(***)

The *Ebony concerto* sounds strikingly vivid in an apt compilation centred on Benny Goodman's other comparable recordings.

Violin concerto in D.
*** DG Dig. 423 696-2 [id.]. Mutter, Philh. O, Sacher – LUTOSLAWSKI: *Chain II; Partita.****
(M) *** Decca 425 003-2 [id.]. Kyung Wha Chung, LSO, Previn – PROKOFIEV: *Concertos 1 – 2.****
*** DG 413 725-2 [id.]. Perlman, Boston SO, Ozawa – BERG: *Concerto.****
(M) *** Ph. 422 136-2 [id.]. Grumiaux, Concg. O, Bour – BERG: *Concerto.****

Mutter gives a strikingly characterful reading of the Stravinsky *Concerto*, neither brittle nor over-romanticized, with playing and recording of the very finest. There is no more recommendable version, and the coupling – an invigorating rather than a popular choice – is equally fine.

Kyung Wha Chung is at her most incisive in the spikily swaggering outer movements, which with Previn's help are presented here in all their distinctiveness, tough and witty at the same time. In the two movements labelled *Aria*, Chung brings fantasy as well as lyricism, less overtly expressive than Perlman but conveying instead an inner, brooding quality. Brilliant Decca recording, the soloist diamond-bright in presence, but with plenty of orchestral atmosphere.

Perlman's precision, remarkable in both concertos on this disc, underlines the neo-classical element in the outer movements of the Stravinsky. The two *Aria* movements are more deeply felt and expressive, presenting the work as a major twentieth-century concerto. The balance favours the soloist, but no one will miss the commitment of the Boston orchestra's playing, vividly recorded.

A lithe and beautifully refined account of the *Concerto* from Grumiaux. In some respects this is the most thoroughly enjoyable account on record and compares favourably with the Perlman. It is enormously vital but its energy is controlled and the tone never becomes unduly aggressive or spiky. The remastered recording is faithful and preserves an excellent balance between violin and orchestra.

Danses concertantes; Pulcinella (ballet): *suite.*
*** Chan. Dig. CHAN 8325 [id.]. ECO, Gibson.

Gibson and the ECO are very well recorded on Chandos and give highly enjoyable accounts of both works. The *Pulcinella* suite does not quite eclipse the Marriner (see below), but it is still very lively, and the *Danses concertantes* scores even over the composer's own in terms of charm and geniality. The CD is especially impressive in its firmness of detail.

Complete ballets: *The Firebird; Petrushka; The Rite of spring.*
*** Decca 421 079-2 (2) [id.]. Detroit SO, Dorati.

Dorati's set of the three great Stravinsky ballets is economically laid out here (although at full price). The Decca recording is consistently spectacular and realistic throughout. In *The Firebird* the clarity and definition of hushed passages is remarkable, while string tremolandos down to the merest whisper are uncannily precise. The performance is very precise too; although Dorati's reading has not changed a great deal from his previous versions with London orchestras, overall it is strong and beautiful. Dorati's account of *Petrushka* is based on the 1947 version, though at certain points he reverts to the original 1911 scoring, in accordance with his recollections of a conversation he had with Stravinsky himself. The recording sounds breathtakingly vivid and clean, yet remains naturally balanced and transparent. The performance does not always have the refinement of Abbado's, but it is immensely dramatic, as is *The Rite of spring.* Here the only let-down is the final Sacrificial dance, which needs greater abandon. Yet this account belongs with the very best, and the sound is exceptionally lifelike and has stunning clarity and presence.

The Firebird (ballet; complete).
(*) Delos Dig. D/CD 3051 [id.]. Seattle SO, Schwarz – *Chant du rossignol.*(*)
(B) **(*) Pickwick Dig. PCD 921. Nat. Youth O of Great Britain, Christopher Seaman – DUKAS: *L'apprenti sorcier.***(*)
(M) ** Decca Dig. 425 018-2 [id.]. VPO, Dohnányi (with BARTÓK: *2 Portraits, Op. 5***).

The Firebird (ballet; complete); *4 Études; Scherzo à la russe.*
**(*) EMI Dig. CDC7 49178-2. CBSO, Rattle.

The Firebird (ballet; complete); *Fireworks, Op. 4; Scherzo fantastique, Op. 3.*
*** Decca Dig. 414 409-2 [id.]. Montreal SO, Dutoit.

The Firebird (ballet; complete); *Fireworks; Scherzo fantastique; Scherzo à la russe.*
*** CBS MK 42432 [id.]. Columbia SO, composer.

Dutoit's version brings a characteristically colourful and atmospheric reading of Stravinsky's brilliant ballet score, ideally and generously coupled with the two early orchestral pieces which led Diaghilev to spot the young composer's talent. Thanks in part to Decca's sensuously beautiful Montreal recording, this is a reading that brings out the light and shade of the writing, so that even *Kaschei's dance* is not just a brilliant showpiece but part of the poetic and dramatic scheme. The pianissimos are of breathtaking delicacy – very vital in this work: the hushed introduction to the final scene with its lovely horn solo brings a sense of wonder. The fill-ups are sparklingly done, making this a clear first choice.

Stravinsky's own 1961 version of *Firebird* may lack the refinement of sound and the dynamic contrasts that mark the finest digital recordings, but it is of far more than documentary interest, when the composer so tellingly relates it to his later work, refusing to treat it as merely atmospheric. What he brings out more than others is the element of grotesque fantasy, the quality he was about to develop in *Petrushka*, while the tense violence with which he presents such a passage as *Kaschei's dance* clearly looks forward to *The Rite of spring*. His two early and brilliant orchestral pieces make the ideal coupling – as they do in Dutoit's fine version – but in addition the jolly *Scherzo à la russe* of 1944 comes as a bonus, done with infectious bounce.

The Delos version brings brilliant, exceptionally clean ensemble from the Seattle Symphony, showing its paces impressively under its music director, Gerard Schwarz. The recording is brilliant and strikingly sophisticated in its detail.

On Pickwick, *Firebird* is a work which inspires the young players of the current National Youth Orchestra to phenomenal feats of virtuosity. This is played at least as brilliantly as most versions by fully professional orchestras, with ensemble just as precise. Only in *Kaschei's dance*, taken a little cautiously, does the weight of the challenge show itself. The popular Dukas piece makes an attractive fill-up, and the modern digital recording is full and brilliant.

Strong, clean and well played, Rattle's CBSO version of *The Firebird* is forthright and positive rather than atmospheric, looking forward to the *Rite of spring* rather than back to Russian nationalism, and it is not one of his most inspired recordings. The two versions of the *Scherzo à la russe* (one for jazz band, one for full orchestra) are both given with all Rattle's usual flair, infectiously bouncy. The *Four studies* provide another light-hearted makeweight.

For a score as magical as *Firebird* a recording can actually be too clear, and the digital sound in Dohnányi's version tends to be too analytical, separating the threads in a way that prevents the music from making its full evocative effect. In any case, the reading is on the chill side.

(i) *The Firebird* (complete); (ii) *The Rite of spring* (complete).
(B) *** ASV CDQS 6031 [id.]. (i) RPO, Dorati; (ii) Nat. Youth O of Great Britain, Simon Rattle.

The ASV CD coupling of the two complete ballets is made possible because Dorati's tempi in the *Firebird* are comparatively fast. But this matches his dramatic approach, as does a recording balance which is rather close, although there is no serious lack of atmosphere in the score's gentler pages of evocation. Not surprisingly with Simon Rattle at the helm, the performance of the National Youth Orchestra in the once-feared showpiece coupling is not just 'good considering', but 'good absolute'; the youngsters under their young conductor (the recordings here date from 1976/7) produce warm and spontaneous playing, and the penalty of having a few imprecisions and errors is minimal. The sound here is slightly more atmospheric than in the coupling, but again there is plenty of bite and the timpani make a fine effect.

The Firebird: suite (1919 version).
*** EMI CDC7 47099-2 [id.]. Phd. O, Muti – MUSSORGSKY: *Pictures.****
(*) Telarc Dig. CD 80039 [id.]. Atlanta SO, Shaw – BORODIN: *Prince Igor:* excerpts.*

Muti gets excellent playing from the Philadelphia Orchestra and, though their response is admirably disciplined, there is delicacy and poetry in the *Dance of the princesses* and the *Berceuse* in *Firebird*, and the colours of this score are heard in full splendour.

Robert Shaw, a thoroughly musical conductor, achieves an atmospheric and vivid reading of Stravinsky's famous suite. The *Round dance of the princesses* is played very gently to maximize the shock of the entry of Kaschei. The very wide dynamic range of the digital recording achieves the most dramatic impact both here and in the closing pages of the finale.

The Firebird: suite (1919); *Petrushka:* complete (1947 score).
(B) *(**) CBS MYK 42540 [MYK 37221]. NYPO, Bernstein.

Bernstein's performance of *Petrushka* is one of the most involved and warm-hearted ever recorded. Bernstein goes to the emotional heart of the score, without violating Stravinsky's expressed markings except in a couple of minor instances. The panoply of the fair music, the inbred hysteria of the puppet's rage, and above all the tragedy of his death are here conveyed with unrivalled intensity and with splendidly vivid recording. *Firebird* is warmly done, if without quite the same superb precision. The digital remastering has smoothed the treble, taking some of the aggressive edge off the recording as well as removing the background; however, the engineers let the top back in for the fierce climax of *Kaschei's dance* in *The Firebird*.

The Firebird suite (1919 version); *The Rite of spring.*
(M) *** DG 415 854-2 [id.]. LSO, Abbado.

Abbado's *Firebird suite* is a performance of great vitality and sensitivity; the conductor's feeling for colour and atmosphere is everywhere and the CD transfer loses nothing of the evocation of the analogue original. There is a degree of detachment in *The Rite of spring*; but on points of detail it is meticulous. There is a hypnotically atmospheric feeling at the opening of Part Two, emphasizing the contrast with the brutal music which follows. The drama is heightened by the wide dynamic range of the recording, and the effect is forceful without ever becoming ugly.

Jeux de cartes (ballet) complete; (i) *Pulcinella* (ballet after Pergolesi) complete.
(M) *** DG 423 889-2 [id.]. (i) Berganza, Davies, Shirley-Quirk; LSO, Abbado.

Abbado gives a vividly high-powered reading of the neo-classical score of *Pulcinella*. If he is in danger of over-colouring, the bite and flair are entirely and convincingly Stravinskian, with rhythms sharply incisive. Not just the playing but the singers too are outstandingly fine. The 1979 recording in its digital remastering has become slightly drier and more acerbic in timbre, adding point to the playing. *Jeux de cartes*, recorded five years earlier, also sounds somewhat drier than it did originally, but the detail, presence and impact remain very telling. The LSO plays with superb virtuosity and Abbado's feeling for atmosphere and colour is everywhere in evidence, heard against an excellently judged perspective.

Petrushka (ballet; 1911 score) complete.
*** DG Dig. 423 901-2 [id.]. LSO, Abbado – MUSSORGSKY: *Pictures.****

Petrushka (1911 score); *4 Études.*
*** Decca Dig. 417 619-2 [id.]. Montreal SO, Dutoit – *Chant du rossignol.****

Petrushka (1947 score); *Circus polka; Fireworks, Op. 4.*
** ASV Dig. CDDCA 542 [id.]. RPO, Bátiz.

Dutoit in his Montreal version, benefiting from superb, atmospheric but well-detailed sound, gives a sparkling performance that brings out the light and shade of *Petrushka*, its poetry and its rhythmic effervescence. As in other brilliant showpieces, the refinement of Montreal pianissimos adds to the atmospheric thrill, but there is no lack of either power or bite in this subtle telling of the story. The coupling of *Le Chant du rossignol* and the *Four Studies* is both generous and apt.

Abbado combines refinement and a powerful sense of dramatic atmosphere (he is especially sympathetic in the central tableaux) with a kaleidoscopic brilliance. The recording has impressive range and colour, but there is a degree of digital edge on the upper strings which is certainly not entirely natural. It is now reissued, generously coupled with an equally impressive account of Mussorgsky's *Pictures at an exhibition*, and holds its competitive place in the current listings of both works.

With bright, forward, well-detailed recording, the Bátiz issue brings a performance of comparatively little sparkle or charm, more emphatic than usual, but therefore looking forward illuminatingly to the *Rite of spring*. The crispness of ensemble, the resilence of rhythms and the distinction of much of the solo work (notably the first flute) lightens what could have been too heavy, with some speeds slower than usual. The two lightweight fill-ups are certainly too heavily done, but are worth having as makeweights.

Petrushka (1911 version); *The Rite of spring.*
⊛ *** CBS MK 42433 [id.]. Columbia SO, composer.
(M) *** Ph. 420 491-2 [id.]. LPO, Haitink.

Petrushka (1947 version); *The Rite of spring.*
*** Ph. 416 498-2 [id.]. Concg. O, C. Davis.
** EMI Dig. CDC7 47408-2 [id.]. Phd. O, Muti.
(M) ** DG Dig. 429 493-2 [id.]. Israel PO, Bernstein.

Stravinsky's own reading of *The Rite of spring* has never been surpassed on record. Over and over again, one finds passages which in their balancing and pacing (generally fast) give extra thrust and resilience, as well as extra light and shade. The whole performance is magnetic, with the argument and tension held together superbly; that is so, despite the obvious limitations of a 1960 recording. The digital transfer may be on the bright side, and there is some slight background noise, but brass and percussion have thrilling impact, sharply terraced and positioned in the stereo spectrum. The recording of *Petrushka* has generally been underrated; it may lack something in lightness and sparkle on the one hand, and poetry on the other – largely a question of recording balance – but the composer presents a very convincing case for a basically fierce approach, full of malevolent grotesquerie; it is as though he has a malicious smile on his face. Even though the result may be relentless, the frenetic element is tellingly made to reflect the pathetic neurosis of the puppet-figure at the centre of the story. The digital remastering has brought coarser sound than in *The Rite*; interestingly, the phrase 'Columbia Symphony Orchestra' denotes two quite different groups of players: while *Petrushka* was recorded in Los Angeles, *The Rite of spring* with its greater magnetism was done in New York.

Haitink's 1974 *Petrushka* has been remastered with great success. There is a sense of expansion of the dynamic range and the performance is given added projection by the vivid sense of presence. It is a very involving account, with detail imaginatively delineated. The rhythmic feeling is strong, especially in the Second Tableau and the finale, where the fairground bustle is vivid. The LPO wind playing is especially fine; the recording's firm definition and the well-proportioned and truthful aural perspective make it a joy to listen to. The natural, unforced quality of Haitink's *Rite* also brings real compulsion. Other versions may hammer the listener more powerfully, thrust him or her along more forcefully; but the bite and precision of the playing here is most impressive.

From first to last Sir Colin Davis makes it clear that he regards *Petrushka* as fun music, drawing brilliantly precise playing from the Concertgebouw, making a striking case for the use of the 1947 score, and rarely if ever forcing the pace, though always maintaining necessary excitement. The piano solo starts a little cautiously in the Russian dance, but that is exceptional in an unusually positive reading. Davis also has his idiosyncrasies in *The Rite of spring* (one of them is his strange hold-up on the last chord), but generally he takes an unusually direct view, and the result is strong, forthright and powerful. Some will prefer a more obviously involving reading but, with the opulent sound of the Concertgebouw Orchestra boldly transferred, the physical impact of this version is still irresistible.

Muti secures playing of stunning virtuosity from the Philadelphians in *Petrushka* and, while their response is breathtaking, his reading can best be described as breathless. There is unremitting drive here, with the *Danse russe* taken at breakneck speed and everything far too regimented; there is too little tenderness and magic in this overdriven account. Similarly Muti's *Rite of spring* offers a performance which is aggressively brutal yet presents the violence with red-blooded conviction. Muti generally favours speeds a shade faster than usual, and arguably the opening bassoon solo is not quite flexible enough, for metrical precision is a key element all through. The recording, not always as analytically clear as some rivals, is strikingly bold and dramatic, with brass and percussion caught exceptionally vividly.

Sonic limitations qualified the enthusiasm with which Bernstein's digital version of *Le Sacre* could be greeted; his *Petrushka* was recorded in the same unglamorous acoustic of the Mann Auditorium, Tel Aviv. However, the results are by no means as uncongenial, though still too dry and unventilated. Bernstein coaxes some highly responsive playing from the Israel Philharmonic and secures much pleasing string tone – not always to be found from this body. Perhaps this *Petrushka* is not as touching as his earlier New York account made in the 1960s, surely one of the most vital and sensitively characterized versions of the work, but it is still vividly projected and keenly felt.

Petrushka (1947 version); *Symphony in 3 movements*.
*** EMI Dig. CDC7 49053-2 [id.]. CBSO, Rattle.

Using the revised, 1947 scoring, Rattle gives a reading which brings out powerfully the sturdy jollity of the ballet, contrasting it with the poignancy of the puppet's own feelings. The full and brilliant recording is beefy in the middle and bass, but Rattle and his players benefit in clarity from the 1947 scoring, finely detailed to bring out many points that are normally obscured. The *Symphony in three movements*, done with comparable power, colour and robustness, makes an unusual but attractive coupling. With his jazz training, Rattle brings out the syncopations and pop references with great panache.

(i) *Pulcinella* (ballet; complete); *Danses concertantes*.
*** Virgin Dig. VC 790767-2 [id.]. (i) Murray, David Thomas, Hill; City of L. Sinfonia, Richard Hickox.

(i) *Pulcinella* (ballet; complete); *Dumbarton Oaks concerto.*
*** Decca Dig. 425 614-2 [id.]. Bernadette Manca di Nissa, Gordon, Ostendorf, Howard, St Paul CO, Hogwood – GALLO: *Trio sonata movements*; PERGOLESI: *Sinfonia.****

(i) *Pulcinella* (ballet; complete); *Suites Nos. 1–2.*
(M) **(*) EMI CDM7 69204-2 [id.]. (i) J. Smith, J. Fryatt, M. King; N. Sinfonia, Rattle.

Pulcinella (ballet): *suite.*
(M) *** Decca 417 734-2 [id.]. ASMF, Marriner – BIZET; PROKOFIEV: *Symphonies.****

Richard Hickox emphasizes the colour in *Pulcinella*, to bring this neo-classical work rooted in the eighteenth century into the full light of the twentieth. So with sound that gives weight and body as well as plenty of detail he relishes the joke behind the *Vivo*, for example, with its trombone raspberries and lumbering double-bass. Equally he gives plenty of balletic bounce to the allegro movements and expressive warmth to the vocal numbers, phrasing in a romantic rather than a classical way. Among the soloists the tenor, Martyn Hill, stands out, though all are good. Hickox similarly gives a strong reminder that the *Danses concertantes* are, above all, ballet music, colourful and vigorous. Warm, full sound.

Christopher Hogwood has here not just gone back to Stravinsky's own score, in order to iron out various inconsistencies with the diligence of a classical scholar, but has also investigated Stravinsky's own sources. The composer used material from 21 different sources, all of them attributed to Pergolesi at the time, but in fact written by five different composers. As a delightful appendix, Hogwood adds some of the originals. The Pergolesi *Sinfonia* provides in its finale the idea for the *Vivo*, while the four movements from *Trio sonatas* by Domenico Gallo provide the themes for the opening overture, among other things. In keeping with this approach, Hogwood directs refined, deliberately lightweight performances of the two Stravinsky works, as much classical as neo-classical. Yet comparison with the eighteenth-century originals consistently makes you understand how Stravinsky's additions transform rather plain ideas. Of the three vocal soloists in *Pulcinella* the most striking is the firm-toned mezzo-soprano, Bernadette Manca di Nissa.

Simon Rattle, within a somewhat dry recording acoustic, conveys far more than usual the links between this score and the much later neo-classical opera *The Rake's Progress*. With lively and colourful playing from the Northern Sinfonia (the solos strong and positive) and with first-rate contributions from the three soloists, the high spirits of this score come over superbly. The CD transfer, however, has increased the effect of dryness and lost a little of the recording bloom.

Those wanting merely the orchestral suite can rest content with Marriner's vintage version, one of the first recordings by which the Academy spread its wings in the music of the twentieth century. The results are superb and the sound of the digitally remastered CD has all the bite one could ask for. It remains a demonstration disc with its sharp separation of instruments, particularly the trombones against double basses in the *Vivo*.

The Rite of spring (complete ballet) (see also above, under *Petrushka*).
(B) *** DG 429 162-2 [id.]. BPO, Karajan – MUSSORGSKY: *Pictures.****
*** DG 415 979-2 [id.]. BPO, Karajan – *Apollo.****
(M) *** Decca 417 704-2 [id.]. Chicago SO, Solti – DEBUSSY: *Prélude à l'après-midi*; RAVEL: *Boléro.***
**(*) Telarc Dig. CD 80054 [id.]. Cleveland O, Maazel.

The Rite of spring; Circus polka; Fireworks; Greeting prelude: Happy birthday.
(M) *** EMI Dig. CD-EMX 9517. LPO, Mackerras.

The Rite of spring; 4 Norwegian moods.
**(*) Decca Dig. 417 325-2 [id.]. Cleveland O, Chailly.

The Rite of spring; Symphonies of wind instruments.
** Decca Dig. 414 202-2 [id.]. Montreal SO, Dutoit.

Both of Karajan's DG stereo recordings are now available on CD and make a fascinating comparison. The earlier, 1966 version (now offered at mid-price, coupled with Mussorgsky's *Pictures*) came in for criticism from the composer, who doubted whether Berlin Philharmonic traditions could encompass music from so different a discipline. Yet listening to the vibrant sounds coming from the remastered CD, one cannot fully accept the composer's response. Certainly the playing of the Berlin Philharmonic is marvellously polished and civilized, yet it is not without bite or excitement, and the lack of malignancy serves to increase the feeling of symphonic strength, while the beauty of the sound created in the lyrical sections brings a potent nostalgia. Nevertheless, in his 1977 version (coupled with *Apollo*), tougher, more urgent, less mannered, Karajan goes a long way towards rebutting Stravinsky's complaints, and the result is superb, above all powerfully dramatic.

Solti's is a powerful, unrelenting account of Stravinsky's revolutionary score, with virtuoso playing from the Chicago orchestra and recording that demonstrates with breathtaking clarity the precision of inner detail. Some of the gentler half-tones of the score are presented rather glaringly, but this view of the work is magnificently consistent, showing Solti at his most tautly dramatic.

Mackerras's version is also at mid-price on the Eminence label and brings a powerful, often spacious performance, recorded in opulent and finely textured, if slightly distanced sound. The weight of the recording adds powerfully to the dramatic impact, though it is a pity that timpani are backward and less sharply focused than they might be. Though short measure, the three little orchestral trifles are done by Mackerras with delectable point and wit.

With speeds faster than usual – markedly so in Part Two – Chailly's taut and urgent reading brings one of Decca's sound spectaculars. The bass drum, so important in this work, leaps out with a power, precision and resonance to startle the listener, although the fast speeds in Part Two provide less contrast than usual before the onslaught of the final *Sacrificial dance.* The unpretentious little *Norwegian moods* make a contrasting coupling.

The sound on the Cleveland Orchestra version conducted by Lorin Maazel is also pretty spectacular. However, there are a number of sensation-seeking effects, such as excessive ritardandi in the *Rondes printanières* so as to exaggerate the trombone glissandi, which are vulgar. Compare, too, the opening of Part Two in this version with that of Karajan, and one is in a totally different world.

Dutoit's Montreal CD offers sumptuous, finely detailed sound with a realistic balance and plenty of presence and body and, of course, a marvellous dynamic range. Yet Dutoit has little of that blazing intensity which one finds in the composer's own record. In short, this Montreal version is outstanding as a recording, but the performance falls short of the highest voltage.

The Soldier's Tale (complete).
*** Nimbus Dig. NI 5063 [id.]. Christopher Lee, SCO, Lionel Friend.

With the actor Christopher Lee both narrating and taking the individual parts, the Nimbus issue brings an attractively strong and robust reading, lacking the last degree of refinement but with some superb solo playing – from the violinist, for example. The recording is vivid and full of presence, with the speaking voice related to instruments far better than is usual. For a version in English, it makes an excellent investment.

The Soldier's tale: suite.
*** Delos Dig. D/CD 3021 [id.]. LACO, Schwarz – PROKOFIEV: *Symphony No. 1****; SHOSTAKOVICH: *Piano concerto No. 1.**(*)*

This made a splendid CD début for a work which is surprisingly little recorded. The acoustic is ideal for the music and the sound is wonderfully realistic and present. The performance makes a nice balance between pungency and the underlying lyricism; there is some splendid solo playing from Paul Shure (violin) and the superb trumpeter, Tony Plog, whose easy virtuosity and fine timbre add much to the music's appeal. Recommended, especially as the couplings are imaginative.

Suites Nos. 1 and 2 for small orchestra.
*** RCA Dig. RD 85168 [RCD1 5168]. Dallas SO, Mata – PROKOFIEV: *Lieutenant Kijé* etc.***

Arranged by the composer from piano duets – 'Easy pieces' that are not so easy – these eight witty orchestral miniatures are a delight. They are played with marvellous finesse and point, and superbly recorded.

Symphony in E flat, Op. 1; Symphony in C; Symphony in 3 movements; Ode (Elegiacal chant in 3 parts).
*** Chan. Dig. CHAN 8345/6 (2) [id.]. SNO, Gibson.

Even compared with the composer's own performances, this collection by the Scottish National Orchestra – in excellent form – under Sir Alexander Gibson stands up well. The vividness of the digital recording makes up for any slight lack of sparkle, and while the *Symphonies for wind instruments* might have seemed a more obvious makeweight for the three major works, it is good to have the *Ode* in memory of Natalia Koussevitzky, which has an extrovert, rustic scherzo section framed by short elegies.

Symphony in C; Symphony in 3 movements.
*** Decca Dig. 414 272-3 [id.]. SRO, Dutoit.

Although the Suisse Romande Orchestra is not in the very first rank, the brilliant recording it now receives from the Decca team and the alert direction of Charles Dutoit make this a very winning coupling. These are both exhilarating pieces and Dutoit punches home their virile high spirits and clean-limbed athleticism.

Symphony in C; Symphony in 3 movements; (i) Symphony of Psalms.
*** CBS MK 42434 [id.]. CBS or Columbia SO, composer; (i) with Toronto Fest. Singers.

The composer's performance of the *Symphony in three movements* is an object lesson to every conductor who has tried to perform the work: he shows how, by vigorous, forthright treatment of the notes, the implicit emotion is all the more compelling. The Columbia Symphony Orchestra plays superbly and the recording is vivid. The *Symphony in C*, with its extraordinarily bleak ending, is splendidly done, and it is only the *Symphony of Psalms* that offers a degree of disappointment, with Stravinsky as interpreter at less than maximum voltage. But this CBS CD offers an invaluable triptych and the digital remastering has been highly successful in clarifying the original recordings without loss of body.

CHAMBER AND INSTRUMENTAL MUSIC

Divertimento.
*** Ph. Dig. 426 254-2 [id.]. Viktoria Mullova, Bruno Canino – PROKOFIEV: *Sonata No. 2 in D***; RAVEL: *Sonata in G.****

Divertimento (from *Le baiser de la fée*); *Duo concertante; Suite italienne.*
*** EMI CDC7 49322-2 [id.]. Itzhak Perlman, Bruno Canino.

The *Divertimento* is an arrangement Stravinsky made in 1933 of his orchestral score, *Le Baiser de la fée*. Quite simply, it is played marvellously by Viktoria Mullova and Bruno Canino and most vividly and naturally recorded.

The *Italian suite* was arranged from the Pergolesi-based ballet, *Pulcinella*, while the *Duo concertante* was written after the *Violin concerto* and for the same artist, Samuel Dushkin. Needless to say, Perlman plays all this music with warmth and understanding, and his achievement in the *Duo concertante*, which has often seemed a dry work, is particularly remarkable. Bruno Canino makes a sympathetic partner and the 1976 recording, originally excellent, has been clearly and cleanly transferred to CD.

Suite italienne.
*** BIS Dig. CD 336 [id.]. Torleif Thedéen, Roland Pöntinen – SCHNITTKE: *Sonata*; SHOSTAKOVICH: *Sonata.****

Stravinsky made several transcriptions of movements from *Pulcinella*, including the *Suite italienne* for violin and piano. The performances by Torleif Thedéen and Roland Pöntinen, Swedish artists both in their mid-twenties, are felicitous and spontaneous, and they are afforded strikingly natural recording.

PIANO MUSIC

Concerto for 2 solo pianos; Petrushka (ballet): arr. for 2 pianos.
*** Ph. Dig. 420 822-2 [id.]. Katia and Marielle Labèque.

The *Petrushka* transcription is exhilarating in the hands of the Labèque sisters and, like the *Concerto for two pianos*, sounds brilliant and lifelike in the acoustic of The Maltings at Snape. The latter work with its self-conscious neo-classicism is very much in sparkling monochrome, as opposed to the vivid, brittle, kaleidoscopic colours of the *Petrushka* arrangement. With a playing time of just over a half an hour, however, this is very short measure indeed.

3 Movements from Petrushka.
*** DG 419 202-2 [id.]. Maurizio Pollini – *Recital.****

Staggering, electrifying playing from Pollini, creating the highest degree of excitement. This is part of an outstandingly generous recital of twentieth-century piano music.

VOCAL MUSIC

(i) *Mass;* (ii) *Les Noces.*
*** DG 423 251-2 [id.]. (i) Trinity Boys' Ch., E. Bach Fest. O; (i, ii) E. Bach Fest. Ch.; (ii) Mory, Parker, Mitchinson, Hudson; Argerich, Zimerman, Katsaris, Francesch (pianos), percussion; cond. Bernstein.

Bernstein reinforces the point that both the *Mass* and the much earlier ballet illustrating a folk wedding ceremony are intensely Russian in their inspiration. In the *Mass* the style is overtly expressive, with the boys of Trinity Choir responding freshly, but it is in *Les Noces* that Bernstein conveys an electricity and a dramatic urgency which give the work its rightful stature as one of Stravinsky's supreme masterpieces, totally original and – even today – unexpected, not least in its black-and-white instrumentation for four pianos and percussion. The star pianists here make a superb, imaginative team. The atmospheric recording now sounds even more vivid in its CD format.

Renard.
*** Decca Dig. 421 717-2 [id.]. Langridge, Jenkins, Hammond-Stroud, Lloyd, L. Sinf., Chailly – WALTON: *Façade.***(*)

(i) *Renard. The Soldier's tale;* (ii) *3 Pieces for clarinet solo; Ragtime;* (iii) *3 Japanese lyrics.*
(BB) *** Hung. White Label HRC 078. Budapest Chamber Ens., András Mihály, (i) Gulyás, Keonch, Polgar, Bordas; (ii) Berkes; (iii) Adrienne Csengery.

Chailly and the London Sinfonietta give a colourful and brilliantly characterized performance of Stravinsky's fable, *Renard*, not an easy work to bring off. Here the humour of the piece comes over well. The British soloists are most convincing in Russian, making a well-contrasted team, and the recording is very vivid indeed, but it is a pity that no text or translation is given.

Mihály's well-planned Stravinsky collection, colourfully performed and recorded, makes an outstanding bargain in Hungaroton's extremely inexpensive White Label series. The oddity is that *The Soldier's tale* has the full text of the entertainment, over half an hour long, but without any dramatic dialogue. Both in the dramatic scena, *Renard* – with four excellent soloists – and in *Ragtime*, the cimbalom plays a prominent part and, aptly in Budapest performances, Marta Fabian's brilliant, idiomatic playing of that Hungarian instrument is put well to the fore. The clear, silvery soprano, Adrienne Csengery, gives delightful performances of the *Japanese lyrics* and Kálmán Berkes is an agile clarinettist in the unaccompanied pieces.

Symphony of Psalms.
⊛ (M) *** CBS MK 44710 [id.]. E. Bach Fest. Ch., LSO, Bernstein – POULENC: *Gloria;* BERNSTEIN: *Chichester Psalms.****

Bernstein's account of the *Symphony of Psalms* ranks among his very finest records, though his view of the work is not as austere and ascetic as the composer's own. Indeed the setting of Psalm 150 with its *Alleluias* and *Laudates* produces ravishing singing from the English Bach Festival Chorus, restrained in its sensuousness, but frisson-creating in the glorious closing section. Both the orchestral playing and the singing are first class and the recording, distinguished by its clarity and range, approaches the demonstration standard in its CD format.

The Rake's progress (complete).
**(*) Decca Dig. 411 644-2 (2) [id.]. Langridge, Pope, Walker, Ramey, Dean, Dobson, L. Sinf. Ch. & O, Chailly.

Riccardo Chailly draws from the London Sinfonietta playing of a clarity and brightness to set the piece aptly on a chamber scale without reducing the power of this elaborately neo-classical piece. Philip Langridge is excellent as the Rake himself, very moving when Tom is afflicted with madness. Samuel Ramey as Nick, Stafford Dean as Trulove and Sarah Walker as Baba the Turk are all first rate, but Cathryn Pope's soprano as recorded is too soft-grained for Anne. Charming as the idea is of getting the veteran Astrid Varnay to sing Mother Goose, the result is out of style. The recording is exceptionally full and vivid but the balances are sometimes odd: the orchestra recedes behind the singers and the chorus sounds congested, with little air round the sound.

Suk, Josef (1874–1935)

Asrael symphony, Op. 27.
*** Sup. Dig. SUP 007404 [id.]. Czech PO, Neumann.

It is astonishing that a work of this stature has been so neglected outside Czechoslovakia. In its organization it owes a good deal to the 'cyclic' principle, fashionable at the end of the last century. A sense of numbness in the face of grief comes across, yet there is much that is fiery, vigorous and exciting. Asrael is the Angel of Death – hence the title – and touches real depths; but it is more than a moving human document, it is a great work. The performance is a very fine one; this is its first recording for almost thirty years and a must for all serious collectors.

A Fairy-tale, Op. 16; Praga (symphonic poem), Op. 26.
*** Sup. Dig. SUP 007509 [id.]. Czech PO, Libor Pešek.

Suk's *A Fairy-tale* is a concert suite drawn from the incidental music to Julius Zeyer's fairy-tale drama, *Raduz and Nahulena*. The invention is full of charm and originality, and it is persuasively played here. On this compact disc it is coupled with *Praga*, a patriotic tone-poem reflecting a more public, out-going figure than *Asrael*, which was to follow it. Libor Pešek secures an excellent response from the Czech Philharmonic; the recordings, which date from 1981–2, are reverberant but good.

Fantasy in G min. (for violin and orchestra), *Op. 24.*
(B) *** Sup. 110601-2. Josef Suk, Czech PO, Ančerl – DVOŘÁK: *Violin concerto.****

Suk's *Fantasy* is a brilliant piece which relates to the traditional essays in violin wizardry as well as to the Czech nationalist tradition. The work has music of characteristic fantasy, though the rhetorical brilliance is equally strong. Suk's playing is refreshing and the orchestral accompaniment under Ančerl is no less impressive. Good remastered 1960s sound.

(i) *Fantasy in G min.* for violin and orchestra, *Op. 24; Symphony in E, Op. 14.*
*** Sup. Dig. SUP 007540 [id.]. Czech PO, Neumann; (i) with Josef Suk.

The *Symphony* sounds marvellously fresh; though much of it is Dvořákian in outward appearance, there is much that one recognizes from Suk's maturity. This is a delightfully inventive and astonishingly accomplished *Symphony* that will captivate all who enjoy Dvořák. The *G minor Fantasy*, Op. 24, is an ardent, life-loving work – a kind of one-movement concerto, full of imaginative ideas and variety of invention. The soloist is placed rather forwardly, but the somewhat reverberant recording is generally well balanced and Suk's performance is very good indeed.

Serenade for strings in E flat, Op. 6; (i) Under the apple tree, Op. 20.
**(*) Sup. SUP 001372. (i) Eva Depoltova; Czech PO, Libor Pešek.

Libor Pešek gives an unhurried and dignified reading of the *Serenade*, though, as in so many recordings made in the House of Artists, the sound is a bit top-heavy. Suk's suite, *Under the apple tree*, written a few years later, is a charming work indebted to Dvořák and the Czech nationalists, but with a distinctive feel to it. It is very well performed and the recording, though not in the demonstration class, is well balanced.

Sullivan, Arthur (1842–1900)

Overtures: *Di ballo; The Gondoliers; HMS Pinafore; Iolanthe; Patience; The Pirates of Penzance; Princess Ida; Ruddigore; The Sorcerer; The Yeomen of the Guard* (all arr. Geoffrey Toye).
*** Nimbus Dig. NI 5066 [id.]. SCO, Alexander Faris.

A well-played and well-recorded collection of Sullivan overtures. Mostly they are little more than pot-pourris, but *The Yeomen of the Guard* is an exception, and the gay *Di Ballo* is vivacious and tuneful and shows Sullivan's scoring at its most felicitous.

Pineapple Poll (ballet music, arr. Mackerras).
*** Ara. Z 8016 [id.]. RPO, Mackerras.

Mackerras's record was considered definitive in its day (1962); it is still striking for its sheer brio. The RPO is in excellent form and the EMI recording still sounds extremely well; the playing has a real feeling of the ballet theatre. As can be seen, the enterprising Arabesque company have made a CD of this earlier account for the American market and this is available in the UK as an import. The transfer is remarkably successful; however, the fortissimos have a degree of hardness on top, the string sound is tighter and there is a touch of shrillness at times, though not beyond control.

Songs: *The absent-minded beggar; The Dove song; Gone!; Let me dream again; The lost chord; The Marquis de Mincepie; Mary Morison; The moon in silent brightness; Shakespeare songs: O mistress mine; Orpheus with his lute; Willow song; St Agnes' Eve; Sweethearts; What does the little birdie say?; Winter.*
*** Conifer Dig. CDCFC 156 [id.]. Jeanne Ommerle, Sanford Sylvan, Gary Wedow.

It has taken a pair of American singers (with a pianist who is also chorus master of the Sante Fe Opera) to discover the delights of these Sullivan songs and bring them to our attention in an admirably planned recital which offers singing to catch their style superbly. The ballads have all the melodic resource of the Savoy Operas and the duet *Sweethearts* could almost have come from *Patience*, although it has an appropriate link with Victor Herbert in its added sentimentality. The Shakespeare settings are memorable, particularly the unexpected soaring line of *Orpheus with his lute*, though the gentle *Willow song* is equally lovely. *What does the little birdie say?* is a children's lullaby, while the splendid Kipling narrative of *The absent-minded beggar* reminds one of the repertoire Peter Dawson made famous. Jeanne Ommerle sings with full involvement with the words and her voice gives consistent pleasure in her simplicity of line and tonal beauty. Sanford Sylvan is very good, too, and, after opening restraint in *The lost chord*, then builds a resplendent climax, aided and abetted by spectacular accompaniment from the pianist, Gary Wedow; one understands how the Victorians could be bowled over by the sheer eloquence of the piece. Elsewhere the reverberant acoustic of the recording is less than ideal, but the words come over clearly and certainly there is plenty of bloom on the voices. A most involving and entertaining collection without one dull number.

OPERAS

As can be seen below, both Decca and – more particularly – EMI have been regrouping their major Gilbert and Sullivan recordings to make them attractively economical in their CD layout. The distinction of both the Godfrey/D'Oyly Carte series and the rather different and more operatic Sargent recordings means that newer competition (linked to current live performances) can seldom match the earlier versions in panache and style, to say nothing of overall polish.

(i) *Cox and Box* (libretto by F. C. Burnand) complete; (ii) *Ruddigore* (complete, without dialogue).
(M) *** Decca 417 355-2 (2). (i) Styler, Riordan, Adams; New SO of L.; (ii) J. Reed, Round, Sandford, Riley, Adams, Hindmarsh, Knight, Sansom, Allister, D'Oyly Carte Op. Ch., ROHCG O, Godfrey.

Cox and Box is a superb performance in every way. It is given a recording which, without sacrificing clarity, conveys with perfect balance the stage atmosphere. It was written in 1867 and thus pre-dates the first G & S success, *Trial by Jury*, by eight years. One must notice the lively military song *Rataplan* – splendidly sung by Donald Adams, an ideal Bouncer – which was to set the style for many similar and later pieces with words by Gilbert, and also the captivating *Bacon 'Lullaby'*, so ravishingly sung by Joseph Riordan. Later on, in Box's recitative telling how he 'committed suicide', Sullivan makes one of his first and most impressive parodies of grand opera, which succeeds also in being effective in its own right.

Ruddigore, too, comes up surprisingly freshly though it was a pity the dialogue was omitted. The performance includes *The battle's roar is over*, which is (for whatever reason) traditionally omitted. There is much to enjoy here (especially Gillian Knight and Donald Adams, whose *Ghosts' high noon* song is a marvellous highlight). Godfrey is his inimitable sprightly self and the chorus and orchestra are excellent. A fine traditional D'Oyly Carte set, then, brightly recorded, even if in this instance the Sargent version is generally even finer.

The Gondoliers (complete, with dialogue).
(M) *(**) Decca 417 254-2 (2) [id.]. Reed, Skitch, Sandford, Round, Styler, Knight, Toye, Sansom, Wright, D'Oyly Carte Op. Ch., New SO of L., Godfrey.

One welcomes back *The Gondoliers* to the catalogue. Isidore Godfrey's conducting is vividly alive and Decca provided a large and excellent orchestra. The solo singing throughout is consistently good. Jeffrey Skitch and Jennifer Toye are a well-matched pair of lovers, and the two Gondoliers and their wives are no less effective. Thomas Round sings *Take a pair of sparkling eyes* very well indeed. The ensemble singing is very well balanced and always both lively and musical. The *Cachucha* is captivating and goes at a sparkling pace. Kenneth Sandford, who is a rather light-voiced Don Alhambra, makes much of his spoken part, as well as singing his songs with fine style. John Reed is a suitably dry Duke of Plaza-Toro: he makes the part his own and is well partnered by Gillian Knight. The drawback lies in the digitally remastered recording, which has been miscalculated – the treble is fierce, making the strings edgy and the female voices peaky.

The Gondoliers (complete, without dialogue).
**(*) EMI CDS7 47775-8 (2) [Ang. CDCB 47775]. Evans, Young, Brannigan, Lewis, Cameron, Milligan, M. Sinclair, Graham, Morison, Thomas, Watts, Glyndebourne Fest. Ch., Pro Arte O, Sargent.

The snag to the Sargent set of *The Gondoliers* is the curiously slow tempo he chooses for the *Cachucha*, while the long opening scene is rather relaxed and leisurely. At the entrance of the Duke of Plaza-Toro things wake up considerably and, early in the opera, Owen Brannigan as a perfectly cast Don Alhambra sings a masterly *No possible doubt whatever*. From then on and throughout the rest of the opera, there is much to captivate the ear. Edna Graham's Casilda is charmingly small-voiced. The age of the 1957 recording shows in the orchestra, but the voices sound fresh, and there is a pleasing overall bloom – sonically this is far preferable to the Decca D'Oyly Carte version.

HMS Pinafore (complete, with dialogue).
⊛ (M) *** Decca 414 283-2 [id.]. Reed, Skitch, Round, Adams, Hindmarsh, Wright, Knight, D'Oyly Carte Op. Ch., New SO of L., Godfrey.

It would be difficult to imagine a better-recorded performance than the 1960 Decca D'Oyly Carte set, complete with dialogue. Donald Adams is a totally memorable Deadeye and his larger-than-life personality underpins the whole piece. Among the others, Jeffrey Skitch is a first-class Captain; Jean Hindmarsh is absolutely convincing as Josephine, and she sings with great charm. Thomas Round is equally good as Ralph Rackstraw. Little Buttercup could be slightly more colourful, but this is a small blemish; among the minor parts, George Cook is a most personable Bill Bobstay. The choral singing is excellent, the orchestral playing good, and Isidore Godfrey conducts with marvellous spirit and lift. The recording has splendid atmosphere and its vintage qualities are very apparent in this remastered form.

HMS Pinafore (complete, without dialogue).
*** That's Entertainment Dig. CDTER2 1150 [MCA MCAD2 11012]. Grace, Sandison, Ormiston, Ritchie, Roebuck, Gillett, Lawlor, Parfitt, Thomson, New Sadler's Wells Ch. & O., Phipps.

The digital recording of the New Sadler's Wells Opera production has a splendid theatrical atmosphere. It is consistently well cast, with Linda Ormiston a particularly characterful Buttercup and Nickolas Grace making an appropriately aristocratic Sir Joseph Porter. Simon Phipps paces the music fluently, if without quite the unerring timing of Godfrey, and this is very enjoyable from first to last. Alongside the classic Godfrey set, however, the characterization is just that bit less sharp; if you want a fine modern recording, this new one is very entertaining.

HMS Pinafore (complete, without dialogue); *Trial by Jury.*
*** EMI CDS7 47798-8 (2). G. Baker, Cameron, Lewis, Brannigan, Milligan, Morison, Thomas, M. Sinclair, Glyndebourne Fest. Ch., Pro Arte O, Sargent.

It is to Owen Brannigan's great credit that, little as he had to do here, without the dialogue, he conveyed the force of Deadeye's personality so strongly. George Baker is splendid as Sir Joseph, and John Cameron, Richard Lewis and (especially) Monica Sinclair, as Buttercup, make much of their songs. Elsie Morison is rather disappointing; she spoils the end of her lovely song in Act I by singing sharp. The whole of the final scene is musically quite ravishing; throughout, if Sir Malcolm fails to find quite all the wit in the music, he is never less than lively. The coupling with *Trial by Jury* makes this a fine bargain. The recording is bright and lively and does not lack atmosphere.

Iolanthe (complete, with dialogue).
(M) *** Decca 414 145-2 (2) [id.]. Sansom, Reed, Adams, Round, Sandford, Styler, Knight, Newman, D'Oyly Carte Op. Ch., Grenadier Guards Band, New SO, Godfrey.

This was the first (1960) stereo *Iolanthe*, not the later and generally inferior remake under Nash. Even though Decca's budget had not yet stretched to the Royal Philharmonic Orchestra, the production was given added panache by introducing the Grenadier Guards Band into the *March of the Peers*, with spectacular effect. John Reed's characterization is wittily immediate, and the famous *Nightmare song* undoubtedly has greater freshness. Mary Sansom is a convincing Phyllis, and if her singing has not the sense of style Elsie Morison brings to the Sargent EMI set, she is marvellous with the dialogue. Her Act II discourse with the two Earls – portrayed to perfection by Donald Adams and Thomas Round – is sheer delight. Alan Styler makes a vivid personal identification with the role of Strephon. Iolanthe's final aria (sung by Yvonne Newman) is a shade disappointing: here the voice does not sound quite secure. But this is a minor lapse in a first-rate achievement. The chorus is excellent, and the orchestral detail has the usual light Godfrey touch. The remastering is very successful, the sound bright but with an admirable acoustic ambience which allows every word to project clearly.

(i) *Iolanthe* (complete, without dialogue); (ii) *Overture Di ballo*.
*** EMI CDC7 47831-8 (2) [Ang. CDCB 47831]. (i) G. Baker, Wallace, Young, Brannigan, Cameron, M. Sinclair, Thomas, Cantelo, Harper, Morison, Glyndebourne Fest. Ch., Pro Arte O, Sargent; (ii) Royal Liverpool PO, Groves.

There is much to praise in this EMI set, and EMI have refurbished the recording very successfully; it suits the studio-based performance and projects the music brightly without loss of inner warmth. The climax of Act I, the scene of the Queen of the Fairies' curse on members of both Houses of Parliament, shows most excitingly what can be achieved with the 'full operatic treatment': this is a dramatic moment indeed. George Baker too is very good as the Lord Chancellor; however, for some listeners John Cameron's dark timbre may not readily evoke an Arcadian Shepherd. The two Earls and Private Willis are excellent, the famous *Nightmare song* is very well and clearly sung, and all of Act II (except perhaps Iolanthe's recitative and ballad near the end) goes very well. The famous *Trio* with the Lord Chancellor and the two Earls is a joy. The *Di ballo overture* acts as an attractive encore at the end of the opera.

The Mikado (complete, without dialogue).
(M) *** Decca 425 190-2 (2) [id.]. Ayldon, Wright, J. Reed, Sandford, Masterson, Holland, D'Oyly Carte Op. Ch., RPO, Nash.
**(*) EMI CDS7 47773-8 (2). Brannigan, Lewis, Evans, Wallace, Cameron, Morison, Thomas, J. Sinclair, M. Sinclair, Glyndebourne Fest. Ch., Pro Arte O, Sargent.

The 1973 stereo re-recording of *The Mikado* by the D'Oyly Carte company directed by Royston Nash is a complete success in every way and shows the Savoy tradition at its most attractive. The digital remastering for CD adds to the brightness: its effect is like a coat of new paint, so that the G & S masterpiece emerges with a pristine sparkle. Musically this is the finest version the D'Oyly Carte company have ever put on disc. The choral singing is first rate, with much refinement of detail. The glees, *Brightly dawns* and *See how the fates*, are robust in the D'Oyly Carte manner but more polished than usual. The words are exceptionally clear throughout. Of the principals, John Reed is a splendid Ko-Ko, a refined and individual characterization. Kenneth Sandford gives his customary vintage projection of Pooh-Bah and Valerie Masterson is a charming Yum-Yum. Colin Wright's vocal production has a slightly nasal quality; but one soon adjusts to it, and his voice has the proper bright freshness of timbre for Nanki-Poo. John Ayldon's Mikado has not quite the satanic glitter of Donald Adams's classic version, but he provides a laugh of terrifying bravura. Katisha (Lyndsie Holland) is commanding, and her attempts to interrupt the chorus in the finale of Act I are superbly believable and dramatic. On CD the singers are given striking presence, though the bright lighting of the sound has brought more sibilance.

The Sargent set, the first of his series, dates from as early as 1957 and the recording has been given remarkable vividness and presence by the digital remastering. Words are crisp and clear and there is much to enjoy. The grand operatic style to the finales of both Acts, the trio about the 'death' of Nanki-Poo and the glee that follows are characteristic of the stylish singing, even if the humour is less readily caught than in the D'Oyly Carte production. Owen Brannigan is a fine Mikado, but the star performance is that of Richard Lewis, who sings most engagingly throughout as Nanki-Poo. Elsie Morison is a charming Yum-Yum and Monica Sinclair a generally impressive Katisha, although she could sound more convinced when she sings *These arms shall thus enfold you.*

The Mikado: highlights.
**(*) That's Entertainment CDTER 1121 [MCA MCAD 6215]. Angas, Bottone, Idle, Garrett, Van Allan, Palmer, E. Nat. Op. Ch. & O, Peter Robinson.

This selection includes virtually all the important music; but it will appeal primarily to those wanting a memento of the English National Opera production. As is normal, the performance is dominated by Ko-Ko, and Eric Idle's characterization will not be to all tastes; moreover the libretto is often considerably altered – most notably in the 'little list' – not always to advantage. Without the stage action, the performance is less than racy and Peter Robinson generally adopts very relaxed tempi; although there are memorable moments, the choral singing is at times surprisingly slack.

Patience (complete, with dialogue).
(M) *** Decca 425 193-2 (2) [id.]. Sansom, Adams, Cartier, Potter, J. Reed, Sandford, Newman, Lloyd-Jones, Toye, Knight, D'Oyly Carte Op. Ch. & O, Godfrey.

Patience comes up superbly in its digitally remastered format. The military numbers are splendidly projected and vividly coloured – *When I first put this uniform on* and *The soldiers of our Queen* have an unforgettable vigour and presence, with Donald Adams in glorious voice. Everything seems to be freshened, and the D'Oyly Carte soloists, chorus and orchestra have never sounded better. Mary Sansom takes the lead charmingly and she is especially good in the dialogue. Both Bunthorne and Grosvenor are very well played. The dialogue is at a slightly lower dynamic level than the music, but that only reflects the reality of the theatre. Overall, this is irresistible.

(i) *Patience* (complete, without dialogue); (ii) *Symphony in E (Irish).*
*** EMI CDC7 47783-8 (2) [Ang. CDCB 47783]. (i) Morison, Young, G. Baker, Cameron, Thomas, M. Sinclair, Harper, Harwood, Glyndebourne Fest. Ch., Pro Arte O, Sargent; (ii) Royal Liverpool PO, Groves.

It seems a curious idea to couple *Patience* with Sullivan's *Irish symphony.* Yet it is a pleasing work, lyrical, with echoes of Schumann as much as the more predictable Mendelssohn and Schubert. Groves and the Royal Liverpool Philharmonic give a fresh and affectionate performance.
Patience was another of the great successes of the Sargent series and (like the Decca set) emerges freshly minted in its new transfer. Although there is no dialogue, there is more business than is usual from EMI and a convincing theatrical atmosphere. The chorus is a strong feature throughout, and where the men and women sing different melodic lines the clarity of each is admirable. Elsie Morison's Patience, George Baker's Bunthorne and John Cameron's Grosvenor are all admirably characterized, while the military men are excellent too. All in all, this is the sort of production we anticipated when EMI first began their 'Glyndebourne' series, and it can be heartily recommended.

The Pirates of Penzance (complete, with dialogue).
(M) *** Decca 425 196-2 [id.]. J. Reed, Adams, Potter, Masterson, Palmer, Brannigan, D'Oyly Carte Op. Ch., RPO, Godfrey.

For compact disc issue, Decca have chosen the second (1968) D'Oyly Carte recording, and Isidore Godfrey is helped by a more uniformly excellent cast than was present on the earlier set. The dialogue is included, theatrical spontaneity is well maintained, and the spoken scenes with the Pirate King are particularly effective. Christene Palmer's Ruth is not quite so poised, but her singing is first rate – her opening aria has never been done better. John Reed's characterization of the part of the Major-General is strong, while Valerie Masterson is an excellent Mabel; if her voice is not creamy throughout its range, she controls it with great skill. Her duet with Frederic, *Leave me not to pine alone*, is enchanting, sung very gently. Godfrey's conducting is as affectionate as ever; but perhaps the greatest joy of the set is Owen Brannigan's Sergeant of Police, a part this artist was surely born to play. It is a marvellously humorous performance, yet the humour is never clumsy; the famous *Policeman's song* is so fresh that it is almost like hearing it for the first time. The recording is superbly spacious and clear throughout, with a fine sense of atmosphere. While a slight degree of edge appears on the voices at times, the sense of theatrical feeling is greatly enhanced and the dialogue interchanges have an uncanny realism.

(i) *The Pirates of Penzance* (complete, without dialogue); *Overtures: Cox and Box; Princess Ida; The Sorcerer.* (ii) *Overture in C (In Memoriam).*
*** EMI CDS7 47785-8. G. Baker, Milligan, Cameron, Lewis, Brannigan, Morison, Harper, Thomas, M. Sinclair, Glyndebourne Fest. Ch., Pro Arte O, Sargent; (ii) CBSO, Dunn.

Besides a performance which is stylish as well as lively, conveying both the fun of the words and the charm of the music, the EMI recording has more atmosphere than usual in this series. Undoubtedly the star of the piece is George Baker; he is a splendid Major-General while, as in the Decca D'Oyly Carte set, Owen Brannigan gives a rich portrayal of the Sergeant of Police. The performance takes a little while to warm up: Sargent's accompaniment to the Pirate King's song is altogether too flaccid. Elsie Morison is a less than ideal Mabel: her opening cadenza of *Poor wandering one* is angular and over-dramatic. However, elsewhere she is much more convincing, especially in the famous duet, *Leave me not to pine alone*. The choral contributions are pleasingly refined, yet have no lack of vigour. *Hail poetry* is resplendent, while the choral finale is managed with poise and a balance which allows the inner parts to emerge pleasingly. The CDs include some overtures as fillers on the second disc, including *In Memoriam*, a somewhat inflated religious piece written for the 1866 Norwich Festival.

Ruddigore (complete recording of original score, without dialogue).
*** That's Entertainment CDTER2 1128 [MCA MCAD2 11010]. Hill Smith, Sandison, Davies, Ayldon, Hillman, Innocent, Hann, Ormiston, Lawlor, New Sadler's Wells Op. Ch. & O, Simon Phipps.

What is exciting about the New Sadler's Wells production of *Ruddigore* is that it includes the original finale, created by the logic of Gilbert's plot which brought *all* the ghosts back to life, rather than just the key figure. The opera is strongly cast, with Marilyn Hill Smith and David Hillman in the principal roles and Joan Davies a splendid Dame Hannah, while Harold Innocent as Sir Despard and Linda Ormiston as Mad Margaret almost steal the show. Simon Phipps conducts brightly and keeps everything moving forward, even if his pacing is not always as assured as in the classic Sargent version. The recording is first class, with fine theatrical atmosphere.

(i) *Ruddigore* (complete, without dialogue); (ii) *The Merchant of Venice* (suite); *The Tempest* (incidental music).

*** EMI CDS7 47787-8 (2). (i) Lewis, G. Baker, Brannigan, Blackburn, Morison, Bowden, M. Sinclair, Harwood, Rouleau, Glyndebourne Fest. Ch., Pro Arte O, Sargent; (ii) CBSO, Dunn.

Sargent's essentially lyrical approach emphasizes the associations this lovely score so often finds with the music of Schubert. The performance is beautifully sung and the excellence is uniform. Perhaps George Baker sounds a little old in voice for Robin Oakapple, but he manages his 'character transformation' later in the opera splendidly. Pamela Bowden is a first-class Mad Margaret, and her short Donizettian scena is superbly done. Equally Richard Lewis is an admirably bumptious Richard. Perhaps, surprisingly, Owen Brannigan does not make quite as much of the *Ghosts' high noon* song as Donald Adams on the D'Oyly Carte set, but his delicious Act II duet with Mad Margaret has an irresistible gentility. The drama of the score is well managed too: the scene in the picture gallery (given a touch of added resonance by the recording) is effectively sombre. A superb reissue, sounding splendid on CD, which brings some interesting bonuses.

The suite of incidental music for *The Tempest* displays plenty of flair and orchestral confidence. The *Banquet dance* is charmingly scored and the *Dance of the Nymphs and Shepherds* is already anticipating *Iolanthe*. The shorter *Merchant of Venice* suite begins to anticipate the lively style which was so soon to find a happy marriage with Gilbert's words. The performance here is highly infectious, and the sound is first class, bright yet with plenty of depth and a spacious ambience.

The Yeomen of the Guard (complete, without dialogue).
*** EMI CDS7 47781-2 (2) [Ang. CDCB 47781]. Dowling, Lewis, Evans, Brannigan, Morison, M. Sinclair, Glyndebourne Fest. Ch., Pro Arte O, Sargent.

(i) *The Yeomen of the Guard* (complete, without dialogue); (ii) *Trial by Jury*.
*** Decca 417 358-2 [id.]. Hood, J. Reed, Sandford, Adams, Raffell; (i) Harwood, Knight; (ii) Round; D'Oyly Carte Op. Ch.; (i) RPO, Sargent; (ii) ROHCG O, Godfrey.

Sir Malcolm Sargent recorded *The Yeomen of the Guard* in stereo twice very successfully. The later Decca set has marginally the finer recording and Sir Malcolm's breadth of approach is at once apparent in the overture, and when the chorus enters (*Tower warders*) the feeling of opera rather than operetta is striking. Indeed one has seldom heard the choruses expand with such power, nor indeed has the orchestra (especially the brass) produced such a regal sound. As the work proceeds the essential lyricism of Sargent's reading begins to emerge more and more, and the ensemble singing is especially lovely. There is no lack of drama either, and indeed the only aspect of the work to be played down somewhat is the humorous side. The pathos of the famous Jester's song in Act II is played up, and the only moment to raise a real smile is the duet which follows, *Tell a tale of cock and bull.* But with consistently fine singing throughout from all the principals (and especially Elizabeth Harwood as Elsie), this *Yeomen* is unreservedly a success with its brilliant and atmospheric Decca recording. The CD transfer has splendid presence and immediacy.

The singing on Sargent's EMI recording (which dates from 1960) is very persuasive. As on his Decca set, the trios and quartets with which this score abounds are most beautifully performed and skilfully balanced, and the ear is continually beguiled. Owen Brannigan's portrayal of Wilfred is splendidly larger than life and Monica Sinclair is a memorable Dame Carruthers. The finales to both Acts have striking breadth, and the delightfully sung trio of Elsie, Phoebe and the Dame in the finale of Act II is a good example of the many individual felicities of this set. *Strange adventure*, too, is most beautifully done. As in the Decca recording, there is very little feeling of humour, but the music triumphs. The sound is excellent, with the CDs bringing greater presence and definition. However, the Decca set also includes Godfrey's immaculately stylish and affectionate *Trial by Jury* with John Reed as the Judge.

'The best of Gilbert & Sullivan': excerpts from: *The Gondoliers; HMS Pinafore; Iolanthe; The Mikado; The Pirates of Penzance.*
(B) *** EMI CDZ7 62531-2. Morison, Graham, Sinclair, Marjorie Thomas, Lewis, Young, George Baker, Cameron, Brannigan, Sir Geraint Evans, Milligan, Wallace, Glyndebourne Fest. Ch., Pro Arte O, Sargent.

With a maximum amount of music included, this makes a fine bargain sampler of Sargent's G & S series. The longest selection comes from *The Mikado* (with nine items included), not the strongest of the performances but with many felicities. The slow tempo for the *Cachucha* remains a curious drawback in the excerpts from *The Gondoliers*; but the items from *Iolanthe*, *The Pirates* and *Pinafore* have plenty of zest, and the lyrical singing is a pleasure throughout when the cast is so strong. The transfers are fresh and clear, with an abundance of ambience.

'A Gilbert & Sullivan Gala': Arias, duets and trios from: *The Gondoliers; The Grand Duke; Haddon Hall; HMS Pinafore; Iolanthe; The Mikado; Patience; The Pirates of Penzance; Ruddigore; The Sorcerer; The Yeomen of the Guard.*
*** EMI Dig. CDC7 47763-2. Masterson, Armstrong, Tear, Luxon, Bournemouth Sinf., Alwyn, or N. Sinfonia, Hickox.

This superb collection combines the best part of two recitals of G & S, the first made by Valerie Masterson and Robert Tear with Kenneth Alwyn in 1982, and the second with Sheila Armstrong, Tear and Benjamin Luxon under the direction of Richard Hickox in 1984. The result is one of the most successful anthologies of this repertoire ever put on disc. Quite apart from the excellence of the singing and the sparkling accompaniments, the programme is notable for the clever choice of material, with items from different operas engagingly juxtaposed instead of being just gathered together in sequence. The singing from the first group is particularly fine. Valerie Masterson's upper range is ravishingly fresh and free, and she sings Yum-Yum's famous song from *The Mikado*, *The sun, whose rays*, with a captivating, ingenuous charm. Robert Tear is also in excellent form and his *A wandering minstrel* is wonderfully stylish, while *A magnet hung in a hardware shop* has fine sparkle. The *Prithee, pretty maiden* duet (also from *Patience*) is hardly less endearing. In the second recital it is the ensemble items that score, notably the duets from *Ruddigore*, *The Gondoliers* and the vivacious *Hereupon we're both agreed* from *The Yeomen of the Guard*; the star here is Benjamin Luxon. He is splendid in the principal novelty, *I've heard it said*, from *Haddon Hall*, and he is left to end the concert superbly with a bravura account of *My name is John Wellington Wells* from *The Sorcerer*, and a splendidly timed, beguilingly relaxed account of *When you find you're a broken-down critter* from *The Grand Duke*, in which Richard Hickox and the Northern Sinfonia make the very most of Sullivan's witty orchestral comments.

Suppé, Franz von (1819–95)

Overtures: *Beautiful Galathea; Boccaccio; Light Cavalry; Morning, noon and night in Vienna; Pique dame; Poet and peasant.*

(M) **(*) Ph. 420 892-2 [id.]. LPO, Marriner.

An amiably elegant collection of Suppé overtures from Marriner. Other versions of *Light Cavalry* are rhythmically more exhilarating (and more polished), while the opening of *Poet and peasant* is a shade too broad. But *Beautiful Galathea* and *Boccaccio* are stylishly done and there is no lack of energy elsewhere. The remastering has freshened the sound attractively.

Overtures: *Beautiful Galathea; Fatinitza; Flotte Bursche; Jolly robbers; Light Cavalry; Morning, noon and night in Vienna; Pique dame; Poet and peasant. March: O du mein Österreich.*
(BB) **(*) LaserLight Dig. 15 611 [id.]. Hungarian State Op. O, János Sándor.

Sándor's LaserLight collection is most generous of all and the Hungarian State Opera Orchestra know just how to play this repertoire: the zigeuner section in the middle of *Light Cavalry* is most winning, while the cello solo in *Morning, noon and night* has an attractive, romantic simplicity. There is plenty of sparkle, and if the playing has not quite the final polish of the RPO the smaller group of first violins ensures that the ensemble is clean and agile in the music's racier moments. Sándor duplicates Dutoit's programme and offers two extra novelties in *Flott Bursche* (which brings an amiable quotation of *Gaudeamus igitur*) and a vivid Viennese-style march. The digital recording is basically full-bodied but has brilliance too, and this is a real bargain.

Overtures: *Beautiful Galathea; Fatinitza; Jolly robbers; Light cavalry; Morning, noon and night in Vienna; Pique dame; Poet and peasant.*
*** Decca Dig. 414 408-2 [id.]. Montreal SO, Dutoit.

Dutoit's pacing is splendid, combining warmth and geniality with brilliance and wit, as in the closing *galop* of *Fatinitza*. The orchestral playing is admirably polished, the violins sounding comfortable even in the virtuoso passages of *Light cavalry*, one of the most infectious of the performances here. It is difficult to imagine these being bettered, while the Decca sound is superb, well up to the usual Montreal standards.

Overtures: *Beautiful Galathea; Jolly robbers; Light cavalry; Morning, noon and night in Vienna; Pique dame; Poet and peasant.*
*** RCA Eurodisc RD 69037. RPO, Gustav Kuhn.

Kuhn's performances are like no others. He takes this music very seriously indeed, lavishing care over every detail. Tempi are spacious, consistently slower than normal, but the effect is not to rob the music of vitality, merely to add to its stature. In the lyrical sections he conjures the most beautiful, expansive playing from the RPO, yet he can be racy in the galops, while not rushing the music off its feet. *Beautiful Galathea* is a striking example of this approach, with the gentle waltz theme played with great elegance, yet retaining its light, rhythmic lilt. *Morning, noon and night* is superb and the opening of *Poet and peasant* sounds wonderfully rich and sonorous, and it has a remarkable dignity too. It is a pity that the programme is not generous, but this disc makes up in quality for anything it may lack in quantity. The richly upholstered recording, made in St Barnabas' Church, London, seems exactly right for the music-making.

Overtures: *Light cavalry; Morning, noon and night in Vienna; Poet and peasant.*
(*) DG 415 377-2 [id.]. BPO, Karajan – ROSSINI: *Overtures.*(*)

Karajan's performances are taken from a 1970 collection and are coupled with four

Rossini overtures. The playing is swaggeringly brilliant, but the sound is just a little fierce at fortissimo level, although the overall balance is warm and natural.

Svendsen, Johan Severin (1840–1911)

Symphonies Nos. 1 in D, Op. 4; 2 in B flat, Op. 15.
*** EMI Dig. CDC7 49769-2 [id.]. Oslo PO, Mariss Jansons.

Symphonies Nos. 1–2; 2 Swedish folk-melodies, Op. 27.
*** BIS Dig. CD 347 [id.]. Gothenburg SO, Neeme Järvi.

Svendsen excelled (where Grieg did not) in the larger forms and, as befits a conductor, was a master of the orchestra. Listening to the two symphonies, one can't help feeling regret that his creative fires burned themselves out and that, after the famous *Romance* for violin and orchestra, he became what we would call nowadays a 'star' conductor. The *D major Symphony* is a student work of astonishing assurance and freshness, in some ways even more remarkable than the *B flat*. Neeme Järvi is a splendid guide to this terrain; these are first-class performances, sensitive and vital, and the excellent recordings earn them a strong recommendation.

The performances from Mariss Jansons and the Oslo Philharmonic are also distinguished by first-rate ensemble, alert rhythms and keenly articulated phrasing. They have much the same enthusiasm and relish as their Gothenburg rivals, who offer a bonus in the form of a transcription for strings of two *Swedish folk-melodies*. But though there is not much to choose between the two recordings, the Oslo orchestra has the richer sonority.

Sweelinck, Jan (1562–1621)

Ballo del Granduca; Echo fantasia; Engelsche Fortuyn; Puer nobis nascitur.
*** Chan. Dig. CHAN 0514 [id.]. Piet Klee (organ of St Laurens Church, Alkmaar) –
BUXTEHUDE: *Collection.****

It is fascinating to have Sweelinck's music, played on a superb Dutch organ, juxtaposed with that of Buxtehude, who was born sixteen years after Sweelinck died and was a direct onward link with Bach. Sweelinck lived during the Dutch Golden Age and was a contemporary of Rembrandt. His music is colourful and appealing, and it could hardly be better represented than in this engaging 'suite' of four contrasted pieces, three of which are based on melodies by others. The first as played here derives from an English ballad, *Fortune my foe*, and will sound familiar to many ears. Piet Klee is a very sympathetic advocate and he is given a recording of demonstration standard.

Szymanowski, Karol (1882–1937)

(i) *Violin concertos Nos. 1, Op. 35; 2, Op. 61;* (ii) *Violin sonata in D min., Op. 9; King Roger: Roxana's song.*
** Polskie Nagrana PNCD 064 [id.]. Wanda Wilkomirska, (i) Warsaw Nat. PO, Rowicki;
(ii) Tadeusz Chmielewski.

It is good to see the long-overdue resurgence of interest in Poland's greatest twentieth-century composer. The *Violin concertos* are Szymanowski at his finest. No. 1 is arguably his masterpiece: it comes from 1917, the vintage year which saw the *Third Symphony* and *Masques*, and creates a sound-world all its own. There is an exotic luxuriance, a sense of ecstasy and longing, a heightened awareness of colour and glowing, luminous textures. It is as if one were perceiving the world in a dreamlike state which, while it lasts, seems more vivid than the reality of everyday life. Wilkomirska's record comes from the early 1960s, but at present there is no CD alternative. Her performances are excellent and, though both scores cry out for the most opulent recorded sound, the performances could not be more idiomatic.

Symphonies Nos. 2, Op. 19; (i) *3 (Song of the night), Op. 27.*
(M) *** Decca Dig. 425 625-2 [id.]. (i) Ryszard Karczykowski, Jewell Ch.; Detroit SO, Dorati (with BARTÓK: *2 Pictures****).

This 1980 Decca coupling was the first Western commercial recording of either of these symphonies. The *Second* is not as rewarding a score as the *Third*, but it is unusual formally: there are only two movements, the second being a set of variations culminating in a fugue. The influences of Strauss and Scriabin are clearly audible and not altogether assimilated. *The Song of the night* is one of the composer's most beautiful scores, and much of its heady, intoxicated – and intoxicating – atmosphere is captured here, together with its extraordinarily vivid colouring and sense of rapture; the detail and opulence of the orchestral textures are fully revealed and the chorus is clear and well balanced. A most valuable reissue, and the Bartók coupling is apt, though here the recording has an analogue master.

Symphonies Nos. 2 in B flat, Op. 19; (i) *4 (Sinfonia concertante), Op. 60; Concert overture in E, Op. 12.*
Polskie Nagrana PNCD 062 [id.]. Warsaw Nat. PO, Rowicki; (i) with Zmudzinski.

The early *Concert overture* proclaims its allegiance to Richard Strauss, and Reger is clearly a model in the *Second Symphony*, but both fill in our picture of his growth. Tadeusz Zmudzinski is a capable player who makes the most of the intractable but haunting *Sinfonia concertante*, but the 1977 recording is constricted (the 1980 account of the *Concert overture* is worse). Definitely not recommended.

Symphony No. 3 (Song of the Night), Op. 27; Demeter, Op. 37 bis; Litany to the Virgin Mary, Op. 59; Stabat mater, Op. 53.
*(*) Polskie Nagrana PNCD 063 [id.]. Woytowicz, Szeczepanska, Hiolski, Szostek-Radkowa, Warsaw Nat. PO Ch. & O; or Polish R. Ch. & SO, Rowicki.

In the *Third Symphony* the late Witold Rowicki brought a sense of vision and a hallucinatory ecstasy which transcend the undoubted sonic limitations. By its side, Dorati's version has a less heady atmosphere, but the Decca recording is far finer and much more agreeable to listen to. Stefania Woytowicz is quite ethereal in the *Stabat mater*, surely one of the great choral works of the century; but the sound leaves a good deal to be desired, even though the CD transfer improves detail.

(i) *Symphony No. 3 (Song of the Night);* (ii) *Symphony No. 4 (Sinfonia concertante); Concert overture.*
**(*) Marco Polo Dig. 8.223290 [id.]. (i) Ochman, Polish State Philharmonic Ch.; (ii) Tadeusz Zmudzinski, Katowice Polish State PO, Karol Stryja.

The Marco Polo version of the *Third Symphony* (but not the *Fourth*) has the advantage of good, well-detailed sound in a resonant hall. The recordings are very recent (1988–9) and Karol Stryja succeeds in getting plenty of atmosphere in No. 3 (not as much as Rowicki but more than Dorati). He, too, uses a tenor rather than a soprano, but his choir is not first class. The *Sinfonia concertante* is not ideally balanced as a recording (the acoustic is too reverberant and the image is not always well focused) but the pianist,

Taduesz Zmudzinski, is at least not too forward and he plays with refinement and sensitivity, as witness the opening of the *Andante*, which is quite magical. This is the best stereo *Sinfonia concertante* to date. The Straussian *Concert overture* makes a useful makeweight, though the recording is over-resonant and the balance synthetic.

String quartets Nos. 1 in C, Op. 37; 2, Op. 56.
*** Olympia OCD 328 [id.]. Varsovia Qt – LUTOSLAWSKI: *Quartet*; PENDERECKI: *Quartet No. 2.****

The *First Quartet* is a beautifully wrought three-movement piece. It has a great deal of exposed and demanding writing, which the Varsovia Quartet play with impeccable intonation and splendid sonority. Theirs is a subtle and deeply felt performance, and the same must be said of their account of No. 2. Again the heady perfume and exotic luxuriance of the *Third Symphony* and the two *Violin concertos* can be discerned in this more monochrome medium; however, the finale has slight overtones of Bartók. There are glorious things in both works, and the Varsovia play marvellously throughout.

(i) *Étude in B flat min., Op. 4/3;* (ii) *Masques, Op. 34;* (iii) *Mazurkas, Op. 50/1, 2, 4, 7, 13, 15, 18–20;* (ii) *Piano sonata No. 2 in A, Op. 21.*
(*) Polski Nagrana PNCD 066 [id.]. (i) Malcuzynski; (ii) Stefański; (iii) Hesse-Bukowska.

Andrzej Stefański is recorded dryly in the astonishing *Masques*, which does not do full justice to the extraordinary refinement of dynamics this score calls for. He copes well with the impossible demands of the *Sonata*, but the recording is pretty grim. Barbara Hesse-Bukowska conveys the strange, elusive quality of the late *Mazurkas*, but again the recording needs to be more of an improvement on the 1968 original. At present there is no better alternative.

Songs

(i) *3 Fragments of the poems by Jan Kasprowicz, Op. 5;* (ii) *Love songs of Hafiz, Op. 24;* (iii) *Songs of the fairy-tale princess, Op. 31;* (iv) *Songs of the infatuated muezzin, Op. 42.*
*** Schwann Dig. CD 314 001 [id.]. (i) Krystyna Szostek-Radkova; (ii) Krystyna Rorbach; (iii) Izabella Klosińska; (iv) Barbara Zagórzanka, Polish Nat. Op. O, Satanowski.

Szymanowski's vocal output has been virtually ignored until quite recently. It is really well worth taking the trouble to explore it. The Schwann and Marco Polo discs have the advantage of presenting these songs in their orchestral form. In the *Songs of the fairy-tale princess*, one feels that Szymanowski must have known Stravinsky's *Le Rossignol* – Izabella Klosińska certainly sings like one. All the singing is very good, but Barbara Zagórzanka in the imaginative *Songs of the infatuated muezzin* deserves special mention. Satanowski achieves marvellously exotic and heady atmosphere throughout, and the recording is excellent.

(i) *3 Fragments of the poems by Jan Kasprowicz, Op. 5;* (ii) *Love songs of Hafiz, Op. 24;* (iii) *Songs of the fairy-tale princess, Op. 31;* (iv) *Songs of the infatuated muezzin, Op. 42;* (v) *King Roger: Roxana's Song.*
**(*) Marco Polo Dig. 8.223294. (i) Anna Málewicz-Madej; (ii & iv) Ryszard Minkiewicz; (iii) Jadwiga Gadulanka; (v) Barbara Zagórzanka; Katowice Polish State PO, Karol Stryja.

On Marco Polo, both the *Songs of the infatuated muezzin* and the *Love songs of Hafiz* are sung by a tenor (Ryszard Minkiewicz) with impressive insight, but the 1989 recording is more resonant and does not flatter him. Jadwiga Gadulanka is hardly less impressive than Klosińska in the extraordinary *Songs of the fairy-tale princess* and one would be hard put to choose between them. What fantastic pieces they are, and how well Stryja and the Katowice orchestra support her. Barbara Zagórzanka sings the famous *Chant de Roxane* beautifully, and both she and Anna Málewicz-Madej in the Kasprowicz songs are very well balanced.

(i) *3 Fragments of the poems by Jan Kasprowicz, Op. 5;* (ii) *5 Songs, Op. 13: Zuleika. Love songs of Hafiz, Op. 24;* (iii) *Songs of the fairy-tale princess, Op. 31;* (iv) *Songs to the words of James Joyce, Op. 54.*
* Polski Nagrania PNCD 067 [id.]. (i) Zylis-Gara; (ii) Lukomska; (iii) Gadulanka; (iv) Bachlada; (i–iii) Marchwinski (pf), (iv) Sulikowski.

The Polski Nagrania CD offers recordings from 1971–8 and all the songs are with piano accompaniment. Teresa Zylis-Gara gives an expressive account of the early Kasprowicz songs and is quite well recorded, but Andrzej Bachlada in the late Joyce settings is not (the acoustic is dry), and he suffers from an unacceptably wide vibrato. Jadwiga Gadulanka sings the high-lying Op. 31 songs with memorable purity and Halina Lukomska gives a lovely account of the Hafiz songs. But the acoustic is distinctly unglamorous and, generally speaking, the sound-quality ranges from undistinguished to very indifferent.

(i) *Mythes, Op. 30;* (ii) *Cradle song, Op. 52; Harnasie, Op. 55: Dance. Kurpian song; Nocturne & tarantella, Op. 28; Romance in D, Op. 23;* (iii) *String quartet No. 2, Op. 56.*
Polski Nagrana PNCD 065 [id.]. (i) Kulka, Marchwińska; (ii) Wilkomirska, Chmielewski; (iii) Wilanów Qt.

The beautiful *Mythes* (which starts with *The Fountain of Arethusa)* are a write-off. The mysterious pianissimo piano accompaniment is up-front and much too loud. The balance in the *Nocturne and Tarantella* is also pretty awful. A pity, because the performances are good; but the disc might be worth considering for the lovely *Second Quartet* (the cover calls it No. 3) which is well played by the Wilanów Quartet (now known as the Varsovia), but again the recording has too little air round the sound.

Tallis, Thomas (c. 1505–85)

Absterge Domine; Candidid facti sunt; Nazareri; Derelinquat impius; Dum transsiset sabbatum; Gaude gloriosa Dei Mater; Magnificat and Nunc dimittis; Salvator mundi.
*** CRD CRD 3429 [id.]. New College, Oxford, Ch., Higginbottom.

The performances by the Choir of New College, Oxford – recorded in the splendid acoustic of the College Chapel – are eminently well prepared, with good internal balance, excellent intonation, ensemble and phrasing. The *Gaude gloriosa* is one of Tallis's most powerful and eloquent works. It has been suggested that it was intended to glorify Queen Mary as well as the Virgin Mary. An invaluable addition to the Tallis discography, and excellently recorded.

Audivi vocem de celo a 4; Candidi facti sunt Nazarei eius a 5; Dum transisset sabbatum a 5; Hodie nobis celorum rex a 4; Homo quidam fecit cenam magnam a 6; Honor, virtus et potestas a 5; In pace in idipsum a 4; Loquebantur variis linguis a 7; Spem in alium a 40; Videte miraculum a 6.
*** EMI Dig. CDC7 49555-2 [id.]. Taverner Ch. and Cons., Andrew Parrott.

Gaude gloriosa Dei Mater a 6; In jejunio et fletu a 5; Lamentations of Jeremiah I and II a 5; Miserere nostri a 7; O nata lux de lumine a 5; O sacrum convivium a 5; Salvator mundi I

and II a 5; Suscipe, quaeso Domine a 7; Te lucis ante terminum (Procol recedant somnia) I a 5.
*** EMI Dig. CDC7 49563-2 [id.]. Taverner Ch. and Cons., Andrew Parrott.

Parrott's two discs of the Latin church music of Tallis are warmly recommendable, a superb collection. The Taverner style is brighter and more abrasive than we are used to in this often ethereal music, but, quite apart from the scholarly justification, the polyphonic cohesion of the writing comes out the more tellingly. The first of the two discs is the obvious one to investigate initially, containing as it does Tallis's most elaborate and most celebrated choral-piece, the 40-part motet, *Spem in alium*, as well as *Videte miraculum* and *Dum transisset sabbatum* – almost as extended in argument. The second of the two discs has the two magnificent *Lamentations of Jeremiah*, as well as an even more expansive motet which Tallis wrote early in his career, *Gaude gloriosa Dei Mater*.

Anthems: *Blessed are those that be undefiled; Christ, rising again; Hear the voice and prayer; If ye love me; A new commandment; O Lord, in Thee is all my trust; O Lord, give thy holy spirit; Out from the deep; Purge me; Remember not, O Lord God; Verily, verily I say: 9 Psalm Tunes for Archbishop Parker's Psalter.*
*** Gimell Dig. CDGIM 007 [id.]. Tallis Scholars, Phillips.

This disc collects the complete English anthems of Tallis and is thus a valuable complement to the discs listed above. Here, of course, women's voices are used instead of boys', but the purity of the sound they produce is not in question, and the performances could hardly be more committed or more totally inside this repertoire. Strongly recommended.

Gaude gloriosa; Loquebantur variis linguis; Miserere nostri; Salvator mundi, salva nos, I and II; Sancte Deus; Spem in alium (40-part motet).
⊛ *** Gimell CDGIM 006 [id.]. Tallis Scholars, Phillips.

Within the admirably suitable acoustics of Merton College Chapel, Oxford, the Tallis Scholars give a thrilling account of the famous 40-part motet, *Spem in alium*, in which the astonishingly complex polyphony is spaciously separated over a number of point sources, yet blending as a satisfying whole to reach a massive climax. The *Gaude gloriosa* is another much recorded piece, while the soaring *Sancte Deus* and the two very contrasted settings of the *Salvator mundi* are hardly less beautiful. The vocal line is beautifully shaped throughout, the singing combines ardour with serenity, and the breadth and depth of the sound is spectacular.

The Lamentations of Jeremiah the Prophet; Spem in alium (40-part motet).
(B) ** Pickwick Dig. PCD 806 [MCA MCAD 25847]. Pro Cantione Antiqua, Mark Brown – ALLEGRI: *Miserere.***

On Pickwick, a strong, generally well-sung performance (although there are moments in the motet when intonation is not absolutely secure). The microphone balance brings a thickening of tone to the expansive climax of *Spem in alium* and less than ideal transparency of texture. But this CD comes at bargain price and may be counted good value.

Taneyev, Sergei (1856–1915)

Symphonies Nos (i) *2 in B flat;* (ii) *4 in C min., Op. 14.*
(M) *(**) Chant du Monde LCD 278 931. USSR RSO, (i) Fedoseyev; (ii) Rozhdestvensky.

Taneyev was a composer of wide-ranging talents whose creative achievements were to some extent overshadowed by his prodigious pianistic talents – he gave the first performance of Tchaikovsky's *First Concerto* – as well as his academic attainments. He was made a professor at the Moscow Conservatoire in his twenties and his pupils included Scriabin, Medtner, Rachmaninov and Glière. However, his symphonies are of uneven appeal. The unfinished *Second*, orchestrated by a Soviet musicologist, Vladimir Blok, even with only three movements is too long for its material and is heavily laden with academic devices. The *Fourth* has a linking theme, which opens the first movement and appears in the others, and is altogether more coherent; its *Andante* has undoubted eloquence and the scherzo has something of Glazunov in its scoring, plus an anticipation of Rachmaninov in its lyrical contrasts. Both performances have great commitment and fervour; no one could fail to respond to the passion of Rozhdestvensky and his players in the C minor work, even if sometimes the orchestral sounds are unrefined (notably the trombones). The recording is immensely vivid, although it is overlit and has moments of coarseness.

Piano quartet in E, Op. 20.
**(*) Pro Arte Dig. CDD 301 [id.]. Cantilena Chamber Players.

The *Piano quartet* is a finely wrought and often subtle work. Its language is closer to that of Brahms or Fauré than to the Russians, though Taneyev's piano writing is highly original. What a superbly sensitive pianist the Cantilena Chamber Players have in the person of Frank Glazer! The performance is altogether first rate, though the acoustic in which it is recorded is not quite big enough.

Piano quintet in G min., Op. 30.
*** Ara. Dig. Z 6539 [id.]. Jerome Lowenthal, Rosenthal, Kamei, Thompson, Kates.

The *Piano quintet* is a powerfully made and ambitious score running to nearly 43 minutes. Not only is it well structured and its motivic organization subtle, its melodic ideas are strong and individual. It is arguably the greatest Russian chamber work between Tchaikovsky and Shostakovich. The recording is not in the demonstration bracket, but it is very good; and the playing, particularly of the pianist Jerome Lowenthal, is excellent. Strongly recommended.

Piano trio in D, Op. 22.
*** Chan. Dig. CHAN 8592 [id.]. Borodin Trio.

This *Trio* is a big, four-movement work: the first is in the usual sonata form, though Taneyev restates the themes in reverse order in the recapitulation; the second is a scherzo which also includes a set of variations; then an *Andante espressivo* leads into the finale. The invention is attractive – and so, too, is the excellent performance and recording. Strongly recommended.

String quartets Nos. 8 in C; 9 in A.
**(*) Olympia OCD 128 [id.]. Leningrad Taneyev Qt.

Both these *Quartets* are large-scale works in the classical mould, and both are beautifully crafted, though they are not strongly personal. The minuet of No. 8 and the scherzo of No. 9 are highly attractive. They are well played, though the violin tone above the stave has a tendency to harden.

String quintet in D, Op. 14.
* Olympia OCD 138 [id.]. Leningrad Taneyev Qt with Benjamin Morozow –
BORODIN: *String quartet No. 2.******

This *String quintet* reveals a strong and resourceful musical mind. It is beautifully proportioned, in three movements, the last of which is a theme and variations. (One of them is quite magical and has enormous delicacy and atmosphere.) The performance by the eponymous quartet and the cellist, Benjamin Morozow, is extremely fine and so, too, is the recording. A rewarding disc.

The Oresteia (opera): complete.
*(*) Olympia OCD 195 A/B [id.]. Chernobayev, Galushkina, Bukov, Dubrovin, Belorussian State Ch. & O, Kolomizheva.

Taneyev's reputation as an academic must be reassessed in the light of this piece, for this is not only a finely wrought work; it is full of imaginative touches and effective musical drama. Rimsky-Korsakov spoke of its 'pages of unusual beauty and expressiveness'. This performance, recorded in 1978, was briefly available on DG in a rather smoother transfer than on these Olympia CDs, vivid though they are. There are some splendid singers. There is a tendency for the sound to coarsen on climaxes, though some of the blame for this must be laid at the feet of the orchestra. A most worthwhile issue.

Tarrega, Francisco (1852–1909)

Music for guitar: *Adelita; La Cartagenera; Columpio; Danza mora; Endecha; Estudio de velocidad; Estudio en forma de minuetto; Jota; Lagrima; La Mariposa; Minuetto; Oremus; Pavana; Preludio in G; Recuerdos de la Alhambra; Sueno.*
* DG Dig. 410 655-2 [id.]. Narciso Yepes.

Although much of Tarrega's music is slight, he was a key figure in the movement to restore the guitar to its rightful place as a concert instrument, and stands as the link between Sor and the composers of the early part of our own century. Narciso Yepes made a special study of Tarrega's manuscripts (there is more than one version of each piece) and plays them very persuasively. The recording has fine definition on CD.

Tartini, Giuseppe (1692–1770)

Concertino for clarinet (arr. Jacob).
* ASV Dig. CDDCA 585 [id.]. Emma Johnson, ECO, Yan Pascal Tortelier – CRUSELL: *Introduction, theme and variations*; DEBUSSY: *Rapsodie*; WEBER: *Concerto No. 1.******

Gordon Jacob's arrangement of sonata movements by Tartini as a brief, four-movement *Clarinet concerto* is a delightful oddity. Inevitably it seems strange to have such baroque ideas associated with clarinet tone; but, with sprightly, characterful playing, it is an attractive and unusual makeweight in Emma Johnson's mixed collection of concertante pieces, well recorded.

Cello concerto in A.
(M) ***** DG 429 098-2 [id.]. Rostropovich, Zurich Coll. Mus., Sacher – BOCCHERINI; VIVALDI: *Concertos.*

As with the other works in this fine 1978 collection, Rostropovich's view of Tartini's *A major Concerto* is larger than life; but the eloquence of the playing disarms criticism, even when the cellist plays cadenzas of his own that are not exactly in period. The lively accompaniment is matched by bright, vivid recording that sounds splendid on CD.

Tavener, John (born 1944)

Funeral Ikos; Ikon of Light; Carol: The Lamb.
*** Gimell CDGIM 005 [id.]. Tallis Scholars, Chilingirian Qt, Phillips.

Both the major works on the disc, *Funeral Ikos* and *Ikon of Light*, represent Tavener's more recent style at its most compelling, simple and consonant to the point of bareness but with sensuous overtones. *Ikon of Light* is a setting of Greek mystical texts, with chant-like phrases repeated hypnotically. The string trio provides the necessary textural variety. More concentrated is *Funeral Ikos*, an English setting of the Greek funeral sentences, often yearningly beautiful. Both in these and in the brief setting of Blake's *The Lamb*, the Tallis Scholars give immaculate performances, atmospherically recorded in the chapel of Merton College, Oxford.

Taverner, John (c. 1495–1545)

Missa gloria tibi Trinitas.
**(*) EMI CDC7 49103-2. Taverner Ch., Andrew Parrott.

Missa gloria tibi Trinitas; Audivi vocem (responsory); ANON.: *Gloria tibi Trinitas.*
*** Hyp. CDA 66134 [id.]. The Sixteen, Harry Christophers.

Missa gloria tibi Trinitas; Dum transisset sabbatum; Kyrie a 4 (Leroy).
*** Gimell Dig. CDGIM 004 [id.]. Tallis Scholars, Phillips.

This six-voice setting of the Mass is richly varied in its invention (not least in rhythm) and expressive in a deeply personal way very rare for its period. Harry Christophers and The Sixteen underline the beauty with an exceptionally pure and clear account, superbly recorded and made the more brilliant by having the pitch a minor third higher than modern concert pitch.

Peter Phillips and the Tallis Scholars give an intensely involving performance of this glorious example of Tudor music. The recording may not be as clear as on the rival Hyperion version, but Phillips rejects all idea of reserve or cautiousness of expression; the result reflects the emotional basis of the inspiration the more compellingly. The motet, *Dum transisset sabbatum*, is then presented more reflectively, another rich inspiration.

Parrott performs the *Mass* at only a semitone above modern pitch. He argues that falsettists were not used and opts for tenors, where both of his rivals have used male altos. The acoustic is drier and, though there is much fine musicianship in evidence and well-balanced recording, the Tallis Scholars have greater fervour. The *Mass* is performed within the framework of the plainchant for High Mass on Trinity Sunday.

Tchaikovsky, Peter (1840–93)

Andante cantabile, Op. 11; Nocturne, Op. 19/4; Pezzo capriccioso, Op. 62 (1887 version); *2 Songs: Legend; Was I not a little blade of grass; Variations on a rococo theme, Op. 33* (1876 version).
*** Chan. Dig. CHAN 8347 [id.]. Wallfisch, ECO, Simon.

This delightful record gathers together all of Tchaikovsky's music for cello and orchestra – including his arrangements of such items as the famous *Andante cantabile* and two songs. The major item is the original version of the *Rococo variations* with an extra variation and the earlier variations put in a more effective order, as Tchaikovsky wanted. Geoffrey Simon draws lively and sympathetic playing from the ECO, with Wallfisch a vital if not quite flawless soloist. Excellent recording, with the CD providing fine presence and an excellent perspective.

Capriccio italien, Op. 45.
(B) *** RCA Dig. VD 87727 [7727-2-RV]. Dallas SO, Mata (with *Concert****).

Capriccio italien, Op. 45; 1812 overture, Op. 49; Francesca da Rimini, Op. 32; Marche slave, Op. 31.
(M) **(*) Ph. 422 469-2 [id.]. Concg. O, Haitink.

Capriccio italien; 1812 overture; Marche slave; Nutcracker suite.
**(*) Decca Dig. 417 300-2 [id.]. Montreal SO, Dutoit.
(M) **(*) DG 423 225-2 [id.]. BPO, Karajan (with Don Cossack Ch.).

Capriccio italien; 1812 overture; Mazeppa: Cossack dance.
** Telarc Dig. CD 80041 [id.]. Cincinnati SO, Kunzel.

Tchaikovsky's *Capriccio italien* was given an extraordinarily successful compact disc début on Mata's Dallas disc. The concert-hall effect of the recording is very impressive indeed, with the opening fanfares as sonically riveting as the silences when the reverberation dies away naturally. The performance is colourful and exciting, and the piece is issued within an attractive compilation of favourite orchestral showpieces (see Concerts section below).

Dutoit's *Capriccio italien* is particularly successful, with even a touch of nostalgia in the string tune that follows the opening fanfare, but there are also high spirits and elegance, and the coda is well prepared and nicely paced. In the *Nutcracker suite* there is almost a chamber-music refinement; the *Waltz of the flowers* is pleasing but rather restrained. *Marche slave* is sombre and dignified, while *1812* (complete with cannon) is exciting without making one sit on the edge of one's chair. The sound is refined and luminous but lacks the sumptuous weight which is needed to give Tchaikovsky's climaxes a physical thrill.

Karajan's *1812 overture* is very professional and quite exciting, although the chorus used to open the piece is not ideally sonorous, and the closing pages have the cannon balanced in a calculated fashion rather than showing a touch of engineering flair. The *Capriccio italien* is played with splendid panache and the *Nutcracker suite* offers similar polish, spick-and-span and vividly coloured; only the *Waltz of the flowers* seems a shade glossy. *Marche slave* has a fine combination of dignity and flair. The remastered recording is brilliant, yet does not lack depth, and the brass fanfares of the *Capriccio* are superbly telling.

Haitink's *Capriccio italien* is warm-blooded, with the string-playing elegantly turned. The restatement of the main theme at the end is given striking weight and thereafter the coda is rather slow in getting under way; but otherwise this is distinctly successful, as is *1812*, which has brilliance and momentum and a touch of dignity at the end, with the bangs well integrated into the orchestral texture. *Francesca da Rimini* is finely played – the central clarinet solo beautifully done – but lacks a sense of high nervous tension in its closing section. The sound is vividly remastered.

If you need a recording of cannon, plus *1812*, and your speakers can accommodate the dynamic range and amplitude, both impressively wide, then the Telarc issue is for you. In the *Capriccio* there are no cannon – so the engineers substitute the bass drum, which is very prominent. The orchestral contribution throughout is lively but not memorable, and the playing simply does not generate enough adrenalin to compensate for the relative lack of projection of the orchestral tone. At the end of *1812*, Tchaikovsky's carefully contrived climax, with its full-blooded scalic descent, seriously lacks weight. The most enjoyable item here is the lively *Cossack dance*.

Capriccio italien, Op. 45; Élégie for strings; Francesca da Rimini, Op. 32; Romeo and Juliet (fantasy overture).
*** Decca Dig. 421 715-2 [id.]. RPO, Ashkenazy.

Capriccio italien is superb, spectacular, elegant and possessed of exhilarating impetus. *Romeo and Juliet* takes a little while to generate its fullest excitement with the love-theme introduced a little coolly, but its climax has great ardour. *Francesca da Rimini* is very exciting too, with much fine wind-playing from the RPO in the lyrical central section. Ashkenazy does not quite match Stokowski in depicting the lovers' frenzied passion, but his demonic closing evocation of the whirlwinds of Hell is overwhelming in impact. Then the programme ends with Tchaikovsky's haunting *Élégie*, a lovely, wistful string melody played with a wonderful feeling of nostalgia. What makes this concert especially successful is the superb recording. It is a real Tchaikovskian sound, as fine as any on record.

Piano concerto No. 1 in B flat min., Op. 23.
⊛ (M) (***) RCA mono GD 87992 [7792-2-RG]. Horowitz, NBC SO, Toscanini – BEETHOVEN: *Piano concerto No. 5*.(***)
*** RCA RD 85912 [RCA 5912-2-RC]. Van Cliburn, RCA SO, Kondrashin – RACHMANINOV: *Concerto No. 2*.***
*** DG 415 062-2 [id.]. Martha Argerich, RPO, Dutoit – PROKOFIEV: *Concerto No. 3*.***
(M) *** Decca 417 750-2 [id.]. Ashkenazy, LSO, Maazel – CHOPIN: *Concerto No. 2*.***
*** Decca 417 555-2 [id.]. Ashkenazy, LSO, Maazel – SCHUMANN: *Concerto*.***
*(**) RCA Dig. RD 89968 [RCA 5708-2-RC]. Barry Douglas, LSO, Slatkin.
(M) *(**) DG Dig. 415 122-2 [id.]. Ivo Pogorelich, LSO, Abbado.
*(**) Ph. Dig. 411 057-2 [id.]. Martha Argerich, Bav. RSO, Kondrashin.
(M) **(*) Decca 417 676-2 [id.]. Curzon, VPO, Solti – GRIEG: *Concerto*.*(**)
** Decca Dig. 417 294-2 [id.]. Schiff, Chicago SO, Solti – DOHNÁNYI: *Variations*.**(*)
* DG Dig. 427 485-2 [id.]. Kissin, BPO, Karajan (with SCRIABIN: *4 Pieces; Étude in C sharp min., Op. 42/5*(**)).

(i) *Piano concerto No. 1 in B flat min., Op. 23. Theme and variations, Op. 19/6.*
(M) **(*) EMI CDM7 69125-2 [id.]. Gavrilov, (i) Philh. O, Muti (with LISZT: *La Campanella*) – BALAKIREV: *Islamey*.***

Horowitz's famous account of the *B flat minor Concerto*, recorded at a concert in Carnegie Hall in 1943 with his father-in-law conducting, has dwarfed every record of the work made since. Somehow the alchemy of the occasion – which raised eleven million dollars in War Bonds! – was unique, and the result is unforgettable. The recording of the orchestra is confined and lacks body, some surface rustle remains from the 78-r.p.m. pressings, while the violins need a judicious degree of filtering, and even then don't sound very rich. But the piano itself is gloriously full and bold. Such is the magnetism of the playing, however, that the ear forgets the sonic limitations within moments. Toscanini's accompaniment is remarkable not only for matching the adrenalin of his soloist but for the tenderness he finds for the lyrical passages of the first movement. The powerful cadenza becomes its climax, wonderfully varied in colour, and with one passage in which there almost seem to be two pianists in duet, rather than just one pair of human hands. Toscanini's moments of delicacy extend to the *Andantino*, which is truly *simplice* (as the composer indicated), even when accompanying the coruscating pianistic fireworks of the central section. The finale carries all before it, with Horowitz's riveting octave passage-work leading on to a tremendously exciting restatement of the big tune and then storming off furiously to the coda. The applause at the end is welcome for once, if only as a release of tension.

The Van Cliburn is also one of the most brilliant recordings of this work ever made. The young American pianist lives up to his reputation as Moscow Prize-winner with playing which has great virtuosity, but much else besides. There is spontaneity and a natural feeling for the phrasing which usually comes only with long experience. Van Cliburn and the Soviet conductor Kondrashin in short give an inspired performance with as much warmth as glitter. The 1958 recording is forward and could do with more atmosphere, but the digital remastering has brought a firmer orchestral image, and the piano timbre is also improved. Coupled with an equally outstanding version of the Rachmaninov *C minor*, this is a very distinguished reissue indeed, even if the piano timbre here is shallower than in the coupling.

Argerich's 1971 recording of the Tchaikovsky *First Piano concerto* with Dutoit remains a strong recommendation. The sound is firm, with excellent presence, and its ambience is more attractive than the later version. The weight of the opening immediately sets the mood for a big, broad performance, with the kind of music-making in which the personalities of both artists are complementary. Argerich's conception encompasses the widest range of tonal shading. In the finale she often produces a scherzando-like effect; then the orchestra thunders in with the Russian dance theme to create a real contrast. The tempo of the first movement is comparatively measured, but satisfyingly so; the slow movement is strikingly atmospheric, yet delicate, its romanticism light-hearted.

Ashkenazy's performance is offered in alternative couplings: the Chopin is the more attractive, being at mid-price. This is not high-powered but it is lyrically satisfying. The soloist refuses to be stampeded by Tchaikovsky's rhetoric, and the biggest climaxes of the first movement are made to grow naturally out of the music. In the *Andantino* too, Ashkenazy refuses to play flashily and he uses the middle section rather as a contrasting episode to set in the boldest relief the delicate return of the opening tune. The finale is very fast and brilliant, yet the big tune is broadened at the end in the most convincing way. The remastering is highly successful: the piano sounds splendidly bold and clear while the orchestral balance is realistic.

Barry Douglas proves an admirable soloist and he provides many imaginative touches, especially in the first-movement cadenzas and the *Andante*, which is beautifully done. Slatkin accompanies capably but the orchestral contribution is altogether more routine, with a rather heavy reprise of the big tune in the finale. The sound is excellent, well balanced and full, with a concert-hall ambience; but until this is coupled with another work it remains uncompetitive.

Gavrilov is stunning in the finale of the *Concerto*; however, the final statement of the big tune is broadened so positively that one is not entirely convinced. Similarly in the first movement, contrasts of dynamic and tempo are extreme, and the element of self-consciousness is apparent. The *Andante* is full of tenderness and the *prestissimo* middle section goes like quicksilver, displaying the vein of spontaneous imagination that we recognize in Gavrilov's other records. The recording is full and sumptuous with a big, bold forward piano-image, so that the work's famous opening makes an immediate impact. In the *Variations*, Opus 19, Tchaikovsky's invention has great felicity. Gavrilov's playing is stylishly sympathetic here and the Liszt *Paganini study*, *La Campanella*, which is his final encore, is dazzling.

The opening of the Pogorelich/Abbado account has an impressive sweep and, provided one accepts the forward balance of the piano, the recording is superbly full-bodied and wide-ranging. The dramatic contrasts of the first movement are thus underlined, with the poetic secondary material beautifully and thoughtfully played by soloist and orchestra alike. But Pogorelich's ruminative (some might say narcissistic) introspection holds up the music's forward flow. The movement overall takes 23 minutes 18 seconds, which must be something of a record. The *Andante* is a delight, with the delicately agile LSO strings matching the soloist's nimbleness in the central *Prestissimo*; and the finale is similarly exhilarating in its crisp articulation. The charisma of the performance is undeniable, but many will find the first movement too wilful to live with – and with no fill-up, the CD seems poor value, running for only 37 minutes.

Argerich's Philips issue comes from a live performance given in October 1980, full of animal excitement, with astonishingly fast speeds in the outer movements. The impetuous virtuosity is breathtaking, even if passage-work is not always as cleanly articulated as in her superb studio performance for DG. Again, this is unrecommendable without a coupling.

Clifford Curzon's 1969 recording with Solti has resurfaced on a Decca CD, but the remastering makes the orchestral sound rather dated, although the piano retains its fullness. It is a characteristically fine version. Curzon matches thoughtfulness to unostentatious bravura, and Solti ensures that the performance overall has fine zest and spontaneity.

Both Schiff and Solti make the most of the lyrical side of the first movement but, with the cadenzas introspective rather than flamboyant, there is a missing dimension. The *Andantino* opens with the most hushed of pianissimos and the soloist is fastidiously delicate throughout – the scherzando middle section is very light and graceful, and the essentially lightweight approach extends to the finale, too, which is underpowered.

After his successful Chopin and Rachmaninov records, Kissin's account of the Tchaikovsky comes as a surprise. But perhaps the fault lay with Karajan, perhaps not. In any case, the first movement must be among the slowest put on record (nearly 24 minutes) and the performance never really recovers.

Piano concertos Nos. 1 in B flat min.; 3 in E flat, Op. 75.
(M) **(*) EMI CD-EMX 2001. Gilels, New Philh. O, Maazel.
** EMI Dig. CDC7 49667-2. Peter Donohoe, Bournemouth SO, Barshai.
** EMI Dig. CDC7 49632-2 [id.]. Gavrilov, BPO, Ashkenazy.

At medium price the Gilels/Maazel coupling from 1973 leads the field for those wanting these two concertos together. The recording is first class; though the piano is placed well forward, the sound is much better than in Gilels's CBS version. The *Third Concerto* is not lacking in memorable ideas and Gilels plays it with authority and freshness. The account of No. 1 is in many ways distinguished too, and it is certainly exciting, but it has a very fast opening that is exhilarating in its way. Many Tchaikovskians will feel, however, that this – one of his broadest melodies – needs a more expansive treatment.

Peter Donohoe's coupling of the *First* and *Third Concertos* doesn't repeat the great success he had with the *Second*. The *B flat minor Concerto* is a spaciously weighty account, with the lyrical secondary material of the first movement presented poetically; but the performance, strong as it is and with a beautifully played *Andante* and with the

Russian dance elements of the finale well brought out, remains obstinately unmemorable. The *Third Concerto* has greater spontaneity and its volatile qualities are well realized. This is enjoyable in its own right; and both works are well recorded.

For Gavrilov's digital remake of the *B flat minor Concerto*, EMI teamed him up with Ashkenazy and recorded the Berlin Philharmonic in their old analogue venue, the Jesus-Christus-Kirche. The balance is not entirely convincing, with the orchestra often sounding rather recessed. After opening impressively, the first movement flows rather more convincingly than before, but the alternation of gentle poetry with sudden bursts of pianistic bravura still fails to sound entirely spontaneous. The slow movement has a scintillating middle section, but the finale was even more gripping in the analogue version. The coupling is much less successful and structually fails to knit convincingly together as it does in the Donohoe version.

(i) *Piano concerto No. 1 in B flat min., Op. 23;* (ii) *Violin concerto in D, Op. 35.*

(B) **(*) DG 429 166-2 [id.]. (i) Lazar Berman; (ii) Christian Ferras, BPO, Karajan.

(M) **(*) CBS Dig. MDK 44643 [id.]. (i) Gilels, NYPO; (ii) Zukerman, Israel PO; Mehta.

(BB) **(*) LaserLight 15 516 [id.]. (i) Jenö Jando, Budapest PO, Andras Ligeti; (ii) Emmy Verhey, Budapest SO, Arpad Joo.

(M) **(*) Ph. 420 717-2 [id.]. (i) Claudio Arrau, Boston SO; (ii) Accardo, BBC SO; C. Davis.

Berman's 1976 recording with Karajan makes a formidabe bargain issue, well coupled with Christian Ferras' much earlier version of the *Violin concerto*. Berman's character is firmly established in the massive chords of the introduction; from there his revelling in dramatic contrast – whether of texture, tone-colour, dynamic or tempo – makes this one of the most exciting readings ever put on record. It is not just a question of massive bravura but of extreme delicacy too, so that in the central scherzando of the slow movement it almost sounds as though Berman is merely breathing on the keyboard, hardly depressing the notes at all. The ripe playing of the Berlin Philharmonic backs up the individuality of Berman's reading, and the recording is massively brilliant to match. Ferras' characteristic tone, with its rather close vibrato in lyrical passages, will not be to all tastes. But his is a well-conceived reading, with Karajan shaping the work as a whole very convincingly. The recording is excellent, rather warmer and more atmospheric than that provided for the *Piano concerto*.

CBS's digital coupling costs slightly more than the DG disc. There are more reservations about the Gilels performance than the Zukerman. The former offers less than first-class orchestral playing and not very distinguished sound, but Gilels's own playing is masterly. In Israel, the sound is much better, and Mehta secures generally good results from the Israel orchestra. The soloist is balanced closely and is made very tangible; Zukerman's warmth is most attractive, and the performance overall has both excitement and spontaneity.

Although their names are unknown in the West, both soloists on the LaserLight super-bargain coupling are excellent players and the performances give real satisfaction. The overall balance in the *Piano concerto* is forward, which means some reduction in dynamic range, but the recording is admirably full and the performance has a direct spontaneity and power, with a strong forward momentum and plenty of excitement in the outer movements, while Jando's controlled virtuosity in the *Prestissimo* section of the *Andantino* is matched by his exciting bravura in the finale. The work's lyrical side is well realized too, more delicately in the *Andantino*, but the orchestral reprise of the big tune in the last movement is powerfully spontaneous. The *Violin concerto* is equally impressive. Emmy Verhey plays with a full tone, sparkling virtuosity and a sense of fantasy, while the slow movement has a tender simplicity and warmth. The recorded balance is natural and the orchestral texture is given plenty of body and ambient warmth yet is rather more open than the *Piano concerto*.

Arrau, splendidly accompanied, gives a direct and unexaggerated performance of the *B flat minor Concerto* which is in general most refreshing. The temperature is not high and, with a seventy-year-old soloist, double octaves do not run quite so freely as once they did. There is also a strange agogic hesitation in Arrau's enunciation of the main theme of the finale, but with clean recording this version will appeal to those who like a thoughtful reading. Salvatore Accardo's account of the *Violin concerto* combines poise and freshness with flair. He has a keen lyricism and a fine sense of line, as one would expect, and he is sensitively accompanied by Sir Colin Davis and the BBC Symphony Orchestra. But he is a shade too close to the microphone to do his tone full justice; otherwise the remastered sound is very good.

(i) *Piano concerto No. 1;* (ii) *Violin concerto;* (iii) *Variations on a rococo theme for cello and orchestra.*
(B) ** Pickwick DUET 12 CD (2). (i) Graffman, Cleveland O, Szell; (ii) Isaac Stern; (iii) Leonard Rose, Phd. O, Ormandy.

This bargain-price Pickwick set is not especially generous, with the *Piano concerto* (at 34 minutes) alone on the first disc. However, Graffman's partnership with Szell produces a performance in which the electricity crackles, with the spirit of Horowitz and Toscanini evoked at the finale. Its atmosphere may be tense but the impact is undeniable, and lyrical contrast is not forgotten; an engaging delicacy pervades the outer sections of the *Andante*. The snag is the over-brilliant recording. Similarly in Stern's powerfully romantic reading of the *Violin concerto* the balance is too forward: his tone is rich but pianissimos consistently become *mezzo fortes*. Rose gives a warm, slightly reticent but admirably eloquent account of the *Rococo variations* and the sound here is quite good, though throughout this disc orchestral tuttis are without a desirable Tchaikovskian opulence.

Piano concerto No. 2 in G, Op. 44.
⊛ *** EMI Dig. CDC7 49124-2 [id.]. Peter Donohoe, Bournemouth SO, Barshai.

This superb recording of the full original score in every way justifies the work's length and the unusual format of the slow movement, where the piece temporarily becomes a triple concerto, with its extended solos for violin and cello. Here these are played with beguiling warmth by Nigel Kennedy and Steven Isserlis. Barshai's pacing is not only perfectly calculated but he gives the opening tune an engaging rhythmic lift. The whole movement goes with a splendid impetus, yet the central orchestral episode is broadened effectively. The slow movement has one of Tchaikovsky's very best tunes, and the performance is a delight from beginning to end. Peter Donohoe plays marvellously in the first two movements – he is quite melting in the *Andante* – and in the finale he is inspired to bravura which recalls Horowitz in the *B flat minor Concerto*. The main theme, shooting off with the velocity of the ball in a pinball machine, is exhilarating and the orchestral response has a matching excitement. The coda, with its cascading octaves, is a *tour de force* and brings one to the edge of one's seat in admiration. The recording has a fine, spacious ambience and is admirably realistic and very well balanced. Tchaikovsky's work has never before received such convincing advocacy on record.

Piano concertos Nos. 2 in G, Op. 44; 3 in E flat, Op. 75.
*** Ara. Dig. Z 6583 [id.]. Jerome Lowenthal, LSO, Comissiona.

In an obviously attractive coupling of two unjustly neglected works, the energy and flair of Lowenthal and Comissiona combine to give highly spontaneous performances, well balanced and recorded. If the *G major Concerto* has not quite the distinction of the EMI version, it is still satisfyingly alive; the soloist brings an individual, poetic response as well as bravura. With very good sound, this is well worth investigating, as the account of the *Third Concerto* is comparably spontaneous.

(i) *Piano concerto No. 2 in G, Op.44* (arr. Siloti); (ii) *Concert fantasia in G, Op. 56.*
*** Olympia OCD 229 [id.]. (i) Gilels, USSR Ac. SO, Svetlanov; (ii) Zhukov, USSR Ac. SO, Kitaenko.

The Russian recording of the abridged Siloti version, made at a public concert in the Moscow Conservatoire in 1972, is hugely exciting and, taken on its own merits, is a great success. Gilels's playing is masterly and Svetlanov brings plenty of vigour to the first movement; and the performance has all the excitement and spontaneity one would expect of a live occasion. The orchestral soloists make the most of the section of concertante music which is left to them, and in the finale the glittering brilliance of Gilels's articulation is matched by his witty restraint in the treatment of the secondary material. The recording balances the piano well forward, but the orchestra remains in the picture and the piano timbre is bold and full. The coupling is a splendid account of the *Concert fantasia*, an engaging and much underrated piece, demanding comparable technical virtuosity from its soloist, which Igor Zhukov provides in full measure. He is sympathetically accompanied, and this is another exciting and involving performance, given very good (1979) sound. The remastering for CD is highly effective.

Violin concerto in D, Op. 35.
*** Decca Dig. 410 011-2 [id.]. Kyung Wha Chung, Montreal SO, Dutoit – MENDELSSOHN: *Concerto.****

(M) *** Decca 417 707-2 [id.]. Kyung Wha Chung, LSO, Previn – BRUCH: *Concerto No. 1;* SAINT-SAENS: *Havanaise.****

(B) *** Ph. 422 473-2 [id.]. Grumiaux, New Philh. O, Krenz – MENDELSSOHN: *Concerto.****

*** Decca Dig. 421 716-2 [id.]. Joshua Bell, Cleveland O, Ashkenazy – WIENIAWSKI: *Violin concerto No. 2.****

(M) *** DG 419 067-2 [id.]. Milstein, VPO, Abbado – MENDELSSOHN: *Concerto.****

(*) Ph. Dig. 416 821-2 [id.]. Mullova, Boston SO, Ozawa – SIBELIUS: *Concerto.**

(M) **(*) Decca 417 687-2 [id.]. Ricci, Netherlands R. PO, Fournet – MENDELSSOHN: *Concerto.***(*)

(*) EMI Dig. CDC7 47623-2 [id.]. Nigel Kennedy, LPO, Kamu – CHAUSSON: *Poème.*(*)

(B) **(*) CBS CD 42537 [MYK 36724]. Stern, Phd. O, Ormandy – MENDELSSOHN: *Concerto.***(*)

Violin concerto in D; Sérénade mélancolique.
**(*) EMI CDC7 47106-2 [id.]. Perlman, Phd. O, Ormandy.

Violin concerto in D, Op. 35; Sérénade mélancolique, Op. 26; String serenade: Waltz.
(*) RCA RD 85933 [RCA 5933-2-RC]. Heifetz, Chicago SO, Reiner, or CO – MENDELSSOHN: *Concerto.*(*)

Chung is engagingly volatile as a performer, responding to the inspiration of the moment, yet she is a deeply thoughtful interpreter. Here, as in her earlier version with Previn, she refuses to sentimentalize the central *Canzonetta*, choosing a flowing, easily songful speed. The result is the more tenderly affecting, though this time the violin is balanced more closely than before. The finale has, if anything, even more exhilaration, with technical problems commandingly overcome at a very fast speed.

Those preferring the alternative coupling with Bruch and Saint-Saëns should be well satisfied with Chung's 1970 version, which is still among the finest in the catalogue and in which Previn's accompanying is highly sympathetic and responsive. This has warmth, spontaneity and discipline; every detail is beautifully shaped and turned without a trace of sentimentality. The recording is well balanced and detail is clean, though the acoustic is warm.

Grumiaux's playing has the usual aristocratic refinement and purity of tone to recommend it. His reading, too, is beautifully paced and has a particularly fine slow movement, less overtly emotional than some; both here and in the brilliant finale he shows superb aplomb and taste. With an excellent accompaniment from Krenz, this ranks among the finest budget versions, for the 1970s recording has a wide range and is firmly focused in its CD format.

Joshua Bell plays with an expressive warmth which is generally kept within a relatively steady pulse. The symphonic strength of the work is brought out without any loss of excitement, rather the opposite. Bell may not have quite the fantasy of a version like Chung's, but it is an outstanding account nevertheless, very recommendable if you fancy the unusual coupling of Wieniawski. In the finale of the Tchaikovsky, Bell does not open out the tiny cuts in the passage-work that until recently have been traditional. Full, brilliant recording, with the soloist well balanced.

Milstein's fine 1973 version with Abbado is coupled with the Mendelssohn *Concerto* and remains one of the best mid-price reissues.

Viktoria Mullova's performance of the Tchaikovsky *Concerto* is immaculate and finely controlled – as is the coupling – but she does not always succeed in achieving the combination of warmth and nobility that this score above all requires. However, her playing has an undeniable splendour and an effortless virtuosity. Ozawa and the Boston orchestra give excellent support and the recording is exemplary.

With the upper range of the 1957 recording smoothed and the orchestral presence enhanced, the magic of Heifetz can now be enjoyed more fully. There is some gorgeous lyrical playing and the slow movement marries deep feeling and tenderness in ideal proportions, while the finale scintillates. Reiner accompanies understandingly, producing fierily positive tuttis. A fine performance of the *Sérénade mélancolique* makes an attractive encore.

Perlman's expressive warmth goes with a very bold orchestral texture from Ormandy and the Philadelphia Orchestra, and anyone who follows Perlman – in so many ways the supreme violin virtuoso of our time – is not likely to be disappointed. The coupling is not very generous, though beguilingly played. The vivid analogue sound is balanced more naturally than are many of Perlman's discs.

Ricci's characteristic, intense vibrato may not be to all tastes, but the ear readily submits to the compulsion and colour of the playing, which shows a rock-steady technique and a splendid lyrical feeling, so that the rich stream of tone is always securely based and the larger-than-life image is attractive, when the orchestral impact and detail are so vividly conveyed. The CD transfer is full and clear.

Nigel Kennedy gives a warmly romantic reading of the Tchaikovsky *Concerto*, full of temperament, with one of the most expansive readings of the first movement ever put on disc. Though the sound is ample, his idiosyncrasies will not please everyone. For all his many *tenutos* and *rallentandos*, however, Kennedy is not sentimental, and his range of tone is exceptionally rich and wide, so that the big moments are powerfully sensual. Okku

Kamu and the LPO do not always match their soloist; the accompaniment sometimes sounds a little stiff in tuttis, though the final coda is thrilling.

Stern was on peak form when he made his first stereo recording with Ormandy, and it is a powerfully lyrical reading, rich in timbre and technically immaculate. The playing has undoubted poetry but is not helped by the very close balance of the soloist, so that pianissimos consistently become mezzo fortes. The orchestral sound is vivid but lacks amplitude.

Violin concerto; Sérénade mélancolique, Op. 35; Souvenir d'un lieu cher, Op. 42: (Méditation; Scherzo; Mélodie; orch. Glazunov).
(BB) *(**) Naxos Dig. 8.550124. Mariko Honda, Slovak PO or CSR SO, Keith Clark.

It was an excellent idea for Naxos to put all Tchaikovsky's music for violin and orchestra on a single super-bargain CD. In fact the *Souvenir d'un lieu cher* includes the *D minor Méditation*, originally intended as the slow movement for the *Concerto*, plus two other pieces, a *Scherzo* and a *Mélodie*, here orchestrated by Glazunov. Together they almost form another miniature concerto (though with the fast movement at the centre). Mariko Honda is wholly in sympathy with the specifically Tchaikovskian melancholy which permeates these shorter, lyrical pieces, and even in the *Concerto* her account of the slow movement and the lyrical episodes of the finale bring a darker colouring than with many soloists. Yet her playing can sparkle too, though overall her chosen tempi are comparatively relaxed. These are all performances of considerable intensity, well accompanied, and it is a pity that the brilliant digital recording balances her so closely, so the microphones do not always flatter her tone in the more histrionic upper tessitura. The orchestral sound is also brightly vivid.

(i) *Violin concerto;* (ii) *The Tempest, Op. 18; The Voyevoda, Op. 78.*
*(**) Olympia Dig./Analogue OCD 180. (i) Viktor Tretyakov; USSR RSO, Fedoseyev; (ii) cond. Ovchinnikov.

This is a curious coupling. The *Violin concerto* is recorded digitally and, although the soloist is forward and rather near the microphone, his playing stands up to such a close scrutiny. It is a strong, powerfully romantic account, with easy virtuosity in the outer movements and a natural sympathy for the folksong element in the gentle *Canzonetta*, while in the finale the lyrical interludes are more virile than usual, yet not less colourful. The orchestral contribution is excellent and brilliantly recorded. When one turns to the symphonic poems, however, the 1979 analogue sound is much more pungent, with tuttis becoming fierce and harsh, such is the ferocity of the playing in the emotional climaxes. In *The Tempest* the great love-theme has enormous Russian ardour – the violins produce amazing intensity in the great upward leap – and the brass chorale at the end has genuine majesty. But in *The Voyevoda*, a much less inspired piece, the unrestrained fervour becomes brutal when the cruder scoring is made to sound unrestrainedly blatant.

1812 Overture, Op. 49; Francesca da Rimini, Op. 32; Marche slave, Op. 31; Eugene Onegin: Polonaise.
**(*) EMI Dig. CDC7 47375-2 [id.]. BPO, Ozawa.

1812 Overture; Francesca da Rimini; Marche slave; Romeo and Juliet (fantasy overture).
(M) *** EMI Dig. CD-EMX 2152. Royal Liverpool PO, Sian Edwards.

1812 Overture; Francesca da Rimini; Romeo and Juliet.
**(*) EMI Dig. CDC7 49141-2 [id.]. Oslo PO, Jansons.

1812 Overture; Hamlet (fantasy overture), *Op. 67; Romeo and Juliet* (fantasy overture).
**(*) Collins Dig. EC 1009-2. LPO, Gibson.

1812 Overture; Hamlet (fantasy overture), *Op. 67; The Tempest, Op. 18.*
*** Delos Dig. D/CD 3081 [id.]. Oregon SO, James DePreist.

1812 Overture; Marche slave; Romeo and Juliet.
**(*) EMI CDC7 47843-2 [id.]. LSO, Previn.

1812 Overture; Nutcracker (ballet): *suite; Romeo and Juliet.*
**(*) Decca Dig. 417 400-2 [id.]. Chicago SO, Solti.

(i) *1812 Overture; Romeo and Juliet;* (ii) *Eugene Onegin: Polonaise; Waltz; Écossaise. The Oprichnik: Dances.*
*** Ph. 411 448-2 [id.]. (i) Boston SO, with Tanglewood Fest. Ch. (in *1812*); (ii) ROHCG O; C. Davis.

(i) *1812 Overture; Serenade for strings, Op. 48; Eugene Onegin: Polonaise and waltz.*
(M) **(*) DG 415 855-2 [id.]. (i) Don Cossack Ch.; BPO, Karajan.

Sian Edwards's reading of *Francesca da Rimini* can be spoken of in the same breath as Stokowski's famous version. The control of the music's emotional ebb and flow shows her as an instinctive Tchaikovskian, moving through the work surely and compulsively, after the doom-laden opening stroke of the tam-tam has created an impending sense of nemesis. Francesca's clarinet entry is melting and the work's middle section has a Beechamesque sense of colour. The passionate climax, representing the discovery of the lovers, falls only just short of the vehement force of the Stokowski version, while the spectacular recording gives great impact to the closing whirlwind sequence and the despair-laden final chords, where the tam-tam makes its presence felt very pungently. *1812* is also very enjoyable indeed, full of vigour and flair, with the lyrical Russian folk melodies on strings and woodwind relished colourfully, and a majestic final sequence with superbly resounding cannon. In *Romeo and Juliet*, the love-theme is ushered in very naturally and blossoms with the fullest ardour, while the feud music combined with the Friar Lawrence theme reaches a very dramatic climax; again the final chords carry a real sense of tragedy. *Marche slave,* resplendently high-spirited and exhilarating, makes a perfect foil. The full-bodied recording is well balanced and thrilling in the proper Tchaikovskian way, with plenty of sonority and weight from the brass and a full string patina. Anything these performances lack in final polish they make up for in commitment and vitality.

The Oregon orchestra show their paces in this vividly colourful triptych, and James DePreist is a highly sympathetic Tchaikovskian. Moreover the Arlene Schnitzer Hall in Portland has excellent acoustics for this repertoire, giving the orchestra fine depth and resonance and a true, unexaggerated brilliance. In *1812*, the cannon are perfectly placed and their spectacular entry is as precise as it is commanding. The performance overall is highly enjoyable, energetic but with the pacing unforced, though the ritenuto before the final peroration is not quite convincing. The performances of both *Hamlet* and *The Tempest* are passionately dramatic, the latter generating more intensity (and more melodrama) than Yondani Butt's ASV version, the former approaching yet not quite equalling Stokowski's account in imaginative vividness. But overall this is an impressive CD début.

Sir Colin Davis is not renowned as a Tchaikovskian, yet here he provides one of the most satisfying versions of *1812* ever recorded. Though he departs from the original score

– to great effect – by including a chorus, it is musical values rather than any sense of gimmickry that make this version so successful. Men's voices alone are used to introduce the Russian hymn softly at the opening, with the ladies freshening the reprise. In the closing spectacle, the chorus soars above the bells; the effect is exhilarating and the very believable cannon are superbly placed. *Romeo and Juliet* is a slightly reserved performance, but one which in its minor degree of introversion misses neither the noble passion of the lovers nor the clash of swords in the feud sequences. The elegiac closing pages are particularly telling. The colourful operatic dances are a generous makeweight and are played with élan, even if the recording balance has lost just a degree of sparkle in the upper range with the removal of virtually all the background noise.

Sir Alexander Gibson's *Overture 1812*, spectacularly recorded at Barking Assembly Hall, compares favourably with available versions and is more impressive than most, while the two Shakespearean *Overtures* (symphonic poems in all but name) are sympathetically shaped and very well played. *Hamlet* has not quite the imaginative force of Stokowski's famous version but is very dramatic nevertheless, and Gibson's depiction of Ophelia shows attractive delicacy and grace. Similarly in *Romeo and Juliet* the shaping of the famous love-theme is eloquently managed, and in both works the LPO playing has plenty of bite and conviction. The use of Watford Town Hall for these two latter works brings sound which is both weighty and expansive.

Previn takes a clear-headed, totally unsentimental view of three of Tchaikovsky's most popular orchestral works. As a result the music emerges stronger in design and no less exciting than usual. On CD the upper range seems slightly restricted, yet there is a striking gain in ambience and warmth, with a resonant bass providing the necessary sumptuousness and the massed violins singing richly. However, with only 47 minutes of music offered, this record is overpriced.

Jansons' *Romeo and Juliet* has genuine breadth and the love-theme shows characteristic Oslo eloquence. The main allegro lacks the last degree of physical excitement but there is plenty of vigour. The one idiosyncrasy is Jansons' interpolation of a tam tam alongside the explosive timpani roll in the coda. In *Francesca da Rimini* there is a frenzied evocation of Dante's Inferno in the outer sections of the work and the orchestral imitation of the whirlwinds in the reprise is very telling; the idyllic central section, too, is beautifully played. However, the overwhelming passion of the lovers does not communicate here with the power of Stokowski's famous performance. *1812* combines brilliance with a rather dignified grandiloquence, but the orchestral response is not specially gripping.

Characteristically, Solti provides an exciting and spectacular *1812*, and the bold immediacy of the Chicago sound – thrusting violins in the allegro, powerful, sonorous brass at climaxes – brings compulsive music-making throughout. At the end the cannon-shots are placed precisely but the bells are curiously blurred; however, the conductor's overall tautness in holding the piece together is undoubtedly commanding. *Romeo and Juliet* has an unexpected element of restraint and the love-theme, very tender and gentle when it first appears on the cor anglais, finds a yearning passion without histrionics; the battle sequences have plenty of bite in the strings, and at the climax the trumpets ring out resplendently. The *Nutcracker suite* produces marvellously characterful solo playing and much subtle detail.

Ozawa's *1812* has the advantage of strikingly vivid digital recording, full-bodied but not without a degree of edge on the brass. The reading is thrustful and certainly exciting, with the Berlin Philharmonic strings singing their lyrical melodies eloquently. The cannon are very spectacular: their first fusillade is so engulfing that one is surprised to discover the orchestra still sitting in their places afterwards, to reassert the musical line!

In the final cannonade, however, the joyous bells are drowned. Ozawa's *Marche slave* is nicely paced, dignified yet spirited, and the *Eugene Onegin Polonaise* is attractively buoyant. The reading of *Francesca da Rimini*, however, is essentially neurotic. At the end of the middle section Ozawa begins his accelerando much too early (at the cor anglais scalic figure) and, while what follows is undeniably thrilling, it turns Tchaikovsky's construction into melodrama.

Karajan's *1812* (with chorus) is also available with different couplings. His earlier reading of the *Serenade* is brilliantly played. The two central movements are superb, the *Waltz* bringing masterly control of rubato and colour (the strings make a lovely sound) while the *Élégie* is freely passionate. The brightness of the sound brings a slight feeling of aggressiveness to the outer movements and especially to the finale. The *Polonaise* and *Waltz* from *Eugene Onegin* have fine panache.

Festival coronation march in D; (i) *Romeo and Juliet:* duet (orch. Taneyev).
*** Chan. Dig. CHAN 8476 [id.]. (i) Murphy, Lewis, Wilson-Johnson; SNO, Järvi – RACHMANINOV: *The Bells* etc.**(*)

Tchaikovsky's *Festival coronation march* was written for open-air performance before the Tsar in 1883. It is suitably grandiloquent but has a rather engaging trio, plus a whiff of the Tsarist hymn we recognize from *1812*. It is very well played here and superbly recorded. The vocalization of *Romeo and Juliet*, with the music drawn from the famous fantasy overture, was left in the form of posthumous sketches, which Taneyev completed and scored. The effect is more like a symphonic poem with vocal obbligatos, rather than operatic. It is well sung here but is mainly of curiosity value.

Festival overture on the Danish national anthem, Op. 15; (i) *Hamlet: Overture and incidental music, Op. 67 bis. Mazeppa: Battle of Poltava and Cossack dance; Romeo and Juliet* (fantasy overture; 1869 version); *Serenade for Nikolai Rubinstein's saint's day.*
⊛ *** Chan. Dig. CHAN 8310/1 (2) [id.]. LSO, Simon, (i) with Janis Kelly, Hammond-Stroud.

Tchaikovsky himself thought his *Danish Festival overture* superior to *1812*, and though one cannot agree with his judgement it is well worth hearing. The *Hamlet* incidental music is another matter. The overture is a shortened version of the *Hamlet fantasy overture*, but much of the rest of the incidental music is unknown, and the engaging *Funeral march* and the two poignant string elegies show the composer's inspiration at its most memorable. Ophelia's mad scene is partly sung and partly spoken, and Janis Kelly's performance is most sympathetic, while Derek Hammond-Stroud is suitably robust in the *Gravedigger's song*. The music from *Mazeppa* and the tribute to Rubinstein make engaging bonuses, but the highlight of the set is the 1869 version of *Romeo and Juliet*, very different from the final, 1880 version we know so well. It is fascinating to hear the composer's early thoughts before he finalized a piece which was to become one of the most successful of all his works. The performances here under Geoffrey Simon are excitingly committed and spontaneous; the orchestral playing is nearly always first rate, and the digital recording has spectacular resonance and depth to balance its brilliance. Edward Johnson, who provided the initial impetus for the recordings, writes the excellent notes and a translation of the vocal music, which is sung (as the original production of *Hamlet* was performed) in French.

Francesca da Rimini, Op. 32.
(*) Ph. Dig. 426 437-2 [id.]. LPO, Gergiev – MUSSORGSKY: *Pictures.*(*)

After the brief introductory *Andante lugubre*, Gergiev's frenzied, almost hysterical treatment of the opening section is matched by comparable intensity in the work's closing pages with much thrilling orchestral bravura. By contrast he paces the central *Andante cantabile*, with its glowing LPO woodwind playing, rather too affectionately and almost loses the music's momentum. The Philips recording provides an agreeable bloom here and there is no lack of spectacle, especially in the biting dissonance of the coda with its flaring tam-tam.

Francesca da Rimini; Hamlet (fantasy overture), *Op. 67a*.
⊛ *** Dell'Arte CDDA 9006 [id.]. NY Stadium O, Stokowski.

Stokowski's famous Everest coupling – one of his greatest records – is here remastered for CD with great success, with the sound cleaner and clearer, yet remarkably expansive in the bass in *Hamlet*. Stokowski's inspired performance is quite sensational. He plays the central lyrical tune so convincingly that, if it has not quite the romantic panache of *Romeo and Juliet*, it has instead the proper sombre passion suitable to the altogether different atmosphere of Shakespeare's *Hamlet*. It is the dignity of the music and its close identification with the play that come over so strikingly. And, fascinatingly, Stokowski shows us how intensely Russian the music is; the funeral march at the end is extremely moving. *Francesca* is hardly less exciting. Surely the opening whirlwinds have seldom roared at such tornado speeds before. The central section is played with the beguiling care for detail and balance for which this conductor was famous. When the great polyphonic climax comes, and the themes for the lovers' passion intertwine with music to suggest they are discovered, the tension is tremendous. The recording throughout is astonishingly vivid when one considers that it was made well over thirty years ago: this is an outstanding reissue in every way. The New York Stadium Orchestra drew on the New York Philharmonic for its players and the tremendous commitment of their response more than makes up for any slight imperfections of ensemble. An indispensable record for all Tchaikovskians.

Manfred symphony, Op. 58.
⊛ *** Chan. Dig. CHAN 8535 [id.]. Oslo PO, Jansons.
*** Decca Dig. 421 441-2 [id.]. Concg. O, Chailly.
*** EMI Dig. CDC7 47412-2 [id.]. Philh. O, Muti.
(M) (*) DG 429 718-2 [id.]. LSO, Yuli Ahronovich.

Jansons' performance of *Manfred* with the Oslo Philharmonic crowns his outstanding series in an electrifying account of this difficult, unconventionally structured work. Except in a relatively relaxed view of the *vivace* second movement, Jansons favours speeds flowing faster than usual, bringing out the drama but subtly varying the tensions to press each climax home to the full and always showing his mastery of Tchaikovskian rubato: his warmly expressive phrasing never sounds self-conscious when it is regularly given the freshness of folksong. The performance culminates in a thrilling account of the finale, leading up to the entry of the organ, gloriously resonant and supported by luxuriant string sound. The Chandos recording is among the finest in the Oslo series, atmospheric but with fine inner detail.

The Chailly version of *Manfred* brings a spectacular display of hi-fi sound and a strong, sympathetic performance, beautifully played, which favours spacious speeds in the outer movements, with tension finely controlled. Only in the final coda, after the organ has entered with thrilling resonance, does Chailly dissipate some of the tension at a very slow speed. Considering the vividness, breadth and brilliance of the sound, it is surprising that the horns sound relatively recessed, but this is a small flaw in a spectacular display record.

Muti's reading is forceful and boldly dramatic throughout. His Scherzo has a quality of exhilarating bravura, rather than concentrating on delicacy; the lovely central melody is given a sense of joyous vigour. The *Andante*, after a refined opening, soon develops a passionate forward sweep; in the finale the amplitude and brilliant detail of the recording, combined with magnificent playing from the Philharmonia Orchestra, brings a massively compulsive projection of Tchaikovsky's bacchanale and a richly satisfying dénouement. The CD adds to the weight and definition of the recording, but the result is slightly less sumptuous than the original LP, and sonically the new Decca version is even more spectacular.

One wonders why DG chose to issue the Ahronovich version, which received a poor press when it first appeared. The recording is spectacular, but his narcissistic ritenuto style, with constant agogic distortion of the rhythmic pulse, is totally unsatisfactory for repeated listening.

Méditation (for violin and orchestra, arr. Glazunov), *Op. 42/1.*
*** EMI CDC7 47087-2 [id.]. Perlman, Israel PO, Mehta – KHACHATURIAN: *Violin concerto.***(*)

A charming Tchaikovskian trifle, arranged for violin and orchestra by Glazunov, which makes an agreeable balm to the ear.

The Nutcracker (ballet), *Op. 71* (complete).
*** EMI Dig. CDS7 47267-8 (2) [Ang. CDCB 47267]. Amb. S., RPO, Previn.
*** Telarc Dig. CD 8137 (2) [id.]. LSO & Ch., Mackerras.
*** EMI Dig. CDS7 49399-2 (2) [Ang. CDCB 49399]. Amb. S., Philh. O, Lanchbery.
*** CBS Dig. M2K 42173 (2) [id.]. Philh. O & Ch., Tilson Thomas.
(*) ROH Dig. ROH 304/5 [id.]. ROHCG O, Mark Ermler – ARENSKY: *Variations.**
(M) **(*) Decca 425 450-2 (2) [id.]. Nat. PO, Richard Bonynge – OFFENBACH: *Le Papillon.****
** Chant du Monde Dig. LDC 278 959/60. USSR RSO & Children's Ch., Fedoseyev.

The Nutcracker (ballet) complete; *Eugene Onegin: Introduction; Waltz; Polonaise.*
*** Ph. Dig. 420 237-2 (2) [id.]. BPO, Bychkov.

Splendid versions of Tchaikovsky's enchanting Christmas ballet come in profusion and it is almost impossible to suggest a clear first choice. Previn's digital version is played superbly and its freshness is immediately apparent in the opening children's party. With the magic beginning at the growth of the Christmas tree there is a fine toy bang to set off the sparkling battle sequence. The Snowflakes scene is captivating, with lovely vocal timbre from the Ambrosians in the delectable *Waltz*. When we arrive at the series of dances which form the *Divertissement* of Act II, the orchestral playing is marvellously elegant and polished, with rhythms lifted and colours glowing. The EMI recording, made at EMI's No. 1 Studio at Abbey Road, has warm ambience, yet detail is cleanly focused and the orchestra is given fine presence.

The Telarc set was recorded in Watford Town Hall, bringing the extra resonance of the concert hall, which adds a little glamour to the violins and a glowing warmth in the middle and lower range. When the magic spell begins, the spectacularly wide dynamic range and the extra amplitude make for a physical frisson in the climaxes, while the glorious climbing melody, as Clara and the Prince travel through the pine forest, sounds richly expansive. Before that, the battle has some real cannon-shots interpolated but is done good-humouredly, for this is a toy battle. In the earlier party scene, Mackerras presses forward more than Previn and this creates added intensity in Act I; but in the Act II *Divertissement* Mackerras's sparkling vivacity is sometimes less telling than Previn's easy elegance, and here the latter is preferable. Yet the great *Pas de deux* brings the most sumptuous climax, with superb sonority from the brass on the Telarc version. The Telarc presentation, too, with a detailed synopsis, is far superior to the much more meagre EMI documentation.

Semyon Bychkov has the services of the Berlin Philharmonic (an orchestra that always identifies readily with Tchaikovsky) and they offer superlative playing, of striking flair and character. Although a concert-hall ambience is favoured, the strings seem more forward, inner detail is very clear and the cymbals have a thrilling metallic clash. There is some superbly stylish playing in the *Divertissement*, and there are many moments when the extra vividness of the Berlin recording is especially compelling; and, of course, Bychkov offers a bonus, for the *Eugene Onegin* excerpts are brilliantly done. The Philips notes are extensive but not so conveniently matched to the CD cues.

Lanchbery has the feeling of ballet music in his very bones, and his account, if not pictorially as evocative in Act I as some of his competitors, nevertheless has an attractive momentum and sweep, so that the narrative line is strongly projected. There are many nuances and touches of detail that could only come from a conductor who knows the score inside out, yet the freshness of his performance is a consistent pleasure too. The Philharmonia Orchestra is on its topmost form and the consistent vitality of the playing is striking when the digital recording is brilliant in a glittering way (yet without edge), while there is no lack of bloom.

Michael Tilson Thomas also has the advantage of fine Philharmonia playing, recorded in rather similar acoustics to the EMI set. The CBS balance is very good too, and this account lies between those of Previn and Mackerras, with a touch more spectacle than the former. Tempi are generally a fraction brisker on CBS, but the brighter rhythmic feeling often pays dividends. Generally, however, this would not be a first choice and the CBS documentation is inadequate, with only a brief synopsis.

Mark Ermler's version was recorded as one of the first issues on the new Royal Opera House label. As in the companion recording of *Swan Lake*, the players respond warmly and idiomatically to Tchaikovsky's ballet music, but the orchestral ensemble is not quite so crisp here, and the warmly reverberant recording tends to inflate the performance, undermining the piece's delicacy, its fairy-tale atmosphere. Detail is obscured too, notably in rapid string passage-work, with heavy brass putting a gauze over the whole ensemble. It is an enjoyable version nevertheless, recommendable to those who expressly want the engaging Arensky coupling.

Bonynge's set is made the more attractive by its rare and substantial Offenbach coupling. His approach is sympathetic and the orchestral playing is polished, even if in the opening scene he misses some of the atmosphere. With the beginning of the magic, as the Christmas tree expands, the performance becomes more dramatically involving, and in the latter part of the ballet Bonynge is at his best, with fine passion in the Act II *Pas de deux* and plenty of colour in the characteristic dances. The Decca recording is brilliant and vivid, but not as expansive as the Mackerras Telarc set. However, it is good value at mid-price.

The newest Russian performance combines balletic grace with rhythmic verve. It has the feel of live music-making and there is plenty of atmosphere and drama. The orchestral playing is vital, and Act I springs fully to life. The snag is the digital recording, bright, rather dry and without the expansive amplitude that makes Tchaikovsky's scoring glow with warmth and colour.

(i) *The Nutcracker* (ballet) complete. (ii) *Sleeping Beauty* (ballet): *suite*; *Swan Lake* (ballet): *suite*.

(B) ** CBS M2YK 45619 (2). (i) Toronto SO, Andrew Davis; (ii) Phd. O, Ormandy.

Taken individually, the CBS performances are impressive, but the coupling is ill-matched. Andrew Davis's complete *Nutcracker* comes from the late 1970s and is given good, modern recording. The performance very much evokes the ballet theatre; the playing has a neat sense of stylish elegance, yet readily matches Tchaikovsky's more expansive moments. Ormandy's pair of suites, sumptuously recorded more than a decade earlier, conversely are ripely spectacular, full of life but not refined or subtle, although the orchestral playing – with plenty of rhythmic life – is polished as well as enthusiastic. The music is enjoyable in an opulently colourful way.

(i) *The Nutcracker* (ballet) complete; (ii) *Swan Lake* (ballet): highlights.
(B) **(*) Pickwick DUET 20 CD. (i) LPO, Artur Rodzinski; (ii) Utah SO, Abravanel.

Rodzinski's *Nutcracker* derives from the old Westminster label and dates from the earliest days of stereo. It must be one of the most involvingly dramatic and exciting accounts of the complete score ever recorded. The tingling vitality of the playing brings infectious zest to the party scene of Act I – and a smile to the face of the listener, when the clock striking midnight to herald the beginning of the magic is recognized, incongruously, as none other than Big Ben! Later the gorgeous *Journey through the pine forest* brings a frisson of pleasure in its breadth and intensity, while the great Act II *Pas de deux* has even greater passion. The studio recording – immensely improved in the CD transfer – is not always completely refined (the percussion and brass sometimes too forward) nor is there a great deal of transparency in the characteristic dances. Yet it has a glowing richness of string texture, so effective in the lilting *Waltz of the flowers*. The rather robust contribution of the chorus robs the *Waltz of the snowflakes* of some of its essential delicacy; yet the whole performance is so grippingly involving that reservations are of less moment, with the set in the bargain range. Fortunately the coupling has comparable vividness and excitement; the recording here is less opulent, brighter and with better internal definition. In a generous selection from *Swan Lake* Abravanel produces often electrifying playing from his splendid Utah orchestra – the *Scène final* is thrilling, yet there is much that is elegant and stylish too, not least the charming *Dance of the little swans* and the eloquently played violin/cello duet in the *Danse des cygnes*.

The Nutcracker (ballet): excerpts, *Op. 71.*
*** Telarc Dig. CD 80140 [id.]. Tiffin School Boys' Ch., LSO, Mackerras.
(M) *** CBS Dig. MDK 44656 [id.]. Amb. S., Philh. O, Tilson Thomas.
*** Ph. Dig. 420 483-2 [id.]. Leningrad PO, Mravinsky – PROKOFIEV: *Romeo and Juliet: Suite No. 2.****
(B) ** Ph. 426 177-2 [id.]. Concg. O & Ch., Dorati.

On the face of it, the Tilson Thomas CD would seem to be the strongest recommendation: it offers considerably more music (70 minutes) than the Telarc disc; the bright-eyed Philharmonia playing is always alive and zestful; and the CBS recording is brilliant and well balanced. Moreover the selection is offered at mid-price.

But when one turns to the Telarc disc, which plays for some 55 minutes only, one enters a different, more expansive Tchaikovskian sound-world: the flair of the Battle sequence between the Nutcracker and the Mouse King immediately captures the imagination. Mackerras misses out much of Act I, but not the famous *Marche* nor the sequence called *The Magic Spell begins*, which is superbly expansive. Similarly, the *Scene in the Pine Forest* with Tchaikovsky's great climbing, scaling melody has a frisson-creating tension, and the *Waltz of the snowflakes* sets the mood for the famous characteristic dances of Act

II, all splendidly done, and recorded in Telarc's most spectacular manner. Nevertheless the CBS disc is undoubtedly a bargain in its own way.

Mravinsky starts with a lengthy sequence from Act I: the departure of the guests and the children, the return of Clara, the coming to life of the Dolls, the gingerbread Soldiers and the battle of the Mice, through to the journey to the Kingdom of the Sweets and the *Waltz of the snowflakes*. Then follow two excerpts from Act II: the *Pas de deux* between the Sugar Plum Fairy and Prince Charming and the final *Waltz and apotheosis*. Mravinsky began his career as a ballet conductor and his performance of these excerpts is quite magical, possessing all the warmth and enchantment one could wish for. The sound is full and expansive.

Dorati's selection comes from his 1975 complete set and, with refined playing and warm attention to detail, is attractive enough, though the selection (41 minutes) is ungenerous.

The Nutcracker (ballet): highlights; *Swan Lake* (ballet): highlights.
(B) * Pickwick Duet 6 CD (2). Phd. O, Ormandy.

These recordings come from the same CBS source as the selections joined with the complete *Nutcracker* – see above. The sound is glossily over-brilliant and, although the playing is polished and often exciting, it hasn't much allure, as presented here. Moreover there is little point in joining these two discs together when the overall playing time of 102 minutes still leaves ample room for more music.

Nutcracker suite, Op. 71a.
*** Ph. Dig. 412 559-2 [412 556-2]. Boston Pops O, John Williams – PROKOFIEV: *Peter and the wolf.****

A vividly crisp performance from John Williams and the Boston Pops. Tempi are brisk and the style is rather metrical but the playing has plenty of rhythmic lift, and only in the closing *Waltz of the flowers* is there a slight lack of lyrical freedom, but not of flair.

Nutcracker suite; Romeo and Juliet.
**(*) DG Dig. 410 873-2 [id.]. BPO, Karajan.
**(*) Telarc Dig. CD 80068 [id.]. Cleveland O, Maazel.

Karajan's suite is delicate and detailed, yet perhaps lacking a little in charm, notably the *Arab dance* which, taken fairly briskly, loses something of its gentle sentience. The overture is both polished and dramatic, but Karajan draws out the climax of the love-theme with spacious moulding, and there is marginally less spontaneity here than in his earlier recordings. The digital sound, characteristic of Berlin, is balanced truthfully; but alongside greater clarity, the CD brings a degree of hardness on the high violins in the *Nutcracker*, although the wind and brass solos have good definition and presence.

Maazel's *Nutcracker suite* is enjoyably colourful. His manner is affectionate (especially in the warmly lilting *Waltz of the flowers*), and the only idiosyncrasy is the sudden accelerando at the close of the *Russian dance*. *Romeo and Juliet* is given a spaciously romantic performance, reaching a climax of considerable passion. However, the almost overwhelming impact of the percussion in the (undoubtedly exciting) feud music is obviously designed for those who like to say, 'Listen to that bass drum!'

Nutcracker suite; Sleeping Beauty: suite; Swan Lake: suite.
⊛ (M) *** DG 429 097-2 [id.]. BPO, Rostropovich.
(M) *** EMI CDM7 69044-2 [id.]. LSO, Previn.
(M) **(*) Decca 417 700-2 [id.]. VPO, Karajan.

*(**) DG 419 175 [id.]. BPO, Karajan.

Rostropovich's triptych of Tchaikovsky ballet suites is very special. His account of the *Nutcracker suite* is enchanting: the *Sugar plum fairy* is introduced with ethereal gentleness, the *Russian dance* has marvellous zest and the *Waltz of the flowers* combines warmth and elegance with an exhilarating vigour. The *Sleeping Beauty* and *Swan Lake* selections are hardly less distinguished. There is plenty of Slavonic intensity in the sweeping climaxes, and in the former the glorious *Panorama* melody is floated over its gently syncopated rocking bass with magical delicacy. Equally, the whimsical portrait of the cats is matched by the sprightly fledgling swans. The 1979 recording, with full strings and a lustrous ambience, expands spectacularly at climaxes, the CD remastering entirely beneficial, combining bloom with enhanced detail. 69 minutes of sheer joy, and at mid-price too.

The digital remastering has been very successful on the EMI disc, freshening the sound of the excellent recordings, taken from Previn's analogue complete sets (which means that the *Dance of the Sugar Plum Fairy* in *The Nutcracker* has the longer coda rather than the ending Tchaikovsky devised for the *Suite*). The performances are at once vivid and elegant, warm and exciting.

The VPO triptych was made during Karajan's Decca period in the 1960s. As sound, this is much preferable to the DG; if tuttis in the latter are rather sharply focused by the digital transfer, overall this record offers fine playing, even if the VPO textures seem more leonine, less sumptuous than those of the Berlin Philharmonic under Rostropovich.

For DG, Karajan immediately creates an electrifying climax in the *Introduction* to *The Sleeping Beauty* and, throughout, the orchestral solos are wonderfully polished and beguiling, though perhaps the *Little Swans* are made to sound rather reserved. But with the excessively bright treble and a meagre supporting bass response, sonically this is less than the whole Tchaikovskian sound-picture.

Nutcracker suite, Op. 71a; Symphony No. 4 in F min., Op. 36.
(M) *** EMI mono CDM7 63380-2 [id.]. RPO, Sir Thomas Beecham.

Beecham himself praised the balance in the *Nutcracker suite*, one of his own favourite records. It was recorded for American Columbia in Walthamstow Assemby Hall in 1953; when it was later reissued on LP, however, a wrong take was used for the *Dance of the flutes*. This has now been rectified by the skilful dubbing of the correct take from a commercial 78-r.p.m. pressing. It was a missing percussion condiment that caused the retake and, endearingly, the tambourine player in the characteristically zestful account of the *Trépak* almost gets left behind at the end. The performance overall has a Mozartian elegance; the *Dance of the flutes*, seductively slow, is ravishing and so is the closing *Waltz of the flowers*. It is a great pity that Sir Thomas was unenthusiastic about stereo in its early days and so allowed his performance of the *Fourth Symphony* to be recorded in mono, though it was made as late as 1957/8. Even so, the sound is outstandingly vivid, and the ear could easily be fooled into thinking it was stereo, so full are the strings and so rich the brass, with their glorious depth of sonority. The performance is unforgettably full of charisma. In the famous rocking crescendo in the first movement, Beecham manages to be urbane while at the same time building up the tension spontaneously; it is his cultivated approach to Tchaikovsky's marvellous orchestration that makes the reading so individual, while the account is second to none in generating excitement, with the thrilling coda of the last movement creating all the adrenalin of a live occasion.

Romeo and Juliet (fantasy overture).
(M) **(*) Decca 417 722-2 [id.]. VPO, Karajan – GRIEG: *Peer Gynt***(*) (with R. STRAUSS: *Till Eulenspiegel***(*)).
*(*) EMI Dig. CDC7 49115-2 [id.]. Phd. O, Muti – SCRIABIN: *Symphony No. 3.***(*)

Karajan's Decca recording of *Romeo and Juliet* comes from the early 1960s. The performance is marvellously shaped and has superb ardour and excitement: his later DG accounts never quite recaptured the spontaneous freshness of this version. The remastered sound is full, firm and clear.

Muti's account opens promisingly, with beautifully moulded wind phrasing and a finely disciplined orchestral response. However, he drives it too hard and at times it comes near to hysteria.

Serenade for strings in C, Op. 48.
*** DG Dig. 400 038-2 [id.]. BPO, Karajan – DVOŘÁK: *Serenade.****
(M) **(*) Ph. 420 883-2 [id.]. ECO, Leppard – DVOŘÁK: *Serenade.***(*)
(M) **(*) Decca 417 736-2 [id.]. ASMF, Marriner – DVOŘÁK: *Serenade** (with SIBELIUS: *Valse triste.****)
(M) ** DG Dig. 429 488-2 [id.]. Orpheus CO – DVOŘÁK; ELGAR: *Serenades.*(*)
(B) ** Van. VNC 7532 [VCD 72012 with ARENSKY & BORODIN: *Nocturne*]. ECO, Somary – ARENSKY: *Variations***(*); PROKOFIEV: *Classical symphony.***

A vigorously extrovert reading from Karajan, with taut, alert and superbly polished playing in the first movement, an elegant *Waltz*, a passionately intense *Élégie* and a bustling, immensely spirited finale. The compact disc is one of the finest to come from DG. Although there is just a hint of digital edge on the violins, this is offset by the extension of the middle and lower range which is gloriously full and resonant.

Leppard's remastered Philips recording sounds more leonine than before, yet his warm, direct manner is very attractive, and the *Waltz* is beautifully done. In general this is preferable to the Marriner alternative.

Marriner's 1969 performance came from the Academy's vintage years, and the unanimity of phrasing of the violins in the intense slow movement is breathtaking in its expressiveness; but the brightening of the treble response inherent in the digital remastering draws the ear to notice the lack of sheer tonal weight that a bigger body of strings can afford. The performance overall is now made to sound more athletic, less warmly expansive.

No one could accuse the Orpheus Chamber Orchestra of lack of energy in the outer movements; indeed the finale has tremendous vigour, the sheer nervous energy communicating in exhilarating fashion. Overall it is an impressive performance, even if the problems of rubato without a conductor are not always easily solved. Yet there is much that is fresh here, and one cannot but admire the precision of ensemble. The sound is first class, with the acoustics of the Performing Arts Center at New York State University providing plenty of warmth as well as clarity and a full, firm bass-line, very important in this work.

The acoustic of Somary's ECO recording is a trifle cool, but the performance generates much bustle in the first movement and the *Élégie* comes off rather well. A more expansive sound would have been welcome here, but this is still very vivid music-making.

Sérénade mélancolique, Op. 26; Valse-scherzo, Op. 34.
*** Ph. Dig. 420 943-2 [id.]. Midori, LSO, Slatkin – PAGANINI: *Violin concerto No. 1.***(*)

Lovely performances of these two short concertante works of Tchaikovsky from Midori: the cantilena of the *Serenade* is meltingly *mélancolique*.

The Sleeping Beauty (ballet), *Op. 66* (complete).
*** EMI CDC7 49216-2 (2) [Ang. CDCB 49216]. Philh. O, John Lanchbery.
(M) **(*) Decca 425 468-2 (3). Nat. PO, Richard Bonynge – MEYERBEER: *Les Patineurs*.***
** ROH Records Dig. ROHCD 306/8 [id.]. ROHCG O, Mark Ermler.

Lanchbery's splendid Philharmonia recording has been economically reissued on a pair of CDs. His performance combines a gracious classical feeling with a theatrical sense of drama which is tellingly projected, yet never forced. He shows a fine concern for detail and the Philharmonia playing is first class. The recording balance is slightly forward but the wide dynamic range is well judged, the brass has genuine splendour and the orchestral textures combine sparkle with bloom.

Bonynge secures brilliant and often elegant playing from the National Philharmonic Orchestra and his rhythmic pointing is always characterful. As recorded, however, the upper strings lack sumptuousness; otherwise, the sound is excellent and there is much to give pleasure, notably the drama of the awakening scene and the Act III *Divertissement*. The Decca sound has a fine sparkle here, and the solo violin (Mincho Minchev) and cello (Francisco Gabarro) provide most appealing solo contributions.

The account by the Royal Opera House Orchestra, playing very elegantly under Mark Ermler, runs to three full-priced CDs, indicating that tempi are often relaxed and leisurely. Although the performance is not without drama, the combination of amiable warmth in the music-making with a body of orchestral sound that is little short of voluptuous inevitably brings an element of blandness. Although it is easy to sit back and wallow in Tchaikovsky's richly coloured scoring and melodic fecundity, rival versions offer a greater feeling of vitality.

The Sleeping Beauty (ballet): highlights.
**(*) ROH Records Dig. ROH 003 [id.] (from above recording, cond. Ermler).

Those wishing to sample the Ermler set will find this disc contains 72 minutes of well-chosen key items. One can certainly appreciate the polish and grace of the orchestral playing here, when the recording – made in St Jude-on-the-Hill, Hampstead – is so flattering.

Sleeping Beauty (ballet): suite.
(BB) ** Naxos Dig. 8.550079 [id.]. Czech RSO (Bratislava), Ondrej Lenard – GLAZUNOV: *The Seasons*.**(*)

The Czech Radio Orchestra under Ondrej Lenard play Tchaikovsky's ballet suite with spirit and colour, and the recording has plenty of weight and ambience and no lack of brilliance. The *Waltz* goes especially well, but before that the *Panorama* is disappointing, taken fast and with a lack of subtlety in the rocking bass rhythm.

Sleeping Beauty: extended suite; *Swan Lake:* extended suite.
** Telarc Dig. CD 80151 [id.]. RPO, Mackerras.

Sleeping Beauty: suite; *Swan Lake:* suite.
** EMI Dig. CDC7 47075-2 [id.]. Phd. O, Muti.

Those who enjoy Telarc recording of Tchaikovsky with its wide dynamic range, rich, sweet violins, ripe middle sonorities, spectacular brass (and the bass drum never forgotten) will enjoy this greatly. The richly resonant sound-picture adds much to the recording. But Mackerras's penchant for brisk tempi does not always find all the magic and colour. The gorgeous *Panorama* from *Sleeping Beauty*, with its melody floated over a rocking bass, sounds much more beguiling at Rostropovich's relaxed tempo; similarly the famous oboe theme of *Swan Lake* is attractively nubile but could be more serene. The violin/cello duet of the *Dance of the Swans* is a highlight; but overall an element of routine hovers over this music-making, for all its surface vivacity.

The snag (if it is that) of Muti's coupling is the very wide dynamic range, which means that when one achieves a satisfactory level for the violin/cello duet the spectacular climaxes are almost overwhelming. The order of items in *Swan Lake* is unconventional, ending with the Act III *Mazurka* instead of the (perhaps more suitable) grandiloquent finale. Muti's approach is essentially spacious and he concentrates on the elegance of the music, achieving an excellent response from his orchestra; but there is plenty of excitement, too, strongly projected by the extremely vivid sound.

Suites Nos. 1 in D min., Op. 45; 4 (Mozartiana), Op. 61.
*** Olympia Dig. OCD 109 [id.]. USSR Academic SO, Svetlanov.

Tchaikovsky's *Orchestral suites* are directly descended from the dance suites of the Baroque era. Svetlanov shows his understanding of this link by his engagingly light touch. He is particularly successful in *Mozartiana*, where Tchaikovsky's neat scoring is always respectful of the music. Even so, the *Preghiera*, based on Mozart's *Ave verum*, can sometimes sound too opulent, but not here. The *Variations* which end the suite are a delight. The highlight of the earlier D minor work is a deliciously orchestrated *Marche miniature* which tends to dwarf everything else, except perhaps the *Introduction* where Tchaikovsky's innate melancholy at the opening is effectively dispersed by the following fugato. With such sympathetic playing and excellent digital sound, this is a prime recommendation for all keen Tchaikovskians.

(i) *Suite No. 2 in C, Op. 53;* (ii) *Symphony No. 2 in C min. (Little Russian), Op. 17.*
*** Olympia OCD 153 [id.]. (i) USSR Academic SO, Svetlanov; (ii) USSR RSO, Fedoseyev.

Svetlanov's inspirational recording of the *Second Suite* is doubly distinctive for making the listener realize that this is a far more substantial and attractive work than was previously thought. The *Scherzo burlesque* has a part for accordions in its central section, but here they are covered with folksy woodwind sounds: the effect is highly piquant. The finale is a vivacious *Danse baroque* where the energy of the performance bubbles right over. The Russian orchestral playing is full of character and affection throughout, and the vivid recording is a joy in projecting this multi-coloured music.

Fedoseyev's version of the *Little Russian symphony* may not be the most brilliant available: the finale is paced in a very relaxed way and the further broadening at the end is overdone. But the very Russian character of the woodwind and the bright, clean string articulation give the music-making plenty of character and impulse.

Suite No. 3 in G, Op. 55.
*** Olympia Dig. OCD 106 [id.]. USSR Academic SO, Svetlanov – ARENSKY: *Violin concerto.****

Svetlanov treats Tchaikovsky's finest suite very freely, supported by the most eloquent response from one of the premier Soviet orchestras. The first movement is lyrically rhapsodic, then comes a bitter-sweet *Valse mélancolique*, its nostalgia curiously dark for all its grace and lightness of form; the Scherzo, deliciously scored, is almost too purposefully gay; but the work is capped by the masterly final theme and variations, which quite outbalances the structure, but justifies itself by its inspired melodic invention and in its unsurpassed use of orchestral colour. Here some of Svetlanov's tempi are unexpected, and the finale *Polacca* is less overwhelming than in some previous versions, Svetalanov emphasizing its dance rhythms rather than seeking to be grandiose. With excellent, vivid digital recording and an attractive concert-hall ambience, this is highly recommendable, particularly in view of the tempting Arensky coupling.

Swan Lake (ballet), *Op. 20* (complete).
*** ROH Dig. ROH 301/3 [id.]. ROHCG O, Mark Ermler.
*** EMI Dig. CDS7 49171-2 (2) [Ang. CDCB 49171]. Philh. O, Lanchbery.
(M) **(*) Decca 425 413-2 (3) [id.]. Nat. PO, Richard Bonynge – MASSENET: *Cigale.****
**(*) EMI CDS7 49531-2 (2) [id.]. LSO, Previn (with Ida Haendel).
**(*) Olympia Dig. OCD 210 A/B [id.]. USSR RSO, Fedoseyev.
* RCA Dig. RD 87804 (2) [7804-2-RC]. St Louis SO, Slatkin.

Mark Ermler's fine version, opulently recorded, makes an impressive first issue on the new Royal Opera House label. Released from the Covent Garden pit to record in the warm acoustic of All Saints', Tooting, the players have responded to Ermler's deeply sympathetic direction with both refinement and red-blooded commitment, and one is constantly aware of the idiomatic feeling born of long acquaintance. The sound is exceptionally full and open, with the brass in particular giving satisfying weight to the ensemble without hazing over the detail. Ermler's speeds are often – though by no means always – on the slow side, but it is a pity that the decision was taken to stretch the work on to an extra CD, three instead of two, making it far less competitive. Nor does that bring any advantage in breaks between the discs, with the division between the second and third discs coming distractingly in the middle of the Act III *Pas de six*. Nevertheless Ermler's broad speeds consistently convey, more than most rivals', the feeling of an accompaniment for dancing, as in the great andante of the Act I *Pas de deux*. This is a set to have you sitting back in new enjoyment of a gorgeous score.

Lanchbery's 1982 *Swan Lake* sounds excellent in its CD format. The digital sound is a shade drier than we would expect now, but there is no lack of fullness to the string timbre, and overall the effect is vivid, with natural perspective and a wide (but not uncomfortably wide) dynamic range. The orchestral playing is first class, with polished, elegant string phrasing matched by felicitous wind solos. Lanchbery's rhythmic spring is a constant pleasure; everything is alert, and there is plenty of excitement at climaxes. Other conductors – notably Fistoulari – have made this score sound more romantically passionate, but there is no lack of emotional commitment here, even if Lanchbery seldom overwhelms the listener. The score's marvellous detail is revealed with long theatrical experience.

Bonynge's approach is essentially strong and vigorous, bringing out all the drama of the score, if less of its charm. The forward impulse of the music-making is immediately striking. As in the other sets of his Decca Tchaikovsky series, the string timbre is somewhat leonine; overall there is fullness without sumptuousness. The brass sounds are open and vibrant and the upper range is brightly lit. The balance is managed well although the (very well-played) violin solos sound rather larger than life. While this lack of ripeness may not appeal to all ears, there is a consistent freshness here, and the moments of spectacle often make a thrilling impact.

Previn's set, like his recordings of the other Tchaikovsky ballets, offers extremely polished orchestral playing, with beautiful wind solos. Ida Haendel's contribution is first class, and there is much refined detail and no lack of drama when the music calls for it. As in his recording of *The Nutcracker*, Previn is at his finest in the Act III *Divertissement* with its variety of national dances where the orchestral soloists all excel themselves. The recording has been opened out admirably by the digital remastering and sounds very fresh, with little loss of ambient warmth. But it would have been more sensible of EMI to reissue this 1976 set at mid-price; the focus is not always absolutely clear.

Fedoseyev is also given a fine modern digital recording, not quite as expansive as Lanchbery's (made in EMI's No. 1 Studio), but full enough, as well as bright and vivid. The Russian way is essentially dramatic; tempi are brisk and there is less of an air of geniality than with Lanchbery. Yet there is warmth too, as in the famous *Waltz*. The vigour of Fedoseyev's approach is infectious if at times a little unrelenting. The set is well documented, and this can be recommended as the Russian timbres have their own unique character, even if the wind solos are not as refined in colour as the Philharmonia.

Slatkin and the St Louis Orchestra have made some impressive records, but their account of *Swan Lake* is disappointingly cool and uncommitted, at times perfunctory. With dance-rhythms too stiff, rarely given the lift they need, this emerges as an efficient but loveless run-through. The performance is not helped by the sound, which is thinner than usual from this source, with dry violin tone.

Swan Lake (ballet), *Op. 20:* highlights.
(B) *** CfP CD-CFP 4296. Sir Yehudi Menuhin, Philh. O, Efrem Kurtz.
**(*) ROH Records ROH 001 [id.]. ROHCG O, Mark Ermler.
(M) **(*) Ph. 420 872-2 [id.]. LSO, Monteux.

A fine bargain selection on CfP with Menuhin present for the violin solos. He finds a surprising amount to play here; besides the famous duet with cello in the *Danse des cygnes*, which is beautifully done, he includes a ravishing account of the *Danse russe* as a postlude to the main selection. The 1960 recording matches the exuberance which Kurtz brings to the music's climaxes with an expansive dynamic range, and it has atmosphere as well as brilliance. The Philharmonia are on top form and the woodwind acquit themselves with plenty of style, while the string playing is characteristically elegant.

The selection from Mark Ermler's Covent Garden recording is generous and played with plenty of character. But the famous oboe tune which, for most listeners, encapsulates the very essence of Tchaikovsky's score does not appear until towards the end, played quickly and melodramatically. The sound matches the complete set in sumptuousness.

Monteux is also a master of this repertoire and his 1962 recording has been made to seem more vivid, while the weight of the sound remains especially effective in the finale, which Monteux takes broadly and grandly. The LSO playing is lively and responsive.

Symphonies Nos. 1–6.
(M) *** DG 429 675-2 (4) [id.]. BPO, Karajan.

Symphonies Nos. 1–6; Capriccio italien; Manfred symphony.
⊛ (M) *** Chan. Dig. CHAN 8672/8 (7) [id.]. Oslo PO, Jansons.

Jansons' outstanding Tchaikovsky series, which includes *Manfred*, is self-recommending. The full romantic power of the music is consistently conveyed and, above all, the music-making is urgently spontaneous throughout, with the Oslo Philharmonic Orchestra always committed and fresh, helped by the richly atmospheric Chandos sound. The seven separate CDs offered here are packaged in a box priced as for five discs.

Karajan's set, however, offers a quite outstanding bargain. Without *Manfred* (a work he never recorded), the six symphonies are fitted on to four mid-priced CDs, the only drawback being that Nos. 2 and 5 are split between discs. From both a performance and a technical point of view, the accounts of the last three symphonies are in every way preferable to his later, VPO digital versions. They date from 1975–6, whereas the first three symphonies were recorded in 1979, and all offer peerless playing from the Berlin Philharmonic which the Oslo Philharmonic cannot always quite match, for all their excellence.

Symphonies Nos. 1–3.
(M) *** Ph. 420 751-2 (3) [id.]. Concg. O, Haitink.

Haitink's readings are satisfyingly consistent and they have genuine symphonic strength. His special advantage, in addition to the superb Concertgebouw playing, is the Philips recording, which sounds splendid in its remastered form: rich yet fresh, refined in detail and not lacking weight. Haitink's choice of speeds, though not always conventional, always seems apt and natural, and in the *First Symphony* it is typical of his flair for balance that the big horn solo which comes at the end of the slow movement has nothing vulgar in it. Similarly in the *Little Russian*, the solemn nobility of the opening introduction has nothing of pomposity about it and, in the finale, the long and loud coda is given genuine joyfulness, with no blatancy. The *Polish symphony* has a disarmingly direct freshness of approach. The slow movement is not as passionate as in some readings, but the delicacy of the scherzo is capped by a finale in which the rhetoric is minimized.

Symphony No. 1 in G min. (Winter daydreams), Op. 13.
*** Chan. Dig. CHAN 8402 [id.]. Oslo PO, Jansons.

Symphony No. 1 in G min., (Winter daydreams), Op. 13; Francesca da Rimini, Op. 32.
* Teldec/WEA Dig. 2292 44939-2. Leipzig GO, Kurt Masur.

Symphony No. 1; Marche slave, Op. 31; Eugene Onegin: Polonaise and Waltz.
*** DG 419 176-2 [id.]. BPO, Karajan.

Refreshingly direct in style, Jansons with his brilliant orchestra gives an electrically compelling performance of this earliest of the symphonies. The focus is sharp, both of the playing and of the recording, which is both brilliant and atmospheric, not least in the lyrical outpouring of the slow movement. Structurally strong, the result tingles with excitement, most of all in the finale, faster than usual, with the challenge of the complex fugato passages taken superbly. The recording is highly successful.

The playing of the Berlin Philharmonic is marvellous and it is typical that, although Karajan takes the opening *Allegro tranquillo* of the first movement quite fast, there is no feeling of breathlessness: it is genuinely *tranquillo*, though the rhythmic bite of the syncopated passages, so important in these early symphonies, could hardly be sharper. The high polish may give a hint of the ballroom to some of the dance movements, with the folk element underplayed, but the fugato in the last movement is given classical strength, and the peroration has regality and splendour. The sound is excellent, brilliant and with a wide dynamic range. However, the quality is very much brasher in all three fill-ups.

Though there is much to be said for bringing out the symphonic weight of Tchaikovsky's writing, Masur and his superb Leipzig orchestra with their smooth manner and rhythmically four-square approach, go too far in removing all hints of Slavonic temperament. Even in this first and lightest of the Tchaikovsky cycle, the result is heavy, and the *Overture* also lacks excitement.

Symphony No. 2 in C min. (Little Russian), Op. 17 (original 1872 score).
*** Chan. Dig. CHAN 8304 [id.]. LSO, Simon.

This is the first recording of Tchaikovsky's original score of the *Little Russian symphony* and probably the first performance outside Russia, prompted by the enterprising enthusiasm of Edward Johnson, who provides an admirably exhaustive sleeve-note. Although the original format gained considerable success at its early performances, it gave the composer immediate and serious doubts, and so in 1879 Tchaikovsky retrieved the score and immediately set to work to rewrite the first movement. He left the *Andante* virtually unaltered, touched up the scoring of the Scherzo, made minor excisions and added repeats, and made a huge cut of 150 bars (some two minutes of music) in the finale. He then destroyed the original. (The present performance has been possible because of the surviving orchestral parts.) There can be no question that he was right. The reworked first movement is immensely superior to the first attempt, and the finale – delightful though it is – seems quite long enough shorn of the extra bars. However, to hear the composer's first thoughts (as with the original version of *Romeo and Juliet*) is fascinating, and this is an indispensable recording for all Tchaikovskians. Geoffrey Simon secures a committed response from the LSO, and the recording is striking in its inner orchestral detail and freshness, although the lower range is without the resonant richness of some CDs.

Symphony No. 2 in C min. (Little Russian), Op. 17 (see also above, under *Suite No. 2*).
*** Telarc Dig. CD 80131 [id.]. Pittsburgh SO, Maazel – RIMSKY-KORSAKOV: *Antar.****

Symphony No. 2 (Little Russian); Capriccio italien, Op. 45.
*** Chan. Dig. CHAN 8460 [id.]. Oslo PO, Jansons.

Symphony No. 2 (Little Russian); Overture 1812, Op. 49.
*** DG 419 177-2 [id.]. BPO, Karajan.

Symphony No. 2 (Little Russian); The Tempest, Op. 18.
**(*) CBS Dig. MK 39359 [id.]. Chicago SO, Abbado.

Like other Soviet conductors, Jansons prefers a fastish speed for the *Andantino* second movement, but what above all distinguishes this version is the joyful exuberance both of the bouncy Scherzo – fresh and folk-like in the Trio – and of the finale. Jansons' handling of the syncopated idea in the development section of that movement is a delight, and the final coda brings a surge of excitement, making most others seem stiff. The coupling is a fizzing performance of the *Capriccio italien*, bringing a gloriously uninhibited account of the coda with its deliberately vulgar reprise of the Neapolitan tune. With some edge on violin tone, this is not the finest of the Chandos Oslo recordings, but is still fresh and atmospheric.

Karajan's performance of the *Little Russian symphony* is played superbly. Everything is in perfect scale; the tempo for the engaging *Andante* is very nicely judged and the outer movements have plenty of drama and fire. The articulation in the finale is a joy, and the sound balance is excellent. The ambient effect seems slightly drier than in the *First Symphony*, but there is no lack of weight. Karajan's *1812* is also exciting and brilliantly transferred, but many will not count this an ideal coupling.

Maazel's slow introduction is weightier and much more measured than with his competitors. From then on, he believes in treating Tchaikovsky directly and without sentimentality, incisive of attack, refined of texture. The undistracting freshness of his view – never too tense – is enhanced by excellent, well-balanced recording. If the fine *Antar* coupling is suitable, this is thoroughly worth while.

The advantage of Abbado's CBS version over direct rivals is the interest of its fill-up, Tchaikovsky's large-scale *Fantasy* on Shakespeare's *The Tempest*. In that work, Abbado's performance, dramatic and passionate as well as evocative in the opening seascape, is likely to be unrivalled on record; in the *Symphony*, too, he is most persuasive, with virtuoso playing from the Chicago orchestra. With speeds generally faster than usual, he conveys lightness and sparkle, so that in the Scherzo the cross-rhythms are incisively sprung. Only in the finale does he adopt a restrained basic speed; effectively so, except that he slows perceptibly in the jaunty syncopated counter-subject. The recording is warm with the sound a little distanced, natural and undistracting but not ideally clear on detail, with the lower range not too well focused and the bass drum balanced too prominently at times. There are no dividing bands for individual movements.

Symphonies Nos. (i) *2 (Little Russian);* (ii) *4 in F min.*
⊛ (B) *** DG 429 527-2 (i) New Philh. O, or (ii) VPO, Abbado.

Abbado's coupling of Tchaikovsky's *Second* and *Fourth Symphonies* is one of the supreme bargains of the current catalogue. His account of the *Little Russian symphony* is very enjoyable, although the first movement concentrates on refinement of detail and is a shade too deadpan. The *Andantino* is very nicely done and the scherzo is admirably crisp and sparkling. The finale is superb, with fine colour and thrust and a memorably spectacular stroke on the tam-tam before the exhilarating coda. The 1967 recording still sounds excellent. But this is merely a bonus for an unforgettable account of the *Fourth Symphony*, unsurpassed on record and sounding marvellous in its remastered CD format, brilliant yet atmospheric, with a balancing resonance and depth. Abbado's control of the structure of the first movement is masterly. The superbly graduated exposition climax is built from a fragile pianissimo of gently rocking violins and erupts into a blazing culmination from the horns. The secondary material is refined and colourful, the counter-melody graceful in the strings, yet Abbado maintains the intensity to the end of the movement. The *Andantino*, with its gentle oboe solo, really takes wing in its central section. Its delectable reprise is followed by a wittily crisp scherzo, while the finale has sparkle as well as power, epitomizing the Russian dance spirit which was Tchaikovsky's inspiration.

Symphony No. 3 in D (Polish), Op. 29.
*** Chan. Dig. CHAN 8463 [id.]. Oslo PO, Jansons.

Symphony No. 3 in D (Polish); Capriccio italien, Op. 45.
*** DG 419 178-2 [id.]. BPO, Karajan.

Symphony No. 3 in D (Polish); Capriccio italien; Eugene Onegin: Polonaise.
*** Virgin Dig. VC 790761-2 [id.]. Bournemouth SO, Litton.

Tchaikovsky's *Third* is given a clear, refreshingly direct reading by Jansons, totally unsentimental, yet conveying the warmth as well as the exuberance of Tchaikovsky's inspiration. The likeness with *Swan Lake* in the first movement is delectably pointed, but it is the irresistible sweep of urgency with which Jansons builds the development section that sets his performance apart, with the basic tempo varied less than usual. The second movement is beautifully relaxed, the *Andante elegiaco* heartwarmingly expressive, tender and refined, and the Scherzo has a Mendelssohnian elfin quality; but it is the swaggering reading of the finale, always in danger of sounding bombastic, which sets the seal on the whole performance. Even the anthem-like second subject has a lightness of touch, avoiding any sense of squareness or coarseness. Though the recording does not convey a genuinely hushed pianissimo for the strings, it brings full, rich and brilliant sound.

Karajan's first movement is full of flair and in the central movements he is ever conscious of the variety of Tchaikovsky's colouring. He even finds an affinity with Brahms in the second movement, and yet the climax of the *Andante* is full of Tchaikovskian fervour. In the finale, the articulation of the *Polacca* is both vigorous and joyful, and it brings a sense of symphonic strength, often lacking in other versions. The recording is bold, brilliant and clear. After the close of the symphony, the spectacular entry of the brass in the *Capriccio* brings a certain glare to the sound, but this is a sparkling performance and the recording is generally well balanced.

Andrew Litton elected to start his Tchaikovsky cycle for Virgin Classics with the most equivocal and intractable of the symphonies, and the results are impressive. In the outer movements he challenges the players to the limit in his fast speeds, but the clean, purposeful manner is very satisfying, weighty without coarseness, even if some other versions spring rhythms more infectiously. Litton's finesse comes out impressively in the *Andante elegiaco*, where he chooses a flowing speed which needs no basic modification for the broad melody which follows. He then moulds that with satisfyingly Elgar-like nobility. In the *Capriccio italien*, the playing and recording display to the full the dramatic contrasts of texture and dynamic, while the *Eugene Onegin Polonaise* brings an even more infectiously rhythmic performance.

Symphonies Nos. 4–6 (Pathétique).
⊛ *** DG 419 745-2 (2) [id.]. Leningrad PO, Mravinsky.

Few reissues give greater cause for rejoicing than this, the last three Tchaikovsky symphonies by the late Yevgeny Mravinsky and the Leningrad Philharmonic Orchestra. They have never been surpassed – save, perhaps, by their classic 1956 mono accounts – and rarely equalled. The DG remastering produces a much cleaner and better-defined sound than we have ever had before. These are very exciting performances which bring one closer to the soul of this music than almost any other accounts, and it is good to have them with several layers of murkiness removed. They cannot be recommended too strongly.

Symphonies Nos. 4–6; Manfred symphony.
(M) *** Decca 425-586-2 (3) [id.]. Philh. O, Ashkenazy.

Ashkenazy's set makes a genuine bargain on three mid-priced discs, although the CD layout splits No. 5 between the second and third movements. Apart from the emotional power and strong Russian feeling of the readings, the special quality which Ashkenazy conveys is spontaneity. The freshness of his approach, his natural feeling for lyricism on the one hand and drama on the other, is consistently compelling, even if at times the orchestral ensemble is not as immaculate as with Karajan or Haitink. The inclusion of the superb, inspirational account of *Manfred* sets the seal on his achievement. The remastering has brought just a degree of digital brightening to the fortissimo violins but adds to the transparency and tangibility of the sound picture overall. The recording quality remains outstandingly full and atmospheric, with the brass gloriously sonorous and a satisfying weight in the bass.

Symphonies Nos. 4–6; The Nutcracker; Sleeping Beauty; Swan Lake: ballet suites.
(M) *** EMI mono/stereo CMS7 634560-2 (3). Philh. O, Karajan.

The Philharmonia in the early 1950s was an extraordinary body, and these early records are worth having even if you already possess Karajan's later accounts with the

Berlin Philharmonic. Nos. 4 and 5 are mono, but the 1959 *Pathétique* is stereo. Exhilarating performances that still sound amazing for their period.

Symphony No. 4 in F min., Op. 36.
*** Chan Dig. CHAN 8361 [id.]. Oslo PO, Jansons.
**(*) DG Dig. 415 348-2 [id.]. VPO, Karajan.
**(*) Telarc Dig. CD 80047 [id.]. Cleveland O, Maazel.

Symphony No. 4; Capriccio italien.
(M) *** DG 419 872-2 [id.]. BPO, Karajan.

Symphony No. 4; Marche slave.
(B) **(*) Pickwick Dig. PCD 867 [MCA MCAD 25171]. LSO, Rozhdestvensky.

Jansons conducts a dazzling performance of the *Fourth*, unusually fresh and natural in its expressiveness, yet with countless subtleties of expression, as in the balletic account of the second-subject group of the first movement. So idiomatic-sounding is Jansons' handling that the transitions between sections are totally unobtrusive, with steady rather than fluctuating speeds. The *Andantino* flows lightly and persuasively, the Scherzo is very fast and lightly sprung, while the finale reinforces the impact of the whole performance: fast and exciting, but with no synthetic whipping-up of tempo. That is so until the very end of the coda, which finds Jansons pressing ahead just fractionally as he would in a concert, a thrilling conclusion made the more so by the wide-ranging, brilliant and realistic recording in which the reverberant background brings warmth of atmosphere and little or no obscuring of detail. The CD adds impressively to the orchestra's sense of presence within the characterful ambience of the Oslo Philharmonic Hall.

Karajan's 1977 version is undoubtedly more compelling than his previous recordings and is in most respects preferable to the newer Vienna version too. After a dramatically robust fanfare at the start of the first movement, the theme of the *Allegro* steals in and its atmosphere has a tinge of melancholy. Yet it is the vitality and drive of the performance as a whole that one remembers, although the beauty of the wind playing at the opening and close of the slow movement can give nothing but pleasure. The finale has tremendous force to sweep the listener along, and the wide dynamic range of the recording makes the most dramatic effect. The CD transfer is extremely vivid. The ubiquitous *Capriccio italien* is offered as a filler.

The *Fourth* is the most successful of the last three Tchaikovsky symphony recordings which Karajan remade digitally in 1985. Although the playing of the Vienna orchestra does not match that of the Berlin Philharmonic in earlier versions, the freer control of tempo in the first movement brings a more relaxed second-subject group, while in the *Andantino* the Vienna oboist is fresher (though the timbre is edgier) than his Berlin counterpart, the phrasing less calculated. The Scherzo is attractively bright, if less precise, and the finale has splendid urgency and excitement. With the extra depth in the bass that CD can provide, the sound is fuller than before, and the warmly resonant acoustic is attractive, even if detail remains a little clouded.

Maazel's Telarc Cleveland disc established a reputation for sound of spectacular depth and brilliance within natural concert-hall acoustics. Maazel's reading is very similar to his very successful 1965 Decca record, and only in the finale does the new version differ markedly from the old, by seeking amplitude and breadth in preference to uninhibited extrovert excitement. Maazel's approach generates a strong forward momentum in the first movement and is consistently involving in its directness. Yet he lightens the tension effectively (like Jansons) by his balletic approach to the second-subject group. The slow movement, with a plaintive oboe solo, is distinctly appealing, and at the *Più mosso*

Maazel makes a swift, bold tempo change. In the finale the Cleveland Orchestra produces a thrillingly rich body of timbre in the upper strings and the fullest resonance from the lower strings and brass.

After the fanfare, Rozhdestvensky's performance takes a little while to warm up but, when the first climax arrives, it is very impressive. The lyrical secondary material is presented very beguilingly and the rocking string theme at the *Ben sostenuto* is positively sensuous. The slow movement is basically simple, although Rozhdestvensky allows himself a mannered emphasis at its climax. The Scherzo, light and gentle, has the feeling of an arabesque, and the finale is strongly articulated and expansive. With first-class digital recording and a powerful response from the LSO in both the *Symphony* and the coupled *Marche slave*, this is certainly worth considering in the bargain-price range.

Symphony No. 5 in E min., Op. 64.
*** Chan. Dig. CHAN 8351 [id.]. Oslo PO, Jansons.
*** Olympia OCD 221 [id.]. Leningrad PO, Mravinsky (with LIADOV: *Baba Yaga, Op. 56.* MUSSORGSKY: *Khovanshchina: Prelude.* WAGNER: *Tristan: Prelude and Liebstod***).
*** Telarc Dig. CD 80107 [id.]. RPO, Previn – RIMSKY-KORSAKOV: *Tsar Saltan: March.****
** DG Dig. 415 094-2 [id.]. VPO, Karajan.
(M) ** DG Dig. 427 822-2 [id.]. LSO, Karl Boehm.

Symphony No. 5; Capriccio italien.
(B) **(*) Pickwick Dig. PCD 875. LSO, Rozhdestvensky.

Symphony No. 5; 1812 Overture, Op. 49.
* Erato/WEA Dig. 2292 45415-2. Nat. SO, Rostropovich.

Symphony No. 5; Hamlet (fantasy overture), *Op. 67.*
** Decca Dig. 425 503-2. Montreal SO, Dutoit.

(i) *Symphony No. 5 in E min.;* (ii) *Marche slave.*
(M) *** DG 419 066-2 [id.]. BPO, Karajan.
(BB) **(*) LaserLight 15 620 [id.]. (i) Prague Fest. O, Pavel Urbanek; (ii) Hungarian State O, Adám Fischer.

Symphony No. 5; Swan Lake (ballet): *suite.*
**(*) Decca Dig. 425 516-2 [id.]. Chicago SO, Solti.

This was the first symphony to be recorded in an outstanding Tchaikovsky series, in which Jansons, Leningrad-trained, revealed something of the debt he owed to the example of Yevgeny Mravinsky, a master among Russian interpreters. Jansons is notably less wilful than Mravinsky tended to be but is no less intense and electrifying. In the first movement, Jansons' refusal to linger never sounds anything but warmly idiomatic, lacking only a little in charm. The slow movement again brings a steady tempo, with climaxes built strongly and patiently but with enormous power, the final culmination topping everything. In the finale, taken very fast, Jansons tightens the screw of the excitement without ever making it a scramble, following Tchaikovsky's notated slowings rather than allowing extra rallentandos. The sound is excellent, specific and well focused within a warmly reverberant acoustic, with digital recording on CD reinforcing any lightness of bass.

Karajan's 1976 recording stands out from his other recordings of the *Fifth*; for many, this will be a first choice. The first movement is unerringly paced and has great romantic flair; in Karajan's hands the climax of the slow movement is grippingly intense, though with a touchingly elegiac preparation for the horn solo at the opening. The *Waltz* has character and charm too – the Berlin Philharmonic string playing is peerless – and in the finale Karajan drives hard, creating an electrifying forward thrust. The remastered recording brings a remarkable improvement; the bass is more expansive and, although the overall sound-picture is brilliantly lit, it has depth and weight too, besides strong projection and impact. The CD at mid-price makes a fine bargain.

Mravinsky's Olympia recording of Tchaikovsky's *Fifth* was recorded in Leningrad in 1973; the remaining pieces come from a concert at the Moscow Conservatoire. If anything, the *Symphony* is even more electrifying than either of the earlier DG versions. Climaxes are still somewhat rough on this version – but this is easily overlooked, given the excitement of the playing. Another factor prompting a strong recommendation is the other material on the disc. Liadov's *Baba Yaga* is given a virtuoso performance and is also well recorded; the Mussorgsky is predictably atmospheric, and the Wagner leaves no doubt that Mravinsky must have been a great interpreter of this composer.

Previn's fine concern for detail is well illustrated by the way that the great horn melody in the slow movement (superbly played by Jeff Bryant) contains the implication of a quaver rest before each three-quarter group, where normally it sounds like a straight triplet. In the first movement, rhythms are light and well sprung, and the third movement is sweet and lyrical yet with no hint of mannerism, for Previn adopts a naturally expressive style within speeds generally kept steady, even in the great climax of the slow movement which then subsides into a coda of breathtaking delicacy. The finale, taken very fast indeed, crowns an outstandingly satisfying reading. The Telarc recording is full and wide-ranging, not as detailed as some, but very naturally balanced.

Though less brightly recorded than its companions in Rozhdestvensky's LSO series for Pickwick, with strings a little cloudy, this version of the *Fifth* brings a strong, passionate performance, with the middle movements in particular beautifully done. The *Capriccio italien* is also given a sunny and relaxed reading at relatively spacious speeds.

Although the orchestral ensemble is not immaculate, the Prague Festival Orchestra's super-bargain version is very exciting. The tension slowly builds through the first movement and is then maintained to the end. Moreover, the slow movement has a quite glorious horn solo, spacious and warm-timbred. The *Marche slave*, which serves for an encore, not unexpectedly has plenty of sombre Slavonic feeling. The digital recording is well balanced to give a ripe brass sound and plenty of weight to the strings.

Solti's 1987 recording of the *Fifth* brings a striking contrast with his earlier (1975) version, also with the Chicago orchestra. In all four movements the speeds are now faster, the manner more spontaneous-sounding and exuberant. What prevents this version from being a first choice, despite brilliant playing, is the recorded sound, immediate and brightly lit but not ideally clear on detail. The *Swan Lake suite* was also recorded in Symphony Hall, but a year later when the engineers were able to cope with its problems, to produce more vivid sound with greater presence.

Karajan's latest VPO version of the *Fifth* brings a characteristically strong and expressive performance; however, neither in the playing of the Vienna Philharmonic nor even in the recorded sound can it quite match his earlier Berlin Philharmonic version for DG.

Dutoit's introduction, taken at a slow *Andante*, sets the subdued pattern of his reading, and the rest of the movement also fails to attain quite as high a voltage as usual with these performers. The slow movement is sweet and easy, with the great horn solo beautifully withdrawn and with radiant tone from the Montreal violins at climaxes, but with weight replacing dramatic cutting edge, when the motto theme intrudes. One appreciates just what has been missing in dramatic bite when it comes to the finale. There the performance suddenly communicates with new immediacy, and the *Hamlet Overture*, too, has the same electricity, perhaps a question of being recorded at a different session. The sound is full and atmospheric in the Montreal manner, but not quite as detailed as usual in big tuttis.

Boehm's 1981 account of the *Fifth*, given really excellent digital sound, has a splendid first movement, full of character and warm, romantic colour. But Boehm refuses to press the music ahead from his very steady basic start in the slow movement and the result is disappointingly heavy, and the finale too is wanting in thrust and ardour.

Tension is surprisingly low in Rostropovich's Washington version. He completely fails to convince in the way he did in his LPO version for EMI. The first movement is surprisingly slow and metrical, but the *Andante* is on the fast side, with the horn solo too square. Only the finale rises above the rest. The *1812 Overture*, too, fails to bring any rush of adrenalin.

Symphony No. 6 in B min. (Pathétique), Op. 74.
*** Chan. Dig. CHAN 8446 [id.]. Oslo PO, Jansons.
*** Decca 411 615-2 [id.]. Philh. O, Ashkenazy.
(M) (***) DG 419 486-2 [id.]. BPO, Karajan.
(M) *(**) EMI CDM7 69043-2 [id.]. BPO, Karajan.
(M) **(*) DG Dig. 431 046-2 [id.]. NYPO, Bernstein.
**(*) DG Dig. 415 095-2 [id.]. VPO, Karajan.

(i) *Symphony No. 6 in B min. (Pathétique), Op. 74;* (ii) *Overture 1812.*
(BB) *(*) LaserLight Dig. 15 524 [id.]. (i) Prague Fest. O, Pavel Urbanek; (ii) Hungarian State O, Adám Fischer.

Symphony No. 6 (Pathétique); (i) *Francesca da Rimini, Op. 32.*
(B) *** EMI CDZ7 62603-2. Philh. O, Giulini; (i) New Philh. O, Barbirolli.

(i) *Symphony No. 6 (Pathétique);* (ii) *Hamlet* (fantasy overture), *Op. 67a.*
(B) *** Ph. 422 478-2 [id.]. (i) LSO, (ii) New Philh. O, Markevitch.

Symphony No. 6 (Pathétique); Romeo and Juliet (fantasy overture).
(M) *** DG 423 223-2 [id.]. BPO, Karajan.

Symphony No. 6 (Pathétique); The Storm, Op. 76.
(B) **(*) Pickwick Dig. PCD 878. LSO, Rozhdestvensky.

Mariss Jansons and the Oslo Philharmonic crown their magnetically compelling Tchaikovsky series with a superbly concentrated account of the last and greatest of the symphonies. It is characteristic of Jansons that the great second-subject melody is at once warm and passionate yet totally unsentimental, with rubato barely noticeable. The very fast speed for the third-movement *March* stretches the players to the very limit, but the exhilaration is infectious, leading to the simple dedication of the slow finale, unexaggerated but deeply felt. Fine, warm recording as in the rest of the series.

After an arresting account of the sombre introduction, the urgency with which Ashkenazy and his Philharmonia players attack the *Allegro* of the first movement of the *Pathétique* belies the composer's *non troppo* marking. The emergence of the beautiful second subject offers the more striking contrast, with Ashkenazy's characteristic lyrical ardour bringing a natural warmth to the great melody. As in his other Tchaikovsky records, this whole performance is pervaded by freshness and spontaneity, through the balletic 5/4 movement, with its essentially Russian quality of melancholy, and the vigorous Scherzo/march, rhythmically buoyant and joyful rather than relentlessly high-powered, as under Karajan. The finale combines passion with tenderness, and the total absence of expressive hysteria brings a more poignant culmination than usual. The CD retains the analogue atmosphere while detail is clarified and intensified.

Giulini's performance was recorded with the Philharmonia at its peak in 1959, and this bargain reissue still sounds excellent in the CD transfer. It comes most generously coupled with Barbirolli's colourful and intense 1969 version of *Francesca da Rimini* with the New Philharmonia, one of his very finest recordings from his last years. Giulini takes a spacious view of the *Pathétique*. There is a degree of restraint in the way he interprets the big melodies of the first and last movements, which are given an almost Elgarian nobility. Yet passionate intensity is conveyed by the purity and concentration of the playing, which equally builds up electric tension and excitement without hysteria. Giulini's 1981 DG digital *Pathétique*, now reissued at mid-price (427 823-2), is curiously lightweight. The recording is also rather closely balanced. The finale does not lack eloquence; but his Philharmonia recording of two decades earlier has more individuality than this.

Karajan has a very special affinity with Tchaikovsky's *Pathétique symphony*. He has recorded it five times in stereo. For many, the 1976 version is the finest – but the current issue on CD of this performance must be treated with extreme caution. The bright recording has been remastered fiercely and the upper range is so sharp-edged as to make the ear cringe in the louder passages. Undoubtedly the impact of Tchaikovsky's climaxes – notably those of the first and third movements – is tremendously powerful, the articulation of the Berlin players precise and strong. In the 5/4 movement Karajan allows the middle section to increase the elegiac feeling, against a background of remorseless but distanced drum-beats, like a tolling bell. The finale has great passion and eloquence, with two gentle sforzandos at the very end to emphasize the finality of the closing phrase. We must hope that DG will consider a further remastering of this recording.

Turning back to Karajan's 1964 CD, one finds a reading that is no less exciting but more consistent in its overall control of tension. At the climactic point of the first movement, the deeply committed playing creates a quality of expressive fervour to send shivers down the spine, with a noble resolution from the Berlin brass. The march/Scherzo has an exhilaratingly consistent forward momentum and, with demonic playing from the Berlin orchestra, wonderfully sharp in ensemble, the aggressive force of the climaxes communicates the greatest excitement. Karajan's consistency is carried through to the passionate last movement, concluded, as in the later version, with those gentle stabbing chordal emphases. It is overall an engulfing experience; the remastered sound is brilliant but with a balancing warmth and weight, the violin timbre bright, but full too. Now offered paired with Karajan's 1967 version of *Romeo and Juliet*, also a very fine performance, this mid-priced CD is very good value.

In between his two DG versions, in 1972 Karajan returned to the Jesus-Christus Kirche in Berlin to record the work yet again, this time for EMI. It is another superlative performance, in some ways the most spontaneous of all in its deep feeling and onward flow. In the first movement the beautiful second subject is less consciously moulded than in the 1964 version, and the *Allegro con grazia* is gentler and has a poignant combination of warmth and nostalgia. The Scherzo/march has enormous energy, yet remains exuberantly joyful; the finale brings the deepest intensity of feeling. The snag again is the recording itself, which in its remastered format is uncomfortably shrill in fortissimos: massed violins don't sound like this in real life. But otherwise there is plenty of body and the ambience of the famous Berlin church adds to the overall sonority.

Markevitch also brings great intensity to his account of the first movement. He takes the *Allegro* at a fast pace and drives hard throughout, producing a *stringendo* that further tautens the climax at the reprise of the second subject. The effect is undoubtedly powerful but, with a touch of harshness to the recording, some might feel that Markevitch is too aggressive, even though the performance is always under emotional control. The second movement has both warmth and elegance, and the march is treated broadly, providing suitable contrast before a deeply felt performance of the finale, where the second subject is introduced with great tenderness. The close of the *Symphony* has an elegiac quality to complete a reading which has a wide emotional range and is gripping from first to last. The performance of *Hamlet* is exciting, with a particularly telling closing section. The portrayal of Ophelia is rather striking, but the remastered recording produces less than ideal fullness for the massed violins.

The timings in Bernstein's version make you suspect that someone has made a mistake with the stopwatch. At 59 minutes overall, it is the slowest *Pathétique* ever, over a quarter of an hour longer than Jansons' (by no means rushed) version. To an amazing degree the conductor's magnetism and his ability to sustain electric tension, not least in hushed pianissimos of fine delicacy, justify his view, but this is an eccentric version by any count, a live recording that is fascinating to hear once but which is not for repeated listening. The wide-ranging DG recording is one of the best made in Avery Fisher Hall.

Karajan's latest version of the *Pathétique* has many characteristically strong points; however, although the reading is not without intensity or spontaneity, it lacks the grip of the earlier Berlin Philharmonic recordings and, with the Vienna ensemble noticeably slacker than that of the Berliners, it is a flawed experience.

Rozhdestvensky's performance with the LSO on the bargain-price Pickwick label, generously coupled and very well recorded in modern digital sound, makes an obvious bargain. His passionate reading fails to match the finest in precision of ensemble – the slow finale is warm rather than tense or tragic – but the sense of spontaneity is most compelling.

The LaserLight *Pathétique* is disappointingly lightweight after the Prague orchestra's successful *Fifth*. This is a symphony that needs maximum intensity and one wishes that it had as much as the coupled *1812*, which is enjoyably exciting and has a spectacular close, with Adám Fischer broadening the final peroration to achieve maximum grandiloquence.

The Tempest (fantasy), *Op. 18* (see also above, under *Symphony No. 2*).
(*) ASV Dig. CDDCA 586 [id.]. LSO, Yondani Butt – LISZT: *Ce qu'on entend sur la montagne*.(*)

The Tempest is a comparatively early work (1873) but its opening seascape, with its highly evocative horn passage, is matched later by the passionate intensity of Miranda and Ferdinand's love-theme, with its soaring upward leap. Yondani Butt gives an impressively controlled performance, holding back for the final climax, and on CD the spectacular digital recording produces some thrilling sounds within its resonant acoustic – the effect is not unlike a Telarc recording.

Variations on a rococo theme for cello and orchestra, Op. 33.
*** DG 413 819-2 [id.]. Rostropovich, BPO, Karajan – DVOŘÁK: *Concerto*.***
*** RCA Dig. RD 71003. Ofra Harnoy, Victoria SO, Freeman – OFFENBACH: *Concerto*; SAINT-SAENS: *Concerto No. 1*.***
(M) *** EMI CDM7 69169-2 [id.]. Tortelier, N. Sinfonia, Yan Pascal Tortelier – DVOŘÁK: *Concerto*.***
*** ASV Dig. CDRPO 8012 [id.]. Tortelier, RPO, Groves – ELGAR: *Concerto***(*); DVOŘÁK: *Rondo*.***

No grumbles about Rostropovich's performance in partnership with Karajan. He plays as if this were one of the greatest works for the cello, and he receives glowing support from Karajan and the Berlin Philharmonic. Rostropovich (in common with all his competitors here) uses the published score, not Tchaikovsky's quite different, original version as played by Wallfisch on Chandos (see above, under *Andante cantabile*). The recording is rich and refined and sounds fresh in its digitally remastered form.

Ofra Harnoy's scale is smaller, the style essentially elegant, not missing its colour or ardour but never forgetting the word 'rococo' in the title. It is a considerable performance, stylish yet emotionally responsive, and Paul Freeman's accompaniment is first class, too. The CD gives a forward balance to the cello, but this is more than acceptable when the playing is so enticing.

A finely wrought account from Tortelier *père*, accompanied by the Northern Sinfonia under Tortelier *fils*. This is very enjoyable, if perhaps not quite so distinguished as Rostropovich on DG. Well worth considering at mid-price.

Tortelier's version on the RPO label is warm and red-blooded, if technically not as flawless as his earlier reading, but the recording is pleasantly atmospheric, slightly distanced so that the tenderness of the performance is brought out the more.

CHAMBER AND INSTRUMENTAL MUSIC

Album for the young, Op. 39: (i) original piano version; (ii) trans. for string quartet by Dubinsky.
*** Chan. CHAN 8365 [id.]. (i) Luba Edlina; (ii) augmented Borodin Trio.

These twenty-four pieces are all miniatures, but they have great charm; their invention is often memorable, with quotations from Russian folksongs and one French, plus a brief reminder of *Swan Lake*. Here they are presented twice, in their original piano versions, sympathetically played by Luba Edlina, and in effective string quartet transcriptions arranged by her husband, Rostislav Dubinsky. The Borodin group play them with both affection and finesse. The CD has plenty of presence.

Piano trio in A min., Op. 50.
*** EMI Dig. CDC7 49865-2 [id.] Chung Trio – SHOSTAKOVICH: *Piano trio No. 1.****
*** Ph. Dig. 422 400-2 [id.]. Beaux Arts Trio.
*** EMI CDC7 47988-2 [id.]. Ashkenazy, Perlman, Harrell.
(*) Delos Dig. DE 3056 [id.]. Cardenes, Solow, Golabek – ARENSKY: *Trio No. 1.**
(*) Olympia OCD 157 [id.]. Leningrad Philharmonic Trio – GLAZUNOV: *String quartet No. 1.**

An ardent and committed performance comes from the Chung Trio. Myung-Whun is very much the dominant partner (at times his virtuosity would seem more at home in a concerto) but he plays with great delicacy and charm. Some of the variations (Nos. 2 and 8) are played better here than in any of the rival versions, and the recording is splendidly truthful and realistic. Moreover they give us the whole work uncut (as did Perlman, Ashkenazy and Harrell). The only snag is the somewhat reticent playing of Myung-Wha Chung: she is a refined cellist, but her sound is not as big or her personality as strong as either her brother or sister. All the same, this is so likeable a performance that we have been tempted to give it three stars. Moreover it includes a worthwhile coupling.

The Beaux Arts give an impressive and imaginative account of this elegiac yet romantically powerful *Piano trio*, which seems to be coming into its own on record. Some ears – though not ours – seem to find it overlong, and many artists observe the optional cuts the composer indicated. The Beaux Arts, who omitted the fugue in their earlier, LP record, now restore it but still make the sizeable cut in the final coda. All the same, theirs is a very fine reading – arguably the best now before the public, though we have a soft spot for the Chungs. It is a pity that there is no fill-up since, at full price, this will be regarded by many collectors as short measure. The Beaux Arts are superbly recorded, although some ears may find the sound almost too vivid and present.

The dominating keyboard role of the first movement of Tchaikovsky's *Piano trio* can so easily sound rhetorical, as well as gripping and commanding – and that element is not entirely avoided by Ashkenazy, Perlman and Harrell. But the *Variations* which form the second part of the work are very successful, with engaging characterization and a great deal of electricity in the closing pages. Indeed, generally this group carry all before them, with their sense of artistic purpose and through their warmth and ardour. The sound is on the dry side, with the digital remastering increasing the sharpness of focus, where a little more ambience would have been a more attractive addition.

The Cardenes group do not always seem absolutely at home in the repetitive rhetoric of the first movement, but in all other respects theirs is an appealing performance, polished and warmly spontaneous. In the strongly characterized set of variations they lead the listener on most communicatively; they include the *Fugue*, and they make a good case for it. Very attractively coupled, this is well worth considering, particularly as the recording is naturally balanced and realistic – not as forward as the Beaux Arts version, and all the better for it.

The balance of the Leningrad trio is much more integrated than in the EMI version, with the piano placed among the strings rather than taking a concertante role. While Tamara Fidler can play boldly when required, she does not dominate the tuttis in quite the way Ashkenazy does. But the intimacy of the performance has its own appeal – the very opening is enticing – and this is a real performance, albeit much more relaxed in the first movement. The *Variations* are done with sparkle and a good deal of charm, and the *Fugue* is not left out. The recording is modern (1986), balanced a shade closely but truthful, and it does not make the strings sound edgy. With its handsome Glazunov coupling, this is excellent value.

String quartets Nos. 1 in D, Op. 11; 2 in F, Op. 22; 3 in E flat min., Op. 30; (i) *Souvenir de Florence* (string sextet), *Op. 70.*
*** EMI Dig. CDS7 49775-2 (2). Borodin Qt, (i) with Y. Bashmet, N. Gutman.

This set assembles all three Tchaikovsky *Quartets* together with the glorious *Souvenir de Florence*. Given performances of this distinction and music of this quality of inspiration, the set is self-recommending. The digital recording is very nearly as outstanding as the performances, and there is no reason to qualify the strength and warmth of our recommendation.

String quartet No. 1 in D, Op. 11.
(M) **(*) Decca 425 541-2 [id.]. Gabrieli Qt – BORODIN; SHOSTAKOVICH: *Quartets.***(*)

The coupling of Tchaikovsky's *D major Quartet* (including the famous *Andante cantabile*) with the Borodin work containing the comparable *Nocturne* is good planning, especially with Shostakovich added to provide a touch of twentieth-century acerbity. The Gabrielis give a finely conceived performance of the Tchaikovsky, producing well-blended tone-quality, and the 1977 recording is clean and alive; but ideally the upper range could be less forcefully projected.

PIANO MUSIC

The Seasons, Op. 37a.
**(*) Chan. Dig. CHAN 8349 [id.]. Lydia Artymiw.

Tchaikovsky's twelve *Seasons* (they would better have been called 'months') were written to a regular deadline for publication in the St Petersburg music magazine, *Nuvellist*. They are lightweight but attractively varied in character and style. It is the gentler, lyrical pieces that are most effective in the hands of Lydia Artymiw, and she plays them thoughtfully and poetically. Elsewhere, she sometimes has a tendency marginally to over-characterize the music. The digital recording is truthful, and on CD the fairly close balance (pedal noises are faintly audible) gives striking presence to the piano which might ideally have been a little further back; but the image is real.

CHORAL MUSIC

Liturgy of St John Chrysostom.
(M) *** AVM AVMCD 1020 [id.]. Svetoslav Obretenov Bulgarian Ch. with soloists, Georgi Robev.

This Bulgarian recording claims to be the first ever complete one of Tchaikovsky's unaccompanied choral work, *The Liturgy of St John Chrysostom*. With its 15 sections lasting a full 75 minutes, it presents a fascinating light on the composer, ending in exultation. Georgi Robev conducts the Svetoslav Obretenov Bulgarian Choir in a dedicated performance. The only snag is that there are no separate tracks to identify different sections on this very long CD.

The Snow Maiden (Snegourotchka): complete incidental music.
**(*) Chant du Monde LDC 278 904 [id.]. Simonova, Martinov, Elnikov, Lomonossov, USSR R. & TV Ch. & O, Provatorov.

This single disc conveniently and generously includes all the 80 minutes of incidental music Tchaikovsky wrote for *The Snow Maiden*, and much of it is vintage material, very delightful, bringing reminders of *Eugene Onegin* in the peasant choruses and some of the folk-based songs, and of the later Tchaikovskian world of *The Nutcracker* in some of the dances. It is true that Tchaikovsky's *Dance of the tumblers* cannot quite match the one from Rimsky-Korsakov's opera in memorability, but, with fine, idiomatic performances, this work is a most cherishable rarity. The soloists are characterfully Slavonic, better caught in the recording than the chorus, which is not helped by backward balance; the bite of their fine singing does not come over fully. Though the digital recording is bright and full-bodied, there is occasional coarseness in the orchestral sound too.

OPERA

Eugene Onegin (complete).
*** Decca 417 413-2 (2) [id.]. Kubiak, Weikl, Burrows, Reynolds, Ghiaurov, Hamari, Sénéchal, Alldis Ch., ROHCG O, Solti.
**(*) DG Dig. 423 959-2 (2) [id.]. Freni, Allen, Von Otter, Schicoff, Burchuladze, Sénéchal, Leipzig R. Ch., Dresden State O, Levine.

Solti, characteristically crisp in attack, has plainly warmed to the score of Tchaikovsky's colourful opera, allowing his singers full rein in rallentando and rubato to a degree one might not have expected of him. The Tatiana of Teresa Kubiak is most moving – rather mature-sounding for the *ingénue* of Act I, but with her golden, vibrant voice rising most impressively to the final confrontation of Act III. The Onegin of Bernd Weikl may have too little variety of tone, but again this is firm singing that yet has authentic Slavonic tinges. Onegin becomes something like a first-person story-teller. The rest of the cast is excellent, with Stuart Burrows as Lensky giving one of his finest performances on record yet. Here, for the first time, the full range of musical expression in this most atmospheric of operas is superbly caught, with the Decca CDs capturing every subtlety – including the wonderful off-stage effects.

The DG version brings a magnificent Onegin in Thomas Allen. The voice may be on the noble side for the role, hardly implying caddishness; however, not only the sheer beauty and firmness of sound but also the range of detailed expression, the facial communication implied, make this the most satisfying account of the title-role yet recorded. It is matched by the Tatiana of Mirella Freni, even at a late stage in her career readily conveying girlish freshness in her voice. The maturing of the character is most convincingly conveyed. The other parts are also strongly taken. The tautened-nerves quality in the character of Lensky comes out vividly in the portrayal by Neil Schicoff, and Anne Sofie von Otter with her firm, clear mezzo believably makes Olga a younger sister, not the usual over-ripe character. Paata Burchuladze is a satisfyingly resonant Gremin and Michel Sénéchal, as on the Solti set, is an incomparable Monsieur Triquet. What welds all these fine components into a rich and exciting whole is the conducting of James Levine with the Dresden Staatskapelle: passionate, at times even wild in Slavonic excitement, yet giving full expressive rein to Tchaikovskian melody, allowing the singers to breathe. The Leipzig Radio Choir sings superbly as well. The snag is that the DG recording is unevocative and studio-bound, with sound close and congested enough to undermine the bloom on both voices and instruments. In every way the more spacious acoustic in the Solti set is preferable.

Queen of Spades (complete).
** Ph. 420 375-2 (3) [id.]. Atlantov, Milashkina, Fedoseyev, Levko, Bolshoi Theatre Ch. & O, Ermler.

The sense of presence and atmosphere here makes up for shortcomings in the singing, with Vladimir Atlantov as Herman too taut and strained, singing consistently loudly, and with Tamara Milashkina producing curdled tone at the top, not at all girlish. Both those singers, for all their faults, are archetypally Russian, and so – in a much more controlled way – is Valentina Levko, a magnificent Countess, firm and sinister.

Opera ballet music: *Eugene Onegin: Écossaise; Polonaise; Waltz. The Maid of Orleans: Entr'acte; Danse des bohémiens; Dans des polichinelles et des histrions. The Oprichnik: Danses. The Sorceress: Introduction; Danse des histrions et scène. Oxana's Caprices: Introduction; Danse russe; Danse des cosaques.*
(M) *** Ph. 422 845-2. ROHCG O, C. Davis.

An engaging collection of mostly lesser-known Tchaikovsky, revealing no new masterpieces but showing the composer's vigorous melodic resource and his brilliant use of the orchestral palette even when his melodies are less memorable. The opening items from *Eugene Onegin* tend to overshadow what follows in their tuneful inspiration, especially when they are played with such *brio* and commitment, but Tchaikovskians will not be disappointed with the rest of the programme. The lively, characterful playing is matched by full yet lively sound, with plenty of ambience, very well balanced.

Telemann, Georg Philipp (1681–1767)

Concertos: for 2 chalumeaux in D min.; for flute in D; for 3 oboes, 3 violins in B flat; for recorder & flute in E min.; for trumpet in D; for trumpet & violin in D.
*** DG Dig. 419 633-2 [id.]. Soloists, Col. Mus. Ant., Goebel.

As Reinhard Goebel points out, Telemann 'displayed immense audacity in the imaginative and ingenious mixing of the colours from the palette of the baroque orchestra', and these are heard to excellent effect here. Those who know the vital *B flat concerto* – or, rather, A major, for that is how it actually sounds – for three oboes and violins, from earlier versions, will find the allegro very fast indeed and the slow movement quite thought-provoking. The chalumeau is the precursor of the clarinet, and the concerto for two chalumeaux recorded here is full of unexpected delights. Marvellously alive and accomplished playing, even if one occasionally tires of the bulges and nudges on the first beats of bars.

Concerto for flute, oboe d'amore and viola d'amore in E; Concerto polonois; Double concerto for recorder and flute in E min.; Triple trumpet concerto in D; Quadro in B flat.
*** O-L Dig. 411 949-2 [id.]. AAM with soloists, Hogwood.

'An attentive observer could gather from these folk musicians enough ideas in eight days to last a lifetime,' wrote Telemann after spending a summer in Pless in Upper Silesia. Polish ideas are to be found in three of the concertos recorded here – indeed, one of the pieces is called *Concerto polonois*. As always, Telemann has a refined ear for sonority, and the musical discourse with which he diverts us is unfailingly intelligent and delightful. The performances are excellent and readers will not find cause for disappointment in either the recording or presentation.

Horn concerto in D; Double horn concerto in D; Triple horn concerto in D; Suite in F for 2 horns and strings; Tafelmusik, Book 3: Double horn concerto in E flat.
*** Ph. Dig. 412 226-2 [id.]. Baumann, Timothy Brown, Hill, ASMF, Iona Brown.

The *E flat Concerto* comes from the third set of *Tafelmusik* (1733) and is the best-known of the four recorded here. The playing here and in the other concertos is pretty dazzling, not only from Hermann Baumann but also from his colleagues, Timothy Brown and Nicholas Hill. Mention should also be made of the concertante contributions from the two violinists. Telemann's invention rarely fails to hold the listener, and the recording has warm ambience and excellent clarity.

Double concerto in F for 2 horns; Concerto in B flat for 3 oboes & 3 violins; Double concerto in F for recorder, bassoon & strings; Concerto in G for 4 violins.
(M) *** Teldec/WEA 2292 43543-2 [id.]. Soloists, VCM, Harnoncourt.

One of the best Telemann discs currently available. The *Concerto for two horns* shows the composer at his most characteristic (natural horns are used), and the performances are most persuasive. The oboes also sound splendidly in tune, which is not always the case with the baroque instrument, and phrasing is alive and sensitive. Indeed these 1966 performances are extremely fine, and only the *Concerto for recorder and bassoon* lets the disc down a little; it is also not as well played as the others. The quality is good and the digital remastering has not tried to clarify artificially what is basically a resonant recording with inner detail mellowed by the ambience.

Oboe concertos: in C min.; D; D min.; E min.; F min.
*** Ph. Dig. 412 879-2 [id.]. Holliger, ASMF, Iona Brown.

The *C minor Concerto* with its astringent opening dissonance is the most familiar of the concertos on Holliger's record, and the *E minor* has also been recorded before, but the remaining three are all new to the catalogue. Telemann was himself proficient on the oboe and wrote with particular imagination and poignancy for this instrument. The performances are all vital and sensitively shaped and a valuable addition to the Telemann discography. Well worth investigation.

(i) *Oboe concertos: in C min.; D min.; E min.; F min.;* (ii) *Sonatas: in G; E min. (from Essercizii Musici); G min. (from Tafelmusik, Part 3).*
(M) **(*) EMI Dig. CDM7 63068-2. Hans de Vries; (i) Amsterdam Alma Music; (ii) Van Asperen, Moller.

Hans de Vries is a fine player and he produces an attractively full timbre on his baroque oboe; the accompaniments for him in the four *Concertos* are alert and stylish. The snag is the very forward balance of the solo instrument, which makes everything sound on one dynamic level. All four *Concertos* are characteristically inventive – but the three *Sonatas* are a delight; in the work taken from the *Tafelmusik*, Telemann offers no fewer than seven movements, all full of character. Apart from the balance, the sound is very vivid and the harpsichord image in the *Sonatas* is particularly pleasing.

Recorder concerto in C; (i) *Double concerto for recorder and bassoon.*
*** BIS Dig. CD 271 [id.]. Pehrsson, (i) McGraw; Drottningholm Bar. Ens. – VIVALDI: *Concertos.****

Clas Pehrsson and Michael McGraw are most expert players, as indeed are their colleagues of the Drottningholm Baroque Ensemble; the recordings are well balanced and fresh.

Double concerto in F, for recorder, bassoon & strings; Double concerto in E min., for recorder, flute & strings; Suite in A min., for recorder & strings.
*** Ph. Dig. 410 041-2 [id.]. Petri, Bennett, Thunemann, ASMF, Iona Brown.

The *E minor Concerto* for recorder, flute and strings is a delightful piece and is beautifully managed, even though period-instrument addicts will doubtless find William Bennett's tone a little fruity. The playing throughout is highly accomplished and the *Suite in A minor*, Telemann's only suite for treble recorder, comes off beautifully. Excellently played and recorded throughout. The compact disc brings out the forward balance of the soloists in the *Double concerto*, but the effect is not unattractive. The orchestral focus is not absolutely clean, though quite agreeable.

(i) *Double concerto in A min. for recorder, viola & strings; Duet in C for recorder & violin.*
(ii) *Trio in C for recorder, violin & continuo; Trio in F for recorder, viola & continuo.*
*** Ph. Dig. 420 243-2 [id.]. Petri, Zukerman, (i) St Paul CO; (ii) James (with HERBERLE: *Recorder concerto in G***).

The liveliness of Telemann's invention is heard at its finest here, not only in the two *Trios*, which are further enlivened by some deliciously nimble decoration from Michala Petri, but also in the *Duet*. Here one is amazed at the diversity of colour and interplay of timbre Telemann achieves in this exceedingly entertaining four-movement piece. Of course the partnership of Petri and Zukerman is a joy: they play with a smiling vivacity and elegance that it is impossible to resist. The forward, truthful recording helps with good projection. The concert is completed with a *Concerto* by Anton Herberle, an obscure musician who lived around the turn of the nineteenth century. His *galant* three-movement work is undeniably engaging and it has a winning virtuoso finale in the form of a fast Minuet with two Trios – the sort of infectious piece that James Galway might wish he had discovered before Ms Petri. Needless to say, she plays it with enormous flair: it is the kind of lollipop that remains in the memory.

Trumpet concerto in D; Double trumpet concerto in E flat; 2 Concertos in D for trumpet, 2 oboes & strings; Concerto in D for 3 trumpets, 2 oboes, timpani & strings.
*** Ph. Dig. 420 954-2 [id.]. Hardenberger, Laird, Houghton, Nicklin, Miller, ASMF, Iona Brown.

The effortless higher tessitura of Hardenberger and his admirable sense of style dominate a concert where all the soloists are expert and well blended by the engineers. The concertos with oboes offer considerable variety of timbre and have fine slow movements; there is for instance an engaging *Poco andante* where the oboes are given an *Aria* to sing over a simple but effective continuo, given here to the bassoon (Graham Sheen). That same work is structured unusually in five movements, with two short *Grave* sections to provide pivots of repose. Telemann is always inventive and, with such excellent playing and recording, this can be recommended to anyone who enjoys regal trumpet timbre.

(i) *Viola concerto in G;* (ii) *Suite in A min. for recorder and strings; Tafelmusik,* Part 2: (iii) *Triple violin concerto in F;* Part 3: (iv) *Double horn concerto in E flat.*
⊛ (BB) *** Naxos Dig. 8.550156 [id.]. (i) Kyselak; (ii) Stivín; (iii) Hoelblingova, Hoelbling, Jablokov; (iv) Z. & B. Tylšar, Capella Istropolitana, Richard Edlinger.

Our Rosette is awarded for enterprise and good planning – to say nothing of good music-making. It is difficult to conceive of a better Telemann programme for anyone encountering this versatile composer for the first time and coming fresh to this repertoire, having bought the inexpensive Naxos CD on impulse. There must be a vibrant musical life in Bratislava, for the excellent Capella Istropolitana consists of members of the Slovak Philharmonic, which is based there, and the soloists here are drawn from its ranks. Ladislav Kyselak is a fine violist and is thoroughly at home in Telemann's splendid four-movement concerto; Jiří Stivín is an equally personable recorder soloist in the masterly *Suite in A minor;* his decoration is a special joy. The *Triple violin concerto* with its memorable *Vivace* finale and the *Double horn concerto* also show the finesse which these musicians readily display. Richard Edlinger provides polished and alert accompaniments throughout: he is especially good at pacing the eight diverse movements of the *Suite,* which has so much in common with Bach's similarly scored *Suite in B minor.* The digital sound is first class.

Darmstadt overtures (suites): in C, TWV 55: C 6; in D, TWV 55: D 15; in D min., TWV 55: D 3; in G min., TWV 55: G 4; Tafelmusik, Part 1: *Overture (suite) in E min.; Concerto in A for flute and violin;* Part 2: *Overture (suite) in D; Concerto for three violins in F;* Part 3: *Overture (suite) in B flat. Concerto for 2 horns in E flat.*
(M) *** Teldec/WEA 2292 42723-2 (3) [id.]. Concerto Amsterdam, Brüggen; VCM, Harnoncourt.

What strikes one with renewed force while listening to these once again is the sheer fertility and quality of invention that these works exhibit. This is music of unfailing intelligence and wit and, although Telemann rarely touches the depths of Bach, there is no lack of expressive eloquence either. Renewing acquaintance with this music has been a pleasure, for it is easy to forget how rewarding these pieces are. The performances are light in touch and can be recommended with real enthusiasm. This would make an excellent start to any Telemann collection.

Tafelmusik: Overtures (suites): in E min. (from Part 1); *in D* (from Part 2); *in B flat* (from Part 3).

(M) *** Teldec/WEA 2292 43546-2 [id.]. Concerto Amsterdam, Brüggen.

Essentially, these works are made up of French dance-movements of considerable diversity, and the *E minor Suite* is engagingly scored for a pair of recorders with strings; although it has no *Badinerie*, its sound is not unlike Bach's B minor work; while Telemann's *D major*, with its forthright use of a trumpet, similarly reminds one of the Bach *Third Suite*, even though its invention has nothing in it as memorable as Bach's famous *Air*. The third suite here is perhaps the most agreeable of all, using two oboes with considerable flair. All this music is expertly played by the Concerto Amsterdam under Frans Brüggen, and the remastered 1970 recording is fresh and full, so that the disc sounds hardly dated at all. Offered at mid-price, it represents first-rate value.

Water Music (Hamburg Ebb and Flow); Concertos in A min.; B flat; F.
*** DG Dig. 413 788-2 [id.]. Col. Mus. Ant., Goebel.

Telemann's *Water Music* was written for the centenary celebrations of the Hamburg Admiralty in 1723, and this lively and inventive suite was performed during the festivities. It is one of Telemann's best-known works and, save for the opening *overture*, is given a very lively performance, with sprightly rhythms and vital articulation. The eccentric opening is less than half the speed of Marriner's (deleted) version on Argo or Wenzinger's famous old Archiv account. Of particular interest are the three *Concertos* which form the coupling, two of which (in F major and A minor) are new to records. The invention is of unfailing interest, as is the diversity of instrumental colouring. The balance is admirably judged and the recording excellent.

CHAMBER MUSIC

Der getreue Musik-Meister: Nos. 4, 7, 13, 20, 28, 31, 35, 50, 53, 59, 62.
*** Denon Dig. C37 7052 [id.]. Holliger, Thunemann, Jaccottet.

This compact disc offers three of the most important works from *Der getreue Musik-Meister* for oboe and continuo, two *Sonatas* and a *Suite*, as well as the *F minor Sonata*, designated for recorder or bassoon and played here by Klaus Thunemann. They are interspersed with various miniatures, all well played and recorded. Holliger's playing is unusually expressive and his eloquence alone makes this selection worth having.

Paris quartets, First Series, *Nos. 1: Concerto in G; 3: Sonata in A; 4: Sonata in G min.; 5: Suite in E min.*
(B) ** Hung. White Label HRC 087 [id.]. Kovács, Hungarian Baroque Trio, Nagy.

These are most inventive works, and the level of inspiration is extraordinarily even. No doubt Brüggen's recordings with the Amsterdam Quartet will return soon on Teldec; meanwhile these Hungarian performances are fresh and enjoyable. They are well recorded, too, though the close balance means that the range of dynamic is limited.

Sonatas for two recorders Nos. 1–6.
*** RCA Dig. RD 87903. Michala Petri and Elisabeth Selin.

Sonatas for two recorders Nos. 1–6; Duetto in B flat.
*** BIS Dig. CD 334 [id.]. Clas Pehrsson, Dan Laurin.

Canon sonatas Nos. 1–6; Duettos Nos. 1–6.
*** BIS Dig. CD 335 [id.]. Clas Pehrsson, Dan Laurin.

All the *Duet sonatas* are in four movements, the second being a fugue; the *Canon sonatas* are for two flutes, violins or bass viols. Needless to say, listening to two recorders for longer than one piece at a time imposes a strain on one's powers of endurance, however expert the playing – and expert it certainly is.

The RCA and BIS versions can be recommended alongside each other, although the BIS disc does contain one extra work. The playing of Michala Petri and Elisabeth Selin is particularly felicitous and the recording first class. However, although it is good to have the two treble recorders blending so well together, a clearer degree of separation would have been advantageous in the imitative writing.

Tiomkin, Dimitri (1894–1979)

Film music: *The Fall of the Roman Empire: Overture: Pax Romana. The Guns of Navarone: Prologue-Prelude; Epilogue. A President's country. Rhapsody of steel. Wild is the wind.*
**(*) Unicorn DKPCD 9047 [id.]. Royal College of Music O, Willcocks; D. King (organ).

Dimitri Tiomkin was one of a number of émigré musicians who made a considerable contribution to the music of Hollywood. He contributed scores to some of the most famous movies of all time, for Hitchcock and Frank Capra among others. But it was Carl Foreman's *High noon* that produced his most memorable idea, and he quotes its famous theme, among others, in *A President's country*, a well-crafted medley used as background music for a documentary about President Johnson's Texas. *Wild is the wind* is another familiar melody; Christopher Palmer's arrangement makes a tastefully scored showcase. The latter has arranged and orchestrated all the music here except *Rhapsody of steel*, a complex pseudo-symphonic score written for another documentary, which lasts some 22 minutes. The music of *Pax Romana* has the robust character of a typical Hollywood epic costume spectacular, featuring a bold contribution from the organ. All the music is played with obvious enjoyment by the Orchestra of the Royal College of Music; no apologies need be made for their technique, which is fully professional. Sir David Willcocks conducts with understanding of the idiom and great personal conviction. The recording is very impressive too, though the balance gives brass and percussion rather too much prominence.

Tippett, Michael (born 1905)

Concerto for double string orchestra.
** Nimbus Dig. NI 5097 [id.]. E. String O, Boughton – STRAVINSKY: *Apollo.***

Like the Stravinsky ballet with which it is coupled, Boughton's account of the Tippett *Concerto* is fresh, warm and punchy, marginally faster in all three movements than the composer himself on his Virgin Classics disc. It is just as sympathetic, with idiomatically jazzy rhythms brought out in the outer movements, as well as the tender poetry of the middle movement, and with the opening viola solo very beautiful indeed. Though the violin ensemble is a little edgy, the reverberant recording smooths it acceptably.

Concerto for double string orchestra; Fantasia concertante on a theme of Corelli; Little Music for strings.
(M) *** Decca 421 389-2 [id.]. ASMF, Marriner.

Concerto for double string orchestra; Fantasia concertante on a theme of Corelli. (i) *Songs for Dov.*
*** Virgin Dig. VC 790701-2 [id.]. SCO, composer; (i) Nigel Robson.

It is particularly valuable to have the *Concerto for double string orchestra*, which Tippett had never previously recorded himself. Interpreting his own youthful inspiration, the octogenarian gives delightfully pointed readings of the outer movements, bringing out the jazzy implications of the cross-rhythms, not taking them too literally, while the lovely melody of the slow movement has never sounded more warmly expressive. The Scottish Chamber Orchestra plays with comparable passion in the *Fantasia concertante*, a related work from Tippett's middle period, while Nigel Robson is a wonderfully idiomatic and convincing tenor soloist in the difficult vocal lines of the three *Songs for Dov*. Warm, full recording.

The ASMF playing is utterly committed. Marriner and his colleagues allow the idiomatic inflexions of the outer movements to have their lightening effect on the rhythm, and in the heavenly slow movement the slowish tempo and hushed manner display the full romanticism of the music without ever slipping into sentimentality. The *Corelli fantasia*, a similarly sumptuous work but without quite the same lyrical felicity, and the *Little Music* provide an ideal coupling. The transfer is first class; the upper string timbre has a touch of astringency but the ambient fullness remains.

Concerto for orchestra; (i) *Triple concerto for violin, viola and cello.*
*** Ph. 420 781-2 [id.]. (i) Pauk, Imai, Kirshbaum; LSO, C. Davis.

In 1979 when the *Concerto* was first heard – with this same conductor and soloists – the new, more exuberantly lyrical style represented an important development in Tippett's career. The digital recording is naturally balanced. The *Concerto for orchestra* was a by-product of the opera *King Priam* and, even more successfully than the opera, it exploits his thorny style, tough and sinewy, hardly at all lyrical in the manner of its coupling. To study such a piece on record is immensely rewarding. The recording dates from the mid-1960s but still sounds well, if not ideally expansive.

Fantasia concertante on a theme of Corelli.
** ASV Dig. CDDCA 518 [id.]. ASMF, Marriner – ELGAR: *Serenade***; VAUGHAN WILLIAMS: *Tallis fantasia* etc.**(*)

The *Fantasia concertante on a theme of Corelli* is certainly successful here, but the composer's account is finer still and has preferable couplings.

Praeludium for brass, bells & percussion; Suite for the birthday of Prince Charles. The Midsummer marriage: (i) *Ritual dances;* (ii) *Sosostris's aria.*
**(*) Nimbus Dig. NI 5217 [id.]. (i; ii) Alfreda Hodgson, (i) Ch. of Opera North; E. N. Philh. O, Tippett.

Tippett in his eighties draws a committed performance from the English Northern Philharmonia, well rehearsed to play this showpiece as part of the Opera North production. This is not the most brilliant account but, quite apart from the composer's insight, it brings an obvious advantage in including the vocal parts in the fourth dance. *Sosostris's aria* makes another good concert item, but the soloist, Alfreda Hodgson, like the chorus, is balanced much too far behind the orchestra. The *Praeludium* is a sustained ceremonial piece, marked by sharp contrasts of dynamic and texture, wayward and distinctive. The *Prince Charles suite* offers another example of Tippett's occasional music, idiosyncratically bringing together echoes of Elgar, Vaughan Williams and Holst in a very Tippett-like way. The composer's direction is rather less persuasive in the *Praeludium* than in the rest, but with warm, atmospheric recording this is more than just an invaluable document.

Symphonies Nos. (i) *1 – 2;* (ii; iii) *3; 4; Suite for the birthday of Prince Charles.*
(M) *** Decca 425 646-2 (3) [id.]. (i) LSO, C. Davis; (ii) Chicago SO, Solti; (iii) Heather Harper.

All the symphonies have previously been available separately, the *First* and *Third* on Philips, the *Second* on Argo and the *Fourth* on Decca. The Polygram merger permits all four to be accommodated in a box of three CDs (since possessing the *First* and *Fourth* originally involved duplication, as they were both coupled with the *Suite for the birthday of Prince Charles*, this new format is obviously attractive). The transfers are splendidly vivid.

String quartets Nos. 1 – 3.
(M) *** Decca 425 645-2 [id.]. Lindsay Qt.

As with the symphonies, the three *Quartets* are now brought together, but on a single disc. The performances carry the composer's imprimatur and are faithfully recorded.

String quartet No. 4.
*** ASV Dig. CDDCA 608 [id.]. Lindsay Qt – BRITTEN: *Quartet No. 3.****

Tippett's *Fourth Quartet* develops even more rigorously the birth-to-death theme of his *Fourth Symphony*, written at about the same time. The emotional core lies in the slow and still abrasive movement which comes third, bringing no easy solution. The Lindsay Quartet give a powerful, deeply committed reading of music far thornier than the late Britten *Quartet* with which it is coupled. Fine, vivid recording, with the players presented rather close, so that extraneous playing noises sometimes intrude.

VOCAL MUSIC

A Child of our time (oratorio).
**(*) Ph. 420 075-2 [id.]. Norman, J. Baker, Cassilly, Shirley-Quirk, BBC Singers, BBC Ch. Soc., BBC SO, C. Davis.
**(*) ASV Dig. CDRPO 8005 [id.]. Armstrong, Palmer, Langridge, Shirley-Quirk, Brighton Fest. Ch., RPO, Previn.

Davis's speeds tend to be on the fast side, both in the spirituals (taking the place which Bach gave to chorales) and in the other numbers. He may miss some of the tenderness; by avoiding all suspicion of sentimentality, however, the result is incisive and very powerful, helped by excellent solo and choral singing. The CD transfer of 1975 analogue sound is fuller and more atmospheric than the much later Previn recording.

Previn's is a colourful and winning performance, warmer and more expressive than Davis's, predictably helped by the conductor's natural understanding of jazz rhythms. This is a reading which leaves you in no doubt as to the depth of emotion felt by the composer; but ensemble is not always ideally crisp, the chorus is set rather backwardly and the soloists, a less polished if just as characterful team as Davis's, have uneven moments. The digital recording is unobtrusively natural, if slightly recessed.

The Mask of Time.
*** EMI Dig. CDS7 47707-8 (2). Robinson, Sarah Walker, Tear, Cheek, BBC Singers, BBC Ch., BBC SO, Andrew Davis.

The Mask of Time is a piece bursting with exuberant invention. There is richness, generosity and overwhelming vigour in this Seven Days of Creation for a Nuclear Age, astounding in a composer who was nearing eighty when he wrote it. With his BBC forces,

Andrew Davis brilliantly clarifies and sharpens the ever-busy score, and the fine discipline brings out a creative, purposeful control behind the wildness, while the poetry of the piece emerges the more intensely, culminating in the lovely setting for soprano and humming chorus of lines by Anna Akhmatova in *Hiroshima, mon amour.* The final wordless chorus then projects the role of music into eternity, under the title, *The singing will never be done.* Davis draws incandescent singing from the BBC Symphony Chorus and attendant professionals. The quartet of soloists too is outstanding, three of them in the original Boston performance. No finer recording has ever been made in the difficult acoustics of the Royal Festival Hall.

King Priam (complete).
*** Decca 414 241-2 (2) [id.]. Tear, Allen, Bailey, Palmer, Minton, Langridge, Robert, Harper, L. Sinf. Ch., L. Sinf., Atherton.

In this superb performance under David Atherton, with an outstanding cast and vivid, immediate recording, the power of Tippett's opera, offbeat as the treatment often is, both musical and dramatic, comes over from first to last. Norman Bailey, thanks to his long association with Wagner, sounds agedly noble to perfection. Robert Tear is a shiningly heroic Achilles and Thomas Allen a commanding Hector, vocally immaculate, illuminating every word.

Tishchenko, Boris (born 1939)

Symphony No. 5.
*** Olympia OCD 213 [id.]. USSR MoC SO, Rozhdestvensky.

Boris Tishchenko's *Fifth Symphony* was composed in 1976, the year of Shostakovich's death, and is a grave, serious – and often painful – work. It opens with a long cor anglais monologue and it pays tribute to Shostakovich not only in the various quotations but at a deeper level; throughout these strong resonances Tishchenko still speaks his own language. A powerful document, this is played with enormous conviction by the Ministry of Culture Symphony Orchestra under Gennady Rozhdestvensky, and is vividly recorded.

Tomasi, André (1901–71)

Trumpet concerto.
(*) CBS MK 42096 [id.]. Wynton Marsalis, Philh. O, Salonen – JOLIVET: *Concertos.**

Like the Jolivet couplings, this is essentially crossover music, if with a neo-classical flavour. The structure is chimerical, but not without spontaneity and, with Wynton Marsalis offering scintillating bravura throughout and an easy affinity with the swiftly changing moods, the result is quite attractive. In playing time, however, this issue is singularly ungenerous.

Tosti, Francesco (1846–1916)

Songs: *L'alba sepàra della luce l'ombra; Aprile; 'A vucchella; Chanson de L'adieu; Goodbye; Ideale; Malia; Marechiare; Non t'amo; Segreto; La serenata; Sogno; L'ultima canzone; Vorrei morire.*
(M) *** Ph. 426 372-2 [id.]. José Carreras, ECO, Muller.

Tosti (knighted by Queen Victoria for his services to music) had a gently charming lyric gift in songs like these, and it is good to have a tenor with such musical intelligence – not to mention such a fine, pure voice – tackling once-popular trifles like *Marechiare* and *Goodbye*. The arrangements are sweetly done, and the recording is excellent.

Tubin, Eduard (1905–82)

(i) *Ballade for violin and orchestra;* (ii) *Double-bass concerto;* (i) *Violin concerto No. 2; Estonian dance suite; Valse triste.*
*** BIS Dig. CD 337 [id.]. (i) Garcia; (ii) Ehren; Gothenburg SO, Järvi.

The repertoire for double-bass is hardly over-endowed, but Tubin's highly imaginative *Concerto* must surely be numbered as one of the most successful ever written for this intractable instrument. The work has an unflagging sense of momentum and is ideally proportioned; the ideas never outstay their welcome and one's attention is always held. The *Second Violin concerto*, though not the equal of his finest symphonies, is of much greater substance than its predecessor. It has an appealing lyricism, is well proportioned and has a strong sense of forward movement. The *Ballade* is a work of gravity and eloquence; it is never static, moves purposefully and holds the listener's interest throughout. *Valse triste* is a short and rather charming piece, while the *Dance suite* is the Estonian equivalent of the *Dances of Galánta*. Splendid performances from both soloists in the *Concertos* and from the orchestra under Järvi throughout, and excellent recording.

(i) *Balalaika concerto; Music for strings; Symphony No. 1.*
*** BIS Dig. CD 351 [id.]. (i) Sheynkman; Swedish RSO, Järvi.

The opening of the *First Symphony* almost puts one in mind of Bax, and there is a Sibelian breadth; but for the most part it is a symphony apart from its fellows. The quality of the musical substance is high and the feeling for form is every bit as strong; its presentation is astonishingly assured for a young man still in his twenties; indeed, the scoring is quite masterly. The *Balalaika concerto* was written for Nicolaus Zwetnow, not only a leading exponent of the balalaika but professor of neurosurgery in Oslo! Emanuil Sheynkman's account with Neeme Järvi is first class, both taut and concentrated. Excellent recording.

Violin concerto No. 1; Suite on Estonian dances for violin and orchestra; Prélude solennel.
** BIS Dig. CD 286 [id.]. Lubotsky, Gothenburg SO, Järvi.

No one approaching this *Suite* or the empty and bombastic *Prélude solennel* without foreknowledge of any of Tubin's other music should judge him on either of these pieces. The *Violin concerto No. 1* is a good deal better – though, again, it is no match for the *Fourth Symphony*, composed only a year later. The solo line is lyrical and the melodic ideas are not unappealing or lacking in character, but the orchestra often provides rather simple harmonic support and the writing is somehow wanting in interest. It was recorded at a public concert in Gothenburg, and both the performance and sound engineering are eminently acceptable.

Symphonies Nos. 2 (The Legendary); 6.
*** BIS CD 304 [id.]. Swedish RSO, Järvi.

The opening of the *Second Symphony* is quite magical: there are soft, luminous string chords that evoke a strong atmosphere of wide vistas and white summer nights, but the music soon gathers power and reveals a genuine feeling for proportion and of organic growth. If there is a Sibelian strength in the *Second Symphony*, the *Sixth*, written after

Tubin had settled in Sweden, has obvious resonances of Prokofiev – even down to instrumentation – and yet Tubin's rhythmic vitality and melodic invention are quietly distinctive. The Swedish Radio Symphony Orchestra play with great commitment under Neeme Järvi, and the engineers have done a magnificent job.

Symphonies Nos. 3; 8.
*** BIS Dig. CD 342 [id.]. Swedish RSO, Järvi.

The first two movements of the wartime *Third Symphony* are vintage Tubin, but the heroic finale approaches bombast. The *Eighth* is his masterpiece; its opening movement has a sense of vision and mystery, and the atmosphere stays with you. This is the darkest of the symphonies and the most intense in feeling, music of real substance and importance. Järvi and the Swedish orchestra play it marvellously and the recording is in the demonstration bracket.

Symphonies Nos. (i) *4 (Sinfonia lirica);* (ii) *9 (Sinfonia semplice); Toccata.*
⊛ *** BIS Dig. CD 227 [id.]. (i) Bergen SO, (ii) Gothenburg SO, Järvi.

The *Fourth* is a highly attractive piece, immediately accessible, the music well argued and expertly crafted. The opening has a Sibelian feel to it but, the closer one comes to it, the more individual it seems. The recording comes from a concert performance and has an exceptionally well-behaved audience. The *Ninth Symphony* is in two movements: its mood is elegiac and a restrained melancholy permeates the slower sections. Its musical language is direct, tonal and, once one gets to grips with it, quite personal. If its spiritual world is clearly Nordic, the textures are transparent and luminous, and its argument unfolds naturally and cogently. It is strong in both concentration of feeling and melodic invention; the playing of the Gothenburgers under Järvi is totally committed in all sections of the orchestra. The performances are authoritative and the recording altogether excellent.

Symphony No. 5 in B minor; Kratt (ballet suite).
*** BIS Dig. CD 306 [id.]. Bamberg SO, Järvi.

The *Fifth* makes as good a starting point as any to investigate the Tubin canon. Written after he had settled in Sweden, it finds him at his most neo-classical; the music is finely paced and full of energy and invention. The ballet suite is a work of much character, tinged with folk-inspired ideas and some echoes of Prokofiev.

Symphony No. 7; (i) *Concertino for piano and orchestra; Sinfonietta on Estonian motifs.*
*** BIS Dig. CD 401 [id.]. (i) Roland Pöntinen; Gothenburg SO, Järvi.

The *Seventh* is a marvellous work, powerfully conceived and masterly in design, and it receives a concentrated and impressive reading. As always with Tubin, the music has great sureness of purpose and a firm sense of direction: you are never in doubt that this is a real symphony which sets out purposefully and reaches its goal. The ideas could not be by anyone else and the music unfolds with a powerful logic and inevitability. Neeme Järvi inspires the Gothenburg orchestra with his own evident enthusiasm. The *Concertino for piano and orchestra* has some of the neo-classicism of the *Fifth Symphony*. In the course of the three interlinked movements there is the same distinctive sense of momentum one finds in all his best music. Roland Pöntinen gives a dashing account of the solo part. The *Sinfonietta* is a fresh and resourceful piece, a Baltic equivalent of, say, Prokofiev's *Sinfonietta*, with much the same lightness of touch and inventive resource. Superb recording – a quite indispensable disc.

Symphony No. 10; (i) *Requiem for fallen soldiers.*
*** BIS Dig. CD 297 [id.]. Gothenburg SO, Järvi; (i) with Lundin, Rydell, Hardenberger, Lund Students' Ch., Järvi.

Tubin's *Requiem*, austere in character, is for two soloists (a contralto and baritone) and male chorus. The instrumental forces are merely an organ, piano, drums, timpani and trumpet. The simplicity and directness of the language are affecting and the sense of melancholy is finely controlled. The final movement is prefaced by a long trumpet solo, played here with stunning control and a masterly sense of line by the young Håkan Hardenberger. It is an impressive and dignified work, even if the quality of the choral singing is less than first rate. The *Tenth Symphony* is a one-movement piece that begins with a sombre string idea, which is soon interrupted by a periodically recurring horn call – and which resonates in the mind long afterwards. The recordings are absolutely first class and in the best traditions of the house.

Complete piano music: *Album leaf; Ballad on a theme by Maat Saar; 3 Estonian folk-dances; 4 Folksongs from my country; A little march for Rana; Lullaby; 3 Pieces for children; Prelude No. 1; 7 Preludes; Sonatas Nos. 1–2; Sonatina in D min.; Suite on Estonian shepherd melodies; Variations on an Estonian folk-tune.*
*** BIS Dig. CD 414/6 [id.]. Vardo Rumessen.

Tubin's first works for piano inhabit a world in which Scriabin, Ravel and Eller were clearly dominant influences but in which an individual sensibility is also to be discerned. The first disc comprises the charming six *Preludes* and the *First Sonata*, as well as a number of miniatures. The second offers the resourceful *Variations on an Estonian folk-tune*, a lovely work that deserves a place in the repertoire, and the *Sonatina in D minor* where the ideas and sense of momentum are on a larger scale than one would expect in a sonatina. The third disc includes the *Seven Preludes* (which bring harmonic fingerprints familiar from the later symphonies) and, most importantly, the *Second Sonata*, a key work in Tubin's development. It opens with a shimmering figure in free rhythm, inspired by the play of the aurora borealis, and is much more concentrated than his earlier piano works. Vardo Rumessen makes an excellent case for it, and even if the work is not as powerful as, say, the very finest of the symphonies, it is impressive stuff. The performances are consistently fine, full of understanding and flair, and the recording is very natural.

Turina, Joaquín (1882–1949)

Rapsodia sinfónica, Op. 66.
*** Decca Dig. 410 289-2 [id.]. De Larrocha, LPO, Frühbeck de Burgos – FALLA: *Nights in the gardens of Spain**** (with ALBÉNIZ: *Rapsodia****).

Turina's *Rapsodia sinfónica* has been recorded by others, but in the hands of Alicia de Larrocha it is played with such éclat that it becomes almost memorable and thoroughly entertaining. The Falla coupling is poetic and atmospheric, while the delightfully chimerical Albéniz companion piece glitters most engagingly. Excellent, vivid sound out of Decca's top drawer.

Tye, Christopher (*c.* 1505 – *c.* 1572)

Mass: Euge bone; Peccavimus patribus nostris.
*** Proudsound Dig. PROUCD 126 [id.]. Clerkes of Oxenford, David Wulstan –
SHEPPARD: *Collection.****

Christopher Tye was a clerk at King's College, Cambridge, before moving on to Ely
Cathedral in the 1540s. Mass settings of the period were often based on a setting of a
votive antiphon, using the opening to provide a motto for each Mass section. Tye's *Euge
bone* belongs to this genre, and Paul Doe surmises that it was composed at about the time
of Edward VI's accession. It is a work of great beauty not otherwise available on CD; it is
sung here with characteristic tonal sophistication by the Clerkes of Oxenford under David
Wulstan, and splendidly recorded in a spacious but not over-reverberant acoustic.

Vaňhal, Jan (1739 – 1813)

(i) *Double bassoon concerto in F; Sinfonias: in A min.; F.*
** BIS CD 288 [id.]. (i) Wallin, Nilsson; Umeå Sinf., Saraste.

The best thing here is the *Concerto*, which is an arresting and inventive piece. The
opening allegro is conceived on a broader canvas than one expects, and the slow
movement has real distinction, touching a deeper vein of feeling than anything else on
this record. It is not too fanciful to detect in some of the harmonic suspensions the
influence of Gluck, with whose music Vaňhal came into contact in the late 1760s. The
two *Sinfonias* are less musically developed but far from uninteresting: the minuet of the *F
major* has a distinctly 'Sturm und Drang' feel to it: Vaňhal's symphonies may well have
paved the way for Haydn at this period; they were certainly given by Haydn while
Kapellmeister at the Esterhazy palace. The recording is good, as one has come to expect
from this source, even if the acoustic is on the dry side. The playing of the Umeå
ensemble is eminently respectable. The balance is well judged, though perhaps the
accomplished young soloists are placed just a little too forward.

Violin concerto in G.
**(*) Sup. Dig. SUP 007571 [id.]. Josef Suk, Suk CO, Vlach – HAYDN: *Concerto in
G.***(*)

Jan Vaňhal's *G major Concerto* is every bit as good as Haydn's in the same key –
which, of course, is not saying a great deal. In fact, it is quite an engaging little work, with
a busy first movement, a rather solemn *Adagio* which Suk plays with characteristic
warmth, and a brilliant *presto* finale, which both soloist and orchestra dive into with great
vivacity and spirit. The recording is truthful if forwardly balanced, but this is short
measure for CD – room could easily have been found for a third concerto.

Varèse, Edgar (1883 – 1965)

Ameriques; Arcana; Density 21.5; Intégrales; Ionisation; Octandre; Offrandes.
(M) *** Sony Analogue/Dig. SK 45844 [id.]. Yakar, NYPO, Ensemble
InterContemporain, Boulez.

This welcome mid-priced reissue combines two previous LPs, bringing together all of
Varèse's most important works. In the inter-war period he was regarded as a wild man of
the avant-garde in writing a work like *Ionisation* for percussion alone and abandoning

conventional argument in favour of presenting blocks of sound. Yet performances like these show what a genius he had – not for assaulting but for tickling the ear with novelty. Boulez brings out the purposefulness of his writing, not least in the two big works for full orchestra, the early *Ameriques* and *Arcana*, written for an enormous orchestra in the late 1920s. Those two works are here played by the New York Philharmonic and are not digitally recorded. The selection recorded more recently in digital sound covers his smaller but just as striking works for chamber ensembles of various kinds, with Rachel Yakar the excellent soprano soloist in *Offrandes*.

Vaughan Williams, Ralph (1872–1958)

Concerto grosso; (i) *Oboe concerto; English folksongs suite; Fantasia on Greensleeves;* (ii) *Romance* (for harmonica and strings).
(M) **(*) Decca 421 392-2 [id.]. (i) Nicklin; (ii) Reilly; ASMF, Marriner.

A somewhat mixed bag of lightweight Vaughan Williams. Celia Nicklin gives a most persuasive account of the elusive *Oboe concerto*, while the *Concerto grosso* is lively and polished. The atmospheric *Romance* is not one of the composer's most inspired works, but it is still worth having on disc. The recordings generally sound well, if with a touch of astringency in the string timbre.

Concerto grosso; (i) *Oboe concerto; Fantasia on Greensleeves; Fantasia on a theme of Thomas Tallis; Five variants of Dives and Lazarus.*
**(*) Nimbus Dig. NI 5019 [id.]. (i) Bourgue; E. String O, Boughton.

Recorded in the spacious acoustic of the Great Hall of Birmingham University, Boughton's sympathetic performances of an attractive group of Vaughan Williams works are presented amply and atmospherically. That is particularly effective in the *Tallis fantasia*, and the *Greensleeves fantasia* – with the flute solo nicely distanced – is equally beautiful. More questionable is the *Oboe concerto* with the superb French soloist, Maurice Bourgue, balanced too close, so that the strings in the background do little more than comment distantly.

(i) *Oboe concerto;* (ii) *The Lark ascending.*
*** DG 419 748-2 [id.]. (i) Neil Black; (ii) Zukerman, ECO, Barenboim – DELIUS: *Aquarelles* etc.; WALTON: *Henry V.****

Neil Black's creamy tone is particularly suited to Vaughan Williams's *Oboe concerto* and he gives a wholly persuasive performance of what is not one of the composer's strongest works. Zukerman's account of *The Lark ascending* is full of pastoral rapture – even if perhaps not totally idiomatic, the effect is ravishing. The recordings from the late 1970s have not lost their allure or atmospheric warmth in the digital remastering.

(i) *Concerto for 2 pianos in C; Symphony No. 5 in D.*
*** Virgin Dig. VC 790733-2 [id.]. (i) Markham, Broadway; RPO, Menuhin.

VW's arrangement of his thornily inspired *Piano concerto* of 1931 for two pianos and orchestra has never sounded so convincing as here, thanks to the inspired duo of Ralph Markham and Kenneth Broadway, making light of the technical problems of piano writing that rarely fits under the fingers and gives few lyrical rewards. In the *Fifth Symphony* Sir Yehudi Menuhin, rather than dwelling on pastoral Englishry, takes a thrustful, purposefully symphonic view, with little lingering yet with warm expressiveness in each movement and with climaxes pressed home with satisfying power. It is an individual version, superbly recorded.

English folksongs suite; Toccata marziale.
(b) *** ASV CDQS 6021 [id.]. London Wind O, Denis Wick – HOLST: *Military band suites* etc.***

As in the Holst suites, the pace of these performances is attractively zestful, and if the slow movement of the *English folksongs suite* could have been played more reflectively, the bounce of *Seventeen come Sunday* is irresistible. The first-class analogue recording has been transferred vividly to CD.

Fantasia on Greensleeves; Fantasia on a theme of Thomas Tallis.
*** EMI CDC7 47537-2 [id.]. Sinf. of L., Allegri Qt, Barbirolli – ELGAR: *Introduction and allegro; Serenade.****
(b) **(*) Pickwick Dig. PCD 930. LSO, Frühbeck de Burgos – ELGAR: *Cello concerto.****

Fantasia on Greensleeves; Fantasia on a theme of Thomas Tallis; Five Variants of Dives and Lazarus; (i) *The Lark ascending.*
*** Argo 414 595-2 [id.]. ASMF, Marriner (i) with Iona Brown.
**(*) Ara. Dig. Z 6568 [id.]. (i) Garcia; ECO, Menuhin.

Fantasia on Greensleeves; Fantasia on a theme by Thomas Tallis; (i) *The Lark ascending.*
⊛ *** Virgin Dig. VCy 790819-2 [id.]. (i) Christopher Warren-Green; LCO, Warren-Green – ELGAR: *Introduction and allegro* etc.*** ⊛

Fantasia on a theme of Thomas Tallis; Five variants of Dives and Lazarus; In the Fen Country; Norfolk rhapsody.
*** Chan. Dig. CHAN 8502 [id.]. LPO, Bryden Thomson.

Fantasia on a theme of Thomas Tallis; (i) *The Lark ascending.*
(*) ASV Dig. CDDCA 518 [id.]. (i) Iona Brown; ASMF, Marriner – ELGAR: *String serenade*; TIPPETT: *Fantasia concertante.*

To Barbirolli's famous EMI coupling of English string music Christopher Warren-Green and his newly re-formed London Chamber Orchestra have added a radiant account of *The Lark ascending*, in which Warren-Green makes a charismatic solo contribution, very free and soaring in its flight and with beautifully sustained true pianissimo playing at the opening and close. For the *Tallis fantasia*, the second orchestra (2.2.2.2.1) contrasts with the main group (5.4.2.2.1) and here, though the effect is beautifully serene, Warren-Green does not quite match the ethereal, other-worldly pianissimo that made Sir John's reading unforgettable. But that is a minor quibble; the performance overall has great ardour and breadth, almost to match the coupled *Introduction and allegro* of Elgar in its intensity. The recording, made at All Saints' Church, Petersham, is quite ideal in its resonant warmth and atmosphere, yet has good definition. This is an altogether superb disc.

The rich projection of the Tallis theme on which Vaughan Williams based his *Fantasia* when it first appears in full, after the pizzicato introduction, sets the seal on Barbirolli's outstanding performance of the *Tallis fantasia*, one of the great masterpieces of all music. The wonderfully ethereal and magically quiet playing of the second orchestra is another very moving feature of this remarkable performance. On CD the sound retains its warmth, amplitude and bloom, but the disposal of background has also taken off a little of the recording's upper range, which is slightly restricted. The delightful *Greensleeves fantasia* makes an attractive bonus, and here the quality is pleasingly fresh.

The Chandos collection is generous. It offers a well-recorded anthology of (save for the *Tallis fantasia*) lesser-known Vaughan Williams. Boult recorded *In the Fen Country* and the *Norfolk rhapsody* successfully, but neither is otherwise available in modern digital sound. Bryden Thomson is a thoroughly persuasive guide in all this repertoire, and in the other two pieces more than holds his own with most of the opposition.

On Argo, superbly balanced and refined performances of four favourite Vaughan Williams works, which with the help of full and clear recorded sound here have great power and intensity. A rewarding record, made in 1972, but enhanced in its CD format; detail is more refined and the fullness retained, but the massed upper strings now have a slight edge in climaxes.

On ASV, Iona Brown offers her second recording of *The Lark ascending* and she has the advantage here of digital recording. The present version, though not finer than the old, is both eloquent and evocative. The *Tallis fantasia* is beautifully played too, but the effect here is relatively bland beside the earlier Argo account. The acoustic is warm but not quite as expansive as the Virgin and EMI versions.

Although Menuhin's performance of the *Tallis fantasia* has plenty of dramatic contrast, his spacious manner brings some lack of inner tension. José-Luis Garcia's simplicity of approach to *The Lark ascending* makes for a very appealing performance, and the *Dives and Lazarus variants* are warmly played. The recording is full and clear, but the violins sound a little thin on top.

Though Frühbeck is rather heavy-handed in his treatment of these Vaughan Williams favourites, the playing of the LSO is refined and the recording first rate. On the bargain-price Pickwick label, it makes an unconventional coupling for Felix Schmidt's outstanding reading of the Elgar *Cello concerto*.

Fantasia on Greensleeves; Fantasia on a theme of Thomas Tallis; Five variants of Dives and Lazarus; (i) *Flos Campi.*
(B) *** Van. VECD 7520 [id.]. (i) Sally Peck, Utah University Chamber Ch.; Utah SO, Maurice Abravanel.

The string works here are given broad, lyrical performances and the warm, spacious, 1968 recording matches them. *Greensleeves* is slow and gracious, and there are more passionate versions of the *Tallis fantasia* available; but the noteworthy point is the way Abravanel catches the inner feeling of the music. The second orchestra makes a luminous sound and the contrasts are well made. Both here and in *Dives and Lazarus* the full strings create a gloriously rich sonority, and the only criticism in the latter variations is that the balance does not position the harp so that its contribution (not a concertante one) emerges very clearly. Sally Peck, the violist, is also placed with her colleagues rather than as a soloist in *Flos Campi* (following the composer's expressed intention), yet her personality still emerges well. Abravanel, always a warm, energetic conductor, displays real understanding, allowing the music to relax as it should in this evocation of the Song of Solomon, but never letting it drag either. The CD transfer is excellent, retaining the naturalness of the original recording.

(i) *Fantasia (quasi variazione) on the Old Hundredth;* (ii; iii) *Flos campi;* (iv) *Magnificat;* (iii; v) *Oxford elegy.*
(M) *** EMI CDM7 69962-2. (i) Katin, LPO Ch. & O, Boult; (ii) Aronowitz; (iii) King's College Ch., Jacques O, Willcocks; (iv) Helen Watts, Amb. S., O Nuova of L., Meredith Davies; (v) with John Westbrook.

The weakest work here is the *Fantasia on the Old Hundredth*, but Peter Katin and Boult do their best for it in an eloquent performance. *Flos campi*, with its deeply expressive solo for the viola (here beautifully played by Cecil Aronowitz) also needs persuasive treatment, and that it receives in Willcocks's hands. The *Magnificat* has strong reminders of *Flos campi* and shows Vaughan Williams in his most Holstian vein. The *Oxford elegy* (1949) is an occasional work which rises well above its original commission, mellifluous music characteristic of the composer's ripe Indian summer. The spoken quotations from Matthew Arnold are effectively presented by John Westbrook, while the Cambridge choir is admirable in its words of tribute to Oxford. Altogether a valuable and generous anthology, very well recorded and impressively transferred to CD.

Fantasia on Sussex folk tunes for cello and orchestra.
*** RCA Dig. RD 70800. Lloyd Webber, Philh. O, Handley – DELIUS: *Cello concerto*; HOLST: *Invocation.****

The *Fantasia on Sussex folk tunes* has lain neglected since its first performance by Casals, and it proves something of a discovery. This is a highly appealing work, most persuasively performed too. The recording is first class.

Five variants of Dives and Lazarus; (i) *The Lark ascending; The Wasps: Overture and suite.*
(M) *** EMI Dig. CD-EMX 9508 [Ang. CDM 62018]. (i) David Nolan; LPO, Handley.

The immediacy of the recording allows no mistiness in *The Lark ascending*, but it is still a warm, understanding performance. The overture is spaciously conceived and it leads to charming, colourful accounts of the other, less well-known pieces in the suite, tuneful and lively. The *Five Variants of Dives and Lazarus* finds Vaughan Williams using his folksong idiom at its most poetic, here superbly played and recorded. The sound is fresh and clear, if rather brightly lit.

Hymn-tune preludes: Nos. 1, Eventide (arr. of Monk); *2, Dominus regit me* (arr. of Dykes); *The Poisoned Kiss: Overture; The Running Set; Sea Songs: Quick march.*
*** Chan. CHAN 8432 [id.]. Bournemouth Sinf., Hurst – ELGAR: *Adieu* etc.***

The overture to the opera *The Poisoned Kiss* is merely a pot-pourri, but it is presented most persuasively here. *The Running Set* is an exhilarating fantasy on jig rhythms, while the *March on sea songs*, with its bounding rhythms and surging melody in the trio, would make an ideal Prom item. Ripe performances and recording. There is some lack of weight in the upper strings, but otherwise this sounds splendid.

Job (masque for dancing).
⊛ (M) *** EMI Dig. CD-EMX 9506 [Ang. CDM 62016]. LPO, Handley.

Job is undeniably one of Vaughan Williams's very greatest compositions. It shows his inspiration at its most deeply characteristic and at its most consistently noble. The breadth of dynamic range of the recording is used to enormous effect by Handley to increase the dramatic effect – the organ entry representing Satan enthroned in heaven has overwhelming impact and power. The ravishingly luminous espressivo playing in the work's quieter lyrical pages is movingly beautiful, with the music's evocative feeling memorably captured. Even at full price this CD would be irresistible, one of Handley's major achievements in the recording studio.

Suite for viola and orchestra; (i) *Flos campi.*
**(*) Chan. CHAN 8374 [id.]. Riddle, Bournemouth Sinf., Del Mar; (i) with Ch.

Neither work here is over-familiar, and the evocation of the Song of Solomon contained in *Flos campi* shows Vaughan Williams at his most rarefied and imaginative. The *Suite* is lightweight but engaging, unpretentious music to be enjoyed, with its charming *Carol* and quirky *Polka mélancolique*. Frederick Riddle is an eloquent soloist, even if the playing is not always technically immaculate, and Norman Del Mar directs sympathetically.

Symphonies Nos. 1–9; English folksongs suite; Fantasia on Greensleeves; Fantasia on a theme by Thomas Tallis; In the Fen Country; The Lark ascending; Norfolk rhapsody No. 1; Serenade to music; The Wasps: Overture and suite.
(M) *** EMI CMS7 63098-2 (7) [id.]. LPO, New Philh. O or LSO, Boult.

Boult's approach to Vaughan Williams was firmly symphonic rather than evocative, and his cycle of the symphonies for EMI, here supplemented by many of the shorter orchestral pieces, brings warm and mature readings, which benefit from full-bodied, well-focused sound. EMI's mid-price offer gathers in a box the seven full-price CDs as originally issued, without any modification of format. Between them they present a comprehensive portrait of the composer, unmatched by any other single issue.

A Sea symphony (No. 1).
(M) **(*) EMI CD-EMX 2142. Joan Rodgers, William Shimell, Liverpool PO Ch., Royal Liverpool PO, Handley.
*** EMI Dig. CDC7 49911-2 [id.]. Lott, Summers, LPO Ch. & O, Haitink.
(M) *** RCA GD 90500. Harper, Shirley-Quirk, LSO Ch., LSO, Previn.
**(*) Virgin Dig. VC 790843-2 [id.]. Marshall, Roberts, LSO Ch., Philh. O, Richard Hickox.
(M) (***) Decca mono 425 658-2 [id.]. Isobel Baillie, Cameron, LPO Ch., LPO, Boult.
** Chan. Dig. CHAN 8764 [id.]. Kenny, Rayner-Cook, LSO Ch., LSO, Bryden Thomson.

Vernon Handley conducts a warmly idiomatic performance, which sustains relatively slow speeds masterfully. The emotional thrust of the work is caught powerfully from the very start, both in the big dramatic moments and in the tenderness of the quieter passages. The reading is crowned by Handley's rapt account of the slow movement, *On the beach at night alone*, as well as by the long duet in the finale, leading on through the exciting final ensemble, *Sail forth*, to a deeply satisfying culmination in *O my brave Soul!*. Joan Rodgers makes an outstandingly beautiful soprano soloist, with William Shimell drier-toned but expressive. There are two reservations: the first section of that long finale is less tense than the rest of the performance, and the recording, full and warm, presents problems in its extreme dynamic range, while placing the two soloists rather distantly. EMI has promised a remastering. That could well help to eliminate the problems, which in any case will not worry everyone – the organ, for example, is better defined here than in any other version. To have such a performance in modern digital sound on a mid-price issue is self-recommending.

As in the rest of his Vaughan Williams series, Bernard Haitink takes what to traditional English ears may seem a very literal view, not at all idiomatic but strong and forthright, to present this colourful work with its Whitman text as a genuine symphony, not just as a colourful cantata. Speeds are almost all unusually spacious, making this (at well over 70 minutes) the slowest version on record; but Haitink sustains that expansive manner superbly. The reading loses in atmosphere, but in its ruggedness it presents an exceptionally strong musical experience. It is the nobility of the writing, rather than its emotional warmth, that is paramount. The final calm epilogue, *O my brave Soul!*, after the excitement of the chorus, *Sail forth*, may be less affectionate and less hushed than in some other versions, lacking a sense of homecoming, but in its more detached way it makes a fine culmination. The recording is the fullest and weightiest yet given to this work, with the orchestra well defined in front of the chorus. Felicity Lott and Jonathan Summers are both excellent.

Previn's is a fresh, youthful reading of a young composer's symphony. Previn's nervous energy is obvious from the very start. He does not always relax even where, as in the slow movement, he takes a rather measured tempo. In the Scherzo, Previn is lighter and cleaner, holding more in reserve. The finale similarly is built up over a longer span, with less deliberate expressiveness. The culminating climax with Previn is not allowed to be swamped with choral tone, but has the brass and timpani still prominent. The *Epilogue* may not be so deliberately expressive, but it is purer in its tenderness and exact control of dynamics. Previn has clear advantages in his baritone soloist and his choir. The recording has been digitally remastered and detail clarified, yet the rich ambience remains, with the performers set slightly back.

If Haitink's performance is by far the most spacious, Richard Hickox's is the briskest in its speeds. The urgency of his view, very idiomatic within the English tradition, can be heard even in the grand opening chorus. With the choir which he has long trained himself and with his two soloists he is particularly responsive to Whitman's words, the passage *The vast similitude interlocks all* in the slow movement given a moving, hushed momentum. Both soloists have excellent diction, with Margaret Marshall bright and clear and Stephen Roberts rather thin-toned, not quite warm or rounded enough. In Virgin's characteristic manner, the sound is slightly distanced, set in a sympathetic acoustic with ample clarity. The timpani at the very start are caught dramatically.

It is good to have Boult's 1954 Decca mono recording of the *Sea symphony* back again on CD. In its original LP form it was one of the first really spectacular demonstration records (once used in the Royal Albert Hall) and it has not lost its power to surprise in the famous opening sequence. As for the performance, Boult was at his most inspired. However diffuse the argument may be, conveyed here is the kind of urgency one normally gets only at a live performance. What comes out above all in a rehearing is the way the work forecasts later Vaughan Williams and what a striking achievement it was for a composer who has been far too readily dubbed a 'late developer'. He was present at the recording sessions.

In his Vaughan Williams series for Chandos, Bryden Thomson conducts a warm-hearted reading, not as clean of ensemble as its direct rivals. This is the same chorus as that used by Hickox on his Virgin version, but here it is far less crisp of attack, though still weighty and dramatic. The full and forward Chandos recording helps, though the definition of detail is not as sharp as in the Virgin version or in Haitink's EMI. Yvonne Kenny makes a dramatic, full-toned soprano, but the microphone captures a distracting unevenness in Brian Rayner-Cook's baritone, with firmness undermined.

A London symphony (No. 2); (i) Concerto accademico; The Wasps: Overture.
(M) *** RCA GD 90501. LSO, Previn; (i) with James Buswell.

A London symphony (No. 2); Concerto grosso.
*** Chan. Dig. CHAN 8629 [id.]. LSO, Bryden Thomson.

A London symphony (No. 2); Fantasia on a theme of Thomas Tallis.
*** EMI CDC7 49394-2 [id.]. LPO, Haitink.

A London symphony (No. 2); (i) The Lark ascending.
*** Telarc Dig. CD 80158 [id.]. RPO, Previn; (i) with Barry Griffiths.

Previn's Telarc version brings an exceptionally spacious reading, marked by a vivid and refined sound-balance. The atmospheric beauty of this lovely score has rarely been brought out more intensely, and the slow movement in particular brings a radiant, deeply poetic performance, caressing the ear. The faster movements consistently bring out the conductor's natural idiomatic feeling for this music, with rhythms nicely sprung – not least the sharp syncopations – and with melodies warmly moulded, though without sentimentality. Barry Griffiths' account of *The Lark ascending* is a welcome bonus, but it is not as instinctively rapturous a performance as those by Iona Brown or Warren-Green.

On RCA, though the actual sonorities are subtly and beautifully realized by Previn, the architecture is presented equally convincingly, with the great climaxes of the first and last movements powerful and incisive. Most remarkable of all are the pianissimos which here have great intensity, a quality of frisson as in a live performance. The LSO play superbly and the digitally remastered recording, made in Kingsway Hall, still sounds well with its wide range of dynamic. The fill-ups are welcome, especially James Buswell's fine account of the *Concerto*.

Like Haitink's other readings of British music, this one is more literal in its rhythmic manners, less obviously idiomatic; but many will find it the more refreshing for that, and the incisiveness certainly makes a powerful impact. In jaunty themes Haitink's straight manner at times brings an unexpected Stravinskian quality, and the expansively serene handling of the lovely melodies of the slow movement brings elegiac nobility rather than romantic warmth. Syncopated themes at times sound a little stiff with this treatment, and the *Lento* sections in the last movement are taken dangerously slowly; but that is set against a fast, intense treatment of the allegro, and the tension is powerfully maintained. In the *Tallis fantasia* the straight rhythmic manners make the result sound somewhat unidiomatic too, but very powerful in its monumental directness. The recording has spectacular range, though it is not quite as transparent or as atmospheric as Previn on Telarc.

Bryden Thomson draws superb playing from the LSO in the *London symphony*, sustaining spacious speeds with a natural feeling for phrasing and rubato that leads the ear on. This is a warmly expressive reading rather than a strongly structural one, helped by the characteristically rich Chandos recording, which in moments of biting attack may be too reverberant for some. The most controversial speed is the one which Thomson chooses for the third-movement Scherzo, subtitled *Nocturne*. Taken slowly like this, it becomes a jolly galumphing dance. The *Concerto grosso* makes a worthwhile coupling, and the LSO's immaculate string section under Thomson's persuasive direction here shows in glowing sound how its easy, unforced inspiration can transcend its utilitarian background and bring it close to the world of the *Tallis fantasia*.

(i) *A Pastoral symphony (No. 3);* (ii) *Oboe concerto.*
**(*) Chan. Dig. CHAN 8594 [id.]. (i) Yvonne Kenny; (ii) David Theodore; LSO, Bryden Thomson.

Bryden Thomson's version of the *Pastoral* is finely paced and powerfully argued. There is no danger here of thinking that VW's predominantly measured writing is merely evocative or rambling. The menace behind it, as well as the implied poignancy, is tellingly conveyed; but the warmly reverberant recording places the orchestra rather close, so undermining the delicacy of pianissimos; and the offstage soprano soloist in the finale is a fraction too close, too specific rather than disembodied, with a hint of vibrato that is distracting. David Theodore's plangent tones in the *Oboe concerto* effectively bring out the equivocal character of this highly original work, making it far more than just another pastoral piece, sharply emphasizing the contrasts of mood and manner.

(i) *A Pastoral symphony (No. 3); Symphony No. 4 in F min.*
(M) *** RCA GD 90503. (i) Heather Harper; LSO, Previn.

One tends to think of Vaughan Williams's pastoral music as essentially synonymous with the English countryside, and it is something of a shock to discover that in fact the *Pastoral symphony* was sketched in Northern France while the composer was on active service in 1916, and the initial inspiration was a Corot-like landscape in the sunset. But the music remains English in essence, and its gentle rapture is not easily evoked. Previn draws an outstandingly beautiful and refined performance from the LSO, the bare textures sounding austere but never thin, the few climaxes emerging at full force with purity undiminished. In the third movement the final coda – the only really fast music in the whole work – brings a magic tracery of pianissimo in this performance, light, fast and clear. In the *F minor Symphony* only the somewhat ponderous tempo Previn adopts for the first movement lets it down. But on the whole this is a powerful reading, and it is vividly recorded.

Symphony No. 4 in F min.; Concerto accademico.
**(*) Chan. Dig. CHAN 8633 [id.]. LSO, Bryden Thomson.

Bryden Thomson conducts a powerful, individual reading of the *Fourth*, rugged rather than biting in the dramatic opening movement, wistful rather than tragic in the second, and cheeky rather than malevolent in the scherzo. Where many performances of the *Concerto accademico* make the composer's neo-classical manner sound like Stravinsky with an English accent, Thomson and Sillito find a rustic jollity in the outer movements, very characteristic of Vaughan Williams, and a delicate, withdrawn quality in the central slow movement. The recording of both *Concerto* and *Symphony* is warm and full in the Chandos manner.

Symphony No. 5 in D; The England of Elizabeth: 3 Portraits (arr. Mathieson).
(M) *** RCA GD 90506. LSO, Previn.

Symphony No. 5 in D; Fantasia on a theme by Thomas Tallis.
** Telarc Dig. CD 80138 [id.]. RPO, Previn.

Symphony No. 5 in D; (i) Flos campi (suite).
⊛ (M) *** EMI Dig. CD-EMX 9512 [Ang. CDM 62029]. Royal Liverpool PO, Handley; (i) with Christopher Balmer & Liverpool Philharmonic Ch.

Symphony No. 5 in D; The Lark ascending.
**(*) Chan. Dig. CHAN 8554 [id.]. LSO, Bryden Thomson.

Vernon Handley's disc is outstanding in every way, a spacious yet concentrated reading, superbly played and recorded, which masterfully holds the broad structure of this symphony together, building to massive climaxes. The warmth and poetry of the work are also beautifully caught. The rare and evocative *Flos campi*, inspired by the Song of Solomon, makes a generous and attractive coupling, equally well played, though the viola solo is rather closely balanced. The sound is outstandingly full, giving fine clarity of texture.

If anyone ever doubted the dedication of Previn as an interpreter of Vaughan Williams, his glowing RCA disc will provide the clearest rebuttal. In this most characteristic – and, many would say, greatest – of the Vaughan Williams symphonies, Previn refuses to be lured into pastoral byways. His tempi may be consistently on the slow side, but the purity of tone he draws from the LSO, the precise shading of dynamic and phrasing, and the sustaining of tension through the longest, most hushed passages produce results that will persuade many not normally convinced of the greatness of this music. It is some tribute to Previn's intensity that he can draw out the diminuendi at the ends of movements with such refinement and no sense of exaggeration. This is an outstanding performance, very well transferred to CD. The *England of Elizabeth suite* is a film score of no great musical interest but undoubtedly pleasant to listen to.

Thomson's version with the LSO, very beautifully played and recorded in spacious sound, brings out the darkness behind this work, inspired by, and dedicated to, Sibelius. It may be less warm and sympathetic than more outward-going readings, less beautiful than others, but it stands as a strong, refreshing reading, superbly recorded, if not quite as cleanly as the very finest. Michael Davis makes a rich-toned soloist in *The Lark ascending*, presented as more than a pastoral evocation.

Previn's performance with the RPO is beautifully played and opulently recorded; but, in a symphony that has long been a favourite with him, he has to contend with his own earlier achievement. His earlier, LSO version for RCA has in addition a raptness and an emotional thrust that are rather missing here when speeds are consistently slower than before. The *Tallis fantasia* makes a very apt coupling, but some of the same reservations apply there too. However much one admires, one is less involved.

Symphony No. 6 in E min.; (i) *Tuba concerto.*
*(*) Chan. Dig. CHAN 8740 [id.]. (i) Patrick Harrild; LSO, Bryden Thomson.

The bluff good humour of the *Tuba concerto* is beautifully caught in Patrick Harrild's rumbustious account on Chandos, rather showing up the lack of bite and tension in the performance of the symphony, a serious flaw in this chill work conceived in wartime. Not only is tension poorly sustained, as though this were a run-through, the ensemble is often surprisingly slack. The Chandos recording is full and warm, and that suits the *Concerto* much better than the *Symphony*, which would benefit from more sharply focused sound. The outstanding tuba soloist plays with wit and panache, but the instrument as recorded sounds rather muffled.

Symphonies Nos. 6 in E min.; 9 in E min.
(m) *** RCA GD 90508. LSO, Previn.

The *Sixth Symphony*, with its moments of darkness and brutality contrasted against the warmth of the second subject or the hushed intensity of the final other-worldly slow movement, is a work for which Previn has a natural affinity. In the first three movements his performance is superbly dramatic, clear-headed and direct, with natural understanding. His account of the mystical final movement with its endless pianissimo is not, however, on the same level, for the playing is not quite hushed enough, and the tempo is a little too fast. The *Ninth*, Vaughan Williams's last symphony, stimulates Previn to show a freshness and sense of poetry which prove particularly thought-provoking and rewarding. The RCA recording is highly successful, and the string tone is expansive and well balanced in relation to the rest of the orchestra.

Sinfonia Antartica (No. 7).
*** EMI Dig. CDC7 47516-2 [id.]. Sheila Armstrong, LPO Ch., LPO, Haitink.

With stunningly full and realistic recording, Haitink directs a revelatory performance of what has long been thought of as merely a programmatic symphony. Based on material from VW's film music for *Scott of the Antarctic*, the symphony is in fact a work which, as Haitink demonstrates, stands powerfully as an original inspiration in absolute terms. Only in the second movement does the 'penguin' music seem heavier than it should be, but even that acquires new and positive qualities, thanks to Haitink.

Sinfonia Antartica (No. 7); Toward the unknown region.
*(*) Chan. Dig. CHAN 8796 [id.]. Catherine Bott, LSO Ch., LSO, Bryden Thomson.

With full and immediate sound, Thomson's version lacks mystery in presenting this colourfully atmospheric score. The lovely oboe melody in the fourth-movement *Intermezzo* is faster and less gently expressive than usual, leading to a rugged account of the finale. If the ominous echoes of No. 6 are muted, Thomson finds more fun than most in the penguin play of the second-movement scherzo. This version will appeal chiefly to those who want the rare choral work, *Toward the unknown region*, a setting of Whitman that antedates the *Sea symphony*. The choral sound is beautiful, with Catherine Bott a radiant soloist; but this early work really needs tauter treatment than Thomson and his team provide.

(i) *Sinfonia Antartica (No. 7); Symphony No. 8 in D min.*
(M) *** RCA GD 90510. (i) Heather Harper, Ralph Richardson, LSO Ch.; LSO, Previn.

The coupling of the *Sinfonia Antartica* with the *Eighth* is the most generous in Previn's cycle. In the former, the RCA recording in its relatively distant balance, as well as Previn's interpretation, concentrates on atmosphere rather than drama in a performance that is sensitive and literal. Because of the recessed effect of the sound, the portrayal of the ice fall (represented by the sudden entry of the organ) has a good deal less impact than on Haitink's version. Before each movement Sir Ralph Richardson speaks the superscription written by the composer on his score. Previn's account of the *Eighth* brings no reservations, with finely pointed playing, the most precise control of dynamic shading, and a delightfully Stravinskian account of the bouncing Scherzo for woodwind alone. Excellent recording, which has been opened up by the digital remastering and made to sound more expansive. At mid-price, this makes a very desirable coupling.

Symphony No. 8 in D min.; Fantasia on Greensleeves; 2 Hymn-tune Preludes: (Eventide; Dominus regit me); Partita for double string orchestra.
**(*) Chan. Dig. CHAN 8828 [id.]. LSO, Bryden Thomson.

In a warm and generally easy-going performance of No. 8, Bryden Thomson underlines the work's pastoral element at relatively slow speeds in three of the four movements. The exception is the third-movement *Cavatina*, which at a flowing speed is similarly easy-going, rather lacking the searching undertones which some other readings find. That approach leads on naturally to *Greensleeves* and the *Hymn-tune Preludes*, similarly pastoral in tone; but then the *Partita* finds the composer in more abrasive mood, less easily sympathetic. This curiously angular work sounds more convincing in a more purposeful performance than this, but in the *Fantasia* finale – a replacement movement that VW wrote after the rest – Thomson effectively brings out the foretastes of the dark first movement of the *Sixth Symphony*. The string sound has more edge on it than in most Chandos issues with Thomson, but that may reflect the LSO rather than the recorded sound, which is full and with plenty of body.

The Wasps: Overture. Serenade to music (orchestral version).
*** Chan. CHAN 8330 [id.]. LPO, Handley – DELIUS: *Collection.****

Exceptionally well recorded and vividly impressive on CD, Handley's readings of the *Wasps overture* and the *Serenade to music* in its orchestral version are most sympathetically done. The *Overture* is more urgent here than in Handley's more recent version for Eminence (as part of the complete suite), and though the *Serenade* inevitably lacks a dimension without voices, this is most persuasive, beautifully played by the LPO.

6 Studies in English folksong for clarinet and piano.
*** Chan. Dig. CHAN 8683 [id.]. Hilton, Swallow – BAX: *Sonata* **(*); BLISS: *Quintet.*
***

These *Folksong studies*, which Vaughan Williams published in arrangements for the viola and cello, come from the mid-1920s and are really very beautiful; they can be recommended even to those normally allergic to this kind of repertory. They are played with the utmost sensitivity by Janet Hilton and Keith Swallow.

VOCAL MUSIC

(i) *Dona nobis pacem;* (ii; iii) *Mass in G min.;* (iii) *O clap your hands.*
(M) *** EMI CDM7 69820-2. (i) Sheila Armstrong, John Carol Case, LPO, Sir Adrian Boult; (ii) King's College, Cambridge, Ch.; (iii) ECO, Sir David Willcocks.

Dona nobis pacem; (i) *5 mystical songs.*
*** Chan. Dig. CHAN 8590 [id.]. Wiens, (i) Rayner-Cook, LPO Ch., LPO, Bryden Thomson.

The *Dona nobis pacem* is powerful music and it is well performed on this Chandos disc by Edith Wiens and Bryan Rayner-Cook. The latter gives an eloquent account of the much earlier *Five mystical songs.* Bryden Thomson seems to be assuming the mantle of Sir Adrian Boult and gets playing of total commitment from the London Philharmonic Orchestra. The recording is made in an appropriately resonant acoustic and the orchestral detail registers well.

Sir Adrian's recording of *Dona nobis pacem* comes from 1973 and still sounds as fresh as the day it was made; in fact it does not compare at all unfavourably with the new Chandos digital account. The sound has space, the range of colour and dynamics is wide, and the performance itself carries a rather special authority. The recording of the *G minor Mass* for *a cappella* forces again more than holds its own against more recent versions in both the quality of the performance and the spacious, atmospheric recording. This is a very welcome and useful reissue.

(i) *In Windsor Forest* (cantata); (ii) *Towards the unknown region.*
*** EMI CDC7 49738-2. (i) Helen Fields, Bournemouth SO Ch. & SO; (ii) CBSO Ch. & O; Del Mar – ELGAR: *From the Bavarian Highlands.****

The cantata *In Windsor Forest*, which Vaughan Williams adapted from his Falstaff opera, *Sir John in Love*, makes the perfect coupling for Elgar's suite of part-songs. Del Mar directs warmly sympathetic performances, given excellent sound. *Towards the unknown region*, digitally recorded, is an early (1907) cantata to words of Walt Whitman; aptly, the chorus is presented at an evocative distance, although the work's big climax is admirably vivid.

Mass in G min.; Te Deum in C.
*** Hyp. CDA 66076 [id.]. Corydon Singers, Best – HOWELLS: *Requiem.****

Matthew Best and the Corydon Singers give as committed an account of the *Mass* as King's College Choir and, despite the spacious acoustic, there is admirable clarity of texture.

(ii) *On Wenlock Edge* (song-cycle from A. E. Housman's *A Shropshire Lad*); (i) *10 Blake songs for voice and oboe.*

❉ (M) *** EMI CDM7 69170-2. Ian Partridge, (i) Janet Craxton; (ii) Music Group of London – WARLOCK: *The Curlew.****

The EMI mid-price CD is an outstandingly beautiful record, with Ian Partridge's intense artistry and lovely individual tone-colour used with compelling success in Vaughan Williams songs both early and late. The Housman cycle has an accompaniment for piano and string quartet which can sound ungainly, but here, with playing from the Music Group of London which matches the soloist's sensitivity, the result is atmospheric and moving. The *Ten Blake songs* come from just before the composer's death, bald, direct settings that with the artistry of Partridge and Craxton are darkly moving. The tenor's sister accompanies with fine understanding in two favourite songs as a welcome extra.

(i) *On Wenlock Edge;* (ii) *Songs of travel* (song-cycles)
*** EMI Dig. CDC7 47220-2 [id.]. (i) Robert Tear; (ii) Thomas Allen, CBSO, Rattle.

The orchestral version of the *Songs of travel* brings home the aptness of treating the nine songs as a cycle, particularly when the soloist is as characterful and understanding a singer as Thomas Allen. The Housman settings in the other cycle are far better known, and Robert Tear – who earlier recorded this same orchestral version with Vernon Handley and the Birmingham orchestra – again proves a deeply perceptive soloist, with his sense of atmosphere, feeling for detailed word-meaning and flawless breath control. Warm, understanding conducting and playing, and excellent sound.

Songs of travel; The House of Life (6 sonnets); *4 Poems by Fredegond Shove; 4 Last songs: No. 2, Tired;* Songs: *In the spring; Linden Lea.*
**(*) Chan. Dig. CHAN 8475 [id.]. Benjamin Luxon, David Williams.

Though Benjamin Luxon's vibrato is distractingly wide, the warmth and clarity of the recording help to make his well-chosen collection of Vaughan Williams songs very attractive, including as it does not only the well-known Stevenson travel cycle but the Rossetti cycle, *The House of Life* (including *The Water mill*), as well as the most famous song of all, *Linden Lea.*

Verdi, Giuseppe (1813–1901)

Ballet music from: *Aida* (including *Triumphal march*); *Don Carlos; Macbeth; I vespri siciliani: (The Four seasons).*
*** Decca Dig. 425 108. Teatro Communale, Bologna, O, Chailly.

Verdi wrote all this ballet music – with more professionalism than enthusiasm – because of the demands of the Paris Opéra for an interpolated dance-sequence in his operas, however inappropriate to the narrative. He was hardly stimulated to write at his highest level and his *Four seasons* in *I vespri siciliani* (which runs for 28 minutes) is no match in imaginative response for Vivaldi's famous work, even though a full orchestral palette is used with some skill. There is much deft scoring, however, in the *Otello* sequence (which he did not want included in the published score), and *La Peregrina* from *Don Carlos* features a romantic scena for concertante violin. There is also a good deal of conventional music; but it is all presented with gusto and polish, and a proper sense of style. Clearly Chailly and his players are enjoying the innocuous rum-ti-tum, and so do we when Decca's recording is so richly coloured and sumptuously brilliant.

Overtures and Preludes: *Aida; La forza del destino; Giovanna d'Arco; Luisa Miller; La Traviata* (Acts I & III); *I vespri siciliani. Macbeth: Ballet music.*
(B) ** Ph. 426 078-2 [id.]. New Philh. O, Markevitch.

A good bargain collection with strongly dramatic performances and excellent CD transfers. *Giovanna d'Arco* and *I vespri siciliani* are especially vivid, and the *Traviata Preludes* are well done too. The sonorous brass tends at times almost to overwhelm the strings, but generally the sound is impressive.

Overtures and Preludes: *Un ballo in maschera* (prelude); *La Battaglia di Legnano; Il Corsaro* (sinfonias); *Ernani* (prelude); *La Forza del destino; Luisa Miller* (overtures); *Macbeth; I Masnadieri* (preludes); *Nabucco* (overture); *Rigoletto; La Traviata* (preludes); *I vespri siciliani* (sinfonia).
*** DG 419 622-2 [id.]. BPO, Karajan.

Overtures and Preludes: *Aida* (prelude); *Un ballo in maschera* (prelude); *La Forza del destino* (overture); *Nabucco* (overture); *La Traviata* (prelude to Act I); *I vespri siciliani* (sinfonia).
(B) *** DG 429 164-2 [id.]. BPO, Karajan – ROSSINI: *Overtures.****

Make no mistake, this playing is in a class of its own and has an electricity, refinement and authority that sweep all before it. Some of the overtures are little known (*Il Corsaro* and *La Battaglia di Legnano*) and are given with tremendous panache and virtuosity. These are performances of real spirit and are vividly recorded, even if the climaxes could expand more.

Overtures and Preludes: *Aida; Attila; Un ballo in maschera; La Forza del destino; Luisa Miller; Nabucco; La Traviata: Preludes, Acts I and III; I vespri siciliani.*
*** DG 411 469-2 [id.]. VPO, Sinopoli.

Overtures: *Aroldo; La Forza del destino; Giovanna d'Arco; Luisa Miller; Nabucco; Oberto, Conte di San Bonifacio; I vespri siciliani.*
*** Decca Dig. 410 141-2 [id.]. Nat. PO, Chailly.

Sinopoli's preference for sharp contrasts and precise rhythms makes for dramatic accounts of these Verdi overtures and preludes, which (like other rivals) include the four finest: *Forza, Vespri siciliani, Luisa Miller* and *Nabucco. Forza*, the finest of all, brings a less fierce account than one would have expected from this conductor, with delicate textures, rhythms and phrasing, but *Luisa Miller* is very characteristic, finely chiselled and exciting in its contrasts, with the Vienna cellos in particular adding lustre. The refined music-making is matched by warm recorded sound.

In his collection, Chailly has the advantage of brilliant Decca recording, with the four most obviously desirable plus three rarities, including the overture to Verdi's very first opera, *Oberto*, and the most substantial of the early ones, *Aroldo*. Crisp and incisive, Chailly draws vigorous and polished playing from the National Philharmonic.

String quartet in E min.
*** CRD CRD 3366 [id.]. Alberni Qt – DONIZETTI: *Quartet No. 13*; PUCCINI: *Crisantemi.****
(*) Hyp. Dig. CDA 66317 [id.]. Delmé Qt – R. STRAUSS: *Quartet.(*)*

The *String quartet* is a unique work in Verdi's output, with a distinctive tone of voice and only one excursion into a recognizably vocal style: in the Neapolitan tune of the trio in the third movement. The Alberni Quartet's performance is strong and compelling, and it is most imaginatively and attractively coupled with the Puccini and Donizetti pieces. The excellent recording has transferred vividly to CD.

The Delmé are not a 'high-powered', jet-setting ensemble and they give a very natural performance of the Verdi which will give much pleasure: there is the sense of music-making in the home among intimate friends, and it is refreshingly unforced, even if the sound is just a shade on the dry side.

Requiem Mass.
*** Decca 411 944-2 (2) [id.]. Sutherland, Horne, Pavarotti, Talvela, V. State Op. Ch., VPO, Solti.
**(*) DG Dig. 415 091-2 (2) [id.]. Tomowa-Sintow, Baltsa, Carreras, Van Dam, V. State Op. Concert Assoc. Ch., Sofia Nat. Op. Ch., VPO, Karajan.
(M) **(*) DG 413 215-2 (2) [id.]. Freni, Ludwig, Cossuta, Ghiaurov, V. Singverein, VPO, Karajan.
(B) ** EMI CZS7 62892-2 (2). Caballé, Cossotto, Vickers, Raimondi, New Philh. Ch. & O, Barbirolli – MOZART: *Requiem.***(*)
* DG Dig. 423 674-2 (2) [id.]. Sweet, Quivar, Cole, Estes, Senff Ch., BPO, Giulini.

(i) *Requiem Mass;* (ii) *Four Sacred pieces.*
**(*) EMI CDS7 47257-8 (2) [Ang. CDCB 47257]. (i) Schwarzkopf, Ludwig, Gedda, Ghiaurov; (ii) J. Baker; Philh. Ch. & O, Giulini.
(M) (***) DG mono 429 076-2 (2) [id.]. Stader, Dominguez, Carelli, Sardi, St Hedwig's Cathedral Ch., Berlin RIAS Chamber Ch. & RSO, Fricsay.
(M) **(*) Decca 421 608-2 (2) [id.]. (i) L. Price, Elias, Bjoerling, Tozzi, V. Musikverein, VPO, Reiner; (ii) Minton, Los Angeles Master Ch., LAPO, Mehta.

(i) *Requiem Mass.* Choruses from: *Aida; Don Carlo; Macbeth; Nabucco; Otello.*
⊛ *** Telarc Dig. CD 80152 (2) [id.]. (i) Dunn, Curry, Hadley, Plishka; Atlanta Ch. & SO, Shaw.

Robert Shaw, who first made his name in the recording world as the chorus-master for some of Toscanini's finest recordings, here in the finest of his Atlanta recordings reflects consistently what he learned from the great maestro in the Verdi *Requiem*. It may not have quite the same searing electricity as Toscanini's rough old NBC recording, but it regularly echoes it in power and the well-calculated pacing. In the *Dies irae* for example, like Toscanini he gains in thrust and power from a speed marginally slower than usual. With sound of spectacular quality, beautifully balanced and clear, the many felicities of the performance, not least the electricity of the choral singing and the consistency of the solo singing, add up to an exceptionally satisfying reading, more recommendable than those of even the most eminent conductors. Only the Giulini has choral singing that might be counted finer; and Shaw also has the advantage of outstanding modern digital recording. Though none of the singers are international stars, their clear, fresh, well-focused voices are beautifully suited to recording, and they make a fine team. The fill-up of five Verdi opera choruses is not as generous as Giulini's but is more colourful, and again brings superb choral singing. This is a fine tribute to Shaw's training with this chorus and orchestra over twenty years. An outstanding issue.

By its side Giulini's EMI set is technically rather less satisfactory as a recording. Yet Giulini's combination of refinement and elemental strength remains totally memorable. What Giulini proves is that refinement added to power can provide an even more intense experience than the traditional Italian approach. In this concept a fine English chorus and orchestra prove exactly right: better disciplined than their Italian counterparts, less severe than the Germans. The array of soloists could hardly be bettered. Schwarzkopf caresses each phrase, and the exactness of her voice matches the firm mezzo of Christa Ludwig in their difficult octave passages. Gedda is at his most reliable, and Ghiaurov with his really dark bass actually manages to sing the almost impossible *Mors stupebit* in tune without a suspicion of wobble. Giulini's set also finds space to include the *Four Sacred pieces* and there is no doubt that in a performance as polished and dramatic as this the element of greatness in these somewhat uneven works is magnified. The CD transfer does its best to freshen the sound and is successful enough in the *Sacred pieces*; but it tends to emphasize the occasional roughness of the heavy climaxes in the *Requiem*, even though generally the quality is fully acceptable.

Fricsay's version (not to be confused with his studio recording of 1950) is of a live performance given in 1960, the very last he conducted before his untimely death. It is a commanding account, often at measured speeds but with a biting sense of drama and a gravity that plainly reflect the conductor's own emotions during his last illness. Like him, the two male soloists are Hungarian, and both are first rate, with the tenor, Gabor Carelli, pleasingly Italianate of tone. Maria Stader, also Hungarian-born, sings with a pure, clear tone, very occasionally suffering intonation problems. Oralia Dominguez is the fruity mezzo, and the chorus is superbly disciplined, with the mono recording remarkably full and spacious. The *Four Sacred pieces* were also recorded live, but ten years earlier. Fricsay gives another dedicated performance. This duplicates the coupling EMI provides for Giulini's classic 1964 account of the *Requiem*, and it comes remarkably close to matching that peerless set.

There is little or nothing reflective about Solti's account, and those who criticize the work for being too operatic will find plenty of ammunition here. The team of soloists is a very strong one, though the matching of voices is not always ideal. It is a pity that the chorus is not nearly as incisive as the Philharmonia on the EMI set – a performance which conveys far more of the work's profundity than this. But if you want an extrovert performance, the firmness of focus and precise placing of forces in the Decca engineering of 1967 make for exceptionally vivid results on CD.

Though Karajan's smooth style has altered relatively little since he recorded this work before for DG, the overall impression is notably fresher – and would be even more so, were the recording more sharply focused and more consistent. The lack of brilliance in the recording also diminishes the element of Italian fire, so that the *Dies irae* is less sharply dramatic than in the finest versions. Soloists are good, naturally and warmly expressive. Though Tomowa-Sintow's un-Italian soprano timbre sometimes brings a hint of flutter, she sings most beautifully in the final rapt account of *Libera me*.

Reiner's opening of the *Requiem* is very slow and atmospheric. He takes the music at something like half the speed of Toscanini and shapes everything very carefully. Yet as the work proceeds the performance quickly sparks into life, and there is some superb and memorable singing from a distinguished team of soloists. The recording has a spectacularly wide dynamic range, enhanced by the CD format, and, with the chorus singing fervently, the *Dies irae* is almost overwhelming. Mehta's performance of the *Sacred pieces* has much more brilliant, sharply focused recording than Giulini's, but in every other way Giulini's performance of Verdi's last work (or group of works) provides a deeper, more searching experience.

Karajan's earlier recording of the *Requiem* has been greatly enhanced in its CD transfer, with the whole effect given greater presence and immediacy. He has a fine team of soloists, too. However, Karajan's reading still smooths over the lines of Verdi's masterpiece. The result is often beautiful, but, apart from the obvious climaxes, such as the *Dies irae*, there is a lack of dramatic bite.

Barbirolli favours slow tempi, but his concentration is not enough to sustain the necessary drama. It is an enjoyably lyrical approach, but more is needed; though the solo quartet is strong, Montserrat Caballé is well below her finest form.

Giulini's Berlin version of the *Requiem* – made 25 years after his first classic EMI recording with Philharmonia forces – is most disappointing. With a flawed quartet of soloists, not only does it lack the fire of the vintage 1964 version, but also the reverberant, rather recessed recording tends to take away what bite remains in this thoughtfully reflective, sensitive reading.

4 Sacred pieces.
(M) **(*) Decca 425 844-2 (2) [id.]. Chicago Ch. & SO, Solti – BEETHOVEN: *Missa solemnis.**

Solti's brand of dedication is one of brightness and tension: he draws finely shaded performances from his forces and the electricity is never in doubt. The climaxes in the *Stabat Mater* and *Te Deum* are thrilling, and their effect is enhanced by the bold, brilliant recording. However, many will demand a more spiritual and more devotional manner in this music.

4 Sacred pieces: Te Deum (only).
** Telarc Dig. CD 80109 [id.]. Morehouse-Spelman Ch., Atlanta Ch. & SO, Shaw – BERLIOZ: *Requiem*; BOITO: *Mefistofele: Prologue.***

Shaw conducts a finely disciplined reading of the Verdi *Te Deum* as the second of two generous fill-ups on the CD version of his recording of the Berlioz *Requiem*. As in the rest of the set, however, tension and mystery are lacking, despite firmly focused recording.

OPERA

Aida (complete).
(M) *** EMI CMS7 69300-2 (3) [Ang. CDMC 69300]. Freni, Carreras, Baltsa, Cappuccilli, Raimondi, Van Dam, V. State Op. Ch., VPO, Karajan.
*** Decca 417 416-2 (3) [id.]. Leontyne Price, Gorr, Vickers, Merrill, Tozzi, Rome Op. Ch. & O, Solti.
(M) *** Decca 414 087-2 (3). Tebaldi, Simionato, Bergonzi, MacNeil, Van Mill, Corena, V. Singverein, VPO, Karajan.
(M) (***) RCA mono GD 86652 (3) [6652-2-RG]. Milanov, Bjoerling, Barbieri, Warren, Christoff, Rome Op. Ch. & O, Perlea.
**(*) DG Dig. 410 092-2 (3) [id.]. Ricciarelli, Domingo, Obraztsova, Nucci, Raimondi, Ghiaurov, La Scala, Milan, Ch. & O, Abbado.
** Decca Dig. 417 439-2 (3). Chiara, Pavarotti, Dimitrova, Nucci, Burchuladze, La Scala, Milan, Ch. & O, Maazel.
** EMI CDS7 47271-8 (3) [Ang. CDCC 47271]. Caballé, Domingo, Cossotto, Ghiaurov, Cappuccilli, ROHCG Ch., New Philh. O, Muti.
** RCA RD 86198 (3) [6198-2-RC]. Leontyne Price, Domingo, Bumbry, Milnes, Raimondi, Alldis Ch., LSO, Leinsdorf.
(**) EMI mono CDS7 49030-8 (3) [id.]. Callas, Tucker, Barbieri, Gobbi, La Scala, Milan, Ch. & O, Serafin.

Karajan's is a performance of *Aida* that carries splendour and pageantry to the point of exaltation. At the very end of the Triumphal Scene, when the march resumes with brass bands, there is a lift, a surge of emotion, such as is captured only rarely on record. For all the power of the pageantry, Karajan's fundamental approach is lyrical. Arias are often taken at a slow speed, taxing the singers more, yet Karajan's controversial choice of soloists is amply justified. On record at least, there can be little question of Freni lacking power in a role normally given to a larger voice, and there is ample gain in the tender beauty of her singing. Carreras makes a fresh, sensitive Radames, Raimondi a darkly intense Ramphis and Van Dam a cleanly focused King, his relative lightness no drawback. Cappuccilli here gives a more detailed performance than he did for Muti on EMI, while Baltsa as Amneris crowns the whole performance with her fine, incisive singing. Despite some overbrightness on cymbals and trumpet, the Berlin sound for Karajan, as transferred to CD, is richly and involvingly atmospheric, both in the intimate scenes and, most strikingly, in the scenes of pageant, which have rarely been presented on record in greater splendour.

Leontyne Price is an outstandingly assured Aida on Decca, rich, accurate and imaginative, while Solti's direction is superbly dramatic, notably in the Nile Scene. Merrill is a richly secure Amonasro, Rita Gorr a characterful Amneris, and Jon Vickers is splendidly heroic as Radames. Though the digital transfer betrays the age of the recording (1962), making the result fierce at times to match the reading, Solti's version otherwise brings full, spacious sound, finer, more open and with greater sense of presence than most versions since.

There is also a place in the catalogue for Karajan's early stereo version from Decca, which stood unrivalled for many years for its spectacle in this most stereophonic of operas. On Decca, as again on EMI, Karajan was helped by having a Viennese orchestra and chorus; but most important of all is the musicianship and musical teamwork of his soloists. Bergonzi in particular emerges here as a model among tenors, with a rare feeling for the shaping of phrases and attention to detail. Cornell MacNeil too is splendid. Tebaldi's creamy tone-colour rides beautifully over the phrases and she too acquires a new depth of imagination. Vocally there are flaws too: notably at the end of *O patria mia*, where Tebaldi finds the cruelly exposed top notes too taxing. Among the other soloists Arnold van Mill and Fernando Corena are both superb, and Simionato provides one of the very finest portrayals of Amneris we have ever had in a complete *Aida*. The recording has long been famous for its technical bravura and flair. CD enhances the overall projection and helps the pianissimos register in a recording with a very wide dynamic range for its period (late 1950s), but the brightness on top at times strikes the ear rather too forcibly. Nevertheless this remains a remarkable technical achievement.

All four principals on the historic RCA set are at their very finest, notably Milanov, whose poise and control in *O patria mia* are a marvel. Barbieri as Amneris is even finer here than in the Callas set, and it is good to hear the young Christoff resonant as Ramfis. Perlea too conducts with great panache.

Fresh and intelligent, unexaggerated in its pacing, Abbado's version from La Scala lacks a little in excitement. It is stronger on the personal drama than on the ceremonial. Domingo gives a superb performance as Radames, not least in the Nile Scene, and the two bass roles are cast from strength in Raimondi and Ghiaurov. Leo Nucci makes a dramatic Amonasro, not always pure of line, while Elena Obraztsova produces too much curdled tone as Amneris, dramatic as she is. In many ways Ricciarelli is an appealing Aida, but the voice grows impure above the stave, and floating legatos are marred. The digital recording fails to expand for the ceremonial, and voices are highlighted, but it is acceptably fresh.

Based on a production at La Scala, the Decca set conducted by Maazel conveys surprisingly little of the feeling of operatic drama. Its great glory is the singing of Luciano Pavarotti, his first recording of the role of Radames. The voice is magnificent, and the superstar tenor's pointing of word-meaning consistently adds illumination, with the character strongly projected. He dominates the performance. Sadly Maazel, adopting speeds on the slow side, is often disappointingly square and metronomic, lacking Verdian warmth and forward thrust. Nevertheless, with a strong cast there is much to enjoy besides Pavarotti. Maria Chiara uses her lovely soprano with fine feeling for Verdian line, even if the characterization is generalized. Gena Dimitrova is a dull Amneris, and Leo Nucci a reliable Amonasro, helping to make the Nile scene the most animated sequence of the whole set. Paata Burchuladze sings with sepulchral darkness, but with little feeling for the Italian language. The recording is not ideally spacious in the big ensembles, but it is still full and brilliant in the Decca manner, the best sound accorded to any recent digital set.

Caballé's portrait of the heroine is superb, full of detailed insight into the character and with countless examples of superlative singing. The set is worth having for her alone, and Cossotto makes a fine Amneris. Domingo produces glorious sound, but this is not one of his most imaginative recordings, while the Amonasro of Piero Cappuccilli is prosaic. So is much of Muti's direction, and the CD transfer, though faithful enough, brings out the relatively small scale of the sound.

There is much to commend in Leontyne Price's 1971 recording of *Aida*. But inevitably it comes into direct comparison with her earlier Decca set, and by that standard it is a little disappointing. Price's voice is not as glowing as it was, and though there are moments where she shows added insight, it is the earlier performance which generates more electricity and has more dramatic urgency. Domingo makes a warm and stylish Radames, Milnes a strong if hardly electrifying Amonasro and Bumbry a superb, imaginative Amneris. However, most of the earlier sets are more impressive in sound.

The Nile Scene has never been performed more powerfully and characterfully on record than in this vintage La Scala set. Though Callas is hardly as sweet-toned as some will think essential for an Aida, her detailed imagination is irresistible, and she is matched by Tito Gobbi at the very height of his powers. Tucker gives one of his very finest performances on record, and Barbieri is a commanding Amneris. The mono sound is more than acceptable.

Aida: highlights (scenes & arias).
(M) *** Decca 417 763-2 [id.]. Tebaldi, Bergonzi, Simionato, MacNeil, V. Singverein, VPO, Karajan.
(M) *** Decca 421 860-2 [id.] (from above recording, cond. Solti).

Aida: highlights.
(M) (***) RCA mono GD 60201 [60201-2-RG] (from above recording with Milanov, Bjoerling; cond. Perlea).
**(*) DG 415 286-2 [id.] (from above set, cond. Abbado).

Although DG have gathered together a generous collection of highlights from Abbado's set, lasting well over an hour, by far the most interesting compilation is the Decca 'Scenes and arias' from John Culshaw's Karajan recording from the early stereo era. The RCA highlights disc is valuable above all for providing a sample of one of Milanov's most compelling performances on record, poised and commanding.

A fairly generous mid-priced reminder of Solti's excellent set, with Price an outstandingly assured Aida.

Alzira (complete).
*** Orfeo CO 57832 (2) [id.]. Cotrubas, Araiza, Bruson, George, Bonilla, Bav. R. Ch., Munich R. O, Gardelli.

Alzira is the shortest of the Verdi operas, but its concision is on balance an advantage on record. In musical inspiration it is indistinguishable from other typical early operas, with Verdian melodies less distinctive than they became later, but consistently pleasing. Gardelli is a master with early Verdi, and the cast is strong, helped by warm and well-balanced recording supervised by Munich Radio engineers.

Aroldo (complete).
** CBS CD 79328 [M2K 39506] (2). Caballé, Cecchele, Lebherz, Pons, NY Oratorio Soc., Westminster Ch. Soc., NY Op. O, Queler.

Aroldo is Verdi's radical revision of his earlier unsuccessful opera, *Stiffelio*: he translated the story of a Protestant pastor with an unfaithful wife into this tale of a crusader returning from the Holy Land. Less compact than the original, it contains some splendid new material such as the superb aria for the heroine, beautifully sung by Caballé. The final scene too is quite new, for the dénouement is totally different. The storm chorus (with echoes of *Rigoletto*) is most memorable – but so are the rum-ti-tum choruses common to both versions. This recording of a concert performance in New York is lively, though the tenor is depressingly coarse.

Attila (complete).
(M) *** Ph. 426 115-2 (2) [id.]. Raimondi, Deutekom, Bergonzi, Milnes, Amb. S., Finchley Children's Music Group, RPO, Gardelli.
** EMI Dig. CDS7 49952-2 [Ang. CDCB 49952]. Ramey, Studer, Shicoff, Zancanaro, La Scala, Milan, Ch. & O, Muti.
** Hung. Dig. HCD 12934/35 (2). Nesterenko, Miller, Sass, Nagy, Kovats, Hungarian R. & TV Ch., Hungarian State O, Gardelli.

With its dramatic anticipations of *Macbeth*, the musical anticipations of *Rigoletto* and the compression which (on record if not on the stage) becomes a positive merit – all these qualities, helped by a fine performance under Gardelli, make this Philips version of *Attila* an intensely enjoyable set. Deutekom, not the most sweet-toned of sopranos, has never sung better on record, and the rest of the cast is outstandingly good. The 1973 recording is well balanced and atmospheric, but the remastering for CD has been able to make only a marginal improvement in definition, with the chorus less sharply focused than one would expect on a modern digital set.

Recorded – like the latest Decca sets of *Aida* and *Simon Boccanegra* – in the Studio Abanella, the digital sound on the Muti set is more agreeable than on most of his La Scala recordings; but it has less presence than the much earlier Gardelli analogue recording, and the voices are so spotlit that they lose much of their natural bloom. The team of American principals is a strong one, with Ramey bringing out the nobility of the central character, hardly the barbarian of history. Cheryl Studer makes an outstanding Odabella, consistently imaginative, to have one regretting that the voice is not caught more sweetly. Neil Shicoff sings strongly in the tenor role of Foresto, and so does Giorgio Zancanaro as Ezio, but they cannot match their opposite numbers in the Philips set, Carlo Bergonzi and Sherrill Milnes.

The Hungaroton set, also conducted by the ever-responsive Gardelli, brings the advantage of clean, brilliant digital sound of a quality now expected from Budapest. There is also the magisterial Evgeni Nesterenko in the name-part, and in this bass role a Slavonic rather than an Italianate timbre helps to characterize the invading barbarian. Lajos Miller is a strong Ezio, and Sylvia Sass a characterful Odabella though, like Deutekom on the Philips set, she has her squally moments. The snag is the principal tenor, the strained and unstylish Janos B. Nagy as Foresto, the knight from Aquileia. He is no match at all for Carlo Bergonzi on the earlier set.

Un ballo in maschera (complete).
*** Decca Dig. 410 210-2 (2) [id.]. Margaret Price, Pavarotti, Bruson, Ludwig, Battle, L. Op. Ch., Royal College of Music Junior Dept Ch., Nat. PO, Solti.
*** DG Dig. 427 635-2 (2) [id.]. Domingo, Barstow, Nucci, Quivar, Sumi Jo, V. State Op. Konzertvereinigung, VPO, Karajan.
*** DG 415 685-2 (2) [id.]. Ricciarelli, Domingo, Bruson, Obraztsova, Gruberová, Raimondi, La Scala, Milan, Ch. & O, Abbado.
(M) *** RCA GD 86645 (2) [6645-2-RG]. L. Price, Bergonzi, Merrill, Grist, Verrett, Flagello, RCA Italiana Op. Ch. & O, Leinsdorf.
(M) *** EMI CMS7 69576-2 (2) [Ang. CDMB 69576]. Arroyo, Domingo, Cappuccilli, Grist, Cossotto, Howell, ROHCG Ch., New Philh. O, Muti.
(***) EMI mono CDS7 47498-8 (2) [Ang. CDCB 47498]. Callas, Di Stefano, Gobbi, Barbieri, Ratti, La Scala, Milan, Ch. & O, Serafin.
(M) * Decca 425 655-2 (2). Bergonzi, Nilsson, MacNeil, Simionato, St Cecilia Ac., Rome, Ch. & O, Solti.

Shining out from the cast of Solti's set of *Ballo* is the gloriously sung Amelia of Margaret Price in one of her richest and most commanding performances on record, ravishingly beautiful, flawlessly controlled and full of unforced emotion. The role of Riccardo, pushy and truculent, is well suited to the extrovert Pavarotti, who swaggers through the part, characteristically clear of diction, challenged periodically by Price to produce some of his subtlest tone-colours. Bruson makes a noble Renato, Christa Ludwig an unexpected but intense and perceptive Ulrica, while Kathleen Battle is an Oscar whose coloratura is not just brilliant but sweet too. Solti is far more relaxed than he often is on record, presenting a warm and understanding view of the score. The recording is extremely vivid within a reverberant acoustic.

Recorded in Vienna early in 1989, *Un ballo in maschera* was Karajan's last opera recording. It was done in conjunction with the new production at that year's Salzburg Festival, which Karajan was scheduled to conduct. He died only days before the first night, while the production was already in rehearsal. The recording makes a fitting memorial, characteristically rich and spacious, with a cast – if not ideal – which still makes a fine team, responding to the conductor's single-minded vision. Karajan's underlining of dynamic contrasts in the final assassination scene, for example, is thrilling, demonstrating his undiminished sense of drama. Standing out vocally is the Gustavo of Placido Domingo, strong and imaginative, dominating the whole cast. He may not have the sparkle of Pavarotti in this role, but the singing is richer, more refined and more thoughtful. Karajan's unexpected and controversial choice of Josephine Barstow as Amelia certainly makes for a striking and characterful performance, even if vocally it is flawed, with the tone growing raw under pressure. Nevertheless this is Barstow's finest achievement on record, and dramatically she is most compelling. Leo Nucci, though not as rough in tone as in some of his other recent recordings, is over-emphatic, with poor legato in his great solo, *Eri tu*. Sumi Jo, a Karajan discovery, gives a delicious performance as Oscar, the page, coping splendidly with Karajan's slow speed for her Act I solo. Florence Quivar produces satisfyingly rich tone as Ulrica. Though the sound is not as cleanly focused as in the Decca recording for Solti, it is warm and full.

Abbado's powerful reading, admirably paced and with a splendid feeling for the sparkle of the comedy, remains highly recommendable. The cast is very strong, with Ricciarelli at her very finest and Domingo sweeter of tone and more deft of characterization than on the Muti set of five years earlier. Bruson as the wronged husband Renato (a role he also takes for Solti) sings magnificently, and only Obraztsova as Ulrica and Gruberová as

Oscar are less consistently convincing. The analogue recording clearly separates the voices and instruments in different acoustics, which on CD is distracting only initially and after that brings the drama closer.

The reissued RCA set makes a fine bargain. All the principals are in splendid voice, and Leinsdorf's direction – too often inflexible in Italian opera – here has resilience as well as brilliance and urgency. Leontyne Price is a natural for the part of Amelia and, with one notable reservation, hers comes near to being a model interpretation, spontaneous-sounding and full of dramatic temperament. Only in the two big arias does Price for a moment grow self-conscious, and there are one or two mannered phrases, overloaded with the wrong sort of expressiveness. Robert Merrill, sometimes thought of as an inexpressive singer, here seems to have acquired all sorts of dramatic, Gobbi-like overtones to add to the flow of firm, satisfying tone. Bergonzi is a model of sensitivity, while Reri Grist makes a light, bright Oscar, and the Ulrica of Shirley Verrett has a range of power, richness and delicacy coupled with unparalleled firmness that makes this one of her most memorable recorded performances. Excellent recording, hardly showing its age, with the voices rather forward.

On EMI the quintet of principals is also unusually strong, but it is the conductor who takes first honours in a warmly dramatic reading. Muti's rhythmic resilience and consideration for the singers go with keen concentration, holding each Act together in a way he did not quite achieve in his earlier recording for EMI of *Aida*. Arroyo, rich of voice, is not always imaginative in her big solos, and Domingo rarely produces a half-tone, though the recording balance may be partly to blame. The sound is vivid, but no translation is provided for this mid-price reissue.

The 1957 EMI recording, with voices as ever set rather close but with a fair amount of space round them, is among the best of the sets with Callas from La Scala, and CD focuses its qualities the more sharply. Cast from strength with all the principals – notably Gobbi and Giuseppe di Stefano – on top form, this is indispensable for Callas's admirers.

In spite of an impressive cast, Solti's earlier version is very disappointing, with its opera-house atmosphere only adding to the impression of uninterested singing and playing.

La Battaglia di Legnano (complete).
(M) *** Ph. 422 435-2 (2) [id.]. Ricciarelli, Carreras, Manuguerra, Ghiuselev, Austrian R. Ch. & O, Gardelli.

La Battaglia di Legnano is a compact, sharply conceived piece, made the more intense by the subject's obvious relationship with the situation in Verdi's own time. One weakness is that the villainy is not effectively personalized, but the juxtaposition of the individual drama of supposed infidelity against a patriotic theme brings most effective musical contrasts. Gardelli directs a fine performance, helped by a strong cast of principals, with Carreras, Ricciarelli and Manuguerra all at their finest. Excellent recording, with the depth of perspective enhanced on CD.

Il Corsaro (complete).
(M) *** Ph. 426 118-2 (2) [id.]. Norman, Caballé, Carreras, Grant, Mastromei, Noble, Amb. S., New Philh. O, Gardelli.

By the time he had completed the score, Verdi had fallen out of love with his subject, an adaptation of Byron. Only latterly has the composer's own poor view of *Il Corsaro* been revised in the light of closer study, and Piave's treatment of Byron turns out to be not nearly so clumsy as had been thought. Though the characterization is rudimentary, the contrast between the two heroines is effective, with Gulnara, the Pasha's slave, carrying conviction in the *coup de foudre* which has her promptly worshipping the Corsair, an early example of the Rudolph Valentino figure. The rival heroines are taken splendidly here, with Jessye Norman as the faithful wife, Medora, actually upstaging Montserrat Caballé as Gulnara. Gardelli, as in his previous Philips recordings of early Verdi, directs a vivid performance, with fine singing from the hero, portrayed by José Carreras. Gian-Piero Mastromei, not rich in tone, still rises to the challenge of the Pasha's music. Excellent, firmly focused and well-balanced Philips sound.

Don Carlos (complete).
*** EMI CDS7 47701-8 (3) [Ang. CDCC 47701]. Domingo, Caballé, Raimondi, Verrett, Milnes, Amb. Op. Ch., ROHCG O, Giulini.
(M) *** EMI CMS7 69304-2 (3) [Ang. CDMC 69304]. Carreras, Freni, Ghiaurov, Baltsa, Cappuccilli, Raimondi, German Op. Ch., Berlin, BPO, Karajan.
**(*) DG Dig. 415 316-2 (4) [id.]. Ricciarelli, Domingo, Valentini Terrani, Nucci, Raimondi, Ghiaurov, La Scala, Milan, Ch. & O, Abbado.
**(*) Decca 421 114-2 (3) [id.]. Tebaldi, Bumbry, Bergonzi, Fischer-Dieskau, Ghiaurov, ROHCG Ch. & O, Solti.

Giulini conducts the same orchestra as Solti directed in the earlier, Decca set and predictably he is more affectionate in his phrasing, while conveying the quiet, dramatic intensity which made his direction so irresistible in the opera house. There is extra joy in the *Auto da fè* scene as it is pointed by Giulini. Generally the new cast is a little stronger than the old, but each is admirably consistent. The only major vocal disappointment among the principals lies in Caballé's account of the big aria *Tu che le vanità* in the final Act. Like the Decca set, this one uses the full, five-Act text. The CD transfer of the 1971 analogue recording brings astonishing vividness and realism, a tribute to the original engineering of Christopher Parker. Even in the big ensembles of the *Auto da fè* scene, the focus is very precise, yet atmospheric too, not just analytic. The extra bite of realism enhances an already fine version to make it the finest, irrespective of age.

Karajan opts firmly for the later, four-Act version of the opera, merely opening out the cuts he adopted on stage. The results could hardly be more powerfully dramatic, one of his most involving opera performances, comparable with his vivid EMI *Aida*. The *Auto da fè* scene is here superb, while Karajan's characteristic choice of singers for refinement of voice rather than sheer size consistently pays off. Both Carreras and Freni are most moving, even if *Tu che le vanità* has its raw moments. Baltsa is a superlative Eboli and Cappuccilli an affecting Rodrigo, though neither Carreras nor Cappuccilli is at his finest in the famous oath duet. Raimondi and Ghiaurov as the Grand Inquisitor and Philip II provide the most powerful confrontation. Though the sound is not as analytically detailed as the earlier, EMI version with Giulini, it is both rich and atmospheric, giving great power to Karajan's uniquely taut account of the four-Act version.

For the dedicated Verdian, Abbado's set brings new authenticity and new revelation. This is the first recording to use the language which Verdi originally set, French; in addition to the full five-Act text in its composite 1886 form including the Fontainebleau scene (recorded twice before), there are half a dozen appendices from the original 1867 score, later cut or recomposed. By rights, this should be the definitive recording of the opera for, as has often been promised, the French text brings an apt darkening of tone compared with the open sounds of Italian, and Abbado is a masterly interpreter of Verdi. The first disappointment lies in the variable quality of the sound, with odd balances, so that although the Fontainebleau opening, with its echoing horns, is arrestingly atmospheric, the *Auto da fè* scene lacks bite, brilliance and clarity. In addition, large-scale flair and urgency are missing; once that is said, however, the cast of singers is a strong one. Domingo easily outshines his earlier recording with Giulini (in Italian), while Katia Ricciarelli as the Queen gives a tenderly moving performance, if not quite commanding enough in the Act V aria. Ruggero Raimondi is a finely focused Philip II, nicely contrasted with Nicolai Ghiaurov as the Grand Inquisitor in the other black-toned bass role. Lucia Valentini Terrani as Eboli is warm-toned if not very characterful, and Leo Nucci makes a noble Posa.

The Decca version includes the important passages often excised, notably the Fontainebleau scene, and that may underline the one major deficiency of the set, that the dramatic temperature fails to rise as it should until the duet between Philip and Rodrigo at the end of Act II (Act I in the four-Act version). Tebaldi in this most exacting Verdian role warms up well and gives a magnificent account of *Tu che le vanità*. Bumbry and Bergonzi both sing splendidly, and after some rather gritty singing early on, Fischer-Dieskau rises fittingly to Rodrigo's great death scene, sounding almost (but not quite) as moving as Gobbi in the old EMI set (mono). Ghiaurov as Philip brings a nobility, a sense of stoic pride, that is most compelling. The recording is of Decca's usual high standard, and though with such a marvellous array of talent one might feel the result should be still more overwhelming, there is no doubt that this version has a great deal to commend it.

Don Carlos: highlights.
(M) *** EMI CDM7 63089-2 (from complete set with Domingo, Caballé, Verrett, Milnes; cond. Giulini).
*** DG Dig. 415 981-2 [id.] (from above recording, cond. Abbado).

Giulini's disc of highlights can be highly recommended. In selecting from such a long opera, serious omissions are inevitable; nothing is included here from Act III, to make room for the *Auto da fè* scene from Act IV – some 37 minutes of the disc is given to this Act. With vivid sound this is most stimulating; the only reservation concerns Caballé's *Tu che le vanità*, which ends the selection disappointingly.

A generous selection from the impressive Abbado set follows the narrative throughout all five Acts. There is well over an hour of music here.

I due Foscari (complete).
(M) *** Ph. 422 426-2 (2) [id.]. Ricciarelli, Carreras, Cappuccilli, Ramey, Austrian R. Ch. & SO, Gardelli.

I due Foscari brings Verdian high spirits in plenty, erupting in swinging cabalettas and much writing that anticipates operas as late as *Simon Boccanegra* (obvious enough in the Doge's music) and *La forza del destino* (particularly in the orchestral motifs which act as labels for the principal characters). The cast here is first rate, with Ricciarelli giving one of her finest performances in the recording studio to date and with Carreras singing tastefully as well as powerfully. The crispness of discipline among the Austrian Radio forces is admirable, but there is less sense of atmosphere here than in the earlier, London-made recordings in the series; otherwise the Philips sound is impressively present and clear.

Ernani (complete).
(M) **(*) RCA GD 86503 (2) [6503-2-RG]. Leontyne Price, Bergonzi, Sereni, Flagello, RCA Italiana Op. Ch. & O, Schippers.
**(*) EMI Dig. CDS7 47083-2 (3) [Ang. CDC 47082]. Domingo, Freni, Bruson, Ghiaurov, La Scala, Milan, Ch. & O, Muti.
** Hung. Dig. HCD 12259/61 [id.]. Lamberti, Sass, Kováts, Miller, Takács, Hungarian State Op. Ch. and O, Gardelli.

At mid-price in RCA's Victor Opera series on two CDs instead of three LPs, Schippers' set, recorded in Rome in 1967, is an outstanding bargain. Leontyne Price may take the most celebrated aria, *Ernani involami*, rather cautiously, but the voice is gloriously firm and rich, and Bergonzi is comparably strong and vivid, though Mario Sereni, vocally reliable, is dull, and Ezio Flagello gritty-toned. Nevertheless, with Schippers drawing the team powerfully together, it is a highly enjoyable set, with the digital transfer making voices and orchestra sound full and vivid.

The great merit of Muti's set, recorded live at a series of performances at La Scala, is that the ensembles have an electricity rarely achieved in the studio, even if the results may not always be so precise and stage noises are often obtrusive. The singing, generally strong and characterful, is yet flawed. The strain of the role of Elvira for Mirella Freni is plain from the big opening aria, *Ernani involami*, onwards. Even in that aria there are cautious moments. Bruson is a superb Carlo and Ghiaurov a characterful Silva, but his voice now betrays signs of wear. As Ernani himself, Placido Domingo gives a commandingly heroic performance, but under pressure there are hints of tight tone such as he rarely produces in the studio. The recording inevitably has odd balances which will disturb some more than others. The CD version gives greater immediacy and presence, but also brings out the inevitable flaws of live recording the more clearly.

Gardelli's conducting is most sympathetic and idiomatic in the Hungarian version and, like Muti's, it is strong on ensembles. Sylvia Sass is a sharply characterful Elvira, Callas-like in places, and Lamberti a bold Ernani, but their vocal flaws prevent this from being a first choice. Capable rather than inspired or idiomatic singing from the rest. The digital recording is bright and well balanced, although the recording acoustics are very resonant.

Ernani: highlights.
** Hung. Dig. HCD 12609 [id.] (from above recording, cond. Gardelli).

A useful selection of items from the complete Hungaroton set, flawed but most sympathetically conducted.

Falstaff (complete).
*** DG Dig. 410 503-2 (2) [id.]. Bruson, Ricciarelli, Nucci, Hendricks, Egerton, Valentini Terrani, Boozer, LA Master Ch., LAPO, Giulini.
*(**) EMI CDS7 49668-2 (2) [Ang. CDCB 49668]. Gobbi, Schwarzkopf, Zaccaria, Moffo, Panerai, Philh. Ch. & O, Karajan.
**(*) Ph. Dig. 412 263-2 (2). Taddei, Kabaivanska, Perry, Panerai, Ludwig, Araiza, V. State Op. Ch., VPO, Karajan.

Giulini's reading combines the tensions and atmosphere of live performance with a precision normally achieved only in the studio. This was Giulini's first essay in live opera-conducting in fourteen years, and he treated the piece with a care for musical values which at times undermined the knockabout comic element. On record that is all to the good, for the clarity and beauty of the playing are caught superbly on CD, and though the parallel with Toscanini is an obvious one – also recorded at a live performance – Giulini is far more relaxed. Bruson, hardly a comic actor, is impressive on record for his fine incisive singing, giving tragic implications to the monologue at the start of Act III after Falstaff's dunking. The Ford of Leo Nucci, impressive in the theatre, is thinly caught, where the heavyweight quality of Ricciarelli as Alice comes over well, though in places one would wish for a purer sound. Barbara Hendricks is a charmer as Nannetta, but she hardly sounds fairy-like in her Act III aria. The full women's ensemble, though precise, is not always quite steady in tone, though the conviction of the whole performance puts it among the most desirable of modern readings.

This earlier (1956) Karajan recording presents not only the most pointed account orchestrally of Verdi's comic masterpiece (the Philharmonia Orchestra at its very peak) but the most sharply characterful cast ever gathered for a recording. If you relish the idea of Tito Gobbi as Falstaff (his many-coloured voice, not quite fat-sounding in humour, presents a sharper character than usual), then this is clearly the best choice, for the rest of the cast is a delight, with Schwarzkopf a tinglingly masterful Mistress Ford, Anna Moffo sweet as Nannetta and Rolando Panerai a formidable Ford. Unfortunately the digital remastering has been mismanaged. While the precision and placing of voices on the stereo stage, a model even today, comes out the more clearly on CD, the transfer itself, at a low level and with high hiss, has lost the bloom and warmth of the original analogue master which was outstanding for its time.

Karajan's second recording of Verdi's last opera, made over twenty years after his classic Philharmonia set, has lower standards of precision, yet conveys a relaxed and genial atmosphere. With the exception of Kabaivanska, whose voice is not steady enough for the role of Alice, it is a good cast, with Ludwig fascinating as Mistress Quickly. Most amazing of all is Taddei's performance as Falstaff himself, full and characterful and vocally astonishing from a man in his sixties. The digital sound is faithful and wide-ranging. The CD version captures the bloom of the original, reverberant recording so vividly that one worries less about any oddities of balance.

La Forza del destino (complete).
*** DG Dig. 419 203-2 (3) [id.]. Plowright, Carreras, Bruson, Burchuladze, Baltsa, Amb. Op. Ch., Philh. O, Sinopoli.
*** RCA RD 81864 (3) [RCD3-1864]. Leontyne Price, Domingo, Milnes, Cossotto, Giaiotti, Bacquier, Alldis Ch., LSO, Levine.
(M) *** RCA GD 87971 (3) [4515-2-RG]. Leontyne Price, Tucker, Merrill, Tozzi, Verrett, Flagello, Foiani, RCA Italiana Op. Ch. & O, Schippers.
(M) ** Decca 421 598-2 (3) [id.]. Tebaldi, Del Monaco, Bastianini, Siepi, St Cecilia Academy, Rome, Ch. & O, Molinari-Pradelli.
*(*) EMI Dig. CDS7 47485-8 (3) [Ang. CDCC 47485]. Freni, Domingo, Zancanaro, Zajic, Bruscantini, Plishka, La Scala, Milan, Ch. & O, Muti.

Sinopoli's is an exceptionally spacious view of *Forza*, in many ways akin to the similarly distinctive reading of *Il Trovatore* recorded for DG by Giulini. Sinopoli draws out phrases lovingly, sustaining pauses to the limit, putting extra strain on the singers. Happily, the whole cast seems to thrive on the challenge, and the spaciousness of the recording acoustic not only makes the dramatic interchanges the more realistic, it brings out the bloom on all the voices, above all the creamy soprano of Rosalind Plowright. Though José Carreras is sometimes too conventionally histrionic, even strained, it is a strong, involved performance. Renato Bruson is a thoughtful Carlo, while some of the finest singing of all comes from Agnes Baltsa as Preziosilla and Paata Burchuladze as the Padre Guardiano, uniquely resonant. Though the speeds will not please all Verdians, Sinopoli's is a distinctive, deeply felt view which in its breadth conveys the epic nobility of the piece with great authority.

James Levine directs a superb performance of an opera which in less purposeful hands can seem too episodic. The results are electrifying, and rarely if ever does Levine cut across the natural expressiveness of an outstanding cast. Leontyne Price recorded the role of Leonora in an earlier RCA version made in Rome in 1956, but the years have hardly touched her voice, and details of the reading have been refined. The roles of Don Alvaro and Don Carlo are ideally suited to the regular team of Placido Domingo and Sherrill Milnes so that their confrontations are the cornerstones of the dramatic structure. Fiorenza Cossotto makes a formidable rather than a jolly Preziosilla, while on the male side the line-up of Bonaldo Giaiotti, Gabriel Bacquier, Kurt Moll and Michel Sénéchal is far stronger than on rival sets. In a good, vivid transfer of the mid-1970s sound, this strong, well-paced version will for many provide a safe alternative to Sinopoli, with an exceptionally good and consistent cast.

No soprano of her generation had natural gifts more suited to the role of Leonora in *Forza* than Leontyne Price. Her admirers will cherish this early recording quite as much as her later one with James Levine, also from RCA. The voice in 1964 was fresher and more open; though the clearer, less ambient recording from the Rome studio exposes it in greater detail, on balance this is a more tender and delicate performance than the weightier one she recorded with Levine. Richard Tucker as Alvaro is here far less lachrymose and more stylish than he was earlier in the Callas set, producing ample, heroic tone, if not with the finesse of a Domingo. Robert Merrill as Carlo also sings with heroic strength, consistently firm and dark of tone; while Shirley Verrett, Giorgio Tozzi and Ezio Flagello stand up well against any rivalry. The sound is remarkably full and vivid for its age, with a fine illusion of presence which quickly makes one forget any analogue hiss.

Tebaldi, as always, makes some lovely sounds, and the *mezza voce* in the soaring theme (first heard in the overture) in *Madre, madre, pietosa Vergine* is exquisite. Mario del Monaco never really matches this. He sings straight through his part – often with the most heroic-sounding noises – with little attention to the finer points of shading that Verdi expects. That the whole performance fails to add up to the sum of its parts is largely the fault of the conductor, Molinari-Pradelli. He is exciting enough in the proper places but his control of ensemble is a marked weakness. Fortunately this deficiency in the conducting is not nearly enough to mar enjoyment of the performance. The brilliance and atmosphere of the recording add much to the listener's pleasure.

Placido Domingo is the glory of the Muti set, recorded at La Scala, giving a performance even more commanding and detailed than in the earlier, RCA version with Levine. Mirella Freni is an appealing Leonora, though she is vocally stressed; like the rest of the cast, she is not helped by the recording, which is depressingly boxy and presents the voices unflatteringly in close-up.

La Forza del destino (slightly abridged).
(***) EMI mono CDS7 47581-8 (3) [Ang. CDCC 47581]. Callas, Tucker, Tagliabue, Clabassi, Nicolai, Rossi-Lemeni, Capecchi, La Scala, Milan, Ch. & O, Serafin.

Callas was at her very peak when she took the role of Leonora in the Scala recording. Hers is an electrifying performance, providing a focus for an opera normally regarded as diffuse. Though there are classic examples of Callas's raw tone on top notes, they are insignificant next to the wealth of phrasing which sets a totally new and individual stamp on even the most familiar passages. Apart from his tendency to disturb his phrasing with sobs, Richard Tucker sings superbly; but not even he – and certainly none of the others (including the baritone Carlo Tagliabue, well past his prime) – begin to rival the dominance of Callas. Serafin's direction is crisp, dramatic and well paced, again drawing the threads together. The 1955 mono sound is less aggressive than many La Scala recordings of this vintage and has been freshened on CD.

Un giorno di regno (complete).
(M) *** Ph. 422 429-2 (2) [id.]. Cossotto, Norman, Carreras, Wixell, Sardinero, Ganzarolli, Amb. S., RPO, Gardelli.

Un giorno di regno may not be the greatest comic opera of the period, but this scintillating performance under Gardelli clearly reveals the young Verdi as a potent rival even in this field to his immediate predecessors, Rossini and Donizetti. The Rossinian echoes are particularly infectious, though every number reveals that the young Verdi is more than an imitator, and there are striking passages which clearly give a foretaste of such numbers as the duet, *Si vendetta*, from *Rigoletto*. Despite the absurd plot, this is as light and frothy an entertainment as anyone could want. Excellent singing from a fine team, with Jessye Norman and José Carreras outstanding. The recorded sound is even more vivid on CD.

I Lombardi (complete).
(M) *** Ph. 422 420-2 (2) [id.]. Deutekom, Domingo, Raimondi, Amb. S., RPO, Gardelli.
**(*) Hung. Dig. HCD 12498/500 [id.]. Kováts, Sass, Lamberti, Misura, Gregor, Jász, Jánosi, Hungarian R. & TV Ch., Hungarian State Op. O, Gardelli.

If you are looking for sophisticated perfection, *I Lombardi* is not the opera to sample, but the directness of Verdi's inspiration is in no doubt. *Otello* is anticipated in the arias, with Pagano's evil *Credo* and the heroine Giselda's *Salve Maria*. The work reaches its apotheosis in the famous *Trio*, well known from the days of 78-r.p.m. recordings. By those standards, Cristina Deutekom is not an ideal Verdi singer: her tone is sometimes hard and her voice is not always perfectly under control, yet there are some glorious moments too and the phrasing is often impressive. Domingo as Oronte is in superb voice, and the villain Pagano is well characterized by Raimondi. Among the supporting cast Stafford Dean and Clifford Grant must be mentioned, and Gardelli conducts dramatically. The recording's atmosphere is well transferred and the action projects vividly.

The Hungaroton set makes a very acceptable alternative to the earlier Philips set. One of the principal glories of the Budapest performance is the brilliant and committed singing of the chorus, turning the Crusaders' Hymn of Act II into a sort of Verdian *Csárdás*. The big ensembles have a warmth and thrust to suggest stage experience, and in the line-up of principals there is no serious weakness; Sylvia Sass, singing with a new evenness and purity, is certainly preferable to the fluttery Deutekom on Philips. Giorgio Lamberti as the hero is no match for Placido Domingo, heroic of tone but unsubtle; similarly, Kolos Kováts as the Hermit has a glorious natural voice, a really firm bass, but musically he is no rival to Raimondi on the earlier set. The sound is excellent, clean and well balanced.

Luisa Miller (complete).
*** Decca 417 420-2 (2) [id.]. Caballé, Pavarotti, Milnes, Reynolds, L. Op. Ch., Nat. PO, Maag.
*** DG 423 144-2 (2) [id.]. Ricciarelli, Obraztsova, Domingo, Bruson, ROHCG Ch. & O, Maazel.
(M) *** RCA GD 86646 (2) [6646-2-RG]. Moffo, Bergonzi, Verrett, MacNeil, Tozzi, Flagello, RCA Italiana Op. Ch. & O, Cleva.

On Decca, Caballé, though not as flawless vocally as one would expect, gives a splendidly dramatic portrait of the heroine and Pavarotti's performance is full of creative, detailed imagination. As Federica, Anna Reynolds is distinctly preferable to Obraztsova, and Maag's sympathetic reading, by underlining the light and shade, consistently brings out the atmospheric qualities of Verdi's conception. Vividly transferred, this Decca recording has the balance of advantage.

Though taut in his control, Maazel uses his stage experience of working with these soloists to draw them out to their finest, most sympathetic form. Ricciarelli gives one of her tenderest and most beautiful performances on record, Domingo is in glorious voice and Bruson as Luisa's father sings with velvet tone. Gwynne Howell is impressive as the Conte di Walter and Wladimiro Ganzarolli's vocal roughness is apt for the character of Wurm. The snag is the abrasive Countess Federica of Elena Obraztsova.

The RCA set has a substantial price advantage, and in many ways it provides a performance to compete with the full-price versions and is just as stylish, with Moffo at her very peak, singing superbly, Carlo Bergonzi unfailingly intelligent and stylish, and Verrett nothing less than magnificent in her role as a quasi-Amneris. MacNeil and Tozzi are also satisfyingly resonant, and Fausto Cleva, though not as compelling as Maag or Maazel, tellingly reveals his experience directing the opera at the Met. Good recording.

Macbeth (complete).
*** Ph. Dig. 412 133-2 (3) [id.]. Bruson, Zampieri, Shicoff, Lloyd, German Op. Ch. & O, Berlin, Sinopoli.
*** DG 415 688-2 (3) [id.]. Cappuccilli, Verrett, Ghiaurov, Domingo, La Scala, Milan, Ch. & O, Abbado.
(M) *** EMI CDS7 47954-8 (3) [id.]. Milnes, Cossotto, Raimondi, Carreras, Amb. Op. Ch., New Philh. O, Muti.
(M) **(*) RCA GD 84516 (2) [4516-2-RG]. Warren, Rysanek, Bergonzi, Hines, Met. Op. Ch. & O, Leinsdorf.

Even more than his finest rivals, Sinopoli presents this opera as a searing Shakespearean inspiration, scarcely more uneven than much of the work of the Bard himself. In the Banqueting scene, for example, Sinopoli creates extra dramatic intensity by his concern for detail and his preference for extreme dynamics, as in the vital stage-whispered phrases from Lady Macbeth to her husband, marked *sotto voce*, which heighten the sense of horror and disintegration over the appearance of the ghost. Detailed word-meaning is a key factor in this, and Renato Bruson and Mara Zampieri respond vividly. Zampieri's voice may be biting rather than beautiful, occasionally threatening to come off the rails, but, with musical precision an asset, she matches exactly Verdi's request for the voice of a she-devil. Neil Schicoff as Macduff and Robert Lloyd as Banquo make up the excellent quartet of principals, while the high voltage of the whole performance clearly reflects Sinopoli's experience with the same chorus and orchestra at the Deutsche Oper in Berlin. CD adds vividly to the realism of a recording that is well balanced and focused but atmospheric.

At times Abbado's tempi are unconventional, but with slow speeds he springs the rhythm so infectiously that the results are the more compelling. Based on the Giorgio Strehler production at La Scala, the whole performance gains from superb teamwork, for each of the principals – far more than is common – is meticulous about observing Verdi's detailed markings, above all those for *pianissimo* and *sotto voce*. Verrett, hardly powerful above the stave, yet makes a virtue out of necessity in floating glorious half-tones, and with so firm and characterful a voice she makes a highly individual, not at all conventional Lady Macbeth. As for Cappuccilli, he has never sung with such fine range of tone and imagination on record as here, and José Carreras makes a real, sensitive character out of the small role of Macduff. Excellent, clean recording, impressively remastered for CD.

Muti's 1976 CD version may now seem extravagantly laid out on three discs, but it includes three important appendices: one aria for Lady Macbeth and two for Macbeth himself, written for the original 1847 version of the opera. Also the three-disc layout means that the breaks between discs come at the end of Acts. Quite apart from that, the set offers a performance – with warm, full-bodied sound well transferred – that is above all dramatic, colourful and sharply rhythmic. Milnes gives a searching account of the title-role, and Fiorenza Cossotto, in what is perhaps her finest performance on record, is commandingly firm-toned and abrasive as Lady Macbeth. Carreras and Raimondi add to the strong team, with the British chorus outshining Italian rivals.

On two mid-price discs in the Victor Opera series, the Leinsdorf version also makes a good bargain, bringing a large-scale performance featuring three favourite principals from the Met. Leonie Rysanek here gives one of her finest performances on record, producing her firmest, creamiest sound for the Sleepwalking scene, even though the coloratura taxes her severely. Leonard Warren, much admired in this part before his untimely death (on stage, singing this very role) gives a strong, thoughtful reading, marred by the way the microphone exaggerates his vibrato. Carlo Bergonzi is a stylish, clear-toned Macduff. Good sound for its period.

I Masnadieri (complete).
(M) *** Ph. 422 423-2 (2). Caballé, Bergonzi, Raimondi, Cappuccilli, Amb. S., New Philh. O, Gardelli.

As this excellent Philips recording makes plain, the long neglect of *I Masnadieri* is totally undeserved, despite a libretto which is a bungled adaptation of a Schiller play. Few will seriously identify with the hero-turned-brigand who stabs his beloved rather than lead her into a life of shame; but, on record, flaws of motivation are of far less moment than on stage. The melodies may only fitfully be out of Verdi's top drawer, but the musical structure and argument often look forward to a much later period in hints of *Forza*, *Don Carlo* and even *Otello*. With Gardelli as ever an urgently sympathetic Verdian, and a team of four excellent principals, splendidly recorded, the set can be warmly welcomed.

Nabucco (complete).
*** DG Dig. 410 512-2 (2) [id.]. Cappuccilli, Dimitrova, Nesterenko, Domingo, Ch. & O of German Op., Berlin, Sinopoli.
*** Decca 417 407-2 (2) [id.]. Gobbi, Suliotis, Cava, Previdi, V. State Op. Ch. & O, Gardelli.
**(*) EMI CDS7 47488-8 (2) [Ang. CDCB 47488]. Manuguerra, Scotto, Ghiaurov, Luchetti, Obraztsova, Amb. Op. Ch., Philh. O, Muti.

Sinopoli makes Verdi sound less comfortable than traditional conductors, but he never lets the 'grand guitar' accompaniments of early Verdi churn along automatically. One keeps hearing details normally obscured. Even the thrill of the great chorus *Va, pensiero* is the greater when the melody first emerges at a hushed pianissimo, as marked, sound almost offstage. Strict as he is, Sinopoli encourages his singers to relish the great melodies to the full. Dimitrova is superb in Abigaille's big Act II aria, noble in her evil, as is Cappuccilli as Nabucco, less intense than Gobbi was on Gardelli's classic set for Decca, but stylistically pure. The rest of the cast is strong too, including Domingo in a relatively small role and Nesterenko superb as the High Priest, Zaccaria. Bright and forward digital sound, less atmospheric than the 1965 Decca set with Gobbi and Suliotis, conducted by Gardelli.

The vividly real and atmospheric sound in the 1965 Decca recording comes up very three-dimensionally on CD, even though tape-hiss is at a higher level than usual. There is more presence than in Sinopoli's DG, but that digital recording copes better with big ensembles. The Viennese choral contribution was less committed than one would ideally like in a work which contains a chorus unique in Verdi's output, *Va, pensiero*; but in every other way this is a masterly performance, with dramatically intense and deeply imaginative contributions from Tito Gobbi as Nabucco and Elena Suliotis as the evil Abigaille. Gobbi was already nearing the end of his full career, but even he rarely recorded a performance so full of sharply dramatic detail, while Suliotis made this the one totally satisfying performance of an all-too-brief recording career, wild in places but no more than is dramatically necessary. Though Carlo Cava as Zaccaria is not ideally rich of tone, it is a strong performance, and Gardelli, as in his later Verdi recordings for both Decca and Philips, showed what a master he is at pointing Verdian inspiration, whether in the individual phrase or over a whole scene, simply and naturally, without ever forcing.

Muti's 1978 set does not match either Sinopoli's newest DG version or the Gardelli set on Decca. The EMI cast, as impressive as could be gathered at the time, with Manuguerra an imaginative choice as Nabucco, failed nevertheless to equal the three-dimensional characterizations of its competitors. Renata Scotto sang well but was not entirely inside her role; Manuguerra proved strong and reliable but lacked something in flair.

Nabucco: highlights.
*** DG Dig. 413 321-2 [id.] (from above recording; cond. Sinopoli).
(M) ** EMI CDM7 63092-2 (from above recording; cond. Muti).

A useful collection of highlights from Sinopoli's strong, dramatic and individual complete set, brightly recorded, which, even at full price, is preferable to the highlights from the Muti version. Though this EMI disc offers generous measure (nearly 65 minutes) and has an impressive cast-list, it is much less involving, although the famous chorus, *Va pensiero*, sounds well enough.

Oberto (complete).
*** Orfeo C 105843 F (3) [id.]. Dimitrova, Bergonzi, Panerai, Baldani, Bav. R. Ch., Munich R. O, Gardelli.

In every way this issue matches the success of Gardelli's earlier, Philips recordings, despite the change of venue to Munich. There is much in *Oberto* that reflects the manners and style of Donizetti, but the underlying toughness regularly provides a distinctive flavour. Gardelli successfully papers over the less convincing moments, helped by fine playing from the orchestra, an outstanding chorus and first-rate principals. Ghena Dimitrova makes a very positive heroine, powerful in attack in her moment of fury in the Act I finale, but also gently expressive when necessary. Only in cabalettas is she sometimes ungainly. The veterans, Carlo Bergonzi and Rolando Panerai, more than make up in stylishness and technical finesse for any unevenness of voice, and Ruza Baldani is a warm-toned Cuniza, the mezzo role. First-rate recording.

Otello (complete).
*** RCA RD 82951 (2) [RCD2-2951]. Domingo, Scotto, Milnes, Amb. Op. Ch., Nat. PO, Levine.
(M) *** RCA GD 81969 (2) [1969-2-RG]. Vickers, Rysanek, Gobbi, Rome Op. Ch. & O, Serafin.
(M) *** EMI CMS7 69308-2 (2) [Ang. CDMB 69308]. Vickers, Freni, Glossop, Ch. of German Op., Berlin, BPO, Karajan.
**(*) EMI Dig. CDS7 47450-8 (2) [Ang. CDCB 47450]. Domingo, Ricciarelli, Diaz, La Scala, Milan, Ch. & O, Maazel.
**(*) Decca 411 618-2 (2). Del Monaco, Tebaldi, Protti, V. State Op. Ch., VPO, Karajan.

Otello: highlights.
(M) **(*) EMI Dig. CDM7 69059-2 (from above recording, cond. Maazel).

Levine's is the most consistently involving *Otello*; on balance, it has the best cast and is superbly conducted as well as magnificently sung. Levine combines a Toscanini-like thrust with a Karajan-like sensuousness, pointing rhythms to heighten mood, as in the Act II confrontation between hero and heroine over Cassio. Domingo as Otello combines glorious heroic tone with lyrical tenderness. Scotto is not always sweet-toned in the upper register, and the big ensemble at the end of Act III brings obvious strain; nevertheless, it is a deeply felt performance which culminates in a most beautiful account of the all-important Act IV solos, the *Willow song* and *Ave Maria*, most affecting. Milnes too is challenged by the role of Iago. His may not be a voice which readily conveys extremes of evil, but his view is far from conventional: this Iago is a handsome, virile creature beset by the biggest of chips on the shoulder. In the digital transfer for CD of the 1977 analogue original, the voices are caught vividly and immediately and with ample bloom. The orchestral sound too is fuller and cleaner than in many more recent versions, though there is an occasional hint of roughness in big tuttis.

The alternative Serafin version in RCA's Victor Opera series makes an outstanding bargain on two mid-priced discs. No conductor is more understanding of Verdian pacing than Serafin and, with sound that hardly begins to show its age (1960), it presents two of the finest solo performances on any *Otello* recording of whatever period: the Iago of Tito Gobbi has never been surpassed for vividness of characterization and tonal subtlety; while the young Jon Vickers, with a voice naturally suited to this role, was in his prime as the Moor. Leonie Rysanek is a warm and sympathetic Desdemona, not always ideally pure-toned, but tender and touching in one of her very finest recorded performances. The sense of presence in the open, well-balanced recording is the more vivid on CD, thanks to a first-rate transfer.

Karajan directs a big, bold and brilliant account, for the most part splendidly sung and with all the dramatic contrasts strongly underlined. There are several tiny, but irritating, statutory cuts, but otherwise on two mid-price CDs this is well worth considering. Freni's Desdemona is delightful, delicate and beautiful, while Vickers and Glossop are both positive and characterful, only occasionally forcing their tone and losing focus. The recording is clarified on CD, with better focus and more bloom than on the much more recent EMI set under Maazel.

Maazel's version, used as soundtrack for the Zeffirelli film but with the text uncut (unlike that of the film), brings a fine performance from Domingo and taut, subtle control from Maazel, particularly good in the spacious, tenderly emotional treatment of the final scene. In many ways Domingo shows how he has developed since he made his earlier recording with Levine; but with a disappointingly negative, unsinister Iago in Justino Diaz, the result often loses in dramatic bite, and Maazel's direction occasionally sags, as in the closing pages of Act II at the end of the oath duet. Ricciarelli, though not the ideal Desdemona, sings most affectingly, with pianissimos beautifully caught in the *Willow song* and *Ave Maria*. One snag is the sound, which is curiously recessed, with the voices often not quite in focus and with little sense of presence.

Karajan's 1961 version, flawed as it is in its casting, yet brings remarkably fine sound to match and even outshine any version since – a tribute to the artistry of the producer, John Culshaw, and his team of Decca engineers. Protti is admittedly not as inadequate an Iago as one had expected. He is always reliable, if never imaginative and never sinister – and that is a drawback in an opera whose plot hinges on Iago's machinations. Del

Monaco is hardly a subtle Otello, although both he and Tebaldi give one of their finest gramophone performances.

Otello: highlights.
(M) *** EMI CDM7 63454-2 [id.] (from above recording, cond. Karajan.).

A generally well-managed selection (though of less than an hour), including excerpts from all four Acts, with a substantial excerpt from Act IV including Freni's touching *Willow song* and *Ave Maria*, then moving on to the tragic finale. The sound is full, appropriately weighty in the score's more spectacular moments.

Otello (complete; in English).
(M) **(*) EMI CMS7 63012-2 (2). Charles Craig, Plowright, Howlett, Bottone, E. Nat. Op. Ch. & O, Mark Elder.

Recorded live at the Coliseum in London, the ENO version of *Otello* is flawed both vocally and in the sound; but those who seek records of opera in English need not hesitate, for almost every word of Andrew Porter's translation is audible, despite the very variable balances inevitable in recording a live stage production. Less acceptable is the level of stage noise, with the thud and rumble of wandering feet all the more noticeable on CD. The performance itself is most enjoyable, with dramatic tension building up compellingly. Charles Craig's Otello is most moving, the character's inner pain brought out vividly, though top notes are fallible. Neil Howlett as Iago may not have the most distinctive baritone, but finely controlled vocal colouring adds to a deeply perceptive performance. Rosalind Plowright makes a superb Desdemona, singing with rich, dramatic weight but also with poise and purity. The Death scene reveals her at her finest, radiant of tone, with flawless attack.

Rigoletto (complete).
*** Ph. Dig. 412 592-2 (2) [id.]. Bruson, Gruberová, Shicoff, Fassbaender, Lloyd, St Cecilia Ac., Rome, Ch. & O, Sinopoli.
*** Decca 414 269-2 (2) [id.]. Milnes, Sutherland, Pavarotti, Talvela, Tourangeau, Amb. Op. Ch., LSO, Bonynge.
**(*) DG 415 288-2 (2) [id.]. Cappuccilli, Cotrubas, Domingo, Obraztsova, Ghiaurov, Moll, Schwarz, V. State Op. Ch., VPO, Giulini.
(M) **(*) RCA GD 86506 (2) [6506-2-RG]. Merrill, Moffo, Kraus, Elias, Flagello, RCA Italiana Op. Ch. & O, Solti.
(***) EMI mono CDS7 47469-8 (2) [Ang. CDCB 47469]. Gobbi, Callas, Di Stefano, Zaccaria, La Scala, Milan, Ch. & O, Serafin.
(M) ** RCA GD 60172 (2) [60172-2-RG]. Merrill, Peters, Bjoerling, Tozzi, Rome Op. Ch. & O, Perlea.
** Decca Dig. 425 864-2 (2) [id.]. Nucci, Anderson, Pavarotti, Ghiaurov, Verrett, Ch. & O of Teatro Comunale di Bologna, Chailly.
* EMI Dig. CDS7 49605-2 (2) [Ang. CDCB 49605]. Zancanaro, Dessi, La Scola, Burchuladze, La Scala, Milan, Ch. & O, Muti.

Sinopoli here has close concern for his singers, with full potential drawn from each in what is the most consistent cast yet on record. Edita Gruberová might have been considered an unexpected choice for Gilda, remarkable for her brilliant coloratura rather than for deeper expression, yet here she makes the heroine a tender, feeling creature, emotionally vulnerable yet vocally immaculate. As a stickler for the text, Sinopoli eliminates a top note or two, as in *Caro nome.* Similarly, Renato Bruson as Rigoletto does far more than produce a stream of velvety tone, detailed and intense, responding to the conductor and combining beauty with dramatic bite. Even more remarkable is the brilliant success of Neil Shicoff as the Duke, more than a match for his most distinguished rivals. Here the *Quartet* becomes a genuine climax as it rarely has been in complete recordings. Brigitte Fassbaender as Maddalena is sharply unconventional but vocally most satisfying. Sinopoli's speeds, too, are unconventional at times, but the fresh look he provides makes this one of the most exciting of recent Verdi operas on disc, helped by full and vivid recording, consistently well balanced.

Just over ten years after her first recording of this opera, Sutherland appeared in it again – and this set was far more than a dutiful remake. From the very start Richard Bonynge shows his feeling for the resilient rhythms; the result is fresh and dramatic, underlining the revolutionary qualities in the score which nowadays we tend to ignore. Pavarotti is an intensely characterful Duke: an unmistakable rogue but an unmistakable charmer, too. Thanks to him and to Bonynge above all, the *Quartet*, as on the Sinopoli set, becomes a genuine musical climax. Sutherland's voice has acquired a hint of a beat, but there is little of the mooning manner which disfigured her earlier assumption, and the result is glowingly beautiful as well as being technically supremely assured. Milnes makes a strong Rigoletto, vocally masterful and with good if hardly searching presentation of character. The digital transfer is exceptionally vivid and atmospheric, underlining the excellence of the original engineering with its finely judged balances, but also enhancing the superimposed crowd noises and the like, which not everyone will welcome.

Giulini, ever thoughtful for detail, directs a distinguished performance. He seems determined to get away from any conception of *Rigoletto* as melodrama; however, in doing that he misses the red-blooded theatricality of Verdi's concept, the basic essential. Although it may be consistent with Giulini's view, it further reduces the dramatic impact that Cappuccilli (with his unsinister voice) makes the hunchback a noble figure from first to last, while Domingo, ever intelligent, makes a reflective rather than an extrovert Duke. Cotrubas is a touching Gilda, but the close balance of her voice is not helpful, and the topmost register is not always comfortable. The recording, made in the Musikverein in Vienna, has the voices well to the fore, with much reverberation on the instruments behind, an effect emphasized by the CD transfer.

Anna Moffo makes a charming Gilda in the Solti set of 1963, well transferred on two mid-price CDs in the Victor Opera series. Solti at times presses too hard, but this is a strong and dramatic reading, with Robert Merrill producing a glorious flow of dark, firm tone in the name-part. Alfredo Kraus is as stylish as ever as the Duke, and this rare example of his voice at its freshest should not be missed. A good bargain, though there are statutory cuts in the text.

There has never been a more compelling performance of the title-role in *Rigoletto* than that of Gobbi on his classic Scala set of the 1950s. At every point, in almost every single phrase, Gobbi finds extra meaning in Verdi's vocal lines, with the widest range of tone-colour employed for expressive effect. Callas, though not naturally suited to the role of the wilting Gilda, is compellingly imaginative throughout, and Di Stefano gives one of his finer performances. The transfer of the original mono recording is astonishingly vivid in capturing the voices, which are sharply focused and given a fine sense of presence, so that you miss stereo spread remarkably little.

This RCA set is mainly of interest for Jussi Bjoerling's contribution. It opens well and generally the conductor, Jonel Perlea, controls the music effectively. But he is hampered by Robert Merrill's rather hammy Rigoletto and the fact that Roberta Peters, although singing nicely, does not project the character of Gilda at all. Indeed the whole atmosphere of the set is of a concert performance, and the close of the opera degenerates into melodrama. The 1956 recording has no lack of vividness.

Chailly's new digital version has the benefit of full and vivid Decca sound, but the performance cannot match the finest existing versions. Pavarotti, recorded very close, undermines the vivacity of his singing by coarse vocal tricks. His earlier recording opposite Sutherland is far preferable. June Anderson makes a strong Gilda but the voice, as recorded, often sounds too heavy; and Leo Nucci, well below form, is far too rough of tone in the title-role, with the voice often unsteady. Chailly's direction is sympathetic, but lacks the individuality of such Italian rivals as Giulini or Sinopoli.

Muti deliberately chose young singers for the roles of Gilda and the Duke, but both Daniela Dessi and Vincenzo La Scola are pale and disappointing, with the flutter in Dessi's soprano exaggerated by the microphone. They are not helped by Muti holding them to the strict letter of the score, allowing none of the usual moments of individual display in concluding top notes. Muti characteristically is also a stickler for obeying metronome markings, which often seem too fast, making for rigidity, while the recording is strangely muffled, taking the edge off the performance. Giorgio Zancanaro in the title-role has a fine voice, but he uses it squarely and with little imagination; and Paata Burchuladze as Sparafucile is out of style.

Rigoletto: highlights.
*** Decca 421 303-2 [id.] (from above recording, cond. Bonynge).
**(*) DG 423 114-2 [id.] (from above recording, cond. Giulini).

Two useful and generous sets of highlights for those who do not want to go to the expense of a complete set. On Decca, it was a pity that *Questa o quella* had to be given an edited fade.

Rigoletto (complete; in English).
(M) **(*) EMI Dig. CMS7 69369-2 (2) [id.]. Rawnsley, Field, Davies, Tomlinson, Rigby, E. Nat. Op. Ch. & O, Elder.

The intensity and fine pacing of the stage performances are splendidly caught in this studio recording, thanks to Mark Elder's keenly rhythmic conducting, making this the most successful of the English National Opera Verdi sets. Outstanding vocally is the heady-toned Duke of Arthur Davies and, though neither John Rawnsley as Rigoletto nor Helen Field as Gilda has a voice so naturally beautiful, they too sing both powerfully and stylishly. Excellent recording, clean, full and well balanced.

Simon Boccanegra (complete).
⊛ *** DG 415 692-2 (2) [id.]. Cappuccilli, Freni, Ghiaurov, Van Dam, Carreras, La Scala, Milan, Ch. & O, Abbado.
(M) (***) EMI mono CMS7 63513-2 (2). Gobbi, Christoff, De los Angeles, Campora, Monachesi, Dari, Rome Op. Chor & O, Santini.
** Decca Dig. 425 628-2 (2) [id.]. Nucci, Te Kanawa, Burchuladze, Aragall, La Scala, Milan, Ch. & O, Solti.

Abbado's 1977 recording of *Simon Boccanegra*, directly reflecting the superb production which the La Scala company brought to London at the time, is one of the most beautiful Verdi sets ever made, and the virtual background silence of the CDs enhances the warmth and beauty of the sound, the orchestra fresh and glowing in ambient warmth, the voices vivid and the perspectives always believable. From this, one can appreciate not just the vigour of the composer's imagination but also the finesse of the colouring, instrumental as well as vocal. Under Abbado the playing of the orchestra is brilliantly incisive as well as refined, so that the drama is underlined by extra sharpness of focus. The cursing of Paolo after the great Council Chamber scene makes the scalp prickle, with the chorus muttering in horror and the bass clarinet adding a sinister comment, here beautifully moulded. Cappuccilli, always intelligent, gives a far more intense and illuminating performance than the one he recorded for RCA earlier in his career. He may not match Gobbi in range of colour and detail, but he too gives focus to the performance; and Ghiaurov as Fiesco sings beautifully too. Freni as Maria Boccanegra sings with freshness and clarity, while Van Dam is an impressive Paolo. With electrically intense choral singing as well, this is a set to outshine even Abbado's superb *Macbeth* with the same company.

Tito Gobbi's portrait of the tragic Doge of Genoa is one of his greatest on record and emerges all the more impressively, when it is set against equally memorable performances by Boris Christoff as Fiesco and Victoria de los Angeles as Amelia. The Recognition scene between father and daughter has never been done more movingly on record; nor has the great ensemble, which crowns the Council Chamber scene, been so powerfully and movingly presented, and that without the help of stereo recording. The transfer is full and immediate, giving a vivid sense of presence to the voices, though tape-hiss is on the high side.

The glory of Solti's set is the singing of Dame Kiri Te Kanawa as Amelia, a beautiful, touching performance. The freedom and absence of strain in the voice go with an almost Straussian quality in her characterization, with the widest dynamic and expressive range. Giacomo Aragall makes a strong, unforced Gabriele, but the others are less distinguished. As a cast, this line-up hardly matches that of Abbado on his rival DG set. That was also recorded with forces from La Scala, Milan, but in conjunction with a celebrated stage production. Leo Nucci is most disappointing, with the voice showing signs of wear, not nearly steady enough. He sings powerfully, but Boccanegra's solo in the great Council Chamber scene finds the voice spreading. Burchuladze also is surprisingly less steady than usual, and Paolo Coni as Paolo is capable but undistinguished. What also makes this a less compelling reading compared with the DG is Solti's obsession with observing the metronome markings in the score very precisely, laudable in theory but often questionable in practice; so the great recognition scene between Boccanegra and his daughter is powerfully dramatic at a speed far faster than usual, but it lacks tenderness and fails to convey the joy of recognition, which Abbado finds so movingly. The sound of the DG analogue version is preferable, though less wide-ranging, with the voices more realistically focused.

Simon Boccanegra: highlights.
** Hung. Dig. HCD 12611 [id.]. Kincses, Nagy, Miller, Gregor, Hungarian State Op. Ch. & O, Patanè.

Though the complete set from which these excerpts are taken (LP only) is a non-starter compared with Abbado's masterly DG version, this makes a useful collection on CD, bringing together some of the finest passages of a still-undervalued masterpiece. Lajos Miller as Boccanegra gives the only performance of real stature, strong and expressive if not always smooth of tone; and the admirable bass, József Gregor, sings Fiesco. Disappointing singing from soprano and tenor, but excellent recording.

Stiffelio (complete).
(M) *** Ph. 422 432-2 (2) [id.]. Carreras, Sass, Manuguerra, Ganzarolli, V. ORF Ch. & SO, Gardelli.

Coming just before the great trio of masterpieces, *Rigoletto*, *Il Trovatore* and *La Traviata*, *Stiffelio* was a total failure at its first performance in 1850. To make *Aroldo* six years later, the score was in effect destroyed, and only through the discovery of two copyists' scores in the 1960s was a revival made possible. Though it lacks some of the beauties of *Aroldo*, *Stiffelio* is still a sharper, more telling work, largely because of the originality of the relationships and the superb final scene in which Stiffelio reads from the pulpit the parable of the woman taken in adultery. Gardelli directs a fresh performance, at times less lively than Queler's of *Aroldo* but with more consistent singing, notably from Carreras and Manuguerra. First-rate recording from Philips, typical of this fine series.

La Traviata (complete).
*** Decca Dig. 410 154-2 (2) [id.]. Sutherland, Pavarotti, Manuguerra, L. Op. Ch., Nat. PO, Bonynge.
**(*) EMI Dig. CDS7 47538-8 (2) [Ang. CDC 47538]. Scotto, Kraus, Bruson, Amb. Op. Ch., Philh. O, Muti.
(M) **(*) Decca 411 877-2 (2) [id.]. Sutherland, Bergonzi, Merrill, Ch. & O of Maggio Musicale Fiorentino, Pritchard.
(**) EMI mono CDS7 49187-8 (2) [Mov. Musica 051-021]. Callas, Kraus, Sereni, Ch. & O of San Carlos Op., Lisbon, Ghione.

Sutherland's second recording of the role of Violetta has a breadth and exuberance beyond what she achieved in her earlier version of 1963, conducted by John Pritchard. Some of the supremely tender moments of her earlier recording – *Ah dite alla giovine* in the Act II duet with Germont, for example – are more straightforward this time, but the mooning manner is dispelled, the words are clearer, and the richness and command of the singing put this among the very finest of Sutherland's later recordings. Pavarotti too, though he overemphasizes *Di miei bollenti spiriti*, sings with splendid panache as Alfredo. Manuguerra as Germont lacks something in authority, but the firmness and clarity are splendid. Bonynge's conducting is finely sprung, the style direct, the speeds often spacious in lyrical music, generally undistracting. The digital recording is outstandingly vivid and beautifully balanced but the CD booklet is not ideal.

Muti has no concern for tradition; at the start of the Act I party music, he is even faster than Toscanini, but the result is dazzling; and when he needs to give sympathetic support to his soloists, above all in the great Act II duet between Violetta and Germont, there is no lack of tenderness. Overall, it is an intensely compelling account, using the complete text (like Bonynge), and it gains from having three Italy-based principals. Scotto and Kraus have long been among the most sensitive and perceptive interpreters of these roles, and so they are here; with bright digital recording, however, it is obvious that these voices are no longer young, with Scotto's soprano spreading above the stave and Kraus's tenor often sounding thin. Scotto gives a view of Violetta which even amid the gaiety of Act I points forward to tragedy. Bruson makes a fine, forthright Germont, though it does not add to dramatic conviction that his is the youngest voice. Small parts are well taken, and the stage picture is projected clearly on CD, with the pleasant reverberation clarified.

In Sutherland's earlier (1963) recording of *La Traviata* it is true that her diction is poor, but it is also true that she has rarely sung on record with such deep feeling as in the final scene. The *Addio del passato* (both stanzas included and sung with an unexpected lilt) merely provides a beginning, for the duet with Bergonzi is most winning, and the final death scene, *Se una pudica vergine*, is overwhelmingly beautiful. This is not a sparkling Violetta, true, but it is vocally closer to perfection than almost any other in a complete set. Bergonzi is an attractive Alfredo and Merrill an efficient Germont. Pritchard sometimes tends to hustle things along with too little regard for shaping Verdian phrases, but the recording quality is outstandingly good in its CD format.

Recorded at a live performance in March 1958, Callas's Lisbon-made version, far more than in her earlier Cetra recording of this opera, lets one appreciate the intensity which made this one of her supreme roles, conveying fleeting emotions even in such an obvious passage as the *Brindisi*. Kraus is a fresh, stylish Alfredo, Sereni a positive Germont, more characterful than in the (deleted) EMI set with De los Angeles. However, the extraneous noises in this live recording – like the prompter's constant groaning – as well as the tape background and the crumbling at climaxes, are made all the clearer on CD.

La Traviata: highlights.
*** Decca Dig. 400 057-2 [id.] (from above set with Sutherland, cond. Bonynge).
(M) *** EMI CDM7 63088-2 (from above recording; cond. Muti).

On this Decca highlights CD, one item is omitted compared with the LP – Germont's *Di Provenza* – but it still includes nearly an hour of music.

Muti's complete set is at full price and it isn't a first choice, so many will be glad to have this fairly generous (61 minutes) mid-price disc of highlights, including both the Act I and Act III *Preludes* and a well-balanced selection from each of the three Acts, with most of the key numbers included.

La Traviata (complete, in English).
(M) **(*) EMI CMS7 63072-2 (2). Masterson, Brecknock, Du Plessis, E. Nat. Op. Ch. & O, Mackerras.

Mackerras directs a vigorous, colourful reading which brings out the drama, and Valerie Masterson is at last given the chance on record she has so long deserved. The voice is caught beautifully, if not always very characterfully, and John Brecknock makes a fine Alfredo, most effective in the final scene. Christian Du Plessis' baritone is less suitable for recording. The conviction of the whole enterprise is infectious – but be warned, Verdi in English has a way of sounding on record rather like Gilbert and Sullivan.

Il Trovatore (complete).
⊛ *** RCA RD 86194 (2) [6194-2-RC]. Leontyne Price, Domingo, Milnes, Cossotto, Amb. Op. Ch., New Philh. O, Mehta.
*** DG Dig. 423 858-2 (2) [id.]. Plowright, Domingo, Fassbaender, Zancanaro, Nesterenko, Ch. & O of St Cecilia Academy, Rome, Giulini.
(M) (***) RCA mono GD 86643 (2) [6643-2-RG]. Milanov, Bjoerling, Warren, Barbieri, Robert Shaw Ch., RCA Victor O, Cellini.
(M) (***) EMI CDS7 49347-2 (2). Callas, Barbieri, Di Stefano, Panerai, La Scala, Milan, Ch. & O, Karajan.
(M) **(*) EMI CMS7 69311-2 (2) [Ang. CDMB 69311]. Leontyne Price, Bonisolli, Obraztsova, Cappuccilli, Raimondi, German Op. Ch., Berlin, BPO, Karajan.
** Decca 417 137-2 (3) [id.]. Sutherland, Pavarotti, Horne, Wixell, Ghiaurov, L. Op. Ch. & Nat. PO, Bonynge.
(M) ** Ph. Dig. 426 557-2 (2) [id.]. Ricciarelli, Carreras, Mazurok, Toczyska, ROHCG Ch. & O, C. Davis.

The soaring curve of Leontyne Price's rich vocal line (almost too ample for some ears) is immediately thrilling in her famous Act I aria, and it sets the style of the RCA performance, full-bodied and with the tension consistently held at the highest levels. The choral contribution is superb; the famous *Soldiers'* and *Anvil choruses* are marvellously fresh and dramatic. When *Di quella pira* comes, the orchestra opens with tremendous gusto and Domingo sings with a ringing, heroic quality worthy of Caruso himself. There are many dramatic felicities, and Sherill Milnes is in fine voice throughout; but perhaps the highlight of the set is the opening section of Act III, when Azucena finds her way to Conte di Luna's camp. The ensuing scene with Fiorenza Cossotto is vocally and dramatically quite electrifying. The CDs are transferred vibrantly to make one of the most thrilling of all early Verdi operas on record.

In an intensely revelatory performance, one which is richly red-blooded but which transforms melodrama into a deeper experience, Giulini flouts convention at every point. The opera's white-hot inspiration comes out in the intensity of the playing and singing, but the often slow tempi and refined textures present the whole work in new and deeper detail, product of the conductor's intense study of the work afresh. Inspired casting presents Rosalind Plowright triumphantly in her first international opera recording. Sensuous yet ethereal in *Tacea la notte*, she masterfully brings together the seemingly incompatible qualities demanded, not just sweetness and purity but brilliant coloratura, flexibility and richly dramatic bite and power. Placido Domingo sings Manrico as powerfully as he did in the richly satisfying Mehta set on RCA, but the voice is even more heroic in an Otello-like way, only very occasionally showing strain. Giorgio Zancanaro proves a gloriously firm and rounded Count di Luna and Evgeny Nesterenko a dark, powerful Ferrando, while Brigitte Fassbaender, singing her first Azucena, finds far greater intensity and detail than the usual roaring mezzo, matching Giulini's freshness. The recording is warm and atmospheric with a pleasant bloom on the voices, naturally balanced and not spotlit. Now on a pair of CDs, it sounds all the firmer and more vivid.

Though dating from 1952, using a cut text as in the Met. production, the Cellini version brings a vivid reminder of that great opera house at a key period. Milanov, though at times a little raw in Leonora's coloratura, gives a glorious, commanding performance, never surpassed on record, with the voice at its fullest. Bjoerling and Warren too are in ringing voice, and Barbieri is a superb Azucena, with Cellini – rarely heard on record – proving an outstanding Verdian.

The combination of Karajan and Callas is formidably impressive. There is toughness and dramatic determination in Callas's singing, whether in the coloratura or in the dramatic passages, and this gives the heroine an unsuspected depth of character which culminates in Callas's fine singing of an aria which used often to be cut entirely – *Tu vedrai che amore in terra*, here with its first stanza alone included. Barbieri is a magnificent Azucena, Panerai a strong, incisive Count, and Di Stefano at his finest as Manrico. On CD the 1957 mono sound, though dry and unatmospheric, is one of the more vivid from La Scala at that period.

The Karajan set with Leontyne Price promised much but proved disappointing, largely because of the thickness and strange balances of the recording, the product of multi-channel techniques exploited over-enthusiastically. So the introduction to Manrico's aria *Di quella pira* provides full-bodied orchestral sound, but then the orchestra fades down for the entry of the tenor, who in any case is in coarse voice. In other places he sings more sensitively, but at no point does this version match that of Mehta on RCA. CD clarifies the sound, but makes the flaws in the original recording all the more evident.

Bonynge's account of *Il Trovatore* is at an altogether lower level of intensity, with elegance rather than dramatic power the dominant quality. Nor does the role of Leonora prove very apt for the present-day Sutherland; the coloratura passages are splendid, but a hint of unsteadiness is present in too much of the rest. Pavarotti for the most part sings superbly; but he falls short, for example, in the semi-quaver groups of *Di quella pira*, and, like Sutherland, Marilyn Horne as Azucena does not produce consistently firm tone. Wixell as the Count sings intelligently, but a richer tone is needed.

Sir Colin Davis offers a fresh and direct reading which in many ways is the antithesis of Karajan's Berlin version with its overblown sound. The refinement of the digital recording makes for a wide, clean separation but, with the backward placing of the orchestra, the result does not have the dramatic impact of the Mehta RCA version. The

Anvil chorus sounds rather clinical and other important numbers lack the necessary swagger. Ricciarelli's Leonora is most moving, conveying an element of vulnerability in the character, but Carreras lacks the full confidence of a natural Manrico. He is less effective in the big, extrovert moments, best in such inward-looking numbers as *Ah si ben mio.* Toczyska's voice is presented rather grittily in the role of Azucena. Mazurok similarly is not flattered by the microphones but, with clean, refined ensemble, this emerges as the opposite of a hackneyed opera.

Il Trovatore: highlights.
*** DG Dig. 415 285-2 [id.] (from above recording, cond. Giulini).
(M) **(*) Decca 421 310-2 [id.] (from above recording, cond. Bonynge).

This generous and well-chosen DG collection of excerpts celebrates Giulini's masterly and highly individual interpretation, with the sound again excellent; but the warning given in the *Gramophone* review might be repeated: 'listening to these highlights may make you regret not having invested in the whole set'.

The selection from Bonynge's Decca set is especially valuable as a reminder of Sutherland's Leonora. The size of the voice and its flexibility are splendidly caught, though a latterday beat afflicts the more sustained passages, and Bonynge does not conduct with his usual urgency. Pavarotti may be stretched by the role of Manrico, but he is nearly always magnificent. Horne is represented by her powerful *Stride la vampa*, Wixell by an undernourished *Il Balen*.

I vespri siciliani (complete).
** RCA RD 80370 (3) [0370-2-RC]. Arroyo, Domingo, Milnes, Raimondi, Ewing, Alldis Ch., New Philh. O, Levine.

This opera, epic in scale to please the Parisian audiences for whom it was written, is a transitional piece, following the firmly confident middle-period Verdi of *Rigoletto*, *Trovatore* and *Traviata*, but not quite achieving the dramatic intensity and musical richness of later operas. The work's great merit is not so much its grandeur as its searching portrayal of the father–son relationship between Monforte, the tyrannical governor of Sicily, and Arrigo, the son he has never known. Their Act II duet, using a melody well known from the overture, is nothing short of magnificent, with Domingo and Milnes at their very peak. The rest of the singing is good, if rarely inspired, and though James Levine's direction is colourful and urgent, such a score needs more persuasiveness. Good recording, vividly remastered.

COLLECTIONS

Arias: *Aida: Se quel guerrier io fossi! . . . Celeste Aida; Pur ti riveggo, mia dolce Aida . . . Tu! Amonasro! Don Carlos: Fontainebleau! Forêt immense et solitaire . . . Je l'ai vue; Écoute. Les portes du couvent . . . Dieu, tu seras dans nos âmes. Nabucco: Che si vuol? Il Trovatore: Quale d'armi . . . Ah! si, ben mio . . . Di quella pira.*
*** DG Dig. 413 785-2 [id.]. Placido Domingo (with various orchestras & conductors) –
PUCCINI: *Arias.****

Domingo's Verdi recital, supplemented by Puccini items from *Manon Lescaut* and *Turandot*, brings an excellent collection of recordings, taken from different sources. When working on a complete opera recording there is no danger of big arias like this simply being churned out without apt characterization. The sound is most vivid throughout.

Arias: *Aida: Ritorna vincitor . . . l'insana parola . . . I sacri nomi; Qui Radamès verra . . . O patria mia. Un ballo in maschera: Morrò, ma prima in grazia. Ernani: Sorta e la notte . . .*

Ernani, volami. La Forza del destino: Pace, pace, mio Dio! Don Carlos: Tu che le vanità. Macbeth: Una macchia è qui tuttora! Otello: Mi parea . . . Piange cantando . . . Ave Maria. Il Trovatore: Tacea la notte placida.
**(*) EMI Dig. CDC7 47396-2 [id.]. Aprile Millo, LPO, Patanè.

Acclaimed as the successor of Leontyne Price, Aprile Millo in this first major recording gives an impressive display of her generous soprano, rich, vibrant and masterfully controlled, with fearless attack on exposed notes. She tackles each of these formidable arias in total confidence, with only the occasional slight uncertainty – as in the final item, *O patria mia* – to reflect her relative inexperience. All the items – a generous collection lasting 73 minutes – bring warmly satisfying singing, and when the repertory is so wide, that itself indicates the only significant shortcoming, a lack of variety in the approach. But this is an impressive début record.

Arias: *Aida: Celeste Aida. Un ballo in maschera: La rivedrà; Di, tu se fedele; Ma se m'è forza perderti. I due Foscari: Dal più remote esilio. Luisa Miller: Quando le sere. Macbeth: Ah, la paterna mano. Rigoletto: Questa o quella; Parmi veder; La donna è mobile. La Traviata: De' miei bollenti. Il Trovatore: Di quella pira.*
(M) *** Decca 417 570-2. Luciano Pavarotti (with various orchestras & conductors).

Taken mainly from a recital which Pavarotti recorded early in his career with Edward Downes and the Vienna State Opera Orchestra, this Verdi collection on the mid-price Opera Gala label can be warmly recommended, a generous collection of favourite items, plus one or two rarer arias.

'Heroines': *Aida: Ritorna vincitor! O patria mia. Un ballo in maschera: Ma dall'arido. Ernani: Ernani involami. La Forza del destino: Madre, pietosa; La Vergine; Pace, pace, mio Dio. Macbeth: Sleepwalking scene. Otello: Willow song; Ave Maria. La Traviata: Addio del passato. Il Trovatore: Tacea la motte; D'amor sull'ali rosee.*
*** RCA RD 87016 [RCD1 7016]. Leontyne Price (with various orchestras & conductors).

Leontyne Price, peerless in her generation in the more dramatic Verdi roles, is here at her finest in a generous collection of arias, recorded at the peak of her career, with the glorious voice well caught in the transfers.

Arias: *Aida: Ritorna vincitor. Un ballo in maschera: Ecco l'orrido campo. Don Carlos: Tu che le vanità. Ernani: Ernani involami. I Lombardi: O Madre dal cielo. Macbeth: Nel di della vittoria; La luce langue una macchia. Nabucco: Anch'io dischiuso un giorno. I vespri siciliani: Arrigo! Oh parli.*
*** EMI CDC7 47730-2 [id.]. Maria Callas, Philh. O, Rescigno.

In this first of two Verdi recital records issued to commemorate the tenth anniversary of Callas's death, the great soprano is at her most commanding, not flawless but thrilling, both in her creative musicianship and in her characterizations, powerfully Shakespearean in the Lady Macbeth arias presented as a sequence, and holding tension masterfully in the long *Don Carlos* scene. Both those performances date from the late 1950s, when the voice was still in fine condition. Though the later items here come from a period when the voice had deteriorated (done in the 1960s but issued only in 1972), Aida's *Ritorna vincitor*, vehemently done, is magnificent for one. Generally good transfers and clean sound.

Arias (Vol. 2): *Aroldo: Ciel! ch'io respiri! . . . Salvami, salvami; O Cielo! Attila: Liberamente or piangi . . . Oh! nel fuggente nuvolo. Un ballo in maschera: Morrò, ma prima in grazia. Il Corsaro: Egli non riede ancora . . . Non so le tetre immagini; Ne sulla*

terra . . . Vola talor dal carcere. Don Carlos: Non pianger, mia compagna; O don fatale.
Otello: Mia madre aveva una povera ancella; Piangea cantando; Ave Maria piena di
grazia. Il Trovatore: Tacea la notte placida . . . Di tale amor.
** EMI CDC7 47943-2 [id.]. Maria Callas, Paris Conservatoire O, Rescigno.

Though this second of the two Callas commemorative issues of Verdi is essential for the
singer's devotees, it can be recommended to others only with severe reservations. The
Shakespearean challenge of the Desdemona sequence from *Otello* is commandingly taken,
very distinctive, and all the singing is dramatic, but too many allowances have to be
made, particularly in the items recorded as late as 1969. Good transfers.

Arias & duets: *Un ballo in maschera: Teco io sto. Il Corsaro: Egli non riede ancora! Don*
Carlos: Non pianger, mia compagna. Giovanna d'Arco: Qui! Qui! Dove più s'apre libero il
ciela; O fatidica foresta. Jérusalem: Ave Maria. I Masnadieri: Dall'infame banchetto io
m'involai; Tu del mio; Carlo vive. Otello: Già nella notte densa; Ave Maria. Il Trovatore:
Timor di me; D'amor sull'ali rosee; Tu vedrai che amor in terr. I vespri siciliani: Arrigo!
Ah, parli a un cor.
(M) *** RCA GD 86534 (6534-2-RG]. Katia Ricciarelli, Placido Domingo, Rome PO or
St Cecilia Ac. O, Gavazzeni.

At mid-price this collection of Verdi arias and duets from two star singers, both in fresh
voice, makes a good bargain. The inclusion of rarities adds to the attractions, and though
the sound is not the most modern, it is more than acceptable in the digital transfer. The
quality is very bright; although the orchestral timbre is a bit thin, both voices are given a
good presence.

Arias: *Don Carlos: Tu che le vanità. La Traviata: Ah fors'è lui. Il Trovatore: Timor di me.*
*** CBS Dig. CD 37298 [id.]. Kiri Te Kanwa, LPO, Pritchard – PUCCINI: *Arias.****

The Verdi part of Kiri Te Kanawa's Verdi–Puccini recital brings three substantial
items, less obviously apt for the singer, but in each the singing is felt as well as beautiful.
The coloratura of the *Traviata* and *Trovatore* items is admirably clean, and it is a special
joy to hear Elisabetta's big aria from *Don Carlos* sung with such truth and precision.
Good recording, enhanced on CD.

Choruses: *Aida: Triumphal march and ballet music. Attila: Urli rapine. La Battaglia di*
Legnano: Giuriam d'Italia. I Lombardi: O Signore dal tetto natio. Nabucco: Gli arredi
festivi; Va pensiero. Otello: Fuoco di gloria. Il Trovatore: Vedi! le fosche; Squilli, echeggi.
(M) ** Decca 417 721-2 [id.]. Ch. & O of St Cecilia Ac., Rome, Carlo Franci.

Although the basic recording seems too brightly lit, in all other respects the quality is
very good, inner detail is sharp and the big climaxes open up well. The performances are
vivid, with a willingness to sing softly and, indeed, sometimes a degree of refinement in
the approach surprising in an Italian chorus. The *I Lombardi* excerpts are especially
appealing, but all the little-known items come up freshly. The trumpets in the *Aida*
Triumphal scene get the full stereo treatment.

Choruses and ballet music: *Aida: Gloria all'Egitto and Ballet. Don Carlos: Ce jour*
heureux; Ballet of the Queen. Macbeth: Ballet music. Nabucco: Va, pensiero. Il Trovatore:
Vedi! le fosche notturne, spoglie (Anvil chorus).
(M) **(*) DG 419 487-2 [id.]. La Scala, Milan, Ch. & O, Abbado.

A lively selection taken from various complete sets. The remastering has brightened the
sound and the choral timbre is clean and incisive – in *Va, pensiero* the climax has a touch

of fierceness, and here as elsewhere the ear notices that the bass is dry too. Both the *Anvil chorus* and the *Grand march* from *Aida* have impressive vividness and projection.

Victoria, Tomás Luis de (c. 1548–1611)

Ascendens Christus (motet); *Missa Ascendis Christus in altum; O Magnum mysterium* (motet); *Missa O Magnum mysterium.*
*** Hyp. Dig. CDA 66190 [id.]. Westminster Cathedral Ch., David Hill.

Missa Ave maris stella; O quam gloriosum est regnum (motet); *Missa O quam gloriosum.*
⊛ *** Hyp. CDA 66114 [id.]. Westminster Cathedral Ch., David Hill.

The Latin fervour of the singing is very involving; some listeners may initially be surprised at the volatile way David Hill moves the music on, with the trebles eloquently soaring aloft on the line of the music. *Ave maris stella* is particularly fine, Hill's mastery of the overall structure producing a cumulative effect as the choir moves towards the magnificent closing *Agnus Dei.* On the companion disc the spirited presentation of the motet *Ascendens Christus in altum* prepares the way for a performance of the Mass that is similarly invigorating. The spontaneous ebb and flow of the pacing is at the heart of David Hill's understanding of this superb music. The recording balance is perfectly judged, with the Westminster acoustic adding resonance (in both senses of the word) to singing of the highest calibre, combining a sense of timelessness and mystery with real expressive power. Throughout, the choral line remains firm without clouding.

Ave Maria; Ave Maris stella (hymn). *Missa Vidi speciosam. Ne timeas, Maria; Sancta Maria, succurre miseris; Vidi speciosam* (motets).
*** Hyp. Dig. CDA 66129 [id.]. Westminster Cathedral Ch., David Hill.

An outstanding collection of some of Victoria's most beautiful music celebrating the Virgin Mary. The four-part *Ave Maria* may not be authentic, but the composer would surely not be reluctant to own it; and the hymn *Ave maris stella* is also a memorable setting. *Vidi speciosam* derives from the Song of Songs and its secular language inspires a special kind of expressive radiance which could only come from a Latin composer. The Westminster Choir again show their flexibly volatile response to this music with that special amalgam of fervour and serenity that Victoria's writing demands. The acoustics of Westminster Cathedral add the right degree of resonance to the sound without clouding, and the choral textures are gloriously rich and yet refined too.

Officium defunctorum.
*** Gimell Dig. CDGIM 012 [id.]. Tallis Scholars, Phillips (with LOBO: Motet: *Versa est in luctum****).
*** Hyp. Dig. CDA 66250 [id.]. Westminster Cathedral Ch., David Hill.

Victoria's *Officium defunctorum* was his last publication; it comprises his *Requiem for six voices,* the Responsory *Libera me* and two motets. He spoke of it in his dedication as a swan-song, not in regard to his own composing but for the dedicatee – though in fact he died only six years later. It is a work of great serenity and beauty. Honours are fairly evenly divided between the Westminster Cathedral Choir on Hyperion and the Tallis Scholars under Peter Phillips. The Westminster Choir has the advantage of boys' voices and larger forces; they are recorded in a warmer, more spacious acoustic. By comparison with the Gimell recording, the sound seems a little less well focused, but on its own terms it is thoroughly convincing. They permit themselves greater expressiveness, too. Moreover the *Requiem* is set in the wider liturgical context by the use of some chants.

The Tallis Scholars achieve great clarity of texture; they are twelve in number and, as a result, the polyphony is clearer and so, too, are their words. The lines are slightly harder-etched, as indeed are those of Spanish choirs, and their intonation is always true. There are no chants but they offer a short and deeply felt motet by Alonso Lobo (c. 1555–1617). The recording has a warm, glowing sound which almost persuades you that you are in the imperial chapel.

Mass and Motet – O quam gloriosum.
(*) Argo Dig. 410 149-2 [id.]. King's College Ch., Cleobury – PALESTRINA: *Tu es Petrus.*(*)

This coupling with Palestrina offers eloquent, if slightly reserved performances in the King's tradition, the voices finely blended to produce an impressive range of sonority. The recording is admirably faithful and, while there is an element of introspection here, the singing also offers moments of affecting serenity.

Vierne, Louis (1870–1937)

Pièces en style libre, Op. 31/11, 14, 15, 19, 20, 21 & 24; Pièces de fantaisie, Op. 53/2 & 5; Op. 54/2.
*(**) Unicorn Dig. DKPCD 9064 [id.]. Jennifer Bate (organ of Beauvais Cathedral).

Jennifer Bate makes a perceptive selection from Vierne's two sets of organ pieces, mixing popular items with others less familiar; and her playing is particularly appealing in the gentle numbers such as the *Berceuse*, Op. 31/19, and the *Arabesque*, Op. 31/15, which are registered with subtlety and charm. However, in the more complex pieces – the opening and very noisy *Carillon de Longpont*, for instance, or the fleeting *Scherzetto*, Op. 31, Nos. 21 and 14 respectively – her bravura is seriously muddied by the wide Beauvais reverberation.

Suite No. 3, Op. 54: Carillon de Westminster.
*** DG Dig. 413 438-2 [id.]. Simon Preston (organ of Westminster Abbey) – WIDOR: *Symphony No. 5.****

The Vierne *Carillon de Westminster* is splendidly played by Simon Preston and sounds appropriately atmospheric in this spacious acoustic and well-judged recording. It makes an attractive makeweight to the Widor *Fifth Symphony*.

Symphony No. 1 in D min., Op. 14. Pièces de fantaisie, suite No. 3, Op. 54: Carillon de Westminster; Dedicace, Étude de soir, Impromptu.
*** Ph. Dig. 422 058-2 [id.]. Daniel Chorzempa (Cavaillé-Coll organ, St Sernin, Toulouse).

The Vierne *First Symphony* is more of an extended suite on the lines of the Widor *Organ symphonies*; its six movements originally appeared separately. Chorzempa's recording is made on an authentic enough instrument, a Cavaillé-Coll, and is splendidly recorded in the generous acoustic of St Sernin, Toulouse. There is no reason for disappointment here; the *Symphony* comes with some of the *Pièces de fantaisie*, all played with conviction and dedication.

Symphonies Nos. 1 in D min., Op. 14; 2 in E min., Op. 20.
*** Mer. CDE 84192 [id.]. David Sanger (organ of La Chiesa Italiana di San Pietro, London).

The *D minor Symphony* dates from the turn of the century and was dedicated to Guilmant. Its sense of power and its quiet originality make it well worth having. The *Second* is a finely wrought piece, perhaps more concentrated than its predecessor. Both are played with much sympathy by David Sanger and the recording has excellent depth and range.

Symphonies Nos. 3 in F sharp min., Op. 28; 4 in G min., Op. 32.
*** Mer. CDE 84176 [id.]. David Sanger (organ of La Chiesa Italiana di San Pietro, London).

In the *Third Symphony*, which is both technically and musically demanding, David Sanger again proves the equal of the challenge on this remarkably attractive organ. Though this is not generally as dark a work as the wartime *Fourth*, it is distinguished by moments of genuine depth. Sanger's feeling for colour in his choice of registration gives special pleasure, especially in the inner movements, the engaging *Intermezzo* from No. 3, for instance, or the equivalent in No. 4, a disarmingly simple minuet. There is no cause to complain of the sound quality, which maintains the high standards Meridian have set themselves: the resonance of the pedals is very telling without muddying the overall sound-picture.

Symphonies Nos. 5 in A min., Op. 47; 6 in B min., Op. 59.
*** Mer. CDA 84171 [id.]. David Sanger (organ of La Chiesa Italiana di San Pietro, London).

David Sanger's No. 5 was originally coupled with the Op. 31 *Pièces en style libre*, but this generous CD offers the splendid *Sixth Symphony* instead. Sanger has genuine commitment to this repertoire and though he is playing an instrument somewhat removed from the Cavaillé-Coll sound-world – the effect is sweeter but not bland – he succeeds in conveying an authentic feeling. The recording is vivid and the impressive finales of both works are spectacular.

Vieuxtemps, Henri (1820–81)

Violin concerto No. 5 in A min., Op. 37.
*** Ph. Dig. 422 332-2 [id.]. Mullova, ASMF, Marriner – PAGANINI: *Concerto No. 1.****
*** RCA RD 86214 [RCA 6214-2-RC]. Heifetz, New SO of L., Sargent – BRUCH: *Concerto No. 1; Scottish fantasia.****
(*) CBS Dig. CD 37796 [id.]. Cho-Liang Lin, Minnesota SO, Marriner – HAYDN: *Concerto.*

Like her Paganini No. 1, Viktoria Mullova's account of the *A minor Concerto* is remarkable for its breathtaking virtuosity and its great fire and style. Sir Neville Marriner and the Academy are supportive and the Philips recording, though a bit bass-resonant, is first class and very vivid and present.

The quicksilver of Heifetz is well suited to the modest but attractive *Fifth Concerto* of Vieuxtemps, and Sir Malcolm provides a musical and well-recorded accompaniment. The balance of the soloist is rather close, but the digital remastering is successful and the couplings are both attractive and generous.

Cho-Liang Lin plays with flair and zest and is well supported by Sir Neville Marriner and the Minnesota orchestra. The recording is first class, and the enhancement provided by the CD is striking. However, the coupling, though well played, is not a very appropriate one.

Villa-Lobos, Heitor (1887–1959)

Bachianas Brasileiras Nos. (iii) *1;* (i; iii) *5;* (i; ii) *Suite for voice and violin.* (iii) arr. of BACH: *The Well-tempered clavier: Prelude in D min., BWV 583; Fugue in B flat, BWV 846; Prelude in G min., BWV 867; Fugue in D, BWV 874.*
*** Hyp. Dig. CDA 66257 [id.]. (i) Jill Gomez, (ii) Peter Manning, (iii) Pleeth Cello Octet.

Jill Gomez is outstanding in the popular *Fifth Bachianas Brasileiras* and with the violinist, Peter Manning, in the *Suite* (1923). Villa-Lobos' favourite 'orchestra of cellos' produce sumptuous sounds in both the *Bachianas Brasileiras*, and an added point of interest is the effective transcriptions for cellos of unrelated Bach preludes and fugues. An eminently attractive introduction to this most colourful of composers.

Bachianas Brasileiras Nos. 1; 2 (includes *The little train of the Caipira*); (i) *5* (for soprano & 8 cellos); (ii) *6* (for flute & bassoon); *9.*
(**) EMI mono CDH7 61015-2 [id.]. French Nat. R. O, composer, with (i) De los Angeles; (ii) Fernand Dufrêne, René Plessier.

It is good to have on EMI's historic Références label this generous collection of the composer's own recordings, not immaculate in performance and with depressingly dry and boxy recording, but full of colour and life. Though even Victoria de los Angeles' golden voice loses some of its bloom, her account of the famous No. 5 is ravishing, and no one has been more persuasive than the composer himself in the other favourite, the *Little train of the Caipira*.

Guitar concerto.
*** Ph. Dig. 416 357-2 [id.]. Pepe Romero, ASMF, Marriner – CASTELNUOVO-TEDESCO: *Concerto;* RODRIGO: *Sones en la Giralda.********

(i) *Guitar concerto; 12 Études; 5 Preludes.*
**(*) DG 423 700-2 [id.]. Yepes, (i) LSO, Navarro.

Guitar concerto; 5 Preludes.
(M) ******* RCA GD 86525 [6525-2-RG]. Bream, LSO, Previn – RODRIGO: *Concierto.********

Helped by attractively atmospheric recording, Romero and Marriner join to give an outstanding account of the Villa-Lobos *Concerto* and make it seem more substantial than usual while losing nothing of its poetic atmosphere. With equally recommendable couplings, this is first choice in this repertoire.

Bream's highly distinguished account of the *Guitar concerto* with Previn has now been reissued at mid-price, coupled with Rodrigo, an excellent idea.

Yepes' performance is a good one too, if without quite the individuality of Bream. The accompaniment is vividly managed and the 1976 recording has been remastered to retain its full bloom and atmosphere. What makes this collection especially attractive is the inclusion of the solo items. Some of the *Preludes* here have a dark intensity which is quite haunting; but at times in the *Études* (not all of which are of equal interest) Yepes sounds a little detached, almost prosaic. But this reservation applies to only a handful of the studies and should not inhibit recommendation of playing of such aristocratic distinction.

PIANO MUSIC

Alma brasileira, Bachiana brasileira No. 4; Ciclo brasileiro; Chôros No. 5; Valsa da dor (Waltz of sorrows).
*** ASV Dig. CDDCA 607 [id.]. Alma Petchersky.

Alma Petchersky is a refined player who produces a wide range of colour and tone, and her articulation is eminently clean. Villa-Lobos's piano music is not generously represented on CD at present, but this issue is as good as any. The sound is very well focused, though there could have been a little more space round the instrument. Alma Petchersky's style is more romantic than that of Cristina Ortiz, and some might find her thoughtful deliberation in the *Preludio* of the *Bachianas Brasileira No. 4* overdone. Her very free rubato is immediately apparent in the *Valsa da dor* which opens the recital. Yet she clearly feels all this music deeply, and the playing is strong in personality and – with fuller piano than on the Decca collection – her timbre is often richly coloured. She is at her finest in the *Brazilian cycle*. The recording is first class, with more body and resonance than in the Decca collection.

As três Maria; Bachianas Brasileiras No. 4; Caixinha de música quebrada; Ciclo Brasileiro; Cirandas Nos. 4 & 14; Cuia prático; Poema singelo; Saudades das selvas Brasileiras No. 2; Valsa da dor.
*** Decca Dig. 417 650-2 [id.]. Cristina Ortiz.

Cristina Ortiz, herself Brazilian, is a natural choice for this repertoire. Her anthology embraces the piano version of the *Bachianas Brasileiras No. 4* and a well-chosen collection of other pieces, the main work on her well-filled disc being the *Ciclo Brasileiro*. She has a good ear for sonority and her phrasing is subtle and sensitive. The piano sound is clean and bright.

Bachianas Brasileiras No. 5 for soprano and cellos.
*** Decca Dig. 411 730-2 [id.]. Te Kanawa, Harrell and instrumental ens. –
CANTELOUBE: *Songs of the Auvergne.***(*)
(M) *** RCA GD 87831 [7831-2-RG]. Anna Moffo, American SO, Stokowski –
CANTELOUBE: *Chants d'Auvergne;* RACHMANINOV: *Vocalise.****

The Villa-Lobos piece makes an apt fill-up for the Canteloube songs completing Kiri Te Kanawa's recording of all five books. It is, if anything, even more sensuously done, well sustained at a speed far slower than one would normally expect. Rich recording to match.

Anna Moffo gives a seductive performance of the most famous of the *Bachianas Brasileiras*, adopting a highly romantic style (matching the conductor) and warm tone-colour.

Viotti, Giovanni Battista (1755–1824)

Violin concerto No. 13 in A.
*** Hyp. Dig. CDA 66210 [id.]. Oprean, European Community CO, Faerber –
FIORILLO: *Violin concerto No. 1.****

Viotti wrote a great many violin concertos in much the same mould, but this is one of his best. Its first movement has agreeable facility; the charming central *Andante* is more ambitious than that in the coupled Fiorillo *Concerto*, and the jaunty rondo/polonaise finale is quite infectious, having much in common with a Paganini finale. Adelina Oprean's quicksilver style and light lyrical touch give much pleasure – she has the exact measure of this repertoire and she is splendidly accompanied and well recorded. The measure, though, is short.

Vivaldi, Antonio (1675–1741)

L'Estro armonico (12 Concertos), Op. 3.
*** DG Dig. 423 094-2 (2) [id.]. Standage & soloists, E. Concert, Trevor Pinnock.
*** O-L 414 554-2 (2) [id.]. Holloway, Huggett, Mackintosh, Wilcock, AAM, Hogwood.
*** Ph. Dig. 412 128-2 [id.]. Carmirelli, I Musici.

Vivaldi's *L'Estro armonico* was published in 1711. The set includes some of his finest music and had great influence. This new chamber version from Pinnock (with one instrument to a part) seems instinctively to summarize and amalgamate the best features from past versions: there is as much sparkle and liveliness as with Hogwood, for rhythms are consistently resilient, ensemble crisp and vigorous. Yet in slow movements there is that expressive radiance and sense of enjoyment of beauty without unstylish indulgence that one expects from the ASMF. The only aspect that one might cavil at is the use of harpsichord continuo throughout (Hogwood used organ as well; Marriner additionally featured the lute). However, this is a small point; everything else here gives delight, not least the sound itself, which is totally free from vinegar. The recording was made in EMI's Abbey Road studios and the balance and ambient effect are judged perfectly: there is bloom and internal clarity and a realistic but not exaggerated sense of presence.

There is no question about the sparkle of Christopher Hogwood's performance with the Academy of Ancient Music. The captivating lightness of the solo playing and the crispness of articulation of the accompanying group bring music-making that combines joyful vitality with the authority of scholarship. Textures are always transparent, but there is no lack of body to the ripieno (even though there is only one instrument to each part). Hogwood's continuo is first class, varying between harpsichord and organ, the latter used to add colour as well as substance. The balance is excellent, and the whole effect is exhilarating. The extra range that the compact disc can encompass helps to give the aural image the impression of greater definition.

Readers allergic to the Academy of Ancient Music are well served, too. I Musici are thoroughly fresh and alive, and few will find much to quarrel with in their interpretation. They may not have the dash and sparkle of the Academy – but they do not have any rough edges either. The Philips recording has great warmth and the texture is well ventilated, allowing detail to register clearly within a realisic perspective. The non-specialist collector will find much to enjoy here.

L'Estro armonico: Double violin concerto in A min.; Quadruple violin concerto in B min.; Triple concerto in D min., for 2 violins and cello, Op. 3/8, 10 and 11. Triple violin concerto in F.
(B) **(*) Pickwick Dig. PCD 809 [MCA MCAD 25854]. Soloists, SCO, Laredo.

The three concertos from *L'Estro armonico* are among Vivaldi's finest; they receive vigorous performances from members of the Scottish Chamber Orchestra, with their director, Jaime Laredo, again creating the lively spontaneity that informs his successful version of *The Four Seasons*. While the solo playing occasionally lacks the last touch of polish, there is excellent team spirit, and the phrasing has more light and shade than in Laredo's companion collection of wind concertos. The recording is a shade overbright, but there is a firm supporting bass line and the acoustic is attractive, adding ambience and warmth without blurring detail. On Pickwick's bargain-price CD label, this seems excellent value.

VIVALDI

La Stravaganza (12 Violin concertos), Op. 4.
*** O-L Dig. 417 502-2 (2) [id.]. Huggett, AAM, Hogwood.

Five of the concertos of Op. 4 look, not to the concerto grosso form of Corelli, but to the true solo concerto form of Torelli and Albinoni, which Vivaldi himself presaged in *L'Estro armonico*. Monica Huggett brings not only virtuosity but also considerable warmth to the solo concertos, and the Academy are both spirited and sensitive. Those who think of Vivaldi's music as predictable will find much to surprise them in *La Stravaganza*; his invention is unflagging and of high quality. Strongly recommended.

The Trial between harmony and invention (Il Cimento dell'armonia e dell'invenzione) (12 Concertos), Op. 8.
**(*) O-L Dig. 417 515-2 (2) [id.]. Bury, Hirons, Holloway, Huggett, Mackintosh, Piguet, AAM, Hogwood.
(*) CRD CRD 3325 (Nos. 1–4); CRD 3410 (Nos. 5–10); CRD 3411 (Nos. 11–12 and *Cello concerto in B min., RV 424; Flute concerto in D, RV 429*) [id.]. Simon Standage, Pleeth, Preston, E. Concert, Pinnock – C. P. E. BACH: *Harpsichord concerto.*(*)

The first four concertos of Op. 8 are a set within a set, forming what is (understandably) Vivaldi's most popular work, *The Four Seasons*. Their imaginative power and their eloquence and tunefulness tend to dwarf the remaining eight concertos, but there is some splendid music throughout the complete work, well worth exploring.

There is no want of zest in the Academy of Ancient Music's accounts of Op. 8. These are likeable and, generally speaking, well-prepared versions and differ from some rivals in choosing the oboe in two of the concertos, where Vivaldi has indicated an option. There are moments where more polish would not have come amiss, and intonation is not above reproach either. However, admirers of the Academy will find much to enjoy here – as, indeed, will those who are not always in tune with period-instrument performances. In *The Four Seasons*, Pinnock is not displaced, however. The recordings are well up to standard and are given fine presence, complete on a pair of CDs.

CRD have anticipated the needs of many collectors, who either may not wish to duplicate *The Four Seasons* or may prefer to choose an alternative account, by making available the remaining eight concertos on two CDs, filling up the available space with two other Vivaldi works, and on CD offering a harpsichord concerto by C. P. E. Bach as a bonus. The *Flute concerto* (played by Simon Preston on a baroque flute) is particularly attractive. These 1981 performances are alert and full of character. A chamber organ is used in the continuo to add extra colour and slow movements remain expressively eloquent, although the playing is a little short on charm. The sound did have a certain astringency, but in the remastering for CD this has been slightly smoothed off, and in tuttis there is at times some loss of focus. The separate concertos are banded, but there is no cueing of individual movements. *The Four Seasons* from this set are available on CD also, well transferred; but buying all twelve concertos is uneconomical since it involves three discs, even if you do get a good deal of extra music.

The Four Seasons, Op. 8/1–4.
*** Virgin Dig. VCy 791081-2 [id.]. Christopher Warren-Green with LCO – ALBINONI: *Adagio;* PACHELBEL: *Canon.***
*** ASV Dig. CDDCA 579 [id.]. José Luis Garcia, ECO (with HANDEL: *Water music: suite No. 1 in F***).
*** Argo 414 486-2 [id.]. Alan Loveday, ASMF, Marriner.
*** DG Dig. 400 045-2 [id.]. Simon Standage, E. Concert, Pinnock.

*** BIS Dig. CD 275 [id.]. Nils-Erik Sparf, Drottningholm Bar. Ens.
*** EMI Dig. CDC7 49557-2 [id.]. Nigel Kennedy, ECO.
*** DG Dig. 419 214-2 [id.]. Stern, Zukerman, Mintz, Perlman, Israel PO, Mehta.
(M) *** EMI CDM7 69046-2 [id.]. Itzhak Perlman, LPO.
*** Ph. Dig. 410 001-2 [id.]. Pina Carmirelli, I Musici.
(B) *** Pickwick Dig. PCD 800 [MCA MCAD 25843]. Jaime Laredo, SCO.
**(*) DG 413 726-2 [id.]. Gidon Kremer, LSO, Abbado.
(M) **(*) CBS Dig. MDK 44644 [id.]. Zukerman, St Paul CO – PURCELL: *Theatre music.***(*)
*** O-L Dig. 410 126-2 [id.]. Hirons, Holloway, Bury, Mackintosh, AAM, Hogwood.
*** Ph. Dig. 420 216-2 [id.]. Viktoria Mullova, COE, Abbado.
**(*) EMI CDC7 47319-2 [id.]. Perlman, Israel PO.
(B) **(*) CfP CD-CFP 9001. Kenneth Sillito, Virtuosi of England, Davison.
(B) ** RCA VD 87732 [7732-2-RV]. Accardo, O de Camera Italiana.
(M) **(*) Decca 417 712-2 [id.]. Konstanty Kulka, Stuttgart CO, Münchinger – ALBINONI: *Adagio****; PACHELBEL: *Canon.****
** Collins Dig. 1006-2 [id.]. David Nolan, LPO.

The Four Seasons, Op. 8/1–4 (with sonnets in Italian and English).
*** Helios/Hyp. CDH 88012 [id.]. Bruni, Edwards (readers), Adelina Oprean, European Community CO, Faeber.

The Four Seasons, Op. 8/1–4; L'Estro armonico: Concerto in A min., RV 356, Op. 3/6.
**(*) RCA Dig. RD 87979 [7979-2-RC]. Uto Ughi, I Virtuosi di Santa Cecilia.

The Four Seasons, Op. 8/1–4; L'Estro armonico: Concertos in A min., RV 356; D, RV 230, Op. 3/6 & 9.
(B) *** Ph. 422 479-2 [id.]. Henryk Szeryng, ECO.

The Four Seasons, Op. 8/1–4. Violin concerto in E (L'amoroso), RV 271.
**(*) Ph. 416 611-2 [id.]. Ayo, I Musici.

The Four Seasons; Violin concertos: in B flat (La Caccia), Op. 8/10; in A (per eco in lontana), RV 552.
(M) **(*) Ph. 420 356-2 [id.]. Roberto Michelucci, I Musici.

The Four Seasons, Op. 8/1-4; Violin concertos: in E flat (La tempesta di mare),RV 253; in C (Il piacere), RV 180, Op. 8/5–6.
**(*) Ph. Dig. 426 847-2 [id.]. Federico Agostini, I Musici.

The Four Seasons, Op. 8/1–4; Triple violin concerto in F, RV 551; Quadruple violin concerto in B min., RV 580.
⊕ *** Ph. Dig. 422 065-2 [id.]. Accardo and soloists with CO.

The Four Seasons; Concerto for strings (Alla rustica) in G, RV 151.
(BB) ** Naxos Dig. 8.550056 [id.]. Takako Nishizaki, Capella Istropolitana, Gunzenhauser.

(i) *The Four Seasons, Op. 8/1–4*; (ii) *Concertos: in C, per la Solemnita di San Lorenzo, RV 556; in G min., per l'orchestra di Dresda, RV 577.*
(M) *** Ph. 422 484-2 [id.]. (i) Felix Ayo, Berlin CO; (ii) Dresden State O (members); Negri.

(i) *The Four Seasons;* (ii) *Flute concertos, Op. 10/1–3.*
(M) *** RCA GD 86553 [Pro Arte CDD 214]. (i) La Petite Bande, Kuijken; (ii) Brüggen, O of 18th Century.

Salvatore Accardo's is a version with a difference. Recorded in live performances at the 1987 Cremona Festival, it is of particular interest in that Accardo uses a different Stradivarius for each of the four concertos – period instruments with a difference! Thanks to this aristocrat of violinists, the sounds are of exceptional beauty, both here and also in the two multiple concertos which are added as a bonus. The performances are much enhanced, too, by the imaginative continuo playing of Bruno Canino. The recording itself is a model of fidelity and has plenty of warmth; it must rank very high in the Vivaldi discography.

Christopher Warren-Green makes a brilliantly charismatic soloist with the re-formed London Chamber Orchestra providing delectably pointed bird-imitations in *Spring* and *Summer.* Tempi of allegros are very brisk, but the effect is tinglingly exhilarating when the soloist's bravura is so readily matched by the accompanying ensemble. Certainly this account of Vivaldi's *Four Seasons* is memorable, and its sheer brio is impossible to resist. Slow movements offer the widest contrast, with delicate textures and subtle use of the continuo, as in *Winter* where Leslie Pearson makes a delightful surprise contribution to the finale, having already embroidered the opening allegro and prevented it from being too chilly. Needless to say, the storms approach gale force, while the peasants are hardly less rumbustious, enjoying their autumn hunting and bacchanale. The recording, made in All Saints' Church, Wallington, has plenty of ambient fullness, but remains bright and fresh. With its equally attractive couplings, this can be strongly recommended to those who like their Vivaldi to be dashing and vital, and yet imaginatively pictorial at the same time.

The ASV version of *The Four Seasons*, with José Luis Garcia as soloist and musical director, was chosen on BBC Radio 3 as ideal for 'Building a Record Library'. That was before some of the current versions listed above made their appearance, but one can understand the reasons for its choice. The recording acoustic (All Hallows Church, London) is particularly pleasing, with the violins of the accompanying group sweetly fresh and the soloist nicely balanced. The overall pacing is beautifully judged, and each movement takes its place naturally and spontaneously in relation to its companions. The effects are well made, but there are no histrionics and, although the continuo does not always come through strongly, the unnamed player makes a useful contribution to a performance that is very easy to live with. The one drawback to this issue is that there is only one track for each of the *Four Seasons*.

Marriner's 1970 Academy of St Martin-in-the-Fields version with Alan Loveday still remains near the top of the list of recommended compact discs. It was made during a vintage Argo recording period and the digital remastering has been completely successful, retaining the fullness and bloom of the original, besides slightly refining its inner detail. The performance is as satisfying as ever, and will surely delight all but those who are ruled by the creed of authenticity. It has an element of fantasy that makes the music sound utterly new; it is full of imaginative touches, with Simon Preston subtly varying the continuo between harpsichord and organ. The opulence of string tone may have a romantic connotation, but there is no self-indulgence in the interpretation, no sentimentality, for the contrasts are made sharper and fresher, not smoothed over.

For his 1975 recording, Felix Ayo chose a talented accompanying group from East Berlin (with Jeffrey Tate at the harpsichord). The playing has microscopic precision and plenty of atmosphere; slow movements are often delicately ethereal in their lightness of texture. Ayo's playing is as sweetly lyrical as ever and, although the result is not as sensuously beautiful as his earlier, I Musici set, the reading is rather more strongly characterized, notably the opening movement of *Winter* which is quite fast and sharply articulated. What makes this issue doubly attractive is the inclusion of the two orchestral concertos. The complicated orchestrations suggested by the composer are not followed to the letter, with clarinos (trumpets) introduced very effectively to celebrate the 'solemnity of San Lorenzo'. The *G minor concerto* also produces some aurally fascinating textures and was dedicated to its Dresden performers, though not the present group! Negri ensures throughout that all the playing is alert and polished and chooses apt tempi. The sound is bright, yet not lacking fullness.

The Archiv version by Simon Standage with the English Concert, directed from the harpsichord by Trevor Pinnock, has the advantage of using a newly discovered set of parts found in Manchester's Henry Watson Music Library – which has additionally brought the correction of minor textual errors in the Le Cène text in normal use. The Archiv performance also (minimally) introduces a second soloist and is played on period instruments. The players create a relatively intimate sound, though their approach is certainly not without drama, while the solo contribution has impressive flair and bravura. The overall effect is essentially refined, treating the pictorial imagery with subtlety. The result is less voluptuous than with Marriner and less vibrant than Christopher Warren-Green, but it finds a natural balance between vivid projection and atmospheric feeling. The digital recording is first class. Authenticists should be well satisfied.

The BIS recording by Nils-Erik Sparf and the Drottningholm Baroque Ensemble is in a rather special category. As a recording, it has astonishing clarity and presence; and as playing, it is hardly less remarkable in its imaginative vitality. These Swedish players make the most of all the pictorial characterization without ever overdoing anything: they achieve the feat of making one hear this eminently familiar repertoire as if for the very first time.

Nigel Kennedy's version of Vivaldi's *Four Seasons* not only shot up into the pop charts and held its position there for an unprecedented length of time, but it has now become the best seller of all records of this best-selling of all classical works. Its success was certainly helped by an unprecedented degree of hype, but no less by Kennedy's gift for communication with the public at large, and especially with the younger generation, both in his laid-back TV and radio manner and in his chosen style in clothes and spiky hair. Good for him, if it helps to draw more listeners into the world of 'classical' music, which is clearly his intention. The time was also ripe for Vivaldi to enjoy a comparable success, for his masterpiece (and notably *Spring*) had already received remarkable exposure in TV and film commercials, to say nothing of radio programmes. Kennedy's account of it is certainly among the more spectacular in conveying its picaresque imagery; only *Autumn* brings a degree of real controversy, however, with weird special effects, including glissando harmonics in the slow movement and percussive applications of the wooden part of the bow to add rhythmic pungency to the hunting finale. There is plenty of vivid detail elsewhere. In the slow movement of *Spring* the tail almost wags the dog in his enthusiasm, and in *Summer*, after Kennedy's inspirationally free account of the *Adagio*, very operatic in feeling, the ferocity of the storm transports one half way to the Antarctic. One certainly arrives there at the bleak opening of *Winter*; then comes an engaging contrast when, after a cadenza-like flourish, Kennedy plays the songful *Largo* with ravishing espressivo. The continuo includes lute (delicately evocative in the slow movement of *Spring*) as well as harpsichord; the overall balance places everything in reasonable perspective, within the flattering ambience of the Church of St John-at-Hackney, in East London. Though (not surprisingly) Kennedy dominates the sound-picture, the strings have body and fullness to add weight to a gleamingly bright upper range. The ECO's playing is always responsive, to match the often very exciting bravura of its soloist, and allegros have an agreeable vitality. However, at 41 minutes, with no fillers, this is not generous and, while this is undoubtedly a memorable experience, it would not be our first choice for repeated listening, particularly in such a competitive field.

The recording made at the 1982 Huberman Festival in Tel Aviv took the opportunity offered by a stellar gathering of fiddlers to give each of the four concertos to a different soloist. The result is an unqualified success, with each artist revelling in writing that offers equal opportunities for bravura and espressivo playing, plus a chance for the imagination to find a similar balance between the musical and pictorial aspects of Vivaldi's remarkable conception.

The novelty of the Helios issue is the inclusion of the sonnets which Vivaldi placed on his score to give his listeners a guide to the illustrative detail suggested by the music. Before each of the four concertos, the appropriate poem is read, first in a romantically effusive Italian manner and then in BBC English (the contrast quite striking). On CD, of course, one can programme out these introductions; one would hardly want to hear them as often as the concertos. The performances are first class, full of energy and with wide dynamic contrasts used to increase the drama. The difference between the gently inebriated, somnolent peasants in the slow movement of *Autumn* and the hunting music of the finale is very striking; while similarly the opening of *Winter* is *sotto voce*, leaving room for later expansion. Adelina Oprean is an excellent soloist, her reading full of youthful energy and expressive freshness; her timbre is clean and pure, her technique assured. Faeber matches her vitality, and the score's pictorial effects are boldly characterized in a vividly projected sound-picture. The sound is first rate: the violins of the accompanying group have the right Italianate gleam.

Those looking for an outstanding mid-priced CD should be well satisfied with Perlman and the LPO. His finesse as a great violinist is evident from first to last. Though some will demand more reticence in baroque concertos, Perlman's imagination holds the sequence together superbly, and there are many passages of pure magic, as in the central *Adagio* of *Summer*. The digital remastering of the 1976 recording is managed admirably, the sound firm, clear and well balanced, with plenty of detail.

On RCA, La Petite Band (soloist unnamed, but presumably Kuijken) offer an authentic version of considerable appeal. Although the accompanying group can generate plenty of energy when Vivaldi's winds are blowing, this is essentially a small-scale reading, notable for its delicacy. The small, pure violin line is particularly appealing in slow movements and one notes how closely the soloist follows Vivaldi's instructions in the second movement of *Spring*: *Largo e pianissimo sempre*. But this mid-priced issue offers not just the four concertos of Op. 8 but also three favourite *Flute concertos* from Op. 10: *Tempesta di mare*, *La notte* and *Il gardinello*. With the master-instrumentalist, Frans Brüggen, playing a period instrument and directing the Orchestra of the 18th Century, the excellence of these performances, vividly recorded, can be taken for granted.

A first-rate bargain version comes from Szeryng, and the only reservation is that the very soft-grained tone of the harpsichord in the continuo does not come through readily because of the reverberation; the chamber proportions of the recording are retained however, and the digital remastering has improved definition. Szeryng's performances are eloquent and beautifully played, and the alert, resilient accompaniments are stylish. The balance places the violin well forward, but the resonance gives the orchestra plenty of body. As a considerable bonus, Szeryng offers two concertos from Op. 3, also played immaculately.

The Philips digital recording with Pina Carmirelli is the third out of the four made in stereo by I Musici, and it is undoubtedly the finest of all. Musical values as ever are paramount; this time, however, there is more vitality and the programmatic implications are more strikingly realized (indeed, the bark of the shepherd's dog in *Spring* is singularly insistent). Yet Carmirelli's expressive playing maintains the lyrical feeling and beauty of tone for which I Musici versions are remembered and combines it with attractively alert and nimble bravura in the allegros. The gentle breezes are caught as effectively as the summer storms, and the slow movement of *Autumn* (helped by especially atmospheric recording) makes an elegiac contrast. The opening of *Winter* is certainly chilly. The recording is outstandingly natural.

Jaime Laredo's Pickwick CD is another fine bargain. The performance has great spontaneity and vitality, emphasized by the forward balance which is nevertheless admirably truthful. The bright upper range is balanced by a firm, resonant bass. Laredo plays with bravura and directs polished, strongly characterized accompaniments. Pacing tends to be on the fast side; although the reading is extrovert and the lyrical music – played responsively – is made to offer a series of interludes to the vigour of the allegros, the effect is exhilarating rather than aggressive.

In the DG version by Gidon Kremer with the LSO under Claudio Abbado, it is obvious from the first bar that Abbado is the dominant partner. This is an enormously vital account, with great contrasts of tempo and dynamic. The dramatization of Vivaldi's detailed pictorial effects has never been more vivid; the vigour of the dancing peasants is surpassed by the sheer fury and violence of the summer storms. Yet the delicacy of the gentle zephyrs is matched by the hazy somnolence of the beautiful *Adagio* of *Autumn*. After a freezingly evocative opening to *Winter*, Abbado creates a mandolin-like pizzicato effect in the slow movement (taken faster than the composer's marking) to simulate a rain shower. The finale opens delicately, but at the close the listener is almost blown away by the winter gales. Kremer matches Abbado's vigour with playing that combines sparkling bravura and suitably evocative expressive moments. Given the projection of a brilliantly lit recording, the impact of this version is considerable. But without a fill-up this now seems too highly priced.

Federico Agostini is flexible in his detailed approach to the solo line and he has a fine, singing tone. His impressively free technical command is equal to all Vivaldi's pictorial histrionics, and in the slow movement of *Summer* and again in the *Largo* of *La tempesta di mare* he produces a serene cantilena of considerable beauty. But overall there is nothing specially memorable about this set, although the recording is first rate. The one individual touch is the use of a chamber organ in the main string group. The player is unnamed but he adds a special touch of dolorous colour to the *Adagio* of *Autumn*, and his contribution increases the bustle of the *Summer* storm. This is by no means a first choice in a crowded field and, considering it is a full-priced issue, one would have expected the documentation to be more elaborately detailed concerning the main work.

Now reissued at mid-price and generously coupled with suites of Purcell's theatre music directed by Raymond Leppard, Zukerman's digitally recorded set is among the best of the modern versions, finding a nice balance between the work's musical and programmatic features; the full recording, however, may be a shade too ample in the bass for some tastes.

Ughi's refined, sweet timbre is always expressive without becoming romantic; there is grace in the phrasing and plenty of vitality too. There is not the strongest individuality in his image – but that can be as much advantage as disadvantage when the music is presented so convincingly, with an alert and sensitive accompanying group who make the most of the score's detail and are dramatic when required without overdoing the histrionics. Modern instruments are used and a chamber scale is preserved. Ughi offers one bonus concerto from *L'Estro armonico* and plays it splendidly – but then Szeryng offers two, and although he does not have the advantage of digital recording, his version, which is in many ways comparable, costs less.

With a different soloist for each of the four concertos, Hogwood directs the Academy of Ancient Music in lively performances with exceptionally imaginative use of continuo contrasts, guitar with harpsichord in *Spring* and *Autumn*, lute and chamber organ in *Summer* and *Winter*. These performances have a high place among authentic versions, a shade more abrasive than most; however, they cannot quite match the subtly responsive approach of Trevor Pinnock's Archiv set with the English Concert. The CD has striking presence – a state-of-the-art transfer.

Viktoria Mullova's Philips record with the Chamber Orchestra of Europe under Claudio Abbado is well worth considering. As one would expect, she is vibrant and vital in the outer movements and imaginative and eloquent in the slow movements. She is given excellent support by Abbado and his players, and the recording, as always from this source, is very well balanced. There is a bonus in the form of the *G minor concerto*, RV 577, one of two Vivaldi composed for Dresden, whose orchestra boasted a strong wind department.

Fine as was Perlman's 1976 recording of *The Four Seasons*, he decided he wanted to record the four concertos again. There are certainly gains, in that the harpsichord continuo is more readily audible, but the closeness of sound, as recorded in the Mann Auditorium in Tel Aviv, is less appealing. As an interpretation, this is a masterly example of a virtuoso's individual artistry, but the account does not convey quite the warmth and spontaneity of the earlier set.

Felix Ayo's performance with I Musici dates from 1959, but the warm, reverberant recording still sounds beautiful. Ayo produces lovely tone throughout; while the account is certainly not without vitality and has stood the test of time, it will be enjoyed most by those for whom richness of sound is paramount. However, to reissue it at full price seems unaccountable.

Among versions in the mid-price and bargain range, that by Kenneth Sillito with the Virtuosi of England under Arthur Davison stands out for its bold, clear sound, beautifully focused and full of presence. Indeed the soloist is a shade too present, and this detracts a little from gentler expressiveness. Yet Sillito's playing is both poetic and assured and, with such vivid projection, this music-making is full of personality in its CD format.

Philips have also reissued Michelucci's 1970 version at mid-price, sounding extremely well. I Musici must have played this work countless times and probably find it more difficult than most groups to bring freshness to each new recording. Roberto Michelucci is a first-class soloist, displaying bursts of bravura in the outer movements but often musingly thoughtful in the slower ones. His expressiveness is finely judged, and the group are naturally balanced, with the harpsichord coming through in the right way, without exaggeration. The last degree of spontaneity is sometimes missing, but this is certainly enjoyable. This version is made the more tempting by the inclusion of two extra named *Violin concertos*, both very well played and recorded.

Not unexpectedly, Accardo on his earlier, RCA Victrola record makes an accomplished and appealing soloist and the Orchestra de Camera Italiana offer full, bright supporting textures. The programmatic drama is conveyed well, but musical values are paramount and this is enjoyable in its fresh, direct manner, if not especially memorable. The sound is vivid, and this might be considered at bargain price, even though it has no couplings; but there are many other more striking versions.

On Decca, Kulka gives a first-class solo performance, while Münchinger and the

Stuttgart Chamber Orchestra, whose early LPs did so much to reawaken interest in Vivaldi, bring a stylish and lively manner to the accompaniments. This was always a strong recommendation in the mid-price range but, with digital remastering, the brightly lit recording has become vivid to the point of astringency in its CD format, and the ear is drawn to this when the bonus items sound much mellower.

David Nolan on Collins provides a fresh, unidiosyncratic account, musically aware and with detail well realized. The solo timbre is sweet and the soloist is integrated very believably into the main group. There is spontaneity here and truthful sound, but this is in no way distinctive; at 38 minutes, without couplings, it cannot be considered competitive, although it is undoubtedly enjoyable.

The super-bargain Naxos version is given first-class digital sound, warm, fresh and well balanced (though the continuo does not come through very impressively). Takako Nishizaki plays beautifully, displaying an appropriate degree of bravura, and the accompaniment under Stephen Gunzenhauser is modest in scale and pleasingly finished. These are amiably musical performances, but Vivaldi's pictorial imagery is understated: the shepherd's dog has obviously just returned from an exhausting spring walk and *Winter* has seemingly been mellowed by the depletion of the ozone layer.

The Four Seasons, Op. 8/1 – 4 (arr. for flute and strings).
*** RCA RD 70161 [RCD1 2264]. Galway, I Solisti di Zagreb.

James Galway's transcription is thoroughly musical and so convincing that at times one is tempted to believe that the work was conceived in this form. The playing itself is marvellous, full of detail and imagination, and the recording is excellent, even if the flute is given a forward balance, the more striking on CD.

The Four Seasons, Op. 8/1 – 4 (arr. for recorder); *Recorder concerto in C, RV 443.*
*** RCA Dig. RD 86656 [6656-2-RC]. Michala Petri, Guildhall String Ens., Malcolm.

No question as to the virtuosity of Michala Petri or the excellence and musicianship of the Guildhall Strings. The question is not how but why. Who wants to hear this eminently violinistically conceived music played on any other instrument, even if by as accomplished an artist as Galway or Petri? Well, those who do are unlikely to be disappointed by the results here, even if there are some ear-piercing moments.

La Cetra (12 violin concertos), Op. 9.
*** EMI Dig. CDS7 47829-8 (2) [Ang. CDCB 47829]. Huggett, Raglan Bar. Players, Kraemer.
*** O-L Dig. 421 366-2 (2) [id.]. Standage, AAM, Hogwood.

La Cetra (The Lyre) was the last set of violin concertos Vivaldi published. Monica Huggett and the Raglan Baroque Players, as in the case of her recording of *La Stravaganza* on the Oiseau-Lyre label, offer performances so accomplished and in such good style that they are unlikely to be surpassed. She is in excellent form and her virtuosity always appears effortless. The Raglan Baroque Players are of the same size as the Academy of Ancient Music, and some players are common to both this and the Oiseau-Lyre Op. 4. First-class recording on CD.

Simon Standage gives an almost equally attractive and fluent account of the set, and honours are so evenly drawn that one is tempted to recommend either or both. Those who have already invested in the Huggett set need not change their allegiance; both recordings are excellent, but perhaps the EMI scores on warmth and naturalness. The Oiseau-Lyre is slightly drier but very clean. Without tempering enthusiasm for the newcomer, we have a marginal preference for the EMI sound.

6 Flute concertos, Op. 10.
* DG Dig. 423 702-2 [id.]. Liza Beznosiuk, E. Concert, Pinnock.
* O-L 414 685-2 [id.]. Stephen Preston, AAM.
(M) ***** Ph. 422 260-2. Gazzelloni, I Musici.
* Ph. 412 874-2 [id.]. Michala Petri, ASMF, Marriner.
(M) ***(*)** EMI Dig. CD-EMX 9504 [Ang. CDM 62014]. William Bennett, ECO, Malcolm.
*(*) Ph. Dig. 420 188-2 [id.]. Aurèle Nicolet, I Musici.

There is some expressive as well as brilliant playing on the DG Archiv CD, which should delight listeners. Try track 8 (the *Largo* movement of *Concerto No. 2 in G minor, La Notte*) for an example of the beautifully refined and cool pianissimo tone that Liza Beznosiuk can produce – and almost any of the fast movements for an example of her virtuosity. Her playing in *Il gardellino* is a delight, and Trevor Pinnock and the English Concert provide unfailingly vital and, above all, imaginative support. The DG recording is exemplary in its clarity. Recommended with enthusiasm: this goes to the top of the list.

Stephen Preston also plays a period instrument, a Schuchart, and the Academy of Ancient Music likewise play old instruments. Their playing is eminently stylish, but also spirited and expressive, and they are admirably recorded, with the analogue sound enhanced further in the CD format.

Severino Gazzelloni's version of the six *Concertos*, Op. 10, has been in circulation throughout the 1970s and its merits are well established; it is a safer recommendation for the general collector than the authentic rivals, good though the best of these is. With fresh, remastered sound this is an excellent mid-price recommendation.

Michala Petri uses a modern recorder and plays with breathtaking virtuosity and impeccable control, and she has the advantage of superb recording. In the slow movements – and occasionally elsewhere – there is more in the music than she finds, but the sheer virtuosity of this gifted artist is most infectious. She uses a sopranino recorder in three of the concertos.

Though beefier in approach than some rival versions, William Bennett's issue on the mid-price Eminence label brings highly enjoyable performances, marked by fine solo playing and sparkling and imaginative continuo from George Malcolm. Good, warm, modern recording.

Like Bennett's set with Malcolm, Aurèle Nicolet's with I Musici is, of course, a modern instrument version, and there is no lack of expertise. There are some touches which will not please purists (some flutter-tonguing in *Il gardellino* sounds out-of-period) but there is no want of virtuosity and charm. The recording is very well balanced.

Bassoon concertos: in C, RV 466; in C, RV 467; in F, RV 486; in F, RV 491; in A min., RV 499; in A min., RV 500.
*(*) ASV Dig. CDDCA 565 [id.]. Daniel Smith, ECO, Ledger.

Bassoon concertos in C, RV 469; in C, RV 470; in C, RV 474; in C, RV 476; in F, RV 487; in G, RV 494.
*(*) ASV Dig. CDDCA 571 [id.]. Daniel Smith, ECO, Ledger.

Bassoon concertos: in C, RV 472; in C, RV 477; in C, RV 479; in D min., RV 481; in F, RV 488; in B flat (La notte), RV 501.
*(*) ASV Dig. CDDCA 662 [id.]. Daniel Smith, ECO, Ledger.

Bassoon concertos: in C, RV 473; in E flat, RV 483; in F, RV 485; in G, RV 492; in A min., RV 497; in B flat, RV 503.
* Ph. Dig. 416 355-2 [id.]. Klaus Thunemann, I Musici.

The bassoon seems to have uncovered a particularly generous fund of inspiration in Vivaldi, for few of his concertos for that instrument are in any way routine and they number almost forty. None of the six recorded on Philips is second rate: they are all inventive, fresh and at times inspired, and Klaus Thunemann and I Musici give most appealing accounts of them. No complaints either about the quality or balance of the Philips recording. Even those not usually responsive to Vivaldi will find these refreshing and original.

Daniel Smith is a genial and personable player and he has considerable facility; even if some of the more complicated roulades are not executed with exact precision, his playing has undoubted flair. He is balanced well forward, but the orchestral accompaniment has plenty of personality and registers well enough. He appears to be working his way steadily through the Vivaldi concertos for his instrument and this (on the second volume, particularly) has led to the juxtaposition of several concertos in the same key, something Thunemann avoids. Even so, this is enjoyably spontaneous music-making, although the concertos should be approached singly, a facility which CD readily provides. The striking work of the third volume is *La notte*, RV 501, which is quite a different piece from the concerto with the same sobriquet for flute and bassoon in G minor. This is a highly original piece, opening with an almost operatic recitative, as if Vivaldi was clearing his throat. Next comes a *Presto* (*Ghosts*), followed by *Sleep* and *Dawn*, all highly evocative in the best *Four Seasons* manner. Smith and Ledger are obviously taken with it and provide an outstandingly characterful performance. Elsewhere the solo playing is spontaneously vigorous and expressive, making up in flair for any final lack of polish. The accompaniments are alert and the recording very lively.

Bassoon concerto in F, RV 485; (i) *Double concerto in G min., for recorder and bassoon (La Notte), RV 104.*
*** BIS Dig. CD 271 [id.]. McGraw, (i) Pehrsson, Drottningholm Bar. Ens. – TELEMANN: *Concertos.****

The concerto subtitled *La Notte* exists in three versions: one for flute (the most familiar), RV 439; another for bassoon, RV 501; and the present version, RV 104. Clas Pehrsson, Michael McGraw and the Drottningholm Baroque Ensemble give a thoroughly splendid account of it, and the *Bassoon concerto in F major* also fares well. Excellent recording.

Cello concertos: in C, RV 398; in G, RV 413.
(M) *** DG 429 098-2 [id.]. Rostropovich, Zurich Coll. Mus., Sacher – BOCCHERINI; TARTINI: *Concertos.****

Performances of great vigour and projection from Rostropovich. The playing is superbly brilliant and immensely strong in character; it may be somewhat large-scale for Vivaldi's two quite short concertos, but undoubtedly every bar comes fully to life. Spendidly lively accompaniments and excellent CD transfers, bright and clean with no lack of depth. Like Tortelier's collection – see below – with which there is no conflict of repertoire, this is for those who primarily care about the communication of joy in great music.

Cello concertos: in C, RV 399; in C min., RV 401; in D min., RV 405; in B flat, RV 423; in F, RV 538; Largo. (i) *Concerto in E min. for cello and bassoon, RV 409.*
*** RCA Dig. RD 87774 [7774-2-RC]. Harnoy, (i) McKay, Toronto CO, Robinson.

Ofra Harnoy's are traditional performances with modern instruments, and none the worse for that; she plays with style, impeccable technique and eloquence: in short, she is a first-class artist with a good lyrical sense. Three of the concertos recorded here are new to the catalogue. One is an arrangement for cello and bassoon of a concerto for two horns. She is given good support from the Toronto Chamber Orchestra under Paul Robinson, and very well recorded.

Cello concertos: in C, RV 400; C min., RV 401; B min., RV 424; (i) for 2 cellos in G min., RV 531; (ii) for violin & 2 cellos in C, RV 561.
(M) *** EMI CDM7 69835-2 [id.]. Paul Tortelier, with (i) Maude Tortelier & (ii) Jacques Manzone; L. Mozart Players, Ledger.

This is one of Tortelier's finest records. The performances here are strong and alive, the slow movements expressive without being over-romanticized. Philip Ledger directs the full-bodied accompanying group and provides a continuo with some flair. The playing is undoubtedly stylish, though the overall effect is not aimed at the 'authentic' lobby, rather at those who seek primarily a warmly understanding response to the composer's inspiration and readily communicated musical enjoyment. The sound is excellent, with the CD remasterings highly successful.

Cello concertos: in C min., RV 402; in D, RV 403; in D min., RV 406; in F, RV 412; in G, RV 414; in A min., RV 422; in B min., RV 424.
*** RCA Dig. RD 60155 [60155-2-RC]. Ofra Harnoy, Toronto CO, Paul Robinson.

There are 27 *Cello concertos*, and the present CD is the second volume in Ofra Harnoy's survey with the Toronto Chamber Orchestra. Her strength lies not so much in her tone, which is not big, but in her selfless approach to this repertoire. She does not regard this music as a vehicle for her own personality but plays it with an agreeable dedication and a delight in its considerable felicities. Again three of the concertos are new to records.

Chamber concertos: in A min., RV 86; in C, RV 87; in D, RV 92 & 95 (La Pastorella); in G, RV 101; in G min., RV 103 & RV 105; in A min., RV 108.
*** Ph. Dig. 411 356-2 (2) [id.]. Petri, Holliger, Ayo, Pellegrino, Jaccottet, Thunemann, Demenga, Rubin.

These are what later generations might have called concertante works, concertos exploiting the interplay of several soloists. They are all given performances of the highest accomplishment and recordings that are natural in both timbre and perspective. As usual, Philips give us warm, excellently focused sound with admirable detail and realism.

Flute concertos: in A min., RV 108; in D, RV 427 & 429; in G, RV 436 & 438; in A min., RV 440.
** RCA Dig. RD 87928. James Galway, I Solisti Veneti, Scimone.

James Galway plays beautifully, of course. He is especially winning in the delightful slow movement of RV 427 and in the infectious finale of the same work. But the forward balance, within a warmly resonant acoustic, means that there is not enough dynamic contrast between the solo instrument and the ripieno, which brings a sense of blandness. Scimone's accompaniments are polished and easy-going rather than ear-grabbing.

Flute concertos in D, RV 427; in D (Il gardellino), RV 428; in D, RV 429; in G, RV 436; in G, RV 438; in A min., RV 440; (i) in C, for 2 flutes, RV 533.
*** HM Dig. HMC 90 5193 [id.]. Janet See, (i) S. Schultz; Philh. Bar. O, McGegan.

Janet See is not only a first-class player but also a real artist whose phrasing is alive and imaginative. Her good musical judgement and taste are matched by a splendid technique and control. Moreover the Philharmonia Baroque Orchestra, a West Coast American group, give her excellent support under Nicholas McGegan, who allows the music to unfold at a natural, unforced pace. Vivaldi also deserves some of the credit for all this, too. The diversity and range of these pieces is astonishing. Highly enjoyable.

Concertos for flute, oboe, violin, bassoon and continuo: in C, RV 88; in D (Il gardellino), RV 90; in D, RV 94; in F, RV 99; in G min., RV 107; Concerto for flute, violin, bassoon and continuo, RV 106.
*** Unicorn Dig. DKPCD 9071 [id.]. Magyer, Francis, Stevens, Jordan, London Harpsichord Ens., Sarah Francis.

A highly engaging group of chamber concertos, suitable for the late evening. Vivaldi's felicitous interplay of wind-colours is ever imaginative. In RV 88, 90 and 106, the flute predominates, while RV 94 creates a partnership between flute and violin; in its central *Largo* the oboe rests while the two main participants recall the slow movement of *Winter* from *The Four Seasons. Il gardellino* (The goldfinch) has similar pictorial evocations to that famous work which are charmingly effective here. The players persuasively work together as a team, creating a most attractive intimacy, and the truthful and well-balanced recording adds to the listener's pleasure in nearly an hour of music in which the composer's invention never flags.

Concertos for flute and strings: in G, RV 435; in F, RV 442; Chamber concertos with flute or recorder: in D (Il Gardellino), RV 90; in F (La Tempesta di mare), RV 98; in G, RV 101; in G min. (La Notte), RV 104.
*** RCA RD 70951 [Pro Arte CCD 229]. Brüggen, O of 18th Century.

An interesting disc. When Vivaldi prepared his set of six concertos, Op. 10, he drew on earlier works (except in the case of the *G major*, RV 435), and on this record Frans Brüggen presents the composer's earlier working of the material. The results are uniformly fresh and delightful and both his solo playing on treble recorder or transverse flute and that of the Orchestra of the 18th Century is remarkably alive and vibrant, completely attuned to the sensibility of the period. Good recording too.

Guitar concertos: in D, RV 93; in A min. (from Op. 3/6), RV 356; in C, RV 425. Double guitar concerto in G, RV 532; Quadruple guitar concerto in B min. (from Op. 3/10), RV 580.
**(*) Ph. Dig. 412 624-2 [id.]. Los Romeros, ASMF, Iona Brown.

Two of these concertos are transcriptions from *L'Estro armonico* and, though they are in themselves pleasing, they are probably more enjoyable in their original form, particularly the slow movements with their sustained melodic lines. The other concertos for lute and mandolin come off excellently. Probably not an issue that would have high priority in a Vivaldi collection, but none the less enjoyable. The *Largo* of RV 93, which ends the programme, is particularly haunting.

Guitar concertos in D, RV 93; in B flat, RV 524; in G min., RV 531; in G, RV 532. Trios: in C, RV 82; in G min., RV 85.
*** DG Dig. 415 487-2 [id.]. Söllscher, Bern Camerata, Füri.

Four of these works are for two mandolins (RV 532) or lute (RV 82, 85, 93), and the other two are for two violins (RV 524) and two cellos (RV 531). Göran Söllscher further enhances his reputation both as a master-guitarist and as an artist on this excellently recorded issue, in which he has first-class support from the Camerata Bern under Thomas

Füri. In RV 532, Söllscher resorts to technology and plays both parts. The DG balance is admirably judged.

Guitar concertos: in C, RV 425; for 2 guitars in G, RV 532; for 4 guitars in D, RV 93; in B min., RV 580 (from L'Estro armonico, Op. 3/10); for guitar, violin, viola & cello in A, RV 82.
(M) ** Ph. 426 076-2 [id.]. Los Romeros, San Antonio SO, Alessandro.

Though their composer did not conceive these works with guitars in mind, they sound quite effective in their present formats. Vivaldi's concertos of this kind are often more enjoyable when grouped in a miscellaneous collection with varying solo timbres. However, guitar and mandolin enthusiasts should find this satisfactory, for the recording is truthful, if a little studio-ish in feeling.

Mandolin concerto in C, RV 425; Double mandolin concerto in G, RV 532; (Soprano) Lute concerto in D, RV 93; Double concerto in D min. for viola d'amore and lute, RV 540. Trios: in C, RV 82; in G min., RV 85.
*** Hyp. CDA 66160 [id.]. Jeffrey, O'Dette, Parley of Instruments, Goodman and Holman.

These are chamber performances, with one instrument to each part, and this obviously provides an ideal balance for the *Mandolin concertos*. There are other innovations, too. An organ continuo replaces the usual harpsichord, and very effective it is; in the *Trios* and the *Lute concerto* (but not in the *Double concerto*, RV 540) Paul O'Dette uses a gut-strung soprano lute. This means that in passages with the lute doubling the violin, the two instruments play in unison and the effect is piquant, with the lute giving a delicate edge to the more sustained string articulation. The delightful sounds here, with all players using original instruments or copies, are very convincing. Certainly the mandolin concertos are more telling (plucked with a plectrum) than they are in guitar transcriptions. The recording is realistically balanced within an attractively spacious acoustic.

Oboe concertos: in C, RV 446 & RV 452; in D min. (from Op. 8), RV 454; in G for oboe and bassoon, RV 545.
*** Ph. Dig. 411 480-2 [id.]. Holliger, Thunemann, I Musici.

Holliger is in superb form, matching his expressive flexibility with infectious bravura in allegros and providing nicely judged ornamentation. All the music is attractively inventive, especially the *Double concerto for oboe and bassoon*, which is nicely scored and has a memorable slow movement. The recording is balanced most realistically.

Recorder concertos: in C min., RV 441; in F, RV 442; in C, RV 443 & RV 444; in A min., RV 445.
*** DG Dig. 415 275-2 [id.]. Copley, Bern Camerata, Füri.

The first two concertos (RV 441–2) are for alto recorder and strings, the remaining three are for an instrument Vivaldi called the *flautino*, which the majority of expert opinion believes to be the sopranino recorder. This plays an octave above the alto recorder. The music is not to be taken at one sitting but, as always with this composer, one is often taken by surprise by the quality and range of the invention. These performances by Michael Copley and the Camerata Bern lack nothing in virtuosity and dash; and the recording is excellent in every way, well balanced and truthful in perspective.

Concertos for strings: in D, RV 121; in D min., RV 127; in E min., RV 133; in F, RV 142; in G, RV 145; in G, RV 151; in G min., RV 152; in A min., RV 161; in B flat, RV 166.
*** Ph. 411 035-2 [id.]. I Musici.

There are nine string concertos on this excellent anthology. Although Vivaldi is often thought to be routine, more often than not he is unpredictable and one is surprised by the freshness of his inspiration. The present disc is one such case and finds I Musici in excellent form.

6 Viola d'amore concertos, RV 392/7.
**(*) Ph. Dig. 422 051-2 [id.]. Massimo Paris, I Musici.

The viola d'amore was a six-stringed instrument with six sympathetic strings under the fingerboard. The instrument must have struck a responsive chord in Vivaldi, as these are imaginative works. Massimo Paris is the fine soloist and plays on a 1748 Florentine instrument by Lorenzo Carcassi with an original Baroque bow. I Musici give bright and lively support on the whole and produce a rich, full-bodied sonority. There is perhaps a touch of routine about their playing, but nevertheless this is an enjoyable and excellently recorded disc.

Violin concertos: L'Estro armonico: in A min., Op. 3/6; La Stravaganza: in A, Op. 4/5; in C min. (Il Sospetto), RV 199; in G min., Op. 12/1.
**(*) EMI Dig. CDC7 47076-2 [id.]. Perlman, Israel PO.

Virtuoso performances of a representative set of Vivaldi violin concertos, given with Perlman's customary aplomb and effortless virtuosity. He scales down the virtuoso display, and those who want sweet, modern string-tone and warmth in the slow movements need look no further. The string playing of the Israel Philharmonic is expressive without becoming overladen with sentiment. The only handicap is the somewhat dryish acoustic.

Violin concertos: in C min. (Il sospetto), RV 199; in D (L'inquietudine), RV 234; in E (Il riposo), RV 270; in E (L'amoroso), RV 271; in E min. (Il favorito), RV 277.
(M) **(*) Ph. 422 493-2 [id.]. Vicari, Gallozi, Cotogni, Ayo, Michelucci, I Musici.

Recorded in 1958 and still sounding well (though the attempt to clarify the warmly resonant sound has brought a minor loss of refinement in tuttis), this attractive collection of five named violin concertos features five different soloists, all of them members of I Musici. The style of Vivaldi performances has generally grown more subtle since this record was made, but it is still attractive, a fair medium-price issue with reasonable sound.

Violin concertos: in D min. for 2 violins and cello, RV 565, Op. 3/11; in E flat (La tempesta di mare), RV 253; in C (Il piacere), RV 180, Op. 8/5 – 6; in E (L'amoroso), RV 271; in A min. for 2 violins, RV 523; in F for 3 violins, RV 551.
(B) *** RCA Dig. VD 87741. Fontanarosa, Agostini, Vernikov, Filippini, I Nuovi Virtuosi di Roma.

I Nuovi Virtuosi di Roma use modern instruments but are recorded in a drier acoustic than that usually afforded to their illustrious colleagues, I Musici, on Philips; the rather more athletic style of their playing brings brighter and quite sharply defined textures, which will appeal to ears already weaned on authenticity. There is certainly no lack of expressive feeling in the *Cantabile* slow movement of *L'amoroso* or indeed in the memorable *Largo e spiccato* of Op. 3, No. 11, while the clean articulation of the accompanying group is striking in the spirited finale of the former work, and indeed in the fugato which closes the first movement of the latter. All the soloists are drawn from the group itself, and the overall standard of playing is high. At bargain price and with modern digital sound, this is excellent value, with a playing time of just over an hour.

Triple concerto for 2 violins and cello in C min. (San Lorenzo), RV 556.
(*) ASV Dig. CDCOE 803 [id.]. COE, Schneider – BACH: *Double concerto*; MOZART: *Sinfonia concertante.*(*)

Vivaldi's *San Lorenzo concerto* for two violins and cello makes an attractive makeweight for the two other multiple concertos on the Chamber Orchestra of Europe's disc. In a performance recorded live at St John's, Smith Square, the outer movements are inflated in scale but bring winningly resilient playing.

Double concerto for violin and oboe in G min., RV 576; Violin concerto in D (per la S.S.ma Assontione di Maria Vergine), RV 582.
(*) Ph. Dig. 411 466-2 [id.]. Holliger, Kremer, ASMF – BACH: *Double concerto* and *Sinfonia.**

As in the Bach coupling, Holliger dominates the performance of the *Double concerto*, especially in the slow movement where Kremer's timbre is less expressively expansive. But Kremer comes into his own in the delightful *D major concerto*, showing Vivaldi at his most inspired and imaginative. This features a double orchestra in the accompaniment, sometimes used antiphonally, and, although the effects are brought off well here, the stereo separation is not as clear as might have been expected. Otherwise the sound, clear and resonant, is finely judged; Kremer's sparkling articulation in the allegros is balanced by his serenely beautiful playing in the delicate cantilena of the central *Largo*.

MISCELLANEOUS CONCERTO COLLECTIONS

Bassoon concerto in A min., RV 498; Cello concerto in C min., RV 401; Oboe concerto in F, RV 455; Concerto for strings in A, RV 158; Violin concerto in E min., RV 278; Concerto for 2 violins and 2 cellos, RV 575.
*** Novalis Dig. 150 016-21 [id.]. Camerata Bern.

The majority of the concertos on this disc are not otherwise available, and most of them are highly inventive. The Camerata Bern is an excellent ensemble, playing on modern instruments with great expertise and a sure sense of style. There is some particularly good playing from the bassoon soloist in the *A minor Concerto*, RV 498; but throughout the disc there is much to divert and delight the listener, and there is no cause for complaint so far as the recording is concerned.

Bassoon concerto in A min., RV 498; Flute concerto in C min., RV 441; Oboe concerto in F, RV456; Concerto for 2 oboes in D min., RV 535; Concerto for 2 oboes, bassoon, 2 horns and violin in F, RV 574; Piccolo concerto in C, RV 444.
(M) *** Decca 417 777-2 [id.]. ASMF, Marriner.

The playing here is splendidly alive and characterful, with crisp, clean articulation and well-pointed phrasing, free from overemphasis. The *A minor Bassoon concerto* has a delightful sense of humour. Altogether the musical substance may not be very weighty; but Vivaldi was rarely more engaging than when, as here, he was writing for wind instruments, particularly if he had more than one in his team of soloists. Well-balanced and vivid recording; this is highly recommendable for all those who do not insist on original instruments in this repertoire. The recordings were made in 1976/7 and have been transferred to CD with pleasing freshness.

Basson concerto in E min., RV 484; Flute concerto in G, RV 436; Concerto for oboe and bassoon in G, RV 545; Concerto for strings in A, RV 159; Concerto for viola d'amore and lute in D min., RV 540; Violin concerto in E (L'Amoroso), RV 271.
*** DG Dig. 419 615-2 [id.]. Soloists, E. Concert, Pinnock.

Entitled 'L'Amoroso' after the fine *E major Violin concerto* which is one of the six varied concertos on the disc, this collection brings lively, refreshing performances with fine solo playing from wind and string players alike, using period instruments in the most enticing way. The *Concerto for oboe and bassoon* is particularly engaging. The recording is well balanced within a pleasingly warm acoustic.

Cello concerto in B min., RV 424; Oboe concerto in A min., RV 461; Double concerto in C min. for oboe and violin, RV Anh. 17; Violin concerto in D, RV 208; Sinfonia in B min., RV 169; Sonata à 4 in E flat for 2 violins, viola and continuo, RV 130.
(M) ** Teldec/WEA 2292 43436-2 [id.]. Soloists, Concerto Amsterdam, Schröder.

There is an element of too much rectitude here, and the forward balance seems to emphasize the somewhat stiff approach, although allegros are alert and lively. The recording readily captures the robust and somewhat plangent timbres, and those who favour Vivaldi played on baroque instruments will certainly find the sound faithful; the digital remastering is clean without loss of ambience, and the 1978 analogue recording sounds quite modern.

Concerto in G min. for 2 cellos, RV 531; Flute concerto in C min., RV 441; Concerto in G min., for flute and bassoon (La notte), RV 104; Concerto in F for flute, oboe and bassoon (La Tempesta di mare), RV 570; Guitar concerto in D, RV 93; Concerto in F for 2 horns, RV 539; Concerto in B flat for violin and cello, RV 547.
*** ASV Dig. CDDCA 645 [id.]. Soloists, ECO, Malcolm.

With George Malcolm in charge it is not surprising that this 65-minute collection of seven diverse concertos is as entertaining as any in the catalogue. *La Tempesta di mare* has plenty of descriptive energy, with the interplay of flute (William Bennett), oboe (Neil Black) and the genial bassoon of Robin O'Neill bringing an attractive range of colour. The ear is struck by the spacious acoustic at the opening of the work for violin and cello, RV 547, while the more intimate *Guitar concerto* makes a nice contrast. The pair of horns (Frank Lloyd and Tony Chidell) sound gloriously robust in sonority in RV 539, while William Bennett chirps cheekily in his bird-like decorations of the solo line in the *C minor Flute concerto*. Perhaps most striking of all is the *Double cello concerto*, vigorously energetic in outer movements, but with a short, serene central *Largo*, with overlapping phrases at the beginning, to remind one of the slow movement of Bach's *Double violin concerto*. The concert ends with the duet version of *La notte*, which has much to charm the ear. Accompaniments are sympathetic and stylish, and the whole programme beams with vitality and conveyed enjoyment. The digital sound is vivid and realistic.

Double concertos: for 2 cellos in G min., RV 531; 2 flutes in C, RV 533; 2 oboes in D min., RV 535; 2 mandolins in G, RV 532; 2 trumpets in C, RV 537; 2 violins, RV 523.
(M) *** Ph. 426 086-2 [id.]. I Musici.

This makes an attractively diverse collection. Most of these concertos are admirably inventive and the performances show I Musici at their very best, on sparkling form. The sound is good too.

Double cello concerto in G min., RV 531; Double flute concerto in C, RV 533; Concertos for strings in D min. (Madrigalesco), RV 129; in G (Alla rustica), RV 151; Double trumpet concerto in C, RV 537; Concerto for 2 violins and 2 cellos in D, RV 564.
*** O-L 414 588-2 [id.]. AAM, Hogwood.

Not everything in this issue is of equal substance: the invention in the *Double trumpet concerto*, for example, is not particularly strong; but for the most part it is a rewarding and varied programme. It is especially appealing in that authenticity is allied to musical spontaneity. The *Concerto for two flutes* has great charm and is dispatched with vigour and aplomb. Performances and recording alike are first rate, with added clarity and presence on CD.

Concertos for 2 cellos in G min., RV 531; 2 mandolins in G, RV 532; recorder in C min., RV 441; C, RV 443; Trio for violin, lute & continuo in G min., RV 85.
(M) *** DG Dig. 427 824-2 [id.]. Demenga, Häusler, Söllscher, Copley, Camerata Bern, Füri.

An excellent mid-priced digital collection, assembled from various records made by the Camerata Bern, which will especially suit those who like their Vivaldi on original instruments. Söllscher's account of the *Duet concerto* for mandolins (in which he takes both solo roles) is quite outstanding, and there is some breathtaking virtuosity from Michael Copley in the *Recorder concerto*. Further variety is provided by the *Trio* which is also an attractive work. The well-balanced recording has splendid presence and realism.

(i) Flute concerto in F (La Tempesta di mare), Op. 10/1; (ii) Oboe concertos: in C (from Op. 8/12), RV 449; in D min., RV 454; (i) Recorder concerto in C, RV 444; Concertos for strings: in D min., RV 127; in A, RV 158.
**(*) Chan. Dig. CHAN 8444 [id.]. (i) Hutchins, (ii) Baskin; I Musici di Montreal, Turovsky.

I Musici di Montreal are recorded in the resonant acoustic of St Madeleine's Church, Montreal, and the balance produces a fresh, bright sound from the fourteen strings, just a shade lacking in body. Their spirited musicianship brings plenty of life to the two attractive string concertos, while the rather beautiful *Largo* of the *A major*, RV 158, enjoys a nicely judged, expressive response. The programme opens buoyantly with Timothy Hutchins's brilliant account of *La Tempesta di mare*, expertly presented on a sopranino recorder; but the highlight of the concert is the pair of oboe concertos, beautifully played by Theodore Baskin. Like Hutchins, he is a principal of the Montreal Symphony. The recording places him realistically in relation to the accompaniment; allowing for the reverberation, the sound is first class.

Flute concerto in G min. (La Notte), Op. 10/2, RV 439; Concertos for strings: in D min. (Madrigalesco), RV 129; in G (Alla rustica), RV 151; Violin concertos: in D (L'Inquietudine), RV 234; in E (L'Amoroso), RV 271; Double violin concerto in A, RV 523; Sinfonia in B min. (Al Santo Sepolcro), RV 169.
(B) **(*) DG 429 167-2 [id.]. Soloists, BPO, Karajan.

This collection dates from 1971 (except for the *Flute concerto*, which was recorded a decade later) and shows Karajan indulging himself in repertoire which he clearly loves but for which he does not have the stylistic credentials. Yet the sheer charisma of the playing and the glorious body of tone the orchestra creates within a resonant acoustic, notably in the extraordinary *Sinfonia al Santo Sepolcro*, is difficult to resist. The orchestra dominates even the solo concertos and the soloists seem to float, concertante style, within the resonantly glowing ambience.

Double flute concerto in C, RV 533; Double oboe concerto in D min., RV 535; Double horn concerto in F, RV 539; Double trumpet concerto in C, RV 537; Concerto for 2 oboes, 2 clarinets and strings, RV 560.
(B) **(*) Pickwick Dig. PCD 811 [MCA MCAD 25960]. Soloists, Scottish CO, Laredo.

An attractive bargain-priced compilation, with soloists and orchestra set back in good perspective in a believable acoustic. The resonance tends to make the trumpet timbre spread, but otherwise the sound is very good. The solo playing is accomplished, although rather more light and shade between phrases would have made the performances even more enticing, while Jaime Laredo's direction of the slow movements is not especially imaginative.

Double flute concerto in C, RV 533; Double horn concerto in F, RV 539; Double mandolin concerto in G, RV 536; Double oboe concerto in A min., RV 536; Concerto for oboe and bassoon in G, RV 545; Double trumpet concerto in D, RV 563.
*** Ph. Dig. 412 892-2 [id.]. Soloists, ASMF, Marriner.

Apart from the work for two horns, where the focus of the soloists lacks a degree of sharpness, the recording often reaches demonstration standard. On CD, the concerto featuring a pair of mandolins is particularly tangible, with the balance near perfect, the solo instruments in proper scale yet registering admirable detail. The concertos for flutes and oboes are played with engaging finesse, conveying a sense of joy in the felicity of the writing. Throughout, the accompaniments are characteristically polished and especially imaginative in their use of light and shade in alternating phrases. Once again Marriner makes a very good case for the use of modern wind instruments in this repertoire.

Concerto in C for 2 flutes, 2 salmò, 2 violins 'in tromba marina', 2 mandolins, 2 theorbos, cello & strings, RV 558; Guitar concerto in D, RV 93; Mandolin concerto in C, RV 425; Double mandolin concerto in G, RV 532; Concerto for viola d'amore and guitar, RV 540.
(B) ** DG 429 528-2 [id.]. Yepes, Takashi, Ochi, Fransca-Colombier. Paul Kuentz CO, Kuentz.

An intimate programme, suitable for the late evening, given mellow recording which is retained in the CD transfer. The *Mandolin concertos* are beautifully recorded, the miniature imagery of the solo instruments truthfully captured in relation to the orchestra. The *Duet concerto* has a gentle charm. RV 93 and RV 540 were intended for lute rather than guitar, but Yepes is persuasive here, particularly in the memorable *Largo* of the latter piece. The concertante work rounds off the programme with a burst of colour. A pleasant rather than a distinctive concert.

Double mandolin concerto in G, RV 532; Oboe concertos: in A min., RV 461; in B flat, RV 548; Concertos for strings: in G (Alla rustica), RV 151; in C (con molti stromenti), RV 558; Double violin concerto in G, RV 516.
*** DG Dig. 415 674-2 [id.]. Soloists, E. Concert, Pinnock.

This collection of six varied Vivaldi concertos finds Pinnock and the English Concert at their liveliest and most refreshing. Outstanding in a nicely balanced programme is the *C major Concerto*, RV 558, involving an astonishing array of concertino instruments, including two violins (curiously labelled *in tromba marina*) and pairs of recorders, mandolins and theorbos, plus one cello. Excellent recording, giving a most realistic impression on CD.

Double concerto for oboe and violin in B flat, RV 548; Triple concerto in C for violin, oboe and organ, RV 554; Double concertos for violin and organ: in D min., RV 541; in C min. & F, RV 766–7.
*** Unicorn Dig. DKPCD 9050 [id.]. Francis, Studt, Bate, Tate Music Group, Studt.

An engaging clutch of concertos, two of which (RV 766–7) are first recordings. The works featuring the organ in a concertante role are in the concerto grosso tradition and are notable for their imaginative juxtaposition of colours – which is not to say that they lack vitality of invention. The recording is very attractive in ambience and the balance is admirable, with the sound first class.

Concertos for strings: in D min. (Concerto madrigalesco), RV 129; in G (Alla rustica), RV 151; in G min., RV 157. (i) Motet: *In turbato mare irato, RV 627;* Cantata: *Lungi dal vago volto, RV 680. Magnificat, RV 610.*
*** Hyp. Dig. CDA 66247 [id.]. (i) Kirkby, Leblanc, Forget, Cunningham, Ingram, Tafelmusik Ch. & Bar. O, Lamon.

Mingling vocal and instrumental items, and works both well-known and unfamiliar, Jean Lamon provides a delightful collection, with Emma Kirkby a sparkling, pure-toned soloist in two items never recorded before: the motet, *In turbato mare irato,* and the chamber cantata, *Lungi dal vago volto.* The performance is lively, with fresh choral sound. The Tafelmusik performers come from Canada, and though the use of period instruments has some roughness, their vigour and alertness amply make up for that. Good, clear recorded sound.

CHAMBER AND INSTRUMENTAL MUSIC

Cello sonatas Nos. 1–9, RV 39/47.
*** CRD Dig. CRD 3440 [id.] (*Nos. 1–4*); CRD 3441 [id.] (*Nos. 5–9*). L'École d'Orphée.

Cello sonatas Nos. 1–6, RV 40–41, 43, 45–7.
*** O-L Dig. 421 060-2 [id.]. Christophe Coin, Hogwood, Zweistra, Ferre, Finucane.

All nine *Sonatas* are given highly musical performances on CRD; they do not set out to impress by grand gestures but succeed in doing so by their dedication and sensitivity. Susan Sheppard is a thoughtful player and is well supported by her continuo team, Lucy Carolan and Jane Coe. The CRD recording is well focused and very present.

On Oiseau-Lyre, Coin and Hogwood offer only six of the nine *Sonatas*: the half-dozen that were collected together and published in 1740, towards the end of Vivaldi's life, as Op. 14. Compared to the CRD version, Coin is the more authoritative player, whose technique is effortless, and the continuo support is more varied in colour. In addition to Christopher Hogwood's harpsichord, there is baroque guitar and an archlute to lend a diversity of colour and texture that is most welcome. The Oiseau-Lyre sound is excellent.

VOCAL MUSIC

Beatus vir, RV 597; Credo, RV 592; Magnificat, RV 610.
(M) *** Ph. 420 651-2 [id.]. Soloists, Alldis Ch., ECO, Negri.

Beatus vir, RV 598; Dixit Dominus in D, RV 594; Introduzione al Dixit: Canta in prato in G, RV 636 (ed. Geigling); *Magnificat in G min., RV 611* (ed. Negri).
(M) *** Ph. 420 649-2 [id.]. Lott, Burgess, Murray, Daniels, Finnie, Collins, Rolfe-Johnson, Holl, Alldis Ch., ECO, Negri.

Crediti propter quod, RV 105; Credo, RV 591; Introduction to Gloria, RV 639; Gloria, RV 588; Kyrie, RV 587; Laetatus sum, RV 607.
(M) *** Ph. 420 650-2 [id.]. M. Marshall, Lott, Finnie, Rolfe-Johnson, Alldis Ch., ECO, Negri.

Dixit dominus, RV 595; In exitu Israel, RV 604; Sacrum, RV 586.
(M) *** Ph. 420 652-2 [id.]. Alldis Ch., ECO, Negri.

Introduction to Gloria, RV 642; Gloria in D, RV 589; Lauda Jerusalem in E min., RV 609; Laudate Dominum in D min., RV 606; Laudati pueri Dominum in A, RV 602.
(M) *** Ph. 420 648-2 [id.]. Marshall, Lott, Collins, Finnilä, Alldis Ch., ECO, Negri.

These recordings come from the late 1970s. Vittorio Negri does not make use of period instruments, but he penetrates as deeply into the spirit of this music as many who do. When they first appeared, we found them lively, stylish performances, beautifully recorded – and they come up splendidly in their new format, digitally refurbished. Any lover of Vivaldi is likely to be astonished that not only the well-known works but the rarities show him writing with the keenest originality and intensity. There is nothing routine about any of this music, or any of the performances either.

Beatus vir, RV 597; Dixit dominus, RV 594.
*** Argo Dig. 414 495-2 [id.]. Buchanan, Jennifer Smith, Watts, Partridge, Shirley-Quirk, King's College Ch., ECO, Cleobury.

Dixit dominus cannot fail to attract those who have enjoyed the better-known *Gloria*. Both works are powerfully inspired and are here given vigorous and sparkling performances with King's College Choir in excellent form under its latest choirmaster. The soloists are a fine team, fresh, stylish and nimble, and the reverberant recording remains atmospheric, without detail becoming clouded. There is plenty of clean articulation from the choristers, nicely projected in the CD format with its extra sharpness of definition.

Dixit dominus, RV 594; Gloria in D, RV 589.
*** DG Dig. 423 386-2 [id.]. Argenta, Attrot, Denley, Stafford, Varcoe, E. Concert & Ch., Pinnock.

Pinnock's versions of the better-known of Vivaldi's two settings of the *Gloria* and the grander of his two settings of the psalm, *Dixit dominus* (the one for double chorus), make an attractive and strong coupling. His fresh, vigorous performances, beautifully recorded, add impressively to his developing reputation as a choral conductor on record, with first-rate playing and singing.

Gloria in D, RV 589.
*** O-L 414 678-2 [id.]. Nelson, Kirkby, Watkinson, Christ Church Cathedral Ch., AAM, Preston – BACH: *Magnificat.****
*** DG Dig. 423 386-2 [id.]. Argenta, Attrot, Denley, Ch. & E. Concert, Pinnock – A. SCARLATTI: *Dixit Dominus.****
(M) *** Decca 421 146-2. Vaughan, J. Baker, King's College, Cambridge, Ch., ASMF, Willcocks – HAYDN: *Nelson Mass.****

The freshness and point of the Christ Church performance of the *Gloria* are irresistible; anyone who normally doubts the attractiveness of authentic string technique should sample this, for the absence of vibrato adds a tang exactly in keeping with the performance. The soloists too keep vibrato to the minimum, adding to the freshness, yet

Carolyn Watkinson rivals even Dame Janet Baker in the dark intensity of the Bach-like central aria for contralto, *Domine Deus, Agnus Dei*. The choristers of Christ Church Cathedral excel themselves, and the recording is outstandingly fine.

Trevor Pinnock directs a bright, refreshing account of the grander and better known of Vivaldi's *Gloria* settings, with excellent playing and singing from the members of the English Concert. Unlike many advocates of period performance, Pinnock is not afraid to give spacious treatment to slow and reflective movements, bringing out the marked contrasts between the twelve movements. Unusually but attractively coupled with the rare Scarlatti setting of *Dixit Dominus*, and very well recorded, it makes a first-rate recommendation.

The CD remastering of the stylish 1962 Willcocks recording of Vivaldi's *Gloria* is strikingly vivid and, with excellent choral and solo singing, this makes a fine and generous bonus for the Haydn *Nelson Mass*.

Gloria in D, RV 588; Gloria in D, RV 589.
*** Argo Dig. 410 018-2 [id.]. Russell, Kwella, Wilkens, Bowen, St John's College, Cambridge, Ch., Wren O, Guest.

The two settings of the *Gloria* make an apt and illuminating coupling. Both in D major, they have many points in common, presenting fascinating comparisons, when RV 588 is as inspired as its better-known companion. Guest directs strong and well-paced readings, with RV 588 the more lively. Good, warm recording to match the performances.

Gloria in D, RV 589; Kyrie, RV 587 and Credo, R 591; Magnificat, RV 610.
*** Erato/WEA 2292 45122-2 [id.]. Jennifer Smith, Staempfli, Rossier, Schaer, Lausanne Vocal & Instrumental Ens., Corboz.

Michel Corboz, a fine choral conductor, gives a lively performance of the *Gloria*, and his version is aptly coupled with three other richly rewarding liturgical settings by Vivaldi. The *Magnificat* is given in its simpler first version on a relatively small scale, with the chorus singing the alto solo, *Fecit potentiam*. The *Kyrie* with its double chorus and double string orchestra, plus four soloists, makes a fine contrast in its magnificence. The professional singers of the Lausanne choir are generally admirable, and the soloists are sweet-toned. Good, clear recording.

Laudate pueri dominum, RV 601; Nisi Dominus, RV 608.
*** Mer. Dig. CDE 84129 [id.]. Lynne Dawson, Christopher Robson, King's Consort, Robert King.

The present setting of Psalm 113, RV 601, is a strong work whose inspiration runs at a consistently high level; Lynne Dawson sings with an excellent sense of style and is given splendid support. The coupling, the *Nisi Dominus*, a setting of Psalm 126, is much better known but makes an attractive makeweight. It is also given an excellent performance by Christopher Robson. Good recording.

(i) *Nisi Dominus (Psalm 126), RV 608; Stabat Mater, RV 621; Concerto for strings in G min., RV 153.*
**(*) O-L Dig. 414 329-2 [id.]. AAM, Hogwood; (i) with Bowman.

These performances are vital enough and there is no want of stylistic awareness. James Bowman is a persuasive soloist. The *Concerto* is an engaging work whose charms benefit from the authentic instruments. The CD is altogether excellent; the sound is marvellously fresh and present.

OPERA

L'Incoronazione di Dario (complete).
** HM Dig. HMC 901235/7 [id.]. Elwes, Lesne, Ledroit, Verschaeve, Poulenard, Mellon, Visse, Nice Bar. Ens., Bezzina.

Vivaldi's opera here receives a lively performance, generally well sung. John Elwes as Darius himself, though stylish, does not sound as involved as some of the others, notably the male alto, Dominique Visse, who is superb both vocally and dramatically as the female confidante, Flora. Reliable singing from the whole cast, and first-rate recording. The full libretto is provided only in Italian, with translated summaries of the plot in English, French and German.

L'Olimpiade: highlights.
(BB) **(*) Hung. White Label HRC 078 [id.]. Kováts, Takács, Zempleni, Miller, Horvath, Kaplan, Gati, Budapest Madrigal Ch., Hungarian State O, Szekeres.

In the very inexpensive White Label series of Hungaroton recordings, a generous collection of highlights from Vivaldi's opera, *L'Olimpiade*, is well worth investigating. An early delight in this selection is the work's most attention-grabbing number, a choral version of what we know as *Spring* from *The Four Seasons*. Ferenc Szekeres' conducting of the Hungarian State Orchestra is too heavy by today's standards, now that we are attuned to period performance, but the singing of soloists and choir is good, and the recording is brightly focused, with clean directional effects.

Orlando Furioso (complete).
*** Erato/WEA 2292 45147-2 (3) [id.]. Horne, De los Angeles, Valentini Terrani, Gonzales, Kozma, Bruscantini, Zaccaria, Sol. Ven., Scimone.

Scimone has heavily rearranged the order of items as well as cutting many, but, with stylish playing and excellent recording, it is a set well worth a Vivaldi enthusiast's attention. Outstanding in a surprisingly star-studded cast is Marilyn Horne in the title-role, rich and firm of tone, articulating superbly in divisions, notably in the hero's two fiery arias. In the role of Angelica, Victoria de los Angeles has many sweetly lyrical moments, and though Lucia Valentini Terrani is less strong as Alcina, she gives an aptly clean, precise performance. The remastering has somewhat freshened a recording which was not outstanding in its analogue LP form.

Wagenseil, George (1715–77)

Harp concerto in G.
(B) *** DG 427 206-2 [id.]. Zabaleta, Paul Kuentz CO – HANDEL: *Harp concerto*; MOZART: *Flute and harp concerto*.***

Wagenseil's *Harp concerto* is a pleasant example of the *galant* style; the felicity of the writing in the first two movements is capped by a very jolly finale. Both performance and recording here can be commended and the remastering is fresh and clear.

Wagner, Richard (1813–83)

Siegfried idyll.
*** DG 419 196-2 (2) [id.]. BPO, Karajan – BRUCKNER: *Symphony No. 8*.***
*** Decca Dig. 410 111-2 [id.]. ECO, Ashkenazy – SCHOENBERG: *Verklaerte Nacht*.**(*)

*** Ph. 412 465-2 (2) [id.]. Concg. O, Haitink – BRUCKNER: *Symphony No. 8.****
(B) *** Pickwick Dig. PCD 928. SCO, Jaime Laredo – DVOŘÁK: *String serenade* etc.***
(M) **(*) EMI CMS7 63277-2 (2) [id.]. Philh. O, Klemperer – MAHLER: *Symphony No. 9.****

Karajan's account of Wagner's wonderful birthday present to Cosima is unsurpassed and is available, coupled with Bruckner's *Eighth*. Ashkenazy makes a fine alternative, its flow of melodies and textures caressing the ear. Warm, full recording to match the playing. Haitink gives a simple, unaffected reading and draws playing of great refinement from the Concertgebouw Orchestra. Like Karajan's version, this has a simplicity of expression and a tenderness that will leave few listeners unmoved.

A beautiful performance too, from Jaime Laredo and the Scottish Chamber Orchestra, warm and poised and ending serenely, yet moving to a strong central climax. The recording, made in Glasgow City Hall, has a pleasingly expansive ambience, yet textures are clear.

Klemperer favours the original chamber-orchestra scoring and the Philharmonia players are very persuasive, especially in the score's gentler moments. However, the balance is forward and, although the sound is warm, the ear craves a greater breadth of string tone at the climax.

Siegfried idyll. Der fliegende Holländer: Overture. Lohengrin: Preludes to Acts I and III. Die Meistersinger: Overture.
*** DG Dig. 419 169-2 [id.]. NYPO, Sinopoli.

Superbly spacious performances from Sinopoli, with *Der fliegende Holländer* seeming less melodramatic than usual, yet played with free rubato in the most effective way. The emotional arch of the *Lohengrin* Act I *Prelude* is superbly graduated, with the New York violins finding radiant tone for the closing pianissimo. *Die Meistersinger* is massively stately. Sinopoli opens and closes the *Siegfried idyll* with the greatest delicacy, and the end is wonderfully serene and romantic; the middle section is fast and volatile, moving to its climax with passionate thrust.

Siegfried idyll. Der fliegende Holländer: Overture. Lohengrin: Prelude to Act I. Die Meistersinger: Overture. (i) *Tannhäuser: Overture and Venusberg music.*
(M) *** CBS MPK 45701 [id.]. Columbia SO, Bruno Walter, (i) with Occidental College Ch.

Bruno Walter draws a lovingly warm account of the *Siegfried idyll* from his players, and the poise of the opening of the *Pilgrims' chorus* is equally full of quiet tension, while the reprise of this famous melody, before the introduction of the Venusberg section, is wonderfully gentle. With the central section thrillingly sensuous, the closing pages – the Occidental College Choir distantly balanced – bring a radiant hush. In digitally remastered form, the recording is most impressive. The detail in the fugato middle section of *Die Meistersinger* is characteristically affectionate, and all the threads are satisfyingly drawn together in the expansive closing pages. The *Lohengrin Prelude* is rather relaxed, but beautifully controlled. With fine orchestral playing throughout, this stands among the most rewarding of all available compilations of Wagnerian orchestral excerpts.

Siegfried idyll. Lohengrin: Preludes to Acts I and III. Die Meistersinger: Prelude to Act I. Parsifal: Prelude to Act I. Tristan und Isolde: Prelude and Liebestod.
(M) *** Ph. 420 886-2 [id.]. Concg. O, Haitink.

The addition of Haitink's simple, unaffected reading of the *Siegfried idyll* to his 1975 collection of *Preludes* enhances the appeal of a particularly attractive concert. The rich acoustics of the Concertgebouw are surely ideal for *Die Meistersinger*, given a memorably spacious performance, and Haitink's restraint adds to the noble dignity of *Parsifal*. The *Lohengrin* excerpts are splendidly played. The digital remastering is almost entirely beneficial.

Siegfried idyll. Lohengrin: Prelude to Acts I & III. Die Meistersinger: Overture. Die Walküre: Ride of the Valkyries; (i) *Wotan's farewell and Magic fire music.*
*** ASV Dig. CDDCA 666 [id.]. Philh. O, Francesco d'Avalos, (i) with John Tomlinson.

Francesco d'Avalos may not be a Furtwängler, but his pacing of this attractively assembled Wagner concert is most convincing. The opening *Siegfried idyll* has all the requisite serenity and atmosphere; here, as elsewhere, the Philharmonia play most beautifully. The boldly sumptuous recording brings a thrilling resonance and amplitude to the brass, especially trombones and tuba, and in the expansive *Meistersinger overture*, and again in *Wotan's farewell* the brass entries bring a physical frisson. John Tomlinson's noble assumption of the role of Wotan, as he bids a loving farewell to his errant daughter, is very moving here, and the response of the Philharmonia strings matches the depth of feeling he conveys. With the Valkyries also given a splendid sense of spectacle, this collection should have a wide appeal.

Siegfried idyll. Tannhäuser: overture. (i) *Tristan: Prelude and Liebestod.*
*** DG Dig. 423 613-2 [id.]. (i) Jessye Norman; VPO, Karajan.

This superb Wagner record was taken live from a unique concert conducted by Karajan at the Salzburg Festival in August 1987. The *Tannhäuser overture* has never sounded so noble, and the *Siegfried idyll* has rarely seemed so intense and dedicated behind its sweet lyricism; while the *Prelude and Liebestod*, with Jessye Norman as soloist, bring the richest culmination, sensuous and passionate, but remarkable as much for the hushed, inward moments as for the ineluctable building of climaxes. The recording gives little or no idea of a live occasion, thanks to rather close balance, but the glow of the Vienna Philharmonic at its peak is beautifully captured.

Siegfried idyll. Tristan und Isolde: Prelude and Liebestod. Die Walküre: (i) *Act I, scene iii; Act II: Ride of the Valkyries.*
(***) RCA mono RD 84751 [RCA 5751-2-RC]. (i) Helen Traubel, Lauritz Melchior; NBC SO, Toscanini.

It is sad that Toscanini never recorded a Wagner opera complete. Despite harsh, limited, mono recording, this CD makes it clear just how incandescent were the Toscanini performances of Wagner and how, with his ear for balance, he brought brightness and transparency to the scores.

ORCHESTRAL EXCERPTS FROM THE OPERAS

Der fliegende Holländer: Overture. Die Meistersinger: Overture. (i) *Tannhäuser: Overture and Venusberg music. Tristan: Prelude and Liebestod.*
(M) *** EMI CDM7 69019-2 [id.]. BPO, Karajan; (i) with German Op. Ch.

All the music here is played excellently, but the *Overture and Venusberg music* from *Tannhäuser* (Paris version, using chorus) and the *Prelude and Liebestod* from *Tristan* are superb. In the *Liebestod* the climactic culmination is overwhelming in its sentient power, while *Tannhäuser* has comparable spaciousness and grip. There is an urgency and edge to

The Flying Dutchman overture, and *Die Meistersinger* has weight and dignity, but the last degree of tension is missing. Moreover the digitally remastered sound produces a touch of fierceness in the upper range of these pieces; the *Tannhäuser* and *Tristan* excerpts are fuller, though some of the original bloom has gone.

Der fliegende Holländer: Overture. Die Meistersinger: Overture. Tristan und Isolde: Preludes, Acts I & III; Liebestod. Die Walküre: Ride of the Valkyries.
(M) * DG Dig. 427 825-2 [id.]. O de Paris, Daniel Barenboim.

Barenboim's collection does not lack intensity, but the snag is that the Orchestre de Paris – particularly the brass section, with its excessive vibrato – does not sound authentic and the recording acoustic is not helpful, failing to give the necessary resonance to the deeper brass sounds.

Götterdämmerung: Dawn and Siegfried's Rhine journey; Funeral march. Lohengrin: Preludes to Acts I & III. Die Meistersinger: Overture; Dance of the apprentices. Die Walküre: Ride of the Valkyries.
(B) *** CfP Dig. CD-CFP 9008. LPO, Rickenbacher.

Karl Anton Rickenbacher, formerly principal conductor with the BBC Scottish Symphony Orchestra, here makes an impressive recording début. He secures first-class playing from the LPO with the strings at their peak in the radiant opening of the *Lohengrin Prelude*. Rickenbacher's tempi are far from stoically Teutonic and he presses the music on convincingly, yet retains a sense of breadth. Some might feel his pacing of the *Die Meistersinger overture* is fractionally fast. The CD improves remarkably on the sound of the original LP: the sound is firmer and fuller, with a more expansive bass response; indeed the *Prelude to Act III* of *Lohengrin* makes a splendid demonstration recording; an exciting performance, particularly vividly projected.

Götterdämmerung: Dawn music; Siegfried's Rhine journey, death and funeral music; Finale. Die Meistersinger: Prelude, Act III; Dance of the apprentices; Entry of the masters. Das Rheingold: Entry of the gods into Valhalla. Tannhäuser: Overture and Venusberg music.
**(*) Delos Dig. D/CD 3040 [id.]. Seattle SO, Schwarz.

The excerpts are well chosen and well tailored. The Seattle orchestra – particularly the strings, who can produce a rich sensuous sheen – play this repertoire most convincingly; and Gerard Schwarz's pacing is convincing, except perhaps in the *Prelude to Act III* of *Die Meistersinger*, where he presses on a shade too strongly. The recording, made in Seattle Opera House, is expansive and clear, with the proper spacious ambience. It is a pity there is no chorus for the *Venusberg music* in *Tannhäuser*.

Götterdämmerung: Dawn and Siegfried's Rhine journey; Siegfried's death and funeral march. Das Rheingold: Entry of the gods into Valhalla. Siegfried: Forest murmurs. Die Walküre: Ride of the Valkyries; Wotan's farewell and Magic fire music.
(M) **(*) Decca 417 775-2 [id.]. Nat. SO of Washington, Dorati.
**(*) EMI Dig. CDC7 47007-2 [id.]. BPO, Tennstedt.
(M) **(*) CBS CD 44769 [MYK 36715]. Cleveland O, Szell.

Dorati's selection from *The Ring* is essentially dramatic. The *Ride of the Valkyries* comes off especially well, as do the three excerpts from *Götterdämmerung* (with a superbly played horn solo in *Siegfried's Rhine journey*). But in the final scene from *Die Walküre* the lack of richness and body of the string-tone that this orchestra can produce limits the effect of Dorati's eloquence.

This EMI Berlin Philharmonic CD was recorded with demonstrable brilliance and the sense of spectacle is in no doubt. There is weight too: the climax of *Siegfried's funeral march* has massive penetration. There is also fine detail, especially in the atmospheric *Forest murmurs*. The playing itself is of the finest quality throughout and Tennstedt maintains a high level of tension. But the brass recording is rather dry and at times the ear feels some lack of amplitude and resonance in the bass.

Breathtaking orchestral playing and very exciting performances from Szell, with some really spectacular moments. The recording could ideally be more opulent, but it has body as well as brilliance, and there is no doubt about the adrenalin running here.

Lohengrin: Preludes to Acts I & III. Die Meistersinger: Overture. Rienzi: Overture. Tannhäuser: Overture.
**(*) EMI Dig. CDC7 47030-2 [id.]. BPO, Tennstedt.

Klaus Tennstedt here shows something of the Klemperer tradition with these essentially broad and spacious readings, yet the voltage is consistently high. The opening and closing sections of the *Tannhäuser overture* are given a restrained nobility of feeling without any loss of power or impact. Similarly the gorgeous string melody at the opening of *Rienzi* is elegiacally moulded, and later when the brass enter in the allegro there is no suggestion of the bandstand. In the Act I *Lohengrin Prelude*, Tennstedt lingers in the pianissimo sections, creating radiant detail, then presses on just before the climax. The Berlin Philharmonic are on top form throughout and the digital recording is both refined and brilliant, if without a glowing resonance in the middle and bass frequencies.

Lohengrin: Preludes to Acts I & III. Parsifal: Preludes to Acts I & III.
(M) *** EMI CMS7 63469-2 (2) [Ang. CDMB 63469]. BPO, Karajan – BRUCKNER: *Symphony No. 8.****

Karajan's Act I *Lohengrin Prelude* is graduated superbly; the *Parsifal* excerpts, too, are nobly shaped, yet here the tension is held at a slightly lower level. Nevertheless this is magnificent playing and the 1975 recording has an attractively wide amplitude.

Lohengrin: Preludes to Acts I & III with Bridal chorus. Parsifal: Prelude and Good Friday music. Tristan: Prelude and Liebestod.
(B) *** EMI CDZ7 62856-2 [id.]. V. State Op. Ch., VPO, Rudolf Kempe.

The glowing nobility of line in Kempe's *Parsifal* excerpts is wonderfully expansive and the *Tristan Prelude and Liebestod* has comparable rapt intensity. Superbly sustained playing from the VPO strings and brass: the *Lohengrin* Act I *Prelude* has never sounded more radiant. These *Lohengrin* excerpts are drawn from the complete set, so that the *Bridal chorus* brings a gentle fade at its close. The sound is full and atmospheric, with only a minimal loss in the lower range.

Die Meistersinger: Prelude to Act III. Tannhäuser: Overture and Venusberg music. Tristan und Isolde: Prelude and Liebestod.
**(*) DG Dig. 413 754-2 [id.]. BPO, Karajan.

In Karajan's digital concert the orchestral playing is altogether superlative; artistically there need be no reservations here. But the upper strings lack an ideal amount of space in which to open out and climaxes are not altogether free. The overall effect is slightly clinical in its detail, instead of offering a resonant panoply of sound. But Brangaene's potion still remains heady, and the playing is eloquent and powerful.

Parsifal: Prelude and Good Friday music.
(B) *** CBS MYK 44872 [id.]. Columbia SO, Bruno Walter – DVORÁK: *Symphony No. 8.****

A glorious account of the *Prelude and Good Friday music* from Walter, recorded in 1959, but with the glowingly rich recording never hinting at its age. The digital remastering is a superb achievement.

'The Ring without words': orchestral excerpts from *The Ring.*
** Telarc Dig. CD 80154 [id.]. BPO, Maazel.

This record offers a series of linked orchestral episodes from the four *Ring* operas, with the scoring left to Wagner but with the linking sometimes dovetailed unconvincingly. The accompanying notes tell the listener what is going on, relating to the 20 cued tracks. The recording is spectacular and the Berlin Philharmonic playing is always powerful; but the special effects (from the hammering dwarfs of *Das Rheingold* to Donner's thunderbolt) are not very sophisticated. The highlights are, predictably, the *Ride of the Valkyries* and *Wotan's* passionate *farewell* to Brünnhilde. Maazel keeps the tension up by pressing on urgently, and at times there is a touch of coarseness to the sound-picture, but overall there is plenty of spectacle.

VOCAL MUSIC

Wesendonk Lieder.
*** Decca 414 624-2 [id.]. Kirsten Flagstad, VPO, Knappertsbusch – MAHLER: *Kindertotenlieder; Lieder eines fahrenden Gesellen.***

Wesendonk Lieder. Tristan und Isolde: Prelude und Liebestod.
**(*) Ph. 412 655-2 [id.]. Jessye Norman, LSO, C. Davis.

Flagstad's glorious voice is perfectly suited to the rich inspiration of the *Wesendonk Lieder. Im Treibhaus* is particularly beautiful. Fine accompaniment, with the 1956 recording sounding remarkable for its vintage, and skilfully remastered.

The poised phrases of the *Wesendonk Lieder* drew from Jessye Norman in this 1976 recording a glorious range of tone-colour, though in detailed imagination she falls short of some of the finest rivals on record. Though the role of Isolde would no doubt strain a still-developing voice, and this is not the most searching of *Liebestods*, it is still the vocal contribution which crowns this conventional linking of first and last in the opera. Good, refined recording.

Wesendonk Lieder: Der Engel; Stehe still; Im Treibhaus; Schmerzen; Träume. Götterdämmerung: Starke Scheite schichet mir dort. Siegfried: Ewig war ich. Tristan: Doch nun von Tristan?; Mild und leise.
(M) (***) EMI mono CDH7 63030-2 [id.]. Kirsten Flagstad, Philh. O, Furtwängler, Dobrowen.

Recorded in the late 1940s and early '50s, a year or so before Flagstad did *Tristan* complete with Furtwängler, these performances show her at her very peak, with the voice magnificent in power as well as beautiful and distinctive in every register. Not that there is as much bloom on the voice here as in the complete *Tristan* recording. The *Liebestod* (with rather heavy surface noise) may be less rapt and intense in this version with Dobrowen than with Furtwängler but is just as expansive. For the *Wesendonk Lieder* she shades the voice down very beautifully, but this is still monumental and noble rather than intimate Lieder-singing. Like other Références issues, this single CD gives no texts or even notes on the music.

Der fliegende Holländer: Senta's ballad. Götterdämmerung: Immolation scene. Tannhäuser: Elisabeth's greeting; Elisabeth's prayer. Tristan und Isolde: Prelude and Liebestod.
*** EMI Dig. CDC7 49759-2 [id.]. Jessye Norman, Amb. Op. Ch., LPO, Tennstedt.

As a Wagnerian, Tennstedt tends to take a rugged view, and it is a measure of his characterful, noble conducting that his contribution is just as striking as that of the great soprano who is the soloist in these items. After a poised and measured account of *Isolde's Liebestod*, Norman is at her most commanding as Elisabeth, both in the outburst of the *Greeting* and in the hushed, poised legato of the *Prayer. Senta's ballad* is also superb, and Brünnhilde's *Immolation scene* brings thrilling singing over a daringly wide range of tone and dynamic, conveying feminine warmth, vulnerability and passion, as well as nobility.

OPERA

Die Feen (complete).
*** Orfeo Dig. C063833 (3) [id.]. Gray, Lovaas, Laki, Studer, Alexander, Hermann, Moll, Rootering, Bracht, Bav. R. Ch. & SO, Sawallisch.

Wagner was barely twenty when he wrote *Die Feen*. The piece is composed continuously in what had become the new, advanced manner, and even when he bows to convention and has a buffo duet between the second pair of principals, the result is distinctive and fresh, delightfully sung here by Cheryl Studer and Jan-Hendrik Rootering. This first complete recording was edited together from live performances. Sawallisch gives a strong and dramatic performance, finely paced; central to the total success is the singing of Linda Esther Gray as Ada, the fairy-heroine, powerful and firmly controlled. John Alexander as the tenor hero, King Arindal, sings cleanly and capably; the impressive cast-list boasts such excellent singers as Kurt Moll, Kari Lovaas and Krisztina Laki in small but vital roles. Ensembles and choruses – with the Bavarian Radio Chorus finely disciplined – are particularly impressive, and the recording is generally first rate.

Der fliegende Holländer (complete).
*** Ph. Dig. 416 300-2 (2) [id.]. Estes, Balslev, Salminen, Schunk, Bayreuth Fest. (1985) Ch. & O, Nelsson.
**(*) Decca 414 551-2 (3) [id.]. Bailey, Martin, Talvela, Kollo, Krenn, Isola Jones, Chicago SO Ch. & O, Solti.
(M) ** Decca 417 319-2 (2) [id.]. London, Rysanek, Tozzi, ROHCG Ch. & O, Dorati.
(M) ** EMI CMS7 63344-2 (3). Adam, Silja, Talvela, Kozub, Unger, Burmeister, BBC Ch., New Philh. O, Klemperer.

Woldemar Nelsson, with the team he had worked with intensively through the season, conducts a performance even more glowing and responsively paced than those of his starrier rivals. The cast is more consistent than any, with Lisbeth Balslev as Senta firmer, sweeter and more secure than any current rival, raw only occasionally, and Simon Estes a strong, ringing Dutchman, clear and noble of tone. Matti Salminen is a dark and equally secure Daland and Robert Schunk an ardent, idiomatic Erik. The veteran, Anny Schlemm, as Mary, though vocally overstressed, adds pointful character, and the chorus is superb, wonderfully drilled and passionate with it. Though inevitably stage noises are obtrusive at times, the recording is exceptionally vivid and atmospheric. On two discs only, it makes an admirable first choice.

What will disappoint some who admire Solti's earlier Wagner sets is that this most atmospheric of the Wagner operas is presented with no Culshaw-style production whatever. Characters halloo to one another when evidently standing elbow to elbow, and even the Dutchman's ghostly chorus sounds very close and earthbound. But with Norman Bailey a deeply impressive Dutchman, Janis Martin a generally sweet-toned Senta, Martti Talvela a splendid Daland, and Kollo, for all his occasional coarseness, an illuminating Erik, it remains well worth hearing. The brilliance of the recording is all the more striking on CD, but the precise placing so characteristic of the new medium reinforces the clear impression of a concert performance, not an atmospheric re-creation.

The outstanding quality of Dorati's set is the conducting and the general sense of teamwork. Both orchestra and chorus are on top form, the recording is splendidly clear and vivid and the reissue is offered on two mid-price CDs. George London's Dutchman is the drawback; the voice is comparatively ill-defined, the phrasing sometimes clumsy. Rysanek is not always the steadiest of Sentas but she sings with character, and the rest of the cast is vocally reliable.

Predictably Klemperer's reading is spacious in its tempi – involving a third disc in its CD reissue – and the drama hardly grips you by the throat. But the underlying intensity is irresistible. This could hardly be recommended as a first choice, but any committed admirer of the conductor should try to hear it. It is a pity that Anja Silja was chosen as Senta, even though she is not as squally in tone here as she can be. Otherwise a strong vocal cast, much beautiful playing (particularly from the wind soloists) and a lively if not particularly atmospheric recording, made to sound drier still in its CD format.

Der fliegende Holländer: highlights.
(M) *** EMI CDM7 63449-2 [id.] (from above set, cond. Karajan).

The selection here (67 minutes) offers the key numbers and includes the Dutchman's Act I monologue and the powerful closing scene. The remastered transfer is vivid but has plenty of atmosphere.

Götterdämmerung (complete).
*** Decca 414 115-2 (4) [id.]. Nilsson, Windgassen, Fischer-Dieskau, Frick, Neidlinger, Watson, Ludwig, V. State Op. Ch., VPO, Solti.
*** DG 415 155-2 (4) [id.]. Dernesch, Janowitz, Brilioth, Stewart, Kelemen, Ludwig, Ridderbusch, German Op. Ch., BPO, Karajan.
*** Ph. 412 488-2 (4) [id.]. Nilsson, Windgassen, Greindl, Mödl, Stewart, Neidlinger, Dvořáková, Bayreuth Fest. (1967) Ch. & O, Boehm.
(M) **(*) RCA/Eurodisc Dig. GD 69007 (4) [69007-2-RG]. Altmeyer, Kollo, Salminen, Wenkel, Nocker, Nimsgern, Sharp, Popp, Leipzig R. Ch., Berlin R. Ch., Dresden State Op. Ch., Dresden State O, Janowski.

In Decca's formidable task of recording the whole *Ring* cycle under Solti, *Götterdämmerung* provided the most daunting challenge of all; characteristically, Solti, and with him the Vienna Philharmonic and the Decca recording team under John Culshaw, were inspired to heights even beyond earlier achievements. Solti's reading had matured before the recording was made. He presses on still, but no longer is there any feeling of over-driving, and even the *Funeral march* is made into a natural, not a forced, climax. There is not a single weak link in the cast. Nilsson surpasses herself in the magnificence of her singing: even Flagstad in her prime would not have been more masterful as Brünnhilde. As in *Siegfried*, Windgassen is in superb voice; Frick is a vivid Hagen, and Fischer-Dieskau achieves the near impossible in making Gunther an interesting and even sympathetic character. As for the recording quality, it surpasses even

Decca's earlier achievement, and the CDs bring added weight to balance the brilliant upper range.

Recorded last in Karajan's *Ring* series, *Götterdämmerung* has the finest, fullest sound, less brilliant than Solti's on Decca but glowing in the CD transfer to match the relatively lyrical approach of the conductor, with Helga Dernesch's voice in the Immolation scene given satisfying richness and warmth. Karajan's singing cast is marginally even finer than Solti's, and his performance conveys the steady flow of recording sessions prepared in relation to live performances. But ultimately he falls short of Solti's achievement in the orgasmic quality of the music. Karajan is a degree less committed, beautifully as the players respond, and warm as his overall approach is. Dernesch's Brünnhilde is warmer than Nilsson's, with a glorious range of tone. Brilioth as Siegfried is fresh and young-sounding, while the Gutrune of Gundula Janowitz is far preferable to that of Claire Watson on Decca. The matching is otherwise very even.

Boehm's urgently involving reading of *Götterdämmerung*, very well cast, is crowned by an incandescent performance of the final Immolation scene from Birgit Nilsson as Brünnhilde. It is an astonishing achievement that she could sing with such biting power and accuracy in a live performance, coming to it at the very end of a long evening. The excitement of that is matched by much else in the performance, so that incidental stage noises and the occasional inaccuracy, almost inevitable in live music-making, matter hardly at all. This recording has been transformed in its CD version. The voices are well forward of the orchestra, but the result gives a magnetically real impression of hearing the opera in the Festspielhaus, with the stage movements adding to that sense of reality. Balances are inevitably variable, and at times Windgassen as Siegfried is treated less well by the microphones than is Nilsson. Generally his performance for Solti is fresher – but there are points of advantage, too. Josef Greindl is rather unpleasantly nasal in tone as Hagen, and Martha Mödl as Waltraute is unsteady; but both are dramatically involving. Thomas Stewart is a gruff but convincing Gunther and Dvořáková, as Gutrune, strong if not ideally pure-toned. Neidlinger as ever is a superb Alberich.

With sharply focused digital sound, Janowski's studio recording hits refreshingly hard, at least as much so as in the earlier *Ring* operas. Speeds rarely linger but, with some excellent casting – consistent with the earlier operas – the result is rarely lightweight. Jeannine Altmeyer as Brünnhilde rises to the challenges not so much in strength as in feeling and intensity, ecstatic in Act I, bitter in Act II, dedicated in the Immolation scene. Kollo is a fine heroic Siegfried, only occasionally raw-toned, and Salminen is a magnificent Hagen, with Nimsgern again an incisive Alberich on his brief appearances. Despite an indifferent Gunther and Gutrune and a wobbly if characterful Waltraute, the impression is of clean vocalization matched by finely disciplined and dedicated playing, all recorded in faithful studio sound with no sonic tricks. On the four CDs the background silence adds to the dramatic presence and overall clarity, which is strikingly enhanced, and this mid-priced reissue is well worth considering.

The Twilight of the Gods (Götterdämmerung): Act III: excerpts in English.
*** Chan. CHAN 8534 [id.]. Rita Hunter, Alberto Remedios, Norman Bailey, Grant, Curphey, Sadler's Wells Opera Ch. & O, Goodall.

This single Chandos CD brings an invaluable reminder of Reginald Goodall's performance of the *Ring* cycle when it was in its first flush of success, covering the closing two scenes. In many ways it possesses an advantage over even the complete live recording of the opera, made at the Coliseum five years later, when Rita Hunter and Alberto Remedios are here obviously fresher and less stressed than at the end of a full evening's performance. Fresh, clear recording, not as full as it might be.

Lohengrin (complete).

⊛ *** Decca Dig. 421 053-2 (4) [id.]. Domingo, Norman, Nimsgern, Randová, Sotin, Fischer-Dieskau, V. State Op. Concert Ch., VPO, Solti.

*** EMI CDS7 49017-2 (3) [Ang. CDCC 49017]. Jess Thomas, Grümmer, Fischer-Dieskau, Ludwig, Frick, Wiener, V. State Op. Ch., VPO, Kempe.

(M) **(*) EMI CMS7 69314-2 (4) [Ang. CDMD 69314]. Kollo, Tomowa-Sintow, Nimsgern, Vejzovic, Ridderbusch, German Op. Ch., Berlin, BPO, Karajan.

With its massive ensembles, *Lohengrin* presents special problems, and the engineers here excel themselves in well-aerated sound that still has plenty of body. Solti presents those ensemble moments with rare power and panache, but he also appreciates the chamber-like delicacy of much of the writing, relaxing far more than he might have done earlier in his career, bringing out the endless lyricism warmly and naturally. It is Placido Domingo's achievement singing Lohengrin that the lyrical element blossoms so consistently, with no hint of Heldentenor barking; at whatever dynamic level, Domingo's voice is firm and unstrained. In the Act III aria, *In fernem Land*, for example, he uses the widest, most beautiful range of tonal colouring, with ringing heroic tone dramatically contrasted against a whisper of head voice, finely controlled. Jessye Norman, not naturally suited to the role of Elsa, yet gives a warm, commanding performance, always intense, full of detailed insights into words and character. Eva Randová's grainy mezzo does not take so readily to recording, but as Ortrud she provides a pointful contrast, even if she never matches the firm, biting malevolence of Christa Ludwig on the Kempe set. Siegmund Nimsgern, Telramund for Solti as for Karajan, equally falls short of Fischer-Dieskau, his rival on the Kempe set; but it is still a strong, cleanly focused performance. Fischer-Dieskau here sings the small but vital role of the Herald, while Hans Sotin makes a comparably distinctive King Henry. Radiant playing from the Vienna Philharmonic, and committed chorus work too. This is one of the crowning glories of Solti's long recording career.

Kempe's is a rapt account of *Lohengrin* which has been surpassed on record only by Solti's Decca set and which remains one of his finest monuments in sound. After all, Kempe looked at Wagner very much from the spiritual side, giving *Lohengrin* perspectives deeper than is common. The intensity of Kempe's conducting lies in its very restraint, and throughout this glowing performance one senses a gentle but sure control, with the strings of the Vienna Philharmonic playing radiantly. The singers too seem uplifted, Jess Thomas singing more clearly and richly than usual, Elisabeth Grümmer unrivalled as Elsa in her delicacy and sweetness, Gottlob Frick gloriously resonant as the king. But it is the partnership of Christa Ludwig and Fischer-Dieskau as Ortrud and Telramund that sets the seal on this superb performance, giving the darkest intensity to their machinations in Act II, their evil heightening the beauty and serenity of so much in this opera. Though the digital transfer on CD reveals roughness (even occasional distortion) in the original recording, the glow and intensity of Kempe's reading come out all the more involvingly in the new format. The set is also very economically contained on three CDs instead of the four for all rivals, though inevitably breaks between discs come in the middle of Acts.

Karajan, whose DG recording of *Parsifal* was so naturally intense, failed in this earlier but related opera to capture comparable spiritual depth. So some of the big melodies sound a degree over-inflected and the result, though warm, expressive, dramatically powerful and with wide-ranging recording, misses an important dimension. Nor is much of the singing as pure-toned as it might be, with René Kollo too often straining and Tomowa-Sintow not always able to scale down in the necessary purity her big dramatic voice. The booklet offers the libretto without an English translation but with a synopsis instead.

Lohengrin: highlights.
(M) **(*) EMI CDM7 63453-2 [id.] (from above set, cond. Karajan).

Another fairly generous sampler (69 minutes) of a set which cannot be counted among Karajan's most successful Wagner recordings. The sound is vivid, with strong forward projection.

Die Meistersinger von Nürnberg (complete).
*** DG 415 278-2 (4) [id.]. Fischer-Dieskau, Ligendza, Lagger, Hermann, Domingo, Laubenthal, Ludwig, German Op. Ch. & O, Berlin, Jochum.
**(*) Decca 417 497-2 (4) [id.]. Bailey, Bode, Moll, Weikl, Kollo, Dallapozza, Hamari, Gumpoldskirchner Spatzen, V. State Op. Ch., VPO, Solti.
(M) (***) EMI mono CHS7 63500-2 (4). Schwarzkopf, Edelmann, Kunz, Hopf, Unger, Bayreuth Fest. Ch. & O, Karajan.
**(*) EMI CDS7 49683-2 (4) [Ang. CDCD 49683]. Adam, Evans, Kelemen, Ridderbusch, Kollo, Schreier, Donath, Hess, Leipzig R. Ch., Dresden State Op. Ch. & State O, Karajan.
(M) ** RCA GD 69008 (4). Wiener, Hotter, Watson, Thomas, Thaw, Hoppe, Kusche, Metternich, Bav. State Op. Ch., Bav. State O, Keilberth.

Jochum's is a performance which, more than any, captures the light and shade of Wagner's most warmly approachable score, its humour and tenderness as well as its strength. With Jochum the processions at the start of the final Festwiese have sparkling high spirits, not just German solemnity, while the poetry of the score is brought out radiantly, whether in the incandescence of the Act III *Prelude* (positively Brucknerian in hushed concentration) or the youthful magic of the love music for Walther and Eva. Above all, Jochum is unerring in building long Wagnerian climaxes and resolving them – more so than his recorded rivals. The cast is the most consistent yet assembled on record. Though Caterina Ligendza's big soprano is a little ungainly for Eva, it is an appealing performance, and the choice of Domingo for Walther is inspired. The key to the set is of course the searching and highly individual Sachs of Fischer-Dieskau, a performance long awaited. With detailed word-pointing and sharply focused tone he gives new illumination in every scene, and Horst Laubenthal's finely tuned David matches this Sachs in applying Lieder style. The recording balance favours the voices, but on CD they are made to sound slightly ahead of the orchestra. There is a lovely bloom on the whole sound and, with a recording which is basically wide-ranging and refined, the ambience brings an attractively natural projection of the singers.

The great glory of Solti's set is not the searing brilliance of the conductor but rather the mature and involving portrayal of Sachs by Norman Bailey. The set is well worth investigating for his superb singing alone, but there is much else to enjoy, not least the bright and detailed sound which the Decca engineers have obtained with the Vienna Philharmonic. Kurt Moll as Pogner, Bernd Weikl as Beckmesser and Julia Hamari as Magdalene are all excellent, but the shortcomings are comparably serious. Both Hannelore Bode and René Kollo fall short of their far-from-perfect contributions to earlier sets, and Solti for all his energy gives a surprisingly square reading of this most appealing of Wagner scores, pointing his expressive lines too heavily and failing to convey real spontaneity. It remains an impressive achievement for Bailey's marvellous Sachs, and the Decca sound comes up very vividly on CD.

Recorded live at the 1951 Bayreuth Festival, Karajan's earlier EMI version has never quite been matched since for its involving intensity. The mono sound may be thin and the stage noises often distracting, but, with clean CD transfers, the sense of being present at a great event is irresistible, with the great emotional moments – both between Eva and Walther and, even more strikingly, between Eva and Sachs – bringing a gulp in the throat. The young Elisabeth Schwarzkopf makes the most radiant Eva, singing her Act III solo, *O Sachs, mein Freund!*, with touching ardour before beginning the Quintet with flawless legato. Hans Hopf is here less gritty than in his other recordings, an attractive hero; while Otto Edelmann makes a superb Sachs, firm and virile, the more moving for not sounding old. There are inconsistencies among the others but, in a performance of such electricity, generated by the conductor in his early prime, they are of minimal importance. The four mid-price CDs are generously indexed and come with a libretto but no translation. EMI should have indicated the index points not just in the libretto, but in the English synopsis as well.

EMI fell down badly in the choice of Sachs. Theo Adam, promising in many ways, has quite the wrong voice for the part, in one way too young-sounding, in another too grating, not focused enough. After that keen disappointment there is much to enjoy, for in a modestly reverberant acoustic Karajan draws from the Dresden players and chorus a rich performance which retains a degree of bourgeois intimacy. Donath is a touching, sweet-toned Eva, Kollo here is as true and ringing a Walther as one could find today, Geraint Evans an incomparably vivid Beckmesser, and Ridderbusch a glorious-toned Pogner. The extra clarity of CD gives a new realism and sense of presence to a recording not specially impressive on LP.

The Keilberth set was recorded at the very first performance given in the rebuilt Opera House in Munich in November 1963. That brings inevitable flaws, but the voices are generally bright and forward, and the atmosphere is of a great occasion. The team of masters includes such distinguished singers as Hans Hotter as Pogner and Josef Metternich as Kottner; but Otto Wiener in the central role of Hans Sachs is too unsteady to be acceptable on record. Jess Thomas makes a ringing and accurate if hardly subtle Walther, and Claire Watson a fresh-toned but uncharacterful Eva. Keilberth paces well but tends to bring out the rhythmic squareness. Like Karajan's inspired Bayreuth recording of 1951, this comes on four mid-price CDs, but has the advantage of stereo sound.

Die Meistersinger: highlights.
(M) **(*) EMI CDM7 63455-2 (from above set, cond. Karajan).

Many will prefer to have a sampler rather than investing in the complete Karajan stereo set, which is let down by the casting of Theo Adam as Sachs. The selection runs to nearly 68 minutes.

Parsifal (complete).
⊛ *** DG Dig. 413 347-2 (4) [id.]. Hofmann, Vejzovic, Moll, Van Dam, Nimsgern, Von Halem, German Op. Ch., BPO, Karajan.
*** Decca 417 143-2 (4) [id.]. Kollo, Ludwig, Fischer-Dieskau, Hotter, Kelemen, Frick, V. Boys' Ch., V. State Op. Ch., VPO, Solti.
**(*) Ph. Dig. 416 842-2 (4) [id.]. Hofmann, Meier, Estes, Sotin, Salminen, Mazura, Bayreuth Fest. (1985) Ch. & O, Levine.
**(*) Ph. 416 390-2 (4). Jess Thomas, Dalis, London, Talvela, Neidlinger, Hotter, Bayreuth Fest. (1962) Ch. & O, Knappertsbusch.

Communion, musical and spiritual, is what this intensely beautiful Karajan set provides, with pianissimos shaded in magical clarity and the ritual of bells and offstage choruses heard as in ideal imagination. The playing of the Berlin orchestra is consistently beautiful; but the clarity and refinement of sound prevent this from emerging as a lengthy serving of Karajan soup. Kurt Moll as Gurnemanz is the singer who, more than any other, anchors the work vocally, projecting his voice with firmness and subtlety. José van Dam as Amfortas is also splendid. The Klingsor of Siegmund Nimsgern could be more sinister, but the singing is admirable. Dunja Vejzovic makes a vibrant, sensuous Kundry who rises superbly to the moment in Act II when she bemoans her laughter in the face of Christ. Only Peter Hofmann as Parsifal leaves any disappointment; at times he develops a gritty edge on the voice, but his natural tone is admirably suited to the part and he is never less than dramatically effective. He is not helped by the relative closeness of the solo voices, but otherwise the recording is near the atmospheric ideal, a superb achievement. The four CDs are still among DG's finest so far.

Solti's singing cast could hardly be stronger, every one of them pointing words with fine, illuminating care for detail; and the complex balances of sound, not least in the *Good Friday music*, are beautifully caught; throughout, Solti shows his sustained intensity in Wagner. There remains just one doubt, but that rather serious: the lack of a rapt, spiritual quality. The remastering for CD, as with Solti's other Wagner recordings, opens up the sound, and the choral climaxes are superb, although the break between the second and third discs could have been better placed. Cueing is generous but the libretto is poor, the typeface minuscule and in places no pleasure to read.

Of all the Wagner operas, this is the one that gains most and loses least from being recorded live at Bayreuth, and the dedication of Levine's reading comes over consistently, if not with quite the glow that so marks Karajan's inspired studio performance. Unfortunately the singing is flawed. Peter Hofmann, in far poorer voice than for Karajan, is often ill-focused, and even Hans Sotin as Gurnemanz is vocally less reliable than usual. The rest are excellent, with Franz Mazura as Klingsor, Simon Estes as Amfortas and Matti Salminen as Titurel all giving resonant, finely projected performances, well contrasted with each other. Waltraud Meier is an outstanding Kundry here. The recording, though not the clearest from this source, captures the Bayreuth atmosphere well.

Knappertsbusch's expansive and dedicated reading is caught superbly in the Philips set, arguably the finest live recording ever made in the Festspielhaus at Bayreuth, with outstanding singing from Jess Thomas as Parsifal and Hans Hotter as Gurnemanz. Though Knappertsbusch chooses consistently slow tempi, there is no sense of excessive squareness or length, so intense is the concentration of the performance, its spiritual quality; and the sound has undoubtedly been further enhanced in the remastering for CD. The snag is that the stage noises and coughs are also emphasized, with the bronchial afflictions particularly disturbing in the *Prelude*. However, the recording itself is most impressive, with the choral perspectives particularly convincing and the overall sound warmly atmospheric.

Das Rheingold (complete).
*** Decca 414 101-2 (3). London, Flagstad, Svanholm, Neidlinger, VPO, Solti.
**(*) DG 415 141-2 (3) [id.]. Fischer-Dieskau, Veasey, Stolze, Kelemen, BPO, Karajan.
**(*) Ph. 412 475-2 (2) [id.]. Adam, Nienstedt, Windgassen, Neidlinger, Talvela, Böhme, Silja, Soukupová, Bayreuth Fest. (1967) Ch. & O, Boehm.
(M) **(*) RCA/Eurodisc Dig. GD 69004 (2) [69004-2-RG]. Adam, Nimsgern, Stryczek, Schreier, Bracht, Salminen, Vogel, Buchner, Minton, Popp, Priew, Schwarz, Dresden State O, Janowski.
** EMI Dig. CDS7 49853-2 (2) [Ang. CDCB 49853]. Morris, Lipovšek, Zednik, Adam, Haage, Bav. RSO, Haitink.

** DG Dig. 427 607-2 (3). Morris, Ludwig, Jerusalem, Wlaschiha, Zednik, Met. Op. O, Levine.

The first of Solti's cycle, recorded in 1958, *Rheingold* remains in terms of engineering the most spectacular on CD. The immediacy and precise placing are thrilling, while the sound-effects of the final scenes, including Donner's hammer-blow and the Rainbow bridge, have never been matched since. The effect remains of demonstration quality, to have one cherishing all the more this historic recording with its unique vignette of Flagstad as Fricka. Solti gives a magnificent reading of the score, crisp, dramatic and direct. He somehow brings a freshness to the music without ever overdriving or losing an underlying sympathy. Vocally, the set is held together by the unforgettable singing of Neidlinger as Alberich. He vocalizes with wonderful precision and makes the character of the dwarf develop from the comic creature of the opening scene to the demented monster of the last. Flagstad learned the part of Fricka specially for this recording, and her singing makes one regret that she never took the role on the stage. Only the slightest trace of hardness in the upper register occasionally betrays her, and the golden power and richness of her singing are for the rest unimpaired. As Wotan, George London is sometimes a little rough, but this is a dramatic portrayal of the young Wotan. Svanholm could be more characterful as Loge, but again it is a relief to hear the part really sung. An outstanding achievement.

Karajan's account is more reflective than Solti's; the very measured pace of the *Prelude* indicates this at the start and there is often an extra bloom on the Berlin Philharmonic playing. But Karajan's very reflectiveness has its less welcome side, for the tension rarely varies. One finds such incidents as Alberich's stealing of the gold or Donner's hammer-blow passing by without one's pulse quickening as it should. There is also no doubt that the DG recording managers were not as painstaking as John Culshaw's Decca team, and that too makes the end result less compellingly dramatic. On the credit side, however, the singing cast has hardly any flaw at all, and Fischer-Dieskau's Wotan is a brilliant and memorable creation, virile and expressive. Among the others, Veasey is excellent, though obviously she cannot efface memories of Flagstad; Gerhard Stolze with his flickering, almost *Sprechstimme* as Loge gives an intensely vivid if, for some, controversial interpretation. The 1968 sound has been clarified in the digital transfer, but generally the lack of bass brings some thinness.

Boehm's preference for fast speeds (consistently through the whole cycle) here brings the benefit that the whole of the *Vorabend* is contained on two CDs, a considerable financial advantage. The pity is that the performance is marred by the casting of Theo Adam as Wotan, keenly intelligent but rarely agreeable on the ear, at times here far too wobbly. On the other hand, Gustav Neidlinger as Alberich is superb, even more involving here than he is for Solti, with the curse made spine-chilling. It is also good to have Wolfgang Windgassen as Loge; among the others, Anja Silja makes an attractively urgent Freia. Though a stage production brings nothing like the sound-effects which make Solti's set so involving, the atmosphere of the theatre in its way is just as potent.

Marek Janowski's performance is treated to a digital recording totally different from Solti's. The studio sound has the voices close and vivid, with the orchestra rather in the background. With Solti, Donner's hammer-blow is overwhelming; but the Eurodisc set comes up with only a very ordinary 'ping' on an anvil, and the grandeur of the moment is missing. Theo Adam as Wotan has his grittiness of tone exaggerated here, but otherwise it is a fine set, consistently well cast, including Peter Schreier, Matti Salminen, Yvonne Minton and Lucia Popp, as well as East German singers of high calibre. Complete on two mid-priced CDs, it is certainly good value.

Haitink's version of *Rheingold*, the second instalment in his EMI *Ring* cycle made in conjunction with Bavarian Radio, follows the same broad pattern as the first to be issued, *Die Walküre*, strong and expansive rather than dramatic, with tension often not quite keen enough. Vocally too the performance has its flaws. Marjana Lipovšek makes a superb Fricka, rich and well projected, but James Morris – also the Wotan in the rival Levine cycle for DG – sounds grittier than before; the fascinating choice of a noted Wotan of the past for the role of Alberich, Theo Adam, proves a mixed blessing. The often unconventional characterization is magnetic, but Adam can no longer sustain a steady note. One powerful point in favour of the EMI set is that it requires only two CDs instead of the usual three. The recording is warm and full rather than brilliant or well focused.

Recorded in conjunction with the latest production of *The Ring* at the Met. in New York, the Levine version brings a strong cast, and it will appeal mainly to those who have had experience of the opera-house performances. Yet neither in sound nor in pacing does the performance capture the sense of live experience very vividly. Though the quality is acceptable, there is too little sense of presence, and the voices lose some of their bloom. James Morris as Wotan, for example, sounds rougher than he does for Haitink; but Ekkehard Wlaschiha is a far firmer Alberich than Theo Adam, and Christa Ludwig makes a characterful Fricka, if not as rich as Lipovšek. Zednik translates very effectively from Loge in the EMI set to Mime at the Met., with Siegfried Jerusalem a powerful if undercharacterized Loge. The balance of advantage lies with the Haitink version, and Levine's slow speeds mean that, unlike the EMI, the DG takes three discs. Levine paces Donner's hammer-blow more dramatically – but neither can compare with the vintage Solti set; for Levine, the sword theme on the trumpet is disappointingly obscured.

Der Ring des Nibelungen (complete).
⊛ (M) *** Decca 414 100-2 (15) [id.]. Nilsson, Flagstad, Windgassen, Fischer-Dieskau, Hotter, London, Ludwig, Neidlinger, Frick, Svanholm, Stoltze, Böhme, Hoffgen, Sutherland, Crespin, King, Watson, VPO, Solti.
(M) *** RCA Dig. GD 69003 (14) [69003-2-RG]. Altmeyer, Kollo, Adam, Schreier, Nimsgern, Vogel, Minton, Wenkel, Salminen, Popp, Jerusalem, J. Norman, Moll, Studer, Leipzig R. Ch., Dresden State Op. Ch. & O, Janowski.

The Decca set – one of the great achievements of the gramophone – has at last been reissued on CD in a special edition of 15 discs at medium price, a bargain of bargains for those who have not already invested in the separate issues, which are all discussed above and below.

Dedication and consistency are the mark of the Eurodisc *Ring*, a studio recording made with German thoroughness by the East German record company, VEB. Originally packaged cumbersomely by Eurodisc on 18 CDs, RCA here reissue it on 14 mid-price discs, to make it much more attractive. Voices tend to be balanced well forward of the orchestra, but the digital sound is full and clear to have one concentrating on the words, helped by Janowski's direct approach to the score. Overall this is a good deal more rewarding than many of the individual sets that have been issued at full price over the last five years.

The Ring 'Great scenes': Das Rheingold: Entry of the Gods into Valhalla. Die Walküre: Ride of the Valkyries; Magic fire music. Siegfried: Forging scene; Forest murmurs. Götterdämmerung: Siegfried's funeral march; Brünnhilde's immolation scene.
(M) *** Decca 421 313-2 [id.]. Nilsson, Windgassen, Hotter, Stolzel, VPO, Solti.

These excerpts are often quite extended – the *Entry of the Gods into Valhalla* offers some ten minutes of music, and the *Forest murmurs* from *Siegfried* starts well before the orchestral interlude. Only *Siegfried's funeral march* is in any sense a 'bleeding chunk' which has to be faded at the end; and the disc closes with twenty minutes of Brünnhilde's Immolation scene.

Der Ring: excerpts: *Das Rheingold: Zur Burg führt die Brucke* (scene iv). *Die Walküre: Ein Schwert verhiess mir der Vater; Ride of the Valkyries; Wotan's farewell and Magic fire music. Siegfried: Notung!; Brünnhilde's awakening. Götterdämmerung: Brünnhilde, heilige Braut! Siegfried's death and Funeral music.*
(B) *** DG 429 168-2 [id.] (from complete recording, cond. Karajan).

The task of selecting highlights to fit on a single disc, taken from the whole of the *Ring* cycle, is an impossible one. But the DG producer of this record has managed to assemble 70 minutes of key items, mostly nicely tailored, with quick fades. The one miscalculation was to end with *Siegfried's funeral march* from *Götterdämmerung*, which leaves the listener suspended; it would have been a simple matter to add the brief orchestral postlude which ends the opera. Nevertheless there is much to enjoy, and this makes a genuine sampler of Karajan's approach to the *Ring* – even the *Ride of the Valkyries* is comparatively refined. The late-1960s sound is excellent.

Siegfried (complete).
*** Decca 414 110-2 (4). Windgassen, Nilsson, Hotter, Stolze, Neidlinger, Böhme, Hoffgen, Sutherland, VPO, Solti.
*** Ph. 412 483-2 (4) [id.]. Windgassen, Nilsson, Adam, Neidlinger, Soukupová, Köth, Böhme, Bayreuth Fest. (1967) Ch. & O, Boehm.
(M) **(*) RCA/Eurodisc Dig. GD 69006 (4) [69006-2-RG]. Kollo, Altmeyer, Adam, Schreier, Nimsgern, Wenkel, Salminen, Sharp, Dresden State O, Janowski.
** DG 415 150-2 (4) [id.]. Dernesch, Dominguez, Jess Thomas, Stolze, Stewart, Kelemen, BPO, Karajan.

Siegfried has too long been thought of as the grimmest of the *Ring* cycle, with dark colours predominating. It is true that the preponderance of male voices till the very end, and Wagner's deliberate matching of this in his orchestration, gives a special colour to the opera, but a performance as buoyant as Solti's reveals that, more than in most Wagner, the message is one of optimism. Each of the three Acts ends with a scene of triumphant optimism – the first Act in Siegfried's forging song, the second with him in hot pursuit of the woodbird, and the third with the most opulent of love duets. Solti's array of singers could hardly be bettered. Windgassen is at the very peak of his form, lyrical as well as heroic. Hotter has never been more impressive on record, his Wotan at last captured adequately. Stolze, Neidlinger and Böhme are all exemplary, and predictably Joan Sutherland makes the most seductive of woodbirds. Only the conducting of Solti leaves a tiny margin of doubt. In the dramatic moments he could hardly be more impressive, but that very woodbird scene shows up the shortcomings: the bird's melismatic carolling is plainly intended to have a degree of freedom, whereas Solti allows little or no lilt in the music at all. With singing finer than any opera house could normally provide, with masterly playing from the Vienna Philharmonic and with Decca's most vivid recording, this is a set likely to stand comparison with anything the rest of the century may provide. The CD transfer is of outstanding quality.

The natural-sounding quality of Boehm's live recording from Bayreuth, coupled with his determination not to let the music lag, makes his account of *Siegfried* as satisfying as the rest of his cycle, vividly capturing the atmosphere of the Festspielhaus, with voices well ahead of the orchestra. Windgassen is at his peak here, if anything more poetic in Acts II and III than he is in Solti's studio recording, and vocally just as fine. Nilsson, as in

Götterdämmerung, gains over her studio recording from the extra flow of adrenalin in a live performance; and Gustav Neidlinger is unmatchable as Alberich. Erika Köth is disappointing as the woodbird, not sweet enough, and Soukupová is a positive, characterful Erda. Theo Adam is at his finest as the Wanderer, less wobbly than usual, clean and incisive.

With Janowski, direct and straight in his approach, securing superb playing from the Dresdeners, the RCA/Eurodisc set lacks a degree of dramatic tension, for he does not always build the climaxes cumulatively. Thus the final scene of Act II just scurries to a close, with Siegfried in pursuit of a rather shrill woodbird in Norma Sharp. The singing is generally first rate, with Kollo a fine Siegfried, less strained than he has sometimes been, and Peter Schreier a superb Mime, using Lieder-like qualities in detailed characterization. Siegmund Nimsgern is a less characterful Alberich, but the voice is excellent; and Theo Adam concludes his portrayal of Wotan/Wanderer with his finest performance of the series. The relative lightness of Jeannine Altmeyer's Brünnhilde comes out in the final love-duet more strikingly than in *Walküre*. Nevertheless the tenderness and femininity are most affecting as at the entry of the idyll motif, where Janowski in his dedicated simplicity is also at his most compelling. Clear, beautifully balanced digital sound, with voices and instruments firmly placed.

When Siegfried is outsung by Mime, it is time to complain, and though the DG set has many fine qualities – not least the Brünnhilde of Helga Dernesch – it hardly rivals the Solti or Boehm versions. Windgassen on Decca gave a classic performance, and any comparison highlights the serious shortcomings of Jess Thomas. Even when voices are balanced forward, the digital transfer helps little to make Thomas's singing as Siegfried any more acceptable. Otherwise, the vocal cast is strong, and Karajan provides the seamless playing which characterizes his cycle. Recommended only to those irrevocably committed to the Karajan cycle.

Tannhäuser (Paris version; complete).
*** DG. Dig. 427 625-2 (3) [id.]. Domingo, Studer, Baltsa, Salminen, Schmidt, Ch. & Philh. O, Sinopoli.
*** Decca 414 581-2 (3) [id.]. Kollo, Dernesch, Ludwig, Sotin, Braun, Hollweg, V. State Op. Ch., VPO, Solti.

Tannhäuser (Dresden version; complete).
**(*) Ph. 420 122-2 (3) [id.]. Windgassen, Waechter, Silja, Stolze, Bumbry, Bayreuth Fest. (1962) Ch. & O, Sawallisch.
** EMI Dig. CDS7 47296-8 (3) [Ang. CDC 47295]. König, Popp, Weikl, Meier, Moll, Jerusalem, Bav. R. Ch. & O, Haitink.

Following up his fine Lohengrin with Solti for Decca, Placido Domingo here makes another Wagnerian sortie, bringing balm to ears wounded by the general run of German heroic tenors. Pressured as he is by the jet-set life of a superstar, it is amazing that he can produce sounds of such power as well as such beauty. In the narration of Act III, it is a joy to hear such a range of tone, dynamic and expression, even if he cannot match his rival, René Kollo, on Solti's Decca set in the agony of the culminating word, '*verdammt*', 'damned'. Following up his experience conducting this opera at Bayreuth (though that was the Dresden, not the Paris, version) Giuseppe Sinopoli here makes his most passionately committed opera recording yet, warmer and more flexible than Solti's Decca version, always individual, with fine detail brought out, always persuasively, and never wilful. Recorded not with Bayreuth forces but in the studio with his own Philharmonia Orchestra, the extra range and beauty of the sound brings ample compensation for a recording that does not attempt to create the sound-stage of Solti's version. Agnes Baltsa is not ideally opulent of tone as Venus, but she is the complete seductress. Cheryl Studer – who sang the role of Elisabeth for Sinopoli at Bayreuth – gives a most sensitive performance, not always ideally even of tone but creating a movingly intense portrait of the heroine, vulnerable and very feminine. Matti Salminen in one of his last recordings makes a superb Landgrave and Andreas Schmidt a noble Wolfram, even though the legato could be smoother in *O star of Eve*.

Solti provides an electrifying experience, demonstrating beyond a shadow of doubt how much more effective the Paris revision of *Tannhäuser* is, compared with the usual Dresden version. The differences lie mainly – though not entirely – in Act I in the scene between Tannhäuser and Venus. Wagner rewrote most of the scene at a time when his style had developed enormously. The love music here is closer to *Walküre* and *Tristan* than to the rest of *Tannhäuser*. Solti gives one of his very finest Wagner performances to date, helped by superb playing from the Vienna Philharmonic and an outstanding cast, superlatively recorded. Dernesch as Elisabeth and Ludwig as Venus outshine all rivals; and Kollo, though not ideal, makes as fine a Heldentenor as we are currently likely to hear. The compact disc transfer reinforces the brilliance and richness of the performance. The sound is outstanding for its period (1971), and Ray Minshull's production adds to the atmospheric quality, with the orchestra given full weight and with the placing and movement of the voices finely judged.

Sawallisch's version, recorded at the 1962 Bayreuth Festival, comes up very freshly on CD. Though the new medium brings out all the more clearly the thuds, creaks and audience noises of a live performance (most distracting at the very start), the dedication of the reading is very persuasive, notably in the Venusberg scene where Grace Bumbry is a superb, sensuous Venus and Windgassen – not quite in his sweetest voice, often balanced rather close – is a fine, heroic Tannhäuser. Anja Silja controls the abrasiveness of her soprano well, to make this her finest performance on record, not ideally sweet but very sympathetic. Voices are set well forward of the orchestra, in which strings have far more bloom than brass; but the atmosphere of the Festspielhaus is vivid and compelling throughout.

Haitink consistently refines the piece, until you can hardly believe that this is an opera which deeply shocked early Victorians with its noisy vulgarity. His performance tends to sound like a studio run-through, carefully done with much intelligence, but largely uninvolved. It is not helped by a strained hero in Klaus König and a shrewish-sounding Venus in Waltraud Meier. Lucia Popp, stretched to the limit in a role on the heavy side for her, produces some characteristically beautiful singing as Elisabeth. Bernd Weikl is an intelligent but uningratiating Wolfram. Finely balanced sound, the more impressive on CD, beautifully atmospheric in the processional scenes.

Tristan und Isolde (complete).
(M) *** EMI CMS7 69319-2 (4) [Ang. CDMD 69319]. Vickers, Dernesch, Ludwig, Berry, Ridderbusch, German Op. Ch., Berlin, BPO, Karajan.
*** DG 419 889-2 (3) [id.]. Windgassen, Nilsson, Ludwig, Talvela, Waechter, Bayreuth Fest. (1966) Ch. & O, Boehm.
**(*) Ph. Dig. 410 447-2 (5) [id.]. Hofmann, Behrens, Minton, Weikl, Sotin, Bav. R. Ch. & SO, Bernstein.
(***) EMI mono CDS7 47322-8 (4) [Ang. CDC47321]. Suthaus, Flagstad, Thebom, Greindl, Fischer-Dieskau, ROHCG Ch., Philh. O, Furtwängler.
**(*) DG Dig. 413 315-2 (4) [id.]. Kollo, Margaret Price, Fassbaender, Fischer-Dieskau, Moll, Dresden State O, Carlos Kleiber.

Karajan's is a sensual performance of Wagner's masterpiece, caressingly beautiful and with superbly refined playing from the Berlin Philharmonic. He is helped by a recording (not ideally balanced, but warmly atmospheric) which copes with an enormous dynamic range. Dernesch as Isolde is seductively feminine, not as noble as Flagstad, not as tough and unflinching as Nilsson; but the human quality makes this account if anything more moving still, helped by glorious tone-colour through every range. Jon Vickers matches her, in what is arguably his finest performance on record, allowing himself true pianissimo shading. The rest of the cast is excellent too. Though CD brings out more clearly the occasional oddities of balance, the 1972 sound has plenty of body, making this an excellent first choice, with inspired conducting and the most satisfactory cast of all.

Boehm's Bayreuth performance, recorded at the 1966 Festival, has a cast that for consistency has seldom been bettered on disc. Now on only three CDs, one disc per Act, the benefit is enormous in presenting one of the big Wagner operas for the first time on disc without any breaks at all, with each Act uninterrupted. Boehm is on the urgent side in this opera and the orchestral ensemble is not always immaculate; but the performance glows with intensity from beginning to end, carried through in the longest spans. Birgit Nilsson sings the *Liebestod* at the end of the long evening as though she was starting out afresh, radiant and with not a hint of tiredness, rising to an orgasmic climax and bringing a heavenly pianissimo on the final rising octave to F sharp. Opposite Nilsson is Wolfgang Windgassen, the most mellifluous of Heldentenoren; though the microphone balance sometimes puts him at a disadvantage to his Isolde, the realism and sense of presence of the whole set have you bathing in the authentic atmosphere of Bayreuth. Making up an almost unmatchable cast are Christa Ludwig as Brangaene, Eberhard Waechter as Kurwenal and Martii Talvela as King Mark, with the young Peter Schreier as the Young Sailor.

Bernstein's five-disc set is not only expensive but cumbersome in five separate 'jewel-boxes'. Nevertheless, the fine quality of the recording is all the more ravishing in the transfer, the sound rich, full and well detailed, a tribute to the Bavarian engineers working in the Herkulessaal in Munich. The surprise is that Bernstein, over-emotional in some music, here exercises restraint to produce the most spacious reading ever put on disc, more expansive even than Furtwängler's. His rhythmic sharpness goes with warmly expressive but unexaggerated phrasing, to give unflagging concentration and deep commitment. The love-duet has rarely if ever sounded so sensuous, with supremely powerful climaxes. Nor in the *Liebestod* is there any question of Bernstein rushing ahead, for the culmination comes naturally and fully at a taxingly slow speed. Behrens makes a fine Isolde, less purely beautiful than her finest rivals but with reserves of power giving dramatic bite. The contrast of tone with Yvonne Minton's Brangaene (good, except for flatness in the warning solo) is not as great as usual, and there is likeness too between Peter Hofmann's Tristan, often baritonal, and Bernd Weikl's Kurwenal, lighter than usual. The King Mark of Hans Sotin is superb. However, this set needs remastering on to four discs.

It was one of the supreme triumphs of the recording producer, Walter Legge, when in 1952 with his recently formed Philharmonia Orchestra he teamed the incomparable Wagnerian, Wilhelm Furtwängler, with Kirsten Flagstad as the heroine in *Tristan und Isolde*. The result has an incandescent intensity, typical of the conductor at his finest. The concept is spacious from the opening *Prelude* onwards, but equally the bite and colour of the drama are vividly conveyed, matching the nobility of Flagstad's portrait of Isolde. The richly commanding power of her singing and her always distinctive timbre make it a uniquely compelling performance. Suthaus is not of the same calibre as Heldentenor, but he avoids ugliness and strain, which is rare in Tristan. Among the others, the only remarkable performance comes from the young Fischer-Dieskau as Kurwenal, not ideally cast but keenly imaginative. One endearing oddity is that – on Flagstad's insistence – the top Cs at the opening of the love-duet were sung by Elisabeth Schwarzkopf. The Kingsway Hall recording was admirably balanced, catching the beauty of the Philharmonia Orchestra at its peak. The CDs have opened up the original mono sound and it is remarkable how little constriction there is in the biggest climaxes, mostly shown in the *fortissimo* violins above the stave.

Kleiber directs a compellingly impulsive reading, crowned by the glorious Isolde of Margaret Price, the most purely beautiful of any complete interpretation on record. Next to more spacious readings, Kleiber's at times sounds excitable, almost hysterical, with fast speeds tending to get faster, for all his hypnotic concentration. But the lyricism of Margaret Price, feminine and vulnerable, is well contrasted against the heroic Tristan of Kollo, at his finest in Act III. Kurt Moll makes a dark, leonine King Mark, but Fischer-Dieskau is at times gritty as Kurwenal and Brigitte Fassbaender is a clear but rather cold Brangaene.

Die Walküre (complete).
*** Decca 414 105-2 (4) [id.]. Nilsson, Crespin, Ludwig, King, Hotter, Frick, VPO, Solti.
*** Ph. 412 478-2 (4) [id.]. King, Rysanek, Nienstedt, Nilsson, Adam, Burmeister, Bayreuth Fest. (1967) Ch. & O, Boehm.
(M) (***) EMI mono CHS7 63045-2 (3) [id.]. Mödl, Rysanek, Frantz, Suthaus, Klose, Frick, VPO, Furtwängler.
(M) *** RCA/Eurodisc Dig. GD 69005 (4) [69005-2-RG]. Altmeyer, Norman, Minton, Jerusalem, Adam, Moll, Dresden State O, Janowski.
**(*) EMI Dig. CDS7 49534-2 (4) [Ang. CDCD 49534]. Eva Marton, Studer, Morris, Goldberg, Salminen, Meier, Bav. RSO, Haitink.
**(*) DG 415 145-2 (4) [id.]. Crespin, Janowitz, Veasey, Vickers, Stewart, Talvela, BPO, Karajan.
** DG Dig. 423 389-2 (4) [id.]. Behrens, Norman, Ludwig, Lakes, Morris, Moll, NY Met. Op. O, Levine.

Solti's conception is more lyrical than one would have expected from his recordings of the other three *Ring* operas. He sees Act II as the kernel of the work, perhaps even of the whole cycle, with the conflict of wills between Wotan and Fricka making for one of Wagner's most deeply searching scenes. That is the more apparent when the greatest of latterday Wotans, Hans Hotter, takes the role, and Christa Ludwig sings with searing dramatic sense as his wife. Before that, Act I seems a little underplayed. This is partly because of Solti's deliberate lyricism – apt enough when love and spring greetings are in the air – but also (on the debit side) because James King fails both to project the character of Siegmund and to delve into the word-meanings as all the other members of the cast consistently do. Crespin has never sung more beautifully on record, but even that cannot cancel out the shortcoming. As for Nilsson's Brünnhilde, it has grown mellower, the emotions are clearer, and under-the-note attack is almost eliminated. Some may hesitate in the face of Hotter's obvious vocal trials; but the unsteadiness is, if anything, less marked than in his EMI recordings of items done many years ago.

When Siegmund pulls the sword, Nothung, from the tree – James King in heroic voice – the Sieglinde, Leonie Rysanek, utters a shriek of joy to delight even the least susceptible Wagnerian, matching the urgency of the whole performance as conducted by Boehm. Rarely if ever does his preference for fast speeds undermine the music; on the contrary, it adds to the involvement of the performance, which never loses its concentration. Theo Adam is in firmer voice here as Wotan than he is in *Rheingold*, hardly sweet of tone but always singing with keen intelligence. As ever, Nilsson is in superb voice as Brünnhilde. Though the inevitable noises of a live performance occasionally intrude, this presents a more involving experience than any rival complete recording. The CD transfer transforms what on LP seemed a rough recording, even if passages of heavy orchestration still bring some constriction of sound.

In this superb reissue on three mid-price CDs Furtwängler's 1954 recording of *Die Walküre*, made in Vienna only months before the conductor's death, stands as the keenest possible competitor to the latest digitally recorded versions – in most ways outshining them. Except for those totally allergic to mono sound even as well balanced as this, the EMI Références set could well be the answer as a first choice, when not only Furtwängler but an excellent cast and the Vienna Philharmonic in radiant form match any of their successors. Even more than in *Tristan*, Ludwig Suthaus proves a satisfyingly clear-toned Heldentenor, never strained, with the lyricism of *Wintersturme* superbly sustained. Neither Léonie Rysanek as Sieglinde nor Martha Mödl as Brünnhilde is ideally steady, but the intensity and involvement of each is irresistible, classic performances both, with detail finely touched in and well contrasted with each other. Similarly, the mezzo of Margarete Klose may not be very beautiful, but the projection of words and the fire-eating character match the conductor's intensity. Rather in contrast with the women soloists, both bass and baritone are satisfyingly firm and beautiful. Gottlob Frick is as near an ideal Hunding as one will find, sinister but with the right streak of arrogant sexuality; while the Wotan of Ferdinand Frantz may not be as deeply perceptive as some, but to hear the sweep of Wagner's melodic lines so gloriously sung is a rare joy. The 1954 sound is amazingly full and vivid, with voices cleanly balanced against the inspired orchestra. Far more than Furtwängler's live recording of *The Ring* from Rome, this *Walküre* (the first of a *Ring* project which sadly went no further) is a superb memorial to his Wagnerian mastery. The only snag of the set is that, to fit the whole piece on to only three CDs, breaks between discs come in mid-Act.

Janowski's direct approach matches the relative dryness of the acoustic, with voices fixed well forward of the orchestra – but not aggressively so. That balance allows full presence for the singing from a satisfyingly consistent cast. Jessye Norman might not seem an obvious choice for Sieglinde, but the sound is glorious, the expression intense and detailed, making her a superb match for the fine, if rather less imaginative Siegmund of Siegfried Jerusalem. The one snag with so commanding a Sieglinde is that she overtops the Brünnhilde of Jeannine Altmeyer who, more than usual, conveys a measure of feminine vulnerability in the leading Valkyrie even in her godhead days. Miss Altmeyer may be slightly overparted, but the beauty and frequent sensuousness of her singing are the more telling, next to the gritty Wotan of Theo Adam. With its slow vibrato under pressure, his is rarely a pleasing voice, but the clarity of the recording makes it a specific, never a woolly sound, so that the illumination of the narrative is consistent and intense. Kurt Moll is a gloriously firm Hunding, and Yvonne Minton a searingly effective Fricka. On CD, the drama and urgency of the recording have even greater bite; and, as with the others in this series, the mid-priced reissue (on four CDs instead of the original five) makes this set far more competitive.

Haitink's is a broad view, strong and thoughtful yet conveying monumental power. That goes with searching concentration and a consistent feeling for the detailed beauty of Wagner's writing, glowingly brought out in the warm and spacious recording, made in the Herkulessaal in Munich. The outstanding contribution comes from Cheryl Studer as Sieglinde, very convincingly cast, giving a tenderly affecting performance to bring out the character's vulnerability in a very human way. At *Du bist der Lenz* her radiant singing brings an eagerly personal revelation, the response of a lover. Despite some strained moments Rainer Goldberg makes a heroic Siegmund, far finer than most today; and Eva Marton is a noble, powerful Brünnhilde, less uneven of production than she has often been on record. Waltraud Meier makes a convincingly waspish and biting Fricka and Matti Salminen a resonant Hunding. James Morris is a fine, perceptive Wotan, and the voice, not an easy one to record, is better focused here than in Levine's rival DG version of this opera from the Met.

The great merits of Karajan's version are the refinement of the orchestral playing and the heroic strength of Jon Vickers as Siegmund. With that underlined, one cannot help but note that the vocal shortcomings here are generally more marked, and the total result does not add up to quite so compelling a dramatic experience: one is less involved. Thomas Stewart may have a younger, firmer voice than Hotter, but the character of Wotan emerges only partially; it is not just that he misses some of the word-meaning, but that on occasion – as in the kissing away of Brünnhilde's godhead – he underlines too crudely. A fine performance, none the less; and Josephine Veasey as Fricka matches her rival, Ludwig, in conveying the biting intensity of the part. Gundula Janowitz's Sieglinde has its beautiful moments, but the singing is ultimately a little static. Crespin's Brünnhilde is impressive, but nothing like as satisfying as her study of Sieglinde on the Decca set. The voice is at times strained into unsteadiness, which the microphone seems to exaggerate. The DG recording is good, but not quite in the same class as the Decca – its slightly recessed quality is the more apparent in the CD transfer – and the bass is relatively light.

Though Levine's speeds are often very slow, his conducting consistently reflects the timing of a stage performance, and the playing of the Met. orchestra is brilliant. Unfortunately the sound, though wide-ranging in frequency and dynamic and with spectacular brass and timpani, has little bloom on it, lacking depth of focus from front to back. Though Hildegard Behrens makes a fascinating and distinctive Brünnhilde, bringing out an element of vulnerability, the unevenness in the voice under pressure is often exaggerated. Gary Lakes makes a throaty, limited Siegmund, and his weaknesses are underlined by the power of the Sieglinde of Jessye Norman, magnetically compelling in every phrase but, in contrast to Behrens, conveying little vulnerability and not quite fitting the role, however intense and powerful the expression. The DG recording brings out the lack of sweetness in James Morris's voice as Wotan, but it is a noble, highly intelligent reading, while Kurt Moll is a magnificent Hunding; Christa Ludwig as Fricka sings with just as much heartfelt intensity here as she did thirty years earlier, taking the same role in the Decca *Ring* cycle with Solti. Compared with that classic version, with its vivid production by John Culshaw for stereo, the new one – for all the glories of wide-ranging digital sound – is shallow and even coarse.

Die Walküre, Act I (complete).
(M) (***) EMI mono CDH7 61020-2 [id.]. Lehmann, Melchior, List, VPO, Bruno Walter.
(M) **(*) Decca 425 963-2 [id.]. Flagstad, Svanholm, Van Mill, VPO, Knappertsbusch.

Though in the days of 78-r.p.m. discs the music had to be recorded in short takes of under five minutes, one is consistently gripped by the continuity and sustained lines of Walter's reading, and by the intensity and beauty of the playing of the Vienna Philharmonic. Lotte Lehmann's portrait of Sieglinde, arguably her finest role, has a depth and beauty never surpassed since, and Lauritz Melchior's heroic Siegmund brings singing of a scale and variety – not to mention beauty – that no Heldentenor today begins to match. Emanuel List as Hunding is satisfactory enough, but his achievement at least has latterly been surpassed.

Flagstad may not have been ideally cast as Sieglinde, but the command of her singing with its unfailing richness, even after her official retirement, crowns a strong and dramatic performance, with Svanholm and Van Mill singing cleanly. The early stereo still sounds vivid.

VOCAL COLLECTIONS

Choruses from: *Der fliegende Holländer; Götterdämmerung; Lohengrin; Die Meistersinger; Parsifal; Tannhäuser.*
(B) **(*) DG 429 169-2 [id.]. Elisabeth Schärtel, Josef Greindl, Bayreuth Fest. Ch. & O, Wilhelm Pitz.

This 1958 collection was recommended in our very first hardback *Stereo Record Guide* and it still sounds remarkably fresh. The female voices are not quite as impressive as the men's, but the tenors sing lustily and usually with fine, crisp discipline under their famous Bayreuth chorus master. Even though this was very early stereo, the spread and depth of the sound is remarkably realistic and in the *Parsifal* excerpt the distanced perspective for the female voices is expertly managed. The singing has ample conviction throughout and it is good to have such a vivid *Grand march* scene from *Tannhäuser*, with brilliant trumpets and an exhilarating sense of joy. The soloists (who have not very much to sing) are not overwhelmingly good. Josef Greindl has a somewhat heavy vibrato in his *Hoi-ho!* piece, but he has the right sort of voice. The remastering has added to the projection and sharpness of choral focus and has lost very little of the original atmosphere.

Choruses from: *Der fliegende Holländer; Lohengrin; Die Meistersinger; Parsifal; Tannhäuser.*
(M) *** Decca 421 865-2 (from complete sets, cond. Solti).

Solti's choral collection is superb, with an added sophistication in both performance and recording – especially in the subtle use of ambience and perspectives – to set it apart from the DG Bayreuth disc, good though that is. The collection opens with a blazing account of the *Lohengrin Act III Prelude*, since of course the *Bridal chorus* grows naturally out of it. But the *Pilgrims' chorus*, which comes next, creates an electrifying pianissimo and expands gloriously, while the excerpts from *Die Meistersinger* and *Parsifal* show Solti's characteristic intensity at its most potent.

Arias from: *Götterdämmerung; Lohengrin; Die Meistersinger; Rienzi; Siegfried; Tannhäuser; Tristan; Die Walküre.*
(M) (***) EMI mono CDH7 69789-2. Lauritz Melchior, LSO, Barbirolli; or Berlin State Op. O, Leo Blech.

No Heldentenor on record has outshone Lauritz Melchior in this Wagner repertory. This collection in the Références series brings together fifteen items recorded in his first full maturity between 1928 and 1931, when the magnificent voice was at its freshest. Not that the *Walküre* excerpts here improve on his incomparable performance as Siegfried in Bruno Walter's complete Act I of 1936 (also on Références CD – see above); but, fascinatingly, Barbirolli in the second of the three excerpts, *Wintersturme*, relaxes him more than Leo Blech did on the other two. The selection ends with Melchior's glorious singing of Walther's two arias from *Meistersinger*, noble and shining. Excellent transfers, with the voice given astonishing presence.

Götterdämmerung: Dawn and Siegfried's Rhine journey; Siegfried's funeral march. Parsifal: Ich sah' das Kind. Tristan und Isolde: Prelude; Liebestod. Die Walküre: Wotan's farewell and Magic fire music.
**(*) Decca 414 625-2 [id.]. Flagstad, Nilsson, London, VPO, Knappertsbusch.

This is a splendid reminder of Hans Knappertsbusch's mastery as a Wagnerian, recorded in the period when Decca was working up to the idea of tackling a complete *Ring* cycle. The much younger Solti was finally chosen for that big project, but the veteran Knappertsbusch in the preliminary period did these glowing performances, collaborating with the two greatest Wagnerian sopranos of their generations, Nilsson in the *Liebestod*, Flagstad in the *Parsifal* item. George London is the Wotan, firmer than he later became. Though the digital transfers are bright, the vividness of sound is amazing, with the voices particularly well caught.

Waldteufel, Emil (1837–1915)

Waltzes: *Acclamations; España; Estudiantina; Les Patineurs.*
(M) *** EMI CDM7 63136-2 [id.]. Monte Carlo Nat. Op. O, Boskovsky – OFFENBACH: *Gaîté parisienne.***

Boskovsky's collection has the advantage of including, besides the three favourites, *Acclamations*, which he opens very invitingly. His manner is *echt*-Viennese, but *The Skaters* responds well to his warmth and there is no lack of sparkle here. The remastering of the mid-1970s recording is admirably fresh.

Walton, William (1902–83)

Capriccio burlesco; Coronation marches: Crown imperial; Orb and sceptre. Funeral march from Hamlet; Johannesburg festival overture; Richard III: Prelude & suite; Scapino overture; Spitfire prelude & fugue.
(M) **(*) EMI CDM7 63369-2 [id.]. Royal Liverpool PO, Sir Charles Groves.

The 1969 collection of Walton's shorter orchestral pieces was made in Studio 2 (EMI's hi-fi-conscious equivalent of Decca's Phase 4) and now seems slightly over-bright with its digital remastering. The sound tends to polarize, with a lack of opulence in the middle range, so necessary in the *nobilmente* of the big tunes of the stirring *Spitfire Prelude and fugue* and *Crown imperial*. The Shakespearean film music was recorded much later (1984) and the quality is fuller, more warmly atmospheric. Although the two *Coronation marches* could do with a little more exuberance, Groves is otherwise a highly sympathetic interpreter of this repertoire, and the playing of the Liverpool orchestra is excellent.

Cello concerto.
*** CBS MK 39541 [id.]. Yo-Yo Ma, LSO, Previn – ELGAR: *Concerto.***
(M) *** EMI CDM7 63020-2. Tortelier, Bournemouth SO, Berglund – SHOSTAKOVICH: *Cello concerto No. 1.***

Yo-Yo Ma and Previn give a sensuously beautiful performance. With speeds markedly slower than usual in the outer movements, the meditation is intensified to bring a mood of ecstasy, quite distinct from other Walton, with the central allegro becoming the symphonic kernel of the work, far more than just a scherzo. In the excellent CBS recording, the soloist is less forwardly and more faithfully balanced than is common. The CD is one of CBS's most impressive.

Tortelier's version of Walton's *Cello concerto* is more openly extrovert in its emotional response, offering a highly involving alternative approach. After the haunting melancholy of the first movement, the central scherzo emerges as a far weightier piece than with Ma and Previn, while the final variations are developed with a strong sense of compulsion. At mid-price and with full, vivid recording, Tortelier's reading remains very competitive.

Viola concerto; Violin concerto.
*** EMI Dig. CDC7 49628-2 [id.]. Nigel Kennedy, RPO, Previn.

Few works written this century can match Walton's two pre-war string concertos in richness and warmth of melody. Kennedy's achievement in giving equally rich and expressive performances of both works makes for an ideal coupling, helped by the unique insight of André Previn as Waltonian. Kennedy on the viola produces tone as rich and firm as on his usual violin. His double-stopping is wonderfully firm and true, and though in the first movement of the *Viola concerto* he opts for a dangerously slow tempo, drawing the lovely first melody out more spaciously than the score would strictly allow, he justifies it with his concentration at a steady, undistorted pace. The Scherzo has never been recorded with more panache than here, and the finale brings a magic moment in the return of the main theme from the opening, hushed and intense. In the *Violin concerto* too, Kennedy gives a warmly relaxed reading, in which he dashes off the bravura passages with great flair. He may miss some of the more searchingly introspective manner of Chung in her 1971 version, but there are few Walton records as richly rewarding as this, helped by warm, atmospheric sound.

Violin concerto.
(M) *** Decca 421 385-2 [id.]. Kyung Wha Chung, LSO, Previn – ELGAR: *Cello concerto.****
(M) (***) RCA mono GD 87966 [7966-2-RG]. Heifetz, Philh. O, composer – ELGAR: *Concerto.*(***)

In the brooding intensity of the opening evocation, Kyung Wha Chung presents the first melody with a depth of expression, tender and hushed, that has never been matched on record, not even by Heifetz. With Previn as guide and with the composer himself a sympathetic observer at the recording sessions, Chung then builds up a performance which must remain a classic, showing the *Concerto* as one of the greatest of the century in this genre. Outstandingly fine recording, sounding the more vivid in its CD format.

It was Heifetz who commissioned the Walton *Concerto* and who gave the first performances, as well as making a wartime recording in America. This is the later version, first issued in 1951, which Heifetz made with Walton conducting, using the revised score. Speeds are often hair-raisingly fast, but few Heifetz records convey as much passion as this. The mono recording is dry, with a distracting hum in the transfer, but the high-voltage electricity has never been matched in this radiant music.

Façade (complete, including *Façade 2*).
(B) *** CfP CD-CFP 4564. Fenella Fielding, Michael Flanders, ASMF (members), Marriner.
**(*) ASV Dig. CDDCA 679 [id.]. Prunella Scales, Timothy West, L. Mozart Players (members), Jane Glover.
(*) Decca Dig. 421 717-2 [id.]. Dame Peggy Ashcroft, Jeremy Irons, L. Sinf., Chailly – STRAVINSKY: *Renard.**

(i) *Façade* (complete); (ii) *Siesta; Overtures: Portsmouth Point; Scapino.*
⊛ (M) *** Decca mono 425 661-2 [id.]. (i) Sitwell, Pears, E. Op. Group Ens., Collins; (ii) LPO, Boult – ARNOLD: *English dances.*(***).

Anthony Collins's 1954 recording of *Façade* is a gramophone classic, sounding miraculously vivid and atmospheric in a CD transfer that seems almost like modern stereo. Dame Edith Sitwell had one of the richest, most characterful of speaking voices and here she recites her early poems to the masterly, witty music of the youthful Walton with glorious relish. Peter Pears is splendid too in the fast poems, rattling off the lines like the *grande dame* herself, to demonstrate how near-nonsense can be pure poetry. Of course there are flaws in Dame Edith's contribution over rhythm. She has no idea whatever of offbeat accentuation or jazz syncopation in *Old Sir Faulk*, but even so the voice itself is incomparable. The Boult mono versions of *Scapino* and *Siesta* make a valuable coupling, although *Portsmouth Point* misses some of the rhythmic bite of his first 78-r.p.m. disc. Malcolm Arnold's own première recording of his masterly *English dances*, full of exuberance and colour, completes a fascinating programme that no lover of English music should miss.

Those seeking a stereo recording of *Façade* should be well satisfied with the CfP reissue. Fenella Fielding and Michael Flanders make a characterful pair of reciters, the one relishing in echo the *grande dame* quality of the poetess, the other, wonderfully fleet of tongue, is not quite so miraculously deft as Peter Pears. The balance favours the reciters against Neville Marriner's wittily pointed accompaniment and, with excellent 1972 sound, this makes a fine alternative choice.

Jane Glover and the London Mozart Players in unaccustomed repertory match the wit of the agile and characterful reciters in a pointed account of the *Façade* entertainment, well recorded, though with the usual bias in favour of the voices. Scales and West as a husband-and-wife team are inventive in their shared roles, and generally it works well. *Scotch rhapsody* is hilariously done as a duet, with West intervening at appropriate moments, and with sharply precise Scots accents. Regional accents may defy Edith Sitwell's original prescription – and her own example – but here, with one exception, they add an appropriate flavour. The exception is *Popular song*, where Prunella Scales's cockney accent clashes horribly with the allusive words, with their 'cupolas, gables in the lakes, Georgian stables'. For fill-up the reciters have recorded more Sitwell poems, but unaccompanied.

Dame Peggy Ashcroft and Jeremy Irons get the fun right in reciting Edith Sitwell's poems, characterizing well but retaining an element of formality, with rhythms crisp. They are matched by a scintillating performance of the young Walton's brilliant score from the London Sinfonietta, and Chailly is unerring over the timing and rhythmic control of the different popular idioms which Walton parodies. The snag is that co-ordination between voices and instruments is flawed: not just a question of the occasional rhythmic freedom from the reciters but rather the balance, which presents the voices very far forward in a different, drier acoustic. That underlines the fact that Dame Peggy in her eighties has to take a breath every few words, while the music too often gets obscured. It is good to have *Façade 2* as supplement, the suite of eight sparer movements that had been discarded originally and which were then resurrected by the composer in 1979.

Film music: *As you like it: Suite. The Battle of Britain: Suite. Henry V: Suite. History of the English speaking peoples: March. Troilus and Cressida* (opera): *Interlude.*
*** EMI Dig. CDC7 47944-2 [id.]. LPO Ch. & O, Carl Davis.

Here, with many items never recorded before, is a heartwarming celebration of Walton's commissioned incidental music, helped by red-blooded performances from the LPO under the tireless advocate, Carl Davis. *The Battle of Britain suite* presents the music that was rejected for the original film. Another vintage Walton march here was written for a television series based on Churchill's history but, again, was never used. It is a pity the *Henry V suite* does not include the Agincourt charge, but it is good to have the choral contributions to the opening and closing sequences. Best of all, perhaps, is the long-buried music for the 1926 film of *As you like it*. Walton, having just had great success with his *First Symphony*, here exuberantly does some joyful cribbing from Respighi, Ravel and others, but remains gloriously himself. Warm, opulent recording.

Film scores: *As you like it; Hamlet.*
*** Chan. Dig. CHAN 8842 [id.]. Catherine Bott, Sir John Gielgud, ASMF, Marriner.

Next to his two other great film-scores for Sir Laurence Olivier, Walton's music for *Hamlet* has been poorly treated, both on record and in concert performance; now, thanks to the diligence of Christopher Palmer, this fine disc in Chandos's Walton series gathers together some 40 minutes of music, most of it previously unrecorded. Some proves to be relatively slight – *The Ghost* for example is little more than bogey-bogey atmosphere-making – and nothing quite matches the magnificent *Funeral march*, but this is still a rich and colourful suite, superbly played and recorded, and much enhanced by the contribution of Sir John Gielgud in two of Hamlet's soliloquies, 'O that this too, too solid flesh' and 'To be or not to be'. The selection of music from the pre-war film of *As you like it* makes a valuable fill-up. It omits four tiny passages, previously recorded by Carl Davis on his EMI disc of Walton film music, but adds the splendid setting of *Under the greenwood tree* in a radiant performance by Catherine Bott, a most valuable addition. Marriner and the Academy draw out all the romantic warmth of both scores, and the sound is richly atmospheric to match.

Henry V (film music): *Passacaglia; The Death of Falstaff; Touch her soft lips and part.*
*** DG 419 748-2 [id.]. ECO, Barenboim – DELIUS: *Aquarelles* etc.; VAUGHAN WILLIAMS: *Lark ascending; Oboe concerto.****

These two fine Walton string pieces make an admirable complement to a sensuously beautiful collection of English music, with Barenboim at his most affectionately inspirational and the ECO very responsive, and with the 1975 recording retaining its warmth and bloom.

Sinfonia concertante for piano & orchestra (original version).
*** Conifer Dig. CDCF 175 [id.]. Kathryn Stott, RPO, Handley – BRIDGE: *Phantasm*; IRELAND: *Piano concerto.****

It is high time that Walton's *Sinfonia concertante* was treated to a good modern recording, and Kathryn Stott, warmly and strongly accompanied by Vernon Handley and the RPO, gives an outstanding reading, the more interesting for bringing the first ever recording of the work's original version. It was in 1943, just before making the very first recording with Phyllis Sellick as soloist – also a superb performance – that Walton revised the score, simplifying the solo part and thinning the orchestration. Responding to a remark that Walton made not long before he died (suggesting that his initial conception was perhaps superior to the revision) and with the active agreement of Lady Walton, Stott and Handley opted to go back to the original, and the result seems to strengthen what is a consistently memorable work, built from vintage Walton material. This was his first full-length piece using orchestra, and – with each movement characterizing one of the three Sitwells, Walton's early sponsors, in turn Osbert, Edith and Sacheverell – it stands up remarkably well, even next to Walton's later masterly concertos for viola, violin and cello. First-rate recorded sound, and a coupling both generous and apt.

Symphonies Nos. (i) *1;* (ii) *2.*
(M) *** EMI Dig. CD-EMX 2151. (i) LPO, (ii) LSO, Sir Charles Mackerras.

(M) ** EMI CDM7 63269-2 [id.]. (i) New Philh. O, Sargent; (ii) LSO, Previn.

Sir Charles Mackerras in coupling Walton's two symphonies makes a particularly strong case for No. 2, with the LSO sharply incisive, helping to bring out both its consistency with No. 1 and a new sensuousness of expression. Where too often No. 2 has been dismissed as Walton imitating himself, saying nothing new, Mackerras firmly establishes the work's distinction, above all in its control of argument and its brilliant use of a very large orchestra. The thematic material may not be as striking as in the high-voltage *First Symphony*, with its eruption of youthful inspiration, but there is consistent lyrical warmth. Mackerras's reading of No. 1, using the LPO, adopts broader speeds than usual. It may not be as bitingly dramatic as the very finest versions, but the richness and strength of the symphony, one of the key British works of its period, come over powerfully. Warm, full recording in both symphonies. An outstanding bargain.

Previn's outstanding version of No. 2, if anything even more intense than the superb Mackerras reading on EMI Eminence, sounds very vivid and immediate in its CD transfer, with the 1974 sound providing a keen sense of presence. Sadly, Sargent's 1966 recording of No. 1 seems tepid beside it, generally a well-behaved reading, but one which lacks Waltonian bite, an essential ingredient in this work.

Symphony No. 1 in B flat min..
(M) *** RCA GD 87830 [7830-2-RG]. LSO, Previn (with VAUGHAN WILLIAMS: *Wasps overture***).

Symphony No. 1 in B flat min.; Coronation marches: Crown Imperial; Orb and sceptre.
** Telarc Dig. CD 80125 [id.]. RPO, Previn.

Symphony No. 1; Portsmouth Point overture.
** Virgin Dig. VC 790715-2 [id.]. LPO, Slatkin.

Symphony No. 1; Variations on a theme by Hindemith.
**(*) EMI Dig. CDC7 49671-2 [id.]. Bournemouth SO, Handley.

On RCA Previn gives a marvellously biting account of the magnificent *First Symphony*. His fast tempi may initially make one feel that he is pressing too hard, but his ability to screw the dramatic tension tighter and tighter until the final resolution is most assured, and certainly reflects the tense mood of the mid-1930s, as well as the youthful Walton's own personal tensions at that time. '*Presto con malizia*' says the score for the scherzo, and malice is exactly what Previn conveys, with the hints of vulgarity and humour securely placed. In the slow movement Previn finds real warmth, giving some of the melodies an Elgarian richness; and the finale's electricity here helps to overcome any feeling that it is too facile, too easily happy a conclusion. The bright recording – made by Decca engineers in the vintage 1960s – has splendid focus in its CD remastering, yet does not lack body. Previn has rarely made a record as powerfully intense as this, and as a performance it is unsurpassed.

With a more sumptuous sound than in most versions, Handley's reading is above all red-bloodedly romantic, with Walton's melodies given their full expressive warmth. Equally, the jazzy spring that Handley gives to the rhythms, with their jaggedly misplaced accents, conveys a consistent buoyancy; nerves jangle less than usual, and the *Presto con malizia* of the scherzo has a *Till*-like sense of fun about it. The lovely flute melody of the slow movement is not as cool as it usually is, leading on warmly to a climax that is weighty rather than bitingly tragic. It is a very valid view, beautifully achieved by Handley and the Bournemouth orchestra. Before the *Symphony*, Handley presents the first CD version of Walton's *Hindemith variations*, one of the most satisfying of his later orchestral works, full of strong invention and finely wrought.

Slatkin does not have quite the rhythmic mastery in giving a jazzy lift to syncopations or in moulding Waltonian melody that you find in both Previn's versions, and the scherzo is almost breathlessly fast. But the finale is magnificent, bringing thrust and power and culminating superbly in the uninhibited triple timpani passage near the end. Slatkin takes an equally electric view of the *Overture*, again played brilliantly by the LPO.

Previn's view of Walton's electrifying *First Symphony* grew broader and less biting with the years. The sumptuous Telarc recording also makes for warmth rather than incisiveness. There is an element of disappointment here even though, with fine playing from the RPO, the slow movement is more richly luxuriant than before. The two *Coronation marches* make a colourful and welcome fill-up.

Symphony No. 2, Suite: Troilus and Cressida (arr. Palmer).
** Chan. Dig. CHAN 8772. LPO, Thomson.

Bryden Thomson in *Symphony No. 2* takes a characteristically broad view, leading up to a rugged account of the *Passacaglia* finale with its nose-thumbing twelve-note theme. The weight of the reading is reinforced by the warmly reverberant recording. It has far less electricity than either the Mackerras or Previn versions of the symphony. In the large-scale symphonic suite which Christopher Palmer has drawn from the opera *Troilus and Cressida*, the four movements broadly follow the layout of a regular symphony. The first scene-setting movement may lack symphonic argument, but the second is an effective scherzo and trio, with the Pandarus music framing Cressida's memorable aria, *At the haunted end of the day*. The slow movement is based on the Act II love scene with its central interlude of love-making followed by poignant farewells. The last is framed by Cressida's two big solos in Act III, ending as the opera does. Though inevitably one misses the voices, it is good to have such rich Walton inspirations so warmly played and recorded.

Passacaglia for solo cello.
*** Chan. Dig. CHAN 8499 [id.]. Raphael Wallfisch – BAX: *Rhapsodic ballad*; BRIDGE: *Cello sonata*; DELIUS: *Cello sonata.****

William Walton's *Passacaglia* for solo cello was composed in the last year of his life. It has restraint and eloquence, and Raphael Wallfisch gives a thoroughly sympathetic account of it. Excellent recording.

(i) *Piano quartet; String quartet in A min.*
**(*) Mer. Dig. CDE 84139 [id.]. John McCabe, English Qt.

The *Piano quartet* is a work of Walton's immaturity, though there are many indications of what is to come. It is coupled with the mature *String quartet*; this is a substantial piece with stronger claims on the repertoire. McCabe and the English Quartet give a convincing enough account of the early piece, but the latter's account of the *String quartet* does not present a strong challenge to that of the Gabrielis on Chandos. If you want this particular coupling rather than the Elgar, however, this is certainly worth investigating.

String quartet in A min.
*** Chan. Dig. CHAN 8474 [id.]. Gabrieli Qt – ELGAR: *String quartet.****

Walton's only *String quartet* must rank as one of his best works and, in hands such as these, sounds far more effective than in the version for full strings that he made in the early 1970s. The performance was given at The Maltings, Snape, and the excellence of both the playing and the recorded sound must earn this a strong recommendation on CD, which is in the demonstration bracket.

Violin sonata.
(*) ASV Dig. CDDCA 548 [id.]. Lorraine McAslan, John Blakely – ELGAR: *Sonata.*(*)

Lorraine McAslan gives a warmly committed performance of Walton's often wayward *Sonata*. The romantic melancholy of the piece suits her well, and though the recording does not make her tone as rounded as it should be, she produces some exquisite pianissimo playing. John Blakely is a most sympathetic partner, particularly impressive in crisply articulated scherzando passages.

CHORAL MUSIC

All this time; Cantico del sole; Jubilate Deo; King Herod and the cock; A Litany; Magnificat and Nunc dimittis; Make we joy now in this feast; Missa brevis; Set me as a seal (antiphon); The Twelve; What cheer?; Where does the uttered music go?.
*** Conifer Dig. CDCF 164 [id.]. Trinity College Ch., Richard Marlow.

Richard Marlow conducts his Cambridge choir of mixed voices in a delectable collection of Walton's sacred choral music, both unaccompanied and with organ. Item after item – the majority from late in the composer's career – brings home how brightly the spirit of *Belshazzar* still burned in his writing right to the end. The *Missa brevis* for Coventry Cathedral in its spareness strikes a darker, deeper note. The *Cantico del sole*, idiomatically setting Italian words of St Francis, is warmly distinctive, and the longest piece, *The Twelve*, to words specially written by W. H. Auden, is far more than an occasional piece. Marlow draws phenomenally responsive singing from his talented choir, with matching and ensemble that approach the ideal. The recording is just as alive and immaculate.

Belshazzar's Feast; Coronation Te Deum; Gloria.
**(*) Chan. Dig. CHAN 8760 [id.]. Howell, Gunson, Mackie, Roberts, Bach Ch., Philh. O, Willcocks.
(M) (**(*)) EMI CHS7 63376-2 [Ang. CDHB 63376]. Milligan, Huddersfield Ch. Soc., Royal Liverpool PO, Sargent – ELGAR: *Dream of Gerontius.*(**(*))
** Telarc Dig. CD 80181 [id.]. William Stone, Atlanta Ch. & SO, Robert Shaw – BERNSTEIN: *Chichester psalms* etc.**

(i) *Belshazzar's Feast; Henry V (film score): Suite.*
*** ASV Dig. CDRPO 8001 [id.]. (i) Luxon, Brighton Fest. Ch., L. Coll. Mus., RPO, Previn.

Belshazzar's Feast; In honour of the City of London.
*** EMI Dig. CDC7 49496-2. Wilson Johnson, LSO Ch., LSO, Hickox.

Richard Hickox not only conducts the most sharply dramatic account of *Belshazzar's Feast* currently available, even crisper and keener if less jazzy than Previn's superb 1971 EMI version (still awaited on CD), but couples it with the one major work of Walton left unrecorded: his cantata, *In honour of the City of London*. With forces almost as lavish as those in the oratorio, its vitality and atmospheric colour come over on this record to a degree generally impossible in live performance. As for *Belshazzar* under Hickox, its voltage has never seemed higher on record, thanks not just to the LSO and Chorus – in far sharper form than for Previn seventeen years earlier – but to the full and brilliant digital recording. The dramatic soloist is David Wilson Johnson, colouring his voice with chilling menace in the writing-on-the-wall sequence.

André Previn's new digital version of Walton's oratorio brings a performance in some ways even sharper and more urgent than his fine earlier version for EMI with the LSO. The recording is very clear, revealing details of Walton's brilliant orchestration as never before. The chorus, singing with biting intensity, is set realistically behind the orchestra, and though that gives the impression of a smaller group than is ideal, clarity and definition are enhanced. Benjamin Luxon – who earlier sang in Solti's Decca version – is a characterful soloist, but his heavy vibrato is exaggerated by too close a balance. The five-movement suite from Walton's film-music for *Henry V* makes an attractive coupling. Previn was the first conductor on record since Walton himself to capture the full dramatic bite and colour of this music, with the cavalry charge at Agincourt particularly vivid.

Willcocks's version of *Belshazzar's Feast* came as the first issue in Chandos's big Walton series, a very promising start. He scores over most rivals in his pacing which, far more than is common, follows the example set by the composer himself in his two recordings. Speeds tend to be a degree faster, as in *By the waters of Babylon*, which flows evenly yet without haste. The soloist, Gwynne Howell, firm and dark of tone, is among the finest of all exponents but, with the Bach Choir placed rather more distantly than in most versions, this is not as incisive as its finest rivals. The *Coronation Te Deum* receives a richly idiomatic performance, and Willcocks also gives weight and thrust to the *Gloria*, with the tenor, Neil Mackie, outstanding among the soloists. The microphone unfortunately catches an unevenness in Ameral Gunson's mezzo. The recording is warmly reverberant, not ideally clear on choral detail but easy to listen to.

The Sargent version, dating from the late 1950s, brings a good example of his 'Hudderspool' work in other than the traditional repertory. This is no match in electric tension for the very first ever recording of *Belshazzar*, made with the same choir and orchestra in 1943 under the composer; but, with generally brisk speeds, it is still fresh and dramatic. James Milligan, a singer cut off in his early prime, is an excellent soloist. The coupling is a generous and apt one, though it would have been far better to have had the earlier versions, Walton's own of *Belshazzar* and Sargent's earlier one of *Gerontius*.

Robert Shaw with his superb chorus achieves a precision of choral ensemble that has hardly been achieved on record before. With a well-balanced recording which gives the chorus detailed clarity with no spotlighting, there is an attractive freshness in this account. Yet the result is not as electrifying as the opening promises, when – curiously, in an American performance – Shaw's passion for precision prevents him from interpreting Walton's jazz rhythms with the necessary degree of rhythmic freedom to make them sound idiomatic. It all sounds too literal. The most damaging flaw is Shaw's inexplicable addition of full chorus singing *Ah!* on the final chord of the orchestral coda, totally unauthorized and not very effective.

Ward, John (1571–1638)

Madrigals: *Come sable night; Cruel unkind; Die not, fond man; Hope of my heart; If heaven's just wrath; If the deep sighs; I have retreated; My breast I'll set; Oft have I tender'd; Out from the vale; Retire, my troubled soul; Sweet Philomel.*
*** Hyp. Dig. CDA 66256 [id.]. Consort of Musicke, Anthony Rooley.

Ward's music speaks with a distinctive voice, free from the self-conscious melancholy that afflicts some of his contemporaries. This is not to say that his output is wanting in depth of feeling or elegiac sentiment, but rather that his language is freer from artifice. He chooses poetry of high quality and his music is always finely proportioned and organic in conception. These settings appeared at the end of the period in which the madrigal flourished (in 1613, to be exact) and can be regarded as representing the tradition at its finest. These new performances have a distinct tonal blend; such is the quality of this music and the accomplishment with which it is presented that collectors who respond to this repertoire should not hesitate.

Warlock, Peter (1894–1930)

Capriol suite for strings.
(M) *** Decca 421 391-2 [id.]. ASMF, Marriner – BRITTEN: *Variations on a theme of Frank Bridge*; BUTTERWORTH: *Banks of green willow* etc.***

The playing of the St Martin's Academy under Marriner is lively, polished and stylish here and readily reveals the freshness of Warlock's invention, based on Elizabethan dances. The recording is first rate: it dates from 1970 and has added realism and presence without loss of body. The Britten and Butterworth couplings are equally attractive.

Serenade for strings (for the sixtieth birthday of Delius).
(M) *** Decca 421 384-2 [id.]. ASMF, Marriner – ELGAR: *Elegy for strings* etc.**(*)

Warlock's gentle *Serenade*, written for Delius, is beautifully played and recorded here, an unjustly neglected work receiving its due.

Songs: *As ever I saw; Autumn twilight; The bachelor; The bayly berith the bell away; Captain Stratton's fancy; First mercy; The fox; Hey, trolly, loly lo; Ha'nacker Mill; I held love's head; The jolly shepherd; Late summer; Lullaby; Milkmaids; Mourne no more; Mr Belloc's fancy; My gostly fader; My own country; The night; Passing by; Piggesnie; Play-acting; Rest, sweet nymphs; Sleep; Sweet content; Take, o take those lips away; There is a lady sweet and fair; Thou gav'st me leave to kiss; Walking the woods; When as the rye; The wind from the west; Yarmouth Fair.*
*** Chan. Dig. CHAN 8643 [id.]. Benjamin Luxon, David Willison.

A remarkably generous recital of 32 Warlock songs, ranging wide, from the melancholy and drama to 'hey-nonny-nonny' Elizabethan pastiche. Songs like *Autumn twilight*, the powerfully expressive *Late summer* and *Captain Stratton's fancy* are appealing in utterly different ways, and there is not a single number in the programme that does not show the composer either in full imaginative flow or simply enjoying himself, as in *Yarmouth Fair*. Luxon's performances are first class and David Willison provides sensitive and sparkling accompaniments. The recording is first class.

The Curlew (song-cycle for tenor, flute, cor anglais & strings).
(M) *** EMI CDM7 69170-2-[id.]. Ian Partridge, Music Group of London – VAUGHAN WILLIAMS: *On Wenlock Edge; 10 Blake Songs.*** ⊛

The Curlew is Warlock's most striking and ambitious work, a continuous setting of a sequence of poems by Yeats, which reflect the darker side of the composer's complex personality. Ian Partridge, with the subtlest shading of tone-colour and the most sensitive response to word-meaning, gives an intensely poetic performance, beautifully recorded and transferred to CD with striking presence.

The Curlew (song-cycle). Songs: *The Birds; Chopcherry; The fairest May; Mourne no more; My ghostly fader; Nursery jingles (How many miles to Babylon?; O, my kitten; Little Jack Jingle; Suky, you shall be my wife; Jenny Gray); Sleep; The Water Lily.*
**(*) Pearl SHECD 510 [id.]. Griffet, Haffner Qt, Murdoch, Ryan.

Each one of these songs is a miniature of fine sensitivity, and James Griffett sings them with keen insight, pointing the words admirably, though his performance of *The Curlew* is not so beautiful or quite so imaginative as Ian Partridge's version. Good recording.

Wassenaer, Unico (1692–1766)

6 Concerti armonici.
(M) **(*) DG 427 138-2 [id.]. Camerata Berne, Thomas Füri.
** Chan. Dig. CHAN 8481 [id.]. I Musici di Montreal, Turovsky.

The Swiss ensemble give performances of impeccable style and accuracy, though in the slow movements they miss something of the breadth and spaciousness in the writing. But they are certainly involved in this music, and they involve the listener too. The remastered DG recording is excellent and at mid-price this is well worth considering.

For years these eloquent concertos were attributed to Pergolesi. In 1981, however, an autograph manuscript came to light in the hand of a Dutch nobleman, which would appear to have settled the matter. I Musici de Montreal have admirable spirit and produce a rich, robust sonority. In terms of finesse, however, they do not displace the best of earlier versions.

Weber, Carl Maria von (1786–1826)

Clarinet concertino in C min., Op. 26.
*** ASV Dig. CDDCA 559 [id.]. Emma Johnson, ECO, Groves – CRUSELL: *Concerto No. 2*** ⊛; BAERMANN: *Adagio***; ROSSINI: *Introduction, theme and variatons.***

Emma Johnson is in her element in Weber's delightful *Concertino*. Her phrasing is wonderfully beguiling and her use of light and shade agreeably subtle, while she finds a superb lilt in the final section, pacing the music to bring out its charm rather than achieve breathless bravura. Sir Charles Groves provides an admirable accompaniment, and the recording is eminently realistic and naturally balanced.

Clarinet concerto No. 1 in F min., J.114.
*** ASV Dig. CDDCA 585 [id.]. Emma Johnson, ECO, Yan Pascal Tortelier – DEBUSSY: *Rapsodie*; CRUSELL: *Introduction, theme and variations*; TARTINI: *Concertino.***
(M) **(*) RCA GD 60035. Stolzman, Mostly Mozart Fest. O, Schneider (with ROSSINI: *Theme and variations in C***; MOZART: *Andante in C, K.315**).

In this fine, inspired version of the Weber *First Concerto* the subtlety of Emma Johnson's expression, even in relation to most of her older rivals is astonishing, with pianissimos more daringly extreme and with distinctively persuasive phrasing in the slow movement, treated warmly and spaciously. In the sparkling finale she is wittier than any, plainly enjoying herself to the full, and is given natural sound, set in a helpful acoustic.

Stolzman's account of the *F minor Clarinet concerto* displays plenty of character, an easy bravura and a succulent tone in the *Adagio*. Here too the orchestra accompanies warmly, with some fine horn playing; but some might feel that in the outer movements the tuttis are too overwhelming in their expansiveness. Although the *Introduction* is a shade bland, the coupled Rossini *Variations* sparkle operatically once they get fully underway; but the Mozart *Andante*, conceived for the flute, needs a lighter touch if it is to be heard on the clarinet.

Clarinet concertos Nos. 1 in F min., J.114; 2 in E flat, J.118; Clarinet concertino, J.109.
*** Virgin Dig. VC 790720-2 [id.]. Antony Pay, O of Age of Enlightenment.
**(*) Chan. CHAN 8305 [id.]. Hilton, CBSO, Järvi.
**(*) HM Orfeo CO 67831A. Brunner, Bamberg SO, Caetani.

Clarinet concerto No. 2.
*** Hyp. CDA 66088 [id.]. Thea King, LSO, Francis – CRUSELL: *Concerto No. 2.********

Antony Pay and the Orchestra of the Age of Enlightenment offer period-instrument performances. Pay uses a copy of a seven-keyed clarinet by Simiot of Lyons from 1800. The sonority is cleaner and less bland than can be the case in modern performances, and the solo playing is both expert and sensitive. A further gesture to authenticity is the absence of a conductor; however, the ensemble might have been even better and the texture more finely judged and balanced had there been one. The recording is vivid and truthful.

Stylish, understanding performances of both *Concertos* from Janet Hilton, spirited and rhythmic (particularly in No. 1), but erring just a little on the side of caution next to her finest virtuoso rivals, given full yet clear and well-balanced digital recording.

Eduard Brunner's performances are often more romantically ardent, with a firmer line. Both slow movements come off especially well, with the horn chorale in the *Adagio* of the *First Concerto* producing some lovely playing from the Bamberg orchestra. However, articulation of the fast running passages is sometimes less characterful, and Janet Hilton finds rather more humour in the finales, especially the *Alla Polacca* of No. 2. Yet Brunner is at his best in the last movement of the *Concertino*, his bravura agreeably extrovert here. On the Orfeo CD orchestral textures are thick in tuttis.

Thea King with her beautiful range of tone-colours gives a totally delightful account of the *Second Concerto*, particularly lovely in the G minor slow movement and seductively pointed in the *Polacca* rhythms of the finale, never pressed too hard. She is accompanied admirably by Alun Francis and the LSO in a warmly reverberant recording that CD makes very realistic indeed.

Horn concertino in E min., Op. 45.
*** Ph. Dig. 412 237-2 [id.]. Baumann, Leipzig GO, Masur – R. STRAUSS: *Horn concertos.*****(*)**

Baumann plays Weber's opening lyrical melody so graciously that the listener is led to believe that this is a more substantial work than it is. At the end of the *Andante* Baumann produces an undulating series of chords (by gently singing the top note as he plays) and the effect is spine-tingling, while the easy virtuosity of the closing *Polacca* is hardly less breathtaking. Masur's accompaniment has matching warmth, while the Leipzig Hall adds its usual flattering ambience.

Piano concertos Nos. 1 in C, J.98; 2 in E flat, J.155; Konzertstück in F min., J.282.
*** EMI Dig. CDC7 49177-2 [id.]. Peter Rösel, Dresden State O, Blomstedt.

The Weber *Piano concertos* are mercurial and well merit an occasional hearing; it is clear that Peter Rösel is a most nimble and intelligent player who is well able to meet the demands of these attractive showpieces. The playing of the Staatskapelle, Dresden, under Herbert Blomstedt is hardly less admirable and should make many friends for this often underrated repertoire. No grumbles about the recording, which is truthfully balanced and well detailed. Recommended.

Introduction, theme and variations (for clarinet and orchestra).
*** Denon C37 7038 [id.]. Meyer, Berlin Philh. Qt – MOZART: *Clarinet quintet.****

This essentially lightweight display piece, attributed to Weber, is now known to be the work of Joseph Küffner (1777–1856) and is listed here for convenience. The recording by Sabine Meyer and the Berlin Philharmonia is first rate, very well balanced and recorded.

Invitation to the dance (orch. Berlioz).
*** Decca Dig. 411 898-2 [id.]. Nat. PO, Bonynge – BERLIOZ: *Les Troyens ballet***; LECOCQ: *Mam'zelle Angot.****

Bonynge's account has elegance and polish and the waltz rhythms are nicely inflected. The Kingsway Hall recording is first class, if slightly sharp in focus.

Konzertstück in F min., Op. 79.
*** Ph. 412 251-2 [id.]. Brendel, LSO, Abbado – SCHUMANN: *Piano concerto.****

This Philips version of Weber's programmatic *Konzertstück* is very brilliant indeed, and finds the distinguished soloist in his very best form: Brendel is wonderfully light and invariably imaginative. In every respect, including the recording quality, this is unlikely to be surpassed for a long time. On CD, Weber emerges in brighter, firmer focus than on LP; collectors wanting this delightful work in the new format need not hesitate.

Overtures: *Abu Hassan; Der Beherrscher der Geister; Euryanthe; Der Freischütz; Oberon; Peter Schmoll; Invitation to the dance* (orch. Berlioz), *Op. 65.*
⊛ *** Nimbus Dig. NI 5154 [id.]. Hanover Band, Roy Goodman.
(M) *** DG 419 070-2 [id.]. BPO, Karajan.

Goodman and the Hanover Band give delectable performances of the six Weber overtures plus *Invitation to the dance* in Berlioz's arrangement. This is among the most persuasive records of period performance, likely to convert even those who resist new-style authenticity. The rasp of trombones at the start of *Euryanthe* has a thrilling tang, and the warm acoustic ensures that the authentic string-players sound neither scrawny nor abrasive, yet present rapid passage-work with crystal clarity. Of feathery lightness, the scurrying of violins in the *Abu Hassan overture* is a delight, and each item – including a rarity in *Der Beherrscher der Geister* – brings its moments of magic, with Goodman, both fresh and sympathetic, securing consistently lively and alert playing from his team.

Karajan's performances have great style and refinement. Weber's overtures are superbly crafted and there are no better examples of the genre than *Oberon* and *Der Freischütz*, both epitomizing the spirit of the operas which they serve to introduce. Needless to say, the Berlin horn playing is peerless in these two pieces. Karajan's stylish performance of another Weberian innovation, the *Invitation to the dance* (in Berlioz's orchestration), makes a valuable bonus. On CD the sound is drier and brighter than originally, with a loss of weight in the bass.

Overtures: *Der Freischütz; Oberon.*
(M) *** DG 415 840-2 [id.]. Bav. RSO, Kubelik – MENDELSSOHN: *Midsummer Night's Dream.****

Kubelik offers Weber's two greatest overtures as a fine bonus for his extended selection from Mendelssohn's *Midsummer Night's Dream* incidental music. The playing is first class and compares favourably with the Karajan versions.

Symphonies Nos. 1 in C; 2 in C.
*** ASV Dig. CDDCA 515 [id.]. ASMF, Marriner.
**(*) Orfeo C 091841A [id.]. Bav. RSO, Sawallisch.

Curiously, both Weber's *Symphonies* are in C major, yet each has its own individuality and neither lacks vitality or invention. Sir Neville Marriner has their full measure; these performances combine vigour and high spirits with the right degree of gravitas (not too much) in the slow movements. The orchestral playing throughout is infectiously lively and catches the music's vibrant character. The recording is clear and full in the bass, but the bright upper range brings a touch of digital edge to the upper strings.

Sawallisch's is also a fine, well-played coupling. His approach is more romantic, with rather more atmosphere. Allegros are alert; and both slow movements go well, although there is heaviness in the minuet of No. 2, taken rather ponderously. On the whole, Marriner is fresher and the Academy playing has greater resilience. The Orfeo recording is smoother on top but not so clear.

Clarinet quintet in B flat, Op. 34.
*** DG Dig. 419 600-2 [id.]. Eduard Brunner, Hagen Qt – MOZART: *Clarinet quintet.***(*)

Clarinet quintet; Flute trio in G min., Op. 63 (for flute, cello and piano).
*** CRD CRD 3398 [id.]. Nash Ens.

(i) *Clarinet quintet;* (ii) *Grand Duo concertante, Op. 48; 7 Variations on a theme from Silvana, Op. 33.*
**(*) Chan. Dig. CHAN 8366 [id.]. Hilton, (i) Lindsay Qt; (ii) Keith Swallow.

While the Mozart *Quintet* is in the great Austro-German tradition, this belongs, as John Warrack's notes put it, to 'the tradition of the Parisian *quatuor brillant*'. Eduard Brunner, the principal clarinet of the Bavarian Radio Symphony Orchestra, and the Hagen Quartet are completely inside this style, and it tells in their fluency and naturalness. Brunner produces a mellifluous tone and the overall sonority is well integrated. The DG recording is first class.

On the CRD version, Antony Pay makes the very most of the work's bravura, catching the exuberance of the *Capriccio* third movement (as unlike a classical minuet as could possibly be managed) and the breezy gaiety of the finale. The Nash players provide an admirable partnership and then adapt themselves readily to the different mood of the *Trio*, another highly engaging work with a picturesque slow movement, described as a *Shepherd's lament*. The recording is first class, vivid yet well balanced.

Janet Hilton plays with considerable authority and spirit though she is not always as mellifluous as her rivals. This version does not entirely sweep the board even though it is very good indeed. However, Janet Hilton's account of the *Grand Duo concertante* is a model of fine ensemble, as are the *Variations on a theme from Silvana* of 1811, in both of which Keith Swallow is an equally expert partner. At times the acoustic seems almost too reverberant in the two pieces for clarinet and piano, but the sound in the *Quintet* is eminently satisfactory.

Grand Duo concertante in E flat, Op. 48.
*** Virgin Dig. VC 791076-2. Michael Collins, Mikhail Pletnev – BRAHMS: *Clarinet sonatas.****

Michael Collins and Mikhail Pletnev play the *Grand Duo concertante* with the greatest delicacy. It makes a refreshingly contrasting makeweight to their masterly accounts of the two Brahms *Sonatas*.

7 Variations on a theme from Silvana in B flat, Op. 33.
*** Chan. Dig. CHAN 8566 [id.]. Gervase de Peyer, Gwenneth Pryor – SCHUBERT: *Arpeggione sonata*; SCHUMANN: *Fantasiestücke* etc.***

These engaging Weber *Variations* act as a kind of encore to Schubert's *Arpeggione sonata* and with their innocent charm they follow on naturally. They are most winningly played by Gervase de Peyer who is on top form; Gwenneth Pryor accompanies admirably. The recording is first class.

Piano sonatas Nos. 1 in C, J.138; 2 in A flat, J.199; 3 in D min., J.206; 4 in E min., J.287. Invitation to the dance, J.260; Momento capriccioso in B flat, J.56 (La gaîtê); Rondo brillante in E flat, J.252.
**(*) Ara. Dig. Z 6584 2 [id.]. Garrick Ohlsson.

The main interest of Weber's *Piano sonatas* resides in the fantasy, the almost operatic qualities, the ardent freshness of so much of their invention. Garrick Ohlsson is elegant and persuasive in their support, and he is a fleet-fingered advocate of the companion pieces, including the perennially high-spirited *Invitation to the dance*. Good, though not outstanding, piano recording.

Folksong settings: The gallant troubadour; John Anderson; My love is like a red, red rose; O poor tithe cauld and restless love; Robin is my joy; A soldier am I; The soothing shades of gloaming; True hearted was he; Yes, thou may'st walk; Where ha'e ye been a' the day.
*** EMI Dig. CDC7 47420-2. Robert White, Sanders, Peskanov, Rosen, Wilson – BEETHOVEN: *Folksongs.****

It was an inspiration for Robert White to unearth, as an ideal coupling for Beethoven, ten of the folksong settings which Weber in the last months of his life composed (like Beethoven before him) for the Scottish publisher, George Thomson. This first recording, winningly sung with heady tenor tone and fine characterization, brings out the poetry and imagination that the dying composer gave to his well-paid commission, including a honeyed setting of *My love is like a red, red rose*. Warm, helpful recording on CD.

Euryanthe (complete).
(M) *** EMI CDM7 63509-2 (3). Jessye Norman, Hunter, Gedda, Krause, Leipzig R. Ch., Dresden State O, Janowski.

Much has been written about the absurdity of the plot of *Euryanthe*, as unlikely a tale of chivalry and troubadours as you will find; as this fine recording bears out, however, the opera is far more than just a historic curiosity. The juxtaposition of two sopranos, representing good and evil, is formidably effective, particularly when the challenge is taken by singers of the stature of Jessye Norman and Rita Hunter. Hunter may not be the most convincing villainess, but the cutting edge of the voice is marvellous; and as for Jessye Norman, she sings radiantly, whether in her first delicate cavatina or in the big aria of Act III. Tom Krause as the villain, Lysiart, has rarely sung better and Nicolai Gedda, as ever, is the most intelligent of tenors. Good atmospheric recording (as important in this opera as in *Freischütz*) and vivid remastering, while the direction from Marek Janowski makes light of any longueurs.

Der Freischütz (complete).
(M) *** EMI CMS7 69342-2 (2). Grümmer, Otto, Schock, Prey, Wiemann, Kohn, Frick, German Op. Ch., Berlin, BPO, Keilberth.
*** DG 415 432-2 (2) [id.]. Janowitz, Mathis, Schreier, Adam, Vogel, Crass, Leipzig R. Ch., Dresden State O, Carlos Kleiber.

Keilberth's is a warm, exciting account of Weber's masterpiece which makes all the dated conventions of the work seem fresh and new. In particular the *Wolf's glen* scene on CD acquires something of the genuine terror that must have struck the earliest audiences and which is far more impressive than any mere scene-setting with wood and cardboard in the opera house. The casting of the magic bullets with each one numbered in turn, at first in eerie quiet and then in crescendo amid the howling of demons, is superbly conveyed. The bite of the orchestra and the proper balance of the voices in relation to it, with the effect of space and distance, helps also to create the illusion. Elisabeth Grümmer sings more sweetly and sensitively than one ever remembers before, with Agathe's prayer exquisitely done. Lisa Otto is really in character, with genuine coquettishness. Schock is not an ideal tenor, but he sings ably enough. The Kaspar of Karl Kohn is generally well focused, and the playing of the Berlin Philharmonic has plenty of polish. The overall effect is immensely atmospheric and enjoyable.

The DG set marked Carlos Kleiber's first major recording venture and this fine, incisive account of Weber's atmospheric and adventurous score fulfilled all expectations. With the help of an outstanding cast, excellent work by the recording producer, and transparently clear recording, this is a most compelling version of an opera which transfers well to the gramophone. Only occasionally does Kleiber betray a fractional lack of warmth, but the full drama of the work is splendidly projected in the enhanced CD format.

Webern, Anton (1883–1945)

5 Movements, Op. 5; Passacaglia, Op. 1; 6 Pieces for orchestra, Op. 6; Symphony, Op. 21.
(M) *** DG 427 424-2 (3) [id.]. BPO, Karajan – BERG: *Lyric suite; 3 Pieces;* SCHOENBERG: *Pelleas und Melisande; Variations; Verklaerte Nacht.****
(M) *** DG 423 254-2 [id.]. BPO, Karajan.

Available either separately or within Karajan's three-CD compilation of music of the Second Viennese School, made in the early 1970s, this collection, devoted to four compact and chiselled Webern works, is in many ways the most remarkable of all. Karajan's expressive refinement reveals the emotional undertones behind this seemingly austere music, and the results are riveting – as for example in the dramatic and intense *Funeral march* of Op. 6. Opus 21 is altogether more difficult to grasp, but Karajan still conveys the intensity of argument even to the unskilled ear. Indeed, if Webern always sounded like this, he might even enjoy real popularity. Karajan secures a highly sensitive response from the Berlin Philharmonic, who produce sonorities as seductive as Debussy. Incidentally, he plays the 1928 version of Op. 6. A strong recommendation, with excellent sound.

Passacaglia, Op. 1.
(*) Chan. Dig. CHAN 8619 [id.]. SNO, Bamert – SCHOENBERG: *Pelleas und Melisande.*(*)

An eminently serviceable account of Webern's relatively lush *Passacaglia*, harnessed to

Matthias Bamert's version of *Pelleas* with the Scottish National Orchestra. Excellent playing and good, if somewhat recessed, recording.

6 Pieces for orchestra, Op. 6.
*** EMI Dig. CDC7 49857-2 [id.]. CBSO, Rattle – SCHOENBERG: *5 Pieces*; BERG: *Lulu: suite.****
*** DG Dig. 419 781-2 [id.]. BPO, Levine – BERG: *3 Pieces*; SCHOENBERG: *5 Pieces.****

Rattle and the CBSO bring out the microcosmic strength of the six Webern *Pieces*, giving them weight and intensity without inflation. Warmth is rightly implied here, but no Mahlerian underlining. This superb performance, given sound of demonstration quality, comes ideally coupled with equally compelling performances of two equivalent masterpieces by Webern's two Second Viennese School colleagues. An outstanding issue in every way.

Levine brings out the expressive warmth of Webern's writing, with no chill in the spare fragmentation of argument and with much tender poetry. With the longest of the six tiny movements, the *Funeral march*, particularly powerful, it complements the other works on the disc perfectly. Ripe recording, with some spotlighting of individual lines.

6 Bagatelles for string quartet, Op. 9; 5 Movements for string quartet, Op. 5; Slow movement for string quartet (1905); *String quartet* (1905); *String quartet, Op. 28.*
(M) *** Ph. 420 796-2 [id.]. Italian Qt.

Readers who quail at the name of Webern need not tremble at the prospect of hearing this record. The early music in particular is most accessible, and all of it is played with such conviction and beauty of tone that its difficulties melt away or at least become manageable. The recording is of outstanding vividness and presence, and it is difficult to imagine a more eloquent or persuasive introduction to Webern's chamber music than this.

(i) *Piano quintet; String trio, Op. 20; Movement for string trio, Op. posth.; Rondo.*
*** DG Dig. 415 982-2 [id.]. Stefan Litwin, LaSalle Qt – SCHOENBERG: *Ode to Napoleon.***

The LaSalle Quartet's collection of miscellaneous chamber works makes a valuable supplement to the Philips record of the quartet music. The *String trio* is one of Webern's strongest and most characteristic chamber works. The *Movement* of 1927 was written in preparation for the full-scale *Trio*; while the two early works are fascinating too, particularly the single-movement *Piano quintet*, in a powerful, post-romantic style. The LaSalle performance brings out the emotional thrust without compromise, but the commitment of the players in all these pieces will immediately help the new listener to respond. First-rate recording.

Weill, Kurt (1900–1950)

(i) *Violin concerto; Kleine Dreigroschenmusik* (suite for wind orchestra from *The Threepenny Opera*).
(M) *** DG 423 255-2 [id.]. (i) Lidell; L. Sinf., Atherton.

Weill's *Concerto* for violin and wind instruments is an early work, resourceful and inventive, the product of a fine intelligence and a good craftsman. The style is somewhat angular (as was that of the young Hindemith) but the textures are always clear and the invention holds the listener's attention throughout. It is splendidly played by Nona Lidell and the wind of the London Sinfonietta, and well recorded too. The *Suite* from *The Threepenny Opera* is given with good spirit and élan.

American and Berlin theatre songs: *Aufstieg und Fall der Stadt Mahagonny: Havanna song; Alabama song; Wie man sich bettet. Die Dreigroschenoper: Die Moritat von Mackie Messer; Der Song vom nein und ja* (Barbara-song); *Seeräuber-Jenny. The Firebrand of Florence: Sing me not a ballad. Happy End: Bilbao song; Surabaya-Johnny. Knickerbocker Holiday: September song; It never was you. Lady in the Dark: Saga of Jenny. Lost in the Stars: Stay well; Trouble time; Lost in the stars. Love Life: Green-up time. One Touch of Venus: Foolish heart; Speak low. Street Scene: Lonely house; A boy like you.*
(***) CBS mono MK 42658 [id.]. Lotte Lenya, Ch. & O, Maurice Levine or Roger Bean.

This collection combines American and German theatre songs, recorded by Lotte Lenya in the 1950s; her vocal range may be limited but her timbre is unique in repertoire she uniquely understood. The recording is bright, clean and clear.

Theatre songs: *Aufstieg und Fall der Stadt Mahagonny: Alabama song; Wie man sich bettet. Das Berliner Requiem: Zu Potsdam unter den Eichen. Die Dreigroschenoper: Die Moritat von Mackie Messer; Salomon song; Die Ballade von der sexuellen Hörigkeit. One Touch of Venus: I'm a stranger here myself. Der Silbersee: Ich bin eine arme Verwandte; Rom war eine Stadt; Lied des Lotterieagenten.* Songs: *Je ne t'aime pas; Nannas-Lied; Speak low; Westwind.*
*** Decca Dig. 425 204-2 [id.]. Ute Lemper, Berlin R. Ens., John Mauceri.

Ute Lemper is nothing if not a charismatic singer, bringing a powerful combination of qualities to Weill: an ability to put over numbers with cabaret-style punch as toughly and characterfully as Lotte Lenya herself, as well as a technical security that rarely lets her down. The choice of items is both attractive and imaginative, bringing together popular favourites and relative rarities like the brilliant *Lied des Lotterieagenten* from *Der Silbersee*. Lemper is not the least troubled with singing in English as well as in German, and the recording vividly captures the distinctive timbre of her voice. Many will find her singing more seductive than that of Lotte Lenya, and the accompaniments are a pleasure in themselves, most atmospherically recorded.

The Ballad of Magna Carta; Der Lindberghflug.
*** Capriccio Dig. 60012-l [id.]. Henschel, Tyl, Calaminus, Clemens, Cologne Pro Musica Ch. & RSO, Latham-König; Wirl, Schmidt, Feckler, Minth, Scheeben, Berlin R. Ch. & O, Scherchen.

Der Lindberghflug ('The Lindbergh Flight') is a curiosity. While collaborating for the first time on the *Mahagonny* Songspiel Weill and Bertolt Brecht conceived the idea of a radio entertainment on the subject which was then (in 1927) hitting the headlines: the first solo flight across the Atlantic by Charles Lindbergh. Brecht wrote the text, and Weill started on the music, but for the Baden-Baden Festival it was diplomatic to ask Hindemith to set some of the numbers, and that is how it first appeared. Only later did Weill set the complete work, and that is how it is given in this excellent – Cologne recording. As a curiosity, a historic 1930 performance of the joint Weill – Hindemith version, conducted by Hermann Scherchen, is given as an appendix, recorded with a heavy background roar but with astonishingly vivid voices. One can understand why Weill was so enthusiastic about the fine, very German tenor who sang Lindbergh in 1930, Erik Wirl. The tenor in the new recording is not nearly so sweet-toned, and the German narrator delivers his commentary in a casual, matter-of-fact way, where in 1930 they had well-delivered narrations in French and English as well as in German. Otherwise the performance under Jan Latham-König fully maintains the high standards of Capriccio's Weill series; and the other, shorter item, *The Ballad of Magna Carta*, another radio feature, written in America in 1940 to fanciful doggerel by Maxwell Anderson, is most enjoyable too, a piece never recorded before. The sharp style is again very characteristic of Weill, though the choruses tend to soften into his Broadway idiom. Clear, if rather dry, recording with voices vivid and immediate.

Die Dreigroschenoper (The Threepenny Opera): complete.
*** Decca Dig. 430 075-2 [id.]. Kollo, Lemper, Milva, Adorf, Dernesch, Berlin RIAS Chamber Ch. & Sinf., Mauceri.
*** CBS MK 42637 [id.]. Lenya, Neuss, Trenk-Trebisch, Hesterberg, Schellow, Koczian, Grunert, Ch. & Dance O of Radio Free Berlin, Brückner-Rüggeberg.

By cutting the dialogue down to brief spoken links between numbers and omitting instrumental interludes which merely repeat songs already heard, Decca's all-star production is fitted on to a single, generously filled CD. The aim has been to return to the work as conceived before Brecht exaggerated its propagandist political overtones. As recorded, with John Mauceri drawing incisive playing from the RIAS Sinfonietta and with bright, full, close-up sound, its saltiness and bite are enhanced, together with its musical freshness. The opening is not promising, with the Ballad-singer's singing voice – as opposed to his tangy spoken narration – sounding very old and tremulous. There are obvious discrepancies too between the opera-singers, René Kollo and Helga Dernesch, and those in the cabaret tradition, notably the vibrant and provocative Ute Lemper (Polly Peachum) and the gloriously dark-voiced and characterful Milva (Jenny). That entails downward modulation in various numbers, as it did with Lotte Lenya, but the changes from the original are far less extreme. Kollo is good – but even more compelling is Dernesch, whose *Ballad of sexual obsession* in Act II is the high spot of the whole entertainment. A pity the third verse had to be omitted for reasons of space, though it was also cut before the first (1928) stage performance. The co-ordination of music and presentation makes for a vividly enjoyable experience, even if committed Weill enthusiasts will inevitably disagree with some of the controversial textual and interpretative decisions.

The CBS alternative offers a vividly authentic recording of *The Threepenny Opera*, Weill's most famous score, darkly incisive and atmospheric, with Lotte Lenya giving an incomparable performance as Jenny. All the wrong associations, built up round the music from indifferent performances, melt away in the face of a reading as sharp and intense as this. Bright, immediate, real stereo recording, made the more vivid on CD.

The Rise and fall of Mahagonny (complete).
**(*) CBS MK 77341 (2) [M2K 37874]. Lenya, Litz, Gunter, Mund, Gollnitz, Markworth, Saverbaum, Roth, Murch (speaker), NW German R. Ch. and O, Brückner-Rüggeberg.

Though Lotte Lenya, with her metallic rasping voice, was more a characterful *diseuse* than a singer, and this bitterly inspired score had to be adapted to suit her limited range, it remains a most memorable performance. The recording lacks atmosphere, with voices (Lenya's in particular) close balanced. Yet even now one can understand how this cynical piece caused public outrage when it was first performed in Leipzig in 1930.

Der Silbersee (complete).
*** Capriccio Dig. 60011-2 (2) [id.]. Heichele, Tamassy, Holdorf, Schmidt, Mayer, Korte, Thomas, Cologne Pro Musica Ch., Cologne RSO, Latham-König.

Till now *Der Silbersee*, containing some of Weill's most inspired theatre music and many memorable tunes, has been known on record through the 'recomposed' version in English which was prepared for the New York City Opera in 1980, incorporating material from other Weill sources. This restoration of the original, written just before Weill left Nazi Germany, aims to cope with the basic problem presented by having his music as adjunct, not to a regular music-theatre piece, but to a full-length play by Georg Kaiser. Between Weill's numbers a smattering of the original dialogue is here included to provide a dramatic thread and the speed of delivery adds to the effectiveness. Led by Hildegard Heichele, bright and full-toned as the central character, Fennimore, the cast is an outstanding one, with each voice satisfyingly clean-focused, while the 1989 recording is rather better-balanced and kinder to the instrumental accompaniment than some from this source, with the voices exceptionally vivid. Particularly telling is the finale with its haunting slow waltz bearing a timely 'green' message. The Overture and Act I are complete on the first disc, Acts II and III on the second. Libretto, notes and background material are first rate, as in the rest of Capriccio's Weill series.

Der Zar lässt sich Photographieren (complete).
**(*) Capriccio Dig. 60 007-1 [id.]. McDaniel, Pohl, Napier, Cologne R. O, Latham-König.

This curious one-act *opera buffa*, first heard in 1928, is Weill's first comic opera, but his last theatre-piece that is through-composed. With the playwright Georg Kaiser, his collaborator on several previous pieces, he produced a wry little parable about assassins planning to kill the Tsar when he has his photograph taken. Angèle, the photographer, is replaced by the False Angèle, but the Tsar proves to be a young man who simply wants friendship, and the would-be assassin, instead of killing him, plays a tango on the gramophone, before the Tsar's official duties summon him again. Jan Latham-König in this 1984 recording directs a strong performance, though the dryly recorded orchestra is consigned to the background. The voices fare better, though Barry McDaniel is not ideally steady as the Tsar.

Weinberger, Jaromir (1896–1967)

Svanda the Bagpiper (opera): complete.
*** CBS CD 79344 (2) [M2K 36926]. Prey, Popp, Jerusalem, Killebrew, Malta, Nimsgern, Bav. R. Ch., Munich R. O, Wallberg.

The famous polka set the seal on the immediate international success of this colourful updating of the *Bartered Bride* formula. Weinberger wrote it when he was thirty, but he never acquired anything like the same popularity again. He went to America, where in disillusion he committed suicide in 1967. None of that sadness comes out in the frothy mixture of *Svanda*, a folk-tale involving a robber charmer who woos beautiful young Dorotka, wife of Svanda. The supernatural is lightly invoked in a trip to hell (Svanda the charmer there) with the devil introduced. Prey (as Svanda), Popp (as his wife) and Jerusalem (as Babinsky, the charmer) make a first-rate team of principals, lending musical flair as well as vocal glamour. Ensemble work is first rate too, most important in this opera, with the polka taken rather slowly and bouncily. Excellent, vivid sound.

Widor, Charles-Marie (1844–1937)

Organ symphony No. 5 in F min., Op. 42/1.
*** DG Dig. 413 438-2 [id.]. Simon Preston (organ of Westminster Abbey) – VIERNE: *Carillon de Westminster.****

Organ symphonies Nos. 5 in F, Op. 42/1; 6 in G, Op. 42/2.
*** Novalis Dig. 150015-2 [id.]. Günther Kaunzinger (Klais organ of Limburg Cathedral).

Organ symphonies Nos. 5; 10 (Romane), Op. 73.
*** Ph. Dig. 410 054-2 [id.]. Chorzempa (organ of Saint-Sernin Basilica, Toulouse).

Günther Kaunzinger's Novalis coupling is now a clear first choice in this repertoire. He plays with great vigour and commitment and makes Widor's opening allegro of the *Fifth Symphony* more substantial and involving than usual; similarly the *Andante quasi allegretto* does not sound in the least bland. The famous *Toccata* is second to none in its rhythmic vivacity. In his hands, the *Sixth Symphony* is an equally impressive piece; in the two slow movements, the *Adagio* and *Cantabile*, he produces some delicious sounds from his woodwind stops. The West German organ has plenty of bite, even a hint of harshness in its fortissimos which help to add character to this music. But the clarity of detail permitted by the acoustics of Limburg Cathedral lets one relish Kaunzinger's bravura and his limpid articulation, especially in the outer movements and *Intermezzo* of No. 6.

Daniel Chorzempa provides a massive demonstration of CD opulence which should send the neighbours scurrying for cover if this CD is played at full volume. He chooses some agreeable registration for the amiable earlier music of the *Fifth Symphony* and the gentle music is distanced and atmospheric to a great degree. Nevertheless, he provides a highly energetic account of the famous *Toccata*, which exudes a nice mixture of power and exuberance. The *Tenth Symphony* has its structure bound together by the Easter plainchant, *Haec Dies*, and after a pleasant *Cantilène* third movement the composer gathers up the threads of the music for another weighty finale; then the rhetoric suddenly evaporates and the piece ends gently. Chorzempa makes much of this effect and seems entirely at home in this repertoire. The Cavaillé-Coll organ is well chosen.

Organ symphony No. 5: Toccata.
*** Argo Dig. 410 165-2 [id.]. Hurford (organ of Ratzeburg Cathedral) – *Recital.****

Those wanting the *Toccata* alone could not do better than choose Peter Hurford's exhilarating version, recorded with great presence and impact on a most attractive organ, and giving demonstration quality.

Wieniawski, Henryk (1835–80)

Violin concerto No. 2 in D min., Op. 22.
*** Decca Dig. 421 716-2 [id.]. Joshua Bell, Cleveland O, Ashkenazy – TCHAIKOVSKY: *Violin concerto.****
(*) Ara. Dig. Z 6597 [id.]. Mark Kaplan, LSO, Miller – PAGANINI: *Violin concerto No. 1.*(*)

Joshua Bell gives a masterly performance, full of flair, even if he does not find quite the same individual poetry in the big second-subject melody or in the central *Romance* as Itzhak Perlman did in his currently deleted version. Excellent recording, brilliant and full.

Mark Kaplan's reading is comparably assured and brilliant, with the *Zigeuner* element of the finale relished equally by soloist and conductor. The close balance of the soloist and the clear recording here lets the fast *moto perpetuo* of the solo part register brilliantly. Mitch Miller with the LSO provides a warmly spontaneous accompaniment.

Wikmanson, Johan (1753–1800)

String quartet No. 2 in E min., Op. 1/2.
*** CRD CRD 33123 (2) [id.]. Chilingirian Qt – ARRIAGA: *String quartets Nos. 1–3.***

Although he did not possess the natural inborn talents of an Arriaga, with whom he is coupled here, Wikmanson was a cultured musician. Little of his music survives, and two of his five *Quartets* are lost. The overriding influence here is that of Haydn and the finale of the present quartet even makes a direct allusion to Haydn's *E flat Quartet*, Op. 33, No. 2. The Chilingirian make out a persuasive case for this piece and are very well recorded.

Wolf, Hugo (1860–1903)

Lieder: *Frage nicht; Frühling übers Jahr; Gesang Weylas; Kennst du das Land? (Mignon); Heiss mich nicht reden (Mignon I); Nur wer die Sehnsucht kennt (Mignon II); So lasst mich scheinen (Mignon III); Der Schäfer; Die Spröde.*
*** DG Dig. 423 666-2 [id.]. Anne Sofie von Otter, Rolf Gothoni – MAHLER: *Das Knaben Wunderhorn* etc.***

It is astonishing that so young a singer can tackle even the most formidable of Wolf's *Mignon* songs, *Kennst du das Land?*, a culminating peak of Lieder for women, with such firm, persuasive lines. Her gradation of the climaxes in the three successive stanzas is masterly – even though she will doubtless be finding even greater insights in a few years' time. The gravity of such a song is then delightfully contrasted against the delicacy of *Frühling übers Jahr* or *Die Spröde*. Eight of the songs are Goethe settings, the ninth, the haunting *Gesang Weylas*, to a Mörike poem. The sensitivity and imagination of Rolf Gothoni's accompaniment add enormously to the performances in a genuine two-way partnership. Well-balanced recording.

Goethe-Lieder: Anakreons Grab; Erschaffen und Beleben; Frech und Froh I; Ganymed; Kophtisches Lied I & II; Ob der Koran; Der Rattenfänger; Trunken müssen wir alle sein. Mörike-Lieder: Abschied; An die Geliebte; Auf ein altes Bild; Begegnung; Bei einer Trauung; Denk' es, O Seele!; Er ist's; Der Feuerreiter; Fussreise; Der Gärtner; In der Frühe; Jägerlied; Nimmersatte Liebe; Selbstgeständnis; Storchenbotschaft; Der Tambour; Verborgenheit.
*** DG 415 192-2 [id.]. Dietrich Fischer-Dieskau, Daniel Barenboim.***

This collection of seventeen of Wolf's Mörike songs and nine Goethe settings was issued on CD to celebrate the singer's sixtieth birthday, a masterly example of his art. Barenboim's easily spontaneous style goes beautifully with Fischer-Dieskau's finely detailed singing, matching the sharp and subtle changes of mood. The mid-1970s analogue recording has been transferred very well, with the voice vividly immediate.

Mörike Lieder: An die Geliebte; Auf ein altes Bild; Auf eine Christblume I & II; Auf einer Wanderung; Auftrag; Begegnung; Bei einer Trauung; Er ist's; Der Gärtner; Gebet; In Frühling; Der Jäger; Jägerlied; Lied eines Verliebted; Neue Liebe; Nimmersatte Liebe; Peregrina I & II; Schlafendes Jesuskind; Selbstgeständnis; Storchenbotschaft; Verborgenheit; Zum Neuen Jahr.

*** EMI Dig. CDC7 49054-2 [id.]. Olaf Bär, Geoffrey Parsons.

Wolf's songs to words by Mörike include many of his finest and most memorable. This generous collection presents the youthful but refined artistry of Olaf Bär in this challenging repertory. Bär's is an exceptionally intelligent and unforced view of these songs, helped by a superb natural voice. Geoffrey Parsons is an ever-helpful accompanist, and the recording is beautifully balanced.

Das spanische Liederbuch (complete).
(M) *** DG 423 934-2 (2). Schwarzkopf, Fischer-Dieskau, Moore.

In this superb medium-priced CD reissue the sacred songs provide a dark, intense prelude, with Fischer-Dieskau at his very finest, sustaining slow tempi impeccably. Schwarzkopf's dedication comes out in the three songs suitable for a woman's voice; but it is in the secular songs, particularly those which contain laughter in the music, where she is at her most memorable. Gerald Moore is balanced rather too backwardly – something the transfer cannot correct – but gives superb support. In all other respects the 1968 recording sounds first rate, the voices beautifully caught. A classic set.

Wyner, Yehudi (born 1929)

Intermezzi (for piano quartet).
** Pro Arte Dig. CDD 120 [id.]. Frank Glazer, Cantilena Chamber Players – FOSS: *Round a common center*; COPLAND: *Piano quartet.***

Wyner, Canadian-born, became a pupil of Walter Piston at Harvard before teaching at Yale (1964–77). The composer calls the *Intermezzi* 'in a curious way a museum piece', assembling as it does numerous allusions to music of the past (Schubert, Chausson, Brahms, Schoenberg and so on) without indulging in any direct quotations. A serious, often deeply felt piece, with very committed playing.

Ysaÿe, Eugène (1858–1931)

6 Sonatas for solo violin, Op. 27.
*** Chan. Dig. CHAN 8599 [id.]. Lydia Mordkovich.

Sonata in D min. (Ballade), Op. 27/3.
(M) *** Ph. 420 777-2 [id.]. D. Oistrakh – DEBUSSY; RAVEL: *Sonatas*; PROKOFIEV: *5 Melodies.***

The six *Sonatas* were all written for the great virtuosi of the time (Szigeti, Thibaud, Enescu and so on) and make cruel demands on the player – and, one is often tempted to add, the listener. Not in this instance, however, for Lydia Mordkovich plays with great character and variety of colour and she characterizes No. 4 (the one dedicated to Kreisler, with its references to Bach and the *Dies Irae*) superbly. These *Sonatas* can seem like mere exercises, but in her hands they sound really interesting. Natural, warm recorded sound. Recommended.

David Oistrakh won the first prize at the International Ysaÿe Concours in Brussels in 1937, and it would be difficult to imagine his account of the best-known of Ysaÿe's six solo *Sonatas* being surpassed even by the composer himself.

Zelenka, Jan (1679–1745)

Capriccios Nos. 1–6; Concerto in G; Hipocondrie in A; Overture in F; Sinfonia in A min..
⊛ *** DG 423 703-2 (2) [id.]. Camerata Bern, Van Wijnkoop.

In this superb orchestral collection, as in the companion Archiv issue of Zelenka *Sonatas* (see below), this long-neglected composer begins to get his due, some 250 years late. On this showing he stands as one of the most distinctive voices among Bach's contemporaries, and Bach himself nominated him in that role, though at the time Zelenka was serving in a relatively humble capacity. As in the sonata collection, it is the artistry of Heinz Holliger that sets the seal on the performances, but the virtuosity of Barry Tuckwell on the horn is also a delight, and the music itself regularly astonishes. One of the movements in the *Capriccio No. 5* has the title *Il furibondo (The angry man)* and, more strikingly still, another piece has the significant title *Hipocondrie* and sounds amazingly like a baroque tango. What comes out from this is that, in this period of high classicism, music for Zelenka was about emotion, something one recognizes clearly enough in Bach and Handel but too rarely in lesser composers. And in his bald expressiveness Zelenka often comes to sound amazingly modern, and often very beautiful, as in the slow *Aria No. 2* of the *Fourth Capriccio*. Superb recording, to match Van Wijnkoop's lively and colourful performances, makes these CDs very welcome indeed.

6 Sonatas for 2 oboes and bassoon with continuo.
⊛ *** DG 423 937-2 (2) [id.]. Holliger, Bourgue, Gawriloff, Thunemann, Buccarella, Jaccottet.
*** Capriccio 10074/5 [id.]. Glaetzner, Goritzki, Sonstevold, Beyer, Pank, Bernstein.

This second outstanding DG Archiv collection offers yet more music by the remarkable contemporary of Bach, Jan Zelenka, born in Bohemia but who spent most of his musical working life in Dresden. In these *Trio sonatas* it is almost as though Zelenka had a touch of Ives in him, so unexpected are some of the developments and turns of argument. The tone of voice is often dark and intense, directly comparable to Bach at his finest; and all through these superb performances the electricity of the original inspiration comes over with exhilarating immediacy. Fine recording, admirably remastered. Another set to recommend urgently to any lover of Baroque music.

The superb performances from East German musicians make light of the technical problems in six striking works, all but one of them in the four-movement *sonata da chiesa* form, and their lively advocacy makes very clear that the chromatic writing, quite different from Bach's, is nevertheless amazingly advanced for its time. First-rate recording. Highly recommended as an alternative to the DG set.

Requiem in C min.
**(*) Claves Dig. CD 50-8501 [id.]. Brigitte Fournier, Balleys, Ishii, Tüller, Berne Chamber Ch. and O, Dahler.

This record of the *Requiem in C minor*, like the settings of the *Lamentations of the Prophet Jeremiah* which Supraphon recorded in the late 1970s, confirms Zelenka's originality. *The Last Trump*, for example, is a thoughtful soprano solo without any of the dramatic gestures one might expect; and the *Agnus Dei* is quite unlike any other setting of his period – or of any other – austere, intent and mystical. There is hardly a moment that is not of compelling interest here; the only minor qualification that needs to be made concerns the balance, which places the solo singers too forward. The performance is well prepared and thoroughly committed. On CD one might have expected the choral focus to be sharper, but in all other respects the sound is very good, with the ambience nicely judged.

Zeller, Carl (1842–98)

Der Vogelhändler (complete).
(M) *** EMI CMS7 69357-2 (2). Rothenberger, Holm, Litz, Dallapozza, Berry, Unger, Forster, Dönch, V. Volksoper Ch., VSO, Boskovsky.

Boskovsky's vivacious and lilting performance of Zeller's delightfully tuneful operetta is in every way recommendable. The cast is strong; Anneliese Rothenberger may be below her best form as Princess Marie, but Renate Holm is a charmer as Christel, and Adolf Dallapozza sings the title-role with heady virility. There are many endearing moments, and the combination of infectious sparkle and style tempts one to revalue the score and place it, alongside *The Merry Widow* and *Die Fledermaus*, among the finest and most captivating of all operettas. For English-speaking listeners some of the dialogue might have been cut, but this is an international set and it is provided with an excellent libretto translation (not always the case in this kind of repertoire). The recording is excellent, combining atmosphere with vividness and giving lively projection of the principal characters.

Zemlinsky, Alexander von (1871–1942)

Symphony No. 2 in B flat; (i) *Psalm 23.*
*** Decca Dig. 421 644-2 [id.]. Berlin RSO, (i) with Ernst Senff Chamber Ch.; Chailly.

Relatively conservative as the idiom is, this *Symphony* is a striking and warmly expressive work that richly deserves revival, particularly in a performance as strong, committed and brilliantly recorded as this. The slow introduction, with Wagnerian echoes from *Siegfried's funeral march*, leads to a bold *Allegro* based on strong and colourful themes, bringing hints of Brahms in Hungarian mood along with touches of Dvořák. The jagged rhythms of the scherzo are delightfully kaleidoscopic, and the slow movement is then relatively conventional in warm, solid, Brahmsian style, before the 45-minute work is rounded off with a *Passacaglia* paying obvious tribute to Brahms's *Fourth Symphony*. The piece inspires Chailly and the Berlin Radio Symphony Orchestra to one of their finest performances on record, helped by vivid sound, full of presence. The setting of *Psalm 23* – placed first on the disc – dates from later in Zemlinsky's career; it is in a rather more advanced harmonic idiom but is just as warm in expression, airy and beautiful. But do not expect a religious atmosphere: this is sensuous music, beautifully played and sung, which uses the much-loved words of the Psalm as an excuse for musical argument, rather than illuminating them.

Lyric symphony, Op. 18.
*** DG Dig. 419 261-2 [id.]. Varady, Fischer-Dieskau, BPO, Maazel.

Zemlinsky's *Lyric symphony* is essentially a symphonic song-cycle, modelled on *Das Lied von der Erde* and based on Eastern poetry; its lush textures and refined scoring make it immediately accessible. The idiom is that of early Schoenberg (*Verklaerte Nacht* and *Gurrelieder*), Mahler and Strauss. Yet it is not just derivative but has something quite distinctive to say. Its sound-world is imaginative, the vocal writing graceful and the orchestration masterly. Both soloists and the orchestra seem thoroughly convinced and convincing, and Maazel's refined control of texture prevents the sound from cloying, as does his incisive manner. Varady and Fischer-Dieskau make an outstanding pair of soloists, keenly responsive to the words, and the engineering is first class, the voices being well balanced against the orchestra.

String quartets Nos. 1, Op. 4; 2, Op. 15; 3, Op. 19; 4, Op. 25.
(M) *** DG Dig. 427 421-2 (2). LaSalle Qt.

The *First Quartet* gained the imprimatur of Brahms, to whom Zemlinsky had shown some of his other early compositions, and the last, which was written at exactly the same time as Schoenberg's *Fourth*, pays his erstwhile pupil the double compliment of a dedication and an allusion to *Verklaerte Nacht*. None of the four is in the least atonal: the textures are full of contrapuntal interest and the musical argument always proceeds with lucidity. There is diversity of mood and a fastidious craftsmanship, and the listener is always held. The musical language is steeped in Mahler and, to a lesser extent, Reger, but the music is undoubtedly the product of a very fine musical mind and one of considerable individuality. Collectors will find this a rewarding set: the LaSalle play with polish and unanimity, and the recording is first class, as is the admirable documentation.

Die Seejungfrau (The Mermaid); Psalm 13, Op. 24.
*** Decca Dig. 417 450-2 [id.]. Ernst Senff Chamber Ch., Berlin RSO, Chailly.

Zemlinsky's three-movement symphonic fantasy, based on the Hans Andersen story of the mermaid, is comparable with Schoenberg's high-romantic *Pelleas and Melisande*, written at the same period, an exotic piece full of sumptuous orchestral writing. It is beautifully performed here, with ample recording to match. The choral setting of Psalm 13 dates from three decades later, but still reveals the urgency of Zemlinsky's inspiration – never a revolutionary in the way Schoenberg was, but always inventive and imaginative. The choral sound is not as full as that of the orchestra.

Gesänge Op. 5, Books 1–2; Gesänge (Waltz songs on Tuscan folk-lyrics), Op. 6 ; Gesänge, Opp. 7–8, 10 & 13; Lieder, Op. 2, Books 1–2; Op. 22 & Op. 27.
*** DG Dig. 427 348-2 (2) [id.]. Barbara Bonney, Anne Sofie von Otter, Hans Peter Blochwitz, Andreas Schmidt, Cord Garben.

Thanks to recordings, the art of Alexander von Zemlinsky is coming to be ever more widely appreciated, and this two-disc DG collection of songs can be warmly recommended for the fresh tunefulness of dozens of miniatures. When in the 1890s he first got to know his future brother-in-law, Schoenberg, he was writing songs that would hardly have shocked Schubert; and even later, so far from following Schoenberg, he adopted in his songs a more conservative style than in his orchestral works or operas. With Cord Garben accompanying four excellent soloists, the charm of these chips from the workbench comes over consistently. Best of all is von Otter, more sharply imaginative than the others, making the one consistent cycle that Zemlinsky ever wrote, the six Maeterlinck Songs, Opus 13, the high point of the set.

Eine florentinische Tragödie (opera; complete).
*** Schwann Dig. CD 11625 [id.]. Soffel, Riegel, Sarabia, Berlin RSO, Albrecht.

A Florentine Tragedy presents a simple love triangle: a Florentine merchant returns home to find his sluttish wife with the local prince. Zemlinsky in 1917 may have been seeking to repeat the shock tactics of Richard Strauss in *Salome* (another Oscar Wilde story) a decade earlier; but the musical syrup which flows over all the characters makes them far more repulsive, with motives only dimly defined. The score itself is most accomplished; it is compellingly performed here, more effective on disc than it is in the opera house. First-rate sound.

Der Gerburtstag der Infantin (opera; complete).
*** Schwann Dig. CD 11626 [id]. Nielsen, Riegel, Haldas, Weller, Berlin RSO, Albrecht.

The Birthday of the Infanta, like its companion one-Acter, was inspired by a story of Oscar Wilde, telling of a hideous dwarf caught in the forest and given to the Infanta as a birthday present. Even after recognizing his own hideousness, he declares his love to the princess and is casually rejected. He dies of a broken heart, with the Infanta untroubled: 'Oh dear, my present already broken.' Zemlinsky, dwarfish himself, gave his heart to the piece, reproducing his own rejection at the hands of Alma Mahler. In this performance, based on a much-praised stage production, Kenneth Riegel gives a heartrendingly passionate performance as the dwarf declaring his love. His genuine passion is intensified by being set against lightweight, courtly music to represent the Infanta and her attendants. With the conductor and others in the cast also experienced in the stage production, the result is a deeply involving performance, beautifully recorded.

Zielensky, Mikolaj (c. 1550–post 1615)

(i) *Communiones;* (ii) *Fantasia Secunda, Fantasia Tertia;* (iii) *Magnificat; Offertoria.*
** Olympia OCD 321 [id.]. (i) Capella Bydgostiensis Pro Musica Antiqua, Galonski; (ii) Ens. Ochlewski; (iii) Polish R. Ch., Wroclaw, Kajdasz.

Little is known about Mikolaj Zielensky – not even his dates of birth and death – though more of his work has been preserved than of any other of his Polish contemporaries. The style is clearly Venetian and makes use of the sumptuous antiphonal choral textures favoured by the Gabrielis. The *Offertories* are eight-voice motets and the *Magnificat* a twelve-part polychoral piece of some grandeur. The music is of considerable interest and merit, and well worth the attention of those with a specialist interest in the period. However, the performances are very much of the 1960s and the recordings wanting in clarity and body.

Collections

A selective list — we have included only the outstanding compilations from the many whcih are available

Concerts of
Orchestral and Concertante Music

Academy of St Martin-in-the-Fields, Sir Neville Marriner

'The French connection': RAVEL: *Le Tombeau de Couperin*. DEBUSSY: *Danses sacrée et profane* (with Ellis, harp). IBERT: *Divertissement*. FAURÉ: *Dolly suite, Op. 56.*
*** ASV Dig. CDDCA 517 [id.].

An excellent collection. The spirited account of Ibert's *Divertissement* is matched by the warmth of Fauré's *Dolly suite* in the Rabaud orchestration. The remainder of the record is hardly less appealing. Ravel's *Le Tombeau de Couperin* is nicely done, as is the Debussy *Danses sacrée et profane*. One would welcome more space round the orchestra and, considering the disc was made in Studio One, Abbey Road, greater use could have been made of the location's ambience. This apart, however, everything is very clear, with the sound even more refined and present on CD.

'The English connection': ELGAR: *Serenade for strings, Op. 20.* TIPPETT: *Fantasia concertante on a theme of Corelli.* VAUGHAN WILLIAMS: *Fantasia on a theme of Thomas Tallis; The Lark ascending* (with Iona Brown).
**(*) ASV Dig. CDDCA 518 [id.].

Sir Neville Marriner's newer performances of the Elgar *Serenade* and the *Tallis Fantasia* are less intense (and less subtle) than his earlier, Decca versions; the highlight of this concert is Iona Brown's radiant account of *The Lark ascending*. The sound is rich and very well defined, especially in its CD format.

MOZART: *Serenade: Eine kleine Nachtmusik, K.525; German dance (Sleigh ride), K.605/3.* ALBINONI: *Adagio* (arr. Giazotto). MENDELSSOHN: *Octet: Scherzo.* PACHELBEL: *Canon.* BACH: *Suite No. 3: Air.* FAURÉ: *Pavane, Op. 60.* BOCCHERINI: *Minuet from Op. 13/5.* TCHAIKOVSKY: *Andante cantabile.* GRIEG: *Elegiac melodies: Heart's wounds; Last spring.*
*** EMI CDC7 47391-2 [id.].

A fresh and engaging concert taken from recordings made between 1974 and 1980. Mozart's *Night music* is played with much grace, and the Mendelssohn *Scherzo* has an appealing lightness of touch. The account of Albinoni's *Adagio* must be the most refined in the catalogue, as also is the gravely measured performance of Pachelbel's *Canon*. The Fauré, Grieg, Boccherini and Tchaikovsky items come from an early – and highly successful – digital concert (1980) and are most beautifully played. Altogether this is excellent value in every respect, and the programme is most appealingly laid out.

VAUGHAN WILLIAMS: *Fantasia on Greensleeves; English folksongs suite.* ELGAR: *Serenade for strings in E min., Op. 20.* BUTTERWORTH: *The Banks of green willow.*

WARLOCK: *Capriol suite.* DELIUS: *On hearing the first cuckoo in spring. A Village Romeo and Juliet: The walk to the Paradise Garden.*
(M) *** Decca 417 778-2.

All these vintage performances are available in other formats and couplings, discussed within these pages. If the present assembly is attractive, there are no grounds for withholding a strong recommendation, for the recordings are first class and the digital remastering most successful.

Trumpet concertos (with (i) Alan Stringer; (ii) John Wilbraham): (i) HAYDN: *Concerto in E flat.* (ii) HUMMEL: *Concerto in E flat.* ALBINONI: *Concerto in C.* L. MOZART: *Concerto in D.* TELEMANN: *Concerto in D.*
(M) *** Decca 417 761-2.

Alan Stringer favours a forthright, open timbre for the Haydn *Concerto*, but he plays the famous slow movement graciously. John Wilbraham is superbly articulate and stylish in the rest of the programme, and his partnership with Marriner in the captivating Hummel *Concerto* makes for superb results. Albinoni's *Concerto* divides the spotlight between trumpet and three supporting oboes to add textural variety, and both the Leopold Mozart and Telemann works are among the finest of their genre. Throughout, the orchestral accompaniments have striking elegance and finesse, and plenty of vitality too; and the recording is bright, with plenty of presence for the soloists.

André, Maurice (trumpet)

Concertos (with Philh. O, Muti.): BACH: *Brandenburg concerto No. 2 in F, BWV 1047.* TELEMANN: *Concerto in D.* TORELLI: *Concerto in D.* HAYDN: *Concerto in E flat.*
*** EMI Dig. CDC7 47311-2 [id.].

André is a big star on the continent, which accounts for the allocation of many compact discs to him in EMI's CD catalogue. It seems a curious idea to include the Bach *Brandenburg*, for, although André plays the solo part most stylishly and the balance with his Philharmonia colleagues is expertly managed, most collectors will have already acquired this work within a complete set. Otherwise this is an admirable concert, for André's performance of the Haydn is particularly pleasing, with a gentle *Andante* to offset the sparkle of the outer movements; the Telemann is also a fine piece. With first-class accompaniments throughout and an excellently balanced recording, the CD is striking for its added presence.

'Trumpet concertos' (with BPO, Karajan): HUMMEL: *Concerto in E flat.* L. MOZART: *Concerto in C.* TELEMANN: *Concerto in D.* VIVALDI: *Concerto in A flat.* (arr. Thilde).
**(*) EMI CDC7 49237-2 [id.].

Another attractive collection of trumpet concertos, brilliantly played by André. His security in the upper register in the work by Leopold Mozart and the fine Telemann *Concerto* is impressive. The jaunty quality of the Hummel is not missed, and the finale of this work, taken at breakneck pace, is certainly exhilarating. The Vivaldi work, arranged from the *Sonata in F major for violin and continuo*, RV 20, makes a very effective display piece. The 1974 recording has generally been well transferred to CD. However, this reissue would have been even more tempting at mid-price, with only 47 minutes of music on offer.

Trumpet concertos (with various orchestras & conductors): HAYDN: *Concerto in E flat.* M. HAYDN: *Concerto in D.* HANDEL: *Concerto in G min.* (from *Oboe concerto No. 3*). VIVALDI: *Double trumpet concerto in C, RV 537.* VIVIANI: *Sonata in C.* TELEMANN: *Concerto/Sonata in D.*
*** DG 415 980-2 [id.].

Michael Haydn's *Concerto*, a concertante section of a seven-movement *Serenade*, has incredibly high tessitura, with the D trumpet taken up to high A (the fourth ledger-line above the treble stave), the highest note in any classical trumpet concerto. It is just a peep but, characteristically, Maurice André reaches up for it with consummate ease. He is completely at home in all this repertoire: his version of the Joseph Haydn *Concerto* is stylish and elegant, with a memorably eloquent account of the slow movement, the line gracious and warmly serene. These are the earliest of the recordings included and the sound is slightly less clean than in the three works accompanied by Mackerras and the ECO.

Trumpet concertos (with LPO, López-Cobos): HAYDN: *Concerto in E flat.* TELEMANN: *Concerto in F.* ALBINONI: *Concerto in D min.* MARCELLO: *Concerto in C min.*
(M) *** EMI CDM7 69189-2 [id.].

Maurice André's cultured playing gives much pleasure throughout this collection. Slow movements are elegantly phrased and communicate an appealing, expressive warmth. The stylishness and easy execution ensure a welcome for the Albinoni and Marcello works, which are transcriptions but are made thoroughly convincing in this format. Excellent, lively accompaniments from the LPO under López-Cobos, and good sound, the more vivid on CD.

BBC Symphony Orchestra, Sir Colin Davis

'*The Last Night of the Proms*' (with BBC Chorus & Choral Society, Jessye Norman): ELGAR: *Cockaigne overture, Op. 40; Pomp and circumstance march No. 1, Op. 39.* BERLIOZ: *Les Troyens: Hail, all hail to the Queen.* WAGNER: *Wesendonk Lieder: Schmerzen; Träume.* MENDELSSOHN: *Octet: Scherzo.* WOOD: *Fantasia on British sea-songs.* HANDEL: *Judas Maccabaeus: See, the conqu'ring hero comes.* ARNE: *Rule Britannia.* PARRY: *Jerusalem* (arr. Elgar).
(M) *** Ph. 420 085-2.

Although the vociferous clapping is sometimes almost overwhelming, this CD (recorded on two 'last nights', in 1969 and 1972) fully captures the exuberant atmosphere of the occasion. Only the *Cockaigne overture* is slightly below par. The full humour of the *Sea songs* extravaganza is well caught, with the clapping coming totally to grief in the *Sailor's hornpipe.* But the fervour of the singing in *Land of hope and glory* and *Rule Britannia* is caught superbly, and the entry of the organ crowns a frisson-making version of Parry's *Jerusalem.*

Berlin Philharmonic Orchestra, Herbert von Karajan

'*Encore*': WEBER: *Invitation to the dance, Op. 65* (arr. Berlioz). SMETANA: *Má Vlast: Vltava.* ROSSINI: *William Tell: Overture.* LISZT: *Les Préludes, G.97; Hungarian rhapsody No. 5, G. 359.*
**(*) DG Dig. 413 587-2 [id.].

Karajan is at his finest in *Vltava*: there is some radiant playing from the Berlin orchestra in the moonlit stillness before the river approaches the St John's Rapids. *Les Préludes* is vibrant, but a little brash; however, the dark colouring of the *Fifth Hungarian rhapsody* is finely caught. The *William Tell overture* has great panache, and *Invitation to the dance* a characteristically suave elegance. The Berlin Philharmonie provides a less flattering ambience than in some of Karajan's earlier analogue recordings.

Opera intermezzi and ballet music: PONCHIELLI: *La Gioconda: Dance of the hours*. Intermezzi from: MASCAGNI: *Cavalleria Rusticana; L'amico Fritz*. GIORDANO: *Fedora*. SCHMIDT: *Notre Dame*. MUSSORGSKY: *Khovanshchina*. MASSENET: *Thaïs: Méditation* (with Schwalbé). VERDI: *Aida: ballet suite*. BERLIOZ: *Damnation de Faust: Danse des Sylphes; Menuet des Follets*. SMETANA: *Bartered bride: Polka*. GOUNOD: *Faust: Waltz*.
(M) *** DG 415 856-2 [id.].

This attractive programme is assembled from recordings made between 1968 and 1972. The playing is marvellous and Karajan consistently displays both warmth and flair: the *Dance of the hours* is captivating, as are the two Berlioz pieces and the *Polka* from the *Bartered Bride* with its affectionate rubato. The various intermezzi sound wonderfully fresh and vivid, and in the *Thaïs Méditation* Michel Schwalbé plays the violin solo exquisitely. In short, this is more than the sum of its parts; and the analogue recordings, although brightly lit in their digitally remastered form, have the advantage of a more flattering and congenial ambience than many of Karajan's more recent sessions made digitally in the Philharmonie.

Christmas concertos: CORELLI: *Concerto grosso in G min., Op. 6/8*. MAREDINI: *Concerto grosso in C, Op. 3/12*. TORELLI: *Concerto a 4 in forma di pastorale per il santissimo natale*. LOCATELLI: *Concerto grosso in F min., Op. 1/8*. G. GABRIELI: *Canzona a 8*. SCHEIDT: *In dulci jubilo*. ECCARD: *Vom Himmel hoch; Es ist ein Ros' entsprungen*. GRUBER: *Stille Nacht*.
(M) **(*) DG 419 413-2.

Karajan's collection of baroque Christmas concertos brings first-class playing from the Berlin Philharmonic; but concentration on sensuous beauty of texture (the string sonorities are often ravishing) does tend to be self-defeating when four pieces with a similar pastoral inspiration are heard together. So DG had the bright idea of interspersing the concertos with carol-like chorales, played by the Berlin Philharmonic brass, ending the concert with Gruber's *Silent Night*. While purists and authenticists are warned to stay clear, others may find a good deal to enjoy here. The remastered 1970s recording is still very good.

GRIEG: *Holberg suite, Op. 40*. SIBELIUS: *Finlandia, Op. 26*. SMETANA: *Má Vlast: Vltava*. LISZT: *Les Préludes*.
(M) *** DG Dig. 427 808-2 [id.].

Four characterful performances, digitally recorded, superbly played and showing the Karajan charisma at its most impressive. At mid-price this is self-recommending, although Karajan's earlier, EMI recording of the Liszt symphonic poem is even more telling.

Boskovsky Ensemble, Willi Boskovsky

'Viennese bonbons': J. STRAUSS Snr: *Chinese galop; Kettenbrücke Waltz; Eisele und Beisele Sprünge. Cachucha galop; Gitana-galop; Hofball-Tänz; Seufzer galop.* J. STRAUSS Jnr: *Weine Gemüths waltz; Champagne galop; Annen polka.* LANNER: *Styrian dances; Die Weber & Abendsterne waltzes; Neue Wiener Ländler.* MAYER: *Schnofler Tänz'.* HAYDN: *Zingarese Nos. 1, 6 & 8.* STELZMÜLLER: *Stelzmüller Tanz'.* SCHUBERT: *Ecossaisen.*
(B) *** Van. VCD 72016 [id.].

This is a captivating selection of the most delightful musical confectionery imaginable. Over an hour of music is gathered here from a much-praised pair of Boskovsky LPs from the early 1970s. The ensemble is a small chamber group, similar to that led by the Strausses, and the playing has an appropriately intimate Viennese atmosphere. Not surprisingly, Boskovsky shows a strong personality as leader and soloist, and this colourful writing bubbles with good spirits and attractive melodies. The programme is almost entirely made up of rare repertoire and makes one realize what an inexhaustible wealth of rare vintage there is in the Viennese musical cellars. The recording is fresh, smooth and clear, with a nice bloom on sound which is never too inflated. At bargain price, this is not to be missed.

Boston Pops Orchestra, John Williams

'On stage': BERLIN: *There's no business like show business.* HAMLISCH: *A Chorus line: Overture.* MANN/WEIL: *Here you come again.* ELLINGTON: *Sophisticated lady; Mood indigo; It don't mean a thing.* STRAYHORN: *Take the 'A' train.* LLOYD WEBBER: *Cats: Memory.* BERLIN: *Top hat, white tie and tails.* YOUMANS: *The Carioca.* SCHWARZ: *Dancing in the dark.* KERN: *I won't dance.* CONRAD: *The Continental.* RODGERS: *On your toes: Slaughter on 10th Avenue* (arr. Bennett).
*** Ph. 412 132-2 [id.].

John Williams is especially good in bringing out detail in the *Overture* for *A Chorus line,* and in the ballet score, *Slaughter on 10th Avenue,* which is heard complete and contains two of the most memorable tunes the composer ever wrote – fully worthy of Gershwin. The other items are offered in groups, tailored sophisticatedly as tributes to Duke Ellington and Fred Astaire; but equally enjoyable is the highlight of Bob Fosse's *Dancin',* the engaging *Here you come again.* Splendid orchestral playing and excellent sound, although the body of strings is not made to seem sumptuous.

'That's entertainment': excerpts from: *That's Entertainment; Fiddler on the Roof; A Little Night Music; Chorus Line; Annie; Evita; Gigi.* RODGERS: *Waltz medley.*
*** Ph. Dig. 416 499-2 [id.].

This is music John Williams does splendidly and there are plenty of really memorable tunes here which many will enjoy in full orchestral dress, not least those by Richard Rodgers and Stephen Sondheim.

'Pops on the march': J. F. WAGNER: *Under the Double Eagle.* ELGAR: *Pomp and circumstance march No. 4, Op. 39.* TCHAIKOVSKY: *Festival coronation march.* WALTON: *Orb and sceptre (Coronation march).* GERSHWIN: *Strike up the band.* HANDY: *St Louis Blues march.* WILLIAMS: *Midway march.* WILLSON: *76 Trombones.* BAUDUC: *South Rampart Street Parade.* NEWMAN: *Conquest.*
*** Ph. Dig. 420 804-2 [id.].

An outstanding early (1980) digital recording made by Soundstream engineers captures the acoustics of Symphony Hall, Boston, with splendid fullness, resonance and brilliance in this exhilarating concert. With only 42 minutes of music offered, this is not generous; but there are few collections of marches nearly as entertaining and gripping as this. John Williams is as at home in Elgar and Walton (with the big central melodies of each gloriously warm) as he is in the sparkling Gershwin *Strike up the band*. *Seventy-six Trombones* wittily quotes from other famous marches and is played with great zest, while the opening *Under the Double Eagle* has an irresistible lilt. The sound is in the demonstration class throughout.

Bournemouth Sinfonietta, Hurst

'*English music for strings*': HOLST: *St Paul's suite, Op. 29/2*. ELGAR: *Serenade for strings, Op. 20*. WARLOCK: *Capriol suite*. IRELAND: *Concertino pastorale*.
**(*) Chan. CHAN 8375 [id.].

The novelty here is Ireland's *Concertino pastorale*, a gently persuasive piece. It is very sympathetically presented. The rest of the programme is well played but less strongly characterized. There are better versions of the Elgar and Warlock suites available, although the *St Paul's suite* of Holst is most enjoyable, with the outer sections of the *Intermezzo* beautifully done. The 1977 sound has plenty of body and atmosphere, but detail at pianissimo level is not as clear as one would have in a modern digital recording, and this is especially true of the pizzicato section of the *Capriol suite*.

Bournemouth Sinfonietta or Symphony Orchestra, Norman Del Mar

HOLST: *Brook Green suite; A Somerset rhapsody*. DELIUS: *Air and dance*. VAUGHAN WILLIAMS: *Concerto grosso; The Wasps: Overture and suite*. WARLOCK: *Serenade*.
*** EMI CDC7 47812-2 [id.].

This CD combines the contents of two previously issued LPs of English music, omitting only one work. Holst's *Brook Green suite* was originally written for the St Paul's School for Girls. It emerged as far more than an exercise for students, as Del Mar's dedicated performance demonstrates, most strikingly in the vigorous final dance. The *Concerto grosso* of Vaughan Williams was also written primarily for amateurs; here it is given as a straight work for double string orchestra. The enchanting Delius miniatures, the hazily atmospheric Warlock and the evocative Holst *Somerset rhapsody* make an excellent contrast, while the *Wasps overture* is dashingly performed and the other items in the suite are delightful, too. Del Mar brings out the wit in the *March of the kitchen utensils* with his mock pomposity. The recording throughout is splendid.

Brüggen, Frans (recorder)

Recorder concertos (with VCM, Harnoncourt): VIVALDI: *Concerto in C min., RV 441*. SAMMARTINI: *Concerto in F*. TELEMANN: *Concerto in C*. NAUDOT: *Concerto in G*.
(M) *** Teldec/WEA 2292 43547-2 [id.].

Frans Brüggen is an unsurpassed master of his instrument, and he gives the four assorted concertos his keen advocacy on this excellent record, reissued from 1968. (In the Vivaldi he even takes part in the tutti.) In his hands, phrases are turned with the utmost sophistication, intonation is unbelievably accurate and matters of style exact. There is spontaneity too and, with superb musicianship, good recording and a well-balanced orchestral contribution, this mid-priced CD can earn nothing but praise.

Burns, Stephen (trumpet)

'Music for trumpet and strings' (with Ensemble): PURCELL: Sonata No. 1 in D. STANLEY: Trumpet voluntary (from Organ Voluntary, Op. 6/5, arr. Bergler). CLARKE: Suite in D. CORELLI: Sonata in D. BALDASSARE: Sonata in F. TORELLI: Sonata a cinque in D, G.1. *** ASV Dig. CDDCA 528 [id.].

Stephen Burns plays a rotary piccolo trumpet in the East German style by Scherzer, and his freedom and smoothness of timbre in the instrument's highest tessitura are breathtaking. With crisp ornamentation (often florid, in short, decorative bursts of filigree), the playing is attractively stylish: the timbre gleams and the exhilarating articulation of the allegros is balanced by a natural expressive lyricism in slow movements. Whether in the beautiful Grave sections of the Corelli and Torelli Sonatas or in the faster movements of the latter piece, this is playing to delight the ear with its combination of sensitivity and bravura, and the Purcell and Clarke works are equally persuasive. The recording balances the soloist well forward and the CD projects him almost into the room, although it also emphasizes the rather insubstantial sound of the accompaniment and the ineffective harpsichord balance. But this collection is Stephen Burns' triumph, and it would be churlish to withhold the fullest recommendation.

Chamber Orchestra of Europe, Judd

'Music of the Masters': BEETHOVEN: Creatures of Prometheus overture, Op. 43. MOZART: Divertimento No. 1 in D for strings, K.136. ROSSINI: Il Barbiere di Siviglia: Overture. FAURÉ: Pavane, Op. 50. WAGNER: Siegfried idyll.
(B) **(*) Pickwick Dig. PCD 805.

An enjoyable and well-balanced programme with first-class ensemble from these young players and excellently balanced digital recording. The presence and naturalness of the sound are especially striking in the Fauré Pavane (with a beautiful flute solo) and the Siegfried idyll, using only a small string group. James Judd brings stylish, thoroughly musical direction, although the overall presentation is a shade anonymous.

Chicago Symphony Orchestra, Barenboim

SMETANA: Má Vlast: Vltava. DVORÁK: Slavonic dances, Op. 46/1 and 8. BRAHMS: Hungarian dances Nos. 1, 3 & 10. BORODIN: Prince Igor: Polovtsian dances. LISZT: Les Préludes.
(M) *** DG 415 851-2 [id.].

The Polovtsian dances have splendid life and impetus. Indeed one hardly misses the chorus, so lively is the orchestral playing. Both Vltava and Les Préludes show Barenboim and the Chicago orchestra at their finest. Vltava is highly evocative – especially the moonlight sequence – and beautifully played; Les Préludes has dignity and poetry, as well as excitement. The Brahms and Dvořák Dances make attractive encores. The only slight snag is that, in the digital remastering, the recording has lost some of its original glow and the strings sound thinner above the stave. But this is striking only in the violin timbre of the big tune of Vltava.

'Children's Weekend'

'Children's Weekend' (played by (i) LSO, Sargent, with Richardson; (ii) SRO, Ansermet; (iii) Pascal Rogé): (i) PROKOFIEV: Peter and the wolf.⊛ (ii) BIZET: Jeux d'enfants. DUKAS: The sorcerer's apprentice. (iii) DEBUSSY: Children's corner.
(B) *** Decca 421 626-2.

Sir Ralph Richardson's account of Peter and the wolf is indispensable, and this nicely chosen supporting programme of music for or about children is all well worth having. Ansermet is characteristically neat in Bizet's Jeux d'enfants and his performance of L'apprenti sorcier – among the best of the analogue LP era – has a cumulative effect; one has the feeling of real calamity before the magician hurriedly returns to put right the mischief his apprentice has wrought. Both recordings show how well the Decca engineers worked with the famous Swiss conductor: they are vivid, full and suitably atmospheric. Pascal Rogé's Children's corner suite is more modern: it is played with appropriate neat elegance. This collection is more than the sum of its parts, one of the highlights of Decca's bargain Weekend catalogue.

Cincinnati Pops Orchestra, Erich Kunzel

'Time warp': DORSEY: Ascent. R. STRAUSS: Also sprach Zarathustra: Opening. GOLDSMITH: Star Trek the Movie: Main theme. The Alien: Closing title. COURAGE: The Menagerie: suite. PHILIPS: Battlestar Galactica: Main theme. WILLIAMS: Superman: Love theme. Star Wars: Throne room and end-title. J. STRAUSS Jnr: Blue Danube waltz. KHACHATURIAN: Gayaneh: Adagio.
*** Telarc Dig. CD 80106 [id.].

This sumptuously recorded CD is well established as a demonstration disc par excellence and needs no fillip from us. Sufficient to say that the playing is first class and the sound superb, the rich ambient effect just right for this music, with particularly gorgeous string and brass timbres, Telarc's concert-hall balance at its most impressive. There are plenty of indelible tunes too and John Williams's music for Superman and Star Wars (the latter in the Elgar/Walton nobilmente tradition) has never been recorded to more telling effect. The collection opens with an electronic spectacular to put the Cincinnati orchestra in orbit.

'Orchestral spectaculars': RIMSKY-KORSAKOV: Mlada: Procession of the nobles. Snow Maiden: Dance of the Tumblers. DUKAS: L'apprenti sorcier. WEINBERGER: Svanda the Bagpiper: Polka and fugue. SAINT-SAENS: Samson et Dalila: Bacchanale. LISZT: Les Préludes.
**(*) Telarc Dig. CD 80115 [id.].

The title is not belied by the sound, which has a sparkling but not exaggerated percussive constituent. The side drum which introduces the colourful Rimsky Procession of the nobles is strikingly well focused, and this clarity comes within a believable overall perspective. There is much fine orchestral playing, with the string detail in the Svanda Polka and fugue particularly pleasing, and the horns sounding agreeably strong and rich-timbred in the introductory Rimsky-Korsakov piece. The Saint-Saëns Bacchanale has plenty of adrenalin, with the timpani and bass drum adding to the climax without swamping it. The account of Les Préludes is lightweight until the end, which is almost solemn in its spacious broadening. The one disappointment is *The Sorcerer's apprentice*, here bright and well paced but lacking cumulative excitement.

'The Stokowski sound' (orchestral transcriptions): BACH: *Toccata and fugue in D min., BWV 565; Fugue in G min., BWV 578.* BOCCHERINI: *Quintet in E: Minuet.* DEBUSSY: *Suite bergamasque: Clair de lune; Prélude: La cathédrale engloutie.* BEETHOVEN: *Piano sonata No. 14 (Moonlight): 1st movement.* ALBÉNIZ: *Sevilla.* RACHMANINOV: *Prelude in C sharp min., Op. 3/2.* MUSSORGSKY: *Night on the bare mountain.*
⊛ *** Telarc Dig. CD 80129 [id.].

Stokowski began his conducting career in Cincinnati in 1909, moving on to Philadelphia three years later; so a collection of his orchestral transcriptions from his first orchestra is appropriate, particularly when the playing is so committed and polished and the recording so sumptuous. Indeed, none of Stokowski's own recordings can match this Telarc disc in sheer glamour of sound. The *'Little' G minor Fugue* of Bach hardly sounds diminutive here, matching the famous *D minor Toccata and fugue* at its resplendent climax. By contrast, Boccherini's *Minuet* is played as a miniature, tenderly and gracefully. Spectacle is paramount in the Albéniz and Rachmaninov pieces, the latter vulgarly larger than life but irresistible. Schoenberg apparently thought Stokowski's sentient arrangement of *Clair de lune* so convincing that he decided it was Debussy's original version; no wonder he liked it, with its element of ecstasy, complete with shimmering vibraphone. The arrangement of *La cathédrale engloutie* is very free and melodramatically telling. Most interesting is *Night on the bare mountain*, which has a grandiloquent brass chorale added as a coda. Any admirer of Stokowski should regard this superbly engineered CD as an essential purchase.

'Pomp and Pizazz': J. WILLIAMS: *Olympic fanfare.* SUK: *Towards a new life.* ELGAR: *Pomp and circumstance march No. 1.* IRELAND: *Epic march.* TCHAIKOVSKY: *Coronation march.* BERLIOZ: *Damnation de Faust: Hungarian march.* J. F. WAGNER: *Under the Double Eagle.* FUČIK: *Entry of the gladiators.* SOUSA: *The Stars and Stripes forever.* HAYMAN: *March medley.*
*** Telarc Dig. CD 80122 [id.].

As enjoyable a march collection as any available, with characteristically spectacular and naturally balanced Telarc recording, with its crisp transients and wide amplitude. The performances have comparable flair and sparkle. The inclusion of John Ireland's comparatively restrained *Epic march* and the Tchaikovsky *Coronation march*, with its piquant trio and characteristic references to the Tsarist national anthem, makes for attractive contrast, while the Hayman medley (including *Strike up the band, 76 Trombones, South Rampart Street Parade* and *When the Saints go marching in*) makes an exuberant, peppy closing section. By comparison the Berlioz *Rákóczy march* is quite dignified. The sound is in the demonstration class. Most entertaining.

'Symphonic spectacular': SHOSTAKOVICH: *Festival overture, Op. 96.* WAGNER: *Die Walküre: Ride of the Valkyries.* FALLA: *El amor brujo: Ritual fire dance.* BIZET: *L'Arlésienne: Farandole.* JÄRNEFELT: *Praeludium.* CHABRIER: *España.* TCHAIKOVSKY: *Marche slave, Op. 31.* HALVORSEN: *Entry of the Boyars.* ENESCU: *Rumanian rhapsody No. 1, Op. 11.* KHACHATURIAN: *Gayaneh: Sabre dance.*
*** Telarc Dig. CD 80170 [id.].

With spectacular recording, well up to Telarc's best standards, this is a highly attractive collection of orchestral lollipops. Everything is played with the special flair which this orchestra and conductor have made their own in this kind of repertoire. Most entertaining, and technically of demonstration standard.

City of Birmingham Symphony Orchestra, Louis Frémaux

French music: RAVEL: *Boléro.* DEBUSSY: *Prélude à l'après-midi d'un faune.* DUKAS: *L'apprenti sorcier.* SAINT-SAENS: *Danse macabre.* CHABRIER: *España.* OFFENBACH: *Overture: La vie parisienne.* HONEGGER: *Pacific 231.* SATIE: *Gymnopédies 1 & 3.* LITOLFF: *Concerto symphonique: Scherzo* (with John Ogdon).
(M) **(*) EMI CDM7 63023-2 [id.].

A generous programme from a successful earlier CBSO era when Frémaux gave the orchestra something of a French accent. The Offenbach *Overture* is as racy as anyone could desire; *The sorcerer's apprentice* also has plenty of sparkle and Chabrier's *España* is hardly less vivid, while *Danse macabre* is both lively and exciting. Contrasts come with the Debussy *Prélude* and the fresh melancholy of the Satie. Ogdon is a brilliant if not a subtle soloist in the famous Litolff *Scherzo.* The recordings were originally very reverberant, and the remastering has generally improved definition, most effectively in the powerful evocation of Honegger's *Pacific 231,* now sounding massive yet not oppressive at its spectacular climax.

Cleveland Symphonic Winds, Fennell

'Stars and stripes': ARNAUD: *3 Fanfares.* BARBER: *Commando march.* LEEMANS: *Belgian Paratroopers.* FUCIK: *Florentine march, Op. 214.* KING: *Barnum and Bailey's favourite.* ZIMMERMAN: *Anchors aweigh.* J. STRAUSS Snr: *Radetzky march.* VAUGHAN WILLIAMS: *Sea songs; Folk songs suite.* SOUSA: *The Stars and stripes forever.* GRAINGER: *Lincolnshire posy.*
*** Telarc Dig. CD 80099 [id.].

This vintage collection from Frederick Fennell and his superb Cleveland wind and brass group is one of the finest of its kind ever made. Severance Hall, Cleveland, has ideal acoustics for this programme and the playing has wonderful virtuosity and panache. What is unusual about the programme is its variety. Both the Barber and Leemans pieces mix subtlety with spectacle; the Barnum and Bailey circus march is predictably exuberant, while *The Stars and stripes* is not overblown, with the piccolo solo in natural perspective. Add to all this digital engineering of Telarc's highest calibre, and you have a very special issue, with the Grainger and Vaughan Williams suites adding just the right amount of ballast.

Czech Philharmonic Orchestra, Neumann

'Festival concert': Bohemian polkas, waltzes and marches by NOVÁCEK; KRÁL; KOMZÁK; LABITSKY; BISKUP; HILMAR; HAŠLER; LABSKÝ; KAŠPAR; VACKAR; NEDBAL; FUCÍK; KMOCH.
*** HM C 107101A; C 107201A (2 CDs, available separately).

These recordings are the Bohemian equivalent of the music of the Strauss family. Although the discs contain no masterpieces of the calibre of *The Blue Danube,* the music is consistently tuneful and agreeably inventive in its scoring. Performances and recording are excellent. If you want something lightheartedly different, try one or other of these two CDs, which are available separately.

Dallas Symphony Orchestra, Eduardo Mata

TCHAIKOVSKY: *Capriccio italien, Op. 45.* MUSSORGSKY: *Night on the bare mountain.* DUKAS: *L'apprenti sorcier.* ENESCU: *Rumanian rhapsody No. 1.*
(B) *** RCA Dig. VD 87727 [7727-2-RV].

One of the outstanding early digital orchestral demonstration CDs. The acoustic of the Dallas Hall produces a thrilling resonance without too much clouding of detail. The Mussorgsky piece is rather lacking in menace when textures are so ample. *The Sorcerer's apprentice* is spirited and affectionately characterized, yet there is no sense of real calamity at the climax. But the Tchaikovsky and Enescu are richly enjoyable, even if the latter lacks the last degree of unbuttoned exuberance in its closing pages.

Dichter, Misha (piano), Philharmonia Orchestra, Marriner

Concertante works: ADDINSELL: *Warsaw concerto.* GERSHWIN: *Rhapsody in blue.* LITOLFF: *Concerto symphonique, Op. 102: Scherzo.* CHOPIN: *Fantasia on Polish airs, Op. 13.* LISZT: *Polonaise brillante* (arr. of WEBER: *Polacca brillante, Op. 72*).
*** Ph. Dig. 411 123-2 [id.].

Never before has the orchestral detail of Addinsell's indelible pastiche emerged so beguilingly on record as it does here under Marriner; he and Misha Dichter combine to give the music genuine romantic memorability, within a warmly sympathetic acoustic. Gershwin's famous *Rhapsody* is hardly less successful, the performance spirited yet glowing. To make a foil, the Litolff *Scherzo* is taken at a sparkingly brisk tempo and projected with great flair. The Chopin *Fantasia* has a lower voltage, but the closing Liszt arrangement of Weber glitters admirably. The sound is first rate and is very believable in its CD format.

Dresden State Orchestra, Varviso

Overtures and intermezzi: ROSSINI: *La gazza ladra: overture.* PONCHIELLI: *La Gioconda: Dance of the hours.* MASCAGNI: *Cavalleria Rusticana: Intermezzo.* PUCCINI: *Manon Lescaut: Intermezzo.* BIZET: *Carmen: Prelude to Act I.* SAINT-SAENS: *Samson et Dalila: Bacchanale.* SCHMIDT: *Notre-Dame: Intermezzo.* MASSENET: *Thaïs: Méditation* (with Mirring). OFFENBACH: *Contes d'Hoffmann: Barcarolle.*
**(*) Ph. Dig. 412 236-2 [id.].

The highlight here is a splendid version of the *Dance of the hours*, the most beguiling in the catalogue. The rich Dresden ambience adds to the colour of the elegant woodwind chirruping, and the recording provides a fine dynamic expansion for the climax before the scintillating finale. Otherwise, the mood is very relaxed and atmospheric; in the ripely romantic account of the *Thaïs Méditation* (with a fine violin solo from Peter Mirring), the Dresden State Opera Chorus creates a soupily religiose backing. The atmospheric timbre of the strings and the warmly sentient playing are certainly very agreeable; and if the Saint-Saëns *Bacchanale* becomes unbuttoned only at the very close, the *Carmen Prelude* does not lack dash. With the background silence especially telling in the Ponchielli ballet, the CD enhances refinement of detail.

Du Pré, Jacqueline (cello)

'Impressions': ELGAR: *Cello concerto in E min., Op. 85* (with LSO, Barbirolli). HAYDN: *Cello concerto in C* (with ECO, Barenboim). BEETHOVEN: *Cello sonata No. 3 in A, Op. 69* (with Barenboim): *Piano trio No. 5 in D (Ghost), Op. 70/1* (with Barenboim and Zukerman).
(M) *** EMI CMS7 69707-2 (2).

A medium-priced anthology that is self-recommending if the mixed programme is of appeal. The chamber-music performances have the same qualities of spontaneity and inspiration that have made Du Pré's account of Elgar's *Cello concerto* come to be treasured above all others; if some find her approach to Haydn too romantic, it is nevertheless difficult to resist in its ready warmth. The sound-quality is fairly consistent, for all the remastered transfers are successful.

English Chamber Orchestra, Raymond Leppard

ALBINONI: *Sonata a 5 in A, Op. 2/3; Sonata a 5 in G min., Op. 2/6.* VIVALDI: *Concertos: in D, P.175; in G min., P.392; Sonata in E flat (Al Santo sepolcro), P.441.* CORELLI: *Concerto grosso in F, Op. 6/9.*
(B) *** CfP CD-CFP 4371.

An outstanding collection of Italian string concertos, recorded in 1970 and sounding first class in digitally remastered form: there is fullness, yet everything sounds fresh. The two Albinoni *Sonatas* are particularly attractive: the four contrasted movements of Op. 2, No. 3, are individually characterized, with the richness of the five-part ensemble obvious in the two slow movements and the fugal allegros sprightly and resilient, and with Leppard adding some witty harpsichord comments in the finale. The Corelli *Concerto grosso* has six equally diverse movements and, while Vivaldi's *Al Santo sepolcro* has only two, they are strongly contrasted. The standard of invention throughout the concert is high and the playing is polished and committed. Except for those who can accept only original instruments, this is a fine concert for the late evening.

'Baroque favourites': M.-A. CHARPENTIER: *Te Deum in D: Introduction.* PACHELBEL: *Canon in D.* BACH: *Chorale preludes: Ich ruf' zu dir; Wir Eilen mit Schwachen; Erbarm' dich. Cantata No. 156: Sinfonia. Suite No. 3 in D: Air. Suite No. 2 in B min.: Badinerie.* HANDEL: *Solomon: Arrival of the Queen of Sheba. Harpsichord suite in D min.: Sarabande. Berenice: Minuet.* GLUCK: *Orfeo: Dance of the Blessed Spirits.* MARCELLO: *Oboe concerto in D min.:* 2nd movement. VIVALDI: *Violin concerto in D, Op. 3/9:* Slow movement. PURCELL: *Abdelazer: suite.*
(M) **(*) CBS Dig. MDK 44650 [id.].

Opening regally with trumpets, Leppard's concert includes many of the usual baroque lollipops, including an engagingly elegant version of the famous Pachelbel *Canon*, and some fine solo oboe contributions from Neil Black, notably in the cantilena from the Bach *Sinfonia* and the slow movement from Alessandro Marcello's *D minor Oboe concerto*. The original programme has been filled out by a substantial suite of Purcellian theatre music from *Abdelazer*, which includes a brisk presentation of the famous tune Britten used as the basis for his *Young person's guide to the orchestra*. Excellent, vivid digital recording.

English Concert, Pinnock

PACHELBEL: *Canon and gigue in D.* VIVALDI: *Sinfonia in G min., RV 149.* ALBINONI: *Concerto a 5 in D min. for oboe and strings, Op. 9/2.* PURCELL: *Chacony in G min.* HANDEL: *Solomon: Arrival of the Queen of Sheba.* AVISON: *Concerto grosso No. 9 in A min.* HAYDN: *Concerto for harpsichord in D, Hob. XVIII/2.*
*** DG Dig. 415 518-2 [id.].

The English Concert is one of the acceptable faces of the authentic-instrument movement, and these vital accounts will give unalloyed pleasure. There are many good things here, particularly the Albinoni *Concerto* (with David Reichenberg the eloquent soloist) and the Avison. Although there are popular items too, such as Handel's *Arrival of the Queen of Sheba* from *Solomon* and the Pachelbel *Canon*, there are others of considerable substance: the Purcell *Chacony* and Haydn's *D major Concerto* brilliantly played on the harpsichord by Trevor Pinnock. The performances are crisp and thoroughly alive, and beautifully recorded.

'The best of Baroque': HANDEL: *Water music: excerpts. Solomon: Arrival of the Queen of Sheba.* PACHELBEL: *Canon and Gigue.* VIVALDI: *Concerto all rustica, RV 151; Concerto for 2 mandolins, RV 532.* BACH: *Brandenburg concerto No. 3 in G, BWV 1048; excerpts from Suites Nos. 2–3, BWV 1067/1068.*
**(*) DG Dig. 419 410-2 [id.].

Anyone wanting to try a representative baroque programme, played in authentic style on original instruments, should find this a good sampler. The playing has much spirit and polish and does not shirk expressive feeling; witness the *Air* from the Bach *Suite No. 3 in D*. The brass sounds in Handel's *Water music* are much less opulent than in performances on modern instruments; and certain items, like Pachelbel's *Canon*, seem just a trifle bleak; but the recording is clean and believable, and this is excellent of its kind.

English Sinfonia, Sir Charles Groves

'Entente cordiale': FAURÉ: *Masques et bergamasques, Op. 112; Pavane, Op. 50.* ELGAR: *Chanson de nuit; Chanson de matin, Op. 15/1–2.* DELIUS: *On hearing the first cuckoo in spring.* RAVEL: *Pavane pour une infante défunte.* WARLOCK: *Capriol suite.* BUTTERWORTH: *The Banks of green willow.* SATIE: *Gymnopédies Nos. 1 & 3* (orch. Debussy).
(B) *** Pickwick Dig. PCD 926.

Having given us some attractive Haydn recordings with the English Sinfonia, Sir Charles Groves now offers a happy juxtaposition of French and British music. He opens with a performance of Fauré's *Masques et bergamasques* which is sheer delight in its airy grace, and later he finds passion as well as delicacy in the Butterworth rhapsody, very effectively followed by Debussy's languorous orchestrations of the Satie *Gymnopédies*. Groves's approach to Warlock's *Capriol* dances is essentially genial (Marriner's version has more zest); but all this music-making is easy to enjoy. The playing is polished and spontaneous and the recording, made at Abbey Road, quite splendid.

Equale Brass

'*Baccanales*': WARLOCK: *Capriol suite* (arr. Gout). POULENC: *Suite* (arr. Jenkins): *Mouvement perpétuel No. 1; Novellette No. 1 in C; Impromptu No. 3; Suite française.* ARNOLD: *Brass quintet.* F. COUPERIN: *Suite* (arr. Wallace). BARTÓK: *4 Hungarian pictures* (arr. Sears).
*** Nimbus NI 5004 [id.].

This offers sound of striking presence and realism, and the programme is certainly imaginative. The arrangements are cleverly scored and produce highly diverting results. Warlock's *Capriol suite* and the music of François Couperin seem unlikely to adapt well for brass, yet they are the highlights of the programme, alongside the engaging Poulenc *Mouvement perpétuel* and the colourful Bartók *Hungarian pictures*. The Equale Brass is a quintet (two trumpets, horn, trombone and tuba); besides immaculate ensemble, their playing is infectiously spirited and readily conveys the enjoyment of the participants, so that the music-making has the atmosphere of a live concert. Each of the twenty-one items is banded. A demonstration issue.

Film classics

'*Film Classics*': WAGNER: *Ride of the Valkyries* (*Apocalypse Now*) O de Paris, Barenboim. MYERS: *Cavatina* (*Deerhunter*) Söllscher. BACH: *Double violin concerto: Vivace; Harpsichord concerto No. 5 in F min.* (*Hannah and her Sisters*) Soloists, E. Concert, Pinnock. R. STRAUSS: *Also sprach Zarathustra*: opening. J. STRAUSS: *Blue Danube* (*2001*) VPO, Maazel/Boehm. DONIZETTI: *L'Elisir d'amore: Una furtiva lagrima* (*Prizzi's Honor*). PUCCINI: *Turandot: Nessun dorma* (*Killing Fields*) Placido Domingo. MOZART: *Clarinet concerto: Adagio* (*Out of Africa*) Prinz, VPO, Boehm. PACHELBEL: *Canon* (*Ordinary People*) E. Concert. Pinnock. BARBER: *Adagio for strings* (*Elephant Man*; *Platoon*) LAPO, Bernstein. RAVEL: *Boléro* (*10*) LSO, Abbado.
**(*) DG 419 630-2 [id.].

The main purpose of a collection like this is to identify music for those who 'know the tune' but not the title. Most of the items included were used to good effect in the films with which they are identified, and no one could fault the performances. The sound too is uniformly good. Newcomers to classical music will find this a useful starting point for further exploration.

Galway, James (flute)

'*Serenade*' (with various orchestras & artists): SCHUBERT: *Serenade* (*Ständchen*), *D.957.* CHOPIN: *Nocturne in E flat, Op. 9/2.* DEBUSSY: *Rêverie; La fille aux cheveux de lin; Le plus que lente.* CIMAROSA: *Serenade* (*Alla siciliana*). BACH: *Suite 3: Air.* MOZART: *Concerto for flute & harp: Andantino* (with Marisa Robles). LISZT: *Consolation No. 3.* KHACHATURIAN: *Spartacus: Adagio of Spartacus and Phrygia.* MASSENET: *Thaïs: Méditation.* VILLA-LOBOS: *Bachianas brasileiras No. 5: Aria.* NARITA: *Song of the seashore.* RACHMANINOV: *Vocalise.* FAURÉ: *Fantaisie.* DRIGO: *I Milioni d'Arlecchino: Serenade.*
** RCA RD 60033 [60033-2-RC].

Galway fans will find this very agreeable and his charisma all but redeems the more outrageous transcriptions. Good sound.

'In the Pink' (with Nat. PO Mancini): MANCINI: *The Pink Panther. The Thorn Birds: Meggie's theme; Theme. Breakfast at Tiffany's. The Molly Maguires: Pennywhistle jig; Theme. Victor Victoria: Crazy world. The Great Race: Pie in the face polka. Baby elephant walk. Two for the road. Speedy Gonzales.* Medley: *Days of wine and roses – Charade – Moon River. Cameo for flute 'for James'.*
✪ *** RCA Dig. RCD 85315 [RCD1-5315].

Henry Mancini has provided a whole string of superb musical ideas. Mancini's tunes are often unashamedly romantic (*Moon River* and *Charade* are superb examples); but the delicate *Meggie's theme* from *The Thorn Birds* or the similar *Theme* from *The Molly Maguires* (which Galway phrases with magical Irish inflexion) have an agreeable understated lyricism. Other no less striking examples make their impact with a quirky rhythmic felicity: no one easily forgets *The Pink Panther* or *The Baby elephant walk.* Mancini is served admirably here by Galway's superb artistry. His advocacy is wonderfully stylish and sympathetic to the melodic lines, while he can add an attractive touch of Irish whimsy to a piece like the *Pennywhistle jig.* Mancini himself directs the accompaniment, using an orchestra of top London sessions players and creating an appropriately silky string timbre. The atmospheric recording is nicely balanced, Galway forwardly miked in the Pop manner, and the whole concoction makes a delightful entertainment, with an encore especially written for the soloist.

'Greatest hits' (with orchestral or instrumental accompaniments): MANCINI: *Pink Panther theme; Thorn Birds theme; Pennywhistle jig.* LLOYD WEBBER: *Angel of music; Memory.* HAMLISCH: *Jean.* KHACHATURIAN: *Sabre dance.* DEBUSSY: *Clair de lune.* LEIGH: *Don't it make my brown eyes blue.* GRAINER: *I know now.* TRAD.: *Belfast hornpipe; Danny Boy; Shenandoah; Greensleeves; Brian Boru's march.* DENVER: *Annie's song; Perhaps love.* RIMSKY-KORSAKOV: *Flight of the bumble-bee.* GIBB: *I started a joke.* PACHELBEL: *Canon.*
*** RCA RD 87778 [7778-2-RC].

The inimitable James Galway here provides a most entertaining crossover collection, full of good tunes and charismatic playing. Whether in Mancini's indelible film-themes, popular classics, traditional melodies like *Shenandoah*, hits by John Denver or Andrew Lloyd Webber, Galway's playing has great personality and charm, and the closing arrangement of *Brian Boru's march* is particularly appealing. Excellent, vivid sound.

Gothenburg Symphony Orchestra, Neeme Järvi

'Intermezzo': Intermezzi from: MASCAGNI: *Cavalleria Rusticana; L'amico Fritz.* CILEA: *Adriana Lecouvreur.* PUCCINI: *Manon Lescaut; Suor Angelica.* LEONCAVALLO: *Pagliacci.* WOLF-FERRARI: *Jewels of the Madonna.* SCHMIDT: *Notre Dame.* MUSSORGSKY: *Khovanshchina.* MASSENET: *Thaïs: Méditation.* VERDI: *La Traviata: Preludes to Acts I & III.* OFFENBACH: *Contes d'Hoffmann: Barcarolle.* PONCHIELLI: *La Gioconda: Dance of the hours.*
(M) *** DG Dig. 429 494-2 [id.].

At mid-price this has obvious attractions, though the modern digital sound could ideally be more sumptuous. But these are distinctive performances: there is plenty of temperament in the more passionate interludes and a balancing restraint in the splendidly shaped *Traviata* Preludes. The vivacious excerpt from *The Jewels of the Madonna* sparkles, and only the *Dance of the hours* gives cause for raised eyebrows with some curiously mannered, hesitant rhythmic distortions.

Hallé Orchestra, Maurice Handford

'Hallé encores': COPLAND: Fanfare for the Common Man. KHACHATURIAN: Spartacus: Adagio of Spartacus and Phrygia. GOUNOD: Mors et Vita: Judex. MACCUNN: Overture: Land of the Mountain and the Flood. SATIE: Gymnopédies Nos. 1 and 3 (orch. Debussy). MASSENET: Thaïs: Méditation. TRAD.: Suo Gan. BARBER: Adagio for strings.
(B) *** CfP CD-CFP 4543.

Maurice Handford and the Hallé offer an exceptionally attractive collection of miscellaneous pieces, beautifully recorded. Many of the items have achieved popularity almost by accident through television and the other media (how else would the MacCunn overture have come – so rightly – to notice?), but the sharpness of the contrasts adds to the charm. The Hallé violins sound a little thin in Barber's beautiful Adagio, but otherwise the playing is first rate. What is particularly attractive about this concert is the way the programme is laid out so that each piece follows on naturally after its predecessor. The CD transfer is vivid.

Harvey, Richard (recorder)

'Italian recorder concertos' (with L. Vivaldi O, Huggett): VIVALDI: Concerto in C min., RV 441; Concerto in C, RV 444. SAMMARTINI: Concerto in F. A. SCARLATTI: Sinfonia di concerto grosso No. 3.
*** Gaudeamus CDGAU 111 [id.].

Richard Harvey plays with persuasive style and flair. Moreover the accompaniments are unusually authentic and in exactly the right scale. The Sammartini Concerto is a charmer and, of the two Vivaldi works, RV 444, for sopranino recorder, is especially engaging. The Scarlatti Sinfonia in five movements is hardly less winning. The recording has excellent presence and a good balance. Highly recommended.

Heifetz, Jascha (violin)

American concertos (with (i) LAPO, Wallenstein; (ii) Dallas SO, Hendl; (iii) Piatigorsky and CO; (iv) RCA Victor SO, Voorhees): (i) KORNGOLD: Violin concerto, Op. 35. (ii) RÓZSA: Violin concerto, Op. 24; (iii) Theme and variations, Op. 29a. (iv) WAXMAN: Fantasy on Bizet's 'Carmen'.
(M) *** RCA mono/stereo GD 87963 [7963-3-RD].

Heifetz's playing in this 1953 mono recording of the Korngold Violin concerto is dazzling, the lyrical music sounds gorgeous and the material, drawn from film scores, is always appealing – and especially when presented like this. The Rózsa Concerto is slightly less memorable but still worth hearing in such a performance. In the Theme and variations he is joined by Piatigorsky, also in very good form. Waxman's 'Carmen' fantasy is simply a string of Bizet's hit tunes, and they are presented with a panache that is little short of astonishing. Few reservations have to be made about the recording; the Rózsa pieces are in stereo, but the Korngold mono sounds just as good. Anyone who cares about fabulous violin-playing should not miss this disc.

Heifetz, Jascha (violin), RCA Victor SO, William Steinberg or Izler Solomon

LALO: *Symphonie espagnole, Op. 21.* SAINT-SAENS: *Havanaise, Op. 83; Introduction and Rondo capriccioso, Op. 28.* SARASATE: *Zigeunerweisen, Op. 20.* CHAUSSON: *Poème.*
(B) (***) RCA mono GD 87709 [7709-2-RG].

These recordings come from 1951–2 and are inevitably limited in range and body. Heifetz plays the Lalo *Symphonie espagnole* without the central *Intermezzo* movement, as was the custom before the war – and how he plays it! The virtuosity is dazzling and quite transcends the period sound. The Chausson *Poème*, in which the conductor is Izler Solomon, is quite unlike other versions: stripped of sentimentality, it is curiously affecting.

Holliger, Heinz (oboe), I Musici

Oboe concertos: MARCELLO: *Concerto in D min.* SAMMARTINI: *Concerto in D.* ALBINONI: *Concerto a 5 in G min., Op. 9/8.* LOTTI: *Concerto in A.* CIMAROSA (arr. Benjamin): *Concerto in C.*
*** Ph. Dig. 420 189-2.

A collection like this is self-recommending, with five concertos offered, all of them attractive. The Lotti has a very agreeable extended *Affettuoso* slow movement, and the *Adagio* of the Sammartini is richly memorable too, while the central movement of Albinoni's Op. 9, No. 8, is wonderfully serene here. The Cimarosa – Benjamin concoction is an unalloyed delight. Holliger's timbre is enticingly coloured throughout and his phrasing is always supple and sensitive; some might feel that his ornamentation is at times a shade prolix, but this is a small point. I Musici accompany with characteristic finesse and Italian warmth.

Hungarian State Orchestra, Mátyás Antal

'Hungarian festival': KODÁLY: *Háry János: suite.* LISZT: *Hungarian rhapsodies for orchestra Nos. 1, 2 & 6* (arr. Doeppler). HUBAY: *Hejre Kati* (with Ferenc Balogh). BERLIOZ: *Damnation de Faust: Rákóczy march.*
(BB) *** Naxos Dig. 8.550142 [id.].

The Hungarian State Orchestra are in their element in this programme of colourful music for which they have a natural affinity. There is no more characterful version of the *Háry János suite* (we have already mentioned it in the Composer index) and Hubay's concertante violin piece, with its gypsy flair, is similarly successful, even if the violin soloist is not a particularly strong personality. The special interest of the Liszt *Hungarian rhapsodies* lies in the use of the Doeppler orchestrations, which are comparatively earthy, with greater use of brass solos than the more sophisticated scoring most often used in the West. The performances are suitably robust and certainly have plenty of charisma. The brilliant digital recording is strong on primary colours but has atmosphere too, and produces plenty of spectacle in the Berlioz *Rákóczy march*.

Johann Strauss Orchestra, Rothstein

'Vienna première': MILLOCKER: *Die Sieben Schwaben* (march). *Jonathan* (march). J. STRAUSS Jnr: *Concurrenzen waltz; L'Inconnue* (polka); *Hoch Osterreich!* (march); *Alexandrine polka; Die Fledermaus: New Csárdás.* E. STRAUSS: *Knall und Fall* (polka); *Leuchtkäferln waltz; Hectograph* (polka). JOSEF STRAUSS: *Frohes Leben* (waltz). *Vorwärts!* (polka); *Nachtschatten* (polka); *Elfen* (polka).
** Chan. Dig. CHAN 8381 [id.].

The present record was sponsored by the Johann Strauss Society of Great Britain. Jack Rothstein gives polished, spirited performances, with rhythms well sprung and touches of rubato nicely sophisticated. He uses a comparatively small orchestral group; the recording is balanced fairly well forward so that, even though the ambient effect is good, the strings are made to sound very bright and not too full-bodied, though detail is admirably clear. The result tends to be aurally tiring and this is best taken a few items at a time. Not all the music is inspired, although the highlights (such as the *Vorwärts!* and *Elfen* polkas of Josef Strauss) are well worth a hearing. Marilyn Hill Smith makes a brief appearance to sing an alternative *Csárdás* for *Die Fledermaus* (distinctly inferior to the famous one); the microphone is not too kind to her voice, although the performance has plenty of character.

(Philip) Jones Brass Ensemble

'Lollipops': LANGFORD: *London miniatures.* RIMSKY-KORSAKOV: *Flight of the bumble bee.* ARBAN: *Variations on a Tyrolean theme.* KOETSIER: *Little circus march, Op. 79.* GRIEG: *Norwegian dance, Op. 35/2.* JOPLIN: *Bethena.* PARKER: *A Londoner in New York.* TRAD. (arr. Iveson): *Song of the Seahorse.*
*** Claves CD 50 8503 [id.].

Recorded in St Luke's Church, Hampstead, this Claves CD makes an ideal demonstration showcase for the superb British group that is in some ways the brass equivalent of the Academy of St Martin-in-the-Fields. Offering music written or arranged specifically for these players, the concert is admirably framed by two suites of descriptive miniatures, both considerable additions to the brass repertoire. In between come many entertaining examples of musical bravura, including Rimsky's descriptive piece, sounding like a jumbo-sized bumble-bee on John Fletcher's incredibly nimble tuba, and Arban's more conventional, but no less breathtaking *Variations on a Tyrolean theme*, where Frank Lloyd is the featured horn player, while Jan Koetsier's *Kleiner Zirkusmarsch* has wonderfully deft articulation from the whole group. Gordon Langford's set of six *London miniatures* shows this composer at his most inventive and Jim Parker's *A Londoner in New York* provides a transatlantic mirror-image in his five-movement suite, with lively jazzy imagery. Tony Faulkner, the recording producer, deserves a credit for the wonderful tangibility of the sound-balance, which combines bite and clarity with fine, rich sonority. The presence of the instrumentalists on CD is very real.

'PJBE Finale': PREVIN: *Triolet for brass.* M. BERKELEY: *Music from Chaucer.* LUTOSLAWSKI: *Mini overture.* DURKÓ: *Sinfonietta.* RAUTAVAARA: *Playgrounds for angels.*
*** Chan. Dig. CHAN 8490 [id.].

As usual, the Jones Brass play these complex scores with superb musicianship and with often breathtaking freedom from any suggestion of technical problems. The writing of both the avant-garde works, Zsolt Durkó's *Sinfonietta,* and Einojuhani Rautavaara's *Playgrounds for angels,* with its separate clustering of different brass textures, is very complex; but both are presented with an easy virtuosity which is most compelling. The Previn *Triolet,* in eight, often brief sections, is amiably diverse. The finale of Berkeley's *Music from Chaucer* is even catchier, and this too is very agreeable in its inventiveness. The recording is very much in the demonstration bracket.

'*Weekend brass*': CLARKE: *Trumpet voluntary.* PURCELL: *Trumpet tune and air.* G. GABRIELI: *Canzona: Sol, sol, la sol; Sonata pian' e forte* (both ed. Gardiner). SUSATO: *Suite* (arr. Iveson). BYRD: *Earl of Oxford's march.* LOCKE: *Music for His Majesty's sackbuts and cornetts.* TRAD.: *Greensleeves.* HANDEL: *La Rejouissance.* SCHEIDT: *Battle suite.* C. P. E. BACH: *March.*
(B) *** Decca 421 633-2.

For those who like superbly alive and polished brass-playing and spectacular sonorities, this collection of Baroque and Renaissance music on Decca's Weekend bargain label should prove excellent value. The recordings are taken from various anthologies made for Argo/Decca, and the remastering is bright and clean. There are some striking antiphonal effects, as in the *Galliard battaglia* of Scheidt and C. P. E. Bach's *March,* and the melodic invention of the programme is consistently striking.

Kremer Ensemble

Viennese dance music: LANNER: *Die Weber, Op. 103; Marien Waltz; Steyrische-Tänze.* J. STRAUSS Snr: *Eisele und Beisele Sprünge* (polka). *Kettenbrücke Waltz; Beliebte Annen-Polka; Wiener Gemüts Waltz; Schwarz'sche Ball-Tänze.* KLAUSER: *Nationalländler Nos. 1, 2, 5 – 6, 12.*
*** Ph. 410 395-2 [id.].

Gidon Kremer, not just a brilliant and individual virtuoso, is a devotee of chamber playing. It is good to have such superb performances of this charming Viennese dance repertoire using an authentic small-scale group. Much of the music is slight, and Johann Strauss Senior emerges as the strongest musical personality, with his *Eisele und Beisele Sprünge polka* – delivered here with great élan – and the engaging *Kettenbrücke Waltz* among the more memorable items. The recording is most realistic in its CD format, although somewhat dry.

Laskine, Lily (harp)

Concertos for harp (with Paillard CO; or (i) Lamoureux O, Mari): HANDEL: *Concerto in B flat, Op. 4/8.* BOIELDIEU: *Concerto in C.* KRUMPHOLZ: *Concerto No. 6.* (i) BOCHSA: *Concerto No. 1.*
(M) ** Erato/WEA 2292 45084-2 [id.].

Although not quite as distinctive as Zabaleta's bargain DG disc (which duplicates the Handel), this is still an enjoyable collection for those who enjoy the concertante harp. Lily Laskine produces much delicate embroidery to entice the ear, and her accompaniments are well managed and atmospherically recorded even if the orchestral sound is not especially transparent. All three of the lesser-known works are agreeably inventive in an undemanding way.

Lloyd Webber, Julian (cello)

'Travels with my cello' (with ECO, Cleobury): J. STRAUSS Jnr: Pizzicato polka. LEHÁR: Vilja. DEBUSSY: Golliwog's cakewalk. SCHUMANN: Träumerei. ALBÉNIZ: Puerta de tierra. SAINT-SAENS: The swan. BACH/GOUNOD: Ave Maria. LLOYD WEBBER: Andante. ALBINONI: Adagio. KHACHATURIAN: Sabre dance. GRAINGER: Londonderry air. RIMSKY-KORSAKOV: Flight of the bumble bee.
**(*) Ph. Dig. 412 231-2 [id.].

This collection is issued in connection with Julian Lloyd Webber's autobiographical book, which shares the same title. The colourful orchestral arrangements were specially made by Christopher Palmer; the recording balance, by not projecting the cello too far forward, ensures that orchestral detail is very good. The solo playing has considerable flair, although the swooping lyrical style in Vilja and, notably, The swan may not appeal to all tastes. But there is no lack of personality here.

'Encore: Travels with my cello, Vol. 2' (with RPO, Cleobury): GERSHWIN: Bess, you is my woman. DEBUSSY: Clair de lune. MOZART: Turkish Rondo. TAUBE: Nocturne. BIZET: Habañera. LEHÁR: You are my heart's delight. VANGELIS: Après-midi. BACH: Jesu, joy of man's desiring. BERNSTEIN: Somewhere. MCCARTNEY: When I'm sixty-four. RIMSKY-KORSAKOV: Song of India, etc.
*** Ph. Dig. 416 698-2.

If anything, Julian Lloyd Webber's second travel album is even more attractive than the first. His warm, singing cantilena always gives pleasure and there are some effective crossover items, notably Vangelis's synthesized Un après-midi and the McCartney song. The orchestra clearly enjoy themselves, and the recording is suitably vivid and atmospheric. Very entertaining of its kind.

London Collegiate Brass, Stobart

ELGAR: Severn suite, Op. 87 (arr. Geehl and Brand). VAUGHAN WILLIAMS: Henry V overture. HOLST: A Moorside suite. IRELAND: A comedy overture.
*** CRD Dig. CRD 3434 [id.].

Elgar's Severn suite is heard in an edition that takes into account the composer's own revisions made for his orchestral arrangement. The result is very convincing, and here the opening theme is given a swagger and feeling of pageantry that remain obstinately in the memory. The rest of the work is also impressive, though the quality of the music is uneven. Vaughan Williams's Henry V overture stirringly quotes both French and English traditional melodies. Holst's Moorside suite demonstrates the composer's usual mastery when writing for wind and brass; while John Ireland's jaunty Comedy overture, played with striking rhythmic felicity, also shows the composer at his finest. The performances here (by a group drawn mainly from the London music colleges, and using trumpets rather than cornets, French horns rather than the tenor horns of the brass band world) produce a fine rich sonority and the execution has impressively polished ensemble. CRD's recording is spacious and realistic, although the upper range at times seems not absolutely clean, probably an effect created by the reverberation.

WALTON: The First shoot. TIPPETT: Festal brass with blues. BRITTEN: Russian funeral music. IRELAND: A Downland suite.
*** CRD Dig. CRD 3444 [id.].

Only the John Ireland suite is (deservedly) well known. Walton's *First shoot*, a mock ballet originally part of a C. B. Cochran review, is characteristically witty – the composer made the brass arrangement not long before he died. In spite of its title, the Tippett piece is stronger and more ambitious; and Britten's *Funeral music* makes a good foil. All the music is played expertly and with considerable intensity, if not always with the greatest subtlety. The recording is excellent.

London Gabrieli Brass Ensemble

'*The splendour of baroque brass*': SUSATO: *La Danserye: suite.* G. GABRIELI: *Canzona per sonare a 4: La Spiritata.* SCHEIDT: *Suite.* PEZEL: *Ceremonial brass music.* BACH: *The Art of fugue: Contrapunctus IX.* CHARPENTIER: *Te Deum: Prelude in D.* arr. James: *An Elizabethan suite.* CLARKE: *The Prince of Denmark's march.* HOLBORNE: *5 Dances.* STANLEY: *Trumpet tune.* LOCKE: *Music for His Majesty's sackbutts and cornetts.* PURCELL: *Trumpet tune and ayre. Music for the funeral of Queen Mary* (with Chorus).
⊛ (B) *** ASV CDQS 6013 [id.].

This is one of the really outstanding brass anthologies and the digitally remastered analogue recording is very realistic. The brass group is comparatively small: two trumpets, two trombones, horn and tuba; and that brings internal clarity, while the ambience adds fine sonority. The opening Susato *Danserye* is splendid music, and the Scheidt *Suite* is similarly inventive. Pezel's *Ceremonial brass music* is also in effect a suite – it includes a particularly memorable *Sarabande*; while Matthew Locke's *Music for His Majesty's sackbutts and cornetts* opens with a very striking *Air* and offers six diverse movements overall. With the Gabrieli *Canzona*, Purcell's *Trumpet tune and ayre* and the Jeremiah Clarke *Prince of Denmark's march* (better known as the *Trumpet voluntary*) all familiar, this makes a superb entertainment to be dipped into at will. The closing *Music for the funeral of Queen Mary* brings an eloquent choral contribution. Introduced by solemn drum-beats, it is one of Purcell's finest short works and the performance here is very moving. The arrangements throughout the concert (usually made by Crispian Steele-Perkins, who leads the group both sensitively and resplendently) are felicitous and the documentation is excellent. This is a very real bargain.

London Symphony Orchestra, Ahronovich

'*Russian spectacular*': KHACHATURIAN: *Gayaneh: Sabre dance. Spartacus: Adagio of Spartacus and Phyrigia. Masquerade: Waltz.* PROKOFIEV: *Lieutenant Kijé: Troika. Love of 3 Oranges: March.* BORODIN: *Prince Igor: Polovtsian dances.* GLINKA: *Overture: Russlan and Ludmilla.* MUSSORGSKY: *Night on the bare mountain.* SHOSTAKOVICH: *The Gadfly: Folk festival.*
(B) **(*) Pickwick Dig. PCD 804.

An excellent collection of characteristically vivid Russian orchestral genre pieces, played with plenty of spirit and polish by the LSO, who are in excellent form. Yuri Ahronovich may not be a subtle conductor, but his pacing here is notably convincing in Mussorgsky's *Night on the bare mountain*, while the piquant Prokofiev *March* is crisply rhythmic and nicely pointed. The *Sabre dance* and *Polovtsian dances* have no lack of energy and fire. The recording combines brilliance with weight; this CD is excellent value in Pickwick's bargain-priced series, even though the ambience is a little dry.

London Symphony Orchestra, Rafael Frühbeck de Burgos

'Spanish spectacular': RIMSKY-KORSAKOV: *Capriccio espagnol.* ALBÉNIZ: *Suite española: Granada* (arr. Frühbeck de Burgos). FALLA: *El amor brujo: Pantomime; Ritual fire dance. Three-cornered hat: 3 dances.* RAVEL: *Alborada del gracioso.* GRANADOS: *Goyescas: Intermezzo.*
(B) **(*) Pickwick Dig. PCD 924.

Rafael Frühbeck de Burgos is obviously completely at home in this repertoire and there is much here that is vividly coloured and exciting. He finds an extra degree of languor in the central section of Ravel's *Alborada* and a Mediterranean eloquence for the Granados *Intermezzo*. Rimsky-Korsakov's *Capriccio* has plenty of glitter and does not lack vitality; however, one does wish the performance could have generated the same degree of unbuttoned exuberance in its final section that Frühbeck finds for the three dances from *The Three-cornered hat*, which make a really exciting end to the concert. Vivid and certainly spectacular sound throughout.

London Symphony Orchestra, André Previn

'Classical favourites': BERNSTEIN: *Overture: Candide.* BARBER: *Adagio for strings.* WALTON: *Orb and sceptre (Coronation march).* DUKAS: *The sorcerer's apprentice.* HUMPERDINCK: *Overture: Hansel and Gretel.* ALBINONI: *Adagio* (arr. Giazotto). DVOŘÁK: *Slavonic dance No. 9, Op. 72/1.* ENESCU: *Rumanian rhapsody No. 1.*
(M) *** EMI CD-EMX 2127.

A most enjoyable and generous collection of favourites, recorded between 1972 and 1977, demonstrating Previn's charisma at the peak of his success with the LSO. The playing sparkles and the musical characterization is strong. This is one of the most attractive accounts of *The sorcerer's apprentice* available, while the *Candide overture* rivals the composer's own version. The delectable Enescu *Rumanian rhapsody* and the Dvořák *Slavonic dance* have splendid life and colour, while the account of Barber's *Adagio* is movingly intense. The sound-quality varies a little between items but is always vivid and often first rate.

Los Angeles Chamber Orchestra, Schwarz

'American string music': BARBER: *Serenade, Op. 1.* CARTER: *Elegy.* DIAMOND: *Rounds.* FINE: *Serious song.*
*** None. Dig. CD 79002 [id.].

The Barber *Serenade* was first recorded in the 1960s, but its long absence from the catalogue is at last rectified by this excellent issue. It is a winning piece with all the freshness of youth. The *Rounds* for strings by David Diamond is another fertile and inventive piece, which has not been available since the early days of LP. Elliot Carter's *Elegy* was originally written for cello and piano, then arranged for string quartet, and dates from 1939. It is a long-breathed and noble piece, while Irving Fine, like Carter a pupil of Boulanger and Walter Piston, composed his *Serious song* in the mid-1950s. A worthwhile issue for all who have inquiring tastes, excellently played and recorded.

Los Angeles Philharmonic Orchestra, André Previn

French music: DEBUSSY: *Prélude à l'après-midi d'un faune.* IBERT: *Escales.* DUKAS: *L'apprenti sorcier.* RAVEL: *Daphnis et Chloé: suite No. 2.*
** Ph. Dig. 426 255-2 [id.].

Previn's *Daphnis et Chloé* suite is probably the best thing in his anthology of French music, though the *Pantomime* could be held together on a tauter rein. The account of *L'apprenti sorcier* is of curiously low voltage and, though well recorded, the playing does not rise much above routine. It communicates relatively little sense of sparkle or pleasure in the music-making. A good rather than an outstanding *Prélude à l'après-midi.* Overall there is little sense of atmosphere, though the recording is very clear and clean.

Ma, Yo-Yo (cello)

'Great cello concertos': HAYDN: *Concerto in D, Hob VIIb/2* (with ECO, Garcia). SAINT-SAENS: *Concerto No. 1, Op. 33* (with O Nat. de France, Maazel). SCHUMANN: *Concerto in A min., Op. 129* (with Bav. RSO, C. Davis). DVORÁK: *Concerto in B min., Op. 104* (with BPO, Maazel). ELGAR: *Concerto in E min., Op. 85* (with LSO, Previn).
(M) *** CBS M2K 44562 (2) [id.].

An enticing mid-priced package, offering at least two of the greatest of all cello concertos, in Yo-Yo Ma's characteristic and imaginatively refined manner. Only the performance of the Haydn gives cause for reservations and these are slight; many will enjoy Ma's elegance here. He is also lucky in his accompanists, and the CBS sound gives no reasons for complaint. The performances are discussed individually under their respective composer entries.

Marsalis, Wynton (trumpet), Edita Gruberová (soprano)

'Let the bright Seraphim' (with ECO, Leppard): FASCH: *Concerto for trumpet and 2 oboes in D.* TORELLI: *2 Sonatas for trumpet and strings a 5.* HANDEL: *Samson: Let the bright Seraphim. Birthday Ode for Queen Anne: Eternal source of Light divine.* PURCELL: *Come ye sons of art: Sound the trumpet; Chaconne. Indian Queen: Trumpet overture; Intrada; Air. King Arthur: Trumpet tune.* MOLTER: *Concerto No. 2 in D.*
*** CBS Dig. MK 39061 [id.].

Although Edita Gruberová makes an important contribution to the success of this anthology, it must be listed here, rather than in the vocal section, for Wynton Marsalis is clearly the star. His superb, sometimes slightly restrained virtuosity is ideal for this programme and his cool sense of classical style brings consistently memorable results. Marsalis scales down his tone superbly to match the oboes in the delightful Fasch *Concerto* (especially as they are backwardly balanced), and he plays the *Sonatas* of Torelli and the sharply characterized Purcell miniatures with winning finesse. With Edita Gruberová he achieves a complete symbiosis in *Sound the trumpet* from *Come ye sons of art*, with the voice and instrumental melismas uncannily imitative; and he forms a comparable partnership in the two Handel arias, where Gruberová's agile and beautifully focused singing is hardly less admirable. The recording balance is excellent and its presence makes the trumpet very tangible, especially in the upper tessitura of the Molter *Concerto*, where the solo playing makes the hairs at the nape of one's neck tingle.

Menuhin, Sir Yehudi and Stéphane Grappelli (violins)

'Top Hat' (with O, Nelson Riddle): BERLIN: *Puttin' on the Ritz; Isn't this a lovely day?; The piccolino; Change partners; Top hat.* KERN: *The way you look tonight.* GERSHWIN: *He loves and she loves; They can't take that away from me; They all laughed; Funny face.* GRAPPELLI: *Alison; Amanda.* CONRAD: *The Continental.* YOUMANS: *Carioca.*
(B) *** CfP Dig. CD-CFP 4509.

This was their fifth collection and here Menuhin and Grappelli are joined by a small orchestral group directed by Nelson Riddle. Aficionados may fear that this will dilute the jazz element of the playing, and perhaps at times it does a little; but Riddle's arrangements are witty and understanding and some of these tunes undeniably have an orchestral feeling. The result is just as lively and entertaining as previous collections in this series. The music itself is associated with Fred Astaire, although Grappelli contributes two numbers himself. The sound is as crisp and lively as ever. On CD the effect is rich and smooth, with no edginess on the forwardly balanced solo violins. There are some superb melodies here and the effect is very entertaining, not least for the marvellous rhythmic crispness of Riddle's brass section.

Messiter, Malcolm (oboe), Guildhall String Ens.

Baroque oboe concertos: VIVALDI: *Concertos: in C, RV 447; in D min., RV 454.* HANDEL: *Concerto No. 3 in G min., HWV 287.* MARCELLO: *Concerto in D min.* J. S. BACH: *Concerto in G min., BWV 1056.* ALBINONI: *Concerto in D min., Op. 9/2.*
*** RCA Dig. RD 60224 [60224-2-RC].

Although authenticists will resist the warm string textures, this is a generous collection with solo playing of great finesse. Messiter's timbre and phrasing in slow movements are quite ravishing, notably in the Marcello, the Vivaldi, RV 454, and in the Albinoni, but also in the superb central cantilena of the Bach transcription.

Montreal Symphony Orchestra, Charles Dutoit

'Fête à la française': CHABRIER: *Joyeuse marche; España* (rhapsody). DUKAS: *L'apprenti sorcier.* SATIE: *Gymnopédies 1 and 2.* SAINT-SAENS: *Samson et Dalila: Air and Danse bacchanale.* BIZET: *Jeux d'enfants.* THOMAS: *Overture: Raymond.* IBERT: *Divertissement.*
*** Decca Dig. 421 557-2 [id.].

A nicely organized programme, opening vivaciously with Chabrier's *Joyeuse marche* and closing with a gloriously uninhibited account of the finale of Ibert's *Divertissement*, police-whistle and all. *L'apprenti sorcier* has a genial warmth rather than the last degree of excitement, although no one could complain that Saint-Saëns's *Bacchanale* lacked adrenalin. The *Gymnopédies* have a wistfully gentle melancholy, and Bizet's *Jeux d'enfants* a fine sense of style; while Thomas's *Raymond Overture* has all the gusto of the bandstand. The performance of *España* does not erase memories of Sir Thomas Beecham, but it certainly does not lack rhythmic élan. First-class Decca sound, brightly vivid to suit the music.

I Musici

ALBINONI: *Adagio in G min.* (arr. Giazotto). BEETHOVEN: *Minuet in G, WoO 10/2.*
BOCCHERINI: *Quintet in E, Op. 11/5: Minuet.* HAYDN (attrib.): *Quartet, Op. 3/5;
Serenade.* MOZART: *Serenade No. 13 in G (Eine kleine Nachtmusik), K.525.* PACHELBEL:
Canon.
*** Ph. Dig. 410 606-2 [id.].

An exceptionally successful concert, recorded with remarkable naturalness and realism.
The compact disc is very believable indeed. The playing combines warmth and freshness,
and the oft-played Mozart *Night music* has no suggestion whatsoever of routine: it
combines elegance, warmth and sparkle. The Boccherini *Minuet* and (especially) the
Hofstetter (attrib. Haydn) *Serenade* have an engaging lightness of touch.

Christmas concertos: CORELLI: *Concerto grosso in G min., Op. 6/8.* MANFREDINI:
Concerto in C, Op. 3/12. TORELLI: *Concerto in G min., Op. 8/6.* LOCATELLI: *Concerto in
F min., Op. 1/8.*
(B) *** Ph. 426 175-2 [id.].

Serenely expressive slow movements are a strong feature of these performances, with
phrasing of considerable finesse. The warm acoustic, with an organ continuo filling out
the textures, adds to the richness and beauty of the sound and, if allegros are not as
sprightly here as in some performances, the relaxed atmosphere is easy to enjoy.

NBC Symphony Orchestra, Arturo Toscanini

BRAHMS, orch. RUBBRA: *Variations & fugue on a theme by Handel, Op. 24.* ROGER-
DUCASSE: *Sarabande (Poème symphonique).* SIBELIUS: *Legend: Lemminkäinen's
homecoming, Op. 22/4.* HARRIS: *Symphony No. 3.* PAGANINI: *Moto perpetuo, Op. 11.*
KABALEVSKY: *Overture: Colas Breugnon, Op. 2.*
(M) (**) Dell'Arte CDDA 9020 [id.].

The great surprise of this collection is Roger-Ducasse's beautiful *Sarabande*, and the
disappointment is the legendary account of Roy Harris's *Third Symphony*. The strings do
not have the sonority of the Koussevitzky account, made during the same period (which
we still await on CD), and there is not a comparable authority. Some of the other items
are more characteristic – the Sibelius and the *Colas Breugnon* find the great conductor on
form. It is odd that both Toscanini and Ormandy should have recorded Edmund
Rubbra's orchestration of the Brahms *Handel variations*, which is not really convincing.
The quality calls for no small measure of tolerance.

(i) New Philharmonia or (ii) ROHCG O, Sir Charles Mackerras

French ballet music: (i) DELIBES: *Coppélia:* excerpts; *Sylvia:* suite. (ii) MESSAGER: *Les
deux pigeons:* suite. (i) GOUNOD: *Faust (ballet):* suite.
(M) **(*) EMI CDZ7 62515-2.

Mackerras is at his sprightly and exhilarating best in this programme of French ballet
music, securing polished and often elegant playing from both orchestras. *Les deux pigeons*
dates from as early as 1958, yet the recording has been remastered most successfully. The
rest of the programme is much later (1970) and only in the massed violins is the quality

noticeably dated. There is a good balance and an attractive ambient effect. Excellent value at medium price.

New York Trumpet Ensemble, 'Y' Chamber Orchestra, Schwarz

'The sound of trumpets': ALTENBURG: *Concerto in D for 7 trumpets.* VIVALDI: *Double trumpet concerto, RV 537.* BIBER: *Sonata (Sancti Polcarpi).* TORELLI: *Sonata a 5.* TELEMANN: *Concerto in D.*
**(*) Delos Dig. D/CD 3002 [id.].

As we know from his outstanding version of the Haydn *Trumpet concerto*, Gerard Schwarz is an accomplished soloist and musician, and both the Telemann and Vivaldi performances (where he is joined by Norman Smith) are first class. The Altenburg *Concerto* features seven soloists, the Biber *Sonata* eight in two antiphonal groups. Both come off splendidly: neither is too long to outstay its welcome. The balance places the brass well forward, but the chamber orchestra is backward, and detail might have been better defined. Otherwise the sound is very good.

Orchestra of St John's, Smith Square, John Lubbock

'On hearing the first cuckoo in spring': VAUGHAN WILLIAMS: *Fantasia on Greensleeves. Rhosymedre.* GRIEG: *Peer Gynt: Morning.* RAVEL: *Pavane.* DELIUS: *On hearing the first cuckoo in spring.* FAURÉ: *Masques et bergamasques: Overture. Berceuse, Op. 56.* SCHUBERT: *Rosamunde: Entr'acte No. 2; Ballet music No. 2.* MOZART: *Divertimento in D, K.136: Presto.*
(B) **(*) ASV Dig. CDQS 6007 [id.].

An enjoyable bargain collection of essentially atmospheric music for late evening. Fine playing throughout: tempi are very relaxed, notably in the Grieg, Fauré and Schubert items, but the evocation is persuasive. The digital recording is first class, full and clear, yet not too clinical in its detail. Some might feel that the music-making here verges on the somnolent in its consistently easy-going manner – the Delius piece is indicative of the conductor's style – but the closing Mozart *Presto* ends the concert with a sparkle.

Parley of Instruments, Roy Goodman

'Purcell's London': KELLER: *Trumpet sonata No. 1 in D.* MATTEIS: *Divisions on a ground in D min.* BALTZAR: *Pavan and Galliard in C.* BLOW: *Chaconne a 4 in G.* ECCLES: *The Judgement of Paris: Symphony for Mercury.* CROFT: *The Twin rivals: suite.* PURCELL: *Trumpet tune in C (Cibell).* ANON.: *Sonata in D (con concertino).*
*** Hyp. Dig. CDA 66108 [id.].

All this music emerged in London towards the close of the seventeenth century and the fascinating titles do not disappoint: Croft's suite is most attractive, as is Eccles' *Symphony for Mercury.* Purcell makes his own appearance in a characteristic trumpet piece, splendidly played (as is the Keller *Sonata*) by Crispian Steele-Perkins. The Matteis variations are highly inventive and Blow's *Chaconne* is equally individual. All in all a diverse and entertaining mix, very well presented, though the recording could be better defined in the bass.

Petri, Michala (recorder), ASMF

Recorder concertos (directed I. Brown): VIVALDI: *Sopranino recorder concerto in C, RV 443.* SAMMARTINI: *Descant recorder concerto in F.* TELEMANN: *Treble recorder concerto in C.* HANDEL: *Treble recorder concerto in F* (arr. of *Organ concerto, Op. 4/5*).
*** Ph. 400 075-2 [id.].

Michala Petri plays her various recorders with enviable skill, and her nimble piping creates some delightful sounds in these four attractively inventive concertos. This is not a record to be played all at once; taken in sections, it has unfailing charm; the sound is of demonstration quality. The CD retains the analogue ambient warmth, while detail seems marginally cleaner.

'English concertos' (directed K. Sillito): BABEL: *Concerto in C for descant recorder, Op. 3/1.* HANDEL: *Concerto in B flat for treble recorder and bassoon, Op. 4/6* (with G. Sheene). BASTON: *Concerto No. 2 for descant recorder in D.* JACOB: *Suite for treble recorder and strings.*
⊛ *** Ph. Dig. 411 056-2 [id.].

The *Concerto* by William Babel (*c.* 1690–1723) is a delight, with Petri's sparkling performance of the outer movements full of good humour and high spirits, matched by Kenneth Sillito's alert accompaniments. The Handel is yet another arrangement of Op. 4/6, with the organ part felicitously re-scored for recorder and bassoon. The two instruments are nicely balanced and thus a familiar work is given an attractive new look. John Baston's *Concerto* has individuality and charm, and the finale is quirkily infectious. Gordon Jacob's *Suite* of seven movements balances a gentle bitter-sweet melancholy in the lyrical writing with a rumbustious, extrovert quality in the dances. Altogether a highly rewarding concert, beautifully played and recorded.

Recorder concertos (directed K. Sillito): VIVALDI: *Concerto in C, RV 44.* MARCELLO: *Concerto in D min.* TELEMANN: *Concerto in F.* NAUDOT: *Concerto in G.*
**(*) Ph. 412 630-2 [id.].

The Vivaldi *Concerto* is the most familiar work for sopranino recorder and has been recorded frequently, though never more winningly than here. The Marcello is better known in its original format for oboe; Michala Petri plays it convincingly on the descant recorder and makes it her own. The Telemann is also a good piece, but the Naudot is rather less memorable. Admirers of this fine artist will be glad to have this new collection, notable for splendid accompaniments, with slow movements particularly attractive in their expressive warmth, without being romanticized. Overall, however, this is a less memorable programme than the collection listed above. The recording is excellent, with the compact disc adding marginally to the clarity of detail within a pleasing ambience.

Philharmonia Orchestra, Herbert von Karajan

BALAKIREV: *Symphony No. 1 in C.* BERLIOZ: *Symphonie fantastique.* MOZART: *Sinfonia concertante, K.297b; Clarinet concerto.* ROUSSEL: *Symphony No. 4.* R. STRAUSS: *Don Juan; Till Eulenspiegel; Death and transfiguration.* STRAVINSKY: *Jeu de cartes.*
(M) (***) EMI mono CMS7 63316-2 (3).

Karajan's classic accounts of the Balakirev and Roussel *Symphonies*, which appeared originally on 78s, were the very first recordings of either work and the former has never been surpassed, even by Beecham. In the Roussel, too, Karajan is completely persuasive, and the playing of the Philharmonia is pretty impressive here and in the *Jeu de cartes*, which for some reason Walter Legge never published at the time. The soloists in the Mozart are the Philharmonia principals – and wonderful they were. A marvellous set and not to be missed.

BARTÓK: *Concerto for Orchestra; Music for strings, percussion and celesta.* BRITTEN: *Variations on a theme of Frank Bridge.* DEBUSSY: *La Mer.* HANDEL arr. HARTY: *Water music.* KODÁLY: *Háry János suite.* RAVEL: *Rapsodie espagnol.* SIBELIUS: *Finlandia; Symphonies Nos. 4, 6 & 7; Tapiola.* VAUGHAN WILLIAMS: *Fantasia on a theme of Thomas Tallis.*
⊛ *** EMI mono CMS7 63464-2 (4).

Of these two Karajan/Philharmonia compilations this is the one that you should on no account miss. The Vaughan Williams and the Britten have hardly ever been played more beautifully, and they are recorded marvellously. Karajan's mid-1950s Sibelius is leaner and more austere than his later versions with the Berlin orchestra (and earned the composer's plaudits). Only No. 7 disappoints, and it is a pity that his earlier No. 5 did not replace it. Also there is something special about the Bartók, which was almost (but not quite) a first recording: Harold Byrns just beat him to it; but, like the Bartók *Concerto*, it has the excitement of discovery.

Ragossnig, Konrad (lute), Ulsamer Collegium, Ulsamer

'Terpsichore': Renaissance dance music by: ATTAINGNANT; DALZA; PETRUCCI; NEUSIDLER; SUSATO; GERVAISE; PHALESE. Early Baroque dance music by: MAINERIO; RESARD; MOLINARO; DA VENOSA; CAROSO; CAROUBEL; HOLBOURNE; DOWLAND; SIMPSON; GIBBONS; PRAETORIUS; HAUSSMANN.
*** DG 415 294-2 [id.].

There are in all 43 items on this compact disc which collects material from the recordings made by this ensemble, issued on two LPs in 1971 and 1972. Although on the face of it this music is of specialist interest, it is in fact highly attractive and could (and should) enjoy wide appeal. The performances are crisp and vital, and the DG engineers have made a first-class job of the digital remastering. Readers who recall the originals will not hesitate, and newcomers will find it full of delights.

Reilly, Tommy (harmonica), ASMF Chamber Ensemble

'Serenade': MOODY: *Bulgarian wedding dance; Sonata* (arr. from HANDEL: *Flute sonatas*). FAURÉ: *Pavane, Op. 50; Romance; Au bord de l'eau, Op. 8/1.* GRIEG: *Norwegian dance, Op. 35/2.* MARTIN: *Adagietto.* D. REILLY: *Aviator.* T. REILLY: *Serenade.* DEBUSSY: *Bruyères.* MENDELSSOHN: *On wings of song.* TRAD.: *My Lagen love.* MCCARTNEY: *2 Beatle girls: Eleanor and Michelle.*
*** Chan. Dig. CHAN 8486 [id.].

The slightly acerbic edge of the harmonica can add piquancy to a romantic programme like this, and Tommy Reilly is a very stylish player. Moody's two contributions are particularly engaging and so is Reilly's own *Serenade*, while all the other light pieces are predictably appealing, if you like the harmonica timbre, projected against a small accompanying group. The effect is consistently refined (even in the Handel arrangement, which is the very opposite of 'authentic') and the pleasingly atmospheric sound makes this a very agreeable concert.

VAUGHAN WILLIAMS: *Romance.* TAUSKY: *Concertino.* MOODY: *Little suite.* Gordon JACOB: *5 Pieces.*
*** Chan. CHAN 8617 [id.].

The atmospheric sound certainly suits the Vaughan Williams, not thematically one of the composer's strongest works but quite haunting in its way. The Tausky *Concertino* is extremely well made, and it is seductively played; in the last analysis it is not really memorable. James Moody's *Little suite* consists of five lightweight miniatures, nicely conceived and expertly scored; but the highlight of the collection is the Gordon Jacob *Suite*, also offering five vignettes: the quality of invention here is of a consistently high standard. Throughout the concert the playing and recording balance are wholly admirable and the remastered sound retains all the bloom of the original recording, made by Decca engineers in St John's, Smith Square.

Richter, Sviatoslav (piano)

Piano concertos (with var. orchestras & conductors): MOZART: *Concerto No. 20 in D min., K.466.* BEETHOVEN: *Concerto No. 3 in C min., Op. 37; Rondo for piano & orchestra in B flat, G.151.* RACHMANINOV: *Concerto No. 2 in C min., Op. 18.* TCHAIKOVSKY: *Concerto No. 1 in B flat min., Op. 54.* SCHUMANN: *Piano concerto in A min., Op. 54.* PROKOFIEV: *Concerto No. 5 in G min., Op. 55.*
(B) **(*) DG 429 918-2 (3).

Although there are severe reservations about the Tchaikovsky *Concerto*, where Richter and Karajan fail to see eye to eye over choice of tempi, and though the Beethoven does not show the great pianist at his very best, there are some outstanding performances here, not least the Prokofiev, which is a classic of the gramophone. At bargain price this is quite tempting.

Royal Liverpool Philharmonic Orchestra, Sir Charles Groves

'*Meditation*': CHOPIN, arr. JACOB: *Les Sylphides: Nocturne in A flat, Op. 32/2.* MASSENET: *Thaïs: Méditation.* ALBINONI/GIAZOTTO. *Adagio in G min.* (both with Clifford Knowles). BORODIN/SARGENT: *Nocturne for strings.* MENDELSSOHN: *A Midsummer Night's Dream: Nocturne.* GLUCK: *Orfeo: Dance of the Blessed Spirits.* FAURÉ: *Pavane, Op. 50.*
(B) ** CfP CD-CFP 4515.

Recorded in Liverpool's Philharmonic Hall in the late 1960s, the remastering has been beneficial in removing any soupiness from the sound, and nearly all these pieces come up fresh, particularly Sir Malcolm Sargent's famous string arrangement of the *Nocturne* from Borodin's *D major Quartet*. Gordon Jacob's scoring of Chopin, too, makes a welcome change from the usual Roy Douglas version. All the performances are alive and well played, and Clifford Knowles is an excellent soloist in the two items needing a concertante violin. The principal flautist of the orchestra at that time was Atarah Ben-Tovin, who went on to become famous in the North-west, arranging special concerts to introduce children to the world of music. She plays beautifully in the Gluck and Fauré pieces, though, in the former, Groves's tempo is slow and the style on the heavy side.

'*Rule Britannia*': ELGAR: *Pomp and circumstance marches Nos. 1 & 4.* HOLST: *Marching song.* VAUGHAN WILLIAMS: *Coastal Command: Dawn patrol.* WALFORD DAVIES: *RAF March past.* WALTON: *Henry V: Touch her soft lips and part; Agincourt song.* WOOD: *Fantasia on British sea songs: Hornpipe.* COATES: *Dambusters march.* BLISS: *Processional.* ALFORD: *On the quarterdeck.* ARNE: *The British Grenadiers; Rule Britannia* (with Anne Collins & RLPO Ch.).
(B) ** CfP CD-CFP 4567.

A genial patriotic collection, nicely varied in content, with Holst, Vaughan Williams and Walton items to contrast with the breezy vitality of the Coates *Dambusters* and the Walford Davies *RAF March past* – a truly splendid march. Anne Collins's consonants seem to be somewhat overemphasized by the microphone in the closing spectacular, a favourite, like Sir Henry's Wood's *Hornpipe*, at the Proms. Sir Charles Groves directs throughout with spirit and affection, if with no striking individuality. Clean, bright, vividly remastered sound (from 1977).

Royal Philharmonic Orchestra, Alan Barlow

'*This England*': ELGAR: *Serenade for strings in E min., Op. 20.* DELIUS: *Irmelin: Prelude; On hearing the first cuckoo in spring; Summer night on the river.* HOLST: *St Paul's suite, Op. 29/2; Brook Green suite.* WARLOCK: *Capriol suite.*
*** ASV Dig. CDDCA 623 [id.].

A very enjoyable concert of mostly string music, well played and given first-class, natural recording, approaching demonstration standard. The performances are all freshly spontaneous. The Delius pieces have agreeably flowing lines, and the *Capriol suite* (nearer to Sargent's version in style than to Marriner's more chimerical approach) is also strongly characterized.

Royal Philharmonic Orchestra, Sir Thomas Beecham

French music: BIZET: *Carmen suite No. 1.* FAURÉ: *Pavane, Op. 60; Dolly suite, Op. 56.* DEBUSSY: *Prélude à l'après-midi d'un faune.* SAINT-SAENS: *Le rouet d'Omphale.* DELIBES: *Le Roi s'amuse* (ballet suite).
⊛ (M) *** EMI CDM7 63379-2 [id.].

No one conducts the *Carmen Prelude* with quite the flair of Sir Thomas, while the last movement of the *Dolly suite, Le pas espagnole,* (in Rabaud's orchestration) has the kind of dash we associate with Beecham's Chabrier. But for the most part the ear is beguiled by the consistently imaginative and poetic phrasing that distinguished his very best performances. The delicacy of string textures and wind playing (notably the flute) in *Le rouet d'Omphale* and the other *Dolly* numbers – the *Berceuse, Le jardin de Dolly* and *Tendresse* – is exquisite, and Debussy's *Prélude à l'après-midi d'un faune* brings a ravishingly diaphanous web of sound. Delibes' pastiche ballet-score, *Le Roi s'amuse*, is given the special elegance that Sir Thomas reserved for music from the past unashamedly rescored to please the ear of later generations. The remastering is marvellously managed and all the recordings (from between 1957 and 1961) sound wonderfully vivid and fresh.

St Louis Symphony Orchestra, Leonard Slatkin

'Classic marches': BERLIOZ: *Damnation de Faust: Rákóczy march.* BEETHOVEN: *Ruins of Athens: Turkish march.* MEYERBEER: *Le Prophète: Coronation march.* MENDELSSOHN: *Midsummer Night's Dream: Wedding march.* IPPOLITOV-IVANOV: *Caucasian sketches: Procession of the Sardar.* J. STRAUSS Snr: *Radetzky march.* PIERNÉ: *Marche des petits faunes.* TCHAIKOVSKY: *Nutcracker suite: March.* ELGAR: *Pomp and circumstance march No. 1.* VERDI: *Aida: Triumphal march.* GOUNOD: *Funeral march of a marionette.* PROKOFIEV: *Love of three oranges: March.* SIBELIUS: *Karelia: Alla marcia.* HERBERT: *Babes in Toyland: March of the Toys.* GANZ: *St Louis Symphony march.* SOUSA: *Stars and stripes forever.*
**(*) RCA Dig. RD 87716 [7716-2-RC].

A generously varied collection of concert marches, with the lighter novelties like the Pierné and Victor Herbert items especially welcome. Slatkin's approach is essentially serious and his spacious tempi (rather too spacious in the Prokofiev and Gounod pieces, which need a touch more bite and wit) seek the grand manner which, coupled to the resonant large-scale recording, suits the more expansive pieces by Meyerbeer, Mendelssohn and Elgar best.

Savijoki, Pekka (saxophone), New Stockholm Chamber Orchestra, Panula

LARSSON: *Concerto for saxophone and string orchestra, Op. 14.* GLAZUNOV: *Concerto in E flat, Op. 109.* PANULA: *Adagio and allegro for string orchestra.*
*** BIS CD 218 [id.].

The find here for most collectors outside Scandinavia will be Lars-Erik Larsson's *Saxophone concerto.* It is a very fine and inventive work; the slow movement with its beautiful canonic opening is of particular distinction. The Glazunov, written at the same time, is more original and imaginative than it at first appears. Accomplished performances and good recording.

Scandinavian Brass Ensemble, Jorma Panula

HALLBERG: *Blacksmith's tune.* HOLMBOE: *Concerto for brass, Op. 157.* MADSEN: *Divertimento for brass and percussion, Op. 47.* GRIEG: *Funeral march.* ALMILA: *Te Pa Te Pa, Op. 26.* DANIELSSON: *Suite No. 3.*
*** BIS Dig. CD 265 [id.].

The sound is quite spectacular and has superb presence and body: in short, a demonstration disc. However, not all the music is spectacular, but the collection is worth having for Holmboe's *Concerto,* a short but finely wrought piece that towers over everything else here. Grieg's *Funeral march* was originally intended for piano, though Grieg arranged it for military band. The Norwegian Trygve Madsen's piece begins attractively enough with some lively syncopation but turns out to be pretty cheap. Christer Danielsson is a Swedish trombonist of note and his *Suite* is craftsmanlike and musicianly.

Scottish Chamber Orchestra, Laredo

'String masterpieces': ALBINONI: *Adagio in G min.* (arr. Giazotto). HANDEL: *Berenice: Overture. Solomon: Arrival of the Queen of Sheba.* BACH: *Suite No. 3, BWV 1068: Air. Violin concerto No. 1 in A min., BWV 1041: Finale.* PACHELBEL: *Canon.* PURCELL: *Abdelazer: Rondo. Chacony in G min.*
(B) *** Pickwick Dig. PCD 802.

An excellent issue. The playing is alive, alert, stylish and committed without being overly expressive, yet the Bach *Air* has warmth and Pachelbel's *Canon* is fresh and unconventional in approach. The sound is first class, especially spacious and convincing on CD, well detailed without any clinical feeling. The Purcell *Rondo* is the tune made familiar by Britten's orchestral guide; the *Chaconne* is played with telling simplicity.

Scottish National Orchestra, Gibson

'Land of the mountain and the flood': MENDELSSOHN: *The Hebrides overture (Fingal's Cave), Op. 26.* BERLIOZ: *Waverley overture, Op. 2.* ARNOLD: *Tam O'Shanter overture.* VERDI: *Macbeth: Ballet music.* MACCUNN: *Overture: Land of the Mountain and the Flood.*
**(*) Chan. Dig. CHAN 8379 [id.].

The MacCunn overture here provides an attractive foil for the Scottish National Orchestra's collection of short pieces inspired by Scotland. These performances are not as refined as the best available versions – significantly, the most dashing performance is of Arnold's difficult and rumbustious overture – but make an attractive recital. On CD, the spectacularly vivid orchestration of *Tam O'Shanter* produces sound that is in the demonstration bracket; and the MacCunn piece is pretty impressive, too. The Berlioz is vivid, and Gibson's approach to *Fingal's Cave* attractively romantic.

Scottish National Orchestra, Neeme Järvi

Music from Estonia, Vol. 2: LEMBA: *Symphony in C sharp min.* TOBIAS: *Julius Caesar overture.* ELLER: *Twilight.* TORMIS: *Overture No. 2.* PÄRT: *Cantus in memoriam Benjamin Britten.*
*** Chan. Dig. CHAN 8656 [id.].

Easily the best thing here is Lemba's *Symphony* (already mentioned under its composer); it is astonishingly accomplished for a 23-year-old: the invention is fresh and memorable and it is played here with evident enthusiasm. The Heino Eller piece is less impressive than his *Elegy*; the *Julius Caesar overture* by Rudolf Tobias (1873–1918) – the very first Estonian orchestral piece – is of less interest, as is the repetitive Tormis work (inspired by the opening of Tubin's *Fifth Symphony*). The Pärt is an effective and haunting little work. But these works are all short and the *Symphony* is long (40 minutes) and altogether delightful. Strongly recommended.

Slovak Philharmonic Orchestra

'Russian Fireworks' (cond. (i) Richard Hayman; (ii) Kenneth Jean; (iii) Stephen Gunzenhauser; (iv) Michael Halász): (i) IPPOLITOV-IVANOV: *Caucasian sketches: Procession of the Sardar.* (ii) LIADOV: *8 Russian folksongs.* KABALEVSKY: *Comedian's galop.* MUSSORGSKY: *Sorochinski Fair: Gopak. Khovanshchina: Dance of the Persian*

slaves. (iii) LIADOV: *Baba Yaga; The enchanted lake; Kikimora.* (iv) RUBINSTEIN: *Feramor: Dance of the Bayaderes; Bridal procession. The Demon: Lesginka.* (ii) HALVORSEN: *Entry of the Boyars.*
(BB) *** Naxos Dig. 8.550328 [id.].

A vividly sparkling concert with spectacular digital sound, more than making up in vigour and spontaneity for any lack of finesse. The Liadov tone-poems are especially attractive and, besides the very familiar pieces by Ippolitov-Ivanov, Halvorsen and Mussorgsky, it is good to have the Rubinstein items, especially the *Lesginka* which has a rather attractive tune.

Smedvig, Rolf (trumpet)

Trumpet concertos (with Scottish CO, Jahja Ling): HAYDN: *Concerto in E flat.* TARTINI: *Concerto in D.* HUMMEL: *Concerto in E flat.* TORELLI: *Concerto in D.* BELLINI: *Concerto in E flat.*
*** Telarc Dig. CD 80282 [id.].

Rolf Smedvig, a native of Seattle, joins the ranks of international virtuosi who offer outstanding versions of the Haydn and Hummel *Concertos.* The easy elegance of his style and his warm phrasing of slow-movement cantilenas is a constant pleasure to the ear, and in the finales the bravura is almost self-effacing in its natural command. Yet in the Haydn *Rondo* he changes his articulation imaginatively when a phrase is repeated. The performances are not quite as exciting as those of Hardenberger (whose projection has rather more extrovert sparkle), but he plays the Hummel in the key of E major, which adds to its brilliance of effect. One of the highlights of the present disc is the wholly engaging Tartini work, a transcription of a violin concerto, which is so effective that one is tempted to dismiss the original as second-best. Bellini's *Concerto,* originally conceived for oboe, is also a delight, heard on the trumpet, when the playing is so sophisticated and so readily catches its operatic feeling. Accompaniments by the SCO under Jahja Ling are admirably cultivated, if with an occasional suspicion of blandness. But that is partly the effect of the richly resonant acoustics of City Hall, Glasgow, where this record was made, with the natural realism characteristic of the Telarc label.

Steele-Perkins, Crispian (trumpet)

Six Trumpet concertos (with ECO, Anthony Halstead): HAYDN: *Concerto in E flat.* TORELLI: *Concerto in D.* M. HAYDN: *Concerto No. 2 in C.* TELEMANN: *Concerto for trumpet, two oboes and strings.* NERUDA: *Concerto in E flat.* HUMPHRIES: *Concerto in D, Op. 10/12.*
(B) *** Pickwick PCD 821.

Collectors who have relished Håkan Hardenberger's famous collection of trumpet concertos (Philips 420 203-2) might well go on to this equally admirable concert, which duplicates only the Haydn – and that in a performance hardly less distinguished. Crispian Steele-Perkins has a bright, gleaming, beautifully focused timbre and crisp articulation, with easy command of the high tessitura of the Michael Haydn work and all the bravura necessary for the sprightly finales of all these concertos. His phrasing in the slow movement of Joseph Haydn's shapely *Andante* is matched by his playing of the *Largo* of the Neruda and the *Adagio–Presto–Adagio* of the Torelli, another fine work. Anthony Halstead with the ECO gives him warmly sympathetic support. The recording balance gives the soloist plenty of presence, but the orchestra is recorded rather reverberantly, an effect similar to that on the Hardenberger record.

Stockholm Sinfonietta, Salonen

'A Swedish serenade': WIRÉN: Serenade for strings, Op. 11. LARSSON: Little serenade for strings, Op. 12. SODERLUNDH: Oboe concertino (with A. Nilsson). LIDHOLM: Music for strings.
**(*) BIS Dig. CD 285 [id.].

The most familiar piece here is the Dag Wirén Serenade for strings. By far the best movement of Lille Bror Söderlundh's Concertino for oboe and orchestra is the lovely Andante, whose melancholy is winning and has a distinctly Gallic feel to it. By contrast, the finale is rather thin and naïve, but the piece is still worth hearing and is certainly played with splendid artistry by Alf Nilsson and the Stockholm Sinfonietta, one of the best small chamber orchestras in the Nordic countries. The Lidholm Music for strings is somewhat grey and anonymous though it is expertly wrought. Esa-Pekka Salonen gets good results from this ensemble and the recording lives up to the high standards of the BIS label. It is forwardly balanced but has splendid body and realism.

Stockholm Sinfonietta, Jan-Olav Wedin

'Swedish pastorale': ALFVÉN: The Mountain King, Op. 37: Dance of the Cow-girl. ATTERBERG: Suite No. 3 for violin, viola and string orchestra. BLOMDAHL: Theatre Music: Adagio. LARSSON: Pastoral suite, Op. 19; The Winter's Tale: Four vignettes. ROMAN: Concerto in D, for oboe d'amore, string orchestra and harpsichord, BeRI 53. ROSENBERG: Small piece for cello and string orchestra.
*** BIS Dig. CD 165 [id.].

A charming record. The Stockholm Sinfonietta is an expert ensemble and play with sensitivity under Jan-Olav Wedin. In addition to affectionate accounts of the Pastoral suite and the charming vignettes for The Winter's Tale, they include Atterberg's Suite No. 3, which has something of the modal dignity of the Vaughan Williams Tallis fantasy. It has real eloquence and an attractive melancholy, to which the two soloists, Nils-Erik Sparf and Jouko Mansnerus, do ample justice. The Blomdahl and Roman works are also given alert and sensitive performances; they make one think how delightful they are. Hilding Rosenberg's piece is very short but is rather beautiful. A delightful anthology and excellent (if a trifle closely balanced) recording. Confidently recommended.

Stuttgart Chamber Orchestra, Karl Münchinger

Baroque music: PACHELBEL: Canon. GLUCK: Orfeo: Dance of the Blessed Spirits. HANDEL: Water music: suite No. 3; Organ concerto in F (Cuckoo and the nightingale; with M. Haselböck). L. MOZART: Toy symphony. ALBINONI: Adagio in G min. (arr. Giazotto). BACH: Suite No. 3, BMV 1068: Air. BOCCHERINI: Minuet (from String quintet in E. Op. 13/5).
**(*) Decca Dig. 411 973-2 [id.].

Beautifully recorded, this is an attractive concert with a very well-played suite from Handel's Water music, and the engaging Cuckoo and the nightingale Organ concerto (with Martin Haselböck an excellent soloist) to give some ballast. The performance of Pachelbel's Canon is a little heavy-handed, but the strongly expressive account of

Albinoni's *Adagio* is convincing. The *Toy symphony* has some piquant special effects, and the shorter lollipops are quite elegantly played. The overall mood is a trifle serious, but that is Münchinger's way.

PACHELBEL: *Canon and gigue.* ALBINONI: *Adagio* (arr. Giazotto). BACH: *Jesu, joy of man's desiring; Sheep may safely graze; Suite No. 3: Air. Fugue in G min., BWV 542.* BOCCHERINI: *Minuet* from *Op. 13/5.* HOFSTETTER: *Serenade.* HANDEL: *Concerto grosso, Op. 6/6: Musette. Solomon: Arrival of the Queen of Sheba. Organ concerto, Op. 4/4. Overture: Berenice.*
(M) **(*) Decca 417 781-2 [id.].

The recording quality of Münchinger's earlier analogue concert is first class and the programme generous; the performances, as before, will suit those who prefer their Baroque lollipops played expansively on modern instruments. The balance is close, which does not permit much dynamic contrast in the Pachelbel *Canon*, although the *Gigue* certainly sounds gracious. The Boccherini *Minuet* and the famous *Serenade* once attributed to Haydn are pleasingly done, and among the Handel items the *Organ concerto* (with Ulrich Bremsteller) is nicely registered. The other Handel excerpts produce rich textures from the strings, and the Albinoni *Adagio* is sumptuous. Those who prefer something more authentic can turn to the Taverner Players on EMI – see below.

Taverner Players, Andrew Parrott

PACHELBEL: *Canon and gigue.* HANDEL: *Solomon: Arrival of the Queen of Sheba. Harp concerto in B flat, Op. 4/6* (with A. Lawrence-King, harp). PURCELL: *3 Parts upon a ground; Suite of Theatre music.* BACH: *Sinfonias from Cantatas 29, 31, 106, 156, 174* and *Christmas oratorio. Cantata 147: Jesu, joy of man's desiring.*
(M) *** EMI Dig. CDM7 69853-2 [id.].

This really outstanding collection of Baroque favourites shows that authentic performance can produce both charm and charisma: there is not a whiff of sterile, scholarly rectitude here. Indeed Pachelbel's famous *Canon* sounds delightfully fresh, heard in its original chamber scoring, while Handel's *Queen of Sheba* arrives in exhilarating fashion. The *Harp concerto*, too, sounds delectable when the effect is so neat and stylish. The Bach *Sinfonias* are varied in content (that from No. 29 includes a bravura organ obbligato, played with considerable flair by John Toll), with No. 174 bringing a real novelty in being a different version of Bach's *Brandenburg concerto No. 3*, attractively expanded in scoring to include horns and oboes. First-class digital recording makes this a highly desirable compilation at a very reasonable price.

Thames Chamber Orchestra, Michael Dobson

'The baroque concerto in England' (with Black, Bennett): ANON. (probably HANDEL): *Concerto grosso in F.* BOYCE: *Concerti grossi: in E min. for strings; in B min. for 2 solo violins, cello and strings.* WOODCOCK: *Oboe concerto in E flat; Flute concerto in D.*
*** CRD CRD 3331 [id.].

A wholly desirable collection, beautifully played and recorded. Indeed the recording has splendid life and presence and often offers demonstration quality – try the opening of the Woodcock *Flute concerto*, for instance. The music is all highly rewarding. The opening concerto was included in Walsh's first edition of Handel's Op. 3 (as No. 4) but was subsequently replaced by another work. Whether or not it is by Handel, it is an uncommonly good piece, and it is given a superbly alert and sympathetic performance here. Neil Black and William Bennett are soloists of the highest calibre, and it is sufficient to say that they are on top form throughout this most enjoyable concert.

Touvron, Guy and Bernard Soustrot (trumpets)

Trumpet concertos (with Lucerne Fest. Strings, Baumgartner): HAYDN: *Concerto in E flat.* MANFREDINI: *Double concerto in D.* M. HAYDN: *Concerto in C.* ALBINONI: *Concerto a cinque, Op. 9/9.*
(*) Denon Dig. C37 7544 [id.].

A generally attractive collection, recorded in Zurich. Both soloists are French, and the style of their playing is admirable in all respects, with no intrusive vibrato. Guy Touvron's account of Joseph Haydn's famous *Concerto* is fresh, lightly articulated and pleasingly stylish. Bravura is always at the service of the music, the nicely paced *Andante* has a hint of melancholy and the finale is contrastingly gay. The Manfredini is a more conventional piece but, like Michael Haydn's two-movement work, also has a memorable finale, dispatched with easy flair by Soustrot. Albinoni's *Concerto a cinque* was intended for a pair of solo violins, but the trumpets make it seem otherwise, and the overlapping imitation of the *Adagio* and finale is particularly effective. The Denon recording is well balanced and orchestral detail is good (although the harpsichord is almost inaudible), while the soloists are given a fine presence against a suitably resonant acoustic.

Tuckwell, Barry (horn)

'Baroque horn concertos from the Court of Dresden' (with ASMF, Iona Brown): KNECHTL: *Concerto in D.* REINHARDT: *Concerto in E flat.* QUANTZ: *Concertos Nos. 3 in E flat; 9 in E flat.* GRAUN: *Concerto in D.* ROLLIG: *Concertos Nos. 14 in E flat; 15 in D.*
*** Decca Dig. 417 406-2 [id.].

None of this is great music, but it is all played by a master-soloist, and electricity is readily created from the bravura demands of the writing, so easily met by Barry Tuckwell. There is plenty of high tessitura (as in the Knechtl and both the Rollig *Concertos*) while Reinhardt's florid writing, with leaps as well as prolix textures, is very testing indeed. This *Concerto*, like those of Quantz and Rollig, favours a *siciliano* slow movement, which brings lyrical contrast. Probably the best works here are the Graun, short and strong in character (particularly the finale with its crisp decoration), and Quantz's No. 9. This features a concertante oboe soloist, who echoes the horn's solo line most appealingly. Polished and stylish accompaniments from the Academy under Iona Brown, and bright, clear recording, with the overall balance managed well and the harpsichord continuo not lost.

Vienna Philharmonic Orchestra, Claudio Abbado

'New Year Concert 1988' (with Vienna Boys' Ch.): REZNICEK: *Donna Diana: overture.* STRAUSS, Josef: *Brennende Liebe; Auf Ferienreisen; Im Fluge* (polkas). STRAUSS, Johann Jnr: *Die Fledermaus overture; Neue pizzicato polka; Freut euch des Lebens* (waltz); *Chit-chat polka; Un Ballo in maschera: Quadrille on themes from Verdi's opera. Liechtes Blut polka; Seid unschlungen Millionen* (waltz); *Perpetuum mobile; Banditen-Galopp; An der schönen blauen Donau.* STRAUSS, Johann Snr: *Radetzky march.*
*** DG Dig. 423 662-2.

If this record, which also includes the Vienna Boys' Choir, does not quite match Karajan's, it still has a real sense of occasion and offers some delectable performances. Obvious favourites like *The blue Danube, Die Fledermaus overture* and, of course, the *Radetzky march* are duplicated, but most of the programme is new. With Rezniček's *Donna Diana* opening the proceedings vivaciously, the mixture is nicely varied to include the familiar and the unfamiliar, and both playing and recording are excellent. Audience participation is taken for granted and is seldom too intrusive but adds to the feeling of enjoyment and spontaneity.

Vienna Philharmonic Orchestra, (i) Sir Georg Solti or (ii) Willi Boskovsky

'Light Cavalry': Overtures: (i) SUPPÉ: *Light Cavalry; Poet and peasant; Morning, noon and night; Pique dame;* (ii) *Beautiful Galatea.* NICOLAI: *The merry wives of Windsor.* REZNIČEK: *Donna Diana.* STRAUSS, Johann Jnr: *Die Fledermaus.*
(B) **(*) Decca 421 170-2.

Suppé overtures represented some of the first repertoire recorded by Solti for Decca in the days of mono LP (when he wanted to record Wagner!). These are his later, stereo versions, first issued in 1960. They generate characteristic intensity and excitement, and the recording has a spectacularly wide dynamic range – too wide for the cello solos in *Morning, noon and night* and *Poet and peasant*, where the instrument is backwardly balanced and sounds more like a viola. Boskovsky's performances are altogether more mellow, yet in *Donna Diana* the exhilarating but relaxed forward impulse is nicely judged. The sound is appropriately bright and vivid, especially brilliant in the four favourite Suppé overtures conducted by Solti.

Vienna Volksoper Orchestra, Bauer-Theussl

'Famous waltzes': WEBER: *Invitation to the dance, Op. 65* (arr. Berlioz). LANNER: *Die Schönbrunner.* IVANOVICI: *Donauwellen (Waves of the Danube).* KOMZAK: *Bad'ner Mad'ln.* JOSEF STRAUSS: *Dynamiden.* ZIEHRER: *Herreinspaziert* (arr. Schönnherr).
**(*) Ph. Dig. 400 013-2 [id.].

'Famous waltzes', Vol. 2: ZIEHRER: *Faschingskinder; Wiener Burger.* LEHÁR: *Gold and silver; Ballsirenen.* ROSAS: *Uber den Wellen.* LANNER: *Hofballtänze; Der Romantiker.*
**(*) Ph. Dig. 412 883-2 [id.].

These two records conveniently gather together some waltzes from contemporaries of the Johann Strauss family. Each has a striking main theme and the performances, if sometimes lacking the last degree of vitality, have an agreeable warmth. Franz Bauer-Theussl's rubato is not always subtle but is often effective in its way. He is good with the atmospheric openings – indeed, he shapes the main theme of Ivanovici's *Donauwellen* (*Danube waves*) very persuasively. This should bring a ready response from listeners, familiar with the music of the Strauss family and wanting to do a little exploring in the Viennese hinterland. Ziehrer and Lanner were accomplished tune-masters, and the Lehár waltzes are first rate. The recording is within an attractively resonant acoustic and yet provides good detail.

Wallace, John (trumpet)

'Man – the measure of all things' (with Philh. O, Warren-Green): MONTEVERDI: Orfeo: Toccata. TORELLI: Sinfonia a 4 in C. ALBINONI: 2 Concerti a 6 in C; Sonata di concerto a 7 in D. VIVALDI: Double concerto in C. FRANCHESCINI: Sonata in D. PURCELL: Sonata in D. BONONCINE: Sinfonia decima a 7. ALBERTI: Sinfonia teatrale a 4.
**(*) Nimbus Dig. NI 5017 [id.].

The title of this collection aims to epitomize the spirit of the Italian Renaissance, which produced a great flowering of the arts. The collection, covering a period of nearly two centuries of trumpet music, almost defeats its own object of showing the diversity of baroque style since, during this period, trumpet devices did not change very much. The music explores all the possibilities of one, two and four trumpets, and the ear finds welcome relief in Albinoni's Concerto a 6 for trumpet, oboes and bassoon. John Wallace is a splendid soloist; in the multiple works he is joined by John Miller, David Mason and William Stokes, who play with comparable bravura. The recording was made in the resonant acoustics of All Saints', Tooting, which tend to blur the opening Monteverdi Toccata and the following Torelli Sinfonia, which features all four soloists. But for the most part the reverberation colours the music attractively.

'Weekend at the Zoo'

'Weekend at the Zoo': SAINT-SAENS: Carnival of the animals (Katchen, Graffman, LSO, Skitch Henderson). RAMEAU: La Poule. DAQUIN: Le coucou. F. COUPERIN: Le moucheron. D. SCARLATTI: Cat fugue. SCHUMANN: Waldszenen: The prophet bird. MUSSORGSKY: Pictures: Ballet of the unhatched chicks. LISZT/SCHUBERT: Die Forelle. DEBUSSY: Images: Poissons d'or. DUTILLEUX: The Blackbird. IBERT: Le petite âne blanc. BARTÓK: Mikrokosmos: From the diary of a fly. COPLAND: The cat and the mouse (Varda Nishry). RIMSKY-KORSAKOV: Flight of the bumble-bee (SRO, Ansermet). ROSSINI: The thieving magpie: overture (LSO, Gamba).
(B) **(*) Decca 425 505-2 [id.].

The performance of Saint-Saëns's zoological fantasy is somewhat larger than life yet has great vitality and a starry solo contribution. Then comes an agreeable pianistic menagerie, played with some flair by Varda Nishry; and the two familiar orchestral items round off a concert/recital to be dipped into rather than played all at one go. Decca's sound is characteristically brilliant.

Wickens, Derek (oboe)

'The classical oboe' (with RPO, Howarth): VIVALDI: Oboe concerto in A min., RV 461. ALESSANDRO MARCELLO: Oboe concerto in D min. HAYDN: Oboe concerto in C.
*** ASV CDDCA 1003 [id.].

During his years with the RPO, Wickens repeatedly demonstrated in yearningly beautiful solos that he was one of the most characterful of London's orchestral players. Though at times he seems to be looking for his back desk rather than his solo spot, his artistry comes out vividly on this well-recorded disc, with the CD providing believable projection for the oboe against Howarth's sympathetic accompaniments.

Instrumental Recitals

Amsterdam Loeki Stardust Quartet

'Virtuoso recorder music': ANON.: Istampita: Tre Fontane. PALESTRINA: Ricercar del secundo tuono. FRESCOBALDI: Canzon prima. MERULA: Canson: La Lusignuola. VIVALDI: Recorder concerto in C, RV 443. LOCKE: Suite in G min. GIBBONS: In Nomine. SIMPSON: Ricercar: Bonny Sweet Robin. BLACK: Report upon When shall my sorrowful sighing slake. JOHNSON: The Temporiser. BYRD: Sermone blande.
*** O-L Dig. 414 277-2 [id.].

The Amsterdam Loeki Stardust Quartet are superbly expert players: their blend is rich in colour and their ensemble wonderfully polished. There are many piquant sounds here: the virtuosity of Robert Johnson's transcribed lute piece, The Temporiser, is a delicious tour de force, with the following Sermone blande of Byrd aptly named; the Vivaldi Concerto transcribes successfully to an all-recorder group. It is surprising – although this is not a collection to be played all at once – that the ear does not readily weary of the timbre, even after several pieces heard consecutively. The recording has striking presence and realism.

Arnowitt, Michael (piano)

'Constellation': J. S. BACH: Well-tempered Clavier, Book 1; Fugue in D sharp min.; Book 2: Fugues in E flat & F sharp min. SHOSTAKOVICH: 24 Preludes & fugues, Op. 87: Fugues in G sharp min. & B flat. MOZART: Symphony No. 41 (Jupiter): Finale. MILHAUD: La création du monde. MESSIAEN: Vingt regards sur l'Enfant-Jésus: Par lui tout à été fait.
*** Ursa Minor Dig. UM 88101 [id.].

Michael Arnowitt, the brilliantly talented young American pianist, is founder of the 'Ideational' school of music interpretation, where 'the elusive search for the unitary, perfect, all-aspects-balanced, homogeneous performance is replaced by a more modest pluralistic goal. Each performer will highlight a specific aspect of the composer's craft; a listener will only attain a full understanding of the work by examining many recordings or live performances of the piece, each illuminating a new, previously hidden glory.' Americans love to intellectualize, and there is a degree of truth here about almost all performances. But Arnowitt declines to practise what he preaches, for this fine music-making is nothing if not all-embracing. It was an ingenious idea to assemble a recital based on the fugue in its various forms, and the Bach and Shostakovich examples are given splendidly lucid and responsive performances. Mozart's Jupiter finale, too, is strong in impetus but laid out clearly in front of the listener, who can certainly examine how it is structured. Milhaud's ballet, like the Messiaen excerpt, deals with the subject of creation, and both employ a fugal treatment with the listener scarcely realizing it. Arnowitt's transcription of the ballet sounds marvellous on the piano and his performance, full of colour and atmosphere and rhythmically riveting, is as fine as any orchestral version. The Messiaen too is a tour de force of brilliant pianism.

Barenboim, Daniel (piano)

'Träumerei': BEETHOVEN: Sonata No. 14 (Moonlight): 1st movt. Sonata No. 8 (Pathétique): Adagio. CHOPIN: Nocturnes: in E flat, Op. 9/2; in F sharp, Op. 15/2. LISZT:

Années de pèlerinage: Au lac de Wallenstadt; Petrarch sonnet No. 123. MENDELSSOHN: *Songs without words: Venetian gondola song; Spring song; Spinning song; Cradle song.* SCHUMANN: *Kinderszenen: Träumerei. Arabesque, Op. 18.* SCHUBERT: *Moments musicaux, D.780/2–3; Impromptu in G flat, D.899/3.* LISZT: *Liebestraum No. 3; Consolation No. 3.*
*** DG 419 408-2 [id.].

It would be difficult to imagine a more attractive collection of piano lollipops than this. Purists may object to the Beethoven sonata movements being extracted, but otherwise the choice makes an admirable programme, with favourite pieces by Liszt, Chopin and Schubert, beautifully played and recorded, nicely placed within the recital, and with Mendelssohn's *Songs without words* and Schumann's *Arabesque* bringing variety to an essentially romantic programme. The recordings were made between 1974 and 1986, and the transfers achieve remarkable consistency of sound-quality.

Bate, Jennifer (organ)

Organ of St James's Church, Muswell Hill, London: *'Two centuries of British organ music':* STANLEY: *Voluntary in F.* RUSSELL: *Voluntary in A min.* SAMUEL WESLEY: *A Scrap.* SAMUEL SEBASTIAN WESLEY: *Holsworthy Church bells; Introduction and fugue in C sharp min.* WOOD: *Prelude on St Mary's.* STANFORD: *Prelude and postlude on a theme of Orlando Gibbons, Op. 105/2; Andante tranquillo; Allegro non troppo e pesante, Op. 101/4 & 2.*
*** Hyp. Dig. CDA 66180 [id.].

French organ music is currently very fashionable, but this fine collection of British repertoire can stand alongside most French compilations for quality and variety of invention. The *Voluntaries* of Charles John Stanley (1713–86) and William Russell (1777–1813) are most personable, and their cheerfulness is striking. Samuel Wesley's *Scrap for organ*, a delightful *moto perpetuo* in binary form, is even more fetching; and the set of rather gentle variations on *Holsworthy Church bells* by his son, Samuel Sebastian, has great charm. Charles Wood's *Prelude on St Mary's* opens elegiacally and brings an association with the opening of Elgar's *First Symphony*. The three Stanford pieces are strongly characterized and round off the collection satisfyingly. The organ of St James, Muswell Hill, is perfectly chosen for the programme, the effect warmly atmospheric yet vivid and clear; and Jennifer Bate's choice of tempi and registration is admirable, with all the music sounding spontaneous.

Organ of Beauvais Cathedral: *'Virtuoso French organ music':* BOELLMANN: *Suite gothique.* GUILMANT: *Cantilène pastorale; March on 'Lift up your heads'.* SAINT-SAENS: *Improvisation No. 7.* GIGOUT: *Toccata in B min.; Scherzo; Grand choeur dialogué.*
**(*) Unicorn Dig. DKPCD 9041 [id.].

The playing here has enormous flair and thrilling bravura. Jennifer Bate's imaginative touch makes Boëllmann's *Suite gothique* sound far better music than it is. In the closing *Toccata*, as in the spectacular Guilmant march based on Handel's famous chorus, the panache and excitement of the playing grip the listener firmly, and the clouding of the St Beauvais acoustic is forgotten. But in the swirling Saint-Saëns *Improvisation* and the Gigout *Scherzo*, detail is masked. In the massive *Grand choeur dialogué*, the clever timing makes the firm articulation register, but although the Unicorn engineers achieve a splendidly sumptuous sound-image, elsewhere there is blurring caused by the wide reverberation of the empty cathedral.

(Organ of Beauvais Cathedral): *'Jennifer Bate and friends'*: DURUFLÉ: *Suite, Op. 5.* LANGLAIS: *Triptyque.* PEETERS: *Aria, Op. 51; Chorale Prelude: Nun sei willkommen, Jesu, lieber Herr, Op. 39/3. Paraphrase on Salve Regina, Op. 123.*
**(*) Unicorn Dig. DKPCD 9077 [id.].

A good deal of this music is highly atmospheric, but the resonance in Beauvais Cathedral does not help to give very clean detail. Even though Jennifer Bate is clearly a master of this repertoire, at times the ear craves a sharper focus, though the recording is realistic. Flor Peeters wrote his *Paraphrase on Salve Regina* especially for her, and this riveting account of the piece, with its cadenza-like writing for the pedals, makes a spectacular conclusion: the sheer amplitude of sound almost overwhelms the listener.

Bell, Joshua (violin), Samuel Sanders (piano)

'Presenting Joshua Bell': WIENIAWSKI: *Variations on an original theme, Op. 15; Scherzo tarantelle, Op. 16.* SIBELIUS: *Romance, Op. 78/2; Mazurka, Op. 81/1.* BRAHMS: *Hungarian dance No. 1.* PAGANINI: *Cantabile.* BLOCH: *Nigun.* NOVÁCEK: *Moto perpetuo.* SCHUMANN: *The Prophet bird.* FALLA: *La vide breve: Spanish dance.* GRASSE: *Waves at play.* SARASATE: *Carmen fantasy.*
*** Decca Dig. 417 891-2 [id.].

Bell's début recital was issued at the same time as his coupling of the Bruch and Mendelssohn *Concertos*; the recording has a similar forward balance, which brings striking presence but also just a hint of edge to the violin timbre. He plays all these pieces with an equal measure of style and easy bravura; often the playing is dazzling, and in the lyrical melodies he produces a comparable amalgam of warmth and elegance.

Bergen Wind Quintet

BARBER: *Summer music, Op. 31.* SAEVERUD: *Tunes and dances from Siljustøl, Op. 21a.* JOLIVET: *Serenade for wind quintet with principal oboe.* HINDEMITH: *Kleine Kammermusik, Op. 24/2.*
*** BIS CD 291 [id.].

Barber's *Summer music* is a glorious piece dating from the mid-1950s; it is in a single movement. Saeverud's *Tunes and dances from Siljustøl* derive from piano pieces of great charm and sound refreshing in their transcribed format. Jolivet's *Serenade* is hardly less engaging, while Hindemith's *Kleine Kammermusik*, when played with such character and finesse, is no less welcome. Throughout, the fine blend and vivacious ensemble give consistent pleasure, and the recording seems ideally balanced within an ambience that brings bloom and atmosphere without being too reverberant. On CD, the illusion of realism is very striking. Highly recommended.

Béroff, Michel (piano)

Music for piano, left hand: BACH, trans. BRAHMS: *Partita in D min., BWV 1004: Chaconne.* SAINT-SAENS: *6 Études, Op. 35.* BARTÓK: *Study.* SCRIABIN: *2 Preludes, Op. 9.* GODOWSKY: *6 Études after Chopin.*
** EMI Dig. CDC7 49079 [id.].

Masterly pianism from Michel Béroff, but the recording is less than ideal, with not quite enough bloom in the dryish and forward piano timbre. (There is also an ugly edit at

11 minutes 52 seconds in the Bach *Chaconne*.) The Saint-Saëns *Études* have lots of charm and the playing is, as one might expect, neither wanting in brilliance nor artistry. The Godowsky transcriptions are pretty dazzling. The unflattering and artificial sound is a drawback, however.

Bolet, Jorge (piano)

'*Encores*': MENDELSSOHN: *Rondo capriccioso, Op. 14; Song without words (Jägerlied), Op. 19/3.* CHOPIN: *Nocturnes: in F sharp, Op. 15/2; in E flat, Op. 9/2; Waltzes: in D flat (Minute), Op. 64/1; in E min., Op. posth. Études: in A flat; F min., Op. 25/1–2; in A min., Op. 25/11.* DEBUSSY: *Prélude: La fille aux cheveux de lin.* SCHUBERT: *Rosamunde: Ballet music* (arr. Godowsky). ALBÉNIZ: *Tango, Op. 165/2* (arr. Godowsky). GODOWSKY: *Élégie* (for left hand). R. STRAUSS: *Ständchen* (arr. Godowsky). BIZET: *L'Arlésienne: Adagio* (arr. Godowsky). MOSZKOWSKI: *En automne, Op. 36/4; La Jongleuse, Op. 52/4.* SCHLOZER: *Étude, Op. 1/2.*
*** Decca Dig. 417 361-2 [id.].

An attractively generous and imaginatively varied recital which, if in essence lightweight, is certainly not without substance and offers much to delight the ear. In the opening Mendelssohn *Rondo capriccioso* Bolet immediately establishes his credentials of easy bravura applied with the lightest of touch. Later in the Chopin *Études* he offers even more dazzling playing but never employs virtuosity for its own sake, while the decorative element in Godowsky's attractive arrangement of Strauss's *Ständchen* is deliciously articulated. Debussy's lovely portrait of the flaxen-haired maid is beautifully done, and the Schubert *Rosamunde ballet music* has considerable charm (again with Godowsky's additions). The sound is most realistic, and this can be recommended strongly on all counts.

Bream, Julian (guitar)

'*Homage to Segovia*': TURINA: *Fandanguillo, Op. 36; Sevillana, Op. 20.* MOMPOU: *Suite compostelana.* TÓRROBA: *Sonatina.* GERHARD: *Fantasia.* FALLA: *Homenaje pour le tombeau de Claude Debussy; Three-cornered hat: Miller's dance.* OHANA: *Tiento.*
*** RCA Dig. RD 85306 [RCD1 5306].

Readers who have already acquired Bream's earlier digital recital concentrating on the music of Albéniz and Granados (see the Composer section, above) will find this hardly less impressive, both musically and technically. The programme here is even more diverse, with the Gerhard *Fantasia* adding a twentieth-century dimension while Ohana's *Tiento* has a comparable imaginative approach to texture. Throughout, Bream plays with his usual flair and spontaneity, constantly imaginative in his use of a wide dynamic range and every possible colouristic effect. The recording has the most tangible realism and presence.

'*Guitarra*': MUDARRA: *Fantasias Nos. 10 and 14.* MILAN: *Fantasia No. 22.* NARVAEZ: *La canción del Emperador; Conde Claros.* SANZ: *Galliardas; Pasacalles; Canarios.* GUERAU: *Villano; Canario.* MURCIA: *Prelude and allegro.* SOR: *Variations on a theme by Mozart, Op. 9.* AQUADO: *Rondo in A, Op. 2/3.* TARREGA: *Prelude in A min; Recuerdos de la Alhambra.* GRANADOS: *La Maja de Goya. Danza española No. 5.* ALBÉNIZ: *Suite española: Cádiz.* TÓRROBA: *Sonata in A.* TURINA: *Fandanguillo.* FALLA: *Homenaje pour le tombeau de Claude Debussy. Three-cornered hat: Miller's dance.*
*** RCA Dig. RD 86206.

A wholly admirable survey of Spanish guitar music covering four hundred years and featuring four different instruments, all especially built by José Ramanillos: a Renaissance guitar, vihuela, baroque guitar and a modern classical guitar. Bream's natural dexterity is matched by his remarkable control of colour and unerring sense of style. Many of the early pieces are quite simple but have considerable magnetism. Three of the items included in the latter part of the recital come from his Albéniz/Granados coupling, reviewed in the Composer section, others from the shorter collection above, dedicated to Segovia, notably the exciting Turina *Fandanguillo*, a real highlight. The presence of the recordings is remarkable, the focus sharp and believable.

Bream, Julian and John Williams (guitars)

'Together': LAWES: *Suite for 2 guitars*. CARULLI: *Duo in G, Op. 34*. SOR: *L'Encouragement, Op. 34*. ALBÉNIZ: *Córdoba*. GRANADOS: *Goyescas: Intermezzo*. FALLA: *La vida breve: Spanish dance No. 1*. RAVEL: *Pavane pour une infante défunte*.
*** RCA RD 83257.

'Together again': CARULLI: *Serenade, Op. 96*. GRANADOS: *Danzas españolas Nos. 6 and 11*. ALBÉNIZ: *Bajo la Palmera, Op. 32. Iberia: Evocación*. GIULIANI: *Variazioni concertanti, Op. 130*.
*** RCA RD 80456.

In this case two guitars are better than one; these two fine artists clearly strike sparks off each other. In the first recital, Albéniz's *Córdoba* is hauntingly memorable and the concert closes with a slow, stately version of Ravel's *Pavane* which is unforgettable. Here Bream justifies a tempo which he did not bring off so effectively in his solo version (now deleted). On the second disc, it is again music of Albéniz that one remembers for the haunting atmosphere the two artists create together. The sound of these reissues is truthful and atmospheric, although the digital remastering for CD does not succeed in removing all the background hiss. This is distinctly noticeable in the first collection but in the second is only very slight, and the effect is not intrusive.

'Live': JOHNSON: *Pavane and Galliard*. TELEMANN: *Partie polonaise*. SOR: *Fantaisie, Op. 54*. BRAHMS: *Theme and variations, Op. 18* (trans. Williams). FAURÉ: *Dolly suite, Op. 56*. DEBUSSY: *Rêverie. Children's Corner: Golliwog's cakewalk. Suite bergamasque: Clair de lune*. ALBÉNIZ: *Castilla*. GRANADOS: *Spanish dance No. 2 (Oriental)*.
**(*) RCA RD 89654.

This recital was recorded live in Boston and New York during a North American tour. The recording is well balanced and eminently realistic, but the drawback is the applause which, though shortened in the editing, is still very intrusive on repeated hearings. The playing is of the highest quality although perhaps at times slightly self-conscious (the Granados encore has an almost narcissistic tonal beauty). As a whole there is not quite the electricity of this team's other recitals. Fauré's *Dolly suite* sounds a little cosy and the transcription of the *Variations* from Brahms's *B flat major Sextet* is not entirely effective. But the *Golliwog's cakewalk* and the Albéniz *Castilla* are highly enjoyable. The compact disc transfer provides a very quiet but not absolutely silent background; it offers the contents of the pair of LPs or tapes on a single disc.

Brendel Alfred (piano)

'The art of Alfred Brendel' Vol. 1: CHOPIN: *Polonaises in F sharp min., Op. 44; in A flat, Op. 53. Andante spianato and Grande polonaise, Op. 22.* LISZT: *Hungarian rhapsodies Nos. 3, 8, 13, 15 (Rácóczy March); 17; Czárdás obstiné.*
(M) **(*) Van. VMCD 7701 [id.].

'The art of Alfred Brendel' Vol. 2: MOZART: *Variations on a minuet by Dupont, K.573.* SCHUMANN: *Symphonic studies, Op. 13.* CHOPIN: *Polonaise in C min., Op. 40/2; Polonaise fantaisie, Op. 61.* LISZT: *Hungarian rhapsody No. 2.*
(M) **(*) Van. VMCD 7702 [id.].

These recordings date from 1968/9 and, if the sound is less full and realistic than we expect nowadays from Brendel's Philips records, this is often more volatile music-making than this very distinctive artist gives us now. The Chopin and Liszt pieces show this readily: the most famous of the *Hungarian rhapsodies* has splendid panache; indeed the Liszt pieces are all done superbly. The Schumann *Symphonic studies* are no less welcome, and admirers of this artist cannot fail to enjoy these discs.

Britton, Harold (organ)

Organ of Royal Albert Hall: *'Organ spectacular'*: SUPPÉ: *Light Cavalry overture.* LEMARE: *Andantino in D flat.* VERDI: *Aida: Grand march.* ALBINONI: *Adagio* (arr. Giazotto). WAGNER: *Ride of the Valkyries.* BACH: *Toccata and fugue in D min., BWV 565.* TCHAIKOVSKY: *None but the lonely heart.* ELGAR: *Pomp and circumstance march No. 1.* SOUSA: *Liberty Bell.* WIDOR: *Symphony No. 5: Toccata.*
(B) *** ASV CDQS 6028.

If one is to have a collection mainly of arrangements of orchestral lollipops on an organ, the instrument at the Royal Albert Hall is surely an ideal choice: it offers the widest dynamic range, including an effective recession of quieter passages readily at the player's command – used to good purpose in *Light Cavalry* – but can also produce truly spectacular fortissimos, with a wide amplitude and a blaze of colour from its multitude of stops. Harold Britton is obviously fully at home on the instrument and plays in an aptly extrovert style for such a recital, obviously enjoying himself. The CD is in the demonstration class – there are few problems of muddying from reverberation.

Chung, Kyung Wha (violin), Phillip Moll (piano)

'Con amore': KREISLER: *La Gitana; Liebeslied; Praeludium and allegro in the style of Pugnani. Liebesfreud.* POLDINI: *Dancing doll.* WIENIAWSKI: *Scherzo-Tarantelle; Caprice in A min.* ELGAR: *Salut d'amor, Op. 12; La Capricieuse, Op. 17.* TCHAIKOVSKY: *Valse sentimentale.* NOVACEK: *Moto perpetuo.* DEBUSSY: *Beau soir.* CHOPIN: *Nocturne in C sharp min.* GOSSEC: *Gavotte.* CHAMINADE: *Sérénade espagnole.* SAINT-SAENS: *Caprice (after a study in the form of a waltz), Op. 52/6.* BRAHMS: *Hungarian dance No. 1.*
*** Decca Dig. 417 289-2 [id.].

Kyung Wha Chung's collection, *'Con amore'*, reflects that title in a delightfully varied choice of items, sweet as well as brilliant. When she claims in all seriousness that she does not think of herself as a virtuoso violinist, she really means that technical brilliance is only an incidental for her; and the poise and flair of all these items show her at her most winningly characterful, helped by Phillip Moll's very sympathetic accompaniment and well-balanced recording, which has fine presence on CD.

Clarion Ensemble

'Trumpet collection': FANTINI: *Sonata; Brando; Balletteo; Corrente.* MONTEVERDI: *Et e pur dunque vero.* FRESCOBALDI: *Canzona a canto solo.* PURCELL: *To arms, heroic prince.* A. SCARLATTI: *Si suoni la tromba.* BISHOP: *Arietta and Waltz; Thine forever.* DONIZETTI: *Lo L'udia.* KOENIG: *Post horn galop.* ARBAN: *Fantasia on Verdi's Rigoletto.* CLARKE: *Cousins.* ENESCU: *Legende.*
⊛ *** Amon Ra CD-SAR 30 [id.].

The simple title '*Trumpet collection*' covers a fascinating recital of music for trumpet written over three centuries and played with great skill and musicianship by Jonathan Impett, using a variety of original instruments, from a keyed bugle and clapper shake-key cornopean to an English slide trumpet and a posthorn. Impett is a complete master of all these instruments, never producing a throttled tone; indeed in the Purcell and Scarlatti arias he matches the soaring soprano line of Deborah Roberts with uncanny mirror-image precision. Accompaniments are provided by other members of the Clarion Ensemble, including Paul Nicholson who plays a fortepiano with great flair and with the slightly dry timbre particularly suited to act as a foil to the brass sounds. The Frescobaldi *Canzona* brings a duet for trumpet and trombone, with a background harpsichord filigree, which is most effective. With demonstration-worthy recording – one could readily believe the instrumentalists to be at the other end of one's room – this is as enjoyable as it is interesting, with the *Post horn galop* and Arban's *Rigoletto variations* producing exhilarating bravura.

Davies, Philippa (flute), Thelma Owen (harp)

'The Romance of the flute and harp': HASSELMANS: *La Source, Op. 44; Feuilles d'automne.* GODARD: *Suite, Op. 16: Allegretto.* GODEFROID: *Étude de concert.* FAURÉ: *Berceuse, Op. 16; Impromptu, Op. 86.* DOPPLER: *Mazurka.* MENDELSSOHN: *Spring song, Op. 62/3.* THOMAS: *Watching the wheat.* SAINT-SAENS: *Le Cygne.* BIZET: *Fair maid of Perth: Intermezzo.* PARISH-ALVARS: *Serenade.* DEBUSSY: *Syrinx; Suite bergamasque: Clair de lune.*
(B) *** Pickwick Dig. PCD 835.

An unexpectedly successful recital which effectively intersperses harp solos with music in which the flute takes the leading role. The playing is most sensitive and the recording is very realistic indeed. The programme, too, is well chosen and attractively laid out. Highly recommended for playing on a pleasant summer evening.

Drake, Susan (harp)

'Echoes of a waterfall': HASSELMANS: *La Source, Op. 44; Prelude, Op. 52; Chanson de mai, Op. 40.* ALVARS: *Divertissement, Op. 38.* GODEFROID: *Bois solitaire; Étude de concert in E flat min., Op. 193.* GLINKA: *Variations on a theme of Mozart.* THOMAS: *Echoes of a waterfall: Watching the wheat; Megan's daughter.* SPOHR: *Variations on Je suis encore, Op. 36.*
*** Hyp. CDA 66038 [id.].

The music is lightweight and sometimes facile, but the young Welsh harpist, Susan

Drake, is a beguiling exponent, and her technique is as impressive as her feeling for atmosphere. Those intrigued by the title of the collection will not be disappointed by the sounds here (the recording is excellent) which balance evocation with a suitable degree of flamboyance when the music calls for it. The Thomas evocation of watery effects is certainly picturesque, as is Hasselmans' charming *La Source*, and both the Spohr and (especially) the Glinka *Variations* have considerable appeal.

Du Pré, Jacqueline (cello)

Early BBC recordings, Vol. 1 (with Stephen Bishop-Kovacevich, Ernest Lush): BACH: (Unaccompanied) *Cello suites Nos. 1 in G; 2 in D min., BWV 1007/8.* BRITTEN: *Cello sonata in C, Op. 65; Scherzo; Marcia.* FALLA: *Suite populaire espagnole* (arr. Maréchal).
(M) (***) EMI mono CDM7 63165-2.

Early BBC recordings, Vol. 2 (with Ernest Lush, (i) William Pleeth): BRAHMS: *Cello sonata No. 2 in F, Op. 99.* F. COUPERIN: (i) *13th Concert a 2 instrumens (Les Goûts-réunis).* HANDEL: *Cello sonata in G min.* (arr. Slatter).
(M) (***) EMI mono CDM7 63166-2.

These two discs on the mid-priced Studio label gather together some of the radio performances which Jacqueline du Pré gave in her inspired teens. Her 1962 recordings of the first two Bach *Cello suites* may not be immaculate, but her impulsive vitality makes phrase after phrase at once totally individual and seemingly inevitable. In two movements from Britten's *Cello sonata in C*, with Stephen Bishop-Kovacevich as her partner, the sheer wit is deliciously infectious, fruit of youthful exuberance in both players. The first of the two discs is completed by Falla's *Suite populaire espagnole*, with the cello matching any singer in expressive range and rhythmic flair. The second has fascinating Couperin duets played with her teacher, William Pleeth; the Handel *Sonata* is equally warm and giving. Best of all is the Brahms *Cello sonata No. 2*, recorded at the 1962 Edinburgh Festival. Though there are incidental flaws, the broad sweep of this magnificent work is conveyed masterfully. Few of Du Pré's later records give a more vivid portrait of her than these. The quality of the mono sound varies but, with clean transfers, the vitality of the performances is unimpaired.

Eden, Bracha and Alexander Tamir (piano duet)

'Dances around the world': RACHMANINOV: *Polka italienne.* MOSZKOWSKI: *Spanish dances, Op. 65/1–2.* GRIEG: *Norwegian dances Nos. 2–3.* BRAHMS: *Hungarian dances and Waltzes.* DVOŘÁK: *Slavonic dances, Op. 46/6–7; Op. 72/8.* SCHUBERT: *Waltzes.* BARBER: *Souvenirs: Pas de deux.* DEBUSSY: *Petite suite: Menuet and ballet.*
(B) *** Pickwick Dig. PWK 1134.

Eden and Tamir travel the world as a piano duo, and this record is exactly like going to one of their concerts: it is both exhilarating and beguiling, full of variety and spontaneity. They sound as if they are enjoying everything they play, and so do we. Very good sound too.

Fábián, Márta (cimbalom)

Baroque music for cimbalom (with Ágnes Szakály, cimbalom, Imre Kovács, flute, Béla Sztankovits, guitar): BACH: *French suites Nos. 2 in C min., BWV 813; 3 in B min., BWV 814; 5 in G, BWV 816.* PACHELBEL: *Partita in C min.* TELEMANN: *Trio sonata.*

(BB) *** Hung. White Label HRC 097.

In order to play Bach's *French suites* on the cimbalom, two instruments and four hands are needed, and here Hungary's most famous virtuoso on the national instrument is joined by her colleague to do just that. The effect is piquantly effective. To make the recital even more rewarding, the solo cimbalom is also joined by flute and guitar to play a winningly tuneful six-movement *Partita* by Pachelbel and a no less engaging *Trio sonata* by Telemann. With excellent recording this is a disc that is as rewarding as it is unusual.

Fowke, Philip (piano)

'*Virtuoso transcriptions*': BACH/RACHMANINOV: *Suite from the Solo violin partita in E min., BWV 1006.* SCHUBERT/RACHMANINOV: *Wohin.* KREISLER/RACHMANINOV: *Liebeslied; Liebesfreud.* BUSONI: *Sonatina No. 6 (Fantasy on 'Carmen').* WEBER/TAUSIG: *Invitation to the dance.* GLINKA/BALAKIREV: *The Lark.* J. STRAUSS Jnr/SCHULZELVER: *Arabesque on themes from 'The Blue Danube'.*
*** CRD CRD 3396 [id.].

Philip Fowke plays with prodigious bravura but treats these display pieces with obvious seriousness of purpose. The presentation, while perhaps a little lacking in fun, still brings freshness to everything included here. It is amazing how pianistic Bach's violin music becomes in Rachmaninov's hands. It is a sparkling collection, bringing out of the cupboard music which still has the power to delight and amaze. The recording is excellent.

'French Impressions'

'*French impressions*' (played by: Er'ella Talmi, flute; Avigail Amheim, clarinet; Gad Levertov, viola; Alice Giles, harpsichord; Kaminkovsky Quartet): RAVEL: *Introduction and allegro.* DEBUSSY: *Sonata for flute, viola & harp.* ROUSSEL: *Trio, Op. 58.* CAPLET: *Conte fantastique.*
(B) *** Pickwick/CDI Dig. PWK 1141.

Excellent, highly sensitive playing throughout an interesting and rewarding programme. This is one of the finest modern versions of Ravel's magically atmospheric *Introduction and allegro*, and the improvisatory nature of the lovely Debussy *Sonata* is captured equally well. The Roussel is of a drier vintage, but the programme ends in high drama with André Caplet's imaginative story in music based on Edgar Allan Poe's *Masque of the Red Death*. As always in this fine series, the recording has a remarkable illusion of presence and realism, and the ambience is perfectly judged.

Fretwork

'*In nomine*': 16th-century English music for viols: TALLIS: *In nomine a 4, Nos. 1 & 2; Solfaing song a 5; Fantasia a 5; In nomine a 4, No. 2; Libera nos, salva nos a 5.* TYE: *In nomine a 5 (Crye); In nomine a 5 (Trust).* CORNYSH: *Fa la sol a 3.* BALDWIN: *In nomine a 4.* BULL: *In nomine a 5.* BYRD: *In nomine a 4, No. 2. Fantasia a 3, No. 3.* TAVERNER: *In nomine; In nomine a 4.* PRESTON: *O lux beata Trinitas a 3.* JOHNSON: *In nomine a 4.* PARSONS: *In nomine a 5; Ut re mi fa sol la a 4.* FERRABOSCO: *In nomine a 5; Lute fantasia No. 5; Fantasia a 4.*
*** Amon Ra CD-SAR 29 [id.].

This was Fretwork's début CD; it immediately demonstrates their special combination of musical understanding, warmth and refinement in this repertoire. They play with polish and elegance and there is a certain aristocratic melancholy here that gives this music great character. The collection is not so obviously of strong popular appeal as the later collection for Virgin but is nevertheless very rewarding and distinguished, and it includes the complete consort music of Thomas Tallis. The sound is naturally pleasing in a fairly rich acoustic and readers can be assured that there is no vinegar in the string-timbre here; indeed, the sound itself is quite lovely in its gentle, austere atmosphere.

'Heart's ease': HOLBORNE: *The Honiesuckle; Countess of Pembroke's paradise; The Fairie round.* BYRD: *Fantasia a 5 (Two in one); Fancy in C.* DOWLAND: *Mr Bucton, his galliard; Captaine Digorie Piper, his galliard; Lachrimae antiquae pavan; Mr Nicholas Gryffith, his galliard.* BULL: *Fantasia a 4.* FERRABOSCO: *In nomine a 5.* GIBBONS: *In nomine a 5; Fantasia a 4 for the great dooble base.* LAWES: *Airs for 2 division viols in C: Pavan of Alfonso; Almain of Alfonso. Consort sett a 5 in C: Fantasia; Pavan; Almain.*
*** Virgin Dig. VC 790706-2 [id.].

An outstanding collection of viol consort music from the late Tudor and early Stuart periods; the playing is both stylish and vivacious, with a fine sense of the most suitable tempo for each piece. The more lyrical music is equally sensitive. This is a tuneful entertainment, not just for the specialist collector, and Fretwork convey their pleasure in all this music. The William Byrd *Fancy* (from *My Ladye Nevells Booke*) is played exuberantly on the organ by Paul Nicholson, to bring some contrast before the closing Lawes *Consort set.* The recording is agreeably warm, yet transparent too.

Galway, James (flute), Kazuhito Yamashita (guitar)

'Italian serenade': GIULIANI/MOSCHELES: *Grand duo concertante in A, Op. 85.* ROSSINI: *Andante with variations.* BAZZINI: *La ronde des lutins, Op. 25.* CIMAROSA: *Serenade.* PAGANINI: *Sonata concertata.*
*** RCA Dig. RD 85679.

This is a lightweight concert; the clear, realistic recording and the polished, elegant playing, plus the fine rapport between these two artists, make for music-making of the highest quality, realistically projected. The Cimarosa *Serenade* is in fact the *Concerto* arranged for oboe by Arthur Benjamin, but it sounds beguiling enough in this alternative scoring for flute and harp. Both the Giuliani and Paganini works are quite extended pieces and, with attractive if ingenuous invention, they do not outstay their welcome; and the Rossini and Bazzini show Galway's easy virtuosity. The CD has very striking presence.

Gilels, Emil (piano)

LISZT-BUSONI: *Fantasia on 2 themes from Mozart's Nozze di Figaro.* LISZT: *Hungarian rhapsody No. 6 in D flat.* SCRIABIN: *Piano sonatas Nos. 3 in F sharp min., Op. 23; 4 in F sharp, Op. 30; 5 Préludes, Op. 74; Étude in C sharp min., Op. 2/1.* DEBUSSY: *Nocturnes, No. 2: Fêtes. Suite bergamasque: Clair de lune.* RAVEL: *Toccata.*
(***) Olympia mono OCD 166.

These recordings come from the period ranging from 1930 to 1984 and naturally vary enormously in quality. Gilels's virtuosity in the *Nozze di Figaro Fantasy* is pretty transcendental (there is fairly heavy surface-noise here) and in the *Hungarian rhapsody* the sound is shallow. The *Third Sonata* of Scriabin and the Op. 74 *Préludes* were recorded in the Soviet Union in 1984, only a few days before his last London recital. Superb performances of the latter, though the recordings are not absolutely first class. The *Fourth Sonata*, marvellously played, was recorded in 1957 and the sound is papery in tone and somewhat wanting in range and colour. Debussy's *Fêtes* is a pre-war recording, and the Ravel suffers from distortion. Some remarkable playing, but the recordings call for much tolerance.

Hardenberger, Håkan (trumpet)

'The virtuoso trumpet' (with Roland Pöntinen): ARBAN: *Variations on themes from Bellini's 'Norma'.* FRANÇAIX: *Sonatine.* TISNÉ: *Héraldiques.* HONEGGER: *Intrada.* MAXWELL DAVIES: *Sonata.* RABE: *Shazam!.* HARTMANN: *Fantasia brillante on the air Rule Britannia.*
*** BIS CID 287 [id.].

This collection includes much rare and adventurous repertoire, not otherwise available and very unlikely to offer frequent access in live performance. Moreover, Hardenberger plays with electrifying bravura in the Maxwell Davies *Sonata* and the virtuoso miniatures. Antoine Tisné's five *Héraldiques* are eclectic but highly effective on the lips of such an assured player; *Scandé* and the following *Élégiaque* are notably characterful. But easily the most memorable item is the Françaix *Sonatine* (originally for violin and piano) in which two delicious brief outer movements frame a pleasing central *Sarabande*. Honegger's improvisatory *Intrada* is an effective encore piece. The recording is eminently realistic, with the CD giving superb presence.

HANSEN: *Cornet sonata in E flat, Op. 18.* ENESCU: *Legend.* HINDEMITH: *Trumpet sonata.* SCHMITT: *Trumpet suite, Op. 133.* LIGETI: *Mysteries of the macabre* (arr. Howarth).
*** Ph. Dig. 426 144-2 [id.].

A mixed bag. Hansen's piece is amiable, and Hindemith's otherwise unmemorable *Sonata* has a fine, elegiac slow movement, while the Schmitt *Suite* has great variety and is very demanding technically. Enescu's *Legend* has an engaging melancholy, while Ligeti's *Mysteries of the macabre* inhabits the world of the outrageous avant-garde and comes complete with rhythmic vocal noises. The reason for its composition remains as mysterious as its title. The three stars are for the playing and the very real recording, but there is not much music here that one would wish to return to very urgently.

Headington, Christopher (piano)

'Pictures & pleasures': SINDING: *Rustle of spring.* GRIEG: *To the spring; Butterfly, Op. 43/1 & 6.* MENDELSSOHN: *Spring song, Op. 62/6.* TCHAIKOVSKY: *Chant sans paroles, Op. 2/3.* DEBUSSY: *Clair de lune.* LISZT: *Liebestraum No. 3.* SCHUBERT: *Moment musical No. 6.* CHOPIN: *Nocturne in E flat, Op. 9/2; Waltz in C sharp min., Op. 54/2.* RACHMANINOV: *Prelude in C sharp min., Op. 3/2.* ELGAR: *Salut d'amour.* BEETHOVEN: *Für Elise.* GRANADOS: *Spanish dance No. 5 (Andaluza).* CHAMINADE: *Autumn.* DVORÁK: *Humoresque in G flat, Op. 101/7.* GODOWSKI: *Alt Wien.* SCHUMANN: *Träumerei.* RAVEL: *Pavane pour une infante défunte.*
** Kingdom Dig. KCLCD 2002 [id.].

An attractively diverse collection with many favourites, well played and recorded. But the overall effect is agreeable rather than memorable.

Horowitz, Vladimir (piano)

Recital: SCHUMANN: *Kinderszenen, Op. 15; Toccata in C, Op. 7.* D. SCARLATTI: *Sonatas: in G, Kk. 455; in E, Kk. 531; in A, Kk. 322.* SCHUBERT: *Impromptu No. 3 in G flat, D. 889.* SCRIABIN: *Poème, Op. 32/1; Études: in C sharp min., Op. 2/1; in D sharp min, Op. 8/12.*
(B) **(*) CBS MYK 42534.

Horowitz's 1968 recital offers marvellous playing of repertoire he knew and loved, recorded when he was still at his technical peak. The recording is dry (there is a hint of wow, but it appears only once or twice); even so, this is magical playing: the Schumann and Scarlatti are superb – but then so is the Scriabin, and Schubert's *G flat Impromptu* is infinitely subtle in its gradations of dynamic and colour.

'At the Met.': D. SCARLATTI: *Sonatas: in A flat, Kk. 127; in F min., Kk. 184 & 466; in A, Kk. 101; in B min., Kk. 87; in E, Kk. 135.* CHOPIN: *Ballade No. 4 in F min., Op. 52; Waltz No. 9 in A flat, Op. 69/1.* LISZT: *Ballade No. 2 in B min., G. 171.* RACHMANINOV: *Prelude No. 6 in G min., Op. 23/5.*
*** RCA Dig. RCD 14585 [RCD1 4585].

The playing is in a class of its own, and all one needs to know is that this recording reproduces the highly distinctive tone-quality Horowitz commanded. This recital, given at the Metropolitan Opera House and issued here at the time of his London Festival Hall appearance in 1982, comes closer to the real thing than anything else on record, except his DG recitals – see below. The quality of the playing is quite extraordinary.

'In London': God save the Queen (arr. Horowitz). CHOPIN: *Ballade No. 1 in G min., Op. 23; Polonaise No. 7 in A flat (Polonaise-Fantasie), Op. 61.* SCHUMANN: *Kinderszenen, Op. 15.* SCRIABIN: *Étude in D sharp min., Op. 8/12.*
*** RCA Dig. RD 84572.

Highlights from the memorable London recital Horowitz gave in 1982, though omitting the elegant Scarlatti sonatas he played on that occasion, doubtless because it would duplicate *'Horowitz at the Met.'* – see above. However, room could surely have been found for the Rachmaninov *Sonata*, or his encores, as the CD is not generously filled. As those who attended this electrifying recital will know, there were idiosyncratic touches, particularly in the *Kinderszenen* (and also in the Chopin *Ballade*), but this is remarkable testimony to his wide dynamic range and his refined *pianopianissimo*. There are many fascinating points of detail in both works (but notably the Chopin) which give one the feeling of hearing the music for the first time.

Recital: BACH/BUSONI: *Chorale prelude: Nun komm der Heiden Heiland.* MOZART: *Piano sonata No. 10 in C, K. 330.* CHOPIN: *Mazurka in A min., Op. 17/4; Scherzo No. 1 in B min., Op. 20; Polonaise No. 6 in A flat, Op. 53.* LISZT: *Consolation No. 3 in D flat.* SCHUBERT: *Impromptu in A flat, D. 899/4.* SCHUMANN: *Novellette in F, Op. 21/1.* RACHMANINOV: *Prelude in G sharp min., Op. 32/12.* SCRIABIN: *Étude in C sharp min., Op. 2/1.* MOSZKOWSKI: *Étude in F, Op. 72/6* (recording of performances featured in the film *Vladimir Horowitz – The Last Romantic*).
*** DG Dig. 419 045-2 [id.].

Possibly the best recording Horowitz ever received, though his RCA compact discs have also given a splendid sense of his *pp* tone. Recorded when he was over eighty, this playing betrays remarkably little sign of frailty. The Mozart is beautifully elegant and the Chopin *A minor Mazurka*, Op. 17, No. 4, could hardly be more delicate. The only sign of age comes in the *B minor Scherzo*, which does not have the leonine fire and tremendous body of his famous 1950 recording. However, it is pretty astonishing for all that.

'The studio recordings': SCHUMANN: *Kreisleriana, Op. 16.* D. SCARLATTI: *Sonatas: in B min., Kk. 87; in E, Kk. 135.* LISZT: *Impromptu (Nocturne) in F sharp; Valse oubliée No. 1.* SCRIABIN: *Étude in D sharp min., Op. 812.* SCHUBERT: *Impromptu in B flat, D. 935/3.* SCHUBERT/TAUSIG: *Marche militaire, D. 733/1.*
⊛ *** DG 419 217-2 [id.].

Horowitz plays in the studio just as if he were in front of an audience, and the freshness and accuracy would be astonishing if we had not already heard him repeating the trick. The subtle range of colour and articulation in the Schumann is matched in his Schubert *Impromptu*, and the Liszt *Valse oubliée* offers the most delicious, twinkling rubato. Hearing Scarlatti's *E major Sonata* played with such crispness, delicacy and grace must surely convert even the most dedicated authenticist to the view that this repertoire can be totally valid in terms of the modern instrument. The Schubert–Tausig *Marche militaire* makes a superb encore, played with the kind of panache that would be remarkable in a pianist half Horowitz's age. With the passionate Scriabin *Étude* as the central romantic pivot, this recital is uncommonly well balanced to show Horowitz's special range of sympathies. Only Mozart is missing, and he is featured elsewhere. The recording is extremely realistic and present in its CD format.

'In Moscow': D. SCARLATTI: *Sonata in E, Kk. 380.* MOZART: *Sonata No. 10 in C, K. 330.* RACHMANINOV: *Preludes: in G, Op. 32/5; in G sharp min. Op. 32/12.* SCRIABIN: *Études: in C sharp min., Op. 2/1; in D sharp min., Op. 8/12.* LISZT/SCHUBERT: *Soirées de Vienne; Petrarch Sonnet 104.* CHOPIN: *Mazurkas, Op. 30/4; Op. 7/3.* SCHUMANN: *Kinderszenen: Träumerei.*
*** DG Dig. 419 499-2 [id.].

This is familiar Horowitz repertoire, played with characteristic musical discernment and spontaneity. Technically the pianism may not quite match his finest records of the analogue era, but it is still both melting and dazzling. The sound too is really excellent, much better than he ever received from his American engineers in earlier days.

Hough, Stephen (piano)

'The Piano Album': MACDOWELL: *Hexentanz, Op. 12.* CHOPIN: *Chant polonaise No. 1.* QUILTER: *The crimson petal; The fuchsia tree.* DOHNÁNYI: *Capriccio in F min., Op. 28/8.* PADEREWSKI: *Minuet in G, Op. 14/1. Nocturne in B flat, Op. 16/4.* SCHLOZER: *Étude in A flat, Op. 1/2.* GABRILOWITSCH: *Mélodie in E; Caprice-burlesque.* RODGERS: *My favourite things.* WOODFORDE-FINDEN: *Kashmiri song.* FRIEDMAN: *Music box.* SAINT-SAENS: *Carnival: The Swan.* ROSENTHAL: *Papillons.* GODOWSKI: *The gardens of Buitenzorg.* LEVITZKI: *Waltz in A, Op. 2.* PALMGREN: *En route, Op. 9.* MOSZKOWSKI: *Siciliano, Op. 42/2; Caprice espagnole, Op. 3.*
⊛ *** Virgin Dig. VC 790732-2 [id.].

There are few young pianists who can match Stephen Hough in communicating on record with the immediacy and vividness of live performance; this dazzling recital of frothy showpieces presents the perfect illustration. This Virgin Classics collection captures more nearly than almost any other recent record – even those of Horowitz – the charm, sparkle and flair of legendary piano virtuosos from the golden age of Rosenthal, Godowski and Lhévinne. So many of the twenty items are frivolous that it may be surprising that any serious pianist can stomach them; yet the very first item, MacDowell's *Hexentanz* (*Witches' dance*), launches the listener into pure pianistic magic, with playing totally uninhibited and with articulation and timing that are the musical equivalent of being tickled up and down the spine. One would hardly expect Hough's own arrangements of sentimental little songs by Roger Quilter or Amy Woodforde-Finden to be worth hearing at all – yet, in their tender expressiveness, they are most affecting. In the grand tradition, Hough does a Valse-caprice arrangement he himself has made of *My favourite things* from *The Sound of Music*, as well as firework pieces by Rosenthal and Moszkowski, among others, along with old-fashioned favourites like Paderewski's *Minuet in G* and Godowski's arrangement of the Saint-Saëns *Swan*. It is a feast for piano-lovers, very well recorded in venues in both London and New York.

Hurford, Peter (organ)

Ratzeburg Cathedral organ: *'Romantic organ music':* WIDOR: *Symphony No. 5, Op. 42: Toccata.* VIERNE: *Pièces en style libre: Berceuse.* ALAIN: *Litanies.* FRANCK: *Chorale No. 3.* KARG-ELERT: *Marche triomphale; Nun danket alle Gotte, Op. 65.* BRAHMS: *Chorale preludes: O wie selig, seid, ihr doch; Schmücke dich; Es ist ein' Ros' entsprungen, Op. 122.* MENDELSSOHN: *Organ sonata in A, Op. 65/3.* REGER: *Introduction and passacaglia in D min.*
*** Argo Dig. 410 165-2 [id.].

There are not many records of Romantic organ music to match this in colour, breadth of repertory and brilliance of performance, superbly recorded. The ever-popular Widor item leads to pieces just as efficient at bringing out the variety of organ sound, such as the Karg-Elert or the Alain. These are performances which defy all thought of Victorian heaviness, and the Ratzeburg organ produces piquant and beautiful sounds. On CD the presence and range are breathtaking.

Ratzeburg Cathedral organ: *'Romantic organ music'*, Vol. 2: LISZT: *Prelude and fugue on BACH.* REGER: *Benedictus, Op. 59/9.* WIDOR: *Symphony No. 6, Op. 42: Allegro.* BRAHMS: *Chorale preludes: O Welt, ich muss dich lassen; Herlich tutt mich verlangen.* VIERNE: *Symphony No. 1: Finale.* PETERS: *Suite modale, Op. 43.* LANGLAIS: *Hymne d'action.* SCHUMANN: *Allegretto, Op. 58/4.* BOELLMAN: *Suite gothique.*
*** Decca Dig. 421 296-2 [id.].

This successor is equally well recorded and the organ seems as effective in the spectacle of Liszt's venture into Bach polyphony as it is in Langlais and Vierne. The balance between French and German repertoire is similar, and this can be recommended with confidence to all those who enjoyed Volume One.

Sydney Opera House organ: *'Great organ works':* BACH: *Toccata and fugue in D min., BWV 565; Jesu, joy of man's desiring.* ALBINONI: *Adagio* (arr. Giazotto). PURCELL: *Trumpet tune in D.* MENDELSSOHN: *A Midsummer Night's Dream: Wedding march.* FRANCK: *Chorale No. 2 in B min.* MURRILL: *Carillon.* WALFORD DAVIES: *Solemn melody.* WIDOR: *Organ symphony No. 5: Toccata.*
(M) **(*) Decca Dig. 425 013-2 [id.].

Superb sound here, wonderfully free and never oppressive, even in the most spectacular moments. The Widor is spiritedly genial when played within the somewhat mellower registration of the magnificent Sydney instrument (as contrasted with the Ratzeburg Cathedral organ – see above), and the pedals have great sonority and power. The Murrill *Carillon* is equally engaging alongside the Purcell *Trumpet tune*, while Mendelssohn's wedding music has never sounded more resplendent. The Bach is less memorable, and the Albinoni *Adagio*, without the strings, is not an asset to the collection either.

Israeli Flute Ensemble

'Flute Serenade': BEETHOVEN: *Serenade in D, Op. 25*⊛. MOZART: *Flute quartet No. 1 in D, K.285.* SCHUBERT: *String trio in B flat, D.471.* HOFFMEISTER: *Flute quartet in A.*
(B) *** Pickwick/CDI PWK 1139.

We have already praised this delightful account of Beethoven's *D major Serenade* in our composer index. The rest of the concert is hardly less winning, including not only one of the more memorable of Mozart's *Flute quartets* but also Hoffmeister's ingenious transcription of a favourite Mozart piano sonata, with its *Rondo Alla turca* finale sounding very sprightly in the arrangement for flute, violin and piano. The Schubert *String trio* makes a graceful interlude and an attractive change of texture; and the recording adds to the listener's pleasure by its complete naturalness of timbre and balance: one can readily imagine the players sitting at the end of one's room.

Johnson, Emma (clarinet)

'La clarinette française' (with Gordon Back, piano): SAINT-SAENS: *Clarinet sonata, Op. 167.* DEBUSSY: *Prélude: La fille aux cheveux de lin.* MILHAUD: *Duo concertante.* POULENC: *Clarinet sonata.* RAVEL: *Pièce en forme de habañera; Pavane pour une infante défunte.* PIERNE: *Canzonetta.* MILHAUD: *Brazileira.*
**(*) ASV Dig. CDDCA 621.

Emma Johnson's collection is enjoyable but comes into direct competition with Gervase de Peyer's very similar recital on Chandos, and the latter is superior in almost all respects. Whereas he, understandably, seems totally inside all the music, occasionally one feels that Johnson needs to live with it a little longer before being able to offer total interpretative fluency. She finds the charm of the Saint-Saëns *Sonata*, but when the engaging opening idea returns to close the finale, her timing of the pause before its reappearance is not quite perfectly judged; and in the Poulenc, although the *Très calme* centrepiece is seductive, it misses the serenity that De Peyer finds. She is cooler in the famous Debussy *Prélude* than he – and many may enjoy her restraint here and in the closing Milhaud *Brazileira*, when she can be infectiously unbuttoned; but the Milhaud *Duo concertante* is less strikingly characterized. The ASV recording is faithful.

Kayath, Marcelo (guitar)

'Guitar classics from Latin America': PONCE: *Valse.* PIAZZOLA: *La muerte del angel.* BARRIOS: *Vals, Op. 8/3; Choro de saudade; Julia florida.* LAURO: *Vals venezolanos No. 2; El negrito; El marabino.* BROUWER: *Canción de cuna; Ojos brujos.* PERNAMBUCO: *Sons de carrilhões; Interrogando; Sono de maghia.* REIS: *Si ela perguntar.* VILLA-LOBOS: *5 Preludes.*
(B) *** Pickwick Dig. PCD 853 [MCA MCAD 25963].

Marcelo Kayath studied in Rio de Janeiro and is a master of this repertoire – indeed his flexibly inspirational accounts of the Villa-Lobos *Preludes* can stand comparison with the finest performances on record. He has the rare gift of playing in the studio as at a live recital; obviously he soon becomes unaware of his surroundings, for he plays everything here with consummate technical ease and the most appealing spontaneity. His rubato in the Barrios *Vals* is particularly effective, and he is a fine advocate too of the engaging Lauro pieces and the picaresque writing of João Pernambuco, a friend of Villa-Lobos. The recording, made in a warm but not too resonant acoustic, is first class, and there is a fine illusion of presence. Even though this is a budget-priced issue, it carries excellent notes.

'*Guitar classics from Spain*': TARREGA: *Prelude in A min.; Capricho arabe; Recuerdos de la Alhambra.* GRANADOS: *La Maja de Goya.* ALBÉNIZ: *Granada; Zambra; Grandina; Sevilla; Mallorca.* TORROBA: *Prelude in E; Sonatina; Nocturno.* RODRIGO: *Zapateado.* TRAD.: *El Noy de la mare.*
(B) *** Pickwick Dig. PCD 876.

Following the success of his first, Latin-American recital, Marcelo Kayath gives us an equally enjoyable Spanish collection, full of colour and spontaneity. By grouping music by several major composers, he provides a particularly revealing mix. The two opening Tarrega pieces are predominantly lyrical, to bring an effective contrast with the famous fluttering *Recuerdos de la Alhambra*, played strongly. Then after the Granados come five of Albéniz's most colourful and tuneful geographical evocations, while the Torroba group includes the *Sonatina*, a splendid piece. After Rodrigo he closes with the hauntingly memorable *El Noy de la mare*. There is over an hour of music and the recording has a most realistic presence; but take care not to set the volume level too high.

Koopman, Ton (harpsichord)

Fitzwilliam Virginal Book: PICCHI: *Toccata.* GIBBONS: *Pavana.* MORLEY: *Fancie.* BULL: *Ut re mi fa so la.* FARNABY: *Up tails all.* BYRD: *Pavana; Galiarda.* PHILIPS: *Amarilli di Julio Romano; Pavana dolorosa; Galiarda dolorosa.* ANON.: *Pakington's Pownde.* BYRD: *Fantasia.*
** Capriccio Dig. 10 211 [id.].

Ton Koopman is very naturally recorded in a pleasing acoustic and his programme is well planned. His style is thoughtful and he is completely at home in the gentle melancholy that pervades much of this repertoire. But when the music is more energetic the projection is not very vivid and tempi often seem too restrained. *Pakington's Pownde* should surely sound more robustly vigorous, and there is not a suspicion of humour in Farnaby's *Up tails all.*

Kremer, Gidon (violin), Elena Bashkirova (piano)

SCHUBERT: *Fantasia in C, D.934.* STRAVINSKY: *Duo concertante.* PROKOFIEV: (Solo) *Violin sonata, Op. 115.* RAVEL: *Sonate posthume.* SATIE: *Choses vues droite et à gauche (sans lunettes).*
(M) *** Ph. 426 387-2 [id.].

This is perhaps the finest of all Gidon Kremer's records: he is superbly partnered by Elena Bashkirova and given a (1980) Philips recording of great realism and presence. The disc is worth having just for Ravel's posthumously published *Sonata*, a youthful work in a single movement that is surprisingly mature and with many magical anticipations of the future. It is a delightful piece, played marvellously. So too are the Prokofiev and

Stravinsky works, full of bravura, yet with the latter displaying an agreeably cool lyrical element; while the Satie miniatures combine wit and sparkle with an attractive finesse. The Schubert *Fantasia* is full of spontaneous romantic flair, and the recital ends with another surprise, Milhaud's delicious *Printemps*, a real lollipop, yet not in the least trivial.

Labèque, Katia and Marielle (piano duet)

'Glad rags': GERSHWIN/DONALDSON: *Rialto ripples.* MAYERL: *Honky-tonk.* JOHNSON: *Carolina shout.* JOPLIN: *The Entertainer; Antoinette; Magnetic rag; Maple leaf rag; Elite syncopations; Strenuous life; Stop-time; Bethena.*
*** EMI Dig. CDC7 47093-2 [id.].

The Labèque duo play with irresistible bravura and dash. Scott Joplin may have frowned on their tempi (he favoured slow speeds), but the playing has such wit and conveyed enjoyment that criticism is silenced. The recording has sparkle, but depth too, and fine presence in CD. This is by far the most recommendable collection of this repertoire.

Larrocha, Alicia de (piano)

'Favourite Spanish encores': MATEO ALBÉNIZ: *Sonata in D.* ISAAC ALBÉNIZ: *Recuerdos de Viaje, Nos. 5, Puerta de Tierra (Bolero); 6, Rumores de la Caleta (Malaguena). Pavana – Capricho, Op. 12. Tango, Op. 165/2; Malaguena, Op. 165/3; Suite espagnole: No. 3, Sevillanas.* SOLER: *Sonatas in G min.; in D.* GRANADOS: *Danzas espanolas Nos. 5 (Andaluza); 7 (Valenciana O Calesera).* TURINA: *5 Danzas Gitanas,* 1st series. *No. 5, Sacro-monte, Op. 55. 3 danzas Andaluzas, No. 3, Zapateado, Op. 8.* MOMPOU: *Impresiones intimas.*
*** Decca 417 639-2 [id.].

This compilation has been made from various recital records Mme de Larrocha made over the years. The Mompou *Impresiones intimas* is the most recent (1984) but the others come from the mid-1970s. She plays the *Impresiones* and the Albéniz and Soler superbly, with finesse and subtlety; and the recordings are very natural and lifelike. In every way a delightful record.

'Spanish fireworks': FALLA: *3 Dances.* M. ALBÉNIZ: *Sonata.* I. ALBÉNIZ: *Iberia: Trianna. Navarra; Sevilla; Asturias.* MOMPOU: *Secreto.* GRANADOS: *Zapateado; Allegro de concierto; Danzas españolas No. 5 (Andaluza); Quejas o la majas el Ruisenor; El Pele.* TURINA: *Sacro-monte; Zapateado.*
(M) *** Decca Dig./Analogue 417 795-2 [id.].

Although the title is slightly misleading, for this is essentially cultivated playing, Alicia de Larrocha can certainly provide bravura when called for, as in the glittering Granados *Allegro de concierto*. But this is a recital that relies for its appeal on evocation and colour – as in the same composer's haunting *Quejas o la majas el Ruisenor*, the excerpts from the Isaac Albéniz *Suite española*, or the atmospheric Mompou *Secreto* – and the sheer distinction and character of its pianism, coolly shown in the delectable *Sonata* of Mateo Albéniz. With 71 minutes, the programme is even more generous than Miss de Larrocha's companion recital (which duplicates one or two items) and the recording, partly digital and partly analogue, is consistently realistic.

LaSalle Quartet

Chamber music of the Second Viennese School: BERG: *Lyric suite; String quartet, Op. 3.*
SCHOENBERG: *String quartets: in D; No. 1 in D min., Op. 7; No. 2 in F sharp min., Op.
10/3* (with Margaret Price); *No. 3, Op. 30; No. 4, Op. 37.* WEBERN: *5 Movements, Op. 5;
String quartet* (1905); *6 Bagatelles, Op. 9; String quartet, Op. 28.*
(M) *** DG 419 994-2 (4) [id.].

DG have compressed their 1971 five-LP set on to four CDs, offering them at a reduced
and competitive price. They have also retained the invaluable and excellent documentary
study edited by Ursula Rauchhaupt – which runs to 340 pages! It is almost worth having
this set for the documentation alone. Now that the Juilliard version on CBS is out of
circulation, this is the only complete survey of the Schoenberg *Four Quartets* plus the
early *D major* before the public. The LaSalle Quartet give splendidly expert
performances, even if at times their playing seems a little cool; and they are very well
recorded. An invaluable issue for all who care about twentieth-century music.

Ledger, Philip (organ of King's College Chapel, Cambridge)

'*Organ music from King's*': BACH: *Toccata and fugue in D min., BWV 565.* BRAHMS:
Chorale prelude: Es ist ein' Ros' entsprungen, Op. 122/8. LISZT: *Prelude and fugue on the
name BACH, G.260.* VAUGHAN WILLIAMS: *Rhosymedre.* FRANCK: *Choral No. 3 in A
min.* VIERNE: *Pièces en style libre: No. 19, Berceuse.* WIDOR: *Symphony No. 5, Op. 42/1:
Toccata.*
(M) *** EMI CD-EMX 2137.

A well-praised recital dating from 1976 has been very successfully remastered: the
sound is clearly defined, yet attractively retains the King's ambience. Philip Ledger is less
flamboyant than some in the famous Bach *Toccata and fugue* and the Widor, but his Liszt
and Franck are particularly impressive, and the Brahms, Vaughan Williams and Vierne
pieces make attractively serene interludes.

'*Organ voluntaries from King's*': CLARK: *Prince of Denmark's march.* SWEELINCK:
Variations on Mein juges Leben. BOYCE: *Voluntary in D.* BACH: *Chorales: Wachet auf;
Wenn wir in hochsten Nothen sein; In dulci jubilo.* BRAHMS: *Schmücke dich, O liebe Seele.*
KARG-ELERT: *Marche triomphale: Now thank we all our God.* WHITLOCK: *Folk tune;
Paen.* STANFORD: *Postlude in G min.* ALAIN: *Litanies.* JONGEN: *Chant de May.* DUPRÉ:
Toccata: Placare Christe servulis.
(M) *** EMI Dig. CD-EMX 2149.

This early digital recital is splendidly recorded with the most spectacularly wide
dynamic range. In a piece like Alain's *Litanies* the contrasts are thrilling. Overall the
programme is highly diverting and well balanced to provide variety. The three closing
French items form an engaging triptych, with the rhythmically quirky *Litanies* leading on
to Jongen's lyrical *May song*, and Dupré's *Toccata* making a riveting end-piece. Before
that, the Bach and Brahms chorales are colourfully registered and the music of Karg-Elert,
Stanford and Whitlock brings comparable diversity. This repertoire has wide musical
interest – it is not just for organ fanciers – and it is all played with imagination and
spontaneity. The recording is in the demonstration class throughout, with the King's
acoustics offering no problems of clouding.

Leonhardt, Gustav (clavichord)

'Clavichord recital': C. P. E. BACH: *Sonatas: in D min.; G min., Wq. 51/4 & 6; in B min./F sharp min., Wq. 63/4.* RITTER: *Suite in F sharp min.* J. S. BACH: *Fantasia & fugue in A min., BWV 904; French suite No. 2 in C min., BWV 813.* W. F. BACH: *3 Polonaises (in E flat min., E min. & F min.).*
*** Ph. Dig. 422 349-2.

A fine recital from the distinguished Dutch scholar-musician. The actual clavichord used is not specified, but it reproduces well on this disc, which must be played at a very low level indeed if it is to give anything like a truthful impression of the instrument. Leonhardt plays with the authority of the scholar and the imagination of the artist. Apart from the two J. S. Bach pieces, probably the most interesting things on the disc are the three *Polonaises* of Wilhelm Friedemann. Leonhardt opens with a *Suite in F sharp minor* by Christian Ritter (c. 1645–c. 1717) who was, like Wilhelm Friedemann, an organist at Halle, but a composer of moderate interest. The C. P. E. Bach *Sonata*, Wq. 63/4, is tonally unusual for its period: its three movements are all in different keys: B minor, D major and F sharp minor. First-rate sound.

'Liebesträume'

'Romantic piano music': (i) Bolet; (ii) Ashkenazy; (iii) De Larrocha; (iv) Lupu: (i) LISZT: *Liebestraum No. 3; Étude de concert No. 3 (Un sospiro).* (ii) RACHMANINOV: *Prelude in C sharp min., Op. 3/2.* CHOPIN: *Nocturne in F min., Op. 55/1; Étude in E, Op. 10/3.* BEETHOVEN: *Piano sonata No. 14 in C sharp min. (Moonlight).* (iii) CHOPIN: *Prelude No. 15 in D flat (Raindrop).* SCHUBERT: *Impromptu in A flat, D. 899/4.* SCHUMANN: *Romance, Op. 28/2.* (iv) BRAHMS: *Rhapsody in G min., Op. 79/2.*
*** Decca 411 934-2 [id.].

Jorge Bolet's warmly romantic account of Liszt gives this specially assembled compact disc its title and is also the only true digital recording included in the programme. But the sound is generally excellent and the digital remastering, if producing a rather forward image, offers truthful quality throughout. The performances are distinguished and there is passionate contrast in Ashkenazy's Rachmaninov. Lupu's Brahms is rather less extrovert in feeling; generally, the recital has a nicely relaxed atmosphere.

Lin, Cho-Liang (violin), Sandra Rivers (piano)

'Bravura': FALLA: *Suite populaire espagnole.* KREISLER: *Liebeslied; Liebesfreud. Tambourin chinois.* MOZART: *Serenade, K. 250: Rondo.* RACHMANINOV: *Vocalise.* WIENIAWSKI: *Capriccio-valse in E, Op. 7.* SARASATE: *Introduction and Tarantella, Op. 43.*
*** CBS Dig. MK 39133 [id.].

Some first-rate playing here from this remarkable young virtuoso. He tosses off these pieces with great aplomb and brilliance. But besides his pyrotechnics, he is also able to find poetry in these miniatures and is well supported by Sandra Rivers. A most attractive recital, as well recorded as it is played.

Lipatti, Dinu (piano)

BACH: *Partita No. 1 in B flat, BWV 825; Chorale preludes: Nunn komm' der Heiden Heiland, BWV 599; Ich ruf' zu dir, Herr Jesu Christ, BWV 639; Jesu, joy of man's desiring* (arr. Hess); *Flute sonata No. 2, BWV 1031: Siciliana.* D. SCARLATTI: *Sonatas, Kk.9 & Kk.380.* MOZART: *Sonata No. 8 in A min., K.310.* SCHUBERT: *Impromptus: in E flat and G flat, D.899/2 & 3.*
(M) *** EMI mono CDH7 69799-2 [id.].

No collector should overlook this Lipatti CD. Most of the performances have scarcely been out of circulation since their first appearance: the haunting account of the Mozart *A minor Sonata* and the Bach *B flat Partita* have both had more than one incarnation on LP. The remastering is well done, and one notices that, among his other subtleties, Lipatti creates a different timbre for the music of each composer.

CHOPIN: *Sonata No. 3 in B min., Op. 58.* LISZT: *Années de pèlerinage: Sonetto del Petrarca, No. 104.* RAVEL: *Miroirs: Alborada del gracioso.* BRAHMS: *Waltzes, Op. 39/1, 2, 5, 6, 10, 14 & 15* (with Nadia Boulanger). ENESCU: *Sonata No. 3 in D, Op. 25.*
(M) (***) EMI mono CDH7 63038-2.

The Chopin *Sonata*, the Liszt and the Ravel were recorded in 1947–8, the Brahms *Waltzes*, with Nadia Boulanger, as long ago as 1937; while the Enescu *Sonata* comes from a 1943 wartime broadcast from Swiss Radio. The Chopin is one of the classics of the gramophone, and it is good to have it on CD in this excellent-sounding transfer. The Brahms *Waltzes* are played deliciously with tremendous sparkle and tenderness; they sound every bit as realistic as the post-war records. The Enescu *Sonata* is an accessible piece, with an exuberant first movement and a rather atmospheric *Andantino*, but the sound is not as fresh as the rest of the music on this valuable CD. A must for all with an interest in the piano.

Lloyd Webber, Julian (cello)

'British cello music' (with (i) John McCabe, piano): (i) RAWSTHORNE: *Sonata for cello and piano.* ARNOLD: *Fantasy for cello.* (i) IRELAND: *The Holy Boy.* WALTON: *Passacaglia.* BRITTEN: *Teme (Sacher); Cello suite No. 3.*
*** ASV Dig. CDDCA 592 [id.].

A splendid recital and a most valuable one. Julian Lloyd Webber has championed such rarities as the Bridge *Oration* at a time when it was unrecorded and now devotes this present issue to English music that needs strong advocacy; there is no alternative version of the Rawsthorne *Sonata*, in which he is most ably partnered by John McCabe. He gives this piece – and, for that matter, the remainder of the programme – with full-blooded commitment. Good recording.

'The romantic cello' (with Yitkin Seow, piano): POPPER: *Elfentanz, Op. 39.* SAINT-SAENS: *Carnival of the animals: The Swan. Allegro appassionato, Op. 43.* FAURÉ: *Après un rêve.* MENDELSSOHN: *Song without words, Op. 109.* RACHMANINOV: *Cello sonata, Op. 19: slow movt.* DELIUS: *Romance.* CHOPIN: *Introduction and polonaise brillante, Op. 3.* ELGAR: *Salut d'amour, Op. 12.*
(B) **(*) ASV CDQS 6014 [id.].

Julian Lloyd Webber has gathered together a most attractive collection of showpieces for the cello, romantic as well as brilliant. Such dazzling pieces as the Popper – always a favourite with virtuoso cellists – is on record a welcome rarity. The recording, a little edgy, if with undoubted presence, favours the cello and is vivid, with good body and range.

Lympany, Moura (piano)

'Best-loved piano classics': CHOPIN: *Fantaisie-impromptu, Op. 66; Études, Op. 10/4 & 5.* BRAHMS: *Waltz, Op. 39/15.* MOZART: *Sonata No. 11, 'Alla Turca', K.331.* BEETHOVEN: *Minuet in G; Für Elise.* SCHUMANN: *Kinderszenen: Träumerei.* LISZT: *Concert study: Un sospiro.* DVOŘÁK: *Humoresque. Op. 101/7.* MACDOWELL: *To a wild rose.* CHAMINADE: *Autumn.* DEBUSSY: *Suite bergamasque: Clair de lune. Children's corner: Golliwog's cakewalk.* RACHMANINOV: *Prelude in C sharp min., Op. 3/2.* RUBINSTEIN: *Melody in F, Op. 3/1.* GRANADOS: *Goyescas: The Maiden and the nightingale.* FALLA: *El amor brujo: Ritual fire dance.* ALBÉNIZ: *Tango, Op. 165/2.*
(M) *** EMI Dig. CDZ7 62523-2.

The popularity and generosity of the programme here speaks for itself. Moreover these are not old recordings rehashed but a brand-new recital, digitally recorded at Abbey Road in 1988. Miss Lympany has lost none of the flair and technical skill which earned her her reputation: the whole programme has the spontaneity of a live recital. At times the playing has a masculine strength, and pieces like *Träumerei* and *Clair de lune* emerge the more freshly through a total absence of sentimentality. Liszt's *Concert study: Un sospiro* is played with commanding passion, and even the more trivial items sound newly minted. At medium price this is very good value, with the Spanish pieces ending the collection memorably, the bold Falla *Fire dance* contrasting with the more lyrical Granados and Albéniz items. The piano timbre is faithful and realistic, if a little dry.

Menuhin, Sir Yehudi and Stéphane Grappelli (violins)

'Menuhin and Grappelli play Berlin, Kern, Porter and Rodgers & Hart': BERLIN: *Cheek to cheek; Isn't this a lovely day; The Piccolino; Change partners; Top Hat; I've got my love to keep me warm; Heat wave.* KERN: *The way you look tonight; Pick yourself up; A fine romance; All the things you are; Why do I love you?* C. PORTER: *I get a kick out of you; Night and day; Looking at you; Just one of those things.* RODGERS: *My funny valentine; Thou swell; The lady is a tramp; Blue moon.*
(M) **(*) EMI CDM7 69219-2 [id.].

'Jealousy and other great standards': Jealousy; Tea for two; Limehouse blues; These foolish things; The Continental; A Nightingale sang in Berkeley Square; Sweet Sue; Skylark; Laura; Sweet Georgia Brown; I'll remember April; April in Paris; The things we did last summer; September in the rain; Autumn leaves; Autumn in New York; Button up your overcoat.
(M) **(*) EMI CDM7 69220-2 [id.].

The partnership of Menuhin and Grappelli started in the television studio; their brief duets (tagged on to interviews) were so successful that the idea came of recording a whole recital, which between 1973 and 1985 became a series of five. These two CDs offer some of the best numbers extracted from all five. One of the secrets of the partnership's success lies in the choice of material. All these items started out as first-class songs with striking melodies which live in whatever guise; and here with ingenious arrangements they spark off the individual genius of each violinist, both as a challenge and towards the players' obvious enjoyment. The high spirits of each occasion are caught beautifully with no intimidation from the recording studio ambience; while the playing styles of each artist are different, they are also complementary and remarkably close in such matters as tone and balance. The result is delightful. The snag is that the digital remastering, in an attempt to add presence, has made the overall sound drier and, more noticeably in the second collection (entitled '*Jealousy*'), there is a degree of edge on the violin timbre.

'*Strictly for the birds*' (with Instrumental Ens., Max Harris): *A Nightingale sang in Berkeley Square. Lullaby of Birdland. When the red, red robin. Skylark. Bye, bye, blackbird. Coucou. Flamingo. Dinah. Rosetta. Sweet Sue. Once in love with Amy. Laura. La Route du Roi. Sweet Georgia Brown.* -
(B) *** CfP Dig. CD-CFP 4549.

This digitally recorded collection dates from 1980. It is the lyrical tunes like the famous opening song, the atmospheric *Laura* and Grappelli's own engaging *Coucou* that are the most memorable, although in pieces like *Bye, bye, blackbird* and *Sweet Georgia Brown* the high spirits of the collaboration are caught well.

Ortiz, Cristina (piano)

'*French impressionist piano music*': DEBUSSY: *2 Arabesques; Prélude: La Cathédrale engloutie. Images: Reflets dans l'eau. Children's corner: Golliwog's cakewalk. Suite bergamasque: Clair de lune; L'isle joyeuse.* CHABRIER: *Pièce pittoresque No. 7: Danse villageoise.* SATIE: *Gymnopédie No. 1.* FAURÉ: *Impromptu No. 3, Op. 34.* IBERT: *10 Histoires: Le petite âne blanc.* POULENC: *Mélancolie.* MILHAUD: *Saudades de Brasil: Copacabana, Op. 67/4.* RAVEL: *Jeux d'eau; Alborada del gracioso.*
(B) **(*) Pickwick Dig. PCD 846 [MCA MCAD 25969].

As usual with Pickwick, this is a very generous recital and it is most realistically recorded. Cristina Ortiz shows her versatility in this wide-ranging French repertoire and projects plenty of charm – Ibert's *Little white donkey* is a notable highlight, while Ravel's *Jeux d'eau* is full of evocative feeling. Sometimes in the bravura her playing goes a little over the top, and one would have liked more poise, but there is no lack of commitment and spontaneity, and there is much to reward here. The Debussy pieces come off especially well, and *Reflets dans l'eau* and *La Cathédrale engloutie* are as atmospheric as the Ravel pieces.

Parker-Smith, Jane (organ)

Organ of Coventry Cathedral: '*Popular French Romantics*': WIDOR: *Symphony No. 1: March pontifical. Symphony No 9 (Gothique), Op. 70: Andante sostenuto.* GUILMANT: *Sonata No. 5 in C min., Op. 80; Scherzo.* GIGOUT: *Toccata in B min.* BONNET: *Elfes, Op. 7.* LEFÉBURE-WÉLY: *Sortie in B flat.* VIERNE: *Pièces de fantaisie: Clair de lune, Op. 53/5; Carillon de Westminster, Op. 54/6.*
*** ASV Dig. CDDCA 539 [id.].

The modern organ in Coventry Cathedral (built by Harrison and Harrison of Durham) is surprisingly well suited to French repertoire. Its bright, full-bodied tutti, with just a touch of harshness, adds a nice bite to Jane Parker-Smith's very pontifical performance of the opening Widor *March* and creates a blaze of splendour at the close of the famous Vierne *Carillon de Westminster*, the finest performance on record. The detail of the fast, nimble articulation in the engagingly Mendelssohnian *Elfes* of Joseph Bonnet is not clouded; yet here, as in the splendid Guilmant *Scherzo* with its wider dynamic range, there is also a nice atmospheric effect. Hardly less enjoyable is the robustly jocular *Sortie* of Lefébure-Wély, which is delivered with fine geniality and panache. Overall, a most entertaining recital.

Organ of Beauvais Cathedral: *'Popular French Romantics' Vol. 2:* FRANCK: *Prélude, fugue et variation, Op. 18.* GUILMANT: *Grand choeur in D* (after Handel). MULET: *Carillon-sortie.* RENAUD: *Toccata in D min.* SAINT-SAENS: *Prelude and fugue.* VIERNE: *Symphony No. 1: Finale. Stèle pour un enfant défunt.* WIDOR: *Symphony No. 4: Andante and Scherzo.*
*** ASV Dig. CDDCA 610 [id.].

The organ at Beauvais is even more suitable for this repertoire and the programme is admirably laid out. With his *Prélude and fugue*, Saint-Saëns is in more serious mood than usual but showing characteristic facility in fugal construction; Widor is first mellow and then quixotic – his *Scherzo* demands the lightest articulation and receives it. High drama and great bravura are provided by the Vierne *Finale* and later by Albert Renaud's *Toccata* and Henri Mulet's *Carillon-sortie*, while Franck's *Prélude, fugue et variation* and the poignant Vierne *Stèle pour un enfant défunt* (written after the death of a child of close friends, to whom the composer was greatly attached) bring attractive lyrical contrast: here Jane Parker-Smith's registration shows particular subtlety. The organ is splendidly recorded, its hint of harshness in tutti giving a proper French tang; and detail is not muddied.

Perahia, Murray (piano)

'Portrait': BEETHOVEN: *Sonata No. 23 (Appassionata), Op. 57.* SCHUBERT: *Impromptu in G flat, D.899/3.* SCHUMANN: *Papillons, Op. 2.* CHOPIN: *Fantaisie-Impromptu, Op. 66; Preludes, Op. 28 Nos. 6, 7 & 15.* MENDELSSOHN: *Rondo capriccioso, Op. 14.* MOZART: *Rondo for piano and orchestra in D, K.382* (with ECO).
*** CBS MK 42448 [id.].

A self-recommending recital, with the single proviso that being a sampler it includes excerpts from a number of CDs which many readers may wish to consider separately. Bearing in mind the variety of sources and that some are remastered analogue and some digital, the sound is remarkably consistent and, for the most part, excellent.

Petri, Michala (recorder or flute)

'Greensleeves' (with Hanne Petri, harpsichord, David Petri, cello): ANON.: *Greensleeves to a grounde; Divisions on an Italian ground.* EYCK, Jacob van: *Prins Robberts Masco; Philis Schoon Herderinne; Wat Zal Men op den Avond Doen; Engels Nachtegaeltje.* CORELLI: *Sonata, Op. 15/5: La Folia.* HANDEL: *Andante.* LECLAIR: *Tambourin.* F. COUPERIN: *Le rossignol vainqueur; Le rossignol en amour.* J. S. BACH: *Siciliano.* TELEMANN: *Rondino.* GOSSEC: *Tambourin.* PAGANINI: *Moto perpetuo, Op. 11.* BRUGGEN: *2 Studies.* CHRISTIANSEN: *Satie auf hoher See.* HENRIQUES: *Dance of the midges.* SCHUBERT: *The Bee.* MONTI: *Czárdás.* HERBERLE: *Rondo presto.* RIMSKY-KORSAKOV: *Flight of the bumble-bee.*
(M) *** Ph. Dig. 420 897-2.

Marvellously nimble playing from Michala Petri, and 71 minutes, digitally recorded at mid-price, so one can afford to pick and choose. Some of the music opening the recital is less than distinctive, but the Couperin transcriptions are a delight and Paganini's *Moto perpetuo* vies with Henriques' *Dance of the midges* for sparkling bravura. There are some attractively familiar melodies by Bach and Handel, among others, to provide contrast, and Henning Christiansen's *Satie auf hoher See* is an unexpected treat. Monti's *Czárdás* ends the programme infectiously.

Petri, Michala (recorder), George Malcolm (harpsichord)

Recorder sonatas: VIVALDI: *Il Pastor fido: Sonata No. 6 in G min., RV 58.* CORELLI: *Sonata in C, Op. 5/9.* D. BIGAGLIA: *Sonata in A min.* BONONCINI: *Divertimento da camera No. 6 in C min.* SAMMARTINI: *Sonata in G, Op. 13/4.* B. MARCELLO: *Sonata in F, Op. 2/1.*
(M) *** Ph. Dig. 412 632-2 [id.].

Six recorder sonatas in a row might seem too much of a good thing, but the playing is so felicitous and the music has such charm that the collection is immensely enjoyable, even taken complete, and if sensibly dipped into is a source of much delight. There are many individual highlights. The Corelli *Sonata* has a memorable *Tempo di gavotta* as its finale which reminds one a little of Handel's *Harmonious blacksmith*; the work in A minor by the composer with the unlikely name of Diogenio Bigaglia (*c.* 1676–*c.* 1745) is a winner, with a nimble minuet and sparkling finale. Bononcini's *Divertimento da camera* alternates slow and fast sections, and in the third-movement *Largo* George Malcolm makes the delicate accompaniment sound like a harp. Sammartini's *Sonata* is enchanting, with its opening *Andante* in siciliano form and three more delectable movements to follow. Throughout, Michala Petri's playing is wonderfully fresh: she has made many records for Philips, but none more enticing than this. George Malcolm proves an equally imaginative partner, and both artists embellish with admirable flair and taste, never overdoing it. The Philips recording is quite perfectly balanced and wonderfully tangible.

Petrov, Nikolai (piano)

French music: RAMEAU: *Cyclope; La poule.* BIZET: *Nocturne No. 1 in D; Variations chromatiques in C min.* SAINT-SAENS: *Toccata (Étude No. 6 in F, Op. 111); Étude en forme d'une valse. Piano concerto No. 2: Scherzo* (arr. Bizet). DUKAS: *Variations, interlude et final.* DEBUSSY; *Images oubliées.* RAVEL: *L'enfant et les sortilèges: Foxtrot (5 o'clock).*
**(*) Olympia OCD 122 [id.].

Nikolai Petrov is a big player and (to judge from the present compilation) an enterprising one. This recital includes some rarities, including the splendid Dukas *Variations, interlude et final*, and is probably worth getting for that alone. There are also the Bizet *Variations* and his remarkable transcription of the *Scherzo* of the Saint-Saëns *Second Piano concerto*. Although Petrov has formidable technical equipment and does produce too big a tone, he is far from insensitive to dynamic nuance. All the same, his *Images oubliées* do not match those of Kocsis (Philips) for sheer beauty and refinement of sound. His companion recital of *Fantaisies* by C. P. E. Bach, Brahms, Liszt, Mendelssohn and Mozart (Olympia OCD 198) is less beguiling, for all its easy virtuosity (most impressive in Liszt's *Don Juan* paraphrase).

Peyer, Gervase de (clarinet), Gwenneth Pryor (piano)

French music for clarinet and piano: SAINT-SAENS: *Sonata, Op. 167.* DEBUSSY: *Première rhapsodie; Arabesque No. 2; Prélude: La fille aux cheveux de lin.* POULENC: *Sonata.*

SCHMIDT: *Andantino, Op. 30/1.* RAVEL: *Pièce en forme de habañera.* PIERNÉ: *Canzonetta, Op. 19.*
⊛ *** Chan. Dig. CHAN 8526.

A gorgeous record. Gervase de Peyer has already made some thirty or so records, but none more attractive than this, and he is accompanied by Gwenneth Pryor with wonderful sympathy. In Debussy's *Rhapsodie* she provides a subtle background tapestry for his languorous opening cantilena (marked *Rêveusement lente*); she then opens up for the work's climax yet lets the clarinet dominate as it must. The Saint-Saëns *Sonata* is an attractively crafted piece, full of engaging invention, with the opening melody returning neatly to close the work at the end of the fourth movement. Poulenc's *Sonata* is characteristically witty, with contrast in its lovely central *Romanza* (*très calme*); and the other short pieces wind down the closing mood of the recital, with De Peyer's luscious timbre drawing a charming portrait of *The girl with the flaxen hair* before the nimbly tripping closing encore of Pierné. This is a quite perfect record of its kind, the programme like that of a live recital and played with comparable spontaneity. The recording is absolutely realistic; the balance could hardly be improved on.

Pinnock, Trevor (harpsichord)

'*The harmonious blacksmith*': HANDEL: *Suite 5: The Harmonious blacksmith.* FISCHER: *Urania: Passacaglia in D min.* COUPERIN: *Les baricades mystérieuses.* BACH: *Italian concerto in F, BWV 971.* RAMEAU: *Gavotte in A min.* D. SCARLATTI: *2 Sonatas Kk.380/1.* FIOCCO: *Suite 1: Adagio in F.* DAQUIN: *Le Coucou.* BALBASTHE: *La Suzanne in E min.*
**(*) DG 413 591-2 [id.].

A delightful collection of harpsichord lollipops, superbly and stylishly played and brilliantly – if aggressively – recorded. If one samples the famous title-piece, being careful to set the volume control at a realistic level, in the CD format the presence and tangibility of the instrument are spectacular. However, the bright sharpness of focus can become just a little tiring if the recital is taken all at once.

Pollini, Maurizio (piano)

PROKOFIEV: *Piano sonata No. 7 in B flat, Op. 83.* STRAVINSKY: *Three movements from Petrushka.* BOULEZ: *Piano sonata No. 2.* WEBERN: *Variations for piano, Op. 27.*
*** DG 419 202-2.

The Prokofiev is a great performance, one of the finest ever committed to disc; and the Stravinsky *Petrushka* is electrifying. Not all those responding to this music will do so quite so readily to the Boulez, fine though the playing is; but the Webern also makes a very strong impression. This is the equivalent of two LPs and is outstanding value.

Pöntinen, Roland (piano)

Russian piano music: STRAVINSKY: *3 Movements from Petrushka.* SCRIABIN: *Sonata No. 7 in F sharp (White Mass), Op. 64.* SHOSTAKOVICH: *3 Fantastic dances.* RACHMANINOV: *Études-tableaux, Opp. 33 & 39.* PROKOFIEV: *Toccata.* KHACHATURIAN: *Toccata.*
*** BIS Dig. CD 276 [id.].

Roland Pöntinen gives a suitably ardent and inflammable account of the *Seventh*

Sonata, the so-called '*White Mass*', and is fully attuned to the Scriabin sensibility, conveying its wild, excitable character to good effect. His playing has real temperament and sense of colour, and this well-recorded recital shows his very considerable technique and prowess to advantage. A very enjoyable programme.

Prometheus Ensemble

'*French impressions*': RAVEL: *Introduction & allegro for harp, flute, clarinet and string quartet.* DEBUSSY: *Danses sacrée et profane; Sonata for flute, viola and harp.* ROUSSEL: *Serenade.*
*** ASV Dig. CDDCA 664 [id.].

This young group gives eminently well-prepared and thoughtful accounts of all these pieces. Although these performances do not displace earlier versions, no one investing in them will be disappointed. The *Danses sacrée et profane* sound particularly atmospheric and the Debussy *Sonata* is played with great feeling and sounds appropriately ethereal. The Roussel, too, is done with great style and, even if the *Introduction and allegro* does not supersede the celebrated Melos account, the Prometheus do it well.

Rawsthorne, Noel (organ)

Organ of Coventry Cathedral: '*Organ spectacular*': VERDI: *Aida: Grand march.* CLARKE: *Trumpet voluntary.* BACH: *Suite No. 3 in D; Air.* SCHUBERT: *Marche militaire.* SULLIVAN: *The lost chord.* MENDELSSOHN: *Midsummer Night's Dream: Wedding march.* SOUSA: *The Stars and stripes forever.* ELGAR: *Pomp and circumstance march No. 1.* TRAD.: *Londonderry air.* HANDEL: *Messiah: Hallelujah.* WAGNER: *Die Walküre: Ride of the Valkyries.*
*** EMI Dig. CDC7 47764-2 [id.].

This collection is aptly named, for the digital recording captures some splendid sounds from the modern Coventry organ. With all the transcriptions arranged by Rawsthorne himself, obviously with the instrument in mind, he shows great flair in both playing and registration. It is a frankly popular programme, well laced with marches, balancing expansive tunes with opportunities for bravura, as in the *Aida* march or the boisterous *Stars and stripes*. The resonance is well controlled by player and engineers alike, and this is very impressive on CD.

Rév, Lívia (piano)

'*For children*': BACH: *Preludes in E, BWV 939; in G min., BWV 930.* DAQUIN: *Le coucou.* MOZART: *Variations on Ah vous dirai-je maman, K.265.* BEETHOVEN: *Für Elise.* SCHUMANN: *Album for the young Op. 63: excerpts.* CHOPIN: *Nocturne in C min., Op. posth.* LISZT: *Etudes G. 136/1 & 2.* BIZET: *Jeux d'enfants: La Toupie.* FAURÉ: *Dolly: Berceuse.* TCHAIKOVSKY: *Album for the young, Op. 39: Maman; Waltz.* VILLA-LOBOS: *Prole do bebê: excerpts.* JOLIVET: *Chansons naïve 1 & 2.* PROKOFIEV: *Waltz, Op. 65.* BARTÓK: *Evening in the country; For Children: excerpts.* DEBUSSY: *Children's corner: excerpts.* MAGIN: *3 Pieces.* MATACIC: *Miniature variations.*
*** Hyp. CDA 66185.

A wholly delectable recital, and not just for children either. The whole is more than the sum of its many parts, and the layout provides excellent variety, with the programme stimulating in mixing familiar with unfamiliar. The recording is first class. Highly recommended for late evening listening.

Richter, Sviatoslav (piano)

CHOPIN: *Préludes, Op. 28/2; 4–11; 13; 19; 21 & 23.* TCHAIKOVSKY: *Nocturne in F, Op. 10/1; Valse-scherzo in A, Op. 7.* RACHMANINOV: *Études-tableaux, Op. 33/3, 5 & 6; Op. 39 1–4; 7 & 9.*
*** Olympia OCD 112 [id.].

Some marvellous playing here from Richter. He plays an odd assortment of Chopin *Preludes*, Nos. 4 through to 10 in the published sequence, then 23, 19, 11, 2, 23 and 21! These obviously derive from a public concert, as there is applause. He is distinctly ruminative and wayward at times. The two Tchaikovsky pieces are done with extraordinary finesse and the Rachmaninov is masterly. The piano does not sound fresh, either in the *C sharp minor Étude-tableau* of Op. 33 or (not surprisingly) in the last of Op. 39, where one or two octaves sound 'tired', but it is all right elsewhere in the set. There is some magical playing in the *A minor* piece and some dazzling virtuosity elsewhere. The recordings are not top drawer and the disc gives no details of their provenance; but the sound is perfectly acceptable.

DEBUSSY: *Estampes; Préludes, Book I: Voiles; Le vent dans la plaine; Les collines d'Anacapri.* PROKOFIEV: *Visions fugitives, Op. 22, Nos. 3, 6 & 9; Sonata No. 8 in B flat, Op. 84.* SCRIABIN: *Sonata No. 5 in F sharp, Op. 53.*
⊛ (M) *** DG 423 573-2 [id.].

The Debussy *Préludes* and the Prokofiev *Sonata* were recorded at concerts during an Italian tour in 1962, while the remainder were made the previous year in Wembley Town Hall. The former sound more open than the rather confined studio acoustic – but what playing! The Scriabin is demonic and the Debussy could not be more atmospheric. The performance of the Prokofiev *Sonata* is, like the legendary Gilels account, a classic of the gramophone.

Rogé, Pascal (piano)

French music: SATIE: *3 Gymnopédies.* POULENC: *3 Novelettes.* DEBUSSY: *Suite bergamasque. Prélude: La fille aux cheveux de lin. Children's corner: Golliwog's cakewalk. L'isle joyeuse.* RAVEL: *Pavane pour une infante défunte; Gaspard de la nuit.*
(M) **(*) Decca 417 768-2 [id.].

A generous mid-priced sampler of Pascal Rogé's talents in French repertoire, to which he is highly suited. Both the Satie *Gymnopédies* and the Poulenc *Novelettes* come from records that have been praised highly by us, and the Debussy is very fine too. There are occasional moments, especially in the Ravel, when one feels the need for a greater sense of drama, but there is a keen intelligence and a sensitivity to atmosphere and colour here; and the Decca recording matches the finesse of the playing.

Rubinstein, Artur (piano)

'A French programme': RAVEL: *Valses nobles et sentimentales Nos. 1–8; La vallée des cloches. Le tombeau: Forlane.* POULENC: *Mouvements perpetuels (Assez modéré; Très*

modéré; Alerte); Intermezzo in A flat; Intermezzo No. 2 in D flat. FAURÉ: *Nocturne in A flat, Op. 33/3.* CHABRIER: *10 Pièces pittoresques: Scherzo-Valse.*
*** RCA RD 85665.

This recital dates from the mid-1960s. The playing is eminently aristocratic and the Ravel pieces and the Poulenc could hardly be bettered. The recording, like the rest of Rubinstein's analogue records, has been enhanced in its new format and is fully acceptable; admirers of this artist need have no qualms about investigating this disc.

Schiller, Allan (piano)

'Für Elise': Popular piano pieces: BEETHOVEN: *Für Elise.* FIELD: *Nocturne in E (Noontide).* CHOPIN: *Mazurka in B flat, Op. 7/1; Waltz in A, Op. 34/2. 3 Écossaises, Op. 72/3; Fantaisie-impromptu, Op. 66.* MENDELSSOHN: *Songs without words: Venetian gondola song, Op. 19; Bees' wedding, Op. 67.* LISZT: *Consolation No. 3 in D flat.* DE SEVERAC: *The music box.* DEBUSSY: *Suite bergamasque: Clair de lune. Arabesques Nos. 1 and 2. Prélude: The girl with the flaxen hair.* GRIEG: *Wedding day at Trodhaugen; March of the dwarfs.* ALBÉNIZ: *Granada; Tango; Asturias.*
(B) *** ASV CDQS 6032 [id.].

A particularly attractive recital, diverse in mood, spontaneous in feeling and very well recorded. The acoustic is resonant, but the effect is highly realistic. There are many favourites here, with Allan Schiller at his most personable in the engaging Field *Nocturne*, De Severac's piquant *Music box* and the closing *Asturias* of Albéniz, played with fine bravura. The Chopin group, too, is particularly successful, with the Scottish rhythmic snap of the *Écossaises* neatly articulated and the famous *B flat Mazurka* presented most persuasively.

Scott Whiteley, John (organ)

Organ of York Minster: *'Great Romantic organ music':* TOURNEMIRE: *Improvisation on the Te Deum.* JONGEN: *Minuet-Scherzo, Op. 53.* MULET: *Tu es Petra.* DUPRÉ: *Prelude and fugue in G min., Op. 3/7.* R. STRAUSS: *Wedding prelude.* KARG-ELERT: *Pastel in B, Op. 92/1.* BRAHMS: *Chorale prelude: O Gott, du frommer Gott, Op. 122/7.* LISZT: *Prelude and fugue on BACH, G.260.*
*** York CD 101.

A superb organ recital, with the huge dynamic range of the York Minster organ spectacularly captured on CD and pianissimo detail registering naturally. John Scott Whiteley's playing is full of flair: the attractively complex and sparklingly florid *Prelude and fugue* of Marcel Dupré is exhilarating and reaches a high climax, while the grand Liszt piece is hardly less overwhelming. The shorter lyrical pieces add serenity and proper contrast at the centre of a recital that is as well planned as it is played and recorded. The opening Tournemire *Improvisation* is very arresting indeed, while Jongen's *Minuet-Scherzo* displays Scott Whiteley's splendidly clear articulation.

Söllscher, Göran (guitar)

'Cavatina': MYERS: *Cavatina; Portrait.* ALBÉNIZ: *Granada.* TÁRREGA: *Maria; Rosita.* BARRIOS: *Villancico de Navidad.* YOCOH: *Sakura.* LLOBET: arr. of Catalan folksongs: *La filla del marxant; La cançó del lladre; El noi de la mare.* LAURO: *El Marabino.* CRESPO:

Norteña. PATIÑO: *Nevando está.* NEUMANN: *Karleksvals.* CARMICHAEL: *Georgia on my mind.* ANON.: *Romance d'amour.*
*** DG Dig. 413 720-2 [id.].

Göran Söllscher is at his finest here. The programme is essentially Romantic and very tuneful and atmospheric. The indelible opening Myers *Cavatina* is of course the justly famous *Deerhunter* theme, while even the anonymous *Romance* will be familiar. Whether in the attractive Llobet arrangements of Catalan folksongs, the two evocative portraits from Tárrega, or Yocoh's colourful *Sakura* (from Japan), this is the kind of music-making that remains in the memory, for even while the playing is relaxed there is no doubt about Söllscher's magnetism. Hoagy Carmichael's *Georgia on my mind* gives the feeling of a final lollipop as the stylish closing encore. The sound is most naturally balanced, and the immediacy and realism are apparent.

Stringer, Alan (trumpet), Noel Rawsthorne (organ)

Organ of Liverpool Cathedral: *'Trumpet and organ':* M.-A. CHARPENTIER: *Te Deum: Prelude.* STANLEY: *Voluntary No. 5 in D.* PURCELL: *Sonata in C. Two Trumpet tunes and Air.* BOYCE: *Voluntary in D.* CLARKE: *Trumpet voluntary.* BALDASSARE: *Sonata No. 1 in F.* ROMAN: *Keyboard suite in D: Non troppo allegro; Presto (Gigue).* FIOCCO: *Harpsichord suite No. 1: Andante.* BACH: *Cantata No. 147: Jesu, joy of man's desiring.* attrib. GREENE: *Introduction and trumpet tune.* VIVIANI: *Sonata No. 1 in C.*
**(*) CRD CRD 3308.

This collection is extremely well recorded. The reverberation of Liverpool Cathedral is under full control and both trumpet and organ are cleanly focused, while the trumpet has natural timbre and bloom. Alan Stringer is at his best in the classical pieces, the *Voluntary* of Boyce, the *Trumpet tunes* and *Sonata* of Purcell and the stylishly played *Sonata* of Viviani, a most attractive little work. He also gives a suitably robust performance of the famous *Trumpet voluntary.* Elsewhere he is sometimes a little square: the Bach chorale is rather too stiff and direct. But admirers of this repertoire will find much to enjoy, and the *Andante* of Fiocco has something in common with the more famous *Adagio* attributed to Albinoni in Giazotto's famous arrangement. The CD transfer improves definition satisfactorily.

Turovsky, Eleonora (violin), Yuli Turovsky (cello)

French music for violin and cello: RAVEL: *Sonata.* J. RIVIER: *Sonatine.* HONEGGER: *Sonatine.* MARTINŮ: *Duo.*
*** Chan. Dig. CHAN 8358 [id.].

The most substantial piece here is the Ravel *Sonata,* which opens magically and is beautifully played by these two artists. Jean Rivier's *Sonatine* is slight but charming, while the Honegger and Martinů works are more challenging. There is over an hour's music here, repertoire that one seldom encounters in the concert hall. A very well-recorded programme, designed rather for the connoisseur of French music than for the wider record-collecting public, but well worth investigating.

Vaidman, Vera (violin), Emanuel Krasovsky (piano)

'Romantic strings': TCHAIKOVSKY: *Méditation; Mélodie, Op. 42/1 & 2; Valse-Scherzo, Op. 34.* DVOŘÁK: *Violin sonatina in G.* SCHUBERT: *Violin sonatina in A min., D.835.* KREISLER: *Schön Rosmarin; Liebeslied; Liebesfreud.*
(B) *** Pickwick/CDI PWK 1137.

Misguidedly mistitled, this collection is a recital of the highest calibre. Though the three memorable Tchaikovsky pieces are played superbly, the highlight is the wonderfully spontaneous account of the Dvořák *Sonatina*, written during the composer's American period and with a melodic inspiration to match the *New World symphony*. It is played here with all the freshness of new discovery. The charm of the Schubert work is equally well caught, and the three Kreisler lollipops make splendid bonnes-bouches at the end. This is an outstanding partnership in every way, and the recording is absolutely real and natural.

Wild, Earl (piano)

'Showpieces for piano': HERZ: *Variations on 'Non più mesta from Rossini's La Cenerentola'.* THALBERG: *Don Pasquale fantasy, Op. 67.* GODOWSKY: *Symphonic metamorphosis on themes from Johann Strauss's Kunsterleben (Artist's life).* LISZT: *Réminiscences de Don Juan. Réminiscences de Robert le Diable.*
(B) *** Van. VNC 7704 (from VCD 72010).

Earl Wild's famous performances from the late 1960s re-emerge on CD with their scintillating brilliance given even greater projection by the digital remastering. The piano sound is slightly dry but not lacking in depth of sonority, especially in the two Liszt operatic paraphrases, which are splendidly authoritative here. Wild's technique is prodigious and his glittering bravura in the engaging Herz *Rossini variations* and Thalberg's equally entertaining *Don Pasquale fantasy* is among the finest modern examples of the grand tradition of virtuoso pianism. Godowsky's piece may have a heavy title, but in Earl Wild's hands, for all the decorative complexities, the lilting waltz-rhythms are still paramount.

Vocal Recitals

Ambrosian Singers, RPO, Elmer Bernstein

'Musical spectacular' (Songs and production numbers from MGM Musicals, with Nick Curtis and Mary Carewe): Excerpts from: *Kismet; Band Wagon; Meet me in St Louis; Gigi; Singin' in the rain; The Pirate; Brigadoon; Ziegfeld Follies.*
*** Chan. Dig. CHAN 8781 [id.].

An indispensable wallow for MGM film-buffs, given Chandos's most spectacular recording, sumptuous yet brilliant in the most exciting way without being too fierce. If Judy Garland's voice seems inseparable from *The Trolley song*, Mary Carewe provides a pretty impressive cover version here, showing plenty of spirit and warm vocal colour in her own right; Nick Curtis makes an equally personable stand-in for Gene Kelly in *Singin' in the rain.* They have the right voices and peppy style for this repertoire, and the Ambrosian Singers follow them across the Atlantic with a convincing twang to their diction. Elmer Bernstein conducts with great zest and, in the *Gigi* sequence, a voluptuous feeling for the lyrical tunes. Of its kind, this is hard to beat.

Ameling, Elly (soprano)

'Soirée française' (with Rudolf Jansen, piano): DEBUSSY: *Beau soir.* FAURÉ: *Mandoline.* GOUNOD: *Chanson de printemps.* POULENC: *Métamorphoses: C'est ainsi que tu es.* CANTELOUBE: *Chants d'Auvergne: Baïlèro; Oi Aä.* ROUSSEL: *Réponse d'un épouse sage.* MESSIAEN: *La fiancée perdue.* CHAUSSON: *Le temps des lilas.* CAPLET: *Le corbeau et le renard.* HONEGGER: *Trois chansons de la Petite Sirène.* FRANCK: *Nocturne.* BIZET: *Chanson d'Avril.* DUPARC: *Romance de Mignon.* SATIE: *Ludions.*
*** Ph. Dig. 412 628-2 [id.].

Elly Ameling's collection of French mélodies is a charming selection, linking well-known songs by Debussy and Fauré to much rarer, just as delightful items, all performed in the consistently pure style which makes this artist a timeless singer. The sweet songs are nicely contrasted with the lighter, more pointed items by Bizet, Gounod, Roussel and Satie, while it is fascinating to have Duparc's setting of *Mignon's song*, originally withdrawn by the composer. Well-balanced recording.

Angeles, Victoria de los (soprano)

'On wings of song': MENDELSSOHN: *Auf Flügeln des Gesanges.* GRIEG: *Ich liebe dich.* BRAHMS: *Wiegenlied.* DVORÁK: *Als die alte Mutter (Songs my mother taught me).* MARTINI: *Plaisir d'amour.* HAHN: *L'enamourée.* DELIBES: *Les filles de Cadiz.* MONTSALVATGE: *5 Canҫiones negras.* SADERO: *Irish lullaby.* YRADIER: *Era la vo.* OVALLE: *La paloma.* LUNA: *Azulao.* CHAPI: *De españa vengo.* RODRIGO: *Carceleras; Madrigales amatorios: Econ qué la lavaré?; Vos me metasteis; De donde vénis, amores?; De los alamos vengo, madre.*
(M) *** EMI CDM7 69502-2 [id.].

Opening with a glorious performance of Mendelssohn's *On wings of song*, followed by a delightfully lyrical *Ich liebe dich*, both of which immediately take wing, Victoria de los Angeles goes on to cover a wide range of repertoire, not all of which suits her quite so well: *Les filles de Cadiz*, for instance, needs a frothier approach than she manages. But later in the recital there are some delicious moments, especially in the Spanish repertoire in which she is so naturally idiomatic. The good things here easily outweigh the lesser and everything is sung with ravishing tone and fine musicianship, the voice vividly projected by the CD remastering.

Angeles, Victoria de los, Elisabeth Schwarzkopf (sopranos), Dietrich Fischer-Dieskau (baritone), Gerald Moore (piano)

'Gerald Moore: A tribute': MOZART: *Più non si trovano.* SCHUBERT: *Nachtviolen; Schwanengesang; Abschied; Im Abendroth; An die Musik.* ROSSINI: *Cats' duet; Serate musicale: La Regata Veneziana; La Pesca.* BRAHMS: *Der Gang zum Liebchen; Vergebliches Ständchen.* SCHUMANN: *Tanzlied; Er und Sie.* WOLF: *Sonne der Schlummerlosen; Das verlassene Mägdlein; Der Zigeunerin; Kennst du das Land.* MENDELSSOHN: *Ich wollt' meine Lieb'; Gruss; Lied aus Ruy Blas; Abendlied; Wasserfahrt.* HAYDN: *An den Vetter; Daphnens einziger Fehler.*
*** EMI CDC7 49238-2.

This masterly collection, at once superbly stylish yet sparkling and at times comic too, comes from the live concert which these artists gave at the Festival Hall on Moore's retirement. The full recital set of two discs is long deleted, but this selection has most of the finest and most delectable items, including Schwarzkopf's unforgettable account of Wolf's greatest song, *Kennst du das Land.* The recital is perhaps most famous for the performance of the *Duetto buffo di due gatti*, attributed to Rossini. The recording, slightly distanced, sounds very real in its digitally remastered CD format, and it is good that a speech by Gerald Moore is included before the recital ends with *An die Musik.*

Atlanta Chorus and Symphony Orchestra, Robert Shaw

'The many moods of Christmas' (arr. R. Russell Bennett): *Good Christian men, rejoice; Patapan; O come all ye faithful; O Sanctissima; Away in a manger; Fum fum fum; March of the Kings; What Child is this?; Bring a torch, Jeanette, Isabella; Angels we have heard on high; The first nowell; I saw three ships; Deck the halls.* GRUBER: *Silent night.* MENDELSSOHN: *Hark! the herald angels sing.* BACH: *Break forth, O beauteous heav'nly light.* REDNER-BROOKS: *O little town of Bethlehem.*
*** Telarc CD 80087 [id.].

The carols here are arranged into four groups, each lasting about 12 minutes, and the scoring and use of both chorus and orchestra is as flamboyantly imaginative as one would expect from a musician of the calibre of Robert Russell Bennett. Moreover the dynamic range of the recording is dramatically wide and the expansion of sound for the climaxes of *O come all ye faithful* and *Hark the herald angels sing*, with thrillingly realistic brass, is almost overwhelming. The chorus is backwardly balanced and with some choral pianissimos the words are barely audible, but the musical effect remains impressive. Technically, this is vintage Telarc, with the hall's ambience seen as of primary importance in its warm colouring of the rich-hued sounds from voices and instrumentalists alike. Highly recommended on all counts.

Augér, Arleen (soprano)

'Love songs' (with Dalton Baldwin, piano): COPLAND: *Pastorale; Heart, we will forget him.* OBRADORS: *Del Cabello más sutil.* OVALLE: *Azulao.* R.STRAUSS: *Ständchen; Das Rosenband.* MARX: *Selige Nacht.* POULENC: *Fleurs.* CIMARA: *Stornello.* QUILTER: *Music, when soft voices die; Love's philosophy.* O.STRAUS: *Je t'aime.* SCHUMANN: *Widmung; Du bist wie eine Blume.* MAHLER: *Liebst du um Schönheit.* TURINA: *Cantares.* LIPPE: *How do I love thee?* COWARD: *Conversation Piece: I'll follow my secret heart.* GOUNOD: *Serenade.* SCHUBERT: *Liebe schwärmt auf allen Wegen.* BRIDGE: *Love went a-riding.* FOSTER: *Why, no one to love.* DONAUDY: *O del mio amato ben.* BRITTEN (arr.): *The Salley Gardens.* LOEWE: *Camelot: Before I gaze at you again.*
⊛ *** Delos Dig. D/CD 3029 [id.].

This extraordinarily wide-ranging recital is a delight from the first song to the last. Arleen Augér opens with Copland and closes with *Camelot*, and she is equally at home in the music by Roger Quilter (*Love's philosophy* is superbly done), Noël Coward and the *Rückert* song of Mahler. Britten's arrangement of *The Salley Gardens*, ravishingly slow, is another highlight. The layout of the recital could hardly have been managed better: each song creates its new atmosphere readily, but seems to be enhanced by coming after the previous choice. Dalton Baldwin's accompaniments are very much a partnership with the singing, while the playing itself is spontaneously perceptive throughout. With a good balance and a very realistic recording, this projects vividly like a live recital.

'Ave Maria'

'Ave Maria': Sacred arias (sung by Leontyne Price, Sutherland, Pavarotti, Horne, Te Kanawa): SCHUBERT: *Ave Maria.* MOZART: *Exsultate jubilate.* GOUNOD: *O divine redeemer.* Arias from: HANDEL: *Samson; Messiah.* VERDI: *Requiem.* BERLIOZ: *Requiem.* BRAHMS: *German requiem.* ROSSINI: *Stabat Mater.* BACH: *Christmas oratorio.*
(M) *** Decca 425 016-2 [id.].

Decca are very good at creating anthologies of this kind and this 70-minute collection, superbly sung and splendidly recorded, makes a most enjoyable recital, with plenty of contrast between items. The programme is framed by Leontyne Price in rich voice in Schubert and admirably flexible in Mozartian coloratura; while Joan Sutherland's *Let the bright seraphim* also shows her in outstanding form. Pavarotti's golden tones bring distinction to the *Ingemisco* and *Sanctus* from the *Requiems* of Verdi and Berlioz respectively; and he is equally impressive in the livelier *Cujus animam* from Rossini's *Stabat Mater.* Kiri Te Kanawa contributes a memorable *I know that my Redeemer liveth*, taken from Solti's complete *Messiah*, and is in ravishing voice in Brahms's *Ihr habt nur Traurigkeit.*

Bach Choir, Sir David Willcocks

'Family carols' (with Philip Jones Brass Ens.): *O come, all ye faithful; Gabriel's message; Angelus and Virginem; Ding dong merrily on high; A virgin most pure; God rest ye merry gentlemen; In dulci jubilo; Unto us a son is born; Once in Royal David's city; Hush, my dear, lie still and slumber.* WILLCOCKS: *Fanfare.* RUTTER: *Shepherd's pipe carol; Star carol.* KIRKPATRICK: *Away in a manger.* GRUBER: *Stille Nacht.* Arr. VAUGHAN WILLIAMS: *Sussex carol.* MENDELSSOHN: *Hark! the herald angels sing.*

(M) *** Decca Dig. 417 898-2.

An admirably chosen and beautifully recorded collection of traditional carols. Fresh simplicity is the keynote here; the brass fanfares bring a touch of splendour but the music is not over-scored. *Silent night* has seldom sounded more serene, and Rutter's infectiously rhythmic *Shepherd's pipe carol* makes a refreshing contrast. The digital sound is in no way clinical; indeed the resonance is perfectly judged.

Battle, Kathleen (soprano)

'Salzburg recital' (with James Levine, piano): PURCELL: *Come all ye songsters; Music for a while; Sweeter than roses.* HANDEL: *O had I Jubal's lyre.* MENDELSSOHN: *Bei der Wiege; Neue Liebe.* R. STRAUSS: *Schlagende Herzen; Ich wollt'ein Sträusslein binden; Säusle, liebe Myrte.* MOZART: *Ridente la calma; Das Veilchen; Un moto di gioia.* FAURÉ: *Mandoline; Les roses d'Ispahan; En prière; Notre amour.* Spirituals: *Honour, honour; His name so sweet; Witness; He's got the whole world in his hands.*
*** DG Dig. 415 361-2 [id.].

Kathleen Battle is at her most characterful and provocative in this recital with Levine, recorded live in the Mozarteum in Salzburg as part of the 1984 Festival. Her singing of Susanna's little alternative aria from *Figaro, Un moto di gioia*, is a particular delight, and Levine – from Ohio, like Battle herself – proves a splendidly pointed and provocative accompanist. Helpfully atmospheric recording.

Berganza, Teresa (mezzo-soprano)

Venetian concert (with Yasunori Imamura, lute, theorbo, chitarra; Joerg Ewald, harpsichord or organ; and continuo): STROZZI: *Non ti doler mio cor; Rissolvetevi pensieri.* SANCES: *Misera, hor si ch'il pianto; O perduti diletti.* MONTEVERDI: *Confitebor tibi Domine.* MILANUZZI: *Ut re mi.* FONTEI: *Auree stelle.* MINISCALCHI: *Fuggir pur mi convien; Fuggir voglio.* LAMORETTI: *Bell'il vana tua beltade.* (Instrumental): MOLINARO: *Fantasia nono.* PALESTRINA: *Vestiva i colli.* RORE: *Anchor che col partire.*
*** Claves CD 8206 [id.].

Teresa Berganza is the star of this attractive concert of Venetian music, with little of the included repertoire at all familiar. The vocal contributions are characteristically intelligent and stylish – but expressively telling, too. The instrumental numbers provide suitable contrast and are very well done; the recording has fine presence. The collection is well documented.

Operatic arias (with ROHCG O or LSO, Gibson) from: GLUCK: *Orfeo ed Euridice; Alceste; Elena e Paride.* PERGOLESI: *La serva padrona.* CHERUBINI: *Medea.* PAISIELLO: *Nina pazza per amore.* ROSSINI: *Il Barbiere di Siviglia; L'Italiana in Algeri; Semiramide; La Cenerentola; Stabat Mater.*
(M) *** Decca 421 327-2 [id.].

This wide selection from Berganza's repertory comes mainly from recordings of the 1960s, when the voice was at its most beautiful, although the *Cenerentola* excerpt is from 1959. The musical intensity combines formidably with an amazing technique (shown throughout the Rossini excerpts), and only occasionally in the classical arias does one sense a lack of warmth. First-rate recording, vividly transferred.

Bergonzi, Carlo (tenor)

Operatic arias from: VERDI: *Aida; Luisa Miller; La forza del destino; Il Trovatore; Un ballo in maschera; Don Carlo.* MEYERBEER: *L'Africaine.* GIORDANO: *Andrea Chénier.* CILEA: *Adriana Lecouvreur.* PUCCINI: *Tosca; Manon Lescaut; La Bohème.*
(M) *** Decca 421 318-2 [id.].

This recital of his early stereo recordings shows Bergonzi on peak form. He does not attempt the rare pianissimo at the end of *Celeste Aida*; but here among Italian tenors is a thinking musical artist who never resorts to vulgarity. The recording (of whatever vintage) has transferred well and retains the bloom on the voice. This is essentially a programme of favourites, but everything sounds fresh.

Berlin German Opera Chorus and Orchestra, Sinopoli

Opera choruses: MOZART: *Die Zauberflöte.* BEETHOVEN: *Fidelio.* WEBER: *Der Freischütz.* WAGNER: *Tannhäuser.* VERDI: *Nabucco; I Lombardi; Macbeth; Il Trovatore; Aida.*
*** DG Dig. 415 283-2 [id.].

A splendid collection of choruses, full of character, the atmosphere of each opera distinctive. The pianissimo at the beginning of the famous *Fidelio Prisoners' chorus* has striking intensity, while the exuberant *Hunting chorus* from *Freischütz* is irresistible in its buoyancy. On the other hand, Sinopoli's broadening of the sustained tune in the short *Aida* excerpt may for some seem too deliberate. Needless to say, the orchestral playing is first class; the balance, with the orchestra placed vividly forward and the chorus set back within a warmly resonant acoustic, is most convincing, although words are not always sharply clear.

Bjoerling, Jussi (tenor)

Operatic recital: Arias from: PONCHIELLI: *La Gioconda.* PUCCINI: *La Fanciulla del West; Manon Lescaut.* GIORDANO: *Fedora.* CILEA: *L'Arlesiana.* VERDI: *Un Ballo in maschera; Requiem.* MASCAGNI: *Cavalleria Rusticana* (with Tebaldi). LEHÁR: *Das Land des Lächelns.*
(M) *** Decca 421 316-2 [id.].

John Culshaw's autobiography revealed what an unhappy man Jussi Bjoerling was at the very end of his career, when all these recordings were made by Decca engineers for RCA. You would hardly guess that there were problems from the flow of headily beautiful, finely focused tenor tone. These may not be the most characterful renderings of each aria, but they are all among the most compellingly musical. The recordings are excellent for their period (1959–60). The Lehár was the last solo recording he made before he died in 1960. The transfers to CD are admirably lively and present.

Bowman, James (alto), King's Consort, Robert King

VIVALDI: *Salve regina in C min., RV 616.* TELEMANN: *Weg mit Sodoms gift'gen Fruchter.* PERGOLESI: *Salve regina in F min.* BACH: *Cantata No. 54; Widerstehe doch der Sunde.*
*** Mer. Dig. CDE 84138.

James Bowman's collection of four varied items suited to the counter-tenor voice makes for an unusual and attractive mixture, beautifully performed by singer and instrumentalists alike. Maybe beauty is brought out too much in the Bach *Cantata* with its severe text, but the singer's artistry is consistent throughout, helped by full, well-balanced recording.

Callas, Maria (soprano)

Operatic recital: Arias from: CILEA: *Adriana Lecouvreur.* GIORDANO: *Andrea Chénier.* CATALANI: *La Wally.* BOITO: *Mefistofele.* ROSSINI: *Il barbiere di Siviglia.* MEYERBEER: *Dinorah.* DELIBES: *Lakmé.* VERDI: *I vespri siciliani.* CHERUBINI: *Medea.* SPONTINI: *La vestale.*
⊛ (***) EMI mono CDC7 47282-2 [id.].

This fine recital disc is a conflation of two of Callas's most successful earlier LPs. The *Medea* and *Vestale* items were originally coupled with extracts from complete opera sets and might otherwise have been left in limbo. These are recordings from the 1950s, when the voice was still in fine condition and the artistry at its most magnetic. Callas's portrait of Rosina in *Una voce* was never more sparklingly viperish than here, and she never surpassed the heartfelt intensity of such numbers as *La mamma morta* and *Poveri fiori.* Some items may reveal strain – the *Bell song* from *Lakmé*, for example – but this has many claims to be the finest single Callas recital on CD, very well transferred.

'Mad scenes and Bel canto arias' (with Philh. O, Rescigno) from: DONIZETTI: *Anna Bolena; La figlia del reggimento; Lucrezia Borgia; L'Elisir d'amore.* THOMAS: *Hamlet.* BELLINI: *Il Pirata.*
*** EMI CDC7 47283-2 [id.].

If, as ever, the rawness of exposed top-notes mars the sheer beauty of Callas's singing, few recital records ever made can match, let alone outshine, her collection of mad scenes in vocal and dramatic imagination. This is Callas at her very peak; Desmond Shawe-Taylor suggested this as the collection which, more than any other, summed up the essence of Callas's genius. For the CD reissue further arias have been added, notably excerpts from Donizetti's *La figlia del reggimento, L'Elisir d'amore* and *Lucrezia Borgia* (from the mid-1960s), a fair example of the latterday Callas, never very sweet-toned, yet displaying the usual Callas fire. Nevertheless, the main part of the recital is indispensable; the digital remastering has enhanced the originally excellent recordings and given the voice striking presence.

'Callas à Paris' (with French Nat. R. O, Prêtre): Arias from: GLUCK: *Orphée et Eurydice; Alceste.* BIZET: *Carmen.* SAINT-SAENS: *Samson et Dalila.* MASSENET: *Manon; Le Cid.* GOUNOD: *Roméo et Juliette.* THOMAS: *Mignon.* CHARPENTIER: *Louise.*
*** EMI CDC7 49059-2.

The original LP collection, *'Callas à Paris'*, dating from 1961 with the singer at her most commanding and characterful, is here augmented with five items from the sequel disc of two years later, when the voice was in decline. The vocal contrast is clear enough, and the need at the time to patch and re-patch the takes in the later sessions makes the results sound less spontaneous and natural. But the earlier portraits of Carmen, Alceste, Dalila and Juliette find Callas still supreme. Her mastery of the French repertory provides a fascinating slant on her artistry.

'The unknown recordings': WAGNER: *Tristan: Liebestod*. Arias from: VERDI: *Don Carlos; I Lombardi; I vespri siciliani; Attila*. BELLINI: *Il Pirata*. ROSSINI: *La Cenerentola; Guglielmo Tell; Semiramide*.
*** EMI CDC7 49428-2 [id.].

The collection brings together unpublished material from several sources, mainly alternative recordings of arias which appeared earlier in other versions, but also live recordings made in Athens and Amsterdam. The alternative readings all bring fresh illumination of a supreme artist who was both deeply thoughtful and spontaneous in that she never merely repeated herself. These items of early Verdi, Rossini and Bellini are all most cherishable, but just as fascinating is her very early Athens account of Isolde's *Liebestod* in Italian and her 1959 Holland Festival performances of passages from Bellini's *Il Pirata* and Verdi's *Don Carlos*. Variable recording, helped by skilled and refined EMI transfers.

Arias from: ROSSINI: *Il barbiere di Siviglia*. VERDI: *Macbeth; Don Carlos*. PUCCINI: *Tosca*. GLUCK: *Alceste*. BIZET: *Carmen* (with Nicolai Gedda). SAINT-SAENS: *Samson et Dalila*. MASSENET: *Manon*. CHARPENTIER: *Louise*.
(M) *** EMI CD-EMX 2123.

This compilation on the EMI Eminence label brings together at budget price some of Callas's most cherishable performances, mostly taken from recital material. An excellent sampler, well recorded and satisfactorily transferred on to a mid-priced CD.

'The incomparable Callas' (Arias from): BELLINI: *Norma*. DONIZETTI: *Lucia*. VERDI: *Ernani; Aida*. PONCHIELLI: *La Gioconda*. PUCCINI: *Tosca*. GLUCK: *Orphée et Eurydice*. GLUCK: *Roméo et Juliette*. THOMAS: *Mignon*. MASSENET: *Le Cid*. BIZET: *Carmen*. SAINT-SAENS: *Samson et Dalila*.
(M) *** EMI CDM7 63182-2 [id.].

One might quibble whether the title 'The incomparable Callas' is apt when applied to these particular items, mostly taken from complete operas and recitals recorded in the 1960s. Her later sets of *Lucia* and *Norma* are both well represented here, but even finer is the *Suicidio!* from her second version of Ponchielli's *La Gioconda*, among her finest achievements. The *Carmen* items taken from the complete set are more questionable in their fierceness but are totally individual – as indeed, flawed or not, is the last-recorded item here, Aida's *Ritorna vincitor*, made in 1972. The transfers capture the voice well. This recital is now available at mid-price.

Arias from ROSSINI: *Semiramide; Il Barbiere di Siviglia*. CHERUBINI: *Medea*. BELLINI: *Norma*. DONIZETTI: *Lucia di Lammermoor*. VERDI: *La Traviata*. MOZART: *Il Seraglio*.
(BB) (*(*)) LaserLight 15 096 [id.].

These LaserLight CDs appear to derive from recordings taken from radio broadcasts that were made live from the operatic stage. Although *Bel raggio lusinghier* from *Semiramide* (1956) is impressive, the highlight here is Callas's 1958 performance of Rossini's *Une voce poco fa* at the Paris Opéra: her creamy coloratura will be a revelation for those who know only her later recordings; she adds the most engaging decoration towards the end. There is also a 1955 *Casta diva* and a powerful *Dei tuoi figli la madre* from *Medea*, conducted by Bernstein two years earlier. Unfortunately the excerpts from *Lucia di Lammermoor* and *La Traviata* are spoilt by poorly focused sound; but there is a fascinating coda in a wild but exciting performance, in Italian, of Constanze's Act II aria from Mozart's *Il Seraglio*.

Volume 1: Arias from: VERDI: *Macbeth; Ernani; Don Carlo; Un ballo in maschera.* DONIZETTI: *Poliuto; Anna Bolena.* CHERUBINI: *Medea.*
(BB) (*(*)) LaserLight 15 223 [id.].

Vieni t'affretta from *Macbeth* (1959) opens with a rare moment of spoken dialogue; although the following *Ah! non credea mirarti . . . Ah! non giunge* (from a 1957 La Scala performance of *La Sonnambula*) is impressive, especially the introduction, and a similar comment might be made about the 1962 *Surta lè la notte . . . Ernani, Ernani,* the highlight here is the fine 1963 *Tu che le vanità* from *Don Carlo*, impressively accompanied by Prêtre and the French National Radio Orchestra, though they are recorded very shrilly. A rare *Di quai soavi lagrime* from Donizetti's *Poliuto* (1960) is also worth having, though the excerpts from *Un ballo, Anna Bolena* and *Medea* are more variable.

Cambridge Singers, John Rutter

'Portrait': BYRD: *Sing joyfully; Non vos relinquam.* FAURÉ: *Cantique de Jean Racine; Requiem: Sanctus.* RUTTER: *O be joyful in the Lord; All things bright and beautiful; Shepherd's pipe carol; Open thou mine eyes; Requiem: Out of the deep.* PURCELL: *Hear my prayer, O Lord.* STANFORD: *Beati quorum via; The Bluebird.* TRAD.: *This joyful Eastertide; In dulci jubilo.* HANDEL: *Messiah: For unto us a child is born.* FARMER: *A pretty bonny lass.* MORLEY: *Now is the month of maying.* DELIUS: *To be sung of a summer night on the water.* VICTORIA: *O magnum mysterium.* TERRY: *Myn lyking.*
(M) *** Coll. Dig./Analogue CSCD 500 [id.].

This splendid mid-priced sampler makes a wonderfully rewarding concert in its own right; but we hope it will also tempt readers to explore the other collections in Rutter's imaginatively planned series, listed below. He has arranged the items here with great skill so that serene music always makes a contrast with the many exuberant expressions of joy, his own engaging hymn-settings among them. Thus the bright-eyed hey-nonny songs of John Farmer and Thomas Morley are aptly followed by the lovely wordless *To be sung of a summer night on the water* of Delius, and Stanford's beautiful evocation of *The Bluebird* (one of Rutter's own special favourites). The sound, vivid and atmospheric, suits the colour and mood of the music quite admirably. Not to be missed!

'There is sweet music' (English choral songs): STANFORD: *The blue bird.* DELIUS: *To be sung of a summer night on the water I & II.* ELGAR: *There is sweet music; My love dwelt in a Northern land.* VAUGHAN WILLIAMS: *3 Shakespearean songs: Full fathom five; The cloud-capp'd towers; Over hill, over dale.* BRITTEN: *5 Flower songs, Op. 47.* Folksongs: arr. MOERAN: *The sailor and young Nancy.* Arr. GRAINGER: *Brigg Fair: Londonderry air.* Arr. CHAPMAN: *Three ravens.* Arr. HOLST: *My sweetheart's like Venus.* Arr. BAIRSTOW: *The oak and the ash.* Arr. STANFORD: *Quick! We have but a second.*
⊛ *** Coll. Dig. COLCD 104 [id.].

Opening with an enchanting performance of Stanford's *The blue bird* and followed by equally expressive accounts of Delius's two wordless summer evocations, this most attractive recital ranges from Elgar and Vaughan Williams, both offering splendid performances, to various arrangements of folksongs, less fashionable today than they once were, but giving much pleasure here. The recording, made in the Great Hall of University College, London, has an almost ideal ambience: words are clear, yet the vocal timbre is full and natural. A highly recommendable anthology.

'*Flora gave me fairest flowers*' (English madrigals): MORLEY: *My bonny lass she smileth; Fyer, fyer! Now is the month of Maying*. EAST: *Quick, quick, away dispatch!* GIBBONS: *Dainty fine bird; Silver swan*. BYRD: *Though Amaryllis dance in green; This sweet and merry month of May; Lullaby*. WEELKES: *Hark, all ye lovely saints*. WILBYE: *Weep, weep, mine eyes; Flora gave me; Draw on sweet night; Adieu sweet Amaryllis*. TOMKINS: *Too much I once lamented; Adieu ye city-prisoning towers*. FARMER: *Little pretty bonny lass*. BENNETT: *Round about*. WEELKES: *Ha ha! this world doth pass; Death hath deprived me*. RAMSEY: *Sleep, fleshly birth*.
*** Coll. Dig. COLCD 105 [id.].

John Rutter's Cambridge Singers bring consistent unanimity of ensemble and a natural expressive feeling to this very attractive programme of madrigals. Perhaps the first group, devoted to love and marriage, may be thought rather consistently mellifluous; but the second, '*Madrigals of times and season*', is nicely contrasted, with the clean articulation of Morley's *Now is the month of Maying* made the more telling by the lightness of the vocal production. John Wilbye's lovely *Draw on sweet night*, which follows, makes a perfect contrast. After two items about '*Fairies, spirits and conceits*', the concert closes in a mood of moving Elizabethan melancholy with a group devoted to mourning and farewell. Superb recording in a most flattering acoustic makes this collection the more enjoyable, though one to be dipped into rather than heard all at once.

'*Faire is the Heaven*' (Music of the English Church): PARSONS: *Ave Maria*. TALLIS: *Loquebantur variis linguis; If ye love me*. BYRD: *Misere mei; Haec dies; Ave verum corpus; Bow thine ear*. FARRANT: *Hide not thou thy face; Lord, not thou thy face; Lord for thy tender mercy's sake*. GIBBONS: *O clap your hands; Hosanna to the Son of David*. PURCELL: *Lord, how long wilt thou be angry; Thou knowest, Lord; Hear my prayer, O Lord*. STANFORD: *Beati quorum via*. Arr. WOOD: *This joyful Eastertide*. HOWELLS: *Sing lullaby; A spotless rose*. WALTON: *What cheer?* VAUGHAN WILLIAMS: *O taste and see*. BRITTEN: *Hymn to the Virgin*. POSTON: *Jesus Christ the apple tree*. HARRIS: *Faire is the Heaven*.
*** Coll. COLCD 107 [id.].

These recordings were made in the Lady Chapel of Ely Cathedral, and the ambience adds beauty to the sound without in any way impairing clarity of focus. The music ranges from examples of the Roman Catholic Rite as set by Tallis, Byrd and Robert Parsons (with a touch of almost Latin eloquence in the presentation), through widely varied Reformation music, to the Restoration, represented by three Purcell anthems, and on to the Anglican revival and the twentieth century. The Reformation group is particularly successful, with the opening Tallis and closing Gibbons works rich in polyphony and Byrd's *Bow thine ear* wonderfully serene. Of the modern items, the Howells pieces are quite lovely and Walton's *What cheer?*, with its engaging imitation, is attractively genial. The Britten and Poston items, both well known, are hardly less engaging; and the concert ends with the ambitious title-number, William Harris's *Faire is the Heaven*, sung with great feeling and considerable power. There is no more successful survey of English church music in the current catalogue and certainly not one presented with more conviction.

Carreras, José (tenor)

Neapolitan songs (with ECO, Muller): DENZA: *Funiculi, funicula; I'te vurria vasà*. CARDILLO: *Core 'ngrato*. D'ANNIBALE: *'O paese d'o sole*. FALVO: *Dicitencello vuie*.

LAMA: *Silenzio cantatore.* MARIO: *Santa Lucia luntana.* DI CURTIS: *Tu, ca nun chiagne!*
Torna a Surriento. DI CAPUA: *'O sole mio.* BOVIO/TAGLIAFERRI: *Passione.* CIOFFI: *'Na
sera 'e maggio.* CANNIO: *'O surdato 'nnamurato.*
**(*) Ph. Dig. 400 015-2 [id.].

José Carreras produces refined tone here. The performances have plenty of lyrical
fervour and are entirely lacking in vulgarity. The opening *Funiculi, funicula* is attractively
lilting, but elsewhere some listeners will wish for a more gutsy style. The recording is first
class. The compact disc combines naturalness with added presence, yet the sound remains
warmly atmospheric.

Spanish songs (with Martin Katz, piano): FALLA: *7 Spanish popular songs.* MOMPOU:
Combat del somni. GINASTERA: *Canción al arbol del olivido.* GUASTAVINO: *La rosa y el
sauce; Se equivicó la paloma.* OBRADORS: *Corazón, porqué pasáis; Del cabelle mas sutil.*
TURINA: *Poema en forma de cançiones, Op. 19.*
*** Ph. Dig. 411 478-2 [id.].

José Carreras's collection of Spanish songs provides an attractive slant on repertory
both rare and well known. It is interesting to have the Falla *Spanish popular songs* sung by
a male voice, predictably with new insights; and there is much lively and imaginative
singing in the rest too, with the voice recorded in close-up.

Arias from: PUCCINI: *Manon Lescaut; Turandot.* LEONCAVALLO: *Zaza; I Pagliacci; La
Bohème; I Zingara.* GIORDANO: *Andrea Chénier.* PONCHIELLI: *La Gioconda; Il Fioliuol
Prodigo.* MASCAGNI: *L'amico Fritz.* GOMES: *Fosca.* CILEA: *L'Arlesiana.* MERCADANTE:
Il Giuramento. BELLINI: *Adelson e Salvini.*
(M) **(*) Ph. 426 643-2 [id.].

Including some attractive rarities, this is an impressive recital. Carreras is never less
than a conscientious artist, and though one or two items stretch the lovely voice to its
limits, there is none of the coarseness that most tenors of the Italian school would indulge
in. Excellent sound and vivid transfers.

Caruso, Enrico (tenor)

'Opera arias and songs': Arias from: VERDI: *Rigoletto; Aida.* MASSENET: *Manon.*
DONIZETTI: *L'Elisir d'amore.* BOITO: *Mefistofele.* PUCCINI: *Tosca.* MASCAGNI: *Iris;
Cavalleria Rusticana.* GIORDANO: *Fedora.* PONCHIELLI: *La Gioconda.* LEONCAVALLO: *I
Pagliacci.* CILEA: *Adriana Lecouvreur.* BIZET: *Les pêcheurs de perles.* MEYERBEER: *Les
Huguenots.* Songs.
(M) (***) EMI mono CDH7 61046-2 [id.].

The EMI collection on the Références label brings together Caruso's earliest recordings,
made in 1902 and 1904 in Milan with misty piano accompaniment. The very first were
done impromptu in Caruso's hotel, and the roughness of presentation reflects that; but
the voice is glorious in its youth, amazingly well caught for that period. It was the sound
of these very recordings which, more than anything else, first convinced a wide public
that the gramophone was more than a toy.

'21 Favourite arias': from LEONCAVALLO: *I Pagliacci.* PUCCINI: *Tosca; La Bohème.*
VERDI: *Rigoletto; Aida; La Forza del destino; Otello; Il Trovatore.* MEYERBEER:
L'Africana. HALÉVY: *La Juive.* GIORDANO: *Andrea Chénier.* DONIZETTI: *La Favorita;*

L'Elisir d'amore. BIZET: *Les Pêcheurs de perles; Carmen.* PONCHIELLI: *La Gioconda.* GOUNOD: *Faust.* FLOTOW: *Martha.* HANDEL: *Serse.*
(***) RCA RD 85911 [RCA 5911-2-RC].

Taken from RCA's earlier Caruso reissue series using the digital Soundstream system (which sought to eliminate the unnatural resonances of the acoustic recording horn, well before the age of general digital recording), these transfers are often surprisingly real and convincing. The selection, unlike EMI's Références disc of Caruso, ranges widely over the great tenor's career, with some fine examples of his work in the French repertory as well as in popular Italian items. An outstanding disc, with the voice remarkably fresh; few technical apologies need to be made here.

'Prima voce': Arias from: DONIZETTI: *L'Elisir d'amore; Don Sebastiano; Il duca d'Alba.* GOLDMARK: *La regina di Saba.* GOMEZ: *Lo schiavo.* HALÉVY: *La juive.* LEONCAVALLO: *Pagliacci.* MASSENET: *Manon.* MEYERBEER: *L'Africana.* PUCCINI: *Tosca; Manon Lescaut.* VERDI: *Aida; Un ballo in maschera; La forza del destino; Rigoletto; Il Trovatore.*
(M) (***) Nimbus mono NI 7803 [id.].

The Nimbus method of transfer to CD, reproducing ancient 78s on a big acoustic horn gramophone of the 1930s, tends to work best with acoustic recordings, when the accompaniments then emerge as more consistent with the voice. There is an inevitable loss of part of the recording range at both ends of the spectrum, but the ear can often be convinced. This Caruso collection, very well chosen to show the development of his voice, ranges from early (1904) recordings of Massenet, Puccini and Donizetti with piano accompaniment to the recording that the great tenor made in 1920, not long before he died, of his very last role, as Eleazar in Halévy's *La juive*, wonderfully characterized.

'Caruso in Song': Popular songs & ballads; Neapolitan songs. Arias by HANDEL and ROSSINI.
(M) (***) Nimbus mono NI 7809 [id.].

Caruso knew all about 'crossover' records generations before the term was invented. As the supreme Italian tenor of his time, perhaps of all time, he had the popular touch. A whole collection of drawing-room ballads – *For you alone* in English, *Because* in French – as well as Neapolitan songs like *Santa Lucia* and *O sole mio*, are sung here with transparent, heartfelt sincerity, and the voice even on these pre-electric recordings seems to ring out with extra amplification, not least in the riotous account of the American wartime song, *Over there* – one verse English, one verse French. But why did he wait till June 1918 to do it, when the war was nearly over? The recordings of the two arias, Handel's *Ombra mai fu* and Rossini's *Domine Deus*, date from 1920, only months before the great tenor's death, and there the weighty, baritonal quality comes over impressively.

Chaliapin, Feodor (bass)

Russian opera arias: MUSSORGSKY: *Boris Godunov: Coronation scene; Clock scene; Farewell and Death of Boris.* Excerpts from: GLINKA: *Life for the Tsar; Russlan and Ludmilla.* DARGOMINSKY: *Russalka.* RUBINSTEIN: *The Demon.* BORODIN: *Prince Igor.* RIMSKY-KORSAKOV: *Sadko.* RACHMANINOV: *Aleko.*
⊛ (M) (***) EMI mono CDH7 61009-2 [id.].

Not only the glory of the voice, amazingly rich and consistent as recorded here between 1908 (aged 35) and 1931, but also the electrifying personality is vividly caught in this superb Références CD. The range of expression is astonishing. If posterity tends to think of this megastar among basses in the role of Mussorgsky's *Boris* (represented here in versions previously unissued), he is just as memorable in such an astonishing item as *Farlaf's Rondo* from *Russlan and Ludmilla*, with its tongue-twisting chatter made thrilling at such speed and with such power. The presence of the singer is unwaveringly vivid in model transfers, whether the original recording was acoustic or electric.

Clare College, Cambridge, Choir and Orchestra, John Rutter

'Carols from Clare': RUTTER: *Shepherd's pipe carol; Nativity carol.* TRAD., arr. Rutter: *Infant holy, infant lowly; Angel tidings; Quelle est cette odeur agréable; Once in Royal David's city; Il est né le divin enfant; I saw three ships; In dulci jubilo; Quem pastores Laudavere; Rocking; The twelve days of Christmas; Here we come a-wassailing; The coming of our King; O come, O come, Immanuel; The infant king; Noël nouvelet; O little town of Bethlehem; Gabriel's message; Sans day carol; Flemish carol; Past three o'clock.* CANTELOUBE: *Shepherd's noël.* GRUBER: *Silent night.*
(M) *** EMI CDM7 69950-2 [id.].

This generous collection combines the contents of two LPs, recorded in 1967 and 1970. The sustained mood is pastoral, to evoke the Christmas Eve atmosphere, the shepherds in the fields and the Baby in the manger. Rutter's own *Shepherd's pipe carol* is delightful and here, as throughout, the discreet yet colourful use of the orchestral palette frames each set of words most tastefully. Rutter's own arrangements are very effective. The charming French carol *Il est né le divin enfant*, has a rustic dance flavour, and the presentation of *I saw three ships*, *In dulci jubilo*, *Rocking*, *Past three o'clock* and Grüber's *Silent night* is equally colourful. The recorded sound, while lacking a little in sharpness of focus, remains warmly atmospheric. An ideal collection for Christmas Eve: it plays for nearly 75 minutes.

'The Holly and the ivy' (Carols): RUTTER: *Donkey carol; Mary's lullaby.* TRAD., arr. RUTTER: *King Jesus hath a garden; Wexford carol; (Flemish) Cradle song; Child in a manger; In dulci jubilo; I saw three ships; The holly and the ivy.* TRAD., arr. WOODWARD: *Up! Good Christian folk.* TRAD., arr. WILLCOCKS: *Gabriel's message; Ding! dong! merrily on high; Quelle est cette odeur agréable.* TRAD., arr. PETTMAN: *I saw a maiden.* DARKE: *In the bleak mid-winter.* PRAETORIUS: *The noble stem of Jesse; Omnis mundus jocundetur.* TCHAIKOVSKY: *The crown of roses.* POSTON: *Jesus Christ the apple tree.* TRAD., arr. VAUGHAN WILLIAMS: *Wassail song.*
⊛ (M) *** Decca 425 500-2 [id.].

This outstanding collection, recorded by Argo in the Lady Chapel at Ely Cathedral in 1979, is a model of its kind. The freshness of the sound, its warm ambience combined with natural detail, has been enhanced even further by digital remastering and the effect is far more transparent and real than Rutter's companion EMI carol record (although that offers 15 minutes' more music). There is surprisingly little duplication and Rutter's admirers, among whom we can be counted, will surely want both discs for the Christmas season. If only one is needed, then this Decca reissue is first choice. The opening arrangement of *King Jesus hath a garden*, using a traditional Dutch melody, immediately sets the mood with its pretty flute decorations. Moreover Rutter's own gentle syncopated *Donkey carol*, which comes fourth, is indispensable to any Christmas celebration, melodically as memorable as any of the great traditional examples of the genre. The whole programme is a delight – not always especially ecclesiastical in feeling, but permeated throughout by the spirit of Christmas joy. Some of the loveliest of seasonal melodies are included and the lyrical style of the music-making is very persuasive, especially when the sound is so refined.

Crespin, Régine (soprano)

French songs: BERLIOZ: *Nuits d'été.* RAVEL: *Shéhérazade* (with SRO, Ansermet). DEBUSSY: *3 Chansons de Bilitis.* POULENC: *Banalities: Chansons D'Orkenise; Hôtel. La courte paille: Le carafon; La reine de coeur. Chansons villageoises: Les gars qui vont à la fête. 2 Poèmes de Louis Aragon.* (with J. Wustman).
*** Decca 417 813-2 [id.].

Régine Crespin's outstanding performances of the Berlioz and Ravel song-cycles with Ansermet are discussed under their composer entries. The Debussy and Poulenc *mélodies* come from a recital made four years earlier with John Wustman. The Poulenc songs are particularly vivid, robust in feeling and with an attractive bravura in *Le carafon* (*The water jug*). The Debussy *Chansons de Bilitis* are also strongly characterized by a singer at her peak at the time of making these recordings. John Wustman accompanies sympathetically and is given striking presence in the piano-accompanied section of the programme.

Dawson, Peter (baritone)

GERMAN: *Merrie England: The Yeomen of England. Glorious Devon.* PHILLIPS: *Fishermen of England.* COWAN: *Waltzing Matilda.* WOOD: *Roses of Picardy.* TRAD.: *The mountains of Mourne.* MURRAY: *I'll walk beside you.* SPEAKS: *On the road to Mandalay.* MCCALL: *Boots.* ADAMS: *The holy city.* BRAHE: *Bless this house.* MOSS: *The floral dance.* NOTON: *Chu Chin Chow: Cobbler's song.* LONGSTAFFE: *When the sergeant-major's on parade.* MOLLOY: *The Kerry dance.* SAMUEL: *Jogging along the highway.* FRENCH: *Phil the Fluter's ball.* HILL: *Waiata poi.* TATE: *Maid of the mountains: A bachelor gay.* O'HAGEN: *O Father Thames.*
(M) *** EMI mono CDH7 63107-2.

Peter Dawson was famous for the clarity of his diction, and in these excellent transfers every word comes over in the sharpest focus. His forthright production and complete vocal security go with natural, characterful warmth, and this makes the more lyrical numbers like *I'll walk beside you* or *Roses of Picardy* especially appealing. By concentrating on the ballads and the more dramatic descriptive songs, of which the two Kipling settings, *On the road to Mandalay* and *Boots*, are both unforgettably alive, this collection provides only a limited survey. Nevertheless there is much to relish here, not least the opening *Yeomen of England* (1929), the lilting *Phil the Fluter's ball* and the celebrated *Floral dance. The Cobbler's song* from *Chu Chin Chow* is another highlight, as is *A bachelor gay* from *The Maid of the mountains*, now sounding engagingly dated.

Domingo, Placido (tenor)

Operatic recital (1970–80 recordings): Arias from: VERDI: *Aida; Giovanna d'Arco; Un ballo in maschera; Don Carlos.* GOUNOD: *Faust.* BOITO: *Mefistofele.* PUCCINI: *Manon Lescaut; Tosca.*
(M) *** EMI Dig. CDM7 63103-2 [id.].

Compiled from Domingo's contributions to EMI opera sets in the 1970s, this mid-price CD includes some 71 minutes of music. The remastering brings the advantage of negligible background noise, but otherwise there is no great gain in presence; however, the sound is admirably clear and well balanced. If Domingo has recorded such items as the *Manon Lescaut* excerpt more perceptively, and if his singing of *Faust* is less stylish here than it usually is in French music, the range of achievement is formidable and the beauties great. The Puccini arias sound especially real, combining a fresh clarity with a pleasing atmosphere.

'Vienna, city of my dreams' (with Amb. S., ECO, Rudel): Arias from: LEHÁR: *Paganini; Merry Widow; Land of smiles.* ZELLER: *Vogelhändler.* KÁLMÁN: *Gräfin Mariza.* FALL: *Rose von Stambul.* O. STRAUSS: *Walzerträume.* J. STRAUSS: *Nacht in Venedig.* SIECZYNSKI: *Wien, du Stadt.*
*** EMI Dig. CDC7 47398-2 [id.].

Having such a golden tenor sound in Viennese operetta makes a winning combination, and Domingo, always the stylist, rebuts the idea that only a German tenor can be really idiomatic. A delightful selection including one or two rarities, very well recorded.

'Ave Maria' (with Vienna Boys' Choir, VSO, Froschauer): HERBECK: *Pueri concinite.* TRAD.: *Adeste fidelis.* FRANCK: *Panis angelicus.* SCHUBERT: *Ave Maria.* KIENZL: *Der Evangelimann: Selig sind, die Verfolgung leiden.* HANDEL: *Xerxes: Ombra mai fù.* EYBLER: *Omnes de Saba venient.* BACH/GOUNOD: *Ave Maria.* FAURÉ: *Crucifix.* BIZET: *Agnus Dei.* LUTHER: *A mighty fortress is our God (Ein feste Burg).*
*** RCA RD 70760 [RCD1 3835].

This collection dates from 1979 and can be recommended unreservedly. Domingo is in freshest voice and these famous religious 'pops' are sung with golden tone and a simple eloquence that is most engaging. Nothing sounds routine and the Vienna Boys make a considerable contribution, notably in the dialogue of the excerpt from Kienzl's *Evangelimann*. In the closing chorale (*Ein feste Burg*) the Chorus Viennensis join the group to excellent effect. Attractively atmospheric recording, with Domingo's voice given fine presence and bloom.

'Bravissimo, Domingo': Arias from: VERDI: *Il Trovatore; Un ballo in maschera* (with Leontyne Price). *Rigoletto; Otello; Don Carlos* (with Sherrill Milnes). *Aida; La Traviata.* PUCCINI: *Tosca; Manon Lescaut* (with Leontyne Price). *Turandot.* LEONCAVALLO: *Pagliacci.* CILEA: *Adriana Lecouvreur.* GOUNOD: *Roméo et Juliette; Faust.* GIORDANO: *Andrea Chènier.* MASCAGNI: *Cavalleria Rusticana.* BIZET: *Carmen.*
*** RCA RD 87020 [RCD1 7020].

This selection of recordings ranges wide over Domingo's recording career. The opening items come from complete sets and *Di quella pira* immediately establishes the ringing vocal authority. The excerpts from *Cav.* and *Pag.* are equally memorable, as are the duets with Sherrill Milnes. With over 72 minutes offered, this is generous enough; although the remastered recordings sometimes show their age in the orchestra, the voice always remains fresh.

'Bravissimo Domingo!', Vol. 2: Arias from: VERDI: *Rigoletto; I vespri siciliani; Il Trovatore; Luisa Miller; La Forza del destino.* PUCCINI: *Tosca; La Bohème.* BELLINI: *Norma* (with Amb. Op. Ch.). MASCAGNI: *Cavalleria Rusticana* (with John Alldis Ch.). WAGNER: *Lohengrin.* MASSENET: *Werther.* DONIZETTI: *L'Elisir d'amore.* TCHAIKOVSKY: *Eugene Onegin.* FLOTOW: *Martha.* GIORDANO: *Andrea Chènier.*
*** RCA RD 86211 [RCA-6211-2-RC].

Opening stylishly with *Questa o quella*, and always establishing his sense of Verdian line, this second RCA collection is if anything even more attractive than the first. There is not a single below-par performance, and Domingo seems as at home in Tchaikovsky's and Wagner's lyricism as he is in the Italian repertoire. *Che gelida manina* (after an engaging little gasp from Mimi) is noble as well as eloquent, and the Donizetti and Flotow arias show the warm timbre of this remarkably consistent artist. Excellent remastering throughout the 72 minutes of music offered.

'Great love scenes' (with Renata Scotto, Kiri Te Kanawa, Ileana Cotrubas) from: PUCCINI: *Madama Butterfly; La rondine.* CILEA: *Adriana Lecouvreur.* MASSENET: *Manon.* GOUNOD: *Roméo et Juliette.* CHARPENTIER: *Louise.*
*** CBS MK 39030 [id.].

This compilation from various CBS opera sets brings an attractively varied group of love duets, with Domingo matched against three splendid heroines. Scotto is the principal partner, better as Adriana than as Butterfly, Juliette or Manon, but still warmly individual, responding to the glory of Domingo's singing which is unfailingly beautiful and warmly committed. The wonder is that his exceptional consistency never falls into routine; these are all performances to have one wanting to go back to the complete operas. Good recording.

'Gala opera concert' (with LAPO, Giulini): Arias from: DONIZETTI: *L'Elisir d'amore; Lucia di Lammermoor.* VERDI: *Ernani; Il Trovatore; Aida.* HALÉVY: *La Juive.* MEYERBEER: *L'Africaine.* BIZET: *Les Pêcheurs de perles; Carmen* (with R. Wagner Chorale).
*** DG Dig. 400 030-2 [id.].

Recorded in 1980 in connection with a gala in San Francisco, this is as noble and resplendent a tenor recital as you will find. Domingo improves in detail even on the fine versions of some of these arias he had recorded earlier, and the finesse of the whole gains greatly from the sensitive direction of Giulini, though the orchestra is a little backward. Otherwise excellent recording, with tingling digital brass in the *Aida* excerpt.

'The best of Domingo': Arias from: VERDI: *Aida; Rigoletto; Luisa Miller; Un ballo in maschera; La Traviata.* BIZET: *Carmen.* FLOTOW: *Martha.* DONIZETTI: *L'Elisir d'amore.* OFFENBACH: *Contes d'Hoffmann.*
*** DG 415 366-2 [id.].

A popular recital showing Domingo in consistent form, the voice and style vibrant and telling, as the opening *Celeste Aida* readily shows, followed by an agreeably relaxed *La donna è mobile.* In the lyric arias, the *Flower song* and the excerpts from *Martha* and *L'Elisir d'amore* there is not the honeyed sweetness of a Gigli, but in the closing *Hoffmann* scena the sheer style of the singing gives special pleasure. The sound is vivid throughout.

Volume 1: Arias from: LEONCAVALLO: *I Pagliacci.* MASCAGNI: *Cavalleria Rusticana.* PUCCINI: *Il Tabarro.* VERDI: *Il Trovatore; La Traviata.* WAGNER: *Lohengrin.*
(BB) (**) LaserLight 15 230.

Although the voice projects vibrantly, the effect here is of being in a seat in the gallery. The highlights are some red-blooded excerpts from a performance of *Il Trovatore*, recorded in New Orleans in 1958 with Caballé and Sordello, and a quite impressive (1967) *Traviata* with Maralin Niska, recorded at the New York City Opera, also the source of the performances of *Pagliacci* (1967), *Cavalleria Rusticana* and *Il Tabarro*

(1968). The excerpts from a Hamburg *Lohengrin*, made in the same year, bring very indifferent sound.

Early Music Consort of London, Munrow

'*Music of the Gothic era*': Notre Dame period: LEONIN: *Organum Viderunt omnes.* PEROTIN: *Organum Viderunt omnes.* Ars Antiqua: *Motets from the Bamberg and Montpellier Codices* by Petrus de Cruce, Adam de la Halle and Anon. Ars Nova: *Motets from the Roman de Fauvel. Chantilly/Ivrea Codices* by Machaut; De Vitry.
*** DG 415 292-2.

This issue draws on the fine three-LP set, '*Music of the Gothic Era*', made by the late lamented David Munrow just before his death in 1976. It offers two items from the first LP, one each by Leonin and Perotin, and gives us more from the other two, from the so-called *Ars antiqua* (1250–1320) and includes two motets of Adam de la Halle, and the *Ars nova* (1320–80), representing such figures as Philippe de Vitry and Machaut. David Munrow had exceptional powers both as a scholar-performer and as a communicator, and it is good that his work is remembered on compact disc. The performances are wonderfully alive and vital, and the digital remastering as expert as one would expect. A strong recommendation.

Elizabethan Singers, Simon Halsey

'*Nowell*': TRAD., arr. JOUBERT: *God rest you merry, gentlemen; Here we come a-wassailing.* TRAD., arr. RUBBRA: *Infant holy.* TRAD., arr. WILLIAMSON: *Ding dong merrily on high; Good King Wenceslas.* TRAD., arr. COLE: *Away in a manger; Deck the hall.* TRAD., arr. BRITTEN: *The holly and the ivy.* TRAD., arr. RIDOUT: *The old year now away is fled.* MCCABE: *Coventry carol.* TRAD., arr. PRESTON: *I saw three ships.* TRAD., arr. EASTWOOD: *Unto us is born a son.* TRAD., arr. GARDNER: *We wish you a merry Christmas; The first nowell.* GRÜBER, arr. RIDOUT: *Silent night.*
(M) *** Decca 425 515-2 [id.].

A further outstanding collection from the old Argo catalogue, recorded with characteristic sophistication in the early 1960s. It draws on *Sing Nowell*, an imaginative collection of 50 carol arrangements, newly published by Novello at that time, and shows us how very alive the carol tradition is among modern composers. All the examples here are immensely enjoyable; they were recorded by the Elizabethan Singers at a vintage period when Simon Halsey trained them to sing with gloriously fresh and focused tone. The digital remastering confirms the beauty and clarity of the original recording.

Ferrier, Kathleen (contralto)

Lieder, arias and songs: MAHLER: *Kindertotenlieder* (with VPO, Walter). GLUCK: *Orfeo ed Euridice:* excerpts including *Che faro.* PURCELL: *Ode for Queen Mary: Sound the trumpet. Indian Queen: Let us not wander* (with I. Baillie). HANDEL: *Ottone: Spring is coming; Come to me.* GREEN: *O praise the Lord; I will lay me down in peace.* MENDELSSOHN: *I would that my love* (with I. Baillie, G. Moore).
(M) (***) EMI mono CDH7 61003-2.

It was especially tragic that Kathleen Ferrier made so few recordings in which the technical quality matched her magical artistry. This disc includes many of her EMI mono records, which generally sound much better than the Decca repertoire listed below. The

Gluck *Orfeo* excerpts (deriving from a broadcast) have undoubtedly been enhanced and the 1949 *Kindertotenlieder* also comes over very well. Particularly worth having are the duets with Isobel Baillie, as these artists obviously worked especially well together. Generally, the new transfers are vivid and show a considerable enhancement of their previous LP incarnations.

'*Blow the wind southerly*' (with Phyllis Spurr, piano): arr. WHITTAKER: *Ma bonny lad; The Keel Row; Blow the wind southerly.* Arr. HUGHES: *I have a bonnet trimmed with blue; I will walk with my love; The stuttering lovers; Down by the Sally gardens; The lover's curse.* Arr. SHARPE: *My boy Willie.* HUGHES/GRAY: *I know where I'm going.* Arr. JACOBSON: *Ca' the yowes.* Arr. BRITTEN: *O Waly Waly.* Arr. ROBERTON: *The fidgety bairn.* Arr. WARLOCK: *Willow, Willow.* QUILTER: *Now sleeps the crimson petal; Fair house of joy; To daisies; Over the mountains.* Arr. QUILTER: *Ye banks and braes; Drink to me only.* Arr. GREW: *Have you seen but a white lillie grow?*
(***) Decca mono 417 192-2 [id.].

This is Ferrier at her most magical. Apart from the famous *Blow the wind southerly*, songs like *I will walk with my love* show her artistic radiance to the full, and throughout she makes the words tell wonderfully. Her consistent freshness and warmth give enormous pleasure. Technically, this is the best of her Decca recitals on CD and, if the sound itself is variable, the voice comes over with beauty and presence . . . and what a voice!

Ferrier, Kathleen (contralto), Bruno Walter (piano)

Edinburgh Festival recital, 1949: SCHUBERT: *Die junge Nonne. Rosamunde: Romance. Du liebst mich nicht: Der Tod und das Mädchen; Suleika; Du bist die Ruh'.* BRAHMS: *Immer leiser wird mein Schlummer; Der Tod das ist die kuhle Nacht; Botschaft; Von ewiger Liebe.* SCHUMANN: *Frauenliebe und Leben, Op. 42.*
(M) (***) Decca mono 414 611-2 [id.].

Though the mono recording – taken from a BBC tape of 1949 – leaves much to be desired, with the piano sound often hazy, this historic issue gives a wonderful idea of the intensity of a Ferrier recital. Her account here of *Frauenliebe* is freer and even more compelling than the performance she recorded earlier. Walter's accompaniments may not be flawless, but they are comparably inspirational. The recital is introduced by a brief talk on Walter and the Edinburgh Festival, given by Ferrier. The CD transfer does not seek to 'enhance' the sound, but most of the background has been cleaned up. There are moments when the vocal focus slips – and this is not exactly hi-fi, even in mono terms – but the ear adjusts readily.

French Operatic favourites

'*French Operatic favourites*' (sung by Obraztsova, Gedda, Freni, Schwarzkopf and Jeannine Collard, Freni, Massard, Callas, Vanzo and Sarabia; Paris Opéra Ch., Prêtre): Arias and choruses from: BIZET: *Carmen; Les pêcheurs de perles.* GOUNOD: *Faust.* OFFENBACH: *Contes d'Hoffmann.* MEYERBEER: *L'Africaine.* SAINT-SAENS: *Samson et Dalila.* MASSENET: *Manon.* THOMAS: *Mignon.*
(B) ** CfP CD-CFP 4562.

Elena Obraztsova is certainly a vibrant Carmen and the *Habanera* and *Seguidilla* have plenty of character; her Delilah, however, lacks sensuality. Gedda offers sensitive accounts of *O paradiso* from *L'Africaine* (not lacking fervour) and *Salut! Demeure chaste et pure* from *Faust*. Mirella Freni adds a sparkling *Jewel song* and there are two favourite choruses from the same opera; Freni also contributes a charming *Adieu notre petite table* from Masssenet's *Manon*; both her arias were recorded in 1968 when the voice was strikingly fresh. However, the chosen *Pearl-fishers' duet* (Alain Vanzo and Guillermo Sarabia) is taken from the 1863 original score and culminates not in a rich reprise of the big melody but in an insubstantial waltz theme. The highlights here are Callas's characterful 1961 recording of the *Polonaise* from *Mignon* and Schwarzkopf's ravishing account of Offenbach's languorous *Barcarolle* in duet with Jeannine Collard, which comes from an unsuccessful 1965 complete set of *Tales of Hoffmann*.

Galli-Curci, Amelita (soprano)

'*Prima voce*': Arias from: AUBER: *Manon Lescaut*. BELLINI: *I Puritani; La Sonnambula*. DONIZETTI: *Don Pasquale; Linda di Chamounix; Lucia di Lammermoor*. GOUNOD: *Roméo et Juliette*. MEYERBEER: *Dinorah*. ROSSINI: *Il Barbiere di Siviglia*. THOMAS: *Mignon*. VERDI: *Rigoletto; La Traviata*.
(M) (***) Nimbus mono NI 7806 [id.].

'Like a nightingale half-asleep,' said Philip Hope-Wallace in a memorable description of Galli-Curci's voice, but this vivid Nimbus transfer makes it much more like a nightingale very wide-awake. More than in most of these transfers made via an acoustic horn gramophone, the resonance of the horn itself can be detected, and the results are full and forward. Galli-Curci's perfection in these pre-electric recordings, made between 1917 and 1924, is a thing of wonder, almost too accurate for comfort, but tenderness is there too, as in the Act II duet from *La Traviata* (with Giuseppe de Luca) and the *Addio del passato*, complete with introductory recitative, but with only a single stanza. Yet brilliant coloratura is what lies at the root of Galli-Curci's magic, and that comes in abundance.

Galway, James (flute), BBC Singers, King's School, Canterbury, Choristers, Galway

'*James Galway's Christmas carol*': GRUBER: *Silent night*. RUTTER: *Shepherd's pipe carol*. BACH: *Suite No. 3: Air. Christmas oratorio: Sinfonia and Chorale. Sheep may safely graze*. OVERTON: *Fantasia on I saw three ships*. TRAD.: *Greensleeves; Zither carol; Patapan; Past three o'clock; I wonder as I wander*. IRELAND: *The holy boy*. BACH/GOUNOD: *Ave Maria*. POSTON: *Jesus Christ the apple tree*. RYAN: *We wish you a merry Christmas*.
*** RCA Dig. RD 85888 [RCD1 5888].

James Galway's silvery timbre introduces Grüber's *Silent night* unaccompanied before the choir joins in and he later adds an obbligato descant. These are all effectively simple arrangements, in which Galway both directs chorus and orchestra and makes regular and attractive solo contributions. John Rutter's engaging *Shepherd's pipe carol* was an obvious choice in a programme that has a happy freshness about its presentation throughout. The interspersed orchestral numbers bring an effective degree of contrast. With clear yet full recorded sound, the ambience mellow but not too ecclesiastical, this is a Christmas compilation that will give a great deal of pleasure.

German Operatic favourites

'German operatic favourites' (sung by: Gedda, Lövberg, Chorus of Bavarian State Opera, Heger, Gruberová, Nilsson, Prey, Lois Marshall, Frick, Moffo). Arias and choruses from: ADAM: *Der Postillon von Lonjumeau.* WAGNER: *Lohengrin; Tannhäuser.* FLOTOW: *Martha.* MOZART: *Die Zauberflöte; Die Entführung aus dem Serail.* WEBER: *Der Freischütz.* BEETHOVEN: *Fidelio.*
(B) **(*) CfP CD-CFP 4561.

This is much the most rewarding of the three Classics for Pleasure 'national' operatic anthologies. It opens enterprisingly with the attractive key aria from Adam's *Der Postillon von Lonjumeau*, and Gedda also contributes a romantically ardent account of the most famous aria from Flotow's *Martha*. Edita Gruberová's Queen of the Night's aria from *Die Zauberflöte* bristles with venom, with glittering upper tessitura; Herman Prey makes an engaging Papageno, and Anna Moffo gives a radiant account of Pamina's *Ach, ich fühls.* Two excerpts from Beecham's 1957 recording of *Die Entführung aus dem Serail* are a joy for the accompaniments alone, but while Gottlob Frick is quite superb in Osmin's *O! wie will ich triumphieren*, Lois Marshall's *Martern alle Arten* is rather less convincing. Two 1959 Wagner contributions from Aase Nordmo Lövberg are not especially congenial in vocal timbre, although Susskind and the Philharmonia give her admirable support. Birgit Nilsson's account of *Agathe's prayer* from *Der Freischütz*, however, is quite breathtaking for the lovely hushed *mezza voce* she provides. The vigorous *Huntsmen's chorus* from this opera is joined by fine accounts of the *Prisoners' chorus* from *Fidelio* and the *Bridal chorus* from *Lohengrin*. On the whole an excellent entertainment, and the sound is consistently vivid and full.

Gigli, Beniamino (tenor)

Opera arias from: GOUNOD: *Faust.* BIZET: *Carmen; Les Pêcheurs de perles.* MASSENET: *Manon.* HANDEL: *Serse.* DONIZETTI: *Lucia di Lammermoor; L'Elisir d'amore.* VERDI: *Rigoletto; Aida.* LEONCAVALLO: *I Pagliacci.* MASCAGNI: *Cavalleria Rusticana.* PUCCINI: *La Bohème; Tosca.* GIORDANO: *Andrea Chénier.* PIETRI: *Maristella.*
⊛ (***) EMI mono CDH7 61051-2 [id.].

No Italian tenor has sung with more honeyed beauty than Beniamino Gigli. His status in the inter-war period as a singing superstar at a time when the media were less keenly organized is vividly reflected in this Références collection of eighteen items, the cream of his recordings made between 1927 and 1937. It is specially welcome to have two historic ensemble recordings, made in New York in 1927 and originally coupled on a short-playing 78-r.p.m. disc: the *Quartet* from *Rigoletto* and the *Sextet* from *Lucia di Lammermoor.* In an astonishing line-up Gigli is joined by Galli-Curci, Pinza, De Luca and Louise Homer. Excellent transfers.

'Prima voce': Vol. 1 (1918–24): Arias from: BOITO: *Mefistofele.* CATALANI: *Loreley.* DONIZETTI: *La Favorita.* FLOTOW: *Martha.* GIORDANO: *Andrea Chénier.* GOUNOD: *Faust.* LALO: *Le roi d'Ys.* LEONCAVALLO: *Pagliacci.* MASCAGNI: *Iris.* MEYERBEER: *L'Africana.* PONCHIELLI: *La Gioconda.* PUCCINI: *Tosca.* Songs.
(M) (***) Nimbus mono NI 7807 [id.].

Gigli's career went on so long, right through the electrical 78-r.p.m. era, that his pre-electric recordings have tended to get forgotten. This collection of 22 items recorded between 1918 and 1924 shows the voice at its most honeyed, even lighter and more lyrical than it became later, with the singer indulging in fewer of the mannerisms that came to decorate his ever-mellifluous singing. In aria after aria he spins a flawless legato line. Few tenor voices have ever matched Gigli's in rounded, golden beauty, and the Nimbus transfers capture its bloom in a way that makes one forget pre-electric limitations. In the one item sung in French, by Lalo, he sounds less at home, a little too heavy; but the ease of manner in even the most taxing arias elsewhere is remarkable, and such a number as the *Serenade* from Mascagni's *Iris* is irresistible in its sparkle, as are the Neapolitan songs, notably the galloping *Povero Pulcinella* by Buzzi-Peccia. One oddity is a tenor arrangement of Saint-Saëns's *The Swan*.

Gomez, Jill (soprano)

'*Cabaret classics*' (with John Constable, piano): WEILL: *Marie Galante: 4 Songs. Lady in the Dark: My ship. Street scene: Lonely house. Knickerbocker glory: It never was you.* ZEMLINSKY: *3 Songs from Op. 27.* SCHOENBERG: *4 Brettl Lieder.* SATIE: *3 Café-concert songs: La Diva de l'Empire; Allons-y, Chochotte; Je te veux.*
⊛ *** Unicorn Dig. DKPCD 9055 [id.].

Jill Gomez here assembles a delectable collection of 'cabaret classics', with Arnold Schoenberg providing the surprise in four songs in popular Viennese style which he wrote at the turn of the century when he was making ends meet as music director of the Uberbrettl Cabaret in Berlin. Jill Gomez's delicious performances make clear that writing these innocently diatonic numbers can have been no chore to the future ogre of the avant-garde. This is the music of love in every sense, delicately provocative, both first-class Schoenberg and excellent light music. The same is true of the two Kurt Weill groups, strikingly contrasted at the beginning and end of the recital. The French-text songs from *Marie Galante* use material adapted from *Happy End*. They are charming in their own right, with his characteristic tanginess given extra subtlety. Weill's mastery is even more strikingly illustrated in the three Broadway songs, ravishing numbers all three: *My ship, Lonely house* and *It never was you*. It is worth getting the record just for Gomez's ecstatic pianissimo top A at the end of that last item. The other groups, as delightful as they are revealing, are from Alexander von Zemlinsky (not quite so light-handed), and the Parisian joker, Satie, in three café-concert songs, including the famous celebration of English music-hall, *La Diva de l'Empire*. John Constable is the idiomatic accompanist. Gomez's sensuously lovely soprano is caught beautifully.

Gothic Voices, Christopher Page

'*The Guardian of Zephirus*' (Courtly songs of the 15th century, with Imogen Barford, medieval harp): DUFAY: *J'atendray tant qu'il vous playra; Adieu ces bons vins de Lannoys; Mon cuer me fait tous dis penser.* BRIQUET: *Ma seul amour et ma belle maistresse.* DE CASERTA: *Amour ma' le cuer mis.* LANDINI: *Nessun ponga speranza; Giunta vaga bilta.* REYNEAU: *Va t'en mon cuer, avent mes yeux.* MATHEUS DE SACTO JOHANNE: *Fortune, faulce, parverse.* DE INSULA: *Amours n'ont cure le tristesse.* BROLLO: *Qui le sien vuelt bien maintenir.* ANON.: *N'a pas long temps que trouvay Zephirus; Je la remire, la belle.*
*** Hyp. CDA 66144 [id.].

Most of this repertoire is unfamiliar, with Dufay the only famous name; but everything here is of interest, and the listener inexperienced in medieval music will be surprised at the strength of its character. The performances are naturally eloquent and, although the range of colour is limited compared with later writing, it still has immediacy of appeal, especially if taken in short bursts. The recording balance is faultless and the sound first rate. With complete security of intonation and a chamber-music vocal blend, the presentation is wholly admirable. There is full back-up documentation.

'The Service of Venus and Mars': DE VITRY: *Gratissima virginis; Vos quie admiramini; Gaude gloriosa; Contratenor.* DES MOLINS: *De ce que fol pense.* PYCARD: *Gloria.* POWER: *Sanctus.* LEBERTOUL: *Las, que me demanderoye.* PYRAMOUR: *Quam pulchra es.* DUNSTABLE: *Speciosa facta es.* SOURSBY: *Sanctus.* LOQUEVILLE: *Je vous pri que j'aye un baysier.* ANON.: *Singularis laudis digna; De ce fol, pense. Lullay, lullay; There is no rose; Le gay playsir; Le grant pleyser; Agincourt carol.*
*** Hyp. Dig. CDA 66283 [id.].

The subtitle of this collection is '*Music for the Knights of the Garter, 1340–1440*'; few readers will recognize many of the names in the list of composers above. But the music itself is fascinating and the performances bring it to life with extraordinary projection and vitality. The recording too is first class, and this imaginatively chosen programme deservedly won the 1988 *Gramophone* award for Early Music. Readers interested in trying medieval repertoire could hardly do better than to start here.

'A song for Francesca': ANDREAS DE FLORENTINA: *Astio non mori mai. Per la ver'onesta.* JOHANNES DE FLORENTINA: *Quando la stella.* LANDINI: *Ochi dolenti mie. Per seguir la speranca.* ANON.: *Quando i oselli canta; Constantia; Amor mi fa cantar a la Francesca; Non na el so amante.* DUFAY: *Quel fronte signorille in paradiso.* RICHARD DE LOQUEVILLE: *Puisquie je suy amoureux; Pour mesdisans ne pour leur faulx parler; Qui ne veroit que vos deulx yeulx.* HUGO DE LATINS: *Plaindre m'estuet.* HAUCOURT: *Je demande ma bienvenue.* GROSSIN: *Va t'ent souspir.* ANON.: *O regina seculi; Reparatrix Maria; Confort d'amours.*
*** Hyp. Dig. CDA 66286 [id.].

No group is more persuasive in presenting medieval music than Gothic Voices under Christopher Page. The title, '*A Song for Francesca*', refers not only to the fourteenth-century French items here, but to the fact that the Italians too tended to be influenced by French style. More specifically, the collection is a well-deserved tribute to Francesca MacManus, selfless worker on behalf of many musicians, not least as manager of Gothic Voices. The variety of expression and mood in these songs, ballatas and madrigals is astonishing, some of them amazingly complex. The Hyperion recording is a model of its kind, presenting this long-neglected music most seductively in a warm but clear setting.

Great Singers

'Prima voce': Great singers 1909–38 (Tetrazzini; Caruso; Schumann-Heink; McCormack; Galli-Curci; Stracciari; Ponselle; Lauri-Volpi; Turner; Tibbett; Supervia; Gigli; Anderson; Schipa; Muzio; Tauber): Arias from: BELLINI: *La Sonnambula; I Puritani; Norma.* LEONCAVALLO: *Pagliacci.* MOZART: *Don Giovanni; Die Zauberflöte.* ROSSINI: *Il Barbiere di Siviglia.* PUCCINI: *Turandot.* VERDI: *Un ballo in maschera.* BIZET: *Carmen.* PUCCINI: *La Bohème.* SAINT-SAENS: *Samson et Dalila.* MASCAGNI: *L'amico Fritz.* Song: REFICE: *Ombra di Nube.*
(M) (***) Nimbus mono NI 7801 [id.].

This was the first of Nimbus's series of archive recordings, taking a radical new view of the problem of transferring ancient 78-r.p.m. vocal recordings to CD. The best possible copies of shellac originals have been played on an acoustic machine with an enormous horn, one of the hand-made Rolls-Royces among non-electric gramophones of the 1930s, with thorn needles reducing still further the need to filter the sound electronically. The results have been recorded in a small hall, and the sound reproduced removes any feeling of boxy closeness. Those who have resisted the bottled or tinny sound of many historic recordings will find the Nimbus transfers more friendly and sympathetic, even if techically there is an inevitable loss of recorded information at both ends of the spectrum because of the absolute limitations of the possible frequency range on this kind of reproducer.

This compilation makes a good starting point, even if the method still does not provide the ideal answer. The Tetrazzini item with which the selection opens, *Ah non giunge* from Bellini's *La Sonnambula*, is one of the supreme demonstrations of coloratura on record, and the programme goes on to a magnificent Caruso of 1910 and an unforgettable performance of the coloratura drinking-song from Donizetti's *Lucrezia Borgia* by the most formidable of contraltos, Ernestine Schumann-Heink. Then follows John McCormack's famous account of *Il mio tesoro* from Mozart's *Don Giovanni*, with the central passage-work amazingly done in a single breath. Other vintage items include Galli-Curci's dazzling account of *Son vergin vezzosa* from Bellini's *I Puritani*, Eva Turner in her incomparable 1928 account of Turandot's aria, Gigli amiably golden-toned in *Che gelida manina* from *La Bohème*, and a delectable performance of the *Cherry duet* from Mascagni's *L'amico Fritz* by Tito Schipa and Mafalda Favero, riches indeed!

'Prima voce': Divas 1906–35 (Tetrazzini; Melba; Patti; Hempel; Galli-Curci; Ponselle; Lehmann; Turner; Koshetz; Norena; Nemeth; Muzio): Arias from: VERDI: *Un ballo in maschera; Rigoletto; Aida; Il Trovatore.* THOMAS: *Mignon.* MOZART: *Die Zauberflöte.* ROSSINI: *Il Barbiere di Siviglia.* MASSENET: *Manon.* PUCCINI: *Madama Butterfly.* BEETHOVEN: *Fidelio.* RIMSKY-KORSAKOV: *Sadko.* BORODIN: *Prince Igor.* GOUNOD: *Roméo et Juliette.* BOITO: *Mefistofele.* Songs: YRADIER: *La Calesera.* DENAUDY: *O del mio amato ben.*
(M) (***) Nimbus mono NI 7802 [id.].

The six supreme prima donnas on this compilation are all very well represented. The soprano voice benefits more than most from the Nimbus process, so that with extra bloom Tetrazzini's vocal 'gear-change' down to the chest register is no longer obtrusive. She is represented by three recordings of 1911, including Gilda's *Caro nome* from *Rigoletto*; and Galli-Curci has three items too, including Rosina's *Una voce poco fa* from *Il Barbiere di Siviglia*. The tragically short-lived Claudia Muzio and the Russian, Nina Koshetz, have two each, while the others are each represented by a single, well-chosen item. They include Melba in *Mimi's farewell*, the 60-year-old Patti irresistibly vivacious in a Spanish folksong, *La calesera*, and Frieda Hempel in what is probably the most dazzling of all recordings of the Queen of the Night's second aria from *Zauberflöte*.

Hebrew Music

'Music on Hebrew themes' (with Nadia Pelle, soprano; Mary Ann Hart, mezzo-sop.; Rodney Nolan, tenor; I Musici de Montreal; Yuli Turovsky): BLOCH: *Baal shem: Nigun. From Jewish life: Prayer; Supplication; Jewish song. Méditation hébraïque.* PROKOFIEV: *Overture on Hebrew themes, Op. 34.* SHOSTAKOVICH: *From Jewish folk poetry* (song-cycle), *Op. 79.*
**(*) Chan. Dig. CHAN 8800 [id.].

Shostakovich wrote his song-cycle in 1948 at the height of a virulent wave of anti-semitism instigated by Stalin. His deep sympathy with the plight of his Jewish compatriots was underpinned by an admiration for Jewish folk music. 'It can appear happy while it is tragic,' he wrote. 'It almost always brings laughter through tears.' Such was the inspiration for his wonderfully vivid set of vocal vignettes, covering almost every kind of human experience, with the accompaniments making a kaleidoscope of matching colours. Some of the songs are for solo voice, others are in a dialogue format; all are sung most imaginatively and movingly here. The other works include a series of melancholy cello pieces, eloquently played by Yuli Turovsky, while the Prokofiev *Overture* makes a suitable contrast. A fine concert but best approached piecemeal. Excellent sound.

Hendricks, Barbara (soprano), Dmitri Alexeev (piano)

Spirituals: *Deep river; Ev'ry time I feel the spirit; Fix me, Jesus; Git on boa'd little child'n; His name is so sweet; Hold on!; Joshua fit de battle of Jericho; Nobody knows de trouble I've seen; Oh what a beautiful city!; Plenty good room; Roun' about de mountain; Sometimes I feel like a motherless child; Swing low, sweet chariot; Talk about a child that do love Jesus; Were you there?; When I lay my burden down.*
*** EMI Dig. CDC7 47026-2 [id.].

So often spirituals can be made to seem too ingenuous, their deep reserve of feeling degraded into sentimentality. Not so here: Barbara Hendricks' vibrant identification with the words is thrilling, the jazz inflexions adding natural sophistication, yet not robbing the music of its directness of communication. Her lyrical singing is radiant, operatic in its eloquence of line, yet retaining the ecstasy of spirit, while the extrovert numbers – *Joshua fit de battle of Jericho* a superb example – are full of joy in their gutsy exuberance. Dmitri Alexeev accompanies superbly and the very well-balanced recording has remarkable presence.

Hilliard Ensemble, Paul Hillier

'The Singing Club': RAVENSCROFT: *A round of three country dances; There were three ravens.* HILTON: *Call George again, boys.* W. LAWES: *Drink to the knight of the moonshine bright; She weepeth sore in the night; Dainty, fine aniseed water; Gather ye rosebuds.* WILSON: *Where the bee sucks.* PURCELL: *'Tis woman makes us love; Sir Walter enjoying his damsel.* BATTISHILL: *Epitaph.* ARNE: *The singing club; To soften care; Elegy on the death of Mr Shenstone; Sigh no more, ladies.* BISHOP: *Foresters sound the cheerful horn.* J. S. SMITH: *The Ancreontick song.* PEARSALL: *There is a paradise on earth; O who will o'er the downs so free.* BARNBY: *Sweet and low.*
**(*) HM Dig HMC 901153 [id.].

The Hilliard Ensemble are particularly at home in the earlier songs here: their blending and intonation cannot be faulted and they show a nice feeling for the gentle melancholy of the period. They manage the more robust glees with panache, notably the *Wedding night song* of Inigo Jones, whose lyrics make a ribald pun on the writer's name, and Purcell's risqué narrative based on a true story of Sir Walter Raleigh's first conquest in the woods. Words are admirably clear throughout and the recording, made in London's Henry Wood Hall, gives a very real impression of the group standing back just behind the speakers. In some of the later nineteenth-century items the style, though not insensitive, is just a little pale.

'Summer is icumen in': ST GODRIC: *Sainte Marie viergene, Crist and Sainte Marie; Saint Nicholas.* Medieval anonymous English songs, including: *Summer is icumen in; Fuweles*

in the Frith; Edi be thu; Worldes blisse; Gabriel fram heven-king; Mater ora filium; Gaude virgo mater Christi. Motets; Mass: excerpts.
*** HM HMC 901154 [id.].

Sumer is icumen in is given twice, in Latin as well as in the Early English version, as is *Campanis cum cymbalis.* Even more valuable are the motets and movements from the Mass, among the earliest transcribed polyphonic works from this country, sung here with persuasive intensity. Paul Hillier gives a helpful, highly informed commentary in the booklet, which also provides full texts. Excellent, well-balanced recording.

'Draw on sweet night' (English madrigals): MORLEY: *O griefe even on the bud; When loe, by breake of morning; Aprill is in my mistris face; Sweet nimphe, come to thy lover; Miraculous love's wounding; Fyer and lightning in nets of goulden wyers.* WEELKES: *Thule, the period of cosmographie; O care thou wilt dispatch mee; Since Robin Hood; Strike it up tabor.* WILBYE: *Sweet hony sucking bees; Adew sweet Amarillis; Draw on sweet night.* J. BENNET: *Weepe O mine eyes.* GIBBONS: *The silver swanne.* TOMKINS: *See, see the shepherd's queene.* WARD: *Come sable night.* VAUTOR: *Sweet Suffolk owle.*
*** EMI Dig. CDC7 49197-2 [id.].

This is an entirely enchanting concert. As might be guessed from the spelling above, Tudor pronunciation is used, which seems to add extra bite to the vocal timbre. Perhaps at times the singing might be a shade more unbuttoned, but it does not lack spontaneity, even when its style is a little lacking in geniality. Intonation and ensemble are flawless, and some of the songs are in five or six parts. The music itself is admirably chosen to cover a wide range of moods; perhaps the singers do not always reflect the lighter moments with enough sparkle; but there is so much here to ravish the ear that few will mind. The balance is slightly recessed in an attractive acoustic: the recording is very real and present.

Hill Smith, Marilyn (soprano), Peter Morrison (baritone)

'Treasures of operetta' (with Concert O, Barry): Excerpts from ZIER: *Der Schatzmeister.* J. STRAUSS Jnr: *Casanova.* KÁLMÁN: *Gypsy Princess.* STRAUS: *Chocolate Soldier.* TAUBER: *Old Chelsea.* MESSAGER: *Veronique.* HERBERT: *Naughty Marietta.* LEHÁR: *The Merry Widow; Giuditta.* ZELLER: *Der Obersteiger.* MONCKTON: *The Arcadians.*
**(*) Chan. Dig. CHAN 8362 [id.].

'Treasures of operetta' Vol. 2 (with Amb. S., Concert O, Barry): Excerpts from: JACOBI: *Sybil.* POSFORD: *Balalaika.* MONCKTON: *The Quaker Girl.* MILLOCKER: *Der arme Jonathan.* ZIER: *Der Schatzmeister; Der Fremdenführer.* GERMAN: *Merrie England.* LEHÁR: *The Merry widow; Paganini.* STOLZ/BENATSKY: *White Horse Inn.* MESSAGER: *Monsieur Beaucaire.* J. STRAUSS Jnr: *Casanova.*
**(*) Chan. Dig. CHAN 8561 [id.].

One has to make an initial adjustment to a style of performance which is very English, evoking memories of the Palm Court tradition of Anne Ziegler and Webster Booth. Marilyn Hill Smith sings freshly and often very sweetly, and she is genially partnered by the warm, easy-going baritone of Peter Morrison. Moreover, the orchestral accompaniments have plenty of flexibility and lilt, and the resonantly rich recording is exactly right for the music. With almost every number a 'hit', this is very attractive of its kind. If anything, the second volume is more successful than the first, with many novelties among the more familiar items, and the charming duet from *The Quaker Girl* an obvious highlight. Extra support is given by the excellent Ambrosian Singers, and the presentation and recording are both of a high standard.

Horne, Marilyn (mezzo-soprano)

'Beautiful dreamer' (The Great American Songbook, with ECO, Carl Davis): FOSTER: Jeannie with the light brown hair; Beautiful dreamer; If you've only got a moustache; Camptown Races. COPLAND: 5 Old American Songs. TRAD.: Sometimes I feel like a motherless child; I've just come from the fountain; Shenandoah, etc.
*** Decca Dig. 417 242-2 [id.].

Marilyn Horne is tangily characterful in this American repertory which draws from her a glorious range of tone, and she bridges the stylistic gaps between popular and concert repertory with supreme confidence. The Copland songs are particularly delightful, and the Decca recording is outstandingly vivid.

(A) Hundred Years of the Gramophone

100 years of the Gramophone (1888–1988): LEONCAVALLO: Pagliacci: Vesti la Giubba (Caruso). MARSHALL: I hear you calling me (John McCormack). KREISLER: Liebslied (Kreisler). CHOPIN: Étude in A (Cortot). BACH: Cello suite No. 1: Prelude (Casals). MUSSORGSKY: Song of the flea (Chaliapin). TARREGA: Recuerdos de la Alhambra (Segovia). ROSSINI: Scala di seta overture (Toscanini). LEONCAVALLO: Mattinata (Gigli). BEETHOVEN: Sonata No. 14 (Moonlight): Adagio (Schnabel). MOZART: Così fan tutte: Soave sia il vento (Schwarzkopf, etc.). DINICU: Hora staccato (Heifetz). PUCCINI: Tosca: Vissi d'arte (Callas). MOZART: Horn concerto No. 4, K.495: Rondo (D. Brain). SCHUBERT: Ave Maria (Menuhin). RACHMANINOV: Prelude in C sharp min. (Rubinstein). BIZET: Carmen: Habañera (De los Angeles). WAGNER: Lohengrin: Prelude, Act III (Boult). VERDI: Aida: Celeste Aida (Domingo). GERSHWIN: Porgy and Bess: Summertime (Te Kanawa). ORFF: Carmina Burana: O Fortuna (LSO Ch., LSO, Previn). SAINT-SAENS: Carnival of animals: The Swan (Du Pré).
(M) *** EMI CDH7 63018-2.

This celebratory sampler inevitably is an arbitrary selection, and every collector will have his or her own ideas about what should have been included. Even more striking is the roster of artists who are not here – Dame Janet Baker, for instance. Nevertheless there is plenty to fascinate the ear and give some idea of what a remarkable recorded legacy is held in the vaults of just one major company. Certain conductors (Beecham, for instance, with de los Angeles) are represented only in accompanying roles.

Italian Operatic favourites

'Italian operatic favourites' (sung by: De los Angeles, Del Monte, Gedda, Moffo, Campora, Grist, ROHCG Chorus, Merrill, Cavalli, Sereni, Corelli). Arias from: VERDI: La Traviata; Rigoletto; Il Trovatore (including Anvil chorus); Aida. ROSSINI: Il Barbiere di Siviglia. PUCCINI: La Bohème; Tosca; Madama Butterfly. PONCHIELLI: La Gioconda. MOZART: Le nozze di Figaro. DONIZETTI: Lucia di Lammermoor.
(B) *(*) CfP CD-CFP 4560.

A disappointing recital. Much of the male singing is undistinguished and often relatively coarse. That comment certainly does not apply to Victoria de los Angeles' excerpts from her 1960 recordings of La Traviata and Madama Butterfly, and Un bel dì *vedremo* is the highlight of the disc. Anna Moffo, recorded in 1961, provides the arias from Rossini's *Il Barbiere di Siviglia*, Mozart's *Voi che sapete* and the Mad scene from *Lucia di Lammermoor*, and there is some lovely singing here also. But while her tone is always creamy and beautiful, there is something too casual about the actual performances.

Jurinac, Sena (soprano)

R. STRAUSS: *Four Last songs (Vier letzte Lieder)*. Opera arias from: MOZART: *Così fan tutte; Idomeneo.* SMETANA: *The Bartered bride; The Kiss.* TCHAIKOVSKY: *Joan of Arc; Queen of Spades.*
(M) (***) EMI mono CDH7 63199-2 [id.].

This EMI Références issue, very well transferred, celebrates a magical, under-recorded singer. It brings together all of Jurinac's recordings for EMI outside the complete operas, and adds a live radio recording from Sweden – with Fritz Busch conducting the Stockholm Philharmonic Orchestra – of Strauss's *Four Last songs*, most beautifully done, if with rather generalized expression. Busch was also the conductor for the Glyndebourne recordings of excerpts from *Così fan tutte* and *Idomeneo.*

Kanawa, Dame Kiri Te (soprano)

'*Come to the fair*' (with Medici Qt; Nat. PO, Gamley): EASTHOPE MARTIN: *Come to the fair.* LAMBERT: *She is far from the land.* TRAD.: *Early one morning; The last rose of summer; Island spinning song; The ash grove; The Keel Row; Comin' thro' the rye; Annie Laurie; O can ye sew cushions; The Sally gardens; Greensleeves; The gentle maiden; I have a bonnet trimmed with blue; Danny Boy.*
*** EMI Dig. CDC7 47080-2 [id.].

Following very much in the Kathleen Ferrier tradition, Dame Kiri Te Kanawa sings this repertoire with infectious charm. She can be exhilaratingly robust, as in the title-piece and *The Keel Row*, yet at the next moment provide a ravishing lyricism, as in *The last rose of summer* or *The Sally gardens*. The orchestral accompaniments are decorative but simple (*Greensleeves*, a highlight, is especially felicitous). The recording has splendid presence. A captivating recital in every way.

'*Portrait*': Arias from: PUCCINI: *Tosca; Gianni Schicchi* VERDI: *La Traviata.* HUMPERDINCK: *Hänsel und Gretel.* MOZART: *Don Giovanni.* R. STRAUSS: *Morgen; Ruhe, meine Seele.* SCHUBERT: *Gretchen am Spinnrade.* SCHUMANN: *Du bist wie eine Blume.* FAURÉ: *Après un rêve.* WALTON: *Façade: Old Sir Faulk; Daphne; Through gilded trellises.*
**(*) CBS MK 39208 [id.].

CBS's sampler portrait of Dame Kiri may not be as representative of her usual repertory as the rival Decca disc (417 645-2), but the rarities – such as the Walton songs – are just as winning as the more predictable items. Recordings are not all of the most vivid, but made reasonably compatible.

'*Ave Maria*' (with St Paul's Cathedral Choir, ECO, Rose): GOUNOD: *Messe solennelle à Sainte Cécile: Sanctus. O divine Redeemer.* MOZART: *Ave verum, K. 618; Solemn Vespers: Laudate Dominum.* FRANCK: *Panis angelicus.* HANDEL: *Solomon: Let the bright Seraphim; Let their celestial concert.* MENDELSSOHN: *On wings of song.* BACH: *Jesu, joy of man's desiring.* SCHUBERT: *Ave Maria.*
**(*) Ph. Dig. 412 629-2 [id.].

Countless music-lovers who heard Dame Kiri sing *Let the bright Seraphim* at the wedding of the Prince and Princess of Wales will be pleased to have this record available, and they will not be disappointed, for the trumpet playing, too, is suitably resplendent. This comes at the end, and the rest of the programme lacks something in variety, although the voice always sounds beautiful and the naturally expressive singing gives much pleasure. The chorus, backwardly balanced, might have been more clearly focused.

'Kiri – A Portrait': CANTELOUBE: *Chants d'Auvergne: Baïlèro.* GAY: *Beggar's opera: Virgins are like the fair flow'r; Cease your funning.* HANDEL: *Messiah: Rejoice greatly; I know that my Redeemer liveth.* BRAHMS: *German Requiem: Ihr habt nun Traurigkeit.* MOZART: *Concert aria: Vado, ma dove? oh Dei!, K.583. Le nozze di Figaro: Dove sono.* BIZET: *Je dis que rien ne m'épouvante.* PUCCINI: *Tosca: Vissi d'arte.* VILLA-LOBOS: *Bachianas brasileiras No. 5.*
*** Decca 417 645-2 [id.].

Decca's portrait of Dame Kiri gathers together many of her most delectable recordings of recent years, a winning compendium of her art, whether seductive in Canteloube and Villa-Lobos, dazzling in Handel, or sparkling in *The Beggar's opera*. The recordings capture the voice at its fullest and most golden.

King's College, Cambridge, Choir, Cleobury

ALLEGRI: *Miserere mei, Deus.* FRESCOBALDI: *Messa sopra l'aria della Monica.* MARENZIO: *Magnificat.* NANINO: *Adoramus te, Christe.* UGOLINI: *Beata es Virgo Maria.*
**(*) EMI CDC7 47065-2 [id.].

An attractively planned concert of Renaissance choral music. Marenzio's fine *Magnificat* and the stirring *Beata es Virgo Maria* of Ugolini (a contemporary of Allegri) make a strong impression – the latter reminding the listener of Andrea Gabrieli. The performances are generally excellent and the King's acoustic provides its usual beautiful aura. The account of Allegri's *Miserere*, although effective, lacks the ethereal memorability of the finest versions; its treble soloist, Timothy Beasley-Murray, is made to sound almost over-confident, with his upward leap commandingly extrovert. The CD gains much from the background silence, but the choral focus is mistier than one might have expected.

King's College, Cambridge, Choir, Ledger

'Festival of lessons and carols' (1979).
*** EMI CDC7 49620-2 [id.].

This most recent version on record of the annual King's College ceremony has the benefit of modern recording, even more atmospheric than before. Under Philip Ledger the famous choir keeps its beauty of tone and incisive attack. The opening processional, *Once in Royal David's city*, is even more effective heard against the background quiet of CD, and this remains a unique blend of liturgy and music.

'Procession with carols on Advent Sunday'.
*** EMI Dig. CDC7 49619-2 [id.].

This makes an attractive variant to the specifically Christmas-based service, though the carols themselves are not quite so memorable. Beautiful singing and richly atmospheric recording; the wide dynamic range is demonstrated equally effectively by the atmospheric opening and processional and the sumptuous closing hymn.

King's College, Cambridge, Choir, Ledger and Willcocks

'Christmas carols from King's College': Once in Royal David's city; O little town of Bethlehem; The first nowell; I saw three ships; Personent Hodie; Myn Lyking; A spotless rose; Away in a manger; I sing of a maiden; O come, O come Emanuel; While shepherds watched; Up! good Christian folk; In the bleak midwinter; Silent night; The holly and the ivy; It came upon a midnight clear; Three kings; On Christmas night; A child is born in Bethlehem; In dulci jubilo; O come all ye faithful; Hark! the herald angels sing.
*** EMI CDC7 47500-2 [id.].

With over an hour of music and twenty-two carols included, this is good value. The recordings were made between 1969 and 1976. The sound is excellent on CD, and the King's acoustic is generally well caught. The closing two carols are made particularly resplendent.

King's College, Cambridge, Choir, Willcocks, Ledger

The Psalms of David, Volume 1: Psalms Nos. 15, 23–4, 42–43, 46, 61, 84, 104, 121–2, 137, 147–50.
(M) *** EMI CDM7 63100-2.

Psalms of David, Volume 2: Psalms Nos. 12, 22, 65–7, 78, 81, 114–15, 126, 133–4.
(M) *** EMI CDM7 63101-2.

Psalms of David, Volume 3: Psalms Nos. 37, 45, 49, 53, 93–4, 107, 130–1.
(M) *** EMI CDM7 63102-2.

In pioneer days the early Christians took over the Psalter along with the Old Testament teachings from the Hebrew Temple, and the Psalms have always been an integral part of Anglican liturgy. Although they are called 'The Psalms of David' it has long been recognized that the original Hebrew collection (some 150 strong) was gathered together over a period of several hundred years, and the writings are from many different anonymous hands. The Anglican settings used on these recordings have offered their composers a fairly wide range of expressive potential, yet the music itself, perhaps because of the stylized metre and the ritual nature of its use, seldom approaches the depth and resonance which are found in the music of the great composers of the Roman Catholic faith, Palestrina, Victoria and so on. The King's College Choir, conducted by Sir David Willcocks from the organ, give an eloquent account of a cross-section of the Psalter on these discs. They are beautifully recorded and well transferred to CD.

Kirkby, Emma (soprano), Consort of Musicke, Rooley

'Madrigals and wedding songs for Diana' (with David Thomas, bass): BENNET: All creatures now are merry-minded. CAMPION: Now hath Flora robbed her bowers. Move now measured sound. Woo her and win her. LUPO: Shows and nightly revels. Time that leads the fatal round. GILES: Triumph now with joy and mirth. CAVENDISH: Come, gentle swains. DOWLAND: Welcome, black night . . . Cease these false sports. WEELKES: Hark! all ye lovely saints. As Vesta was. WILBYE: Lady Oriana. EAST: Hence stars! too dim of light. You meaner beauties. LANIER: Bring away this sacred tree. The Marigold. Mark how the

blushful morn. COPERARIO: *Go, happy man. While dancing rests. Come ashore, merry mates.* E. GIBBONS: *Long live fair Oriana.*
*** Hyp. CDA 66019 [id.].

This wholly delightful anthology celebrates early royal occasions, aristocratic weddings, and in its choice of Elizabethan madrigals skilfully balances praise of the Virgin Queen with a less ambivalent attitude to nuptial delights. Emma Kirkby is at her freshest and most captivating, and David Thomas, if not quite her match, makes an admirable contribution. Accompaniments are stylish and well balanced, and the recording is altogether first rate.

Lehmann, Lotte (soprano)

Opera arias from: BEETHOVEN: *Fidelio.* WEBER: *Der Freischütz; Oberon.* NICOLAI: *Die lustigen Weiber von Windsor.* WAGNER: *Lohengrin; Tannhäuser; Tristan und Isolde.* R. STRAUSS: *Der Rosenkavalier; Ariadne auf Naxos; Arabella.* KORNGOLD: *Die tote Stadt; Das Wunder der Heliane.* J. STRAUSS Jnr: *Die Fledermaus.* LEHÁR: *Eva.*
(M) (***) EMI mono CDH7 610422 [id.].

Lehmann's celebrated account of the Marschallin's monologue from the classic set of *Rosenkavalier* excerpts recorded in Vienna in 1933 is an essential item here. Otherwise this collection of fourteen of her recordings, made in the days of 78s, concentrates on the Parlophone issues done in Berlin in the 1920s and early '30s. The earliest has the young George Szell accompanying her in Korngold (the only pre-electric here), but there are many other treasures. The Richard Strauss items are particularly valuable, with Arabella's *Mein Elemer* recorded within months of the opera's première in 1933. Though Isolde was not a role she would ever have considered singing on stage, the *Liebestod* here has wonderful poise and beauty, while it is good to hear her speaking voice in the 1928 recording of Lehár's *Eva*.

Song recital: CIMARA: *Canto di primavera.* SADERO: *Fà la nana.* GOUNOD: *Vierge d'Athènes.* PALADILHE: *Psyché.* DUPARC: *La vie antérieure.* HAHN: *Infidélité; L'enamourée; D'une prison.* GRECHANINOV: *My native land (Heimat).* WORTH: *Midsummer.* SJOBERG: *Visions (Tonerna).* TRAD.: *Drink to me only; Schlafe, mein süsses Kind.* BALOCH: *Do not chide me.* WOLF: *Nun lass uns Frieden schliessen; Und willst du deinen Liebsten sterben sehen?; Der Knabe und das Immlein.* R. STRAUSS: *Wozu noch, Mädchen; Du meines Herzens Krönelein.* BRAHMS: *Das Mädchen spricht; Mein Mädel hat einen Rosenmund.* SCHUMANN: *Waldesgespräch; Du bist wie eine Blume; Frühlingsnacht.* SCHUBERT: *Im Abendrot; Der Jüngling an der Quelle; An die Nachtigall; Nacht und Träume; An Die Musik.*
(M) (***) RCA mono GD 87809 [7809-2-RG].

Bringing together Lehmann's 78-r.p.m. recordings, made for RCA between 1935 and 1947, this is a fascinating, often unexpected collection, with Italian, French and English songs as well as German Lieder. The transfers bring the singer vividly face to face with the listener, but this is not so full a portrait as the Références collection of her singing opera arias, recorded in the 1920s and early '30s (see above).

Leipzig Radio Chorus, Silvio Varviso

German opera choruses (with Dresden State O) from: WEBER: *Der Freischütz*. NICOLAI: *Merry wives of Windsor*. MOZART: *Die Zauberflöte*. BEETHOVEN: *Fidelio*. WAGNER: *Der fliegende Holländer; Die Meistersinger; Tannhäuser; Lohengrin; Parsifal*.
*** Ph. Dig. 422 410-2 [id.].

Unlike most collections of this kind, this one is not assembled from previous complete sets but has been specially compiled, and great care has been taken with the production values. The recording, made in the warm resonance of the Dresden Lukaskirche, gives a wonderful bloom to the choral sound. Perhaps Weber's huntsmen could have a sharper focus in their throatily stirring opener but, as with Wagner's sailors later, their enunciation is splendidly crisp. Nicolai's *O süsser Mond* (with its lovely melody, familiar from the overture) is magically atmospheric; and if the acoustics in the sombre Prison scene from *Fidelio* are evocative rather of the dungeon than of the open air, this is most moving, with the prisoners' solos included (by able members of the chorus). The women's voices are appealingly fresh, whether as spinners in *Der fliegende Holländer* or adding radiance to the second of the two *Pilgrims' choruses* from *Tannhäuser*. The excerpts from *Die Meistersinger* are richly and thrillingly expansive, and the concert closes with the glorious chorus of the Holy Grail from *Parsifal*, with the Dresden Boys' Choir adding to the frisson of evocative splendour. Varviso's pacing is always aptly judged and the whole programme sounds spontaneous, as if at a live concert. Full translations are included, and technically this fine disc is in the demonstration class for its beauty as well as its realism.

London Symphony Chorus and Orchestra, Richard Hickox

Opera choruses: BIZET: *Carmen: Toreador chorus*. VERDI: *Il Trovatore: Anvil chorus. Nabucco: Gli arredi festivi; Va pensiero. Macbeth: Che faceste?. Aida: Grand march*. GOUNOD: *Faust: Soldiers' chorus*. BORODIN: *Prince Igor: Polovtsian dances*.
(B) *** Pickwick Dig. PCD 908.

Most collections of opera choruses are taken from sets, but this is a freshly minted digital collection of favourites, sung with fine fervour and discipline. The opening *Toreador chorus* from *Carmen* is zestfully infectious and the *Soldiers' chorus* from *Faust* is equally buoyant. The noble line of Verdi's *Va pensiero* is shaped beautifully by Hickox, with the balance between voices and orchestra particularly good. In *Gli arredi festivi* from *Nabucco* and the famous Triumphal scene from *Aida* the orchestral brass sound resonantly sonorous, even if the fanfare trumpets could have been more widely separated in the latter piece. The concert ends with Borodin's *Polovtsian dances* most excitingly done. The recording, made at the EMI Abbey Road studio, has the atmosphere of an idealized opera house, and the result is in the demonstration bracket, with a projection and presence fully worthy of this polished but uninhibited singing.

Lott, Felicity (soprano), Graham Johnson (piano)

Mélodies on Victor Hugo poems: GOUNOD: *Sérénade*. BIZET: *Feuilles d'album: Guitare. Adieux de l'hôtesse arabe*. LALO: *Guitare*. DELIBES: *Eclogue*. FRANCK: *S'il est un charmant gazon*. FAURÉ: *L'absent; Le papillon et la fleur; Puisqu'ici bas*. WAGNER: *L'attente*. LISZT: *O quand je dors; Comment, disaint-ils*. SAINT-SAENS: *Soirée en mer; La*

fiancée du timbalier. M. V. WHITE: *Chantez, chantez jeune inspirée.* HAHN: *Si mes vers avaient des ailes. Rêverie.*
*** HM HMC 901138 [id.].

Felicity Lott's collection of Hugo settings relies mainly on sweet and charming songs, freshly and unsentimentally done, with Graham Johnson an ideally sympathetic accompanist. The recital is then given welcome stiffening with fine songs by Wagner and Liszt, as well as two by Saint-Saëns that have a bite worthy of Berlioz.

McCormack, John (tenor)

Popular songs and Irish ballads. TRAD.: *The garden where the praties grow; Terence's farewell to Kathleen; Believe me if all those endearing young charms; The star of the County Down; Oft in the stilly night; The meeting of the waters; The Bard of Armagh; Down by the Salley Gardens; She moved thro' the fair; The green bushes.* BALFE: *The harp that once through Tara's halls.* ROECKEL: *The green isle of Erin.* SCHNEIDER: *O Mary dear.* LAMBERT: *She is far from the land.* HAYNES: *Off to Philadelphia.* MOLLOY: *The Kerry dance; Bantry Bay.* MARSHALL: *I hear you calling me.* E. PURCELL: *Passing by.* WOODFORD-FINDEN: *Kashmiri song.* CLUTSAM: *I know of two bright eyes.* FOSTER: *Jeannie with the light brown hair; Sweetly she sleeps, my Alice fair.*
(M) (***) EMI mono CDH7 69788-2.

McCormack's voice recorded with wonderful naturalness, partly because he mastered early the art of using the microphone. These 78-r.p.m. transfers, all but one from the 1930s and '40s, sound as fresh and real as the day they were made. In Irish repertoire like *The star of the County Down* McCormack is irresistible, but in lighter concert songs he could also spin the utmost magic. *Down by the Salley Gardens* and Stephen Foster's *Jeannie with the light brown hair* are superb examples, while in a ballad like *I hear you calling me* (an early pre-electric recording from 1908) the golden bloom of the vocal timbre combining with an artless line brings a ravishing frisson on the closing pianissimo. Many of the accompaniments are by Gerald Moore, who proves a splendid partner. Occasionally there is a hint of unsteadiness in the sustained *piano* tone, but otherwise no apology need be made for the recorded sound which is first class, while the lack of 78-r.p.m. background noise is remarkable.

Martinelli, Giovanni (tenor)

'Prima voce': Arias from: GIORDANO: *Andrea Chénier; Fedora.* LEONCAVALLO: *Pagliacci.* MASCAGNI: *Cavalleria Rusticana; Iris.* TCHAIKOVSKY: *Eugene Onegin.* VERDI: *Aida; Ernani; La forza del destino; La Traviata.*
(M) (***) Nimbus mono NIM 7804 [id.].

This collection of 17 fine examples of Martinelli's very distinctive and characterful singing covers his vintage period from 1915 to 1928, with one 1927 recording from Verdi's *La forza del destino* so clear that you can hear a dog barking outside the studio. The other two items from *Forza* are just as memorable, with Martinelli joined by Giuseppe de Luca in the Act IV duet, and by Rosa Ponselle and the bass, Ezio Pinza, for the final duet, with the voices astonishingly vivid and immediate.

Monteverdi Choir, English Baroque Soloists, Gardiner

'Sacred choral music': D. SCARLATTI: *Stabat Mater.* CAVALLI: *Salve regina.* GESUALDO: *Ave, dulcissima Maria.* CLÉMENT: *O Maria vernana rosa.*
*** Erato/WEA Dig. 2292 45219-2 [id.].

This collection is centred round Domenico Scarlatti's *Stabat Mater*, which is praised in the Composer section. The shorter works which fill out this collection are no less worth while, notably the rewarding Gesualdo motet from the *Sacrae cantiones*, whose remarkably expressive opening has few precedents in its harmonic eloquence, and another Marian motet by Jacques Clément, better known as Clemens non Papa. The recording is very good indeed without being in the demonstration bracket.

Muzio, Claudia (soprano)

Arias from: BELLINI: *La Sonnabula; Norma.* VERDI: *Il Trovatore; La Forza del destino.* BOITO: *Mefistofele.* MASCAGNI: *Cavalleria Rusticana.* PUCCINI: *La Bohème; Tosca.* CILEA: *L'Arlesiana; Adriana Lecouvreur.* GIORDANO: *Andrea Chénier. Songs.*
(M) (***) EMI mono CDH7 69790-2.

This is a superb celebration of one of the greatest Italian sopranos of the century, one who died tragically young and whose recording career failed to encompass the very period when she was, by all accounts, at her greatest. All twenty items on this Références CD come from her last years, 1934 and 1935 (she died of a heart complaint in 1936). *Casta diva* here would have expanded more generously a few years earlier; but, once that is said, every single item brings magical communication, highly individual in expression and timbre, with the voice shaded and varied in tone and dynamic so that one is mesmerized by phrase after phrase. There are few accounts of Mimi's arias from *La Bohème* to match these – with the close of the *Farewell* wonderfully veiled in tone; while the Cilea, Giordano and Boito items have a depth of expression never surpassed. The beauty of legato line in the Bellini items and the tonal variety in the Verdi arias, conveying tragic intensity, remain models for all time. Keith Hardwick's superb transfers bring the voice to us wonderfully refreshed and clarified, almost as though Muzio were still in our presence.

New College, Oxford, Choir, Higginbottom

'Carols from New College': *O come all ye faithful; The angel Gabriel; Ding dong merrily on high; The holly and the ivy; I wonder as I wander; Sussex carol; This is the truth; A Virgin most pure; Rocking carol; Once in Royal David's city.* ORD: *Adam lay y-bounden.* BENNETT: *Out of your sleep.* HOWELLS: *A spotless rose; Here is the litle door.* DARKE: *In the bleak midwinter.* MATHIAS: *A babe is born; Wassail carol.* WISHART: *Alleluya, a new work is come on hand.* LEIGHTON: *Lully, lulla, thou little tiny child.* JOUBERT: *There is no rose of such virtue.*
*** CRD CRD 3443 [id.].

A beautiful Christmas record, the mood essentially serene and reflective. Apart from the lovely traditional arrangements, from the Czech *Rocking carol* to the Appalachian *I wonder as I wander*, many of the highlights are more recently composed. Both the Mathias settings are memorable and spark a lively response from the choir; Howells' *Here is the little door* is matched by Wishart's *Alleluya* and Kenneth Leighton's *Lully, lulla, thou little tiny child* in memorability. In some of these and in the opening *O come all ye faithful* and the closing *Once in Royal David's city*, Howard Moody adds weight with excellent organ accompaniments, but fifteen of the twenty-one items here are sung unaccompanied, to maximum effect. The recording acoustic seems ideal and the balance is first class. The documentation, however, consists of just a list of titles and sources – and the CD (using the unedited artwork from the LP) lists them as being divided on to side one and side two!

'O Sing unto the Lord' (with Instrumental Ens. led by Roy Goodman): VAUGHAN WILLIAMS: *O Clap your hands* (motet). STANFORD: *Magnificat and Nunc dimittis in G.* TAVERNER: *Mater Christi* (motet). PURCELL: *O Sing unto the Lord* (Verse anthem). BAINTON: *And I saw a new heaven.* BRITTEN: *Missa brevis.* MONTEVERDI: *Beatus vir.* HARVEY: *I love the Lord.*
⊛ *** Proudsound PROUCD 114 02 [id.].

It is difficult to conceive of a better or more rewarding collection of (mainly British) church music than this, marvellously sung by this fine choir of 16 trebles and 12 men. The recording, made in New College Chapel, is ideally balanced, very real indeed, and offers the most beautiful choral textures, used over the widest range of dynamic. The programme opens quite spectacularly with Vaughan Williams's brief but ambitious setting of Psalm 47 for double chorus, brass, percussion and organ (a demonstration item if ever there was one) and continues with Stanford's inspired *Magnificat and Nunc dimittis in G*, with a memorable treble solo in the former from Daniel Johnson, and with Michael Morton (bass) almost equally impressive in the latter. Then the programme ranges from Taverner's fine motet, *Mater Christi*, written some 400 years earlier, to Harvey's rich modern setting of Psalm 16, with its satisfyingly pungent dissonances. In between come one of Purcell's finest verse-anthems (with a convincing authentic accompaniment led by Roy Goodman), Bainton's glorious *And I saw a new heaven*, Britten's *Missa brevis* (which anyone who enjoys the *Ceremony of carols* will equally relish) and Monteverdi's madrigal-styled *Beatus vir* with its florid polyphony dramatically broadening at the end for the closing *Amen*.

'Rejoice in the Lamb' (with Fiori Musicali): BAIRSTOW: *Blessed city, Heavenly Salem.* DURUFLÉ: *4 Motets on Gregorian themes, Op. 10.* BRITTEN: *Rejoice in the Lamb, Op. 30.* WISE: *The ways of Zion do mourn.* BYRD: *Ave verum corpus.* GIBBONS: *O clap your hands.* HANDEL: *Chandos anthem No. 6, As pants the hart.*
** Proudsound Dig. PROUCD 125 [id.].

There is much to enjoy here, not least the four brief but engaging *Motets sur des thèmes grégoriens* of Maurice Duruflé, the serene Byrd *Motet* and the fine Gibbons *Anthem*. But it was less than ideal planning to feature just one of the *Chandos anthems* when these are usually put on disc grouped together. Good though the performance is, Christophers' account (on the appropriately named Chandos label) using well-known soloists is even better. Britten's *Rejoice in the Lamb* also suffers from the recording's very wide dynamic range so that the solos, not always sung by the strongest voices (notably the famous treble accolade for the mouse, which is certainly diminutive here), are not strongly projected by comparison with the choral contributions.

Norman, Jessye (soprano)

'Sacred songs' (with Amb. S., RPO, Gibson): GOUNOD: *Messe solennelle à Sainte Cécile: Sanctus. O Divine Redeemer.* FRANCK: *Panis angelicus.* ADAMS: *The Holy City.* ANON.:

Amazing grace. Greensleeves. Let us break bread. I wonder. MAGGIMSEY: *Sweet little Jesus Boy.* YON: *Gesù Bambino.*
*** Ph. Dig. 400 019-2 [id.].

Miss Norman's restraint is very telling here; she sings with great eloquence, but her simplicity and sincerity shine through repertoire that can easily sound sentimental. The Gounod *Sanctus* is especially fine, but the simpler traditional songs are also very affecting. The compact disc is very much in the demonstration class, strikingly natural and giving the soloist remarkable presence, especially when she is singing unaccompanied.

French songs (with Dalton Baldwin, piano): DUPARC: *La vie antérieure; Phidylé; Chanson triste; L'invitation au voyage.* RAVEL: *2 mélodies hébraïques.* POULENC: *Voyage à Paris; Montparnasse; La Grenouillère; Les chemins de l'amour.* SATIE: *3 mélodies; Je le veux.*
**(*) Ph. 416 445-2 [id.].

Recorded in 1976, Jessye Norman's delightful collection of French songs reveals the great voice already glowing in its distinctive range of tone and expression. But at that point in her career she was still a shade inhibited in the studio; though the interpretative subtleties are many, she was later to give even deeper and more searching performances in this repertory. The analogue sound has been transferred very well.

Hohenems Festival recital (with Geoffrey Parsons, piano): HANDEL: *Dank sei dir Herr; Lascia ch'io pianga.* SCHUMANN: *Widmung; Du bist wie eine Blume; Schöne Fremde; Auf einer Burg; Wehmut; Frühlingsnacht.* SCHUBERT: *Der Musensohn; Auf dem See; Meeres Stille; Ave Maria; An die Natur; Rastlose Liebe; Gretchen am Spinnrade; Die Liebe hat gelogen; Der Tod und das Mädchen; Erlkönig.* BRAHMS: *Meine Liebe ist grün.* R. STRAUSS: *Wir beide wollen springen.* Spirituals: *He's got the whole world in his hands; Great day.*
**(*) Ph. Dig. 422 048-2 [id.].

Recorded live at the Hohenems Festival in June 1987, this fine disc gives a vivid idea of the atmosphere of excitement at a Jessye Norman recital. It ends in explosions of wild joy and enthusiasm in response to the two spirituals which are given as final encores, exuberant, full-throated singing that communicates with physical impact. Next to this, Jessye Norman's studio-made recordings of Lieder sound reticent – but there are losses as well as gains, particularly when the recording is on the rough side, with piano-tone clangy. The freedom of expressiveness will also strike many Lieder-enthusiasts as excessive, with Schumann's *Widmung*, for example, fluctuating in tempo out of wild urgency. But there are many unique moments, as in the dark intensity of Schubert's *Meeres Stille* or the colourful vocal characterization in *Erlkönig*. Recording balance is not ideal, with the voice sometimes set at a distance.

'Live' (with Geoffrey Parsons, piano): HAYDN: *Arianna a Naxos.* HANDEL: *Rinaldo: Lascia ch'io pianga. Dank sei dir Herr.* MAHLER: *Des Knaben Wunderhorn: Wer hat dies Liedlein erdacht? Das irdische Leben; Rheinlegendchen. Scheiden und Meiden.* BERG: *Liebe; Mignon; Die Nachtigall; Schliesse mir die Augen beid* (2 versions). R. STRAUSS: *Ich trage meine Minne; Seitdem dein Aug'; Kling!; Wir beide wollen springen.* RAVEL: *Étude en forme de habañera.* Spirituals: *Great day; He's got the whole world in his hands.*
*** Ph. Dig. 422 235-2 [id.].

Recorded live at various venues during Jessye Norman's appearances in eleven different cities on her European tour in 1987, this recital record follows up her earlier one from Hohenems, even sharing the same Baroque works and spirituals, though in different performances. Here more than in Hohenems the applause tends to be intrusive, but the glory of the unique voice is more compelling than ever. As before, her free-ranging expressiveness may worry purists, but the intensity of communication is what matters. By far the biggest item is the Haydn at the start, given a highly dramatic performance of extremes. It was a charming idea to interlace an extended sequence of Mahler and Berg songs, all lyrical and accessible. Ravel's *Habañera* setting, an extended wordless *vocalise*, makes an unexpected but satisfying conclusion. The disc comes in a slip-case with a separate booklet of words and translations, plus a note by the singer about her first, seminal visit to Europe in 1968.

Opera Choruses

'*Famous Opera choruses*' (various artists) from: VERDI: *Nabucco; Il Trovatore; Aida; Macbeth.* LEONCAVALLO: *Pagliacci.* PUCCINI: *Madama Butterfly.* GOUNOD: *Faust.* WAGNER: *Tannhäuser.* TCHAIKOVSKY: *Eugene Onegin.* MUSSORGSKY: *Boris Godunov.* (B) ** Decca 421 176-2 [id.].

A generally rewarding bargain collection, given characteristically vivid Decca sound. Many favourites are here, with the *Aida* triumphal scene taken from Karajan's spectacular, early, Vienna set. The Waltz scene from *Eugene Onegin* comes from another early set, made in Belgrade, and includes the Introduction to Act II. The scene from *Boris Godunov* is a studio recording, with the Covent Garden Opera Chorus ably conducted by Edward Downes and with Joseph Rouleau as Boris. The inclusion of items (the Wagner and Leoncavallo excerpts) contributed by the perfectly adequate Kingsway Chorus under Camerata is the only curious choice.

Operatic Duets: 'Duets from famous operas'

Duets sung by: (i) Nicolai Gedda, (ii) Ernest Blanc, (iii) Jussi Bjoerling and Victoria de los Angeles, (iv) Carlo Bergonzi, (v) Maria Callas, (vi) Mirella Freni, (vii) Eberhard Waechter and Graziella Sciutti, (viii) Tito Gobbi, (ix) Gabriella Tucci, (x) Franco Corelli, (xi) Evelyn Lear and D. Ouzounov, (xii) Antonietta Stella; (i; ii) BIZET: *Les Pêcheurs de perles: Au fond du temple saint.* (iii) PUCCINI: *Madama Butterfly: Bimba dagli occhi.* (iv; v) *Tosca: O dolci mani.* (i; vi) *La Bohème: O soave fanciulla.* (vii) MOZART: *Don Giovanni: Là ci darem la mano.* (v; viii) ROSSINI: *Il barbiere di Siviglia: Dunque io son'.* (ix; x) VERDI: *Il Trovatore: Miserere d'un'alma già vicina.* (xi) MUSSORGSKY: *Boris Godunov: O Tsarevich I beg you.* (x; xii) GIORDANO: *Andrea Chénier: Vicini a te.* (B) **(*) CfP CD-CFP 9013.

There are not many operas that hold their reputation in the public memory by means of a male duet, but *The pearl fishers* is one, and a sturdy performance of *Au fond du temple saint* makes a suitable centre-point for this collection of purple duos. The CD, however, opens with the genial lyricism of *Là ci darem la mano*, from the 1961 Giulini set of *Don Giovanni* with Eberhard Waechter and Graziella Sciutti singing most winningly. The star quality of the artists is noticeable through most of these extracts. Highlights include this beautifully relaxed *Là ci darem*, the short Rossini item, and the *La Bohème* duet (which seldom fails). There is also a blaze of melodrama from *Andrea Chénier*. As a programme, the effect of a series of such full-blooded, passionate vocal embraces is perhaps a little wearing. But otherwise, with generally lively recording, few will be disappointed. The CD has been remastered admirably to make the most of the different recording sources – the vocal timbres are particularly smooth and natural, without loss of projection.

Operatic Duets: 'Great love duets'

'Great love duets' (sung by Sutherland, Freni, Pavarotti, Tebaldi, Corelli, M. Price, Cossutta): PUCCINI: Madama Butterfly; La Bohème; Tosca; Manon Lescaut. VERDI: Otello; La Traviata.
(M) *** Decca 421 308-2 [id.].

This collection in Decca's mid-price Opera Gala series is very well chosen, starting and ending with duets from two of Karajan's outstanding Puccini recordings for Decca, Madama Butterfly and La Bohème, both with Freni and Pavarotti. The Bohème item includes not only the duet O soave fanciulla but the two favourite arias which precede it, Che gelida manina and Sì, mi chiamano Mimì. Sutherland is represented by La Traviata, Tebaldi by Manon Lescaut and Margaret Price by Otello, all very well transferred.

Operatic Duets: 'Great operatic duets'

'Great operatic duets' (sung by Sutherland, Pavarotti, Freni, Ludwig, Horne, Bergonzi, Fischer-Dieskau, Del Monaco, Bastianini): from DELIBES: Lakmé. PUCCINI: Madama Butterfly. BELLINI: Norma. VERDI: La Forza del destino; Don Carlo. OFFENBACH: Contes d'Hoffmann.
(M) *** Decca 421 314-2 [id.].

Again at mid-price, Decca provides a further excellent collection of duets, ranging rather more widely, from some of the company's finest recordings of the 1960s and '70s. The choice is imaginative and the transfers excellent, to bring out the fine quality of the original analogue sound.

Operetta: 'Golden operetta'

'Golden operetta': J. STRAUSS, Jnr: Die Fledermaus: Mein Herr Marquis (Gueden); Csardas (Janowitz). Eine Nacht in Venedig: Lagunen waltz (Krenn). Wiener Blut: Wiener Blut (Gueden). Der Zigeunerbaron: O habet Acht (Lorengar). Casanova: Nuns' chorus (Sutherland, Ambrosian Singers). ZELLER: Der Obersteiger: Sei nicht bös (Gueden). LEHÁR: Das Land des Lächelns: Dein ist mein ganzes Herz (Bjoerling). Die lustige Witwe: Vilja-Lied (Sutherland); Lippen schweigen (Holm, Krenn). Schön ist die Welt (Krenn). Der Graf von Luxemburg: Lieber Freund . . . Bist du's, Lachendes Gluck (Holm, Krenn). Giuditta: Du bist meine Sonne (Kmentt). LECOCQ: Le Coeur et la main: Bonsoir Perez le capitaine (Sutherland). OFFENBACH: La Périchole: Letter song. La Grande Duchesse de Gérolstein: J'aime les militaires (Crespin).
(M) *** Decca 421 319-2 [id.].

A valuable and generous anthology, not just for the obvious highlights: Joan Sutherland's Vilja and the delightful contributions from Hilde Gueden – notably a delicious Sei nicht bös – recorded in 1961 when the voice was at its freshest; but also Régine Crespin at her finest in Offenbach (the duchess reviewing her troops) and the charming Letter song from La Périchole. In their winningly nostalgic account of the Merry Widow waltz Renate Holm and Werner Krenn hum the melody, having sung the words, giving the impression of dancing together. The recording throughout is atmospheric, with plenty of bloom and with the voices given a natural presence.

Pavarotti, Luciano (tenor)

'The world's favourite arias' from: LEONCAVALLO: *I Pagliacci.* FLOTOW: *Martha.* BIZET: *Carmen.* PUCCINI: *La Bohème; Tosca; Turandot.* VERDI: *Rigoletto; Aida; Il Trovatore.* GOUNOD: *Faust.*
** Decca 400 053-2 [id.].

As one would expect from Pavarotti, there is much to enjoy in his ripe and resonant singing of these favourite arias, but it is noticeable that the finest performances are those which come from complete sets, conducted by Karajan (*Bohème*), Mehta (*Turandot*) and Bonynge (*Rigoletto*), where, with character in mind, Pavarotti's singing is more intense and imaginative. The rest remains very impressive, though at under 40 minutes the measure is short. *'Tutto Pavarotti'* – see below – is the recital to choose.

'Digital recital' (with Nat. PO, Chailly or Fabritiis): Arias from: GIORDANO: *Fedora; Andrea Chénier.* BOITO: *Mefistofele.* CILEA: *Adriana Lecouvreur.* MASCAGNI: *Iris.* MEYERBEER: *L'Africana.* MASSENET: *Werther.* PUCCINI: *La Fanciulla del West; Manon Lescaut* (with Howlett).
**(*) Decca Dig. 400 083-2 [id.].

The passion with which Pavarotti tackles Des Grieux's Act III plea from *Manon Lescaut* is devastating, and the big breast-beating numbers are all splendid, imaginative as well as heroic. But the slight pieces, Des Grieux's *Tra voi belle* and the *Iris Serenade*, could be lighter and more charming. The compact disc gives the voice even greater projection but it also makes the listener more aware of the occasional lack of subtlety of the presentation.

Neapolitan songs (with Ch. and O of Teatro Comunale, Bologna, Guadagno, or Nat. PO, Chiaramello): DI CAPUA: *O sole mio; Maria, Mari.* TOSTI: *A' vuchella. Marechiare.* CANNIO: *O surdato 'nnamurato.* GAMBARDELLA: *O Marenariello.* ANON.: *Fenesta vascia.* DE CURTIS: *Torna a Surriento. Tu, ca nun chiagne.* PENNINO: *Pecchè . . .* D'ANNIBALE: *O paese d'o sole.* TAGLIAFERRI: *Piscatore 'e pusilleco.* DENZA: *Funiculi, funicula.*
*** Decca 410 015-2 [id.].

Neapolitan songs given grand treatment in passionate Italian performances, missing some of the charm but none of the red-blooded fervour. The recording is both vivid and atmospheric and is digitally remastered most successfully.

'Mamma' (Italian and Neapolitan popular songs with O and Ch., Henry Mancini): BIXIO: *Mamma; Vivere; Mia canzone al vento; Parlami d'amore.* DE CURTIS: *Non ti scordar di me.* BUZZI-PECCIA: *Lolita:* excerpts. GASTALDON: *Musica proibita.* CESARINI: *Firenze sogna.* KRAMER: *In un palco della scala.* RIVI: *Addio, sogni di gloria!* D'ANZI: *Voglio vivere così.* DI LAZZARO: *Chitarra romana.* DE CRESCENZO: *Rondine al nido.* TRAD.: *Ghirlandeina.* CALI-FONA: *Vieni sul mar'.* ARONA: *Campana di San Giusto.*
**(*) Decca Dig. 411 959-2 [id.].

Larger-than-life arrangements by Henry Mancini of popular Italian and Neapolitan songs with larger-than-life singing to match. Vulgarity is welcomed rather than skirted, which is fair enough in this music. Larger-than-life recording, too.

'O Holy night' (with Wandsworth School Boys' Ch., Nat. PO, Adler): ADAM: *Cantique de noël (O holy night).* STRADELLA: *Pieta Signore.* FRANCK: *Panis angelicus.* MERCADANTE: *Parola quinta.* SCHUBERT: *Ave Maria.* BACH/GOUNOD: *Ave Maria.*

BIZET: *Agnus Dei.* BERLIOZ: *Requiem: Sanctus.* TRAD.: *Adeste fidelis.* YON: *Jesù bambino.* SCHUBERT, arr. Melichar: *Mille cherubini in coro.*
**(*) Decca 414 044-2 [id.].

Pavarotti is hardly a model of taste but he avoids the worst pitfalls; and if this sort of recital is what you are looking for, then Pavarotti is a good choice, with his beautiful vocalizing helped by full, bright recording. Note too that one or two of these items are less hackneyed than the rest, for instance the title setting by Adam, Mercadante's *Parola quinta* and the *Sanctus* from Berlioz's *Requiem Mass.*

'*Pavarotti's greatest hits*': from PUCCINI: *Turandot; Tosca; La Bohème.* DONIZETTI: *La fille du régiment; La Favorita; L'Elisir d'amore.* R. STRAUSS: *Der Rosenkavalier.* BIZET: *Carmen.* BELLINI: *I Puritani.* VERDI: *Il Trovatore; Rigoletto; Aida; Requiem.* GOUNOD: *Faust.* PONCHIELLI: *La Gioconda.* LEONCAVALLO: *I Pagliacci* and *Mattinata.* ROSSINI: *La danza.* DE CURTIS: *Torna a Surriento.* FRANCK: *Panis angelicus.* SCHUBERT: *Ave Maria.* DENZA: *Funiculi, funicula.*
*** Decca 417 011-2 (2) [id.].

This collection of 'greatest hits' can safely be recommended to all who have admired the golden beauty of Pavarotti's voice. Including as it does a fair proportion of earlier recordings, the compilation demonstrates the splendid consistency of his singing. Songs are included, as well as many well-chosen excerpts from opera. The sound is certainly vibrant on CD, but this remains at full price; Decca have since issued an even more generous collection on a pair of mid-priced discs, appropriately called '*Tutto Pavarotti*', see below.

'*Passione*' (with Bologna Teatro Comunale O, Chiaramello): TAGLIAFERRI: *Passione.* COSTA: *Era de maggio.* ANON.: *Fenesta che lucive; La Palummella; Te voglio bene assaje.* NARDELIA: *Chiove.* FALVO: *Dicitencello vuie.* DE CURTIS: *Voce 'e notte.* DI PAPUA: *I 'te vurria vasa.* MARIO: *Santa Lucia luntana.* LAMA: *Silenzio cantatore.* CARDILLO: *Core 'ngrato.*
*** Decca Dig. 417 117-2 [id.].

With the advantage of first-class recording, this perhaps is the most attractive of Pavarotti's Neapolitan collections. The voice sounds fresh, the singing is ardent and the programme is chosen imaginatively. The great tenor obviously identifies with this repertoire and sings everything with the kind of natural response that skirts vulgarity. The orchestrations by Giancarlo Chiaramello show a feeling for the right kind of orchestral colour: they may be sophisticated, but they undoubtedly enhance the melodic lines. If the title of the collection suggests hyperbole, there is in fact a well-judged balance here between passionate romanticism and concern for phrasing and detail.

'*Anniversary*': Arias from: PUCCINI: *La Bohème; Tosca.* GIORDANO: *Andrea Chénier.* BELLINI: *La Sonnambula.* PONCHIELLI: *La Gioconda.* VERDI: *La Traviata; Un ballo in maschera.* LEONCAVALLO: *Pagliacci.* BOITO: *Mefistofele.* ROSSINI: *Gugliemo Tell.* MASCAGNI: *Cavalleria Rusticana.*
**(*) Decca 417 362-2 [id.].

Pavarotti's recital celebrated the 25th anniversary of his operatic début. It is a good compilation of mixed items from complete opera sets, some of them relatively rare and mostly imaginatively done, though the *Andrea Chénier* items could be subtler. Good, bright recording of various vintages.

'*Mattinata*': Songs by BELLINI; GIORDANI; ROSSINI; GLUCK; TOSTI; DONIZETTI; LEONCAVALLO; BEETHOVEN and others.
(M) **(*) Decca 417 796-2 [id.].

Pavarotti is at home here in the lightweight items. Giordani's *Caro mio ben* is very nicely done and the romantic songs have a well-judged ardour. Gluck's *Che farò*, the one operatic aria included, is rather less impressive. The tone is not always golden, but most of the bloom remains. Vivid transfers.

'*Volare*' (popular Italian songs, with Ch. & O of Teatro Comunale di Bologna, Mancini): MODUGNO: *Volare*. DENZA: *Occhi di fata*. BIXIO: *La strada nel bosco; Chi è più felice di me; La canzone dell' amore; Cantate con me; Bimmi tu primavera*. SIBELLA: *La girometta*. D'ANZI: *Malinconia d'amore*. BONAGURA: *Luna marinara*. CASSARINI: *Fra tanta gente*. MASCHERONI: *Fiorin fiorello*. DE CURTIS: *Ti voglio tanto bene*. RUCCIONE: *Una chitarra nella notte*. MASCAGNI: *Serenata*. FERILLI: *Un amore così grande*.
**(*) Decca Dig. 421 052-2 [id.].

Supported by Henry Mancini in characteristically colourful arrangements, Pavarotti throws his considerable weight into these popular Neapolitan songs, not the most tasteful renderings but very satisfying for aficionados, helped by aptly ripe recording.

Donizetti and Verdi arias (with Vienna Op. O, Downes) from: DONIZETTI: *Dom Sébastien, roi de Portugal; Il Duca d'Alba; La Favorita; Lucia di Lammermoor*. VERDI: *Un ballo in maschera; I due Foscari; Luisa Miller; Macbeth*.
(M) *** Decca 421 304-2 [id.].

Though not as distinguished as either the Sutherland or the Marilyn Horne (Rossini) recitals in Decca's mid-price series, Pavarotti's 'Opera Gala' issue of Verdi and Donizetti represents the tenor in impressive performances of mainly rare arias, recorded early in his career in 1968, with the voice fresh and golden. Good, full recording.

King of the high Cs': Arias from: DONIZETTI: *La fille du régiment; La Favorita*. VERDI: *Il Trovatore*. R. STRAUSS: *Der Rosenkavalier*. ROSSINI: *Guglielmo Tell*. BELLINI: *I Puritani*. PUCCINI: *La Bohème*.
(M) *** Decca 421 326-2 [id.].

The punning title may not be to everyone's taste, but this is another attractively varied Pavarotti collection, now offered at mid-price, a superb display of his vocal command as well as his projection of personality. Though the selections come from various sources, the recording quality is remarkably consistent, the voice vibrant and clear; the accompanying detail and the contributions of the chorus are also well managed. The Donizetti and Puccini items are particularly attractive.

'*Tutto Pavarotti*': Arias from: VERDI: *Aida; Luisa Miller; La Traviata; Il Trovatore; Rigoletto; Un ballo in maschera*. DONIZETTI: *L'Elisir d'amore; Don Pasquale*. PONCHIELLI: *La Gioconda*. FLOTOW: *Martha*. BIZET: *Carmen*. MASSENET: *Werther*. MEYERBEER: *L'Africana*. BOITO: *Mefistofele*. LEONCAVALLO: *Pagliacci*. MASCAGNI: *Cavalleria Rusticana*. GIORDANO: *Fedora*. PUCCINI: *La Fanciulla del West; Tosca; Manon Lescaut; La Bohème; Turandot*. ROSSINI: *Stabat Mater*. BIZET: *Agnus Dei*. ADAM: *O holy night*. DI PAPUA: *O sole mio*. TOSTI: *A vucchella*. CARDILLO: *Core 'ngrato*. TAGLIAFERRI: *Passione*. CHERUBINI: *Mamma*. DALLA: *Caruso*.
(M) *** Decca 425 681-2 (2).

Opening with Dalla's *Caruso*, a popular song in the Neapolitan tradition, certainly effective, and no more vulgar than many earlier examples of the genre, this selection goes on through favourites like *O sole mio* and *Core 'ngrato* and one or two religious items, notably Adam's *Cantique de Noël*, to the hard core of operatic repertoire. Beginning with *Celeste Aida*, recorded in 1972, the selection of some twenty-two arias from complete sets covers Pavarotti's distinguished recording career with Decca from 1969 (*Cielo e mar* and the *Il Trovatore* excerpts) to 1985, although the opening song was, of course, recorded digitally in 1988. The rest is a mixture of brilliantly transferred analogue originals and a smaller number of digital masters, all or nearly all showing the great tenor in sparkling form. The records are at mid-price, but there are no translations or musical notes.

'The essential Pavarotti': Arias from VERDI: *Rigoletto; Il Trovatore.* PUCCINI: *La Bohème; Tosca; Turandot.* DONIZETTI: *L'Elisir d'amore.* FLOTOW: *Martha.* BIZET: *Carmen.* LEONCAVALLO: *I Pagliacci.* Songs by TOSTI; LEONCAVALLO; DENZA; DI CURTIS and others.
(M) *** Decca 430 210-2 [id.].

This recital, compiled from Decca's back catalogue, was launched with considerable accompanying hype – posters even appeared on the London Underground – and in consequence the disc managed to enter the charts alongside Nigel Kennedy's recording of Vivaldi's *Four Seasons*. Many of the recordings offered here are also included in the mid-priced two-disc set, *'Tutto Pavarotti'*, which offers far more music for only a little more outlay, and thus is more representative of Pavarotti's 'essential' repertoire. However, the present programme, vividly transferred to CD, certainly shows the great tenor in good form, not only in the most popular of popular arias but also in the songs like *O sole mio, Torna a Surriento!* and a sparkling version of Rossini's *La Danza*.

'Live, on stage': excerpts from: VERDI: *Rigoletto; La Traviata.* PUCCINI: *La Bohème.*
(BB) LaserLight 15 104. [id.].

Although the opening of the *Rigoletto* excerpts (with Scotto as Gilda) promises well, with Pavarotti's voice ringing out boldly, the sound soon begins to deteriorate, the *La Traviata* scenes are insecure and distorted, and the focus becomes very fuzzy indeed in *La Bohème*. Not recommended.

Volume 1 (Live recordings: 1964/67): excerpts from: DONIZETTI: *Lucia di Lammermoor* (with Scotto). VERDI: *Rigoletto* (with Rinaldi, Lazzarini, Cappuccilli). *Requiem* (with L. Price, Cossotto, Ghiaurov). MOZART: *Idomeneo* (with Richard Lewis).
(BB) (**) LaserLight 15 225 [id.].

It is good to hear Pavarotti's voice sounding so youthful, gloriously free and strong in these recordings from *Lucia di Lammermoor* and *Rigoletto*, recorded in 1967. His partnership with Renata Scotto in the former is impressive and in the duet, *Sulla tomba che rinserra*, she sings very affectingly. The *Quartet* from *Rigoletto* is also excitingly done, and the 1964 excerpts from *Idomeneo* show how well Pavarotti is suited to an opera he was to record for Decca twenty-five years later. The only write-off here is the excerpt from Verdi's *Requiem*, which is poorly focused. Otherwise the sound is good, if not refined.

Ponselle, Rosa (soprano)

'Prima voce': Arias from: BELLINI: *Norma.* PONCHIELLI: *La Gioconda.* SPONTINI: *La vestale.* VERDI: *Aida; Ernani; La forza del destino; Otello.* Songs by: ARENSKY; RIMSKY-KORSAKOV; DE CURTIS; DI CAPUA; JACOBS-BOND.
(M) (***) Nimbus mono NI 7805.

One of the most exciting American sopranos ever, Rosa Ponselle tantalizingly cut short her career when she was still at her peak. Only the Arensky and Rimsky songs represent her after her official retirement, and the rest make a superb collection, including her classic accounts of *Casta diva* from Bellini's *Norma* and the duet, *Mira o Norma*, with Marion Telva. The six Verdi items include her earlier version of *Ernani involami*, not quite so commanding as her classic 1928 recording, but fascinating for its rarity. Equally cherishable is her duet from *La forza del destino* with Ezio Pinza.

Arias from: VERDI: *Ernani; Otello; La forza del destino; Aida.* MEYERBEER: *L'Africana.* SPONTINI: *La Vestale.* PONCHIELLI: *La Gioconda.* BELLINI: *Norma.* BACH-GOUNOD: *Ave Maria.* RIMSKY-KORSAKOV: *The nightingale and the rose* & Songs.
(M) (***) RCA mono GD 87810 [7810-2-RG].

The clarity and immediacy of the RCA transfers make a complete contrast with the warmly atmospheric Nimbus transfers of the same singer. Though the voice is exposed more, with less bloom on it, the character and technical command are, if anything, even more impressively presented. To sample the greatness of Ponselle, try her dazzling 1928 account of *Ernani involami* or her poised *Casta diva*. Notable too is the final trio from *La forza del destino* with Martinelli and Pinza, even more immediate than on Nimbus's Martinelli disc.

Popp, Lucia (soprano)

Slavonic opera arias (with Munich R. O, Soltesz): from DVOŘÁK: *Armida; Rusalka.* JANÁČEK: *Jenůfa.* SMETANA: *The Bartered bride; Dalibor.* TCHAIKOVSKY: *Eugene Onegin; Pique Dame.* PROKOFIEV: *War and peace.*
**(*) EMI Dig. CDC7 49319-2 [id.].

Lucia Popp, Czechoslovakian born, has seven Czech items out of the ten in her charming collection of Slavonic arias. It is good to have as starter the rare aria from Dvořák's opera, *Armida*, a classical figure who here emerges as first cousin to *Rusalka*, the water-sprite. The other Dvořák scenas and the Janáček are just as appealing, and the contrasted Smetana arias are beautifully characterized. Reflective as most of these excerpts are – including the Russian items – Popp's musical imagination and concern for word-meaning effectively counteract any feeling of sameness. The voice is recorded rather close, which only occasionally exaggerates Popp's tendency to squeeze salient notes. In the Tchaikovsky, the one disappointment on the disc, Tatiana's outbursts in *Onegin* sound rather constricted and the performance has its perfunctory moments, with singer and conductor not letting the music expand enough. Apart from the balance of the voice, the sound is pleasantly atmospheric, with the beauty of orchestral textures well caught, if slightly at a distance.

Price, Leontyne (soprano)

'Christmas with Leontyne Price' (with V. Singverein, VPO, Karajan); GRUBER: *Silent night.* MENDELSSOHN: *Hark! the herald angels.* HOPKINS: *We three kings.* TRAD.: *Angels we have heard on high; O Tannenbaum; God rest ye merry, gentlemen; Sweet li'l Jesus.* WILLIS: *It came upon the midnight clear.* BACH: *Vom Himmel hoch.* BACH/GOUNOD: *Ave Maria.* SCHUBERT: *Ave Maria.* ADAM: *O holy night.* MOZART: *Alleluja, K.165.*
**(*) Decca 421 103-2 [id.].

There is much beautiful singing here, but the style is essentially operatic. The rich, ample voice, when scaled down (as for instance in *We three kings*), can be very beautiful, but at full thrust it does not always catch the simplicity of melodic line which is characteristic of many of these carols. Yet the vibrant quality of the presentation is undoubtedly thrilling, and it can charm too, as in *God rest ye merry, gentlemen*, with its neat harpsichord accompaniment. The sound is admirably full, clear and vivid in its CD format.

Ricciarelli, Katia (soprano), José Carreras (tenor)

'*Duetti d'amore*' from PUCCINI: *Madama Butterfly*. VERDI: *I Lombardi*. DONIZETTI: *Poliuto; Roberto Devereux*.
(M) *** Ph. 426 644-2 [id.].

The two Donizetti duets are among the finest he ever wrote, especially the one from *Poliuto*, in which the hero persuades his wife to join him in martyrdom. This has a depth unexpected in Donizetti. Both these items receive beautiful performances here; the Puccini love duet is made to sound fresh and unhackneyed, and the *Lombardi* excerpt is given with equal tenderness. Stylish conducting and refined recording.

Robeson, Paul (bass)

'*Favourites*': KERN: *Ol' Man River; Roll away, clouds; The lonesome road; Got the south in my soul; Hush-a-bye lullaby; Round the bend of the road; Carry me back to green pastures; Blue prelude; Wagon wheels; So shy; St Louis blues; Little man, you've had a busy day; I ain't lazy, I'm just dreaming; All through the night; Shenandoah.* ELLINGTON: *Solitude. Song of the Volga Boatman; Dear old Southland; Nothin'; A perfect day.*
(***) EMI CDC7 47839-2 [id.].

A welcome reissue from the EMI archives offering recordings made between 1928 and 1939 when the great singer was in his prime, vocally and artistically. There is an innocence in the singing of the simpler songs (*So shy*, for instance) which he would perhaps not have captured so easily later in his life. Throughout, the Robeson magic projects readily and there is little complaint about the technical quality of the originals, although the digital remastering has brought a touch of dryness to the voice in its most resonant low notes.

Rogers, Nigel (tenor), Anthony Bailes (lute)

'*Airs de cour*' (songs from the reign of Louis XIII): MAUDUIT: *Eau vive, source d'amour.* DE COURVILLE: *Si je languis d'un martire incogneu.* ANON.: *C'est un amant, ouvrez la porte.* BATAILLE: *Un jour que ma rebelle; Ma bergère non légère; Qui veut chasser une migraine.* GUÉDRON: *Si jamais mon âme blessée; Césses mortels de soupir; Quel espoir de guarir.* LE FÉGUEUX: *Petit sein où l'amour a bâti son séjour.* MOULINIÉ: *Paisible et ténébreuse nuit; Quelque merveilleuse chose; Je suis ravi de mon Uranie; Enfin la beauté que j'adore.* BOESSET: *Plaignez la rigueur de mon sort; N'espérez plus, mes yeux; Ennuits, désespoirs et douleurs.* GRAND RUE: *Lors que tes beaux yeux, mignonne.*
(M) *** EMI CDM7 63070-2.

A beautifully sung and most naturally recorded recital of *airs de cour* (Court songs) which will give much pleasure to the non-specialist listener who might not normally venture into this repertoire. The songs are simple in style, the settings, usually of popular anonymous verse, follow the text naturally without word repetition but often with a pleasing, elegant freshness. The songs are mostly about *l'amour* and the hedonistic pleasures of eating and drinking. There is sentiment, melancholy (though usually not so overt as in Elizabethan lute songs), gaiety and (cultivated) high spirits. The melodic writing has pleasing spontaneity, often helped by the light rhythmic feeling: *Ma bergère, non légère en amours* may have ingenuous lyrics but it goes with an engaging swing, while *Qui veut chasser une migraine* good-naturedly chooses to cure the headache with a well-laden table (sausages and ham), good wine and good company. The love-songs are nicely expressive, and the recital attractively intersperses the gay settings with the more dolorous expressions of feeling like the lovely *Quel espoir de guarir* or the two closing songs by Étienne Moulinié. The CD has great presence and realism; the balance between voice and the sympathetic lute accompaniments of Anthony Bailes is ideal. It is a great pity that translations are not provided; even so, the French words are easy to follow.

'Sacred arias'

'Sacred arias' (sung by (i) Dame Kiri Te Kanawa; (ii) Lucia Popp; (iii) Elsie Morison; (iv) Richard Lewis; (v) Dame Joan Sutherland; (vi) John Shirley-Quirk; (vii) Dame Janet Baker; (viii) Dietrich Fischer-Dieskau; (ix) Montserrat Caballé and Fiorenza Cossotto; (x) Nicolai Gedda; (xi) Victoria de los Angeles; (xii) Robert Gambill): (i) MOZART: *Mass in C min., K.427: Laudamus te.* (ii) *Exsultate jubilate: Alleluja, K.165.* (iii) HANDEL: *Messiah: I know that my Redeemer liveth.* (iv) *Comfort ye . . . Ev'ry valley. Judas Maccabaeus: Sound an alarm.* (v) BACH: *Cantata No. 147: Bereite dir.* (vi) HAYDN: *The Creation: Now heaven.* (vii) *Elijah: O rest in the Lord*; (viii) *Draw near, all ye people . . . Lord God of Abraham.* (ix) VERDI: *Requiem: Agnus Dei*; (x) *Ingemisco.* (xi) FAURÉ: *Requiem: Piè Jesu.* (xii) ROSSINI: *Stabat Mater: Cujus animam gementem.*
(B) **(*) CfP CD-CFP 4532.

Although the contributions from Fischer-Dieskau and Gedda are impressive enough and Richard Lewis's *Sound an alarm* is vigorously stirring, it is the ladies who shine most brightly here. Joan Sutherland's account of Bach's *Bereite dir*, made in 1958 (an unexpectedly welcome contribution to an EMI record), is particularly lovely. Kiri Te Kanawa and Lucia Popp are also on top form, while Dame Janet's *O rest in the Lord* (from *Elijah*) is wonderfully poised and serene. The male contributions are more uneven, and Robert Gambill's histrionics in the closing Rossini *Cujus animam* has the feeling more of the opera house than of the concert hall.

St George's Canzona, John Sothcott

Medieval songs and dances: *Lamento di Tristano; L'autrier m'iere levaz. 4 Estampies real; Edi beo thu hevene quene; Eyns ne soy ke plente fu; Tre fontane;* PERRIN D'AGINCOURT: *Quant voi en la fin d'este.* Cantigas de Santa Maria: *Se ome fezer; Nas mentes semper teer; Como poden per sas culpas; Maravillosos et piadosos.*
*** CRD CRD 3421 [id.].

As so often when early music is imaginatively re-created, one is astonished at the individuality of many of the ideas. This applies particularly to the second item in this collection, *Quant voi en la fin d'este*, attributed to the mid-thirteenth-century trouvère, Perrin d'Agincourt, but no less to the four Cantigas de Santa Maria. The fruity presentation of *Como poden per sas culpas* ('As men may be crippled by their sins, so they may afterwards be made sound by the Virgin') is admirably contrasted with the strong lyrical appeal of the following *Maravillosos et piadosos*, directly extolling the virtues and compassion of Saint Mary. Among the four *Estampies real* the one presented last (band 11 on the CD) is haunting in its lilting melancholy. The instrumentation is at times suitably robust but does not eschew good intonation and subtle effects. The group is recorded vividly and the acoustics of St James, Clerkenwell, are never allowed to cloud detail. The sound is admirably firm and real in its CD format.

St George's Chapel, Windsor Castle, Choir, Christopher Robinson

20 Christmas carols (with John Porter, organ): *Once in Royal David's city; Hark! the herald angels sing; God rest you merry, gentlemen; The holly and the ivy; Gabriel's message; It came upon the midnight clear; People, look east; There is no rose of such virtue; Away in a manger; A stable in Bethlehem; The first nowell; O come all ye faithful; On Christmas night; Silent night; Jesus Christ the apple tree; In the bleak mid-winter; While shepherds watched their flocks; Ding dong merrily on high; In dulci jubilo; O little town of Bethlehem.*
**(*) Abbey Dig. CD MVP 827 [id.].

The opening *Once in Royal David's city* is treated as a processional, but otherwise these are no-frills performances, the singing direct and eloquent, the arrangements straightforward. With such generous measure and many favourites included, this is very good value – even if some other carol collections are more imaginatively presented. The digital recording is excellent.

St John's College, Cambridge, Choir, George Guest

'*Christmas weekend*': GRUBER: *Silent night.* RUTTER: *Shepherd's pipe carol.* MENDELSSOHN: *Hark the herald angels; O little town of Bethlehem; Born on earth; The twelve days of Christmas; Up! good Christian folk; Good King Wenceslas; While shepherds watched; God rest you merry, gentlemen; The holly and the ivy; Away in a manger; The first nowell; I saw three ships; Suo Gan.*
(B) *** Decca 421 022-2.

This is first rate in every way, a wholly successful concert of mostly traditional carols, in sensitive arrangements without frills. The singing is straightforwardly eloquent, its fervour a little restrained in the Anglican tradition, yet with considerable underlying depth of feeling. The full character of every carol is well brought out; the expressive simplicity of *I saw three ships* and Rutter's *Shepherd's pipe carol* is most engaging. The recording is excellent, and on Decca's inexpensive Weekend label this is a bargain.

Schipa, Tito (tenor)

Opera arias from: GLUCK: *Orfeo ed Eurydice.* A. SCARLATTI: *La Donna ancora e fedele; Pirro e Demetrio* (& Song: *Sento nel core*). BELLINI: *La Sonnambula.* DONIZETTI: *Don Pasquale; L'Elisir d'amore; Lucia di Lammermoor.* VERDI: *Rigoletto; Falstaff.* PONCHIELLI: *La Gioconda.* PUCCINI: *La Bohème; Tosca.* MASCAGNI: *Cavalleria Rusticana; L'amico Fritz.* MASSENET: *Werther; Manon.*
(M) (**(*)) EMI mono CDH7 63200-2 [id.].

This EMI collection is particularly valuable for containing Schipa's first recordings, made in 1913. Whether in *Lucia*, *Rigoletto* or *Cavalleria*, the voice and the interpretations are even fresher than they were later. The disc is also indispensable for containing one of the most delectable of all Schipa records, his delicious account of the

Cherry duet from *L'amico Fritz* with Mafalda Favero. But his RCA account of the aria for which he was most famous, *Una furtiva lagrima* from *L'Elisir d'amore*, is preferable to this (see below), and the transfers are not as immaculate as one expects of this EMI series.

Arias from: MASSENET: *Werther; Manon.* CILEA: *L'Arlesiana.* ROSSINI: *Il Barbiere di Siviglia.* DONIZETTI: *L'Elisir d'amore; Lucia di Lammermoor.* LEONCAVALLO: *Pagliacci.* VERDI: *Rigoletto; La Traviata.* MOZART: *Don Giovanni.* HANDEL: *Xerxes.* BELLINI: *La Sonnambula.* Songs by TOSTI and others.
(M) (***) RCA mono GD 87969 [7969-2-RG].

RCA provides vivid, very immediate transfers of a sparkling collection of Neapolitan songs as well as arias. Few tenors have matched Schipa for the point and personality of his singing within his carefully chosen limits. It is like being face to face with the singer.

Schwarzkopf, Elisabeth (soprano)

'Elisabeth Schwarzkopf sings operetta' (with Philharmonia Ch. and O, Ackermann): Excerpts from: HEUBERGER: *Der Opernball.* ZELLER: *Der Vogelhändler.* LEHÁR: *Der Zarewitsch; Der Graf von Luxembourg; Giuditta.* J. STRAUSS, Jnr: *Casanova.* MILLÖCKER: *Die Dubarry.* SUPPÉ: *Boccaccio.* SIECZYŃSKY: *Wien, du Stadt meiner Träume.*
⊛ *** EMI CDC7 47284-2 [id.].

This is one of the most delectable recordings of operetta arias ever made, and it is here presented with excellent sound. Schwarzkopf's 'whoopsing' manner (as Philip Hope-Wallace called it) is irresistible, authentically catching the Viennese style, languor and sparkle combined. Try for sample the exquisite *Im chambre séparée* or *Sei nicht bös*; but the whole programme is performed with supreme artistic command and ravishing tonal beauty. This outstanding example of the art of Elisabeth Schwarzkopf at its most enchanting is a disc which ought to be in every collection. The compact disc transfer enhances the superbly balanced recording even further, manages to cut out nearly all the background, give the voice a natural presence, and retain the orchestral bloom.

'Romantic opera arias': from WAGNER: *Tannhäuser; Lohengrin* (with Christa Ludwig). SMETANA: *Bartered bride.* TCHAIKOVSKY: *Eugene Onegin.* WEBER: *Der Freischütz.*
(M) *** EMI CDM7 69501-2 [id.].

This CD draws on a pair of LPs but centres on one of them, a classic recital containing Wagner and Weber, with Agathe's two arias from *Der Freischütz* given with a purity of tone and control of line never surpassed, magic performances. So too with the Wagner heroines. The second record found Schwarzkopf less keenly imaginative in more unusual repertoire. This was recorded eight years after the first (in 1967) and the voice had to be controlled more carefully. *The Bartered bride* aria is attractive (though sung in German) but the *Letter scene* from *Eugene Onegin* is less convincing: here the projected vocal personality seems too mature for the young Tatiana. The remastered sound is certainly vivid.

'Carnegie Hall recital': MOZART: *Così fan tutte: Come scoglio. Abendempfindung; Als Luise; Dans un bois solitaire; Un moto di gioia.* SCHUBERT: *An Sylvia; Der Einsame; Der Vollmond strahlt; Die Vögel; Gretchen am Spinnrade; Seligkeit.* GLUCK: *Einem Bach der fliesst.* R. STRAUSS: *Puhe, meine Seele; Schlechtes Wetter; Hat gesacht; Wiegenlied.* WOLF: *Herr, was trägt der Bodem hier; Bedeckt mich mit Blumen; In dem Schatten meiner Locken; Zum neuen Jahr; Philine; Kennst du das Land?; Wir haben beide lange Zeit*

geschwiegen; Was soll der Zorn, mein Schatz; Wiegenlied im Sommer; Elfenlied;
Nachtzauber; Die Zigeunerin. SCHUMANN: *Der Nussbaum.* BRAHMS: *Ich hab' in Penna;*
Vergebliches Ständchen. HANDEL: *Atalanta: Care selve. Swiss folk song: 'S Schätzli.*
(M) (***) EMI (mono) CHS7 61043-2 (2) [id.].

The live recording of Schwarzkopf's 1956 Carnegie Hall recital – long-buried treasure,
finally unearthed – brings a marvellous supplement to her immaculate series of studio
recordings of Lieder and opera. Inevitably, even with such a perfectionist there are tiny
blemishes, not to mention intrusive applause from the enthusiastic New York audience;
but the atmosphere and intensity of a great occasion are vividly conveyed, and with it an
extra dimension in Schwarzkopf's powers of artistic communication. The programme is
astonishingly generous, with substantial encores after each group. So, after the opening
Mozart group, Schwarzkopf adds nothing less than *Come scoglio* from *Così* and, with
piano accompanying her instead of an orchestra, her agility is even more phenomenal
than in her masterly performances from her two complete opera sets. The range of
expression is astonishing, through the items by Schubert, Gluck, Strauss and others, with
inimitable touches of humour in the haunting Swiss folksong, *'S Schätzli*, and Brahms's
Vergebliches Ständchen. The climax comes in the big group of twelve Lieder by Hugo
Wolf, including above all the setting of Goethe, *Kennst du das Land?*, which here more
than ever emerges as the greatest of all Lieder for a woman's voice. With George Reeves a
most sympathetic accompanist, this is one of the most vivid examples of a live Lieder
recital ever put on disc. The mono sound, while inevitably limited, is faithful and clear as
presented on CD.

Schwarzkopf, Elisabeth, Irmgard Seefried (sopranos)

Duets (with Gerald Moore, piano; Philh. O, Josef Krips; VPO, Karajan): MONTEVERDI:
Io son vezzosetta pastorella; Ardo e scoprir; Baci cari; Dialogo di ninfa e pastore.
CARISSIMI: *Detesta la cativa sorte in amore; Lungi amai; Il mio core; A piè d'un verdi*
alloro. DVOŘÁK: *13 Moravian songs, Op. 32.* HUMPERDINCK: *Hansel und Gretel: Dance*
duet. R. STRAUSS: *Der Rosenkavalier: Herrgott im Himmel!.*
(M) (***) EMI mono CDH7 69793-2.

This compilation brings delicious singing from two favourite artists, both in their early
prime. What does it matter stylistically that in the Monteverdi and Carissimi duets a
piano accompaniment is used (as it was in Nadia Boulanger's barrier-breaking collection
of 1937, now also issued on Références) and that the expressive style is anachronistic!
The artistry and vocalism are what matter, and the Dvořák *Duets* (done in German but
with Slavonic élan) bring comparable tenderness and sparkle. Most desirable of all for
devotees of these singers are the two operatic items. Though Karajan was to go on to
conduct even more seductively in his complete recording of *Rosenkavalier* with
Schwarzkopf as the Marschallin, it is marvellous to hear her in the lighter role of Sophie,
next to the ideal Octavian. The Humperdinck duet is even more relaxed and full of fun
here under Krips than it is in the Karajan complete set, when Schwarzkopf as Gretel was
partnered by Elisabeth Grümmer. *Rosenkavalier* specialists might note that Karajan, in
the middle of the *Presentation of the Silver Rose*, follows the traditional reading of E flat
in the little trumpet solo before the second half, instead of the score's E natural, which he
preferred later.

Sopranos

'*Great sopranos of our time*' ((i) Scotto; (ii) Schwarzkopf; (iii) Sutherland; (iv) Nilsson; (v) De los Angeles; (vi) Freni; (vii) Callas; (viii) Cotrubas; (ix) Caballé): (i) PUCCINI: *Madama Butterfly: Un bel dì.* (vi) *La Bohème: Sì, mi chiamano Mimì.* (ii) MOZART: *Così fan tutte: Come scoglio.* (iii) *Don Giovanni: Troppo mi spiace . . . Non mi dir.* (iv) WEBER: *Oberon: Ozean du Ungeheuer.* (v) ROSSINI: *Il Barbiere di Siviglia: Una voce poco fa.* (vii) DONIZETTI: *Lucia di Lammermoor: Sparsa è di rose . . . Il dolce suono . . . Spargi d'amaro.* (viii) BIZET: *Les Pêcheurs de perles: Comme autrefois.* (ix) VERDI: *Aida: Qui Radames . . . O patria mia.*
(M) *** EMI CD-EMX 9519.

An impressive collection, drawn from a wide variety of sources. It is good to have Schwarzkopf's commanding account of *Come scoglio* and Nilsson's early recording of the Weber, not to mention the formidable contributions of Callas and the early Sutherland reading of *Non mi dir*, taken from Giulini's complete set of *Giovanni*. The CD transfers are bright and vivid, and this makes a fascinating mid-priced anthology.

Souzay, Gérard (baritone)

French song recital (with (i) Dalton Baldwin, (ii) Jean-Pierre Rampal, Robert Cordier; (iii) Paris Conservatoire O, Vandernoot): DEBUSSY: (i) *2 chansons de Charles d'Orléans; 3 ballades de François Villon; Le promenoir des deux amants.* RAVEL: (i; ii) *Chansons madécasses;* (iii) *Chanson hébraïque; Don Quichotte à Dulcinée; 2 mélodies hébraïques; 5 mélodies populaires grecques; Ronsard et son âme.*
⊛ (M) *** EMI CDM7 63112-2.

Not to be missed. The Ravel songs come from 1958, when the great French baritone was in wonderful voice; the Debussy from 1971. Having long treasured the French mono LP of the Ravel, it is particularly gratifying to see this return without the inevitable clicks that even the best-cared-for records can acquire. The transfer makes the voice very present and tremendously clear; there is a little (minimal) loss of warmth and a slight hardening in the image. But what performances these are! The Ravel have never been surpassed. A desert-island disc.

Soviet Army Chorus, Soloists and Band, Colonel Boris Alexandrov

DUNAYEVSKY: *Song of youth.* TRAD.: *A birch tree in a field; Volga boat song; Along Peter's Street; Ah! lovely night; Kamarinskaya; Annie Laurie; Kalinka; Bandura; Oh No! John; Snowflakes.* ALEXANDROV: *Ukrainian poem.* SHAPORIN: *The Decembrists: Soldiers' chorus.* MOKROUSOV: *You are always beautiful.* WILLIAMS-JUDGE: *Tipperary.* KNIPPER: *Song of the plains.*
*** EMI CDC7 47833-2 [id.].

This anthology caused something of a sensation on its first issue, and it has still not lost its power to electrify. The sheer vitality of the music-making is at times almost overwhelming, yet there is much magic too. The unnamed tenor's performance of *Annie Laurie* is meltingly lovely and although the words of *Oh No! John* are not sharply clear, the singer's vocal production and bluff humour are memorable. *Tipperary*, learnt especially for the 1956 visit, has irresistible gusto. The Russian items, with the balalaika often to the fore, are generally very exciting too, with *Ah! lovely night* another frisson-creating lyrical number. The recordings come from 1956 and 1963. The remastering has added clarity and presence, plus some fierceness, but has also lost some of the original ambient atmosphere.

Stade, Frederica von (mezzo-soprano)

Opera arias from: ROSSINI: *Otello.* HAYDN: *La fedelta premiata; Il mondo della luna.* MOZART: *La clemenza di Tito.*
*** Ph. 420 084-2 [id.].

Von Stade's Philips recital is a splendid compilation of some of her finest performances from complete sets of rare operas. It is sad that the Philips Haydn series did not achieve wider circulation, when it included such delectable items as those here; it is also valuable to have reminders of her contribution to the Rossini *Otello* set and to Colin Davis's recording of Mozart's *Clemenza di Tito.* Good original sound, well transferred.

Stefano, Giuseppe Di (tenor)

Neapolitan songs (with New SO, Pattacini or Olivieri): DE CURTIS: *Torna a Surriento; Tu ca'nun chiagne; Sona chitarra! A canzone 'e Napule; Ti voglio tanto bene.* BONGIOVANNI: *Lacreme napulitane.* TAGLIAFERRI: *Napule canta; Pusilleco.* CALIFANO: *'O surdato 'nnammurato.* CARDILLO: *Catari, catari.* COSTA: *Era di maggio matenata; Scetate.* NICOLAVALENTE: *Addio, mia bella Napoli.* CESANNI: *Firenze sogna.* DI LAZZARO: *Chitarra romana.* NEN: *Parlami d'amore Mariu.* BARBENS: *Munasterio 'e Santa-Chiara.*
(M) *** Decca 417 794-2.

Di Stefano was still in magnificent voice in the mid-1960s when he recorded these popular Neapolitan songs – including many comparative rarities as well as obvious choices like *Torna a Surriento, Catari, catari,* and *Addio, mia bella Napoli.* Despite the inevitable touches of vulgarity, the singing is both rich-toned and charming. The recording is admirably clear and vivid.

Sutherland, Dame Joan (soprano)

'The art of the prima donna': Arias from: ARNE: *Artaxerxes.* HANDEL: *Samson.* BELLINI: *Norma; I Puritani; La Sonnambula.* ROSSINI: *Semiramide.* GOUNOD: *Faust; Roméo et Juliette.* VERDI: *Otello; Rigoletto; La Traviata.* MOZART: *Die Entführung aus dem Serail.* THOMAS: *Hamlet.* DELIBES: *Lakmé.* MEYERBEER: *Les Huguenots.*
⊛ (M) *** Decca 425 493-2 (2) [id.].

This ambitious early two-disc recital (from 1960) remains one of Joan Sutherland's outstanding gramophone achievements, and it is a matter of speculation whether even Melba or Tetrazzini in their heyday managed to provide sixteen consecutive recordings quite as dazzling as these performances. Indeed, it is the Golden Age that one naturally turns to rather than to current singers when making any comparisons. Sutherland herself by electing to sing each one of the fabulously difficult arias in tribute to a particular soprano of the past, from Mrs Billington in the eighteenth century, through Grisi, Malibran, Pasta and Jenny Lind in the nineteenth century, to Lilli Lehmann, Melba, Tetrazzini and Galli-Curci in this, is asking to be judged by the standards of the Golden Age. On the basis of recorded reminders, she comes out with flying colours, showing a greater consistency and certainly a wider range of sympathy than even the greatest Golden Agers possessed. The sparkle and delicacy of the *Puritani Polonaise,* the freshness and lightness of the Mad scene from Thomas's *Hamlet*, the commanding power of the *Entführung* aria and the breathtaking brilliance of the Queen's aria from *Les Huguenots* are all among the high spots here, while the arias which Sutherland later recorded in her complete opera sets regularly bring performances just as fine – and often finer – than the later versions. The freshness of the voice is caught superbly in the recording, which on CD is amazingly full, firm and realistic, far more believable than many new digital recordings. Reissued at mid-price, it is surely an essential purchase for all who care for beautiful singing.

'*Bel canto Arias*' (with Welsh Nat. Op. O, Bonynge): Arias from: DONIZETTI: *Il castello di Kenilworth; Betley; La Favorita.* VERDI: *Attila.* MEYERBEER: *L'Africaine.* BELLINI: *I Capuleti ed i Montecchi.* ROSSINI: *Guillaume Tell; Il barbiere di Siviglia.*
** Decca Dig. 417 253-2 [id.].

Recorded in the mid-1980s, Sutherland's '*Bel canto*' collection with the Welsh National Opera Orchestra finds the voice in variable form, less firm than when in pristine condition, whether early or late. As long as you are not distracted by the beat on sustained notes, however, there is much to relish of Sutherland at her warmest, here exploring new repertory, even though, for all its brilliance, this *Una voce* is not the most sparkling. Full, vivid recording.

'*Joy to the world*' (Christmas carols) (with Amb. S., New Philh. O, Bonynge) (all arr. Gamley): HANDEL: *Joy to the world.* WILLIS: *It came upon the midnight clear.* ADAM: *O holy night.* GOUNOD: *O Divine Redeemer.* TRAD.: *What child is this?; Adeste Fidelis; The 12 days of Christmas; Good King Wenceslas; The holly and the ivy; Angels we have heard on high; Deck the hall.* REGER: *The Virgin's slumber song.* MENDELSSOHN: *Hark! the herald angels sing.* SCHUBERT: *Ave Maria.*
** Decca 421 095-2 [id.].

These are sugar-coated arrangements of carols made by Douglas Gamley – but who is going to complain when the result cocoons the listener in a web of atmospheric sound? Of its kind this is very good indeed, with an unforgettable, resilient performance of *The 12 days of Christmas*. The brisk carols come off best. The digital remastering offers clear, vivid sound, with the voice caught naturally.

'*Opera gala*': Excerpts from: BELLINI: *Norma.* DONIZETTI: *Lucia di Lammermoor: Mad scene; Linda di Chamounix.* VERDI: *Ernani; I vespri siciliani.*
⊛ (M) *** Decca 421 305-2 [id.].

Sutherland's 'Opera Gala' disc is one of the most cherishable of all operatic recital records, bringing together the glorious, exuberant items from her very first recital disc, made within weeks of her first Covent Garden success in 1959 and – as a valuable supplement – the poised account of *Casta diva* she recorded the following year as part of the '*Art of the Prima Donna*'. It was this 1959 recital which at once put Sutherland firmly on the map among the great recording artists of all time. Even she has never surpassed the freshness of these versions of the two big arias from *Lucia di Lammermoor*, sparkling in immaculate coloratura, while the lightness and point of the jaunty *Linda di Chamounix* aria and the *Boléro* from *I vespri siciliani* are just as winning. The sound is exceptionally vivid and immediate, though the accompaniments under Nello Santi are sometimes rough in ensemble.

'*Coloratura spectacular*': Arias from: PICCINNI: *La Cecchina*. HANDEL: *Alcina*. MOZART: *Die Zauberflöte*. ROSSINI: *La cambiale di matrimonio*. BELLINI: *Beatrice di Tenda; I Puritani; La Sonnambula*. VERDI: *I Masnadieri; Attila*. DONIZETTI: *La fille du régiment*.
(M) *** Decca 417 814-2 [id.].

The title of this Sutherland collection, '*Coloratura spectacular*', could not be more apt. The ten items, imaginatively selected from Sutherland recordings made between 1962 and 1968, give plentiful reminders of her peerless brilliance and agility, the bright clarity of the voice as well as its scale and beauty. It is good to have unpredictable excerpts like the Piccinni, the *Queen of the Night's aria* and the Rossini alongside the Bellini and Donizetti excerpts. Nor is there a lack of variety, when more than just cabalettas are included, with the Verdi and the *Sonnambula* arias given with the preceding aria. The voice is superbly caught on CD, not to mention the instrumental accompaniments, with no distracting discrepancy between the tracks.

'*Greatest hits*': Excerpts from: HANDEL: *Samson*. LEHÁR: *Merry widow*. J. STRAUSS Jnr: *Casanova*. DONIZETTI: *Fille du régiment*. DELIBES: *Lakmé*. BELLINI: *Norma*. GOUNOD: *Faust*. DONIZETTI: *Lucia di Lammermoor: Mad scene*. Song: ARDITI: *Il bacio*.
(M) *** Decca 417 780-2 [id.].

A collection like this, well chosen to entertain, is self-recommending at mid-price. The recordings all come from the period when the voice was at its freshest: *Let the bright seraphim*, the *Bell song* from *Lakmé*, and the vivacious *Jewel song* from *Faust* in 1961; while the luscious version of *Vilja* (with chorus) was made in 1963. The lively excerpt from *La fille du régiment* comes from the complete set, as does the *Mad scene* from *Lucia di Lammermoor* – the 1961 first recording, under Pritchard. The sound is consistently vivid.

'*Prima donna assoluta*': Arias from OFFENBACH: *Contes d'Hoffmann*. DONIZETTI: *Fille du régiment; Lucia di Lammermoor*. GOUNOD: *Faust*. BELLINI: *I Puritani*. VERDI: *La Traviata*.
(B) *** Decca 425 605-2 [id.].

Issued on Decca's cheapest label, this captivating recital concentrates on excerpts from Sutherland's complete sets. However, the closing *Lucia di Lammermoor* Mad scene derives from her famous 1959 Decca début record, conducted by Nello Santi, representing one of the most magical and thrilling displays of coloratura ever recorded: the luminous freshness of the voice is unforgettable. The other recordings come from between 1960 and 1972, and this disc is in every way a bargain. The documentation, however, is entirely biographical.

Sutherland, Dame Joan (soprano), Marilyn Horne (mezzo-soprano) and Luciano Pavarotti (tenor)

'*Duets and trios from the Lincoln Center*' (with NY City Op. O, Bonynge): excerpts from VERDI: *Ernani; Otello; Il Trovatore*. BELLINI: *Norma*. PONCHIELLI: *La Giaconda*.
**(*) Decca Dig. 417 587-2 [id.].

Not all gala concerts make good records, but this is an exception; almost every item here puts an important gloss on the achievements of the three principal stars in the concerted numbers. It is good to have a sample not only of Sutherland's Desdemona but of Pavarotti's Otello in their account of the Act I duet. The final scene from *Il Trovatore* is more compelling here than in the complete set made by the same soloists five years earlier. The microphone catches a beat in the voices of both Sutherland and Horne, but not as obtrusively as on some studio discs. Lively accompaniment under Bonynge; bright, vivid digital recording, but over-loud applause.

Sutherland, Dame Joan and Luciano Pavarotti (tenor)

Operatic duets (with Nat. PO, Bonynge) from: VERDI: *La Traviata; Otello; Aida* (with chorus). BELLINI: *La Sonnambula.* DONIZETTI: *Linda di Chamounix.*
*** Decca 400 058-2 [id.].

This collection offers a rare sample of Sutherland as Aida (*La fatale pietra . . . O terra, addio* from Act IV), a role she sang only once on stage, well before her international career began; and with this and her sensitive impersonations of Desdemona, Violetta and the Bellini and Donizetti heroines, Sutherland might have been expected to steal first honours here. In fact these are mainly duets to show off the tenor, and it is Pavarotti who runs away with the main glory, though both artists were plainly challenged to their finest and the result, with excellent accompaniment, is among the most attractive and characterful duet recitals. The recording is admirably clear and well focused.

Operatic duets from: DONIZETTI: *Lucia di Lammermoor; L'elisir d'amore; Maria Stuarda; La fille du régiment.* VERDI: *Rigoletto.* BELLINI: *I Puritani.*
*** Decca 417 815-2 [id.].

Taken from the complete opera recordings they made together from the late 1960s onwards, this collection of operatic duets finds both superstars in glowing form, with Decca recordings of the finest vintage for the period, beautifully transferred to CD.

Tallis Scholars, Peter Phillips

'*Christmas carols and motets*': *Ave Maria* settings by JOSQUIN DES PRES; VERDELOT; VICTORIA. *Coventry carol* (2 settings). BYRD: *Lullaby.* PRAETORIUS: *Es ist ein Ros'entsprungen; Joseph lieber, Joseph mein; In dulci jubilo; Wachet auf.* BACH: *Wachet auf.* Medieval carols: *Angelus ad virginem; There is no rose; Nowell sing we.*
*** Gimell Dig. CDGIM 010 [id.].

Wonderfully serene singing from the Tallis Scholars, recorded with superb naturalness and presence, makes this a very special Christmas record. There is something unique about a carol, and even the very early music here has that special intensity of inspiration which brings memorability. There are some familiar melodies too, notably those set by Praetorius; but much of this repertoire will come as refreshingly new to most ears. The singing has a purity of spirit. The CD is very much in the demonstration class for the clear choral image, heard against the ideal acoustics of St Pierre et St Paul, Salle, Norfolk.

Tenors

'*Great tenors of our time*' (with (i) Carlo Bergonzi; (ii) Franco Corelli; (iii) Placido Domingo; (iv) Nicolai Gedda; (v) James McCracken; (vi) Luciano Pavarotti; (vii) Jon Vickers): (iii) VERDI: *Aida: Se quel guerrier . . . Celeste Aida.* (v) *Otello: Niun mi tema.* (i) *La Forza del destino: O tu che in seno.* (iv) BIZET: *Les Pêcheurs de perles: Je crois entendre.* (vii) *Carmen: Flower song.* (i) PUCCINI: *Tosca: E lucevan le stelle.* (ii) *Turandot:*

Nessun dorma. (iii) *Manon Lescaut: Donna non vidi mai.* (ii) GIORDANO: *Andrea Chénier: Come un bel di.* (vi) MASCAGNI: *L'Amico Fritz: Ed anche . . . oh amore.* (iv) GOUNOD: *Faust: Salut! Demeure.* (vii) SAINT-SAENS: *Samson et Dalila: Arrêtez, o mes frères.*
(M) **(*) EMI CD-EMX 2114.

EMI compiled this anthology ingeniously from many sources; for example, Luciano Pavarotti, an exclusive Decca artist from early in his international career, had earlier still taken part in EMI's complete set of *L'Amico Fritz*, so providing the excerpt which completes this constellation of great tenors. Not that each is necessarily represented in the most appropriate items, and the compilation does have one wishing (for example) that Vickers rather than McCracken was singing *Otello*, though that excerpt is valuable for preserving a sample of Barbirolli's complete set of that opera. And although Vickers does not make an ideal Don José, it is useful to have his *Flower song*, since the set from which it comes is one of the less recommendable versions. The transfers are clear and fresh, the voices given immediacy, the orchestral backing suitably atmospheric. Considering the variety of the sources (dating from 1959 – Placido Domingo's fine *Salut! Demeure* – to 1974 – the same artist's stirring *Celeste Aida*, which opens the programme), the recording is remarkably consistent.

Tetrazzini, Luisa (soprano)

'*Prima voce*': Arias from: BELLINI: *La Sonnambula.* DONIZETTI: *Lucia di Lammermoor.* ROSSINI: *Il Barbiere di Siviglia.* THOMAS: *Mignon.* VERACINI: *Rosalinda.* VERDI: *Un ballo in maschera; Rigoletto; La Traviata; Il Trovatore; I vespri siciliani.* Songs.
(M) (***) Nimbus mono NI 7808 [id.].

Tetrazzini was astonishing among coloratura sopranos not just for her phenomenal agility but for the golden warmth that went with tonal purity. The Nimbus transfers add a bloom to the sound, with the singer slightly distanced. Though some EMI transfers make her voice more vividly immediate, one quickly adjusts. Such display arias as *Ah non giunge* from *La Sonnambula* or the *Bolero* from *I vespri siciliani* are incomparably dazzling, but it is worth noting too what tenderness is conveyed through Tetrazzini's simple phrasing and pure tone in such a tragic aria as Violetta's *Addio del passato*, with both verses included. Lieder devotees may gasp in horror, but one of the delightful oddities here is Tetrazzini's bright-eyed performance, with ragged orchestral accompaniment, of what is described as *La serenata inutile* by Brahms – in fact *Vergebliches Ständchen*, sung with a triumphant if highly inauthentic top A at the end, implying no closure of the lady's window!

Thill, Georges (tenor)

French opera arias (with orchestras conducted by Bigot; Heurteur; Gaubert; Szyfer; Frigara) from: BERLIOZ: *La Damnation de Faust; Les Troyens à Carthage.* BIZET: *Carmen.* GLUCK: *Alceste.* GOUNOD: *Faust; Roméo et Juliette* (with Germaine Feraldy, soprano). MASSENET: *Le Cid; Werther.* ROSSINI: *Guillaume Tell.* SAINT-SAENS: *Samson et Dalila.*
(M) (***) EMI mono CDM7 69548-2.

Georges Thill left an enormous discography, and this selection of 78-r.p.m. discs made between 1927 and 1936 will come as a revelation to younger collectors unacquainted with his work. He made his début at the Paris Opéra in 1924 and soon established himself as the greatest French tenor of his day. The tone is splendidly full and round and the phrasing masterly. In an age when one is lucky to make out what language is being sung, let alone the actual words, his diction is an object-lesson. Every word resonates, and yet it is the musical line which remains paramount. At 74 minutes, this is a generous sampling of his recorded legacy, very well transferred and absolutely indispensable to anyone who cares about singing.

Tibbett, Lawrence (baritone)

Arias from: LEONCAVALLO: *Pagliacci.* ROSSINI: *Il Barbiere di Siviglia.* VERDI: *Un ballo in maschera; Simon Boccanegra; Falstaff.* PUCCINI: *Tosca.* BIZET: *Carmen.* GOUNOD: *Faust.* WAGNER: *Die Walküre.* GRUENBERG: *Emperor Jones.* HANSON: *Merry Mount.* GERSHWIN: *Porgy and Bess.*
(M) (***) RCA mono GD 87808 [7808-2-RG].

The glorious, characterful timbre of Tibbett's baritone is superbly caught in RCA's clear, immediate transfers, with the vibrato never obtrusive as it can be on some records. It is sad that so commanding a singer was heard relatively little outside America; but this is a superb memorial, not just for the classic arias but for such an item as the excerpt from Louis Gruenberg's *Emperor Jones,* a role he created.

Turner, Dame Eva (soprano)

Opera arias and songs: Arias from VERDI: *Il Trovatore; Aida.* PONCHIELLI: *La Gioconda.* PUCCINI: *Tosca; Madama Butterfly; Turandot.* MASCAGNI: *Cavalleria Rusticana.* WAGNER: *Lohengrin; Tannhäuser.* Songs: GRIEG: *I love thee.* TOSTI: *Goodbye.* RONALD: *O lovely night.* DEL RIEGO: *Homing.* D'HARDELOT: *Because; Sometime in my dreams.*
(M) (***) EMI mono CDH7 69791-2.

The art of Eva Turner is superbly celebrated in this generous selection of recordings made between 1928 and 1933. They include not only her celebrated 1928 recording of Turandot's *In questa reggia* but also magnificent samples of her portrayals of Aida, Leonora in *Trovatore* and La Gioconda, as well as half a dozen songs and ballads. Most fascinating of all are her two Wagner recordings, of *Elsa's dream* from *Lohengrin* and *Elisabeth's greeting* from *Tannhäuser,* sung in English. These were never issued, and Dame Eva's copy of the latter, the only one surviving, was broken into three pieces. It was lovingly reassembled so that it could be played, if with persistent clicks. The CEDAR process (Computer Enhanced Digital Audio Restoration) was then used to eliminate the clicks, automatically filling in each microscopic gap with surrounding material in a way impossible if the process is to be done laboriously by hand. The finished result is among the most thrilling of all the recordings ever made by Dame Eva, rich and intense. It is a delight also to have Dame Eva's spoken introduction, recorded in June 1988 when she was in her ninety-eighth year. Keith Hardwick's transfers, quite apart from the help from CEDAR, are models of their kind, with the voice astonishingly vivid.

Vienna Boys' Choir

'Folksongs and songs for children' (with V. CO, Harrer; Farnberger, Miller).
*** Ph. Dig. 400 014-2 [id.].

Here are some two dozen songs, many traditional, and all of great charm. They are presented artlessly, but the singing is polished and the simply scored accompaniments are very effective. The recording is admirably natural, with the CD offering a marginal improvement in definition. There is a good deal of moderately paced music here, and sometimes one feels that the direction could be more spirited; yet the overall effect is undoubtedly beguiling and, not taken all at once, this recital will give much pleasure. With the CD comes an excellent booklet, complete with all translations.

Walker, Sarah (mezzo-soprano)

'Blah, blah, blah' (with Roger Vignoles, piano, in cabaret at the Wigmore Hall): GERSHWIN: Blah, blah, blah; They all laughed; Three times a day; Boy, what love has done to me. PORTER: Tale of the oyster; Where O where?. BERNSTEIN: Who am I?. NICHOLAS: Place settings; Usherette's blues. DRING: Song of a nightclub proprietress. BOLCOM: Lime jello, marshmallow, cottage-cheese surprise. FLANDERS and SWANN: A word on my ear. LEHMANN: There are fairies at the bottom of my garden. WRIGHT: Transatlantic lullaby. BAKER: Someone is sending me flowers. SCHOENBERG: 3 Brettl Lieder.
*** Hyp. Dig. CDA 66289 [id.].

Recorded live at the Wigmore Hall in London, Sarah Walker's recital of trifles is one of the happiest records you could wish to find, as well as one of the funniest. Her comic timing is masterly in such delectable revue numbers as Cole Porter's Tale of the oyster or William Bolcom's culinary patter-song, Lime jello, marshmallow, cottage-cheese surprise. Perhaps surprisingly, she does such a song as There are fairies at the bottom of my garden straight, restoring its touching quality in defiance of Beatrice Lillie's classic send-up. Also, by treating a popular number such as Transatlantic lullaby as a serious song, she not only underlines purely musical qualities but touches a deeper vein than one might expect in a cabaret sequence. Three of Schoenberg's Brettl Lieder, in deft English translations by Michael Irwin, are sung just as delightfully – and more provocatively than the German versions which were recorded by Jill Gomez in her delectable 'Cabaret classics' recital. The title, Blah, blah, blah, comes from the opening number, a witty concoction by George Gershwin with words by his brother, Ira, which reduces the popular love-song lyrics to the necessary – and predictable – rhymes. Roger Vignoles, always an understanding accompanist, here excels himself with playing of flair and brilliance, exuberantly encompassing every popular idiom in turn. The recording, unlike most made at the Wigmore Hall, captures some of the bloom of its acoustic; but that means that the voice is set slightly at a distance. Texts are provided but, with such clear diction from the singer, they are needed only occasionally.

Walker, Sarah (mezzo-soprano), Thomas Allen (baritone)

'The Sea' (with Roger Vignoles, piano): IRELAND: Sea fever. HAYDN: Mermaid's song; Sailor's song. DIBDIN: Tom Bowling. WALTON: Song for the Lord Mayor's table; Wapping Old Stairs. WOLF: Seemanns Abschied. FAURÉ: Les Berceaux; Au cimetière; L'horizon chimerique. SCHUBERT: Lied eines Schiffers an die Dioskuren. BORODIN: The Sea; The Sea Princess. DEBUSSY: Proses lyriques: De grève. IVES: Swimmers. SCHUMANN: Die Meerfee. BERLIOZ: Nuits d'été: L'ile inconnue. MENDELSSOHN: Wasserfahrt. BRAHMS: Die Meere. TRAD.: The Mermaid. Arr. BRITTEN: Sail on, sail on.
⊛ *** Hyp. CDA 66165 [id.].

With Roger Vignoles as master of ceremonies in a brilliantly devised programme, ranging wide, this twin-headed recital celebrating 'The Sea' is a delight from beginning to end. Two outstandingly characterful singers are mutually challenged to their very finest form, whether in solo songs or duets. As sample, try the setting of the sea-song, *The Mermaid*, brilliantly arranged by Vignoles, with hilarious key-switches on the comic quotations from *Rule Britannia*. Excellent recording.

Welitsch, Ljuba (soprano)

Arias from: TCHAIKOVSKY: *Eugene Onegin*. VERDI: *Aida*. PUCCINI: *Tosca; La Bohème*. WEBER: *Der Freischütz*. R. STRAUSS: *Salome: Closing scene*.
(M) (***) EMI mono CDH7 61007-2 [id.].

It is sad that Ljuba Welitsch's career was far shorter than it should have been. The voice itself, strikingly individual in its timbre, conveys fire and intensity and, as these classic recordings consistently show, the vibrant personality matches that. This immaculately transferred collection gathers together the handful of studio recordings she made for EMI after the Second World War (notably *Tatiana's letter song* from 1948, done in German). As a splendid bonus comes the radio recording, made in Vienna in 1944, of the closing scene from Strauss's *Salome*, where the extra vibrancy of live performance is caught vividly, despite the fuzziness of sound, here reasonably clarified in the digital transfer.

Westminster Abbey Choir, Preston

Christmas carols: TRAD.: *Up! awake; There stood in heaven a linden tree; The holly and the ivy; Ding dong merrily on high; Up! good Christian folk; In dulci jubilo; Rocking; Illuminare Jerusalem; Good King Wenceslas*. OLDHAM: *Remember O thou man*. WISHART: *Alleluya, a new work*. CHARPENTIER: *Salve puerule*. POSTON: *Jesus Christ the apple tree*. PRAETORIUS: *Resonet in laudibus*. MAXWELL DAVIES: *Nowell (Out of your sleep arise)*. HAMMERSCHMIDT: *Alleluja! Freuet euch*. MENDELSSOHN: *Hark! the herald angels sing*. SCHEIDT: *Puer natus*. GARDNER: *Tomorrow shall be my dancing day*. BRITTEN: *Shepherd's carol*.
*** DG Dig. 413 590-2.

An excellent concert in every way. The programme is nicely balanced between old favourites and rewarding novelty, the traditional material spiced with modern writing, which readily captures the special essence that makes a carol instantly recognizable as a Christmas celebration. Fresh singing of fine vigour, expressively responsive, is combined with first-class sound, the ambience nicely judged.

Westminster Cathedral Choir, Hill

'*Treasures of the Spanish Renaissance*': GUERRERO: *Surge propera amica mea; O altitudo divitiarum; O Domine Jesu Christe; O sacrum convivium; Ave, Virgo sanctissima; Regina coeli laetare*. LOBO: *Versa est in luctum; Ave Maria; O quam suavis est. Domine*. VIVANCO: *Magnificat octavi toni*.
*** Hyp. CDA 66168 [id.].

This immensely valuable collection reminds us vividly that Tomas Luis de Victoria was not the only master of church music in Renaissance Spain. Francisco Guerrero is generously represented here, and the spacious serenity of his polyphonic writing (for four, six and, in *Regina coeli laetare*, eight parts) creates the most beautiful sounds. A criticism might be made that tempi throughout this collection, which also includes fine music by Alonso Lobo and a superb eight-part *Magnificat* by Sebastian de Vivanco, are too measured, but the tension is held well, and David Hill is obviously concerned to convey the breadth of the writing. The singing is gloriously firm, with the long melismatic lines admirably controlled. Discreet accompaniments (using Renaissance double harp, bass dulcian and organ) do not affect the essentially a cappella nature of the performances. The Westminster Cathedral acoustic means the choral tone is richly upholstered, but the focus is always firm and clear.

White, Robert (tenor)

'Favourite Irish songs of Princess Grace' (with Monte Carlo PO, Stapleton): *Danny Boy; Pretty Kitty Kelly; Galway Bay; MacNamara's Band; Oft in the stilly night; Molly Malone; The last rose of summer; The foggy dew; Mother Machree; Off to Philadelphia; I hear you calling me; My wild Irish rose; The Sally gardens; She is far from the land; The star of County Down; Macushla; Mistress Biddy was a giddy little witch; The Rose of Tralee; I'll take you home again, Kathleen.*
*** Virgin VC 790705-2 [id.].

Princess Grace of Monaco was the sponsor for a Foundation to support a comprehensive archive of Irish music in Monte Carlo, from which these songs are taken; the colourful orchestral arrangements are by Peter Hope and Robert Docker. Among contemporary singers, Robert White is unsurpassed in this repertoire. His golden tenor and wonderfully free upper range make the lyrical numbers, like *I hear you calling me* and *The Sally gardens*, sound quite ravishing, while the light-hearted *MacNamara's Band* and *The star of the County Down* sparkle splendidly. The total lack of artifice in the singing, combined with an obvious emotional response, brings consistent pleasure. A superb voice, naturally caught by the engineers and very well balanced with the warmly recorded orchestral accompaniments, sympathetically directed by Robin Stapleton. This is outstanding of its kind.

Winchester Cathedral Choir, Martin Neary

'A solemn musick' (with Baroque Brass of London): PURCELL: *Funeral music for Queen Mary and Motets; Jehova, quam multi sunt hostes.* CROFT: *Burial service.* BACH: *O Jesu Christ, mein Lebens Licht, BWV 118.* BLOW: *Salvator mundi.* HUMFREY: *Hymne to God the Father.* GREENE: *Lord, let me know mine end.* BATTISHILL: *O Lord, look down from heaven.*
*** EMI Dig. CDC7 47772-2 [id.].

Martin Neary's splendid new version of Purcell's *Funeral music* is discussed under its composer entry. The rest of the programme, music with similar associations by other composers, is also very rewarding, usually elegiac in mood but sometimes with dramatic contrasts, as in Croft's *Burial service*. Particularly fine are Greene's *Let me know mine end* and Pelham Humfrey's *Hymne to God the Father*, with the solo beautifully sung by the counter-tenor, David Hurley. The recording is diffuse but pleasingly atmospheric.